THE HISTORY OF PARLIAMENT

THE HOUSE OF COMMONS 1660-1690

THE HISTORY OF PARLIAMENT

THE
HOUSE OF COMMONS
1660-1690

Basil Duke Henning

II

MEMBERS

C–L

PUBLISHED FOR THE HISTORY OF PARLIAMENT TRUST
BY SECKER & WARBURG, LONDON
1983

First published in England 1983 by
Martin Secker & Warburg Limited
54 Poland Street, London W1V 3DF
© Crown copyright 1983
ISBN 0-436-19274-8

Printed in Great Britain by Fletcher & Son Ltd, Norwich
and bound by Richard Clay (The Chaucer Press) Ltd, Bungay, Suffolk

Contributors

P.A.B.   P. A. Bolton

B.M.C.   B. M. Crook

E.C.   Eveline Cruickshanks

I.C.   Irene Cassidy

J.S.C.   J. S. Crossette

E.R.E.   E. R. Edwards

J.P.F.   J. P. Ferris

B.D.H.   B. D. Henning

G.H.   Gillian Hampson

M.W.H.   M. W. Helms

G.J.   Geoffrey Jaggar

A.M.M.   A. M. Mimardière

V.C.D.M. V. C. D. Moseley

L.N.   Leonard Naylor

E.R.   Edward Rowlands

P.W.   Paula Watson

MEMBERS
C – L

CAESAR, Sir Charles (1653–94), of Bennington, Herts.

HERTFORD 1679 (Mar.)
HERTFORDSHIRE 1679 (Oct.), 1681, 1689

b. 22 Feb. 1653, 2nd but o. surv. s. of (Sir) Henry Caesar*.
educ. St. Catharine's, Camb. 1668–71; M. Temple,
1669. *m.* 3 Nov. 1672, Susanna (*d.* 29 Mar. 1693), da.
and h. of Sir Thomas Bonfoy, Dyer, of Hammersmith,
Mdx., 3s. 1da. *suc.* fa. 1668. Kntd. 4 Oct. 1671.[1]
   Commr. for assessment, Herts. 1673–80, 1689–90;
j.p. and dep. lt. Hunts. Apr. 1688–*d.*, Herts. ?Oct.
1688–*d.*

Caesar was knighted during Charles II's visit to
Cambridge University in 1671. But according to
the antiquary Chauncy he 'declined all public employments ... and affected not the Roman party
nor their proselytes'. He was reported to have given
£100 towards the renewal of the Hertford charter
in 1678, and in the following February he was
returned for the borough with Sir Thomas Byde*.
Marked 'honest' on Shaftesbury's list, he was inactive in the first Exclusion Parliament, in which
he was appointed only to the committee for the
habeas corpus amendment bill, and abstained in the
division on the exclusion bill. On the evening of the
dissolution he went to Hertford, but, as he told
William Hale*, found three other candidates
already in the field 'soliciting their interests there.
I offered them my service, but whether I shall go
on to make an interest there I am not fully
resolved'. His dilemma was solved by Hale's withdrawal from the county election, leaving Caesar to
defeat the exclusionist Byde, despite the efforts of
the intriguer Sir Robert Peyton* to smear him as a
supporter of the Duke of York. As knight of the
shire in the second Exclusion Parliament he was
appointed to the committee of elections and privileges and to that to inquire into Peyton's conduct.
The Earl of Essex and the Earl of Salisbury (James
Cecil*) recommended Silius Titus* for the county
in 1681, but a gentry meeting resolved upon Caesar
and Hale, who were returned. He left no trace on
the records of the Oxford Parliament.[2]

Caesar is unlikely to have stood in 1685, but as a
moderate and sober Anglican he was appointed to
local office in 1688. He regained his seat in the
Convention, but he was not active, being appointed
to only 11 committees, including those to inquire
into the authors and advisers of recent grievances,
and to consider the bill to prevent excessive election
expenses. He was teller against the Tory candidate
in the Mitchell by-election, and, as one of the committee to bring in a bill for restoring corporations,
supported the disabling clause. But he was defeated
by the Tory Ralph Freman* at the next general
election. He died on 13 Aug. 1694 and was buried
at Bennington. Chauncy described him as

> very regular in his life and orderly in his family. ... He
> was very generous to all whom he employed, but
> seldom pardoned a slight to his person, or a contempt
> of his business. ... He would not contract any friend-
> ship or acquaintance with any he thought scandalous,
> and abhorred those who would purchase the favour of
> their prince with the price of the rights of the people.
> He would not willingly quarrel with his neighbours,
> nor spare any cost or charge to obtain his point.

A benefactor of his college in his will, he also left
generous sums to his younger sons and £3,500 to
his daughter, as well as annuities during their
minorities. His son Charles, a zealous Jacobite, sat
for either borough or county from 1701 to 1741
with three short intervals.[3]

[1] Clutterbuck, *Herts.* ii. 286–7; St. Catharine's, Camb. Adm.
Reg.; J. R. Woodhead, *Rulers of London*, 34. [2] Chauncy, *Herts.* ii.
82; L. Turnor, *Hertford*, 115; Grey, viii. 140; Add. 33573, f. 127;
Herts. RO, D/ELw/F29/4, James to Sir Jacob Wittewronge, 2
Feb. 1681. [3] Chauncy, ii. 82; *CJ*, x. 395–6; Clutterbuck, ii. 86;
W. H. S. Jones, *Hist. St. Catharine's, Camb.*, 248, 386; PCC 189
Box.

E.R.E./G.J.

CAESAR, Henry (1630–68), of Bennington, Herts.

HERTFORDSHIRE 1660, 3 Apr. 1666–6 Jan. 1668

b. 2 Oct. 1630, 2nd s. of Sir Charles Caesar†, master of the
rolls 1639–42, by 2nd w. Jane, da. of Sir Edward Barkham, ld. mayor of London 1621–2, of Southacre, Norf.
educ. Jesus, Camb. 1646; I. Temple 1647. *m.* 6 Nov.
1649, Elizabeth (*bur.* 30 Aug. 1670), da. and h. of
Robert Angel, merchant, of London, 2s. (1 *d.v.p.*) 1da.

suc. bro. 1642; kntd. 7 July 1660.[1]

Asst. Society of Mineral and Battery Works 1649–51; commr. for militia, Herts. Mar. 1660; j.p. Herts. Mar. 1660–d., St. Albans July 1660–d.; dep. lt. Herts. c. Aug. 1660–d., commr. for assessment Aug. 1660–d.[2]

Caesar was descended from an Italian physician, Cesare Adelmare, who came to England about 1550, acquired property in Hertfordshire by marriage, and became medical adviser to Mary Tudor and Elizabeth. His grandfather, Sir Julius Caesar[†], who sat in every Parliament from 1589 to 1621, acquired Bennington and became master of the rolls in 1614. Caesar was 'a true assertor of the reformed religion', which probably implies Presbyterian sympathies, and held no local office until the eve of the Restoration. He was the first of his family to sit for Hertfordshire, for which he was returned at the general election of 1660. Though he made no recorded speeches in the Convention, and was rewarded for his loyalty with a knighthood, it is said that he was 'active . . . to suppress the court of wards and liveries and to ease the people of hardships and charges which accrue to them by the tenures of knight service, and from the compositions which were yearly paid for corn and victual'. A moderately active committeeman, he was appointed to 16 committees, including those for the cancellation of grants, for inquiring into the state of the queen mother's jointure, for settling the militia, and for the supplementary poll bill.[3]

It is not known whether Caesar stood for re-election in 1661, but he regained his seat at a by-election in April 1666 in spite of the furious opposition of Thomas Fanshawe*, an Exchequer official, who declared that he would 'make all those gentlemen sheriffs successively that gave their voices for Sir Henry Caesar'. A very active Member, he served on 38 committees in two sessions, though most were of secondary importance. He served on the parliamentary delegation ordered to attend the King with the resolutions against French imports. He was also appointed to consider the bills for establishing a public accounts commission, for receiving information on the increase in Popery, and for the relief of poor prisoners. He may have welcomed the fall of Clarendon, who had warned him through Sir Harbottle Grimston* against appearing to favour conventicles. He was among those appointed to inquire into the miscarriages of the war, to report on the proceedings in Mordaunt's impeachment, and to consider the public accounts bill. He died of smallpox, like his father and elder brother before him, on 6 Jan. 1668, and was buried at Bennington. The county historian described him as a man 'endowed with good learning . . . and a clear and discerning

judgment. He was very loyal to the King, faithful to his trust, always ready to ease the subjects of their grievances.'[4]

[1] Clutterbuck, *Herts.* ii. 286. [2] BL Loan 16. [3] E. Lodge, *Sir Julius Caesar*, 8; *VCH Herts.* iii. 75; Chauncy, *Herts.* ii. 81. [4] *HMC Verulam*, 63, 70, 72; *The Gen.* n.s. ix. 43; Clutterbuck, ii. 286; Chauncy, ii. 81.

M.W.H./E.R.E./G.J.

CALMADY, Josias I (1619–83), of Langdon, Wembury, Devon.

OKEHAMPTON 27 Apr. 1660

bap. 10 Oct. 1619, 3rd but 1st surv. s. of Sir Shilston Calmady of Wembury, being 1st s. by 2nd w. Honora, da. of Edmund Fortescue of Fallapit, wid. of Humphrey Prideaux of Soldon. *educ.* Exeter, Oxf. 1638; M. Temple 1640. *m.* (1) 16 Aug. 1647, Thomasine, da. of Sir Richard Buller[†] of Shillingham, Cornw., 2da.; (2) 11 Nov. 1652, Elizabeth, da. of John Coffin of Portledge, Devon, wid. of William Gay of Chittlehampton, Devon, 2s. *d.v.p.* 2da. *suc.* fa. 1646.[1]

Commr. for assessment, Devon 1647–8, 1652, 1657, Aug. 1660–80, j.p. 1650–3, Mar. 1660–d., commr. for militia Mar. 1660, recusants 1675.

Calmady's ancestors had been seated in Devon since the 14th century, first entered Parliament in 1554, and acquired Langdon in the following year. Calmady's father, who stood unsuccessfully for Okehampton in 1641, fought for Parliament in the first Civil War and was killed at the siege of Ford House in February 1646. Although Calmady himself was not politically active during the Civil Wars, he came to terms with the new regime and served as a justice and assessment commissioner intermittently during the Interregnum. At the general election of 1660 he was involved in a double return for Okehampton, near his property of Bratton Clovelly. He was seated on the merits of the return, and marked as a friend on Lord Wharton's list. He was an inactive Member of the Convention, though his four committees included that for the indemnity bill. His only speech was on the bill of sales on 11 July, when he proposed 'to cast it out or put it in the fire, or else to commit it to the necessary house above, if it must be committed'. For making a motion so 'unbefitting such an assembly' he was immediately rebuked by Arthur Annesley*, and eight days later he was given leave to go into the country.[2]

Calmady was allowed to decline the office of sheriff of Devon in 1675 on the grounds of being 'scorbutical and hydropsical', but may have been admitted to the Green Ribbon Club, with his nephew Josias Calmady II*, during the exclusion crisis. In his will, dated 7 Mar. 1683, his gift to the curate of Wembury was conditional upon his being 'a conformable man to the doctrine and discipline of the Church of England'. He was buried at Wembury nine days later.[3]

[1] Vivian, *Vis. Devon*, 130, 210; *Vis. Cornw.* 57; W. K. H. Wright, *Hist. Okehampton*, 98. [2] B. H. Williams, *Ancient Westcountry Fams.* 44; Wright, 99; Bowman diary, f. 72v. [3] *CSP Dom.* 1675–6, p. 137; PCC 148 Drax.

M.W.H./J.S.C.

CALMADY, Josias II (c.1652–1714), of the Inner Temple and Leawood, Bridestowe, Devon.

OKEHAMPTON 1679 (Mar.), 1679 (Oct.)

b. c.1652, 3rd but 1st surv. s. of Shilston Calmady of Leawood by Elizabeth, da. and coh. of Humphrey Gayer of Plymouth. *educ.* Trinity, Oxf. matric. 5 May 1668, aged 16; I. Temple 1669, called 1676. *m.* (1) lic. 29 Dec. 1680, Elizabeth (*d.* 27 Feb. 1695), da. and coh. of Sir Edward Waldo, Clothworker, of Cheapside, London and Pinner, Mdx., 4s. (2 *d.v.p.*) 2da.; (2) 1699, Jane. da. of Thomas Rolt of Milton Ernest, Beds., 1da. *suc.* uncle Josias Calmady I* in Langdon estate 1683, fa. 1688.[1]

Commr. for assessment, Devon 1679–80, 1689–*d.*, j.p. June 1688–?*d.*, sheriff 1694–5; freeman, Plymouth 1696; lt.-col. of militia ft. Devon by 1697–*d.*, dep. lt. 1701–*d.*[2] Commr. for drowned lands 1690.[3]

Calmady's father served on the assessment commissions in 1652 and 1657. Calmady himself, a lawyer, first stood for Parliament at a by-election in 1677 for Okehampton, six miles from his home, but he was defeated by Henry Northleigh* by a sizeable margin. He was successful in both elections of 1679, when the returning officer was a kinsman, Benjamin Gayer. He was considered 'honest' by Shaftesbury, joined the Green Ribbon Club, and voted for exclusion, but he did not speak and was named to no committees. Despite the efforts of his colleague, (Sir) Arthur Harris*, he was rejected by his constituency in 1681, but he became a Whig collaborator under James II. He was approved as court candidate for Okehampton in 1688, but is not known to have contested the borough again, though he stood unsuccessfully for Plymouth in 1698. He continued to sit on the Devon taxation commission throughout Queen Anne's reign, his will being proved on 20 Nov. 1714. His son served for Saltash as a Tory from 1715 to 1722.[4]

[1] Vivian, *Vis. Devon*, 130; *Vis. Cornw.* 172; *Western Antiquary*, ix. 178; *Mar. Lic.* (Harl. Soc. xxx), 50. [2] *CSP Dom.* 1696, p. 424; Eg. 1626, f. 11. [3] *Cal. Treas. Bks.* ix. 794. [4] W. K. H. Wright, *Hist. Okehampton*, 103–4; *Prot. Dom. Intell.* 8 Feb. 1681; PCC 216 Aston.

J.S.C.

CALTHORPE, Sir Christopher (c.1645–1718), of East Barsham, Norf.

NORFOLK 10 Feb.–21 Apr. 1679

b. c.1645, 1st surv. s. of James Calthorpe of East Barsham by 2nd w. Catherine, da. of Sir Edward Lewkenor of Denham, Suff. *educ.* Christ's, Camb. adm. 5 Apr. 1659, aged 14; M. Temple 1660. *m.* 19 Sept. 1664, Dorothy (*d.* 7 Feb. 1715), da. of Sir William Spring, 1st Bt.†, of Pakenham, Suff., 5s. *d.v.p.* 9da. *suc.* fa. 1652; KB 23 Apr. 1661.[1]

Commr. for assessment, Norf. 1661–80, 1689, j.p. 1668–Feb. 1688, dep. lt. 1669–Feb. 1688, Nov. 1688–9, col. of militia ft. 1672–83, freeman, King's Lynn 1682.[2]

Calthorpe's ancestors had held manorial property in Norfolk since 1376 and first represented the county under Henry VI. His father was a parliamentary sympathizer in the Civil War and held local office under the Commonwealth.[3]

Although Calthorpe was akin to Lord Townshend (Sir Horatio Townshend*) through his mother, he joined the rival faction in Norfolk politics headed by Lord Yarmouth (Robert Paston*). On 19 Apr. 1676 Yarmouth wrote that Calthorpe

despite of his mother, brothers, and all the machines in the world to divert, sticks to me in the principle of serving his prince; he is a most popular man, and has given me more credit than can be imagined.

In February 1679 he was recommended by (Sir) Joseph Williamson* and put up by Yarmouth with Sir Nevill Catelyn* as court candidate for the county as men 'that will meddle with ministers of state'. He was returned after a bitter contest, and was appointed to the committee of elections and privileges. Classed as 'base' by Shaftesbury, his election was declared void on the petition of Sir John Hobart*, and he was defeated at the ensuing by-election. At the second general election of the year he was again asked to stand by Yarmouth, but he 'earnestly desired to be excused' on the entreaties of his wife, who had told him 'that he would ruin himself and his family by running into debt, and bid him consider that his estate was small, and he had debts upon it before and had increased them much by his charges the two last elections'. But at a county meeting called by Yarmouth, the gentlemen 'would hear no excuse' and undertook to raise a subscription to meet his and Catelyn's expenses. They were defeated by the country candidates, and did not stand in 1681. As foreman of the grand jury, he signed the loyal address in 1682 abhorring the 'Association'.[4]

In 1688 Calthorpe bluntly declared that he could not give his assent to the repeal of the Test Act and Penal Laws, and he was removed from local office. When he was restored in 1688 he followed the example of Sir John Holland* in refusing to act with

Roman Catholics. A non-juror after the Revolution, he was disarmed in September 1689 at the behest of Sir Henry Hobart*, who had inherited a grudge against him, and in the following summer he was placed in confinement as a person 'suspected to be dangerous to the peace of the kingdom'. Hobart again had him arrested after the assassination plot in 1696, when Dean Prideaux described him as:

a man of strong zeal and weak judgment, and totally bigoted to Toryism, but one whom I reckon a harmless man, and not otherwise inclined to the cause he is in but by suffering for it.

He died on 7 Feb. 1718, aged 75, the last surviving knight of the Bath and the last of his family to enter Parliament, and was buried at Fakenham.[5]

[1] Le Neve's Knights (Harl. Soc. viii), 10; East Anglian Misc. (1916), 10, 12. [2] Add. 36988, f. 305; Norf. Ltcy. Jnl. (Norf. Rec. Soc. xxx), 9; Lynn Freemen, 193. [3] Norf. Arch. ix. 153–4, 171. [4] HMC 6th Rep. 377; CSP Dom. 1679–80, pp. 59, 75; Add. 36988, ff. 143–4, 180; HMC Lothian, 142. [5] Norf. Ltcy. Jnl. 89, 109, 115, 143; Prideaux Letters (Cam. Soc. n.s. xv), 172–3, 176–81.

E.C.

CALVERLEY, Sir Henry (c.1641–84), of Eryholme, Yorks.

NORTHALLERTON 1679 (Mar.), 1679 (Oct.), 1681

b. c.1641, 2nd s. of John Calverley of Eryholme by Margaret, da. of Thomas Jenison of Irchester, Northants. educ. Queen's, Oxf. 1655; G. Inn 1658; M. Temple 1659, called 1664. m. 18 Dec. 1669, Mary, da. of Sir Henry Thompson* of Marston, Yorks., 1s. d.v.p. 2da. suc. bro. 1668; kntd. 24 Dec. 1675.[1]

J.p. Yorks (N. Riding) 1670–7, co. Dur. 1671–80; commr. for assessment (N. Riding) 1673–80, co. Durham 1677–80, recusants (N. Riding) 1675.

Calverley came from a cadet branch of a 15th century family which was granted the Eryholme estate by the crown in 1580. His father does not seem to have taken any part in the Civil War, though his uncle was a Royalist. Succeeding his brother in the estate in 1668, Calverley was soon afterwards appointed to the North Riding magistracy, only to be removed in 1677 for having maintained that smiths' forges ought not to be subject to hearth-tax; though it was later alleged that his real offence was an attempt to enforce the recusancy laws.[2]

Calverley was returned to the Exclusion Parliaments for Northallerton, eight miles from Eryholme, doubtless on the Lascelles interest. Classed as 'honest' by Shaftesbury in 1679, he was moderately active, being appointed to eight committees, of which the most important was for security against Popery. He also helped to draft an address for calling out the militia in and around London, and showed an interest in three matters which continued to preoccupy him in the next Parliament: abuses in the Post Office, the collection of hearth-tax, and the import of cattle. He was absent from the division on the exclusion bill. In June 1680 under Shaftesbury's leadership he sought to indict the Duke of York as a popish recusant. An active Member of the second Exclusion Parliament, he was appointed to 15 committees, including the committee of elections and privileges. He was among those ordered to receive information about the Popish Plot and to draft the address for the removal of Jeffreys. He acted as teller for the second reading of the bill to prohibit imports of Scottish cattle, and was named to the committee to inquire into the proceedings of the judges. In the Oxford Parliament he was named only to the elections committee.[3]

Calverley suffered in the reaction that followed disclosure of the Rye House Plot when his house was searched and arms were seized. Sometime before, however, he had left the country. He was in Rome in April 1683 and not expecting to quit Italy until June. Therefore his travels took him to Paris, where a court spy described him as 'certainly a dangerous person' and where he seems to have engaged in many of the Whig plots abroad. He died there on 14 June 1684, the last of the family.[4]

[1] Clay, Dugdale's Vis. Yorks. i. 251. [2] VCH Yorks. N. Riding, i. 78; Cal. Comm. Comp. 1386; HMC Finch, ii. 45; Reresby Mems. 125; State Trials, vii. 1313. [3] HMC Ormonde, n.s. v. 340; CJ, ix. 657. [4] HMC Var. ii. 174; E. Riding RO, DDFA39/38; HMC 7th Rep. 397, 400.

P.A.B./P.W.

CALVERLEY, William (c.1622–60), of Holborn, London.

NEWCASTLE-UPON-TYNE 11 Apr.–4 July 1660

b. c.1622, o.s. of Sheffield Calverley, merchant, of Newcastle by Barbara, da. of William Hall, merchant, of Newcastle. educ. L. Inn 1640, called 1647. unm. suc. fa. 1623.[1]

Freeman, Newcastle 1660.[2]

Calverley was descended from an ancient and widespread Yorkshire gentry family. His father, a younger son, was apprenticed to a Newcastle alderman and married his master's daughter, but died young. Calverley himself, a lawyer, was occasionally consulted by the great Newcastle companies, but avoided all political commitment or office. He was probably elected to the Convention as substitute for his stepfather Ralph Grey, a prominent member of the corporation, who at the age of 76 could legitimately be excused the long journey to Westminster. He made no speeches and was named to no committees, but he probably supported the Government. Given leave of absence on 29 June 1660, he died in the parish of St. Andrew, Holborn five days later, and was buried in St. Nicholas, Newcastle.[3]

[1] Clay, *Dugdale's Vis. Yorks.* i. 247. [2] *Reg. of Freemen* (Newcastle Recs. Committee iii), 76. [3] *Newcastle Merchant Adventurers* (Surtees Soc. xciii), 184; (ci), 232, 245; *Newcastle Hostmen* (Surtees Soc. cv), 249, 250; *Northumb. Vis. Peds.* ed. Foster, 65; Rylands Lib. mss. 299, f. 382.

M.W.H./G.H.

CAMPDEN, Visct. *see* **NOEL, Wriothesley Baptist**

CAMPION, William (1640–1702), of Combwell, Goudhurst, Kent.

SEAFORD   1689, 1690, 1695, 31 Dec. 1698
KENT   1701 (Dec.)

bap. 6 Feb. 1640, 1st s. of Sir William Campion of Combwell by Grace, da. of Sir Thomas Parker[†] of Ratton, Suss. *educ.* Trinity Coll. Camb. 1655; M. Temple 1657; Padua 1660. *m.* lic. 1 Nov. 1662, Frances, da. of (Sir) John Glynne* of Henley Park, Surr., 2s. (1 *d.v.p.*) 7da. *suc.* fa. 1648.[1]

Commr. for assessment, Kent 1665–80, 1689–90, Seaford and Pevensey 1690; j.p. Kent 1669–87, 1689–*d.*, dep. lt. 1685–?Feb. 1688, 1689–*d.*; sub-commr. for prizes, Dover 1690–8, June–Oct. 1702; asst. Mines Co. 1693.[2]

Campion claimed descent from an Essex gentry family. His great-grandfather bought the former monastic estate of Combwell under Elizabeth and sat for Haslemere in 1586. His father commanded the royalist garrison of Boarstall House in the Civil War, for which he was knighted. After compounding for £1,354, he took up arms again in 1648 and was killed in a sortie from Colchester. Although his estates lay in Kent, Essex and Norfolk, and he owned valuable house property in London, he was connected by marriage with so many Sussex families that Herbert Morley* regarded him as a fellow-countryman. Campion himself was born in Sussex and probably brought up in the Presbyterian Parker family after his father's death. His marriage was to reinforce this leaning to the opposition, and he became a member of the Green Ribbon Club. His bust in Goudhurst church suggests a strong character, but he took no part in national politics until he was nearly 50. Although removed from the commission of the peace in 1687 he remained a deputy lieutenant, and replied to the lord lieutenant's questions on the repeal of the Test Act and Penal Laws that 'until he hears the debates in Parliament he cannot resolve'. With regard, presumably, to the Kent elections, he declared himself 'already engaged to two persons he has a confidence in'.[3]

At the general election of 1689, Campion was returned as senior Member for Seaford on the interest of his uncle Sir William Thomas*. His only committee in the Convention was for the attainder of those in rebellion in Ireland. Although clearly a Whig, he was not reckoned a supporter of the disabling clause in the bill to restore corporations, but he acted as teller against the return of John Beaumont* for Hastings. He remained a Court Whig under William III, signing the Association in 1696. He died on 20 Sept. 1702, and was buried at Goudhurst. His son Henry sat for Sussex as a Tory under Queen Anne.[4]

[1] *Suss. Arch. Coll.* x. 3, 34–35. [2] *CSP Dom.* 1689–90, p. 172; 1693, p. 207; *Cal. Treas. Bks.* xvii. 364. [3] *Danny Archives* ed. J. A. Wooldridge, xv–xvi; *Suss. Arch. Coll.* x. 4; Hasted, *Kent,* vii. 80–81. [4] *CJ,* x. 335; *Misc. Gen. et Her.* (ser. 4), ii. 264.

B.D.H.

CANN, Sir Robert, 1st Bt. (c.1621–85), of Small Street, Bristol and Stoke Bishop, Westbury-on-Trym, Glos.

BRISTOL   11 Feb 1678, 1679 (Mar.), 1679 (Oct.)–
28 Oct. 1680

b. c.1621, 1st s. of William Cann, merchant, of Bristol and Compton Greenfield by Margaret, sis. of Robert Yeamans, merchant, of Wine Street, Bristol. *m.* (1) lic. 17 July 1642, Cicely, da. of Humphrey Hooke[†], merchant, of Bristol, 1s. 1da.; (2) 10 Feb. 1647, Anne, da. of Derrick Popley, merchant, of the Red Lodge, Bristol, 1s. 1da. *suc.* fa. 1658; *kntd.* 22 Apr. 1662; *cr.* Bt. 13 Sept. 1662.[1]

Member of merchant venturers, Bristol 1646, treas. 1653–4, master 1658–9; freeman, Bristol 1646, common councilman 1649–63, sheriff 1651–2, mayor 1662–3, 1675–6, alderman 1663–*d.*; commr. for militia, Bristol Mar. 1660, assessment, Bristol Aug. 1660–4, 1679–80, Glos. 1673–80; sheriff, Glos. 1670–1, j.p. 1679–*d.*; dep. lt. Bristol June 1685–*d.*[2]

Cann was alleged to have persuaded his father not to jeopardize his estate by joining in his uncle's plot to betray Bristol to Prince Rupert in 1643. His father continued to hold municipal office till his death; as mayor he proclaimed the Commonwealth in 1649 and served on the assessment commission during the Interregnum. Cann inherited or acquired land both in the Bristol area and in the West Indies, where he owned a sugar plantation. He welcomed the Restoration, urging the corporation to offer the King £1,000, twice what the majority considered adequate, and was created a baronet as one 'ready to express his loyalty and good affection'. The distinction was perhaps felt too keenly, since it led to 'furious animosities' about precedence. Clarendon wrote to Ormonde of a 'ridiculous contention between women for place', but Cann's delight in parading the streets with six footmen in rich liveries suggests that, although Bristol husbands at this time were notoriously hen-pecked, he was not far behind his wife in the desire to 'shine'. On a complaint from John Knight I* that Cann had not only neglected his civic duties, but countenanced and cherished the Quakers and sectaries, he was severely reprimanded by the King. On the death of his first wife's nephew, Sir Humphrey Hooke*, he was elected to the Cavalier Parliament with the support of the dissenters, and marked 'worthy' on Shaftesbury's list. A moderately active Member, he was appointed to 20 committees, the majority of which were for private bills or commercial matters, including five intended to assist the cloth industry. On 12 Nov. 1678 he was added to the committee to inquire into the mistranslation in the French edition of the *London Gazette*.[3]

Cann was re-elected, probably unopposed, to the first Exclusion Parliament, and again marked 'worthy' by Shaftesbury. He was appointed to no committees and on 1 May 1679 was given leave to go into the country for a week; but he was still absent for the division on the exclusion bill, and had probably already gone over to the Court. He was appointed a county magistrate, and at the next general election he was opposed by a Whig, Robert Henley, who petitioned. Before the case could be heard or Cann appointed to any committees, he was denounced to the House for declaring that there was no Popish Plot, only a Presbyterian Plot. It was alleged that he 'took his measure from the Marquess of Worcester' (Henry Somerset*). The charge was attested by his colleague Knight, who had also changed front, and was now an exclusionist. Defending himself in the House, Cann exclaimed: 'As for the credit of Sir John Knight in Bristol, it is such that a jury of twelve men, his neighbours, will not believe his testimony', adding in a too audible aside: 'God damme, 'tis true'. Despite his humble apologies for his rash words, the House decided that he had added impiety to incredulity and voted unanimously to expel him and send him to the Tower. He now told the Speaker: 'I ever did, and ever shall believe this to be a Popish Plot, as sure as you are in the chair', and was released after a few days, but never stood again. His position in municipal life was unaffected, and his assistance was sought for electing a Tory mayor in 1682. His failure to oppose the election of a new alderman conducted by (Sir) Robert Atkyns* in the mayor's absence earned him inclusion in the court list of the ill-disposed on the bench, but he voted

for the surrender of the charter, and was nominated to the new corporation. According to Roger North*, however, whose brother had married Cann's daughter, his life was shortened by a brush with Jeffreys during the Bloody Assizes. The lord chief justice's humanity was outraged by the activities of the 'spirits', who provided the West Indian Plantations with labour by kidnapping; Cann was implicated, but the crown intervened to save him from prosecution in consideration of his loyalty and good service. Shaken by 'journeys, troubles and perplexities', Cann unwisely switched from Bristol milk, 'morning, noon and night', to small beer; 'but nature would not long bear so great a change'. He was buried at St. Werburgh's in November 1685, the only member of the family to sit in Parliament.[4]

[1] *Bristol and Glos. Arch. Soc. Trans.* xlix. 204; *Deposition Bks.* (Bristol Rec. Soc. vi) 65; (xiii), 202; *Merchants and Merchandise* (Bristol Rec. Soc. xix), 125; *Le Neve's Knights* (Harl. Soc. viii) 338; Rudder, *Glos.* 801; *Glos. N. and Q.* ii. 594; Wards 7/85/74. [2] *Merchant Venturers* (Bristol Rec. Soc. xvii), 29; A. B. Beavan, *Bristol Lists*, 281; *Deposition Bks.* (Bristol Rec. Soc. xiii), 202; *CSP Dom.* 1685, p. 189. [3] SP29/92/91, 110; 397/86; J. Latimer, *Bristol in the 17th Century*, 225, 315; *CSP Dom.* 1651–2, p. 324; *CSP Col.* vii. 32; Bristol RO, common council proceedings 1659–75, f. 20; *Pepys Diary*, 11 June 1668; North, *Lives*, ii. 186. [4] Grey, vii. 380–5; *CJ*, ix. 642, 648; *CSP Dom.* 1682, p. 382; SP29/422/218; Bath mss, Thynne pprs. 22, f. 8; *Bristol Charters* (Bristol Rec. Soc. xii), 194; SP44/71/186, 336/265–6; North, op. cit. ii. 196–7.

J.P.F.

CAPEL, Hon. Henry (1638–96), of Kew, Surr.

TEWKESBURY	1660, 1661, 1679 (Mar.), 1679 (Oct.), 1681
COCKERMOUTH	1689
TEWKESBURY	1690–11 Apr. 1692

bap. 6 Mar. 1638, 3rd s. of Arthur Capel†, 1st Baron Capell of Hadham (*d.*1649), by Elizabeth, da. and coh. of Sir Charles Morrison, 1st Bt.†, of Cassiobury, Herts.; bro. of Arthur, 1st Earl of Essex. *m.* settlement 16 Feb. 1659, Dorothy (*d.* 7 June 1721), da. and coh. of Richard Bennet of Chancery Lane, London and Kew, *s.p.* KB 23 Apr. 1661; *cr.* Baron Capell of Tewkesbury 11 Apr. 1692.

Commr. for assessment, Glos. and Surr. Aug. 1660–80, Glos., Herts. and Surr. 1689–90, Cumb. 1690; dep. lt. Glos. c. Aug. 1660–?81; commr. for loyal and indigent officers, Surr. 1662; feodary of Ogmore, Glam. 1662–92; j.p. Surr. 1672–81; commr. for recusants, Glos. and Surr. 1675; chief steward, manor of Richmond 1689–?92; high steward, Tewkesbury by 1695–*d.*[1]

PC [I] 1673–85, 1693–*d.*; first ld. of Admiralty 1679–80; PC 21 Apr. 1679–31 Jan. 1680, 14 Feb. 1689–*d.*; ld. of Treasury 1689–90; gov. Society of Mineral and Battery Works 1689–*d.*; member, Society of Mines Royal 1690; one of the lds. justices [I] 1693–5; ld. dep. [I] 1695–*d.*

The fortunes of the Capel family were made by Sir William Capel, a younger son from Suffolk, who became a London Draper. He was elected for the city in 1491, 1512 and 1515, twice served as lord mayor, and acquired considerable landed property in Essex and Hertfordshire. Capel's father was returned for the latter county in both elections of 1640 as a supporter of the popular party. But he was raised to the peerage in 1641 and, after fighting for the King in both wars, beheaded in 1649 as one of the commanders of the Colchester garrison, his executors later compounding at £4,706 17s.11d.[2]

Capel inherited the manor of Tewkesbury Barton from his paternal grandmother, and was returned for the borough, apparently unopposed, at the general election of 1660, in flagrant violation of the final ordinance of the Long Parliament forbidding the return of Cavaliers' sons. An inactive Member of the Convention he was named to the committee for the militia bill and three others of little significance. At the Restoration his eldest brother was made lord lieutenant of Hertfordshire and created Earl of Essex, while Capel himself, after re-election, was made a knight of the Bath for the coronation. But neither brother was prominent in politics under the Clarendon administration and the Cabal. On 15 June 1661 Capel acted as teller against a proviso to the bill confirming the Act of Indemnity, but he took no part in the Clarendon Code, except by twice helping to consider additional corporations bills. On 3 May 1662 he opposed the adjournment of the debate on the militia bill. He was listed as a court dependant in 1664, though probably only as the friend and brother-in-law of Lord Cornbury (Henry Hyde*). His most important committees during this period were to consider the prohibition of cattle imports (20 Oct. 1665), to inquire into the insolence of Popish priests and Jesuits (20 Oct. 1666), and to hear the petition from the merchants trading with France (17 Jan. 1667). He was one of the delegation which presented the petition to the King. He took no part in the proceedings against Clarendon, though in 1668 he was among those who considered restraints on jurors and presented an address for wearing English manufactures. Sir Thomas Osborne* included him in 1669 among the Members to be engaged for the Court by the Duke of York, but the evidence of the Journals suggests that he seldom attended the next two sessions. His chief interest at this time was his notable garden at Kew, the nucleus of the Royal Botanic Garden, from which he produced, according to Evelyn, 'the choicest fruit of any plantation in England, as he is the most industrious and understanding in it'.[3]

It was probably the drift towards Popery, as evidenced by the third Dutch war, the Declaration of Indulgence, and the Duke of York's conversion, that stimulated Capel into an active political role. He also gained prestige by the appointment of his brother as lord lieutenant of Ireland in 1672. On 18 Mar. 1673 he helped to draw up the address on the condition of Ireland; but his first recorded speech, in the autumn session, shows that he was moving towards opposition. He would vote no further supply for the war, though he would not expressly refuse it, trusting that the King would redress their grievances:

> If this war was for the maintenance of the Crown and nation, would venture all he has, life and fortune, for it. He is descended from one that lost his life for maintaining of both. Would know how we came into this war before we give money to it.

In the debate on grievances which followed he made the first of many attacks on the standing army:

> You have been told how difficult it is for armies and properties to stand together. Is not of that opinion that they are a security to us at home; knows nothing of affairs abroad. Our security is the militia, that will defend us and never conquer us. Our defence abroad is our ships. . . . Moves to vote this army a grievance. Is indifferent whether this army be disbanded now or after the war. Abroad they are of little use, and at home wholly useless.

Capel's motion was accepted, and he was named to the committee to draft an address accordingly. His activity did not go unnoticed, and in December Sir William Temple* wrote to Essex that his brother was now

> much more known in the nation than you left him, and much more considered at Court as well as in the country since the last session, though in different kinds. I think your lordship need not trouble yourself much about it, but leave him to his good senses and his good stars. He is yet very young in the busy world, and must have many such heats and colds as these before he is at his journey's end.

During the attack on the Cabal in the next session the Essex group, headed by Capel and William Harbord*, defended Arlington. Capel spoke against an address for his dismissal, acted as teller against a motion for candles, and proposed a vote on impeachment, which was bound to be rejected. He was named to the committees to consider the habeas corpus bill and the general test bill, and to inquire into allegations of parliamentary corruption. On 7 Feb. 1674 he declared that he was 'happy to harangue against a standing army, which he is satisfied is of no great use in war or peace', but demanded the disbandment of the new-raised forces only. This line displeased the extremists, but proved acceptable to the House. He was added to the committee to draw up the articles of Arlington's impeachment, and appointed to those to consider the Scottish army law, illegal exactions, and the condition of Ireland.[4]

At the opening of the spring session of 1675 Capel acted as teller against adjourning the debate on the vote of thanks for the speech from the throne. But he voted for the first article of the impeachment of Osborne (now Lord Treasurer Danby). He was named to the committees to bring in a bill appropriating the customs to the use of the navy and to consider an explanatory bill against Popery. He helped to prepare reasons on the Four Lawyers' case, and was sent to the Lords to desire a conference. On 4 June he said:

> you are told not to send them to the Tower because of the Lords' order. He thinks our privilege, as well as our property, involved in this matter. If we have no satisfaction from this conference, then shall be as forward as any man to send them to the Tower but he would waive it for the present.

It was reported that the court defeat on supply on 19 Oct. was due to the Essex group led by Capel and William Harbord*. On 21 Oct. he was again appointed to the committee for an appropriations bill, but on the next day he spoke against setting a precedent by lodging the funds in the chamber of London instead of the Exchequer, describing it as 'a blow to the best of Governments'. He feared that it would lead to a distinction between trusting the King, 'whom we ought to trust', and trusting the City. Perhaps because of speeches such as this, Capel's name appears on the working lists as to be influenced by his brother and on the list of government speakers. Nevertheless it was the Essex group that was given the credit for the defeat of the supply resolution. Capel was named to the committees for the bills to prevent illegal exactions, to extend habeas corpus, and to recall British subjects from the French service, and his was the first name on the committee to consider relieving Sir Edmund Jennings* of his duties as sheriff. Sir Richard Wiseman* reported that Capel 'was a very ill man the last session, and spoiled Sir Francis Russell* and some others', including Sir Rowland Berkeley* and William Banks I*.[5]

After the long prorogation Capel was hot for war with France, and was marked 'worthy' on Shaftesbury's list. On 28 Mar. 1677 he urged an address promising assistance in such a war, and was placed on the committee to prepare it. He acted unsuccessfully as teller against a perpetual ban on the import of Irish cattle. On 11 Apr. he spoke of his hope that the King would be pressed to form an alliance against France, and helped to prepare an address. After the adjournment on 29 Jan. 1678 he seconded the motion of Lord Cavendish (William

Cavendish*) against any treaty that failed to reduce France to the boundaries set by the Treaty of the Pyrenees, and was again named to the committee to prepare an address. On supply he proposed a compromise sum of £800,000 to support a war with France, and on 14 Mar. helped prepare another address for a declaration of war. But his old fear of the connexion of an army with Popery persisted.

> This is a great army now raising, and to be employed against the French King. . . . The muster-master must obey the law, and no man to be [en]listed, without having taken the oaths of allegiance and supremacy, and the Tests against Popery. . . . We are under great jealousies, and have great reason for it.

He was named to the committee to summarize foreign commitments and spoke against those ministers who had advised the King's answer to the recent addresses of the Commons:

> I will pay the ministers all respect without doors. . . . But within these walls we may speak our thoughts. . . . I move that you will put the question for the removal of the ministers, and I will give my affirmative.

He was among those entrusted with drafting the address for the removal, and preparing reasons for a conference on disbanding the army.[6]

In the final session of the Cavalier Parliament, Capel was named to almost all the committees concerned with the Popish Plot, including that to translate Coleman's letters. He twice interrogated Coleman and reported the results to the House. On 4 Nov. 1678, in the debate on the motion of Lord Russell (Hon. William Russell*) for removing the Duke of York from the King's person and councils, Capel took a more moderate and cautious stance.

> The Duke has made the advance to the Parliament by his behaviour in informing the Lords he will retire, etc. Let us not cast him out of our arms. It is entirely necessary that we be unanimous. If we once divide, we give him all the advantage against us imaginable. I have great respect for his person. His father, with my father, suffered in the rebellion, but if I cannot separate my interest from his person, I must divide from him. We all agree as to making such laws, that should the Duke be King, it might not be in his power to prejudice the Protestant religion. I move, therefore, not to lose the fruit of this debate; and as you have been told he has removed himself from the King's councils, you may agree to that and as for removing him from the King's person, adjourn that debate to another time.

The debate was, in fact, adjourned. Throughout the remainder of the session Capel continued to speak out against standing armies and the danger of Popery. When the House was informed that orders had been given for the seizure of the papers of Ralph Montagu*, Capel was among those sent to the King to desire details of his offence. He seconded the motion of Sir John Lowther III* to send for the papers immediately, and assisted Harbord in fetching them from their place of concealment. When they were read to the House, sufficient evidence was obtained of the negotiations with France to enable Capel to impeach the lord treasurer at the bar of the Lords. A moderately active Member of the Cavalier Parliament, he had been named to 178 committees, acted as teller on nine occasions, and made 59 recorded speeches.[7]

Capel was re-elected to the three Exclusion Parliaments, and again marked 'worthy' by Shaftesbury. He approved the drafting of an address on the right of the Commons to choose their Speaker, and served on the delegation that presented it. He was appointed to the committee on matters depending in the last Parliament and the secret committee on the Popish Plot, and helped to draft the address asking the King to entrust the informer Bedloe to the care of the Duke of Monmouth. He spoke four times against Danby's pardon, and was among those ordered to prepare an address and manage a conference on the subject. He reported from the committee which inspected the Lords' Journals on 24 Mar. 1679. His appointment to the remodelled Privy Council did not preclude his continued involvement in arrangements for the trial of Danby and the Popish lords. On 27 Apr. he moved a resolution 'that the Papists have had all their encouragement from the Duke's being a Papist', but he both spoke and voted against exclusion.

> I do agree that laws made to declare the succession are to be obeyed when made, but they are not yet made. . . . The safest way to preserve us is not to take away the duke's right to the crown. Should you take it away, do you not put all the Protestant princes upon it to preserve his right? If he has his right, they can have no pretence on his behalf. But parliamentarily, this day's consideration is to take care of the life of the King. Therefore I move not to close the debate, but appoint a bill be drawn that there may be a Parliament every three years, and a Parliament in being at the demise of the King. A few days will pass it and bind us in all the security imaginable against the consequences we apprehend.

As first lord of the Admiralty he insisted on the appointment of the venal Harbord as secretary, while he himself undertook the thankless task of coaxing a grant for the fleet out of a hostile House. When he alleged that every man cried out, 'Let us have a fleet', his voice was drowned in shouts of 'No', and it proved impossible even to fix a day for a debate on supply. A very active Member of the first Exclusion Parliament, he had been appointed to 23 committees and made 15 speeches.[8]

Capel's first period of service at the Council board was short and stormy. After the autumn election, in which according to Harbord he was sure of election for Tewkesbury and Breconshire, and perhaps also for Shoreham, he asked who had advised the prorogation of the new Parliament, but was abruptly silenced by the King. He again tried to raise the matter in November, together with his brother, Lord Russell, and Lord Cavendish (William Cavendish*). Finally on 31 Jan. 1680 in obedience to Shaftesbury's instructions, he asked leave to withdraw, which the King granted 'with all my heart'. By now a convert to exclusion, he became 'the instrument to beget correspondence' between Sunderland and the Duchess of Portsmouth on the one hand, and Shaftesbury and the chief managers of the Commons on the other.[9]

When the second Exclusion Parliament at last met, Capel followed the opposition line. On 26 Oct. he delivered a long and eloquent speech, in the course of which he attributed all the grievances of the nation to France and Popery, referred favourably to Protestant dissenters, and called for consideration 'of the prevention of Popery and a Popish successor'. On the next day he was named to the committees to inquire into abhorring and to draw up an address for preserving the Protestant religion. After recanting his views on exclusion, he was appointed to the committee to bring in the bill:

> I have formerly given some proof that I have been for moderation, and (God willing) shall always be for it when it may do some good. In the last two Parliaments I did so argue for moderation that many of my friends told me that I had deserted the true interest of my King and country. . . . I am of opinion this is a case in which there is no room for moderation, if by moderation be meant the making of any other law for the security of our religion. Because . . . all other bills that can be desired, without this bill, will not prove effectual, but will leave us in the unhappy condition of contesting with a Popish successor during this King's life and with the power of a Popish king hereafter.

Four days later he spoke in favour of comprehension, saying 'We are now to enlarge the Church as far as we can and make the pale of the Church as wide as we can; we need help against the Papists', and he was named to the committee to repeal the Elizabethan law against Protestant dissenters. Ormonde had evidence, in the shape of a letter from Capel to his colleague Sir Francis Russell, that he was the chief promoter of belief in an Irish plot, and he was one of the managers of a conference on the subject. He helped to draw up the answer to the King's message insisting on the legal succession. In an impassioned speech on the following day he declared that exclusion was the only means of protecting posterity from Popery, slavery and bloodshed, concluding with the prediction that 'the English are of a quiet nature, but should we be so unfortunate as to have a Popish King, it would bring us all into confusion and blood. If this bill pass not, all the nation will be in blood.' He regarded exclusion as the prime business of the House, and when the King broached the subject of aid for Tangier Capel's position was that 'we will support him when we are safe, but till then, no money'. He helped to prepare the address for the removal of Lord Halifax (Sir George Savile*), whom he regarded as chiefly responsible for the defeat of exclusion in the Lords. He attacked Lord Chief Justice Scroggs for his dismissal of the Middlesex grand jury before they could present the Duke of York for recusancy, and was named to the committee of inquiry into the proceedings of the judges. He was among those ordered to draw up the impeachment of Edward Seymour*, who had argued for 'expedients' to avoid exclusion. He supported the resolution that 'all considerable Papists be banished from England', and on 6 Jan. 1681, after reaffirming his belief in the Irish plot, was named to the committee to draw up reasons. On the next day he inquired into why the Lords had produced no alternative to exclusion, and attacked Halifax as an enemy to King and country. Again very active, he had been named to 21 committees and made 23 speeches.[10]

Capel was returned unopposed at the general election of 1681. During the brief Oxford Parliament he was named only to the committee of elections and privileges. On 25 Mar. he asked why the Lords had taken no action on the Commons' bill repealing the Elizabethan law against Protestant dissenters, and rebuked Sir Leoline Jenkins* for his refusal to carry Fitzharris's impeachment to the Lords. He was becoming repetitious, however, and Anchitell Grey* abruptly terminated his account of another speech because it was 'mostly what he had said in the last Parliament'.[11]

After the Rye House Plot, Essex was arrested and cut his throat in the Tower. It was rumoured that a warrant would be issued for Capel, but he hastened to present his duty to the Duke of York and no action was taken against him. Like his sister-in-law, he gave no countenance to the absurd story put about by the Whigs that his brother had been murdered. Richard Coote* believed that in consequence he was 'like to be laid aside' at Tewkesbury, and he did not stand in 1685. During the Revolution he came in to William at Berwick St. Leonard on 3 Dec. 1688 together with his brother-in-law, now 2nd Earl of Clarendon, who described Capel, Harboard and Sir John Hotham* as demanding the cancellation of James II's election writs, 'fearing, as I have reason to believe, that they could not get into the House of Commons'. At the meeting of Members of Charles II's Parliaments he helped to draft the address to the Prince for new writs. This gave him time to secure the Percy interest at Cockermouth through his sister-in-law, Lady Essex, the sister of the 5th Earl of Northumberland.[12]

Capel was a very active Member of the Convention, in which he was named to 61 committees and made more than 50 recorded speeches. On the opening day of the session he urged a speedy debate on the state of the nation, declaring, contrary to the opinion of (Sir) Thomas Clarges*, that 'we are a full House'. He was appointed to the committee to bring in a list of essentials for securing religion, the laws and liberty. On 28 Jan. he urged the House to vote that the throne was vacant, and was named to the committee to prepare reasons for a constitutional conference, which he helped to manage. He was among those appointed to amend the Lords' version of the declaration of rights. As first lord of the Treasury and a Privy Councillor he carried several messages to and from the King, who said privately that 'Sir Henry Capel was weak, but he believed he would not rob him'. In the debate on the Corporations Act he declared that though he would 'live and die for the Church of England', he favoured removing the sacramental Test for officeholders. He chaired the committee reversing Russell's attainder, reporting to the House on 15 Mar. He also chaired the committee for the Lords' bill for the naturalization of Prince George of Denmark, carrying it to the Upper House on 28 Mar. In the debate on the establishment of the succession, on 8 May, Capel opposed the proviso of Charles Godolphin* that nothing in the bill should prejudice the hereditary succession, saying that 'either a foreign minister is in it, or a stratagem from France'. He was not on the committee for the toleration bill, but was named to that appointed to manage the conference with the Lords on the bill. On 1 June he was named to the committee to inquire into the delays in the relief of Londonderry, one object of which was to fasten the responsibility on Halifax, and eventually drove him to resign. Lord Cornbury (Edward Hyde*) found his uncle 'very warm' against Halifax during the debate in the committee of the whole House on the state of the nation on 3 Aug. William told Halifax that 'he did not intend to show any countenance to Sir Henry Capel, and seemed to say that whatever happened he should not continue in his employment'. After the recess Capel was ordered to bring in an account of the charges of the war during the past year. The first Member appointed to prepare the bill for restoring and confirming corporations, he supported the disabling clause, and on 10 Jan. 1690 urged its retention in the bill. On 16 Jan., on the motion to commit the indemnity bill to a committee of the whole House, Capel said that:

If we go so fast on with the indemnity, and leave the pains and penalties [bill] asleep, it will go slowly on. . . . You may incorporate them into the same bill, and I hope we shall be unanimous.

The motion was defeated and the bill of pains and penalties was given its second reading.[13]

When the Convention was dissolved William kept his promise to Halifax by dismissing Capel from the Treasury. Nevertheless he regained his Tewkesbury seat at the general election, and sat as a court Whig both in the Commons and after his elevation to the peerage. He was made lord deputy of Ireland in 1695, and died there on 30 May 1696. He was buried at Little Hadham. His property descended to his nephew, the 2nd Earl of Essex.

Lord Dartmouth described Capel as 'a very weak, formal, conceited man; had no other merit than being a violent party man', and Burnet wrote that he was 'naturally a vain, as well as a weak man . . . set on to anything that gained him applause'. Certainly he became 'a violent party man', though his shift to a passionate espousal of exclusion was shared by many moderates. He spoke frequently and often at great length, and though the quality of his oratory was not outstanding, on several occasions he seems to have influenced the decisions of the House. His stance was essentially negative: he feared Popery and standing armies, and accordingly he opposed those ministers who, he thought, did not share those fears.[14]

[1] R. Somerville, *Duchy of Lancaster Official Lists*, 228; Foxcroft, *Halifax*, ii. 230; *Cal. Treas. Bks.* ix. 627; 1682–3; *CSP Dom.* 1694–5, p. 462. [2] Copinger, *Suff. Manors*, i. 227; *VCH Herts. Fams.* 83–84, 94–95; Keeler, *Long Parl.* 126. [3] *VCH Glos.* viii. 136; *Cal. Cl. SP*, v. 366–9; *CJ*, viii. 685; ix. 87; *Evelyn Diary*, iv. 144. [4] Grey, ii. 204, 218, 324, 394; *CJ*, ix. 286, 295, 307; *Essex Pprs.* (Cam. Soc. n.s. xlvii), 154. [5] *CJ*, ix. 315, 354; *Essex Pprs.* (Cam. Soc. ser. 3, xxiv), 6; Grey, iii. 250, 362; iv. 25; *HMC Hastings*, ii. 383. [6] Grey, iv. 312, 346–7; v. 31, 134, 177, 179, 241–2, 357–8; *CJ*, ix. 408, 424, 428, 477. [7] *CJ*, ix. 524, 534, 559, 562; Grey, vi. 147–8, 281–2, 345–7; *HMC Lords*, i. 85. [8] Grey, vi. 423; vii. 88–89, 95, 135–6, 149, 252–3, 276; *HMC Ormonde*, n.s. iv. 356, 505; *CJ*, ix. 574, 584. [9] *Sidney Diary*, i. 79; *HMC Ormonde*, n.s. iv. 545; v. 238, 312, 346; *HMC 7th Rep.* 476; Burnet, ii. 249. [10] Grey, vii. 360–2, 398–9, 423, 455–7; viii. 13, 55–56, 280–1; *CJ*, ix. 645, 647, 648, 655; *HMC Ormonde*, n.s. v. 302, 328; *Faithful Reg.* 28–29; Jones, *First Whigs*, 139; *Exact Coll. Debates*, 29; *HMC 12th Rep. IX*, 112. [11] *Prot. Intell.* 15 Feb. 1681; Grey, viii. 302, 307, 328. [12] Luttrell, i. 266; *HMC Ormonde*, n.s. vii. 83; Add. 34730, f. 91; *HMC 7th Rep.* 407; *HMC Astley*, 60; *Clarendon Corresp.* ii. 212, 214, 221. [13] Grey, ix. 4–5, 21, 111, 151, 239–40, 520, 521–2; *IHR Bull.* xlix. 252, 259; Foxcroft, ii. 81, 227, 230, 231; R. Morrice, *Entering Bk.* 2, p. 590; *Clarendon Corresp.* ii. 285; Luttrell, i. 565. [14] Burnet ed. Routh, iv. 285; *Burnet Supp.* ed. Foxcroft, 412.

B.D.H.

CAREW, Sir John, 3rd Bt. (1635–92), of Antony, Cornw.

CORNWALL	1660
BODMIN	16 May 1661
LOSTWITHIEL	1679 (Mar.), 1679 (Oct.), 1681
CORNWALL	1689
SALTASH	1690–1 Aug. 1692

bap. 6 Nov. 1635, 3rd but 1st surv. s. of Sir Alexander Carew, 2nd Bt.[†], of Antony by Jane, da. of Robert Rolle of Heanton Satchville, Devon; bro. of Richard Carew*. *m.* (1) bef. 1664, Sarah (*bur.* 28 Mar. 1671), da. of Anthony Hungerford of Farleigh Castle, Som., 2s. *d.v.p.* 2da.; (2) Elizabeth (*d.* 9 Aug. 1679), da. of Richard Norton* of Southwick, Hants, 2da.; (3) lic. July 1681, Mary, da. of Sir William Morice, 1st Bt.*, of Werrington, Devon, 2s. 1da. *suc.* fa. 23 Dec. 1644.[1]
    Commr. for militia, Cornw. 1659, Mar. 1660, assessment Jan. 1660, 1661–80, 1689–90, j.p. Mar. 1660–80, 1687–?*d.*, col. of militia ft. Apr. 1660, lt.-col. by 1679–?80; commr. for oyer and terminer, Western circuit July 1660; dep. lt. Cornw. 1662–80; stannator, Foymore 1673, Penwith and Kerrier 1686; freeman, Portsmouth 1674; commr. for recusants, Cornw. 1675.[2]
    Commr. for drowned lands 1690.[3]

Carew came from a junior branch of the Devonshire family. His ancestors acquired Antony in the 15th century and represented the neighbouring borough of Saltash under Elizabeth. His father, who sat for Cornwall in the Long Parliament, initially opposed the King, but while in command of one of the Plymouth forts in 1643 he attempted to defect to the Cavaliers, and was executed. Carew himself was too young to take any part in the Civil War, but in religion he seems to have been a Presbyterian. He held no offices under the Protectorate, but was appointed to both the militia commissions of 1659 and 1660. He was one of the group of Cornish gentry who met in Truro from 27 to 31 Dec. 1659 and issued a proclamation in favour of a free Parliament.[4]

At the general election of 1660 Carew was involved in a double return at Bodmin, which was eventually decided against him; but he was successful for the county at the top of the poll. Marked as a friend by Lord Wharton, he was not active in the Convention. He was named to four committees, including those on the bills to prevent marital separation and profanity. After another contest at Bodmin in 1661 he was seated on the merits of the return. Wharton again listed him as a friend, and he took no part in the Clarendon Code. He was not active in the Cavalier Parliament, being appointed to only 27 committees, including that to inquire into the shortfall in the revenue in the first session. He defaulted on a call of the House on 13 Feb. 1668, but was excused on production of a medical certificate, and appointed for the first and only time to the committee of elections and privileges in the next session. In 1674 he was elected to represent the Cornish tin miners in negotiations with the Government about the duty and other grievances. Sir Richard Wiseman* included him among the Cornish Presbyterians from whom the Court could expect no support. Shaftesbury marked him 'doubly worthy' in 1677, when he was among those ordered to bring in a bill to repeal the ban on cattle imports. In 1678 he was appointed to the committees for settling the stannary laws, improving the navigability of the Fal river, and enabling the King to make leases of Duchy of Cornwall property. But on 18 Dec. he was again in default on a roll call.[5]

Carew was returned to the Exclusion Parliaments for Lostwithiel together with his brother-in-law Walter Kendall*, the dominant figure on the corporation. Shaftesbury marked him 'worthy' in 1679, but he was again inactive. He was appointed to the elections committee, and to those to report on matters undetermined in the previous Parliament, and to consider a bill establishing fixed times for the coinage of tin. He voted for the first exclusion bill, and was removed from local office. A moderately active Member of the second Exclusion Parliament, he was appointed to five committees, of which the most important was on the bill for religious comprehension. He must have attended the Oxford Parliament, since he was one of the Members ordered to recommend a more suitable place for the House to meet, and he joined the Cornish syndicate for victualling Tangier. He is not known to have stood in 1685; but in the following year, together with the sheriff, Bishop Trelawny of Bristol, and the Roman Catholic Sir John Arundell, he urged the King to summon a convocation of tinners, which they undertook would be favourable to reform of the stannaries. He was himself chosen as one of the stannators, and restored to the commission of the peace. To the questions on the repeal of the Test Act and Penal Laws in 1688 he was reported as answering doubtfully

> till it be debated in Parliament how the religion established by law may be otherwise secured. . . . He will assist and contribute his utmost endeavours to the election of such members of Parliament, and no others, but such as he either knows or believes to be loyal subjects, and who will most faithfully serve his Majesty in all things with security to our said religion.

Despite these answers, the Earl of Bath, as the lord lieutenant, recommended him as court candidate for Saltash.[6]

Carew was returned for the county at the general election of 1689, presumably as a Whig. A moderately active Member of the Convention, he was appointed to 18 committees, and acted as teller for the Whig candidate in the Mitchell by-election case. He was named to the committee on the bill to restore corporations, but not listed as a supporter of the disabling clause. At the general election of 1690 he had to step down to a borough seat. He died on 1 Aug. 1692 and was buried at Antony. His younger son, the fifth baronet, was a Jacobite who represented the county from 1713 till his death over 30 years later.[7]

[1] The Gen. n.s. xxiv. 23; Soc. of Genealogists, Exeter mar. lic. [2] Parl. Intell. 9 Apr. 1660; CSP Dom. 1679–80, p. 61; Add. 6713, ff. 121, 377. [3] Cal. Treas. Bks. ix. 687. [4] Vivian, Vis. Cornw. 143; Keeler, Long Parl. 126–7; M. Coate, Cornw. in Gt. Civil War, 308, 311. [5] Paroch. Hist. Cornw. i. 101; CJ, viii. 87, 250; Cal. Treas. Bks. iv. 227. [6] Cal. Treas. Bks. vii. 148–9; viii. 832. [7] Trans. Plymouth Inst. ix. 293.

M.W.H./P.W.

CAREW, Sir Nicholas (1635–88), of Beddington, Surr.

GATTON 29 Nov. 1664, 1679 (Mar.), 1679 (Oct.), 1681

bap. 30 June 1635, o.s. of Sir Francis Carew[†] of Beddington by Susan, da. of Sir William Romney, Haberdasher, of London. *educ.* Hayes, Mdx. (Dr Thomas Triplett); Lincoln, Oxf. 1651. *m.* 4 May 1656 (with £4,000), Susanna, da. of Sir Justinian Isham, 2nd Bt.*, of Lamport, Northants., 3s. 4da. *suc.* fa. 1649; kntd. by 3 Oct. 1660.[1]

Commr. for militia, Surr. Mar. 1660, j.p. Mar. 1660–70, capt. of militia horse Apr. 1660–at least 1661, dep. lt. c. Aug. 1660–70, commr. for assessment Aug. 1660–80, corporations 1662–3, inquiry, Richmond Park 1671, recusants, Surr. 1675, rebuilding, Southwark 1677.[2]

Carew was the grandson of Sir Nicholas Throckmorton[†], a younger son of the Warwickshire family, who changed his name on succeeding to the Beddington estate in 1611. His father pleaded that he had been obliged as a sworn servant to attend the King during the Civil War, but had not fought; and in view of his debts he was fined only £1,000 for his delinquency, though he was further assessed at £800 by the committee for the advance of money and the fine was still unpaid at his death. Carew became the ward of Carew Ralegh[†], who doubtless instilled in him a distrust of the Stuarts. At his marriage his estate was valued at £2,200 p.a., but land worth £600 p.a. had to be sold soon afterwards. He was involved in Booth's rising in 1659, and his property still lay under sequestration at the Restoration. He accompanied Lord Berkeley, one of the peers sent to The Hague to invite Charles II to return in 1660, and was knighted. On the Fifth Monarchist rising in London in 1661, he was ordered to quarter his militia troop in Southwark 'that so they may be on hand to suppress any insurrection'.[3]

Carew seized the opportunity afforded by the death of William Oldfield* in 1664 without an adult heir to win a seat at Gatton, eight miles from his home. An active Member of the Cavalier Parliament, he was appointed to 188 committees, acted as teller in 23 divisions, and made over 150 recorded speeches. In his first session he was named to the committee for the Brixton canal bill and acted as teller against the bill to make the Wey navigable. But the only measure of political importance with which he was associated during the Clarendon administration was the five mile bill. In 1667, however, he was appointed to the committees of inquiry into the miscarriages of the second Dutch war and the sale of Dunkirk. After helping to consider the bill to banish the fallen minister, he acted with Sir Robert Carr* as teller both for putting the question on the report stage and against the amendments. He later accused some speakers in a debate on miscarriages on 15 Feb. 1668 of fearing that the results of the inquiry would justify the Banishment Act, and was teller for the motion to condemn the delay in ordering Rupert's squadron to rejoin Albemarle in 1666. His proposal to ease the crown's financial difficulties by the sale of cathedral lands evoked no response; but a second expedient, for laying a tax on 'those that have cheated the King', brought him into prominence for the first time. He carried three messages to the public accounts commissioners, and on 11 Apr. was ordered with (Sir) Robert Brooke* to convey the House's thanks for their report on the embezzlement of prize goods. He cited evidence that it was (Sir) William Penn* who had first advised Lord Sandwich (Edward Montagu I*) to break bulk on the rich East India prizes, and helped to prepare and deliver the articles of impeachment. He was among those sent to the King with a message for encouraging the wearing of English manufactures, and acted as teller for the proviso to the conventicles bill requiring the laws against Papists to be put into execution. He was so scornful of the defence offered by Sir George Carteret* over his accounts that he provoked Sir Charles Wheler* into a breach of order. He consistently obstructed supply; but he was equally hostile to measures against nonconformists and was removed from the commission of the peace on the passing of the renewed Conventicles Act. He wanted the lord mayor's commitment of the prominent dissenter Jekyll condemned as illegal and arbitrary. After the assault on Sir John Coventry*he proposed the deferment of all other business until a bill to banish the culprits had passed both Houses:

His reason is, that we may have freedom of speech till this bill be done. Without a better guard than Coventry had, he cannot speak freely to anything else. Perhaps this may be a new way of frightening people, that they may be alarmed and afraid. Hopes you will add more 'to maim', and let some general law be included in this particular occasion, for our safety in future.

On 21 Jan. 1671 he remarked that he hoped never to hear it said in the House that the necessities of the King were above the abilities of the people, and three days later he carried to the Upper House the bill to encourage the export of beer, ale and mum.[4]

When Parliament met again in February 1673, Carew acted as teller against searching for precedents for the issue of election writs by the lord chancellor during the recess without warrant from the Speaker. In the debate on relieving Protestant dissenters, he said that he 'would have the Church of England as strong as you can against the Church of Rome. Would be loath to ask toleration of them. Would take in those that dissent not in matters of doctrine.' He was opposed to a sacramental test for office-holders, which would have excluded many nonconformists; renunciation of transubstantiation should suffice. In the autumn session he was appointed to the committees to devise a general test to 'clear the House of Lords and the Court of Papists', and to draw up the addresses against the Modena marriage and the standing army. The militia, he claimed, was fully as serviceable as the new-raised forces. In the next session he joined in the attack on the remaining members of the Cabal. He proposed that the King should be asked to prevent Lauderdale from returning to England. On 16 Jan. 1674 he told the House that:

Lord Arlington has confessed enough to condemn him. He told you of a statue that might have been erected for him, for maintaining the Triple League. Knows not by whom, unless at Rome. He says he had a hand in the prorogation. The war and the Declaration were only to introduce a standing army, without which Popery could not be secured. Arlington has told you he had a hand in all these. It is fit he should fare no better than others. Would have no root of the Cabal to grow; every little weed will grow.

He helped to draw up the impeachment, and was teller against seeking the concurrence of the Lords to the address for the dismissal of Buckingham. Although not named to the drafting committee, he brought in a bill on 23 Feb. for a test to be taken by Members of both Houses, but the session was suddenly prorogued before the second reading. Thereupon, as one of the 'guilty Commons', he took refuge in the City, where, as the grandson of a Jacobean alderman, he was sure of a welcome.[5]

In the succeeding sessions Carew was associated with all the favourite measures of the Opposition. 'He is no friend to the Court,' wrote his sister-in-law, 'and is apt to speak his mind,' a tendency which was probably reinforced by his sufferings from gout. He was particularly determined to incapacitate Papists from sitting in Parliament; but he was also appointed to committees for recalling British subjects from French service, appropriating the customs revenue to the use of the navy, hindering the growth of Popery, providing for the Protestant education of the royal children, and securing the liberty of the subject. One of his favourite themes was the enrichment of officials at the expense of the landowner, and on 22 Apr. 1675 he acted as teller, with Andrew Marvell*, for a place bill. During the disputes between the Houses in the summer he helped to manage a conference and to prepare reasons for three others. In the autumn session he originated the proposal that the money to be raised for building warships should be paid, not into the Exchequer, but into the chamber of London, a suggestion no doubt prompted by his City connexions. In 1677 he was marked 'thrice worthy' on Shaftesbury's list, and helped to draw up the addresses promising to assist the King in the event of a war with France, and urging the conclusion of alliances. He was also on the committee for the address of 10 May 1678 for the removal of counsellors. He was appointed to the committee to inquire into the Popish Plot, and moved for a warrant from the lord chief justice for the arrest of those accused by Titus Oates. Unmollified by the grant of a licence to erect water-mills on his estate for grinding dyes, he helped to draw up reasons for believing in the plot and excluding the Duke of York from the House of Lords. In the debate on disbanding the army on 27 Nov. he told the House: 'I will not say this army was raised for this plot, but the more loyal this army is, the more surely they might take away the King's life and place the crown on his successor.' He was among those ordered to prepare instructions for the disbandment commissioners and the address on the dangers confronting the nation. When Ralph Montagu* announced that he had letters of great consequence to produce, Carew exclaimed:

> Let the papers in Montagu's hands be brought now, and if they concern any man, under his Majesty himself, I would prosecute the thing now. I know not whether we shall be here to-morrow morning or no; it may be we shall all be clapped up by to-morrow.

When the letters were read, he was among those ordered to prepare Danby's impeachment.[6]

Carew was re-elected to the Exclusion Parliaments, though in February 1679 he probably had to overcome the Oldfield interest, now exercised by Sir John Thompson*. Shaftesbury marked him 'worthy', but he was only moderately active in the first Exclusion Parliament, with ten committee appointments and 13 speeches. He proposed the impeachment of the Queen's physician. He said on 11 May: 'I shall be glad to be shown any bands and fetters that a prince, when he comes to the crown, shall not easily break'. One of the 'hot and violent conductors', he helped to draft the exclusion bill, and voted for the second reading. He and his associates, according to Danby, were much praised 'for their great earnestness to have a successor named'. He was again moderately active in the second Exclusion Parliament, in which he was named to seven committees and made 25 speeches. He considered that Lord Halifax (Sir George Savile*) should be removed from Court because he would change his religion when Popery came in, and he was among those appointed to draft an address on the dangerous state of the kingdom. When the charges against Edward Seymour* were questioned he said:

> If you put so great a discouragement upon Members that bring in impeachments against great men, what use are you of, unless to give money? We know the condition of the nation; if we go this way to work, we give up all. You must mistrust the honour and wisdom of your Members, that they bring in this charge maliciously, if you refer it to a committee, and rest not upon their undertaking to make it good.

Though he differed from William Sacheverell* in believing that to cure Popery was to cure all, he had no faith in the expedients proposed after the Lords had rejected the second exclusion bill:

> These bills will signify nothing, unless you can remove your popish successor and your popish interest. These bills will not reach your Papists in masquerade, who will certainly continue as long as there is a popish successor, and make your banishing bill, and your association bill too, as ineffectual as white paper. Let such as I could name to you have the command of the sea-ports ... and when the present heat is over, let the Papists come back when they will, they will have no cause to doubt having a kind reception. For you must not expect to have plain rustic country gentlemen in such commands, but well-bred courtiers, and some good, easy, credulous gentlemen, that will soon be persuaded there is no danger in Popery; and then of what use will your banishing or association bill be? As long as the Duke hath so many friends at Court (between whose interest and Popery I cannot hear there is any distinction), I think no laws that we can make against Popery will do us any good, because all the laws we have already have done us none.

Although Carew's logic was not generally accepted, he was appointed to the committee to draw up the address insisting on exclusion. On the comprehension bill he was 'for uniting, and parting with ceremonies, but never will part with the liturgy of the Church, nor a reverend habit'. In the Oxford Parliament he was appointed only to the elections committee. On 24 Mar. 1681 he proposed the reintroduction of the exclusion bill, 'the same bill which passed the last Parliament'. On the proposal for a regency, he inquired what would happen if the Duke would not submit to it; would not those who opposed him be traitors in law?[7]

Carew did not stand in 1685, and in 1687 was included among the eminent Parliament men in opposition to James II. He died on 9 Jan. 1688 and was buried at Beddington. He seems to have been a crotchety but honest politician. Almost the only government action which he went on record as approving was the withdrawal of the Declaration of Indulgence in 1673. Unlike William Harbord* he did not allow gout to control his temper, or appetite for office his policy. His son did not survive him long, but his grandson sat for Haslemere, and later for the county, as an independent Whig.[8]

[1] Manning and Bray, Surr. ii. 523; Vis. London (Harl. Soc. xvii), 212; Vis. Northants. (Harl. Soc. lxxxvii), 252; Duppa-Isham Corresp. (Northants. Rec. Soc. xvii), 177; Q. Sess. Recs. (Surr. Rec. Soc. xxxv), 33. [2] Duppa-Isham Corresp. 183; Parl. Intell. 23 Apr. 1660; Add. 6167, f. 207; Cal. Treas. Bks. iii. 1161. [3] VCH Surr. iv. 170; Cal. Comm. Comp. 841, 3253; Cal. Comm. Adv. Money, 335; Grey, iii. 94; Duppa-Isham Corresp. 121; Add. 29597, f. 21. [4] CJ, viii. 602; ix. 40, 42, 78, 80, 87, 90; Grey, i. 75, 108, 167, 187, 299, 336, 364; Milward, 223; Dering, 45, 47. [5] CJ, ix. 248, 303; Grey, ii. 38, 86, 197, 220, 237, 281; Williamson Letters (Cam. Soc. n.s. ix), 157. [6] Northants. RO, IC982a; Grey, i. 315; vi. 116, 175, 279, 346; Bulstrode, 316; CSP Dom. 1678, p. 510. [7] Hatton Corresp. (Cam. Soc. n.s. xxii), 174; Grey, vii. 74, 238; viii. 22, 88, 100, 295, 316; HMC Ormonde, n.s. v. 561; Browning, Danby, ii. 83; Exact Coll. Debates, 166. [8] Manning and Bray, ii. 527; Grey, ii. 92; iii. 64; vi. 175; vii. 337.

J.S.C.

CAREW, Richard (1641–91), of Abertanat, Salop.

CALLINGTON   1679 (Oct.), 1681
SALTASH   1690–Sept. 1691

bap. 21 Apr. 1641, 6th but 4th surv. s. of Sir Alexander Carew, 2nd Bt.[†], of Antony, Cornw., and bro. of Sir John Carew, 3rd Bt.* m. lic. 31 July 1674, Penelope, da. of Rice Tanat of Abertanat, and coh. to her bro. Owen, s.p.[1]

Commr. for assessment, Salop 1679–80, Devon and Salop 1689–d.; sub-commr. for prizes, Plymouth ?1689–d.[2]

Carew received a portion of £500 under his father's will, enough to cover his premium as apprentice to a Levant merchant and stock in trade besides. He went out to Smyrna in 1661, joining two of his brothers who both died there. He probably returned to England in 1673, and in the following year married the sister-in-law of Sidney Godolphin II*. Although an uncle of the same name survived until 1685 or 1686 it was probably Carew who unsuccessfully contested Saltash at the first general election of 1679 on the family interest. His petition was referred to the committee of elections and privileges, but never reported. He or his uncle sat for Callington in the second and third

Exclusion Parliaments on the Rolle interest. Probably a supporter of exclusion like his brother, he was not appointed to any committees and made no recorded speeches in either Parliament. Although a placeman after the Revolution he was listed among the Opposition in 1690. He was buried at Antony on 18 Sept. 1691. He bequeathed his Shropshire property to his brother's family.[3]

[1] The Gen. n.s. xxiv. 23–24; xxv. 154; Mont. Colls. xiii. 119. [2] Cal. Treas. Bks. ix. 1307. [3] Information from Miss Sonia P. Anderson; Courtney, Parl. Rep. Cornw. 151, 273; HMC Downshire, i. 387; PCC 5 Fane.

P.W.

CAREW, Thomas I (1624–81), of the Inner Temple and Barley, nr. Exeter, Devon.

CALLINGTON   1659
MITCHELL   6 May 1660
EXETER   1681

bap. 19 July 1624, 4th but 3rd surv. s. of Sir Richard Carew, 1st Bt.[†], of Antony, Cornw., being 2nd surv. s. by 2nd w. Grace, da. of Robert Rolle of Heanton Satchville, Devon; bro. of John Carew[†] and half-bro. of Sir Alexander Carew, 2nd Bt.[†] educ. I. Temple 1641, called 1651. m. lic. 26 Aug. 1661, Elizabeth (d. 23 Nov. 1677), da. of John Cupper, merchant, of Barley, 5s. (1 d.v.p.) 3da. Kntd. 21 July 1671.[1]

J.p. Cornw. Mar. 1660–1, Devon 1662–d., Tiverton 1680–d.; commr. for militia, Cornw. Mar. 1660, assessment, Devon Aug. 1660–80, Cornw. 1664–80, Exeter 1673–80; bencher, I. Temple 1667; commr. for recusants, Devon 1675, dep. lt. 1676–d.; recorder, Exeter 1676–d.[2]

Carew, a professional lawyer, was too young to take an active part in the Civil War like his elder brothers, though he admitted to 'being once misled in the times of confusion', presumably referring to his membership of Richard Cromwell's Parliament. 'A worthy, loyal gentleman', he was presented to George Monck*, his kinsman, on his arrival in London in 1660, and signed the declaration of the King's party in Devon. He stood for Mitchell at the general election and was involved in a double return. Seated in the Convention as a court supporter on the merits of the return, he was named only to the committee of elections and privileges. He made no attempt to safeguard his interests when his brother was attainted as a regicide, 'choosing rather to cast himself upon your Majesty's royal favour'. He was rewarded with the grant of the forfeited properties of Bowhill and Higher Barley, and he acquired further property in the Exeter neighbourhood by marriage. Bishop Sparrow wrote in 1671:

The chief man in this country for skill and courage and diligence, and who is the oracle of the county, by whom this city is kept in good order, is Mr Thomas Carew, barrister, a man neither covetous nor ambitious, one who professes himself bound to endeavour what he can to make satisfaction for being once misled in the times of confusion. He is our true friend in all our concerns, and deserves encouragement.

On behalf of the corporation he negotiated with the chapter over the bill to unite Exeter parishes in 1673, and a timely loan of £500 for the extension to the ship canal in March 1676 cannot be dissociated from his election as recorder two months later. He was ordered to examine at Plymouth, the imprisoned General John Lambert† who was suspected of complicity in the Popish Plot. As recorder of Exeter, he was 'prevailed upon by the loyal party to stand' at short notice at the first general election of 1679, but he was defeated by the candidates of 'the fanatic party'. He was returned as an opponent of exclusion in 1681, but was appointed to no committees and made no speeches in the Oxford Parliament. He died on 25 July 1681 and was buried at St. Thomas near Exeter. His son Thomas sat for Saltash as a Tory from 1701 to 1705.[3]

[1] The Gen. n.s. xxv. 155; Vivian, Vis. Devon, 142; Soc. of Genealogists, Exeter mar. lic.; PCC 300 Wootton. [2] Trans. Devon Assoc. lxi. 213. [3] SP29/36/68; HMC Popham, 213; Exeter corp. act bk. II, ff. 128, 159, 162; CSP Dom. 1678, pp. 511–12; HMC Montagu, 174, 175; C. Worthy, Suburbs of Exeter, 163; W. P. Courtney, Parl. Rep. Cornw. 272; Devon and Cornw. N. and Q. xxii. 48.

M.W.H./J.S.C.

CAREW, Thomas II (1632–73), of Haccombe, Devon.

TIVERTON 1661–Sept. 1673

bap. 21 June 1632, 1st s. of Thomas Carew of Haccombe by Anne, da. of Thomas Clifford, DD, of Ugbrooke, Chudleigh. educ. M. Temple, entered 1649; Exeter, Oxf. 1650, BA 1653, MA 1655. m. (1) c.1650, Elizabeth, da. and coh. of Sir Henry Carew of Bickleigh, 3s (2 d.v.p.) 3da.; (2) lic. 20 June 1672, Martha, da. and coh. of Arthur Duck†, DCL, of South Cadbury, Som., wid. of Nicholas Duck of Mount Radford, nr. Exeter, Devon, 1da. suc. fa. 1656; cr. Bt. 2 Aug. 1661.[1]
J.p. Devon Mar. 1660–d., commr. for militia Mar. 1660, capt. of militia horse Apr. 1660, commr. for assessment 1661–d., oyer and terminer, Exeter 1664, inquiry into Newfoundland govt. 1667; dep. lt. Devon 1670–d.; sub-commr. of prizes, Plymouth 1672–d.[2]
Gent. of the privy chamber 1668–d.[3]

Carew's ancestors settled in Devon about the beginning of the 14th century. Other branches produced knights of the shire in Tudor times, but the Haccombe family was less prominent. Carew's father took no part in public life, and he may have owed his return for Tiverton at the general election of 1661 to his father-in-law, the last of the elder branch of the family, whose imposing residence lay

some four miles away. An inactive Member of the Cavalier Parliament, Carew was appointed to 23 committees, the most important being to consider restraints on juries in 1668 and to receive information about conventicles in the following year. His court appointment of 1668 reflects the rise to power of his cousin Thomas Clifford*, who was no doubt also responsible for his excise pension of £400. But he was not listed as a court supporter in 1669–71. During the second Dutch war he was given a post in the prize office, and he was also discharged the £1,500 for which he stood liable when a Devonshire tax-collector absconded. Nevertheless, according to his nuncupative will dated 13 Sept. 1673 he left a personal estate of only £480, half of it arrears of salary as sub-commissioner of prizes, and debts over £1,000. One creditor came to the house where he died on the day of the funeral 'and made some disturbances to hinder the corpse from being carried out', until the young heir agreed to renew the bond. Carew was the only member of the Haccombe branch of his family to sit in Parliament.[4]

[1] Trans. Devon Assoc. lvii. 333. [2] Parl. Intell. 7 May 1660; APC Col. i. 433; C6/35/47. [3] Carlisle, Privy Chamber, 181. [4] Trans. Devon Assoc. lvi. 313; J. Prince, Worthies of Devon, 164; Lysons, Devon, 45; Browning, Danby, i. 170; Letters to Williamson (Cam. Soc. ix), 54; C6/35/47.

J.P.F.

CAREY, Anthony, 5th Visct. Falkland [S] (1656–94), of Great Tew, Oxon.

OXFORDSHIRE	1685
GREAT MARLOW	1689
GREAT BEDWYN	1690–24 May 1694

b. 15 Feb. 1656, o.s. of Henry Carey*, 4th Visct. Falkland. educ. Winchester 1668; Christ Church, Oxf. 1672. m. 1681, Rebecca (d. 30 Sept. 1709), da. of Sir Rowland Lytton* of Knebworth, Herts., 1da. suc. fa. 2 Apr. 1663.[1]
Treas. of the navy 1681–9; groom of the stole to Prince George 1687–90; ld. of the Admiralty 1691–3, first ld. 1693–d.; PC 17 Mar. 1692–d.[2]
Freeman, Portsmouth 1682; j.p. Essex, Hants, Kent, Mdx., Suff., Surr., Suss. and Westminster 1687–?d., Oxon. ?Mar. 1688–d., Bucks. 1689–d.; dep. lt. Oxon. 1685–d., Bucks. 1689–d.; commr. for assessment, Bucks. and Oxon. 1689–90, Kent and Westminster 1690.[3]

Although Clarendon described Falkland as having 'nothing left to keep him' on his father's death, his marriage to 'a great fortune' enabled him to purchase for £15,000 the lucrative post of treasurer of the navy. 'Too youthful for so difficult a trust', it was suspected that he would only draw the salary of £500 p.a., while Edward Seymour* continued to do the work and rake in the perquisites. Evelyn, however, a friend of the family, called him 'a pretty, brisk, understanding, industrious young gentleman', though admitting that he was 'faulty' in his youth. He was not on the Oxfordshire commission of the peace when returned for the county in 1685. Although a Tory he later claimed that he had 'never followed the orders of the Court in King James's time, nor gave my consent to bring a person into that Parliament, though I was promised I should be a peer of England'. A very active Member of James II's Parliament, he was appointed to 22 committees, including that to inspect the disbandment accounts. In the second session he voted against the employment of Roman Catholic officers, and was appointed to the committee for the address. His financial position further improved when he took a share in the syndicate formed by the 2nd Duke of Albemarle (Christopher Monck*) to recover the wreck of a Spanish treasure-ship, which turned out to be highly profitable, and he acquired an interest at Great Marlow by purchasing the manor from (Sir) Humphrey Winch*. Presumably he gave satisfaction on the repeal of the Test Act and Penal Laws, since he succeeded the Earl of Scarsdale (Robert Leke*) in Prince George's household in 1687, and was confirmed as deputy lieutenant in February 1688.⁴

Falkland was returned to the Convention for Marlow, and was again a very active Member, serving on 64 committees, acting twice as teller, and making 17 recorded speeches. In an early debate he spoke on behalf of the Admiralty, and was clearly prepared to accept the Revolution. On 29 Jan. 1689 he moved for a declaration of rights before the throne was filled:

> It concerns us to take such care, that, as the Prince of Orange has secured us from Popery, we may secure ourselves from arbitrary government. The Prince's declaration is for a lasting foundation of the Government. . . . Before the question be put, who shall be set upon the throne, I would consider what powers we ought to give the Crown to satisfy them that sent us hither. We have had a Prince that did dispense with our laws, and I hope we shall never leave that doubtful. The King set up an ecclesiastical court, as he was supreme head of the Church, and acted against law, and made himself head of the charters. Therefore, before you fill the throne, I would have you resolve what power you will give the King and what not.

He was then appointed to the committee to draw up the declaration. Three days later he was one of five Members deputed to convey the thanks of the House to the army and navy officers for their steady support of Protestantism and their part in delivering the nation from Popery. On 2 Feb. he spoke in the debate in favour of the view that James had abdicated and the throne was vacant, saying that 'if this vote be grounded merely upon the King's leaving the kingdom, he may come again and resume the Government'. Shortly after this he was appointed to committees to prepare reasons and to manage a conference on the state of the throne, and to amend the Lords' resolution declaring William and Mary King and Queen. On 12 Feb. Falkland returned to the Lords their amendments to the declaration of rights. On 20 Feb. he spoke in favour of clarifying the position of the Convention so that the urgent problems outlined in the King's speech might be speedily dealt with:

> If we have not the power of a Parliament, we can go upon nothing. There are precedents to justify the Lords' bill that they have sent us. We have great works upon our hands; as that of the relief of Ireland, and to assist our allies etc., and the nation is in an unsettled condition. The Lords' bill is a foundation for us to build upon, and I move that we follow the Lords' example.

He was appointed to the committee for the declaratory bill. In further speeches of 26 Feb. he emphasized the importance of settling affairs at home before the wider issues requiring substantial financial aid could be dealt with, and to clear any doubts regarding royal revenue he believed that this should be settled quickly by Act of Parliament. Other important committees on which he served during the early weeks of the Convention were those to draw up an address for assisting the King in defence of the Protestant religion, to suspend habeas corpus, to prepare a bill for the abolition of the hearth-tax and to inquire into the authors and advisers of grievances. In April he served on committees to consider lack of confidence in government credit and to draw up an address for the declaration of war against France. He may have gone over to the Opposition when he was displaced as treasurer of the navy in April, for William complained to Halifax that he both spoke and voted against supply. On 8 May he spoke on the necessity for strengthening the Protestant succession by ensuring that a proviso to the bill of succession effectively barred any heirs of James II's son. He was appointed to the committees to examine the Journals relating to the Popish Plot and to draw up an address for permission to inspect the Privy Council registers and the books of the Irish committee.⁵

Falkland was scarcely less active in the second session, in which his committees included those to report on bills depending, to inquire into the miscarriages of the war, and to consider the bill for punishing mutiny and desertion. He acted as teller on 20 Nov. 1689 against a second reading of the bill to reverse the attainder of Thomas Walcot*, and in December sat on the committee for the bill to restore corporations. He spoke against the disabling clause on 10 Jan. 1690, declaring:

This clause is a contradiction of the whole bill. This clause takes away the rights of those you would save. The clause takes away the rights that were restored by the Prince of Orange's circulary letters. It is dangerous now the King is going out of the kingdom to discontent such a body of people. I am more afraid of the consequence of this now people are generally dissatisfied. This bill is a restoring of corporations, and not a bill of pains and penalties. This clause is improper for this bill, and for the present circumstances of affairs, and I would have it rejected.

On the same day he acted as teller against a Whig attempt to make the clause acceptable by modifying its terms, and, when the clause was finally rejected, carried the bill to the Lords. On the question of indemnity, he declared on 16 Jan.:

It is absolutely necessary to express whom you will except before you inflict pains and penalties. If you design such a bill to ease the minds of the subjects, the sooner you do it, the sooner you will ease them. If anything makes people against the Government, it is the uncertainty of passing this bill.

In the last week of the Convention he clashed with the Whigs William Williams* and John Arnold*, and was appointed to the committee on the bill for restoring university charters. At the general election he transferred to Great Bedwyn, and was appointed to the Admiralty board in the following year. Evelyn considered him 'very much reclaimed' from his former faults; but he died of smallpox on 24 May 1694 and was buried in Westminster Abbey. His heir was a Jacobite, and the next member of the family to enter Parliament was Lucius Ferdinand Cary, MP for Bridport 1774–80.[6]

[1] Her. and Gen. iii. 40; Cal. Treas. Bks. x. 838. [2] Luttrell, ii. 51. [3] R. East, Portsmouth Recs. 366. [4] Bodl. Carte 47, f. 48; 222, f. 288; HMC Ormonde, n.s. vi. 51; Evelyn Diary, v. 182; Grey, ix. 500; Cal. Treas. Bks. viii. 1426, 2042–3; Ellis Corresp. ii. 294–6; Add. 28875, f. 426; VCH Bucks. iii. 71. [5] Grey, ix. 26, 29–30, 33, 48, 92, 241; CJ, x. 20; Hatton Corresp. (Cam. Soc. n.s. xxiii), 130; Foxcroft, Halifax, ii. 238. [6] Grey, ix. 512, 522; Evelyn Diary, v. 182; Her. and Gen. iii. 40.

L.N./G.J.

CAREY, Henry, 4th Visct. Falkland [S] (1634–63), of Great Tew, Oxon.

OXFORDSHIRE	7 Feb. 1659
OXFORD	1660
OXFORDSHIRE	1661–2 Apr. 1663

bap. 21 Nov. 1634, 2nd s. of Lucius Carey†, 2nd Visct. Falkland [S], sec. of state 1642–3, by Lettice, da. of Sir Richard Morison† of Tooley Park, Leics. educ. Hayes, Mdx. (Dr Thomas Triplett); travelled abroad (France) 1650. m. 14 Apr. 1653, Rachel (d. 24 Feb. 1718), da. of Anthony Hungerford† of Blackbourton, Oxon., 1s. suc. bro. 17 Sept. 1649.[1]

J.p. Oxon. Mar. 1660–d., Oxford Aug. 1660–d.; freeman, Oxford Mar. 1660; commr. for militia, Oxon. Mar. 1660, oyer and terminer, Mdx. and Oxf. circuit July 1660–d.; ld. lt. Oxon. July 1660–d.; commr. for assessment, Oxon. and Oxford Aug. 1660–d.; custos rot. Oxon. Dec. 1660–d., commr. for loyal and indigent officers 1662.[2]

Col. of horse, June–Dec. 1660; col. of ft., Dunkirk garrison 1661–2; capt. of horse [I] 1662–d.[3]

Gent. of privy chamber June 1660–d.; PC [I] 1662–d.[4]

MP [I] 1662–d.

Lord Falkland came from a widespread west country family established in Somerset by the 12th century, which first sent Members to Parliament in 1362. His father, the second Viscount, was the first of the family to settle in Oxfordshire, making Great Tew the centre of the brilliant intellectual circle described by Clarendon. Although he at first concurred in the Long Parliament's attempts to curb royal power, he supported the Court over the root and branch bill. He was appointed secretary of state, but his hatred of the war soon led him to a death 'scarcely distinguishable from suicide'. Although himself an ardent Royalist, who had been secretly commissioned as colonel of horse with John Talbot* in 1654, Falkland sat for the county in Richard Cromwell's Parliament, when he was described as 'the most active young man in the House'. After the dissolution he was engaged in plans for a royalist rising, but on 12 Aug. 1659 he was arrested and sent to the Tower, where he remained till November. In the following February he led those who presented the Oxfordshire address for a free Parliament.[5]

Falkland's parliamentary service excluded him from the scope of the Long Parliament ordinance, and at the general election of 1660 he was returned for Arundel probably on the Howard interest, as well as for Oxford, for which he chose to sit. Lord Wharton listed him as a friend to be managed by Thomas Wenman*, Lord Wenman. A moderately active Member, he served on 28 committees, acted as teller five times and made 17 recorded speeches from a high Anglican and Cavalier viewpoint. On 1 May he helped manage a conference on the great affairs of the kingdom, and sat on the committee to consider legal forms of the Restoration. Shortly after, he was appointed to committees to prepare the bill for abolishing the court of wards and to consider land purchases. On 7 May, he was listed second of the 12 Members chosen to attend the King in Holland. On his return he delivered to the House a letter sent by the King from Canterbury, and was given a regiment of horse. On 2 June he acted as teller for hearing accounts under the indemnity bill for the Civil War period as well as the Interregnum. With regard to individual offenders, he opposed the limited penalty proposed for Francis Lascelles*, and wished to render William Sydenham† and John Pyne† liable to any punishment short of death. He spoke in favour of excluding from the House any Members who had sat in the High Court of Justice, and against the proviso to impose the oaths of allegiance and supremacy on the Roman Catholics. He favoured the motion of (Sir) Allen Brodrick* to refer doctrinal matters to a national synod. Falkland served on the committee to inquire into the state of the queen mother's jointure lands on the second reading of the bill to confirm land purchases, and on 9 July proposed that her position should be considered by an ad hoc committee. On 1 Aug. he acted as teller for the first reading of the bill brought in by William Prynne* appointing commissioners to take accounts. Next day he proposed reducing the interest rate to six per cent. He brought in a bill to this effect on 4 Aug. and was appointed to the committee. He defended Sir Arthur Hesilrige† and was sent to the Lords on 24 Aug. to desire a free conference on the regicides who had surrendered themselves on the proclamation. Early in the next month he served on the committee for the disbandment bill.[6]

In the second session Falkland was appointed to the committees for the attainder bill and for a supplementary poll bill. He remarked that 'the settling of the militia heretofore occasioned all their last mischief', and advised a second reading of the bill introduced by Richard Knightley*. He agreed with the Worcester House declaration for modified episcopacy, but opposed the bill to give 'liberty to tender consciences'. He spoke for restoring the dukedom of Norfolk, on the grounds that the head of the Howard family was 'as powerful to do mischief as an earl or a duke'. In the debate on William Drake's seditious pamphlet *The Long Parliament Revived*, Falkland favoured condemning Drake first, and then leaving him to the King's mercy. He was deputed to carry up the articles of impeachment on 4 Dec. As further evidence of his unyielding royalist attitude, on 7 Dec. he moved that estates acquired during the Civil War as well as those during the Interregnum should be forfeit.[7]

Falkland moved up to the county seat in 1661, with his satellite Sir Anthony Cope*. He was a very active Member in the opening sessions of the Cavalier Parliament, serving on 36 committees. He sat on the committee for the security bill, and on 17 May 1661 was teller for the resolution to burn the Covenant, which he carried to the Lords. Other committees included those for settling the claims of the Marquess of Winchester out of the estate of

Robert Wallop*, for improving the revenue and for the corporations bill. On 25 June he was given leave to go to his regiment at Dunkirk, but he had returned temporarily by 26 July, when the two Houses were at issue over the corporations bill. He proposed the printing of a remonstrance to show their reasons for differing with the Lords, but the motion was badly received. He helped manage a conference on the regicides bill on 27 July and delivered a petition to the King recommending favourable consideration of Lord Winchester's case. He also helped to inspect the accounts of disbandment commissioners and to bring in the militia bill. In 1662 he twice carried messages to the King, once to thank him for arresting Wither for libelling the House, and again with Henry Coventry* to ask that the money collected for releasing English slaves in North Africa should be used solely for that purpose. If a report of Morrice's is to be believed, Falkland made a great stir during the debate on the uniformity bill by declaring that 'Popery comes in with such an evil torrent upon us that, upon my conscience, we that have all in land shall not have time left us to consult for our state'. A proposal was made to call him to the bar, but it was thought wise not to draw more attention to a Member 'that can speak excellently well and cares for no man'. But he was not appointed to the committee and was said to be 'all the time after under a cloud'. Falkland was less active in the second session, due to his military commitments. Before his regiment at Dunkirk was disbanded, he was appointed captain of a troop of horse in Ireland, probably as compensation. 'I would think myself happier to oblige his father's son,' wrote Clarendon, 'than in compassing anything for my own.' He was also elected to the Irish Parliament, in which he proved a 'hornet' to the Opposition. But his friends in England were assured that he had grown grave as well as severe. Described as 'a most violent, indefatigable promoter of the Act of Uniformity', he was appointed on his return to the committees to consider its defects and to bring in a bill against the growth of Popery. He died on 2 Apr. 1663 and was buried at Great Tew. 'His heart was broke,' according to Clarendon, 'with the pure despair of his fortune. . . . When a little age had worn away some heats and passions, he would have proved an extraordinary man.'[8]

[1] *Her. and Gen.* iii. 40; *Evelyn Diary*, iii. 168; *Verney Mems.* i. 467. [2] *Oxford Council Acts* (Oxf. Hist. Soc. xcv), 254. [3] *HMC Ormonde*, i. 241. [4] Carlisle, *Privy Chamber*, 170. [5] Add. 10115, f. 97; *Cal. Cl. SP*, iv. 177; *CSP Dom. 1659-60*, pp. 103, 157, 241, 242, 361. [6] *CJ*, viii. 47, 86; Bowman diary, ff. 5, 6, 53v, 65v, 68v, 111, 115v; *Old Parl. Hist.* xxii. 444. [7] *Old Parl. Hist.* xxiii. 15, 20, 28, 36, 43; *CJ*, viii. 201. [8] *Conway Letters*, 188; *CJ*, viii. 315,

396, 398; R. Morrice, Entering Bk. 1, p. 112; Bodl. Carte 47, ff. 10, 44; HMC 15th Rep. VII, 165.

M.W.H./L.N./G.J.

CAREY (CARY), John (1612–85), of Stanwell, Mdx.

NEW WINDSOR   1679 (Oct.)–4 Nov. 1680

bap. 23 Dec. 1612, 1st s. of Sir Philip Cary† of Hunslet, Yorks. and Silver Street, London by Elizabeth, da. of Richard Bland of Carleton, Rothwell, Yorks. *educ.* St. John's, Oxf. 1627. *m.* (1) Mary (*bur.* 29 Dec. 1657), da. and coh. of Sir Charles Montagu† of Cranford, Essex, wid. of Edward Baesh† of Stanstead Bury, Herts., *s.p.*; (2) Catherine (*bur.* 1 Sept. 1673), *s.p. suc.* gt-uncle in Stanwell estate 1622, fa. 1631.[1]

Master of the buckhounds to the Prince of Wales 1638–bef. 1642, (as King) June 1660–85; gent. of the privy chamber ?1641–6, 1681–5.[2]

Keeper of Marylebone Park, Mdx. 1631–42, j.p. Mdx. July 1660–d., dep. lt. c. Aug. 1660–d., commr. for assessment 1661–3, 1673–4; alderman, New Windsor 1685–d.[3]

Carey's father, a younger brother of the 1st Viscount Falkland, sat for Woodstock in four early Stuart Parliaments. Carey was granted the reversion of the keepership of Marylebone Park in 1623, though he seems to have lost this before the Civil War. But he became master of the Prince of Wales's buckhounds, a post worth £120 p.a., and joined the King at Oxford in 1642. He was never in arms, and in 1649 compounded for his delinquency at £600 on the Oxford articles. His particular showed an income of £1,677 p.a. but debts of over £13,000. He made good his claim to a moiety of Stanwell in the following year, and paid a further £600 fine. After the Restoration his appointment as master of the buckhounds was confirmed at an increased salary 'in consideration of many years of service', and he received compensation for loss of Marylebone Park. In 1678, with the partition of the Knyvett estates, he became sole owner of Stanwell.[4]

Carey stood for Windsor, six miles from his home, as a court candidate in the second election of 1679. He was involved in a double return; but he was unseated without leaving any trace on the records of the second Exclusion Parliament and is unlikely to have stood again. He died on 18 Oct. 1685 and was buried at Stanwell. This estate, and other lands in Kent and Lincolnshire worth £2,000 p.a. in all, eventually passed by chancery decree to the 6th Lord Falkland.[5]

[1] *The Gen.* (n.s.) xxiii. 202–3; *VCH Mdx.* iii. 37. [2] *CSP Dom.* 1638–9, p. 56; 1660–1, pp. 75, 239; Lysons, *Environs*, iii. 246; *Cal. Treas. Bks.* i. 616; LC3/1; Carlisle, *Privy Chamber*, 194. [3] *CSP Dom.* 1685, p. 69. [4] F. Harrison, *Devon Carys*, ii. 403; *CSP Dom.* 1619–23, p. 515; 1625–6, p. 582; 1667, p. 408; *Cal. Comm. Comp.* 1402–3; *Cal. Treas. Bks.* ii. 546; iii. 881; *VCH Mdx.* iii. 37. [5] *CJ,*

ix. 638, 646; *HMC Lords*, iii. 92–95; *Her. and Gen.* iii. 133–4.

L.N./G.J.

CARR, Sir Ralph (1634–1710), of Newcastle-upon-Tyne, Northumb. and Coken, Houghton-le-Spring, co. Dur.

NEWCASTLE-UPON-TYNE   1679 (Oct.), 1681, 1689, 1690

b. 14 July 1634, 1st s. of William Carr, merchant, of Newcastle by Jane, da. and coh. of Ralph Cock, merchant, of Newcastle. *educ.* St. John's, Camb. 1652; G. Inn 1654. *m.* (1) Jane (*d.* 20 Aug. 1667), da. of Sir Francis Anderson* of Newcastle, 1s. *d.v.p.* 2da.; (2) Isabella, da. of Hon. James Darcy* of Sedbury Park, Yorks., 1s. *d.v.p. suc.* fa. 1660; *kntd.* 26 June 1676.[1]

Freeman, Newcastle 1660; commr. for assessment, Newcastle Aug. 1660–1, 1663–4, 1677–80, co. Dur. 1664–79, co. Dur. and Newcastle 1689–90; member, hostmen's co., Newcastle 1663; j.p. co. Dur. 1664–Apr. 1688, Oct. 1688–d., Durham 1698; alderman, Newcastle by 1677–87, Oct. 1688–d., mayor 1677–8, 1693–4, 1705–6; commr. for recusants, co. Dur. 1675; dep. lt. Newcastle by 1678–Feb. 1688, Oct. 1688–d., commr. for carriage of coals 1679, capt. of militia ft. to Feb. 1688.[2]

Carr's family had been merchants in Newcastle since the 15th century, first representing the town in 1491. Carr's father, although one of the ruling oligarchy in the town, was probably a parliamentary sympathizer in the Civil War. He served on the common council during the Interregnum, and was appointed to the assessment committee in 1652 and the militia committee in March 1660, shortly before his death. Carr himself bought an estate in Durham from a cousin in 1665, adding the valuable mineral rights six years later. He supported the enfranchisement of the bishopric, but continued to reside chiefly in Newcastle, where he was particularly diligent in the militia, and was the natural successor to his first wife's father as leader of the court party on the corporation. He was returned for the borough to the second and third Exclusion Parliaments, but left no trace on their records, and as one of the Durham grand jury, together with (Sir) William Bowes* and Sir Ralph Cole*, signed the loyal address in 1681 approving their dissolution. He apparently did not stand in 1685, and was removed from the Newcastle corporation in 1687. To the lord lieutenant's questions he replied bluntly:

I am not of the opinion for taking away the Penal Laws and the Test. . . . I would not be thought so ill a man or deserve such a censure as to be an accessory to or vote for any person to do an act which I cannot in my judgment approve of. . . . When I was in authority, I used all the mildness imaginable to those which differed from me in judgment, always thinking that conscience neither ought nor could be forced. I intend always to live in obedience to the established laws of the nation and in loyalty to my King. These, my lord, are my thoughts, and I the rather deliver them so plainly and without ambiguity because I think in a thing of this nature every one ought to act in the sun.[3]

Carr was returned unopposed at the general election of 1689. According to Anthony Rowe* he voted to agree with the Lords that the throne was not vacant. But he was not active in the Convention. His six committees included that on the bill to establish a 'court of conscience' in Newcastle. In the second session he was named to the committees for inquiring into war expenditure and restoring corporations. His 'mildness' did not extend to Quakers, on whom he favoured the imposition of double taxation. In his only recorded speech he said:

They would not fight for the King. They were heretics, and if they had risen in primitive times would have been judged so by the Councils.

He was re-elected in 1690, together with William Carr[†], probably a nephew, who was to represent the town for 20 years. He himself remained active in local affairs until his death on 5 Mar. 1710. He was buried at Houghton-le-Spring.[4]

[1] Surtees, *Dur.* i. 209; J. Brand, *Hist. Newcastle*, i. 281. [2] *Reg. of Freemen* (Newcastle Recs. iii); 76; *Arch. Ael.* (ser. 4), xxiii. 145–6; *CSP Dom.* 1678, p. 140; PC2/72/561; *Cal. Treas. Bks.* v. 1205. [3] Surtees, i. 206; R. Howell, *Newcastle and the Puritan Revolution*, 185; *Council Minute Bk.* (Newcastle Recs. Soc. i), 161; Durham Cathedral Lib. Allan mss 7/194; *CSP Dom.* 1678, p. 140; 1680–1, p. 386. [4] *HMC Le Fleming*, 234; Morrice, Entering Bk. 3, p. 32; *CJ*, x. 303; Surtees, i. 154.

G.H.

CARR, Sir Robert (c.1637–82), of Aswarby, Lincs.

LINCOLNSHIRE   2 Jan. 1665, 1679 (Mar.), 1679 (Oct.), 1681

b. c.1637, o.s. of Sir Robert Carr, 2nd Bt., of Aswarby by Mary, da. and coh. of Sir Richard Gargrave[†] of Nostell, Yorks. *educ.* St. John's, Camb. adm. 6 Mar. 1654, aged 16. *m.* (1) 13 July 1662, Isabel Falkingham; (2) ?bigamously, aft. Mar. 1664, Elizabeth, da. of Sir John Bennet of Dawley, Harlington, Mdx., 2s. (1 *d.v.p.*) 2da. Kntd. by 1664; *suc.* fa. as 3rd Bt. 14 Aug. 1667.[1]

Commr. for militia, Lincs. Mar. 1660, sewers Aug. 1660, assessment, Lincs. 1661–3, Lincs. and Mdx. 1665–80, Westminster 1667–80, Lancs. 1673–80; dep. lt. Lincs. by 1665–?*d.*; j.p. Lincs. 1666–*d.*, Glos. by 1680–*d.*; recorder, Boston 1670–*d.*; bencher, G. Inn 1672; freeman, King's Lynn 1675, Preston 1682.[2]

Capt. Lord Gerard's Horse 1666–7.[3]

Commr. for union with Scotland 1670–1; gent. of the privy chamber 1671–?78; chancellor, duchy of Lancaster 1672–*d.*; PC 14 Feb. 1672–12 June 1678, 15 Oct. 1680–*d.*; commr. for Tangier 1673–80; member, R. Fishery Co. 1679.[4]

Carr was descended from a merchant of the staple who acquired a Lincolnshire manor in 1503. The estate was considerably enlarged at the dissolution of the monasteries, and Robert Carr sat for Boston in 1559. Carr's father, though 'deeply distempered with melancholy', was seized at Aswarby by a guard of musketeers in May 1644, and imprisoned by Parliament. He was not required to compound; but at the Restoration he was recommended for the order of the Royal Oak, with an estate of £4,000 p.a. By then, however, it was alleged that Carr had 'risen up' against his parents, 'and in a terrifying, if not warlike, way has prevailed upon some of their tenants to pay the rents to him'. Carr countercharged that his mother was keeping his father under restraint, guarded by the soldiers of his cousin (Sir) Edward Rossiter*, and obtained an order of the House of Lords that he was to be allowed to visit his father in the company of two local justices. In 1662 Carr married at Sleaford a certain Isabel Falkingham, described in *Flagellum Parliamentarium* as 'his mother's maid, to whom he gave £1,000 that she should not claim him' when a couple of years later he was successfully 'courting' the sister of Sir Henry Bennet*. This second marriage brought him a valuable court connexion; but it was probably debt as well as ambition that prompted him to contest the county seat left vacant by the death of (Sir) Charles Hussey*. Though 'neither appearing in the country nor certainly known to stand for it till within very few days before the election', he was pitched upon to oppose the Presbyterian interest. He defeated Hussey's nephew by 600 votes, and a government correspondent wrote:

We think ourselves very happy that our interests are placed in the hands of a gentleman from whose qualities, abilities, and integrity we do most confidently assure ourselves of all honourable and correspondent offices and respects.[5]

Carr became a very active Member of the Cavalier Parliament, being appointed to 391 committees, acting as teller in 22 divisions, and making over a hundred speeches. He fulfilled his constituents' expectations by having himself immediately added to the committees considering a local enclosure bill, a local estate bill, and the bills for draining salt marshes and Deeping fen. But his first care was to improve his own financial position by selling off some of his imbecile father's land. On 26 Jan. 1665 a bill for this purpose was referred to a committee. When a paper was 'framed, printed, and published at the door of the House ... with arguments and reasons' against the bill, it was voted a great abuse and breach of privilege. Carr's mother refused to attend the committee, which was chaired by Robert

Milward*, later to be described as his brother, although the relationship has not been established. Nor would she allow Henry Williams* to see her husband, as the committee had ordered. The bill passed the Commons on 16 Feb., and received the royal assent at the end of the session. In the Oxford session Carr was appointed to his first committees of political importance, those for the five mile bill and the attainder of English officers in enemy service. So ardent was he for the prohibition of cattle imports that he was twice named to the committee for the bill, and it was on this issue that he made his mark in the 1666 session. He twice acted as teller against Lords' amendments designed to reduce the impact of the measure on Ireland, and was sent to desire a conference, which he helped to manage. On 24 Sept. he was one of those appointed to ask Drs Dolben and Outram to preach before the House on a fast day, and was afterwards ordered to thank them and ask them to print their sermons. He was named to the abortive parliamentary accounts commission, again opposed the Lords over easing nonconformists of double taxation, and took part in three more conferences, on the encouragement of coinage, the accounts bill, and the charges against Clarendon's friend Mordaunt.[6]

Carr inherited the Aswarby estate, with an annual value of about five or six thousand pounds, in August 1667. He had already taken a London house which became notorious for heavy drinking, especially when Sir Henry Belasyse* was killed in a duel arising from a drunken quarrel. Doubtless his hospitality helped to win him friends, and to prepare for the attack on Clarendon, in which he took a leading part. He helped to draw up the address of thanks for the lord chancellor's dismissal, to prepare a public accounts bill, to consider a bill to prevent the growth of Popery, and to inquire into restraints on jurors, the miscarriages of the second Dutch war, and the sale of Dunkirk. He was among those appointed to reduce into heads the charges against the fallen minister, and supported the motion for his impeachment both in debate and division. When the Lords refused to comply without specific charges, Carr was named to the committee to draw up reasons, and also to those to examine the accounts of the French merchants and the indigent officers fund, of which his brother in-law Sir John Bennet* was treasurer. Although he twice acted as teller against banishing Clarendon 'because you are confirming what the Lords have done', he was appointed to the committee for the bill. During the Christmas recess he was among those employed to continue the audit of Bennet's accounts, but he is unlikely to have shown him any

favour. The two men had been on bad terms since Carr had been 'so busy in the House of Commons' when the Royal Adventurers into Africa came under scrutiny, and Bennet (wearing his other hat as post-master-general) went so far as to dismiss two of his brother-in-law's clients, the postmistress of Stilton, ostensibly because of her sex, and (more seriously) the postmaster of Grantham, the nearest stage to Aswarby, where Carr was anxious to establish a parliamentary interest. When Parliament met again Carr served on the deputation to demand satisfaction from the lord chief baron ((Sir) Matthew Hale*) about easing sheriffs in their accounts. He was also twice sent to ask the Duke of York to order Sir John Harman to give evidence to the miscarriages committee, and to the public accounts commissioners to desire them to expedite their proceedings. He supported the triennial bill brought in by Sir Richard Temple* on 18 Feb. 1668, and throughout the session opposed 'with very much reason' the project for draining the Lindsey level in which the Earl of Lindsey (Robert Bertie I*) was 'the chief undertaker'. When proposals for religious comprehension came before Parliament, Carr feared that 'his Majesty is possessed that the House of Commons is fond of toleration, and that we are possessed that his Majesty is fond of it'. He was among those instructed to receive information of nonconformist insolence and to consider the bill to prolong the Conventicles Act, though John Milward* interpreted his speech as hostile to the measure. On 30 Mar. 1668 he carried back to the Lords the bill to stiffen the penalties for importing foreign cattle. He helped to prepare the impeachment of (Sir) William Penn* and to manage a conference, and on 23 Apr. he was again sent to Brooke House to inquire whether the commission was satisfied with the naval accounts brought in by Sir George Carteret*. He served on the deputation from both Houses to ask the King to encourage the wearing of English manufactures, and was named to the committee on the bill to prevent the refusal of writs of habeas corpus. He was listed among Ormonde's friends at this time.[7]

On 12 Nov. 1669 Carr complained to the House that the attorney-general had put a stop to proceedings by (Sir) John Morton* against Henry Brouncker*, and he was sent with Sir Thomas Meres* to inquire the reason. He was the first Member named to attend the Duke of Albemarle (George Monck*) with the thanks of the House for preserving law and order. In the debate on the charges against Lord Orrery (Roger Boyle*) he was teller for putting the question, and a fortnight later he urged the House to protect Orrery's witnesses against possible reprisals from Ormonde. His most important committee in this session was on the bill to prevent exorbitances and abuses in parliamentary elections. Always an intolerant Anglican at heart, in the next session he was among those ordered to consider the second conventicles bill, to report on the Lords' amendments, and to see that they were correctly inserted. On 30 Mar. 1670 he was sent to desire a conference on the bill, for which he helped to prepare reasons. He took the chair in committee on the bills for the Waveney navigation canal and for severing the entail on a minor Lincolnshire estate. His other committees included those for the bills against transporting English subjects overseas and for appointing commissioners to negotiate union with Scotland. He helped to manage a conference on the addition of names to a naturalization bill and to prepare reasons for allowing teams of up to five draught animals on public highways without restriction.[8]

Carr was one of the five prominent country Members who went over to the Court in November 1670. A hostile account alleged that he gave in a list of his debts to (Sir) Thomas Clifford*, the government bribe-master, who paid out no less than £7,000. Carr seems to have been a remarkably unsuccessful speculator on the turf; but it is not clear that Clifford ever received value for money. During the session his new recruit twice spoke in favour of a land-tax rather than the additional excise sponsored by the Government. He was among those appointed to draw up reasons for a conference on regulating juries, which never met. In the debate on the assault on Sir John Coventry* he adopted the moderate position of advocating a stop to all other business only until the bill to punish such offences should pass the Commons. He took the chair for bills to reform the collection of fines, to remove the Cornish assizes from Launceston to Bodmin, and to consider a bill to establish a land registry. His record of hostility to the Upper House ensured him prominence in the dispute culminating in the Commons resolution against alterations of supply bills by the Lords; he was three times sent to demand conferences, which he helped to prepare and manage. At the end of the session in May 1671 the Opposition listed him among the court party, and in 1672 Arlington obtained for him a life patent as chancellor of the duchy of Lancaster, 'an honourable place, worth some £1,200 p.a., and admitting of much ease and quiet'. Almost immediately he was compelled to swallow the Declaration of Indulgence, writing to (Sir) Joseph Williamson*:

I pray God they make no ill return for this gracious declaration of his Majesty, which, it being his pleasure, I

am highly satisfied with. But I know no other thing could have made it relish well with me, who have upon all acts of grace found them highly ungrateful. But, whatever my private opinion was before the Declaration, I am sure now I am of opinion with it.

When Parliament met again he sought to allay the storm among his fellow-Anglicans by proposing to ask the King for a proclamation that the ecclesiastical laws should remain in being, and pointing out that the reluctance of magistrates to enforce them had amounted to a tacit dispensation to nonconformists. Nevertheless he was twice named to committees to draft addresses against the suspending power. By virtue of his office it fell to him to assist Secretary Henry Coventry* in conducting Edward Seymour* to the Speaker's chair, to bring two messages from the King, and to serve on the deputation with the address for encouraging British manufactures. He was named to the committees that produced the test bill and considered a bill of ease for nonconformists, though neither measure was altogether congenial to him. 'Likes neither the Papists nor the dissenters', he told the House. 'But the Papists have fought for the King, the others have not; therefore would have more kindness for them', and consequently refrain from imposing the test on Roman Catholic pensioners. When it was proposed on the last day of the session to ask the King to print the grievances presented by the House, he argued that this implied 'a mistrust of the King, that he will not do what he has promised'.[9]

During the summer Carr frequently deputized for Arlington at the department of state; but he was profoundly disturbed by the appointment of Sir Thomas Osborne*, Lindsey's brother-in-law, to the Treasury. Nevertheless in the autumn debates he and Temple, another turncoat, were the only Members to afford consistent support to the official spokesmen, Coventry and the lord keeper Heneage Finch*, though they were 'the worst heard that can be in the House*'. Carr seconded the motion for thanks for the speech from the throne, and tried to divert the attack on the Modena marriage. But he was laughed down when he told the Commons to 'proceed to your grievances (if you have any), and the King will give you redress'. He denied that the army constituted a grievance:

No man can say that a standing army in time of peace was ever attempted. Most of the forces were about Norfolk and Suffolk, where the Dutch have attempted landing. Your addresses formerly were to disband them when the war should be ended, and will you do it now, the war in being?

His name figured on the Paston list, and before the 1674 session the French embassy reported that

Arlington hoped to use Carr's prestige in the House to win support for the continuance of the alliance against Holland. In fact there is evidence that Carr's sympathies were with the Dutch at this time, and he may have provided du Moulin with valuable background information about the factions in Whitehall. In Parliament all his efforts had to be devoted to saving his brother-in-law from impeachment. He produced a letter to the Speaker from Arlington, asking to be heard in his own defence, and undertook that 'any question this House will ask this noble lord he will answer'. Though he did not fail to mention their relationship, he was appointed to the committee to consider the charges; but Arlington's successful defence would probably have obliged them to acquit him, had not 'Sir Robert Carr's modesty cooled it by crying for an adjournment'. He was also appointed to the committees to consider a general test, to inspect the Scottish Army Act, and to inquire into the condition of Ireland.[10]

Carr further inflamed the suspicions of Osborne (now Lord Treasurer Danby) by supporting an independent candidate in the King's Lynn by-election against his son-in-law Robert Coke*. In a memorandum on Arlington's faction in the Commons he wrote that Carr had

> alleged that the King ought not to be trusted, for that he had no sooner passed his word (though in print) but he broke it. Observe his sauciness to the King, and yet his cowardice to all others. His reporting that I was farming the customs, and that this was the last trick I had to put off Parliament by making a shift with that advance money. (My lord keeper told me this came from Sir Robert Carr.) His telling my Lord Mordaunt that now the Parliament was to sit, for that my Lord Arlington had prevailed with his Majesty, notwithstanding all the opposition I had made to it. Besides all the liberties he has taken not only at his own table but at Secretary Coventry's and elsewhere to report falsehoods and undervaluing discourses against me.

During the quarrel between the Houses in the summer of 1675, Carr proudly announced that he was reputed one of the three principal incendiaries in the Commons (the others being Seymour and Coventry). After suggesting that the Lords could only have produced their reasons while suffering from a collective hangover, he was appointed to prepare or manage three conferences that did nothing to bridge the gap. He was also named to the committees for both appropriation bills. He was included among the officials in Parliament at this time, and shown on the working lists as possessing interest over the Lancashire, Cheshire and Leicestershire Members as well as his direct subordinates. His personal friends in the House included Sir John Newton* and Robert Apreece*; but Sir

Richard Wiseman*, the government whip, hoped to detach Lionel Walden I* and William Broxholme*, writing of Carr himself: 'assuredly if the King please to turn off this gentleman it would be for his service; but if not that, in the next place I wish he might be employed abroad'. Heavy losses at Newmarket in 1676 obliged Carr to mortgage most of his estate for £20,000. Later in the year Carr and Sir Philip Monckton* accused each other of fomenting demands for a new Parliament in their respective counties, and Monckton was imprisoned by order of the Privy Council. When Parliament met again, Shaftesbury classed him as 'doubly vile', while Carr defended the committal of Shaftesbury's cousin and agent Harrington by the Council. He spoke repeatedly for supply, and was named to the committees to consider the bills recalling British subjects from the French service and strengthening habeas corpus. He helped to prepare the addresses desiring the King to withstand the danger from France and promising a credit of £200,000, and to manage conferences on foreign policy and the naval programme. He advised the House against entrenching on the prerogative by demanding an alliance with Holland, and was named to the committee to draw up an address in less specific terms.[11]

Meanwhile Lindsey, with government support, was striving to undermine Carr's interest in the Lincolnshire boroughs. His recordership at Boston bore little electoral fruit. But at Grantham, where the death of the aged Sir William Thorold* was long and impatiently expected, Carr used his crony Newton to form an incongruous alliance with the veteran Presbyterian judge William Ellys* in support of the latter's namesake and heir. Though 'commanded by the King not to endeavour to bring into Parliament a person disaffected to the Government that he might gratify his private animosity against my Lord Lindsey and his relatives', he had the satisfaction of driving the first Bertie nominee from the field. But at Westminster he was still officially regarded as one of the court party during the opening months of 1678, and his speeches justified his inclusion in the much abbreviated list of government speakers. When Seymour was under attack, Carr took the heat out of the issue by moving that the House should proceed as usual to consider the speech from the throne as soon as a day had been fixed for a full-scale debate on the Speaker's irregular adjournments. He helped to draw up addresses demanding the reduction of France to her 1659 frontiers and an immediate declaration of war, seconded the motion of (Sir) Thomas Clarges* for supply, and was among those instructed to prepare a summary of England's international commitments. After Seymour's brief retirement from the speakership, he helped to conduct him back to the chair. The Grantham election had been narrowly lost to a last-minute court candidate, but there were good grounds for a petition, and Carr, who was nervous of an attack from the Opposition over the Monckton case, could hardly refuse his support. From the committee of elections Meres reported in favour of the country candidate, but the Government made a supreme effort, and the House reversed the decision. Carr was blamed by both sides, by the Court for 'appearing very high in the House of Commons for bringing in Sir William Ellys*' and by the Opposition for flinching from charging Lindsey with using the militia to threaten the voters. This time the King and the courtiers who shared his sporting interests were unable to save him. He was turned out of the Council, and Danby sought to reduce the perquisites of his office by nominating Roger Bradshaigh I* as sheriff of Lancashire. Nevertheless after the Popish Plot Carr defended Williamson over the signing of commissions to Roman Catholic officers, and supported the proviso to allow the Duke of York to retain his seat in the Lords:

> I fear, if you reject this proviso, it will hurt what you would preserve. If hereafter there should be occasion for this, let it be in a bill by itself. Till I have better reason than I have yet heard, I must give my vote for the proviso.

His last important committee in the Cavalier Parliament was to find a way round the royal veto on the militia bill, and he took no part in the debate on the impeachment of Danby.[12]

Carr continued to sit as knight of the shire in the Exclusion Parliaments. At the first general election of 1679 he repulsed a challenge from the Lindsey candidate Sir Thomas Hussey* without difficulty, though he took the precaution of using his duchy interest to secure another seat at Preston. Shaftesbury classed him as a 'worthy' Member for Lincolnshire and 'vile' for Preston. A very active Member of the first Exclusion Parliament, he was named to 23 committees and delivered about a dozen speeches. Somewhat chastened by his experience, he no longer sought the limelight, and when William Sacheverell* proposed him as 'a person of eminence' to inform the King that the Commons desired further time to consider his rejection of Seymour as Speaker, he begged in vain to be excused. He was again sent to the King on 21 Mar. in a deputation to ask that the safety of the informer Bedloe should be entrusted to the Duke of Monmouth. He was among those appointed to consider the bill for security against Popery, and

took a full part in the proceedings against his old enemy Danby, helping to manage two conferences, to consider the attainder bill and to draft an address for a proclamation summoning him to surrender. On 17 Apr. he was named to the secret committee to prepare evidence for the trial of the fallen treasurer. Still loyal to his old friends, he declared himself surprised at the aspersions cast on Henry Coventry. Together with two eminent lawyers, John Maynard I* and William Williams*, he was given special responsibility for bringing in a bill to regulate parliamentary elections. He helped to prepare reasons for invalidating Danby's pardon, saying on 7 May:

> Those without doors think Danby as deep in the Plot as any of the five Popish lords.... 'Tis apparent this lord's friends are numerous above, and compassion hath gained him many friends here. I move for going by sure steps, and that a committee be appointed to search precedents.

He was among those instructed to prepare for and manage conferences on the disbandment bill and the trial of the lords in the Tower. He did not speak in the exclusion debate, and according to Roger Morrice he was absent from the division; but in the state papers he was listed as voting against the commitment of the bill. He was defeated at Preston in September, though he had not been blacklisted in the 'unanimous club'; but two months later he snubbed the Duke of York, who passed through Grantham on his way to Scotland, by not even deigning to leave his coach.[13]

Nevertheless Carr was restored to the Privy Council just before the second Exclusion Parliament met. He was selected to convey to the Commons the King's intention to veto the bill, but like Sidney Godolphin I* refused to do so. French diplomatic intelligence, improved out of all recognition under Ruvigny, noted regretfully that he had always been violent against the Roman Catholics, but enjoyed powerful protection in the Lords. Presumably this was an oblique reference to Lord Halifax (Sir George Savile*), for on 22 Nov. 1680 Carr assured the House that Halifax had disliked the repeated prorogations. Although granted leave to go into the country on 18 Dec. he was named later in the day to the committee for drafting an address insisting on exclusion, and ten days later he was one of six Members ordered to prepare the repeal of the Corporations Act. Moderately active in this Parliament, he was appointed in all to 14 committees and made four speeches. When the King announced the dissolution to the Privy Council, Carr rose to his feet to protest, but was forbidden to speak. In 1681 he was again returned for both Lincolnshire and Preston, but apart from his nomination to the committee of elections and privileges he left no trace on the records of the Oxford Parliament. Though still a comparatively young man, he was taken seriously ill in May 1682, when a false report of his death delighted the Papists. He died on 14 Nov. and was buried at Sleaford. His only son died unmarried and under age in the following year, and on the death of his mad uncle Rochester the baronetcy became extinct. Under the 1664 Act half the Aswarby estate went to Charles Fox*, who had married Carr's niece, the other half to his daughter Isabella, who brought it to her husband John Hervey† (later 1st Earl of Bristol), heavily encumbered with debt.[14]

[1] *Lincs. Peds.* (Harl. Soc. l), 230; Lincs. AO, Monson mss 7/14/25. [2] *CSP Dom.* 1665-6, p. 36; P. Thompson, *Hist. Boston*, 458; *Lynn Freemen*, 187; *Preston Guild Rolls* (Lancs. and Cheshire Rec. Soc. ix.), 183. [3] *CSP Dom.* 1665-6, p. 557. [4] Carlisle, *Privy Chamber*, 188; Sir Robert Somerville, *Duchy of Lancaster Office Holders*, 3; *HMC 12th Rep. IX*, 69; *Williamson Letters* (Cam. Soc. n.s. viii), 149; *Sel. Charters* (Selden Soc. xxviii), 198. [5] *The Gen.* iii. 104; *Her. and Gen.* ii. 120; *HMC 6th Rep.* 95, 100, 106; *HMC 7th Rep.* 112, 127; *LJ*, xi. 132; *Evelyn Diary*, iii. 372; *CSP Dom.* 1670, p. 698; *The News*, 12 Jan. 1665; C. Holmes, *17th Cent. Lincs*, 235. [6] *CSP Dom.* 1664-5, p. 196; *CJ*, viii. 598, 601, 603, 654, 658, 661, 670, 672, 674, 683, 690; Holmes, 239-40; *Dering Pprs.* 13. [7] *Her. and Gen.* ii. 120; *Pepys Diary*, 29 July 1667; *Milward*, 118, 140, 190, 254-5; *Clarendon Impeachment*, 137-8; *CJ*, ix. 18, 40, 42, 53, 59, 70, 72, 87; *CSP Dom.* 1671-2, p. 2; Add. 35865, f. 18; Grey, i. 115. [8] Grey i. 167, 212; *CJ*, ix. 106, 112, 137, 139, 150. [9] *Marvell* ed. Margoliouth, i. 305; Harl. 7020, f. 35; *CSP Dom.* 1671-2, pp. 149, 215; 1675-6, p. 28; *Hatton Corresp.* (Cam. Soc. n.s. xxiii), 12; Grey, i. 275, 315, 413; ii. 23, 35, 84, 176; *Dering*, 47, 116; *CJ*, ix. 198, 214, 230, 232, 233, 234, 239, 253, 258, 279; Clarke, *Jas. II*, i. 434. [10] *CSP Dom.* 1673, pp. 241, 266; *Essex Pprs.* (Cam. Soc. n.s. xlvii), 132; *Williamson Letters* (Cam. Soc. n.s. ix), 52, 115, 155; Grey, ii. 183-4, 204, 220, 271, 274, 285; PRO31/3, bdle. 130, f. 3; K. W. D. Haley, *Wm. of Orange and the Eng. Opp.* 119-21; CJ, ix. 296. [11] *CSP Dom.* 1675-6, pp. 28, 42; *HMC Lords*, iii. 268; Browning, *Danby*, iii. 1; Grey, iii. 244, 267; iv. 110, 271, 381; *CJ*, ix. 344, 352, 398, 418; *Marvell*, ii. 323. [12] *CSP Dom.* 1675-6, p. 249; 1678, p. 205; *HMC Rutland*, ii. 44, 48, 50; *Hatton Corresp.* (Cam. Soc. n.s. xxii), 166; E. Turner, *Colls. Hist. Grantham*, 14; Grey, v. 6, 159, 226-7; vi. 222, 244; *CJ*, ix. 476; PRO31/3, bdle. 139, f. 262v; *HMC Ormonde*, n.s. iv. 429, 431, 433; R. Morrice, Entering Bk. 1, pp. 86-87; Finch diary, 4, 25 Nov. 1678. [13] Beaufort mss, Ld. to Lady Worcester, 22 Feb. 1679; Grey, vi. 411-12; vii. 146, 298; *HMC Ormonde*, n.s. iv. 347; Add. 28046, f. 194; *CJ*, ix. 616, 618; *HMC 9th Rep.* pt. 1, p. 456. [14] *Temple Mems.* ed. Courtenay, ii. 69; PRO31/3, bdle. 146, f. 59v; Grey, viii. 46; *HMC Ormonde*, n.s. v. 563; Morrice, 1, p. 345; *HMC Kenyon*, 141; *HMC Lords*, iii. 268.

J.S.C.

CARR *see also* **KERR**

CARTER, John (c.1619–76), of Kinmel, Denb.

DENBIGHSHIRE 1654, 1656, 1659
DENBIGH BOROUGHS 1660

b. c.1619, 2nd s. of Thomas Carter, vicar of Dinton, Bucks. 1610-46, by Anne, da. of William Curtis of Chesterton, Cambs. *m.* c.1647, Elizabeth, da. and coh. of David Holland of Kinmel, 3s. (1 *d.v.p.*) 4da. Kntd. 7 June 1660.[1]

Lt.-col. of horse (parliamentary) 1644-5, col. 1645-7; gov. Conway Castle 1646-61, Holyhead Nov. 1660-1.[2]

Commr. for N. Wales association, Caern. and Denb. 1648, militia 1648, N. Wales Mar. 1660; j.p. Denb. 1648-*d.*, Caern. 1650-July 1660, Anglesey 1656-*d.*, Flints. Mar.-July 1660; commr. for assessment, Merion. 1649-52, Caern., Denb., Flints. and Anglesey 1649-52, 1657, Jan. 1660-1, Denb. 1665-74, sequestration, N. Wales 1649, propagation, Wales 1650; sheriff, Caern. Feb.-Nov. 1650, Denb. 1664-5; custos rot. Caern. 1651-6, Denb. 1656-Mar. 1660, Merion. Mar.-July 1660; commr. for scandalous ministers, N. Wales 1654, security 1655-6; freeman, Denbigh 1655-61; col. of militia, N. Wales Mar. 1660; steward, lordship of Denbigh July 1660-*d.*[3]

Member, high court of justice 1651.[4]

Carter's father sat in the Westminster Assembly and was presumably a Presbyterian. Carter is said to have been a linen-draper, but nothing certain is known of his career before his arrival in Wales in 1644 as second-in-command of a London cavalry regiment. He served under Sir Thomas Myddelton*, and acquired Kinmel by marriage, dividing the Holland estate with the Cavalier William Price*, who had married the other coheir. Nevertheless Carter became the mainstay of the republican cause in North Wales. He defeated Sir John Owen at Llandegai in the second Civil War, sat for Denbighshire under the Protectorate, and received a Cromwellian 'knighthood' in 1658. Although retained in office both by the Rump and the succeeding military regime, he may have begun to trim his sails. He took no known part against Myddelton's royalist rising in 1659, and George Monck* must have considered him favourable to the Restoration, entrusting to him in March 1660 the slighting of Denbigh Castle, which had 'long heavily burdened the neighbouring gentry'.[5]

In the following month Carter was returned for the Boroughs, doubtless with the support of the Myddelton interest. He was listed as a friend by Lord Wharton, who reserved him for his own management. An inactive Member of the Convention, he was named to the committee of elections and privileges and to eight others, including that responsible for the assessment ordinance. Despite a very unfavourable account of his career since 1648, probably prepared by Owen, he was knighted soon after Charles II's arrival, and signed the North Wales petition for justice on the regicides. He was appointed to the committee for recovering the queen mother's jointure. A proviso to the indemnity bill was offered in the Lords to make Carter liable for £1,200 extorted by duress in 1648, but it was rejected. He served on the committee to consider a similar clause directed against John Hut-

chinson*, and also on those to appoint commissioners for disbanding the army, to settle the
revenue, and to state the debts of the army and
navy. He was granted the stewardship of the crown
manor of Denbigh, but his unsuccessful application
for the constableship of Beaumaris provoked a
bitter comment from Thomas Bulkeley*, who
compared him to the serpent which fell upon the
friends who had saved it from death. As some compensation he was made governor of Holyhead,
which aroused some alarm among the Bulkeley interest in Anglesey; but both garrisons were soon
withdrawn. During the recess Carter was ordered
to extend his demolition work to Caernarvon
Castle, with the assistance of William Griffith*, but
the task was apparently beyond them. Wharton sent
him a copy of the case for modified episcopacy, but
he took no part in the debate. On 17 Nov. he presented a petition to the House, alleging royal support
for the renewal of his lease of Gresford rectory,
which he claimed as an 'ancient tenant to the dean
and chapter of Winchester', and a resolution was
passed in his favour.[6]

Carter did not stand again, although he was said
to be working for the Glynne interest in Caernarvonshire in 1661. Together with Mutton Davies*,
he appeared at the bar of the House in 1668 to ask
for protection against two alleged importers of Irish
cattle, who were suing for recovery of their property. He died on 28 Nov. 1676, aged 57, and was
buried at St. George's, Kinmel. The next member
of the family to sit was William Carter†, who was
elected for Hull in 1741.[7]

[1] *Le Neve's Knights* (Harl. Soc. viii), 65; Lipscomb, *Bucks.* ii.
145; *HMC 6th Rep.* 86; *Cambs. Par. Regs.* vii. 110. [2] *CSP Dom.*
1644-5; p. 181; 1645-7, pp. 563-4; 1660-1, p. 367; *Cal. Treas.
Bks.* i. 206; W. R. Williams, *Parl. Hist. Wales*, 74. [3] J. Williams,
Recs. of Denbigh, 134; *Thurloe*, iii. 216; *CSP Dom.* 1660-1, p. 138;
Cal. Treas. Bks. v. 392. [4] *CSP Dom.* 1651, p. 523. [5] J. Williams,
Ancient and Modern Denbigh, 250; A. H. Dodd, *Studies in Stuart
Wales*, 120, 139, 163; *CSP Dom.* 1660-1, p. 488. [6] *HMC 2nd Rep.*
86; *Merc. Pub.* 14 June 1660; *HMC 7th Rep.* 98; *Cal. Wynn Pprs.*
360, 361; *Arch. Camb.* i. 150. [7] *Cal. Wynn Pprs.* 364; *Milward*,
189; *CJ*, ix. 52; *Caern. Hist. Soc. Trans.* xiii. 6.

M.W.H./A.M.M.

CARTER, Lawrence (c.1641–1710), of Clement's
Inn and The Newarke, Leicester.

LEICESTER   1689, 1690, 1701 (Dec.)

b. c.1641, 1st s. of Lawrence Carter of Paulerspury, Northants. by Eleanor, da. and h. of John Pollard, yeoman,
of Leckhampstead, Bucks. *educ.* Clement's Inn. *m.* (1)
by 1667, Elizabeth (*d.* 29 Sept. 1671), da. and coh. of
Thomas Wadland, attorney, of The Newarke, 2s.; (2)
lic. 5 July 1675, aged 33, Mary, da. of Thomas Potter
of London, 2s. 4da. *suc.* fa. 1669.[1]

Commr. for assessment, Leics. 1677-9, 1690, Leic-

ester 1679-80, 1689; freeman, Leicester 1689; j.p.
Leics. 1689-*d.*; steward, honour of Leicester 1697-
1702.[2]

Receiver-gen. duchy of Lancaster Mar.–July 1702.[3]

Carter, the son of a prosperous gentleman
farmer, was articled to a Leicester attorney, whose
daughter he married. He was man of business to
the Earls of Stamford and Huntingdon, and it was
alleged that his advice impelled the latter to go over
to the Court in 1681. It was Huntingdon who tried
to persuade the Leicester corporation to surrender
their charter in 1684, and when they refused a writ
of quo warranto was sent to Carter, upon which
resistance ceased. Huntingdon became recorder
under the new charter. Carter was one of the first
to kiss hands on the accession of James II, and
wrote optimistically to the mayor on 14 Feb. 1685:
'We are got into the most peaceable age that men
have yet lived in'. In the following month, with
Huntingdon's support, he obtained letters patent to
provide the town with a piped water supply from
the Soar. The works, which cost him about £4,000,
were constructed by John Wilkins, one of the
aldermen and a man of 'most mechanical genius'.[4]

Unlike his master Huntingdon, Carter survived
the Revolution with exemplary smoothness. In 1689
he was returned unopposed for Leicester as a
moderate Whig, probably on the interest of his
other patron Lord Stamford. A moderately active
Member of the Convention, he was appointed to 27
committees and made four recorded speeches. On 6
Feb. he spoke in favour of proceeding against the
London alderman who had bailed Robert Brent, the
'popish solicitor' and regulator. He was among
those to whom the Lords bill for new oaths of supremacy and allegiance was committed, and he
strongly opposed the exemption of the bishops:

> all the subjects of England are under one King: and there
> is but one allegiance, according to our law. It was sug-
> gested here that the bishops had taken an oath to King
> James, and therefore their consciences would not bear
> to swear to King William, and I think that the strongest
> reason why it should be tendered them. We must not
> set two heads on one Church, and divide the bishops.
> Some have taken it and some not; and as to the govern-
> ment, we have taken it. How can we be true to the
> King, if all do not? We have done it, and they ought to
> do it.

He was appointed to the committee to prepare
reasons for conferences on this subject and on the
seizure of horses belonging to Roman Catholics.
During the committee stage of the indemnity bill
he opposed the wholesale exceptions proposed by
the hottest Whigs. 'There is some discourse without
doors', he told the House, 'that if we go about things
we shall set the whole nation on fire. I hope the

King's directions will be most acceptable to the nation.' He moved unsuccessfully against excepting Huntingdon.

> I hope this will not appear to be the greatest offender. He came in to act in this commission when the lawyers and bishops thought it safe to act. He was well assured, before he acted, and advised with several lawyers, who gave him encouragement to proceed. (He was called upon to name those lawyers.) He dissented in divers things that they acted against the Church.

He was particularly prominent over the succession issue, reporting reasons for disagreeing with the Lords, amendments to the clause on 9 July, and two conferences which followed. He also helped to consider the bill to reverse the quo warranto against London, and to prepare reasons for a conference on Titus Oates. On 18 July he was given leave to go into the country, though only after a division. He was less active after the recess, and needless to say was not listed as a supporter of the disabling clause in the bill to restore corporations. Local loyalties outweighed party with him, and he was teller for the election of John Beaumont* at Hastings. He sat in the next Parliament as a court Whig, but it was his son, later a judge, who was first returned for Leicester as a Tory in 1698. Carter himself was buried at St. Mary, Leicester on 1 June 1710, aged 69, with a memorial inscription recording that he had been three times elected for the borough.[5]

[1] *Leckhampstead Par. Reg.* 11; H. R. Moulton, *Cat.* (1930), 91; Baker, *Northants.* ii. 206; Nichols, *Leics.* i. 318; *London Mar. Lic.* ed. Foster, 248; *Recs. Bor. Leicester* ed. Stocks, iv. 379. [2] *Reg. Leicester Freemen*, i. 172; Sir Robert Somerville, *Duchy of Lancaster Official Lists*, 180. [3] Somerville, 19. [4] PCC 17 Coke; Grey, ix. 387; *Huntington Lib. Q.* xv. 376; *Recs. Bor. Leicester*, iv. 379; J. Thompson, *Leicester*, 437; PC2/71/16; *Cal. Treas. Bks.* vii. 23, 47, 179; Nichols, 318. [5] Grey, ix. 67, 212–13, 245, 386–7; *CJ*, x. 93, 211, 213, 215, 223, 335.

E.C.

CARTERET, Sir George, 1st Bt. (c.1610–80), of Whitehall and Hawnes, Beds.[1]

PORTSMOUTH 1661

b. ?6 May 1610, 1st s. of Élie de Carteret of Metesches, Jersey by Elizabeth, da. of Hugh Dumaresq of Sark. *m.* 6 May 1640, his cos. Elizabeth (*d.*1697), da. of Sir Philippe de Carteret of St. Ouen, Jersey, 3s. (2 *d.v.p*) 5da. *suc.* fa. 1634; kntd. 21 Jan. 1645; *cr.* Bt. 9 May 1645.

Lt. RN 1629, capt. 1633–9; lt.-gov. Jersey 1643–51, v.-adm. 1644–7.

Comptroller of the navy 1641–2, treas. July 1660–7; v.-chamberlain June 1660–*d.*; PC 11 July 1660–21 Apr. 1679; commr. for trade Nov. 1660–7, plantations Dec 1660–70, trade and plantations 1671–4; jt. farmer, French shipping duty 1661–7; elder bro. Trinity House 1661–*d.*, master 1664–5; agent R. Adventurers into Africa 1661–3, asst. 1664–71; commr. for Tangier 1662–*d.*; ld. prop. Carolina 1663–*d.*; asst. R. Fishing Co. 1664; commr. for prize appeals 1665–7; v.-treas. [I] 1667–70; ld. of Admiralty 1673–9.[2]

J.p. Essex, Hants, Kent and Mdx. 1639–44, Aug. 1660–*d.*; bailiff, Jersey 1643–51, May 1660–1; commr. for assessment, Westminster 1661–3, 1677–9, Berks. 1665–*d.*, Devon and Hants 1665–79, Mdx. 1673–9, Beds. 1673–*d.*, loyal and indigent officers, London and Westminster 1662, oyer and terminer, Mdx. 1662; freeman, Portsmouth 1662; ranger, Cranborne chase 1664–*d.*[3]

Carteret's ancestors had held property in Jersey since the 12th century. But his father was a younger son, and he was himself bred to the sea without ever acquiring more than the rudiments of a gentleman's education. He distinguished himself in the expedition that smoked out the Sallee corsairs in 1637, and was promised the post of comptroller of the navy in reversion in 1639. He married the daughter of the head of his family, whom he succeeded as bailiff of Jersey in 1643. After suppressing the parliamentarian militia, he turned the island into a base for privateers, from which a steady supply of munitions flowed to the royalist forces in the west of England. Sir Edward Hyde†, accompanying the future Charles II on his visit to the island in 1646, described Carteret as:

> a worthy and most excellent person, of extraordinary merit towards the crown and nation of England; the most generous man in kindness, and the most dexterous man in business ever known; and a most prudent and skilful lieutenant-governor, who reduced Jersey not with greater skill and discretion than he kept it. And besides his other parts of honesty and discretion, undoubtedly a good, if not the best seaman in England.

In 1649 Charles wrote to Carteret, promising never to forget his good services, and he appears to have kept his word. He 'had the honour to hold the last sword for the King'; it was not until December 1651 that the Commonwealth forces were able to subdue Jersey, and then only by granting Carteret generous terms. He was not required to compound for his privateering gains, and took service in the French navy until Mazarin's alliance with Cromwell, when he was briefly sent to the Bastille. After the death of the great Protector he resumed contact with the exiled Court, signing his letters, mischievously, with the name of the author of *Eikonoklastes*.[4]

Carteret had not been impoverished by his loyalty. At his own computation he was worth £50,000 at the Restoration, including his claims for reimbursement, for which provision was at once made by means of crown leases in Devon and elsewhere. Together with Daniel O'Neill* he farmed the duty on French shipping at an annual rent of £1,000. He was made vice-chamberlain, treasurer of the navy, and a Privy Councillor. In his administrative capacities his loyalty, industry and integrity were beyond cavil, even his adversary William Coventry* acknowledging that 'he is a man that doth take the most pains, and gives himself the most to do business of any man about the Court, without any desire of pleasure or divertisements'. Essentially a family man, he was disgusted by 'the baseness and looseness of the Court' to the point of reminding his former guest of 'the necessity of having at least a show of religion in the government, and sobriety'. Hyde, now Lord Chancellor Clarendon, declared that Carteret was 'a punctual officer and a good accountant'; but Samuel Pepys* found his ignorance in financial matters perverse and ridiculous, complaining that he argued 'like a mad coxcomb, without reason or method'. 'The most passionate man in the world, ... it was always his humour to have things done his way', and his accounts were so idiosyncratic that no serious audit was possible. On such occasions he took care to provide the navy board with an excellent dinner to lubricate proceedings.[5]

At the general election of 1661 Carteret was returned for Portsmouth on the Admiralty interest. An inactive Member of the Cavalier Parliament, he was named to 41 committees, almost all of them during the administration of Clarendon, whose great confidant he was. But conscious no doubt of the 'ill English' at which Andrew Marvell* scoffed, he seldom spoke except in self-defence. As a senior Household official, he helped to conduct (Sir) Edward Turnor* to the Speaker's chair, and attended a conference to hear a loyal message from the Scottish Parliament. His committees in the first session included those for restoring the bishops to the House of Lords, making reparations to the Marquess of Winchester, inquiring into the shortfall in the revenue, and considering the corporations and uniformity bills. He was naturally named to the committees to consider the naval regulations bill and the proviso on behalf of the lord high admiral. On 21 Nov. he was among those sent to ask the King when he would receive an address about disarming the disbanded soldiers, and a week later he was desired to attend the commissioners appointed to state the debts of the army and navy. He helped to present the vote of thanks for the King's speech of 1 Mar. 1662, and was added to the committee for the relief of loyalists. He was much vexed at the appointment of Coventry to the navy board in May, and it was not long before they were in dispute over the victualling accounts, on which Carteret was charging 3d. in the £.[6]

In the 1663 session Carteret was named to the committees to hear a petition from the loyal and indigent officers and to enlarge the power of martial law in the fleet. He found Parliament 'in a very angry, pettish mood at present, and not likely to be better'. He was one of the four Privy Councillors sent on 12 May to the King with four resolutions of the House regarding postal contracts, trade with Scotland and Ireland, the export of geldings, and the appointment of consuls. His most important committee in this session was on the bill for preventing abuses in the sale of offices; Coventry believed him to be responsible for the outcry over this matter, though Carteret had claimed the credit for dissuading William Prynne* from raising it in the previous session. He was among those appointed to consider the bill for improving the revenue, and was the first Member named to the committee to hear a petition from naval creditors. By the end of the year he was able to boast that the navy was quite out of debt, a laudable achievement attained by the use of his personal credit. His aim, he confided to Pepys, was that 'the King should not be able to whip a cat but I must be at the tail of it'. Listed as a court dependant in 1664, he was appointed to consider the bills to prevent the surrender of English merchantmen to pirates, to increase the authority of the navy board, and to preserve the timber in the Forest of Dean. On 25 Nov. he was among those instructed to present thanks to the King and the City for defending the nation against the Dutch. He had predicted that commercial rivalry would lead to another war, and was described by Coventry as the principal intermediary (together with Thomas Grey*) between the Royal Adventurers into Africa and the Court, 'Carteret (though underhand) governing the merchants by their dependence on him for trade and payment in the navy'. He had long been interested in the profits to be realized from colonial projects, and on the conquest of the New Netherlands the Duke of York assigned to him and Lord Berkeley all the land between the Hudson and the Delaware, to be named New Jersey in honour of his native island. On 20 Feb. 1665 he was the first Member named to the committee on the bill for raising the level of interest on government loans.[7]

Carteret, who was morbidly nervous of infection, does not appear to have attended the Oxford session during the plague. This was a mistake, for in his absence the supply bill was passed with provisions that curtailed his profits considerably. Pepys feared that when Parliament met again they would 'fall hard upon him' for the ill-success of the naval war. At Court he was neglected, with enemies working to undermine his position. While at the Treasury Sir Philip Warwick* 'endeavours hard to come to a good understanding of Sir George Carteret's accounts'; but Pepys feared that 'our method of accounting, though it cannot I believe be far wide from the mark, yet [it] will not abide a strict examination if the Parliament should prove troublesome'. Carteret offered to produce his accounts as soon as the House met in September 1666, and was named to the committee to bring in a bill for preventing the embezzlement of gunpowder and ammunition. Nevertheless, according to Coventry, 'the House hath a great envy at Sir George Carteret', and by the following summer he had come to recognize that he must quit the navy 'on any good terms'. He was fortunate to be able to exchange offices with Lord Anglesey (Arthur Annesley*), whose post as vice-treasurer of Ireland was considered to be worth £5,000 p.a., to which the King added a pension of £500 on the Barbados sugar duty. He told Pepys at this time that he was worth £65,000 in all, though 'he was not, all expenses and things paid, clear in estate £15,000 better than he was when the King came in'. This presumably excluded the £15,487 that he had claimed from the crown for disbursements in Jersey during the Civil War, and perhaps also the Hawnes estate, which he had just purchased as a residence for his eldest son.[8]

Fortunately for Carteret, in the session following the fall of Clarendon the Opposition concentrated on those immediately responsible for the failures to follow up the victory off Lowestoft and to defend the Medway. In the miscarriages debate of 22 Feb. 1668 he told the House 'that it was ever against his judgement and advice to pay seamen by tickets', which was no more than the truth. On 5 Mar. he was ordered to give an account of what moneys were assigned for the navy, and how they were afterwards employed and issued by him. On 24 Apr. (Sir) Robert Brooke* tabled the exceptions taken by the public accounts commission to Carteret's accounts; but nothing further was done that session. His ordeal began on 8 Nov. 1669 when Sir Robert Carr* accused him of reflecting on the commissioners of accounts, 'as if they had given a false account of things', and Carteret asked leave to read his reply to their observations 'by reason he is an ill expresser of himself'. On 17 Nov. he told the House:

He has attended the commissioners to give them all satisfaction, which it seems he has not, and they have made observations on his proceedings. He protests he has not paid one penny without sufficient vouchers for the use of the war. It seems they say he has done nothing well, after all his pains and hazard of his person and fortune in the plague. He came then, and with his credit kept the fleet abroad and borrowed upon his own credit

without security £280,000 and has done all that he possibly could; but he will not talk of what he has done further, though he knows many can justify it. They cannot say he ever took bribes, but has kept his Majesty's fleet abroad, when it must else have come home.

The Commons found him guilty of misdemeanours on nine of the ten observations submitted by the commissioners, of which the most important was his high-handed disregard of the appropriations stipulated in the Additional Aid of 1665; while a Lords committee acquitted him on the only charges they had time to discuss. As Edmund Waller I* pointed out, if he had been guilty he would have fled, like Clarendon, two years before, and it was only by three votes that the House resolved to suspend him. During the recess he resigned his Irish post and retired into comparative obscurity. The King told the Brooke House commissioners that he was satisfied with Carteret's handling of naval expenditure, repeating this in his speech from the throne on 14 Feb. 1670, and, much to the irritation of the Buckingham faction, the inquiry lapsed. Carteret's name appeared on both lists of the court party in this period, but there is no evidence that he attended again until the third Dutch war. His position at Court was unaffected. He received a grant of land in the Bahamas, and in September was sent to France to receive the first instalment of the subsidy payable under the treaty of Dover.[9]

Carteret was added to the committee of elections and privileges on 22 Feb. 1673, but he left no further trace in the Journals. However he was appointed to the board of admiralty when the Duke of York was forced out of office by the Test Act, and named on the Paston list. He attended at least two naval debates, telling the House of his own experiences before the Civil War in compelling the Dutch to salute the flag, and supporting Pepys on the classification of warships. He was listed as a court dependant in 1675 and classed as 'vile' by Shaftesbury. In *A Seasonable Argument* he was described as:

once treasurer of Ireland and the navy, in which two places he cheated the crown of £40,000, as upon account was made apparent. He has wisely conveyed great part of his estate beyond seas.

His name was on both lists of the court party in 1678, and as one of the 'unanimous club' it is unlikely that he stood in the following year. He died on 14 Jan. 1680, and was buried at Hawnes. His eldest son had been killed at Sole Bay, but in 1681 his grandson was given the peerage that had been intended for him. His great-grandson was the distinguished Georgian statesman, while a younger grandson, Edward, was returned for Huntingdon in 1698, Bedford in 1702, and Bere Alston in 1717.[10]

[1] This biography is based on G. R. Balleine, *All for the King.* [2] *Cal. Treas. Bks.* i. 258; *Sel. Charters* (Selden Soc. xxviii), 175, 182; *Pepys Diary*, 27 Oct. 1662; *Williamson Letters* (Cam. Soc. n.s. viii), 149; *Cal. Col. SP*, 1661–8, p. 126; *CSP Dom.* 1666–7, p. 355; 1667, p. 347. [3] R. East, *Portsmouth Recs.* 357; *CSP Dom.* 1664–5, p. 50. [4] *Fanshawe Mems.* 42; S. E. Hoskins, *Chas. II in the Channel Is.* i. 79; *Cal. Comm. Comp.* 2329; Grey, i. 214; *Cal. Cl. SP*, iv. 84, 110. [5] *Cal. Treas. Bks.* i. 532; *Pepys Diary*, 30 Oct. 1662, 6 Apr., 11 May, 22, 24 June 1663, 29 Mar. 1664, 1 Apr., 24, 31 July 1665, 6 Feb., 27 July 1667; Clarendon, *Life*, iii. 130. [6] *Pepys Diary*, 8 May, 12 June 1662, 23 July 1664; Marvell ed. Margoliouth, i. 146; *CJ*, viii. 245. [7] *Pepys Diary*, 13 June 1662, 14 Apr., 2 June, 19 Nov., 3 Dec. 1663, 14 Aug. 1665; *Camb. Hist. Jnl.* xii. 113. [8] *Pepys Diary*, 6, 7 Nov., 8 Dec. 1665, 9 Jan., 2 Mar., 21, 23 Sept. 1666, 12 Apr., 17 May, 18, 28 June 1667; *Cal. Treas. Bks.* i. 532; v. 60; vi. 172. [9] *Milward*, 196; *Pepys Diary*, 1 Apr. 1665; Grey, i. 158, 164, 166, 170–1, 178–9, 214; *CJ*, ix. 105, 116, 120; *HMC 8th Rep.* 128–33; D. T. Witcombe, *Cav. House of Commons*, 92–94; *Bulstrode Pprs.* 130; Browning, *Danby*, i. 75; PRO31/3, bdle. 125, f. 253; *CSP Col.* 1669–74, pp. 122–3; Marvell, ii. 311. [10] Grey, ii. 340; iii. 379.

P.W.

CARY, Sir George (c.1653–85), of Clovelly, Devon.

OKEHAMPTON   1681

b. c.1653, 1st s. of George Cary, DD, dean of Exeter, by Anne, da. of William Hancock of Combe Martin; bro. of William Cary*. *m.* (1) lic. 30 June 1676, Elizabeth (*d.*1677), da. and coh. of James Jenkyn of Trekenning, St. Columb Major, Cornw., 1s. *d.v.p.*; (2) 30 Oct. 1679, Martha, da. and h. of William Davie of Canonteign, Devon, *s.p.* Kntd. c.1679; *suc.* fa. 1680.[1]
J.p. Devon 1678–*d.*; recorder, Okehampton 1681–*d.*[2]

Cary came from a cadet branch of the great Devonshire family that had held land in the county in the 12th century, and represented it in two of Edward III's Parliaments. Although his father remained rector of Clovelly throughout the Interregnum, his uncle Robert, the lord of the manor, took up arms for the King during the Civil War, serving as governor of Bideford, and was knighted at the Restoration. Cary himself was knighted shortly before succeeding to the estate in 1680. He was returned to the third Exclusion Parliament for Okehampton, but was totally inactive. Shortly afterwards he replaced the exclusionist (Sir) Arthur Harris* as recorder of the borough.[3]

As recorder of Okehampton, Cary presented a loyal address in June 1681, signed by 230 residents of the borough, thanking the King for his declaration upon the dissolution of Parliament. When the surrender of the charter was demanded Cary carried it up without complaint. In the new charter he was appointed recorder for life, in accordance with a request from the corporation. But he died on 6 Jan. 1685, aged 31. He was buried at Clovelly,

leaving an encumbered estate to his brother William.[4]

[1] Vivian, *Vis. Devon*, 159, 441; Eg. 2753, p. 78. [2] W. K. H. Wright, *Okehampton*, 104. [3] W. G. Hoskins, *Devon*, 469; F. Harrison, *Devon Carys*, i. 185–6. [4] *CSP Dom.* July–Sept. 1683, pp. 423, 424; 1683–4, p. 217; Wright, 105; *HMC Lords*, n.s. v. 356.

J.S.C.

CARY, William (c.1661–1710), of Clovelly, Devon.

OKEHAMPTON   1685, 1689, 1690
LAUNCESTON   1695, 1698, 1701 (Feb.), 1701 (Dec.), 1702, 1705, 1708

b. c.1661, 2nd s. of George Cary, DD, dean of Exeter, and bro. of Sir George Cary*. *educ.* Queen's, Oxf. matric. 23 Mar. 1678, aged 16; M. Temple 1679. *m.* (1) aft. 1683, Joan (*d.* 4 Feb. 1687), da. of (Sir) William Wyndham*, 1st Bt., of Orchard Wyndham, Som., *s.p.*; (2) lic. 28 Mar. 1694 (with £5,000), Mary (*d.*1701), da. of Thomas Mansel I* of Briton Ferry, Glam., 3s. (1 *d.v.p.*) 2da. *suc.* bro. 1685.[1]
Recorder, Okehampton 1685–?Jan. 1688; j.p. Devon 1687–July 1688, Oct. 1688–96, 1700–*d.*, commr. for assessment 1689–90, dep. lt. 1703–*d.*[2]
Commr. for drowned lands 1690.[3]

In January 1685 Cary succeeded his brother in the Clovelly estate, in the recordership of Okehampton (after considerable opposition), and in the representation of the borough at the general election two months later. But he was totally inactive in James II's Parliament. A Tory and a High Churchman, he returned the same negative answers as Sir Edward Seymour* on the repeal of the Test Act and Penal Laws. He was removed from local office, went over to William of Orange after his landing in the west, and was re-elected to the Convention. An inactive Member, he probably served on six committees, including the committee of elections and privileges, and voted to agree with the Lords that the throne was not vacant. On 24 Jan. 1690 he was added to the committee to investigate the complaints of two 'discoverers of seditious persons' who had been committed to prison while in attendance on the House. He was returned again for Okehampton in 1690 and for Launceston to the seven succeeding Parliaments. He voted consistently Tory, and was again removed from the commission of the peace for refusing the Association. Cary made out his will in September 1710, and it was proved in January 1711. His two sons, who both died without issue in 1724, did not sit in Parliament.[4]

[1] Vivian, *Vis. Devon*, 159; Collinson, *Som.* iii. 495; *Cat. Penrice and Margam Mss*, ser. 4, iii. 144. [2] W. K. H. Wright, *Okehampton,*

105; PC2/76, f. 263. [3] *Cal. Treas. Bks.* ix. 794. [4] Luttrell, i. 477; H. Horwitz, *Parl. Policy and Pols.* 338.

J.S.C.

CARY *see also* **CAREY, John.**

CASTLETON, 5th, Visct. [I] *see* **SAUNDERSON, George.**

CATELYN, Sir Neville (1634–1702), of Kirby Cane, Norf. and Wingfield Castle, Suff.

NORFOLK   10 Feb.–21 Apr. 1679, 5 May 1679
NORWICH   1685, 1689

bap. 3 Mar. 1634, 2nd but o. surv. s. of Richard Catelyn[†] of Kirby Cane, being o.s. by 2nd w. Dorothy, da. of Sir Henry Neville of Billingbear, Berks. *educ.* King's, Camb. 1650. *m.* (1) Dorothy, da. and coh. of Sir Thomas Bedingfield[†] of Darsham, Suff., 1s. *d.v.p.* 1da.; (2) Elizabeth (*bur.* 5 Feb. 1681), da of Robert Houghton of Ranworth, Norf., 1s. *d.v.p.*; (3) Mary, da. of Sir William Blois of Grundisburgh Hall, Suff., *s.p. suc.* fa. 1662; kntd. 11 Oct. 1662.[1]

Capt. of militia horse, Norf. Apr. 1660, maj. by 1676–?79; commr. for assessment, Norf. and Suff. 1661–80, Norf., Norwich and Suff. 1689–90; j.p. Norf. 1668–Feb. 1688, 1689–d., Suff. 1680–5; dep. lt. Norf. by 1676–Feb. 1688, Nov. 1688–?d., Suff. 1680–5.[2]

Catelyn was descended from a Norwich family which had represented the city in several Tudor Parliaments. His grandfather established himself as a country gentleman with the purchase of Kirby Cane in 1604. The family was royalist in the Civil War. Catelyn's half-brother was killed in action, and his father was disabled from sitting in the Long Parliament in 1644 for deserting the service of the House, and his estate sequestrated. But he was discharged without fine by order of the House in 1647. He signed the petition for a free Parliament in 1660.[3]

Catelyn entered Norfolk politics in 1675 as an adherent of Lord Yarmouth (Robert Paston*), and was defeated by Sir Robert Kemp* in a county by-election, at a cost of not less than £600. When a vacancy occurred at Norwich in February 1678 William Wyndham, the brother-in-law of Yarmouth's rival, Lord Townshend, thought it unwise to oppose 'so popular and notable a knight' as Catelyn; but before the poll he made way for Yarmouth's son, William Paston*. At the first general election of 1679 he was recommended for the county by (Sir) Joseph Williamson*, and nominated by Yarmouth as a candidate 'devoted to the crown' who would not 'meddle with ministers of state'. He was returned after a bitter contest, classed as 'base' by Shaftesbury, and appointed to the committee of

elections and privileges. He was unseated when the election was declared void, but re-elected a fortnight later. He was not named to any further committees in the first Exclusion Parliament, but voted against the bill. He 'earnestly' desired Yarmouth to excuse him from standing again in the autumn, assuring him he would exercise to the utmost his interest in favour of any other court candidate, but at length agreed to stand with Sir Christopher Calthorpe* when a county subscription was raised to meet their expenses. An agent of Yarmouth's reported that he had spoiled his chances by going home the day before the poll 'to the great dissatisfaction and discouragement of his friends', adding 'I cannot as yet understand that Sir Nevill did withdraw for any other reason but only that the rabble did asperse him with being popishly affected'. His 'timorousness' so disappointed his friends, the same correspondent went on, that they resolved not to support him again in the future. In March 1682 he subscribed to the loyal address from Norfolk disavowing the 'Association'.[4]

Catelyn was elected for Norwich unopposed in 1685, and was listed among the Opposition. A moderately active Member of James II's Parliament, he was appointed to four committees of no political importance. In 1688 he told the lord lieutenant:

If he should be chosen a Member of Parliament when the King shall think fit to call one, he can by no means consent to the taking off the Penal Laws and the Tests, though he is of opinion that in the Penal Laws some things may be reviewed and amended.

He was removed from local office, and when he was restored in October 1688 he followed the example of Sir John Holland* in refusing to sit with the Roman Catholics. He was re-elected in 1689, and, according to Anthony Rowe*, voted to agree with the Lords that the throne was not vacant. Again moderately active in the Convention, he was appointed to 15 committees, including those to hear a petition from dealers in Norwich stuffs (11 May) and to consider the establishment of a 'court of conscience' for small claims in the city (16 Nov.). Granted leave of absence for a fortnight on 7 Dec., he was added to the elections committee on the next day. He died in July 1702 and was buried at Kirby Cane, the last of his family. His widow married Sir Charles Turner, MP for King's Lynn from 1695 to 1738.[5]

[1] *Vis. Norf.* (Harl. Soc. lxxxv), 49; *Le Neve's Knights* (Harl. Soc. viii), 161–2. [2] *Parl. Intell.* 9 Apr. 1660; *Cal. Treas. Bks.* i. 77; *HMC Lothian*, 127; *Norf. Ltcy. Jnl.* (Norf. Rec. Soc. xxx), 7, 104. [3] Blomefield, *Norf.* viii. 31–35; Keeler, *Long Parl.* 128; *Cal. Comm. Comp.* 113, 942; W. Rye, *Address from the Gentry of Norf.* (1660). [4] *HMC 7th Rep.* 532; Add. 36988, ff. 143–6, 149, 180; Ketton-

Cremer mss, Hobart to Windham, 22 Feb. 1678; *CSP Dom.* 1679–80, pp. 59, 66. [5] *Norf. Ltcy. Jnl.* 88; Blomefield, viii. 32.

E.C.

CAVE, Sir Roger, 2nd Bt. (1655–1703), of Stanford Hall, Leics.

COVENTRY 1685, 1689

bap. 21 Sept. 1655, 3rd but 1st surv. s. of Sir Thomas Cave, 1st Bt., of Stanford by 2nd w. Penelope, da. and coh. of Thomas Wenman*, 2nd Visct. Wenman of Tuam [I]. *educ.* Christ's, Camb. 1671. *m.* (1) lic. 24 Feb. 1676, Martha, da. and h. of John Browne of Eydon, Northants., clerk of Parliament 1638–49, May 1660–91, 4s. (2 *d.v.p.*) 2da.; (2) Mary, da. of Sir William Bromley of Baginton, Warws., 1s. 2 da. *suc.* fa. Nov. 1670.[1]

Commr. for assessment, Northants. 1677–80, Leics. and Northants. 1689–90; sheriff, Northants. 1679–80; j.p. Northants. 1680–7, 1689–d., Leics. by 1700–d.; dep. lt. Northants. 1685–7.[2]

Cave's ancestors had resided at Stanford, on the borders of Leicestershire and Northamptonshire, as tenants of Selby Abbey in the 15th century. They purchased the freehold on the dissolution of the monasteries; but they were not a regular parliamentary family, although a younger son, Sir Ambrose Cave, sat for Leicestershire and Warwickshire and became chancellor of the duchy under Elizabeth. Cave's father was created a baronet on the eve of the Civil War; it was alleged that he had acted as commissioner of array and furnished the King with horses, arms and money, but, although the estate was under sequestration for a time, there are no records of compounding.[3]

Cave was given the baronetcy fee of his brother-in-law, Orlando Bridgeman*, in 1673, and sued out a pardon for homicide in 1677; the circumstances are unknown. With Bridgeman's help he and the local Tory Sir Thomas Norton* defeated the Whig John Stratford* at Coventry in 1685. He was moderately active in James II's Parliament, being appointed to the committees for expiring laws, a naturalization bill, and the bill for the suppression of simony. He was removed from local office in 1687, and during the Revolution joined Princess Anne's escort at Nottingham. He was re-elected to the Convention, and voted to agree with the Lords that the throne was not vacant. An inactive Member, he was named to the committee of elections and privileges, and to those to inquire into the authors and advisers of grievances, to prepare a bill for the abolition of hearth-tax, and to consider the toleration bill. In the second session he was appointed only to the committee to examine the state of the revenue. He is not known to have stood again. He died on 11 Oct. 1703, and was buried at Stan-ford. His son, the third baronet, sat for Leicestershire as a Tory from 1711 till his death in 1719.[4]

[1] *Vis. England and Wales Notes* ed. Crisp, viii. 128–37. [2] Northants. RO, FH 2226. [3] Bridges, *Northants.* i. 579; *Cal. Comm. Adv. Money*, 1048–9; *Cal. Comm. Comp.* 98. [4] *CSP Dom.* 1673–5, p. 16; 1677–8, p. 175; 1685, p. 72; Bath mss, Thynne pprs. 28, f. 92; information from G. H. Jones.

A.M.M.

CAVENDISH, Henry, Visct. Mansfield (1630–91), of Bolsover, Derbys. and Welbeck Abbey, Notts.

DERBYSHIRE   1660
NORTHUMBERLAND   1661–25 Dec. 1676

b. 24 June 1630, 4th but o. surv. s. of Sir William Cavendish†, 1st Duke of Newcastle-upon-Tyne, by 1st w. Elizabeth, da. and h. of William Bassett of Blore, Staffs., wid. of Hon. Henry Howard; bro. of Charles Cavendish†, Visct. Mansfield. *educ.* privately; travelled abroad 1644–7. *m.* by 1652, Frances (*d.* 23 Sept. 1695), da. of Hon. William Pierrepont* of Thoresby, Notts., 4s. *d.v.p.* 5da. *styled* Visct. Mansfield June 1659, Earl of Ogle 16 Mar. 1665; *suc.* fa. as 2nd Duke of Newcastle 25 Dec. 1676; KG 17 Feb. 1677.

Master of the robes June 1660–2; gent. of the bedchamber 1662–85; PC 15 June 1670–Dec. 1688; c.j. in eyre (north) 1677–89.[1]

J.p. Notts. July 1660–89; dep. lt. Notts. c. Aug. 1660–70, Derbys. by 1662–70; commr. for assessment, Derbys. Aug. 1660–74, Northumb. Aug. 1660–1, Northumb. and Notts. 1663–74, sewers, Hatfield chase Aug. 1660; col. of vol. horse, Notts. 1661; commr. for loyal and indigent officers, Northumb. 1662; jt. c.-in-c. of militia, Cumb., Westmld., Northumb. and co. Dur. 1667; ld. lt. Northumb. (jt.) 1670–6, (sole) 1676–89, Notts. 1677–89, Yorks. Oct. 1688–9; commr. for recusants, Derbys. 1675; custos rot. Northumb. 1675–89, Derbys. and Notts. 1677–89; recorder, Berwick-upon-Tweed 1685–6, Newcastle-upon-Tyne and East Retford 1685–Oct. 1688; col of militia ft. York Oct. 1688–*d.*[2]

Capt. indep. tp. 1666; gov. Newcastle 1666–?74, Berwick 1675–86, col. of ft. 1667, 1673–4, Oct.–Dec. 1688.[3]

Lord Mansfield was grandson to a younger brother of the 1st Earl of Devonshire, who acquired an estate in Northumberland by marrying Lord Ogle's heiress. His father, the commander of the Cavalier army in the north, was exiled after the Civil War and his estates, worth over £22,000 a year, were sold by the treason trustees. Mansfield himself, who had been with the royalist forces at Marston Moor, stood for Derbyshire at the general election of 1660. He was probably encouraged to defy the Long Parliament ordinance by his father-in-law, who considered all these measures void since the death of Charles I. According to Mansfield's father, still in exile, 'the Anabaptists, believing his passion to serve the King, threatened to take him, dead or alive'; but, aided by 'a trick of returning the writs' and a troop of horse from Nottingham, he was successful after a contest. He presented himself to the King at Dover, and was rewarded with the mastership of the robes. He made no recorded speeches in the Convention, and his committee work was limited to the bill for restoring his father's title and estates and the petition for a fast.[4]

Mansfield transferred to Northumberland in 1661, and was probably returned unopposed. Lord Wharton listed him as a friend, but he was again inactive in the Cavalier Parliament. He was appointed to 22 committees, including the committee of elections and privileges in eight sessions, and made 11 recorded speeches. He took little part in controversial measures, his most important committees in the first session being for restoring the bishops to the House of Lords and executing those under attainder; but in view of the deplorable condition of his father's eight parks after the despoliation of the Civil War and Interregnum, he was probably more interested in the bill to prevent the poaching of deer. His 'melancholy, splenetic apprehensions' induced him to resign his office to Laurence Hyde*, and though he was given a less exacting post in the bedchamber he was always eager for an excuse to avoid attendance at Court. Nevertheless he was listed as a court dependant in 1664, and seconded the motion of Sir John Goodricke* in the Oxford session for the gift of £120,000 to the Duke of York for his naval services. In 1667 he was entrusted, together with the 1st Earl of Carlisle (Charles Howard*), with the defence of the northern counties, and in his constituency, where he was apparently a stranger, he gained the character of 'a prudent, well-tempered nobleman'. On 20 Sept. he wrote to Sir George Savile*: 'I am very sorry for the fall of my lord chancellor, and truly I am not resolved whether to go to the beginning [of the next session] of the Parliament'. A friend of Sir Thomas Osborne*, who, he already predicted, would be 'a great man in business', he was included in both lists of the court party in 1669-71 and made joint lord lieutenant of Northumberland (with his father) and a Privy Councillor. On 14 Feb. 1671 he informed the House that the King had cancelled the patent for lighthouses in Ireland, which had been declared a grievance.[5]

Mansfield, styled Lord Ogle since his father's dukedom, was again under arms in the third Dutch war, but his officers caused alarm, and his defence was clumsy:

> He must choose some Roman Catholics or he cannot raise the King a good regiment. . . . He has but two officers Papists in his whole regiment, and one was put upon

him. It does not become us to think of so great danger of Popery. . . . Northumberland . . . is divided betwixt Papists and such as have fought against the King. He is the son of a father that has fought for him, and so are they also; therefore it cannot be thought amiss to employ them.

He probably introduced the bill for the enfranchisement of Durham, since he was the first Member named to the committee on 10 Mar. 1673. In the next session he was among those appointed to consider the revival of the Border Act. His name appeared on the Paston list, and on 1 Apr. 1675 his friend Osborne, now Lord Treasurer Danby, wrote to him: 'I am by the King's command to let you know that he will take it kindly if you would take the trouble to be here the first session of Parliament'. This tactful summons was effective. Ogle was in his place on the first day of the session and again moved for the representation of Durham. He confidently denied the charge against Danby of declaring at the council board that a new proclamation was better than an old law. He defended the Newark charter and opposed a second address against Lauderdale. A court dependant and a government speaker in the autumn session, his last in the Commons, he was among those appointed to consider illegal exactions and the duties on coal exports. During the ensuing recess he succeeded to the Newcastle peerage.[6]

Newcastle remained loyal to the Stuarts all his life, though with decreasing enthusiasm. His electoral interest in Nottinghamshire and Northumberland remained a potent factor, and he voted against exclusion in 1680. But his sufferings from gout increasingly rendered him 'fit for no place but what is very private and retired'. He made little attempt to canvass support for James II's religious policy, and was easily gulled by Danby in 1688. He evaded taking the oaths to the new regime after the Revolution on the grounds of ill health. He died on 26 July 1691 and was buried at Bolsover. The bulk of his estate, valued at £9,000 p.a., was inherited by his son-in-law, the 4th Earl of Clare (John Holles*).[7]

[1] CSP Dom. 1660-1, p. 26; 1661-2, p. 365; Cal. Treas. Bks. v. 573. [2] C181/7/20; Kingdom's Intell. 7 Mar. 1661; CSP Dom. 1667, p. 214; 1670, p. 353; 1677-8, p. 13; 1685, 54, 67, 86; 1686-7, p. 263; 1687-9, p. 297; Yorks. Arch. Jnl. xxix. 284. [3] CSP Dom. 1665-6, p. 476; 1666-7, p. 384; 1667, p. 179; 1671-2, p. 270; 1675-6, p. 450; 1686-7, p. 260; HMC Portland, ii. 149. [4] M. Cavendish, Duchess of Newcastle, Life of Newcastle, 127, 143-5, 253; Cal. Cl. SP, v. 1. [5] Life of Newcastle, 135-6; HMC Portland, ii. 146; Browning, Danby, ii. 13; CSP Dom. 1667, p. 357; Spencer mss. [6] HMC Portland, ii. 150; Grey, ii. 75-76; iii. 44, 191; Dering, 59, 95. [7] HMC 14th Rep. IX, 417; Reresby Mems. 320; HMC Lords, ii. 14, 37, 114, 279; Luttrell, ii. 270.

M.W.H./E.R.E.

CAVENDISH, William, Lord Cavendish (1641–1707), of Chatsworth, Derbys.

DERBYSHIRE 1661, 1679 (Mar.), 1679 (Oct.), 1681

b. 25 Jan. 1641, 1st s. of William, 3rd Earl of Devonshire by Lady Elizabeth Cecil, da. of William Cecil†, 2nd Earl of Salisbury. *educ.* privately; travelled abroad (France, Italy) 1657–60. *m.* 26 Oct. 1662, Lady Mary Butler (*d.* 31 July 1710), da. of James, 1st Duke of Ormonde, 3s. 1da.; at least 1da. illegit. *suc.* fa. as 4th Earl of Devonshire 23 Nov. 1684; KG 3 Apr. 1689; *cr.* Duke of Devonshire 12 May 1694.[1]

Dep. lt. Derbys. c. Aug. 1660–80; commr. for assessment, Derbys. 1661–80, Mdx. and Westminster 1679–80, loyal and indigent officers, Derbys. 1662, capt. of militia horse ?1669–80; steward, honour of High Peak ?1684–d., Tutbury 1692–d.; ld. lt. Derbys. 1689–d., Notts. 1692–4; high steward, Kingston-upon-Thames 1689–d.; custos rot. Derbys. 1689–d.; recorder, Nottingham 1697–d.[2]

PC 22 Apr. 1679–31 Jan. 1680, 14 Feb. 1689–d.; ld. steward 1689–1702; commr. for reforming abuses in the army 1689; c.j. in eyre (north) 1690–d.; one of the lds. justices 1695–1701; gov. Society of Mineral and Battery Works 1696–d.[3]

FRS 1663–85.

Lord Cavendish's ancestor had sat for Suffolk in two of Richard II's Parliaments, but the real architect of the family fortunes was Sir William Cavendish, treasurer of the chamber to Henry VIII, who acquired a vast estate in the North Midlands by his marriage to 'Bess of Hardwick'. Cavendish's great-grandfather was created Earl of Devonshire in 1618. His father, a pupil of Hobbes, was impeached as a Royalist in 1642 and sat in the Oxford Parliament.[4]

Cavendish was still under age when he was nominated at a meeting of the gentry as court candidate for Derbyshire at the general election of 1661, and returned after a contest. In the first session of the Cavalier Parliament he was appointed to 15 committees, including those for the corporations and uniformity bills, and the bill of pains and penalties; but he left no trace on the records of the next four sessions, though listed as a court dependant in 1664. He served as a volunteer aboard the fleet under the Duke of York during the second Dutch war, giving the first proofs of the courage that was to stand him in good stead both in politics and private life. He was appointed to the committee of elections and privileges for the first time in 1666, but achieved no prominence in the House till the fall of Clarendon. On 13 Dec. 1667 he complained that the bill to banish the fallen minister 'enables him to spend the estate he has gotten by our ruins in another country', and spoke very well, in the judgment of John Milward*. He was sent to ask for the Lords' concurrence in a proclamation calling on Clarendon

to give himself up, and acted as teller against the banishment bill. He was among those ordered on 23 Apr. 1668 to attend the King with the resolution of the House for the wearing of English manufactures. In the same session he acted as teller for a motion to appropriate supply to the use of the navy, the first of many such measures which he was to support. 'A libertine both in principle and practice' and a lover of display, he ran himself into debt, and a month after the House rose in March 1669, 'the privilege being out, he dare not trust his creditors'. He left for France, where he was involved, not discreditably, in a brawl in a theatre with several drunken French officers. When Parliament met again in the autumn he was listed by Sir Thomas Osborne* among the Members who had usually voted for supply. He was appointed, for the first time for eight years, to two important committees, those to consider prolonging the Conventicles Act and to receive information about seditious conventicles, and intervened in the debate on the impeachment of Lord Orrery (Roger Boyle*), no doubt with the aim of protecting his father-in-law Ormonde from the threatened counter-attack. He was among those who spoke on 10 Jan. 1671 in favour of deferring all other business for the bill to punish the assailants of Sir John Coventry*. Consequently when his brother-in-law Lord Ossory (Thomas Butler*) laid down his military command in 1672, Cavendish's application to succeed him was vetoed by the King. 'Ambitious and resentful', he bore a lasting grudge against those who had baulked him in the career to which his temperament was so well suited.[5]

Cavendish's parliamentary activity sharply increased in the next session. On 10 Feb. 1673 he successfully moved for the reading of the resolution of 1663 against the Declaration of Indulgence. He was sent to the Lords to desire a conference on the test bill, although in private he criticized the tactics of the country party; 'when so much money was given to buy a law against Popery, the force of the money would be stronger in order to the bringing it in than the law could be for keeping it out'. On 22 Mar. he moved for a debate on grievances, saying that 'it was now fit to give satisfaction to the people by considering who were the King's evil counsellors', and he desired that the revenue might not be 'disposed of or managed by the lord treasurer [Thomas Clifford*], a person so much suspected of Popery'. Sir William Temple* reckoned him among the most violent group in the Opposition, and in the autumn he supported his friend, the Hon. William Russell*, in advising a refusal of supply. Despite his suspicions of Dutch bribery among the

Opposition, his speech was almost a paraphrase of Dutch propaganda;

> Here is money asked of us to carry on a war we were never advised about, and what we have given is turned to raising of families, and not paying the King's debts. There is so little fruit of the addresses of the last session that we now find greater grievances, as articles of war and martial law. The nation's interest is laid aside for private interest.

When Parliament resumed in 1674 he acted as teller against debating the speech from the throne. He declared himself in favour of removing the Duke of Buckingham both from office and from Court, and presented a petition against the pressing of seamen. Although on the committee for the general test bill, he was prepared to consider a petition from Bernard Howard as a Papist who professed a desire to 'live quiet'. He was also appointed to the committee on the bill to prevent illegal exactions.[6]

In the spring session of 1675 Cavendish again expressed dissatisfaction with the King's opening speech, and took a leading part in the attack on ministers. He helped to draft the address for the removal of Lauderdale and to consider a bill to prevent illegal imprisonment. But, thanks to his contacts with foreign embassies, these domestic matters did not blind him to the international situation. 'The danger of Flanders falling into French hands is what he most apprehends', he said. 'If one prince has been able to manage a war against Christendom with such success, we may justly apprehend it.' He helped to plan the impeachment of Osborne (now Lord Treasurer Danby), and undertook to prove the charge of misusing secret service funds. A week later, in grand committee, he queried the official estimate of a mere two thousand British troops in French service. When the motion for a further address for their recall was lost on the chairman's casting vote Cavendish demanded a recount, spluttering so abundantly in his indignation that Sir John Hanmer* spat back at him. Challenges had been exchanged and swords all but unsheathed when Edward Seymour* resumed the chair, restored order, and swept the principals off in his coach to enforce a reconciliation over dinner. Cavendish was added to the committee on the bill to hinder Papists from sitting in Parliament; but he still had Lauderdale in his sights. He seconded the proposal to invite Burnet, who had been forbidden the Court for testifying against the Scottish favourite, to preach to the House on the King's birthday, and on 31 May he acted as teller for a second address. As soon as the session ended, Cavendish and Richard Newport*, 'brisk House of Commons men who made so bold with his Majesty in Parlia-

ment', were in their turn forbidden the Court, and Lauderdale was brazen enough to insult Cavendish in the theatre in the King's presence. During the summer recess public attention was redirected to the role of English mercenaries in the expansion of France by the death in action at Strasbourg of Col. John Howard, the youngest brother of the 1st Earl of Carlisle (Charles Howard*). A discussion of the event between Cavendish and Sir Thomas Meres* in St. James's Park was reported to another brother, a notorious Roman Catholic, who distributed 'a very cursed paper' denouncing the 'two bold and busy Members' as 'barbarous incendiaries'. When the House met again in the autumn Sir Trevor Williams* produced a copy, and Russell moved that Seymour should again intervene to prevent a duel, though Howard was so gouty that he could not wield a pen, much less a sword. Cavendish denied the words attributed to him, though he was sorry that Howard's brother should have died fighting against his country's honour. Enjoined not to prosecute the quarrel he was provoked into posting up a flysheet describing Howard as a poltroon, and the House sent him to the Tower, but he was discharged two days later. Meanwhile he had moved for a debate on anticipation of revenue, and on 26 Oct. acted with Russell as teller for lodging it in the chamber of London. 'Let those that think not this a good way propose another that's better', he said. The first Member named to conduct the inquiry into the assault on the Anglican convert Luzancy, he called on Sir John Reresby* to testify, and helped to draft the address complaining of the failure to apprehend the principal culprit, the Jesuit St. Germain. He was also among those appointed to consider the bill for the liberty of the subject. He took a moderate line on the revival of the differences between the Houses over the jurisdiction of the Lords, and helped to manage a conference.[7]

Cavendish was now recognized as one of the leaders of the Opposition, and in 1676 Sir Richard Wiseman* included him among those Members he had no hopes of gaining for the Court. In another duel Lord Mohun, one of the country peers who was acting as his second, was mortally wounded. When Parliament met again, Cavendish queried the legality of the long recess, and complained that he was denied access to Shaftesbury and the other peers who had been sent to the Tower for expressing the same view, though less cautiously. He was again appointed to committees for recall from the French service, liberty of the subject, and preventing the growth of Popery. On 6 Mar. 1677 he told the House:

Parliaments have been prorogued without doing anything, and money has been refused for our better strength at sea; and now we have had a long prorogation and officers notoriously known to raise men for the French service, and much countenanced here at Court. When he considers these things he still thinks we have creatures and pensioners of France in our councils.

He helped to manage conferences on the danger from France and the naval programme, and to draft addresses promising aid for defence and urging the formation of alliances. But he was determined that the Commons should retain control of the purse-strings. ' 'Tis an ill precedent to charge the people because the King may have a war', he said on 23 May, a few days before the session came to an abrupt end. At the next brief meeting in July he 'modestly moved in a few words . . . that they might have the order read whereby they were last adjourned'. He visited Shaftesbury in the Tower in November, and was marked 'thrice worthy'. He seconded William Sacheverell* in his attack on Seymour on 28 Jan. 1678 for his irregular adjournments, and supported the address for reducing France to her frontiers of 1659, which he helped to draw up. He acted as teller against going into committee on supply, saying

Prerogative protects us, but those abuse it who speak of it without telling us how 'tis for our safety. I am for it as it is by law, but not for prerogative to be swayed by ill counsels. I am not for the ministers having money to employ it, either for a short war, or no war. Let us be showed that a war is intended in earnest. I am sorry I cannot [but] suspect otherwise. Till that be plain, I cannot give money. Till it be showed us, I cannot give a penny.

During the spring and summer sessions Cavendish helped to draw up the address for war with France, to prepare reasons on the growth of Popery, to summarize foreign commitments, to draw up another address for the removal of counsellors, and to consider the revived bill for hindering Papists from sitting in Parliament. The speech from the throne on 18 June provoked from him the derisive suggestion that the opposition firebrand Michael Malet* should be yoked with Secretary Williamson in returning thanks 'for the gracious expressions'. More seriously, he demanded the removal of those ministers who had advised a further demand for supply. 'Our liberality has brought upon us the fears of Popery and arbitrary power.'[8]

In the last session of the Cavalier Parliament, Cavendish was appointed to the committee of inquiry into the Popish Plot and to those to examine Coleman and to translate his letters. He helped to draw up reasons for belief in the plot. Nevertheless his real target was Danby, for he had been convinced by Lord Faversham and John Churchill II* that it was the lord treasurer who denied him employment, whereas the Duke of York, mindful of his good conduct at the battle of Lowestoft, was disposed to grant him a command. 'I have an extreme veneration for the Duke', he said on 4 Nov., 'for I think the Duke had not the least hand in the plot.' But he recognized the force of public opinion. 'If I had the honour to be near the Duke, I would advise him to withdraw. . . . I think we cannot answer our duty to the King, nor our country, if we do not address that the Duke may be removed from the King.' When Williamson was proved to have signed commissions to Roman Catholic officers, Cavendish declared his opinion that 'a standing army in time of peace, whether the officers be Popish or Protestant, is illegal'. He also noted that Monmouth was described as the King's son; 'have we a Prince of Wales?' he inquired ironically. He favoured the impeachment of the unfortunate secretary for his lapses, and helped to draft the address for his imprisonment. When the Lords proposed to except the Duke of York by name from the bill to exclude Papists from Parliament, Cavendish said:

I cannot agree to the Duke's being declared a Papist by Act of Parliament till I hear the Lords' reasons for the proviso. If we agree to the proviso, we cannot hear the Lords' reasons. Possibly I may be convinced by the Lords, but I am not by anything I have heard yet.

He helped to draft the instructions for disbanding the army and the address on the dangers facing the nation. He was clearly familiar with the contents of the papers of Ralph Montagu* before they were produced in the House, and headed the Commons delegation sent to ask the King for details of the charges against him. Responsibility for Danby's impeachment was specially imposed on Cavendish and William Williams*, and he defended their conduct in concealing the place and time of meeting from Members 'who would come only to spy what we did'. He was among those instructed to examine the articles of impeachment. Altogether he had been a moderately active Member of the Cavalier Parliament, in which he had been appointed to 81 committees, acted as teller in ten divisions, and made about 120 recorded speeches.[9]

Cavendish was re-elected unopposed to the Exclusion Parliaments. An active Member in 1679, with eight committees and 18 speeches, he was marked 'worthy' on Shaftesbury's list. Nevertheless, from the first he showed himself, to his father's delight, one of the most moderate of the Opposition, and was brought to Court by Ossory at the King's request. He was anxious to find an expedient for breaking the deadlock over the speakership, and seconded Russell's nomination of William Gregory* as compromise candidate. He spoke twice in the debate occasioned by Bedloe's evidence, and brought the King's answer to the request of the House for entrusting the informer's safety to Monmouth. On the humiliation of Edward Sackville* for expressing disbelief in the plot, he remarked, 'I like any opinion of the House that looks like justice, and not animosity', but found little support. But towards Danby he was implacable. 'It is cruelty to the public to let this pardon pass', he said. He helped to manage a conference and to draft the summons to the fallen minster to give himself up. He acted as teller against the court candidates at Windsor, and, on the rumour that Tangier, like Dunkirk, was to be sold to the French, he moved to attach it formally to the crown. His name stood first on the committee appointed to prepare a bill to this effect. Although his popularity in the country was such that a spurious speech was published over his name, he could no longer 'keep pace' with the Opposition, especially after his nomination to the remodelled Privy Council. When the King reminded the House of the need to send out a fleet, Cavendish said:

> I see no reason to abandon all thoughts of public safety because all things are not yet done. No man in this House can say so much of ill management, etc., as I can think. . . . But, because you have not everything done on a sudden, will you put a negative on the King's message? There is no reason for that, or why we should be ruined whilst we consider [how] to punish offenders. I have examined myself, and if I were not in the state I am, I should be of the same opinion.

On 17 May he informed the House that the King would receive their loyal address, promising to revenge his possible assassination on the Papists. He considered exclusion a desperate measure, calculated to provoke foreign interference, and voted against the bill.[10]

During the summer Cavendish's military ambitions seemed at last on the point of fulfilment, for he was commissioned colonel of foot against the rebels in Scotland, an embarrassing appointment since he had publicly declared that Lauderdale's enemies, to his personal knowledge, were 'of as great loyalty, honour and estates as any are in that country'. He declined the offer, and in January 1680 was given leave, together with Russell, to withdraw from the Privy Council. After pointedly ignoring the Duke of York at Newmarket, he was again forbidden the King's presence. He was among those who sought to obtain the Duke's conviction for recusancy in June. Secretary Jenkins, however, was told that if the King persuaded Lord Devonshire to pay Cavendish's debts and grant him a

more liberal maintenance, he would 'return to his duty . . . to the King, as well as to his father'. He was less active in the second Exclusion Parliament, being appointed to only two committees and making 11 speeches. Although now a convert to exclusion, he would have nothing to do with Monmouth's claims, and 'took occasion sometimes to show his dislike of the violence and virulence of the prosecutors'. Speaking 'much beyond himself' in the debate on Halifax, he abandoned his defence of rumour as a ground for action, 'urging it as mere nonsense that common fame should publish what counsels were clandestinely and secretly delivered', and desiring that the address for his removal might lie upon the table 'until fortified with better reasons'. When William Harbord* and Miles Fleetwood* asserted that Seymour had been guilty of malversation, Cavendish sarcastically expressed his confidence that they would not be 'exposed'. During the attack on Laurence Hyde* he inquired: 'What becomes of liberty of speech if he may be questioned for what he does here?' On 18 Dec. he moved, despite calls to proceed to a vote, for a numerous committee to draw up an address insisting on exclusion, to which he was appointed. 'He inveighed against French mistresses and said he doubted of the success of their endeavours, because they ought not to prosecute any actions in themselves just by unjust means.' Nevertheless he carried the impeachment of Lord Chief Justice Scroggs to the Lords on 5 Jan. 1681. Two days later he proposed that the House should pass a resolution declaring resistance to a Popish successor to be lawful, since he would be incapable of performing the office of a King, but was forced to agree that it would be no substitute for a statute. In the Oxford Parliament he helped to prepare for a conference on the loss of the bill of ease for dissenters and to draw up the third exclusion bill. He was willing to overlook Jenkins's fault after he had begged the House's pardon for refusing to carry up the impeachment of Fitzharris, and objected to explanations from Members of their change of attitude on exclusion.[11]

Cavendish kissed the King's hand at Newmarket in 1681, but in other respects his life altered little. His father feared that his late hours in town might destroy him, and complained that he could not obtain a clear list of his debts, though he was in danger of arrest. He sought vainly to bring Königsmarck to account for the murder of Thomas Thynne II*. He was not involved in the Rye House Plot, and offered to help Russell to escape from Newgate by changing clothes with him. As Earl of Devonshire he led the Opposition in the Lords in

1685. He quarrelled with a courtier named Cole-peper and was provoked into striking him in Whitehall, for which he was sentenced to pay a fine of £30,000. He signed the invitation to William of Orange, and took a prominent part in the Revolu-tion. One of the leading Whig peers, though not a member of the Junto, he was created a duke in 1694. He died on 18 Aug. 1707, and was buried at All Saints, Derby. Burnet's description has already been quoted in part. After alluding to the defects of his character, he credits him with 'the courage of a hero, with a much greater proportion both of wit and learning than is usual in men of his birth'. His youngest son sat for Derby with two intervals from 1701 to 1742, and one of the county seats was usually at the disposal of the family throughout the 18th century.[12]

[1] HMC 15th Rep. VII, 161, 166; Pepys Diary, 11 May 1660. [2] Sir Robert Somerville, Duchy of Lancaster Office Holders, 162, 170; Cal. Treas. Bks. ix. 1509; x. 273; HMC Buccleuch, ii. 107; Manning and Bray, Surr. i. 342; Nottingham Bor. Recs. vi. 36. [3] CSP Dom. 1689-90, p. 97; BL Loan 16. [4] Copinger, Suff. Manors, i. 60-61; Lysons, Derbys. 147-8; DNB; Cal. Comm. Adv. Money, 402. [5] HMC Hastings, ii. 141; CSP Dom. 1665-6, p. 431; Grey, i. 66, 183; Milward, 165; CJ, ix. 40, 92; Burnet, ii. 91; HMC Rutland, ii. 11; CSP Ven. 1669-70, p. 72; Dering, 45; PRO31/3, bdle. 127, f. 189. [6] Dering, 110, 148; CJ, ix. 265, 292; Burnet, ii. 16-17; Grey, ii. 152, 200, 247, 329, 362, 374; CSP Ven. 1673-5, p. 39; Essex Pprs. (Cam. Soc. n.s. xlvii), 131. [7] Dering Pprs. 59, 77, 82, 89; Grey, iii. 4, 83, 120, 128-9, 291-3, 299, 316, 356; iv. 39; vii. 191; Haley, Shaftesbury, 389; Essex Pprs. 319; Bramston Autobiog. (Cam. Soc. xxxii), 199; Bulstrode Pprs. 302-3, 316-19; Reresby, 101. [8] Browning, Danby, i. 229; HMC Rutland, ii. 34, 39; Grey, iv. 65, 101, 200, 368, 391; v. 6-7, 31, 81-82, 95, 98; CSP Dom. 1676-7, p. 564; 1677-8, pp. 149, 268; CJ, ix. 398, 418, 428, 432; HMC Portland, iii. 355. [9] Browning, iii. 8; Grey, vi. 141, 218, 225, 236, 253, 347, 370; CJ, ix. 542, 561. [10] De-vonshire mss IH, letter of 28 Jan. 1679; HMC Ormonde, n.s. iv. 347, 356; v. 5, 38, 98; Grey, vi. 426; vii. 2, 14, 15, 30, 54, 98, 247, 274-5; CJ, ix. 573, 588, 602. [11] HMC Ormonde, n.s. iv. 522; v. 137, 142, 503, 561-2; vi. 2, 8; CSP Dom. 1679-80, p. 177; 1680-1, pp. 38-39; Grey, vii. 198; viii. 44, 90, 198, 268, 283, 308; HMC 7th Rep. 479; PRO31/3, bdle. 146, f. 26v; bdle. 147, f. 85; Exact Coll. Debates, 154, 256; CJ, ix. 683. [12] Luttrell, i. 132, 174; HMC Ormonde, n.s. vi. 161, 328; Browning, i. 374; Burnet, ii. 92, 382.

E.R.E.

CAWLEY, William (c.1628–aft. 1700), of Chich-ester, Suss.

CHICHESTER 1659, 3–21 May 1660

b. c.1628, 1st s. of William Cawley[†] of Chichester by 1st w. Catherine, da. of William Walrond of Isle Brewers, Som. educ. I. Temple 1645, called 1652. m. by 1655, Elizabeth. suc. fa. 1667.[1]

J.p. Suss. 1652–July 1660; commr. for assessment 1652, 1657, Jan. 1660, militia 1659.

Cawley was the grandson of a prominent Chich-ester brewer. His father sat for the city in 1628-9 and for Midhurst in the Long Parliament and Richard Cromwell's Parliament. A regicide and a Rumper, he fled to Switzerland before the Restora-tion. But his mother came from a royalist family, his younger brother became an archdeacon and he himself married the daughter, not otherwise identi-fied, of a sequestrated Cavalier.[2]

Cawley sat for Chichester in 1659, and was involved in a double return at the general election of 1660. Seated on the merits of the return, he was displaced by John Farrington[*] on the merits of the election without leaving any other trace on the re-cords of the Convention. The family estate was granted to the Duke of York, who sold it to Henry Brouncker[*] for £2,100. Brouncker bequeathed it to Sir Charles Lyttelton[*]. After the Revolution, when it was rumoured that Edmund Ludlow[†] was to be brought back from exile to suppress the Irish re-bellion, Lyttelton, like other holders of regicides' lands, feared that they might be restored to the heirs. In order to confirm his title to the manor of Rumboldswyke he paid Cawley and his wife £400. But by 1700 Cawley was reduced to poverty and was granted £5 by the Inner Temple. The date of his death is not known, and he was the last of his family to sit in Parliament.[3]

[1] DNB; Som Wills, v. 106. [2] Cal. Comm. Comp. 834; CSP Dom. 1660-1, p. 338. [3] Fines for Manors (Suss. Rec. Soc. xx), 376; A. Hay, Chichester, 351-2; Cal. I.T. Recs. 356.

B.M.C./B.D.H.

CECIL, James, Visct. Cranborne (1646–83), of Hatfield, Herts.

HERTFORDSHIRE 4 Apr.–3 Dec. 1668

b. bef. 27 Mar. 1646, 1st s. of Charles Cecil[†], Visct. Cran-borne (d. Dec. 1660) by Lady Diana Maxwell, da. and coh. of James, 1st Earl of Dirletoun [S]. m. lic. 25 Sept. 1661 (with £11,000), Lady Margaret Manners (d. Aug. 1682), da. of John Manners[†], 8th Earl of Rutland, 5s. 5da. suc. gdfa. as 3rd Earl of Salisbury 3 Dec. 1668; KG 31 Aug. 1680.[1]

Capital steward, Hertford 1668–d.[2]

PC 3 Jan. 1679–18 Jan. 1681.

Lord Cranborne, like his cousin Lord Burghley (John Cecil[*]), was the great-great-grandson of the Elizabethan statesman. His great-grandfather, the 1st Earl of Salisbury, acquired the royal manor of Hatfield in 1607 in exchange for Theobalds, and this became the principal seat of the family. Cran-borne's father supported Parliament in the Civil War as MP for Hertford, but was secluded at Pride's Purge, and died soon after the Restoration.[3]

Cranborne was returned for the county, appar-ently with Quaker support, at the cost of £1,200 at a by-election in 1668. He sat in the Lower House for just over a month before the recess as a sup-porter of the Cabal. During this time he attended the King with an address for wearing English manufactures, was appointed to a committee for an estate bill, and acted as teller against a proviso in the bill for appropriating the customs for the navy. He also presented a petition from the wife of Brome Whorwood* complaining of hard usage by her husband. In the Upper House he became one of the Opposition 'hotspurs' and a close associate of Shaftesbury. His appointment to the Privy Council was widely welcomed, but as a strenuous supporter of exclusion he was given leave to retire in 1681. He died in May 1683 and was buried at Hatfield. His death caused a serious financial crisis, for though his income was estimated at £12,200 p.a., it was encumbered by debts, trust funds, annuities, and legacies to children of over £78,000. The parliamentary tradition of the Cecil family was temporarily interrupted by the 4th Earl, who became a Roman Catholic under James II, but a younger son was returned for Castle Rising in 1701 as a Whig.[4]

[1] *VCH Herts. Peds.* 118–19, 126; *Northern Gen.* iv. 144; L. Stone, *Family and Fortune*, 153–4; Luttrell, i. 215–16. [2] L. Turnor, *Hertford*, 107, 120. [3] *VCH Herts.* iii. 92; *CSP Dom.* 1638–9, p. 622; Keeler, *Long Parl.* 130; A. Kingston, *Herts. during the Civil War*, 145–8. [4] *Pepys Diary*, 4 Apr. 1668; *EHR*, lxxi. 387–8; *Milward*, 297; *Letters to Williamson* (Cam. Soc. n.s. ix), 156–7; *CSP Dom.* 1679–80, p. 15; Luttrell, i. 253, 260; Stone, 154–6.

E.R.E./G.J.

CECIL, John, Lord Burghley (c.1648–1700), of Burghley House, Northants.

NORTHAMPTONSHIRE   29 Apr. 1675–1 Feb. 1678

b. c.1648, 1st s. of John, 4th Earl of Exeter by 1st w. Lady Frances Manners, da. of John Manners†, 8th Earl of Rutland. *educ.* Stamford g.s.; St. John's, Camb. 1667. *m.* lic. 4 May 1670, aged 21, Lady Anne Cavendish, da. of William, 3rd Earl of Devonshire, wid. of Charles, Lord Rich, 4s. 4da. *suc.* fa. as 5th Earl of Exeter 1 Feb. 1678.[1]

J.p. Northants. and Peterborough 1670–c.84; commr. for assessment, Northants. and Rutland 1677–8; recorder, Stamford 1682–5, Oct. 1688–97.[2]

Lord Burghley was the great-great-grandson of the Elizabethan statesman. His grandfather died early in the Civil War, leaving his father too young to take any part in it, though he welcomed the Restoration and became lord lieutenant of Northamptonshire. Burghley himself was returned for the county at a by-election in 1675, probably unopposed. He was moderately active during his three sessions in the Cavalier Parliament, being named to ten committees, of which the most important were to appropriate the customs to the use of the navy and to prevent illegal exactions from the subject. His only speech was in defence of his brother-in-law, William Cavendish*, Lord Cavendish, on 2 Mar. 1677. He probably brought in Lord Cullen's

estate bill eight days later, as his name heads the committee, and the election petition of Thomas Hatcher.* He was marked 'doubly worthy' by Shaftesbury, and secured the return of the country candidates at Stamford in the first general election of 1679. But in the Upper House he proved more interested in art than politics, usually leaving his proxy with his cousin, the 2nd Earl of Bridgwater, a moderate country peer. On 24 Oct. 1679 he obtained a pass to go beyond the seas with his wife, his heir, 22 servants and 30 horses, and was of course absent from the division in the Upper House on the second exclusion bill and from the trial of Lord Stafford. He went on a second tour of Europe in 1683, accompanied by Charles Fitzwilliam* and William Hyde*. On his return 46 pictures which he had bought in Italy were seized by the customs, but released without payment shortly after the accession of James II. Lord Exeter acted as lord high almoner at the coronation, but was noted as in opposition in 1687, and is said to have joined the Prince of Orange in the following year. Nevertheless he was a non-juror after the Revolution. He left with his wife and three younger sons on a third visit to the Continent in 1699, but died of peritonitis near Paris on 29 Aug. 1700, and was buried at St. Martin's, Stamford. His eldest son was Tory MP for Rutland at his death, while two of the younger sons sat for Stamford under William III and Anne.[3]

[1] *Life of Richard Kidder* (Som. Rec. Soc. xxxvii), 6. [2] *CSP Dom.* 1682, p. 559; 1697, p. 477. [3] Grey, iv. 172, 317; *HMC 13th Rep. VI*, 13; *CSP Dom.* 1679–80, p. 352; 1683–4, p. 192; 1689–90, p. 528; 1699–1700, p. 259; *Cal. Treas. Bks.* vii. 1350–1, 1424; *Ellis Corresp.* ii. 320; *Ailesbury Mems.* 237.

J.P.F.

CHADWICK, James (c.1660–97), of Ludgate Street, London, and The Deanery, Canterbury, Kent.

NEW ROMNEY   1689
DOVER   1690, 1695–11 May 1697

b. c.1660, 1st s. of James Chadwick, Merchant Taylor, of King Street, London and Enfield, Mdx. by w. Elizabeth. *m.* lic. 29 July 1682, aged 22, Mary (*d.*1687), da. of John Tillotson, dean of Canterbury 1672–91, 2s. 1da. *suc.* fa. 1678.[1]

Commr. for assessment, Kent and New Romney 1689–90, Mdx. 1690; freeman, Dover 1690; dep. lt. Kent 1694–*d.*, lt.-col. of militia ft. by 1697–*d.*[2]

Asst. Mines Co. 1693; commr. for customs 1694–*d.*[3]

Chadwick claimed descent from a Lancashire gentry family. His grandfather, a lawyer, was in arms for Parliament and sat for Nottingham under the Protectorate. His father, a prosperous merchant, was probably a member of a London Independent congregation, bequeathing £40 to its minister and £10 to its poor out of an estate of some £19,300; but Chadwick must have become an Anglican at an early age. He inherited property in Romney Marsh and a house in London, but after his wife's death he lived principally with his father-in-law at Canterbury. No doubt this improved his interest at New Romney. On 6 Oct. 1688 he thanked the corporation for their 'favour in designing me for one of the burgesses . . . when there shall be occasion, and I esteem the favour the greater because I am wholly a stranger to you'. He further undertook to 'preserve our religion and laws', and his record in the Revolution shows that this was not merely a form of words. He accompanied Lord Winchilsea to Faversham on 12 Dec., and was sent by the deputy lieutenants to seek the instructions of the Privy Council for the disposal of the captive King.[4]

Chadwick was returned to the Convention for New Romney after a contest with Sir Charles Sedley*, and also represented the port at the coronation. An inactive Member of the Convention, he was named to the committee of elections and privileges and to seven others, including those for preventing the illegal export of wool, relieving Huguenot refugees, and reversing the quo warranto against London. He was not recorded as speaking, but he supported the disabling clause in the bill to restore corporations, and was appointed to the committee on the bill for regulating elections in the Cinque Ports. He lost his seat to Sedley at the general election, but sat for Dover as a country Whig until he became a placeman in 1694. He died on 11 May 1697, and was buried at St. Lawrence Jewry. His family were left in financial straits, and none of his descendants appears to have entered Parliament.[5]

[1] PCC 93 Reeve, 114 Pyne; *Mar. Lic.* (Harl. Soc. xxx), 102; T. Birch, *Life of Tillotson* (1753), 125. [2] Add. 29625, f. 122v; Eg. 1626, f. 23. [3] *Sel. Charters* (Selden Soc. xxviii), 239; *Cal. Treas. Bks.* x. 739; xii. 44, 206. [4] *Vis. Notts.* (Thoroton Soc. rec. ser. xiii), 48; A. C. Wood, *Notts. in the Civil War*, 133; Merchant Taylors apprentice bk. 1635–9, p. 175; PCC 93 Reeve; information from H. Horwitz; Birch, 251; Kent AO, NR/AEp, f. 6; *N. and Q.* (ser. 3), vi. 2, 22; *Ailesbury Mems.* 207. [5] Add. 33923, f. 462; *Suss. Arch. Colls.* xv. 209; *CSP Dom.* 1697, p. 162; Birch, 347, 349; *St. Lawrence Jewry* (Harl. Soc. Reg. lxxi), 195.

B.D.H.

CHAFE, Thomas I (c.1611–62), of Sherborne, Dorset and the Middle Temple.

TOTNES 1660

b. c.1611, 1st s. of John Chafe, merchant, of Exeter, Devon by Anne, da. of William May of North Molton, Devon. *educ.* M. Temple 1631, called 1638. *m.* lic. 28 Dec. 1641 aged 30, Catherine, da. of Sir Thomas Malet†, j.K.b. 1641–2, May–Dec. 1660, of St. Audries, Som., 1s. 5da. *suc.* fa. 1619.[1]

Bencher, M. Temple 1659; j.p. Dorset July 1660–d., commr. for assessment Aug. 1660–d.

Chafe's grandfather, of Somerset origin, migrated to Exeter where he was twice mayor. Chafe became a lawyer, and, though doubtless an Anglican and a Royalist in sympathy, took no part in the Civil War. His father-in-law, the father of John Malet* and Michael Malet*, was associated with the 1st Earl of Bristol over the Kent petition of 1642, and Chafe, as one of the earl's trustees, helped to buy back and manage the forfeited estate during the Interregnum.[2]

The first of his family to enter Parliament, Chafe was returned for Totnes, presumably on the Seymour interest, at the general election of 1660, when Cavaliers and their sons were forbidden to stand. A moderately active Member of the Convention he was appointed to 29 committees, including those to draft the assessment ordinances, and made 12 recorded speeches, mostly in defence of the Church against Popery and fanaticism. He wished to impose the oath of supremacy on recusants, and the 39 Articles on incumbents, and he supported the ousting of the intruded dons at Oxford by Lord Hertford, the head of the younger branch of the Seymour family. He was named to the committees for the navigation bill and for settling ecclesiastical livings, and he was among those ordered to give directions on engrossing the latter bill. He was of course named to the committee to consider reparations to his employer, Lord Bristol. He was active in taxation measures, helping to draw up an assertion of the sole right of the Commons to name local commissioners. He was also named to the committees to fix the Dunkirk establishment and to consider a bill for endowing vicarages, a matter which concerned him personally, since his wife's dowry was charged on a Cornish rectory.[3]

In the second session, Chafe attacked the 'indulgence and remissness' of the poll-tax commissioners, and was named to the committee to examine defects in the Act. He was among those appointed to consider the attainder bill. In the debate on the militia bill he moved for a limitation on the powers of imprisonment granted to deputy lieutenants. He was among those appointed to draft the clauses for compensating the crown for the loss of feudal revenue by means of the excise and for repealing Henry VIII's Statute of Liveries, though he insisted on proper compensation for officials of the court of wards. He opposed such local Puritans as Sir Walter Erle* and Denzil Holles* in preferring mothers to grandfathers as guardians.[4]

Chafe was replaced by Sir Edward Seymour* at the general election of 1661. He was buried in the Temple Church on 3 July 1662.[5]

[1] Vivian, *Vis. Devon*, 536; PCC 74 Parker; *Mar. Lic.* (Harl. Soc. xxvi), 262–3. [2] *Trans. Devon Assoc.* xix. 531; *Cal. Comm. Comp.* 2170; *CSP Dom.* 1656–7, p. 10; Dorset RO, KG2655; *CJ*, ii. 507. [3] Bowman diary, ff. 25v, 53, 69, 109; PCC 138 Laud. [4] *Old Parl. Hist.* xxiii. 2, 22, 47, 61; *CJ*, ix. 177. [5] *Temple Church Recs.* 16.

M.W.H./J.P.F.

CHAFE, Thomas II (c.1642–1701), of West Hall, Folke, Dorset.

BRIDPORT 1685

b. c.1642, o.s. of Thomas Chafe I*. *educ.* Sherborne sch.; Wadham, Oxf. 1657. *m.* 13 Apr. 1662, Susanna, da. and h. of Edward Moleyns of West Hall, 1s. *d.v.p.* 5da. *suc.* fa. 1662.[1]

J.p. Dorset 1670–June 1688, Nov. 1688–96, 1700–*d.*; commr. for assessment 1673–80, 1689–90, recusants 1675; freeman, Lyme Regis 1683; dep. lt. Dorset 1685–May 1688, Oct. 1688–96, 1701–*d.*; alderman, Bridport aft. 1685–Jan. 1688.[2]

Chafe no doubt owed his return for Bridport in 1685 chiefly to the recorder, Hugh Hodges*, with whom he must have been on intimate terms, since their fathers had been trustees for the Digby estates during the Interregnum, and they had been schoolfellows at Sherborne. Chafe probably held property in Bridport in the right of his wife, whose ancestor had sat for the borough as long ago as 1491. He left no trace on the records of James II's Parliament.[3]

Chafe's answers to the lord lieutenant's questions on the repeal of the Test Act and the Penal Laws were negative. He was displaced from the corporation of Bridport, and omitted from the commission of the peace and the lieutenancy in the summer of 1688. Although he continued to act as a j.p. under the new regime, he refused the Association in 1696, and was removed from local office. But he was restored to the commission of the peace before he died on 25 Nov. 1701, aged 59. He was buried at Folke.[4]

[1] Hutchins, *Dorset*, iv. 181; *Misc. Gen. et Her.* (ser. 5), viii. 297. [2] C. A. F. Meekings, *Dorset Hearth Tax*, 116; Dorset RO, KG 1147, 1148, 1496; Lyme Regis court bk. 1672–92, f. 333v; PC2/72/567. [3] Dorset RO, KG 2655; *CSP Dom.* 1656–7, p. 10; PCC 108 Barrington; Bridport corp. mss 21, no. 2244. [4] Hutchins, iv. 183; PC 2/72/567; 76, f. 256; *CSP Dom.* 1689–90, p. 248.

J.P.F.

CHAFFIN see CHAFIN

CHAFIN (CHAFFIN), Thomas (1650–91), of Chettle, Dorset.

POOLE	1679 (Mar.), 1679 (Oct.), 1681, 1685
DORCHESTER	9 Dec. 1689
HINDON	1690–17 Jan. 1691

b. 15 July 1650, 2nd surv. s. of Thomas Chafin of Chettle by 2nd w. Amphillis, da. of Laurence Hyde† of Heale, Wilts. and coh. to her gt.-gdfa. Richard White of Alton, Hants. *educ.* Magdalen Hall, Oxf. 1666. *m.* 23 Jan. 1674, Anne, da. of John Penruddock of Compton Chamberlayne, Wilts., 5s. (2 *d.v.p.*) 6da. *suc.* bro. 1660.[1]

J.p. Dorset 1678–June 1688, Nov. 1688–*d.*, capt. of militia ft. by 1679–Feb. 1688, major Oct. 1688–*d.*; freeman, Poole 1679, Salisbury 1683; commr. for assessment, Dorset, Poole, Wilts. and Salisbury 1679–80, Dorset and Som. 1689–90; dep. lt. Dorset 1680–Feb. 1688, Oct. 1688–*d.*[2]

Commr. for drowned lands 1690.[3]

Chafin's family was of Wiltshire origin, producing a Member for Salisbury in 1475. The Dorset branch was established in Elizabethan times, and Chafin's grandfather was elected for Bridport in 1628. His father, a royalist commissioner, valued his estate in his composition at £500 p.a. By his marriage, incidentally a very happy one, to the daughter of the leader of the Cavalier rising in 1655, Chafin strengthened his royalist background and his family connexions.[4]

Chafin was recommended to the corporation of Poole by Thomas Strangways* and sat in the three Exclusion Parliaments. Shaftesbury regarded his political attitude as doubtful, but he was marked as a country Member on Huntingdon's list. In 1679 he was named only to the committee of elections and privileges, but he voted for the exclusion bill. After re-election to the second Exclusion Parliament he was one of the Members appointed to receive information about the Popish Plot on 13 Nov. 1680, but on 8 Jan. 1681 he was granted leave of absence. He left no trace on the records of the Oxford Parliament or James II's Parliament.[5]

Chafin's regiment was not involved in the rout of the Dorset militia at Bridport in 1685, but Chafin and his friend Thomas Erle* fought as volunteers at Sedgemoor. After the battle they were presented to the King by John Churchill II*, but no tangible acknowledgment of their services was offered. He gave negative answers on the repeal of the Test Act and Penal Laws, lost office, and probably assisted Erle in the Revolution.[6]

Chafin's electoral expenses in 1689 must have been heavy. He first stood for Poole, where he was involved in a double return with Sir Nathaniel Napier*. The elections committee found in Chafin's favour, but their recommendation was reversed by the House, to whom 'Mr Chafin was obnoxious . . . being a notorious Tory'. Then in December Chafin stood for Dorchester at a by-election, and defeated Nathaniel Bond*. His opponent petitioned, but the committee made no report before the dissolution of the Convention.

Chafin was allowed to sit, though he was not named to any committee. On 29 Jan. 1690 he wrote to his wife:

> The Parliament is prorogued, and most are of the opinion it will be dissolved. . . . Mr Freke [Thomas Freke I*] went down this day; I shall stay here till next week, partly by his direction, and partly by my own inclination. . . . The prick-eared party are much troubled at this prorogation; things seem of better complexion here than formerly.

Chafin sat for Hindon in the next Parliament, but died on 17 Jan. 1691, and was buried at Chettle. Two of his sons sat for the county as Tories.[7]

[1] VCH Hants, ii. 477; Hutchins, Dorset, iii. 570; St. Andrew Undershaft par. reg. [2] CSP Dom. 1679–80, p. 61; Hoare, Wilts. Salisbury, 478; Hutchins, i. 24; Poole archives, B17; Churchill College, Cambridge, Erle-Drax mss. [3] Cal. Treas. Bks. ix. 794. [4] SP23/179/264–274. [5] Dorset RO, D124, Strangways to Poole corp. 29 Jan. 1679. [6] Hutchins, iii. 566. [7] J. Sydenham, Hist. Poole, 263; CJ, x. 13, 24; Hutchins, iii. 566.

J.P.F.

CHAPLIN, Thomas (1591–1672), of Bury St. Edmunds, Suff.

BURY ST. EDMUNDS   1659, 3–14 May 1660

bap. 21 Oct. 1591, 3rd s. of William Chaplin (d.1629) of Semer by 1st w. Agnes. m. Elizabeth, da. of Robert Ignis alias Hynes, goldsmith, of Bury St. Edmunds, 2s. d.v.p. 2da.[1]
Alderman, Bury St. Edmunds by 1643–?62; commr. for execution of ordinances, Bury 1643, eastern association 1643, assessment, Bury 1645–52, Suff. 1649–52, Suff. and Bury 1657, Jan. 1660; elder, Bury classis 1647; commr. for militia, Suff. 1648, 1659, Bury Mar. 1660; j.p. Suff. 1650–Mar. 1660, commr. for security 1655–6.[2]
Member, high court of justice 1650.

Chaplin came of Suffolk yeoman stock. His grandfather had farmed at Long Melford, and his father was bailiff of Semer manor at his death. Chaplin himself set up as a linen-draper in Bury St. Edmunds. A Presbyterian and a parliamentary supporter in the Civil War, he held local office throughout the Interregnum, besides sitting in one of the high courts of justice. He represented Bury in Richard Cromwell's Parliament and contested the borough at the general election of 1660, when he was involved in a double return. On 3 May he and John Clarke I* were allowed to take their seats on the merits of the return, only to be unseated a few days later when the committee reported adversely on the merits of their election. During his short stay in the Convention he made no recorded speeches and was not appointed to any committees. He does not seem to have taken any further part in public life. His will, in which he mentioned lands in Wyverstone and several houses in Bury, was dated 24 Apr. and proved on 25 Nov. 1672. His direct descendants remained nonconformists and did not enter Parliament; but his great-nephew Robert sat for Grimsby from 1715 until expelled as a South Sea Company director.[3]

[1] J. J. Muskett, Suff. Manorial Fams. iii. 109–10, 114. [2] Suff. and the Gt. Rebellion (Suff. Green Bks. iii), 27, 40, 132; County of Suff. Divided (1647), 7; Thurloe, iii. 223. [3] Muskett, 109.

M.W.H./P.W.

CHAPMAN, William (c.1647–at least 1687), of St. James's Street, Westminster.

DOVER   1685

m. (1) lic. 25 Nov. 1672, 'aged 23', Amy, da. of Robert Mildmay of Terling, Essex; (2) lic. 3 Oct. 1684, 'aged 40', Honora, da. of Joseph Roberts of St. Thomas Hill, Canterbury, Kent.[1]
Freeman, Dover and Sandwich 1684.[2]

Chapman's origins are obscure, though he may have been akin to William Chapman, a hempdresser, who became a freeman of Dover in 1656 and captain of two bulwarks in the town defences. Presumably an attorney, he acquired an interest in the port by his second marriage, and procured the new charter at the cost of £141 19s.8d. He was returned to James II's Parliament as a non-official Member in the following year and helped to support the canopy at the coronation. He was doubtless a Tory; but his only committee was on the bill for the new parish of St. James Piccadilly, where he was a vestryman. He was marked 'gone away' in the rate book for 1687, and nothing further is known of him or his family.[3]

[1] Mar. Lic. (Harl. Soc. xxiii), 209; (xxx), 178; Vis. Kent (Harl. Soc. liv), 140. [2] Add. 29625, f. 94; Sandwich corp. year bk. E/F, f. 244. [3] Add. 29625, f. 84; J. B. Jones, Annals of Dover, 386; Suss. Arch. Colls. xv. 297; CSP Dom. 1684–5, p. 191; Westminster City Lib. St. James Piccadilly vestry bks. and rate bks.

B.D.H.

CHARLTON, Francis (1651–1729), of Whitton Court, Salop.

LUDLOW   1679 (Mar.), 1679 (Oct.), 1681
BISHOP'S CASTLE   1685

b. 27 June 1651, 1st s. of (Sir) Job Charlton* (1st Bt.) by 1st w.; bro. of William Charlton*. educ. Shrewsbury 1662; L. Inn, entered 1662; St. Edmund Hall, Oxf. 1666. m. (1) bef. 1682, Dorothy, da. and coh. of Lancelot Bromwych, rector of Enville, Staffs., 1s.; (2) 13 Mar. 1707, Mary, da. of Joseph Came, merchant, of London, 2s. 1da. suc. fa. as 2nd Bt. 27 May 1697.[1]
Freeman, Ludlow 1679, common councilman 1680–5, alderman 1685–Dec. 1688, 1689, mayor 1689–90; j.p. Salop June 1688–9, commr. for assessment 1689–90; sheriff, Salop 1698–9, Herefs. 1708–9.[2]

On his grandfather's death in 1670, Charlton took up residence at Whitton. He has to be distinguished from the Whig conspirator, who came from the Apley branch of the family. He was returned for Ludlow, where his father was recorder, as a court supporter in all three Exclusion Parliaments. Classed as 'base' by Shaftesbury, he was absent from the division on the first exclusion bill, and was appointed to no committees. In James II's Parliament he was chosen for Bishop's Castle, where his father had acquired substantial property by marriage, but he again took no recorded part in parliamentary proceedings. He must have been regarded as favourably inclined to James II's ecclesiastical policy, since he was added to the commission of the peace in the summer of 1688. After succeeding to a rent-roll of £1,748 p.a. he received three castaway votes at Ludlow in the first general election of 1701, but he never stood again as a serious candidate, nor does he appear to have sat on the county bench after the Revolution. He died on 21 Apr. 1729 and was buried at Ludford. His nephew, Job Staunton Charlton, sat for Newark as a Whig from 1741 to 1761.[3]

[1] *Trans. Salop Arch. Soc.* (ser. 2), vii. 33; (ser. 4), vi. 64. [2] *Ludlow Charters*, 205. [3] *Ludlow Charters*, 329; *Trans. Salop. Arch. Soc.* (ser. 2), vii. 104; (ser. 4), iii. 4; ix. 59, 61.

E.C.

CHARLTON, Job (c.1614–97), of Lincoln's Inn and Ludford, Herefs.

LUDLOW   1659, 1660, 1661

b. c.1614, o. surv. s. of Robert Charlton, Fishmonger, of Mincing Lane, London and Whitton Court, Salop by 1st w. Emma, da. of Thomas Harby of Adstone, Northants. *educ.* Magdalen Hall, Oxf. matric. 20 Apr. 1632, aged 17; L. Inn 1633, called 1640. *m.* (1) 31 Mar. 1646, Dorothy (*d.* 21 Feb. 1658), da. and h. of William Blunden[†] of Bishop's Castle, Salop, 4s. (1 *d.v.p.*) 3da.; (2) 12 Nov. 1663, Lettice, da. of Walter Waring of Owlbury, Salop, 1s. 1da. Kntd. 14 Mar. 1662; *suc.* fa. 1670; *cr.* Bt. 12 May 1686.[1]

Commr. for assessment, Herefs. 1649–50, Salop 1650–2, Herefs. and Salop. Jan. 1660–80, 1689–90; j.p. Herefs. 1649–53, Mar. 1660–80, Salop 1650–3, July 1660–86, Glos. 1662–?80; alderman, Ludlow by 1659–75, recorder 1675–92; commr. for militia, Salop 1659, Salop and Herefs. Mar. 1660; bencher L. Inn 1660; commr. for oyer and terminer, Oxford circuit July 1660; second justice, Chester circuit 1661–80, c.j. 1662–80; 1686–9; commr. for corporations, Salop 1662–3, recusants 1675.[2]

Serjeant-at-law Oct. 1660, King's serjeant 1668–80; chairman, committee of elections and privileges 11 May 1661–22 Apr. 1671, ways and means 22–27 Nov. 1661, 29 Nov. 1664; j.c.p. 26 Apr. 1680–26 Apr. 1686.

Speaker of House of Commons 4–18 Feb. 1673.

Charlton's father, a thriving London goldsmith, claimed descent from a Shropshire gentry family which dated from the 13th century and had represented the county under Mary Tudor. He acquired Ludford, just outside Ludlow across the Teme, in 1607. As one of the farmers of the crown right of pre-emption on tin in Devon and Cornwall, he advanced £3,843 to Charles I in 1643, and after the Civil War he was obliged to pay £720 to the committee for the advance of money; but he was not an active Royalist, and in 1653 he was able to enlarge his estate by the purchase of Whitton Court for £3,700.[3]

Charlton himself was named after his uncle Sir Job Harby, one of Charles I's customs farmers. He became a lawyer and an alderman of Ludlow, for which he was first returned to Richard Cromwell's Parliament. After its dissolution he assisted Andrew Newport* in preparing for a royalist revolt in Shropshire. Re-elected in 1660, he was one of the leaders of the royalist junto in the early days of the Convention and a very active Member throughout. He was named to 82 committees, in six of which he took the chair, and made 35 recorded speeches. Before the Restoration he was appointed to the committee of elections and privileges, the drafting committee, and those to prepare an answer to the King's letter, and to consider the indemnity bill, in the passage of which he played an important part. He was 'very violent' against Sir Anthony Ashley Cooper* as a Cromwellian, seconding the motion to except all who had served in the high courts of justice, and desired to extend the proviso to those who had petitioned against Charles I, or sat in the Rump, abjured, contrived the Instrument of Government, or imposed taxation under the Protectorate, together with major-generals and decimators. 'He never pressed for the death of any, yet to serve the future peace of the nation he could not be silent.' On individual offenders, however, he spoke 'but moderately' against his fellow-lawyer Bulstrode Whitelocke[†] and altogether opposed excepting the Salopian Richard Salwey[†]. He took the chair of the committee to report amendments to the bill, and supported the proposal to oblige Protectorate office-holders to refund their salaries, though he admitted that the proviso might require amendment. He was chairman of the grand committees for religion and for tunnage and poundage. When the ejection of scandalous ministers was discussed he 'hoped the House would not be more cruel than Henry VIII, who allowed maintenance for their lives'; but he insisted on conformity, and from the committee on settling ministers reported a proviso to the bill imposing penalties for recalcitrance. These high matters did not prevent him from steering through committee a local charity bill to establish a hospital at Newport. His uncle wrote proudly:

> Job is the most leading man in the House of Commons, and carries all before him when he appears and speaks. . . . He is the highest man in the House for the King's interest.

His services were rewarded with the coif at the first call of the reign. Wharton sent him the case for modified episcopacy with objections and answers, and after the recess he was among those appointed to bring in a bill to give statutory effect to the Worcester House declaration. He spoke repeatedly for expediting the militia bill. He supported the grant of excise rather than a land tax as compensation for the abolition of the court of wards, and took the chair in the committee to draft clauses accordingly. On the post office bill on 15 Dec. he argued for 'letters to all Members of Parliament to go free during their sitting'.[4]

Charlton was re-elected in 1661 and listed by Lord Wharton as a friend, despite his resolute Anglicanism. Again very active in the Cavalier Parliament, he was appointed to 266 committees, taking the chair in seven of them, managed seven conferences with the Lords and made 31 reported speeches. He was in the chair of the elections committee for the first nine sessions, and twice acted as chairman of ways and means. In 1661 he was appointed to the committees for the security, uniformity and corporations bills, the bill of pains and penalties, and the bill for the execution of those under attainder. He was sent to ask Bruno Ryves, formerly chaplain to Charles I to preach on the unseasonable weather 'showing how the neglect of exacting justice on . . . the old King's murderers . . . was a main cause of God's punishing a land'. He reported on the Lords' amendments to the corporations bill on 30 Apr. 1662, and also took the chair for the militia bill. He was rewarded with the much-coveted post of chief justice of Chester, and given an additional £500 p.a. in 1664 'in order to his support and for his services'. His father's claims on the crown were settled by a payment of £3,700. Listed as a court dependant, he is said to have played a leading part in the repeal of the Triennial Act, and chaired the conventicles bill. In the Oxford session he was appointed to the committee for the five mile bill, and spoke in its favour. Andrew Marvell*, in his account of the court party in 1666, wrote:

> Charlton advances next, whose coif does awe
> The mitre troop, and with his looks give law.
> He marched with beaver cocked of bishop's brim,
> And hid much fraud under an aspect grim.

When John Ashburnham I* was charged with re-ceiving a bribe from the French merchants, Charlton said they 'were like the devil, both tempters and accusers'. In November 1667 he defended Clarendon, saying: 'I know not one precedent where words or intentions were treason at common law, for they are not treason where no act follows'; but he took the chair of the committee on the banishment bill. He was listed among the court supporters as a friend of Ormonde, and he supported the attempt to impeach the Earl of Orrery (Roger Boyle*) in November 1669. He was in the chair on a supply bill on 8 Dec. 1670, when he suggested 'we might read the order by which we had enlarged the time twice already and we might make this third enlargement in the same terms, which was agreed to'. When Parliament was to meet again in 1673 after repeated prorogations, the Privy Council decided that Charlton should be chosen Speaker, though Robert Milward* feared 'his zeal to run with his own opinion against the King's measures'. He was proposed to the House by Henry Coventry* as a

> very fitting person in respect of his experience in the order of the House, and long service to his Majesty; which choice was immediately assented to, without any contradiction or dispute.

Only ten days later Charlton fell ill. The House had to adjourn, and he resigned. This may have been a diplomatic illness since he had been faced with parliamentary storms over the Declaration of Indulgence and the issue of writs by Lord Chancellor Shaftesbury without the warrant of the House. He was given £1,000 from secret service money by (Sir) Stephen Fox* 'for quitting the chair'. After this, Charlton ceased to take a leading part in the proceedings of the Commons though he was named on the Paston list and sent the goverment whip in 1675 in a personal letter from Coventry. He was listed as an official and a government speaker in that year, and was classed as 'thrice vile' by Shaftesbury in 1677. In the debates on making alliances to reduce the power of France in that year, Charlton was derided by William, Lord Cavendish, for declaring that 'if the King were a Mahommedan, we ought to obey him'. The only committee of importance to which he was appointed under the Danby administration was on the bill for preserving the liberty of the subject on 3 Mar. 1678. On 18 June following, Grey reported, Charlton supported the grant of an additional £300,000 to the King, saying 'the King denies you no bills you present him, only *le Roi s'avisera*. And I would not have you do anything indecent to the King.' The speech was interrupted by laughter in the House. In November he was one of the Welsh judges reflected on in the House for not bringing priests and Jesuits to trial, whereupon Silius Titus* remarked

> I believe the character that is given of Sir Job, that he is a good Protestant, but ... Sir Job is a gentleman of the long robe and did desire to be in a better condition than he was, and as things were like to be, this is the way to rise, not to persecute that party.

He was classed as a court supporter in both the court and opposition lists of 1678.[5]

In 1680 the King decided to replace Charlton as chief justice of Chester by Sir George Jeffreys, who had lost his post of recorder of London for opposing exclusion. Roger North* wrote that Jeffreys

> laid his eye on the place of chief justice of Chester which was full of Sir Job Charlton, than whom there was not a person better qualified for his Majesty's favour; an old Cavalier, loyal, learned, grave and wise. He had a considerable estate towards Wales and desired to die in that employment. But Jeffreys, with his interest on the side of the Duke of York, pressed the King so hard that he could not stand it, but Sir Job Charlton must be a judge of the common pleas and Jeffreys at Chester in his place. ... Sir Job laid this heavily upon his heart and desired only that he might speak to the King and receive his pleasure from his own mouth, but was diverted as a thing determined. But once he went to Whitehall and placed himself where the King, returning from his walk into St. James's Park, must pass, and there he set him down like a hermit poor. When the King came in and saw him at a distance, sitting where he was to pass, concluded he intended to speak with him, which he could not by any means bear: he therefore turned short off and went another way. Sir Job seeing that, pitied his poor master, and never thought of troubling him more but buckled to his business in the common pleas. And may Westminster hall never know a worse judge than he was.

Six years later, Charlton was removed from the common pleas for giving his opinion against the dispensing power, but he remained on good terms with James II, who restored him to his old place at Chester and stayed with him at Ludford in 1687. He was finally dismissed from office after the Revolution, presumably as a non-juror. The list of East India stockholders at this time shows him as probably the largest investor outside the London merchant community, with a holding of £5,350. He died on 24 May 1697, aged 83, and was buried at Ludford.[6]

[1] *Vis. London* (Harl. Soc. xv), 155; F. A. Crisp, *Frag. Gen.* n.s. i. 83. [2] C. B. Brown, *New Guide to Ludlow*, 187–9; *Trans. Salop Arch. Soc.* (ser. 2), vii. 30; *CSP Dom.* 1675–6, p. 247. [3] *Trans. Salop Arch. Soc.* (ser. 4), ix. 58–60; *Cal. Comm. Adv. Money*, 289–90. [4] *Cal. Cl. SP*, iv. 205, 238, 681; D. Underdown, *Royalist Conspiracy*, 236–7, 240; Bowman diary, ff. 4v, 41v, 43, 50v, 78v, 108, 138; *HMC 5th Rep.* 168, 205; *CJ*, viii. 84, 95, 131, 148, 199; *Old Parl. Hist.* xxiii. 2, 15, 18, 25, 26. [5] D. R. Witcombe, *Cav. House of Commons*, 32, 95; *CJ*, viii. 424, 549; ix. 42; *Trans. Salop Arch. Soc.* (ser. 4), ix. 60; *Cal. Treas. Bks.* i. 517, 601; *CSP Dom.* 1661–2, pp. 324, 360; Bodl. Carte mss 80, ff. 757–8; 130, f. 288; *Marvell* ed. Margoliouth, i. 145; Grey, i. 46, 184; vi. 102, 201–3; *Clarendon Impeachment*, 36; Harl. 7020, f. 37; K. W. D. Haley, *Shaftesbury*, 315; *Dering Diary*, 23, 103–4, 120–1; Add. 28091, ff. 59–60.

[6] North, *Lives*, i. 276–7; *Reresby Mems.* 420–1; Eg. 2882, f. 271; *Trans. Salop Arch. Soc.* (ser. 4), ix. 61, Add. 22185, f. 14.

M.W.H./E.C.

CHARLTON, William (c.1652–85), of Ludford, Herefs.

LUDLOW   15–18 Apr. 1685

b. c.1652, 2nd s. of (Sir) Job Charlton* by 1st w., and bro. of Francis Charlton*. *educ.* Shrewsbury 1662; St. Edmund's Hall, Oxf. matric. 30 Mar. 1666, aged 14; L. Inn, entered 1667, called 1674. *unm.*[1]
Freeman, Ludlow 1676, common councilman 1676–d., town clerk 1679–80, 1681–d.; commr. for assessment, Salop 1679–80.[2]

Charlton became a lawyer like his father. His appointment by the Ludlow corporation as town clerk in April 1679 was initially approved by the crown, but quashed on a technicality at the instance of Lord Newport. However, Charlton's father used his extensive interest at Court to procure a royal veto on the rival candidate, and he regained the post in February 1681. A Tory, he was reappointed under the 1685 charter and elected to James II's Parliament. But he died three days later on 18 Apr. before it met, and was buried at Ludford.[3]

[1] *Trans. Salop Arch Soc.* (ser. 2), vii. 85; (ser.4), vi. 64; [2] Ludlow corp. ledger bk.; *CSP Dom.* 1679–80, p. 123; 1680–1, p. 158. [3] *CSP Dom.* 1679–80, pp. 514, 602–3; 1680–1, p. 23; 1685, pp. 50–51; *Trans. Salop Arch. Soc.* (ser. 2), vii. 34.

E.C.

CHARNOCK see CHERNOCK

CHEALE, John (*d.* 1685), of Shermanbury, Suss.

NEW SHOREHAM   1679 (Mar.), 1679 (Oct.)

o.s. of Richard Cheale, yeoman, of Clapham. *unm. suc.* fa. 1652.[1]
Commr. for assessment, Suss. 1673–80.

Cheale's family took no known part in the Civil War. He inherited an inn at Shoreham, which he sold in 1664, as well as the manor of Sakenham in Shermanbury. He acquired further property in Shermanbury and elsewhere in 1668, but seems to have resided chiefly with his cousin, John Cheale the younger, at Findon. It was his cousin who obtained a grant of arms in 1672, in which Cheale was comprised. As 'John Cheale senior' he defeated Sir Anthony Deane* at Shoreham in the first election of 1679. Shaftesbury marked him 'doubtful', but he voted against the bill, though otherwise he took no known part in the first Exclusion Parliament. He defeated the country candidate Robert Fagg* in August, but he was only slightly more active in the next Parliament. He was named to the committees to consider a petition against the Royal Africa Company and the bill for removing Papists from the London area. Apparently he did not stand in 1681, when Fagg took the seat, and it was probably his cousin, 'Capt. Cheale', who was approved by the dissenters as a candidate for the next election in September. Neither stood in 1685, and on 28 Aug. Cheale was buried at Findon, the only member of the family to enter Parliament.[2]

[1] Comber, *Suss. Genealogies Horsham*, 55–57; PCC 103 Bowyer, 111 Cann. [2] E. Cartwright, *Paroch. Top. Bramber*, ii. pt. 2, p. 88; H. Cheal, *Hist. of the Marlipans*, 5; *Fines of Manors* (Suss. Rec. Soc. xix), 45; *Grantees of Arms* (Harl. Soc. lxvi), 51; *CSP Dom.* 1680–1, p. 473; Comber, 57.

B.M.C./B.D.H.

CHENEY *see* CHEYNE

CHERNOCK (CHARNOCK), Sir Villiers, 2nd Bt. (c.1641–94), of Holcot, Beds.

BEDFORDSHIRE   1685

b. c.1641, 3rd but o. surv. s. of Sir St. John Chernock, 1st Bt., of Holcot by 1st w. Audrey, da. of Sir William Villiers, 1st Bt., of Brokesby, Leics. *educ.* Winchester 1656; Queens', Camb. 1661. *m.* by 1667, Anne (*bur.* 19 Sept. 1684), da. and coh. of John Pynsent, protonotary of c.p., of Carleton Curlieu, Leics. and Combe, Croydon, Surr., 5s. (2 *d.v.p.*) 6da. *suc.* fa. 1681.[1]

Commr. for assessment, Beds. 1667–80, 1689–90, j.p. 1670–Feb. 1688, Oct. 1688–*d.*, commr. for recusants 1675, sheriff 1680–1, dep. lt. 1685–Feb. 1688, 1689–*d.*

Chernock came from a cadet branch of a Lancashire family which twice sat for Newton in early Stuart Parliaments. His own ancestors had held Holcot since 1541. Despite kinship with the St. Johns of Bletso, his father seems to have avoided commitment during the Civil War, but held local office throughout the Interregnum. Though he was created a baronet in 1661, he was not a j.p. after the Restoration. Chernock's own career was undistinguished. He was returned for the county as a Tory on the Bruce interest in a contested election in 1685, but left no trace on the records of James II's Parliament. His cousin Robert became notorious as the King's Roman Catholic nominee for the presidency of Magdalen College, but Chernock himself followed the example of Sir Anthony Chester* in refusing to assent to the first two questions on the repeal of the Test Act and Penal Laws and was removed from local office. He is not known to have stood again. He was buried at Holcot on 27 Oct. 1694, aged 53. His heir, who married a daughter of William Boteler*, twice represented the county between 1705 and 1715.[2]

[1] Burke, *Commoners*, ii. 104; F.A. Blaydes, *Gen. Bed.* 154, 399. [2] *VCH Beds*. iii. 387; *Vis. Beds*. (Harl. Soc. xix), 92; *Ailesbury Mems*. i. 100; Blaydes, 154.

L.N./G.J.

CHESTER, Sir Anthony, 3rd Bt. (c.1633–98), of Chicheley, Bucks. and Lidlington Park, Beds.

BEDFORD   1685

b. c.1633, 2nd but 1st surv. s. of Sir Anthony Chester, 2nd Bt., of Chicheley by Elizabeth, da. of Sir John Peyton[†] of Doddington, Cambs. *m.* 21 May 1657, Mary (*d.* 21 May 1710), da. of Samuel Cranmer, Brewer, of London and Astwoodbury, Bucks., 7s. (2 *d.v.p.*) 9da. *suc.* fa. Feb. 1652, uncle Sir Henry Chester[†] in Beds. estate 1666.[1]

J.p. Bucks. July 1660–Feb. 1688, Sept. 1688–?*d.*, Beds. 1676–Feb. 1688, Oct. 1688–93, Bedford Nov. 1688; commr. for oyer and terminer, Norfolk circuit July 1660; dep. lt. Bucks. c. Aug. 1660–Feb. 1688, Oct. 1688–?*d.*, Beds. 1672–Feb. 1688; commr. for assessment, Bucks. Aug. 1660–80, Beds. 1673–80, Bucks. and Beds. 1689–90, corporations, Bucks. 1662–3, sheriff 1668–9; commr. for recusants, Beds. 1675; freeman, Bedford 1677.[2]

Chester was descended from a London merchant family which was granted arms in 1467. Chicheley and Lidlington were acquired in Elizabethan times. Chester's father succeeded to the baronetcy and to a reduced estate in 1635, and became a zealous Royalist in the Civil War. He distinguished himself at Naseby, after which he went into exile. The estate was made over to Chester's uncle, who sat for the borough under the Protectorate, to save it from sequestration. Chester himself made a fortunate marriage, and reunited the family estates on his uncle's death in 1666.[3]

Chester was considered as a possible candidate for Buckinghamshire in 1679, but did not stand, though he supported the Tory candidate in 1685. A henchman and neighbour of the Bruces, he was elected to James II's Parliament for Bedford. A moderately active Member he served on four committees, of no political significance, including those to prevent the export of wool and to improve tillage. Though a strong Tory, his Anglicanism was stronger, for he refused two of the questions on the repeal of the Test Act and Penal Laws, declaring:

> He has not at present any thoughts of standing for knight or burgess in Parliament, but if his country thinks fit to choose him, that then he cannot give his consent to take away such laws as do support the Church of England.

Nor could he support any candidate willing to do so. He was removed from local office, but his reappointment as deputy lieutenant in 1689 indicates support for the Revolution. He contested Bedford unsuccessfully in 1690. Chester died on 15 Feb.

1698, aged 65, and was buried at Chicheley. His grandson, the sixth baronet, represented the county from 1741 to 1747.[4]

[1] *Vis. Bucks.* (Harl. Soc. lviii), 25–27; R.E.C. Waters, *Chesters of Chicheley*, i. 349–59. [2] Huntington Lib. Stowe mss, 452/2; Beds. RO, Ch. 16/6. [3] Waters, i. 9, 114–15, 161–5, 343–4; *VCH Bucks.* iv. 312–13; *VCH Beds.* iii. 306, 434. [4] Bodl. Carte 79, f. 185; *Bucks. Recs.* xix. 467; Waters, i. 346.

L.N./G.J.

CHETWYND, John (c.1643–1702), of Rudge, Standon, Staffs.

STAFFORD	1689, 1690
TAMWORTH	1698–17 Mar. 1699
STAFFORD	1701 (Feb.), 24 July–9 Dec. 1702

b. c.1643, 1st s. of John Chetwynd of Rudge by Susan, da. of John Broughton of Withington. *m.* by 1678, Lucy (*d.* 28 Feb. 1738), da. of Robert Roane of Tullesworth, Chaldon, Surr., 3s. 1da. *suc.* fa. 1674, cos. Walter Chetwynd* 1693.[1]
Capt. of ft. [I] 1674–8.[2] Receiver of taxes, Staffs. 1677–8, commr. for assessment 1689–90, sheriff 1695–6, j.p. and dep. lt. by 1700–*d.*[3]

Chetwynd's father played no known part in the Civil War. He himself purchased a commission in the Irish army, though he never set foot in the country. Although only distantly related to Walter Chetwynd*, he apparently stood next in the entail of the Ingestre estate, and was made a local tax official in 1677 in order to secure his cousin's support for the Danby administration. In the Convention he replaced him as Member for Stafford. Presumably a Tory, he was blacklisted by Anthony Rowe* among those who voted to agree with the Lords that the throne was not vacant. An inactive Member, his 11 committees included those to consider the bill restoring corporations (2 May) and to inquire into the delay in relieving Londonderry (1 June) and the sale of offices (19 June). After the recess he was among those entrusted with the petition from the widow of Sir Thomas Armstrong*, his cousin's fellow-Member in the first Exclusion Parliament. Re-elected in 1690, his later political career was erratic. 'An immoderate taker of snuff', he sneezed himself to death on 9 Dec. 1702. His son succeeded him as Member for Stafford; an equally versatile politician, he represented the borough with two short intervals until his death in 1734, acquiring an Irish peerage after the Hanoverian succession.[4]

[1] H.E.C. Stapylton, *Chetwynds of Ingestre*, 225–6. [2] *HMC Ormonde*, ii. 210; n.s. iv. 84. [3] *Cal. Treas. Bks.* v. 615, 951, 1099. [4] *Staffs. Parl. Hist.* (Wm. Salt Arch. Soc.), ii. 168–9.

A.M.M.

CHETWYND, Walter (1633–93), of Ingestre, Staffs.

STAFFORD	3 Feb. 1674, 1679 (Mar.), 1685, 1690–21 Mar. 1693

b. 1 May 1633, o.s. of Walter Chetwynd of Ingestre by Frances, da. and h. of Edward Hesilrige of Arthingworth, Northants. *m.* 14 Sept. 1658, Anne (*d.* 1671), da. of Sir Edward Bagot†, 2nd Bt. of Blithefield, Staffs., 1da. *d.v.p. suc.* fa. 1669.[1]
Commr. for assessment, Staffs. 1661–80, Warws. 1673–80, Staffs. and Warws. 1689–90; dep. lt. Staffs. 1662–87, 1689–*d.*, Warws. 1686–7; j.p. Staffs. by 1665–*d.*, sheriff 1684–5.[2]
FRS 1678.

Chetwynd's ancestors took their name from a property in Shropshire that they were holding in 1180, and acquired Ingestre, four miles from Stafford, by marriage about 1263. His father was probably a royalist sympathizer; it was alleged in 1650 that he had assisted the Cavaliers with horses and men. But he took no part in public life after the Restoration. Chetwynd himself was appointed to the lieutenancy when he was described as 'loyal and orthodox, sober and prudent', with an income of £600 p.a. at present and £2,000 in reversion to his father. His chief interests were scholarly, though he never completed his history of Staffordshire. On succeeding to Ingestre he rebuilt the church to a design supplied by Sir Christopher Wren* and increased its endowment.[3]

Chetwynd was returned for Stafford, probably unopposed, in 1674, and shared the representation of the borough with his cousin William for the remainder of the Cavalier Parliament. His neighbour, the Roman Catholic Lord Aston, commended him to (Sir) Joseph Williamson* as being 'so faithful a subject, and so gallant, knowing and obliging a person to all persons of merit, that you cannot ... but be most perfectly informed of all things of this country'. But he was not active in Parliament, being appointed by full name to only four committees, of which the first was the committee of elections and privileges in the spring session of 1675. Williamson sent him the government whip for the autumn, but he was unable to attend owing to a severe attack of the stone and the stranguary. 'If it pleases God to enable me to undertake a journey to London', he wrote, 'I shall hasten to pay my duty to his Majesty and my country.' He was noted as 'ill at present' and included on the working lists among the Members 'to be remembered'. In 1677 his cousin and heir John Chetwynd* was made receiver of taxes for the county, Sir Richard Wiseman* listed him among the government supporters and Shaftesbury marked him 'vile'. In *A Seasonable Argument* he was said to have been 'courted, treated, and complimented out of his vote', and he was included in the government list of the court party in May 1678.[4]

Chetwynd was one of the principal supporters of the court candidates for Staffordshire before the first general election of 1679, in which he was himself re-elected for the borough. Shaftesbury again marked him 'vile'; but in the first Exclusion Parliament he was appointed only to the elections committee. On 4 Apr. he was obliged by William Sacheverell* to admit that he had heard of some compromising expressions of Lord Stafford's about the Popish Plot in a letter intercepted by a fellow magistrate; but he is not known to have spoken in the House on any other occasion, and he was absent from the division on the exclusion bill. His cousin Charles, a servant of the Duke of Monmouth and a member of the Green Ribbon Club, gave evidence to a Commons committee of a plot to discredit his friend Dugdale, the informer; but he was not believed. Nevertheless this connexion may have secured Chetwynd's omission from the 'unanimous club' of court supporters, though it did not save his seat in the autumn election, and it can have been little consolation that he was proposed by William Leveson Gower* for the county, where there was no prospect of ousting Sir John Bowyer*. A very good friend of Sir Leoline Jenkins*, he was prevented by an attack of fever from reporting on Monmouth's progress through Staffordshire and Cheshire in 1682; but on 25 Sept. he wrote:

> Though the mayor and aldermen of Stafford are (most of them) truly loyal, yet the inferior burgesses so far outnumber them that my old fellow-Member Sir Thomas Armstrong* may with reason expect to carry the election there against all opposition.[5]

Chetwynd was serving as sheriff of his county during the general election of 1685. But he had prudently obtained a dispensation to leave it, and hence was free to serve his borough again, on the recommendation of Lord Ferrers, the high steward. The execution of Armstrong and the death of Edwin Skrymsher had left both seats vacant, and he was probably returned unopposed. Listed by Danby among the Opposition in James II's Parliament, he was again inactive, being appointed only to the elections committee and to consider the bill for the relief of poor prisoners. To the lord lieutenant's questions in 1688 he replied that 'he was never a friend to Penal Laws, much less to Tests, but, as to consenting or dissenting to the taking them away, he doubts'. Nor would he commit himself to the court candidates; indeed the royal electoral agents warned their master that if Bowyer and

Sir Charles Wolseley* stood for the county in support of his ecclesiastical policy, Chetwynd would join with Sir Walter Bagot* to defeat them. It is not known whether he stood in 1689, but he regained the borough seat as a Tory in 1690. He died in London of smallpox on 21 Mar. 1693, and was buried at Ingestre.[6]

[1] *Vis. Staffs.* (Wm. Salt Arch. Soc. v, pt. 2), 84. [2] *Gentry of Staffs.* (Staffs. Rec. Soc. ser. 4, ii), 9; *Staffs. Hist. Colls.* (Wm. Salt Arch. Soc. 1912), 338. [3] H.E.C. Stapylton, *Chetwynds of Ingestre*, 8, 42, 203–13; *Cal. Comm. Adv. Money*, 1184; *Gentry of Staffs*, 9; *DNB*. [4] *CSP Dom.* 1675–6, pp. 87, 323. [5] Grey, vii. 78; *Staffs. Peds.* (Harl. Soc. lxiii), 50; *CSP Dom.* 1679–80, pp. 196, 214; 1680–1, p. 687; 1682, pp. 144, 370, 380, 426. [6] *CSP Dom.* 1684–5, p. 235; 1685, p. 31.

A.M.M.

CHETWYND, William (c.1628–91), of Rugeley, Staffs. and Grendon, Warws.

STAFFORD 1661

*b.*c.1628, 1st s. of William Chetwynd, merchant, of Bristol by Elizabeth, da. of one Long of Bristol. *educ.* Oxf.; M. Temple 1650. *unm. suc.* fa. 1651, uncle Walter at Rugeley 1653.[1]

Commr. for assessment, Staffs. 1657, Aug. 1660–80, 1689–90, j.p. July 1660–?*d.*, capt. of militia horse by 1662–bef. 1680, commr. for corporations 1662–3, loyal and indigent officers 1662.[2]

The Rugeley branch of the family was founded by Chetwynd's grandfather Thomas, and its wealth was chiefly derived from the iron industry. A great-uncle was dean of Bristol from 1617 to 1639, and Chetwynd's father became a merchant and ship-owner in the city. He was apparently hostile to the Stuarts, for his election as chamberlain just before the Civil War was initially vetoed by the Council, and he retained office after the execution of Charles I. Although Chetwynd was named to the Staffordshire assessment commission under the Protectorate after succeeding to the Rugeley estate of £500 p.a., he was clearly an Anglican and a Royalist. Shortly after the Restoration, he was noted as 'well-moneyed, . . . loyal and orthodox, [and] an ingenious, sober man'. Too much reliance should not be placed on these epithets, as he was wrongly described as 'burgess for Lichfield' and 'aged about 38'. But 'well-moneyed' he certainly was. Some of his money was ploughed back into the family business; he began the manufacture of garden-rollers at Madeley, and purchased several mills along the Trent, where he ground corn and produced starch and paper. But he did not neglect land purchases, and by his death the value of his estate had risen to £2,700 p.a.[3]

Chetwynd became the first of the family to enter Parliament when he was returned for Stafford, nine miles from Rugeley, at the general election of 1661. A moderately active Member of the Cavalier Parliament, he was probably appointed to 219 committees, including the committee of elections and privileges in 11 sessions. In the opening session he was named to the committees for restoring the bishops to the House of Lords, inquiring into the shortfall in revenue, preventing mischief from Quakers, and considering the uniformity bill and the bill of pains and penalities. During the prolonged debate of 28 Jan. 1662 on cancelling the conveyances fraudulently extorted from Lady Powell, he acted as teller against bringing in candles, and on 18 Feb. he was among those assigned to prepare reasons for disagreeing with the Lords on the bill for confirming ministers in their livings. On the third reading of the Stour and Salwarp navigation bill, intended to serve the Droitwich saltworks, his name was inserted as a commissioner. In the 1663 session he was named to the committee for defining the mines royal. On 12 May he wrote to (Sir) Edward Bagot*:

The Commons House have seriously set themselves to inspect the several branches of the King's revenue. His lands, his customs, the excise, the chimneys [hearthtax], post office, etc. are under the consideration of several committees. The customs they have gone through, and agreed them, *communibus annis*, worth £400,000, though brought in at a lower estimate. Crown lands (*viz.* fee-farm rents and the King's demesne, besides parks, forests and chases) they have agreed them to be £100,000, given in but at £68,000 p.a. Post Office, now set at £21,000, will be raised to £27,000 p.a. But the chimneys is the thing that amazes us, whose value from the 'Chequer is but £162,882 p.a., supposed by all never to be less than £300,000. This branch is now under hand; and, besides the great frauds in the City of London (whose chimneys amount but to £18,000), many abuses will be discovered in the country, as the leaving out some townships. The House, upon complaint from several places of the harm the Irish cattle do, have read a bill twice to prohibit their being brought into England betwixt 1 June and 25 Dec.; so those that are brought in must of necessity come lean. I am of opinion no money will be given this session, the House totally declining all overtures made obscurely to try them; and yet I'll promise for nothing. There is a bill that you will wonder at [that] will be brought in this week to exclude all persons from civil and military employment who have acted with the late times. Of this there is thought to be a great need, for some reasons too large to tell you.

Two days later he was added to the committee on the bill to prevent sectaries' meetings. On 5 Oct. 1666 he acted as teller against recommitting the bill to prohibit the import of foreign cattle.[4]

Chetwynd took no part in the proceedings against Clarendon, though he was named to the committees to consider the additional bill against Irish cattle (13 Dec. 1667) and to inspect the Militia Acts (3

Apr. 1668). Five days later he moved the bill to transfer the guardianship of the heir to the Leveson estate, which his colleague Richard Milward* had introduced, and he served on the committee. He was appointed to both committees for extending the Conventicles Act, and he was one of the Members to whom the bill to prevent electoral abuses was committed on 8 Dec. 1669. He was reckoned a friend to Ormonde, and Sir Thomas Osborne* included him among the independent Members who usually voted for supply. He had probably known Joseph Williamson* at Oxford, for he addressed him on the most familiar terms: 'Joseph', he began on 24 Oct. 1670,

without either 'dear' or 'honest', you neither visit nor write to me, and I hate you. . . . You are a monster, for there are monsters in morality as well as nature, and it was a poor, ill-natured trick to come to Northampton and not to Stafford, to prefer [Henry] O'Brien* before sack and rare cider, and old women before young. You may therefore now walk in Tothill Fields, dine at your taverns, and treat your friends at your coffee-house in Scotland Yard, but I will not join you; I am resolved to stay at home next session.

He appears to have been as good as his word, for he is next mentioned in the Journals on 23 Jan. 1671, when his absence from the call of the House a fortnight earlier was excused.[5]

In 1673 Chetwynd helped to produce the Test Act and the bill of ease for dissenters. He also served on the deputation that presented the address for encouraging British manufactures. In the following year he was joined in the House by his cousin Walter, who had succeeded Milward at a by-election, a remarkable tribute to the strength of his interest in a comparatively open borough. It is assumed that 'Mr Chetwind' in the Journals continues to refer to the more experienced Member. In the spring session of 1675 he was among those ordered to draw up an address for the recall of British subjects from the French service. Williamson atoned for his neglect by sending him a hamper of German wine (claret was acquiring unfortunate political implications) to accompany the government whip for the next session. Chetwynd assured him (perhaps not altogether convincingly) that he had scarcely been sober for five days in consequence, drinking Williamson's health with his cousin, Sir Robert Holte*, the dean of Lichfield, and 'the cripple captain' (perhaps Richard Dyott*). He came up to town, unlike his cousin, and was named to the committee on the bill for the better preservation of the liberty of the subject. But his name appeared in no more court lists, and by 1677, when Shaftesbury marked him 'worthy', he had gone over to the Opposition. His activity further decreased, however, and on 18 Dec. 1678 he was sent for in custody for another default on a call of the House.[6]

It was reported in January 1679 that Chetwynd had declined an invitation from his constituency to stand again; but it seems that in fact the corporation, under pressure from their high steward, the Duke of Monmouth, asked him to make way for Sir Thomas Armstrong*. 'When Stafford cast off Mr Chetwind and would none of him, [he] presently took his horse and called for drink, declaring he would there bury his wife, meaning the town', and he took no further part in politics. To the lord lieutenant's questions in 1688 he replied that 'he should be for taking off several Penal Laws, [but] he is not for parting with all of them', and like his cousin he refused to promise his vote to candidates pledged to James II's ecclesiastical policy. He died of apoplexy at Grendon on 9 Apr. 1691, aged 63, and was buried at Rugeley. His heir was his sister, who put up a memorial mentioning his service in the militia, the commission of the peace, and Parliament, and describing him as 'conspicuous for intelligence, prudence, and constancy . . . and faithful to Church, King and country'.[7]

[1] *Vis. Staffs.* (Wm. Salt Arch. Soc. v, pt. 2), 82–83; Le Neve, *Mon. Angl.* 1690–9, p. 112. [2] *Gentry of Staffs.* (Staffs. Rec. Soc. ser. 4, ii), 37; T. Pape, *Restoration Govt. of Newcastle-under-Lyme*, 17. [3] *Merchants and Merchandise* (Bristol Rec. Soc. xix), 211, 213; *Dep. Bks.* (Bristol Rec. Soc. xiii), 203; *Gentry of Staffs.* 9; H.E.C. Stapylton, *Chetwynds of Ingestre*, 168. [4] *CJ*, viii. 379; William, Lord Bagot, *Mems. Bagot Fam.* 71–72. [5] *Milward*, 246; *CSP Dom.* 1670, p. 452. [6] *CSP Dom.* 1675–6, pp. 283, 335–6. [7] *HMC Ormonde*, n.s. iv. 315; Bath mss, Thynne pprs. 27, ff. 21–22, Powell to Thynne, 12 Feb. 1681; Le Neve, 112.

A.M.M.

CHEYNE (CHENEY), Charles (1625–98), of Chesham Bois, Bucks., and Chelsea, Mdx.

AMERSHAM	1660
GREAT MARLOW	5 Mar. 1666
HARWICH	1690
NEWPORT	1695–30 June 1698

b. Oct. 1625, 4th but 1st surv. s. of Francis Cheyne of Chesham Bois, being 3rd s. by 2nd w. Anne, da. of Sir William Fleetwood[†] of Great Missenden, Bucks.; bro. of William Cheyne.[†] *educ.* Brasenose, Oxf. 1640; L. Inn 1642; travelled abroad (Spain, Italy) 1643–50. *m.* (1) 1654, Lady Jane Cavendish (*d.* 8 Oct. 1669), da. of William Cavendish[†] 1st Duke of Newcastle, 1s. 3da.; (2) lic. 8 June 1688, Isabella (*d.* 9 July 1714), da. of Sir John Smythe of Bidborough, Kent, wid. of John, 1st Earl of Radnor, *s.p. suc.* fa. 1644; *cr.* Visct. Newhaven [S] 17 May 1681.

J.p. Bucks. 1652–3, Mar. 1660–85, Westminster 1665–Feb. 1688, Mdx. by 1680–?87, commr. for assessment, Bucks. Jan. 1660–80, Mdx. Aug. 1660–80, 1689–90, militia, Bucks. Mar. 1660; dep. lt. Bucks. c. Aug. 1660–?87, Mdx. 1689–96; commr. for corporations, Bucks. 1662–3.[1]

Commr. of customs 1675–87, inquiry into the Mint 1677–9.[2]

Cheyne's ancestors acquired the Buckinghamshire manor of Drayton Beauchamp in 1364 and first represented the county under Richard II. The family seems to have avoided involvement in the Civil War, though Cheyne's long residence in Roman Catholic countries was made the grounds for an accusation of Popery in 1650. He certainly returned with a pronounced taste for the baroque, but his religious and political affiliations were no bar to his nomination as j.p. in 1652. He probably never took the oaths to the Commonwealth, and was removed even before his marriage to the daughter of a leading Cavalier exile. With her dowry he was able to purchase a valuable estate in Chelsea; but he made no response to Mordaunt's appeal for funds for the exiled Court in 1659. In the following year he was returned for Amersham, two miles from his principal residence at Chesham Bois. An inactive Member of the Convention, he was appointed only to a private bill committee, but doubtless supported the Court.[3]

Cheyne is not known to have stood in 1661, when the dominant Drake interest regained control of Amersham. He may have been occupied in the development of his Chelsea property, to which he had just added the manorial rights. He sued out a pardon in 1663, and was returned for Marlow at a by-election in 1666. A moderately active Member of the Cavalier Parliament, he was appointed to 137 committees, including the committee of elections and privileges in seven sessions, acted as teller on five occasions, and made 33 recorded speeches, many of them on financial matters. It may be presumed that he was not well disposed to Sir Henry Bennet*, whom he had recently been obliged to dissuade from usurping the title of Lord Cheyne. After the fall of Clarendon he was added to the committee to consider the miscarriages of the war. He was sent to the Lords on 10 Dec. 1667 to desire a conference on freedom of speech in Parliament. He opposed unsuccessfully the adjournment of the debate on woodmongers till after Christmas. Sir Thomas Osborne* included him among the Members who might be engaged for the Court by the Duke of York and his friends. He was teller against the adjournment of the supply debate on 2 Mar. 1670, and in the following month was sent to the Lords to desire a conference on the conventicles bill. His parliamentary activity reached a peak in the next session. He was appointed to the committee to examine the accounts of the navy. He spoke in favour of deferring all other business until the bill for punishing the assailants of Sir John Coventry* had passed both Houses, and was appointed to the committee. He helped to manage a conference on the growth of Popery on 3 Mar. 1671, and acted as teller against a proviso on behalf of Roman Catholics who had borne arms for the King or lost their estates in consequence of their loyalty. He was particularly concerned with the bill to prevent fraudulent cattle sales at Smithfield, which he carried to the Lords, later returning to request a conference. He took the chair for the game preservation bill, and acted as teller against the Putney Bridge bill, which might have subjected his Chelsea property to an imposition. He spoke in favour of the conventicles bill on 5 Apr. On 8 Feb. 1673 he moved for a bill to naturalize foreign Protestants. Two days later, he supported a motion asking for the withdrawal of the Declaration of Indulgence, and he was appointed to the committee to prepare an address accordingly. In the same month he spoke for the bill for the ease of Protestant dissenters. He strongly attacked the marriage of the Duke of York to Mary of Modena, and moved for a call of the House in October to make sure that all Members had taken the Test. On 31 Jan. 1674 he opposed the removal of Buckingham and Lauderdale.[4]

Cheyne was one of the court caucus who met to concert parliamentary measures at Lord Treasurer Danby's in the spring of 1675, when he and Sir Edward Dering* spoke repeatedly against Danby's impeachment. He was appointed to the committees on the bill to prevent the growth of Popery (27 May), and to prevent Papists from sitting in Parliament (23 Oct.). His support of the Court was rewarded in December, when he and Dering were both appointed commissioners of the customs, at a salary of £1,200 p.a. He was classed as an official in 1675, and a government speaker. Sir Richard Wiseman* hoped in 1676 that he would 'endeavour to merit that favour the King hath showed him' and take particular care of Henry Monson* in the lobby. However, he became much less active in Parliament than before, and his silence was unfavourably noted on the working lists. In the spring of 1677 he was appointed to the committee on the bill to recall the King's subjects in French service, and he moved for the supply by way of an 18 months' tax. He was classed as 'thrice vile' by Shaftesbury at this time. In 1678, when he was again classed as a court supporter, he moved (15 Mar.) for the Lords concurrence with the Commons address for an immediate declaration of war against France, and on 28 May he asked the House to proceed with measures for disbanding the army. Although not included in the opposition list of the 'unanimous club' he did not sit in any of the Exclu-

sion Parliaments, and was granted a Scottish peerage in 1681.[5]

In February 1685 Cheyne was suspended as commissioner of the customs for expressing doubts about the legality of continuing to levy customs after the death of Charles II before any parliamentary re-grant, but he was reinstated. The crown purchased from him in 1687, for £1,869, 21 acres of meadowland on which Chelsea hospital was eventually built. In the same year he retired as commissioner of the customs, but was granted out of the customs of Berwick-upon-Tweed a pension of £1,200 p.a., which ceased with the Revolution. He was a follower of Danby, now Lord Carmarthen, in the 1690 Parliament, and refused the Association in 1696. He died on 30 June 1698 and was buried at Chelsea.[6]

[1] Huntington Lib. Stowe mss 2/452. [2] HMC Lindsey, 172–4; Cal. Treas. Bks. v. 751, 986; CSP Dom. 1689–90, p. 53; 1691–2, p. 163; [3] VCH Bucks. iii. 219, 341; T. Faulkner, Chelsea, i. 328–9; Cal. Comm. Adv. Money, 1370; Cal. Cl. SP. iv. 157; CSP Dom. 1663–4, p. 61. [4] Clarendon, Life, ii. 358–9. CJ, ix. 40, 130, 215, 227, 229, 236; Dering, 47, 112, 119, 156; Grey, i. 420; ii. 25, 191, 373. [5] Dering Pprs. 63; Add. 28091, f. 35; Grey, v. 248; vi. 27. [6] HMC Ormonde, n.s. vii. 322; CSP Dom. 1685, p. 22; 1686–7, p. 368; Luttrell, i. 329; Cal. Treas. Bks. viii. 1262, 1321; xxi. 287; HMC 11th Rep. VII, 152.

M.W.H./L.N./E.C.

CHEYNE, William (1657–1728), of Chesham Bois, Bucks.

AMERSHAM	1681, 1685
APPLEBY	25 July 1689, 1690
BUCKINGHAMSHIRE	24 Feb. 1696, 1698, 1701 (Feb.)
AMERSHAM	1701 (Dec.)
BUCKINGHAMSHIRE	1702
AMERSHAM	1705–1 May 1707

bap. 14 July 1657, o.s. of Charles Cheyne*, 1st Visct. Newhaven [S], by 1st w. educ. Brasenose, Oxf. 1671. m. (1) 16 Dec. 1675, Elizabeth (bur. 10 Aug. 1677), da. of Edmund Thomas of Wenvoe, Glam., s.p.; (2) 6 May 1680, Gertrude (d. 11 June 1732), da. of Robert Pierrepont of Thoresby, Notts., s.p. suc. fa. as 2nd Visct. Newhaven [S] 30 June 1698.

Dep. lt. Bucks. 1677–Feb. 1688, Sept. 1688–June 1702, Dec. 1702–12, j.p. 1680–Feb. 1688, Sept. 1688–?d., col. of militia ft. by 1697–?1714, ld. lt. June–Dec. 1702, 1712–14.[1]

Commr. of privy seal 1690–2; clerk of the pipe 1703–6, 1711–d.[2]

Unsuccessful at the first general election of 1679, Cheyne was returned for Amersham as a Tory in 1681 but was totally inactive both at Oxford and in James II's Parliament. He was absent when the King's questions on the repeal of the Test and Penal Laws were put, but he was removed from the local commissions. Before the Revolution, he broke with the family tradition by attaching himself to the Hon.

Thomas Wharton*, with whom he shared a passion for racing, and who secured his return to the Convention at a by-election for Appleby at the cost of £2,200. Cheyne was not an active Member, being appointed only to the committee of elections and privileges and another on a private bill. Anthony Rowe* listed him as voting to agree with the Lords that the throne was not vacant, six months before he could have taken his seat. He quarrelled with Wharton before the general election of 1698, and reverted to Toryism. He died on 26 May 1728, the last of his family, and was buried at Drayton Beauchamp.[3]

[1] Eg. 1626, f. 5. [2] Luttrell, ii. 15, 326; *Cal. Treas. Bks.* xviii. 353–4; xxi. 118; xxv. 433. [3] Sir Richard Steele, *Wharton Mems.* (1715), 29–31; *Verney Mems.* ii. 462; T. Faulkner, *Chelsea,* i. 336.

L.N./E.C.

CHICHELEY, Sir John (c.1640–91), of Southampton Square, Bloomsbury, Mdx.

NEWTON   1679 (Mar.), 1679 (Oct.), 1681, 1685, 1689, 1690–20 Mar. 1691

b. c.1640, 2nd s. of Thomas Chicheley* by 1st w. *educ.* I. Temple 1657. *m.* c.1667, Isabella (*d.* 29 Nov. 1709), da. and coh. of Sir John Lawson of Alresford, Essex, wid. of Daniel Norton of Southwick, Hants, 5s. (2 *d.v.p.*) 4da. Kntd. June 1665.[1]

Ltd. RN 1662, capt. 1663, r.-adm. 1673–5.[2]

Envoy, Spanish Netherlands 1670; commr. for navy 1675–80, ordnance 1679–82; ld. of Admiralty 1682–4, 1689–90.[3]

Freeman, Portsmouth 1675, Liverpool 1686; j.p. Essex, Hants, Kent, Mdx., Norf., Suff., Suss. and Westminster by 1679–87, Lancs. and Mdx. 1689–*d.*; commr. for assessment, Cambridge 1679–80, Lancs. 1689; conservator, Bedford level 1683–*d.*[4]

As a younger son, Chicheley was bred to a naval career, but on his going to sea in 1659 his father had to borrow £300 for the outfit. In October 1661, his stepmother wrote that he had been 'seasoned with a sea fight against the Turk towards the making him a seaman'. Promotion quickly followed. He served under the Duke of York against the Dutch and was knighted shortly after the battle of Lowestoft in June 1665. On his marriage to a wife with an estate of £800 p.a., his father allowed him £400 p.a. and his salary as a flag-officer brought his income up to £1,400 p.a. Between 1668 and 1671 he saw service in the Mediterranean, and in the third Dutch war was taken prisoner during the action at Sole Bay, but soon released. Promoted rear-admiral soon afterwards, he distinguished himself at the action off Texel. In 1675 on his appointment as a commissioner of the navy at a salary of £500 p.a., he retired from active service, though he sometimes thought of returning to sea when his finances were straitened. For some two years he and his wife lived in Montpellier for reasons of health and economy.[5]

Chicheley first entered Parliament in 1679 as Member for Newton, on the interest and at the expense of his brother-in-law, Richard Legh*, and retained the seat for the rest of his life. An adherent of the Duke of York, he voted against the bill, and was marked as a court supporter on Huntingdon's list. Otherwise inactive in the first Exclusion Parliament, he wrote to Legh two days after its dissolution:

> This place affords not much news, only much talk, neither fit to be writ or said, but I find now all tongues at liberty to that degree, that few or none scruples talking treason when they please. What will the end or issue of this be none knows or can imagine: affairs has [*sic*] so ill an aspect that it is hard to say what one thinks.

When the ordnance was put into commission in June he was appointed a commissioner, in place of his father, though he had earlier been granted the reversion of the mastership. He was totally inactive in the second and third Exclusion Parliaments. Like his father, he suffered from the enmity of George Legge*, who in 1682 became master of the ordnance over his head, but the blow was softened by his appointment as a lord of the Admiralty at a salary of £1,000 p.a. In James II's Parliament he was an active Member. He was named to 13 committees, of which the most important were those to inspect the accounts of the disbandment commissioners, to provide carriages for the navy and ordnance, to repeal a clause in the Act for draining the Great Level of the fens, and to encourage shipbuilding. In 1686 he was granted a pension of £800 p.a. 'in consideration of good and faithful service'.[6]

Chicheley was re-elected in 1689, but in the Convention he served on only two committees on naval matters, those to consider the petition of the *Greenwich* seamen and to examine complaints about the press. According to Ailesbury's list he voted to agree with the Lords that the throne was not vacant and on 9 Feb. he wrote to his nephew Peter Legh*:

> Nothing will satisfy some but placing the crown on the Prince, which will be a precedent for placing it on another whenever the Lords and Commons please, and so consequently make this kingdom, which has never been elective, into a commonwealth, if they please, which God forbid. I am sure for my own part, it's the last Government I should choose to live under, but when necessity may force a man, that one must submit to.

He was reappointed to the Admiralty board in March but his submission cannot have carried great weight. Lord Halifax (Sir George Savile, 4th Bt.*), his stepbrother, was concerned to find that Chicheley had been 'ill represented' to William III, and noted in August: 'I must tell him to speak to the King'. But he was removed from the Admiralty in the following year. He continued to represent Newton until his death on 20 Mar. 1691. He was buried at St. Giles in the Fields, the last of the family to sit in Parliament.[7]

[1] *Le Neve's Knights* (Harl. Soc. viii), 234; E. C. Legh, Lady Newton, *Lyme Letters*, 18, 33, 98; W.F.C. Plowden, *Chicheley Plowdens*, 125. [2] *Lyme Letters*, 18, 25–26, 56. [3] *Bulstrode Pprs.* 159; *Cal. Treas. Bks.* vi. 140. [4] R. East, *Portsmouth Recs.* 361; Wahl-strand thesis, 58; Lancs. RO, QSC 102–5; Mdx. RO, MJP/CP5a; S. Wells, *Drainage of the Bedford Level*, i. 463–5. [5] *Lyme Letters*, 9, 14, 25, 46–48, 56–57, 69–70, 114; *CSP Dom.* 1672, pp. 177, 331; *Cal. Treas. Bks.* iv. 850; Legh, *House of Lyme*, 284. [6] *House of Lyme*, 292–3; *CSP Dom.* 1673–5, p.411; 1690–1, p.21; *Bulstrode Pprs.* 272; *Lyme Letters*, 80; *Cal. Treas. Bks.* viii. 517. [7] *Lyme Letters*, 160, 184; Foxcroft, *Halifax*, ii. 213.

I.C./G.J.

CHICHELEY, Thomas (1614–99), of Wimpole, Cambs. and Great Queen Street, St. Giles in the Fields, Mdx.

CAMBRIDGESHIRE   1640 (Nov.)–16 Dec. 1642, 1661
CAMBRIDGE   1679 (Mar.), 1679 (Oct.), 1681, 1685, 1689

b. 25 Mar. 1614, 1st s. of Sir Thomas Chicheley[†] of Wimpole by Dorothy, da. and coh. of Sir Thomas Kempe of Olantigh, Kent. *educ.* I. Temple 1632. *m.* (1) 13 Aug. 1635, Sarah (*d.* 19 Jan. 1654), da. of Sir William Russell[†], 1st Bt., of Chippenham, Cambs., 3s. *d.v.p.* 2da.; (2) c.1655, Anne (*bur.* 31 July 1662), da. of Sir Thomas Coventry[†], 1st Baron Coventry of Aylesborough, wid. of Sir William Savile, 3rd Bt.[†], of Thornhill, Yorks., 2s. (1 *d.v.p.*) *suc.* fa. 1616; kntd. 2 June 1670.[1]

Sheriff, Cambs. 1637–8, dep. lt. by 1639–42, c. Aug. 1660–85; j.p. Cambs. by 1641–2, Cambs. and Ely July 1660–87, Cambridge 1679–?87, 1689–?d., Westminster by 1687–Feb. 1688; commr. for disarming recusants, Cambs. 1641; custos rot. Cambs. 1642, Cambs. and Ely July 1660–87; commr. for oyer and terminer, Norfolk circuit July 1660, assessment, Cambs. Aug. 1660–80, Cambridge and Cambridge Univ. 1673–80, Ely 1677–80, Cambs., Cambridge, Cambridge Univ. and Ely 1689–90, corporations, Cambs. 1662–3, loyal and indigent officers 1662, sewers, Bedford level 1662–3; bailiff, Bedford level 1663–5, 1666–7, 1670–93, conservator 1667–70, 1693–*d.*; commr. for pontage, Cambridge 1663, 1673; freeman, Portsmouth 1668, Liverpool 1686; high steward, Cambridge 1670–May 1688, 1689–*d.*; master, Grocers' Co. 1686–7.[2]

Commr. for ordnance 1664–70, master 1670–9; treas. of seamen's prize-money 1665–7; PC 10 June 1670–2 Mar. 1687; commr. for inquiry into land settlement [I] 1671, Tangier 1673–80; master of ordnance [I] 1674–9, member, R. Fishery Co. 1677; chancellor, duchy of Lancaster 1682–7.[3]

Lt. Duke of Richmond's Horse 1666–7; capt. of ft. Portsmouth 1669–71, the Tower 1677–9; capt. of Life Gds. [I] by 1677–80.[4]

Chicheley was descended from a London Grocer, the elder brother of the future Archbishop of Canterbury, who represented the City in 1397. His ancestors had held Wimpole, nine miles from Cambridge, under Henry VI, but his father, who sat in the Addled Parliament, was the first of the family to represent Cambridgeshire. Extravagant by nature, Chicheley incurred debts at an early age and spent almost £40,000 on Wimpole in the 1630s. A ship-money sheriff, he was returned to the Long Parliament for the county, sat at Oxford and lent the King a considerable sum during the Civil War. He compounded for £1,985 10s. 8d. on the Oxford articles in 1647, his estate being valued at £1,100 5s.4d. p.a. Little is known of his activities during the Interregnum, but in November 1659 Sir Edward Hyde[†] described him as 'a very worthy person and my good friend'. After the Restoration he was nominated a knight of the Royal Oak with an estimated income of £2,000.[5]

Chicheley was returned for Cambridgeshire in 1661, and was a moderately active Member of the Cavalier Parliament, being appointed to 68 committees. In the first session he was given special responsibility for the security bill and named to the committees for confirmation of public acts, for restoring the bishops to the House of Lords, and for the corporations bill. But his principal concern in the opening sessions was the drainage of the Bedford level. As one of the new Adventurers, he served on three committees, twice acted as teller, and acted as second to Lord Gorges (Richard Gorges*) in his quarrel with (Sir) William Tyringham* and Samuel Sandys*, although the House intervened to prevent bloodshed. Despite the professed friendship of Hyde (now Lord Chancellor Clarendon), Chicheley seems to have joined the rival faction formed by Sir Henry Bennet*, two branches of whose family were established in his constituency. They shared in the grant of a modest reversion of £200 p.a. in 1663, and when the Ordnance was put into commission on the death of the borough Member, Sir William Compton*, he took his first step into the official world by purchasing a seat on the board with a salary of £134 13s.4d. Mindful of his family connexions with the city, he contributed to the construction of a new barge for the Grocers' Company and to the rebuilding of St. Stephen's Walbrook after the Great Fire. In the 1666–7 session he was named to two committees of local interest, for the plague bill, to which a clause for the benefit of Cambridge had been added, and for the bill to unite the two parishes in Swaffham. He was teller for the Court on 4 Jan. 1667 in an unsuccessful attempt to prevent the description of Irish cattle as a nuisance. He took no part in the attack on Clarendon, though he was added to the committee to establish a public accounts commission.[6]

The ordnance office was by no means blameless for the miscarriages of the second Dutch war, but, rather to the chagrin of Samuel Pepys*, they seem to have escaped the grilling that befell the navy board. Chicheley was in high favour at Court, thanks in part to his prowess at tennis. His promotion was less rapid than in the case of his colleague Sir John Duncombe*; but he was able to secure repayment of £12,000 advanced to the royal cause during the Civil War, and to impress Pepys with his affluence. After a visit to Chicheley's house in Great Queen Street on 11 Mar. 1668, the diarist wrote:

> A very fine house, and a man that lives in mighty great fashion, with all things in a most extraordinary manner noble and rich about him, and eats in the French fashion all; and mighty nobly served with his servants, and very civil, that I was mighty pleased with it; and good discourse. He is a great defender of the Church of England and against the Act for Comprehension, which is the work of this day, about which the House is like to sit till night.

He was named to the committees to receive information about conventicles (18 Nov. 1669) and to consider the continuance of the Conventicles Act (2 Mar. 1670). As a court dependant he was included in both lists of the government supporters in 1669–71. His appointment as master of the ordnance in 1670 at the much increased salary of £1,500 was followed by a knighthood, a seat on the Privy Council, and preferment to other public offices. He attended the meeting of the court caucus on 21 Dec. 1672 to prepare for the next session, though he did not play a prominent part in it, and he was named on the Paston list of 1673–4. Prince Rupert declared himself 'satisfied and extremely pleased with the punctual performance of the master of ordnance' during the third Dutch war; and when he was given a similar appointment in Ireland, where 'all matters relating to the ordnance were in confusion', the lord lieutenant declared that the office could not be 'in a more worthy person's hands'. Chicheley was included in the working lists, and as a government supporter in 1676. But Sir Richard Wiseman* blamed him for the absence from the House of his son-in-law, Richard Legh*, and desired that the King 'would please to let him and other of his servants know that he expects from them all a diligent attendance and a faithful and honest discharge of their duty'. Shaftesbury marked him 'thrice vile'. In his sole recorded speech on 14 Feb. 1678 he gave an estimate of the expenditure on the ordnance. He came to blows with Lord Ibrackan (Henry O'Brien*) in a division of the House and both were committed to the custody of the serjeant-at-arms on 10 May, but the cause of their quarrel is not recorded. He was appointed to the committees to examine the arrears due to the forces to be disbanded, and to take account of the additional excise. He was not active in the last session, though he was on both lists of the court party, and on 23 Dec. delivered a curt message to the House from the King on their importunate anxiety for his safety. He was further rewarded with the grant of a market and three annual fairs at Soham, a Cambridgeshire manor which he had drained and developed.[7]

One of the 'unanimous club', Chicheley had to step down from the county seat in the Exclusion Parliaments, despite vigorous canvassing, but as high steward of Cambridge he was returned for the borough. Again marked 'vile' by Shaftesbury, he was named to no committees in 1679, but on 27 Mar. he brought a message from the King about the inquiries into the Popish Plot, and he voted against exclusion. When the King resolved to return the ordnance to commission in June, Chicheley was offered a seat on the board, but preferred to pass it on to his son. His Irish office went to Lord Longford (Francis Aungier*), who also purchased his Irish regiment, but he remained a Privy Councillor. He left no trace on the records of the second and third Exclusion Parliaments. His stepson, Lord Halifax (Sir George Savile,*) was now one of the leading figures in the Government, and in 1682 obtained for him the dignified and influential post of chancellor of the duchy. Lord Preston (Sir Richard Grahme*), who had also coveted the office and was hopeful of an imminent vacancy, was told that Chicheley was 'threescore and ten years old, but as vigorous and healthy as most men of his age, only sometimes troubled with the gout'.[8]

In 1685 Chicheley was returned for Preston on the duchy interest, but remained faithful to his old constituency. An inactive Member of James II's Parliament, he was appointed only to the committee of elections and privileges and to that to take the accounts of the disbandment commissioners. He was listed among the opposition. His strongly Anglican views were no passport to favour in the new reign, and it was an additional misfortune that during his years in the Ordnance he had fallen out with Lord Dartmouth (George Legge*), the most reliable of the King's Protestant advisers. As his son-in-law observed, 'Whilst he has so great an enemy as the Lord Dartmouth, there is small hopes for him, poor man. He must sink under his burden.' Remarking on Ormonde's removal as lord lieutenant of Ireland, Chicheley compared the Duke's hard usage with his own.

> When I see how that honourable good man my Lord of Ormonde is used, I hope I shall pass by my usage with

great ease and follow the example of a man that had got a neat's tongue in one hand and a piece of bread in the other, and went up and down the town and told everybody he held his tongue and ate his bread.

By this time his finances were also in a depressed state, partly due to electoral expenses, and he was obliged to retrench his expenditure, a difficult task for one of his nature. He reduced his household and moved into his son's house in Southampton Square, but in 1686 he was forced to sell Wimpole to Sir John Cutler.[9]

Chicheley, when closeted by the King, refused to agree to the repeal of the Penal Laws and Test. Accordingly he was requested to deliver up the seal of the duchy. According to Roger Morrice, Chicheley told the King's messenger 'to give his most humble duty to his Majesty and to tell him he hoped he should never suffer so much for his Majesty ... as he had for his father King Charles I. But this is so great it cannot be true.' He was removed as *custos rotulorum*, and in May 1688 was replaced as high steward of Cambridge by Lord Dover. Dover, however, fled the country at the Revolution, and Chicheley not only regained the stewardship but was re-elected to the Convention. Though presumably a Tory, he left no trace on its records, and retired from politics at the dissolution. He resumed his drainage activities, this time on Humberside, but he was heavily in debt when he died on 1 Feb. 1699, and was buried at Wimpole.[10]

[1] Wards 7/55/175; *Le Neve's Knights* (Harl. Soc. viii), 234; E. C. Legh, Lady Newton, *Lyme Letters*, 5, 17. [2] Keeler, *Long Parl.* 133; C. H. Cooper, *Annals of Cambridge*, iii. 316, 513, 546, 557, 639–40; iv. 41; *CSP Dom.* 1689–90, p. 181; *Camb. Antiq. Soc. Procs.* xvii. 105; S. Wells, *Drainage of Bedford Level*, i. 350, 456–70; R. East, *Portsmouth Recs.* 359; Wahlstrand thesis, 58; B. Heath, *Grocers' Co.* 211–12. [3] *CSP Dom.* 1664–5, pp. 49, 413; 1670, p. 224; 1671, p. 358; 1673–5, p. 185; 1679–80, p. 288; Sir Robert Somerville, *Duchy of Lancaster Office Holders*, 3; *Williamson Letters* (Cam. Soc. n.s. viii), 149. [4] *CSP Dom.* 1677–8, p. 437; 1679–80, pp. 229, 372; *HMC Ormonde*, n.s. ii. 208. [5] Buckler, *Stemmata Chicheleana*, 13; *VCH Cambs.* v. 265; *Lyme Letters*, 9; Keeler, 133; *CSP Dom.* 1670, p. 387; SP 23/192/865, 868; *CJ*, v. 313; *Cal. Cl. SP*, iv. 439, 471, 508, 534; P. Barwick, *Life of Dr John Barwick* (1724), 454. [6] *CJ*, viii. 249; Foxcroft, *Halifax*, i. 29; *CSP Dom.* 1663–4, p. 241; 1664–5, p. 187; Heath, 212. [7] *Pepys Diary*, 2 Sept., 25 Oct. 1667, 11 Mar. 1668; *Cal. Treas. Bks.* v. 539–40; *R. Hist. Soc. Trans.* (ser. 4), xxv. 60; *CSP Dom.* 1670, pp. 259, 587; 1672–3, p. 630; 1673, pp. 280, 301, 575; 1677–8, pp. 516–17; *Lyme Letters*, 8–9, 130; Grey, v. 148; *CJ*, ix. 480, 563. [8] *Case of Many Protestant Freeholders* (1680); *CSP Dom.* 1673–5, p. 411; 1679–80, pp. 320, 372; 1680–1, p. 186; Cooper, iii. 577; *HMC Ormonde*, n.s. v. 96, 122; *HMC 7th Rep.* 366, 373. [9] *Lyme Letters*, 130; *VCH Cambs.* v. 265; *Case of Many Prot. Freeholders*. [10] *Bramston Autobiog.* (Cam. Soc. xxxii), 278; R. Morrice, Entering Bk. 2, p. 82; *CSP Dom.* 1689–90, pp. 132, 475, 506; *Lyme Letters*, 205; W.F.C. Plowden, *Chicheley Plowdens*, 119–21.

E.R.E./G.J.

CHICHESTER, Sir Arthur, 3rd Bt. (c.1662–1718), of Youlston, Devon.

BARNSTAPLE 1685, 1689, 1713, 1715–3 Feb. 1718

b. c.1662, 2nd s. of Sir John Chichester, 1st Bt.*, by 2nd w. *m.* 15 Apr. 1684, Elizabeth, da. and coh. of Thomas Drewe† of Broadhembury Grange, 4s. 6da. *suc.* bro. Sept. 1680.[1]

Freeman, Barnstaple 1684; commr. for assessment, Devon 1689–90, j.p. ?1689–96, 1700–*d.*, dep. lt. 1703–?*d.*[2]

Chichester sold the family estate at Raleigh and resided at Youlston, three miles from Barnstaple. Sworn in as a freeman of the borough in 1684 under the new charter, he was returned to Parliament in the following year. His only committee in James II's Parliament was on a bill to enable an Exeter gentleman to change his name. Although the corporation would not accept him as recorder in 1686, he was re-elected to the Convention in 1689. According to Anthony Rowe* he voted to agree with the Lords that the throne was not vacant, but he was appointed to no committees and made no recorded speeches. He obtained leave to go into the country at the second attempt on 19 Mar. 1689, and probably did not return till his re-election as a Tory nearly a quarter of a century later. He died on 3 Feb. 1718, and was buried at Pilton. His son, a Jacobite, sat for Barnstaple from 1734 till his death six years later.[3]

[1] W. R. Drake, *Devon Notes and Notelets*, 250; Vivian, *Vis. Devon*, 307. [2] PC 2/76/263. [3] T. Wainwright, *Barnstaple Recs.* i. 74, 82; *Trans. Devon Assoc.* lxii, 264.

J.S.C.

CHICHESTER, Sir John, 1st Bt. (1623–67), of Raleigh, nr. Barnstaple, Devon and the Strand, Westminster.

BARNSTAPLE 1661–2 Nov. 1667

b. 23 Apr. 1623, 1st s. of Sir Robert Chichester of Raleigh by Mary, da. of Robert Hill of Shilston. *educ.* Exeter, Oxf. 1638–40. *m.* (1) 28 Jan. 1647, Elizabeth (bur. 30 Nov. 1654), da. of Sir John Rayney, 1st Bt., of Wrotham, Kent *s.p.* (2) 18 July 1655, Mary, da. of Theodore Colly, wid. of George Warcup, merchant, of London, 4s. 3da. *suc. fa.* 1627; *cr.* Bt. 4 Aug. 1641.[1]

J.p. Devon July 1660–*d.*, dep. lt. c. Aug. 1660–*d.*, commr. for assessment Aug. 1662–*d.*, jt. farmer of excise 1662–5; recorder, Barnstaple 1665–*d.*[2]

Chichester's ancestors had been landowners in Devon since at least the 14th century, and first sat for Barnstaple, two miles from Raleigh, in 1559. Chichester himself, who was created a baronet in 1641 and 'heretofore smiled at the troubles of others', began to feel the effects of civil war in 1644 when hundreds of troops were quartered at his house in Raleigh. Spending prolonged periods in France, by leave of Parliament, he claimed to have suffered severe losses at the hands of the royal forces, and was assessed at a mere £500 by the committee for the advance of money. He held no office until the Restoration.[3]

Returned for Barnstaple at the general election of 1661, Chichester was an inactive Member of the Cavalier Parliament, being appointed to only three committees. The first (25 June 1661) was for a private bill in which a fellow-Devonian, Sir Peter Ball†, was concerned. On 3 July he was mentioned as one of the Members who had not yet received the sacrament according to the order of the House, apparently having been ill. Together with Sir James Smyth* he was nominated by the Devon justices to farm the county excise in 1662 for £8,600 p.a.; but after three years he was replaced by the father of Sir Peter Colleton*. He was among those appointed to consider the Medway navigation bill on 8 Feb. 1665, and in the next session he was named to the committee of elections and privileges. On the evening of 2 Nov. 1667 he killed a young woman whom he 'kept and conversed with as his wife', while in a frenzy. He died of smallpox later in the evening.[4]

[1] W. R. Drake, *Devon Notes and Notelets*, 248–50; PCC 31 Alchin; Vivian, *Vis. Devon*, 174; *Reg. Coll. Exon.* ii. 58. [2] *Cal. Treas. Bks.* i. 425, 639; *Merc. Pub.* 30 Aug. 1660; T. Wainwright, *Barnstable Recs.* i. 255. [3] Wainright, i. 239; *HMC 4th Rep.* 308; *Cal. Comm. Adv. Money*, 641; *CSP Dom.* 1657–8, p. 549; 1658–9, p. 578. [4] *Bulstrode Pprs.* 6; Westmld. RO, Fleming mss, 924; *HMC 6th Rep.* 186.

J.S.C.

CHIFFINCH, William (d.1691), of Whitehall and Philberts, Bray, Berks.

NEW WINDSOR 1685

> ?2nd s. of Thomas Chiffinch, innholder, of Salisbury, Wilts. *m.* by 1662, Barbara Nunn, 1da.[1]
> Page of the backstairs to Queen Catherine of Braganza 1662; page of the bedchamber and keeper of the closet 1666–85; jt. master of the hawks by 1675–d.[2]
> Commr. for assessment, Berks. 1673–80; freeman, New Windsor 1677, chamberlain 1681, alderman 1681–9, mayor 1685–6; j.p. Berks. by 1680–d.; keeper, Hyde Park by 1681–d.; master, Cutlers' Co. 1685–6.[3]

Chiffinch was probably born in Salisbury like his brother, Thomas, who had entered the royal service as page of the bedchamber by 1644, joined the exiled Court, and was granted arms in 1664. Two years later he died, and Chiffinch succeeded to most of his offices. Over the years he made himself indispensable to both Charles II and James II in their secret dealings. On the death of William Willoughby* he was granted a joint lease of Bestwood Park 'as a mark of the King's favour and bounty in consideration of many and faithful services'. An adept at backstairs intrigue, he handled payments under the secret treaty of Dover. His wife was a Roman Catholic and their only child was brought up in the same religion, but Chiffinch willingly undertook that she should become a Protestant

when an advantageous match with Sir William Clifton* was proposed.[4]

Chiffinch owned property in the Windsor neighbourhood, and had held municipal office since 1681. He was returned unopposed in 1685, and became a moderately active Member of James II's Parliament, serving on seven committees, including those to recommend expunctions in the Journals, to inspect expiring laws and to regulate hackney coaches. In 1688 the King's electoral agents reported that he was proposed as candidate for the borough by the corporation, but he did not stand again. Presumably he accepted the Revolution, for he continued in local office, retained his position as master of the hawks, and was confirmed in his appointment as keeper of Hyde Park, but he was replaced on the Windsor corporation in August 1689. Chiffinch was buried at Bray on 26 Nov. 1691. His daughter married the first Earl of Jersey of the Villiers family and became an active Jacobite.[5]

[1] Add. 5520, f. 4; *Wilts. Par. Reg.* ix. 25; *Salisbury Mar. Lic. 1615–82*, p. 163. [2] *CSP Dom.* 1661–2, p. 498; 1665–6, p. 354; *Cal. Treas. Bks.* iv. 326; ix. 1733. [3] *First Hall Bk.* (Windsor Hist. Recs. i), 30, 37, 48, 74, 178; *HMC Finch*, ii, 123; *CSP Dom.* 1685, pp. 46, 69, 102; 1689–90, p. 76. [4] Add. 5520, f. 4; Hoare, *Wilts.* Salisbury, 473, 595; *Grantees of Arms* (Harl. Soc. lxvi), 51; *Cal. Treas. Bks.* iv. 185, 386; v. 1317–23; *HMC Finch*, ii. 81, 83. [5] PCC 5 Fane; J. M. Dalton, *Cal. of St. George's Chapel, Windsor*, 147, 411–12; *First Hall Bk.* 13, 74; Berks. RO, Bray par. reg.

L.N./G.J.

CHILD, Josiah (c.1630–99), of Wanstead, Essex.[1]

PETERSFIELD 22 Dec. 1658–22 Mar. 1659
DARTMOUTH 1–6 Feb. 1673, 15 Feb. 1673
LUDLOW 6 June 1685

> b. c.1630, 2nd s. of Richard Child, merchant, of Fleet Street, London by Elizabeth, da. of one Roycroft of Weston Wick, Salop. *m.* (1) 26 Dec. 1654, Hannah, da. of Edward Boate†, shipbuilder, of Portsmouth, Hants 2s. (d.v.p.) 1da.; (2) lic. 14 June 1663 (aged 32), Mary, da. of William Atwood, merchant, of Hackney, Mdx., wid. of Thomas Stone, merchant, of London, 1s. 2da.; (3) lic. 8 Aug. 1676, Emma, da. and coh. of Sir Henry Barnard, merchant, of London and Bridgnorth, Salop, wid. of Francis Willoughby of Middleton, Warws. 2s. *cr.* Bt. 16 July 1678.[2]
> Dep. treas. of the navy, Portsmouth 1655–60; freeman, Portsmouth 1655, alderman 1656–62, mayor 1658–9; member, R. Africa Co. 1672, asst. 1675–6; committee, E. India Co. 1674–6, 1678–d., gov. 1681–3, 1686–8, dep. gov. 1684–6, 1688–90; commr. for assessment, London and Warws. 1677–80, Essex 1679–80, 1689–90, Warws. 1689; j.p. Essex 1679, 1687–d., dep. lt. Apr. 1688–?d., sheriff Nov. 1688–9.[3]
> Commr. for trade 1668–72.

Although Child was removed from office by the commissioners for corporations in 1662, the Restoration had little effect on his meteoric rise from humble origins. The market for naval stores may have contracted somewhat, though Child, as a good mercantilist, pointed out that he drew his supplies entirely from the New England colonies, but on his second marriage he returned to London and built a new brewery in Southwark. 'Much of the beer was small and stinking, and the rest ill-tasted and unfit for the sea'; but it was good enough for the navy and the royal household. Already in 1665 he was canvassing among his friends in Parliament his theory of a low rate of interest as the prime requisite for an expanding economy. His signature occupies a prominent place on the Southwark by-election return in the following year, and he was recommended by the King for membership of the Brewers' Company. The publication in 1668 of his *Brief Observations concerning Trade and Interest of Money* was timed to coincide with a parliamentary debate. The book, advocating toleration as well as cheap money, caused a considerable stir, though its originality and consistency have been overrated, and its author was proposed by Buckingham for a seat on the Navy Board. Meanwhile Child had formed a syndicate with Sir Thomas Littleton, 2nd Bt.* and Thomas Papillon* to bid for the victualling contract for the navy, but their tender was rejected in favour of Sir Denis Gauden, from whom the all-powerful surveyor-general of victualling, Samuel Pepys*, had received so many gratifications. Pepys's offence was not to be forgiven; for the moment, however, Child confined himself to proposing the establishment of a victualling commission, and in 1671 the rival syndicates merged (as the Duke of York had wished six years before), under the chairmanship of (Sir) Denny Ashburnham*.[4]

Meanwhile, Child and another business associate, William Love*, described by Roger North* as the leading fanatics in the City, had been appointed to the council of trade. Unfortunately material interests soon disrupted their spiritual unity, and with it the council itself, allegedly a sinister machination of the republicans to infiltrate the government machine; for Love was a member of the Levant Company, while Child was embarking on purchases of East India Company stock which were before long to give him virtual control. In 1673, however, he was far from exclusively occupied with the Eastern trade. He bought for £11,500 from the trustees of Robert Brooke* the estate at Wanstead where he had been living for some years, 'a cursed and barren spot, as commonly these over-grown and suddenly moneyed men for the most part seat themselves', and adorned it at prodigious cost with walnut trees and fish ponds many miles in circuit. He was a founder-member of the Royal Africa Company,

and part-owner of 1,330 acres in Jamaica. Although he never visited Dartmouth, he acquired an interest there by entering into a partnership with a local ship-owner, presumably one who felt himself threatened by the expansion of the London-based firm of (Sir) John Frederick*. One of the Dartmouth seats had been vacant since October 1671 and, aided by a lavish expenditure of money and court pressure on the customs officials, Child defeated Frederick's partner Nathaniel Herne* in a by-election on 1 Feb. 1673. The election was among those quashed by the House because writs had been issued by Lord Chancellor Shaftesbury during a recess, but Child's majority was impregnable, and he was again returned a fortnight later.[5]

Child naturally prepared to defend himself against Herne's petition by adding his name to the committee of elections, but his other 18 committees in the Cavalier Parliament were almost wholly concerned with trade. The Dutch agent du Moulin, who approached him about this time, was dismayed at his hostility. But with the collapse of the Cabal and the advent to power of the Anglican Danby, Child's support for the Government rapidly disappeared. He withdrew from the victualling contract with Papillon; his accounts had still not been passed at his death a quarter of a century later. In the 1674 session he took a prominent part in two opposition manoeuvres, the attack on the press-gang and the whispering campaign against Pepys. In the debate on impressment, Child declared sarcastically that he was glad to hear from Pepys that 'so few have been oppressed. He has conversed all his time with seafaring men; knows of hundreds of masters of ships etc. that have been pressed.' He was less effective when named as the authority for Pepys's Popish practices, when he shuffled and prevaricated.[6]

In April 1675 Child, Papillon, Littleton and Henry Powle* were active in collecting evidence for the impeachment of Danby. He served on the committee for appropriating the customs to the use of the navy, and in a debate on the growth of London he delivered himself of the remarkable assertion that 'sixty years' experience has made it evident, in fact, that rents have increased the more for building houses'. It was probably the conspiracy against Danby rather than the breakdown of the victualling contract that led (Sir) Joseph Williamson* to inform Herne, the outgoing governor of the East India Company, that the King would be highly offended if either Child or Papillon were chosen as his successor, 'both men having behaved very ill towards him'. 'I am loath to speak plain English', Sir Richard Wiseman* wrote of Child in 1676, 'but if he were well observed he might be proved to be a capital offender', and Shaftesbury marked him 'worthy' in 1677.[7]

Sobered perhaps by his temporary exclusion from the East India board, Child made no more speeches in the Cavalier Parliament. He was probably required to earn his baronetcy only by abstention from overt opposition, for his name appears on no list of court supporters in 1678. He was added to the commission of the peace in 1679, but seems never to have acted, presumably because he scrupled the oaths. He virtually withdrew from English politics during the exclusion crises, though it was reported in February 1679 that he was engaged, with his third wife's brother-in-law Chandos, in an attempt to reconcile Shaftesbury and Danby. He was quick to sense the Tory reaction in the autumn of 1681, and on behalf of the East India Company began the policy of sweetening the Court with a present of 10,000 guineas. This entailed a feud with Papillon which was to dominate the rest of his career. By his third wife (the widow of the eminent naturalist) he had resumed his ancestral connexions with the Welsh marches, and he proceeded to strengthen his interest by marrying his daughter to Charles Somerset*, characteristically improving the occasion by unloading on the bridegroom a large quantity of East India stock, which promptly depreciated.[8]

Child had acquired a poor opinion of Parliament and the 'ignorant country gentlemen, who hardly knew how to make laws for the good government of their own families, much less for the regulating of companies and foreign commerce'. But with the mounting criticism of his expensive and ambitious Indian policy, and the tightening links between the company and the Court, he may have thought it advisable to strengthen his position with a seat in Parliament. He was returned for Ludlow at a by-election in 1685 on the interest of Somerset's father, the Duke of Beaufort. He sat on only one committee in James II's Parliament, and made no recorded speeches. Nevertheless he was regarded by James (whose investments he supervised) as a valuable potential recruit to the Court. On 6 Aug. 1687, Roger Morrice reported that Child, 'a man of parts and of great estate (though his principles are not known) was pressed exceeding hard by the King himself, who sent for him twice to Hampton Court who used many arguments to him, but peremptorily refused to be an alderman'. Although Child thus avoided acknowledging the new London charter, the same objection could not apply to taking county office in Essex. In spite of the outraged reaction of Tory country gentleman like (Sir) John

Bramston* when such 'commonwealthsmen' were appointed to the bench, Child went on to announce his candidature for the county seat in 1688. Hostility towards his Indian policy increased in the City as the year wore on, but Child steadfastly refused adoption as a court candidate, and by September James's electoral agents had given up hope of him. Child did not stand in 1689, when he was sheriff of Essex, nor so far as is known for any later Parliament. But with a holding computed at £51,000 at the Revolution he remained active in the affairs of the East India Company till his death on 22 June 1699, aged 69. Two of his sons entered Parliament, the younger representing Essex (with one break) from 1710 to 1734.[9]

Contemporary notices of Child are mostly unfavourable. The most balanced estimate comes from Burnet:

> A man of great notions as to merchandise, which was his education, and in which he succeeded beyond any man of his time; he applied himself chiefly to the East India trade, which by his management was raised so high, that it drew much envy and jealousy both upon himself and upon the company; he had a compass of knowledge and apprehension beyond any merchant I ever knew; he was vain and covetous and thought too cunning, though to me he seemed always sincere.[10]

[1] This biography is based on W. Letwin, *Sir Josiah Child, Merchant Economist.* [2] *Inhabitants of London in 1638* ed. Dale, 171. [3] *CSP Dom.* 1655, p. 431; 1658–9, p. 326; 1665–6, p. 371; 1687–9, p. 187; R. East, *Portsmouth Recs.* 328; Add. 38871, ff. 7–12; *Cal. Ct. Mins. E.I. Co.* ed. Sainsbury, x. 47, 175; *Bramston Autobiog.* (Cam. Soc. xxxii), 304. [4] *CSP Dom.* 1661–2, p, 18; 1664–5, p. 540; 1665–6, p. 371; 1668–9, p. 642; 1671, p. 481; 1672–3, p. 264; Morant, *Essex,* i. 30; *Cal. Treas. Bks.* ii. 387; *Pepys Diary,* 25 Sept. 1668. [5] R. North, *Examen,* 461–2; *CSP Col.* 1669–74, pp. 99, 410; *Cal. Treas. Bks.* iii. 451; *Cal. Ct. Mins. E.I. Co.* ix. 307; *VCH Essex,* vi. 324; *Evelyn Diary,* iv. 305–6; *CSP Dom.* 1672–3, pp. 488–9, 511, 559, 577. [6] K. H. D. Haley, *Wm. of Orange and the Eng. Opp.* 54; *CSP Dom.* 1673–5, p. 41; Grey, ii. 331, 432. [7] *Dering Pprs.* 78–79; *HMC Lindsey,* 10–11; Grey, iii. 9; *CSP Dom.* 1676–7, p. 75. [8] *HMC 9th Rep.* pt. 2, p. 456; Luttrell, i. 435; Scott, *Joint Stock Cos.* i. 321; A. C. Wood, *Levant Co.* 114; *Ailesbury Mems.* 673. [9] R. Morrice, Entering Bk. 2, p. 164; *Ellis Corresp.* ii. 119–20; Add. 22185, f. 14. [10] Burnet ed. Routh, iv. 414.

J.P.F.

CHISENHALL, Sir Edward (1646–1727), of Chisnall Hall, Coppull, Lancs.

WIGAN	1689
PRESTON	5 Dec. 1690

b. 14 Oct. 1646, 3rd but 1st surv. s. of Edward Chisenhall of Chisnall and Gray's Inn by Elizabeth, da. of Alexander Rigby of Layton. *m.* (1) bef. Apr. 1665, Anne, da. of Thomas Adkinson of Blew Hall, Essex, 1da.; (2) 25 Apr. 1671, Elizabeth, illegit. da. of Sir William Playters, 2nd Bt., of Sotterley, Suff., 2s. 1da.; (3) 21 Sept. 1683, Elizabeth, da. and coh. of Hon. Richard Spencer* of Orpington, Kent, *s.p. suc.* fa. 1654; kntd. 24 Apr. 1671.[1]

Commr. for assessment, Lancs. 1673–80, Lancs. and

Norf. 1689–90, recusants, Lancs. 1675, j.p. 1672–Apr. 1688, 1689–95, 1702–15, dep. lt. 1689–1715.[2]

Chisenhall's ancestors had held the manor from which they took their name since the 13th century. His father obtained a post in the Prince of Wales's household, and fought for the King in both wars. He petitioned to compound in 1648 for property valued at £120 p.a., including Chisenhall Buildings in Gray's Inn, and, upon proof that he had never practised as a barrister, was fined £480, which he had paid off by 1651. He retired to Chisnall, where he wrote a defence of the Church of England published shortly before his death under the title *Catholike History*. Little is known of Chisenhall's early life. He acquired property in Norfolk by his second marriage which he wished to dispose of to purchase an estate at Preston, but two private bills for this purpose failed in 1678 and 1680. He took a lively interest in the affairs of Wigan, four miles from Chisnall, opposing the surrender of the charter in 1681. In 1685 he was persuaded to withdraw his candidacy in favour of Lord Charles Murray*. A convinced Anglican like his father, he was omitted from the commission of the peace in 1688. At the mayoral election of September 1688 in Wigan, he and William Banks II* actively supported the successful candidate, a strong Whig, who duly signed their return to the Convention four months later. But according to Anthony Rowe* Chisenhall voted to agree with the Lords that the throne was not vacant, and he declared the comprehension bill 'so destructive to the Church of England [that] he desired it [to] lie on the table till Doomsday'. He was appointed to the committees to consider the bill for disarming Papists and the Wye and Lugg navigation bill, but was given leave to go into the country on 4 June, and may not have returned. He lost his seat at the general election, but came in for Preston later in the year. He was buried at Standish on 1 Apr. 1727, the only member of his family to sit in Parliament.[3]

[1] *Reg. of Standish* (Lancs. Par. Reg. Soc. xliv), 104; *Vis. Lancs.* (Chetham Soc. lxxxiv), 79; *Le Neve's Knights* (Harl. Soc. viii), 247–8; *St. Dunstan in the East* (Harl. Soc. Reg. lxxxiv), 63; *St. Margaret's Westminster* (Harl. Soc. Reg. lxiv), 182; *VCH Lancs.* vi. 227. [2] Croxton, *Lancs.* iv. 237; Lancs. RO, QSC 81 et seqq. [3] *Cal. Comm. Comp.* 1860; *Royalist Comp. Pprs.* (Lancs. and Cheshire Rec. Soc. xxvi), 35–38; *HMC 9th Rep.* pt. 2, p. 101; *CJ*, ix. 684; *HMC Le Fleming*, 181–2; *HMC Kenyon*, 178, 196; *Hatton Corresp.* (Cam. Soc. n.s. xxiii), 128; Lancs. RO, Standish par. reg.

I.C.

CHIVERS, Henry (c.1653–1720), of Fiddington, Ashchurch, Glos. and Quemerford, nr. Calne, Wilts.

CALNE 1689, 1690, 1698, 23 Mar. 1702, 1702

b. c.1653, o.s. of Seacole Chivers of Quemerford by Eleanor, da. and coh. of John Roberts of Fiddington. *m.* Bridget (*d.* 1724), da. of Duke Stonehouse* of Great Bedwyn, Wilts., 1da. *suc.* fa. 1657.[1]

Commr. for assessment, Wilts. 1677–80, 1689–90, sheriff 1677–8; j.p. Glos. 1683–?96, Wilts. June 1688–96, 1700–5; dep. lt. Wilts. 1683–?96, 1701–?*d.*; alderman, Malmesbury 1685–7; col. of militia ft. Wilts. by June 1688–at least 1697.[2]

Capt. of ft. regt. of Duke of Beaufort (Henry Somerset*) 1685–7, Queen Dowager's Ft. (later 2 Ft.) 1687–9; lt.-col. R. Ft. Gds. (later Grenadier Gds.) 1689–90.

Chivers came of a prosperous family of clothiers which had been settled in Calne since the mid-16th century, and had acquired considerable property in the county. His father was probably a Royalist at the outset of the Civil War, but, together with Henry Bayntun I* and George Lowe* he gave himself up to the parliamentary forces at Calne in 1644, and escaped financial penalty. Chivers succeeded in early childhood to an estate of £1,000 p.a., and his wardship was contested between William Duckett* and James Ashe†, the case eventually reaching the House of Lords in 1668.[3]

Chivers stood for Calne, one mile from Quemerford, in the first election of 1679 against his cousin Walter Norborne*, but his petition was not reported from the committee of elections. It is not known whether he stood in the next three elections, but he probably opposed exclusion. In 1685 he was nominated 'capital burgess' of Malmesbury in the new charter and commissioned in one of the new regiments formed to resist Monmouth's rebellion. He transferred to 'Kirke's Lambs' two years later. He was removed from the Malmesbury corporation in December 1687, but a few months later the King's agents reported that he enjoyed one of the principal interests at Calne, and recommended him as a j.p. Lord Yarmouth (William Paston*), the joint lord lieutenant, described how

with great entreaties and persuasions I prevailed with Mr Chivers to be for the taking off of the Penal Laws and Tests, and [he] will rely solely upon his Majesty. His chiefest scruple was that he should be hanged hereafter for what he does at present, and [he] desired great security.

In 1689 he was returned for Calne. Anthony Rowe* listed him among those who voted to agree with the Lords that the throne was not vacant. Nevertheless he was commissioned in the Grenadier Guards under Henry Sidney*. His only committee in the Convention was on the estate bill promoted by the Earl of Radnor (Charles Bodvile Robartes*) on 21 Jan. 1690. He was returned for Calne to four more Parliaments and voted with the Tories. He died on 30 Apr. 1720, aged 67, and was buried at Leigh

Delamere, the only member of his family to enter Parliament.[4]

[1] *Wilts. Arch. Mag.* xxiv. 218; Sir T. Phillipps, *Monumental Inscriptions*, pt. 2, p. 41. [2] *CSP Dom.* 1685, p. 297. [3] *VCH Wilts.* iv. 149; A. E. W. Marsh, *Calne*, 119; H. Bull, *Hist. Devizes*, 200; C5/45/2; *LJ*, xii. 232; Aubrey and Jackson, *Wilts. Colls.* 38. [4] PC2/72, f. 555; SP44/165/222.

B.D.H.

CHOLMLEY, Sir Henry (1609–66), of West Newton Grange, Yorks.

MALTON   8 Jan. 1641[1]
APPLEBY   1660

bap. 2 Feb. 1609, 4th but 2nd surv. s. of Sir Richard Cholmley[†] (*d.* 1631) of Whitby by 1st w. Susan, da. of John Legard, merchant, of London and Ganton, Yorks.; bro. of Sir Hugh Cholmley[†], 1st Bt. *educ.* I. Temple 1628; travelled abroad 1633. *m.* c.1638, Katharine (*d.* 1672), da. of Henry Stapleton of Wighill, wid. of Sir George Twisleton, 1st Bt., of Barley, 2s. (1 *d.v.p.*) 1da. Kntd. 27 Dec. 1641.[2]

Lt.-col. of militia ft. Yorks, by 1640; j.p. Yorks. (W. Riding) 1642–8, (N. and W. Ridings) Mar. 1660–*d.*, Westmld. Mar.–July 1660; commr. for levying money, Yorks, 1643, assessment (N. and W. Ridings) 1644–8, Aug. 1660–1, (N. Riding) 1661–*d.*, northern assoc., (N. and W. Ridings) 1645, militia, Yorks. 1648, Mar. 1660, oyer and terminer, Northern circuit July 1660; dep. lt. (N. Riding) 1661–*d.*[3]

Col. of ft. (parliamentary) 1642–4, 1648, June–Oct. 1660.[4]

Commr. for regulating excise 1645, abuses in heraldry 1646, exclusion from sacrament 1646, scandalous offences 1648.

Cholmley was intended for the legal profession, but he was expelled from the Temple after the Christmas disorders in 1634, and his marriage a few years later to a wealthy widow made him financially independent. Unlike his elder brother, he remained faithful throughout the Civil War to the Long Parliament, in which he represented Malton, and in 1648 he directed the siege of Pontefract. But his conduct was not sufficiently vigorous to please the radicals, and he did not sit after Pride's Purge. Out of office during the Interregnum, he had become an active Royalist in 1659, when he persuaded his nephew Barrington Bourchier* to join in Booth's rising, and he took a prominent part under Thomas Fairfax*, 3rd Lord Fairfax, in the overthrow of the military junta. The Rump ordered his arrest on 18 Feb. 1660, but he returned to the House when the secluded Members were readmitted three days later.[5]

Cholmley was not popular in his own county, and at the general election of 1660 he was returned for Appleby chiefly by means of the dowager countess of Pembroke, whom he had assisted in her dispute with her tenants in Craven. A moderately active

Member of the Convention, he was appointed to 14 committees, twice acted as teller, and made eight recorded speeches. A court supporter, he was sent to the Lords on 2 May with the King's letter, and was one of the four Members to count the votes for the deputation to carry the reply, to which he was himself elected. On returning to Westminster he was appointed to the committee for the recovery of the queen mother's jointure, and acted as teller for the motion to impose only a moderate fine on Francis Lascelles*, one of the Yorkshire regicides. He intervened several times in the indemnity debates, proposing Maj.-Gen. James Berry[†] as one of the persons to be excepted from the bill, and opposing the reading of a petition from Oliver St. John[†], but urging favour for Bulstrode Whitelocke[†]. On 2 July he said that he supported 'in part' the formidable list of categories proposed for political disablement. After the recess he described the militia bill as unnecessary, because the King was already in control; the issue 'had set them together by the ears once before, and [he] desired it might be let alone'. Nevertheless he was added to the committee for the bill. Lord Wharton sent him a copy of the case for modified episcopacy. He presented Bourchier's petition on 9 Nov., and spoke in its favour. On 19 Nov. he said: 'If the King's present revenue was made up [to] £1,200,000 a year, the court of wards might be spared without any further trouble'.[6]

Cholmley is not known to have stood in 1661. He was rewarded for his services with a grant of £1,000 out of the Bourchier estates, which were otherwise guaranteed against forfeiture. An active magistrate and deputy lieutenant, he was prevailed on in the spring of 1666 'to leave a plentiful fortune and great reputation in his own country' in order to deputize for his nephew, Sir Hugh Cholmley*, as superintendent of the harbour works at Tangier. It was thought that his military experience would be useful in man-management, but Henry Norwood*, the deputy governor, found his excessive zeal and uncontrollable temper intolerable, and it was fortunate that he died after a few months. His body was brought home for burial in his private chapel at West Newton Grange on 30 June 1666. His children were all dead without issue by 1680.[7]

[1] Did not sit after Pride's Purge 6 Dec. 1648, readmitted 21 Feb. 1660. [2] Clay, *Dugdale's Vis. Yorks.* ii. 254; PC2/43/53. [3] *Cholmley Mems.* (1787), 60; *W. Riding Sess. Recs.* (Yorks. Arch. Soc. rec. ser. liv), 363; H.B. M'Call, *Fam. of Wandesford*, 291. [4] E. Peacock, *Army Lists*, 36. [5] Keeler, *Long Parl.* 134; *Cal. I. Temple Recs.* ii. 221; *Cholmley Mems.* 29; D. Underdown, *Pride's Purge*, 211–12; *Cal. Cl. SP*, iv. 310, 598; *CSP Dom. 1659–60*, pp. 293, 373; 1660–1, p. 446; *Monckton Pprs.* ed. Peacock, 26. [6] *Cal. Cl. SP*, iv. 643; G. C. Williamson, *Lady Anne Clifford*, 214, 255; *CJ*, viii. 14, 60, 181; Bowman diary, ff. 5, 7, 28, 42v; *Old Parl. Hist.* xxiii. 2, 8, 17. [7] *Cal. Treas. Bks.* i. 196; *CSP Dom. 1663–4*,

pp. 463, 474; Sir Hugh Cholmley, *Account of Tangier* (1787), 252, 255–6; Clay, ii. 254.

M.W.H./L.N.

CHOLMLEY, Sir Hugh, 4th Bt. (1632–89), of the Inner Temple and Whitby, Yorks.

NORTHAMPTON   1679 (Mar.)
THIRSK   1685

b. 21 July 1632, 3rd but 2nd surv. s. of Sir Hugh Cholmley†, 1st Bt., of Whitby by Elizabeth, da. of Sir William Twysden, 1st Bt.†, of Roydon Hall, East Peckham, Kent. *educ.* St. Paul's c.1642–5; travelled abroad (France) 1645–9; I. Temple, entered 1647, 1656; Camb. 1649–50. *m.* 19 Feb. 1666, Lady Anne Compton (*d.* 26 May 1705), da. of Spencer Compton†, 2nd Earl of Northampton, 2da. (1 *d.v.p.*). *suc.* nephew 2 July 1665.[1]

Gent. usher to Queen Catherine of Braganza 1662–at least 1679; commr. for Tangier 1662–80, surveyor-gen. of the mole 1669–76; jt. farmer of alum works 1665–79; asst. R. Fishery Co. 1677.[2]

Capt. of militia ft. Yorks. (N. Riding) by 1665–?60, dep. lt. 1666–Feb. 1688; j.p. (N. Riding) 1668–Feb. 1688 Nov. 1688–*d.*, Peterborough 1682; commr. for assessment (N. Riding) 1673–80, Northants. 1679–80; common councilman, Scarborough aft. 1684–Mar. 1688.[3]

Cholmley was descended from a cadet branch of the Cholmondeleys of Cheshire which acquired lands in Yorkshire in the late 15th century, and represented the county in 1558. His father, who sat for Scarborough in five Parliaments, took a prominent part in resisting ship-money, and raised a regiment for Parliament in 1642. A strong churchman, he went over to the King in the following year and became governor of Scarborough. He took his family abroad in 1645, returning after the execution of Charles I to compound for his estates. He was fined £850 on property estimated at £1,000 p.a. Cholmley himself, who had been promised a place in the bedchamber, later claimed that only illness had prevented him from taking part in the Worcester campaign. He went abroad again in 1658, and on his return to England a royalist agent wrote: 'The young gentleman does the King very good service; his principles are right, and he is well esteemed by moderate Presbyterians'.[4]

On the disablement of Luke Robinson* in 1660, the Duke of York recommended Cholmley to fill the vacancy at Scarborough, but he was not elected. In 1662 he was given a post in the Queen's household and appointed to the Tangier committee. His colleague Samuel Pepys*, who described him as 'a fine, worthy, well-disposed gentleman', recorded Cholmley's growing irritation with the frivolity and extravagance of the Court and his belief that the kingdom would 'of necessity . . . fall back again to a Commonwealth'. In 1663 Cholmley, in partnership with Sir John Lawson, the admiral, and the Earl of Teviot, governor of Tangier, was granted a contract to build a mole across the harbour there. He had made a special study of the subject and had gained practical experience in the construction of a pier at Whitby. Even after succeeding to the family estate on which he developed the alum deposits, he spent a large part of his time at Tangier supervising the work. The project ran into financial difficulties, and in 1669, when he was the only surviving contractor, the contract was cancelled and a department for the mole set up under Cholmley as surveyor general with a salary of £1,500 p.a. Severe storms caused serious damage to the mole in the winter of 1674–5, and in 1676 he was replaced as surveyor-general by his assistant, Henry Shere. Cholmley wrote a journal of his life and an account of his work at Tangier, to which he prefixed a memoir of his early years.[5]

According to this memoir, Cholmley's childhood had been passed mainly in Northamptonshire, where he formed a close friendship with his contemporary, [Sir] Henry Yelverton*, and these ties had been strengthened by his marriage. Lord Manchester [Robert Montagu*] and Yelverton's son, Lord Grey de Ruthin, encouraged him to stand for Northampton at the first general election of 1679. He was successful, and marked 'base' on Shaftesbury's list. In the first Exclusion Parliament he was appointed to only three committees, of which the most important was for the prevention of illegal exactions; but he made seven speeches. He spoke evasively in the debate of 12 Mar. on the King's rejection of Edward Seymour* as Speaker, arguing that 'the matter . . . is of the nature of those things, which had better lie undetermined, than be decided either way', and moved to proceed to the choice of a new Speaker. On 17 Apr. he opposed a motion to place the money voted for disbanding the army in the chamber of London instead of the Exchequer, on the grounds that this would offend the King at a time when they needed his help to pass laws to protect the country in the event of a Popish successor. He spoke against the address for the removal of Lauderdale on 6 May, saying

> all the great officers, and those most in affairs, have been removed and changed no less than four, five and six times over; and yet neither have complaints lessened, nor . . . affairs at all mended.

He shocked the House by reflecting on the foreign ideas acquired by the King whilst in exile abroad, and blaming the lack of vigilance of the post-Restoration Parliaments. He went on to suggest the prevention of

> that great familiarity and access, which the ministers of foreign princes and more especially those of France [have] unto His Majesty's privacies and solitudes.

He spoke twice against exclusion. First on 27 Apr. when he urged that

> it must be . . . the steady endeavours of this House to make things so much more uneasy to the Papists after the King's death than they are whilst he is living, that it shall be the interests of all the Papists, and of the Duke himself, to wish the continuance of the King's life.

To this end he moved 'that the debates of the House may be at this time so to limit the power of the successor, as to make the people safe'. He repeated these arguments in a later debate on 11 May, when he maintained that putting aside the Duke of York would be

> so full of inconvenience that we ourselves should not agree to it: for besides that there are many doubting men that will question the very validity of such an Act of Parliament; so if we put by the Duke, whom shall we give the sceptre to?

He moved for a committee to prepare a bill for their protection against a Popish successor 'by taking out of his hands all power that may in any kind be held prejudicial to our safety and by placing such authority in successive Parliaments'. Ten days later he voted against the exclusion bill. He also spoke twice in debates concerning the Earl of Danby. First, on the dispute with the Lords who wished to proceed with the trial of the five Popish lords before considering the question of Danby's pardon, he supported the Lords in urging no further delay in the trial and disputing the claims of those who considered the pardon threatened Parliament's control over supply, saying: 'the right of money is one of the pillars of the Government, so inherent in the people [that] an Act of Parliament cannot take it from them'. In a later debate he made a long speech warmly defending Danby and particularly praising his opposition to the interests of France and the Roman Catholic Church, whose machinations he blamed for the Treasurer's overthrow. He had proved himself so formidable in debate that at the following general election Ralph Montagu* stepped down from a county seat to keep him out.[6]

In July 1683 Cholmley assured Secretary Jenkins of his loyalty:

> I have some reason to hope there will be changes both in the persons and the minds of those that compose the next House of Commons, that they may act more according to the sense of the nation than did some of our late representatives . . . I now hope the whole nation will find that an honest loyalty is the best policy, and that the way to prevent all fears from the growth of our neighbours is not to pinch and straiten His Majesty's affairs, but to support him with such cheerful supplies as may let the world see he is master of their hearts and purses.

He was elected for Thirsk in 1685, probably on the recommendation of the Roman Catholic Lord Belasyse, a kinsman by marriage under whom he had served at Tangier. On 26 May he presented a petition from some of the York electorate against Sir John Reresby*. A moderately active Member of James II's Parliament, he was appointed to five committees, including that for taking the disbandment accounts. In view of the interest on which he sat, he could hardly object to the employment of Roman Catholics in the army, but after the recess he stressed the usefulness of the militia and criticized the liberality of earlier grants of supply. Danby listed him among the Opposition, and to the lord lieutenant's questions on the Test Act and Penal Laws he replied:

> As I never used previous meetings to lead my votes, so I always voted as I thought upon hearing the debate, and therefore cannot give a certain answer to the question undiscussed. . . . It is still more difficult to know how another man will give his vote. I shall endeavour to choose such Members as will act and vote as I myself would do. . . . No man can differ more in opinion from myself than I differ at the same time from him, and in equal causes the living fairly seems to me a debt so justly due to human nature [that] I must think meanly of anyone [who] should either slacken his kindness or other friendly office merely on account of religion or opinion.

He was removed from municipal and county office, and when the Dutch invasion became imminent the lord lieutenant was ordered to seize his horses. No doubt he welcomed the Revolution, but he died on 9 Jan. 1689 and was buried at Whitby. His only surviving daughter had married a London merchant called Nathaniel Cholmeley, whose parentage is unknown, and their elder son inherited the estate and sat for Hedon as a Whig from 1708 to 1721.[7]

[1] This biography is based on Sir Hugh Cholmley, *Account of Tangier* (1787). [2] *Pepys Diary*, 6 Aug., 27 Oct. 1662; R. B. Turton, *Alum Farm*, 187, 191; *CJ*, ix. 457; *Williamson Letters* (Cam. Soc. n.s. ix), 149; E. M. G. Routh, *Tangier*, 348, 354; *Sel. Charters* (Selden Soc. xxviii), 198. [3] Add. 41254, ff 5, 28v; *HMC Var.* ii. 169; PC2/72/640; *Fenland N. and Q.* vi. 215. [4] *VCH N. Riding*, ii. 496, 503, 517; *Cal. Comm. Comp.* 2062; *CSP Dom.* 1658–9, p. 576; *Cal. Cl. SP*, iv. 560. [5] Adm. 2/1745, f. 2; *Pepys Diary*, 6 Mar., 21 June, 12 July, 9 Aug. 1667; Routh, 37, 343–54; Turton, 183. [6] Add. 29557, f. 94; Grey, vi. 434; vii. 139–40, 189–90, 191, 244; *HMC Ormonde* n.s. v. 84; BL, M636/33, John to Sir Ralph Verney, 11 Aug. 1679. [7] *CSP Dom.* July–Sept. 1683; Grey, viii. 357, 367; *HMC Var.* ii. 404; Clay, *Dugdale's Vis. Yorks.* ii. 256.

P.A.B./P.W.

CHOLMONDELEY, Francis (1636–1713), of Vale Royal, Cheshire.

NEWTON   1689

> *bap.* 10 Jan. 1636, 6th but 3rd surv. s. of Thomas Cholmondeley of Vale Royal by Elizabeth, da. and h. of John Minshull of Minshull; bro. of Thomas Cholmondeley*. *educ.* Brasenose, Oxf. MA 1669.[1]

Freeman, Liverpool 1686; j.p. Lancs. 1689–Mar. 1690, Aug. 1690–1.[2]

Cholmondeley joined the exiled Court in 1655, but as a devout student of divinity is unlikely to have remained there long. He was taken prisoner after the rising of Sir George Booth* in 1659. When James II expressed his determination to retain the Roman Catholic officers in November 1685, he wrote to Richard Legh* to express his anxiety about the security of the Church,

which must certainly fail in great measure if the Test be violated. . . . If this fence be broke, I know not where it will end. . . . Pray God avert the feared consequence . . . that our confidence in the King's word may not be shaken, which has been so much extolled.

He was returned on the Legh interest for Newton in 1689, entering Parliament at the age of 53. He took no part in the Convention except to vote to agree with the Lords that the throne was not vacant, and shortly afterwards fell 'dangerously ill of a pleurisy'. On 22 May (Sir) Henry Capel* told the Commons that he wished to resign his seat, since he could not take the oaths to the new regime; but his request was ignored, and he was given three weeks to attend. On 7 Jan. 1690 the House was informed that he was in town, looking after his dying cousin William Banks II*, though he had not attended Parliament all that session. He resolutely refused the oaths, and was sent to the Tower, but the Convention was adjourned before further action could be taken against him. His 'scruple of conscience' met with scant sympathy, even from his own family, who told him that he was suffering from 'the disease of a Quaker'. Although a friend of Joseph Addison† he remained a non-juror all his life. He was buried at Minshull on 3 July 1713.[3]

[1] Ormerod, *Cheshire*, ii. 157. [2] Wahlstrand thesis, 58; Lancs. RO, QSC 106. [3] *CSP Dom.* 1655, p. 599; 1689–90, pp. 208, 241; Ormerod, i. p. lxvi; ii. 157; Evelyn Legh, Lady Newton, *Lyme Letters*, 137, 181; *HMC Kenyon*, 264; Add. 36707, ff. 59, 68; *CJ*, x. 143, 325, 328; *Clarendon Corresp.* ii. 301.

I.C.

CHOLMONDELEY, Thomas (1627–1702), of Vale Royal, Cheshire.

CHESHIRE   17 Jan. 1670, 1685

b. 15 Sept. 1627, 3rd but 1st surv. s. of Thomas Cholmondeley of Vale Royal; bro. of Francis Cholmondeley*. *m.* (1) bef. 1651, Jane (*d.* 14 Apr. 1666), da. of Sir Lionel Tollemache, 2nd Bt.†, of Helmingham, Suff., 5s., *d.v.p.* 7da.; (2) 20 May 1684, Anne (*d.*1742), da. of Sir Walter St. John, 3rd Bt.*, of Lydiard Tregoze, Wilts., 4s. (1 *d.v.p.*) 1da. *suc.* fa. 1653.[1]

Commr. for militia, Cheshire Mar. 1660, capt. of militia ft. Apr. 1660, sheriff June 1660–1, j.p. July 1660–?89, dep. lt. c. Aug. 1660–Nov. 1688, commr. for assessment Aug. 1660–80, 1689, corporations 1662–3,

loyal and indigent officers 1662; alderman, Chester by 1664–84; commr. for maintenance of poor clergy, I.o.M. 1675; freeman, Liverpool 1686.[2]

Cholmondeley's ancestors had been established on the Cheshire estate from which they took their name since the late 12th century, and first sat for the county in 1547. His father bought Vale Royal early in the 17th century, served as a ship-money sheriff and a royalist commissioner of array, and compounded for his delinquency on a fine of £450. Cholmondeley inherited his father's politics and was involved in the rising of Sir George Booth* in 1659. At the Restoration he was made sheriff of Cheshire, holding office until November 1661, and consequently presiding over the general election. He was proposed for the order of the Royal Oak with an estate of £2,000 p.a. His neighbour and political adversary, Sir John Crewe, described him as

a proper handsome gentleman of a strong constitution, of good natural parts and of a solid judgement. He was a kind husband, an indulgent parent, a loving and affectionate master; a cried-up landlord, a constant and generous housekeeper. He got esteem without seeking it and without pride; a good justice of the peace, patiently giving ear to all who came before him; a very faithful trustee and careful in those matters in which he was employed .. He was of a generous disposition, of an universal affability; a composer of differences; apt to do kindnesses to his countrymen; remarkable for his temperance, liberality and hospitality.[3]

Cholmondeley stood as court candidate for the county at a by-election in 1670, and defeated Sir Philip Egerton*. He was a moderately active Member of the Cavalier Parliament, being named to 63 committees, most of which were for private bills, and acting as teller in three divisions. In his first session he was appointed to the committees for both conventicles bills, for authorizing commissioners to treat for union with Scotland and for the bill preventing the growth of Popery. About this time his name appears on a list of court supporters drawn up by the Opposition. After the long prorogation he was named to the committees which produced the test bill (6 Mar. 1673) and considered a bill of ease for Protestant dissenters. In 1674 he was on the committees for the bills to prevent illegal exactions and to reform the collection of the hearthtax.[4]

Despite his relative inconspicuousness Cholmondeley was named on the Paston list. In April 1675 he was summoned to the court caucus which met Danby to arrange the business of the House, and in September he received the government whip as well as a personal letter from Henry Coventry*. He was noted as a court supporter 'to be remembered', but

Sir Richard Wiseman* 'doubted' his reliability, blamed him and (Sir) Henry Capel* for leading William Banks I* astray, and hoped that Roger Werden* might 'undeceive Mr Cholmondeley, or inform how it can be done'. Probably the author of *A Seasonable Argument* was not far from the truth when he alleged that Cholmondeley had been 'promised a great place at Court, but not only deceived, but laughed at, poor gentleman'. Although he was inactive in the closing sessions of the Cavalier Parliament, Shaftesbury marked him 'doubly vile' and he was included in the 'unanimous club' of court supporters; but his name does not appear on the list drawn up by the Government.[5]

There is no evidence that Cholmondeley sought election to the Exclusion Parliaments. When Monmouth toured Cheshire in 1682, Cholmondeley twice wrote to Secretary Jenkins to purge the Cheshire commission of the peace without delay, adding:

> I find many are, by what has happened to the Duke of Monmouth, brought to consider, and some to repent, of what they did, and to hold them on in a good way, the removing from employment of such as encouraged them to wander may be a good inducement.

In 1685 Cholmondeley was returned again for Cheshire after a hotly contested election, but was named to only two committees of no political importance. He was listed by Danby as one of those in Parliament opposed to James II. In May 1687 the bishop of Chester prepared the address thanking James for his promises to maintain the Established Church in his Declaration of Indulgence. Roger Morrice noted that

> it is said the address was proposed to Mr Thomas Cholmondeley of Vale Royal who is reported to answer to the dean that he would never thank the King for breaking the laws, or words to that purpose, who is therefore complained of, and some say taken into custody.[6]

In October 1688 Cholmondeley wrote to Lord Dartmouth (George Legge*) that he prayed 'for a right understanding between his Majesty and the Prince of Orange to prevent the effusion of blood'. He did not stand in 1689, though he actively supported the Tory candidates at Chester. A non-juror and an active Jacobite, he was arrested in May but released on £3,000 bail. He accepted a commission from the exiled King, and was probably one of those who assured him in 1694 that 'the people of England are very much disposed to receive him'. He died on 26 Feb. 1702 and was buried at Church Minshull, Cheshire. 'Had he not lived in times of difficulties and divisions', wrote his Whig neighbour, 'he had been the most popular commoner at home and abroad.' His son Charles sat for Cheshire

as a high Tory in the last two Parliaments of Queen Anne and again from 1722 to his death in 1751.[7]

[1] Ormerod, *Cheshire*, ii. 157–8; *Cheshire Vis. Peds.* (Harl. Soc. xciii), 27–28. [2] *Parl. Intell.* 16 Apr. 1660; *Cal. Treas. Bks.* xvii. 128; Chester corp. assembly bk. 2, ff. 137v, 150; SP29/420/131; 44/70/75; Wahlstrand thesis, 58. [3] *Thurloe*, iii. 348; Ormerod, i. p.lxvi; iii. 156. [4] *CSP Dom.* 1670, p. 30. [5] *Dering Pprs.* 63; *CSP Dom.* 1675–6, p. 304. [6] *CSP Dom.* 1682, pp. 383, 434, 439; R. Morrice, Entering Bk. 2, pp. 137, 138. [7] *HMC Dartmouth*, i. 139; Bodl. Eng. C711, f. 100, *HMC Buccleuch*, ii. 91; *Hatton Corresp.* (Cam. Soc. n.s. xxiii), 146; *HMC Lords*, iii. 92; *Orig. Pprs.* ed. Macpherson, i. 475; Ormerod, ii. 156.

G.H./B.D.H.

CHOWNE, Henry (c.1613–68), of Horsham, Suss.

HORSHAM   1661–Oct. 1668

> *b.* c.1613, 4th but 2nd surv. s. of Thomas Chowne (*d.* 1639) of Place House, Alfriston by Rachel, da. of William Campion of Combwell, Goudhurst, Kent. *m.* 26 Apr. 1642, Barbara (*bur.* 29 Sept. 1688), da. of Thomas Middleton* of Horsham, 7s. 1da. *suc.* nephew William 1651.[1]
> Commr. for assessment, Suss. Aug. 1660–*d.*, j.p. 1662–*d.*

Chowne came of a family settled in Kent since the early 15th century. His great-grandfather sat for Wilton in 1553 and for London in 1555, and his grandfather represented Rochester in 1593. His father sold the Kentish property and moved to Alfriston. The family played no part in the Civil War. As a younger son, Chowne was apprenticed to the father of Sir Robert Cordell*, and by 1639 was acting as his factor at Smyrna, where he entertained George Courthope* 'very magnificently'. He succeeded to the family estate, which included property in Horsham, in 1651, but continued to hold stock in the East India Company, and later procured a post at Surat for his son.[2]

Chowne was involved in a double return for Horsham in 1659, but he was not allowed to sit, and the election was declared void. He is not known to have stood in 1660, but he succeeded his aged father-in-law in the following year, and was included in Lord Wharton's list of friends. A moderately active Member of the Cavalier Parliament, he was named to 33 committees, including those for the corporation bill, the bill against unlawful meetings of dissenters, the five mile bill and the preservation of prize goods. He twice claimed privilege: on 6 Dec. 1666 the House ordered a servant of a hackney coachman into custody 'for his affront and abuse offered to Dr [Thomas] Burwell*, Mr [Edward] Rigby*, and Mr Chowne ... and for uttering reproachful words tending to the dishonour of the House'. No more appears in the Journals. On 14 Jan. of the next year he petitioned for relief against Thomas White, 'an attorney who had arrested him at the church on a Sunday (for £10,000) for words' which Chowne had supposedly spoken. The case occasioned considerable debate about whether privilege had been violated, the arrest having taken place when Parliament was not in session, but the House found in Chowne's favour and fined White £1,000. On 28 Jan. 1667 he acted as teller against disposing, for rebuilding other churches, of the materials and sites of London churches not to be rebuilt after the Great Fire. Clearly a high churchman, his only recorded speech attacked the comprehension measures sponsored by Lord Keeper Bridgeman:

> Mr Chowne made a long formal speech in which he told them that they were all born within the church; had received their rights and dues from the church; what then should cause them to dissent and separate from their mother? It was the devil that first moved them to dissent, and then a rebellious Parliament that did countenance and justify them in that rebellion, to the spilling of the blood of his sacred Majesty. It was this pretended conscience that murdered the King, dissolved the Parliament and enslaved the liberty of the nation, and that did tyrannize over the orthodox clergy.

Chowne was buried at Horsham on 22 Oct. 1668, and Bridgeman's son was returned at the by-election. Chowne's grandson Thomas was returned for Seaford as a Tory in 1702 and 1710.[3]

[1] *The Gen.* n.s. xxiv. 73–78; *Vis. Suss.* (Harl. Soc. liii), 168; (lxxxix), 24–25; Add. 5698, pp. 302, 407; PCC 64 Harvey, 280 Brent, 166 Hene. [2] *Courthope Mems.* (Cam. Soc. ser. 3, xiii), 116–17; *Cal. Ct. Mins. E.I. Co.* ed. Sainsbury, vii. 432; Add. 49696, f. 165; *Danny Archives* ed. Woolridge, 34. [3] *Milward*, 63, 69, 78, 217.

B.M.C./B.D.H.

CHRISTIE, Thomas (1622–97), of Bedford.

BEDFORD 1685, 1689, 1690

bap. 30 Jan. 1622, 1st s. of Thomas Christie of Bedford by Jane, da. of William Faldo of Bedford. *m.* (1) aft. 29 June 1646, Alice (*bur.* 9 Oct. 1666), da. and h. of John Poole, Brewer, of London, wid. of Charles Bainbrigge, Brewer, of Clerkenwell, Mdx., 1s. 2da. *d.v.p.*; (2) 15 Oct. 1667, Anne (*bur.* 4 Sept. 1709), da. of Oliver Luke of Woodend, Cople, Beds., *s.p.*[1]

Commr. for militia, Beds. Mar. 1660; j.p. Bedford Sept. 1660–at least 1661, Nov. 1688–*d.*, Beds. 1685–*d.*; commr. for assessment, Bedford 1661–80, Beds. and Bedford 1689; dep. steward, honour of Ampthill by 1662–?*d.*[2]

Christie's family had lived in Bedford since Elizabethan times, and provided a mayor for the borough in 1590. He became an attorney, and either he or his father was appointed to the county assessment committee in 1652. But from the Restoration he attached himself to the Bruce interest. A Churchman and a Tory, he 'often argued with Parliament men and others about the unreasonableness

and unlawfulness of the Exclusion', and helped to secure the surrender of the charter in 1684. He was returned for the borough in the following year, and became a very active Member, despite his lack of status and experience. He was named to 19 committees in James II's Parliament, including that for the private bill to relieve the creditors of the Earl of Cleveland, the last of the Bedfordshire Wentworths, and took the chair on a bill for the better recovery of tithe. With two barristers, William Wogan* and Roger North*, he was entrusted with preparing a bill for registering the deaths, burials, marriages and issue of the nobility and gentry, and he was appointed to the committee on the bill for the general naturalization of Huguenot refugees. After the recess he went into opposition with an impressive speech on supply wrongly attributed by Anchitell Grey* to Thomas Coningsby*.

> We owe . . . a duty to our country, and by that are bound to leave our posterity as free in our liberties and properties as we can. . . . There being officers now in the army that have not taken the Test flats greatly my zeal for it. . . . They debauch the manners of the people, their wives, daughters and servants. Men dare not to go to church where they quarter for fear of mischief to be done to their houses in their absence. Ploughmen and servants quit all country employment to turn soldier, and then a court martial in times of peace is most terrible. . . . The Guards I am not against; . . . I only speak of those that have been new raised.[3]

Christie replied to the questions put to him by Lord Ailesbury (Thomas Bruce*) on the repeal of the Tests and Penal Laws:

> [If he] be chosen, which he does not at present design, then he will comply with the King's inclination so far as he can with a good conscience and with the safety of the Protestant religion of the Church of England. . . . He has always been civil and moderate both towards the Catholic and Protestant dissenters. . . . He will give his vote for such as have always been of fixed and steady loyalty.

Nevertheless as one of Ailesbury's 'votaries' he was retained on the commission of the peace. Re-elected in 1689, he was even more active in the Convention, in which he was appointed to 93 committees, taking the chair in 18, acted as teller in four divisions, and carried nine bills to the Lords. Presumably this remarkable record was due to his efficiency as chairman, coupled with a certain amount of political indifference; he did not vote to agree with the Lords that the throne was not vacant, though he called for a 'new Magna Carta' in the debate of 29 Jan., and was appointed to the committees to report on the essentials for preserving religion, laws and liberties, to recommend alterations to the coronation oath, and to inquire into the authors and advisers of recent grievances. On 29 Apr. he delivered a report on the bailing of Brent, the 'Popish solicitor', and he was appointed to the committee on the bill for restoring corporations. The legislation with which Christie was most prominently connected included the two leather bills, two estate bills, the tithe bills, three bills for establishing local 'courts of conscience' for small claims, the bill to encourage woollen manufactures, and a naturalization bill. On 24 June he expressed doubt whether the opinion given by (Sir) Henry Bedingfield* in the last reign favoured the dispensing power. He helped to draw up the address requesting permission to inspect the records of the Irish committee of the Privy Council. On 4 July he acted as teller for a proviso to the Wye and Lugg navigation bill offered on behalf of a leading Bedfordshire Whig, the Earl of Kent. He helped to manage a conference on the attainder bill on 2 Aug.[4]

After the recess Christie was added to the committee to inspect war expenditure, and reported on the petition from the widow of Sir Thomas Armstrong* on 19 Nov. He helped to draft the address seeking to establish responsibility for the employment of Commissary Shales. With (Sir) William Williams*, John Arnold* and Sir Matthew Andrews*, he was ordered to draw up a list of Brent's papers. On 21 Dec. he reported on several complaints from merchantmen about the navy. He took the chair on the bill for the preservation of captured French salt, and carried it to the Lords on 10 Jan. 1690. He reported the bills to reverse Armstrong's attainder and the judgements *de scandalis magnatum* obtained by the Duke of Beaufort (Henry Somerset*). He was re-elected in 1690, and sat in the Officers' Parliament as an independent Tory. He was buried at St. Paul's, Bedford on 9 July 1697, the only member of his family to enter Parliament. He died rich, though not worth the £20,000 with which some credited him, and endowed eight almshouses which he had already built in his lifetime.[5]

[1] *Beds. Par. Reg.* xxxv. 9; PCC 93 Lee, 97 Twisse; *St. James Clerkenwell* (Harl. Soc. reg. xvii), 291; G. A. Blaydes, *Gen. Bed.* 24, 29, 86. [2] Add. 33590, f. 158. [3] *Beds. N. and Q.* iii. 351; *True Relation of What Happened at Bedford* (1672); *CSP Dom.* 1677–8, p. 489; *VCH Beds.* ii. 58; *CJ,* ix. 736, 751; Lowther diary, ff. 43–46. [4] *Hardwick SP,* ii. 115; *CJ,* x. 110, 204, 205, 246; Grey, ix. 359. [5] *CJ,* x. 296, 325, 337, 342; Blaydes, 39; *HMC Lords,* n.s. iv. 292; *Beds. N. and Q.* iii. 110–11; *VCH Beds.* iii. 33.

L.N.

CHUDLEIGH, Thomas (*b.* c.1649), of Golden Square, Westminster.

NEW ROMNEY 3 May 1685

b. c.1649, 1st s. of Thomas Chudleigh, surgeon, of Castle Close, Exeter, Devon by Agnes Vaughan. *educ.* Christ Church, Oxf. matric. 7 Apr. 1666, aged 16; M. Temple

1668. *m.* lic. 10 July 1671, his cos. Elizabeth, da. of Gregory Cole of the Middle Temple and Buckish Mills, Devon, *s.p. suc.* fa. 1668.[1]

Sec. of embassy, Madrid 1671, Paris 1672–3, Köln 1673, The Hague 1673–4, Nymwegen 1675–8; surveyor-gen. of customs 1679–82; ambassador extraordinary, The Hague 1682–5; commr. of customs 1684–Feb. 1688.[2]

Dep. lt. London 1687–Oct. 1688.

Chudleigh came of a Devon family which had first represented the county in the 14th century. In the Civil War his grandfather Sir George Chudleigh, 1st Bt.[†], originally fought for Parliament, but resigned his commission in 1643 and took up arms for the King. Chudleigh's father, a younger son, served under Sir Charles Vavasour first in Ireland and then in England against the parliamentary forces. He compounded in 1648, his fine being only £30, and became a surgeon in Exeter.[3]

Chudleigh inherited little in the way of wealth or prospects, but his cousin Thomas Clifford* was able to launch him on an official career, though he still needed financial assistance. He served under Lord Sunderland and Sir Leoline Jenkins*, who found in him 'all the accomplishments that can be desired in a gentleman for business'. As ambassador at The Hague, he succeeded in apprehending and extraditing Sir Thomas Armstrong*, but in his more strictly diplomatic functions he was a failure. He infuriated William of Orange by tampering with the English regiments in the Dutch service to induce them to refuse the normal courtesies to the Duke of Monmouth. William complained that Chudleigh had 'behaved, on several occasions, very impertinently with regard to me, being a very foolish and impertinent man', and he had to be recalled.[4]

As early as December 1683 Chudleigh had sought a seat in Parliament through the Trelawny interest. He was not successful at the general election of 1685, but James II nominated him to fill the vacancy at New Romney caused by the decision of Sir Benjamin Bathurst* to sit for Bere Alston. Although a stranger, he took the opportunity of urging the corporation to surrender their charter. A moderately active Member, he was named to five committees of secondary importance, and summoned to the meeting of the court caucus in the autumn session. In April 1687 it was reported (probably accurately) that Chudleigh had become a Roman Catholic. In February of the next year he lost his place in the customs, though he was given a pension of £1,200 p.a. in lieu of his salary, and in the same month was considered for the position of envoy to Portugal. He did not receive the post and in September left England 'in discontent'. Perhaps his knowledge of foreign affairs prompted his departure; he may have foreseen the outbreak of hostilities and anticipated William's intentions sooner than James. It was said that he was 'going to France to be a Carthusian monk' together with his secretary. The date of his death is not known.[5]

[1] H. C. Hardwick, *Chudleigh Mems.* 9; Vivian, *Vis. Devon*, 215. [2] *CSP Dom.* 1671, p. 503; 1673, pp. 105, 212; 1675–6, p. 448; 1680–1, p. 53; 1682, p. 454; *HMC Buccleuch*, i. 506; *Clarendon Corresp.* i. 624; *Cal. Treas. Bks.* vi. 53, 294; vii. 1464; viii. 1689. [3] *Cal. Comm. Comp.* 1879; Hardwick, 9. [4] C. H. Hartmann, *Clifford of the Cabal*, 8, 43; *Despatches of Plott and Chudleigh* ed. Middlebush, 118; *CSP Dom.* 1680–1, p. 53; Dalrymple, *Mems.* i. app. 123–4. [5] Add. 28894, f. 280; Kent AO, NR/JB, f. 115; NR/AC2, f. 637; *Cal. Treas. Bks.* viii. 430; Luttrell, i. 398; *Ellis Corresp.* i. 251; ii. 152, 162, 193; BL, M636/43, John to Sir Ralph Verney, 30 Aug. 1688.

B.D.H.

CHURCHILL, George (1654–1710).[1]

ST. ALBANS 1685, 1689, 1690, 1695, 1698, 1701 (Feb.), 1701 (Dec.), 1702, 1705

PORTSMOUTH 1708–8 May 1710

bap. 17 Mar. 1654, 3rd but 2nd surv. s. of Winston Churchill*; bro. of John Churchill II* and Charles Churchill†. *unm.*; 1s.[2]

Lt. RN 1666–8, 1672–4, capt. 1678–93, adm. 1702–3; ensign, Duke of York's Dgns. 1676, lt. 1678–9; capt. King's Dgns. 1685–Dec. 1688; cornet and maj. 3 Life Gds. 1691–2.

Commr. for assessment, Herts. and St. Albans 1689; j.p. Herts. by 1698–*d.*, Dorset by 1701–*d.*; dep. ranger, Windsor Little Park 1702–*d.*; elder bro. Trinity House 1704–*d.*, master 1705–7.[3]

Groom of the bedchamber to Prince George of Denmark 1689–1708; ld. of Admiralty 1699–1702; member of council 1702–8; commr. for naval sick and wounded 1707.[4]

Churchill accompanied the Earl of Sandwich (Edward Montagu I*) on his mission to Madrid as a page at the age of 12, though he was commissioned as a lieutenant in the navy. On his return he became a draper's apprentice, but was rescued from this humdrum occupation by the outbreak of the third Dutch war. His elder brother's success at Court ensured that from 1676 he was seldom out of employment, military or naval. He was returned on his brother's interest for St. Albans in 1685 under the new charter, when he was described as 'a person never before seen or known by the townsmen'; but he was completely inactive in James II's Parliament. Sunderland recommended him for re-election as court candidate in 1688.[5]

Churchill was one of the first naval officers to join William of Orange, and, as captain of the frigate *Newcastle*, stood by to assist the seizure of Plymouth citadel on 27 Nov. 1688. Lord Bath reported him 'a very worthy gentleman and much devoted to your Highness's service'. He was re-elected to the Convention, in which he made three recorded speeches and was appointed to only four committees, including those for the habeas corpus suspension bill, and for considering a petition from the Greenwich seamen. He was absent at sea for some time, and on 18 Nov. 1689 he was charged with extorting money for convoying merchantmen. In his defence he declared that 'it was a voluntary gift from them, and I compelled no man'. But the House found him guilty and sent him to the Tower. He was released on his petition ten days later, and resumed his seat, being appointed to the committee to recommend provision for wounded seamen and their dependants. He continued to sit as a Tory under William III, although until his brother's disgrace he was on active service in the navy. Under Anne, when he was chiefly occupied in naval administration, he became a Whig. He died on 8 May 1710 and was buried in Westminster Abbey. His moderate fortune, estimated at £24,000, was divided between his illegitimate son and his nephew, Francis Godfrey†.[6]

[1] Unless otherwise stated this biography is based on A. L. Rowse, *The Early Churchills*, 352–64. [2] Musbury par. reg. [3] *Cal. Treas. Bks.* ix. 1494; xiv. 185. [4] LS 13/231/24. [5] Churchill, *Marlborough*, i. 47; Soc. of Genealogists, London Drapers' Apprentices; *HMC Verulam*, 101; *CSP Dom.* 1687–9, p. 276. [6] *CSP Dom.* 1687–9, p. 364–5; *CJ*, x. 289, 290, 297; *HMC Downshire*, i. 319; Grey, ix. 430–1; Luttrell, vi. 580.

E.R.E./G.J.

CHURCHILL, John I (1622–82), of Colliton House, Dorchester, Dorset.

DORCHESTER 20 May 1661

b. 1622, 1st s. of William Churchill of Muston Manor, Piddlehinton by Mary, da. of George Yarde of Churston Ferrers, Devon, *educ.* M. Temple 1647. *m.* (1) 30 Jan. 1650, Bridget, da. of Charles Vaughan† of Ottery St. Mary, Devon, 1da.; (2) July 1664, Frances, da. of John Hooke* of Bramshot, Hants, *s.p. suc.* fa. 1681.[1]

J.p. Dorset July 1660–*d.*, commr. for assessment 1661–80; freeman, Poole and Lyme Regis 1662; commr. for corporations, Dorset 1662–3, recusants 1675.[2]

The Churchills were prominent merchants in Dorchester in Tudor times, and built their town house on ex-chantry land acquired under Edward VI. In 1609 they bought a country seat some three miles out of town. They owned much property in Dorchester and had a special interest in brewing. Whether their own residence, a stone's throw from the High Street, lay within the borough became the subject of controversy between Churchill and the corporation.[3]

Churchill was the first of his family to enter Parliament. His father, having unwillingly served as high constable in 1634, sheriff in 1640, and, at the entreaty of the townsmen, deputy governor of Dorchester during the royalist occupation, is unlikely to have coveted further public office. Churchill was elected to the Cavalier Parliament for the borough, on the elevation of Denzil Holles* to the peerage. There is some possibility of confusion with Winston Churchill* in the early sessions, but he was clearly inactive. Only 41 committees can be positively assigned to him, and none of these was of much political or religious importance. He helped to prepare an estate bill for (Sir) Ralph Bankes* and the bill to naturalize Lady Holles, his predecessor's third wife.[4]

Through the Hunton family Churchill was related to Sir Edward Nicholas, the secretary of state, and was probably a court supporter at first. He was noted in 1675 as to be influenced by Sir John Churchill*; but his position on Wiseman's list in 1676 suggests that he was believed to be inclining to the country party, and in the following year Shaftesbury marked him 'worthy'. Churchill was buried at Piddlehinton on 22 Dec. 1682; his will shows him to have been in financial difficulties, but most of his property seems to have gone eventually to his brother, William Churchill*.[5]

[1] Hutchins, *Dorset*, ii. 415; Eg. 2753, f. 141; *Mdx. Par. Reg.* i. 10. [2] Hutchins, i. 22, 32; C. A. F. Meekings, *Dorset Hearth-Tax*, 115–17; Dorset RO, KG 1148; Lyme Regis mss. B6/11, f. 25. [3] Hutchins, ii. 415, 804; C. H. Mayo, *Dorchester Recs.* 470–7; Oldfield, *Boroughs*, i. 260. [4] Dorset RO, Q. Sess. order bk. 1625–37; *CSP Dom.* 1655–6, p. 334. [5] Dorset RO, D.60/T.103, f. 4; PCC 13 Hare.

J.P.F.

CHURCHILL, John II (1650–1722).[1]

NEWTOWN I.o.W.   1679 (Mar.)

b. 24 June 1650, 2nd but 1st surv. s. of (Sir) Winston Churchill*; bro. of Charles Churchill† and George Churchill*. *educ.* Dublin free g.s. 1662; St. Paul's c.1664. *m.* 1 Oct. 1678, Sarah (*d.* 19 Oct. 1744), da. of Richard Jennings* of Sandridge, Herts. and coh to her bro., 2s. *d.v.p.* 5da. *cr.* Lord Churchill of Eymouth [S] 21 Dec. 1682, Baron Churchill of Sandridge 14 May 1685; *suc.* fa. 1688; *cr.* Earl of Marlborough 9 Apr. 1689; KG 14 Mar. 1702; *cr.* Duke of Marlborough 14 Dec. 1702.

Page to the Duke of York by 1667, gent. of bedchamber 1673–85, (as King) 1685–Nov. 1688; master of the wardrobe 1679–85; ambassador, Paris Mar.–Apr. 1685, The Hague 1701–12; PC 14 Feb. 1689–23 June 1692, 19 June 1698–30 Dec. 1711, 1715–*d.*; ld. of the bedchamber 1689–92; master of the horse and governor to the Duke of Gloucester 1698–1700; one of the lds. justices 1698–1700; master of the Ordnance 1702–11, 1715–*d.*

Ensign, 1 Ft. Gds. 1667; capt. of ft. Admiralty Regt. 1672, lt.-col. 1675–83; lt.-col. 2 R. English Regt. (French army) 1674–7; brig. of ft. 1678; col. 1 Dgn. Gds. 1683, 3 Horse Gds. 1685–Nov. 1688, (later 7 Ft.) 1689–92, (24 Ft.) 1702–4, 1 Ft. Gds. 1704–11, 1714–*d.*; maj.-gen. 1685–6; lt.-gen. Nov. 1688; c.-in-c. English

forces in the Netherlands 1690–2, allied forces 1701–11; capt.-gen. 1702–11, 1715–*d.*

J.p. Herts. 1683–?92, Dorset 1685–at least 1689, Mdx. and Westminster 1687–?92; high steward, St. Albans 1685–*d.*; dep. lt. Dorset 1685–May 1688; gov. Hudson's Bay Co. 1685–91; custos rot. Oxon. 1706–12; gov. Chelsea hospital 1715–*d.*[2]

Churchill began his career as page to the Duke of York, who became aware of his martial ambitions and obtained for him a pair of colours in the guards. After service in Tangier he became the lover of the Duchess of Cleveland, from whom he extracted £4,500. In 1671 he fought duels with Sir John Fenwick* and Henry Herbert*, and in the third Dutch war served under Turenne with great distinction. In 1678 he accompanied Sidney Godolphin I* as military adviser on a mission to William of Orange. At the general election in the following year he was returned with Sir John Holmes* for Newtown on the government interest, and marked 'base' on Shaftesbury's list. But he went into exile in Flanders with the Duke of York before the first Exclusion Parliament met, and was given leave on 1 May 1679 to go into the country 'for this whole session, in order to the recovery of his health'. Nevertheless Roger Morrice listed him as voting against the exclusion bill.

Churchill acquired one moiety of the Jennings estate by marriage, and bought the other in 1684. He thus enjoyed the principal interest at St. Albans, and in 1685 the mayor announced his candidature for the borough. In the event, however, his brother George was elected, perhaps because James II had made known his intention to give him an English peerage. He was by far the most important of the army deserters who went over to William of Orange in November 1688. The rest of his career, which has made him perhaps the most celebrated soldier in English history, is well-known. He died on 16 June 1722 and was buried in Westminster Abbey.[3]

[1] This biography is based on W. S. Churchill, *Marlborough*; A. L. Rowse, *The Early Churchills*. [2] A. E. Gibbs, *Corp. Recs. of St. Albans*, 85, 112. [3] *Som. Arch. and Nat. Hist. Soc. Proc.* xxx, pt. 2, p. 44; *HMC Verulam*, 100–1.

P.W.

CHURCHILL, Sir John (c.1620–85), of Lincoln's Inn and Churchill, Som.

BRISTOL   30 Mar.–Oct. 1685

b. c.1620, 1st s. of Jasper Churchill, Cutler, of London by w. Alice. *educ.* L. Inn 1639, called 1647. *m.* 16 May 1654 (with £2,500), Susan, da. of Edmund Prideaux† of Forde Abbey, Devon, 4da. *suc.* fa. 1648; kntd. 12 Aug. 1670.[1]

Deputy registrar, Chancery c.1639–45; solicitor-gen. to the Duke of York 1670, attorney-gen. 1673–85; master of the rolls Jan. 1685–*d.*[2]

J.p. Mdx. July 1660–*d.*, Som. 1662–*d.*; commr. for sewers, Som. Aug. 1660, assessment Som. Aug. 1660–80, Mdx. 1673–9; bencher, L. Inn 1662, reader 1670, treas. 1670–1; freeman, Bristol 1676, Bath 1679; recorder and alderman, Bristol 1682–*d.*, dep. lt. June 1685–*d.*[3]

Churchill was the first cousin of Winston Churchill*, whose father he succeeded as deputy registrar of Chancery before the Civil War. He took no part in the Civil War, but during the Interregnum built up a thriving practice at the Chancery bar. In 1652 he bought for £5,900 the manor of Churchill, from which presumably his ancestors took their name, though no connexion has been proved, and two years later married the daughter of the Protector's attorney-general. By 1662 he was regarded as 'a sure and faithful workman' in election business, but he cherished no parliamentary ambitions for himself, preferring to rise in the service of the Court, and not disdaining a courtesy to Lady Castlemaine. He succeeded Edward Thurland* as legal adviser to the Duke of York in 1670. His most noteworthy contact with Parliament during the reign of Charles II was as a victim of the dispute between the Houses in 1675, when he was ordered to explain why he had accepted a brief to prosecute Thomas Dalmahoy* in the House of Lords. Quite undaunted he replied that he was too busy a man to concern himself about orders of the Lower House, and that 'he saw little of privilege of Parliament in the case'. He was later seized by the serjeant-at-arms, backed by a force of 30 Members, while pleading in Chancery, and lodged in the Tower for the remainder of the session.[4]

It was probably the boldness of Churchill's speech on this occasion that marked him out as a future court spokesman in the Commons, and in the nearer future as a replacement for (Sir) Robert Atkyns* as recorder of Bristol, some 15 miles from his Somerset residence. He was given the freedom of the city in 1676 at the instance of Sir Robert Cann*, but it was not until 1682 that Atkyns could be manoeuvred out of the recordership. As one of the four Tories on the corporation his first task was to secure the surrender of the charter, upon which he was reappointed, and on the death of Sir Harbottle Grimston* he was appointed master of the rolls. Two months later the Duke of Beaufort (Henry Somerset*) recommended the Bristol corporation 'to elect him a representative for this city in the ensuing Parliament, a thing that will be both for the honour and vanity of the city'. Churchill was returned unopposed, but he was not an active Member of James II's Parliament. He was appointed to the committee for the bill to settle the estate of the Earl of Ossory (who was about to marry Beaufort's daughter), and he was also one of six Members ordered to bring in a bill for a tax on new buildings on 17 June. He died during the recess and was buried at Churchill on 11 Oct. 1685. Despite his extensive practice, his executors seem to have had some difficulty in making adequate provision for his daughters' portions.[5]

[1] *Som. and Dorset N. and Q.* xxvii. 185–93; *Dorset Par. Reg.* ii. 125. [2] T. D. Hardy, *Principal Officers of Chancery*, 120–1; SP23/186/410. [3] Bristol RO, Common Council Proceedings 1670–87, f. 93; Beaven, *Bristol Lists*, 187, 204, 232; *CSP Dom.* 1673, p. 571; 1685, p. 189. Bath council bk. 2, f. 750. [4] North, *Lives*, i. 260–1; *Som. Arch. Soc. Proc.* xxxi. 34–35; Bristol RO, AC/C74/76, Ames Poulett to Sir Hugh Smith, 27 Feb. 1662; J. Latimer, *Annals of Bristol*, 367–8; Grey, iii. 219; *CJ*, ix. 351. [5] SP44/68/180; SP29/422/218; Common Council Proceedings 1670–87, f. 214; J. Evans, *Hist. Bristol*, 232; *Glos. N. and Q.* iv. 461; *Som. Arch. Soc. Proc.* xxxi. 36.

J.P.F.

CHURCHILL, William (1627–1702), of Colliton House, Dorchester and Muston Manor, Piddlehinton, Dorset.

DORCHESTER 1685

bap. 15 Jan. 1627, 2nd s. of William Churchill of Muston, and bro. of John Churchill I*. *m.* 26 Feb. 1652, Grace, da. of Sir John Meller† of Little Bredy, Dorset, 3s. *suc.* bro. 1682.[1]

Commr. for assessment, Dorset 1673–80, 1689–90, j.p. June 1688–9.

Nothing is known either of the circumstances of Churchill's election or of his activities in the House, though he was doubtless a Tory. He did not even serve on the committee for the estate bill introduced by his colleague and nephew Edward Meller*. After the Revolution he was probably a non-juror. He was buried at Piddlehinton in August 1702. His second son John was elected for Dorchester in 1708.

[1] Hutchins, *Dorset*, ii. 414; F. Brown, *Som. Wills.* vi. 48–9; Add. 41620, f. 84.

J.P.F.

CHURCHILL, Winston (1620–88), of Minterne Magna, Dorset and Whitehall.[1]

WEYMOUTH AND MELCOMBE REGIS 1661
LYME REGIS 1685

bap. 18 Apr. 1620, 2nd but 1st surv. s. of John Churchill of Wootton Glanville, Dorset by 1st w. Sarah, da. and coh. of Sir Henry Winston of Standish, Glos. *educ.* St. John's, Oxf. 1636–8; L. Inn 1637, called 1652. *m.* 26 May 1648 (with £1,500), Elizabeth, da. of Sir John Drake† of Ashe, Musbury, Devon, 8s. (5 *d.v.p.*) 3da. *suc.* fa. 1659; kntd. 22 Jan. 1664.[2]

Capt. of horse (royalist) 1643–5.

J.p. Dorset July 1660–*d.*, Mdx. 1680–*d.*; commr. for assessment, Dorset Aug. 1660–80, Mdx. 1664–9, Westminster 1679–80; freeman, Poole Nov. 1660; Lyme

Regis 1685; commr. for loyal and indigent officers, Dorset 1662, dep. lt. 1664–d.[3]

Commr. for settlement [I] 1662–9; clerk-comptroller of the green cloth 1664–d.[4]

FRS 1664–85.

Churchill constructed for himself an impressive pedigree, but he was in fact the grandson of a Dorset copyholder. His father studied law at the Middle Temple, and became deputy registrar of Chancery, in which capacity he acted as jackal, and later Judas, to Bacon. Churchill himself became an undergraduate at St. John's during the period of Laud's greatest munificence to the college; but a few years later, as a law student, he was haled before the Privy Council for publicly drinking confusion to the Archbishop. During the Civil War his father, who had resigned his Chancery post to his cousin (Sir) John Churchill*, was active as commissioner of array, compounding for £440 in 1646 on property valued at £245 p.a. Churchill himself saw service with the King's forces in the west until wounded in the arm in December 1645. Although called to the bar in 1652, as a Cavalier he was forbidden to practise; but he is not known to have engaged in royalist conspiracy during the Interregnum, living quietly with his wife's relatives until his father's death.[5]

Churchill was returned for Weymouth in 1661 as a follower of the Earl of Bristol. He took little interest in his constituency; alone among its four Members he made no contribution to the cost of rebuilding the harbour bridge. But at Westminster he was quick to make his mark. Though in the earlier sessions of the Cavalier Parliament there is some possibility of confusion with John Churchill I*, he was probably appointed to all the committees of major political significance, including those for the corporations and uniformity bills. As chairman of the committee of inquiry into a seditious pamphlet attacking the former measure, he reported on 15 July that William Prynne* had admitted responsibility. He also took the chair for the bill to reduce to 3 per cent the interest payable on loans to Cavaliers, and helped to manage conferences on the corporations bill and the bill of pains and penalties. Churchill received no encouragement from Clarendon, possibly owing to the absence in Guernsey of Sir Hugh Pollard*, who was expected to manage the west country Members. Accordingly he attached himself to the rising interest of Sir Henry Bennet*, who observed that he 'spoke confidently and often, and upon some occasions seemed to have credit in the House', though but 'of ordinary condition and mean fortunes'. It was under Bennet's patronage that he first appeared at Court and

became one of the government managers in the Commons, while Lord Wharton seems to have regarded him as a moderate. Nevertheless, after the autumn recess he served on the committee for the execution of those under attainder, and was among those sent to the King to ask for the return of Vane and Lambert for this purpose. Charles was so much impressed that he personally ordered an augmentation to Churchill's somewhat dubious arms, on the grounds of his war service and his 'present loyalty as a Member of the House of Commons'. He spent the Christmas recess in Dorset, where he was reported as speaking 'very disrespectfully' of Clarendon. On his return to Westminster he took the chair for an estate bill. He helped to prepare reasons on confirming ministers in their livings and compensating the loyal and indigent officers, and on 10 May 1662 he was sent to the Lords to desire a conference on the militia bill.[6]

Churchill was rewarded with a seat on the Irish land commission, in which capacity he was regarded as one of the King's men, bent on resisting the excessive claims of the Cromwellian settlers, though this position was compromised by his strenuous and successful efforts to secure a large forfeited estate for Bennet. He was never again so active at Westminster, though he continued to take an acute interest in parliamentary affairs. On 12 Nov. 1662 he wrote to Bennet about a bill drawn up together with his friend Thomas Clifford* 'which had not been so long laid aside, but to give way to greater matters. I could heartily wish myself engaged with all the lawyers in the quarrel of that bill.' In the following January Bennet sent for him to defend the Declaration of Indulgence. Nevertheless he continued to serve on the committees for the Clarendon Code. In 1664 he was listed as a court dependant and helped to manage the conference on injuries sustained at the hands of the Dutch. Still in high favour he was knighted and made clerk-comptroller of the green cloth, though Ormonde, as lord steward, objected to the intrusion of an outsider into a senior Household appointment. On 6 Feb. 1665 he acted as teller with his colleague Bullen Reymes* and against the son of another colleague, Giles Strangways*, in a division on a bill to assert the rights of the crown over salt-marshes, and in the autumn he again opposed Strangways, in debate and division, over the import of Irish cattle.[7]

Churchill seems to have been unable to attend the succeeding sessions owing to his work in Ireland, in the course of which he became involved in a violent quarrel with one of the Duke of York's agents, an awkward incident, since the Duke was now on the most intimate terms with Churchill's daughter. In the 1669 session, Churchill defended the second conventicles bill, denouncing the influence of 'seditious people whispering with many of the House', and was appointed to the committee. He attempted to obstruct the proceedings against Ormonde's arch-enemy Orrery (Roger Boyle*), and acted as teller for the acquittal of Clarendon's confidant Sir George Carteret* on a charge of falsifying accounts. He was one of the delegation sent by the House to thank the dying Albemarle for preserving the peace of the kingdom.[8]

The decline in Churchill's position in the House from this time forward is described by A. L. Rowse:

> He was now, first and foremost, an official of the Royal Household; he was there to defend the King's policy and his wishes. As Charles's Government became more unpopular and lost command of any majority in the Commons, so Sir Winston was considered simply a placeman of the Crown. ... As a leading spokesman of the Court in the House throughout the whole period, he incurred unpopularity when opinion turned more and more against the Court, and in the public prints he was traduced for the undignified situation he was placed in by his daughter's relation to the heir to the throne..

He still served on some important committees, intended to prevent electoral abuses (8 Dec. 1669) and to supply defects in the Conventicles Act (21 Nov. 1670); but his speech on the Lord's amendments to the latter, seeming to justify each and every exercise of the prerogative in ecclesiastical matters, was seriously at variance with the feeling of the House. Nor was it tactful in discussing the assault on Sir John Coventry* to express surprise that some Members seemed more afflicted by the injury to his colleague's nose than to Charles I's neck. As a court dependant he was on both lists of government Members at this time and on the Paston list in 1673–4. He made an effective defence of his department against Sir Thomas Byde* in 1674, and sat on the important committee on Irish affairs in the same year. It is notable that he did nothing to save Bennet (now Lord Arlington) from impeachment. It was in this year that his historical work *Divi Britannici* was at last published; in view of Churchill's position in the royal household, he was not required to submit it to censorship, but unfortunately it contained a passage so high in defence of the King's prerogative of taxation that it had to be recalled and amended for fear of Parliament.[9]

Churchill was listed among the officials in the Commons in 1675. Speaking about the jurisdiction of the Lords, he urged the House to 'go as high in proof, and as low in words as you can'; and when the conduct of Sir John Churchill* became matter

for impassioned debate he confined himself to a technical point in his cousin's favour. But he did not shrink from affirming his belief that those who contrived the dispute were the men who did not own the King's supremacy. When the session was resumed in the autumn the debate on English officers in the French service took an embarrassingly personal turn, and he had to undertake to recall his son (John Churchill II*). Nor could the proposal for a test for pensioners be approved by one who had so long helped to manage the court party: 'there can be no greater infamy ... in casting reflection, suspicion and self-condemnation', he said, and proposed instead the punishment of those who cast aspersions on Parliament. There seems to have been no reference in the House to the misadventure of *Divi Britannici*, unless perhaps the setting up of a committee to investigate publications scandalous to Church and State (20 Oct. 1675) on which Churchill served; but revenue questions bulked large in debate. Churchill was twice teller for unsuccessful government motions; and on being challenged for his views on the appropriation of revenue to the use of the navy, he said that he would accept it when misuse of funds was proved. But he would have no truck with the proposal to pay taxes into the chamber of London; the economic supremacy of the capital was a grievance, he asserted, especially to ship-building constituencies like his own. A further decline in his prestige in the House was signalized when his speech on the pricking of (Sir) Edmund Jennings* as sheriff was laughed down.[10]

Although listed among the government speakers, Churchill was less loquacious in the 1677 session. Shaftesbury classed him as 'thrice vile', but he helped to draw up the address for the formation of an alliance against France. The author of *A Seasonable Argument* wrote of him: 'He proffered his own daughter to the Duke of York, and has got in boons £10,000. He has published in print that the King may raise money without his Parliament.' He took no part in debate in the early sessions of 1678; (Sir) Joseph Williamson* noted that he was to be questioned, and his salary was reduced from £600 to £200 p.a. He told (Sir) Stephen Fox 'that he must be forced to retire to his estate in the country', and the cut was restored; but it was perhaps while he was suffering from a sense of grievance that he was appointed to the committees to summarize treaty obligations and to draft a bill to exclude Papists from Parliament (12 June). After the Popish Plot he helped to manage a conference on the bill; but he was still listed among the court party, and when he supported the Lords' proviso to exempt the

Duke of York he was shouted down, in spite of his protestation that he was obliged to speak in discharge of his conscience. An attempt to discredit Titus Oates failed no less lamentably. He had been an active Member of the Cavalier Parliament, perhaps serving on 224 committees, acting as teller in 18 divisions, and making about 40 recorded speeches. As one of the 'unanimous club' he is unlikely to have stood during the exclusion crisis. After the Rye House Plot he informed Secretary Jenkins about the disaffected speeches and writings of a Dorset attorney.[11]

Churchill was elected in 1685 for Lyme Regis, probably on the Drake interest. A very active Member of James II's Parliament, he was appointed to 16 committees, including those to examine the disbandment accounts and to recommend expunctions from the Journals. On 6 June he was named to two committees on private bills, to enable respectively Ormonde's grandson to make a jointure for his wife, and Edward Meller[†] to sell land for payment of debts. He carried the latter bill to the Lords a week later. On 18 June he acted as teller for the bill to prevent clandestine marriages, and was appointed to the committee. The speeches in defence of the Government sometimes attributed to him in the second session were delivered by Sir William Clifton[*]. He was probably out of sympathy with the King's religious policy, advising the bishop of Bristol not to deal too harshly with an impudent sermon at Dorchester about the dangers of Popery. He died on 26 Mar. 1688, and was buried at St. Martin in the Fields. Despite his years of court service, he had increased his estate by only a couple of small purchases, and he died in debt. His youngest surviving son, Charles Churchill[†], inherited Minterne, and sat for Weymouth from 1701 to 1710.[12]

[1] This biography is based on A. L. Rowse, *The Early Churchills*. [2] *St. Stephen Walbrook* (Harl. Soc. Reg. xlix), 59; *St. Peter, Paul's Wharf* (Harl. Soc. Reg. xxxiii), 22; *Cal. Comm. Adv. Money*, 1092; *HMC Bath*, ii. 175. [3] Hutchins, *Dorset*, i. 32; Lyme Regis court bk. 1672–92, f. 384; Dorset RO, D84 (official). [4] *CSP Ire.* 1660–2, p. 577; *CSP Dom.* 1668–9, p. 163; *HMC Ormonde*, n.s. vii. 185; *Cal. Treas. Bks.* viii. 1950. [5] *N. and Q. for Som. and Dorset*, xxvii. 190–2; *Gen. Mag.* xv. 110; *Black Bk. L. Inn*, ii. 458–63; SP23/186/410–16; *Cal. Comm. Adv. Money*, 1092. [6] *Cal. Cl. SP*, v. 208; Hutchins, ii. 442; *CJ*, viii. 302, 308, 311, 314, 356; Clarendon, *Life*, ii. 207–10; *CSP Ire.* 1666–9, p. 99; *CSP Dom.* 1661–2, p. 176. [7] *CSP Ire.* 1660–2, p. 616; 1663–5, pp. 42–43, 89, 231; Lister, *Clarendon*, iii. 232; *HMC Ormonde*, n.s. vii. 185; *CJ*, viii. 548, 620; Carte, *Ormond*, iv. 243; Bodl. Carte mss 34, ff. 448v, 452v; Stowe 744, f. 81; *Milward*, 233–4. [8] *Bulstrode Pprs.* 64; Stowe 745, f. 10; *CJ*, ix. 108, 111; Grey, i. 161–2, 174, 186. [9] Grey, i. 248, 337; ii. 377–9; Arber, *Term Catalogues*, i. 187; Wood, *Athenae*, iv. 235. [10] Grey, iii. 154, 236, 266, 335, 359–60, 367, 455; iv. 23; *CJ*, ix. 370, 373. [11] *CJ*, ix. 472, 543; Dorset RO, D124, box 235, bdle. 1, Fox to Marlborough, n.d.; *Wood's Life and Times* (Oxf. Hist. Soc. xxi), 428; *CSP Dom.* July–Sept. 1683, p. 239. [12] *CSP Dom.* 1686–7, p. 134; Hutchins, iv. 471.

J.P.F.

CHUTE, Chaloner (1632–66), of The Vine, Hants.

DEVIZES   1659
HASLEMERE   17–20 May 1661

bap. 15 Dec. 1632, 2nd but o. surv. s. of Chaloner Chute[†] of the Middle Temple and Sutton Court, Chiswick, Mdx. by 1st w. Anne, da. and coh. of Sir John Scory of Wormesley, Herefs., wid. of William Place of Dorking, Surr. *educ.* M. Temple 1645, called 1656. *m.* 1654, Catharine, da. of Richard, 13th Lord Dacre, 3s. 1da. *suc.* fa. 1659.[1]

J.p. Hants 1659–July 1660; militia, Hants and Mdx. 1659, Mdx. Mar. 1660; commr. for assessment, Wilts. Jan. 1660, Hants 1665–d.

Chute was, like his father and grandfather, a lawyer. His father established the wealth and position of the family, purchasing The Vine in 1653 and serving as Speaker for two months during Richard Cromwell's Parliament, though he had been a defender of the Church throughout the Interregnum, and was regarded as a friend by the Cavaliers. Chute himself was not an active politician, but he had a strong motive for entering Parliament as a purchaser of part of Lady Powell's estate, which had been alienated by dubious means during the Interregnum by her husband and nephew (William Powell[*]). He stood for Haslemere in 1661, probably on the More interest, and was involved in a double return. He was seated on 17 May on the merits of the return, but was unseated three days later on the merits of the election. On 28 Jan. 1662, a proviso to the bill to annul Lady Powell's fine was introduced on his behalf, but was rejected. During one of the divisions he was overheard by Bullen Reymes[*] in the lobby of the House to observe bitterly, 'Well, gentlemen, I hope ere long to be of a Parliament wherein I may give away some of your estates as well as you give away mine'. For this remark Chute was brought in custody to the bar of the House for having 'spoken reproachful words against the honour and justice and in breach of the privilege of this House'. Chute died in 1666, aged 34. His son stood unsuccessfully for Ludgershall in 1685, but the family was next represented in Parliament by his grandson, who sat for two Isle of Wight constituencies as a Whig from 1737 to 1747.[2]

[1] Guildhall Lib., St. Andrew Holborn par. reg.; Berry, *Hants Gen.* 118–19; C. J. Robinson, *Mansions of Herefs.* 314; PCC 77 Skynner. [2] W. Chute, *Hist. of The Vine*, 78; J. Waylen, *Hist. Devizes*, 294, 303; Reymes diary.

J.S.C.

CLAPHAM, Christopher (c.1608–86), of Uffington, Lincs.

STAMFORD   1659
APPLEBY   1660

b. c.1608, 1st s. of George Clapham of Beamsley, Skipton,

Yorks. by Martha, da. of Reginald Heber of Marton, Yorks. *m.* (1) by 1627, Mary (*d.* 1 Aug. 1637), da. of John Lowden of Wrenthorpe, Yorks., 2s. *d.v.p.* 1da.; (2) 14 May 1639, Margaret (*d.* 1674), da. of Anthony Oldfield, attorney, of Spalding, Lincs., wid. of Robert Moyle, protonotary of c.p., of Twyford, Mdx., 4s. (2 *d.v.p.*) 4da.; (3) lic. 26 Apr. 1678, Mary (*d.* 28 Nov. 1702), da. of Robert Needham†, 2nd Visct. Kilmorey [I], of Shavington, Salop, *s.p. suc.* fa. 1629. Kntd. 8 June 1660.[1]

Freeman, Stamford 1658; j.p. Yorks. (W. Riding) July 1660–70, 1672–bef. 1680, 1685–*d.*, Lincs. (Kesteven) 1663–*d.*; commr. for assessment, Westmld. and Kesteven Aug. 1660–1, (W. Riding) Aug. 1660–80, Lincs. 1661–3, 1665–80, oyer and terminer, Lincoln 1661; capt. vol. horse, Lincs. ?1663; commr. for recusants (W. Riding) 1675; dep. lt. Lincs. 1681–*d.*, sheriff 1682–3.[2]

Clapham's ancestors derived themselves from 'Pharamond, king of France' and claimed to have been lords of Clapham for several generations before the Norman Conquest. Their pedigree can be traced more confidently to the early 15th century, when they acquired Beamsley by marriage and became retainers of the Cliffords. Three of Clapham's brothers fought for the King in the Civil War, but he avoided commitment himself, though his sympathies were obviously royalist. As steward of the Clifford manors in Westmorland, he assisted the dowager countess of Pembroke in her dispute with her tenants in 1650. But after his second marriage he seems to have made over Beamsley to his son. He leased Uffington, two miles from Stamford, from the Duke of Buckingham, and sat for the borough in Richard Cromwell's Parliament.[3]

At the general election of 1660 Clapham was returned for Appleby on Lady Pembroke's interest. A court supporter, he was moderately active in the Convention, in which he was named to 13 committees, including the committee of elections and privileges, and acted as teller in three divisions. He was among those appointed to consider the King's letter and the draft assessment ordinance. On 2 June he told the House of regicide sentiments alleged to have been uttered by William White*; but his informant was found to be 'distempered'. He was teller against putting the question on excluding Bulstrode Whitelocke† from the indemnity, and against setting up a committee, to which he was none the less appointed, to examine the petition from the intruded dons at Oxford. He was among those ordered on 30 June to inquire into unauthorized Anglican publications, and three days later he appeared as teller, in the unexpected company of Denzil Holles*, against the abatement clause in the poll bill. Perhaps it was through Holles that he made the acquaintance of the veteran Dorset radical Sir Walter Erle*, who moved for privilege

on his behalf when he was served with a subpoena. His proviso to the indemnity bill on behalf of Sir Jordan Crosland* charging Sir Wilfred Lawson* with plundering Rydal was rejected. On 25 Aug. he reported to Sir Anthony Ashley Cooper* from Wakefield that 20 pictures from Charles I's art collection were in Lady Sussex's Yorkshire residence, and another had been purloined from the Queen's closet by the mother of Sir Richard Temple*. In the second session he was concerned only with private bills. On 18 Dec. he successfully petitioned the crown for confirmation of the extensive manorial rights in Wakefield which he had purchased from the Earl of Holland's trustees.[4]

Clapham was included by Lord Wharton among his Lincolnshire friends in 1661, but there is no other indication that he stood. As a Lincolnshire j.p. his zeal against the local Presbyterians could not avert a stinging rebuke from the Treasury in 1663 'in vindication of his Majesty's revenue'. Probably he and Francis Wingfield* had failed to assist the excise farmers. In 1667 he was again in trouble for prosecuting a Northamptonshire taxcollector who had distrained his cattle. He was mentioned as a possible candidate for Appleby in 1668, and made several efforts to promote an enclosure bill. He doubtless opposed exclusion, for he was recommended as 'a Church of England sheriff' in 1682. The lord lieutenant of Lincolnshire (Robert Bertie I*) wrote that 'his loyalty has been conspicuous enough'. He was buried at St. Mary's, Stamford on 16 Aug. 1686, the only member of the family to sit in Parliament.[5]

[1] Clay, *Dugdale's Vis. Yorks.* ii. 475. [2] F. Peck, *Antiqs. of Stamford*, i. 229; SP29/26/73; *CSP Dom.* 1663–4, p. 296; 1680–1, p. 515. [3] *Hunter's Peds.* (Harl. Soc. lxxxviii), 34–38; Whitaker, *Craven*, 443; G. C. Williamson, *Lady Anne Clifford*, 196, 214; F. E. D. Willis, *Hist. Uffington*, 43. [4] Williamson, 402; *CJ*, viii. 64, 74; Bowman diary, ff. 62v, 89; *CSP Dom.* 1660–1, pp. 200, 417; 1661–2, p. 38. [5] SP29/233/85; *Cal. Treas. Bks.* i. 495; *CSP Dom.* 1663–4, p. 296; 1682, p. 514; PC2/59/434; *Milward*, 157; *CJ*, ix. 164; Clay, ii. 475.

M.W.H./L.N.

CLARGES, Thomas (c.1618–95), of Westminster and Stoke Poges, Bucks.

SUTHERLAND, ROSS AND CROMARTY	1656
ABERDEEN BURGHS AND LAUDER BURGHS	1659
WESTMINSTER	1660
SOUTHWARK	13 Mar. 1666
CHRISTCHURCH	1679 (Mar.), 1679 (Oct.), 1681, 1685
OXFORD UNIVERSITY	1689, 1690–4 Oct. 1695

b. c.1618, o.s. of John Clargis, farrier, of Drury Lane, Westminster by Anne Leaver. *m.* by 1653, Mary, da. of George Procter, yeoman, of Norwell Woodhouse, Notts. and coh. to her bro. Edward, 1s. *suc.* fa. 1648; kntd. 8 May 1660.[1]

Commr. for assessment, Westminster 1657, 1661–3, 1664–80, Aberdeen 1657, Jan. 1660, Bucks. 1661–74, Mdx. 1663–9, Berks. 1664–74, Surr. 1673–4, Mdx. and London 1677–80, Southwark 1677–9, Berks. and Surr. 1679–80, Berks., Bucks., Mdx., London, Westminster and Oxf. Univ. 1689–90, sewers, Westminster Aug. 1660; dep. keeper, Hampton Court, Mdx. Aug. 1660–70; freeman, Preston 1662; j.p. Bucks. Mdx. and Westminster 1662–71, Surr. 1667–71, Mdx. 1689–*d.*; commr. for inquiry, Richmond Park, Surr. 1671, recusants, Mdx. and Surr. 1675; bailiff, Oxford 1687–Feb. 1688.[2]

Commissary-gen. of musters Feb. 1660–71; clerk of the hanaper Mar.–June 1660; commr. for maimed soldiers Dec. 1660–1; PC [I] 1663; commr. of public accounts 1691–*d.*[3]

Clarges, the son of an obscure London craftsman, was apprenticed (according to Anthony à Wood) to an Oxford apothecary, and served in the royalist army in that capacity 'as long as any army was'. After his sister's marriage to George Monck* he became his principal agent in London, and as 'Dr Clarges' an active Member of the second Protectorate Parliament. His royalist sympathies were never in doubt, and he is credited by Burnet with winning his brother-in-law's support for the Restoration. At the general election of 1660 he was rejected at Tamworth, and involved in a double return at Tregony which was decided against him, but he was successful at Westminster. In the Convention he was moderately active, being appointed to 30 committees, and making 26 recorded speeches. On 26 Apr. he was sent to ask Monck's chaplain to preach to the House, and on 2 May given leave to carry a letter from Monck to the King. Edward Montagu I*, also en route to The Hague, confided to Samuel Pepys* his low opinion of Clarges's intelligence. He was knighted at Breda, and confirmed as commissary-general of musters, although not altogether trusted. On his return to the House he took a generally moderate line over the indemnity bill, acting as teller against the exception of William Lenthall†, but speaking against Richard Deane, an Anabaptist who had distributed dangerous papers in Scotland. On 22 June he moved that the grant previously voted for Monck should be made effectual, and was sent to the Lords to ask their concurrence in ordering payment out of current taxation. He favoured hearing the petition from the intruded dons at Oxford. On 26 June he reported from the committee set up to recommend ways and means of paying Monck's arrears. Three days later he proposed that the whole army

should take the oaths. He was in favour of committing the complaint about unauthorized Anglican publications. He rebuked the clerk for reading without order a 'most dangerous' proviso drafted by William Prynne* to disable abjurors under the indemnity bill. It was 'an indulgence not to inquire who brought it in', he said, 'but [he] did deserve to be called to the bar'. He also urged the House to reject the proposal for the refunding of salaries received during the Interregnum. He defended William Boteler†, the most unpopular of the major-generals, but moved against a preacher who had written a book to justify the execution of Charles I. On 23 Aug. he reminded the Commons of Monck's promise to save the life of Sir Arthur Hesilrige†, and spoke in conference to the same effect on the following day. Before the autumn recess he reported the Dunkirk establishment and a proviso to the college leases bill, and was appointed to the disbandment committee.[4]

When Parliament met again in November, Clarges said that he would not oppose reading the Book of Common Prayer in the House, though it had never yet been done. He wanted the Worcester House declaration for modified episcopacy to be confirmed by statute. He reported the Helston election case, and as chairman of the committee to estimate the debts of the army and navy presented Lockhart's petition. He warned the House against the excise, which had caused Masaniello's rebellion in Naples. He was teller against the proviso to exclude from benefit under the college leases bill those who had been purged in the royal visitation of the universities. He wanted to make provision for imposing the assessment on Scotland. He proposed fixing wine prices at a level which, he was assured by an eminent vintner, would still leave an ample profit margin. He concluded the session by recommending payment of Lockhart's claim.[5]

Clarges was granted a lease of Reading Abbey in 1661 and a perpetual pension of £500 p.a. on the Newcastle coal duties, but he was defeated in the general election, and it was several years before he could find a seat in the Cavalier Parliament. A 'busy gentleman', he crossed over to Ireland in 1663 to look after some property in Galway which he had acquired during the Protectorate. He took the opportunity of opening a correspondence with Sir Henry Bennet*, whose policy of toleration he endorsed; though his distaste for Papists in general and Irish Papists in particular was only increased by his experiences. He was alarmed to hear of a measure under discussion in the Commons which would have threatened his pension. When a vacancy occurred at Salisbury, Monck (now Duke of Albemarle) suggested that his brother-in-law could be very useful in Parliament over the bill for army discipline; but Clarendon, who wanted the seat for his son, ignored the suggestion. Clarges was wealthy enough to spend over £700 on a by-election at Southwark in 1666, according to his defeated opponent, and soon became a very active Member. He was appointed to 286 committees, presented 18 reports, acted as teller in five divisions, and made about 130 speeches. On 11 Dec. he was named by the House to the abortive public accounts commission. He acted as teller for a discriminatory tax on aliens on 5 Jan. 1667, and a week later reported reasons for a conference on the subject. Later in the month he was among those ordered to attend the King with a petition from the merchants trading to France, and he carried to the Upper House the bill to prevent disturbances among the seamen. He helped to draw up the address of thanks for the dismissal of Clarendon, and was appointed to the committees to inquire into the miscarriages of the war and the sale of Dunkirk. He was among those ordered to consult Albemarle about security against highway robbery. He drafted the bill against Popery which received a second reading on 30 Oct. He accused Sir William Batten* of designing the discharge of seamen by ticket, and was sent, with other Members, to ask Lord Anglesey (Arthur Annesley*) about it. He bore no grudge against the fallen minister, saying that words might be heresy, but not treason, and acting as teller for the motion to refer the charges to a committee. Nevertheless he was among those appointed to consider the banishment bill. He was one of the Members ordered to take the accounts of the indigent officers fund during the Christmas recess. When the investigation into the miscarriages of the war was resumed, he was reported to be particularly hot over the business of tickets, which compared unfavourably with his own administration of the army. He was teller for the motion, aimed principally at Bennet (now Lord Arlington), that the failure to send Albemarle and Rupert timely intelligence in 1666 was a miscarriage. He was chairman of the committee for the bill to prevent thefts and robberies. In the debate on the conduct of (Sir) William Penn* on 14 Apr. 1668 he described the distribution of the prize-goods as 'the most arrogant thing that was ever done'. On 23 Apr. he proposed stricter financial control of the indigent officers fund, of which Arlington's brother Sir John Bennet* was treasurer. In spite of Clarges's attacks on the administration of the navy, Sir Thomas Osborne* included him among the Members to be gained for the Court by the Duke of York.[6]

Clarges took the principal part in the enactment of the Highway Repair Act of 1670. As chairman of the committee appointed on the second reading he was entrusted with inserting the provisos agreed on the report stage and with carrying the bill to the House of Lords, and he was equally prominent as chairman in preparing for and reporting from the conferences which followed. On 29 Nov. he returned to the Upper House the estate bill introduced on behalf of his nephew, the 2nd Duke of Albemarle (Christopher Monck*). It was the assault on Sir John Coventry* that brought Clarges into conflict with the Government. As a resident of Piccadilly, he was probably the nearest active j.p. to the scene of the outrage, and he took the depositions which showed that the culprits were guards officers. When Parliament reassembled he gave a narrative to the House, was appointed to the committee for the bill, and on 11 Feb. 1671 was sent to desire a conference with the Lords. Later in the session he reported the bills for continuing the powers of the London Fire Court and securing the stipends of City incumbents. But when Parliament rose Clarges, no longer protected by his brother-in-law, soon felt the weight of the King's displeasure and was dismissed from all his offices.[7]

In the debate of 6 Feb. 1673 on the issue of election writs during the recess, Clarges pointed out that the real issue was whether the lord chancellor or the House of Commons was to decide when a seat was vacant. On the Declaration of Indulgence he considered that the King's good intentions had been abused by the Papists. He was appointed to the committee for the test bill, although he was doubtful of its efficacy because of the Pope's dispensing power. He led the attack on the Cabal's handling of Irish affairs, notably the latitude accorded to the Roman Catholic swashbuckler, Colonel Talbot. In the autumn session, faced by the imminent marriage of the Duke of York to Mary of Modena, he reminded the House that Louis XIV's brother had just married a Protestant princess, but she had been required to change her religion on her entry into France. He helped to draw up the addresses against the marriage and against the new-raised forces, which he considered another grievance. He also complained of large donations to the King's mistresses. He was chairman of the committee which drafted the petition for a fast to reconcile differences and divisions 'chiefly occasioned by the undermining contrivances of popish recusants', and on 3 Nov. carried it to the Lords for their concurrence. In a major speech on 12 Jan. 1674 he mentioned the universal hatred felt for the French alliance, and attacked the evil counsellors who had persuaded the King to declare war on the Dutch without consulting Parliament. 'The best thing to rivet the King and his people is mutual confidence', he declared. He was chosen to ask Dr Lloyd (later one of the Seven Bishops) to preach to the House on the anniversary of Charles I's execution. His appointment to the committee for the habeas corpus bill in this session began his association with the most important reform of the reign. In the course of several attacks on the Duke of Buckingham, he threw out the suggestion that 'no Member for the future, whilst Parliaments sit, should have the temptation of offices', and on 18 Feb. he reported from the committee which drafted a bill to improve attendance.[8]

It might have been expected that under the Danby administration, combining firm churchmanship at home with a patriotic anti-French policy in Europe, Clarges would have reverted to the Court. But he seems to have distrusted the new lord treasurer from the first. In the spring session of 1675 he took the chair for the first time on the habeas corpus bill. He described default in attendance by Members as a grave breach of trust, and proposed sending letters to their constituencies 'to give them notice how they are represented'. He was the first Member named to the committee to draft the letters, and was also appointed to the committee on the bill for the suppression of Popery. He helped to prepare reasons for one conference on the dispute over the judicature of the Lords, and to manage two others, and had just reported to the House on precedents for writs of habeas corpus returnable to Parliament when the session was abruptly terminated. In the autumn he helped to prepare the bill imposing penalties on British subjects who remained in French service, to draw up the address on the failure to apprehend the Jesuit St. Germain and to manage a conference to avoid the revival of differences between the Houses. When Parliament reassembled in 1677 he was marked 'thrice worthy' on Shaftesbury's list, and at once reverted to the question of British subjects in French service. He was appointed to the committee for the revived bill, and also to those for securing the liberty of the subject and preventing the growth of Popery. On 6 Mar. he told the House:

> I intended to have said something to you about the passes for ships, which is raising money by order of Council, of the judges being pensioned, and the like, but waive all for that of France. ... This grievance of France is a matter of so great consequence, that if there be no tendency of redressing it this day we are lost.

He helped to draw up the three addresses on foreign policy that followed.[9]

On 28 Jan. 1678 Clarges pungently criticized the conduct of Edward Seymour* in the chair:

> This adjourning the House has been usurped by you more than by any Speaker before you. Gentlemen stand up to speak, and you adjourn the House and will not hear them. ... 'Tis our birthright to speak, and we are not so much as a part of a Parliament if that be lost.

He helped to draw up the addresses for reducing France to her 1659 frontiers and for a declaration of war, though characteristically thinking that 'we need not be at so vast an expense'. Clarges, who 'had his whole estate almost on new foundations', bitterly opposed the tax on new buildings, acting as teller for the unsuccessful motion of 23 Mar. to hear counsel for the Hon. William Russell* plead at the bar of the House against taxing the development of the Bedford estate. 'Why may not a man make the best of his own land?' he asked. He was among those appointed on 29 Apr. to attend the lord chancellor about alterations in the commissions of the peace and to summarize foreign commitments. The lack of visible action against France provoked him to blunter criticism of ministers, some of whom, he believed, were in French pay:

> I am of opinion ... that 'tis to no purpose to advise the King any further till we have assurance that the fruits of our former addresses are executed. This is strange to me, after the King lays the whole matter before us and calls for our advice, and tells us he would follow it; and I thought he would have done it because he had distrusted the advices of those who had plunged him into these inconveniences.

From the committee for the removal of counsellors he reported on 8 May an address asking the King to remove from his presence the Duke of Lauderdale, whose harshness seemed calculated to produce a rebellion in Scotland. He helped to draw up reasons for a conference on burial in woollen two days later, and took the chair on the bill for forming a separate parish of St. James Piccadilly. As the session drew to its close he acted as manager of conferences on disbanding the army, fixing the dimensions of colliers and requiring burial in woollen.[10]

The last session of the Cavalier Parliament confirmed Clarges in his worst suspicions, both of the Roman Catholics and of the ministry. He was appointed to the committees to inquire into the Popish Plot, to examine Coleman, and to translate his letters, and helped to draw up the resolution affirming belief in the 'damnable and hellish plot'. He was concerned in the drafting of eight addresses, and proposed the impeachment of Secretary Williamson for signing commissions for Roman Catholic officers. Despite his habitual parsimony with public money, he declared that he would have £200,000 given to Titus Oates. 'The saving the King's life by the discovery of the plot', he declared generously, 'is above the restoration of the King; he cannot be too well rewarded.' He was appointed to the committee to prepare instructions for disbandment. 'If the King be not happy in this Parliament', he remarked prophetically, 'he will never be in any. Those that make a difference in this matter are no friends to the crown.' He was appointed to the committee for the impeachment of Danby, and defended the conduct of its chairman, William Williams*. He was among those ordered to draw up reasons for a conference on supply, and acted as teller against recommitting the articles of impeachment.[11]

Clarges sat for Christchurch in the Exclusion Parliaments on the interest of the 2nd Earl of Clarendon (Henry Hyde*), whose brother, Laurence Hyde*, was his tenant in St. James's Square. Shaftesbury marked him 'worthy', and in 1679 he made 43 speeches, including four firm but moderate contributions to the debate on the choice of a Speaker. He was appointed to 40 committees, in five of which he took the chair, and had a hand in drafting six addresses, reporting on 21 Mar. that for a solemn day of humiliation, which he carried to the Lords for their concurrence. He expressed dismay at the issue of a pardon to Danby, and helped to draft the summons for him to surrender himself for trial, or face a bill of attainder. He was chairman of the committee for security against Popery, which produced a bill 'of so prodigious a length' that it never received a second reading. But he was more successful over habeas corpus, reporting the bill on 4 Apr. and carrying it to the Lords four days later. He helped to draw up reasons for a conference on the attainder of Danby, and on 25 Apr. was added to the secret committee to draw up articles against him. He was on the committees to consider the Lords' amendments on the habeas corpus bill and to prepare for a conference on the disbandment bill. After reporting on the existence of precedents, he was assigned to the joint committee for the trials of the lords in the Tower. On 9 May he moved for a standing order to forbid the Speaker to carry up a money bill without consent of the House, and was again appointed to a committee to search for precedents. He reported the bill for the removal of Papists from the metropolitan area on 19 May, carrying it to the Lords two days later, and he also helped to prepare a message to the Lords asking for concurrence in a demand for the execution of two convicted priests. But he parted company with the opposition in 'a long and considerate speech' on exclusion:

I desire that there may be no further proceeding in this bill. If I did think that the person of the King, laws, or religion were in danger without this bill, I would give my consent to it with as great alacrity as anybody; but this bill seems to me to hazard the King's life. Religion is of great moment to provide for hereafter, and to secure it by all means lawful and just; but I am taught to do no evil that good may come of it, and through the consequences of the bill I would not disgrace the Protestant religion. . . . A certain unjust thing is not to be done for any just. No human policy can give you an absolute security of religion. Are we sure that the Lords will pass the bill? The King never will. If he does, when this law is passed, we must have a standing army to maintain it [against] a prince exasperated to the highest degree, . . . and then what security can you have for your laws? . . . If there be confusions and dislike of the Government, the King goes after the Duke, and all is confusion. . . . Consider what condition you are in; you have passed a law to-day against Popery, and another that all Papists shall be convicted by name, and if twenty be together, they may be knocked on the head; that no Papist shall sit in either House of Parliament; the habeas corpus bill; bill against illegal exactions; and will you, by this bill of incapacitating the Duke, lose all these good bills that could never yet be arrived at?

Clarges's arguments were not answered, but the division, which followed immediately, showed that the House was unconvinced by them. He had not forfeited its respect, however, and was twice sent to the Lords to desire conferences on the habeas corpus bill, which at last received the royal assent.[12]

Clarges must have been well enough pleased with the results of this Parliament, but it was believed that, like other friends of Lord Halifax (Sir George Savile*), he might not stand again. Like other Members formerly thought 'warm enough', he enjoyed 'no vogue' in the second Exclusion Parliament, and his activity declined perceptibly. He was appointed to 23 committees and made 12 speeches. He helped to draw up the addresses promising support for the King and the Protestant religion and asking for a pardon to be proclaimed for all informers about the Popish Plot. He was appointed to the committee to inquire into abhorring, but strove to avert the expulsion of Sir Robert Cann* and Sir Francis Wythens*. He seconded the motion of Sir Thomas Stringer* for describing the Duke of York as heir presumptive in the exclusion bill. When John Trenchard* reported the address for the removal of Halifax on 22 Nov., Clarges insisted on 'free liberty to exercise my reason against it'. He commended Halifax's services in the last Parliament in obtaining the King's consent to the abolition of quartering and the reform of habeas corpus, and, despite calls of order, described it as unconstitutional in principle to forbid a man the King's presence. He was eventually silenced by Silius Titus*, who recalled the identical address for the removal of Lauderdale reported to the House in 1678 by Clarges himself. Nevertheless he acted as teller for the unsuccessful motion to recommit the address. He took little further part in the second Exclusion Parliament, except for a rather perfunctory defence of the position of Laurence Hyde on the Treasury board. Every endeavour, including the label of Papist, was made to hinder his re-election because he had opposed exclusion. Although he defeated his Whig opponents, there is no evidence that he attended the Oxford Parliament.[13]

Clarges was re-elected in 1685 and became a very active Member of James II's Parliament, in which he was appointed to 19 committees. According to Thomas Bruce*, he was 'discontented' from the opening of Parliament, and was accordingly hissed by the loyal majority, but this is unlikely with Halifax in the Government. His principal concern in the first session was to establish St. James Piccadilly as a separate parish, for which purpose he was given leave to bring in a bill on 27 May. His name stands first on the committee for inspecting the disbandment accounts, and he was among those instructed to prepare bills for licensing hackney coaches and the general naturalization of Huguenot refugees. When, on the news of Monmouth's invasion, Bruce revived the proposal for a tax on new buildings, Clarges called it 'a very young notion' and left the House 'foaming at mouth' to complain to Hyde, now Lord Treasurer Rochester, who persuaded the King that it was unsound. He reported the St. James Piccadilly bill on 20 June, carried it to the Lords three days later and returned it after amendment on the last day of the month. He went into open opposition in the second session after the dismissal of Halifax. Speaking with unwonted moderation he claimed that a further grant of supply was unnecessary; if his nephew Albemarle had been properly supported, Monmouth's rebellion could have been suppressed by the militia. Confidence between King and people was essential, but it could not survive the intention announced in the speech from the throne of breaking the Test Act, which bore out the argument of the exclusionists that a Popish successor entailed a Popish army:

> I am afflicted greatly at this breach of our liberties, and, seeing so great difference between this speech and those heretofore made, cannot but believe this was by some other advice. This struck at here is our all, and I wonder there have been any men so desperate as to take any employment not qualified for it; and I would therefore have the question: 'That a standing army is destructive to the country'.

He was teller for the motion to discuss the Roman Catholic officers before supply, and was the first Member nominated to draw up the address for their dismissal.[14]

Clarges was described in the list of eminent parliamentarians in opposition as considerable for parts, but not to be trusted. He was present at the Bishop of London's trial before the ecclesiastical commission in 1686, and helped in the defence of the Seven Bishops. He sent his son to attend William of Orange at Exeter, and was among those appointed to draw up the address of thanks of 26 Dec. 1688. He was returned for Oxford University, no doubt on the Hyde interest, in the abortive election held under James's writ, and again in the following month. He was very active in the Convention, in which he was named to 108 committees and made about a hundred recorded speeches. He was again one of the Members entrusted with drafting an address of thanks on the first day of the session. He sought to embarrass the Whigs by reading William's declaration. On the constitutional issue he defined his position in the following words:

> To say that the crown is void is a consequence of an extraordinary nature. The consequence must be, we have power to fill it, and make it from a successive monarchy an elective; and whether a commonwealth, or alter the descent, is yet ambiguous.

He was appointed to the committee to bring in a list of the essentials for securing religion, laws and liberties. He hoped that in the interests of unity the House would agree with the Lords that the King had deserted the throne rather than abdicated; but he was appointed nevertheless to the committee to draw up reasons for adhering to the Commons resolution, and added to that to manage the conference of 5 Feb. 1689. He considered that the crown had devolved automatically on the next Protestant heir in succession, and therefore voted to agree with the Lords that the throne was not vacant. Nevertheless he accepted the majority decision: 'since it has been voted here that the throne is vacant, I am satisfied, though I was then against it'. But he urged the House to maintain control of the new regime by granting revenue for no more than three years. In the debate of 5 Mar. he said: 'I wish the committee after discovery of all these grievances had named the persons who occasioned them'. He was appointed to the committee for that purpose, and also to those for the bill to punish mutiny and desertion and the bill of rights and settlement. He failed to convince the House that the sovereign should swear to maintain the established Protestant religion, but helped to draft the coronation oath. Despite his defence of the sacramental test, he was the first Member nominated to the committee for the repeal of the Corporations Act. He attacked the professed Protestants who had collaborated with the Papists in the last reign; but he was named to the committee for the comprehension bill. On 8 Apr. he reported reasons for retaining the proviso about Queen Catherine of Braganza in the bill for the removal of Papists, and was sent to desire a conference. He seconded the motion for an address promising aid for a war with France, which he helped to draft. He desired toleration only as a temporary measure, till the nonconformists should be convinced of their errors, but his name stands first on the committee for the bill. He described the bill for the suspension of habeas corpus as 'the most unreasonable and destructive that ever was made in Parliament. We have had a struggle for it these fourteen years, and now upon suggested necessities to dispense with this law!' He was appointed to the committee of inquiry into the delays in relieving Londonderry. He was the only Member to defend Robert Wright*, though he had himself no doubt of the illegality of the dispensing power, and was among those appointed to bring in an indemnity bill. He doubted whether the case presented to the House on 24 June against certain Jacobite propagandists were sufficient to satisfy a jury. Three days later he tabled the answers of Lord Nottingham (Daniel Finch*) about the arrest of Peregrine Osborne*.[15]

After the recess Clarges was sent to ask Dr Peter Birch, a high church convert from Presbyterianism, to preach to the House on the anniversary of the Gunpowder Plot. His activity in the second session of the Convention was chiefly directed towards exposing the failures of the war administration, especially in Ireland. He was appointed to the committee to inquire into the expenses of the war, and declared that the nation could not afford an army of 70,000. In the debate on 26 Nov. he blamed the failure to send baggage-horses and the negligence of the officers over clothing for the heavy loss of life in Ireland; but no improvement could be expected without a strong executive, and the lack of experience at the Treasury was particularly unfortunate, he thought, no doubt with Rochester in mind. He was appointed to the committee to draw up the address asking who had recommended Commissary Shales. He described the access of foreigners in the army as another great discouragement. But he agreed with William Sacheverell* that the House should not nominate Members to the King for employment in Ireland. He favoured the grant of an independent income to Princess Anne. In the debate on restoring corporations he may have been responsible for the attempt to extend the disabling clause to the regulators; but

on 10 Jan. 1690 he moved for its rejection as 'destructive to the peace and quiet of the kingdom; instead of reconciliation it lays the foundation of perpetual division'. He opposed the bill to reverse the attainder of Sir Thomas Armstrong*, though Morrice's allegation that he described it as countenancing the Rye House Plot is not confirmed by Anchitell Grey*, and he pointed out that (Sir) Thomas Pilkington* could obtain relief by ordinary course of law.[16]

Clarges was re-elected in 1690, and sat until his death. Burnet described him as

an honest but haughty man, who valued himself upon opposing the Court, and on his frugality in managing the public money. . . . Many thought he carried this too far, but it made him very popular. After he was become very rich himself by the public money, he seemed to take care that nobody else should grow as rich as he was in the same way.

He owed his wealth to the chance of his connexion with Monck; but his influence survived his brother-in-law's death. His greatest achievement was habeas corpus, though Sir Robert Howard* declared that he would always be honoured for his speech in 1685 exposing the contradictions in James II's professions. Although in a minority in the Convention on most issues, his willingness to accept the decisions of the House secured its continued respect, shown by his nomination in 1691 to the public accounts committee, on which he served for the rest of his life. He died of apoplexy on 4 Oct. 1695, in the 78th year of his age, leaving an estate of about £5,000 p.a. to his son.[17]

[1] IHR Bull. vi. 189 [2] Preston Guild Rolls (Lancs. and Cheshire Rec. Soc. ix), 142; Mdx. RO, MJP/CP5a; Cal. Treas. Bks. iii. 1161; Oxf. Council Acts (Oxf. Hist. Soc. n.s. ii), 191, 196. [3] CJ, vii. 828, 873; viii. 213; CSP Dom. 1660–1, p. 432; CSP Ire. 1663–5, p. 49. [4] Wood's Life and Times (Oxf. Hist. Soc. xxi), 216; Grey, vi. 309; Ludlow Mems. ii. 160, 278; Burnet ed. Foxcroft, 53; Cal. Cl. SP, v. 24; Pepys Diary, 6 May 1660; CJ, viii. 61, 135, 141; Bowman diary, ff. 6v, 20v, 25, 32, 36v, 43, 50, 60v, 105v; Old Parl. Hist. xxii. 444, 447. [5] Old Parl. Hist. xxiii. 5, 22, 62, 68, 70, 80; CJ, viii. 177, 182, 235. [6] Cal. Treas. Bks. i. 222; CSP 1665–6, p. 397; PCC 170 Irby; CJ, viii. 280, 686; ix. 11, 15, 52, 62; x. 108; CSP Ire. 1660–2, p. 610; 1663–6, pp. 118, 119, 243; Cal. Cl. SP, v. 393; N. and Q. (ser. 12), x. 28; HMC 5th Rep. 347–8; Pepys Diary, 30 Oct. 1667, 11 Feb. 1668; Add. 36916, f. 11; Grey, i. 31, 135; Milward, 272. [7] CJ, vii. 23, 219, 313–14; CJ, ix. 582, 615, 626, 627, 634. [13] Foxcroft, Halifax, i. 175; HMC Ormonde, n.s. v. 561; Grey, vii. 382, 386, 432; viii. 42–43; CJ, ix. 660; HMC 12th Rep. IX, 114; Clarendon Corresp. i. 182. [14] Ailesbury Mems. 105–6; Bramston Autobiog. (Cam. Soc. xxiii), 213–14; Grey, viii. 355–6; CJ, ix. 757. [15] Cumb. RO, Fleming mss 3024; Clarendon Corresp. ii. 179; IHR Bull. xlix, 256; Grey, ix. 15, 47, 55, 88, 112, 123, 139, 190, 197, 253, 268, 344, 354, 356, 459; CJ,

x. 18, 42, 65, 74, 91, 133; R. Morrice, Entering Bk. 2, p. 536.
[16] *CJ*, x. 274; Grey, ix. 388, 446–7, 449–50, 467, 478, 482, 511,
525, 547; Morrice, 2, p. 675; 3, p. 74; Bath mss, Thynne pprs. 24,
f. 77, Clarges to Weymouth, 6 Nov. 1689. [17] *Wood's Life and
Times* (Oxf. Hist. Soc. xxvi), 490; Burnet, i. 179; Grey, ix. 295;
Luttrell, iii. 534.

M.W.H./L.N.

CLARGES, Sir Walter, 1st Bt. (c.1654–1706), of
Piccadilly, Westminster.

COLCHESTER   1679 (Mar.), 1679 (Oct.), 1685
WESTMINSTER   1690, 1702

b. c.1654, o.s. of Thomas Clarges*. *educ.* Merton, Oxf.
matric. 3 Feb. 1671, aged 17. *m.* (1) Jane, da. of Sir
Dawes Wymondsold of Putney, Surr., 1da.; (2) by 1682,
Jane (*d.* 17 Sept. 1690), da. of Hon. James Herbert* of
Tythrop House, Kingsey, Bucks., 2s. (1 *d.v.p.*) 2da.;
(3) 15 Dec. 1690, Elizabeth, da. and coh. of Sir Thomas
Gould, Draper, of Aldermanbury, London, wid. of Sir
Robert Wymondsold of Putney, 6s. 3da. *cr.* Bt. 30 Oct.
1674; *suc.* fa. 1695.[1]
   Commr. for assessment, Westminster 1677–80, Colchester 1679–80, Bucks. and Westminster 1689–90,
Lincs. and Mdx. 1690; freeman, Maldon 1679, Oxford
1687–Feb. 1688; j.p. Essex 1683–Apr. 1688, Westminster ?1690–6, Mdx. by 1701–*d.*; dep. lt. Mdx. 1692–6,
1701–*d.*, Surr. 1702–*d.*[2]
   Capt. Duke of Monmouth's Ft. 1678–9, R. Dgns.
1679–81; maj. 1 Horse Gds. 1681–5.

As soon as Clarges came of age his father sought
a seat for him at a by-election at Clitheroe; but his
cousin, the 2nd Duke of Albemarle (Christopher
Monck*) ordered him to make way for Sir Thomas
Stringer*. He became an army officer in 1678, and
in the following year was returned for Colchester,
where Albemarle also enjoyed an interest. Shaftesbury considered him 'doubtful', but Huntingdon
marked him as country. He was an inactive
Member of the first Exclusion Parliament, in which
he was named only to the committee of elections
and privileges and to that for the bill to disable
those who had not taken the oaths from sitting in
Convocation. He voted against the committal of the
first exclusion bill. Re-elected in August, he was
totally inactive in the second Exclusion Parliament,
and lost his seat in 1681 through the intervention
of Titus Oates, who told the Colchester electors that
he was a Papist. In the following year he seconded
Albemarle in his duel with Lord Grey of Warke,
but he was wounded and disarmed by Charles Godfrey*, 'so here the Whigs had the better of it'.[3]
   Clarges regained his seat in 1685, but his only
committee in James II's Parliament was on the bill
for the new parish of St. James Piccadilly. Listed
among the Opposition by Danby, he had laid down
his commission by October, presumably as a protest
against the employment of Roman Catholic officers.
When the lord lieutenant asked about his attitude

to the repeal of the Test Act and Penal Laws, he
said that he had already given his answer and
thought a repetition needless. He was removed
from the Essex commission of the peace, and was
sent by his father 'at great expense' to attend the
Prince of Orange at Exeter during the Revolution.
Nevertheless he was defeated at Colchester at the
general election of 1689, and his petition was
rejected. He sat for Westminster as a Tory from
1690 to 1695 and again from 1702 to 1705, but died
in March 1706. The second baronet sat for Lostwithiel in Anne's last Parliament, and a younger
son represented Reading under George I.[4]

[1] Trinity Coll. Dublin, 749/2/189, 4/414; Prob. 10/1401. [2] Essex
RO, DB3/12/13; C18/17/37; *Oxford Council Acts* (Oxf. Hist. Soc.
n.s. ii), 191, 196; Luttrell, iv. 89. [3] *HMC Kenyon*, 100; Bodl. Carte
223, f. 256; *HMC 7th Rep.* 371, 429. [4] *Bramston Autobiog.* (Cam.
Soc. xxxii), 307; Grey, ix. 459; *CJ*, x. 11; Le Neve, *Mon. Angl.
1700–15*, p. 106; Luttrell, vi. 33.

G.H.

CLARKE, George (1661–1736), of All Souls College, Oxford.[1]

OXFORD UNIVERSITY   23 Nov. 1685
WINCHELSEA   1702
EAST LOOE   1705
LAUNCESTON   29 May 1711
OXFORD UNIVERSITY   4 Dec. 1717,   1722,   1727,
                             1734–22 Oct. 1736

b. 7 May 1661, o.s. of Sir William Clarke, sec. at war, of
Pall Mall, Westminster by Dorothy, da. and coh. of
Thomas Hilyard *alias* Hall of Hebburn, co. Dur. *educ.*
Jermyn Street academy (Mr Gordon) to 1672; privately
1672–5; Brasenose, Oxf. 1675, BA 1679, MA 1683,
BCL 1686, DCL 1708; I. Temple 1676. *unm. suc.* fa.
1666.[2]
   Fellow of All Souls, Oxford 1680–*d.*; judge-advocate-
gen. 1682–1705; sec. at war [I] 1690–2; jt. sec. at war
1693–1702; jt. sec. of Admiralty 1702–5; ld. of Admiralty 1710–14.[3]

Clarke's father, a Londoner of obscure parentage,
joined the army secretariat under John Rushworth*
about 1646. An efficient secretary and an outstanding record-keeper, he served George Monck* from
1654 until he died of wounds received on board his
flagship in the Four Days' battle, leaving Clarke,
'that sweet child', to the care of his mother and
his friend, Samuel Barrow, who became her second
husband. A private bill became necessary to settle
the estate, which was steered through committee
by their neighbour, Sir Cyril Wyche*. Clarke continued to enjoy the happiest of homes, and grew up
a cultivated and sociable man, with a wide circle of
friends in the literary and political worlds. He was
elected fellow of All Souls in 1680, and succeeded
his step-father as judge-advocate-general, an
agreeable post as 'there were not very frequent oc-

casions for courts martial'. He intended to join the royal army in the west in 1685, but was detained in London on the King's orders, though he did take part in the trial of some soldiers who had deserted to Monmouth. He was returned for Oxford University on the Duke of Ormonde's recommendation at a contested by-election in November. 'The potmen and juniors carry all before them', commented Wood; but Parliament had already been prorogued, and he never took his seat. He spent the remainder of the reign successfully avoiding the questions on the repeal of the Test Act and Penal Laws, but he attended James II at Salisbury during the Revolution, of which he left a graphic account.[4]

Clarke's commission was confirmed by the new regime, and he held office till 1705, when he was dismissed for voting against John Smith* as Speaker. A lord of the Admiralty in Queen Anne's last administration, he was removed on the Hanoverian succession. He represented the University again as a Hanover Tory from 1717 till his death on 22 Oct. 1736. He was buried in the chapel of All Souls, to which he was a generous benefactor, though he bequeathed much of his wealth and his important collection of manuscripts to the new foundation of Worcester.[5]

[1] This biography is based on Clarke's own account of his life in *HMC Popham*, 259–89. [2] C. J. Feret, *Fulham Old and New*, i. 170. [3] *CSP Dom.* 1682, p. 69. [4] G. E. Aylmer, *State's Servants*, 261–2; PCC 95 Mico; *CJ*, ix. 225; *Wood's Life and Times* (Oxf. Hist. Soc. xxvi), 171. [5] Feiling, *Tory Party*, 389.

L.N.

CLARKE, Sir Gilbert (c.1645–1701), of Somershall Hall, Brampton, Derbys.

DERBYSHIRE   1685, 1689, 1690, 1695

b. c.1645, o. surv. s. of Godfrey Clarke of Somershall by 1st w. Elizabeth, da. of Sir Thomas Milward of Eaton Dovedale. *educ.* Univ. Coll. Oxf. matric. 12 July 1661, aged 16; I. Temple 1667. *m.* (1) Jane (d. 18 May 1667), da. and h. of Robert Byerley of Hornby, Yorks., 1da.; (2) 6 July 1671, Barbara (d. Aug. 1687), da. of George Clerke* of Watford, Northants., 2s. 2da.; (3) Frances, da. of Richard Legh* of Lyme, Cheshire, wid. of Robert Tatton of Wythenshawe, Cheshire, *s.p. suc.* fa. 1670; kntd. 2 Mar. 1671.[1]

J.p. Derbys. 1672–6, 1685–Mar. 1688, 1689–96, 1700–d., commr. for assessment 1673–80, 1689–90, recusants 1675, sheriff 1675–6, dep. lt. 1683–Feb. 1688, Oct. 1688–96, by 1701–d.[2]

Clarke's ancestors acquired the Somershall estate near Chesterfield in Elizabethan times, but none of them entered Parliament. His father was accused of raising men for the King in the Civil War, but the charge was never made good, and he was appointed to the assessment committee in 1657 and to the militia committee just before the Restoration.

Clarke acquired most of the Milward estate by purchase or inheritance. The Chesterfield area was already a centre of heavy industry, and it was presumably to avoid involvement in the imposition of the hearth-tax on forges and furnaces that Clarke resigned from the commission of the peace in 1676 on the rather unlikely grounds of age and infirmity. Having recovered from these complaints he was returned as a Tory for Derbyshire in 1685 with the support of the Duke of Newcastle (Henry Cavendish*). He was a moderately active Member of James II's Parliament, in which he was appointed to three committees, those to report on expiring laws, to estimate the yield of a tax on new buildings, and to consider an estate bill. He 'would not promise' his consent to the repeal of the Test Act and Penal Laws, or to vote for the court candidates, and was removed from local office. He was again moderately active in the Convention. According to the Ailesbury list he voted to agree with the Lords that the throne was not vacant. Among his 30 committees were those to recommend alterations in the coronation oath, to inquire into the authors and advisers of recent grievances, to consider the bill to prevent mutiny and desertion, and to report on the political prisoners. He helped to consider the toleration bill and the bill of rights and settlement. He remained a Tory in the next two Parliaments, refusing the Association in 1696. He died on 30 May 1701 and was buried at Brampton. His son Godfrey sat for Derbyshire as a Tory from 1710 to 1734.[3]

[1] *Fam. Min. Gent.* (Harl. Soc. xxxvii), 335–7; *Vis. Northants.* (Harl. Soc. lxxxvii), 53. [2] J. C. Cox, *Derbys. Annals*, i. 183; *HMC Coke*, ii. 358. [3] *Cal. Comm. Adv. Money*, 1074; Lysons, *Derbys.* 89, 131; *HMC Finch*, ii. 43; *HMC Rutland*, ii. 86; *CSP Dom.* 1685, p. 105.

J.P.F.

CLARKE, John I (d.1681), of Bury St. Edmunds, Suff.

SUFFOLK   1653
BURY ST. EDMUNDS   1654, 1656, 1659, 3–14 May 1660

s. of John Clarke of Bocking, Essex. *m.* Margaret, da. of one Bourne of Bury St. Edmunds, 1s. 1da.[1]

Elder, Bury St. Edmunds classis 1645; alderman, Bury by 1648–?62; collector of assessments, Suff. 1648; commr. for assessment, Bury 1648–52, Suff. 1649–52, Suff. and Bury 1657, Suff. Jan. 1660, militia, Suff. 1648, 1659, Bury Mar. 1660; j.p. Suff. 1650–Mar. 1660, commr. for scandalous ministers 1654, security 1655–6, sheriff 1670–1.[2]

Commr. for high court of justice 1650.

Clarke's father was descended from a Kentish family. He himself settled in Bury St. Edmunds, of which he was an alderman by 1648. He does not seem to have taken any active part in the Civil War, but he held local office continuously during the Interregnum and sat in the Barebones and Protectorate Parliaments. He was involved in a double return for Bury at the general election of 1660. He was allowed to sit on the merits of the return, but unseated 11 days later. During his few days in the Convention he was not appointed to any committees and made no recorded speeches. He made no further attempts to enter Parliament. In 1672 his house in Bury was licensed for Presbyterian worship. He died in November 1681 and was buried in St. Mary's churchyard, Bury. In his will he mentioned lands in Suffolk and Cambridgeshire, and left legacies totalling £4,200. His son Samuel was proposed as court candidate for Cambridgeshire in 1688 and created a baronet in 1698.[3]

[1] Dorm. and Ext. Baronetcies, 117. [2] County of Suff. Divided (1647), 11; Thurloe, iii. 225. [3] Parl. Intell. 21 Apr. 1660; CJ, viii. 9, 25; CSP Dom. 1671–2, pp. 410, 435; PCC 179 North.

M.W.H./P.W.

CLARKE, John II (d.1675), of Chirton, Northumb.

COCKERMOUTH   29 Mar. 1670–6 May 1675

s. of Roger Clarke of Great Torrington, Devon by Honor, da. of Christopher Hockin, clothier, of Frithelstock, Devon. m. Jane, s.p.[1]

J.p. Northumb. July 1660–d.; commr. for assessment, Northumb. 1661–3, Northumb. and Newcastle-upon-Tyne 1664–74; freeman, Newcastle 1662, dep. lt. 1670–d.; commr. for recusants, Cumb. 1675.[2]

Clarke's father was twice mayor of Torrington; but nothing certain is known of his own career before the Restoration, when he was probably about 40. He had presumably already entered the service of the Earl of Northumberland, perhaps through the agency of his fellow-Devonian, Hugh Potter*. As auditor, he carried out a survey of Corbridge in 1663, and he was returned for Cockermouth on his employer's interest in 1670. As lessee of a colliery he spoke against taxing mines on 23 Jan. 1671. In 1672 he bought Chirton, where he built a mansion. By agreement with the dowager countess, he obtained materials from Warkworth Castle and labour from the Percy estate. 'A long cavalcade of 272 wains' was needed to carry the spoil. He also held a lease of the Alnwick demesnes during the infancy of the heiress. On 9 Feb. 1673 he claimed privilege against a claimant to the earldom, a trunk-maker, who desired to summon him as a witness. Clarke admitted that he was now seized in fee-simple of some of the Northumberland estates:

He stood bound at the last Earl's death for £40,000, and

this estate is for his security. . . . Now if you will think fit that the gentleman that brought this petition shall lay down £40,000, he will waive his privilege.

Although fully competent to defend his own interests in the House, he was not active as a committeeman. He may have been appointed to 13 committees, of which perhaps the likeliest to concern him was on the bill for the enfranchisement of Durham; but most of these references are probably to George Clerke*. He died on 6 May 1675 'after ten days' sickness, mostly of a lethargy'. His widow married Philip Bickerstaffe*.[3]

[1] Exeter Mar. Lic. 20; Trans. Devon Assoc. lxxvi. 175; J. Brand, Hist. Newcastle, i. 380; PCC 108 Dycer. [2] Reg. of Freemen (Newcastle Rec. Soc. iii), 78; CSP Dom. 1670, p. 383. [3] Trans. Devon Assoc. lxxvi. 176; HMC 3rd Rep. 94; Hist. Northumb. v. 75; viii. 322; x. 133; PCC 108 Dycer; Dering, 60; Grey, ii. 400–1; CSP Dom. 1675–6, p. 108.

E.C./J.P.F.

CLARKE see also CLERKE.

CLAYTON, John (c.1620–at least 1694), of Oakenshaw, Yorks. and the Inner Temple.

LOSTWITHIEL   1659, 4 June 1660

b. c.1620, 1st s. of John Clayton of Oakenshaw, recorder of Leeds 1626–61, by 1st w. Elizabeth, da. of Gerard Fitwilliam of Bentley. educ. Clare, Camb. 1638; I. Temple 1639, called 1648. m. lic. 20 Mar. 1674, 'aged 48', Thomasine, da. of Sir Samuel Owfield[†], Fishmonger, of Covent Garden, Westminster and Upper Gatton, Surr., wid. of Deane Goodwin of Bletchingley, Surr., s.p. suc. fa. 1671.[1]

Capt. of ft. (parliamentary) 1643, major bef. 1650.[2]

Commr. for northern association, Yorks. (W. Riding) 1645, assessment 1647–52, 1657, Jan. 1660, Sept. 1660–1, j.p. 1649–52, 1655–July 1660; capt. of militia ft. Yorks. 1650, commr. for militia Mar. 1660.[3]

Clayton and his father were both lawyers and both zealous Parliamentarians in the Civil War. At the capture of Leeds in 1643 Clayton took the colours of the royalist governor Sir William Savile, 3rd Bt.[†], and he later distinguished himself in the defence of Hull. At the Restoration he reckoned that he had been 'serviceable' to the hundred of Askrigg and Morley for 14 years. He probably owed his election for Lostwithiel to the family of his fellow-Member, Walter Moyle*, another Inner Temple lawyer, though many years his junior. But in 1660 he was involved in a double return with Henry Ford*, which was not resolved in his favour till 4 June. Lord Wharton assigned him to the management of Sir Wilfrid Lawson*. On 24 July Clayton wrote to Sir George Savile*:

I hope what was concluded the last night at the House (which sat late) will be acceptable news to the clothiers, which I shall send down by this night's post ... viz. that the customs of all woollen manufactures for the King's life shall be but 3s.4d.

He was an inactive Member of the Convention, serving, as 'Major Clayton', only on the committee for settling ministers before the autumn recess, and on four others afterwards, including that for taking accounts of public moneys; but he probably voted with the Opposition, for all his protestations of loyalty to the King and detestation of Oliverians and Rumpers. He held no office, not even the humblest, after 1660, though his younger brother was on the West Riding commission of the peace, and he seems to have made no particular mark at the bar. He was imprisoned in 1662 for four months on a charge of treasonable words. A bachelor on the wrong side of 50 when his father died, he had to marry within three years a virtuous wife with a portion of at least £800 or lose the inheritance. He chose a Surrey widow of 13 years' standing, whose son, Deane Goodwin*, bequeathed her an annuity on condition that her second husband should not meddle with it, but there is no mention of the marriage on her memorial. Clayton assisted William Jephson* at East Grinstead in 1679 by introducing him to the Goodwins, but he took no known part in the politics of the Exclusion crisis, or later. He was still alive in 1694, when he addressed a petition to the benchers of his Inn about his chambers, which had been sub-let to a 'blackamoor', but the date of his death has not been ascertained.[4]

[1] Clay, *Dugdale's Vis. Yorks.* iii. 394–5; *London Mar. Lic.* ed. Foster, 289. [2] *HMC 5th Rep.* 110. [3] *CSP Dom.* 1650, p. 506. [4] Notts. RO, DDSR221/94/16, Clayton to Savile; *HMC Portland*, i. 139; PC2/56/159, 262; PCY 52, f. 380; Bodl. Carte 103, f. 221; *I. Temple Recs.* iii. 300.

J.P.F.

CLAYTON, Sir Robert (1629–1707), of Old Jewry, London and Marden Park, Godstone, Surr.

LONDON	1679 (Mar.), 1679 (Oct.), 1681, 1689
BLETCHINGLEY	1690
LONDON	1695
BLETCHINGLEY	1698
LONDON	1701 (Feb.), 1701 (Dec.)
BLETCHINGLEY	1 Dec. 1702
LONDON	1705–16 July 1707

b. 29 Sept. 1629, 1st s. of John Clayton, carpenter, of Bulwick, Northants. by Alice, da. of Thomas Abbott of Gretton, Northants. *m.* 26 Dec. 1659, Martha (*d.* 25 Dec. 1705), da. and coh. of Perient Trott, merchant, of London, 1s. *d.v.p.* Kntd. 30 Oct. 1671; *suc.* partner John Morris* in Bucks. estate 1682.[1]

Member, Scriveners' Co. 1658–79, asst. 1670, master 1671–2; member, Drapers' Co. 1679–*d.*, master

1680–1; alderman of London 1670–83, 1689–*d.*, sheriff 1671–2, ld. mayor 1679–80; asst. R. Africa Co. 1672–at least 1681; commr. for assessment, London 1673–80, Bucks. and Surr. 1677–80, Essex 1679–80, Bucks., London and Surr. 1689–90, Norf. 1690; j.p. Surr. 1674–82, 1689–*d.*, Essex 1680–?82; commr. for recusants, Surr. 1675; dep. lt. London 1676–81, 1689–1702; asst. Hudson's Bay Co. 1676, treasurer 1678; col. orange regt. of militia ft. London 1680–1, 1689–90, 1694–1702; pres. Hon. Artillery Co. 1690–1703; gov. Irish Soc. 1692–1706; pres. St. Thomas's hosp. 1692–*d.*[2]

Commr. of customs 1689–97; director, Bank of England (with statutory intervals) 1702–*d.*[3]

FRS 1688.

Clayton's father was 'a poor man of no family', but he had an uncle Robert Abbott, a thriving scrivener, with whom he took service 'in a very low capacity'. Despite his lack of formal education he rose to be Abbott's chief clerk, inheriting from him in 1658 a house and shop in Cornhill and an annuity of £100. He went into partnership with John Morris*, another of Abbott's clerks, their firm combining the functions of modern land agents, conveyancers, brokers and bankers. As former servants of Abbott, who had been condemned to death as a commissioner of array in 1643, they enjoyed an excellent connexion with the Cavalier party, and greatly prospered by unravelling the complexities of land ownership after the Interregnum. Among their most considerable clients were the Duke of Buckingham, the Earl of Peterborough, and Sir George Jeffreys (for whom Clayton secured the post of common serjeant of London), as well as Sir Frescheville Holles*, Lord Cornbury (Henry Hyde*) and his brother Laurence Hyde*, Sir Francis North*, (Sir) Stephen Fox*, Sir Eliab Harvey*, and Sir William Pritchard*. Clayton and Morris lent money on the security of deeds, which did not always find their way back to their original possessors. It was the general belief that as trustees they had swallowed up most of Peterborough's and Buckingham's estates. In 1672 they obtained a royal pardon 'for all usurious contracts in taking interest more than 6% ... though not conscious of any ground of offence'. Hence the portrait of Clayton in *Absalom and Achitophel* as 'extorting Ishban ... pursued by a meagre troop of bankrupt heirs'. Clayton and Morris purchased in 1672 the manor of Marden, which Clayton transformed from a 'despicable farm' into a magnificent seat for himself 'at extraordinary expense', and in 1677 they purchased the borough and manor of Bletchingley three miles away, together with five other Surrey manors sold under a private Act to pay Peterborough's debts. All the Surrey estates devolved on Clayton under a division of property made in 1678, and he inherited

Morris's share four years later. He acquired through his wife one of the largest plantations in Bermuda, leased Kennington manor from the Duchy of Cornwall, and purchased the island of Brownsea in Poole Harbour with the copperas works there, and iron works in Ireland. He acquired fame in London, not only as its wealthiest citizen but also by securing the foundation of the Royal Mathematical School at Christ's Hospital, opened in 1673, for the training of boys to a knowledge of navigation 'to the great increase of seamen and the benefit of trade'. He also rebuilt the southern front of the Hospital at a cost of £10,000. The house he built for himself in Old Jewry had a banqueting hall more splendid than anything in the royal palaces, and as sheriff he entertained the King and most of the nobility there. Evelyn wrote of him as 'this prince of citizens, there never having been any, who, for the stateliness of his palace, prodigious feasting, and magnificence, exceeded him'. He was an active member of the common council, and a member of the committees administering the city lands, the Ulster plantation, and the London markets. He was believed to hanker after a peerage, and was intimate with (Sir) Joseph Williamson* and (Sir) John Robinson I*; but he went over to the country party in 1673 when he promoted the London petition of grievances on trade with Sir Thomas Player*. Thereafter, he became an associate of Shaftesbury and a political ally in London of the nonconformists, whom he would never prosecute, though he remained an Anglican and declared himself 'never to have been in a conventicle'.[4]

Clayton represented London in the Exclusion Parliaments. An active Member in 1679, he was classed as 'honest' by Shaftesbury, and appointed to 14 committees, including those to inquire into the recent fires in the City of London and the state of the navy, to examine the disbandment accounts, and to consider the bills to prevent illegal exactions and reform the bankruptcy law. He voted for the exclusion bill and spoke twice about pensioners. He told the House on 23 May that Fox was 'regular in his accounts, and you may see the same things in his ledger with as much ease as if you had his book of secret service'. Four days later Clayton was engaged in giving the House an account of the excise pensioners when Black Rod appeared. He was chosen lord mayor without opposition in September of that year, and was again elected MP for London in October. He spent £6,955 on his mayoralty, entertaining Shaftesbury and other leaders of the country party in splendid style on several occasions. At the request of Shaftesbury, Lord Huntingdon and Lord Grey of Warke he summoned the common council in January 1680 to support a citizens' petition for the meeting of Parliament, but the proposal was defeated by one vote through the efforts of Jeffreys, now recorder. He was more successful in September, when the King assured him that Parliament would meet within a couple of months. On 20 Oct. the common council voted their thanks to him on his mayoralty 'for his watchful care during his whole time for the preservation of his Majesty's person and this City, together with our religion and liberties, in the midst of those wicked and desperate Popish Plots', for 'his asserting the right of petitioning his Majesty for the calling and sitting of Parliaments, notwithstanding all opposition to the contrary', and for the 'kind and affectionate reception he has constantly given to the citizens of London in all their humble application to him as well in this court as in the common hall'.[5]

A very active Member of the second Exclusion Parliament, Clayton was appointed to 29 committees, including the committee of elections and privileges, and made 15 recorded speeches. He served on the inquiries into abhorring and the conduct of Sir Robert Peyton*, and on 14 Nov. 1680 he reported the address for the removal of Jeffreys. 'What sticks with me', he said, 'is his officiousness at the council table.' He was appointed to the committee on the bill for regulating the coinage (9 Dec.). On 13 Dec. he moved that all Papists should be banished 20 miles from London, and five days later he spoke in favour of the exclusion and association bills, and was among those ordered to draft an address accordingly. He was also entrusted with bringing in bills to regulate the post office and to repeal the Corporations Act. He served on most of the committees to investigate the Popish Plot, and on 6 Jan. 1681 moved for a debate on the new evidence from the Irish witnesses before the next report.[6]

Before the Oxford Parliament met Clayton and (Sir) George Treby* examined the Roman Catholic conspirator Fitzharris in Newgate. By the prisoner's own account he was promised an acquittal if he would accuse the Queen, the Duke of York, and Danby of complicity in the murder of Godfrey, and Lord Halifax (Sir George Savile*) and Lawrence Hyde of receiving pensions from France. But Clayton told the House that Fitzharris had asked whether he had said enough to save his life.

We told him we thought not, but if he would ingenuously confess what counsel he had for drawing and modelling his treasonable paper, and be ingenuous in the whole, we would take his further examination, and wished him to consider it.

Clayton was appointed to five committees in the Oxford Parliament, including the committee of elections and privileges, and those to report on the progress of Danby's impeachment, to prepare for a conference with the Lords on the loss in the previous Parliament of the bill of ease for Protestant dissenters, and to draw up Fitzharris's impeachment, a move to get him out of the hands of the King and into those of the House. On 26 Mar. he declared:

> We can discharge our trust no better than to observe the directions of those that sent us hither. We, who represent the City of London, have received an address from the body of that City in the matter of the bill for excluding the Duke of York. I could heartily wish that some expedient may be found rather than that bill; but if there be none, I must pursue my trust and humbly move that a bill may be brought in to disable James, Duke of York from inheriting the imperial crown of this realm.

He was appointed to the committee to draw up the bill, over which he would have presided had Parliament not been dissolved.[7]

In April a government informer reported that Clayton, like Player and Thomas Pilkington*, was in favour of 'a free state and no other government', whereas Shaftesbury wanted to make Monmouth King. On 13 May he was appointed to the committee of the common council to draw up the petition for the calling and sitting of a Parliament. In the following October he brought to Sir Leoline Jenkins* papers purporting to show that 'there is little justice to be had in Ireland against Romish priests'. It was presumed that his intentions were to influence the jury at Shaftesbury's forthcoming trial for high treason, and to secure Ormonde's removal as lord lieutenant of Ireland. There were rumours that Clayton was also to be charged with high treason at this time, but through Jeffreys, now lord chief justice, he secured immunity from the harassment to which other Whigs were subjected, and he was able to make his peace with the Court.[8]

Clayton was appointed on 18 Jan. 1682 to the committee to prepare the defence of the London charter against the quo warranto issued against it, and he was one of the Whig aldermen removed on the forfeiture of the charter in 1683. He was defeated at Bletchingley in 1685, but in 1688 the King's agents reported that the borough was under his influence, and that he in turn might be influenced by Jeffreys. On the restoration of the London charter in October, Clayton was reinstated as alderman, but refused to act until the Revolution. In December, he presented a common council address to the Prince of Orange, then on his way to London. After the Prince's arrival, James asked the City for protection, but 'Sir Robert Clayton so in-

fluenced the common council that this security was denied'. He attended the meeting of Members of Charles II's Parliaments on 26 Dec., and was among those entrusted with drawing up an address to the Prince. He also persuaded the common council to lend him £200,000.[9]

Clayton regained his seat in the Convention and was made commissioner of customs by the new regime. An active Member, he was named to 53 committees, including the committee of elections and privileges in both sessions, and made 13 recorded speeches. Together with Sir John Holt* he was sent to examine the late treasury solicitors in the Tower; but they laid all the responsibility on the attorney-general. On 25 Feb. 1689 he acted as teller for appointing a special committee of inquiry into the violation of the liberties and franchises of the City of London and other corporations in 1682–3, and he was among those appointed to discover the authors and advisers of these and other grievances. He opposed the proposal for the indefinite suspension of the Habeas Corpus Act, asking:

> When you have taken these people, how will you hold them in prison? Had it not been for the Habeas Corpus Act, there had not been many of us here now; we had been dead and rotten in prison. . . . I would have this a temporary bill for a short time, and not to be drawn into example.

During March he was appointed to committees to draw up an address of thanks for the abandonment of the hearth-tax, to devise new oaths of allegiance and supremacy, to reverse the attainder of the Hon. William Russell*, and to consider a bill for the speedier conviction and disarming of Papists. He seldom served on private bill committees, but on 20 Mar. he was among those ordered to consider the claim of Edmund Prideaux* against Jeffreys's estate, which, as one of the trustees, he was instrumental in saving for the family. In April he was named to committees to report on petitions against the customs commissioners and the East India Company. He was among those ordered to inquire into the delay in relieving Londonderry (1 June), and draw up the request for leave to inspect the Privy Council registers (1 July). He was also one of the Members appointed to bring in a bill for the relief of London widows and orphans, and to prepare reasons for a conference on Titus Oates. He made three reports from the committee for an embargo on imports from France, and carried the bill to the Lords on 7 Aug.[10]

After the recess Clayton served on the committees of inquiry into the expenses and miscarriages of the war. He complained that it was cheaper for London merchants to hire Dutch capers to protect them than to pay the convoy money demanded by the navy. He supported the disabling clause in the bill to restore corporations, but did not trouble to vote for it, though he was in the Palace of Westminster at the time. He was appointed to the committee for imposing a general oath of allegiance, and acted as teller against naming people for exception from indemnity.[11]

Clayton sat alternately for Bletchingley and London as a court Whig for the rest of his life. He died on 16 July 1707, father of the City, and was buried beneath a sumptuous memorial at Bletchingley. Apart from charitable bequests, the estate was inherited by a nephew, who sat for the borough from 1715 to 1744 as a Whig.[12]

[1] J. R. Woodhead, *Rulers of London*, 48; *Le Neve's Knights* (Harl. Soc. viii), 270; Manning and Bray, *Surr.* ii. 310–11; *Reg. St. Botolph Bishopsgate*, i. 485. [2] *Scriveners Common Ppr.* (London Rec. Soc. iv), 122, 125; Woodhead, 48; Guildhall Lib. Gregory mss, 1103; *CSP Dom.* 1682, p. 548; *HMC Ormonde*, n.s. vi. 32; *HMC Lords*, i. 179; iii. 47; Luttrell, i. 83; v. 193; *Sel. Charters* (Selden Soc. xxviii), 188; G. A. Raikes, *Hist. Hon. Artillery Co.* ii. 474. [3] *Cal. Treas. Bks.* ix. 82; xii. 158; *N. and Q.* clxxix. 59–60. [4] Guildhall Lib. Noble coll.; PCC 305 Wootton; Manning and Bray, ii. 302–3; *Evelyn Diary*, iv. 121, 147, 185–6; Guildhall Lib. mss 6428; *Econ. Hist. Rev.* (ser. 2), iv. 221–43; *HMC Lords*, i. 305–6, (n.s.) i. 175; *Clarendon Corresp.* i. 196, 199–200; *Cal. Treas. Bks.* v. 1402; 1680–1, pp. 490–1; 1682, pp. 29–30; H. Wilkinson, *Adventurers of Bermuda*, 338, 363; *Poems on Affairs of State*, iii. 293–4; *Bulstrode Pprs.* 230; *Gent. Mag.* xxxix. 517; *Williamson Letters* (Cam. Soc. n.s. viii), 114. [5] Grey, vii. 318, 345; *CSP Dom.* 1679–80, pp. 296, 597; *Hatton Corresp.* (Cam. Soc. n.s. xxii), 207–8; Add. 27447, f. 496; Luttrell, i. 29; London Corp. RO, common council jnl. [6] Grey, vii. 471; viii. 35, 133; *HMC 12th Rep. IX*, 100, 107. [7] *HMC Ormonde*, n.s. vi. 91; Grey, viii. 303, 309–10; *CJ*, ix. 709. [8] *CSP Dom.* 1680–1, pp. 232, 280; *HMC Ormonde*, n.s. vi. 180, 182, 200, 273; Luttrell, i. 106; Manning and Bray, ii. 303. [9] Luttrell, i. 471; Surr. RO, 60/9/6; Clarke, *Jas. II*, ii. 271; *Clarendon Corresp.* ii. 224. [10] *CJ*, x. 34, 132, 223, 241, 252; Grey, ix. 134, 139. [11] Grey, ix. 411, 412; R. Morrice, Entering Bk. 3, p. 84; *CJ*, x. 338. [12] Manning and Bray, ii. 310–11; PCC 165 Poley.

E.C.

CLAYTON, Thomas (c.1612–93), of Oxford and The Vache, Chalfont St. Giles, Bucks.

OXFORD UNIVERSITY   1660

b. c.1612, 1st s. of Thomas Clayton, MD, master of Pembroke 1624–47, by Alice, da. of Bartholomew Warner, MD, of Oxford. *educ.* Pembroke, Oxf. matric. 25 May 1627, aged 15, BA 1629, MA 1631, BM 1635, MD 1639; G. Inn 1633. *m.* bef. 1650, Bridget (*d.* 11 Dec. 1687), da. of Sir Clement Cottrell[†], groom-porter, of South-repps, Norf., 1s. 1da. *suc.* fa. 1647; kntd. 27 Mar. 1661.[1]

Fellow of Pembroke, Oxf. ?1629–49; regius professor of medicine and master of Ewelme hospital 1647–65; j.p. Oxon. July 1660–Mar. 1688, Oxford 1661, Bucks. 1663–Feb. 1688, Bucks. Sept. 1688–*d.*, Oxon. Oct. 1688–*d.*; commr. for visitation, Oxf. Univ. July 1660–2, assessment, Oxon. Aug. 1660–80, Oxf. Univ. Aug. 1660–1, 1673–9, Oxford 1661–9, Bucks. 1663–74, 1679–80, Oxon. and Oxf. Univ. 1689–90; warden of Merton, Oxf. 1661–*d.*; commr. for recusants, Bucks. and Oxon. 1675.[2]

Clayton's father, a Yorkshireman, married the daughter of the regius professor of medicine at Oxford and succeeded to his chair. A Laudian in religion, he became the first master of Pembroke and died while preparing to resist the parliamentary visitation of the university after the Civil War. Clayton's brother was a Cavalier officer, but he himself, a practising physician, took no known part in the war. He submitted to the parliamentary visitors, and was allowed to inherit the professorship, which was augmented during the Protectorate 'on account of his merit and the trouble attending his office'. But the ungrateful recipient 'hazarded his life and spent much money for the Restoration', at least by his own account.[3]

Clayton defeated William Lenthall[†], the former Speaker, at the general election of 1660, and became a moderately active Member of the Convention, in which he was appointed to 26 committees and made 11 recorded speeches, mostly on the religious issue. He spoke against receiving the petition of the intruded dons on 25 June, but was the first to be nominated to the committee to report on it. He was among those instructed on 4 July to prepare for a conference on three orders issued by the House of Lords. He was as violent in supporting the referral of the religious settlement to a synod as Denzil Holles* was in opposing it, and he considered the bill inadequate because it failed to mention the Thirty-Nine Articles as well as scripture. Religion must be founded on the law of God, but must also conform with the law of the land. 'Discipline [was] as necessary with doctrine as life in a natural body.' He was no more enthusiastic about the bill for settling ministers in livings, proposing to defer the second reading for ten days, but was appointed to the committee. He supported the proposal to except Sir Arthur Hesilrige[†] from the indemnity. On 24 Aug. he was added to the committee to recommend measures for regulating printing. He was teller for the bizarre motion that the serjeant-at-arms should assist in searching for smuggled tobacco. He was appointed to the committee to examine defects in the Disbandment Act and helped to manage the conference on settling ministers. In the second session he moved for an additional tax on all who had accepted Cromwellian titles or falsely assumed the style of Doctor of Physic, and his name was the first on the committee list. He was among those ordered on 17 Nov. to bring in a bill for modified episcopacy. He supported the proviso introduced by his colleague John Myles* to exempt the university letter-carriers from the nationalization of the postal services.[4]

Clayton prepared to contest the general election

of 1661, but was bought off through the intervention of his brother-in-law, Sir Charles Cotterell*. He was knighted, made warden of Merton, and allowed to buy a forfeited regicide estate in Buckinghamshire for £9,500. Unfortunately for his posthumous reputation, his position as warden brought him into frequent conflict with the university chronicler, Anthony à Wood, who described him as impudent and lascivious, and one who had 'sided with all parties'. He was regarded by the local Quakers as a persecutor; but his record of compliancy was ended by James II. To the lord lieutenant's questions in 1688, he answered:

> He shall think fit that the Penal Laws against the dissenters in matters of religion be repealed, but not the Tests till he shall be convinced that he ought to do so. . . . He is not able to assist at any elections of persons of what judgment or persuasion soever by reason of his very great age and the many infirmities thereby.

He was removed from the commission of the peace, and apparently accepted the Revolution. He died on 4 Oct. 1693. His only son had no parliamentary ambitions and died without issue in 1714.[5]

[1] *Wood's Life and Times* (Oxf. Hist. Soc. xix), 132; D. Macleane, *Hist. Pemb. Coll.* (Oxf. Hist. Soc. xxxiii), 213–15; PCC 76 Essex; information from Miss J. K. Cordy. [2] *Restoration Visitation of Oxf.* (Cam. Misc. xviii), 57. [3] *Grantees of Arms* (Harl. Soc. lxvi), 54; Macleane, 237; *Reg. Visitors Oxf.* (Cam. Soc. n.s. xxix), 539; *CSP Dom.* 1658–9, pp. 11, 264; 1660–1, p. 262. [4] Bowman diary, ff. 25, 55v, 55, 67, 81, 98; *Voyce from the Watch Tower*, 171; *CJ*, viii. 106, 154, 163, 182; *Old Parl. Hist.* xxii. 444; xxiii. 12, 60. [5] *CSP Dom.* 1660–1, pp. 512, 525, 526; *Wood's Life and Times* (xix) 312, 385, 394; (xxvi) 432; *VCH Bucks.* iii. 188.

L.N.

CLERKE, Sir Francis (c.1624–86), of Rochester and Ulcombe, Kent.

ROCHESTER   1661, 1681, 1685–25 Feb. 1686

b. c.1624, 2nd but 1st surv. s. of Henry Clerke†, serjeant-at-law, of Rochester by Grace, da. and h. of George Morgan of Crow Lane House, Rochester; bro. of John Clerke†. *educ.* M. Temple, entered 1641, called 1656; Univ. Coll. Oxf. matric. 1 July 1642, aged 18. *m.* (1) 17 Oct. 1646, Mary (*d.* bef. 1663), da. of Sir Robert Darell of Calehill, Kent, 3s. (1 *d.v.p.*) 2da.; (2) Elizabeth, da. and h. of John Cage of Brightwell Court, Bucks., wid. of John Hastings of Woodlands, Dorset, 1s.; (3) lic. 6 Dec. 1670, Elizabeth, da. of John Turner of Canterbury, Kent, wid. of Nathaniel Hardy, DD, dean of Rochester, *s.p. suc.* fa. 1648; kntd. 28 May 1660.[1]

J.p. Kent July 1660–*d.*; commr. for assessment, Kent Aug. 1660–80, Rochester 1663–4; sewers, Medway marshes Dec. 1660; warden, Rochester bridge 1661, 1669, 1676, 1683, asst. 1661–84; commr. for corporations, Kent 1662–3, loyal and indigent officers 1662; sub-commr. for prizes, Dover 1665–7; receiver of hearth-tax, Kent 1664–7, dep. lt. 1665–8, 1680–*d.*, commr. for recusants 1675; freeman, Maidstone 1683–*d.*[2]

Gent. of privy chamber by June 1660–*d.*[3]

Clerke's father, a second cousin of George Clerke*, had represented Rochester in 1621, 1625 and 1626, and his elder brother John had been returned for the city to the Short Parliament. Clerke raised a regiment for the King during the Kentish rising of 1648, and was fined £200. In 1656 his name appeared on lists of royalist suspects. At that time he was living mostly in London, first in Gray's Inn and then in the Middle Temple, but he made frequent trips to Ulcombe. Charles II, on his return to England, spent the night of 28 May 1660 with the Dukes of York and Gloucester at Clerke's house in Rochester, on which occasion he was knighted. He later claimed that he gave the royal brothers 'the first dish of meat they had from any private person'.[4]

Returned for Rochester in 1661 on his family interest, Clerke was a moderately active Member, being named to 154 committees and acting as teller on four occasions. In the first session of the Cavalier Parliament he was appointed to the committees on the bills for the confirmation of public acts, for restoring the bishops to the House of Lords, for preventing mischiefs from schismatics, and for pains and penalties. He was teller for the Lindsey level bill in 1662 and for the bill to regulate the manufacture of tobacco pipes in 1665. At Oxford he was named to the committee for the five mile bill, and, together with the Hon. William Coventry* and William Prynne*, presented to the King an address for the relief of sick and maimed prisoners. As one of the Members who had usually voted for supply, he figures in both lists of court supporters in 1669–71. Together with Sir Thomas Peyton*, he was accused in the House on 17 Mar. 1670 of irregularities as a prize commissioner during the second Dutch war; but the matter was dropped after full debate. He was teller for the amendment to except existing holders of pluralities from paying £10 for a dispensation, and on 8 Dec. was appointed to the committee for the conventicles bill. He was named to the committees for the habeas corpus amendment bill in 1674 and for the appropriation bill in the spring session of 1675. He received the government whip in the autumn and was named as a member of the court party on the working lists and in Wiseman's account. His only speech was on 15 Feb. 1677, when Sir John Holland* accused William Ashburnham* of misrepresenting one of his speeches to the King, and cited Clerke as a witness, but he said that he remembered nothing of the matter. He was named to the committee for the bill to ensure the Protestant education of the royal children. Shaftesbury listed Clerke as 'doubly vile', and his name is on the government list of 1678. While he was not named as a member of the 'unanimous club', in *Flagellum Parliamentarium* he was called 'a cheating commissioner of the prize office, and gave £600 to be so', and in *A Seasonable Argument* he appears as 'a constant receiver of all public money and constant diner at court tables'.[5]

At the first general election of 1679, Clerke was defeated by Sir John Banks*, also a government supporter, but one who 'hath the better way of guinea kissing'. In August it was reported that 'every one confesseth Sir Francis Clerke to be wiser by much than all the other candidates, but his fault, as they call it, is that he votes for the Court', and there is no evidence that he went to the poll. He regained his seat in 1681, but left no trace on the records of the Oxford Parliament. He was re-elected in 1685, and became a very active Member of James II's Parliament. He was appointed to 19 committees, including those to calculate the yield of a tax on new buildings and to consider the bill to provide Rochester and Chatham with fresh water. He died suddenly on 25 Feb. 1686. His son Francis was returned for Rochester in 1690.[6]

[1] *Vis. Kent* (Harl. Soc. liv), 36; *Little Chart Reg.* 114; *Vis. Northants.* (Harl. Soc. lxxxvii), 54; Lipscomb, *Bucks.* iii. 29; F. F. Smith, *Hist. Rochester*, 108, 112. [2] *Cal. Treas. Bks.* i. 687; ii. 52; iii. 23; C181/7/70; *Twysden Ltcy. Pprs.* (Kent Recs. x), 24; *Arch. Cant.* xvii. 173; Eg. 2985, f. 66; *CSP Dom.* 1666–7, p. 246; Smith, 119; K. C. Martin, *Maidstone Recs.* 161. [3] Carlisle, *Privy Chamber*, 166, 197. [4] *Arch. Cant.* xv. 112; xxiii. 77; *CSP Dom.* 1682, p. 19. [5] *CJ*, viii. 394, 584; ix. 141, 178, 383; Grey, iv. 76. [6] BL, M636/33, John Verney to Sir Ralph Verney, 4 Aug. 1679; *CJ*, ix. 570.

B.D.H.

CLERKE (CLARKE), George (c.1626–89), of Watford, Northants.

NORTHAMPTONSHIRE 1661

> *b.* c.1626, 1st s. of Sir George Clarke, Grocer, of London and Watford by Barbara, da. of Robert Palmer, Grocer, of London and Hill Warden, Beds. *educ.* Queens', Camb. 1639; L. Inn 1646; travelled abroad. *m.* (1) lic. 9 June 1648, Mary (*d.*1668), da. of Philip Holman, scrivener, of Warkworth, Northants., 2s. *d.v.p.* 6da.; (2) Sarah, da. of (Sir) Edward Turnor* of Little Parndon, Essex, *s.p. suc.* fa. 1649.[1]
>
> Commr. for militia, Northants. Mar. 1660; j.p. Mar. 1660–87, 1689–*d.*, commr. for assessment Aug. 1660–80, 1689, loyal and indigent officers 1662, dep. lt. 1662–bef. 1680.[2]

Clerke's father, of Warwickshire descent, was one of the leading City Royalists, serving as sheriff of London in 1641–2. 'The new, honest, stout sheriff' was chiefly responsible for the election of the loyal Richard Gurney as lord mayor. He was allegedly imprisoned as a delinquent in 1642–3 for refusal to pay his assessment. On his release he went to live on his country property, and at the height of the Civil war, it is stated, enclosed four-fifths of his manor of Watford. He was appointed to several commissions after the Civil War until a few months before his death, when he retired on grounds of ill-health, and suffered no further financial penalties for his loyalty.[3]

Clerke travelled extensively in most European countries, but held no local office before March 1660. He was proposed as a knight of the Royal Oak, with an estate of £3,000 p.a. He was returned for the county in 1661 after a contest. His record in the Cavalier Parliament cannot always be distinguished from those of Henry Clerke I* and John Clarke II*, but he was regular in attendance and probably moderately active with at least 62 committee appointments, including those for the uniformity bill and the bill for execution of those under attainder in 1661. In the following year he carried a message from the House to the bishop of Ely. He was named to the committee for the impeachment of Lord Mordaunt in 1667. He was probably teller against the motion for the impeachment of Lord Orrery (Roger Boyle*) in 1669, and later in the session was authorized to bring in a bill for the punishment of vandalism. He was listed by Sir Thomas Osborne* among the Members who usually voted for supply, though in connexion with the excise he wrote to his absent colleague Sir Justinian Isham, 2nd Bt.*: 'We are in great care, as becomes us, to defend our houses and private families from the mischief of inspection'. In 1670 he was appointed to the committees for the conventicles bill and inspecting the Treasury and navy estimates. On 26 Nov. he was given leave to bring in a bill for building an assize in Northampton. In 1675 he was probably appointed to the committee for appropriating the customs to the use of the navy. On 8 Nov. he acted as teller for the unsuccessful motion to read the bill for rebuilding Northampton, but 11 days later he had the satisfaction of carrying it to the Lords. Shaftesbury first noted Clerke as 'worthy' in 1677, but later altered this to 'vile', though his name appears on no court lists after 1669. Clerke probably acted as teller for the bill, directed against (Sir) Edward Harley*, to decrease control of incumbents by patrons, and against the repeal of the bill forbidding imports of cattle, and served on the committee for educating children of the royal family as Protestants. On 29 Apr. 1678 he was added to the committee to draw up reasons for a conference on the growth of Popery, and on 14 June he carried a Northamptonshire estate bill to the Lords. Clerke does not seem to have stood again, but he opposed exclusion, remaining on the commission of the peace till 1687, when he did not appear to answer the lord lieutenant's questions on the repeal of the Test Act and Penal Laws. He accepted the Revolution, and was reappointed to the county bench, but he was buried at Watford on 29 May 1689. His heir was his nephew Robert, a Roman Catholic, and no later member of the family entered Parliament.[4]

[1] *Vis. Northants.* (Harl. Soc. lxxxvii), 53; Bridges, *Northants.* i. 590. [2] Northants. RO, FH2226. [3] Bridges, i. 585, 627; V. Pearl, *London and the Outbreak of the Puritan Revolution*, 114, 124, 295–6. [4] *Genealogists Mag.* xiii. 41; *CJ*, ix. 112, 119, 389, 413.

E.R.E.

CLERKE, (CLARKE), Henry I (1621–81), of Enford, Wilts.

GREAT BEDWYN 17 May 1661

b. bef. 6 Sept. 1621, 2nd *s.* of Sir Henry Clarke of Avington, Hants, being 1st *s.* by 2nd *w.* Margaret, da. of Richard Percey of Lee Court, Greatham, Hants. *m.* settlement 7 June 1639 (with £1,000), Isabella, da. of Thomas Warwick, organist of Westminster Abbey, Mdx., at least 5s. 5 other ch. *suc.* fa. at Enford 1654.[1]
Major of horse (royalist) by 1646.[2]
J.p. Wilts. July 1660–*d.*, commr. for assessment Aug. 1660–74, corporations 1662–3, loyal and indigent officers 1662, capt. of militia 1661–?71; freeman, Winchester by 1663, Portsmouth 1675; sub-commr. of prizes, Bristol 1672–3; commr. for recusants, Wilts. 1675; receiver of recusant forfeitures, Norf., Suff., Cambs. and Hunts. 1680–*d.*[3]

Four generations of Clerke's family had served the crown, and in the Civil War his father's royalist sympathies were unquestionable, but timely advances to the county committee averted sequestration, 'which saddens the well-affected'. Clerke himself was in arms, finishing the war as a major of horse at the surrender of Oxford, and compounded on his own discovery for clothes and horses worth £30, £100 out on loan and his expectations in Enford, which had been settled on him at his marriage with the sister of Sir Philip Warwick*. He was 'in no manner engaged in the latter war', and went abroad in 1649, but returned on his father's death, and 'on a glimmering of hope' took part in Penruddock's rising in association with the 1st Lord Rochester. He was tried for his life, but, to the attorney-general's chagrin, Warwick's brother-in-law, a barrister, came down from London to defend him, and he was acquitted, though not released until the following year, and then only on heavy bail. Clerke may have enjoyed Lady Rochester's interest at Great Bedwyn at the general election of 1661. There was a double return, but Clerke was allowed to take his seat, and no further report was made. He is known to have served on the committee for the uniformity bill and seven others, but probably

most of the references in the Journals are to George Clerke*. His chief concern was to provide for his large family, for which his income, estimated at £800 p.a. in 1667, was insufficient. One son obtained a post in the alienations office, another became a barrister and a third a don. Clerke's name appears on both lists of the court party in 1669–71, and on the King's instructions he was given a pension of £400 p.a. on the excise by 1675. He received the government whip in September, and he was named on the working lists and in Wiseman's account in December. Shaftesbury marked him 'thrice vile', and in *A Seasonable Argument* he was described as 'an indigent commissioner of the prizes, [with] a place in the customs house at Bristol worth £200 p.a.'. This last appointment cannot be confirmed, though he may have been given a temporary appointment as compensation for the suppression of the prize office in 1673. He probably handed over the Enford property to his son Henry Clerke II* about the same time, when his name ceased to appear on the assessment commissions. He was again noted as a court supporter in both lists in 1678.[4]

It is not known whether Clerke stood at the first election of 1679. He was named as a pensioner by (Sir) Stephen Fox* in the first Exclusion Parliament, and in July was reported to have 'spent highly' at Bedwyn without much prospect of regaining his seat. In June 1680 he was appointed receiver of recusants' estates in East Anglia, but died in the following year.[5]

[1] *Wilts. Arch. Mag.* xxiii. 336; *Vis. Hants.* (Harl. Soc. lxiv), 189; *CSP Dom.* 1656–7, p. 2; 1671–2, p. 53; *Wilts. N. and Q.* ii. 534; *Al. Ox.* 282, 284, 285. [2] *CSP Dom.* 1654, f. 114. [3] Hoare, *Wilts. Salisbury* 449; Winchester corp. assembly bk. 5, f. 1; R. East, *Portsmouth Recs.* 362; *CSP Dom.* 1671–2, p. 53; 1673, p. 594; *Cal. Treas. Bks.* vi. 583. [4] G. N. Godwin, *Civil War in Hants*, 73, 339; *Cal. Comm. Comp.* 104–5; *Wilts. Arch. Mag.* xxvi. 357; SP23/74, f. 962; SP23/215/420–3; *Thurloe*, iii. 308, 371; *CSP Dom.* 1656–7, p. 2; 1671–2, p. 53; 1673, p. 594; Hoare, *Repertorium Wiltonense*, 16. [5] *HMC Ormonde*, n.s. iv. 518; *HMC Finch*, ii. 55; *Cal. Treas. Bks.* vi. 583; vii. 207.

J.P.F.

CLERKE, Henry II (c.1640–89), of Enford, Wilts. and the Inner Temple, London.

LUDGERSHALL 1685

b. c.1640, 1st *s.* of Henry Clerke I*. *educ.* I. Temple 1657. *m.* 3 Feb. 1673 (with £3,500), Hester, da. of Sir Erasmus de la Fountaine of Kirby Bellars, Leics., 1s. 1da. *suc.* fa. 1681.[1]
Clerk of entries, alienation office July 1660–*d.*[2]
Commr. for assessment, Wilts. 1664–80, 1689, j.p. 1674–June 1688, Oct. 1688–*d.*, dep. lt. 1683–June 1688, Oct. 1688–*d.*; freeman, Calne 1685–June 1688.[3]

Clerke's estate lay some seven miles from Ludgershall, where, as a Tory and a high churchman, he no doubt enjoyed the support of Lord Ailesbury (Robert Bruce*) in 1685. He served on no committees in James II's Parliament and made no recorded speeches, but was summoned to the meeting of the court caucus on 17 Nov. He avoided the lord lieutenant's questions on the repeal of the Penal Laws and Test Act in 1688 by going to London, but the King's electoral agents described him as 'a very ill man, and not to be reconciled to your Majesty's interest, except the fear of losing his office in the alienation office will engage him'. Though they expected him to be returned, Clerke was not elected to the Convention. He was confirmed in his office by the new regime on 10 June 1689, but he was buried at Enford on 30 Oct., the last of his family to sit in Parliament.[4]

[1] *Westminster Abbey Reg.* (Harl. Soc. x), 8; Wilts. RO, 413/151; *Cal. Treas. Bks.* vii. 207. [2] *CSP Dom.* 1660–1, p. 117. [3] *CSP Dom.* 1685, p. 128; PC2/72, f. 678. [4] *Cal. Treas. Bks.* viii. 431; ix. 153, 452; Wilts. RO, Enford par. reg.

J.P.F.

CLIFFORD, Thomas (1630–73), of Ugbrooke, Chudleigh, Devon.

TOTNES 1660, 1661–22 Apr. 1672

b. 1 Aug. 1630, 1st s. of Hugh Clifford of Ugbrooke by Mary, da. of Sir George Chudleigh, 1st Bt.[†], of Ashton. *educ.* Exeter, Oxf. 1647; M. Temple 1648. *m.* 27 June 1650 (with £1,000), Elizabeth (*d.* 21 Sept. 1709), da. of William Martin of Lindridge, Bishop's Teignton, and coh. to her bro. William, 7s. (4 *d.v.p.*) 8da. *suc.* fa. 1640; kntd. *c.* June 1664; *cr.* Baron Clifford of Chudleigh 22 Apr. 1672.[1]

J.p. Devon Mar. 1660–73, commr. for militia Mar. 1660, maj. of militia horse Apr. 1660–at least 1661; commr. for assessment, Devon Aug. 1660–9, Westminster 1666–9, the Household 1671; dep. lt. Devon 1661–73, commr. for loyal and indigent officers 1662; sub-commr. for prizes, London 1665–7.[2]

Gent. of the privy chamber June 1660–*d.*; commr. for sick and wounded 1664–7; asst. R. Fishing Co. 1664; commr. for Duke of Monmouth's estates 1665–70; envoy extraordinary, Denmark and ambassador extraordinary, Sweden 1665; PC 5 Dec. 1666–19 June 1673; comptroller of the Household 1666–8, treas. 1668–72; ld. of Treasury 1667–72, ld. treas. 1672–3; commr. for trade 1668–72, union with Scotland 1670–1, inquiry into land settlement [I] 1672.[3]

Clifford claimed descent from a baronial family prominent in the north country during the Middle Ages. His ancestors were living in Wiltshire in the 15th century, and produced a Member for Salisbury in 1547, but from the reign of Henry VII they also held land in Devon. His father is said to have died of an illness contracted as a colonel in the Bishops' Wars. Clifford's wardship was sold for £250, an experience which seems to have imbued him with a lasting hatred for the court of wards, 'taking

away the child and heir of the house from the mother's breast'. His maternal grandfather took up arms for the Parliament in 1642, but laid down his commission in the following year.[4]

Clifford's hereditary estate, though possibly underestimated by Samuel Pepys* at seven score pounds a year, was small and until 1663 burdened with his grandmother's jointure. His wife's family was a cadet branch of the recusant Martins of Dorset, and there is some suggestion that her uncle and guardian (who with Clifford and Henry Ford* formed a locally famous 'triumvirate of topping wits' during the Interregnum) was a crypto-Catholic. 'While the sun of monarchy was under an eclipse, these stars of the first magnitude in our hemisphere sparkled only among themselves and their familiars in their own dark orbs.' Clifford himself in later years told his astrologer that it was in October 1659 that he 'first appeared on a public account at Exeter, and gained great esteem among the people', but nothing more is known of his political activities, either local or national, till he was elected to the Convention for Totnes, some 12 miles from Ugbrooke. A moderately active Member, he was named to 16 committees, of which the most important were for the abolition of the court of wards and the attainder bill. He soon achieved prominence as a financial expert, and was appointed chairman of the committee for satisfying the public debt. In this capacity he carried to the Lords the report on moneys owing to Anthony Buller.* His maiden speech was against the imposition of double taxation on recusants, and on 15 Aug. 1660 he reverted to this theme, saying 'it was like the Egyptians to lay a double task and take away the straw'. In a debate on supply on 19 Nov. he proclaimed himself in favour of any kind of taxation, provided that the court of wards was abolished. Evidently his performance had attracted favourable attention at Court, for on 21 Dec. he was sworn a gentleman of the privy chamber.[5]

Re-elected for Totnes in 1661 with the aid of a letter from the Duke of York, though apparently not without opposition, Clifford was listed by Lord Wharton as a friend, and at once became one of the most active Members of the Cavalier Parliament. By the time of his promotion to the Upper House, he had been named to 325 committees, besides acting as teller on 20 divisions. He was concerned with the principal measures of the opening session, the corporations and uniformity bills and the bill of pains and penalties. He acted as teller (with his colleague's son, Edward Seymour*) for an unsuccessful proviso to the bill of oblivion, against which he is said to have made a notable speech, attacking the royal prerogative. When William Love* refused the sacrament, Clifford feared that he might have imbibed 'Popish principles' abroad. On 24 July he reported to the House as chairman of the committee drawing up regulations for the navy. After the recess he was named to the committee for the execution of those under attainder, and on 4 Dec. he brought in a petition on behalf of the patentees for wine licences. In 1662 he was added to the committee to consider a pamphlet against the excise, and both in this session and the next he took a leading part in preparing compensation for loyal and indigent officers. On 18 Mar. he came to blows in the House with Andrew Marvell*, who was apparently the aggressor; the occasion of their dispute is not known, though Marvell was later to describe Clifford as 'a tall louse'. Clifford's parliamentary standing was not affected by the incident; he reported the bill to prevent customs frauds and three days later carried it to the Lords. On 8 Apr. he was entrusted with an address against the Merchant Adventurers, and on 28 Apr. with managing a conference on the uniformity bill. In May he was chiefly active over the militia bill, acting as teller in two divisions and being ordered to bring in amendments, and as chairman of the committee on customs administration.[6]

By the autumn of 1662, Clifford had engaged 'the particular friendship' of Sir Henry Bennet*. Burnet's story that he had previously offered his services to Clarendon, who rejected him as a secret Papist, is improbable. In Clarendon's own account, Clifford and his friend Winston Churchill* are described as 'country gentlemen of ordinary condition and mean fortunes' who had hitherto followed the directions of Sir Hugh Pollard*, but nothing is said about his religion. Clifford's commonplace book reveals him at this date and for some years to come as an orthodox Anglican, though with strong High Church proclivities. According to one of Pepys's informants, his intimacy with Bennet arose solely from 'Clifford's coming to him and applying himself to him for favours, when he came first up to town to be a Parliament man'. Evelyn described Clifford as Bennet's creature, 'and never from him'. It was certainly Bennet who drew attention to his influence as a speaker in the House, obtained for him a grant of the logwood farm (worth about £100 p.a.), procured his admission to the inner circle of managers for the Court, and assigned him some responsibility for intercepting letters. In the 1663 session he came out against relaxing the legal penalties for eating meat in Lent and in favour of increasing clerical stipends in those hot-beds of dissent, the corporate towns. But he was also in favour

of toleration; he was named to the committees to consider defects in the Act of Uniformity and the Corporations Act, and on 25 Feb. he acted with the crypto-Catholic (Sir) Solomon Swale* as teller for the small minority of 30 who, in a House of 300, favoured the Declaration of Indulgence. As a reward, Clifford was granted the first reversion of a tellership of the Exchequer, presumably without payment, for later in the same session he took part in preparing a bill to forbid the purchase of offices. Meanwhile, he was more concerned to protect his parliamentary position among the Anglicans; he was named to the first conventicles bill, and on 4 Apr. he joined in a message of thanks to the King for his proclamation against Jesuits and popish priests. In this session he was ordered to bring in a bill for the encouragement of trade and to draft a clause restraining imports of cattle from Scotland and Ireland, a specially sore point with the west country Members whom he aspired to lead. On 10 July he attended the King with a petition from the Merchant Adventurers of Exeter for the enforcement of the Navigation Act—a sighting shot for his great campaign against the Dutch in the following year. In the spring session of 1664 he was listed as a court dependant, and took the chair in a committee on the state of trade, though many years later he was to admit to the House that 'he may probably speak out of his compass in trade, having no knowledge in it but what he has learned here'. Nevertheless on 21 Apr. he confidently reported that the 'wrongs, dishonours and indignities done to his Majesty by the subjects of the United Provinces [are] the greatest obstruction to our foreign trade', and was sent to the Lords to desire a conference on the subject. He was again named to the committees on the conventicles bill and the additional corporations bill.[7]

Clifford was knighted during the summer, and in the session that followed he was teller for the grant of £2,500,000 for war with the Dutch, describing the debate in detail in a long letter to the Hon. William Coventry*. His animosity against the Merchant Adventurers of London, who drove their principal trade with the Low Countries, was undiminished, and he opposed a bill for their relief. After the Christmas recess he was chosen to carry the estate bill of Sir Robert Carr*, Arlington's brother-in-law, to the Lords, and to ask the King to proclaim a day of fasting and prayer for victory over the Dutch. Having done as much as any man (except perhaps Sir George Downing*) to start the war, Clifford did not personally shirk the consequences. He served as a volunteer in the naval campaign of 1665, and followed it up with a diplomatic mission to the northern courts. Coventry regretted 'the absence of so considerable a man from Parliament . . . where he may be the most useful Member in the House', and he resumed his seat in the 1666 session. He again served on the committee for the Irish cattle bill under Seymour's chairmanship, but on 6 Oct. he reported to Bennet (now Lord Arlington):

> Keen as the House of Commons is for the bill against Irish cattle, yet on report of it from the committee it is ordered to be re-committed, there being some clauses so extravagant and severe as to the seizing and conviction.

He was active over the proposed prohibition of imports from France, being charged with preparing reasons for a conference with the Lords and with attending the King with the Commons' vote. He succeeded Pollard as comptroller on 28 Nov. and a few days later, by the King's command, read a despatch from Scotland announcing the defeat of the rebels there. On 11 Dec. he was approved by the House as commissioner of public accounts, and on 29 Jan. 1667 he was one of the Members appointed to attend the King with an address on behalf of merchants trading with France. He intervened unsuccessfully in the Dartmouth by-election in favour of Joseph Williamson*.[8]

Clifford was not particularly prominent in the stormy debates which followed the dismissal of Clarendon. He was named to the committees considering public accounts and restraints on juries. To the latter he gave evidence of the harshness of (Sir) John Kelyng* at the Devon assizes. On 25 Oct. 1667 Clifford and Richard Kirkby* were ordered to obtain a statement on naval intelligence from Arlington, and later he defended his patron in debate on this subject. Always reckoned a reliable friend by Lord Sandwich (Edward Montagu I*), he seems to have defended the admiral's conduct at Bergen (of which he had been an eye-witness) and to have pitched eagerly on the unfortunate Peter Pett* as general scapegoat. Clifford served on the committees for the impeachment and banishment of Clarendon, but he was against pressing the dispute with the Lords over the failure to prevent his flight. On 6 Dec. he was ordered to bring in a bill for free trade with Scotland, and three days later by the King's command he tabled a statement of arrears of poll-tax. He attacked the proposal of Sir Richard Temple* for the frequent holding of Parliaments as 'a bill of ill consequence, breeding jealousy between the King and his people'. He took part in examining the militia laws, and he was twice entrusted with drafting clauses in the wine duties bill.[9]

Clifford was now much in the public eye, but in spite of his consistent support for toleration and his hostility to the Protestant Triple Alliance, no suspicions of his religion appear to have been yet uttered, even by his enemy Marvell in private correspondence. Indeed it was not till 1671 that his guileless Anglican friend Evelyn 'suspected him a little warping to Rome'. But on 25 Jan. 1669 the King revealed his own secret conversion to Arlington and Clifford as well as to the recusant Lord Arundell of Wardour, and bade them prepare for a public declaration 'as wise men and good Catholics ought to do'. At this stage Clifford seems to have been hoping for a voluntary reunion between Canterbury and Rome, though his conversation with Arundell overheard by Sir William Bucknall* is certainly susceptible of a more sinister interpretation. In foreign affairs, he was undoubtedly the chief architect of the alliance with France. His reckless courage at this stage enabled him to outstrip the cautious Arlington in royal favour. According to the Duke of York he was 'the only minister of Charles II that served him throughout faithfully and without reproach'. In a pamphlet called *The Alarum*, which was found scattered in Westminster Hall when Parliament reassembled on 20 Oct. 1669, he was depicted as whispering absolute power to the King. In a debate on the conventicles bill on 10 Nov. he recalled the promise of toleration in the declaration of Breda. More controversial was his reference to the Swedes, partners in the Triple Alliance, as 'a mercenary people', and he was forced to explain that he used the adjective in no pejorative sense. When Ormonde's friends proposed the impeachment of Lord Orrery (Roger Boyle*), Clifford 'would not have the sword of this House . . . blunted upon offences of this nature'. On the return of the conventicles bill from the Lords with a questionable amendment reserving the royal supremacy in religion, Clifford remarked: 'We shall be puzzled when we come to the Lords at a conference if they should ask us why we will not recognise the King's supremacy'. On 10 Mar. 1670 he was instructed to inform the Lords that the Lower House agreed in principle to union with Scotland. Two days later he announced that the King had promised effective measures against both conventicles and recusants.[10]

Shortly after the end of the session Clifford left for Dover, where on 22 May he and Arlington signed the secret clauses providing for the conversion of England. Parliament met again on 24 Oct. 1670 for what was to be Clifford's last session in the Lower House. About this time he was described by an opposition satirist as 'the grandson of a Devonshire vicar, now treasurer of the Household, a commissioner of the Treasury, and chief commissioner for managing the bribe money wherewith to buy votes in the Parliament house'. As the leading figure in the Treasury commission he was no doubt responsible for an increase of 50 per cent in secret service payments between 1666 and 1671, and he was also extremely active in debate:

> We struggled with a debt after the war between two and three millions. . . . in all these straits the King spent not above half his revenue; whatever wanted, the King kept his navy in repair. The King was sensible how lands fell everywhere, and was unwilling to press you.

He was against a tax on new buildings, pointing out to his fellow cattle-breeders that the growth of London had produced a most gratifying increase in prices at Smithfield. A subsidy, he revealed, brought in only £45,000, and he favoured a land-tax, which he was forced to withdraw by 'the zeal which transports gentlemen' against it. On the re-presentations of Sir Edward Dering* he also abandoned the excise on home brewing. His attitude to bankers showed an interesting development; in April 1670 he thought they 'ought to be commended and encouraged', by the following January they had become merely 'necessary evils'. He did not neglect local interests, defending the continued exemption of tin-mines from the subsidy on the grounds that they provided many of the small vessels of Devon with cargoes as far afield as Alexandria. Clifford's horror at the proposal of John Birch* to tax church dignitaries was not his only gesture to the Anglican majority in this session; on 23 Nov. he moved to have the dissenter Jekyll sent for in custody. On the assault on Sir John Coventry* which so inconveniently delayed supply, he protested against excepting the culprits from pardon as an infringement of the prerogative. For a court spokesman he was remarkably forthcoming in the debate on the Devon by-election on 18 Jan. 1671; perhaps he was not displeased at the enforced withdrawal as court candidate of the Earl of Bath's nominee in favour of Sir Coplestone Bampfylde*, under whom he had served in the militia. As the session drew towards its close, Clifford was twice appointed to draw up reasons for conferences on supply, and on 20 Apr. he informed the House of its forthcoming prorogation.[11]

Clifford, with Seymour's co-operation as chairman of ways and means, had produced 'by far the richest harvest since the revenue had first been established.' During the long recess which followed, his influence over policy increased. He was primarily responsible for the Stop of the Exchequer, the Declaration of Indulgence and the third Dutch war. His appointment as lord treasurer ended his old friendship with Arlington. When Parliament met again in 1673 Clifford had moved to the Upper House. The test bill, which he attacked in the Lords in an impassioned speech, revealed his religious allegiance. He laid down his offices on 19 June

> before he had formed wide political connexions. What he unquestionably lacked in administrative talent, he made up in courage and sympathy; his influence was based on readiness to disburse bribes that he did not touch himself, on naturally high prerogative notions, and on a close intimacy with the royal brothers, by whom he was instructed in the Catholic secret. He was ever foremost in the imminent deadly breach . . . and his own apparently self-inflicted death merely followed a political suicide.

Clifford, whose health had begun to give way as early as 1670, died on 17 Oct., perhaps by his own hand, within four months of his retirement, and was buried in his private chapel at Ugbrooke. His descendants, as recusants, were excluded from political life till the Emancipation.[12]

[1] C. H. Hartmann, *Clifford of the Cabal*, 14, 15, 35. [2] *Parl. Intell.* 16 Apr. 1660; *Cal. Treas. Bks.* iii. 841; Nat. Maritime Mus. Southwell mss, 17/15. [3] Hartmann, 25, 26, 38; *CSP Dom.* 1664–5, p. 173; 1672, p. 40; Barbour, *Arlington*, 172; *Sel. Charters* (Selden Soc. xxviii), 183. [4] Hartmann, 6–8; J. Prince, *Devon Worthies*, 221; *CSP Dom.* 1640–1, p. 230; Grey, i. 275. [5] *Pepys Diary*, 26 Apr. 1667; Hartmann, 19–21, 24–25; Bowman diary, ff. 117, 140; *Old Parl. Hist.* xxiii. 18. [6] Adm. 2/1745, f. 30; *CSP Dom.* 1666–7, p. 518; Prince, 223; Hartmann, 26–27; Reymes diary; *Marvell* ed. Margoliouth, i. 141. [7] Hartmann, 3–5, 27, 30; Clarendon, *Life*, ii. 207–10; Burnet, i. 402; *Pepys Diary*, 26 Apr., 24 June 1667; *Cal. Cl. SP*, v. 318; *CSP Dom.* 1663–4, p. 50; Grey, i. 402; [8] Add. 32094, ff. 24–27; *CSP Dom.* 1664–5, p. 547; 166–7, pp. 187, 379. [9] *Milward*, 168; Grey, i. 78, 83; *Pepys Diary*, 25 Feb. 1666, 13 Nov. 1667; *CSP Dom.* 1668–9, p. 542; *Clarendon Impeachment*, 121. [10] *Evelyn Diary*, iii. 577; Clarke, *Jas. II*, i. 441–2; ii. 638; *CSP Dom.* 1668–9, p. 542; Hartmann, 191; Grey, i. 160, 176–7, 200, 250; ii. 397. [11] Harl. 7020, f. 42v; Witcombe, *Cavalier House of Commons*, 111; Grey, i. 267, 301, 303, 314, 316, 322, 343, 353–4, 360–1, 366, 398–9; *Dering*, 83; Browning, *Danby*, i. 274; R. Granville, *Hist. Granville Fam.* 357. [12] Witcombe, 125; Barbour, 184, 185, 204; Hartmann, 261–3; *Evelyn Diary*, iv. 21, n. 1.

J.P.F.

CLIFFORD, Lord see **BOYLE, Charles.**

CLIFTON, Clifford (1626–70), of Clifton-on-Trent, Notts.

East Retford   1659, 1661–June 1670

bap. 22 June 1626, 2nd s. and h. of Sir Gervase Clifton*, being o.s. by 2nd w. *educ.* G. Inn 1647. *m.* 4 July 1650, Frances, da. of Sir Heneage Finch,† Speaker of the House of Commons 1626, of Kensington, Mdx., 3s. (2 *d.v.p.*), 4da. Kntd. 27 Dec. 1661; *suc.* fa. in Clifton estate 1666.[1]

Commr. for militia, Notts. Mar. 1660; j.p. Notts. July 1660–d., liberties of Southwell and Scrooby 1669; dep. lt. Notts. 1661–d., capt. vol. horse 1661; commr. for assessment, Notts. 1661–d., Nottingham 1663–4, Mdx. 1663–d.[2]

FRS 1667.

Although Clifton had presumably exempted himself from the Long Parliament ordinance against Cavaliers and their sons by sitting in Richard Cromwell's Parliament, he did not stand in 1660, but in the following year he regained his seat at East Retford, where his father was high steward. He was a very active committeeman in the first half of the Cavalier Parliament, being appointed to 253 committees and acting as teller in 12 divisions. He took part in considering the corporations bill and the bill of pains and penalties, and on 17 July 1661 acted as teller against a proviso to the militia bill. He was also teller against a proviso to the poor relief bill about soldiers and their families on 17 Feb. 1662. He was appointed to carry to the Lords the estate bill of the Earl of Huntingdon, his step-mother's nephew, and served on the committee for the sectaries bill. In 1663 he was teller for committing to the whole House the bill for the better maintenance of clergymen in towns, and for the bill to reform the collection of hearth-tax. The high standing which his constant attendance and industry had earned him in the House was shown by his selection to ask the chaplain of Gray's Inn to preach on the 16th anniversary of the martyrdom of Charles I. In the Oxford session in the autumn of 1665 he supported the Government over supply, acting as teller on a motion for candles. With his father, he was thanked by the lord lieutenant for his services in securing fanatics. On the fall of Clarendon he was appointed to the committees to inquire into the sale of Dunkirk and to prepare the public accounts bill, but he was teller against the first article of the impeachment. He was appointed to the committees to examine the relief given to loyal and indigent officers as well as to the committee of public accounts, but he was still not unhelpful to the Government, acting as teller for the motion on 30 Mar. 1668 to debate supply every day. He was named to the committees on the militia laws and habeas corpus, and acted as teller against the wrecking amendment to include Roman Catholics in the conventicles bill. He was listed among the Members to be engaged for the Court by the Duke of Buckingham in 1669, and on 1 Dec. acted as teller for the Buckingham faction in rejecting the case against Lord Orrery (Roger Boyle*). He was buried at Clifton on 22 June 1670. His father's kindness to his tenants and generosity to the poor had somewhat impaired the estate, and the family trustees had to obtain a private Act to sell land and raise £4,000 portions for each of his surviving daughters.[3]

[1] J. Raine, *Par. of Blyth*, 139; *Vis. Notts.* (Thoroton Soc. rec. ser. xiii), 68; *St. Stephen Walbrook* (Harl. Soc. Reg. xlix), 63;

Thoroton, *Notts.* i. 109. [2] *Kingdom's Intell.* 7 Mar. 1661. [3] *CJ*, viii. 393, 451, 526, 584, 647; ix. 18, 90, 114; *HMC Var.* vii. 428; *HMC 8th Rep.* pt. 1 (1881), 149; *Dering*, 30.

E.R.E.

CLIFTON, Sir Gervase, 1st Bt. (1587–1666), of Clifton-on-Trent, Notts.

NOTTINGHAMSHIRE	1614, 1621, 1624, 1625
NOTTINGHAM	1626
NOTTINGHAMSHIRE	1628
EAST RETFORD	1640 (Apr.), 1640 (Nov.)–1 Jan. 1646 [new writ]
NOTTINGHAMSHIRE	1661–28 June 1666

b. 25 Nov. 1587, o. (posth.) s. of George Clifton of Clifton-on-Trent by Winifred, da. of Sir Anthony Thorold† of Marston, Leics. *educ.* St. John's, Camb. 1603; M. Temple 1607. *m.* (1) c.1608, Lady Penelope Rich (*d.* 26 Oct. 1613), da. of Robert, 1st Earl of Warwick, 1s.; (2) c.1614, Lady Frances Clifford (*d.* 22 Nov. 1627) da. of Francis Clifford†, 4th Earl of Cumberland, 1s. 4da.; (3) 5 May 1629, Mary (*d.* 19 Jan. 1631), da. of John Egioke of Egioke, Worcs., wid. of Sir Francis Leeke†, of Newark, Notts., *s.p.*; (4) 17 May 1632, Isobel (*d.* 1637), da. of Thomas Meeke of Wolverhampton, Staffs., wid. of John Hodges, Grocer, of London, *s.p.*; (5) c.1638, Anne (*d.* 1639) da. of Sir Francis South of Kelsterne, Lincs., *s.p.*; (6) 17 Feb. 1639, Jane (*d.* 17 Mar. 1656) da. of Anthony Eyre of Rampton, Notts. 2s. 3da.; (7) 17 Dec. 1656 (with £4,000), Lady Alice Hastings, da. of Henry, 5th Earl of Huntingdon, *s.p. suc.* gdfa. 1588; KB 25 July 1603; *cr.* Bt. 22 May 1611.[1]

J.p. Notts. 1609–46, July 1660–*d.*, liberties of Southwell and Scrooby 1664; sheriff, Notts. 1610–11; high steward, East Retford 1616–47, 1660–*d.*; county treasurer (north), Notts. 1625–6, dep. lt. 1626–46, c.Aug. 1660–*d.*; commr. of array, Lincs. and Notts. 1642, oyer and terminer, Midland circuit July 1660; assessment, Notts. Aug. 1660–*d.*, Nottingham 1663–4, loyal and indigent officers, Notts. 1662.[2]

Clifton was the most illustrious member of a family whose authentic history extends back to the reign of Henry II, and who provided one of the knights for Nottinghamshire in the Model Parliament. With an estate worth an easy £3,000 p.a. before the Civil War, he 'generously, hospitably and charitably entertained all, from the King to the poorest beggar', and was reckoned 'an extraordinary kind landlord and good master'. His cousin Gervase Holles* described him as

a gentleman every way worthy of his ancient extraction and deserving ancestors, having lived with as much lustre and love in his country as any in my time whatsoever, being of a nature. . . . most affable and courteous, of a disposition most noble, of good erudition, and (throughout this long and damned rebellion) of a most unshaken and unsullied loyalty to his lawful sovereigns.

A Straffordian in the Long Parliament, he sat at Oxford during the Civil War and served as commissioner of array in the Newark garrison. His heavy fine of £7,625 was paid off by 1650, and he took no part in Cavalier conspiracy during the Interregnum. His son by his first marriage was described as 'his father's greatest foil', and at the Restoration he offered £2,500 for a viscountcy with special remainder to his second son, Clifford Clifton*.[3]

At the age of 73 Clifton was returned to his ninth Parliament as knight of the shire, and listed by Lord Wharton as a friend. On 3 July 1661 the House was informed that he had received the sacrament, though not at the time appointed. A moderately active Member of the Cavalier Parliament, he was appointed to 21 committees in eight sessions, of which the most important were for security against seditious practices in 1661 and for amending the Corporations Act in 1664. As a deputy lieutenant, he was officially thanked for his services in securing fanatics during the second Dutch war. His medical attendant in his last years was the county historian Thoroton, who describes how, though 'of a sound body and a cheerful, facetious spirit . . . he left the choicest things of this world with as great pleasure as others enjoy them. He received from me the certain notice of his near approaching death, as he was wont to do an invitation of good friends to his own bowling-green.' His deathbed was attended by the rector, his former chaplain, 'to do the office of his confessor', his children, 'whom patriarch-like he particularly blessed and admonished, with the smartness and ingenuity of an excellent and well-studied orator', and his friends, 'who were not so sensible of his danger, because he entertained them after his usual manner'. He died of suppression of urine on 28 June 1666, and was buried with appropriate ceremony at Clifton, the mourners including all the principal nobility and gentry of the county, irrespective of politics.[4]

[1] C142/216/22; Vis. Notts. (Thoroton Soc. rec. ser. xiii), 68; J. T. Godfrey, Notts. Churches, Rushcliffe, 57–58, 62; CSP Dom. 1656–7, p. 279. [2] Notts. County Recs. ed. Copnall, 9, 10, 13; Foedera, viii. pt. 2, p. 145; HMC Var. vii. 390, 395; A. C. Wood, Notts. in the Civil War, 175; Hutchinson Mems. 96. [3] Trans. Thoroton Soc. xxxvii. 36–40; Thoroton, Notts. i. 108–9; CSP Dom. 1635–6, p. 11; Mems. Holles Fam. (Cam. Soc. ser. 3, lv), 181; Keeler, Long Parl. 135–6; Cal. Comm. Comp. 1318; Cal. Cl. SP, v. 3. [4] HMC Var. vii. 428; Thoroton, Notts. i. 109; Add. 38141, f. 22; Dugdale, Diary, 109.

E.R.E./J.P.F.

CLIFTON, Sir William, 3rd Bt. (1663–86), of Clifton-on-Trent, Notts.

NOTTINGHAMSHIRE 1685–May 1686

bap. 7 Apr. 1663, 3rd but o. surv. s. of (Sir) Clifford Clifton*. educ. Trinity Coll. Camb. 1677. unm. suc. fa. in Clifton estates 1670, uncle Sir Gervase Clifton, 2nd Bt., 14 Jan. 1675.
Dep. lt. Notts. 1683–d., j.p. 1685–d.
Col. (later 15 Ft.) 1685–d.[1]

Clifton, a clever, precocious and self-willed youth, was placed under the joint guardianship of his mother, the family steward, and his kinsman William Sacheverell*, who arranged a brilliant marriage with one of the daughters of the Duke of Newcastle (Henry Cavendish*). The lady was not to his taste, however, and he extricated himself from the match by making difficulties over the settlement and writing anonymous letters to Newcastle accusing himself of terrible debauchery. At the same time he assisted the elopement of his sister with a penniless Anglo-Irish baronet. His uncle, the lord chancellor (Heneage Finch I*), could only wring his hands over 'so wilful and so uncounsellable a young man . . . very skilful in dissembling'. But worse was to follow; on his mother's death, Clifton, whose conduct had so outraged the local gentry that they threatened to cudgel him, made his way to Court, where he rapidly became 'very familiar and conversant'. Still only 17, he arranged a match for himself with the daughter of William Chiffinch*, blithely undertaking to convert her to Protestantism, a task for which the lord chancellor considered him totally unequipped. Sacheverell commented that by a marriage with a Papist or reputed Papist 'he will infallibly lose both his interest and friends in these parts', and nothing came of it.[2]

With the same impetuous energy Clifton turned to politics. He was described to Lord Halifax (Sir George Savile*) as 'a young gentleman of almost incomparable natural parts, and very good acquired, accompanied with an excellent resolution, and takes all the pains imaginable to make himself popular'. Newcastle was apparently prepared to overlook Clifton's treatment of his daughter, and expressed his delight at the manner in which he confuted the elderly Whig lawyer, Edward Bigland*, in a discussion at Welbeck. A few months after the King had ordered Clifton to be added to the lieutenancy, he was urging on Secretary Jenkins the necessity of electoral preparations; but on 3 Nov. 1683 Jenkins replied that 'His Majesty thinks it not seasonable at this time for his friends to move of themselves or to join with others in order to the election of Parliament men'. Undeterred, Clifton built up such a formidable interest at Nottingham that at the next general election he was considered certain to be chosen with little or no expense. Instead, on the sudden refusal of Lord Eland he consented, at the importunity of Newcastle and Secretary Sunderland, to contest the county. Sir Scrope Howe* at once withdrew, and the other opposition candidate Richard Slater* stood down before the poll, so that in 'the most factious county in the kingdom' both seats went to the Court.[3]

Clifton was moderately active in James II's Parliament, serving on the committee of elections and privileges and on four others. Characteristically, he seconded the over-enthusiastic motion for supply on the first day of the session. On the outbreak of Monmouth's Rebellion he raised a regiment of foot, but returned to Westminster in November. He made two speeches in this session, often wrongly attributed to (Sir) Winston Churchill*. In the first he pointed out that England already had a standing army in the shape of the beefeaters – a slang expression for which the youthful colonel was gravely reproved by Thomas Howard II*. In the supply debate of 16 Nov. 1685 Clifton objected: '£200,000 is much too little. Soldiers move not without pay. No penny, no paternoster.' His regiment had been ordered to Holland in September, but on 3 Dec. Clifton was granted extended leave, which he used to court an unidentified 'great lady' in France. 'They say he had lost his nose', wrote the Puritan Roger Morrice, 'which was the occasion of his going beyond the seas.' On 10 May 1686 Whitehall was shocked by the news of his death at the early age of 23. His cousin and heir was a Roman Catholic, but the 5th baronet sat for East Retford from 1727 to 1741.[4]

[1] CSP Dom. Jan.–June 1683, p. 65. [2] HMC 8th Rep. pt. 1 (1881), 149; HMC Finch, ii. 81, 83–85. [3] Spencer mss, Millington to Halifax, 27 Aug. 1681; Clifton to Halifax, 21 Mar. 1685; Notts. RO, DDSR 219/1/14, Newcastle to Halifax, 18 Oct. 1682; CSP Dom. 1683–4, p. 73; 1685, pp. 104, 105. [4] Bramston Autobiog. (Cam. Soc. xxxii), 198; Lowther diary, ff. 26, 40; HMC 7th Rep. 499; CSP Dom. 1685, p. 400; R. Morrice, Entering Bk. 1, p. 534; HMC Downshire, i. 165.

E.R.E.

CLINKARD, Archibald (d.1696), of Sutton Valence, Kent.

MAIDSTONE   1685

s. of Gabriel Clinkard of Westminster. m. (1) 1654, Anne, da. of Sir John Mayne, 1st Bt., of Linton, 3s. (2 d.v.p.) 2da. (2) lic. 21 Jan. 1675, Margaret, da. of Thomas Tyndall of Sutton Valence, wid. of Maximilian Taylor of Sutton Valence, s.p.[1]

Capt.-lt. vol. horse, Kent Oct. 1660, capt. by 1672–bef. 1680, commr. for assessment 1673–80, j.p. ?1675–8, 1679–89, sheriff 1681–4, dep. lt. 1682–9; freeman, Maidstone 1683.[2]

Clinkard's father, head bailiff of Westminster before the Civil War, claimed kinship with the Buckinghamshire gentry. According to his own account after the Restoration he was 'plundered and tried for his life, and deprived of his place' for his loyalty, while Clinkard himself was taken prisoner at Worcester; but this is improbable, for only four days before the battle he was in custody at Gravesend, and the Council of State ordered him to be sent up to London for questioning. He may have

attended the exiled Court for a time, but he had returned to England by 1654, when he married the daughter of a zealous Kentish Royalist with Buckinghamshire connexions. His name appears on a list of royalist suspects at this time, and he was probably the 'John Clinkard' who was proposed for the order of the Royal Oak at the Restoration, with an income of £600. His father was granted arms in 1664, and Clinkard himself entered the service of the Duke of Richmond, witnessing his will in 1671.[3]

After Clinkard's second marriage he was appointed a j.p., but as a follower of Sir Vere Fane* he signed the protest against government support for Sir John Banks* at Winchelsea in 1677, and was removed from the county bench. He was restored a year later, and made a deputy lieutenant in 1682, the King having 'received a good testimony' of his loyalty. He held the shrievalty for three consecutive years, but the reason for this unusual extension of tenure is not known. In 1685 he was returned for Maidstone, six miles from Sutton Valence. A moderately active Member of James II's Parliament, he was appointed to the committees for two naturalization bills, and to those to estimate the yield of a tax on new buildings and to provide for the conveyance of fresh water to Rochester and Chatham. In 1688 he gave affirmative answers on the repeal of the Test Act and Penal Laws, and the lord lieutenant recommended his retention in local office. It was reported that he had a 'good interest' at Maidstone, but he was not named as a court candidate. His attitude towards the Revolution is not known, but though his son served as captain under Edward Dering* in Ireland, Clinkard himself was not again appointed to local office. His will, dated 24 Feb. 1696, was proved at Canterbury a month later. No other member of his family entered Parliament.[4]

[1] Harl. 1172, f. 60; Misc. Gen. et Her. (ser. 5), ix. 120; St. Paul Covent Garden (Harl. Reg. xxxi), 1; Canterbury Mar. Lic. iii. 98; London Mar. Lic. ed. Foster, 1319; Vis. Kent (Harl. Soc. liv), 172; Eton Coll. Reg. ed. Sterry, 76; M. Temple Adm. Reg. 213; Kent AO, PRC 17/79/19; London Mar. Lic. (Harl. Soc. xxiv), 184; Hasted, Kent, v. 371. [2] Stowe 744, f. 51; Harl. 1172, f. 60; Add. 21948, ff. 340, 384; Maidstone Recs. ed. Martin, 161. [3] Harl. 1172, f. 60; CSP Dom. 1651, p. 395; 1671–2, p. 283; Bodl. Rawl. A3, f. 204; Arch. Cant. xi. 271; Add. 21948, ff. 340, 384; Cal. Ct. Mins. E.I. Co. ed. Sainsbury, ix. 234. [4] Kent AO, Sa/ZB3/1; HMC Finch, ii. 44; CSP Dom. 1682, p. 370; 1683–4, p. 341.

B.D.H.

CLOBERRY, John (c.1625–88), of Upper Eldon, King's Somborne and Parchment Street, Winchester, Hants.

HEDON	3 Apr.–29 June 1660
LAUNCESTON	29 June 1660
WINCHESTER	1679 (Mar.), 1679 (Oct.), 1681

b. c.1625, 2nd s. of John Cloberry (d. 1657) of Bradstone, Devon, being 1st s. by 2nd w. Catharine, da. and h. of George Drake of Spratshayes, Littleham, Devon, wid. of Henry Ford of Bagtor, Ilsington, Devon; half-bro. of Henry Ford*. educ. M. Temple 1647. m. (1) by 1649, Margery, da. and coh. of Robert Riggs of Fareham, Hants, wid. of John Erlisman of Calbourne, I.o.W., s.p.; (2) lic. 7 Apr. 1662, Anne (d. 25 Jan. 1667), da. of William Cranmer, Merchant Adventurer, of Rotterdam, Holland, wid. of Nathaniel Wyche, merchant, of Surat, India, 1s. d.v.p. 6da. Kntd. 7 June 1660.[1]

Maj. of ft. by 1651, lt.-col. by 1659; col. of horse 1659–Oct. 1660; capt. Prince Rupert's Horse 1667; lt.-col. Queen Dowager's Horse (later 6 Dgn. Gds.) 1685–6.[2]

Commr. for assessment, Devon 1657, Aug. 1660–1, Clackmannan and Stirling 1657, Jan. 1660, Hants 1667–80, Winchester 1679–80, militia, Cornw. Mar. 1660, sewers, Westminster Aug. 1660; freeman, Winchester 1669; j.p. Hants 1679–d., dep. lt. 1680–d.[3]

Cloberry was descended from an undistinguished gentry family which had held Bradstone since the 15th century, and claimed kinship with George Monck*. He entered the Commonwealth army after the execution of Charles I and, serving under Monck in Scotland, achieved rapid promotion. He was brought over to the Stuart cause by his brother-in-law, John Otway*, in the summer of 1659. He assisted in the purge of republican officers, and was sent with Ralph Knight* to negotiate with the committee of safety in London in November. On the second return of the Rump Monck sent him to demand the readmission of the secluded Members. His popularity in the army, due to his support of the soldiers' demands for an indemnity and the confirmation of land purchases, was particularly useful to Monck at this juncture.[4]

At the general election of 1660 Cloberry was elected at Hedon, presumably on the interest of Hugh Bethell*, and was involved in double returns at Launceston and St. Mawes. Marked as a friend on Lord Wharton's list to be managed by Sir Wilfred Lawson*, he was not active in the Convention, though recognized as one of Monck's mouthpieces in the House. He was named to only 12 committees, but these included the important drafting committee to prepare bills in accordance with the delaration of Breda and the committee to consider the land purchases bill. Doubtless a court supporter, he was given a pension of £600 p.a. and knighted at the Restoration. On 22 June he seconded the motion of (Sir) Thomas Clarges* for putting into effect the grant of £20,000 already voted for Monck, and was appointed to the committee to recommend 'the surest and speediest way'. A week later the Launceston election was resolved in his favour, whereupon he gave up his seat at Hedon. He continued to concern himself with his

men, serving on the committees to state the debts of the army and navy and to consider the bill enabling soldiers to exercise trades in corporate towns. After the recess his committees included those on the bills for the suppression of profanity, the prevention of marital separation, and the taking of public accounts. On 15 Dec. he acted as teller against a proviso to the bill abolishing the court of wards intended to safeguard a claim of William Powell*.[5]

Cloberry is unlikely to have stood in 1661. His first wife came from a minor Hampshire gentry family, and by 1667 he had acquired manorial property in the county and a house in Winchester. He may have considered standing for the city as early as 1669, when he took out his freedom, and he was eventually returned unopposed to all three Exclusion Parliaments. Shaftesbury marked him 'base' in 1679 and on 10 Mar. he questioned the validity of the House's claim to choose their own Speaker without a right of veto by the crown:

> I will not say that we have no power in this matter, but that we have right is not yet proved. I had rather give my eyes, hands and head than part with this power if it be your right; but if it be a flower of the crown, I would rather die than take it away. . . . Therefore, I move that the thing may be thoroughly debated, and see our own title to it, and not carry a dough-baked representation to the King that we cannot maintain.

When the King remained obdurate against Edward Seymour* Cloberry urged the House to choose another Speaker. An active Member of the first Exclusion Parliament, he was appointed to 18 committees, including the committee of elections and privileges, and those to review expiring laws, to bring in a bill for regulating elections, to consider the bill summoning Danby to give himself up, and to inspect the Journals daily. On 12 Apr. he was given leave to go into the country, but he seems to have returned by the end of the month, for he was appointed to committees for examining the disbandment accounts, preventing illegal exactions and inquiring into the shipping of artillery to Portsmouth. Presumably, therefore, he either paired or deliberately abstained from the division on the first exclusion bill. He was moderately active in the second Exclusion Parliament, with no speeches and only seven committees, including those to draft the address undertaking to defend the Protestant religion at home and abroad, and to bring in a bill for uniting Protestants. In the Oxford Parliament he was named only to the elections committee.[6]

Cloberry stood for re-election in 1685 with the support of the lord lieutenant of Hampshire (Edward Noel*), but was persuaded to desist on the eve of the poll in favour of the official court candidate, Roger L'Estrange*. He served as a volunteer against the Duke of Monmouth's forces at Sedgemoor, and Lord Lumley chose him as second-in-command of a new cavalry regiment. Ill health obliged him to resign his commission in the following year. He died of fever and dropsy at the age of 63, and was buried in Winchester Cathedral on 31 Jan. 1688 beneath a grotesquely ugly memorial. The claims to a great share in the Restoration made in his epitaph have also been derided, perhaps with less justice. His two eldest daughters were already married to the Tory politicians Sir Charles Holte* and William Bromley†, the future Speaker, and the others also made good matches with the aid of £4,000 portions. A nephew was returned for Truro in 1695.[7]

[1] *Vis. Devon*, ed. Vivian, 201; *Hants Mar. Lic.* 1607–40, p. 82; *Vis. Hants* (Harl. Soc. lxiv), 155; Guildhall RO, 10091/25; R. E. C. Waters, *Chesters of Chicheley*, 418–20. [2] *CSP Dom.* 1685, p. 290. [3] C181/7/37; Winchester corp. assembly bk. 6, f. 45. [4] Lysons, *Devon*, 61; *Devon Protestation Returns* ed. Howard, 366; Barwick, *Life*, 161–2, 187–8, 222. [5] *Cal. Cl. SP*, v. 20; *Cal. Treas. Bks.* i. 242; Bowman diary, f. 20v; *CJ*, viii. 72. [6] *VCH Hants*, iii. 212; iv. 477; v. 219; J. Milner, *Winchester*, ii. 216; Grey, vi. 420, 433. [7] *CSP Dom.* 1685, pp. 96, 97; Barwick, 275–7; Waters, 419; *Hants Par. Reg.* iv. 17.

P.W.

CLOPTON, Sir John (1638–1719), of Clopton, Stratford-on-Avon, Warws.

WARWICK 1679 (Mar.)

b. 14 Oct. 1638, 1st s. of Thomas Clopton of Clopton by Eglantine, da. of John Keyte of Ebrington, Glos. *m.* 1662, Barbara (*d.* 10 Dec. 1692), da. and h. of Sir Edward Walker, garter king of arms 1645–77, 6s. (3 *d.v.p.*) 4da. *suc.* fa. 1643; kntd. 6 July 1662.[1]

Commr. for assessment, Warws. 1661–80, 1689–90, j.p. 1668–*d.*, dep. lt. by 1680–7, 1689–?*d.*; recorder, Stratford 1684–1709.[2]

Clopton's family had resided on the estate from which they took their name since the 13th century. They provided a knight of the shire for Gloucestershire in 1346, but their parliamentary record was intermittent. Clopton's father died early in the Civil War, and he himself came of age only in 1659. He married the daughter of a Cavalier exile and was clearly a court supporter; but before the exclusion crisis he was on friendly terms with Thomas Mariet*, and he was involved with the republican engineer Yarranton in an ambitious scheme to revive the ill-fated project of William Sandys* for canalizing the Avon in order to develop Stratford as a port and an industrial centre.[3]

Clopton was returned for Warwick at the first general election of 1679 with the support of Lord Brooke (Fulk Greville*). Shaftesbury classed him as 'doubtful' for the first Exclusion Parliament. He

was appointed to no committees and given leave to go into the country on 29 Apr., but he is said to have voted against committing the bill. He is not known to have stood again, though he succeeded Thomas Lucy* as recorder of Stratford under the new charter. Presumably he opposed James II's religious policy, for he signed the letter to Sunderland of 16 Oct. 1688 in which the deputy lieutenants declared their inability to resume office. 'A person of eminent loyalty and of great interest in his country', he died on 13 Apr. 1719 and was buried with his ancestors at Stratford, the last of the family to sit in Parliament.[4]

[1] *Vis. Warws.* (Harl. Soc. lxii), 88–89; R. B. Wheler, *Hist. Stratford*, 48–49. [2] Warws. RO, QS1/1/26; *VCH Warws.* iii. 253. [3] Dugdale, *Warws.* 697–9; Add. 34730, f. 105; *VCH Warws.* iii. 238. [4] SP31/4/131; Dugdale, 700; Wheler, 49.

A.M.M.

COATES, Thomas (*d.*1686), of Reading, Berks.

READING 13 Mar.–23 June 1685, 27 June 1685–c. June 1686

m.(1) 10 Apr. 1655, Elizabeth Johnson of Reading, 1da.; (2) by 1669, Mary (*d.* May 1701), da. of John Millingate of the Grange, Dummer, Hants, wid. of Henry Doyley of Turville, Bucks., *s.p.*[1]

Asst. Reading 1659, alderman 1662–*d.*, mayor 1666–7, freeman 1681.[2]

Coates was an innkeeper who acted as postmaster of Reading under the Protectorate, and later provided a coach service to London. Presumably a Royalist in the first Civil War, he declared in 1656 that 'he had drawn his sword these 13 years against the Presbyterians and would not sheath it yet'. He was appointed to the bench by the commissioners for corporations, and was active in the government interest during the exclusion crisis. He was court candidate in 1681, but gave up the contest owing to 'the great disparity of votes'. In 1683 when he had 'the reputation of a loyal man', he took part in dispersing a Whig meeting called by Lord Lovelace (John Lovelace*) and attended by John Blagrave* and Nathan Knight*. He stood again in 1685 and was returned with John Breedon*. However, the Whig candidates Sir Henry Fane and Sir William Rich* petitioned, and the House declared the election void. At the ensuing by-election Coates headed the poll, but he left no trace on the records of James II's Parliament. In March 1686 Coates, as senior alderman, together with the recorder, brought down the new charter, but he died soon afterwards, letters of administration being granted to his daughter on 8 July.[3]

[1] Berks. RO, Reading, St. Lawrence par. reg.; *VCH Hants*, iii. 370; W. D. Bayley, *House of D'Oyly*, 75. [2] *Thurloe*, v. 314; *CSP*

Dom. 1660–1, p. 98, July–Sept. 1683, p. 389; Berks. RO, Reading corp. diary, 14 Feb. 1659, 27 May 1662; freedoms reg. f. 385. ³ *Thurloe*, v. 314; information from Miss Maplesden, Reading; *CSP Dom.* 1680–1, pp. 136–7, 166–7; July–Sept. 1683, p. 389; corp. diary, 9 Feb. 1681, 8 Mar. 1686; *CJ*, ix. 716, 746; *HMC 11th Rep. VII*, 199; Prob. 6/62/116.

L.N./G.J.

COKE, John I (1635–71), of Holkham, Norf.

KING'S LYNN   18 Mar. 1670–1 Aug. 1671

bap. 8 Sept. 1635, 6th but o. surv. s. of John Coke of Mileham by Merriel, da. and h. of Anthony Wheatley of Hill Hall, Holkham. *educ.* I. Temple 1652–7; travelled abroad c.1657–64. *unm. suc. fa.* 1661.[1]

J.p. Norf. July 1660–*d.*, commr. for oyer and terminer, Norfolk circuit 1661, assessment Norfolk 1661–9, loyal and indigent officers 1662; freeman, King's Lynn 1670.[2]

Coke's great-grandfather was granted arms in 1566, but it was of course his grandfather, Sir Edward Coke† (1552–1634), who founded the fortunes of the family and began a notable parliamentary record as MP for Aldeburgh in 1589. His father took the side of Parliament during the Civil War, serving on local commissions during the Commonwealth and Protectorate, and in 1653 inherited most of the family estate, comprising 60 manors in Norfolk alone, besides large estates in Hertfordshire, Suffolk and Berkshire, valued at £8,200 p.a. They were, however, heavily mortgaged through the extravagance and mismanagement of his predecessors. At the Restoration he was proposed as a knight of the Royal Oak, when his Norfolk estate was grossly undervalued at £1,000 p.a. Coke himself was a great traveller, telling Philip Skippon*, who met him at Florence in 1664, that he was on his way to Constantinople. Meanwhile he entrusted the stewardship of his estate to his 'close friend', Andrew Fountaine*, who was said to have saved him from drowning. But when Coke embarked on marriage negotiations in 1669 for the daughter of Sir Nicholas Crisp*, many of the title-deeds could not be produced, and Fountaine was discovered to have converted £20,000 to his own use. In the following year Coke was returned unopposed for Lynn on the family interest; but he took no known part in the Cavalier Parliament. He died on 1 Aug. 1671, and was buried at Holkham. He bequeathed Holkham as well as the property entailed by his great-grandfather to his cousin Robert Coke*.[3]

¹ *Vis. England and Wales Notes* ed. Crisp, viii. 110–12; *HMC Lords*, i. 115. ² *Lynn Freemen*, 178. ³ Blomefield, *Norf.* ix. 238; C. W. James, *Coke Fam. and Descendants*, 96–107; *HMC Lords*, ii. 255; Churchill, *Coll. Voyages and Travels*, (1746), vi. 646; PCC 129 Penn.

E.C.

COKE, John II (c.1653–92), of Melbourne, Derbys. and Melton Mowbray, Leics.

DERBY   1685, 1689

b. c.1653, o.s. of Thomas Coke† of Gray's Inn and Melbourne by Mary, da. of Richard Pope of Woolstaston, Salop. *educ.* Christ Church Oxf. 1669; G. Inn 1669. *m.* 15 June 1672, Mary (*d.* 1680), da. and h. of Sir Thomas Leventhorpe, 4th Bt., of Shingehall, Sawbridgeworth, Herts., 3s. (1 *d.v.p.*) 4da. *suc. fa.* 1656.[1]

Commr. for assessment, Derbys. 1673–80, Derbys., Herts. and Leics. 1689–90; dep. lt. Derbys. and Leics. 1680–?86, Leics. 1689–*d.*, Derbys. 1690–?*d.*; capt. of militia ft. Derbys. aft. 1680–?86, j.p. 1682–7, ?1689–*d.*[2]

Gent. usher to Queen Catherine of Braganza 1685–?89.[3]

Capt. Princess Anne's Ft. June–Dec. 1685; lt.-col. of horse, regt. of William, Lord Cavendish† Dec. 1688–9.[4]

Coke's ancestors, who were not related to Chief Justice Coke and the Longford family, were established in Derbyshire by the reign of Edward III. His grandfather, Sir John Coke, first entered Parliament in 1621 and served as secretary of state from 1625 to 1640. His father, a younger son, was returned for Leicester at both elections of 1640; a Royalist, he sat at Oxford in 1644 and was fined £500 for his delinquency. He was arrested as a conspirator in 1651, and saved his life by a voluminous and detailed confession of his activities and associates. On succeeding to the Melbourne estate, valued at £850 p.a., he paid a further £2,200 as composition. During Coke's long minority the manor of Melton Mowbray was purchased, and the Hertfordshire property which his wife inherited in 1679 brought his annual income up to £3,000. An opponent of exclusion, he was defeated by Sir William Hartopp* in the Leicestershire by-election of April 1679, and again at Derby, eight miles from Melbourne, in 1681. After the Rye House Plot he forwarded to the Government charges of dangerous words said to have been uttered by George Vernon*, one of his opponents.[5]

On the accession of James II Coke's loyalty was recognized with a place at Court. He prepared to contest Leicestershire again, but probably withdrew before the poll. He was successful at Derby, but he did not become an active Member of James II's Parliament. He was appointed only to the committees to report on expiring laws and to estimate the yield of a tax on new buildings. On the Duke of Monmouth's invasion he was commissioned in the regiment of Lord Ferrers; but when he returned to Westminster he went into opposition. When James insisted on retaining the Roman Catholic officers in the army, Coke seconded the motion of the Hon. Thomas Wharton* for a debate, saying: 'We are all Englishmen, and we ought not to be frighted out of our duty by a few high words'. None ventured to excuse this remark, though he asked pardon of the King and the House, and his loyalty was attested by Sir Hugh Cholmley* and other Members. On the motion of Lord Preston (Sir Richard Grahme*), he was sent to the Tower, but released on the prorogation of Parliament a few days later.[6]

Coke was of course deprived of his commission, but his name still appears in the court list of 1687, and when he was recommended by the royal electoral agents, rather desperately, as a candidate for the abortive election of 1688, they declared that he was 'under the influence of the queen dowager, as holding another place or pension from her'. At the Revolution he raised a troop of horse for the Protestant cause, and was made second-in-command of Lord Cavendish's regiment. He was re-elected for Derby at the modest cost of some £25, and voted to agree with the Lords that the throne was not vacant. No committee work in the Convention can be certainly assigned to him, though he was still in London as late as May 1689; but the possibility of confusion with William Cooke* cannot be ruled out. William III gave him a regiment, but he resigned his commission in the summer, either through ill health or inability to accept the change in regime. He went abroad soon afterwards and died in Geneva in 1692. His son represented the county in five Parliaments under William and Anne.[7]

[1] J. T. Coke, *Coke of Trusley*, 69–70; Clutterbuck, *Herts.* iii. 209. [2] *HMC 7th Rep.* 409; *HMC Cowper*, ii. 358. [3] *Wood's Life and Times* (Oxf. Hist. Soc. xxvi), 170. [4] *HMC Downshire*, i. 54; *HMC Cowper*, ii. 350. [5] Keeler, *Long Parl.* 137; *Cal. Comm. Comp.* 1844–9; D. Underdown, *Royalist Conspiracy*, 20, 47; Nichols, *Leics.* iii. 784*; *Reresby Mems.* 398; Coke (Melbourne) mss 111b/1; Add. 6705, f. 101; *CSP Dom.* July–Sept. 1683, p. 182. [6] *HMC Rutland*, ii. 85; *Reresby Mems.* 398, 403; Grey, vii. 369–70; *CJ*, ix. 760; *Wood's Life and Times*, 170; *HMC Downshire*, i. 54. [7] *Hatton Corresp.* (Cam. Soc. n.s. xxiii), 120; *HMC Cowper*, ii. 350–7; Coke, 70.

E.R.E.

COKE, Richard (1622–69), of Thorington, Suff.

DUNWICH   1661–Nov. 1669

bap. 8 Sept. 1622, 2nd but 1st surv. s. of Henry Coke† of Thorington by Margaret, da. and h. of Richard Lovelace of Kingsdown, Kent. *educ.* King's, Camb. 1637. *m.* lic. 26 June 1647, Mary, da. of Sir John Rous of Henham, Suff., 1s. 1da. *suc.* fa. 1661.[1]

J.p. Suff. July 1660–*d.*, commr. for assessment Aug. 1660–*d.*; freeman, Dunwich 1661; dep. lt. Suff. by 1667–*d.*[2]

Coke's father was the fifth son of Sir Edward Coke†, who settled Thorington on him in 1620. He represented Dunwich, four miles from Thorington, in the Short and Long Parliaments until disabled as a Royalist and fined £300. Nothing is known of

the activities of Coke himself during this period, but he was later described as 'an active honest Royalist', and proposed for the order of the Royal Oak, when his income was estimated at £1,000 p.a.[3]

Coke was returned for Dunwich with his brother-in-law, John Rous I*, in 1661, doubtless as a court supporter. An inactive Member of the Cavalier Parliament, he was appointed to the committee of elections and privileges in two sessions, and to 16 others, of which the most important were to consider the uniformity bill (3 July 1661) and the charges against Lord Mordaunt (25 Oct. 1667). His three recorded speeches in 1668 show that he was a strong Churchman. In Suffolk, he said,

> many parsons there had altered the liturgy from 'as *many* as are here present' to 'as *few* as are here present'.

During a debate on the King's speech on 8 Apr. he moved that 'dissenters should bring in their proposals to the House and show their reasons why they do dissent from the government established'. On 7 May he pointed out that Sir Robert Howard*, in a list of bills left unfinished by the House, had omitted the conventicles bill. He was buried at St. Peter Hungate, Norwich on 11 Nov. 1669.[4]

[1] *Vis. Eng. and Wales Notes* ed. Crisp, viii. 108–11. [2] *CSP Dom.* 1667, p. 85. [3] Keeler, *Long Parl.* 136–7; C. W. James, *Coke Fam. and Descendants*, 112–20; *Cal. Comm. Adv. Money*, 246; *Cal. Comm. Comp.* 96. [4] Grey, i. 97; *Milward*, 248, 299.

P.W.

COKE, Robert (c.1651–79), of Thorington, Suff. and Holkham, Norf.

KING'S LYNN   21 Apr. 1675

b. c.1651, o.s. of Richard Coke*. *educ.* Queens', Camb. 1667. *m.* 26 Nov. 1674 (with £7,000), Lady Anne Osborne (*d.* 5 Aug. 1722), da. of Sir Thomas Osborne*, 1st Duke of Leeds, 2s. 1da. *suc.* fa. 1669, cos. John Coke I* 1671.[1]

Commr. for assessment, Norf. 1673–*d.*, Suff. 1677–*d.*; j.p. Norf. 1673–*d.*, Suff. 1674–*d.*; dep. lt. Norf. 1673–*d.*; freeman, King's Lynn 1674; sheriff, Norf. 1676–7.[2]

On succeeding to the vast Holkham estate, Coke embarked on prolonged litigation with Andrew Fountaine*, his cousin's unfaithful steward. He married 'for perfect love' in 1674, allowing his father-in-law, the lord treasurer, to name his own terms for the settlement, and consequently imposing on the estate a jointure of £1,500 p.a., more than twice the usual rate for a portion of £7,000. When Sir Francis North* was made a judge, thereby creating a vacancy in the family borough of King's Lynn, Coke at once took out his freedom and stood in the ensuing by-election as a court candidate against Simon Taylor*, a prominent local vintner. After an expensive campaign which lasted five months he was elected to the Cavalier Parliament, and Lord Treasurer Danby induced Taylor to drop his petition in return for the reimbursement of his electoral expenses. The double burden, amounting to £10,000, was too much for Coke's finances, and, according to *A Seasonable Argument*, he could, only evade his creditors by claiming parliamentary privilege. Eventually Danby lent him £5,000 at the standard rate of 6 per cent, and personally supervised the reorganization of his estate.[3]

Coke naturally appeared as a potential court supporter in the working lists. Shaftesbury marked him 'doubly vile', but Sir Richard Wiseman* found that he needed 'to be spoke to to attend', and he was named to only four committees. His estate bill was steered through committee by his colleague, Robert Wright*. He was appointed to the committee of elections and privileges in the penultimate session of the Parliament, and was included in both lists of the court party. With his brother-in-law Lord Latimer (Edward Osborne*) he acted as teller for the unsuccessful motion of 21 Dec. 1678 to omit the word 'treacherously' from the impeachment of Danby. He died of smallpox on 19 Jan. 1679, and was buried at Tittleshall, leaving £4,000 of election bills still unpaid. The next Coke of Holkham to enter Parliament was his grandson, who sat for the county as a Whig from 1722 until raised to the peerage six years later.[4]

[1] *Vis. England and Wales Notes* ed. Crisp, viii. 110–12; *Bulstrode Pprs.* 271–2. [2] *Lynn Freemen*, 182. [3] C. W. James, *Coke Fam. and Descendants*, 111–17; North, *Lives*, i. 121; *HMC Hastings*, ii. 166; Browning, *Danby*, ii. 36–37; *HMC 6th Rep.* 389. [4] James, 127–8; *CJ*, ix. 433; Add. 37911, f. 3.

E.C.

COKE, Sir Robert, 2nd Bt. (1645–88), of Longford, Derbys.

DERBYSHIRE 1685

bap. 29 Apr. 1645, 2nd but 1st surv. s. of Sir Edward Coke, 1st Bt., of Longford by Catherine, da. and coh. of Sir William Dyer of Great Staughton, Hunts. *educ.* Jesus, Camb. 1662. *m.* settlement 2 Sept. 1663, Sarah (*d.* 1686), da. and coh. of Thomas Barker of Albrightlee, Salop, *s.p. suc.* fa. by 1669.[1]

J.p. Derbys. 1670–*d.*, dep. lt. 1671–*d.*, sheriff 1671–2, commr. for assessment 1673–80, recusants 1675, capt. of militia ft. by 1680–*d.*, commr. for charitable uses 1682.[2]

Coke's grandfather, the sixth son of Sir Edward Coke†, married the heiress of Longford. His father, created a baronet in 1641, appears to have aimed at neutrality in the Civil War. He was named to the committee for the midland association in 1642, but was subsequently sequestrated by the county com-

mittee. He never compounded, however, and in 1646 was appointed sheriff and assessment commissioner. But he took no further part in local government till 1657, after which he served on taxation commissions till his death. Coke himself was a Tory, who forwarded to the Government in 1683 a charge of dangerous words against George Vernon*. He was returned for the county in 1685 with the support of the Duke of Newcastle (Henry Cavendish*), but was probably listed among the Opposition. His only committee in James II's Parliament was on the bill to encourage shipbuilding. He was buried at Longford on 15 Jan. 1688, leaving under his will an endowment for 12 almshouses. His brother, the last of this branch of the family, never entered Parliament.[3]

[1] *Vis. Eng. and Wales Notes* ed. Crisp, viii. 114. [2] J. C. Cox, *Three Centuries of Derbys. Annals.* i. 40, 173; *HMC 7th Rep.* 409; Add. 36663, f. 348. [3] Cox, *Churches of Derbys.* iii. 195; *Cal. Comm. Comp.* 47; *CSP Dom.* July–Sept. 1683, p. 182; 1685, p. 105.

E.R.E.

COKER, Robert (c.1617–98), of Mappowder, Dorset.

DORSET 1656, 1660

b. c.1617, 1st s. of William Coker of Mappowder by Jane, da. of William Williams of Herringston. *educ.* Magdalen Hall, Oxf. 1635; M. Temple 1638. *m.* (1) 6 Jan. 1642, Joan (*d.* 29 Oct. 1653), da. of John Browne† of Frampton, 1da.; (2) Mary, da. of Edward Hooper of Boveridge, wid. of John Brune of Athelhampton, 5s. 1da. *suc.* fa. 1656.[1]

Capt. of ft. (parliamentary) 1643, lt.-col. 1645; gov. Weymouth 1645–7; commr. for sequestration, Dorset by 1646–50, j.p. by 1646–July 1688, Nov. 1688–*d.*, sheriff 1646–7; freeman, Weymouth 1648; commr. for militia, Dorset 1648, 1649, 1655, 1659, Mar. 1660, assessment 1649, 1657, Jan. 1660–80, 1689–90, oyer and terminer, Western circuit July 1660; pressing seamen, Dorset 1665, capt. of militia horse 1667–at least 1678, dep. lt. 1672–June 1688, Oct. 1688–*d.*, commr. for recusants 1675.[2]

Coker's ancestors had resided at Mappowder since the reign of Henry V, but their parliamentary record was limited to providing an MP for Shaftesbury in 1559. Coker's father, a royalist commissioner, was fined £280 on an estate valued at £220 p.a.; but Coker himself, perhaps under the influence of his first wife's family, took the other side; hence most of his father's fine was appropriated to his own arrears of pay.[3]

Coker was returned for the county at the general election of 1660, but in the Convention he served only on the committees for confirming the privileges of Parliament and for the prevention of profanity. He obtained leave to go down to the country on 29 Aug. and showed no further interest in Parliament, though he remained very active as j.p. and militia officer, not without an acid comment on the inconvenience caused by the absence of so many deputy lieutenants in Parliament time. With George Fulford*, Coker was officially commended by the Council for his good work in mustering the militia to repel an imaginary French invasion during the Popish Plot hysteria; but the Government's real opinion of this unnecessary efficiency is shown by the comment against his name on a militia list some two years later: 'to be suspected'. His standing in the county is illustrated by the choice of his house for the meeting of gentlemen both of the eastern and western parts which resulted in the unanimous adoption of Thomas Strangways* and Thomas Freke I* for the first Exclusion Parliament. His replies to James II's questionnaire on the repeal of the Test Act and Penal Laws were negative, and he was dropped from the lieutenancy and the commission in 1688. He took an active part in bringing over the Dorset militia to William of Orange. He died on 19 Sept. 1698, aged 82, and was buried at Mappowder. His son stood unsuccessfully for Dorchester in 1700, but no later member of this branch of the family entered Parliament.[4]

[1] Hutchins, *Dorset*, ii. 303; iii. 723, 731; *Vis. Dorset*, (Harl. Soc. xx), 30. [2] C. H. Mayo, *Dorset Standing Committee*, 8, 9, 208, 301–2; Christie, *Shaftesbury*, i. p. xxxviii; *Weymouth Minute Bk.* (Dorset Recs. Soc. i), 204; PR030/23, bdle. 7, no. 560; Add. 31948, f. 116; *Som. and Dorset N. and Q.* xxviii. 78. [3] Hutchins, iii. 723; *Cal. Comm. Comp.* 799, 1072. [4] C. A. F. Meekings, *Dorset Hearth-Tax*, 117; Add. 31947, f. 176; Dorset RO, D124, letter of Thomas Strangways, 29 Jan. 1679; Hutchins, i. 606; iii. 731; Churchill College, Camb., Erle-Drax mss.

M.W.H./J.P.F.

COLCHESTER, Sir Duncombe (1630–94), of Westbury-on-Severn and the Wilderness, Abbinghall, Glos.

BERE ALSTON 1681
GLOUCESTER 1689

b. 26 Sept. 1630, 1st s. of Richard Colchester of Westbury by 1st w. Jane, da. of John Duncombe of Deddington, Oxon. *educ.* Northampton (Mr Denton) 1638–40; Charterhouse 1640–1; Camberwell (Mr Caradine) 1641. *m.* 19 July 1655 (with £2,500), Elizabeth, da. of John Maynard I* of Gunnersbury, Mdx., 2s. 3da. *suc.* fa. 1643; kntd. 9 Nov. 1674.[1]

Commr. for militia, Glos. and Gloucester Mar. 1660, capt. of militia horse, Glos. Apr. 1660; commr. for assessment, Glos. 1661–80, Gloucester 1677–80, Glos. and Gloucester 1689–90; j.p. Glos. Sept. 1660–82, 1689–*d.*, dep. lt. 1670–81, 1689–*d*; verderer, Forest of Dean 1668–*d.*, commr. for inquiry 1673, 1679, 1683, 1692; alderman, Gloucester 1672–*d.*, mayor 1674–5; commr. for recusants, Glos. 1675.[2]

Capt. of ft. regt. of Marquess of Worcester (Henry Somerset*) 1667.

Colchester came of a minor gentry family of Worcestershire origin. His grandfather acquired lands in Gloucestershire, and his father, a cursitor and later a six clerk in Chancery, who had his arms confirmed in 1636, added to the estate, buying the manor of Westbury in 1641 with the profits derived from his offices and judicious money-lending. He was apparently in arms for the King at the siege of Gloucester and a payment of £600 to the county committee failed to save the estate from sequestration. Colchester himself was accused of fighting for the King in the second Civil War but the charge may have been merely due to the malice of a litigious relative, and no composition was exacted. At the Restoration Colchester signed the address of welcome to the King and was nominated a knight of the Royal Oak, his estate being valued at £800 p.a. He was one of the four signatories to the proposals for redefining the rights of the crown and the commoners in the Forest of Dean, which were largely embodied in the Act of 1668. Appointed alderman of Gloucester under the new charter of 1672, he was knighted during his mayoralty two years later.[3]

In 1681 Colchester was returned for Bere Alston, his father-in-law's borough, but left no trace on the records of the Oxford Parliament. Nevertheless in June 'an immediate order' was received from the King for the dismissal of Colchester from the lieutenancy. There is no evidence that he stood in 1685, but in 1688 he put himself forward for the county. As early as February the Duke of Beaufort reported 'that the general vogue was for Sir John Guise* and Sir Duncombe Colchester', and at the county court in September Colchester was 'amongst the freeholders in person'. The results of his efforts are not known, but in 1689 he was returned for Gloucester unopposed. He was a moderately active member of the Convention, being named to 12 committees, of which the most important was to report on the state of the revenue. On 21 Nov. he acted as teller for the motion adjourning all committees in order to expedite supply. When (Sir) William Leveson Gower* declared that he was 'for taking out all the deer in this King's park that were in King James's park', such as Commissary Shales, Colchester added: 'If you turn out the deer, it will do you no good unless you turn out the keeper too', whereupon some Members asked, 'Does he mean the King?'. He was named to the committee on the bill to restore corporations, and supported the disabling clause.[4]

Colchester probably did not stand again. He died on 25 May 1694 and was buried at Westbury. His eldest son represented Gloucestershire in the Whig interest in 1701 and 1702.[5]

[1] Glos. RO, D36/A1, Colchester jnl. 1, ff. 9, 14, 34, 41, 45; D36/F/A3–4; Kensington Par. Reg. 75; Vis. Glos. ed. Fenwick and Metcalfe, 45. [2] Parl. Intell. 9 Apr. 1660; Cal. Treas. Bks. vi. 196, 470; vii. 962; ix. 1156; C.E. Hart, Royal Forest, 169, 173, 180, 181, 187; Gloucester Guildhall, common council bks. 1656–86, ff. 498, 621; 1690–1700, f. 99. [3] G. E. Aylmer, King's Servants, 295–300; Cal. Comm. Adv. Money, 648, 727, 837–840; Glos. N. and Q. i. 165–6; Hart, 166. [4] CSP Dom. 1680–1, p. 319; Bath mss, Thynne pprs. 15, f. 110; 24, f. 41; Grey, ix. 464. [5] Rudder, Glos. 794.

B.D.H.

COLCHESTER, Visct. see SAVAGE, Richard.

COLCLOUGH, Sir Caesar, 2nd Bt. (1623–84), of Greenham, Thatcham, Berks. and Tintern Abbey, co. Wexford.

NEWCASTLE-UNDER-LYME 1661

bap. 23 Nov. 1623, 1st s. of Sir Adam Colclough, 1st Bt. [I] of Tintern Abbey by Anne, da. of Sir Robert Rich, master in Chancery. *m.* 5 June 1647, Frances, da. of Sir Francis Clarke of Hitcham, Bucks. and North Weston, Thame, Oxon., 1s. 1da. *suc.* fa. 4 Apr. 1637.[1]

Commr. for assessment, Berks. 1661–9, Staffs. 1661–3; j.p. Berks. 1662–d., commr. for recusants 1675.[2]

Colclough's ancestors sat regularly for Newcastle from 1360 to 1407. But his great-grandfather obtained the site of the dissolved abbey of Tintern in Ireland from Henry VIII and made it the family's principal seat. Colclough was apparently regarded as a parliamentary supporter in 1647, when his Irish estates, valued at £680 p.a., were sequestrated by Ormonde. He was probably living in England at the time, on a Berkshire manor leased from Lord Lucas, but nothing more is heard of him until the general election of 1661, when he was returned for Newcastle, the first of the family for two hundred years to sit for the borough. He owned property there, but he must have owed his election chiefly to his cousins, who were substantial townsmen. In a list of the Staffordshire gentry he is described as a stranger to the county, though 'reported loyal and orthodox' and 'a sober man', with an estate of £600 p.a. Lord Wharton listed him as a friend, to be managed by Sir Richard Onslow*. In the first session of the Cavalier Parliament he was named to the committee for the corporations bill, but he served on only six others throughout. On 9 Oct. 1666 he was among those appointed to hear a petition from the Gloucestershire cloth-workers, but sat on no further committees after this session. In 1670 Bishop Ward included him in his list of justices for the Newbury division of Berkshire, but noted him as being in Ireland. He was one of the court dependants absent in 1675, and he was again listed as absent by Sir Richard Wiseman*. Shaftesbury marked him 'vile'

in 1677. During the last session he was among those to be sent for in custody. He did not stand again, and died at Tintern on 22 June 1684. The baronetcy became extinct in 1687, but later members of the family sat for Irish constituencies both before and after the Act of Union.[3]

[1] Coll. Top. et Gen. v. 373. [2] Vis. Berks. (Harl. Soc. lvii), 30. [3] J. Ward, Stoke-on-Trent, 337–40; HMC Ormonde, ii. 107; CSP Ire. 1633–47, p. 659; VCH Berks. iii. 320; Staffs. RO, D593/3/16/2/1; Staffs. Parl. Hist. (Wm. Salt Arch. Soc.), ii. 126; Staffs. Gentry (Staffs. Rec. Soc. ser. 4, ii), 8; Salisbury Cathedral Lib. Bp. Seth Ward, Liber Notitiae, f. 56.

A.M.M.

COLE, Sir Ralph, 2nd Bt. (1629–1704), of Brancepeth Castle, co. Dur.

DURHAM 27 Mar. 1678, 1679 (Mar.)

bap. 3 Nov. 1629, 2nd but 1st surv. s. of Sir Nicholas Cole, 1st Bt., of Newcastle-upon-Tyne, Northumb. and Brancepeth Castle by 1st w. Mary, da. of Sir Thomas Liddell, 1st Bt., of Ravensworth, Northumb. *m.* (1) by 1651, Margaret (*d.*1657), da. of Thomas Windham of Felbrigg, Norf., wid. of one Shouldham, 3s. *d.v.p.* 1da.; (2) by 1664, Catherine (*d.*1704), da. of Sir Henry Foulis, 2nd Bt., of Ingleby, Yorks., *s.p. suc.* fa. Dec. 1669.[1]

Freeman, Newcastle 1660, Durham 1673; commr. for assessment, co. Dur. 1661–80, 1689–90; lt.-col. of militia by 1662, col. by 1685, dep. lt. 1668–?d.; j.p. 1670–?d.; commr. for recusants 1675, carriage of coals, Newcastle 1679.[2]

Cole was descended from an insignificant Gateshead tradesman who died in 1583. But his grandfather invested some of the enormous wealth which he had acquired as a merchant adventurer of Newcastle in the purchase of Kepyer, at the gates of Durham, in 1630 and Brancepeth Castle six years later. As one of the leaders in the prolonged defence of Newcastle against the Scots in the Civil War, he was imprisoned and savagely fined. Cole's father, three times mayor of Newcastle and a commissioner of array, was in arms for the King and also forced to compound for his delinquency. His losses were estimated at £50,000.[3]

Cole was the first of the family to abandon trade. As a child he is said to have studied painting under van Dyck, and he was to paint the portrait of Thomas Wyndham II*. He retained several Italian painters in his service, an extravagance which forced the sale of Kepyer in 1674. Unlike his father, he supported the enfranchisement of Durham, and was returned at the head of the poll at the first election for the city in 1678. An inactive Member of the Cavalier Parliament, he was appointed only to the committee for the explanatory bill on the prohibition of imports from France, and to two others of less importance. He was marked 'doubly vile' on

Shaftesbury's list and included in the 'unanimous club' of government supporters. Nevertheless he was re-elected to the first Exclusion Parliament. Shaftesbury marked him 'vile' and according to Roger Morrice he voted against the bill; but he left no other trace on the records. He is not known to have stood again, though he signed the address approving the dissolution of Parliament in 1681.[4]

Cole apparently accepted the Revolution, but in 1701 he had to sell the Brancepeth estate for £16,000, plus an annuity of £500. He died on 9 Aug. 1704 and was buried at Brancepeth, the only member of his family to sit in Parliament.[5]

[1] C. Surtees, *Castle of Brancepeth*, 36. [2] *Reg. of Freemen* (Newcastle Recs. iii), 76; Surtees, *Dur.* iv (2), p. 22; *Arch. Ael.* i. 187; Durham Univ. Lib., Mickleton Spearman mss 8/69–72; *Cal. Treas. Bks.* v. 1205. [3] R. Howell, *Newcastle and the Puritan Revolution*, 15, 124, 162; *Dur.* iv. (2), p. 66; Hutchinson, *Dur.* iii. 314; *Cal. Comm. Comp.* 971, 1978. [4] *Cosin Corresp.* (Surtees Soc. lv), 212, 249, 256; *CSP Dom.* 1680–1, p. 386. [5] Hutchinson, 314.

G.H.

COLE, Thomas (1622–81), of Liss, Hants.

HAMPSHIRE 1656
PETERSFIELD 1660

bap. 15 Jan. 1622, 1st s. of Thomas Cole of Liss by Mary, da. of Thomas Waller of Beaconsfield, Bucks. *educ.* G. Inn 1641. *m.* (1) Dec. 1651, Elizabeth (*d.* 1659), da. and coh. of Sir Stephen Harvey of Colchester End, Hardingstone, Northants., *s.p.*; (2) lic. 23 Apr. 1662, Judith, da. of Abraham Cullen, merchant, of Great St. Helens, London, wid. of Peter Tryon of Bulwick, Northants., 1s. 1da. *suc.* fa. 1641.[1]

Commr. for execution of ordinances, Hants 1645, assessment, Hants 1647–52, 1657, Jan. 1660–80, Northants. 1663–4, 1673–4, militia, Hants 1648, 1659, Mar. 1660; j.p. Hants by 1650–July 1660, 1662–*d.*, Northants. 1670–*d.*; commr. for security, Hants 1655–6; freeman, Portsmouth and Winchester by Apr. 1660; capt. of militia ft. Hants Nov. 1660, sheriff 1663–4, dep. lt. 1667–*d.*, commr. for recusants 1675.[2]

Cole claimed to be a distant cousin of Edward Cole[†], registrar to the bishop of Winchester, who sat for the city in 1601 and 1604. His grandfather, however, was a Londoner who married into the Dering family, and from them his father bought Liss, four miles from Petersfield, in 1612. Cole was appointed to the county committee in 1645, held local office throughout the Interregnum, and sat for Hampshire in 1656. At the general election of 1660 he defeated the republican Thomas Muspratt at Winchester, but chose to sit for Petersfield, thereby leaving a seat vacant for Lord St. John (Charles Powlett I*). He was an inactive Member of the Convention. He made no recorded speeches, but may have been appointed to two unimportant committees, though on both occasions his name was mis-spelt. After his second marriage he resided principally in Northamptonshire, and Lord Montagu of Boughton hoped that he might stand for Stamford in the country interest in 1679. However, he was not removed from local office before his death. He was buried at Liss on 4 Mar. 1681, the only member of this branch of the Cole family to sit in Parliament.[3]

[1] J. E. Cole, *Gen. of Cole Fam.* 29–31; *London Mar. Lic.* ed. Foster, 307. [2] R. East, *Portsmouth Recs.* 356; *Thurloe*, iii. 363; Winchester corp. assembly bk. 4, f. 137; *Cal. Treas. Bks.* i. 82; SP29/225/101. [3] *Misc. Gen. et Her.* ii. 240–1; *VCH Hants*, iv. 85; *CSP Dom.* 1663–4, p. 386; Add. 29557, f. 91.

M.W.H./J.P.F.

COLERAINE, 2nd Baron [I] *see* **HARE, Henry.**

COLES, William (c.1616–97), of Woodfalls, nr. Downton, Wilts.

DOWNTON 1659, 3–9 May 1660

b. c.1616, 2nd but 1st surv. s. of Barnabas Coles of Woodfalls by w. Katherine Barnes. *educ.* Brasenose, Oxf. 1635; M. Temple 1637, called 1645. *m.* (1) settlement 25 Mar. 1647, with £1,500, Eleanor, da. of Leweston Fitzjames[†] of Leweston, Dorset, 3s. (1 *d.v.p.*); (2) bef. 1657, Joyce, 2s. *d.v.p.* 2da.; (3) 21 July 1690, Elizabeth, da. of James Goddard of South Marston, Wilts., wid. of Gilbert Raleigh* of Downton, *s.p. suc.* fa. 1653.[1]

Commr. for militia, Wilts. 1648, 1659, Mar. 1660, j.p. 1653–July 1660, commr. for scandalous ministers 1654, assessment 1657, Jan. 1660, sequestrations 1659.[2]

Coles's ancestors had leased Woodfalls, about a mile from Downton, since the reign of Elizabeth. Their status lay on the fringes of the gentry and the professional classes; a namesake and contemporary, who resided in the Close at Salisbury, serving as steward to Edmund Ludlow* and clerk of the peace for Wiltshire during the Interregnum, entered his pedigree at the heralds' visitation of 1677. Coles himself, 'an honest gentleman', according to his cousin's employer, represented Downton in Richard Cromwell's Parliament, and stood for re-election in 1660. After a double return he was allowed to sit on the merits of the return, but he was unseated six days later on the merits of the election, without leaving any other trace on the records of the Convention. He never again held local office, even the most minor, and died in 1697, leaving to his grandson and heir Barnaby an estate of about £350 p.a. No other member of the family sat in Parliament.[3]

[1] *Misc. Gen. et Her.* (ser. 5), ix. 20, 108, 110, 174–5; Dorset RO, 173; Hoare, *Wilts. Downton*, 55; PCC 289 Brent, adm. act. bk., 27 Nov. 1697. [2] *Cal. Comm. Comp.* 755. [3] *Voyce from the Watchtower*, 104, 119; C5/232/14.

M.W.H./J.P.F.

COLLETON, Sir Peter, 2nd Bt. (1635–94), of Exmouth, Devon and Golden Square, Westminster.

BOSSINEY 1681, 1689, 1690–24 Mar. 1694

bap. 17 Sept. 1635, 1st s. of Sir John Colleton, 1st Bt., of Exeter, Devon and London by Catherine, da. of William Amy of Exeter. *m.* c.1669, Elizabeth, sis. of John Leslie of Barbados, wid. of William Johnston, 1s. 3da.; 1s. illegit. *suc.* fa. c. May 1667.[1]

Member of council, Barbados 1664–84, dep. gov. and pres. of council 1672–7; ld. prop. Carolina 1666–*d.*, high steward 1669, chancellor 1670–*d.*; member, R. Adventurers into Africa 1667–72, asst. 1670–1; ld. prop. Bahamas 1670–*d.*; member, Hudson's Bay Co. 1670–*d.*; asst. R. Africa Co. 1672–*d.*; commr. for assessment, Westminster 1677–80, 1689–90, Devon 1690; freeman, Exeter 1678; j.p. Mdx. and Westminster 1677–80, Westminster 1689–*d.*; dep. lt. Westminster 1689–*d.*[2]

Commr. for public accounts 1691–*d.*

FRS 1677.

Colleton came from a merchant family established in Exeter in the early 16th century. His father fought in the Cavalier army in the first Civil War and compounded on the Exeter articles in 1646 with a fine of £244. Altogether he computed his losses in the King's service at £4,000. He became a planter in Barbados in 1650 and accepted the Protectorate regime; but he returned to England at the Restoration. As a kinsman of the Duke of Albemarle (George Monck*) he was given a baronetcy and appointed commissioner for wine licences, and he stood unsuccessfully for Dartmouth shortly before his death.[3]

Meanwhile Colleton himself had been managing the family plantation, one of the largest in Barbados. Together with Albemarle and Lord Ashley (Sir Anthony Ashley Cooper*), he became one of the eight lords proprietors of Carolina, and was entrusted with recruiting settlers from Barbados. He was consulted about the origins of the Hudson's Bay Company, and inherited £1,800 stock in the Africa Company. On behalf of the Barbados planters he gave evidence to the House of Lords against the proposed sugar duties in 1671. On the death of William Willoughby* in 1673 he temporarily assumed the government of the island. But he finally returned to England in or before 1677, when he visited Ashley (now Earl of Shaftesbury) in the Tower. On 15 May he advanced £1,500 to the crown on the security of the second Disbandment Act.[4]

Colleton stood unsuccessfully at the second general election of 1679, but the Journal, which records his petition, does not name the constituency. He was returned in 1681 for Bossiney, where the returning officer, Edward Amy, was presumably a kinsman. Though clearly an exclusionist, he left no trace on the records of the Oxford Parliament. His name was found on the papers of a Whig conspirator arrested after the Rye House Plot, apparently as a contributor to Titus Oates's pension, and he is unlikely to have stood in 1685. He regained his seat in 1689, but with only seven committee appointments he was not an active Member of the Convention. He was one of five Members instructed on 9 Aug. to prepare a bill to ease the plantations of the duties imposed in 1685. After the recess he was appointed to the committees to inquire into war expenditure and to consider the second mutiny bill. In his only recorded speech, on miscarriages in the navy, he said:

> As soon as they had the victuals out of these ships, all their men fell sick. I am fully convinced that your men have been ill-used by the victuallers, and unless it be remedied you will have no fleet next year.

He was named to the committees on the bills for restoring corporations, in which he supported the disabling clause, and for imposing a general oath of allegiance. Re-elected as a country Whig, he became a member of the first public accounts commission. But he died on 24 Mar. 1694, and was buried at St. James Piccadilly. The next member of the family to sit was James Edward Colleton, returned in 1747 for Lostwithiel as a government supporter.[5]

[1] Vivian, *Vis. Devon*, 218; PCC 72 Box; *CSP Dom.* 1666–7, p. 575. [2] *CSP Col.* 1661–8, p. 692; 1669–74, pp. 43–44, 52, 120, 122, 143, 1065, 1070; 1677–80, p. 403; 1681–5, pp. 36, 675, 938; K. H. D. Haley, *Shaftesbury*, 233, 242; *HMC 6th Rep.* 412; B. Willson, *Great Company*, i. 47; *Caribbeana*, iv. 312; *Exeter Freemen* (Devon and Cornw. Rec. Soc. extra ser. i), 169; Mdx. RO, WJP/CP3; *CSP Dom.* 1689–90, p. 54; 1691–2, p. 164. [3] *Cal. Comm. Comp.* 1356; *CSP Dom.* 1660–1, pp. 95, 322; 1666–7; p. 440, 450, 453, 473; V. Harlow, *Barbados*, 199–221. [4] *Caribbeana*, iii. 299; Harlow, 214–15; *CSP Dom.* 1663–4, p. 485; 1677–8, p. 268; *CSP Col.* 1661–8, pp. 153, 157; 1669–74, pp. 141, 496, 499; Haley, 231, 233, 237–42; *HMC 9th Rep.* pt. 2, p. 11; PCC 91 Carr; *Cal. Treas. Bks.* vi. 815. [5] *CJ*, ix. 638; J. Maclean, *Trigg Minor*, iii. 209–10; SP29/430/34; Grey, ix. 442; *Cal. Treas. Bks.* ix. 1151.

E.C.

COLLINGWOOD, Daniel (c.1634–81), of Branton, Eglingham, Northumb. and Whitehall.

BERWICK-UPON-TWEED 10 Jan. 1665
MORPETH 1679 (Oct.), 1681

b. c.1634, 1st s. of Sir Robert Collingwood of Branton by 1st w. Margaret, da. of Sir John Delaval of North Dissington, Northumb. *educ.* Warkworth g.s.; Christ's, Camb. adm. 6 Mar. 1650, aged 16; G. Inn 1650. *unm. suc.* fa. 1666.[1]

Commr. for militia, Northumb. Mar. 1660, assessment, Northumb. Aug. 1660–1, 1663–80, co. Dur. 1673–9, Berwick 1673–80, loyal and indigent officers, Northumb. 1662; j.p. Northumb. 1666–*d.*, dep. lt. 1670–*d.*; asst. R. Fishery Co. 1677; commr. for carriage of coals, port of Newcastle 1679.[2]

those ordered to draft a new clause in the poll bill and to bring in bills for encouraging exports and controlling prices. He was one of the managers of Lord Mordaunt's impeachment.[3]

During the proceedings against Clarendon in the autumn of 1667, Colman showed courage and discretion, as well as forensic skill. He intervened only in the major debates, observing on 6 Nov.: 'What is laid before you is only by hearsay, but no assurance that it will be made good'. His principal speech, three days later, on the first charge was so crushing that Anchitell Grey* suppressed it altogether from his account of the debate:

> The question is, whether it be in your power to declare this article treason by 25 *Ed.* 3.... Your enacting power is a kind of omnipotency, but in a declaratory power you can declare no more than is committed to you, and with safety to the subject you cannot declare this treason. Then, what must be our rule in declaring I dare not say. For scarce a man can tell what was treason, before 25 *Ed.* 3 was made to bring things to a certainty, and what was uncertain to them who made the law can [not] be certain to us now.

On the dispute between the Houses, he observed on 2 Dec.: 'No man can commit in capital matters without taking examinations beforehand; otherwise no man can justify a commitment. Therefore I am not satisfied that the Lords had not reason to deny'.[4]

Colman's defence of Clarendon was very far from damaging his status in the House. He was chosen chairman of the committee to consider the petition of Alexander Fitton against Lord Gerard of Brandon about the Gawsworth estate, presented two reports, and was named to the committee to consider the claim of the Upper House to jurisdiction. He helped to draw up the impeachment of (Sir) William Penn* and was ordered to attend a conference. On 7 May 1668 he was among the Members entrusted with emending the articles against Henry Brouncker*. In 1669 Sir Thomas Osborne* regarded him as one to be engaged for the court by the Duke of York and his friends, and he gave his opinion that the charges against Lord Orrery (Roger Boyle*) fell within the Statute of Treasons. In this session he was asked to recommend changes in the poor law, and was appointed to the committee for the continuance of the Conventicles Act. He opposed the divorce bill introduced on behalf of Lord Roos (John Manners*): 'In all laws of divorce the woman is not deprived of her estate ... We must be satisfied somewhat further in matter of fact.' He intervened in the debate on the sale of fee-farm rents on behalf of his constituency. On 7 Apr. 1670 he was appointed to the committee to consider the privilege case brought by Sir John Pretyman*,

and he was one of five Members selected to ensure that the resolution of the House was correctly entered in the Journal. He was also ordered to attend a conference on shipping.[5]

Colman achieved his greatest prominence in his last session. He was ordered to report on defects in the Conventicles and Militia Acts, and on 19 Dec. 1670 he was named to the committee to examine protections granted by Members. His name stands first on the committee for the continuance of Acts for coal prices and to prevent delays in extending property for debt, where he took the chair. After Christmas he acted as chairman of the committee of the whole House to punish the assault on Sir John Coventry*, and both in the House and in conference he spoke in favour of the bill to make nose-slitting a felony. He took part in four other conferences, on the subsidy bill, the growth of Popery, the excise bill, and the increase in import duties, stoutly resisting any claim by the Upper House to emend money bills. On 21 Apr. 1671 he reported from the conference on fee-farm rents. Colman was marked out for preferment, and it was said that but for his early death while still in his thirties he would have been appointed solicitor-general instead of Sir William Jones*. He was buried at Brent Eleigh on 29 Oct. 1672, leaving the tithes to augment the living under the Act of 1665 which he had helped to prepare. None of his sons entered Parliament, and the family became extinct in the male line in 1740.[6]

[1] *Misc. Gen. et Her.* (ser. 2), i. 373–4; *Vis. Essex* (Harl. Soc. xiii), 209; Westminster City Lib. St. Mary le Strand par. reg.; J. Harris, *Epitaphs in Salisbury Cathedral*, 58; *Wilts. N. and Q.* vi. 435; Copinger, *Suff. Manors*, i. 41; PCC 147 Eure. [2] Hoare, *Wilts*. Salisbury, 449, 711. [3] Copinger, i. 40–42; Harl. 1560, f. 250; North, *Lives*, i. 61; *VCH Hants*, iv. 541; A. G. Matthews, *Walker Revised*, 69; *CJ*, viii. 623, 627, 656, 671, 681. [4] *Clarendon Impeachment*, 28, 34, 92. [5] *CJ*, ix. 54, 88, 100, 157; Grey, i. 184, 255, 259, 266. [6] *CJ*, ix. 181, 189, 211, 214, 235; Grey, i. 345, 382–3, 465; North, loc. cit.; *Misc. Gen. et Her.* (ser. 2), i. 350, 373.

J.P.F.

COLMAN, Roger (c.1623–60), of Gornhay, Tiverton, Devon.

TIVERTON 14 July–6 Nov. 1660 [new writ]

> *b.* c.1623, 1st s. of Francis Colman of Gornhay by Bridget, da. of Lewis Cruwys of Cruwys Morchard. *educ.* Exeter, Oxf. matric. 9 Apr. 1641, aged 18. *m.* Elizabeth, da. of William Drewe of Broadhembury Grange, 1s. 4da. *suc.* fa. 1650.[1]
> Commr. for assessment, Devon 1657.

Colman's first known ancestor, a Tiverton merchant, died in 1553. The family bought one-eighth of the manor, which had been divided among the coheirs of the Courtenay Earls of Devon, and established themselves among the minor gentry;

they recorded their pedigree at the heralds' visitation of 1620, though they still employed apprentices as late as 1674. Neither Colman himself nor any of the family is known to have taken part in the Civil War.[2]

Colman was returned for Tiverton at a by-election in 1660. He made no speeches, but was named to the committee for the Dunkirk establishment on 1 Sept. Nothing is known of his politics, but his appointment to a local commission under the Protectorate suggests that he may have followed the Presbyterian opposition line of his colleague Robert Shapcote* and his predecessor Thomas Bampfield*. His will, dated 27 Oct. 1660, was proved at Exeter on 10 November.[3]

[1] Vivian, *Vis. Devon*, 221, 257, 862. [2] M. Dunsford, *Hist. Mems. Tiverton*, 325; Lysons, *Devon*, 511. [3] Rylands Lib. Eng. mss 299, f. 539.

M.W.H./J.P.F.

COLMAN, William (*b.* c.1655), of Gornhay, Tiverton, Devon.

TIVERTON   1685, 1689

> *b.* c.1655, o.s. of Roger Colman*. *m.* (1) 19 Dec. 1676, Mary, da. of Peter Prideaux* of Netherton, *s.p.*; (2) 3 Oct. 1680, Jane, da. of Sir Edmund Fortescue* of Fallapit, *s.p.*; (3) 3 Nov. 1684, Elizabeth, da. of William Bogan of Gatcombe, Little Hempston, 1s. 1da. *suc.* fa. 1660.[1]
> Capt. of militia ft. Devon by 1680; j.p. Tiverton 1680–1, Devon 1687–July 1688, Oct. 1688–?*d.*; j.p. and alderman, Tiverton 1684–7; commr. for assessment, Devon 1689–90.[2]

Colman was still under age when his mother drew up her will in 1674. Whereas his ancestors had been satisfied to marry into the lesser gentry, his first and second wives both came from leading Tory families. He was undoubtedly a Tory and probably a persecutor of dissenters. As one of the grand jury at the summer assizes of 1680, he was held responsible by the House for an abhorring presentment. Nothing is known of his election to James II's Parliament, nor of his activities in it. He was removed from the corporation in 1687, and came in to William of Orange at Exeter in November 1688. He was re-elected to the Convention, and according to Anthony Rowe* voted to agree with the Lords that the throne was not vacant. He sat on two committees in the first session, one to prevent the export of wool and the other to consider the affairs of the East India Company, and on the committee to prepare a bill of indemnity after the recess. He is not known to have stood again, though he was active as trustee in various family settlements till at least 1712. His grandson Edward sat for Orford as a

stop-gap in the Seymour interest from 1768 to 1771.[3]

[1] Vivian, *Vis. Devon*, 221. [2] M. Dunsford, *Hist. Mems. Tiverton*, 193; PC2/72/535. [3] PCC 15 Dycer; *Trans. Devon Assoc.* xcviii. 214; Dunsford, 193, 372, 457; *CJ*, ix. 656; *HMC 7th Rep.* 416; *HMC Lords*, n.s. v. 178; vi. 239; ix. 240.

J.P.F.

COLMORE, William (c.1649–1723), of Old Deanery House, Warwick.

WARWICK   1689, 1690

> *b.* c.1649, 3rd s. of William Colmore, merchant, of Birmingham, being 1st s. by 2nd w. *educ.* Magdalen Coll. Oxf. matric. 3 May 1667, aged 18; I. Temple 1669. *m.* Jan. 1676, Elizabeth (*d.* 27 May 1731), da. and coh. of Edmund Waring† of Humphreston Hall, Donington, Salop, 10s. (6 *d.v.p.*) 3da. *suc.* fa. 1675.[1]
> Commr. for assessment, Warws. 1677–80, 1689–90, j.p. 1690–?*d.*, sheriff 1699–1700.

Colmore came from a Birmingham merchant family, one of whom was on the original board of governors of King Edward VI's school. His father served on the county committee in the Civil War, and continued to hold local office during the Interregnum. Though he retained a valuable estate in Birmingham, he seems to have moved to Warwick in later life. Colmore himself married the daughter of a Shropshire republican, who was lucky to escape exclusion from the Act of Indemnity at the Restoration. Nevertheless he was a Tory who joined with William Digby*, Lord Digby at the general election of 1689. He voted to agree with the Lords that the throne was not vacant; but his only committee in the Convention was to consider the petition against the East India Company of an interloping merchant. He was re-elected, but lost his seat in 1695. His eldest son of the same name sat for Warwick as a Tory from 1713 until his early death in 1722. Colmore himself died eight months later, on 16 July 1723, and was buried in St. Mary's, Warwick. No member of the family subsequently sat in Parliament.[2]

[1] A. L. Reade, *Johnsonian Gleanings*, vii. 122–4. [2] Ibid. 115; *Warws. Recs.* v. 140; vi. 201.

A.M.M.

COLT, John Dutton (1643–1722), of Stafferton House, Leominster, Herefs.

LEOMINSTER   1679 (Mar.), 1679 (Oct.), 1681, 1689, 1690, 1695, 8 Jan.–3 Apr. 1701

> *bap.* 16 Mar. 1643, 1st s. of George Colt of Colt Hall, Cavendish, Suff. by Elizabeth, da. and coh. of John Dutton† of Sherborne, Glos.; bro. of Sir Henry Dutton Colt, 1st Bt.†. *educ.* Hayes, Mdx. (Dr Thomas Triplett). *m.* (1) 31 Aug. 1671, Mary (*d.* 15 Feb. 1703), da. and h.

of John Booth* of Letton, Herefs., 5s. 4da.; (2) Margaret, da. of William Cooke* of Highnam, Glos., wid. of John Arnold* of Llanvihangel Crucorney, Mon., *s.p. suc.* fa. 1659.[1]

Alderman, Leominster c.1673–85, 1689–*d.*, bailiff 1680–1; j.p. Herefs. 1678–80, ?1689–at least 1702, Som. 1699–1700, Mon. 1699–at least 1702; dep. lt. Herefs. 1678–c.80, 1689–at least 1701; commr. for assessment, Leominster 1679–80, Herefs. Leominster and Bristol 1689–90; collector of customs, Bristol 1689–1700, dep. lt. 1689–?1700, commr. for port regulation 1690, lt.-col. of militia ft. by 1697–?1700; paymaster of the first classis lottery 1715–17.[2]

Colt's family originally hailed from Cumberland, but his 15th-century ancestor Thomas Colt†, 'the great commoner of the Yorkist revolution', acquired considerable estates in Suffolk and Essex, and there the Colts resided, without much distinction, till the reign of Charles I. By then they were deeply entangled in financial difficulties, and Colt's father found himself 'heir to very little'. His marriage to the daughter of one of the richest commoners in England ought to have eased his position, especially as he hopefully gave each of his nine sons the middle name of 'Dutton'; he compounded in 1650 for two horses worth £40 and no less than £100 worth of clothes. But his decision to take up arms for the King again in the second Civil War is said to have lost Colt his inheritance, which descended unimpaired to his cousin Sir Ralph Dutton*. He was driven to living by his wits, with such success that he was known as 'the great cheat', and in 1661 a bill was introduced to make void divers judgments and conveyances obtained from James Scudamore* by George and Thomas Colt as a consequence of his losses at play. Colt claimed to have been present as a small boy at the battle of Worcester, where his father was 'almost cut to pieces'; he withdrew first to Ireland and then to the Low Countries, where he was accidentally drowned in January 1659, according to family tradition while about to set out on a secret mission to Ireland.[3]

Colt had accompanied his father to the exiled Court, but he received no reward at the Restoration. The personal intervention of the King in a lawsuit which his uncle brought against him in the House of Lords in 1670 may have further embittered him. It was presumably the Dutton connexion that introduced him into Herefordshire county society and enabled him to marry an heiress in the following year. He took up residence in Leominster, where he acted as steward to John Wildman I*. 'The head of the fanatic party' in the town, he 'managed them at his pleasure'. Elected for the borough in 1679 at the first opportunity, little was known of him elsewhere except his Cavalier background, and Shaftesbury marked him as 'doubtful'.

But he soon distinguished himself in opposition as 'a hot, disobliged and fierce-speaking man against the Court'. A very active Member of the first Exclusion Parliament, he was named to 24 committees, acted as teller in two divisions, and spoke three times, getting off the mark by calling no less a person than Secretary Coventry to order for reflecting on the Roundhead background of John Birch*. He took part in drawing up the address for the immediate execution of the Jesuit Pickering, and on 27 Apr. he said:

> If the Duke be found to have had a hand in the conspiracy, I know no reason but that the Duke may be impeached, though absent, and then there is good ground for a bill to provide for a Protestant succession.

On 7 May he was added to the committee for the security of the King and kingdom, and he was one of the four Members appointed to prepare a message to the Lords urging the speedy implementation of the death sentences passed on Popish priests. He both spoke and voted for the exclusion bill.[4]

Colt was re-elected in September, but in the long interval before the second Exclusion Parliament met he was involved in a violent altercation with Jeremiah Bubb* at the assizes, which he called a breach of privilege. Colt's vindictiveness contributed to the alienation of moderates like Scudamore's son John Scudamore*, Lord Scudamore, from the country party. He was even more active in this Parliament, in which he was named to 47 committees and made five speeches. He was a manager of the conference on the alleged Irish plot. On 17 Nov. 1680 he seconded the motion for the impeachment of Halifax, and added to it the name of Lord Chief Justice Scroggs for disparaging the evidence against Mrs Cellier, the Popish midwife. He took part in preparing the address of 20 Dec. insisting on exclusion.[5]

In the Oxford Parliament Colt helped to prepare for the conferences on the loss of the bill to repeal the laws against Protestant dissenters and on the impeachment of Fitzharris. On the dissolution he is reported to have been offered by Shaftesbury a captaincy in a revolutionary army, but he was in a violent temper when he returned to Leominster, indiscreetly declaring before potentially hostile witnesses: 'I will be hanged at my own door before such a damned Popish rascal as the Duke of York shall ever inherit the crown of England'. Colt led the opposition to the surrender of Leominster's charter, but the two parties in the corporation were almost equal. The Tories gained control when the Duke of York began an action for *scandalum magnatum* against Colt, forcing him to take refuge from the sheriff's writ at the house of his wife's kinsman

Richard Williams*, just over the border in Radnorshire. The case was allowed to languish for a year, but Colt persisted in opposing the quo warranto, although now in a minority on the corporation. On 3 May 1684 the jury awarded damages against him of £100,000, an outrageous punishment on a man who cannot have been more than moderately well-off. In October he was reported to be a prisoner, and he remained in the King's Bench or on parole, under threat of a similar action by the Duke of Beaufort (Henry Somerset*). He petitioned Parliament unavailingly in 1685, and was excepted from the general pardon in the following year. Even when released on bail in March 1687, he resolutely refused to collaborate with James II; but he took no part in the Revolution.[6]

At the general election of 1689, Colt refused to stand for Leominster until he was assured that (Sir) Edward Harley* was safe for the county. He was again returned, though this time as junior Member and probably not without a contest. He was again active in the Convention, being appointed to 42 committees, and making two recorded speeches. He was teller in six divisions, opposing the Lords over retaining a reference to the vacancy of the throne. He served on the committees for amending the coronation oath, suspending habeas corpus, inquiring into the authors and advisers of grievances and considering the first mutiny bill. On 15 Mar. he petitioned for the collectorship of customs at Bristol in consideration of his sufferings for the Protestant religion. On 27 Mar. he had leave to go into the country for a fortnight; his business was probably to produce the old Leominster charter and expel the nominated aldermen. On his return he was very suitably appointed to the committee to consider a bill for restoring corporations. He helped to draw up reasons for a conference on disarming Papists. On 1 June he demanded an inquiry into the delay in relieving Londonderry. He took part in the impeachment of the Jacobite propagandists on 13 June, and two days later he was one of four Members to commend the case of Mrs Fitzharris to the King. In the second session, he supported the government on supply, but acted as teller against bailing the victualling commissioners. He was listed as supporting the disabling clause in the bill to restore corporations. When a bill was introduced to prevent Beaufort from pursuing the charge of *scandalum magnatum*, Colt declared that he preferred to rely on the duke's honour.[7]

Colt remained a Whig, but in 1700 he lost his place in the customs on a variety of charges, including malversation and trading with the enemy. Soon afterwards he lost his seat at Leominster to

the Harley interest; three attempts to regain it were unsuccessful. Colt died on 19 Apr. 1722; his brother sat for Newport (I.o.W.) and Westminster, but none of his descendants entered Parliament.[8]

[1] Wotton, *Baronetage*, iv. 48; *Cal. Cl. SP*, iv. 138; Howard, *Vis. Suff*. ii. 35–37; PCC 105 Penn (will of Thomas Triplett). [2] G. F. Townsend, *Leominster*, 149, 295; BL Loan 29/182/290v, Sir Edward to Lady Harley, 11 June 1678; *Cal. Treas. Bks*. ix. 10, 620; xv. 279; xxix. 758; xxxi. 40; Eg. 1626, f. 18. [3] Copinger, *Suff. Manors*, i. 64–65; Morant, *Essex*, ii. 492; Howard, ii. 31, 36; Keeler, *Long Parl*. 162–3; Wotton, iv. 48; SP23/218/397; *CSP Dom*. 1655. p. 595; 1657–8, p. 311; *CJ*, viii. 305, 307, 378; *Thurloe*, vii. 255. [4] *HMC 8th Rep*. pt. 1 (1881), 144; *CSP Dom*. 1682, p. 576; J. Price, *Leominster*, 88; *HMC Ormonde*, n.s. v. 547; Grey, vii. 146, 151, 286; *CJ*, ix. 626; Add. 28046, f. 153. [5] BL Loan 29/140, Sir Edward to Robert Harley, 30 July 1680; *Ailesbury Mems*. i. 47; *CJ*, ix. 645, 648, 683; Grey, viii. 22. [6] *CSP Dom*. 1682, pp. 326, 426, 576; 1683–4, p. 280; 1684–5, p. 174; 1686–7, pp. 243, 386; Wotton, iv. 49; Luttrell, i. 374; *HMC Portland*, iii. 397; *CJ*, ix. 720; *London Gazette*, 15 Mar. 1686. [7] BL Loan 29/184/123, Colt to Harley, 14 Jan. 1689; Wotton, iv. 50; *CSP Dom*. 1689–90, p. 25; *CJ*, x. 299, 302, 343. [8] Luttrell, iv. 535; *Cal. Treas. Bks*. xiv. 74; Price, 121.

E.R.

COMPTON, Sir Charles (c.1624–61), of Grendon and Sywell, Northants.

NORTHAMPTON   4 Nov.–bef. 30 Nov. 1661

b. c.1624, 2nd s. of Spencer Compton†, 2nd Earl of Northampton, by Mary, da. of Sir Francis Beaumont of Cole Orton, Leics.; bro. of Sir Francis Compton* and Sir William Compton*. *educ*. Eton 1633–6. *m*. (1) Mary, da. of Sir Hatton Fermor of Easton Neston, Northants., 3s. 2da.; (2) c. June 1661, Felicia, da. of Thomas Pigott of Chetwynd, Salop, wid. of William Wilmer of Sywell, 1da. (posth.). Kntd. 12 Dec. 1643.[1]

Lt.-col. of horse (royalist) 1642–5, col. 1645–6; capt. R. Horse Gds. (The Blues) 1661–*d*.[2]

J.p. Northants. July 1660–*d*., dep. lt. c. Aug. 1660–*d*., capt. vol. horse Aug. 1660.[3]

Surveyor and receiver of greenwax fines 1661–*d*.[4]

Compton's ancestors took their name from Compton Wynyates in Warwickshire, where they resided from the 12th century, first representing the county under Edward III. But after buying Castle Ashby in 1512 they gradually transferred their principal interest to Northamptonshire, and when Compton's grandfather was made an earl in 1618 he took his title from the county town. Compton's father was killed at the head of the Cavalier forces at Hopton Heath in 1643. Compton and his three eldest brothers were also prominent Cavalier leaders in the Midlands. His most notable achievement was the surprise of Beeston Castle. With his share of the £30,000 settled on the seven younger children of the 2nd Earl, a small property was purchased for him at Grendon. He came under suspicion during the second Civil War, but he compounded for £127 in December 1648, taking the Covenant and the negative oath. Compton and his brother-in-law Sir William Fermor*, reported to

have good interest among the royalist townsmen of
Northampton, were summoned before the Council
of State in 1653. But for all these natural suspicions
he seems to have been less active a Royalist than his
brother William. At the Restoration it was recognized that he was 'of a noble family, and a very
deserving person'. He received a commission in the
Blues, a grant of part of the greenwax fines, and a
warrant to fell timber in four coppices. More profitable was his second marriage to a well-dowered
widow, who brought him an estate about seven
miles from Northampton, valued in 1682 at £1,000
p.a. A by-election occurring a few months later, he
was successful, but died before taking his seat owing
to a fall from his horse. He was buried at Sywell on
30 Nov. 1661. His widow married John Beaumont*.
His eldest son Hatton Compton was recommended
as knight of the Royal Oak with an income of £600
p.a., but none of his descendants entered Parliament.[5]

[1] W. B. Compton, *Compton of Compton Wynyates*, 118; *Diary of
Thomas Isham of Lamport*, 148. [2] Compton, 65, 117; W. H. Black,
Docquets of Letters Patent, 283; *Kingdom's Intell.* 18 Feb. 1661.
[3] SP29/11/52. [4] *Cal. Treas. Bks.* i. 185–6; *CSP Dom.* 1663–4, p.
675. [5] Compton, 24, 104; *Cal. Comm. Comp.* 1879; *CSP Dom.*
1648–9, p. 251; 1652–3, p. 477; 1663–4, p. 477; *HMC Portland*, i.
581; D. Underdown, *Royalist Conspiracy*, 38, 80, 270–1; *Cal.
Treas. Bks.* i. 7, 136, 185–6, 198; SP29/421/216.

E.R.E.

COMPTON, Sir Francis (c.1629–1716), of
Hamerton, Hunts. and Kew, Surr.

WARWICK   28 Mar. 1664

> *b.* c.1629, 5th s. of Spencer Compton†, 2nd Earl of Nor-
> thampton; bro. of Sir Charles Compton* and Sir Wil-
> liam Compton*. *educ.* privately (Dr Peter Gunning) *m.*
> (1) Elizabeth, da. and coh. of Sir Capel Bedell, 1st Bt.†,
> of Hamerton, *s.p.*; (2) lic. 20 June 1664, Jane (*d.* Apr.
> 1677), da. of Sir John Trevor† of Trevalun, Denb., wid.
> of Arthur Elmes of Lilford, Northants., 2s. 3da.; (3)
> Mary, da. of Samuel Fortrey of Kew, wid. of Sir
> Thomas Trevor, 1st Bt.†, of Enfield, Mdx. and Leam-
> ington, Warws., *s.p.*; (4) 16 Aug. 1699, Sarah, niece of
> Anthony Rowe* of Whitehall, 1da. Kntd. 27 Dec.
> 1661.[1]
> Lt. R. Horse Gds. (The Blues) Feb. 1661, capt. Nov.
> 1661, maj. 1676, lt.-col. 1678–Dec. 1688, 1689–*d.*
> J.p. Hunts, July 1660–?85, Surr. 1680–3, by 1700–
> ?*d.*, Warws. 1690–1, by 1701–?*d.*; commr. for assess-
> ment, Hunts. Aug. 1660–80, Northants. and Warws.
> 1664–80, Denb. and Warws. 1689, Denb. 1690; dep. lt.
> Hunts. c. Aug. 1660–?84; commr. for loyal and indigent
> officers, Hunts. 1662, complaints, Bedford level 1663.
> Jt. surveyor and receiver of greenwax fines 1677–9.[2]

Compton's first marriage and purchase of the
other moiety of the Bedell estate presumably took
place before the Restoration, for he was credited on
the list of proposed knights of the Royal Oak with
an income of £2,000 p.a. In the words of Sir Philip
Warwick* he

was of so tender age that he came not into play till his
present Majesty's happy restitution; but since showed
himself in the command he hath of a troop of horse in
his Majesty's guard here at home, and abroad in Flanders, equal to his brothers.

His eldest brother, the third earl, was lord lieutenant of Warwickshire, and presumably arranged
his return for Warwick at a by-election in 1664 with
Lord Brooke, the patron of the borough. He celebrated his election by carrying off the wealthy
widow Elmes under the noses of his rivals Sir John
Chicheley* and (Sir) Thomas Crew*. He was not
an active Member, serving on only five committees
of elections, nine for private bills and 12 others. He
was appointed to the committee for the continuance
of the Conventicles Act in 1669, and his name
appeared on both lists of the court party. He
received the government whip for both sessions in
1675, perhaps unnecessarily, as he was to introduce a private bill of his own for the sale of his first
wife's estate, presumably to meet the expenses of a
career in The Blues. (Sir) John Berkenhead* took
the chair in the committee, and the bill received the
royal assent on 9 June. On 21 Oct. Compton was
appointed to the committees for appropriating the
customs for the use of the navy and preventing
illegal exactions. He also acted as teller for the
adjournment of the supply debate on 6 Nov. His
name appears on the list of officials in the Commons, and Shaftesbury marked him 'doubly vile'.
He was noted in *Flagellum Parliamentarium* and *A
Seasonable Argument* as a captain in the guards; but
before the next session he had moved towards the
Opposition on foreign policy. Owing to a mistake
in his estate Act, a supplementary bill had to be
introduced in the Lords, and when it was sent down
to the Commons (Sir) John Malet*, a prominent
country spokesman, took the chair instead of the
courtier Berkenhead. Nevertheless his bill received
the royal assent, on the same day that his second
wife's death set him free to hunt out another
wealthy widow, so that he was not obliged to sell
Hamerton till six years later. In the division on 23
May 1677 Compton was one of the Members who
voted against the Court on naming Holland as an
ally. Danby seems to have bought him off with a
grant to him, as one of a syndicate headed by the
Earl of Peterborough, of the profits of the fines of
court, and included him among the court party in
1678, though noting that he was 'in the country'
for the spring session. He took little part in proceedings in Parliament, except when it was alleged
that his sister, the wife of Sir Hugh Cholmley*,
could throw some light on the Popish Plot. 'All
know our family to be Protestant', he said, 'and I

believe my sister would not conceal anything she knew.'[3]

Compton does not seem to have stood at the general election, though it was reported that there was 'great labouring' for him in Warwickshire, and he was not blacklisted in the 'unanimous club'. The grant of the fines of court was cancelled as 'prejudicial to the King's subjects', but the syndicate received some compensation. Compton fought at Sedgemoor, where he was wounded, but under the influence of his brother, the bishop of London, he became increasingly hostile to James II's policy, and was listed by Danby among the Opposition. He undertook to lead his regiment over to William of Orange in November 1688, but he was less successful than Lord Cornbury (Henry Hyde*), partly owing to his 'want of head or heart' according to Burnet, and returned to James. His career in the army was only briefly interrupted, and he was still a serving soldier when he died in his Pall Mall lodgings on 20 Dec. 1716, aged 87. He was buried next to his brother at Fulham.[4]

[1] *London Mar. Lic.* ed. Foster, 317; *HMC Buccleuch*, i. 326; *St. James Duke's Place Par. Reg.* iii. 340; Luttrell, iv. 577. [2] *Cal. Treas. Bks.* v. 795; vi. 121. [3] *VCH Hunts.* iii. 67; *Warwick*, *Mems.* 286; *HMC Buccleuch*, i. 315; 326; *CJ*, ix. 325; 416; Foxcroft, *Halifax*, i. 129; Grey, vi. 393–4. [4] Add. 34730, f. 36; *Cal. Treas. Bks.* vii. 361; *HMC Sackville*, i. 17; *Burnet Supp.* ed. Foxcroft, 530; Clarke, *Jas. II*, ii. 217; PCC 205 Whitfield.

A.M.M.

COMPTON, Sir William (c.1625–63), of Linton, Cambs. and Drury Lane, Westminster.

CAMBRIDGE 1661–18 Oct. 1663

b. c.1625, 3rd s. of Spencer Compton†, 2nd Earl of Northampton; bro. of Sir Charles Compton* and Sir Francis Compton*. *educ.* Eton 1634–6; travelled abroad 1646–8. *m.* c.1651, Elizabeth, da. of Sir Lionel Tollemache, 2nd Bt.†, of Helmingham, Suff., wid. of William, 1st Baron Alington [I], of Horseheath, Cambs., *s.p.* Kntd. 12 Dec. 1643.[1]

Maj. of ft. (royalist) 1643, lt.-col. 1644–5; lt.-gov. Banbury Castle 1644–6; col. of horse 1645–6; maj.-gen. 1648.[2]

Master of the Ordnance June 1660–d.; PC 3 Apr. 1662–d.; commr. for Tangier 1662–d.; treas. loyal and indigent officers fund 1662–d.[3]

J.p. Cambs. July 1660–d., dep. lt. c. Aug. 1660–d.; commr. for assessment, Cambs. Aug. 1660–d., Warws. 1661–d.; chairman, corporations commission, Cambs. 1662–3; commr. for loyal and indigent officers, Cambs. London and Westminster 1662.[4]

Of the six remarkable royalist brothers, Compton was probably the ablest and certainly bore the highest character. He was well-endowed for a younger son, his grandfather, the 1st Earl, having settled on him the Kentish manor of Erith. His defence of Banbury Castle during a three-month siege in 1644, when he was still in his teens, was remarkable not only for physical determination and courage but for the simple Anglican piety which he enforced in the garrison. His moral courage was no less; he alone dissented from his eldest brother's unjust and irregular cashiering of one of his officers in 1645. He surrendered on honourable terms on 8 May 1646, but, as a Kentish landowner, he could not refuse to take up arms in the second Civil War and served during the siege of Colchester as a major-general. Cromwell is said to have described him as 'the sober young man and godly Cavalier', and he escaped with the moderate fine of £660. He settled in Cambridgeshire on his marriage, and as a member of the Sealed Knot was engaged in most Cavalier plots until the last phase of the Interregnum, when his refusal to credit the treachery of Sir Richard Willys led to his exclusion. At the Restoration he crossed to Holland with the fleet, led a troop in the King's escort from Dover to London, and was appointed master of the Ordnance.[5]

Compton was returned for Cambridge, ten miles from Linton, at the general election of 1661, probably without a contest. He was an active Member in the first and second sessions of the Cavalier Parliament, in which he was appointed to 64 committees, managed three conferences (none of major importance) and carried eight messages to the King. In the summer of 1661 he was named to the committees for the security, corporations and uniformity bills and the bill of pains and penalties. Apart from these government measures, he also took part in considering the bill for drainage of the Bedford level. After the recess he was appointed to the committees considering the annulling of the conveyance of Lady Powell's estate, the bill for ease of sheriffs, ways of relieving loyalists, and the militia bill. He was teller for candles in the debate on the Powell estate bill, and on 14 Mar. 1662 he was instructed to carry the militia bill to the Upper House and to remind their lordships of the sheriffs bill. When the militia bill returned in May, he was appointed to the small committee to consider a proviso about the assessment of peers, and he also served on the committee for the additional corporations bill. In the same month he attended the King with two messages, asking him to prevent a duel between Lord Ossory (Richard Butler*) and Philip Howard* and to arbitrate between the old and the new adventurers in the Bedford level.[6]

In the second session of the Cavalier Parliament, Compton brought a reply from the King to the address against the Declaration of Indulgence. It is clear from his letters that he had little sympathy for the nonconformists. He was appointed to the committees to consider the petition of the loyal and indigent officers and the bill for hindering the growth of Popery. On 4 Apr. 1663 he was one of 12 Members ordered to join with the Lords in returning thanks for the proclamation against Popish priests and Jesuits. He served on the committee to consider defects in the law against sale of offices. On 12 May he was among the Members entrusted with an address on improving the revenue, and four days later he was appointed to the committee to consider amendments to the Bedford level bill. When the King revealed the proposal of Sir Richard Temple* to act as 'undertaker', Compton was sent to thank him for his message and, a week later, to ask who had been the intermediary. He served on the committee for the bill for the loyal and indigent officers, and was one of six Members appointed to draw up an additional clause on 10 July. He carried the subsidy bill to the Lords, and on 25 July was sent to ask the King to allow the export of horses to the plantations and to preserve the timber in the Forest of Dean. His last appearance in the Commons was to convey the King's answer two days later. Compton died after a short illness at his home in Drury Lane on 18 Oct. 1663, aged 38. Samuel Pepys*, usually no admirer of Cavaliers, wrote of the general, if transient, regret:

> all the world saying that he was one of the worthiest men and best officers of state now in England; and so in my conscience he was—of the best temper, value, abilities of mind, integrity, birth, fine person, and diligence of any one man he hath left behind him in the three kingdoms.

Of not one courtier in a thousand, Pepys added, could it be said, as of Compton, that no man spoke ill of him; and it is clear that with his death the Government lost a steadying influence in the House of Commons which would have been increasingly valuable in the subsequent sessions of the Cavalier Parliament.[7]

[1] W. B. Compton, *Compton of Compton Wynyates*, 120; D. Underdown, *Royalist Conspiracy*, 85; *Cal. Comm. Comp.* 1831. [2] P. Young, *Edgehill*, 231; W. H. Black, *Docquets of Letters Patent*, 282–3; Compton, 89; *List of Officers Claiming* (1663), 30; Add. 29570, f. 57. [3] *CSP Dom.* 1660–1, p. 44; Add. 1660–85, p. 92; *Pepys Diary*, 27 Oct. 1662. [4] *Camb. Antiq. Soc. Procs.* xvii. 105. [5] Warwick, *Mems.* 286; Add. 29570, f. 57; Underdown, 290; *Pepys Diary*, 6 May 1660; *HMC 5th Rep.* 207. [6] Add. 32324, f. 53; *CJ*, viii. 352, 423, 427, 435. [7] Add. 15948, f. 112; *CJ*, viii. 443, 502, 507, 525; *Pepys Diary*, 19 Oct. 1663.

E.R.E.

CONINGSBY, Thomas (1657–1729), of Hampton Court, Herefs.

LEOMINSTER 1679 (Oct.), 1681, 1685, 1689, 1690, 1695, 1698, 1701 (Feb.), 1701 (Dec.), 1702, 1705, 1708, 1715–18 June 1716

b. 2 Nov. 1657, o.s. of Humphrey Coningsby† of Hampton Court by Lettice, da. of Sir Arthur Loftus of Rathfarnham, co. Dublin [I]. *educ.* L. Inn, entered 1671. *m.* (1) lic. 18 Feb. 1675, Barbara (*div.* 1697), da. of Ferdinando Gorges, merchant, of Barbados and Eye Manor, Herefs., 3s. *d.v.p.* 3da.; (2) Apr. 1698, Lady Frances Jones, da. and coh. of Richard Jones*, 1st Earl of Ranelagh [I], 1s. *d.v.p.* 2da. *suc.* fa. 1671; *cr.* Baron Coningsby of Clanbrassil [I] 7 Apr. 1692, Baron Coningsby 18 June 1716, Earl of Coningsby 30 Apr. 1719.[1]

Commr. for assessment, Herefs. 1677–80, Herefs. and Leominster 1689–90; j.p. Herefs. 1678–c.81, 1687–July 1688, Oct. 1688–1721, dep. lt. 1689–1714, capt. of militia 1689–?90; high steward, Hereford 1695–*d.*; custos rot. Herefs. 1696–1721, Rad. 1714–21; ld. lt. Herefs. and Rad. 1714–21; steward of crown manors, Rad. 1714–21.[2]

Commr. for excise appeals [I] 1689–90; jt. paymaster-gen. [I] 1690–8; one of the lds. justices [I] 1690–2; v.-treas. [I] 1692–1710; PC [I] 1693–?1724; PC 13 Apr. 1693–7 Nov. 1724.

Coningsby's ancestors had been landholders in the West Midlands since the reign of Edward I. Sir Humphrey Coningsby, a judge, bought Hampton Court, four miles from Leominster, about 1510, and between the accession of Elizabeth I and the Civil War his descendants were seven times elected for the county. Coningsby's grandfather, Fitzwilliam Coningsby, was expelled from the Long Parliament as a monopolist; he was replaced in the House by Humphrey Coningsby, who was likewise soon disabled as a Royalist. The estate valued at £4,000 p.a. was heavily mortgaged; Coningsby described his grandfather as 'a man of great extravagancy and expense, as well as beyond description negligent in the management of his affairs'. Their fine was set at £4,000 on a declared rental of just over £800 p.a., but much of it was seemingly never paid. When Fitzwilliam Coningsby stood for Leominster in 1661 he was denied the poll because he was in prison for debt; he was not on good terms with his eldest son, from whom he alienated whatever he could, including the furniture and the title-deeds. Coningsby's mother escaped from her husband's creditors for a time by obtaining a post at Court, but by 1675 she was a prisoner in the King's Bench, and her steward, without her knowledge or consent, arranged the marriage of Coningsby, who was only just turned 17, with the daughter of Ferdinando Gorges, a notorious slaver called the 'King of the Blacks'. The marriage to a woman equally lacking in sense and breeding turned out quite as badly as might have been expected, though the financial acumen of Coningsby's father-in-law soon pulled the estate round. A local historian describes Coningsby as 'contending against the disadvantages of a neglected education, although he never overcame the evil effects of a want of early discipline and self-control. . . . Upright, courageous and high-principled, though vain, impulsive and impatient of control, Lord Coningsby's greatest enemy was himself.'[3]

Coningsby was first returned for Leominster at the second general election of 1679 in place of James Pytts* who had voted against exclusion. Henceforward he was to be invariably elected 'whether absent or present, without trouble or expense'. When he left for Westminster, Gorges, who was a cousin of Shaftesbury, urged him 'to write to him all the proceedings of Parliament . . . to encourage the people to choose him again, seeing him stand up for the good of the subject so much, and advising the *mobile* of that corporation every post'. An active Member, he was named to ten committees in the second Exclusion Parliament, of which the most important was to prepare an address insisting on exclusion, but he did not speak. He was duly re-elected to the Oxford Parliament, which he 'very nobly attended with good horses and men', according to his brother-in-law. He was appointed to the committee of elections and privileges, and secured an unexpected success with his maiden speech, when he proposed that the hapless Secretary Jenkins should carry Fitzharris's impeachment to the Lords. Writing to Gorges, he complained that 'instead of sitting like a free Parliament, he thought they sat more like a company of slaves in a garrison. . . . The King's guards were the greatest grievance of the nation.' At a meeting in the lodgings of John Scudamore*, Lord Scudamore, Shaftesbury is said to have offered Coningsby a captaincy in a revolutionary army. As the most moderate of the Herefordshire Whigs, Coningsby and Scudamore were on excellent terms until Mrs Coningsby discovered—through the keyhole—an intrigue between her husband and Lady Scudamore. The humiliating outcome was the elopement of the guilty pair, followed by the forced surrender of the lady to her husband's servants at pistol-point. The Tories were naturally delighted: 'these two were Parliament men in the last two Parliaments . . . and both great sticklers for the sober or godly party and the good old cause'. However, Gorges managed to patch up the marriage. The local Whig leader (Sir) Edward Harley* sent Coningsby a letter 'much more like a fatherly than a friendly advice', to which he replied that his constituents' support was unshaken, with the unspoken implication that the second seat might be available for Harley's son Robert.[4]

Coningsby remained under suspicion of holding Whig cabals at his home, attended by John Birch* and John Dutton Colt*. Laurence Hyde* advised

him not to stand in 1685 unless with the approval of the Duke of Beaufort (Henry Somerset*). Nevertheless he was re-elected. In James II's Parliament he was named to two unimportant committees, and a speech sometimes attributed to him was probably delivered by Thomas Christie*. He was restored to the commission of the peace in 1687, but he returned negative answers in 1688 on the repeal of the Test Act and Penal Laws, and was again removed.[5]

In the Convention, Coningsby was again an active Member, serving on 47 committees, acting as teller in eight divisions and making eight recorded speeches. According to Ailesbury's list he voted to agree with the Lords that the throne was not vacant, and he took part in the inquiry into the authors and advisers of grievances ordered on 5 Mar. 1689. He was appointed to the committee for the Wye and Lugg navigation, and with Paul Foley* acted as teller against adjourning the debate. He showed a keen interest in Irish affairs, being appointed to the committees to inquire into the delays over the relief of Londonderry and to consider raising money from the forfeited estates of Irish Jacobites. He took part in preparing the bill of attainder, but was against mass exceptions to the bill of indemnity. 'This is lumping indeed!' he exclaimed. He acted as teller with Sir Patience Ward* on an amendment to the bill for restoring corporations on 23 July, and Sir Edward Harley wrote with evident relief: 'Mr Coningsby carried himself very worthily'. Harley was probably less satisfied with Coningsby in the second session. His concern with Ireland continued; he was appointed to the committee for the relief of refugees, but he acted as teller for adjourning the debate on Commissary Shales on 26 Nov., and commended the modesty of George Churchill* in the sums he took for convoys. He was teller for adjourning the debate on the bill for restoring corporations on 2 Jan. 1690, and probably voted against the disabling clause. A few days later he told the House: 'Surrenderers were the scaffolds, and regulators were the builders: will you leave them out?'[6]

Coningsby remained a firm Whig, nevertheless. He was in high favour with William III after bandaging the latter's wound at the battle of the Boyne. His last years were darkened by domestic bereavement, unsuccessful litigation and political reverses. He died on 1 May 1729, and his grandson, the last of the family, survived him by only a few months.

[1] *St. Paul's Covent Garden* (Harl. Soc. Reg. xxxiii), 9; C. J. Robinson, *Mansions and Manors of Herefs.* 146–8; *L. Inn Reg.* i. 311. [2] *Symonds's Diary* (Cam. Soc. lxxiv), 195; BL Loan 29/74, letter to Sir Edward Harley, 28 Sept. 1689; *CSP Dom.* 1689–90, p. 455; *Arch. Camb.* (ser. 3), iii. 189. [3] *Vis. Salop* (Harl. Soc. xxviii), 130; *Cal. Comm. Comp.* 2064–71; Keeler, *Long Parl.* 139–

40; *CJ*, viii. 392; *CSP Dom. Add.* 1660–85, p. 319; G. F. Townsend, *Leominster*, 157, 171; T. Coningsby, *Manor of Marden*, i. 261–3, 327, 407, 411, 467, 480; C5/51/9. [4] *CSP Dom.* 1680–1, p. 225; 1682, pp. 290–1, 506; Add. 5822, f. 122; BL Loan 29/183, f. 96v, Sir Edward Harley to Robert Harley, 19 Aug. 1681, f. 100, Coningsby to Sir Edward Harley, 27 Aug. 1681. [5] *CSP Dom.* 1682, p. 292; N. Ireland PRO, Duros mss, DOD 638/3(1); Grey, viii. 365–6. [6] *CJ*, x. 205; BL Loan 29/140, Sir Edward to Robert Harley, 23 July 1689; Grey, ix. 379, 432, 522.

J.P.F.

CONNOCK, John I (1631–c.75), of Treworgey, St. Cleer, Cornw.

LISKEARD 5 May 1660

b. 31 July 1631, 1st s. of Nicholas Connock of St. Cleer by Joan, da. of Hannibal Vivian[†] of Trelowarren, Cornw. *educ.* M. Temple 1649. *m.* (1) by 1654, Bridget, da. and coh. of Walter Hele of Wimpston, Modbury, Devon, 1s.; (2) Elizabeth, da. of John Courtenay of Molland, Devon, wid. of John Tremayne of Collacombe, Cornw., 2s. 5da. *suc.* fa. 1641, uncle John in Treworgey estate 1658.[1]

Commr. for assessment, Cornw. 1661–74, sheriff 1669–70.

Connock was descended from a Wiltshire tanner who was appointed receiver of the duchy of Cornwall, and at the dissolution of the monasteries acquired extensive property in and around Liskeard, which he first represented in 1554. Connock's uncle, the head of the family, was also a duchy official; he served in the royalist army as major of horse in the first Civil War, and Treworgey was sequestrated in 1648, but no composition proceedings are recorded.

Connock was involved in a double return at Liskeard, two miles from his home, at the general election of 1660, and seated on the merits of the return. He made no recorded speeches in the Convention and was named to no committees, but was presumably a court supporter. He is not known to have stood again. His will dated 3 Dec. 1674 was proved at Bodmin on 27 Mar. 1676.[2]

[1] Vivian, *Vis. Cornw.* 93, 618; PCC 433 Ruthen, 46 Wootton. [2] *Paroch. Hist. Cornw.* i. 202; iii. 151; M. Coate, *Cornw. in Gt. Civil War*, 182, 267–8; *Cal. Comm. Comp.* 117, 2980; *List of Officers Claiming* (1663), 121; Cornw. RO, will.

M.W.H./P.W.

CONNOCK, John II (c.1654–1730), of Treworgey, St. Cleer, Cornw.

LISKEARD 1679 (Mar.), 1685

b. c.1654, 1st s. of John Connock I* by 1st w. *educ.* Christ Church, Oxf. matric. 16 Dec. 1670, aged 16. *m.* Maria, da. of Robert Burgoyne of South Tawton, Devon, 2s. 3da. *suc.* fa. 1676.

Commr. for assessment, Cornw. 1677–80, 1689–90, j.p. 1680–?d.; alderman, Liskeard 1685–Oct. 1688.

Connock was returned for Liskeard at the first general election of 1679. Classed as 'honest' by Shaftesbury, he made no speeches and was appointed to no committees in the first Exclusion Parliament; but he voted for the bill, probably under the influence of his colleague John Buller*. He soon went over to the Court, however, making way for Jonathan Trelawny I* in the autumn election, and he was added to the commission of the peace in 1680 and named to the corporation of Liskeard in the new charter. He regained his seat in 1685, but left no trace on the records of James II's Parliament. The Earl of Bath recommended him for re-election as court candidate in 1688, but he is not known to have stood again, though he accepted the Revolution and remained on the commission of the peace. The last of the family to sit in Parliament, he was buried at St. Stephen's by Saltash on 17 July 1730.

Vivian, *Vis. Cornw.* 93; *CSP Dom.* 1685, p. 66.

P.W.

CONWAY, Sir Henry, 1st Bt. (1635–69), of Bodrhyddan, Flints.

FLINTSHIRE 1661–4 June 1669

bap. 22 Feb. 1635, 2nd but 1st surv. s. of William Conway of Bodrhyddan by Lucy, da. of Thomas Mostyn of Rhyl. *m.* 7 Apr. 1661, Mary, da. of Sir Richard Lloyd I* of Esclus Hall, Denb., 2s. 2da. *suc.* fa. c.1654; *cr.* Bt. 25 July 1660.[1]

Sheriff, Flints. 1656–7, commr. for militia, Mar. 1660, j.p. Mar. 1660–d., dep. lt. c. Aug. 1660–d., commr. for assessment Aug. 1660–d., oyer and terminer, Wales, 1661, loyal and indigent officers, Flints. 1662.

The estate of Bodrhyddan had been in the hands of the Conways since the 13th century, but their only previous parliamentary experience had been for the county in 1558 and the boroughs in 1563. Conway's father, reputed to be a Roman Catholic, was added to the commission of array in 1643, and fortified Rhuddlan Castle for the King. After the war, he took the Covenant and the negative oath, and petitioned to compound, although too weak and old to travel to London. No further proceedings are recorded.[2]

Conway himself, probably an Anglican, was created a baronet at the Restoration and returned for the county in 1661. So far as can be ascertained, he was a totally inactive Member of the Cavalier Parliament. He was given leave to go into the country on 16 Nov. 1666, and died on 4 June 1669.[3]

[1] *Jnl. Flints. Hist. Soc.* xix. 77, 79, 86. [2] J. E. Griffith, *Peds. of Anglesey and Caern. Fams.* 260–1; *Jnl. Flints. Hist. Soc.* xviii. 54;

Cal. Comm. Comp. 1632; *Wood's Life and Times* (Oxf. Hist. Soc. xxvi), 46. [3] *Jnl. Flints. Hist. Soc.* xx. 1.

A.M.M.

CONWAY, Sir John, 2nd Bt. (c.1663–1721), of Bodrhyddan, Flints.

FLINTSHIRE	1685, 1695, 1698, 1701 (Feb.)
FLINT BOROUGHS	2 Feb.–2 July 1702
FLINTSHIRE	1705
FLINT BOROUGHS	1708, 1710
FLINTSHIRE	1713
FLINT BOROUGHS	1715–27 Apr. 1721

b. c.1663, 1st s. of Sir Henry Conway*. *educ.* Eton 1678; Christ Church, Oxf. matric. 10 June 1679, aged 16. *m.* (1) c.1687, Maria Margaretta (*d.* June 1690), da. and coh. of John Digby of Gayhurst, Bucks., 1s., *d.v.p.* 2da.; (2) Sept. 1701 (with £20,000), Penelope, da. of Richard Grenville of Wotton Underwood, Bucks., 2da. *suc.* fa. 4 June 1669.[1]

Freeman, Denbigh 1679; sheriff, Flints. Jan.–Nov. 1688, dep. lt. 1689–?96, j.p. by 1691–6, 1700–*d.*; commr. for assessment Denb. and Flints. 1689–90.[2]

Conway inherited his family's traditional loyalty to the crown, but in his case it was tempered by an equal loyalty to the Church of England and the established institutions of the country. He accompanied the Duke of York to Oxford in 1683, receiving an honorary degree on the occasion, and he was returned for the county to the Parliament of 1685 as a Tory. He was appointed only to the committee of elections and privileges and to that to recommend ways of keeping up the price of wool and corn. He seems to have been a somewhat wild young man about town, and although his first wife came from a well-known Roman Catholic family, he was pricked as sheriff in 1688 to prevent him from standing for re-election. After regaining his seat in 1695 he voted consistently with the Tories, refusing to sign the Association of 1696. He died at Bath on 27 Apr. 1721, aged 58, and was buried at Rhuddlan, the last male of his family.[3]

[1] *Jnl. Flints. Hist. Soc.* xx. 3–5; Luttrell, v. 92. [2] J. Williams, *Recs. of Denbigh*, 139; *CSP Dom.* 1687–9, p. 143. [3] Luttrell, ii. 238; *HMC Downshire*, i. 286.

A.M.M.

CONYERS, Tristram (1619–84), of Walthamstow, Essex.

MALDON	1660

b. 5 Sept. 1619, 1st s. of William Conyers of Walthamstow, serjeant-at-law, by 1st w. Mary, da. and coh. of Sir Francis Harvey†, j.c.p., of Cotes, Northants. *educ.* Merchant Taylors' 1631; St. John's, Oxf. 1635; M. Temple 1635, called 1643. *m.* bef. 1650, Winifred, da.

of Sir Gilbert Gerard, 1st Bt.*, of Flambards, Mdx., 5s. 6da. *suc.* fa. 1659.[1]

J.p. Essex by 1653–70, 1673–*d.*, commr. for assessment 1657, Jan. 1660–80, militia Mar. 1660; sewers, Havering and Dagenham levels Sept. 1660, Essex Oct. 1660; bencher, M. Temple 1664, reader 1669, treas. 1672–3; commr. for recusants, Essex 1675; steward, Waltham forest ?1676–*d.*

Serjeant-at-law 1674–*d.*

Conyers's family left Boltby in Yorkshire to settle at Walthamstow at the beginning of the 17th century. His grandfather was a London merchant, and his father, a wealthy lawyer from the Middle Temple, acted as judge of assize on the Norfolk circuit in 1654.

Conyers, a successful lawyer, was involved in a double return at Maldon in the general election of 1660, but was allowed to take his seat. Lord Wharton marked him as a friend, to be managed by his father-in-law. An inactive Member of the Convention he was appointed to nine committees, of which the most important in the first session was to consider legal forms of the Restoration. After the recess he was among those entrusted with the bill for endowing vicarages out of impropriate rectories and the clause repealing the Statute of Livery. Wharton sent him a copy of the case for modified episcopacy with objections and answers. He never stood again. He was removed from the commission of the peace in 1670 as a sympathizer with dissenters, but was restored three years later, and retained during the Exclusion crisis. He died on 6 Aug. 1684 and was buried at Walthamstow. His son John contested East Grinstead in 1685 and 1689, and sat for the borough as a Tory almost continuously from 1695 to his death 30 years later.[2]

[1] *Vis. Essex* ed. Howard, 24; Morant, *Essex*, i. 48–49. [2] *M. Temple Bench Bk.* 210; Essex RO, T 2/26; assize rolls 35/121/2, D/DCV3/9; C191/7/48, 59.

M.W.H./G.H.

COOK, Sir William, 2nd Bt. (c.1630–1708), of Broome Hall, Norf. and Mendham, Suff.

GREAT YARMOUTH	1685
NORFOLK	1689, 1690, 1698

b. c.1630, o.s. of Sir William Cook, 1st Bt., of Broome Hall by 1st w. Mary, da. of Thomas Astley of Melton Constable, Norf. *educ.* Emmanuel, Camb. 1647; G. Inn 1648. *m.* settlement 1664, Jane (*d.* 1698), da. and coh. of William Steward of Barton Mills, Suff., 7da. *suc.* fa. Feb. 1681.[1]

J.p. Norf. Sept. 1660–Feb. 1688, 1689–*d.*, capt. of militia ft. c. Oct. 1660–at least 1679; commr. for assessment, Norf. 1661–80, Suff. 1679–80, Norf. and Suff. 1689–90, recusants, Norf. 1675, dep. lt. by 1676–Feb. 1688, Nov. 1688–*d.*; freeman, Yarmouth 1685.[2]

Cook's grandfather, from a minor Suffolk gentry

family settled at Linstead by the 15th century, acquired Broome by marriage in 1603. His father apparently avoided commitment in the Civil War, though he was named to the assessment commission in 1652. He signed the Norfolk address for a free Parliament in 1660 and was created a baronet in 1663. Cook himself was 'very well versed in every kind of learning, but especially distinguished by the suavity of his manners', and already 'venerable' in his forties. An active militia officer and a strong loyalist, he was much distressed at the dissension between Court and Commons revealed in the 1677 session. As an adherent of Lord Yarmouth (Robert Paston*), he was regarded as a suitable court candidate in 1679, should Sir Christopher Calthorpe* decline to contest the county again, and he was again mentioned in 1681 as a possible compromise candidate, having 'always been accounted of the loyal party', but not 'violent'. In 1682 he signed the address abhorring the 'Association'.[3]

Cook was returned for Yarmouth in 1685 on the Paston interest, though, as he wrote to Archbishop Sancroft, he felt himself

> very incompetent for so great a trust in this critical juncture. There is nothing can sweeten this service but the thoughts of Lambeth being so near Westminster and the pleasure I shall receive by waiting on your grace will smooth the roughness of that province which is put upon me. It would still add to my happiness if I might (without offence) beg the care of one of your grace's servants to procure me a small quiet lodging on Lambeth side of the river with a bed in some near chamber for my servant, and what is ordinary in the kind will suit well with my circumstances, which highly incite me to frugality and to wish for a short but happy Parliament.

A moderately active Member of James II's Parliament, he was appointed to nine committees, none of which was of major political importance. He probably introduced the bill to renew the Yarmouth Harbour Act, since he was the first Member appointed to the committee.[4]

In 1688 Cook agreed that 'some of the Penal Laws may require a review and amendment', but he was determined 'not to part with the Tests', and he was removed from local office. Like Sir John Holland* and most of the other county magistrates he refused to act with Roman Catholics on the bench in October 1688. He was returned for the county in 1689, and, according to Anthony Rowe*, voted to agree with the Lords that the throne was not vacant. He had leave to go into the country for his health on 18 Feb. but returned to become again a moderately active Member. He was appointed to 20 committees in the Convention, including those to consider the abolition of the hearth-tax, to adopt new oaths of allegiance and supremacy, to repeal

the Corporations Act and to inquire into the reasons for the fall in rents. In both sessions he was among those ordered to consider the bill for the better recovery of tithe.[5]

Cook returned from the recess in the company of the Whig Members for Yarmouth, George England* and Samuel Fuller*. He was named to the committees to restrain election expenditure, to inquire into the miscarriages of the war, to establish a 'court of conscience' for small claims at Norwich, and to draft the address to ask who was responsible for the appointment of Commissary Shales. He was added to the committee of elections and privileges on 9 Dec., but a week later he again applied for leave, and was probably absent from the division on the disabling clause in the bill to restore corporations.[6]

Cook, who remained a Tory under William III, was obliged to sell Broome. He died at Mendham in January 1708, aged 78, the only member of his family to enter Parliament, and was buried at Cranworth. His epitaph proclaims him an avowed defender of monarchy and hierarchy, 'equally unaffected by the wicked artifices of rabid Papists and schismatics'.[7]

[1] Vis. Norf. (Harl. Soc. lxxv), 54; Vis. Norf. Notes (Norf. Rec. Soc. xxvii), 64. [2] Cal. Treas. Bks. i. 64; CSP Dom. 1679–80, p. 32; HMC 6th Rep. 382; Norf. Ltcy. Jnl. (Norf. Rec. Soc. xxx), 7, 92, 154; Yarmouth corp. assembly bk. 1680–1701, p. 84. [3] Vis. Suff. ed. Metcalfe, 19, 128; Blomefield, Norf. x. 109; W. Rye, Address from the Gentry of Norf. (1660); CSP Dom. 1675–6, p. 323; 1682, p. 56; Add. 36988, ff. 145–6, 180; E. Bohun, Autobiog. 24–25. [4] Bodl. Tanner mss 31, f. 17. [5] Norf. Ltcy. Jnl. 88–89. [6] Diary of Dean Davies (Cam. Soc. lxviii), 57. [7] Blomefield, x. 110; Le Neve, Mon. Angl. 1650–1715, p. 226.

E.C.

COOKE, John (c.1648–1726), of Petworth, Suss.

MIDHURST   1681
ARUNDEL   22 Feb. 1694, 1698, 1701 (Feb.), 1701
                             (Dec.)

b. c.1648, 1st s. of Edward Cooke of Field Place, Goring by 1st w. Katherine, da. of Thomas Fry of Battlehurst, Kirdford. educ. M. Temple 1667. m. lic. 17 Oct. 1671, Susan (d. 19 Apr. 1707), da. of John Whitehead of Clandon, Surr., wid. of her cos. George Stringer of the Middle Temple and coh. to her uncle Richard Stringer of Petworth, 2s. 1da. d.v.p. suc. fa. 1662.[1]
    Commr. for assessment, Suss. 1673–80, 1689, j.p. 1674–c.81, May 1688–d., dep. lt. 1692–?d.

Cooke came from a minor gentry family of 16th century date that had apparently avoided involvement in the Civil War. He alienated his inheritance to the Shelleys in 1669, but his marriage two years later brought him property in Petworth, eight miles from Midhurst. He was returned for the borough, presumably as a supporter of exclusion, in 1681, but left no trace on the records of the Oxford Parliament. In the following September he was reported to be the choice of 'the dissenting party' for Arundel at the next election, and he was removed from the commission of the peace. There is no evidence that he stood in 1685. He was looked upon as a Whig collaborator, and in May 1688 James II's agents recommended him to be restored as j.p. He sat for Arundel as a Whig under William III and was buried at Goring on 1 Oct. 1726, the only member of his family to sit in Parliament.[2]

[1] *Suss. Arch. Colls.* lxxviii. 66–67; Add. 5699, pp. 128, 131; PCC 16 Laud. [2] *Suss. Arch. Colls.* lxii. 202; PCC 225 Plymouth; *CSP Dom.* 1680–1, p. 473.

B.M.C./B.D.H.

COOKE, William (c.1620–1703), of Highnam Court, Glos.

GLOUCESTER   1679 (Mar.), 1689, 1690

b. c.1620, 1st s. of Sir Robert Cooke[†] of Highnam by 1st w. Dorothy, da. of Sir Miles Fleetwood[†] of Aldwinkle, Northants.; bro. of Edward Cooke[†]. *educ.* G. Inn 1636. *m.* lic. 30 Mar. 1648, Anne, da. and coh. of Dennis Rolle of Stevenstone, Devon, 9s. (5 *d.v.p.*) 7da. *suc.* fa. 1643.[1]

Commr. for assessment, Glos. 1648–52, 1657, Aug. 1660–80, Gloucester 1661–3, 1666–80, Glos. and Gloucester 1689–90, militia, Glos. 1648, Glos. and Gloucester Mar. 1660; lt.-col. of militia ft. Glos. Apr. 1660, j.p. 1648–?64, 1670–?79, ?1689–bef.1701, dep. lt. July 1660–?64, 1670–?79, 1689–bef. 1701, commr. for corporations 1662–3; verderer, Forest of Dean 1668–?d.; alderman, Gloucester 1672–d., mayor 1673–4, Nov. 1688–9; commr. of inquiry, Forest of Dean 1673, 1679, 1683, 1691.[2]

Cooke was descended from a cadet branch of the Essex puritan family seated at Gidea Hall which figured so prominently in Tudor Parliaments. His grandfather acquired the manor of Highnam just outside Gloucester by marriage in about 1597, and represented Gloucestershire in the Addled Parliament. His father and younger brother Edward were both in arms for the Parliament, but Cooke is not known to have played any part in the Civil War, though he held local office throughout the Interregnum. He signed the Gloucestershire address of welcome to the King, and was nominated to the proposed order of the Royal Oak, with an income estimated at £1,000 p.a.[3]

It is not known why Cooke was removed from local office after serving as commissioner for corporations. As he was restored in 1670 he presumably had no qualms about enforcing the Conventicles Act, and he was nominated alderman for life under the new Gloucester charter of 1672, at which time he was, with Duncombe Colchester*, regarded as a principal agent of the high steward,

Lord Worcester (Henry Somerset*), on the corporation. In April 1675 he was defeated by his fellow-alderman, Henry Norwood*, in the by-election occasioned by the death of (Sir) Edward Massey*. Either Cooke or some of the electors petitioned, but on 7 Mar. 1678 the elections committee reported in Norwood's favour, to which, after a division, the House agreed. But 12 months later Cooke was returned for the city at the first general election of 1679 with the unanimous approval of the corporation and apparently unopposed. Shaftesbury marked him 'base'. A moderately active Member of the first Exclusion Parliament, he was appointed to the committee of elections and privileges and three others of secondary importance. He was given leave for a month on 1 May, and was absent from the division on the first exclusion bill. 'A worthy gentleman of a plentiful estate', he fought the next election as an exclusionist, but was defeated by the lord lieutenant's candidate, Sir Charles Berkeley III*. He was removed from local office, and his petition was never reported from the elections committee. He left the country party when 'his eyes were opened' to the villainy of John Arnold*, and it is unlikely that he stood at the next two elections.[4]

When the Roman Catholic mayor of Gloucester resigned in November 1688, Cooke was chosen in his place. He was returned unopposed to the Convention as a Tory, and voted to agree with the Lords that the throne was not vacant. Again moderately active, he was named to 31 committees, of which the most important were to inquire into the authors and advisers of recent grievances, to examine the late solicitors to the Treasury, to prepare a militia bill and to consider the toleration bill. But some of these entries may refer to John Coke II*. He was also appointed to committees for the bills to abolish the court of the marches and to establish 'courts of conscience' for small claims for Bristol and Gloucester. After the recess his committees included those to reverse the attainder of Sir Thomas Armstrong*, to restore corporations, and to deprive Lord Worcester (now Duke of Beaufort) of actions *de scandalis magnatum* against his principal Whig opponents. Re-elected in 1690, Cooke was reckoned a government supporter. He died early in 1703. His grandson represented Gloucester as a Whig from 1705 to 1710.[5]

[1] *Vis. Glos.* ed. Fenwick and Metcalfe, 47–48. [2] *Parl. Intell.* 9 Apr. 1660; *Bristol and Glos. Arch. Soc. Trans.* lviii. 260–3; Gloucester Guildhall, council bk. 1656–80, pp. 498, 581; 1681–99, p. 221; 1700–60, p. 89; *Cal. Treas. Bks.* ii. 594; iii. 262; iv. 150; vi. 196; vii. 962; ix. 1156. [3] Keeler, *Long Parl.* 141; *Cal. Cl. SP,* iv. 553, 685; *Glos. N. and Q.* i. 166–7. [4] Rudder, *Glos.* 117; *CSP Dom.* 1672, p. 444; *Ailesbury Mems.* 30–31; *HMC Ormonde,* n.s. iv. 346. [5] Gloucester Guildhall, council bk. 1700–60, p. 89.

B.D.H.

COOPER, Sir Anthony Ashley, 2nd Bt. (1621–83), of Wimborne St. Giles, Dorset and The Close, Salisbury, Wilts.[1]

TEWKESBURY	1640 (Apr.)
WILTSHIRE	1653, 1654, 1656,[2] 1659
DOWNTON	7 Jan. 1660[3]
WILTSHIRE	1660

b. 22 July 1621, 1st s. of Sir John Cooper, 1st Bt.[†], of Rockbourne, Hants by 1st w. Anne, da. and h. of Sir Anthony Ashley, 1st Bt.[†], of Wimborne St. Giles; bro. of George Cooper*. *educ.* privately (Aaron Guerdon) 1627–37; Exeter, Oxf. 1637–8; L. Inn 1638. *m.* (1) 25 Feb. 1639, Margaret (*d.* 11 July 1649), da. of Sir Thomas Coventry[†], 1st Baron Coventry of Aylesborough, *s.p.*; (2) 15 Apr. 1650, Lady Frances Cecil (*d.* 31 Dec. 1652), da. of David Cecil[†], 3rd Earl of Exeter, 2s. (1 *d.v.p.*); (3) 30 Aug. 1655, (with £4,000) Margaret, da. of William Spencer[†], 2nd Baron Spencer, *s.p. suc.* fa. 23 Mar. 1631; *cr.* Baron Ashley 20 Apr. 1661; Earl of Shaftesbury 23 Apr. 1672.

Dep. lt. Dorset 1642–4, July 1660–72; sheriff, Dorset 1643, Wilts. Dec. 1646–Feb. 1648; j.p. Dorset 1643–?74, Wilts. 1646–?74, Mdx. 1653–?59; commr. for assessment, Dorset and Wilts. 1647–52, 1657, Jan. 1660–1, Mdx. 1652, Jan. 1660–1, militia, Dorset and Wilts. 1648, 1659, Mar. 1660, administering engagement, Dorset 1650; freeman, Poole 1651, Salisbury 1654; commr. for oyer and terminer, Mdx. 1653–4, Western circuit 1654–5, July 1660, scandalous ministers, Dorset, Poole and Wilts. 1654; v.-adm. Hants Apr. 1660–1; commr. for sewers, Som. Aug. 1660, highways and sewers, London and Westminster 1662; ld. lt. Dorset 1672–4; high steward, Salisbury 1672–*d.*; bencher, L. Inn 1673.[4]

Col. of ft. and capt. of horse (royalist) 1643–4; gov. Weymouth 1643; field-marshal-gen. Dorset (parliamentary) 1644; brig. 1644; col. of horse Jan.–Nov. 1660; gov. I.o.W. Feb. 1660–1.

Commr. for law reform 1652–3; judge of probate 1653–4; Councillor of State 14 July 1653–Dec. 1654, May–Oct. 1659, 2 Jan.–31 May 1660; commr. for the army (acting) Dec. 1659–Jan. 1660; PC 31 May 1660–19 May 1674, ld. pres. Apr.–Oct. 1679; commr. for trade Nov. 1660–72, plantations Dec. 1660–70; chancellor of Exchequer 1661–72; treas. of prizes 1664–7; ld. of Treasury 1667–72; commr. for union with Scotland 1670; pres. council of trade and plantations 1672–4; ld. chancellor 1672–4.

Member, Society of Mines Royal and Mineral and Battery Works 1662, gov. 1663–*d.*; asst. R. Adventurers into Africa by 1664–71; ld. prop. Carolina 1663–*d.*; member, Hudson's Bay Co. 1668–73, dep. gov. 1673–4, committee 1674–5; sub-gov. Royal Africa Co. 1672–4, asst. 1674–7; member, Skinners' Co. 1681–*d.*[5]

FRS 1663.

Cooper was descended on both sides from gentry families which came to the fore under the Tudors. His paternal grandfather sat for Whitchurch in 1586. His father, one of the country party in the 1628–9 Parliament, left over £35,000 debts, but even after considerable sales of land by direction of the court of wards, an enduring grievance, Cooper was enjoying an income of £2,350 p.a. before the

Civil War. He was not eager to take up arms in the Civil War, and changed sides at the beginning of 1644. He was closely associated with the Government in Barebones's Parliament and the opening months of the Protectorate, but withdrew from the Council of State at the end of 1654, on the defeat of the motion to offer Cromwell the crown, and was excluded from the 1656 session of Parliament. He took a prominent part in the overthrow of the military regime in 1659, and supported the return of the secluded Members.

Cooper never sat for his native county, where he was unpopular as a harsh and unscrupulous landlord. He controlled one seat at Poole, his father's constituency, but he preferred to stand again as knight of the shire for Wiltshire. Though he owned two manors in the county, he visited them only to hold courts and collect rents, and when he was appointed sheriff in 1646 he had to take a house in Salisbury. Nevertheless he was probably returned unopposed. As a Privy Councillor he acted as a government spokesman in the Convention, but with an exceptionally powerful treasury bench, he was required to be no more than an active Member, serving on 45 committees and making 24 recorded speeches. He was one of the committee of seven to draw up an answer to the King's letter on 1 May. He was named to the delegation of 12 Members sent to the King at Breda and helped to draw up their instructions. He took part in no less than ten conferences with the Lords, covering most of the principal business of the session. On 4 June he acted as one of the commissioners for administering the oath of allegiance. He spoke against the proviso to the indemnity bill aimed at compelling Edmund Prideaux* to surrender the enormous profits made by his father during the Interregnum:

> He was free to speak because he never received any salary; but looked upon the proviso as dangerous to the peace of the nation, saying it reached Generals [George] Monck* and Montagu [Edward Montagu I*] after the House had given them thanks, and thousands more.

Though closely associated with the Presbyterians, Cooper was well known to be totally devoid of any religious belief other than faith in his stars; but he found widespread support when he declared on 16 July:

> Our religion was too much intermixed with interest, neither was it ripe now to handle religion. But he moved the whole committee might be adjourned for three months.

He twice acted as teller for the Government on supply, in favour of continuing the debate on tunnage and poundage on 16 July and against resuming the debate on Irish cattle five days later. On 23 July he brought a message from the King about exports of cloth. When the fate of the regicides was under discussion, Cooper signed a certificate in favour of John Hutchinson* and presented the petition of George Fleetwood†, who had married his brother George's sister-in-law. He spoke against making Sir Arthur Hesilrige† liable to the death penalty, saying that 'he thought this man not considerable enough'. On 10 Sept., he was one of the Members instructed to draft an amendment to the disbanding bill. With his old enemy, Denzil Holles*, he acted as teller against the Lords' amendments to the bill for settling ministers, and on 13 Sept. he had the satisfaction of informing the House that the King had agreed to that bill and also to the abolition of his bugbear, the court of wards, which had sold two of the Cooper estates to Holles a quarter of a century before.[6]

Cooper was a commissioner for the trial of the regicides, and in the second session was named to the committee for the attainder of Oliver Cromwell, who had once, according to report, nearly become his father-in-law. He spoke against the court of wards (21 Nov.) and a few days later, mindful of the importance to Poole of the tobacco-pipe manufacture, moved against the export of pipeclay. When Sir Walter Erle* complained of the misconduct of the militia, Cooper replied that it was not approved by the King but reprimanded. On 19 Dec. he spoke against giving public money to those—many of them Dorset electors—who had helped Charles to escape after Worcester.[7]

Cooper did not stand at the general election, when his parliamentary interest reached its nadir. Even at Poole his brother lost his seat, and though two of his associates were eventually declared elected there they had to endure the tribulations of a double return. On 20 Apr. 1661 he was raised to the peerage as Lord Ashley, and two days later he became chancellor of the Exchequer. For the next six years he was primarily concerned with routine financial administration, though as a west country landowner he could not avoid supporting the Irish cattle bill in the Lords in 1666. But he remained loyal to the Clarendon administration till, and even beyond, the end, twice speaking against the impeachment of the fallen lord chancellor. Through Bullen Reymes* he was able to undermine the Strangways interest at Weymouth, which returned Ashley's former ward Sir John Coventry* at a by-election in 1667 and his son in 1670. But he was never a territorial magnate, and in 1670 neighbouring Downton rejected his business associate John Man* and Poole gave him some offence in its choice of Thomas Trenchard I*. Meanwhile his title had

contributed to the initials of the Cabal, and he had become one of the makers of policy, though the religious clauses of the Treaty of Dover were concealed from him. The Stop of the Exchequer, the third Dutch war and the Declaration of Indulgence all belong to his period of power, though later he denied responsibility for all save the last. It was this that gave the occasion for his appointment as lord chancellor, for Lord Keeper Bridgman had qualms about extending the royal prerogative so far, and was otherwise ill-qualified for office in a crisis. At the same time he was advanced two steps in the peerage as Earl of Shaftesbury. His new office gave him the opportunity greatly to extend his interest. Owing to the long recess there were a number of vacant seats, and before Parliament reassembled the new lord chancellor issued on his own authority writs for at least 15 by-elections. Of the Members returned, ten were court dependants, and not more than three (Josiah Child, George Cooper and John Man) were personally associated with the lord chancellor. Unfortunately it was the last two that attracted most attention, because Giles Strangways* believed, no doubt correctly, that the writs had been so timed as to ensure the defeat of his son Thomas* at both Poole and Weymouth, and exaggerated estimates of the total number of seats involved were made. When the House of Commons ordered new elections to be held on the Speaker's warrant, only three results were changed. Thomas Strangways came in by agreement at Poole, and at Dover and Wendover respectively the officials Sir Edward Spragge and Edward Backwell were unseated on petition by Thomas Papillon* and Thomas Wharton*, both later to be closely linked with Shaftesbury. The other by-elections for which writs were issued on the same day produced seven courtiers and at most two Shaftesburians—Sir Scrope Howe* and Sir Samuel Barnardiston*, both county Members.

Meanwhile, in the Lords, this error of judgment—for such it was, in view of the Commons' jealousy of their privileges and suspicion of the executive, although the lord chancellor had ample precedent on his side—had been compounded by another, his famous *delenda est Carthago* speech against the Dutch. The withdrawal of the Declaration of Indulgence on 8 Mar. was a confession of the failure of Shaftesbury's policy, though he was not actually dismissed until November. Almost at once he began to associate with the 'Hotspurs' of the Upper House, and on 20 Apr. 1675 he signed the protest against the non-resisting test. In October his candidate Thomas Moore* was humiliatingly defeated in the Dorset by-election; but it was not through a conventional territorial interest that Shaftesbury presented a threat to the Government. His London house was suspect as a focal point of sedition and intrigue, and on 16 Feb. 1676 Secretary Williamson, disturbing a colloquy with (Sir) Edward Harley*, brought him a message 'that his Majesty thought it were much better he were at home in the country'. Far from heeding the warning, Shaftesbury took up residence at Thanet House within the jurisdiction of the corporation. Thanks to his extensive commercial interests, and the adaptability which had first won him a seat in Parliament, he talked the same language as the City magnates, and henceforward was in almost daily contact with their leaders, Sir Robert Clayton,* Sir Thomas Player*and Thomas Pilkington*. His immediate aim was to force a dissolution of the Cavalier Parliament, in which Danby had succeeded in forming a relatively stable court majority, by appealing over its head to the City and country at large. When it reassembled in 1677, Shaftesbury supported the argument that its legal existence had been automatically terminated by its long recess. He found few sympathizers in the House of Lords, which committed him to the Tower, where he remained till February 1678. Thanks to his steadfastness in imprisonment, he emerged the principal figure among the country peers, and through his influence over the Hon. William Russell* he was in a good position to co-ordinate opposition tactics in both Houses. Moreover, his secretary Thomas Bennett* had entered the Commons, where he acted as Shaftesbury's mouthpiece, whipping up the excitement over the Popish Plot and the revelations of Ralph Montagu*.

Shaftesbury's interest was not much in evidence at the Exclusion elections; even in the borough from which he took his title, Bennett owed his return to his own local influence, aided by a modest subvention from the county Member, Thomas Freke I*. But the list of Members of the new Parliament which Shaftesbury drew up confirms Burnet's view that his real strength lay in his profound knowledge of the political nation. His estimate of the opposition strength was over-sanguine, judged by the severe test of readiness to vote against the court in the vital division on the exclusion bill; nevertheless only 28 Members deserted the Whigs, while 18 marked as 'base' or 'vile' voted for the bill, an error of some 8 per cent. Meanwhile, in a fruitless attempt to reduce the political temperature, the King had named Shaftesbury president of the council, taking good care, however, that this hybrid body should know nothing of affairs of state. It was not consulted over the dissolution of Parliament,

which it had singularly failed to control. The second general election of 1679 greatly strengthened the Whigs, and soon afterwards Shaftesbury was dismissed. Adjournment followed adjournment in the hope that the excitement would diminish; the press was muzzled, but Shaftesbury was astonishingly successful in keeping up the ferment by means of the Green Ribbon Club and its lesser brethren, the pope-burnings, the presentation of the Duke of York as a recusant, and the organization of petitions, aided by the continued reverberations of the Popish Plot. When Parliament at last met, the exclusion bill passed through the Commons without a division and was brought up to the Lords on 15 Nov. 1680. There followed the famous oratorical duel between Halifax and Shaftesbury, though the rejection of the bill was a foregone conclusion. Hitherto, Shaftesbury's concentration on the single issue of exclusion had been a source of strength; now, faced with the impossibility of reviving the bill in the current session, a section of the more selfish and opportunist Whigs, led by Montagu and Sir William Jones*, threatened defection, but were easily crushed. At the 1681 elections the Whigs were better organized than ever before, though once again Shaftesbury's advice was ignored or rejected by the neighbouring boroughs (Downton, Christchurch and Shaftesbury). But he probably approved, if he did not originate, the instructions delivered to many Members by their constituents to reject all 'expedients'.

The dissolution of the Oxford Parliament may have prompted Shaftesbury to consider an armed revolt; if so, the cold reception of his proposals by the more respectable Whigs, such as John Scudamore*, Lord Scudamore, deterred him. The execution of Fitzharris frightened many of the Popish Plot witnesses into offering their services against Shaftesbury, and on 2 July he was arrested and his papers impounded. On 24 Nov. 1681, the Middlesex grand jury, empanelled by Pilkington as sheriff and including Barnardiston, Papillon, John Dubois* and Edward Rudge* returned a verdict of *ignoramus*. But in the following year the Whigs lost control of the City, and the day before the new Tory sheriffs were sworn in Shaftesbury went into hiding. His judgment clouded by ill health, he urged on his allies the necessity of immediate insurrection, but neither Russell and his fellow-aristocrats on the Council of Six nor his west-country associates like John Trenchard* and Sir William Courtenay* responded. He slipped across to Holland in a small boat; fortunately for him, Carthage was still undestroyed, and the Amsterdam patriciate accorded him sanctuary. He died there on 21 Jan. 1683.

No attempt can be made here to assess as a whole the political career of so controversial a figure. Unlike Pym, he had to contend with a government backed by foreign subsidies, and the tiny standing army of the Restoration was sufficient to limit the coercive effect of the mob. Forced to restrict himself to constitutional methods, he made important contributions to the development of Parliament, but rather outside its walls than within, skilful debater though he undoubtedly was. The Opposition could not hope to emulate the discipline of the government benches, as it had been developed by Danby. But Shaftesbury's detailed knowledge of England and flair for publicity in all its forms enabled him to enlarge the political nation and produce the remarkable election results of 1679–81. It was not without reason that the Tory counter-attack of the ensuing years concentrated on the electorates.

[1] Factual information in this biography is based on K. H. D. Haley, *The First Earl of Shaftesbury*. [2] Excluded. [3] Double return of 23 Dec. 1640 decided in his favour. [4] W. D. Christie, *Life of Shaftesbury*, i. pp. xxvii. liv; Hutchins, *Dorset*, i. 32; Hoare, *Wilts.* Salisbury, 445; C181/7/24; *Tudor and Stuart Proclamations* ed. Steele, i. 405. [5] BL Loan 16; E. E. Rich, *Hudson's Bay Co.* i. 85. [6] Christie, p. xli; Bowman diary, ff. 51, 85v, 154v; *Old Parl. Hist.* xxii. 444. [7] *Old Parl. Hist.* xxiii. 21, 32, 53, 59.

J.P.F.

COOPER, George (1626–89), of Farley, Wilts.

POOLE   24 Oct. 1654, 1660, 3–6 Feb. 1673

bap. 15 Dec. 1626, 2nd s. of Sir John Cooper, 1st Bt.[†], of Rockbourne, Hants, and bro. of Sir Anthony Ashley Cooper*. *educ.* Exeter, Oxf. 1642. *m.* July 1647, Elizabeth, da. and coh. of John Oldfield, Fishmonger and sugar refiner, of London, 2s. (1 *d.v.p.*) 6da.[1]
Capt. (parliamentary) by 1644; maj. 1646.
Commr. for militia, Tower Hamlets 1648–9, Wilts. 1659, Mdx. and Wilts. Mar. 1660; j.p. Mdx. 1648–July 1660, Dorset by 1649–52, Wilts. 1653–bef. 1657; commr. for assessment, Mdx. 1650, 1652, Wilts. 1657, Mdx. and Wilts. Jan. 1660, Wilts. 1673–80, scandalous ministers, Wilts. 1654, oyer and terminer, Western circuit 1655; freeman, Poole Apr. 1660; treas. of prizes, Dover 1666.[2]
Trustee for maintenance of ministers 1649–Feb. 1660; member, high court of justice 1650, 1654; commr. of Admiralty Feb.–July 1660, revenue arrears [I] 1671.[3]

Cooper, in the judgment of Edmund Ludlow*, was 'an honest gentleman, though brother to Sir Anthony', by whom he was completely overshadowed. He held office throughout the Interregnum, but his career reached its apogee with his appointment to the admiralty board by the Rump. He was returned for Poole on his brother's interest at the general election of 1660, and marked by Lord Wharton as a friend. He may have voted with the Opposition, but he withdrew from the ballot for the delegation to The Hague, and his only known

positive action in the Convention was to claim privilege to extract his servant from the Counter, and even this may have been James Cowper*. His chief concern was to retain the crown lands in Clarendon Park, which he had bought for £3,000 in debentures, in which he hoped for support from the Presbyterian peers, but his petition was unsuccessful. The park was granted to the Duke of Albemarle (Gen. George Monck*) in 1665, but Cooper continued to reside at Farley, in the neighbourhood.[4]

In any case Cooper's growing family must have pressed on his resources. It was no doubt his brother, as treasurer of prizes, who obtained for him a post at Dover in the second Dutch war. His seat on the Irish revenue commission brought him into contact with the Earl of Ranelagh (Richard Jones*), with whom he later entered into financial transactions. He was elected for Poole on 3 Feb. 1673, but his return was declared void at the instance of the indignant Giles Strangways*, the writ having been issued by Cooper's brother, then lord chancellor, during the recess without authority from the House. Cooper's willingness to lend himself to this dubious procedure may have been induced by a loan from Shaftesbury, the interest on which was forgiven five years later.[5]

Cooper survived his brother, and on 25 Aug. 1683 assigned the £1,200 owed to him by Ranelagh, John Bence* and others to his daughter Catherine. Having mortgaged his estate, he was described as 'lately deceased' in July 1689. His two sons died childless without achieving parliamentary careers, but his daughter, Lady Hanham, broke with the family political tradition, and was sent to the Tower for Jacobite activities.[6]

[1] Collins, *Peerage*, iii. 546; Wimborne St. Giles par. reg. [2] *Som. and Dorset N. and Q.* xiii. 67; *CSP Dom.* 1668–9, p. 47; Poole archives, B17; G. E. Aylmer, *State's Servants*, 131–2. [3] *CSP Dom.* 1671, pp. 479–80. [4] *Voyce from the Watch Tower*, 117, 122; *CJ*, viii. 138, 146; *CSP Dom.* 1658–9, pp. 23–4; 1660–1, p. 290; Hoare, *Wilts.* Alderbury, 144, 147. [5] *HMC Ormonde*, n.s. iv. 445; PCC admon. act. bk. 1705, f. 142; PRO 30/24, bdle. 6A, no. 321. [6] Dorset RO, D124, box 236, bdle. 9, Trippet to Fox, 20 July 1689; *CSP Dom.* 1689–90, p. 245; Luttrell, i. 585.

M.W.H./J.P.F.

COOPER, *see also* ASHLEY

COOTE, Richard, 2nd Baron Coote of Coloony [I] (c.1655–1701).

DROITWICH   1689, 1690

b. c.1655, 2nd but 1st surv. s. of Richard, 1st Baron Coote of Coloony [I] by Mary, da. of Sir George St. George of Carrick Drumrusk, co. Leitrim. *m.* lic. 19 Aug. 1680, aged 25, Catherine, da. and h. of Bridges Nanfan* of Birtsmorton, Worcs., 3s. *suc.* fa. 10 July 1683; *cr.* Earl of Bellomont [I] 2 Nov. 1689.[1]

   Capt. of horse, Dutch army by 1687–Mar. 1688.[2]
   Treas. to Princess Mary of Orange Mar. 1688, (as Queen) 1689–94; gov. of Leitrim 1689–93, Massachusetts 1695–7, New York 1697–*d*.[3]
   Commr. for assessment, Worcs. 1689, j.p. and dep. lt. by 1700–*d*.

Coote was descended from an Elizabethan soldier who settled in Connaught. His father, a younger son, was a Parliamentarian in the Civil War like the rest of the family. An ardent Protestant he took a distinguished part in the Cromwellian conquest, but by 1659 he had become a Royalist. He was raised to the Irish peerage at the Restoration, and by 1677 his estate was valued at £2,500 p.a. Coote himself has to be distinguished from his cousin, a captain in the Irish Guards. After killing a Scottish colonel in a duel in 1677, he married a Worcestershire heiress without her parents' consent, and became an ardent Whig. Under James II he enlisted in the Dutch army. 'I doubt he makes little of his Irish estate', wrote his father-in-law, 'and chooses rather to retreat into a cheaper country.' He declared himself 'afflicted at the misrepresentation of his loyalty', but James II considered him 'most disaffected to the King and kingly government'. Letters patent were issued commanding him to return to Ireland, but instead he was given a post in Mary's household and accompanied William to England in November.[4]

Although Coote was 'not satisfied whether I rightly account myself a freeholder of England', he was returned for Droitwich at the general election of 1689, probably on the Earl of Shrewsbury's interest. A moderately active Member of the Convention, he was appointed to 14 committees, including the committee of elections and privileges, and those considering the suspension of habeas corpus, the toleration bill, and Schomberg's naturalization. When he was made treasurer to the Queen, Morrice described him as 'a most worthy person', which probably implies strong Presbyterian sympathies. 'His estate almost all lies in Ireland in the enemy's hands', and on 15 Apr. he was appointed to the committee for the relief of Protestant refugees. He was added to the committee to consider an address sent down from the Lords, and on 13 Aug. carried a message to desire a conference about Titus Oates. He gave evidence in the Lords about miscarriages in Ireland. In the second session he was named to the inquiry into war expenditure, as well as to three more committees concerning Irish affairs, and he was given an Irish earldom. A member of the committee on the bill for restoring corporations, he was reckoned a supporter of the

disabling clause. Re-elected in 1690, he impeached Thomas Coningsby* and (Sir) Charles Porter* for maladministration in Ireland. But after the Queen's death his career lay entirely in the colonies, where he is best remembered for his well-intentioned but unfortunate undertaking with the privateer Captain Kidd. He died on 5 Mar. 1701, the only member of this branch of the Coote family to sit at Westminster.[5]

[1] *Mar. Lic.* (Harl. Soc. xxx), 39. [2] *HMC Downshire*, i. 286. [3] Dalrymple, *Mems.* ii. bk. 5, p. 172; LS15/231/20; *HMC Portland*, iii. 535. [4] *Cal. Cl. SP*, iv. 601; v. 682; Add. 34730, ff. 89, 91; *CSP Dom.* 1677–8, pp. 510, 522; 1683–4, p. 68; 1687–9, pp. 66, 84–85; Bodl. Carte 217, ff. 194–5; *HMC Downshire*, i. 286. [5] Add. 34730, f. 95; *CSP Dom.* 1689–90, p. 456; Morrice, Entering Bk. 2, p. 475; *HMC Lords*, ii. 139–40, 142, 183; *HMC Portland*, viii. 70.

E.R.

COPE, Sir Anthony, 4th Bt. (1632–75), of Hardwick and Hanwell, Oxon.

BANBURY   1660

OXFORDSHIRE   1661–11 June 1675

b. 16 Nov. 1632, 1st s. of Sir John Cope, 3rd Bt., of Hanwell by 2nd w. Lady Elizabeth Fane, da. of Francis Fane[†], 1st Earl of Westmorland; bro. of Sir John Cope, 5th Bt.* *educ.* Oriel, Oxf. c.1649. *m.* c.1652, Mary (*d.* 1714), da. of Dutton, 3rd Baron Gerard of Gerard's Bromley, Staffs., 3s. 1da. *d.v.p. suc.* fa. 13 Oct. 1638.[1]

   Commr. for assessment, Oxon. Jan. 1660–*d*., militia Mar. 1660, j.p. Mar. 1660–*d*., col. of militia ft. Apr. 1660–?61; dep. lt. Sept. 1660–?*d*.; freeman, Oxford 1661; commr. for corporations, Oxon. 1662–3, loyal and indigent officers 1662, oyer and terminer, Oxford circuit 1665, recusants, Oxon. 1675.[2]
   Capt. of ft., regt. of Lord Falkland (Henry Carey*) 1661–2.

Cope came from a cadet branch of a family which settled in Northamptonshire in the late 14th century, and which first represented that county in 1397. His ancestors acquired Hanwell in 1498. Cope, an Anglican, employed the royalist agent Richard Allestry as his chaplain during the Interregnum, and together with Lord Falkland came under suspicion himself in 1659. He was among those who presented the Oxfordshire address for a free Parliament in February 1660, and was elected to the Convention for Banbury, three miles from his residence. He was classed among Wharton's friends to be managed by Lord Wenman (Thomas Wenman*). He was appointed to only eight committees, of which the most important was to consider the legal forms of the Restoration. On 12 Sept. he acted as teller for the Lords' proviso for assessing themselves under the poll bill. He was presumably the 'Sir Jonathan Cope' who opposed the bill for modified episcopacy on 28 Nov., but made no other recorded speeches. He was nominated to the proposed order of the Royal Oak with an estate of £4,000 p.a., and was described as 'of known honour and loyalty'.[3]

Cope was returned for the county with Falkland in 1661, and became a moderately active Member of the Cavalier Parliament, serving on 83 committees and acting as teller in three divisions. As an associate of Falkland, he was probably a 'country Cavalier'. In 1661 he was among those chosen to keep account of Members receiving the sacrament, and he served on committees for reporting the shortfall in revenue, for the corporations bill and for inspecting accounts of the disbandment commissioners. His committees in 1663 included those to consider the petition of the loyal and indigent officers, to consider defects in the hearth-tax, to examine and report on the subsidy rolls, and to inquire into the conduct of Sir Richard Temple*. In March 1664, Cope acted as teller with (Sir) Charles Hussey* for the motion to read a proviso for the repeal of the Triennial Act. His activity declined after this session, but he was appointed to the committee for the banishment of Clarendon. On 8 Apr. 1668 he was teller against the motion that the King should seek advice for uniting Protestants. He was listed by Sir Thomas Osborne* among the Members who had usually voted for supply. In the debate of 18 Mar. 1670 against transporting prisoners overseas, he intervened to say that he 'would have no man out of reach of Westminster Hall'. His interest in the old and new wool quays brought him in £473 13s.4d. p.a., and he was allowed to present his case to the House by counsel when the clause in the bill for rebuilding London to assess wharfage rates was discussed. He was appointed to the committee for the test bill, and in the debate on the Lords' amendments of 21 Mar. 1673, declared that he had 'heard of many Catholics that would take the oath of allegiance, but not of obedience'. Together with Sir John Pakington, 2nd Bt.* he led a great pope-burning procession on the anniversary of Gunpowder Plot, later in the year. Among later committees were those for inquiring into charges of corruption against Members and for better collection of the hearth-tax. He died on 11 June 1675 and was buried at Hanwell.[4]

[1] *Misc. Gen. et Her.* (n.s.) i. 240–1; *VCH Oxon.* ix. 116; C. L. Shadwell, *Reg. Orielense*, i. 259. [2] Hants RO, 43M48/449–50; *Parl. Intell.* 16 Apr. 1660; *Oxford Council Acts* (Oxf. Hist. Soc. xcv), 280; A. Ballard, *Chrons. Woodstock*, 92. [3] *Misc. Gen. et Her.* (ser. 3), iv. 203; *VCH Oxon.* ix. 114–16; *Cal. Cl. SP*, iv. 386; D. Underdown, *Royalist Conspiracy*, 265; *CSP Dom.* 1659–60, p. 361; *Kingdom's Intell.* 25 Mar. 1661; *Old Parl. Hist.* xxiii. 30. [4] *CJ*, viii, 538; ix. 77, 143; Grey, i. 237; ii. 145; PCC 12 Bence; P. E. Jones, *The Fire Court*, ii. 207–8; *Williamson Letters* (Cam. Soc. n.s. ix), 71; *Wood's Life and Times* (Oxf. Hist. Soc. xxi), 316.

M.W.H./L.N./G.J.

COPE, Sir John, 5th Bt. (1634–1721), of Hanwell, Oxon. and Chelsea, Mdx.

OXFORDSHIRE   1679 (Mar.), 1679 (Oct.), 1689

BANBURY   23 Feb. 1699

b. 19 Nov. 1634, 3rd but 2nd surv. s. of Sir John Cope, 3rd Bt., of Hanwell, and bro. of Sir Anthony Cope, 4th Bt.* *educ.* Queen's, Oxf. 1651; travelled abroad (France, Italy, Germany, Low Countries). *m.* bef. 1673, Anne (*d.* 1713) da. of Philip Booth, 7s. (3 *d.v.p.*) 1da. *suc.* bro. 11 June 1675.[1]

Lt. of ft. regt. of Henry Carey*, Visct. Falkland, July 1660–2; July 1660–2; capt. of ft. 1667.[2]

J.p. Oxon. 1676–81, 1689–*d.*, Oxford by 1700–*d.*; dep. lt. Oxon. 1676–?83, 1689–?*d.*; commr. for assessment, London 1677–80, Oxon. and Oxford 1679–80, London, Oxon. and Oxford 1689–90; freeman, Oxford 1679–June 1688.[3]

Director, Bank of England (with statutory intervals) 1695–1702.[4]

Cope travelled extensively in his youth, though apart from two brief spells of military service little is known of his means of subsistence. His wife, whom he described as 'a neighbouring gentlewoman', is said to have been the daughter of a lodging-house keeper at Dunkirk who engaged in royalist intrigue. His brother, displeased at the *mésalliance*, left him only a life interest in Hanwell. He was elected to the first Exclusion Parliament for the county after a lengthy poll, and marked 'honest' on Shaftesbury's list; but he was an inactive Member, making no recorded speeches and sitting only on the committee for the reform of the bankruptcy laws which the Whigs desired. He was absent from the division on the exclusion bill. He defeated Sir Philip Harcourt* at the next general election, and in the following July sought to have the Duke of York presented as a recusant by the grand jury of Middlesex. His only traceable activity in the second Exclusion Parliament was as a member of the committee of elections and privileges. Despite a letter of support from Shaftesbury, he was defeated by Harcourt in 1681, and in July was removed from the commission of the peace. His name was sent to William of Orange on a list of the Opposition to James II, and he was removed as freeman of Oxford in June 1688.[5]

Cope represented the county in the Convention, but his record was undistinguished. He served on only six committees, including those for continuing proceedings at law, for considering the affairs of the East India Company and for prohibiting trade with France. He supported the disabling clause in the bill to restore corporations. His support for the Revolution is evident from the loans exceeding £8,000 which he made to the Government. He seems to have acquired considerable wealth, for his investments in Bank of England stock alone were worth £12,500. He was defeated at the Oxfordshire election in 1690, and thereafter sat only briefly for Banbury in one Parliament. He died on 11 Jan. 1721 at Bramshill Park, his son's Hampshire seat, and was buried at Eversley. The family retained an interest at Banbury, but his son, a supporter of Walpole, sat for various constituencies in Devonshire and Hampshire, representing the latter county from 1727 to 1734.[6]

[1] *Misc. Gen. et Her.* (ser. 3), iv. 214; n.s. i. 240; PCC 93 Plymouth. [2] *HMC Portland*, iii. 228; *CSP Dom.* 1661–2, p. 278; 1667–8, p. 38. [3] SP 44/29/158; Bodl. Carte 79, f. 680; *CSP Dom.* July–Sept. 1683, p. 162; *Oxford Council Acts* (Oxf. Hist. Soc. n.s. ii), 117; PC 2/72, ff. 677–8. [4] *N. and Q.* clxxix. 41. [5] T. E. Sharpe, *A Royal Descent*, ii. 56, 117; PCC 12 Bence; *HMC 7th Rep.* 479; Bodl. Locke mss, c 7/76. [6] *Cal. Treas. Bks.* ix. 1971, 1976, 1980, 1981, 1987; x. 910, 915; PCC 93 Plymouth.

L.N./G.J.

COPLEY, Sir Godfrey, 2nd Bt. (c.1653–1709), of Sprotborough, Yorks.

ALDBOROUGH   15 May 1679, 1679 (Oct.), 1681
THIRSK   1695, 1698, 1701 (Feb.),
                             1701 (Dec.), 1702, 1705,
                             1708–9 Apr. 1709

b. c.1653, 1st s. of Sir Godfrey Copley, 1st Bt., of Sprotborough by 1st w. Eleanor, da. of Sir Thomas Walmesley[†] of Dunkenhalgh, Lancs. *educ.* L. Inn 1674. *m.* (1) lic. 15 Oct. 1681, Catherine, da. and coh. of John Purcell* of Nantribba, Mont., 3s. *d.v.p.* 2da.; (2) c. June 1700, Gertrude, da. of Sir John Carew, 3rd Bt.*, of Antony, Cornw., *s.p. suc.* fa. 17 Feb. 1678.[1]

Sheriff, Yorks. Feb.–Nov. 1678; commr. for assessment, Yorks. (W. Riding) 1679–80, 1689–90, j.p. by 1690–*d.*, dep. lt. by 1700–?*d.*[2]
Commr. for public accounts 1702–4.[3]
FRS 1691–*d.*

Copley came from a cadet branch of a 15th-century Yorkshire family. His father, a royalist major of horse during the Civil War compounded on a fine of £1,366, and was created a baronet at the Restoration. He died while serving as sheriff of Yorkshire in 1678, and through Sir John Reresby* Copley obtained from Lord Treasurer Danby (a kinsman of the family) a patent 'to be continued in that office for the remaining part of the year'. In return Copley was expected to assist Reresby in his disputed election at Aldborough by persuading John Wentworth, whose son had married his sister, to drop his petition. But after he had 'discoursed the business with Mr Wentworth and urged his promises and engagement', he could report little success. A few months later he stood himself against Reresby at the general election on the Wentworth interest. Defeated at the poll he was seated on petition on 15 May, just in time to vote for exclusion.

His only committee during his 11 days in the first Exclusion Parliament was on a naturalization bill. Re-elected in the autumn, he was again moderately active in the second Exclusion Parliament. He was appointed to three committees, including those to prohibit the import of cattle from Scotland and to reform the collection of the hearth-tax. In his only recorded speech he declared that he believed the charges against the Marquess of Worcester (Henry Somerset*) to be more than common fame. The Aldborough electors commended Copley's 'care and civility whilst in the House', but warned Wentworth that if he failed to 'discharge his arrears upon the last election ... 'twill be somewhat hard for him to have an entertainment like to his former'. Although he was re-elected without a contest in 1681, he left no trace on the records of the Oxford Parliament.[4]

Copley does not seem to have stood in 1685, and on 24 July he was licensed to travel abroad. Nevertheless his name appeared on a list of the Yorkshire Opposition in 1687. He returned to the House in 1695 as a Tory, though he signed the Association in 1696. He died of quinsy on 9 Apr. 1709, and was buried at Sprotborough.[5]

Copley took an active interest in the sciences, and made a valuable collection of prints and mathematical instruments. In his will he left £100 to the Royal Society for the improvement of natural knowledge, which since 1736 has been used for an annually awarded gold medal. He bequeathed his estate to a distant cousin, Lionel Copley of Wadworth.[6]

[1] Clay, *Dugdale's Vis. Yorks.* ii. 52; *Nonconformist Reg.* ed. Turner, 55; Luttrell, iv. 656. [2] *Reresby Mems.* 132; Add. 29674, f. 160. [3] *Cal. Treas. Bks.* xix. 178. [4] *Royalist Comp. Pprs.* (Yorks. Arch. Soc. rec. ser. xviii), 117–19; Reresby, 132, 155; *HMC 12th Rep. IX*, 114; *HMC Var.* ii. 396. [5] PC2/71/121; Luttrell, vi. 428. [6] *DNB*; Clay, ii. 53.

P.W.

CORBET, Sir Richard, 2nd Bt. (1640–83), of Leighton, Mont. and Longnor Hall, Salop.

SHREWSBURY   17 Mar. 1677, 1679 (Mar.), 1679
                          (Oct.), 1681

bap. 2 Sept. 1640, 1st s. of Edward Corbet (*d.*1649) of Leighton by Anne, da. of Sir Richard Newport[†], 1st Baron Newport of High Ercall. *educ.* Christ Church, Oxf. 1658. *m.* lic. 5 Jan. 1664, Victoria, da. and coh. of Sir William Uvedale[†], treas. of the chamber, of Wickham, Hants, 4s. (3 *d.v.p.*) 6da. *suc.* gdfa. Apr. 1653.[1]

J.p. Mont. 1662–*d.*, Salop by 1670–81; dep. lt. Salop by 1670–?81, capt.-lt. of militia ft. to 1682; commr. for assessment, Salop and Mont. 1673–80, recusants, Salop 1675; freeman, Shrewsbury 1675.[2]

FRS 1665.

Corbet came from a cadet branch of the family which settled at Longnor in the reign of Henry VI, and acquired a Welsh estate by marriage in 1617. His grandfather, created a baronet in 1642, was described as a delinquent in 1648, but his estate was not sequestrated, and he never compounded. His father appears to have taken no active part in the Civil War.[3]

On Corbet's return for Shrewsbury in a contested by-election in 1677, Shaftesbury first classed him 'worthy' later altering it to 'vile'. But his name figures on no government lists of the court party. A moderately active Member of the Cavalier Parliament, he was appointed to 16 committees. On 29 Apr. 1678 he was added to the committee of inquiry into the growth of Popery, and he was among those appointed to consider the bill to hinder Papists from sitting in Parliament (12 June). In the final session he was appointed to the committee of elections and privileges, and to that to draw up instructions for disbanding the army. He was re-elected to the Exclusion Parliaments, and again marked 'vile' on Shaftesbury's list, though he was not included in the 'unanimous club'. A very active Member in 1679, he was appointed to 20 committees, including those to inspect the disbandment accounts, to consider the extension of habeas corpus, to draw up a bill to continue the prohibition of imported cattle and fish, to regulate parliamentary elections, and to prevent illegal exactions. On 5 May he moved to declare Danby's pardon 'illegal and void in law', a proposition which Silius Titus* found ridiculous and contradictory, and acted as teller against allowing all Members to vote on the committee stage of the bill against cattle imports. According to the list in the State Papers he voted against the committal of the first exclusion bill, but it is more likely that he abstained, as Roger Morrice thought.[4]

Corbet probably became an exclusionist under the influence of William Forester*, with whom he travelled from Coventry to Westminster for the second Exclusion Parliament, although the informants admitted that Corbet, unlike his companions, 'had no arms visible'. Again a very active Member, he was named to 11 committees, deputizing for George Treby* to deliver reports on the Eye, Reigate, and Bury St. Edmunds elections. He was among those ordered to draft addresses for the preservation of the Protestant religion at home and abroad and for the removal of Jeffreys. He was also appointed to the committees to receive information

about the Popish Plot, and to consider the bills to abolish the court of the marches and to unite Protestants. As chairman of the committee of inquiry into the proceedings of the judges, he presented a long report on 23 Dec. and ten days later introduced articles of impeachment against Scroggs. In the Oxford Parliament he was named only to the elections committee.[5]

Corbet, together with Forester, accompanied the Duke of Monmouth on his northern progress in 1682. At the time of the Rye House Plot he was seriously ill, and Lord Russell (Hon. William Russell*), on the morning of his execution asked Dean Tillotson for news of his friend's health. He died on 1 Aug. 1683 and was buried at St. Margaret's, Westminster. His grandson, the fourth baronet, represented Shrewsbury as a Whig under the first two Georges.[6]

[1] A. E. Corbet, *Corbet Fam.* ii. 208; *Trans. Salop. Arch. Soc.* (ser. 4), xii. 217–18. [2] *CSP Dom.* 1682, p. 81; *Shrewsbury Burgess Roll* ed. Forrest, 65. [3] Corbet, ii. 196; *Mont. Colls.* xiii. 349; *Cal. Comm. Adv. Money*, 725. [4] Grey, vii. 184. [5] *CSP Dom.* July–Sept. 1683, p. 175; *CJ*, ix. 688, 697. [6] *CSP Dom.* 1682, p. 428; *Mont. Colls.* xiii. 345.

E.C.

CORBET, Sir Vincent, 2nd Bt. (c.1642–81), of Moreton Corbet, Salop.

SHROPSHIRE   1679 (Mar.), 1679 (Oct.)

b. c.1642, 2nd but 1st surv. s. of Sir Vincent Corbet, 1st Bt.†, of Moreton Corbet by Sarah, da. and coh. of Sir Robert Monson† of North Carlton, Lincs. *m.* by 1668, Elizabeth, da. and coh. of Francis Thornes of Shelvock, Salop, 3s. (2 *d.v.p.*) 1da. *suc.* fa. 28 Dec. 1656.[1]

Capt. of militia horse, Salop 1661, commr. for assessment 1661–80, dep. lt. by 1670–d., j.p. 1672–d., commr. for recusants 1675.[2]

Corbet was the head of an eminent Shropshire family which had regularly represented the county since the Model Parliament. His father, knight of the shire in the Short Parliament, raised a regiment of foot for the King during the Civil War, and compounded in 1646 on the Bridgnorth articles on a fine of £2,822 at one-sixth, reduced by £433 on account of debts totalling £9,200. He was said to be willing to participate in a plan to seize Shrewsbury for the King in 1654, but did not take part in Penruddock's rising the following year. Corbet inherited as a minor an estate further encumbered by the need to raise portions for his five sisters. He fell under the control of Francis Thornes, the principal trustee, who received most of the profits from his estates and to whose daughter he was married off at the earliest opportunity.[3]

Returned for Shropshire at both elections of 1679, Corbet was classed as 'honest' by Shaftesbury, but was absent from the division on the exclusion bill. He was appointed to no committees in either the first or second Exclusion Parliaments. It was later alleged that he offered William Forester* 100 muskets to defend the Protestant interest against the Papists. He died in London of smallpox on 4 Feb. 1681, and was buried at Moreton Corbet. His daughter and heir married the son of Edward Kynaston I*.[4]

[1] Trans. Salop. Arch. Soc. (ser. 4), xi. 172–3. [2] SP29/41/85. [3] Cal. Comm. Comp. 1370–1; Cal. Comm. Adv. Money, 736; A. E. Corbet, Corbet Fam. ii. 339; Underdown, Royalist Conspiracy, 91, 146. [4] CSP Dom. July–Sept. 1683, p. 137; Prot. Dom. Intell. 8 Feb. 1681.

E.C.

CORDELL, Sir John, 2nd Bt. (1646–90), of Long Melford, nr. Sudbury, Suff.

SUDBURY   1685
SUFFOLK   1689

b. 10 Nov. 1646, 1st s. of Sir Robert Cordell, 1st Bt.* educ. Bury St. Edmunds g.s. 1656; travelled abroad 1663–6. m. by 1674, Elizabeth, da. of Thomas Waldegrave* of Smallbridge, Suff., 1s. 2da. suc. fa. Jan. 1680.[1]

Commr. for assessment, Suff. 1673–80, 1689–d., maj. of militia ft. 1677–?Apr. 1688, j.p. 1683–July 1688, 1689–d., Sudbury 1684; dep. lt. Suff. 1685–?Apr. 1688, 1689–d.; alderman, Sudbury 1685–Mar. 1688.[2]

Cordell, unlike his father, was a Tory. In June 1680 he and his brother-in-law, Thomas Waldegrave, whose father had represented Sudbury in the Cavalier Parliament, were instructed to search the house of the mayor of Sudbury, the electoral agent of Sir Gervase Elwes, 1st Bt.*, for seditious letters and papers. When shortly afterwards a quo warranto was issued against the corporation, Cordell and Waldegrave petitioned the King that no new charter should be issued until they had been heard, since they had been informed that the corporation intended to surrender their charter and obtain a new one with the aim of continuing the government of the town in the same hands. He appears to have achieved some success, since when the new charter was granted in March 1685 he was appointed one of the aldermen and at the subsequent parliamentary election he was returned for the borough. But he was not active in James II's Parliament. He was appointed only to the committee on the bill for the repair of Yarmouth harbour before being given leave to go into the country in June.[3]

Cordell probably opposed James II's religious policy, being removed from the Sudbury corporation in March 1688. He represented the county in the Convention and, according to Anthony Rowe*, voted to agree with the Lords that the throne was not vacant. An inactive Member, he was appointed only to the committees to hear a petition from army creditors and to consider a bill to develop the grounds of Arundel House. He twice obtained leave to go into the country, no doubt for his health, for he was buried on 9 Sept. 1690 at Long Melford. The baronetcy passed to his eldest son, who was returned for Sudbury in 1701.[4]

[1] CSP Dom. 1663–4, p. 226; Bury St. Edmunds G.S. List (Suff. Green Bks. xiii), 86. [2] CSP Dom. 1676–7, p. 587; 1685, pp. 68, 166. [3] CSP Dom. 1684–5, pp. 48, 269; F.C.D. Sperling, Hist. Sudbury, 174; Leeds Central Library, Marlborough mss 12/79. [4] PC2/72/627.

P.W.

CORDELL, Sir Robert, 1st Bt. (c.1616–80), of Long Melford, Suff.

SUDBURY   24 Mar. 1662, 1679 (Mar.)

b. c.1616, 1st s. of Sir John Cordell, Mercer, of London by Sarah, da. of Robert Bankworth, scrivener, of London. educ. Exeter, Oxf. matric. 21 June 1633, aged 16; travelled abroad 1635; G. Inn 1636. m. c.1643, Margaret, da. and coh. of Sir Edmund Wright of Swakeleys, Ickenham, Mdx., ld. mayor of London 1641–2, 2s. 1da. suc. fa. 1649; cr. Bt. 22 June 1660.[1]

Sheriff, Suff. 1653–4, commr. for militia Mar. 1660, j.p. July 1660–70; commr. for assessment, Suff. Aug. 1660–d., Sudbury 1677–8, recusants, Suff. 1675.

Cordell was a collateral descendant of Sir William Cordell, a distinguished lawyer who acquired the ex-monastic property of Long Melford in 1554 and sat for Suffolk in the last Marian Parliament, of which he was Speaker. Long Melford passed to the Savage family by marriage, and was mortgaged to Cordell's father, a prosperous London merchant and master of the Mercers' Company, who was imprisoned in November 1642 for refusing to lend Parliament £1,000. Subsequently, however, he served on the committee for the new model ordinance before retiring from the aldermanic bench in 1647. Cordell himself paid £500 to the committee for the advance of money in 1643, and by 1647 was a creditor of Parliament for over £2,600. Nothing else is known of him until he was appointed sheriff of Suffolk under the Commonwealth. In 1654 he bought Long Melford from the trustees of the 2nd Earl Rivers for £28,959, but held no further office until the Restoration.[2]

Cordell was involved in double returns for Sudbury, three miles from his home, at the general elections of 1660 and 1661, but both were decided against him. Though he was given a baronetcy at the Restoration, Lord Wharton classed him as a friend. But when he was at last successful at a by-election in 1662, he was described as a 'loyal gentleman'. An inactive Member of the Cavalier Parliament, he was appointed to only 15 committees, including the committee of elections and privileges in four sessions. In May 1662 he was nominated to the committee on the additional bill to regulate corporations. On 17 Feb. 1665 a bill on his behalf was ordered to be read, but this has not been identified. He was absent from a call of the House in February 1668. He was twice appointed to committees for the relief of the widow and children of Sir Henry Williams*, and helped to consider three measures aimed at preventing the export of raw wool. His omission from the commission of the peace after the second Conventicles Act in 1670, indicates that he probably supported toleration. Henceforth he voted with the Opposition, since his name does not appear on any of the lists of court supporters, except that in *A Seasonable Argument* he was described as 'a poor gentleman that has almost spent all'. Shaftesbury considered him a friend, classing him as 'doubly worthy' in his list of the House of Commons.[3]

Returned for Sudbury at the first general election of 1679, Cordell was classed as 'worthy' by Shaftesbury and duly voted for exclusion. He was not appointed to any committees and made no recorded speeches. He did not stand for re-election in September, either on account of ill-health, or because his interest had been undermined by Sir Gervase Elwes*. He was buried on 3 Jan. 1680 at St. Lawrence Jewry, London.[4]

[1] PC2/44/585. [2] Copinger, *Suff. Manors*, i. 133, 138; *CSP Dom.* 1640, p. 171; 1641–3, p. 403; 1647–8, p. 35; 1649–50, p. 301; 1650, p. 157; *Suff. Inst. Arch. Procs.* ii. 53–58; V. Pearl, *London and the Outbreak of the Puritan Revolution*, 114, 297–8; SP19/63/13; *CJ*, viii. 240. [3] *CJ*, viii. 35, 253; *Merc. Pub.* 24 Apr. 1662. [4] F.C.D. Sperling, *Hist. Sudbury*, 74.

P.W.

CORIE, Francis (c.1596–1678), of Bramerton, Norf.

NORWICH   1661–19 Feb. 1678

b. c.1596, 1st s. of Robert Corie of Bramerton by 1st w. *educ.* Pembroke, Camb. 1612; G. Inn 1613, called 1618, ancient 1638. *m.* (1) Bridget (*d.* 10 Mar. 1653), *s.p.*; (2) Anne, da. of Sir John Corbet, 1st Bt.†, of Sprowston, Norf., 1s. 1da. *suc.* fa. 1629.[1]

J.p. Norf. by 1641–54, 1659–?d.; recorder, Norwich 1642–4, July 1660–77; commr. for assessment, Norf. Jan. 1660, Norf. and Norwich Aug. 1660–d., oyer and terminer, Norfolk circuit July 1660; dep. lt. Norf. Sept. 1660–d.; commr. for voluntary gift, Norwich 1662, corporations, Norf. 1662–3, recusants 1675.[2]

Corie's ancestors had held property at Bramerton, five miles from Norwich, since 1403, and a cadet branch of the family was prominent on the corporation under the Stuarts. Corie himself, a practising lawyer, was clearly out of sympathy with

the parliamentary cause in the Civil War, but he remained on the commission of the peace till 1654, and was reappointed by the Rump in 1659. After the Restoration he regained his post as recorder of Norwich, and was returned for the city after a contest at the general election of 1661. An inactive Member of the Cavalier Parliament, he was appointed to 45 committees, including that for preventing mischiefs from Quakers in the first session. He took the chair for the bill to regulate the manufacture of Norfolk stuffs, and on 4 Feb. 1662 he reported several amendments and a proviso, to all of which the House agreed without a division. In 1663 he was among those called on to recommend remedies for dissenters' meetings, and he also helped to consider the staple bill, a bill for the repair of Wells quay, and a petition from the Suffolk spinning industry. He was confirmed as recorder in the new charter of the same year. In November 1669 he was detained on 'mesne process' in Norwich Castle, but the House of Commons ordered the sheriff to release him. Nothing further is known of the incident, which does not seem to have affected his standing either at Westminster or in his own county. On behalf of his constituency he acted as teller with the Hon. William Coventry* on 4 Apr. 1670 for a Lords' proviso to the Yarmouth pier bill, and helped to prepare reasons for a conference. In the following year he welcomed the King to Norwich during the royal tour of Norfolk. He was sent the government whip in 1675, but he was now in his eightieth year, and he did not attend the autumn session. Danby included him in his working-lists among those to be influenced by (Sir) Joseph Williamson*, who corresponded with his cousin Thomas, and Sir Richard Wiseman* listed him among the court supporters. On the other hand Shaftesbury marked him 'thrice vile', and the author of *A Seasonable Argument* thought him no better than his colleague, Christopher Jay*, a pensioner . A new recorder was elected in 1677, and Corie died intestate and heavily in debt on 19 Feb. 1678, aged 82. He was buried at Bramerton, the only member of the family to sit in Parliament.[3]

[1] Blomefield, *Norf.* v. 472–3. [2] *Q. Sess. Order Bk.* (Norf. Rec. Soc. xxvi), 5, 63; Blomefield, iii. 384, 405; H. Le Strange, *Norf. Official Lists*, 127; PC2/55/20; *Norwich Vol. Gift* (Norf. Rec. Soc. i), 73. [3] Blomefield, iii. 384, 388; v. 473; *CJ*, viii. 357; ix. 112, 153; *Corie Letters* (Norf. Rec. Soc. xxvii), 13; PCC 32 Drax; *CSP Dom.* 1677–8, p. 660.

P.W.

CORNBURY, Visct. *see* **HYDE, Edward** and **Henry**

CORNEWALL, Henry (c.1654–1717), of Bredwardine Castle, Herefs. and East Bailey Lodge,
Enfield, Mdx.

WEOBLEY	1685
HEREFORD	11 June 1689, 1690
HEREFORDSHIRE	1698
WEOBLEY	1701 (Feb.), 1702, 1705, 1710

b. c.1654, o.s. of Edward Cornewall of Moccas Court,
Herefs. by Frances, da. of Sir Walter Pye[†] of The
Mynde, Much Dewchurch, Herefs. wid. of Henry
Vaughan of Bredwardine; half-bro. of Roger Vaughan*.
m. (1) 11 Oct. 1683, Margarita (d. 26 Nov. 1692), da.
and h. of Laurentius Huyssen, Lord of Weelde, Zeeland, 2s. (1 d.v.p.); (2) lic. 27 Apr. 1695, Susanna, da.
and coh. of Sir John Williams, 2nd Bt.[†], of Pengethley,
Herefs., 3s. (1 d.v.p.) 1da. suc. fa. 1709.[1]

Page of honour to the Duke of York c.1669; equerry
to Princess Mary 1677, master of the horse by 1683–5.[2]

Ensign, Admiralty (Duke of York's) regt. 1672, lt.
by 1676; capt. of ft. R. Eng. Regt. (French army) 1675–
6, Holland Regt. (later The Buffs) 1677–82; capt.-lt. R.
Horse Gds. (The Blues) 1682, capt. 1682–5; col. (later
9 Ft.) 1685–Nov. 1688.[3]

Commr. for assessment, Herefs. and Hereford 1689–
90; j.p. Herefs., Brec. and Rad. 1699–?d.; dep. lt.
Herefs. 1701–?d.

Cornewall's father, like his uncle Humphrey,
fought as a Royalist in the Civil War. Compounding
before his marriage to a wealthy widow, he was
fined a nominal £5. Soon after the Restoration
he was made sub-commissioner of excise at the
unanimous request of the Herefordshire Members.
He was expected to be returned for Leominster in
1670, but the vacancy did not materialize. Cornewall was bred a courtier. When his half-brother was
killed at Sole Bay, he cleared his debt to the crown
and took over the remainder of the Vaughan estates.
He was probably the Captain Cornewall serving
under Monmouth in the French army in 1676; in
that year his English commission was respited because he had not taken the oaths. There seems no
reason to suppose that he was anything but an Anglican, however, and he took them in 1677, when
he accompanied Princess Mary to Holland on her
marriage. His duties carried him backwards and
forwards between the two countries, and he is
unlikely to have seen much more active service until
1685. In that year he took a crown lease of one of
the lodges in Enfield chase. He was returned for
Weobley, some six miles from Moccas, at the general election. Probably a moderately active Member
of James II's Parliament, he may have served on
six committees, including those to recommend expunctions from the Journals and to consider a
naturalization bill. Although his wife was included
in this measure, he can hardly have attended the

sittings of the committee, since he was engaged in
raising a regiment in Herefordshire to resist the
Duke of Monmouth's invasion. His recruiting activities were regarded as little short of trespass by
the Duke of Beaufort (Henry Somerset*), who was
outraged to find his own regiment compelled to
yield precedence. It is noteworthy that all Cornewall's officers, including the second-in-command,
Sir John Morgan*, Sir Francis Edwards* and Jeremiah Bubb*, were firm Protestants, and by the
spring of 1687 he himself had become so uneasy
about James's policy that he determined to send in his
papers. Nevertheless he was recommended as court
candidate for Weobley, and his resignation was not
accepted until after William's landing in 1688.[4]

In the Revolution Cornewall took no part, his
personal loyalties being deeply committed to both
sides, although he was probably the 'Captain Cornwall' mentioned in French dispatches as William's
chief agent in the army. Under Bubb, most of his
regiment went over to William without opposition.
Cornewall did not defend his seat at the general
election which followed. Anthony Rowe* blacklisted him as voting to agree with the Lords that
the throne was not vacant, but he did not enter the
House till four months later, when his success at
the Hereford by-election dismayed the local Whigs.
He was an inactive Member, acting as teller for a
proviso in the interests of the Earl of Kent to the
Wye and Lugg navigation bill, and being named
only to the committees to inquire into war expenditure and to consider a naturalization bill. Cornewall
held neither military nor court office after the Revolution, and in Parliament he was usually reckoned
a Tory; some inconsistency in his record may be
ascribed to unfulfilled hopes of a place. He died on
22 Feb. 1717 in his 64th year and was buried in
Westminster Abbey. His surviving son by the first
marriage was elected for Hereford as a Whig in
1747, while by his second marriage he was father of
Velters Cornewall, who sat for the county as a Tory
in seven Parliaments from 1722 to 1768, and of
James Cornewall, twice returned for Weobley as a
government supporter.[5]

[1] Foljambe and Reade, House of Cornewall, 102–5; Lysons, Environs, ii. 290; C. J. Robinson, Mansions and Manors of Herefs.
119; Reg. of Dutch Church, Austin Friars, 205. [2] Robinson, Castles
of Herefs. 20; CSP Dom. 1677–8, p. 532; PCC 87 Fane. [3] CSP
Dom. 1676–7, p. 412; J. Childs, Army of Charles II, 246. [4] Cal.
Comm. Comp. 2024; Cal. Treas. Bks. i. 329–30, 333; vii. 373; CSP
Dom. 1672–3, p. 342; 1677–8, p. 244; 1680–1, pp. 387–8; Denizations and Naturalisations (Huguenot Soc. xviii), 169; Hatton
Corresp. (Cam. Soc. n.s. xxiii), 67; Ellis Corresp. i. 302; Bodl. Carte
130, f. 24. [5] J. R. Jones, Revolution of 1688 in England, 286;
Browning, Danby, i. 417; BL Loan 29/75, Mary Foley to Sir
Edward Harley, 10 May 1689; D. Rubini, Court and Country, 46,
58–59; IHR Bull. xxxiii. 227; Westminster Abbey Reg. (Harl. Soc.
x), 289.

E.R.

CORNEWALL, Humphrey (1616–88), of Berrington, Herefs. and Barneby House, Ludlow, Salop.

LEOMINSTER 1661

bap. 14 July 1616, 1st s. of John Cornewall of Berrington by Mary, da. of William Barneby of Hull, Bockleton, Worcs. *m.* Theophila, da. of William Skinner of Thornton College, Lincs., 5s. 4da. *suc.* fa. 1645.[1]

Capt. of ft. (royalist) c.1645–6, Admiralty Regt. 1672–8.

J.p. Herefs. July 1660–*d.*; commr. for assessment, Herefs. Aug. 1660–80, Salop 1677–80; maj. of militia, Herefs. by 1662–*d.*, commr. for loyal and indigent officers 1662, dep. lt. 1662–*d.*; member, council in the marches of Wales 1670–*d.*; commr. for recusants, Herefs. 1675; freeman, Ludlow 1676, alderman 1685–*d.*, mayor 1686–7.[2]

Cornewall was head of a family descended from an illegitimate son of Richard, Earl of Cornwall, brother of Henry III. Their previous parliamentary experience for marcher constituencies goes back to 1369. Cornewall served under Sir Henry Lingen* in the Civil War; he claimed that he originally took up arms to defend himself and his neighbours from plundering Cavaliers. Edward Harley* and others of the county committee certified that he had acted under constraint in the attack on Stokesay Castle and in sitting on a royalist grand jury. His fine was set at £222, and he successfully pleaded debt to avoid paying more than £21 16s. to the committee for the advance of money. He was suspected of complicity in Booth's rising, though his name does not appear in any royalist correspondence during the Interregnum. He was recommended for a knighthood of the Royal Oak at the Restoration, when his income was set down at £6,000 p.a. Indeed, he laid claim to a share in the fund for loyal and indigent officers.[3]

At the general election of 1661, Cornewall stood for Leominster, three miles from his principal residence, in partnership with Fitzwilliam Coningsby† against the Duke of Buckingham's candidate. Cornewall, assisted by the deputy lieutenants and the militia, was duly elected, but he was unable to carry Coningsby, to whom the returning officer refused the poll because he was a prisoner for debt. Nothing daunted, Cornewall and the other Herefordshire Members proposed that the sub-commissioners of excise for the county should be replaced by Coningsby and his own brother Edward, but even under the lax control of Southampton the Treasury jibbed at this proposal. An unrepentant Cavalier, Cornewall let it be known that he intended to secure Robert Harley I* as a former parliamentarian officer if he visited Herefordshire, but Lord Herbert of Raglan (Henry Somerset*) dissuaded him. He

was appointed to only 31 committees throughout the Cavalier Parliament, none of major importance, and made no speeches. For this inactivity he had various excuses: in 1664 he and Sir Edward Hopton* were the only deputy lieutenants on duty in the county, and in the following year he complained that he was 'hindered from attending the services of this House' by the suit of a Ludlow attorney, presumably in the court of the marches. His interventions in local affairs continued to be unfortunate; in 1666 his tactless handling of a dispute over hearth-tax in Hereford nearly caused a riot.[4]

Nevertheless, Cornewall remained in favour with the Court, becoming a member of the council in the marches in 1670, and receiving the first of several payments of royal bounty in 1671. 'Old Cornewall of the House of Commons' was given a commission in the Duke of York's regiment at the age of 56, after the death of Roger Vaughan* at Sole Bay, when the Cornewall brothers and Herbert Aubrey* became liable for his debts to the crown. Danby granted him an excise pension of £200 p.a., but refused to discharge the debt so long as Cornewall remained in Parliament. Cornewall received the government whip in 1675, and his name appears in the list of officials. He was one of the Herefordshire Members not doubted by Sir Richard Wiseman*, and he was noted as 'doubly vile' by Shaftesbury. But in 1678 his name does not occur in the list of court supporters drawn up by the Opposition, and he may have ceased to attend after the winter session.[5]

Cornewall is not known to have contested Leominster in any of the Exclusion Parliaments, and in 1685 he stood down in favour of his son Robert. He became mayor of Ludlow under the new charter of 1685, and gave affirmative answers on the repeal of the Test Act and Penal Laws. He died at Ludlow and was buried on 7 July 1688. News of his death cannot have reached Sunderland immediately for on 13 July he recommended Cornewall as court candidate for Ludlow.[6]

[1] C. J. Robinson, *Manors and Mansions of Herefs.* 118; *Salop. Hearth-Tax* ed. Pitchford, 164; Foljambe and Reade, *House of Cornewall*, 87–89, 279. [2] Add. 16178, f. 81; *CJ*, viii. 376; BL Loan 29/49, accounts of Nicholas Philpott, 1662–8; 29/141, Sir Edward Harley to Robert Harley, 19 June 1691; *CSP Dom.* 1670, p. 190; 1672, p. 218; 1678, p. 151; 1685, p. 51; Ludlow Ledger Bk. 1648–80, f. 302. [3] SP23/202/758–67; *Cal. Comm. Adv. Money*, 1057; *List of Officers Claiming* (1663), 34 [4] BL Loan 29/79, Thos. Harley to Sir Edward Harley, 18 Mar. 1661; *CJ*, viii. 392, 590–1; *Cal. Treas. Bks.* i. 329–30, 333; *HMC Portland*, iii. 269; *CSP Dom.* 1663–4, p. 454; 1666–7, p. 321. [5] *Cal. Treas. Bks.* iii. 757, 1183; iv. 704; v. 1239–40; *Hatton Corresp.* (Cam. Soc. n.s. xxii), 92. [6] T. Wright, *Hist. Ludlow*, 498; *Ludlow Reg.* (Salop. Par. Reg. Soc. xiii), 535; Bodl. Carte 130, f. 24.

E.R.

CORNEWALL, Robert (1647–1705), of Berrington, Herefs.

LEOMINSTER 1685

bap. 17 June 1647, 1st s. of Humphrey Cornewall*. *educ.* I. Temple 1666. *m.* lic. 24 July 1668, Edith, da. of Sir Francis Cornwallis of Abermarlais, Carm., 8s. (4 *d.v.p.*) 3da. *suc.* fa. 1688.[1]

Ensign, regt. of Lord Worcester (Henry Somerset*) 1667; capt. of dgns. regt. of (Sir) John Talbot* 1678–9; capt. indep. tp. 1685; capt.-lt. Queen Dowager's Horse (later 6 Dgn. Gds.) 1685–7, capt. 1687–Dec. 1688.[2] J.p. Herefs. 1675–?89, commr. for assessment 1677–80, 1689; freeman, Ludlow 1681; capt. of militia, Herefs. by 1683–?89.[3]

Gent. waiter to Prince George of Denmark 1683–9.

Cornewall's father seems to have made over his Herefordshire estates to his son some time before his death, though as an army officer and a courtier he can seldom have resided on them. He was returned for Leominster on the family interest to James II's Parliament, in which he was appointed only to the committee of elections and privileges and to that for establishing the parish of St. James Piccadilly. Like his father, he answered all three questions on the repeal of the Test Act and Penal Laws in the affirmative, and was recommended for re-election as court candidate. His regiment was one of the last to disband in 1688, and Cornewall was probably a Jacobite under William III, when he appears to have taken no part in local or national affairs, losing both his commission and his place at Court. In March 1689, Robert Harley II* wrote:

> Robert Cornewall is come down, and talks high that the rebellious soldiers were increased and could not be beat, but would fight to the last man, and that the Scots would bring in the late King.

Early in the next reign, however, he applied to Harley for a place; 'his affairs have not succeeded according to expectation; he hopes that the Prince [George] will not forget him, for his inclination and desires are fixed upon employment'. But apparently Cornewall's hopes were unfulfilled. He died suddenly on 9 Nov. 1705, and was succeeded by his eldest son Charles, who was elected for Bewdley in 1709 and for Weobley in 1715.[4]

[1] Foljambe and Reade, *House of Cornewall*, 90, 280; C. J. Robinson, *Mansions and Manors of Herefs.* 118. [2] *CSP Dom.* 1666–7, p. 180. [3] Ludlow Ledger Bk. 1680–90, f. 11; *CSP Dom.* Jan.–June 1683, p. 94; Portland mss BL Loan 29/141, Sir Edward Harley to Robert Harley, 19 June 1691. [4] Bodl. Carte 130, f. 24; *HMC Portland*, iii. 435; viii. 102.

E.R.

CORNWALLIS, Charles I (c.1619–75), of High Holborn, Mdx. and Rock, Worcs.

EYE 20 Jan. 1662–28 Aug. 1675

b. c.1619, 3rd s. of Sir Charles Cornwallis[†] (*d.*1629) of Beeston St. Andrew, Norf. and Harborne, Staffs., being o.s. by 3rd w. Dorothy, da. of Richard Vaughan, bp. of London, wid. of John Jegon, bp. of Norwich; half-bro. of Sir William Cornwallis[†]. *m.* lic. 20 June 1640, aged 21, Edith, da. of John Newce of Rock, and coh. to her bro. John, 1s. 2da.[1]

Commr. for assessment, Worcs. 1648–52, 1657, 1665–73, Mdx. and Suff. 1663–73, Westminster 1665–73, militia, Worcs. 1648, Mar. 1660, j.p. 1648–53; collector of customs, London aft. 1661–9; commr. for oyer and terminer, Norfolk circuit 1665, recusants, Suff. 1675.[2]

Gent. of privy chamber June 1660–*d.*[3]

Cornwallis was the son of a Jacobean courtier and diplomat, and the first cousin of Sir Frederick Cornwallis*. He acquired a small estate in Worcestershire by marriage, but lived chiefly in London. Although both sides of the family were royalist in the Civil War he was appointed to the county committee in 1648 and held local office under the Commonwealth. At the Restoration he was given a post at Court and petitioned jointly with Sir Henry Bennet* for the office of postmaster-general. In this he was unsuccessful, but he was given a post in the customs and granted £2,000 from secret service.[4]

Cornwallis was returned on the family interest for Eye at a by-election in 1662. A moderately active Member of the Cavalier Parliament, he was appointed to 55 committees, of which 25 were for estate bills. Although without formal legal qualifications, he seems to have been in demand as a trustee, and his chief motive for election was probably to forward the estate bill of John Coplestone[†], the Cromwellian sheriff of Devon. On 6 Feb. he was added to the committee with three other Suffolk Members, and the bill was reported by (Sir) Robert Brooke* nine days later. But Coplestone's part in the suppression of Penruddock's rising must have left him with many enemies, and on third reading it was defeated by seven votes in a thin House. It was reintroduced with a slight variation of title in April, and passed without a division. Cornwallis was instructed to carry it to the Lords, where it was refused a third reading. In the next session it was first introduced in the Upper House and Cornwallis, together with Sir Francis Vincent* and Thomas Waldegrave*, was named as a trustee. It was sent down to the Commons on 2 May 1663, but finally rejected on third reading by 77 votes to 38. Two months later Cornwallis, together with (Sir) Thomas Fanshawe* and (Sir) Ralph Bankes*, successfully claimed privilege against subpoenas issued against them by the Papist Sir George Wakeman, later physician to the Queen. A more awkward responsibility was laid on him as security for an £8,000 mortgage obtained by Sir Kenelm Digby, another notable Roman Catholic, who died in Paris in 1665, and made him executor. In this capacity he conveyed the Leicestershire and Rutland estates to the creditors, much to the indignation of the heir. From October 1667 to his death Cornwallis was regularly named to the committee of elections and privileges, though when Digby's efforts to recover the property reached their climax in 1670, he relied principally on evasion. However, on 25 Feb. 1671 his privilege was affirmed, and he does not seem to have suffered any material loss. In the same session he was added to the committee to consider a petition concerning the burden of the poor on his parish, St. Giles in the Fields, though he is not known to have served on the vestry. He was not listed among the court party at this time. In the 1674 session he was named to the committees to report on the dispute between Sir Thomas Byde*, a fellow privy-chamberman, and the board of green cloth, and to inquire into the condition of Ireland. He died on 28 Aug. 1675 and was buried in his parish church nine days later. The next member of the family to sit was his great-grandson, a Jacobite sympathizer, who represented the Cardigan constituencies from 1722 to 1729.[5]

[1] Add. 19124, f. 457; Malcolm, *Londinium Redivivum*, i. 305; Blomefield, *Norf.* vi. 285; Foster, *London Mar. Lic.* 18, 333, 1164. [2] *CSP Dom.* 1668–9, p. 353. [3] Carlisle, *Privy Chamber*, 167. [4] *VCH Worcs.* iv. 321, 324; R. W. Ketton-Cremer, *Norf. in the Civil War*, 52; *CSP Dom.* 1660–1, pp. 445, 559; *Cal. Treas. Bks.* i. 451. [5] *CJ*, viii. 408, 515; ix. 163, 209; *HMC 7th Rep.* 168; *LJ*, xi. 461, 501; *HMC Lords*, n.s. vi. 346–9; *CSP Dom.* 1670, p. 374; 1671–2, p. 35; *Private Corresp. of Jane, Lady Cornwallis*, p. xl.

P.W.

CORNWALLIS, Charles II (1632–73), of Brome Hall, Suff.

EYE 1660, 1661–7 Jan. 1662

bap. 19 Apr. 1632, 1st s. of Sir Frederick Cornwallis*, 1st Baron Cornwallis, by 1st w. *m.* Margaret, da. of Sir Thomas Playsted of Arlington, Suss., 8s. (3 *d.v.p.*) 2da. KB 23 Apr. 1661; *suc.* fa. as 2nd Baron Cornwallis 7 Jan. 1662.
Capt. of militia horse, Suff. Apr. 1660; commr. for assessment, Suff. Aug. 1660–*d.*, Mdx. 1661–2; j.p. Suff. 1662–*d.*; alderman, Thetford by 1669–?*d.*; steward, honour of Eye 1671–*d.*[1]

Although Cornwallis's eligibility under the Long Parliament ordinance must have been dubious, he was returned for Eye at the general election of 1660. An inactive Member of the Convention, he was appointed in the first session only to the committee of elections and privileges and made no recorded speeches, but he was teller in five divisions. On 1 Aug. he opposed the bill for inquiring into embezzlements during the Interregnum. After the recess he was added to the committee for the militia bill,

and appointed to two other committees of less importance. A court supporter, he was teller for the grant of the second moiety of the excise to the King for life. Re-elected in 1661, he was a very active Member in the first session of the Cavalier Parliament. He was appointed to 39 committees, including the committee of elections and privileges and the committee for the security bill, and acted as teller on three occasions. He was named to the committee for the corporations bill, and opposed the motion that all Members who attended it should be allowed to vote. He was also among those named to consider the bill of pains and penalties and to ask the lord treasurer for a report on the condition of the Forest of Dean. His career in the Commons was cut short by the death of his father at the end of the Christmas recess. He himself died on 13 Apr. 1673, aged 41, and was buried at Culford. His grandson was returned for Eye as a Whig in 1695.[2]

[1] *Cal. Treas. Bks.* iii. 888. [2] *CJ*, viii. 188, 277; *CSP Dom.* 1660–1, p. 559.

M.W.H.

CORNWALLIS, Sir Frederick, 1st Bt. (1611–62), of Culford, Suff.

EYE 1640 (Apr.), 1640 (Nov.)–23 Sept. 1642

IPSWICH 29 Oct. 1660

b. 14 Mar. 1611, 3rd but o. surv. s. of Sir William Cornwallis† of Brome Hall, Suff. being o.s. by 2nd w. Jane, da. of Hercules Mewtas of West Ham, Essex. *educ.* privately. *m.* (1) c.1630, Elizabeth (*d.*1644), da. of Sir John Ashburnham of Ashburnham, Suss., 3s. (2 *d.v.p.*) 1da.; (2) 1646 (with £2,000), Elizabeth, da. of Sir Henry Crofts* of Little Saxham, Suff., 1da. *suc.* fa. 1611; *cr.* Bt. 4 May 1627; *kntd.* 1 Dec. 1630; *suc.* half-bro. Nicholas Bacon at Culford 1660; *cr.* Baron Cornwallis of Eye 20 Apr. 1661.[1]
Gent. usher of the privy chamber 1633–45; treas. of the Household to Charles II (as Prince of Wales) 1645, (as King) 1649, May 1660–*d.*; PC 4 July 1660–*d.*[2]
Steward, honour of Eye 1639–49, May 1660–*d.*; freeman, Ipswich June 1660; j.p. Suff. July 1660–*d.*, Mdx. Aug. 1660–*d.*; commr. for oyer and terminer, Norfolk circuit July 1660, assessment, Suff. Aug. 1660–1, sewers, Westminster Aug. 1660; dep. lt. Suff. c. Aug. 1660–*d.*[3]
Lt. of horse 1639–40.[4]

Cornwallis was descended from a London merchant whose son married a Suffolk heiress in the reign of Richard II. One of the family first represented the county in 1439. Cornwallis himself, a courtier like his father and grandfather before him, sat for Eye in both the Short and Long Parliaments. A Straffordian, he crossed over to Holland in 1642 and was disabled from sitting for recruiting mercenaries for the King. He held no commission himself, though he is said to have been in action at Cropredy Bridge. He accompanied the Prince of Wales into the west country, and was in Exeter when it surrendered. Most of the Cornwallis estate was out in jointure to his mother, and the remainder, valued at £800 p.a., had been mortgaged to her. His fine was set at one year's income, but he was 'obliged by the violence of his creditors to withdraw himself into parts beyond the seas'. He was with Charles II in Jersey in 1649, but had returned to England by 1655, when he was arrested for assisting in the escape of royalist agents. His financial position was transformed when his mother died in 1659, and in addition to her jointure he inherited the Culford estate a few months later.[5]

Under the Long Parliament ordinance against the candidature of Cavaliers, Cornwallis was ineligible at the general election of 1660, though the family borough had no scruples about electing his son. At the Restoration he was confirmed as treasurer of the Household, and recommended as court candidate for a by-election at Haverfordwest. He does not seem to have gone to the poll there, but he was given the freedom of Ipswich, and returned for the borough a few months later. A court supporter, he was appointed to no committees in the Convention; but on the day of its dissolution he urged the Commons to agree with the Lords that they should be assessed for the poll-tax by their peers. He did not stand again, being raised to the peerage in the coronation honours. But he did not enjoy his title long; he died of apoplexy on 7 Jan. 1662, and was buried at Brome. He was described as

> a man of so cheerful a spirit, that no sorrow came near his heart, and of so resolved a mind, that no fear came into his thoughts; so perfect a master of courtly and becoming raillery, that he could do more with one word in jest than others could do with whole harangues in earnest; a well-spoken man, competently seen in modern languages, of a comely and goodly personage.

But Samuel Pepys*, who was less well-disposed towards Cavaliers, dismissed him as 'a bold, profane-talking man'.[6]

[1] Reg. St. Botolph Bishopsgate, i. 179; Private Corresp. of Jane, Lady Cornwallis, xxviii, xxxv, xliii; HMC Portland, iii. 150; Cal. Comm. Adv. Money, 656; Copinger, Suff. Manors, i. 285; Chamberlain Letters ed. McClure, i. 306. [2] Carlisle, Privy Chamber, 134; LC3/1; Cal. Comm. Comp. 1389. [3] Cornwallis Corresp. 293; East Anglian, vi. 316; C181/7/37. [4] CSP Dom. Add. 1625–49, p. 607. [5] Copinger, iii. 238; HMC 10th Rep. VI, 89–92; SP23/204/591–9; Cal. Cl. SP, i. 397, 403; iii. 79; HMC Ormonde, n.s. i. 240–1; S. E. Hoskins, Chas. II in the Channel Is. ii. 315; Thurloe, iii. 339; CSP Dom. 1655, pp. 204, 588; 1657–8, p. 6. [6] NLW, Haverfordwest corp. mss 388; Old Parl. Hist. xxiii. 79; HMC 5th Rep. 159; D. Lloyd, Mems. (1668), 663; Pepys Diary, 16 Jan. 1662.

M.W.H./P.W.

CORRANCE, John (c.1616–94), of St. Martin's Lane, Westminster, and Rendlesham, Suff.

ALDEBURGH 1679 (Oct.), 1681

b. c.1616, o.s. of Allen Urren alias Corrance, Merchant Taylor, of London and Wimbish Hall, Essex by Catherine, sis. of Richard Bell of York. educ. Christ Church, Oxf. matric. 15 Feb. 1633, aged 16; I. Temple 1636; Padua 1640. m. Margaret, da. of Sir John Hare[†] of Stow Bardolph, Norf., 1s. 2da. suc. fa. 1649.[1]

Sheriff, Bucks. 1661–2, Suff. 1686–7; commr. for sewers, Bedford level 1662–3; j.p. Westminster by 1680–9; commr. for assessment, Suff. 1689–90.[2]

Corrance's father, of Warwickshire origin, was granted arms in 1620, while serving as sheriff of Radnorshire, and acquired a small estate in Essex. Neither Corrance nor his father seems to have taken any part in the Civil War. As mortgagee of the Lucy property of Haversham he was pricked as sheriff of Buckinghamshire in 1661, but he sold the manor shortly afterwards to the father of Sir John Thompson*, and acquired from his own brother-in-law two manors in Rendlesham, about seven miles from Aldeburgh. Although he lived chiefly in Westminster and held no office in Suffolk at the time, he was 'esteemed by the country gentlemen', and was returned for Aldeburgh at the second general election of 1679, probably as an opponent of exclusion, for he remained a Westminster magistrate. In the second Exclusion Parliament he was appointed only to the committee for repealing the Corporations Act. He was re-elected in 1681, but left no trace on the records of the Oxford Parliament, and there is no evidence that he stood in 1685.[3]

Corrance improved his interest by the purchase of Parham Hall in 1687 and was immediately selected as sheriff. In 1688 James II's electoral agents reported that the Aldeburgh electorate proposed to choose him again, adding that they 'could give no good account' of his attitude to the King's religious policy. Another prospective candidate was told:

> I could not learn how Mr Corrance had been beneficial to them any other way than by showing them common respects, and having gained an opinion amongst them of being firm to the Church of England.

But Corrance refused to stand 'upon pretence of age and the gout', and took no further part in public life. His will was dated 17 Nov. 1693 and proved on 7 May 1694. His grandson sat for Orford as a Tory from 1708 to 1722.[4]

[1] Vis. London (Harl. Soc. xv), 211; Burke, Commoners, iii. 370–1; PCC 120 Fairfax, 95 Box. [2] S. Wells, Drainage of the Bedford Level, i. 350; Mdx. RO/WJP/CP1, 2. [3] Grantees of Arms (Harl. Soc. lxvi), 260; Morant, Essex, ii. 558; Lipscomb, Bucks. iv. 188; Copinger, Suff. Manors, iv. 322; E. Suss. RO, Winterton mss, Godfrey to Turnor, 5 Dec. 1688. [4] Copinger, v. 156; Winterton mss, Godfrey to Turnor, 3 Dec. 1688; PCC 95 Box.

P.W.

CORYTON (CORITON), John 1 (1621–80), of Newton Ferrers, Cornw.

CALLINGTON   21 June 1660
CORNWALL   1661
CALLINGTON   1679 (Mar.)
LAUNCESTON   1679 (Oct.)–Aug. 1680

bap. 29 July 1621, 3rd but o. surv. s. of William Coryton†
of Newton Ferrers by Elizabeth, da. of Sir John
Chichester of Raleigh, Devon. *m.* (1) 27 Dec. 1643, Eli-
zabeth (*d.* 27 Sept. 1677), da. and coh. of John Mills of
Colebrooke, Devon, 2s. 2da.; (2) lic. 24 May 1680,
Anne, da. of one Bradford, wid. of Daniel Wayte of the
Inner Temple and Acton, Mdx., *s.p. suc.* fa. 1651; *cr.*
Bt. 27 Feb. 1662.[1]

Capt. of ft. (royalist) 1642, col. by 1646.[2]

J.p. Cornw. July 1660–*d.*; recorder, Launceston c. Nov.
1660–*d.*; commr. for assessment, Cornw. 1661–*d.*,
corporations 1662–3, loyal and indigent officers 1662,
dep. lt. 1662–*d.*; stannator, Foymore 1663, 1673; sub-
commr. of prizes, Plymouth 1665–7, 1672–4; commr.
for recusants, Cornw. 1675.[3]

Commr. for accounts, loyal and indigent officers
1671.[4]

Coryton's ancestors were established in Devon
by the reign of Henry III. They acquired Newton
Ferrers, two miles from Callington, in the 16th
century, and a younger son of the family sat for
Liskeard in 1558. Coryton's father was one of the
leaders of the Opposition in Charles I's early Parliament, but he was expelled from the Long Parliament for administrative abuses as vice-warden of
the stannaries and mayor of Bossiney, and fought
for the King as colonel of foot. Coryton himself,
after serving under John Berkeley†, also seems to
have been in command of a Cavalier regiment when
he and his father surrendered to (Sir) Thomas
Fairfax, 3rd Lord Fairfax* early in 1646. They
escaped fairly lightly, the father's fine being
formally granted to Coryton's unmarried sister,
who had negotiated their surrender, while Coryton
himself to avoid 'being troubled' compounded at
£297 after succeeding to the estate. He came under
suspicion after Booth's rising 'for having a store of
stately horses and letting his house at rack-rent for
three years on pretence of living in London'.
According to the informer, he was 'esteemed a
fighting man, and one of great influence'; but the
depositions were too vague to permit any action
against him.[5]

As a Cavalier Coryton was excluded from standing at the general election of 1660, but was returned
for Callington when Edward Herle* chose another
seat. In the Convention he was inactive, being appointed only to the committee to consider a petition
from the serjeant-at-arms. He seems to have
returned both Members for Callington in 1661,
when he was himself elected knight of the shire. An
active Member of the Cavalier Parliament, he was
appointed to 265 committees and acted as teller in
ten divisions, but he did not speak. In the opening
session he was named to the committees for the
security and uniformity bills. He acted as chairman
of the committee to consider the petition from
English slaves in North Africa, and, as one of the
delegation which presented the address on this subject, reported the King's answer to the House on 5
Apr. 1662. He was teller for the second reading of
the additional corporations bill on 30 Apr. 1664,
and was appointed to the committee. He took the
chair in the committee on the bill for building a
church at Falmouth, and helped to manage the
conference. In 1665 he was granted a patent to erect
lighthouses on the Channel coast in 1665, levying
6*d.* a ton on all foreign ships anchoring between the
Isle of Wight and Mount's Bay. He appears to have
owed his appointment as prize commissioner in the
second Dutch war and an award of £400 to the influence of John Evelyn, the diarist. He twice represented the Cornish tinners in negotiations with
the Government.[6]

In 1667 Coryton was appointed to consider the
petition against Lord Mordaunt and the bill establishing a public accounts commission, but his attitude to the fall of Clarendon cannot be assessed.
On 11 Dec. he was among those instructed to bring
in a bill regarding the loyal and indigent officers
fund, and he was later appointed one of the commissioners to take the accounts. His name occurs
on both lists of the court party in 1669–71, Sir
Thomas Osborne* including him among the Members to be engaged by the Duke of Buckingham.
But he was appointed to the committees to prevent
illegal imprisonment and to inspect the Conventicles and Militia Acts, and seems to have acted
as teller against the Court in a minor division on
supply on 10 Dec. 1670. His chief concern, however, was to prevent the transfer of the summer
sessions for Cornwall to Bodmin from Launceston,
where he was recorder. After telling in three divisions against the bill he was forced to admit defeat,
but it failed to pass the House of Lords. He was
named on the Paston list of court supporters in
1673–4. His application for appointment as additional navy commissioner at Plymouth in 1674 was
unsuccessful, but in the following year he was
granted a long lease of a crown manor in Cornwall
on exceptionally favourable terms. He received the
government whip for the autumn session, and was
appointed to the committee for the bill to hinder
Papists from sitting in Parliament. His name appears on the working lists, and Sir Richard Wiseman* included him among the Cornish Members

whom the Earl of Bath and Lord Arundell of Trer-ice (Richard Arundell*) 'can certainly make sure of'. In 1677 he was granted an excise pension of £400 p.a., and Shaftesbury marked him 'doubly vile'. The author of *Flagellum Parliamentarium* noted his lighthouse patent, and accused him, like his county colleague Jonathan Trelawny I*, of cheating the Prize Office. His name was on both lists of the court party in 1678.[7]

Coryton was returned for Callington at the general election, and his two sons were elected at Newport and Bossiney. Marked 'vile' on Shaftesbury's list, he became a moderately active Member of the first Exclusion Parliament. The most important of his 11 committees was to bring in a bill for banishing Papists from the metropolitan area and confining them to the neighbourhood of their homes. He voted against the exclusion bill. He was returned for Launceston in the autumn, but died before the second Exclusion Parliament met, being buried at St. Mellion on 23 Aug. 1680.[8]

[1] Lysons, *Environs*, ii. 9. [2] *List of Officers Claiming* (1663), 11, 31; SP23/200/621. [3] R. and O. B. Peter, *Launceston*, 406; *HMC Var.* i. 333; Add. 6713, f. 377; Nat. Maritime Museum, Southwell mss 17/15. [4] *CSP Dom.* 1671, p. 255. [5] Vivian, *Vis. Cornw.* 101; Keeler, *Long Parl.* 143; M. Coate, *Cornw. in Civil War*, 26, 29, 103, 206–7, 226; *Cal. Comm. Comp.* 1679. [6] SP29/115/21; *CJ*, viii. 395, 554, 561, 564; *CSP Dom.* 1664–5, p. 205; Add. 15857, f. 186; *Cal. Treas. Bks.* ii. 142; iv. 227. [7] *CJ*, ix. 214, 224, 233; *LJ*, xii. 485; *Cat. Pepysian Mss* (Navy Rec. Soc. lvii), 22; *Cal. Treas. Bks.* iv. 841. [8] *CJ*, ix. 605.

M.W.H./P.W.

CORYTON, John II (1648–90), of Newton Ferrers, Cornw.

NEWPORT	1679 (Mar.)
CALLINGTON	6 May–17 Nov. 1685, 1689, 28 Feb.–July 1690

bap. 21 Jan. 1648 1st s. of John Coryton I*, and bro. of William Coryton*. *educ.* Exeter, Oxf. 1666. *m.* lic. 22 Feb. 1672, Elizabeth, da. and coh. of Sir Richard Chiverton, Skinner and merchant, of Clerkenwell Green, Mdx., 2 da. *d.v.p. suc.* fa. as 2nd Bt. Aug. 1680.[1]

Commr. for assessment, Cornw. 1673–80, 1689; j.p. Cornw. 1681–July 1688, Oct. 1688–?*d.*, Devon 1682–July 1688; sheriff, Cornw. 1683–4; freeman, Saltash 1683; mayor, Callington 1684–5; alderman 1685–Oct. 1688; alderman, Liskeard 1685–Oct. 1688; stannator, Foymore 1686.[2]

Coryton first stood for Newport at a by-election in 1678. He was defeated by Ambrose Manaton*, and his petition was never reported. But he was successful at the next general election, when he may also have contested Launceston. Shaftesbury marked him 'base', but no committees can be definitely allotted to him, and he was absent from the division on the first exclusion bill. At the autumn election he stood down in his brother's

favour. As mayor of Callington in 1685, he returned himself and his brother, but he probably never took his seat, owing to illness, and his election was eventually declared void. He followed the lead of Sir John Carew* in returning negative answers to the lord lieutenant's questions on the Tests and the Penal Laws, and was removed from county office. James II's electoral agents noted that he controlled one seat at Callington, which he was to represent for the rest of his life. According to Antony Rowe* he voted to agree with the Lords that the throne was not vacant, but otherwise he was totally inactive in the Convention. Re-elected in 1690, he was buried at St. Mellion on 30 July.[3]

[1] Vivian, *Vis. Cornw.* 101. [2] *CSP Dom.* 1685, pp. 66, 257; *HMC Var.* i. 328; J. Tregoning, *Laws of the Stannaries*, 57. [3] *CJ*, ix. 518, 731.

G.H.

CORYTON, William (1650–1711), of Newton Ferrers, Cornw. and the Middle Temple.

BOSSINEY	1679 (Mar.)
NEWPORT	1679 (Oct.)
CALLINGTON	1681, 1685
MITCHELL	18 Sept.–12 Dec. 1689
CALLINGTON	1695, 1698, 1701 (Feb.), 30 Nov. 1703, 1708, 1710–6 Dec. 1711

bap. 24 May 1650, 2nd s. of John Coryton I*, and bro. of John Coryton II*. *educ.* Exeter, Oxf. 1666; M. Temple 1669, called 1675. *m.* (1) lic. 11 Dec. 1688, Susanna (*d.* 6 Aug. 1695), da. of Sir Edward Littleton, 2nd Bt.* of Pillaton, Staffs., 1s.; (2) Sarah, wid. of Thomas Williams, banker, of London, *s.p. suc.* bro. as 3rd Bt. July 1690.

Commr. for assessment, Cornw. 1679–80, 1689–90, Kent 1690; freeman, Saltash 1683, Bodmin and Callington 1685; alderman, Lostwithiel 1685–Oct. 1688; j.p. and dep. lt. Cornw. by 1701–*d.*[1]

Coryton, a younger son, became a professional lawyer and clearly more of a committed politician than his brother. For the first general election of 1679 he may have relied on an old family interest at Bossiney, of which his grandfather had twice been mayor. He was marked 'base' on Shaftesbury's list. An inactive Member of the first Exclusion Parliament, he was appointed to the committee of elections and privileges and probably to two committees for private bills. He voted against exclusion, and at the next election he was defeated at his father's borough of Callington, but replaced his elder brother at Newport. He was moderately active in the second Exclusion Parliament, being appointed to the committees to hear complaints against the ecclesiastical courts, to provide relief against arbitrary fines, and to repeal the Corporations Act. At the general election of 1681 he was returned for Callington, but left no trace on the records of the Oxford Parliament. In 1682 he was granted the reversion of some duchy of Cornwall property, at a fine reduced from £380 to £100 in consideration of his father's loyalty and service.[2]

Coryton was re-elected with his brother, the mayor, in 1685, and became a very active Member of James II's Parliament, being named to 17 committees. On 30 May he was given leave to bring in a bill to revive the 'coinage' of tin, which passed both Houses. He was appointed to the committee to recommend expunctions from the Journals, and acted as chairman on the bill to provide carriages for the navy and ordnance, which he carried to the Lords on 15 June. The lord lieutenant of Cornwall noted that the questions on the repeal of the Test Act and Penal Laws were to be put to him, as a lawyer, by Lord Chancellor Jeffreys. Presumably he refused, unlike Nicholas Courtney*, as he was not included among the Templars who concurred. He is not known to have stood at the general election of 1689, but was returned for Mitchell at the by-election caused by the discharge of Charles Fanshawe*, Viscount Fanshawe, as a non-juror. He was named to the elections committee for the second session of the Convention, and also to that for the reversal of the attainder of Sir Thomas Armstrong. But on 12 Dec. he was unseated in favour of Humphrey Courtney*. After succeeding to the baronetcy, he sat for the family borough of Callington as a Tory, refusing the Association in 1696. He died on 6 Dec. 1711. His son sat for Callington as a Tory (with one break) from 1713 to 1734.[3]

[1] *CSP Dom.* 1685, p. 256; *HMC Var.* i. 328; J. Wallis, *Bodmin Reg.* 169. [2] *CJ*, ix. 641; *Cal. Treas. Bks.* vii. 418, 473. [3] *CJ*, ix. 735.

G.H.

COTTERELL, Sir Charles (1615–1701), of St. Martin's Lane, Westminster.

CARDIGAN BOROUGHS   6 Apr. 1663

b. 16 Apr. 1615, o.s. of Sir Clement Cotterell†, groom porter, of Southrepps, Norf. by Anne, da. and h. of Henry Alleyne of Wilsford, Lincs. *educ.* Queens', Camb. 1629–32. *m.* 1642 (with £400) Frances, da. of Edward West of Marsworth, Bucks., 2s. (1 *d.v.p.*) 3da. *suc.* fa. 1631; kntd. 6 Mar. 1645.[1]

Asst. master of ceremonies, 1641–6, master June 1660–86; steward to Elizabeth, Queen of Bohemia c.1652–5; secretary to the Duke of Gloucester 1655–Sept. 1660; master of requests 1667–86.[2]

Capt. of ft. (royalist) 1642, maj. 1643–6.[3]

Freeman, Portsmouth 1662; commr. for assessment, Westminster 1663–9, 1677–80, Mdx. 1664–9, Mdx. and Westminster 1689–90; dep. lt. Mdx. by 1680–Jan. 1688.[4]

Cotterell's father, from an obscure Norfolk family, became groom-porter to James I, married a Lincolnshire heiress, and sat for Boston in 1624. But her small property, valued at only £160 p.a., had to be sold before the Civil War. Cotterell also became a courtier, and served in the Cavalier army. On the execution of Charles I he went to Antwerp, where he was able to accord hospitality to royalist fugitives, and took service successively with two members of the royal family in exile. Returning at the Restoration he became master of ceremonies. A man of some culture and learning, he translated works from French, Italian and Spanish, and joined the literary circle which gathered round 'the matchless Orinda'. He helped to save her husband, James Philipps*, from the worst consequences of his membership of two High Courts of Justice. When the election of Philipps for Cardigan Boroughs was declared void, he brought in Cotterell in his place, hoping, as his wife explained, that Cotterell would not

> despise this little instance, since 'tis all his misfortunes have left him capable to give of his esteem and gratitude to you, for whom I am certain he has as profound a respect and veneration as for any man living. I know you are not fond of being a Parliament man; yet since you are elected so much without your seeking that I am sure it was not so much as thought of by you, and, since it was intended as a testimony of the eternal value and friendship that Antenor and Orinda must ever have for the noble Poliarchus, I hope he will not be angry to be sent into the House without his own consent or knowledge.

Cotterell survived a petition from his opponent and became an inactive Member of the Cavalier Parliament, sitting on only 44 committees. In his first session he was named to those to provide remedies against meetings of dissenters, to consider a bill for the prevention of profanity, to relieve persons who for various reasons had been unable to subscribe to the Act of Uniformity, and to consider a petition from the inhabitants of Westminster about the poor. Together with Edward Progers* he was thanked by the House on 18 July for obtaining from the King a promise of preferment for their chaplain. In 1664 he served on a committee for establishing St. James Piccadilly as a separate parish. He was noted as a court dependant in that year and on both lists in 1669–71. His name appeared on the Paston list and the list of King's servants in 1675. Marked 'thrice vile' on Shaftesbury's list in 1677, he was named to the committee for educating children of the royal family as Protestants. In *A Seasonable Argument* he was said to have obtained £11,000 by virtue of his offices, and he was again noted as a court supporter on both lists in 1678. In the last two sessions, he was appointed to the committees to summarize foreign commitments and to translate Coleman's letters. His was the first name on the committee to consider the access of ambassadors to the Court. On 28 Nov. 1678, in his only recorded speech, he conveyed to the House information about the Plot derived from Dutch intelligence in Frankfort, which he was ordered to communicate to the Lords.[5]

Cotterell did not stand again, but remained as master of ceremonies until allowed to resign in favour of his son in 1686. He died on 7 June 1701, and was buried in St. Martin in the Fields, the only member of his family to sit in Parliament.[6]

[1] Wards 7/82/104; F. G. Lee, *Church of Thame*, 517-8; Cottrell-Dormer (Rousham) mss, 'Advice to my son'. [2] *CSP Dom.* 1641-3, p. 66; Cottrell-Dormer mss, court offices. [3] *HMC Downshire*, i. 284-5. [4] R. East, *Portsmouth Recs.* 357. [5] P. W. Souers, *The Matchless Orinda*, 111, 120; K. Philipps, *Letters of Orinda to Poliarchus* (1705), 133-4; Grey, vi. 285; *CJ*, ix. 544, 550. [6] *CSP Dom.* 1686-7, p. 328; A. Wood, *Fasti*, ii. 324-5; Cottrell-Dormer mss, family account.

L.N./G.J.

COTTON, John I (1621-1702), of Conington, Hunts. and Cotton House, Westminster.

| HUNTINGDON | 1661 |
| HUNTINGDONSHIRE | 1685 |

b. 9 Mar. 1621, 1st s. of Sir Thomas Cotton, 2nd Bt.[†], of Conington, being o.s. by 1st w. Margaret, da. of Lord William Howard of Naworth Castle, Cumb. *educ.* Magdalene, Camb. 1637; travelled abroad 1639-42. *m.* (1) 8 June 1644, Dorothy, da. and h. of Edmund Anderson of Stratton, Beds., 7s. *d.v.p.* 2da.; (2) 20 Oct. 1658, Elizabeth, da. of Sir Thomas Honeywood[†] of Markshall, Essex, and h. to her bro. John Lamott Honeywood*, 1 surv. s. 2da. *suc.* fa. as 3rd Bt. 13 May 1662.[1]

J.p. Hunts. July 1660-Apr. 1688, Oct. 1688-*d.*, Beds. 1680-Feb. 1688, Oct. 1688-93; commr. for assessment, Hunts. Aug. 1660-80, Westminster 1661-3, 1664-80, Huntingdon 1663-80, Beds. 1664-80, 1689-90, Hunts. and Westminster 1689; oyer and terminer, Norfolk circuit July 1660, dep. lt. Hunts. c. Aug. 1660-Mar. 1688, Oct. 1688-?96, Beds. 1670-Feb. 1688; commr. for loyal and indigent officers, Hunts. 1662, recusants 1675, col. of militia ft. by 1680-Feb. 1688.[2]

Cotton's ancestor, a younger son of the Cheshire family, inherited Conington in 1460, and Thomas Cotton first sat for Huntingdonshire in 1554. Cotton's grandfather, Sir Robert Cotton[†], was the favourite antiquary of the Opposition in the early Stuart Parliaments, despite his descent from the royal house of Scotland. His father was named to the county committee in 1642-3, but concentrated on improving and extending his estate, valued shortly before his death at £3,000 p.a. Cotton took no part in the Civil War, though there can be no doubt where his sympathies lay: he was 'devoted to the prerogative, even to slavery', according to

Burnet, and frankly told the House that there were great mistakes in his grandfather's work. The second Lord Dartmouth called him 'a very worthy, honest gentleman, that understood and loved the constitution of his country'. Shortly after his second marriage, he is said to have attempted suicide. Returned for Huntingdon at the general election of 1661, he was a moderately active Member of the Cavalier Parliament, in which he was appointed to 84 committees, acted as teller in eight divisions and made seven recorded speeches. In the first session he was appointed to the committees for the security bill and the bill of pains and penalties. On 30 June 1663 he acted as teller for the bill against Quakers and other sectaries, and he objected to the Lords' amendments to the explanatory uniformity bill of the same year. 'Sir John Cotton, knight' was noted as a court dependant in 1664, but this may have been due to confusion with his Cambridge-shire namesake (father of John Cotton III*), who was a gentleman of the privy chamber. His devotion to the Church was recognized in his selection to ask Dr Stillingfleet to preach to the House in 1666.[3]

Cotton's recorded speeches were plentifully adorned with classical tags. According to Evelyn, Cotton was only 'a pretended great Grecian, but had by no means the parts or genius of his grand-father'; but Cotton's letters suggest that this verdict was too harsh. On 27 Feb. 1668 he moved to raise £300,000 upon the luxury of eating and drinking, which reminded him of the decadence of Rome. But his major effort was reserved for the debate on toleration of 11 Mar. when he attacked such Pres-byterian tenets as that the King was *maior singulis* but *universo minor*; that he was but *minister bonorum*; that he was only to command as he is good (*dominium in gratia*); the principle of self preservation (*salus populi, suprema lex*); 'and many more such'. He served on committees considering the petitions of his college in 1669 and of Henry Williams* in 1670. Sir Thomas Osborne* listed him as usually voting for supply, but he was sufficiently outraged by the attack on Sir John Coventry* to wish to lay aside all other business, and on 13 Feb. 1671 he moved that the preamble to the supply bill should provide for the money to be applied to maintaining the Triple Alliance. In 1673 he served on the com-mittee that produced the test bill. But with the break-up of the Cabal, Cotton moved back to the Court. In the debate on the standing army of 7 Feb. 1674 he objected to the removal of necessary guards. He received the government whip for the autumn session of 1675, and made an important speech:

Princes may be mistaken, councils may err, but the King cannot do ill. Three things hinder supply. First, the fear that what they give may be spent in luxury. . . . Secondly, the fear that Popery should be brought in; we see Papists placed in military employment. Thirdly, the fear of being governed in an arbitrary way by a standing army. But now he comes to the great point. Is really of opinion that at this time we should give the King supply for the fleet. Virgil calls us in scorn *divisos orbe Britannos*. Our ships are our walls, to which the King has a natural affection, and more employs his mind on than any of his predecessors. Would have us give him something now. Moves for £500,000.

Cotton served on the committee to hinder the growth of Popery, and acted as teller against the motion to adjourn debate on Shirley v. Fagg on 17 Nov. Late-night sittings had no terrors for him, as his Westminster home adjoined the two Houses. His name appears on the working lists, and Sir Richard Wiseman* described him as 'a very good man, and rarely misseth in his vote, and then by mistake only. Some person (trusty) should always sit near him.' On the other hand the author of *A Seasonable Argument* called him 'a madman who cut his own throat, and now cuts his country's by his vote', and Shaftesbury marked him 'thrice vile'. He probably abandoned his residence in Huntingdonshire in 1676, when he took out a game licence for within ten miles of Stratton. In 1677 he was appointed to the committees for recalling British subjects from the French service and hindering the growth of Popery, as well as to that for the estate bill of Lord Manchester (Robert Montagu*). He was marked as a court supporter in both lists of 1678, during which he was appointed to the committee to summarize the foreign commitments undertaken by the Government, and added to the committee to prevent the growth of Popery. He seems to have been unaffected by the Popish Plot agitation, except when the Lords nervously desired him to remove his coals and faggots from their cellars.[4]

Cotton is not known to have stood for any of the Exclusion Parliaments. In 1681 he was hoping for a peerage, but nothing came of it. Although he had left Conington to fall into decay, he was still one of the largest landowners in Huntingdonshire, for which he was returned to James II's Parliament. He was moderately active, serving on the committee to review the accounts of the disbandment commissioners and probably on three others. But he was no less hostile to Popery than to dissent, and in 1687 offered shelter to one of the ejected fellows of Magdalen; his 'little villa at Stratton', during the Civil War, had sufficed to accommodate not only his own household and his father's second family, but also his grandfather's famous library. To the

lord lieutenant's questions on the repeal of the Test Act and Penal Laws he replied:

> With all humility and duty he answers that if he be chose (for he does not design to stand), then he will come into the House with a design to be convinced with the best argument which he hopes may be given for the repealing the laws. . . . He must be of consequence for electing such Members as are of the same mind.

Cotton's ingenious phraseology did not save him from dismissal from all local office. He took no part in the Revolution, but accepted the new regime: 'as for the public affairs', he wrote in 1693, 'I desire wholly to acquiesce in God's providence'. His ascetic life earned for him a healthy and cheerful old age, occupied by learned correspondence, the composition of Latin verse, and the writing of an autobiography which does not seem to have survived. He died on 12 Sept. 1702, aged 81, and was buried at Conington. In accordance with his desires, the Cottonian Library was sold to the nation for £4,500. His grandson was elected for Huntingdon in 1705 and for the county in 1710 as a Tory.[5]

[1] *Misc. Gen. et. Her.* (n.s.), i. 340; *PC Reg.* vi. 445; F. A. Blaydes, *Gen. Bed.* 110. [2] *CSP Dom.* 1679–80, p. 70; *HMC Lords*, ii. 173. [3] *VCH Hunts.* iii. 148; *D'Ewes Autobiog.* ed. Halliwell, ii. 43; Burnet, ii. 107; Grey, v. 373; R. Vaughan, *Protectorate*, ii. 460, 462, 464; Carlisle, *Privy Chamber*, 164; *CJ*, viii. 533, 627. [4] *Evelyn Diary*, iii. 443; *Milward*, 199–200, 219; Grey, i. 113; ii. 393; iii. 323; *Dering*, 45, 76; *Bulstrode Pprs.* 318; *CSP Dom.* 1676–7, p. 222; *HMC Lords*, ii. 17. [5] *VCH Hunts.* iii. 145; *CSP Dom.* 1680–1, p. 647; *Letters Written by Eminent Persons* (1813), i. 18, 20, 22.

E.R.E.

COTTON, John II (1628–1703) of Botreaux Castle, Cornw.

BOSSINEY 1685

bap. Dec. 1628, 3rd s. of William Cotton, precentor of Exeter Cathedral, by Elizabeth, da. and coh. of John Hender† of Botreaux Castle; bro. of William Cotton*. *m.* Sarah (*d.* 6 Mar. 1677), da. and coh. of John Fuljames of Woodbrooke, Som., *s.p. suc.* bro. Edward 1675; kntd. 9 July 1685.[1]
Commr. for assessment, Cornw. 1677–80, 1689–90, j.p. 1678–?*d.*, sheriff 1679–80; freeman, Tintagel 1685–Sept. 1688; dep. lt. Cornw. by 1701–*d.*[2]

Cotton was returned to James II's Parliament for Bossiney on the strong property interest that he had inherited from his maternal grandfather; but he was probably wholly inactive. In July he was knighted at Whitehall 'in recognition of the constant and unshaken loyalty of himself and his family'. He was recommended for re-election as court candidate by the Earl of Bath in the summer of 1688, but shortly afterwards he was displaced from the corporation by order in council. He probably never stood again, though he must have accepted the Revolution, for he remained on the county bench and was appointed to the lieutenancy. He died on 2 Feb. 1703 and was buried at Minster, the last of his family.[3]

[1] J. Maclean, *Trigg Minor*, i. 607, 652–3; Vivian, *Vis. Devon*, 240–1. [2] Maclean, iii. 207; PC2/72/734. [3] B. H. Williams, *Ancient West Country Fams.* 62–65.

E.C.

COTTON, John III (c.1647–1713), of Madingley Hall, Cambs.

CAMBRIDGE   1689, 1690, 6 Nov. 1696, 1698, 1701 (Feb.), 1701 (Dec.), 1705

b. c.1647, 1st s. of Sir John Cotton, 1st Bt., of Landwade by Jane, da. and h. of Edward Hinde of Madingley. *educ.* Trinity, Camb. 1663. *m.* 14 Jan. 1679, Elizabeth (*d.* 3 Dec. 1714), da. and coh. of Sir Joseph Sheldon, Draper, of St. Paul's Churchyard, London, 2s. (1 *d.v.p.*) at least 7da. *suc.* fa. as 2nd Bt. 25 Mar. 1689.[1]

Commr. for pontage, Cambridge 1673, assessment, Cambs. 1679–80, Cambs. and Cambridge 1689–90; freeman, Cambridge 1679; j.p. Cambs. 1680–7, ?1689–d., dep. lt. 1685–7, by 1701–?d.; gamekeeper, Newmarket 1689–d.; recorder, Cambridge 1702–d.[2]

Cotton was descended from a wealthy London mercer who acquired Landwade soon after 1420, and was not akin to Sir Robert Cotton*. The family first represented the county in 1439. As sheriff of Cambridgeshire, Cotton's father attempted to carry the university plate to Charles I in 1642, but took no further part in the Civil War. In view of 'the smallness of his offence', he was fined only £350, a year's value of his estate. Although he married an heiress, he was compelled to mortgage his inheritance, and lived abroad during the Interregnum.[3]

Cotton doubtless opposed exclusion, for he was made a j.p. in 1680 in his father's lifetime. Though his answers on the repeal of the Penal Laws and Test are not extant, he was apparently hostile to James II's ecclesiastical policy, and was removed from local office. He was first returned for Cambridge, three miles from Madingley, in 1689, and two days after the Convention met was recorded as waiting on William III with the solemn engagement of the county gentry to stand by him. But according to one list he voted to agree with the Lords that the throne was not vacant. A moderately active Member, he was appointed to 16 committees but he made no recorded speeches. Early in the first session he was named to committees to prevent disputes concerning the present Parliament, and to bring in a bill for better regulating the Exchequer. He was among those appointed to consider the bill for the speedier conviction and disarming of Papists, to inspect the Journals about the Popish Plot, to consider the Lords' proviso to the bill of rights and settlement, and to draw up an address for permission to inspect the Privy Council regis-

ters and the books of the Irish committee. Among his committees in the second session were those for the second mutiny bill and for granting indemnity to persons helping to bring in William and Mary. He continued to sit for the borough as a Tory with but two short intervals until he retired in his son's favour in 1708. He died on 16 Jan. 1713, aged 66, and was buried at Landwade. His son, described as the last active Jacobite in England, sat for Cambridge and Cambridgeshire from 1708 to 1741.[4]

[1] *East Anglian*, i. 343–4; J. R. Woodhead, *Rulers of London*, 147; J. P. Hore, *Sporting Recs. of Cheveley*, 21. [2] C. H. Cooper, *Annals of Cambridge*, iii. 557, 582; iv. 52, 110. [3] *Camb. Antiq. Soc. Procs.* xxxviii. 5, 7, 18, 46; VCH Cambs. ii. 411; A. Kingston, *East Anglia and the Civil War*, 301; Hore, 20; *Cal. Comm. Comp.* 891; *Cal. Comm. Adv. Money*, 558; *CSP Dom.* 1663–4, p. 245; *Cal. Treas. Bks.* iii. 217. [4] *Camb. Antiq. Soc. Procs.* xxxviii. 7; *East Anglian*, i. 344.

E.R.E./G.J.

COTTON, Sir Robert (1644–1717), of Hatley St. George, Cambs.

CAMBRIDGESHIRE   1679 (Oct.), 1681, 1685, 1689, 1690
NEWPORT I.o.W.   1695, 1698
TRURO   12 Feb. 1702

bap. 2 May 1644, 3rd s. of Sir Thomas Cotton, 2nd Bt.[†], of Conington Castle, Hunts., being 1st surv. s. by 2nd w. Alice, da. and h. of Sir John Constable of Dromanby, Yorks., wid. of Edmund Anderson of Eyworth, Beds.; half-bro. of John Cotton I*. *m.* lic. 4 July 1663, 'aged 21', Gertrude (*d.* 17 Aug. 1701), da. of William Morice I* of Werrington, Devon, 1s. *d.v.p.* 1da. Kntd. 3 June 1663.[1]

Commr. for assessment, Cambs. 1664–80, 1689–90, j.p. 1672–Mar. 1688, 1689–d., commr. for recusants 1675; freeman, Cambridge 1679; dep. lt. Cambs. 1685–Mar. 1688, Oct. 1688–d.; sheriff, Cambs. and Hunts. Jan.–Nov. 1688; commr. for pontage, Cambridge 1692.[2]

Jt. postmaster gen. 1691–1708.[3]

Although Cotton settled in Cambridgeshire on his marriage, he appears, like Sir Levinus Bennet*, to have taken no part in politics before the exclusion crisis. At the second election of 1679 they defeated the country candidates Gerard Russell* and Edward Partherich*. As 'Mr Cotton' he may have been moderately active, with three committees in the second Exclusion Parliament, the most important being for relief from arbitrary fines. He took no known part in the Oxford Parliament, and in James II's Parliament he was named only to the committee on the bill for exporting leather. His answers on the repeal of the Test Act and Penal Laws are not extant, but his attitude cannot have been satisfactory to the Government, for the King's agents recommended his removal from local office. After the Revolution Lord Danby (Sir Thomas

Osborne*) unsuccessfully recommended Cotton for employment. In the Convention he voted to agree with the Lords that the throne was not vacant. In other respects his record cannot be entirely distinguished from that of the Cheshire Member, but he was probably very active, making some 20 speeches, serving on up to 80 committees, and telling in four divisions. If so, he was appointed to the committees for securing religion, laws and liberties, to consider the suspension of habeas corpus, and to inquire into the authors and advisers of grievances. He helped to draw up the address for the suppression of the mutiny at Ipswich. The first recorded speech definitely ascribed to the Member for Cambridgeshire was on 28 Mar. 1689, when he opposed the proviso to the coronation oath to permit alterations in religion. He was named to the committees for the repeal of the Corporations Act and for the toleration bill. He wished to agree to the Lords' amendment exempting the clergy from the new oath of allegiance, and was appointed to a small committee on 24 Apr. to search for precedents. He recommended himself to the new regime by praising the King's leniency and serving on all the committees to naturalize his Dutch cousins and advisers. He took the chair for the bill naturalizing Auverquerque and Zuylestein, and on 29 Apr. carried it to the Upper House. On the question of exclusion from indemnity he urged specifying offenders rather than offences, which would

> leave such jealousies in people as that they will not think themselves safe; it will go so large I fear it will hazard the peace and safety of the nation. The great wheels, the *primum mobiles*, that have gone so violently and brought us into this confusion, I move that you will proceed against them.

Cotton took the chair in the committee considering the petition of George Speke.* He acted as teller for the bill for better ordering the forces on 21 May, but against the suspension of habeas corpus, which he had strongly opposed both on second and third readings:

> As an Englishman, I am jealous of our liberties, and will not give my vote to betray them.... If this was for suspicion of fact by words, or any ground of reasonable suspicion; but when the suspicion has no ground but upon private resentments, and that not so open, and not known why suspected, this alters the very reason of the law of habeas corpus.

He agreed that the verdict on Titus Oates had been illegal, but opposed 'clogging' the resolution with allegations of corruption. 'Nothing will more settle the nation than a quiet, peaceable spirit among ourselves', he told the House on 12 June, and he defended the records of (Sir) Robert Sawyer* and Bishop Sprat of Rochester in the last reign. He was

appointed to the committee for the bill of rights and settlement, and helped to draw up the address for leave to inspect the entries about Ireland in the Privy Council registers and to consider the charges of malversation against William Harbord*.[4]

In the second session Cotton was named to the committees on the expenses and miscarriages of the war and for the mutiny bill. He helped to draw up the address to ask who was responsible for the appointment of Commissary Shales and to prepare a report on the state of the revenue. He spoke against reducing Princess Anne's income, and acted as teller against the disabling clause in the bill to restore corporations. He continued to defend Sawyer's conduct, even in the trial of Sir Thomas Armstrong*; 'as Sawyer did his duty to the King, so he did to the prisoner', he told the House on 20 Jan. 1690, though the Whigs suspected that 'all this fencing' was less to save Sawyer than the Hon. Heneage Finch I*.[5]

With Thomas Frankland*, Cotton became joint postmaster-general on the dismissal of John Wildman I* in 1691, and as a placeman voted with the Government. He retired from office in 1708 on the grounds of age, though he did not die until 12 Sept. 1717. He seems to have been distressed for money in his last years. His daughter brought the Hatley property, on which he had erected a fine house, to her husband, Samuel Trefusis†.[6]

[1] F. A. Blaydes, *Gen. Bed.* 110; *London Mar. Lic.* ed. Foster, 337; *Le Neve's Knights* (Harl. Soc. viii), 171; *Top. and Gen.* iii. 40. [2] C. H. Cooper, *Annals of Cambridge*, iii. 582; iv. 19. [3] *Cal. Treas. Bks.* ix. 1037; xxii. 345. [4] Browning, *Danby*, ii. 160; *CJ*, x. 49, 100, 110, 139, 151, 204; Grey, ix. 202, 212, 246, 266–7, 274, 293, 296, 361, 384. [5] *CJ*, x. 296, 329; Grey, ix. 497, 535. [6] *Pol. State*, xiv. 303; *Cal. Treas. Pprs.* iv. 363.

J.P.F.

COTTON, Sir Robert, 1st Bt. (c.1635–1712), of Combermere, Cheshire.

CHESHIRE   1679 (Oct.), 1681, 1689, 1690, 1695, 1698, 1701 (Feb.), 1701 (Dec.)

b. c.1635, 2nd but 1st surv. s. of Thomas Cotton of Combermere, being 1st s. by 2nd w. Elizabeth, da. of Sir George Calveley of Lea and coh. to her bro. Sir Hugh. *educ.* travelled abroad (France) 1651–5. *m.* c.1666, Hester, da. of Sir Thomas Salusbury, 2nd Bt.†, of Llewenni, Denb. and h. to her bro. Sir John Salusbury*, 5s. (4 *d.v.p.*) 11da. *suc.* gdfa. 1649; kntd. 25 June 1660; *cr.* Bt. 29 Mar. 1677.[1]

J.p. Cheshire Mar. 1660–82, ?1689–*d.*, Denb. 1689–*d.*, Flints. by 1701–*d.*; commr. for militia, Cheshire Mar. 1660; dep. lt. Cheshire 1661–82, Nov. 1688–*d.*, Denb. and Flints. by 1701–*d.*; commr. for corporations, Cheshire 1662–3, loyal and indigent officers 1662, assessment, Cheshire 1663–80, Cheshire and Denb. 1689–90, Flints. 1690; alderman, Chester by 1664–84; freeman, Denbigh 1665, 1700; steward, lordship of

Denbigh 1689–1702; custos rot. Denb. June–Oct. 1689, 1699–1702, col. of militia by 1699.[2]

Cotton's ancestor, of a Shropshire family, received a grant of the former Cistercian monastery of Combermere from Henry VIII. A younger brother sat for Cheshire in the reign of Mary, but they were not a regular parliamentary family. Cotton's octogenarian grandfather contributed arms and plate to the royalist cause, and compounded for £666 13s.4d. 'Known to bear a royalist name', Cotton himself was included in the list drawn up by Roger Whitley* in 1658, and took part in the rising led by Sir George Booth*. He was knighted at the Restoration, and granted the reversion of the office of chamberlain of Chester to take effect on the death of Heneage Finch*. But this grant was invalidated by Finch's resignation in 1677 in favour of the 9th Earl of Derby. Cotton's baronetcy was no doubt intended as compensation, but he went into opposition nevertheless. He was returned for the county as a Whig in the second general election of 1679, and in the second Exclusion Parliament probably served on the committees for repealing the Irish Cattle Act and reforming the collection of hearth-tax. At Oxford he was appointed to the committee for the exclusion bill. During the Duke of Monmouth's 'progress' in Cheshire in 1682, Cotton was described as 'his almost constant attendant'. He was dismissed from local office, and presented by the grand jury in 1683 as dangerous to the peace and security.[3]

At the general election of 1685 Cotton stood with John Mainwaring* against two Tories. They were defeated, but petitioned, very fortunately for Cotton, since his attendance at the committee of elections, although productive of no positive result, enabled him to prove an alibi, with the aid of such unexceptionably Tory witnesses as John Ashburnham II* and Sir William Twysden*, when he was accused of conspiring with Lord Delamer (Henry Booth*) to send assistance to Monmouth. He was noted as a member of the opposition to James II, though considerable only for his interest, and undoubtedly welcomed the Revolution. He regained his seat in 1689, but was considerably less active in the Convention than his namesake Sir Robert Cotton*. In the debate on the bailing of Robert Brent, the regulator, on 6 Feb. 1689, he rather irrelevantly reminded the House of excessive bail taken from Delamer, for whom he had stood surety. The only two committees which can definitely be assigned to him were for the naturalization of Marshall Schomberg and the repeal of the Corporations Act. Lord Brandon (Hon. Charles Gerard*) complained of him to the Earl of Shrewsbury as a 'busy' person, whose information should be disregarded, and he was removed as custos rotulorum of Denbighshire, where he had inherited the important Llewenni estate. He supported the disabling clause in the bill to restore corporations, and remained a country Whig under William III. He died on 17 Dec. 1712, aged 77. His grandson, the third baronet, was returned for Cheshire as a Whig in 1727.[4]

[1] Ormerod, *Cheshire*, iii. 415; *Verney Mems.* i. 502; ii. 28. [2] Chester corp. mss. assembly bk. 2, ff. 137v, 150; J. Williams, *Ancient and Modern Denbigh*, 109; *Recs. of Denbigh*, 143; Ormerod, iii. 405; *CSP Dom.* 1689–90, p. 31; A. L. Cust., *Chrons. of Erthig*, 62. [3] Ormerod, i. pp. lxvii, 61; iii. 414–15; *Cal. Comm. Comp.* 898, 2576; *CSP Dom.* 1682, pp. 408, 441. [4] *CJ*, ix. 721; *CSP Dom.* 1685, pp. 326, 336; 1689–90, p. 151; Luttrell, i. 366, 369; *Reresby Mems.* 406–7; *HMC 7th Rep.* 499; *State Trials*, xi. 571–4; Grey, ix. 66.

G.H.

COTTON, William (c.1608–73), of Botreaux Castle, Cornw.

CAMELFORD 3 Aug. 1660

b. c.1608, 1st s. of William Cotton, precentor of Exeter Cathedral 1606–46; bro. of John Cotton II*. *educ.* Exeter, Oxf. 1629, BA 1632, MA 1635. *m.* (1) c.1639, Catherine (*d.*1649), wid. of John Rawlinson, DD, principal of St. Edmund Hall, Oxf., *s.p.*; (2) 27 May 1657, Eleanor Larder of Saltash, Cornw., *s.p. suc.* fa. 1656.[1]

Fellow of Exeter 1629–39; mayor, Tintagel 1646–?50; j.p. Cornw. Aug. 1660–*d.*, commr. for assessment Aug. 1660–9.[2]

Cotton's grandfather, a notorious nepotist who claimed descent from the Cheshire family, became bishop of Exeter in 1598 and established his sons in the diocese. His father was deprived of all his possessions during the Civil War, both spiritual and temporal, and was reduced to living in a small rented house near Silverton. Although Cotton was fellow of his college for ten years, he was never ordained. Presumably he resigned in order to marry, a change of status he could well afford since through his mother he was heir to a moiety of the Hender estate. Although he had taken no known part in the Civil War, he did not stand at the general election of 1660. But after the Restoration he was involved in a double return at Camelford, which was resolved in his favour. He was appointed to no committees and made no recorded speeches in the Convention, but doubtless supported the Court. He did not stand again. He died on 25 Dec. 1673, leaving an estate of £800 p.a., and was buried at Minster.[3]

[1] J. Maclean, *Trigg Minor*, i. 652–3; PCC 74 St. John; Vivian, *Vis. Devon*, 240–1. [2] Maclean, iii. 210. [3] Maclean, i. 643–6; iii. 216, 262; Add. 18448, f. 30.

M.W.H.

COURTENAY, Francis (1652–99), of Powderham Castle, Devon.

DEVON   1689, 1690, 1695, 1698–1 Apr. 1699

bap. 27 Feb. 1652, 2nd s. of Sir William Courtenay, 1st Bt.*, and bro. of Richard Courtenay* and George Courtenay†. m. settlement 26 Nov. 1670 (with £4,000), Mary, da. of William Boevey, merchant, of Little Chelsea, Mdx., 3s. (2 d.v.p) 9da.[1]

Commr. for assessment, Devon 1677–80, 1689–90, j.p. June–July 1688, 1689–96, col. of militia by 1699.[2]

Courtenay's wife, of Flemish extraction, was a step-daughter of Sir James Smyth*; her half-sister married Sir Levinus Bennet*. As Courtenay was still under age at the time of their marriage, his father promoted a private bill to enable him to settle the estate, to which he had become the heir on his elder brother's death. Sir Charles Harbord* reported that the bill required no amendments, and it received the royal assent in the same session.[3]

Courtenay joined William of Orange in November 1688, and was elected for the county in 1689 owing to the physical incapacity of his father. He may have been appointed to the committee of elections and privileges in the first session of the Convention, but he left no other trace on its records. In later Parliaments he voted Tory, refusing the Association in 1696. He died before his father on 1 Apr. 1699 and was buried at Chelsea. His son, who succeeded as second baronet, sat for Devon as a Tory (with one interval of two years) from 1701 till his death.[4]

[1] Vivian, Vis. Devon, 248–9; A. W. Crawley-Boevey, Mems. Boevey Fam. 19, 156. [2] Post Boy, 4 Apr. 1699. [3] PC2/76/263; CJ, ix. 176; E. Cleaveland, Noble Fam. of Courtenay, 305. [4] Bodl. Fleming newsletter, 3334; Top. and Gen. iii. 130; Luttrell, iv. 500.

J.P.F.

COURTENAY, Richard (c.1655–96), of Colyton, Devon and Fetcham, Surr.

HONITON   1689

b. c.1655, 4th s. of Sir William Courtenay*, and bro. of Francis Courtenay* and George Courtenay†. m. (1) aft. 26 Mar. 1676, (with £2,000) Jane, da. of Sir Thomas Southwell, 1st Bt., of Castle Mattress, co. Limerick [I], 1s.; (2) Catharine, da. of Sir William Waller II* of Strutton Ground, Westminster, 2da.[1]

Capt. of ft. (Dutch army) May 1688–9, 2 Marine Regt. 1690–d.

Gent. of privy chamber 1689–d.[2]

Commr. for assessment, Devon 1689–90.

On his marriage to the sister of Sir Robert Southwell* Courtenay was described as 'a regular, sober and very hopeful man' and endowed by his father with lands worth £1,000 p.a. He remarried after

her death in 1681, and probably accompanied his second wife's father into exile in Holland, where he was commissioned in the regiment of Philip Babington*. Returned unopposed for Honiton in 1689 on his father's interest, Courtenay leaves no certain trace on the records of the Convention, though he was presumably a Whig. He may have been too busy job-hunting to attend often. He fancied himself as collector under the Navigation Act or alternatively surveyor-general of customs, but he was not above applying for a grant of post-groats at a rent of £10 p.a. 'in consideration of his steadfastness to Protestantism'. The King was 'graciously disposed', but Courtenay ended his parliamentary career as he began, a captain of foot. He was drowned with his only son on active service in the Mediterranean in January 1696.[3]

[1] Vivian, Vis. Devon, 248; PCC 198 Bond. [2] Carlisle, Privy Chamber, 202. [3] HMC Egmont, ii. 40–41; Cal. Treas. Bks. ix. 106, 146; CSP Dom. 1689–90, p. 190; 1696, pp. 33, 79.

J.P.F.

COURTENAY, Sir William, 1st Bt. (1628–1702), of Powderham Castle, and Ford House, Newton Abbot, Devon.

ASHBURTON   1660
DEVON   1679 (Mar.), 1679 (Oct.), 1681

bap. 7 Sept. 1628, 1st s. of Francis Courtenay† of Powderham by 2nd w. Elizabeth, da. of Sir Edward Seymour, 2nd Bt.†, of Berry Pomeroy. m. c.1643, Margaret, da. of Sir William Waller I* of Osterley Park, Mdx. and h. to her gdfa. Sir Richard Reynell of Ford House, 9s. (2 d.v.p.) 8 da. suc. fa. 1638; cr. Bt. Feb. 1645; suc. cos Lady Howard in Fitzford estate 1671, cos. Sir William Courtenay, Bt. at Newcastle, co. Limerick [I] by 1674.[1]

Commr. for assessment, Devon 1657, Aug. 1660–80, 1689–90, militia Mar. 1660, j.p. Mar. 1660–80, July 1688–d., col. of militia horse Apr. 1660, dep. lt. 1661–70, 1676–80, ?1689–d., commr. for loyal and indigent officers 1662, sheriff 1664–5; commr. for inquiry into Newfoundland government 1667; freeman, Exeter 1674, Totnes by 1684, Plymouth 1696; commr. for recusants, Devon 1675; portreeve, Bere Alston 1680–1; commr. for inquiry into recusancy fines, Cornw. Devon, Exeter and Dorset Mar. 1688.[2]

'This ancient family', wrote a contemporary, 'of itself is enough to ennoble a county.' Courtenay's ancestor came to England with Eleanor of Aquitaine in 1152, and acquired the great barony of Okehampton. From 1335 to 1556 the head of the family enjoyed the title of Earl of Devon, while junior members represented the county regularly from 1377. Courtenay later claimed to have begun political life as a Cavalier 'which name I own to the last drop of blood . . . and there will I stick in spite of fate and all the enemies that I have upon earth'. He tried to hold aloof from political life in the Interregnum, though he gave shelter to the dean of Exeter at Powderham. When he was 'drawn in to be a grandjuryman', he told Henry Seymour I* in March 1658 that if he could be assured of the King's forgiveness and favour, he would hazard all in his service; he had already undertaken more than any three in his county. Courtenay kept his word, and on 13 Feb. 1660 with Sir John Northcote* and Simon Leach* was arrested for stirring up tumultuous demands in Exeter for a free Parliament. He was elected to the Convention for Ashburton, where he owned property. Lord Wharton, perhaps confusing him with his cousin, the recusant leader of the Hampshire Cavaliers, expected his election to be disallowed, but he took his seat, and on 12 July 1660 with Northcote was charged to desire George Monck* to withdraw the guard from the House. Otherwise he leaves no trace on the records of this Parliament, being principally engaged in suppressing disaffection in the west country with Sir Coplestone Bampfylde*. Courtenay was named to the projected order of the Royal Oak, with an estate valued at £3,000 p.a., but failed to secure re-election in 1661, though he put up his father-in-law at Honiton, and his characteristic large and shapely signature attests the returns for Devon and Totnes.[3]

In the following year Courtenay joined Bampfylde and Northcote in searching the guildhall at Exeter for arms in 1662. As sheriff, he secured the release of the deprived rector of Honiton, a Presbyterian and a kinsman by marriage whom he had himself presented during the Commonwealth, and established him in safety at Powderham. He refused the offer of a seat at Plympton in 1667. He formed the triumvirate (with Sir Edward Seymour* and (Sir) John Rolle*) to oppose the court candidate at the by-election for Devon in 1671, declaring that

> he would not have stirred in the business if the Earl of Bath had not appeared in opposition to Sir Coplestone Bampfylde, and if he should receive a baffle in this election, he would sell all his estate in Devonshire and leave the country.

Courtenay had the satisfaction of defeating Bath not only in the election, but also in the contest for the inheritance of Lady Howard (mother of George Howard*), consisting of the Fitz property in Devon and Cornwall and over £9,000 personal estate. Shortly afterwards he inherited 35,000 acres in Ireland from his cousin. With his name, his wealth, his loathing of 'new damned French tricks', and his friendship with the Hon. William Russell*, he now became the leader of the country party in Devon. 'The present Sir William', wrote Prince, 'hath

wanted nothing but his health to have rendered him as illustrious as most of his ancestors.' Much of his political activity took place behind the scenes, as Sir John Fowell* implies. As lord of the manor, he could nominate the returning officer at Honiton. Though he asserted that he always left people 'to their own dispose', he gave his interest to Thomas Reynell* at Ashburton and to Henry Northleigh* at Okehampton in the 1677 by-elections.[4]

Courtenay was duly returned for Devon to the Exclusion Parliaments. At the first election of 1679 he joined forces with the trimmer, Edward Seymour*, against the court supporter Bampfylde. A member of the Green Ribbon Club, he was marked 'honest' on Shaftesbury's list. He was inactive in the first Exclusion Parliament, serving only on two committees, those for the security bill and the export of leather, but he voted for exclusion, and was re-elected in September. During the summer of 1680, he tried to organize a petition at quarter sessions for the immediate sitting of Parliament, and acted as host to Monmouth at Exeter during his western progress. He was removed from local office, and Sir Leoline Jenkins* lamented (quite correctly, granted his premisses):

> An ancient, noble name will look odd in story, when its glorious ancestors shall appear to have placed their highest honours and merit in serving the crown, and a descendant standing alone with the blemish of having disserved it.

In the second Exclusion Parliament, Courtenay was moderately active, serving on the committee of elections and privileges and on the inquiries into abhorring and the conduct of Sir Robert Peyton*. With Sir Walter Yonge, 3rd Bt.*, he was preparing to present a petition to the King from Devon for the continuation of Parliament, when it was dissolved. He was returned unopposed to the Oxford Parliament, in which he was appointed to the committee for the exclusion bill and is said to have begun a speech on the subject, only to be shouted down before he had completed three sentences. He remained active in local politics, exercising 'commanding persuasion' on Richard Duke* to purchase the borough of Ashburton. Courtenay and Samuel Rolle* were the only Devonshire magnates who failed to sign the loyal address approving the dissolution in September 1681.[5]

According to Lord Grey of Warke, Courtenay promised Russell to support Monmouth by force of arms. He was implicated by Monmouth's confession in the Rye House Plot, and his old comrade Bampfylde was ordered to take his deposition. It is probable that he was already disabled by the stroke which paralysed one side of his body. Further evidence was provided by William Howard* who stated that he was to be engaged by Reynell, and it was not denied that he had received a visit from Walcot, allegedly on private business. Courtenay was summoned to attend the King in Sir Leoline Jenkins's office on 4 July 1683, but he seems to have been allowed to put his disclaimer in writing, and no further proceedings were taken.[6]

Courtenay did not oppose the Honiton charter of 1684, on the assurance that his rights would be reserved. But apparently this condition was not kept, and he lost the right to nominate the returning officer for the 1685 elections. He was ordered to be apprehended during Monmouth's rebellion, but in 1688 he was restored to local office. He was 'supposed to be right' on the repeal of the Test Act and Penal Laws, and was expected to stand for Devon in spite of his infirmity. He was conspicuously inactive when William of Orange landed. Even when the prince spent the night in Courtenay's house near Newton Abbot he 'gave no countenance to the enterprise, either in his own name or by his tenants'. However, it was reported on 20 Nov. that his two sons had joined the prince, and in April 1689 he was offered a peerage, 'as one of those who have contributed . . . to the settling of the nation'. This was one of William's genealogical blunders, for Courtenay considered himself the rightful Earl of Devon, and would not be satisfied with any title other than this one, which could hardly be granted to him without offence to the Earl of Devonshire (William Cavendish*, Lord Cavendish). Courtenay's loyalty to William III appears to have been doubted, but he signed the Association, unlike his eldest son, and was described as 'zealous for the government' in 1696. He died on 1 Aug. 1702 and was buried at Wolborough.[7]

[1] *Trans. Devon Assoc.* xxii. 106; *Devon N. and Q.* ii. 8. [2] *Parl. Intell.* 16 Apr. 1660; *HMC 14th Rep. IX*, 274; *APC Col.* i. 433; A. Jenkins, *Hist. Exeter*, 178; *HMC 9th Rep.* pt. 1, p. 282; *Trans. Devon. Assoc.* viii. 367; *Cal. Treas. Bks.* viii. 1804. [3] J. Prince, *Worthies of Devon*, 263; *Devon N. and Q.* iv. 40; W. G. Hoskins, *Devon*, 75; Eg. 3330, f. 39; *Cal. Cl. SP*, iv. 19; *CSP Dom.* 1659–60, p. 366; *Trans. Devon Assoc.* xcviii. 212; D. Underdown, *Royalist Conspiracy*, 30, 268; E. Cleaveland, *Noble Fam. of Courtenay*, 303. [4] A. G. Matthews, *Calamy Revised*, 452; SP29/188/22; *HMC Popham*, 193; R. Granville, *Hist. Granville Fam.* 362; *Trans. Devon Assoc.* xxii. 106; Eg. 3330, f. 39; Dalrymple, *Mems.* ii. bk. vi, 196; Prince, 263; *CSP Dom.* 1675–6, p. 512. [5] *CSP Dom.* 1679–80, pp. 567, 570; 1680–1, p. 199; 1697, p. 90; *Trans. Devon Assoc.* xlviii. 327; xciv. 453; xcviii. 214; *HMC 11th Rep. VII*, 13; *HMC 15th Rep. VII*, 106; *HMC Lords*, i. 177; Bodl. Carte mss 39, f. 198; Luttrell, i. 61; Grey, viii. 432; *HMC Portland*, iv. 122; *HMC Ormonde*, n.s. vi. 148. [6] Ford Grey, *Secret Hist.*; Clarke, *Jas. II*, i. 742; *CSP Dom.* Jan.–June 1683, p. 353; July–Sept. 1683, pp. 25, 70, 92, 145–6; *State Trials*, ix. 373, 380, 403. [7] *CSP Dom.* 1684–5, p. 159; 1685, p. 157; 1689–90, pp. 49, 122; 1697, pp. 90, 116; Dalrymple, *Mems.* ii. bk. vi, 195; *HMC Dartmouth*, i. 189; Bodl. Fleming newsletter 3334; *HMC 13th Rep. VI*, 39, 41; Luttrell, v. 202.

M.W.H./J.P.F.

COURTENAY *see also* **COURTNEY**

COURTHOPE, George (1616–85), of Whiligh, Ticehurst, Suss.[1]

SUSSEX   1656[2]
EAST GRINSTEAD   1659, 1660, 1661

b. 3 June 1616, 1st s. of Sir George Courthope of Whiligh by 1st w. Alice, da. of Sir George Rivers† of Chafford, Kent. *educ.* Westerham g.s. (Mr Walter) 1623–30; Merchant Taylors' 1630–2; Univ. Coll. Oxf. 1632–6, BA 1635; travelled abroad (Italy, Near East) 1636–9. *m.* 12 July 1643, Elizabeth, da. and h. of Edward Hawes, merchant, of London, 4s. (2 *d.v.p.*) 2da. *suc.* fa. 1642; kntd. 24 Apr. 1661.
    Commr. for alienations 1642–53, 1654–77; gent. pens. June 1660–*d.*[3]
    J.p. Suss. 1646–9, 1656–*d.*, dep. lt. Aug. 1660–*d.*, commr. for assessment Aug. 1660–80, sewers, Rother marshes Oct. 1660, Wittersham marshes Dec. 1660, loyal and indigent officers, Suss. 1662.

Courthope's ancestors were living on the Kent-Sussex borders by the end of the 13th century and acquired Whiligh by marriage in 1515. The family served on the alienations commission from the reign of Elizabeth until its abolition in 1833. Although Courthope's sympathies were royalist, he remained in London with the King's permission throughout the Civil War to save his office. In 1656 he became the only member of this branch of his family to be elected to Parliament. He was returned for East Grinstead at the general election of 1660, but he was not an active Member of the Convention. He was named to eight committees, including those to consider the legal forms of the Restoration and the militia bill. He made no recorded speeches, but doubtless voted with the Court, having sued out a pardon under the great seal. He was re-elected in 1661, but he was again inactive in the Cavalier Parliament, in which he was appointed to the committee for the corporations bill and to 39 others of less importance. He was marked as a court dependant in 1664, and obtained the King's permission to accompany his son to France in the following year only on condition of returning in time for the autumn session. But he defaulted in attendance in 1671, and was noted as absent in the list of officials in 1675. His name appeared on the working lists, and was marked 'vile' by Shaftesbury in 1677. Feeling the weight of his years, he was allowed to hand over his office to his son. He was unable to attend in 1678 for reasons of health, though he was included in the government list of court supporters. On 17 Dec. he was ordered to be sent for in custody. The serjeant-at-arms accepted a gratuity of £20 and promised to report to the House that he could not undertake the journey to London without danger to his life. Convinced that 'retiredness is more safe than business', Courthope did not stand again, and applied himself to studying 'the art of dying well'. He died on 18 Nov. 1685, and was buried at Ticehurst. The next member of the family to enter Parliament was Sir George Loyd Courthope, first returned for Rye in 1906 and ultimately Father of the House.[4]

[1] This biography is based on Courthope's memoirs (*Cam. Misc.* xi. 95–157). [2] Excluded. [3] *Cal. Treas. Bks.* v. 647; Beaufort mss. 600–2. [4] J. A. Wooldridge, *Danny Archives*, xiv; J. Comber, *Suss. Genealogies Lewes*, 85; *CJ*, ix. 197.

M.W.H./B.M.C.

COURTNEY (COURTENAY), Humphrey (1641–96), of Tremeer, Lanivet, Cornw.

MITCHELL 17 Dec. 1689, 12 Nov. 1690, 14 Dec. 1695–Mar. 1696

bap. 4 Aug. 1641, o.s. of Richard Courtney of Tremeer by Philippa, da. of Humphrey Prouze of Chagford, Devon. *educ.* Balliol, Oxf. 1659; I. Temple 1659, called 1677. *m.* 27 Dec. 1666, Alice, da. of Sir Peter Courtney* of Trethurfe, Cornw. and h. to her bro. William, 2s. 9da. *suc.* fa. 1660.[1]

Commr. for assessment, Cornw. 1665–80, 1689–90, recusants 1675; j.p. Cornw. to 1680, Devon and Cornw. July 1688, Oct. 1688–*d.*; freeman, Bodmin 1685–Sept. 1688; stannator of Blackmore 1686.[2]

Courtney came from a junior branch of the Trethurfe family. His father fought for the King in the West Country in the first Civil War, compounded in May 1646 on a fine of £457 at one-sixth, and left him an estate valued at £1,200 p.a., including property in Mitchell. Unlike his uncle Nicholas Courtney*, who arranged for his call to the bar, he does not seem to have been a practising lawyer, though he was described as 'a knowing justice' and 'of great estate' when he was removed in 1680 from the Cornish commission of the peace, after contesting West Looe as an exclusionist. His interest at Mitchell was strengthened when his wife inherited Trethurfe in 1683, and he again became a j.p. under James II. But he gave the same negative answers as Sir John Carew* on the repeal of the Test Act and Penal Laws in 1688, and was removed from local office. Nevertheless Lord Bath recommended him as court candidate for Lostwithiel, and suggested that he should be 'treated with' for his interest.[3]

Courtney stood unsuccessfully for Mitchell in 1689, and petitioned against the return of Charles, Viscount Fanshawe*. After Fanshawe's expulsion from the House, he did not prosecute his petition, preferring to fight a by-election. He was defeated by William Coryton* and again petitioned. On 12 Dec. the elections committee reported that Court-

ney had been duly elected and should have been returned, and after two divisions carried by ultra-Whig tellers the House agreed. An inactive Member of the Convention, he was appointed to two committees, one for the sale of the Duke of Buckingham's estates and the other to allow surgeons to administer medicine. He represented Mitchell, after protracted election contests, in the next two Parliaments as a Tory, though he signed the Association shortly before his death. He was buried in the Temple Church on 25 Mar. 1696, leaving his estates mortgaged up to the hilt. His son William was returned for Mitchell in December 1701, but eventually had to sell everything except Tremeer.[4]

[1] Vivian, *Vis. Cornw.* 115; Gilbert, *Paroch. Hist. Cornw.* iii. 19. [2] J. Wallis, *Bodmin Reg.* 169; PC2/72/235; J. Tregoning, *Laws of the Stannaries*, 57. [3] Gilbert, iii. 11; *Cal. Comm. Comp.* 1278; M. Coate, *Cornw. in Gt. Civil War*, 370; PCC 107 Nabbs; Add. 18448, f. 31. [4] 4 & 5 Anne, cap. 63.

E.C.

COURTNEY (COURTENAY), Nicholas (c.1630–1722), of the Inner Temple, and St. Breock, Cornw.

SALTASH 1679 (Mar.)
CAMELFORD 1685

b. c.1630, 4th s. of William Courtney (*d.*1642) of Tremeer, nr. Camelford by Jane, da. of James Bassett of Tehidy, Illorgan; bro. of Hugh Courtney†. *educ.* I. Temple 1660. *m.* 28 Apr. 1656, Jane, da. of Sir George Granville of Penheale, wid. of John Tregagle of Trevorder, St. Breock, *s.p.*[1]

Commr. for assessment, Cornw. 1664–80, 1689, Mdx. 1677–9, Westminster 1679–80; steward of Helston manor by 1669–?*d.*, East Greenwich 1714–?*d.*; j.p. Devon and Cornw. 1673–98; attorney-gen. duchy of Cornw. 1673–98; commr. for recusants, Cornw. 1675; bencher, I. Temple 1677, treas. 1694–5; recorder, Saltash 1677–83; freeman, Saltash 1683, Plymouth 1684, Bodmin and Liskeard 1685–Sept. 1688; asst. Camelford to Sept. 1688.[2]

Courtney, a lawyer 'of a true Cavalier suffering family once steady to the crown', was an uncle of Humphrey Courtney*. He signed the Cornish declaration for a free Parliament in December 1659. At the Restoration he secured the release of his radical brother, who had represented Wales in Barebones's Parliament. A kinsman of the Earl of Bath through his wife, Courtney successfully petitioned for the office of attorney-general of the duchy of Cornwall in 1673 with an annual fee of £20, raised to £50 in the following year. In 1675 he was granted £100 as the King's free gift and in 1677 he was chosen recorder of Saltash on the special recommendation of the King at the time of the renewal of the borough's charter.[3]

Courtney successfully contested Saltash at the

first general election of 1679. Classed as 'base' by Shaftesbury, he duly voted against the exclusion bill. An inactive Member of the first Exclusion Parliament, he was appointed to the committee of elections and privileges, and those to inspect the poor laws, and to inquire into the causes of the decay of the leather trade. He also acted as a teller in favour of a motion for adjournment during the hearing of the Leicester election case. He was defeated in September and no action was taken on his petition. In 1685 he was given the freedom of Liskeard and Bodmin under their new charters. Returned to James II's Parliament for Camelford as a Tory, he was moderately active, being appointed to two committees on private bills and that to estimate the yield of the proposed tax on new buildings. He was one of the Templars who were reported to have concurred with the King's religious policy 'under the lord chancellor's examination', and in 1688 he was recommended as court candidate for Camelford. But in September he was removed from office in all his boroughs, and he did not stand again. Under William III he was constrained to surrender his duchy office 'to prevent the same being taken from him', presumably as a non-juror. In 1702 he petitioned

> before he leaves the stage (being above three score and twelve years old) that his long and steady service to the Crown and Government may be honoured in such preferment as your lordship shall think fit.

In 1709 and 1710 he petitioned unsuccessfully for a reversionary lease of the duty of 4d. per cwt. upon all tin coined in the stannaries, but in 1714 his request for the stewardship of East Greenwich was granted. His anxiety to obtain an office was doubtless increased by his financial difficulties. As early as 1691 the scientist Robert Boyle remitted a debt of £150 and interest which Courtney could not pay. He died on 26 Oct. 1722 and was buried in the Temple Church.[4]

[1] Vivian, *Vis. Cornw.* 115; B. Spooner, *John Tregagle*, 18–19. [2] *Cal. Treas. Bks.* iii. 289; iv. 39, 68; xiii. 69; *CSP Dom.* 1677–8, pp. 182–3, 513; 1685, p. 66; J. Wallis, *Bodmin Reg.* 169; *Cal. Plymouth Mun. Recs.* ed. Worth, 8; PC2/72/735. [3] Vivian, 105–18; PCC 107 Nabbs; PC2/55/256; *Cal. Wills Cornw.* (Index Lib. lvi), 75; *Cal. Treas. Bks.* iv. 315, 321, 599, 765; *CSP Dom.* 1677–8, pp. 182–3, 578. [4] *Cal. I. Temple Recs.* 206, 215; 80, 86; *Cal. Treas. Bks.* xxiii. 440; xxiv. 30; xxvii. 407, 419; *Cal. Treas. Pprs.* 1708–14, p. 405; W. P. Courtney, *Parl. Rep. Cornw.* 151; PCC 3 Fane.

P.W.

COURTNEY (COURTENAY), Sir Peter (c.1616–70), of Trethurfe, Ladock, Cornw.

MITCHELL	24 Apr. 1640
TREGONY	22 Oct. 1660

b. c.1616, 2nd but 1st surv. s. of Edward Courtney of Trethurfe by Elizabeth, da. of Tristram Gorges of Butshead, St. Budeaux, Devon. *educ.* Exeter, Oxf. matric. 21 June 1633, aged 16; L. Inn 1636. *m.* (1) 27 Dec. 1638, Alice (*d.* 18 Nov. 1659), da. of Jonathan Rashleigh[†] of Menabilly, Cornw., 1s. 4da.; (2) Amy, da. of Peter Courtney of Penkivel, Cornw., *s.p. suc.* fa. by 1636; kntd. 28 June 1642.[1]

Commr. of array, Cornw. 1642; portreeve, Mitchell by Apr. 1660–at least 1661; j.p. Cornw. July 1660–*d.*, commr. for assessment Aug. 1660–9.

Lt.-col. of ft. (royalist) 1642, col. 1643–?46.[2]

Courtney was descended from a younger son of the Devonshire Courtenays who married a Cornish heiress in the late 15th century. The family regularly sat for Cornish boroughs from Tudor times. Courtney was knighted on the eve of the Civil War at York, to which he had travelled at great hazard to inform the King of the good affection of the Cornish people. He served under Sir Bevil Granville[†], and compounded in 1648 for a fine of £326. An active royalist conspirator during the Interregnum, he was a member of the western association in 1650 and in the following year he was described as 'one that is ready to serve upon any insurrection'. The Cornish committee suspected him of complicity in the Booth rising. He himself claimed that throughout this period he had lost some £7,000 by plunder and compositions and undergone 'seven or eight imprisonments'.[3]

After the Restoration Courtney was added to the Cornish commission of the peace, but his only other reward was a grant of the farm of the Cornish tin customs at a rent of £3,000 p.a., shortly afterwards rescinded on the discovery of an earlier grant to someone else. Returned to the Convention at a by-election for Tregony in October 1660 he was probably a court supporter, but he made no speeches and was appointed to no committees. In 1665 he petitioned for a pension from the tin farm, mentioning his services and losses for the royalist cause and complaining that he was a prisoner for debt in his own house. Nothing seems to have been done for him. His will was proved on 3 May 1670. His only son died without issue in 1683, leaving his estates to his cousin and brother-in-law, Humphrey Courtney*.[4]

[1] Vivian, *Vis. Cornw.* 117–18. [2] W. H. Black, *Docquets of Letters Patent*, 74. [3] *Cal. Comm. Comp.* 1234; D. Underdown, *Royalist Conspiracy*, 35; *CSP Dom.* 1665–6, p. 143; *HMC Portland*, ii. 588. [4] *CSP Dom.* 1665–6, p. 143.

M.W.H./P.W.

COVENTRY, Hon. Henry (c.1618–86), of Piccadilly Hall, The Haymarket, Westminster and West Bailey Lodge, Enfield, Mdx.[1]

DROITWICH 1661, 1679 (Mar.), 1679 (Oct.), 1681

b. c.1618, 4th s. of Sir Thomas Coventry[†], 1st Baron Coventry of Aylesborough, ld. keeper 1625–40, being 3rd s. by 2nd w. Elizabeth, da. of John Aldersey, merchant, of London, wid. of William Pitchford, Grocer, of London; half-bro. of Thomas Coventry[†], 2nd Baron Coventry and bro. of John Coventry[†] and William Coventry*. *educ*. Queen's, Oxf. matric. 20 Apr. 1632, aged 14, BA 1633, MA 1636, BCL 1638; I. Temple 1633; travelled abroad (Italy, France, Netherlands) 1640–Apr. 1660; Padua 1643. *unm*.[2]

Fellow of All Souls, Oxf. 1634–48, June 1660–?72; chancellor, Llandaff diocese ?1638–40; j.p. Worcs. June 1660–*d*.; freeman, Droitwich ?1661; asst. R. Fishing Co. 1664; commr. for encroachments, Windsor 1671, assessment, Mdx. 1673–80, Worcs. 1677–80; chief ranger, Enfield chase 1675–*d*.[3]

Capt. of ft. (Dutch army) by 1654–63.[4]

Groom of the bedchamber 1662–9, 1670–2; commr. for settlement [I] 1662–3; envoy extraordinary, Sweden 1664–6, 1671–2; plenip. congress of Breda 1667; sec. of state (north) 1672–4, (south) 1674–80; PC 3 July 1672–*d*.; commr. for prizes 1672–4, Tangier 1673–84; ld. of Admiralty 1673–9.[5]

Coventry was destined for the civil law, and his father's interest procured for him a Welsh ecclesiastical office at a very early age. But he was given leave to travel on his father's death and remained abroad throughout the Civil War and Interregnum. He obtained a commission in one of the Zeeland regiments, but from 1655 he was in touch with the exiled Court. He returned in April 1660, carrying letters from the King to Sir Anthony Ashley Cooper* and Sir John Holland*. Sir John Granville was asked to use his interest on Coventry's behalf in the Cornish boroughs, since he was not comprised in the Long Parliament ordinance against the candidature of Cavaliers and their sons; but he failed to find a seat in the Convention.[6]

Having qualified himself for the freedom of Droitwich by the purchase of a minimum share in the salt-works from his brother-in-law Sir John Pakington, 2nd Bt.*, Coventry was returned for the borough at the general election of 1661, probably without a contest. He already held the promise of a place at Court, and in the Cavalier Parliament he was clearly both active and popular from the first. In the Journals he was not always distinguished from his brother William, with whom he worked closely as long as the Clarendon administration lasted. Andrew Marvell* believed that 'Hector Harry steers by Will the wit'; his bluff military manner might have been more to the taste of a House dominated by ex-soldiers in its early sessions than was his brother's conscious intellectual superiority. Altogether he may have served on 279 committees, made 477 speeches, carried 55 bills or messages, and told in ten divisions. It was probably he who was appointed to the committee for the security bill and carried the thanks of the House

for the King's birthday sermon. Although he received no wages from his corporation, unlike his colleague Samuel Sandys II*, he was named to the committee for the bill to unite two Droitwich parishes. He was also among those to whom the most important political measures of the first session were committed, those for restoring the bishops to the House of Lords, the corporations and uniformity bills, and the bill of pains and penalties. On 15 July he was sent to remind the Lords of the corporations bill, and he helped to manage the subsequent conference. He was also probably a manager of conferences on the bill of pains and penalties and the Westminster highways bill. After the recess he was added to the committee for the execution of those under attainder, and on the House's instructions obtained from the King a promise of preferment for the chaplain. Together with Lord Falkland (Henry Carey*) he was sent to the King on 5 Apr. 1662 to ask that directions should be given for the redemption of English slaves in North Africa, a charitable activity to which his brother William was particularly devoted. He probably helped to manage five more conferences before the session ended, and was named to the committee for the additional corporations bill. He was among those sent on 19 May to ask the King to give himself the trouble to hear the rival claims to the Lindsey level.[7]

Coventry was made a commissioner for the Irish land settlement, in which capacity he was expected to hold the balance between the three who favoured the Roman Catholics and the three who favoured the Cromwellian settlers. The position was very little to his taste, and he was recalled to Westminster for the 1663 session and replaced by (Sir) Allen Brodrick*. On his arrival he wrote to Ormonde: 'We have not, I am afraid, hitherto used the arts necessary to the keeping our House here in temper. We are upon the necessary points of revenue and the militia, but proceed in neither with the vigour and zeal as [in] the last session. . . . The Declaration [of Indulgence] hath hitherto had a very bad effect in both Houses.' A stronger Anglican than his brother, he was among those instructed to bring in a bill for the maintenance of the urban clergy, to consider a measure for hindering the growth of Popery, and to provide remedies for meetings of dissenters. He was also named to the committees to bring in a bill to restrict public office to loyalists, and to consider an estate bill promoted on Pakington's behalf, and the bill, aimed chiefly at his brother, to regulate the sale of offices. He reported again to Ormonde at considerable length on 12 May:

I am for my own part as assiduous both at Court and in the House as I can be, and as inquisitive as my temper will give me leave; and yet I can neither tell you what the House intends nor what we at Whitehall wish they should. . . . We are daily upon the King's revenue, and pretend to great vigour in inspecting the mis-demeanours of the management. A vote this day passed to pray the King not to grant a patent of the Post Office till he had received an address from the House of Com-mons in the behalf of some that offer a greater rent. There is a bill coming in against the sale of offices, and another to incapacitate such as have borne arms against the King, some few excepted. This day a bill was brought in against the importation of any fat cattle from Ireland, and it is after a long debate committed. What fate it will have I know not. Bills against Popery, Qua-kers, presbyters, conventicles, and what not; and yet the revenue and the militia where they were; only this much, there is a vote passed in order to the method of the management that the committee shall bring in a bill to appropriate each considerable expense to a particular branch of the revenue, as the customs [to] the navy and garrisons.

Coventry delivered the message from the King denouncing Sir Richard Temple* as an 'under-taker', and he was the first Member named to the inquiry into Temple's conduct. Both the brothers were appointed to the committee for the relief of those who had been unable to subscribe to the dec-laration in the Act of Uniformity, but only Co-ventry took part in the conference. On the other hand his brother was chiefly responsible for the bill to settle the post office and wine licences on the Duke of York; but it was Coventry who acted as teller for agreeing to a Lords' amendment, and was sent to the Upper House to desire a conference. Both the brothers, together with Sir William Comp-ton*, attended the King to ask that horses might be freely exported to the plantations. After the pro-rogation he wrote apologetically to Ormonde: 'I believe the vote concerning Irish cattle hath not come to you with any great applause. It was not to be avoided; the complaint of the fall of rents from all gentlemen whose estates lie in pastures was so great, and so many even in the House concerned, that there was no stopping it.'[8]

During the recess Coventry visited the Low Countries in an effort to convince the authorities in Zeeland that a commission in their forces was not incompatible with the post at Whitehall. Listed as a court dependant in 1664, he spoke for the repeal of the Triennial Act. He was named to the committees for the conventicles bill and the additional corpora-tions bill, and helped to manage a conference on grievances against the Dutch. On 5 May he brought up to the Lords the bills to prevent the surrender of merchantmen to pirates and to facilitate the en-closure of Malvern chase, as well as a Glouc-estershire estate bill, and it was probably he who

acted as manager of a conference on the conventicles bill. He was absent for the next two sessions as envoy at Stockholm, in which capacity he registered considerable success at the cost of undermining his health by the heavy drinking indispensable to dip-lomacy in the northern capitals. In October 1666 he acted as teller for the adjournment in a supply debate, and was among those appointed to receive information on the insolence of Popish priests and Jesuits. In the following January he twice divided the House in favour of hearing the petition from the English merchants trading with France, and served on the deputation that presented a joint address on their behalf. After proposing a confer-ence on the impeachment of Lord Mordaunt on 6 Feb. 1667, he was added to the committee of man-agement.[9]

During the summer Coventry and Denzil Holles* were responsible for the negotiations at Breda that ended the second Dutch war. But the fall of Clarendon and the advent of the Cabal reduced his role as government spokesman in the Commons, besides separating him politically from his brother, though without damaging their per-sonal relationship. He spoke against the unprece-dented vote of thanks for the lord chancellor's dis-missal, though he helped both to draft the address and to summarize the charges against him. He urged the House not to 'trample' on the fallen minister, and spoke against the proposal to demand his commitment. He might have involved himself in serious trouble when he drew his sword on Edward Seymour* only just outside the precincts, but the House accepted an assurance that the quarrel was quite unconnected with Seymour's speeches against Clarendon. 'Scolded severely at by the King' for his defence of the fallen minister, Coventry replied 'that if he must not speak what he thought in this business in Parliament, he must not come thither. . . . By this very business', Samuel Pepys* was told, 'Harry Coventry hath got more fame and common esteem than any gentleman in England hath at this day.' After the Christmas recess he was sent with Sir Robert Howard* to receive the testimony of the dying Duchess of Albemarle for a private bill. He was one of four Members who thanked the King for his proclama-tion against conventicles, and in the debate on com-prehension 'Mr Henry Coventry said that a union was good and to be wished, but not such a union as would destroy the Church'. He spoke against ex-pelling (Sir) William Penn* from the House before anything had been proved against him. In the next session he similarly came to the defence of Sir George Carteret*. After denouncing attendance at conventicles as no less a crime than 'cozening the King's money', he was among those appointed to receive information about nonconformist insolence. A supporter of the Triple Alliance, he rebuked (Sir) Thomas Clifford*, who had served under him in Stockholm, for undiplomatic language in describing the Swedes as a mercenary people, and his proposal to give three days to the discussion of grievances for every day spent on supply temporarily lost him his post in the bedchamber. He acted as teller against an export levy on coal on 14 Mar. 1670; but the King's acceptance of the necessity for renewing the Conventicles Act removed one important difference between him and the Court. 'Never was there a more merciful bill,' he said, 'that punishes neither with blood nor banishment a people that have punished us with both.' He helped to prepare reasons for a conference with the Lords. In the following month he was teller for a private bill promoted by (Sir) John Heath* and for the sale of fee-farm rents. In December he urged the House to provide for repayment of a debt owed by the King to William of Orange, and he was not prepared to defer supply because of the assault on his nephew Sir John Coventry*, though they were personally on the best of terms, and he of course served on the bill to banish the culprits. In April 1671 he helped to manage a conference on and to prepare reasons for the additional excise, and his name appeared on both lists of the court party at this time.[10]

In August Coventry returned to Stockholm to persuade the Swedish government, by not entirely unmercenary methods, to join the alliance against the Dutch, and on the death of John Trevor* he succeeded as secretary of state. He lost £3,000 on the Stop of the Exchequer, which his brother vainly sought to extract from the Treasury. When Parliament met again in February 1673 it fell to Coventry to propose first Job Charlton* and then Edward Seymour* as Speaker, and during the remaining sessions of the Cavalier Parliament he carried no less than 37 messages from the King to the Commons. On the third Dutch war he said:

> It shows good prudence in the House of Commons to have refused to meddle with advising war; it is the King's just prerogative. . . . We have found the dangers of being against the King of France, therefore we joined him, and he has succeeded beyond expectation. If we had a war with France, it would give Holland much advantage both here and in the Indies, their sea monarchy. The Hollanders are more formidable to us than it was thought, if first we should not be sure of the French.

His speech was sufficiently convincing to be followed by an almost immediate grant of supply.

He dutifully defended the Declaration of Indulgence, arguing that 'either the King must have the liberty of dispensing, or else is always obliged to put the Penal Laws in execution'. Nevertheless he helped to draw up two addresses against the suspending power, and served on the committee to prevent the increase of Popery, though he did not approve of the test bill that it produced. He was even more doubtful about the bill of ease for Protestant dissenters: 'a man would give something to get something, but would not give something to get nothing. . . . If we are to increase our garrison, would not do it with those that have the plague.' Nevertheless he was appointed to the committee, and hoped that the bill might be amended in the Lords. In the autumn session he had the odious task of informing the House that the King would not interfere with the Modena marriage. He denied that the forces in being could be termed a standing army in time of war, nor could they be a grievance because they were not unlawful.[11]

With the elevation of Heneage Finch* to the House of Lords and in the absence of (Sir) Joseph Williamson* at the conference of Cologne, Coventry became virtually leader of the House in 1674, and his name headed the Paston list. The inexperienced Sir Francis North* was well content to leave the management of the court interest to him, recognizing that:

> no man was ever better qualified for that post, for he was an ancient Member, and had the nice step of the House, and withal was wonderfully witty and a man of great veracity. He had never said anything in the House which afterwards proved a lie, and had that credit there that whatever he affirmed the House believed.

He was named to the committees to prevent imprisonment and illegal exactions. In the debate on the new-raised forces he reminded the House of the London apprentices' riots before the Civil War. 'He can remember crowns and heads of princes lost for want of guards.' He helped to prepare for a conference with the Lords on peace with the Dutch and to inquire into imprisonment by order of the Privy Council. He spoke against the bill to give security of tenure to the judges during good behaviour, but he was the first Member appointed to the committee. He brought the debate on Samuel Pepys* to an end with the dry remark that he believed 'there are a great many more Catholics than think themselves so, if having a crucifix will make one'. Williamson was told that 'Mr Secretary Coventry is at present somewhat ill, and 'tis no wonder, considering the vast pains he takes in the House, being like the cherubim with the flaming sword, turning it every way to defend his master's cause'. In the spring session of 1675 he was among those to whom the bill to prevent the growth of Popery was committed. He opposed his brother's place bill, reminding the House:

> You are pleased to make use of the Privy Councillors to carry your messages to the King. Formerly they had cushions to sit on, but were thrown out of doors, and must they be thrown out of doors too? This bill is not consistent with the government, and he would lay it by.

The recall of all British subjects from French service, he observed, would subject them to the death penalty for desertion and stain the King's honour. Moreover, it was unnecessary:

> There is not one English pair of colours in Holland, and yet more men gone over into Holland by thrice the number than into France.... More of our men have come over to Holland from the French army than we have sent into France.

His relations with the Court were unaltered by the emergence of Danby as chief minister, though their relations were never cordial, and Coventry played no part in defending him against impeachment, observing only that 'sometimes a minister of state, in favour, carried things higher than other men have done in their place'. He was anxious to compose the dispute between the Houses over the jurisdiction of the Lords, though he helped to manage a conference about Shirley v. Fagg, and attended a conference on the Four Lawyers, after which he was among those ordered to prepare reasons. Before the autumn session Coventry and Williamson sent out a 'government whip' to reliable court supporters living out of London, which was heavily criticized as tending to faction. He replied with a story about a scholar from the other university who wore only one spur, believing that if his horse went on one side, the other would not be left behind. He was prepared to accept appropriation of the customs to the use of the navy, though not payment into the chamber of London, and was named to the committee for the bill. He was also among those instructed to bring in a bill of recall from French service. He had been, he claimed, as much for appeasing the differences with the Lords as any man, and was among those appointed to prepare reasons for a conference to prevent their revival.[12]

When Parliament met again in February 1677 it was Coventry's first task to defend the legality of the long prorogation, and Shaftesbury marked him 'doubly vile'. In the supply debate he challenged William Cavendish*, Lord Cavendish: 'If the King has any ministers that advise him to raise money without a Parliament, 'tis more than he knows. And there are none, and he is assured the King has no

such thoughts, and that he has more understanding than to rule so. If any man knows such ministers, let them be named.' He was named to the committees to consider the recall bill, illegal exactions, habeas corpus, and the growth of Popery. He helped to manage a conference on building warships and to draft addresses promising support against foreign enemies and urging the need for allies. Only further supply, he emphasized, would enable England to pursue an independent foreign policy: 'the King cannot have money without us, nor we alliances without him'. Even Marvell admitted: 'yet have we one Secretary honest and wise', and William Sacheverell* exempted him from a savage attack on the Privy Council.

> I did not mean to reflect upon that gentleman, for although he has the figure of a great officer, yet in my conscience he has not the management of anything, nor has he the least influence in business. It is our misfortune, sir, that it is so, for I am persuaded he is a good Protestant and a true Englishman.

Sacheverell's estimate was soon to be proved correct. Nevertheless at this juncture Coventry was more uneasy about the invasion of the prerogative in foreign affairs: 'There was never such a precedent as to tell the King terms of leagues, offensive and defensive.... He is not afraid of any counsel he has ever given the King; as a Privy Councillor he has taken his oath and as a Parliament man he has his opinion, and he is of opinion that the King is not obliged to follow either his Privy Council or Parliament.' When the debate on the speech from the throne of 28 Jan. 1678 about the threat to Flanders was interrupted by an opposition attempt to censure Seymour for irregularly adjourning the House, Coventry exclaimed: 'I vow to God, though I hate murder, yet I had rather be guilty of twenty murders than hinder our proceedings now'. He was named to the committee to draw up the reply, but he strongly disapproved of its terms, especially the stipulation that France must be reduced to her frontiers of 1659:

> 'Tis vain to make new treaties when we are put back to old ones. If the King has arms sufficient ... he will not weary of them till he has restored Christendom to such a peace.

The ignorance of protocol shown by such leading Members as Sir Thomas Littleton, 2nd Bt.*, justified Coventry in his reluctance to communicate diplomatic documents to 500 men. He described the efforts of the Commons to find sources for supply that would not affect their personal fortunes as 'leaping from twig to twig'. He was named to the committee of 14 Mar. that produced an address asking for an immediate declaration of war. When the exhaustion of the continental allies became apparent, he secured a supply for disbanding the new-raised forces, with the assistance of his brother and the more reasonable Members of the Opposition.[13]

Coventry was not favourably impressed with Oates at first, but eventually wrote: 'I am entirely convinced there was a most desperate design'. In the last session of the Cavalier Parliament he was appointed to the committees to inquire into the Popish Plot and to translate Coleman's letters. He succeeded in warding off an address demanding the removal of the Duke of York from Court by proposing a measure to fine magistrates who failed to enforce the recusancy laws. On 16 Nov. he was sent to remind the Lords of the bill to exclude Papists from both Houses of Parliament, and when the Upper House added a proviso to exempt the Duke of York he warned the Commons not to jeopardize the bill by rejecting it. When Williamson was sent to the Tower for signing commissions for Roman Catholic officers, Coventry was among those ordered to draw up an address asking the King not to release his colleague. His last known appearance in the Cavalier Parliament was on 9 Dec. and, 'having for some time been a prisoner in my chamber with gout', he may not have heard the reading of the letter from Danby to Ralph Montagu* warning him not to mention to Coventry a syllable about the money which the King had sought to obtain from France.[14]

Hence Coventry's reputation remained high after the dissolution, even if Shaftesbury marked him 'vile'. 'Standing fair with my old borough, and not affecting to change old masters', he was able to refuse the offer of a seat at Oxford University, and was re-elected unopposed to the three Exclusion Parliaments. In 1679 he was named to no committees, but brought six messages from the King, and made 24 speeches. His efforts to divert the attack on Danby were rather slight, but the effrontery displayed by Oates at the bar of the Commons revived all his initial distrust of a young man who had already changed his religion twice. 'The House expects not expostulations nor answers from him, but obedience', he said. He was retained on the remodelled Privy Council, though sceptical of the benefits to be derived by bringing in the Opposition leaders. 'To be well heard at Court and well-spoken of in Parliament is a great good fortune, if our new ministers can acquire it', he wrote to Ormonde. 'But though they have as yet done neither good nor evil, I find the bare being preferred maketh some of them suspected.' He spoke against the exclusion bill as 'the most ruinous to law and the property of the subject imaginable. . . . I never saw a lawful

successor of the crown disappointed, but, first or last, he came back to the crown again.' He argued unconvincingly that the King might still have legitimate children, or the duke revert to the religion of his baptism, and voted against the bill. Attacked by John Birch* as an instrument to deceive the previous Parliament into believing that a war with France was intended, he replied that if an angel from heaven were to charge him with lying, it must be a fallen angel. Unimpressed by the evidence offered against Pepys, he wished the case to be heard at the bar of the House, not in committee. Re-elected in the autumn, he was laid up for much of the winter with gout. He sold his office to Sir Leoline Jenkins* for £6,500, retiring to the sporting delights of Enfield chase, and to 'converse with neighbours that have no more cunning than myself'. A long indisposition probably prevented him from attending the second Exclusion Parliament. His constituents remained loyal, and sent him as a private gentleman to represent them again in the Oxford Parliament, where he delivered a last appeal for an expedient to resolve the exclusion issue:

> All men believe that the religion of the Duke is as fatal a thing as can be to the nation. . . . If it be our opinion that excluding the Duke, etc., be the best way, this House cannot do it alone; . . . we are but one of the legislative power. . . . A grand committee is most proper for this debate. . . . Find out a way to secure us from Popery and preserve the King's life, be it what it will. When men press on too fast, many times they tire their horses and come late into their inn. Let a committee try expedients.

His speech was heard out patiently, but produced no effect, and he took no further part in politics. He died on 7 Dec. 1686, and was buried at St. Martin in the Fields. He left most of his property for Droitwich charities, endowing the workhouse and founding schools for both sexes.[15]

[1] This biography is based on D. T. Witcombe, 'Parl. careers of Sir William and Mr Henry Coventry' (Oxf. Univ. B. Litt. thesis, 1954). [2] *Survey of London*, xxxi. 42; W. Robinson, *Hist. Enfield*, i. 228; *Vis. Cheshire* (Harl. Soc. lix), 5; PCC 19 Dorset; *CSP Dom.* 1640, p. 162; *Jesuit Recs.* ed. Foley, vi. 623; *Cal. Cl. SP*, iv. 612. [3] Wood, *Fasti*, i. 500; *Sel. Charters* (Selden Soc. xxviii), 183; *Cal. Treas. Bks.* iii. 923; Sir Robert Somerville, *Duchy of Lancaster Office Holders*, 209. [4] *Cal. Cl. SP*, ii. 316; *CSP Ire.* 1663–5, p. 8. [5] *Cal. Treas. Bks.* i. 387; *CSP Ire.* 1660–2, p. 577; 1663–5, p. 64; *CSP Dom.* 1670, pp. 1, 88; 1671, p. 376; *Bulstrode Pprs.* 242; *Williamson Letters* (Cam. Soc. n.s. viii), 149. [6] *Cal. Cl. SP*, iii. 12; iv. 47, 173, 600, 607, 612, 660; v. 16. [7] Worcs. RO, 261/4/698, f. 29; Clarendon, *Life*, ii. 349; *Marvell* ed. Margoliouth, i. 146; *CJ*, viii. 261, 311, 314, 315, 390, 401, 402, 418, 423, 425. [8] *Milward*, 274; *Cal. Cl. SP*, v. 282, 296; *CSP Ire.* 1663–5, pp. 48, 64; *CJ*, viii. 527, 532, 533; *HMC Ormonde*, n.s. iii. 47, 52–53, 58. [9] *Add.* 35865, f. 212; *Cal. Cl. SP*, v. 327; *CJ*, viii. 548, 562, 634, 678, 680, 685, 690; *LJ*, xi. 607–8; Clarendon, ii. 425; Burnet, i. 549; *Milward*, 79. [10] *Milward*, 95, 101, 105, 220, 279; *Pepys Diary*, 12 Oct., 16 Nov. 1667; *Clarendon Impeachment*, 45, 126; *CJ*, ix. 59, 61, 139, 152, 155, 233; Grey, i. 174, 186, 227; *CSP Dom.* 1670, pp. 1, 88; *Dering*, 28. [11] *Cal. Treas. Bks.* iii. 1009, 1012; *CJ*, ix. 245, 253, 263, 264; Burnet, i. 548–9; Grey, ii. 3, 10–11, 18, 39, 43, 104, 135; *Dering*, 136, 160. [12] North, *Lives*, i. 119; Grey, ii.

392–3, 415, 421; iii. 45, 71, 126, 149, 361, 370; iv. 35; *CJ*, ix. 308, 344, 361; *Williamson Letters* (Cam. Soc. ix), 131; *Dering Pprs.* 65. [13] Grey, iv. 82–84, 126, 194, 366, 377, 385; v. 9, 43, 62–63, 68, 199; vi. 28; *CJ*, ix. 418, 428; *Marvell*, i. 195; Eg. 3345, ff. 60v, 63. [14] *HMC Ormonde*, n.s. iv. 267, 290, 303; Grey, vi. 134, 291, 304; *CJ*, ix. 560; Finch diary, 4 Nov. 1678. [15] Burnet, ii. 187; *HMC Ormonde*, n.s. iv. 314, 325; v. 57, 393, 528; Grey, vii. 33, 41, 49, 143, 145–6, 242–3, 312; viii. 311–12; *Bramston Autobiog.* (Cam. Soc. xxxii), 251; Nash, *Worcs.* i. 328; *VCH Worcs.* iii. 88.

E.R.

COVENTRY, Sir John (c.1636–85), of Mere, Wilts. and Suffolk Street, Westminster.

WEYMOUTH AND   8 Feb. 1667, 1679 (Mar.),
MELCOMBE REGIS   1679 (Oct.), 1681

> b. c.1636, o.s. of Hon. John Coventry[†] of Barton, Pitminster, Som. by Elizabeth, da. and coh. of John Colles of Barton, wid. of Herbert Dodington[†] of Breamore, Hants. *educ.* travelled abroad (France, Italy, Hungary, Germany, Low Countries) 1655–9; Padua 1659; Queen's, Oxf. 1660. *unm. suc.* fa. 1652; KB 23 Apr. 1661.[1]
>
> Commr. for sewers, Som. Dec. 1660, assessment, Som. and Wilts. 1661–80; j.p. Wilts. 1667–70, Som. 1668–70; dep. lt. Wilts. 1668–75; bailiff of Burley Walk, New Forest 1674–*d.*; freeman, Lymington 1679.[2]

Coventry's father, a younger son of the lord keeper, sat for Evesham in the Long Parliament and fought for the King in the Civil War. He was one of the leaders of the western association in 1650 and took some part in helping Charles II to escape after Worcester, but died of drink a few months later. Coventry's aunt, Lady Savile, engaged as tutor an impoverished Cavalier, Edward Sherburne, eminently suitable in every respect but religion. When William Coventry* appealed against the decimation of his nephew's estate in 1656, the Somerset commissioners agreed that Sherburne's pupil was under age, but alleged that he 'lives beyond seas, and is suspected to be brought up in the Popish religion'. Their suspicions were well-founded, for in his will dated 7 Apr. 1667 he declared himself 'a true son of the Church of Rome, and so have been several years'. Nevertheless they were prepared to discharge the estate (valued at £3,000 p.a.) if he were 'taken into the tuition of some honest and well-affected person'. Coventry accordingly became the ward of his uncle Sir Anthony Ashley Cooper*, whose politics he followed, and in 1662 he was described as 'loyal and orthodox; a very hopeful man'. At the Weymouth by-election of 1667, the full weight of the court interest was put behind him. His former guardian, now chancellor of the Exchequer, wrote to the corporation in his support and Bullen Reymes* used his influence with the mayor (whose mother was his business partner) while Sir Roger

Cuttance, flag captain to the Earl of Sandwich (Edward Montagu I*), accused his opponents of provoking disorder. On the other side, the canvassers 'did not say Sir John Coventry will swear a thousand oaths in an hour, or rant, or be drunk, and that he is a courtier'; but the electorate were left to draw their own conclusions from these careful negatives. However, with the returning officer on his side, Coventry was safe, and on 8 Feb. he was allowed to take his seat on the merits of the return. On 20 Nov. the committee of elections reported him duly elected and the House accepted this recommendation.[3]

A moderately active Member of the Cavalier Parliament, Coventry was named to 87 committees, seldom failing to give his attention to such subjects as the export of beer, the import of brandy, and the adulteration of wines. His hereditary weakness did not render him incapable as teller in nine divisions (usually with a leading member of the country party as colleague), and he took part in five conferences with the Lords. A follower of Ormonde, he was teller for the motion to impeach his rival Lord Orrery (Roger Boyle*). On the other hand he was in favour of proceeding with the charges against Sir George Carteret*. Sir Thomas Osborne* included him among those to be gained for the Court by the Duke of York. Despite his conversion, he was one of six Members instructed on 8 Mar. 1670 to bring in a bill against recusants, and received an anonymous letter threatening to pistol him unless he desisted. In the same session he took part in a conference on the conventicles bill, to which his opposition was sufficiently marked to cause his exclusion from the commission of the peace. He was prominent, and perhaps obstructive, in the supply debates in the autumn. He served on the committee to consider the debts of the navy, and the day before the House adjourned for Christmas he moved for a tax on theatres. 'Sir John Berkenhead* to excuse them said they had been of great service to the King, upon which Sir John Coventry desired that gentleman to explain whether he meant the men or women players.' The implication that Charles's appreciation of Nell Gwyn and her colleagues extended beyond the purely aesthetic infuriated Coventry's 'dearly beloved friend' Monmouth, who was naturally concerned to prove that his father begat no children outside the nuptial bond. An ambush, consisting of gentlemen of Monmouth's troop in the guards, was set for Coventry as soon as Parliament adjourned, and when he returned from the tavern at two in the morning his assailants seized him and cut his nose to the bone. The damage was not permanent, and Coventry had the uncommon satisfaction of giving his name to the Act that was passed against nose-slitting.[4]

Henceforward, Coventry was a somewhat erratic member of the Opposition. Although not a few of his 29 recorded speeches contain sensible remarks, pithily expressed, he was a political lightweight, and his tongue would never earn him so much fame as his nose. On 3 Mar. 1671, and again two years later, he was one of the Members appointed to manage a conference with the Lords on the growth of Popery, a subject of which he had a great deal more personal knowledge than his colleagues could have suspected. In the 1673 session he raised the question of grievances, and proposed that no supply be granted till the bill against Popery was passed. He was also teller against the Court on two election petitions. At this juncture Charles found it expedient to be reconciled with him, perhaps as a friendly gesture from one crypto-Catholic to another, for in the recess rumours about Coventry's religion began to circulate, and there was talk of obliging him to take the Test.[5]

Coventry's response was to increase his activity and hostility in the 1674 session. 'The French league is so infamous that we cannot name it without odium', he proclaimed. He attacked Buckingham as one who 'has made it his business to sow dissension between the King and this House', and, though he was too contemptible to be worth impeaching, desired that he might 'be removed from the King's person for ever'. He was one of the five Members charged with procuring evidence against Arlington, and three days later he was teller for the address demanding the secretary of state's removal.[6]

Shortly before the spring session of 1675, Coventry's uncle Henry Coventry*—'most of the House know our relation, and that we live well together'—drafted a frank letter recommending him to marry to clear the debts he had accumulated, in spite of his ample fortune, and to choose as his bride

> a Protestant and of Protestant relations, for silencing your enemies and satisfying your friends in their jealousies, which have risen partly by your conversation and familiarity with those of a contrary religion, and partly from your difficulty in receiving the sacrament upon the last Act of Parliament.

Coventry's intemperate habits disqualified him from marriage, his debts from the more heroic step of proclaiming his change of faith, and he had to fall back on the difficult course of dissimulation. Presumably he took the oath against transubstantiation under the Test Act. On 23 Apr. he moved the address for the dismissal of Lauderdale,

pointing out 'that we are not so much looking into Scotland but our own safety.' He spoke in favour of Danby's impeachment, in spite of a well-grounded distrust of the process—'we have not had good success in them hitherto'—and undertook to prove malversation in the Exchequer. But his accusation that the lord treasurer had improperly interfered in Irish affairs misfired when William Harbord*, on whom Coventry had relied for proof, denied all knowledge of it. He was one of the Members charged with preparing an address for the recall of English subjects from French service, with the bill for appropriating the customs to the use of the navy, and—inevitably—with measures for suppressing Popery. The King showed his renewed displeasure by silently refusing to approve his nomination as deputy lieutenant of Wiltshire.[7]

In the autumn session of 1675, Coventry condemned the 'affront' given to William Cavendish*, Lord Cavendish, by Thomas Howard; not without reference to his own misadventure he added, 'some course must be taken, or we shall be hectored by every life-guardsman, and be obliged to fight him'. He seconded the motion for an inquiry into the bribery of Members and the despatch of letters to secure the attendance of the court party, and was named to the inquiry into the release of priests and Jesuits. In short, he played his full part in the unruliness of the session, which resulted in an exceptionally lengthy recess. When Parliament reassembled, he refused to join his former guardian, now Earl of Shaftesbury, in declaring it automatically dissolved by the length of the recess, but declared 'we have sat so long the people are weary of us', and seconded the motion for an address to the King requesting a dissolution. He did not fail to get his name on the usual committee for the suppression of Popery, but was otherwise not very active in the 1677 session. Shaftesbury marked his nephew as 'thrice worthy' at this time. In the earlier sessions of 1678 there is also little recorded of him, except an attempt to base a charge of breach of privilege on another unfortunate clash with the military, involving his servant and a Captain Arundell, which ended rather ignominiously with the Speaker administering a reproof to Coventry for casting a slur on a Member's family.[8]

But with the Popish Plot disclosures in the autumn, Coventry's activity reached a new climax, no doubt in self-defence. He was named to the committee of inquiry, and helped to manage the conference with the Lords on this 'damnable and hellish plot'. He was particularly concerned with Coleman's letters, declaring that 'whoever is against printing them, has either taken money for his vote, or is popishly affected'. On 6 Nov. 1678 he was among those Members who presented an address to the King to this effect. He was one of the committee of seven charged with searching the lodgings of a French Papist employed on the *London Gazette*, though his attack on Secretary Williamson in this connexion was so clumsy that he had to apologize instead to Williamson's colleague, his own uncle. On the next day, however, he went further still, in a speech worthy of the new Whigs:

> We talk of Popery, and the heir of the Crown protects Papists. I move for the business of the day, about removing the Duke from the King's presence and councils.[9]

Whatever the rumours about Coventry's religion, his reputation as a martyr was unaffected, and he was returned for Weymouth in all three Exclusion Parliaments. It is significant that Shaftesbury did not include his nephew among his 'worthy men', but he was marked as a supporter on Huntingdon's list, and voted for the first exclusion bill. He sat on eight committees in 1679, but made no speeches. On 4 Apr. he was ordered to bring in a clause to prevent any of the royal family from marrying Papists, and on 24 May to draw up an answer to the Upper House on the trials of Danby and the five Popish lords. For the second Exclusion Parliament, he was returned at the top of the poll. He was described rather absurdly by the French ambassador at this time as 'one of the most considerable Members, an enemy of the Court and even more of Monmouth'. On 25 Feb. 1680

> Sir John Coventry was so unfortunately drunk that at a great coffee house in the City he publicly spoke very rude and barbarous words reflecting on his Highness . . . that the Duke was a Papist and a traitor, and that he would prove him one.

The duke wisely decided to overlook the transgression. When Parliament met, Coventry again became very active over the Popish Plot. He was named to the committee to receive information and the committee of ten which examined Sheridan's papers, as well as to the committee of elections and privileges. He was defeated at Lymington in 1681, but retained his seat at Weymouth, though he left no trace in the records of the Oxford Parliament.[10]

A man with Coventry's weaknesses was not likely to be trusted with any Whig secrets in the years that followed. Nevertheless, he came under suspicion in 1683, and in September he was brought to make decent apologies to the King and Duke of York, and sufficient promises for the future. It seems probable that his health was now giving way under the influence of his excesses. At the time of Monmouth's landing in the west he was at Bath,

showing no disposition to join his former friend in rebellion, and on 14 Nov. 1685 he died, leaving his ailing uncle, Sir William, to tackle such awkward testamentary dispositions as a legacy of £100 to the English College at Rome and an injunction to 'bury me in the first Catholic church they can find'. It was suggested that Sir William's headaches were 'increased by disentangling the snarled accounts of Sir John's officers'.[11]

[1] *Gentry of Staffs.* (Staffs. Rec. Soc. ser. 4, ii), 8; *Procs. Som. Antiq. and Nat. Hist. Soc.* lxxvii. 110; *Cal. Cl. SP*, ii. 131; Hoare, *Wilts.* Mere, 25; Wood, *Fasti*, ii. 31. [2] C181/7/26; *CSP Dom.* 1675–6, p. 161; 1684–5, p. 127; *HMC 3rd Rep.* 94; *Q. Sess. Recs.* (Som. Rec. Soc. xxxiv), p. xi; *Cal. Treas. Bks.* iv. 477; E. King, *Old Times Revisited*, 191. [3] *Cal. Comm. Comp.* 1382, 1678; D. Underdown, *Royalist Conspiracy*, 30, 54; Christie, *Shaftesbury*, i. p. xx; Notts. RO, DDSR 221/96; *DKR*, xxxviii. 49; PCC 132 Cann; *Thurloe*, iii. 481; *Gentry of Staffs.*, 8; Burnet, i. 488; Hoare, *Repertorium Wiltonense*, 15; Hutchins, *Dorset*, ii. 436; *CJ*, viii. 692; ix. 23. [4] *CJ*, ix. 112, 120, 150, 186; Add. 36916, f. 203; Burnet, i. 488; *Dering*, 43–44; *Marvell* ed. Margoliouth, ii. 307; 22 & 23 Car. II, cap. 1. [5] *CJ*, ix. 260, 261, 263; *Dering*, 142; Grey, ii. 137; *Essex Pprs.* (Cam. Soc. ser. 2, xlvii), 131; *HMC 4th Rep.* 229. [6] Grey, ii. 247, 343, 382; *CJ*, ix. 295. [7] Grey, ii. 382; iii. 28, 44, 84, 91; vi. 160; Add. 32094, f. 251; *CSP Dom.* 1675–6, pp. 147, 161. [8] Grey, iii. 337, 368; iv. 72; v. 287–9. [9] *CJ*, ix. 530, 533, 537; Jones, *First Whigs*, 26; Grey, vi. 159–60, 165. [10] PRO 31/3, bdle. 146, ff. 26v–27; *HMC Ormonde*, n.s. v. 281, 285. [11] *CSP Dom.* July–Sept. 1683, p. 151; *Savile Letters* (Cam. Soc. lxxi), 275; *HMC 4th Rep.* 229; R. Morrice, *Entering Bk.* 1, p. 496; *HMC Downshire*, i. 37, 59; PCC 132 Cann; Spencer mss, Ld. Weymouth to Ld. Halifax, 26 Apr. 1686.

J.P.F.

COVENTRY, Hon. Thomas (c.1630–99), of Croome D'Abitot, Worcs. and Snitterfield, Warws.

DROITWICH	1660
CAMELFORD	16 May 1661
WARWICK	1681, 1685

b. c.1630, 2nd s. of Thomas Coventry†, 2nd Baron Coventry of Aylesborough (*d.*1661) by Mary, da. of Sir William Craven, Merchant Taylor, of Watling Street, London, ld. mayor 1610–11. *m.* (1) by 1661, Winifred (*d.* 11 June 1694), da. of Piers Edgcumbe* of Mount Edgcumbe, Maker, Cornw., at least 2s.; (2) 16 July 1695, his domestic servant, Elizabeth, da. of Richard Grimes, turner, of London, *s.p. suc.* nephew as 5th Baron 25 July 1687; *cr.* Earl of Coventry 26 Apr. 1697.[1]

J.p. Worcs. July 1660–Mar. 1688, 1689–*d.*, Warws. 1690–*d.*; commr. for assessment, Mdx. 1663–9, Warws. 1673–80, Warws. and Worcs. 1689–90, recusants, Cornw. 1675; high steward, Worcester 1687–*d.*, Evesham 1687–Feb. 1688, Oct. 1688–*d.*; custos rot. Worcs. 1689–*d.*[2]

Coventry's great-grandfather, a successful lawyer, acquired Croome D'Abitot in 1592, and his grandfather sat for Droitwich in 1621 before becoming lord keeper. His father supported the King at the outset of the Civil War, but had made his peace with Parliament by 1643. Information that Coventry and his elder brother had been under arms for Charles II at Worcester in 1651, though supported by the republican projector Andrew Yarranton, was adroitly stifled by Richard Dowdeswell I*. Hence he was eligible under the Long Parliament ordinance at the general election of 1660, though his royalist sympathies cannot have been in doubt. He was returned for Droitwich as a court supporter, but left no trace on the records of the Convention.[3]

Coventry made way for his uncle Henry in the family borough in 1661, but stood for Camelford, probably on his father-in-law's interest. He was involved in a double return with Bernard Granville* but seated on the merits of the return. Though there is some possibility of confusion with his uncles' records in the Cavalier Parliament he was appointed by full name to only 20 committees, including the committee of elections and privileges in four sessions, and it is clear that he was not an active Member. In the first session he was named to the committees for the bill to restore bishops to the House of Lords, the uniformity bill, and the bill for a canal to connect Droitwich to the Severn, and in 1663 to those for the staple bill and the Duke of York's revenue. His last legislative committee was on a private bill in 1668, and in the same year he bought Snitterfield, five miles from Warwick, for £14,500. Sir Thomas Osborne* listed him among the Members to be engaged for the Court by the Duke of York, but he defaulted on a call of the House in 1671. Sir Richard Wiseman* was confident that 'he will vote well if he be only managed' by his brother-in-law (Sir) Richard Edgcumbe* and his uncle Henry, who sent him the government whip in 1675; but by 1677 he had gone over to the Opposition, his former brother-in-law Lord Shaftesbury (Sir Anthony Ashley Cooper*) classing him as 'worthy'.[4]

Coventry is not known to have stood in 1679, but he probably came to oppose exclusion, for in 1681 he was returned for Warwick with the support of Lord Brooke (Fulke Greville*). He left no trace on the records of the Oxford Parliament, but he was re-elected in 1685, presumably as a Tory, though he was sufficiently moderate to lend some support to Sir Richard Newdigate* in the county election. An inactive Member of James II's Parliament, he was appointed only to the elections committee and the committee to recommend expunctions from the Journals, and on 4 June he was granted two months' leave of absence on account of ill health. In the second session he spoke in favour of supply, but would reward the Roman Catholic officers 'some other way'. After the Revolution he was reckoned among the opposition peers; but he signed the

Association in 1696 and was created Earl of Coventry, with special remainders to three distant cousins. He died on 15 July 1699 in his seventieth year, and was buried at Croome D'Abitot. The next member of the family to sit was his cousin William, who was returned for Bridport as a Whig in 1708.[5]

[1] *Her. and Gen.* vii. 97–98; *Vis. Warws.* (Harl. Soc. lxii), 13–14. [2] *Townshend's Diary* (Worcs. Rec. Soc.), iii. 276; *Warws. Recs.* viii. p. xli; Worcs. RO, Evesham corp. order bk.; *CSP Dom.* 1689–90, p. 140. [3] *VCH Worcs.* iii. 314; *Townshend's Diary*, ii. 65, 70, 76, 133; *Cal. Comm. Adv. Money*, 1363, 1369. [4] *CJ*, viii. 250; ix. 205; Dugdale, *Warws.* 662. [5] *CSP Dom.* 1685, pp. 62, 72; Grey, viii. 357 (ascribed to Thomas Coningsby); Lowther diary, f. 17; Nash, *Worcs.* i. 261.

M.W.H./E.R.

COVENTRY, Hon. William (1627–86), of Whitehall and Bampton, Oxon.[1]

GREAT YARMOUTH 1661, 1679 (Mar.)

bap. 4 Oct. 1627, 5th s. of Sir Thomas Coventry†, 1st Baron Coventry of Aylesborough, being 4th s. by 2nd w.; bro. of Henry Coventry* and John Coventry† and half-bro. of Thomas Coventry†, 2nd Baron Coventry. *educ.* Queen's, Oxf. 1642; travelled abroad (France) by 1649–52. *unm.* Kntd. 26 June 1665.[2]

Capt. of ft. (royalist) c.1645.[3]

Sec. to the Duke of York May 1660–7; commr. for trade Nov. 1660–9, plantations Dec. 1660–9, navy 1662–7, Tangier 1662–9; PC 26 June 1665–5 Mar. 1669; ld. of Treasury 1667–9.[4]

Freeman, Yarmouth 1660, Portsmouth 1661, 1666; agent, R. Adventurers into Africa Dec. 1660–3; j.p. Essex, Kent, Mdx. and Suss. 1662–7, Oxon, by 1669–bef. 1680; asst. R. Fishing Co. 1664; commr. for assessment, Oxon. 1673–80, Norf. 1677–80, Glos. 1679–80.[5]

The youngest of a large family, Coventry returned from his travels to fight for the King, and at the age of 18 commanded a company of foot. He was not required to compound, but joined the royalist exiles in Paris, and gained a great reputation as a collector of intelligence. In 1652 Sir Edward Nicholas† wrote: 'Mr William Coventry is doubtless of the Presbyterian faction, and so may upon good hopes of advancement be anything else', while Sir Edward Hyde† concluded that he had 'good parts, but is void of religion'. Despite his family background, he was a professed enemy of the lawyers, and spoke as disparagingly of the great seal 'as if it had been a common scroll of no significance'. He returned to England in the same year ostensibly on a royalist mission, but soon made his peace with the regime, probably through his brother-in-law, Sir Anthony Ashley Cooper*, and took little part in conspiracy, though after Penruddock's rising he was arrested at Rufford, the home of his nephew, Sir George Savile*.[6]

Recommended by Sir Philip Warwick as 'honest and useful', Coventry crossed over to The Hague on the eve of the Restoration and offered himself as secretary to the Duke of York, who had been appointed lord high admiral. His political career was to bring him into the keenest conflict with Hyde, who wrote of him:

> He was a sullen, ill-natured, proud man, whose ambition had no limits, nor could be contained within any. His parts were very good, if he had not thought them better than other men's; and he had diligence and industry, which men of good parts are too often without. . . . He was without those vices which were too much in request, and which make men most unfit for business, and the trust that cannot be separated from it.

He led the royal entry into London on 29 May 1660, and at the general election of 1661 he was returned for Yarmouth, where the Admiralty interest was important as an employer of labour and a source of government contracts. A very active Member of the Cavalier Parliament, he was named to at least 398 committees, in 12 of which he took the chair, made 353 recorded speeches, carried 14 bills and messages, and acted as teller in nine divisions. In the opening session he was appointed to the committees for restoring bishops to the House of Lords, for the uniformity bill, and for the bill of pains and penalties. He took the chair for the first time on 24 July to consider a proviso to the naval regulations bill, which he carried to the Lords. After the recess he attended conferences on traitorous designs and the execution of the attainted republicans. Bullen Reymes* noted that he spoke very well in favour of cancelling the conveyances extorted from Lady Powell during the Commonwealth, though it was his brother Henry who was teller against adjourning the debate. For some years to come they worked very closely together, with the younger brother taking the lead, and it is not always possible to distinguish them in the Journals. It was Coventry who was on the first delegation to the King for recovering money collected for the redemption of English slaves in Africa, a lifelong interest of his, and his brother who served on the second. Formal recognition of his position in the Admiralty was accorded by his appointment as extra commissioner of the navy in 1662. The House gave him leave on 18 Apr. to bring in a bill for requisitioning transport for naval and military stores, which in due course he reported and carried to the Lords. He was also named to the committee for the additional corporations bill.[7]

Coventry was persuaded by William Pierrepont* that it was necessary to enlarge the use of martial law in the fleet. He reported a bill to this purpose on 17 Mar. 1663, which in the opinion of his friend and admirer Samuel Pepys* gave the Admiralty tyrannical power over under-officers. He was named to the committee for the bill to restrain abuses in the sale of offices, though it was primarily aimed at himself; by his own calculations his position was worth something like £25,000 in the first three and a half years. The attack was nominally led by the 'undertaker', Sir Richard Temple*, but it was clearly inspired by some of the lord chancellor's friends, for example Sir George Carteret*, who were alarmed at Coventry's growing ascendancy in Parliament and his alleged intimacy with Sir Henry Bennet*. Clarendon himself wrote of Coventry after his own downfall:

> He had sat a Member in the House of Commons from the beginning of the Parliament, with very much the reputation of an able man. He spoke pertinently, and was always very acceptable and well heard; and was one of those with whom they who were trusted by the King in conducting his affairs in the Lower House consulted very frequently; but not so much, nor relied equally upon his advice, as upon some few others who had much more experience, which he thought was of use only to ignorant and dull men, and that men of sagacity could see and determine at a little light, and ought rather to persuade and engage men to do that which they judged fit than consider what themselves were inclined to do: and so did not think himself to be enough valued and relied upon and only to be made use of to the celebrating the designs and contrivances of other men, without being signal in the managery, which he aspired to be.

With his less tolerant brother, he was named to the committee for the relief of those who had inadvertently failed to subscribe to the declaration in the Act of Uniformity, and promoted the bill to vest in his employer the revenue from wine licences and the Post Office. He probably acted as teller against a proviso on behalf of the haberdashers and vintners' apprentices, and was sent to the Lords on 23 July to desire a conference. Two days later he attended the King with recommendations from the House for the free transport of horses to the plantations and the preservation of the Forest of Dean.[8]

Coventry was listed among the court dependants in 1664, and appointed to the committees for the conventicles bill and the additional corporations bill. He took the chair for the bill to prevent the handing over of merchantmen to pirates. He was sent to the Lords on 16 May to desire a conference on the conventicles bill, which he helped to manage. In 1665 he twice acted as teller with his colleague Sir William Doyley* in the interests of his constituency to oppose the incorporation of its suburb of Little Yarmouth, and the grateful corporation rewarded him with £25. On 9 Feb. he helped to manage a conference on the supply bill, and four days later he was sent with Sir Maurice Berkeley*,

Edmund Progers* and John Frescheville* to thank the King for his constant favours to the Commons. He accompanied the Duke of York on board the fleet during the summer campaign, and after the battle of Lowestoft he was knighted and sworn of the Privy Council, despite Clarendon's objections to his lack of status. In the Oxford session he helped to prepare the bill attainting English fugitives in the service of the enemy and to present an address for an inquiry into the management of the Chatham chest for disabled seamen and their dependants. He also served on the deputation to present the joint address for the prohibition of French imports, and was nominated to the abortive parliamentary accounts commission. Andrew Marvell* regarded him at this time as the virtual leader of the court party in the House. On the death of the Earl of Southampton he was appointed to the treasury board, and supported the proposal of Sir George Downing* to strengthen government credit by repaying loans in course. During the brief session of July 1667, he was the only speaker to oppose the motion of (Sir) Thomas Tomkyns* for the immediate disbandment of the new-raised forces on the grounds that the peace (which his brother was engaged in negotiating) was not certainly known.[9]

Before the next session Coventry resigned from the Duke of York's service 'that he might be the more free to prosecute the Earl of Clarendon', and took up residence in a new house in Pall Mall which he bought from (Sir) Thomas Clarges* for £1,400. When Parliament met he defended the lord chancellor's dismissal:

> When the Kingdom was in such consternation I made it my request to the King that if I were anyway obnoxious to him or the nation he would remove me; and so thought I did no man injury to let them be exposed to that which I offered myself, thinking none fitting for his service that was not liking to him and his people, and those most proper that the nation most liked.

Coventry's successive posts in the Admiralty and the Treasury left him wide open to attack for the mismanagement of the war. Indeed he was sometimes credited with advising it, though such a suggestion cannot survive a scrutiny of his own papers. He was among those ordered to bring in a public accounts bill, to report on freedom of speech in Parliament, and to summarize the charges against Clarendon. But, by what he later admitted to be an 'unfortunate mistake', he tried to divert the accusation of faulty intelligence in the 1666 campaign, for which he and Bennet (now Lord Arlington) were chiefly responsible, by reading 'a letter from the Duke of Albemarle [George Monck*] touching the good condition of all things at Chatham just before

the Dutch came up and did that fatal mischief'. Albemarle's dogged courage in the Four Days' battle, though hard to justify in terms of the losses sustained, had raised him above criticism, and his friends in the House now joined with the Clarendonians against Coventry. He was sent with Lord Ancram (Charles Kerr*), Sir Robert Brooke* and Sir Philip Musgrave* to ask the Duke of York what orders had been given for the fortification of Sheerness; but he was by now so alarmed about his own position that he absented himself from the debates on Clarendon, much to the King's displeasure. To his friend and admirer Samuel Pepys* he said: 'I have done my do in helping to get him out of the administration of things for which he is not fit; but for his life or estate, I will have nothing to say to it'. According to Marvell, who failed to perceive the delicacy of Coventry's position both at Court and in the House in this session, he 'miscarried far against his expectation in the bill he offered for the repair of Yarmouth pier'. But after the Christmas recess he 'gave good satisfaction to the House' over the failure to recall Rupert in time to assist Albemarle at the start of the Four Days' battle, and an attempt by Sir Richard Temple* and Sir Frescheville Holles* to reopen the inquiry into the sale of offices in the navy came to nothing. Coventry had prudently surrendered his claim to gratuities in return for a pension of £500 p.a., and this arrangement continued under his successor, Matthew Wren*. He was named to the committees to prevent the refusal of habeas corpus and to appropriate the wine-tax to the navy.[10]

The King disliked Coventry as a 'visionaire' and a melancholy man, and was only awaiting an excuse to dismiss him. This was afforded by the Duke of Buckingham, who caricatured Coventry as 'Sir Cautious Trouble-all' in his play The Country Gentleman; Coventry sent a challenge to his fellow Privy Councillor, and was removed from all his offices. Despite frequent reports to the contrary, he was never employed again. Nevertheless Sir Thomas Osborne* still for a time included him among those who might be engaged for the Court by the Duke of York. As a private Member he took the chair for two naturalization bills, and was named to several committees in 1669–71 concerned with conventicles, the growth of Popery, and illegal imprisonment. Although his standing in the House must have been second to none, he was twice defeated in divisions on the revived Yarmouth pier bill; but on 4 Apr. 1670 he reported reasons for disagreeing with a Lords proviso on behalf of Norwich, and was sent to request a conference. His warning to the Commons against usurping the judicial powers of the Lords persuaded them to drop their attempt to punish the dissenter Jekyll. He was at one with his brother in urging the House to enable the King to repay William of Orange, and not to make the assault on his nephew Sir John Coventry* an excuse for deferring supply, though he himself drafted the bill to punish the culprits. When the Lords sought to reduce the sugar duties Coventry helped to manage one conference and to prepare reasons for another. During the recess that followed he sold his town house to Nell Gwyn and went to live in Oxfordshire as a country gentleman.[11]

Coventry remained on the best of terms with his brother, despite the divergence in their politics, and in January 1673 his nephew Thomas Thynne II* wrote to assure him that the Court wished for his attendance in the next session. Nevertheless he proposed the motion of 10 Feb. 'that the laws for uniformity of the Church of England cannot be suspended but by Act of Parliament', and helped to draw up both addresses to this effect. On 21 Feb. he introduced a bill to enable young people to be apprenticed to gentlemen as cooks and gardeners. He steered the bill through committee, and it was ordered to be engrossed ten days later, but never reached the statute book. As one of the committee that brought in a bill of ease for dissenters, he opposed an amendment disqualifying them from sitting in the Commons, asking whether it was intended to imitate the Rump 'by narrowing their party and garbling the Parliament with oaths and tests'. Nevertheless, he helped to manage a conference on the growth of Popery and served on the committee that produced the test bill, which he supported in debate. Fearing an outright attack on the ministry, he left Westminster before the end of the session, and found himself, to use his own expression, 'out with all sides'. Nevertheless Sir William Temple* seems to have regarded him as the leader of the most radical opposition group in the Commons in the autumn session, including William Garway*, Robert Thomas*, William Sacheverell*, the Hon. William Russell*, and William Cavendish*, Lord Cavendish. This party, he wrote,

> would run up to the height and fall upon the ministers, especially Buckingham, Arlington and Lauderdale, and their carriage, particularly in the business of the war, so as absolutely to break all the present set both of men and business at Court and bring some of themselves in their room.

He thought Coventry would be 'very busy this session, but his carriage in the last and extreme ambition, so generally believed, has lost him a good deal of credit in the House of Commons'. When Parliament met, he spoke against the Modena marriage and helped to draw up the address. He was among those directed 'to show how this standing army is a grievance', and his speech on supply obliged the Court to accept a conditional offer as the best they could hope to get. When a bill was proposed in the next session to withhold the franchise from Papists and nonconformists, Coventry objected that Convocation would become the arbiters of election, since they alone could decide what conformity entailed. He supported addresses for the removal of the surviving ministers of the Cabal from the King's counsels in 1674, but would go no further, opposing proposals to expel Lauderdale from the country, to cancel Buckingham's patent as master of the horse, and to impeach Arlington. 'It was never a good time when the subject has been for breaking and infringing pardons.' He was given special responsibility for devising a general test. On the war with Holland he perceived that 'it is our interest to have peace before our neighbours, if we can'; but he pointed out that 'we are wholly in the dark as to the affairs of Christendom, since few of us have the means of knowing how intelligence and reasons of state are abroad'. He helped to draw up the address for peace, took the chair in the committee to prepare reasons, and reported a conference with the Lords. He defended Pepys against charges of Popery, and as chairman of the small committee of inquiry insisted that the accused should be present when they interrogated Shaftesbury, from whom the reports had been found to emanate. The humiliated intriguer gave out that Coventry was aiming at recall to office, and he was indeed received at Court in August for the first time since his dismissal, when he found the Duke of York considerably more cordial than the King.[12]

When Burnet first became acquainted with English politics in 1675 he recognized that

> Sir William Coventry had the greatest credit of any man in the House. He never meddled personally with any minister; he had a perfect understanding of affairs. So he laid open the affairs of government with the more authority, because he mixed no passion or private resentments with it. His brother, the secretary [of state], usually answered him with much life in a repartee, but not with the weight and force with which he spoke.

In the spring session he spoke in favour of impeaching Lauderdale, and helped to draft the address for his removal. He was reluctant to admit claims of privilege by spendthrifts like Sir John Pretyman*; 'this may tend to sending hither the most unfit men in England'. He had long outgrown his youthful cynicism and become a very religious man, believing that 'our Church has preserved more decency of ceremonies than any church whatso-ever'. He disliked the proposal for a register of Papists, but was named to the committee to draw up a bill. On 22 Apr. he brought in a place bill that anticipated the Act of 1707 in requiring Members to seek re-election when appointed to offices of profit under the crown. He was reported as arguing that such a measure was essential because

> at the beginning of this Parliament there were but about forty pensioners to the Court by offices, places, etc., and that now there were about 200, and he feared that, except this or a like bill did pass, or this Parliament [were] dissolved and the Triennial [Act] revived, we should shortly be at the French lock, that an edict from the King would pass here for an Act of Parliament.

The second reading was carried in a thin House, with Marvell and Sir Nicholas Carew* acting as tellers, but the bill was rejected a week later by 145 votes to 113. While admitting that the patent granted to Richard Kent* as cashier of excise provided no grounds for impeaching the lord treasurer, Coventry complained that:

> The end of this patent is that trick of making new credit for the King. . . . The anticipation of the King's revenue, and the facility of it, [is] an inducement to spend more than the revenue, and to entrap men by such securities is the ruin of themselves, wives, and children.

He was among those ordered on 14 May to draw up a further address for the recall of British subjects from the French service, and five days later to consider an appropriation bill. He described himself as 'of the coolest side' in the dispute between the Houses over the Lords' jurisdiction, though he helped to manage or to prepare reasons for the principal conferences. In the autumn session he was named to the committee on the bill for preventing Papists from sitting in either House of Parliament. The debate on the naval programme was almost monopolized by 'the two professors', Pepys and Coventry, the House eventually accepting the latter's recommendation of a total grant of £300,000. Costs, he considered, could be reduced by encouraging a native sailcloth industry, and he was given leave, with John Birch*, to bring in a bill for this purpose. He complained of the arbitrary conduct as Speaker of Edward Seymour*, who retaliated (in his capacity as treasurer of the navy) by alleging that the 'vermin' to whom Coventry had 'sold' office had not yet been weeded out, and were costing the taxpayer dear. He took the chair in the committee to draw up reasons for avoiding a revival of the dispute with the Upper House, and was sent to desire a conference.[13]

When Parliament met in 1677 Coventry was eager to debate the constitutional issue whether the long recess entailed an automatic dissolution, and Shaftesbury originally marked him 'worthy'. He opposed the doubling of the estimates to provide for an expansion of the naval programme from 20 to 30 ships, pointing out that his constituents were likely to be better informed over such matters than Seymour's. He was named to the committees for the recall bill, the prevention of illegal exactions, and habeas corpus. It was probably his efforts to convince the House of the overwhelming gravity of the international situation that prompted Shaftesbury to alter his rating to 'vile'. He opened the debate on grievances on 6 Mar. with the chilling injunction:

> Consider the posture we are in with respect to France, the greatest grievance that can be to the nation. In respect of France and Popery, all other things are but trifles. Popery may be here without France, but 'tis impossible that France should be here without Popery. Four or five years since we had the notion of France's greatness, but we see the thing not better. . . . He alone [Louis XIV] can contend with all Europe. . . . The end and purpose of France's conquests is not for trade. The whole bent of France (a stirring people) is to consider what next thing he'll undertake if he get rest again. Having almost swallowed Flanders, will he not begin again? . . . If once France gets peace, nothing is so feasible and practicable as [an attack on] England.

He was the first Member named to the committee to draft an address for an alliance against France. On 11 Apr. he carried up the Yarmouth pier bill, and was among those appointed to manage a conference on the naval programme. He helped to draw up the address promising an immediate credit of £200,000, and reported another asking for a short adjournment, so that further supply could be debated in a full House.[14]

Coventry was still a hawk during the earlier sessions of 1678. On 29 Jan., in one of his longest and most effective speeches, he was reported as showing

> the great inconvenience of raising a land army, the danger that might follow on it, the little use that could be made of it, the great charge it must put the nation to. He was for hiring bodies from the German princes, and for assisting the Dutch with money; and he moved to recall our troops from France, and to employ them in the Dutch service. He thought that which did more properly belong to England, was to set out a great fleet, and to cut off the French trade everywhere.

He was the first Member named to the committee to draw up an address for reducing France to her 1659 frontiers, and on 30 Apr. he was among those ordered to summarize the alliances communicated to the House by (Sir) Joseph Williamson*. Almost alone in the Commons, he remained undaunted by the increasing war-weariness among the confederate powers:

Does any man know why the States of Holland draw out of the war? Not that they like the peace, but from their inability to support so vast a charge with so little help; and perhaps they are jealous of the Prince of Orange's power amongst them. . . . If that jealousy of Holland be of the Prince, some means must be thought of to remove that jealousy. If indeed the States cannot carry on the war on account of their poverty and inability, I am sorry we must stretch our purses; but rather than leave them out we must do it. . . . I am of opinion that the French King has a weak side, and, if the war be held on a while, that weak side would be seen. He has, we see, quitted Sicily; and there's some defect surely, and he hastens his project of peace at Nymwegen. . . . As soon as the confederacy is dissolved, France has you at his mercy. Let no man think the confederacy can be raised again when once dissolved. It would be the most joyful thing to all the princes of the Continent for the King of France to employ his arms upon an attempt against England; they then may breathe awhile. The danger is so near us, and so irresistible, because we have so few friends. I could wish we had clearer lights in this matter; but yet we had better go into a war than be swallowed up by a peace.

In the debate on councillors of 10 May, he declared that 'there was not a cobbler in the street but could have told what would save England'. Later in the month he spoke for disbanding the army, observing: 'I cannot come up now to matter of war, though formerly I was as much for it as any man'. He agreed with his brother against some of the more impractical Members of the Opposition that a further supply would be required to pay off the new-raised forces, despite the 'fears and jealousies . . . that the pretence of a truce from time to time would be still an occasion of keeping up the army'. On 18 June he moved for an inquiry into corruption of Members. Two days later he attended a conference to hear a dispatch from Nymwegen about a hitch in the negotiations, and on 22 June he helped to draw up an expedient to be offered to the Lords over their proviso to the disbandment bill.[15]

It was probably Coleman's letters, confirming his belief that Popish intrigues were based on French support, that persuaded Coventry to give credence to the Popish Plot. He proclaimed himself an enemy to the Roman Catholics 'not because they are erroneous in religion, but because their principles are destructive to the government where I live'. In the final session of the Cavalier Parliament he helped to draw up seven addresses, including that for the continued imprisonment of his brother's colleague, (Sir) Joseph Williamson*, whose casual attitude to the signing of commissions for Roman Catholic officers he condemned. On 19 Nov. he reported an address for the offer of rewards to encourage further information on plots to assassinate the King. Prejudiced, as he admitted, by his obligations to the Duke of York, he supported the Lords' pro-

viso to exempt his former patron from the bill excluding all Papists from both Houses of Parliament. He asked the House to bear in mind the duke's services to the navy, and his concurrence in the marriage of his daughter to the Prince of Orange. The proviso was carried by two votes, and Coventry was among those instructed to prepare for a conference on two less important provisos concerning the servants of the Queen and the duchess. Another address that he had helped to draft was for calling out the militia, and he was dismayed by the King's rejection of the militia bill. 'The most considerable and the most remarkable man' in the Commons, according to Daniel Finch*, he left Westminster 'on purpose that he might be turned out of the House' for not taking the oaths in the bill against Papists. But he was recalled in time to hear of the attempt by the Government to seize the diplomatic papers of Ralph Montagu*, which he considered a most sinister move. After they had been read to the Commons he was among those appointed to draw up Danby's impeachment.[16]

Coventry was reluctant to stand again, but the corporation of Yarmouth would not be 'prevailed with to part with him', and he was returned to the first Exclusion Parliament without attending the election. Shaftesbury apparently believed that he was also a candidate for Oxfordshire. Temple, who had been out of England for the greater part of Danby's administration, considered that at this period

> Sir William Coventry had the most credit of any man in the House of Commons, and, I think, the most deservedly, not only for his great abilities, but for having been turned out of the Council and Treasury to make way for my Lord Clifford's greatness and the designs of the Cabal. He had been ever since opposite to the French alliances, and bent upon engaging England in a war with that crown and [with the] assistance of the confederates, and now extremely dissatisfied with the conclusion of the peace, and with the ministry that he thought either assisted, or at least might have prevented it; and in these dispositions he was like to be followed by the best and soberest part of the House of Commons.

Sobriety, however, was not much in evidence in this Parliament, and Shaftesbury classed him as 'vile'. An active Member, he delivered 26 speeches, and was named to 23 committees, including those to draw up the addresses remonstrating against Danby's pardon, and demanding a proclamation for his apprehension. He also helped to manage a conference on the attainder bill, and to examine the disbandment accounts. When the Lords sent down a bill 'for the better discovery and more speedy conviction of Popish recusants', he was named to the committee, and defended it in debate against those who considered it too lenient as a bill with 'a very good title ... and a good aim'. When Oates accused (Sir) John Robinson I* of threatening to rack a prisoner, Coventry brought a message from his brother, who was too ill to attend, undertaking to secure the King's permission to inform the House more fully; and he was appointed to the committee to inquire into Robinson's alleged miscarriages. He helped to draw up the bill prolonging the ban on cattle imports, although he was dubious of its merits:

> Gentlemen are to consider the general and universal good, which must take place of the more particular good. ... As to the common people, there is no comparison who receives advantage or disadvantage by it. It is plain, if Irish cattle be kept out, it makes flesh dearer.

In the debate on the militia he reminded the House of the French King's appetite for glory; 'and nothing will fill his sails with more glory ... like the accession of such a spot of ground as this to the Catholic religion'. He helped to draw up reasons for asserting the illegality of Danby's pardon, though he does not seem to have been convinced of it himself, and he boldly resisted the demand of the extremists that the fallen statesman should be denied counsel to plead for him. On 11 May he reported a conference on the trial of the lords in the Tower, whose prolonged imprisonment he contrasted with the professed zeal of the House for habeas corpus. According to (Sir) Allen Brodrick* Coventry 'very dexterously' foreclosed the republican position before the main debate on exclusion, in which he said:

> I hope the whole carriage of my life will make me need no apology for myself as to my sincerity for the Protestant religion ... Whenever it comes to pass that the Duke shall be disinherited, and they in Scotland set him up for a king whom you acknowledge not, they will set up such a thorn in your sides, by the help of France, that you will never be able to get it out; and how France has formerly played that game we all know ... Let us not throw another strength into the King of France's hand by making the Duke desperate.

Like his brother, he voted against the commitment of the bill, and he warned the House against accepting the evidence of his former butler against Pepys.[17]

It is hardly surprising that Coventry could not be persuaded to stand again in the autumn, and finally retired from public life. He died 'calmly and piously' at Tunbridge Wells, where he had gone to take the waters, 23 June 1686, and was buried at Penshurst. During his lifetime he had given £2,000 for the redemption of slaves, to which he added £3,000 in his will and another £2,000 for the relief of Huguenot refugees. His epitaph describes him as

energetic, sagacious and indefatigable in business, far-sighted, steadfast and fearless in war and conflict.

In the Privy Council and in Parliament his singular wisdom and keenness of intelligence were admirable and conspicuous; and, what is very difficult in times of variance, he was most careful in all his offices to combine the loyalty due to his prince with zeal for his country's safety. A pious adherent of the reformed religion and its strenuous and successful champion, the ornament of his own age and an example for ages to come, ... he redeemed many prisoners and succoured the needy.[18]

[1] This biography is based on D. T. Witcome, 'Parl. Careers of Sir William and Mr Henry Coventry' (Oxf. Univ. B. Litt. thesis, 1954). [2] Lysons, *Environs*, iii. 155; *Evelyn Diary*, ii. 564. [3] Clarendon, *Life*, ii. 201. [4] *Pepys Diary*, 22 May 1660, 27 Oct. 1662, 2 Sept. 1667, 6 Mar. 1669. [5] *Yarmouth Freemen*, 92; R. East, *Portsmouth Recs.* 357, 359; *Sel. Charters* (Selden Soc. xxviii), 173, 183. [6] Nicholas Pprs. (Cam. Soc. xl), 208, 297, 309; *Cal. Cl. SP*, ii. 138; iv. 593; *Thurloe*, iv. 598; *CSP Dom.* 1655-6, p. 228; *Camb. Hist. Jnl.* xii. 111-12. [7] *Cal. Cl. SP*, iv. 611; Clarendon, *Life*, ii. 104, 202; *CJ*, viii. 341, 355, 395, 420, 428; Reymes diary, 28 Jan. 1662. [8] *Pepys Naval Mins.* (Navy Rec. Soc. lx), 400; Bodl. Carte 47, f. 403; *Pepys Diary*, 12 Oct. 1663; Clarendon, ii. 203; *HMC Le Fleming*, 225; *Camb. Hist. Jnl.* xii. 114-15; *CJ*, viii. 518. [9] *CJ*, viii. 549, 564, 623, 644, 661; C. J. Palmer, *Hist. Yarmouth*, 214; Clarendon, ii. 460, iii. 11; *Marvell* ed. Margoliouth, i. 146; *Milward*, 83. [10] Clarke, *Jas. II*, i. 431; *Savile Corresp.* (Cam. Soc. lxxi), 20; Add. 35865, f. 10v; *Camb. Hist. Jnl.* xii. 113; P. Fraser, *Intell. of Secs. of State*, 79-80; *Pepys Diary*, 28 Oct. 1667; *CJ*, ix. 18, 107, 140; *Marvell*, ii. 248. [11] *Pepys Diary*, 7 Dec. 1668, 6 Mar. 1669; *CJ*, ix. 119, 140, 146, 153, 233; *Dering*, 11, 28; *Survey of London*, xxix. 377; *Hatton Corresp.* (Cam. Soc. n.s. xxii), 103. [12] Bath mss, Thynne pprs. 16, ff. 53-54, 104-5; E. C. Legh, Lady Newton, *Lyme Letters*, 52; *Dering*, 126; *Essex Pprs.* (Cam. Soc. n.s. xlvii), 121; Grey, ii. 223, 243, 267, 321, 356; *CJ*, ix. 259, 260, 263, 300, 307, 309; *Williamson Letters* (Cam. Soc. n.s. ix), 69; Foxcroft, *Halifax*, i. 113. [13] Burnet, i. 479; ii. 89-90; Grey, iii. 13, 16, 63, 72-73, 264, 320, 397-8, 407, 410-11, 416; *CJ*, ix. 320, 321, 344, 352, 371, 380; *Dering Pprs.* 65, 68; *HMC 7th Rep.* 492. [14] Grey, iv. 93, 130, 188-9; Burnet, ii. 124. [15] Burnet, ii. 133; Grey, v. 18-22, 299-300, 325, 377; vi. 13, 70, 103-4. [16] Grey, vi. 235-6, 249, 301, 330, 344, 391; Finch diary, 19 Nov., 11 Dec. 1678. [17] Foxcroft, i. 141; Courtenay, *Temple Mems.* ii. 27; *CJ*, ix. 584, 587, 592; *HMC Ormonde*, n.s. v. 95; Grey, vii. 66, 102-3, 107-8, 207, 256-8, 295. [18] *Works of Sir Thomas Browne* ed. Wilkin, i. 257-8; Foxcroft, i. 465; *Ellis Corresp.* i. 131, 136; PCC 92 Lloyd; *Reg. Roff.* 918.

E.C.

COVERT, Sir John, 1st Bt. (1620–79), of Slaugham, Suss.

HORSHAM 1661

b. 3 June 1620, 3rd but 2nd surv. s. of Sir Walter Covert of Maidstone, Kent by Anne, da. of John Covert of Ewhurst, Suss., and h. to her uncle Sir Walter Covert† of Slaugham. *educ.* Jesus, Camb. 1637. *m.* aft. 1641, Isabella, da. of Sir William Leigh of Longborough, Glos., wid. of Gervase Warmestry, registrar of Worcester dioc., 1s. *d.v.p.* 4da. *suc.* bro. 1643; *kntd.* 19 June 1660; *cr.* Bt. 2 July 1660.[1]

J.p. Suss. July 1660–*d.*, dep. lt. c. Aug. 1660–*d.*, commr. for sewers, W. Suss. Oct. 1660, assessment, Suss. 1661–*d.*, loyal and indigent officers 1662, recusants 1675.[2]

Covert was the last of a Sussex family which can be traced back in the county to the early 13th century, first entering Parliament in 1384. Their prosperity increased with the growth of the local iron industry. Covert was in arms for the King in the first Civil War, and he was imprisoned in Warwick Castle after the fall of Chichester in 1643. His annual income was then said to be only £92, though he had considerable expectations under family settlements. He compounded for £300 in 1645, and took no part in royalist conspiracy, appealing against the decimation tax imposed on Cavaliers in 1656. In 1660 he signed the declaration of the London Royalists, abjuring animosity towards the other party, and he was created a baronet at the Restoration.[3]

Covert was returned for Horsham, six miles from his home, at the general election of 1661. A moderately active Member of the Cavalier Parliament, he was appointed to 167 committees, including the committee of elections and privileges in 11 sessions; but he made no recorded speeches. In the first session he was named to the committees on the bills for restoring the bishops to the House of Lords and preventing mischief from Quakers; but he took no part in the principal measures of the Clarendon Code, though he helped to consider the bill of pains and penalties and the bill for the execution of those under attainder. In 1663 he was among those ordered to hear a petition from the loyal and indigent officers and to devise remedies for the meetings of sectaries. In 1666 on the death of his great-uncle's widow, the second wife of Denzil Holles*, he inherited an estate of £900 p.a.[4]

Covert was appointed to the committee on the bill for the extension of habeas corpus in 1668, and in the following year Sir Thomas Osborne* included him among the independent Members who had usually voted for supply, but later transferred his name to the list of court dependants. No office has been traced, but he was in receipt of an excise pension of £300 p.a. in 1677. He was teller in a thin House on 4 Dec. 1669 for granting privilege to a servant of Sir John Pretyman*, and was named to the committees to authorize negotiations for union with Scotland and to consider an additional conventicles bill in 1670. In 1673 he was among those appointed to the committees to prevent abuses at elections and the growth of Popery, the latter of which produced the test bill. In 1674 he helped to consider a measure for the relief of insolvent debtors, and in 1675 those to prevent illegal exactions, to promote the liberty of the subject and to abolish the penalty of burning for heresy. In the autumn he was among those instructed to devise a test against corruption of Members, and acted as teller against the bill to establish a 'court of conscience' for small claims for Westminster. His name appeared on the working lists, and Sir Richard Wiseman* regarded him as a government supporter in

1676. Shaftesbury naturally marked him 'doubly vile' in 1677, but the author of *A Seasonable Argument*, perhaps ignorant of his excise pension, described him as 'wheedled with promises' and 'much in debt'. He was on both lists of the court party in 1678, and is unlikely to have stood again. He died on 11 Mar. 1679, and was buried at Slaugham. His two surviving daughters brought the Covert property to their husbands, Sir James Morton* and Henry Goring II*.[5]

[1] J. Comber, *Suss. Genealogies, Ardingly*, 186. [2] Kent AO, U269/022; C181/7/58. [3] *Suss. Arch. Colls.* xlvi. 172; E. Straker, *Wealden Iron*, 416; C. T. Sanford, *Suss. in Great Civil War*, 56; *Cal. Comm. Comp.* 858; *CSP Dom.* 1656-7, p. 24; Bodl. Wood mss 276A/168. [4] *Cal. Comm. Comp.* 858. [5] *Cal. Treas. Bks.* v. 1318; *CJ*, ix. 378; *VCH Suss.* vii. 182-3, 190.

B.M.C.

COWARD, William (1634–1705), of Chamberlain Street, Wells, Som. and Totteridge, Herts.

WELLS   1679 (Mar.), 1679 (Oct.), 1681, 17 Jan. 1690, 1695, 1698, 1701 (Feb.), 1701 (Dec.), 1702

bap. 19 July 1634, 1st s. of William Coward of Wells and East Pennard, Som. by Catherine, da. of John Dodington of Dodington, Som. *educ.* Lyons Inn; L. Inn 1655, called 1662. *m.* (1) by 1666, Bridget (*d.* 22 Mar. 1682), da. of Sir Thomas Hall of Bradford-on-Avon, Wilts., 1s. 1da.; (2) Lady Philippa Annesley, da. of Arthur Annesley*, 1st Earl of Anglesey, wid. of Charles, 3rd Baron Mohun of Okehampton, 1s. *suc.* fa. 1664.[1]

Commr. for excise appeals Oct. 1660–79; serjeant-at-law 1692–*d*.[2]

Dep. recorder, Wells 1663, recorder by 1670–83, Aug.–Oct. 1688, 1689–*d*.; commr. for assessment, Som. 1664–80, 1689–90, Wells 1679–80, 1690; bencher, L. Inn 1680, treas. 1689–90; j.p. Som. Feb. 1688–*d*., chairman of quarter sessions, Apr. 1688, dep. lt. 1691–*d*.[3]

Coward came from a family which had risen rapidly in the social scale after acquiring property in Wells by marriage, and entered their pedigree at the heralds' visitation of 1623. His father married the sister of Sir Francis Dodington, a prominent Cavalier commander, and his uncle, a militia officer, had to compound for delinquency in attending the King at Exeter. At the Restoration Coward, a lawyer, was nominated a commissioner of excise appeals in trust for Dodington, who had become a Roman Catholic, and the commissioners for corporations appointed him deputy to the 2nd Lord Poulett as recorder of Wells. His father died in office as mayor of the city in the following year. Coward was returned for Wells to the three Exclusion Parliaments, the first of his family to sit. Marked 'doubtful' on Shaftesbury's list, he was appointed to the committee of elections and privileges in 1679 and voted for exclusion, but left no other trace on the records of these Parliaments. His 'subtle and canting insinuations' prevailed on 'the factious party' in Wells to authorize the sale of the corporation lands to finance the defence of their charter. He lost his office in 1683, and did not stand in 1685.[4]

Although a firm Anglican, Coward became a Whig collaborator in the later years of James II, and was included among the dissenters and Roman Catholics recommended for the commission of the peace in 1687. At the quarter sessions of April 1688 he 'gave a charge to the grand jury second to none but Cicero himself'. He was approved as court candidate for Wells, but probably did not stand at the general election of 1689. On the suicide of Thomas Wyndham II*, Coward succeeded him both as recorder and as MP for Wells. But he is unlikely to have taken his seat in the Convention, and was defeated at the general election in the following month. After regaining his seat in 1695 he sat till his death as a Tory, though he signed the Association in 1696. He died on 8 Apr. 1705, and was buried in St. Cuthbert's, where his memorial inscription describes him as a most learned and esteemed lawyer and a vindicator of the Anglican Church in Parliament. His son sat for Wells as a Whig from 1708 to 1710 and again for a few weeks in 1716.[5]

[1] A. J. Jewers, *Wells Cathedral*, 132–4; Sir T. Phillipps, *Vis. Som.* 56; PCC 133 Gee. [2] *Cal. Treas. Bks.* i. 75; v. 1263; *CSP Dom.* 1691–2, p. 247. [3] Wells corp. mss., T. Serel, Roll of Recorders; act bk. 1662–5, f. 33; *CSP Dom.* 1670, p. 165; 1687–9, pp. 192, 252; 1690–1, p. 358; Som. RO, Q/JC99 et seq. [4] *Vis. Som.* (Harl. Soc. xi), 30; *Cal. Comm. Comp.* 1234; *CSP Dom.* 1670, p. 272; 1682, p. 544. [5] *CSP Dom.* 1687–9, pp. 191–2; Collinson, *Som.* iii. 407.

I.C.

COWPER, James (1622–83), of Westminster.

HERTFORD   1656, 24 Mar. 1659, 1660

bap. 8 Dec. 1622, 5th s. of Sir William Cowper, 1st Bt. (*d.*1664) of Ratling Court, Nonington, Kent by Martha, da. of James Master of East Langdon, Kent. *educ.* Emmanuel, Camb. 1640; L. Inn 1643, called 1650. *m.* 9 May 1657, Anne (*d.* 2 July 1710), da. of John Wroth of Loughton, Essex, 2s. 1da.[1]

    Commr. for militia, Herts. Mar. 1660, j.p. Mar. 1660–78; commr. for oyer and terminer, Home circuit July 1660, assessment, Herts. Aug. 1660–1.[2]

Cowper's great-grandfather was a London Dyer who died in 1569. His father, 'an eminent lover of the Church', obtained a lease of Hertford Castle from James I and a baronetcy and office from Charles I. He was imprisoned as a Royalist during the Civil War and claimed to have lost £17,000,

although all that can be traced is a payment of £500 at Haberdashers' Hall. Cowper himself took no part in the Civil War, during which he qualified as a lawyer, but he became a property developer during the Interregnum in association with the father of Andrew Henley*. In 1656 he became the first member of his family to sit in Parliament. Hence he was outside the scope of the Long Parliament ordinance against the candidature of Cavaliers and their sons, and was re-elected for Hertford at the general election of 1660. He was totally inactive in the Convention, although he probably voted with the Court. He never stood again, and was buried at St. Michael's, Cornhill on 8 Aug. 1683. His widow married the fourth Earl of Suffolk, but none of his descendants entered Parliament.[3]

[1] *VCH Herts. Fams.* 136; Clutterbuck, *Herts.* ii. 194. [2] *Herts. County Recs.* vi. 321. [3] *L. Inn Black Bks.* ii. 415–23, 467, 469.

M.W.H./E.R.E.

COWPER, Sir William, 2nd Bt. (1639–1706), of The Castle, Hertford.

HERTFORD   1679 (Oct.), 1681, 1689, 1690, 1695, 1698

bap. 14 Dec. 1639, o.s. of John Cowper (*d.*1643) of Hertford by Martha, da. of George Hukeley, merchant, of London. *educ.* G. Inn 1659. *m.* lic. 8 Apr. 1664, Sarah (*d.* 3 Feb. 1720), da. of Samuel Holled, merchant, of London, 4s. (2 *d.v.p.*) *suc.* gdfa. 20 Dec. 1664.[1]

    Commr. for inquiry into recusancy fines, Herts. 1687–Oct. 1688; j.p. Herts. by Apr. 1688–*d.*, Mdx. 1689–*d.*; dep. lt. Herts. 1689–*d.*; commr. for assessment, Herts. and Mdx. 1689–90.[2]

Cowper's father, the elder brother of James Cowper*, died in Ely House under imprisonment as a Royalist. Little is known of Cowper's early life; he was accepted by the Earl of Shaftesbury (Sir Anthony Ashley Cooper*) as a kinsman, though no relationship can be established, and frequently visited him in the Tower in 1678 as one of his trustees. A member of the Green Ribbon Club, he stood for Hertford at the second election of 1679, probably with the support of the dissenters, since his election agent was one of the leading Quakers in the town. He was returned top of the poll, and with his colleague Sir Thomas Byde* launched the Hertfordshire petition against the delays in the assembly of the second Exclusion Parliament. When it met he was moderately active, serving on five committees, of which the most important were to consider the bill regulating parliamentary elections, and to inspect the pardon given to the informer Dangerfield. He made three speeches. On 15 Dec. 1680 he denied that it was the expulsion of the

Roman Catholic heir to the throne which required Sweden to keep up a standing army. 'Unless you banish the Duke as well as the Papists', he told the House, 'we can have no hope of preserving the Protestant religion and the quiet of the nation.' But in view of the rejection of the exclusion bill in the Lords, he supported as 'the next best thing' the Association proposed by William Cavendish*, Lord Cavendish. He favoured the dismissal of Lawrence Hyde I*, because whoever was against exclusion was against their religion and their liberty. He was re-elected to the Oxford Parliament, in which he seconded the motion of Sir John Hotham* for publishing the resolutions agreed by the House:

> Let men think what they please, the weight of England is the people, and the world will find that they will sink Popery at last.

He was appointed to the committee to draw up the third exclusion bill, and back in London served on the Middlesex grand jury which indicted Danby for the Godfrey murder. He was himself indicted later in the year for reflecting on some of the Hertford magistrates, and was alleged to have said that if Parliament voted a supply, the King would bring in arbitrary government and Popery. Already a marked man, he was not deterred from standing bail for Shaftesbury; and after the Rye House Plot he was himself required to find bail of £3,000.[3]

Cowper probably became a Whig collaborator under James II, as he acted in the commission to inquire into recusancy fines and as a j.p. He regained his seat at the general election of 1689, and became a moderately active Member of the Convention, in which he was named to 14 committees. In the debate on the state of the nation on 28 Jan., he proposed going into grand committee. A week later he joined in the complaint about the bailing of Brent, the 'Popish solicitor'. He was among those appointed to inquire into the authors and advisers of grievances, to examine James II's treasury solicitors, and to consider the toleration bill. In the second session he served on the committees to inquire into the miscarriages of the war and to hear a petition from three informers. He was listed as supporting the disabling clause in the bill to restore corporations, and remained a court Whig under William III. He died of apoplexy on 26 Nov. 1706, leaving an estate of £2,500 p.a. to his elder son, MP for Hertford 1695–1700 and subsequently lord chancellor. His younger son, Spencer Cowper†, also served in Parliament as MP for Bere Alston and Truro before receiving a judgeship in 1727.[4]

[1] VCH Herts. Fams. 138. [2] Mdx. RO, MJP/CP5a; Cal. Treas. Bks. viii. 1695, 1983. [3] CSP Dom. 1677–8, p. 235; 1680–1, pp. 363,

524; July–Sept. 1683, p. 318; 1684–5, p. 39; Dom. Intell. 5 Sept. 1679; HMC Lindsey, 30; Grey, viii. 160, 162, 293; ix. 50; Somers Tracts, viii. 407; Luttrell, i. 148. [4] HMC Downshire, i. 287; Grey, ix. 50; Luttrell, vi. 109, 111.

E.R.E.

CRADOCK, Joseph (c.1605–86), of Evenwood, co. Dur. and Cradock Hall, Richmond, Yorks.

RICHMOND   1661–17 Jan. 1662

> b. c.1605, 5th but 4th surv. s. of John Cradock, DD (d.1627), spiritual chancellor of Durham, by Margaret, da. of William Bateman of Wensleydale, Yorks., wid. of one Robinson. educ. Newcastle-upon-Tyne g.s.; Sidney Sussex, Camb. 1622, BA 1625, MA 1628; DCL by 1636. m. (1) Elizabeth (d.1643), da. of Robert Cruse, Grocer, of London, 2s. 3da.; (2) Jane (d. 18 Dec. 1676), da. and coh. of Anthony Maxton, preb. of Durham, 5da. Kntd. 11 May 1661.[1]
> Commissary, archdeaconry of Richmond 1636–46, c. July 1660–81; j.p. co. Dur. July 1660–d., Yorks. (N. Riding) 1664–d.; commr. for assessment (N. Riding) 1661–79, co. Dur. 1661–3, 1679–80, corporations, Yorks. 1662–3, loyal and indigent officers 1662, recusants (N. Riding) 1675.[2]

Cradock claimed descent from the Staffordshire family, but his ancestors appear to have lived in Yorkshire for several generations. His father had a successful career in the Church, and as a younger son he was himself ordained deacon in 1625; but after his father's death he was recommended by the bishop for membership of an ecclesiastical commission. Later he acquired a doctorate of civil law, presumably at a university abroad, and in 1636 he was appointed commissary in the archdeaconry of Richmond. A Royalist in the Civil War, he compounded in 1648 with a fine of £112. But by his second marriage he acquired an estate in county Durham, and during the Interregnum he built Cradock Hall in Richmond, which became his residence.[3]

Cradock was returned for Richmond in a contested election in 1661, the first of his family to sit in Parliament, and asserted his status as a layman by accepting a knighthood. A moderately active Member, he was named to nine committees, eight of which were in the first five weeks of the Cavalier Parliament. They included the committee of elections and privileges, and those for confirming public Acts and providing for the repair of highways. In June he was appointed to the committees for restoring the temporal jurisdiction of the clergy and ascertaining the fees chargeable by masters in Chancery. His last committee was for the uniformity bill on 3 July. But on the petition of his opponent, John Wandesford*, the elections committee reported that Cradock was disqualified by his orders, and he was unseated. He remained active in local government, and it was reported that he and Humphrey Wharton* incited a mob to attack a collector of the unpopular hearth-tax. During the exclusion crisis, however, he supported the Court, and in May 1684 Sunderland referred to the King's satisfaction 'with the affection and zeal you bear towards him and the Government on all occasions'. He died on 6 Apr. 1686 and was buried at Richmond, leaving an estate of £600 p.a., including colliery interests, and the butlerage and prizage of wine imports in the five northern counties.[4]

[1] Clay, *Dugdale's Vis. Yorks.* iii. 339; PCC 125 Clarke. [2] C. Clarkson, *Richmond*, 176; R. Holmes, *Pontefract Bk. of Entries*, 77; *N. Riding Recs.* vi. 90; vii. 70. [3] *Arch. Ael.* (ser. 3), xv. 44–49; *CSP Dom.* 1629–31, p. 237; *Royalist Comp. Pprs.* (Surtees Soc. cxi), 178; Clarkson, 176–7; *Durham Cathedral Reg.* (Harl. Soc. Reg. xxiii), 86. [4] *CJ*, viii. 346; *EHR*, li. 635; *CSP Dom.* 1683–4, pp. 39, 62; 1684–5, p. 33.

P.A.B./P.W.

CRADOCK, Thomas (1633–90), of Harperley, co. Dur. and Cradock Hall, Richmond, Yorks.

RICHMOND   1679 (Mar.), 1679 (Oct.), 1685

bap. 8 Apr. 1633, 1st s. of (Sir) Joseph Cradock* by 1st w. *educ.* G. Inn 1650, called 1658; Trinity Hall, Camb., BA 1654, MA 1657. *m.* (1) 1662, Sibilla (*d.* 2 Mar. 1669), da. and coh. of Gabriel Clarke, DD, archdeacon of Durham, 1da.; (2) 21 Dec. 1671, Dorothy, da. of Nicholas Heath of Little Eden, co. Dur., 1s. *d.v.p. suc.* fa. 1686.[1]

Fellow of Trinity Hall, Camb. 1658–62; attorney-gen. to bp. of Durham 1664–72; j.p. co. Dur. 1666–?83, Yorks. (N. Riding) 1677–80; commr. for assessment, co. Dur. 1667–80, (N. Riding) 1679–80, co. Dur. and N. Riding 1690; recorder, Richmond 1669–84, ?Oct. 1688–d.; commr. for recusants, co. Dur. 1675; commissary, archdeaconry of Richmond 1681–d.[2]

Cradock broke with the ecclesiastical tradition of his family to the extent of becoming a common lawyer; but he married the daughter of a church dignitary who brought him a substantial fortune. He became recorder of Richmond in 1669 and was returned for the borough at the next general election ten years later. Shaftesbury classed him as 'honest', but he left no trace on the records of the first Exclusion Parliament, and probably paired on the bill. Nevertheless he was removed from the North Riding bench in 1680. His only committee in the second Exclusion Parliament was to examine the disbandment accounts. He was replaced by the court supporter John Darcy* in the Oxford Parliament, and lost his recordership under the new charter. However he succeeded his father as commissary, and regained his seat in 1685 on the corporation franchise. A moderately active Member of James II's Parliament, he was appointed to five committees, including those on the bills to prevent

theft and rapine on the northern border, to prohibit the import of tallow candles, and to relieve insolvent debtors. He succeeded to his father's estate, valued at £600 p.a. in the following year. In September 1688 the King's agents reported that he would be elected at Richmond and was considered favourable to the repeal of the Test Act and Penal Laws. In fact Cradock does not seem to have stood in 1689, possibly because of failing health, since he died on 25 Feb. 1690 and was buried in Durham Cathedral. In his will he mentioned £10,085 in money and investments. The next member of the family to sit in Parliament was Sheldon Cradock, who was returned for Camelford in 1830.[3]

[1] Clay, *Dugdale's Vis. Yorks.* iii. 339. [2] Hutchinson, *Dur.* i. 554; C. Clarkson, *Richmond*, 176, App. xlvii, lxxv; SP44/135/144; *Arch. Ael.* (ser. 3), xv. 44–46; *N. Riding Recs.* vii. 5, 30. [3] *Arch. Ael.* (ser. 3), xv. 44–49; SP44/135/144.

P.A.B./P.W.

CRAMOND, 2nd Baron [S] *see* **RICHARDSON, Thomas**

CRANBORNE, Visct. *see* **CECIL, James**

CRAWFORD, Robert (c.1657–1706), of Bobbing Court, Kent.

QUEENBOROUGH   1689, 1690, 1695, 1698, 1701 (Feb.), 1701 (Dec.), 1702

b. c.1657. *m.* lic. 27 July 1687, aged 30, Frances (*d.* 18 Dec. 1693), da. and h. of Henry Sandford of Bobbing Court, wid. of Sir George Moore, 1st Bt., of Maids Moreton, Bucks., and of Edward Digges of Chilham Castle, Kent, *s.p.*[1]

Lt. of ft. Admiralty Regt. 1673, capt.-lt. 1684, capt. 1686–9; lt.-gov. Sheerness 1684, gov. 1690–d.; brevet col. 1694.

J.p. Kent Apr.–Oct. 1688, 1689–d., dep. lt. Feb.–Oct. 1688; jurat, Queenborough June 1688–?d.[2]

Crawford, an army officer of unknown origin, became second-in-command of the Sheerness garrison in 1684. His marriage to the heiress of the Bobbing Court estate, on the opposite shore of the Swale, strengthened his interest at Queenborough, for which he was recommended as court candidate in 1688. He headed the poll at the abortive election in September, and was again successful in January. A totally inactive Member of the Convention, he left no trace in the Journals except for two applications for leave, but he was probably a court Tory. Unlike most of his regiment he accepted the Revolution and was promoted to governor in 1690. A consistent government supporter under William III, he signed the Association; but he rejoined the

Tories in the first Parliament of Queen Anne. He died in November 1706.[3]

[1] Hasted, *Kent*, vi. 198; *Canterbury Mar. Lic.* iv. 169; *Mar. Lic.* (Harl. Soc. xxxi), 7. [2] Kent AO, Qb/RPp/1; *CSP Dom.* 1687–9, p. 274. [3] *CSP Dom.* 1687–9, p. 274; 1689–90, pp. 553, 555; *Ailesbury Mems.* 376; Le Neve, *Mon. Angl.* 1700–15, p. 123.

B.D.H.

CREW, John (c.1598–1679), of Steane, Northants. and Lincoln's Inn Fields, Mdx.

AMERSHAM	May 1624, 1625
BRACKLEY	1626
BANBURY	1628
NORTHAMPTONSHIRE	1640 (Apr.)
BRACKLEY	1640 (Nov.)[1]
NORTHAMPTONSHIRE	1654, 1660

b. c.1598, 1st s. of Sir Thomas Crew[†] of Nantwich, Cheshire and Steane by Temperance, da. and coh. of Reynold Bray of Steane. *educ.* G. Inn, entered 1615, called 1624; Magdalen Coll. Oxf. matric. 26 Apr. 1616, aged 18. *m.* c.1623, Jemima, da. and coh. of Edward Waldegrave of Lawford Hall, Essex, 6s. 2da. *suc.* fa. 1634; *cr.* Baron Crew of Stene 20 Apr. 1661.[2]

J.p. Northants. 1634–49, 1656–*d.*, commr. for defence 1642, assessment 1643–8, 1657, Jan. 1660–1, sequestration 1643, execution of ordinances 1643, accounts 1643, levying of money 1643, appeals, Oxf. Univ. 1647, militia, Northants. 1648, Northants. and Westminster Mar. 1660, drainage, Great level of the fens 1649, visitation, Oxf. Univ. 1654, scandalous ministers, Northants. 1654, statutes, Durham college 1656, oyer and terminer, Midland circuit July 1660. Member, committee of Both Kingdoms 1644–8; commr. for treaty of Uxbridge 1645, abuses in heraldry 1646, exclusion from sacrament 1646, bishops' lands 1646, scandalous offences 1648, trade 1655–7, relief of Piedmontese Protestants 1656; Councillor of State 25 Feb.–31 May 1660.[3]

Crew's grandfather was a tanner of Nantwich, who put his two sons to the law. Both became Speakers of the House of Commons, a record which remains unique. Crew, a moderate Parliamentarian in the Civil War, was imprisoned at Pride's Purge. Though summoned to Cromwell's 'Other House', he never took his seat. He returned to Westminster with the secluded Members, and moved the resolution condemning the execution of Charles I.[4]

Crew was returned for Northamptonshire for the third time at the general election of 1660. It is probable that most of the 19 references in the Journals are to him rather than to his son. He derived additional political weight from the part played by his son-in-law Edward Montagu I* in the Restoration. His only known speech was unfortunate; Samuel Pepys* records on 29 Apr. 1660 that, according to Montagu, 'Mr Crew did go a little too far the other day in keeping out the young lords from sitting'. He served on the committees for the abolition of the court of wards and the continuance of the Convention, and took part in drawing up the instructions for the messengers to the King and the conference on the King's reception. He was one of the delegation that met Charles II at The Hague. After the King's return, as a leading Presbyterian he seems to have been chiefly interested in the bill for settling ministers, helping to draw up a proviso on crown livings on 1 Sept. and to manage a conference on 10 Sept.[5]

Crew received a peerage in the coronation honours, and retired from public life. His Northamptonshire estate was estimated at £1,660 p.a. Pepys describes his household as 'the best family in the world for goodness and sobriety'. There is no evidence that he conformed, and on Christmas Eve 1662 he lamented the fate of 'the poor ministers who are put out, to whom, he says, the King is beholden for his coming in, and that if any such thing had been foreseen, he had never come in'. He was reckoned an opposition peer from 1675 till his death. He died on 12 Dec. 1679 and was buried at Steane.[6]

[1] Secluded at Pride's Purge, 6 Dec. 1648, and readmitted 21 Feb. 1660. [2] Baker, *Northants.* i. 685. [3] *CSP Dom.* 1655–6, pp. 1, 100, 218. [4] Ormerod, *Cheshire*, iv. 310; Keeler, *Long Parl.* 147. [5] *Pepys Diary*, 29 May 1660. [6] Add. 34222, f. 38v; *Pepys Diary*, 24 Dec. 1662, 5 Nov. 1666; *Survey of London*, iii. 75.

M.W.H./J.P.F.

CREW, Thomas (c.1624–97), of Steane, Northants.

| NORTHAMPTONSHIRE | 1656 |
| BRACKLEY | 1659, 1660, 18 July 1661, 1679 (Mar.) |

b. c.1624, 1st s. of John Crew*. *educ.* G. Inn 1641; Padua 1647. *m.* (1) May 1650, Mary, da. of Sir Roger Townshend, 1st Bt.[†], of Raynham, Norf., 1s. *d.v.p.* 3da.; (2) 1674, Anne, da. and coh. of Sir William Armine, 2nd Bt.[†], of Osgodby, Lincs., wid. of Sir Thomas Wodehouse of Kimberley, Norf., 2da. Kntd. 26 Sept. 1660; *suc.* fa. as 2nd Baron Crew of Stene 12 Dec. 1679.[1]

J.p. Northants. 1656–at least 1666, commr. for militia 1659, Mar. 1660, assessment Aug. 1660–79, dep. lt. c. Aug. 1660–2; high steward, Banbury 1683–Oct. 1688.[2]

Crew was re-elected in 1660 to the family borough, two miles from Steane, without a contest. He seems to have been completely inactive in the Convention, in which his father also sat, though Lord Wharton regarded him as a friend. In the following election he was involved in a double return with Sir William Fermor, decided in his favour on 18 July 1661. He does not appear to have held county office for long, and his committee record suggests that he was one of the least active Members of the Cavalier Parliament; he was added to the committee of elections and privileges in 1666 and 1673 and to that for an estate bill in 1678. Perhaps his health was poor; he was suffering from continued apoplectic fits in 1662 and troubled with the vapours and dizzy spells in the following year. Nevertheless, Samuel Pepys* found him 'mighty busy' to save his brother-in-law, Lord Sandwich (Edward Montagu I*) from the committee for miscarriages in 1668, and with his father 'bemoaning my lord's folly in leaving his old interest, by which he hath now lost all'. Although he appears on the list drawn up by Sir Thomas Osborne* in 1669 as one who might be engaged for the Court by the Duke of York, he probably remained in opposition. He was noted as 'thrice worthy' by Shaftesbury in 1677.[3]

Crew was re-elected at Brackley in February 1679, and again appears as 'worthy' on Shaftesbury's list. He justified this description by voting for the exclusion bill, but otherwise leaves no trace on the records of the first Exclusion Parliament. He again voted for the bill in 1680, having meanwhile succeeded to the peerage, and was reckoned an opponent of James II in 1687. But he voted for a regency in 1689, and was considered hostile to the new government in the following year. He died on 30 Nov. 1697, and was buried at Steane, leaving £20,000 each to his three surviving daughters. His widow married Arthur Herbert*. His brother, the Jacobite bishop of Durham, succeeded to the title and an estate of £6,000 p.a., and with him the male line of the Crews of Steane ended.[4]

[1] Baker, *Northants.* i. 685. [2] SP44/66/307. [3] *Pepys Diary*, 31 Mar. 1662, 15 May 1663, 12 Feb., 15 Apr. 1668. [4] Northants. RO, FH 2893D; *Clarendon Corresp.* ii. 256; Luttrell, iv. 313.

M.W.H./J.P.F.

CRISP, Sir Nicholas (c.1598–1666), of Hammersmith, Mdx.

WINCHELSEA   1640 (Apr.), 1640 (Nov.)–2 Feb. 1641, 1661–26 Feb. 1666

b. c.1598, 1st s. of Ellis Crisp, Salter, of Bread Street, London by Hester, da. of John Ireland, Salter, of London. *m.* by 1619, Anne, da. and coh. of Edward Prescott, Salter and goldsmith, of London, 5s. (3 *d.v.p.*) 5da. *suc.* fa. 1625; kntd. 1 Jan. 1640; *cr.* Bt. 14 Apr. 1665.[1]

Member, Salters' Co. 1619, master 1640–1; member, Artillery Co. 1621; Merchant Adventurer; member, Barbary Co., Guinea Co. 1631; capt. of militia ft. London by 1632–?42, common councilman by 1640–1; j.p. Mdx. by 1641–2, July 1660–*d.*, Cornw. 1644–6; commr. of array, London 1642, loyal and indigent officers, London and Westminster 1662, assessment, London 1661–3, Mdx. 1661–*d.*; dep. lt. London 1662–*d.*; asst. R. Adventurers into Africa 1663–6.[2]

Jt. farmer of customs 1638–40, 1662–*d.*; commr. for customs Sept. 1660–2, trade Nov. 1660–*d.*, plantations Dec. 1660–*d.*; gent. of privy chamber 1664–*d.*; jt.-farmer of alum works 1665–*d.*[3]

Col. of horse (royalist) 1643–5.

FRS 1663.

Crisp's grandfather, a native of Leicestershire, acquired the manor of Marshfield and other property in Gloucestershire, and his father was one of the richest merchants in Jacobean London. Crisp invested in numerous projects and built himself a magnificent house at Hammersmith for £25,000. He was largely responsible for opening up the Guinea trade, and contracted for the great farm of the customs in 1638. Expelled from the Long Parliament as a monopolist, he joined the King at Oxford, and executed the London commission of array. He raised a regiment for the King's service, and supplied him with 'thousands of gold'. In 1647 he retired to France. He compounded on the Exeter articles, a fine of £1,000 imposed in 1649 being reduced to £356 two years later, when his interest in the Guinea trade and personal estate valued at £140,000 was set in the balance against debts amounting to £300,000 incurred in the late King's service.[4]

Crisp was active in the royalist conspiracies prior to the Restoration, and signed the declaration of London Royalists in support of George Monck* in April 1660, disclaiming 'any thoughts of revenge for past mischiefs'. The following July he petitioned from a debtors' prison

for an order for payment of £20,000. . . . This is his own special portion of the great debt of £100,000 due to him and other farmers of the customs from the Long Parliament who promised to pay the King's debts on their advancing money to discharge the two armies.

He was soon at liberty, and became one of the customs commissioners at a salary of £2,000 p.a. Nominated for London by the court party in 1661, he was 'stiffly cried down' by the dissenters as a friend to the bishops. But he was returned for Winchelsea on the lord warden's interest, and listed by Lord Wharton as a friend. A moderately active Member of the Cavalier Parliament, he was appointed to 42 committees, including the committee of elections and privileges in five sessions, and several concerned with the revenue. In 1661 he was appointed to the committees for the restoration of bishops to the House of Lords, the uniformity bill, and the bill of pains and penalties. After the Christmas recess he was added to the committee to consider abuses in the customs and appointed to that for the additional corporations bill. On the last day of the session he was given special responsibility, with William Morice I* and (Sir)

Robert Brooke*, for recommending the case of a merchant's widow to the King. During this period he obtained for himself a moiety in the farm of sea-coal exports, two-thirds of the customs duties on spices until the repayment of £20,000 due to him for his factories in Guinea, and a special grant of £10,000 for his services in compounding the debt owed by Charles I to the East India Company; while his son was granted the reversion of the office of collector of customs outwards in the port of London. After 1663, when he helped to consider a petition from the loyal and indigent officers and an additional bill for their relief, his activity declined. Nevertheless he was listed as a court dependant in 1664, and attended the Oxford session, acting as teller on the third reading for the bill to encourage the planting of hemp and flax. He formed a syndicate with Sir Hugh Cholmley* which was granted the alum farm for 21 years on payment of a yearly rent of £5,260. He died on 26 Feb. 1666, aged 67, and was buried in St. Mildred's, Bread Street. At his request, his heart, enclosed in an urn, was placed on the pedestal of the bronze bust 'of that glorious martyr, King Charles I, of blessed memory' erected by him in his chapel at Hammersmith. The family never fully recovered from his losses in the Civil War, but his grandson Charles sat for Woodstock in 1721–2.[5]

[1] F. A. Crisp, *Crisp Colls.* iv. 4–5; C. J. Feret, *Fulham Old and New*, iii. 68. [2] S. Watson, *Salters' Co.* 145; *Ancient Vellum Bk.* ed. Raikes 32; *CSP Dom.* 1631–3, pp. 186, 237; Keeler, *Long Parl.* 147; T. K. Rabb, *Enterprise and Empire*, 273; V. Pearl, *London and the Outbreak of the Puritan Revolution*, 121; SP29/61/5; *Sel. Charters* (Selden Soc. xxviii), 179. [3] R. B. Turton, *Alum Farm*, 187; Carlisle, *Privy Chambers*, 174. [4] Crisp, iv. 2–5; Feret, iii. 60–61; Clarendon, *Life*, ii. 232–3; *Vis. London* (Harl. Soc. xv), 201; *DNB*; *Cal. Comm. Comp.* 1651; K. G. Davies, *R. African Co.* 40. [5] D. Underdown, *Royalist Conspiracy*, 37; *A Declaration of the Nobility and Gentry that adhered to the late King now residing in and about the City of London* (1660); *CSP Dom.* 1660–1, pp. 122, 538, 605; 1661–2, pp. 14, 25, 320, 331, 608; 1663–4, p. 639; 1665–6, pp. 79, 400; *Cal. Treas. Bks.* i. 226, 446, 553; *CJ*, viii. 436, 620; Turton, 182; Crisp, iv. 3; T. Faulkner, *Fulham and Hammersmith*, 128.

E.C.

CRISPE, Henry (c.1650–1700), of Aldermanbury, London.

LANCASTER 1685

b. c.1650, 1st s. of Henry Crispe, Haberdasher, of London by Elizabeth, da. of Anthony Biddulph, Haberdasher, of London. *educ.* St. Paul's; Christ's, Camb. adm. 18 June 1666, aged 16; I. Temple 1666, called 1676. *unm. suc.* fa. 1654.[1]

Common serjeant, London 1678–d.; member, Hon. Artillery Co. 1681; dep. lt. London 1685–7, Oct. 1688–9; bencher, I. Temple 1697, reader 1698.[2]

Crispe's paternal ancestry has not been ascertained beyond one generation. He was born in Hamburg, where his father was one of the Merchant Adventurers commissioned to administer the engagement to the Commonwealth in 1650. He became a lawyer, and succeeded Jeffreys as common serjeant in 1678, during the mayoralty of his stepfather Sir James Edwards, 'a right loyal man' even by the exacting standards of the Duke of York. The post, held in conjunction with the clerkship of the orphans, was worth £700 p.a. Crispe soon revealed himself as a high-flyer for the prerogative, and became the principal agent of the Court in the City. He gave evidence on behalf of Jeffreys before a parliamentary committee in 1680. By April 1682 Secretary Jenkins was consulting him about securing the surrender of the charter, and in September he nominated Peter Rich* as Tory candidate for sheriff. In the following month he was manager for Sir William Pritchard* in the election for lord mayor, and he urged the prosecution of Thomas Pilkington* as ringleader in the riots at these elections. In 1683 he recommended that 'our justices, especially the lord mayor, might be a little quickened in the execution of the laws against conventicles, it being certain that, as long as those nurseries of rebellion are kept open, we shall have designs against the monarchy'.[3]

Crispe had no known connexion with Lancaster, but as a court candidate to oppose Lord Brandon (Hon. Charles Gerard*) in 1685 he was very warmly recommended to the corporation by Lord Keeper Guilford (Francis North*), Jeffreys and Sunderland. He fought the election in person, defying the mob much as in London three years earlier. 'Crispe caused the mayor to commit one of the rabble for saying he had a Pope in his belly', Sir Daniel Fleming* was told. Crispe was a moderately active Member of James II's Parliament, being appointed to nine committees, most of which chiefly concerned the City. He took part in estimating the revenue likely to arise from a tax on new buildings and in considering the bills for rebuilding St. Paul's, supplying defects in the bankruptcy laws and regulating hackney coaches. Of particular interest to him was the bill for the relief of widows and orphans in the City.[4]

It was rumoured in October 1685 that Crispe would be promoted to the office of recorder, but this never took place. In 1687 'Mr. Chiffinch sent for him by the King's direction to his lodgings in Whitehall, where he found his Majesty alone, who asked him some questions concerning the Penal Laws and the Test'. Roger North* described Crispe as 'an honest, reasonable gentleman, and very loyal, but it seems was not one that would go into all measures'. He was removed from the lieutenancy, and, though he was restored in October 1688, the Revolution soon ended his political career. He was in some danger of Whig reprisals, but no doubt his firmness over the Penal Laws saved him. Besides his city office, he had some private practice, appearing as counsel before the House of Lords. He died a bachelor in 1700, administration being granted to two cousins on 6 Nov.[5]

[1] F. A. Crisp, *Crispe Fam.* i. 26, 99. [2] *CSP Dom.* 1685, p. 86; *HMC Lords*, iii. 45; *Ancient Vellum Bk.* ed. Raikes, 112. [3] *CSP Dom.* 1649–50, p. 496; 1682, pp. 149, 412, 486, 561; Jan.–June 1683, p. 100; Bodl. Carte 216, f. 214; Grey, vii. 462; *Vis. Warws.* (Harl. Soc. lxii), 21; *HMC Dartmouth*, i. 59. [4] Westmorland RO D/Ry 2899, letter of William Kirkby, 9 Apr. 1685; 2902, letter of William Fleming, 13 Apr. 1685; *CSP Dom.* 1685, p. 63. [5] *CSP Dom.* 1685, p. 343; *LJ*, xiv. 384; North, *Lives*, i. 281; Luttrell, iv. 699; R. Morrice, *Entering Bk.* 2, p. 84.

I.C./J.P.F.

CROFT, Sir Herbert, 1st Bt. (c.1652–1720), of Croft Castle, Herefs.

HEREFORDSHIRE 1679 (Mar.), 1690, 1695

b. c.1652, 1st s. of Herbert Croft, bp. of Hereford, by Anne, da. of Jonathan Brown, dean of Hereford. *educ.* Magdalen Coll. Oxf. matric. 27 Apr. 1668, aged 16; M. Temple 1668. *m.* c. Oct. 1675, Elizabeth, da. of Thomas Archer* of Umberslade, Warws., 6s (4 *d.v.p.*) 5da. *cr.* Bt. 18 Nov. 1671; *suc.* fa. 1691.[1]

Commr. for assessment, Herefs. 1673–80, 1689–90, j.p. 1673–Mar. 1688, Oct. 1688–?*d.*, dep. lt. 1673–Feb. 1688, by 1694–at least 1701, commr. for recusants 1675, lt.-col. of militia ft. ?1682–Feb. 1688, Oct. 1688–?1701; high steward, Leominster 1704–*d.*[2]

Croft's ancestors had been at Croft Castle since the 11th century and had represented the county as early as 1307; but their Herefordshire interest had lapsed in 1617 when Croft's grandfather declared himself a Roman Catholic and retired to the Benedictine monastery at Douai. Three of Croft's uncles fought for the King in the Civil War. In 1659 his father succeeded to the estate, valued at £2,000 p.a., becoming bishop of Hereford in 1661, and dean of the Chapel Royal in 1668. Charles II admitted that he was an excellent preacher, but his denunciations of the royal morals proved unpalatable and in 1670 he retired to his diocese. As a convert from Rome, he was alleged by Titus Oates to have been singled out by the Jesuits for assassination.[3]

It was clear that Croft would have a strong claim to sit for the county when the Cavalier Parliament should come to an end, but the country party made the mistake of trying to fob him off with Leominster. Croft was duly returned for Herefordshire in February 1679, and marked 'honest' on Shaftesbury's list. A moderately active Member of the first Exclusion Parliament, he twice acted as teller, and was named to three committees, including those to inspect expiring laws and to consider the bill ex-

cluding from Convocation all who had not taken the oaths and renounced transubstantiation. On 17 Apr. in his only speech he opposed the payment into the chamber of London of taxes voted for disbanding the army, as a proposal 'setting the King's Exchequer different from our own, as if his concerns and ours had not coherence': the interest of the nation would not be maintained 'without a mutual correspondence and concurrence of King and people'. He was named to the committee of inquiry into the shipping of artillery, voted against the first exclusion bill, and on the last day of the Parliament acted as teller against the return of the exclusionist Philip Foley* for Bewdley.[4]

Croft did not attempt to stand for re-election in the autumn, as Foley joyfully reported on 2 Aug., but promised his assistance to (Sir) Edward Harley*. During Monmouth's rebellion he interrogated Harley and commanded the county militia, which, however, does not seem to have been in action. His answers on the repeal of the Test Act and Penal Laws were negative, and he was dropped from the lieutenancy. He promised his electoral interest to the country party in 1688, but appears to have considered standing himself, either for the county or for Leominster. Although he subscribed £40 to the loan to William of Orange in December 1688, his father's acceptance of the Declaration of Indulgence had weakened his position, and he does not seem to have gone to the poll in either constituency in the following month. He soon accommodated himself to the new regime, serving as foreman of the grand jury which presented a loyal address to William and Mary at the summer assizes of 1689. He regained his seat in the following year as a court Whig. He died on 30 Nov. 1720 and was buried at Croft. His son, the second baronet, was returned for Leominster as a Whig in 1722.[5]

[1] O.G.S. Croft, *Croft of Croft Castle*, 105–8. [2] *CSP Dom.* 1673, p. 462; 1696, pp. 488–9; G. F. Townsend, *Leominster*, 291; BL Loan 29/141, Sir Edward to Robert Harley, 19 June 1691. [3] Croft, 56–85; *Symonds's Diary* (Cam. Soc. lxxiv), 196. [4] *CJ*, ix. 634; Grey, vii. 119. [5] Add. 29910, f. 141; *HMC Portland*, iii. 149, 417, 484; BL Loan 29/140, Sir Edward to Robert Harley, 22 June 1685.

E.R.

CROFTS, Sir Henry (c.1590–1667), of Little Saxham, Suff.

EYE 1624
DERBY 1626
BURY ST. EDMUNDS 14 May 1660

b. c.1590, 1st s. of Sir John Crofts† of Little Saxham and West Stow by Mary, da. of Sir Thomas Shirley† of Wiston, Suss. *m.* (1) settlement 1 Nov. 1610, Elizabeth (*d.* 1 Oct. 1643), da. of Sir Richard Wortley of Wortley, Yorks., 5s. (2 *d.v.p.*) 5da.; (2) Margaret (*d.* 26 May 1674), 1s. *d.v.p.* 3da. Kntd. 3 Feb. 1611; *suc.* fa. 1628.[1]

Commr. of array, Suff. 1642, j.p. July 1660–*d.*, dep. lt. c. Aug. 1660–*d.*, commr. for assessment Aug. 1660–*d.*[2]

Crofts's ancestors are said to have held manorial property in the reign of Edward I, but they were of little account until the 16th century, when they acquired Little Saxham, which became their principal residence. The first of the family to enter Parliament was his father, who sat for Thetford in 1597. Although Crofts, a strong Anglican, was named to the Suffolk commission of array, he remained inactive during the Civil War. On the introduction of the Covenant in 1643 he wrote:

> I hope God will in his mercy direct me to some place of retreat, whereby I may avoid the having that tendered to me which I am resolved and am bound in conscience never to subscribe unto.

In 1646 he had to surrender to the sequestrators the portion due to his daughter, who had married the Cavalier Sir Frederick Cornwallis* without his consent; but this was returned to him when the sequestration was lifted in 1648. His sister was the mother of Sir Henry Bennet*, and three of his sons were also in exile with Charles II. The eldest, William, who took charge for a time of the upbringing of the future Duke of Monmouth, then called 'James Crofts', was raised to the peerage in 1658.[3]

Crofts, who owned property in Bury St. Edmunds, five miles from his home, stood for the borough at the general election of 1660 with Sir John Duncombe, another royalist sympathizer. After a double return they were seated on the merits of the election. Doubtless a court supporter, he was not an active Member of the Convention. He was appointed to nine committees, including those for settling the revenue in July and the Dunkirk establishment in September. On 28 Dec. he acted as teller for the bill empowering the corporation of London to raise money by assessment for the militia. He did not stand again, and made over the estate to his son, Lord Crofts, in 1664, reserving an annuity of £600 p.a. for himself and £5,000 for his widow. He was buried at Little Saxham on 31 Mar. 1667. On his son's death in 1677 the estate passed to William Crofts*.[4]

[1] T. Gage, *Hundred of Thingoe*, 133; *Little Saxham Par. Reg.* (Suff. Green Bks. v), 156–7, 179, 183–9. [2] Add. 39246, f. 12. [3] Copinger, *Suff. Manors*, i. 267, 272, 273, 404, 412–13; vii. 100–5; *Verney Mems.* i. 292. [4] Copinger, vii. 103; *Little Saxham Par. Reg.* 182.

M.W.H./P.W.

CROFTS, William (c.1639–95), of Little Saxham, Suff.

BURY ST. EDMUNDS 1685

b. c.1639, 2nd s. of Anthony Crofts† (*d.* 1657) of West Stow by Mary, da. of Richard Franklin of Willesden, Mdx., wid. of Sir John Smith of Leeds Castle, Kent. *m.* (1) 1675, Mary (*d.* Oct. 1680), da. and h. of Philip, 3rd Visct. Wenman of Tuam [I], *s.p.*; (2) Anne, da. and coh. of William Alington, Fishmonger, of London, 5s. 2da. *suc.* bro. 1664, cos. William, 1st Baron Crofts in Little Saxham estate 1677.[1]

Ensign, Coldstream Gds. 1673; lt. of ft. regt. of Mq. of Worcester (Henry Somerset*) 1673–4.

Maj. of militia ft. Suff. by 1677, lt.-col. 1689–*d.*, commr. for assessment, Suff. 1679–80, 1689–90, j.p. and dep. lt. 1685–?*d.*[2]

Crofts's father, the younger brother of Sir Henry Crofts* inherited the manor of West Stow and sat for Bury St. Edmunds in 1624. He probably sympathized with the Royalists like the rest of his family, but he does not seem to have taken any part in the Civil War and lived quietly during the Interregnum mainly on his wife's property at Willesden. Crofts's elder brother was created a baronet in 1661, and died three years later; but Crofts did not inherit West Stow, which was bequeathed to his widow, from whom it passed to Edward Progers*. This may explain why he entered the army during the third Dutch war, rather late in life. He was posted to Ireland, where he was recommended for promotion, as the lord lieutenant explained, not only as a cousin of Lord Arlington (Sir Henry Bennet*), but because 'I hear from all sides [that he] is a very diligent man and constantly at his duty'. His regiment was disbanded at the end of the war; but in 1675, on his first marriage, the Little Saxham estate was entailed on him by his childless cousin, Lord Crofts, and he inherited it two years later.[3]

Crofts was added to the Suffolk commission of the peace in 1685 and returned to James II's Parliament for Bury St. Edmunds. Presumably a Tory, he was not active, being appointed only to the committee on the bill to provide carriages for the navy and ordnance. He did not stand again, and was buried at Little Saxham on 29 Jan. 1695. The next member of the family to enter Parliament was his great-grandson Richard Croftes, who was returned for Petersfield in 1767.[4]

[1] *Little Saxham Par. Regs.* (Suff. Green Bks. v), 188, 208–10; *West Stow Par. Reg.* (Suff. Green Bks. vii), 187–9; *Vis. England and Wales Notes* ed. Crisp, vii. 29. [2] E. Suff. RO, 105/2/11. [3] T. Gage, *Hundred of Thingoe*, 135–8; Copinger, *Suff. Manors*, vii. 104–5; *CSP Dom.* 1673, pp. 350, 385. [4] *Little Saxham Par. Reg.* 209.

P.W.

CROKE, Richard (c.1625–83), of the Inner Temple and Marston, nr. Oxford.

OXFORD 1654, 1656, 1659, 1661

b. c.1625, 2nd but 1st surv. s. of Unton Croke[†] of Marston by Anne, da. and h. of Richard Hore of Marston. *educ.* Winchester 1636, aged 11; I. Temple, entered 1636, called 1646. *m.* by 1654, Elizabeth (*d.* 27 Mar. 1683), da. of Martin Wright, goldsmith, of Oxford, 5s. (3 *d.v.p.*) *suc.* fa. 1671; kntd. 16 Mar. 1681.[1]

Commr. for sale of Woodstock manor 1649; freeman, Oxford 1653, dep. recorder 1653–60, recorder June 1660–*d.*; j.p. Oxford 1655–Aug. 1660, 1665–*d.*, Abingdon 1655, Woodstock 1656–Aug. 1660, Oxon. Mar. 1660–*d.*; commr. for security, Oxon. 1655–6, assessment, Oxon. 1657, Jan. 1660, 1661–3, 1664–80, Oxford 1661–80, militia, Oxon. 1659, Oxford Mar. 1660; bencher, I. Temple 1662, reader 1670; commr. for recusants, Oxon. 1675.[2]

Serjeant-at-law 1675–*d.*

Croke's ancestors were established in Buckinghamshire in the early 15th century, and first represented the county in 1572. His grandfather was Speaker in 1601 and later a judge. His father sat for Wallingford in 1626, supported Parliament during the Civil War, and was made serjeant-at-law by Cromwell. His younger brother took a prominent part in the suppression of Penruddock's rising, but Croke himself, according to Anthony à Wood, 'always ran with the times'. He married into a prominent Oxford family and sat for the city in the three Protectorate Parliaments.[3]

Croke was defeated in the general election of 1660, but he composed a loyal address from the corporation at the Restoration, and regained his seat after a contest in 1661. On 11 May 1663 he reported a bill for the benefit of his cousins, the children of Bulstrode Whitelocke[†]; but he was not an active Member of the Cavalier Parliament. He probably served on less than 50 committees, though before 1671 his record can seldom be distinguished from that of Robert Croke*, his second cousin. Probably, however, he was appointed to the committees for preventing abuses in the courts of justice, the conventicles bill, and the prohibition of Irish cattle imports, and was listed by the Opposition as a court supporter. In the first of his seven recorded speeches, on 9 Feb. 1674, he urged caution over defining illegal exactions, since customary levies, for example in corporations, were recognized by common law. He favoured committing the bill, and was named to the committee. He was given the coif in 1675, though he supported the bill to extend habeas corpus. 'This bill', he said, 'may be done without prejudice to the King's evidence and prerogative, and with great safety to the subject.' He was among those ordered to prepare reasons for resisting the claim of the House of Lords to hear appeals involving a Member of the Lower House. He was included in the working lists among the lawyers to be influenced by the lord keeper. In the debate of 21 Mar. 1677 on the Newark election dispute, Croke advanced legal arguments in support of the King's right to enfranchise boroughs. 'A charter is a flower of the crown', he declared, 'and the King's undoubted right.' He conceded the inconvenience of the grant when Parliament was in session, but, in view of the precedents, 'who can dispute the King's right in doing it?' Nevertheless, he moved for a committee of inquiry. When John Hatcher*, the serving sheriff of Lincolnshire, petitioned against the return of Henry Noel* for Stamford, Croke declared:

> A writ of summons to choose Members of Parliament is an original thing, and not an iota can be altered without Act of Parliament. He hears it said that the corporation makes the return of the writ. No; they elect, but the sheriff makes the return, and it is against the law of nature for the same man to be both agent and patient. . . . If they might return themselves, most of the sheriffs of England would sit here. There is reason in it, and it is against a rule of law and a dangerous precedent for a sheriff to return himself against all ancient usage.

Croke was changed from 'worthy' to 'vile' on Shaftesbury's list. On 21 Dec. 1678, he moved unsuccessfully to omit the word 'traitorously' from the first article of Danby's impeachment.[4]

Croke did not stand again, though he received three 'castaway' votes at the second general election of 1679. 'A very loyal person', he opposed exclusion, and on 31 May 1681 the corporation thanked him for drafting the address approving of the dissolution of Parliament, for which he was knighted. He is described in his epitaph as a 'devoted son' of the Church of England, but Anthony à Wood declared that 'his religion was as venal as his tongue'. He died on 14 Sept. 1683 and was buried at Marston, the last of that branch to sit in Parliament.[5]

[1] *Vis. Oxon.* (Harl. Soc. v), 280–1; Bodl. mss, Wood F4, f. 124. [2] A. Croke, *Croke Fam.* ii. 514; *Oxford Council Acts* (Oxf. Hist. Soc. xcv), 201, 262; *Thurloe*, iii. 595. [3] Burke, *Commoners*, i. 355–7; Croke, 391, 511–515, 521–525; M. Toynbee and P. Young, *Strangers in Oxford*, 138; *Wood's Life and Times* (Oxf. Hist. Soc. xix), 196; *Oxford Council Acts* (Oxf. Hist. Soc. xcv), 255. [4] Grey, ii. 404; iii. 105; iv. 297–8, 315–16; vi. 385–6; *CJ*, ix. 341. [5] *Oxford Council Acts* (Oxf. Hist. Soc. n.s. ii), 119, 139; *Wood's Life and Times* (Oxf. Hist. Soc. xix), 196; *HMC Ormonde*, n.s. v. 618; *Par. Colls.* (Oxon. Rec. Soc. iv), 204.

L.N./G.J.

CROKE, Robert (c.1636–71), of Chequers, Ellesborough, Bucks.

WENDOVER 1661–30 July 1671

b. c.1636, 1st s. of Sir Robert Croke[†] (*d.*1681), clerk of the pipe, of Hampton Poyle, Oxon. by Susanna, da. and coh. of Sir Peter Van Lore, 1st Bt., of Tilehurst, Berks. *educ.* Queen's, Oxf. 1653; I. Temple 1655, called 1661. *unm.*[1]

Commr. for assessment, Bucks. 1661–9, loyal and indigent officers 1662.

Croke's branch of the family had a strong legal tradition. His grandfather, a younger son, acquired Chequers by marriage. His father was Member for Wendover in both Parliaments of 1640, but was disabled as a royalist commissioner of array, and compounded for £772. Elected for Wendover two-and-a-half miles from his home, in 1661, Croke was an inactive Member, with probably no more than 22 committees. In the opening session of the Cavalier Parliament he was named to the committees for the corporations bill and for considering ways of relieving loyalists. In July 1669 he was granted the reversion to his father's office, but he did not live to claim it. He died on 30 July 1671, aged 35, and was buried at Ellesborough. His father was the last of this branch of the family, after whom Chequers eventually came to John Thurbarne*.[2]

[1] Lipscomb, *Bucks.* ii. 189; A. Croke, *Croke Fam.* ii. 502.
[2] Keeler, *Long Parl.* 147–8; *Cal. Comm. Comp.* 1471; *CSP Dom.* 1668–9, p. 413; *Cal. Treas. Bks.* iii. 249; Lipscomb, ii. 189; *VCH Bucks.* ii. 336.

L.N./G.J.

CROMWELL (afterwards WILLIAMS), Henry (1625–73), of Bodsey House, Ramsey, Hunts.

HUNTINGDONSHIRE 1654, 1656, 1659, 1660, 1661–3 Aug. 1673

bap. 22 June 1625, 3rd but o. surv. s. of Henry Cromwell of Ramsey Abbey by 2nd w. Anne, da. of Sir Richard Dyer of Place House, Great Staughton, wid. of Sir Edward Carr, 1st Bt., of Sleaford, Lincs. *m.* his cos. Anne, da. and h. of Richard Cromwell of Upwood, Hunts., *s.p. suc.* fa. 1657.[1]

Commr. for assessment, Hunts. 1657, Aug. 1660–9, Huntingdon 1663–9, militia, Hunts. Mar. 1660; col. of militia ft. Hunts. Apr. 1660–?72, j.p. July 1660–d., dep. lt. Aug. 1660–d., commr. for loyal and indigent officers 1662, appeals, Bedford level 1668.[2]

Gent. of the privy chamber 1671–d.; capt. R. Ft. Gds. 1672–d.[3]

Cromwell was descended from Morgan Williams, who married the sister of Henry VIII's great minister. The founder of the family dropped his Welsh patronymic in favour of his uncle's surname, acquired extensive monastic lands in Huntingdonshire and represented the county in 1539. His descendants in the senior line were profuse and extravagant, and their interest was already declining before the Civil War. Cromwell's grandfather and father were both active Royalists, though their fines were remitted in consideration of their kinship to the future Protector. Notwithstanding this cle-

mency, he succeeded to a much diminished estate and manner of life. Though the son of a Cavalier officer he had demonstrated his good affection to Parliament by sitting for Huntingdonshire under the Protectorate, and, being thus within the qualifications imposed by the Long Parliament, he was re-elected in 1660, probably unopposed. He was not an active Member of the Convention, though he may, as 'Mr Williams', have helped to prepare the bill for the abolition of the court of wards. He obtained leave to go into the country on 8 May, but returned to be nominated to the committee on maimed soldiers. At the Restoration he obtained the King's consent to drop the name of Cromwell, and was named to the order of the Royal Oak, with an income probably over-estimated at £2,000 a year. On 7 July he made a speech on a question of privilege. On 11 Sept. he presented a petition on behalf of himself and his tenants, 'being two hundred families', against the fen drainage bill; a proviso was read to provide for the better safety of the country, but rejected by 99 to 84. When the bill was revived in the second session, Williams was appointed to the committee.[4]

Williams was re-elected to the Cavalier Parliament, in which he was a moderately active Member, serving on 102 committees, acting as teller in 17 divisions, and making six recorded speeches. He served on the committee for the corporations bill in 1661. Although presumably an Anglican, he acted as teller with one of the Boscawens on 16 Apr. 1662 for debating the amendments made by convocation in the Book of Common Prayer, and in 1663 he was in favour of an address to mitigate the observance of Lent. He supported the first turnpike bill, acting as teller in two divisions. He continued to oppose every bill brought forward for the drainage of the fens, and on 3 May 1664 leave was given to bring in a provisio for his especial benefit. He was reckoned a court dependant at this time, though it is not clear why. His name stands first among those authorized to bring in a highways bill on 26 Nov. As a member of the committee for the private bill of Sir Robert Carr*, he was given the delicate task of interviewing his unfortunate half-brother, the 2nd baronet. 'Surly Williams' apparently missed the Oxford session, but his activities in 1666 earned him from Andrew Marvell* the sobriquet of 'the accountants' bane'. He sat on the committees inquiring into the embezzlement of military stores and the hearth-tax returns, and on 18 Oct. seconded the proposal for raising money from office-holders by privy seal. He was one of the 11 Members appointed on 8 Jan. 1667 to propose reasons for a conference on the poll bill. He was teller for the country party on the Winchelsea election division, and, with Thomas Lee I*, against allowing counsel to Lord Mordaunt.[5]

Although Williams was named to the committees of inquiry into the miscarriages of the war and the sale of Dunkirk he took no part in the impeachment of Clarendon. On 22 Apr. 1668 he spoke in support of lowering the maximum rate of interest, and two days later he was teller with Jonathan Trelawny I* for a proviso to the conventicles bill authorizing distraint for unpaid fines. In 1669 Sir Thomas Osborne* noted him as one of the independent Members who usually voted for supply, but he was in favour of proceeding with the inquiry into the suppression of the case brought by (Sir) John Morton* against Henry Brouncker* in the King's bench, and on 17 Feb. 1670 he was actually teller against the supply bill. Meanwhile some of the chickens hatched by his obstinate resistance to the Bedford level project were coming home to roost. The commissioners, Williams complained, had marked out the boundaries of his manor of Ramsey in the newly-drained fenland very inequitably. Although he had been made a commissioner of appeals, nothing short of a private Act could right him. His bill was introduced on 4 Nov. 1670, but made slow progress; twice additional names had to be added to the committee, and when Giles Hungerford* reported on 5 Dec. it was ordered to be re-committed after prolonged debate. It did not pass the Lower House till 19 Dec., only to be rejected by the Lords on the first reading. Meanwhile Williams had confirmed his position as an Anglican stalwart by moving for the punishment of the prominent London dissenter Jekyll for reflecting on the lord mayor. He seconded the motion for the publication of the names of Members absent from their duties, although he had himself twice made default in attendance, in 1666 and 1668. On 10 Dec., probably with the best intentions, he threw the government timetable on supply into chaos by proposing a tax on new buildings. Williams's attitude to defaulters had not passed unnoticed, and when he applied for leave to go into the country on 7 Feb. 1671 it was refused without a division. Nevertheless he went, and was presented for absence from a call of the House; but the Commons, having enjoyed the joke, voted to excuse him by 185 to 86, Carr and Lionel Walden I* acting as tellers for the majority.[6]

The failure of his private bill had certainly not eased Williams's financial situation, and he was no doubt glad to evade his creditors by a post at Court. More bizarre was his transformation, at the age of 47, from a militia colonel to a regular captain, a commission in the Grenadiers being apparently obtained for him by his nephew Sir Robert Carr, although of course late vocations to the military life might be held to run in the family. He attended the first session of 1673, being named on 7 Mar. to the committee of elections and privileges and to that for relieving Protestant dissenters. According to tradition he died of a stroke when his candidate was defeated at a by-election in the same year. If so (and the details are muddled and unconvincing), he must have lingered for some time, for the only possible election, when (Sir) Nicholas Pedley* was returned for the county, had been held on 15 Feb. and Williams did not die till 3 Aug. His heirs were his sisters, who sold Ramsey Abbey to Silius Titus*. Williams's career as a Member of Parliament is chiefly of interest in illustrating by its sheer eccentricity the difficulty of welding the loyalist Anglican backwoods squires into a stable government majority.[7]

[1] M. Noble, *Mems. Cromwell Fam.* i. 67–72. [2] *Parl. Intell.* 30 Apr. 1660. [3] Carlisle, *Privy Chamber*, 188; *CSP Dom.* 1671–2, p. 249; 1673, p. 483. [4] *VCH Hunts.* ii. 193–4; *Cal. Comm. Comp.* 978–9; *Merc. Pub.* 19 July 1660; Bowman diary, f. 59v. [5] *CJ*, viii. 427, 437, 472, 476, 505, 589, 601, 673, 686; *Marvell* ed. Margoliouth, i. 147; *Milward*, 27. [6] *Milward*, 270; *CJ*, ix. 106, 178, 202; *LJ*, xii. 397; Grey, i. 299; *Dering*, 22, 27. [7] *CSP Dom.* 1671–2, p. 233; PRO 30/53/7, f. 98; Noble, 70.

M.W.H./E.R.E.

CROSLAND, Sir Jordan (1618–70), of Newby, nr. Ripon, Yorks.

SCARBOROUGH 1661–Aug. 1670

bap. 31 Dec. 1618, 1st s. of John Crosland of Canon Garth, Helmsley by Jane, da. of Henry Atkinson of Little Cattall. *m.* by 1651, Bridget, da. of John Fleming of Rydal, Westmld., and coh. to her bro. William, 4s. 6da. *suc.* fa. 1635; kntd. 14 July 1642.[1]

Col. of horse (royalist) 1642–6; gov. Helmsley Castle 1644; constable, Scarborough Castle July 1660–*d.*[2]

Commr. for assessment, Yorks. (N. Riding) Aug. 1660–9, (W. Riding) 1661–9; j.p. (N. and W. Ridings) July 1660–*d.*, York 1663, (E. Riding) 1666–*d.*; dep. lt. (W. Riding) c. Aug. 1660–*d.*, (N. Riding) 1666–*d.*; lt. vol. horse (W. Riding) 1661–at least 1663; col. of militia ft. (N. Riding) 1661–*d.*; commr. for corporations, Yorks. 1662–3, loyal and indigent officers 1662; sub-commr. for prizes, Hull 1665–7.[3]

Crosland's ancestors seem to have been of little account before the 16th century, and he himself inherited only a lease of Helmsley rectory, valued at £100 p.a. Knighted on the eve of the Civil War, he held the neighbouring castle, the property of the Duke of Buckingham, for the King until forced to surrender to Fairfax, and then joined the garrison of Worcester. He was again in arms in the second Civil War, but compounded at one-sixth on 20 Apr. 1649. Shortly afterwards he married a Roman

Catholic heiress who brought him property in Lancashire, and in 1653 he was returned as a Papist by the county committee, though he denied the charge. He involved himself in plans for a Cavalier rising in the north in 1655, and was imprisoned at Hull in the spring of 1658.[4]

In the Convention Christopher Clapham* introduced a proviso to the indemnity bill requiring Sir Wilfred Lawson* to make reparations to Lady Crosland for the plunder of Rydal, but it was rejected. Crosland himself, 'a fine gentleman and a good soldier', was appointed constable of Scarborough and returned for the borough at the general election of 1661. A moderately active Member of the Cavalier Parliament, he was appointed to 37 committees, including the committee of elections and privileges in seven sessions. None of them was of major political significance, but in the first session he was named to those to consider the shortfall in revenue (18 June) and the militia bill (3 Dec.). When the latter measure was returned from the Lords he was among those to whom the proviso for the assessment of peers was referred. He took no part in legislation against Protestant nonconformists, but on 17 Mar. 1663 he was appointed to the committee to hinder the growth of Popery, although soon afterwards he was maintaining a priest, presumably for the use of his wife and children. He was active as a militia officer in the suppression of the Derwentdale Plot, and was rewarded with the forfeited estate of one of the conspirators, a leasehold worth £300 p.a., though he had to pay £2,000 compensation to Sir Thomas Osborne*, the landlord. He was twice appointed to committees concerned with the plight of the loyal and indigent officers, and listed as a court dependant in 1664, though he was probably a client of Buckingham, under whom he served in the West Riding volunteers. In partnership with Sir Thomas Gower* he tendered unsuccessfully for the Yorkshire excise farm in 1665, but he served as sub-commissioner for prizes in the second Dutch war at a salary of £400 p.a. In this capacity he was involved in an international incident over the detention of a Swedish ship, and taken into custody, but he was released after Lords Arlington and Berkeley had pacified the irate resident. In May 1666 he received as the King's gift a prize ship called the *Black Bear*. His last important committee was to receive information about the insolence of Popish priests and Jesuits on 20 Oct. 1666, but Osborne listed him as a court dependant in 1669 and he continued to be named to the elections committee. He died on 20 Aug. 1670 and was buried in Ripon Minster, the only member of his family to sit in Parliament. His younger sons all became priests and his grandson was registered as a Catholic non-juror in 1715.[5]

[1] Clay, *Dugdale's Vis. Yorks.* i. 184–5. [2] *List of Officers Claiming* (1663), 34; *Townshend's Diary* (Worcs. Rec. Soc.), 144; *Fairfax Corresp.* iii. 120–1; *Merc. Pub.* 12 July 1660. [3] *Reresby Mems.* 40, 43; *CSP Dom.* 1663–4, p. 393; 1666–7, p. 124; H. B. M'Call, *Fam. Wandesford*, 291; *HMC 8th Rep.* pt. 1 (1881), 275; Nat. Maritime Mus. Southwell mss 17/15. [4] *Royalist Comp. Pprs.* (Yorks. Arch. Soc. rec. ser. xviii), 198; *Cal. Comm. Comp.* 1696; D. Underdown, *Royalist Conspiracy*, 141, 221, 276. [5] *CJ*, viii. 84; Bowman diary, f. 62 v; *Reresby Mems.* 43, 48–49; *CSP Dom.* 1660–1, p. 327; 1664–5, pp. 4, 208; 1665–6, pp. 396, 443; 1670, p. 694; PC 2/58/303, 312, 320; H. Aveling, *Northern Catholics*, 343; Browning, *Danby*, i. 29; ii. 30.

P.A.B./P.W.

CROUCH, Thomas (1607–79), of Trinity Hall, Cambridge.

CAMBRIDGE UNIVERSITY 1660, 1661

bap. 18 Oct. 1607, 2nd s. of Thomas Crouch (*d.*1616) of Corneybury, Wyddial, Herts., fellow of King's 1585–98, by Sarah, da. of Henry Galliard, mercer, of Norwich, Norf. *educ.* Eton 1622–6; King's, Camb. 1626, BA 1630, MA 1633. *unm.*[1]

Fellow of King's 1629–50; proctor, Camb. Univ. 1643, 1649–50; commr. for assessment, Camb. Univ. and Cambridge Aug. 1660–3, 1664–74, 1677–9, loyal and indigent officers, Cambs. 1662, complaints, Bedford level 1663, recusants, Cambs. 1675.

Crouch's grandfather, a London Clothworker, bought the manor of Corneybury in 1583. Though only minor gentry, they achieved two notable marriages into the Montagu family. Although Crouch inherited an inn at Buntingford and the leases of two local farms, he became a fellow of King's, like his father before him. At the outbreak of the Civil War he was said to have 'maligned Parliament' and helped to convey the college plate to the King, but he was not ejected until 1650, when he was received as a fellow commoner at Trinity Hall. He was returned at the general election of 1660 as a Royalist and a staunch Anglican. As befitted a university representative he was much concerned with ecclesiastical matters. A moderately active Member of the Convention, he was named to 21 committees, including that on the indemnity bill, and made six recorded speeches. He 'spoke excellently' on 23 June against the petition from the intruded dons at Oxford, and was named to the committee to consider it. On 4 July he was among those appointed to prepare for a conference on three orders issued by the Lords. Two days later he spoke in favour of consulting with divines over the religious settlement, and in grand committee he spoke against the bill drafted by the Presbyterian Thomas Bampfield*. He favoured committing the bill for settling ecclesiastical livings and was named to the committee. He spoke against the proposal to exclude 'scandalous' or 'ignorant' ministers, asking who was to be the judge of scandal, and attacked the Presbyterian practice of restricted admission to the sacrament, which should be open to 'all but such as were very notorious and not [merely] suspected'. He took a prominent part in the college leases bill, helping to transpose the wording at one point and to insert a clause confirming fellows and scholars. On 1 Sept. he carried up the bill to provide a maintenance for the vicar of Royston. After the recess he supported the committal of the bill to endow vicarages out of impropriate rectories and was named to the committee. He was added on 17 Nov. to the committee to bring in the bill for modified episcopacy. He chaired the committee to confirm the grant of a Suffolk advowson to Emmanuel College, and carried up the bill. He also took the chair for a Bedfordshire estate bill. He was appointed to the committee to report on bills depending on the Lords, of which the most important was the college leases bill. On 20 Dec. he supported the exemption of the universities from the nationalization of postal services.[2]

Despite a recommendation from his kinsman, the Earl of Manchester, who became chancellor of the university at the Restoration, Crouch never regained his fellowship at King's. Nevertheless he was re-elected unopposed in 1661, and listed as a moderate by Lord Wharton. He must have already made his mark as an efficient chairman in the Convention, for his record in the Cavalier Parliament was prodigious. Of his 742 committees, he took the chair in 47, apparently specializing in estate bills, though he had no formal legal training. In public affairs he remained an indefatigable defender of his university and his Church. He was also active in the routine business of the House, such as examining the Journals and reporting on bills depending. He acted eight times as teller and carried 15 bills to the Lords; but he was less prominent in debate: only 24 of his speeches (apart from reports) were recorded. In the opening session he was appointed to the committees for the uniformity bill and the bill of pains and penalites. He took the chair for the bill to prevent mischiefs from Quakers and carried it up on 19 July. He also steered through committee the bill under which the father of James Scudamore* was enabled to endow several churches. As one of those entrusted with perfecting the bill for regulating printing, he successfully defended the university press against the London printers. After Christmas he chaired the bills to confirm three Acts of the Convention and to increase the stipends of the urban clergy. He was among those ordered to expedite a report on measures for the relief of

loyalists. On 10 Apr. 1662 he carried up a bill to give effect to the charitable bequests of Sir Robert Hitcham[†], a great benefactor of Pembroke College. He helped to check the text of the Prayer Book, to draft a new paragraph for the uniformity bill, and to prepare reasons for a conference on it. Before Parliament was prorogued he was able to report that he had extracted the records of the triers and ejectors from Philip Nye, and helped to manage a conference on the printers' bill. When the House met again in 1663, he was among those appointed to bring in the urban clergy bill again, and to report on defects in the Act of Uniformity. He took the chair for a leaseholds bill and for the bill to establish turnpikes on the Cambridge road. He helped to inquire into the conduct of Sir Richard Temple* and to manage a conference on the Duke of York's revenue. Although he was appointed to the committees to prevent the growth of Popery and meetings of sectaries, on 18 July he carried up a bill to grant relief from the Act of Uniformity to those who had been prevented by circumstances from subscribing to it, and he was sent to invite the witty Presbyterian minister, Vincent Alsop, to preach to the House. He was listed as a court dependant in 1664, when his most important committee was to manage a conference on Falmouth church. He reported another Herefordshire highways bill on 1 Feb. 1665 and took the chair for the bill to unite city churches in both sessions of 1665. At Oxford he helped to consider the five mile bill and acted as teller against the bill to encourage the growth of hemp and flax. He invited Dr Perrinchief to preach to the House on 9 Nov., and was afterwards ordered to thank him. An authority on relations between town and gown in Cambridge, he was teller on 24 Nov. 1666 for giving precedence to the vice-chancellor over the mayor in the plague bill. In another division three days later, he favoured deleting the description of Irish cattle imports as a nuisance. On 10 Dec. 1666 he was sent to thank the rector of St. Margaret's, one of the best and ablest of the conformists, for his sermon. He reported on 22 Jan. 1667 in favour of a petition from certain merchants who had imported prohibited French wines.[3]

Crouch's work in the session which followed the fall of Clarendon was particularly important. Among his major committees were those to draw up the address of thanks for the lord chancellor's dismissal, to inquire into the miscarriages of the second Dutch war and the sale of Dunkirk, and to consider the charges against Lord Mordaunt. He showed particular concern over the hearth-tax, which had aroused great resentment in both universities. After he had reported on abuses in its collection on 7 Dec. 1667, his committee was ordered to bring in a bill to reform them. When Crouch reported the bill on 27 Mar. he had to fend off a motion for recommittal; but he was able to carry it up four days later. He opposed the enfranchisement of Durham, saying that the Midlands were over-rated because of their under-representation in Par-liament. He also acted as chairman and teller for extending the Conventicles Act, and was appointed to the committee on the bill to prevent the refusal of habeas corpus. With Sir Charles Wheler*, the other Member for the university, he was teller on 5 May for confirming the allotments made for the rebuilding of Thames Street after the fire of London; and in the following year he took the chair for the bill to enable a house to be built for the dean of St. Paul's. He was also among those ordered to consider a petition from Magdalene College, but the committee never reported. His name was on both lists of the court party at this time among those to be engaged by the Duke of York. He feared that the bill for the divorce of Lord Roos (John Man-ners*) might be against divine law, and suggested consulting Convocation. He was given special re-sponsibility on 7 Apr. 1670 for investigating a letter of protection given by Sir John Pretyman*, and on the following day reported that 'the House had been ill dealt with'. He was anxious to ensure that jurors were not fined for non-attendance, and after the summer recess he helped to prepare reasons for a conference on regulating juries. In a debate on aug-menting vicarages on 22 Nov. he declared:

> All the revenues of Trinity College in Cambridge are impropriations. Henry VIII took away all their revenue in lands, leaving them but three manors. Henry VIII, called them 'the Trinity in Unity'. Would have laymen used as you will use churchmen and begin when you please.

An additional bill for regulating hearth-tax was ordered on 2 Mar. 1671, and Crouch was the first Member appointed to bring it in; but even after receiving orders to expedite the matter 12 days later he failed to galvanize the committee into activity. He again chaired a committee for renewing the Conventicles Act, reporting three times, and speak-ing on 30 Mar. 1671 in support of the clause to indemnify those whose zeal against dissent had led them to exceed their powers:

> You have made a law to indemnify persons for treasons and murders and robberies, etc. This is for indemnify-ing persons for executing the laws. Suits are com-menced upon account of this law; you are tied in justice to do it.

He carried up the bill on 5 Apr., and later in the month returned to the Lords the important in-testacy bill (the Statute of Distribution) which he had chaired in committee, together with a bill for the maintenance of the clergy in the London parishes affected by the Great Fire.[4]

In the debate on the Declaration of Indulgence, Crouch moved on 8 Feb. 1673 to proceed with the consideration of the King's speech. On 10 Feb. he was appointed to the committee to prepare an address against the Declaration, and on the report stage opposed any reference to Protestant unity. As a staunch Anglican he was not entirely happy over the concessionary bill to ease Protestant dissenters, declaring on 19 Feb.

> Ease implies a burden of some weight. Would any phy-sician advise with a patient without knowing what he ails? Would know what it is would satisfy these people before we proceed any farther.

He was particularly concerned over where dis-senters should be allowed to meet, protesting that they were certainly not wanted at Cambridge, where they would 'be disturbed by the youths there with disputing'. Shortly afterwards he was ap-pointed to the committee to draw up an address for preventing the growth of Popery, and was among those named to manage a conference on the test bill. On 28 Jan. 1674 he spoke against reading the peti-tion of Bernard Howard, brother of the Duke of Norfolk, declaring:

> This petition is to dispense with a Papist contrary to the law. Can you repeal a law upon a particular man's ac-count by petition?

He was named to the committee to prepare a gen-eral test bill, and attained the summit of his political career as chairman of the committee appointed to consider the charges against Arlington. On 17 Feb. he reported that 'some difficulties had occurred' and nothing further was done. As chairman of the com-mittee on bills depending when Parliament met again, he recommended proceeding with the bill for the repair of churches and the recovery of small tithes. In both sessions of 1675 he was appointed to the committees for recalling British subjects from the French service, appropriating the customs to the use of the navy and hindering Papists from sitting in Parliament. He helped to draw up reasons for a conference on the Four Lawyers on 3 June. In the autumn session he was one of the five Mem-bers sent to ask Col. Thomas Howard if he were responsible for publishing a violent attack on Wil-liam Cavendish*, Lord Cavendish, and he appears, like Sir Thomas Hatton*, to have voted against the Danby administration. Although earmarked for special attention by Sir Richard Wiseman* during the long recess which followed, he was included among the government speakers, and he appears on the working lists as under the influence of Peter Gunning, the Arminian bishop of Ely. A hostile account describes him as 'the priests' mad jade who rides without fear or wit, preserved by the Court into whose interest he long since has matriculated'. In the 1677 session Crouch opposed the bill to abolish payment of wages to Members, though to reassure his constituents he signed on 3 Mar. a formal release of all claims before Sir Harbottle Grimston*. In the House he stated that:

He never received wages for the place he serves for, and never will. But the bill is not fit to pass. Will you take away any man's land? Why will you take away his wages?

He was appointed to the committees for preserving the liberty of the subject, preventing the growth of Popery, and ensuring a Protestant education for the royal children, and took the chair for the bill to enable small vicarages to be augmented. He carried this bill to the Lords, together with those to prevent simony and to facilitate the taking of affidavits in the country. Shaftesbury, who had originally marked Crouch 'doubly vile', saw reason later to halve this assessment, and in fact he probably went over to the Opposition in 1678, for his name appears in neither list of the court party. On 30 Apr. he reported a bill to increase the endowments of St. Asaph's Cathedral, and was appointed to the committee to summarize foreign commitments. In the closing session he was named to the committees to inquire into the Popish Plot and to disable Papists from sitting in Parliament. He offered himself for re-election, but apparently withdrew before the poll. He was buried in King's College Chapel on 30 Aug. 1679, the only member of his family to sit in Parliament. He bequeathed his library to the college.[5]

[1] Clutterbuck, *Herts.* iii. 430; *Mdx. Par. Reg.* ix. 17; *HMC 1st Rep.* 67. [2] *VCH Herts.* iv. 116–17; PCC 127 King; *Cal. Comm. Adv. Money*, 1029–30; L. J. Saltmarsh, *King's Coll.* 57; Bowman diary, ff. 25, 56 v, 64 v, 117 v; *CJ*, viii. 74, 204; *Old Parl. Hist.* xxiii. 6, 60. [3] Saltmarsh, 58; *CJ*, viii. 299, 303, 313, 356, 396, 428, 456, 472, 526, 527, 620; *Fanshawe Mems.* 589; *CSP Dom.* 1667–8, p.5. [4] *CJ*, ix. 87, 90, 102, 208, 223, 227, 230, 233; Grey, i. 120, 231, 251, 301, 413. [5] Grey, ii. 13, 28, 39, 70, 358; iv. 238; *CJ*, ix. 263, 317, 413, 472; Harl. 7020, f.33v; Old Schools Cambridge, Cambridge Univ. Registry 50/22; Clutterbuck, iii. 430; Blomefield, *Cambridge*, 135; PCC 127 King.

M.W.H./E.R.E./G.J.

CRUMPE, Sir Richard (c.1628–1700), of Ballan Street, Bristol.

BRISTOL   1685

b. c.1628, s. of Robert Crumpe, yeoman, of Rodley, Westbury-on-Severn, Glos. *m.* Margaret, da. and coh. of William Crabbe, merchant, of Bristol, 1s. 2da. Kntd. 18 Oct. 1681.[1]

Freeman, Bristol 1653, common councilman 1661–75, sheriff 1665–6, alderman 1675–*d.*, mayor 1677–8; commr. for assessment, Bristol 1673–80, 1689–90, dep. lt. 1685–Feb. 1688, member of merchant venturers 1692, warden 1694–5.[2]

Crumpe was described as a gentleman's son when he was apprenticed to a Bristol soap-boiler in 1646. He was a founder member of the royalist Gloucestershire Society during the Interregnum, and was knighted as a Tory in 1681. By this time he had become the leading figure in the West Indies trade. One of the 'good' aldermen, in the eyes of a court supporter in 1683, he supported the surrender of the Bristol charter, and was reappointed. An anonymous letter charged him with defrauding the customs in 1684, but the commissioners were apparently satisfied with his explanation. He was returned unopposed to James II's Parliament, in which he was appointed only to the committee to revive the Leather Export Act. He received £17 13s. 4d. in parliamentary wages from the corporation, who made it clear to him that they expected a 'sedulous care' in their concerns, which he duly exercised by persuading Thomas Bruce*, Lord Bruce that excessive taxation on the West Indian plantations would be 'of fatal consequence'. He failed, however, to secure the reimbursement of the £470 spent by the city during Monmouth's rebellion. He gave negative replies on the repeal of the Test Act and Penal Laws, and was removed from the lieutenancy. However, he was reported 'right' by the King's electoral agents and recommended as an alternative court candidate in 1688. He died on 14 Jan. 1700, and was buried at St. Thomas's, the only member of his family to sit in Parliament.[3]

[1] J. Smith, *Men and Armour for Glos.* 73; Bristol RO, apprenticeship bk. 1640–58, f. 99; *Le Neve's Knights* (Harl. Soc. viii), 358; PCC 20 Noel. [2] Bristol RO, burgess bk. 1651–62, f. 10 v; A. B. Beaven, *Bristol Lists*, 186, 201, 224, 284; *Merchant Venturers* (Bristol Rec. Soc. xvii), 33. [3] Bristol RO, Jeffries Coll. 2, p. 101; SP29/422/127, 218; *Ailesbury Mems.* 106; *Cal. Treas. Bks.* vii. 997, 1213; J. Evans, *Hist. Bristol*, 232; J. Latimer, *Bristol in the 17th Century*, 427; T. Garrard, *Edward Colston the Philanthropist* (1852), 371.

J.P.F.

CULLEN, Abraham (c.1624–68), of East Sheen, Surr.

EVESHAM   1661–28 Aug. 1668

b. c.1624, 1st s. of Abraham Cullen, merchant, of Great St. Helens, London by 1st w. Abigail, da. of Martin Moonens, hosier, of Norwich, Norf. *m.* 10 Dec. 1650 (aged 26), Abigail, da. of John Rushout, Fishmonger, of London and Marylords, Essex, 4s. (1 *d.v.p.*) 6da. *suc.* fa. 1658; *cr.* Bt. 17 June 1661.[1]

Capt. of militia ft. Surr. Apr. 1660, j.p. July 1660–*d.*; commr. for assessment, London and Surr. 1661–*d.*, Evesham 1663–4.[2]

Both Cullen and his wife, a sister of Sir James Rushout*, were of purely Flemish extraction. His grandfather Richard Van Cuelen, a religious refugee from Breda, became a hosier in Norwich, dying at Wandsworth in 1644. His father took out a patent with another Fleming in 1626 for the manufacture of stone pots, jugs and bottles at Lambeth. When it lapsed in 1641 he was still not reckoned more than moderately well off. None of the family seems to have taken any part in politics during the Civil War and Interregnum, but its prosperity dated from this period. The father bought several valuable City freeholds, while the son began to acquire land in several counties, moving out to East Sheen on his father's death, though he was still described as a Londoner when returned for Evesham in 1661, presumably on the Rushout interest. An inactive Member of the Cavalier Parliament, he was appointed to only 22 committees, most of them of commercial or financial interest. He was among the Members appointed to inspect the accounts of the disbandment commissioners. In 1664 he served on the committee for the Wey navigation bill promoted by his colleague William Sandys. His name stands first on the committee to bring in a bill for the preservation of prize goods on 13 Oct. 1665, which suggests opposition sympathies. He was appointed to the committee to inspect the accounts of navy, ordnance and stores on 26 Sept. 1666, but he took no part in the attack on Clarendon. His only recorded speech occurred in the grand committee on supply on 6 Mar. 1668, when he proposed a tax on coaches, but found no seconder. He died intestate on 28 Aug. and was buried at Mortlake. His personal and real estate was inventoried at over £20,000. His youngest son and eventual successor, Sir Rushout Cullen, sold the Sheen estate about 1679 and moved to Cambridgeshire, which he represented as a Whig from 1697 to 1710.[3]

[1] *Vis. Surr.* (Harl. Soc. lx), 34; *Walloons at Norwich* (Huguenot Soc. i), pt. ii. 191; PCC 526 Wootton; *Mortlake Par. Reg.* 25–29. [2] *Parl. Intell.* 23 Apr. 1660. [3] *Wandsworth Par. Reg.* 314; *CSP Dom.* 1625–6, p. 575; 1638–9, p. 620; *VCH Surr.* ii. 283; iv. 71; *Misc. Gen. et Her.* (ser. 2), ii. 110; Grey i. 107; Worcs. RO, Rushout mss.

E.R./J.P.F.

CULLIFORD, Robert (1617–98), of Encombe, Dorset.

WAREHAM　1660, 16 May 1661

b. 22 Feb. 1617, o. (posth.) s. of Robert Culliford of Encombe by Margaret, da. of Robert Hyde of West Hatch, Wilts. m. (1) 14 May 1638, Elizabeth, da. of Sir Edward Lawrence† of Creech Grange, Steeple, Dorset, 6s. (1 *d.v.p*) 5da; (2) bef. 10 Oct. 1676, Jane, da. and h. of John Williams of Tyneham, Dorset, wid. of Sir Robert Lawrence of Creech Grange, *s.p. suc.* fa. at birth.[1]

J.p. Dorset July 1660–June 1688, Nov. 1688–*d.*, Poole 1665; commr. for assessment, Dorset Aug. 1660–3, 1666–80, 1689–90; dep. lt. I. of Purbeck 1661–?76; freeman, Lyme Regis 1662; commr. for corporations, Dorset 1662–3, recusants 1675.[2]

Culliford was the sixth of his name to own Encombe, a depopulated tithing in the Isle of Purbeck. The estate was valued at £400 p.a. by the sequestrators during the Civil War, but the farmstock was worth £800. His grandmother, who was still enjoying her jointure in 1643, contributed £100 to Parliament; but his step-father, Thomas Veale, became a royalist colonel and Culliford probably shared his sympathies. His activity, however, was directed solely at the preservation of his property, particularly his cattle, and in this cause he assisted the royalist capture of Wareham in 1644 and raised a force of 250 men from his neighbours in 1646 to blockade the Cavalier garrison of Corfe Castle. This service exempted him from compounding for his delinquency and from the decimation tax in 1656. But his real sentiments are clear from his eager acceptance of a post at the exiled Court 'as attendant to the young gallant there' for one of his sons.[3]

Culliford was returned for Wareham at the general election of 1660, though his candidature must have been dubious under the Long Parliament ordinance against Cavaliers. A moderately active Member of the Convention, he made no recorded speeches, but was named to 16 committees, of which the most important were for the navigation bill and the bills to settle ministers in their livings and to reduce interest to 6 per cent. He also helped to consider bills for compensation to two great Dorset landowners, the Marquess of Winchester and the Earl of Bristol. He was given leave on 30 Aug., and there is no evidence that he returned to Westminster for the second session.

Although Culliford could add to his personal popularity in the neighbourhood his kinship through his mother's family with Lord Chancellor Clarendon, a connexion that was not forgotten in the next generation, he was involved in a double return at the general election of 1661 with his brother-in-law Robert Lawrence, who had at one time commanded the royalist garrison of Corfe Castle. There may have been a personal flavour about the contest, for he was later to marry Lawrence's widow. Although the House seated him on the merits of the return as early as 16 May, and their decision was confirmed on the merits of the election on 15 June, he had been granted leave on the previous day, and was not appointed to his first committee in the Cavalier Parliament till 26 Nov. Thereafter he was moderately active, with 185 committees. In the adjourned first session these included those for the bills to prevent customs frauds, to restrain exports of leather and rawhide, and to regulate abuses in the packing and weighing of butter, and for the additional corporations bill. In March 1663 he was among those ordered to consider a petition from the loyal and indigent officers, and bills were referred to him to prevent the growth of Popery and to cancel several judgments and securities obtained by practice against his colleague George Pitt*, whose grandfather had been one of his guardians. Later in the session he was one of the Members called on to devise remedies for meetings of sectaries and to inspect the Corporations Act. Legislation with which he was concerned included the staple bill, and the bills to regulate the sale of offices and titles and to prevent butchers from selling live fat cattle. He was an active and successful recruiting officer for the navy during the second Dutch war, and attended the Oxford session, in which he was appointed to the committee for the five mile bill.[4]

Culliford's activity naturally diminished after his kinsman's fall, though with five sons to place in the customs service his loyalty to the Government of the day was not easily undermined. He was named to the committees to consider an additional bill against Irish cattle and to inquire into customs fees, and his name appears on both lists of the court party in 1669–71 as one of the Members to be engaged by Clarendon's son-in-law, the Duke of York. Nevertheless he was appointed to the committee that produced the test bill in 1673. In the following year he was named to the inquiry into the state of Ireland, and he was also among those entrusted with the bill to reform the pressing of seamen. His name was included in the working lists among those Members to be influenced by Edward Seymour* through his son, presumably William Culliford[†]. But the position of his name on Wiseman's list suggests that he was in opposition under Danby, and Shaftesbury marked him 'worthy' in 1677, when he was appointed to the committee on the bill for the recall of British subjects from the French service. His chief interests seem to have been ecclesiastical legislation and local estate bills, and his last committee was on a bill to enable the executors of (Sir) Ralph Bankes* to sell land for payment of debts (4 Mar. 1678). Nevertheless he was in London in September, when his wife sent him an account of the rumoured French landing in Purbeck that had greatly increased the Popish Plot hysteria.[5]

It is unlikely that Culliford stood again. His answers to the questions on the repeal of the Test Act and Penal Laws were negative, and he was removed from the commission of the peace. But during the Revolution he saved his Roman Catholic neighbours at Lulworth Castle from a threatening mob: 'God has been pleased to raise up a friend of almost an enemy', was how one of them described the incident. He was buried at Corfe Castle on 10 Feb. 1698. His son William sat for Corfe from 1690 to 1699.[6]

[1] Wards 5/11/1946; Hutchins, *Dorset*, i. 516; Add. 29976, f. 5; PCC 67 Lort. [2] Hutchins, i. 22; Lyme Regis mss B6/11, f. 24. [3] *Cal. Comm. Adv. Money*, 986; Add. 8845, pp. 11, 12; SP23/152/665–9; C. H. Mayo, *Dorset Standing Committee*, 16; *CSP Dom.* 1645–7, p. 348; 1656–7, p. 151; Bodl. Rawl. A41, f. 210. [4] *CJ*, viii. 251, 271; *Ellis Corresp.* i. 227; Shaftesbury (Wimborne St. Giles) mss, Culliford to Ashley, 10 Apr. 1665. [5] *Cal. Treas. Bks.* i. 524, 726; ii. 244; vi. 711; vii. 1324; x. 945; Add. 28053, f. 126. [6] Dorset RO, D10/C3/1, Joseph Tomes to Clara Weld, 25 Dec. 1688; Soc. of Genealogists, Corfe Castle par. reg.

M.W.H./J.P.F.

CURWEN, Sir Patricius, 1st Bt. (c.1602–64), of Workington, Cumb.

CUMBERLAND 1625, 1626, 1628, 1640 (Apr.), 1640 (Nov.)–15 Mar. 1643, 1661–15 Dec. 1664

b. c.1602, 1st s. of Sir Henry Curwen[†] of Workington by 1st w. Catherine, da. of Sir John Dalston of Dalston, and coh. to her gdfa. Thomas Tyrell of Birdbrook, Essex. *educ.* Queens', Camb. matric. 18 Apr. 1620, aged 18. *m.* 28 Feb. 1620, Isabella (*d.* Jan. 1667), da. and coh. of Sir George Selby[†] of Whitehouse, co. Dur., 1s. *d.v.p. suc.* fa. 1623; *cr.* Bt. 12 Mar. 1627.[1]

J.p. Cumb. 1625–44, July 1660–*d.*, dep. lt. by 1627–42, c. Aug. 1660–*d.*; commr. for oyer and terminer 1630, Northern circuit July 1660; piracy Cumb. 1631, sheriff 1636–7, commr. for assessment 1640, Aug. 1660–*d.*, array 1642; lt. honour of Cockermouth by Mar. 1660–*d.*; lt.-col. of militia ft. Cumb. Oct. 1660–*d.*, commr. for loyal and indigent officers 1662.[2]

Col. of ft. (royalist) 1642–4.[3]

Curwen's ancestors had held Workington since the 12th century, and first represented Cumberland in the reign of Edward III. Curwen served as knight of the shire in all the Parliaments of Charles I, voting against the attainder of Strafford before being disabled as a Royalist. 'A pious and peaceful man', according to the Cavaliers' eulogist, he was 'master of a great wit and a vigorous discourse, outdoing most in action', and of a 'clear and heroic mind'. By his own account he served reluctantly and obstructively both on the local commission of array and in the Oxford Parliament. He was the first in the county to submit and take the Covenant, whereupon he was plundered by a party of Cavalier horse. He valued his estate at only £620 p.a., including his profits from coal mines, the manufacture of salt, and a salmon fishery. His fine was fixed at £2,000 in 1645, but he was in arms again in the second Civil War, and was sentenced to pay a further £1,152 6s.8d. in 1649. After this he appears to have held aloof from royalist conspiracy.[4]

Under the last ordinance of the Long Parliament Curwen was ineligible at the general election of 1660, nor could he appear openly to support the return of Lord Broghill (Roger Boyle*) for Cockermouth. It was considered, moreover, that he was 'basely abused' in the salt excise. He regained his seat in 1661 against slight opposition, and was listed by Lord Wharton among the moderates in the Cavalier Parliament. A patron of Joseph Williamson* and his brother, he was probably a country Cavalier. But he was not an active Member, taking no part in the Clarendon Code and being named only to the committees for the highways bill (13 June 1661), the preservation of freshwater fish (9 Apr. 1663), and three estate bills. He applied for a farm of the local customs, chiefly in order to divert Irish cattle imports from the Lowthers' port at Whitehaven to Workington. He behaved 'very handsomely' in rounding up the local Quakers after the Derwentdale plot, and applied for some long promised compensation for his losses, computed at £23,000. But neither the Lilburne lands in Abbey Hulme nor the farm of the Cumberland hearth-tax appear to have come his way before his death on 15 Dec. 1664. He was buried at Workington on 12 Apr. 1665, at the cost of £680. One of the pallbearers, Sir Philip Musgrave*, described him as a loss to the county, where he had 'a long time lived with much reputation among them and loved just ways'. In his will Curwen declared:

> I utterly abhor and renounce all idolatry and superstition, all heresy and schism, and whatever is contrary to sound religion and the word of God, professing myself with my whole heart to believe all the articles of the Christian faith and the whole doctrine of the Protestant religion taught and maintained in the Church of England.

His heir was his brother Thomas, an equally firm Anglican, who had been nominated for the order of the Royal Oak with an estate, presumably in expectation, of £1,000 p.a. But his step-mother, the widow of one of the Gunpowder plotters, and his half-brother Eldred, who inherited Workington in 1672, were recusants, and the next member of the family to enter Parliament was his cousin Eldred of the Stella Park branch, who sat for Cockermouth from 1738 to 1741.[5]

[1] J. F. Curwen, *House of Curwen*, 142–51; *Vis. Cumb.* (Harl. Soc. vii), 5; *Vis. Essex* (Harl. Soc. xiv), 661. [2] Keeler, *Long Parl.* 149; *Foedera*, viii. pt. 2, p. 144; *CSP Dom.* 1660–1, p. 313; Cumb.

RO, D/Lec. 107. [3] *Cal. Comm. Comp.* 1240; *List of Officers Claiming* (1663), 35. [4] Curwen, 7, 231; Keeler, 148–9; SP23/179/582–602; *HMC Portland*, i. 186. [5] *CSP Dom.* 1660–1, pp. 424, 515; 1663–4, pp. 315, 360, 577; *CSP Ire.* 1660–2, pp. 626–7; *HMC Lonsdale*, 93; Curwen, 148–58.

E.C.

CUST, Sir Richard, 1st Bt. (1622–1700), of The Black Friars, Stamford, Lincs.[1]

LINCOLNSHIRE 1653
STAMFORD 1679 (Mar.), 1679 (Oct.), 1681

b. 23 June 1622, o.s. of Samuel Cust of Boston by Anne, da. of Richard Burrell, Grocer, of London and Dowsby. *educ.* Trinity Coll. Camb. 1638; I. Temple 1641, called 1650. *m.* lic. 29 Dec. 1644, Beatrice, da. and h. of William Pury of Kirton, Lincs., 7s. *d.v.p.* 5da. *suc.* fa. 1663; *cr.* Bt. 29 Sept. 1677.

Capt. of ft. (parliamentary) 1642.
J.p. Lincs. (Holland) 1649–July 1660, (Lindsey) 1651–July 1660, (Kesteven) 1653–July 1660, Lincs. 1670–81, Feb. 1688–*d.*, Northants., Warws. and Rutland to 1681; treas. Holland 1649–50; commr. for assessment, Lincs. 1652, 1657, 1673–80, 1689–90, militia 1659, capt. of militia horse 1659, dep. lt. 1677–81; commr. for inquiry into recusancy fines, Derbys., Lincs. and Notts. Mar. 1688.[2]
Commr. for army 1653.

Cust's ancestors had held land in the Lincolnshire village of Pinchbeck since the 14th century, but it was not until the Civil War that they became armigerous. His father served on the county committee, and he was himself in arms for Parliament. He became the first of the family to enter Parliament when he was nominated to represent Lincolnshire in 1653, and in the same year he was appointed to the army committee. He acquired his house in Stamford in 1654. At the Restoration he sued out a pardon, no doubt through the good offices of his kinsman, Sir Edward Nicholas†, and after succeeding to an estate which his own purchases increased to £1,000 p.a. took pains to ingratiate himself with the royalist Berties. Evidently he had no scruples about the Conventicles Act, for in 1670 he was restored to the commission of the peace. In return for a baronetcy, he used his influence with the Stamford corporation on behalf of Charles Bertie* in the 1678 by-election. But at the next general election Cust agreed to stand with William Hyde* on the interest of the Earl of Exeter (John Cecil*), which obliged Bertie and his brother to beat an ignominious retreat. His 'vigorous assistance' for Sir Thomas Hussey* in the county election was not enough to atone for this, and the Earl of Lindsey (Robert Bertie I*) wrote to him:

> My relations have such a resentment of your late proceedings that, as affairs now stand, I judge the interview of our families at present very unseasonable, both upon that score, and also it may create a jealousy in your new

friends, who are too considerable to be lost upon such a trifle. But possibly a little time may allay all hearts and bring things to a happy composure.

Cust was classed as 'doubtful' on Shaftesbury's list, but in the Exclusion Parliaments he acted uniformly with the country party. Despite two periods of leave, he was moderately active in 1679, with three speeches and 13 committees, including the committee of elections and privileges. On 21 Mar. he urged that the £500 reward promised for the discovery of Godfrey's murderers should be given to Bedloe. He was among those instructed to bring in a bill for removing Papists from London and confining them to within five miles of their homes. During the debate of 29 Apr. on the bill to secure the King against Popish assassination plots he asked:

What if, for your present security you made an address to the King, with an humble proposal that all offices may be put into such hands for the people's satisfaction as shall be recommended to his Majesty in Parliament, and that those offices should not become void, nor be filled up, upon the death of the King, but by Parliament? I see nothing can render such a proposal undutiful in presenting it, the present state of things considered; and by this means you will be sure of a Parliament upon demise of the King.

He was later added to the committee for the bill. On 2 May he reported to the House 'the utmost truth' about the disbandment accounts that 'the committee could find out in so short a time' as four days. He helped to draw up reasons for two conferences on the trials of the lords in the Tower, and an address promising to defend the King and the Protestant religion, and he duly voted for the committal of the first exclusion bill.[3]

Cust made no speeches in the second Exclusion Parliament, but he was very active as a committeeman. His 19 committees included those to draft addresses asking for a fast and insisting on exclusion, to consider the bill for religious comprehension, to prepare the repeal of the Corporations Act, and to bring in bills for security against arbitrary power. He left no trace on the records of the Oxford Parliament, though he is said to have attended. On 7 Apr. 1681 information was given that he had declared himself in favour of a 'free state and no other government' at a 'grand cabal at the *King's Head* tavern' in Shaftesbury's presence, and he was removed from the commission of the peace. Lindsey ordered his house to be searched for arms after the Rye House Plot, describing him to Secretary Jenkins as one of the leaders of the disaffected in the county, and adding: 'I suppose you have heard him often in the House'. No arms were found, and no further action was taken.[4]

Cust soon resumed friendly relations with Lindsey. He did not stand again, and was able to secure the release of one of his kinsmen detained on suspicion during Monmouth's invasion in 1685. He was listed among the Opposition in 1687, and Pury Cust, his only surviving son, was active in the Revolution, though he was defeated at Stamford in 1689. Cust himself died on 30 Aug. 1700 and was buried at St. George, Stamford. The next member of the family to enter Parliament was his great-grandson, the third baronet, who sat for Stamford from 1743 to 1770, for the last nine years as Speaker.

[1] This biography is based on Lady E. C. Cust, *Recs. Cust Fam.* [2] *Cal. Treas. Bks.* viii. 1806. [3] Grey, vii. 14, 142–3, 213; *CJ*, ix. 609, 614, 615, 697. [4] *CSP Dom.* 1680–1, p. 232; July–Sept. 1680, pp. 32, 180.

P.W.

CUTLER, Sir John, 1st Bt. (c.1608–93), of Tothill Street, Westminster and Upper Brockley, Deptford, Kent.

TAUNTON   1679 (Oct.)–8 Dec. 1680
BODMIN   1689, 1690–15 Apr. 1693

b. c.1608, *s.* of Thomas Cutler, Grocer, of London. *m.* (1) 11 Aug. 1642, Elizabeth (*bur.* 28 May 1650), da. and coh. of Sir Thomas Foote†, 1st Bt., ld. mayor of London 1649–50, 1da. *d.v.p.*; (2) 27 July 1669, Alicia (*bur.* 10 May 1685), da. of Sir Thomas Tipping of Wheatfield, Oxon., 1da. Kntd. 17 June 1660; *cr.* Bt. 12 Nov. 1660.[1]
    Member, Grocers' Co. by 1651, master 1652–3, 1685–6, July 1688–9; alderman, London 2–5 Aug. 1651, common councilman 1654–5, 1658–9, 1661–2; commr. for assessment, London 1657, Jan. 1660–1, Kent and Westminster 1678–80, Mdx. 1689, Cambs., Kent, Mdx. and Yorks. (W. Riding) 1689–90; jt. receiver-gen., Notts. and Derbys. Dec. 1660–73; dep. lt. London 1662–Oct. 1688, 1690–*d.*, Kent 1680–Feb. 1688, Mdx. 1689–*d.*; receiver of contributions, St. Paul's Cathedral 1663–6; member, Hon. Artillery Co. 1663; j.p. Kent, Mdx. and Westminster 1672–Feb. 1688, Mdx. and Westminster Sept. 1688–*d.*; sheriff, Kent 1675–6; commr. for recusants, Mdx. 1675.[2]
    FRS 1664.

Cutler's father never became warden of his company, and in 1640 was reckoned only in the fourth rank of 'ability'. Cutler himself married well, and probably abandoned trade for finance at an early stage of his career. He took no part in the Civil War, and fined for alderman in 1651, though he served inconspicuously on the common council. Like (Sir) Robert Clayton*, he specialized in the largest kind of mortgage business, and during the Interregnum he acquired considerable property in Yorkshire from the 2nd Lord Strafford, as well as the manor of Brockley, which he retained. At the Restoration a timely loan of £5,000 to the crown earned him a baronetcy and a receivership. In 1663 he gave £1,500 towards the repair of St. Paul's, and was made receiver of voluntary contributions for the same purpose, 'which they say will be worth three times as much money'. After the Great Fire he rebuilt his Company's hall at his own expense, and acquired a reputation for a combination of public munificence and personal frugality, though he had always time for serious discourse in coffee-houses. By 1671 he had moved to Westminster, a more convenient address than Gracechurch Street for most of his clientèle, and built a gallery in his new parish church. He is said to have lent £40,000 to the 6th Baron de la Warr, and the unfortunate William Lenthall* lived to see over £20,000 against his name in Cutler's books on the security of his land and office.[3]

During the Popish Plot Cutler was active as a j.p. in suppressing a Roman Catholic school in Westminster. Although a generous landlord to his distant Yorkshire tenants, he was reputed an 'old curmudgeon' by his neighbours, and he was defeated in September 1679 by the country candidate, Sir William Pulteney*. He was temporarily successful, however, as court candidate for Taunton, presumably on the interest of his former son-in-law, Sir William Portman*. In June 1680 he was foreman of the jury that acquitted Lord Castlemaine (Roger Palmer*). When the second Exclusion Parliament met he took no part in its proceedings, and, having informed the House through his counsel that he was satisfied that he was not duly elected, he was unseated. In 1686 he bought the great Cambridgeshire estate of Wimpole from (Sir) Thomas Chicheley*. As a Kent j.p. he replied to the lord lieutenant's questions on the repeal of the Test Act and Penal Laws:

He does not intend to stand for Parliament man, nor to elect any. . . . When it comes to a trial he shall show himself an honest man to all intents and purposes.

Honesty, however, was not the quality that was required, and Cutler was removed from public office.[4]

Cutler was returned for Bodmin at the general election of 1689 on the interest of the 2nd Earl of Radnor (Charles Bodvile Robartes*), who married his only surviving child. An inactive Member of the Convention, he did not vote to agree with the Lords that the throne was not vacant. He was appointed to 11 committees, including those to inquire into deficiencies in government credit and abuses in the coinage, to restore corporations, and to receive proposals for raising money on forfeited Irish estates. On 31 Oct. he told the House that expenditure might be easily and substantially reduced

by diminishing the salaries given to the commissioners of the customs house and to most other commissioners

and officers, for those commissioners had above £1,000 a man, and he would find sufficient men every way well qualified to discharge that office for £200 a piece salary per annum.[5]

Cutler was re-elected in 1690, but died on 15 Apr. 1693, aged 85, and was buried in St. Margaret's, Westminster, the only member of his family to enter Parliament. His wealth was popularly reckoned at £100,000 in cash and £6,000 p.a. in land. After extensive charitable bequests, the principal beneficiary in his will was his nephew Edmund Boulter†, who sat for Boston from 1698 to 1701.[6]

[1] *Stepney Mar. Reg.* ed. Ferguson, ii. 28, 136; *St. Margaret Westminster* (Harl. Soc. Reg. lxiv), 116; *Par. Colls.* (Oxf. Rec. Soc. xi), 337. [2] W. W. Grantham, *Wardens of Grocers' Co.* 28, 33; J. R. Woodhead, *Rulers of London*, 55; *CSP Dom.* 1660–1, p. 429; 1663–4, p. 115; *HMC Lords*, iii. 46; *Cal. Treas. Bks.* i. 78; v. 350; *Ancient Vellum Bk.* ed. Raikes, 87. [3] *Misc. Gen. et Her.* (ser. 2), ii. 57; Guildhall RO, common council jnls.; J. B. Heath, *Grocers' Co.* 298–307; *HMC Var.* ii. 378; H. H. Drake, *Hundred of Blackheath*, 30, 34; *Cal. Treas. Bks.* i. 78, 501, 507, 653; x. 271; *Pepys Diary*, 23 Jan., 22 Dec. 1663; *HMC Egmont Diary*, iii. 311; Luttrell, iii. 126; *CSP Dom.* 1693, p. 215; *HMC Lords*, n.s. vii. 547. [4] *CSP Dom.* 1678, p. 490; Grey, vi. 179; *Ellis Corresp.* ii. 216; *Thoresby Diary*, i. 233–4; *State Trials*, vii. 1067; *CJ*, ix. 672; *VCH Cambs.* v. 265. [5] R. Morrice, *Entering Bk.* 2 p. 640. [6] Luttrell, iii. 81; *HMC Ancaster*, 433.

E.C.

DACRES, Sir Thomas (1587–1668), of Cheshunt, Herts.

HERTFORDSHIRE	1626, 1628, 26 Aug. 1641[1]
HIGHAM FERRERS	16 May 1660

b. 19 Oct. 1587, 1st s. of Sir Thomas Dacres of Cheshunt by 2nd w. Dorothy, da. of Thomas Pigott of Doddershall, Bucks. *educ.* St. John's, Camb. 1603. *m.* c.1609 (with £2,000), Martha, da. of Thomas Elmes of Lilford, Northants., 9s. (3 *d.v.p.*) 4da. *suc.* fa. 1615, kntd. 22 Feb. 1617.[2]

Sheriff, Herts. Aug.–Nov. 1615, j.p. c.1621–49, 1656–*d.*, dep. lt. by 1627–42, commr. for assessment 1643–8, Aug. 1660–*d.*, Hunts. 1647–8, Northants. Aug. 1660–1, sequestration, Herts. 1643, defence 1643, accounts 1643, levying of money 1643, eastern association 1643; treas. Cromwell's regt. 1644; commr. for new model ordinance, Herts. 1644; member, council of war, Kent 1645; commr. for militia, Herts. and Hunts. 1648, Herts. Mar. 1660, oyer and terminer, Northern circuit July 1660.[3]

Commr. for exclusion from sacrament 1646, appeals, Oxf. Univ. 1647, scandalous offences 1648, adventurers [I] 1654.

Dacres was the great-grandson of one of Henry VIII's masters of requests, who acquired the college and advowson of Higham Ferrers as well as the property at Cheshunt where the family lived. His grandfather sat for Castle Rising in 1571. Dacres, a Presbyterian, felt the weight of Archbishop Laud's displeasure, and supported Parliament throughout the first Civil War, but was turned back by the soldiers, to his great indignation, at Pride's Purge. He was involved in a double return with Edward Harby† for Higham Ferrers at the general election of 1660, which was resolved in his favour on 16 May. An inactive Member of the Convention, he was named to only nine committees, of which the most important was for confirming civil marriages. His chief concern in the House was to obtain repayment of the £250 he had advanced for the suppression of the Irish rebellion in 1642. On 8 Nov. he obtained leave of the House 'to attend certain commissioners' in the afternoon; and four days later Arthur Annesley* presented a report from the committee for debts of the army and navy, recommending that he should receive £180 interest; but the House would only vote him the principal, which they charged on the excise. Dacres's activity over revenue matters naturally increased; he was appointed to the committees for settling wine licences and for excise and accounts. But he was probably reckoned an opponent of the Court, and at the dissolution he had still received nothing. His estate was valued at £1,000 p.a. at this time, but the effort of launching his numerous offspring on the world without court assistance had probably strained his resources, and he suffered further loss in the Great Fire of London. He was buried at Cheshunt on 26 Dec. 1668, 'without funeral solemnity or other expenses, according as these times of humiliation require'. His grandson became a gentleman pensioner to Charles II, and sold the Cheshunt estate in 1675. But the Higham Ferrers property was reserved, and in 1724 the borough was unsuccessfully contested by his great-grandson, who revived the fortunes of the family, though not their parliamentary record, by marrying one of the coheirs of Richard Brett*.[4]

[1] Secluded at Pride's Purge 6 Dec. 1648, readmitted 21 Feb. 1660. [2] Clutterbuck, *Herts.* ii. 101; Keeler, *Long Parl.* 151. [3] J. Chamberlain, *Letters*, i. 612; Keeler, 150; *HMC Hatfield*, xxii. 311; *Foedera*, viii. pt. 2, p. 144. [4] Clutterbuck, ii. 100, 102; Bridges, *Northants.* ii. 173–4; *VCH Northants.* iii. 278; *HMC Lords*, n.s. xi. 403–4; Underdown, *Pride's Purge*, 151–2; *CJ*, viii. 243; PCC 31 Coke.

M.W.H./J.P.F.

DALMAHOY, Thomas (d. 1682), of The Friary, Guildford, Surr.

GUILDFORD   5 Dec. 1664, 1679 (Mar.)

3rd s. of Sir John Dalmahoy of Dalmahoy, Ratho, Midlothian by Barbara, da. of one Bernard. m. (1) 19 June 1655, Lady Elizabeth Maxwell (*bur.* 2 Sept. 1659), da. and coh. of James, 1st Earl of Dirletoun [S], wid. of William, 2nd Duke of Hamilton [S], *s.p.*; (2) 19 Feb. 1681, Elizabeth, da. of William Muschamp of Rowbarns, East Horsley, Surr., wid. of Sir William Clerke, 2nd Bt., of Shabbington, Bucks., *s.p.*[1]

Commr. for assessment, Surr. 1661–80; freeman, Guildford 1664; j.p. Surr. 1664–*d.*, dep. lt. by 1665–*d.*, commr. for recusants 1675, rebuilding of Southwark 1677.[2]

Lt. indep. tp. 1667.[3]

Dalmahoy came from a 13th century Scottish knightly family. He was in the service of the Hamiltons by 1632, but later claimed to have 'suffered for my constant loyalty and duty to his Majesty [Charles II] and to his father of blessed memory'. As master of the horse to the second Duke, who was mortally wounded at Worcester in the Stuart cause, Dalmahoy arranged his funeral, and subsequently married his widow. The Hamilton estates in Scotland remained sequestrated; but as coheir to her father she brought him property and interest at Guildford, though her daughters apparently disputed some part of the settlement. Samuel Pepys*, meeting the 'Scotch gentleman' on his way to the exiled Court in May 1660, found him 'a very fine man', and Speaker Onslow, whose family was akin to Dalmahoy's second wife, called him genteel and generous. He was proposed for the order of the Royal Oak, with an income of £1,200 p.a.[4]

Dalmahoy was returned for Guildford at a by-election in 1664, with the personal support of the Duke of York, who was said in *A Seasonable Argument* to have voted for him. A moderately active Member of the Cavalier Parliament, he was appointed to 49 committees, acted as teller in three divisions, and made ten recorded speeches. Although a consistent supporter of the Government, he joined forces with Sir Nicholas Carew* of the country party to oppose the Wey navigation bill in 1665, and secured its rejection on first reading. He was appointed to the committee for the continuation of the Conventicles Act in 1668. A friend of Ormonde, he appeared on both lists of the court party in 1669–71. When the Wey navigation bill was reintroduced in 1670, he submitted a proviso and was appointed to the committee. His name appears on the Paston List. Lauderdale's brother, Lord Halton, had acquired the property next to his ancestral home, and so it was not merely a countryman but a neighbour whom he had to defend against the increasingly vociferous demands for his removal. He pointed out on 13 Jan. 1674 that Lauderdale was not even in Scotland when the Scottish Parliament gave the Government the power to use the militia outside their own country. In the spring session of 1675, he was appointed to the committee to consider an alleged assault by Lauderdale's servants on a witness, and reminded the House that:

the Duke of Lauderdale has been banished and imprisoned by the late usurped powers from 1648 till the

King's Restoration; and hopes he deserves not such severity.

In the same session he became involved in a case in the House of Lords concerning his first wife's mother, though only as a legatee. The four lawyers who had appeared for the appellant were sent to the Tower, and it was moved that Dalmahoy, like John Fagg I*, should join them for betraying the privileges of the Commons; but he protested that he had neither directly nor indirectly applied himself to the Lords, or owned their power, and the motion was rejected without a division.[5]

Dalmahoy was named on the working lists and included by Sir Richard Wiseman* among the government supporters, while Shaftesbury in 1677 marked him 'doubly vile'. In *A Seasonable Argument* he was described as 'a Scotch serving-man' and 'a creature of Lauderdale's'. When the Duke of Norfolk's estate was debated on 9 Mar. Dalmahoy defended the character of his absent colleague Arthur Onslow*, one of the trustees, although they were of opposite parties. When complaint was made of Scots regiments in the French army, he pointed out that there were three times as many in the Dutch service. On 7 May 1678 he was appointed to the committee to draw up the address for the removal of counsellors, but he twice acted with Lord Ancram (Charles Kerr*) as teller for the adjournment in order to avoid a debate on Lauderdale. His name appeared on both lists of the court party for this year.[6]

Dalmahoy stood for re-election on the corporation interest at the first general election of 1679, and defeated the republican Algernon Sidney†, despite energetic canvassing by the Quakers. Shaftesbury marked him 'vile' and he voted against exclusion. His only committees in the first Exclusion Parliament were to inquire into the decay of the woollen manufactures and the abuses of the post office. In his only recorded speech, he again defended Lauderdale:

> No man in his station has defeated the designs of the Papists more than the Duke. When ten or twelve thousand were up in rebellion in Scotland, all at a time, did not the Duke show himself a good subject? . . . I never saw the French Ambassador with him, and I frequent his house.

As one of the 'unanimous club' he did not stand again, and sold his Guildford property in 1681. He died on 24 May 1682, and was buried at St. Martin in the Fields. No other member of his family sat in Parliament, either north or south of the border.[7]

[1] *Vis. Surr.* (Harl. Soc. lx), 34; *Scots Peerage*, iii. 130; *Her. and Gen.* v. 380. [2] *CSP Dom.* 1664–5, p. 527; Add. 6167, f. 208. [3] *CSP Dom.* 1667, p. 183. [4] *Statistical Account*, i. 83; *HMC Hamilton*, 183; PCC 69 Cottle; *CSP Dom.* 1651, p. 455; 1660–1, p. 380;

Pepys Diary, 11 May 1660; Burnet, i. 350. [5] *CJ*, viii. 602; ix. 152, 350; *Statistical Account*, i. 83; Grey, ii. 238; iii. 214; *Dering Pprs.* 97, 98. [6] Grey, iv. 217, 259; *CJ*, ix. 477, 479. [7] A. Collins, *Mems. Sidney Fam.* 153–4; Grey, vii. 191–2; *Her. and Gen.* v. 380.

J.S.C.

DALSTON, John (1611–92), of Acorn Bank, Temple Sowerby, Westmld. and Milrig, Cumb.

APPLEBY 1661

bap. 15 Oct. 1611, 2nd but 1st surv. s. of Sir Christopher Dalston of Acorn Bank by Anne, da. of Sir William Hutton of Penrith, Cumb. *educ.* Queen's, Oxf. 1631; G. Inn, entered 1631. *m.* settlement 20 Oct. 1634, Lucy (*d.* 1682), da. and h. of Richard Fallowfield of Great Strickland, Westmld., 6s. 5da. 10 other ch. *d.v.p. suc.* fa. 1634.[1]

J.p. Westmld. ?1642–4, July 1660–*d.*; sheriff, Cumb. c.1643; commr. for assessment, Westmld. Aug. 1660–80, 1689–90, corporations 1662–3, charitable uses 1670, recusants 1675, dep. lt. by 1685–Feb. 1688, Nov. 1688–*d.*[2]

Lt.-col. of ft. (royalist) ?1642–4.[3]

Dalston's ancestors took their name from a Cumberland manor where the senior branch of the family had resided at least since the 13th century, first representing the county in 1383. The Westmorland branch was established on the grant in 1543 of the former property of the Hospitallers in Temple Sowerby, some seven miles from Appleby. During the Civil War Dalston accepted a commission as second-in-command to his wife's cousin Sir John Lowther I* in the royalist army 'for fear of losing his estate and not for any desire he had to oppose the Parliament', and the county committee testified that he had never been in actual service in the field. A further point in his favour was that he had apprehended a seminary priest and committed him to the common gaol. He declared an income of £96 p.a. with reversions totalling £140, and was fined £290. But with only the first moiety paid, he engaged in the second Civil War, and incurred a further penalty of £315. He was not involved in royalist conspiracy, but at the Restoration he was recommended for the order of the Royal Oak, with an estate valued at £600 p.a.[4]

At the general election of 1661 Dalston was returned for Appleby, together with Lowther's son, on Lady Pembroke's interest. Lord Wharton listed him as a friend, and he may have been a country Cavalier, but he was not an active Member of the Cavalier Parliament. He was appointed to only ten committees, of which the most important was for the border bill (22 Nov. 1666), and he left no trace in the Journals after the fall of Clarendon. Together with Daniel Fleming* he was the subject of a complaint to the Treasury from the excise farmers in

1669. Shaftesbury marked him 'worthy' in 1677, but he had probably ceased to attend, for his epitaph credits him with only 15 years as 'envoy to Parliament from the borough of Appleby'. To the lord lieutenant's questions in 1688, he stoutly replied in writing

> I do not (in my weak judgment) think that the taking away of the Penal Laws would be for the general good of the nation, these laws being the great security and support of the Government; and therefore I cannot in conscience either vote [for] the taking of them away, or give any vote to the electing such Members as would take them away. ... To live peaceably under the Government with my fellow subjects of what persuasion soever is a duty which I owe both to God and the King, and I am steadfastly resolved (*Deo volente*) to perform it accordingly.

He was removed from the lieutenancy, and signed the petition sponsored by Sir John Lowther III* for a free Parliament on 1 Dec. 1688. He died on 13 Apr. 1692, and was buried at Kirkby Thore. His memorial describes him as

> especially fit for public affairs; but he preferred to confine himself to private life, taking the lead in promoting hospitality among his neighbours, enlarging his estate, and attaining knowledge of himself and his household.

His great-grandson sat for Westmorland from 1747 till his death in 1759.[5]

[1] *Trans. Cumb. and Westmld. Antiq. Soc.* n.s. x. 242–5; SP 23/186/414. [2] SP23/186/408; *Trans. Cumb. and Westmld. Antiq. Soc.* n.s. x. 245; Westmld. RO, Appleby memo. bk. 1662–85, D/Ry 1124, 3314. [3] SP23/186/408. [4] *Trans. Cumb. and Westmld. Antiq. Soc.* n.s. x. 204; Nicolson and Burn, *Westmld. and Cumb.* i. 382–4; SP23/186/396–412. [5] *Trans. Cumb. and Westmld. Antiq. Soc.* n.s. x. 245; Westmld. RO, D/Ry 1055, 3363.

L.N.

DALTON, John (c.1610–79), of Derby.

DERBY 1659, 1660, 1661

b. c.1610, o.s. of John Dalton, vintner, of Nottingham by w. Isabel. *m.* Anne, da. of Richard Pyott of Streetly, Staffs., 2s. (1 *d.v.p.*) *suc.* fa. 1618.[1]
Alderman, Derby 1645–70, mayor 1646–7, 1652–3, 1668–9; commr. for assessment, Derbys. 1657, Aug. 1660–d., Derby 1663–4, militia, Derbys. Mar. 1660, capt. of militia ft. Mar. 1660–?61, j.p. Mar. 1660–70.[2]

Dalton entered a very brief pedigree at the heralds' visitation of 1662. He had probably lived in Derby since his mother's second marriage, and by 1641 he was established there as a draper. Presumably he sympathized with the parliamentary cause in the Civil War, as he was first appointed to municipal office in 1645. The only member of his family to enter Parliament, he was first elected in 1659. In the Convention he obtained leave to go into the country on 11 July 1660, but was named to the committees to enable soldiers to exercise trades in corporate towns without apprenticeship and

to take accounts of public moneys received. He probably voted with the Opposition. He was again inactive in the Cavalier Parliament, serving on only six committees throughout, three of which were for private bills. He was among those appointed to consider the regulation of the hallage duty on woollen cloth in 1664, and was added to the committee on the bill to regulate printing on 26 Oct. 1666. On 18 Jan. 1667 his colleague Anchitell Grey* 'made a fair excuse for him, as that he was an old man and lame of the gout', but he was still absent on 13 Feb. and only appeared towards the end of the month when his fine was remitted because of his illness. He was added to the committee for the drainage of Deeping fen in 1668. As a sympathizer with dissenters, he was removed from the commission of the peace in 1670. Sir Richard Wiseman* had no hopes of gaining his vote for the court in 1676, and Shaftesbury marked him 'thrice worthy' in the following year. He died, the senior alderman of the borough, on a visit to Nottingham on 30 Aug. 1679, and was buried in St. Werburgh's chancel, Derby.[3]

[1] Glover, *Derbys.* ii. 487; PCY, 35A, ff. 261–2. [2] W. Hutton, *Derby*, 84–85. [3] Lysons, *Derby*, clviii; *Reliquary*, xxv. 26; *Milward*, 65; *CJ*, ix. 56; Add. 6705, f. 102.

M.W.H./J.P.F.

DANBY, Thomas (1631–67), of Farnley, Yorks.

MALTON Apr.–18 Dec. 1661

b. 17 Aug. 1631, 1st s. of Sir Thomas Danby† of Thorpe Perrow by Catherine, da. of Sir Christopher Wandesford† of Kirklington. *m.* Nov. 1659, Margaret, da. and coh. of Hon. William Eure of Malton, 2s. 1da. *suc.* fa. 1660.[1]
Commr. for militia, Yorks. Mar. 1660; assessment (W. Riding) 1661–d., mayor, Leeds 1661–2; commr. for corporations, Yorks. 1662–3.[2]

Danby was descended from a mercer who sat for York in 1453. By the end of the century the family had become landed and they continued to increase their estates in the county. His father, who represented Richmond in the Long Parliament, raised forces for the King during the Civil War and compounded on a fine of £4,780. Danby's expectations at the time were computed at £2,000 p.a., including collieries in Marhamshire. He was appointed the first mayor of Leeds by the new charter of 1661. In the same year he was returned for Malton on his wife's interest, and listed as a friend by Lord Wharton. But he was unseated on 18 Dec. without having been appointed to any committees in the Cavalier Parliament. He did not stand again and was killed on 31 July 1667 during a brawl in a London tavern. No later member of the family entered Parliament.[3]

[1] *Christopher Danby* (Thoresby Soc. xxxvii), 2; T. D. Whitaker, *Richmondshire*, ii. 98–99. [2] *Leeds Corp. Court Bks.* (Thoresby Soc. xxxiv), 203–4; *HMC 8th Rep.* pt. 1 (1881), 275. [3] Keeler, *Long Parl.* 152–3; *Royalist Comp. Pprs.* (Yorks. Arch. Soc. rec. ser. xx), 86–87; *Verney Mems.* ii. 71, 319; *Thornton Autobiog.* (Surtees Soc. lxii), 163.

P.A.B./P.W.

DANBY, Earl of *see* OSBORNE, Peregrine

DANIEL, Jeffrey (1626–81), of St. Margaret's, Preshute, Wilts.

MARLBOROUGH 1660, 1661

bap. 29 June 1626, 1st s. of William Daniel of St. Margaret's by Frances, da. of William Wilmot of Wantage, Berks. *educ.* Magdalen Coll. Oxf. 1642. *m.* (1) lic. 25 Apr. 1648, Catherine, da. of John Southby† of Carswell, Buckland, Berks., *s.p.*; (2) 5 Nov. 1649, Rachel (*d.* 1667), da. of John Ernle of Whetham House, Calne, Wilts., 4s. (3 *d.v.p.*) 3da.; (3) lic. 4 Oct. 1672, Susanna, da. of Matthew Nicholas, DD, dean of St. Paul's, 1s. *d.v.p. suc.* fa. by 1648.[1]

Commr. for assessment, Wilts. 1649–52, 1657, Jan. 1660–80, j.p. Mar. 1660–d., commr. for corporations 1662–3.[2]

Daniel was descended from a younger son of the Cheshire family who migrated to Wiltshire under Henry VIII, acquired a former Gilbertine monastery just outside Marlborough, and sat for Devizes in 1545. Nothing is known of his father or himself during the Civil War, but Daniel was nominated to the Wiltshire assessment committee by the Rump shortly after his first marriage into a prominent radical family. He continued to serve throughout the Interregnum, but his views may have changed under the influence of his second wife, the sister of John Ernle*, and he probably welcomed the Restoration. He was returned at the top of the poll for Marlborough in 1660 and marked by Lord Wharton as a friend. An inactive Member of the Convention, he was appointed to only seven committees, including those to insert the excise clauses in the bill for the abolition of the court of wards and to consider rules for disbanding the army.[3]

Daniel was again top of the poll in 1661, but he was not recorded as attending the Cavalier Parliament until 26 Nov., when he was named to the committee for restoring the dukedom of Somerset to the Seymour family. Charles Seymour* sent him a barrel of oysters for Christmas, which he found 'indifferently good'. A moderately active Member, he was appointed to 192 committees. As a magistrate he interested himself locally in the plight of the industrious poor, and he was appointed to the committees for the additional poor relief bill in 1663 and 1664. Presumably an Anglican, he helped to consider the conventicles bill in 1664 and the bill to repress the insolence of Popish priests in 1666. His estate was valued at £700 p.a. about this time. In 1670 he was teller for a motion to postpone consideration of supply until the House had heard the report of the public accounts commission, and he was appointed to the committees to consider the second conventicles bill and the bill to prevent the transportation of English subjects overseas. He was also among those instructed to examine the deficiencies in the Conventicles and Militia Acts. He may, therefore, have been in opposition during the Cabal, and his third marriage, which brought him into the loyal Nicholas family, did not immediately strengthen his links with the Court. In the spring session of 1675 he was named to the committees to prevent illegal exactions and to hinder Papists from sitting in Parliament, and he was twice appointed to committees to prevent the growth of Popery. He acted as teller with (Sir) Giles Hungerford* for denying parliamentary privilege to the court supporter, Sir Robert Holte*, in 1677. Shaftesbury marked him 'doubly worthy', but altered it to 'doubly vile', perhaps because he suspected the influence of Danby's lawyer, George Johnson*, noted in the working lists. But he was not mentioned on either list of the court party in 1678. His last committee was on 20 June, and he may not have attended the final session of the Cavalier Parliament.[4]

Daniel did not stand again, although he was present at the second Marlborough election of 1679. He died on 22 Apr. 1681 and was buried at Preshute. The trustees named in his will included Ernle and Sir Henry Goodricke*. His son William sat for Marlborough as a Tory from 1695 till his death in 1698.[5]

[1] *Coll. Top. et Gen.* v. 346, 349; *Wilts. Vis. Peds.* (Harl. Soc. cv), 43; *London Mar. Lic.* ed. Foster, 374; Bromham par. reg.; PCC 103 Drax; information from Mr. M. G. Rathbone, Wiltshire County Archivist. [2] Hoare, *Wilts.* Salisbury, 444. [3] *Wilts. Arch. Mag.* xxxiv. 253, 264. [4] Add. 32324, f. 162; *HMC Var.* i. 147; Hoare, *Repertorium Wiltonense*, 16; *CJ* ix. 124, 411. [5] J. Waylen, *Marlborough*, 335; *Coll. Top. et Gen.* v. 349; PCC 103 Drax.

M.W.H.

DANIEL, Sir Peter (*d.*1700), of London Bridge, and Clapham, Surr.

SOUTHWARK 1685

1st s. of William Daniel, Haberdasher, of Southwark by Mary, da. of John Delanoy of Southwark. *m.* 1659, Elizabeth, da. of William Greene, merchant, of London, 3s. 2da. *suc.* fa. 1678; *kntd.* 13 Apr. 1684.[1]

Member, Haberdashers' Co. 1656, master 1683–4, 1689–90; common councilman, London 1672–3, deputy 1674–82, alderman 1682–*d.*, sheriff 1683–4; commr. for assessment, Surr. 1679–80, 1689–90, j.p. 1681–*d.*, sheriff 1681–2; dep. lt. London 1681–9; committee, E. I. Co. 1683–5; gov. Irish Soc. 1687–8; col. blue regt. of militia ft. London 1687–9, 1692–d.[2]

Daniel's maternal uncle, Peter Delanoy, an alderman of London, had represented Southwark in the 1656 Parliament. His father fined for alderman in 1670. Daniel was put in nomination as alderman for Bridge ward, where he lived, by Sir William Pritchard*, the Tory lord mayor, and was elected in December 1682. On 5 Sept. 1683 Pritchard nominated him as sheriff, 'the Whig party not appearing'. After the seizure of the London charter, he was reappointed to both offices by royal commission, and as sheriff attended the execution of Algernon Sidney[†] in December 1683. He had substantial holdings of East India stock, usually buying and selling £500 worth at a time, and was admitted to the governing body of the company at this time.[3]

Daniel was returned for Southwark to James II's Parliament. A moderately active Member, he was among those ordered to estimate the yield of a tax on new buildings and to consider bills to encourage woollen manufactures and to relieve poor debtors. In 1686 he subscribed £2,500 to a government loan on the security of the linen duty. He must have supported James's policy of religious toleration, since he survived the purge of Tory aldermen in March 1687 and was appointed governor of the Irish Society, which administered the City's plantation in Ulster. In October 1688 he presented to James a loyal address from the London lieutenancy, pledging their lives and fortunes to the King's defence. After the Revolution, though the senior alderman below the chair, the Whigs three times effectively blocked his election as lord mayor after bitter contests. In 1690 he subscribed £500 to a government loan. He died on 9 May 1700 and was buried at Clapham. No other member of the family sat in Parliament.[4]

[1] *Vis. London* (Harl. Soc. xlii), 48; *Vis. Surr.* (Harl. Soc. lx), 71; PCC 70 Noel. [2] J. R. Woodhead, *Rulers of London*, 56; Luttrell, i. 278, 283; ii. 610; *HMC Lords*, iii. 45. [3] *Verney Mems.* ii. 340; *CSP Dom.* July–Sept. 1683, pp. 373–4. [4] *Cal. Treas. Bks.* viii. 2176; ix. 2007; *HMC Lords*, ii. 69; Luttrell, ii. 46–47, 569, 578, 581; iv. 432–3; Lysons, *Environs*, iv. 586.

E.C.

DANVERS *alias* **VILLIERS** (formerly **WRIGHT** and **HOWARD**), **Robert** (1624–74), of Bassetsbury, High Wycombe, Bucks. and Knighton, Rad.

WESTBURY   4 Jan.–12 Feb. 1659
MALMESBURY   1660

b. 19 Oct. 1624, illegit. s. of Frances, da. of Sir Edward

Coke[†], l.c.j.K.b. 1613–16, of Stoke Poges, Bucks., w. of John Villiers, 1st Visct. Purbeck, prob. by Sir Robert Howard[†] of Clun Castle, Salop. *educ.* in France c.1633–41. *m.* 23 Nov. 1648, Elizabeth (*d.*1709), da. and coh. of Sir John Danvers[†] of Dauntsey, Wilts., 2s. 3da. *suc.* mother 1645; *summ.* to Lords as Visct. Purbeck 15 June 1660.[1]

Col. of ft. (royalist) 1643–4; gov. Oswestry 1643–4.[2]
Freeman, Chipping Wycombe 1668.[3]

Danvers, the offspring of a notorious liaison at the Jacobean Court, was baptized Robert Wright. After conviction for adultery in High Commission, his parents fled to France, changed their religion, and brought him up as a Roman Catholic under the name of Howard. They returned to England on the eve of the Civil War, and rejoined the Court. Lord Purbeck, who was feeble-minded, was persuaded to recognize the young Howard as his son, which he certainly was not, and he took the name of Villiers. After serving as a volunteer at Edgehill, he was commissioned as a colonel through his mother's influence, but dismissed when Rupert took over responsibility for Shropshire in 1644. He submitted to Parliament, abjured Rome, and became a Presbyterian. After inheriting from his mother an estate of close on £3,000 p.a., he paid fines for his delinquency totalling £2,650, 'which money he borrowed at interest', but the property was not finally cleared from sequestration till 1653. Meanwhile he had married the daughter of a regicide, and declared that he would himself have been ready to act as the King's executioner. On the death of his father-in-law he was given leave by the Protector to assume the name and arms of Danvers 'because those of the name of Villiers had sided' with the fallen monarchy, and he produced such good testimony of his affection to the new regime that he was exempted from decimation. On Purbeck's death in 1658 he renounced the peerage and sat in Richard Cromwell's Parliament as Member for Westbury until expelled as a Cavalier.[4]

Danvers was returned for Malmesbury in 1660 on his wife's interest and took his seat at once, but was appointed to no committees. On 17 May 'standing up in his place, [he] denied the matters objected against him', which were apparently based on his remarks at the time of Charles I's trial; and the case against him collapsed when the principal witness admitted that his evidence was only hearsay. A month later, however, the charges were renewed in the House of Lords, and he was ordered to attend as 'Viscount Purbeck'. Although he at first stood on his privilege as a Member of the Commons, he was brought to the bar, and charged with treasonable and atheistical words in 1649. Danvers did not deny the words, but insisted that he was not a peer, or, if he was, that with five small children and £5,000 of debts, his estate, reduced to under £1,000 p.a., was inadequate to support the title. He was discharged on £10,000 bail on 27 July. Meanwhile in the Lower House, the elections committee was asked to recommend whether a new writ should be issued for Malmesbury, but no report was made and no writ issued, although Danvers was alleged to have said that 'he only sits in the present Parliament for formality's sake, and never goes, for he can do his country no good'. During Michaelmas term he levied a fine to the King for all his titles, and on 27 Dec. he took the oaths to the restored monarchy and entered into a further bond of £5,000 to attempt nothing against it.[5]

A few days before Venner's revolt Danvers 'said the Anabaptists would prevail, and he should adhere to his former principles, absolutely disliking monarchy'. His horses were seized but returned by order in council. At this stage his career becomes hard to distinguish from that of Col. Henry Danvers, also an Anabaptist and a suspected plotter. He was certainly in the Tower on 2 July 1662 when his wife was given leave to visit him, and they were licensed to assume the name and arms of Danvers. He was later transferred to York, but escaped in 1664. Presumably he was recaptured, for during the second Dutch war he was held in custody in the Isle of Wight. He was given the freedom of Wycombe in 1668, but had to leave the country to escape his creditors, and died at Calais in 1674. He must have become a Roman Catholic again, for he was buried in the church of Nôtre Dame. His descendants revived the claim to the title from time to time, and in 1678 the House of Lords declared, in spite of precedent, that it could not be extinguished by fine; but none of them succeeded in entering either House.[6]

[1] CP; Burke, Dormant and Extinct Peerages, 559; Cal. Comm. Comp. 1075. [2] W. H. Black, Docquets of Letters Patent, 46; SP23/180/138. [3] First Wycombe Ledger Bk. (Bucks. Rec. Soc. xi), 185. [4] [T. Longueville], Curious Case of Lady Purbeck, 137–9; SP23/180/138; Cal. Comm. Comp. 1075–6, 1639; HMC 7th Rep. 110. [5] CJ, viii. 26, 34, 84; LJ, xi. 64, 65–66, 93–94, 107; HMC 7th Rep. 110, 117, 126–7; HMC 9th Rep. pt. 2 (1884), p. 58; CSP Dom. 1660–1, pp. 419, 425. [6] CSP Dom. 1660–1, p. 477; 1661–2, p. 320; 1663–4, pp. 652–3; 1664–5, p. 355; 1673–5, p. 407; PC2/55/114, 56/40; SP29/217/35.

M.W.H./B.D.H.

DARCY, Hon. Conyers (1622–92), of Hornby Castle, Yorks.

BOROUGHBRIDGE 1660
YORKSHIRE 1661

bap. 3 Mar. 1622, 3rd but 1st surv. s. of Conyers, later 5th Baron Darcy, by Grace, da. and h. of Thomas Rokeby of Skiers. educ. Univ. Coll. Oxf. 1637; G. Inn 1640. m. (1) 14 May 1645, Lady Catherine Fane (bur. 30 Aug. 1649), da. of Francis Fane†, 1st Earl of Westmorland, s.p.; (2) 6 Feb. 1650, Lady Frances Howard (d. 9 Apr. 1670), da. of Thomas Howard†, 1st Earl of Berkshire, 3s. 3da.; (3) 19 May 1672, Lady Frances Seymour (bur. 5 Jan. 1681), da. of William Seymour†, 2nd Duke of Somerset, wid. of Richard, 2nd Visct. Molyneux, and of Thomas Wriothesley†, 4th Earl of Southampton, s.p.; (4) 8 Jan. 1685, Elizabeth, da. and coh. of John Frescheville*, 1st Baron Frescheville of Staveley, wid. of Philip Warwick of Frognal, Chislehurst, Kent, s.p. summ. to Lords in fa.'s barony as Lord Conyers 1 Nov. 1680; suc. fa. as 2nd Earl of Holdernesse 14 June 1689.[1]

Commr. for northern assoc. Yorks. (W. Riding) 1645; j.p. (N. Riding), 1646–9, 1661–Feb. 1688, Nov. 1688–d., (W. Riding) 1647–9, 1671–Sept. 1688, Nov. 1688–?d.; commr. for assessment (N. Riding) Aug. 1660–80, (W. Riding) 1661–80; col. of militia ft. (N. Riding) by 1661–81; dep. lt. (N. Riding) 1661–Feb. 1688, (W. Riding) 1677–81; commr. for loyal and indigent officers, Yorks. 1662, corporations 1662–3; constable, Middleham Castle 1671–d.; bailiff, Richmond liberty 1672–d.; commr. for recusants (W. and E. Ridings) 1675.[2]

Capt. indep. tp. 1667.

Darcy could trace his descent from a Domesday tenant-in-chief with substantial holdings in Lincolnshire. A later member of the family, with the not inappropriate Christian name of Norman, represented that county in three Parliaments of Edward III, and two medieval baronies were created by writs of summons to the Upper House. In 1641 one of them was called out of abeyance, together with the barony of Conyers which was claimed in the female line, for Darcy's grandfather. His father, a royalist commander in the Civil War, compounded on a fine of £2,992 for his delinquency, though the value of his estate was computed at over £4,000 p.a.[3]

Although Darcy himself was nominated in 1645 to the committee for the northern association, and to the commission of the peace in the following year, he is unlikely to have served. However, it may have been believed that this was sufficient to put him outside the scope of the Long Parliament ordinance against the candidature of Cavaliers and their sons, and at the general election of 1660 he was returned for Boroughbridge on the interest of his brother-in-law, (Sir) Henry Stapleton*. His only possible committee in the Convention was the committee of elections and privileges. In the following year he was returned for the county. An inactive Member of the Cavalier Parliament, he was appointed to 32 committees at most, including the elections committee in six sessions. He was appointed by full name to 18 committees, including those to consider the bill of pains and penalties (4 July 1661) and to report on defects in the Corporations Act (6 Mar. 1663). Thereafter his career in the House is noteworthy only for his membership of successive election committees. In 1669 Sir Thomas Osborne* included him among the Members to be gained for the Court by the Duke of Buckingham. His name was included on the working lists, but it was noted that he had been missing from an important debate. However, Sir Richard Wiseman* listed him among the court supporters, and Shaftesbury classed him as 'doubly vile'. According to *A Seasonable Argument* he had been 'assisted by the Court in stealing the Lord Lexinton's sister from her guardian for his son' (John Darcy*). He was on both lists of the court party in 1678, and petitioned for a cornetcy in the yeoman of the guard for his son Philip Darcy*. Forwarding the petition to (Sir) Joseph Williamson*, Osborne (now Lord Treasurer Danby) commented:

> Besides his quality, you are enough witness of his constant and faithful serving of the crown; and since his Majesty has promised him a kindness, I know not how he can receive one more easy for the King to grant. If additional arguments be needed in his behalf, it is no ill one that he does not only serve the crown well but at his own expense.[4]

As one of the 'unanimous club', Darcy did not contest the elections of 1679, and when the second Exclusion Parliament met he was called up to the House of Lords in his father's second barony. He opposed the policies of James II, and seems to have been involved, in a minor way, with the preparations for the northern uprising in 1688. He died at Aston on 13 Dec. 1692 and was buried at Hornby.[5]

[1] Clay, *Dugdale's Vis. Yorks.* ii. 83–84; Soc. of Genealogists, Coventry St. Michael bishops' transcripts. [2] *HMC Var.* ii. 165; C. Clarkson, *Richmond*, p. xcix; *CSP Dom.* 1671, p. 158; 1685–6, p. 116; Yale Univ. Lib. Osborn mss; *HMC Astley*, 49. [3] *Parl. Rep. Yorks.* (Yorks. Arch. Soc. rec. ser. xcvi), 87; *VCH Yorks. N. Riding*, i. 79, 315; J. T. Cliffe, *Yorks. Gentry*, 99–100; *Royalist Comp. Pprs.* (Yorks. Arch. Soc. rec. ser. xx), 7–8. [4] *CSP Dom.* 1678, p. 458; SP29/407/22. [5] Browning, *Danby*, ii. 137.

M.W.H./P.A.B./P.W.

DARCY, Hon. James (1617–73), of Sedbury Park, nr. Richmond, Yorks.

RICHMOND   1660

bap. 30 Nov. 1617, 6th s. of Conyers, 4th Baron Darcy (*d.*1654) by Dorothy, da. of Sir Henry Belasyse, 1st Bt.†, of Newburgh Priory; bro. of Conyers, later 1st Earl of Holdernesse, and Hon. Marmaduke Darcy*. *m.* by 1650, Isabel, da. of Sir Marmaduke Wyvill, 2nd Bt.†, of Burton Constable, 3s. 4da.[1]
Commr. for militia, Yorks. Mar. 1660; j.p. Yorks. (N. Riding) July 1660–6, commr. for assessment Aug. 1660–*d.*; receiver of free gift, Yorks. 1661–5, commr. for corporations 1662–3, loyal and indigent officers 1662.[2]
Master of the stud 1661–*d.*[3]

Darcy inherited under a family settlement a small estate of his own at Patrick Brompton, but preferred to live on his wife's property, three miles from Richmond. Having taken no part in the Civil War, he was eligible to stand for the borough on the family interest at the general election of 1660, and was returned with his brother-in-law, Sir Christopher Wyvill*. He was classed as a friend by Lord Wharton, who entrusted him with the management of a dozen Yorkshire Members; but if he took any part in the Convention it was doubtless as a court supporter. He does not seem to have stood for re-election, but in June 1661 he was appointed master of the royal stud at £200 p.a., under contract to supply 12 horses a year for £800. His salary was abolished in the Household reforms of 1668, and his contract was reduced to £500 for five horses of his own breeding. His will, dated 13 Oct. 1673, was proved on 5 Feb. 1674. His son James sat for Richmond under William III and Anne, and was given an Irish peerage in 1721.[4]

[1] Clay, *Dugdale's Vis. Yorks.* ii. 81. [2] *Cal. Treas. Bks.* i. 666; *HMC 8th Rep.* pt. 1 (1881), 275. [3] *CSP Dom.* 1660–1, p. 606; *Cal. Treas. Bks.* iv. 564. [4] *Royalist Comp. Pprs.* (Yorks. Arch. Soc. rec. ser. xx), 7; *VCH N. Riding*, i. 79–80; *Cal. Treas. Bks.* i. 303, 445; ii. 239, 528; iii. 220; *York Wills* (Yorks. Arch. Soc. rec. ser. lxviii), 31.

M.W.H./P.A.B./P.W.

DARCY, Hon. John (1659–89), of Hornby Castle, Yorks.

RICHMOND   1681, 1685, [1689]

bap. 5 Nov. 1659, 1st s. of Hon. Conyers Darcy*, later 2nd Earl of Holdernesse, by 2nd w.; bro. of Philip Darcy*, *educ.* G. Inn 1675. *m.* 5 Feb. 1674, Bridget, da. of Robert Sutton†, 1st Baron Lexinton of Aram, 5s. (3 *d.v.p.*) 2da.[1]
J.p. Yorks. (W. Riding) 1680–Sept. 1688, Nov. 1688–*d.*; dep. lt. (W. Riding) 1680–Feb. 1688, (N. Riding) 1685–Feb. 1688, Oct. 1688–*d.*; col. of militia ft. (W. Riding) 1681–7.[2]
Major, Queen's Life Gds. 1681–5; lt.-col. Earl of Shrewsbury's Horse (later 5 Dgn. Gds.) July–Dec. 1685.

At the age of 15, Darcy with the help of his father abducted and married Lord Lexinton's only daughter, 'not eleven years old and having a great portion left her by her father'. Her guardian petitioned the House of Lords on 23 Feb. 1674 but the hearing of the case was prevented by the prorogation the following day. An opponent of exclusion, Darcy was appointed to county office in 1680 and commissioned in the guards. He was returned for Richmond, seven miles from his father's residence at Hornby, in 1681, but left no trace on the records of the Oxford Parliament. Re-elected to James II's Parliament, he may have been appointed to the

Darcy Family of Yorkshire

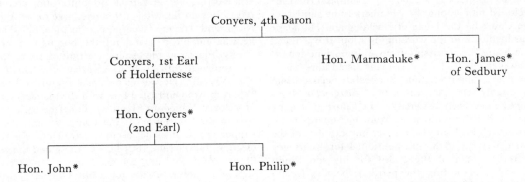

Conyers, 4th Baron

Conyers, 1st Earl
of Holdernesse

Hon. Marmaduke*

Hon. James*
of Sedbury

Hon. Conyers*
(2nd Earl)

Hon. John*

Hon. Philip*

committee of elections and privileges. He voted against the Court in the second session, together with Charles Fox*. Both offenders were reported to have been suspended the King's presence at the prorogation and dismissed from their employment, though on their 'humble submission' they were permitted to kiss the King's hand.[3]

To the lord lieutenant's questions in 1688 Darcy replied:

> If I am chosen a Member of Parliament, I will give my opinion according to the debate of the House; but my present opinion is not to repeal the Penal Laws and the Test. If I do give my interest to any to serve in Parliament, it shall be to such as I think knowing men and well-affected to the King and government as established.

Though he was removed from local office, the King's electoral agents, who expected him to be returned for Richmond, described him in September as 'right'. It was probably about this time, however, that he succeeded in reconciling Lord Danby (Sir Thomas Osborne*) and the Earl of Devonshire (William Cavendish*), thereby laying the foundations for the bi-partisan rising in the north. Still unsuspected, he was restored to the lieutenancy by the Duke of Newcastle (Henry Cavendish*), and ordered to arrest Lord Lumley, one of the signatories to the invitation to William of Orange. Darcy pretended that he was unable to find his fellow-conspirator, though, according to Sir John Reresby*, 'it appeared afterwards that he was not far off, and [Darcy] might have seized him if he pleased'. Another account claims that Lumley escaped across the border into county Durham. Darcy played a direct part in Danby's seizure of York on 22 Nov., and was expected to swell the number of Danby's Tory followers in the Convention; but although he was returned for Richmond on 10 Jan. 1689 he had died of quinsy four days earlier. He was buried in Westminster Abbey.[4]

[1] Clay, *Dugdale's Vis. Yorks.* ii. 84; *HMC 9th Rep.* pt. 2, p. 46. [2] *Reresby Mems.* 345; *CSP Dom.* 1679–80, p. 456; *HMC Astley*, 49; *Yorks. Arch. Jnl.* xxix. 266. [3] *HMC 9th Rep.* pt. 2, p. 46; *LJ*, xii. 648; *Reresby Mems.* 401–2, 502; PRO 31/3, bdle. 162, f. 189v. [4] Browning, *Danby*, i. 389; *HMC 7th Rep.* 420; *Reresby Mems.* 524; Add. 41805, f. 213.

P.A.B./P.W.

DARCY, Hon. Marmaduke (1615–87), of Whitehall.

RICHMOND   9 Feb. 1665

bap. 4 June 1615, 5th s. of Conyers, 4th Baron Darcy; bro. of Conyers, later 1st Earl of Holdernesse, and Hon. James Darcy*. *educ.* Trinity Coll. Camb. 1631; L. Inn 1633. *unm.*[1]

Lt.-col. of ft. (royalist) 1642–4; col. of horse 1644–5.[2]

Gent. usher of the privy chamber by 1656–*d.*; surveyor of gt. wardrobe 1672–*d.*[3]

Commr. for assessment, Yorks. (N. Riding) 1673–4, 1679–80, (W. Riding) 1677–9, recusants (N. Riding) 1675; recorder, Richmond 1684–*d.*[4]

Darcy, always 'Duke' to his friends, served in the King's army under his cousin Lord Belasyse until the surrender of Newark. He was one of Charles II's followers expelled from Scotland in 1650, and lived peacefully in exile at Ratisbon until 1655. Then, as 'a gallant gentleman and nobly allied in the northern parts', he was selected to lead a royalist rising in Yorkshire. After its failure he joined the exiled Court and was given a post in the privy chamber, which he retained for the rest of his life.[5]

Darcy returned to England with the King at the Restoration, and was elected for Richmond on the family interest in 1665. An inactive Member of the Cavalier Parliament, he was appointed to 19 committees at most, but only the committee of elections and privileges in three sessions and two private bill committees can be certainly assigned to him. In consideration of his 'services and sufferings' he was given £1,050 in 1667, but a further

£3,000 long remained unpaid. As a court dependant, his name appeared on both lists of the court
party in 1669–71, and also in *Flagellum Parliamentarium*, though the author confused him with
his brother James, the master of the royal stud. In
1672 he succeeded Bullen Reymes* as surveyor of
the great wardrobe, with a salary of £300 p.a. He
was noted as one of the officials in the Commons in
1675, classed as 'thrice vile' by Shaftesbury, and
listed as a government supporter by the Court in
1678.[6]

Although not blacklisted in the 'unanimous club',
Darcy was overwhelmingly defeated by Humphrey
Wharton* at the general election and never stood
again, though he presented the loyal address from
Richmond in 1681 and succeeded the exclusionist
Thomas Cradock* as recorder under the new char-
ter. With strong support from Ormonde, his claims
on the crown were settled in 1684 by the grant of
£3,600 spread over six years. He died in his bed in
Windsor Castle on 3 July 1687, and was buried in
St. George's chapel.[7]

[1] Clay, *Dugdale's Vis. Yorks*. ii. 81; *HMC Var.* viii. 66. [2] *List of
Officers Claiming* (1663); *HMC Ormonde*, n.s. ii. 390. [3] *Archaeologia*, xxxv. 338; *CSP Dom.* 1672–3, p. 306. [4] SP44/335/144.
[5] C. Brown, *Hist. Newark*, i. 114; *Cal. Cl. SP*, ii. 69, 324, 395;
Clarendon, *Rebellion*, v. 374; *Nicholas Pprs.* (Cam. Soc. n.s.l), 327;
D. Underdown, *Royalist Conspiracy*, 139–41; *Archaeologia*, xxxv.
338; *CSP Dom.* 1657–8, pp. 292, 311. [6] *Pepys Diary*, 24 May 1660;
CSP Dom. 1667, p. 139; 1671–2, p. 22. [7] C. Clarkson, *Richmond*,
115; *London Gazette*, 22 Aug. 1681; *HMC Ormonde*, n.s. vii. 277–
9; *CSP Dom.* 1684–5, p. 210; *HMC Downshire*, i. 253; Ashmole,
Berks. iii. 174.

P.A.B./P.W.

DARCY, Hon. Philip (1661–94), of Aston, Yorks.

NEWARK   1685
RICHMOND   15 Feb. 1689

bap. 1 May 1661, 2nd s. of Hon. Conyers Darcy*,
later 2nd Earl of Holdernesse, by 2nd w.; bro. of
Hon. John Darcy*. *unm.*[1]

Commr. for assessment, Yorks. (N. Riding) 1677–
80, 1689–90, j.p. by 1690–*d.*[2]

Cornet and major, Duke of York's 3 Life Gds. 1680–
5.

Commr. for prizes 1690–*d.*[3]

Darcy bought a commission in the guards for
£2,000, and was returning for Newark in 1685 as a
serving officer on the interest of the recorder Lord
Lexinton, whose only child was married to his
brother John. A moderately active Member of
James II's Parliament, he was appointed to the
committee of elections and privileges and to those
on the bills for exporting leather and licensing
hackney coaches. He was obliged to surrender his
commission during the recess, in return for a pension of £400, and presumably followed his brother
into opposition in the second session. He lost his

seat at the general election of 1689, but his brother's
unexpected death two days before had created a
vacancy in the family borough of Richmond, for
which he was returned at a by-election. His only
committee in the Convention was for the relief of
Huguenot refugees. A court Tory, he received £900
as royal bounty, most of which went to pay off his
debts, and shortly after the dissolution he was made
chief commissioner for prizes. He never stood
again, and died in the summer of 1694.[4]

[1] *Top. and Gen.* iii. 335. [2] *Add.* 29674, f. 161. [3] *Cal. Treas. Bks.*
ix. 377; x. 763. [4] *CJ*, x. 230; *Secret Service Moneys* (Cam. Soc. lii),
120; *HMC Buccleuch*, ii. 113; PCC 190 Box.

E.R.E.

DARCY, Sir Thomas, 1st Bt. (1632–93), of
Braxted Lodge, Essex.

MALDON   1679 (Oct.), 1681, 1685, 1689, 1690–
Apr. 1693

b. 1 Jan. 1632, o. (posth.) s. of Thomas Darcy of Tip-
tree Priory by Mary, da. of Sir Andrew Astley of
Writtle. *educ.* Jesus, Camb. 1650; G. Inn 1652. *m.* (1)
Cicely (*d.* 29 May 1661), da. of Sir Simonds D'Ewes,
1st Bt.[†], of Stowlangtoft Hall, Suff. and h. to her gdfa.
Sir William Clopton, 1da. *d.v.p.*; (2) lic. 12 Feb. 1663,
Jane, da. and h. of Robert Cole, barrister, of the Middle
Temple, 5s. (4 *d.v.p.*) 3da. *suc.* gdfa. 1638; *cr.* Bt. 19
June 1660.[1]

J.p. Suff. 1656–70, 1680–7, Essex 1680–Apr. 1688,
Oct. 1688–*d.*; commr. for assessment, Suff. 1657, Jan.
1660–79, Essex and Maldon 1689–90, militia, Suff.
1659, recusants 1675.[2]

Gent. of the privy chamber (extraordinary) July
1660.[3]

The Darcy family of Essex were descended from
a London Vintner who became lord mayor and
represented the city in 1337. The senior line first
sat for the county in 1416 and were advanced to the
peerage in 1551. Darcy, 'puritan bred and born',
came from a cadet line; his great-grandfather was a
notable Elizabethan witch-hunter and his grandfather, a lawyer, died insane. At the Restoration
Darcy obtained an honorary post at Court, too late
to avoid serving as foreman of the grand jury on
the regicides. He acquired by his first marriage a
Suffolk estate valued at £518 p.a. when he sold it in
1677. He bought Braxted Lodge, six miles from
Maldon, from John Cotton I* and was returned
for the borough after a contest at the second election
of 1679. Presumably he opposed exclusion, since he
was added to the commission of the peace. He was
re-elected in 1681 without a contest, but served on
no committees in the second or third Exclusion
Parliaments. He had lost his interest at Maldon by
1685, but the Duke of Albemarle (Christopher
Monck[†]) procured his return in order to secure his

support for the county election. A moderately active Member of James II's Parliament, he was appointed to the committees on the bills to suppress simony, to encourage shipbuilding and to establish a land registry.[4]

To the questions on the repeal of the Test Act and Penal Laws, Darcy replied that he did not intend to stand for Parliament himself, and could not promise to vote for candidates willing to comply with James II's policy. He was removed from local office, but the King's electoral agents continued to take his candidature seriously. He was returned to the Convention, of which he became an active Member, with 42 committees. Though presumably a Tory, he did not vote to agree with the Lords that the throne was not vacant. His most important committees in the first session were for the removal and disarming of Papists and the attainder bill. He was among those added to the inquiry into the expenses of the war on 15 Jan. 1690, and appointed to consider the bill imposing a general oath of allegiance. He was re-elected to the next Parliament, but died in April 1693, and the baronetcy became extinct a few years later.[5]

[1] Wards 7/92/116; Morant, *Essex*, i. 459; ii. 140; *Vis. Essex* (Harl. Soc. xiv), 44; Wright, *Essex*, ii. 777; PCC 50 Coker. [2] *HMC Lords*, i. 179; Essex RO, Q/SR399/10. [3] LC 3/2. [4] *State Trials*, vi. 187; Morant, *Essex*, ii. 139–41; Copinger, *Suff. Manors*, i. 142–3; *Bramston Autobiog.* (Cam. Soc. xxxii), 172–5. [5] *Bramston*, 345, 374.

G.H.

DARELL, Sir John (1645–94), of Calehill, Little Chart, Kent.

MAIDSTONE   1679 (Mar.)
RYE   1679 (Oct.), 1681, 1689, 1690–
             24 Jan. 1694 [new writ]

bap. 20 Aug. 1645, 1st s. of Edward Darell of Gray's Inn by Dorothy, da. of Robert Kipping of Tudeley. *educ.* G. Inn, entered 1658; Corpus, Oxf. 1663. *m.* 4 Aug. 1670, Elizabeth, da. and h. of his uncle Sir John Darell of Calehill, *s.p. suc.* fa. 1665; kntd. 26 July 1670; *suc.* uncle 1675.[1]

Member, Society of Mines Royal 1666, asst. 1669–74, 1675–7, 1682–3; member, Society of Mineral and Battery Works 1667, asst. 1671–7.[2]

J.p. Kent 1671–8, 1679–80, Feb. 1688–*d.*; commr. for assessment, Kent 1673–80, 1689–90, Rye 1690, recusants, Kent 1675; recorder, Canterbury 1687–Oct. 1688; dep. lt. Kent Feb. 1688–*d.*[3]

Darell's ancestor, a Yorkshireman, acquired Calehill by marriage in the reign of Henry IV, and sat for Kent in seven Parliaments between 1407 and 1429; but they were not a regular parliamentary family. Darell's uncle and his father, a lawyer, were Royalists in the second Civil War, and paid respectively £400 and £250 to the county committee for their compositions. On succeeding to his uncle's

estate, Darell became associated with the country party. He signed the protest against the candidature of Sir John Banks* at Winchelsea in 1677, and was removed from the commission of the peace by the King's command. He was returned for Maidstone on the Fane interest at the first election of 1679 and marked 'honest' on Shaftesbury's list. A moderately active Member he was appointed to five committees, including those for the habeas corpus amendment bill and for security against Popery, and voted for the exclusion bill. At the next election Darell was returned for Rye, where he was 'recommended as a burgess by the fanatics of Canterbury', and probably also by his neighbour and kinsman Edward Dering*. He was again removed from the commission of the peace as leader of the Kentish petitioners in 1680. He remained moderately active in the second Exclusion Parliament, being named to the committees to regulate elections, to reform the collection of the hearth-tax and to bring in a bill for the naturalization of foreign Protestants. He was re-elected in 1681, but left no trace on the records of the Oxford Parliament.[4]

Darell probably did not stand in 1685, but became a Whig collaborator later in the reign of James II, to whom he would be the more acceptable because his heir, a distant cousin, was being educated as a Roman Catholic at St. Omer. He was nominated recorder of Canterbury in the new charter, and recommended by the King's electoral agents as j.p. and deputy lieutenant. They also approved his candidature at Canterbury, with the support of the dissenters; but he is unlikely to have stood there in 1689. He was returned unopposed for Rye in a contested election, and also chosen to represent the Cinque Ports at the coronation of William and Mary. He was inactive in the Convention, in which he was named to only three committees. He was teller against excepting Hereford from the bill for restoring corporations, but did not vote for the disabling clause. He was appointed to the committee for the bill declaring the right of election in the Cinque Ports. Re-elected in 1690, he remained a court Whig, but he died early in 1694 and was buried at Little Chart on 2 Feb. The Calehill estate, valued at £1,035 p.a., was registered as the property of a Catholic non-juror in 1715, and no later member of the family entered Parliament.[5]

[1] *Little Chart Reg.* 50, 116, 148; *Vis. Kent* (Harl. Soc. liv), 45; *Le Neve's Knights* (Harl. Soc. viii), 240. [2] BL Loan 16. [3] Hasted, *Kent*, xii. 611. [4] *Arch. Cant.* xvii. 46–48; A. M. Everitt, *Community of Kent and the Great Rebellion*, 257; *Cal. Comm. Comp.* 458; Kent AO, 5a/ZB3/1; *HMC Finch*, ii. 44; *CSP Dom.* 1679–80, p. 526; Bath mss. Coventry pprs. 6, f. 230. [5] *CSP Dom.* 1691–2, p. 535; *CJ*, x. 322; *Little Chart Reg.* 153; PCC 30 Box; *English Catholic Nonjurors*, 88.

B.D.H.

DASHWOOD, Sir Robert, 1st Bt. (1662–1734), of Northbrook, Kirtlington, Oxon.

BANBURY   1689, 1690, 1695
OXFORDSHIRE   29 Nov. 1699

b. 6 Oct. 1662, 1st s. of George Dashwood, merchant, of Hackney, Mdx. by Margaret, da. of William Perry of Thorpe, Surr. educ. Eton c. 1675–9; Trinity, Oxf. 1679; I. Temple 1679. m. lic. 9 June 1682, Penelope (bur. 22 Feb. 1735), da. and coh. of Sir Thomas Chamberlayne, 2nd Bt., of Wickham, Oxon., 5s. (4 d.v.p.) 4da. suc. fa. 1682; kntd. 4 June 1682; cr. Bt. 16 Sept. 1684.[1]

Sheriff, Oxon. 1683–4; freeman, Woodstock 1684, Oxford 1685–Feb. 1688; dep. lt. Oxon. 1684–Feb. 1688, 1689–?d., j.p. 1685–Mar. 1688, Oct. 1688–d.; asst. Banbury by 1689; commr. for assessment, Oxon. and Oxford 1689–90.[2]

Gent. of the privy chamber 1685–Dec. 1688; commr. for preventing export of wool 1689–92.[3]

Dashwood was a cousin of Sir Samuel Dashwood*. His father, a wealthy revenue farmer, was promised a baronetcy in 1682, but died before the patent passed the great seal. Dashwood inherited an estate of £2,300 p.a. and acquired by marriage property in Oxfordshire valued at a further £1,700 p.a. A courtier under James II, he nevertheless lent Edmund Prideaux* £10,000 to buy his pardon after Monmouth's rebellion, and stood security for the remaining £5,000, no doubt as a strictly business transaction. A churchman, he refused the first two questions on the repeal of the Test Act and Penal Laws, and was removed from local office. It was reported at this time that he 'hates Popery, [and] loves the Church of England, but cannot swallow the doctrine of passive obedience'. He was returned for Banbury as 'a member of this borough' at the general election of 1689. An inactive Member of the Convention, he voted to agree with the Lords that the throne was not vacant, according to Ailesbury's list, but he was appointed to only four committees, of which the most important was for the repeal of the Corporations Act. He voted as a Tory under William, refusing the Association in 1696. He died on 14 July 1734 and was buried at Kirtlington. His grandson represented the county from 1740 to 1754, and again from 1761 to 1768, as a Tory.[4]

[1] J. Townsend, Oxon. Dashwoods, 8, 13. [2] Woodstock council acts 1679–99 (17 Sept. 1684); Oxford Council Acts (Oxf. Hist. Soc. n.s. ii), 170, 196; CSP Dom. 1684–5, p. 193. [3] Carlisle, Privy Chamber, 198. [4] Cussans, Herts. Hitchin, 52–53; Cal. Treas. Bks. iii. 235; v. 532; vi. 46; Townsend, 6–8; Add. 36707, f. 38; HMC Lords, n.s. v. 309, 310; CSP Dom. 1684–5, p. 123; CJ, x. 116; Hearne's Colls. (Oxf. Hist. Soc. lxxii), 363.

L.N./G.J.

DASHWOOD, Sir Samuel (c.1643–1705), of Bishopsgate, London and Mortlake, Surr.

LONDON   1685, 1690

b. c.1643, 1st s. of Francis Dashwood, merchant, of London by 1st w. Alice, da. of Richard Sleigh of Pilsbury, Derbys. m. lic. 17 May 1670 (aged 27), Anne (d. 16 June 1721), da. of John Smith of South Tidworth, Hants, 3s. (1 d.v.p.) 7da. suc. fa. 1683; kntd. 30 July 1684.[1]

Member, Vintners' Co. 1663, master 1684–5, asst. to 1687; member, Levant Co. 1663, asst. 1680–91; asst. R. Africa Co. 1672–4, 1677–9, 1682–4, 1687–9, 1692–3, 1698–9, 1701–3, 1705–d.; sheriff, London 1683–4; alderman 1683–7, Oct. 1688–d., ld. mayor 1702–3; committee, E.I. Co. 1684–6, 1690–5, 1698–1703, dep. gov. 1700–2; dep. lt. London 1685–7, Oct. 1688–?95, London and Surr. 1702–d.; commr. for assessment, London 1689–90, Surr. 1690; col. yellow regt. of militia ft. London 1702–d.; j.p. Bucks. 1702–d.; pres. Bethlehem and Bridewell hospitals 1704–d.[2]

Jt. farmer of excise 1677–83, commr. 1689–96; commr. for preventing export of wool 1689–92.[3]

Dashwood's grandfather was a Somerset yeoman. His father established himself in business in London, and with Dashwood's uncle (the father of Sir Robert Dashwood*) formed a syndicate to farm the excise in 1677. Dashwood himself was elected Tory sheriff of London in June 1683. He applied through (Sir) Stephen Fox* for permission to fine off, but the King replied that he could not 'dispense with Mr Dashwood being sheriff this year', and he was continued in office after the forfeiture of the charter. He was also appointed to the excise commission on the abolition of farming in the same year.[4]

Dashwood was elected for London in 1685, and became a moderately active Member of James II's Parliament. He was appointed to six committees, including those on expiring laws (26 May), on the bill to rebuild St. Paul's (22 June) and for the general naturalization of Huguenot refugees (1 July). He also sat on a committee on a bill to amend the bankruptcy laws, which did not reach the statute book before the prorogation. On 19 Dec. he supported a petition against a defaulting banker, and urged a reform in the law. He had himself been defrauded of £5,000, and when the case was judged the following year the only penalty which could be imposed on the banker under a statute of James I was the pillory. Between July 1685 and August 1686 he made loans to the crown amounting to £32,500 at 7 per cent on the security of the linen duty.[5]

Dashwood was one of the six Tory aldermen removed in the summer of 1687 for opposing the London address for liberty of conscience. Reinstated as alderman on the restoration of the charter in October 1688, he became an active member of the common council and a member of its committees to administer the city lands and the Ulster Plantation. He was among those appointed on 11 Dec. 1688 to draw up the address to the

Prince of Orange, and to raise a loan of £200,000, of which he subscribed £60,000 himself. At this time he held £2,725 East India stock. He also sat on the committees to procure the reversal of the judgement of quo warranto against the City, and to produce a scheme for restoring the solvency of the widows' and orphans' fund. Still a Tory, he was defeated at a by-election in May 1689, but he was appointed to the excise board, and regained his seat at the general election of 1690. He died on 10 Sept. 1705, aged 63, and was buried at Mortlake. His younger brother, who bought West Wycombe from the father of Thomas Lewes* and sat for Winchelsea from 1708 to 1713 as a Whig, founded a major parliamentary dynasty.[6]

[1] Cussans, *Herts*. Hitchin, 52. [2] J. R. Woodhead, *Rulers of London*, 56; PC2/72/507; *HMC Lords*, iii. 45; Guildhall Lib. Stocken and Noble Colls.; Luttrell, v. 193. [3] *Cal. Treas. Bks.* v. 532; vi. 46; vii. 665, 772; ix. 253; xi. 164. [4] North, *Lives*, ii. 202–4; Luttrell, i. 278, 283; *Clarendon Corresp.* i. 90–91; *CSP Dom.* July–Sept. 1683, pp. 373, 386; 1683–4, p. 16. [5] Christ Church Oxf. Evelyn mss; *CSP Dom.* 1685, p. 64; 1686–7, p. 165. [6] Luttrell, i. 411; *Cal. Treas. Bks.* viii. 2177–81; *Ellis Corresp.* ii. 350; London Corp. RO, common council jnl.; Add. 22185, f. 14; R. Morrice, Entering Bk. 2, p.556; Maitland, *Hist. London*, i. 490; *Sewall Diary*, i. 216.

E.C.

DAVENANT, Charles (1656–1714), of Westminster.[1]

ST. IVES	1685
GREAT BEDWYN	1698, 1701 (Feb.)

b. 17 Nov. 1656, 2nd s. of Sir William Davenant (*d.*1668) of Lincoln's Inn Fields, being 1st s. by 3rd w. Henriette Marie du Tremblay, wid. of St. Germain Beaupré of Anjou, France. *educ.* Cheam g.s. Surr. 1665; Balliol, Oxf. 1671–3; travelled abroad (Holland) c. 1673–5; LL.D. Camb. 1675; advocate, Doctors' Commons 1675. *m.* c.1678, Frances, da. and h. of James Molins, MD, of Shoe Lane, London, 2s. (1 *d.v.p.*) 6da.

Commr. for excise 1678–89, hearth-tax 1684–Jan. 1685, July 1685–9; sec. to commrs. for union with Scotland 1703; inspector-gen. of imports and exports 1705–*d.*[2]

Dep. lt. London 1687–Oct. 1688, Herefs. Apr. 1688–9.[3]

According to Aubrey, Davenant's father was Shakespeare's son by the wife of an Oxford innkeeper. He became a courtier and playwright, and was implicated in the army plot of 1641. He acted as lieutenant-general of the ordnance in the royalist army of the Marquess of Newcastle during the first Civil War, and then joined Henrietta Maria in exile. He is said to have become a Roman Catholic, but his conversion must have been of short duration. During the second Civil War he was captured while on a mission to the Virginian Royalists, and on his release he was able, despite 'the nicety of the times' to return to the entertainment world as producer of the first operas in England. At the Restoration he became manager and part-owner of the Duke of York's Theatre. Davenant took over this interest from his mother with a 16½ per cent holding while still an undergraduate, but his only play, *Circe*, was not a success. He owed his doctorate at Cambridge, which qualified him for practice as a civilian, to 'money and favour', the latter presumably being due to the Duke of Monmouth as chancellor of the university. He offered (Sir) Joseph Williamson*£500 for 'some post of business', but his seat on the excise board, which enabled him to marry, was apparently due to some other interest. A rival, Thomas Prise*, described him as a spy of Shaftesbury and Monmouth on the Court, but he retained his posts, at a salary rising to £1,000 p.a., until the Revolution.[4]

Davenant was elected for St. Ives in 1685 on the government interest. A moderately active Member of James II's Parliament he was appointed to nine committees, including those on the bills for establishing the new parish of St. James Piccadilly, preventing clandestine marriages, and relieving poor debtors. He was summoned to the meeting of the court caucus on 18 Nov., and presumably opposed the address against the employment of Roman Catholic officers. In 1687 he sold his theatrical interests to his brother Alexander for £2,400. He was approved by the King's electoral agents as court candidate for St. Ives in June 1688, but he is not likely to have stood in 1689, and was deprived of office under the new regime. He became a prominent Tory pamphleteer and economist under William III, and sat for Bedwyn. He lost his seat in 1701, when he was one of the three Tory Members who were discovered at supper with the French minister on the evening of the declaration of war, but Queen Anne gave him office as inspector-general of imports and exports. He died on 6 Nov. 1714, and was buried at St. Bride's, Fleet Street. His son held minor diplomatic appointments under the Hanoverians, but no other Member of the family entered Parliament.[5]

[1] This biography is based on D. Waddell, 'Career and Writings of Charles Davenant' (Oxford D. Phil. thesis, 1955). [2] *Cal. Treas. Bks.* v. 1055; vii. 1074; viii. 247; ix. 190. [3] *CSP Dom.* 1687–9, pp. 62, 186. [4] A. Harbage, *Sir William Davenant*, 104–6, 120, 147; L. Hotson, *Commonwealth and Restoration Stage*, 222, 231; *CSP Dom.* 1677–8, p. 616; 1678, p. 371; 1682, p. 617. [5] Hotson, 285; *Cal. Treas. Bks.* viii. 430.

E.C.

DAVERS, Sir Robert, 2nd Bt. (c.1653–1722), of Rougham, nr. Bury St. Edmunds, Suff.

BURY ST. EDMUNDS	1689, 1690, 1695, 1698, 1701 (Feb.), 22 Nov. 1703
SUFFOLK	1705, 1708, 1710, 1713, 1715, 30 Mar.–1 Oct. 1722

b. c.1653, o.s. of Sir Robert Davers, 1st Bt., of Barbados by Eleanor Luke of Barbados. *m.* 2 Feb. 1682, Mary, da. and coh. of Thomas Jermyn*, 2nd Baron Jermyn of St. Edmundsbury, 4s. 5da. *suc.* fa. June 1684.[1]

Member of council, Barbados 1682–?87, baron of the Exchequer 1683–?87; commr. for assessment, Suff. and Bury St. Edmunds 1689–90; j.p. Suff. 1700–?*d.*[2]

Gent. of privy chamber 1691–1714.[3]

Davers may have been the son of the Robert Davers who emigrated to Barbados at the age of 14 in 1635; but according to the contemporary Suffolk historian, Sir Richard Gipps, his father was the younger son of a Buckinghamshire family who served in the royalist army and only went out to the West Indies after the execution of Charles I. By 1673 he was one of the leading planters in Barbados, with 600 acres, worth £30,000. About 1680 he returned to England, bought the estate of Rougham, four miles from Bury St. Edmunds, and was created a baronet. Davers himself was born in Barbados, and held office in the island until 1687, when he finally settled in England. In May 1688 he petitioned unsuccessfully for some allowance for his services.[4]

Davers was originally selected by his wife's uncle, Lord Dover, as court candidate for Bury in 1688; but he excused himself 'upon the account of his presence being so very necessary now he is pulling down his house', and it was clear to the royal electoral agents that he would oppose the repeal of the Test Act and Penal Laws. He defeated John Hervey[†] at the general election of 1689, and voted to agree with the Lords that the throne was not vacant. A moderately active Member of the Convention, he was appointed to 36 committees, including those to repeal the Corporations Act, to regulate the administration of oaths to army officers, and to consider an attainder bill. In June he acted as chairman for an estate bill. He was one of five Members ordered on 9 Aug. to prepare a bill to ease the plantations of the duties imposed in 1685. After the recess he was named to the committee of inquiry into war expenses, and in his only recorded speech opposed supply. After 1690 he became a friend of Robert Harley II* and usually voted with the Tories. Although he signed the Association in 1696, he was later a member of the October Club, and in 1721 his name was included in a list of leading Jacobites sent to the Pretender. He died on 1 Oct. 1722, aged 69, and was buried at Rushbrooke. His younger son, the 4th baronet, was returned for Bury as a Tory in 1722 and for the county in 1727.[5]

[1] *Rushbrooke Par. Reg.* (Suff. Green Bks. vi), 349–66. [2] *CSP Col.* 1681–5, pp. 248, 556, 565; 1689–92, p. 146; 1693–6, pp. 33, 444. [3] Carlisle, *Privy Chamber,* 207, 211 [4] *List of Persons who Went to*

Amer. Plantations ed. Hotton, 63; *Suff. Inst. Arch. Procs.* viii. 152–3; *Cal. Treas. Bks.* viii. 1820, 1836. [5] *IHR Bull.* liv. 200; R. Morrice, *Entering Bk.* 2, p. 675; Stuart mss 65/10; *Rushbrooke Par. Reg.* 353–66.

P.W.

DAVIE, Sir John, 2nd Bt. (1612–78), of Creedy, Devon.

TAVISTOCK   16 May–17 Dec. 1661

bap. 6 Dec. 1612, 1st s. of Sir John Davie, 1st Bt.[†], of Sandford by Juliana, da. of Sir William Strode[†] of Newnham. *educ.* Exeter, Oxf. 1631; I. Temple 1631. *m.* (1) Eleanor, da. of Sir John Acland, 1st Bt., of Columbjohn, *s.p.*; (2) by 1645, Triphena (*bur.* 1 Feb. 1659), da. and coh. of Richard Reynell[†] of Creedy, wid. of Nicholas Hunt of Chudleigh, 1s. *d.v.p.* 1da.; (3) 17 Apr. 1661, Margaret (*d.* 25 Apr. 1670), da. of Sir Francis Glanville[†] of Kilworthy, nr. Tavistock, wid. of William Kelly of Kelly, *s.p.*; (4) lic. 3 Oct. 1671, Amy, da. of Edmund Parker of Burrington, wid. of Walter Hele of South Poole, *s.p. suc.* fa. Oct. 1654.[1]

J.p. Devon 1656–65, commr. for assessment 1657, Jan. 1660–*d.*, militia Mar. 1660, dep. lt. Aug. 1660–?65, 1676–?*d.*[2]

Davie's grandfather, a merchant, was three times mayor of Exeter. His father sat for Tiverton in 1621, was created a baronet by Charles I and was later appointed to the Devon commission of array. His estates were sequestrated in 1649 on a charge of lending the King £400 and assisting him with horses, but the sequestration was taken off in the following year. Davie himself, though a Presbyterian, held local office during the Interregnum. But at the Restoration he was proposed for the order of the Royal Oak with an annual income of £2,000. At the general election of 1661 he challenged the Russell interest in Tavistock, and was returned by the portreeve on the broader franchise of 'the freeholders generally'. There was a double return, but he was allowed to take his seat on the merits of the return. He was appointed to no committees in the Cavalier Parliament, however, and was unseated by the Hon. William Russell* seven months later, when the House declared in favour of confining the franchise to the 'freeholders of inheritance only'.[3]

Davie kept a Presbyterian chaplain, and in 1663 headed the list of Devon justices who were 'arrant Presbyterians'. According to the bishop of Exeter his mansion at Creedy was their 'chief place of resort'. He was removed from local office, though he later acted as deputy lieutenant. He was buried at Sandford on 31 July 1678. His widow married Sir Nicholas Slanning*.[4]

[1] Vivian, *Vis. Devon,* 270, 412, 462, 645, 712, 719. [2] *CSP Dom.* 1675–6, p. 498. [3] *Trans. Dev. Assoc.* lxvii. 320; *Cal. Comm. Adv.*

Money, 1127. [4] D. R. Lacey, *Dissent and Parl. Pols.* 388; PCC 109 Reeve; *Devon and Cornw. N. and Q.* xxi. 284.

J.S.C.

DAVIE, Sir John, 3rd Bt. (c.1660–92), of Creedy, Devon.

SALTASH 1679 (Oct.), 1681

b. c.1660, 1st s. of William Davie, barrister, of the Inner Temple by Margaret, da. of Christopher Clarke, merchant, of Exeter. *educ.* Exeter, Oxf. matric. 21 Mar. 1678, aged 17. *unm. suc.* fa. 1663, uncle Sir John Davie, 2nd Bt.* July 1678.[1]

J.p. Devon 1687–*d.*, dep. lt. May–July 1688, sheriff Mar.–Nov. 1689, commr. for assessment 1689–90.

Davie was returned to the second and third Exclusion Parliaments for Saltash, doubtless as a supporter of the country party, although there is no record of his activity. He followed the example of Sir Edward Seymour* in returning negative answers on the repeal of the Penal Laws and Test Act in 1688. He was removed from the lieutenancy only two months after appointment, but allowed to remain on the commission of the peace. He was the first sheriff of Devon appointed after the Revolution, but died on 30 Sept. 1692, aged 32. He was buried at Sandford, the last of the family to sit in Parliament.

[1] Vivian, *Vis. Devon*, 270; *London Vis. Peds.* (Harl. Soc. xvii), 40.

J.S.C.

DAVIES, Mutton (1634–84), of Gwysaney, Flints. and Llannerch, Denb.

FLINTSHIRE 18 Nov. 1678, 1679 (Mar.), 1679 (Oct.)

b. 19 Feb. 1634, 1st s. of Robert Davies of Gwysaney by Anne, da. and coh. of Sir Peter Mutton† of Llannerch. *educ.* I. Temple 1652; travelled abroad (France, Italy) 1654–7. *m.* 27 May 1658, Elizabeth, da. of Sir Thomas Wilbraham, 2nd Bt., of Woodhey, Cheshire, 5s. 5da. *suc.* fa. 1666.[1]

Commr. for assessment, Flints. Aug. 1660–80, Denb. 1661–80; freeman, Denbigh 1665, common councilman 1667–*d.*, alderman 1676–7, 1679–80; j.p. Denb. and Flints. 1669–*d.*; sheriff, Flints. 1669–70; dep. lt. Denb. and Flints. 1674–*d.*; commr. for encroachments, Denb. 1684.[2]

Davies came from a minor gentry family which could trace its descent to the early 13th century. His father, an active Royalist, compounded in 1648 for £646. Davies himself went abroad during the Interregnum, gaining military experience in France and the Low Countries. He took part in the royalist rising of 1659 led by Sir George Booth* as a captain of horse under Roger Whitley*. With the failure he was imprisoned in Chester Castle, from

which he was released on 28 Jan. 1660. At the Restoration his father was proposed for the order of the Royal Oak, with an estate valued at £2,000.[3]

Davies himself assisted (Sir) John Carter* in an affray with two alleged smugglers of Irish cattle, and obtained the protection of the House in 1667. He gained the Flintshire seat on the death of Sir Thomas Hanmer* in 1678, when none of the more influential families of the shire was in a position to provide a candidate of its own. Shaftesbury saw no reason to alter the rating of 'doubly vile' which he had given to his predecessor. During the last weeks of the Cavalier Parliament he was named only to the committee for the bill to facilitate the conviction of Popish recusants. Classed as 'vile' in Shaftesbury's list he nevertheless voted for the committal of the exclusion bill on 11 May, but was otherwise inactive in the first Exclusion Parliament. He retained his seat in the second election of 1679, although challenged by Sir John Hanmer*. Moderately active in the second Exclusion Parliament, he was appointed to the committee of elections and privileges and to those on bills for burial in woollen and the regulation of hackney coaches. He did not stand in 1681, feeling it better not to affront the Court by opposing Hanmer again; but a few days after the election he was present at a dinner at which the King (he informed a Welsh friend) expressed his desire to see not only the Papists suppressed, but also the Presbyterians. He died on 29 Oct. 1684 and was buried at Mold, the only member of his family to sit in Parliament.[4]

[1] *Arch. Camb.* (ser. 4), i. 178; *Frag. Gen.* xi. 59; Add. 34015, f. 145. [2] J. Williams, *Recs. of Denbigh*, 136, 138–9, 141; *Cal. Treas. Bks.* vii. 1132. [3] *Cal. Comm. Comp.* 1717. [4] *CJ*, ix. 52; *HMC 3rd Rep.* 259; *HMC 4th Rep.* 425; *HMC Portland*, i. 684; A. H. Dodd, *Studies in Stuart Wales*, 204, 206.

A.M.M.

DAWLEY, Henry (c.1646–c.1703), of Lainston House, Sparsholt, Hants.

LYMINGTON 1 Nov. 1680, 1681

b. c.1646. o.s. of Henry Dawley of Lainston by Anne, da. of John Worsley of Gatcombe, I.o.W. *educ.* Wadham, Oxf. 1659. *m.* lic. 10 Sept. 1670 (aged 24), Mary, da. of Anthony Collins of the Middle Temple and Newport, I.o.W., 1s. 3da. *suc.* fa. 1654.[1]

Freeman, Winchester 1677, Lymington 1680; commr. for assessment, Hants 1679–80, 1689–1702, j.p. 1679–87, ?1689–*d*; commr. of inquiry, New Forest 1691; dep. lt. Hants 1689–?*d.*, col. of militia ft. by 1697–?*d.*[2]

Dawley's great-grandfather bought the manor of Lainston in 1613. Nothing is known of the family's politics before Dawley stood as a court supporter at the Lymington by-election in 1680. He again defeated an exclusionist at the next general election, but in neither the second nor the third Exclusion Parliaments was he appointed to any committee. He was probably a high Anglican, since he was removed from local office in 1687. But he accepted the Revolution, and stood for Stockbridge in 1693. The date of his death is unknown, but his name does not appear on either the assessment commission or the Winchester electorate after 1702. He was the only member of the family to sit in Parliament. His son sold Lainston in 1711.[3]

[1] T. Phillips, *Vis. Hants*, 20; *London Mar. Lic.* ed. Foster, 387; PCC 197 Alchin. [2] Winchester corp. assembly bk. 6, f. 100; C. St. Barbe, *Recs. of Lymington*, 9; *Cal. Treas. Bks.* ix. 1384; *CSP Dom.* 1699–1700, p. 235; Eg. 1626, f. 45. [3] *VCH Hants*, iv. 445.

P.W.

DAWNAY, John (1625–95), of Cowick, Yorks.

YORKSHIRE	1660
PONTEFRACT	1661, 1679 (Mar.), 1679 (Oct.), 1681, 1685, 1689

bap. 25 Jan. 1625, 2nd s. of John Dawnay of Cowick by Elizabeth, da. of Sir Richard Hutton, j.c.p. 1617–39, of Goldsborough. *educ.* G. Inn, entered 1641; Jesus, Camb. 1641. *m.* (1) 4 Aug. 1645, Elizabeth (*bur.* 21 Feb. 1663), da. of Sir John Melton[†] of York, sec. to council of the north, 5s. *d.v.p.* 3da.; (2) lic. 14 May 1663, Dorothy (*bur.* 28 May 1709), da. of William Johnson of Wickham, Lincs., 2s. 1da. *suc.* nephew 1644; kntd. 2 June 1660; *cr.* Visct. Downe [I] 19 Feb. 1681.[1]

J.p. Yorks. (W. Riding) 1647–Mar. 1657, Aug. 1657–Sept. 1688, Nov. 1689–*d.*; commr. for militia, northern counties 1648, Yorks. Mar. 1660, assessment (W. Riding) 1657, Jan. 1660–80, 1690, (N. Riding) Aug. 1660–1, 1664–80, 1689–90; dep. lt. (W. Riding) c. Aug. 1660–77; commr. for sewers, Hatfield chase Aug. 1660, (E. Riding) Sept. 1660, oyer and terminer, Northern circuit 1661, corporations, Yorks. 1662–3; steward, honour of Cowick and Snaith 1669–*d.*; commr. for recusants (W. Riding) 1675.[2]

Dawnay's ancestors settled at Cowick, 12 miles from Pontefract, in the reign of Henry VII. His great-grandfather represented Thirsk under Elizabeth. No member of the family appears to have fought in the Civil War, but after succeeding an infant nephew in the estate Dawnay was appointed to the county committee and held local office throughout the Interregnum. But on 17 Feb. 1660 he and Sir Thomas Wharton* presented George Monck* with the declaration of the Yorkshire gentlemen for a free Parliament, and he was returned unopposed for the county a few weeks later. Wharton's brother classed him as a friend, but he doubtless earned his knighthood by steady support of the Court in the Convention. He was

not active, however, though his eight committees included the committee of elections and privileges and the drafting committee. On 30 June he acted as teller against a proviso to the bill of indemnity annulling releases and discharges extorted from Cavaliers. He was also appointed to the committee to state the debts of the army and navy.[3]

Dawnay stepped down to Pontefract, where he owned a large number of burgages, for the general election of 1661, and continued to represent this borough for the remainder of the period. Wharton again listed him as a friend in the Cavalier Parliament, in which he was moderately active. His 69 committees included the committee of elections and privileges in 11 sessions; but he took no part in the Clarendon Code. He was principally responsible for the defeat of the Lords bill for settling the Hatfield level in 1662. Sir Thomas Osborne* listed him in 1669 among the Members to be engaged for the Court by the Duke of Buckingham, and his uncle Sir Philip Musgrave* suggested that he should be given an Irish peerage. In 1670 he was appointed to the committees for preventing illegal imprisonment and nominating commissioners for union with Scotland, and in the spring session of 1675 to those for hindering Papists from sitting in Parliament and preventing the growth of Popery. He received the government whip for the autumn session, in which his committees included those to consider the bills preventing illegal exactions and recalling British subjects from the French service. Shaftesbury classed him 'worthy' in 1677, but although now clearly in opposition he was not prominent in the closing sessions of this Parliament.[4]

Dawnay was again classed as 'worthy' in 1679. An inactive Member of the first Exclusion Parliament, he was appointed to the committees for regulating elections, receiving proposals for the royal fisheries, and investigating abuses in the Post Office. He voted for exclusion, but probably changed sides under the influence of his friend Lord Halifax (Sir George Savile*) in the second Exclusion Parliament, in which he was named to no committees. He was alleged to have offered Lord Sunderland £25,000 for a peerage, but it was Halifax who obtained an Irish viscountcy for him just before the 1681 election. Nevertheless it was as Sir John Dawnay and not Lord Downe that he was appointed to the committee of elections and privileges in the Oxford Parliament.[5]

Downe was moderately active in James II's Parliament with eight committees of secondary importance, and was listed among the Opposition. In 1688 he gave the lead to 12 other West Riding justices in returning negative answers on the repeal of the Test Act and Penal Laws:

We judge we ought not to pre-engage ourselves by consenting to the demand before arguments may be heard and considered in Parliament, and we are further sensible that the Protestant Church may be deeply concerned herein as to its security, which Church we are bound to support by all lawful means.

As the King's electoral agents expected, he was re-elected to the Convention. He did not vote to agree with the Lords that the throne was not vacant. An inactive Member, he was named only to the committees for continuing legal proceedings, removing Papists from the London area, examining prisoners of state, and repealing the Corporations Act. But on 29 May 1689 he obtained leave to go into the country for a month, and there is no evidence that he ever returned to Westminster. At the general election he stood down in favour of his son Henry, who sat for Pontefract as a Tory in the next Parliament and for the county from 1698 to 1700 and 1707 to 1727.[6]

[1] Clay, *Dugdale's Vis. Yorks.* ii. 334–5. [2] Add. 29674, f. 160; C181/7/20, 44; *HMC 8th Rep.* pt. 1 (1881), 275; Sir Robert Somerville, *Duchy of Lancaster Official Lists*, 158. [3] *Letter and Declaration of Yorks.* (1660); *CJ*, viii. 79. [4] J. Hunter, *South Yorks.* i. 167; *CSP Dom.* 1671, p. 239. [5] *Reresby Mems.* 217–18; Eg. 1169, f. 19. [6] *HMC Var.* ii. 403.

M.W.H.

DEANE, Sir Anthony (1633–1721), of Crutched Friars, London.

NEW SHOREHAM   24 Oct. 1678
HARWICH   1679 (Mar.), 1685

b. 3 Dec. 1633, 2nd s. of Anthony Deane of London by (?)Elizabeth, da. of William Wright, Barber Surgeon, of London. *educ.* Merchant Taylors' 1646. *m.* (1) Anne (*d.*1677), 4s. (3 *d.v.p.*) 1da.; (2) 23 July 1678, 'aged 40', Christian (*d.*1687), da. and h. of William Lyons of Bocking, Essex, wid. of Sir John Dawes, 1st Bt., of Putney, Surr., 3s. (2 *d.v.p.*) 6da. Kntd. 3 July 1675.[1]

Asst. shipwright, Woolwich by Nov. 1660; master shipwright, Harwich 1664, Portsmouth 1668–75; commr. resident at Portsmouth 1672–5; comptroller of victualling 1675–80, stores Mar.–June 1680; member, R. Fisheries Co. 1677; special commr. of the navy 1685–Oct. 1688; elder bro. Trinity House 1685–9.[2]

Capt. of ft. Harwich 1667.[3]

Freeman, Harwich 1673, Portsmouth 1675; alderman, Harwich 1674–?89, mayor 1675–6, 1681–2; j.p. Essex 1676–80, Essex, Hants, Kent, Mdx., Suff., Surr., Suss. and Westminster 1687–9; commr. for assessment, Harwich 1677–9; member of shipwrights' co. Rotherhithe, Surr. 1686.[4]

FRS 1681–d.

Deane, who was born in Gloucestershire, was probably a cousin of Richard Deane, the regicide and Commonwealth admiral; but nothing is known of his father's career or of his own before the Restoration, though Clarendon, in a moment of pardonable exasperation, called him 'the veriest fanatic that is in England'. He is first heard of in government service as a shipwright at Woolwich, and in 1664 he was put in charge of Harwich dockyard. He owed his promotion to Samuel Pepys*, who described him as 'a conceited fellow, and one that means the King a great deal of service, [and] more of disservice to other people that go away with profits he cannot make'. Even after his transfer to Portsmouth in 1668, and his appointment as navy commissioner, he maintained his interest at Harwich, presenting a pulpit-cloth to the parish church and taking out the freedom of the borough in 1673. He contributed about £60 in money and timber (presumably not his own) to build a new town hall, and was elected to the corporation. In 1677 he accepted from the borough a deposit of £90 to be invested by him at interest.[5]

However, before the dissolution of the Cavalier Parliament a vacancy occurred at Shoreham, where Deane was known as a purchaser of plank for the Portsmouth dockyard. He was enthusiastically recommended to the borough by the Dukes of York and Monmouth, and Samuel Fortrey, an ordnance official, was ordered to promote his election. He was duly returned, and marked 'doubly vile' on Shaftesbury's list; but he was not an active Member of the Cavalier Parliament. During the Popish Plot, he was appointed to the committees to investigate noises in Old Palace Yard and to examine Coleman's papers, but he did not speak.[6]

Deane was defeated by John Cheale* at Shoreham in the first general election of 1679, but was returned unopposed for Harwich together with Pepys. A moderately active Member he was named to the elections committee, but given leave on 9 Apr. to go into the country. On his return he was appointed to the committees to receive proposals concerning the royal fisheries, to inquire into the shipping of artillery from Portsmouth, and to consider the reform of the bankruptcy law. On 20 May he and Pepys were committed to the custody of the serjeant-at-arms on various charges trumped up by William Harbord*, ranging from the 'piratical proceedings' of the privateer *Hunter* during the third Dutch war to the betrayal of naval secrets to the French. In his own defence he said that the French

had no need of learning from England, they had got into so excellent a method. . . . I have twelve children to take care of, and I to think of a better way than that happy station I was in! . . . For these nineteen years I have faithfully served the navy, and more regulations have been under my hand than were ever before.

Roger Morrice alleged that he voted against exclusion on the following day, before being sent to the

Tower. On the dissolution of Parliament Deane and Pepys were released on bail, 'and if my lord chief justice hang 500 Jesuits he will not regain the opinion he hath thereby lost with the populace'. It was reported that they would stand for re-election, 'but all rational men blame them for it'. Curiously enough, Deane was not included in the black list of the 'unanimous club'. He remained in office until June 1680, when he resigned, presumably in anticipation of the meeting of the second Exclusion Parliament, and returned to private life. He was granted arms in 1683.[7]

On the accession of James II Deane accepted the seat on the navy board which was pressed on him by Pepys, but with some reluctance, because in private practice he could earn more than double the offered salary of £500. His imprisonment had only briefly interrupted his favourite leisure activity, and his family had increased (by his own estimate) to 15, 'not without expectation of more', he added complacently. He regained his seat at Harwich, and became an active Member of the 1685 Parliament, in which he was appointed to 14 committees, including those to examine the disbandment accounts, to provide carriages for the navy and ordnance offices, to prohibit the import of gunpowder, to encourage ship-building, to finance the construction of St. Paul's, and to relieve London widows and orphans. The King's electoral agents reported no opposition to him in Harwich in 1688, but unlike Pepys he decided not to contest the general election of 1689. He was not employed again after the Revolution, and was imprisoned for some months as a Jacobite suspect. Very little is known of the last 30 years of Deane's life, or of his family, though one of his sons died in Russia working as a shipwright for Peter the Great. He died at his house in Charterhouse Square, London on 11 June 1721, 'aged 96', and was buried at St. Olave's, Hart Street. His will shows him to have been in comfortable, though scarcely opulent circumstances, with no land other than house property in Ipswich.[8]

[1] Greenwich Par. Reg. 66; Grantees of Arms (Harl. Soc. lxvi), 72; East Anglian, n.s. iii. 147; St. Olave Hart Street (Harl. Soc. Reg. xliv), 82–89, 216–31; St. Martin Outwich (Harl. Soc. Reg. xxxiii), 41; CSP Dom. 1675–6, p. 197. [2] CSP Dom. 1660–1, p. 359; 1664–5, p. 311; 1667–8, p. 492; Sel. Charters (Selden Soc. xxviii), 199; Cat. Pepysian Mss (Navy Recs. Soc. xxvi), 89–90. [3] CSP Dom. 1667, p. 43. [4] S. Dale, Harwich and Dovercourt, 221, 223, 224; R. East, Portsmouth Recs. 361; CSP Dom. 1675–6, p. 478; 1686–7, p. 21. [5] Essex Review, xxxiv. 196–205; Pepys Diary, 6 June 1663, 14 July 1664; Essex Arch. Soc. Trans. n.s. xxii. 395; Dale, 221; Harwich bor. recs. 98/4/133. [6] CSP Dom. 1668–9, p. 354; 1678, p. 438; Adm. 2/1746, f. 152; Cal. Treas. Bks. v. 830, 854. [7] CJ, ix. 570, 629; Grey, ix. 627; Hatton Corresp. (Cam. Soc. n.s. xxii), 187; Newdegate, Cavalier and Puritan, 130. [8] Cat. Pepysian Mss, 75–76; HMC Dartmouth, i. 155; Bodl. Rawl. mss A179, f. 161; Pepys Corresp. i. 27–28; Luttrell, iv. 535; Pol. State, xxi. 671; Essex Review, xxxiv. 204; PCC 112 Buckingham.

B.M.C.

DEANE, John (c.1632–94), of Oxenwood, Tidcombe, Wilts.

GREAT BEDWYN	1679 (Mar.)
LUDGERSHALL	1689, 1690–31 Dec. 1694

b. c.1632, 1st surv. s. of James Deane of Deanland, Basing, Hants by 2nd w. Frances, da. of Thomas Baynard of Lackham, Wilts. educ. M. Temple 1650. m. (1) Margaret, da. of Thomas Garrard of Lambourn, Berks., 1s.; (2) bef. 1665, Magdalene, da. of John Stroughill of Barkham, Berks., at least 1s. 3da. suc. fa. 1652.[1]

Commr. for assessment, Hants 1661–80, Wilts. 1677–80, Berks. 1679–80, 1689, Hants and Wilts. 1689–90, loyal and indigent officers, Wilts. 1662, recusants, Berks. and Hants 1675; dep. lt. Hants ?1676–Feb. 1688, col. of militia ft. by 1679–Feb. 1688; j.p. Hants 1680–Apr. 1688, 1689–d., Wilts. 1680–June 1688, Oct. 1688–d., Berks. 1680–?d.; freeman, Portsmouth 1683.[2]

Lt. of ft. Sir William Killigrew's regt. 1662.[3]

Deane's grandfather obtained a grant of arms in 1598 with a list of seven generations of ancestors. Yet although the family was widespread in northeast Hampshire, they do not seem to have been of any account before. Deane's father leased Oxenwood from the Seymours shortly before the Civil War, in which he appears to have take no part. Deane himself was of course too young to fight, but was drawn into Penruddock's rising 'through the influence of his malignant neighbours rather than his own inclination'. He returned to his mother's house after only three days, but he was condemned to death and only obtained a reprieve at great expense. He was released on bail in 1656, and on a certificate of his penitence allowed to redeem his estate (practically all of which would only come to him on his mother's death) for £200. At the Restoration Deane and other survivors, with the widows of their less fortunate companions, offered a proviso to the indemnity bill excepting their judges, but it did not pass. He obtained a regular commission in 1662, but did not hold it long, and retired to live the life of a country gentleman of modest means, serving in 'several chargeable places of honour in the country', and possibly sometimes entrusted by Prince Rupert with private business.[4]

Oxenwood lies near the meeting-point of Wiltshire, Berkshire and Hampshire. Deane held office in all three counties, though as deputy lieutenant and militia officer he was most prominent in the last. It was as a country candidate and possibly on the Powlett interest that he was defeated by Charles West* in the Andover by-election of 1678. At the next general election he stood for Great Bedwyn, only four miles from his home, and his success deprived Daniel Finch*, one of the leading government spokesmen, of a seat in the first Exclusion Parliament. An inactive Member, he was appointed only to the committee of elections and privileges and to that for examining the disbandment accounts. Shaftesbury marked him 'honest', but, to use his own words, he voted against 'the horrid and hellish bill of exclusion'. Though supported by the Bruce interest in the autumn, he was unsuccessful, and his petition was not reported. His loyalty was not in question, however, for he was added to the commissions of the peace both in Hampshire and Wiltshire. It is not known whether he stood in 1681, but four years later he unsuccessfully opposed the Whig candidates at Whitchurch, about midway between his Hampshire and Wiltshire properties. Claiming to have spent £10,000 in the King's service, he petitioned for an office of profit. James II, who retained a gracious sense of his 'constant loyalty and good services', recommended him to the lord treasurer; but whatever was done for him, he was soon 'turned out of all he had for refusing to take away the Penal Laws', and even Finch magnanimously described him as a great sufferer. To the lord lieutenant of Wiltshire, Deane 'sent a civil excuse for not coming, and said he had given his answer to the Duke of Berwick', who noted him among the Hampshire deputy lieutenants as negative on the first and second questions.[5]

Deane came in to William of Orange at Hungerford, only eight miles from Oxenwood, and was returned to the Convention for Ludgershall. He voted to agree with the Lords that the throne was not vacant, but did not hesitate to petition the new Government for employment. He was again an inactive Member; of his four committees, the most important was for the bill to restore corporations. He was re-elected in 1690, but died of smallpox at Westminster at the end of 1694. He was buried at Tidcombe on 4 Jan. 1695. His younger son went out to the West Indies as a preacher, while his heir James obtained a private Act in 1701 for the sale of Oxenwood, said to be worth not above £150 p.a., and Deanland followed not long after.[6]

[1] *Vis. Hants* (Harl. Soc. lxiv), 199; *Wilts. Vis. Peds.* (Harl. Soc. cv), 16; *Vis. Berks.* (Harl. Soc. lvi), 214, 291; *Al. Ox.* 389; M. B. Deane, *Bk. of Dene*, 20; *Coll. Top. et. Gen.* viii. 188–9. [2] *CSP Dom.* 1679–80, p. 60; R. East, *Portsmouth Recs.* 366. [3] *CSP Dom.* 1661–2, p. 516. [4] *Grantees of Arms* (Harl. Soc. lxvi), 72; Wilts. RO, 562/1; PCC 289 Brent; *Thurloe*, iii. 372; *CSP Dom.* 1656–7, pp. 24–25; 1658–9, pp. 251–2; 1673–5, p. 509; *HMC 7th Rep.* 98, 123–4; *HMC Laing*, i. 448–9. [5] *HMC Finch*, ii. 54–55, 289; *CSP Dom.* 1685, p. 178; 1689–90, p. 181. [6] *CSP Dom.* 1689–90, p. 181; *Wood's Life and Times* (Oxf. Hist. Soc. xxvi), 476; PCC adm. act bk. 1695, f. 13; *Wilts. Arch. Mag.* vi. 303; *Magd. Coll. Reg.* vi. 119; St. 13 Wm. III c.40; Deane, 21.

J.P.F.

DEEDES, Julius (1635–92), of Hythe, Kent.

HYTHE   1679 (Mar.), 3 Apr.–4 June 1685, 1689

bap. 6 Sept. 1635, o.s. of William Deedes, mercer, of Hythe by 1st w. Bennet, da. of Robert Smith, mercer, of Margate. *m.* Anne (*d.*1698), da. of Richard Bate of Lydd, 4s. 4da. *suc. fa.* 1653.[1]
    Capt. of militia ft. Cinque Ports by 1673–82, 1689–d.; commr. for assessment, Kent 1673–80, Hythe 1679–80, Kent, Hythe and Lydd 1689–90, Pembroke 1690; j.p. Kent 1676–80, 1689–92; freeman, Hythe by 1679, mayor 1680–1, 1684–5, 1690–1, jurat 1682–3.[2]

Deedes came of a family settled in Kent by the end of the 16th century. His father appears to have been the first to live at Hythe where he became a jurat and captain of militia under the Commonwealth. Deedes himself was granted arms in 1653, and married into a leading Cinque Ports family. He first became active in parliamentary politics at a by-election at Hythe in 1673. He defeated Sir William Honeywood* at the first general election of 1679, and was marked 'worthy' on Shaftesbury's list. But in the first Exclusion Parliament he was appointed only to the committees to report on a petition from five foreign merchants and to consider the security bill. He was absent from the division on the exclusion bill, and stood down at the next election for personal reasons. Nevertheless he was removed from the county magistracy in 1680 and lost his militia commission two years later. When a smuggler was killed by a customs official early in 1685, Deedes falsified evidence at the inquest and secured parliamentary privilege by returning himself to James II's Parliament. But the lord high steward vetoed his nomination as one of the bearers of the canopy at the coronation, his election was declared void without his having taken any part in the proceedings of the House, and on 21 July he resigned as mayor.[3]

Deedes was re-elected in 1689, and allowed to officiate at the coronation of William and Mary. He helped to apprehend two Jacobite propagandists in the summer. In the Convention he served on no committees, though on 31 July 1689 he acted as teller against the adjournment of the debate on free trade in woollen manufactures, and he supported the disabling clause in the bill to restore corporations. He lent £250 to the Government in 1690, but continued to give practical expression to his free trade views. In May 1692 it was reported that 14 persons in his employ beat and wounded customs officers who tried to prevent the transport of 16 bags of wool from his barn. According to a Treasury minute 'the seizure was legal as being of reasonable suspicion, and the rescuing thereof was a transgression of the law'.[4]

Deedes was buried at Hythe on 9 Sept. 1692. His will indicates that he was in comfortable circumstances. He left portions of £1,500 for his two surviving daughters and bequeathed to his wife and sons considerable properties in and around Hythe, lands in Oxfordshire, and six Pembrokeshire advowsons. But it was not until 1807 that another member of the family was returned for Hythe.[5]

[1] Cussans, *Herts.* Hertford, 42; Hasted, *Kent*, vii. 238; *Canterbury Mar. Lic.* ii. 278. [2] Hythe assembly bk. 1649–83, f. 437; G. Wilks, *Cinque Port Barons*, 88–89; W. Boys, *Hist. Sandwich*, ii. 813; Stowe 745, f. 67; *CSP Dom.* 1682, p. 172; 1689–90, p. 235. [3] *CSP Dom.* 1650, p. 511; 1685, p. 164; Stowe 746, ff. 14–19; *Cal. Treas. Bks.* viii. 391; *Suss. Arch. Colls.* xv. 193. [4] *Cal. Treas. Bks.* ix. 1623, 1699, 2001; *Suss. Arch. Colls.* xv. 209; *HMC Finch*, ii. 224. [5] PCC 183 Fane.

B.D.H.

DE GREY, William (1652–87), of Merton, Norf.

THETFORD 1685–27 Feb. 1687

b. 21 Oct. 1652, o.s. of James de Grey of Merton by Elizabeth, da. of Sir Martin Stuteville of Dalham, Suff., and coh. to her bro. John. *educ.* Thetford g.s.; Caius, Camb. 1668; M. Temple 1671. *m.* settlement 5 Jan. 1675 (with £3,600), Elizabeth, da. of Thomas Bedingfield of Darsham, Suff., and coh. to her bro. Thomas, 7s. (5 *d.v.p.*) 1da. *suc.* fa. 1665.[1]

Commr. for assessment, Norf. 1673–80, Suff. 1679–80; j.p. and dep. lt. Norf. 1676–*d.*, maj. of militia ft. 1677–*d.*, freeman, Thetford 1681, Dunwich 1683.[2]

De Grey's ancestors were Suffolk landowners by the middle of the 13th century, acquiring Merton (ten miles from Thetford) by marriage about a hundred years later. A member of the family sat for King's Lynn in 1545. De Grey's grandfather was a Royalist, but his father, served on the committee of the eastern association, and on local commissions during the Commonwealth and Protectorate. He signed the Norfolk address for a free Parliament presented to General George Monck* in 1600. De Grey was himself a Tory, signing as a grand juryman the loyal address from Norfolk in March 1682 to express abhorrence at the 'treacherous artifices' of Shaftesbury and his associates. He was elected for Thetford in 1685; the election was contested, but his own return was unopposed. A moderately active Member of James II's Parliament, he was appointed to the committees to propose remedies for the low prices of wool and corn, and to consider the bills for the repair of Yarmouth pier, the improvement of tillage, and the relief of imprisoned debtors. He attended the second session, but his attitude to the King's religious policy is not known. He died on 27 Feb. 1687 and was buried at Merton. His son Thomas sat for Thetford under Queen Anne and for Norfolk under George I as a Whig.[3]

[1] *Norf. Antiq. Misc.* i. 74–76, 80–85, 93, 98; Norf. RO, Walsingham mss 42/1. [2] Add. 28082, f. 79; *Norf. Antiq. Misc.* i. 93; *HMC Lothian*, 127; East Suff. RO, EE6/1144/13. [3] *Address from Gentry of Norf.* ed. Rye, 29; Add. 36988, f. 180; *Norf. Antiq. Misc.* i. 92.

E.C.

DEINCOURT, Lord *see* LEKE, Robert

DELAVAL, Ralph (1622–91), of Seaton Delaval, Northumb.

NORTHUMBERLAND 1659, 1660, 15 Mar. 1677, 1679 (Mar.), 1679 (Oct.), 1681

b. 13 Oct. 1622, o.s. of Robert Delaval (*d.*1623) of Seaton Delaval by Barbara, da. and coh. of Sir George Selby† of Whitehouse, co. Dur. *educ.* Queen's, Oxf. 1638; L. Inn 1639. *m.* 2 Apr. 1646, Lady Anne Leslie (*d.*1696), da. of Alexander, 1st Earl of Leven [S], wid. of Hugh Fraser, Master of Lovat [S], 7s. (4 *d.v.p.*) 6da. *suc.* gdfa. 1628; *cr.* Bt. 29 June 1660.[1]

Dep. lt. Northumb. 1644, c. Aug. 1660–July 1688, commr. for northern assoc. 1645, militia 1648, 1659, Mar. 1660, assessment Northumb. 1649–52, 1657, Jan. 1660–80, 1689–*d.*, co. Dur. Aug. 1660–1, 1673–4; sheriff, Northumb. 1649–50, j.p. 1652–87, commr. for oyer and terminer, Northern circuit, July 1660, carriage of coals, Newcastle 1679.[2]

Farmer of salt duties to 1667.[3]

Delaval was descended from a Hexham stonemason called John Woodman, whose grandson changed his name to Delaval on succeeding to the estate in 1471. The family welcomed the Reformation, but did not enter Parliament until 1626. Delaval was a Parliamentarian in the Civil War and held local office throughout the Interregnum. He was returned for the county to Richard Cromwell's Parliament, but became a royalist conspirator, chiefly valued for his supposed influence over Charles Howard*. He was re-elected in 1660 and doubtless supported the Court in the Convention, though he left no trace on its records. He sued out his pardon, and was rewarded with a baronetcy and a lease of the duties on Scottish salt, which competed with the produce of his own works. At the general election of 1661 he was replaced as knight of the shire by Lord Mansfield (Henry Cavendish*). His chief interest lay in improving his estate, rated at £1,610 p.a., and in particular his collieries, for which he obtained expensive pumping machinery and built a new harbour at Seaton Sluice. 'The profit did not answer the account', according to Roger North*; but Delaval derived exquisite pleasure from designing and executing his projects, and had an opportunity of displaying his stoic temperament when disaster struck. He was accused of encouraging the Derwentdale plot in 1663, and his Presbyterian chaplain dedicated to him a discourse against conformity. But Delaval himself certainly conformed, and did not resign from the bench after the passing of the second Conventicles Act, probably because he was engaged in negotiating simultaneously for government help for the harbour project, and for the marriage of his invalid heir to an 'over-forward beauty' of the Court, to whom the King gave £2,000 as royal bounty.[4]

Delaval was successful at the double by-election caused by the death of Sir William Fenwick* and the succession of Mansfield to the peerage in 1676. An inactive Member of the Cavalier Parliament in its later sessions, he was named to only four committees, including that for the border rapine bill. Noted as 'to be fixed' on the working lists, he was given £500 a year for three years to assist in his harbour construction works, and marked 'doubly vile' by Shaftesbury. He was added to the committee to prepare reasons for a conference on the growth of Popery on 15 Apr. 1678, and served on the Commons delegation to inform the lord chancellor, among other things, that a recent addition to the Northumberland commission of the peace was a suspected Papist. He was on both lists of court supporters at this time.[5]

Delaval retained his seat in the Exclusion Parliaments. The only serious challenge came from the Roman Catholic courtier, Ralph Widdrington*, at the first general election of 1679, which cost £1,000 to defeat, but Delaval's colleague, Sir John Fenwick*, footed the bill. Nevertheless Shaftesbury marked him 'vile'. A moderately active Member of the first Exclusion Parliament he was named to five committees, none of much political importance, and voted against the bill. After Delaval's re-election in the autumn, despite blacklisting in the 'unanimous club' of court supporters, he was given responsibility for the salaries of the customs staff at Seaton Sluice, whereby he became 'collector and surveyor of his own port, and no officer to intermeddle there'. In the second Exclusion Parliament he was appointed only to a committee on a private bill, and added to that to take the disbandment accounts. There is no evidence that he attended the Oxford Parliament. In the years that followed he supported Fenwick against Widdrington, and was replaced in James II's Parliament by the latter's henchman, William Ogle*. In 1686 the Privy Council ordered his removal from the commission of the peace, and he was listed among the Opposition in the following year. Presumably he remained a deputy lieutenant, for in February 1688 he and Philip Bickerstaffe* replied on the repeal of the Test Act and Penal Laws:

1. If we or any of us should be chosen knight of the shire or burgess of a town, when the King shall think fit to call a Parliament, it shall be our chiefest care and study to do nothing there contradictory to our duty to God or our loyalty to our dread sovereign.

2. In all places where we are any way qualified we will modestly assist to the election of such Members as we conceive will faithfully discharge their duty to God, and with their lives and fortunes will preserve and maintain their fidelity to their prince, and carefully and sedulously watch all their opportunities to perform that great trust reposed in them both for the good of the King and the whole kingdom.

3. The principles of the religion in which we have been educated do teach us a firm obedience to the King and a brotherly love to our fellow-subjects; so that we readily comply to live friendly with those of all persuasions as subjects of the same prince and good Christians ought to do.

He never stood again. He died in embarrassed circumstances on 22 Aug. 1691 and was buried at Seaton Delaval. His namesake, the admiral, who was elected for Bedwyn as a Tory in 1695, came from another branch of the family; but his youngest son, the third baronet, sat for Morpeth from 1701 to 1705 as a Whig.[6]

[1] *New Hist. Northumb.* ix. 170-1. [2] *CJ*, iii. 657; *Cal. Treas. Bks.* v. 1205. [3] *Cal. Treas. Bks.* iii, 255-6. [4] *New Hist. Northumb.* ix. 157-8, 160, 169; *Cal. Cl. SP*, iv. 177, 198, 202; *Cal. Treas. Bks.* iii. 256, 500, 701, 965; Hodgson, *Northumb.* pt. 3, i. 340; North, *Lives*, i. 176-8; *CSP Dom.* 1663-4, p. 615; A. G. Matthews, *Calamy Revised*, 257. [5] Add. 47608, f. 183; *Cal. Treas. Bks.* v. 721; *CJ*, ix. 470. [6] *Cal. Treas. Bks.* vi. 616; North, i. 176; *New Hist. Northumb.* ix. 161-2.

M.W.H./G.H.

DELVES, Nicholas (1618–90), of Friday Street, London and Camberwell, Surr.

HASTINGS   1659, 1660

b. 2 Dec. 1618, 3rd s. of Thomas Delves, grazier, of Hollington, Suss. *m.* 1644, Mary, da. and coh. of Edmund Warnett, Cutler and haberdasher, of London Bridge, 5s. (4 *d.v.p.*) 2da.[1]

Commr. for sewers, Surr. and Kent Aug. 1660, assessment, London Sept. 1660-1; alderman, London Apr.–June 1661, common councilman 1663-5, 1667-70; master, Merchant Taylors' Co. 1662-3; dep. gov. Irish Soc. 1668-9.[2]

Delves came from a Sussex yeoman family. He was apprenticed to a London Merchant Taylor in 1635, and became a London tradesman, but retained his connexion with the county of his birth, and in particular the Hastings area, where his father farmed. His wife was also of a Sussex family, and in 1659 he bought the manor of Hoseland, three miles north of Hastings, where his brother Thomas acted as returning officer in both his successful elections. He himself held no office during the Interregnum, and probably had Anglican and royalist sympathies. In the Convention he was an inactive Member. He was appointed to seven committees, including those for drafting a clause in the book of rates concerning foreign ships and for the encouragement of English woollen manufactures and shipping. His only committee of political importance was for the attainder of Oliver Cromwell.[3]

Delves probably did not stand in 1661. In that year he fined for alderman, and, although elected to the common council, he seems to have resided in a large house in Camberwell, probably as tenant of the Muschamp estate, which had come to his kinsman, Edward Eversfield*, by marriage. He received a grant of lands in Devon to pay off a loan of £350 made to a distressed loyalist, Sir Henry Norton[†], during the Interregnum, and in 1664 he sold out an investment of £600 in the East India Company; but his was evidently not one of the large mercantile fortunes of the day. He served on the Camberwell vestry, and was buried in the parish church on 3 Nov. 1690, the only member of the family to sit in Parliament.[4]

[1] Add. 5697, f. 70v; Soc. of Genealogists, Boyd's London Units, 16532, 48931. [2] C181/7/31; J. R. Woodhead, *Rulers of London*, 59. [3] *Fines of Manors* (Suss. Rec. Soc. xix), 229; Bodl. Rawl. D682, f. 51; W. G. Moss, *Hist. Hastings*, 136; HMC 7th Rep. 151. [4] *CSP Dom.* 1661–2, pp. 159, 193; *Cal. Ct. Min. E.I. Co.* ed. Sainsbury, vii. 477; W. H. Blanch, *Parish of Camerwell*, 52, 144, 156–7; J. Comber, *Suss. Genealogies Horsham*, 93; Greater London RO, Camberwell St. Giles par. reg.

M.W.H./J.P.F.

DENHAM, John (1615–69), of Middle Scotland Yard, Whitehall.[1]

OLD SARUM   1661–20 Mar. 1669

b. 1615, o.s. of Sir John Denham of Inworth, Egham, Surr., baron of the Exchequer 1617–39, by 2nd w. Eleanor, da. of Gerald, 1st Visct. Moore of Drogheda [I]. *educ.* Trinity, Oxf. 1631; L. Inn 1631, called 1639. *m.* (1) 25 June 1634, Anne (*d.* c.1646), da. of Don Coton of Whittington, Glos. and coh. to her gdfa., 1s. *d.v.p.* 2da.; (2) 25 May 1665, Margaret, da. and coh. of Sir William Brooke[†] of Cooling Castle, Kent, *s.p. suc.* fa. 1639; KB 23 Apr. 1661.[2]

J.p. Surr. c.1641–6, sheriff 1642–3, commr. of array 1642; j.p. Mdx. Aug. 1660–*d.*, Westminster Sept. 1660–*d.*; commr. for sewers, Westminster Aug. 1660, assessment, Westminster 1661–4, Wilts. 1661–3, oyer and terminer, Mdx. 1662, loyal and indigent officers, London and Westminster 1662, highways and sewers 1662; clerk of works, Tower of London 1662–*d.*; bailiff, Bedford level 1664–5, conservator 1665–6.[3]

Gov. Farnham Castle, Surr. 1642.

Surveyor-gen. of works, June 1660–*d.*; commr. for plantations Dec. 1660–*d.*; member, R. Adventurers into Africa Dec. 1660–3, R. Fishing Co. 1664.[4]

FRS 1663–6.

Denham could trace his ancestry no further than his grandfather, a London goldsmith. His father

held judicial office both in England and Ireland; one of his last judgments was against the legality of ship-money in Hampden's case. Denham shared his father's opinion, and expressed it, both in his play *The Sophy* (performed in 1641) and in his poem *Cooper's Hill*, published at Oxford during the Civil War. An only child, he succeeded to a competent estate, which, together with his first wife's inheritance, brought in £680 p.a., but he soon gambled it away. He was in arms for the King in 1642, but his defence of Farnham Castle was inglorious, and on his release he took no further part in the fighting. Captured again at Dartmouth in 1646, he became acquainted with Hugh Peter, the radical cleric, who obtained permission for him to attend on Charles I at Hampton Court. Falling under suspicion, he fled abroad in 1648, and entered the service of the Prince of Wales, who employed him on diplomatic missions to Scotland and Poland. In spite of his denials he was regarded as a follower of Henrietta Maria's party. Further ill luck at the gaming table compelled him to return to England, where he was thought to be more in danger from his creditors than from the Government; his debts already exceeded £4,000 in 1647. He managed to rescue Little Horkesley from the treason trustees, but soon had to surrender it to the mortgagee. But the 5th Earl of Pembroke took him under his protection at Wilton, though he continued to correspond with the exiled court. In 1658 he took Pembroke's son (William Herbert*, Lord Herbert) abroad, but returned in the following year, and became more directly involved in Cavalier plotting as head of a faction opposed to Lord Mordaunt, though his links with the Independents proved of little use.[5]

At the Restoration, Denham was made surveyor of works in accordance with a patent obtained in exile, though his knowledge of architecture was purely theoretical. At the general election of 1661, Pembroke returned him for his borough of Old Sarum. He was a moderately active committeeman, serving on 62 committees in 11 sessions. He soon put his membership to practical use, claiming privilege against an attorney who had sued him to outlawry. Denham was responsible for initiating the paving of Holborn, and he took a prominent part in the legislation for improving highways in and around London and Westminster. On 8 Apr. 1662, he was among those ordered to draw up reasons for a conference on the subject. In the following year he was on a small committee appointed to consider a proviso for widening London streets, and in 1665 he was one of the Members to bring in an additional bill. He served on no committees of political importance, except one for an additional corporations bill, but was regarded as a court dependant. His second marriage, in which there was great disparity of age and even more of appearance, subjected him to much ridicule, especially as the lady, who had been brought forward by Lord Bristol, was hotly pursued by the Duke of York. Shortly afterwards Denham went out of his mind; jealousy was popularly supposed to be the cause, but it was more probably tertiary syphilis. When Denham had recovered sufficiently to attend Parliament as a court supporter, Andrew Marvell* wrote:

Of early wittols first the troop marched in,
For diligence renowned, and discipline:
In loyal haste they left young wives in bed,
And Denham these by one consent did head.

In a debate on 13 Oct. 1666, he attacked the proposed ban on Irish cattle imports. (Sir) Allen Brodrick* to the Duke of Ormonde: 'Jack Denham presents his duty to your grace, who alas hath not recovered his former understanding in any measure, yet spoke very good sense this morning in opposition to the bill'. Shortly afterwards Lady Denham was taken ill, and died on 6 Jan. 1667; the post mortem, held to refute suspicions of poison, gave inflammation of the bowels as cause of death, and revealed incidentally that her virginity was intact; but neither finding dissipated the atmosphere of scandal in which Denham now moved, though he continued to attend and speak regularly in Parliament. In the same month, he was given leave to attend the House of Lords as witness for the defence of his old enemy Mordaunt and ordered to bring in a proviso about the rebuilding of London.[6]

Denham was one of the Members appointed to confer with the Duke of Albemarle (George Monck*) about highway robberies on 26 Oct. 1667. He opposed stiffening the penalties for recusancy during the Dutch war with 'a merry story' from Boccaccio. He took part in the attack on Clarendon, though not appointed to the impeachment committee. To the evident surprise of John Milward*, he made 'a most rational and excellent speech' justifying, though only at second hand, the charge that the lord chancellor had described the King as 'indisposed for government'. When Clarendon was accused of advising the King 'never hereafter to think of Parliaments', John Birch* sarcastically suggested on 9 Nov. that such words must be due to 'distraction'; but Denham, no doubt from his own experience of the condition, declared this explanation unlikely. On the same day he and Sir Charles Harbord* were asked to put into execution the laws restraining the excessive fares demanded by hackney coachmen. He spoke twice in favour of

the conventicles bill, saying: 'It is true Holland and France did tolerate several religions amongst them, but it is as true that they keep a standing army in pay to keep them under'. He asserted that the evidence of the cowardice of Henry Brouncker* was demonstrably false. Denham died on 20 Mar. 1669, and was buried in Westminster Abbey. Though long accounted a sceptic in religion, he declared himself in his will a true Christian of the Church of England 'as by law it is now established . . . whose doctrine and discipline I do and ever have embraced and adhered to, not only as being born and bred within it, but (after diligent search and inquiry both at home and abroad) have chosen for the best and most apostolic in the Christian world'.[7]

[1] Unless otherwise stated, this biography is based on the introduction by T. H. Banks to *Poetical Works of Sir John Denham.* [2] *Glos. Inquisitions* (Index Lib. ix), 56; Hasted, *Kent*, iii. 520. [3] C181/7/38; *Tudor and Stuart Proclamations* ed. Steele, i. 405; S. Wells, *Drainage of the Bedford Level*, i. 457. [4] *Sel. Charters* (Selden Soc. xxviii), 173, 183. [5] Morant, *Essex*, i. 235; Manning and Bray, *Surr.* iii. 250; SP23/80/169–72; *Nicholas Pprs.* (Cam. Soc. n.s. xl), 300; D. Underdown, *Royalist Conspiracy*, 243, 305; *Clarendon SP*, iii. 740. [6] *Cal. Cl. SP*, v. 13; *CJ*, viii. 393, 602, 681, 687; *Pepys Diary*, 15 Aug. 1664, 12 Dec. 1666; *Marvell* ed. Margoliouth i. 144; Bodl. Carte 35, f. 101. [7] *Milward*, 104, 116, 216, 225, 262; Grey, i. 30; *Clarendon Impeachment*, 27; *Bulstrode Pprs.* 96; PCC 57 Penn.

J.P.F.

DENNE, Vincent (c.1628–93), of Denne Hill, Kingston, Kent.

CANTERBURY 1656, 1681

b. c.1628, 1st s. of Thomas Denne of Canterbury by Susan, da. and coh. of Arthur Honeywood of Lenham. *educ.* Queens', Camb. 1645–8; Magdalen Hall, Oxf. BA 1648, MA 1651; G. Inn 1648, called 1655. *m.* c.1655, Mary, da. and coh. of Thomas Denne† of Denne Hill, 4da. *suc.* fa. 1657.[1]

Student of Christ Church, Oxf. 1648; freeman, Canterbury 1656, commr. for assessment 1657, Jan. 1660, 1679–80, Kent and Canterbury 1689–90; j.p. Kent 1657–July 1660, 1689–*d.*; commr. for militia, Canterbury Mar. 1660, sewers, Walland marsh, Dec. 1660; surveyor of customs, Deal 1661–?66; bencher, G. Inn 1677; recorder, Canterbury Oct. 1688–*d.*, Dover 1689–*d.*; steward of chancery court, Cinque Ports 1689–*d.*[2]

Serjeant-at-law June 1688–*d.*

Denne came of a family long settled in Kent and armigerous since at least the reign of Henry III. One of them represented the county in 1320 and his father-in-law sat for Canterbury in 1624. His own return to the second Protectorate Parliament and his inclusion on the commission of the peace in the following year would indicate no great hostility to the regime. After the Restoration, however, in his petition for the surveyorship of the customs at Deal, he claimed that he had served Charles I by conveying letters to and from the fleet and that he had been obliged to leave the country. He also asserted that his father, 'who was servant to the last two Kings' had been imprisoned and lost £600 'to their utter ruin'. The customs commissioners recommended that the petition should be granted in view of Denne's 'long fidelity and activity'.[3]

Denne was removed from the commission of the peace after the Restoration, though he did receive the surveyorship at Deal. A practising lawyer, in April 1664 at the quarter sessions at Dover he defended two dissenters and 'pleaded . . . so vehemently that some threatened to throw him over the bar'. Returned for Canterbury, five miles from his home, to the Oxford Parliament, probably as an exclusionist, he left no trace on its records. He did not stand again, though he may have become a Whig collaborator, being raised to the coif in 1688. He died on 8 Oct. 1693 and was buried at Kingston. No later member of the family entered Parliament.[4]

[1] *Vis. Kent* (Harl. Soc. liv), 47; M.I. St. Giles, Kingston. [2] *Roll of the Freemen* ed. Cowper, 115; Kent AO, Q/JC, 19, 20, 21; *Cal. Treas. Bks.* i. 8, 369; C181/7/73; *CSP Dom.* 1665–6, p. 286; 1689–90, p. 355; J. B. Jones, *Annals of Dover*, 347; Luttrell, i. 446. [3] Hasted, *Kent*, ix. 345–6; *CSP Dom.* 1660–1, p. 153. [4] *CSP Dom.* 1663–4, pp. 565–6.

B.D.H.

DENNYS, Nicholas (1616–92), of Barnstaple and Derworthy, Milton Damerel, Devon.

BARNSTAPLE 1660, 1661

bap. 13 Nov. 1616, 3rd s. of Thomas Dennys, yeoman (*d.*1632), of Ilfracombe, by 2nd w. Joan Rice. *educ.* Pembroke, Oxf. 1634; I. Temple 1635, called 1646. *m.* (1) c.1647, Jane (*bur.* 1 July 1674), da. of William Squire of South Molton, 1s. *d.v.p.* 3da.; (2) 6 July 1675, Jane, da. of one Richards of Dunkeswell, wid. of Sir Benjamin Oliver of Exeter, *s.p.*[1]

Deputy recorder, Barnstaple ?1656–74, freeman Mar. 1660; commr. for assessment, Devon Aug. 1660–80, 1689–90, corporations 1662–3; bencher, I. Temple 1662–9; commr. for charitable uses, Devon 1667, recusants 1675; recorder, Bideford bef. 1682–at least 1685.[2]

Dennys may have been descended from a gentry family which provided a Member for Barnstaple in 1449, but the descent has not been traced, and his grandfather described himself as a mere husbandman. At his father's death Dennys inherited property in Ilfracombe and elsewhere, but he became a professional lawyer in practice at Barnstaple. He did not openly take sides during the Civil War, although his brother was removed from the mayoralty as a Royalist in 1651. Returned for the borough at the general election of 1660, doubtless as a supporter of the Restoration, Dennys was inactive in the Convention. He made no recorded speeches,

and was named to only five committees. He was among those ordered to prepare a clause on foreign vessels for the book of customs rate, and served on the committee that produced the navigation bill.[3]

Re-elected in 1661, Dennys was again inactive, being appointed to only 31 committees of secondary importance in the Cavalier Parliament. In the opening session he took the chair in the large committee to consider a confirmatory bill for draining the Great level of the fens, and also reported a Devonshire estate bill. His most important committee politically was on the bill to prevent mischiefs from Quakers. Thereafter his activity declined, though he was among those ordered to consider bills to regulate the manufacture of Devon stuffs in 1663 and to prevent legal delays in 1664. In 1669 he was disbenched at his own request upon payment of a fine of 100 marks, 'having declared to the treasurer his resolution not to come any more to the bench table nor to read'. He seems henceforward to have devoted himself to local affairs. He defaulted on a call of the House in 1671. After his first wife's death he retired from practice and settled in Milton Damerel. He was named to the committees on the bill for uniting Exeter parishes both in 1673 and 1674. It was hoped to recruit him for the court party in 1675 through the lord keeper, but Shaftesbury marked him 'worthy' in 1677. As recorder of Bideford he signed loyal addresses following the Rye House Plot and the accession of James II. He was buried at Milton Damerel on 31 May 1692. He was the only member of this family to sit in Parliament; but a grandson, William Fortescue, sat for Newport, I.o.W. from 1727 to 1736.[4]

[1] *Devon and Cornw. N. and Q.* xxiii. 148–51; Soc. of Genealogists, Exeter Mar. Lic. Feb. 1671. [2] *HMC 5th Rep.* 371; T. Wainwright, *Barnstaple Recs.* i. 231; *Cal. I. T. Recs.* iii. 63; *Devon and Cornw. N. and Q.* xxiii. 149; *Trans. Devon Assoc.* xlvii. 318–21. [3] *Devon and Cornw. N. and Q.* xxiii. 116–17, 145–7; J. B. Gribble, *Mems. Barnstaple*, 271. [4] *CJ*, viii. 270, 302; *Cal. I. T. Recs.* ii. 273; *Trans. Devon Assoc.* xlvii. 318–21; information from Mr R. O. Dennys, Somerset Herald.

M.W.H./J.S.C.

DERING, Edward (1650–89), of Surrenden Dering, Kent.

KENT 1679 (Mar.), 1679 (Oct.), 1681

b. 18 Apr. 1650, 1st s. of Sir Edward Dering, 2nd Bt.*. *m.* 9 June 1677, Elizabeth (*d.* 20 Oct. 1704), da. of Sir William Cholmeley, 2nd Bt., of Whitby, Yorks., 7s. (4 *d.v.p.*) 2da. *suc.* fa. 1684.[1]

Commr. for assessment, Kent 1673–80, 1689, j.p. 1679–80, 1689–d., col. of militia by 1680–1, dep. lt. Feb. 1688–d.

Col. (later 27 Ft.) Mar. 1689–d.[2]

Dering entered politics in 1677 as a follower of Sir Vere Fane*, signing the protest against government support for Sir John Banks* in the Winchelsea by-election. His own return for the county in three successive elections was regarded by his father as an almost unprecedented honour for the family, but in fact resulted from the exclusion crisis, and at both elections of 1679 he had to face a poll. He was listed as 'honest' by Shaftesbury, and voted for exclusion, but he was named to no committees and made no speeches in the first Exclusion Parliament. After re-election he was removed from the commission of the peace. In the second Exclusion Parliament he was named only to the committee on the bill for the banishment of Papists. On 15 Nov. 1680, during the debate on the Lords' bill for regulating trials of peers, he moved that the bill might be temporary. 'If it be a good bill, you may continue it.' On 21 Dec. he presented a petition against committal by the Privy Council, which was referred to the committee of grievances. He was returned unopposed to the Oxford Parliament, but left no trace on its records.[3]

In 1681 Sir John Tufton* and several other Kentish gentlemen attested a series of accusations against Dering, which were laid before the King. Among these were that he had drunk confusion to lawn sleeves, and had declared that a limited monarchy 'was a —— in a chamber pot'. It was said that he was favoured by the 'fanatics', and Lord Winchilsea, the lord lieutenant, alleged that he was 'the principal person who obstructs your Majesty's service, and hinders us in our addresses'. Dering denied the charges, which his father attributed to envy and malice, though admitting privately that Dering had 'taken more liberty in words than could well consist with the dutiful respect owing his King', but the words were 'rather irreverent than malicious . . . much less mischievous'. He was more concerned about Dering's debts, amounting to some £2,800.[4]

In July 1683, after the discovery of the Rye House Plot, Dering's house was searched for arms, and though none were found Winchilsea was confident that Dering had hidden them, 'for I had notice two or three years past', he wrote, 'that he had in one chamber 15 or 16 cases of pistols and five or six blunderbusses'. A few weeks later Dering and his father waited upon the King and the Duke of York to express their detestation of the plot.[5]

Dering did not stand in 1685, but it was reported that he gave his interest to Lewis Watson*, who did not go to the poll. He was presumably a Whig collaborator, being recommended for the lieutenancy in February 1688, but 'contributed more than any man in Kent towards bringing about the Revolution', urging the militia to concentrate

at Faversham to prevent any attempt to rescue James II. But he was defeated at Hythe, and Sir Vere Fane refused him his support in the county election for the Convention. 'Much in King William's interest', he raised a regiment of foot and took it to Ireland. On 6 Oct. 1689, when it was probable that MPs in the army might be sent back to Westminster, he added a postscript to a letter from Henry Wharton* to his brother Thomas*:

> I never repented my not being a Parliament man till now; but, however, when others move, pray let me pass for a Member.

He died, however, 'of a flux' on 15 Oct. at Dundalk, and was buried at Pluckley. His son sat for Kent in the second and fourth Parliaments of Queen Anne.[6]

[1] Information from P. H. Blake; F. Haslewood, *Pluckley Mems.* 7. [2] Kent AO, Q/JC/16, 17, 19. [3] Kent AO, Sa/ZB3/1; Grey, vii. 474; *HMC 12th Rep. IX*, 101. [4] *Dering Pprs.* 130–2; SP29/416/92; *CSP Dom.* 1680–1, p. 395. [5] *CSP Dom.* July–Sept. 1683, p. 117; *Dering Pprs.* 145. [6] BL Loan 29/86, Abigail Stephens to Lady Harley, n.d.; *N. and Q.* (ser. 3), vi. 41, 122; Boyer, *Hist. Wm. III*, ii. 139; Add. 33923, ff. 461, 463; *Arch. Cant.* x. 341; R. Morrice, Entering Bk. 2, p. 623; Bodl. Carte 79, f. 261; G. Story, *Hist. Wars in Ireland*, pt. 1, p. 29.

B.D.H.

DERING, Sir Edward, 2nd Bt. (1625–84), of Surrenden Dering, Kent and Bloomsbury, Mdx.

KENT	1660
EAST RETFORD	8 Nov. 1670
HYTHE	1679 (Mar.), 1679 (Oct.), 1681

b. 12 Nov. 1625, 1st s. of Sir Edward Dering, 1st Bt.†, of Surrenden Dering by 2nd w. Anne, da. of Sir John Ashburnham of Ashburnham, Suss. *educ.* Heathfield 1632, Cripplegate, London (Thomas Farnaby) 1633, Throwley (Mr Craig) 1634–7, Woodford (Mr Copping) 1637–9; Sidney Sussex, Camb. 1640, Emmanuel 1642, BA 1643; Middle Temple, entered 1641; Leyden 1644; travelled abroad (Netherlands and France) 1644–6. *m.* 5 Apr. 1648, Mary da. of Daniel Harvey, merchant, of Croydon, Surr., 8s. (3 *d.v.p.*) 9da. *suc.* fa. 22 June 1644.[1]

Commr. for militia, Kent Mar. 1660, j.p. July 1660–*d.*, dep. lt. July 1660–2, 1668–*d.*; commr. for oyer and terminer, Home circuit July 1660, assessment, Kent Aug. 1660–80, Mdx. and Notts. 1677–9, for sewers Rother marshes Oct. 1660, Walland marsh Dec. 1660, recusants, Kent 1675.

Commr. for settlement [I] 1662–9; PC [I] 1667–9; commr. of privy seal 1669–73, customs 1675–9; gov. Merchant Adventurers 1675–*d.*; commr. for inquiry into the Mint 1677–8; chairman, committees of supply and ways and means 4–23 Feb. 1678; ld. of Treasury 1679–*d.*[2]

MP [I] 1662–6.

Dering's ancestors, said to have been resident in Kent since Saxon times, had held Surrenden since the 15th century, and provided a Member for New

Romney in 1547. His father sat for the county in the Long Parliament, and as an advocate of 'primitive episcopacy' moved the first reading of the root and branch bill. He joined the King at the outbreak of the Civil War, but soon laid down his commission and submitted to Parliament. On an estate valued at £800 p.a. it was recommended that he should be allowed to compound for £1,000, but the fine was discharged on his death.[3]

Dering's father died in financial straits, and Dering, with his large family, was always eager for office to reduce his debt. Nevertheless he 'most carefully and resolutely refused, during the time of the usurped power, all manner of public employment'. When George Monck* declared for a free Parliament, Dering seized 'the first opportunity since the last King's death of doing service to my country . . . went down to Kent and declared to stand for knight of the shire'. He was returned after a contest, and became a moderately active Member of the Convention. He made no recorded speeches, but was appointed to 26 committees, including that to prepare the bill for abolishing the court of wards. He helped to manage the conference on the declaration about the Irish rebellion on 26 May, and to prepare for a conference on three orders issued by the Lords. He was also appointed to the committees for settling ecclesiastical livings and preparing a report on the revenue. On 27 Aug. the Earl of Winchilsea wrote to Dering desiring him

> to get the Act for settling my estate in the north . . . for the payment of my debts, etc., to be passed your House with all the speed you can. As also to entreat you to use your endeavours for my lord Marquess of Hertford's business, and to be to-morrow at two in the afternoon at the committee, where you will find occasions enough to assist my lord.

Clearly Winchilsea relied chiefly on Dering's influence with his 'brother solicitor', (Sir) Heneage Finch*. Dering was promptly added to the committees for the bill restoring the dukedom of Somerset and for the Winchilsea estate bill. Shortly thereafter Winchilsea wrote that Dering had been 'very industrious in assisting me upon all occasions to serve his Majesty before the King came into England', praised his work as deputy lieutenant and 'in all other things which concerned his Majesty's service'. After the recess he was added to the committees to bring in the militia bill and the bill for modified episcopacy.[4]

Dering did not stand in 1661, 'thinking of nothing more than settling myself quietly at home to govern my small fortune and many children as well as I could'. He was not allowed to rusticate for long, being appointed in July 1662 one of the six commissioners for executing the Act of Settlement in Ireland. He was returned to the Dublin Parliament for Lismore, and won the respect of the lord lieutenant, the Duke of Ormonde, as a 'loyal servant' who was also 'knowing and able in business'. By 1665 his sights were set again on a seat at Westminster. Sir Robert Southwell* asked Sir Thomas Peyton* to let him know of any vacancy in Kent or the Cinque Ports, 'so that his father-in-law, Sir Edward Dering, a man of talent, might serve his Majesty in the House of Commons'. He was proposed for Winchelsea, but the Duke of York preferred to nominate Baptist May*. When the Irish claims commission was wound up in 1669, Dering returned to England as a commissioner of the privy seal. He received the 'court commendation' for a seat at East Retford, where he was 'totally a stranger', and was unanimously elected on the Duke of Newcastle's interest.[5]

Dering was a very active Member of the Cavalier Parliament, being named to 207 committees, in eight of which he took the chair. Over 60 of his speeches were recorded by other diarists, the first being on 5 Apr. 1671 when, in the debate on the third reading of the conventicles bill, he argued that the bill would 'involve the justices in many inconveniences'. As a placeman he was already regarded as a court supporter by the Opposition. At the beginning of the next session, on 6 Feb. 1673, when the debate on the issue of the writs by the lord chancellor during the prorogation had become 'warm', he displayed the moderation which was to be his hall mark, and seconded the unsuccessful motion of Sir Anthony Irby* to refer the matter to a committee to consider precedents, 'which was certainly regular and parliamentary'. Again taking a moderate stance, he argued on 10 Feb., with others of the court party, for proceeding against the Declaration of Indulgence by petition, as in 1628, rather than by resolution:

> I was no advocate for that clause in the Declaration which was now under debate because that I did not see any material difference between a universal, indefinite, unlimited suspension of laws, as this seemed to be by the Declaration, and a total repeal and abrogation, which no man had yet affirmed the King had power to do. But yet I did most willingly join with these gentlemen who had made it their desires that it might be suffered at least *decenter cadere*, that there might pass no vote upon this occasion which might so much as in appearance lessen the entire happy harmony that was between the King and this House. . . . No man could yet say that anybody's liberty or property had been invaded in the least, or that suffered to the value of a hair of his head. That what we complained of was rather what we feared than what we felt; that I would not deny but these fears were worthy of our consideration by men in the trust under which we were.

Though the resolution against the suspending power was passed by a large majority, Dering was named to the committee to draw up the address. He was more successful in persuading the House to accept the King's 'gracious assurances and promises' on 24 Feb. With regard to the exclusion of dissenters from Parliament, he opposed tacking a clause to the bill of ease or any other measure, and the House again accepted his preference for 'a distinct bill by itself, it being the speediest, safest, and most effectual way'. But his attempt to exempt the existing members of the Queen's household from the oaths against Popery by a 'moderation' of the Lords' proviso was wrecked by an indiscreet speech from Lord Ancram (Charles Kerr*). Soon after the adjournment Dering, to his dismay, lost his post when the privy seal was taken out of commission. 'You had ill offices done you by my Lord Clifford [Thomas Clifford*]', wrote Finch, 'as being a zealot in the House upon imaginations of Popery.' He failed to secure another appointment, but after much agony he was granted a pension. A great friend of Danby, whom he in no way blamed for his disappointment, he spoke in favour of supply in the autumn session. In 1674 he was named to 16 committees, including those to bring in a bill for regulating elections and to provide relief under habeas corpus. He also helped to consider the general test bill and the bill to prevent illegal exactions. His name appears on the Paston list.[6]

In his diary for 1675, Dering describes several meetings of the government caucus under Danby's chairmanship. In the spring session he was among those appointed to bring in a bill for preventing Papists from sitting in Parliament, and on 3 May he defended Danby against the charge of misusing the royal prerogative. He took a prominent part in the debates on the recall of British subjects from French service, moving unsuccessfully for the adjournment on 10 May and proposing the omission of the word 'all'. Though he opposed making an address, he was named to the committee to prepare it. He took the chair for two bills of concern to churchmen, those for the augmentation of small vicarages and the better recovery of tithes. He tried to reduce the tension between the Houses, urging that Arthur Onslow* and Thomas Dalmahoy* would suffer hardship if their appeals were not heard by the Lords, and counselling moderation over Shirley v. Fagg. He helped to manage a conference on this case, and to draw up reasons on the Four Lawyers. In the autumn he was given leave to reintroduce the vicarages bill. In accordance with Danby's tactics he sought to defer the debate on supply until more of the court supporters had

reached Westminster. He twice unsuccessfully moved to increase the vote from £300,000 to £380,000. On 11 Nov. he was appointed to the committee to annex an appropriation clause to the bill for building 20 warships. When complaint was made that (Sir) Edmund Jennings* had been pricked as sheriff, Dering considered that it was sufficient to address the King requesting that no more Members should be thus disabled from attending the House; but he was named to the committee to find a way of superseding the appointment. He reported the vicarages bill on 19 Nov., but it was lost on the prorogation four days later. Understandably Dering's name appears on the government lists of court supporters, including that labelled 'officials', for on 22 Dec. 1675 he was, at last, given employment as a commissioner of customs with an annual salary of £1,200. In the following spring Dering's brother-in-law, now Lord Chancellor Finch, hoped that he would succeed Sir John Duncombe* as chancellor of the Exchequer, but the post went to Sir John Ernle*.[7]

When Parliament met, after the long prorogation, Dering continued his support of the Court, and was marked 'doubly vile' on Shaftesbury's list. On 5 Mar. 1677 he spoke against the opposition motion appropriating the customs (which was defeated) and on the next day, in the debate on alliances against France, he said that 'he thinks we are not fully apprized of how things stand abroad, and therefore he would leave treaties to the King'. He argued for the second reading of the bill for the education of the royal children as Protestants, a measure which the country party opposed, since it admitted the possibility of a Catholic successor. He again took the chair on the bill for the better repair of churches. He was named to the committee to consider the petition of the creditors of the Merchant Adventurers, of which he was governor. He helped to draw up the address promising assistance for a war and took the chair of the committee of the whole House in the debate on the Irish cattle bill. He was among those appointed to manage the conference on the building of the 20 warships, and on 16 Apr. reported the bill for the relief of insolvent debtors.[8]

Dering acted as chairman of the supply committee during the first session of 1678, presiding over 14 days of debate. On 16 Feb. he spoke in support of the bill to prevent the export of wool:

If we vent our wool beyond sea, we cannot vent our cloth. I would have this committee empowered to find a way of securing the wearing of it at home. Sumptuary laws here have lately had no effect. The people have been in jollity and gaiety since the Restoration of the King, and it is no wonder they are wanton in their plenty.

When Dering reported from the committee of ways and means in favour of a poll-tax, he was ordered, together with Sir Francis Winnington*, Sir Thomas Meres* and Sir Charles Harbord*, to bring in a bill accordingly, and he took the chair in grand committee on its second reading. He reported on 27 Feb. in favour of an additional clause to prohibit the import of French goods, and was among those ordered to bring it in. He carried two messages to the Lords, to remind them of the bill against Popery on 8 Mar. and six days later to inform them that the Commons agreed with their amendments to the supply bill. On the same day he was among those appointed to draw up the address for declaring war on France. On 7 May, during the attack on Lauderdale, he said:

> We never judge a man without hearing him. . . . In what is past, the Act of Indemnity has pardoned some, and Lauderdale has been here now two years, and all this has passed in silence. If any man be ready with articles against him, I am ready for impeachment against him; and I would have him sent for to answer here, but not condemn him unheard.

He was again summoned to a caucus meeting on 29 May, presumably to prepare for another debate on supply, in which however he is not recorded as speaking. On 5 June he was named to the revived committee to consider the petition of the Merchant Adventurers' creditors. He again took the chair on the bill for the relief of insolvent debtors. He was appointed to the committee for the bill to prevent Papists from sitting in Parliament, and on 20 June managed the conference on disbanding the army.[9]

When the last session of the Cavalier Parliament opened in the fevered atmosphere of the Popish Plot, Dering was named to the committees to inquire into the plot, to consider the bill disabling Papists from sitting in Parliament, and to translate Coleman's letters. He furnished two of the translations himself. He helped to draw up reasons for the conference of 1 Nov. on the plot, and a fortnight later he complained:

> The Lords promised their concurrence for remedies for preservation of the King's person, etc. Nothing yet is done in it; nor is the King's speech considered, though we sat upon an unusual day. Are we bolder than we were, or safer? I think not. . . . I declare, if nothing be done this session for the Protestant religion . . . nothing remains but to make our graves and lie down in them.

But he urged the House to exempt the Duke of York from the disabling bill:

> If we disagree with the Lords in this proviso, and leave it out, and the King give not his consent to the bill, your bill must fall, or runs a great hazard. I would agree; and when that is done, move the King to give an immediate consent to the bill. You have then but one Popish peer in the Lords' House (if the Duke be one).

The proviso was accepted by a majority of two. Dering both took the chair in the committee to draw up reasons and reported from the subsequent conference on 26 Nov. On the proposed address to represent the state and danger of the nation, he remarked that 'the present danger is not so much from principles of government as from Popery and the army', and wished to proceed with the disbandment bill. He was one of the few friends of Danby named to the committee to prepare his impeachment, and, though included in the government list of court supporters, was not mentioned in the 'unanimous club'.[10]

Dering sat for Hythe in the Exclusion Parliaments, while his son represented the county. Both elections of 1679 were contested, but his return was unopposed. He was again marked 'vile' by Shaftesbury. In the dispute between King and Commons over the Speakership he warned the House against proceeding with normal business until the authority of the chair was beyond cavil, and considered that the best expedient was to choose a third person, as was eventually done. On his appointment to the Treasury board on 26 Mar. at a salary of £1,600 p.a. he wrote in his diary that he

> was never more surprised at anything than the news I was to be one, having not made the least application to the King or any person at the Court for it, nor ever having entertained a thought of it.

The appointment was made 'solely upon the recommendation and good character' given of him by Sidney Godolphin I*, 'an absolute stranger'. His work at the Treasury may have reduced his attendance at the House, and he was only moderately active, being named to the committee of elections and privileges, and to six others, including those for the amendment of habeas corpus and the speedier conviction of recusants. He voted against the exclusion bill, and on 14 May, in the violent debate on supply, moved successfully for the adjournment. Dering was again only moderately active in the second Exclusion Parliament, being named to five committees. On 3 Nov. 1680 he was among those given leave to bring in a bill for uniting Protestants and was put on the committee. Ironically enough he was himself labelled a Papist in a pamphlet written by Dr Tonge, and on 9 Nov. invoked, for the only time in his parliamentary career, his privilege.

> The compliment he gives me, of 'wise and learned', is like poison boiled in wine, to operate the more violently. . . . In this libel I am accused plainly of no less than Popery, and of the worst of crimes, of being 'an active and seditious Papist, a correspondent of the Pope and the nuncio'.

The House voted the allegation 'false, scandalous

and libellous'. He was named to the committee appointed to draw up the address for the removal of Halifax. In the debate on a supply for Tangier he urged the House to ascertain the facts before taking any action. He was named to the committee to examine the proceedings of the judges in dismissing grand juries. It was not until two days before the end of the Parliament that Dering announced his conversion to exclusion, and even then he couched the announcement in his usual moderate tones. 'I think the bill the best expedient', he said, 'as I always did', conveniently forgetting his vote against the first bill.

> You have been told of a conference with the Lords about it, if it may be done in a parliamentary way. . . . The King's denial of the bill in his message is very favourable and gentle to us. . . . If the King lays his reasonable refusal upon the Lords, and if once you give reasons to satisfy the Lords, if they be with us, the argument is very favourable for the King's consent.

Dering accordingly moved for an address to the King for a conference with the Lords on exclusion, but the motion did not find a seconder.[11]

Dering was returned unopposed in 1681. He attended the Oxford Parliament, but was named only to the committee to prepare for a conference with the Lords on the loss of the bill repealing the Elizabethan statute against dissenters. Despite his swing to exclusion and his son's hostility he remained at his post at the Treasury and on the commission of the peace. He died on 24 Apr. 1684 in his town house and was buried at Pluckley.[12]

Dering was an inveterate diarist, keeping both personal and parliamentary diaries. The former reveal his constant preoccupation with his finances and indicate how dependent he was on office. When he drew up his accounts for the period 1648–79 he calculated his receipts at £39,989 and his expenses at £42,057. This deficit was reduced, he wrote 'out of some moneys I had saved out of my employment in Ireland', and in 1680 he calculated that if he lost his post at the Treasury his income would be reduced to less than half. In his parliamentary diaries he shows more interest in procedure and precedents than Anchitell Grey*. Like John Milward* he gains in clarity by not attempting to report each speech separately. He apparently took notes during sittings, and very shortly thereafter worked them up into narrative accounts of each day's proceedings, which, since he regarded each debate as a whole, are easy to follow.[13]

[1] Blake mss, Dering diary and acct. bk. 1625–8. [2] Kent AO, Q/JC 10–15; Twysden Ltcy. Pprs. (Kent Recs. x), 13, 23, 37; CSP Ire. 1660–2, p. 577; 1666–9, pp. 347, 823; Cal. Treas. Bks. iv. 788, 869; v. 751, 986; vi. 4, 265, 728; Dering Pprs. 113–14. [3] Hasted, Kent, i. 136; Keeler, Long Parl. 156. [4] Dering Pprs. 110; Stowe 744, ff. 42, 48. [5] Dering Pprs. 111, 112; CSP Ire. 1666–9, p. 331; CSP Dom. 1665–6, p. 121; Stowe 744, f. 105; Savile Corresp. (Cam. Soc. lxxi), 25. [6] Grey, i. 421; Dering, 108–9, 116–18, 132–3, 135, 147–8; Dering Pprs. 62, 64; Stowe 745, f. 73; Kent AO, U1713/A18–26; CSP Dom. 1673, p. 359. [7] Bulstrode, 316; Dering Pprs. 63; Grey, ii. 391; iii. 293–4, 300, 410, 413–14; iv. 26; CSP Dom. 1676–7, p. 480; Browning, Danby, i. 197n. [8] Grey, iv. 186, 198, 295; CSP Dom. 1678, pp. 193–4. [9] Grey, v. 157, 360. [10] Ibid. vi. 204, 246, 310, 336. [11] Ibid. vi. 414, 430; vii. 433–4; viii. 277; Dering Pprs. 115. [12] Kent AO, U1713/B37; HMC Egmont, ii. 139. [13] Blake mss, diary and acct. bk. 14 Sept. 1675, 28 Apr. 1680, 2 Oct. 1681; Dering Pprs. 28, 111, 115, 130.

B.D.H.

DEVEREUX, Hon. Walter (c.1621–83), of Butley Priory, Suff.

ORFORD   1660, 1661

b. c.1621, 3rd but 2nd surv. s. of Sir Walter Devereux†, 2nd Bt., of Leigh, Worcs., later 5th Visct. Hereford, by 2nd w. Elizabeth, da. of Thomas Knightley of Burgh Hall, Staffs., wid. of Matthew Martin of Barton, Cambs. m. c.1648, Anne (d. c.1666), da. and h. of William Forthe of Butley, 1s. d.v.p. 3da.[1]

Commr. for sewers, Norf. and Suff. 1658–9; freeman, Orford Mar. 1660; j.p. Suff. July 1660–d.; commr. for assessment, Suff. Aug. 1660–80, Orford 1661–79, recusants, Suff. 1675; steward of crown manors, Card. and Carm. 1678–d.[2]

The Devereux family can be traced back on the Welsh marches to the reign of Henry II, and regularly represented Herefordshire from 1378. Devereux's father, like the head of the family the Earl of Essex, supported Parliament in the Civil War. He served on the Worcestershire county committee, but retired into private life on the execution of Charles I. Devereux and his elder brother, later the sixth viscount, both married Suffolk heiresses. By his marriage he acquired a life interest only in an encumbered estate three miles from Orford and an interest in the borough. Until the Restoration he held only minor local office.[3]

Devereux was granted the freedom of Orford on 1 Mar. 1660, aged 38, and returned to the Convention for the borough. An inactive Member, he was appointed to the committee of elections and privileges and added to that to examine discoveries of debts owed to the public. He was given leave to go into the country on 2 Aug. and may not have returned to Westminster after the recess. Two applications for minor offices were unsuccessful.[4]

Devereux was re-elected in 1661, but was equally inactive in the Cavalier Parliament. He was appointed to 46 committees, including the committee of elections and privileges in six sessions. He took no part in the major measures of the Clarendon Code, but was among those named to the committees to consider the execution of those under attainder (26 Nov. 1661) and the defects in the Corporations Act (6 Mar. 1663). He was on both lists of the court party in 1669–71 among those who had usually voted for supply, and was named to the committee for renewing the Conventicles Act (2 Mar. 1670). He was appointed to a committee for a local charity bill in the spring session of 1675, and in the autumn made his only recorded speech, telling the House the wording of the paper that William Cavendish*, Lord Cavendish, had posted up at Whitehall in defiance of its orders. In the same session he was appointed to the committees for appropriating the customs to the use of the navy and for extending habeas corpus. Shaftesbury classed him as 'vile' in 1677, when his most important committee was on the bill for the recall of British subjects from the French service. After obtaining the stewardship of three crown manors in South Wales, he was included in the court list of government supporters in 1678, and on 30 Oct. was added to the committee to translate Coleman's letters.[5]

Although not included in the 'unanimous club' of court supporters, Devereux did not stand for the Exclusion Parliaments. His affairs were embarrassed, and after his wife's death he went to live with Thomas Glemham*. He was involved in litigation with his eldest daughter, whom he sought unsuccessfully to cut out of the succession to Butley after an unsuitable marriage. He died at Glemham in December 1683.[6]

[1] *Vis. Worcs.* (Harl. Soc. xc), 30; *VCH Northants. Fams.* 187; *East Anglian,* n.s. iii. 143. [2] C181/6/292, 341–2, 360; *HMC Var.* iv. 268. [3] Collins, *Peerage,* vi. 2; *East Anglian,* n.s. iii. 140. [4] *HMC Var.* iv. 268; *CSP Dom.* 1660–1, p. 91; *Cal. Treas. Bks.* i. 23–24. [5] Grey, iii. 313; *Cal. Treas. Bks.* v. 1021–2. [6] *East Anglian,* n.s. iii. 141.

M.W.H.

DIGBY, John, Lord Digby (1634–98), of Sherborne Castle, Dorset.

DORSET   18 Oct. 1675–24 Mar. 1677

bap. 26 Apr. 1634, 1st s. of George Digby[†], 2nd Earl of Bristol, by Lady Anne Russell, da. of Francis, 4th Earl of Bedford. *educ.* privately. *m.* (1) 26 Mar. 1656, Alice (*d.*1658), da. and h. of Robert Bourne of Blake Hall, Essex, *s.p.*; (2) lic. 13 July 1663, Rachel, da. and coh. of Sir Hugh Wyndham, j.c.p. 1673–84, of Silton, Dorset, *s.p. suc.* fa. as 3rd Earl 24 Mar. 1677.[1]

J.p. Dorset July 1660–June 1688, 1689–*d.*, Som. July 1660–79; commr. for oyer and terminer, Western circuit July 1660, sewers Som. Dec. 1660, assessment Dorset 1661–74, Som. 1664–74; dep. lt. Dorset 1672–4, ld. lt. 1679–June 1688, Oct. 1688–*d.*; custos rot. Dorset 1680–June 1688, 1689–*d.*; freeman, Lyme Regis 1683.[2]

Digby's grandfather, the 1st Earl of Bristol, came from a cadet branch of the Midland family. He was granted the Sherborne Castle estate as a reward for diplomatic services in 1616. His father sat for the county in both Parliaments of 1640 before being called up to the Lords, having made the Lower House too hot to hold him by his unexpected and well-publicized opposition to Strafford's attainder. During the Interregnum, when his father in exile became a convert to Rome, Digby seems to have lived with his Puritan mother, whose 'zeal cannot suffer a Catholic under her roof'. She bought back the estates from the Treason Trustees by selling her own jointure, and settled it on Digby on his marriage. Digby showed little desire to emulate his ancestors in high politics, and he certainly took no part in his father's increasingly futile opposition to the Clarendon administration. He was himself 'naturally inclined to avoid the hurry of public life', or, less politely 'every way a weak man'. His abuse of Shaftesbury when he learnt that his candidature for the county in 1675 was to be opposed must be ascribed to a conviction that the seat appertained to his estate, rather than to political animosity. Digby won the election handsomely, but lost the action for *scandalum magnatum*; the damages and costs, however, were more than covered by a subscription from the gentlemen of the county.[3]

Digby took part in only two sessions of the Cavalier Parliament, during which he was an active Member, being named to 20 committees. In considering the bill to restrict the growth of Popery on 15 Nov. 1675, he might, as the son of a notorious convert, be expected to contribute special knowledge; his own religion, as his episcopal obituarist expresses it, 'was that which by law is established'. He was also on the committee for the bill to recall English subjects from French service on 10 Nov. 1675, and took part in the conference on a joint address to urge the formation of an alliance to defend the Netherlands on 13 Mar. 1677. Sir Richard Wiseman* listed him among the government supporters, and he wrote to (Sir) Joseph Williamson* between sessions, offering his services.[4]

After his succession to the peerage as Earl of Bristol, Digby can be reckoned a follower of Danby, to whom he sold his father's house at Wimbledon; but after some hesitation he voted for his attainder on 14 Apr. 1679. He abstained from the division on the exclusion bill, but voted for the condemnation of Lord Stafford. In June 1681 Bristol had the satisfaction of presenting, and Charles of receiving, a loyal petition from Shaftesbury's own county. By 1687, however, he appears as an opponent of the Court on Danby's list. His canvass of the deputy lieutenants and justices of the peace was singularly unsuccessful; favourable replies were received only from the four Roman Catholics on the commission and two others of little weight in the county. When he was ordered to dismiss the remainder, he replied desiring Sunderland (who was his brother-in-law) 'to beg the King to excuse me from acting as his lieutenant'. But on 28 Sept. 1688 he received the writ for the sheriff to hold the elections for James's abortive second Parliament, and on inquiry he found that he had been restored on his own conditions. Nevertheless, he led the gentlemen of the county over to William in November, a service rewarded with a pension of £5,500. Even before the Convention met he was in favour of the transfer of the crown, and appears to have been active (doubtless through Thomas Erle*) in securing the return of like-minded candidates. In the Convention he signed the protest of the minority in the Upper House against the narrow defeat of a resolution affirming that the throne was vacant (4 Feb. 1689). Bristol died on 18 Sept. 1698, and was buried at Sherborne Abbey. His estate passed to his cousin William Digby*, whose descendants continued to represent the county in the 20th century.[5]

[1] *St. Martin in the Fields* (Harl. Soc. Reg. lxvi), 103; *Mar. Lic.* (Harl. Soc. xxiv), 72. [2] *CSP Dom.* 1671-2, p. 236; 1679-80, p. 269; *Q. Sess. Recs.* (Som Rec. Soc. xxxiv), p. xi; Lyme Regis court bk. 1672-92, f. 336. [3] PRO 31/8, ff. 922, 1067; Clarendon, *Life*, 393; Hutchins, *Dorset*, iv. 254; *Guise Mems.* (Cam. Soc. ser. 3, xxviii), 149-150; Christie, *Shaftesbury*, ii. 216; *HMC 15th Rep. VII*, 178; *Hatton Corresp.* (Cam. Soc. n.s. xxii), 123, 126. [4] Hutchins, iv. 254; *CSP Dom.* 1675-6, p. 580. [5] *CSP Dom.* 1680-1, p. 656; 1687-9, pp. 213, 287, 293-4, 302; Browning, *Danby*, i. 125; R. Morrice, Entering Bk. 2, pp. 201-2; *Burnet Supp.* ed. Foxcroft, 531; *HMC Lords*, iii. 381.

J.P.F.

DIGBY, Robert, 3rd Baron Digby of Geashill [I] (1654-77), of Coleshill, Warws.

WARWICK   30 May-29 Dec. 1677

> *b.* 30 Apr. 1654, 2nd but 1st surv. s. of Kildare, 2nd Baron Digby [I], by Mary, da. of Robert Gardiner of London; bro. of Simon Digby* and William Digby*. *educ.* privately; Magdalen Coll. Oxf. 1670, MA 1676; travelled abroad 1673-6. *unm. suc.* fa. 11 July 1661.
> Commr. for assessment, Warws. 1677-*d.*

Lord Digby's ancestors first sat for Leicestershire in 1373. The Warwickshire branch was founded in 1495 and represented that county under the Tudors. Digby's father was too young to take part in the Civil War, and died soon after the Restoration, leaving him the Coleshill estate, worth £1,500 p.a., and lands in Ireland which brought in £2,000 more, though encumbered with annuities. Digby's mother, although still a young woman, did not remarry, but devoted herself to the upbringing of her children. Her sons' education was confided to her chaplain, William Rawlins, described (theologically) as 'a very primitive man'. Digby was returned for Warwick, no doubt with the support of Lord Brooke (Fulke Greville*), at

the first election after his return from his travels, and three days after the adjournment of the 1677 session. Shaftesbury marked him 'doubly worthy', but he never took his seat. He died during the recess on 29 Dec. and was buried at Coleshill.

> *VCH Warws.* iv. 51; *CSP Ire.* 1660-2, p. 381; *Letters of 2nd Earl of Chesterfield*, 281; J. Kettlewell, *Works*, i. 31.

A.M.M.

DIGBY, Simon, 4th Baron Digby of Geashill [I] (1657-86), of Coleshill, Warws.

WARWICK   1685-19 Jan. 1686

> *b.* 18 July 1657, 3rd but 2nd surv. s. of Kildare, 2nd Baron Digby [I]; bro. of Robert Digby* and William Digby*. *educ.* privately; Magdalen Coll. Oxf. 1674; L. Inn 1676. *m.* 27 Aug. 1683, Lady Frances Noel (*d.* 29 Sept. 1684), da. of Edward Noel*, 1st Earl of Gainsborough, 1da. *suc.* bro. 29 Dec. 1677.
> Commr. for assessment, Warws. 1679-80, dep. lt. by 1680-*d.*

Lord Digby first stood as a court candidate for Coventry in August 1679, but finished at the foot of the poll. As patron of the Coleshill living he was 'one of those few who thought a cure of souls too great a trust to be given upon any other consideration than pure merit'. In consequence he was 'under the greatest concern imaginable that he might be found a faithful steward in the disposal of that trust', and select one 'as might be a constant friend and monitor to him, in all the difficulties of the spiritual life, during his pilgrimage here'. His eventual choice was the future non-juror, John Kettlewell. Digby was returned for Warwick at the general election of 1685, probably with the assistance of Lord Brooke (Fulke Greville*). A very active Member of James II's Parliament, he was named to 20 committees. The most important in the first session were the committee of elections and privileges, and those to recommend expunctions from the Journals, to estimate the yield of a tax on new buildings, and to provide for the general naturalization of Huguenot refugees. He was 'very much against establishing an army', and spoke in the debate after the recess to such effect that he was appointed to the small committee to draft the address against the employment of Roman Catholic officers. He was listed among the Opposition, but died on 19 Jan. 1686, and was buried at Coleshill. Kettlewell's funeral sermon naturally dwells on his 'many notable virtues', which included the proselytization of his friends.

> He would follow them with good counsels, which he would manage discreetly and time seasonably, laying wait for them in their most impressive moods, especially after any great danger, or in time of sickness; and wherein he would reason clearly, endeavouring to con-

vince and persuade them, both from the cogent reason of things, and from the more affecting argument of his own experience.

His sins were few, and even though he occasionally indulged in games of chance he made it a rule that what he lost should go as the price of his pleasure, what he won, to the poor.

J. Kettlewell, *Works*, i. 21–22, 797, 800–2; *HMC Lindsey*, 31; R. Morrice, Entering Bk. 2, p. 518.

A.M.M.

DIGBY, William, 5th Baron Digby of Geashill [I] (c.1662–1752), of Coleshill, Warws.

WARWICK 1689, 1690, 1695

b. c.1662, 4th but 3rd surv. s. of Kildare, 2nd Baron Digby [I]; bro. of Robert Digby* and Simon Digby*. *educ.* privately; Magdalen Coll. Oxf. matric. 16 May 1679, aged 17, BA 1681, DCL 1708. *m.* lic. 22 May 1686, Lady Jane Noel (*d.* 10 Sept. 1733), da. of Edward Noel*, 1st Earl of Gainsborough, 4s. *d.v.p.* 8da. *suc.* bro. 19 Jan. 1686, cos. John Digby*, 3rd Earl of Bristol, in Dorset estate 1698.
    Dep. lt. Warws. 1686–7, ?1689–96, commr. for assessment 1689–90, j.p. 1690–6, 1700–?*d.*; gov. St. Bartholomew's hosp. 1729–*d.*; member of common council, Georgia 1733.[1]
    Member, Society for Propagation of the Gospel 1701.[2]

Lord Digby was appointed one of the deputy lieutenants of Warwickshire by the 4th Earl of Northampton, and was the first to sign the letter to Sunderland of 16 Oct. 1688 thanking him for his intention to continue them, but indicating that several militia officers would not serve with those who had not taken the Test. He was returned for Warwick at the general election of 1689, probably, like his brothers before him, with the support of Lord Brooke (Fulke Greville*). A Tory, he voted to agree with the Lords that the throne was not vacant. A moderately active Member of the Convention, he was named to 28 committees, including those to inquire into the authors and advisers of recent grievances, to prepare cases against prisoners of state, to draft the coronation oath, to consider the new oaths of allegiance and supremacy, and to repeal the Corporations Act. He helped to prepare the addresses thanking the King for his declaration that he would maintain the Church and promising him support for a war with France. He was also appointed to the committee for the toleration bill. As an Irish landowner, he was attainted by the Dublin Parliament, and was naturally concerned about the plight of refugees from that country. He was among those instructed to draft an address asking for permission to inspect the Privy Council records about Irish affairs (3 July). Five days later he was given leave to go into the country for three weeks. But he returned after the recess, and was named to the committees to recommend the Irish nobility and gentry for the royal bounty, and to draft the address seeking to establish the responsibility for the appointment of Commissary Shales. He was added to the committee of elections and privileges on 9 Dec., and appointed to the committee to consider the bill to provide for the security of Protestants in Ireland. He also served on two committees of Warwickshire interest, to provide for the endowment of Astley vicarage and to examine a petition from Birmingham about King Edward VI's School. His last committee was for the restoration of the university charters.[3]

Digby was re-elected to the next two Parliaments as a Tory, but, as one of the instigators of the opposition to the Association, he never sat again after 1698. The rest of the long life of 'the good Lord Digby' was spent in charitable activities and the encouragement of literature. He made Coleshill a haven for non-jurors, but is perhaps best known as a patron of Pope. 'A noble specimen of ancient, uncorrupted English virtue', he died on 29 Nov. 1752, aged 90, and was buried in Sherborne Abbey. He had survived his sons, two of whom sat for Warwickshire as Tories, but his grandsons continued the family parliamentary record.[4]

[1] *CSP Dom.* 1686–7, p. 261; SP31/4/131; Warws. RO, QS1/1/16–20, 22–34. [2] *CSP Dom.* 1700–2, p. 358. [3] SP31/4/131; *VCH Warws.* iv. 52. [4] *HMC 13th Rep. IV*, 372.

A.M.M.

DILLINGTON, Edward (c.1655–90), of Westover, I.o.W.

NEWPORT I.o.W. 25 June 1689

b. c.1655, 2nd s. of Sir Robert Dillington, 1st Bt.[†], of Knighton, being o.s. by 2nd w. Catherine, da. of Edward, 1st Baron Gorges of Dundalk [I]. *educ.* Trinity, Oxf. matric. 14 Mar. 1673, aged 17. *unm.*[1]
    Commr. for assessment, Hants 1677–80, 1690.

Dillington was returned for Newport at a by-election in 1689 caused by the death of Sir Robert Dillington, 3rd Bt.* He was probably a Whig, but he made no speeches and was appointed to no committees. He was buried at Stetchworth, the seat of his uncle, Richard Gorges*, on 11 Feb. 1690.[2]

[1] *Misc. Gen. et Her.* (ser. 2), i. 381; Hoare, *Wilts.* Cawden, 30. [2] *Mon. Inscriptions from Cambs.* 155.

P.W.

DILLINGTON, Robert (c.1634–87) of Knighton, I.o.W.

NEWPORT I.o.W. 1659, 1660, 8 Nov. 1670, 1679 (Mar.), 1679 (Oct.), 1681 *b.* c.1634, 1st s. of Robert Dillington (*d.*1654) of Mottistone by Frances, da. of William Collier of Piddletrenthide, Dorset. *educ.* Queen's, Oxf. 1653; G. Inn 1654. *m.* (1) July 1659, Jane (*d.*1674), da. of John Freke[†] of Cerne Abbey, Dorset, 2s. 1da. 8 other ch. *d.v.p.*; (2) lic. 28 May 1678, Hannah, da. and coh. of William Webb, Grocer, of Throgmorton Street, London, 1s. 2da. *suc.* gdfa. Sir Robert Dillington[†] as 2nd Bt. 1664.[1]

Commr. for militia, Hants 1659; j.p. Hants July 1660–80, Dorset and Wilts. 1676–80; commr. for assessment, Hants Aug. 1660–3, 1664–9, I.o.W. Aug. 1660–1, 1663–4, wastes and spoils, New Forest 1672–3, 1679, recusants, Hants 1675; freeman, Lymington 1679; verderer, New Forest by 1686–*d.*[2]

The founder of the Dillington family, a customs official, sat for Poole in two Marian Parliaments before acquiring the manor of Knighton, four miles from Newport, about 1564, to which were later added six others in the island. During the Civil War Dillington's father was on the county committee, while his grandfather accepted local office during the Interregnum and sat for Newport in 1654. Dillington took over the seat in Richard Cromwell's Parliament, and retained it at the general election of 1660. He was listed by Lord Wharton as a friend, but he was inactive in the Convention, making no speeches and being appointed to no committees. His name was mentioned only on 24 July when he was given leave to go into the country. He did not stand in 1661. During the second Dutch war he wrote to Joseph Williamson*, with whom he had corresponded in his university days, asking for additional forces to defend the island and reporting on the state of the militia.[3]

Dillington regained his seat at a by-election in 1670. He was excused default in attendance on 21 Jan. 1671, and became a moderately active Member of the Cavalier Parliament. He was named to 40 committees, including that for the bill to prevent the growth of Popery six weeks later. On 4 Feb. 1673, during a debate on a motion to ask for a speedy acknowledgment by the King that penal statutes in ecclesiastical matters could only be suspended by Act of Parliament, Dillington called for more respect in the wording of the motion, saying: 'Possibly His Majesty may have forgotten our address, and desires he may be reminded of it, in all humbleness, for a gracious answer'. During a debate on grievances on 17 Mar. 1673, when Lord St. John (Charles Powlett I*) had complained that a regiment had been quartered in Hampshire at a cost of 5*d.* a meal, Dillington corrected the statement by saying that he was informed 'in Hampshire that they must either allow 5*d.* a day or keep the soldiers in the houses'. In 1674 he was appointed to the committees for regulating parliamentary elections and considering the state of Ireland. He received the government whip from Williamson for the autumn session of 1675, but was marked 'doubly worthy' on Shaftesbury's list in 1677. During the Popish Plot panic he was appointed to the committee to investigate noises heard in Old Palace Yard. After a violent scene in the House on 21 Nov. 1678 between the courtier Jonathan Trelawny I* and William Ashe* of the country party, he said that he had overheard the quarrel and that Ashe had given no provocation which could justify a blow.[4]

Dillington continued to represent Newport in the Exclusion Parliaments, and Shaftesbury again marked him 'worthy'. He was moderately active in 1679, being appointed to 11 committees, including those to take the disbandment accounts, to consider the bill for preventing illegal exactions, to continue the Act against the import of Irish cattle, and to inquire into the state of the navy. He voted for the exclusion bill, and was removed from local office. In the second Exclusion Parliament he was appointed only to the committee for a naturalization bill, and in the third only to the committee of elections and privileges. He probably did not stand in 1685. He died on 25 Apr. 1687, aged 53, and was buried at Newchurch.[5]

[1] *Misc. Gen. et Her.* (ser. 2), i. 366, 381–2; PCC 81 Alchin; C10/108/45. [2] *Cal. Treas. Bks.* iii. 875, 1204; iv. 124, 697; vi. 199; viii. 758; E. King, *Old Times Revisited*, 191. [3] *Oglander Mems.* ed. Long, 127; *VCH Hants.* v. 142, 163, 181, 183, 219, 252; PCC 76 Foot; *CSP Dom.* 1665–6, pp. 533–4, 548, 589. [4] Grey, ii. 49, 131; vi. 257. [5] *Misc. Gen. et Her.* (ser. 2), ii, 124–5.

P.W.

DILLINGTON, Sir Robert, 3rd Bt. (c.1664–89), of Knighton, I.o.W.

NEWPORT I.o.W. 11 Jan.–13 May 1689

b. c.1664, 1st s. of (Sir) Robert Dillington*, 2nd Bt., by 1st w. *educ.* Queen's, Oxf. matric. 1 June 1682, aged 17. *unm. suc.* fa. 25 Apr. 1687.

Commr. for assessment, Hants 1689.

Dillington was returned for Newport in 1689. He was probably a Whig like his father, but in the short time he sat in the Convention he was appointed to no committees, though on 30 Apr. he charged Sir Robert Holmes* with breach of his privilege by quartering soldiers on his house. He died on 13 May 1689, aged 25, and was buried at Newchurch. His brother, the fifth baronet, was returned for Newport in 1707 and again in 1717 as a government supporter.

Misc. Gen. et Her. (ser. 2), ii. 367.

P.W.

DIXWELL, Sir Basil, 2nd Bt. (1665–1750), of Broom House, Barham, Kent.

DOVER 1689, 1695, 1698

b. 11 Dec. 1665, o.s. of Sir Basil Dixwell, 1st Bt., of Broom House by Dorothy, da. and coh. of Sir Thomas Peyton, 2nd Bt.*, of Knowlton. *educ.* Christ Church, Oxf. 1682. *m.* (1) Dorothy (*d.* c.1718), da. and coh. of Sir John Temple of East Sheen, Surr., *s.p.*; (2) 25 Apr. 1720, his cos. Catharine, da. of William Longueville of the Inner Temple, *s.p. suc.* fa. 7 May 1668.

Col. of militia horse, Kent by Dec. 1688, j.p. and dep. lt. 1689–?*d.*; commr. for assessment, Kent, Dover and Folkestone 1689–90, court of lodemanage, Cinque Ports 1689, col. of militia ft. by 1697.[1]

Auditor of excise 1691–1713, 1714–*d.*[2]

Capt. Sandgate Castle 1694–6; lt.-gov. Dover Castle 1696–1702, 1714–?*d.*[3]

Dixwell's family was of Warwickshire origin, but one of them inherited considerable property around Folkestone and elsewhere in 1622, and sat for Hythe four years later. His great-uncle was John Dixwell[†] the regicide, but his grandfather died before the Civil War and his father came of age only after the Restoration, when he was given a baronetcy. Dixwell acted as spokesman for the Kentish deputy lieutenants at Faversham during the Revolution. The loyal Earl of Ailesbury (Thomas Bruce*) called him 'silly, malign and busy', and did not overlook his regicide connexion, while the King, who was compelled to accept the escort of Dixwell's militia, complained of his 'rude and rebellious carriage'. On his return to Kent on 29 Dec. 1688 Dixwell collected signatures for the Association to stand by the Prince of Orange, and he was elected for Dover a few days later. He was among those chosen to carry the canopy at the coronation, but played no known part in the Convention. Although clearly a Whig, he was not listed as supporting the disabling clause in the bill to restore corporations, and he lost his seat to James Chadwick* at the general election. In the two succeeding Parliaments he sat as a court Whig. He died on 25 Mar. 1750, the last of his family, and was buried at Barham.[4]

[1] Hasted, *Kent*, vi. 350; Add. 29625, f. 120; *CSP Dom.* 1689–90, p. 210; Eg. 1626, f. 24. [2] *Cal. Treas. Bks.* ix. 1202; xxvii. 92; xxix. 35, 193. [3] *Arch. Cant.* xxi. 256; *CSP Dom.* 1696, p. 152; 1702–3, p. 162. [4] Hasted, *Kent*, vi. 350–1; viii. 160–1; *N. and Q.* (ser. 3), vi. 23, 42, 82, 121; *Ailesbury Mems.* 210–12; Clarke, *Jas. II*, ii. 259; Add. 28037, f. 50; *Arch. Cant.* xxi. 254.

B.D.H.

DOCWRA, Thomas (1624–by 1706), of Putteridge, Offley, Herts.

ST. ALBANS 1685

b. 7 Oct. 1624, 1st s. of Periam Docwra of Putteridge by Martha, da. of Oliver, 3rd Baron St. John of Bletso. *educ.* Eton c.1635; Trinity Coll. Camb. 1636, BA 1642.

m. (1) Margaret, da. of Robert Cherry, 1da.; (2) lic. 14 Sept. 1671, Dorothy Stone of Pirton, 1s. *d.v.p. suc.* fa. 1643.[1]

J.p. Herts. 1646–Mar. 1660, 1662–Feb. 1688, Beds. 1680–Feb. 1688, Beds. and Herts. Oct. 1688–90; commr. for assessment, Herts. 1647–52, 1657, Aug. 1660–80, St. Albans 1661–9, Ely 1673–4, Beds. 1689, militia, Herts. 1648, Mar. 1660; dep. lt. Herts. 1681–7, Beds. 1685–Feb. 1688, Beds. and Herts. Oct. 1688–90.[2]

Docwra's great-grandfather, of north country stock, bought Putteridge in 1525. Docwra succeeded his father early in the Civil War, and held local office throughout the Interregnum, which he regained after a brief interval in 1662. But he probably opposed exclusion, being added to the lieutenancy in 1681. Lord Bruce (Thomas Bruce*) regarded him as 'a most worthy friend', and perhaps recommended him for St. Albans in 1685 as a Tory. An inactive Member of James II's Parliament, he was appointed only to the committee on the bill for exporting leather. He gave evasive answers to the questions on the Test Act and Penal Laws, declaring:

> If I am chosen a Member, my resolution shall be to come into the House absolutely with a most loyal temper, and no wise prepossessed. . . . My intentions are to act in every sense according to honour and conscience, hoping that the King can never be able to ask anything but what I can cheerfully concur with.

His friend Bruce, now Earl of Ailesbury, observed that Sunderland regarded Docwra's answers as 'impertinent'.[3]

Despite his answers, Docwra proved loyal to James II, moving into the Jacobite camp. By 1690 he was a non-juror and had been removed from local office. Though an associate of Sir William Parkins, he does not seem to have been involved in the Jacobite conspiracy of 1696. In 1700 he settled his estates, said to be worth £3,000 p.a., on his grandson, Sir George Warburton, 3rd Bt.[†] Two weeks after James II's death in 1701 he was reported to have taken the oaths of allegiance. His will, dated 4 June 1700, was proved on 26 Oct. 1706.[4]

[1] Clutterbuck, *Herts.* iii. 83; *The Gen.* n.s. xiv. 273; *London Mar. Lic.* ed. Foster, 407; PCC 209 Eades. [2] *CSP Dom.* 1680–1, p. 182; *Herts. Recs.* i. 386. [3] Clutterbuck, iii. 82–83; *VCH Herts.* iii. 42; *Ailesbury Mems.* i. 164, 165. [4] *Herts. Recs.* i. 386; *Ailesbury Mems.* ii. 369–70; Clutterbuck, iii. 83; Luttrell, v. 92; PCC 209 Eades.

E.R.E./G.J.

DOLBEN, Gilbert (c.1658–1722), of Finedon, Northants.

RIPON	1685
PETERBOROUGH	1689, 1690, 1695, 1701 (Feb.), 1701 (Dec.), 1702, 1705, 1708
YARMOUTH I.o.W.	1710, 1713

b. c.1658, 1st s. of John Dolben, archbishop of York 1683–6, by Catherine, da. of Ralph Sheldon of Stanton, Derbys.; bro. of John Dolben†. *educ.* Westminster 1671; Christ Church, Oxf. matric. 18 July 1674, aged 15; I. Temple 1674, called 1681. *m.* by 1683, Anne, da. and coh. of Tanfield Mulso of Finedon, 1s. *suc.* fa. 1686; *cr.* Bt. 1 Apr. 1704.

Attaché, Nymwegen 1676; gent. of privy chamber 1689–1702; j.c.p. [I] 1701–20; chairman, elections committee 2 Mar.–27 May 1714.[1]

J.p. Yorks. (W. Riding) 1684–Sept. 1688, Northants. 1686–Feb. 1688, 1689–96, 1700–?*d.*; commr. for assessment, Northants. 1689–90; bencher, I. Temple 1706, treas. 1720–1.[2]

Dolben came of a clerical family on both sides. His grandfather, who was of Welsh extraction, held a living in Northamptonshire and was bishop-designate of Bangor at his death. His father, the half-brother of Sir Thomas Meres*, rose from ensign to major in the royalist army, and was twice seriously wounded. Taking Anglican orders during the Interregnum, he married the niece of Gilbert Sheldon, later archbishop of Canterbury. He became dean of Westminster in 1662, which he combined with the bishopric of Rochester from 1666. His outspoken loyalty to Clarendon interrupted his career only temporarily, and in 1683 he was translated to York. In the House of Lords, according to Sir William Trumbull*, he commanded more interest and authority than all the rest of the bench of bishops. After an early venture into diplomacy Dolben preferred to follow his uncle Sir William into the legal profession. Fortunately he married an heiress, since he was slow to build up a practice. Five years after his call to the bar, Trumbull was told that 'Gil is grown the fustiest old gentleman you ever saw. Even to a sight he is some way discontented, I presume for want of business . . . He is more troubled with vapours than ever you were.' Returned for Ripon in 1685 on his father's interest, he was an active Member of James II's Parliament, in which he was appointed to 14 committees. He was selected to ask the eminent high church divine, Dr Sherlock, to preach and to thank him for his sermon. He was appointed to the committees for preventing clandestine marriages, rebuilding St. Paul's, repairing Bangor Cathedral and naturalizing Protestant refugees, and acted as chairman on the bill to prohibit the import of buttons. He returned negative answers on the repeal of the Test Act and Penal Laws to the lord lieutenant of Northamptonshire, and was dismissed from local office.[3]

The Revolution found Dolben well placed to command support in both parties. His episcopal background would always recommend him to the Tories, while his uncle, who had lost a judgeship

for expressing doubts on the quo warranto proceedings, was much respected by the Whigs. He had probably already reunited the Finedon estate by buying out his brother, who had married the other Mulso coheir but wasted her fortune and his own by 'profligate gaming'. At the general election of 1689 he was returned for Peterborough, no doubt with the support of the dean and chapter. He was again an active Member, with 51 committees and nine recorded speeches. On 28 Jan. Dolben became the first Member to declare publicly in the House that James's reign was at an end:

> I tell you freely my opinion that the King is demised, and that James II is not King of England. For I lay it down as an undoubted proposition that when the king does withdraw himself from the administration of the government, without any provision to support the commonwealth, when, on the contrary, he stops the use of the great seal by taking it away with him, this amounts to what the law calls 'demise'.

As a Tory he was anxious to avoid any suggestion of elective monarchy, and wished it to be understood that the next heir had succeeded automatically. 'The speech was very long, and very learned, and well delivered.' When Henry Pollexfen* suggested that James's departure had been involuntary, Dolben interjected that 'no one can deny that he might have stayed if he would'. On the next day he declared that 'there is nothing in statute or common law against a popish prince, but it is against the interest of the nation'. On 1 Feb. he proposed a vote of thanks to all who had opposed the ecclesiastical commission. He considered the resolution of the Commons that the throne was vacant more logical than the alternative proposed by the Lords, and was among those entrusted with drawing up reasons. On 6 Feb. he was sent to desire a conference accordingly; but in the end he voted to agree with the Lords. He was appointed to the committees to inquire into the authors and advisers of grievances, to draw up the declaration of rights, to alter the oaths of allegiance and supremacy, and to draw up an address of thanks for the King's promise of a general pardon. He took the chair in the grand committee for the new oaths and presented eight reports. He was appointed to the committees for the repeal of the Corporations Act and to consider the comprehension bill, and on 15 Apr. he carried the bill for the new oaths to the Lords. On the next day he was the first to be nominated to the committee for putting the great seal in commission. He helped to draw up reasons for the conferences on disarming Papists and on the poll-tax. Dolben's uncle had been reinstated as judge, and was responsible for bringing Titus Oates's writ of error to the House; but Dolben took no part in the discussion of this case, though he was added to the committee considering the proceedings against the Whig clergyman Johnson. He was among those ordered to bring in an indemnity bill on 22 June. He spoke in defence of his father's successor in the see of Rochester, Bishop Sprat, who, he asserted, had 'acted with great zeal for the Protestant religion'.[4]

When the Government met for its second session, Dolben was appointed to the committees to consider the petition from the widow and daughters of Sir Thomas Armstrong* and to reverse his attainder. He acted as chairman for the address inquiring who had advised the appointment of Commissary Shales, and on 2 Dec. he reported the King's curt answer. He defended the part of (Sir) Robert Sawyer* in the condemnation of Armstrong, saying that he had clearly not prosecuted the whole indictment. He acted as teller for the second reading of the bill confirming university charters. In the debate on exceptions to the indemnity bill on 21 Jan. 1690, he supported the proposal of William Sacheverell* to name individual culprits since specifying crimes had failed. Presumably reflecting on William Williams*, he said: 'Some, like Cain, bear their brands about them. You will find enough to satisfy the concerned.' Dolben continued to sit in the Commons as a Tory, even after his appointment as an Irish judge. He died on 22 Oct. 1722. His only son took orders, but his grandson, the third baronet, sat for Northamptonshire from 1768 to 1774 as an independent, and also for Oxford University.[5]

[1] *Clarendon Corresp.* i. 624; Carlisle, *Privy Chamber*, 205; *HMC Portland*, v. 146. [2] Northants. RO, FH2226. [3] *Pepys Diary*, 24 Feb. 1668; *Cal. Wynn Pprs.* 429; *HMC Downshire*, i. 151; *CJ*, ix. 718, 721, 754. [4] *HMC Downshire*, i. 389; *IHR Bull.* xlix. 249, 251; *CJ*, x. 12, 16, 18, 64, 81, 124, 127; Macaulay, *Hist.* 1274; Grey, ix. 7, 28, 40, 48, 385; Simpson thesis, 225. [5] *CJ*, x. 298, 337; Grey, ix. 529, 539.

J.P.F.

DOLMAN, Sir Thomas (1622–97), of Shaw, Berks.

READING   1661

b. 13 Jan. 1622 o.s. of Humphrey Dolman of Shaw by Anne, da. and h. of John Quarles, merchant, of London. *educ.* Lincoln, Oxf. 1638; L. Inn 1641. *m.* 1651, Margery (*d.* 21 Jan. 1687) da. and h. of John Hobday of Thornton, Warws., 5s. (3 *d.v.p.*) 3da. Kntd. 2 Feb. 1661; *suc.* fa. 1666.[1]

Commr. for assessment, Berks. Jan. 1660–80, 1689–90, Leics. 1673–80, Warws. 1677–80, militia, Berks. Mar. 1660; j.p. Berks. July 1660–87, Newbury 1664, 1671, 1685, Leics. 1669–87, dep. lt. Berks. c. Aug. 1660–?87; freeman, Reading 1661; commr. for recusants, Berks. 1675.[2]

Gent. of the privy chamber 1672–85; clerk to the Privy Council extraordinary 1676, ordinary 1677–85.[3]

Dolman's ancestors were prosperous Newbury clothiers. His great-grandfather bought Shaw manor in 1554, and is said to have spent £10,000 in building. Although his father was named to the commission of array and Shaw became a royalist garrison in the Civil War, the property escaped sequestration. Dolman himself is said to have fought at the second battle of Newbury, but his father held local office during the Interregnum, and there is no evidence that either was active in royalist conspiracy. Dolman's knighthood was perhaps intended to enhance his status at Reading where the Royalists feared 'an ill election' in 1661. He was granted the freedom of the borough and apparently returned unopposed. A moderately active Member of the Cavalier Parliament, he was appointed to 167 committees, acted as teller in 11 divisions, and made eight recorded speeches. During the Clarendon administration his most important committees were to consider the uniformity bill, the five mile bill, and the public accounts bill. A zealous Anglican, he was teller against allowing a debate on the order for receiving the sacrament on 9 Dec. 1666. Shortly afterwards he succeeded to the Shaw estate, which was probably somewhat over-valued by Bishop Ward at £2,000 p.a. In 1667 he was appointed to the committee to prevent the growth of Popery, and was teller for the unsuccessful proviso of 28 Apr. 1668 that the conventicles bill was intended against the Roman Catholics. He was one of the deputation sent on 23 Nov. 1669 to thank the Duke of Albemarle (George Monck*) for taking measures to prevent disturbances by the disaffected. Ten days later he was teller against accepting one of the charges of misdemeanour brought by the public accounts commissioners against Sir George Carteret*. He was appointed to all the committees directed against conventicles in this session, and acted as teller for the bill on 9 Mar. 1670. He appeared in both lists of the court party in 1669–71 as one to be engaged by the Duke of York. Dolman's activity was most marked during the session of 1670–1, when he was among those named to manage a conference on the growth of Popery, and served on some 40 other committees. In debates on supply he acted as stalking-horse for the Government, proposing, to the horror of Sir Thomas Meres*, an additional excise on beer and ale, and during the recess he was given a post at Court. When Parliament reassembled, he again took the lead over supply. He declared that the third Dutch war was just and prudent and Parliament no less loyal than before, and therefore proposed a land tax of £70,000 a month for 18 months. He opposed dispensations either for Protestant dissenters from the oaths of allegiance and supremacy, or the Roman Catholic Bernard Howard from the recusancy laws. On Howard's petition he declared:

> If the little thief gets in at the window of the house, he will soon open the great door to let in the rest of the thieves. Let one in by such a petition and you may let in the rest.

His name appeared on the Paston list of court supporters in 1673-4.[4]

As one of the executors of the will of Thomas Rich*, Dolman was appointed to the committee to confirm his son's marriage settlement. After the Abingdon by-election in 1675 he assured Sir Richard Wiseman* that Sir John Stonhouse* would vote for the Court, and he received the government whip from Secretary Coventry. After the autumn session, however, Wiseman wrote of Dolman that it 'goes against his mind if he votes ill, and if he does do so, I am sure he is deluded by promises'. On the working lists, therefore, he was included among those 'to be remembered', and when Parliament reassembled after the long recess he was granted one of the Privy Council clerkships, valued in *A Seasonable Argument* at £500 p.a. The author of *Flagellum Parliamentarium* alleged that he was 'flattered with belief of being made secretary of state', and Shaftesbury marked him 'thrice vile'. Among his committees in the 1677 session were those on the bills for preventing illegal exactions, and for educating the children of the royal family as Protestants. Although (Sir) Joseph Williamson* included him among the government speakers, he made only two more speeches in the House, and neither was helpful to the Government. On 1 Feb. 1678, he advocated sending the court supporter Thomas Wancklyn* to the Tower for issuing fraudulent protections. He was more reliable as a teller, opposing that part of the address of 10 May 1678 which called for the removal of evil counsellors, and supporting compensation to the crown for the loss of customs revenue arising from the prohibition of imports from France. During the last session of the Parliament he was appointed to the committees to inquire into the Popish Plot, to translate Coleman's letters and to search Langhorne's papers. As clerk to the Council he was present when Coleman's letters were shown to Oates, and on 2 Nov. he said that 'Mr Oates saw but one line of these letters, and he told us presently whose hands they were'. His acceptance of the Popish Plot no doubt accounts for his exclusion from the 'unanimous club' of court supporters, though his name is first in the government list of 1678. But he did not stand again.[5]

Dolman surrendered his clerkship to William Bridgeman* in January 1685, though retaining the profits. Shortly afterwards, he petitioned for over four years' arrears of salary. Apparently opposed to James II's policies, he was removed from the bench in 1687. William of Orange stayed a night at Shaw on his way to London in December 1688, but Dolman's attitude to the Revolution is not known. He died on 18 July 1697 and was buried at Shaw, the only member of his family to sit in Parliament.[6]

[1] Reading Univ. mss, H. C. Cherry, Bercherienses Prosapiae, 1, p. 479; *Vis. Berks.* (Harl. Soc. lvi), 193; *VCH Berks.* iv. 90; PCC 138 Pyne; *VCH Warws.* v. 80. [2] Berks. RO, Reading corp. diary, 6 Apr. 1661; *CSP Dom.* 1685, p. 38. [3] Carlisle, *Privy Chamber*, 190; *CSP Dom.* 1676-7, p. 570; 1684-5, p. 284; PC2/65/231, 486. [4] *VCH Berks.* i. 389-90; iv. 89-90; W. Money, *Battles of Newbury*, 216; *HMC Portland*, iii. 250; Salisbury Cathedral Lib., Bp. Seth Ward, Liber Notitiae, f. 53; *CJ*, ix. 212; Grey, i. 272, ii. 8-9, 39, 362; *Dering*, 111. [5] Grey, v. 56; vi. 165; *CJ*, ix. 479, 500; *HMC Lords*, i. 10, 15. [6] *CSP Dom.* 1684-5, pp. 282, 284; *Cal. Treas. Bks.* viii. 705; *HMC 14th Rep. IX*, 452; Money, 23.

L.N./G.J.

DONE, Thomas (c.1651-1703), of Park Street (Queen Anne's Gate), Westminster.

NEWTOWN I.o.W.   1685, 1689, 1690, 1695

> *b.* c.1651, 6th s. of Sir Ralph Done (*d.*1660) of Duddon, Cheshire, being 3rd s. by 2nd w. Elizabeth, da. of Sir John Savage of Clifton, Cheshire. *educ.* L. Inn 1672; G. Inn 1672, called 1677. *m.* lic. 2 July 1678, aged 27, Jane, da. of Sir Thomas Griffith, merchant, of Bishopsgate, London, 1s. 3da.[1]
>
> Auditor of imprests 1677-*d.*; commr. of inquiry into abuses in the Mint 1678; j.p. Westminster 1682-9; commr. for assessment, Mdx. and Westminster 1689-90.[2]

Done was descended from a cadet branch of a family established in Cheshire since the 13th century. His great-uncle sat for the county in 1593. His father, a Royalist, was taken prisoner at Nantwich in 1644, but was not required to compound for his estate. After qualifying as a barrister, Done obtained a grant for life of an Exchequer office, valued at £1,000 p.a. or more and served on the jury which awarded the Duke of York £10,000 for *scandalum magnatum* against Titus Oates. He was elected for Newtown on the government interest in 1685, and became a very active Member of James II's Parliament, serving on 19 committees, including that to recommend expunctions from the Journals. He took the chair for the inspection of the disbandment accounts. In the second session he was instructed with Charles Bonython* to see that the streets between Temple Bar and Westminster Hall were kept clear for Members to pass to and from the House, and he presented a petition against a defaulting banker. Although he was clearly a strong Anglican, he was one of the Middlesex justices who asked for a dispensation in 1687. He was on the jury which acquitted the Seven Bishops; nevertheless he was told on 15 Sept. 1688 that 'the King thinks fit you should stand for Newtown', and recommended by Sunderland to Sir Robert Holmes* as court candidate. He was duly returned at the general election after the King's flight.[3]

Done was again a very active Member in the Convention, being appointed to 57 committees and acting as teller in six divisions. He was one of the Members appointed to thank Burnet for his sermon on the day of thanksgiving, 31 Jan. 1689. As one of the champions of the Church, he was sent with William Leveson Gower* to thank the archbishops for the steadfast refusal of most of the Anglican clergy to read the Declaration of Indulgence. A Tory, he voted to agree with the Lords that the throne was not vacant. The accounts of the Treasury solicitors of the previous reign were in his hands, and on 22 Feb. 1689 he was added to the committee to search for evidence of tampering with the courts of justice. He was appointed to the committees to inquire into the authors and advisers of recent grievances, to bring in the first mutiny bill, to draft new oaths of supremacy and allegiance, to repeal the Corporations Act and to prepare a comprehension bill. Although he was not named to the committee to draw up the address of thanks for the King's message of 12 Apr. on religion, he took the chair and presented the report, and on 16 Apr. was sent to the Lords to agree to their amendments. On 6 May he acted as teller for the unsuccessful motion that the auditor of the receipt should be paid £4,000 for his pains over the poll-tax. He was also teller for putting the Tory motion to replace the word 'hereafter' in the Bill of Rights. He was proposed as chairman of the grand committee on the bill of indemnity, but was defeated by Sir Thomas Littleton, 3rd Bt.* He was appointed to the committee for the toleration bill, but acted as teller against reading the London petition for admitting dissenters to office. He took the chair in the committee to consider the petition from the creditors of the army, but although the report was said to be ready at the end of May he did not present it till 28 June, when the petitioners had promised him a gratuity of 1d. in the £ on their claims. On 19 Aug. he was sent to the Lords to desire a conference on the bill for the better recovery of tithe.[4]

When the House reassembled on 19 Oct. Done seconded the motion of (Sir) Joseph Tredenham* for an adjournment to Monday week. He was appointed to the committees to inspect war expenditure and examine miscarriages. On 30 Dec. he was teller for the unsuccessful motion to debate the Lords' amendments to the tithe bill. He was sent to

desire Dr Scott to preach to the House on the anniversary of Charles I's execution. He continued to represent Newtown as a Tory in the next two Parliaments. His refusal to sign the Association, however, caused some surprise. He died in January 1703.[5]

[1] Ormerod, *Cheshire*, ii. 249; *London Mar. Lic.* ed. Foster, 411; PCC 5 Degg. [2] *Cal. Treas. Bks.* v. 627, 641, 791, 810, 986. [3] *State Trials*, x. 131; *CJ*, ix. 751; Christ Church Oxf. Evelyn mss; Luttrell, i. 396, 446; *CSP Dom.* 1687–9, p. 276. [4] *CJ*, x. 16, 86, 126, 197, 199; Simpson thesis, 175; R. Morrice, Entering Bk. 2, p. 556; Add. 29564, f. 66. [5] Morrice, 3, p. 617; *CJ*, x. 339; *HMC Lords*, n.s. ii. 211; Luttrell, v. 258; *Cal. Treas. Bks.* xviii. 111.

P.W.

DORMER, John (1612–79), of Lee Grange, Quainton, Bucks.

BUCKINGHAM   c. May 1646, 1660

bap. 6 Jan. 1612, 1st s. of Sir Fleetwood Dormer of Lee Grange by Mary, da. of Sir Euseby Isham of Pytchley, Northants., wid. of Edward Reade of Cottesbrooke, Northants. *educ.* Magdalen Hall, Oxf. ?1625, BA 1628, MA 1630; L. Inn 1629, called 1636; travelled abroad 1635–8. *m.* by 1640, Katherine (*bur.* 23 Aug. 1691), da. and h. of Thomas Woodward of Saxons Lode, Ripple, Worcs., 3s. (1 *d.v.p.*) 3da. *suc.* fa. 1639.[1]

J.p. Bucks. by 1640–d., Worcs. 1647–8, 1649–July 1660, Buckingham 1654, 1660, 1663; commr. for defence, Worcs. 1644, assessment, Worcs. 1644, 1648–52, Jan. 1660, Bucks. 1647–52, 1657, Jan. 1660–d., militia, Bucks. and Worcs. 1648, 1659, Mar. 1660, Northants. 1659, oyer and terminer, Norfolk circuit July 1660, recusants, Bucks. 1675.

Commr. for removing obstructions 1651–2, Admiralty Feb.–July 1660.

Dormer's family had been established in Buckinghamshire since the 13th century. One of them sat for Wycombe in the Reformation Parliament, and the Lee Grange branch benefited greatly from the dissolution of the monasteries. Dormer was a passive Parliamentarian during the Civil War, and was first returned for Buckingham, seven miles from his home, as a recruiter. Although an Independent in religion, he was neither an active Rumper nor a supporter of the Protectorate. By June 1659 he had come to favour a Restoration, for he lent the exiled King £100, and on the return of the secluded Members he was appointed to the board of Admiralty.[2]

Dormer was re-elected in 1660, surviving a petition from Francis Ingoldsby†, but he was an inactive Member of the Convention, in which he was named only to the committee of elections and privileges and to consider the bill restoring the dukedom of Norfolk. Lord Wharton sent him a copy of the case for modified episcopacy, but he took no part in the debates. He withdrew before the poll in 1661 in favour of the Cavalier William Tyringham*, and was rewarded with a baronetcy for his son. He died on 22 May 1679 and was buried at Quainton, leaving debts of some £3,000. A younger son, Robert, twice represented the county as a Whig before becoming a judge in 1706.[3]

[1] Lipscomb, *Bucks*. i. 415; PC2/44/596. [2] F. G. Lee, *Church of Thame*, 505–6; *VCH Bucks*. iv. 95; D. Underdown, *Pride's Purge*, 371; B. Worden, *The Rump*, 98–99, 376; *HMC 8th Rep*. pt. 3 (1881), p. 6. [3] *CJ*, viii. 87; BL M636/17, Smith to Verney, 27 Dec. 1660; PCC 77 Exton; Lee, 507.

M.W.H./L.N./G.J.

DORRINGTON, Francis (1619–93), of Westminster and Sidney, Alfold, Surr.

HASLEMERE   11 Nov. 1680

bap. 2 Sept. 1619, s. of Richard Dorrington, rector of West Stoke, Suss. 1615–30. *m*. lic. 22 Apr. 1642, Anne, da. of William Danson, Clothworker, of Westminster, 4s. (2 *d.v.p.*) 4da.[1]

Freeman, Clothworkers' Co. 1641, master 1672–3, asst. to 1687; lt. of militia ft. Westminster Apr. 1660; commr. for sewers Aug. 1660, assessment, Westminster 1661–9, Surr. and Suss. 1679–80; alderman, London 1668–9.[2]

Dorrington was apprenticed to a London Clothworker, and married his master's daughter as soon as he was out of his time. His own interests, however, lay chiefly in the shipping and brewing trades. He took no known part in the Civil War, but was joint owner of a London ship, the *Constant Ann*, licensed to sail to royalist Virginia in 1650. He probably supported the Restoration, serving as a juror on two of the regicide trials. During the second Dutch war his frigate, the *Leicester*, about to sail with a cargo of brimstone, was sunk as a blockship at Blackwall, for which the Privy Council awarded him £1,500 compensation in 1668. In the same year he tendered against Sir Dennis Gauden and Josiah Child* for a naval victualling contract. He was allowed to fine off for alderman at £213 13s.4d., and for the wardenship of his company, but served as master in 1672–3.[3]

By 1676 Dorrington had acquired a small estate on the borders of Surrey and Sussex, seven miles east of Haslemere. When he first stood for the borough as a country candidate in February 1679 he received only three votes; but Lord Treasurer Danby was galvanized into ordering the immediate payment of his 12-year-old claim. Nothing was done, however, and Dorrington stood again in August in partnership with Denzil Onslow*. Although he had apparently retired from business, he remained a Middlesex ratepayer, and served on the jury for the trial of Lord Castlemaine (Roger Palmer*). He was seated on petition on 11 Nov., but took no known part in the second Exclusion Parliament. He and Onslow were defeated in 1681, and their petition could not be reported during the

brief life of the Oxford Parliament. Though Dorrington welcomed the Revolution, advancing £1,100 to the new regime in 1689, he is unlikely to have stood again. He died on 12 June 1693 and was buried at Alfold. None of his descendants sat in Parliament.[4]

[1] Information from Prof. H. Horwitz and Mrs P. Gill; Guildhall Lib. mss, 10091/23/69; *Mems. St. Margaret's Westminster*, 182–250, 620, 627; PCC 108 Coker. [2] Information from Mr J. Reed, clerk to the Clothworkers' Co.; *Merc. Pub*. 26 Apr. 1660; C181/7/39; PC2/72/506; J. R. Woodhead, *Rulers of London*, 61. [3] *CSP Dom*. 1650, p. 238; 1667, p. 493; 1667–8, p. 206; PCC 108 Coker; *State Trials*, v. 1115, 1195; *Pepys Diary*, 14 Feb., 26 Aug. 1668; *Cal. Treas. Bks*. v. 1384; information from Mr J. Reed. [4] *Surr. Musters* (Surr. Rec. Soc. iii), 344; *Cal. Treas. Bks*. v. 1205; vi. 480; vii. 706; ix. 1983; *Moneys for Secret Services* (Cam. Soc. lii), 28; *State Trials*, v. 1680; *CJ*, ix. 650, 707; Manning and Bray, *Surr*. ii. 72.

J.P.F.

DOWDESWELL, Richard I (1601–73), of Pull Court, Bushley, Worcs.

TEWKESBURY   1660, 1661–25 Sept. 1673

bap. 24 Feb. 1601, 1st s. of Roger Dowdeswell of New Inn, London and Pull Court by Martha, da. of Richard Blomer of Eastleach Martin, Glos. *educ*. New Inn. *m*. 1628, Anne (*d*. 2 June 1680), da. of Sir Charles Pleydell of Midgehall, Lydiard Tregoze, Wilts., 3s. (1 *d.v.p.*) 5da. *suc*. fa. 1633.[1]

Freeman, Tewkesbury 1641; j.p. Worcs. July 1660–d., Glos. 1662–d.; commr. for assessment, Glos. and Worcs. Aug. 1660–d., corporations, Worcs. 1662–3, loyal and indigent officers 1662.[2]

Dowdeswell's family had been living in Bushley, the next parish to Tewkesbury, since Elizabethan times, and held office in the borough. His father, a successful lawyer, bought Pull Court and other property in the village. Dowdeswell himself, an attorney, was clearly a Royalist in the Civil War, and was accused of assisting in the commission of array and of supplying the Royalists in the second War. But by a variety of shifts and subterfuges he avoided punishment until the pardon ordinance was passed in 1653. He was thus eligible for the general election of 1660. He was returned for the borough, apparently unopposed, and selected to present the borough's address of welcome to Charles II. He was an inactive Member of the Convention, being named to only ten committees. On 4 May he was appointed to the committee for the bill concerning land purchases. On 18 June he spoke in favour of postponing debate on the indemnity bill. He opposed the motion of William Prynne* to exclude his countryman Richard Salway† from the bill and presented Salway's petition. He was appointed to the committees to examine unauthorized Anglican publications, to prepare for a conference on orders issued by the Lords, to examine the public debt, and to consider the bill reducing interest to six per cent. On 9 Aug. he moved successfully to defer for a week the second reading of the Lords' bill for compensation to the royalist Marquess of Winchester. Further postponement followed but after Dowesdwell had been given leave to go to the country on 20 Aug. the bill was committed though never reported. After the recess Dowdeswell was appointed to the committees for the attainder bill and supplying defects in the poll-tax.[3]

Dowdeswell was re-elected in 1661, again apparently without opposition. He was a moderately active Member of the Cavalier Parliament, being named to 124 committees, including that for the execution of those under attainder. In 1664 he was named to the committee for the conventicles bill, and his name stands first on the committees for the bill disafforesting Malvern chase and to consider grievances over the administration of justice. From the latter emanated the two bills that he carried to the Lords on 16 Feb. 1665. In the Oxford session he was ordered, with (Sir) John Maynard I* and Richard Colman* to bring in a tithe bill. He was named to the committees for the five mile bill and the bill to prevent the import of Irish cattle. On 12 Oct. 1666 he was, with William Prynne*, ordered to bring in a bill to rectify attorneys' abuses.

Dowdeswell was one of the Members who objected to including the dismissal of Clarendon in the address of thanks to the King in 1667, 'intimating that it was precondemning him before any crime was laid to his charge'. Dowdeswell again spoke in defence of the fallen minister on 6 Nov., moving to have the heads of the accusations committed 'to inquire the truth', arguing that 'common fame is not sufficient to bring him upon the stage'. Five days later he stated that there was 'a violent stream against the chancellor', words for which he was almost called to the bar. Allowed to remain in his place, Dowdeswell 'professed no reflective intention, and humbly craved the pardon of the House'.[4]

Meanwhile, having been appointed to the committee to bring in the public accounts bill on 15 Oct., Dowdeswell was named to the committee to consider it. On the next day he was appointed to three committees, including that for the bill to prevent the growth of Popery, and was active in the routine business of the House for the remainder of the session. Sir Thomas Osborne* included him among those to be engaged for the Court by the Duke of York, but he was named to no committees in the next short session. He resumed his activity in 1670, taking the chair for the bill to prevent arrests of judgments. In the debate on the subsidy bill of 27 Jan. 1671, he urged that the assessors

should be placed upon oath, to which the House agreed. On 6 Feb., in the debate in the grand committee on the bill of registers,

> Mr Dowdeswell moved that instead of entering of judgments as they now do in the courts of Westminster, which is now extremely chargeable to search for, and difficult to find, all judgments, statutes, and recognizances might be entered in the country where the lands do lie.

According to Sir Edward Dering* this came 'nearest to the sense of the House' but the debate ended without a resolution. When the House reassembled after the long prorogation Dowdeswell is not recorded as taking part in the debates on the Declaration of Indulgence; but on 7 Mar. 1673 he was named to the committee for the bill of ease for Protestant dissenters. The last mention of him in the Journal was his appointment on 10 Mar. to the committee for the bill enfranchising Durham. He died on 25 Sept. 1673 and was buried the same day at Bushley.[5]

[1] *Vis. Eng. and Wales Notes*, ed. Crisp, vii. 64–67. [2] M. F. Redmond, 'Bor. of Tewkesbury 1575–1714' (Birmingham Univ. MA thesis, 1950), 42, 53. [3] *VCH Worcs.* iv. 478; *CJ*, ii. 729, 746, 749, 782; iv. 66; *Cal. Comm. Adv. Money*, 857–9; *Cal. Comm. Comp.* 2306; J. Bennett, *Tewkesbury*, 439–40; Redmond, 51; Bowman diary, ff. 5, 6v, 130. [4] *Milward*, 86; Grey, i. 16, 34. [5] *Dering*, 71; *Worcs. Par. Reg. Soc.* (Bushley), 80.

M.W.H./B.D.H.

DOWDESWELL, Richard II (c.1653–1711), of Pull Court, Bushley, Worcs.

TEWKESBURY   1685, 1689, 1690, 1695, 1698, 1701
                (Feb.), 1701 (Dec.), 1702, 1705,
                1708

b. c.1653, 1st s. of William Dowdeswell of Pull Court by Judith, da. of Elkin Wymonsold of Putney, Surr. *educ.* Christ Church, Oxf. matric. 27 July 1669, aged 16. *m.* 1676, Elizabeth, da. of Sir Francis Winnington of the Middle Temple and Stanford Court, Stanford-on-Teme, Worcs., 5s. (3 *d.v.p.*) 3da. *suc.* fa. 1683.[1]

Commr. for assessment, Worcs. 1677–80, Glos. and Worcs. 1689–90; j.p. Glos. and Worcs. 1677–81, 1689–*d.*; sheriff, Worcs. 1688–9; freeman, Preston 1682; dep. lt. Glos. 1689–?*d.*, Worcs. by 1702–?*d.*; capt. of militia ft. Worcs. by 1697–?*d.*[2]

Dowdeswell was the grandson of Richard Dowdeswell I*. His father seems to have taken no part in national politics. When (Sir) Henry Capel* decided not to stand for Tewkesbury in 1685, Dowdeswell was returned, apparently unopposed. Probably a Whig, he left no trace on the records of James II's Parliament. In 1688, the King's electoral agents listed him, almost certainly erroneously, as a 'dissenter' who should be added to the commission of the peace for Worcestershire. When he was pricked as sheriff of Worcestershire in November,

Brent, 'the popish attorney', pointed out that his father had held the same expensive office as recently as 1677, and urged an alteration; but no political objections were made, and Dowdeswell was still sheriff during the general election of 1689. However, the coroners acted as returning officers for the county, in accordance with the letter from the Prince of Orange, and Dowdeswell was himself re-elected for Tewkesbury, again without apparent opposition. In the Convention he was named only to the committee of elections and privileges, and to that for the bill to abolish the hearth-tax. He was listed as a supporter of the disabling clause in the bill to restore corporations. He continued to represent the borough in the next eight Parliaments, voting consistently with the Whigs. He died on 17 Oct. 1711 and was buried at Bushley. His son, also a Whig, sat for Tewkesbury from 1711 until 1722, and members of the family continued to represent the borough until the late 19th century.[3]

[1] Vis. Eng. and Wales Notes ed. Crisp, vii. 64–67. [2] Preston Guild Rolls (Lancs. and Cheshire Rec. Soc. ix), 198; Eg. 1626, f. 52. [3] HMC Astley, 60.

B.D.H.

DOWNE, 1st Visct [I] see DAWNAY, John.

DOWNING, Sir George (1623–84), of St. Stephen's Court, Westminster and East Hatley, Cambs.

EDINBURGH	1654
CARLISLE	1656, 1659
MORPETH	8 June 1660, 1661, 1679 (Mar.), 1679 (Oct.), 1681

b. Aug. 1623. 2nd s. of Emmanuel Downing, attorney, of Fleet Street, London and Salem, Mass., being 1st s. by 2nd w. Lucy, da. of Adam Winthrop of Groton, Suff. educ. Harvard 1639, BA 1642. m. 1654, Frances (d.1683), da. of Sir William Howard of Naworth Castle, Cumb., 3s. 5da. Kntd. 21 May 1660; cr. Bt. 1 July 1663.[1]
Chaplain, New Model Army 1646–7; scoutmaster-gen. 1649–57.[2]
Envoy to Swiss cantons 1655; commr. for security 1656, registers [S] 1656; teller of the Exchequer 1656–d.; resident, Holland 1658–May 1660, envoy extraordinary 1661–5, ambassador 1671–2; commr. for trade Nov. 1660–72; sec. to the Treasury 1667–71; commr. for trade with Scotland 1668, customs 1671–d.; freeman, E.I. Co. 1672; commr. for marine treaty with Holland 1674.[3]
J.p. Mdx. and Westminster 1656–?58, Cambs. 1674–d.; commr. for statutes, Durham college 1656, assessment, Cumb., co. Dur., Westmld. and Westminster 1657, Northumb. Aug. 1660–1, 1673–80, Cambs. 1663–80, Westminster 1667–80.[4]

Downing's ancestors can be traced in Suffolk back to the opening years of Elizabeth's reign, and one of the family sat for Orford in 1586. His grandfather was master of Ipswich grammar school, but his father, a puritan lawyer who practised chiefly in the court of wards, emigrated to New England in 1638. Downing, one of the first graduates of Harvard, was educated for the ministry and became preacher to the regiment of John Okey[†]. He came into the north as secretary to Sir Arthur Hesilrige[†], and Cromwell made him director of military intelligence. As an ardent advocate of the offer of the crown in 1656, he was rewarded with the post of resident in Holland, with special responsibility for penetrating royalist organizations. He succeeded in suborning the Hon. Thomas Howard*, through whom he made his peace with the King in May 1660. He was confirmed as teller of the Exchequer and knighted on board ship. About this time Thomas Widdrington* died at The Hague, thereby creating a vacancy at Morpeth. Downing's brother-in-law Charles Howard* enjoyed the dominant interest in the borough, and he was returned at a by-election in June, retaining the seat for the rest of his life.[5]

Downing became an active Member of the Convention, in which he was appointed to 34 committees, taking the chair in five. He carried seven bills to the Lords, and made nine speeches. On 27 July he urged the House to 'pass the bill for money, and not by way of condition, but trust his Majesty to hasten the bill of indemnity', and four days later he was named to the revenue committee. But for the most part he confined himself to commercial matters, on which his residence in Holland gave him expert status. On 15 Aug. he was ordered to seek the concurrence of the Lords in asking for a proclamation to forbid the export of raw materials used for the cloth industry. He was chiefly responsible for the re-enactment of the Commonwealth Navigation Act, taking the chair in the committee, and later carrying the bill to the Lords. On 31 Aug. he reported the bill to regulate the Colchester bay trade. He was the first Member appointed to the committee for the disbandment bill, and helped to draft the amendment deferring the withdrawal of garrisons. After the recess he moved to revive the committee for the cloth industry, 'and desired they might also consider the state of the herring fishery and the settlement of the East India Company', two particularly sore points in Anglo-Dutch relations. On 16 Nov. he spoke in support of his brother-in-law's bill to prevent theft and rapine on the northern borders. Lord Wharton sent him the case for modified episcopacy with objections and answers, but this debate he took no part in. On 24 Nov. he reported a petition from the surveyor-general of the customs, and was among those sent to ask the lord chief justice and the lord chief baron to enforce the laws against smuggling. As self-appointed adviser to the Government, he played a key role in the financial settlement, helping to draft the clause settling half the excise on the crown as compensation for the loss of feudal revenues, and moving on 27 Nov. that the other half should be settled on the King for life. He told the House two days later that there were at least 80,000 people in France employed in working up English and Irish wool, and had the satisfaction of carrying up the bill to prohibit its export. Another mercantilist measure which he steered through the House was the bill to prevent the planting of tobacco in England. He supported the restoration of the dukedom of Norfolk to the head of the Howard family, and, with characteristic stinginess, the privilege of free postage for Members during sessions. On 21 Dec. he urged the House to lay aside the bill for compensation to officials of the court of wards and proceed with the bill to encourage fishing, to such good effect that this bill too he reported and carried to the Lords before the dissolution. His last speech in the Convention was to urge the payment of the debts incurred by the Queen of Bohemia during her long exile in Holland.[6]

In the opening session of the Cavalier Parliament Downing was appointed to the committee of elections and privileges and that for confirming the Act of Indemnity. 'From a pedagogue and a fanatic preacher, not worth a groat', he was, as Evelyn noted, 'becoming excessive rich'. He purchased an estate in Cambridgeshire, which he steadily expanded. In his absence it was entrusted to his mother's management on an allowance of £23 p.a. 'I really believe one of us two is indeed covetous', she wrote to her American kinsfolk, and certainly neither believed in cosseting the tenants, even at Christmas. After the coronation Downing returned to The Hague, where he succeeded in capturing Okey and two other regicides, and sending them over to England for execution. Though Samuel Pepys*, once his deputy in the Exchequer, wrote that 'all the world takes notice of him for a most ungrateful villain for his pains', he was rewarded with a baronetcy. 'Almost the sole source of initiative making for a solution of the crown's financial problems', he was given leave to attend the session of 1663, in which he again made his mark in mercantilist legislation. 'A very voluminous speaker, who would be thought wiser than any of the merchants', according to Clarendon, he was the first Member named to the committee to bring in

measures for the advancement of trade, and on the same day acted as teller for the recall of a proclamation against the export of geldings. As chairman of the trade committee he recommended an increase in the duty levied on cattle imports during the second half of the year. Two further reports were necessary before the bill was ready for engrossment, but on 13 June he was able to carry it to the Lords. 'A fertile legislator', he also steered through the Commons, the bill to regulate the herring fishery and served on the deputation sent to ask the King for the punctual and effectual observance of the Navigation Act. He was listed as a court dependant in 1664, though he was at his post throughout the session. Convinced of English superiority in strength and of the Dutch propensity to bluff, he fomented the rivalry between the two peoples. Remaining at The Hague for several months after the second Dutch war had broken out, he was able to forward naval intelligence obtained with 'the keys taken out of De Witt's pocket when he was a-bed'. But his expectation that the Dutch economy would collapse under the strain of war proved unfounded; on the contrary he witnessed with envy the oversubscription of the Dutch war-loan at a mere 4 per cent. On his return to England he set himself to improve government credit, much to the disgust of Clarendon, who believed that he was chiefly concerned to increase the income from his tellership. Resuming his seat for the Oxford session, he was named to the committee for attainting English officers in the enemy forces, and gave the Commons 'a speech of an hour painting forth the Dutch and their conditions in all their colours'. Supported by Arlington and the King he took over from Heneage Finch* the management of supply, in which his principal achievement was the additional aid bill. Aiming to revolutionize public borrowing by appealing to the small investor, he revived the principle of appropriating the revenue to specified purposes; but his great innovation, resisted by Clarendon as an entrenchment on the prerogative, provided for the repayment of loans 'in course' instead of by treasury whim or favour. Returning to London, which was still infected by the plague, he used every publicity device available, including advertisements in the *Gazette* and personal application to his acquaintances, to make the loan a success. Exhausted by his volubility and pertinacity, one reluctant investor confessed: 'the beginning, end, and every part of it is to be imputed to him'. In the next session he again took the chair of a committee on trade, which on 8 Oct. 1666 recommended a total prohibition of French imports. After seeking the Lords' concurrence, he helped to manage one conference and to prepare reasons for another, and acted as teller against a hostile merchants' petition. He was named to the committee of inquiry into the insolence of Popish priests. On 10 Nov. he carried up a bill to encourage coinage, later taking the chair for consideration of the Lords' amendments and reporting a conference. He was less prominent in supply in this session, telling Pepys that 'it is not the fault of the House but the King's own party that hath hindered the passing of the bill for money by their popping in of new projects'. On 5 Dec. he 'excellently made good' the justice of a bill for the total exclusion of Irish cattle from England, later helping to prepare and manage conferences on the subject. He was named to the committee to prepare reasons for cancelling the Canaries Company patent. Another recommendation from the trade committee was for compulsory burial in woollen to reduce imports of linen; Downing reported a bill for this purpose on 2 Jan. 1667, and acted as teller on third reading a week later.[7]

On the death of Lord Treasurer Southampton in May 1667, Downing became secretary to the new treasury commissioners, 'rough and ill-natured men, not to be moved with civilities or importunities in the payment of money', whose appointment marks an epoch in financial administration. Downing's contribution has been the subject of controversy, but there can be no doubt that he established and regularized procedure, producing a great blossoming of Treasury records into a systematic series, and it was almost certainly on his suggestion that payment in course was extended to cover loans secured on the ordinary revenue, 'the most important financial experiment of the period'. He became known as the bankers' enemy, who by his own admission would have no bank in England but the Exchequer. Doubtless he welcomed the fall of Clarendon, who had publicly 'given some very sharp reprehensions to Downing for his presumption in undertaking to set such a design on foot that concerned the whole fabric of the Exchequer, in which he was an inferior officer'. But he took no known part in the proceedings against the fallen minister. His principal concern was to legalize the assignment of Exchequer orders, an essential element in the expansion of government credit. He brought in a bill for this purpose on 15 Oct., and despite the political excitement reported it from committee three weeks later. He had been granted £5,000 for the relief of English prisoners-of-war in Holland, but 'so well did he husband the money' that not more than £3,500 was spent. Nevertheless he expressed concern at the failure of the peace treaty to provide for their release, and was one of

five Members sent to ask the King to relieve them. He brought in a bill to balance trade with Ireland, and recommended a commission on Scottish trade for the same purpose. He also introduced a bill to promote tillage, navigation, and the breeding of cattle, and took the chair for the leather export bill. 'He labours very worthily to advance our trade', Pepys admitted, 'but doth it with mighty vanity and talking.' As a mercantilist he favoured taxing wine, brandy, and linen on entry into the country, not at the point of sale, which other Members believed would reduce smuggling. He was on both lists of the court party in 1669–71 as a dependant, and acted with (Sir) Thomas Clifford* as the chief government spokesman on supply. A hostile writer described him as

> formerly Okey's little chaplain, and a great promoter of the Dutch war. A teller in the Exchequer, of the council of trade, and secretary to the Treasury, he keeps six whores in pay, and yet has got £50,000. A great driver of the law tax.

His frank statements of accounts were generally well received by the Commons. On 27 Oct. 1670 he claimed that the Treasury commission had redeemed one-third of the three million pound debt which they had inherited. But on 12 Dec. he 'gave great offence to the House' by alleging that of the residue a significant proportion was due from official Members 'who pleaded their privilege and would not pay it'. Ordered to produce details, he was able to name only Walter Strickland*, Thomas Prise*, Lionel Walden I*, and Thomas Harlackenden* as principals, with Richard Kirkby* and Anthony Gilby* as sureties, while the total sum involved was less than a fifth of the £110,000 he had estimated. Not for the first time he had proved 'a mighty talker, more than is true'. After the Christmas recess, as one of the leading government spokesmen on supply, he opposed the deferment of all other business for the bill to punish the assault on Sir John Coventry*. He was teller for committing the subsidy bill on 16 Jan. 1671, and took the chair for the bills to confirm the Duke of York's surrender of wine licensing and to prevent the planting of tobacco in England. He also helped to prepare or manage conferences on the additional excise, the tobacco bill, and the export of wool.[8]

Downing's credit operations foundered on the inability of the Exchequer to compete with private banks, and in 1671 he was replaced by Sir Robert Howard* as secretary to the Treasury. He was compensated with a seat on the customs board at a salary of £2,000 p.a. His return to Holland as ambassador later in the year was widely and correctly interpreted as a prelude to another war. In fact he exceeded his instructions by breaking off relations before the King was ready for war, and returning hastily for fear of the mob. He was sent to the Tower, but released before the next session. On 10 Feb. 1673, in the debate on the Declaration of Indulgence, he defended the suspending power with disarming autobiographical candour. 'Gentlemen that make account of their loyalty may give their votes freeely', he said; 'he, that has done otherwise, cannot be so free.' Nevertheless he was appointed to the committee to draft an address. He was named to the committee to prevent moor-burning in the north, and took the chair for bills to extend the Coinage Act and to regulate the trade with Greenland and the plantations, which he considered of great consequence. In expectation of a flood of useful Dutch refugees, he proposed the general naturalization of Protestant aliens, and acted as teller for committing the bill. His name appeared on the Paston list of court supporters in 1673–4. In the next session he vigorously opposed the address for the removal of Arlington:

> Let him stand or fall, as he shall appear. Several have aggravated his crimes with circumstances, and yet are for the address to the King. Should not your proceedings be higher? ... To aggravate the crimes, and not proceed upon them, agrees not with reason. ... Articles against him are entered, and you vote him not fit to come into the King's presence ... and he keeps his offices of freehold still. Can this be honorable for you, the grand inquest of the kingdom? Why must you do this? Because the gentleman has a pardon, you must try him! No pardon hinders proceedings of justice. After sentence, then possibly a pardon is pleadable, but then, and not before. ... God forbid that men should not be accused by common fame, but not condemned! Lord Arlington, an old Cavalier, who served the King, was with him abroad, was never suspected to be a villain, and now must be sequestered from the King upon common fame!

He was among those ordered to bring in an impeachment accordingly. On the proposals for peace with Holland, he said that he would not tell the House his opinion of the war, which most Members knew; although he could not consent to the treaty as it stood, the articles were too intricate for detailed debate, and he would simply have the King desired to procure peace. He was appointed to the committees to prevent illegal exactions and to consider the condition of Ireland.[9]

In the spring session of 1675 Downing's committees included those for enlarging the scope of habeas corpus and extending the Border Act. Although he supported the abolition of the levy on coal exports, he was teller against a second reading for a bill to ease the trade. From the customs figures he was convinced of 'the mischief we

suffered by the French trade', and he produced a highly influential report showing an adverse balance of £800,000 p.a., though it seems that he over-valued the silk and linen imports. He was twice named to committees for appropriating the customs to the use of the navy; but a further proposal to lodge in the chamber of London the revenue granted for the building of warships brought him to his feet in defence of the department in which he had served, in person or by deputy, for 20 years.

> What was done to stop the Exchequer was by order of Council and by the great seal, not orders of the Exchequer. That place that gives accounts most sure and constantly is the best place. Money was paid in to London at the beginning of the rebellion, and [he] dreads everything that may have its likeness. Would [expect] devils from Hell to say: 'Destroy the Exchequer, and take this way', which is one of the best securities. With it you destroy property. The Exchequer is one of the fundamental pillars of monarchy, the easiest and cheapest. In the year 1660 money was paid into the chamber of London, not yet accounted for, for disbanding the army, and no man can ever find out how it can be accounted for, nor ever will. Had it been in the Exchequer, it might. Shall it be said we put it in such hands, nay voted it in such hands? Some are hot enough that the Exchequer is not to be trusted; when that trust is gone, the government is gone. Has anything been misplaced in the Exchequer? Mend it. Resolve that the money be appropriated, and refer it to the committee to make it effectual.

Though the distinction between a political and an administrative decision was too subtle for the House, the opposition proposal was rejected, and an attempt to tack a clause for the bankers to the warships bill was also unsuccessful. 'When you go in such an untrodden way', he warned them, 'you may repent when it is too late. Things of this kind are altering the government.' Downing's name was included in the lists of officials and government speakers in the Commons, and with the other customs commissioners on the working lists. In 1677 Shaftesbury marked him 'thrice vile', and in *A Seasonable Argument* he was described as

> a poor child bred up on charity. Like Judas, betrayed his master; what then can his country expect? He drew and advised the oath of renouncing the King's family, and took it first himself. For his honesty, fidelity, etc., rewarded by his Majesty with £80,000 at least, and is commissioner of the customs. The House bell to call the courtiers to vote at six o'clock at night.

In this session he spoke against the illegal exactions bill because it deprived customs officials of the power to make 'contingent and necessary variations' while extending the penalties for treason to a new range of offences. In addition, the injunction to 'withstand' exactions would 'let in all outrages, which this sort of men are too inclined to already'. He was nevertheless appointed to the committee.

He supported the naval programme, observing that:

> Whatever is bestowed on building ships makes a Parliament still more necessary; for the King must have supply to support them, and so there is no danger of our not meeting. Here is not one that says thirty ships are not necessary. This great fleet of France can intend no other neighbour than we.

The addition of an appropriation clause, on the other hand, he regarded as 'going by an ill way to a good end. . . . The just prerogative of the crown is as necessary as the being of the House of Commons. He takes tacking to be of the most mischievous consequence imaginable.' Although anxious to end dependence on imported linen, he ridiculed the bill introduced by John Birch* for the compulsory growing of hemp and flax in every parish, attacking the poor law in the course of his speech as a 'specious pretence . . . For mankind . . . hoot them out of the parish; but for foxes . . . spare them to make more sport.' When it was proposed to bring the mad Duke of Norfolk home from Italy, he warned the House that the Lords would take exception to removing his guardians. He helped to draft the addresses on the danger from French power and the need to form alliances against it. 'The way now is to make war and declare it afterwards', he told the House, drawing on his experience in Holland. 'You should block up the river of Bordeaux, Rochelle, and the Seine that France may vent nothing by sea. Now is the time or never.' A member of the committee for the recall of British subjects from the French service, he denounced the recruitment and despatch of mercenaries: 'If any by order, trick or connivance have suffered these men to go over, he would have them declared enemies to their King and country'. But he protested that the customs board was unable to prevent it. He opposed the bill brought in by Thomas Neale* to establish the ballast shore on the Tyne estuary because it was not supported by Newcastle, and denied that exports of corn had been increased by the bounty. He served on the committee for the bill to suppress pedlars, hawkers, and petty chapmen, defending them 'tooth and nail' against the corporations.[10]

Downing was on both lists of the court party in 1678. He was appointed to the committee to draft the address for reducing France to her frontiers of 1659. In support of Birch's land registry bill, he observed: 'Every man's estate is the worse for the fraud and deceit of another; something of this kind is necessary'. He resumed his own activity as a legislator, taking the chair in seven committees in the spring and summer sessions, including that for the border bill. He introduced and chaired bills for the export of coal and cider, burial in woollen, and the encouragement of woollen manufactures, the last of which he carried to the Lords on 16 Mar. When the Opposition demanded the removal of Councillors responsible for the rejection of addresses on foreign policy, he offended the House by inquiring whether it was apparent that the King had acted on their advice. He took part in drafting the address for an immediate war with France, and was sent to the Lords to desire a conference. After helping to summarize foreign commitments he declared his dislike of them, principally because of his mistrust of the Dutch. Meanwhile a conference had been arranged on his bill for burial in woollen, and he helped to prepare reasons; but all these measures were lost by the short prorogation in May. When Parliament met again he urged the retention of the new-raised forces. 'Let all jealousies be laid aside', he said, 'and let common safety be looked upon only.' He was summoned to a meeting of the government caucus, acted as teller for the Court on this issue on 11 June, and helped to manage a conference. He took part in the inquiry into the distribution of leaflets attacking the bill for burial in woollen. He reported the revived bill on 18 June, and also those to enforce the measurement of colliers and to encourage the woollen industry. After returning them to the Lords, he reported the subsequent conferences, and had the satisfaction of witnessing the royal assent to all except the last measure. In the final session of the Cavalier Parliament, he was among those ordered to draw up an address for the removal of Papists from the metropolitan area, to consider the bill for hindering them from sitting in Parliament, and to prepare reasons for belief in the Plot. For positive measures he was at a loss, though he affirmed that a law for castrating priests and Jesuits had been highly successful in Sweden. But he would agree with the Lords' proviso to allow the Duke of York to retain his seat. His last speech was in defence of Danby, who, he affirmed, required no patent to authorize him to issue instructions to ambassadors. A very active Member, Downing had been appointed to 289 committees, carried 18 messages, and acted as teller in 14 divisions. Over a hundred of his speeches to the Commons are recorded, in addition to 37 reports from committee.[11]

Despite Downing's inclusion on the 'unanimous list' circulated by the Opposition, he was re-elected to all the Exclusion Parliaments. A moderately active Member in 1679, with 11 committees, he was marked 'vile' on Shaftesbury's list. On the Lords bill against Popery, he remarked:

It will never be well till you settle the minds of the people by a clause that no treaty of marriage shall be for the future with a Papist, and so you will give no countenance to priests to be at Whitehall.

William Garway*, however, jeered at his claim that the matter had lain long upon his spirits, and he did not speak again in this Parliament. On 15 Apr. 1679 he reported that only a minute saving was possible on the disbandment estimates. He voted against exclusion. He was given leave to bring in a bill to simplify the taking of the affidavits required for burial in woollen, but he was unable to do so before the prorogation. In the second Exclusion Parliament he was very active as a committeeman. He was named to 19 committees, though none of them was of greater political significance than that to draw up the address for a fast. He took the chair for the burial affidavit bill, and the bills to encourage woollen manufactures and to prohibit the import of cattle from Scotland. The first and last of these measures he carried to the Lords. He supported the general naturalization of foreign Protestants, though only so far as to 'enable them to buy land and exercise their trades', and was appointed to the committee to bring in a bill. On 7 Jan. 1681 he enraged William Harbord* by speaking well of Laurence Hyde*. He left no trace on the records of the Oxford Parliament, but remained active as commissioner of customs until a few weeks before his death. It was during these years that he developed the famous street in Westminster that bears his name. He was buried, of course in woollen, in the Cambridgeshire village church of Croydon on 24 July 1684. His eldest son was feeble-minded, but his grandson, the third baronet, sat for Dunwich as a Whig with one interval from 1710 to 1749.[12]

Downing's character has usually been painted to match his only surviving portrait, which reveals him as a phenomenally ugly man. The first of the Yankee go-getters, he valued himself 'upon having things do well under his hand', as another notable adminstrator observed. There was not much originality in his ideas, according to the historian of the Treasury, 'but he was surely unique in the energy and practicality with which he applied them'. As secretary of the Treasury he played a vital part in professionalizing the staff. His pulpit training stood him in good stead as a debater, despite occasional lapses of grammar and a candour which sometimes shocked the House but makes for excellent reading.[13]

[1] DNB; J. Beresford, Godfather of Downing Street, 24, 138; J. J. Muskett, Suff. Man. Fams. i. 99. [2] Beresford, 48, 52, 63. [3] CSP Dom. 1655, p. 606; 1657-8, pp. 62, 222; 1660-1, p. 74; 1671, p. 505; 1673-5, p. 287; Old Parl. Hist. xxi. 5; Cal. Treas. Bks. i. 308, 672; iii. 1125, 1281; Bulstrode Pprs. 17; Cal. Ct. Mins. E.I. Co. ed. Sainsbury, ix. 142. [4] CSP Dom. 1655-6, p. 297. [5] Beresford, 18, 24, 41, 51; Thurloe, vii. 429; Carte, Orig. Letters, ii. 319-23. [6] Bowman diary, f. 99; L. A. Harper, Eng. Navigation Laws, 57; CJ, viii. 142, 151, 194, 199, 218, 222, 228; Old Parl. Hist. xxiii. 7, 15-16, 25, 32, 36, 56, 61, 64; Pepys Diary, 28 June 1660; C. D. Chandaman, Eng. Pub. Revenue, 38. [7] Beresford, 125, 130; Evelyn Diary, iii. 445; Pepys Diary, 17 Mar. 1662, 6 Nov. 1665, 12 May, 23 Nov. 1666, 27 Feb. 1668; H. Roseveare, Treasury: Foundations of Control, 23, 25-26; Cal. Cl. SP, v. 125-6; Clarendon, Life, 594, 599, 606; Roseveare, Treasury: Evolution of a British Inst. 60-62; CJ, viii. 494, 496, 515, 519, 632, 637, 665, 670, 673, 674, 675; Milward, 55. [8] Clarendon, Life, 609, 793; Chandaman, 214-17; Treasury Evolution, 62, 71; Treasury Foundations, 27; Milward, 87, 139, 202, 236; CJ, ix. 16, 26, 36, 182, 200, 224, 233, 238; Beresford, 198-9; Cal. Treas. Bks. i. 693; ii. 474-5; Pepys Diary, 10 Jan. 1666, 27 Feb., 28 May, 8 Sept. 1667; Harl. 7020, f. 37; Grey, i. 271, 322-3; Dering, 31, 46. [9] Hatton Corresp. (Cam. Soc. n.s. xxii), 70, 78; CSP Ven. 1671-2, p. 116; HMC 6th Rep. 368; Grey, i. 286; ii. 18, 313-14, 350; Dering, 112, 115; CJ, ix. 275, 296. [10] Grey, iii. 333, 360, 450; iv. 125, 134-5, 162, 183-4, 220, 256; CJ, ix. 373, 387, 392; Dering Pprs. 320; Bulstrode Pprs. 17; HMC Lords, n.s. x. 155; Treasury Evolution, 66-67; Eg. 3345, ff. 34, 39, 45v; HMC 7th Rep. 468. [11] Grey, v. 147, 246-7, 308-9; vi. 7, 204, 244-5, 376; CJ, ix. 439, 443, 446, 451, 453, 459, 495, 502-5, 513-15; CSP Dom. 1678, pp. 154-4, 194. [12] Grey, vii. 80; viii. 226; CJ, ix. 627, 656, 682, 683, 695, 696; HMC 12th Rep. IX, 113; HMC 5th Rep. 187; Beresford, 134, 287; Luttrell, i. 313. [13] Beresford, 16; Pepys Diary, 27 May 1667; Treasury Evolution, 60, 71.

J.P.F.

DOYLEY, Sir John, 1st Bt. (1640-1709), of Chiselhampton, Oxon.

NEW WOODSTOCK 1689

bap. 17 Nov. 1640, 2nd but 1st surv. s. of John Doyley† of Greenland House, Hambleden, Bucks. by Mary, da. and coh. of Sir John Shirley† of Isfield, Suss. educ. Wadham, Oxf. 1657. m. lic. 11 July 1666, Margaret (d.1704), da. and coh. of Sir Richard Cholmley† of Grosmont, Yorks., 8s. (4 d.v.p.) 4da. suc. fa. c.1660; cr. Bt. 7 July 1666.[1]

Commr. for oyer and terminer, Oxford circuit July 1660, assessment, Oxon. ?1661-80. and Oxford 1689-90; j.p. Oxon. 1674-Mar. 1688, Oxford 1682-Mar. 1688, Oxon. and Oxford Oct. 1688-?96, by 1701-d.; dep. lt. Oxon. 1676-Feb. 1688, 1689-?96, 1700-d.; freeman, Woodstock 1681, Oxford 1684-Feb. 1688; sheriff, Oxon. 1684-5, capt. of militia horse 1687-9.[2]

Doyley was descended from a Norman baron established in Oxfordshire under William the Conqueror. His ancestors had acquired Chiselhampton manor by 1536 and prospered at the dissolution of the monasteries. Henry Doyley, a younger son, sat for Wallingford in 1601, and Doyley's great-grand-father represented Oxfordshire in 1604. They were strongly Puritan in sympathy. Doyley's father was governor of Newport Pagnell for Parliament during the Civil War, and was elected for Oxfordshire as a recruiter. He was secluded at Pride's Purge and did not again hold local office until January 1660. He probably died later in the year.[3]

Doyley owed his baronetcy to his marriage to the daughter of a prominent Cavalier, and became a Tory and a churchman. He stood unsuccessfully for Oxfordshire at the first election of 1679 as an opponent of exclusion, accompanied Lord Norris with the loyal addresses from Oxfordshire and Woodstock in 1681, and helped to regulate the corporation of Oxford in 1684. To the lord lieutenant's questions on the repeal of the Test Act and Penal Laws in 1688, he replied that 'he has no thought of standing, but if chosen ... he cannot determine what way he shall give his vote until he hath heard it fairly debated on both sides'. He may have owed his election for Woodstock in 1689 to Norris. An active Member of the Convention, he voted to agree with the Lords that the throne was not vacant. His 37 committees included those to consider the Lords' proviso on the succession in the bill of rights and to draw up the address for permission to inspect the Privy Council registers and the books of the Irish committee. In the second session he was named to the committees for the second mutiny bill, for examining public accounts, and for attainting Irish rebels. He made no recorded speeches, but acted as teller against the election of the Whig John Southby* at Abingdon. In the closing weeks of the Convention he was appointed to the committees to restore the university charters and to report on the poor laws.[4]

Doyley probably did not stand again. According to the historian of the family, he was a patron of learning and a man of much worldly wisdom, but proud and extravagant. His later years were marked by financial difficulty. Provision had to be made for a large family, and costly lawsuits depleted the estate. He died on 13 Apr. 1709 and was buried at Stadhampton. His son and grandson both stood for Abingdon, but he was the last of the family to sit in Parliament.[5]

[1] Bodl. mss, Stadhampton par. reg.; W. D. Bayley, *House of D'Oyly*, 30–35. [2] Woodstock council acts, 1679–99 (3 Feb. 1681); *Oxford Council Acts* (Oxford Hist. Soc. n.s. ii), 163, 196; SP44/29/158; *CSP Dom.* 1689–90, p. 125; Bayley, 33. [3] *Top. and Gen.* i. 368; *VCH Oxon.* vii. 10; Bayley, 30–31; W. H. Black, *Docquets of Letters Patent*, 147; *CJ*, iv. 235, 246. [4] *EHR*, xl. 255; *Wood's Life and Times* (Oxf. Hist. Soc. xxi), 442; *CJ*, x. 327. [5] Bayley, 33–36.

L.N.

DOYLEY, Sir William (c.1614–77), of Shotesham, Norf.

NORFOLK	1654, 1656,[1] 1659
GREAT YARMOUTH	18 May 1660, 1661–Nov. 1677

b. c.1614, 1st s. of William Doyley of Pond Hall, Hadleigh, Suff. by Elizabeth, da. of Richard Stokes, archdeacon of Norwich 1587–1619. *m.* 1637, aged 23, Margaret, da. of John Randolfe, yeoman, of Pulham St. Mary Magdalene, Norf., 4s. (1 *d.v.p.*) 6da. *suc.* fa. 1637, cos. Susan Doyley in Shotesham estate 1640; kntd. 2 July 1641; *cr.* Bt. 29 July 1663.[2]

Commr. of array, Norf. 1642, new model ordinance 1645, assessment, Norf. 1645–52, 1657, Jan. 1660–*d.*, Suff. 1657, Aug. 1660–*d.*, Yarmouth Aug. 1660–1, Westminster 1667–*d.*, militia, Norf. 1648, 1659, Mar. 1660; j.p. Norf. 1649–*d.*, col. of militia ft. Apr. 1660–*d.*; freeman, Yarmouth 1660, Portsmouth 1661; commr. for oyer and terminer, Norfolk circuit July 1660, corporations, Norf. 1662–3; receiver of taxes, London and Mdx. 1671–*d.*, hearth-tax, Surr. and Southwark 1671; commr. for recusants, Norf. 1675.[3]

Commr. for disbandment Aug. 1660–1, excise appeals Oct. 1660–*d.*, sick and wounded 1664–7, 1672–4, revenue wagons 1665–7, exchange office 1667–70, loyal and indigent officers' accounts 1671.[4]

The East Anglian branch of the Doyley family was established about the middle of the 15th century. Doyley, who could expect little from his father, took service in the Swedish army as a young man, and on his return to England married into an obscure local family. In 1641 his position was transformed by the death of an infant cousin, from whom he inherited the Shotesham estate. At the outbreak of the Civil War he was appointed to the commission of array, but in East Anglia he was powerless to assist the royalist cause, and he took refuge in the Netherlands. He obeyed an order from the Long Parliament to return in 1645, serving on the county committee and representing Norfolk under the Protectorate.[5]

On 23 Jan. 1660 Doyley wrote to Sir Horatio Townshend*, leader of the royalist conspirators in Norfolk, undertaking to do anything in his power 'for the country's peace, ease of grievances, and settlement of the nation', and he signed the address for a free Parliament presented to George Monck*. Honourably defeated in the county election, with over 2,000 votes, he was returned for Yarmouth on the open franchise, although the corporation would have preferred the regicide Miles Corbet. Seated in the Convention on the merits of the election, he was marked as a friend by Lord Wharton, to be managed by his colleague Sir John Potts*. They were asked by their constituents to secure a frigate to guard the Yarmouth herring fleet off Orkney from the Ostend privateers. Doyley was an active Member, with four tellerships, seven recorded speeches, and 44 committees, including the inquiry into unauthorized Anglican publications. In the debate on the indemnity bill he urged that all provisos should be referred to a select committee, and when it was proposed to require the refund of official salaries received during the Interregnum he moved that the judges should be exempted. On 26 July he was teller against a levy of 8*d.* a head on live cattle imported from Scotland, many of which were fattened on Norfolk pastures. He opposed the bill to enable Sir George Booth* to sever the entail on his estates, preferring to reward him for his services to the Restoration with a grant of £10,000. A member of the revenue committee, he complained that Norfolk was extremely over-assessed, and moved for the more equitable method of a national pound rate. On 16 Aug. he was added to the managers of a conference on the poll-tax. It was probably Townshend's interest with Lord Treasurer Southampton, the lord lieutenant of the county, that obtained for Doyley a seat on the excise appeals board. In his case the post was at first no sinecure, for in this capacity he sought and obtained authority from the Commons for the levy of excise on calico and raw silk. He reported frequently to the House from the army committee, and on 31 Aug. brought in the disbandment bill, subsequently helping to manage a conference. He was also among those to whom the proposed establishment for Dunkirk was committed, and before the adjournment the Commons unanimously accepted his lengthy report on payments due from Parliament for supplies and services. As disbandment got under way during the recess, he asked for the retention of two companies of foot in Yarmouth, which could not be 'trusted without a guard, as the Anabaptists try to foment differences between the Episcopalians and Presbyterians'. When Parliament reassembled in November, Doyley wrote:

> The poll bill falls so strangely short of what was expected that the want of that money hath run us into great debts, which we are now considering how to satisfy. The bill of attainder is almost finished; their lives are spared, their estates confiscated. . . . The Queen is suddenly to return with her fair daughter, who is the greatest beauty in the world; but what do I talk of beauties, who, through age and a load of business, such as makes me groan under it, am scarce able to sleep or eat in quiet.

He was among those entrusted with preparing the excise clauses in the bill to abolish the court of wards. He served on the committee for the bill to encourage the fishing industry and acted as teller for making Wednesday a meatless day. When one Member protested that this would cause hardship to travellers, Doyley 'said jestingly that it was fit (Sir) Samuel Jones* and his family should be excepted'. He was teller for authorizing innkeepers to hold wine licences, and against enabling the corporation of London to impose a two months' assessment for the militia.[6]

Doyley was re-elected in 1661 with the support of both Presbyterians and Independents, though he had little sympathy with their beliefs. It was later declared that '[Richard] Huntington* and his cabal were the only instruments of Sir William Doyley's being made a burgess'. James Johnson* acted as his agent, and he was described as the 'father' of the

partial conformists in the borough. Wharton again listed him among his friends in the House, and he took no part in the Clarendon Code. An active Member of the Cavalier Parliament, nevertheless, he was appointed to 198 committees, in six of which he took the chair, and helped to manage three conferences. He made six recorded speeches, carried five bills to the Upper House, and acted as teller in eight divisions. On 14 May he asked the Lords for their concurrence in the printing of the speech from the throne, and was appointed to the committee for the security bill. He took the chair for a Somerset estate bill in which Francis Wyndham* was named as principal trustee, and was appointed to the committees to prevent tumultuous petitioning and mischief from Quakers, and to consider the bill of pains and penalties. On 11 July he delivered his last report on disbandment, tabling a summary of the charges and expenses incurred in paying off the navy. He carried the fen drainage bill to the Lords, and after the recess acted as teller with John Birch* for an unsuccessful motion to impose a general excise on beer and ale. He reported a bill to penalize the import of adulterated madder, and on 28 Feb. 1662 he was teller against hearing the report of Francis Goodricke* on the alnage bill. With Sir Baynham Throckmorton, 2nd Bt.*, and (Sir) William Lowther* he was asked to expedite the lord treasurer's report on the Forest of Dean, which he tabled on 13 Mar. Eight days later Doyley and Birch were again unsuccessful in an attempt to strengthen the excise, when a bill to regulate frauds and abuses was rejected on second reading.[7]

Although Doyley acted as commissioner for corporations in Norfolk, he was unable to protect Johnson and his other friends in Yarmouth. He may have obtained his baronetcy in an attempt to compensate for this blow to his local prestige, and he remained attentive both to local needs and to the requirements of the Exchequer. In the 1663 session he acted as teller with Thomas Clifford* against a motion to 'mitigate the rigour of the law as to the strict observation of this Lent and prohibiting the eating of flesh'. He carried up the Wells quay bill, and reported an explanatory bill about arrears of excise. A court dependant in 1664, he was authorized by the House on 29 Apr. to bring in another bill to prevent excise frauds. When a bill to incorporate the suburb of Little Yarmouth was introduced on behalf of (Sir) Robert Paston* in the autumn session, Doyley desired that his constituency 'should have timely notice of it to make their objections', and with his colleague William Coventry* he twice acted as teller against it. They were each rewarded by the corporation with a gift of £25.

On 15 Dec. he again failed to secure a reduction in the county assessment. He was sent to thank the Presbyterian conformist Dr Owtram for his sermon on the anniversary of Charles I's execution, and on 9 Feb. 1665 he attended a conference on the Lords' proviso to the royal aid bill. During the second Dutch war he was given the responsibility, together with (Sir) Henry Vernon* and Robert Scawen*, of bringing up revenue payments to the Exchequer from the provinces, and he also took charge of the sick and wounded, including prisoners, in Essex, Norfolk and Suffolk. He complained to Samuel Pepys*

> of the great neglect of our masters, the great officers of state, about all business, and especially that of money, having now some thousands prisoners, and no money provided almost for the doing of it.

A naval surgeon reported to Joseph Williamson* that:

> Sir William Doyley has personally visited every sick and hurt person on shore in these quarters, so that 400 are cleared off and none will now be a burden longer than needs be, through orders issued by him, which the several agents are to execute exactly. He is indefatigable in his service, and not a penny is spent that could be saved.

He led the opposition on behalf of the Norfolk farmers to the ban on Irish cattle imports, disingenuously pretending to John Milward* in committee that 'if they might be supplied for one year with cattle out of Ireland, they being at present in want of stock, they would desire no more'. The expense of a large family had by now compelled him to mortgage his whole estate, and the acquisition of a tellership in the Exchequer for his extravagant eldest son must have required further outlay. He went down with a stroke in April 1666, and his colleagues considered his recovery little short of miraculous.[8]

Doyley probably welcomed the fall of Clarendon, serving on the committee of inquiry into the miscarriages of the war. He also helped to consider the measure to improve government credit by legalizing the transfer of Exchequer bills. On 27 Oct. 1667 he reported an undertaking from the Dutch ambassador that the English prisoners of war in Zeeland would be released immediately, but a month later he formed one of the Commons deputation sent to ask the King to make provision for their speedy relief and enlargement. He was awarded a pension of £300 p.a. for his pains over the revenue, and appointed to the new exchange commission to which was entrusted the general supervision of the processes of tax collection. On 21 Feb. 1668 he was among those ordered to ascertain how much of the revenue voted for the war had actually been applied

to that purpose. He managed the bill to authorize the collection of duties by Yarmouth corporation for the upkeep of the port, drawing up trade statistics for use in committee, and acting as teller on the report stage on 26 Mar. 1670. Four days later he carried back to the Lords the bill to enable Anthony Ashley* to make a jointure for his wife. He was chairman for the bill promoted by Henry Williams* to overturn a decree by the Bedford level commissioners, and carried it up. He also carried the bill to enable the estate of the defaulting tax-official Thomas Harlackenden* to be sold. The exchange office was suppressed towards the end of 1670, but Doyley's name appears on both lists of the court party at this time, and in 1671 he joined the syndicate formed by Lord St. John (Charles Powlett I*) to farm the customs.[9]

During the third Dutch war, Doyley again served as commissioner for the sick and wounded. According to A Seasonable Argument he 'got £7,000 out of the Dutch prisoners' allowance and starved many of them to death'; but in fact he was unable to extract from the Treasury the money owing in his constituency for quartering the sick and wounded after the battle of Sole Bay, totalling nearly £1,000, and his experience as hearth-tax receiver for Surrey was disastrous owing to frauds by 'pretended agents'. When Clifford was exposed as a Papist in 1673, Doyley made a feeble attempt to defend him, and even suggested that there was no danger in his remaining lord treasurer, since 'the King concerns himself in all things of the Treasury'. He was named on the Paston list, and in 1674 he was among those appointed to consider the charges against Lord Arlington, to bring in a general test bill, and to inquire into the state of Ireland. His affairs were becoming steadily more involved, and in the spring session of 1675 he was obliged to claim privilege for three of his servants. Nevertheless he took the chair for a highways bill, and was named to the committee for appropriating the customs to the use of the navy and for preventing the growth of Popery. Listed among the officials in the House and on the working lists, he received the government whip for the autumn session, and promised (Sir) Joseph Williamson* to attend. He was again appointed to the appropriation committee, but denied the contention of Sir Nicholas Carew* that the proceedings of the disbandment commissioners in 1660–1 afforded a precedent for paying the revenue for the navy into the chamber of London instead of the Exchequer. During the long recess, he was listed among the government supporters by Sir Richard Wiseman* and as a government speaker by Williamson, while Shaftesbury marked him 'thrice vile'. On 9 Sept. 1676 he wrote to Danby that he had 'sold as much land as I shall receive £4,000 for', and he was retained on the excise appeals commission. On 12 Mar. 1677 he defended the additional excise and the corn bounty:

> The subject has advantage by this additional duty of excise. As to the Act for Exportation of Corn, he appeals whether any man of £5 p.a. gains not by it. The King has deducted out of his customs £80,000 for abatements, according to that Act.

His last important committee was on the bill to ensure the Protestant education of the royal children. During the summer his son was found to have misused his office for private gain, though he contrived to shield himself from the worst consequences by turning King's evidence against his superior, Sir Robert Howard*. Doyley himself was buried at Hadleigh in November 1677, although he was posthumously included in the 'unanimous club', doubtless in confusion with his son. His will was never proved, and it was not until 1790 that another member of the family entered Parliament.[10]

[1] Excluded. [2] W. D. Bayley, *House of D'Oyly*, 110, 117–18; Norf. RO, Norfolk consistory court wills, 93 Trotter. [3] *Parl. Intell.* 9 Apr. 1660; *Cal. Treas. Bks.* i. 74; ii. 206; iii. 567, 1134; *Norf. Ltcy. Jnl.* (Norf. Rec. Soc. xxx), 9; *HMC Lothian*, 125; *Cal. Yarmouth Freemen*, 191; R. East, *Portsmouth Recs.* 356; Blomefield, *Norf.* iii. 405. [4] *CJ*, viii. 116; *Cal. Treas. Bks.* i. 75, 671; iv. 433; v. 197; *CSP Dom.* 1663–4, p. 112; 1667, p. 288; 1671, p. 324; 1671–2, pp. 94, 241. [5] Bayley, 99; Copinger, *Suff. Manors*, iii. 160–1; Blomefield, v. 506–7; *HMC Portland*, i. 149; *CJ*, ii. 884; iii. 129, 332. [6] *HMC Townshend*, 23; *Address from Gentry of Norf.* ed. Rye, 29; *Cal. Cl. SP*, iv. 639–40; *CSP Dom.* 1660–1, pp. 68, 309; Bowman diary, ff. 43, 50, 104v, 122; *CJ*, viii. 124, 128, 134, 165–6, 222, 224, 231; *HMC 6th Rep.* 363; *Old Parl. Hist.* xxiii. 68. [7] *CSP Dom.* 1668–9, p. 77; 1670, pp. 473–4; 1677–8, p. 519; Bayley, 118; *CJ*, viii. 262, 304, 368, 371. [8] *CSP Dom.* 1666–7, pp. 103, 568; *CJ*, viii. 437, 511, 531, 578, 592, 594, 598; C. J. Palmer, *Hist. Yarmouth*, 214; Add. 32094, f. 24; *Pepys Diary*, 9 Sept. 1665; *Milward*, 4, 9; Bayley, 119; *Evelyn Diary*, iii. 433, 448. [9] *Milward*, 94; *CJ*, ix. 26, 184, 185, 235; *Cal. Treas. Bks.* ii. 611; iii. 1122; C. D. Chandaman, *Eng. Pub. Revenue*, 182; H. Swinden, *Yarmouth*, 899. [10] *HMC 6th Rep.* 374; *Cal. Treas. Bks.* iv. 405; Grey, ii. 153; iii. 363; iv. 227; Dering, 149; *CJ*, ix. 326, 345; *CSP Dom.* 1675–6, p. 332; 1677–8, p. 448; Add. 28051, f. 35; *Hatton Corresp.* (Cam. Soc. n.s. xx), 155.

M.W.H./E.C.

DRAKE, Sir Francis, 2nd Bt. (1617–62), of Buckland Abbey, Devon.[1]

BERE ALSTON   29 June 1646[2]
NEWPORT   1660, 1661–6 Jan. 1662

bap. 25 Sept. 1617, 1st s. of Sir Francis Drake, 1st Bt.†, of Buckland Abbey by 2nd w. Joan, da. of Sir William Strode† of Newnham, Plympton St. Mary, Devon. *educ.* I. Temple 1633; travelled abroad (Italy) 1638–40. *m.* 18 Jan. 1641 (with £2,500), Dorothy, da. of John Pym† of Brymore, Som., *s.p. suc. fa.* 11 Mar. 1637.

Col. of ft. (parliamentary) 1642–4; commr. for assessment, Devon 1643–9, 1657, Aug. 1660–*d.*, sequestrations 1643, sheriff 1645–6, j.p. 1647–57, Mar. 1660–*d.*, commr. for militia 1648, Mar. 1660.

Drake's great-uncle, the famous admiral, sat in three Elizabethan Parliaments. By upbringing and family connexions Drake was unsympathetic to the Court, and his marriage to Pym's daughter brought him even closer to the leaders of the parliamentary Opposition to Charles I. On the outbreak of the Civil War he joined the parliamentary army and became colonel of the Plymouth regiment, but was forced to sue out a pardon in 1644. Elected as recruiter for Bere Alston, where he owned some of the burgages, he abstained from sitting after Pride's Purge. He played no active part in politics during the Interregnum, but signed the Exeter declaration for a free Parliament on 11 Jan. 1660.[3]

In April 1660, Drake stood again for Bere Alston, but the double return was decided in favour of George Howard*. However, he had been returned for Newport, where as former lord of the manor of Werrington he retained a property interest. He was totally inactive in the Convention, though Lord Wharton listed him as a friend. Drake was re-elected for Newport in 1661, but his health was failing, and apart from an application for leave in June he left no trace on the records of the Cavalier Parliament. He died on 6 Jan. 1662, and was buried at Buckland, leaving his estates to his nephew, Sir Francis Drake, 3rd Bt.*

[1] This article is based on E. F. Eliott-Drake, *Fam. and Heirs of Drake*. [2] Abstained after Pride's Purge 6 Dec. 1648, readmitted 21 Feb. 1660. [3] W. H. Black, *Docquets of Letters Patent*, 156; Devon RO, 346M/T1–20.

M.W.H./G.H.

DRAKE, Sir Francis, 3rd Bt. (1647–1718), of Buckland Abbey, Devon.

TAVISTOCK   26 Mar. 1673, 1679 (Mar.), 1679 (Oct.), 1681, 1689, 1690, 10 Nov. 1696, 1698

bap. 1 May 1647, 2nd but 1st surv. s. of Thomas Drake of Brendon Barton, Week St. Mary, by Susan, da. of William Crymes of Buckland Crymes. *educ.* Exeter, Oxf. matric. 3 June 1663, aged 16. *m* (1) 6 Feb. 1665, Dorothy (*bur.* 30 Jan. 1679), da. of Sir John Bampfield, 1st Bt.†, of Poltimore, 4da.; (2) lic. 21 Oct. 1680, Anne (*bur.* 22 Dec. 1685), da. of Thomas Boone† of Mount Boone, and coh. to her bro. Charles Boone*, *s.p.*; (3) 18 Feb. 1690, Elizabeth, da. of (Sir) Henry Pollexfen* of Woodbury, 7s. 1da. *suc.* fa. c.1653, uncle Sir Francis Drake, 2nd Bt.*, 6 Jan. 1662.[1]

J.p. Devon 1670–5, 1689–*d.*, commr. for assessment 1673–80, 1689–90, recusants 1675, inquiry into recusancy fines, Devon, Cornw. and Dorset 1688; recorder, Plymouth 1696–*d.*; col. of militia ft. Devon by 1697–?*d.*; dep. lt. Devon and Plymouth 1701–*d.*; v.-adm. Devon 1715–*d.*[2]

Drake's father joined the parliamentary army at the beginning of the Civil War, but later went over to the Royalists. After his death, Drake was brought up by his uncle, and subsequently by William Strode I* and a brother of Sir John Davie, 2nd Bt.*, though his first marriage to the sister of the high Anglican loyalist, Sir Coplestone Bampfylde*, was concluded without their knowledge. He was first returned for Tavistock four miles from his home on his own interest at a by-election to the Cavalier Parliament, and became an active opposition Member. He was appointed to 66 committees, made at least 13 speeches, and acted as teller in five divisions. In his maiden speech, on 20 Jan. 1674, he complained that the House had spent five days discussing the charges against Lord Arlington, and proposed an address for his removal. In the spring session of 1675 he acted as teller for including the Scottish army law in the charges against Lauderdale, whom he thought 'not a fit companion for the King'. He was appointed in both sessions to the committees on the bills to appropriate the customs to the use of the navy and to hinder Papists from sitting in Parliament.[3]

On the Earl of Bath's request Drake was removed from the commission of the peace during the long recess, and Sir Richard Wiseman* was informed by a local correspondent that he was 'dejected' in consequence. Although he was marked 'thrice worthy' on Shaftesbury's list, and (Sir) John Malet* referred to his case as a grievance, he took no ascertainable part in the 1677 session, and on 31 May was given permission to go abroad with his family and servants 'for the benefit of his health'. When he returned he was even more vocal in opposition. On 7 May 1678 he remarked:

> We are in a declining age, and [have] one foot in the grave. Nothing can remove jealousies at home and abroad but removing these counsellors.

On the same day he was teller for presenting an address for the removal of Lauderdale. He asserted that 'a standing army and a Parliament are inconsistent', and on 17 June acted as teller against the naval estimates. In the ensuing debate on supply he argued:

> Let us . . . get these men removed from [about] the throne that have endeavoured to break trust and confidence betwixt the King and us. They are uneasy with a Parliament, and would have such a revenue granted the King that they may have no more. No Englishman can give this money demanded, and I would give none.

During the concluding session of the Cavalier Parliament he was added to the committee of inquiry into the Popish Plot and moved the impeachment of Secretary Williamson for signing commissions for Roman Catholic officers. He was teller on 26 Nov. against adjourning the debate on disabling Papists from sitting in Parliament, and was among those entrusted with drafting instructions for disbanding the army. He acted as teller for an address against private advices, which he helped to draft.[4]

Drake was re-elected to the Exclusion Parliaments and marked 'worthy' on Shaftesbury's list. A very active Member in 1679, he was appointed to 35 committees and twice acted as teller. Among his committees were those to summon Danby to surrender, to extend habeas corpus, and to provide for security against Popery. He was teller against paying into the Exchequer the revenue intended for disbandment, and voted for exclusion. In his only speech, on 23 May, he attacked those Members of the previous Parliament who 'came up to give money to betray their public trust'. After re-election he took part in petitioning for the meeting of Parliament, but he seems to have been absent until the closing days of the second Exclusion Parliament, when he became moderately active. He was named to five committees and moved for an address for the dismissal of Laurence Hyde*. He was probably selected by Sir William Courtenay* as his colleague for the county in 1681, but stood down for the more moderate (Sir) Samuel Rolle* and served again for his borough. In the Oxford Parliament he was appointed to the committee of elections and privileges, and to those to prepare for a conference on the loss of the bill of ease for dissenters and to bring in the exclusion bill.[5]

In the Tory reaction after the Exclusion Parliaments, Drake's continued opposition eventually led him into exile. According to Lord Grey of Warke, he was to be approached about a rising in the West, and he was accused of cognizance of the Rye House Plot. An action at law was actually commenced against him for saying that 'it would never be well with England till the Duke of York was excluded'. Before the writ could be served he made over his estates in trust to Sir John Davie, 3rd Bt.*, and escaped overseas. He was pardoned by James II, and in April 1688 the King's electoral agents concluded that he was 'undoubtedly right' on the religious issue and might stand for Devon in the proposed Parliament if your Majesty will lay an obligation on him so to do'. They also noted his interest at Bere Alston, where he owned several burgages. However, by September they had come to realize that he could not be 'prevailed upon to stand or concern himself in public business'. Two months later he joined William of Orange at Exeter.[6]

Elected again for Tavistock to the Convention, Drake was moderately active, being appointed to 26 committees and acting as teller in three divisions. During the first session he was appointed to the committees to inspect the coronation oath and to consider the bill from the Lords to prevent 'all questions and disputes concerning the assembling and sitting of this present Parliament'. In his only recorded speech in this Parliament, during the debate on revenue of 27 Feb. 1689, he exclaimed:

> I thank God we are delivered from these men; now we are under a Prince who has deserved well of the nation in delivering us, and I would give him the best acknowledgment we can, but not to prejudice the people. The same reasons for not giving formerly make me for it now, for our Prince to support the honour of the nation.

After the recess he was named to the committee of inquiry into war expenditure, and helped to draw up the address about the appointment of Commissary Shales. He acted as teller against recommending Members for service in Ireland, and was appointed to the committee on the bill for restoring corporations, in which he supported the disabling clause. After its defeat he was named to the committee on the bill to indemnify those who had taken part in the Revolution, and was a teller against the second reading of the bill to restore the university charters.[7]

Drake sat in three more Parliaments as a court Whig. He was buried at Meavy on 15 June 1718. His son, the fourth baronet, sat for Tavistock as an independent Whig from 1715 to 1734.[8]

[1] Vivian, *Vis. Devon*, 301; E. F. Eliott-Drake, *Fam. and Heirs of Drake*, i. 400; ii. 30, 65. [2] *HMC Finch*, ii. 43; *Cal. Treas. Bks.* viii. 1804; *CSP Dom.* 1696, p. 424; Eg. 1626, f. 11; Ind. 24577. [3] Eliott-Drake, i. 293; ii. 4; PCC Laud 8; Bodl. Carte 78, f. 610; *Devon and Cornw. N. and Q.* xv. 322; Grey, ii. 318; iii. 215; *CJ*, ix. 322. [4] Grey, iv. 138; v. 354; vi. 86, 99, 230; *CSP Dom.* 1677–8, p. 162; *CJ*, ix. 551. [5] *CJ*, ix. 598; Grey, vii. 315; *CSP Dom.* 1679–80, p. 567; *HMC 12th Rep. IX*, 113; *True Prot. Merc.* 9 Mar. 1681. [6] Ford Grey, *Secret Hist.* 16, 18; Clarke, *Jas. II*, i. 742; *HMC Downshire*, i. 259; R. Morrice, *Entering Bk.* 1, p. 421; Eliott-Drake, ii. 40; Luttrell, i. 307, 477. [7] Grey, ix. 125; *CJ*, x. 300, 337. [8] *HMC 13th Rep. VI*, 33, 40.

J.S.C.

DRAKE, John (1625–69), of Great Trill, Axminster, Devon.

BRIDPORT 1660

bap. 4 Apr. 1625, 1st s. of Sir John Drake[†] of Ashe House, Musbury, by Ellen, da. of Sir John Boteler[†], 1st Baron Boteler, and coh. to her bro. William, 2nd Baron Boteler. *educ.* I. Temple 1664. *m.* (1) Jane (*d.* 31 July 1652), da. of Sir John Yonge* of Colyton, Devon, 2s. 1da.; (2) Dionise, da. of Sir Richard Strode[†] of Newnham, Devon, 3s. *suc.* fa. 1636; kntd. 5 June 1660; *cr.* Bt. 31 Aug. 1660.[1]

J.p. Devon 1646–*d.*, Dorset 1666–*d.*; commr. for assessment, Devon 1647–52, 1657, Jan. 1660–*d.*, militia 1648, 1659, Mar. 1660, oyer and terminer, Western circuit 1655, 1662; capt. of militia ft. Devon Apr. 1660, col. Sept. 1660–*d.*, sheriff 1662–3.[2]

The Drakes acquired Ashe by marriage in 1415. Drake's grandfather was four times Member for Devon, and his father served for Lyme Regis in 1624 and 1625. Drake is first heard of as a prisoner in Prince Maurice's hands, vowing vengeance on Lord Powlett for the burning of Ashe House by the Cavaliers. He may have been taken in arms for Parliament, though he was only 18 at the time. His mother claimed £6,000 compensation, and succeeded in extracting close on £1,500 from the Powletts. Drake's politics seem to have been sufficiently obscure or accommodating for him to accept county office under every government established during the Interregnum, and a baronetcy at the Restoration. He probably owed this honour to his mother, a kinswoman of William Howard*, and said to be 'a great actor for the King'. He was even recommended for the order of the Royal Oak, when his estates were reckoned at £800 *p.a.* He sat in the Convention for Bridport, but did nothing, either by way of speeches or committee work, and on 16 June 1660 he obtained leave to go into the country. He is unlikely to have stood again. He died on 6 July 1669 and was buried at Axminster. His youngest son was unsuccessful at Lyme in 1689, but sat for Honiton from 1690 to 1715 as a Tory.[3]

[1] Vivian, *Vis. Devon*, 297; *Devon and Cornw. N. and Q.* vi. 114. [2] *Parl. Intell.* 16 Apr. 1660; *Merc. Pub.* 17 Sept. 1660; C. A. F. Meekings, *Dorset Hearth-Tax*, 117; *CSP Dom.* 1668–9, p. 399; *Trans. Devon Assoc.* x. 309–14; *Thurloe*, ii. 296. [3] *Cal. Comm. Comp.* 866, 1053; *Cal. Cl. Sp*, iv. 319.

M.W.H./J.P.F.

DRAKE, Sir William (c.1651–90), of Shardeloes, nr. Amersham, Bucks.

AMERSHAM 1 Nov. 1669, 1679 (Mar.), 18 Dec. 1680, 1681, 1685, 1689, 14 Feb.–Sept. 1690

b. c.1651, 1st s. of Francis Drake[†] of Walton-on-Thames, Surr. by 2nd w. Dorothy, da. of Sir William Spring, 1st Bt.[†], of Pakenham, Suff.; bro. of John Drake[†]. *educ.* St. John's, Oxf. matric. 22 Nov. 1667, aged 16; M. Temple 1669. *m.* c.1670, Elizabeth, da. and coh. of Hon. William Montagu* of Boughton, Northants., 3s. (2 *d.v.p.*) 4da. *suc.* fa. c.1660; kntd. 2 Sept. 1668; *suc.* to estates of uncle Sir William Drake, 1st Bt.* 1669.[1]

Dep. lt. Bucks. 1672–Feb. 1688, Sept. 1688–*d.*; commr. for assessment, Bucks. 1673–80, 1689–90, Cheshire 1690.[2]

Drake's father sat for Amersham in the Long Parliament until Pride's Purge, when, as a leading supporter of the Treaty of Newport, he was imprisoned. He represented Surrey under the Protectorate, and supported the offer of the crown to Cromwell. Drake himself succeeded under age to his uncle's estate and parliamentary seat, though he defeated an outsider, Sir Ralph Bovey, by a mere six votes, after profuse expenditure. Nevertheless, he was an inactive Member of the Cavalier Parliament, in which he was appointed to only three committees. He appeared in the opposition list of 1671 as a court supporter, and in *A Seasonable Argument* he was said to be 'under the command of his father-in-law'. Though he became a deputy lieutenant in 1672, he was never included in the Buckinghamshire commission of the peace. In the working lists he was assigned to Danby's own management. Sir Richard Wiseman* marked his name with a query in 1676, but considered that he 'may be certainly managed by Mr. Attorney Montagu' (his father-in-law). When Parliament reassembled he duly seconded in his only recorded speech a grant of £600,000 for the navy. Shaftesbury marked him 'worthy' in 1677, though he was named as a court supporter in both lists of 1678. His sole committee in that year was to consider relief for the creditors of the Merchant Adventurers.[3]

Drake sat in all the Exclusion Parliaments after contested elections, but he was totally inactive in committee and debate. Shaftesbury again marked him 'worthy' in 1679, and he voted for the first exclusion bill. Nevertheless he was included in the 'unanimous club', and in August he was opposed by the republican Algernon Sidney[†]. The contest must have been costly, for Drake was compelled to retrench his household expenditure. When the second Exclusion Parliament met, the House declared the election void, but Drake was successful at the subsequent by-election, and also in 1681. He fortified his interest at Amersham by building a stately market-hall for the town in the following year. Returned again in 1685, he was a moderately active Member of James II's Parliament, but none of his four committees was of political importance. In 1688 the King's electoral agents expected Drake to be re-elected at Amersham, 'and it is not doubted but he will go right'. No answers are recorded from him on the repeal of the Penal Laws and Tests, and he was removed from the lieutenancy. He was returned to the Convention, but was again inactive, with only two committees. He was listed as a supporter of the disabling clause in the bill to restore corporations, and was re-elected, but he was buried at Amersham on 24 Sept. 1690. His son Montagu sat as a Tory for Amersham from 1695 to 1698.[4]

[1] Lipscomb, *Bucks.* iii. 21, 154–5; Guildford Muniment Room, Walton-on-Thames par. reg.; *HMC 7th Rep.* 487. [2] *CSP Dom.* 1671–2, p. 266. [3] Keeler, *Long Parl.* 159; D. Underdown, *Pride's Purge*, 110, 147, 168; *HMC 7th Rep.* 488; *CJ*, ix. 103, 126; *Bucks. Recs.* xvii. 11; Grey, iv. 104. [4] *HMC 13th Rep. VI*, 19; *7th Rep.* 475; *CJ*, ix. 638, 646; *VCH Bucks.* iii. 141; Lipscomb, iii. 155.

L.N./G.J.

DRAKE, Sir William, 1st Bt. (1606–69), of Shardeloes, nr. Amersham, Bucks.

AMERSHAM 1640 (Apr.), 1640 (Nov.),[1] 1661–
          28 Aug. 1669

bap. 28 Sept. 1606, 1st s. of Francis Drake[†], gent. of the privy chamber, of Esher, Surr. by Joan, da. and coh. of William Tothill, a six clerk in Chancery, of Shardeloes. *educ.* Amersham (Dr Charles Croke); Christ Church, Oxf. 1624; M. Temple 1626; G. Inn 1629; travelled abroad 1630–?37; Leyden 1634. *unm. suc.* fa. 1634; kntd. 14 July 1641; *cr.* Bt. 17 July 1641.[2]
   Commr. for defence, midland assoc. 1642; j.p. Bucks. by 1647–53, 1661–*d.*, commr. for militia 1648, Mar. 1660, dep. lt. c.Aug. 1660–1, commr. for assessment 1661–*d.*, corporations 1662–3.[3]
   Chirographer of common pleas 1652–9.[4]

Drake's grandfather, a younger son of the Ashe family, became in 1572 its first Member of Parliament. Of puritan stock on both sides of the family, Drake inherited Shardeloes from his maternal grandfather, a wealthy chancery official, and added to it the manor of Amersham in 1637, thereby acquiring an impregnable interest in the borough, which he represented in the Short and Long Parliaments. A bibliophile and a classical scholar, he took no active part in politics during the Civil War and Interregnum. He spent many years abroad, even after he was appointed by the Rump to the valuable office of chirographer, or *custos brevium*, in the common pleas, which he doubtless exercised by deputy.[5]

Although Drake resumed his seat with the secluded Members in February 1660, he is not known to have stood at the general election; but he was returned to the Cavalier Parliament in 1661 and listed by Lord Wharton as a friend. An inactive Member, he was appointed six times to the committee of elections and privileges; but his only legislative committee was on the bill to cancel the fines extorted from Lady Powell (see William Powell*), for which he may have borne some official responsibility. He died in London on 28 Aug. 1669 and was buried at Amersham, where he endowed the almshouses. He was succeeded in his estates and in Parliament by his nephew.[6]

[1] Abstained after Pride's Purge, 6 Dec. 1648, readmitted 21 Feb. 1660. [2] Lipscomb, *Bucks.* iii. 154–5, 168; A. Croke, *Hist. Croke Fam.* i. 509; *APC*, 1630–1, p. 26; PC2/44/35. [3] Huntington Lib. Stowe mss, 2/452; T. Langley, *Hundred of Desborough*, 17. [4] *HMC 10th Rep. IV*, 217; G. E. Aylmer, *State's Servants*, 98. [5] *VCH Bucks.* iii. 147, 149; Lipscomb, 168; Keeler, *Long Parl.* 159–60; *CJ*, v. 235; vi. 34; D. Underdown, *Pride's Purge*, 209; Aylmer, 98; *Shardeloes Pprs.* ed. Eland, 55–56. [6] Lipscomb, iii. 154, 168; *VCH Bucks.* iii. 141, 155.

L.N./G.J.

DRAPER, Cresheld (1646–94), of May Place, Crayford, Kent.

WINCHELSEA   7 Mar. 1678, 1679 (Mar.), 1679
              (Oct.), 1681, 1685

bap. 8 Nov. 1646, o.s. of William Draper of Crayford by 2nd w. Mary, da. and coh. of Richard Cresheld[†], serjeant-at-law, of Mattishall, Norf. *educ.* Sevenoaks g.s.; St. John's, Camb. 1661, *m.* lic. 24 Mar. 1666, Sarah, da. of Sir Dennis Gauden, surveyor-gen. of victualling, of Clapham, Surr., 1s. 2da. *suc.* fa. 1651.[1]

Member, Hon. Artillery Co. 1670; commr. for assessment, Kent 1673–80, 1689–90, j.p. 1675–Feb. 1688, lt.-col. of militia by 1679–Feb. 1688, dep. lt. 1683–Feb. 1688.[2]

Draper's grandfather, a London Merchant Taylor, bought most of the parish of Crayford in the reign of James I. His father served on three local committees between 1648 and his death, but his maternal grandfather, who had been made a judge by the Long Parliament, laid down office on the execution of the King, and his step-father, John Egioke*, was hostile to the Protectorate. Draper was nominated by Robert Austen* to oppose the obnoxious *nouveau riche*, Sir John Banks*, at Winchelsea in 1678, and won the seat on petition at the cost, it was later alleged, of £11,000.

Although Draper's estate was worth not much more than £1,000 p.a., he may have raised most of this large sum himself; at his death mortgages of £13,000 were outstanding. His motive can only be conjectured; but it may have arisen from the break-up of his marriage. His father-in-law was now little more than a dependant of Banks, who may have used his wealth and power to compel Draper to a legal separation with generous alimony of £300 p.a. Shaftesbury marked Draper 'worthy', but he was an inactive Member of the Cavalier Parliament, serving on only five committees, of which the most important was on the Lords bill on behalf of foreign Protestant artisans. He was re-elected to the next four Parliaments. Shaftesbury marked him 'worthy' again in 1679, and he was listed as voting for exclusion, although he had obtained leave to go into the country on 27 Apr. His last parliamentary committee was for a local estate bill in the second Exclusion Parliament. By 1682, when he went into partnership with Lord Windsor and George Pitt* to patent an invention for the construction of wet docks, he was presumably a court supporter, and in the next year he was made a deputy lieutenant. He was re-elected in 1685, and with his son took part in the coronation of James II, but was totally inactive in Parliament. He claimed to be too ill to answer the lord lieutenant's questions on the repeal of the Test Act and Penal Laws in 1688, and was removed from local office. He was probably in serious financial difficulties, for in the same year he was compelled to sell the Oxfordshire property that had come to him from his mother, and he was not reappointed to the lieutenancy or the commission

of the peace. He died on 15 Mar. 1694, the only member of the family to sit in Parliament. Overgenerous legacies completed the ruin of his estate, which was sold to Sir Clowdisley Shovell[†] for £20,500.[3]

[1] Soc. of Genealogists, Crayford par. reg.; *Reg. Roff.* 999; PCC 43 Box. [2] *Ancient Vellum Bk.* ed. Raikes, 98; *CSP Dom.* Jan.–July 1683, pp. 134, 155; *CJ*, ix. 605. [3] PCC 83 Sadler; Hasted, *Kent*, ii. 272; Defoe, *Tour*, 130–1; PC2/69/16; D. C. Coleman, *Sir John Banks*, 104, 163; *CSP Dom.* July–Sept. 1683, p. 218; *Suss. Arch. Colls.* xv. 193; *Wheatley Recs.* (Oxf. Rec. Soc. xxxvii), 71, 75; C10/258/26, 28; 236/29.

B.D.H./J.P.F.

DUBOIS, John (1622–84), of Love Lane, London.

LIVERPOOL 1679 (Mar.), 1679 (Oct.), 1681

bap. 24 Feb. 1622, s. of Jean Dubois, physician, of Canterbury, Kent by Catherine, da. of Jacques de l'Espine of Canterbury. *m.* (1) 11 Jan. 1652, Anne (*d.* 1659), da. of Charles Herle, rector of Winwick, Lancs., 1s.; (2) 1662, Sarah, da. of Daniel Waldo, Clothworker, of Honey Lane, London, 4s. 2da.[1]

Member, Weavers' Co. 1653–*d.*; common councilman, London 1674–82, auditor, bridgehouse accounts 1679–80; commr. for assessment, London 1677–80, Kent 1679–80; committee E. I. Co. 1681–*d.*[2]

Dubois's father was a member of the French Huguenot church in Canterbury, and Dubois himself became an elder of the French church in Threadneedle Street in 1671, though from 1672 to 1674 he was also churchwarden of St. Mary Aldermanbury. His interest in the silk trade was adversely affected by Colbert's tariffs. He joined the group of London merchants who protested against the French alliance, and in 1674, together with Sir Patrick Ward* and Thomas Papillon*, he was among the 14 signatories to the *Scheme of Trade*, which presented evidence of an unfavourable balance of trade with France. In that year he was elected to the common council, becoming a member of the committees administering the city lands and markets, and he promoted the petition to oblige those merchants who had gone to live in the suburbs after the Great Fire to return to the City. In 1679 he was elected auditor of the bridgehouse accounts, an office of considerable profit.[3]

Dubois's brother-in-law and partner Charles Herle (cousin of Edward Herle*) was a merchant in Liverpool, for which Dubois was returned to the Exclusion Parliaments. Classed as 'honest' by Shaftesbury, he was very active in the first Exclusion Parliament, being appointed to 34 committees. Among the most important were those to consider the Lords bill for the better discovery and speedier conviction of Popish recusants and the bill for securing the King and kingdom against Popery, and to draw up an address for the removal of Lauderdale. He supported the exclusion bill in debate and division, saying that it would deprive Papists of any reason to threaten the King's life. As a member of the Weavers' Company, he was appointed to the inquiry into the decay in the cloth industry.[4]

Dubois remained very active in the second Exclusion Parliament, in which he was named to 37 committees. He again spoke for exclusion, saying:

> I have a great many children. . . . I would have their souls saved, that hereafter they may not be in Popery, which we shall be with a Popish successor. If the Catholics have such an influence on the government under a Protestant Prince, what will they have under a Popish?

He was appointed to the committees to prepare a bill for uniting Protestants, to draft addresses to desire the removal of Sir George Jeffreys as recorder of London, and to represent the dangerous state of the nation. On 20 Nov. he was teller against the second reading of the bill forbidding the import of Scottish cattle. He reported an address for the remission of a fine imposed on the exclusionist journalist, Benjamin Harris. On 26 Nov. he spoke in favour of impeaching Edward Seymour* and was appointed to the committee. He was named to the committees to prepare a bill for the naturalization of all foreign Protestants, and to consider a bill for the discovery of estates settled to superstitious uses. During the Oxford Parliament he is not known to have spoken, but he was appointed to five committees, including those to prepare the impeachment of Fitzharris and to bring in the third exclusion bill.[5]

The common council appointed Dubois with Sir Thomas Player* and his East India Company associate Papillon to prepare a petition for a new Parliament on 13 May 1681. In November he served on the *ignoramus* jury that rejected the charge of treason against Shaftesbury. On this occasion he was heard to complain that 'it is a great grief to many good people that it should be treason to call the King a Papist. Why may not a man call a spade a spade?' Dubois and Papillon were the Whig candidates at the shrieval election in the summer of 1682. The outgoing sheriffs declared them elected by large majorities; but the lord mayor, Sir John Moore*, swore in two Tories. The aggrieved candidates sought to obtain a writ of *mandamus* for a false return, and in April 1683 had all the Tory aldermen arrested. Moore's successor, Sir William Pritchard, brought an action against them for wrongful arrest, but Dubois died before the case was heard. He was buried at St. Mary Aldermanbury on 30 Oct. 1684, the sermon being preached, in accordance with his will, by the Lati-

tudinarian Dean Tillotson. Out of a personal estate of £35,205 he left many charitable bequests, including £100 to the French church in Threadneedle Street and £10 to the Liverpool poor. He was the only member of his family to sit in Parliament.[6]

[1] *Reg. of Walloon Church, Canterbury* (Huguenot Soc. v), 121, 472; *Hist. Walloon and Huguenot Church at Canterbury* (Huguenot Soc. xv), 95; *Reg. French Church, Threadneedle St.* (Huguenot Soc. xiii), 33, 44; *Her. and Gen.* ii. 237. [2] J. R. Woodhead, *Rulers of London*, 62. [3] Guildhall RO, common council jnl.; *IHR Bull.* xxix. 207–18. [4] Grey, vii. 238. [5] Grey, vii. 396, 414; viii. 90, 117; *CJ*, ix. 686. [6] *CSP Dom.* 1680–1, pp. 256, 276, 603; *Cal. Ct. Mins. E.I. Co.* ed. Sainsbury, x. 294, 707; Woodhead, 62; Ailesbury, *Mems.* 71; *St. Mary Aldermanbury* (Harl. Soc. Reg. lxi), 202; PCC 169 Hare.

I.C./E.C.

DUCKETT, Lionel (1652–93), of Box, Wilts.

CALNE 1679 (Oct.), 1689

b. 4 Mar. 1652, o.s. of William Duckett* by 1st w. *educ.* St. John's, Oxf. 1668; M. Temple 1669. *m.* lic. 27 Sept. 1680, Martha, da. of Samuel Ashe* of Langley Burrell, 6s. (3 *d.v.p.*). *suc.* fa. 1686.[1]

Dep. lt. Wilts. June 1688–*d.*, j.p. June 1688–*d.*, commr. for assessment 1689.[2]

Duckett was returned for Calne on the family interest at the second general election of 1679. There is no evidence of a contest. He was a totally inactive Member of the second Exclusion Parliament, being named to no committees and making no recorded speeches, and did not stand for re-election. In a long letter to an uncle drafted on 30 July 1683 he explained his reasons, though his chief purpose in writing was to scotch the report that he

> delighted . . . in the company of factious persons and such as are discontented with the Government. Now, sir, I will deal sincerely with you and, as far as the necessary brevity of a letter will admit, shall, I hope, satisfy you and clear myself on this point. That I ever delighted in such company (knowing of them to be such) is an accusation wherein I am infinitely wronged, though I cannot but confess that the debates of that furious Parliament at Westminster whereof I, for want of a better, was a Member, were enough to corrupt the principles of any unwary young man living. Yet this I can say (and a great many others for me) that I never did approve of the heat and passion wherewith things were then carried on. At that time I was so far in ignorance as to think that their great zeal was only bent against Popery; whereas since it is plainly evident that too many of them had at that time designs in hand more wicked than their malice could invent to accuse the Papists of. This was yet further confirmed by the proceedings afterwards at Oxford, of which Parliament (I thank God) I was not a Member, having had a belly full before at the Westminster Parliament; from the time of the dissolution of which I have lived (I can say it) as retired a life as any man in England, very seldom keeping any company at all or going abroad, for I am sure I have not been six miles from home this year and a half, so that I content myself with speculation.
>
> Amongst many others of my serious thoughts I have

often with great sorrow considered the danger I apprehended his Majesty, and consequently the whole nation, to be in from a sort of people who not only pretend to more loyalty than others, calling themselves emphatically the 'True Protestants', and I have often and earnestly prayed God to defend his Majesty and the royal family from all such machinations which it had to be feared were contriving against him by that party. . . . I have not without amazement considered the insolence of these people and what usage they have given his Majesty, not suffering him to take the liberty they have taken themselves; they may have liberty to protest and afterwards publish their protestations. If his Majesty at any time is pleased to let the people know his mind by way of declaration, it is presently followed with a swarm of venomous libels, impudently pretending to undermine the people. If a poor sneaking Papist at any time happens to procure a reprieve after sentence, then presently, forsooth, his Majesty is a favourer of Papists; if a true Protestant comes to be arraigned for treason he need not fear of an ignoramus brought in by a jury of as honest men as himself. Nay, it was thought hard that Stephen, their protomartyr, should run the risk of an Oxfordshire jury after he had been sanctified by an Old Bailey ignoramus. There might be an hundred things said more of the same nature too long for a letter, as the art, the industry used in seducing his Majesty's unwary subjects from their loyalty.

If Duckett's sentiments were sincere he may have supported two Tories, Sir John Ernle* and Thomas Webb*, at the 1685 election. He did not stand, and in 1688 the King's agents made no mention of his interest at Calne, though he was described as 'a favourer of dissenters', and recommended for local office. He was returned for Calne to the Convention, probably unopposed, and was again totally inactive. His only mention in the Journal is when he was given leave to go to the country on 1 Apr. 1689; but he was presumably a Whig. He died on 5 Dec. 1693 and was buried at Kensington. In his will he enjoined his wife to bring up his children 'in the Protestant religion according to the orthodox reformed episcopal Church of England of which communion I profess myself'. His sons George and William represented Calne in the Whig interest under Anne and George I.[3]

[1] T. E. Duckett, Duckett Fam. 55, 59; The Gen. n.s. xxxvii. 213. [2] Wilts. RO A1/1/1. [3] Bodl. Firth mss c.3, f. 29; J. R. Jones, First Whigs, 158; PCC 206 Coker.

B.D.H.

DUCKETT, William (1624–86), of Hartham, Corsham, Wilts.

CALNE 1659, 1660, 1661

bap. 23 May 1624, 1st s. of John Duckett† of Calstone by Jane, da. of William Winter of Colford, Glos. *educ.* St. John's, Oxf. 1640; I. Temple 1642. *m.* (1) by 1651, Elizabeth, da. of Thomas Henshaw of Kensington, Mdx., 1s.; (2) 1655, Anne (*d.* c.1667), da. of George Knight,

mercer, of Bristol, wid. of Walter Chapman of Bath, 1da.; (3) lic. 14 Sept. 1669, Margaret, da. of Sir Henry Moore, 2nd Bt., of Fawley, Berks., *s.p. suc.* fa. 1648.[1]

J.p. Wilts. 1650–4, Mar. 1660–Apr. 1680, July 1680–d., commr. for assessment 1652, Jan. 1660–80, militia Mar. 1660, major of militia ft. Apr. 1660, col. by Apr. 1680, July 1680–d., commr. for loyal and indigent officers 1662, recusants 1675, dep. lt. 1675–Apr. 1680, July 1680–d.; freeman, Calne 1685–d.[2]

Duckett's family acquired the manor of Calne under Elizabeth and first sat for the borough in 1584. Their house at Calstone was burnt down by the parliamentary forces during the Civil War, but there is no evidence that they took any active part. Duckett himself was nominated to the commission of the peace during the Commonwealth and elected to Richard Cromwell's Parliament; but in June 1659 the royalist conspirator Allen Brodrick* reported that he 'seemed ready to assist'.[3]

Duckett was re-elected in 1660, but left no trace on the records of the Convention. He was proposed for the order of the Royal Oak with an estate of £1,000 p.a. He defeated (Sir) Edward Bayntun* at the general election of 1661, but he was scarcely more active in the Cavalier Parliament. He was appointed to ten committees, including the committee of elections and privileges in three sessions, and that to consider an estate bill promoted by (Sir) Edward Hungerford* in 1664. But he twice defaulted on calls of the House, and his name appeared on no lists until he was marked 'doubly worthy' by Shaftesbury in 1677.

Duckett did not stand for the Exclusion Parliaments, but his son was successful in August 1679, and in the following April the Privy Council ordered him to be removed from all county office. He was reinstated in July 1680, however, and must have become a Tory, for he was approved as 'burgess' of Calne in the new charters of 1685. He died on 1 Nov. 1686, and was buried at Calne.[4]

[1] Wilts. Vis. Peds. (Harl. Soc. cv), 52; Sir George Duckett, Ducketiana, 40–42; T. E. Duckett, Duckett Fam. 46; The Gen. n.s. xxxiii. 262. [2] Merc. Pub. 12 Apr. 1660; PC2/68, f. 484; CSP Dom. 1685, p. 535. [3] Calne Guild Stewards Bk. (Wilts. Arch. Soc. vii), p. xii; Cal. Cl. SP. iv. 225. [4] HMC 10th Rep. IV, 115; CSP Dom. 1685, pp. 28, 128.

B.D.H.

DUDLEY, Sir William, 1st Bt. (c.1607–70), of Clopton, Northants.

NORTHAMPTON 9 Mar.–9 Apr. 1663

b. c.1607, 3rd s. of Edward Dudley of Clopton by Elizabeth, da. of Robert Wood of Lambley, Notts. *m.* (1) Hester, da. of Edward de Pleurs of Westminster, *s.p.*; (2) 11 Sept. 1651, Jane, da. of Sir Roger Smith of Edmondthorpe, Leics., *s.p.*; (3) Mary, da. and h. of Paul Pindar of Bishopsgate, London, 2s. 1da. *suc.* bro. 1641; *cr.* Bt. 1 Aug. 1660.[1]

Member, Merchant Taylors' Co. 1630, Hon. Artillery Co. 1635; commr. of array, Northants. 1642; alderman, London July–Aug. 1651, commr. for assessment, Northants. 1657, Jun. 1660, 1661–9; j.p. Northants. July 1660–5, 1670–d., Hunts. 1661–5; sheriff, Northants. Nov. 1660–1; commr. for complaints, Bedford level 1663.[2]

Dudley's ancestors had held land in Clopton astride the Huntingdonshire border since 1395, but had never entered Parliament. As one of six brothers he was expected to carve out a career for himself, and to that end was apprenticed to a London Merchant Taylor in 1623. On his master's death seven years later he took over the business and traded at the sign of the *Black Raven* in St. Paul's Churchyard. Among his customers was Thomas Wentworth[†], the chronically impecunious son of the 1st Earl of Cleveland, who bought 'divers parcels of cloth at hard and dear rates' and found himself dunned before the Privy Council when he failed to pay. Such persistence brought its own reward, and Dudley was already a wealthy man, reckoned in the second class of London citizens, when he succeeded to the family estate. During the Civil War, he was alleged to have escorted the plate sent to the King from the Cambridge colleges, and he was certainly present, with all his tenants, when the commission of array was read at Kettering in 1642. Later he claimed to have acted only under constraint; it was suggested 'that he might have took his horse and rid away, to which he replied not, but hummed'. His youngest brother Gamaliel fought for the King in both wars, and was knighted. Repeated attempts by the informers to have Dudley classified as a delinquent all failed, thanks to mysteriously glowing certificates in his favour from the Northamptonshire and Huntingdonshire committees. His first wife he appears to have obtained by abducting her from the custody of her grand-parents; the Council of State reversed its decision twice, eventually ordering him to return her, but presumably the marriage had already been consummated. He fined for alderman in 1651, and in the following year was elected master of his Company, though he had never taken livery or held any other office, but again he preferred to fine off.[3]

At the Restoration Dudley was created a baronet and pricked sheriff of Northamptonshire, in which capacity he supervised the general election of 1661, and prevented the Presbyterian Richard Knightley[*] from regaining his seat. After his defeat by Sir James Langham[*] in 1662, he seems to have been responsible for purging the Northampton corporation of dissenters and modifying the charter. On petition, Langham's election was declared void, and

Dudley, with the support of the mayor and 'the loyal party', defeated Christopher Hatton[*]. He was unseated a month later without having taken any ascertainable part in the business of the House. Presumably it was the Montagus who procured Dudley's removal from the commission of the peace in 1665. When he was taken seriously ill in 1667 he expressed himself anxious to be reconciled with Lord Montagu, but he was not restored until shortly before his death on 18 Sept. 1670. On the memorial erected by his widow at Clapton he was said to be 73 years of age, probably a mistake for 63. His son Matthew, after contesting Higham Ferrers in 1685, sat for Northampton as a Whig from 1702 to 1705.[4]

[1] *Vis. Northants.* ed. Metcalfe, 86; PCC 187 Twine; *CSP Dom.* 1649–50, p. 475; *St. Clement Eastcheap* (Harl. Soc. Reg. lxvii), 92; Bridges, *Northants.* ii. 372. [2] Information from Col. G. F. H. Archer, clerk of the Merchant Taylors' Co.; *Ancient Vellum Bk. of Hon. Artillery Co.* ed. Raikes, 50. [3] Bridges, 369; *Inhabitants of London* ed. Dale, 65; *CSP Dom.* 1639–40, p. 171; 1649–50, pp. 428, 429, 433, 475; *Misc. Gen. et Her.* (ser. 2), ii. 71; information from Col. Archer; SP19/112/119–20. [4] *Diary of Thomas Isham*, 12–13; Add. 29551, ff. 8, 12, 18; *CSP Dom.* 1663–4, pp. 204, 223, 603; *HMC Buccleuch*, i. 316.

J.P.F.

DUKE, Sir John, 2nd Bt. (1633–1705), of Benhall, Suff.

ORFORD   1679 (Mar.), 1679 (Oct.), 1681, 1689, 4
          May 1697

bap. 3 Jan. 1633, 1st surv. s. of Sir Edward Duke[†], 1st Bt., of Benhall by Ellenor, da. and coh. of John Panton of Westminster. *educ.* Emmanuel, Camb. 1649; travelled abroad 1657. *m.* c.1694, his cos. Elizabeth, da. of Edward Duke, MD, FRCP, 1s. 4da. *suc.* fa. 1671.[1]

Commr. for assessment, Suff. 1661–80, Orford 1679–80, Suff. and Orford 1689–90; j.p. and dep. lt. Suff. 1671–83, 1689–d., commr. for recusants 1675; mayor, Orford 1677–8; alderman, Dunwich June–Oct. 1688.[2]

The Duke family had been settled at Brampton in Suffolk since the time of Edward III, but the manor of Benhall, which became the principal family seat, was not bought until 1610. Duke's father, who represented Orford eight miles away in the Short Parliament, was knighted and made a commissioner of array. He cannot have acted, however, for he was appointed to two parliamentary commissions in 1643–4. His sympathies were probably royalist, for he took no further part in local affairs. He was included in the list drawn up by Roger Whitley[*] in 1658, and created a baronet in 1661.[3]

Returned for Orford to the Exclusion Parliaments, Duke was classed as 'base' by Shaftesbury. In 1679 he was not an active Member, being appointed only to the committees to consider the bill for regulating elections, and to inquire into the shipping of artillery from Portsmouth. He belied Shaftesbury's rating by voting for the exclusion bill; but in the second and third Exclusion Parliaments he was totally inactive. He was removed from the Suffolk commission of the peace in December 1683, and the quo warranto brought against the Orford corporation in March 1684 was intended largely to overthrow Duke's interest. As a result he did not stand in the 1685 election. Although nominated to the Dunwich corporation in June 1688, he probably opposed repeal of the Test Act and Penal Laws, for the King's agents in September reported that they could 'give no good account' of him as a candidate for Aldeburgh. He was returned to the 1689 Convention for Orford in an election held under the old charter, but he was appointed to no committees and made no recorded speeches. According to Ailesbury's list he voted to agree with the Lords that the throne was not vacant. On 28 Feb. he was granted leave to go into the country. He was, however, also listed as supporting the disabling clause in the bill to restore corporations. After 1690 he had only one brief spell in Parliament, although his activity in the county continued. He was buried at Benhall on 24 July 1705. His son, Sir Edward Duke, 3rd Bt., sat for Orford as a Tory in 1721–2.[4]

 [1] Add. 19127, f. 244. [2] Add. 39246, f. 24; *HMC Var.* iv. 269; vii. 104. [3] Copinger, *Suff. Manors*, ii. 27–28; v. 104; vii. 210; *CSP Dom.* 1657–8, p. 553. [4] SP29/437/11; *HMC Var.* vii. 104; Copinger, vii. 192–3, 204–5.

P.W.

DUKE, Richard (1652–1733), of Otterton, Devon.

ASHBURTON   1679 (Oct.), 1695, 1698, 1701 (Feb.)

b. 2 May 1652, 1st s. of Richard Duke of Otterton by Frances, da. of George Southcote of Buckland Tout Saints. *educ.* Colyton sch. 1660; Powderham, Martock, Exeter and Ottery schs.; Exeter, Oxf. 1669–70; I. Temple 1670–1; travelled abroad 1671–2, 1673–5. *m.* (1) 17 May 1673, Isabella, da. of (Sir) Walter Yonge*, 2nd Bt., of Colyton, 2da. *d.v.p.*; (2) 28 Feb. 1705, Elizabeth, da. of John Cholwich of Farringdon, 1s. 1da. *d.v.p. suc.* fa. 1716.[1]

Commr. for assessment, Devon 1679–80, 1689, j.p. 1705–d.[2]

Duke's family owed its fortune to a clerk in the augmentations office who bought Otterton Priory in 1539, and sat for Dartmouth in the Parliament of 1547. Duke's father was in arms for Parliament in the Civil War, but his name appears on the list of proposed knights of the Royal Oak, with an estate of £1,000 p.a.; he was described as 'a busy fanatic . . . a common runner up and down on factious errands', who when the judges of assize lodged at his house, insisted on reading prayers himself in the Presbyterian way. Even by the country party he was regarded as inexcusably indiscreet. It was probably he, rather than Duke, who joined the Green Ribbon Club.[3]

Duke himself, while still a student at the Temple, applied for government employment, but without success. His extended honeymoon in 1673–5 was spent principally at Montpellier. He first stood for Ashburton in February 1679, when he was described by Shaftesbury as 'honest', but he was defeated by William Stawell* and his petition was never heard. He was successful in September, however, and became a moderately active Member of the second Exclusion Parliament. He was named to the committees to consider the proceedings of the judges in Westminster Hall, the regulation of parliamentary elections, and the export of beer, ale and mum, but he did not speak. He was again defeated by Stawell in 1681, but went to Oxford for his petition to be presented. A few months later Duke's father, at the 'commanding persuasion' of Sir William Courtenay*, bought a moiety of the manor and borough of Ashburton from Lewis Watson*, but this was not sufficient to secure his election in 1685.[4]

Duke was reported to have been arrested with his kinsmen Sir Walter Yonge* and Thomas Reynell* and other leading west country Whigs immediately before Monmouth's landing. On his release he embarked on another continental tour, this time to Germany and the Low Countries, where he visited Locke. He returned to England at the end of 1686; but it was probably his father who followed Reynell's lead in answering with a qualified affirmative the lord lieutenant's questions on the repeal of the Test Act and Penal Laws. James II's electoral agents were nevertheless assured that Duke was 'right' on the subject, and approved him as court candidate for Ashburton. He made no move to assist William of Orange in 1688, and probably stood down at the ensuing general election in favour of his brother-in-law Yonge, who had lost his seat at Honiton. When he regained the seat he voted consistently Whig. He was buried at Otterton on 27 Feb. 1733. All his children predeceased him without issue, and he left his estate to a distant cousin. The family became extinct in the male line shortly afterwards without further parliamentary honours.[5]

[1] *Trans. Devon Assoc.* l. 493–4; *Misc. Gen. et Her.* (ser. 4), iii. 31; *Devon and Cornw. N. and Q.* x. 196. [2] *Trans. Devon Assoc.* l. 494, 500. [3] W. G. Hoskins, *Devon*, 448; *Devon and Cornw. N. and Q.* xviii. 316; North, *Lives*, i. 151. [4] *CSP Dom.* 1671, p. 158; *Trans.*

Devon Assoc. xciv. 453; *HMC Portland*, iv. 122. [5]Luttrell, i. 342; M. Cranston, *John Locke*, 257; *Trans. Devon Assoc.* l. 494.

J.P.F.

DUNCH, Hungerford (1639–80), of Down Ampney, Glos. and Little Wittenham, Berks.

CRICKLADE   1660, 1679 (Mar.), 1679 (Oct.)–9 Nov. 1680

bap. 20 Jan. 1639, 1st s. of Edmund Dunch[†] of Little Wittenham by Bridget, da. and h. of Sir Anthony Hungerford of Down Ampney. *educ.* Christ Church, Oxf. 1655. *m.* 30 Apr. 1677, Katherine, da. and h. of William Oxton, Brewer, of Westminster, 1s. *suc.* fa. 1678.[1]

Commr. for militia, Berks. and Oxon. Mar. 1660, assessment, Berks. 1665–*d.*, col. of militia ft. by 1664; j.p. Glos. and Wilts. 1666–*d.*

Dunch was descended from an auditor of the Mint who bought the ex-monastic manor of Little Wittenham in 1552, and sat for Wallingford, five miles away, in 1563. His father, a Parliamentarian in the Civil War, represented the borough in the Long Parliament and Berkshire under the Protectorate before receiving a 'peerage' from his cousin, Oliver Cromwell. From his mother Dunch inherited Down Ampney, two miles from Cricklade. His father withdrew from politics after the collapse of the Commonwealth, and at the general election of 1660 Dunch, who had just come of age, was returned for both Wallingford and Cricklade, choosing to sit for the latter. An inactive Member of the Convention, he was appointed only to the committee to bring in the bill for the abolition of the court of wards. Although he was nominated to the proposed order of the Royal Oak, with an income of £2,000 p.a., his background probably prevented him from standing in 1661, but he regained his seat at the dissolution of the Cavalier Parliament. He was marked 'honest' on Shaftesbury's list and appointed to the committee of elections and privileges in the first Exclusion Parliament, but he was absent from the division on the bill. He was re-elected in August, but probably never took his seat. He died on 9 Nov. 1680, and was buried at Little Wittenham 'without pomp or vain expense, but with a bountiful largesse to the poor'. A distribution of £200 in Cricklade ensured the survival of the family interest, and his son was returned for the borough as a Whig in 1701.[2]

[1]Westminster City Lib. St. Martin in the Fields par. reg.; *Vis. Berks.* (Harl. Soc. lvi), 197; *London Mar. Lic.* ed. Foster, 426; PCC 59 Laud; *Wood's Life and Times* (Oxf. Hist. Soc. xxi), 105, 500. [2]*VCH Berks.* iv. 382; Keeler, *Long Parl.* 161–2; PCC 144 Bath.

M.W.H./L.N.

DUNCOMBE, Charles (1648–1711), of Lombard Street, London and Teddington, Mdx.

HEDON	1685
YARMOUTH I.o.W.	1690
DOWNTON	1695–1 Feb. 1698
IPSWICH	1701 (Feb.)
DOWNTON	1702, 1705, 1708, 1710–9 Apr. 1711

bap. 16 Nov. 1648, 2nd s. of Alexander Duncombe of Drayton Beauchamp, Bucks. by Mary, da. of Richard Pawley of Whitchurch, Bucks.; bro. of Anthony Duncombe[†]. *unm.* Kntd. 20 Oct. 1699.[1]

Member, Goldsmiths' Co. 1672, liveryman 1674, prime warden 1684–5, master 1685–6; member, R. Fishery Co. 1677; freeman, E.I. Co. 1677, Portsmouth 1684; member, Hon. Artillery Co. 1682, treas. 1703–4; alderman, London 1683–6, 1700–*d.*, sheriff 1699–1700, ld. mayor 1708–9; dep. lt. London 1685–7, Oct. 1688–9, Mdx. 1692–?*d.*, Wilts. 1701–?*d.*, commr. for assessment, London and Mdx. 1690; j.p. Wilts. and Yorks. (N. and W. Ridings) by 1701–?*d.*; col. green regt. of militia, London 1702–7; commr. for Greenwich hospital 1704.[2]

Cashier of excise 1680–97, hearth-tax 1684–Nov. 1688; commr. for the Mint 1680–6; six clerk in Chancery 1682–3; commr. for tin coinage 1684–7.[3]

Duncombe, who came from one of the more obscure branches of the family, was apprenticed to Edward Backwell[*] in 1665. According to the 1st Earl of Dartmouth, a timely warning from Lord Shaftesbury in 1672 enabled him to draw out 'a very great sum of his own in the Exchequer, besides thirty thousand pounds of the Marquess of Winchester' [Charles Powlett I[*]] before the Government suspended payment. But Backwell was ruined, and Duncombe took over his premises in Lombard Street at the sign of the Grasshopper, forming with Richard Kent[*], cashier of the excise, from 1674 to 1676, 'perhaps the dominant partnership in the money-market of the time'. Under Danby they founded 'a new type of credit agency, directly fed by the springs of the revenue'. Duncombe and his friend Henry Guy[*] attached themselves to Sunderland, who doubtless assisted in his appointment as cashier of the excise in 1680 at an annual salary of £600 p.a., increased to £1,150 in 1683, over and above what he could make by rigging the market in Exchequer tallies.[4]

Roger North[*] describes 'a slight entertainment' which he and his brothers gave to Duncombe and Guy some time after Sunderland's dismissal for favouring exclusion:

> We thought these had been our good friends as they had furiously professed; but, in truth, being creatures of my Lord Sunderland, who was then entering again at the back door of the Court, they came only to spy how his lordship (their grandee) was resented among us. So without any provocation, they fell to swearing what a

divine man he was . . . and this so long that Sir Dudley North, to take them down a little, asked, but very inadvertently, how he came to be turned out of the Court before. At this they were hush. They had what they came for and said not a word more. But, from that time, Lord Sunderland declared open war against the Lord Keeper [Sir Francis] North* and all his dependants.

During the inquiry into the Rye House Plot, it was alleged that in order to 'keep in with both sides', he had passed information to the plotters. This was evidently disregarded, since in September 1683 he was appointed one of the aldermen of London by royal commission. At this time he was reported as saying of the Government's action on the Rye House Plot that 'he could not see why people should make so much fuss in the matter, for the Court only wanted to hang some nine or ten persons who were obnoxious to them'. The following year he was appointed cashier of the hearth-tax with a salary of £400 p.a. in return for a £50,000 loan to the King at five per cent interest, rather than the usual six per cent.[5]

At the general election of 1685 Duncombe was returned for Hedon as a court supporter with his partner Guy, who had represented the borough since 1670. An active Member of James II's Parliament, he was appointed to 14 committees, including the committee of elections and privileges. He was added to the committees to take the disbandment accounts and to recommend expunctions from the Journals, and helped to estimate the yield of a tax on new buildings. He acted as teller for a bill to continue the levy on coal for the benefit of London widows and orphans, which was rejected, and was named to the committees for the bill for their relief and for the general naturalization of Protestant refugees. He was instrumental in persuading Lord Treasurer Rochester (Laurence Hyde*) to support the extension of the Coinage Acts, which had brought the goldsmiths much profit, despite North's opposition. After the recess he was added to the committee for the reform of the bankruptcy laws, to which was referred a petition from the creditors of two London goldsmiths.[6]

Duncombe eagerly anticipated Rochester's dismissal, thereby confirming Lord Clarendon (Henry Hyde*) in a low opinion of his 'integrity and morality', and was rewarded by Sunderland with a pardon 'for extortion and usurious contracts'. He was confident that the government would secure an ample majority in the abortive elections of 1688, and the King's agents reported that his own seat at Hedon was safe. By October, however, he was becoming anxious about the security for his loans. He was replaced as cashier of the hearth-tax in November, and refused James an advance of £1,500 to facilitate his flight, for which he was subse-

quently excluded from pardon. He served on the deputation from the City sent to invite William of Orange to enter London, and lent him £20,000. He was defeated at the general election of 1689, but returned to the House as Member for Yarmouth in 1690. A court supporter, he signed the Association in 1696. In 1698 he was expelled from the House for falsely endorsing Exchequer bills. A Tory under Queen Anne, he died on 9 Apr. 1711 and was buried at Downton. Probably the wealthiest commoner in England, he was reported to be worth £400,000, of which half went to the 2nd Duke of Argyll, who had married his niece. His nephew Anthony, who succeeded to the Wiltshire property, sat for Salisbury from 1721 to 1734 and then for Downton until raised to the peerage in 1747. His nephew Thomas Browne, who assumed the name of Duncombe, inherited the Yorkshire estate, and, after sitting for Downton as a stop-gap, was elected for Ripon in 1734.[7]

[1] Foster, *Yorks. Peds.* ii; PCC 49 Aylett. [2] J. R. Woodhead, *Rulers of London*, 63; *Cal. Ct. Mins. E.I. Co.* ed. Sainsbury, xi. 56; *Sel. Charters* (Selden Soc. xxviii), 198; R. East, *Portsmouth Recs.* 367; *Ancient Vellum Bk.* ed. Raikes, 112; G. A. Raikes, *Hist. Hon. Artillery Co.* ii. 477; Luttrell, v. 193; vi. 186. [3] *Cal. Treas. Bks.* vi. 449; vii. 1347; viii. 117, 1622, 2125; xii. 5; T. D. Hardy, *Cat. of Chancery*, 111. [4] Woodhead, 63; Burnet, i. 550; J. B. Martin, *The Grasshopper*, 28-31; C. D. Chandaman, *Eng. Pub. Revenue*, 247; *Cal. Treas. Bks.* v. 555; vi. 612; vii. 984; Dalrymple, *Mems.* i, pt. 2, p. 146. [5] North, *Lives*, ii. 195; *CSP Dom.* July-Sept. 1683, p. 57; 1683-4, p. 16; A. F. W. Papillon, *Papillon Mems.* 235; *Cal. Treas. Bks.* vii. 1347; Kenyon, *Sunderland*, 81. [6] *CJ*, ix. 748; North, ii. 213. [7] *Clarendon Corresp.* ii. 66; *HMC Lords*, ii. 307; Luttrell, i. 471; Clarke, *Jas. II*, ii. 486; *Cal. Treas. Bks.* viii. 2093, 2099, 2100, 2140, 2150; Macaulay, *Hist.* 2759; Hoare, *Wilts. Downton*, 39.

P.W.

DUNCOMBE, Sir John (1622–87), of Battlesden, Beds. and Pall Mall, Westminster.

BURY ST. EDMUNDS 14 May 1660, 1661

bap. 20 July 1622, 2nd but 1st surv. s. of William Duncombe of Battlesden by Elizabeth, da. of Sir John Poyntz of South Ockendon, Essex. *educ.* Eton c.1634–8; Christ's, Camb. 1638; travelled abroad 1641–?46; Leyden 1643. *m.* 12 July 1646, Elizabeth, da. of Sir Humphrey May† of Carrow Priory, Norf., chancellor of the duchy of Lancaster 1618–30, 1s. 6 other ch. *Kntd.* 1648; *suc.* fa. 1655.[1]

Commr. for militia, Beds. Mar. 1660, oyer and terminer, Norfolk circuit July 1660; j.p. Beds. July 1660–?83, dep. lt. c. Aug. 1660–80; commr. for assessment, Beds. Aug. 1660–80, Suff. 1661–80, Bury St. Edmunds 1661–9, 1677–80, Bucks. 1673–4, complaints, Bedford level 1663, wastes and spoils, Beds. 1669.[2]

Commr. of the Ordnance 1664–70; ld. of treasury 1667–72; PC 22 May 1667–21 Apr. 1679; commr. for prize appeals 1672–4; chancellor of Exchequer 1672–6.[3]

Duncombe's great-grandfather acquired Battlesden and two other Bedfordshire manors in the Russell sphere of influence about the middle of the

16th century, and his grandfather was twice returned for Tavistock under James I. Although his father was posthumously described as 'of perfect loyalty to his Majesty of blessed memory', he was a parliamentary supporter in the Civil War, serving on the county committee from 1643–48. It was later asserted that Duncombe used to carry his father's papers to the committee as 'a kind of attorney', but in fact he was on his travels, and when he returned to England he married into a strongly royalist family. He was dubbed at Carisbrooke by Charles I, who snatched a sword from one of his startled guards and told him that 'it was to perform a promise to his relations'. At the Restoration he was proposed for the order of the Royal Oak with an income of £1,000 p.a., but the Earl of Cleveland thought his estate was worth double and recommended him for the lieutenancy, adding that 'by reason the late troubles' he had 'lived out of the county of Bedford', but was now returned.[4]

Duncombe's wife had been living at Bury St. Edmunds during the Interregnum, and her sister married (Sir) Thomas Hervey*. It was probably on this interest that Duncombe contested the borough at the general election of 1660. After a double return he and Sir Henry Crofts* were seated on the merits of the election. No doubt he was a court supporter, since his brother-in-law, Baptist May*, stood high in the King's favour; but he was not active in the Convention. His only committee was for the recovery of the queen mother's jointure, but he twice acted as teller. He opposed the motion of 1 June to limit to 20 the number of those to be excepted from indemnity, and that of 20 Dec. to permit taverns to be licensed for the sale of wine.[5]

Duncombe was re-elected in 1661 with Crofts's son-in-law, Sir Edmund Poley*. A very active Member of the Cavalier Parliament, he was appointed to 226 committees, acted as teller in 22 divisions, and made over 120 recorded speeches. One of the tellers for the committal of the corporations bill on 20 June, he was the first Member named to the committee. He was again a teller in the third reading debate in favour of the proviso that the commissioners should not be members of the corporations which they were to regulate, or have stood for the borough in question at the previous election. He served on the committee for the bill of pains and penalties, and helped to manage a conference on 27 July. After the recess he was sent to the Lords to desire a conference on the corporations bill, which he again helped to manage. He was also appointed to the committee for the execution of those under attainder, but he was even more prominent in measures of less overtly political

import. On 6 Feb. 1662 he was teller against an amendment to the bill for settling the poor in their parishes. His only chairmanship was on the estate bill promoted by his brother-in-law, Thomas Knollys*, which he carried up on 21 Feb. He was not long in attaching himself to the faction forming round Crofts's nephew, Sir Henry Bennet*, and attacking the financial policy of the Clarendon administration. On 8 Mar. he took the bold step for a private Member of introducing a bill for returning the receipt of the revenue to the old course of the Exchequer. A second reading was ordered, but never reached. On 24 Apr. he was given leave to bring in a bill to authorize the levying of tolls for the repair of Watling Street between Dunstable and Hockliffe, 'the most dismal piece of ground for travelling that ever was in England', and immediately adjoining his own estate. Before the first session ended he had also taken a conspicuous part in the progress of the bills for settling the militia, relieving sheriffs, confirming ministers in their livings, and cleaning the streets in the capital. He helped to prepare reasons for two conferences on these measures, and three times acted as a manager.[6]

Duncombe was appointed to the principal committees of the 1663 session. His Watling Street bill received its first reading on 23 Feb. and he was the first to be named to the committee, which, however, failed to report. He was also among those appointed to bring in a bill to prevent the growth of Popery and to consider the petition from the loyal and indigent officers. He was sent to the Lords to desire a conference about the expulsion of Jesuits and Popish priests, and to the King to thank him for issuing a proclamation for this purpose. He was also among those ordered to devise remedies for the meetings of sectaries, to consider the bill to prevent abuses in the sale of offices and honours, and to inquire into the conduct of Sir Richard Temple*. He returned to the Lords on 13 July to remind them of the bills against Popery and nonconformity, and helped to manage a conference on a bill to provide relief from the Act of Uniformity. He was appointed to the committees to draft the conventicles bill in 1664 and to consider the five mile bill in the following year. Meanwhile his official career had begun with a seat on the ordnance commission formed after the death of Sir William Compton*. Pepys found him 'a very proper man for business, being very resolute and proud and industrious', and he was clearly the driving force behind the reforms which followed. Andrew Marvell* described him as chief of the 'projectors', and the House rejected by a narrow majority his bill to nationalize the gunpowder trade in times of war. But he was not solely concerned with departmental matters, and acted as teller during the second Dutch war for going into committee of supply and imposing double taxation on dissenters.[7]

The ordnance commission had been so successful that on the death of Lord Treasurer Southampton the King determined to put the Treasury also into commission, and nominated Duncombe to the board. There was jealousy at Court of his rapid rise, and after complaints that the Medway forts had been unable to protect Chatham from the Dutch owing to shortage of gunpowder, Marvell wrote:

> All men admired he to that pitch could fly;
> Powder ne'er blew man up so soon so high,
> But sure his late good husbandry in petre
> Show'd him to manage the Exchequer meeter;
> And who the forts would not vouchsafe a corn,
> To lavish the King's money more would scorn. . . .
> But the true cause was that, in 's brother May,
> Th' Exchequer might the privy purse obey.

On his first visit to the new commission Pepys observed with amusement that 'Duncombe looks so big, and takes as much state on him as if he had been born a lord', lolling at the table with his feet up. He took no part in the attack on Clarendon in the autumn of 1667, though he was appointed to the committees to inquire into restraints on juries and to consider the public accounts bill. As spokesman for the Ordnance, he blamed the negligence of the workmen employed to fortify Sheerness. 'Being reproved for it by Sir Edward Spragge'*, he told the House, 'they fell into a mutiny for want of pay.' He defended the board 'with great imperiousness and earnestness', but Pepys thought that 'the House is resolved to be better satisfied in the business of the unreadiness of Sheerness, and want of arms and ammunition there and everywhere'. Later he declared that there had been everything necessary for the fortifications but time. On 5 Mar. 1668 he attended the King with a resolution from the House demanding the enforcement of the laws against unlawful assemblies of Papists and nonconformists, and in the following month he was appointed to the committee for the continuation of the Conventicles Act. He spoke regularly on finance, declaring on 1 May that the proposal to appropriate the additional customs duties to the fleet would so 'disorder the course of the Exchequer, that no man will know what to do, nor with what safety to act in the greatest emergencies'. He defended Carteret's method of repaying loans on the Privy Seal in three instalments as helping to maintain the Government's credit. He formed a close alliance at the Treasury with the Hon. William Coventry*, and his old patron Bennet (now Lord Arlington) convinced himself 'that these two were his enemies, and

designed his ruin'; but the breach was only temporary. The Duke of Buckingham was also hostile, and in a scene in *The Country Gentleman* (a play written jointly with Sir Robert Howard*) ridiculed him as Coventry's ape, under the name of 'Sir Gravity Empty'. The outcome was to drive Coventry out of office, but Duncombe did not follow him, as was expected. On 28 Mar. 1670 he objected to a clause that nothing in the conventicles bill should affect the royal supremacy in ecclesiastical affairs, on the ground that 'if the King has power of dispensation, he has it without this proviso'. On 20 Dec. he announced that in accordance with the desires of the House the King had reduced the duty on wine. As a government spokesman, he naturally opposed the deferment of supply until the bill to punish the assailants of Sir John Coventry* had passed. He was among those ordered to prepare reasons for a conference on the additional excise (6 Mar. 1671) and to consider the bill for the sale of fee-farm rents. During a further debate on conventicles he declared that he was

> sorry such a stubborn people should be thus countenanced. Did not the City tremble under the menace of these people? And these are the people we must indulge. If you once come to weaken the hands of the deputy lieutenants, the Government will be in danger. Nothing but numbers will content this people; they began the troubles and will do so again. [He] expects nothing from them but misery and ruin; no age nor government that ever trusted them was secure.

Duncombe's name of course appeared on both lists of the court party during these sessions, while an opposition writer described him as one of the managers of the duty on legal proceedings and May's brother-in-law, 'and if that be not enough, Old Nick reward him'.[8]

The Stop of the Exchequer occurred during the ensuing recess, but Lord Shaftesbury (Sir Anthony Ashley Cooper*) later exonerated both himself and Duncombe, his successor as chancellor, from responsibility, all of which he laid at the door of Thomas Clifford*, the lord treasurer. When Parliament reassembled, Duncombe conducted the new Speaker, (Sir) Job Charlton*, to the chair, and on 5 Feb. 1673 he opposed the suspension of all Members elected on Shaftesbury's writs during the recess. The Declaration of Indulgence can hardly have commanded his genuine approval, but, rather as an upholder of the prerogative than an advocate of toleration, he tried to persuade the House that there would be 'no peace now without it'. With more sincerity he spoke against the bill for the ease of Protestant dissenters, since no question of the prerogative was involved, saying that this may sway the very government so as to over-balance it. [He] will never think it fit that those men should have 'ease'.... Their principles are not consistent with honest people; let them not set up a government by themselves, for the Presbyterians will ever be for a Commonwealth.

If a bill were passed he suggested it should be operated for a trial period of a year. On 22 Feb. during a debate on a motion to desire a speedy answer from the King to their address on the suspension of the Penal Laws, he said

Will you precipitate an answer from the King?... Why so hasty? No man in common conversation is pressed at this rate.

When the King's reply was received he spoke in favour of an address of thanks, saying

Could the King say a more kind thing than his message?... How could the King keep all things quiet but by suspending the laws?

He was appointed to the committee to draw up an address on the suspending power. On 3 Mar. he opposed an address to the King to prevent the growth of Popery by making all officials and all army and navy officers take the sacrament because he did not 'like to expose holy things in this manner', and because men pressed for the navy would 'refuse it at sea to avoid the service'. While anxious for the comprehension of all Protestants in the Church, he would give no encouragement to dissent, and supported the exclusion of dissenters from the Commons. When the committee to prevent the growth of Popery, on which he served, produced a test to exclude Roman Catholics from office, he expressed the fear that 'some will let religion and all go, if preferment lies in the way'.[9]

The forced resignation of Clifford under the Test Act and his replacement by Danby eventually undermined Duncombe's position, though he continued as a government spokesman in the autumn session of 1673, and was named on the Paston list. He supported a vote of thanks for the King's speech and defended the Modena marriage. In the debates on the remaining ministers of the Cabal in the New Year, he thought it was hard to condemn Lauderdale unheard and expressed great compassion for Buckingham's misfortunes. But in defence of Arlington he was more eloquent:

Possibly, when you come to examine things, this gentleman will appear of great temper and worth. He had no concealments in his discourse here. Has, in his conversations with him, always heard him speak well of this House.... Must Arlington wash himself in the Thames, night and morning, from suspicions of Popery?... For the 'French war'... knows that the difference betwixt Buckingham and Arlington was pretty high about it. The shaking of the Triple Alliance is laid to his charge. Lord Clifford said 'Arlington did

defend himself in it to the last extremity, and that he was an honest man to his King and country'. Arlington did as great service to the nation as possible by it. Speaks this to show how dark things are in common fame; therefore would have things made clear.... Proceed by impeachment, and he shall be as ready to give his vote as any man.

On 23 Jan. 1674 he supported Coventry's demand for building restrictions, to prevent the construction of too many tenement houses:

At this end of the town whole fields go into buildings, and are turned into alehouses filled with necessitous people.

Six days later he informed the House that it was often necessary for the Treasury to take a man into custody 'for fear of losing the King's money', and to send such a person overseas was better than keeping him in an English prison, where he might be ruined by bad company. Nevertheless he was appointed to the committees for the extension of habeas corpus, the prevention of illegal exactions, and the inquiry into the condition of Ireland. He asserted that there were no complaints about the present judges, and denied that giving them patents to hold office during good behaviour rather than at the royal pleasure would be effective.[10]

Shortly before the next session Danby appointed Richard Kent* as cashier of excise, and authorized him by patent not only to make disbursements on the direct order of the lord treasurer but to provide advances on the credit of the running cash. Duncombe, horrified at this breach of the traditional Exchequer procedure, petitioned the King, while the Opposition, suspecting that the improvement in government credit would facilitate corruption of Members, made it the main charge in the attempt to impeach Danby. As the chief witness, Duncombe said that he would have prevented the sealing of the patent if he had not been ill at the time, but refused to be drawn on the question of its legality. But he could not resist telling the House that 'the order of the Exchequer, if known, would be found to be the greatest beauty and economy in the world'. In the dispute over the jurisdiction of the House of Lords, he urged the Commons not to 'let the Government be torn in pieces by these unfortunate differences'. 'You have been a happy Parliament', he told them and he hoped they would continue so. He was again listed among the officials in the House in the autumn session. Urging a further supply in the autumn session, he suggested that a refusal might 'put extremities to work'. William Sacheverell* demanded the meaning of this portentous phrase, which Duncombe somewhat lamely explained as 'making the crown, and them that depend upon it, uneasy'. He had clearly lost the ear of the House, and when he proffered a statement of revenue and expenditure he was refused a hearing. As an ardent churchman, his contribution to the debate of 25 Oct. on the state of the nation was remarkable:

> Many places are so unprovided that the parson must work for his living, and at this rate the Church will fall of itself. Ill use is made even of the power of the Church; it does the Church no good. Not for the ends intended by the ecclesiastical courts; speaks not to oppose them, nor to lessen the authority of the Church.

He spoke frequently in support of the naval construction programme, though unable to withhold the comment that 'the excise is so anticipated that the King has no profits of it'.[11]

During the recess Danby arranged for a proclamation suppressing all public coffee-houses, which the Opposition used as meeting-places. On 7 Jan. 1676 a petition from the coffee sellers, asking to be allowed time to get rid of their existing stocks, was presented to the Privy Council by Duncombe, which 'looks like an opposition to the treasurer'. Aided by the Duke of York, Danby succeeded in securing Duncombe's removal. On 25 Apr. Christopher Hatton* wrote

> Last Friday night the King told Sir John Duncombe that he must resign his place. He desired to know for what crime. The King told him that he did believe him to be a very honest gentleman, but that he did obstruct his affairs by interfering with the treasurer, and that he would not have his treasurer be uneasy.

Shaftesbury hopefully marked Duncombe and his son as 'worthy', but altered the rating to 'vile', perhaps because of the pension of £2,000 p.a. which had been granted as compensation. There is no evidence that he attended the House again, and in November 1678 his pension was cancelled, no doubt at the instigation of Danby, who at the end of that year included Duncombe's name in a list of his enemies.[12]

Duncombe did not stand in 1679, and was dropped from the Privy Council. In May 1680 there was a rumour that he would be restored to the chancellorship of the Exchequer, but it proved to be unfounded. He contested Eye in 1681 on the Cornwallis interest in partnership with George Walsh*, but their petition was not heard before the dissolution of the Oxford Parliament. He died at Battlesden on 4 Mar. 1687. Burnet described him as

> a judicious man but very haughty, and apt to raise enemies against himself. He was an able Parliament man, but could not go into all the designs of the Court; for he had a sense of religion, and a zeal for the liberty of his country.[13]

[1] *Beds. N. and Q.* ii. 48; *PC Reg.* xii. 195; Westminster City Lib. St. Martin in the Fields par. reg.; *Beds. Par. Reg.* xxxvii (Battlesden), 12. [2] *Cal. Treas. Bks.* iii. 193. [3] *CSP Dom.* 1664–5, p. 41; 1667, p. 115; 1670, p. 224; 1671–2, p. 419; 1672–3, p. 171;

1676–7, p. 91; T. D. Hardy, *Principal Officers of Chancery,* 111. [4] *Beds. N. and Q.* ii. 40; Wood, *Athenae Oxon.* iv. 12; *Pepys Diary,* 31 May 1667; SP29/8/178. [5] *Bristol Letter Bks.* (Suff. Green Bks. i), 15; *CJ,* viii. 59, 224. [6] *CJ,* viii. 291, 314, 315, 331, 368, 382, 402, 433, 434; Burnet, i. 478; Defoe, *Tour,* ii. 524. [7] *CJ,* viii. 459, 466, 533, 669, 672; *Trans. R. Hist. Soc.* (ser. 5), xxv. 58–59; *Pepys Diary,* 24 Apr. 1667; *Marvell* ed. Margoliouth, i. 146. [8] *Pepys Diary,* 31 May, 3, 4 June, 22 Oct. 1667, 29 Jan. 1668; 6, 10 Mar. 1669; *Marvell,* i. 160; *Milward,* 93, 188; *Bulstrode,* 28; Grey, i. 148, 172, 246, 418; Carte, *Ormond,* iv. 353; *Dering,* 45; Harl. 7020, f. 39v. [9] K. H. D. Haley, *Shaftesbury,* 296; *CJ,* ix. 245; *Dering,* 106, 132, 142; Grey, ii. 31, 41, 49, 58, 80, 90, 93, 99, 117. [10] Grey, ii. 183, 193–4, 240–1, 266, 306–7, 337, 366, 416–17; *CJ,* ix. 300. [11] C. D. Chandaman, *English Public Revenue,* 64–65; Grey, iii. 57–58, 64, 66, 255, 264, 304, 309, 317, 321, 347–8, 396; *CJ,* ix. 361. [12] Browning, *Danby,* i. 194; Add. 29555, f. 192; *Hatton Corresp.* (Cam. Soc. n.s. xxii), 122; *Cal. Treas. Bks.* v. 217, 1163. [13] BL M636/32, Lady Gawdy to Sir Ralph Verney, 6 Feb. 1679; *HMC Finch,* ii. 78; *Beds. N. and Q.* ii. 49; Burnet, i. 478.

P.W.

DUNCOMBE, William (c.1647–1704), of Battlesden, Beds.

BURY ST. EDMUNDS   10 Feb. 1673
BEDFORDSHIRE   1689, 1695

b. c.1647, 1st s. of Sir John Duncombe*. *educ.* travelled abroad 1666. *m.* settlement 30 May 1672, Jane (*bur.* 17 Feb. 1701), da. of Sir Frederick Cornwallis*, 1st Baron Cornwallis, 2s. (1 *d.v.p.*) 3da. *suc.* fa. 1687.[1]

Commr. for assessment, Beds., Suff. and Bury St. Edmunds 1673–80, Beds. 1689–90, recusants, Suff. 1675; j.p. Beds. 1680–bef. 1683, Feb. 1688–*d.*; freeman, Eye by 1681; dep. lt. Beds. Feb. 1688–*d.*

Envoy to Sweden 1689–92; one of the lds. justices [I] 1693–5; comptroller of army accounts 1703–*d.*[3]

Duncombe joined his father as MP for Bury St. Edmunds after a by-election in 1673. Inactive in the Cavalier Parliament, he made no recorded speeches and was appointed to only four committees. He was named with his father on the Paston list and the list of King's servants in the House, but Sir Richard Wiseman* doubted his reliability. In the working lists he was noted among those to be 'fixed', but he is not known to have received any personal gratification. After Danby had ousted his father from the Exchequer in 1676, Shaftesbury marked him 'worthy', but later changed his classification to 'vile', perhaps on learning of his father's pension. In April 1677, he acted as teller against a proviso to the bill to prevent abuses in the import of Irish cattle, and in 1678 he was appointed to the committee to translate Coleman's letters.

Duncombe is not known to have stood during the exclusion crisis, but his removal from the commission of the peace suggests Whiggish sympathies, and in the Bedfordshire election of 1685 he gave one of his votes to the Hon. Edward Russell*. He may have been a Whig collaborator, for he was appointed a deputy lieutenant in February 1688. Returned for Bedfordshire in 1689 he was inactive in the Convention, making no recorded speeches and serving only on the committees for the new oaths of supremacy and allegiance, and for the relief of Huguenot refugees. In April he was appointed envoy to Sweden and had arrived in Stockholm by 16 July. He was listed as a supporter of the disabling clause in the bill to restore corporations, but his despatches prove that he was still *en poste* during the debates of January 1690. Though something of a 'trimmer', he signed the Association in 1696. Duncombe died of smallpox on 13 Apr. 1704 and was buried at Battlesden, the last of his family to sit in Parliament. The estate was sold in 1706.[4]

[1] *Beds. N. and Q.* ii. 46; *CSP Dom.* 1665–6, p. 540; F. A. Blaydes, *Gen. Bed.* 344; *Beds. Par. Regs.* xxxvii (Battlesden), 2, 12, 13; Prob. 6/82/245. [2] E. Suff. RO, EE2/D4/2. [3] *Cal. Treas. Bks.* ix. 98; x. 122; xviii. 41; *CSP Dom.* 1693, pp. 134, 175; 1694–5, p. 471. [4] Beds. RO, CH 15/1; SP 95/13/4, 81; 104/153/210; Luttrell, v. 413; *Beds. Par. Regs.* xxxvii. 13; *VCH Beds.* iii. 343.

L.N./G.J.

DUNGARVAN, Visct. [I] *see* BOYLE, Charles, Lord Clifford

DUNMORE, 1st Earl of [S] *see* MURRAY, Lord Charles

DUNSTER, Henry (1618–84), of Mincing Lane, London and Jenningsbury, Hertford.

ILCHESTER 1660, 1661

> *bap.* 6 Sept. 1618, s. of Giles Dunster, yeoman, of Seavington St. Michael, Som. *m.* c. May 1655, Mary (*d.* 10 Oct. 1718), da. of Henry Gardiner of Jenningsbury, and h. to her bro. Edward, 6s. 2da.[1]
> Freeman, Grocers' Co. 1644, warden 1668–9, master 1669–70; 'burgess', Ilchester by Apr. 1660–?74; commr. for assessment, London Aug. 1660–80, Som. 1664–9, Herts. 1664–80, recusants, Som. 1675.[2]

Dunster came from a South Somerset yeoman family, several of whom became merchants in London in the 17th century. He was apprenticed to a London Grocer in 1636, and appears to have taken no part in the Civil War. 'He increased the family fortune by his laudable industry', but little is known of his trading ventures except for the despatch of two consignments of arms to the Barbary corsairs under the Commonwealth. His business was adversely affected by the Cromwellian war with Spain, and he may have become less active after marrying a Hertfordshire heiress, though he retained a London address, and is said to have fined for alderman, but this cannot be confirmed.[3]

Dunster held 52 acres in Ilchester by 1652 and was elected to the corporation. He was returned for the borough at the general election of 1660 as a supporter of the Restoration, probably unopposed; but he took no ascertainable part in 'that Parliament which recalled the King together with the monarchy', as his epitaph expressed it. Re-elected in 1661, when he signed his own indenture, he survived a petition from Robert Hunt*, but never became an active Member of the Cavalier Parliament. He was named to only 18 committees, including the committee of elections and privileges in six sessions. In the opening session he was among those ordered to consider bills for regulating common fields, and preventing abuses in weighing and packing butter, and to inspect the disbandment accounts. His brother Giles became a commissioner for public accounts after the second Dutch war, later serving as surveyor-general of customs; but there is no sign that Dunster's own career was affected, and indeed he may have moved into opposition. He was appointed to the committees to recommend increases in customs rates (29 Feb. 1668), and in 1670 to those to consider the additional bill for the rebuilding of London and a bill to prevent illegal imprisonment. He was absent from a call of the House in 1671, but his excuses were accepted, and later in the session he was named to the committee to prevent the export of wool. His name appears on no lists of the court party, and Shaftesbury marked him 'worthy' in 1677. His last committee (3 June 1678) was on a bill to provide for the son of a London alderman and excise farmer.[4]

Dunster sold his property in Ilchester in 1674 and never stood for the borough again. But he came forward as court candidate for Hertford at the second general election of 1679. After his defeat by Sir Thomas Byde*, though only by a handful of votes,

> he retired into private life, where he conducted himself with devout piety towards his God, severe justice towards his neighbours, singular fidelity in his promises, wonderful foresight and sagacity in business transactions, beneficence towards the poor, and goodness and benevolence towards all.

'Well deserving of his King, his church, and his country', he died of an epidemic fever on 29 July 1684, aged 66. He was buried at All Saints, Hertford, the only member of the family to sit.[5]

[1] Som. RO, Seavington St. Michael par. reg.; Guildhall Lib. mss 11593/1/62; Clutterbuck, *Herts.* ii. 183. [2] Guildhall Lib. mss 11593/1/136; W. W. Grantham, *Wardens of the Grocers*, 30. [3] PCC 167 Clarke, 150 Coventry, 3 Bath, 139 Hare; Clutterbuck, ii. 159; *CSP Dom.* 1651, p. 523; 1651–2, p. 552; Add. 34015, p. 128. [4] E317/Som. 24; *CJ*, viii. 358; ix. 36; Clutterbuck, ii. 159. [5] H. R. Moulton, *Cat.* 234; Clutterbuck, ii. 159–60.

M.W.H./J.P.F.

DUTTON, Sir Ralph, 1st Bt. (c.1645–1721), of Sherborne, Glos.

GLOUCESTERSHIRE 1679 (Mar.), 1679 (Oct.), 1681, 1689, 1690, 1695

b. c.1645, 2nd s. of Sir Ralph Dutton of Standish by Mary, da. and coh. of William Duncombe, Haberdasher, of London. *m.* (1) settlement 13 Aug. 1674, Grizel (*d.*1678), da. of Sir Edward Poole* of Kemble, Wilts., 1da.; (2) 14 Jan. 1679 (with £10,000), Mary, da. and h. of Peter Barwick of Westminster, physician to King Charles II, 4s. (3 *d.v.p.*) 4da. *suc.* bro. 1675; *cr.* Bt. 22 June 1678.[1]

Commr. for assessment, Glos. 1677–80, 1689–90, j.p. and dep. lt. 1689–?1710, col. of militia ft. by 1697–?1710.[2]

Dutton's great-grandfather, a younger son of a Cheshire family, bought the former monastic estate of Sherborne in 1551. Although the family enjoyed a reputation for opulence, Dutton's uncle was the first to enter Parliament, representing the county until disabled for royalism in 1644. Dutton's father was also a Royalist; as commissioner of array, he raised a regiment for the King in 1642, and went into exile in 1646, but is said to have died on the voyage.[3]

Dutton himself was notable chiefly as an enthusiastic follower of greyhound coursing, to the serious embarrassment of his estate. He was returned for the county to the Exclusion Parliaments, and marked 'honest' by Shaftesbury. He was appointed to three committees in 1679, of which the most important was for the better regulation of elections, and voted for the bill. He was re-elected, though not without opposition, in August, and again named to three committees in the second Exclusion Parliament, including that for repealing part of the Severn Fishing Act. At the general election of 1681 he was accused of a change of heart over exclusion, and in the Oxford Parliament he was named only to the committee of elections and privileges. He remained an exclusionist after the dissolution, entertaining the Duke of Monmouth at his home in November.[4]

Although Dutton was not actively opposed to James II he was compelled to pay £1,100 for his baronetcy, and it was reported that the title to his property was to be queried. With Henry Bertie* he helped to rescue John Lovelace* in December 1688, and was elected to the Convention in the following month. An active Member, he was named to 37 committees and acted as teller in four divisions. He was appointed to the committees to inquire into the authors and advisers of grievances and to draw up the address promising assistance for a war with France. On 30 Apr. 1689 he gave information to the House of a case of treasonable

words, and was thanked for causing the culprit to be arrested. He was appointed to the committee on the bill for restoring corporations. His only recorded speech was on the indemnity bill on 4 June, when he proposed ironically: 'It seems, by the silence of the House, nobody is in fault; therefore, pray let us go home'. On 12 June he was among those instructed to inspect the Journals of both Houses regarding the Popish Plot. He acted as teller for the adjournment of the debate on the Wye and Lugg navigation on 4 July, against going into committee on supply on 30 July, and on 20 Aug. against an amendment concerning the adulteration of wine to the bill prohibiting trade with France. In the second session, he served on three important committees, those to inquire into the miscarriages of the war, to consider the second mutiny bill, and to examine the state of the revenue. He obtained leave for a fortnight on 18 Dec., but was listed as a supporter of the disabling clause in the bill to restore corporations. He remained a Whig under William III, but lost his seat in 1698. He made over his estate to his son in 1710, and took refuge from his creditors in Ireland, where he died between 12 Oct. 1720 and 21 Mar. 1721. His son was returned for Gloucestershire in 1727 as a Whig.[5]

[1] B. Morgan, *Dutton Fam.* 246–7. [2] Eg. 1626, f. 16. [3] *Cal. Sherborne Muns.* 4, 243–4; Keeler, *Long Parl.* 162–3; Morgan, 158. [4] *CSP Dom.* 1680–1, p. 561; 1690–1, p. 548; Morgan, 223; *HMC Ormonde*, n.s. vi. 8. [5] R. Morrice, Entering Bk. 1, p. 562; *Cal. Treas. Bks.* viii. 746; *Univ. Intell.* 11 Dec. 1688; Grey, ix. 281; *Cal. Sherborne Muns.* 29.

J.P.F.

DYKE, Sir Thomas (1619–69), of Horeham, Waldron, Suss.

SEAFORD 1660, 1661–13 Dec. 1669

b. 10 Dec. 1619, 3rd s. of Thomas Dyke (*d.*1632), of Cranbrook, Kent by Joan, da. and coh. of Thomas Walsh of Horeham. *educ.* St. John's, Camb. 1635; I. Temple 1636. *m.* 7 Aug. 1639, Catherine (*d.*1695), da. of Sir John Bramston, l.c.j.K.b., of Skreens, Roxwell, Essex, 3s. (1 *d.v.p.*) 9da. *suc.* bro. 1638; *kntd.* 19 June 1641.[1]

Commr. for militia, Suss. Mar. 1660, oyer and terminer, Home circuit July 1660; j.p. Suss. July 1660–*d.*, dep. lt. Aug. 1660–*d.*, commr. for assessment Aug. 1660–*d.*, sewers, Wittersham marshes Dec. 1660.[2]

Dyke's family, though widespread in the south east, was of little account before his father acquired the manor of Horeham, 15 miles from Seaford, by marriage. His own marriage and his knighthood on the eve of the Civil War suggest royalist sympathies, but he managed to avoid involvement either in the war or in Cavalier plotting during the Interregnum, devoting himself to the improvement of his iron works. He held no local office before the return of the secluded Members, but became the first of the family to enter Parliament when he was returned for Seaford at the general election of 1660. He was an inactive Member of the Convention, being named only to the committee of elections and privileges. But he had given enough support to the Court for his candidature in 1661 to be endorsed by the lord warden. He was moderately active in the first eight sessions of the Cavalier Parliament, with 39 committees. He was among those appointed to hear the petition against iron imports on 19 Feb. 1662; but his only committee of political significance was for the additional corporations bill in 1664. He died on 13 Dec. 1669, and was buried at Waldron, leaving to his son an encumbered estate.[3]

[1] Vis. Suss. (Harl. Soc. lxxxix), 38. [2] C181/7/71. [3] Suss. Arch. Colls. xxxii. 30; Adm. 2/1745, f. 38.

M.W.H./B.D.H.

DYKE, Sir Thomas, 1st Bt. (c.1650–1706), of Horeham, Waldron, Suss.

SUSSEX   1685
EAST GRINSTEAD   1689, 1690, 1695

b. c.1650, 2nd but 1st surv. s. of Sir Thomas Dyke*. educ. Westminster 1660–1; Christ Church, Oxf. matric. 1 June 1666, aged 16; M. Temple 1667; travelled abroad. m. Philadelphia, da. and coh. of Sir Thomas Nutt of Mays, Selmeston, Suss., 2s. (1 d.v.p.) 3da. suc. fa. 1669; cr. Bt. 3 Mar. 1677.[1]
    Commr. for assessment, Suss. 1677–9, 1689–90, enclosure, Ashdown Forest 1677; j.p. 1680–July 1688, Nov. 1688–96, 1700–d., dep. lt. 1685–May 1688, Oct. 1688–?1701.[2]
    Commr. for public accounts Apr.–June 1696.

During the reign of Charles II, Dyke seems to have taken no active part in politics. He was probably fully occupied in paying off his father's debts. He sold Hodesdale Forge to William Ashburnham* in 1678. He was returned as knight of the shire to James II's Parliament, where he at once made his mark by thirding the motion for supply on 22 May 1685. He was an active committeeman, being appointed to 12 committees, including those for the bills to prohibit clandestine marriages, to reform bankruptcy proceedings, and to provide for the rebuilding of St. Paul's. A Tory and an Anglican, he was soon noted by Danby as an opponent of James II's religious policy. In February 1687 he had to present a petition on behalf of a kinsman, and the King seized the opportunity to 'closet' him, with mutually unsatisfactory results. James 'pressed him hard and closely, but he desired to be excused from promising his vote, which he could not in conscience perform'. At the King's threat of

'other courses', Dyke 'seemed troubled . . . and hoped he should never see [him] use force, saying he was sure those of the Church of England would never make resistance, or rebel against his Majesty'. The King hoped for a change of mind, and did not remove him from local office until he failed to attend the lord lieutenant on the same subject. Nevertheless James's electoral agents warned him that Dyke would probably be returned at East Grinstead, where he had property, on the interest of the Earl of Dorset (Charles Sackville*). At the Revolution he was ordered, with Sir William Thomas*, to seize all Jesuits and other suspects in Sussex.[3]

Dyke was duly elected to the Convention for East Grinstead, although the return was disputed. He was allowed to sit on the merits of the return, and, according to Ailesbury's list, voted to agree with the Lords that the throne was not vacant. On 20 Mar. 1689 he was added to the committee to examine the cases of the political prisoners. A week later John Birch* reported against the validity of Dyke's election, but the House reversed the decision without a division. He became a moderately active Member, with 14 committees, including those for the comprehension bill and restoring corporations. On 19 Apr. he spoke in favour of exempting the bishops from the oath of allegiance unless the King was advised to the contrary. On 23 May he acted as teller for the motion to ask the King to make further necessary provision for Protestant refugees from Ireland. There is no evidence that he attended the second session.[4]

Dyke was regarded as one of the High Church leaders in the second and third Parliaments of William III, but he refused the Association in 1696 and retired from political life. He died on 31 Oct. 1706, and was buried at Waldron. The parliamentary history of the family was not resumed till Victorian times.

[1] Bramston Autobiog. (Cam. Soc. xxxii), 26, 105. [2] Suss. Arch. Colls. xiv. 59. [3] Bramston Autobiog. 198, 269; R. Morrice, Entering Bk. 2, p. 52; CSP Dom. 1687–9, p. 379; W. H. Hills, Hist. East Grinstead, 42. [4] Grey, ix. 211.

B.M.C.

DYOTT, Richard (c.1619–77), of Lichfield, Staffs.

LICHFIELD   5 Dec. 1667–5 Nov. 1677

b. c.1619, 2nd s. of Sir Richard Dyott† (d.1660) of Lichfield by Dorothy, da. and h. of Richard Dorington of Stafford. m. (1) 7 Feb. 1665, Katherine (d. 29 June 1667), da. of Thomas Gresley of Lullington, Derbys., 1s.; (2) 28 Apr. 1670, Mary, da. of Richard Greene† of Wyken, Warws., 2s. 1da. suc. bro. 1662.[1]
    Capt. of horse (royalist) 1642–?46.[2]
    Capt. of militia ft. Lichfield 1663–d.; commr. for assessment, Lichfield 1663–d., Staffs. 1673–d.[3]

Dyott's great-grandfather was granted arms in 1563, and his grandfather sat for Lichfield in 1602. His father, who served on the Council in the North, and was knighted by Strafford in Ireland, 'for his exemplary loyalty suffered frequent imprisonment' during the Civil War and Interregnum, though he was eventually discharged without compounding, while Dyott himself and three of his brothers were in arms for the King. He is said to have been in exile under the Commonwealth, but returned before the Restoration. Shortly after succeeding to the estate, valued at £500 p.a., he was described as 'loyal and orthodox and valiant; of ability sufficient; a good fellow'.[4]

Dyott was returned for Lichfield at a by-election in 1667, probably unopposed. An inactive Member of the Cavalier Parliament, he was named to only six committees in nine sessions. He was three times appointed to the committee of elections and privileges. In 1669 Sir Thomas Osborne* included him among the government supporters who generally voted for supply. He was appointed to a committee on the bill for the preservation of fishing in the Severn and its tributaries in 1674, and to committees for the relief of poor debtors in the spring session of 1675, and again in the autumn, for which he received the government whip and promised to attend. His name appears on the working lists and he was reckoned a court supporter by Sir Richard Wiseman*, though Shaftesbury seems to have marked him 'doubly worthy'. In *A Seasonable Argument* he was described as a sea-captain and a kinsman of Sir Robert Carr* with a pension of £400 p.a. Baxter described him as 'one that professed himself no Papist, but was their familiar'. He died on 5 Nov. 1677, and was buried at St. Mary, Lichfield, but his name was posthumously included in the 'unanimous club' of court supporters. His son sat for Lichfield as a Tory in eight Parliaments between 1690 and 1715.[5]

[1] *Vis. Staffs.* (Wm. Salt Arch. Soc. v, pt. 2), 118–19; Staffs. RO, D661/1/787; *Vis. Warws.* (Harl. Soc. lxii), 118; *Gresleys of Drakelow* (Wm. Salt Arch. Soc. n.s. i), 251. [2] *Staffs. Parl. Hist.* (Wm. Salt Arch. Soc.), ii. 131. [3] *Gentry of Staffs.* (Staffs. Rec. Soc. ser. 4, ii), 13. [4] Shaw, *Staffs.* i. 335; *Cal. Comm. Comp.* 89, 547; *Staffs. Parl. Hist.* (Wm. Salt Arch. Soc.), ii. 131. [5] M. Sylvester, *Reliquiae Baxterianae*, iii. 179; *Gresleys of Drakelow*, 251.

A.M.M.

EARLE, Thomas (c.1629–96), of Bristol and Eastcourt House, Crudwell, Wilts.

BRISTOL   Jan. 1681, 1681

b. c.1629, s. of William Earle, yeoman, of Patney by Joan, da. of Robert Dickenson, yeoman, of Chirton. *m.* bef. 1658, Elinor, da. of Joseph Jackson† of Small Street, Bristol, and Sneyd Park, Glos., 4s. 5da. *suc.* uncle Giles in Crudwell estate 1677; kntd. 4 Dec. 1681.[1]

Freeman, Bristol 1656, common councilman 1668–84, Oct. 1688–90, sheriff 1671–2, alderman 1681–3, 1689–90, 1691–*d.*, mayor 1681–2; member of merchant venturers, Bristol 1663, warden 1670–1, master 1673–4; j.p. Wilts. 1676–80, 1681–7, 1690–*d.*, Som. 1681–7, Glos. 1685–7; commr. for assessment, Bristol 1677–80, 1689–90; sheriff, Wilts. 1679–80; dep. lt. Bristol 1685–?86, 1689–*d.*[2]

Earle came from a Wiltshire yeoman family which farmed at Eastcourt from the middle of the 16th century, ultimately purchasing the freehold from the Pooles. He was apprenticed to a Bristol merchant in 1647, and continued to trade to New England and the Peninsula after succeeding to the family estate in 1677. After the election of Sir Robert Cann* had been declared void, Earle, a moderate Tory, narrowly defeated Sir Robert Atkyns*, but probably never took his seat in the second Exclusion Parliament. He was re-elected two months later after another contest with the Whigs, and attended the Oxford Parliament, but made no speeches and was appointed to no committees. His election as mayor later in the year was welcomed by the Court, and he was knighted. But he was reluctant to persecute the dissenters, took no part in the intrigues against Atkyns, and voted against the surrender of the charter in 1683. He was restored to the bench of aldermen after the Revolution. But at the general election of 1690 he was accused by Sir John Knight* of exporting munitions to France, and again removed until he obtained a writ of restitution from the King's bench. He died on 24 June 1696, aged 67, and was buried at St. Werburgh's. His eldest son, who succeeded to the family business, sat for Bristol as a Whig from 1710 to 1727, while his youngest, who inherited the family estate, sat for two Wiltshire boroughs from 1715 to 1747 as a dependant first of the Duke of Argyll and then of Walpole.[3]

[1] A. B. Beaven, *Bristol Lists*, 287; F. A. Brown, *Som. Wills*, ii. 125; *Merchants and Merchandise* (Bristol Rec. Soc. xix), 58; PCC 16 Hale. [2] Bristol RO, burgess rolls 1651–62, f. 41; A. B. Beaven, op. cit. 124, 186, 187, 202, 208, 224; *Merchant Venturers* (Bristol Rec. Soc. xvii), 31; *Q Sess. Recs.* (Som. Rec. Soc. xxxiv), p. xi; *CSP Dom.* 1685, p. 189. [3] Aubrey and Jackson, *Wilts. Colls.* 215; Bristol RO, apprenticeship bks. 1640–58, f. 132; *Merchants and Merchandise*, 161–3, 266–7, 272–3; SP44/62/288; *CSP Dom.* 1682, pp. 100, 228; Jan.–June 1683, p. 150; J. Latimer, *Bristol in the 17th Century*, 454; *Glos. N. and Q.* iv. 561.

J.P.F.

EDEN, Sir Robert, 1st Bt. (c.1644–1720), of West Auckland, co. Dur.

DURHAM CO.   1679 (Mar.), 1690, 1698, 1702, 1705, 1708, 1710

b. c.1644, 1st s. of John Eden of West Auckland by Catherine, da. of Sir Thomas Layton of Layton, Yorks. *educ.* Queen's, Oxf. matric. 2 Aug. 1661, aged 17; M. Temple 1664, called 1670. *m.* aft. 7 Apr. 1669, Margaret (*d.* 2

July 1730), da. and h. of John Lambton of Durham, 8s. (at least 2 *d.v.p.*) 6da. *cr.* Bt. 13 Nov. 1672; *suc.* fa. 1675.[1]

J.p. co. Dur. by 1669–Apr. 1688, Nov. 1688–?*d.*, Stockton-on-Tees 1683, Northumb. 1685–July 1688; commr. for assessment, co. Dur. 1673–80, 1689–90, recusants 1675, dep. lt. by 1701–?*d.*[2]

Eden's ancestors were established in the county of Durham by the 15th century, though none had entered Parliament. His grandfather, a Royalist in the first Civil War, compounded for £132 in 1644, and was nominated a knight of the Royal Oak after the Restoration with an estimated income of £1,000; but no evidence has been found to determine the role of his father during the Civil War and Interregnum.[3]

Eden qualified as a barrister, but he was created a baronet in his father's lifetime two years later, and is unlikely to have practised. In the first county election in 1675, he supported Thomas Vane*, the country candidate; but he was himself returned at the first general election of 1679 as a court supporter at the head of the poll and marked 'base' on Shaftesbury's list. A moderately active Member of the first Exclusion Parliament, he was appointed to four committees, including those to investigate the conduct of the sheriff at Eden's own election and to inspect the Journals. He voted against exclusion, and did not stand again until 1690, though in February 1684 he was recommended by Bishop Crew. He gave evasive answers on the repeal of the Penal Laws and Test Act, declaring:

> If I shall be chosen to serve in Parliament when his Majesty thinks fit to call one, I shall give my vote according to the reasons of the debate in such matters as shall there be treated of. ... If I concern myself in electing Members to serve in Parliament, I will vote for those who I hope will consent to such matters as will be for the honour and safety of his Majesty's royal person and welfare of the Government both in Church and State.

He was accordingly among the 'prime justices' removed from the commission of the peace. He sat as a Tory in five further Parliaments under William III and Anne, being succeeded as knight of the shire in 1713 by his son. He was buried at Auckland St. Helen on 17 May 1720.[4]

[1] *Vis. Dur.* ed. Foster, 111; *Pepys Diary*, 7 Apr. 1669; Collins, *Peerage*, viii. 288. [2] Dur. RO, Q. Sess. Order Bk. 6; *HMC Le Fleming*, 210; *CSP Dom.* 1700–2, p. 255. [3] Hutchinson, *Dur.* iii. 339–40; *Cal. Comm. Adv. Money*, 1266; *Royalist Comps.* (Surtees Soc. cxi), 185. [4] *CSP Dom.* 1675–6, p. 184; July–Sept. 1683, p. 435; Durham Cathedral Lib. Sharp mss 82/10; *HMC Le Fleming*, 210.

G.H./G.J.

EDGCUMBE, Piers (c.1610–67), of Mount Edgcumbe, Maker and Cotehele, Calstock, Cornw.

NEWPORT	1628
CAMELFORD	1640 (Apr.), 1640 (Nov.)– 22 Jan. 1644
NEWPORT	c. Feb. 1662–6 Jan. 1667

b. c.1610, 1st s. of Sir Richard Edgcumbe[†] of Mount Edgcumbe by 2nd w. Mary, da. of Sir Thomas Coteel, merchant, of St. Martin's Lane, Cannon Street, London; bro. of Richard Edgcumbe[†]. *educ.* St. John's Camb. 1626; Leyden 1629. *m.* 6 June 1636 (with £3,000), Mary, da. of Sir John Glanville[†] of Broad Hinton, Wilts., 2s. 2da. *suc.* fa. 1639.[1]

Commr. for array, Cornw. 1642, j.p. July 1660–*d.*, Devon 1662–*d.*; commr. for assessment, Cornw. Aug. 1660–*d.*, sheriff Nov. 1660–1; dep. lt. Devon 1661–*d.*, commr. 1662–*d.*; commr. for loyal and indigent officers, Cornw. 1662, oyer and terminer, Western circuit 1665.

Lt.-col. of foot (royalist) 1642–4, col. 1644–6.[2]

Dep. gov. Mines Royal 1654–7, asst. 1657–64.

Edgcumbe's family took their name from a farm near Tavistock, where they were living in the 13th century. After acquiring Cotehele by marriage in 1353, they held property on both banks of the Tamar and represented constituencies in Devon and Cornwall from 1447. Edgcumbe was one of the most energetic of the Cornish Royalists until early in 1646, when he entered into negotiations with (Sir) Thomas Fairfax* (3rd Lord Fairfax), who promised 'immunity, indemnity, and even a reward', and persuaded the committee for compounding to accept a fine of £1,275. He took no part in conspiracy during the Interregnum, concentrating on his mining interests. As a Cavalier he was ineligible at the general election of 1660 under the Long Parliament ordinance, and in the following year he was sheriff of the county. He was proposed as a knight of the Royal Oak, with an income reduced to £2,000 p.a. He returned to the House by defeating Henry Ford* in a by-election at Newport early in 1662. As Ford was a friend of Thomas Clifford*, the rising star at the Restoration Court, Edgcumbe can perhaps be reckoned a Country Cavalier. But he left no record of activity in the House, and was ordered to be sent for as a defaulter on 15 Dec. 1666. He died, however, on 6 Jan. 1667, and was buried at Calstock. His epitaph described him as

> a pattern to posterity and an honour to the age he lived in; a master of languages and sciences, and a lover of King and Church, which he endeavoured to support to the utmost of his power and fortune.[3]

[1] Vivian, *Vis. Cornw.* 141–2; *Coll. Top. et Gen.* iv. 218; C142/579/52. [2] F. T. R. Edgar, *Sir Ralph Hopton*, 208. [3] Keeler, *Long Parl.* 163–4; R. Symonds, *Diary* (Cam. Soc. lxxiv), 51; M. Coate, *Cornw. in Civil War*, 103, 207, 226; *Cal. Comm. Comp.* 1082–3.

G.H.

EDGCUMBE, Richard (1640–88), of Cotehele, Calstock and Mount Edgcumbe, Maker, Cornw.

LAUNCESTON   1661
CORNWALL   1679 (Mar.), 1679 (Oct.), 1681

bap. 13 Feb. 1640, 1st s. of Piers Edgcumbe*. *educ.* Christ Church, Oxf. 1657. *m.* 5 Jan. 1671 (with £5,000), Lady Anne Montagu, da. of Edward Montagu I*, 1st Earl of Sandwich, 3s. (1 *d.v.p.*), 6da. KB 23 Apr. 1661; *suc.* fa. 1667.[1]

Commr. for assessment, Cornw. 1663–80, Devon 1673–80, Hants 1679–8; member, Soc. of Mines Royal 1669, dep. gov. 1670–2, asst. 1678–*d.*; dep. lt. Cornw. 1670–*d.*, Devon 1676–*d.*; stannator, Foymore 1673; j.p. Devon 1674–*d.*, Cornw. 1675–*d.*; commr. for recusants, Cornw. 1675; freeman, Saltash 1683, Plymouth 1684, Bodmin and Liskeard 1685; common councilman, Truro 1685–*d.*[2]
FRS 1676.

Returned for Launceston at the general election of 1661, Edgcumbe became an inactive Member of the Cavalier Parliament, being appointed to only 25 committees. He was included in both lists of the court party in 1669–71 among those who usually voted for supply. In 1670 he served on committees for two bills of local interest, one to enable Peter Killigrew II* to build a quay at Falmouth, the other to empower the King to grant leases of duchy of Cornwall lands. In 1671 he was 'cullied', according to *Flagellum Parliamentarium*, into marrying Lord Sandwich's daughter. His honeymoon was interrupted by a summons to attend the House, and on arrival he was appointed to the committee for removing the Cornish assizes from his constituency to Bodmin. His only committee of political importance was for the appropriation of the customs to the use of the navy in 1675. Sir Richard Wiseman* wanted the Earl of Bath and Lord Arundell of Trerice (Richard Arundell*) to 'make sure' of him. His name continued to appear in the working lists, and he entertained the King at Mount Edgcumbe in 1677 'where he and the whole Court was nobly treated'. Nevertheless he seems to have gone into opposition by this time. Shaftesbury marked him 'worthy', and he was omitted from the 'unanimous club' of court supporters in 1678. (Sir) Joseph Williamson* noted him as absent from a vital debate, though he certainly attended the House, being named to three committees of local interest in the earlier sessions of that year, two for settling the stannary laws and one for the Fal navigation. In December, however, he was again absent on a call of the House, and he may have veered back towards the Court, for when he was elected knight of the shire in March Shaftesbury marked him 'vile'. He was given leave to go into the country on 29 Apr. 1679, and hence was absent from the division on the exclusion bill. He continued to represent Cornwall in the second and third Exclusion Parliaments, but was named to no committees and made no speeches. Nevertheless he was rewarded by the Court. On behalf of the Cornish tinners, he and Francis Robartes* persuaded the crown to revert to the practice of four coinages a year, his petition on behalf of Stonehouse Quay was granted, and his lease of fishing and water rights over two years was extended for his sons. He was also a member of the Cornish syndicate that applied for the Tangier victualling contract in 1681. At the general election of 1685, Sunderland urged him to secure the return of loyal candidates. Edgcumbe expressed his zeal to serve the King, though he did not stand himself, being 'exceedingly afflicted with the gout'. Before his death, however, he had moved into opposition to James II, being noted as one of those most considerable both for interest and estates. He followed the lead of Sir John Carew* in giving negative replies on the repeal of the Tests and Penal Laws, but died before he could be removed from office. He was buried at Maker on 3 Apr. 1688. His son sat for various Cornish constituencies as a Whig from 1701 to 1742, when he was raised to the peerage.[3]

[1] Collins, *Peerage*, v. 231; F. E. Harris, *Life of Sandwich*, ii. 235. [2] BL Loan 16; *HMC 9th Rep.* pt. 1, p. 281; Add. 6713, f. 377; *CSP Dom.* 1685, p. 66, 71; J. Wallis, *Bodmin Reg.* 169. [3] *CSP Dom.* 1677–8, p. 313; 1685, pp. 21, 35; *Cal. Treas. Bks.* vi. 106, 142; vii. 45, 148–9, 404, 1526; viii. 99, 209.

P.W.

EDISBURY, John (c.1646–1713), of Symond's Inn, Chancery Lane, London.

OXFORD UNIVERSITY   1679 (Mar.)

b. c.1646, 2nd s. of John Edisbury (*d.*1677) of Pentreclawdd, Denb. by 1st w. Martha, da. of Joshua Downing of Chatham, Kent. *educ.* G. Inn, entered 1654; Brasenose, Oxf. matric. 9 Nov. 1661, aged 15, BA 1665, MA 1668, DCL 1672; advocate, Doctors' Commons 1672. *unm.*[1]

Commr. for assessment, Oxf. Univ. 1677–80; master in Chancery 1684–1709; chancellor, Exeter dioc. 1692–?1709; j.p. Cornw. by 1701–?9.[2]

Edisbury came of a minor Welsh family resident in Denbighshire from the middle of the 16th century. His grandfather, however, entered the service of the crown as a dockyard official; he received a grant of arms, bought Pentreclawdd in 1630, and was surveyor of the navy from 1632 till his death in 1638. His father was taken prisoner by the parliamentary forces during the Civil War, but was not required to compound for his estate. He became steward to Sir Thomas Myddelton*, and served as protonotary of Denbigh and Montgomery from 1647 to the Restoration.[3]

Edisbury became a civilian, and first stood for the university at the by-election of 1674, but, 'being soundly jeered and laughed at for an impudent fellow, desisted'. He came top of the poll in the next general election, owing his success to 'the juniors and potmen, he being one himself'. Shaftesbury regarded his politics as doubtful, but Huntingdon marked him as a court supporter. A moderately active Member of the first Exclusion Parliament, he made no speeches, but was appointed to the committee of elections and privileges, and instructed to ask Dr Jane, a ritualistic Calvinist and at this time an ardent exponent of passive obedience, to preach a sermon for a fast. On 10 Apr. 1679 he was added to the committee to inquire into the publication of pamphlets defending Danby. Although not appointed by name to the committee for excluding from Convocation those who had not taken the oaths, he sat on it as a university Member and reported the bill. According to the official list he voted against the exclusion bill, but it is more probable that he abstained, as Roger Morrice believed, since he was replaced at the August election by a firmer partisan, and never stood again. He became a master in Chancery in 1684, for which he paid his predecessor £1,500, but must have accepted the Revolution, for he was mentioned as a possible ambassador to Spain in 1692. But in 1708 he was found to have embezzled the funds committed to his charge in order to assist his elder brother, who had ruined himself in building Erddig Hall. He was forced to resign, and died on 16 May 1713. His cousin Kenrick sat for Harwich as a placeman from 1709 to 1713.[4]

[1] A. N. Palmer, *Country Townships of Wrexham*, 224–5. [2] T. D. Hardy, *Principal Officers of Chancery*, 94–96; *Wood's Life and Times* (Oxf. Hist. Soc. xxvi), 403; A. L. Cust, *Chrons. of Erthig*, 143. [3] Palmer, 225–9. [4] *Wood's Life and Times* (Oxf. Hist. Soc. xxi), 441, 443; *CJ*, ix. 579, 600; *HMC Downshire*, i. 31; Luttrell, ii. 326; Cust, 141; Palmer, 224.

L.N.

EDWARDS, Sir Francis, 1st Bt. (1643–90), of St. Chad's College, Shrewsbury, Salop.

SHREWSBURY   1685, 1689

bap. 13 May 1643, 2nd but 1st surv. s. of Sir Thomas Edwards of Greet by Cicely, da. of Edward Brooke of Church Stretton. *educ.* Balliol, Oxf. 1660. *m.* bef. 1665, Eleanor, da. of Sir George Warburton, 1st Bt., of Arley, Cheshire, 1s. 4da. *suc.* fa. 1660; *cr.* Bt. 22 Apr. 1678.[1]

J.p. Salop 1665–June 1688, Nov. 1688–*d.*, commr. for assessment 1665–80, 1689–*d.*, recusants 1675; alderman, Shrewsbury 1685–*d.*, mayor 1685–6; freeman, Portsmouth 1686.[2]

Capt. regt. of Henry Cornewall* (later 9 Ft.) 1685–7; lt.-col. regt. of Charles Herbert* (later 23 Ft.) 1689–*d.*

Edwards was descended from a London mercer, who acquired St. Chad's College in Shrewsbury at the Reformation and helped to found the school. His grandfather was bailiff of Shrewsbury and sheriff of Shropshire 1620–1. His father was a Royalist during the first Civil War, acted as a commissioner of array, and compounded in September 1646 on a fine of £2,060 at one-sixth. On the other hand, his uncle Humphrey Edwards†, who came in for Shrewsbury as a recruiter in 1646, was a regicide. His father had been given a baronetcy by Charles I on 21 Mar. 1645, but as the grant never passed the great seal, Edwards was created a baronet *de novo* 33 years later, though with the precedency of the former creation.[3]

Edwards lived principally in Shrewsbury, where his younger brother was town clerk. He was himself appointed to the corporation under the new charter of 1685 and elected to James II's Parliament, in which he was appointed to no committees. He became an army officer on Monmouth's invasion, but was cashiered in May 1687 for opposing the introduction of Roman Catholic officers. In the following year he gave negative replies to the lord lieutenant's questions on the repeal of the Test Act and Penal Laws. He intended to stand for Shrewsbury at the election to be held in September 1688, and was returned to the Convention. He left no trace on its records apart from voting to agree with the Lords that the throne was not vacant. Nevertheless, he was given command of a regiment of foot on the Dutch establishment, and was sent to Ireland in May 1689. In February 1690 he was recruiting in Chester, but he is said to have fought at the battle of the Boyne. He died intestate in Ireland later in the year, letters of administration being granted to his brother on 23 Dec. on behalf of his only son, then a minor. But no later member of the family entered Parliament.[4]

[1] *Salop. Par. Reg. Lichfield*, xiv. 153; *Trans. Salop Arch. Soc.* (ser. 3), i. 328; (ser. 4), xii. 219. [2] Owen and Blakeway, *Shrewsbury*, i. 493–4, 535; R. East, *Portsmouth Recs.* 368. [3] *Trans. Salop Arch. Soc.* (ser. 3), i. 321–72; (ser. 4), xi. 173–4; *Cal. Comm. Comp.* 1456. [4] Owen and Blakeway, i. 493–4; *CSP Dom.* 1680–1, p. 540; 1686–7, p. 403; 1689–90, pp. 109, 129, 442; *HMC Downshire*, i. 242; *Ellis Corresp.* i. 302; PRO 30/53/8, f. 69; *Trans. Salop Arch. Soc.* (ser. 4), xii. 219.

E.C.

EGERTON, John, Visct. Brackley (1646–1701).

BUCKINGHAMSHIRE   1685–26 Oct. 1686

b. 9 Nov. 1646, 1st s. of John, 2nd Earl of Bridgwater by Lady Elizabeth Cavendish, da. of Sir William Cavendish†, 1st Duke of Newcastle; bro. of Sir William Egerton* and Hon. Charles Egerton†. *m.* (1) 17 Nov. 1664, Lady Elizabeth Cranfield (*d.* 3 Mar. 1670), da. and h. of James Cranfield†, 2nd Earl of Middlesex, 1s. 1da., *d.v.p.*; (2) 2 Apr. 1673, Jane, da. of Charles Powlett I*, Lord St. John of Basing, 7s. (2 *d.v.p.*) 2da. KB 23 Apr. 1661; *suc.* fa. as 3rd Earl of Bridgewater 26 Oct. 1686.[1]

J.p. Bucks. 1668–87, 1689–*d.*; dep. lt. 1668–86, ld. lt. 1686–7, 1689–*d.*; j.p. Herts. by 1676–87; capt. of militia horse, Bucks. by 1680–?6; recorder, Brackley 1686–Sept. 1688.[2]

PC 7 May 1691–*d.*; ld. of trade 1695–9; Speaker of the House of Lords 1697, 1700; one of the lds. justices 1699–1700; first ld. of the Admiralty 1699–*d.*

Lord Brackley's great-grandfather, a natural son of the Cheshire family, rose to be lord keeper under Elizabeth and to represent his county in two Parliaments. In 1604, he bought the ex-monastic estate of Ashridge on the borders of Hertfordshire and Buckinghamshire. The family took no part in the Civil War, but this did not save their property from the parliamentary forces, as their royalist and Anglican sympathies were well known. The second earl, though usually reckoned a member of the country party in the Cavalier Parliament, voted against exclusion in 1680. Though pressed by Sir Ralph Verney* and others, Brackley refused to stand for the county in the Exclusion Parliaments, and showed little enthusiasm for electioneering in 1685. 'I am forced to be a Parliament man for the county of Buckingham', he wrote to his Whig cousin, the 4th Lord Herbert of Chirbury, 'much against my will, but with my father's command.' Not only did the secretary of state, Lord Sunderland, write on his behalf, but the Hon. Thomas Wharton* asked the Whig electors to give Brackley their second votes, and he finished at the top of the poll. Once elected, he proved an active and a conscientious Member, serving on 14 committees, of which the most important was to recommend expunctions from the Journals. In the second session, he probably went into opposition with his father, whom he succeeded in the following year. He was removed from the lord lieutenancy of Buckinghamshire in 1687 as an opponent of James II. He supported the transfer of the crown and enjoyed the confidence of William III, dying in office as first lord of the Admiralty on 19 Mar. 1701. One of his sons sat for Buckinghamshire from 1706 to 1708, and afterwards for Brackley.[3]

[1] Clutterbuck, *Herts.* i. 391–2. [2] *CSP Dom.* 1667–8, p. 301; 1685, p. 235; 1686–7, p. 189; *Herts. Co. Recs.* vi. 520. [3] Chauncy. *Herts.* ii. 481; *HMC 5th Rep.* 90; BL M636/32, Sir Ralph to Edmund Verney, 29 Jan. 1679; PRO 30/53/8, f. 9; Browning, *Danby*, i. 373.

L.N.

EGERTON, Sir Philip, (*d.*1698), of Oulton, Cheshire.

CHESHIRE   1679 (Mar.), 1685

5th but 2nd surv. s. of Sir Rowland Egerton, 1st Bt.[†], of Oulton, and Farthinghoe, Northants. by Bridget, da. of Arthur, 14th Lord Grey de Wilton, and coh. to her bro. Thomas. *m.* by 1656, Catherine (*d.*1707), da. and h. of Piers Conway of Hendre, Flints., 4s. (2 *d.v.p.*) 4da. *suc.* fa. in Cheshire estate 1646; kntd. 23 June 1660.[1]

Sheriff, Cheshire 1654–7, commr. for militia Mar. 1660, j.p. Mar. 1660–2, 1672–?89, capt. of militia horse Apr. 1660, lt.-col. 1661–?89; commr. for assessment, Cheshire Aug. 1660–80, 1689, Chester 1677–80, Flints. 1690, corporations, Cheshire 1662–3, loyal and indigent officers 1662, dep. lt. 1665–?89; freeman, Liverpool 1667.[2]

Egerton's ancestors had held land in Cheshire since the 12th century. A cadet branch, established in Staffordshire, represented that county as early as 1429, but Egerton's grandfather was the first of the family to sit for Cheshire. Egerton's mother was an ardent Puritan. His father lent the King £1,080 early in the Civil War, a little more than half of what was asked, but 'never manifested any malignancy' towards Parliament, which voted him thanks for bringing the news of the surrender of Pontefract in 1645. Egerton succeeded to Oulton on his father's death, when his elder brother inherited the Northamptonshire and Staffordshire property. He raised a troop of horse for the royalist rising of Sir George Booth* in 1659, and was knighted at the Restoration.[3]

Egerton was active in repressing disaffection in the early years of Charles II. He first stood for Cheshire as a country candidate at a by-election in 1670, yielding to the aspiring courtier Thomas Cholmondeley* after three days' polling, but he was successful at the first general election of 1679. Shaftesbury marked him 'honest', and he became an active Member of the first Exclusion Parliament. He made no speeches, but was named to 15 committees, of which the most important were on the bills for security against Popery and to continue the ban on importing Irish cattle. According to Roger Morrice, he disappointed Shaftesbury's expectations by voting against exclusion. It is not known whether he stood in September, when he was replaced by the exclusionist Sir Robert Cotton, Bt.*, but he was defeated in 1681.[4]

After Roger Whitley* lost the mayoral election at Chester in 1682, it was reported that all the windows in Egerton's town house were broken 'by the rabble'. He helped to search the houses of the leading local Whigs after the Rye House Plot, and regained his seat in 1685. He was again active in James II's Parliament, serving on 11 committees, including that to recommend expunctions from the Journals. He was reappointed deputy lieutenant in November 1688, and became a non-juror after the Revolution. In 1690 he was imprisoned in Chester

Castle as a Jacobite suspect. He died on 15 Aug. 1698 and was buried at Little Budworth. The parliamentary record of this branch of the family was not resumed until 1807, when John Egerton was returned for Chester.[5]

[1] Ormerod, *Cheshire*, ii. 222; Baker, *Northants.* i. 621. [2] Ormerod, ii. 221; *HMC 3rd Rep.* 245. [3] Ormerod, ii. 620; *Cal. Comm. Adv. Money*, 999; *Committee at Stafford* (Hist. Colls. Staffs. ser. 4, i), 153; *Whitelocke Mems.* i. 483; *Cal. Comm. Comp.* 3252; *CSP Dom.* 1660–1, p. 440. [4] *HMC 10th Rep. IV*, 371; *CSP Dom.* 1665–6, pp. 8, 47; 1670, p. 30. [5] *CSP Dom.* 1682, p. 472; *HMC 3rd Rep.* 245; *HMC Kenyon*, 244.

G.H.

EGERTON, Randolph (1618–81), of Betley, Staffs.

STAFFORDSHIRE   1661

b. 2 Nov. 1618, 1st s. of Sir Ralph Egerton of Betley by Frances, da. of Sir John Harington of Kelston, Som. *m.* (1) Penelope (*d.* 20 Mar. 1670), da. of Robert Needham[†], 2nd Visct. Kilmorey [I], *s.p.*; (2) settlement 1 May 1673, Elizabeth, da. and coh. of Henry Murray, groom of the bedchamber, of Berkhampstead, Herts., 1s 2da. *suc.* fa. 1624.[1]
    Capt. of ft. (royalist) 1642, maj.-gen. of horse by 1644; lt. 1 Life Gds. 1661, capt. 1666, maj. 1672, lt.-col. 1678–*d.*[2]
    J.p. Staffs. July 1660–*d.*, dep. lt. Aug. 1660–*d.*; jt. farmer of excise, Cheshire and Lancs. by 1661, Staffs. 1662–74; commr. for assessment, Staffs. 1661–80, corporations 1662–3, loyal and indigent officers, Staffs. and Westminster 1662.[3]
    Trustee for country excise 1671–4.[4]

Egerton was descended from a younger son of the Cheshire family. His ancestors had been seated in Staffordshire since early in the 15th century, first representing the county in 1429. He had a distinguished military career in the Civil War, compounding on comparatively easy terms after helping to secure the surrender of Ludlow Castle. He was arrested in June 1650 for holding correspondence with Charles II, but released on bail three months later. He was in arms for the King under Sir George Booth* in 1659. At the Restoration he raised a troop of horse to meet the King at Dover; but for the moment the wartime major-general had to be satisfied with a commission as lieutenant in the guards as reward for his loyalty. He was recommended as knight of the Royal Oak on the London list, with an estate valued at £1,000 p.a.; but a local estimate of £800 p.a. is to be preferred. He was held in high esteem by the Staffordshire gentry as 'very loyal, orthodox and valiant; a wise, prudent man, but a good fellow'. He was returned as knight of the shire in 1661, and listed as a friend by Lord Wharton. But he was not an active Member of the Cavalier Parliament. He was named to 53 committees, and of his five recorded speeches two were

merely brief personal explanations. In the first session he was named to the committee to report on the defects in the revenue, to consider the charges against James Philipps* and to bring in a militia bill. In 1663 he helped to report on defects in the Act of Uniformity, to bring in a bill against Popery, to consider a bill for making the rivers Mersey and Weaver navigable and a petition from the loyal and indigent officers, and to receive proposals for regulating abuses in the excise. As an excise farmer, he was noted as a court dependant in 1664. Thereafter his activity declined, though he continued to take an interest in the loyal and indigent officers. His clumsy effort to procure evidence for the divorce of Lord Roos (John Manners*) suggests that he was no Clarendonian, and in 1667 he was appointed to the committee to inquire into the sale of Dunkirk. On 28 Feb. 1668 he informed the House of the insolence of sectaries in Staffordshire, and was appointed to a committee to investigate the subject. Later in the same session he introduced a petition from the wife of Sir Robert Howard*.[5]

Egerton's name appears on both lists of the court party in 1669–71 as a court dependant. In the latter year he joined a syndicate headed by Sir William Bucknall* for farming the entire excise outside London. When this concession was terminated in 1674, he was granted a pension on the excise as compensation. His last parliamentary committee was on 18 May 1675, when he was appointed to consider a complaint of breach of privilege committed by Lauderdale's servants. But he was included on the list of officials in the autumn, and on the working lists, where he was noted as possessing influence over his colleague Sir Edward Littleton*. On 25 Oct. he protested against the coupling of guardsmen and Popery by Michael Malet*. Shaftesbury marked Egerton 'thrice vile', and in *A Seasonable Argument* he was described as 'a captain in the guards [who] has had in boons £1,000', which understates both his rank and his rewards. He was again on both lists of the court party in 1678, and on 30 Oct. told the House of a vaguely sinister conversation with Lord Castlemaine (Roger Palmer*) about Coleman. Blacklisted in the 'unanimous club', he never stood again. He died on 20 Oct. 1681 and was buried in Westminster Abbey. His only son died in childhood, but his widow married Charles Egerton[†], a younger son of the second Earl of Bridgwater.[6]

[1] Wards 7/70/193; *Misc. Gen. et Her.* (n.s.), iv. 193; *Scots Peerage*, iii. 399; *Westminster Abbey Reg.* (Harl. Soc. x), 218, 354. [2] P. Young, *Edgehill*, 214; *Bulstrode Pprs.* 243. [3] T51/11/17; *Cal. Treas. Bks.* i. 427, 639; iii. 833; vi. 682; T. Pape, *Restoration Govt. and Newcastle-under-Lyme*, 17. [4] *Cal. Treas. Bks.* iii. 832. [5] *Hist. Pirehill* (Wm. Salt Arch. Soc. n.s. xii), 216–17; *Gentry of Staffs.*

(Staffs. Rec. Soc. ser. 4), ii. 14; *Cal. Comm. Comp.* 1521; *CSP Dom.* 1650, pp. 208, 522; 1659–60, pp. 94, 147; *HMC 5th Rep.* 150; *Milward*, 46–47, 201, 281; Grey, i. 147. [6] E. Hughes, *Studies in Admin. and Finance*, 148; Grey, iii. 337; vi. 122; PCC 32 Cottle; *Hist. Pirehill*, 214.

A.M.M.

EGERTON, Sir William (1649–91), of Worsley, Lancs. and Hemel Hempstead, Herts.

BRACKLEY	1679 (Oct.)
AYLESBURY	1685
BRACKLEY	1690–24 Dec. 1691 [new writ]

b. 15 Aug. 1649, 2nd s. of John, 2nd Earl of Bridgwater; bro. of John Egerton*, Visct. Brackley, and Hon. Charles Egerton[†]. *m.* Honora, da. of Sir Thomas Leigh* of Hamstall Ridware, Staffs., 1s. *d.v.p.* 4da. KB 23 Apr. 1661.[1]

Freeman, Chipping Wycombe 1672; commr. for assessment, Lancs. 1677–9, Herts. 1689; dep. lt. Herts. 1689–*d.*[2]

Egerton's father was high steward of Chipping Wycombe when Sir John Borlase, 1st Bt.*, died in 1672. Egerton stood at the by-election against Borlase's son, who allegedly enjoyed the support of the 'fanatics'. There was a double return, but the House decided against Egerton. He was again unsuccessful at the next general election at Brackley, the family borough, but succeeded in August 1679. He served on no committees in the second Exclusion Parliament, but probably opposed exclusion, like his father in the Upper House. It is not known whether he stood in 1681, but together with Richard Anderson* he presented a congratulatory address from Aylesbury on James II's accession, and broke the long Whig domination at the general election. He served only on the committee to inquire into wool and corn prices, and presumably went into opposition with his father in the second session of James II's Parliament. He died at Christmas 1691 and was buried at Hemel Hempstead.[3]

[1] Clutterbuck, *Herts.* i. 392. [2] *First Wycombe Ledger Bk.* (Bucks. Rec. Soc. xi), 195. [3] Browning, *Danby*, i. 373; *London Gazette*, 19 Mar. 1685; Chauncy, *Herts.* ii. 483; Luttrell, ii. 320.

L.N./G.J.

EGIOKE, John (c.1616–63), of Shurnock Court, Feckenham, Worcs.

EVESHAM   1660

b. c.1616, 2nd but 1st surv. s. of Sir Francis Egioke of Shurnock Court, teller of the Exchequer, by Eleanor, da. of Francis Dyneley of Charlton, Cropthorne. *educ.* L. Inn 1634–5. *m.* settlement 6 July 1652, Mary (*d.*1652/3), da. and coh. of Richard Cresheld[†], serjeant-at-law, of Mattishall, Norf., wid. of William Draper of May Place, Crayford, Kent, *s.p. suc.* fa. 1622.[1]

Member of county committee, Worcs. 1645, j.p. 1647–50, 1654–*d.*, commr. for assessment 1648–52, 1657, Jan. 1660–1, militia 1648, Mar. 1660.[2]

Egioke came from an old but undistinguished Worcestershire family. They took their name from a small manor in Inkberrow, and were regarded as gentry from the 15th century, though they did not purchase the freehold till about 1590. A cousin sat for Tamworth in 1601, but the most enterprising of the family was Egioke's father, who acquired a post in the Exchequer and a knighthood from the new dynasty. In 1609 he sold most of his freehold land, but without severing his local connexions. He leased property from the dean and chapter of Worcester, and served as recorder of Evesham till his death.[3]

Egioke, who was allowed to succeed to his father's estate without an inquisition post mortem, took no active part in the Civil War till 1645, when, together with Sir Thomas Rous*, he was added to the county committee by order of the House. He helped to negotiate the surrender of Worcester in the following year, and committed himself to the new order by buying the freehold of Shurnock Court at the sale of capitular lands in 1650. But his father-in-law, Cresheld, resigned from the judicial bench in protest against the King's trial, and Egioke himself was probably a Presbyterian and no friend to the Protectorate. In 1655 the 'teacher of the parish' of Feckenham (later to be Egioke's executor) was described as 'a desperate enemy' of the regime.[4]

Although Cresheld had died in 1652, his long service to Evesham as recorder (in succession to Egioke's father) and as MP in five Parliaments must have been responsible for Egioke's return at the top of the poll in the contested election of 1660. Lord Wharton marked him as a friend, to be influenced by Thomas Foley I*, and he probably voted with the Opposition. He was appointed to the committee of elections and privileges, and added to the committee to bring in two declarations against Papists, but made no recorded speeches. Shurnock of course reverted to the dean and chapter at the Restoration, but Egioke's lease was not affected. His freehold estate was reduced to two or three messuages in Inkberrow, and he was not named to the assessment commission of 1661, though he witnessed the Evesham return at the general election, and remained on the commission of the peace. He was buried at Inkberrow on 22 Dec. 1663. He sought to entail his property on two cousins of his own name, but Shurnock passed to the family of his eldest sister, the Bearcrofts.[5]

[1] *Vis. Worcs.* (Harl. Soc. xxvii), 52; C8/320/61; PCC 215 Brent. [2] *Diary of Henry Townshend* (Worcs. Hist. Soc.), iii. 229. [3] *VCH*

Worcs. iii. 425; Nash, Worcs. ii. 7; CSP Dom. Add. 1580–1625, p. 446; Keeler, Long Parl. 146; PCC 5 Swann. [4] CJ. iv. 55; Diary of Henry Townshend, i. 197; VCH Worcs. iii. 117; Thurloe, iii. 212. [5] Misc. Gen. et Her. (ser. 3), v. 202; Add. 34738, ff. 53–58.

M.W.H./J.P.F.

ELAND, Lord see SAVILE, William

ELDRED, John (1629–1717), of Earl's Colne, Essex.

HARWICH   1689

> b. 2 Oct. 1629, 1st s. of John Eldred of Stanway, Essex by Anne, da. and coh. of Thomas Goodman of Leatherhead, Surr. educ. Colchester g.s.; Bishop's Stortford g.s.; Merchant Taylors' 1644–5; Caius, Camb. 1646; L. Inn 1648, called 1654. m. 15 Dec. 1657, Margaret (d. 27 Jan. 1714), da. of Richard Harlackenden of Earl's Colne, and coh. to her half-bro. Richard, 2s. (1 d.v.p.) 3da. suc. fa. 1682.[1]
>
> Dep. recorder, Colchester ?1658–at least 1668, Harwich by 1663–?84; j.p. Essex July 1660–80, Apr. 1688–?d.; commr. for assessment, Essex Aug. 1660–9, 1677–80, Colchester and Harwich 1663–4, 1667–9, Harwich 1677–9, Essex, Colchester and Harwich 1689–90, L. Inn 1690; freeman, Harwich 1663; bencher, L. Inn 1673, treas. 1671–2; commr. for recusants Essex 1675, dep. lt. 1701–2.[2]

Eldred was descended from Thomas Eldred, an Ipswich merchant who accompanied Thomas Cavendish on his world voyage from 1586 to 1588. His grandfather, also a merchant, settled in Colchester, took out a grant of arms in 1631, and acquired Olivers manor in Stanway. His father supported Parliament during the Civil War, and held local office during the Interregnum. Eldred became a lawyer, and married an heiress. He held office in the municipalities of Colchester and Harwich, and probably joined his father on the Essex commission of the peace after the Restoration. Both served as pall-bearers at the reinterment of the Cavalier martyr Sir Charles Lucas in June 1661.[3]

Nevertheless Eldred, a dissenter, was clearly no friend to the restored monarchy. He served as deputy recorder of Harwich under Sir Harbottle Grimston*, who recommended him to the corporation for Parliament in 1674 'in case (Sir) Capel Luckyn* should happen to die'. He was removed from the county bench in 1680 as an exclusionist, and acted as legal adviser to the City Whigs at the election of sheriffs in 1682. Henry Mildmay* considered him as a possible colleague for the next Essex election, but eventually preferred a churchman. Although Eldred acquired a personal grievance against James II when he was obliged to surrender property in Westminster and Surrey as crown lands, he may have become a Whig col-laborator. In 1688 James II's agents recommended his restoration to the commission of the peace, and reported that Colchester intended to choose him at the proposed election. It is not known whether in fact he went to the poll there, but he defeated Samuel Pepys* at Harwich. A moderately active Member of the Convention, he was appointed to 15 committees, but made no recorded speeches. Among his committees in the first session was that to consider the relief of Irish Protestants. He was chairman of the committee to reverse the judgments against Titus Oates, reporting on 5 July and carrying up the bill to the Lords on the following day. In the second session his committees included those to prevent excessive expenses at elections and to bring in a bill of attainder against all Jacobites in arms. He is not known to have supported the disabling clause in the bill to restore corporations, or to have stood again. He died on 2 Sept. 1717 and was buried at Earl's Colne, the only member of his family to sit in Parliament.[4]

[1] Morant, Essex, ii. 193; Vis. Essex ed. Howard, 31; Coll. Top. et Gen. vi. 295–6; Top. and Gen. i. 235. [2] Harwich bor. recs. 98/4/26; Essex RO, Assize rolls 35/100–25; Q/SR/468–501; T/2/26; Colchester Castle, Colchester Exam. and Recog.; HMC Lords, i. 179; Harwich Charters (1798), 57; CSP Dom. 1700–2, p. 251. [3] Gent. Mag. (1837), pt. 1, pp. 486–7; Grantees of Arms (Harl. Soc. lxvi), 81; Morant, ii. 193; Merc. Pub. 13 June 1661. [4] HMC Lords, iii. 53; The Essexian Triumviri (1684), 7; Cal. Treas. Bks. viii. 877, 885–7; Morant, ii. 193.

G.H./G.J.

ELGIN, 2nd Earl of [S] see BRUCE, Robert, Lord Bruce

ELIOT, Daniel (c.1646–1702), of Port Eliot, St. Germans, Cornw.

ST. GERMANS   1679 (Mar.), 1679 (Oct.), 1681, 1685, 1689, 1690, 1695, 1698, 2 Apr. 1701

> b. c.1646, 3rd but 1st surv. s. of John Eliot*, and bro. of Richard Eliot.* educ. Christ's, Camb. adm. 17 July 1663, aged 17; travelled abroad 1664–7; L. Inn 1668. m. lic. 13 July 1685, Katherine, da. of Thomas Fleming of North Stoneham, Hants, 1da. suc. fa. 1685.
>
> Commr. for assessment, Cornw. 1679–80, 1689–90, j.p. June 1688–d., dep. lt. by 1701–d.

Eliot was returned for the family borough of St. Germans at the first election after he came of age, and continued to sit in the next eight Parliaments. Classed as 'honest' by Shaftesbury, he voted for the exclusion bill, but he was otherwise totally inactive throughout the period. He remained unmarried during his father's lifetime, during which he may also have been less intransigent as an opponent of the Court. He joined the syndicate of 'the knights and burgesses of the present Parliament for Cornwall' which applied for the Tangier victualling contract in 1681. At the general election of 1685, within a month of succeeding to the estate, he agreed to share the representation of St. Germans with (Sir) Thomas Higgons*, the Earl of Bath's brother-in-law, and Bath suggested that he might be 'treated with' again for his interest in 1688. Alternatively the Presbyterian (Sir) Walter Moyle* might be persuaded to stand against him, 'which he always desires'. At the same time the King's agents listed him among the dissenters formerly out of the commission of the peace. He probably sat as a Tory in the Convention, though he did not vote to agree with the Lords that the throne was not vacant, and in subsequent Parliaments he usually voted with the Tories, refusing to sign the Association in 1696. He died on 11 Oct. 1702 and was buried at St. Germans. His only daughter married the antiquary Browne Willis[†], but the estate was inherited by a cousin, Edward Eliot, who was returned for St. Germans as a Tory in 1705.

Vis. England and Wales Notes ed. Crisp, xiii. 122–5; PC2/57/332. *Cal. Treas. Bks.* vii. 148–9.

P.W.

ELIOT, Edward (1618–?1710), of Trebursey, nr. Launceston, Cornw.

LAUNCESTON   5 May–29 June 1660
ST. GERMANS   1661

bap. 9 July 1618, 4th but 2nd surv. s. of Sir John Eliot[†] (*d.* 1632) of Port Eliot, St. Germans by Radigund, da. and h. of Richard Gedie of Trebursey; bro. of John Eliot*. *educ.* Tiverton g.s. 1629. *m.* Anne, da. of Francis Fortescue of Preston, Devon, 5s. (3 *d.v.p.*), 3da.[1]
Commr. for assessment, Cornw. 1644–52, 1657, Jan. 1660–80, 1689–1707, j.p. 1657–62, commr. for militia 1659, Mar. 1660, recusants 1675.[2]

Eliot inherited the Trebursey estate, and held local office during the Civil War and the Interregnum. In December 1659 he was one of the Cornish gentlemen who issued a proclamation at Truro for a free Parliament. After a double return at Launceston in the general election of 1660, he was seated by the House on 5 May on the merits of the return, but unseated on 29 June on the merits of the election. He had been classed as a friend by Lord Wharton, but during his short stay in the Convention he was not appointed to any committees. At the general election of 1661 he was returned for the family borough of St. Germans. An inactive Member, he was appointed by full name only to the committee of elections and privileges in November 1667. An opponent of the Court, his name was included by Sir Richard Wiseman* in his list of 19

Cornishmen from whom he expected no support in 1676, and in 1677 Shaftesbury classed him as 'doubly worthy'. He did not stand for Parliament again, though Lord Bath recommended that he should be 'treated with' for his interest in 1688. He was last named to the Cornish assessment commission in 1707 and his will was proved on 12 June 1710. None of his descendants entered Parliament.[3]

[1] Vivian, *Vis. Cornw.* 147–50; H. Hulme, *Sir John Eliot*, 346. [2] M. Coate, *Cornw. in Gt. Civil War*, 224. [3] Hulme, 382–5; Coate, 308; *Vis. Eng. and Wales Notes* ed. Crisp. xiii. 124.

M.W.H./P.W./J.P.F.

ELIOT, John (1612–85), of Port Eliot, St. Germans, Cornw.

ST. GERMANS   1640 (Apr.), 1660, 1661

bap. 18 Oct. 1612, 1st s. of Sir John Eliot[†] of Port Eliot, and bro. of Edward Eliot*. *educ.* Tiverton g.s. by 1628–9; Lincoln, Oxf. 1629–31; travelled abroad (France) 1631–2. *m.* 28 Nov. 1632 (with £3,000), Honora (*d.*1652), da. of Sir Daniel Norton[†] of Southwick, Hants, 4s. (2 *d.v.p.*) 5da. *suc.* fa. 1632.[1]
Commr. for assessment, Cornw. 1644–8, 1657, 1661–80; v.-adm. Devon 1645–?53, Mar.–Oct. 1660; j.p. Cornw. 1647–53, 1656–70, commr. for militia 1648, Mar. 1660; alderman, Lostwithiel 1655–62; freeman, Liskeard 1661; commr. for recusants, Cornw. 1675.[2]

The fortunes of the Eliot family were founded on privateering under Henry VIII and partially invested in the former priory of St. Germans, renamed Port Eliot. Eliot's grandfather sat for the borough in 1572, and his father was celebrated as the most violent leader of the Opposition in the early Parliaments of Charles I. Eliot himself succeeded under age to an estate of £1,500 p.a., and was heavily fined for marrying without the permission of the court of wards. He was elected to the Short Parliament for St. Germans, but played little part in the Civil War or Interregnum, though he was appointed to the county committee in 1644. His estate suffered severely at the hands of the Royalists, and in 1647 the Long Parliament voted him £7,000 as compensation for his own losses and his father's.[3]

Eliot finished a bad last in the county election in 1660, but succeeded in regaining his seat at St. Germans after 20 years. Lord Wharton marked him as a friend, and sent him a copy of the case for modified episcopacy. His committee record in the Convention cannot be distinguished from that of John Eliott*, but he was probably inactive. He was proposed for the order of the Royal Oak, with the improved income of £2,500. Re-elected in 1661, he was again inactive, being appointed by full name to the committee of elections and privileges in six sessions of the Cavalier Parliament, and probably to 32 others, including those for the execution of the remaining regicides in 1662 and for the inquiry into the miscarriages of the war in 1667. In 1670 he was removed from the commission of the peace, doubtless as an opponent of the Conventicles Act. Sir Richard Wiseman* included him in 1676 among the Cornish Members from whom the Government could expect little good, and in the following year Shaftesbury classed him as 'doubly worthy'. He handed over the representation of the family borough in the Exclusion Parliaments to his two sons, and was buried at St. Germans on 25 Mar. 1685.[4]

[1] Vivian, *Vis. Cornw.* 147–50; H. Hulme, *Sir John Eliot,* 22, 266, 346, 350, 391; *The Gen.* n.s. i. 23. [2] *CSP Dom.* 1649–50, p. 203; 1652–3, p. 522; 1655, p. 541; 1659–60, p. 571; *Add.* 1660–85, p. 121; M. Coate, *Cornw. in Gt. Civil War,* 224; Cornw. RO, Lostwithiel recs.; Liskeard court bk. [3] Gilbert, *Paroch. Hist. Cornw.* ii. 36–64; Hulme, 17–22, 346–53, 382–7, 391–3; *The Gen.* n.s. i. 23. [4] *Buller Pprs.* ed. Worth, 117; *Vis. Eng. and Wales Notes* ed. Crisp, xiii. 122.

M.W.H./P.W.

ELIOT, Richard (1652–85), of Port Eliot, St. Germans, Cornw.

ST. GERMANS   1679 (Mar.), 1679 (Oct.), 1681

bap. 22 Apr. 1652, 4th s. of John Eliot*, and bro. of Daniel Eliot*. *unm.*[1]
  Ensign, Plymouth garrison 1676–8.
  Commr. for assessment, Cornw. 1679–80.

As a younger son Eliot was intended for a military career and in 1676 entered the service at Plymouth garrison under the Earl of Bath. In 1678, however, the justices for the Western circuit received a warrant to suspend the execution of any sentence passed on him should he be found guilty of the death of one John Grimes of Plymouth. Possibly this incident caused him to leave the army, for there is no further evidence of his military career, though he must have been either acquitted or pardoned, since he was returned to the Exclusion Parliaments for his father's borough of St. Germans. Classed as 'honest' by Shaftesbury, he duly voted for the first exclusion bill. Otherwise he was totally inactive. He was buried at St. Germans on 22 Dec. 1685.[2]

[1] Vivian, *Vis. Cornw.* 147–50. [2] *CSP Dom.* 1676–7, p. 466; 1678, p. 14.

P.W.

ELLIOTT, John (c.1633–70), of Winterbourne Earls, Wilts.

DOWNTON   9 May 1660

b. c.1633, 1st s. of Nicholas Elliott of Salisbury by Emily, da. of John Nicholas of Winterbourne Earls. *educ.* Winchester 1645; New Coll. Oxf. 1651, BCL 1658, DCL 1665; advocate, Doctors' Commons 1668. *unm.*
  Fellow of New Coll. 1653–65; commr. for assessment, Wilts. Aug. 1660–d.; chancellor, Salisbury dioc. 1665–d.

Elliott's family had held municipal office in Salisbury since Elizabethan times, and his mother was the sister of Sir Edward Nicholas†. His father, mayor in 1633–4, seems to have avoided commitment in the Civil War; by 1647 he had become one of the principal burgage-holders in Downton. Elliott was an Anglican, but sufficiently flexible to satisfy the visitors at Oxford during the Commonwealth, though he later claimed that he had 'always in these times of delinquency and rebellion lived under a cloud, and hath been all along looked on as a disaffected person . . . in regard of his own and his relations' affections to your Majesty'. Standing in conjunction with his schoolfellow Giles Eyre*, Elliott was seated in the Convention after a double return had been decided in their favour. As nephew to the senior secretary of state, Elliott may have been moderately active, with 13 committees, though there is the possibility of confusion with John Eliot*. He probably served on the committee for the attainder bill, and was added to the revenue committee on 27 Nov. 1660. At the next general election Elliott was willing to stand down in favour of Edward Nicholas*, but, finding that the borough would not accept a 'stranger', he offered himself for re-election with his uncle's support. Again there was a double return, but this time Elliott and Eyre did not press their petition after the charge of fraudulent creation of freeholds had been made on the floor of the House. Elliott died on 10 Aug. 1670, and was buried at Winterbourne Earls. His brother inherited his 'mean and poor estate'; but no other member of the family entered Parliament.

Hoare, *Wilts.* Alderbury, 78, 101, Downton, 19; Eg. 2538, f. 252; Eg. 2539, f. 5; D. Nicholas, *Mr Sec. Nicholas,* 81; *Wilts. Inquisitions* (Index Lib. xxiii), 366–7; SP29/6/89; Wilts. RO, Radnor mss 337, 1025; Bath mss, Thynne pprs. 10, f. 72, Nicholas to Thynne, 7 Mar. 1661.

M.W.H.

ELLIS *see* **ELLYS**

ELLISON, Robert (1614–78), of Newcastle-upon-Tyne, Northumb. and Hebburn, co. Dur.

NEWCASTLE-UPON-TYNE   1 Dec. 1647,[1] 1660

bap. 2 Feb. 1614, 2nd s. of Cuthbert Ellison, merchant (*d.*1628), of Newcastle by Jane, da. of Christopher Ile, merchant, of Newcastle. *m.* (1) 29 Mar. 1635, Elizabeth (*d.* 30 June 1665), da. of Cuthbert Grey, merchant, of Newcastle, 7s. (1 *d.v.p.*) 7da.; (2) 27 July 1672, Agnes, wid. of James Briggs, merchant, of Newcastle, *s.p.*[2]

Member, merchant adventurers of Newcastle 1634, asst. 1645–8, gov. 1676–*d.*; freeman, Newcastle 1635; sheriff, Newcastle 1644, co. Dur. 1658–July 1660; commr. for sequestration, Newcastle 1644, assessment, Newcastle 1645–8, co. Dur. 1657, Newcastle and co. Dur. Aug. 1660–1, Newcastle 1677–*d.*, northern assoc., Newcastle 1645, accounts 1645; member, hostmen's co. of Newcastle 1645; commr. for militia, co. Dur. and Newcastle 1648, co. Dur., Northumb. and Newcastle Mar. 1660; j.p. co. Dur. 1657–9; c.-in-c. militia, Newcastle Jan. 1660, member of Eastland Co. 1663.[3]

Ellison's family had been established as Newcastle merchants since the middle of the 16th century, but had not served in Parliament. Ellison, a Presbyterian, was nominated sheriff when the town was captured by the Scots in 1644. He was returned for the borough as a recruiter after a hot contest, but secluded at Pride's Purge. He appears to have profited by the upheaval in municipal government, and bought an estate in county Durham about 1650. Although very anxious to resume his seat in 1660, he was probably unable to leave his burdensome sheriffdom of the county. But he was re-elected in April, and became a moderately active Member of the Convention. He was appointed to 36 committees, of which the most important were to consider the indemnity bill, to prepare an excise bill, to inquire into unauthorized Anglican publications, and to settle ecclesiastical livings. His only recorded speech was on the indemnity bill on 7 July, when he moved to reject the charge of plunder against Sir Wilfred Lawson*, 'and no mention of his name in the papers'. On 6 Aug. he was ordered to carry to the Lords the bill for the enfranchisement of Durham. He was also on the committee to establish the names of Charles I's judges; but he was less active after the recess, and did not stand again. He presumably remained a dissenter, holding no office between 1661 and 1677, though he was very active in the affairs of the merchant adventurers. He died on 12 Jan. 1678, and was buried at St. Nicholas, Newcastle. The next member of the family to sit was his great-grandson, an army officer, who bought a seat at Shaftesbury in 1747.[4]

[1] Did not sit after Pride's Purge, 6 Dec. 1648. [2] R. E. and C. E. Carr, *Hist. Fam. Carr*, iii. 118–19. [3] *Newcastle Merchant Adventurers* (Surtees Soc. xciii), 136, 146; (ci), 253; *Reg. of Freemen* (Newcastle Recs. iii), 18; R. Welford, *Men of Mark 'twixt Tyne and Tweed*, ii. 168; R. Howell, *Newcastle and the Puritan Revolution*, 187; *Newcastle Hostmen* (Surtees Soc. cv), 269; *Cal. Cl. SP*, iv. 526. [4] Howell, 167–8, 183–4; *HMC Popham*, 161; Bowman diary, f. 62v; *CJ*, viii. 114; *Merchant Adventurers* (Surtees Soc. ci), 112; Surtees, *Dur.* ii. 76.

M.W.H./G.H.

ELLYS (ELLIS), William (1607–80), of Grantham and Nocton, Lincs.

BOSTON	1640 (Apr.), 1640 (Nov.),[1] 1654
GRANTHAM	1656, 1659
BOSTON	25 Feb.–5 May 1679

bap. 19 July 1607, 2nd s. of Sir Thomas Ellis† (*d.*1627) of Wyham, Lincs. by Jane, da. of Gabriel Armstrong of Wishall, Notts. *educ.* Christ's, Camb. 1623, BA 1627; G. Inn 1627, called 1634. *unm.* Kntd. 30 Apr. 1671.[2]

Commr. for sewers, Lincs. 1638–9, Lincs. and Northants. 1654; dep. recorder, Boston 1638, recorder 1639–62; dep. lt. Lincs. 1642; commr. for sequestration, Lincs. (Lindsey) 1643, eastern assoc. Lincs. 1643, assessment Lincs. 1644–52, 1657, 1673–*d.*, Yorks. (W. Riding) 1666–9, Mdx. 1673–4, new model ordinance, Lincs. 1645; elder, Serjeants' Inn classis 1645; commr. for militia, Lincs. 1648, 1659, Mar. 1660; j.p. (Kesteven and Holland) 1650–July 1660, (Kesteven) Sept. 1660–*d.*; commr. for oyer and terminer, Leics., Northants. and Warws. 1653–4; bencher, G. Inn 1654, treas. 1657–66; reader 1664; commr. for statutes, Durham college 1656, sewers, Lincs. Aug. 1660.

Commr. for excise 1645, with Scottish army 1645, for abuses in heraldry 1646, exclusion from sacrament 1646, scandalous offences 1648, obstructions 1651–2; solicitor-gen. 1654–May 1660; serjeant-at-law, 1669, King's serjeant 1671; j.c.p. 1672–6, 1679–*d.*[3]

Ellys's family had been seated at Wyham since Elizabethan times. His father, a lawyer, sat for the county in 1597. Ellys, also a lawyer, and a strong Presbyterian, was an active supporter of Parliament in the Civil War, and became solicitor-general under the Protectorate. At the general election of 1660 he was involved in a double return at Grantham. He was marked as a friend by Lord Wharton, and named to the committee of elections and privileges. However, he probably never took his seat, and lost his post at the Restoration. He remained a Presbyterian at heart, protecting ejected ministers, but must have conformed when his friend Sir Robert Carr* procured the coif for him in 1669. He became a judge three years later, but dissented from the decision in Exchequer chamber on the Suffolk election appeal (see Sir Samuel Barnardiston*). At Danby's insistence, he was removed from the bench in 1676, though 'the lord treasurer declared he was forced to be unmannerly with the King to out Ellys'.[4]

At the first general election of 1679, Ellys was returned for Boston. Classed 'honest' by Shaftesbury, 'Serjeant Ellis' was appointed to eight committees and made 16 speeches, most of them directed at the minister who had secured his dismissal. During the debate on Danby's pardon on 22 Mar., he said:

Consider whether the chancellor, by the duty and trust of his place, ought not to have acquainted the King with the exorbitancy of this pardon; neither fit for the King to grant nor the treasurer to receive in a . . . clandestine manner. I think that you may declare that the chancellor has not done the duty of his place to pass this patent; an illegal patent both in matter and manner. . . . I offer it to your consideration whether the pardon is not absolutely void. The King is the fountain of justice and mercy; he may pardon offenders, but some things the King cannot pardon, though the indictment be in the King's name . . . because all the people are concerned in it and it is *pro bono publico*. . . . This impeachment is at the suit of all the Commons of England; neither the King nor the attorney general are parties to it. It is in the nature of an appeal of rape, which the King cannot pardon.

He moved that the Commons should 'go on to the Lords upon the impeachment and desire that the treasurer may be imprisoned'. He was appointed to the committees to draw up the address and the summons to Danby to surrender himself. On 27 Mar. he called the Lords' bill for banishing Danby 'such a precedent to compound for treason as I never yet saw', but he advised the House not to throw it out, but to continue with their own bill of attainder, for which he was himself appointed to the committee. He urged that the Lords should be told 'that all this ill consequence is come from not committing him'. He helped to consider further articles against Danby, and on 25 Apr. moved for a committee to inquire into the circumstances under which his pardon was sealed. When it reported three days later he again insisted that the pardon was illegal, claiming that

> to pardon before trial, when the King knows not what fact he is to pardon, is a dangerous precedent. A man may destroy the nation, if so, and do what he will. . . . The King cannot pardon a man, an impeachment depending.

He insisted that the lords in the Tower should be denied copies of the evidence against them and that the Roman Catholic Lord Belasyse should appear in person at his trial, though crippled by gout. He was among those appointed to draw up reasons for a conference on Danby's pardon on 5 May, but on the same day he was reappointed to the bench, thereby vacating his seat in the Commons, and depriving the country party of an able debater. There was a rumour in the following February that he might be removed again, but he kept his office until his death on 11 Dec. 1680, leaving an estate of £1,500 p.a. in and around Grantham to his great-nephew, Sir William Ellys*.[5]

---

[1] Did not sit after Pride's Purge 6 Dec. 1648, readmitted 4 June 1649. [2] *Lincs. Peds.* (Harl. Soc. l), 325–6. [3] P. Thompson, *Hist. Boston*, 458; *CSP Dom.* 1645–7, p. 264; 1655–6, p. 218; *HMC Ormonde*, n.s. v. 273; C181/7/77. [4] Keeler, *Long Parl.* 164; *CJ*, vi. 223; Thompson, 542; *Hatton Corresp.* (Cam. Soc. n.s. xxii), 132; *CSP Dom.* 1675–6, p. 249; *Cal. Treas. Bks.* iii. 1247; iv. 699, 734–7; vi. 89; *State Trials*, vi. 1070–74. [5] Grey, vii. 41–2, 61, 95, 114–15, 123–4, 133, 152–3, 154; *Her. and Gen.* ii. 121.

M.W.H./P.W.

ELLYS, Sir William, 2nd Bt. (c.1654–1727), of Wyham and Nocton, Lincs.

GRANTHAM 1679 (Mar.), 1679 (Oct.), 1681, 1689, 1690, 1695, 1698, 1701 (Feb.), 1701 (Dec.), 1702, 1705, 1708, 1710

b. c.1654, 1st s. of Sir Thomas Ellys, 1st Bt. of Wyham by Anne, da. of Sir John Stanhope† of Elvaston, Derbys. *educ.* Lincoln, Oxf. matric 4 Nov. 1670, aged 16. *m.* 2 Oct. 1672, Isabella (*d.* 16 Jan. 1686), da. of Richard Hampden* of Great Hampden, Bucks., 5s. (4 *d.v.p.*) 3da. *suc.* fa. c.1662, gt.-uncle William Ellys* 1680.[1]

Commr. for assessment, Lincs. 1673–80, Leics. and Lincs. 1689–90; freeman, Grantham 1676; j.p. Lincs., Northants. and Rutland 1680–1, Lincs. ?1689–*d.*, Leics. 1694–*d.*; commr. for inquiry into recusancy fines, Lincs., Notts. and Derbys. Mar. 1688.[2]

Ellys's grandfather died on the eve of the Civil War. His father was too young to take part, but was appointed to the Lincolnshire militia committee in March 1660, and created a baronet at the Restoration, possibly as compensation for the grant to Ellys's great-uncle which had failed to pass the seal before Cromwell's death. 'A drunken sot', his name disappears from the assessment commission between 1661 and 1663, and Ellys himself was brought up by his bachelor great-uncle in a Presbyterian environment. With the support of Sir Robert Carr*, a friend of the family, he began canvassing at Grantham in 1677 well ahead of the long-awaited death of the octogenarian Sir William Thorold*. Described as 'a disaffected person' by Lord Lindsey (Robert Bertie I*), who was at daggers drawn with Carr, Ellys was defeated by Sir Robert Markham*, but petitioned. Lord Treasurer Danby, who was Lindsey's brother-in-law, chose to regard the petition as a 'trial of strength, and to decide the fate of the session'. Sir Thomas Meres* reported from the elections committee on 10 June 1678 in Ellys's favour, but the recommendation was reversed by the House under direct pressure from the King, though only by 12 votes. 'In the debates of the House and committee there have been more loose expressions and calling the persons to account for the same than had happened in many years before.'[3]

Ellys was successful for Grantham at the next general election and held the seat with one interval until 1713. On his arrival in London he dined with Shaftesbury, who marked him 'honest', and joined the Green Ribbon Club. He was moderately active in the first Exclusion Parliament, in which he was appointed to five committees, including that on the bill for regulating elections. He duly voted for exclusion, and after re-election in August, like the rest of Carr's followers, pointedly abstained from greeting the Duke of York when he passed through Lincolnshire.[4]

Ellys was an active Member of the second Exclusion Parliament, in which he served on 12 committees, including those to inquire into the conduct of Sir Robert Peyton*, to petition for a full pardon for the informer Dangerfield, to give relief from arbitrary fines, and to promote the discovery of superstitious endowments. In the Oxford Parliament he was appointed only to the elections committee; but Lindsey expected him to stand for the county at the next election as head of the local Presbyterians, and could not believe that his brother-in-law John Hampden* had failed to involve him in the Rye House Plot. At the 1685 election every effort was made to secure 'the exclusion of the excluder', and Ellys and (Sir) John Newton* were defeated at Grantham by two Tories. In the list of the opposition to James II, he was noted as considerable both for interest and estate, his inheritance of Nocton having doubled his income and enabled him to live 'like a prince'. His appointment to the local commission of inquiry into recusancy fines did not turn him into a Whig collaborator. He was again expected to stand for the county in 1688, but, as Lindsey recognized, his real political base was Grantham, where he possessed 'such an influence that he will not only be chosen himself, but his interest will also choose any other', and where he was indeed returned both at the abortive election in December and in the following month.[5]

Ellys was a moderately active Member of the Convention, though he was still no speaker at this stage of his career. He was appointed to 29 committees, including those to recommend the essentials for securing religion, law and liberty, to inquire into the authors and advisers of recent grievances, to draft new oaths of supremacy and allegiance, and to consider the toleration bill. After the recess he served on committees to inquire into war expenditure and to consider the second mutiny bill, and supported the disabling clause in the bill to restore corporations. He remained a country Whig under William III and Anne, equally zealous against placemen and the inflammatory Dr Sacheverell. He died on 6 Oct. 1727, and was succeeded by his son Richard, who had shared with him the representation of Grantham from 1701 to 1705 before sitting for Boston as an opposition Whig.[6]

[1] *Lincs. Peds.* (Harl. Soc. l), 326; *Assoc. Arch. Socs.* xxiv. 362; Lipscomb, *Bucks.* ii. 261. [2] *Grantham corp. minute bk.* 1, f. 632v; *Cal. Treas. Bks.* viii. 1806. [3] *Her. and Gen.* ii. 121; D. R. Lacey, *Dissent and Parl. Pols.* 389–90; E. Turner, *Colls. Hist. Grantham,* 13–14; *CSP Dom.* 1678, p. 205; *Hatton Corresp.* (Cam. Soc. n.s. xxii), 166; *HMC Buccleuch,* i. 328; *HMC Rutland,* ii. 44; *HMC Ormonde,* n.s. iv. 429, 431. [4] *Sir George Sitwell, First Whig,* 55; *Lincs. N. and Q.* xviii. 148–50. [5] *CSP Dom.* July–Sept. 1683, p. 180; *HMC Rutland,* ii. 88; *HMC Portland,* iii. 536. [6] F. Hill, *Tudor*

and Stuart Lincoln, 187; G. A. Holmes, *Politics in the Age of Anne,* 133, 223.

J.S.C.

ELWES, Gervase (c.1657–c.87), of Stoke by Clare, Suff.

SUDBURY 1679 (Mar.), 1679 (Oct.), 1681

b. c.1657, 2nd s. of Sir Gervase Elwes, 1st Bt.* *m.* Isabella, da. of Sir Thomas Hervey* of Ickworth, Suff., 2s. 2da.[1]

Commr. for assessment, Suff. and Sudbury 1679–80; freeman, Preston 1682.[2]

Elwes's eldest brother died young, and he was returned to the Exclusion Parliaments for Sudbury on his father's interest. He was classed as 'honest' by Shaftesbury in 1679, when his only committees were the committee of elections and privileges, and that to inquire into the decay of the woollen industry; but he voted for the bill. He was totally inactive in the next Parliament, but at Oxford he was again appointed to the elections committee. He made no recorded speeches. He was still alive on 13 Apr. 1686 when his father added a codicil to his will, but had probably died before James II's electoral agents reported on Sudbury in September 1688.[3]

[1] *VCH Northants. Fams.* 67–68. [2] *Preston Guild Rolls* (Lancs. and Cheshire Rec. Soc. ix), 185. [3] PCC 139 Pyne, 209 Eedes.

P.W.

ELWES, Sir Gervase, 1st Bt. (1628–1706), of Stoke College, Stoke by Clare, Suff.

SUDBURY 28 May 1677
SUFFOLK 1679 (Mar.)
SUDBURY 1679 (Oct.), 1681
SUFFOLK 1690, 1695
SUDBURY 16 Feb. 1700, 1701 (Feb.), 1701 (Dec.), 1702, 1705–11 Apr. 1706

bap. 21 Aug. 1628, 1st s. of Sir Gervase Elwes, Merchant Taylor, of Blackfriars, London by Frances, da. of Sir Robert Lee of Billesley, Warws.; bro. of Sir John Elwes*, and step-bro. of Sir Richard Everard*. *educ.* travelled abroad (Spain, Italy, France) 1646–51; Padua 1650. *m.* 2 Mar. 1652, Amy, da. and h. of William Trigge of Chiswick, Mdx., 6s. (5 *d.v.p.*) 5da. *suc.* fa. 1652; *cr.* Bt. 22 June 1660.[1]

Commr. for militia, Suff. Mar. 1660; j.p. Suff. July 1660–81, Lancs. 1663–Apr. 1688, Suff. and Lancs. 1689–*d.*, Essex 1666–*d.*; commr. for assessment, Suff. Aug. 1660–80, Lancs. 1673–80, Essex and Yorks. (N. Riding) 1677–80, Sudbury 1679–80, Essex and Suff. 1689–90; protonotary of c.p. duchy of Lancaster Aug. 1660–*d.*; steward, honour of Clare 1661–85, 1691–*d.*; freeman, Preston 1662, 1682; dep. lt. Suff. by 1665–81, 1689–*d.*; commr. for subsidy, Essex 1671, recusants, Suff. and Essex 1675.[2]

Elwes's family was of Nottinghamshire origin. He was a distant cousin of Sir Gervase Helwys, lieutenant of the Tower, who was executed in 1615 for the murder of Sir Thomas Overbury. His grandfather made a fortune in trade and became an alderman of London in 1605. His father took no part in the Civil War, though he paid his parliamentary assessment of £300 with reasonable promptitude, and served as j.p. for Middlesex under the Rump. But Elwes's mother was the sister-in-law of the royalist Sir Francis Seymour†, and he himself associated chiefly with Royalists on his travels, meeting Sir Edward Hyde† in Spain and later corresponding with him. He acquired a small property in Suffolk by marriage, adding to it by purchase the manor of Ashen just across the Stour. At the Restoration he was created a baronet 'upon the desire of Lady Seymour', and given a life patent for a post in the duchy of Lancaster administration at Preston, which he exercised by deputy. Hyde described him as 'a gentleman of good fortune and very honest'.[3]

By 1677 Elwes had acquired a dominant interest at Sudbury, some ten miles down the valley from his home, through his agent Catesby, an attorney who served four terms as mayor. He was returned to the Cavalier Parliament at a by-election, and became a moderately active Member with 17 committees, including four designed to assist the struggling local cloth industry. The most politically significant were those to summarize alliances in April 1678 and to facilitate the conviction of recusants after the Popish Plot. Shaftesbury classed him as 'worthy' in 1677, but in the following year Danby hopefully listed him among the court supporters.[4]

At the first general election of 1679 Elwes was returned for Suffolk, while his son defeated Sir William Spring* at Sudbury. A moderately active Member of the first Exclusion Parliament, he was again marked 'worthy' on Shaftesbury's list, and was appointed to 12 committees, including those to consider the bill for security against Popery and to inquire into the decay in woollen manufactures. He was given leave for a week on 1 May, returning with a picturesque deposition from a local rat-catcher about midnight manoeuvres by troops of Popish cavalry in Lord Petre's park, which he passed on to (Sir) George Treby*. On 13 May he acted as teller against prolonging the prohibition of cattle imports. He was among the Members to whom the bills for reforming the bankruptcy laws and for exporting cloth to Turkey were committed, and he voted for exclusion. In the autumn elections he made way for Spring in the county seat, while he and his son monopolized the representation of Sudbury. He was active in the second Exclusion Parliament, with ten committees, including the committee of elections and privileges, and those to consider the bills for prohibiting Irish cattle and regulating the trial of peers and parliamentary elections. He was also appointed to the committees to receive information about the Popish Plot, to examine the proceedings of the judges, and to inquire into abuses in the Eye election. He was re-elected for Sudbury and also returned for Preston on his duchy interest. He was again named to the elections committee, but had not chosen his seat when the shortlived Oxford Parliament was dissolved.[5]

Elwes held his duchy post on a life patent, but in October 1681 the bishop of Norwich reported that the King had given orders for the removal of 'that busy Sir Gervase Elwes' from the Suffolk commission of the peace, and he also lost his stewardship of the honour of Clare. He remained an Essex j.p., presumably because his political interest did not extend to that county, but complaints were lodged against his henchman Catesby and a new charter was imposed on Sudbury. He did not stand in 1685, and was listed among the Opposition in 1687. But he may have become a Whig collaborator, for in 1688 he was confident that his answers on the repeal of the Test Act and Penal Laws would give satisfaction. From Suffolk it was reported that he would be returned for Sudbury with Catesby 'in case he be not chosen in the county'. But he is not known to have stood in 1689. He regained the county seat in 1690, and was usually reckoned as a court Whig. He died on 11 Apr. 1706 and was buried at Stoke, leaving a heavily encumbered estate to his grandson, the second baronet, who also succeeded him in the representation of Sudbury.[6]

[1] *VCH Northants. Fams.* 67–69; *Evelyn Diary*, iii. 31, 58. [2] SP 29/80/13; Lancs. RO, QSC 63–123; Sir Robert Somerville, *Duchy of Lancaster Official Lists*, 110, 203; Add. 39246, ff. 5, 30; *Cal. Treas. Bks.* iii. 821; vi. 871; Essex RO, O/OA30; *HMC 7th Rep.* 533; *Preston Guild Rolls* (Lancs. and Cheshire Rec. Soc. ix), 144, 185. [3] *Misc. Gen. et Her.* (n.s.), iv. 133–4; *Cal. Comm. Adv. Money*, 326, 840; *VCH Northants. Fams.* 67; *Cal. Cl. SP*, ii. 114, 352–3; Copinger, *Suff. Manors*, v. 286; Morant, *Essex*, ii. 340; *CSP Dom. 1660–1*, pp. 7, 45; *HMC Kenyon*, 407. [4] F. C. D. Sperling, *Short Hist. Sudbury*, 74, 78–79, 83; *VCH Suff.* ii. 269. [5] *HMC 13th Rep. VI*, 152; *CJ*, ix. 621. [6] *HMC 7th Rep.* 533; Sperling, 74; *CSP Dom. 1684–5*, pp. 48, 269; 1685, p. 68.

P.W.

ELWES, Sir John (1635–1702), of Whitehall and Grove House, Fulham, Mdx.

MARLBOROUGH 31 Jan.–6 Feb. 1673, 10 Feb. 1673

bap. 1 Nov. 1635, 4th s. of Sir Gervase Elwes, merchant, of London; bro. of Sir Gervase Elwes*, and step-bro. of Sir Richard Everard*. *educ.* I. Temple 1653; Queen's, Oxf. 1654. *m.* 23 Jan. 1672, Elizabeth, da. and coh. of Sir Walter Raleigh of East Horsley, Surr., *s.p.*

Kntd. by 1667; *suc.* cos. Henry in Fulham estate 1677.[1]

?Lt. King's Ft. Gds. (Spanish army) 1658; capt. of ft. regt. of Sir Allen Apsley* 1667.[2]

Gent. of privy chamber June 1660–Nov. 1688, gent. usher by 1692–*d.*; cup-bearer to Queen Catherine of Braganza 1662, carver by 1669–at least 1679; commr. for excise appeals 1678–9; receiver-gen. duchy of Lancaster 1686–*d.*[3]

Commr. for recusants, Wilts. 1675, assessment Mdx. 1677–80, 1689–90; j.p. Mdx. 1680–Feb. 1688, Westminster 1683–Feb. 1688, Mdx. and Westminster Sept. 1688–*d.*[4]

Elwes has to be distinguished from his cousin, Sir John Elwes of Barton Court, who acquired a Berkshire estate by marriage in 1657 and was knighted at Oxford in 1665. Elwes was brought up at Marlborough Castle by his aunt, the step-mother of Charles Seymour*. Probably one of the English Royalists serving with the Spanish army in Flanders in 1658, he became a courtier at the Restoration, and was granted the reversion of a duchy of Lancaster post. He was returned unopposed for Marlborough on the Seymour interest in 1673, but had to submit himself to the formality of re-election when the writs issued during the recess were invalidated by the House. A moderately active Member of the Cavalier Parliament, he was named to 48 committees and thrice acted as teller, but he did not speak. As soon as he took his seat he was added to the committee of elections and privileges and appointed to that considering the bill to prevent corruption and abuses in elections. His name appears on the Paston list of court supporters. In the autumn session of 1675 he was named to the committees on the bills to prevent illegal exactions and to recall British subjects from the French service, and acted as teller for the adjournment of the debate on the naval estimates. His chief interests were probably ecclesiastical, and he was twice appointed to committees on bills for the augmentation of small livings, as well as to another for the repair of churches and chapels. On the working lists he was included among those 'to be remembered', and he was duly promised during the long recess the reversion of a seat on the board of excise appeals. In *A Seasonable Argument* he was described as an admirer of the Court, very poor, but with a place in Ireland worth £300 p.a., which seems to be a mistake. Sir Richard Wiseman* included him among the government supporters in the House, and Shaftesbury marked him 'thrice vile'. In 1677 he was appointed to the committee on the bill for preserving the liberty of the subject, and acted as teller for Henry Herbert*, the court candidate in the Bewdley election. But at the end of the year he succeeded to a fine estate in Fulham, which reduced his dependence on the Government, and he was

among those Members reported to have gone over to the Opposition over foreign policy in May 1678. On 18 June he acted as teller with John Birch* against the adjournment of the debate on corruption. Nevertheless he was on both lists of the court party. He was defeated at Marlborough at the general election, and did not stand again.[5]

Elwes opposed exclusion, and as a gentleman of the privy chamber thought it his duty to repeat to the Duke of York remarks made in a coffee house by Anthony Rowe* tending to discredit Monmouth's confession after the Rye House Plot. But unlike his brother he could not promise support for the repeal of the Test Act and Penal Laws, and was omitted from the Middlesex commission of the peace of February 1688. He seems to have accompanied James II to Salisbury, but thence he made his way to Nottingham to join the northern rebels. Under the new regime he was promoted to gentleman usher and granted 14 houses in the City which had been forfeited under the law against superstitious uses. He greatly improved his estate, and presented communion rails to Fulham church, where he was buried on 6 Mar. 1702.[6]

[1] *Misc. Gen. et Her.* (n.s.), iv. 133–4; Westminster City Lib. St. Martin in the Fields par. reg.; C. J. Feret, *Fulham Old and New*, iii. 279. [2] Clarke, *Jas. II*, i. 349–50; *CSP Dom.* 1667, p. 191. [3] Carlisle, *Privy Chamber*, 165, 197; SP29/47/116; *Cal. Treas. Bks.* v. 1053; vi. 46; Sir Robert Somerville, *Duchy of Lancaster Office Holders*, 18–19. [4] Mdx. RO, MJ/SBB 446; MJP/CP5a; WJP, CP 1–3. [5] *VCH Berks.* iv. 207; Add. 32324, f. 178; *CJ*, ix. 369, 397; *Cal. Treas. Bks.* v. 123; Feret, iii. 280; Foxcroft, *Halifax*, i. 129; Mexborough mss, Reresby corresp. 1/50. [6] *Ailesbury Mems.* 84, 192; Luttrell, v. 148; *Cal. Treas. Bks.* ix. 630; Feret, i. 195; iii. 280–1.

B.D.H.

ELWILL, John (c.1642–1717), of Polsloe House, nr. Exeter, Devon.

BERE ALSTON 1681, 1689, 1695

b. c.1642, 1st s. of John Elwill, grocer, of Exeter by Rebecca Pole of Exeter. *educ.* Exeter, Oxf. 1659; Leyden 1664. *m.* (1) lic. 14 Mar. 1676, Frances, da. of Sir John Bampfield, 1st. Bt.†, of Poltimore, *s.p.*; (2) 2 Oct. 1682, Anne, da. of Edmund Lee, Saddler, of London, 2s. 2da. *suc.* fa. 1675; kntd. 28 Apr. 1696; *cr.* Bt. 25 Aug. 1709.[1]

Commr. for assessment, Exeter 1679–80, 1689–90; j.p. Devon June–July 1688, 1689–1704, 1705–10, Surr. aft. 1702–10; jt. receiver of taxes, Devon 1689–92, 1695–6, 1699–1701; freeman, Plymouth 1696; capt. of militia horse, Devon by 1697–?*d.*; dep. master of the mint, Exeter 1698; sheriff, Devon Jan.–Nov. 1699.[2]

Elwill's father, who served as bailiff of Exeter in 1659, destined him for the Congregational ministry; but Elwill preferred to make his career in trade. His education at Oxford and Leyden 'gave a philosophic edge' to his correspondence with his Dutch business contacts. By exporting Devonshire serges and importing German linens he built up one of the leading mercantile fortunes of the day in the west of England. His first wife probably shared the religious attitudes of her brother Thomas Bampfield*, and he began to interest himself in politics. He formed a friendship with George Treby* to whom he wrote in 1677

> for information as to the disposition of the Court, and likelihood of a French war, because this is of importance to himself and others who have property abroad and floating on the waves.

He joined the Green Ribbon Club, and on the prorogation of the second Exclusion Parliament wrote:

> Many of your friends are in despair, expecting nothing short of ruin for the nation if destitute of Parliament. Many would wish a petition to be presented first from London, and then from all the counties, that Parliament may sit in January and continue sitting until some terms are made about the King's person and the Protestant religion. All agree that London should lead the dance. None, however, will put this in practice unless it is approved of by you and Mr [Henry] Pollexfen*.

He was returned for Bere Alston on the Drake interest in 1681, but left no trace on the records of the short-lived Oxford Parliament.[3]

Elwill was quick to rally to the Prince of Orange in November 1688 and regained his seat in 1689. A very active Member of the Convention, he was appointed to 62 committees and acted as teller on seven occasions. His chief concern was commercial rivalry with France. He was among those instructed to consider the balance of trade, to investigate complaints against the customs, to draw up an address promising support for the war, to consider the toleration bill, and to inspect the Journals for references to the Popish Plot. On 18 June he asked the House:

> Are we only to fight and have no trade? To be neglected and no convoys for merchants? They make fortifications in France, and we shall have no fear of invasion? There is no militia, and Pendennis Castle is in ill condition, and lies open to the French and Irish too. I would have particular instructions to the committee to inquire into the Navy.

On 1 July he was named to the committees to consider the Lords' proviso to the bill of rights and the bill to prevent the import of French goods. He acted as teller for a bill to allow colliers to continue to use foreign-built ships, and helped to prepare reasons for conferences on Titus Oates and on the duties on coffee, tea and chocolate. He was teller against going into committee on supply on 30 July, and on the following day against adjourning the debate on free trade.[4]

After the recess Elwill was named to the inquiries into the expenses and miscarriages of the war. He kept up the pressure from the trading interest, remarking on 14 Nov. that:

> 'Tis a strange thing we should have so many ships at sea and never meet any French ships; 'tis a strange doctrine to have so much loss by capers of six or ten guns; and if we cannot fortify ourselves against capers, how shall we against men of war? If the committee will enquire into the numbers of ships for stations, that will be your only way to secure trade.

He acted as teller for the motion to ask the King who was responsible for recommending Commissary Shales, and helped to draft the address. He was appointed to the committees to examine the state of the revenue and added to that to request some provision for Princess Anne. A member of the committee for restoring corporations, he warmly supported the disabling clause, acting as teller against extending the provisions to James II's regulators and against bringing in candles to prolong the debate of 10 Jan. 1690. He was also among those entrusted with the bill to enforce a general oath of allegiance, and acted as teller for making reparations to (Sir) Thomas Pilkington*.[5]

Elwill lost his seat at the general election, but regained it in 1695 as a court Whig. By 1704 his fortune was estimated at £50,000. He died on 25 Apr. 1717. The next member of the family to sit was the fourth baronet, who was elected for Guildford in 1747 as a government supporter.[6]

[1] PCC 83 Dycer, 95 Whitfield, 190 Fox, 150 Bath; *Mar. Lic.* (Harl. Soc. Vis. xxxiv), 162; *St. Stephen Walbrook* (Harl. Soc. Reg. xlix), 66; J. R. Woodhead, *Rulers of London*, 106; Manning and Bray, *Surr.* iii. 252. [2] *Cal. Treas. Bks.* ix. 250; x. 934; xiii. 108; xiv. 341; xv. 323; *HMC 9th Rep.* pt. 1, p. 282; Eg. 1626, f. 11. [3] A. Jenkins, *Exeter*, 169; *Al. Ox.* 461; Exeter corp. act bk. 11, ff. 26–28; C. Wilson, *England's Apprenticeship*, 190–1, 197; *HMC 13th Rep. VI*, 7, 8, 21; Lady Eliott-Drake, *Fam. and Heirs of Drake*, ii. 65. [4] *HMC 7th Rep.* 416; Grey, ix. 335; *CJ*, x. 208, 245. [5] Grey, ix. 420; *CJ*, x. 296, 232, 329, 339. [6] *HMC Portland*, iv. 122; *Hist. Reg. Chron.* ii. 21.

J.S.C.

ENGLAND, George (1643–1702), of South Quay, Great Yarmouth, Norf.

GREAT YARMOUTH 1679 (Oct.), 1681, 1689, 1690, 1695, 1698, 1701 (Feb.)

bap. 22 Sept. 1643, 1st s. of Sir George England of Yarmouth by Sarah, da. of Thomas Smith of Runton. *educ.* Emmanuel, Camb. 1660; G. Inn 1661, called 1668. *unm. suc.* fa. 1677.[1]

Freeman, Yarmouth 1663; commr. for assessment, Yarmouth 1677–80, Norf. and Yarmouth 1689–90; j.p. Norf. 1678–80, 1689–*d.*; sub-steward, Yarmouth Oct. 1688–91, recorder 1691–*d.*[2]

England's grandfather was an obscure Yarmouth craftsman, but his father became one of the leading herring merchants in the town. A strong Parliamentarian in the Civil War, he resigned from the corporation after the execution of Charles I but resumed office under the Protectorate. After the Restoration he was said to be worth thirty or forty thousand pounds, and he was knighted on Charles II's visit to Yarmouth in 1671 at the instance of the lord lieutenant, Lord Townshend. England himself, a lawyer, was the first of the family to enter Parliament. A dissenter at heart though an occasional conformist, he was first returned for the borough as an exclusionist at the second general election of 1679, after the retirement of (Sir) William Coventry*, and removed from the Norfolk commission of the peace. A moderately active Member of the second Exclusion Parliament, he chaired the committee of inquiry into the misconduct of the under-sheriff at the Norfolk election of February 1679. He was also among those appointed to consider the bills to rectify the marriage settlement of Sir Charles Hoghton* and to facilitate collection of hearth-tax. Re-elected in 1681, he was named only to the committee of elections and privileges in the Oxford Parliament. Despite the restriction on the franchise in the new charter of 1684 he was elected with Richard Huntington* by the freemen in the following year; but they did not petition against the return of Sir William Cook* and (Sir) John Friend* by the corporation.[3]

England became sub-steward of Yarmouth at the Revolution. With one of his brothers prime bailiff and another captain in the borough militia he was returned unopposed to the abortive Parliament of 1688, and again in 1689. Though he made no recorded speeches he was very active in the Convention. His 59 committees included those to recommend alterations to the coronation oath (25 Feb.), to examine prisoners of state (20 Mar.), to consider new oaths of allegiance and supremacy (28 Mar.), and to prepare a bill for religious comprehension (1 Apr.). He probably introduced the bill to confirm and explain the Yarmouth Harbour Act of 1685, which on 20 Apr. he carried to the Lords. In May he was named to the committees for restoring corporations and the toleration bill. He chaired the bill to enable the Duke of Norfolk to build over the grounds of Arundell House, and carried it up. On 13 June England and his colleague Samuel Fuller* wrote to the corporation to recommend the appointment of the refugee dean of Ross as lecturer at Yarmouth, and six days later they were named to the committee for the relief of the Irish clergy. He was added to the committee to consider the Lords' proviso on the succession to the bill of rights (1 July), and two days later he helped to draft the address for leave to inspect the Privy Council records relating to Ireland. But he

returned to his constituency a few days later.[4]

England and Fuller left Yarmouth for Westminster on 21 Oct., sharing a coach with Dean Davies and the mayor and picking up Cook, now serving as Tory knight of the shire, on the way. This was perhaps a mistake, for the coach 'stuck fast in a slough' in Epping Forest, and they did not reach London till the evening of 23 Oct. Although England thus missed the first day of the new session, he was appointed to the committees of inquiry into the miscarriages and expenses of the war and the state of the revenue. He took the chair for the bill to establish a 'court of conscience' for small claims for Norwich, which he carried to the Lords. He was added to the elections committee on 9 Dec., and reckoned as a supporter of the disabling clause in the bill to restore corporations. He was named to the committees to discharge the Duke of Norfolk's estate and to impose a general oath of allegiance.[5]

Although England remained a Whig under William III, he was liable to take an independent line, especially over trade. He died on 30 June 1702 and was buried at St. Nicholas, Yarmouth. His memorial records that he was several times Member of Parliament, and a true friend both to the town and to the liberty of his country. On the other hand a political opponent described him as 'insolent, shameless and perfidious', apt to boast of his own honour and equity, and very angry when they were questioned. His heir was his brother Benjamin, who sat for Yarmouth as a Tory from 1702 to 1706.[6]

[1] *East Anglian Peds.* (Harl. Soc. xci), 67–68; D. Turner, *Sepulchral Reminiscences,* 30, 110, 113. [2] *Cal. Yarmouth Freemen,* 95; C. J. Palmer, *Hist. Yarmouth,* 345, 351. [3] Palmer, *Perlustration of Yarmouth,* ii. 223–6; *Hist.* 214; *Norf. Arch.* xxx. 156; *CSP Dom.* 1668–9, p. 75; 1679–80, p. 66; *CJ,* ix. 678. [4] Palmer, *Hist.* 215; *CJ,* x. 151, 154; *Diary of Dean Davies* (Cam. Soc. lxviii), 24, 31. [5] *Diary of Dean Davies,* 56–57; *CJ,* x. 306, 313. [6] H. Swinden, *Hist. Yarmouth,* 882; E. Bohun, *Autobiog.* 26

E.C.

ENYS, Samuel (1611–97), of Enys, nr. Penryn, Cornw.

PENRYN 1660

b. 11 Oct. 1611, 3rd s. of John Enys of Enys by Winifred, da. and coh. of Thomas Rise of Trewardreva, Constantine. *m.* 5 July 1647, Elizabeth (*d.* 28 May 1705), da. of Samuel Pendarves of Roskrow, Gluvias, 6s. (3 *d.v.p.*) 1da.[1]

Capt. of militia ft. Cornw. Apr. 1660–4, commr. for assessment 1661–80, 1689–90; jt. farmer of tin coinage, duchy of Cornw. 1661–4; j.p. Cornw. 1670–?*d.*; alderman, Penryn 1685–Oct. 1688.[2]

Enys was descended from a minor gentry family that can be traced back on the property from which they took their name to the reign of Edward III. A younger son, Enys was apprenticed at the age of 16 to an English merchant at San Sebastian. With the approach of the Civil War the factory's political sympathies were divided and Enys fought a duel 'maintaining the King's honour and dignity'. On a visit to England in 1642–3 he equipped a kinsman to fight in the Cavalier army, and he was briefly imprisoned in the parliamentary garrison at Plymouth. He owed his release to the intervention of John St. Aubyn* and a 'loan' of £100. He did not return again until after the surrender of Pendennis, the last royalist stronghold in the county. Enjoying 'the best trade of any merchant in Penryn and Falmouth', he was able to purchase and enlarge the family estate. When Henry Seymour I* visited the west country to raise contributions for the exiled Court, Enys, aided by his brother-in-law William Pendarves* and Jonathan Rashleigh I*, gave him a bill of exchange for £300. In 1659 he arranged for the purchase of 300 firelocks in France, which were stored at Trelawne. Richard Arundell* and Jonathan Trelawny I* employed him to negotiate with John Fox†, the governor of Pendennis, who was less afraid of the Cavaliers than of the anabaptists under his command; but plans to infiltrate the garrison were suspended on the advance of George Monck* into England.[3]

On the return of the secluded Members Enys was commissioned in the Cornish militia under Hugh Boscawen*. He defeated Fox at Penryn, one mile from his home, at the general election of 1660, although it was claimed that his duel in 1642 was sufficient to disqualify him as a Cavalier. An inactive Member of the Convention, he was named only to the committee to examine John Thurloe† and to state the debts of the army and navy. Lord Wharton marked him as a friend, but he was clearly a court supporter. In September he obtained a crown lease of two manors in Sussex, and in January 1661 he was further rewarded with the farm of the tin coinage at a rent of £2,000 p.a. At the general election he gave way to Pendarves.[4]

Enys and his partner were soon involved in serious dissensions with James Robyns*, the saymaster, who feared that the duchy interests would be endangered if the tin were not brought into the coinage halls for assay. Enys objected that these buildings had fallen into disrepair during the Civil War, and insisted that the assay and coinage should continue to be carried out in the blowing-houses, as during the Protectorate. Eventually the farm was sub-let to Sir Richard Ford*, but Arundell secured compensation for the partners in the form of a pension of £500. In 1668 Enys offered Joseph Williamson* £100 for a post in the local customs for his son Richard, who was appointed collector at

Penryn. He was himself made a j.p. in 1670, and nominated to the corporation of Penryn under the new charter of 1685. He was not without local enemies, however, who sought to asperse his loyalty, and in July he was compelled to draw up an interesting and convincing defence of his conduct during the Civil War and Interregnum. His attitude to the Revolution is not known. He died on 8 Nov. 1697 and was buried at Gluvias, the only member of his family to sit in Parliament.[5]

[1] Vivian, Vis. Cornw. 152. [2] Parl. Intell. 9 Apr. 1660; CSP Dom. 1660–1, p. 496; 1685, pp. 73–74. [3] Paroch. Hist. Cornw. ii. 86, 326; Cornw. RO, DDEN1900/2; Glanville, Hamilton and Ward (solicitors, Truro), Enys mss (trans. at Cornw. RO); CSP Dom. 1666–7, p. 397. [4] Cornw. RO, DDEN1900/2; Cal. Treas. Bks. i. 67, 99; CSP Dom. 1661–2, p. 60. [5] Cal. Treas. Bks. i. 129, 211–12, 302; ii. 146, 560; iii. 585; CSP Dom. 1663–4, p. 660; 1667–8, p. 386; Cornw. RO, DDEN1900/2; Paroch. Hist. Cornw. ii. 83.

M.W.H./E.C.

ERLE, Thomas (c.1650–1720), of Charborough, Dorset.[1]

WAREHAM	1679 (Mar.), 1679 (Oct.), 1681, 1685, 1689, 1690, 1695
PORTSMOUTH	1698, 1701 (Feb.)
WAREHAM	1701 (Dec.), 1702, 1705, 1708, 1710, 1713, 1715–28 Mar. 1718

b. c.1650, 2nd s. of Thomas Erle† (d.1650) of Bindon House, Axmouth, Devon by Susanna, da. of William, 1st Visct. Saye and Sele. educ. Trinity, Oxf. matric. 12 July 1667, aged 17; M. Temple 1669, m. 1675, Elizabeth, da. of (Sir) William Wyndham* of Orchard Wyndham, Som., 1da. suc. gdfa. Sir Walter Erle* 1665.[2]

Dep. lt. Dorset 1674–May 1688, Oct. 1688–?d., commr. for assessment 1677–80, 1689–90, j.p. 1678–June 1688, Nov. 1688–?d., capt. of militia ft. by 1679, maj. by 1686, lt.-col. Dec. 1688, commr. for rebels' estates 1686; freeman, Poole 1691; commr. for Chelsea Hosp. 1715–d.[3]

Col. new regt. of ft. 1689–98, (later 19 Ft.) 1691–1709; brig. 1693; gov. Portsmouth 1694–1712, 1714–18; maj.-gen. 1696; c.-in-c. [I] 1701–5, Britain 1708–12; lt.-gen. 1703; col. of dgns. [I] 1704–5; gen. of ft. 1711.

PC [I] 1701; one of the lds. justices [I] 1702–3; PC 3 May 1705–d.; lt. of the Ordnance 1705–12, 1714–18.

MP [I] 1703–13.

Erle's father enjoyed with Sir Anthony Ashley Cooper* 'the nearest friendship imaginable'. He was a Parliamentarian in the Civil War till secluded at Pride's Purge. His mother's second marriage to the brother of Francis Hawley*, however, took him into a Cavalier household, from which his grandfather, after his elder brother's death without issue, was at pains to extract him, committing his education to Thomas Grove*, Thomas Moore*, Henry Whithed* and two other sound puritan trustees.

Nevertheless, for the first 35 years of his life Erle failed to commit himself to the country party attitude traditional in his family.[4]

Erle's father had been elected to the Long Parliament for Wareham, which is six miles from Charborough, and the family may be considered to have possessed a natural interest there. On Erle's entry into the first Exclusion Parliament, Cooper (now Lord Shaftesbury) marked his old friend's son as 'doubtful', but he voted for exclusion. In the second Exclusion Parliament he left no record, apart from the grant of leave of absence on 8 Dec. 1680; but his re-election without opposition or expense in 1681 suggests that his constituents were satisfied that his attitude to exclusion had not changed. He was again totally inactive in the Oxford Parliament. But on 19 Nov. Erle, together with two other justices, Henry Butler* and George Ryves*, asked the Government for guidance in dealing with an opponent of the Court who described all addressers as either fools or rogues. On 3 July 1683 he was ordered with Richard Fownes* to search Poole for arms.[5]

Erle was a little more active in James II's Parliament, being named to the committees for the relief of the Earl of Cleveland's creditors and the suppression of pedlars, but was soon afterwards called away by the news of Monmouth's landing. In the absence of the lord lieutenant, and presumably also of his colonel, Sir William Portman*, he assumed command of the East Dorset militia. With his friend Thomas Chafin* he fought as a volunteer at Sedgemoor, and was presented by Lord Churchill (John Churchill II*) to the King. Due to the coldness of James II's reception or to some other cause, Erle was one of the first to commit himself to William of Orange. In the words of the inscription put up by his great-grandson on the ice-house at Charborough:

> Under this roof in the year 1686 a set of patriotic gentlemen of this neighbourhood concerted the great plan of the Glorious Revolution.

Erle returned adverse answers to the lord lieutenant's questions on the repeal of the Test Act and Penal Laws in 1687, and was removed from the commission and the lieutenancy. On 21 June 1688 he obtained a pass overseas with Samuel Rolle*, but he was back at Charborough by the middle of August. James's agents considered his election assured for Wareham; they had been doubtful of his attitude in April, but by September were assured that he was 'right'. Nevertheless, it is clear from Erle's papers that he took the leading part in securing Dorset for William. One of his correspondents wrote from Lyme Regis on 21 Dec. 1688:

> Places of great trust and advantage will be distributed now, and I hope (as you have well deserved) you will come in for your share.[6]

Erle was very active in the general election of 1689. His interest carried both seats at Wareham, and Portman applied for it at Corfe Castle and Poole. In the latter borough Chafin was defeated by Sir Nathaniel Napier*, and it was suspected that Erle supported Thomas Trenchard II* at Dorchester in the hope of keeping out Napier's son, Gerard Napier*. In the Convention, according to Ailesbury's list, Erle voted to agree with the Lords that the throne was not vacant. His only committee was for preventing the export of wool, and he did not speak. On the death of his colleague Ryves he obtained leave (19 Mar.), no doubt in order to take the writ down, and on 29 Apr. he was given a pass for Bristol on his way to Ireland with his regiment. Erle was described as possessing 'very good sense, a hearty man for his country, brave, and loves his bottle'. For the remainder of his career he seems to have been a fairly consistent Whig. He died on 23 July 1720, and was buried at Charborough. His descendants in the female line continued to sit for Wareham and other Dorset boroughs throughout the 18th century.[7]

[1] This biography is based on the family papers of Admiral of the Fleet the Hon. Sir Reginald Plunkett-Ernle-Erle-Drax, deposited at Churchill College, Camb. and consulted there by courtesy of the Librarian. [2] Hutchins, *Dorset*, iii. 502; Dorset RO, D60/F2; *HMC Portland*, iii. 352; Christie, *Shaftesbury*, i. p. xlix. [3] *CSP Dom.* 1679–80, p. 61; Luttrell, i. 482; *Cal. Treas. Bks.* viii. 546; Poole Archives B17; C. G. T. Dean, *R. Hosp. Chelsea*, 298–9. [4] Christie, i. p. x; PCC 158 Mico; *Cal. Comm. Comp.* 1858. [5] *Prot. Dom. Intell.* 22 Feb. 1681; *CSP Dom.* 1680–1, p. 570. [6] *CSP Dom.* 1685, pp. 191, 200; 1687–9, p. 402; Hutchins, iii. 506, 566; Luttrell, i. 482. [7] *CSP Dom.* 1689–90, p. 82; Mackay, *Mems.* 104.

J.P.F.

ERLE, Sir Walter (1586–1665), of Charborough, Dorset.

POOLE	1614, 1621, 1624
DORSET	1625
LYME REGIS	1626
DORSET	1628
LYME REGIS	1640 (Apr.)
WEYMOUTH AND MELCOMBE REGIS	1640 (Nov.)[1]
DORSET	1654, 1659
POOLE	1660

b. 22 Nov. 1586, 1st s. of Thomas Erle of Charborough by Dorothy, da. of William Pole of Shute, Devon; bro. of Christopher†. *educ.* Queen's Oxf. 1602; M. Temple 1604. *m.* 7 May 1616, Anne (*d.* 26 Jan. 1654), da. and h. of Francis Dymoke of Erdington, Warws., 1s. *d.v.p.* 2da. *suc.* fa. 1597; kntd. 4 May 1616.[2]

Freeman, Poole 1613, Lyme Regis bef. 1631, Weymouth 1640; sheriff, Dorset 1618–19; j.p. Dorset by 1622–6, 1629–48, 1657–d., Devon 1647–8; dep. lt. Dorset 1625–6, by 1642–3, collector of loan 1626, commr. of sewers 1638, oyer and terminer, Western circuit 1640, July 1660, assessment, Dorset 1640–8, 1657, Aug. 1660–d., Poole Aug. 1660–1, suppression of enclosure riots, Dorset 1643, sequestration 1643, accounts 1643, chapter, Westminster Abbey 1645, militia, Dorset 1648, Mar. 1660, scandalous ministers 1654, col. of militia ft. Apr. 1660.[3]

Committee, Virginia Co. 1620; gov. Dorchester New England Co. 1624–7; member, council for Virginia 1621; treas. for reformado officers, 1644; lt. of Ordnance 1644–5, 1647–8; commr. for Admiralty 1645–8, propositions for relief of Ireland 1645, exclusion from sacrament 1646, bishops' lands 1646, indemnity 1647–9, scandalous offences 1648.

Capt. of horse (parliamentary) 1642–3.[4]

The Erles were not of much account in their native Devonshire before they moved to Charborough, which they had acquired by marriage, about the middle of the 16th century. Erle, the first of his family to enter Parliament, was a Presbyterian in religion and a moderate opponent of the Court in politics; his principles remained unaltered throughout his long career. After his dazzling triumph in the county election the previous year, he retired in 1660 to the borough for which he had first been elected nearly half a century before. Although in the sunset of his long and eventful political career, he showed no diminution of energy. Twenty-one of his speeches in the Convention are on record, and he was named to 58 committees. As father of the House he was the first Member appointed to the committee of elections and privileges, and in the opening weeks of the session he was also among those named to the drafting committee and the committees for the land purchases and indemnity bills. He did not take a conspicuous part in the prolonged debates on the exceptions to this bill, but in favouring the naming of individuals rather than categories he reduced the danger of a wholesale proscription. On 12 May he moved that the great officers of state should be chosen by Parliament, subject to confirmation by the King. He spoke in favour of the petition from Oliver St. John[†], and acted as teller in favour of the admission of William Lenthall[†] to pardon.[5]

Erle had not forgotten his youthful exploits as a Low Countries soldier, which gave him a lifelong interest in military affairs, more successfully displayed, perhaps, in administration than on the field of battle. He was on the committees to nominate commissioners for the army (23 July), and to settle the militia (6 Nov.). In these capacities, as so often before, he must have been a thorn in the flesh of the court spokesman. Never, he said, had

he known any bill entrench so much upon the liberty of the subject as the militia bill, which provided for martial law. He was teller in favour of a motion to hear complaints against the militia commissioners, 16 Nov., and cited examples of the unruly and insulting behaviour of the soldiers. He moved 'to do somewhat for the good of the people', instead of making them pay excise to maintain expenditure on defence. He had already opposed excise as a substitute for feudal revenues, preferring instead a perpetual land rate. While at first sight it might seem only fair that compensation for abolishing the court of wards should be borne by the landowners who complained of it, rather than by the public at large, it must be remembered that a substantial imposition on land would have increased the inducements to sell out which Erle was offering at this time to the middling gentry with property adjoining Charborough. His reasons were personal, and explain also his support for Cooper's motion to give the guardianship of a minor to his grandfather rather than to his mother. Erle's daughter-in-law, by her second marriage to the younger brother of Francis Hawley*, Lord Hawley, had taken Erle's grandchildren into a royalist household, and Erle's closing years were dominated by his anxiety to ensure that his heir Thomas Erle* should be brought up in the fear of the Lord, 'not that I have any intention to withdraw him from his duty and all due respects to his mother, but that I have a desire to have him educated by my advice'. The boy must in any case succeed to the settled estate but, by appropriating all his spare cash to the purchase of land, Erle could hold out a substantial bribe to the Hawleys to submit his grandson, in his own interests, to the effective guardianship of such Puritans as Thomas Grove*, Thomas Moore* and Henry Whitehead*, failing which, the unsettled estate was to go to his granddaughter and her husband, Thomas Trenchard I*.[6]

Indeed it was religious issues that moved Erle often to eloquence. He was the only Member to object to the selection of the Royalist Dr Gauden to preach before the House. He wanted a grand committee on the subject (6 July) and protested against the re-imposition of the 39 articles. He justified the attack of Sir John Northcote*, his old comrade-in-arms of Civil War days, on the idleness of cathedral clergy. He rebuked Robert Bruce*, Lord Bruce, son of the Dorset landowner whose enclosures he had been ordered to defend in 1643, for speaking meanly of those who prayed by the spirit. In the vital debate on religion, he favoured separating the discussion of doctrine and discipline (16 July). He was teller for the motion to hear the petition from the intruded ministers (21 July), having postponed the leave of absence which he had obtained two days before. On 17 Nov. he was added to the committee appointed to bring in a bill for modified episcopacy in accordance with the Worcester House declaration.[7]

Erle's long parliamentary experience made him a keen and sometimes cantankerous watchdog in matters of procedure and privilege. In this session he turned a severe eye on the press, whether it was engaged in producing misleading accounts of debates (25 June), specious Anglican propaganda (30 June) or a crack-brained pamphlet called *The Long Parliament Revived*. His report from committee recommending the apprehension of the printer of this last work was accepted on 17 Nov. Nor was he disposed to allow the Upper House to encroach upon the privileges of the Lower; he was responsible for managing the conference on the Lords' order forbidding George Pitt* to cut timber on his wife's property in Gloucestershire (4 July). Already he had been sent to the Lords to encourage them to pass speedily the assessment bill, returning with a dusty answer (25 May). It was the Lords who struck out of the Post Office bill Erle's proviso that Members' letters should be carried free in session time.[8]

In most of these issues, Erle was in the minority, and each of his four tellerships ended in defeat. He had many relatives in the Convention but even in that assembly, from which Royalists and their sons were supposed to be excluded, there could be embarrassing moments for a man with Erle's record. On one occasion he found himself sitting cheek by jowl with young (Sir) Ralph Bankes*, whose father's property at Corfe Castle had been pillaged by Erle's servants to provide material for repairs to Charborough, previously destroyed by the Royalists. 'I was about to have asked you how far forth you thought me in equity obliged to that which you seem to require', he wrote. Erle had emerged from the Civil War with much cleaner hands than the Brownes and Trenchards, for instance, but he was probably well-advised not to seek re-election in 1661. He remained an active justice of the peace till the year of his death, and even when he was too ill to hold a pen the force of his character and the clarity of his mind enabled him to dictate a will complicated in both its testamentary and personal provisions. He was buried at Charborough on 1 Sept. 1665.[9]

[1] Did not sit after Pride's Purge, 6 Dec. 1648, readmitted 21 Feb. 1660. [2] Keeler, *Long Parl.* 165-7; *St. Botolph Bishopsgate Reg.* i. 54. [3] Hutchins, *Dorset*, i. 32; ii. 452; *Merc. Pub.* 12 Apr. 1660; Dorset RO, Q. Sess. Order Bk. 1625-37; *APC*, 1625-6, pp. 305, 329; C181/5/225, 377; Eg. 784, ff. 50, 59v, 72v; Lyme Regis mss. B6/11, f. 16; *Trans. Devon Assoc.* x. 312. [4] E. Peacock, *Army Lists*, 50. [5] Bowman diary, ff. 5v. 28v; *CJ*, viii. 2, 8, 11, 27, 61; *Clarendon SP*, iii. 748. [6] Christie, *Shaftesbury*, i. p. xviii; *Old Parl. Hist.* xxiii. 14, 15, 18; Dorset RO, D60/F 2; PCC 158 Mico. [7] Bowman diary, ff. 56, 65v, 80v; *Cal. Cl. SP*, iv. 319; *Old Parl. Hist.* xxiii. 5. [8] H. Robinson, *Brit. Post Office*, 48-51; *Old Parl. Hist.* xxxiii. 56. [9] G. Bankes, *Story of Corfe Castle*, 256-8; *Dorset Hearth-Tax* ed. Meekings, 115-17; *CSP Dom.* 1663-4, p. 552.

M.W.H./J.P.F.

ERNLE (EARNLEY), John (c.1620-97), of Burytown, Blunsdon, Wilts.

WILTSHIRE		1654, 1660
CRICKLADE		1661
NEW WINDSOR	27 Feb.–5 Apr.	1679
GREAT BEDWYN		1681
MARLBOROUGH		1685, 1689, 1690

b. c.1620, 2nd but o. surv. s. of John Ernle of Whetham House, Calne by Philadelphia, da. of Sir Arthur Hopton of Witham Friary, Som. *m.* (1) settlement 1 Mar. 1646, Susan, da. of Sir John Howe, 1st Bt., of Little Compton, Withington, Glos., 2s. *d.v.p.* 7da.; (2) 19 Sept. 1672, Elizabeth (*d.*1691), da. of William, 1st Baron Allington of Killard [I], wid. of Charles Seymour*, 2nd Baron Seymour of Trowbridge, *s.p.* Kntd. by 4 Apr. 1664; *suc.* fa. 1684.[1]

J.p. Wilts. 1649-52, 1656-89, Essex and Herefs. 1680-?89; commr. for assessment, Wilts. 1657, Jan. 1660-80, 1689-90, Herefs. 1679-80, 1689, militia, Wilts. Mar. 1660; capt. of militia horse, Wilts. Apr. 1660, dep. lt. 1661-83, commr. for corporations 1662-3, loyal and indigent officers 1662, oyer and terminer, Western circuit 1665; sub-commr. for prizes, Bristol 1665-6; commr. for recusants, Essex 1675; freeman, Windsor 1679.[2]

Comptroller of naval stores 1671-6; commr. for accounts, loyal and indigent officers 1671; chancellor of the Exchequer 1676-89; PC 10 May 1676-Dec. 1688; ld. of Admiralty 1677-9, Treasury 1679-85, 1687-9.[3]

Ernle's family migrated about the middle of the 16th century from Sussex, which they had represented in 1324, to Wiltshire, acquiring ex-monastic land and extending their estates by fortunate marriages. Ernle's grandfather was nominated a commissioner of array, and his great-uncle, the royalist governor of Shrewsbury, was killed in action in 1644; but the junior members of the family maintained neutrality. One of the Dorset branch was a neighbour and henchman of Sir Anthony Ashley Cooper*, with whom Ernle was elected to the Convention for Wiltshire. An inactive Member, he made no recorded speeches, and was appointed to only nine committees, including that for the indemnity bill. On 13 July 1660 he was allowed to petition the House of Lords in support of his claim to the estate of Judge Jenkins, a prominent royalist sufferer. He was added to the committees for restoring the dukedom of Somerset (28 Aug.) and preparing a militia bill (10 Nov.). His petition for the reversion of the clerkship of the pells in association with John Norden* bore no fruit, despite his claim to have spent his fortune in promoting the Restoration, and it was probably his father who was proposed for the order of the Royal Oak, with an estate of £1,000 p.a.[4]

Ernle had to move down to a borough seat in 1661, but was returned unopposed for Cricklade, some five miles from Burytown. He eventually became a moderately active Member of the Cavalier Parliament, serving on 152 committees; but the first of these was on a private bill in April 1662, and he took no part in the Clarendon Code. He was appointed to a committee to bring in a clause to prohibit the sale of titles on 18 May 1663; but he seems to have owed his own knighthood to the 'costly preparation' which he made to entertain the King on the progress to Bath a few months later. In 1664 he served on the committees for the estate bills promoted by his neighbours, (Sir) Edward Poole* and (Sir) Edward Hungerford*, the second of which he carried to the Lords. He was appointed to the prize commission in the second Dutch war, but 'laid aside' in 1666, which, with an income of only £800 p.a. and a growing family, must have represented a serious loss. He took no known part in the proceedings against Clarendon, but he was named to the committee for taking public accounts in 1668. His only tellership was against an amendment to the bill to prevent thefts and robberies. In the debate on toleration on 11 Mar., in almost the first of at least 130 recorded speeches, he agreed that the obnoxious ecclesiastical courts should be reformed, but asserted that a few took offence at the authority of the Church itself. He was appointed to the committees for the continuance of the Conventicles Act, and he was also active over the loyal and indigent officers fund. He was noted about this time both as a friend of Ormonde and among the Members to be gained for the Court by the Duke of York. He opposed the bill to allow Lord Roos (John Manners*) to marry again as no fit subject for a secular assembly. A frequent speaker on financial matters, he supported the deferment of supply until the bill to punish the assailants of Sir John Coventry* had been passed. 'Nothing will make the people give more cheerfully than doing ourselves right in this business', he proclaimed on 10 Jan. 1671, adding that he would like the House to 'sit morning and afternoon till it be done'. He helped to draft the bill to prevent the growth of Popery and to manage a conference, and he also took part in preparing reasons on prevent-

ing the export of wool. At the end of the session he was appointed commissioner of the navy, in which his son was serving, and also accounts commissioner for the loyal and indigent officers fund.[5]

Ernle was summoned to the meeting of the government caucus on 21 Dec. 1672, but took little part in the next two sessions, though his name was on the Paston list. He defended Samuel Pepys in the debate of 10 Feb. 1674 against the charge of delivering valuable naval stores to the French allies. But he was much more active in 1675, warning the House of increasing French strength at sea, and speaking frequently on the naval programme. He was listed as an official Member and a government speaker, and for the next few years identified himself with the following of Lord Treasurer Danby. He helped to draw up reasons on the imprisonment of the Four Lawyers, and was appointed in both sessions to the committee for the appropriation bill. In the debate of 21 Oct. he admitted that it was unfitting for a commissioner of the navy to speak against appropriation; but he feared that 'if the King be put to necessity, you take away what is not anticipated. The King may "want bread" in the navy biscuit.' He opposed depositing the proceeds of the tax for building warships in the chamber of the London corporation, which he implied was bankrupt.[6]

When Ernle succeeded Sir John Duncombe* as chancellor of the Exchequer in 1676, and was granted an excise pension to supplement his salary, it was rumoured that he owed his post to a promise to arrange a marriage between his step-son, the 5th Duke of Somerset, and one of Danby's daughters, and Shaftesbury marked him 'thrice vile'. He was among those appointed to consider the bill for the recall of British subjects from the French service, to manage a conference on the proposed alliance against France, and to draw up the address promising support for a war. He continued to press for supply, though sometimes with 'mistaken zeal', drawing an alarming picture of English unpreparedness. 'The King has neither stores, nor money, nor ships', he told the House on 11 Apr. 1677. 'Twenty or thirty privateers may easily burn all our ships and master the Channel.' He helped to manage the conference on the building of 30 warships, and to draw up two further addresses on foreign affairs, though he expressed anxiety lest they should conflict with prerogative. On 28 Jan. 1678 he defended the irregular adjournments of the House in the previous session on the grounds that Edward Seymour* had merely carried out the King's orders. After the discovery of a Jesuit college in Herefordshire, he claimed that 'there have been more convictions in the Exchequer since my time than in any other man's in that office before me; and I shall do my utmost endeavour to suppress the growth of Popery'. In the debates on foreign policy, he repeatedly expressed distrust of the Dutch as allies. 'Worthy Sir John Ernle' was among those appointed to draw up an address for the removal of counsellors, though he defended Lauderdale 'in a most elegant speech'. He told the House on 30 May that 'the charge of land and naval forces have [sic] eaten out all your poll bill'. He was appointed to the committee to report on how much was due to those about to be disbanded, and helped to manage a conference on the subject.[7]

In the last session of the Cavalier Parliament, Ernle was appointed to the committees to inquire into the Popish Plot and to consider the bill for hindering Papists from sitting in Parliament, though he considered it more dangerous to expel the Duke of York than to keep him under the King's eye. He helped to draw up reasons for believing in the Popish Plot, which he thought confirmed by Bedloe's evidence. But after taking part in the examination of Coleman, he was against printing his letters:

> If I knew any persons that are not satisfied that there was a plot, I would be for printing the letters. The Papists will never be satisfied that there was a gunpowder treason, nor will printing these letters convince them that there was a plot. I think you can give no more satisfaction to the Protestants than they have already.

Nor did he care for the proposal to publish the names of those accused by Coleman of receiving money from the French Embassy. His motion for a proclamation to banish priests and Jesuits was derided as inadequate. With Henry Coventry* reluctant to act, and (Sir) Joseph Williamson* discredited by his dispensations to Roman Catholic officers, the burden of handling an increasingly hostile and suspicious House fell almost entirely on Ernle. He had to explain the restraints put on Titus Oates and the seizure of the papers of Ralph Montagu*, who was able to show that he had not been expressly forbidden to communicate with the papal nuncio, as Ernle originally asserted. Though he defended Danby's record of hostility to France and economy at the Treasury, his last committee was to examine the engrossed articles of impeachment against the minister.[8]

Ernle was on both lists of the court party in 1678, and, as one of the 'unanimous club', had great difficulty in finding a seat at the general election. By 10

Feb. 1679 it was clear that no Wiltshire borough could be induced to consider him, and Sir John Kempthorne* refused to stand down in his favour at Portsmouth. Eventually he was returned for the royal borough of Windsor on the corporation franchise, but this election was so dubious that Shaftesbury did not include him in his list of Members, though Lord Huntingdon marked him as a Tory. His position was all the more precarious when it appeared that he was the only debater in the Commons on the Court side. At the very outset of the first Exclusion Parliament he proved unequal to the task. He had been instructed to nominate Sir Thomas Meres* as Speaker, but before he could do so John Birch* had proposed Seymour. When he was rejected by the King, Ernle failed to allay the indignation of the Commons by reminding them that 'election is in one place and approbation in another, as in choice of bishops'. A moderately active Member, he was appointed to four committees, including that deputed to ask the King to entrust Bedloe's safety to the Duke of Monmouth. He spoke twice more after the dispute over the Speaker had been resolved, once to deny that there had been any embezzlement in the Treasury, and again to demand a further reprimand for Oates. He was unseated on 5 Apr., before the division on the exclusion bill. It is not known whether he stood in the autumn, but he was returned for Great Bedwyn in 1681, presumably on his second wife's interest. He made four speeches in the Oxford Parliament, seconding the motion on 24 Mar. 'to think of some expedients' rather than hazard the rejection of another exclusion bill. He was appointed to the committees to prepare reasons for a conference on the loss of the bill in the previous Parliament to repeal the Elizabethan Act against nonconformists, and to draw up articles of impeachment against Fitzharris.[9]

Ernle was returned to James II's Parliament for Marlborough, where his wife had lived during her first marriage. A very active Member, he was appointed to 19 committees, including those to recommend expunctions from the Journals, to draw up the address promising assistance against Monmouth's rebellion, and to consider the bill for the general naturalization of Huguenot refugees. In the second session he insisted that a standing army was a necessity, and asked for a vote for £1,200,000. He was appointed to the committee to draft the address against Roman Catholic officers. In 1687 the French ambassador noted that Ernle had been retained through all the changes in the Treasury for the past 11 years, but only because he was so inconsiderable. In September 1688 he was 'discoursed of' as a candidate for the county. On the Dutch landing he sued out a pardon from James, but on 19 Dec. he was presented to William by Lord Clarendon (Henry Hyde*). He was re-elected after a contest to the Convention, in which he voted to agree with the Lords that the throne was not vacant. But he made no speeches, and his only committee was to report on the fees due to the officers of the House. Although he held his seat in 1690, he seems to have held no office, local or national, under the new regime. He was buried at Calne on 27 June 1697, the last of his family to sit in Parliament. His grandson put up a memorial inscription, describing him as a most obedient son of the Church of England, who was universally beloved on account of his gentle and kindly disposition. But as a politician his frequent blunders suggest that, like most of Danby's appointments, he was essentially second-rate.[10]

[1] *Wilts. Vis. Peds.* (Harl. Soc. cv), 57; *Le Neve's Knights* (Harl. Soc. viii), 200; *Westminster Abbey Reg.* (Harl. Soc. x), 8; *CJ*, viii. 543. [2] *Merc. Pub.* 12 Apr. 1660; Hoare, *Wilts.* Salisbury, 449; Nat. Maritime Mus. Southwell mss 17, p. 15; *HMC 6th Rep.* 338; *HMC Var.* iv. 132. [3] *CSP Dom.* 1671, pp. 288, 324; 1676–7, p. 91; 1677–8, p. 136. [4] *Wilts. Arch. Mag.* xl. 441; *CSP Dom.* 1660–1, p. 447; *Cal. Cl. SP*, iv. 315; *HMC 7th Rep.* 123. [5] *CSP Dom.* 1663–4, p. 264; *CJ*, viii. 579; ix. 64, 212, 244; Hoare, *Repertorium Wiltonense*, 16; Grey, i. 110, 252; *Milward*, 215. [6] *CSP Dom.* 1672–3, p. 630; Grey, ii. 409; iii. 162, 319, 357; *CJ*, ix. 341. [7] *Hatton Corresp.* (Cam. Soc. n.s. xxii), 122; *CJ*, ix. 398, 418, 419, 424, 477, 502; Grey, iv. 345, 381; v. 6, 274, 284; vi. 34; Finch diary, Feb. 1677; *Lauderdale Pprs.* (Cam. Soc. n.s. xxxviii), 135. [8] Grey, vi. 145, 150, 157, 201, 212, 292–3, 337, 353; Finch diary, 19 Dec. 1678. [9] *Further Corresp. Pepys* ed. Tanner, 344–7; Bath mss, Coventry pprs. 6, f. 21; *Hatton Corresp.* 178; *CSP Dom.* 1679–80, p. 98; *HMC Ormonde*, n.s. iv. 346; Grey, vi. 417–18; vii. 45, 48; viii. 296. [10] Grey, viii. 356, 363; PRO 31/3, bdle. 168, f. 105v; Bath mss, Thynne pprs. 24 f. 39; *CSP Dom.* 1687–9, p. 616; *Clarendon Corresp.* ii. 231; PCC 232 Lort; *The Gen.* n.s. xiv. 42; information from Canon Cyril Witcombe.

M.W.H./L.N.

ERNLE, Sir John (1647–86), of Whetham House, Calne, Wilts. and The Homme, Much Marcle, Herefs.

CALNE   1685–25 Oct. 1686

bap. 31 Dec. 1647, 1st s. of John Ernle*. *educ.* Exeter, Oxf. 1664; L. Inn 1666. *m.* 6 Dec. 1674, Vincentia, da. and coh. of Sir John Kyrle, 2nd Bt.*, of Much Marcle, 1s. 1da. Kntd. June/July 1673.[1]

Lt. RN 1664, 1670–2, capt. 1672–80; cornet, Prince Rupert's horse 1667; capt. Barbados Dgns. 1673–at least 1675.[2]

Freeman, Portsmouth 1678; j.p. Glos. and Herefs. 1680–*d.*; conservator, Forest of Dean 1681–*d.*; dep. lt. Herefs. 1685–*d.*[3]

Ernle was one of the gentlemen captains of whom Samuel Pepys* so strongly disapproved, even to the extent of ridiculing an episode in which he saved the life of one of his subordinate officers. His naval service was interrupted by the usual education of an eldest son. Prince Rupert thought highly of his courage, especially after he was wounded at the battle of the Texel. He went on half-pay when peace was made with the Dutch, but was given a company in the Irish army, and was employed in the Mediterranean in 1677–9. Although he lived chiefly in Herefordshire after his marriage, he was returned for Calne as a court supporter in 1685. No committee work can be definitely ascribed to him in James II's Parliament, and he was probably inactive. He died on 25 Oct. 1686 and was buried at Much Marcle. His son, the last of the family, did not enter Parliament.[4]

[1] *Mariner's Mirror*, xxxiii. 100; Cooke, *Herefs.* iii. 28–29; *CSP Dom.* 1673, p. 521. [2] *CSP Com.* 1667, p. 183; 1673–5, pp. 17, 371; *Cal. Treas. Bks.* iv. 724; *Cat. Pepysian Mss* (Navy Rec. Soc. xxvi), 348. [3] R. East, *Portsmouth Recs.* 363; *Cal. Treas. Bks.* vii. 279. [4] *Tangier Pprs.* (Navy Rec. Soc. lxxiii), 156; *CSP Dom.* 1673, p. 521; 1677–8, p. 381; Burke, *Commoners*, iii. 621.

L.N.

ERNLE, Sir Walter, 1st Bt. (c.1628–82), of The Close, Salisbury and Etchilhampton, Wilts.

DEVIZES   1679 (Mar.), 1681

b. c.1628, 1st s. of Edward Ernle of Etchilhampton by Gertrude, da. of John St. Loe of Knighton. *educ.* Leyden 1645; M. Temple 1647. *m.* by 1649, Martha, da. of Edward Tooker* of Maddington, and h. to her bro. Sir Giles Tooker, 1st Bt., 2s. (1 *d.v.p.*) 2da. *suc.* fa. 1656; *cr.* Bt. 2 Feb. 1661.[1]

J.p. Wilts. 1652, July 1660–*d.*; commr. for assessment, Wilts. Jan. 1660–80, Salisbury Aug. 1660–3; capt. of militia horse, Wilts. Apr. 1660–?*d.*; sheriff, Wilts. 1661–2, dep.-lt. 1662–*d.*, commr. for oyer and terminer, Western circuit 1665, recusants, Wilts. 1675.[2]

Ernle's father, a younger son, served as a royalist commissioner in the Civil War and was fined £400. Ernle's marriage presumably earned him his fleeting appearance on the commission of the peace under the Commonwealth, and perhaps encouraged him to stand for Devizes, three miles from Etchilhampton, on the corporation interest in 1661. His estate was valued at £1,500 p.a. in 1667. In the first Exclusion Parliament he was marked 'doubtful' by Shaftesbury. A moderately active Member, he was appointed to four committees, including that for the security bill. He was absent from the division on the exclusion bill, and on the next day was given leave to go into the country. At the general election he apparently stood in conjunction with the court supporter George Johnson*, and he was not removed from local office. He was successful in 1681, but left no trace on the records of the Oxford Parliament. He died on 25 July 1682 and was buried at Bishop's Cannings. His grandson, Sir Edward

Ernle, was returned for Devizes as a Whig in 1695.[3]

[1] PCC 117 Cottle. [2] *Merc. Pub.* 12 Apr. 1660; Add. 32324, ff. 68, 102. [3] *Wilts. Vis. Peds.* (Harl. Soc. cv), 56; *Cal. Comm. Comp.* 950; Bath mss, Thynne pprs. 10, f. 90, Ernle to Sir James Thynne, 19 Mar. 1661; Hoare, *Repertorium Wiltonense*, 15.

J.P.F.

ESTCOURT, Thomas (c.1645–1702), of Chelsea, Mdx. and Sherston Pinkney, nr. Malmesbury, Wilts.

MALMESBURY	3 Nov. 1673, 1685
BATH	1695

b. c.1645, 1st s. of Sir Thomas Estcourt, master in Chancery 1652–83, of Sherston Pinkney by 1st w. Magdalen, da. of Sir John Browne of East Kirkby, Lincs. *educ.* St. Edmund Hall, Oxf. matric. 24 May 1661, aged 16; L. Inn. 1662. *m.* lic. 11 Feb. 1678, Mary, da. of Sir Vincent Corbett, 1st Bt., of Morton Corbett, Salop, 2s. (1 *d.v.p.*) 2da. Kntd. 15 Sept. 1674; *suc.* fa. 1683.[1]

Commr. for assessment, Wilts. 1665–80, 1689–90, Mdx. 1679–80; high steward, Malmesbury 1671, 1673–7; j.p. Mdx. 1675–87, Wilts. aft. 1690–?96, dep. lt. Wilts. aft. 1690–96, 1700–d., sheriff 1692–3.[2]

Examiner in Chancery 1674–82; committee, R. Fishery Co. [I] 1691; asst. Mines Co. 1693.[3]

Estcourt's ancestors had been considerable landowners on the borders of Gloucestershire and Wiltshire since the 14th century, and represented neighbouring boroughs under Elizabeth. His father, a Puritan, served on local commissions during the Interregnum, and was first made a master in Chancery by the Rump, though an uncle served in the royalist army, and Estcourt himself, 'his father's own son', was sure that 'nothing but loyal blood runs in my veins'. Estcourt was elected high steward of Malmesbury and returned to Parliament at a contested by-election in 1673, surviving a petition from his opponent. An inactive Member of the Cavalier Parliament, he was named to only 11 committees of little political importance. Although named on the Paston list, he was expected to propose the impeachment of Danby in April 1675, but he made no recorded speeches. Never called to the bar, he was knighted and given a minor post in Chancery. In the working lists he was assigned to the management of the lord keeper, but it was the Duke of Ormonde, as lord steward, who granted him the reversion of the judgeship of the Household court. Shaftesbury marked Estcourt 'thrice vile' in 1677, and he lost his corporation interest at Malmesbury, but he was not to be relied on as a court supporter. He was noted as absent from a debate in 1678, and omitted from the May government list. He later claimed, perhaps in a moment of alcoholic fantasy, to have headed a 'party volant' in the ensuing session, which 'gained the additional duties on wine for three years, and £600,000, instead of £300,000, for ships, when my Lord of Danby, had his life been at stake, could only have gained the last mentioned sum'. His father's second wife came from a prominent Devonshire recusant family, and in *A Seasonable Argument* Estcourt was described, apparently untruly, as 'converted to the Church of Rome by his young, handsome mother-in-law, with whom he is very inward'.[4]

Estcourt was listed among the 'unanimous club' of court supporters, and did not stand for the Exclusion Parliaments, in which his seat was occupied by Sir William Estcourt*, a distant cousin. He was charged with complicity in the Popish Plot, and prudently withdrew to Flanders with the Duke of York. Though the principal accuser, who seems to have been the nonconformist Roger Morrice, was obliged to recant under his own hand, he was described in a skit of 1680 as 'Estcourt the sot, that knew all the plot, and could only discover his mother's lewd twat'. He regained his seat in 1685 after a contest, but took no ascertainable part in James II's Parliament. In reply to an inquiry about his attitude to the repeal of the Test Act and Penal Laws, he wrote on 5 Mar. 1687:

> I am really against sanguinary laws in controversial points of divinity, it being my opinion that scarce any sect professing Christianity ought to suffer in their persons on that account, especially if they obey the Government in all temporal matters. I shall be pleased to serve the King as far as I can, *salvo contenemento*, as lawyers call it. I served the late King so far that I presumed I was intended for a sacrifice, . . . though I never had a shilling by the Crown, nor by the reversion of the stewardship of the Marshalsea that my Lord of Ormonde gave me . . . and now I hope I shall not be esteemed the less if I do not hereby promise to give my vote to take off the Test, because perhaps I am not a competent judge of the consequences without hearing the debates. . . . I desire this may not prejudice the opinion that I hope is had of me of being a dutiful, loyal subject.

In a postscript to a letter written shortly thereafter, however, he declared that he was 'for taking off the Tests as well as Penal Laws'. But he had already been removed from the Middlesex bench.[5]

Estcourt is not known to have stood in 1689. He was defeated at Malmesbury in 1690 but was returned for Bath in 1695. He refused the Association of 1696 and was removed from the Wiltshire lieutenancy. He died between March and October 1702, the last of the family to sit in Parliament.[6]

[1] Burke, *Gentry* (1952), 1940; T. D. Hardy, *Principal Officers of Chancery*, 92; *Lincs Peds.* (Harl. Soc. l), 181. [2] *Coll. Top. et Gen.* vi. 297; PC2/76/503. [3] Hardy, 125; *CSP Dom.* 1691–2, pp. 3, 4; 1693, p. 207. [4] *HMC Portland*, iii. 34; Beaufort mss; *Poems on Affairs of State*, ii. 309. [5] Beaufort mss. [6] PC2/76/503; H. Horwitz, *Parl. Policy and Pols.* 358; PCC 160 Herne.

B.D.H.

ESTCOURT, Sir William, 3rd Bt. (1654–84), of Long Newnton, Glos.

MALMESBURY 1679 (Mar.), 1679 (Oct.), 1681

b. 16 May 1654, 3rd but 2nd surv. s. of Sir Giles Estcourt, 1st Bt.[†] (*d.*1668), of Long Newnton by Anne, da. of Sir Robert Mordaunt, 2nd Bt., of Massingham Parva, Norf. *educ.* L. Inn 1676. *unm. suc.* bro. as 3rd Bt. 1675.[1]

Commr. for assessment, Wilts. 1677–9, j.p. 1679–*d.*

Estcourt was the third cousin of Thomas Estcourt*. His father, created a baronet in 1622, sat for Cirencester in 1628. He seems to have been in arms against the Parliament and was taken prisoner at the fall of Bath, but apparently neither compounded nor paid the £1,000 at which he was assessed by the committee for the advance of money.[2]

Estcourt succeeded to the title when his elder brother was killed in a duel in Italy. He replaced his cousin in the Exclusion Parliaments as Member for Malmesbury, a borough some three miles from Long Newnton. Shaftesbury marked him 'doubtful'. He was a moderately active Member in 1679, when he was named to seven committees, of which the most important were on the bills for regulating elections, amending habeas corpus, and providing security against Popery. He was not recorded as speaking, and was absent from the division on the first exclusion bill. He was again moderately active in the second Exclusion Parliament with eight committees, including those for the bills to regulate elections (26 Oct. 1680) and to prohibit the import of Irish cattle (3 Nov.). In the Oxford Parliament he was named only to the committee of elections and privileges. As he survived the purge of the commissions of the peace he probably opposed exclusion. He served as foreman of the jury which acquitted Edward Nosworthy II* in November 1684. At the celebration which followed at the *Globe* tavern in Fleet Street, an altercation broke out after 'a discourse arose about leaping horses' between Henry St. John* and Francis Stonehouse*. Politics is unlikely to have played any part, since Estcourt was run through both by the Whig St. John, and the Tory Edmund Webb*. The last of his family, his death, according to Morrice, was 'very much bewailed'. The murderers were pardoned, probably because of Webb's signal loyalty 'in turbulent and staggering times'.[3]

[1] *Wilts. N. and Q.* v. 326. [2] *Cal. Comm. Adv. Money*, 727, 1119. [3] *N. and Q.* (ser. 4, iv), 275, 418; clxii. 57–58; R. Morrice, Entering Bk. 1, p. 448; *Wilts. Arch. Mag.* xxix. 184–5; *Cal. Treas. Bks.* vii. 1473.

B.D.H.

ETTRICK, Anthony (1622–1703), of the Middle Temple and Holt Lodge, Dorset.

CHRISTCHURCH 1685

b. 15 Nov. 1622, 1st s. of William Ettrick of Barford by Anne, da. and h. of William Willis of Pamphill. *educ.* Trinity, Oxf. 1640; M. Temple 1641, called 1652. *m.* Aug. 1651, Ann, da. of Edward Davenant, DD, vicar of Gillingham, Dorset, 3s. 2da. *suc.* fa. 1663.[1]

Commr. for assessment, Dorset Aug. 1660–1, 1664–80, 1689–90, Poole 1663–80; freeman, Lyme Regis 1662; recorder, Poole 1662–82; bencher, M. Temple 1672, reader 1673, treas. 1678–9; j.p. Dorset 1674–96, 1700–?*d.*, chairman, quarter sessions, c. June–Dec. 1688; commr. for inquiry into customs offences, Poole, 1677, visitation 1681.[2]

The Ettricks appear in the Wimborne area of Dorset in Elizabethan times; and the President of Trinity's malicious remark that Ettrick would conjure up a jackanapes to be his great-grandfather reflected simultaneously on the brevity of his stature and his lineage, as well as his eccentricity. Ettrick's father entered his pedigree in the Visitation of 1623, and before the Civil War had become steward to Sir John Bankes[†], lord of the manor of Corfe Castle. He was repeatedly accused of delinquency, but escaped on payment of £24 to the county committee, his estate being valued at £200 p.a. Ettrick himself married the daughter of a wealthy clergyman. Their marriage settlement was set aside by private Act of Parliament in 1662, nominally to enable him to pay his debts, but actually to facilitate his purchase of Holt Lodge. As a practising barrister, he seems to have lived principally in London, where he registered his pedigree in 1666, though he continued to act as steward to the Bankes family.[3]

Ettrick first stood in 1677 for Corfe Castle. Although duly elected he immediately 'surrendered' the seat to Lord Latimer (Edward Osborne*), who was returned accordingly. A few years later, Ettrick appears as agent for Latimer's brother Lord Dunblane (Peregrine Osborne*) on his Dorset estates; but as Dunblane obtained these estates as late as 1682, the origins of Ettrick's connexion with the Osborne family must be sought elsewhere, and may perhaps be found in his brother's post as collector of customs at Sunderland. Sir Leoline Jenkins* referred to him as a good friend when despatching him to Dorset to take charge of investigations after the Rye House Plot. He was generously rewarded, not merely with the venison he asked for but with a third of Kingswood chase.[4]

Ettrick played the chief part in the campaign against Samuel Hardy, the nonconformist minister of Poole. When the surrender of the charter ensured the return of two Tories in 1685 he allowed his son, William Ettrick*, to stand for Poole, while he himself was returned on the Hyde interest at Christchurch, where the Whig agent, Henry Trenchard*, had designs upon his recordership of Poole. No activity in James II's Parliament can positively be attributed to him, and he may not have attended, for he was in Dorset to sign the order for Monmouth's committal on 8 July.[5]

Ettrick and his son were among the ten Templars reported to have given their concurrence to James II's religious policy in 1687. He is not known to have stood again, and was removed from the commission of the peace for refusing the Association in 1696. He occupied his leisure by contributions to local history and by preparing (in unwarranted confidence of an early demise) a tomb which has become the principal tourist attraction of Wimborne Minster, where (more or less) he was 'buried' on 5 Oct. 1703.[6]

[1] *Procs. Dorset Nat. Hist. and Arch. Soc.* xxxvii. 26–39; Hutchins, *Dorset*, iii. 221; J. Aubrey, *Brief Lives*, i. 250. [2] J. Sydenham, *Poole*, 241; C. A. F. Meekings, *Dorset Hearth-Tax*, 117; Dorset RO, KG 1148, 1496, 1147; *Cal. Treas. Bks.* v. 828; SP 44/53/53; Lyme Regis mss B6/11, f. 25. [3] Aubrey, ii. 18; *Cal. Comm. Adv. Money*, 1025; C. H. Mayo, *Dorset Standing Committee*, 296–7, 411, 430; Bankes mss, till 2, no. 2; *CJ*, viii. 423; 13 & 14 Chas. II (private), c. 30; *Misc. Gen. et Her.* (ser. 5), iv. 197. [4] *CSP Dom.* 1677–8, p. 80; Jan.–June 1683, p. 353; July–Sept. 1683, p. 11; *HMC Lindsey*, 40–43; Browning, *Danby*, i. 366; *Cal. Treas. Bks.* i. 222; iv. 762; viii. 962. [5] *Proc. Dorset Nat. Hist. and Arch. Soc.* xxxvii. 33–34; North, *Lives*, iii. 183–4; *Clarendon Corresp.* i. 182; *CJ*, ix. 750; Grey, viii. 364, 367; PC2/76/256. [6] R. Morrice, Entering Bk. 2, p. 71.

J.P.F.

ETTRICK, William (1651–1716), of Holt Lodge, Dorset and the Middle Temple.

POOLE   1685
CHRISTCHURCH   1689, 1690, 1695, 1698, 1701 (Feb.), 1701 (Dec.), 1702, 1705, 1708, 1710, 1713, 1715–5 Dec. 1716

b. 15 Nov. 1651, 1st s. of Anthony Ettrick*. *educ.* Trinity, Oxf. 1667; M. Temple 1669, called 1675. *m.* (1) Elizabeth, da. and coh. of Sir Edmund Bacon, 4th Bt., of Redgrave, Suff., 1da.; (2) Frances, da. of Thomas Wyndham II* of Witham Friary, Som., 1da. *suc.* fa. 1703.[1]

Freeman, Poole 1684, Salisbury 1685; commr. for assessment, Dorset and Somerset 1689–90, Mdx. 1690, bencher, M. Temple 1699, treas. 1711–12.[2]

Attorney to Prince George by 1692–1708; counsel to commr. for land bank 1699; counsel to the Admiralty 1711–14.[3]

While Ettrick's father concentrated on undermining the ecclesiastical independence of Poole, ten miles from Holt, he was himself at work crushing its administrative autonomy; and it can hardly have been with much joy that the cowed electors returned him to James II's Parliament. He soon made his mark, with 15 committees, including the committee of elections and privileges and that to recommend expunctions from the Journals. On 11 June he reported the estate bill of Edward Meller*, though Roger North* claimed the principal credit for its passage. A week later he acted as teller with (Sir) Winston Churchill* for the second reading of the bill to prevent clandestine marriages, and was appointed to the committee. On 27 June he reported from a small committee a clause to forbid any proposal in Parliament for altering the succession to the throne; but it was ordered to lie on the table. It is probable that he rode the circuit with Judge Jeffreys on the Bloody Assizes, for he later remembered how 'it caused compassion in Englishmen when they saw so many men's quarters hanged up upon the western roads'. A speech on supply attributed to Ettrick in the second session was probably delivered by William Hewer*.[4]

Although Ettrick probably concurred with the King's ecclesiastical policy, he succeeded his father in the representation of Christchurch in 1689 on the interest of the 2nd Earl of Clarendon (Henry Hyde*). A moderately active Member of the Convention, he was appointed to 21 committees, including that which produced the list of essentials for the preservation of religion, law, and liberty. He voted to agree with the Lords that the throne was not vacant, a view he was still maintaining as late as 8 May, for King James's 'desertion' could not affect the rights of his heirs. Nevertheless he was among those appointed to inquire into the authors and advisers of grievances and to draft the new coronation oath.[5]

Ettrick's work for the remainder of the Convention was chiefly the prevention of excessive reprisals against James's supporters, or at any rate the churchmen among them. Against Papist converts, like Sunderland, he did not scruple to call for the full rigours of the law. But in general he insisted that there was nothing better than a reconciliation. He spoke against extending the treason laws, and defended James II's judges and the ecclesiastical commissioners. He would include all in the indemnity bill except those who were notorious, and he hoped that those who had made atonement by their present services would be buried in oblivion. Stout churchman though he was, he was pepared to make concessions to the dissenters. 'I am as much for indulgence to tender consciences as anybody', he said on 17 May. He would let them believe as they pleased, so long as they were not allowed to fill the world with endless controversies and disputes through the medium of the press. In the same spirit he spoke against continuing the suspension of habeas corpus. 'You are going into the country', he said on 22 May, 'and I know not how soon some of us may be sent for again and committed, perhaps till November, to a close prison all this summer.' The arrest of Peregrine Osborne* in the next must have seemed to Ettrick to lend point to this remark.[6]

In the second session Ettrick was appointed to the committees for restoring corporations and the attainder bill. On 18 Dec. he reported Lord Hereford's estate bill and carried it to the Lords. He spoke boldly against the disabling clause, and on 10 Jan. 1690 acted as teller for the motion to discuss the indemnity bill in a committee of the whole House. He continued to sit for Christchurch till his death, voting on most issues with the Tories. He died on 5 Dec. 1716 and was buried at Wimborne Minster. His estate descended to his unmarried daughter, but his interest had been based more on his legal ability and his connexion with the Osbornes than on his property.[7]

[1] Aubrey, *Brief Lives*, i. 250; *London Vis. Peds.* (Harl. Soc. xcii), 12. [2] Poole archives B17; Hoare, *Wilts.* Salisbury 483. [3] *Cal. Treas. Bks.* xxiii. 222–3. [4] *CSP Dom.* July–Sept. 1683, p. 431; 1683–4, p. 215; Grey, ix. 210. [5] R. Morrice, Entering Bk. 2, p. 71; *Clarendon Corresp.* i. 181–3; Browning, *Danby*, i. 366, 421, 423, 428–9; Grey, ix. 54–55, 238. [6] Grey, ix. 259–60, 266, 301, 314, 317, 382; J. P. Kenyon, *Sunderland*, 237. [7] Grey, ix. 518; Burke, *Commoners*, iii. 16.

J.P.F.

EVELYN, Sir Edward, 1st Bt. (1626–92), of Long Ditton, Surr.

SURREY 1685

b. 25 Jan. 1626, 5th but o. surv. s. of Sir Thomas Evelyn of Long Ditton by Anne, da. and h. of Hugh Gold *alias* Gawith, Grocer, of London. *m.* 15 Sept. 1659, Mary (*d.*1696), da. and coh. of Charles Balaam of Elm, Cambs., 3s. *d.v.p.* 6da. *suc.* fa. 1659; kntd. 13 Sept. 1676; *cr.* Bt. 17 Feb. 1683.[1]

J.p. Surr. Mar. 1660–Feb. 1688, Nov. 1688–?*d.*, commr. for assessment Sept. 1660–80, 1689–*d.*, loyal and indigent officers 1662, recusants 1675, dep. lt. 1683–? Mar. 1688, Oct. 1688–*d.*; alderman, Kingston-on-Thames 1685–Mar. 1688.[2]

Gent. of the privy chamber 1689–*d.*[3]

Evelyn was a great-grandson of the gunpowder manufacturer who established the family fortune in Tudor times. His father was a commissioner of array in 1642 and was assessed by the committee for the advance of money two years later, but he soon came to terms with the new regime and served as a justice of the peace throughout the Interregnum, though maintaining a 'prelatical' chaplain. Evelyn himself was apprenticed to a London Grocer in 1643, but in 1651 he compounded for

delinquency in both wars and paid a nominal fine. At the Restoration he was one of the proposed knights of the Royal Oak, with an annual income estimated at £600.[4]

Evelyn first stood for Parliament in 1685. Described by his cousin, the diarist, as 'an honest gentleman, much in favour with his Majesty', he was successful for Surrey, though he owed his seat chiefly to the wiles of the sheriff. He was moderately active in James II's Parliament, being appointed to four minor committees, including those on the bills to prevent the importation of tallow candles and to regulate hackney coaches. He presumably opposed James's religious policies, as he was removed from the Kingston corporation in March 1688. He was considered a likely candidate for re-election, but he did not stand again, though he accepted the new regime, and was appointed gentleman of the privy chamber. He died on 3 May 1692 and was buried at Long Ditton, the last of this branch of the family.[5]

[1] *Misc. Gen. et Her.* (ser. 2), iv. 318; PCC 49 Weldon. [2] *CSP Dom.* 1684–5, p. 266; PC2/72/640. [3] Carlisle, *Privy Chamber*, 204. [4] Guildhall Lib. mss 11593/1, f. 132; *Cal. Treas. Bks.* ix. 1321. [5] *Evelyn Diary*, iv. 433; H. Evelyn, *Hist. Evelyn Fam.* 525; PCC 143 Fane.

J.S.C.

EVELYN, George I (1617–99), of Wotton, Surr.

REIGATE	c. Sept. 1645[1]
HASLEMERE	20 May 1661
SURREY	1679 (Mar.), 1679 (Oct.), 1681, 1689

b. 18 June 1617, 1st s. of Richard Evelyn of Wotton by Eleanor, da. and h. of John Stansfield of The Cliff, Lewes, Suss. *educ.* Guildford g.s.; Trinity, Oxf. 1634–7; M. Temple 1637. *m.* 28 May 1640, Mary (*d.* 15 May 1644), da. and coh. of Daniel Caldwell of Horndon on the Hill, Essex, 5s. *d.v.p.*; (2) bef. Oct. 1647, Mary (*d.* 8 Aug. 1664), da. of Sir Robert Offley of Dalby, Leics., wid. of Sir John Cotton of Eltham, Kent, 5s. *d.v.p.* 4da. *suc.* fa. 1640.[2]

Commr. for assessment, Surr. 1643–8, Aug. 1660–80, 1689–90, sequestrations 1643, levying of money 1643, defence 1643, 1645, execution of ordinances 1644, new model ordinance 1645, militia 1648, Mar. 1660, j.p. Mar. 1660–6, 1681–7, by 1690–?*d.*, dep. lt. c. Aug. 1660–75, by 1694–*d.*; freeman, Guildford 1662; commr. for recusants, Surr. 1675, rebuilding of Southwark 1677.[3]

Gent. of the privy chamber (extraordinary) June 1660–?85.[4]

Evelyn, the elder brother of the well-known diarist, succeeded to an estate of £4,000 p.a. on the eve of the Civil War. Though he showed no alacrity to contribute to the advance of money for the parliamentary cause, he served on the county committee and was returned as a recruiter to the Long

Evelyn Family

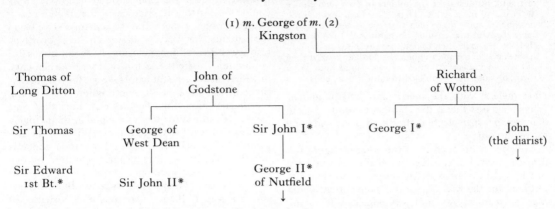

(1) *m.* George of *m.* (2)
Kingston

Thomas of Long Ditton — John of Godstone — Richard of Wotton

Sir Thomas — George of West Dean — Sir John I* — George I* — John (the diarist) ↓

Sir Edward 1st Bt.* — Sir John II* — George II* of Nutfield ↓

Parliament, surviving an allegation 'that he did raise and send horse to the King', only to be removed at Pride's Purge. After the execution of the King he was reported as sympathetic towards a royalist uprising, but he spent most of the Interregnum politically inactive, with his noted garden and fountains.[5]

Evelyn was involved in a double return for Haslemere in 1661 and seated on the merits of the election. In the Cavalier Parliament he was inactive, being named to only 37 committees. It is not known why his name does not appear in the 1666 commission of the peace, particularly since he was listed as a friend of Ormonde. But he may have been reluctant to enforce the Clarendon Code, for he voted to make it more acceptable by fining instead of imprisoning conventiclers. He was appointed to the committee on the bill to hinder Papists from sitting in Parliament in the spring session of 1675. He was assigned to Sir Adam Browne's* management on the working lists, but without effect, and Shaftesbury marked him 'thrice worthy' in 1677.[6]

At the first general election of 1679 Evelyn was 'invited by the country' to stand for the county with Arthur Onslow* against Browne and Lord Longford (Francis Aungier*), the court candidates, and in the words of the diarist

the country coming in to give their suffrages for my brother were so many that I believe they ate and drank him out near £2,000 by a most abominable custom.

He was again considered 'worthy' by Shaftesbury, and was probably moderately active in the first Exclusion Parliament. He may have served on four committees, none of which was of political importance, but he voted for the bill. Opposition was expected in August but failed to develop, and the sitting Members were re-elected, the crowd 'taking

Esquire Evelyn on their shoulders and carried him to the *Crown* door' and, in contrast to the previous election, the freeholders 'were so far from putting the elected knights to any charge that they invited them to the *White Hart* to dinner'. Evelyn was probably more active in the second Exclusion Parliament, in which either he or his cousin was named to ten committees, including those to inquire into the conduct of the judges, to take the disbandment accounts and to repeal the Corporations Act. It was probably he who feared 'lest the House should suffer in making good the articles' against Edward Seymour*, and supported the address for the removal of Laurence Hyde* with the exclamation: 'Is not the Duke of York the public enemy of the kingdom? . . . [I] would not have him under a temptation'. He was re-elected unopposed, but at Oxford he was appointed only to the committee of elections and privileges.[7]

At the accession of James II in 1685 Evelyn wrote to his brother complaining that he had been misrepresented at Court:

But you and all men that know me must witness that I was always loyal to his late Majesty (of blessed memory) and am now to his present Majesty, and shall so continue to my life's end, praying for his long life and the happiness of his government.

With an election imminent the diarist urged Evelyn to transfer his interest to his cousin Sir Edward Evelyn*, since the Court did not wish him to stand, and

I had observed by the account we had weekly, what very mean and slight persons (some of them gentlemen's servants, clerks, persons neither of reputation nor interest) were set up.

Evelyn, however, despite his disfavour at Court, claimed that 'the country would choose him, whether he would or no', and wrote back:

To show you how unwillingly I am persuaded to stand again, I have not solicited one voice either for myself or friend, but leave the freeholders to their own choice at the day of the election. There have been many of my neighbours and countrymen with me to desire I would serve them in this ensuing Parliament. I have desired their excuse, but when I could not prevail with them to let me be at home and in quiet, I told them that, if they did choose me and Mr Onslow, we would both serve them, because we are obliged to do it if once chosen.

Nevertheless, with the sheriff and lord lieutenant actively against them, the country candidates were defeated in a snap election after their party had gone to seek lodging.[8]

Evelyn was dropped from the commission of the peace in 1687, but considered a likely candidate for Surrey in the abortive elections of 1688. He was returned for the last time to the Convention, being then 71 years of age, and was named only to the committee on the bill to restore the London charter on 13 July 1689. In the bill to restore corporations, he supported the disabling clause. Evelyn died on 4 Oct. 1699 and was buried at Wotton. Over 2,000 mourners attended the funeral of 'a most worthy gentleman, religious, sober and temperate, [and] noted for keeping a good house after the ancient English way of hospitality'. His daughter Mary married Sir Cyril Wyche*, but the estate was inherited by his brother the diarist, whose grandson was returned for Helston in 1709.[9]

[1] Did not sit after Pride's Purge, 6 Dec. 1648, readmitted 21 Feb. 1660. [2] Misc. Gen. et Her. (ser. 2), iv. 202–3; H. Evelyn, Hist. Evelyn Fam. 45. [3] Evelyn Diary, v. 170; Surr. RO, QS2/1/6/325; Add. 6167, f. 208. [4] LC3/2. [5] Aubrey, Surr. iv. 116; Underdown, Royalist Conspiracy, 38; Hist. Evelyn Fam. 30, 42. [6] Eg. 2539, f. 208v. [7] HMC Ormonde n.s. iv. 317, 341; Evelyn Diary, iv. 165; True Dom. Intell. 29 Aug. 1679; Grey, viii. 90–91; HMC 12th Rep. IX, 114. [8] Hist. Evelyn Fam. 49; Evelyn Diary, iv. 433. [9] Luttrell, iv. 569; Evelyn Diary, v. 357–60.

J.S.C.

EVELYN, George II (1641–99), of Ventris House, Nutfield, Surr.

BLETCHINGLEY	1679 (Mar.), 1679 (Oct.), 1681
GATTON	5 Nov. 1696

b. 4 Dec. 1641, 4th s. of Sir John Evelyn I*. educ. M. Temple, entered 1657, called 1664; Christ Church, Oxf. 1658; Padua 1664. m. (1) 8 Sept. 1664, Mary (bur. 16 Jan. 1673), ?da. of Richard Longland of Coulsdon, s.p.; (2) lic. 13 June 1673, Margaret (bur. 24 May 1683), da. and coh. of William Webb, Grocer, of Throckmorton Street, London, 3s. 5da.; (3) lic. 15 Aug. 1684, Frances, da. of Andrew Bromehall of Stoke Newington, Mdx., 2s. 1da. suc. fa. at Nutfield 1664, bro. Sir John Evelyn, 1st Bt., at Godstone 1671.[1]

Commr. for assessment, Surr. 1673–80, 1689–90, j.p. 1679–?d., dep. lt. 1694–d.[2]

Evelyn inherited a small estate from his father in 1664, and seven years later the entailed family property, though his elder brother had done all he could to destroy it. Returned for Bletchingley, within a mile of his home, to the three Exclusion Parliaments, he was considered 'honest' by Shaftesbury and voted for exclusion. No committees can be definitely assigned to him in these Parliaments, in which his cousin and namesake sat for the county. Since he remained on the commission of the peace, the presumption must be that he joined the court party. He came at the foot of the poll at Bletchingley in 1685, but sat for Gatton under William III as a country Whig. He died on 19 June 1699 and was buried at Godstone, leaving many children by two of the 'most extraordinary beautiful wives'. His sons John and George later sat for Bletchingley, and his son William, who took the surname of Glanville, sat for Hythe from 1728–66.[3]

[1] Misc. Gen. et Her. (ser. 2), iv. 338; PCC 581 Wootton, 131 Laud; A.R. Bax, Surr. Mar. Lic. 27. [2] Evelyn Diary, v. 170; Surr. RO, QS2/1/6/306. [3] HMC 6th Rep. 489; Surr. RO, Clayton mss 60/9/4–7; H. Evelyn, Hist. Evelyn Fam. 204–6; Evelyn Diary, v. 187.

J.S.C.

EVELYN, Sir John I (1591–1664), of Lee Place, Godstone, Surr.

BLETCHINGLEY	1628, 1640 (Nov.),[1] 1660

bap. 20 Oct. 1591, 2nd s. of John Evelyn (d.1627) of Godstone by Elizabeth, da. and h. of William Stevens of Kingston-upon-Thames. educ. Emmanuel, Camb. 1606; M. Temple 1610. m. 24 Nov. 1618, Thomasine, da. of William Heynes of Chessington, and coh. to her bro. Matthew, 4s. 3da. Kntd. 25 June 1641.[2]

Member, Virginia Co. 1612, E.I. Co. 1624; j.p. Surr. 1627–48, 1659–d.; commr. for assessment 1643–8, Sept. 1660–3, sequestrations 1643, levying of money 1643, new model ordinance 1645, defence 1645, militia 1648, Mar. 1660, sewers, Kent and Surr. Aug. 1660.[3]

Commr. for bishops' lands 1646–8.

Evelyn's family had held the manor of Walkhampstead in Godstone since 1588. His grandfather established the family fortune by a grant of the monopoly of making gunpowder under the Tudors. On his marriage Evelyn built a large house at Godstone, two miles from Bletchingley, at the alleged cost of £9,000. He succeeded to the family business in 1627, but after a protracted dispute with the Government he lost the contract in 1636. A Presbyterian like his more radical nephew, Sir John Evelyn II*, he reluctantly supported Parliament in the Civil War; but he regarded Charles I as 'the best of men', and was secluded at Pride's Purge. He was returned for Bletchingley at the top of the poll in 1660, but he was not active in the Convention. He was probably appointed to six committees, including those to bring in a bill to abolish the court of wards and to investigate unauthorized Anglican publications. On 6 July 'Sir John Evelyn of Surrey' urged that the bill for a religious settlement should be committed and a national synod called. Ten days later he seconded the proposal of Sir Anthony Ashley Cooper* to adjourn the committee for three months. He did not stand again, and was buried at Godstone on 18 Jan. 1664, leaving an estate of over £1,400 p.a. to his eldest son, who had been created a baronet at the Restoration.[4]

[1] Did not sit after Pride's Purge 6 Dec. 1648, readmitted 21 Feb. 1660. [2] Misc. Gen. et Her. (ser. 2), iv. 329, 337; Aubrey, Surr. iii. 90. [3] T. K. Rabb, Enterprise and Empire, 288; C181/7/30. [4] VCH Surr. iv. 286; G. E. Aylmer, King's Servants, 367; Keeler, Long Parl. 168-9; Surr. RO, Clayton mss, 60/9/1; Bowman diary, ff. 55v, 85v; H. Evelyn, Hist. Evelyn Fam. 212.

M.W.H./J.S.C.

EVELYN, Sir John II (1601–85), of West Dean, Wilts.

WILTON	1626
LUDGERSHALL	1640 (Apr.), 1640 (Nov.),[1]
	3–23 May 1660
STOCKBRIDGE	23 May 1660

b. 11 Aug. 1601, 1st s. of George Evelyn, clerk in Chancery, of West Dean by Elizabeth, da. and h. of Sir John Rivers of Chafford, Kent. educ. Merchant Taylors' 1613; Emmanuel, Camb. 1615, BA 1619. m. 2 Apr. 1622, Elizabeth, da. and coh. of Robert Coxe, Grocer, of London, 1s. d.v.p. 4da. Kntd. 8 Aug. 1623; suc. fa. 1636.[2]

J.p. Wilts. 1637–d., Hants 1641–July 1660; commr. for assessment, Wilts. 1643–4, 1649–52, Jan. 1660–80, Hants and Wilts. 1643, levying of money, 1643; execution of ordinances, Hants 1645; gov. Covent Garden precinct 1646; commr. for militia, Wilts. 1648, Hants and Wilts. Mar. 1660, scandalous ministers, Wilts. 1654, oyer and terminer, Western circuit 1655, recusants, Hants 1675.[3]

Commr. for Westminster Assembly 1643, for provision for New Model Army 1645, Admiralty 1645–8, propositions for relief of Ireland 1645, abuses in heraldry 1646, exclusion from sacrament 1646, bishops' lands 1646, managing assessment 1647; member, committee of both kingdoms 1648; Councillor of State 25 Feb.–29 May 1660.

Evelyn was the nephew of Sir John Evelyn I* and cousin of the diarist. His grandfather bought the West Dean estate, nine miles from Stockbridge, in 1618. Evelyn succeeded to a property of £2,000 p.a., encumbered with at least £7,000 debt, and was disappointed in the expectation that his younger brother would be granted the Chancery post held by their father. A Presbyterian, he opposed Charles I before and during the Civil War and was explicitly excluded from pardon in 1642. Although he abstained from the House after Pride's Purge, he

continued to hold local office during the Interregnum, and bought the manor of Bishop's Sutton at the sale of church lands.[4]

Evelyn was appointed to the Council of State on the return of the secluded Members. At the general election of 1660 he was involved in a double return at Ludgershall. After taking his seat on the merits of the return, he was unseated in favour of the Anglican William Thomas* on the merits of the election, but remained in the Convention as Member for Stockbridge. An inactive Member, he probably voted with the Opposition. He made no recorded speeches, but as 'Sir John Evelyn of Wiltshire' was appointed to five committees, including those to bring in a bill for the abolition of the court of wards, to prepare instructions for the messengers to the King, to confer with the Lords about his reception, and to inquire into the state of the queen mother's jointure. He was given leave to go into the country on 27 June, and probably did not return. Although he took no further active part in politics, he conformed to the Church of England and probably opposed exclusion, since he remained a j.p. after 1680. 'A long-lived, happy man', he died on 26 June 1685. He cut off one of his surviving daughters with 5s. because of her marriage to the Tory Lord Castleton (George Saunderson*), and left the whole of his estate, reduced in value by a quarter, to his other daughter Elizabeth, mother of Evelyn Pierrepont*. The grateful legatee erected a sumptuous memorial at West Dean describing him as devoting his life to making new friends and reconciling enemies.[5]

[1] Abstained after Pride's Purge, 6 Dec. 1648, readmitted 21 Feb. 1660. [2] Misc. Gen. et Her. (ser. 2), iv. 329-31; PCC 109 Dale. [3] CSP Dom. 1637, p. 137; Thurloe, iii. 296. [4] H. Evelyn, Hist. Evelyn Fam. 492; Wilts. Arch. Mag. xxii. 259-61; G. E. Aylmer, King's Servants, 367; Keeler, Long Parl. 169-70; VCH Hants, iii. 43; iv. 322, 494; D. Underdown, Pride's Purge, 218. [5] CJ, viii. 9, 42; Hoare, Wilts. Everley, 7; Fanshawe Mems. 306; Hoare, Repertorium Wiltonense, 16; PCC 133 Cann; Wilts. Arch. Mag. xxii. 293-4.

M.W.H./P.W.

EVERARD, Sir Richard (c.1625–94), of Westminster.

WESTMINSTER	1661

b. c.1625, 1st s. of Sir Richard Everard, 1st Bt.†, of Langleys, Great Waltham, Essex by 1st w. Joan, da. of Sir Francis Barrington, 1st Bt.†, of Barrington Hall, Hatfield Broad Oak, Essex; step-bro. of Sir Gervase Elwes, 1st Bt* and Sir John Elwes*. m. (1) c.1654, Elizabeth, da. and coh. of Sir Henry Gibb, 1st Bt., groom of the bedchamber 1611–46, of Falkland, Fife and Westminster, 2s. (1 d.v.p.) 1da.; (2) Jane, da. of Sir John Finet, master of the ceremonies 1626–41, of St. Martin's Lane, Westminster, s.p. Kntd. by 1661; suc. fa. as 2nd Bt. June 1680.[1]

J.p. Westminster Mar. 1660–70, ?1675–87, Mdx. 1661–70, Essex 1664–70, 1675–Apr. 1688, Oct. 1688–d.; commr. for militia, Westminster Mar. 1660, sewers Aug. 1660, assessment, Westminster Aug. 1660–78, Essex 1663–80, 1689, loyal and indigent officers, London and Westminster 1662; dep. lt. Essex 1670–80; commr. for recusants, Mdx. 1675.[2]

Everard's ancestors had held manorial property in Great Waltham since 1482. His father married into the Barrington family, which dominated the county committee in the Civil War, became a Presbyterian elder, and represented Essex under the Protectorate.[3]

Everard probably acquired a residence in Westminster by marriage, and was knighted soon after the Restoration. He was returned for Westminster after a contest at the general election of 1661, and listed as a friend by Lord Wharton. A moderately active Member of the Cavalier Parliament, he was appointed to 171 committees and acted as teller in three divisions, but seldom spoke. He seems to have been most prominent in the opening sessions, probably in opposition, for he took no part in the Clarendon Code. He assumed the chair for the bill to confirm private Acts and carried it to the Lords. He also reported a bill to establish a registry of pawnbrokers, and was appointed to the committee to consider a bill for paving, repairing and cleaning the streets in his constituency. After the summer recess he was the first Member appointed to attend the King with a request that all those under attainder should be brought back to the Tower for trial. He was added to the committee on the bill for restraining the export of leather on 6 Mar. 1662, took the chair, and carried it up. In 1663 he was among those ordered to draft a bill to prevent the growth of Popery, a matter on which he felt strongly, for on 11 Apr. he wrote to Humphrey Weld*, one of his colleagues on the Westminster bench, complaining that a harsh and illegal punishment for the seizure of Popish books and trinkets 'argues more affection to Babylon than to the crown of England'. As a Westminster MP he was added to the committee on the bill for the naturalization of George Willoughby* and others, and reported it to the House. A petition from the inhabitants of Westminster was read in connexion with the additional poor relief bill on 23 June, and Everard was the second Member named to the committee. He was the first to whom was committed, on 2 Apr. 1664, the bill for the continued enjoyment of water brought to Westminster from Hyde Park. On 1 Dec. he complained that he had been affronted and assaulted by John Elwes and Peter Killigrew*; the matter was referred to the committee of privileges, but never reported. His last chairmanship was for

an Essex estate bill, which he reported on 27 Oct. 1666.[4]

Everard's activity declined under the Cabal. He probably favoured toleration, for he was removed from the commission of the peace when the second Conventicles Act became law, and on 7 Mar. 1673 he was appointed to the committee for a bill of ease for protestant dissenters. In a debate on grievances on 17 Mar. he 'complained of the levying half a crown per annum of all licensed alehouses'. Somewhat surprisingly he was included on the working lists, though Sir Richard Wiseman*, who 'doubted' him, wrote to Danby: 'I hope the Duke of Albemarle [Christopher Monck*] will secure him. The King or your lordship may be pleased to mind of it, as likewise (Sir) Thomas Clarges* if any good may be done upon him'. Presumably some was: Shaftesbury listed him as 'thrice vile' and he was classed as a court supporter on the government list of 1678. The author of *A Seasonable Argument* alleged that he had received £500 'and that being near spent, must have more or seek a new way to get bread'. After the Popish Plot his local knowledge was called on for a search of the Commons cellars for gunpowder. On 9 Nov. he informed the House that he had apprehended 'a person mentioned in Mr Coleman's letter', and was among those appointed to examine the prisoner's papers. This was his last committee: he was absent from the call of the House on 11 Dec. and sent for in custody by the serjeant-at-arms, and he was granted leave 12 days later. He never stood again. He gave negative answers on the Test Act and Penal Laws questions. He died on 29 Aug. 1694 'in the seventieth year of his age', and was buried at Great Waltham. His son inherited an estate of only £500 p.a. Langleys was sold to Samuel Tufnell† in 1710, and no other member of Everard's family entered Parliament.[5]

[1] Morant, *Essex*, ii. 86–87; Essex RO, wills 352/ER/23. [2] C181/7/37. [3] *VCH Essex*, ii. 61, 230–1; *HMC 7th Rep.* 549–52. [4] *CJ*, viii. 301, 305, 308, 401, 406, 515, 659; Dorset RO, D10/Cl. [5] *Dering*, 143; Grey, vi. 174; Morant, ii. 87; Bodl. North, b. l. f. 322.

E.C.

EVERSFIELD, Anthony (c.1621–95), of Denne Park, Horsham, Suss.

HORSHAM   1679 (Mar.), 1679 (Oct.), 1685, 1689

b. c.1621, 4th s. of Nicholas Eversfield† of The Grove, Hollington by Dorothy, da. of Edward Goring of Oakhurst; bro. of Edward Eversfield†, John Eversfield* and Sir Thomas Eversfield†. *educ.* St. Alban Hall, Oxf. matric. 31 Mar. 1637, aged 16, BA 1640. *unm. suc.* bro. Edward c.1676.[1]

Commr. for assessment, Suss. 1661–3, 1664–80, 1689–90, j.p. 1677–July 1688, Nov. 1688–d.

Having undertaken not to demand wages, Eversfield was returned for Horsham, where he held at least one burgage, at both elections of 1679. Shaftesbury confused him with his nephew Nicholas*, but probably meant to class him as 'old and vile' (though he had not sat before), and he was marked 'court' on Lord Huntingdon's list. Either uncle or nephew was given leave on 17 Apr. 1679 to go into the country until Friday in Easter week, but as neither voted in the division on the Exclusion Bill they probably agreed to absent themselves. Nevertheless, Eversfield was re-elected in August, but lost his seat to John Machell* in 1681. His success in 1685 suggests that he was a Tory, and he certainly retained local office till 1688. To the lord lieutenant's questions on the repeal of the Test Act and Penal Laws he replied:

> I must remain doubtful until I have considered of the debates in the next Parliament, the most proper place to decide this question. I can give no positive answer to any of the three questions.

He retained his seat in 1689, and on 21 May broke with the family tradition of total inactivity both in committee and debate by having himself added to the committee to inquire into sending children abroad to be educated as Papists. He was buried at Horsham on 24 Oct. 1695. He was succeeded by his great-nephew Charles, who sat for Horsham and Sussex as a Tory under Queen Anne, but went over to the Whigs after the Hanoverian succession.[2]

[1] J. Comber, *Suss. Genealogies, Horsham* 94–96. [2] W. Albery, *Parl. Hist. Horsham*, 509; Add. 5698, f. 206.

B.M.C.

EVERSFIELD, Edward (c.1618–c.1676), of The Grove, Hollington, Suss.

BRAMBER 1660

b. c.1618, 3rd s. of Nicholas Eversfield[†] of The Grove, and bro. of Anthony Eversfield*, John Eversfield* and Sir Thomas Eversfield[†]. *m.* (1) c.1644, Mary, da. of Francis Muschamp of Bredinghurst, Camberwell, Surr. and coh. to her bro. Edmund, *s.p.*; (2) lic. 8 Nov. 1666, 'aged about 35', Frances, da. of Thomas Carleton of Carshalton, Surr., wid. of Richard Roberts of Thorpe Langton, Leics., 1 ch. *d.v.p.*; (3) 23 Oct. 1670, Cecily, da. and coh. of Gervase Warmestry, registrar of Worcester dioc., *s.p. suc.* bro. Sir Thomas 1649, nephew John in Denne Park estate 1669.[1]

J.p. Suss. July 1660–*d.*; commr. for assessment, Suss. Aug. 1660–3, 1673–4, Surr. 1664–9; freeman, Portsmouth 1672.[2]

Gent. of the privy chamber (extraordinary) July 1660–*d.*[3]

Eversfield's great-grandfather acquired considerable estates in Sussex about the middle of the 16th century. His father and elder brother both represented Hastings, the latter being disabled in 1644, and compounding for his estates for £800. Eversfield's name appears on the list of proposed knights of the Royal Oak. His estates, valued at £600 p.a., lay entirely in East Sussex, and he must have owed his seat at Bramber to his wealthy younger brother John and his cousins, the Gorings. He made no speeches in the Convention and served on no committees. He was presumably the 'Mr Ersfield, a Sussex gentleman' who stood for Rye in 1667. He preferred a bill in Chancery on 22 Apr. 1675. His will was proved on 8 Nov. 1676.[4]

[1] *Suss. Inquisitions* (Suss. Rec. Soc. xiv), 84; *Coll. Top. et Gen.* iii. 150; *VCH Surr.* iv. 31; *Suss. N. and Q.* xiv. 256; xvi. 120; *London Mar. Lic.* ed. Foster, 463; Nichols, *Leics.* ii. 671. [2] R. East, *Portsmouth Recs.* 360. [3] LC3/2. [4] J. Comber, *Suss. Genealogies Horsham*, 89–95; Keeler, *Long Parl.* 170; *VCH Surr.* iv. 31; *CSP Dom.* 1667, p. 539; C9/406/58; PCC 137 Bence.

M.W.H./B.M.C.

EVERSFIELD, John (c.1624–78), of Charlton Court, Steyning, Suss.

STEYNING 5 July 1660

b. c.1624, 5th s. of Nicholas Eversfield[†] of The Grove, Hollington, and bro. of Anthony Eversfield*, Edward Eversfield* and Sir Thomas Eversfield[†]. *educ.* Magdalen Hall, Oxf. matric. 8 May 1640, aged 16; I. Temple 1641. *m.* (1) Hester (*d.*1672), da. and coh. of John Knight of Westergate, 1s.; (2) 3 July 1673, Susan, da. and coh. of Francis Norman of Salehurst, wid. of Thomas Foster of Iden, *s.p.*[1]

Commr. for sewers, W. Suss. Oct. 1660, assessment Suss. 1663–*d.*, j.p. 1668–*d.*[2]

Eversfield's first marriage must have been fortunate for a younger son, for in 1652 he was able to buy Charlton Court for £4,500, and in the list of proposed knights of the Royal Oak his income was estimated at £1,500 (more than twice his elder brother's). He was returned to the Convention for Steyning at a by-election when his cousin Henry Goring I* chose to serve for the county. Like his brother Edward, he made no speeches and served on no committees, but presumably supported the Court. He was buried at Steyning on 22 May 1678.[3]

[1] J. Comber, *Suss. Genealogies Horsham* 95–96; *Vis. Suss.* (Harl. Soc. lxxxix), 42; Add. 5698, f. 93v. [2] C181/7/58. [3] Add. 5698, f. 248v.

M.W.H./B.M.C.

EVERSFIELD, Nicholas (c.1646–84), of Charlton Court, Steyning, Suss.

BRAMBER 1679 (Mar.)

b. c.1646, o.s. of John Eversfield* by 1st w. *m.* 29 June

1674, Elizabeth, da. and h. of Nicholas Gildridge of Eastbourne, 1s. 2da. *suc. fa.* 1678.[1]

Commr. for assessment, Suss. 1677–80.

Eversfield was returned to the first Exclusion Parliament for Bramber, probably on the interest of his cousins the Gorings, soon after he succeeded to his father's estate. Unlike the rest of his family, he may have been Whiggish; Shaftesbury confused him with his uncle Anthony Eversfield*, but probably meant to mark him 'honest'. He made no speeches, sat on no committees, and probably paired with his uncle weeks before the division on the exclusion bill. He died in 1684, and was succeeded by his son Charles, who reunited the Eversfield estates in 1695, and at the end of a long parliamentary career sat for Steyning from 1741 to 1747 as an Old Whig.[2]

[1] *Vis. Suss.* (Harl. Soc. lxxxix), 42; J. Comber, *Suss. Genealogies Horsham*, 96; PCC 31 King. [2] PCC 145 Hare.

B.M.C.

EVERY, John (1643–79), of Wootton Glanville, Dorset and Cothays, Som.

BRIDPORT   1679 (Mar.)

bap. 15 Nov. 1643, o.s. of John Every of Symondsbury, Dorset by Anne, da. and h. of George Williams of Wootton Glanville. *educ.* Wadham, Oxf. 1661. *m.* 1666, Elizabeth, da. of Thomas Trenchard† of Wolveton, Dorset, *s.p. suc. fa.* 1658, cos. William Every of Cothays c.1660.[1]

Commr. for assessment, Dorset 1664–9, Som. 1679–*d.*; freeman, Lyme Regis 1666; sheriff, Dorset 1676–7; j.p. Dorset 1677–*d.*, Som. 1678–*d.*[2]

Every's great-grandfather appears to have laid the foundation of the family fortune around the turn of the century by judicious land dealings with the more improvident members of the nobility and gentry. The elder branch of the family transferred themselves to Derbyshire by marriage with an heiress, achieved a seat in the Short Parliament and a baronetcy in the following year, and were notable Royalists in the Civil War and Booth's rising. The west-country branches played a much less conspicuous role in this period even though Every's father was step-son to a Cavalier sheriff of Dorset.[3]

Every seems to have been an ardent sportsman, generous in his bequest to his 'quondam huntsman' and himself receiving perhaps the highest compliment one country gentlemen can pay another when John Strangways* left him his pack of hounds. 'A very loyal man', he displayed proper horror when his radical brother-in-law, John Trenchard* declared that a Trenchard had as much right to the throne as any Stuart. 'Brother, have a care of speaking treason, for if you do I will be sure to

inform against you,' Every warned him. On the other hand his step-brother John Hurding opposed the court candidate at Bridport on 1 Feb. 1677. As sheriff, he was responsible for more than his share of contested by-elections, and his handling of the ding-dong struggle between Thomas Browne* and Sir Nathaniel Napier* and his methodical endorsements of the Bridport writs are creditable to his judgment and commonsense, whatever the legal pundits may have thought. Every joined the Green Ribbon Club, and when he was himself returned for Bridport at the general election, Shaftesbury marked him 'honest'. He fulfilled expectations by voting for the first exclusion bill, but sat on no committees in the first Exclusion Parliament and made no speeches. Every died soon after the end of the session on 8 July 1679 and was buried at Wootton Glanville. His property was partitioned between John Leigh* and Sir Robert Henley*, the latter taking the Dorset property. His widow married William Joliffe†, who sat for Poole from 1698 to 1705.[4]

[1] Hutchins, *Dorset*, iii. 333, 747; *Som. Wills*, i. 73, 76; Wootton Glanville par. reg. [2] *Som. Rec. Soc.* xxxiv. p. xi; Lyme Regis mss B6/11, f. 26. [3] Dorset RO, MW/M4; Bankes mss, till 32, p. 10; C. H. Mayo, *Dorset Standing Committee*, 357, 431; *Som. and Dorset N. and Q.* xv. 134; Hutchins, ii. 264; *Cal. Comm. Comp.* 2448–9. [4] PCC 19 Bath; Dorset RO, D.124 (family); SP29/430/44; *Som. and Dorset N. and Q.* xiii. 67; *CJ*, ix. 439; Hutchins, iii. 743, 747; Vernon, *Cases in Chancery*, i. 37–48; J. R. Woodhead, *Rulers of London*, 100.

J.P.F.

EXTON, Sir Thomas (1631–88), of Trinity Hall, Cambridge.

CAMBRIDGE UNIVERSITY   1679 (Mar.), 1679 (Oct.),
1681, 1685

bap. 2 June 1631, 1st s. of John Exton of Westminster, judge of the Admiralty 1651–68, by Thomasina, da. and coh. of Ralph Brooke, York Herald, of London. *educ.* Merchant Taylors' 1637–43; Trinity Hall, Camb. 1647, LL.B. 1652, LL.D. 1662; G. Inn. 1649, called 1659, ancient 1676; advocate, Doctors' Commons 1664. *m.* 19 Jan. 1664, Isabella, da. of Robert Hore, Apothecary, of London, wid. of Thomas Prujean of Hornchurch, Essex, 1s. 1da. *suc. fa.* 1668; kntd. 23 Nov. 1675.[1]

Fellow of Trinity Hall 1651–63; master 1676–*d.*; chancellor, London dioc. 1663–*d.*; j.p. Essex 1665–87; commr. for assessment, Westminster 1667–9, Cambridge, Camb. Univ. and London 1679–80; vicar-gen. to the abp. of Canterbury 1684–*d.*[2]

Advocate-gen. 1675–86; judge of the Admiralty July–Dec. 1686; dean of the arches 1686–*d.*[3]

Exton's father, a civil lawyer, took no known part in the Civil War, and was sufficiently flexible or uncommitted to earn appointment as judge of the Admiralty court by the Rump and confirmation by the Duke of York at the Restoration. Exton combined his father's profession with a successful career at the university, interrupted only by marriage. He was appointed advocate-general in 1675, and returned to Cambridge in the following year as master of his college. As chancellor to the diocese of London, he enjoyed the useful support of his bishop, Henry Compton, and was returned to all the Exclusion Parliaments for the university. He was marked 'vile' on Shaftesbury's list. Moderately active in the first Exclusion Parliament, he was appointed to five committees and made two recorded speeches. In the dispute over the speakership he counselled moderation to avoid a constitutional crisis, arguing that to waive the Commons' rights at that time was not to renounce them for ever. He was named to committees on the bills for continuing the prohibition of Irish cattle and for security against Popery. On 10 Apr. 1679 he defended Dr John Nalson, a Cambridgeshire clergyman who had been imprisoned for lampooning the leaders of the country party:

> By other books this doctor has writ, he had showed himself loyal, and it was quite contrary to his intention that this pamphlet should be printed. He humbly supplicates your compassion for what he has done.

Exton was added to the committee conducting a languid inquiry into two pamphlets defending Danby, which was given the additional responsibility of considering Nalson's petition. Assuming the chair of this ineffectual body, he produced a report on 1 May recommending Nalson's discharge from confinement. As a sop to the lampoonist's victims, it was added that he should be removed from the commission of the peace, and the recommendations were accepted by the House without a division. Exton duly voted against exclusion, and after his re-election in August he was able through Sir Leoline Jenkins* to secure the withdrawal of a royal nominee for a fellowship of his college. In the second Exclusion Parliament he is mentioned only as receiving leave of absence, and at Oxford he was completely inactive.[4]

Re-elected in 1685, Exton was moderately active in James II's Parliament, being appointed to five committees, including those for the speedier recovery of tithe, the prevention of clandestine marriages, and the relief of London widows and orphans. He was appointed a judge of the Admiralty in July 1686, but his tenure of office was brief. He was accused of giving contradictory advice to the King and to his diocesan over the suspension of Dean Sharp for preaching an anti-Papist sermon whose views were held to reflect on the King, and was dismissed by the ecclesiastical commission. At the trial of the Seven Bishops he gave evidence that their petition was in Archbishop Sancroft's handwriting. Falling ill shortly after the trial, he died on 5 Nov. 1688 and was buried at St. Benet Paul's Wharf, the only member of his family to sit in Parliament.[5]

[1] Guildhall RO, St. Andrew Holborn par. reg.; *DNB*; *Le Neve's Knights* (Harl. Soc. viii), 303; *St. Benet Paul's Wharf* (Harl. Soc. Reg. xxxix), 47; *London Mar. Lic.* ed. Foster, 1099. [2] *DNB*; *Bramston Autobiog.* (Cam. Soc. xxxii), 247; H. E. Malden, *Hist. Trin. Hall*, 161. [3] *CSP Dom.* 1675–6, p. 401; 1686–7, pp. 194, 223; *Cal. Treas. Bks.* iv. 849; Newcourt, *Rep.* i. 446. [4] B. P. Levack, *Civil Lawyers in England*, 229; Grey, vi. 436; vii. 103–4; *CSP Dom.* 1679–80, pp. 526, 530; Bodl. Tanner mss 155, ff. 119, 121. [5] *HMC Downshire*, i. 185–6; *Bramston Autobiog.* 248, 251; R. Morrice, Entering Bk. 1, pp. 629, 637; 2, p. 30; *State Trials*, xii. 287; Luttrell, i. 473; *St. Benet Paul's Wharf* (Harl. Soc. Reg. xli), 81.

E.R.E./G.J.

EYLES, John (*d.*1703), of Great St. Helens, London and Southbroom, nr. Devizes, Wilts.

DEVIZES 1679 (Oct.)

> 1st s. of John Eyles, woolstapler, of Devizes by w. Mary. *m.* Sarah Cowper of London, 2s. 5da. *suc.* fa. 1662; kntd. 15 Aug. 1687.[1]
> Alderman of London 1687–Sept. 1688, dep. lt. 1687–Oct. 1688, ld. mayor Sept.–Oct. 1688; j.p. Wilts. June–Oct. 1688.
> Principal farmer of the alnage by 1680–*d.*[2]

Eyles's family had been prominent in the Devizes mercantile community since the early years of the century. He became a London merchant, engaging in the supply of slaves to Barbados, sometimes by rather questionable methods. By 1680 he had prospered sufficiently to buy for £9,000 a lease of the alnage duty (with his son-in-law), as well as a property just outside his native town which gave him an interest there. A strict Baptist 'of good parts . . . especially of temper', he would have commanded the support of its largest dissenting congregation. With another exclusionist Sir Giles Hungerford*, he was elected by 'the popularity' in September 1679, and returned by the mayor on receiving a bond for £2,000 to protect himself from the consequences of this irregularity. But he remained in good standing with the Government; two months later he was one of the three merchants to whom Henry Guy* referred the examination of the Barbados sugar tax account, and their report in April was accepted and passed to Richard Aldworth* for action. When Parliament met, the Devizes return was challenged by Sir Walter Ernle* and George Johnson*, who had been elected by the corporation. Although the elections committee did not report, Eyles and Hungerford do not appear to have taken their seats. Eyles contested the borough again in 1681, but this time his opponents were returned, and Parliament was dissolved before his petition could be heard. Though he obtained a pass for Holland on 28 Sept. 1683, there is no reason to suppose that this was other than a business journey.[3]

It is not known whether Eyles stood in 1685, but he became one of James II's Whig collaborators later in the reign, receiving a knighthood and local office both in London, where he served briefly as lord mayor, and in Wiltshire. The Devizes corporation had now been so regulated, according to the King's electoral agents, that they would undoubtedly choose Eyles and the mayor, 'very honest and fit persons to serve his Majesty'. But when Eyles came to put this opinion to the test, he was again disappointed. Presumably the dispossessed councilmen had regained power, and their distaste for him was so strong that they preferred another Whig, Sir William Pynsent*. Eyles and William Trenchard* petitioned, claiming that all the 'burgesses' had the right to elect; but the report from the elections committee, delivered by John Birch* was adverse, and the House agreed. Evidence was given to the committee of inquiry into the alnage of Eyles's oppressive conduct, and he retired from public life; but he supported the new regime with loans totalling £18,000 in 1689, and took a leading part in arranging remittances to the English army in Flanders. He was buried at St. Helen's, Bishopsgate on 5 July 1703. In addition to some bequests for general charitable purposes in Devizes, he left £100 to the Baptist chapels there and in London. A younger son, nephew and grandson sat for Devizes in every Parliament from 1715 to 1741.[4]

[1] J. R. Woodhead, *Rulers of London*, 66. [2] *HMC Lords*, iv. 34, 38; PC2/72/668. [3] *Wilts. Arch. Mag.* iv. 162; vi. 134; *Cal. Ct. Mins. E. I. Co.* ed. Sainsbury, x. 174; *HMC Lords*, n.s. iv. 130; *Bramston Autobiog.* (Cam. Soc. xxxii), 315; D. P. Lacey, *Dissent and Parl. Pols.* 391; *Cal. Treas. Bks.* vi. 261, 513; *CSP Dom.* 1683–4, p. 193. [4] *Ellis Corresp.* ii. 150; *CJ*, x. 56–57, 175; *Cal. Treas. Bks.* ix. 405, 1972, 1974, 1983, 1984; PCC 109 Degg.

J.P.F.

EYRE, Anthony (1634–71), of Rampton, Notts.

NOTTINGHAMSHIRE   1661–Nov. 1671

b. 17 Sept. 1634, 2nd but o. surv. s. of Sir Gervase Eyre of Laughton en le Morthen, Yorks. by Elizabeth, da. and coh. of John Babington of Rampton. *educ.* I. Temple 1654. *m.* (1) 9 June 1657, Lucy (*d.* June 1659), da. of Sir John Digby of Mansfield Woodhouse, Notts. 1da.; (2) Elizabeth, da. of Sir John Pakington, 2nd Bt.*, of Westwood, Worcs. 3s. (2 *d.v.p.*), 4da. *suc.* fa. 1644.[1]
Commr. for militia, Notts. Mar. 1660; j.p. Notts. Mar. 1660–d., liberties of Southwell and Scroby 1674; dep. lt. Notts. c. Aug. 1660–d.; commr. for assessment, Notts. Aug. 1660–d., Nottingham and Newark 1663–4,

sewers, Hatfield chase Aug. 1660, loyal and indigent officers, Notts. 1662, capt. of militia by 1662–d., jt. farmer of excise 1665–d.[2]
Cornet, indep. tp. of Sir George Savile* 1666–7.

Eyre's ancestors were landowners in the Peak District in the reign of Henry III. One of them sat for Derbyshire in 1459, but they were not a regular parliamentary family. Eyre's father bought out the other coheiress of Rampton in 1624 and took up residence there; a royalist cavalry officer and commissioner of array, he died in the Newark garrison. The Yorkshire estate was sequestrated at the end of the war until Eyre's guardian John Newton* compounded for it in 1652 for the moderate fine of £580 in order to terminate expensive legal proceedings. Eyre himself has to be distinguished from his uncle, a Cavalier colonel, who served in the Duke of York's household after the Restoration. He was accused of complicity in Booth's rising in 1659. In 1661 he sensationally defeated the opposition candidate William Pierrepont*; but he was not an active Member of the Cavalier Parliament, with only 32 committees in 14 sessions, none of them of prime political importance. He took part in considering ways to relieve loyalist sufferers in 1661, and in 1663 he was appointed to the committee for the estate bill promoted by his father-in-law Pakington. From 1665 he supplemented his rent-roll with the income from the county excise, which he farmed jointly with the father of Sir William Stanhope* for £3,100 p.a., a grant which he probably owed to Pakington's brother-in-law William Coventry*. His attendance at the House was so irregular that he narrowly escaped a fine for default in February 1688; but his name appears on the list drawn up by Sir Thomas Osborne* of Members to be engaged for the Court by the Duke of York. Eyre's own tastes and character were commonplace. He was much away from home, usually on the plea of seeing a man about a horse, and he made little or no profit out of the excise farm, which he left to subordinates. But his second wife was a highly competent business woman. She took over a factory in Gainsborough and began the manufacture of sailcloth for the Admiralty. Her first samples were embarrassingly well received, and Eyre had to explain: 'what I have hitherto made has only been an essay whether our country people could be brought to understand the manufacture'. In December 1670 he was appointed to the committee for the private bill to provide portions for the daughters of (Sir) Clifford Clifton*. His new industrial interests secured his addition to the committee considering petitions for the employment of the poor in the following February. But his health was breaking up, with frequent recurrences of fever; on 1 Mar. he obtained leave to go into the country, and he was buried at Rampton on 11 Nov. He was succeeded by his son Gervase, who sat for the county from 1698 to 1700 as a Tory.[3]

[1] J. Hunter, *South Yorks.* i. 288–9; *Cal. Comm. Comp.* 2744. [2] C181/7/21; *Kingdom's Intell.* 1 Sept. 1662; *Cal. Treas. Bks.* i. 641. [3] A. C. Wood, *Notts. in the Civil War*, 122, 134; *Cal. Comm. Comp.* 769; *Hutchinson Mems.* 96; *CSP Dom.* 1670, pp. 484, 527; Spencer mss, Elizabeth Eyre to Sir William Coventry, 25 Oct. 1670.

E.R.E.

EYRE, Giles (1635–95), of Brickworth, Whiteparish, Wilts. and Lincoln's Inn.

DOWNTON   9 May 1660
SALISBURY   22 Jan.–4 May 1689

bap. 28 May 1635, 1st s. of Giles Eyre of Brickworth by Anne, da. of Sir Richard Norton, 1st Bt.[†], of Rotherfield Park, East Tisted, Hants. *educ.* Winchester 1647; Exeter, Oxf. 1653; L. Inn 1654, called 1661. *m.* (1) lic. 18 Nov. 1662 (with £3000), Dorothy (*d.* 15 Jan. 1668), da. of John Ryves of Ranston, Shroton, Dorset, 3s.; (2) Christabella, da. of Thomas Wyndham I[*] of Tale, Payhembury, Devon, 2s. *d.v.p.* 3da. *suc.* fa. 1685; kntd. 31 Oct. 1689.[1]

Commr. for assessment, Wilts. Aug. 1660–1, 1673–9, Wilts and Salisbury 1679–80, Wilts., Salisbury and Southampton 1689–90; bencher, L. Inn 1675; recorder, Newport I.o.W. 1675–84, Oct. 1688–*d.*, Southampton 1681–90; dep. recorder, Salisbury 1675–81, recorder 1681–4, Oct. 1688–*d.*[2]

J.K.b. 4 May 1689–*d.*

Eyre's father, unlike his uncle Henry, was not politically active, though he was named to the Wiltshire assessment commission in 1657 and probably paid Eyre's election expenses. He owned property at Redlynch, a mile from Downton, where he sometimes resided, for Eyre himself was baptized in Downton church. After a double return for the borough at the general election of 1660 had been settled in his favour, 'Giles Eyre jun.' joined the Opposition in the Convention and was marked as a friend on Lord Wharton's list. He was not active as a committeeman, being appointed presumably to the committee on the Marquess of Winchester's bill (against which he delivered a set speech) and perhaps to nine others. He moved to lay aside the debate on the Thirty-Nine Articles on 2 Aug., and Wharton sent him a copy of the case for modified episcopacy; but he took no part in the debate in the second session, although on 22 Nov. he delivered another set speech against the militia bill. He was again involved in a double return at Downton in 1661, in conjunction with his school-fellow John Elliott. After demonstrating his forensic skill as a newly-qualified barrister by extracting a favourable report from the election committee, he allowed the matter to drop when allegations of fraudulent creation of freeholds were made on the floor of the House.[3]

Eyre was made deputy recorder of Salisbury under the new charter of 1675, which he had procured, and given a tankard worth £10 by the corporation. He apparently did not contest any of the exclusion elections, perhaps out of deference to the court connexions of his second wife's family, though he was active in support of Sir Joseph Ashe[*] at Downton. The Wyndham connexion certainly came in useful for Eyre after he had been elected recorder of Salisbury by 'the popularity' in 1681. An informer wrote that he was 'not a good man, nor are any of his name'; but John Wyndham[*], in spite of the plainest hints from Secretary Jenkins, refused to certify otherwise than that 'Mr Giles Eyre is a person very loyal and well affected to religion and government of the Church as by law established'. Eyre's appointment was confirmed by the crown, but he lost it under the new charter of 1684. His interest remained unbroken, and in 1686 the corporation wished to restore him to the old post of deputy recorder.[4]

Eyre was approved, with some reservations, as court candidate for Downton in 1688. A strong dissenter, according to the King's electoral agents, he could also be recommended because he managed the affairs of the Roman Catholic Lord Arundell of Wardour. He had been 'very violent, but ambitious of honour, and supposed he will be right to reconcile himself to your Majesty'. It is unlikely that he stood for Downton in 1689, when the two sitting Members, both Whigs, were elected; but he was returned for Salisbury, where he was again recorder, by the corporation, and apparently allowed to take his seat. During his three months in the Convention he was an active Member. He made six recorded speeches and was appointed to 19 committees including those to bring in a list of essentials for securing religion, laws and liberties, and to draw up reasons on the state of the throne. He helped to manage the conference, and to draw up amendments to the resolution of the House of Lords. On the declaration of rights, he asked: 'May you not be told that these things are ancient flowers of the crown, and not to be parted with? I would not have our purchase, like the Indians, to give gold for rattles.' But he was not a legal pedant, being willing to avoid delay by agreeing with the Lords to omit the article inserted to cover the case of William Williams[*], and on 20 Feb. he declared:

> If we are not constituted a Parliament under these circumstances now, we may never have one in England more. ... We are an infant government, if I may so

style it; it must be preserved by the hand that brought it up. Are we sure our successors will be of our mind?

He was appointed to the committees for the bill of rights, the coronation oath and the oaths of supremacy, but his obliging speech of 11 Mar. ensured that his stay in the Lower House would be short:

> I see in this matter of the revenue we go on very heavily. In a matter of this moment, to support the honour of the King, whatever you do in this bill, if it goes as is proposed, you do less than nothing, to the joy of your enemies and the sorrow of your friends. Therefore I propose a vote that you give the King a revenue for life of £1,200,000 p.a.

The grateful King determined that Eyre's should be the first judicial appointment of the reign (though either he or Lord Halifax seems to have confused him with his cousin Samuel), and as soon as the formalities of the serjeanthood could be completed, he took his seat on the King's bench.[5]

As an assistant to the Upper House, Eyre's opinions were moderately delivered, though on Titus Oates's case he declared: 'As to the whipping, it is plain it is a villainous judgment, let Bracton say what he pleases'. No doubt he recalled that his own grandfather had been flogged by order of Star Chamber. He gave no opinion on the barring of impeachment by royal pardon, or on the legality of the surrender of the charters. Roger Morrice alleged that he had procured the surrender of the Salisbury charter, presumably in 1675 or 1688. Nevertheless he was looked on by the Government as a safe man, and presided at the trial of the Lancashire Jacobites in 1694. He died on 2 June 1695 and was buried at Whiteparish. His eldest son Giles was a lunatic, but a younger son sat for Downton from 1698 (with one interlude) till his death in 1715.[6]

[1] *Wilts. N. and Q.* v. 100–2; Dorset RO, Jp 389; *Misc. Gen. et Her.* (ser. 5), ix. 109; *Som. Wills*, ii. 43. [2] *CSP Dom.* 1675–6, p. 53; Hoare, *Wilts.* Salisbury, 712; J. S. Davies, *Hist. Southampton*, 185. [3] *Wilts.* RO, Radnor mss 337; Bowman diary, ff. 117, 129v; *Old Parl. Hist.* xxiii. 24. [4] Hoare, 475, 484; Radnor mss 1084, Ashe to John Snow, 1 Feb. 1679, 5 Feb. 1681; *CSP Dom.* 1680–1, pp. 405, 421, 452, 516. [5] Grey, ix. 80, 81–82, 99, 156; Foxcroft, *Halifax*, ii. 213; *CSP Dom.* 1689–90, p. 59. [6] *HMC Lords*, ii. 79, 345, 431; R. Morrice, Entering Bk. 3, p. 99; *HMC Kenyon*, 309.

J.P.F.

EYRE, Henry (1628–78), of Woodlands, Dorset.

SALISBURY   1659, 1660
DOWNTON   22 Apr. 1675–18 July 1678

bap. 23 Oct. 1628, 10th but 6th surv. s. of Giles Eyre of Brickworth, Whiteparish, Wilts. by Jane, da. and h. of Ambrose Snelgrove of Redlynch, Wilts. *educ.* L. Inn 1647, called 1653; Jesus, Oxf. BA 1649, MA 1652. *m.* c.1658, Dorothy, da. of Sir George Hastings† of Woodlands, wid. of Christopher Dodington of Lincoln's Inn

and Horsington, Som., and coh. to her nephew Henry, *s.p.*[1]
Fellow of Jesus 1648–51, Merton 1651–?58; recorder, Salisbury 1656–June 1660; commr. for assessment, Wilts. 1657, Jan. 1660–1, 1677–*d.*, Dorset 1664–9; j.p. Wilts. 1657–66, Dorset 1662–5, 1668–70, 1675–*d.*; commr. for recusants 1675.[2]

Eyre came from the cadet branch of a Wiltshire family which can be traced back to the reign of Edward II, though its parliamentary history begins only in the 16th century. His father was 'much oppressed by public power for his laudable opposition to the measure taken in the reigns of James I and Charles I', and was plundered by the Cavaliers in the Civil War. Eyre, a lawyer by profession, was re-elected for Salisbury, seven miles from the paternal home, in 1660, clearly as an opponent of the Restoration (which deprived him of his recordership). He was not an active committeeman, being appointed to the committee of elections and privileges and perhaps nine others, where he cannot be distinguished from his nephew Giles, and he made two recorded speeches. The first, in the supply debate, was harmless enough; he proposed as a compromise that £800,000 should be raised, half by excise, half by a land tax. But in the debate on the bill authorizing the corporation of London to raise money for celebrations, he asserted that:

> the desire came from a few persons only and not from the major part; and moved to lay the bill aside, or else to read it tomorrow se'nnight (which was the next day after the rising of the House).[3]

Eyre is unlikely to have contested the general election of 1661, and little is heard of him for the next 14 years. One of his brothers, an Independent minister, was ejected from his Salisbury parish in 1662, but Eyre seems to have conformed, though his removal from the Dorset commission of the peace in May 1670 shows that he was hostile to the Conventicles Act. His mother's property at Redlynch, one mile from Downton gave him an interest there which he strengthened by obtaining, together with the sitting Member Sir Joseph Ashe*, the grant of two annual fairs. Returned at a by-election in 1675, he was a very active committeeman, serving on 95 committees in only three years in the Cavalier Parliament. Of these 18 were on legal matters, and he was chairman for five private bills. He lost no time in declaring himself an opponent of the Court, moving on 17 May that no new bills should be introduced till satisfaction had been given on the removal of counsellors and the formation of an anti-French alliance. He helped to prepare reasons for the conferences on Shirley v. Fagg and the Four Lawyers, and was named to two anti-Popish committees. In the autumn session he was appointed to the committees for appropriating the customs to the use of the navy and excluding Papists from Parliament. Sir Richard Wiseman* listed him, by a natural confusion of residence and constituency, among the Dorset Members opposed to the Court, and Shaftesbury marked him 'doubly worthy'. In 1677 he was nominated to the committees for recalling British subjects from French service, preserving the liberty of the subject and preventing the growth of Popery. On 9 Mar. he carried the estate bill of Sir Trevor Williams*, which he had chaired, to the Lords. On 9 Feb. 1678 he acted as teller for continuing the debate on irregular adjournments. Eyre died on 18 July, and was buried at Whiteparish. On the death of his widow some years later the Hastings estate in Dorset was reunited and passed to Samuel Rolle*.[4]

[1] Hoare, *Wilts. Frustfield*, 56; H. N. Bell, *Huntingdon Peerage*, 96; Hants RO, 16M50/7; *Coll. Top. et Gen.* iv. 277–8. [2] Hoare, *Wilts.* Salisbury, 711. [3] *Wilts. N. and Q.* v. 98; Christie, *Shaftesbury*, i. pp. xxxvii, liv; *Old Parl. Hist.* xxiii. 12, 50. [4] A. G. Matthews, *Calamy Revised*, 187; Hoare, *Wilts.* Downton, 22; *Dorset Hearth-Tax* ed. Meekings, 33, 117; Grey, iii. 156; Hutchins, *Dorset*, iii. 155; *Wilts. N. and Q.* v. 99.

M.W.H./J.P.F.

EYTON, Kenrick (c.1607–81), of Lower Eyton, Denb.

FLINTSHIRE   12 Nov. 1660

b. c.1607, 1st s. of Sir Gerard Eyton of Lower Eyton by Elizabeth, da. and h. of Edward Bromfield of Bodulltin. *educ.* I. Temple 1626, called 1634. *m.* (1) 11 Feb. 1636, Eleanor, da. and coh. of Sir Peter Mutton† of Llannerch, 3s. 4da.; (2) bef. 1656, Mary, da. of Sir Francis Bickley, 1st Bt., of Attleborough, Norf., wid. of William Hoo of Hoobury, St. Paul's Walden, Herts., 1s. 2da. *suc.* fa. 1652; kntd. 13 Apr. 1675.[1]
Protonotary and clerk of crown, Denb. and Mont. 1637–46, May 1660–*d.*; j.p. Flints. 1641–4, Chester, Denb. and Flints. July 1660–*d.*; commr. for assessment, Flints. Sept. 1660–1, Denb. 1661–80, Chester and Flints. 1673–80, Caern. 1673–4; attorney-gen. Cheshire and Flints. Aug. 1660–71; second justice, N. Wales circuit 1670–6, c.j. 1676–*d.*; member, council in the marches of Wales 1672–*d.*[2]
Capt. (royalist) 1634–6.

Eyton's ancestors had been established at the property from which they took their name in the 11th century, but their record of parliamentary service began only in 1614. Both Eyton and his father acted for the King from the beginning of the Civil War. They compounded on the Denbigh articles for £457, and Eyton went to France where he corresponded with Evelyn. But in 1656 Maj. Gen. James Berry† recommended that Eyton's estate should not be decimated because he had changed his interest several years before; he had married a godly gentlewoman and frequented the society of

godly men. At the Restoration he petitioned successfully for the office of attorney-general for Cheshire and Flintshire, and was returned to the Convention for the Welsh county at an election long delayed by the death of the sheriff. He took no known part in its proceedings, but he was clearly a court supporter, becoming a Welsh judge ten years later. He was buried at Bangor on 21 Nov. 1681, the last of the family to sit in Parliament.[3]

[1] J. Y. W. Lloyd, *Hist. Powys Fadog*, ii. 161–3; iii. 325; PCC 69 Cottle, 170 Penn. [2] W. R. Williams, *Gt. Sessions in Wales*, 80, 104–5. [3] Lloyd, ii. 152; *Cal. Comm. Comp.* 1236; *Evelyn Diary*, ii. 558; *CSP Dom.* 1655–6, p. 212; 1660–1, pp. 126, 208; *Arch. Camb.* (ser. 5), vii. 114.

M.W.H./A.M.M.

FAGG, John I (1627–1701), of Wiston, Suss.

RYE	3 Oct. 1645
SUSSEX	1654, 1656,[1] 1659
STEYNING	1660, 1661, 1679 (Mar.), 1679 (Oct.)
SUSSEX	1681
STEYNING	1685, 1689, 1690, 1695, 1698, 7–18 Jan. 1701

b. 4 Oct. 1627, o.s. of John Fagg of Rye by Elizabeth, da. of Barnaby Hodgson of Framfield. *educ.* Emmanuel, Camb. 1644; G. Inn 1644. *m.* (1) 19 Mar. 1646, Mary (*d.* 20 Nov. 1687), da. of Robert Morley of Glynde, 9s. (4 *d.v.p.*) 5da.; (2) Anne (*d.* 11 May 1694), da. of Philip Weston of Newbury, Berks., wid. of Thomas Henshaw of Billingshurst, Suss., *s.p. suc.* fa. 1645; *cr.* Bt. 11 Dec. 1660.[2]
Commr. for assessment, Suss. 1645–52, 1657, Jan. 1660–80, 1689–90, Kent Jan. 1660, 1673–80, 1690, militia, Suss. 1648, Kent and Suss. 1659, Suss. Mar. 1660; j.p. Suss. 1649–July 1660, May 1688–*d.*, commr. for scandalous ministers 1654, sewers, rapes of Lewes and Pevensey 1659, Sept. 1660, Denge marsh Oct. 1660, Walland marsh Dec. 1660; dep. lt. Suss. May 1688–*d.*; commr. for derelict lands 1696, col. of militia ft. by 1697–*d.*[3]
Commr. for high court of justice 1649; Councillor of State 31 Dec. 1659–25 Feb. 1660.[4]
Col. of ft. 1659, Feb.–July 1660.[5]

Fagg's father, the wealthiest inhabitant of Rye before the Civil War, served as mayor in 1642–3 and advanced £1,000 to the parliamentary cause. Fagg himself became the ward and brother-in-law of Herbert Morley*, under whose guidance he chiefly acted in his earlier years. He was returned for Rye as a recruiter, the first of his family to enter Parliament. In 1649 he sat for three days as one of the King's judges, and took his seat in the Rump after some hesitation. In the same year he acquired the Shirley estate at Wiston, two miles from Steyning, valued at £1,000 p.a. and carrying with it an unchallengeable interest in the borough. He held local office throughout the Interregnum, though he was excluded from the second Protectorate Parliament in 1656. He was commissioned to raise a regiment of foot by the Rump in 1659, and taken prisoner by forces loyal to the military junta in an attempt to assist Morley at Portsmouth in December. The Rump gave him a vote of thanks, and appointed him to the Council of State.[6]

Fagg was returned for Steyning at every election from 1660 till his death more than 40 years later. Lord Wharton marked him as a friend in the Convention, to be managed by Sir Richard Onslow*, but he was named only to the committee of elections and privileges, and made no recorded speeches. Like his brother-in-law he was slow to perceive the inevitability of the Restoration, and it was not until May that he took steps to obtain a pardon. He was removed from the commission of the peace and his regiment given to Lord Mordaunt, but he was not otherwise molested. He was even created a baronet, and he represented Rye as one of the bearers of the canopy at the coronation. Presumably Wharton was disappointed in him, for his name disappeared from the 1661 list of friends, though he remained a Presbyterian, sheltering ejected ministers and educating his sons at a dissenting academy. He was again inactive in the Cavalier Parliament, in which he was appointed to 41 committees, none of much political significance, and acted as teller in four divisions. His attendance was probably irregular, for he defaulted on a call of the House in 1663, but he was doubtless in opposition to the Clarendon administration. On 29 Apr. 1668 he reminded the House of the Lords bill for the improvement of Ashdown forest, but it was resolved to proceed no further that session. He acted as teller on 1 Mar. 1670 for the total prohibition of imported brandy.[7]

In 1675 Fagg acquired a niche in constitutional history as defendant in an action brought by Thomas Shirley, a court physician, for the lands which (he asserted) his grandfather had no power to sell. Waiving his privilege, Fagg was successful both in Exchequer and Chancery, but Shirley appealed to the House of Lords. Fagg appeared in the Upper House on 3 May, but on the next day he desired the opinion of the House whether his privilege did not excuse him from defending his case in the Lords. In the course of the prolonged struggle between the Houses that followed Fagg was sent to the Tower by order of the Commons for breach of their privileges. He was released after a couple of days, and, with 'the noise of the lions . . . scarce out of his ears', was promised the protection of the House. The unaccustomed limelight may have been otherwise not to his distaste, for when Parliament reassembled for the autumn session he made one of his rare interventions in debate in the character of 'a broken timber-merchant'. He believed that Sussex alone could provide twice the quantity of timber required for the naval programme, and when Samuel Pepys*, on behalf of the Admiralty, offered £55 a load for any of suitable quality, Fagg replied that he sold his produce for far less, though he did not know what the royal dockyards paid. Shirley renewed his appeal to the Lords on 17 Nov. 1676, and for the second time that year the session had to be brought to a premature end to prevent deadlock. In the end, Shirley lost his case in the Upper House.[8]

Shaftesbury marked Fagg 'doubly worthy' in 1677. On 10 May 1678 he acted as teller for continuing the debate on a resolution against Lauderdale. He was again marked 'worthy' in 1679. In the first Exclusion Parliament he was appointed to the elections committee and acted as teller for the adjournment on 10 Apr., apparently hoping to prevent the introduction of a bill extending the prohibition of Irish cattle. He was given leave to go into the country on 17 Apr., and was absent from the division on the first exclusion bill. In the autumn election he stood unsuccessfully for the county, and was described as a 'most zealous' supporter of Algernon Sidney† at Bramber. He remained inactive in the second Exclusion Parliament, in which he was appointed to the elections committee and to that to consider the regulation of the poor. He was returned both for Steyning and the county in 1681, setting out for Oxford 'with a gallant train'. He opted to serve for Sussex and was as usual appointed to the elections committee, but left no other trace on the records of the third Exclusion Parliament. The local dissenters in September chose him as one of their candidates for Sussex, with his two sons for Steyning, and his son-in-law (probably Philip Gell*) for Shoreham. Even in 1682 he was active in the municipal politics of Rye in the country interest.[9]

Fagg returned to his borough at the general election of 1685. On 3 June he applied for leave to go into the country, but this was refused, perhaps to prevent him from joining Monmouth's rebellion. For the rest of the session he was kept more busy with committee work than in any previous Parliament. On the same day he was appointed to the revived committee to recommend expunctions from the Journals, and altogether he served on eight committees in James II's Parliament. In the second session he was added to that to consider reform of the bankruptcy laws. Although included among the Sussex Opposition as one 'considerable for interest', he was a friend of Penn and probably became a Whig collaborator in 1688. He was appointed a j.p. and deputy lieutenant and approved as court candidate for Sussex. But it was again for Steyning that he served in the Convention, though he may not have taken his seat until the summer, for on 3 May 1689 he was reported ill in the country. His only committee in the first session was on the bill for the relief of poor prisoners (22 May). He was listed among the supporters of the disabling clause in the bill to restore corporations, and in the New Year helped to consider the bill of indemnity for the revolution, the illegitimization of children born to the wife of John Lewknor II* during her elopement, and the poor law. He remained a court Whig under William III, and died on 18 Jan. 1701, a few days after he had been returned for the eleventh time.

[1] Excluded. [2] Berry, *Suss. Genealogies, Lewes* 193, 262; C/142/77/95; *Glynde Par. Reg.* (Suss. Rec. Soc. xxx), 18; *Suss. N. and Q.* xv. 21. [3] C181/6/367, 7/55; *Cal. Treas. Bks.* xi. 201; Eg. 1626, f. 41. [4] *CJ*, vii. 799. [5] *CSP Dom.* 1659-70, p. 562. [6] L. A. Vidler, *New Hist. Rye*, 76, 160; *Suss. Arch. Colls.* v. 94; PCC 97 Rivers; *Thurloe*, iv. 161; vii. 712; *Suss. Manors* (Suss. Rec. Soc. xx), 496; Grey, iii. 270; *Cal. Cl. SP*, iv. 481; A. Fletcher, *County Community in Peace and War*, 250, 351. [7] *Cal. Cl. SP*, v. 7-8; Vidler, 80; D. R. Lacey, *Dissent and Parl. Pols.* 391; *CJ*, viii. 477; *Milward*, 283. [8] *Suss. Arch. Colls.* v. 25; Grey, iii. 113-14, 269, 292, 293; *CJ*, ix. 329, 350, 356. [9] G. W. Meadley, *Sidney Mems.* 326-7; *Sidney Diary*, i. 115, 117; *CSP Dom.* 1680-1, p. 473; 1682, pp. 366-8; *Prot. Dom. Intell.* 18 Mar. 1681.

B.M.C.

FAGG, John II (c.1646-72), of Wiston, Suss.

NEW SHOREHAM   24 Oct. 1667-31 July 1672

b. c.1646, 1st s. of John Fagg I*, and bro. of Robert Fagg*. *educ.* St. Catherine's, Camb. 1663; I. Temple 1664. *unm.*

Returned for Shoreham on the family interest while still under age, Fagg was an inactive Member. He was appointed to only five committees, of which the most important was to review the hearth-tax on 2 Mar. 1671. He died on 31 July 1672, and was buried at Glynde.

Vis. Suss. (Harl. Soc. lxxxix), 43; *Glynde Par. Reg.* (Suss. Rec. Soc. xxx), 13.

B.M.C.

FAGG, Robert (c.1649-1715), of Wiston, Suss.

NEW SHOREHAM   1679 (Mar.), 1681
STEYNING   1690, 4 Mar.-10 Apr. 1701, 1701 (Dec.)

b. c.1649, 2nd but 1st surv. s. of John Fagg I*, and bro. of John Fagg II*. *educ.* Steyning academy (William Corderoy) 1662-3; St. Catherine's, Camb. 1663; I. Temple 1664, called 1671. *m.* 21 Sept. 1671, Elizabeth, da. of Benjamin Culpepper of Lindfield, 1s. 2da. *suc.* fa. as 2nd Bt. 18 Jan. 1701.[1]

Commr. for assessment, Suss. 1673-80, 1689-90, j.p. May 1688-*d.*

Fagg was prepared for Cambridge at a boarding school in Steyning kept by an ejected minister. He became a barrister, but his elder brother died in the following year and he is unlikely to have practised. He was returned for Shoreham on the family interest at the first general election of 1679. There was a contest, but Fagg's own return was unopposed. A Whig and a probable dissenter, he was marked 'honest' on Shaftesbury's list. He was named only to the elections committee in the first Exclusion Parliament, but, unlike his father, voted for the bill. He was defeated in the August election by the court candidate John Hales*, and his petition was never reported. He regained the seat in 1681 after a contest, but left no trace on the records of the Oxford Parliament. Later in the year the local Whigs approved him and his younger brother as candidates for Steyning, but he is not known to have stood in 1685. He was probably a Whig collaborator in 1688, when he was appointed to the commission of the peace; but he again failed to go to the poll in 1689. He was a country Whig under William III. He died on 22 Aug. 1715 and was buried at Albourne. Both his son and his grandson were returned for Steyning, the former as a Tory in 1708 and the latter as Whig in 1734.[2]

[1] *Vis. Suss.* (Harl. Soc. lxxxix), 43; D. R. Lacey, *Dissent and Parl. Pols.* 392; PCC 174 Fagg. [2] *CJ*, ix. 638; *CSP Dom.* 1680-1, p. 473.

B.D.H.

FAIRFAX, Henry, 4th Lord Fairfax of Cameron [S] (1631-88), of Denton, Yorks.

YORKSHIRE   1679 (Mar.), 1679 (Oct.), 1681

b. 10 Dec. 1631, 2nd but 1st surv. s. of Henry Fairfax of Oglethorpe, rector of Bolton Percy 1646-62, by Mary, da. of Sir Henry Cholmley† of Whitby. *educ.* G. Inn, entered 1641. *m.* by 1657, Frances (*d.* 14 Feb. 1684), da. of Sir Robert Barwick of Toulson Hall, Thorp Arch, and h. to her bro. Robert, 4s. (1 *d.v.p.*) 6da. *suc.* fa. 1665, cos. Thomas Fairfax*, 3rd Lord Fairfax 12 Nov. 1671.[1]

Commr. for assessment, Yorks. (W. Riding) 1657, Jan. 1660, 1673-80, (E. Riding) 1679-80, militia, York 1659, Yorks. and York Mar. 1660; dep. lt. (W. Riding) 1673-*d.*, j.p. 1675-*d.*; commr. for recusants, Yorks. 1675; col. of militia ft. (W. Riding) by 1678-*d.*[2]

Fairfax took part under his cousin's leadership in the Yorkshire rising in support of George Monck* in January 1660. His father resigned his living under the Act of Uniformity, and he was himself regarded as leader of the East Riding Presbyterians, though he gave information which helped to suppress the Derwentdale conspiracy. Most of the family estate went to the Duke of Buckingham on his cousin's death in 1671, but he succeeded to Denton and three other manors. He was regarded as leader of the West Riding justices who obstructed the collection of the hearth-tax. On the dissolution of the Cavalier Parliament he was at first reluctant to stand, but he eventually joined interests with the Anglican Lord Clifford (Charles Boyle*) and was returned for Yorkshire to all three Exclusion Parliaments as a country Member. On his arrival in London in March 1679 he reported to his wife that it was the general opinion that 'your friend, our lord treasurer [Danby], does not stay the storm that is coming upon him', adding that he had waited on the King, 'who was pleased to ask me how I did, and told me he was glad to see me'. Classed as 'honest' by Shaftesbury, he was moderately active in the first Exclusion Parliament, with six committees. These included the committees to reform the collection of hearth-tax, to prolong the ban on cattle imports, and to encourage the cloth industry by requiring wool to be worn during the winter months. He voted for exclusion. Supported by 'sectaries and fanatics', he was re-elected unopposed. Walking in St. James's Park on the eve of the next Parliament, the Duke of York

> took him by the hand and said to him: 'Well, my Lord, I see you are all come up to do what you can against me'. 'I am the more sorry for the occasion', replied that Lord, 'but we are all resolved to assert the properties of our nation and the Protestant religion', and His Royal Highness replied again, 'I will give you all the assurance you can ask that I will not disturb your property'.

In the second and third Exclusion Parliaments, he was appointed only to the committee of elections and privileges, and he did not stand in 1685. He died on 9 Apr. 1688 and was buried at Denton. At the funeral, according to his friend Thoresby, the nonconformist antiquary, 'there was the greatest appearance of the nobility and gentry that I have ever seen. The poor wept abundantly, a good evidence of his charity'.[3]

[1] Her. and Gen. vi. 399, 405; C. Markham, Fairfax, 389. [2] Yale Univ. Lib. Osborn mss. [3] Parl. Rep. Yorks. (Yorks. Arch. Soc. rec. ser. xcvi), 92–93; CSP Dom. 1678, p. 563; D. R. Lacey, Dissent and Parl. Pols. 393; Reresby Mems. 48, 186–7, 190, 581; Fairfax Corresp. ed. Bell, ii. 163, 233; EHR, li. 643; Markham, 395; HMC Astley, 38–40; Verney Mems. ii. 333.

E.C.

FAIRFAX, Thomas, 3rd Lord Fairfax of Cameron [S] (1612–71), of Nun Appleton, Yorks.[1]

CIRENCESTER	17 Feb. 1649
WEST RIDING	1654
YORKSHIRE	1659, 1660

b. 17 Jan. 1612, 1st s. of Ferdinando Fairfax[†], 2nd Lord Fairfax of Cameron [S], by 1st w. Mary, da. of Edmund Sheffield[†], 1st Earl of Mulgrave. educ. St. John's, Camb. 1626; G. Inn 1628; travelled abroad (Netherlands, France) 1629–32. m. 20 June 1637, Anne (d. 16 Oct. 1665), da. and coh. of Horace, 1st Baron Vere of Tilbury, 2da. Kntd. 28 Jan. 1640; suc. fa. 13/14 Mar. 1648.

J.p. Yorks. (W. Riding) by 1637–d., (E. Riding) 1648–50, 1652–Mar. 1660, liberties of Ripon, Sutton and Marston 1654; commr. for assessment (W. Riding) 1643–52, 1657, Jan. 1660–d., (E. and N. Ridings) 1644–52, 1657, Westminster Jan. 1660, 1663–d., York Jan. 1660–d., levying of money, Yorks. 1643, sequestration (W. Riding) 1643, northern assoc. 1645, martial law, London 1646, militia, Yorks. 1648, 1655, Westminster, Bristol and York 1659, Yorks. and Westminster Mar. 1660; gov. I. of Man 1649–50; commr. for scandalous ministers, Yorks. 1654; custos rot. (W. Riding) July 1660–d.; commr. for oyer and terminer, Northern circuit July 1660, sewers Westminster Aug. 1660, (E. Riding) Sept. 1660.[2]

Capt. of dgns. 1639–40; gen. of horse (parliamentary) 1642–5; capt.-gen. New Model army 1645–50.

Constable of the Tower 1647–50; commr. for high court of justice 1649; Councillor of State 1649–50, May–Oct. 1659, 2 Jan.–25 May 1660; commr. for maimed soldiers Dec. 1660–1.[3]

Fairfax's family had held manorial property in Yorkshire since the 13th century, first representing the county in 1324. Fairfax himself, a devout Presbyterian, served in the Low Countries under Sir Horace Vere, whose daughter he later married, and captained a troop of Yorkshire dragoons in the first Bishops' war. He and his father were the staunchest supporters of the parliamentarian cause in Yorkshire, and his independence of faction, no less than his military expertise, was recognized by his appointment to command the New Model army. He was involved in a double return at Cirencester in 1647, which was not resolved in his favour until after Pride's Purge. His indecisiveness made the King's trial possible, though in the words of his wife's famous outburst, he had more sense than to attend himself. He resigned his command in 1650 in protest against the war with the Scots, and never took his seat in the first Protectorate Parliament. He kept clear of royalist intrigues, even after the marriage of his only surviving daughter to the second Duke of Buckingham, and in Richard Cromwell's Parliament sat with the republicans. After the second expulsion of the Rump he opened negotiations with George Monck* for a free Parliament, and he led the Yorkshire rising which helped to overthrow the military regime.[4]

Fairfax was returned unopposed for Yorkshire at the general election of 1660, and marked as a friend by Lord Wharton. An inactive Member of the Convention, in which he usually sat next to Monck, he was named to the committee of elections and privileges and to only nine others. He was elected to the delegation from both Houses to attend the King, and served on the joint committees to draft their instructions and to prepare for the King's reception. He took no part in the debates on the indemnity bill, though according to Edmund Ludlow* he said in private that

> if they would except any, he knew of one that was fit so to be, and that was himself, for that being then general he hindered it not when he might have done it.

He was among those appointed to consider the petition from the intruded Oxford dons on 25 June and to recommend an establishment for Dunkirk four days later. On 18 Aug. he stammered out a few unintelligible words in defence of his execution of two royalist officers taken at the surrender of Colchester in the second Civil War; but there seems to have been no serious threat of reprisals. Most of his remaining activity was concerned with the welfare of the men who had served under his command. He was appointed to the committee for the Dunkirk establishment bill on 1 Sept., and four days later urged that Monck's Coldstream Guards and the regiments assigned to the Dukes of York and Gloucester should be retained. He was named to the committee for the bill to enable disbanded soldiers to exercise trades without apprenticeship, and added after the recess to the committee to consider a petition from the maimed soldiers pressed for the parliamentary army. His last committee was on the bill for levying arrears of excise.[5]

Fairfax characteristically deferred his decision to stand for re-election in 1661 until six days before the election. He then wrote to Edward Bowles, the most influential Presbyterian minister in the north, to use all honest means on his behalf, but without success. On the discovery of the Anabaptist plot in October 1663 he wrote to Buckingham to condemn those who 'destroy unity by keeping up distinctions which both the King and Parliament in great wisdom have thought fit to bury in oblivion; and this I doubt not hath caused many to seem enemies which are real friends. But I shall plead for no man, but leave such to clear their own integrity.' During the second Dutch war (Sir) William Coventry* reported that Fairfax 'was full of professions of loyalty, and is thought to be a man who does not make professions contrary to his thoughts'. He died on 12 Nov. 1671, and was buried at Bilbrough. Buckingham, despite his scandalous mistreatment of Fairfax's daughter, inherited Nun Appleton and Bolton Percy; but the Denton estate and the Scottish peerage went to his cousin Henry Fairfax*.[6]

[1] This biography is based on M. A. Gibb, *The Lord General.*
[2] *W. Riding Sess. Recs.* (Yorks. Arch. Soc. rec. ser. liv), 32–57;

CSP Dom. 1655, p. 78; C181/7/37, 44. [3] *CJ*, viii. 213. [4] *Her. and Gen.* vi. 385; D. Underdown, *Pride's Purge*, 48, 190–2; Add. 36992, f. 368. [5] *Bramston Autobiog.* (Camden Soc. xxxii), 116–17; Ludlow, *Voyce from the Watch Tower*, 125; Bowman diary, f. 154; *Old Parl. Hist.* xxii. 473. [6] *Fairfax Corresp.* ed. Bell, ii. 175–6; *CSP Dom.* 1660–1, p. 536; 1644–5, p. 506.

M.W.H./E.C.

FAIRFAX, Hon. Thomas (1657–1710), of Denton, Yorks.

MALTON   1685
YORKSHIRE   1689, 1690, 1695, 1698, 1701 (Feb.), 1701 (Dec.), 1 Jan.–1 May 1707

b. 16 Apr. 1657, 1st s. of Henry Fairfax*, 4th Lord Fairfax of Cameron [S]. *educ.* Magdalen Coll. Oxf. 1675. *m.* c.1685, Catherine, da. and h. of Thomas, 2nd Baron Colepeper of Thoresway, 3s. 4da. *suc.* fa. as 5th Lord Fairfax of Cameron [S] 9 Apr. 1688.

J.p. Yorks. (W. Riding) 1675–bef. 1685, 1689–d.; commr. for assessment (W. Riding) 1677–80, York 1677–9, Yorks. 1689–90; capt. of militia horse (W. Riding) 1678–Aug. 1688, Oct. 1688–?d., col. of militia ft. Oct. 1688–?d., dep. lt. (W. Riding) Oct. 1688–d. (E. Riding) by 1701–2, Kent and York by 1701–?d.; c.-in-c. of militia, Yorks. 1689.[1]

Capt. indep. tp. 1685–7; lt.-col. 2 Horse Gds. 1689–94; col. Queen's Dgns. (later 3 Dgn. Gds.) 1694–5.[2]

Fairfax defeated the exclusionist William Palmes* at Malton in 1685 on the interest of the widow of Thomas Danby*. He was listed among the Opposition, but his only committees in James II's Parliament were to devise remedies for the low price of wool and corn and to consider the bill to prevent theft and rapine on the Scottish borders. In June, as part of the measures to resist Monmouth's invasion, he received a commission to command an independent troop of horse, only to lose it in 1687 because of his opposition to the Declaration of Indulgence. He was one of the three captains of militia horse in the West Riding who replied to the questions on the repeal of the Penal Laws and Test Act in August 1688:

> In case any of us shall be chosen Members of Parliament, which we have no prospect of, we will give our vote upon hearing the debates of the House according to the best of our judgment, as becomes loyal subjects and honest men. We will give our vote for such men to be Members of Parliament as we believe to be men of sound judgment [and] understanding, of good principles, and truly loyal.

He took part in the seizure of York, and collected voluntary contributions for William of Orange. He was returned as knight of the shire on 24 Dec. under James's writ, and again in the following month, probably as a Whig. An inactive Member of the Convention, he was among those appointed on 15 Mar. 1689 to consider the Gloucestershire petition against the alnage, but he was given leave of absence for two months on 7 June to join his regiment. After the recess he was appointed only to the committee of elections and privileges, and to three others of minor importance. He is not listed as a supporter of the disabling clause in the bill to restore corporations. He continued to sit for Yorkshire under William III as a court Whig. He regained his seat at a by-election in 1707 but was forced to vacate it a few months later under the provisions of the Act of Union with Scotland. He died on 6 Jan. 1710, and was buried at St. Martin in the Fields. His widow sold the Yorkshire property, but his younger son was twice returned for Maidstone, and sat for Kent from 1754 to 1768.[3]

[1] Add. 29674, f.160; SP31/4/124; Yale Univ. Lib. Osborn ms; *Reresby Mems.* 527, 529; *Yorks. Arch. Jnl.* xxix. 283; Eg. 1626, ff. 56, 57; SP44/165/194. [2] *Verney Mems.* ii. 391. [3] *Reresby Mems.* 585; *Yorks. Arch. Jnl.* x. 162, 164; Browning, *Danby*, i. 403.

P.A.B.

FALKLAND, 4th Visct. [S] *see* **CAREY, Henry**

FALKLAND, 5th Visct. [S] *see* **CAREY, Anthony**

FANE, Charles, Lord le Despenser (1635–91), of Apethorpe, Northants.

PETERBOROUGH 26 May 1660, 1661–12 Feb. 1666

b. 6 Jan. 1635, 1st s. of Mildmay Fane[†], 2nd Earl of Westmorland, being o.s. by 1st w. Grace, da. of Sir William Thornhurst of Agnes Court, Kent; half-bro. of Sir Vere Fane*. *educ.* Emmanuel, Camb. 1649; travelled abroad (France and Low Countries) 1652–4. *m.* (1) 15 June 1665, Elizabeth, da. and h. of Charles Nodes of Shephalbury, Herts., *s.p.*; (2) Lady Dorothy Brudenell, da. of Robert, 2nd Earl of Cardigan, *s.p. suc.* fa. as 3rd Earl of Westmorland 12 Feb. 1666.

J.p. Northants. and Peterborough July 1660–c.86; dep. lt. Northants. c. Aug. 1660–?66; commr. for assessment, Northants. Aug. 1660–6, Hunts. 1664–6, oyer and terminer, Nassaborough July 1660; capt. vol. horse, Northants. Nov. 1660; keeper of Cliff bailiwick, Rockingham forest 1682–*d.*[1]

The Fanes were established as a Kentish family by the 15th century and first entered Parliament in Tudor times. Lord le Despenser's grandfather acquired Apethorpe by marriage in 1617 and was raised to the peerage seven years later. His father, who sat for Peterborough in 1621, was a commissioner of array in the Civil War, but was soon captured by the parliamentary forces, and imprisoned till he took the Covenant and compounded in 1644. Le Despenser, though ineligible under the Long Parliament ordinance, was involved in a double return for Peterborough at the general election of 1660, but allowed to take his seat on 26 May. An inactive Member, he was named to five com-

mittees of which the most important were to amend the order for quiet possession of sequestrated livings and to support the drainage of the fens. He was re-elected to the Cavalier Parliament, in which he was again inactive, with 20 committees in five sessions. He was appointed to the committees for the corporations and uniformity bills in 1661, and in the following year he and Sir Roger Norwich* raised volunteer troops of horse, to ensure that there should be no resistance to the demolition of the defences of Northampton. His father, the joint lord lieutenant, was ordered to forward their names to Sir Henry Bennet* 'so that the King may gratify them as occasion serves'. The only gratification that can be traced is the grant of Willybrook Hundred; but le Despenser was noted as a court dependant in 1664. In the House of Lords he moved into opposition, voting for dissolution in 1675, which presumably earned him a 'worthy' on Shaftesbury's list. In 1680 he voted against exclusion, but for the condemnation of Lord Stafford. Nevertheless the compiler of the list of Northamptonshire Whigs in 1682 appears to have meant to include him under the style of 'Earl of Westminster' with an estate of £2,500 p.a. But he remained on the commission of the peace till at least 1685. Though reckoned among the opponents of James II in 1687, he denied taking up arms for William of Orange in the following year. He died on 18 Sept. 1691 and was buried at Apethorpe. His nephew, the sixth earl, wrote of him that he 'came into the possession of an estate above the double of what he left it, but, being one that cared not for business and having no children of his own, left all to the management of those about him'.[2]

[1] Add. 34222, ff. 12–13. [2] *HMC 10th Rep. IV*, 46; *CSP Dom.* 1661–2, p. 560; SP29/421/216; Add. 29563, f. 352.

M.W.H./E.R.E.

FANE (VANE), Hon. George (c.1616–63), of Basildon, Berks. and Hatton Garden, London.

CALLINGTON 1640 (Nov.)–16 Jan. 1643
WALLINGFORD 1661–Apr. 1663

b. c.1616, 5th but 4th surv. s. of Francis Fane[†], 1st Earl of Westmorland, by Mary, da. and h. of Sir Anthony Mildmay of Apethorpe, Northants.; bro. of Mildmay Fane[†] and Sir Francis Fane[†]. *educ.* Eton 1627–32; Emmanuel, Camb. 1632; travelled abroad (Italy) 1635–8. *m.* by 1650, Dorothy, da. and h. of James Horsey of Honington, Warws., wid. of Thomas Marsh of Cambridge, and Hackney, Mdx., 1s. 1da.[1]

Capt. of ft. [I] 1642, lt.-col. (royalist) by 1643, col. 1644–9.[2]

J.p. Berks. July 1660–*d.*, dep. lt. c. Aug. 1660–*d.*; commr. for assessment, Warws. Aug. 1660–1, Berks.

1661–d., corporations, Berks. 1661–3, loyal and indigent officers 1662.[3]

Fane was disabled for royalism early in the Civil War when he was serving in Ireland. He fought as a colonel at Marston Moor, and was granted the reversion of a clerkship in the court of wards, worth £7,000 p.a. He seems to have returned to Ireland, but compounded on his own discovery in 1649. He possessed nothing but clothing, equipment and a horse, worth in all £60, and escaped with a fine of £3. This was doubtless a preliminary to his marriage to an heiress, whose property would otherwise have become liable to sequestration. He was imprisoned for a few weeks in 1651 on suspicion, but took no part in royalist plots during the Interregnum. As a precaution, however, he purchased his estate at Basildon in 1656 in the names of his sister, Lady Bath (who may have advanced him some of the money) and his nephew, Lord le Despenser (Charles Fane*).[4]

Fane stood for Wallingford, ten miles upstream, in 1661. A few days before the poll, assisted by three other deputy lieutenants, he 'ejected the mayor . . . and established another in his room, upon pretence of an authority from his Majesty'. Secretary Nicholas was instructed on 28 Mar. to prepare a letter for the King's signature, expressing his great dislike of these proceedings, and ordering them to reinstate the mayor; but Fane was duly returned four days later. He was one of the most active Members in the opening sessions of the Cavalier Parliament, serving on 84 committees, including those for the security, corporations and uniformity bills, and the bill of pains and penalties. On 28 May he acted as teller against a Lords amendment. He took a prominent part in private bills, carrying four to the Upper House, probably introducing two others, and reporting on another, that of Anthony Ettrick*. His name stands first in the committees for bills to establish a registry of pawnbrokers, to provide allowances for curates and to reduce the rate of interest on loyalists' debts. He helped to manage conferences on the corporations bill and the bill of pains and penalties. He was one of the Members appointed to attend the lord treasurer about the Forest of Dean on 25 July, and to perfect the bill for the regulation of printing on the next day. After the autumn recess he was named to the committee on the bill for the execution of those under attainder. On 16 Apr. 1662 he was voted £10,000 compensation for the abolition of the court of wards, but his applications for an immediate payment of half this sum out of the Post Office revenue and for a post on the Irish establishment bore no fruit. He was among the Members instructed on 19 May to

present an address on draining Lindsey level. Clearly he was in close touch with the Court, his brother the 2nd Earl of Westmorland using him as an intermediary with Lord Chancellor Clarendon. He was the first Member appointed to consider a petition from Cholsey, a village adjoining his constituency, on 20 Mar. 1663. A fortnight later he was one of the Members ordered to thank the King for his message about priests and Jesuits. But he died in the same month, and was buried on 25 Apr. at St. Bartholomew the Great, Smithfield.[5]

[1] VCH Northants. Fams. 97, 112. [2] P. Young, Marston Moor, 96–97; HMC Ormonde, i. 128, 159, 210. [3] Berks. RO, Wallingford stat. bk. ff. 25–26. [4] Keeler, Long Parl. 172; Cal. Comm. Comp. 2099; VCH Berks. iii. 460–1; CSP Dom. 1651, pp. 113, 209. [5] PC2/55, ff. 180–1; SP29/33/51; CJ, viii. 311, 314, 326; CSP Dom. 1661–2, p. 221; CSP Ire. 1663–5, p. 512; Cal. Cl. SP, v. 240.

L.N.

FANE, Sir Henry (c.1650–1706), of Basildon, Berks.

READING   1689, 1690, 1695

b. c.1650, o.s. of Hon. George Fane*. m. lic. 28 Apr. 1668, aged 18, Elizabeth, da. of Thomas Southcote of Exeter, Devon, and h. to her nephew George Southcote of Calwoodley, Devon, 6s. (2 d.v.p.) 1da. KB 23 Apr. 1661; suc. fa. 1663.[1]

  J.p. Devon 1674–87, Berks. 1675–87, by 1701–d.; commr. for assessment, Berks. 1677–80, Devon 1679–80, Berks. and Devon 1689–90.

  Commr. for excise Apr.–Oct. 1689, forfeited estates [I] 1690; PC [I] 1690–d.[2]

Fane was the favourite nephew of the masterful Countess of Bath, who obtained a KB for him at the coronation of Charles II and settled on him her Irish estates. But he inherited a grievance against the crown, which had failed to give his father any compensation for the abolition of his office in the court of wards, and became a Whig. He first stood for Reading, eight miles downstream from his residence, at the general election of 1685, but the poll was refused on the grounds that he was not a freeman. The election was declared void, but he did not contest the by-election, and was removed from local office in 1687, probably at the instance of Lord Clarendon (Henry Hyde*). His name was sent to William III on a list of the Opposition to James II. He was expected to contest Reading in the summer of 1688, and is said to have accompanied Lord Lovelace (John Lovelace*) in his attempt to join the Prince of Orange in November. At the general election of 1689 he defeated Clarendon's son Cornbury (Edward Hyde*). His appointment as commissioner of excise lasted only six months, and was probably intended to secure the acceptance of a scheme of reform submitted by a syndicate headed by his cousin, Sir Vere Fane*. His only committee in the Convention was for the relief of distressed Irish Protestants, but he supported the disabling clause in the bill to restore corporations. He continued to sit for Reading as a Whig in the next two Parliaments, though his chief interests seem to have lain in Ireland. He was buried at Basildon on 12 Jan. 1706. His son, after sitting in the Lower House of the Irish Parliament, was made an Irish peer, and his grandson sat for Reading from 1754 to 1761.[3]

[1] *VCH Northants. Fams.* 112–13. [2] Luttrell, i. 523; ii. 86, 142; *HMC Finch*, ii. 357. [3] *Clarendon Corresp.* i. 555; R. Morrice, Entering Bk. 2, p. 292; information from Mr G. H. Jones.

L.N./J.P.F.

FANE, Thomas (1626–92), of Burston, Hunton, Kent.

MAIDSTONE 1679 (Oct.), 1681

bap. 7 Sept. 1626, 3rd but 2nd surv. s. of Sir George Fane[†] of Burston by 2nd w. Anne, da. of Sir Oliver Boteler of Teston. *educ.* Padua 1646. *unm. suc.* bro. 1643.[1]

Commr. for assessment, Kent 1673–80, 1689–90, j.p. 1675–?d., dep. lt. by 1680–d.

Fane's father, the younger brother of the first Earl of Westmorland, represented Maidstone, five miles from Burston, in four early Stuart Parliaments. None of the family was of age to take part in the Civil War, and Fane entered politics only in 1677, when he signed the protest drafted by his cousin, Sir Vere Fane*, against government support for the candidature of Sir John Banks* at Winchelsea. He was returned for Maidstone to the second and third Exclusion Parliaments, but he left no trace on their records. He refused to subscribe to the loyal address abhorring the Rye House Plot because 'it might lessen his influence with the people'. Nevertheless he was reappointed to county office in 1685, though he is not likely to have stood for re-election. In 1688 he gave affirmative answers on the repeal of the Test Act and Penal Laws. James II's electoral agents noted him as 'right', and believed that he would be supported by the mayor and the dissenters. Sunderland, however, preferred to nominate Edwin Wyatt* as court candidate for Maidstone. Since Fane's epitaph records that he was three times returned unanimously 'against the restless designs of Popery and arbitrary power', he was presumably successful at an abortive election; but in 1689 the family interest was represented by his cousin, who was defeated by Banks's son. Fane probably did not stand again himself, but he rallied to the new regime and continued to hold local office.

He died on 5 Sept. 1692 and was buried at Hunton. His heir was his cousin, Mildmay Fane[†], who was returned for the county as a Whig in 1715.[2]

[1] *VCH Northants. Fams.* 96 [2] Kent AO, Sa/ZB3/1, U282/o, ff. 2–4; Eg. 2895, f. 244; *VCH Northants. Fams.* 96.

B.D.H./J.P.F.

FANE, Sir Vere (1645–93), of Mereworth, Kent.

PETERBOROUGH 22 Mar. 1671
KENT 1679 (Mar.), 1679 (Oct.), 1681, 1689, 1690–18 Sept. 1691

b. 13 Feb. 1645, 3rd s. of Mildmay Fane[†], 2nd Earl of Westmorland, being 1st surv. s. by 2nd w. Mary, da. and coh. of Horace, 1st Baron Vere of Tilbury, wid. of Sir Roger Townshend, 1st Bt.[†], of Raynham Hall, Norf.; half-bro. of Charles Fane*, Lord le Despenser, and Sir Horatio Townshend, 3rd Bt.*. *m.* 13 July 1671, (with £6,600), Rachel, da. and h. of John Bence* of Bevis Marks, London, 5s. (1 *d.v.p.*) 3da. KB 23 Apr. 1661; *suc.* half-bro. as 4th Earl of Westmorland 18 Sept. 1691.[1]

Dep. lt. Kent 1668–82, 1689–92, j.p. 1669–78, 1679–82, Aug. 1688–d.; asst. Rochester bridge 1672, warden 1673, 1680, 1687; commr. for assessment, Kent 1673–80, 1689–90, jt. ld. lt. 1692–d.[2]

Fane stood for Peterborough in 1666 for the seat vacated by his half-brother Charles, but was unsuccessful. However, the other seat became vacant in 1671, and he represented the city in the last nine sessions of the Cavalier Parliament. An inactive Member, he served on only six committees, but was marked 'doubly worthy' on Shaftesbury's list. He probably composed the letter to the lord lieutenant protesting against government support for Sir John Banks* at Winchelsea in 1677, acted as teller against his election on 7 Mar. 1678, and was removed from the commission of the peace by order of the King in the same month. In the Exclusion Parliaments he sat for Kent, where his family had originated in the 15th century. 'He was a very good-natured man', according to his son, the 6th Earl, 'but affected popularity too much, living in Kent, where he was greatly beloved, far beyond the compass his estate would allow of.' Shaftesbury marked him 'worthy', and he voted for the first exclusion bill. His only committee was on the bill to encourage the export of leather in the second Exclusion Parliament.[3]

Fane objected to the address from the Kentish militia in the spring of 1682, promising loyalty to the King and his heirs 'in the right line', because, he maintained, the Duke of York would be excluded by the next Parliament, and he was again removed from local office. Nothing more is heard of him till the Revolution, in which, according to his son, he was 'very forward and active'. He was again returned for Kent in 1689, though he was defeated at Maidstone by Banks's son. In the Convention he helped to conduct Henry Powle* to the Speaker's chair. He was appointed only to the committee of elections and privileges, but was listed as supporting the disabling clause in the bill to restore corporations. He was re-elected in 1690, but succeeded to the peerage in the following year. In the Upper House he was reckoned a government supporter, but in his expectation of reward as manager of the excise with Thomas Mun* 'he found himself greatly deceived in the short time he had to live'. He died of diabetes on 29 Dec. 1693, and was buried at Mereworth. Two of his younger sons sat for Kent in succession from 1715 to 1722.[4]

[1] C10/300/22. [2] HMC Finch, i. 509; Kent AO, Q/JC 12–21; CSP Dom. 1682, p. 223; information from Mr P. F. Cooper, Bridge Clerk, Rochester Bridge Trust. [3] CJ, ix. 451; Kent AO, Sa/ZB3/1; HMC Finch, ii. 44. [4] Eg. 2895, f. 244; N. and Q. (ser. 3), vi. 121; HMC 10th Rep. IV, 48; Cal. Treas. Pprs. i. 41, 70, 210.

B.D.H.

FANSHAWE, Charles, 4th Visct. Fanshawe of Dromore [I] (1643–1710), of Suffolk Street, Westminster.

MITCHELL   22 Jan.–13 May 1689

b. 6 Feb. 1643, 5th but 3rd surv. s. of Sir Thomas Fanshawe I* by 2nd w.; bro. of Henry Fanshawe* and Thomas Fanshawe*. *educ.* Christ's, Camb. 1663; I. Temple 1664. *unm. suc.* nephew 10 Oct. 1687.[1]

Capt. of ft. Coldstream Gds. 1669–70, regt. of William Alington*, 3rd Baron Alington 1678–9.

Commr. for revenue [I] 1670–6, excise appeals 1676–89; envoy extraordinary to Portugal 1681–5.[2]

Fanshawe began his career in 1667 by attending the peace negotiations at Breda. After two applications from the King on his behalf for a fellowship of his college, the master wrote to Joseph Williamson*:

besides the unfitness of the person, the consequence of his coming in will so disturb the happiness and comfort of all our lives, that, if you will endeavour to satisfy Lord Arlington and take him off from urging Mr Fanshawe upon us, I shall feel bound to serve you while I live.

It was probably he of whom Samuel Pepys* wrote at this time as 'a witty but rascally fellow, without a penny in his purse, that was asking . . . what places there were in the Navy for him'. Rejected both by Cambridge and the Admiralty, he was commissioned in the guards, and given a seat on the Irish revenue board. When the Irish revenue farm was terminated, he was compensated with a pension of £250 p.a. on the Irish establishment, and appointed to a sinecure office in England. In 1678 he

served in Flanders in the regiment of his kinsman, Lord Alington.[3]

Fanshawe was sent on a diplomatic mission to Portugal in 1681, but failed to obtain a renewal of the treaty of commerce with that country. Returned for Mitchell, where he was a stranger, in 1689, he was named to no committees in the Convention, but urged delay on the motion to declare the throne vacant. He insisted that James's flight was not voluntary, and was one of the three Members who voted against the declaration. On 30 Jan. he argued that the clergy who prayed for King James should not be censured by the House as they were 'subject to another jurisdiction'. According to Ailesbury's list he voted to agree with the Lords that the throne was not vacant, and on 13 May he was discharged from sitting for refusing to take the oaths to the new regime. In May 1692 he was arrested for high treason and was sent to the Tower. After his release in the summer he purchased an estate at Little Bedwyn in Wiltshire. He died on 28 Mar. 1710 at his house in Suffolk Street, and was buried at Ware. The next member of the family to sit was Simon Fanshawe, who was brought in on the government interest for Old Sarum in 1751 and for Grampound in 1754.[4]

[1] Vis. Eng. and Wales Notes ed. Crisp, vi. 149. [2] CSP Dom. 1668–9, p. 653; 1671, p. 211; 1679–80, p. 437; Cal. Treas. Bks. iii. 402, 553; Luttrell, i. 534. [3] H. C. Fanshawe, Fanshawe Fam. 122–3; CSP Dom. 1667, pp. 220, 230; 1668–9, p. 318; Cal. Treas. Bks. v. 176–7, 197; Pepys Diary, 23 Feb. 1668. [4] Fanshawe, 122–3; Luttrell, i. 532, 564; ii. 443; Hardwick SP, i. 411; information from Mrs L. Schwoerer; R. Morrice, Entering Bk. 2, p. 444; Grey, ix. 37, 244; HMC Portland, iii. 424; Hatton Corresp. (Cam. Soc. n.s. xxiii), 177.

E.C.

FANSHAWE, Hon. Henry (1634–85), of Dengie Hall, Essex and King Street, Westminster.

PENRYN   19 May–Aug. 1685

bap. 8 June 1634, 3rd but 2nd surv. s. of Sir Thomas Fanshawe I* by his 2nd w.; bro. of Charles Fanshawe* and Thomas Fanshawe*. *educ.* M. Temple 1657. *unm.*[1]

Registrar to King's remembrancer in the Exchequer by 1667–d.; jt. surveyor and receiver of greenwax fines 1677–9; receiver of prize arrears 1677–?79; wine licence arrears 1679; commr. for excise appeals 1679–d.[2]

Freeman, Grimsby 1672; commr. for assessment, Westminster 1677–9; capital burgess, Penryn Mar. 1685.[3]

On his mother's death in 1668, Fanshawe inherited a third share in Dengie Hall, an estate acquired by his great-grandfather in 1561, and £1,000 in money. But his chief source of income was his office in the Exchequer. In 1669 he was granted £20 p.a. 'for his services in keeping, sorting and ordering the hearth-rolls', and five years later was given a

Fanshawe Family

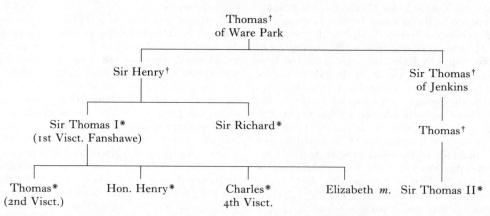

Thomas† of Ware Park

Sir Henry† — Sir Thomas† of Jenkins

Sir Thomas I* (1st Visct. Fanshawe) — Sir Richard* | Thomas†

Thomas* (2nd Visct.) — Hon. Henry* — Charles* 4th Visct. — Elizabeth *m.* Sir Thomas II*

royal bounty of £300 for 'his extraordinary services in recovering the extracts of the late subsidy'. He was mentioned as possible candidate for Grimsby in 1672 and Okehampton in 1676, and in the following year he received £250 on the secret service account, probably to enable him to contest the Isle of Wight borough of Newtown. But he was defeated on the poll and petitioned without result. He was a henchman of Danby, whom he visited in the Tower during the exclusion crisis, and Charles II declared that he had 'a very particular favour' for Fanshawe, being 'very well satisfied of his integrity and intelligence'.[4]

Fanshawe was nominated to the Penryn corporation in the new charter of 1685, and elected to James II's Parliament a couple of months later. An active Member, he was appointed to the committee of elections and privileges, and to 14 others, including those to consider the bills for the better recovery of tithe, the establishment of a land registry, and the general naturalization of Huguenot refugees. He also helped to estimate the yield of the proposed tax on new buildings. He died during the recess and was buried at Ware on 31 Aug.[5]

[1] *Vis. England and Wales Notes* ed. Crisp. vi. 159. [2] *Cal. Treas. Bks.* iii. 215, 221; iv. 831; v. 795, 993, 1105, 1263, 1304; vi. 46, 121; vii. 365; Northants. RO, FH1670. [3] *HMC 14th Rep. VIII*, 285; *CSP Dom.* 1685, p. 74. [4] *Fanshawe Mems.* pp. xii, 304; H. C. Fanshawe, *Fanshawe Fam.* 121, 125; *Cal. Treas. Bks.* iii. 215; iv. 336, 529, 831–2; v. 351, 365, 1328, 1330; *CSP Dom.* 1672, p. 555; Eg. 3330, f. 39; *CJ*, ix. 391; Add. 29560, f. 13. [5] Northants. RO, FH647, 3577.

E.C.

FANSHAWE, Sir Richard, 1st Bt. (1608–66), of Portugal Street, Lincoln's Inn Fields, Mdx.[1]

CAMBRIDGE UNIVERSITY 1661–16 June 1666

bap. 12 June 1608, 6th but 5th surv. s. of Sir Henry Fan-

shawe† of Ware Park, Herts., King's remembrancer in the Exchequer, by Elizabeth, da. of Thomas Smythe† of Westenhanger, Kent; bro. of Sir Thomas Fanshawe I*. *educ.* Cripplegate (Thomas Farnaby) 1620–3; Jesus, Camb. 1623; I. Temple 1626; travelled abroad (France, Spain) 1627–34. *m.* 18 May 1644 (with £10,000), his cos. Anne (*d.* 30 Jan. 1680), da. of Sir John Harrison* of Balls Park, Herts., 6s. (5 *d.v.p.*) 8da. *cr.* Bt. 2 Sept. 1650; kntd. Apr. 1660.[2]

Sec. of embassy, Madrid 1635–8; sec. of war [I] 1640–1; King's remembrancer in the Exchequer 1641–8; sec. of war to the Prince of Wales 1644–6; treas. of the navy (royalist) 1648–50; Latin sec. 1659–*d.*; master of requests 1659–64; envoy extraordinary to Portugal 1661, ambassador 1662–3; PC [I] 1662; PC 2 Oct. 1663–*d.*; ambassador to Spain 1664–6.

Master of Ilford hosp., Essex c.1642–51; freeman, Limerick 1649, Portsmouth 1663.[3]

MP [I] 1640–2.

Fanshawe's mother intended him for the law; but 'it seemed so crabbed a study, and disagreeable to his inclinations' that on her death in 1631 he determined to use the £1,000 she bequeathed him to qualify himself for a diplomatic career. To this he was well-suited by temperament, being 'so reserved that he never showed the thought of his heart in its greatest sense', except to his wife. He regarded argument as 'an uncharitable custom', and 'would never be drawn to the faction of either party, saying he found it sufficient honestly to perform that employment he was in'. His distaste for 'faction' implied an unquestioning loyalty to his King and to his church; he was 'a true Protestant of the Church of England, so born, so brought up, and so died', though crypto-Catholics like Secretary Windebank chose to label him a Puritan. After three years at the Madrid embassy, he served as secretary to the council of war in Ireland and sat in the Dublin Parliament. Returning to England in 1641 he succeeded his brother as King's remembrancer in the Exchequer, which he valued at £600 p.a. But he accompanied the King to Oxford, and was appointed secretary to the council of war designed to attend the Prince of Wales in the west country. Before his departure he married; but his wife's portion and his own sources of income were all in the hands of the enemy. 'We might truly be called merchant adventurers', she wrote to her son many years later, 'for the stock we set up our trading with did not amount to £20 betwixt us. . . . Our stock bought pens, ink, and paper, which was your father's trade; and by it, I assure you, we lived better than those that were born to £2,000 a year, as long as he had his liberty.' Although his employment ceased with the collapse of the royalist cause in the west, he accompanied the Prince to Jersey; but in 1647 he obtained a pass from the Speaker to return to England and compound for his estate, which apart from his post in the Exchequer, on which debts of £1,173 were secured, consisted only of an annuity of £50 in Essex, presumably as master of Ilford hospital. He never compounded, however, the real purposes of his visit being to raise money to support his family in exile and to publish his translation of Guarini's *Pastor Fido*, which won him considerable acclaim. He was summoned to join the royalist fleet in the Downs during the second Civil War, and acted as treasurer so long as Prince Rupert had a base in Ireland. Meanwhile his wife raised nearly £4,000 by selling a property in Essex. Fanshawe assisted Sir Edward Hyde[†], who found him 'a very honest and discreet man', in his negotiations with Spain in 1650, and was given a baronetcy. Summoned to Scotland to attend the King, he acted as secretary of state, though he refused the Covenant. He was taken prisoner after the battle of Worcester, but became seriously ill with scurvy and was set free after ten weeks on £4,000 bail. Until the death of Oliver Cromwell, to whom he chiefly owed his release, he lived quietly in England with his family, publishing a selection from Horace, perhaps his most accomplished work, and a translation of the *Lusiad* which shows a thorough understanding of Portuguese. With his reputation thus established as a linguist and a man of letters, and an unblemished moral character, he was invited by the 5th Earl of Pembroke to undertake the tuition of his eldest son, William Herbert*, for a year. Pembroke's interest with the Protectorate sufficed to secure the cancellation of Fanshawe's bonds, and he was free to accompany his pupil to the Continent. He resumed contact with Hyde, who secured for him the posts of Latin secretary, at a fee of £100 p.a., and master of requests,

by which you have the King's ear three months in [the] year as much as the secretary [of state], and in which

you would very honestly get six or seven hundred pounds a year.[4]

Fanshawe returned to England with the King. The need to conciliate George Monck* ensured that he never secured the post that he really coveted, that of secretary of state, and the profits of his principal office were engrossed by Secretary Nicholas. At the general election of 1661 he was elected in his absence and without his knowledge for Cambridge University, at no more expense to himself than 'a letter of thanks, two brace of bucks, and 20 broad pieces of gold to buy them wine'. He figured prominently in the coronation, at which he represented the Duke of Normandy, attired in 'fantastic habits of the time'. In the opening weeks of the Cavalier Parliament he was named to the committee of elections and privileges, and those for confirming public acts, the fen drainage bill, and a Hertfordshire estate bill. But he never became an active Member, and during the recess he was sent to Catherine of Braganza at Lisbon with the King's letter and picture. He returned to England at Christmas, but after the royal marriage went back to Portugal as ambassador. He was named to the elections committee for the second session in his absence, but never resumed his seat, though he was in England again for the last three months of 1663, before being transferred to Madrid, and listed as a court dependant in 1664. He was superseded in 1666, ostensibly for exceeding his instructions, but actually in order to provide a refuge for the Earl of Sandwich (Edward Montagu I*) from impeachment for embezzling prize goods. 'It was no advantage to him to be known to be in the [lord] chancellor's confidence', commented Hyde, now Lord Chancellor Clarendon, on his dismissal. He died of a violent fever on 16 June while preparing to leave for England, and was eventually buried in the family vault at Ware, with an inscription to which the record of his parliamentary service had to be added as a postscript. His only surviving son, a deaf-mute, died unmarried in 1694.[5]

[1] This biography is based on the *Fanshawe Mems.* [2] *Vis. Eng. and Wales Notes* ed. Crisp, vi. 162. [3] *VCH Essex*, ii. 188. [4] *Cal. Comm. Comp.* 1865; *Cal. Cl. SP*, ii. 70, 92; *DNB*; *HMC Heathcote*, 9. [5] M. Rex, *Univ. Rep.* 344; Eg. 1634, ff. 28–29.

E.R.E./E.C.

FANSHAWE, Thomas (1632–74), of Ware Park, Herts.

HERTFORD 1661–May 1674

bap. 17 June 1632, 1st s. of Sir Thomas Fanshawe I* by 2nd w.; bro. of Charles Fanshawe* and Henry Fanshawe*. *educ.* M. Temple 1657. *m.* (1) 3 Apr. 1648,

Catherine (*bur.* 13 June 1660), da. of Knighton Ferrers of Bayfordbury, and h. to her gdfa. Sir John Ferrers, *s.p.*; (2) Apr. 1665, Sarah, da. of Sir John Evelyn I* of West Dean, Wilts., wid. of Sir John Wray, 3rd Bt.†, of Glentworth, Lincs., 1s. 3da. KB 23 Apr. 1661; *suc.* fa. as 2nd Visct. Fanshawe of Dromore [I] 26 Mar. 1665.[1]

Commr. for oyer and terminer, Home circuit July 1660, assessment, Herts. 1661–*d.*, Lincs. 1673–*d.*; j.p. Herts. 1661–6, St. Albans 1668, Lincs. (Holland and Kesteven) 1670–*d.*; commr. for loyal and indigent officers, Herts. 1662, dep. lt. 1665–?9.

King's remembrancer in the Exchequer 1665–*d.*

Fanshawe was described by his aunt, the wife of Sir Richard Fanshawe*, as 'a handsome gentleman of an excellent understanding and of great honour and honesty'. The Ware Park estate of £1,652 p.a. was made over to him when he came of age, in exchange for his first wife's inheritance, which had to be sold to meet his father's debts. He was involved in plans for a Royalist rising in 1659 and sent to the Tower. As a Cavalier's son he was ineligible at the general election of 1660, but he was returned for Hertford, two miles from Ware, in 1661. A moderately active Member of the Cavalier Parliament, he acted as teller in five divisions and was appointed to at least 116 committees, including the committee of elections and privileges in 11 sessions, and possibly to more as he is not always distinguishable from his father in the first session. He received the order of the Bath at the coronation, and as Sir Thomas Fanshawe junior he was named to the committees for confirming public acts and restoring bishops to the House of Lords. He was teller for committing the corporations bill on 20 June, and was appointed to all the committees for the Clarendon Code. On the bill of pains and penalties he acted as teller against a proviso relating to the estate of Sir John Danvers†. In 1663 he was among those ordered to report on defects in the Corporations Act, to consider a petition from the loyal and indigent officers, and to inspect the laws on the sale of offices. He acted as teller for the bill to authorize the levying of tolls on the Newmarket road, which passed through his estate. Like his father, he was listed as a court dependant.[2]

Fanshawe succeeded in 1665 to an Irish peerage, a post in the Exchequer and an estate burdened with debts and legal complications following his father's intestacy. His financial worries must have aggravated his hereditary tendency to high blood pressure. As acting lord lieutenant during the second Dutch war he sent to gaol as disaffected several gentlemen who had been Parliamentarians during the Civil War, and, when Sir Harbottle Grimston* remonstrated, he replied that Grimston 'has as deep a hand in the late horrid and bloody rebellion as any man'. Clarendon wrote to Grim-

ston deploring the 'unwarrantable folly' of his old friend Fanshawe, adding that his 'passion and animosity' did the King no service. He was among those appointed to inspect the tax returns in the Exchequer on 18 Oct. 1666. His attitude to the fall of Clarendon is not known, but in 1667 he was appointed to the committees to report on the charges against Lord Mordaunt, to consider the bill for assigning debts in the Exchequer, and to examine the accounts of the loyal and indigent officers fund. In the debate on bribery he was among those who 'could not deny that they had wine given them . . . not as bribes, but out of the vintners' own kindness'. On 17 Feb. 1668 he was among those ordered to attend the lord chief baron ((Sir) Edward Turnor*) about easing the passage of sheriffs' accounts through the Exchequer. He was also named to committees to prevent restraints on jurors and to relieve the wives and children of intestates. On 11 Mar. in his only fully recorded speech he bitterly attacked toleration for Protestant dissenters:

> If these tender consciences were so good as is pretended to, then they should live without offence to God and men; but what villainies did these men commit when they had the power in their hands is most notorious. Let us not . . . stand in fear of their number, of which there is so much noise, but let the laws be put in execution against them and they will soon be brought under, as he had the experience of some persons in Hertfordshire who frequented unlawful meetings, and, upon the execution of the laws, they have conformed and come in good order to church.

He was appointed to the committee for extending the Conventicles Act, and told for it on the third reading.[3]

After selling Ware to Sir Thomas Byde* for £26,000 he took up residence with his second wife's father for a time. He wrote to Joseph Williamson* from West Dean on 28 July:

> I am now settled in Wiltshire and, were it not for the entertainment received from Sir John Evelyn, would have to converse with dogs and horses. I know no man living here besides Sir John. It will be kindness to let me have the ordinary news once a week, for the stock of old Cavaliers wish and pray for the prosperity of the King and would be glad to hear of his happiness, although we are not fit for anything but ruin. I wish His Majesty may never find the mischief of it. . . . Let me know whether Parliament will sit in August that I may steer my course accordingly.

Parliament did not in fact sit again till 1669, and Fanshawe moved to Glentworth, his wife's dower, perhaps to keep out of reach of his creditors, though his profits of office, a pension of £600 p.a. inherited from his mother and the expectation of £4,000 on Evelyn's death should have enabled him to stave them off. He was appointed to the committees to consider the conventicles bill and to receive information about conventicles, and acted as teller against the suspension of Sir George Carteret*. As a court dependant his name figures on both government and opposition lists in 1669–71, and in *Flagellum Parliamentarium* he was described as a pensioner and much in debt. His parliamentary activity decreased, his last important committee being to prevent the growth of Popery on 2 Mar. 1671, and he applied unsuccessfully for the embassy at Constantinople. He was named to the committee on the bill for ease of sheriffs on 24 Jan. 1674. His name appeared on the Paston list, but in May he died of apoplexy like his father and grandfather before him, and was buried in the Fanshawe vault at Ware.[4]

[1] *Vis. Eng. and Wales Notes* ed. Crisp, vi. 158; *The Gen.* n.s. xvii. 282. [2] *Fanshawe Mems.* 12, 308; *Cal. Comm. Comp.* 1884; D. Underdown, *Royalist Conspiracy*, 281; *CSP Dom.* 1659–60, p. 191; *CJ*, viii. 306, 476. [3] *HMC Verulam*, 62–65, 68–72; *Milward*, 137, 221; *CJ*, ix. 90. [4] *Fanshawe Mems.* 208, 301–2, 306; *CSP Dom.* 1667–8, p. 464; 1668–9, p. 625; *CJ*, ix. 120; *Hatton Corresp.* (Cam. Soc. n.s. xxii), 100; PCC 72 Bunce.

E.R.E.

FANSHAWE, Sir Thomas I (1596–1665), of Warwick Lane, London.

HERTFORD   17 May 1624, 1625, 1628, 1640
                 (Apr.), 1640 (Nov.)–7 Sept.
                 1642
HERTFORDSHIRE   1661–26 Mar. 1665

b. 16 Nov. 1596, 1st s. of Sir Henry Fanshawe† of Ware Park, Herts., and bro. of Sir Richard Fanshawe*. *educ.* travelled abroad (France) 1618. *m.* (1) 23 Sept. 1627, Anne (*bur.* 19 July 1628), da. of Sir Giles Alington of Horseheath, Cambs., 1da.; (2) 24 June 1629 (with £10,000), Elizabeth, da. of Sir William Cokayne, Skinner, of Broad Street, London and Rushton, Northants., ld. mayor 1619–20, 9s. (5 *d.v.p.*) 7da. *suc.* fa. 1616; KB 2 Feb. 1626; *cr.* Visct. Fanshawe of Dromore [I] 5 Sept. 1661.[1]

King's remembrancer in the Exchequer 1619–41, Aug. 1660–d.[2]

J.p. Herts. by 1625–42, Essex by 1632–42, Herts. July 1660–d., St. Albans Sept. 1660–d.; commr. of array, Herts. 1642, dep. lt. c. Aug. 1660–d.; commr. for oyer and terminer, Home circuit July 1660, assessment, Herts. Aug. 1660–d., loyal and indigent officers 1662.[3]

Fanshawe's ancestors had been tenants on the Derbyshire manor of Holmesfield since at least 1417. They first entered Parliament in Elizabethan times, held office in the Exchequer, and bought Ware Park, 'one of the best seats within twenty miles of London'. Fanshawe was described by his sister-in-law as

a very worthy, valiant, honest, good-natured gentleman, charitable and generous and had excellent natural parts, yet choleric and rash, which was only incommode to his own family; he was a very pretty man, (for he was

but low), of a sanguine complexion, much of a gentleman in his mien and language.

It was estimated that before the Civil War his property in Hertfordshire, Essex and London was worth £2,800 p.a., and his office as King's remembrancer another thousand. But this he was compelled to make over to his brother in 1641 after the discovery of serious irregularities in the appointment of staff. Nevertheless he fought for the King at Edgehill and joined with Sir Gervase Clifton*, Richard Spencer*, and Sir William Walter in advancing a considerable loan in 1643 on the security of the royal forests. A Straffordian in the Long Parliament, he sat at Oxford in 1644. After a brief period of exile at the end of the first Civil War he petitioned to compound on the Barnstaple articles in 1648. He alleged debts of £14,000, and was fined £1,310. During the Interregnum he made over the Hertfordshire estate to his son. His arrest was ordered in 1659 after Booth's rising, and he signed the declaration of the Hertfordshire Cavaliers in April 1660 disclaiming thoughts of revenge, though he was of course ineligible at the general election.[4]

Fanshawe, who is said to have refused an offer from his kinsman Cromwell to reinstate him in the Exchequer, regained his office soon after the Restoration. It was some years before his advance to Charles I could be repaid, and as compensation for the delay he was given an Irish peerage, for which the fees fell little short of £200. Although no longer a Hertfordshire resident or freeholder, he was returned for the county at the general election of 1661, and listed as a friend by Lord Wharton. An active Member of the Cavalier Parliament in its first four sessions, he was appointed each time to the committee of elections and privileges, and probably to 137 others, including seven conferences. He was the first Member appointed to the committee on the bill for confirming public acts (14 May), served on the committee for the security bill, and helped to manage a conference about it. He was also appointed to the committees to consider restoring bishops to the House of Lords, the corporations bill, and the bill to prevent mischief from Quakers. During the debate on the bill promoted by Sir John Pakington, 2nd Bt.*, 'Sir Thomas Fanshawe took occasion to thank the House for showing so much kindness to a Cavalier, it being the first time he ever saw any'. His name again stands first on the committee for the uniformity bill (3 July), and on the following day he was among those entrusted with the bill of pains and penalties. It was probably Fanshawe who drew the attention of the House to the pamphlet of William Prynne* against the corporations bill, since he was the first to be appointed to the committee. Before the autumn recess he may have acted as teller for confirming the election of the royalist candidates at Downton, and as manager of a conference on the uniformity bill. He was the first Member named to the committee for the militia bill (3 Dec.), and before the session ended he was appointed to manage three more conferences, to compare the texts of the Book of Common Prayer, to prepare reasons for a conference on the uniformity bill, and to report whether it was necessary to produce a supplementary bill obliging incumbents to renounce the Covenant.[5]

In the 1663 session Fanshawe was among those appointed to report on defects in the Act of Uniformity and the Corporations Act, to consider a petition from the loyal and indigent officers, and to prepare a bill to prevent the growth of Popery. On 29 Apr. he read to the House a letter from William Willoughby* 'and several other persons of quality of the county of Hertford, complaining of the frequent and numerous conventions of Quakers, Anabaptists, and other dissenters'. His was the first name on the committees 'to provide such further remedies and expedients as they shall find necessary' for this situation, and to consider the bill to regulate vestries. He was among those ordered to prepare a bill restricting office to loyal Anglicans, and on 6 May he carried up the bill to authorize the levying of toll on the highways in Hertfordshire. He was appointed to the committee to prevent abuses in the sale of offices and honours and he was the first Member appointed to consider an explanatory bill on relieving the loyal and indigent officers. On 2 July he carried to the Lords two bills, one against Popery, the other against conventicles, and he helped to manage a conference on relief from the Act of Uniformity. A court dependant in 1664, he was the first Member named to the committee for the conventicles bill, which he carried to the Lords on 28 Apr., later helping to manage a conference. He told the local Quakers in August that they were not punished for their religion, but for assembling in numbers larger than was lawful, and he was prepared to plead the cause of a conventicler who had loyally served Charles I. In the next session he probably introduced the bill to continue the Turnpike Act, since his name once more headed the list of the committee. When he was struck down with apoplexy at his London home on 28 Mar. 1665, Charles II is said to have remarked that he had lost the best of men and subjects. He was buried at Ware, intestate and £28,000 in debt, and his widow was saved from penury only by the grant of a pension of £600 to her and her heirs for 31 years.[6]

[1] Wards 7/54/122; *Vis. Eng. and Wales Notes* ed. Crisp, vi. 157–61; *Fanshawe Mems.* 293–4; *Chamberlain Letters*, ii. 149. [2] *CSP Dom.* 1619–23, p. 78; *Chamberlain Letters*, ii. 264; *Cal. Treas. Bks.* i. 237. [3] Rymer, *Foedera*, viii. pt. 2, p. 9; *HMC 10th Rep. IV*, 503. [4] H. C. Fanshawe, *Hist. Fanshawe Fam.* 1–3; *Fanshawe Mems.* 295–8; Eg. 3328, f. 105; G. E. Aylmer, *King's Servants*, 124, 129; Keeler, *Long Parl.* 172; *Cal. Comm. Comp.* 1864; *CSP Dom.* 1659–60, p. 56. [5] Eg. 3328, f. 105; *Cal. Treas. Bks.* i. 47; *Fanshawe Mems.* 298–300; *CJ*, viii. 261, 288, 311, 355, 358, 367; Reymes diary, 17 June 1661. [6] *CJ*, viii. 533, 562; x. 108; Chauncy, *Herts.* i. 408; *Fanshawe Mems.* 301; Eg. 3328, f. 105.

E.R.E.

FANSHAWE, Sir Thomas II (1628–1705), of Jenkins, Barking, Essex.

ESSEX   1685

bap. 8 June 1628, 1st s. of Thomas Fanshawe† of Jenkins, clerk of the crown in the K.b., by Susan, da. and coh. of Matthias Otten of Putney, Surr. *educ.* I. Temple 1646. *m.* (1) 5 Feb. 1657, Margaret (*d.*1674), da. and h. of Sir Edward Heath of Cottesmore, Rutland, 1da.; (2) Elizabeth (*d.*1729), da. of Sir Thomas Fanshawe I*, 1st Visct. Fanshawe of Dromore [I], of Ware Park, Herts., *s.p. suc.* fa. 1652; kntd. 10 Dec. 1660.[1]

J.p. Essex Mar. 1660–Apr. 1688, Oct. 1688–bef. 1701, commr. for militia Mar. 1660, assessment, Essex Aug. 1660–80, 1689–90, Rutland 1673–80, sewers, Havering and Dagenham levels Sept. 1660, Wittersham marshes Dec. 1660; dep. lt. Rutland 1671–Mar. 1688.[2] Clerk of the crown in the K.b. June 1660–d.[3]

Fanshawe belonged to a younger branch of the family which had acquired the manor of Barking in 1567. His father, who inherited a valuable office in the King's bench, was elected for Lancaster in 1640 and sat at Oxford during the Civil War. He compounded for £1,300 on the Barnstaple articles on an income of £900, of which £200 represented his salary.[4]

Fanshawe was with his father in the west of England in 1645–6 and succeeded to his office at the Restoration. He took no known part in politics until 1685, when he was returned to James II's Parliament for Essex as a Tory at the head of the poll. His only committee was on the bill to prevent the import of tallow candles. In 1688 he gave negative answers on the repeal of the Test Act and Penal Laws, and was removed from county office. The King's agents reported that he would be nominated for re-election in the Church interest. He was restored to the commission of the peace in October, but refused to act until after the Revolution. He did not appear at the general election of 1689 and probably never stood again. He died after several years of 'decrepitude' on 29 Mar. 1705, and was buried at Barking, the last of the Essex Fanshawes to sit in Parliament. He bequeathed Jenkins to his cousin, Thomas Fanshawe of Parsloes, but the will was upset on a technicality and the property passed to his daughter, the widow of Baptist Noel*.[5]

[1] *Vis. Eng. and Wales Notes* ed. Crisp, vi. 150–1. [2] Essex RO, assize rolls 35/102–26, QSR448–52, T2/26; C191/7/48; *CSP Dom.* 1671, p. 273; 1689–90, p. 477. [3] *Cal. Treas. Bks.* i. 630. [4] H. C. Fanshawe, *Fanshawe Fam.* 231–2; Keeler, *Long Parl.* 172–3; *Cal. Comm. Comp.* 1661; *Fanshawe Mems.* 15. [5] *Fanshawe Mems.* 312–14; *Bramston Autobiog.* (Cam. Soc. xxxii), 172, 316–17, 326, 346; Essex RO, DD/Ac2; *R. Hist. Soc. Trans.* (ser. 4), xix. 185; *VCH Essex*, v. 192.

G.H./E.C.

FARRINGTON, John (c.1609–80), of Chichester, Suss.

CHICHESTER   21 May 1660, 1679 (Oct.)–Dec. 1680

b. c.1609, 1st s. of Thomas Farrington of Chichester by Dorothy, da. of Henry Payne of Chichester. *educ.* Brasenose, Oxf. matric. 30 June 1626, aged 17; G. Inn 1633. *m.* lic. 9 June 1638, Anne, da. of John May of Rawmere, 2s. 3da. *suc.* fa. 1654.[1]

J.p. Suss. July 1660–80; commr. for sewers W. Suss. Oct. 1660, assessment, Suss. 1661–4, 1679–*d.*, Chichester 1663–4; sheriff, Suss. 1666–7.[2]

Farrington was descended from a Lancashire family that had been settled for three generations in Chichester, where his father was four times mayor. He took no known part in the Civil War, but led an attempt to rescue three Royalists in the city in 1647. An antiquary and a friend of Selden, he was involved in a double return for Chichester at the general election of 1660 but was seated on the merits of the election. He was appointed to no committees and did not speak. He is not known to have stood in 1661, but later in the year obtained a letter from the King to one of the prebendaries, desiring that two leases should be renewed to him on the grounds of his constant loyalty. But he opposed the courtier Baptist May* at the Midhurst by-election of 1670, though they were closely connected by marriage. A strong Protestant, he was noted for his severities during the Popish Plot hysteria, which earned him an unopposed return for Chichester at the second general election of 1679, and removal from the commission of the peace. He was appointed to the committee of elections and privileges in the second Exclusion Parliament, but was given leave to go into the country for his health on 1 Dec. 1680, and was buried at St. Peter the Great, Chichester on 18 Dec. He died intestate.[3]

[1] *Vis. Suss.* (Harl. Soc. lxxxix), 44. [2] C181/7/58. [3] *VCH Suss.* iii. 88; Stanford, *Suss. in the Gt. Civil War*, 127; *CSP Dom.* 1661–2, p. 135; Bodl. Tanner 149, f. 23; Wood, *Athenae*, iii. 1274; Add. 5699, f. 181v.

M.W.H./B.M.C.

FARRINGTON (FARINGTON), Richard (c.1644–1719), of South Street, Chichester, Suss.

CHICHESTER   4 Jan. 1681, 1681, 1698, 1708, 1710, 1715–7 Aug. 1719

b. c.1644, 2nd s. of John Farrington*. *m.* (1) lic. 28 Feb. 1671, aged 27, Elizabeth, da. of William Marlott of Itchingfield, 3s. *d.v.p.*; (2) lic. 24 May 1687, Elizabeth, da. and h. of John Peachey of Eartham, *s.p. cr.* Bt. 17 Dec. 1697.[1]

Commr. for assessment, Suss. 1679–80, 1690, inquiry into recusancy fines 1687, j.p. May 1688–?*d.*, sheriff 1696–7; capt. of militia ft. Chichester by 1697–*d.*[2]

Although a younger son, Farrington seems to have inherited considerable property in and around Chichester, perhaps because his elder brother (knighted in 1681) was loyal to the Court. He himself adhered to the country party like his father, whom he succeeded as Member for the city, and he was described by the Presbyterian Morrice as a 'fanatic', like his colleague John Braman*, who was also his first wife's step-father. He left no trace on the records of the second and third Exclusion Parliaments, but was recommended for re-election by the local Whigs. His house was searched for arms without result in November 1681. He was also suspected, with better cause, of allowing the house to be used for a conventicle. When an informer was set upon and killed by his coachman Davis in 1682, Farrington was tried for murder on his own brother's information, but acquitted, despite the efforts of Jeffreys for the prosecution. With Braman, he organized the welcome for the Duke of Monmouth on his visit to Chichester in February 1683, and his house was again searched. In 1684 Davis was condemned for highway robbery in Hampshire, but despite several reprieves seems to have confessed nothing material against his former master before the fact.[3]

Farrington was arrested on the eve of Monmouth's invasion in 1685, but no proceedings followed. He probably became a Whig collaborator, and the King's electoral agents expected him to be elected for Chichester in 1688. But he did not regain his seat for another ten years, and held it only intermittently. He continued to vote consistently with the Whigs till his death on 7 Aug. 1719.[4]

[1] *Vis. Suss.* (Harl. Soc. lxxxix) 44; J. Comber, *Suss. Genealogies, Horsham*, 220; PCC 7, 183 Browning. [2] *Cal. Treas. Bks.* viii. 1696; Eg. 1626, f. 41. [3] R. Morrice, *Entering Bk.* 1, pp. 424–5; 2, pp. 20, 28, 49, 52; *CSP Dom.* 1680–1, pp. 472, 473, 585; 1682, p. 545; Jan.–June 1683, pp. 58, 70, 358; 1683–4, pp. 303, 314; Luttrell, i. 228, 230, 237. [4] *CSP Dom.* 1685, p. 157; D. R. Lacey, *Dissent and Parl. Pols.* 394.

B.M.C.

FARWELL (FAREWELL), Arthur (c.1642–87), of Westminster.

DARTMOUTH   1685–May 1687

b. c.1642, 1st s. of Arthur Farewell of Lincoln's Inn by Anne, ?da. of John Winyard, keeper of the Palace of Westminster. *educ.* Magdalen Coll. Oxf. 1658; I.

Temple 1660. *m.* 1 June 1669, Mary, da. and coh. of Nicholas Monck, bishop of Hereford, 3s. *suc.* fa. 1652.[1]

Sec. to Christopher Monck* by 1681–*d.*[2]

Farwell was probably descended from a 14th century Member for Taunton; if so, he was the only other bearer of the name to enter Parliament, though by Tudor times several branches of the family had acquired estates in Somerset. Younger sons, like Farwell's grandfather, showed a predilection for the law, as a result of intermarriage with the family of the celebrated Elizabethan judge Sir James Dyer (previously Speaker in Edward VI's last Parliament). Farwell's father, also a barrister, took no part in the Civil War, though most of the family supported Parliament. In his will he admonished his wife to take especial care of Farwell's education.[3]

However, Farwell owed his career less to his education than to his marriage to the cousin of the 2nd Duke of Albemarle, who made him his secretary, though he had 'very little love and kindness' for him. When Albemarle became chancellor of Cambridge University in 1682, Farwell was given an honorary degree, but was unable to profit from his employer's letter of recommendation to the electors in 1685, and at Harwich he had to make way for a court nominee. He was, however, returned for Dartmouth after a contest, doubtless on the same interest; but he left no trace on the records of James II's Parliament. He was buried at St. Margaret's Westminster on 3 May 1687, and with the death of his patron Albemarle in the following year his family disappeared into obscurity, though his brother, a major in the Dutch army, became deputy governor of the Tower in 1689. His sons had apparently all died childless by 1709.[4]

[1] *CSP Dom.* 1640–1, p. 490; *HMC 5th Rep.* 108; PCC 322 Brent (wrongly calendared as John Farwell); E. F. Ward, *Christopher Monck, Duke of Albemarle*, 14; *St. Margaret's, Westminster* (Harl. Soc. Reg. lxiv), 113, 144; *Mems. of St. Margaret's, Westminster*, 631; C10/492/137. [2] Ward, 69. [3] *N. and Q.* (ser. 5), iv. 413. [4] Ward, 182; C. H. Cooper, *Annals of Cambridge*, iii. 608–10; R. Morrice, *Entering Bk.* 2, p. 126; St. Margaret's, Westminster par. reg.; *Som. Wills*, iv. 66; C5/84/57.

J.P.F.

FAUNT, George (*d.*1697), of Foston, Leics.

LEICESTERSHIRE 1661

2nd s. of Henry Faunt (*d.*1665) of Little Claybrook, Leics. by 2nd w. Barbara, da. of Thomas Love of Leicester. *m.* 30 June 1646, Dorothy, da. of Edward Hanbury of Kelmarsh, Northants., 2s. (1 *d.v.p.*) 4da. *suc.* uncle at Foston 1639.[1]

Sheriff, Leics. 1658–Nov. 1660, commr. for militia Mar. 1660, assessment Aug. 1660–79, dep. lt. c. Aug. 1660–80, j.p. 1661–85, commr. for corporations 1662–3, receiver of taxes 1671–4.[2]

Faunt was the great-grandson of a Huntingdonshire lawyer who bought Foston and sat for Leicestershire in 1555. The younger son of a younger brother, he was designated heir by his uncle, Sir William Faunt, who was fined £4,000 in Star Chamber for enclosing. Faunt petitioned the Long Parliament in 1641, and the judgment was reversed. Nevertheless none of the family took any known part in the Civil War, nor did Faunt himself before the overthrow of the Rump hold any office except the shrievalty. In this capacity he presented the Leicestershire petition for a free Parliament to George Monck* in January 1660, and was taken into custody on the orders of the Council of State. He was released in time to conduct the general election with admirable imperturbability. When news was received that the republican general John Lambert[†] was only 14 miles away with a party of horse 'all the electors left the high sheriff, Col. Faunt, save 16, all he could get to stay with him'. But the formalities were observed, and two supporters of the Restoration duly returned. The purchase of Laughton from a ruined Parliamentarian a few years before may have strained his resources, for in the Convention a private bill to confirm a protectorate ordinance was steered through committee without amendment by Richard Hopkins I* to enable him to sell part of his uncle's entailed estate to pay his debts and to provide for his wife and younger children. The income of £2,000 p.a. with which he was credited in the Leicestershire list for the projected order of the Royal Oak was probably exaggerated.[3]

Nevertheless Faunt was returned unopposed for the county at the general election of 1661. He was appointed to the committee for the uniformity bill, but altogether he was one of the least active Members of the Cavalier Parliament, being named to the committee of elections and privileges in seven sessions and to only seven others. He was granted leave to go into the country on 6 Dec. 1666 and to attend the assizes on 22 Feb. 1668. On the latter occasion he must have returned to Westminster without delay, for on 3 Apr. he was among those ordered to prepare for a conference on fining jurors. He was appointed receiver of the Leicestershire subsidy in 1671, and classed by the Opposition as a government supporter. He was named to his last committee on 7 Dec. 1674, but after the recess in May 1675 he petitioned against the debt-ridden borough Member, Sir John Pretyman*, and claimed privilege himself for the stay of a chancery commission. He received the government whip in the autumn, and was assigned on the working lists to the management of Sir Robert Carr* as chancellor of the duchy. Carr's influence, however, was highly suspect in government circles, and after the recess Sir Richard Wiseman* commented: 'Mr Faunt I think does not go maliciously against us, but I know not which [way] to apply to him'. Danby had no such problem, and on 28 June 1676 a warrant was ordered for a grant of £726 5s. as royal bounty, to be satisfied by tallies on his tax payments. He was replaced as receiver by Sir William Hartopp*, Pretyman's equally indigent colleague; but an opposition pamphlet described him in 1677 as 'a constant receiver of all taxes', who was to have had '£500 out of the last tax', and Shaftesbury classed him 'doubly vile'. Absent from a call of the House on 13 Dec. 1678, he was one of the Members sent for in custody.[4]

Blacklisted in the 'unanimous club', Faunt never stood again. The Opposition complained that he was retained on the Leicestershire commission of the peace in 1680, despite being then 'a prisoner in the King's bench'. He was buried at Foston on 4 Nov. 1697, the last of the family to sit in Parliament.[5]

[1] Nichols, *Leics.* iv. 103, 175; *Diary of Thomas Isham of Lamport,* 186. [2] *Leicester Bor. Recs.* ed. Stock, 480; *Cal. Treas. Bks.* iv. 89, 110; v. 298. [3] Nichols, ii. 694; iv. 169–70; *CJ,* ii. 195, 209, 216; vii. 553, 836, 848; viii. 198; *CSP Dom.* 1659–60, pp. 335–6; 1676–7, p. 178; *Merc. Pol.* 23 Feb. 1660; 12 Car. II cap. 26. [4] *CJ,* ix. 329, 339; *Cal. Treas. Bks.* v. 255, 298. [5] *HMC Lords,* i. 183; Nichols, iv. 172.

E.C.

FAWKENER, Edward (c.1628–91), of Uppingham, Rutland.

RUTLAND 1681

b. c.1628, 1st s. of Kenelm Fawkener of Braunston by Catherine, da. of Thomas Ireland of Preston, Rutland, and coh. to her bro. Edward. *educ.* G. Inn 1648. *m.* bef. 1650, Dorcas (*bur.* 10 Jan. 1713), da. and coh. of William Neville of Holt, Leics., 1s. *suc.* gt.-uncle at Scarlies 1653, fa. 1667.[1]
  Commr. for assessment, Rutland 1649–50, 1657, Aug. 1660–3, 1677–80, 1689–90, lt. of militia horse Apr. 1660, j.p. July 1660–82, ?1690–d., dep. lt. c. Aug. 1660–82, 1690–d.; commr. for enclosures, Deeping fen 1665.[2]

Fawkener's family was established at Stoke Dry in Rutland by the early 16th century, but their claim to a descent from a 15th century lord mayor of London was disallowed by the heralds in 1682. They took no known part in the Civil War, though Fawkener served on local commissions during the Interregnum. He bought the manor of Uppingham in 1658, and presumably supported the Restoration, for he was commissioned in the militia in April 1660, signed the address of congratulation to Charles II, and was proposed as one of the knights

of the Royal Oak, with an income estimated at £600 p.a. He was returned for the county in 1681, but took no known part in the Oxford Parliament. He probably favoured exclusion, for he was removed from local office in the following year. He was buried at Uppingham on 4 Dec. 1691, the only member of his family to sit in Parliament.[3]

[1] *Vis. Rutland* (Harl. Soc. lxxiii), 33–34; Wright, *Rutland,* 130. [2] *Parl. Intell.* 9 Apr. 1660. [3] *VCH Rutland,* i. 201; ii. 97–98.

E.C./B.D.H.

FAWKES, Thomas (c.1640–1707), of Farnley, Yorks.

KNARESBOROUGH 21 Mar. 1689, 17 May 1690

b. c.1640, 1st s. of Michael Fawkes of Farnley by 3rd w. Mary, da. of Sir John Molyneux, 1st Bt., of Tevershall, Notts. *m.* (1) Sarah, da. and h. of Francis Mitchell of Arthington Grange, Yorks., 2s. (1 *d.v.p.*) 1da.; (2) lic. 25 Dec. 1677, Mary, da. of William Welby of Denton, Lincs., 1s. *d.v.p. suc.* fa. 1647.[1]
  J.p. Yorks. (W. Riding) 1672–Aug. 1688, Nov. 1688–d., commr. for assessment 1673–80, 1689–90, capt. of militia horse ?1679–Aug. 1688, Oct. 1688–?d., dep. lt. by 1700–?d.[2]

Fawkes was descended from a steward of Knaresborough forest who was living at Farnley under Henry VII. His grandfather was returned as a recusant in 1604, and in the following year a distant cousin achieved immortality of a sort in the Gunpowder Plot. But his father seems to have conformed. Too old to fight himself during the Civil War, he threatened to flog his tenants if they refused to join the Cavalier army. He compounded at £360 for an estate of £120 p.a., partly at rackrent. Fawkes was an Anglican; he gave the same evasive answers as the Hon. Thomas Fairfax* on the repeal of the Test Act and Penal Laws in August 1688. At the general election of 1689 he was involved in a double return at Knaresborough, ten miles from his home, with Lord Latimer (Edward Osborne*). He was seated on the merits of the election and became the first of his family to enter Parliament in the orthodox way. A moderately active Member of the Convention, he was named to 12 committees. On 10 June he was added to the committee to report on defects in the militia laws, and later in the month he was among those to whom the attainder bill was committed. He was also appointed to consider the bill to reverse the judgments against Titus Oates and to hear a charge of malversation from the tenants of Sir Walter Vavasour, a Yorkshire Papist; but on the same day he was given leave to go into the country for a month. After the recess, he was on the committees to prepare a bill for the more effectual tendering of the new oaths and to consider the second mutiny bill. He did not vote for the disabling clause in the bill to restore corporations, but he was probably a moderate Whig. At the general election of 1690 he defeated Henry Slingsby II*. He died on 7 Aug. 1707 and was buried at Otley. His son Francis was returned for Knaresborough at a by-election in 1714.[3]

[1] Clay, *Dugdale's Vis. Yorks.* i. 207. [2] *Yorks. Arch. Jnl.* xxix. 283; Eg. 1626, f. 57. [3] Clay, i. 204–7; *Royalist Comp. Pprs.* (Yorks. Arch. Soc. rec. ser. xviii), 110–12; *CJ*, x. 205.

P.W.

FEILDE, Edmund (1620–76), of Shephalbury and Marden Hill, Herts.

HERTFORD 28 Apr. 1675–3 June 1676

bap. 11 Sept. 1620, o. surv. s. of Thomas Feilde, rector of St Andrew's, Hertford 1598–1623, by 2nd w. Anne, da. of Charles Nodes of Shephalbury. *educ.* Emmanuel, Camb. 1637; I. Temple 1639, called 1652. *m.* c.1653, Frances (*d.*1690), da. of William Pert of Arnolds Hall, Mountnessing, Essex, wid. of his cos. Charles Nodes of Shephalbury, 2s. 1da. *suc.* fa. 1623.[1]

Commr. for militia, Herts. Mar. 1660, assessment Aug. 1660–1, 1663–74.

Feilde's name, in various spellings, is ancient in Hertfordshire, but of his own direct ancestry little is known. His father, born at Weston where he owned both copyhold and freehold land, obtained his education at Cambridge as a sizar. He was ordained in 1595, and after holding various livings in Hertfordshire and preaching in London was able to provide a portion of £1,500 for Feilde's sister. Feilde's own early maintenance and education was covered by three annuities totalling £135 p.a., and he inherited property in Hertford, lands in Weston and Bengeo, and the rectory of Rushden. Nothing is known of his activities in the Civil War. He may have practised as a lawyer, though he was not called to the bar until 1652. About this time he married his cousin's widow, who came of an armigerous family, and obtained a grant of arms himself. He took up residence on her property, and at the Restoration was proposed as a knight of the Royal Oak, with an income of £600 p.a.; but he was apparently never a j.p. About 1672 he bought the manor of Marden, four miles north-west of Hertford, from the wife and sister-in-law of Arthur Sparke*. He defeated the court supporter Sir John Gore* at a by-election for the borough in 1675 with the support of the sitting Member, Sir Thomas Byde*, whose son was married to Feilde's daughter. Gore petitioned, but Feilde was allowed to take his seat. In his few months in Parliament he was appointed only to the committee for the tithe recovery bill, and he did not speak. Sir Richard Wiseman*

probably assessed him as a sound churchman, despite his country connexions, and believed that 'Mr Feilde may be successfully applied to' on behalf of the Court. But he died on 3 June 1676, aged 56, and was buried in Shephal church, where a memorial described him as a man of strict piety, deep learning and calm and prudent temperament. In the last year of his life he bought Stanstead Abbots, which became the family seat. His son was knighted in 1681, presumably as a Tory, but the next member of the family to enter Parliament was his great-grandson, who sat for Hertford from 1770 to 1780 as an independent Whig.[2]

[1] Herts. RO, Hertford St. Andrew par. reg.; PCC 96 Swann; Clutterbuck, *Herts.* ii. 169; iii. 243. [2] *Al. Cant.* ii. 136; *The Gen.* n.s. xv. 59; Chauncy, *Herts.* i. 382, 541; ii. 416.

E.R.E.

FELTON, Sir Henry, 2nd Bt. (1619–90), of Playford, Suff.

SUFFOLK 1656,[1] 1659, 1660, 1661

b. 27 July 1619, 1st s. of Sir Henry Felton, 1st Bt., of Playford by Dorothy, da. of Sir Nicholas Bacon, 1st Bt., of Redgrave, wid. of Sir Bassingbourne Gawdy† of West Harling, Norf. *m.* 19 Dec. 1637, Susanna, da. of Sir Lionel Tollemache, 2nd Bt.†, of Helmingham, Suff., 12s. (7 *d.v.p.*) 3da. *suc.* fa. 18 Sept. 1624.[2]

J.p. Suff. 1657–July 1671, Dec. 1671–July 1688, 1689–*d.*; commr. for assessment, Suff. 1657, Jan. 1660–80, 1689–*d.*, Ipswich 1663–4, sewers, Norf., Suff., Lincs. and Northants. 1658–9, militia Suff. 1659, Mar. 1660; col. of militia horse, Suff. Apr. 1660, by 1676–at least 1680, capt. by 1664–at least 1671; freeman, Ipswich June 1660, Dunwich 1678; commr. for oyer and terminer, Norfolk circuit July 1660; dep. lt. Suff. c. Aug. 1660–?July 1688, 1689–*d.*, commr. for loyal and indigent officers 1662, v.-adm. 1663–83, commr. for recusants 1675; bailiff, Ipswich 1684–5, portman 1685–July 1688.[3]

Felton was descended from a merchant who acquired the manor of Shotley by marriage early in the 15th century. His own estate, exclusive of his grandmother's jointure, was valued at £797 p.a. on his marriage in 1637. He took no part in the Civil War, but in 1656 he became the first of the family to be elected to Parliament, and he held county office under the Protectorate. By the summer of 1659 he had become an active Royalist. In January 1660 he presented the Suffolk petition for a free Parliament to George Monck*, and his arrest was ordered by the Council of State.[4]

Felton was re-elected to the Convention as knight of the shire, and marked as a friend by Lord Wharton. An inactive Member, he was named only to the committee of elections and privileges and the committee on the bill for confirming parliamentary privilege. At a gentry meeting he was approved for re-election, and invited to choose his colleague. Elected for the county for the fourth time in 1661, he was no more active in the Cavalier Parliament, in which he was appointed to only 19 committees, including the elections committee in seven sessions, and acted as teller in six divisions. In the opening session he was among those to whom the bill to prevent mischief from Quakers was committed, and was teller against a proviso to the militia bill. As 'a person of great integrity and loyalty' he was granted custody of the hundreds of Bosmere, Claydon and Samford. In 1663 he was teller in three divisions on important measures: the bills against Popery and to settle a revenue on the Duke of York and the bill against conventicles, in which he favoured excusing from local office those who refused the sacramental test. On 11 Dec. 1667 he claimed that his cattle had been distrained by the servant of his cousin Anthony Gawdy; but he failed to attend the committee of privileges either in person or by counsel, and (Sir) Job Charlton* reported that the distraint was to recover rent due from his second son Thomas, one of the royal pages. Thomas Waldegrave* was desired to give Felton notice of the report, and a fortnight later the House resolved that his privilege had been infringed; but the servant was released, nevertheless. He acted as teller for the Opposition on supply on 1 Dec. 1670, but was included in a list of the court party at the end of the session. This may be connected with an obscure incident that caused Felton's temporary removal from the bench. In September, however, the attorney-general was directed not to prosecute him for certain words which 'his Majesty is pleased to pardon', presumably because his son was now a groom of the bedchamber.[5]

Felton's only recorded speech was on 18 Feb. 1673, when he sought to obtain a reduction in taxes for his constituency. His name appeared on the Paston list, and on 19 Feb. 1673 he was teller against the return as his colleague for Suffolk of Sir Samuel Barnardiston*, the country candidate who had narrowly defeated his wife's nephew Lord Huntingtower (Lionel Tollemache*). Felton's name was included in the working lists, but Sir Richard Wiseman* noted that he had been absent during the autumn session of 1675, and queried his reliability. Shaftesbury marked him 'doubly vile', and in *A Seasonable Argument* he was described as 'a pensioner, and his son a bedchamber man'. He was on both lists of the court party in 1678.[6]

As one of the 'unanimous club', Felton did not stand again. An opponent of exclusion, he presented the Suffolk address approving the dissolution of Parliament in 1681, and was nominated bailiff of

Ipswich in the new charter. In April 1688 the royal electoral agents reported that he might regain his seat at the next election, 'though he be an infirm man'. They hoped that he might 'go right' on the repeal of the Test Act and Penal Laws, though he had 'answered wrong to the Lord Dover', the Roman Catholic lord lieutenant. But he was removed as portman of Ipswich in July. He accepted county office after the Revolution, but died soon afterwards, being buried at Playford on 20 Oct. 1690. His eldest son, the third baronet, who had stood unsuccessfully for Thetford in 1689, was returned for Orford as a Whig in 1695, while Thomas sat for Orford and Bury St. Edmunds with one short interval from 1690 to 1709.[7]

[1] Excluded. [2] *Suff. Inst. Arch. Procs.* iv. 33–34, 54–56. [3] C181/6/291, 341, 342, 360, 381; *Merc. Pub.* 26 Apr. 1660; Add. 39246, ff. 4, 23; *East Anglian* n.s. vi. 316; *HMC Var.* vii. 102; Ind. 24557; R. Canning, *Principal Charters of Ipswich*, 51–52. [4] *Suff. Inst. Arch. Procs.* iv. 29; D. Underdown, *Royalist Conspiracy*, 269; *Suff. and the Great Rebellion* (Suff. Rec. Soc. iii), 129; *CSP Dom. 1659–60*, p. 568. [5] Add. 32324, f. 53v; *CJ*, viii. 304, 477, 502, 509; ix. 56, 66; *CSP Dom.* 1661–2, pp. 321, 344, 402; 1671, p. 477; *Milward*, 198, 224; *Cal. Treas. Bks.* i. 669; iii. 934. [6] *Dering*, 121; *CJ*, ix. 312. [7] *London Gazette*, 10 Oct. 1681; PC2/72/723; *Suff. Inst. Arch. Procs.* iv. 54.

P.W.

FENWICK, Sir John, 3rd Bt. (c.1644–97), of Wallington, Northumb. and Westminster.[1]

NORTHUMBERLAND   15 Mar. 1677, 1679 (Mar.), 1679 (Oct.), 1681, 1685

b. c.1644, o.s. of Sir William Fenwick, 2nd Bt.* *m.* 14 July 1663, Lady Mary Howard (*d.* 27 Oct. 1708), da. of Charles Howard*, 1st Earl of Carlisle, 3s. 1da. *d.v.p. suc.* fa. bef. 9 July 1676.[2]

Capt. Sayer's Ft. 1667, Duke of Monmouth's Ft. (French army) 1672–4; cornet, Queen's 2 Life Gds. 1672–4, guidon 1674–5, capt. 1676–8, maj. 1679–81, lt.-col. 1681–7; col. of ft. (Dutch army) 1675–7; col. of ft. 1678–9, horse 1687–Dec. 1688, brig. 1678, 1685–Dec. 1688; gov. Holy Island 1681–Dec. 1688.

Capt. of militia horse, Northumb. to 1670; commr. for assessment, Northumb. 1673–80, Berwick-upon-Tweed 1677–80, carriage of coals, Newcastle-upon-Tyne 1679; j.p. Northumb. by 1680–9, Mdx. and Westminster 1687–9; dep. lt. Northumb. by 1680–9; c.-in-c. militia, Northumb. and co. Dur. 1685; common councilman, Berwick 1685–Oct. 1688.[3]

Gent. of the privy chamber 1671–85.[4]

A delicate child, Fenwick was hopelessly spoilt by his mother and grew up totally uneducated and the object of his father's aversion. 'But a young novice when he came to London, [he] married soon after the Earl of Carlisle's daughter, and, neither he nor she taking any care of their affairs, he bought a standard in the Life Guards and lived in town, and they burned their candles at both ends.' On 5 Feb. 1671 he fought a duel with John Churchill II* after a quarrel at a masquerade. He was among the English volunteers who served in the French army under Turenne in the third Dutch war, after which he was warmly recommended to William of Orange, both by the Duke of York and by Danby, as 'a gentleman both of considerable quality and fortune'. He arrived in Flanders at the close of the 1675 campaign and was given a regiment, which he found very much under strength. On William's instructions he returned to Northumberland during the winter to recruit, but the pay and conditions in the Dutch army were considered inferior to those offered by the French agents, who were also active. Reporting on his failure to William when he rejoined the army in the spring, he suggested 'obliging' the English by raising their wages; but, according to Lady Mary's vivid though illiterate account of the incident that determined the relationship for the rest of their lives, the prince replied that he would not go to the door to oblige an Englishman. Fenwick was with difficulty restrained by Sir William Temple* from resigning his commission on the spot, and then only out of regard for his own reputation. He served with distinction in the ensuing campaign and was wounded in the face at the siege of Maastricht, but was obliged to return to England on his father's death. William wrote to Lord Ossory (Thomas Butler*) that he had 'behaved very well for the short time he was here'.[5]

Finding the estate burdened with a debt of £4,000 and £1,900 in annuities, Fenwick sold the lead-mines to William Blackett* 'at a vast undervalue', and prepared to contest a double by-election in Northumberland. According to *A Seasonable Argument* he was given £2,000 for this purpose, and promised a place at Court. However, he was already a gentleman of the privy chamber, and the secret service accounts record payments of only £200, half paid a fortnight after he had been returned and the other half in January 1678. Shaftesbury marked him 'doubly vile', and his name appears among the excise pensioners. In the Cavalier Parliament, he was appointed to only five committees, including that to amend the Border Act of 1662. On 15 Apr. 1678 he was added to the committee to prepare reasons for a conference on the growth of Popery, and during the recess he and his colleague (Sir) Ralph Delaval* gave evidence that they had vainly urged the Duke of Newcastle (Henry Cavendish*) and the lord chancellor not to appoint a suspected Papist to the Northumberland bench. On 29 Apr. they were sent with others to inform the lord chancellor accordingly. His name was on both lists of court supporters, and on 10

May he acted as teller against a paragraph in the address for the removal of counsellors. His regiment, which he had again raised locally for service in Flanders, was now among those scheduled for disbandment, and on 30 May he was appointed to the committee to report on how much was due to these forces.[6]

Though Fenwick 'never saw his estate in many years but when he went to choose a Parliament man, . . . he was always sure to be chose himself with none or little expense'. At the first general election of 1679, the King and the Duke of York solicited his interest for the latter's servant, Ralph Widdrington*, 'reputed a Papist'. Fenwick, however, not only supported Delaval but contributed £1,000 to his expenses and they continued to represent the county in all the Exclusion Parliaments. Shaftesbury marked him 'vile', but he was appointed only to the committee of elections and privileges in 1679, and did not vote on the exclusion bill. In 1680 he was among those instructed to bring in a bill to limit imports of Scottish cattle, which had been presented as a grievance by the Northumberland grand jury. In the Oxford Parliament he was again appointed only to the elections committee. At the summer assizes he refused the address approving the dissolution as sent down by the Duke of Newcastle (Henry Cavendish*), saying that 'he would do nothing but in open court, and would not sign anything but what the grand jury approved'. But he was out of the county in the following year when the feud with the Widdrington faction reached 'a dangerous crisis'. Although denied Newcastle's support in 1685 he retained his seat amid great rejoicings. In James II's Parliament he was named to the committee for the disbandment accounts. But on the news of Argyll's landing in Scotland he was sent north to take command of the local forces, to Widdrington's mortification. He was not in the House during the discussion of Monmouth's attainder, and the allegation that he carried it up to the Lords is a later malicious invention.[7]

To Newcastle's questions on the repeal of the Test Act and Penal Laws, Fenwick replied with studied insolence:

> I shall not need to return my answer, since it is of much less consequence to his Majesty's service to give your grace the trouble of it than your letter would have been to the country, which you were pleased to refuse me, in favour of Mr [William] Ogle* and myself for knights of the shire. I suppose his Majesty's intention in sending these orders to your grace was to know the minds of those gentlemen who live in the country, to whom he has not an opportunity to speak himself, and not of those who have the honour to be always near his person.

Presumably he gave satisfaction when closeted, for he was recommended for re-election as court candidate in September 1688. During the Revolution he was at Windsor in command of 4,000 men, but even before James's flight many of them had gone over to William. His brother-in-law, the 2nd Earl of Carlisle (Edward Howard*), invited him on behalf of the peers to assume responsibility for the preservation of order in the capital, but he refused. He accompanied Lord Feversham to Rochester to escort James back to London, and resigned his commission. Together with (Sir) John Talbot* and Lord Lichfield he took his leave of the King, who 'bade him be sure to get into the next Parliament and as many of his friends as could, believing they designed to fall on his son and exclude the Prince of Wales, which his friends if in the Parliament might prevent'. But he is unlikely to have stood again. He sold Wallington to Sir William Blackett* for £4,000, and an annuity of £2,000 for the joint lives of his wife and himself. Nine-tenths of this went to satisfy his creditors, and henceforth he had no occupation but conspiracy. His fellow Jacobite, Lord Ailesbury (Thomas Bruce*) wrote of him: 'As to the affairs of the times, he had a poor head, and understood them as little as he did those of his family'. He had already endured two short spells of imprisonment when he aroused William's implacable resentment by an insult to the Queen. After the assassination plot of 1696 he was arrested, but he could not be tried for treason because one of the necessary witnesses absconded, and the Government, infuriated by his attempts to incriminate the court Whigs in his confessions, determined to proceed by attainder. After heated debate the bill passed the Commons by 189 to 156 and the Lords by 68 to 61, and received the royal assent on 11 Jan. 1697. Fenwick was beheaded on Tower Hill on 27 Jan. Believing that the Church of England was 'the best and purest of churches', he was attended by a non-juring bishop. What remained of his property was granted to his nephew, the 3rd Earl of Carlisle (Charles Howard*).[8]

[1] This biography is based on Add. 47608, ff. 162–86. [2] Le Neve, *Mon. Angl.* 1680–99, pp. 178–9; W. J. Pinks, *Hist. Clerkenwell*, 46; Blackett mss, Carlisle to Blackett, 9 July 1676. [3] *HMC Portland*, ii. 149; Hodgson, *Northumb.* pt. 1, i. 306; *Cal. Treas. Bks.* v. 1205; *CSP Dom.* 1685, p. 67; 1686–7, p. 231. [4] Carlisle, *Privy Chamber*, 189. [5] *Ailesbury Mems.* 389; *Bulstrode*, 170; HMC Portland, iii. 320; Browning, *Danby*, ii. 386; *CSP Dom.* 1676–7, pp. 238, 334; *Willem III en Portland* (Rijks Geschiedkundige Publicatien, xxvii), 57, 71. [6] *Cal. Treas. Bks.* v. 1330, 1332; *CJ*, ix. 469. [7] *Cal. Treas. Bks.* v. 1217; *CSP Dom.* 1682, p. 321; Jan.–June 1683, p. 98; 1685, p. 222; Spencer mss, Reresby to Halifax, 20 Aug. 1681; Macaulay, *Hist.* 474–6. [8] *CSP Dom.* 1687–9, pp. 273, 277; 1689–90, pp. 11, 71; *Hatton Corresp.* (Cam. Soc. n.s. xxiii), 122; *Ailesbury Mems.* 389; *HMC Finch*, ii. 313; Macaulay, 1999–2000, 2640, 2660, 2678, 2687.

G.H.

FENWICK, Roger (c.1662–by 1701), of Stanton Hall, Long Horsley, Northumb.

MORPETH 1689, 1690

*b.*c.1662, 1st s. of William Fenwick (*d.*1675) of Irthington, Cumb. by Elizabeth, da. of Robert Ellison* of Hebburn, co. Dur. *educ.* St. Edmund Hall, Oxf. matric. 25 June 1678, aged 16; G. Inn 1678, called 1686. *m.* 10 July 1692, Elizabeth, da. and h. of George Fenwick† of Brinkburn, Northumb., 4s. (1 *d.v.p.*) 2da. *suc.* gdfa. 1689.

Commr. for assessment, Northumb. 1689–98, G. Inn 1690–4.

Fenwick came from a cadet branch of the family established at Stanton, four miles from Morpeth, early in the 16th century. His grandfather held local office from 1647 to the Restoration, and his uncle died of wounds after leading the charge of Lockhart's regiment at the battle of the Dunes, perhaps the outstanding feat of the New Model Army in Flanders. Little is known of his father, except that he resided on a family property near Naworth Castle, the Cumberland seat of the earls of Carlisle. But his grandfather remained a Presbyterian, sheltering the covenanter Veitch at Stanton in 1677.

Fenwick, a barrister, was elected for Morpeth in 1689, where he was probably acceptable to the 2nd Earl of Carlisle (Edward Howard*) as a former neighbour. His politics, however, were Tory, for he voted to agree with the Lords that the throne was not vacant. An active Member of the Convention, he was appointed to 46 committees, but made no recorded speeches. In the first session he was among those ordered to examine the prisoners of state in Newgate, to consider the new oaths of allegiance and supremacy, to repeal the Corporations Act, to consider the bill of rights and to inquire into the delay in relieving Londonderry. After the recess he was appointed to the committee of inquiry into the miscarriages of the war. He was re-elected in 1690, but died between 1698, when he was last named to the Northumberland assessment commission, and 1701. No later member of this branch entered Parliament.

Hodgson, *Northumb.* pt. 2, ii. 109, 113–14; *Hist. Northumb.* vii. 474; *Thurloe*, vii. 156.

G.H.

FENWICK, Sir William, 2nd Bt. (c.1617–76), of Wallington, Northumb.

NORTHUMBERLAND 6 Nov. 1645,[1] 1654, 1656, 1659, 1660, 1661–bef. 9 July 1676

*b.*c.1617, 2nd but 1st surv. s. of Sir John Fenwick, 1st Bt.†, of Wallington, being 1st s. by 2nd w. Grace, da. of Thomas Loraine of Kirkharle; half-bro. of John Fenwick[†]. *educ.* Morpeth g.s.; Christ's, Camb. adm. 26 June 1633, aged 16; G. Inn 1636. *m.* by 1644, Jane, da. of Henry Stapilton of Wighill, Yorks., 1s. 2da. *suc.* fa. c.1658.[2]

Dep. lt. Northumb. 1644, c. Aug. 1660–*d.*, commr. for northern association 1645, assessment 1645–52, 1657, Aug. 1660–74, militia 1648, Mar. 1660; j.p. Northumb. 1650–*d.*, Cumb. 1674–*d.*; col. of militia, Northumb. 1659, c.-in-c. Jan. 1660; commr. for oyer and terminer, Northern circuit July 1660; capt. vol. horse, Northumb. 1661.[3]

Commr. for security [S] 1656.

Fenwick's ancestors had held lands in Northumberland since early in the 13th century, and first represented the county in 1378. Fenwick's father, a commissioner of array, sat for Northumberland in the Long Parliament until disabled as a Royalist in 1644; but he was reinstated in 1646 until Pride's Purge. His half-brother was more consistent in his loyalties, for he fell at Marston Moor at the head of the royalist dragoons. Fenwick himself was returned as a recruiter for the other county seat, but abstained from the House after Pride's Purge. He regained local office early in the Commonwealth and again represented Northumberland in the Protectorate Parliaments. He did not resume his seat with the secluded Members in 1660, but was re-elected to the Convention, in which he played no known part, and to the Cavalier Parliament. During his absence on leave in 1661, protection was claimed by an Essex resident as Fenwick's menial servant, but the outcome is not known. His estates were rated in 1663 at £1,500 p.a., but he may have encountered some of the financial difficulties which were to overwhelm his son; in 1670 his cattle were distrained for debt. He was three times added to the committee of elections and privileges, but his only legislative committee was for determining differences about houses destroyed by fire in 1671. At the end of the session he was listed as a government supporter by a hostile critic, and his name appeared again on the working lists. He was dead by 9 July 1676, when canvassing had begun on behalf of his son.[4]

[1] Abstained after Pride's Purge, 6 Dec. 1648. [2] Hodgson, *Northumb.* pt. 2, i. 256–7. [3] *CJ*, iii. 657; Stowe 185, f. 161; *Cal. Cl. SP*, iv. 526; *Merc. Pub.* 16 May 1661. [4] *New Hist. Northumb.* xii. 351; Keeler, *Long Parl.* 174; *CJ*, viii. 297; ix. 149; Hodgson, pt. 3, i. 328–9; Blackett mss, Carlisle to Blackett, 9 July 1676.

M.W.H./G.H.

FERMOR (FARMER), Sir William, 2nd Bt. (1648–1711), of Easton Neston, Northants. and Leicester Fields, Westminster.[1]

NORTHAMPTON   31 Oct. 1670, 1679 (Mar.)

b. 3 Aug. 1648, 2nd but 1st surv. s. of Sir William Fermor, 1st Bt., of Easton Neston by Mary, da. and coh. of Hugh Perry *alias* Hunter, Mercer, of London, wid. of Hon. Henry Noel of North Luffenham, Rutland. *educ.* Magdalen Coll. Oxf. 1664. *m.* (1) 21 Dec. 1671, Jane (*d.* 10 Aug. 1673), da. of Andrew Barker of Fairford, Glos., 1da.; (2) Jane 1682, Catherine, da. of John Poulett*, 3rd Baron Poulett of Hinton St. George, Som., 1da.; (3) 4 Mar. 1692 (with £10,000), Lady Sophia Osborne, da. of Sir Thomas Osborne* of Kiveton, Yorks., 1st Duke of Leeds, wid. of Donough, Lord Ibrackan, of Great Billing, Northants., 2s. 4da. *suc.* fa. 14 May 1661; *cr.* Baron Leominster 12 Apr. 1692.

Commr. for assessment, Northants. 1673–80, 1689–90, dep. lt. 1674–87; commr. for inquiry, Whittlewood and Salcey forests 1679; j.p. Northants. by 1680–Feb. 1688, 1689–*d.*[2]

Fermor was descended from a merchant of the staple who bought Easton Neston about 1530. The family first represented the county in 1553. Fermor's father served as captain of horse in the royalist army for six months, and compounded for £1,400. He contested Brackley unsuccessfully in 1661, just before his death. Fermor stood for Northampton, where he had a 'fair house', at the first vacancy after he came of age; he was opposed by Lord Ibrackan (Henry O'Brien*), but the other seat also became vacant and they were returned without a contest. He was not an active Member of the Cavalier Parliament, serving on only 13 committees. He was added to the committee to consider defects in the Conventicles and Militia Acts in 1670. His name does not appear on any court list, but he was marked 'vile' by Shaftesbury in 1677. His most important committee was in the following year when he helped to summarize foreign commitments. When he was re-elected for Northampton, Shaftesbury marked him 'worthy', but he served on only one committee in the first Exclusion Parliament, that for prohibiting the import of Irish cattle, and was absent from the division on the bill. It is not known whether he stood again, nor was he active in local government, his chief interests being artistic. Nevertheless he was probably regarded as a court supporter, being granted a cattle market in Towcester and three annual fairs in 1684. But he did not appear to answer the lord lieutenant's questions on the repeal of the Test Acts and Penal Laws in 1687, and was removed from local office. He was reappointed after the Revolution, but after his third marriage he sat in the House of Lords as a Tory. He died on 7 Dec. 1711, and was buried at Easton Neston. His son was created Earl of Pontefract in 1721, but no later member of the family was elected to Parliament.[3]

[1] *Survey of London*, xxxiv. 513–14. [2] *CSP Dom.* 1673–5, p. 271; *Cal. Treas. Bks.* vi. 184; Northants. RO, FH 1271, 2226. [3] Baker,

Northants. ii. 142–3; *Cal. Comm. Comp.* 1063; *HMC Portland*, ii. 289, 290; SP29/421/216; *CSP Dom.* 1683–4, p. 275.

E.R.E.

FERRERS, John (1629–80), of Walton-on-Trent, Derbys. and Tamworth Castle, Staffs.

DERBYSHIRE   1660
TAMWORTH   26 Nov. 1669–26 Mar. 1670

> *b.* 26 July 1629, o.s. of Sir Humphrey Ferrers of Tamworth Castle by Anne, da. of Sir John Packington of Hampton Lovett, Worcs. *educ.* Corpus, Camb. 1645. *m.* Anne, da. and coh. of Sir Dudley Carleton, clerk of the Privy Council 1636–43, of Imber Court, Thames Ditton, Surr., 1s. *d.v.p.* 1da. *suc.* fa. 1633.[1]
>
> Commr. for scandalous ministers, Derbys. and Notts. 1654; sheriff, Derbys. 1654–5, commr. for security 1655–6; j.p. Derbys. 1656–*d.*, Warws. July 1660–*d.*; commr. for assessment, Derbys. 1657, Aug. 1660–*d.*, Warws. 1661–3, 1664–*d.*, militia, Derbys. Mar. 1660; c.-in-c. of militia, Derbys. Mar. 1660; dep. lt. Derbys. July 1660–*d.*, Staffs. c. Aug. 1660–1; commr. for oyer and terminer, Midland circuit July 1660, recusants, Derbys. 1675.[2]
>
> Capt. Lord Chesterfield's Ft. 1667.

Ferrers's ancestors registered great estates in Derbyshire and Staffordshire in Domesday Book, and held the title of Earl of Derby from 1138 until it was forfeited after Simon de Montfort's rebellion. The first of the family to sit in the House of Commons was Sir John Ferrers, who represented Staffordshire in 1478. Ferrers held local office during the Interregnum, but signed the Derbyshire petition to General George Monck* for a free Parliament, and was returned for the county at the general election of 1660. An inactive Member of the Convention he was named to ten committees, including that for the indemnity bill. But most of his activity occurred in the second session, during which he made five recorded speeches. He was named to the committees to consider the militia bill, to draft the excise clauses in the bill to abolish the court of wards, and to prepare instructions for disbanding the army. But his chief concern was to prevent the break-up of marriages. On 10 Nov. he brought in a bill to prohibit alimony for wives who left their husbands without consent. He offered a proviso on the second reading, and was the first Member named to the committee. He reported the bill at the end of the month, but it was ordered to be recommitted, and nothing further is heard of it. Ferrers was by no means a complete misogynist, opposing the proposal of Sir Anthony Ashley Cooper* to debar mothers from acting as guardians to their own children, and supporting a reward from public funds for the sister of John Lane*, who had helped the King to escape after the battle of Worcester.[3]

Though 'well-affected' to the monarchy Ferrers did not stand for re-election in 1661, when the Derbyshire gentry agreed to support William Cavendish*, Lord Cavendish, and the Cavalier colonel, John Frescheville*. After skilful nursing of the Tamworth constituency he was elected in 1669 by a majority of the 'populacy and burgesses at large'. During his four months in the Cavalier Parliament, interrupted by the Christmas recess, he probably supported the country party. But he was appointed to only two unimportant committees, and on 26 Mar. 1670 he was unseated in favour of the court candidate, Lord Clifford (Charles Boyle*). His only son was drowned in the Trent in 1678, leaving him the last male heir of this branch of the family. He died on 14 Aug. 1680 and was buried at Tamworth. His epitaph claims no particular qualities, but enumerates the noble families with which he was connected by birth and marriage. An improving landlord, he left an estate valued at £2,000 p.a. His great-granddaughter carried the Tamworth interest into the Compton and Townshend families.[4]

[1] Shaw, *Staffs.* i. 426; *The Gen.* n.s. xvii. 282. [2] *Thurloe*, iii. 212; J. C. Cox, *Three Centuries of Derbys. Annals*, i. 172–3; Stowe 142, f. 70. [3] Dugdale, *Warws.* 1089, 1135; *HMC 9th Rep.* pt. 2, p. 396; *Old Parl. Hist.* xxiii. 9, 14, 33, 48, 59; *CJ*, viii. 195. [4] *The Reliquary*, n.s. vi. 112; *HMC Bath*, iv. 265; *CSP Dom.* 1670, p. 136; *CJ*, ix. 147; *Staffs. Parl. Hist.* (Wm. Salt Arch. Soc.), ii. (1), 133–4.

M.W.H./E.R.E.

FETHERSTONHALGH, Thomas (*d.*1682), of Stanhope Hall, co. Dur.

DURHAM CO.   1679 (Oct.), 1681

> 1st s. of John Fetherstonhalgh of Stanhope Hall by Alice, da. and h. of William Maire of York. *m.* 29 Nov. 1654, Anne, da. of John Clavering of Axwell, co. Dur., at least 1s. *suc.* fa. 1657.[1]
>
> Commr. for assessment, co. Dur. Aug. 1660–3, 1664–9, 1679–80, capt. of militia ft. by 1666–?*d.*; freeman, Durham 1673; commr. for recusants, co. Dur. 1675, j.p. by 1680–*d.*[2]

Fetherstonhalgh's ancestors had resided at Stanhope for many generations, assuming the surname and gaining admission to the gentry in the reign of Edward III. His grandfather sat for Morpeth in 1621, and his father, a Royalist in the second Civil War, compounded for £547 10s. in 1649. Fetherstonhalgh, whose estate was valued for militia purposes at £500 p.a., signed the Durham petition for the re-establishment of the palatinate at the Restoration. On Bishop Cosin's death he petitioned for the office of receiver-general of the bishopric during the vacancy as a reward for his father's sufferings. He was returned for the county at the second general election of 1679, but his only committee was to bring in a bill against importing Scottish cattle. When Dean Granville called on his congregation to re-elect Fetherstonhalgh and his kinsman William Bowes* in 1681, a local nonconformist objected that the two were neither Protestants nor enemies to Popery; but he was returned with an increased majority. He left no trace on the records of the Oxford Parliament, but at the August assizes was awarded £40 damages against an opponent who had called him a Papist. He died on 28 July 1682 and was buried at Stanhope, the last of his family to sit in Parliament.[3]

[1] W. M. Egglestone, *Stanhope*, 91; Dur. RO, Denton par. reg.; *Vis. Dur.* ed. Foster, 71, 119; *CSP Dom.* 1684–5, p. 164; *PCC Admons.* (Index Lib. lxxii), 141; C6/132/235. [2] *HMC Var.* ii. 116; Durham Cathedral Lib. Sharp mss 109/11; *CSP Dom.* 1671–2, p. 231; Surtees, *Dur.* iv. pt. 2, p. 22. [3] *Vis. Dur.* 119; *CSP Dom.* 1671–2, p. 424; *Royalist Comps.* (Surtees Soc. cxi), 200–1; Surtees, i. p. cxliv; Sharp mss 109/11, 41; C. E. Whiting, *Nathaniel, Lord Crewe*, 116–17; *Six N. Country Diaries* (Surtees Soc. cxviii), 45; Egglestone, 92.

G.H./G.J.

FIENNES, Hon. James (c.1602–74), of Broughton Castle, Oxon.

BANBURY   19 July 1625
OXFORDSHIRE   1626, 1628, 1640 (Apr.),
                         1640 (Nov.),[1] 1660

b. c.1602, 1st s. of William, 1st Visct. Saye and Sele by Elizabeth, da. of John Temple of Burton Dassett, Warws. and Stowe, Bucks.; bro. of John Fiennes[†] and Nathaniel Fiennes[†]. *educ.* Queens', Camb. 1618, Emmanuel 1622; travelled abroad 1624–5; L. Inn 1628. *m.* bef. 1631, Frances (*d.* July 1684), da. and coh. of Sir Edward Cecil[†], 1st Visct. Wimbledon, 3s. *d.v.p.* 2da. *suc.* fa. as 2nd Visct. 14 Apr. 1662.[2]

J.p. Oxon. ?1626–35, by 1641–48, aft. 1653–56, Mar. 1660–*d.*, commr. for execution of ordinances 1644, assessment Oxon. 1644, 1657, Jan. 1660–2, appeals, Oxf. Univ. 1647, militia, Glos. and Oxon. 1648, Mar. 1660; dep. lt. Oxon. c. July 1660–8, ld. lt. 1668–*d.*; freeman, Oxford 1668.[3]

Commr. for exclusion from sacrament 1646, scandalous offences 1648.

Fiennes was descended from a Boulonnais baron, Enguerrand, who married an English heiress and was killed at Acre in 1189. One of the family sat for Sussex in 1429, but they migrated to Oxfordshire and acquired a peerage soon afterwards. Fiennes's father, nicknamed 'Old Subtlety', headed the local resistance to ship-money and was one of the most prominent parliamentary peers in the Civil War. Although an Independent in religion, he made strenuous efforts for a peaceful settlement in 1648. Fiennes, who had 'always been reputed an honest Cavalier and a quiet man', did not sit after Pride's Purge, and like his father retired from active politics during the Interregnum, although his brother

Nathaniel became a staunch Cromwellian. He was among those who presented the Oxfordshire address for a free Parliament in February 1660, and was returned for the county a few weeks later. He made no recorded speeches and sat on only three unimportant committees in the Convention. Father and son both sued out their pardons, and in September Fiennes petitioned the King to refuse his assent to the bill to restore the Flintshire estates of the Earl of Derby, part of which had been acquired by his son-in-law. Fiennes probably did not stand in 1661. In the Lords he was an opponent of Clarendon, whom he succeeded as lord lieutenant. He died on 15 Mar. 1674 and was buried at Broughton, the last of the family to sit in the Lower House.[4]

[1] Did not sit after Pride's Purge, 6 Dec. 1648, readmitted 21 Feb. 1660. [2] Keeler, *Long Parl.* 176. [3] *Oxford Council Acts* (Oxf. Hist. Soc. n.s. ii), 27. [4] *The Gen.* n.s. xii. 149–50; A. Wood, *Athenae Oxon.* iii. 550; Keeler, 176–7; *CSP Dom.* 1659–60, p. 361; 1660–1, p. 291; E. T. Rogers, *Protests of the Lords*, i. 36; A. Beesley, *Hist. Banbury*, 475.

M.W.H./L.N./G.J.

FINCH, Daniel (1647–1730), of Kensington, Mdx. and Milton Ernest, Beds.[1]

GREAT BEDWYN   29 Jan.–6 Feb. 1673, 10 Feb. 1673
LICHFIELD   1679 (Oct.), 1681

b. 2 July 1647, 1st s. of Heneage Finch* (later 1st Earl of Nottingham), and bro. of Hon. Edward Finch[†], Hon. Heneage Finch I* and William Finch*. *educ.* Westminster; I. Temple 1658; Christ Church, Oxf. 1662; travelled abroad (Italy, France) 1665–8. *m.* (1) 16 June 1674, Lady Essex Rich (*d.* 23 Mar. 1684), da. of Robert Rich[†], 3rd Earl of Warwick, 2s. *d.v.p.* 6da.; (2) 29 Dec. 1685 (with £12,000), Anne, da. of Christopher Hatton*, 1st Visct. Hatton of Gretton, 6s. (1 *d.v.p.*) 9da. *styled* Lord Finch 12 May 1681; *suc.* fa. as 2nd Earl of Nottingham 18 Dec. 1682, cos. as 7th Earl of Winchilsea 9 Sept. 1729.

Commr. for assessment, Mdx. and Westminster 1673–80, recusants, Wilts. 1675; freeman, Portsmouth 1682.[2]

Ld. of Admiralty 1679, first ld. 1680–4; PC 4 Feb. 1680–12 Mar. 1696, 2 May 1702–7, 23 Sept. 1714–*d.*; sec. of state (south) 1689–93, 1702–4; ld. pres. 1714–16. FRS 1668.

Finch's studious and dutiful conduct, both at Oxford and on the grand tour, gave his parents every satisfaction. In particular they thought it 'a fortunate circumstance' of his travels to have obtained the protection of John Trevor*, the sitting Member for Great Bedwyn, when he was in Paris on a diplomatic mission in 1668. Trevor died in 1672, and Finch succeeded to his seat, probably on the nomination of the dowager duchess of Somerset, who appointed him one of her trustees. He was first elected on 29 Jan. 1673, but the writs issued during the recess were declared void (despite his

Finch Family of Kent and Middlesex

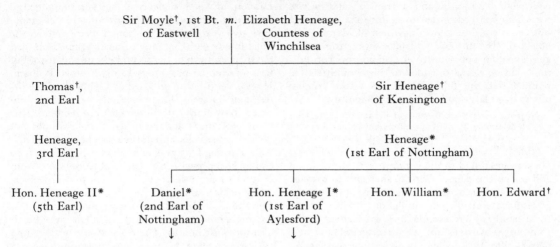

father's powerful argument in their favour), and he had to go through what in his case was probably no more than the tiresome formality of re-election. His record in the House cannot at first be always distinguished from that of Francis Finch*, but he was moderately active, serving on 40 committees or a little less in eight sessions, and making 35 speeches, nine of which are not reported by Anchitell Grey*. In his old age he wrote for the benefit of his children a summary of his parliamentary career:

> In Parliament (my first public appearance in the year 1672/3) I always thought the limits of the prerogative of the crown and the liberties and rights of the people so well settled that those landmarks ought not to be removed.... I did not think it a breach of [the] trust with which every Member is vested to gratify King Charles II with little sums, whose revenue for all services was not above £1,200,000.... I have always been for some indulgence in those who differed in religion from the established Church, so far as was consistent with the safety of the Church and the peace of the state.

His maiden speech was apparently delivered on 27 Oct. 1673, a defence of the conduct of Edward Seymour* as Speaker. He opposed impeachments in general, as invariably leading to 'rage and violence overruling law'. On 19 Jan. 1674 he dealt with the charges against Lord Arlington in detail, commenting: 'Gentlemen say nothing of their own knowledge, nor one witness to prove'. He was named on the Paston list, and in the next session he moved to examine how far the charges against Lord Treasurer Danby were criminal before calling evidence. On the proposal to exclude placemen from the Commons, he said on 29 Apr. 1675: 'We are not to pull feathers thus from the King'. So effective was his speech that (Sir) William Coventry*

could only urge that the bill should not be rejected outright but simply not ordered to be engrossed. He pointed out that the recall of British subjects from French service would aggravate the unemployment problem: 'Most of these men in France [are] such as will have little livelihood here when they return. If they could have stayed, few would have gone.' In a wise and compassionate speech on toleration for dissenters, he showed that, with a settled income of £3,000 p.a., he had outgrown his father's tutelage:

> The last session you considered of indulgence; and because we are safe on shore, shall we have no consideration for them who struggle with the tide? Whatever the case be, 'tis charity and prudence to think on them, so considerable a part of the nation, and would not have them in despair.

Finch had made his mark, and ten days later he was appointed to his first important committee, on the bill for preventing the growth of Popery. He was noted as a court dependant before the autumn session, in which he was appointed to the committees to consider the bill for hindering Papists from sitting in Parliament and to draw up an address for the apprehension of the Jesuit St. Germain. His name appeared in Wiseman's account, on the list of government speakers and on the working lists.[3]

In the 1677 session Finch spoke in favour of supply: 'You have been told by persons that understand the condition of the navy . . . that £600,000 will be necessary to put us in some equality with our neighbours, and that 'tis impossible the money should be embezzled'. When William Williams* attacked the power of Chancery, Finch naturally sprang to his father's defence. ''Tis now a great and expensive jurisdiction', he confessed, adding quite truthfully: 'The present lord chancellor has endeavoured to lessen and restrain it', and he was named to the committee to bring in a regulating bill. To the bill to abolish payment of Members he objected: 'By this bill you take away from every gentleman an opportunity of obliging his corporation', but he was also named to this committee. He pointed out the difficulty of discussing foreign affairs in so large and ignorant an assembly:

> No man can represent the state of all the world here, and, with deference, you are not competent judges. Leave it to the King, whose wisdom and right it is to preserve himself and you.

He was appointed to the committee to draw up an address on the danger from France and to manage a conference on the same subject. He supported the government bill for educating the children of the royal family as Protestants, and was named to the committee; perhaps for this reason Shaftesbury marked him 'thrice vile'. On 23 May he was among those Members charged with drawing up an address for the speedy conclusion of an alliance against France. In the debate on supply on 4 Feb. 1678 he asked: 'Do you expect the thanks of the country for delay? Their rage, rather, and the discontent of Christendom.' He was teller for the motion to go into committee, and three days later he was among the Members appointed to consider the reports from the Ordnance and the Admiralty. He did not take much part in private legislation, but he served on the committee for the Earl of Warwick's estate bill to look after his wife's interests. On 30 Apr. he was named to the committee to summarize foreign commitments. He was among the Members summoned to the caucus of the court party on 30 May. In the last session of the Cavalier Parliament he was appointed to the committees to inquire into the Popish Plot and to impeach Lord Arundell of Wardour. He spoke against the proposed address for the removal of the Duke of York from Court, 'not to the dissatisfaction of the House', he thought, 'but the Duke was very well pleased'. He was one of the Members ordered to prepare reasons for a conference on disabling Papists from sitting in Parliament and to bring in bills to secure the Protestant religion. He helped to draft representations on the dangers arising from non-observance of the laws against recusancy, and sat on the committee for the bill to secure speedier conviction of recusants. On the impeachment of Danby he denied the power of the House to declare treason. His name appeared on both lists of the court party.[4]

At the general election Finch was defeated by John Deane*, who refused the offer of a safe seat elsewhere. Though out of Parliament he was appointed to the newly constituted Admiralty commission, in which capacity he has been adjudged to have fully justified his modest confession of ignorance two years before. Although blacklisted in the 'unanimous club', he might have regained his seat at Great Bedwyn at the second election of 1679, but he preferred to pass it on to his brother William. He was returned unopposed at Lichfield on the interest of Thomas Thynne I*, who described him as entirely at the devotion of Lord Halifax, (Sir George Savile*) and promised that he would not be a courtier. His appointment as first lord of the Admiralty and Privy Councillor in February 1680 could not prevent Sir Charles Lyttelton* from writing: 'I am told that Mr Finch, my lord chancellor's eldest son, is run high into the popular way'. Lyttelton's informant was either malicious or uncomprehending, for when Parliament met Finch 'did the King and the Duke great service'. Arguing against exclusion, he urged the House to

> consider what a miserable prospect we shall have before us, what unextinguishable flames we are kindling in this nation, what wretched confusion we are raising to ourselves and entailing upon our posterity.

So cogent were his arguments that Hugh Boscawen* made no attempt to answer them, but seizing on his incidental remark that Roman Catholics were Christians too, delighted the Opposition with a long and irrelevant diatribe against Popery and Antichrist. With regard to the laws against Protestant dissenters, Finch relied less on rigorous logic than on commonsense: 'No vote of yours is a declaration of the law of England, but you give your opinion, which is not a total suspension of the law, but only to take off the vigorous prosecution of it'. He fastened at once on the weak point in the second exclusion bill: 'I was surprised at the bringing in the bill, but much more that we should leave all things at uncertainty who shall succeed . . . We are going about by this bill to divide Protestants, which will gratify the Papists.' In the debate on Seymour's impeachment on 26 Nov. 1680, Finch set himself to provoke William Harbord*, whose blatant self-interest, once exposed, might serve to divide the country party. Picking up Harbord's accusation of 'dexterity' in managing the House, which of course had no conceivable relevance to the financial irregularities with which Seymour was ostensibly charged, he said:

> I perceive gentlemen manage this matter with very great dexterity, for some speak to the matter of all the articles, and others make other objections against Mr Seymour. . . . We hear of some miscarriages of this gentleman in the chair of the Long [i.e. Cavalier] Parliament; I desire to know whether Harbord did not give his vote for him to be Speaker at the next.

Harbord retaliated with the aspersion that Finch had voted in the Privy Council for retaining the Duke of York in England, to which he replied: 'I can justify myself to every Member, and the most partial'.[5]

Though Finch was one of the most frequent government speakers, with 16 speeches, he was appointed to only three committees in this Parliament. He helped to draw up the address on Tangier, but he was not among the Members entrusted with bringing in a comprehension bill for Protestant dissenters. Nevertheless, he took the chair in the committee, and the draft is almost entirely in his handwriting. On 22 Nov. he obtained permission from the House to bring in a separate toleration bill, which was also largely drafted by him. He defended the comprehension bill on its second reading, and was named to the committee, but no further report was made. He was appointed to the committee for the prevention of superstitious bequests. In the debate on impeaching Lord Chief Justice Scroggs, Finch attacked the opinion of John Maynard I* as 'a doctrine so mischievous that this age, or the next, may rue it. . . . I would have a precedent showed me when ever any offence was declared treason in Parliament that was not felony before; whether ever they did declare or enact a man out of his life?' On 7 Jan. 1681, after the receipt of the King's message ruling out any alteration of the succession, he said: 'I move that you will not spend more time in fruitless debate, but go upon things you have a certain prospect of effecting'. In spite of an unfounded charge by his country opponent that he had voted for the repeal of the Irish cattle bill, Finch was re-elected for Lichfield in 1681. He also had himself returned for Newtown on the Holmes interest, chiefly to keep his Lichfield opponent out of the House. But he was unable to attend the Oxford Parliament as his wife was expecting their sixth child. He asked (Sir) Edward Harley* to take special care of the comprehension bill in his absence, but Parliament was dissolved before anything could be done.[6]

Finch's long and important career after he succeeded to the peerage in 1682 as Earl of Nottingham can only be outlined here. He lost office when the admiralty board was dissolved in 1684, but remained a Privy Councillor, though he absented himself after the Jesuit Father Petre was sworn of the Council in 1687. It was intended that Nottingham should sign the invitation to William of Orange in 1688, but at the last moment he developed scruples of conscience and withdrew. With Lord Halifax and Sidney Godolphin I* he was sent by James II on a futile mission to William at Hun-

gerford. He opposed the transfer of the crown, but agreed to accept William, who thought him an honest man, as king de facto, and was appointed secretary of state. In this capacity he introduced the toleration bill into the House of Lords, but his attempts at comprehension failed. On the loss of the Smyrna fleet in 1693 he was dismissed, though a parliamentary inquiry subsequently exonerated him from blame. He was struck out of the council book in 1696 for refusing the Association, but restored on the accession of Anne both to the Council and to office. But he found it impossible to co-operate with the Whigs and resigned two years later. He bought the estate of Burley-on-the-Hill in Rutland, which became his principal residence, and his eldest surviving son sat for the county from his coming-of-age until he succeeded to the peerage. Nottingham broke with his own party in 1711 on the issue of 'no peace without Spain', which enabled him to obtain the Occasional Conformity Act. As a Hanover Tory he was made president of the Council by George I. This post he lost in 1716 by demanding mercy for the Jacobite peers, and he never held office again, dying on 1 Jan. 1730 at the age of 82. Nottingham's abilities were certainly above average, but he owed his political importance less to them than to his influence over the clergy, obtained by his sound churchmanship and his unimpeachable moral character.

[1] This biography is based on H. Horwitz, *Revolution Politicks*, from which all unacknowledged quotations are taken. [2] R. East, *Portsmouth Recs.* 365. [3] *HMC Finch*, i. 509; ii. 16–19; Grey, ii. 309–10; iii. 73, 135, 163; *CJ*, ix. 375. [4] Grey, iv. 124, 146, 179, 197; v. 73; vi. 139–40; *CJ*, ix. 388, 391, 394, 398, 407, 543; *CSP Dom.* 1678, p. 194; Leics. RO, Finch mss, 4 Nov., 21 Dec. 1678. [5] *HMC Finch*, ii. 54–55; *Hatton Corresp.* (Cam. Soc. n.s. xxii), 224; Ailesbury, *Mems.* 42; Grey, vii. 411, 423, 429, 458; viii. 92–94; Finch mss, 26 Nov. 1680. [6] *CJ*, ix. 683, 687; *Jnl. Eccles. Hist.* xv. 205, 207, 208, 214; Grey, viii. 201–2, 243, 275; Bath mss, Thynne pprs. 17, f. 117; 21, f. 190.

J.P.F.

FINCH, Francis (c.1602–77), of Rushock, Worcs.

WINCHELSEA   1661–Aug. 1677

b. c.1602, o.s. of Henry Finch of Kempley, Glos. by Anne, da. and coh. of Leonard Pigot of Little Horwood, Bucks., wid. of Samuel Danvers of Culworth, Northants. *m.* settlement 1619, Jane (*d.*1680), da. of John Thornborough, bp. of Worcester 1617–41, 5s. (4 *d.v.p.*) 6da. *suc.* fa. 1631.[1]

Commr. of array, Worcs. 1642; freeman, Worcester 1643; j.p. Worcs. July 1660–*d.*, Mdx. Aug. 1660–*d.*; commr. of oyer and terminer, Oxford circuit July 1660, assessment, Worcs. Aug. 1660–*d.*, loyal and indigent officers, London and Westminster 1662, recusants, Worcs. 1675.[2]

Commr. for excise Oct. 1660–8, 1674–*d.*, wine duties retrospect Apr.–Oct. 1670.[3]

According to his grant of arms in 1634, Finch's

grandfather 'went out of Kent' into Buckinghamshire, and he himself was acknowledged as a kinsman by the Earl of Winchilsea, the head of the Kentish Finches. He was married at the age of 17 to the daughter of Bishop Thornborough, a lusty prelate who believed in early marriage, and may have selected him as a sound Protestant husband for a daughter who had already shown inclinations to Popery. Later she was to introduce a Jesuit into the bishop's palace to minister to her sick brother. Finch had interests in the Forest of Dean iron industry; but in 1639 he leased Rushock, valued at £300 p.a., from the Merchant Taylors, and made it his principal residence. A commissioner of array in the Civil War, he claimed a reward at the Restoration for 17 years' faithful service to the monarchy, during which he had 'suffered plunder amounting near unto £10,000'. He came up to London on a safe-conduct from Sir William Waller I* in the summer of 1644, and was promptly arrested as a spy, though Waller had found him 'very ready to give demonstration of his fidelity to the Parliament' by drawing off Sir John Winter, Samuel Sandys I* and other gentlemen of quality in his neighbourhood. Kempley was discharged from sequestration by the Gloucestershire county committee, probably because it was already mortgaged up to the hilt, and in 1649 Finch compounded at one-sixth for stocks of coal, iron, and other materials at Elbridge furnace, and for farm stock and household goods at Rushock, worth in all £300. He was not involved in royalist conspiracy until the autumn of 1659, when in conjunction with the mineralogist Sir John Pettus* he sought to win over Charles Fleetwood†, the republican general.[4]

On 14 Apr. 1660 Finch and Sir John Pakington, 2nd Bt.*, presented George Monck* with a declaration of the Worcestershire Cavaliers disclaiming animosity towards their opponents. At the Restoration he successfully applied for a seat on the excise board with a salary of £250 p.a., doubtless assisted by his 'ancient friend', Lord Chancellor Clarendon, who regarded him as 'a very honest and discreet person'. At the general election of 1661 he was returned as government candidate for Winchelsea, the constituency where the Kentish Finches had begun their parliamentary career in 1337. A moderately active Member of the Cavalier Parliament, he was probably appointed to 81 committees, including the committee of elections and privileges in eight sessions. In the first session he was named to the committees to inquire into the shortfall in the revenue and to consider the bill of pains and penalties and the Stour and Salwarp navigation bill. After the autumn recess he was probably responsible for the bill to regulate imports of madder, since he had applied for the post of searcher and was the third Member named to the committee. With (Sir) Robert Clayton* he took over in 1662 the lease of the royal iron-works in the Forest of Dean, which had 11 years to run. In 1663 he was among those appointed to consider bills for the recovery of arrears of excise and the better regulation of the tax, and attended a conference on 23 July. He was teller against the recommendation of the supply committee that there should be a restriction on the real value of lands for the subsidy. In the next session he was named to the committees on the bills to expedite the payment of vinters' forfeitures and to improve the revenue from the Forest of Dean, and on 29 Apr. 1664 he was among those ordered to bring in a bill for the redress of frauds and abuses in the excise. He was also appointed to the committees for the conventicles bill and the additional corporations bill. In the next session he was granted privilege against Sir Thomas Grobham Howe, the purchaser of Kempley. On 20 Oct. 1666 he was among those ordered to receive information on the insolence of popish priests and Jesuits. 'A very discreet, grave person', he told Samuel Pepys* 'many fine things' about such leading personalities in the Commons as John Vaughan* and William Prynne*.[5]

Finch doubtless regretted the fall of Clarendon in 1667, and an administrative reform in the following year when the new commissioners appointed for London in 1666 ousted their rivals, deprived him of office, together with (Sir) Denny Ashburnham*, though their salaries were continued in the form of a pension until alternative employment should be found. His name appeared on both lists of the court party in 1669–71 among the independent Members who usually voted for supply. He was appointed to the committees to receive information of seditious conventicles (18 Nov. 1669) and to consider a bill to prevent the growth of Popery (2 Mar. 1671). It is doubtful whether he had any practical suggestions to offer, since his wife appears to have brought up his surviving children as Roman Catholics. From 1673 his committee appointments cannot be distinguished from those of Daniel Finch*, who as a rising politician was doubtless more active. His name appears on the Paston list, and a vacancy on the excise board in 1674 enabled him to regain office with double his former salary. Moreover, in consideration of his 'great sufferings', he was allowed to sell three places in the Sandwich customs. He was listed as an official in 1675, and marked 'thrice vile' by Shaftesbury in 1677. On 14 Apr. he claimed privilege for a tenant of his in

Shropshire, and delivered a private bill to the Speaker, which was never read. On 23 Aug. he was reported 'lately deceased'. A priest was apprehended, and later martyred, at Rushock during the Popish Plot. The lease was transferred in 1691, and no other member of the family entered Parliament.[6]

[1] *Vis. Glos.* (Harl. Soc. xxi), 61; *Vis. Eng. and Wales Notes* ed. Crisp, viii. 3; *Glos. Inquisitions* (Index Lib. ix), 159; PCC 38 Bath. [2] *List of Worcester Freemen* (1747). [3] *Cal. Treas. Bks.* i. 75; ii. 559; iv. 579; *CSP Dom.* 1670, p. 178. [4] *Worcs. Recusant,* iii. 36–38; *Townshend's Diary* (Worcs. Rec. Soc.), i. 108, 137, 141; SP29/9/2; *CSP Dom.* 1644, pp. 445–6; *Cal. Comm. Comp.* 86; SP23/213/737–41; *Cal. Cl. SP,* iv. 355, 389, 393, 444; *Mordaunt Letter-Bk.* (Cam. Soc. ser. 3, lxix), 66. [5] *Townshend's Diary,* i. 37; HMC *Popham,* 227; *Mordaunt Letter-Bk.* 63; *Cal. Treas. Bks.* i. 19; C. E. Hart, *Royal Forest,* 158; *CJ,* viii. 508, 601; Atkyns, *Glos.* 256; *Pepys Diary,* 23 June 1665, 3 July 1666. [6] C. D. Chandaman, *Eng. Pub. Revenue,* 57–58; *Cal. Treas. Bks.* ii. 559; iv. 335; *CSP Dom.* 1667–8, p. 467; 1673–5, p. 302; 1677–8, p. 318; PC2/66/208; Nash, *Worcs.* ii. 302; *Worcs. Recusant,* iii. 39.

B.D.H.

FINCH, Heneage (1621–82), of Ravenstone, Bucks. and Kensington, Mdx.[1]

CANTERBURY   1660
OXFORD UNIVERSITY   1661–10 Jan. 1674

b. 23 Dec. 1621, 1st s. of Sir Heneage Finch[†] of Kensington, Speaker 1626, by 1st w. Frances, da. of Sir Edmund Bell[†] of Beaupré Hall, Outwell, Norf. *educ.* Westminster; Christ Church, Oxf. 1636; I. Temple 1638, called 1645. *m.* 30 July 1646, Elizabeth, da. of Daniel Harvey, merchant, of Lawrence Pountney Hill, London, 10s. (3 *d.v.p.*) 4da. *suc.* fa. 1631; kntd. 6 June 1660; *cr.* Bt. 7 June 1660, Baron Finch of Daventry 10 Jan. 1674, Earl of Nottingham 12 May 1681.

Commr. for militia, Mdx. Mar. 1660, assessment, oyer and terminer, Mdx. July 1660, Kent Aug. 1660–1, 1665–74, Mdx. Sept. 1660–74, Westminster 1665–74, Northants. 1673–4; bencher, I. Temple June 1660, treas. 1661–73, reader 1661; commr. for sewers, N. Kent Sept. 1660; freeman, Canterbury Oct. 1660; j.p. Kent, Mdx. and Northants. 1661–d.; commr. for loyal and indigent officers, Mdx., London and Westminster 1662; chamberlain, palatinate of Chester 1673–6; gov. of the Charterhouse 1674.

Solicitor-gen. June 1660–70; asst. R. Fishing Co. 1664; attorney-gen. 1670–3; chairman of ways and means 21 Feb.–14 Mar. 1673; ld. keeper 1673–5; PC 9 Nov. 1673–d.; ld. of admiralty 1673–5; PC [S] 1674, 1676; ld. chancellor 1675–d.[2]

Finch's first certain ancestor in the male line was summoned to attend the Council in 1337 as representative of Winchelsea, and shortly afterwards acquired land in Sussex. The advance of the family to the ranks of the peerage by the early 17th century was due, like Finch's own successful career, to a combination of legal eminence and loyal service to the crown. He took no part in the Civil War, but during the Interregnum built up a successful practice at the bar, specializing in municipal law. His accounts showed average earnings of £1,400 in the last four years before the Restoration. His first appearance in public affairs was as counsel for Thomas Street* in the Worcester election case of 1659. Next year he was returned both for Mitchell and for Canterbury, for which his cousin John, Lord Finch, the unhappy Speaker of 1628-9, had sat. He had already been promised a baronetcy by his namesake, the 3rd Earl of Winchilsea, and from the first played the leading part in the Convention as one of the royalist junto. He was appointed to 111 committees, from which he made 53 reports, including nine from conferences, and at least 70 of his speeches are recorded. He supported Edward Turnor* on 26 Apr. 1660 in urging that the House should render God his due before Caesar's, and on the following day seconded the motion of Edward King* for the suspension of private business. On 1 May he seconded the motion for receiving the King's letter, and was appointed to the committee to answer it and the conference to discuss it with the Lords. Two days later he was named to the committee for drafting bills in accordance with the declaration of Breda, in which most of the important measures in the first phase of the Convention originated. He took the chair, and was given sole responsibility for the bill to abolish the court of wards. He was also chairman of the bill to confirm land purchases. He penned the bill for confirmation of Parliament, and carried it to the Lords on 5 May with most of the amendments of John Maynard I* struck out. He moved the House to concur with the Lords in lifting the sequestration of the Duke of Buckingham's estate. He introduced the indemnity bill, and bills for the confirmation of legal proceedings and for the cancellation of grants made during the Civil War and Interregnum. On 28 May he reported from a conference on the declaration against the Irish rebels, and two days later introduced a petition for a public thanksgiving. He seconded the motion of Roger Palmer* for including John Hutchinson* in the indemnity bill, and brought in the tunnage and poundage bill on 20 June. He was chosen chairman both for the indemnity bill and for the important committee to prepare the clause of exceptions. After his appointment as solicitor-general he took the chair in the committee of four named to draft the form of acceptance of the royal pardon. He seconded the vote of thanks to George Monck* on 29 June, and spoke against enforcing the repayment of salaries by Protectorate officials, which would have included Monck and Edward Montagu I*. His most celebrated speech in the Convention occurred on 9 July in the debate on the ecclesiastical settlement:

The religion of our Church is not to seek, but we have enjoyed it long, and there now should not be [need] to inquire for it; but [he] moved that it be referred to an assembly of divines, for which we ought to petition the King, and [he] said there was no law to alter the government of the Church by bishops.

On 19 July he was instructed to ask the King to postpone the assizes, pending the passing of current legislation. Given special responsibility with Matthew Hale* for bringing in a bill for tunnage and poundage, he reported a new book of rates nine days later. He was named to the committee that produced the navigation bill. Finch's work in August was chiefly concerned with the differences between the Houses over the indemnity bill, though he also brought in a temporary bill to continue the excise. He was chairman of the committee to inquire into the dangerous delays in legislation which these differences entailed, and reported from the conference. He suggested as a compromise that all regicides who not had not been executed should be banished. When the debate on religion was renewed he urged that ordination by presbyters should not be a precedent, but hoped for some moderation in ceremonies. On 14 Aug. he carried the Commons amendments to the indemnity bill to the Lords, who nevertheless insisted on excepting Lambert, Vane and two others. Finch then urged his own House not 'to venture the shipwreck of the whole vessel [rather] than throw a few overboard. . . . The sparing of them was the way to lose the Act of Oblivion, and moved to agree with the Lords.' Two further conferences followed, which Finch reported, and on 30 Aug. he brought in, on instructions, a draft petition for sparing the lives of Lambert and Vane. For the last fortnight before the adjournment, the House was principally occupied with finance. Finch reported from the revenue committee, brought in two assessment bills, took the chair in a committee of the whole House on customs and excise, and reported from the committee for disbandment. On 11 Sept. he reported from the conference on settling ministers. He was chairman of the committee to draft a petition for a commission on purchases of public lands. He opposed the motion that the King be asked to marry a Protestant as a breach of the prerogative.[3]

During the recess Finch led for the crown, as his office required, in the prosecution of the regicides. When Parliament reassembled, he seconded the motion for a land tax. He was greatly disturbed at the publication of *The Long Parliament Revived*, and was chosen chairman of the committee to impeach its author. 'He could not think anything more dangerous than the writing [of] this book at such a

time. . . . Burning the book was too tame a punishment.' On 23 Nov. he proposed granting half the excise to the crown in compensation for the court of wards, and together with William Pierrepont* he drafted a clause accordingly. He reported from the committee for the six months' assessment. He described liberty for tender consciences as Cromwellian cant and wished that the bill to confirm the Worcester House declaration 'had never been brought in', though he had been appointed to the committee. He was ordered to carry up the attainder bill on 7 Dec., and on the following day took the chair in the grand committee on the assessment. In the debate on grievances on 13 Dec. he moved against any remonstrance. On 17 Dec. he was ordered to bring in a bill for £70,000 for the expenses of the coronation. But even Finch's prestige was insufficient to quell the laughter when he proposed a reward for (Sir) Samuel Jones*; whereupon he adroitly moved that no further grants out of the excise should be considered. As the appointed date for dissolution was reached and passed, Finch's burden, in spite of an exceptionally powerful and experienced front bench, grew no less. He was instructed to prepare reasons for conferences on college leases and the prevention of marital separation, and reported from committees considering the Lords' amendments to the bill abolishing the court of wards and the bill for coronation expenses. As if this were not enough he was placed in the chair of the committee drafting a clause to forbid the adulteration of wine. He reported two conferences just before and after Christmas, and on 29 Dec. was appointed one of the managers of a conference on disbandment.[4]

At the general election of 1661 Finch was elected at Beaumaris on the Bulkeley interest, but chose to sit for Oxford University for which he had also been returned, unenthusiastically but without a poll, on the nomination of Lord Chancellor Clarendon. Neither the attorney-general nor the senior secretary of state sat in Parliament, and several of the Privy Councillors were promoted to the Lords at or before the coronation. Hence he is likely to have taken no less prominent a part in the inadequately reported first session of the Cavalier Parliament than in the Convention. With Sir George Carteret* he conducted Turnor to the Speaker's chair. He reported the conference on the King's marriage on 13 May. On the next day he and Job Charlton* were ordered to bring in the militia bill, which was to be his principal responsibility in this session. He was sent to ask Bruno Ryves, formerly chaplain to Charles I, to preach on the King's birthday. After helping to draft a proviso on the third reading of the security bill, he carried it to the Lords and later reported a conference on it. On 1 June, he made the first of 13 reports from grand committee on the militia bill, which yielded to the King sole command of the armed forces. On 7 June, he brought in, according to the instructions of the House, a bill for a free and voluntary contribution to the revenue. He was appointed to the committees for the corporations and uniformity bills, and on 1 July was ordered to bring in a bill for the execution of the attainted prisoners in the Tower. Three days later, he was instructed to bring in the evidence against one of them, Sir Arthur Hesilrige†. He acted as chairman of the committee to ensure that High Commission was excluded from the restoration of the temporal jurisdiction of the clergy. He twice reported conferences on the corporations bill, and was one of the Members entrusted with perfecting the bill for the regulation of printing. He was asked to bring in a bill for the maintenance of incumbents in towns, though this did not receive its first reading till the following March. On 27 July he was desired to draw up a petition recommending the Marquess of Winchester to the royal favour. Two days later the Speaker thanked Finch in the name of the House, 'for his care and discreet carriage' in managing a conference on printing. He reported the conference on conspiracy on 19 Dec. and was appointed to the joint committee to examine it. On 18 Feb. 1662 he was ordered to prepare reasons for the conferences on the bills against schismatics and for confirming ministers in their livings. He was among those to prepare reasons for a conference on the uniformity bill and to manage a conference on the loyal and indigent officers, which he reported. When the militia bill returned from the Lords, he was chairman of the committee to prepare an expedient reconciling the differences between the Houses. He served on four other conferences in this session and reported that on the highways bill on 19 May.[5]

Finch's activity declined as younger men came forward to act as spokesmen for the Court. In the 1663 session he was chiefly concerned with the Declaration of Indulgence, taking the chair of the committee which drafted the address against it. He reported two conferences on priests and Jesuits, for one of which he had acted as chairman in the committee to prepare reasons. With John Kelyng*, he was ordered to take care of the prosecution of those responsible for abusing hackney coachmen. On 2 Apr. he reported the King's message withdrawing the Declaration; he obtained the concurrence of the Upper House to a vote of thanks, with which he, among other Members, attended the King. In an elaborate speech, carefully preserved, he defended the common law against the bill introduced by (Sir) John Bramston* to enlarge the jurisdiction of the Admiralty. He was appointed to the committee to bring in the bill restricting office to loyalists, and he was given sole responsibility for bringing in a subsidy bill 'according to ancient form', and a clause to assert the royal prerogative of erecting or demolishing fortifications. Marked as a court dependant in 1664, Finch was one of four Members charged with examining the title of the Triennial Act, and he spoke at length, in reply to John Vaughan*, in favour of repeal. He was again one of four Members ordered on 30 Mar. to bring in a bill for the better collection of hearth-tax. He was named to the committees for the conventicles and additional corporations bills, and to those to bring in bills for the prevention of profanity and extravagance and for registering conveyances and mortgages (another reform which would have reduced the work available for common lawyers). He was one of the managers of the conference on Dutch depredations on 21 Apr. In October he appeared before the Privy Council on behalf of the Canary merchants who desired a new charter for their company.[6]

Finch brought in the supply bill in the Oxford session, but owing to an unfortunate lack of liaison on the government side, he denounced as 'introductive to a commonwealth' the proposal of Sir George Downing* to appropriate the proceeds to the war effort. He spoke in support of the five mile bill and was named to the committee. He exerted himself so much against the proposed ban on foreign cattle (including those imported from Ireland) that he collapsed with nervous exhaustion. He was named to the committee though he continued to oppose the bill on second and third readings. On 24 Oct. 1665 he was instructed to bring in a bill for one month's assessment for the Duke of York's benefit, but he does not seem to have done so. A week later he was sent with (Sir) John Berkenhead* and Giles Strangways* to thank the university for their loyalty, and was created a DCL. The defence of Irish cattle continued in the next session to engage his best efforts. He was again appointed to the committee on the bill, but the effect of his 'excellent' speech on 5 Oct. 1666 was lessened when Sir Richard Temple* obliged him to withdraw his description of the word 'nuisance' as unprecedented in statute. Finch wrote to Ormonde that he had resorted to 'unreasonable offers' to defeat the bill, but in vain. On the prohibition of imports from France he helped to manage a conference on 17 Oct. and to prepare reasons for a further conference.

With Charlton and (Sir) Edward Thurland* he was
given special responsibility for a bill to redeem the
hearth-tax, and he was one of five Members instructed to bring in a poll bill. Andrew Marvell*
denounced him as leader of 'the lawyers' mercenary
band' in the excise debate. On 10 Dec. he was
among those ordered to prepare reasons for a conference on Irish cattle. After Christmas John Milward* again found him 'excellent' in a conference
on the poll bill, which he reported to the Commons.
He had been denied permission to appear before
the Upper House as counsel for Lord Roos (John
Manners*), but his name stands first in the committee on the bill to illegitimize Lady Roos's children. He helped to manage conferences on public
accounts and the plague bill, and after attacking the
denial of counsel to Lord Mordaunt as 'of dangerous consequence', he was added to the impeachment
committee.[7]

The downfall of the lord chancellor, to whom
Finch owed his seat, placed him in an awkward
position. He helped to draw up the address of
thanks, which he thought necessary, and took part
in the inquiries into restraints on juries, the miscarriages of the war and the sale of Dunkirk. But
his silence was noticed in the House, and the King
ordered him to be active in the impeachment of
Clarendon. He was among those ordered to search
out precedents; but his major speech on 29 Oct.
1667 was little to the taste of the enemies of the
fallen minister:

> I have said nothing with any design to gratify or serve my
> Lord Clarendon or any of his relations. . . . I am not
> my lord's champion, much less a voluntary martyr for
> him. I have only provided for the peace of my own
> heart that I may not die with this guilt upon me, of
> having wanted the courage in a case of blood to speak
> according to the best of my understanding.

He spoke on most of the articles, pointing out that
'there was a great mischief in declaring treason by
Parliament'. Only the alleged betrayal of secrets to
France, he said, must be treason, 'if you have any
inducement to believe it'. He was appointed to draw
up reasons for a conference on 16 Nov., but he
found the refusal of the Lords to commit Clarendon
without specific accusation quite reasonable. 'No
extricating ourselves out of this difficulty', he said
on 2 Dec. 'but by sending up the articles.' Two
days later he reported the conference on Clarendon's letter and flight, and helped to draw up
reasons for a conference on freedom of speech in
Parliament. He was named to the committee on the
bill for the banishment and disablement of Clarendon. When the House returned to normal after
Christmas, Finch was able to settle his old score

with Temple, who in breach of good manners had
brought in a triennial bill without leave. He was
scandalized at the unprecedented breach of prerogative in the proposal to lay the text of the Triple
Alliance before the House. On 18 Mar. 1668 he
made 'a worthy and excellent speech in justification
of bishops and their charitable and pious acts', and
in opposition to the proposal to assess them to a
subsidy like laymen. Instead, he brought in a bill
for raising £100,000 on retailers of wine and
brandy. He was appointed to the committee to state
the case of restraints on juries on 3 Apr. Although
he had appeared as counsel for the defence in Skinner v. the East India Company, he argued 'most
excellently' against the pretensions of the House of
Lords. 'If a cause be originally tried by the Lords
it is barred of all appeal', he pointed out. 'The
Lords have no power to give a remedy where the
law gives none, unless the Commons have a share
in that remedy.'[8]

In the next session Finch carried the House with
him in the debate on the conventicles bill, though
his reasoning seems specious and unconvincing. But
on the next day he was unable to obtain permission
for Carteret to be heard by counsel in his defence
against charges of irregularity in his accounts:

> When the ablest man shall be speechless in the House of
> Commons, will you put this gentleman to answer for
> himself, with all his troubles about him? They may say
> that for him, which he cannot but brokenly and inter-
> ruptedly say for himself.

Legally, he said, in words which seemed to fore-
shadow his greatness as a judge, Carteret might be
guilty of a misdemeanour, but equitably not. With
equal reasonableness he opposed the impeachment
of Lord Orrery (Roger Boyle*): 'No man knows,
when a spirit of accusation is up, when it will rest
again, and he never knew much good done in Parliaments where many impeachments were'. He
firmly rejected the claim of the Lords to be the
fountain of justice. The Wine Duties Act had not
worked well, and on 19 Feb. 1670 Finch was instructed to bring in a new bill to replace it. He
drew up reasons for a conference pointing out the
absurdity of the Lords' proviso to the conventicles
bill restoring all prerogatives at any time enjoyed
by the King or his predecessors, and on 30 Mar.
reported the conference and also one on the naturalization bill. A further conference on the privilege
of peers under the conventicles bill followed, which
he also reported. He acted as chairman for an additional clause to the bill for preventing the surrender
of English ships to pirates and on the bill for the
sale of fee-farm rents. Though Finch was promoted
attorney-general during the summer recess, in the

first part of the next session all his speeches were on supply. He was one of six Members instructed to bring in a bill for an additional excise on beer. 'Would not any man purchase the safety of the kingdom with his blood?' he asked the House, 'Will he not do it with his money?' When it was proposed to defer supply after the assault on Sir John Coventry*, he said: 'Why you should, for an imaginary opinion of the people, set a stop to all things', he knew not. Nevertheless his was the first name on the committees to bring in the bill for the punishment of the assailants and to consider the Lords' amendments to it. When the proposal to establish a land registry was revived, he attacked it in committee in a set speech. He helped to prepare reasons for a conference on the subsidy bill on 1 Mar. 1671, and two days later reported a conference on the growth of Popery. But his principal achievement was the final defeat of the Lords' pretensions to interfere with money bills. He was one of the managers of the conference on 11 Apr., telling the House two days later:

> If the Lords can show a precedent that they ever added or took a mite of what the Commons have given the King, they may impose now; and they may exempt themselves, by the same reason, from paying their proportion.

He was ordered to draw up reasons for another conference, and on the last day of the session the House passed a unanimous vote of thanks to him 'for his great pains and care ... in vindication of their privilege and just and undoubted right of the Commons of England'. His name appeared on both lists of the court party during this session, while an opposition writer described him as

> the great framer of all money Acts, which he stuffs with oaths and ruin; the only contriver of the repeal of the Act for Triennial Parliaments; the corrector of all Irish Acts; and hath thereby got £10,000.[9]

In the turbulent sessions of 1673 Finch and Henry Coventry*, 'who are reckoned to speak as from their places wholly', were the only debaters on the Court side who could command a hearing. Finch defended the issue of election writs during the recess, which he said had never been challenged before the Long Parliament. He declared that the King's counsel knew nothing of the Declaration of Indulgence, 'until it was forth', agreed that it should never happen again, and was the first Member appointed to draw up an address against it. He was also on the committee to consider a further reply on 25 Feb., but he found some of the expressions in it rather shocking. He reported the conference on the growth of Popery on 6 Mar., and his name stands first on the committee for the test

bill. He regarded the bill of ease for Protestant dissenters 'as a pious thing, to reconcile, and not to establish separation.... Would not have the dissenters part of the legislative power, till they be of one body with us in doctrine and discipline.' He reported a conference on the Test and helped to prepare reasons for one on the bill of ease. But he resisted the bill for the general naturalization of Protestant immigrants, bloodsuckers who would starve the poor and destroy the legal system. In October, he advised the House not to protest against the Duke of York's marriage. 'It will be in vain to consider of the form of this address, when the matter will not bear one.' Nevertheless he was named to the committees to draft the address, and to draw up a general test. This was his last session in the Lower House, for on the dismissal of Lord Chancellor Shaftesbury a few days later he was given custody of the great seal and raised to the peerage. He had been named to 245 committees in the Cavalier Parliament and made 47 reports, of which 16 were from conferences and 19 from grand committee. Since the regular reporting of debates began again in 1666, he had made about 130 speeches.[10]

The government at this juncture has been described as a triumvirate, consisting of Lord Treasurer Latimer (Sir Thomas Osborne*), Speaker Edward Seymour*, and Finch, who was presumably cast for the role of Lepidus. His interest in the Lower House, mainly with lawyers and chancery officials, was at Latimer's disposal, and he strongly supported the non-resisting test in 1675, though his request to their lordships not to 'trifle away their time' hardly helped to advance it. But if he was only a second-grade figure in the world of high politics, his legal eminence is unquestioned, and his nine years at the head of his profession marked a revolution in equity, to which he gave for the first time intelligible and permanent principles. His courtesy to junior counsel is vouched for by no less a Whig than John Somers*. While Shaftesbury marked him 'thrice vile' in 1677, William Sacheverell* went out of his way to express his esteem and respect. When Latimer (now Earl of Danby) was sent to the Tower in 1679, Finch was reckoned more his friend than any other minister. Though he refused to seal his pardon, he was censured by the Upper House for remarking—with a considerable divergence from the truth—that the King 'always supports the creatures of his power', and he argued for the right of the bishops to vote in capital cases. But in the Privy Council he gave the lead in speaking 'long and violently' against the King's decision to dissolve the first Exclusion Parliament, and six months later 'he spoke so earnestly against the prorogation' of its successor 'that his Majesty commanded him to desist'. He voted against exclusion and supported a policy of limitations; but as lord high steward he delivered the death sentence on Lord Stafford in what Burnet considered one of the best speeches he ever made. At Oxford he found legal grounds for the rejection of Fitzharris's impeachment, and was made an Earl a few weeks later. He died on 18 Dec. 1682 and was buried at Ravenstone.[11]

Finch's reputation among lawyers has always been of the highest, but he has not fared so well at the hands of historians, though they have noted his remarkable continuity of office and immunity from attack in a time of passion and intrigue. 'In the midst of a corrupt court', wrote Macaulay, 'he had kept his personal integrity unsullied.' His family life was exceptional, his marriage a real partnership, and he guided his children (who all turned out well) through the use of praise rather than terror. Burnet described him as

> a man of probity and well-versed in the law; but very ill-bred, and both vain and haughty. He was long much admired for his eloquence, but it was both laboured and affected, and he saw it as much despised before he died. . . . He was an incorrupt judge, and in his court he could resist the strongest applications from the King himself, though he did it nowhere else.

The last assertion is disproved by Finch's conduct over the impeachment of Clarendon and the handling of Parliament in 1679. It has been suggested (with hindsight) that his condemnation of Stafford was due to fear, but there is no reason to suppose that Finch believed him innocent. He was not a maker of policy, but during 22 years of continuous ministerial office it is hard to trace any serious deviation from his principles of loyalty to the Church and respect for the prerogative.[12]

[1] This biography is based on the introduction by D. E. C. Yale to *Ld. Nottingham's Chancery Cases* (Selden Soc. lxxiii), pp. ix–xxxvi. [2] C181/7/146; *Sel. Charters* (Selden Soc. xxviii), 193; Canterbury Arch. A/C5, f. 30. [3] *Suss. Arch. Coll.* lxx. 22; *Cal. Cl. SP*, iv. 675, 681, 682; v. 20; *CJ*, viii. 11, 16, 26, 38, 45, 55, 57, 115, 119, 132, 137, 150, 158, 159, 160, 167; *Voyce from the Watch Tower*, 123; Bowman diary, ff. 33, 50v, 134, 136, 146; *Old Parl. Hist.* xxii. 477; *Hutchinson Mems.* 326. [4] Bowman diary, f. 66v; *Old Parl. Hist.* xxiii. 12, 17, 20, 30, 52, 58; *CJ*, viii. 192, 219, 221, 222, 224, 225, 228. [5] *CJ*, viii. 245, 255, 256, 261, 296, 312, 313, 415, 423, 431. [6] *CJ*, viii. 442, 458, 459, 460, 466, 476, 509, 524, 537; *Chancery Cases* (Selden Soc. lxxix), 940–58; *Evelyn Diary*, iii. 388. [7] Clarendon, *Life*, 599; Burnet, i. 402–3; *CJ*, viii. 621, 623, 638, 639, 676, 683, 686, 687; Bodl. Carte 34, ff. 452v, 464v; 35, f. 86; Carte, *Ormond*, iv. 243; *Milward*, 15, 40, 62, 73; *Marvell* ed. Margoliouth, i. 145. [8] *CJ*, ix. 1, 4, 5, 8, 33, 41; *Milward*, 86, 231, 236, 289; Carte, *Ormond*, iv. 306–7; *Chancery Cases* (Selden Soc. lxxix), 965; *Clarendon Impeachment*, 41, 43, 46, 52; Grey, i. 84, 85, 119, 154; *Pepys Diary*, 22 Feb. 1668. [9] Grey, i. 162–3, 164, 173, 185, 193, 254, 316, 339, 438; *CJ*, ix. 150–1, 154, 155, 162, 194; *Chancery Cases* (Selden Soc. lxxix), 966–78; Harl. 7020, f. 37v. [10] *Essex Pprs.* (Cam. Soc. n.s. xlviii), 132; E. C. Legh, *Lady Newton, Lyme Letters*, 52; Grey, ii. 3–4, 63, 95, 156, 194; *Dering*,

109–10; *CJ*, ix. 251, 263, 275, 280, 284. [11] Browning, *Danby*, i. 119; *Bulstrode Pprs.* 284; Burnet, ii. 81, 205, 275, 285; *Sydney Diary*, i. 3, 25; *Temple Works* ed. Swift, i. 341. [12] Macaulay, *Hist.* 894; Burnet, ii. 42–43; Ailesbury, *Mems.* 42.

M.W.H./L.N.

FINCH, Hon. Heneage I (c.1649–1719), of Albury, Surr.

OXFORD UNIVERSITY	1679 (Mar.)
GUILDFORD	1685
OXFORD UNIVERSITY	1689, 1690, 1695, 1701 (Feb.), 1701 (Dec.), 1702–15 Mar. 1703

b. c.1649, 2nd s. of Heneage Finch*, and bro. of Daniel Finch*, Hon. Edward Finch[†] and Hon. William Finch*. *educ.* Westminster; I. Temple, entered 1662, called 1673; Christ Church, Oxf. matric. 18 Nov. 1664, aged 15. *m.* 16 May 1678, Elizabeth, da. and coh. of Sir John Banks, 1st Bt.*, of The Friars, Aylesford, Kent, 3s. 6da. *cr.* Baron Guernsey 15 Mar. 1703, Earl of Aylesford 19 Oct. 1714.

Attaché, Breda 1667; KC 1677; solicitor-gen. 1679–86; chairman, committees of supply and ways and means 22 May–20 Nov. 1685; PC 20 Mar. 1703–May 1708, 13 Dec. 1711–*d.*; chancellor, duchy of Lancaster 1714–16.[1]

Bencher, I. Temple 1678; commr. for assessment, Oxford Univ. 1679–80, 1689–90, Surr. 1689–90, I. Temple 1690; j.p. and dep. lt. Surr. by 1701–?*d.*

Finch followed his father's profession with great success, but in the absence of any family interest he found it more difficult to enter Parliament. He was narrowly defeated at Leicester in 1677, when he stood on the Earl of Huntingdon's interest. His brother Daniel wrote that at the dissolution of the Cavalier Parliament 'he was in a very good station, lucrative and quiet'. But against his father's recommendation he was appointed solicitor-general on the dismissal of Sir Francis Winnington* on 13 Jan. 1679, and renewed efforts were made to find him a seat. He was apparently defeated by the country candidate Sir Trevor Williams* at Monmouth, in spite of 'six files of musketeers' ordered into the town by the Marquess of Worcester (Henry Somerset*); but at Oxford University, which his father had represented till he was raised to the peerage, he was successful after a poll. He was marked 'base' by Shaftesbury and voted against the exclusion bill; but was apparently otherwise content to be totally ignored by a House that heaped responsibilities on Winnington. He did not stand for the University at the general election, nor apparently for Monmouth as his brother expected, and was out of Parliament till 1685. 'The smooth-tongued solicitor' showed none of his father's urbanity in prosecuting Lord Russell (Hon. William Russell*) after the Rye House Plot; Burnet condemned his 'vicious elequence and ingenious malice'. Meanwhile he had bought an estate at Albury, four miles from Guildford, for which he was returned to James II's Parliament, though his election was 'disputable', and he was defeated at Newport (I.o.W.). He was a very active Member, with 14 committees. As chairman of the supply committee, from which he made 14 reports, he was given sole responsibility for bringing in five bills. The first of these were the bills to settle on the new King for life all the revenues enjoyed by his brother, and to lay an imposition on wine and vinegar, both of which Finch carried to the House of Lords. He helped to draft the loyal address from the House on the Duke of Monmouth's invasion. His name stands first on the committee for the bankruptcy bill. He was one of ten Members ordered to bring in a clause against exclusion on 26 June. But he took the chair in the committee which drew up the address against the employment of Popish officers in November, and his days in office were numbered. He was retained to conduct the prosecution of Lord Delamer (Henry Booth*) 'with his usual vehemence', but gave occasion for his dismissal by refusing a warrant to the apostate Obadiah Walker to continue to hold the mastership of his Oxford college.[2]

Finch won great applause as counsel for the Seven Bishops in 1688, and on 10 Dec. was elected under James's writ for Oxford University. The result was confirmed in the following month. He was an active Member of the Convention, in which he was appointed to 39 committees and made 28 recorded speeches. He helped to draw up the address of thanks to the Prince of Orange on 22 Jan. 1689, and to bring in the list of essentials for securing religion, laws and liberties. He favoured establishing a regency for James's lifetime, 'as if the King were a minor or in a frenzy'. In the debate on the state of the nation, he concluded:

> For us to limit the succession is plainly to say we may choose a king; and is this called the prudence we ought to act with, to destroy that constitution of the government, which we came here to maintain?

According to Ailesbury's list Finch voted to agree with the Lords that the throne was not vacant. His committees included those to amend the Lords' version of the declaration of rights, to suspend habeas corpus, to inquire into the authors and advisers of grievances and to prepare the bill of rights. On 11 Mar. the Lords sent down a bill for annulling Russell's attainder, and Finch rather ill-advisedly opened the debate: 'I see many gentlemen's eyes are upon me; therefore I stand up to give an account of my reasons for the part I acted in that unfortunate business'. He was repeatedly interrupted by calls to order, and as stout a Tory as Sir Henry Goodricke* coldly observed that it was strange 'to hear the learned gentleman vindicate himself, when nobody accuses him'. Nevertheless he was named to the committee. He helped to draw up the address for the suppression of the Ipswich mutiny, but he may have found the atmosphere of the Lower House increasingly unfriendly, for from then until the end of the Convention he obtained leave to attend the Lords as counsel in no less than 17 cases. However, he was among those ordered to examine precedents for the indemnity bill and to bring in a new coronation oath on 25 Mar. In the debate on comprehension he had the better of the argument with John Birch*, but his antagonist had the last and most damaging word: 'The strength of Finch's arguments, and the smoothness of his discourse, have been known here before'. He was among those Members ordered to draw up addresses of thanks to William for undertaking to maintain the Church of England and of support for the war with France, and took part in a conference on the new oaths of allegiance and supremacy. He was appointed to the committee for the toleration bill and helped to manage a conference. He was added to the managers of a conference on the poll-tax on 27 May, and took part in considering the Lords' amendments to the bill of rights. In July his name was added to the committees to draw up reasons for conferences on Titus Oates and the duties on coffee, tea and chocolate.[3]

In the second session Finch was instructed to search for precedents concerning the Jacobite prisoners in the Tower and appointed to the committee on the bill for restoring corporations. He spoke in favour of Princess Anne's patent and helped to draw up the address on her behalf. He attacked the disabling clause root and branch, declaring it incapable of amendment. If there were Tories who had surrendered charters there were also Whigs who had benefited from the dispensing power. So general was the offence that, if the clause stood, 'you put out the men of estates, and the ancient corporations are put into the hands of men of little or no fortune, and some call them the *mobile*'. In the closing days of the Parliament, he was appointed to the committees for enforcing a general oath of allegiance and for restoring the university charters.[4]

Finch continued to represent Oxford University, except in the 1698 Parliament, till he was raised to the peerage under Queen Anne. He generally followed his brother's line in politics, and on the Hanoverian succession was advanced two steps in the peerage and given office. He died on 22 July

1719 and was buried at Aylesford, where he had succeeded to the Banks property in the right of his wife. His eldest son was sitting for Surrey as a Tory when he succeeded to the peerage.

[1] *HMC Finch*, i. 457, 479. [2] *Recs. Bor. Leicester* ed. Stocks, iv. 546; Leics. RO, Finch mss, Daniel to Sir John Finch, 10 Feb. 1679; *Hatton Corresp.* (Cam. Soc. n.s. xxiii), 198; *HMC Finch*, ii. 54; *HMC Ormonde*, ii. 50; *Evelyn Diary*, iv. 500; Burnet, ii. 376; *VCH Surr.* iii. 74; *CSP Dom.* 1685, pp. 118, 125; *CJ*, ix. 715, 723, 724, 743, 758, 760; Burnet ed. Routh, iii. 96–97; *Reresby Mems.* 407, 424. [3] *Wood's Life and Times* (Oxf. Hist. Soc. xxvi), 287; *IHR Bull.* xlix. 258; Grey, x. 49, 84, 91, 93, 143, 153, 241, 242. [4] Grey, ix. 499, 518–19; *CJ*, x. 312.

L.N.

FINCH, Hon. Heneage II (1657–1726), of Eastwell, Kent.

HYTHE 1685

b. 3 Jan. 1657, 2nd s. of Heneage, 3rd Earl of Winchilsea (*d.*1689) by 2nd w. Lady Mary Seymour, da. of William Seymour[†], 2nd Duke of Somerset. *educ.* Wye g.s. 1663; Chelsea, Mdx. 1665; travelled abroad (France, Italy) 1676–7. *m.* lic. 14 May 1684 Anne (*d.* 5 Aug. 1720), da. of Sir William Kingsmill of Sydmonton, Hants, *s.p. suc.* nephew as 5th Earl of Winchilsea 5 Aug. 1712.[1]

Col. of militia ft. Kent by 1678–89, dep. lt. 1678–89; freeman, Canterbury 1680; j.p. Kent c.1683–9, commr. for assessment 1689–90.[2]

Capt. Coldstream Gds. 1682, lt.-col. 1687–9; groom of the bedchamber to the Duke of York 1683–5, (as King James II) 1685–Dec. 1688.

V.-pres. Soc. of Antiquaries 1724–*d.*[3]

Finch's father was too young to fight in the first Civil War, but he later claimed to have been an active Royalist from the age of 19, and he was certainly one of the leading Cavalier plotters in Kent in 1655. At the Restoration he accepted employment as ambassador to the Porte in order to pay off his debts, an aim in which he was only partly successful, and when he returned he was made lord lieutenant of Kent. Finch became a soldier and a courtier, and married a maid of honour to Mary of Modena. He was returned to James II's Parliament as the King's nominee for Hythe, and at Mary's special request helped to support her canopy at the coronation. He was appointed to seven committees, none of any political importance, though one was for the bill to convey fresh water to Rochester and Chatham. His father was dismissed as lord lieutenant in 1687, and took an active part in the Revolution; but Finch apparently complied with James's policy, later becoming a non-juror. He was captured in 1690 while trying to escape to France. He lived mostly at Eastwell with his nephew, the 4th Earl, where he was able to indulge his antiquarian tastes; but he stood unsuccessfully for Rochester in 1701 and for Maidstone in 1705 and 1710. When he succeeded to the peerage he refused the oaths

and never took his seat, though his wife, a poetess of some merit, was lady of the bedchamber to Queen Anne. He died of inflammation of the bowels on 30 Sept. 1726. Lord Hertford, his friend and fellow antiquarian, wrote that 'for sure he had no enemy, nor was he one to anybody'.[4]

[1] *HMC Finch*, i. 251, 364; ii. 26–29. [2] *CSP Dom.* 1678, p. 354; Jan.–July 1683, p. 134; *Roll of Freemen* ed. Cowper, 317. [3] J. Evans, *Soc. of Antiquaries*, 68. [4] Kent AO, NR/AEp/50; *Suss. Arch. Coll.* xv. 192; *HMC Le Fleming*, 270; R. Morrice, *Entering Bk.* 3, p. 142; Luttrell, ii. 38, 50, 73; *Poems of Anne, Countess of Winchilsea* ed. Reynolds, pp. xxix–xxxi.

B.D.H.

FINCH, Hon. William (c.1651–1726), of the Inner Temple, London.

GREAT BEDWYN 1679 (Oct.)

b. c.1651, 3rd s. of Heneage Finch[*], and bro. of Daniel Finch[*], Hon. Edward Finch[†] and Hon. Heneage Finch I[*]. *educ.* privately; Christ Church, Oxf. matric. 1 June 1666, aged 15; I. Temple 1662, called 1675. *m.* lic. 17 May 1681 (with £3,000), Anne, da. of Sir William Hoskins of Oxted, Surr., 1s. 1da.[1]

Solicitor-gen. to Queen Catherine of Braganza by 1682–92;[2] bencher, I. Temple 1696, reader 1697.

As a child, Finch was too delicate to be sent to Westminster, where the great Dr Busby was at the height of his powers. He became a lawyer, though he is not known to have practised in the courts, and his political career was brief, obscure and involuntary. His brother Daniel secured his return for Great Bedwyn in the autumn of 1679 on the Seymour interest, but he seems to have been totally inactive in the second Exclusion Parliament. On his marriage he was given a court appointment, but for most of his life he was apparently confined by bodily infirmities to his chamber in King's Bench Walk. He died on 26 Feb. 1726 as the result of a fall, so far forgotten that the obituarist, while correctly recording his place in the Finch pedigree, made a mistake in his name. His will, while providing for a jointure, mentions neither wife nor children.[3]

[1] *Mar. Lic.* (Harl. Soc. xxx), 62; Manning and Bray, *Surr.* ii. 391. [2] *Cal. Treas. Bks.* ix. 1391. [3] *HMC Finch*, ii. 55; iii. 139; *I. Temple Recs.* iv. 34; *The Gen.* n.s. vii. 43; *Temple Church Recs.* 40; PCC 97 Plymouth.

J.P.F.

FISHER, Sir Clement, 2nd Bt. (1613–83), of Great Packington, Warws.

COVENTRY 1661

bap. 9 Mar. 1613, 1st s. of Sir Robert Fisher, 1st Bt. of Great Packington by Elizabeth, da. of Sir Anthony Tyringham[†] of Tyringham, Bucks. *m.* 8 Dec. 1662, Jane (*d.* 9 Sept. 1689), da. of Thomas Lane of Bentley, Staffs. *s.p. suc.* fa. 29 Mar. 1647.[1]

J.p. Warws. Mar. 1660–c.73; commr. for oyer and terminer, Midland circuit July 1660, assessment, Warws. Aug. 1660–80, Westminster 1663–4, Coventry 1664–80, loyal and indigent officers, Warws. 1662.[2]

Fisher's great-grandfather, a gentleman pensioner at the court of Henry VIII, acquired Great Packington at the dissolution of the monasteries. His grandfather was returned for Tamworth in 1584. Fisher's father was a commissioner of array, and he himself bore arms in the royalist garrison of Lichfield in the Civil War, though his brother, Thomas, was 'always well-affected to Parliament'. He compounded at one-sixth on an estate of £660 p.a. for £1,711 in 1648. In 1656 he petitioned for exemption from the decimation tax on the grounds that in recent years he had manifested his good will to the regime.[3]

Fisher was returned for Coventry, seven miles from his home, at the general election of 1661. He was not an active Member of the Cavalier Parliament, being named to only 20 committees, most of which were in the first session. He was among those appointed to consider the bill restoring bishops to the House of Lords and the bill of pains and penalties, and to bring in a militia bill. He married the sister of John Lane*, on whom an annuity of £1,000 had been settled in recognition of her part in the King's escape after the battle of Worcester, and was listed as a court dependant in 1664. He was absent from a call of the House on 15 Dec. 1666, and on 13 Apr. 1668 he was given permission to go into the country for the recovery of his health. Sir Thomas Osborne* included him in 1669 among the independent Members who usually voted for supply, but his last committee was on a private bill on 13 Mar. 1671. Not long afterwards he seems to have been removed from the Warwickshire bench, presumably for reasons of health. Secretary Coventry wrote to him to attend the spring session of 1675, but he did not receive the government whip in the autumn, and Sir Richard Wiseman* noted his absence. Though Shaftesbury classed him as 'doubly vile', his name appeared on no further list of court supporters, except to indicate that he was again absent. He did not stand again, and died on 13 Apr. 1683. He was buried at Great Packington. His title was inherited by a nephew, but no later member of the family entered Parliament.[4]

[1] *Vis. Warws.* (Harl. Soc. lxii), 32–33. [2] *Warws. Recs.* v. p. xvii. [3] *VCH Warws.* iv. 36, 182; Dugdale, *Antiqs. Warws.* 989; *Cal. Comm. Comp.* 1548; SP23/204/312–18; *Verney Mems.* ii. 30. [4] T. W. Whitley, *Parl. Rep. Coventry*, 102; D. Ogg, *Reign of Chas. II*, 483; *Life of Dugdale* ed. Hamper, 145.

A.M.M.

FITZGERALD, Wentworth, 17th Earl of Kildare [I] (1634–64), of Kilkea Castle, co. Kildare.

EAST RETFORD   1660

b. 1634, 2nd but 1st surv. s. of George, 16th Earl of Kildare [I], by Lady Joan Boyle, da. of Richard, 1st Earl of Cork [I]. *m.* c. May 1658 (with £6,000), Lady Elizabeth Holles, da. of John Holles†, 2nd Earl of Clare, 1s. 1da. *suc.* fa. c.1657.[1]
J.p. Notts. July 1660–1, commr. for assessment Aug. 1660–*d.*, gov. King's Co. [I] 1661–*d.*[2]
Gent. of the privy chamber 1661–*d.*; PC [I] 1661–*d.*[3]
Capt. of horse [I] 1662–4.[4]

Lord Kildare's ancestors were among the original Anglo-Norman invaders of Ireland in the 12th century. Henry VIII broke the wealth and power of the Geraldines, as they were called, and all but exterminated the family. Kildare's father was brought up in England as a Protestant. He seems to have run through his estate in the first two years of his majority, and in 1642 Maynooth Castle, the old seat of the family, was destroyed by the Catholic rebels, against whom he was in arms as colonel of a regiment. At the Cessation he took service with Parliament, acting as deputy governor of Dublin in 1647. On Cromwell's arrival in Ireland he lost his regiment; he crossed over to England and spent most of the remaining years of his life a prisoner for debt. In January 1656 it was reported that he had been transferred to the poor side in the Upper Bench, and he probably did not long survive.[5]

Kildare himself was named after the great lord deputy, presumably before his father went into opposition in the Irish Parliament of 1634. Various small sums were granted to his mother from time to time, but it seems to have been his uncle Roger Boyle (Lord Broghill as he then was) who contrived Kildare's marriage to a daughter of the wealthy Earl of Clare, probably by arrangement with his political associate William Pierrepont*, whose daughter had married Lady Elizabeth's brother (Gilbert Holles*). Kildare, like his younger brother, may have served in the Cromwellian army in Ireland, as he found it necessary to sue out a pardon after the Restoration. He is not known to have had either property or residence in Nottinghamshire, and must have owed his election at East Retford in 1660 entirely to Pierrepont. The first of his family to sit at Westminster, he was not an active Member of the Convention, in which he was named to only six committees and made no recorded speeches. His most important committee was to examine the public debt, and he also served on that for restoring the Marquess of Ormonde to his estates. Kildare probably did not seek re-election. Broghill (now Lord Orrery) had recommended him for a commission in the Irish army. He took his seat in the Irish House of Lords in 1661, and was active both in Parliament and the Privy Council. He was granted compensation of £10,000 for surrendering his hereditary right to the customs of Strangford and Ardglass, and £2,000 of this was paid to Orrery and other trustees to defray his debts and raise portions for his sisters. Kildare died quite unexpectedly of fever on 5 Mar. 1664. His son John, the 18th Earl, sat for Tregony as a Whig from 1694 to 1695.[6]

[1] *CSP Dom.* 1658-9, p. 12; *Cal. Cl. SP*, iv. 76. [2] *CSP Ire.* 1660-2, p. 381. [3] Carlisle, *Privy Chamber*, 172. [4] *HMC Ormonde*, i. 349. [5] *Letters of Strafford* ed. Knowler, i. 309; *Lismore Paprs.* (ser. 2), iv. 267; *HMC Egmont*, i. 444; *HMC Ormonde*, ii. 107; *CSP Dom.* 1655, p. 349; 1655-6, p. 109. [6] Carte, *Ormond*, i. 132-4; *Thurloe*, vii. 21; *HMC Ormonde*, o.s. ii. 398; *CSP Ire.* 1660-2, p. 537; 1663-5, p. 62; 1669-70, p. 385; *Cal. Treas. Bks.* i. 497.

M.W.H./E.R.E.

FITZHARDINGE, 1st Visct. [I] *see* **BERKELEY, Sir Charles II.**

FITZHARDINGE, 2nd Visct. [I] *see* **BERKELEY, Sir Charles I.**

FITZHARDINGE, 3rd Visct. [I] *see* **BERKELEY, Sir Maurice, 1st Bt.**

FITZHERBERT, John (c.1624-93), of College Green, Bristol and Luckington, Wilts.

MALMESBURY   1685

b. c.1624, 1st s. of William Fitzherbert, merchant, of Bristol. *m.* by 1652, Anne (*d.*1682), ?da. of John Fownes, merchant, of Bristol, at least 4s. 2da. *suc.* fa. 1662.[1]

Commr. for assessment, Wilts. Aug. 1660-80, 1689-90, Bristol 1661-3, Som. 1664-5; customer outwards, Bristol Sept. 1660-89, dep. lt. 1674-?89; j.p. Wilts. 1677-d., Glos. 1680-?89; commr. of inquiry, Forest of Dean 1679; alderman, Malmesbury 1685-7.[2]

Fitzherbert's grandfather, a younger son of a prolific Oxfordshire gentry family, became an eminent Bristol merchant, and his father, who farmed the prisage of wines from the mother of Sir William Waller I*, acquired Luckington, seven miles from Malmesbury, in 1632. At the outbreak of the Civil War Fitzherbert was acting as his father's clerk. Both were active Royalists and claimed losses of £3,000 in the cause. They took temporary refuge in Oxford in 1643 when their design to betray Bristol to the Cavaliers was discovered. When the city was reconquered by the New Model Army in 1645, Fitzherbert's father was thrust into a dungeon in

irons, and forced to buy his liberty from Philip Skippon[†] for £360. It was alleged that he enlisted men and collected money for the Royalists in the second Civil War; but there is no mention of this in Fitzherbert's petition after the Restoration, which earned him a customs post at Bristol. He continued to trade with Newfoundland on his own account, leased an estate in Virginia (together with Sir Humphrey Hooke*), and from 1665 was sending local intelligence to Joseph Williamson*.[3]

Fitzherbert was nominated a 'capital burgess' in the Malmesbury charter of 1685, and returned for the borough as a Tory six weeks later after a contest. He left no trace on the records of James II's Parliament. Though he was removed from the Malmesbury corporation in 1687, no doubt as a sop to the dissenters, he gave affirmative answers on the repeal of the Penal Laws and Test Act in Bristol, Gloucestershire and Wiltshire, and was recommended for re-election as court candidate. But he is unlikely to have stood for the Convention. Although his son Humphrey replaced him as customer of Bristol after the Revolution, he must have taken the oaths to the new regime, for he continued to sit on the Wiltshire bench. He died on 20 Mar. 1693 and was buried at Luckington. No other member of this family is known to have sat in Parliament.[4]

[1] E134/27, 28 Chas. II Hilary 15; *Wilts. N. and Q.* vii. 189; Sir T. Phillipps, *Mon. Inscriptions Wilts.* ii. 51; H. F. Waters, *Gen. Gleanings in Eng.* 1098; PCC 78 Coker. [2] *Cal. Treas. Bks.* i. 54; ix. 196; ix. 121; *CSP Dom.* 1685, p. 64; 1687-9, p. 215; PC2/72/555. [3] *Paroch. Colls.* (Oxon. Rec. Soc. ii), 35-36; *Vis. Oxon.* (Harl. Soc. v), 243; Aubrey and Jackson, *Wilts. Colls.* 105; *Deposition Bks.* (Bristol Rec. Soc. vi), 18; *Soc. of Merchant Venturers* (Bristol Rec. Soc. xvii), 3; *Merchants and Merchandise* (Bristol Rec. Soc. xix), 258; *CSP Dom.* 1660-61, p. 201; 1665-6, p. 116; *Cal. Cl. SP*, v. 256. [4] PC2/72/55; Bodl. Carte 130, f. 24; Phillipps, ii. 51.

B.D.H.

FITZJAMES, John (1619-70), of Leweston, Dorset.

DORSET	1654, 1656
POOLE	24 Jan.-22 Mar. 1659
DORSET	1660
POOLE	15 June 1661-21 June 1670

b. 31 Dec. 1619, 1st s. of Leweston Fitzjames[†] of Leweston by Eleanor, da. and coh. of Sir Henry Winston of Standish, Glos.; bro. of Henry Fitzjames[†] and Thomas Fitzjames*. *educ.* Magdalen Coll. Oxf. 1636. *m.* 7 Aug. 1638, Margaret, da. of Nathaniel Stephens[†] of Eastington, Glos. 2s. *d.v.p.* 5da. *suc.* fa. 1638; kntd. 9 July 1660.[1]

Capt. of militia ft. Dorset by 1641; commr. for assessment, Dorset 1643-9, 1652, Dorset and Som. 1657, Jan. 1660, Dorset Aug. 1660-9, Poole 1661-3, accounts, Dorset 1643, levying of money 1643, execution of ordinances 1644; ranger, Cranborne chase 1645-51; sheriff, Dorset 1645-6; j.p. Dorset 1648-52, 1656-

d., Som. July 1660–d.; commr. for militia, Dorset 1648, Mar. 1660; freeman, Poole 1649; commr. for piracy, Dorset 1653, dep. lt. July 1660–d,; commr. for sewers, Som. Aug. 1660.[2]

Col. of horse (parliamentary) 1644–6.[3]

The Fitzjames family had been established in Somerset by the 15th century; but the Dorset branch acquired their principal estate by bequest from the last of the Lewestons in 1584. The elder line were recusants, but Fitzjames's grandfather, founder of the Leweston branch, was a pillar of the Establishment, both materially and morally. The lack of a nearby borough limited their parliamentary opportunities; nevertheless Fitzjames's father sat for Bridport in 1597. He was dropped from the commission of the peace in 1626 as an opponent of the Court.[4]

Fitzjames's connexions with the Gloucestershire Presbyterians through his wife's family brought him into the circle of Major-General Edward Massey*, under whom his military career in the Civil War concluded, and he was closely associated with Sir Anthony Ashley Cooper*. But if he followed his father's politics he remained faithful to his grandfather's religion. He retained the use of the Book of Common Prayer in the family chapel throughout the Interregnum, insisting even in 1651 on an Anglican ceremony for his sister's marriage, and acquired the reputation of a discreet but reliable protector of Cavaliers. At the Restoration he claimed to have tried to advance the King's service for 12 years.[5]

Returned for his county in 1660, Fitzjames was prevented by illness from 'making a personal submission' to the King at The Hague and from playing much part in the Convention. He was named to the committee for the assessment ordinance, and acted as teller on 27 June against a clause in the indemnity bill on behalf of the maintenance trustees. He was too modest to expect re-election in 1661; 'a burgess's place . . . is as much as (without vanity) I could expect'. He accordingly stood for Poole, doubtless in the Cooper interest, and was declared elected on the votes of non-resident freemen after a double return. He was included in Lord Wharton's list of friends, and probably voted with the Opposition under Clarendon. Though he was named to only 17 committees in the first nine sessions of the Cavalier Parliament, he was far from inactive; according to (Sir) Edward Harley*, writing in 1666, 'he seldom fails in the House'. His ineffectiveness is shown in a matter which concerned him personally, the failure of the committee set up to find some means of encouraging Abraham Forester's invention for repairing highways. Forester's

father, the versatile rector of Folke, was not only Fitzjames's neighbour but his physician, skilled in compounding pills which relieved his wife of her melancholy fits during pregnancy. But in spite of the King's recommendation and the naming of five other Dorset Members to the committee nothing was done.[6]

Fitzjames may have supported the Cabal, in which his patron (now Lord Ashley) played a leading role. He was included by Sir Thomas Osborne* among the Members who had usually voted for supply, and acted as teller for his wife's brother-in-law Peregrine Palmer* in the Bridgwater election case. His record during the Interregnum leaves no doubt possible as to the sincerity of his Anglicanism; but his correspondence with the dean of Salisbury shows that after Bartholomew he maintained one of the ejected ministers in his house, which was later to be licensed to his widow for Presbyterian worship, and opposed the second conventicles bill. In also opposing the bill to enable Lord Roos (John Manners*) to divorce his wife, he no doubt acted on principle, both as a good churchman and a good family man; moreover his brother Henry was connected with the Duke of York's household. He died on 21 June 1670 and was buried at Long Burton.[7]

Fitzjames is revealed in his letters as an attractive, but not a strong character. Once his campaigning days were over, he seems never to have enjoyed good health, nevertheless serving with the militia during the second Dutch war. Tolerant and humane, though conscious of what was due to his position as a gentleman, he was happiest among his family and in his garden or library at 'poor Leweston'. The adjective (which he habitually used) demands an explanation; but if his estimate of £700 as two years' profit of all his lands is correct, his income was hardly equal to his rank. His debts, with which he was obsessed, amounted to less than £3,000, largely incurred on behalf of his brothers and sisters; they contrasted disagreeably with the purses of gold that his father and grandfather had been able to bequeath to their numerous offspring. Moreover, at his death he had not succeeded in making any provision for his daughters, all of or near marriageable age. One of them, however, married Sir George Strode*, who bought out the other coheirs to the Leweston estate.[8]

[1] Som. and Dorset N. and Q. xvi. 248; Glos. Par. Reg. xiii. 96; Northumberland (Alnwick) mss 548, f. 1; HMC Portland, iii. 259. [2] HMC Hatfield, xxii. 354; Northumberland mss 547, ff. 1, 7; 549, f. 100; Christie, Shaftesbury, i. p. xlvii; Hutchins, Dorset, i. 32; CSP Dom. Add. 1660–85, p. 95. [3] CSP Dom. 1644, p. 478; 1645–7, p. 488. [4] Eg. 784, f. 55; Hutchins, iv. 132; RCAM West Dorset, 132–3; A. L. Rowse, Ralegh and the Throckmortons, 177, 180. [5] CSP Dom. 1645–7, p. 38; Northumberland mss 549, f. 101;

Cal. Cl. SP, v. 26. [6] *Cal. Cl. SP*, iv. 684; v. 26; Northumberland mss 552, f. 55; 549, f. 49; 551, f. 77; *HMC Portland*, iii. 301; *CSP Dom.* 1664–5, p. 151. [7] Northumberland mss 550, ff. 85, 87; *CSP Dom.* 1672–3, p. 178; *Add.* 1660–85, p. 140; *CJ*, ix. 119, 136, 150. [8] Northumberland mss 547, f. 79; 550, f. 68.

M.W.H./J.P.F.

FITZJAMES, Thomas (c.1624–1705), of Nursling, Hants.

DOWNTON 1659, 3–9 May 1660

b. c.1624, 2nd s. of Leweston Fitzjames[†] of Leweston, Dorset, and bro. of John Fitzjames* and Henry Fitzjames[†]. *educ.* Lincoln, Oxf. matric. 25 Jan. 1639, aged 15; M. Temple 1642, called 1649. *m.* 14 Feb. 1657, Katherine, da. of Thomas Mill of Fullerton, Hants, at least 2s. (1 *d.v.p.*) 2da.[1]
Clerk of the entries, alienations office 1642–53, 1654–July 1660.[2]
Forester of Battramsley bailiwick, New Forest by 1662–8; freeman, Lymington 1665; commr. for assessment, Hants 1690–1702.[3]

Unlike his brothers, Fitzjames took no part in the Civil War. After the Restoration he claimed to have been 'engaged in Lord Mordaunt's business' in Surrey in 1659, when he had held a commission under Sir Francis Vincent*. He probably owed his election for Downton to his dead sister's husband William Coles*, though he may also have had the support of Sir Anthony Ashley Cooper*, but in 1660 there was a double return. He was allowed to sit on the merits of the return, but unseated six days later on the merits of the election, without, as far as is known, taking any part in parliamentary business. In July he lost his place in the alienations office to Henry Clerke II*. For the rest of his long life he seems to have lived quietly on one or other of the Mill estates in Hampshire, though in 1662 he was unable to attend the Swainmote in the New Forest 'being detained elsewhere on the King's service'. In 1668 he was 'unhandsomely outed' of his bailiwick, but on what grounds is not known. On his elder brother's death he tried unsuccessfully to establish a claim to the Leweston estate. He seems to have succeeded to Fullerton, presumably in the right of his wife, shortly after the Revolution, and was named to all the Hampshire assessment commissions till 1705. He was apparently survived only by one daughter, Catherine, through whom it is probable that Fullerton came to John Chetwynd, MP for Stockbridge 1722–34.[4]

[1] *Som. and Dorset N. and Q.* xvi. 220; C5/160/17. [2] *CSP Dom.* 1660–1, p. 117. [3] Woodward, *Hants*, iii. 41; Northumberland (Alnwick) mss 553, f. 5; E. King, *Old Times Revisited*, 190. [4] *CSP Dom.* 1660–1, p. 102; Northumberland mss, 551, ff 41, 42; PCC 266 Pell, will of Thomas Mill; C10/167/26; *VCH Hants*, iv. 413.

M.W.H./J.P.F.

FITZWILLIAM, Hon. Charles (c.1646–89), of Stamford Baron, Lincs.

PETERBOROUGH 1685, 8 Jan.–Sept. 1689

b. c.1646, 3rd but 2nd surv. s. of William Fitzwilliam[†], 2nd Baron Fitzwilliam of Lifford [I], by Jane, da. and coh. of Hugh Perry *alias* Hunter, Mercer, of London, wid. of Robert Perry, merchant, of London; bro. of William Fitzwilliam*, 3rd Baron Fitzwilliam. *educ.* Westminster; M. Temple, entered 1661; Magdalene, Camb. adm. 21 Jan. 1664, aged 17; Padua 1670; travelled abroad (Italy) 1670–6. *unm.*[1]
Maj. of ft. regt. of Lionel Walden I* 1678–9, R. Fusiliers June–Nov. 1685, regt. of William, Lord Cavendish by Mar. 1689, lt.-col. May 1689–*d.*
J.p. Peterborough 1682–?85, Northants. 1689–*d.*; dep. lt. Lincs. Oct. 1688–*d.*; commr. for assessment, Lincs. and Northants. 1689.[2]

Although Fitzwilliam embarked on a military career, he seems to have been a dilettante by temperament. He matriculated at Padua in 1670, visited Rome in 1676, and accompanied the Earl of Exeter (John Cecil*) on his artistic tour of the Continent in 1683. He was probably less inclined to opposition than his elder brother, whom he suceeded as Member for Peterborough on Exeter's interest in 1685. A moderately active committeeman in James II's Parliament, he was appointed to the committee of elections and privileges and those to recommend expunctions from the Journals and to consider the bills for the Bedford level and for bringing fresh water to Rochester and Chatham. He displeased the King by voting against the dispensations for Roman Catholic officers, and was deprived of his commission after the second session. Re-elected to the Convention, he left no trace on its records, being absent on military service from 16 Mar. 1689, first in England, then in Ireland, where he died in September of the same year. He left all his property to his nephew and niece, the children of Sir Christopher Wren*, whom he made his executor.[3]

[1] *CSP Dom.* 1685, p. 411; 1689–90, pp. 27, 146; SP44/165/293. [2] *Fenland N. and Q.* vi. 215; Northants. RO, FH2226. [3] Northants. RO, F(M)C 414; *CSP Dom.* 1683–4, p. 192; *HMC Downshire*, i. 79; *Reresby Mems.* 402–3; *HMC Coke*, ii. 335, 357; PCC 12 Dyke.

J.P.F.

FITZWILLIAM, William, 3rd Baron Fitzwilliam of Lifford [I] (1643–1719), of Milton, Northants.

PETERBOROUGH 8 Nov. 1667, 1679 (Mar.), 1681

b. 22 Apr. 1643, 2nd but 1st surv. s. of William Fitzwilliam[†], 2nd Baron Fitzwilliam, and bro. of Hon. Charles Fitzwilliam*. *m.* 10 May 1669, Anne (*d.* 14 Feb. 1717), da. and h. of Edmund Cremer of Setchley, Norf., 4s. (3 *d.v.p.*) 6da. *suc.* fa. 21 Feb. 1659; *cr.* Earl Fitzwilliam [I] 21 July 1716.
Commr. for assessment, Northants. 1664–80, 1689,

Norf. 1673–80; dep. lt. Northants. 1666–78, 1715–_d._; j.p. Peterborough 1668–_d._, Norf. 1669–Feb. 1688, Northants. 1676–Feb. 1688, 1689–_d._; custos rot. Peterborough 1715–_d._[1]

Fitzwilliam was descended from a London alderman who bought Milton, three miles from Peterborough, and other property in the Soke in 1502. The family frequently provided Members for the city from 1553. Fitzwilliam's father represented it in the Long Parliament until Pride's Purge; a tepid Parliamentarian, he continued to hold local office under the Commonwealth. When Fitzwilliam came of age, the estate (which had been saved from complete ruin by his father's prudent marriage) was valued at £3,000 p.a. He contested the Peterborough by-election of 1666 with Edward Palmer* and Sir Vere Fane*; although he received most votes he was defrauded of election by chicanery with the scot and lot rolls, but he was successful on petition. He was not an active Member of the Cavalier Parliament, in which he was named to 34 committees, none of them after 1675. He was appointed to the parliamentary committee to take the accounts of poll tax and assessments on 21 Feb. 1668, and to that for the conventicles bill. He acted as teller against the alnage bill, and was among those ordered to attend the King with the resolutions of both Houses for wearing clothes of English manufacture. Sir Thomas Osborne* included him among those who had usually voted for supply.[2]

Like his father, Fitzwilliam married prudently, securing a Norfolk heiress 'worth £1,200 p.a. [in] lands of inheritance, and a good personal estate besides'. He was named to the committees for the second conventicles bill, for the extension of habeas corpus, and for the estate bill promoted on behalf of his friend Henry Williams*. He continued to show concern over the liberty of the subject, and in 1674 was appointed to a committee for the relief of those under writs of habeas corpus. Although clearly in opposition to the administration of Osborne (now Earl of Danby), he did not sever all ties with the Court, prevailing on (Sir) Joseph Williamson* to act as godfather to his eldest daughter. His last important committee was for preventing the growth of Popery in the spring session of 1675. Shaftesbury marked him 'worthy' in 1677, and again when he was re-elected to the first Exclusion Parliament. In this Parliament he was again inactive. He was appointed to the committee of elections and privileges and that for expiring laws, but he voted for the bill. At the August election he lost his seat to Charles Orme*, but he regained it in 1681, though he left no trace on the records of the Oxford Parliament. He was included in the list of

Northamptonshire Whigs about 1682, with an estate that had increased to £3,500 p.a., but he seems to have remained on the commission of the peace, perhaps on condition of renouncing political activities. The family interest at Peterborough in the next two elections was represented by his brother. He gave negative replies on the repeal of the Test Act and Penal Laws, and was removed from local office. Although he doubtless welcomed the Revolution, he does not seem to have returned to politics, and the Irish earldom he received from George I was probably intended more as a reward for his son, Whig MP for Peterborough from 1710 to 1728.[3]

[1] Northants. RO, F(M) 2101–3 (lieutenancy commissions). [2] M. W. Finch, _Five Northants. Fams._ (Northants. Rec. Soc. xix), 101; Keeler, _Long Parl._ 177–8; Bodl. Carte 46, f. 437; Northants. RO, F(M) C412, Henry Williams to Fitzwilliam, 18 Apr. 1666. [3] _HMC 6th Rep._ 487; _CSP Dom._ 1673–5, p. 463; SP29/421/216.

E.R.E./J.P.F.

FLEETWOOD, Edward (1634–1704), of Penwortham Priory, nr. Preston, Lancs.

PRESTON 7 Aug. 1660, 1685

bap. 12 Oct. 1634, 3rd but 1st surv. s. of John Fleetwood of Penwortham by Anne, da. of William Faringdon of Worden Hall, Leyland. _educ._ Padua 1648; Brasenose, Oxf. 1651, BA 1654; G. Inn 1656. _m._ 15 May 1659, Anne, da. of George Purefoy† of Wadley, Berks., _s.p. suc._ fa. 1657.[1]

Freeman, Preston 1642, 1662, 1682; commr. for assessment, Lancs. Jan. 1660–80, 1689–90, j.p. Mar. 1660–6, 1670–7, 1689–92, 1702–_d._, dep. lt. 1662–?66, 1680–6, 1689–?93, commr. for corporations 1662–3.[2]

Fleetwood's ancestors were of little consequence in Lancashire until the dissolution of the monasteries, when John Fleetwood† acquired Penwortham Priory, just across the Ribble from Preston, for which one of the family sat in 1553. The Penwortham branch were less conspicuous than those established in Buckinghamshire, Northamptonshire or Staffordshire. Fleetwood's father, a strong churchman, was a commissioner of array at the outset of the Civil War, but gave himself up to the forces of Parliament in February 1643 and compounded in 1647 for £617. Fleetwood himself may have been brought up in the Earl of Derby's household with his father's ward Roger Bradshaigh I*, and throughout his political career he remained a loyal adherent of the Stanleys.[3]

As a Cavalier's son Fleetwood was ineligible at the general election of 1660, but was returned for Preston at a by-election after the Restoration. His only committee in the Convention was on the Lords bill for reparations to the Marquess of Winchester. Doubtless a court supporter, he was proposed for the order of the Royal Oak, with an estate of £1,000 p.a. With the re-establishment of the duchy interest at Preston he did not sit again till 1685, when he was returned as a Tory. An inactive Member of James II's Parliament, he was appointed only to the committees on the bills to provide carriages for the royal progresses and to prohibit the import of gunpowder. He refused to serve as deputy lieutenant under the Roman Catholic Lord Molyneux in October 1688, but accepted local office after the Revolution. He was buried at Penwortham on 17 Apr. 1704. His heir was his fourth cousin Henry, a Jacobite, who sat for Preston from 1708 to 1722.[4]

[1] *Vis. Lancs.* (Chetham Soc. lxxxv), 110, 156; *Penwortham Priory Docs.* (Chetham Soc. xxx), pp. lxv–lxix. [2] *Preston Guild Rolls* (Lancs. and Cheshire Rec. Soc. ix), 111, 144, 186; Lancs. RO, QSC62–79, 103–6; SP29/61/157. [3] *VCH Lancs.* vi. 56, 58–59; *Royalist Comp. Pprs.* (Lancs. and Cheshire Rec. Soc. xxvi), 321–3. [4] *HMC Kenyon*, 125, 203; *CSP Dom.* 1687–9, p. 323.

I.C.

FLEETWOOD, Miles (c.1630–88), of Aldwinkle All Saints, Northants.

OXFORDSHIRE	1656
NEW WOODSTOCK	1659
NORTHAMPTONSHIRE	28 Feb.1678, 1679 (Oct.), 1681

b. c.1630, 1st s. of Sir William Fleetwood*. *educ.* Queens', Camb. 1646; G. Inn 1648. *m.* (1) by 1651, Elizabeth (*d.*1657), da. and coh. of Nathaniel Still of Hutton Court, Som., 5s. (2 *d.v.p.*); (2) lic. 12 Dec. 1666, Barbara, da. and coh. of John St. Andrew of Gotham, Notts., wid. of Sir Oliver St. John, 1st Bt., of Woodford, Northants., *s.p. suc.* fa. 1674.[1]

J.p. Northants. 1653–80, Oxon. 1652–June 1660; common councilman, Woodstock to 1662; commr. for assessment, Northants. and Oxon. 1657, Northants. 1661–74, 1679–80, militia, Northants. and Oxon. Mar. 1660.[2]

Clerk of the privy seal 1656–8; teller of the receipt 1658–?June 1660; gent. of the privy chamber (extraordinary) June 1660–?80.[3]

Fleetwood's political outlook was apparently derived more from his uncle, the parliamentary general, than from his royalist father. Indeed he inherited nothing more substantial than the manor of Aldwinkle, valued at a mere £140 p.a., and without his second wife's jointure of £600 p.a. his position would have been desperate. Lack of compensation for his father's loss of office when the court of wards was abolished, and the grant of Woodstock Park to the Lovelaces gave him two solid grievances against the crown. However, he was able to entertain his friends, thanks to Lord Hatton (Christopher Hatton*) who supplied him with venison and bottles of sherry, and he may have made a little on the side as a brewer and by recommending grooms, attorneys and even clergymen to his wealthier acquaintances. He re-entered the House as knight

of the shire in February 1678 by defeating the court supporter Sir Roger Norwich*, and was marked 'worthy' by Shaftesbury. With his narrow fortune, he was quite a stranger to Restoration London, despite his honorary post at Court, and he was greatly shocked to find prayers for the dead in use in the chapel of St. James's Palace; Silius Titus* raised the matter in the House on his behalf. If he was still too modest to speak for himself he was not much more forward in committee work, for he was appointed only to consider bills on behalf of foreign Protestant craftsmen, and for settling the stannary laws, and two local estate bills.[4]

At the general election Norwich was returned unopposed, but Fleetwood and another Whig, John Parkhurst*, stood for the junior seat. 'It was hard to distinguish by the view which had the most [*sic*]; but at last to prevent the charges which such an infinite number of people would have cost, it was yielded to Mr Parkhurst, who required a poll.' Fleetwood regained his seat in August 1679 at Norwich's expense, and was removed from the commission of the peace a few months later. In the second Exclusion Parliament Fleetwood not only found his voice, making three recorded speeches, but also became a moderately active committeeman. He was appointed to the committees for the Irish cattle bill, for inspecting the arrangements for the trial of Lord Stafford and for the prevention of superstitious bequests, and three others. On 18 Nov. 1680 he moved that the informer Turberville might 'have such a pardon as Lord Danby has, and it will be full enough', and two days later he and George Vernon* undertook to prove the charges of financial irregularity against Edward Seymour*. 'I confess I understand not how those two gentlemen come to be inspired with the knowledge of his accounts', commented one observer. On 25 Nov. he complained that Seymour had made no answer to his charges, and on the next day he was teller against adding the court supporter (Sir) Christopher Musgrave* to the impeachment committee. He was re-elected unopposed in 1681, an exclusionist triumph that might have had serious consequences for him, for on the hustings Sir Thomas Samwell* presented him with a strongly exclusionist *Address to the Knights of the Shire*, which Fleetwood caused to be read aloud to the electors. At Oxford he was appointed to the committee of elections and privileges, and he was among the Members instructed to recommend a more convenient place for the Commons to sit. On 25 Mar. he demanded that Sir Leoline Jenkins* should ask pardon on his knees for 'reflecting' on the House.[5]

Fleetwood was noted as one of the Northamptonshire Whigs in 1682, and presented as disaffected by the grand jury in the following year. At Norwich's instance he and Samwell were indicted in Hilary Term 1685 for publishing a seditious libel, but they had still not been brought to trial in June, and in April 1686 they were pardoned. Nevertheless, Fleetwood was noted on Danby's list as in opposition to James II. He died before the Revolution, on 28 July 1688, and was 'decently but very privately interred' at Aldwinkle All Saints. His will shows that he retained the Calvinist faith of his forebears. The estate was sold on his son's death ten years later, and no later member of this branch of the Fleetwood family entered Parliament.[6]

[1] *Northants. N. and Q.* n.s. i. 115–16; *London Mar. Lic.* ed. Foster, 492. [2] *HMC Lords*, i. 187; A. Ballard, *Chrons. Woodstock*, 92. [3] Add. 4184, no. 149; E403/2523, nos. 114, 184, 187; LC3/2. [4] SP29/421/216; Add. 29556, f. 400; 29557, f. 126; 29558, f. 22; 29559, f. 316; 29560, f. 486; Grey, vi. 190. [5] Add. 29556, f. 431; Northants. RO, IC 1076a; Grey, viii. 31, 40, 78; *HMC Ormonde*, n.s. v. 504; R. Morrice, Entering Bk. 1, pp. 450–1. [6] SP29/421/216; *Somers Tracts*, viii. 410; Luttrell, i. 325; Morrice, 466; *CSP Dom.* 1686–7, p. 84; *HMC Lords*, ii. 305; PCC 139 Ent; Bridges, *Northants.* ii. 209.

E.R.E.

FLEETWOOD, Sir William (1603–74), of High Lodge, Woodstock Park, Oxon.

NEW WOODSTOCK 1640 (Apr.), 1661–Feb. 1674.

bap. 20 July 1603, 2nd but 1st surv. s. of Sir Miles Fleetwood[†], of Aldwinkle All Saints, Northants. by Anne, da. of Nicholas Luke of Woodend, Beds.; bro. of Charles Fleetwood[†]. *educ.* Emmanuel, Camb. 1619. *m* (1) bef. 1631, Frances, da. and h. of Henry Sture of Maridge, Devon, 3s. 1da.; (2) c.1638, Elizabeth, da. and h. of Thomas Harvey of Twycross, Leics., 4s. 3da. Kntd. 20 July 1624; *suc.* fa. 1641.[1]
Cup-bearer by 1624–46, May 1660–d.; receiver-gen. of the court of wards 1641–3.[2]
J.p. Northants. and Oxon. by 1634–46, Oxon. July 1660–d., Woodstock Aug. 1660–d.; ranger, Woodstock Park by 1642–?50, May 1660–d.; commr. of array, Northants. 1642, assessment, Oxon. Aug. 1660–d., Northants. 1663–d., Beds. 1665–d., loyal and indigent officers, Oxon. 1662; freeman, Woodstock by 1662.[3]
Capt. of ft. (royalist) 1642, col. by 1646.

Fleetwood came from a cadet branch of the Lancashire family which held for three generations an office in the court of wards worth £1,500 p.a. His father, a zealous Puritan in religion but a moderate in politics, sat for Hindon in the Long Parliament till his death in 1641; but Fleetwood, already a courtier, had been involved in a double return at Woodstock, which he had represented in the Short Parliament, and never took his seat. 'Being a servant in ordinary of the late King, he attended his person at Oxford', bringing with him, as he later claimed, £60,000 revenue from the court of wards. Parliament naturally removed him from his post, which

was given to his brother Charles, later a general during the Interregnum. From his father he inherited, beside his office, only a small estate in Northamptonshire bought under James I which he valued at £300 p.a., but he had also a grant for life of Woodstock Park, worth another £120 p.a. He was allowed to compound on the Oxford Articles for £510, which was paid, or at least promised, by his brother.[4]

Fleetwood was awarded £2,000 compensation by the Convention for the abolition of the court of wards, but no provision was made for payment. He was returned for Woodstock in 1661; and listed as a friend by Lord Wharton. A moderately active Member of the Cavalier Parliament, he was named to 94 committees. In the opening session he was appointed to the committees to inquire into the shortfall in the revenue and to consider the corporations bill, and had the rather empty satisfaction of hearing that his compensation ought to be doubled. He was listed as a court dependant in 1664 and named to the committee for the conventicles bill, though his brother was a leading light in the Independent congregation of Dr John Owen at Stoke Newington. He was one of the Members ordered to bring in a supplementary militia bill on 3 Apr. 1668. His name appears on both lists of the court party in 1669–71 and on the Paston list as a court dependant. But on his deathbed he complained that lack of compensation for loss of office 'and his great losses in the late unhappy times have forced him to contract great debts'. He was recommended as 'a fit object of favour' on 2 Feb. 1674, but died before anything could be done for him. He was buried at Aldwinkle All Saints ten days later.[5]

[1] *Northants. N. and Q.* n.s. i. 113–15. [2] *Cal. Treas. Bks.* iv. 471–2. [3] *CSP Dom.* 1641–3, p. 317; Aubrey, *Brief Lives*, ii. 30; Woodstock council acts, 1661–79 (28 Aug. 1662). [4] H. W. Bell, *Court of Wards*, 25; Keeler, *Long Parl.* 178–9; G. E. Aylmer, *King's Servants*, 381; SP23/196/165–7; *VCH Northants.* iii. 165; *Cal. Treas. Bks.* iv. 471–2; *Cal. Comm. Comp.* 1403. [5] *CJ*, viii. 219, 407; Bell, 165; *Cal. Treas. Bks.* iv. 471–2.

L.N.

FLEMING, Sir Daniel (1633–1701), of Rydal, Grasmere, Westmld.

COCKERMOUTH 1685

b. 24/25 July 1633, 1st s. of William Fleming of Coniston, Lancs. and Rydal by Alice, da. of Roger Kirkby[†] of Kirkby Ireleth, Lancs. *educ.* Crosthwaite (Messrs Wheelwright and Radcliff) to 1639; privately (Mr Nathaniel Edgar and Mr Southwick); Irton (Mr Bartle) 1644; Penrith (Mr Thomas Milborne); Crosthwaite (Mr Sanderson) 1648; Bank (Mr Dodgson) 1649; Queen's, Oxf. 1650–2; G. Inn 1652–3. *m.* 27 Aug. 1655, Barbara (*d.* 13 Apr. 1675), da. of Sir Henry Fletcher,

1st Bt., of Hutton Hall, Cumb., 11s. (3 *d.v.p.*) 4da. *suc.* fa. 1653; kntd. 15 May 1681.[1]

J.p. Cumb. and Westmld. Mar. 1660–June 1680, Cumb. Nov. 1680–May 1688, Oct. 1688–*d.*, Westmld. Nov. 1680–*d.*, Lancs. 1663–Apr. 1688, 1689–?*d.*; commr. for militia, Cumb. and Westmld. Mar. 1660, oyer and terminer, Northern circuit July 1660, assessment, Westmld. Aug. 1660–80, Cumb. Aug. 1660–1, 1663–80, Lancs. 1664–80, Cumb., Lancs. and Westmld. 1689–90; sheriff, Cumb. Nov. 1660–1; lt. of militia ft. Cumb. and Westmld. Nov. 1660, capt. 1661, maj. 1668, lt.-col. 1672–Apr. 1688, Oct. 1688–1700, col. 1700–*d.*; commr. for corporations, Westmld. 1662–3; dep. lt. Cumb. and Westmld. 1662–Feb. 1688, Oct. 1688–*d.*, Lancs. 1674–?Apr. 1688; commr. for charitable uses, Cumb. and Westmld. 1670, recusants 1675; freeman, Kendal and Lancaster 1684.[2]

Fleming's ancestors had been powerful landowners in the north-west since the 12th century, and provided an MP for Carlisle in 1326. His father fought for the King in both Civil Wars, but since he had not yet inherited the Rydal estate he escaped with the comparatively modest fine of £160. Fleming was sent to Oxford during the Interregnum, where his tutor was Dr Thomas Smith, subsequently bishop of Carlisle, and his servitor Joseph Williamson*, the future secretary of state. Pricked as sheriff in 1658, he was excused on the intercession of Charles Howard* and his brother-in-law, Sir George Fletcher*. He refused all office before the Restoration, nor would he accept the invitation of Sir John Lowther I* to stand for Westmorland at the general election of 1660. On 21 May he proclaimed Charles II at Cockermouth, and as sheriff of Cumberland he was responsible for the 1661 election. He was proposed for the order of the Royal Oak with an estate of £1,800 p.a.[3]

Fleming's reluctance to enter the parliamentary arena was not due to lack of either capacity or commitment, both of which he demonstrated at county level. A strong churchman and loyalist, he was an active militia officer and took a leading part in the repression of Quakers and other nonconformists. A competent antiquary, he was 'so versed in the northern laws and customs as to be constantly requested by the judges of assize to sit as their assessor on circuit'. Moreover, his correspondence with Smith and Williamson kept him in touch with national politics. When the latter entered Parliament Fleming took the trouble to draw up a whole legislative programme. An Act was needed, he thought, to modify the law on church attendance, so that the fines might be diverted from relieving the poor, 'who are little better for them', to the public service:

> namely, four-fifths to the use of the navy or herring fishery and one-fifth to the use of the train-bands in each county, to be divided among the officers (who have

now no pay) and the soldiers for their encouragement. If all conventiclers were punished as rioters and their fines so disposed of, it would strengthen the King at the charge of his enemies.

Other measures that he proposed concerned legal fees, tithe, heralds' visitations, and the establishment of county land banks and registers. Williamson commented:

> Mr Fleming's discreet and active care expressed in his letters is very well liked here, the King having had the reading of them. Indeed, we want everywhere such steady, sober heads.

In 1675 he wrote to Williamson, listing all 'the chargeable and troublesome offices' he had held:

> I shall not be so vain as to think I deserve anything of his Majesty, since I know the performances of subjects deserve no reward. There are few that have so good a friend as you at Court but they will be encouraged sometimes to act the part of a beggar.... God having blessed me with thirteen hopeful children all living, and my estate being but small, I have as great reason to look after interest for the providing for them as many other persons.

His application brought no results, and in June 1680, after a quarrel with Lord Morpeth (Edward Howard*), he was left out of the Cumberland commission of the peace, but soon restored on the intervention of Sir John Lowther III*. He was presented at Court by (Sir) Christopher Musgrave* on 15 May 1681 and knighted, an honour for which he had expressed little desire.[4]

Fleming appears to have played an active part in the quo warranto proceedings in the north-west in 1684, when he prevailed on the corporations of Kendal and Lancaster to surrender their charters. In 1685 he again declined an invitation to stand for the county, probably because with his large family he could not afford the expense, but he was returned on the Fletcher interest at Cockermouth. The contested election cost him only £10 5s. A very active Member of James II's Parliament, he was appointed to 18 committees, of which the most important was on the bill for the general naturalization of Huguenot refugees (1 July). At a meeting convened at Penrith by Lord Preston (Sir Richard Grahme*) on 24 Dec. 1687, Fleming returned the same negative answers as Lowther on the repeal of the Test Act and Penal Laws. Sir Thomas Strickland* urged him unsuccessfully to 'consider if the best way to preserve the Protestant religion is not to comply with the King'. Lord Thanet (Thomas Tufton*) offered him a seat at Appleby in the next Parliament, but he had found that 'absence from home in London is very prejudicial to [my] large family of young children'. He never stood again, and sought to deter his eldest son William from accepting nomination for Westmorland in 1696, though he had taken the oaths to the new regime. He died on 25 Mar. 1701, and was buried at Grasmere. His son represented the county in three Parliaments as a court Whig, and was rewarded with a baronetcy in 1705.[5]

[1] *Fleming Mems.* (Cumb. and Westmld. Antiq. and Arch. Soc. Tracts, xi), 73–76. [2] Ibid. 78–79; *HMC Le Fleming*, 27, 96, 174, 210, 355, 372, 378, 401–3; *CSP Dom.* 1673–5, p. 246; Eg. 1626, f. 7; Westmld. RO, D/Ry1124. [3] *Fleming Mems.* 5–6, 71–77. [4] Wotton, *Baronetage*, iv. 20; *HMC Le Fleming*, 31–32, 44, 168–9, 174; *CSP Dom.* 1670, p. 60; 1673–5, p. 521. 1681, p. 285. [5] *HMC Le Fleming*, 209, 343, 401, 403; *HMC Kenyon*, 225.

G.H./E.C.

FLEMING, Edward (c.1653–1700) of North Stoneham, nr. Southampton.

SOUTHAMPTON   25 Nov.–31 Dec. 1689

b. c.1653, 1st s. of Edward Fleming of North Stoneham by Katherine, da. of Edward Hooper of Boveridge, Dorset. *educ.* M. Temple 1672. *m.* lic. 16 Nov. 1672, 'aged 23', Margaret, da. of Thomas Bland, Scrivener, of London, 3s. 2da. *suc.* fa. 1664.[1]

J.p. Hants by 1680–Apr. 1688, 1690–*d.*, dep. lt. 1682–Apr. 1688; verderer, New Forest 1686; freeman, Lymington 1686; sheriff, Hants 1688–9, commr. for assessment 1689–90.[2]

Fleming's great-grandfather, a lawyer from the Isle of Wight, sat for Winchester in three Elizabethan Parliaments and bought the manor of North Stoneham in 1595. He subsequently sat for the county and for Southampton before becoming a judge. Fleming's father was too young to take part in the Civil War, but held local office both under the Protectorate and after the Restoration. Fleming himself was probably a Tory since he remained in local office during the exclusion crisis. In 1688 he returned negative answers to the first and second questions on the repeal of the Test Act and Penal Laws, and was removed from local office, but pricked as sheriff after the landing of William of Orange. An American observer reported that he was a candidate at the Hampshire by-election in February 1689, but it is probable that he was only acting as returning officer. After the expiry of his term of office he was returned to the Convention for Southampton on the freeman franchise, but unseated on petition without making any speeches or serving on any committees. He died in 1700, aged 47. His son sat for Southampton as a Tory from 1710 to 1722.[3]

[1] Berry, *Hants Genealogies*, 126; PCC 165 Carr. [2] *CSP Dom.* 1682, p. 81; 1685, p. 144; C. St. Barbe, *Recs. of Lymington*, 10. [3] *VCH Hants*, iii. 479; v. 151, 256; G. N. Godwin, *Civil War in Hants*, 5; *N. and Q.* (ser. 10), ix. 496.

P.W.

FLETCHER, Sir George, 2nd Bt. (c.1633–1700), of Hutton Hall, Hutton-in-the-Forest, Cumb.

CUMBERLAND   1661, 1681, 1689, 1690, 1695, 1698–23 July 1700

b. c.1633, 2nd but o. surv. s. of Sir Henry Fletcher, 1st Bt., of Hutton by Catherine, da. of Sir George Dalston† of Dalston. *educ.* Queen's, Oxf. 1651. *m.* (1) 27 Feb. 1655, Alice, da. of Hugh, 1st Baron Coleraine [I], of Longford Castle, Wilts., 2s. (1 *d.v.p.*) 3da.; (2) c.1664, Lady Mary Johnston, da. of James, 1st Earl of Hartfell [S], wid. of Sir George Grahme, 2nd Bt., of Netherby, Cumb., 2s. 2da. *suc.* fa. 24 Sept. 1645.[1]

Sheriff, Cumb. 1657–8, 1679–80; commr. for assessment, Cumb. 1657, Aug. 1660–80, Westmld. 1661–3, 1673–80, co. Dur. 1666–9, Cumb. and Westmld. 1689–90, militia, Cumb. Mar. 1660; j.p. Cumb. Mar. 1660–80, 1681–May 1688, Oct. 1688–*d.*, Westmld. Mar. 1660–*d.*, dep. lt. Cumb. c. Aug. 1660–80, Cumb. 1681–Feb. 1688, Westmld. 1685–Feb. 1688, Cumb. and Westmld. Oct. 1688–*d.*; capt. of militia horse, Cumb. and Westmld. Oct. 1660, col. of ft. by 1663–80, 1683–Feb. 1688, Oct. 1688–*d.*; alderman, Carlisle 1662–87, mayor 1671–2; commr. for oyer and terminer, Northern circuit 1665, charitable uses, Westmld. 1670, recusants, Cumb. and Westmld. 1675; asst. Linen Corp. 1690.[2]

Fletcher was the grandson of a wealthy Cockermouth merchant, who bought Hutton in 1605. His father raised a regiment for Charles I at the outbreak of the Civil War and was killed at the battle of Rowton Heath, whereupon he was himself imprisoned for a time in Carlisle Castle. His mother compounded for the estates on a fine of £764. This seems to have been lenient, for his inheritance included Hutton, described as 'a prince-like palace', Calder Abbey, and much other property. Under the Protectorate he was appointed to the assessment commission, but declined nomination as knight of the shire in 1659. His record placed him outside the scope of the Long Parliament ordinance against the candidature of Cavaliers' sons in 1660, but he was defeated by Sir Wilfred Lawson* after a bitter contest.[3]

At the general election of 1661 Fletcher defeated Sir William Huddleston, a prominent Cavalier, and became the first of his family to enter Parliament. An inactive Member, he was appointed to only 19 committees in the Cavalier Parliament, including the elections committee in seven sessions, and was three times listed among the defaulters. His most important committee was for restoring bishops to the House of Lords, a matter in which his stepfather, Thomas Smith, was eventually to have a personal interest. Although Lord Wharton listed him as a moderate and he took no part in the Clarendon Code, as a j.p. he was severe on Quakers, whose refusal of tithe threatened his interests as lay impropriator of Brigham rectory, the mother church of Cockermouth. On the other hand, he was one of the Cumberland magistrates accused of trying 'to make themselves popular' by a narrow interpretation of the hearth-tax and stopping the collectors from distraining for arrears. He was elected mayor of Carlisle by a single vote in 1670, and Smith's appointment as dean two years later strengthened his interest there at the expense of Sir Philip Musgrave*, who complained that Fletcher

> for many years has endeavoured to contrive a jealousy between my Lord Carlisle [Charles Howard*] and me, that by my lord's countenance he might make himself head of a faction in this county and Carlisle in opposition to my family and myself.

In the 1673 session he was added to the committee to prevent abuses in parliamentary elections. Meanwhile Lord Carlisle tried to reconcile him with Musgrave, but was 'ill put to it betwixt us'. Sir Richard Wiseman* in 1676 recommended approaching Fletcher through Lord Ogle (Henry Cavendish*), but he twice acted as host to the Scottish covenanting peer, Lord Cassilis, and Shaftesbury marked him 'doubly worthy'. He was among those instructed to summarize foreign commitments on 30 Apr. 1678, but failed to attend the final session, and on 25 Jan. 1679 he wrote to his brother-in-law Daniel Fleming*: 'I intend to be a spectator next Parliament'.[4]

Fletcher's temporary retirement from politics may have been due to a serious quarrel with Lord Carlisle. The reasons for their estrangement are not clear, but may be connected with the seizure on a warrant signed by Fletcher and Sir John Lowther III* of 18 Irish cattle illegally imported by Carlisle's son, Lord Morpeth (Edward Howard*). Relations were no doubt exacerbated by the imposition on him of the burdensome office of sheriff, which he had already filled during the Commonwealth, and in 1680 he was deprived of his militia commission and removed from the lieutenancy and the bench. He was befriended by (Sir) Christopher Musgrave*, who needed Fletcher's 'country interest' to supplement his own interest at Court. In 1681 he had the satisfaction of displacing Morpeth as knight of the shire. He set out for Oxford, where he had the promise of a room in his old college, on 5 Mar., but his intended route was circuitous and there is no evidence that he took his seat before the dissolution. His standing at Court improved, and through his step-son, James Grahme*, and George Legge* the King was brought to intervene personally in his dispute with Lord Carlisle. The settlement restoring Fletcher to office after a formal apology was humiliating to his opponent, who protested vainly:

> I am apprehensive that the manner of carrying this business will give this gentleman's vanity the opportunity of bragging that he has carried this matter over my belly, my authority given him being public, his acknowledgment private.

Together with Musgrave he secured the surrender of the Carlisle charter in 1683, and was appointed to the remodelled corporation.[5]

On 10 Feb. 1685 Musgrave wrote that he supposed Fletcher would stand for re-election to James II's Parliament,

> for it is most absolutely necessary that he takes this opportunity to express his duty to the King, for, if he should decline it, he would gratify his enemies and disable his friends from serving him.

But Fletcher was obdurate, refusing to stand himself or to allow his son to stand for Cockermouth. 'That which weighs most with me is the charge and attendance', he wrote, 'for if it be a good Parliament, it may be a long one, if an ill one, short, and in neither case I would be in. They [that] are upon the place, and have convenience so, cannot judge of the prejudice it is to a country gentleman.' Instead, he recommended his eldest step-son, Lord Preston (Sir Richard Grahme*), who was returned. But to Preston's questions on the repeal of the Test Act and Penal Laws in 1687 he replied:

> It is humbly my opinion that the first question is more proper for the consideration of a Parliament than a private meeting of country gentlemen, who, not having liberty to debate, are unable to arrive at a true understanding of the conveniences or inconveniences that may attend this question; but whenever his Majesty shall be pleased to call a Parliament, if the gentry and freeholders of this county will do me the honour to let me serve them as one of their Members, I shall endeavour to discharge my duty to my God, my King and country as well as my conscience and judgment can direct me.... Wherever I am an elector, and that such persons are present with whom I think I may with confidence trust my religion, liberty and property, they shall freely be my choice.... I have ever been of the King's opinion that conscience ought not to be forced, and when I was a Member of Parliament did act accordingly.

He was again removed from the lieutenancy. In October 1688 he and Musgrave rode into Carlisle at the head of a great cavalcade with the restored charter; but they refused to co-operate with Lowther in calling out the militia in December, and secured the peaceful withdrawal of the Roman Catholic officers. He stood in conjunction with Sir John Lowther II*, at the general election of 1689 and was 'quietly elected'. He had passed York on his way to London by 22 Jan., but left no trace on the records of the Convention, except for an application for leave for six weeks on 6 May 'to settle the militia'. His acceptance of this command was regarded as a sign of his 'great affection to the

Government'. He continued to sit for the county as a court Whig for the rest of his life. He died on 23 July 1700, aged 67, leaving an estate of £1,500 p.a., and was buried at Hutton. According to his epitaph, composed by his daughter, he was

an affectionate husband and an indulgent father, careful of his children's education, regular in his own life and conversation; pious without affectation, and free without vanity, charitable, hospitable, and eminently just; so great a patriot to his country that he was chosen knight of the shire of Cumberland near forty years; much beloved in his lifetime and much lamented at his death.[6]

[1] Hutchinson, *Cumb.* i. 507; *Flemings in Oxford* (Oxf. Hist. Soc. xliv), 358. [2] *HMC Le Fleming*, 170, 174, 181, 212; SP29/445/115; *CSP Dom. Add.* 1660–70, p. 683; 1680–1, p. 362; Jan.–June 1683, pp. 202, 241; Eg. 1626, f. 7; S. Jefferson, *Hist. Carlisle*, 447; Westmld. RO, D/Ry 1124; *Sel. Charters* (Selden Soc. xxviii), 213. [3] Hutchinson, i. 508; *Cal. Comm. Comp.* 1662; Sandford, *Antiqs. and Fams. in Cumb.* 39; *CSP Dom.* 1658–9, p. 247; 1659–60, p. 415; *HMC Le Fleming*, 24. [4] *CSP Dom.* 1660–1, p. 515; 1666–7, p. 145; 1667, pp. 3, 142; 1675–6, pp. 268–9, 489, 573; 1676–7, p. 418; 1678, p. 5; *HMC Le Fleming*, 152; Westmld. RO, D/Ry 2122. [5] *CSP Dom.* 1677–8, p. 415; Jan.–June 1683, pp. 177, 192, 230; Westmld. RO, D/Ry 2285, Fletcher to Fleming, 18 July 1679; *HMC Le Fleming*, 170–1, 191; *Flemings in Oxford* (Oxf. Hist. Soc. lxii), 8, 307. [6] Westmld. RO, D/Ry 2847, 2853, Musgrave to Fleming, 10, 16 Feb. 1685; 2855, Fletcher to Fleming, 16 Feb.; 2857, Lowry to Fleming, 17 Feb.; 3244, 3464, Lowther to Fleming, 4 Aug. 1688, 4 Apr. 1689; Lowther, *Mems.* 52; *HMC Le Fleming*, 223, 234; Hutchinson, i. 509, 512.

M.W.H./E.C.

FLETCHER, Henry (1661–1712), of Hutton Hall, Cumb.

COCKERMOUTH   1689

b. Apr. 1661, 2nd but 1st surv. s. of Sir George Fletcher, 2nd Bt.*, by 1st w.; half-bro. of George Fletcher†. *educ.* Queen's, Oxf. 1678–9. *unm. suc.* fa. as 3rd Bt. 23 July 1700.[1]

Alderman, Carlisle 1684–7, mayor 1687–Mar. 1688; lt. of militia horse, Cumb. by 1685–9, capt. 1689–at least 1690, commr. for assessment 1689–90.[2]

Fletcher was 'civil and studious' during his year at Oxford, distinguishing himself by 'his abundant kindness to his countrymen'. His father refused to let him stand in 1685 for Cockermouth, where the family owned much property, but in July 1687 he wrote to his uncle, Sir Daniel Fleming*: 'I have been staying at Cockermouth, my father wishing me to stand for Parliament for that place'. Like his father he probably opposed James II's religious policy, and was removed from the Carlisle corporation. He was returned for Cockermouth at the general election of 1689. He attended the coronation of William and Mary, but he was totally inactive in the Convention. At the general election of 1690 he supported the candidature of (Sir) Christopher Musgrave* for Westmorland, but, 'falling into a languor and melancholy state of mind', he did not stand again himself, though he entertained lavishly on behalf of his half-brother George, who was returned for Cockermouth in 1698 and sat for the county from 1701 till his death. After succeeding to the baronetcy he settled his estates on a distant cousin of the Moresby branch, declared himself a Roman Catholic and retired to the Benedictine monastery at Douai. The baronetcy became extinct at his death on 19 May 1712.[3]

[1] *Vis. Cumb. and Westmld.* ed. Foster, 49; *Flemings in Oxford* (Oxf. Hist. Soc. xliv), 305, 405, 557. [2] *HMC 9th Rep.* pt. 1, p. 199; R. S. Ferguson, *Royal Charters of Carlisle*, 274; S. Jefferson, *Hist. Carlisle*, 447; PC2/72/651; Westmld. RO, D/Ry 2832, 4077. [3] *Flemings at Oxford* (Oxf. Hist. Soc. xliv), 239, 297; Westmld. RO, D/Ry 2858, Musgrave to Fleming, 21 Feb. 1685; Hutchinson, *Cumb.* i. 509.

G.H.

FLOYD see LLOYD, Sir Richard I

FLYNT, Thomas (c.1614–70), of Allesley, nr. Coventry, Warws. and Gray's Inn.

COVENTRY   1661–28 Aug. 1670

b. c.1614, 1st s. of William Flynt of Allesley. *educ.* G. Inn 1632, called 1637, ancient 1654. *m.* (1) 15 Oct. 1641, Anne, da. of John Thornton of Brookhall, Northants., *s.p.*; (2) Martha, da. of Humphrey Greswold of Greet, Worcs., 1s. (posth.). *suc.* fa. aft. 1632.[1]

J.p. Warws. July 1660–*d.*, commr. for assessment, Warws. Aug. 1660–9, Coventry 1664–9; bencher, G. Inn 1661, reader 1665; recorder, Tamworth 1664–*d.*[2] Serjeant-at-law 1669–*d.*

Flynt, the grandson of a prosperous but illiterate Warwickshire yeoman, became a lawyer, and by 1652 had purchased and enclosed the manor on which he was born. He took no part in the Civil War, but presumably he welcomed the Restoration, when he was proposed as a knight of the Royal Oak with an income of £700 p.a. He assisted the corporation of Coventry to apply for a new lease of Cheylesmore Park, and was returned for the borough, two miles from his home, at the general election of 1661. But he was not active in the Cavalier Parliament, being nominated to only 24 committees. Half of them were in the first session, including those to bring in the bill against schismatics and to consider the corporations bill. He was made a serjeant-at-law in 1669, when Sir Thomas Osborne* included him among the Members who had usually voted for supply. But on 22 Nov. a complaint was made to the House that, as recorder of Tamworth, he was responsible for delaying a by-election by detaining the writ, and he was formally reprimanded. He died at Allesley on 28 Aug. 1670, having 'lain for some time ill of a feverish distemper, much heightened by violent pains of the stone. . . . 'Tis thought the serjeant has left £10,000 debts, which all his estate will scarce satisfy.' His financial problems were due to his extravagant life-style, notably the new house that he had built in Allesley Park. He was the only member of his family to sit in Parliament.[3]

[1] Dugdale, *Warws.* 131; *VCH Northants. Fams.* 305. [2] C. F. Palmer, *Hist. Tamworth*, p. xxiv. [3] *VCH Warws.* vi. 4; PCC 97 Savile; Add. 29265, f. 20; T. W. Whitley, *Parl. Rep. Coventry*, 103; SP29/278/61, 279/75.

A.M.M.

FOLEY, Paul (c.1645–99), of Stoke Edith, Herefs.

HEREFORD   1679 (Mar.), 1679 (Oct.), 1681, 1689, 1690, 1695, 1698–13 Nov. 1699

b. c.1645, 2nd s. of Thomas Foley I*, and bro. of Philip Foley* and Thomas Foley II*. *educ.* Magdalen Hall, Oxf. matric. 19 June 1662, aged 17; I. Temple 1662, called 1669. *m.* lic. 25 Mar. 1668, Mary, da. of John Lane, Clothworker, of Lawrence Pountney Lane, London, 2s.[1]

Member, Society of Mines Royal 1666, asst. 1667–78; member, Society of Mineral and Battery Works 1666, asst. 1673–87; commr. for public accounts 1691–7.[2]

Commr. for assessment, Glos. and Herefs. 1673–80, Hereford 1679–80, Herefs. and Hereford 1689–90, I. Temple 1690; freeman, Bewdley 1673; j.p. Herefs. 1675–80, Mar. 1688–d.; bencher, I. Temple 1687; dep. lt. Herefs. 1689–d.[3]

Speaker of House of Commons 14 Mar. 1695–7 July 1698.

'A learned, though not a practising lawyer', Foley was well versed in constitutional precedent. In 1670 he bought Stoke Edith, six miles from Hereford, from the heirs of Sir Henry Lingen*, though much of his income must have come from his share in the family business. On the false report of the death of Ranald Grahme* in the following year, he was proposed as country candidate for Leominster, John Birch* 'extolling his wealth and bounty in works of charity'. He was acceptable to the dissenters, employing ejected ministers as tutors for his children, and may have been a Presbyterian himself. He again thought of standing in 1675, this time for Weobley, but soon desisted. It was at his house that the local opponents of the Court heard his chaplain deliver a scathing attack on the bishops as a 'dead weight' in the House of Lords, and laid their plans for the next election. Foley was himself nominated for Hereford, which he represented in all three Exclusion Parliaments.[4]

Foley was classed as 'honest' on Shaftesbury's list in 1679, and was not long in making his mark in the first Exclusion Parliament. He was appointed by full name to eight committees, including the committee of elections and privileges, but he was probably very active, with as many as 29 in all. He made eight speeches, 'communicating his observations on the learning of records, to which he applied himself very closely', and was described as 'one newly started up into great vogue in that House'. His probable committees included those to bring in bills for regulating elections, prohibiting the import of Irish cattle, and security against Popery. He helped to draft the address for the removal of Lauderdale (6 May) and to prepare reasons for a conference on the appointment of a lord high steward to preside at the trial of the lords in the Tower. He served on a joint committee to make arrangements for the trial. Most of his speeches were on this subject, but he also spoke in the exclusion debate to assert that it was constitutional to alter the succession, though he was not sanguine about the result:

> The question is now, whether there can be any other way to secure religion than what is proposed. I have observed what has been proposed another way, and had I received any satisfaction in matter of religion, I might possibly have closed with it. . . . Do what you can, all may come to blood, but you will secure the Protestant religion by making the Duke incapable to succession by Act of Parliament.

He duly voted for the committal of the bill. Barillon, who credited him with drafting the bill, described him as an Independent and a republican, and rewarded him with 300 guineas for his services to France.[5]

Again very active in the second Exclusion Parliament, Foley may have served on up to 50 committees, and made 16 speeches. He served on the committee to inquire into abhorring, helped to draw up the second exclusion bill and to manage a conference on the Irish plot. He was on the drafting committees for four addresses, including that for the removal of Lord Halifax, whom he violently attacked as guilty by common fame of advising the dissolution of the previous Parliament. He was among those ordered to prepare the impeachment of Edward Seymour*; nor did he spare his own kinsman Francis North*, allegedly accusing him 'of arbitrary principles, because he had heard him discourse to that purpose at his own table', and moving for his impeachment. On 15 Dec. 1680 he declared ominously: 'I would enable the Protestants to defend themselves against the Papists, or any in their behalf', and he was named to the committee to prepare bills for security against arbitrary power. He was among those ordered on 21 Dec. to consider the bill for uniting Protestants and to bring in a bill correcting ecclesiastical pluralities. Showing remarkable prescience of the form to be taken by the Government's counter-attack on its leading opponents, he warned the House that 'men have been fined, not according to their crimes, but their principles', and he was the first Member appointed to the committees to bring in and to consider a bill to prevent arbitrary fines. In the debate on exclusion on 7 Jan. 1681 he said:

> The King proposed expedients the last Parliament but offers none now. If the King were not biased [by his counsellors] he is confident the King would be convinced. . . . I propose that in his Majesty's presence we debate this exclusion, etc. with the Lords whether any expedient can be found in this matter.

He made no speeches in the Oxford Parliament but was appointed to the elections committee, and to those to recommend a more convenient place for the House to meet, to prepare for a conference on the loss of the bill of ease for dissenters, to impeach Fitzharris, and to bring in the third exclusion bill.[6]

The new charter of 1682 broke Foley's interest at Hereford for a time. In view of his public prognostication of bloodshed and civil war, it is not surprising that he was soon afterwards accused of complicity with (Sir) Edward Harley*, Thomas Coningsby* and John Dutton Colt* in a plot to take over the Herefordshire militia. But no proceedings were taken against him and he remained at liberty until Monmouth's invasion. He was then put under restraint, and on release left the county. Harley, his closest political associate, wrote on 16 Oct. 1685: 'Our friends at Stoke went Monday last towards Oxford, all household broke up, stock dispersed, iron works set for seven years at £500 p.a. rent. The stock sold for £9,000.' During his residence at Oxford he attended the proceedings of the ecclesiastical commission against Magdalen, and witnessed the severity of Sir Thomas Jenner*. He was listed by Danby among the eminent Members of Parliament hostile to James II, but great efforts were made to win him over, for he was made a j.p. in February 1688 and licensed to empark Stoke Edith in June. Although not approved as a court candidate, by September he was sure of regaining his seat. As his mother was to write a few months later: 'I think he hath as great an interest as any man in a regular way can have'. He subscribed £50 to the loan to the Prince of Orange, and was duly returned at the general election of 1689.[7]

Foley was a very active and prominent Member of the Convention. He may have been appointed to 128 committees, taking the chair in seven, and made 35 recorded speeches. He was named to the committee to draw up a list of the essentials for securing religion, law and liberties, and helped to manage the conference of 5 Feb. on the state of the throne. On 22 Feb. he reported the bill to remove all questions and disputes about the status of the Convention and returned it to the Lords. He probably took the initiative over continuing legal actions and reviving expiring laws, since his name stands first on both committees. He was appointed to the committee for the suspension of habeas corpus, and delivered two reports on the authors and advisers of grievances. On matters of local concern, he brought in the Wye and Lugg navigation bill on 15 Mar. and was appointed to the committee on the bill for abolishing the court of the marches. He was named to the committees for the first mutiny bill, the bill of rights, and the new oaths of supremacy and allegiance, to which he was again the first Member appointed. On 1 Apr. he was among those ordered to prepare the repeal of the Corporations Act and to bring in a bill for religious comprehension. He chaired the committees responsible for making arrangements for the House to attend the coronation, and for a local estate bill. He served on the committee for the toleration bill and helped to manage a conference. He was among those ordered to conduct the inquiry into the delay in relieving Londonderry. He disliked the Lords' amendments to the bill of rights, declaring: 'Here is a power in the bill vested in the Privy Council to declare that the next heir shall inherit the crown'. On 22 June he reported the bill to annul the attainder of the Whig martyr, Alderman Cornish, and returned it to the Lords. He was teller with Thomas Coningsby* against the adjournment of the debate on the Wye and Lugg bill on 4 July. Foley's father-in-law had sat on the common council of London for ten years, and he was probably responsible for bringing the malversation of the orphans fund to the attention of the House, since he was the first Member appointed to a committee to bring in a bill for stricter control. He was added on 24 July to the committee to prepare reasons for disagreeing with the Lords about Titus Oates, and reported a fortnight later. With John Hawles* he was ordered to bring in a bill for security against Jacobites. He also helped to prepare reasons for a conference on reserving the power of the spiritual courts in the tithe bill.[8]

After the recess Foley was the first Member appointed to the committee for restraining expenditure at elections, no doubt in consequence of the defeat of the Whig candidate for the other Hereford seat by electors 'not willing to make choice without money'. He was sent to the Lords on 26 Oct. to impeach the Earls of Salisbury and Peterborough as Roman Catholic converts. After a debate on the ill usage of prisoners in Newgate and other gaols, he was appointed to a committee to prepare a bill for the better regulation of imprisonment. On the following morning he brought in a bill 'for establishing the rights of the subject', and carried it to the Lords a week later. On 7 Nov. he delivered a report on the miscarriages of the war. He acted as teller for an address to inquire who was responsible for recommending Commissary Shales, and was appointed to the committee to draft it. On 2 Dec. he told the House: 'It is impossible the King and kingdom should be safe as long as persons are in Council that have sat in King James's Council'. On 10 Dec. he carried up the bill of rights and succession; but, like his brother Thomas, he was veering towards the country Opposition. He was named to the committee of inquiry into the state of the revenue on 14 Dec., and moved for 'an humble representation to the King that things may be managed more to the satisfaction of the people'. He was appointed to the committees to draft an address for provision for Princess Anne and to consider the bill for restoring corporations. At the importunity of his constituents he acted as teller for excluding Hereford from the bill; but he supported the disabling clause.

> It was endeavoured, the last two reigns, to pack a Parliament to subvert all our constitutions. . . . We have ill ministers, and they are concerned that the same thing may be done again. Men have done all they can to annihilate their corporations, and we must not annihilate but restore these men! If there be any in corporations who are sorry for what they have done, they will take this for a very merciful proviso, that they may do no more mischief to corporations and to the King. Therefore, retain this proviso.[9]

Foley continued to sit for Hereford till his death. During the next Parliament he became leader of the country Whigs, his heavy eloquence, unadorned with wit or sparkle, commending him to the backbenchers. He was elected Speaker in 1695 and died of gangrene on 11 Nov. 1699. His son Thomas succeeded to an estate of £4,000 p.a. as well as to the Hereford seat. But his political heir was his son-in-law, Robert Harley II*.[10]

[1] *Vis. Worcs.* ed. Metcalfe, 47; J. R. Woodhead, *Rulers of London*, 105. [2] BL Loan 16; *Cal. Treas. Bks.* ix. 1080; xii. 266. [3] *Univ. Birmingham Hist. Jnl.* i. 109. [4] Burnet ed. Routh, iii. 197; *DNB*; *Econ. Hist. Rev.* (ser. 2), iv. 326; BL Loan 29/79, Thomas to Sir Edward Harley, 12 Jan. 1671; 29/49, Williams to Harley, 25 Feb. 1675; D. R. Lacey, *Dissent and Parl. Pols.* 395; *CSP Dom.* 1675–6, pp. 460–1. [5] *HMC Ormonde*, n.s. v. 97; Grey, vii. 256, 300; *CJ*, ix. 620; PRO31/3, bdle. 146, f. 27v; Dalrymple, *Mems.* i. 383. [6] *CJ*, ix. 648, 655, 656, 696; Grey, viii. 48, 67, 159, 228, 273; North, *Lives*, i. 193; *HMC 12th Rep. IX*, 111. [7] SP29/417/88; *CSP Dom.* 1682, p. 425; 1687–9, p. 211; BL Loan 29/140, Sir Edward to Robert Harley, 16 Oct. 1685; 29/75, Mary Foley to Harley, 10 May 1689; 29/184/120; Grey, ix. 395; *HMC Portland*, iii. 385, 411. [8] *CJ*, x. 20, 51, 82, 89, 143, 156, 254; Grey, ix. 351. [9] BL Loan 29/75, Mary Foley to Sir Edward Harley, 10 May 1689; *CJ*, x. 276, 280, 296, 322; Grey, ix. 422, 473, 480–1, 517–18; R. Morrice, Entering Bk. 3, p. 73. [10] Feiling, *Tory Party*, 311–12; M.I.

E.R.

FOLEY, Philip (1648–by 1716), of Prestwood, Kingswinford, Staffs.

BEWDLEY	1679 (Mar.), 1679 (Oct.), 1681
STAFFORD	1689
DROITWICH	1690
STAFFORD	1695, 1698
DROITWICH	25 Feb. 1701

bap. 12 May 1648, 4th but 3rd surv. s. of Thomas Foley I*, and bro. of Paul Foley* and Thomas Foley II*. *m.* Penelope, da. of William, 6th Lord Paget, 4s. (2 *d.v.p.*) 7da.[1]

Freeman, Bewdley 1675; commr. for assessment, Staffs. and Worcs. 1679–80, Staffs. 1689–1713; j.p. and dep. lt. Staffs. 1689–?*d.*[2]

Member, Society of Mines Royal 1690.[3]

Foley was an active partner in the family iron business, with works in seven counties. His father bought the manor of Prestwood about 1670 and settled it on him. A strong Presbyterian, he was a friend to Philip Henry and a patron to other nonconformist ministers. He sat for the family borough of Bewdley in the Exclusion Parliaments, and was classed as 'honest' by Shaftesbury. With his elder brothers also in the House, the only committee that can be definitely ascribed to him is on the bill for security against Popery, to which he was added on 7 May 1679; but he voted for the committal of the first exclusion bill. He is unlikely to have stood in 1685, but became a Whig collaborator later in James II's reign.[4]

Foley was returned for Stafford in 1689. A moderately active Member of the Convention, he was appointed by full name to 23 committees, including the committee of elections and privileges in both sessions. With his brothers, he was named to the committee on the bill to regulate the Droitwich salt-works. His most important committees were to inquire into the delay in relieving Londonderry and to reverse the quo warranto judgment against London. He supported the disabling clause in the bill to restore corporations, and was obliged to transfer himself to Droitwich at the general election of 1690. Like the rest of his family he was a country Whig in the next two Parliaments, signing the Association in 1696. He did not sit in the next reign, though he continued to be named to the Staffordshire tax commission until 1713. His will was proved on 21 Dec. 1716. The Prestwood branch produced no more Members of Parliament.[5]

[1] Guildhall RO, St. Peter-le-Poer par. reg.; Shaw, *Staffs.* ii. 235. [2] *Univ. Birmingham Hist. Jnl.* i. 110; *Staffs. Dep. Lts.* (Wm. Salt Arch. Soc. 1931), 285. [3] BL Loan 16. [4] *Worcs. Arch. Soc.* n.s. xxvii. 35–37; *Econ. Hist. Rev.* (ser. 2), iv. 326; PCC 136 Fox; Shaw, ii. 234; D. R. Lacey, *Dissent and Parl. Pols.* 395–6; R. Morrice, Entering Bk. 2, pp. 176–7. [5] PCC 136 Fox.

E.R./G.J.

FOLEY, Robert (c.1651–1702), of Stourbridge, Worcs.

GRAMPOUND   1685

> b. c.1651, o.s. of Robert Foley of Stourbridge by 1st w. Anne, da. of John Blurton of Worcester. *educ.* Magdalen Hall, Oxf. 1668; I. Temple 1670. *m.* 16 Feb. 1675 (with £1,500), Anne (d. 4 Apr. 1717), da. of Dudley North I*, 4th Lord North, 4s. 1da. *suc.* fa. 1676.[1]
>
> Member, Hon. Artillery Co. 1673; alderman, Bewdley 1685–?d.; j.p. Worcs. 1685–?86, July 1688–d., commr. for assessment 1689.[2]
>
> Marshal to Sir Francis North* 1675–82; sec. of presentations in Chancery 1682–5.[3]

After the Restoration Foley's father, the brother of Thomas Foley I*, became the chief supplier of ironmongery to the navy and receiver-general of aids in Worcestershire; but by 1674 his financial affairs were in considerable disorder, partly because the Government had failed to pay his bills. A marriage was accordingly arranged for Foley on the basis of a £1,500 portion and a jointure of £400 p.a., nearly three times the standard rate. The bride's brother, Roger North*, wrote that:

> The old father fancied that a friend at Court, so considerable as his lordship [Sir Francis North] was, might be useful, which, together with his lordship's skill in dealing with such a touchy spark, drew a full consent to all. The young man was every way acceptable, and, left to himself, would not have chosen one that was fifteen years older than he was. But finding that his father by negligence, sottishness, and desperate projects was in a fair way to utter ruin, he was glad upon any terms to get the estate settled.

The marriage proved fortunate for Foley. He acted as marshal to his brother-in-law 'which brought in pence' and obviated the necessity of keeping house. When North became Lord Keeper Guilford in 1682 Foley was made 'secretary to the presentations worth (honestly) near £300 a year'. But 'what surmounted all' in Roger North's opinion, was the help Guilford was able to give Foley both

> with his purse, as well as advice and countenance, in working through a most perplexed administration of his father's personal estate. The old man died without a will; and his great dealings of divers kinds [were] all in confusion.

With the help of his brothers-in-law, Foley eventually managed to straighten out his father's affairs, although the appointment of Sir Dudley North II* to the Treasury in 1684 did not suffice to secure priority for his claims on the navy.[4]

Foley was returned for Grampound as a placeman in 1685 on Guilford's recommendation. A moderately active Member of James II's Parliament, he was named to seven committees of no great political importance, including those to consider expiring laws and the bills for the speedier recovery of tithe and the suppression of simony. He lost office with Guilford's death in September, but he petitioned for interest on the £683 due to him for ironwork supplied to the navy. His name appeared on the list of dissenters to be added to the Worcestershire commission of the peace in May 1688, and he was retained after the Revolution at the King's command, though he never stood again. He died on 27 Sept. 1702, aged 51, and was buried at Old Swinford. None of his descendants entered Parliament.[5]

[1] Nash, *Worcs.* ii. 465; Westminster City Lib., St. Martin in the Fields par. reg. [2] *Ancient Vellum Bk.* ed. Raikes, 102; *Univ. Birmingham Hist. Jnl.* i. 112. [3] North, *Lives*, i. 404. [4] Ibid. i. 403–4; ii. 234; Nash, ii. 465; *The Gen.* ii. 37–38; *Cal. Treas. Bks.* vi. 751; vii. 263. [5] North, i. 335; *Cal. Treas. Bks.* viii. 540, 961; *CSP Dom.* 1689–90, p. 145; Nash, ii. 212.

P.W.

FOLEY, Thomas I (1617–77), of Witley Court, Worcs.

WORCESTERSHIRE   1659
BEWDLEY   1660, 7 Nov. 1673–10 Mar. 1677

> b. 3 Dec. 1617, 3rd s. of Richard Foley (d.1657), ironmaster, of Stourbridge, being 2nd but 1st surv. s. by 2nd w. Alice, da. of William Brindley of Willenhall, Staffs. *m.* bef. 1641, Anne, da. and h. of John Browne, gunfounder, of Spelmonden, Kent, 4s. (1 *d.v.p.*) 2da.[1]
>
> Dep. gov. Society of Mineral and Battery Works 1647–75, treas. 1657–76; member, Society of Mines Royal 1653, treas. 1654–76, dep. gov. 1658–76; member, corp. for propagation of the gospel in New England 1661.[2]
>
> Commr. for assessment, Staffs, 1649–52, Worcs. 1657, Aug. 1660–3, 1664–74; j.p. Staffs. 1650–3, Worcs. 1657–July 1660, 1662–d.; commr. for scandalous ministers, Worcs. 1654, militia Mar. 1660; freeman, Portsmouth 1665; commr. for recusants, Worcs. 1675.[3]

Foley's father, who established the family fortune, moved to Stourbridge about 1630, where he set up slitting mills and obtained a virtual monopoly of nail-making in the West Midlands. He seems to have preserved neutrality during the Civil War, though his sympathies were royalist and he supplied ordnance to the King's armies. Foley himself is not known to have taken part in the war, but he was a friend of the Presbyterian divine Baxter, and during the Interregnum he secured valuable naval ordnance contracts and was appointed to county office. 'A religious, faithful man', according to Baxter, 'of unquestioned fidelity and honesty', he bought Witley in 1655 and represented the county in Richard Cromwell's Parliament, the first of the family to sit.[4]

Foley was defeated in the Worcestershire election in 1660, but he was returned for Bewdley, some five miles from Witley. An inactive Member of the

Convention, he was appointed to 11 committees. In his only recorded speech he opposed the exception of the Independent preacher Nye from the benefits of the bill of indemnity. His committees included those to prepare the excise and custom bills, to settle ecclesiastical livings and to prevent profanity. He did not stand in 1661, but defeated Henry Herbert* at a by-election in 1673. His position was vulnerable to charges of bribery, however, and there is no evidence that he ever sat in the Cavalier Parliament, though it was not until the 1677 session that his seat was awarded to his opponent on petition. He died on 1 Oct. and was buried at Witley.[5]

[1] *The Gen.* vi. 119–20; *Vis. Worcs.* ed. Metcalfe, 46–47. [2] BL Loan 16; PC2/55/217. [3] R. East, *Portsmouth Recs.* 358. [4] *Trans. Worcs. Arch. Soc.* n.s. xxi. 2–5; *CSP Dom.* 1645–7, p. 4; 1652–3, p. 486; 1659–60, p. 529; *VCH Worcs.* iv. 372; M. Sylvester, *Reliquiae Baxterianae*, pt. 2, p. 93. [5] *HMC 5th Rep.* 299–300; *HMC Laing*, i. 311; *Cal. Cl. SP*, iv. 642; Bowman diary, f. 9; R. Warner, *Epistolary Curiosities of the Herbert Fam.* 97–98, 100–103; *CJ*, ix. 293, 397; *CSP Dom.* 1677–8, pp. 8, 11; *Vis. Worcs.* 46.

M.W.H./E.R./G.J.

FOLEY, Thomas II (c.1641–1701), of Witley Court, Worcs.

WORCESTERSHIRE 1679 (Mar.), 1679 (Oct.), 1681, 1689, 1690, 1695

DROITWICH 14 Jan. 1699, 13 Jan.–1 Feb. 1701

b. c.1641, 1st s. of Thomas Foley I*, and bro. of Paul Foley* and Philip Foley*. *educ.* Pembroke, Camb. adm. 4 July 1657, aged 16, BA 1660; I. Temple, entered 1657. *m.* Elizabeth (*d.* 6 Jan. 1686), da. of Edward Ashe†, Draper, of Fenchurch Street, London, 4s. 4da. *suc.* fa. 1677.[1]

Member, Society of Mineral and Battery Works 1670, asst. 1678–87, dep. gov. 1693–9; asst. Society of Mines Royal 1689.[2]

Commr. for assessment, Worcs. 1673–80, Glos. 1689, Staffs. and Worcs. 1689–90; sheriff, Worcs. 1673–4; freeman, Bewdley 1673; j.p. Worcs by 1679–85, July 1688–?*d.*, Staffs. ?1689–*d.*; dep. lt. Staffs. 1689–?*d.*[3]

Foley was first returned for the county two years after succeeding to his father's estate, and represented it throughout the exclusion crisis. A Presbyterian conformist, he was marked 'honest' on Shaftesbury's list. In the first Exclusion Parliament he was certainly appointed by full name only to the committee of elections and privileges and to those to consider expiring laws and the bill for security against Popery; but he voted for exclusion. An active Member of the second Exclusion Parliament, he was named to 14 committees, including the elections committee. The most important were to consider the bill prohibiting the import of cattle from Ireland, to bring in a bill to amend the Severn Fishery Act, and to consider the bill for Protestant

unity. Great efforts were made to oust Foley at the general election of 1681, but he was re-elected to the Oxford Parliament, in which he was again appointed to the elections committee and also to that for the impeachment of Fitzharris.[4]

Foley was defeated at the general election of 1685. Although listed among the Opposition in 1687, he probably became a Whig collaborator. He was appointed to the commission of the peace in July 1688 and adopted as court candidate after his brother Philip had assured the local Roman Catholics and dissenters that 'there was no reason to doubt that he stood well in his Majesty's favour'. He adroitly changed sides at the Revolution, occupying Worcester for the Protestant cause, and regained his seat in the Convention. A very active Member, he was appointed to at least 77 committees, including the elections committee in both sessions, and those to bring in a list of the essentials for securing religion, law and liberty, to suspend habeas corpus, to alter the oaths of allegiance and supremacy, and to consider the first mutiny bill. On 1 Apr. 1689 he was among those ordered to prepare the repeal of the Corporations Act and to bring in a bill for religious comprehension. He helped to draw up the address to thank the King for undertaking to maintain the Church and to prepare reasons for a conference on the new oaths of allegiance and supremacy. He was appointed to the committee for the toleration bill, and helped to manage a conference. On 10 July he was added to the committee of inquiry into the delay in relieving Londonderry. He was the first of the family to go over to the Opposition, voting on 8 Nov. to reduce the land tax by 'laying part of it upon the lawyers'. He was named to the committee for restoring corporations (19 Dec.), and supported the disabling clause.[5]

Foley continued to sit for the county in the next two Parliaments as a country Whig, signing the Association in 1696. He died on 1 Feb. 1701. His son sat for Stafford from 1694 to 1712, when he was one of the 12 Tories raised to the peerage to secure a majority in the Upper House.[6]

[1] *Vis. Worcs.* ed. Metcalfe, 47. [2] BL Loan 16. [3] *Univ. Birmingham Hist. Jnl.* i. 109; *Wm. Salt Arch. Soc.* (1931), p. 285. [4] *Bagford Ballads* ed. Ebsworth, ii. 998–1000; D. R. Lacey, *Dissent and Parl. Pols.* 397. [5] *CSP Dom.* 1685, p. 23; R. Morrice, *Entering Bk.* 2, pp. 176–7, 343, 654; *CJ*, x. 143. [6] *CP*, v. 535.

E.R./G.J.

FOOTE, Samuel (c.1626–91), of Tiverton, Devon.

TIVERTON 21 Nov. 1673, 1679 (Mar.), 1679 (Oct.), 1681, 1689, 1690–26 Mar. 1691

b. c.1626. *m.* (1) 1657, Mary Keate (*d.* 17 Jan. 1678),

4 da.; (2) Martha, da. of Thomas Mompesson of Brewham, Som., 1s.[1]

Alderman, Tiverton 1655–Jan. 1688, Oct. 1688–d., mayor ?1662–3; commr. for recusants, Devon 1675, assessment 1677–80, 1689–d.[2]

Foote, a merchant, was already prominent in the religious life of Tiverton by 1654, when he protested against the defective godliness of Robert Shapcote*, and in the following year he was elected to the corporation after it had been purged by Major-General John Disbrowe†. A convert to Anglicanism after the Restoration, as churchwarden and mayor he took a leading part in persecuting his former Independent pastor. He defeated the court candidate Sir Hugh Acland* at a by-election in 1673, and became moderately active as a committeeman in the seven remaining sessions of the Cavalier Parliament, with 29 appointments. None of these was of political importance; five were concerned with the cloth trade, on which his opinion would certainly have been of weight. He exported no less than 22 per cent of the cloth that passed through Exeter in 1676. Sir Richard Wiseman* confused his name with that of Samuel Rolle* in his report to Danby in 1676, but probably meant to describe him as a 'fierce mutineer', while in the following year Shaftesbury put him down as 'worthy'. In 1678, however, Foote joined his colleague (Sir) Henry Ford* against John Birch* and Thomas Papillon* of the country party in opposing the bill to encourage leather exports; this, his only tellership, was presumably dictated by his own or his constituents' economic interests.[3]

Foote was re-elected to all three Exclusion Parliaments. Still classed by Shaftesbury as 'worthy', he voted for the first exclusion bill. A moderately active Member in 1679, he was named to four committees, but to none in the second and third Exclusion Parliaments. In 1682 it was reported that he and his son-in-law Robert Burridge† were engaged in gun-running, but no action seems to have been taken against him. Probably he experienced another timely change of heart, for he was reappointed to the Tiverton bench under the new charter of 1684. But he was unable to save his seat in the general election of 1685, though he witnessed the return, and he was removed from the corporation in January 1688.[4]

Foote was again returned at the general election of 1689. He was an inactive Member of the Convention, being named to only two committees. He supported the disabling clause in the bill to restore corporations. He has to be distinguished from two London namesakes, Samuel Foote, Ironmonger, who made his will on 5 Nov. 1691, and Samuel

Foot, merchant, who died in 1697. It was probably the latter, a connexion of the Onslow family, who advanced money to the new regime; but Foote himself had enough interest to secure Burridge's appointment as receiver-general of Devon and Exeter. Re-elected in 1690, he died intestate on 26 Mar. 1691, aged 65, and was buried at Tiverton. His landed property, including the manor of Wemworthy, was valued at over £500 p.a., and he had already given his eldest daughter £1,500 on her marriage to a local squire of ancient lineage. His only son died childless in 1696 and the property was divided among the daughters.[5]

1 Burke, *Gentry* (1952); J. Blundell, *Mems. and Antiqs. Tiverton*; W. Harding, *Hist. Tiverton*, ii. 56, 58; *Vis. Eng. and Wales Notes* ed. Crisp, vii. 11. 2 M. Dunsford, *Hist. Mems. Tiverton*, 372, 456. 3 *CSP Dom.* 1654, p. 279; Dunsford, 192, 372; *CJ*, ix. 358, 496; W. B. Stephens, *17th Cent. Exeter*, 159. 4 *CSP Dom.* 1682, p. 69; Dunsford, 193; PC2/72/582. 5 J. R. Woodhead, *Rulers of London*, 71; PCC 27 Fane, 73 Pyne; *Cal. Treas. Bks.* ix. 130, 2004; *Trans. Devon Assoc.* lxvii. 326; *Devon and Cornw. N. and Q.* xviii. 261; Lysons, *Devon*, 513, 551.

J.P.F.

FORD, Henry (1617–84), of Nutwell Court, Woodbury, Devon.[1]

TIVERTON 6 Apr. 1664, 1679 (Mar.), 1679 (Oct.), 1681

bap. 19 Jan. 1617, o. (posth.) s. of Henry Ford of Bagtor, Ilsington by Catherine, da. and h. of George Drake of Spratshayes, Exmouth; half-bro. of John Cloberry*. *educ.* Exeter, Oxf. 1634–6. *m.* 25 Feb. 1641, Eleanor (*d.* 3 Feb. 1673), da. of Sir Henry Rowe of Shacklewell, Hackney, Mdx., 3s. (2 *d.v.p.*) 4da. *suc.* fa. at birth; kntd. 20 July 1672.[2]

J.p. Devon 1644, July 1660–d., commr. for oyer and terminer, Western circuit July 1660, assessment, Devon Aug. 1660–80, lt.-col. of militia ft. c. Aug. 1660–?69, commr. for corporations 1662–3, recusants 1675, dep. lt. 1676–d.[3]

Sec. to ld. lt. [I] 1669–70, 1672–3; commr. for sick and wounded 1672–4.[4]

FRS 1663–82.

Ford bore a surname which was ancient and widespread in Devon. An ancestor represented the county in 1348. His uncle, John Ford, was the favourite dramatist at the court of Charles I and Henrietta Maria. After leaving Oxford, Ford spent much of his early youth in litigation with his stepfather. He was present at the trial of Strafford in 1641, but took no part in the Civil War, though his sympathies were undoubtedly royalist, and he was nominated to the commission of the peace at Oxford in 1644. He bought Nutwell for £6,050 in 1649. During the Interregnum he achieved local celebrity as one of the circle of 'topping wits' who revolved round Thomas Clifford*. By 1659 he had gravitated to London and joined the Rota Club.[5]

Ford contested Lostwithiel on the Robartes interest at the general election of 1660, an expensive business, for he induced the mayor to make a double return on condition of saving him harmless. It is not known whether he stood in 1661, but he was again defeated in 1662 at Newport; his petition was never reported to the House. Perhaps he was not a very good candidate; 'his generous mind was above the little creeping arts of insinuation'. But once he entered Parliament at a by-election for Tiverton in 1664, his seat proved impregnable, in spite of adverse political currents. 'He had a very endearing deportment, and was no less successful than ready in serving and befriending others.' Ford was a very active Member of the Cavalier Parliament, sitting on 187 committees and acting as teller in 18 divisions. 'He was an excellent orator, and spoke every thing he had to say with a graceful presence, both of mind and body.' The diarists mention 36 of his speeches. He had not been many months in Parliament before he was chosen chairman of two committees on private bills, one promoted by Lord Strangford (Philip Smythe*), the other by his fellow-Devonian, the Duke of Albemarle (George Monck*). He was named to the committee to consider the miscarriages of the war in 1667, and on 8 May 1668 reproved Richard Hampden* for speaking in favour of a dissolution, which had been one of the charges against Clarendon. In 1669 he went to Ireland as secretary to Lord Robartes. Robartes was not a success as lord lieutenant, and Ford returned to England with him the following year. He first came to the fore in the Commons in 1671 as a warm defender of the Church. When John Birch* proposed a discriminatory tax on church dignitaries, Ford replied that they were not envied by good men, 'and they had better be envied than pitied by Birch'. It was perhaps in the course of this debate that the following incident occurred, unrecorded by Anchitell Grey*:

> 'Mr Speaker', says he, 'I never heard a good motion from that nook of the House' (nodding to it), and then paused; whereupon some of the party called, 'To the bar, to the bar'.... But being permitted once more to speak, he said, 'Mr Speaker, I never heard a good motion from that nook of the House—but I was ready to second it'.

He appears in both court and opposition lists at this time as a supporter of the court party, but he was also careful of his constituents' interests, acting as chairman of the committee for the regulation of serge manufactures, their principal industry.[6]

In the third Dutch war, Ford succeeded Clifford as commissioner for the sick and wounded, but soon returned to Ireland as secretary to Lord Lieutenant Essex. His intention was obviously to look about him, but he was soon complaining: 'I find every place full here'. According to his biographer, 'he was never fortunate in his designs for himself or family; nor may it be concealed that he was sometimes too overweening in his opinion'. His second tenure of office in Ireland lasted little longer than the first, and in December 1673 he was dismissed for disclosing official secrets and replaced by William Harbord*. To make matters worse, his patron Clifford (to whom he had conveyed a friendly message from the Roman Catholic archbishop of Dublin) had revealed himself a Papist and fallen from power. Ford himself came under suspicion, and seems to have been unable to find another patron; perhaps he was already recognizable as that pathetic but familiar figure, the politician with a great future behind him. He flattered Lauderdale publicly without response; he was named on the Paston list, attended the meeting of the court caucus on 14 Apr. 1675, and acted as teller against the first article on the impeachment of Danby, who put him down for an excise pension of £300, but omitted to pay it; he attached himself to Edward Seymour*, and then offended 'the King of the West Saxons' irredeemably by contradicting him on his pet hobby-horse, the ill effects on Devon of the import of Irish cattle. Meanwhile his financial circumstances grew desperate; his paternal estate had to be sold, and the author of *Flagellum Parliamentarium* sneered: 'so much in debt he cannot help taking his bribe and promise of employment'. *A Seasonable Argument* (which seems to have been well informed on all but the most vital point) ascribed to him 'a pension of £300 p.a., which is almost all he has to subsist on'.[7]

Ford was never more active in Parliament than in the five years following his second return from Ireland. He was immediately added to the committee for the impeachment of Arlington, whom he threatened to denounce for attending Mass, and named to the committee to consider the state of Ireland. On alnage, however, a real grievance to the woollen manufacturers of his constituency, 'the House would not endure Sir Henry Ford's project of repealing the law'. Between 1675 and 1678 he served on five committees for the exclusion of Papists from Parliament or the suppression of Popery, two for the appropriation of the customs for the navy, and two for the better preservation of the liberty of the subject. He appears in 1675 on the working lists as to be influenced by Seymour, and as a government speaker. In this capacity he was sometimes quite effective. 'If such sums have been spent for *secret* service', he asked William Cavendish*, Lord Cavendish, 'how does that Lord know they have been misspent? Our addresses take no effect, because what things are alleged are not made good.' On 6 May he was teller for the motion to continue the debate on Lauderdale. He was also prominent in the disputes on jurisdiction with the other House; he was sent to the Lords on 18 May to desire a conference, though he denied that he had accompanied the serjeant-at-arms when the four lawyers were arrested in Westminster Hall. He was teller for the Government on at least three crucial divisions on supply, two in the autumn of 1675 and one on 5 Mar. 1677. But by the latter date, Ford's attitude was already causing anxiety to Danby's managers in the Commons. 'Sir Harry Ford relies upon my friendship to be remembered for something to come in time by your lordship', wrote Sir Richard Wiseman* to Danby. 'Mr Harbord disserves the King and is put in; Sir Henry Ford serves the King and is put out. Truly, my lord, Sir Harry Ford must not be forgotten.' It was in the field of foreign policy that he showed his independence, voting against the Government on the alliance with Holland in May 1677, though he was against immediate war with France. Nevertheless Shaftesbury noted him as 'thrice vile'. His defection from the Court was ascribed to the influence of Seymour, in spite of the brisk exchange between them a few weeks before on the subject of Irish cattle. His speech was well calculated to infuriate his opponent:

> Reason has but a few proselytes both within doors and without. ... 'Tis the populace that makes the value of the land. There is no reason for Irish land being of low value, but the poverty of the people, and not the fifth part of Ireland peopled. Will you take away so beneficial a thing from your fellow-subjects? ... The thing is indifferent to his country, and he will make no motion in it.

His name disappeared from the official lists of government speakers and court supporters from this time, but he was rewarded by a position of new authority in the House, acting as chairman for five bills, though on the bill to prevent the export of wool he had to give way to George Treby*. On 29 Apr. 1678, Ford found himself partnered by none other than Birch in a division for maintaining their disagreement with the Lords on the growth of Popery, and the next day he was named to the committee on foreign policy. But he was still essentially moderate and on 15 June opposed the motion for no further supply. He was sent to the Lords on 27

June to desire a conference on disbanding the army, for which he later prepared reasons. With his colleague, Samuel Foote*, he opposed the bill to encourage export of leather, but they were beaten on the division by 141 votes to 72. Nevertheless he was ordered to carry the bill to the Upper House. He also took part in two conferences on the bill for burial in woollen. In the autumn session Ford was comparatively inactive, but on 21 Dec. 1678 he courageously defied the storm aroused by the revelations of Ralph Montagu*. He would not accept them as proof of treason till he knew whether or not Danby had authority by place or patent to conduct these negotiations.[8]

Perhaps Ford's patriotic stand on foreign policy, coupled with his care for the economic interests of his constituency, was sufficient to scare off opposition there. In any case he was returned to the first Exclusion Parliament, though included in the list of the 'unanimous club' and labelled 'vile' by Shaftesbury. He was again very active, sitting on 18 committees, of which the most important were for the security and habeas corpus bills. He was chairman of the committee to examine the aspersions on the informer Dugdale. He made three speeches, including the perhaps rather uneasy demand that Stephen Fox* should name the recipients of secret service money, and the amounts. Despite voting against the exclusion bill, he was re-elected in August 1679. He still had influence in government circles, and he was still active in the second Exclusion Parliament, being named to 13 committees, of which the most important was to draft the address for the dismissal of Halifax. He spoke out against the second exclusion bill, pointing out that neither Act of Parliament nor attainder had sufficed to exclude Henry VII from the throne:

> I am as fond as any man of the Protestant religion, but I offer to your consideration how far the legality of this bill will be.

He opposed the address for the removal of Laurence Hyde*, whose only crime was to have the Duke of York for a brother-in-law. This may well have been Ford's last appearance in the House, for though he was re-elected in 1681 his name does not appear in the records of the Oxford Parliament.[9]

Ford's biographer describes him as

> of a sanguine, fair complexion, and consequently of a lively, cheerful humour. For stature, he was something above the common standard, of a very graceful, portly presence, a ready elocution and agreeable conversation. His discourse was neat and historical, the subject of it curious, and out of the common road of entertainment. ... He was looked upon as the glory of the west, for his abilities and steady principles both of Church and state.

This might be regarded as a polite return of favours

which Prince acknowledged having received in early life from Ford, but it is in part no more than an echo of the opposition squib, *The Chequer Inn*:

> The western glory, Henry Ford,
> His landlord Bales outeat, outroar'd,
> 　　And did the trenchers lick.
> What pity 'tis a wit so great
> Should live to sell himself for meat.

There was indeed a strong element of pathos in Ford's later years. His one hope lay in an advantageous match for his eldest son, who insisted, however, on marrying a portionless girl. Ford naturally disinherited him, but there was no chance of saving the estate. Ford was buried at Woodbury on 12 Sept. 1684; under his will, his trustees had to raise £1,000 for his daughters' portions, and next year Nutwell was sold by John Kelland* on their behalf to Henry Pollexfen* for £6,318.[10]

[1] This biography is based on J. Prince, *Worthies of Devon* (published in 1701). [2] Vivian, *Vis. Devon*, 350; St. John at Hackney par. reg.; *HMC Dartmouth*, iii. 116. [3] A. Jenkins, *Exeter*, 174; *HMC 14th Rep. IX*, 274. [4] *CSP Dom.* 1671–2, p. 265; 1673–5, p. 63. [5] *Trans. Devon Assoc.* xlv. 259; Grey, vii. 203; Devon RO, 364M/T409; Aubrey, *Brief Lives*, i. 290. [6] *CJ*, viii. 55, 604, 670; ix. 299; *Milward*, 300; Grey, i. 362. [7] *CSP Dom.* 1671–2, p. 265; 1672, p. 528; 1673–5, p. 63; Stowe 204, f. 170v; *Essex Pprs.* (Cam. Soc. n.s. xlvii), 85–86; Grey, iii. 214; iv. 328; Lysons, *Devon*, 292. [8] Stowe 204, ff. 65, 225; *HMC 9th Rep.* pt. 2, p. 54; Foxcroft, *Halifax*, i. 129; Grey, ii. 413; iii. 88, 215, 267; iv. 312, 328; vi. 376. [9] Grey, iv. 238; vii. 322, 426; PC2/69, f. 30; *HMC 12th Rep. IX*, 113. [10] *HMC Lords*, n.s. i. 11; PCC 85 Cann; Lady Eliott-Drake, *Fam. and Heirs of Drake*, ii. 61; Devon RO, 364M/T390.

M.W.H./J.P.F.

FORD, Sir Richard (c.1614–78), of Seething Lane, London and Baldwins, Dartford, Kent.

SOUTHAMPTON　1661–31 Aug. 1678

b. c. 1614, 2nd s. of Thomas Ford, merchant, of Exeter, Devon by ?Elizabeth, da. of William Frank of Ottery St. Mary, Devon. *educ.* Exeter, Oxf. 1631. *m.* Grace, 2s. 3da. Kntd. 16 May 1660.[1]

Freeman, Exeter 1635, Southampton 1661; capt. blue regt. London militia 1659, col. white auxil. regt. 1661–6, common councilman 1659–61; commr. for assessment, London Aug. 1660–*d.*, Kent 1673–*d.*; alderman, London 1661–*d.*, sheriff 1663–4, ld. mayor 1670–1, additional coal-meter c.1661–*d.*; commr. for corporations, Hants 1662–3, loyal and indigent officers, London, Westminster and Hants 1662; jt. farmer of tin coinage, duchy of Cornw. 1664–7; member, Hon. Artillery Co. 1670, commr. for charitable uses 1675, recusants 1675; pres. St. Bartholomew's hospital 1675–*d.*[2]

Member, Merchant Adventurers' Co. by 1644, gov. by Nov. 1660–75; member, Mercers' Co. 1654, master 1661–2, 1674–5; committee, E.I. Co. 1658–63, 1664–5; dep. gov. R. Adventurers into Africa 1663, asst. 1664–71; asst. R. Africa Co. 1672–*d.*[3]

Commr. for trade 1656–7, Nov. 1660–8, for Tangier 1662–73, for marine treaty with United Provinces 1674–5.[4]

FRS 1673–*d.*

Ford did not claim kinship with either of the established Devonshire families of that name, nor does his father appear to have belonged to the Exeter patriciate by birth or marriage. His education was presumably intended to fit him for a career in the Church, but he preferred to go into trade. He impressed Samuel Pepys* as 'a very able man of his brains and tongue, and a scholar', though, like so many merchants, he could not keep a secret. He settled in Rotterdam in 1642, and helped to supply the royalist armies through the western ports. The Earl of Warwick described him as a great 'malignant' who sought to embroil Parliament with the United Provinces, and a vote was passed at Westminster to outlaw him. The Royalist Peter Mews, however, later called him 'a knave in grain ... for when he should have supplied my lord of Ormonde with arms and ammunition, he carried corn to the rebels'. He was allowed to compound on a rather vague particular in 1649 for £129, though the Council of State suspected him of 'some design of special mischief for Charles Stuart, being a principal man in all their councils'. But he was sufficiently reconciled to the regime to return to England in 1652, to act as supplier to the Protectorate navy and to serve on the committee of trade. As an influential member of the common council and 'a very loyal, prudent gentleman', he took a leading part in promoting the Restoration in the City, and on 9 Feb. 1660 the Rump ordered his arrest. At the general election he was involved in a double return at Exeter, which was decided against him. As one of the delegation from the City he was knighted at The Hague, but, despite the Duke of York's recommendation, he was again unsuccessful at Exeter in 1661, presumably because his association with the great London monopoly companies was distasteful to the provincial trading community. In London, on the other hand, he enjoyed considerable popularity, but was unable to overcome the prejudice against 'episcopal men'. At Southampton, however, the Duke of York's letter proved efficacious and he was elected.[5]

Ford was an active Member of the Cavalier Parliament, being appointed to 195 committees, mostly on trade matters, and acting as teller in seven divisions, but despite Pepys's commendation he seldom spoke in the House. In the opening session he was appointed to the committees for the security, corporations and uniformity bills. He was the principal representative of the East India Company in their negotiations with the Dutch, and a strong advocate of the war. Early in 1662 he was twice ordered to attend the King with resolutions of the House concerning the packing of wool and the dearth of corn. He was teller against a proposal to suspend until

Christmas the Merchant Adventurers' monopoly of cloth exports to Holland and Germany, and helped to manage a conference on the customs. The King 'had an inclination to serve Sir Richard', but it was some time before he received any substantial reward for his services, other than his knighthood and some naval contracts. Pepys, however, caught him out in an attempt to pass off 'old stuff that had been tarred, covered over with new hemp, which is such a cheat as hath not been heard of', at any rate by the zealous novice in the Navy Office; but his 'Holland duck' was excellent. Ford's syndicate apparently outbid the customs farmers for the additional duties, and were awarded £8,000 compensation when their tender was rejected. In 1663 he was appointed to the parliamentary committee of inquiry into the effects of the suspension of the Merchant Adventurers' patent. The King gave him £1,500 to cover his expenses as sheriff of London, without which he could not have undertaken the office. In the spring session of 1664, he was marked as a court dependant, and named to the committees for the conventicles bill and for the bill to relieve the creditors of the Merchant Adventurers, which came to nothing; but when it was revived in the autumn he acted as teller against it on the second reading. Later in the same session he took the chair in committees to consider a petition from naval suppliers and to regulate vintners' measures. He formed a syndicate which received a grant of the crown's right of 'coinage' on all tin mined in England and Wales; although his proposal to issue tin farthings was disallowed, the Treasury would not accept his contention that he had been a loser by the contract. As the leading merchant in the Africa company he was chiefly responsible for the second Dutch war. At Oxford he was teller against the second reading of the bill to prohibit the import of Irish cattle, and in the next session he was among those ordered to prepare reasons for a conference on the subject.[6]

Apart from serving on the committee for the bill to establish a public accounts commission, Ford took no part in the measures against Clarendon. He probably introduced the bill for reducing the parishes of Southampton from five to two in March 1668, since his name stands first in the list of the committee. He was also appointed to the committee for the conventicles bill, and acted as teller for the bill to reduce rates of interest. Sir Thomas Osborne* originally included him among the dependants of the Duke of York in 1669, but transferred him, with (Sir) William Coventry*, to the list of those Members who might be 'engaged' for the Court. In 1670 Ford served on the committees to enable a deanery to be built for St. Paul's and to

prevent illegal imprisonment, and was among those ordered to attend a conference on the shipping bill. At the same time he was engaged, on commission, to manage negotiations with Hamburg regarding compensation for six English ships destroyed in the Elbe by the Dutch during the war. But his tender for the customs farm was rejected. On 6 Feb. 1671 he seconded the motion of William Garway* for an inquiry into the conduct of the London Jews. It was alleged that in London in 1670-1 'the laws against conventicles have been laid asleep, and a moderate lord mayor has let the people do what they list'. On laying down office, Ford was compelled to petition the King 'for such largesse as may enable him to end the life spent in his service without contempt in the City'. His claim to have kept London 'tranquil' is substantiated by a report on the corporation in 1672, which stated that while in office he had

> suspended the execution of the laws against nonconformists, by which he gained the applause of all that party, though they had used all the villainous arts imaginable to keep him out of the government. He is a man of excellent parts, and may do his Majesty excellent service in the City.

His financial troubles cannot have been too severe, for he was able to take a lease from Eton of a country house in Kent, and when his London house was destroyed in the Navy Office fire in January 1673, he transferred his business to premises on Tower Hill.[7]

In the debate on the Declaration of Indulgence, Ford moved for a committee of inquiry 'to offer you such an expedient as may be for the good of the nation'. He was among those ordered to bring in a bill for the general naturalization of foreign Protestants, which he opposed as entailing the 'prostitution' of corporations. He was on the committee for rebuilding the Navy Office, and his was the first name among those appointed in 1674 to bring in a bill for paving the streets of the City and completing the rebuilding of churches and other public works. He was named on the Paston list. During the summer the Merchant Adventurers voted to replace him as governor by Sir Edward Dering*, who described his predecessor as 'a man of ill reputation'. In the autumn session of 1675 he was roused from his usual silence in the House by John Ernle*, who impugned the solvency of the City chamber. He was appointed to inquire into the assault by a Jesuit on a Protestant convert and to hear a petition against the East India Company. His name appears on the working lists as one of those 'to be remembered' and was added by Osborne (now Lord Treasurer Danby), though with some hesitation, to the list drawn up by Sir Richard Wiseman* at the end of the session. In

1677 he was among the Members ordered to bring in a bill to regulate the collection of hearth-tax, to consider another petition from the creditors of the Merchant Adventurers, and to abolish the penalty of burning for heresy. Lord Shaftesbury (Sir Anthony Ashley Cooper*), who had been his friend over the tin farm, marked him 'worthy', but in *A Seasonable Argument* he was described as 'the joint contriver of the two Dutch wars, for which he had £10,000, and yet is scarce able to live', and he was posthumously included in the 'unanimous club' of court voters. His last committee in June 1678 was once again on the affairs of the Merchant Adventurers. He died in his sixty-fifth year on 31 Aug. and was buried at Bexley, under a memorial that speaks of his

> great talents and even greater integrity (for he knew everything except deceit). [He was] most skilled in several languages and almost every art ... an exile with his prince (as was seemly) and a leader in his return. How many offices he enjoyed cannot be determined, but they were far fewer than he deserved.... Heaven remained the only reward which he could earn.

But his intestacy, and the obscurity into which his family lapsed, suggest that his career, largely devoted to one of the declining sectors of English trade, had brought him less profit than was merited by his ability.[8]

[1] *Le Neve's Knights* (Harl. Soc. viii), 49; *Exeter Mar. Lic.* 16; C6/32/27. [2] *Exeter Freemen* (Devon and Cornw. Rec. Soc. extra ser. i), 131; J. S. Davies, *Hist. Southampton*, 205; *Mordaunt Letter Bk.* (Cam. Soc. ser. 3, lxix), 150–1; J. R. Woodhead, *Rulers of London*, 71; Stowe 186, f. 15; *CJ*, x. 236; *Ancient Vellum Bk.* ed. Raikes, 98. [3] *CSP Dom.* 1644, p. 320; 1660–1, p. 372; 1663–4, p. 310; Woodhead, 71; *HMC 11th Rep. III*, 55. [4] *CSP Dom.* 1655–6, p. 188; 1663–4, p. 660; 1673–5, p. 287; *Pepys Diary*, 27 Oct. 1662; *Cal. Treas. Bks.* ii. 280. [5] Plymouth City Lib. mss, J. Prince, *Devon Worthies*; *Pepys Diary*, 17 Mar. 1663, 18 Oct. 1664; *CSP Dom.* 1644, pp. 190, 312; 1649–50, p. 370; 1657–8, p. 328; 1660–1, p. 538; *Cal. Cl. SP*, iv. 538; v. 209; *HMC Hodgkin*, 107, 111; *Nicholas Pprs.* (Cam. Soc. n.s. xl), 267; SP23/216, ff. 410, 414; *HMC Popham*, 217, 229; *CJ*, vii. 837; viii. 55; Adm. 2/1745, ff. 31, 33. [6] *Cal. Ct. Mins. E.I. Co.* ed. Sainsbury, vi. 85, 111; *Cal. Cl. SP*, v. 398, 457; *CJ*, viii. 340, 358, 399, 418, 577, 591, 611, 617, 660; *CSP Dom.* 1660–1, p. 331; 1661–2, p. 433; 1663–4, pp. 358, 467; 1668–9, p. 642; 1676–7, p. 258; *Cal. Treas. Bks.* ii. 280; *Camb. Hist. Jnl.* xii. 113. [7] *Milward*, 209; *CJ*, ix. 64, 79, 157; *CSP Dom.* 1670, pp. 446, 457; 1671, pp. 368, 546; 1671–2, p. 541; *Cal. Treas. Bks.* iii. 690, 691; *Dering*, 71; *Gent. Mag.* xxxix. 516; J. Donkin, *Hist. Dartford*, 334; *Bulstrode Pprs.* 259. [8] Grey, ii. 12, 154; iii. 357; Kent AO, U1713/A37; *CJ*, ix. 250; *CSP Dom.* 1664–5, p. 495; Le Neve, *Mon. Angl.* 1650–79, pp. 187–8.

M.H.W./P.W.

FORESTER, William (1655–1718), of Dothill Park, Salop.

MUCH WENLOCK 1679 (Mar.), 1679 (Oct.), 1681, 1689, 1690, 1695, 1698, 1701 (Feb.), 1701 (Dec.), 1702, 1705, 1708, 1710, 1713

b. 10 Dec. 1655, 2nd but 1st surv. s. of Francis Forester of Wellington by Lady Mary Newport, da. of Richard Newport[†], 1st Baron Newport, of High Ercall, wid. of John Steventon of Dothill Park. *educ.* Trinity Coll. Camb. 1673. *m.* lic. 23 Apr. 1684, Lady Mary Cecil, da. of James Cecil*, Visct. Cranborne, 2s. 3da. *suc.* fa. 1684; kntd. 20 Aug. 1689.[1]

Commr. for assessment, Salop 1677–80, 1689–90, Glos. 1690; j.p. Salop 1680–by 1683, ?1689–*d.*, Westminster 1691–?*d.*; capt. of militia ft. Salop c.1680–2.[2]

Clerk of the green cloth 1689–1717.[3]

The Forester family were hereditary foresters of Wellington Hay and had resided in Wellington since at least the 13th century. They built the Old Hall on Watling Street in the 15th century and represented Wenlock in 1529 and 1554. The family's long-lasting parliamentary interest in the borough, however, was not established until the early 17th century when Forester's great-grandfather purchased the manor of Little Wenlock. The family appears to have avoided involvement in the Civil War, though his grandfather was appointed a commissioner of militia in 1648.[4]

Forester was returned to all the Exclusion Parliaments for Wenlock and to 11 of the next 12 Parliaments. Although he was considered 'honest' by Shaftesbury, he took part in the general boycott of the division on the exclusion bill by Shropshire Members and was added to the commission of the peace in February 1680. Nevertheless, he was becoming a staunch exclusionist, and on 26 June he joined with Shaftesbury and other members of his faction in presenting the Duke of York as a Papist to the Middlesex grand jury. His only committee in these Parliaments was to bring in a bill for the naturalization of all alien Protestants (31 Dec.). It was later alleged that Forester met other opposition Members in Coventry and then consulted Shaftesbury in Highgate on his way to the Oxford Parliament. By February 1682 he had lost his position in the Shropshire militia and was soon dropped from the commission of the peace. In September he accompanied the Duke of Monmouth on his northern tour. An informer later stated that he

> was always very zealous for the Duke of Monmouth's interest and the informant has often heard him argue for his title to the crown after the King's death in relation to his legitimacy. He has heard Forester say that if the King should die he would take part with Monmouth against the Duke of York.

The following year Forester was implicated up to his neck in the Rye House Plot, and in July he was forced to give two sureties of £2,000 each to keep the peace. It was reported that in Shropshire a gentleman of £2–3,000 per annum was discovered to have 50 muskets which he concealed and would not own, but by parcels, when he saw they were resolved to search and must find them. And they likewise found 700 weight of powder hid under ground; and when they were upon search one of the company put his stick into an oven and felt something which, upon stirring, jingled, which occasioned the emptying the oven of ashes, among which they found 50 pike heads. It seems Mr Forester, to conceal them, had sawed the pikes into small pieces and privately burnt them in the oven and forgot to take away the iron heads of them.[5]

Forester was not returned to James II's Parliament, and in June 1685, in the wake of the Monmouth rebellion, he was sent to the Tower 'suspected of dangerous and treasonable practices'. He probably bribed his way out, for on 28 June a warrant was issued to apprehend one Edward Goldegay, 'who wilfully suffered Forester to escape out of his custody'. By 1687 Forester was living with his wife at The Hague acting as an intermediary between the English Opposition and the Prince of Orange. In March he was ordered by the King 'to set aside all excuses and within 14 days after the letters are delivered to him to return into England and not to fail thereof upon pain and peril'. His name remained on Bentinck's list of English correspondents, though no letters survive. He regained his seat at the general election of 1689, but he was not active in the Convention. He acted as teller for the Whigs on the motion for the adjournment of 8 Feb. 1689. His four committees included the committee of elections and privileges, and that to consider the security bill. He probably owed his post at Court to his wife, a friend of the Queen's. He remained a supporter of William throughout his reign, signing the Association in 1696, and kept his Household office until shortly before his death. He was buried at Wellington on 22 Feb. 1718. His son sat for Wenlock as a Whig in three Parliaments.[6]

[1] Salop Arch. Soc. Trans. (ser. 2), iii, 167–70; (ser. 3), ii. 333–4. [2] CSP Dom. 1682, p. 81. [3] LS13/231/2; J. M. Beattie, English Ct. in Reign of Geo. I, 186. [4] Salop Arch. Soc. Trans. (ser. 4), vii. 145–8; Blakeway, Sheriffs of Salop, 126–7. [5] HMC Ormonde, n.s. v. 340; CSP Dom. 1682, pp. 386, 428, 429; July–Sept. 1683, pp. 82, 137, 175–6; North, Examen, 389. [6] CSP Dom. 1685, pp. 159, 229, 232; 1686–7, p. 391; Hatton Corresp. (Cam. Soc. n.s. xxiii), 67. Dalrymple, Mems. ii. bk. v. 86; J. R. Jones, Revolution of 1688, 225; Luttrell, v. 416, 417; PCC 58 Tenison.

J.S.C.

FORSTER, Sir Humphrey, 2nd Bt. (1650–1711), of Aldermaston, Berks.

BERKSHIRE   5 Mar. 1677, 1679 (Mar.), 1685, 1690, 1695, 1698, 1701 (Feb.)

b. 21 Dec. 1650, 1st s. of William Forster (d.1661) of Aldermaston by Elizabeth, da. of Sir John Tyrell* of Heron, East Horndon, Essex. educ. Westminster 1663. m. 26 Nov. 1672, Judith (d.1720), da. and coh. of (Sir) Humphrey Winch, 1st Bt.*, of Hawnes, Beds. and Harleyford, Bucks., 2s. 1da. d.v.p. suc. gdfa. as 3rd Bt. 12 Oct. 1663.[1]

J.p. Berks. c.1671–July 1688, 1689–d., commr. for assessment 1673–80, 1689–90, recusants 1675, dep. lt. by 1680–Feb. 1688, 1689–?d.

Forster was descended from an Oxfordshire family settled at Harpsden in the 15th century and first representing the county in 1467. Aldermaston was acquired by marriage in the early 16th century. A Royalist during the Civil War, Forster's grandfather was suspected of heavily mortgaging his estates to contribute to the King's cause, and did not secure their discharge from sequestration on payment of £1,000 till 1653. His father was a Parliamentarian, who was appointed to the militia committees in 1659 and in March 1660.[2]

Forster was returned for Berkshire at a by-election in 1677. According to his own account it cost him £1,500, 'though he had no powerful adversary'. On the working lists he was marked 'to be fixed', but Shaftesbury considered him 'worthy'. An inactive Member, he served on only three committees, of which the most important was for abolishing the writ de heretico comburendo. He made no recorded speeches. On 7 Mar. 1678 he was teller against the election of the court supporter Henry Norwood* at Gloucester. On 30 Jan. 1679 Sir Ralph Verney* wrote that he had been unable to persuade Forster to stand again, but he was returned to the first Exclusion Parliament, and again marked 'worthy' on Shaftesbury's list. He was named to only two committees, neither of which was of political importance. He voted for exclusion, but he was listed in the 'unanimous club', and replaced in August by a steadier country candidate Richard Southby*. Forster evidently came to oppose exclusion, remaining in local office in 1680, but he may have decided to retire temporarily from politics because of the growing violence of the struggle. He returned to the House in 1685, when his sole committee was on the bill for the recovery of tithes. To the lord lieutenant's questions he replied:

He cannot be for repealing the Tests, but, as for the Penal Laws that are not absolutely necessary for the support of the Church of England, he is willing to have them repealed, having been sixteen years in commission, without ever having persecuted any one for their opinion. . . . He will assist those of the same mind. . . . He will ever live friendly with those of all persuasions.

He was removed from local office, and did not sit in the Convention. He regained his seat in 1690, however, and as 'a very honest churchman' represented

Berkshire continuously for 11 years. He died on 13 Dec. 1711 and was buried at Aldermaston, the last of his family.[3]

[1] *Vis. Berks.* (Harl. Soc. lvi), 208; *Cat. Ashmolean Mss,* 330; *Mar. Lic.* (Harl. Soc. xxiii), 209; *VCH Berks.* iii. 394. [2] *VCH Berks.* iii. 389-90; SP23/24/1086, 223/663; *Cal. Comm. Comp.* 880-1. [3] BL, M636/32; *HMC Downshire,* i. 549, 565; Berks. RO, Aldermaston par. reg.; *VCH Berks.* iii. 390.

L.N./G.J.

FORSTER, William (1667-1700), of Bamburgh Castle, Northumb.

NORTHUMBERLAND   1689, 1690, 1695, 1698-1 Sept. 1700

b. 28 July 1667, 1st s. of Sir William Forster of Bamburgh by Dorothy, da. and h. of Sir William Selby of Twizell; bro. of Ferdinando Forster[†]. *m.* settlement 24 June 1693, Elizabeth, da. and h. of William Pert of Arnolds Hall, Mountnessing, Essex, *s.p. suc.* fa. 1674.[1]

J.p. Northumb. ?1689-*d.*; common councilman, Berwick-upon-Tweed 1686-7; commr. for assessment, Northumb. and co. Dur. 1689-90.[2]

Forster was descended from the illegitimate son of an Elizabethan warden of the marches, who had a grant of Bamburgh from the crown. The men of the family were short-lived; his grandfather died before the Civil War and his father became the ward of the royalist Sir Thomas Liddell, but was too young to take any active part. He served on the militia commission of 1659, no doubt through the influence of his guardian's kinsman, Sir Henry Vane[†], and was proposed as knight of the Royal Oak at the Restoration with an income of £1,000 p.a.[3]

Forster was appointed to the corporation of Berwick at the age of 19, but removed a year later for his 'misbehaviour' in promoting an Anglican address. He was returned for Northumberland at the general election as a Tory. An inactive Member of the Convention, he voted to agree with the Lords that the throne was not vacant, and was named to three committees, of which the most important was to inquire into the sending of children overseas to be educated as Roman Catholics. He continued to sit for the county as a Tory for the rest of his life, initially refusing to sign the Association in 1696. He died on 1 Sept. 1700, and was buried at Bamburgh, his brother and heir succeeding him as knight of the shire.[4]

[1] *Hist. Northumb.* i. 156-7; Morant, *Essex,* ii. 45. [2] *CSP Dom.* 1686-7, p. 231. [3] *Hist. Northumb.* i. 156, 164. [4] *CSP Dom.* 1686-7, p. 231; J. Scott, *Berwick-upon-Tweed,* 221; Luttrell, v. 88.

G.H.

FORTESCUE, Sir Edmund, 1st Bt. (1642-66), of Fallapit, East Allington, Devon.

PLYMPTON ERLE   27 Oct.-30 Dec. 1666

bap. 22 Sept. 1642, 2nd s. of Sir Edmund Fortescue (*d.*1647) of Fallapit by Jane, da. of Thomas Southcote of Mohun's Ottery. *educ.* Balliol, Oxf. 1658. *m.* by 1661, Margery (*d.* 10 May 1687), da. of Hon. Henry Sandys of Mottisfont, Hants, 1s. 2da. *suc.* gdfa. 1650; kntd. and *cr.* Bt. 31 Mar. 1664.[1]

Commr. for assessment, Devon 1661-*d.*, corporations 1662-3, j.p. 1664-*d.*; sub-commr. for prizes, Portsmouth 1664-5.[2]

Fortescue came from the elder branch of a family established in Devonshire by the reign of King John, which had first produced a Member of Parliament in 1382. During the Civil War the Fortescues of South Devon, unlike their cousins in the north of the county, were strongly royalist. Fortescue's grandfather compounded for £660, and his father was taken prisoner while executing the commission of array. After his release he became governor of Salcombe Castle, renamed Fort Charles, until its surrender in May 1646, and died in exile at Delft.[3]

At the Restoration Fortescue applied for the governorship of Fort Charles, the key of which was retained in the family, but no appointment was made and the castle fell into disuse. He was created a baronet in 1664 on credit and made a prize commissioner in the second Dutch war. But the post was suppressed in the following year, and in October 1666 he successfully contested Plympton as a country candidate. Another indenture purporting to return the courtier Sir Nicholas Slanning* was disallowed by the House, and Fortescue took his seat. He was appointed only to the committee of elections and privileges before his death on 30 Dec. He was buried at East Allington, the last of the Fallapit branch to sit in Parliament.[4]

[1] Lord Clermont, *Hist. Fortescue Fam.* 41; Stow, *Survey of London,* vi. 90. [2] Exeter city act bk. 9, f. 356; Devon RO, DD63122, 63162; Nat. Maritime Mus. Southwell mss 17/15. [3] Lysons, *Devon,* 343; Hoskins, *Devon,* 195; Clermont, 30-40; *DNB.* [4] *CSP Dom.* 1660-1, p. 88; 1667-8, p. 240; *Cal. Treas. Bks.* iii. 230; *Milward,* 29; Lysons, 5.

J.S.C.

FORTESCUE, Hugh (1665-1719), of Penwarne, Mevagissey, Cornw.

TREGONY	1689, 1690
GRAMPOUND	1695
TRURO	1698
TREGONY	1701 (Feb.), 1701 (Dec.)
MITCHELL	1705, 1708
LOSTWITHIEL	1710

bap. 2 June 1665, 1st s. of Arthur Fortescue of Buckland Filleigh, Devon and Penwarne by Barbara, da. of John Elford of Sheepstor, Devon. *m.* (1) settlement 19 Oct. 1692, Bridget, da. and h. of Hugh Boscawen* of Tregothnan, Cornw., 7s. (5 *d.v.p.*) 2da.; (2) Lucy, da. of Matthew Aylmer†, 1st Lord Aylmer of Balrath [I], 1s. 1da. *suc.* fa. 1693.[1]

J.p. Cornw. July 1688–*d.*, Devon 1689–*d.*; commr. for assessment, Cornw. 1689–90; dep. lt. Devon by 1701–*d.*

The Filleigh branch of the Fortescue family was descended from Sir John Fortescue, author of *The Governance of England*, who sat for various constituencies between 1421 and 1437. In contrast to the South Devon Fortescues, they supported Parliament in the Civil War. Fortescue's father held local office under the Commonwealth and Protectorate, but was removed from the Devonshire commission of the peace after the Restoration as a dissenter. He purchased Penwarne, and had settled in Cornwall when Fortescue was born.[2]

Fortescue himself conformed to the Church of England, but as a Whig collaborator he accepted James II's religious policy and was recommended as court candidate for the county in 1688, probably to keep him out of the Earl of Bath's borough of Plymouth. At the general election of 1689 he was returned for Tregony, six miles from Penwarne, doubtless with the assistance of the Boscawen interest. An inactive Member of the Convention, he was appointed to only three committees, those to consider the petition from the widow of Sir Thomas Armstrong*, to reverse his attainder, and to prepare charges against the former treasury solicitors, all in the second session. He supported the disabling clause in the bill to restore corporations, and remained a court Whig under William III and Anne. He died in the closing months of 1719. His eldest son was raised to the peerage in 1721, and a younger son sat for Barnstaple and Devon under George II as an opposition Whig.[3]

[1] Vivian, *Vis. Devon*, 355. [2] Lysons, *Devon*, 82; Hoskins, *Devon*, 195; *Paroch. Hist. Cornw.* iii. 324. [3] *Hist. Reg. Chron.* 41; *Pol. State*, xviii. 583.

P.W./J.P.F.

FORTH, Hugh (1610–76), of Clapham, Surr.

WIGAN   1659, c. Apr.–31 July 1660

bap. 6 July 1610, 1st s. of Robert Forth, brazier, of Standish Gate, Wigan, Lancs. by Catherine, da. of William Gardiner of Wigan. *m.* (1) Sarah, da. of John Fowle, merchant, of London, 1da.; (2) 8 Sept. 1645, Sarah, da. of William Essington, merchant, of London, *s.p.*; (3) lic. 10 Oct. 1667, Amy, da. of Robert Gurdon of Assington, Suff., *s.p. suc.* fa. 1622.[1]

Commr. for sewers, Kent 1657.[2]

Four generations of Forth's ancestors had resided in Wigan. Their efforts to establish kinship with a neighbouring gentry family called Ford had failed, but Forth's grandfather and uncle were both prominent on the corporation in the reign of James I, and engaged in bitter dispute with the local church authorities. Forth himself, left fatherless at the age of 12, went up to London and became a merchant. On the eve of the Civil War he was lodging in the house of his cousin, Robert Gardiner, in Basinghall Street. Gardiner was one of the leading City Royalists, but Forth was not implicated in his cousin's activities. He was not allowed to draw Gardiner's dividends from the East India Company during the war, but he did secure the desequestration of the house in 1646. He was returned to Richard Cromwell's Parliament for his home town, and in 1660 he was re-elected, this time together with his former landlord's son, William Gardiner*. As one of the small group of Members commissioned on 9 May to raise a loan of £30,000 in the City, he immediately offered £500 from his own resources, for which he was formally thanked by the House. Although presumably a supporter of the Restoration, he was named to no more committees. His principal motive for sitting may have been to exert leverage for a claim on the East India Company, and on 27 June they agreed to pay him and his partner £2,000 on account. His election was declared void on 31 July, and he is not likely to have stood again. He was buried at St. Mary Aldermanbury on 20 Feb. 1676, the only member of the family to sit in Parliament. He does not seem to have been related to the London aldermen and excise farmers, Dannett and John Forth, though he may have shared their religious sympathies, for his widow came from a strongly Presbyterian family and married the eminent nonconformist divine, Dr Thomas Jacombe.[3]

[1] *Wigan Par. Reg.* (Lancs. Par. Reg. Soc. iv), 77, 244, 270; Lancs. RO, will of Robert Forth; *Vis. London* (Harl. Soc. xv), 259; (xcii), 66; *Vis. Lancs.* (Chetham Soc. lxxiv), 95; Soc. of Genealogists, Boyd's London Units 10542; *London Mar. Lic.* ed. Foster, 502. [2] C181/6/228. [3] *Church and Manor of Wigan* (Chetham Soc. n.s. xvi), 213, 259–60, 294; E179/252/2; *Cal. Ct. Mins. E.I. Co.* ed. Sainsbury, ii. 356; vi. 22; *St. Mary Aldermanbury* (Harl. Soc. Reg. lxii), 189; J. R. Woodhead, *Rulers of London*, 71–72; A. G. Matthews, *Calamy Revised*, 293.

M.W.H./I.C.

FOULIS, Sir David, 3rd Bt. (1633–95), of Ingleby Greenhow, Yorks.

NORTHALLERTON   1685

bap. 14 Mar. 1633, 1st s. of Sir Henry Foulis, 2nd Bt., of Ingleby Greenhow by Mary, da. of Sir Thomas Layton of Sexhow. *m. c.* June 1655, Catherine, da. of Sir David Watkins of Covent Garden, Westminster, 6s. (2 *d.v.p.*) 5da. *suc.* fa. 13 Sept. 1643.[1]

Commr. for assessment, Yorks. (N. Riding) 1657, Aug. 1660–80, 1689–90, j.p. 1657–c.1663; commr. for militia, Yorks. Mar. 1660; lt.-col. of militia ft. (N. Riding) by 1665, col. 1670–Feb. 1688, dep. lt. 1666–Feb. 1688, Oct. 1688–d.; freeman, Hartlepool 1671.[2]

Foulis's ancestors had been in the service of the Stuarts since the 15th century, and regularly represented Edinburgh in the Scottish Parliament. His grandfather came south with James I, who made him cofferer to the prince and gave him crown lands in Yorkshire worth £1,000 p.a.; but when his accounts were queried he went into opposition, and was imprisoned in 1633 for instigating resistance to compositions for knighthood. His father gave evidence against Strafford, and took up arms for Parliament in the Civil War. Foulis himself married the daughter of one of the leading compounding officials, and seems to have been removed from the bench about the time of the anabaptist plot. A brief venture into alum mining seems to have brought him little profit. During the exclusion crisis a courtier described him as 'very well-principled', and he was active as a deputy lieutenant in searching the homes of suspects after the Rye House Plot. He was returned as a Tory for Northallerton at the general election of 1685. He was listed among the Opposition, but was given leave of absence on 22 June and left no other trace on the records of James II's Parliament. To the lord lieutenant's questions on the Tests and Penal Laws he replied:

> I have no thoughts of being a Parliament man, so to that particular I can only say (with all duty and submission) that I ever judged divers of the Penal Laws very severe, and if I were a Parliament man should heartily press and wish (as I now do) a review were made of them and the Tests; and when the debate should be argued in the House, for or against them, I should most faithfully declare my judgment according to my conscience and reason.... I shall endeavour that such be chosen as I truly think are undoubtedly loyal and faithful to the crown, of unbiased judgments rightly to understand the Penal Laws and Tests, and fit for the service of their country.... As I ever admired moderation, so I shall always live in full peace and amity with all my fellow subjects that are truly faithful to the King, and shall persuade others to do the like.

He was removed from local office, but restored in the autumn and took an active part in guarding the coast against the Dutch. His attitude to the Revolution is not known. He died on 13 Mar. 1695 and was buried at Ingleby, the only member of his family to sit at Westminster.[3]

[1] Clay, *Dugdale's Vis. Yorks.* i. 148–9; *St. Paul Covent Garden* (Harl. Soc. Reg. xxxv), 7. [2] *Add.* 41254, ff. 37v; *HMC Var.* ii. 165; H. B. M'Call, *Fam. of Wandesford*, 291; *CSP Dom.* 1687–9, p. 315; C. Sharp, *Hist. Hartlepool*, 72. [3] *VCH Yorks. N. Riding*, ii. 245; J. T. Cliffe, *Yorks. Gentry*, 86, 138, 327, 343; Sheepscar Lib. Mexborough mss 15/90; R. B. Turton, *Alum Farm*, 191; *HMC Var.* ii. 169; *HMC 7th Rep.* 415.

P.A.B.

FOUNTAINE, Andrew (c.1637–1707), of Narford, Norf. and Bell Bar, North Mimms, Herts.

NEWTON   1679 (Mar.), 1679 (Oct.), 1681

b. c.1637, 2nd s. of Brigg Fountaine (*d.*1661) of Salle, Norf. and the Inner Temple by Joanna, da. of Andrew Henley of Taunton, Som. *educ.* I. Temple 1655–7; travelled abroad c.1657–61. *m.* (1) Theophila, da. of Edmund Stubbe, rector of Huntingfield, Suff. 1621–59, wid. of William Wells of Halvergate, Norf., 1da.; (2) lic. 29 Apr. 1672, aged 35, Sarah, da. of (Sir) Thomas Chicheley* of Wimpole, Cambs., 3s. (1 *d.v.p.*) 2da.[1]

Commr. for assessment, Herts. 1679–80, 1689–90.

Fountaine came from a Norfolk family which had been of local importance since the 15th century. His father, a barrister, may have had royalist sympathies during the Civil War: he was assessed at £400 at Haberdashers' Hall in 1644. Fountaine became acquainted with John Coke I* at the Temple, and allegedly saved him from drowning. After travelling with him on the Continent he became his steward, and extracted large sums of money from the estate. In 1666 he purchased the estate of Brookmans in Hertfordshire from Sir William Dudley*. But three years later he was dismissed from his stewardship.[2]

Although Fountaine's second wife complained ceaselessly of his boorish, drunken habits, it was she who found him a seat in the Exclusion Parliaments, highly desirable if he were to avoid a debtors' prison. Her brother-in-law Richard Legh*, who controlled Newton, even paid his election expenses. Legh was an opponent of exclusion, and Fountaine was marked as a court supporter on Lord Huntingdon's list; but Fountaine had no compunction in voting for the first exclusion bill. Otherwise he was completely inactive. He does not appear to have sought election in 1685, but in 1689 he appealed to the young Peter Legh* for a seat at Newton. Although his claim was supported by Legh's mother, he was refused and never sat again. Increasing financial difficulties compelled him in 1701 to sell to John Somers* his Hertfordshire estate, including his newly-built house at Bell Bar. He died on 7 Feb. 1707 and was buried at Narford, the only member of his family to enter Parliament.[3]

[1] Blomefield, *Norf.* vi. 234–5; *Vis. Suff.* (Harl. Soc. lxi), 42; *London Mar. Lic.* ed. Foster, 505; *HMC Lords,* i. 115. [2] *Blomefield,* vi. 233; *Cal. Comm. Adv. Money,* 406; Chauncy, *Herts.* ii. 441; Clutterbuck, *Herts.* i. 454; C. J. James, *Coke Fam. and Descendants,* 106–7. [3] E. C. Legh, Lady Newton, *House of Lyme,* 291–2, 310; *Lyme Letters,* 101–2, 161; *Le Neve's Knights* (Harl. Soc. viii), 472.

I.C.

FOWELL (VOWELL), Edmund (c.1598–1664), of Harewood, Calstock, Cornw.

TAVISTOCK	c. Aug. 1646[1]
DEVON	1656
TAVISTOCK	1659
PLYMOUTH	29 Apr.–9 June 1660

b. c.1598, 1st s. of John Fowell of Plymouth, Devon by Anne, da. of John Croker of Lyneham, Yealmpton, Devon. *educ.* Broadgates Hall, Oxf. 1616; M. Temple 1617, called 1625. *m.* (1) by 1632, Jane (*d.*1640), da. of Sir Anthony Barker† of Sonning, Berks, 2s. (1 *d.v.p.*) 1da.; (2) by 1647, Alice, da. of Sir Francis Glanville of Kilworthy, Tavistock, Devon, wid. of John Connock of Harewood, 2s. 2da. *suc.* fa. 1627.[2]

Town clerk, Plymouth 1627–47, coroner 1635; j.p. Devon and Cornw. 1647–9, 1650–Mar. 1660, Devon Apr.–July 1660, 1661–*d.*; commr. for assessment, Devon 1647–8, 1652, 1661–*d.*, Cornw. and Devon 1657, Jan. 1660; bencher, M. Temple 1648; commr. for oyer and terminer, Western circuit 1655, militia, Devon Mar. 1660.[3]

Fowell's father, a younger son of the Fowellscombe family, became town clerk of Plymouth, an office which Fowell inherited. A lawyer like his father, he acquired property there and at Tavistock and an interest in the fishing industry. His second marriage brought him the lease of a duchy of Cornwall estate on the other bank of the Tamar, which he purchased for £555 18s. at the sale of crown lands. A Presbyterian, he did not sit after Pride's Purge, but was allowed to take his seat in the second Parliament of the Protectorate. Although he signed the Devon declaration for a free Parliament, he did not return with the other secluded Members in 1660. At the general election Fowell and John Maynard I* were returned by the corporation and allowed to sit on the merits of the return. He was probably an opponent of the Court. As 'Mr Vowell' he was appointed to two committees, one to prepare for a conference on the regicides and the other to draft a declaration against recusants. On 30 May he was teller against the Lords amendments to the judicial proceedings bill; but he was unseated on 9 June on the merits of the election, and retired from political life. His lease of Calstock was renewed in 1661. He was incapacitated by a stroke in September 1663, when he signed his will with a mark, and was buried at Calstock on 27 Feb. following. Harewood reverted to the Connock family, and nothing further is known of Fowell's descendants.[4]

[1] Did not sit after Pride's Purge, 6 Dec. 1648. [2] Vivian, *Vis. Devon*, 369, 412; *M. Temple Bench Bk.* 197; PCC 92 Harvey, 54 Coke. [3] *HMC 9th Rep.* pt. 1, pp. 283–4; *Trans. Devon Assoc.* x. 312; *Thurloe*, iii. 296. [4] Lysons, *Cornw.* 53; E320/D31; Lady Eliott-Drake, *Fam. and Heirs of Drake*, i. 421; Vivian, *Vis. Cornw.* 93; *Cal. Treas. Bks.* viii. 210; Calstock par. reg.

M.W.H./J.S.C./J.P.F.

FOWELL, John (1623–77), of Washbourne, Harberton, Devon.

ASHBURTON   1659, 1660, 1661–8 Jan. 1677

bap. 14 Aug. 1623, 1st s. of Sir Edmund Fowell†, 1st Bt., of Fowellscombe, Ugborough by Margaret, da. of Sir Anthony Powlett of Hinton St. George, Som. *m.* by 1665, Elizabeth, da. of Sir John Chichester of Hall, Devon, 2s. (1 *d.v.p.*) 3da. *suc.* fa. as 2nd Bt. Oct. 1674.[1]

J.p. Devon 1652–3, 1657–July 1660, Sept. 1660–*d.*, commr. for assessment 1657, Aug. 1660–74, militia Mar. 1660; gov. Dartmouth 1661–*d.*; commr. for corporations, Devon 1662–3, loyal and indigent officers 1662, v.-adm. 1666–*d.*; commr. of inquiry, Newfoundland govt. 1667, pressing seamen, Devon 1672, recusants 1675, v.-warden of the stannaries ?–*d.*[2]

Fowell's family was founded by a lawyer, who sat for Totnes in 1455. His father represented Ashburton from its re-enfranchisement by the Long Parliament till Pride's Purge; a Presbyterian, he was active in sequestration work in Devon, but welcomed the Restoration and was made a baronet. Returned for the family borough in 1659 and 1660, Fowell probably supported the Court in the Convention, in which he was moderately active; he made no speeches, but probably sat on 15 committees, of which the most important were for fixing the maximum rate of interest at 6 per cent and for the attainder bill. He was also concerned with the suppression of profanity and the proclamation of a fast. On 28 Dec. 1660 he obtained the concurrence of the Upper House to a grant of £10,000 to the Duke of York.[3]

Fowell was considered a sufficiently staunch Royalist to retain his seat during the Presbyterian débâcle in 1661; he may have enjoyed the support of George Monck*, who recommended him as governor of Dartmouth. Though lucrative, this post seems to have carried little political weight. He was not an active Member of the Cavalier Parliament, in which he was named to only 35 committees, and twice acted as teller. In the first session he was entrusted with carrying a local estate bill to the Lords; he also served on the committees for the corporations and militia bills. On 19 Mar. 1662 he was teller in favour of excluding tin from the provisions of the bill against customs fraud, and in the following month he attended the King to ask for the suspension of the Merchant Adventurers' monopoly of cloth exports to Germany. A letter written many years later shows Fowell keenly alive to 'the decay of our woollen trade, which falls exceedingly heavy on this poor, populous country', and convinced that government interference could only be harmful. In 1664 he was among the Members appointed to consider a clothiers' petition and to draw up a bill for the better observance of

Sunday. In 1666 the petition against the Canary patent came before him, and he was among those asked to estimate the yield of the hearth-tax.[4]

At the instance of Thomas Clifford* Fowell reluctantly and ineffectively intervened in the Dartmouth by-election of 1667 on behalf of Joseph Williamson*, covering himself beforehand with the remark that the fickle corporation had disappointed him once before, and afterwards with the assurance that his failure was due to want of power, not want of will. About this time he probably succeeded to Clifford's farm of the logwood patent, and in 1669 he was listed by Sir Thomas Osborne* among those who usually voted for supply. In the session of 1670–1, he was named to two committees concerned with woollen manufactures, but after that he probably ceased to attend. He was granted £500 on the hearth-tax in 1675, and on receipt of the government whip, promised Williamson to come up 'in spite of the indisposition which you know I am subject to'. Nevertheless, he retained an intelligent interest in politics, as appears from a letter of 14 Jan. 1676:

> Till we come plainly to believe that what is truly for the interest of the King is for the interest of the people, and whatever is for the good of the people is for his Majesty's advantage, I doubt we shall never enjoy that happiness which is daily prayed for.

Williamson was so impressed that he showed the letter to the King, who returned it without comment. The last reference to him is as a sure man for the Court in the list drawn up by Sir Richard Wiseman* in 1676. Fowell died on 8 Jan. 1677, three days after inheriting his mother's jointure of £900 p.a., and was buried at Ugborough.[5]

[1] Vivian, *Vis. Devon*, 370 [2] *CSP Dom.* 1661–2, p. 311; 1664–5, p. 177; 1671–2, pp. 346, 402; *APC Col.* i. 433; Exeter City Lib. DD 63162; Devon RO, 1392M/L1676/1; Ind. 24557. [3] Keeler, *Long Parl.* 180. [4] *Cal. Treas. Bks.* i. 384; P. Russell, *Dartmouth*, 131; *CSP Dom.* 1675–6, p. 512. [5] *CSP Dom.* 1666–7, pp. 379, 473; 1675–6, pp. 326, 512, 541; 1676–7, p. 500; *Cal. Treas. Bks.* ii. 402; iii. 167; iv. 314.

M.W.H./J.P.F.

FOWELL, Sir John, 3rd Bt. (1665–92), of Fowell-scombe, Ugborough, Devon.

TOTNES   1689, 1690–Nov. 1692.

bap. 12 Dec. 1665, o. surv. s. of John Fowell*. *unm. suc.* fa. 8 Jan. 1677.
    Freeman, Totnes to 1684; j.p. Devon 1687–July 1688, 1689–*d.*, commr. for assessment 1689–90.[1]

Fowell's replies on the repeal of the Test Act and Penal Laws followed the standard negative pattern set by Sir Edward Seymour*. He was apparently in London in November 1688, but slipped away to join William of Orange before the end of the month.

The family borough of Ashburton was securely under Whig control in 1689, but Fowell was successful at Totnes, three miles from his estate at Washbourne, no doubt with the aid of the Seymour interest. An inactive Member of the Convention, he was listed by Anthony Rowe* as voting to agree with the Lords that the throne was not vacant. His only committees before the recess were to draw up the address of thanks for the King's promise to maintain the Church, to consider the bill for restoring corporations and to inquire into the education of Papists' children. In the second session was added to the committee of elections and privileges, and named to a committee on a private bill on 2 Jan. 1690, when he presumably voted against the disabling clause in the bill to restore corporations. He was re-elected two months later, but buried at Ugborough on 26 Nov. 1692. The baronetcy became extinct, and his intention of leaving his estate to a cousin of his name and blood was thwarted by a technicality. Fowellscombe eventually came to his sister, the mother of Arthur Champernowne, MP for Totnes from 1715 to 1717.[2]

[1] *Trans. Devon. Assoc.* viii. 367. [2] *Hatton Corresp.* (Cam. Soc. n.s. xxiii), 110; *HMC 7th Rep.* 416.

J.P.F.

FOWKE, John (c.1596–1662), of Mark Lane, London and Claybury, Essex.

LONDON   1661–22 Apr. 1662

b. c.1596, 3rd s. of William Fowke of Tewkesbury, Glos. by Alice, da. of George Carr of Bushley, Worcs. *m.* (1) bef. 1634 (with £800), Catherine, da. of Richard Briggs, Haberdasher, of Lombard Street, London, 2s. 1da.; (2) lic. 25 Sept. 1638, aged 42, Mary, da. of Edward Basse, Mercer, of Cheapside, London, 1s. *d.v.p.* 5da.[1]
    Freeman, Haberdashers' Co. 1617, master 1642–3, 1652–3, 1655; committee, E.I. Co. 1625–6; asst. Levant Co. 1629–54; common councilman, London 1641, alderman 1642–*d.*, sheriff 1643–4, ld. mayor 1652–3; commr. for militia 1642–Apr. 1647, Sept. 1647–53, 1659, assessment, London 1642, 1647–9, Jan. 1660–*d.*, Glos. 1657; asst. corp. of the poor, London 1647, 1649; j.p. Glos. 1649–Mar. 1660, Essex 1656–Mar. 1660; pres. Christ's Hosp. 1651–2; commr. for oyer and terminer, London July 1660, sewers, Havering and Dagenham levels Sept. 1660.[2]
    Commr. for customs 1643–5; comptroller and trustee, bishops' lands 1646; dean and chapter lands 1649; commr. for high court of justice 1649, regulation of trade 1650–1, relief under articles of war 1652, law reform 1652–3, sale of crown property 1653; judge of probate 1653–4; commr. for adventurers [I] 1654, security [I] 1656.[3]

Fowke claimed descent from the Staffordshire gentry and, through his mother, from a well-known Tyneside merchant family. He was apprenticed to a London Haberdasher, but his chief interest was in the Mediterranean trade, and he wore the livery of his company for a quarter of a century before achieving office. Nor was he particularly successful as a merchant; on the eve of the Civil War he was only in the third rank for 'ability'. Politically, however, he was prominent in opposition to Charles I. In obedience to a resolution of the Commons he refused to pay tonnage and poundage in 1627, and his goods to the value of £5,827 were seized by the customs. A further refusal in 1629 led to his commitment to the Fleet prison until he was able to produce £40,000 bail. After a brief period on the East India board, he also fell out with the company about his liabilities as security for a defaulting merchant. He played a leading part in stimulating petitions from the citizens to the Long Parliament and in organizing the London train-bands. In January 1643 Charles described him as 'notoriously guilty of schism and high treason'. During the Civil War he gladly abandoned trade for the more profitable service of the state. But he was again committed to the Fleet in 1645 for refusing to deliver his accounts as commissioner of customs on oath. Despite these occasional twinges of conscience, his prosperity increased, especially after his appointment as comptroller of bishops' lands. In 1648 he spent £3,819 in buying four of the bishop's manors in his native county, and he acquired an estate in Essex. His rapacity was the delight of royalist propagandists. After persistent petitioning he was awarded £27,615 compensation for his losses over tunnage and poundage, and £7,000 damages against the East India Company. Though regarded as a Presbyterian, he was 'not much noted for religion' and complied with all the changes of the Interregnum.[4]

In the months preceding the Restoration, Fowke, as chairman of the committee of safety, was the most active and influential member of the common council, being anxious to prevent the corporation giving way to the popular pressure for a free Parliament, lest they should produce a direct confrontation between the City of London and the army. He signed the common council petition of 24 Dec. 1659 for the return of the secluded Members and the convening of a free Parliament, and was a member of the delegation to present it. On 19 Jan. 1660 he was one of the three commissioners appointed to treat with Monck in the name of the City. He was on the committee appointed on 22 Feb. to draw up a 'congratulatory petition' to Parliament for restoring the city gates and the common council, and when presenting it he explained that his brethren 'found some persons for a monarchical, some for a Commonwealth, some for no government at

all. The last they did dislike; for the other they would not presume to direct, but should acquiesce and submit to the determination of Parliament.' When the Restoration seemed inevitable he hastened to publish documentary evidence that he had refused to act as one of the King's judges in 1649, and informed a correspondent of Hyde's that he would be delighted to receive a letter from Charles II. He was appointed to the committees of the common council to prepare the City's answer to the Declaration of Breda, to draw up a petition against the excise, and to raise a loan of £100,000 in the City for the disbandment of the army.[5]

At the general election of 1661 Fowke, the senior alderman on the bench, was put up for London by the opponents of the Church, as 'a countenancer of good ministers' and 'deeply engaged in bishops' lands'. On his election Lord Wharton included him in his list of friends in the Cavalier Parliament. An inactive Member, he was appointed to only four committees. With the House about to adjourn on 31 July, he was ordered to bring in a bill after the summer recess to make stealing of children subject to the penalties of felony. He was among those named to the committee on the bill to prevent frauds on the customs (29 Jan. 1662). In the debate on the hearth-tax, he expressed the fear that it 'would set the chimneys, and so the City of London in a flame not easily to be quenched'. On 13 Mar. he moved a proviso for London to the bill for settling the militia. In the course of a long speech he

> let fall several factious and dangerous expressions tending to blemish the honour and justice of this House and their proceedings, and pretending he had direction from the City for bringing in this proviso. But [the House was] informed that the said alderman had solicited and endeavoured to incense the City and beget in them an ill opinion of the proceedings of the House, and that the proviso was contrary to the judgment and without the direction of the City.

A motion to send him to the Tower was rejected, but he received from the Speaker 'a grave and severe reprehension' on his knees at the bar of the House, and his proviso was laid aside. At his request the corporation resolved on 8 Apr. to pay him 4s. a day as parliamentary wages 'due by the statute' and his livery. Two days later he was named to the committee for his kidnapping bill; but on 22 Apr. he died of apoplexy. No other member of the family entered Parliament.[6]

[1] Vis. London (Harl. Soc. xv), 288; Vis. Glos. (Harl. Soc. xxi), 37; PCC 79 Byrde; Guildhall RO, 10091/19/180v; Misc. Gen. et Her. (ser. 5), ii. 219; St. Dunstan in the East (Harl. Soc. Reg. lxix), 85–91, 221. [2] Guildhall RO, 15857/1; J. R. Woodhead, Rulers of London, 72; C191/7/47. [3] G. E. Aylmer, State's Servants, 435; Cal. Cl. SP, ii. 171. [4] DNB; Clarendon, Rebellion, ii. 433; V. Pearl, London and the Outbreak of the Puritan Revolution, 130–1, 138, 316–20; Misc. Gen. et Her. (ser. 2), ii. 115; VCH Essex, v. 194;

CSP Dom. 1660–1, p. 539. [5] G. Davies, *Restoration*, 294; *Cal. Cl. SP*, iv. 526, 538, 597–8. [6] Guildhall RO, common council jnl.; *CSP Dom.* 1660–1, p. 539; D. R. Lacey, *Dissent and Parl. Pols.* 398; *CJ*, viii. 316, 386; *Voyce from the Watch Tower*, 296; *Smyth's Obituary* (Cam. Soc. xliv), 55.

E.C.

FOWNES, Richard (1652–1714), of Steepleton Iwerne, Dorset.

CORFE CASTLE	1681, 1685, 1689, 1690, 1695, 26 Apr. 1699, 1701 (Feb.), 1701 (Dec.), 1702, 1705, 1708, 1710, 1713–July 1714

bap. 25 Aug. 1652, 1st s. of Thomas Fownes of Steepleton Iwerne by Alice, da. of John Mynne of Woodcote, Epsom, Surr. *educ.* Oriel, Oxf. 1668. *m.* (1) aft. 1677, Elizabeth, da. of Gabriel Armstrong of Rempstone, Notts., 2s. (1 *d.v.p.*) 1da.; (2) settlement 21 Nov. 1693, Elizabeth, da. of William Aysh of South Petherton, Som., wid. of Samuel Cabell of Buckfastleigh, Devon, *s.p. suc.* fa. 1670.[1]

Commr. for assessment, Dorset 1679–80, 1689–90, dep. lt. 1680–May 1688, Oct. 1688–*d.*; commr. for visitation, Poole 1681; capt. of militia horse, Dorset 1683–?June 1688, j.p. 1685–June 1688, Nov. 1688–*d.*, commr. for rebels' estates 1686; freeman, Poole 1691; steward of crown estates, Som. 1705–7.[2]

Fownes was the grandson of a Plymouth merchant who served as mayor in 1619–20. His father, who was too young to take part in the Civil War, bought a Dorset estate from George Pitt* in 1654 for £6,000. At the Restoration he was appointed colonel of the East Dorset militia, and acted as sheriff for the general election of 1661 and as a commissioner for corporations. Fownes himself, a churchman and a Tory, threatened to oppose Thomas Bennett* at Shaftesbury in 1681; but Thomas Freke I* found him a seat at Corfe Castle at the expense of a less prominent exclusionist, Nathaniel Bond*. The first of the family to sit, he left no trace on the records of the Oxford Parliament, but he was active in suppressing nonconformity in Poole, and as a deputy lieutenant he helped to search the house of Edward Norton* after the Rye House Plot. He was again totally inactive in James II's Parliament. He gave negative answers on the repeal of the Test Act and Penal Laws, and was removed from local office. The King's electoral agents described his interest at Corfe as dependent on William Culliford†. He supported the Revolution, signing the warrants for raising money for William of Orange on 30 Nov. 1688, and was re-elected to the Convention. He voted to agree with the Lords that the throne was not vacant, and was appointed to the committees for two estate bills. With one brief interval he retained his seat for the rest of his life, voting with the Tories and refusing

the Association in 1696. He was reported dead on 20 July 1714. The defeat of his son at the general election in the following year concluded the parliamentary history of this branch of the Fownes family.[3]

[1] Herts. RO, Cheshunt par. reg.; *Vis. Dorset* (Harl. Soc. cxvii), 4; F. Brown, *Som. Wills*, iv. 98–99; Exeter City Lib. 48/14/76/1. [2] SP44/53/53; Churchill College, Camb., Erle-Drax mss; *Cal. Treas. Bks.* v. 1204; viii. 546; xxii. 270; Poole Archives, B17. [3] Vivian, *Vis. Devon*, 272–3; Hutchins, i. 299; Eg. 2537, f. 264; Pythouse Pprs. ed. Day, 89, 97; *CSP Dom.* Jan.-June 1683, p. 376; Erle-Drax mss; *HMC Portland*, v. 473.

J.P.F.

FOX, Charles (1660–1713), of Chiswick, Mdx. and Farley, Wilts.

EYE	8 Dec. 1680
CRICKLADE	26 May 1685, 1689, 1690, 1695
SALISBURY	1698, 9 July 1701, 1701 (Dec.), 1702, 1705, 1708, 1710, 31 Aug.–21 Sept. 1713

b. 2 Jan. 1660, 3rd s. of (Sir) Stephen Fox* by 1st w. *educ.* travelled abroad (Italy, Germany, Holland, France), 1676–8. *m.* 1679 (with £6,000) Elizabeth (*d.* 1703), da. and h. of Sir William Trollope, 2nd Bt., of Casewick, Lincs., *s.p.*[1]

Commr. for assessment, Wilts. 1679–80, Mdx. 1689, Lincs. and Wilts. 1689–90; freeman, Salisbury 1680, Portsmouth 1684; j.p. Wilts. 1682–June 1688, Oct. 1688–*d.*[2]

Paymaster of the forces (sole) 1682–5, (jt.) 1702–5; jt. receiver-gen. and paymaster [I] 1690–8.[3]

Fox was born at Brussels just before the Restoration, named after Charles II who acted as his godfather, and naturalized in 1670. Both his elder brothers were then dead, and in 1676 he was sent on a tour of the Continent under the charge of Dr Younger, later dean of Salisbury. On his return he was married to a Lincolnshire heiress 'who brings with her (besides a great sum) near, if not altogether, £2,000 p.a.', though in fact her guardian, Sir Robert Carr*, defaulted on part of her portion. The Water Eaton estate, near Cricklade, was settled on him on this occasion, and he probably first stood for the borough at the first general election of 1679. He was not successful, and in the autumn he contested Eye on the interest of his brother-in-law, the 3rd Lord Cornwallis. After a double return had been decided in his favour, he took his seat in the second Exclusion Parliament, still under age. He left no trace on its proceedings, but probably voted with the Court. It was rumoured that he would contest Downton in 1681, but nothing came of it. He was given the lucrative office of paymaster-general in 1682 under the supervision of his father; but he was corpulent and easy-going, and never achieved eminence in either administration or politics.[4]

Fox stood again for Cricklade in 1685, and was seated on the merits of the return. Apart from one short break in 1701, he represented this borough or Salisbury for the rest of his life. 'His modesty made him backward in attempting set speeches', but as a committeeman he was moderately active in James II's Parliament, with seven committees, including those to examine the disbandment accounts, to estimate the yield of a tax on new buildings, and to reform the bankruptcy law. He was much disturbed by the employment of Roman Catholic officers in the army, and was advised by his friends to absent himself from Parliament in order not to displease the King by voting to discuss grievances before supply.

> But, the day being come on which the question was to be put, he found such a concern growing upon him for the cause of the Church ... that, moved by the impulse of his conscience, he could not be easy till he went to the Speaker's chamber. His coming thither occasioned his friends to be again importunate with him to withdraw himself. ... But hearing the debates arising in the House, he could no longer contain himself, but went into it, even after the question was put (a thing that was unusual, but then allowed), and carried it ... by his single vote; for which he was reprimanded by King James, and dismissed from his valuable employments.

The paymastership, which some valued at £9,000 p.a., though his father reckoned the net annual income at £3,164, was given to Lord Ranelagh* (Richard Jones*). But Fox was allowed to kiss the King's hand in the following January, and in 1688 the royal electoral agents, who correctly expected him to be re-elected, hoped that he might 'go right' on James's ecclesiastical policy.[5]

In the Convention Fox voted to agree with the Lords that the throne was not vacant, and he was again moderately active. He was appointed to 17 committees, acted as teller in four divisions, and made two recorded speeches. On 14 June 1689 he strongly denied the old charge that his father had offered bribes from the secret service fund to Members of the Cavalier Parliament. When the naval victuallers were ordered into custody on 23 Nov. he came forward as security for Sir Richard Haddock*, and on 5 Dec. he was teller for the successful motion for their release on bail. A member of the committee on the bill for restoring corporations, he acted as teller for disabling James II's regulators when the measure reached the floor of the House.[6]

A high-church Tory, Fox was far more of a party man than his father, though he regularly voted for supply under William III and Anne. He was dismissed in 1696 for voting against the attainder of Sir John Fenwick* and again under Anne

for voting for the Tack. He died at Chiswick in his father's lifetime on 21 Sept. 1713, considerably indebted, and was buried at Farley.[7]

[1] G. S. Fox-Strangways, Earl of Ilchester, *Life of Henry Fox, 1st Lord Holland*, i. 12–14; C. Clay, *Public Finance and Private Wealth*, 267–8. [2] Hoare, *Wilts*. Salisbury, 477; R. East, *Portsmouth Recs*. 367. [3] Clay, 270. [4] Ilchester, i. 14; *Denizations and Naturalizations* (Huguenot Soc. xviii), 105; Clay, 267–9; *Evelyn Diary*, iii. 219, 248; Wilts RO, Radnor mss 1084, Ashe to Snow, 29 Jan. 1681. [5] *Mems. of Sir Stephen Fox* (1717), 77–78; *Reresby Mems*. 399, 401–2; *Ellis Corresp*. i. 14. [6] Grey, ix. 309, 444; *CJ*, x. 302, 323. [7] Clay, 270–5.

E.C.

FOX, Somerset (1618–89), of Caynham, nr. Ludlow, Salop.

LUDLOW   24 Feb. 1670, 1679 (Mar.)

bap. 18 Jan. 1618, 1st s. of Somerset Fox of Caynham and Gwernygoe, Mont. by Anne, da of Sir Walter Long† of South Wraxhall, Wilts. *educ*. Leyden 1633. *unm. suc*. fa. 1643.[1]

Cornet (royalist) ?1642–4; col. of ft. 1644–5.[2]

Commr. for assessment, Salop 1661–80, 1689–*d*., Herefs. 1673–80; dep. lt. Salop 1662–?87; freeman, Ludlow 1669, alderman by 1671; commr. for recusants, Salop 1675.[3]

Fox's ancestors were prominent in the affairs of Ludlow from the early 15th century, and regularly represented the borough, three miles from Caynham, in Tudor times. During the Civil War Fox's father served on the commission of array, while Fox himself returned from the Continent in 1642 with Prince Rupert, under whom he served in the Bristol garrison. His services to the parliamentary cause in securing the surrender of Ludlow Castle to John Birch* in 1646 were so highly valued that he was not required to compound for his delinquency, though he apparently went into exile. In 1648 he was ordered by the Prince of Wales to take charge of the munitions at Le Havre intended for the use of the Royalists in the second Civil War, and six years later he was involved with a cousin, a brother of Gilbert Gerard II*, in a plot to assassinate the Protector. The death sentence was commuted to transportation in view of his full confession, and he was ordered to be sent to Barbados with Edward Grey* and others. But he was still in England in 1656.[4]

At the Restoration Fox was granted a pension of £300 p.a. as compensation 'for his losses in the cause of the late King', and payment continued even during the 1666 freeze on the ground that he was 'in treaty for a marriage that may repair his fortune; but the chief obstacle thereto is the stop to his pension'. The match did not materialize however, and he seems to have died a bachelor. In 1670 he was returned to the Cavalier Parliament at a by-election for Ludlow, where he retained a strong interest as principal trustee of the family charity, patron of the living, and owner of a large town house. An inactive Member, he was added to the committee of elections and privileges in three sessions, and appointed to 11 others, including those for the relief of loyal and indigent officers (19 Dec. 1670) and to recommend measures for preventing the export of wool (21 Feb. 1671). His name appeared on the opposition list of the court party and on the Paston list of 1673–4. During the debate on recalling British subjects from the French service on 10 May 1675 'some warm expressions' passed between (Sir) Robert Thomas* and Fox, who 'upon command of the House [said that] he would give his honour to proceed no farther thereupon'. In the same session he was added to the committee on the bill for preservation of the Forest of Dean. He received the government whip in the autumn in the shape of a personal letter from Secretary Coventry, and on 3 Nov. contradicted Birch's assertion that there were plentiful supplies of timber in the Forest of Dean, having 'been told by credible persons in the country that there is not timber in all that forest to build two second-rate ships and two third-rates'. His name appeared on the list of dependants, on the working lists, and on the list of government supporters drawn up by Sir Richard Wiseman* during the recess. Shaftesbury classed him as 'thrice vile', and in *Flagellum Parliamentarium* he was described as 'a privy chamber man', though this cannot be confirmed from the official lists, and 'a court cully', which underestimates him, for he was given an additional secret service pension of £200 p.a. on 6 Apr. 1678, though he made no more speeches and served on no committees after 1675. He was on both lists of the court party at this time.[5]

Fox was re-elected at the first general election of 1679, when he was marked 'vile' on Shaftesbury's list. He voted against the first exclusion bill, but took no other known part in this Parliament. Blacklisted in the 'unanimous club', he was replaced by Thomas Walcot* in the autumn, and probably never stood again. In December 1680 he was chosen as town clerk by the corporation, to whom he gave a silver tankard. But this appointment was probably regarded as inimical to the Charlton interest, and was quashed by the Privy Council, which 'did not think fit that Col. Somerset Fox . . . should undergo the burden thereof, as well in regard of his age and infirmity as that he hath formerly served his Majesty in employments of greater dignity'. He was buried at Ludlow on 11 Oct. 1689, the last of his family, leaving a personal estate of £6,000. The land was divided among his four sisters.[6]

[1] *Salop Par. Reg.* Hereford Dioc. xiii. 155, 419; *Mont. Colls.* xxvii. 92–94. [2] Information from Brig. Peter Young; *Royalist Ordnance Pprs.* (Oxf. Rec. Soc. xlix), 329; *Symonds Diary* (Cam. Soc. lxxiv), 271. [3] Ludlow ledger bk. 1648–80, f. 259; *Trans. Salop Arch. and Nat. Hist. Soc.* (ser. 4), ii. 32–33. [4] Ibid. 10; *Mont. Colls.* xxvii. 103; E. Warburton, *Mems. Prince Rupert*, i. 112; *HMC 6th Rep.* 172; *HMC Pepys*, 213; D. Underdown, *Royalist Conspiracy*, 101–2; *Thurloe*, iii. 453–4; *CSP Dom.* 1656–7, p. 584. [5] *CSP Dom.* 1661–2, p. 338; 1665–6, p. 326; Grey, iii. 129–30, 390. [6] *Trans. Salop Arch. and Nat. Hist. Soc.* (ser. 4), ii. 33; *CSP Dom.* 1680–1, p. 158; PC2/69/181; *Salop Par. Reg.* xiii. 541; C8/416/97; *Mont. Colls.* xxvii. 106–8.

E.C.

FOX, Stephen (1627–1716), of Farley, Wilts. and Whitehall.[1]

SALISBURY	30 Nov. 1661
WESTMINSTER	1679 (Mar.)
SALISBURY	1685
WESTMINSTER	9 Nov. 1691, 1695
CRICKLADE	26 Jan. 1699, 1701 (Feb.), 1701 (Dec.)
SALISBURY	15 Mar. 1714

b. 27 Mar. 1627, 6th but 4th surv. s. of William Fox (*d.*1652) of Farley by Elizabeth, da. of Thomas Pavy of Plaitford. *educ.* Salisbury cathedral sch. 1633–40. *m.* (1) 8 Dec. 1651, Elizabeth (*d.* 11 Aug. 1696), da. of William Whittle of London, 7s. *d.v.p.* 3da.; (2) 11 July 1703, Christian (*d.*1718), da. of Francis Hopes, rector of Aswarby, Lincs. 1682–1705, 2s. 2da. Kntd. 1 July 1665.[2]

Gent. of the horse to the Prince of Wales 1646; master of the horse 1649–50; clerk of the stables 1653–4, the kitchen 1654–June 1660; clerk-comptroller of the green cloth June 1660–1, clerk 1661–78, 1679–89; paymaster of the forces 1661–76, May–Nov. 1679; commr. of the stables 1679–82, 1702; ld. of Treasury 1679–85, 1687–9, 1690–1702, first ld. 1696–7.

Freeman, Salisbury 1661; commr. for assessment, Wilts. 1661–80, 1689–90, Salisbury and Westminster 1663–80, Hants 1665–74, Som. 1673–80, Westminster 1689, highways, London and Westminster 1662; j.p. Mdx. 1680–7, ?May 1688–*d.*, Westminster 1680–9, Wilts. by 1682–9; recorder, Boston 1682–5.[3]

In his own words 'a wonderful child of providence', Fox rose to immense wealth and public prominence from genuinely humble origins. The family status lay on the borderline between peasantry and gentry; but he received a sound general education as a chorister in Salisbury cathedral, and his elder brother John, who held a post at Court on the dean's recommendation, brought him into the household of the royal children as supernumerary servant and play-fellow. After acting as page to Lady Stafford, the Countess of Sunderland, and the Earl of Leicester, he entered the service of Lord Percy, master of horse to the Prince of Wales, and under his 'severe discipline' followed the Cavalier army in 1644–5 and then went into exile in France and Jersey. When the royal stables were dispersed in 1650, Fox returned to the modest family home and married. His Wiltshire origins now stood him in good stead; first Hobbes obtained for him the post of keeper of the privy purse to the Earl of Devonshire, and then, on the earnest recommendation of Sir Edward Hyde†, he was appointed to manage the meagre financial resources of the exiled Court, under the modest style of clerk of the kitchen. Hyde found him

> very well qualified with languages and all other parts of clerkship, honesty and discretion that were necessary for the discharge of such a trust. . . . His great industry, modesty, and prudence did very much contribute to the bringing the family [i.e. Household], which for so many years had been under no government, into very good order.

He was granted arms in 1658, and at the Restoration he was promoted to the board of green cloth and given some small Hampshire leaseholds forfeited by one of the regicides. The decisive step in his career was his nomination as paymaster to the guards in January 1661, in order to ensure that morale in this miscellaneous body was not impaired by long delays and heavy arrears.[4]

Fox was first returned for Salisbury on the Hyde interest in a by-election at the end of the year. Farley is only five miles from the city, but he acquired a nominal property interest by leasing a vacant plot in the Close. His election expenditure totalled £87 10s., most of which went on 'an entertainment' for the corporation and a donation to the municipal poor relief fund. An inactive Member of the Cavalier Parliament, he was appointed to 32 committees, including the committee of elections and privileges in nine sessions, and made three recorded speeches. Outside the House his importance was drastically increased by the 'great undertaking' of 1662, under which he assumed personal responsibility for obtaining credit for the Pay Office. As he might have to wait up to 14 months before the Treasury could reimburse him, he was allowed to deduct 8 per cent from the crown and 3½ per cent from the soldiers. His accounts show that up to the third Dutch war and the Stop of the Exchequer he ploughed back most of the profits into the undertaking, only diversifying into well-secured loans to fellow courtiers and the purchase of pensions and offices. Listed as a court dependant in 1664, he was knighted in the following year. In 1666 Andrew Marvell* included him among the government whips:

> His birth, his youth, his brokage all dispraise
> In vain; for always he commands who pays.

The King, Fox recorded, expressed great satisfaction at the efficiency of the Pay Office during the second Dutch war, which contrasted favourably with the chaos of naval finance under Sir George Carteret*.[5]

It is also from Fox's pen that we have an account of his failure to join in the attack on his patron after he had been dismissed as lord chancellor in 1667:

> The King took it ill from me that I went in the Parliament for my lord chancellor against him. I took the liberty to say to his Majesty that I did know my lord chancellor so well that I could not in conscience give my vote against him; at which the King turned from me and left me to myself, saying I was an honest fellow.

He emerged unscathed from the public accounts commission at Brooke House, and was included as a dependant in both lists of government supporters in 1669–71 and the Paston list of 1673/4. His committees in this period included those to consider the bill for the sale of the fee-farm rents (5 Apr. 1670), in which he was to speculate substantially but unremuneratively, and to inquire into the condition of Ireland (20 Feb. 1674). He spoke against the impeachment of Danby on 27 Apr. 1675, acted as teller against taking Serjeant Pemberton into custody for pleading in the Lords, and was again listed among the officials in the House. His duties now included the disbursement of substantial sums 'for secret service', in part at least to avoid the cumbrous, antiquated, and expensive 'course of the Exchequer'. But Danby regarded his virtual monopoly of public credit with suspicion, and during the long recess he was deprived of the paymastership and with it the 'undertaking'; while the secret service account was transferred to the secretary to the Treasury, who was Danby's own brother-in-law, Charles Bertie*. A caustic and unreliable summary of his career up to this point appears in *Flagellum Parliamentarium*:

> Once a link-boy; then a singing -boy at Salisbury; then a servingman; and, permitting his wife to be common beyond sea, at the Restoration was made paymaster to the Guards, where he has cheated £100,000; and is one of the green cloth.

Shaftesbury marked him 'thrice vile' in 1677, and he did not go into open opposition until the last days of the Cavalier Parliament. As mortgagee of Hungerford House, on which he had advanced £3,000 to the spendthrift (Sir) Edward Hungerford*, he enjoyed a substantial interest in Westminster, more particularly as the property was well-situated for high-class commercial redevelopment, and he was named to the committees for bills to establish a 'court of conscience' for small claims (2 Apr. 1677) and to build a new church (4 May 1678). His successors in the 'undertaking' had soon run into difficulties, and on 30 May he was among those ordered to estimate how much pay was owing to the newly-raised forces. Although he was on both lists of the court party, he voted for Danby's impeachment on 19 Dec., and was immediately removed from the board of green cloth 'in as severe words as could be expressed', though the Duke of York intervened to insist that he should retain his Whitehall lodgings, which he had rebuilt at his own expense.[6]

At the first general election of 1679 Fox was returned for Westminster after a contest, and marked 'vile' on Shaftesbury's list. With the eclipse of Danby he was restored to his place in the Household, and the financial collapse of his successors in the 'undertaking' compelled the Government to have recourse again to his credit as paymaster. An inactive Member of the first Exclusion Parliament, he was appointed only to the committees to consider a bill for the sale of a messuage in Lincoln's Inn Fields and to inquire into abuses and exorbitances in the Post Office. According to the official list he voted against the exclusion bill, but it is more probable that he abstained, as Roger Morrice believed. The new Parliament was eager to investigate allegations of wholesale corruption in its predecessor, but Bertie refused to co-operate, and on 23 May William Sacheverell* reminded them that:

> You have a Member within your walls (if you will go to it in good earnest) that can discover to whom money and pensions were paid; and if he will not, he is not fit to be here. It is Sir Stephen Fox, who, though he has delivered up the private books, yet has several books that can discover it.

He was out of the House at the time, and when he arrived he

> seemed resolute, and (as they termed it) trifled with them; till [Hugh] Boscawen* moved that if he would not deal more clearly a bill might be brought in to confiscate his estate and take away his life, language it seems he could not so well relish, and then [he] submitted to answer questions more readily.

He pointed out that he had long handed over his official papers, but William Garway* and Sir Robert Clayton* refused to believe that 'so great a master of accounts' had failed to keep duplicates. He was sent back to Whitehall in the custody of Sir John Hotham, 2nd Bt.*, Sir Robert Peyton* and (Sir) John Holman* to fetch his ledgers, 'great, vast books' as he termed them, in a fruitless attempt to curb the Commons' appetite; but Arlington, the lord chamberlain, told them that no books might be removed or inspected without the King's command. The House then determined to rely on his memory. A list of the Cavalier Parliament was read out to him, and he told the House of payments to 27 Members, from the then Speaker (Edward Seymour*) downwards. He added that secret service

expenditure had greatly increased under Danby's administration, and that 30 other Members had been granted pensions after he had handed over to Bertie. He was blacklisted in the 'unanimous club', and the election expenditure revealed in his accounts failed to win him a seat in the second Exclusion Parliament, even at Cricklade, where he had acquired an interest by the purchase of Water Eaton manor for £20,000. At Court his position never stood higher, as 'the only instrument that has kept things afloat by his credit and supplies', and his contribution to staving off revolution can hardly be exaggerated. Any resentment that the King felt at his disclosures in the first Exclusion Parliament was quickly swallowed, and in November 1679 he was given a seat on the Treasury board, which he occupied for longer than any other contemporary except Sidney Godolphin I*. He retained control of the Pay Office through his sons and kinsmen.[7]

By now Fox was reputedly 'the richest commoner in the three kingdoms'. Although he disparaged the yield on land as compared with other investments, he had acquired a substantial estate in the seventies in his native county and in Somerset at a cost of some £85,000. But he never set up as a country gentleman, his busy official life making it impracticable for him to reside any further from Whitehall than Chiswick. Evelyn dined with him in 1680, and wrote:

> He is believed to be worth at the least £200,000 honestly gotten, and unenvied, which is next to miracle, and that with all this he still continues as humble and ready to do a courtesy as ever he was; nay, he is very generous, and lives very honourably, of a sweet nature, well-spoken and well-bred, and so very highly in his Majesty's esteem and useful that being long since made a knight, he is also advanced to be one of the lords commissioners of the Treasury. . . . In a word, never was man more fortunate than Sir Stephen; and with all this he is an handsome person, virtuous and very religious, and for whom I have an extraordinary esteem.

By 1682 he had been able to install at least ten of his connexions in subordinate posts in the Household, besides those in the Pay Office. His works of charity were particularly notable. He built almshouses and rebuilt the parish church at Farley, and to him should be assigned most of the credit for the founding of Chelsea hospital, popularly attributed to the more glamourous figure of Nell Gwyn.[8]

On the accession of James II the Treasury was taken out of commission and given to Lord Rochester (Laurence Hyde*). Fox had acquired his own interest at Salisbury by purchasing the lease of the nearby manor of Pitton and Farley, including his own birthplace, for £5,200, and he was returned for the city at the general election of 1685. A moderately active Member of this Parliament, he was named to seven committees, including those to examine the disbandment accounts, to recommend expunctions from the Journals, to provide carriages for the royal progresses, and to estimate the yield of a tax on new buildings. In the second session he led the revolt of the royal 'domestics' against the employment of Roman Catholic officers, but unlike his son he was not dismissed, though when the post of cofferer, which he deeply desired, fell in on the death of Henry Brouncker*, the right of reversion which he had acquired from the previous King was not honoured. On the other hand he returned to the Treasury in January 1687 on the fall of Sunderland, and in June 1688 he was recommended for retention on the Wiltshire bench. At the Revolution he lost office for a time, but was restored to the Treasury in 1690 when King William found that he 'must employ such as would advance money'. His political conduct in the succeeding reigns has been described as 'habitually discreet'; he usually supported the government of the day, but abstained from controversial divisions. He died on 28 Oct. 1716, worth over £174,000, and was buried at Farley. He had survived all his numerous first family, but his two sons by his second wife had long and successful careers in both Houses of Parliament.

Fox's career was in several respects the most remarkable of his age. In strictly financial terms he had by 1686, when his income can be assessed at £14,186, far outstripped the East India magnate, Sir John Banks*. A handful of the aristocracy had larger resources, but his had been acquired within a single lifetime. It is remarkable, therefore, that he lived almost free from envy and with a reputation for integrity that recent research confirms. In this respect the simple Anglican piety of his childhood home stood him in good stead. Dr Clay suggests three factors that enabled him to mix easily with those who started far above him on the social ladder; the schooling of a gentleman, introduction at Court during the most impressionable years of his life, and the familiarity with the Continent acquired during the years of exile. Parliament was far from being the most important institution in his career, and he had no aspirations towards swaying its debates by his oratory, though he could make a serviceable contribution from time to time on supply. As a placeman his record is notable for independence; he defied the Government on three such notable occasions as the impeachments of Clarendon and Danby, and the breach of the Test Act.[9]

[1] This biography is based on C. Clay, *Public Finance and Private Wealth*. [2] G. S. Fox-Strangways, Earl of Ilchester, *Life of Henry*

Fox, 1st Lord Holland, 3–15. [3] Salisbury corp. recs. D35, f. 131; *Tudor and Stuart Proclamations* ed. Steele, i. 405; Mdx. RO, MJP/CP5a; WJP/CP1, 2; P. Thompson, *Hist. Boston*, 458. [4] Clarendon, *Rebellion*, v. 337–8; S. E. Hoskins, *Chas. II in the Channel Is.* ii. 315. [5] *Marvell* ed. Margoliouth, i. 145. [6] *CJ*, ix. 350; *HMC Ormonde*, n.s. iv. 290. [7] *CJ*, ix. 629–30; Grey, vii. 317–24; *HMC Ormonde*, n.s. iv. 517–18, 538. [8] *Evelyn Diary*, iv. 218–19. [9] Add. 28875, f. 426; *Ellis Corresp.* ii. 59.

J.P.F.

FOX, Thomas (1622–66), of the Moat House, Tamworth, Staffs. and Whitefriars, London.

TAMWORTH 1659, 1660

b. 4 Mar. 1622, 3rd s. of Edward Fox, mercer (*d.*1640) of Birmingham, Warws. by Elizabeth, da. and h. of Hugh Grasbrook of Hints, Staffs. *educ.* I. Temple 1648, called 1656. *m.* (1) Mary, da. of Richard Mason of Newton, Salop, *s.p.*; (2) 28 Sept. 1654, Judith, da. of Sir Henry Boothby, 1st Bt., of Bradlow Ash, Derbys., *s.p.*[1]

Capt. (parliamentary) ?to 1646.[2]

Agent for sequestrations, Salop 1650–5; town clerk, Tamworth to 1663; commr. for scandalous ministers, Staffs. 1654, assessment, Warws. 1657, Staffs. and Warws. Aug. 1660–1, militia, Staffs. Mar. 1660; j.p. Staffs. Mar.–July 1660.[3]

Fox and his elder brothers were all in arms for Parliament in the Civil War, and he may also have been a kinsman of Col. John Fox, the 'jovial tinker' and commander of the Edgbaston garrison. A scrivener by trade, he settled in Shrewsbury on demobilization and read for the bar, while acting as sequestrator of Royalists' estates. He became town clerk of Tamworth, perhaps on the recommendation of his 'worthy friend' Michael Biddulph*, a Presbyterian like himself, and was returned for the borough to Richard Cromwell's Parliament, and again at the general election of 1660. In the Convention he was appointed only to the committees to investigate the unauthorized publication of parliamentary proceedings and to draft a proviso to the indemnity bill for protecting the purchasers of estates, and after the summer recess to those for the bills to suppress profanity and settle the militia. Although an inactive committeeman and a silent Member, he doubtless voted with the Opposition and did not stand again. A report on the Staffordshire gentry, after recalling his military record and 'violent' religious convictions, described him as 'moneyed', with 'very able and dangerous parts, being bred up to the law'. On removal from office by the commissioners of corporations, he made over his estate, valued at £200 p.a., to his brother-in-law Sir William Boothby, and settled in London. He died in Dublin in 1666, presumably on a visit to his brother, whose grandson George Fox was returned for Hindon as a Tory in 1741.[4]

[1] Glover, *Derbys.* ii. 582; Shaw, *Staffs.* i. 422; Add 28176, f. 224. [2] *Active Parliamentarians* (Staffs. Rec. Soc. ser. 4, ii), 61. [3] *Cal. Comm. Comp.* 319, 725; *CSP Dom.* 1663–4, p. 23. [4] *Gentry of Staffs.* (Staffs. Rec. Soc. ser. 4, ii), 16.

M.W.H./A.M.M.

FOXWIST, William (c.1610–73), of Caernarvon, Caern. and St. Albans, Herts.

CAERNARVON BOROUGHS	13 Jan.	1647[1]
ANGLESEY		1654
SWANSEA		1659
ST. ALBANS		1660

b. c.1610, 3rd but 1st surv. s. of Richard Foxwist of Caernarvon by Ellen, da. of Sir William Thomas of Aber, Caern. *educ.* Jesus, Oxf. matric. 25 Jan. 1628, aged 17; L. Inn 1629, called 1636. *m.* Mary, da. of John Pemberton, Grocer, of London and St. Albans, *s.p. suc.* fa. 1615.[2]

Commr. of array, Caern. 1642; recorder, St. Albans 1645–61; j.p. St. Albans borough 1645–Sept. 1660, liberty 1656–Sept. 1660, Caern. 1650–July 1660, Herts. 1651–July 1660; judge of Admiralty, N. Wales 1646; commr. for assessment, Herts. and St. Albans 1647–52, Caern. 1647, Herts., St. Albans and Caern. 1657, Jan. 1660, St. Albans Sept. 1660–1; commr. for militia, Herts. and Caern. 1648, Herts. and N. Wales Mar. 1660; commr. for N. Wales assoc. Caern. 1648; bencher, L. Inn 1648; second justice, Brecon circuit 1655–9, Chester circuit Mar.–Aug. 1660.[3]
Commr. for security 1656.

Foxwist came from a cadet branch of a 13th century family which took its name from a Cheshire manor. His ancestors had moved to Caernarvon in early Tudor times. Foxwist, a lawyer, took no active part in the Civil War, but began his long association with St. Albans by becoming recorder in 1645. He succeeded a royalist kinsman as Member for Caernarvon Boroughs in 1647 until Pride's Purge, after which he did not sit. He was appointed a Welsh judge under the Protectorate and attended the funeral of Oliver Cromwell as one of the mourners.[4]

Foxwist was appointed second justice of Chester on the return of the secluded Members, and at the general election of 1660 defeated Col. Alban Cox[†] at St. Albans. An inactive Member of the Convention, he was named in the first session only to the committee of elections and privileges, and to those for the indemnity bill and the bill to settle ecclesiastical livings. On 28 July he apparently committed a breach of privilege by testifying before the Lords on the subsidy and excise bills which the Commons were then debating. Two days later he moved that Sir Thomas Myddelton* should be rewarded for assisting in Booth's rising. After the recess he was appointed only to the committee on the bill for settling wine licences. Although, on behalf of his corporation, he congratulated the King 'in a short and pithy speech' on his Restoration, and presented him

with £100 in gold, he was probably in opposition. He lost not only his judgeship but his position as a local magistrate, and he resigned as recorder in January 1661. He is not known to have stood again, confining himself to his legal practice, which does not seem to have been remunerative. In his will, dated 25 Mar. 1673 and proved on 14 Dec., he calculated that after sale of lands in Caernarvonshire and payment of £800 debt, his widow would enjoy an income of only £104 p.a. He was the only member of his family to sit in Parliament.[5]

[1] Did not sit after Pride's Purge, 6 Dec. 1648, readmitted 21 Feb. 1660. [2] W. R. Williams, *Old Wales*, i. 257, 378; Keeler, *Long Parl.* 360; *Vis. Northants.* (Harl. Soc. lxxxvii), 167. [3] W. H. Jones, *Old Karnarvon*, 159; A. E. Gibbs, *Corp. Recs. of St. Albans*, 72–73, 76–77, 297, 298; W. R. Williams, *Gt. Sessions in Wales*, 60–61. [4] *Lancs. and Cheshire Rec. Soc.* xiii. 43; W. H. Jones, op. cit. 62, 159; *Trans. Caern. Hist. Soc.* xiv. 26. [5] *CJ*, viii. 39; *Merc. Pub.* 5 July 1660; Bowman diary, f. 105; *Gt. Sessions*, 61; Gibbs, 76; PCC 158 Pye.

M.W.H./E.R.E./G.J.

FRANCKLYN, Sir William (c.1635–91), of Mavorn, Bolnhurst, Beds.

BEDFORD	1679 (Mar.), 1679 (Oct.), 1681

b. c.1635, 2nd but 1st surv. s. of George Francklyn of Mavorn by Dorothy, da. of William Halsey of Great Gaddesden, Herts. *educ.* Winchester 1650, aged 13; Oriel, Oxf. 1651; L. Inn 1654. *m.* Letitia (*bur.* 15 May 1691), da. of Sir William Hicks, 1st Bt.[†], of Beverstone Castle, Glos., wid. of Arthur, 1st Earl of Donegall [I], *s.p. suc.* fa. 1673; kntd. 30 Aug. 1675.[1]
Commr. for assessment, Beds. 1664–80, 1689–90, Bedford 1679–80; j.p. Beds. 1671–1680, ?1689–*d.*; freeman, Bedford 1677; dep. lt. Beds. 1689–*d.*[2]
Col. of ft. [I] Feb.–July 1689.[3]

Francklyn's ancestors had held Mavorn as tenants of Canons Ashby priory and bought the manor soon after the dissolution of the monasteries, but appear to have cherished neither social nor political ambitions. Francklyn's father took no known part in the Civil War, and his own early career is equally obscure. He was returned to the Exclusion Parliaments for Bedford, six miles from his home, apparently unopposed, and marked 'honest' on Shaftesbury's list. Though he may sometimes have been confused in the Journals with Sir William Frankland*, he was probably moderately active in the first Exclusion Parliament. He was appointed to ten committees, of which the most important was to inquire into the conduct of John Robinson I* as lieutenant of the Tower. A vehement opponent of Popery, he declared in his only recorded speech:

Our laws, liberties and all that should protect us are at stake now, and are fit to be taken care of; and yet there is something more necessary, and that is the life of the King (which God long preserve!). There is danger from the Papists; they get ground upon us to our destruction.

It must be fear that must keep them quiet; and let them see that when that fatal blow is struck, the Kingdom will rise as one man to prevent the effects of that blow. Let the Act of Association of 27 Elizabeth be read, and from thence take some measures for the preservation of the King's person.

On 8 May he was sent to ask the Lords to sit in the afternoon. He voted for exclusion, and took the chair in the committee which drafted a request to the Lords to return the Popish priests condemned on circuit for execution, and was ordered to carry the message to the Lords. When he was removed from the commission of the peace in 1680 he was said to have 'great estates in the county', but this is difficult to reconcile with his later financial position. Moderately active in the second Exclusion Parliament, he was named to five committees, including those for the better collection of the hearth-tax and for preventing superstitious bequests. He was appointed only to the committee of elections and privileges in the Oxford Parliament. He took no known part in the events of James II's reign, but he doubtless supported the Revolution. He was commissioned as a colonel of foot in February 1689 and was sent to Ireland, but returned in July to seek supplies. He unsuccessfully contested Bedford in 1690. A man of extravagant tastes, he left debts of £3,427 and an estate estimated at only £2,461. He was buried at Bolnhurst on 7 Apr. 1691, the only member of his family to sit in Parliament.[4]

[1] Le Neve's Knights (Harl. Soc. viii), 300; Beds. RO, DD/FN 973, 1097. [2] Beds. RO, DD/FN 1101. [3] HMC Lords, ii. 160. [4] Vis. Beds. (Harl. Soc. xix), 31, 110; J. Godber, Hist. Beds. 210, 254; Grey, vii. 142; HMC Lords, ii. 160, 180; CJ, x. 375–6; Beds. RO, DD/FN 1224; Beds. Par. Regs. xi (Bolnhurst), 24.

L.N./G.J.

FRANKLAND, Thomas (c.1665–1726), of Thirkleby, nr. Thirsk, Yorks. and Chiswick, Mdx.

THIRSK	1685, 1689, 1690
HEDON	3 Dec. 1695
THIRSK	1698, 1701 (Feb.), 1701 (Dec.), 1702, 1705, 1708, 1710–7 June 1711 [new writ]

b. c.1665, 2nd but 1st surv. s. of Sir William Frankland, 1st Bt.* educ. Camb. 1680–1; L. Inn 1683. m. lic. 14 Feb. 1683, aged 18, Elizabeth (d. 20 July 1733), da. of Sir John Russell, 4th Bt., of Chippenham, Cambs., 8s. (5 d.v.p.) 3da. suc. fa. as 2nd Bt. 2 Aug. 1697.[1]

  Commr. for excise Apr.–Oct. 1689; jt. postmaster-gen. 1691–1715; commr. for customs 1715–18.[2]

  Commr. for assessment, Yorks. (N. and W. Ridings) 1689–90; j.p. and dep. lt. (N. Riding) by 1701–d.

Frankland's political career began at the age of 13 when he was chaired at a Thirsk election by the supporters of the victorious country candidates as a substitute for his father, who was crippled with

gout. A few months later he was sent south and placed in the charge of his childless uncle Lord Fauconberg, who found him 'a little soft and very studious', wanting assurance more than learning. On his early marriage he took up residence near Fauconberg's house at Sutton Court. When his father deemed it prudent as a known exclusionist not to stand for re-election at Thirsk in 1685, Frankland was returned in his absence, unopposed. Danby seems to have meant to list him among the Opposition. But he feared that he might have some difficulty in discharging his trust to the electors without displeasing the King, and took no known part in James II's Parliament. The royal electoral agents correctly reported in September 1688 that he would be re-elected, but they were 'doubtful' of his attitude to the King's religious policy. In the Convention he was sent to the Lords on 17 Apr. 1689 to ask for a conference on the removal of Roman Catholics from the metropolitan area. But he was named to no committees, made no recorded speeches, and lost his seat on the excise board through inability to subscribe to a government loan. Though doubtless a Whig, he was not listed as a supporter of the disabling clause in the bill to restore corporations, and he told his father that the House was more inclined to mercy than sacrifice. His moderation stood him in good stead in 1691, when he and Sir Robert Cotton* were appointed postmasters-general. He remained a court Whig in the Commons until the post was declared incompatible with a seat in 1711. He died on 30 Oct. 1726 and was buried at Thirkleby. Two of his sons sat for Thirsk between 1713 and 1749.[3]

[1] Clay, Dugdale's Vis. Yorks. ii. 245–6; HMC Astley, 44–45, 52. [2] Cal. Treas. Bks. ix. 82, 1037; xxix. 390, 407; xxxii. 666. [3] HMC Astley, 41, 42, 44, 59, 63, 71, 73; H. Robinson, British Post Office, 78.

P.A.B./P.W.

FRANKLAND, Sir William, 1st Bt. (c.1640–97), of Thirkleby, nr. Thirsk, Yorks.

THIRSK	8 Feb. 1671, 1679 (Mar.), 1679 (Oct.), 1681

b. c.1640, o.s. of Sir Henry Frankland of Thirkleby by Anne, da. of Sir Arthur Herrys† of Creeksea, Essex. m. by 1662, Arabella (d. 26 Feb. 1687), da. of Hon. Henry Belasyse† of Newburgh Priory, Yorks., 6s. (2 d.v.p.) 2da. cr. Bt. 24 Dec. 1660; suc. fa. 1672.[1]

  Commr. for assessment, Yorks. (N. Riding) Sept. 1660–80, (W. Riding) 1673–80, (N. and W. Ridings) 1689–90; dep. lt. (N. Riding) 1662–81, lt.-col. of militia ft. by 1665; col. ?1678–81; j.p. 1665–81, 1689–d.; receiver of hearth-tax W. Riding and York 1671–4; commr. for recusants (N. Riding) 1675.[2]

The Frankland estates in the North Riding were

acquired by a London Clothworker in Elizabethan times. Frankland's grandfather represented Thirsk, four miles from Thirkleby, in 1628–9 and in the Short Parliament. His father, although one of Strafford's knights, fought for Parliament in the Civil War and served as assessment commissioner from 1647 to 1650, but he accommodated himself to the Restoration and sat on the North Riding bench till his death. Frankland himself received a baronetcy at the Restoration, and in 1668 was ordered by the Commons to investigate abuses in the hearth-tax in Yorkshire. Three years later he replaced one of the guilty officials, who had been dismissed. He had strengthened his interest at Thirsk by his marriage, and was returned unopposed to the Cavalier Parliament at a by-election. A moderately active Member, he was appointed to 26 committees. In 1674 he was added to those to consider the impeachment of Arlington and the general test bill, and in the next session he was named to those for preventing the growth of Popery and hindering Papists from sitting in Parliament. According to the working lists it was hoped that the influence of his brother-in-law, Lord Fauconberg, might win him over to the Court, but Shaftesbury was undoubtedly correct in marking him 'worthy' in 1677. He continued to lead the resistance of the Yorkshire magistrates to the hearth-tax, claiming in particular that smiths' forges should be exempt, and on 31 Jan. 1678 he and (Sir) Metcalfe Robinson* complained that one of the collectors had infringed their privilege by serving them with a summons during the session. On 18 Feb., in his only recorded speech, he urged a reduction of £400,000 in the £1,000,000 demanded for maintaining the war with France. He helped to prepare reasons for a conference on the growth of Popery on 29 Apr. and to draw up the address for the removal of counsellors on 7 May. During the summer he was named to the committee on the bill for the better collection of hearth-tax. In the final session he was among those appointed to consider the bill disabling Papists from sitting in Parliament and to translate Coleman's letters.[3]

Frankland was re-elected to the Exclusion Parliaments, in which he was sometimes confused with Sir William Francklyn*. In 1679 Shaftesbury again classed him as 'worthy' and he was moderately active. He voted for exclusion, and probably served on four committees, taking the chair on the hearth-tax bill. His failure to attend the Duke of York on his way to Scotland in the autumn was neither unnoticed nor forgotten. He may again have served on four committees in the second Exclusion Parliament, but at Oxford he was named only to the elections committee. He intended to stand again after

the Duke had succeeded to the throne in 1685, but withdrew in favour of his son when Fauconberg informed him that his candidature would be objectionable to the King, advising him further to send as soon as the election was over 'a submissive letter particularly mentioning your great fit of the gout when his Majesty passed through these parts'. Frankland complied, writing that he had hoped, if elected,

> to have repaired in some measure past errors and mistakes, which were rather of a passive than an active nature. I do not, however, wish to defend them, being much more inclined to give proofs of submission than to offer argument for my justification. Therefore when your lordship intimated that his Majesty did not approve of my standing, I disputed the thing no longer, thinking it better to serve his Majesty in his way rather than my own, and hoping it will be accepted as an earnest of that duty and loyalty of which my heart is full.

Fauconberg replied: 'I this morning showed your letter to his Majesty, by whom it was very well received'. He was still reckoned among the Opposition in 1687, but he never stood again, suffering with 'an admirable patience many years under the affliction of a most painful distemper'. He died on 2 Aug. 1697 and was buried at Thirkleby. His memorial inscription describes him as:

> A true lover of his country, a constant assertor of its liberties, a promoter of its welfare and a defender of its laws in all capacities; as a representative in Parliament, a public magistrate, a friendly, courteous, and charitable neighbour, a prudent and indulgent father. Of a pleasant wit and agreeable conversation, of a sound judgment and unbiased integrity, and of a temper even, cheerful, happy to himself, and delightful to all who knew him. To complete all the rest, in his religion truly Christian, pious, and humble, of a comprehensive and charitable spirit, free from superstition and neglect.[4]

[1] Clay, *Dugdale's Vis. Yorks.* ii. 244–5. [2] H. B. M'Call, *Fam. Wandesford*, 291; Add. 41254, f.49v; *HMC Var.* ii. 165; *N. Riding Recs.* vi. 116; vii. 50, 93; *Cal. Treas. Bks.* iii. 731, 799. [3] *VCH Yorks. N. Riding*, ii. 57; J. T. Cliffe, *Yorks. Gentry*, 359; *CJ*, ix. 66, 429; *Cal. Treas. Bks.* v. 417, 418. [4] *HMC Astley*, 59–62; W. Grange, *Vale of Mowbray*, 196.

P.A.B./G.J.

FRANKLIN, Sir Richard, 1st Bt. (1630–85), of Moor Park, Rickmansworth, Herts. and Charing Cross, Westminster.

HERTFORDSHIRE 1661

bap. 20 July 1630, 1st s. of Sir John Franklin[†] of Willesden, Mdx. by Elizabeth, da. of George Purefoy of Wadley, Berks. *educ.* G. Inn, entered 1648; Balliol, Oxf. 1649. *m.* (1) by 1653, Elizabeth (*bur.* 21 Nov. 1660), da. and coh. of Sir Thomas Cheke[†] of Pirgo, Essex, 3s. (1 *d.v.p.*) 1da.; (2) 30 Apr. 1661, Eleanor, da. of Sir Samuel Tryon, 2nd Bt., of Boys Hall, Halstead, Essex, and h. to her bro., Sir Samuel, 3rd Bt., 3da. *suc.* fa. 1648; kntd. 14 July 1660; *cr.* Bt. 16 Oct. 1660.[1]

J.p. Herts. and St. Albans 1658–d.; commr. for militia, Herts. Mar. 1660; capt.-lt. of militia horse, Herts.

Apr. 1660; commr. for assessment, Herts. and Mdx. Aug. 1660–80, St. Albans 1664–9, Glos. 1673–80; dep. lt. Herts. 1662–d.[2]

Gent. of the privy chamber (extraordinary) June 1660, (ordinary) 1666–85.[3]

Franklin's ancestors achieved gentry status only towards the end of the 16th century. His father represented Middlesex in 1625, and again in the Long Parliament as a parliamentary supporter. On coming of age Franklin bought Moor Park, and at his marriage his estates were valued at £2,300 p.a. He was appointed a j.p. under the Protectorate, but he attached himself to the Court at the Restoration, and was granted a baronetcy.[4]

Franklin was returned for Hertfordshire at the general election of 1661. A moderately active Member of the Cavalier Parliament, he was appointed to 113 committees, including those for the corporations bill and the bill of pains and penalties in the opening session. On the fall of Clarendon he was appointed to the committee to consider the charges against Lord Mordaunt, and added to the committee of inquiry into the miscarriages of the war. On 17 Apr. 1668 he was ordered to carry to the Lords the bill to establish a trust for the children of Richard Taylor*. His tenure of Moor Park, celebrated for its magnificent gardens, was brief. He had already sold the house to the Duke of Ormonde, and the manor followed a few years later. He was listed among Ormonde's friends, but not as a member of the court party at this time. But his activity increased on the dissolution of the Cabal. He was appointed to the committee for the prevention of abuses in elections in 1673, and in 1675 to those for the abolition of de heretico comburendo and for appropriating the customs to the use of the navy. He was named as an excise pensioner, receiving money from the French subsidies, and appeared in three of the working lists, once with a query. Sir Richard Wiseman* noted him as being 'in the care of (Sir) Christopher Musgrave'*. He was marked 'doubly vile' by Shaftesbury in 1677 and appeared in both lists in 1678. Among his committees in that year were those to draw up reasons for a conference on the growth of Popery and to consider the bill excluding Papists from both Houses of Parliament. He did not stand again and died at his house in Charing Cross. He was buried at Willesden on 16 Sept. 1685, the last of his family to sit in Parliament.[5]

[1] Clutterbuck, Herts. i. 194; Letters of Dorothy Osborne ed. Moore Smith, 95; The Ancestor, ii. 185. [2] Parl. Intell. 16 Apr. 1660. [3] LC 3/2; Carlisle, Privy Chamber, 177, 192. [4] Keeler, Long Parl. 181–2; Clutterbuck, i. 194, 196; Letters of Dorothy Osborne, 119. [5] Clutterbuck, i. 194, 196; Morant, Essex, ii. 252; Survey of London, xvi. 71.

E.R.E./G.J.

FREDERICK, John (1601–85), of Old Jewry, London.

DARTMOUTH   1660
LONDON   10 Mar. 1663

bap. 25 Oct. 1601, 5th but 3rd surv. s. of Christopher Frederick, surgeon, of London by 2nd w. Mary, sis. of John Saunders of London. m. 10 Jan. 1637, Mary, da. of Thomas Rous, merchant, of Lime Street, London, 4s. (3 d.v.p.) 8da. Kntd. 26 June 1660.[1]

Member, Barber Surgeons' Co. 1632, livery 1635, asst. 1645, master 1654–5, 1658–9; freeman, E.I. Co. 1647, committee 1657–8, 1660–2; alderman, London 1653–83, sheriff 1655–6, ld. mayor 1661–2, commr. for security 1656, militia 1659, assessment Aug. 1660–80, oyer and terminer Nov. 1660; member, Grocers' Co. 1661, master 1677–8; member, Hon. Artillery Co. 1661; dep. lt. London 1662–70; pres. Christ's Hosp. 1662–83; commr. for recusants, London 1675.[2]

Commr. for trade 1656–7.[3]

Frederick's father, who emigrated from the Low Countries about 1580, became sergeant-surgeon to James I and twice master of the Barber Surgeons. Frederick never practised his father's profession, but by 1656 he had become a leading merchant, interested especially in the Spanish trade, and a shipowner. One of his ships was called the Anne of Dartmouth, and he had probably already entered into partnership with some of the local merchants, and acquired an interest in that port. An elder brother had fought in the parliamentary army in the first Civil War, but Frederick himself scrupulously avoided political commitment, even after Cromwell's war with Spain. In religion he was Presbyterian, though he must have conformed after the Restoration. His name appears on the London list of proposed Knights of the Royal Oak, with an income of £2,000 p.a. Though not yet outstandingly wealthy, his credit status was among the highest in the Convention; he took the leading part in trying to procure a loan of £30,000 in the City in May 1660, and received the thanks of the House. Altogether he was moderately active in 1660, his name being mentioned on 27 occasions in the Journals, and he spoke four times. But he confined himself almost exclusively to mercantile matters, twice opposing as inequitable the replacement of feudal dues on land by an excise on consumers, and, as a leading importer of sherry, seconding the motion of Thomas Chafe I* (from the neighbouring constituency of Totnes) for laying a penalty on the adulteration of wine with lime. Besides his membership of the committee for the excise clause in the bill for abolition of the court of wards, Frederick was asked to take care during the autumn recess of the redemption of English slaves in Barbary, and with (Sir) John Robinson I* to rebuke the lord mayor for his backwardness in collecting London's assessments.[4]

Frederick's election as lord mayor in November 1661 was a sign that the anti-royalist reaction in London manifested so sensationally in the general election eight months before was far from spent. When he himself entered the House shortly after his term of office had expired, the Restoration honeymoon was clearly over. In his first session he took part in considering a bill to hinder the growth of Popery, acted against two court Devonians, Thomas Clifford* and Edward Seymour*, in a division on the wine licences bill, and presented an address to the King for the strict enforcement of the Navigation Act. But his relations with the Government, especially while the tolerant Arlington (Sir Henry Bennet*) was in power, never degenerated into hostility; in 1667 he was asked for advice on paying off the fleet, and he was described as 'the only merchant who has had kindness and most singular favours' from the Post Office. These favours were doubtless of great commercial value to Frederick; on the other hand his extensive correspondence with the Mediterranean and the New World provided the Government with a useful intelligence network, and his credit financed the diplomatic missions of Sir Leoline Jenkins*. His political activity was again directed to forwarding the concerns of the trading community in general and London in particular. He retained an interest at Dartmouth, handling the grant for its fortification in the second Dutch war, but failed to seat his candidates there either in 1667 or 1673, when Nathaniel Herne* was defeated at the poll. In the Cavalier Parliament he was moderately active, acting as teller on six occasions and serving on 90 committees, but he made no recorded speeches. His real political importance in the second half of Charles II's reign was as one of the leaders in the City of the moderate and responsible opposition to the Court. In marked contrast to his predecessor John Fowke*, he returned his parliamentary wages to the corporation, he rebuilt his house after the Great Fire on a palatial scale (though on an old-fashioned plan), and he was a munificent benefactor to Christ's Hospital. Because of his known opposition to the Conventicles Act, he was removed from the lieutenancy in 1670, and two years later the Government received the following unfavourable report on him:

> By reason of his age he is apt to be led by others. . . . A man of little dispatch, very ready to run into mistakes; he hates a soldier, and cannot endure to see any of the King's guards.

This is hardly a convincing portrait of a City magnate, apart from the anti-militarism; in fact it is clear that Frederick was a remarkably active man, both in business and on the bench, and keenly interested in politics till well past his 80th year. He was prominent in the leading committees conducting corporation business and patronage. Some of the best commercial brains of the next generation served their apprenticeship with him, and he was uncommonly ready to delegate authority to his junior partners. Until he was removed from the bench in 1683 he was a firm friend to nonconformists; an informer who applied for a warrant to raid a conventicle in 1675 was told that the alderman was otherwise engaged. On 27 May he was named to his most important parliamentary committee, on the bill to prevent the growth of Popery. Sir Richard Wiseman* wrote to Danby of the four London Members in 1676:

> If there be so good a work in hand as the ascertaining the interest of the bankers' debt (as I hear there is) it may be an inducement for the citizens to give money, though I will not answer for them. But I am sure such a work will be generally very acceptable, and the King will lose nothing by it, but gain undoubtedly both honour and profit, and truly your lordship will gain great repute by it too.

In 1677 Shaftesbury classed Frederick as 'doubly worthy'. There was no perceptible decrease in his attendance record in the closing sessions of the Cavalier Parliament, though in February 1678, (Sir) Joseph Williamson* complained of 'not having had the opportunity of meeting you in the Parliament House'. An Edinburgh correspondent of his remarked about this time on 'your Puritan humour' and grumbled: 'You will always maintain the Presbyterian principles and justify their practices'. In spite of his age he might have been disappointed at his failure to be re-elected to the Exclusion Parliaments; his son-in-law reflected bitterly on the time 'when the City chose men of estates and experience'. Though Frederick's court connexions may have told against him at this time, causing him to be dropped from the main committees of the corporation, his principles were unchanged; he was noted as remaining on the bench with the lord mayor to receive a Whig petition on 27 June 1681, and two months later as one of the dissenting aldermen who were sent for to dine with the Prince of Orange. In 1682 an informer 'going about to deliver warrants to suppress unlawful conventicles' complained to the Privy Council that he had been dragged before Frederick by a rabble, and ignominiously bound over to the next sessions. But in the same year Secretary Jenkins described his company to a fledgling diplomat as 'persons of the chiefest rank and wealth in London, as well as of a general credit all Europe over'.[5]

Frederick was buried at St. Olave Jewry on 19 Mar. 1685. His will shows a personal estate of £42,000. His son was probably a dissenter; but his grandsons achieved parliamentary honours as well as a baronetcy and a country estate. Frederick himself is a recognizable and honourable type of City man; he lacked the showmanship of Sir Robert Viner, and the demagogic appeal of Thomas Papillon*. But his credit was always good, and his business ethics (whatever use he made of his post office connexions) conformed to the standards of his age and class. Nor did he wish to rise above his class in any other way; he bought no country estate, and none of his children married into the gentry or aristocracy. It is fitting that his name should remain in daily use in the City, for the site of his mansion (demolished in 1776) is still called Frederick's Place.

[1] E. H. Fellowes, *Frederick Fam.* 1–21; A. T. Young, *Annals of Barber-Surgeons*, 550–3; *Inhabitants of London in 1638* ed. Dale, 47, 171. [2] J. R. Woodhead, *Rulers of London*, 73; *CSP Dom.* 1655–6, p. 280; 1657–8, p. 330; 1661–2, p. 505; Add. 36916, f. 179; Luttrell, i. 83; *Cal. Ct. Mins. E.I. Co.* ed. Sainsbury, iii. 219; *Ancient Vellum Bk.* ed. Raikes, 85. [3] *CSP Dom.* 1655–6, p. 18. [4] *Aliens in London* (Huguenot Soc. x), 316; *CSP Dom.* 1655, p. 67; 1655–6, p. 200; 1678, p. 353; *APC Col.* i. 462; Fellowes, 5; *Old Parl. Hist.* xxiii. 18, 21, 65–66; *CJ*, viii. 45. 171, 185. [5] *CJ*, viii. 503, 522; *CSP Dom.* 1665–6, p. 374; 1666–7, p. 451; 1667, p. 277; 1667–8, p. 35; 1677–8, p. 680; 1678, pp. 293, 353; 1678–9, p. 77; 1680–1, p. 332; 1682, p. 446; *Cal. Treas. Bks.* ii. 62, 99; *EHR*, li. 35; Add. 36916, f. 179; *Gent. Mag.* xxxix. 515; *HMC 7th Rep.* 353; *HMC Portland*, iii. 349; *HMC Ormonde*, n.s. vi. 118.

M.W.H./J.P.F.

FREEMAN, Ralph (c.1655–86), of East Betchworth, nr. Reigate, Surr.

REIGATE 1679 (Oct.)–9 Dec. 1680, 1681

b. c.1655, 1st s. of Sir George Freeman of East Betchworth by Mary, da. of (Sir) Richard Onslow* of West Clandon. *educ.* M. Temple 1674. *m.* lic. 21 June 1680, Elizabeth, da. of Edward Silvester, merchant, of Thames Street, London, 2s. 1da. *suc.* fa. 1678.[1]

Commr. for assessment, Surr. 1679–80.

Freeman's grandfather married a connexion of the first Duke of Buckingham, sat for Winchelsea in 1626 and 1628–9, and bought East Betchworth manor for £1,080. As master of requests he attended the King during the Civil War and was fined £800 on the Oxford articles, compounding for his interest in the coal tax with an additional £530. The family remained under suspicion as royalist sympathizers during the Interregnum, and Freeman's father was made a knight of the Bath at the coronation of Charles II. Freeman himself was returned for Reigate, about three miles from his home, at the second general election of 1679,

doubtless as a court supporter, for he was unseated in favour of the exclusionist Deane Goodwin* on 9 Dec. 1680. He regained his seat in 1681, but was named to no committees and made no speeches in either the second or third Exclusion Parliaments. He was killed in an affray on Hounslow Heath in August 1686. His assailant, an army officer named William Freeman, was found guilty of manslaughter, but pardoned by James II on 14 Mar. 1687. His sons died unmarried without entering Parliament.[2]

[1] *Mar. Lic.* (Harl. Soc. xxx), 34; Manning and Bray, *Surr.* ii. 208; iii. 54. [2] *Vis. London* (Harl. Soc. xv), 295; *Surr. Arch. Colls.* xiv. 187; Manning and Bray, ii. 207; *Cal. Comm. Comp.* 1522–3; *Verney Mems.* ii. 448; *CSP Dom.* 1686–7, p. 389.

J.S.C.

FREIND *see* **FRIEND**

FREKE, Thomas I (c.1638–1701), of Shroton and Melcombe Horsey, Dorset.

DORSET 1679 (Mar.), 1679 (Oct.), 1681, 1685, 1689, 1690, 1695, 1698, 1701 (Feb.)

b. c.1638, 3rd s. of John Freke[†] of Cerne Abbey, being 2nd s. by 2nd w. Jane, da. and coh. of Sir John Shurley[†] of Isfield, Suss., wid. of Sir Walter Covert[†] of Slaugham, Suss. *educ.* M. Temple 1655. *m.* 19 Sept. 1669, Cicely, da. of Robert Hussey of Stourpaine, Dorset, *s.p. suc.* bro. 1657.[1]

Commr. for militia, Dorset Mar. 1660, j.p. Mar. 1660–*d.*, commr. for assessment Aug. 1660–80, 1689–90, dep. lt. July 1660–at least 1666, 1672–*d.*; freeman, Poole Nov. 1660, Lyme Regis 1666; commr. for loyal and indigent officers, Dorset 1662, sheriff 1663–4, commr. oyer and terminer, Western circuit 1665, for recusants, Dorset 1675; high sheriff, Dorchester 1679–*d.*[2]

Freke's great-grandfather, of yeoman stock, built up an estate of £100,000 in the service of the crown, and the next generation produced a Member for Dorchester in 1584 who was twice subsequently knight of the shire. A series of premature deaths left the Shroton family to be headed by a minor almost throughout the Civil War and Interregnum. Nevertheless Freke was named to the order of the Royal Oak, perhaps as a compliment to his step-father, Denzil Holles*, with an estate valued at £4,000 p.a. While he was officiating as sheriff, four offenders under the Conventicles Act, including a brother-in-law of Henry Henley*, were removed from his custody to safer keeping in Windsor Castle. But as Freke was apparently non-resident his responsibility for the undue leniency alleged was at most indirect, and even before the Act of Uniformity he had shown himself unsympathetic to Independents.[3]

By 1675, Freke had become Shaftesbury's right-hand man in Dorset. He showed his political judgment by refusing to stand against the Sherborne Castle interest that year, and it was not till 1679 that he entered the House. Even then he accepted nomination only on condition that the court supporter Thomas Strangways* agreed to join interests with him; they were duly returned unopposed. Shaftesbury marked him 'honest' and he was moderately active in the first Exclusion Parliament, being appointed to seven committees, including those to bring in a bill for regulating elections, to take the disbandment accounts, to inquire into the shipping of artillery from Portsmouth and to continue the prohibition on importing Irish cattle. He voted for the exclusion bill.[4]

Freke's electoral arrangement was renewed for the next election, and, so far as is known, for all the remaining elections of this period. In the second Exclusion Parliament he was named only to the committee to inquire into the working of the ecclesiastical courts in Surrey. After the dissolution he acted as agent for the country party in Dorset, and took the minutest interest in the elections at Shaftesbury, Dorchester and Corfe Castle. Already he had the kind of local reputation that a political organizer needs: 'no man ever lost yet by offering him a kindness'. He was returned as senior knight of the shire in 1681, and named to the committee of elections and privileges at Oxford.[5]

Freke had probably gone over to the Court before the Rye House Plot, when he helped to search the house of Edward Norton*, who was not only a fellow-member of the Green Ribbon Club but a neighbour of his wife's family. He was moderately active in James II's Parliament, in which he was named to five committees, including those to consider the estate bill promoted by Edward Meller* and the clandestine marriages bill.[6]

Freke's answers to the lord lieutenant's questions on the repeal of the Test Act and Penal Laws were negative. Next to Strangways and Francis Luttrell II*, he was the biggest owner of ex-monastic land in the county, and the hostile pen of a dissenting minister described the three of them at this time in the following terms:

> They are full of consternation and fear, and sit constantly a-drinking when they meet, and then a-talking against Popery, and then somebody is false among them, and repeats their discourse, and then are overcome with fears till the next time.

He was retained in local office, and the King's electoral agents considered him 'moderate' and expected him to be chosen for the county. He took no part in the Revolution, his name being conspicuously absent from the warrants for raising money for William of Orange.[7]

Freke was probably inactive in the Convention. He was appointed to the committee of elections and privileges, but did not vote either to agree with the Lords that the throne was not vacant or for the disabling clause in the bill to restore corporations. He was given leave to go into the country on 16 Apr. 1689, and it is probable that all the later references in the Journals are to his cousin, though at the dissolution his Tory kinsman Thomas Chafin* acknowledged acting under his orders.[8]

Freke continued to be returned for the county and to vote with the Opposition till his death in November 1701. He had greatly augmented his estate by purchases, such as the sporting rights over Cranborne chase, shrewdly calculated to enhance his political interest. On either score he was justly described (though perhaps with a humorous undertone) as 'the great Freke'. Under his will, his estate passed to the wife of his cousin Thomas Freke II*, to revert on her death to the Pitts of Stratfieldsaye.[9]

[1] *The Ancestor*, x. 179–212; Wards 5/11/1951; Shroton parish reg. [2] Hutchins, *Dorset*, i. 32; ii. 362; Lyme Regis mss B6/11, f. 26. [3] *CSP Dom.* 1663–4, pp. 355, 601, 612; Calamy, *Nonconformists' Memorial*, 166. [4] Christie, *Shaftesbury*, ii. 216–17; Dorset RO, D124, corresp. of Thomas Strangways. [5] *Pythouse Pprs.* ed. Day, 96–97; Yale Univ. Lib. Osborn mss, letter of William Bennett, 20 Oct. 1680. [6] *CSP Dom.* Jan.–June 1683, p. 376. [7] R. Morrice, Entering Bk. 2, pp. 201–2. [8] Hutchins, iii. 566. [9] Luttrell, v. 114; *CSP Dom.* 1697, p. 293; PCC 5 Herne.

J.P.F.

FREKE, Thomas II (1660–1721), of Hannington, Wilts.

CRICKLADE	26 May–10 June 1685, 5 Apr. 1689
WEYMOUTH AND	
MELCOMBE REGIS	22 May 1691, 1695, 1698
LYME REGIS	1705, 1708

b. 17 Jan. 1660, 1st s. of Thomas Freke of Hinton St. Mary, Dorset by 2nd w. Elizabeth, da. of Sir William Clarke of Ford Place, Wrotham, Kent. *educ.* Wadham, Oxf. 1675; M. Temple, entered 1675. *m.* (1) 10 Oct. 1683, Elizabeth (*d.*1714), da. and coh. of Thomas Pile of Baverstock, Wilts., *s.p.*; (2) Dec. 1718, Mary Corbett, *s.p. suc.* gt.-uncle at Hannington 1684.[1]

Commr. for assessment, Wilts. 1689; capt. of militia horse by 1697–?1702; j.p. Wilts. by 1701–*d.*, Dorset 1702–*d.*; dep. lt. Dorset 1702–?*d.*; freeman, Lyme Regis 1705.[2]

Freke's grandfather died in 1642, being 'mercifully taken away from the troubles that ensued', as his widow, the sister of a prominent Cavalier, described it. His father, too young to fight in the Civil War, also married into a well-known royalist family; but Freke and his brother William, a law student, joined the Green Ribbon Club at an early age. Their father's modest Dorset leasehold never qualified him for county office, but in 1684 Freke succeeded to Hannington, a compact property of nearly £1,000 p.a. which had been in the family since 1605, and an ample personal estate. In the following year he contested Cricklade, six miles away, as a Whig. On the day of the election he 'brought out of the country forty horse and thirty foot armed', who beat and wounded many of the Tory voters. His supporters were described as 'men of dangerous principles', perhaps an allusion to his brother's Socinianism, though this had not yet become notorious. The bailiff sealed an indenture in Freke's favour, and he was allowed to sit on the merits of the return. He was listed among the Opposition, but Edmund Webb* produced another indenture, and he was unseated on the merits of the election without taking any known part in James II's Parliament. Webb proceeded to rub salt in the wound by prosecuting him and his supporters at the next assizes, and they were fined £143 13s.4d. for the election riot.[3]

The King's electoral agents did not mention Freke as a candidate for Cricklade in 1688, but on 20 Sept. he wrote to Lord Weymouth (Thomas Thynne I*) to ensure due notice of the delivery of the precept. Seated on petition on 5 Apr. 1689, he was probably moderately active in the Convention. As 'Mr Freke junior' he was definitely appointed to the committee to recommend ways of relieving Protestant refugees from Ireland, and subsequently he may have been appointed to 24 others, including those to bring in a bill to control abuses in the sale of offices, to reverse Cornish's attainder, and to consider the Lords' amendments to the bill of rights. In the second session he was added to the committee for the mutiny bill, and appointed to that to exonerate Sir Trevor Williams*, John Dutton Colt* and John Arnold* from the Duke of Beaufort's actions for *scandalum magnatum*. He supported the disabling clause in the bill to restore corporations, and was named to the committee for imposing a general oath of allegiance to the new regime. He did not stand for Cricklade again, but as a representative of two Dorset boroughs he remained a court Whig under William and Anne. Freke died in 1721, leaving the Hannington estate to his brother, but no later member of the family entered Parliament.[4]

[1] *The Ancestor*, xi. 36–37; Hutchins, *Dorset*, iv. 333; PCC 195 Barnes, 129 Buckingham. [2] Lyme Regis mss B6/11, f. 41. [3] C. B. Fry, *Hannington*, 25; Elizabeth Freke, *Diary*, 32; *Cal. Treas. Bks.* viii. 577, 744; *CJ*, ix. 719, 732. [4] Bath mss, Thynne pprs. 24, f. 39; *CJ*, x. 72–73; PCC 129 Buckingham.

J.P.F.

FREMAN, Ralph (1627–1714), of Aspenden, Herts.

HERTFORDSHIRE 1685, 30 Apr. 1690

bap. 29 May 1627, 1st s. of Ralph Freman of Aspenden by Mary, da. of Sir William Hewett[†] of Pishiobury, Sawbridgeworth. *educ.* privately (Seth Ward). *m.* 10 Feb. 1662, Elizabeth, da. of Sir John Aubrey, 1st Bt., of Llantrithyd, Glam., 3s. (1 *d.v.p.*) 7da. *suc.* fa. 1665.[1]

Commr. for assessment, Herts. 1661–80, 1689–90, sewers, Essex Oct. 1660; j.p. Herts. 1663–87, Oct. 1688–d., dep. lt. 1681–7, 1689–?d.[2]

Freman's grandfather and great-uncle, clothiers of London, acquired Aspenden in 1607. His father, according to Chauncy, 'in the time of the rebellion did quit all public employments, affected a retired life, and pleased himself with the conversation of his children'. Nevertheless, he served on every county committee from 1643 to 1650. Freman's tutor was Seth Ward, the future bishop of Salisbury, who had been deprived of his Cambridge fellowship. Dorothy Osborne described Freman as 'a pretty gentleman' with 'a great deal of good nature'.[3]

Freman stood for the county as a court supporter in February 1679, at first 'without opposition, but being observed that 150 or 200 Papists appeared for him in a body, the freeholders took notice of it and chose [William] Hale*.' Shaftesbury evidently believed that he had been returned and listed him as 'base'. He was expected to stand again later in the year, and the moderate Sir Charles Caesar* urged Hale to join forces. But when Hale made it clear that he would not serve, Freman probably desisted. With government backing, he was returned to James II's Parliament, where he was moderately active. He was appointed to five committees, including those for recommending expunctions in the Journals and for the general naturalization of Protestants. He was noted as an opponent of James II in 1687 and removed from the lieutenancy. He was elected for the county again in 1690 after a double return. Freman died on 17 Nov. 1714 and was buried at Aspenden. His son, a Tory, represented the county from 1697 to 1727.[4]

[1] Clutterbuck, *Herts.* iii. 348, 358; Westminster City Lib. St. Mary le Strand par. reg.; *Boyd's London Units*, 2602. [2] C191/7/59; *Herts. Recs.* vi. 522; vii. 375. [3] *VCH Herts.* iv. 19; Chauncy, *Herts.* i. 249; *Letters of Dorothy Osborne* ed. G. C. Moore Smith, 57. [4] Bodl. Carte 228, f. 134; Add. 33573, f. 126; BL, M636/33, John Verney to Sir Ralph Verney, 28 Aug. 1679; *CSP Dom.* 1685, p. 79; 1686–7, p. 314; 1687–9, p. 125; *CJ*, x. 395–6; Clutterbuck, iii. 354.

E.R.E./G.J.

FRESCHEVILLE, John (1607–82), of Staveley, Derbys.[1]

DERBYSHIRE 1628, 1661–16 Mar. 1665

b. 4 Dec. 1607, o.s. of Sir Peter Frescheville[†] of Staveley by 1st w. Joyce, da. of Thomas Fleetwood[†] of The Vache, Chalfont St. Giles, Bucks., wid. of Sir Hewett

Osborne† of Kiveton, Yorks. *educ.* Magdalen Hall, Oxf. 1621; M. Temple 1624. *m.* (1) Bruce (*d.* 10 Apr. 1629), da. of Francis Nicholls, barrister, of the Middle Temple and Ampthill, Beds., *s.p.*; (2) Apr. 1630, Sarah (*d.* 25 June 1665), da. and h. of Sir John Harington of Elmesthorpe, Leics., 3da.; (3) Dec. 1666, Anna Charlotte (*d.* 12 Nov. 1717), da. of Sir Henry de Vic, 1st Bt., chancellor of the Garter, of Windsor Castle, Berks., *s.p. suc.* fa. 1634; *cr.* Baron Frescheville of Staveley 16 Mar. 1665.[2]

Dep. lt. Derbys. by 1630–42, July 1660–*d.*, commr. of array 1642, j.p. July 1660–*d.*, capt. vol. horse Oct. 1660–1, commr. for assessment 1661–5, corporations 1662–3, loyal and indigent officers 1662, oyer and terminer, Northern circuit 1665.[3]

Cornet of the bodyguard 1639; capt. of horse (royalist) 1642, col. 1643–4; gov. Welbeck 1645, York 1670–*d.*; capt. R. Horse Gds. (The Blues) 1661–79.[4]

Gent. of the privy chamber 1639–45.[5]

Frescheville's ancestors had held land in Derbyshire since at least 1225. One of them represented the county in 1301, 1307 and 1313, and was summoned to a Great Council in 1324. Frescheville himself was bred at the Court of Charles I, whom he served as a menial servant. He joined the King's army at Nottingham in 1642, and commanded the royal forces in his own county. He obtained a warrant for a peerage, but his second wife, a great gambler, became impatient at the delay in the patent, and his ardour for the Stuart cause cooled. Though he visited Charles I in captivity at Hampton Court, he had useful contacts on the other side, and his fine of £287 10s.4d., even though conditional on endowing a local chapel with £30 p.a., was very moderate. He successfully claimed exemption from the decimation tax on the grounds of 'good affection' to the Protectorate, and only became involved in royalist conspiracy after the return of the Rump.[6]

Frescheville crossed over to Holland immediately before the Restoration, and obtained a fresh warrant for a peerage with a special remainder to his daughters, but again, much to his wife's indignation, it failed to pass the seal. His wife complained to Ormonde:

As for Mr Frescheville, no injustice can ever make him a rebel, but this is so unkind a thing of the King that it will break his heart. I only heard this fall from him, that if he were unhandsomely used in this he would never make any request but one, that would easily be granted, which is to quit his country.

He was compensated with a commission in The Blues, and the lease without fine of the crown manor of Eckington. As the gentry candidate for Derbyshire in 1661 he easily defeated the Presbyterian, Sir John Curzon†. Resuming his seat after an interval of 32 years, he was a moderately active Member of the Cavalier Parliament, being appointed to 66 committees, including the committee of elections and privileges in four sessions. In the opening session he was among those instructed to consider reparations to the Marquess of Winchester, his eldest daughter's father-in-law, as well as the shortfall in revenue, the corporations and uniformity bills, and the bill for restoring advowsons and impropriations given up by Royalists, like himself, in their compositions. On 10 Jan. 1662 he was added to the committee on the bill for the execution of the remaining regicides, and two months later he acted as teller for a proviso to the hearth-tax bill. He was sent to the Lords to ask them to expedite the impropriations bill. He took a prominent part in the passage of the militia bill, helping to prepare an expedient for the assessment of peers on 16 May and asking the Lords for a conference. He was added to the managers, and on the next day acted as teller for agreeing with the Lords. In the hectic closing days of the session he was also sent to desire a conference on the border bill, and helped to manage a conference on restoring corporations.[7]

In the 1663 session Frescheville was among those appointed to hear a petition from the loyal and indigent officers, to resolve the differences between his son-in-law, Charles Powlett I*, and Lord Winchester, and to provide remedies for the meetings of sectaries. Still only an expectant peer, he was listed as a court dependant in 1664, and on 13 Feb. 1665 he was sent, together with Sir Maurice Berkeley*, William Coventry* and Edward Progers*, to thank the King for his constant grace and favour to the House. His patent at length passed the seal in the following month, but without the special remainder, and his third marriage in 1666 failed to produce a male heir. He remained a reliable court supporter in the Upper House, and was appointed governor of York in 1670. But he suffered severely from the stranguary in his later years, and was absent from the division on the second exclusion bill. He died on 31 Mar. 1682 and was buried at Staveley, the reversion of which he had sold to the Earl of Devonshire for £2,600.[8]

[1] This biography is based on *Jnl. Derbys. Arch. Soc.* n.s. vi. 51–63. [2] *Savile Corresp.* (Cam. Soc. lxxi), 9. [3] *HMC 9th Rep.* pt. 2, p. 389; *HMC Coke*, ii. 259; *HMC 15th Rep. VII*, 162; Add. 34306, f. 10; *Chesterfield Bor. Recs.* 138; J. C. Cox, *Three Centuries of Derbys. Annals*, i. 172–3. [4] *CSP Dom. Add.* 1625–49, p. 607; 1644, p. 191; 1670, p. 204. [5] Carlisle, *Privy Chamber*, 141. [6] Clarendon, *Life*, ii. 359–60; *Cal. Comm. Comp.* 1048; *Thurloe*, iv. 509; D. Underdown, *Royalist Conspiracy*, 242, 276. [7] Bodl. Carte 214, ff. 244–5; *Cal. Treas. Bks.* i. 283, 290; *HMC Hastings*, i. 141; *CJ*, viii. 383, 423, 432, 433. [8] *Coll. Top. et Gen.* iv. 213–18.

E.R.E.

FREWEN, Thomas (1630–1702), of Brickwell House, Northiam, Suss.

RYE 1679 (Mar.), 1679 (Oct.), 1681, 1685, 15 Jan.–1 Apr. 1689, 9 Feb. 1694, 1695 *bap.* 27 Sept. 1630, o.s. of Stephen Frewen, Skinner, of London and Northiam by 1st w. Katherine, da. and coh. of Thomas Scott of Northiam. *educ.* I. Temple, entered 1648, called 1656; Padua 1649; St. John's, Oxf. BA 1650, MA 1653. *m.* (1) c.1656, Judith (*d.* 29 Sept. 1666), da. and h. of John Wolverstone, Fishmonger, of Fulham, Mdx., 2s. (1 *d.v.p.*) 1da.; (2) 1671, Bridget (*d.*1679), da. of Sir Thomas Layton of East Layton Hall, Stanwick St. John, Yorks. and coh. to her bro. Charles, 5s. (2 *d.v.p.*) 1da.; (3) lic. 15 Dec. 1681, Jane (*d.* 20 June 1718), da. of Sir Robert Cooke[†] of Highnam, Glos., wid. of Sir Dawes Wymondsold of Putney, Surr., *s.p. suc.* fa. 1679.[1]

J.p. liberties of Ripon, Sutton and Marston, Yorks. 1662, Kent 1672–89, Suss. 1672–July 1688, Nov. 1688–d., liberty of Cawood, Yorks. 1685; commr. for assessment, Suss. 1673–80, 1690, Mdx. 1689, recusants, Kent 1675; freeman, Portsmouth 1675; dep. lt. Suss. by 1701–d.[2]

John Frewyn sat for Shoreham in two Parliaments of Edward II, but Frewen's grandfather, a zealous Puritan, was of Worcestershire origins. He was rector of Northiam, six miles north-west of Rye, from 1583 to 1628. Frewen's uncle, Accepted, the eldest of a large family, became archbishop of York at the Restoration. A bachelor and a notorious misogynist, he bequeathed to Frewen's father a considerable fortune, including 27,000 guineas in specie, enabling him to retire from trade, take out a grant of arms and purchase property in his native village.[3]

Frewen sat for Rye in the Exclusion Parliaments. Shaftesbury was uncertain about his politics. He listed him first as 'base', then as 'doubtful', and finally as 'honest'. Frewen was absent from the division on the first exclusion bill, though his subsequent activities and attitudes were those of a Tory. He was named only to a naturalization bill committee in the first Exclusion Parliament, and to none in its two successors. According to a correspondent of Sir Leoline Jenkins* he was 'as honest a gentleman as any in the county, and of a plentiful estate'. His own letters to Jenkins clearly reveal his dislike of the powerful Whig faction in his constituency. Before the 1685 election the corporation of Rye accepted the lord warden's claim to nominate one Member, but begged that either Frewen or John Shales, to whose industry and expense they owed their 'present established unity and freedom from malcontents', should be selected. In fact the nomination went to Sir Thomas Jenner*, and Frewen was returned on his own interest. He was again inactive, being named only to the committee for the maintenance of Great Yarmouth pier and harbour. His answers to the lord lieutenant of Sussex on the repeal of the Tests and Penal Laws were flatly negative. He was re-elected to the Convention but unseated on petition by the Whig Sir

John Austen* without leaving any trace on its records. He again sat for Rye from 1694 to 1698, when he signed the Association, but voted consistently against the Court. He died on 8 Sept. 1702, the only member of his family to sit in the Commons before the 19th century.[4]

[1] *VCH Yorks. N. Riding*, i. 132; *London Mar. Lic.* ed. Foster, 515; C. J. Feret, *Fulham Old and New*, ii. 171. [2] *CSP Dom.* 1685, p. 185; R. East, *Portsmouth Recs.* 361. [3] *DNB*; *Grantees of Arms* (Harl. Soc. lxvi), 95; J. R. Woodhead, *Rulers of London*, 74. [4] *CSP Dom.* 1680–1, p. 210; 1682, pp. 229, 350, 367; 1685, p. 24.

B.D.H.

FRIEND (FREIND), John (c.1641–96), of Hackney, Mdx.

GREAT YARMOUTH 1685

b. c.1641, 1st s. of John Friend, Brewer, of The Minories, London by Elizabeth Cole. *m.* (1) by 1660, Joan Butcher, 2s. *d.v.p.* 2da.; (2) lic. 8 Oct. 1679, aged 38, Anne, da. of Robert Huntington of Hackney, commr. for excise 1668–84, *s.p. suc.* fa. 1665; kntd. 3 Aug. 1685.[1]

Member, Brewers' Co. 1662, asst. 1687; member, Hon. Artillery Co. 1667–90; dep. lt. Tower Hamlets by 1680–9, London 1687–Oct. 1688; lt.-col. of militia ft. Tower Hamlets by 1680–9; freeman, Yarmouth 1685; j.p. Mdx. 1685–Feb. 1688, Sept. 1688–9, commr. for assessment 1689.[2]

Jt. farmer of excise 1677–83, commr. 1683–9; commr. for hearth-tax 1684–9.[3]

Friend's family can be traced back in the parish registers of St. Katharine by the Tower for several generations, but little is known of his father apart from his occupation, and he himself is said to have risen 'from mean beginnings to great credit and much wealth'. He built the Phoenix brewhouse in the Minories and joined the syndicate formed by Sir Samuel Dashwood* and his uncle in 1677 to farm the excise. Two years later he married a commissioner's daughter, and when his proposals for the renewal of the lease were rejected in favour of direct administration in 1683 he was himself compensated with a seat on the board. But it was his enthusiasm for part-time soldiering that won him royal favour. He was returned to James II's Parliament for Great Yarmouth, where his wife's uncle Richard Huntington* was an influential citizen. A moderately active Member, he was appointed to five committees, including those to take the disbandment accounts and to consider a bill for the repair and maintenance of Yarmouth pier and harbour. He was knighted during the recess, and doubtless continued to support the Government in the second session, despite his high Anglican views. In April 1688 the King was informed that his constituency would re-elect him only 'if your Majesty shall require it', but Sunderland ignored the hostile attitude of the Yarmouth dissenters and recommended him as court candidate. On the landing of William of Orange, he was ordered to call out the Tower Hamlets militia.[4]

After the Revolution Friend became a non-juror and lost all his offices. In 1694 a Jacobite conspirator reported:

> Sir John Freind answers for a regiment of cavalry and two regiments of militia in the neighbourhood of the Tower of London, and he gives room to hope that . . . he may be able to take possession of the Tower of London for the King.

According to Burnet 'his purse was more considered than his head, and was open on all occasions, as the party applied to him'. In March 1696 he was arrested on a charge of high treason, having kept in his possession 'the most imprudent papers . . . that were ever known upon such occasions'. At his trial he asked for a copy of the indictment against him and for counsel under the provisions of the statute that was about to come into force to regulate treason trials, but the attorney-general would not consent to a postponement. 'He knew of the assassination plot, though he was not to be an actor in it', and he could not deny that he had invited and planned to assist a foreign invasion. Refusing to turn King's evidence to save his life, he was executed at Tyburn on 3 Apr. 1696. In his dying speech he affirmed his belief

> that, as no foreign power, so neither any domestic power can alienate our allegiance. For it is altogether new and unintelligible to me that the King's subjects can depose or dethrone him on any account.

Attended on the scaffold by three eminent nonjuring divines, he died a true member of the Church of England, 'which suffers so much at present for a strict adherence to loyalty, the laws and Christian principles'. His share in the *Phoenix* brewhouse was sold for £5,500. No other member of the family entered Parliament.[5]

[1] *St. Katharine by the Tower* (Harl. Soc. Reg. lxxvi), 77, 79, 100, 182; (lxxx), 6, 82; *Le Neve's Knights* (Harl. Soc. viii), 399; *Mar. Lic.* (Harl. Soc. xxx), 8. [2] Guildhall RO, 5448, 5875; *Ancient Vellum Bk. of Hon. Artillery Co.* ed. Raikes, 91, 126; *Cal. Yarmouth Freemen*, 120. [3] *Cal. Treas. Bks.* v. 532, 862; vii. 782, 1074; ix. 190. [4] Burnet ed. Routh, iv. 311; *Le Neve's Knights*, 399; Foxcroft, *Halifax*, i. 385; D. C. Chandaman, *Eng. Pub. Revenue*, 73; G. Goold Walker, *Hon. Artillery Co.* 98–99; *CSP Dom.* 1687–9, pp. 271, 349. [5] *DNB*; Macpherson, *Orig. Pprs.* i. 473; *HMC Var.* viii. 82; Burnet, iv. 311; Macaulay, 2610–12; *True Copy of Pprs. Delivered by Sir John Friend* (1696); *Cal. Treas. Bks.* xiii. 112.

E.C.

FULFORD, George (c.1619–85), of Toller Fratrum, Dorset.

CHRISTCHURCH 1679 (Oct.), 1681

b. c.1619, 5th but 2nd surv. s. of Sir Francis Fulford[†] of Great Fulford, Dunsford, Devon by Elizabeth, da. and coh. of Bernard Samways of Toller Fratrum. *educ.* M. Temple 1640. *m.* 31 Aug. 1654 (with £2,300), Susanna, da. of John Browne[†] of Frampton, Dorset, *s.p. suc.* fa. in Dorset estates 1664.[1]

J.p. Dorset 1657–May 1670, June 1670–d., commr. for assessment Aug. 1660–80, pressing seamen 1665; freeman, Lymington 1667; dep. lt. Dorset 1672–d., commr. for recusants 1675, sheriff 1683–4.[2]

Fulford came from an old Devonshire family, probably resident at Great Fulford since the reign of Richard I. They first entered Parliament in 1553, but were not a regular parliamentary family. Fulford's father acquired extensive property in Dorset by marriage and took up residence there, but sat for his native county in 1625, his only Parliament. A commissioner of array and a royalist sheriff during the Civil War, he later compounded for his estate. Fulford's eldest brother was killed in the siege of Exeter in 1643, but he himself took no part in the Civil War and in 1654 married the daughter of a prominent Rumper. Nevertheless, the local Quakers denounced him as a Cavalier and a persecutor, and in 1660 he assisted the aged Sir John Strangways* to proclaim the Restoration at Sherborne.[3]

Fulford succeeded in 1664 to his father's Dorset estates, valued by the sequestrators at £600 p.a. His temporary removal from the commission of the peace in 1670 suggests that he was considered out of sympathy with the Conventicles Act, and he was mentioned as a possible country candidate for Dorset in 1675. He founded a school at Lymington following the regulations framed by his father-in-law for a school at Frampton, but when he stood for the borough in February 1678 he finished bottom of the poll, behind the Tory Sir Richard Knight* and the Whig John Button*. With Robert Coker* he was commended by the Privy Council for his prompt action in mustering the militia during the Purbeck invasion alarm. A supporter of Thomas Strangways* at county elections, he probably opposed exclusion. He was returned for Christchurch at the second general election of 1679 on the interest of the 2nd Earl of Clarendon (Henry Hyde*), who had faith in his 'good intentions to church and state'. In the second Exclusion Parliament he was appointed only to a committee for a naturalization bill. He was re-elected in 1681 after a contest with two exclusionists, but left no trace on the records of the Oxford Parliament. He died on 17 May 1685 and was buried at Toller Fratrum. His nephew Francis was returned for Callington in 1690 and 1698.[4]

[1] Hutchins, *Dorset*, ii. 698–9; Dorset RO, 7582. [2] Add. 31948, f. 78; PRO 30/24, bdle. 4, nos. 135–6; C. St. Barbe, *Recs. of Lym-*

ington, 9. ³Hutchins, ii. 698; *Cal. Comm. Comp.* 1311–12; *CSP Dom.* 1656–7, p. 123; *Som. and Dorset N. and Q.* xiii. 179. ⁴Add. 8845, pp. 5, 52; *VCH Hants*, iv. 649; *CSP Dom.* 1675–6, p. 245; 1680–1, p. 165; Hutchins, i. 606; ii. 699; Dorset RO, D124, Fulford to Strangways, 16 Feb. [1681].

P.W.

FULLER, Samuel (1646–1721), of South Quay, Great Yarmouth, Norf.

GREAT YARMOUTH 1689, 1690, 1695, 1701 (Feb.)

bap. 20 Dec. 1646, 1st s. of John Fuller, merchant, of Yarmouth. *m.* 6 May 1673, Rose, da. of Richard Huntington* of Yarmouth, 3s. (2 *d.v.p.*) 3da. *suc.* fa. 1673.¹
Freeman, Yarmouth 1672, alderman 1676–84, Oct. 1688–*d.*, bailiff 1679–80, 1698–9, mayor 1707–8; commr. for assessment, Yarmouth 1679–80, Norf. and Yarmouth 1689–90; capt. of militia ft. Yarmouth 1689–?*d.*; j.p. Norf. by 1690–?*d.*²

Fuller's father, who became a freeman of Yarmouth in 1649, signed the loyal address from the corporation of Yarmouth to Richard Cromwell in 1658, but was confirmed in office as common councilman by Charles II's charter of 1663, and three years later acquired a large house on the quayside. Fuller himself belonged to the Whig party on the corporation, opposing the surrender of the charter in 1683. He was first returned for the borough at the general election of 1689, replacing his father-in-law, who had been elected to James II's abortive Parliament. An active Member of the Convention, he was appointed to 37 committees, including those to examine prisoners of state (19 Mar.), to inquire into the exactions of customs officials (5 Apr.), to hear an interloper's petition against the East India Company (18 Apr.), to prepare a bill regulating Norwich stuffs (11 May), and to consider the toleration bill (15 May). With his senior colleague George England*, Fuller was responsible for recommending the refugee dean of Ross as lecturer at Yarmouth, and a few days later he was the second Member named to the committee for the relief of the Irish clergy. At the beginning of July he was appointed to the committees for prohibiting imports from France, reversing Titus Oates's conviction for perjury, and drafting an address for leave to inspect the Privy Council records relating to Ireland. But he had left Westminster for his constituency before the King's negative answer was reported to the House on 13 July. He came up with England and Sir William Cook* for the second session, and was appointed to the committee for restoring corporations; but he did not support the disabling clause. His other committees included those to inquire into the expenses and miscarriages of the war (1 Nov.), and to consider a general oath of allegiance (21 Jan. 1690). Under William III he

remained a Whig, though sometimes in association with England taking an independent line, especially over matters of commerce. 'Conspicuous for justice, prudence and piety', he died on 19 May 1721, aged 75, and was buried in St. Nicholas, Yarmouth. An inscription recorded that he was 'sent as burgess to that memorable Convention in the year 1688 [old style] and many later Parliaments'. His son John stood unsuccessfully for the borough in 1727, and sat for Plympton Erle from 1728 to 1734.³

¹Gt. Yarmouth par. reg.; C. J. Palmer, *Perlustration of Yarmouth*, ii. 148–9; D. Turner, *Sepulchral Reminiscences.* 35–36. ²*Cal. Freemen*, 105; H. Swinden, *Hist. Yarmouth*, 952–4; *Diary of Dean Davies* (Cam. Soc. lxviii), 24, 56; *Norf. Ltcy. Jnl.* (Norf. Rec. Soc. xxx), 117, 140. ³*Cal. Freemen*, 81; C. J. Palmer, *Hist. Yarmouth*, 215; SP29/422/90; *Diary of Dean Davies*, 57; Swinden, 866.

E.C.

GAPE, John (1623–1703), of Harpsfield Hall, nr. St. Albans, Herts.

ST. ALBANS 1679 (Mar.)

b. 5 Dec. 1623, o.s. of John Gape, tanner, of Fishpool Street, St. Albans by Joan, da. of Giles Marston of Hillend. *educ.* St. Albans g.s. 1631. *m.* 9 Apr. 1646, Anne (*d.* 31 Dec. 1682), ?da. of Thomas Oxton of St. Albans, 2s. 4da. *suc.* fa. 1625.¹
Alderman, St. Albans 1655–*d.*, mayor 1658–9, 1668–9, 1679–80; jt. farmer of excise, Herts. 1658–9, 1668–74; commr. for assessment, St. Albans Aug. 1660–1, 1664–9, 1673–4, Herts. and St. Albans 1679–80, 1689, Herts. 1690; j.p. Herts. 1697–*d.*²

Gape's ancestors, tanners of St. Albans, had held property there since the middle of the 15th century, and became prominent in local politics from the mid-16th century onwards, frequently serving as mayors. Though Gape may have had royalist sympathies he held municipal office during the Interregnum, and even, for a time, supplemented the profits of the family business with the county excise farm. This he resumed after the Restoration with a single partner at an annual rent of £8,800. He was able to purchase the manor of Harpsfield Hall in 1676, and three years later he became the first of the family to enter Parliament, defeating the sitting Member, Samuel Grimston*, at the first general election of 1679. Shaftesbury surprisingly marked him 'honest', but he was totally inactive in the first Exclusion Parliament, and absent from the division on the bill. He is not known to have stood again, and may have been glad to return to local politics, for he became mayor for the third time later in the year. He was granted arms in 1684, contributed to the restoration of the Abbey church and became a governor of the local grammar school. As one of the aldermen who surrendered the borough charter, he retained his seat on the bench under the

1685 charter and was named a standing justice of the peace. He seems to have accepted the Revolution, becoming a county magistrate in 1697. In addition to his Hertfordshire estates, Gape acquired lands in Cambridgeshire worth at least £150 p.a., and property in Lincolnshire. He died on 20 Apr. 1703 and was buried in the Abbey. His eldest son, John Gape[†], who succeeded to most of the estate, sat as a Tory for St. Albans in six Parliaments between 1701 and 1715.[3]

[1] *VCH Herts. Peds.* 159–60; St. Albans Abbey reg. [2] A. E. Gibbs, *Corp. Recs. of St. Albans*, 7, 75, 85, 101; *Cal. Treas. Bks.* i. 153; iii. 833, 836; vi. 861; *CSP Dom.* 1685, p. 73; Clutterbuck, *Herts.* i. 72; *Herts. Recs.* vi. 522. [3] *VCH Herts.* ii. 401–2, 416; A. Kingston, *Herts. during the Civil War*, 131; *Cal. Treas. Bks.* i. 153; iii. 833; *Grantees of Arms* (Harl. Soc. lxvi), 97; Clutterbuck, i. 71–72, 111; appendix, 32; ii. 192; Gibbs, 85, 86; *CSP Dom.* 1685, p. 73; *VCH Herts. Peds.* 160; PCC 91 Degg.

E.R.E./G.J.

GAPE, Thomas (*d.*1678), of the Middle Temple, London and Porton, Wilts.

GREAT BEDWYN   16 May 1660

3rd s. of Hugh Gape, weaver, of Dorchester, Dorset. *educ.* M. Temple 1648, called 1667. *m.* Anne (*d.* 29 Apr. 1686), da. of William Backhouse of London, 2s. 4da.[1]
    Servant to the Mq. of Hertford (later 2nd Duke of Somerset) 1646–Oct. 1660, to the dowager duchess Oct. 1660–74; commr. for assessment, Wilts. Aug. 1660–1, 1664–9; clerk of the peace, Som. Aug. 1660–?73.[2]

Gape's father was a craftsman in a small way who never achieved municipal office. But Francis Gape, the royalist clerk of the peace for Dorset, was probably a kinsman and brought him to the notice of the Seymours. In 1646 he entered the service of the Marquess of Hertford, who doubtless paid for him to improve his knowledge of the law at the Middle Temple. No less an authority than Sir Orlando Bridgeman commended his work, and by 1660 he was steward of the manorial court of Great Bedwyn. Commanded by his employer to stand at the general election, he was blamed by the friends of Sir Ralph Verney* for the 'hot contest' and double return that followed. But his refusal to compromise was no doubt dictated by his loyalty to the Seymour interest. Gape was allowed to sit on the merits of the election, and marked by Lord Wharton as a friend. In the House he concerned himself exclusively with his employer's interests, though doubtless voting with the Court. On 25 June he asked the House not to trouble Hertford, in his capacity as chancellor of Oxford, with the petition of the intruded dons. He was named to committees for two private bills, one of which was for breaking the Seymour entail. When Hertford was appointed *custos rotulorum* of Somerset, he made Gape clerk of the peace.[3]

Gape was unable to attend the general election of 1661, and was defeated at Bedwyn by Henry Clerke I*, although still supported by the Seymour interest. His affairs had not prospered, and in 1666 he wrote that he dared not stir from his employer's town house for fear of a debtors' prison, but his belated call to the bar a year later will at least have enlarged his confines. 'In above twenty years', he wrote on 18 Jan. 1667, 'I have not been able to make any considerable provision for my wife and children, notwithstanding my diligent performances in this noble family. But my deceased brother-in-law left a debt of near £1,500 upon the estate, and all that I have got in my lifetime (except my office) will hardly serve to pay it off.' When his daughter married in 1669, her uncle, a successful apothecary, had to find most of her dowry. Thereafter his circumstances improved; the dowager duchess of Somerset owed him £1,250 at her death, and in 1677 he was able to lay out £3,750 on the purchase of land in Wiltshire. He died at Porton in 1678, leaving £1,000 portions to his two unmarried daughters, and his coach and horses to his wife. Both his sons were entered at the Middle Temple; one apparently died young, the other became a lunatic, and nothing further is known of the family.[4]

[1] *Dorchester Bor. Recs.* ed. Mayo, 410; Hoare, *Wilts.* Everley, 30; PCC 97 Reeve; *M. Temple Reg.* i. 175, 184. [2] *HMC Bath*, iv. 219, 227; *Cal. Treas. Bks.* i. 627; E. Stephens, *Clerks of the Counties*, 155. [3] *CSP Dom.* 1640, p. 323; *HMC 5th Rep.* 586; *Cal. Comm. Comp.* 1468; *HMC Bath*, iv. 258; BL, M636/1; Bowman diary, f. 25. [4] Bath mss, Thynne pprs. 10, f. 104; *HMC 7th Rep.* 460, 462, 488; PCC 97 Reeve, 25 Vere.

M.W.H./J.P.F.

GARDINER, William (1628–91), of Basinghall Street, London and Roche Court, Fareham, Hants.

WIGAN   Apr.–31 July 1660

b. 9 May 1628, 3rd but o. surv. s. of Robert Gardiner, Mercer, of London, being 2nd s. by 2nd w. Mary, da. of Robert Palmer, Grocer, of London, and Hill, Warden, Beds. *educ.* ?Magdalen Coll. Oxf. to 1648. *m.* 28 May 1661, Jane, da. of Robert Brocas of Beaurepaire, Hants, and h. to her bro. Bernard, 2s. *suc.* fa. 1659; *cr.* Bt. 24 Dec. 1660; KB 23 Apr. 1661.[1]
    Freeman, Wigan 1649; member, Mercers' Co. by 1660, capt. green regt. London militia Oct. 1660–2, auxiliary regt. 1662, common councilman 1661–2, commr. for assessment 1661–3, dep. lt. 1662.[2]

Gardiner's grandfather was mayor of Wigan in 1596. His father, a younger son, became a London merchant, one of the wealthiest in Bassishaw ward, and stood unsuccessfully for his native borough in 1628 and both elections of 1640. One of the leading Royalists in the City, he was imprisoned by Parliament for organizing the petition against the militia ordinance of 1642. His house was sequestrated throughout the war, but he was not otherwise financially affected. No record exists of Gardiner's matriculation, but he was probably the commoner of Magdalen who refused to submit to the parliamentary visitation of 1648, and was sent down.[3]

At the general election of 1660 Gardiner and his cousin Hugh Forth* were involved in a double return at Wigan with unidentified opponents. They were allowed to take their seats, but during the four months before the election was declared void Gardiner was totally inactive in the Convention. He is not known to have stood again, and soon became involved in prosecuting his wife's claim to the Brocas estates. It was reported in 1662 that he was 'just ready to break, his bills of exchange being all protested at Leghorn'. Presumably he went bankrupt, for he never again held even the humblest local office. He had not paid his baronet's fee, from which he was discharged in 1686. Meanwhile he had reached a compromise over the Brocas property with the rival claimant. He received a small cash payment and settled down at Fareham, where he was buried on 23 June 1691. He died intestate, with his father's legacies still unpaid, and administration was granted to a creditor. No other member of his family ever entered Parliament.[4]

[1] M. Burrows, *Brocas of Beaurepaire*, 241–2; *St. Michael Bassishaw* (Harl. Soc. Reg. lxxiii), 3; PCC 530 Pell. [2] J. R. Woodhead, *Rulers of London*, 75; *Parl. Intell.* 1 Nov. 1660; *CSP Dom.* 1661–2, p. 559; *Merc. Pub.* 8 Apr. 1662. [3] D. Sinclair, *Hist. Wigan*, i. 196, 215; ii. 3; *Inhabitants of London in 1638* ed. Dale, 141; V. Pearl, *London and the Outbreak of the Puritan Revolution*, 150, 207; *Cal. Comm. Comp.* 1070; *Reg. of Visitors to Oxf. Univ.* (Cam. Soc. n.s. xxix), 97, 104, 107; *Misc. Gen. et Her.* (ser. 2), ii. 36. [4] *VCH Hants*, iv. 167; *Verney Mems.* ii. 201; *Cal. Treas. Bks.* viii. 685, 1047.

M.W.H./I.C./E.C.

GARRARD, John (c.1638–1701), of Clipston, Northants.

LUDGERSHALL 1679 (Oct.)
AMERSHAM 1698, 7–13 Jan. 1701

b. c.1638, 1st s. of Sir John Garrard, 2nd Bt., of Lamer Park, Wheathampstead, Herts. by Jane, da. of Sir Moulton Lambarde of Sevenoaks, Kent. *educ.* Christ Church, Oxf. 1657; I. Temple 1658. *m.* lic. 6 May 1669, 'aged 25', Katherine (*d.* 16 Apr. 1702), da. and coh. of Sir James Enyon, 1st Bt., of Floore, Northants., wid. of Sir George Buswell, 1st Bt., of Clipston, 1da. *suc.* fa. as 3rd Bt. 11 Mar. 1686.[1]

Commr. for assessment, Herts. 1673–80, 1689–90, j.p. and dep. lt. 1689–*d.*, sheriff 1690–1.[2]

Groom-porter 1699–*d.*

Garrard's great-grandfather, of Kentish origin, served as lord mayor of London in 1555–6 and represented the city in 1558. His grandfather bought Lamer in the reign of James I and was created a baronet. His father, an active Parliamentarian, held no local office after 1650, though he lived into the reign of James II. At the Restoration the estate was valued for militia purposes at £750 p.a.[3]

Garrard was returned for Ludgershall at the second general election of 1679 on the interest of his brother-in-law, the courtier Thomas Neale*. A friend and neighbour of the loyal Ishams, he was presumably a court supporter, though he took no part in committee work or debate. He and Neale were involved in an unresolved double return in 1681. A court Tory under William III, he succeeded Neale as groom-porter. He died in his London lodgings on 13 Jan. 1701, aged 62, after an operation for the stone, and was buried at Wheathampstead. His brother, a London Grocer, succeeded both to his estate and to his seat at Amersham, becoming lord mayor in 1710.[4]

[1] *N. and Q.* cciii. 544. [2] *Hertford County Recs.* vi. 522. [3] *VCH Herts.* ii. 299; A. Kingston, *Herts. during the Civil War*, 62; *HMC Verulam*, i. 102. [4] *N. and Q.* cciii. 544; BL, M636/33, Stewkeley to Verney, 21 Aug. 1679; Luttrell, v. 3, 6; Clutterbuck, *Herts.* i. 521.

J.P.F.

GARWAY (GARRAWAY), William (1617–1701), of Ford, Suss.

CHICHESTER 1661
ARUNDEL 1679 (Mar.), 1679 (Oct.), 1681, 1685, 1689

bap. 10 Apr. 1617, 1st s. of Sir Henry Garway, Draper, of Broad Street, London, ld. mayor 1639–40, by Margaret, da. of Henry Clitherow, merchant, of London. *educ.* Pembroke, Camb. 1632; travelled abroad 1635. *unm. suc.* fa. 1646.[1]

Capt. of ft. (royalist) 1642–4.[2]

Gent. of privy chamber c.1642–4; commr. for trade 1668–72, customs 1671–5.[3]

J.p. Suss. July 1660–?70, May 1688–?*d.*; commr. for assessment, Suss. Aug. 1660–74, 1689–90, Chichester 1663–4, sewers, W. Suss. Oct. 1660, loyal and indigent officers, London, Westminster and Suss. 1662, recusants, Suss. 1675, dep. lt. May–Oct. 1688.[4]

Garway's family, of Herefordshire origin, had been London merchants for three generations. His father, one of the leading City Royalists, was imprisoned for resisting parliamentary exactions during the Civil War. Garway himself was in arms for the King; he was taken prisoner and released on parole in November 1644. After succeeding to part of his father's Sussex estates he compounded at one-tenth for his delinquency with a fine of £290. Until his mother's death in 1657 brought him five farms in Sussex, he lived in London, where he apparently owned some rather questionable property, since after the apprentices' attack on the brothels in 1674 he told the House that his losses had been as great as any other Member's. A bachelor of abstemious tastes, who 'abstains from all food at least one day every week, and at other times ordinarily abstains from wine and strong liquors' he was of 'excellent natural endowments and great reading', becoming, in the eyes of a Sussex neighbour, 'a walking library'.[5]

Garway was returned for Chichester at the general election of 1661. He was an active committeeman in the Cavalier Parliament, though he never assumed the chair in any of his 283 committees, and he was even more prominent in debate, with 325 recorded speeches. In the first session he was named to the committee for the corporations bill, and in 1663 to those inquiring into a Sussex commission to discover lands gained from the sea, and to consider the bill to prevent abuses in the sale of offices. By now he was associated with the opposition group led by John Vaughan*. He was named to the committee of inquiry into the conduct of Sir Richard Temple*, who had offered to 'manage' the Commons, and sent with Vaughan to the Earl of Bristol, who had acted as intermediary with the Court. But in the supply debate of 23 Nov. 1664 Vaughan, Garway and Temple all 'chanted to the same tune', and one which the government spokesman found decidedly unmelodious.[6]

By 1666 Clarendon had come to regard Garway as a follower of Buckingham, and his parliamentary activity increased. On 21 Sept. he was sent to desire the concurrence of the Lords in an address of thanks to the King 'for his great care in management' of the second Dutch war. He was teller for the second reading of the bill to preserve naval stores, after which he was appointed to the committee. Samuel Pepys*, who as a witness before the parliamentary accounts committee was meeting Garway for the first time, found him good company, and wrote that he had

> not been well used by the Court, though stout to death, and hath suffered all that is possible for the King from the beginning. But discontented as he is, yet he never knew a session of Parliament but he hath done some good thing for the King before it rose. . . . Sir William Coventry* told me it is much to be pitied that the King should lose the service of a man so able and faithful.

He helped to prepare reasons for a conference on prohibiting French commodities, and served on the Commons delegation to ask for a proclamation, later acting as teller for hearing a petition from the merchants affected by the ban. On 8 Nov. he produced a complete financial programme for raising £1,800,000, and acted as teller for an 11 months' assessment on land at the rate of £12,000 a month. The House preferred a poll bill, however, to which he moved his 'great proviso' for a public accounts

commission. This was accepted, despite great efforts by the Court to flush every possible government supporter out of the theatres and bawdyhouses to vote against it; but later it was agreed that a separate bill was constitutionally necessary. The Lords objected to the proposal as an infringement on the prerogative, and repeated conferences in which Garway participated failed to bring the Houses to an agreement. He acted as teller for another proviso to the supply bill to deny the usual fees to Exchequer officials on money paid out by anticipation. He also helped to prepare reasons for a conference on imports of cattle from Ireland and to manage a conference on Lord Mordaunt's impeachment. Although the accounts bill, in which Garway was named as a commissioner, was lost at the prorogation, he and Sir Thomas Littleton, 2nd Bt.* were among the 12 Members appointed by the King for the same purpose at the Lords' request. They reluctantly agreed to serve, fortified by the judges' opinion in favour of the legality of the commission, but it accomplished nothing. He came up to Westminster for the abortive session in July, and seconded the motion of Thomas Tomkyns* for disbanding the newly-raised forces, though he admitted that it might not be 'convenient' to address the King to this purpose until peace had been concluded.[7]

When Parliament met again in October after the fall of Clarendon, Garway was among those appointed to bring in a public accounts bill. He was not particularly prominent in the attack on the fallen minister, however, being more concerned 'to bring the House to mind the public state of the nation, and to put off these particular piques between man and man'. On 15 Nov. he criticized the refusal of the Lords to imprison Clarendon without a specific charge as a breach of the Commons' privilege. He was among those appointed to prepare reasons for this view and to consider the bill of banishment. Apparently he was absent for the remainder of the session, for he was appointed to no committees and no speeches were recorded. During the summer of 1668, as a member of the Buckingham faction, he was nominated to the Irish accounts commission; but Ormonde, at whom the inquiry was principally aimed, had many friends among the Sussex Cavaliers, and Garway stood down in favour of Sir Thomas Osborne*. He was no loser by his forbearance, however, for in October he was appointed to the reconstituted council of trade.[8]

During the short 1669 session Garway was among those appointed to receive information about seditious conventicles. When the accounts commission reported he was sharply critical of the activities of Sir George Carteret* as treasurer of the navy, and urged that no fresh supply should be considered until the charges had been answered. When Sir John Marlay* described £300,000 as 'a pitiful sum to give the King' Garway retorted:

> Indeed it is a pitiful sum to them that are like to pay none of it. Hopes that we shall not be in the condition of France, when all the money is in one pocket. This sum will set you out a good fleet, and hopes we may have something left in our pockets to get on horseback with, to defend ourselves upon any emergency. Would leave the customs appropriated to the use of the navy.

He moved successfully that supply should not exceed £400,000, and that it should be raised neither by a land tax nor a house excise. Always jealous of the Commons' privilege *vis à vis* the Upper House, on 27 Nov. 1669, during the renewed debate on Skinner's case, he desired that the King should stay the execution of the Lords' order against the East India Company, but 'the motion was laid aside because it would put the King upon too much difficulty between the two Houses'. At this time he was regarded as a possible recruit for the court party, 'to be engaged by the Duke of Buckingham and his friends'. When the House met again after Christmas 'the Garway party appeared with the usual vigour', according to Andrew Marvell*, though they were not well supported by the country gentlemen. He was the first Member named to the inquiry into the wine duties, and was also among those appointed to consider a bill to prevent transportation, and the second conventicles bill; but of the last measure 'he was not fond', and he may have resigned from the county bench at this time.[9]

In the next session Garway was the first to be appointed to the committee to inspect the naval debt (31 Oct. 1670). Five days later he joined in the attack on the bankers, 'the commonwealth men that destroy the nobility and gentry'. On 18 Nov. he 'spoke sharply' against the proposal to collect the duty on imported spices by licensing the retailers, 'calling it arbitrary and tyrannical'. On 3 Dec. during the debate on the financial programme of Sir Robert Howard*, he introduced a red herring by moving that any clergyman holding two livings should pay £10, but admitted at the end of the debate that he did not expect it to pass, 'but only to set a mark upon it'. Now strongly opposed to a land tax as 'a mark of our chains', he succeeded in postponing any discussion until the yield of other taxes could be estimated. Five days later he supported the tax on offices.[10]

After the attack on Sir John Coventry* Garway was one of those who insisted on laying aside all other business until a bill to banish the culprits should pass both Houses. He was named to the small committee to bring it in, and later to prepare reasons for a conference. He retained sufficient City connexions to be given special responsibility for a bill to secure the creditors of the Grocers' Company, one of his rare private bill committees. He acted as teller for agreeing with the committee that the country candidate had been duly elected at Seaford on the broad franchise. He unsuccessfully urged the House to look for an alternative to the subsidy bill, and when (Sir) John Cotton I* proposed to mention in the preamble that supply had been given to maintain the Triple Alliance, Garway objected that

> we should not meddle with those matters of state which were not submitted to us nor of which we were not [sic] all informed; and besides we should be wary of interesting ourselves in those leagues, lest we should be called upon to maintain them.

He reminded the House of their former votes to stand by the King in the Dutch war which had resulted in an obligation to furnish 'very great sums of money'. A week later his request to be given leave 'to further his occasions' was denied.[11]

To the horror of the Opposition, Garway 'the Hector of the House' accepted an offer from his friend Thomas Clifford* in September 1671, and became a customs commissioner with a salary of £2,000 p.a. On the eve of the next session during the third Dutch war he and Thomas Lee I*, the 'bell-wethers of the country party' attended a meeting in which they agreed to propose a supply of £600,000, calculated to be 'enough to procure a peace, but not to continue a war'. But when the House met they proceeded to justify the satirists by carrying a grant for almost double that sum. In other respects, as Burnet noted, they continued to act on the opposite side, and they claimed that their action was necessary to prolong the session. Garway helped to prepare both addresses against the suspending power, and another on the dangerous condition of the Protestants in Ireland. He was among those instructed to bring in bills to naturalize foreign Protestants, and to give ease to dissenters. In debate he seemed to lean in the direction of comprehension, urging relief for 'the better sort' who would subscribe to the 39 Articles, 'or as many of them as relate to the doctrine of the Church of England'. He also favoured eliminating the renunciation of the Covenant, though he admitted that this concerned only 'a few old gentlemen'. He was prepared to grant Papists no more than freedom of worship: 'if you might see them in all their frippery, [he] believes you would not have so many of them'. On 6 Mar. 1673 he was appointed to the committees that produced the test bill and the address against the growth of Popery, and acted as teller for insisting that pensions to Roman Catholics should be withdrawn. In the debate on the Lords amendments he proposed, unsuccessfully, that the test for both navy and army officers should consist only of a denial of transubstantiation, which would, of course, have permitted the retention of nonconformist officers who were particularly valuable in the senior service. When it was argued that the King's necessities required a prompt supply Garway replied sharply that:

> if there were any necessities they were not of our making; that we might have been called together sooner; that if the necessities were such, it was fit to inquire who were the authors of those counsels which had now brought the King to these extremities.

He complained that the House had been 'strangely represented' in the Lords over the test, and acted as teller for the unsuccessful motion to consider the general naturalization bill in grand committee. Together with the Anglican diehard Giles Strangways* he opposed the Lords' proviso to the bill of ease in favour of the suspending power, and helped to draw up reasons for disagreeing.[12]

In the autumn session Garway refused to join in the attack on the new Speaker, Edward Seymour*, but was included by Sir William Temple in the most extreme opposition grouping. He opposed an immediate vote of thanks for the speech from the throne and was among those named to draw up the address against the Duke of York's second marriage. On the same day he proposed a religious test for Members of both Houses, and was appointed to the committee to bring in a bill. With (Sir) William Coventry*, he was considered the only Member capable of inducing the House to attack the French alliance, and fear of losing his post did not, as the King hoped, act as a deterrent. In January 1674 he joined in the attack on the surviving ministers of the Cabal, but defended 'his dead friend' Clifford. More surprisingly, unless he already had his eye on the Arundel constituency, he gave qualified support to the petition of Bernard Howard for relief from the recusancy laws, though not so as to qualify him for employment in the state or militia. When Charles asked for the 'advice and assistance' of the House on the terms of peace proferred by the Dutch, Garway asserted that they were solely the King's concern, since the Commons 'had no hand in advising the war', and he complained of the 'darkness' in which they had been kept. Despite his evident willingness to obstruct business he was on the committee ordered to prepare reasons for the peace and helped to manage the conference with the Lords. He again displayed his aversion to standing armies, saying that 'in all his reading [he] has found that these established guards have been the ruin of most princes', and he moved for an address against them. He supported the bills to prevent transportation and illegal exactions, and was also appointed to the committee on the bill for judges' patents to be irrevocable except for misbehaviour. He appears to have sympathized with Pepys, who had been involved in a disputed return at Castle Rising on the Howard interest, moving to receive the report of the elections committee, demanding that the grounds for the charge of Popery should be clearly stated, and accompanying Coventry and Meres to receive an explanation from Lord Shaftesbury (Sir Anthony Ashley Cooper*) when he was revealed as the originator of the rumours.[13]

Garway began the spring session of 1675 by opposing the usual vote of thanks for the King's speech. On 19 Apr. he denounced the assistance given to French imperialism by British policy. Though his request for 'a representation . . . of the state of this kingdom in reference to France' was not liked by the House, he continued to press for the recall of all British subjects from the French service. He supported the proposal to register the Papists 'and no other dissenters' at quarter sessions. He expressed dissatisfaction at the retention of Lauderdale but defended Osborne, now Lord Treasurer Danby, in the impeachment debate, though bluntly critical of his policies. When the proposal to appropriate the customs revenue to the use of the navy was revived, he was the first Member appointed to bring in a bill. He allowed his hostility to the pretensions of the Upper House to outweigh all other considerations when he supported the commitment of his neighbour John Fagg I* to the Tower for complying with the Lords, and no Member entered more vigorously into the dispute. He helped to draw up reasons for, or to manage, several conferences, and spoke on at least a dozen occasions. In the autumn session he opposed the Government's naval programme, queried Pepys's figures on the strength of the French and Dutch navies, and supported the motion that any money granted should be entrusted to the City rather than the Exchequer. When the Shirley v. Fagg dispute was again brought up he urged the House to proceed 'with such care and tenderness . . . as not to lose the fruits of this session', but he was still firmly against the appellate jurisdiction of the Lords, and when the motion denying it failed, he remarked 'privately' that by this vote you may get your privilege for a few of us and lose the judicature upon the whole commons of England, besides the endangering never raising the spirit of the House in it again.

He was named as usual to the principal committees of political importance, including those to examine dangerous books and to ensure the Protestant education of the royal children.[14]

Soon after Parliament rose Garway met the fate which had been confidently announced for him two years before, and was dismissed from the customs board. His removal, it was subsequently stated, 'lost the King £100,000 a year', and he certainly seems to have understood the significance of the incipient trade boom, which by increasing the revenue threatened parliamentary control. But in 1677 Shaftesbury appears to have marked him initially 'vile', or perhaps 'neutral', because he did not support the contention that the long recess had automatically entailed a dissolution. On 15 Feb. he described himself as 'one who believes this as good a Parliament as when we first sat', though he was 'not very fond of it neither'. He helped to consider another petition from Howard, and cited medical opinion to show that the mad duke of Norfolk could be brought home from Italy without danger. He seconded Sir Harbottle Grimston* in demanding that discussion of supply and grievances should 'go hand in hand, every other day'. He manifested his distrust of the Admiralty, and urged the House to proceed with caution over supply. He voted for a land tax for a year to be the freer to demand the withdrawal of the additional excise, lest it become a perpetuity and 'there shall be no occasion for your meeting when there is none for money'. He spoke out strongly on the danger of French power, and was one of those charged with drafting an address and managing a conference on the subject. When the King's answer proved unsatisfactory, Garway reluctantly proposed a further address, promising assistance in a war, but not to the extent 'of lives and fortunes', and was on the committee to draft it. He appears to have redeemed himself in Shaftesbury's eyes, and his rating was by stages adjusted to 'doubly worthy'.[15]

Garway entered freely into the heated debates on foreign policy in 1678, and helped to draw up the address for reducing France to her frontiers of 1659. Totally reversing his notorious proposal of March 1673, he now urged Members to vote only half the million pounds demanded by the Government to finance a war. After repeatedly reproaching the ministers for keeping the House in ignorance of the true nature of the alliances, he was appointed to the committee to summarize them. He was also among those ordered to bring in bills to reform the bankruptcy laws and to secure the Protestant religion. By 30 May, 'seeing there are no hopes of war, which I would willingly have gone on with', he was urging the immediate disbandment of all forces raised in the preceding eight months. Complaining that he personally was 'taxed to the utmost', he declared the further demand in the King's speech of 18 June to exceed the ability of the country. 'This looks to me of a strange nature', he concluded ominously, 'as if the House of Commons were never to come here more; I know not how to comply with it.' His last recorded attendance in the Cavalier Parliament was three days later, when he acted as teller against the return of the court candidate at Westbury, and he was apparently absent for the whole of the stormy final session after the Popish Plot.[16]

The Howard interest which Garway had cultivated was swept away by the Popish Plot; but he was returned for Arundel, two miles from his home, to the Exclusion Parliaments without known opposition, and marked 'worthy' on Shaftesbury's list. Again an active Member, he was appointed to 15 committees and made 50 speeches in 1679. He advised the House to insist on their choice of Seymour for Speaker. 'I would not give the King offence', he said, 'but [I would] not part with one hair of our right. If you will not stand to it here, you will have a great many things put upon you.' Although he described Danby as his former friend, he helped to draft the summons to him to give himself up and objected to his pardon. He took part in drawing up the address which characterized it as illegal and in managing a conference on the subject. He was also appointed to the committee for the attainder bill and until it should pass the Lords would not even consider supply, complaining that they had reduced the penalty to mere banishment. He was anxious to complete disbandment, and helped to draw up reasons for a conference. While unprepared to lay the blame for the Popish Plot entirely at the Duke of York's door, he had no doubt that his religion had been a great cause of it. On 14 May he laid down further conditions for supply in a resolution

that this House will not enter upon consideration to charge the subjects till effectual security be taken to preserve the King's Protestant subjects, the priests executed, and the lords in the Tower tried.

On 20 May he joined in the attack on Pepys, asserting that 'we have a land plot, this is a sea plot'. But he was absent from the vote on the exclusion bill, and in the last week of the session returned to the attack on Danby's pardon, being among those ordered to prepare the answer on methods of proceedings over impeachments. During the examination of (Sir) Stephen Fox* he had admitted that he was 'conversant' with the method of secret service payments, and after the dissolution he was given 300 guineas by the French ambassador, presumably for his vigour in supporting the disbandment of the army and the impeachment of the lord treasurer.[17]

When the second Exclusion Parliament met, Garway declared that petitioning was 'the undoubted right of the subject', though he had himself been neither Petitioner nor Abhorrer. He was appointed to the inquiries into the conduct of Sir Robert Peyton* and into abhorring, though determined that a hearing should not be denied to individual offenders. He also took part in drafting the addresses asking for a full pardon for informers and representing the dangerous state of the kingdom, and in managing conferences on the Irish plot and the method of trying Lord Stafford. He came out firmly against exclusion on 2 Nov. 1680.

> I hope the prudence of this House may find out some expedient to secure the nation, more likely to be brought to perfection, than this of the exclusion bill. . . . For my part, I am more afraid of an army without a general than a general without an army; and therefore I think that if instead of ordering a committee to bring in a bill for disinheriting the Duke, you bring in a bill for banishing all the Papists out of the nation, and other bills for having of frequent Parliaments, and to secure good judges and justices, that so the laws you have already, as well as what more you may make, may be duly executed, it may do as well, and may be more likely to have success.

In the debate on the second reading he exploited the divisions in the country party over the succession by demanding that the bill should contain

> some general expression that no Protestant heir be excluded [from] the succession. If we will not do something of that nature, it looks like setting up a commonwealth.

He opposed the attack on Lord Halifax and unsuccessfully moved the recommittal of the address for his removal. After commenting on the King's speech of 15 Dec. that he 'would have a real, and not a verbal satisfaction' for property and the security of the Protestant religion, he helped to draft the reply. He strongly supported the introduction of a bill to banish Papists, but warned the House to 'take heed you do not forget Protestants'. He urged unity with dissenters, 'for that disjunction has made you weak'. He again asserted the necessity of disbandment, declaring that 'as long as we have standing forces in the kingdom, I fear they will cut all our throats'. He had again been an active Member of the second Exclusion Parliament, with 12 committees and 25 speeches. But as one of the leading

'men of expedients' in the Oxford Parliament, he was named only to the committee of elections and privileges, and spoke only in the debate on the disappearance of the bill to repeal the Elizabethan statute against Protestant dissenters. This was 'such a breach of the constitution of Parliament', he considered 'that it is in vain to pass any bill if this be not searched into'. But his zeal for Protestant unity was not sufficient, in the eyes of the Sussex dissenters, to outweigh his dislike of exclusion, and they did not adopt him as one of their candidates in 1682.[18]

Garway's interest at Arundel, however, was unshaken, and there is no evidence of a contest in 1685. He was only moderately active in James II's Parliament, with three committees. When the Government broke with precedent by moving for supply on the first day of the session, he told the House that it was customary to follow the King's speech by reading a bill. He was named to the committee of elections and was among those ordered to inspect the accounts of the disbandment commissioners and to bring in the bill for the general naturalization of foreign Protestants. On 22 June, however, he was given leave to go into the country for his health, and there is no evidence that he returned to Westminster after the recess. He was listed among the Opposition as 'considerable for parts' but 'not to be trusted'. Nevertheless he was approved, doubtless on Howard's recommendation, as deputy lieutenant and j.p. in May 1688, and the royal agents reported that his seat was safe. At the Revolution he attended the meeting of Members of Charles II's Parliaments, helped to draft the address to William of Orange for a general election, and expressed his willingness to sign the Association.[19]

Re-elected to the Convention, though relegated to the junior seat, Garway resumed an active rôle, being named to 55 committees and making 95 recorded speeches. When the House first met he opened the debate on William's letter. 'All England is sensible of the great deliverance we have had from Popery and slavery', he said, and moved to desire the Prince 'to take the administration of the Government upon him'. He was appointed to the committee to draft an address accordingly, and on 29 Jan. 1689 initiated another address for stopping ships from sailing to France. It is clear that he supported the transfer of the crown to William, but on the necessity of constitutional guarantees he was forthright:

> We have had such violations of our liberties in the last reigns that the Prince of Orange cannot take it ill if we make conditions to secure ourselves for the future, and in it we shall but do justice to those who sent us hither.

He was among those who prepared the declaration of rights and managed the conference on James II's 'abdication' and the 'vacancy' of the throne. In a debate on supply on 11 Mar. he urged the House to distinguish between a standing revenue and a tax imposed for a limited period. He was appointed to the committees for suspending habeas corpus, the first mutiny bill, and the bill of rights. He repeated his arguments against the sacramental test, especially its effects on the navy, and wished to modify the coronation oath:

> I would have the church doors made wider. . . . In order to that I move that the King . . . swear to maintain the Protestant religion as it is, or shall be, established by law.

But attempts to provide for parliamentary alterations in the Establishment were unacceptable to the House, though he was appointed to the committee to bring in a comprehension bill. He helped to draw up the addresses thanking the King for his promise to maintain the Church and undertaking to support a war with France. He helped to prepare reasons for imposing the new oaths on the clergy and rejecting the Lords' claim to name commissioners for the poll-tax. He was among those ordered to take care of the militia bill, which was designed to set up a counterweight to the professional army, but it failed at the prorogation. When indemnity was debated on 14 May, he followed the Whig line that 'things' should be considered rather than 'persons', for punishment. He would not dabble in blood, 'but from pecuniary penalties I would not exempt them'. He enlarged upon this two days later, saying that he 'would not destroy families, but leave them a livelihood and no more'. After serving on the inquiry into the delay in the relief of Londonderry, however, he came to the conclusion that the main cause of miscarriages was that 'we are not quicker with our money to supply the present emergencies of the Government', and he proposed, unsuccessfully, that the House should give supply priority over indemnity, though he was on the committee for the bill. He sought to resolve differences between the Houses by declaring that a bill to reverse the conviction of Oates would suffice. On 1 July, two days after receiving leave to go into the country he was appointed to the committee to ask permission to inspect the Privy Council records about Ireland, and he was certainly at Westminster on the eve of the recess when he reversed his attitude over supply and told Richard Hampden* that the House had already given enough for one year.[20]

When Parliament reconvened in the autumn Garway was highly critical of the conduct of the war. He was appointed to the inquiry into war expenditure and described the account of forces in being, submitted by Lord Ranelagh (Richard Jones*), as the worst he had ever seen in his life. He now recognized the need for further supply, not exceeding £2,000,000, because 'he would not be cozened', and the House accepted his proposal that two-thirds of the grant should be raised by a land tax. He considered that 'some exemplary thing' should be done to George Churchill* for requiring money for convoying merchantmen, and, after joining vigorously in the attack on Commissary Shales, he helped to draw up the address inquiring who had recommended this disastrous appointment. But when the King replied by asking the Commons to nominate suitable replacements, Garway with the majority evaded responsibility, recommending only that no Members should be named since there were already too many placemen in the House. He was appointed to the committee on the state of the revenue and listed as a supporter of the disabling clause in the bill to restore corporations. On 20 Jan. 1690 he attacked (Sir) Robert Sawyer* for his part in the condemnation of Sir Thomas Armstrong*, and he was named to the committee for imposing a general oath of allegiance. In his last recorded speech, he reiterated his opinion on the indemnity bill: 'Find out things; else you will never find out persons, or come at them as long as you live'.[21]

Garway was defeated by the dissenter James Butler* at the general election of 1690 and retired from political life, though remaining 'very healthful and stout in his body' and 'very inquisitive after more knowledge' into and beyond his eightieth year. A local clergyman described him in 1697 as 'careful to purchase all books of worth as they come from the press, and very curious and attentive in reading and marking them'. It is all the more striking that his recorded speeches, which he invariably delivered extemporarily, are totally free from pedantry and literary allusion, though Morrice's informants accused him of 'constantly clogging all great matters in the Convention'. Throughout his parliamentary career his interest lay almost exclusively in affairs of state. He was named to only 30 committees on private bills, all in the Cavalier Parliament. Except during the supply debate in 1673, and perhaps for the opening months of the Convention, he was consistently in opposition, demanding redress before supply, the abolition of the standing army, and relief for Protestant nonconformists. His tolerance even extended so far as to permit the public exercise of Roman Catholic worship. He cannot be absolved from the charge of venality, despite the apparent simplicity of his life-style; and as a moderate in the exclusion crisis he incurred the hostility of his former associates, and his policy of comprehension was distasteful to many dissenters. He died on 4 Aug. 1701 and was buried at Ford, the only member of his family to sit in Parliament. Subject to the life interest of his nephew Sir William Norris[†], he bequeathed his whole estate to Christ's Hospital.[22]

[1] Guildhall RO, St. Peter le Poer par. reg.; *Vis. Suss.* (Harl. Soc. lxxxix), 52; PC2/45/47. [2] Clarendon, *Rebellion*, iii. 399. [3] *Vis. Suss.* 52; *Cal. Treas. Bks.* iii. 935; iv. 869. [4] C181/7/58. [5] *DNB*; V. Pearl, *London in the Puritan Revolution*, 290–301; *Letter Bks. of Sir Samuel Luke* (Beds. Hist. Rec. Soc. xliii), 404–5; *Cal. Comm. Comp.* 1481; Grey, ii. 393; W. Turner, *Compleat Hist. of Most Remarkable Providences* (1697), ch. 71, p. 90. [6] *CJ*, viii. 511; Add. 32094, f. 26. [7] Clarendon, *Life*, iii. 132–3; *CJ*, viii. 630, 644, 659, 661, 669, 670, 675, 683; *Pepys Diary*, 3, 6 Oct. 1666, 5 June, 25 July 1667; *Milward*, 38, 56, 83. [8] *Pepys Diary*, 17 Nov. 1667; *Clarendon Impeachment*, 51; *CJ*, ix. 21; Carte, *Ormond*, iv. 325; Eg. 2539, f. 260; Browning, *Danby*, i. 64. [9] Grey, i. 159, 176, 188, 189, 195, 230; *Marvell* ed. Margoliouth, ii. 300. [10] Grey, i. 274, 315, 319; *Dering*, 3, 21. [11] *Dering*, 47, 49, 76–77; *CJ*, ix. 189, 191, 200. [12] *Marvell* ed. Margoliouth, i. 185; North, *Examen*, 456; *HMC 13th Rep. VI*, 6; *Poems on Affairs of State*, i. 181; Burnet, ii. 15–16; *Dering*, 112, 126, 139; Grey, ii. 32, 38, 44, 47, 86, 137; *CJ*, ix. 264, 275, 279. [13] *Essex Pprs.* (Cam. Soc. n.s. xlviii), 131; *Dering*, 152, 154, 156; Grey, ii. 185, 196, 205, 241, 257, 282, 327, 338, 359, 392, 404, 407, 420; PRO 31/3, bdle. 129, ff. 40, 62; *CJ*, ix. 300, 302, 304, 305. [14] *Dering Pprs.* 59, 65, 67, 82, 85; Eg. 3345, f. 23; Grey, iii. 8, 17, 42–43, 81, 112, 324, 327, 362; iv. 9, 12, 39; *CJ*, ix. 339, 344. [15] *Williamson Letters* (Cam. Soc. n.s. ix), 67; *Dering Pprs.* 114; *HMC Lindsey*, 45; Grey, iv. 69, 112, 120–1, 176, 190, 218, 228, 313; *CJ*, ix. 385, 398. [16] *CJ*, ix. 428, 472; Grey, v. 37, 76, 78, 100, 106, 167–8, 187; vi. 29, 38, 96. [17] Grey, vi. 407; vii. 45, 67, 85, 92, 149–50, 185, 274, 305, 319; Dalrymple, *Mems.* i. 382. [18] Grey, vii. 370, 388, 394, 398, 428; viii. 50, 160–1, 192, 301; *Exact Coll. Debates*, 26–27, 150; *CJ*, ix. 648, 667; *HMC 12th Rep. IX*, 99; *HMC Ormonde*, n.s. vi. 5; *CSP Dom.* 1680–1, p. 473. [19] R. Morrice, Entering Bk. 1, p. 462; 2, pp. 395, 398, 409; *CSP Dom.* 1687–9, p. 199; *CJ*, x. 6. [20] Grey, ix. 3, 25, 30, 150, 191, 249, 280, 293; *CJ*, x. 9, 20, 112, 192; Morrice, 2, p. 507; A. Boyer, *Hist. Wm. III*, ii. 121. [21] Grey, ix. 389–90, 403, 434, 451, 453, 467, 536, 542; *CJ*, x. 296. [22] Grey, ii. 392; iii. 110; Morrice 2, p. 517; Turner, ch. 48, p. 29; Dalloway, *W. Suss.* ii. pt. 1, p. 48; PCC 126 Dyer.

B.M.C./B.D.H.

GAWDY, Sir Charles, 1st Bt. (c.1635–1707), of Crow's Hall, Debenham, Suff.

EYE   8 Nov. 1678, 1679 (Mar.), 1681, 1685

b. c.1635, 1st s. of Sir Charles Gawdy of Crow's Hall by Vere, da. and coh. of Sir Edward Cooke of Gidea Hall, Romford, Essex. *m.* (1) 4 Sept. 1657 (with £4,000), Lady Mary Feilding (*d.*1691), da. of George, 1st Earl of Desmond [I], 1s. 2da.; (2) by 1699, Elizabeth, *s.p. suc.* fa. 1650; kntd. bef. 1661; *cr.* Bt. 20 Apr. 1661.[1]

J.p. Suff. July 1660–?89; commr. for assessment, Suff. Aug. 1660–80, 1689–92, Orford 1679–80; dep. lt. Suff. 1662–89, capt. of militia ft. by 1664, maj. by 1676–?89; freeman, Eye 1675; commr. for recusants, Suff. 1675, receiver of taxes 1677–9; common councilman, Thetford 1682–Oct. 1688; portman, Orford 1685–Oct. 1688.[2]

Gawdy's grandfather, a younger son of the Norfolk family, inherited Crow's Hall, ten miles from Eye, from the Framlinghams in 1595. His father, 'a

zealous professor of the reformed religion, settled and established in the reign of Elizabeth . . . a lover of monarchy and of an undaunted loyalty', held Household office under Charles I and served as commissioner of array and colonel of horse in the Civil War. His delinquency fine was fixed at £1,789, but reduced to £165 on settling £150 p.a. for his life on four local ministers. This turned out well for the family, since he died only two years later, with a cheerfulness that astonished the beholders. It is clear from the family papers, however, that he had incurred other debts, and the estate was never again on a firm financial footing.[3]

Gawdy probably accompanied his cousin William Gawdy* to The Hague in May 1660, and was knighted there. In the following year he was created a baronet, but he seems to have taken no part in politics until October 1675, when he brought up the Suffolk petition against the Royal Africa Company. He was first returned for Eye at a by-election in 1678. Shaftesbury marked him 'vile', and he was included in the 'unanimous club' of court supporters; but he obtained leave to go into the country on 18 Dec. and is not known to have played any part in the closing weeks of the Cavalier Parliament. At the first general election of 1679 Gawdy joined with (Sir) Robert Reeve* to oppose the Cornwallis interest, by which he was aspersed as a Papist, although nothing could be further from the truth. The other candidates withdrew on the eve of the poll, after putting Gawdy to the expense of a whole year's revenue, or so it was believed in the family. He was again marked 'vile' by Shaftesbury, and voted against exclusion. He was appointed only to the committee of elections and privileges and to that to consider a petition from some foreign merchants. On the dissolution of the first Exclusion Parliament, Gawdy's mother wrote to her lifelong friend and adviser, Sir Ralph Verney*: 'I dread a new election at Eye, for I fear a third part of that way of destruction I shall not be able to prevent'. Lord Cornwallis was determined to oust him, and by August the electors were 'feasting so high' as to double the expense of the last election; but all he could achieve was a double return, and the grant of the fine imposed on the bailiff of Eye for seditious words. The return was decided in favour of the Cornwallis candidates when Parliament met, but Gawdy regained his seat after another contest in 1681, though he was appointed to no committees in the Oxford Parliament.[4]

On the death of Charles II, Verney urged Gawdy to come to town at once, for 'there are certain critical moments when men that observe them may build their fortunes'. Sunderland urged him to secure the return of loyal candidates to James II's Parliament, and he was himself re-elected for Eye. A very active Member, he was appointed to 16 committees. He helped to draw up the loyal address from the House on the news of Monmouth's invasion, and was also concerned with the measures to prevent clandestine marriages, encourage shipbuilding and relieve poor debtors. Presumably he continued to support the Government in the second session, for he was granted the crown's interest in the estate of a neighbour who had hanged himself; but it is not clear that he gained anything material from Verney's recommendation of him as 'a most accomplished gentleman, extremely civil, obliging in all his expressions, and well worthy of his Majesty's favour'. In September 1688 the King's electoral agents reported that Gawdy would probably be chosen for Eye; though his principles could not be depended upon, his circumstances would engage him to serve the Court. He did not stand in 1689, and was dropped from the lieutenancy after the Revolution. His name ceased to appear on the assessment commissions after 1692, when he probably sold his estate. He was buried at Romford on 15 Sept. 1707. The baronetcy expired with his only son, who was of unsound mind.[5]

[1] HMC Gawdy, 153; Verney Mems. ii. 119. [2] Add. 39246, ff. 4, 5, 23; E. Suff. RO, EE2/D5/1; CSP Dom. 1676–7, p. 590; 1685, p. 46; Cal. Treas. Bks. v. 431; SP44/165/61. [3] Copinger, Suff. Manors, vii. 130–3; W. H. Black, Docquet of Letters Patent, 74; Cal. Comm. Comp. 1236–7; HMC Gawdy, 189. [4] HMC 7th Rep. 494; Bulstrode Pprs. 315; BL, M636/32, 33 Lady Gawdy to Verney, 6, 27 Feb., 10 Mar. 1679, 15 July, 12 Aug. 1679; Cary Gardiner to Verney, 20 Aug. 1679; Cal. Treas. Bks. vi. 627; Grey, viii. 228. [5] Verney Mems. ii. 378; CSP Dom. 1685, p. 21; Cal. Treas. Bks. viii. 434, 1152.

P.W.

GAWDY, William (1612–69), of West Harling, Norf. and Bury St. Edmunds, Suff.

THETFORD 1661–Aug. 1669

bap. 24 Sept. 1612, 1st s. of Framlingham Gawdy[†], barrister, of West Harling and Gray's Inn by 1st w. Lettice, da. and coh. of Sir Robert Knollys[†] of Westminster. educ. Bury St. Edmunds g.s.; Caius, Camb. 1629, BA 1632; I. Temple 1633. m. 1 Sept. 1636, Elizabeth (d.1653), da. and h. of John Duffield of East Wretham, Norf., 4s. (2 d.v.p.) 1da. suc. fa. 1654; cr. Bt. 13 July 1663.[1]

J.p. Norf. July 1660–d., Thetford 1666–d.; dep. lt. Norf. c. Aug. 1660–d., maj. of militia ft. 1661–d.; commr. for assessment, Norf. and Thetford 1661–d., Suff. 1663–4, corporations Norf. 1662–3.[2]

Gawdy's ancestors were minor landowners in the Waveney valley until the middle of the 16th century, when they rose to wealth and eminence in the law, and represented King's Lynn and Norwich under Edward VI. His father sat for Thetford, six miles from West Harling, in seven Parliaments. A passive Parliamentarian in the Civil War, he was secluded at Pride's Purge, and did not sit on local commissions after the execution of Charles I. Gawdy himself took no part in public life during the Civil War and Interregnum. After succeeding to the estate he became a flockmaster on a large scale and kept methodical records of all his business transactions, though he seems to have resided chiefly at Bury. On the eve of the Restoration he attended Charles II at The Hague.[3]

Gawdy began his search for a seat before the dissolution of the Convention, and was advised by Sir John Holland* to apply to the Duke of Norfolk's brother, 'disclaiming any interest of his own to be considerable'. However, he was returned for Thetford at the general election of 1661. An active Member of the Cavalier Parliament, he was appointed to 141 committees, including the committee of elections and privileges in six sessions, and acted as teller in five divisions. He was in London almost throughout the first session, being named to the committees to inquire into the shortfall in revenue, and to consider the security, corporations, and uniformity bills, and the bill of pains and penalties. He was also appointed to the committee on the bill to repair Wells quay, and after the recess to two others of local interest, those to confirm the restoration of the dukedom of Norfolk and to regulate the manufacture of Norwich stuffs. He acted as teller on 16 Dec. to lay aside all the remaining provisos to the bill for confirming incumbents, and a month later he was added to the revived committee for the execution of the remaining regicides. In 1663 he was appointed to the committees for hindering the growth of Popery and providing remedies against meetings of sectaries. He helped to consider the bill produced by the latter committee, and, doubtless under the influence of the tolerant Holland, acted as teller for a proviso which allowed for the duties of servants. He was already described in the Journals as 'Sir William', although the patent for his baronetcy did not pass the seals until the following month. He was given leave to go into the country on 10 July, but this appears to have been a tactical move in a factional struggle with Sir Ralph Hare*, for five days later they were on opposite sides in a division on striking out commissioners from the subsidy bill, which was followed by the omission of one of the Norwich names. Still in accord with Holland over the Triennial Act in 1664, he acted as teller against a proviso to the bill of repeal. In the same session he helped to consider the revived conventicles bill, and in the autumn he was among the Members appointed to consider two more bills of special interest to his county, those to resolve disputes over the lading and unlading of herrings at Yarmouth, and to settle the estate of Sir Jacob Astley*. For the remainder of the Clarendon administration he was less active, and he probably did not attend the Oxford session during the plague. But he was named to the committee on the bill for the illegitimization of Lady Roos's children (21 Jan. 1667). On the fall of Clarendon he was appointed to the committees to inquire into the miscarriages of the Dutch war and the sale of Dunkirk, and to consider the charges against Lord Mordaunt. In the same session he was among those to whom were committed private bills to enable Lord Townshend (Sir Horatio Townshend*) to exchange some of his land with the East Raynham glebe, and to provide for the repair of Yarmouth harbour. His last committee was on the bill to prevent the refusal of writs of habeas corpus (24 Apr. 1668). He was buried at West Harling on 18 Aug. 1669. Both his surviving sons were deaf-mutes, and he was the last of this branch of the Gawdy family to enter Parliament.[4]

[1] *Norf. Arch.* xxvi. 352–3. [2] *HMC Gawdy*, 195, 196. [3] *Norf. Arch.* xxvi. 335; Keeler, *Long Parl.* 184; Add. 27396, f. 363; Add. 36990, ff. 145–98; *HMC Gawdy*, 189. [4] *HMC Gawdy*, 190, 192; *CJ*, viii. 514, 524, 538; *Norf. Arch.* xxvi. 371–2.

E.C.

GEE, Orlando (1619–1705), of Petworth, Suss. and Syon Hill, Isleworth, Mdx.

COCKERMOUTH 1679 (Mar.), 1679 (Oct.), 1681, 1685, 1690

b. 1619, 4th s. of John Gee (*d.*1631), vicar of Dunsford, Devon by Sarah Mogridge of Littleham, Devon. *m.* (1) lic. 17 May 1662, Elizabeth, da. of Sir William Maxey of Bradwell-next-Coggeshall, Essex, wid. of Thomas Barker of Sibton, Suff., *s.p.*; (2) Anne, da. and h. of Robert Chilcot of Isleworth, *s.p.* Kntd. 18 Aug. 1682.[1]
    Registrar of Admiralty (jt.) Sept. 1660, (sole) 1662–*d.* Commr. for assessment, Cumb., Essex, Mdx. and Suss. 1679–80.

Gee came from a clerical family of Lancastrian origin that had produced several notable anti-Catholic polemicists in Elizabethan and early Stuart times. He took no known part in the Civil War, but obtained a pass for Holland in 1652, and by 1659 he had entered the service of the 4th Earl of Northumberland. Doubtless he had, like John Clarke II*, been recruited by his fellow-Devonian, Hugh Potter*. He was joined with Potter as registrar of the Admiralty at the Restoration, and when Clarke's death left a vacancy at Cockermouth in 1675, he stood for the borough on the Percy interest, which had been weakened by the death of the 5th Earl without male heirs, and was defeated by an ambitious local squire, Sir Richard Grahme*.[2]

Gee was returned for Cockermouth to the Exclusion Parliaments, and classed 'doubtful' by Shaftesbury. He was named to no committees in 1679, but voted against the bill. In the second Exclusion Parliament he was appointed to the committee of elections and privileges and probably to four others, including those for the bills to prohibit cattle imports, to prevent the imposition of arbitrary fines, and to unite Protestants. There is no evidence that he attended the Oxford Parliament. His knighthood was probably obtained on the recommendation of the 6th Duke of Somerset, who had married the Percy heiress and was materially indebted to Gee for his work in exposing the bogus pedigree of a rival claimant to the estate.[3]

Gee was re-elected for Cockermouth in 1685, when he defeated a brother of the Hon. Thomas Wharton*, sharing expenses with the Tory, Sir Daniel Fleming*. A very active Member of James II's Parliament, he was appointed to 17 committees, including the committee to examine the disbandment accounts in 1679. On 16 June he acted as teller for the Lindsey level bill introduced on behalf of Sir William Killigrew*, which was rejected by a large majority. Other bills with which he was concerned included those for the suppression of simony, the establishment of a land registry, and the general naturalization of Huguenot refugees. He was recommended for re-election as court candidate in September 1688, and stood on his own interest. But after succeeding in the abortive election he stood down in favour of (Sir) Henry Capel*. He regained his seat as a Tory in 1690. He died childless in 1705, aged 86, and was buried at Isleworth, leaving legacies amounting to £10,000. His epitaph commemorates his long service to the Percy family and his charities, including a gift of £500 for rebuilding the church, but makes no mention of his parliamentary activities, and no other member of the family sat in the Commons.[4]

[1] *DNB*; Eg. 2758, f. 107; *London Mar. Lic.* ed. Foster 535; Morant, *Essex*, i. 157; Le Neve, *Mon. Angl.* 1700–15, p. 96. [2] *CSP Dom.* 1651–2, p. 562; 1675–6, p. 115; *HMC 3rd Rep.* 88. [3] G. Brenan, *House of Percy*, ii. 326. [4] *HMC Le Fleming*, 197, 403; *CSP Dom.* 1687–9, p. 273; Yale Univ. Osborn mss, Lowther to Lowther, 29 Dec. 1688; *Misc. Gen. et Her.* (ser. 5), x. 29; Le Neve, 96.

E.C.

GEE, William (c.1648–1718), of Bishop Burton, Yorks.

KINGSTON-UPON-HULL 1679 (Oct.), 1681, 1689
BEVERLEY 1690, 1701 (Dec.), 1702

b. c.1648, 1st s. of William Gee of Bishop Burton by 1st w. Rachel, da. of Sir Thomas Parker[†] of Willingdon, Suss. *m.* (1) 23 Feb. 1664, Elizabeth (*d.*1684), da. of Sir

John Hotham, 2nd Bt.*, of Scorborough, Yorks., 5s. 6da.; (2) settlement 8 Oct. 1685, Eizabeth, da. of Charles Cracroft of Louth, Lincs., wid. of John Ellerker of Risby, Yorks., 1s. 2da. *suc.* fa. 1678.[1]

Commr. for concealments, Yorks. 1671; j.p. Yorks. (E. Riding) 1672–80, ?1689–*d.*, dep. lt. 1673–?80, 1689–?*d.*; commr. for assessment (E. Riding) 1673–80, 1689–90, Hull 1690; lt.-col. of militia ft. (E. Riding) ?1691–*d.*[2]

Gee was descended from an Elizabethan merchant who was three times mayor of Hull. His great-grandfather sat for the borough in 1589. The family were reckoned among the puritan gentry at this time, but Gee's father played little part in politics, being nominated only to the committee for the northern association in 1645 and the militia committees of 1648 before going abroad. On the Continent he associated chiefly with exiled Cavaliers; his second wife was the eldest daughter of Richard Spencer*, and he held no further office until the eve of the Restoration. At the age of 16 Gee married his cousin, who was four years younger, and strengthened his links with the country party. He was defeated for Hull at the first election of 1679, and his petition, although supported by his father-in-law and other friends, brought him no satisfaction. But he was successful in September, and removed as j.p. in the following year. He was probably totally inactive in both the second and third Exclusion Parliaments. He contested Hull again in 1685, but was easily defeated. On Monmouth's landing orders were given for his arrest as a dangerous and disaffected person. Some time before the Revolution he was in Holland with Hotham and William Harbord*, doubtless plotting the success of the projected invasion. 'A bitter enemy to the King', he came over with the Dutch in December 1688, having sworn with his associates 'that they would never lay down arms till they made the Prince of Orange king'. He was returned to the Convention but served only on the committee of elections and privileges, and on 15 May 1689 he was allowed leave of absence for three weeks. He did not support the disabling clause in the bill to restore corporations, but he was listed as a Whig under Anne. He was buried at Bishop Burton on 15 Oct. 1718, the last of his family to sit in Parliament.[3]

[1] Clay, *Dugdale's Vis. Yorks.* iii. 24, 263; *Lincs. Peds.* (Harl. Soc. l) 275. [2] *Cal. Treas. Bks.* iii. 912; Add. 29674, f. 161v; SP44/165/278; Eg. 1626, f. 55. [3] J. T. Cliffe, *Yorks. Gentry*, 269; *Verney Mems.* i. 478, 491–2; ii. 18; *CSP Dom.* 1685, p. 228; *HMC 7th Rep.* 412, 424; Bodl. Fleming mss 3334.

P.A.B.

GEERS, Thomas (c.1643–1700), of Hereford.

HEREFORD 1685

b. c.1643, 1st s. of Thomas Geers of The Marsh, Bridge Sollers, Herefs. by Sarah, da. of Thomas Snowdon of London. *educ.* Wadham, Oxf. matric. 22 Mar. 1661, aged 18; I. Temple 1661, called 1668, *m.* (1) 1671, Sarah, da. and coh. of Timothy Colles of Hatfield, Herefs., 1s.; (2) 1676, Elizabeth, da. and h. of William Cope of Iccomb, Glos., wid. of Thomas Whitney of Whitney, Herefs., 2s. 1da. *suc.* fa. 1675.[1]

J.p. Herefs. 1670–?89, commr. for assessment 1673–80; common councilman, Hereford 1682–3, dep. steward 1683–Oct. 1688, alderman 1683–Oct. 1688; bencher, I. Temple 1685; second justice, S. Wales circuit 1685–6. Brecon circuit 1686–Nov. 1688, c.j. Nov. 1688–9.[2]

Serjeant-at-law 1686–9.

Geers's great-uncle, a proctor of Doctors' Commons, bought the manor of Bridge Sollers, six miles from Hereford, in 1622. The family were inactive during the Civil War and Interregnum, prudently tending and increasing their estates, until Geers's father was appointed an assessment commissioner by the Rump in January 1660. Both Geers's marriages brought him land and connexions. He took up residence in Hereford, no doubt to forward his legal practice, and was named to the corporation in the new charter of 1682. In the following year the Duke of Beaufort (Henry Somerset*) appointed him deputy steward of the borough, and he became a Welsh judge in 1685. Geers was elected as a court supporter to James II's Parliament. He was moderately active, with six committees, of which the most important was on the bill for the general naturalization of Huguenot refugees. Presumably the King was satisfied with his conduct, for he was raised to the coif in 1686. With regard to the Test Act and Penal Laws, Beaufort reported that Geers retained 'the same mind he was of when the King spoke to him', and thought he commanded enough interest at Hereford to stand on a repeal platform, though he was not sanguine of success. He was duly approved by Sunderland for re-election as a court candidate. On 10 Sept. 1688, however, Robert Harley II* wrote that, although the Hereford electors had their reservations about (Sir) William Gregory* 'they like him better than Geers'. On Beaufort's recommendation he was somewhat tardily promoted chief justice of his circuit, but in the following month he subscribed £30 to the loan for William of Orange. He never stood again, losing all his offices under the new regime, and probably becoming a non-juror. He died in November 1700; his grandson was elected for Hereford as a Tory in 1727 and 1741.[3]

[1] C. J. Robinson, *Mansions and Manors of Herefs.* 39, 302; Cooke, *Herefs.* iv. 30. [2] Duncumb, *Herefs.* i. 360–1; *CSP Dom.* Jan.–June 1683, p. 346; W. R. Williams, *Great Sessions in Wales*, 141–2. [3] Cooke, 26; Bodl. Carte 130, f. 24; *HMC 7th Rep.* 348; BL Loan 29/184, f. 121; *HMC Portland*, iii. 417; Beaufort mss, Richard Hopton to Beaufort, 20 Apr. 1683.

E.R.

GELL, Sir John, 2nd Bt. (1612–89), of Hopton, Wirksworth, Derbys. and St. Martin's Lane, Westminster.

DERBYSHIRE   1654, 1656,[1] 1659, Jan.–8 Feb. 1689

bap. 7 Oct. 1612, 1st s. of Sir John Gell, 1st Bt., of Hopton by 1st w. Elizabeth, da. of Sir Percival Willoughby[†] of Wollaton, Notts. *educ.* Magdalen Hall, Oxf. 1632. *m.* by 1648 (with £4,000), Katherine (*d.*1668), da. of John Packer[†], clerk of the privy seal, of Shellingford, Berks., 4s. (2 *d.v.p.*) 3da. *suc.* fa. 26 Oct. 1671.[2]

J.p. Derbys. 1649–51, Mar.–July 1660, 1675–80, Mar. 1688–*d.*, commr. for assessment 1649–52, 1659, Jan. 1660, 1666–80, scandalous ministers, Derbys. and Notts. 1654, militia, Derbys. 1659, Mar. 1660; receiver, honour of Tutbury 1671–*d.*; sheriff, Derbys. 1672–3, dep. lt. Feb. 1688–*d.*; commr. for inquiry into recusancy fines, Notts., Derbys. and Lincs. Mar. 1688.[3]

Gell's ancestors had held Hopton as crown tenants since 1422, and were granted arms in 1575. His father incurred much odium as ship-money sheriff, and was created a baronet on the eve of the Civil War. To avert the consequences he took up arms for Parliament and became one of the most active commanders in the Midlands, while Gell's uncle became the first of the family to enter Parliament, sitting as recruiter for Derby from 1645 until Pride's Purge. Gell himself took no known part in the Civil War, but represented the county in the Protectorate Parliaments after his father had been driven out of public life for concealing a royalist plot. He signed the Derbyshire address for a free Parliament in 1660, but was unsuccessful at the general election.[4]

Although regarded as 'the most rigid Presbyterian in the county', Gell was restored to the commission of the peace after succeeding to the title. He was defeated for the borough at very moderate expense in the first general election of 1679, and removed from the county bench as an exclusionist. A Whig collaborator, he was recommended as court candidate for the county in 1688, but changed sides in December, sending his son to Nottingham with a gift of £100 for Princess Anne. He was elected to the Convention, but died in London on 8 Feb. 1689 without taking any known part in the proceedings, and was buried at Wirksworth.[5]

[1] Excluded. [2] *Jnl. Derbys. Arch. Soc.* xl. 103; *The Reliquary*, xi. 225; *HMC 10th Rep. IV*, 169. [3] *HMC 9th Rep.* pt. 2, p. 398; Sir Robert Somerville, *Duchy of Lancaster Office Holders*, 164; *Cal. Treas. Bks.* viii. 1806. [4] *Jnl. Derbys. Arch Soc.* xxxiv. 150; xxxv. 108, 110; *HMC 9th Rep.* pt. 2, pp. 394–5; Stowe 185, f. 145. [5] D. R. Lacey, *Dissent and Parl. Pols.* 399; *The Reliquary*, n.s. vi. 112; Vernon (Sudbury) mss 13/43; *CSP Dom.* 1687–9, p. 273; *HMC Hastings*, ii. 187; R. Morrice, *Entering Bk.* 2, p. 370; *Jnl. Derbys. Arch. Soc.* xxiv. 149.

E.R.E.

GELL, Philip (1651–1719), of Hopton, Wirksworth, Derbys.

STEYNING   3 Jan. 1681
DERBYSHIRE   18 Apr. 1689

bap. 6 July 1651, 2nd but 1st surv. s. of Sir John Gell, 2nd Bt.*. *m.* 26 Nov. 1678, Elizabeth, da. of John Fagg I* of Wiston, Suss., *s.p. suc.* fa. as 3rd Bt. 8 Feb. 1689.[1]

Freeman, Levant Co. 1676; commr. for assessment, Derbys. 1679–80, 1689–90, Suss. 1690; j.p. Derbys. Mar. 1688–*d.*; receiver, honour of Tutbury 1689–*d.*; dep. lt. Derbys. 1690–*d.*[2]

Gell, after an apprenticeship to a leading Turkey merchant, was living at Smyrna as a factor when his elder brother died in 1674. Ordered home by his father, he was captured by corsairs, and force-marched across the desert from Derna to Tripoli. After brutal treatment from his captors he was released by the English fleet under Sir John Narborough. He stood on his father-in-law's interest for Steyning at the second general election of 1679, and was seated on petition only a week before the prorogation of the second Exclusion Parliament, in which he made no speeches and served on no committees. He does not appear to have stood for re-election, but after the dissolution of the Oxford Parliament he was reported to be the dissenters' choice for Shoreham, though he seems to have been a churchman himself. However, he is not likely to have stood for any constituency in 1685.[3]

Gell may have been reckoned a Whig collaborator like his father, as he was appointed to the commission of the peace in February 1688. He rallied to the Revolution rather late in the day, forming part of Princess Anne's escort on her return to London. On his father's death a few months later he succeeded him as knight of the shire, and became a moderately active Member of the Convention. He was appointed to 21 committees, including those to consider the Lords amendments to the bill of rights, to reverse the judgments against Titus Oates, and to inquire into the delay in relieving Londonderry. After the recess he was among those instructed to prepare charges against the former Treasury solicitors and to inquire into the miscarriages and expenses of the war. He was given leave to go into the country for three weeks on 21 Dec. 1689, but may have returned early, since he is listed as supporting the disabling clause in the bill for restoring corporations, and was named to the committee on the bill to impose a general oath of allegiance.[4]

Gell probably never stood again. It was said of him that 'he thinks to avoid censure by not acting'. He died on 15 July 1719 and was buried at Wirksworth, the last of the family.[5]

[1] *Jnl. Derbys. Arch. Soc.* xxxiv. 149; Add. 5698, f. 263. [2] Sir Robert Somerville, *Duchy of Lancaster Office Holders*, 165; *HMC Cowper*, ii. 358. [3] Information from Miss Sonia P. Anderson; *HMC 9th Rep.* pt. 2, p. 398; *CSP Dom.* 1680–1, p. 473. [4] R. Morrice, *Entering Bk.* 2, pp. 370–2. [5] *HMC Cowper*, iii. 12.

E.R.E.

GEORGE, John (1594–1678), of Baunton, Glos. and the Middle Temple.

CIRENCESTER   1626, 1628, 1640 (Apr.), 1640 (Nov.)– 3 Nov. 1646 [new writ], 1661–Dec. 1678

bap. 15 Sept. 1594, 2nd but 1st surv. s. of Robert George of Baunton by Margaret, da. of Edward Oldisworth of Glos. *educ.* Magdalen Hall, Oxf. ?1611, BA 1614; M. Temple 1615, called 1623. *m.* lic. 18 July 1627, Elizabeth (*bur.* 4 June 1677), da. of John Tirrell of St. Ives, Hunts., 5s. 1da. *d.v.p. suc.* fa. 1623.[1]
    Clerk of the wardrobe 1637–*d.*[2]
    J.p. Glos. by 1639–?44, 1656–bef. Mar. 1660, July 1660–*d.*, commr. for assessment 1643, Jan. 1660–*d.*, sequestrations, Glos. and Gloucester 1643, execution of ordinances, Glos. 1643; bencher, M. Temple 1651, treas. 1658–9; commr. for militia, Glos. 1659, recusants 1675.[3]

George's family had resided in Baunton, two miles from Cirencester, since the 14th century, and became lords of the manor after the dissolution of Cirencester abbey. A cousin represented the borough in 1601. George, who inherited a modest estate, became a lawyer. For two years before the Civil War he held a minor government office in succession to a younger brother, and he acted as agent to the Thames conservancy, set up by patent in 1628. For this he narrowly escaped expulsion from the Long Parliament as a monopolist. Nevertheless he originally took the parliamentary side in the Civil War and helped to garrison Cirencester in August 1642, but he was taken prisoner by Rupert in the following February and carried to Oxford where he changed sides and sat in the Parliament there. It is not clear why he was not treated as a delinquent, especially as he seems to have been a staunch Anglican. In 1654 his only daughter was married according to the rites of the Church of England. He was restored to the bench in 1656, but was named to no local commissions during the Interregnum until the return of the Rump.[4]

In 1660 George was defeated by Henry Powle* at Cirencester. While his petition was under consideration he was listed by Lord Wharton as a friend. He was returned in 1661 apparently unopposed, and was moderately active in the Cavalier Parliament, being named to 81 committees in nine sessions. Many of these concerned legal matters, and in the first session he chaired two private bills; but he was also a strict sabbatarian. He took the chair for the bill for better observation of the Lord's day in 1663, and twice reported amendments, most of which were rejected; and on 7 Apr. he was one of five Members ordered to bring in a fresh bill. In the same session he complained to the House that his signature had been forged on ten bonds, each of £1,000, as surety for a certain William George, a partner in the Bristol excise farm. At the request of the Commons, Lord Treasurer Southampton ordered a certificate to this effect to be entered on the pipe roll.[5]

In the spring of 1664 George was again appointed to the committee for the Lord's day observance bill. He was ordered to take care of the bill to enable his unfortunate neighbour, Henry Poole, to sell the remainder of the Sapperton estate, but it was never reported. He was very active in the Oxford session, in which he was named to ten committees; but subsequently his years and the distance to Westminster began to tell on him, and he defaulted in attendance in 1666 and 1668. He probably presented the petition against hearth-tax from the blacksmiths of his constituency on 6 Nov. 1667, since he was the first Member appointed to consider it. His only recorded speech was in the debate on the misdemeanours of Sir George Carteret* when, drawing on his memories of the punishment of his fellow monopolists by the Long Parliament, he denied that the House had any power of suspension, though this seems to have been merely a quibble over a word. His last committee appointment was to a canal bill on 10 Nov. 1670.[6]

Ever since the Cavalier Parliament met, George had been engaged in a running battle with the benchers of the Middle Temple to avoid the duty, and still more the expense, of reading. On 24 May 1661 he was granted a dispensation on the grounds of age and infirmity, but presumably he was told that neither was a sufficient excuse for not giving a feast, for in the following year he declared that he would read when Parliament was dissolved. On 28 Oct. 1664 it was resolved to ask him to vacate his chamber if he would not read. In 1669 it was assigned to (Sir) Henry Peckham*, who was almost immediately advanced to the degree of the coif. George had already given up his practice, but 'the persons who use his chamber' remained undisturbed for another four years, when it was granted to Francis Barrell*, one of the readers for 1674. On 14 Feb. Powle presented a petition from George accusing Barrell of breach of privilege, and he was reprimanded by the Speaker and ordered to hand over the key. Sir Richard Wiseman*, in his account of the Commons in 1676, noted erroneously but understandably next to George's name, 'I think he is dead'. Nevertheless, in 1677 he was marked 'worthy' by Shaftesbury. He was never called on to fulfil his undertaking to read, dying, probably, in December 1678, and being buried at Baunton on 6 Jan. 1679, 18 days before the dissolution. His estates passed to a nephew, but no member of the family sat in Parliament again.[7]

[1] *Vis. Glos.* (Harl. Soc. xxi), 248–9; *London Mar. Lic.* ed. Foster, 537. [2] *CSP Dom.* 1638–9, p. 617. [3] Gloucester corp. mss, letter bk. 1640–60, f. 3. [4] Rudder, *Glos.* 267; Keeler, *Long Parl.* 184–5; Clarendon, *Rebellion*, ii. 447; *Vis. Glos.* 248. [5] *CJ*, viii. 277, 374, 454, 455, 456, 467, 480; *Cal. Treas. Bks.* i. 573. [6] *CJ*, viii. 552; *Bristol and Glos. Arch. Soc. Trans.* l. 241; Grey, i. 213. [7] *M.T. Recs.* 1161, 1175, 1198, 1242, 1243, 1277; Grey, ii. 421–4, 436; *CJ*, ix. 309, 311; *Vis. Glos.* 248.

M.W.H./B.D.H.

GERARD, Hon. Charles (c.1659–1701), of Halsall, Lancs.

LANCASHIRE 1679 (Mar.), 1679 (Oct.), 1681, 1689, 1690–3 Jan. 1694

b. c.1659, 1st s. of Charles, 1st Baron Gerard of Brandon, by Jeanne, da. of Pierre de Civelle, equerry to Queen Henrietta Maria; bro. of Fitton Gerard*. *m.* 18 June 1683, Anne (*div.* 1698), da. and coh. of Sir Richard Mason* of Bishop's Castle, Salop and Sutton, Surr., *s.p.* legit. *styled* Visct. Brandon 21 July 1679; *suc.* fa. as 2nd Earl of Macclesfield 3 Jan. 1694.
  Lt.-col. Ld. Gerard's Horse 1678–9, col. June–Sept. 1679, Oct.–Dec. 1688, 1694–*d.*; maj.-gen. 1694.
  Commr. for assessment, Cheshire and Lancs. 1677–80, Mdx. 1679–80, Cheshire 1689, Lancs. and Mdx. 1689–90; freeman, Preston 1682; dep. lt. Lancs. 1687–9, Wales 1689–96; j.p. Lancs. Apr. 1688–*d.*, Cheshire by 1701–*d.*; steward of Blackburn hundred 1689–90; ld. lt. Lancs. 1689–*d.*, N. Wales 1696–*d.*; custos rot. Lancs. 1689–*d.*, Mont. 1700–*d.*; freeman, Liverpool 1690; constable of Liverpool Castle and butler, Lancs. 1691–*d.*; v.-adm. Cheshire and Lancs. 1691–*d.*, N. Wales 1696–*d.*; commr. for superstitious uses, Lancs. 1693; col. of militia ft. Lancs. and Denb. by 1697–*d.*[1]
  Envoy, Hanover 1701.

The Lancashire Gerards were major landowners there and intermittently knights of the shire from the middle of the 14th century. The fortunes of the Halsall line, descended from a younger son of the Elizabethan master of the rolls, were made by Gerard's grandfather, who acquired the Gawsworth estate in Cheshire by marrying the heiress of the Fittons. Gerard's father, one of the most prominent royalist commanders in the Civil War, was in exile during the Interregnum. He was attached to the queen mother's party, and married the daughter of one of her attendants. At the Restoration he became captain of the guard until 1668, when he resigned with ample compensation in favour of the Duke of Monmouth, amid rumours of financial malpractices. His reputation was further clouded

by allegations of forgery and intimidation arising out of Alexander Fitton's claim to Gawsworth. He was a court supporter in the House of Lords as late as 1677, when Shaftesbury described him as 'vile'.[2]

Gerard, who was born in Paris, was naturalized in 1660. Embracing the profession of arms, he first saw service under the great Condé. On his return to London he killed a footboy with his bare hands while under the influence of drink, but he was granted a free pardon. By 1679 both Gerard and his father, in spite of innumerable favours from the Court, had become strong Whigs and intimates of Monmouth. Gerard 'had the honour to be chose in three Parliaments without any opposition either from the gentlemen or freeholders' of Lancashire. Noted by Shaftesbury as 'honest', he was moderately active in the first Exclusion Parliament. On 9 Apr. he was sent to the Lords to desire a conference on their amendments to Danby's attainder. He was named to three committees, and voted for the exclusion bill. The advancement of his father to the earldom of Macclesfield failed to win him over, and he was one of the Middlesex grand jury which presented the Duke of York as a popish recusant. As Lord Brandon, he was an active Member of the second Exclusion Parliament, with 13 committees, including those to receive information about the Popish Plot and to inquire into abhorring. He helped to draw up the addresses for the dismissal of Jeffreys and Halifax, and to make preparations for the trial of Lord Stafford. In the Oxford Parliament he was named only to the committee of elections and privileges.[3]

In the summer of 1682 Brandon and his father attended Monmouth on his progress into Cheshire, during which they treated him with quasi-regal honours, and it was reported that they were planning a rising in Cheshire. He was sent to the Tower on the discovery of the Rye House Plot, but no evidence was offered against him, and he was discharged.[4]

The year 1685 was disastrous for Brandon both in public and private life. In March his marriage broke up, in circumstances which his peers were later to find entirely to his discredit. At the general election court pressure was brought to bear against William Leveson Gower*, who contemplated offering Brandon a seat at Newcastle-under-Lyme. None of the gentry except Sir Charles Hoghton* and Edward Rigby* would endorse his candidature for Lancashire, and he was heavily defeated. At Lancaster the handicraftsmen supported him, but their vote was swamped by the 'twopenny freemen' created for the purpose by the servile mayor. On Monmouth's landing a proclamation was issued for the arrest of Brandon and his father. Macclesfield

Gerard Family

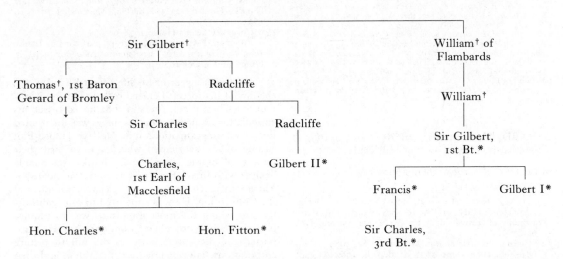

fled abroad, but Brandon found himself again in the Tower. He was convicted of treason largely on the evidence of Lord Grey of Warke, who implicated him in the Rye House Plot. Brandon was condemned to death, but first reprieved, by what a Cheshire acquaintance described as 'a pure act of grace, the object not having the least spark of merit in him', and then in August 1687 pardoned.[5]

Brandon immediately joined the ranks of James II's Whig collaborators. He and his henchman William Spencer* accepted commissions as deputies to the Roman Catholic Lord Lieutenant Molyneux. Gerard became 'a violent assertor of the King's dispensing power to the highest degree', rallying the nonconformists and bullying the mayors of Lancaster, Wigan and Preston into surrendering their charters. As a reward, his father's forfeited estates, valued at £2,000 p.a., but encumbered with a great mortgage, were granted to him.[6]

Macclesfield returned to England with William of Orange in November 1688; but Brandon himself at first miscalculated the situation and appeared in arms for King James. As he later wrote to William:

> Sure your Majesty could not think the worse of me for being faithful to a King to whom I owed my life, and whose commission I therefore believed I ought not to refuse when it was offered me. But this I thought myself obliged in honour to be true to my trust. Both my principles and my inclinations were always on your Majesty's side, and when King James was gone away, I am sure no man came to you with a more sincere intention to serve you than myself.

It is hardly surprising that at the general election of 1689 Lancaster rejected two of Brandon's officers, in spite of 'his lordship personally appearing to manage that election'. Brandon's own election as knight of the shire was for a time in jeopardy, though whether it was his profligate life or his political tergiversations that shocked the nonconformist conscience is not clear. With only 12 committees Brandon was not active in the Convention. In the first session he took part in drawing up the mutiny bill and the new oaths of allegiance and supremacy. The peerage conferred by James II on Alexander Fitton, the rival claimant to Gawsworth, on 1 May perhaps decided William to risk the sincerity of Brandon's conversion. On 13 May Brandon obtained leave from the House 'to go into the country, being so directed by his Majesty', and in the following month, on the resignation of Lord Derby, he was appointed lord lieutenant. A Jacobite invasion from Ireland was thought to be imminent, and, though his list of deputies seems to be directed more to the repayment of old political debts than to efficiency, Brandon was undoubtedly energetic and competent in his defence measures, showing himself ready to harry those Papists whom he had formerly cultivated as allies. He returned to Westminster for the second session of the Convention, serving on the committees to inquire into war expenses and the public revenue, and to consider the bill for restoring corporations, in which he supported the disabling clause. Brandon received no further marks of favour from the new regime till he succeeded to the peerage in 1694, but he remained a court Whig. He died on 5 Nov. 1701, aged 42, and was buried in Westminster Abbey.[7]

[1] *Preston Guild Rolls* (Lancs. and Cheshire Rec. Soc. ix), 180; *CSP Dom.* 1689–90, pp. 335, 472; *Cal. Treas. Bks.* x. 89; xvi. 299;

xix. 457; Eg. 1626, ff. 25, 58. ² Baines, *Lancs*. iv. 376–7; *VCH Lancs*. iii. 195–6; *CSP Dom*. 1667–8, p. 560. ³ *LJ*, xiii. 47; *Dalrymple Mems*. ii. pt. 2, p. 183; *Cal. Treas. Bks*. v. 201, 358; *Hatton Corresp*. (Cam. Soc. n.s. xxii), 127; *Reresby Mems*. 400. ⁴ *CSP Dom*. 1682, p. 383; Jan.–June 1683, p. 385; July–Sept. 1683, p. 35; Luttrell, i. 301. ⁵ *HMC Lords*, n.s. iii. 65–67; *CSP Dom*. 1685, p. 277; 1698, p. 144; Westmld. RO, Fleming mss 2846, Brandon to Lancs. freeholders, 10 Feb. 1685; *HMC 5th Rep*. 186; *Reresby Mems*. 407; Rylands Lib., Legh mss, Thomas to Richard Legh, 5 Dec. 1685; Luttrell, i. 417. ⁶ *HMC Kenyon*, 188, 212, 213; *Cal. Treas. Bks*. viii. 1591, 1677. ⁷ *Dalrymple*, 182; *CSP Dom*. 1689–90, p. 150; 1691–2, p. 64; *HMC Kenyon*, 213; *Jolly's Note Bk*. (Chetham Soc. n.s. xxxiii), 92.

I.C.

GERARD, Sir Charles, 3rd Bt. (1653–1701), of Flambards, Harrow-on-the-Hill, Mdx.

MIDDLESEX 1685, 1689, 1690
COCKERMOUTH 1695

b. 16 Aug. 1653, 1st s. of Francis Gerard*. *m*. 10 Feb. 1676, Honora, da. of Charles Seymour*, 2nd Baron Seymour of Trowbridge, 1s. *d.v.p*. 2da. *suc*. fa. Dec. 1680.[1]

Commr. for assessment, Mdx. 1679–80, 1689–90, j.p. 1681–Feb. 1688, Sept. 1688–*d*., dep. lt. 1692–*d*., capt. of militia horse by 1697–?*d*.[2]

Gerard first stood for Middlesex in 1681, but was defeated by an exclusionist. He headed the list of suitable jurors for Middlesex compiled for the use of the Tory sheriffs in 1683. He was successful for the county in 1685, and became a moderately active Member of James II's Parliament. His nine committees included those to relieve insolvent debtors, to extend expiring laws, to estimate the yield of a tax on new buildings, and to reform the bankruptcy law. But the most important was on the bill for the general naturalization of immigrant Protestants. He presumably opposed the King's religious policy, for he was omitted from the commission of the peace in February 1688. He was re-elected in 1689, and voted to agree with the Lords that the throne was not vacant, but was appointed to no committees in the Convention. For the rest of his political career he voted with the Tories, though he signed the Association in 1696. He died at Harrow in 1701. His daughter brought Flambards to her husband, the son of (Sir) Lancelot Lake*.[3]

[1] *Harrow Reg*. 317; BL Loan 29/183, f. 62v, Sir Edward to Lady Harley. [2] *CSP Dom*. 1691–2, p. 164; Eg. 1626, f. 11. [3] *CSP Dom*. 1683–4, p. 177.

E.C.

GERARD, Hon. Fitton (c.1660–1702), of Chelsea, Mdx.[1]

YARMOUTH I.o.W. 1689
CLITHEROE 20 Nov. 1693–2 Feb. 1694, 17 Apr. 1694
LANCASTER 25 Feb. 1697
LANCASHIRE 1698

b. c.1660, 2nd s. of Charles, 1st Earl of Macclesfield. *educ*. Christ Church, Oxf. entered 1673. *unm*. *suc*. bro. Hon. Charles Gerard* as 3rd Earl of Macclesfield 5 Nov. 1701.

Cornet, Queen's Horse 1678–9.

Freeman, Preston 1682, Liverpool 1698; j.p. Lancs. 1689–*d*., commr. for assessment 1689–90; dep. lt. Lancs. and Wales 1689–*d*.[2]

Until the last year of his life Gerard lived in the shadow of his forceful elder brother. During Monmouth's Cheshire progress in 1682 he expressed his support for exclusion, and his name was mentioned during the investigations into the Rye House Plot as one of the gentlemen who 'came to visit their honest Wapping men' and drank treasonable healths with them. Returned as court candidate for Yarmouth in 1689, he was an inactive Member of the Convention. He was appointed to four committees, of which the most important was to inquire into the failure to relieve Londonderry. He supported the disabling clause in the bill to restore corporations. He remained a court Whig, and died on 26 Dec. 1702.[3]

[1] R. Blunt, *Hist. Handbk. to Old Chelsea*, 124. [2] *Preston Guild Rolls* (Lancs. and Cheshire Rec. Soc. ix), 186; Lancs. RO, QSC 103; Wahlstrand thesis, 58. [3] *CSP Dom*. 1682, p. 396; *State Trials*, ix. 371.

P.W.

GERARD, Francis (1617–80), of Clement's Inn, Mdx.

SEAFORD Feb. 1641[1]
MIDDLESEX 1659
BOSSINEY 1660

b. 12 Oct. 1617, 1st s. of Sir Gilbert Gerard, 1st Bt.*, and bro. of Gilbert Gerard I*. *educ*. G. Inn, entered 1625; St. Catherine's Camb. 1632; travelled abroad 1638–41. *m*. c.1648, Isabel (*d*.1670), da. of Thomas Cheke† of Pirgo, Havering, Essex, 3s. Kntd. 3 June 1660; *suc*. fa. 6 Jan. 1670.[2]

Filazer of c.p. by 1636–45; commr. for maimed soldiers Dec. 1660–1.[3]

Commr. for excise, Worcs. 1644, assessment, Mdx. and Westminster 1647–8, Mdx. Jan. 1660–*d*., Westminster Jan. 1660–1, Surr. 1673–*d*., militia, Mdx. 1648, Mdx., Tower Hamlets and Westminster Mar. 1660; j.p. Mdx. 1658–July 1660, 1667–*d*.; commr. for sewers, Westminster Aug. 1660, loyal and indigent officers, Mdx. 1662.[4]

Gerard, unlike his father and brother, was 'in arms against Parliament', for which he was deprived of his clerkship in the court of common pleas. But his father's interest saved him from compounding, kept him in Parliament until Pride's Purge, and even won him a seat for a time on the county committee. His right to sit in Richard Cromwell's Parliament as knight of the shire was apparently not challenged.[5]

Having thus demonstrated his good affection for

Parliament, Gerard could be regarded as not comprised within the ordinance forbidding Cavaliers to stand at the general election of 1660. He was returned for Bossiney with his brother-in-law Charles Pym*, and was listed as a friend by Lord Wharton. A moderately active Member of the Convention, he made no recorded speeches, but probably served on 36 committees, including the committee of elections and privileges. On 3 May he was appointed to the important committee to prepare bills in accordance with the King's letter, and on the next day he was among those entrusted with the bill to confirm land purchases. He served on most of the committees for taxation. Doubtless a court supporter, he was knighted at the Restoration. He was named to the committees to recover the queen mother's jointure (8 June) and to inquire into unauthorized Anglican publications (30 June). He acted as teller against the proposal to exclude from the indemnity bill all lawyers who had appeared for the Interregnum governments in the high courts of justice. He helped to consider the bills to settle ministers in their livings and to fix an establishment for Dunkirk. On 5 Sept. he carried to the Lords the bill to restore his distant cousin, the royalist general, to his estate, and with it the college leases bill and the petitions on behalf of Vane and Lambert. After the recess he helped to draft the petition for a fast. With (Sir) Lancelot Lake* he was sent to ask the lord chamberlain to keep the Banqueting Hall clear when the House attended to thank the King for the Worcester House declaration on modified episcopacy. He was added to the committee for the militia bill and appointed to those considering the bill to prevent marital separation and to draft the excise clause in the bill abolishing the court of wards.[6]

Gerard is unlikely to have sought re-election. On his father's death he inherited a large plantation in Bermuda, as well as the Middlesex estate. He stood for the county as court candidate in September 1679, but withdrew after one day's poll, having received only 194 votes. He died in December 1680.[7]

[1] Secluded at Pride's Purge 8 Dec. 1648, readmitted 21 Feb. 1660. [2] Harrow Reg. 175; Lysons, Environs, ii. 578; CSP Dom. 1670, p. 553; PC Reg. iii. 327. [3] CSP Dom. 1635–6, p. 461; Cal. Comm. Adv. Money, 504–5; CJ, viii. 213. [4] W. H. Black, Docquets of Letters Patent, 285; C181/7/37 [5] Keeler, Long Parl. 185; Cal. Comm. Adv. Money, 504; D. Underdown, Pride's Purge, 147, 168. [6] CJ, viii. 83, 175. [7] H. Wilkinson, Adventurers to Bermuda, 244, 255, 343; Dom. Intell. 9 Sept. 1679; BL Loan 29/183, f. 62v, Sir Edward to Lady Harley, 28 Dec. 1680.

M.W.H./E.C.

GERARD, Gilbert I (c.1618–83), of Gray's Inn and Harrow-on-the-Hill, Mdx.

WESTMINSTER   1660

b. c.1618, 2nd s. of Sir Gilbert Gerard, 1st Bt.*, and bro. of Francis Gerard*. educ. G. Inn, entered 1625, called 1648, ancient 1650; Emmanuel, Camb. 1634. unm. Kntd. 18 Mar. 1661.

Clerk of council, duchy of Lancaster 1640–53, 1655–d.; commr. for alienations 1656, forest appeals 1657, maimed soldiers Dec. 1660–1.[1]

Commr. for volunteers, Mdx. 1644, militia 1644, Mar. 1660, assessment, Mdx. and Westminster 1647–8, Aug. 1660–1, Mdx. 1663–80, duchy of Lancaster 1663–4; j.p. Westminster July 1660–6, commr. for sewers Aug. 1660; conservator, Bedford level 1663–7, 1668–70, 1673–d., bailiff 1667–8.[2]

Although qualified as a barrister and apparently resident in the chambers built by his grandfather, Gerard spent the whole of his adult life (except for two years under the Commonwealth) as a duchy of Lancaster official in a post worth £600 p.a. Returned unopposed for Westminster at the general election of 1660, he was marked as a friend on Lord Wharton's list, and became a moderately active Member of the Convention. About half the references in the Journals are to 'Colonel Gerard', but it cannot be determined whether he held this rank in the local militia or the clerk confused him with Gilbert Gerard of Crewood. He seems to have been appointed to 26 committees and acted as teller in six divisions; but his only recorded speech was to ask for the collection taken at the thanksgiving service for the Restoration to be given to the poor of his constituency. He was in favour of excepting Major Richard Creed, but against excepting Sir Arthur Hesilrige[†] from the benefits of the indemnity bill. On 30 July he was appointed to the committee for settling ecclesiastical livings, but he opposed the institution of a committee to establish how many livings where the rightful incumbents were dead had been filled by presentations under the great seal. On 1 Sept. he was named to the committee for disbanding the army, and he was appointed a commissioner to discharge the pensioners in Ely House and the Savoy. Among his private bill committees was one for the drainage of the fens, in which he later invested heavily. He opposed the bill empowering the corporation of London to defray the expenses of the militia by a two-month assessment. His knighthood was presumably intended as an inducement not to stand against Sir Philip Warwick* in 1661. He took no further part in politics and was buried at Harrow on 5 Nov. 1683.[3]

[1] Sir Robert Somerville, Duchy of Lancaster Office-Holders, 30; information from Prof. G. E. Aylmer; CJ, viii. 213; Carlisle, Privy Chamber, 166. [2] C181/7/38; S. Wells, Drainage of Bedford Level, i. 456–63. [3] CSP Dom. 1653–4, p. 426; Parl. Intell. 2 Apr. 1660; Bowman diary, f. 3; CJ, viii. 67, 135, 138, 192; Lysons, Environs, ii. 578.

M.W.H./E.C.

GERARD, Gilbert II (*d.*1687), of Fiskerton, Lincs. and Pall Mall, Westminster.

NORTHALLERTON   1661, 1679 (Mar.), 1679 (Oct.),
                 1681

1st s. of Radcliffe Gerard of Barton, Lancs. by Jennet, illegit. da. of Devereux Barrett of Tenby, Pemb. *m.* (1) c.1646, Mary, da. of Sir John Brereton of Brereton Hall, Cheshire, wid. of Sir Michael Hutchinson, gent. pens., of Westminster, 2s. 2da.; (2) by 1660, Mary (*bur.* 5 Dec. 1680), da. of John Cosin, dean of Peterborough 1640, bp. of Durham Dec. 1660–72, 3s. (1 *d.v.p.*) 2da. *suc.* fa. c.1662; *cr.* Bt. 17 Nov. 1666.[1]
    Capt. of ft. (royalist) 1642, horse 1643–6; lt. King's 1 Life Gds. 1661–8.[2]
    Gent. of the privy chamber by June 1660–?85; commr. for disbandment 1679.[3]
    Jt. farmer of excise, Cumb. and Westmld. c.1661, co. Dur. and Northumb. by 1661–5; constable, Durham 1661–76; commr. for assessment, co. Dur. 1661–80, Westminster 1661–3, Mdx. 1665–9, 1679–80, Lincs. 1673–4, Yorks. (N. and W. Ridings) 1673–80, (E. Riding) 1679–80, improvement, Kingswood chase 1661, corporations, Yorks. 1662–3, loyal and indigent officers, co. Dur., London and Westminster 1662; j.p. co. Dur. 1663–80, (N. Riding) 1676–80, Mdx. 1677–80; dep. lt. co. Dur. 1663–?80, (N. Riding) by 1679–?80; master of Greatham hosp. co. Dur. 1663–?*d.*; freeman, Hartlepool 1665; sheriff, co. Dur. 1665–75; commr. for recusants, co. Dur. and N. Riding 1675.[4]

Gerard has to be distinguished not only from his cousins who sat in the Convention, but also from his uncle, the royalist governor of Worcester during the first Civil War, and the parliamentarian colonel, Gilbert Gerard of Crewood. He was the first cousin of Lord Gerard of Brandon, the royalist general, under whom his father served as lieutenant-colonel, while Gerard himself commanded a troop of the Life Guards. On 29 Aug. 1645 a warrant was made out in his favour for a baronetcy, but it never passed the seals. He was captured at St. Neots in the second Civil War, but given a pass overseas a year later. He must have returned to England before Easter 1654, when he came up from Worcestershire to London ostensibly to sell land, and was thrown into the Tower in close custody. He was not brought to trial for the conspiracy to kill 'a certain mechanic fellow by name Oliver Cromwell', for which his brother John was executed, and on 1 Sept. he was banished. He was included in a list of the 'gentlemen that follow the Court' in exile, but returned to England after the death of the 'mechanic', and by May 1659 was described as leader of a party of young Cavaliers, whose zeal might induce them to make a premature attempt on Bristol and Gloucester.[5]
    At the Restoration Gerard hoped to be appointed clerk of the green cloth, but had to be satisfied with an unpaid post in the privy chamber, a share in the

northern excise farm, and a commission in the guards under his cousin. His second wife's father held office as dean of Peterborough for a few months before being raised to the Bishopric of Durham, and in each capacity was able to reward him, first with a lease of Fiskerton and then with the office of constable of Durham. It was to Bishop Cosin's interest also as lord of the manor that he owed his first return for Northallerton as 'Sir Gilbert Gerard, bt.'. Ormonde chose him to administer the oaths at the meeting of the Cavalier Parliament, no doubt in confusion with the experienced Sir Gilbert Gerard, 1st Bt.*, who had not been re-elected. As 'Sir Gilbert Gerard' he was appointed to the committees for the uniformity bill, the Hilton charity bill, and the Weaver navigation bill, and acted as teller for finding that James Philipps* had condemned John Gerard to death in 1654. In the second session he was among those instructed to inspect the excise administration and to consider the staple bill and the petition from the loyal and indigent officers, whose relief continued to be a matter of concern to him. He was listed as a court dependant in 1664. On 7 Feb. 1665 he was given leave to bring in a bill for the repair of Hartlepool pier. It was defeated on first reading, with Gerard twice acting as teller for the minority; but the grateful corporation gave him the freedom of the borough. In the Oxford session he was named to the committees for the five mile bill and the bill to prohibit the import of foreign cattle. He was also among those ordered to devise remedies for the insolence of the Jesuits, who had converted his brother-in-law, the bishop's only son, and carried him off to the Continent. The anomaly over his rank was corrected by a fresh grant of a baronetcy on 17 Nov. 1666, with special remainder to the issue of his second marriage. In the same month he was appointed to the committee on the bill to empower his father-in-law to lease certain flooded lead-mines to Humphrey Wharton*.[6]
    Gerard is unlikely to have welcomed the fall of Clarendon, though he was appointed to the committee for the banishment bill. He carried Wharton's bill to the Lords on 31 Oct. 1667, but much of his energy in this session was devoted to warding off attacks on Lord Gerard and the proposal to enfranchise Durham, which Cosin regarded as an infringement on the bishop's prerogative. When his cousin gave up the command of the guards to the Duke of Monmouth, Gerard sold his commission for £1,200; but he was still included by Sir Thomas Osborne* among the court dependants in the House. Though less active under the Cabal, he was appointed to all the committees against conventicles

at this time, and according to his father-in-law 'did no small service' towards keeping the Commons from imposing a land-tax on 1 Dec. 1670. Cosin granted him a reversion to the manors of Gateshead and Wickham, the King overriding the objections of the dean and chapter, and on the bishop's death in 1672 he inherited the North Riding manor of Brafferton.[7]

On 10 Mar. 1673 Gerard moved for a bill to disable dissenters from becoming Members of Parliament, and was again among those appointed to consider the enfranchisement of Durham. His name appeared on the Paston list, though at this time he was reckoned a satellite of Buckingham. He introduced the charges against Lord Arlington on 13 Jan. 1674, and spoke frequently and vehemently about the minister's Popish proclivities. But he was unable to produce evidence, and Arlington's position was actually strengthened by the appointment of a committee (on which Gerard served) to consider whether there were grounds for impeachment. Gerard was so humiliated by this failure that he did not speak again in the House for four years, though he was named in the same session to the committees to consider illegal exactions, the judges' patents, and the condition of Ireland. He attended the meeting of the court caucus at the beginning of the spring session of 1675, and was among those Members appointed to bring in a bill for preventing Papists from sitting in Parliament and to consider another to prevent the growth of Popery. Henceforward he seldom missed any anti-papal measures. In June he conducted the first Durham county election (apart from those held under the Protectorate). He received the government whip for the autumn session, and promised Secretary Williamson to attend. On 13 Nov. he was among those instructed to prepare an address protesting at the failure to apprehend the Jesuit St. Germain.[8]

During the long recess that followed, the whole Gerard connexion, for reasons that have not been definitely elucidated, went over to the Opposition. Gerard's name appeared on the working lists, and Sir Richard Wiseman* relied on his interest with the Cheshire Members; but he was marked 'doubly worthy' by Shaftesbury in 1677. In this session he was named to the committees for the bills for the recall of British subjects from the French service and the Protestant education of the royal children. He seems to have taken a particular interest in the naturalization of English children born abroad during the Interregnum, and twice carried up a bill for this purpose. He was also appointed to committees to hear a petition from the parish of St. Martin in the Fields and to consider a bill to establish a

'court of conscience' in Westminster for small claims. He broke his long silence on 20 Feb. 1678 to demand a resumption of crown lands in Ireland, where Arlington had received extensive grants. He opened the debate of 14 Mar. on the state of the nation with an important speech:

> The King has had unhappy counsels. I will not exasperate matters, nor ravel into counsels. I will only say that, if the advice of the Parliament had been taken, we had not been in this situation. . . . Our outworks are already taken, the Spanish Netherlands, and I fear the French army is so great that the Prince of Orange cannot make head against it; and the worst of all is, we have jealousies amongst ourselves . . . I will not sit down therefore without a motion, viz. 'that we may humbly move his Majesty to declare war against the French King', the consequence whereof will be the bringing in our allies; and we will venture our hearts and lives, and our purses will be open like Englishmen, and I hope for good success.

He was among those appointed to draw up an address accordingly. On 15 Apr. he supported the motion of Sir John Hotham, 2nd Bt.*, to draw up reasons during the recess for apprehending the growth of Popery, and was named to the committee. On 7 May he said: 'I should examine this, whether the army was not put upon you upon the bare pretence of a war with France', and he helped to draw up the address for removal of counsellors. He was named to the principal committees in the last session arising out of the Popish Plot. On 18 Nov. he moved for an address for 'at least half the militia of England to be in readiness till we are in some measure secure from the attempts of the Papists'. The House resolved that a slightly lesser proportion would suffice, and he helped to draw up the address for a third part of the militia to be called out. He also proposed that (Sir) Joseph Williamson* should be sent to the Tower for counter-signing commissions to Roman Catholic officers, and helped to draft an address asking the King not to release the peccant secretary. He was among those ordered to prepare reasons for disagreeing with the Lords about the Roman Catholic servants of the Queen and the Duchess of York, and to bring in a series of anti-papal bills. He helped to prepare instructions for disbanding the army, and was nominated commissioner for this purpose. When it was announced that the Government had seized the cabinets of Ralph Montagu*, Gerard urged that they should be delivered unopened to the House. An active Member, he had been named to 249 committees, including the committee of elections and privileges in 15 sessions, acted as teller in four divisions, and made 33 recorded speeches.[9]

Gerard was re-elected to the Exclusion Parliaments on the Lascelles interest, and marked 'worthy' on Shaftesbury's list. A very active Member in 1679, he was appointed to 28 committees, including those to report on the state of matters pending in the last Parliament, to investigate the conduct of the sheriff of Durham in the county election, to examine the disbandment accounts, and to consider the habeas corpus amendment bill and the bill for security against Popery. He was again nominated to the disbandment commission, and helped to draw up the address for the removal of Lauderdale. Denounced as an excise pensioner on 9 May, he satisfied the House that his £300 p.a. was not a bribe, but compensation for the loss of his farm. In the debate on the shipping of artillery to Portsmouth he expressed suspicion of the Duke of York. He was appointed to the committee of inquiry, and voted for exclusion.[10]

When Gerard presented a petition from Westminster in January 1680 for the second Exclusion Parliament to be allowed to meet, the King replied that he did not expect to find a Gerard in such a thing, and refused to hear his explanation. In April he was fetched up from Yorkshire under the escort of a gentleman usher, and questioned by the Privy Council about the famous 'black box', alleged to contain the marriage certificate of Monmouth's parents and to have been bequeathed to him by Cosin. He denied on oath all knowledge of the matter, but was removed from local office. Barillon included him in his list of the most considerable Members. When Parliament met in the autumn he initiated the inquiry into abhorring in an able speech:

> I crave leave to remind you of a great infringement which hath been made of the liberty of the subject since the last session of Parliament. Sir, many good Protestants ... resolved to petition his Majesty ... to let the Parliament sit.... But although this was conformable to law and the duty of good subjects, considering what danger his Majesty's person and the Protestant religion was [sic] in, yet it was traduced to his Majesty as seditious and tumultuous, and forbidden by a proclamation, and great affronts and discouragements given to such as either promoted or delivered such petitions; and at last several persons in many places were set up to declare at the assizes and other public places an abhorrency and detestation of such petitioning. Sir, I humbly conceive the subjects of England have an undoubted right to petition his Majesty for the sitting of Parliaments and redressing of grievances. ... I think it is so necessary and material a privilege of the subject as that we ought without loss of time to assert our rights to it, and therefore I humbly move you to make some vote to that purpose.

He was appointed to the committee of inquiry, and helped to prepare the addresses promising to support the Protestant religion at home and abroad, demanding the removal of Jeffreys, and representing to the King the dangerous state of the kingdom. On 20 Nov. he introduced articles of impeachment against Edward Seymour*, served on the committee to examine them, and carried them up to the Lords. After the defeat of the second exclusion bill in the Upper House, he said: 'We shall appear neglectful of our duty if we do not try what security can be contrived by an association bill', and he was appointed to a committee to prepare another address insisting on exclusion. He was a very active Member, with 31 committee appointments and seven speeches. In the Oxford Parliament he was named to five committees, including those to impeach Fitzharris and to bring in the third exclusion bill.[11]

In December 1681 Gerard was wounded and disarmed by Edmund Webb* in a political duel arising out of the exclusion debates. There were rumours in 1683 that he was seeking a reconciliation with the Court, but they seem to have lacked foundation. He stood for Westminster as a Whig in 1685; but 'some people got a black box and carried it about on a pole, crying: "No black box, no excluder!"', and he was unsuccessful. He retired into the country, but was obliged to return to face a parliamentary inquiry into his disbandment accounts, which showed a deficit of £1,589 9s.7d. After Monmouth's rebellion it was reported that he would be tried for conspiracy, but the prosecution was abandoned after the Government had decided to pardon his cousin, the Hon. Charles Gerard*. He was still listed by Danby among the Opposition to James II soon afterwards but he died 'on his travels, at York'. He was buried in the Minster on 24 Sept. 1687. His youngest son Samuel stood unsuccessfully for Lancaster in 1689, but no other member of this branch of the Gerard family sat in Parliament.[12]

[1] Ormerod, Cheshire, i. 653; B. G. Charles, George Owen of Henllys, 43; Cosin Corresp. (Surtees Soc. lv), 2, 298–9; PCC 1 Penn. [2] Information from Brig. Peter Young; CSP Dom. 1673, p. 196. [3] Carlisle, Privy Chamber, 166; Cal. Treas. Bks. vii. 58. [4] Hutchinson, Dur. i. 554; Cal. Treas. Bks. i. 166, 288, 321, 633; iv. 1708; v. 417; HMC 8th Rep. pt. 1 (1881), 275; HMC Var. ii. 165; CSP Dom. 1663–4, p. 151; C. Sharp, Hist. Hartlepool, 71; Cosin Corresp. 11, 133, 249. [5] Ormerod, ii. 132; Royalist Comp. Pprs. (Lancs. and Cheshire Rec. Soc. xxix), 23–25; Add. 38141, f. 176; HMC Portland, i. 478; CSP Dom. 1649–50, p. 542; 1654, pp. 273, 293, 353; Thurloe, iii. 334, 342; D. Underdown, Royalist Conspiracy, 99–102; SP29/26/78; Cal. Cl. SP, iv. 210. [6] CSP Dom. 1659–60, p. 354; 1661–2, p. 378; CJ, viii. 245, 372, 602; Cosin Corresp. 28, 88. [7] Milward, 105, 232, 297; Grey, i. 88; CJ, ix. 69, 88, 95; Dorset RO, D124, box 235, bdle. 1; Cosin Corresp. 260; Hutchinson, i. 539; VCH N. Riding, ii. 100. [8] Dering, 135; Grey, ii. 270–1; Essex Pprs. (Cam. Soc. n.s. xlvii), 163–4; Williamson Letters (Cam. Soc. n.s. ix), 111–12, 115, 125, 135; Yale Univ. Lib. Osborn mss; CSP Dom. 1675–6, pp. 179, 317. [9] CJ, ix. 409, 416, 454, 464, 477, 541, 542; Grey, v. 192, 223–4, 273, 349; vi. 212, 219, 346. [10] CJ, ix. 601, 620; Grey, vii. 110, 213–14, 262–3; HMC Ormonde, n.s. iv. 517. [11] Sidney Diary, i. 230; HMC Ormonde, n.s. iv. 574; v. 510, 511; PRO 31/3, bdle. 146, f. 28; Exact Coll. Debates,

20–21, 177; *CJ*, ix. 658, 684. [12] Bath mss, Thynne pprs. 21, f.337; Leeds Pub. Lib. Mexborough mss, 24/26, 25/11; *HMC Astley*, 61; *CJ*, ix. 722, 751–2; *HMC Portland*, iii. 393; *HMC Downshire*, i. 64; *Northumbrian Docs.* (Surtees Soc. cxxxi), 163; *Yorks. Arch. Jnl.* i. 260.

P.A.B.

GERARD, Sir Gilbert, 1st Bt. (1587–1670), of Flambards, Harrow-on-the-Hill, Mdx.

WIGAN	1614
MIDDLESEX	1621, 1624, 1625, 1626, 1640 (Apr.), 1640 (Nov.)[1]
LANCASTER	1660

b. 23 Oct. 1587, 1st s. of William Gerard of Flambards by Dorothy, da. of Anthony Radcliffe, Merchant Taylor, of London. *educ.* ?Trinity Coll. Camb. 1602. *m.* c.1614, Mary, da. of Sir Francis Barrington, 1st Bt.[†], of Barrington Hall, Hatfield Broad Oak, Essex, 4s. 4da. *suc.* fa. 1609; *cr.* Bt. 13 Apr. 1620.[2]

Clerk of council, duchy of Lancaster 1609–40; treas. at war 1642–5; commr. for W. Indies plantations 1643; member, committee of both kingdoms 1644–8; commr. for regulating excise 1645; trustee for the Elector Palatine 1645; commr. for abuses in heraldry 1646, exclusion from sacrament 1646, indemnity 1647–9, compounding 1647, managing assessment 1647, scandalous offences 1648; chancellor, duchy of Lancaster 1648–July 1649, Mar.–July 1660; commr. for trade 1655–7; treasurer, relief of Piedmontese Protestants 1656; commr. for statutes, Durham College 1656, appeals, survey of forests 1657; Councillor of State 25 Feb.–31 May 1660; gent. of privy chamber June 1660–*d.*; commr. for maimed soldiers Dec. 1660–1; dep.-gov. Bermuda Co. 1661–*d.*[3]

J.p. Mdx. 1615–bef. 1640, 1652–*d.*; sheriff, Bucks. 1626–7; commr. for assessment Mdx. 1643–8, Aug. 1660–9, Bucks. 1644, 1647–8, sequestration, Mdx. 1643, levying of money 1643, volunteers 1643, maintenance of army, 1644, execution of ordinances, Bucks. 1644, defence Mdx. 1644, new model ordinance 1645, Westminster Abbey 1645, appeals, Oxf. Univ. 1647, militia, Bucks., Mdx. and Tower Hamlets 1648, Tower Hamlets and Westminster Mar. 1660; commr. of oyer and terminer Mdx. 1653–4, custos rot. Mar.–July 1660; commr. for sewers, Westminster Aug. 1660.[4]

Gerard's grandfather, a younger brother of the Elizabethan master of the rolls, founded the Middlesex branch of the family. Gerard's own marriage took him into the heart of the puritan cousinage. He was a prominent Parliamentarian in the Civil War, serving as treasurer at war. A 'fierce Presbyterian', he was imprisoned at Pride's Purge and took no part in politics during the Interregnum, though he was summoned to Cromwell's 'Other House'. On the return of the secluded Members he was restored to his post as chancellor of the duchy, and took part in the meetings of the Presbyterian cabal at Suffolk House.[5]

In the general election of 1660 Gerard stood unsuccessfully for Middlesex but was returned for Lancaster, presumably on the duchy interest. His two sons, Francis and Gilbert, also sat in the Convention, in which he was an active but not particularly prominent Member, being named to 49 committees, and acting as teller in two divisions. He made seven recorded speeches. He was on the committees for the abolition of the court of wards, the King's reception, the indemnity bill and the confirmation of parliamentary privilege. He was among those charged with preparing instructions for the messengers to the King, and was made a commissioner for administering the oath of allegiance to Members on 4 June. His name stands first on the list of the committee to inquire into the publication of Anglican pamphlets on 30 June. In the grand committee on religion he said 'he could not give his vote to the question until he heard whether it were against the Covenant'. He was also named to the committees for settlement of the revenue and consideration of the Lords' amendments to the pardon bill. On 22 Aug. he said that he had invited several persons to surrender themselves on the proclamation, and could never give his vote to except them for life. Gerard had already been removed from office, and played little part in the second session of the Convention. On its dissolution, he retired into private life, though he was nominated to the knighthood of the Royal Oak, with an estate of £600 p.a. He died on 6 Jan. 1670 and was buried at Harrow.[6]

[1] Secluded at Pride's Purge, 6 Dec. 1648, readmitted 21 Feb. 1660. [2] C142/308/156. [3] Sir Robert Somerville, *Duchy of Lancaster Official Lists*, 2, 3, 29; *CSP Dom.* 1655–6, pp. 1, 182, 218; H. W. Wilkinson, *Adventurers of Bermuda*, 255, 343. [4] *Mdx. Sessions Recs.* iii. 55; C181/7/37. [5] Keeler, *Long Parl.* 165–6; *Hutchinson Mems.* 220; *Clarendon SP*, iii. 729–30. [6] Bowman diary, f. 84; *Old Parl. Hist.* xxii. 442; *Smith's Obituary* (Cam. Soc. xliv), 50.

M.W.H./I.C.

GEWEN (GOWEN, GUEANE), Thomas (c.1585–1660), of Bradridge Barton, Boyton, Cornw.

BOSSINEY	1624	
NEWPORT	17 Mar. 1626	
LAUNCESTON	4 Jan. 1647[1]	
CORNWALL	1654	
LAUNCESTON	1656,[2] 1659, 5 May–Nov. 1660	

b. c.1585, o.s. of Christopher Gewen of Werrington, Devon. *educ.* Queen's, Oxf. matric. 4 Mar. 1603, aged 18, BA (Exeter) 1604; I. Temple 1605. *m.* (1) by 1617, ?da. of Edward Cosworth of Cosworth, Cornw., 1s.; (2) 23 July 1622, Mary, da. of Matthew Springham of Richmond, Surr., wid. of Arthur Puckell, Leather Seller, of London and Beverley, Yorks., 1s. 2da. *suc.* fa. by 1606.[3]

Jt. auditor, duchy of Cornw. 1627–33, havener, escheator and feodary 1633–48, May 1660–*d.*; stannator,

Foymore 1636; j.p. Cornw. by 1640–8, by 1654–July 1660, Aug. 1660–*d.*; commr. for sequestrations, Cornw. and Devon 1643, levying of money, Cornw. 1643, execution of ordinances 1644, assessment 1644–8, 1657, Jan. 1660; recorder, Launceston 1646–51, 1653–*d.*; commr. for militia, Cornw. 1648, Mar. 1660.[4]

Commr. for obstructions 1648.

Gewen's ancestors had leased duchy of Cornwall estates in and around Launceston for generations, and his great-grandfather had been mayor of the borough in 1545. Gewen himself was carefully educated at Oxford and the Inns of Court in accordance with his grandfather's will; but his career was principally determined by his successive marriages. His first wife's family had long been prominent in the administration of the duchy, in which he himself held office on a life patent; but his second wife was the sister-in-law of Benjamin Valentine†, a violent opponent of Charles I, and it was this connexion which decided Gewen's political and religious stance during the Civil War. A strong Presbyterian, he became a leading member of the county committee until he was imprisoned at Pride's Purge. Though mentioned as a Presbyterian Royalist as early as 1650, he was essentially a pragmatic monarchist with no respect for dynasty. He bought Bradridge at the sale of crown lands, and in the second Protectorate Parliament renewed the offer of the crown to the Protector on 3 Feb. 1658.[5]

At the general election of 1660 Gewen was involved in a double return at Launceston, five miles from his home. To his natural interest in the borough he had added a strong corporation interest as a recorder, and he was allowed to take his seat on the merits of the return. Lord Wharton marked him as a friend, but as official and tenant of the restored duchy of Cornwall he was in no position to oppose the Court. An inactive Member of the Convention, he was added to the committee of elections and privileges, and appointed to six others, including those to draft the assessment and thanksgiving ordinances, and to confer with the Lords about the King's reception. In grand committee on 9 July he spoke for the bill for the maintenance of the true reformed Protestant religion and the suppression of disorders and innovations in worship. He naturally supported the bill to confirm land sales, 'saying it was much for the King's interest'. On 30 July he urged that a book written by a preacher to justify the execution of Charles I should be referred to the committee for settling ministers, to which he was appointed. He petitioned the committee on the land sales bill about his purchase of Bradridge, and on the report of Timothy Littleton* the House agreed to recommend him to the King 'as a fit object of his Majesty's grace and favour'.

After the recess he was named to the committee on the bill for endowing vicarages (7 Nov.); but he died later in the same month. His widow and son obtained a new lease of Bradridge on an entry fine of £300, but no other member of the family entered Parliament.[6]

[1] Secluded at Pride's Purge, 6 Dec. 1648. [2] Excluded. [3] PCC 83 Stafford, 76 Weldon, 5 May; *Bramston Autobiog.* (Cam. Soc. xxxii), 13; *Al. Ox.* 559; *Richmond Par. Reg.* (Surr. Par. Reg. Soc. i), 144. [4] *Foedera*, viii. pt. 2, p. 244; pt. 3, p. 164; pt. 4, p. 60; Add. 6713, f. 167; *CSP Dom.* 1660–1, p. 365; *Western Antiquary*, vii. 138; A. F. Robbins, *Launceston Past and Present*, 193; R. and O. B. Peter, *Launceston*, 406. [5] *Western Antiquary*, ix. 166–7; *CJ*, viii. 152; PCC 83 Stafford; Vivian, *Vis. Cornw.* 104; M. Coate, *Cornw. in the Gt. Civil War*, 29, 225; *HMC Portland*, i. 584; D. Underdown, *Pride's Purge*, 152, 195; *Burton Diary*, ii. 424. [6] Bowman diary, ff. 64v, 72v, 105v; *CJ*, viii. 13, 152; *CSP Dom.* 1660–1, p. 365; *Cal. Treas. Bks.* i. 47, 214, 301.

M.W.H./P.H.

GILBY, Anthony (*d.*1682), of Everton, Notts.

KINGSTON-UPON-HULL 1661

6th s. of Sir George Gilby of Stainton, Lincs. by Elizabeth, da. and h. of Charles Fitzwilliam of Bole, Notts. *m.* c.1637, Ruth, da. and h. of Robert Rogers of Everton, 1s. *d.v.p.*[1]

Lt.-col. of ft. (royalist) 1644, col. by 1646; lt.-col. Lord Belasyse's Ft. July–Oct. 1660; capt. Hull garrison Oct. 1660–?81.[2]

Gent. of the privy chamber June 1660–*d.*[3]

J.p. Notts. July 1660–*d.*, liberties of Southwell and Scrooby 1664; dep. lt. Notts. c. Aug. 1660–1, Yorks. (E. Riding) c. Aug. 1660–*d.*; dep. gov. Hull Oct. 1660–?81; commr. for corporations, Yorks. 1662–3, loyal and indigent officers, Notts., Yorks. and Hull 1662, assessment, Notts. 1663–80, Hull 1664–79; jt.-receiver of hearth-tax, Lincs. (Lindsey) and Hull 1664–9; subcommr. of prizes, Hull 1664–7; commr. for recusants, (E. Riding) 1675.[4]

Gilby, descended from a minor Lincolnshire gentry family, acquired a modest leasehold estate in Nottinghamshire by marrying an heiress. An active Royalist, he served under Lord Belasyse in the Newark garrison and signed the articles of surrender in 1646. In the second Civil War he was again in arms in the garrison of Pontefract, compounding on a nominal fine of £25 in 1650. Described by the local major-general as 'a dangerous enemy', he was imprisoned for complicity in the projected rising of 1655. By January 1660 he was in London, attempting to enlist Presbyterian support for the Restoration.[5]

Gilby was returned in 1661 for Hull, where he was deputy to Belasyse, the governor. Although inactive in debate, and only once a teller, he was appointed to 170 committees, and, with his colleague Andrew Marvell*, kept his constituents regularly informed of developments in the House. He served on the committee of 26 Nov. 1661 on the bill for the execution of those under attainder. In 1663 he helped to consider a petition from the loyal and indigent officers, and a bill to hinder the growth of Popery. He was listed as a court dependant in 1664. During the second Dutch war he took effective measures against conventicles in Hull by placing spies in every street, and suggested to Joseph Williamson* that his presence was more important in the garrison 'whilst the enemy is upon the coast' than at Westminster. Sir Thomas Osborne* listed him as a court dependant in 1669, when he was appointed to the committee to continue the earlier act against conventicles. He was one of the Members in debt to the crown in 1670, though only as surety for William Broxholme*. He had no qualms about the harsh measures taken against Roman Catholics, telling his constituents that 'they may thank themselves for it', and evidently supported the bill to exclude them from Parliament 'that now our laws will be made by those of our own religion'. He received the government whip in 1675, and was listed as an official. He served on the committees for the recall of British officers from the French service (10 Nov. 1675) and the Protestant education of the royal children (27 Mar. 1677). He was marked 'thrice vile' by Shaftesbury, and his name appeared on both lists of the court party in 1678, though in one of them it has been read as 'Gibbs'. His name was mentioned by the informer Bedloe, once Belasyse's servant, in his evidence to the House on the Popish Plot, and in his only recorded speech (assigned by Anchitell Grey* to 'Col. Rigby') he demanded 'a particular examination, that honest men may be vindicated, and others punished'.[6]

After the dissolution Gilby applied by letter to the corporation of Hull offering his services in the coming Parliament, but was turned down. The ordnance commissioners discovered that he had embezzled £650 worth of lead and 12,000 bricks belonging to the Hull garrison. He was dismissed from his posts, but not otherwise proceeded against, 'in consideration of his loyal and eminent services'. He was buried at Everton on 27 Apr. 1682, the only Member of his family to sit in Parliament.[7]

[1] Fam. Min. Gent. (Harl. Soc. xl), 1227–8; Paver's Mar. Lic. (Yorks. Arch. Soc. rec. ser. xl), 117. [2] A. C. Wood, Notts. in the Civil War, 134; Merc. Pub. 19 July 1660; CSP Dom. 1660–1, p. 314; 1682, p. 33. [3] Carlisle, Privy Chamber, 169. [4] HMC 8th Rep. pt. 1 (1881), p. 275; Cal. Treas. Bks. ii. 642; iii. 244; iv. 695; PRO 30/24, bdle. 40, no. 41, f. 9. [5] Wood, 116, 147, 167–9; Cal. Comm. Comp. 2632; Cal. Cl. SP, ii. 122, 337, 356, iv. 535, 555. [6] CSP Dom. 1667, p. 315; 1670, p. 270; Grey, i. 323; vi. 185; Hull corp. letters, 909, 911. [7] Hull corp. letters, 924; Cal. Treas. Bks. vii. 375; Notts. RO, Everton par. reg.

P.A.B./J.P.F.

GLANVILLE, William (1618–1702), of Wonford, Devon and Greenwich, Kent.

QUEENBOROUGH 8 Jan. 1681, 1681

bap. 13 Sept. 1618, 1st s. of William Glanville, merchant, of Heavitree, Devon by w. Anstace. educ. Exeter, Oxf. 1634; M. Temple 1635, called 1642, steward 1677. m. c.1647, Jane (bur. 19 Dec. 1651), da. of Richard Evelyn of Wootton, Surr., 1s. suc. fa. c.1648.[1]

Commr. for alienations 1689–d.[2]

Glanville, according to his brother-in-law John Evelyn, came 'of an ancient family in Devonshire', though presumably of a cadet branch. Nothing is known of his activities during the Civil Wars and Interregnum. It is not clear whether he was a practising lawyer, though 'by his prudent parsimony' he 'much improved his fortune'. By 1665 he was in possession of a house at Greenwich, where Samuel Pepys* concealed some of his prize goods, but two years later, when his son was admitted to the Middle Temple, his address was given as Wonford. He emerges from the pages of his brother-in-law's diary as a strong personality:

> a great friend when he took a fancy, and as great an enemy when he took displeasure; subject to great passions, positive, well-spoken, of good natural parts.... In person handsome; very temperate.

He probably stood for Queenborough on the interest of Edward Hales I*, whose daughter was later to marry his son. At the second election of 1679 he was defeated by the court candidate James Herbert*, but seated on petition two days before the dissolution, whereupon he promised the corporation to 'forget all unkindness showed me at the last election', and took up residence in the house of a notorious local Whig. He was apparently re-elected unopposed, but was appointed to no committees in his brief parliamentary career. A friend of Locke's since at least 1666, he was given minor government office at the Revolution. He was 'not a little proud' that Locke, as well as Sir Walter Yonge* and Edward Clarke†, called him 'father'.[3]

On 7 Aug. 1701 Glanville was given permission, because of ill health, to appoint a deputy for his post in the alienations office, and under date of 12 Apr. 1702 Evelyn wrote in his diary that

> this night died my brother-in-law Glanville, after a very tedious illness, in the 84th year of his age, and willed his body to be wrapped in lead and carried down to Greenwich, where it was put on board in a yacht, and buried in the sea ... which made much discourse, he having no relation at all to the sea.

No doubt this eccentric disposition of his remains was due to his adoption of Socinian principles, which occasioned a quarrel with the diarist, who nevertheless considered that 'he might have been an extraordinary man, had he cultivated his parts'. His son was the last male of the family, but his granddaughter married another Evelyn, who assumed the name of Glanville and sat for Hythe as a government supporter from 1728 to 1766.[4]

[1] Devon RO, Heavitree par. reg.; *Evelyn Diary*, ii. 539; *Misc. Gen. et Her.* (ser. 2), v. 209; PCC 74 Essex. [2] *Cal. Treas. Bks.* ix. 137; LS13/231/8. [3] *Evelyn Diary*, v. 497; *Pepys Diary*, 13 June 1667; *Mar. Lic.* (Harl. Soc. xxxi), 204; *Arch. Cant.* xxii. 184; *CSP Dom.* July–Sept. 1683, p. 411; Bodl. Locke c10, ff. 12–13; c17, f. 20; *Locke–Clarke Corresp.* ed. Rand, 398; information from Dr E. S. de Beer. [4] *Cal. Treas. Bks.* xvi. 349; *Evelyn Diary*, v. 497–8.

B.D.H.

GLASCOCK, William (1617–88), of Kings Langley, Herts.

NEWPORT I.o.W. 1661

b. 30 May 1617, o.s. of William Glascock of Hoo Place, Aldham, Essex by Elizabeth, da. of John Burton of Eastbourne, Suss. *educ.* St. Catherine's, Camb. 1633, LL.B (Trinity Hall) 1640; Leyden 1639. *m.* 17 June 1656, Sarah, da. and coh. of James Mayne of Bovingdon, Herts., 1da. *suc.* fa. 1635; kntd. by 22 Nov. 1676.[1]

Commr. for assessment, Mdx. Aug. 1660–79, Westminster 1661–79, Herts. 1664–80, highways and sewers, London and Westminster 1662; j.p. Herts. 1685–?*d.*[2]

Commr. for plantations Dec. 1660–70; gent. of the privy chamber 1670–85; judge of Admiralty [I] 1670–5; commr. for excise appeals [I] 1671–5; master of requests 1675–85.[3]

Glascock came from a cadet branch of an extensive family which had acquired much property in Essex in Tudor times, received a grant of arms in 1571, and provided an MP for Sudbury in 1601. He must be distinguished from two of his cousins, Sir William Glascock of Wormley, a master in Chancery who was knighted in 1661, and Sir William Glascock of Farnham, who received the same honour as sheriff of Essex in 1682 but died in office. Glascock was described by (Sir) John Bramston* as 'a person of great integrity, quick of apprehension, sagacious, and of a clear and deep judgment'. From his father he inherited 'a pretty seat' in Essex and an income of under £200 p.a. He apparently passed the Civil War studying the civil law at Leyden. He had returned to England by 1656 when he abducted and married a 12-year-old heiress who brought him a Hertfordshire estate worth £125 p.a. He took her to France, where, according to his friend Bramston

she was perverted from the religion she had been bred in and turned Papist, and never returned to our church, though her husband lived and died in the communion of the Church of England.[4]

At the Restoration Glascock was made a commissioner for foreign plantations, subsequently holding a number of other posts, none of which was particularly important or well paid. He owed his election to the Cavalier Parliament to his friend and kinsman, the 2nd Earl of Portland, who as governor of the Isle of Wight brought him in for Newport. Although quite active in the opening session, serving on the committees for the corporation, uniformity and regicides bills, he was appointed to only 52 committees in all. In 1663 he was named to the committees on the bills to settle an annuity on the 3rd Earl of Portland, and to prevent abuses in the sale of offices and titles, and added to that to provide remedies against meetings of dissenters. In the Oxford session he was added to the committee for attainting English officers in the Dutch service. In 1669 Sir Thomas Osborne* included him among the Members to be engaged for the Court by the Duke of York and his friends, and in 1671 he was appointed to the Irish board of excise appeals with a salary of £200 p.a. 'His employment in the Parliament not suffering him to attend there', he was dismissed in 1675, but compensated with one of the masterships of request. He was noted as an official Member, included on the working lists, and knighted. But his new salary was only £100 p.a. and he petitioned for a supplementary pension of £66 on the Irish establishment. Osborne, now Lord Treasurer Danby, disliked the continuance of unnecessary salaries, but admitted to the King that 'your bounty cannot be better placed than on the petitioner'. (Sir) Stephen Fox* later confessed that Glascock received several sums from the secret service accounts, though some of this, like his excise pension, may have been for the benefit of Thomas Prise*. In 1676 Sir Richard Wiseman* (with whom he had studied at Cambridge) recommended that he should 'watch' (Sir) Richard Powle*, whose continued support for the Government was doubtful. Shaftesbury marked him 'doubly vile' in 1677, and he was included in the government list of court supporters in the following year. The management of the Isle of Wight boroughs was now in different hands, and although Glascock was not stigmatized by the Opposition as one of the 'unanimous club', he is unlikely to have stood again.[5]

On the accession of James II Glascock and the other masters of requests were dismissed from office, though his salary was continued. But 'he could never keep his lady in his life to any rules or bounds of expense', and was compelled to sell much of her property. He died on 14 July 1688 and was buried under a marble slab at Kings Langley, his widow spending 'in or about his funeral much beyond what she ought to have done, his estate considered'. Bramston, one of his trustees, found that 'his debts proved very much greater than he did know or think of, I believe, so that the trust could not possibly be performed as he appointed'.[6]

[1] Wards 7/87/243; *Vis. Essex* (Harl. Soc. xiii), 406; Chauncy, *Herts.* ii. 470; *St. Dionis Backchurch* (Harl. Soc. Reg. iii), 32; PCC 106 Exton; *CSP Dom.* 1675–7, p. 429. [2] *Tudor and Stuart Proclamations* ed. Steele, i. 405. [3] Carlisle, *Privy Chamber*, 187; *CSP Dom.* 1671, p. 231; 1673–5, p. 593; Ind. 24557; Chauncy, ii. 470; *Essex Letters* (1770), 119–20. [4] *Vis. Essex.* (Harl. Soc. xiv), 576; *Grantees of Arms* (Harl. Soc. lxvi), 101; *Bramston Autobiog.* (Cam. Soc. xxxii), 313–14; *CSP Dom.* 1655–6, p. 152; *HMC Verulam*, 103; *Herts. Recs.* i. 296. [5] *Bramston*, 313; *Cal. Treas. Bks.* iv. 683; v. 383; *CSP Ire.* 1669–70, p. 84; *HMC Ormonde*, n.s. iv. 518. [6] *Bramston*, 313–14; *Secret Service Moneys* (Cam. Soc. lii), 145, 199; *VCH Herts.* ii. 184, 243; Chauncy, ii. 470.

P.W.

GLEANE, Sir Peter, 1st Bt. (1619–96), of Hardwick, Norf.

NORFOLK   1679 (Oct.), 1681

bap. 1619, 1st s. of Thomas Gleane of Hardwick by Elizabeth, da. and coh. of Thomas Brewse of Topcroft. *m.* c.1650, Penelope (*d.* 17 Feb. 1690), da. and coh. of Sir Edward Rodney† of Rodney Stoke, Som., 2s. 1da. *suc.* fa. 1661; *cr.* Bt. 6 Mar. 1666.[1]

Lt. of ft. (royalist) c.1643, capt. ?by 1645; lt.-col. of ft. regt. of Lord Townshend (Sir Horatio Townshend.*) 1667.[2]

Commr. for assessment, Norf. Aug. 1660–80, 1689–90, maj. of militia ft. c. Oct. 1660, col. 1667–?76, lt. vol. horse c. Oct. 1660, j.p. 1661–76, commr. for loyal and indigent officers 1662, recusants 1675.[3]

Gleane's ancestors were eminent merchants in Tudor Norwich. His great-grandfather acquired Hardwick and his grandfather sat for Norwich in 1628–9. His father avoided involvement in the Civil War, but Gleane himself, by his own account, 'raised and armed two foot companies at his own charge'. In fact he served in the regiment of the Somerset Royalist Sir Thomas Bridges, and he did not compound, presumably because in his father's lifetime he had no estates worth sequestrating. He remained a royalist suspect under the Protectorate. During the second Dutch war he was created a baronet and as second-in-command to Lord Townshend took the leading part in organizing the defence of Yarmouth. Lord Yarmouth (Robert Paston*), the leader of the rival faction in Norfolk politics, admitted Gleane's record of loyalty, but described him as 'a melancholy man', perhaps owing to financial troubles. He was removed from local office with Townshend in 1676.[4]

An active exclusionist, Gleane helped to bring witnesses to Westminster on behalf of the country candidate, Sir John Hobart*, after the county election of February 1679, and he stood jointly with Hobart in the autumn, defeating the court candidates with the support of the dissenters. Yarmouth was told of a speech to the freeholders after the result had been declared in which Gleane promised

> that he would faithfully discharge his trust, by truly serving the King, and his mother the Church of England as it is now established, and his country, which speech did so far displease a great many of that party who did choose him, that if he had declared this as freely before the election, I believe he never had been elected by them, for they stick not to say already they fear he will turn pensioner.

A moderately active Member of the second Exclusion Parliament, he was appointed to five committees, including those to inquire into the responsibility for the proclamation against tumultuous petitioning (19 Nov. 1680) and into abuses during the Eye election (8 Dec.), no doubt because Hardwick was in the honour of Eye. Again successful with Hobart in 1681, he was appointed to no committees at Oxford, and he was never recorded as speaking.[5]

Two contested elections brought Gleane's fortune to the point of no return. He claimed £200 expenses from Townshend, who instructed his agent to 'let Peter know that I would not for £500 be beholden to him for one pennyworth of service, or anything else', and to pay anything Gleane might have been promised before that date, but refused to countenance him any further. Gleane's melancholy now took a morbid and extravagant turn. In the following year he erected a tomb for himself and his wife in the chancel of Hardwick church. The memorial inscription, slightly tinged with his native dialect either by the mason or the transcriber, proclaims:

> He served the crown faithfully above 40 years in military offices. . . . In his civil status he bore the character of a justice of the peace within this county above 20 years, and had the honour twice to be chosen one of the representatives of the same to serve in Parliament, in which several services for his King and country he spent his strength and fortunes, and the wounds which that [sic] received were not healed in the year 1683.

Process was begun in 1686 to exact the fee of £1,095 for his baronetcy, but stayed by Lord Treasurer Rochester. He was forced to sell Hardwick to Sir John Holland*, and when he died on 7 Feb. 1696 he was apparently not buried in his tomb. His eldest son subsisted for a time on a pension of £20 a year from the county rates, and when this was withdrawn he was flung naked and starving into the Fleet prison. No later member of the family entered Parliament.[6]

[1] *E. Anglian Peds.* (Harl. Soc. xcvii), 55. [2] Blomefield, *Norf.* v. 219; *List of Officers Claiming* (1663), 16; *CSP Dom.* 1667, p. 180. [3] *Cal. Treas. Bks.* i. 73; Blomefield, iii. 411. [4] *N. and Q.* (ser. 2), viii. 187; Blomefield, v. 218–20; Add. 34014, f. 80; *CSP Dom.* 1667, pp. 224, 226; Eg. 3229, f. 111. [5] Add. 36988, f. 149; Norf. RO, Windham mss, Hobart to Windham, 27 Mar. 1679, 14 Jan.

1682. [6]Add. 41654, ff. 31–32; *CSP Dom.* 1682, p. 55; Blomefield, v. 219–20; *Cal. Treas. Bks.* viii. 795; *E. Anglian,* iii. 24–25; (n.s.) v. 18–19.

E.C.

GLEMHAM, Thomas (c.1647–1704), of Glemham Hall, Little Glemham, Suff.

ORFORD 1681, 1685, 1689, 1690

b. c.1647, 1st s. of Sir Sackville Glemham of Glemham Hall by Frances, da. of Sir Thomas Gardiner[†] of Cuddesdon, Oxon., attorney-gen. 1645–6. *educ.* Trinity, Oxf. matric. 11 May 1665, aged 18; I. Temple 1667. *m.* (1) 24 June 1673, Dorothy, da. and coh. of Borowdale Mileson of Norton, Suff., wid. of John Stuteville of Dalham, Suff., *s.p.*; (2) lic. 19 Dec. 1685, 'aged 30', Elizabeth, da of Sir John Knyvett of Ashwellthorpe, Norf., 1s. *suc.* fa. by 1664.[1]

Commr. for assessment, Suff. 1673–80, Suff. and Orford 1689–90; j.p. Suff. 1678–*d.*; portman, Orford 1685–Oct. 1688, common councilman 1693–?*d.*; dep. lt. Suff. 1689–*d.*; freeman, Dunwich 1694.[2]

Glemham's ancestors were living in the village from which they took their name in 1419, but they did not acquire the manor, together with considerable monastic property, until Tudor times. His great-grandfather represented the county in the last Parliament of Elizabeth, but his grandfather impaired his fortune and became a professional soldier. He took a prominent part in the Civil War as royalist governor of York and Carlisle, and compounded in 1647 on a fine of £951. His father, who was also in arms, was imprisoned in King's Lynn as a suspected plotter in 1655. The estate was valued at £400 p.a. for decimation. After the Restoration Glemham's second cousin, Lady Castlemaine, obtained a bishopric for his great-uncle; but this was apparently the limit of the royal bounty towards the family.[3]

Glemham doubtless opposed exclusion, remaining on the Suffolk commission of the peace in 1680. On the death of Henry Parker II* he was elected to the Oxford Parliament for Orford, eight miles from his home, and nominated to the corporation in the new charter of 1685. He was re-elected to James II's Parliament, but neither in 1681 nor 1685 was he appointed to any committees. His attitude to James II's religious policy is not known, but he was re-elected as a Tory to the Convention, in which he voted to agree with the Lords that the throne was not vacant. But he did not speak, and was only slightly more active as a committeeman. His first committee was not until 14 Dec. 1689, when he was among those named to consider a bill to enable Lord Hereford, the owner of Orford Castle, to make a jointure. In the closing weeks of this Parliament, he was appointed to eight more committees,

including those to consider the bill for restoring corporations and imposing a general oath of allegiance. He was re-elected for the last time in 1690. He died intestate on 24 Sept. 1704, 'a gentleman endowed with great civility as inheritor of the virtue and estate of . . . his ancestors', and the last of the family to sit in Parliament.[4]

[1]Add. 19132, ff. 53–54; *Vis. Suff.* (Harl. Soc. lxi), 30; *Mar. Lic.* (Harl. Soc. xxx), 220; *CJ*, viii. 535. [2]*CSP Dom.* 1685, p. 46; SP44/165/282; E. Suff. RO, EE6/1144/13, p. 81. [3]Add. 19132, ff. 50–51; Copinger, *Suff. Manors*, v. 127, 140; Clarendon, *Rebellion,* ii. 286; *Cal. Comm. Comp.* 1579; *CSP Dom.* 1655, p. 368; *Thurloe,* iv. 327; *Pepys Diary,* 29 July 1667. [4]Le Neve, *Mon. Angl.* 1700–15, p. 92; Prob. 6/80/227; W. Suss. RO, Shillinglee mss, Morgan to Turner, 25 Sept. 1704; *HMC Egmont,* ii. 197; Add. 19101, f. 7.

J.P.F.

GLYD, John (c.1651–89), of Gray's Inn.

BLETCHINGLEY 14 Jan.–23 Nov. 1689

b. c.1651, o.s. of Richard Glyd (*d.*1658) of Pendhill, Bletchingley, Surr. by Anne, da. of Anthony Stoughton[†] of Worplesdon, Surr. *educ.* St. Edmund Hall, Oxf. matric. 12 July 1667, aged 15; G. Inn 1667, called 1674, ancient 1688. *unm. suc.* gdfa. 1665.[1]

Commr. for assessment, Surr. 1679–80, 1689.

Glyd's grandfather, a tallow-chandler of Sussex origins, married a Bletchingley heiress, and built a fine house there in 1636. The family took no known part in the Civil War. Pendhill was settled on Glyd's mother, who survived him, and Glyd himself, a bachelor, lived in chambers at Gray's Inn, 'a lawyer of sound judgment, good learning, and very fair reputation, as well for his morals as for his religion'. In October 1679 he cast his vote at Bletchingley for the exclusionist candidates, George Evelyn II* and John Morris*, though he hedged his bets in 1685 by voting for the Tory Ambrose Browne*, together with Morris's partner, Sir Robert Clayton*. He himself was returned for the borough to the Convention as a Whig. He was named to no committees and it is not recorded that he spoke. He died unmarried on 23 Nov. 1689, the only member of the family to sit in Parliament.[2]

[1]*Vis. Surr.* (Harl. Soc. lx), 49. [2]*Vis. London* (Harl. Soc. xv), i. 317; *VCH Surr.* iv. 253, 263; *Surr. Arch. Coll.* v. 219; xxv. 84–86; U. Lambert, *Bletchingley,* 313–15; PCC 71 Dyke; Surr. RO, Clayton mss, 60/9/4, 6.

J.S.C.

GLYDE, William (*d.*1710), of Exeter, Devon.

EXETER 1679 (Mar.), 1679 (Oct.)

1st s. of William Glyde, chandler, of Exeter by 1st w. Elizabeth. *m.* by 1665, Margaret Hillard (*d.* 15 Aug. 1704), at least 3s. (2 *d.v.p.*).[1]

Capt. of militia ft. Exeter by 1667, maj. by 1697, freeman and common councilman 1667, receiver 1673–

4, commr. for assessment 1673–80, 1689–90, sheriff 1674–5, alderman 1675–84, 1687–d., mayor 1676–7, dep. lt. 1701–3.[2]

Glyde's father, an Exeter tradesman, 'trailed a pike for the King' in the Civil War, and compounded at £15 on the Exeter articles. Glyde himself, 'a person of turbulent spirit', was the leader of the nonconformists in the city after the Restoration, but was elected to the corporation by recommendation of the Duke of Albemarle. In 1669 the mayor complained of his 'important and indiscreet appearance in the council chamber of the city with a pretended message from his Majesty', which gave 'affront to the established worship or government of the Church'. Nevertheless he leased the city brewhouse in 1671 for 14 years at the rent of £110 p.a., and became a prominent figure on the corporation. After laying down office as mayor in 1677 he 'made it his labour *per fas aut nefas* to be elected' to Parliament.[3]

Glyde defeated the court candidate at the first general election of 1679, with the support, it was alleged, of 'factious nonconformist ministers' and the rabble. A hostile account describes how during the election Glyde 'gets on the table among the clerks that took the poll, seizes some of the poll books, kicks the mayor on the shins, and assaults the sheriff'. Despite these credentials, Shaftesbury marked him 'doubtful'. His only committee in the first Exclusion Parliament was to inquire into miscarriages in the navy, and he voted against the bill. Re-elected in the autumn, he organized a petition for the assembly of Parliament, but when it met he took no active part in its proceedings. He was given leave on 2 Nov. 1680 to go into the country 'for recovery of his health', and apparently never returned to Westminster, for in January 1681 he was absent at a call of the House, and he was not re-elected to the Oxford Parliament.[4]

Glyde was expelled from the bench in 1684 for 'opprobrious language and abuse of the mayor and justices in open court'. Restored as alderman by James II in 1687, he started an action against the corporation for his parliamentary wages. Orders were given for his arrest as a Jacobite in June 1690, but he appears to have accepted the new regime. He died on 20 Aug. 1710 and was buried in Exeter Cathedral, the only member of his family to enter Parliament.[5]

[1] *Exeter Cath. Reg.* (Devon and Cornw. Rec. Soc. v), 32, 69, 155; *Al. Ox.* 572, 573; *Som. Wills*, iii. 36. [2] Exeter corp. act bk. 11, f. 65; Eg. 1626, f. 12; R. Izacke, *Exeter*, 176, 177; A. Jenkins, *Exeter*, 181; *Trans. Devon Assoc.* lxi. 213; *HMC Montagu*, 174. [3] *Cal. Comm. Comp.* 1416; Exeter corp. act bk. 11, ff. 71, 115; *HMC Montagu*, 174, 175; *CSP Dom.* 1668–9, p. 550; 1679–80, p. 567. [4] *CSP Dom.* 1679–80, pp. 566–7; PC2/67/123. [5] *CSP Dom.* 1690–1, p. 31; *HMC Finch*, ii. 294; *EHR*, lxvi. 48; R. Polwhele, *Hist. Devon*, ii. 26.

J.S.C.

GLYN, Nicholas (1633–97), of Glynn, Cardinham, Cornw.

BODMIN 1679 (Mar.), 1679 (Oct.), 1681, 1685, 1689, 1690

bap. 3 Oct. 1633, 1st s. of William Glyn of Glynn by Alice, da. of Arthur Harris* of Hayne, Devon. *educ.* Exeter, Oxf. 1652. *m.* settlement 21 June 1664, Gertrude, da. and coh. of Anthony Dennys of Orleigh, Devon, 3s. (2 *d.v.p.*) 2da. *suc.* fa. 1664.[1]

Commr. for militia, Cornw. Mar. 1660, assessment Aug. 1660–80, 1689–90, j.p. 1666–July 1688, Oct. 1688–d., sheriff 1674–5, maj. of militia ft. by 1679–Feb. 1688; freeman, Bodmin 1685–June 1688; stannator, Foymore 1686; asst. Camelford to June 1688.[2]

Glyn belonged to a minor Cornish family settled on the property from which they took their name since at least the 14th century. They had not previously entered Parliament, though they had provided mayors of Bodmin in the 15th and 16th centuries, and his grandfather was sheriff of Cornwall in 1620. His father appears to have taken no part in the Civil War, but served on the county assessment commissions of 1647 and 1648.[3]

Returned for Bodmin, three miles from his home, to the Exclusion Parliaments, Glyn was classed by Shaftesbury as 'honest', but he did not vote on the committal of the first exclusion bill. He was presumably a court supporter, however, since he remained a j.p. But he was named to no committees throughout the period and was fined for defaulting on a call of the House on 4 Jan. 1681. Nevertheless he joined the syndicate of 'the knights and burgesses of the present Parliament for Cornwall' which applied for the Tangier victualling contract. He was named to the Bodmin corporation in the new charter, and re-elected unopposed. According to Anthony Rowe* he voted to agree with the Lords that the throne was not vacant. He was twice granted leave of absence, but left no other trace on the records of the Convention. Re-elected for the last time in 1690, he was buried at Cardinham on 27 Mar. 1697. His son sat for Camelford as a Tory from 1698 to 1705.[4]

[1] Burke, *Gentry* (1952), 994; Gilbert, *Paroch. Hist. Cornw.* i. 196, 199; Vivian, *Vis. Cornw.* 178–9 [2] *CSP Dom.* 1679–80, p. 61; J. Wallis, *Bodmin Reg.* 169; PC2/72/694; J. Tregoning, *Laws of the Stannaries*, 57. [3] J. Maclean, *Trigg Minor*, ii. 58–62; Gilbert, i. 200. [4] *Cal. Treas. Bks.* vii. 148–9; *CJ*, ix. 703; x. 67, 216; PCC 93 Pyne.

E.C.

GLYNNE, John (c.1603–66), of Portugal Row, Westminster; Henley Park, Ash, Surr. and Hawarden, Flints.

CAERNARVON BOROUGHS	1640 (Apr.)
WESTMINSTER	1640 (Nov.)[1]
CAERNARVONSHIRE	1654
FLINTSHIRE	1656–10 Dec. 1657
CAERNARVONSHIRE	1660

b. c.1603, 2nd s. of Sir William Glynne (*d.*1620) of Glynllifon, Caern. by Jane, da. of John Griffith of Caernarvon; bro. of Thomas Glynne†. *educ.* Westminster 1615; Hart Hall, Oxf. matric. 9 Nov. 1621, aged 18; L. Inn 1621, called 1628. *m.* (1) 2 May 1633, Frances (*bur.* 17 Nov. 1646), da. of Arthur Squibb, later Clarenceux King of Arms, of Henley Park, 2s. 5da.; (2) Anne, da. of John Manning of London, and coh. to her bro. John Manning of Cralle Place, Warbleton, Suss., wid. of Sir Thomas Lawley, 1st Bt.†, of Spoonhill, Salop, 1s. 1da. Kntd. 16 Nov. 1660.[2]

Dep. steward, Westminster by 1639–48; bencher, L. Inn 1641; commr. for sequestrations, Westminster 1643, assessment, Westminster 1643, Mdx. 1644–7, Aug. 1660–3, Surr. 1645–7, London and Caern. 1647, Oxon., Surr., Anglesey, Caern., Denb. and Flints. 1657, Anglesey and Flints. Jan. 1660–1, Caern. Aug. 1660–1, Oxon., Caern. and Flints. 1665–*d.*, accounts, Westminster 1643; recorder, London 1643–9; commr. for volunteers, Mdx. 1644, new model ordinance, Mdx. and Surr. 1645, defence, Surr. 1645, Westminster Abbey 1645; protonotary and clerk of the crown, Denb., Flints. and Mont. 1646–7; j.p. Mdx. and Westminster 1648–9, Caern. 1650–*d.*, Anglesey, Denb. and Merion. Mar.–July 1660, Mdx., Westminster, Surr. and Flints. Mar.–July 1660, 1662–*d.*, Oxon. 1662–*d.*; commr. for North Wales association, Caern. 1648, militia, Cheshire, Mdx., Westminster, Caern. and Merion. 1648, Mdx., Westminster, Oxon., Surr. and North Wales Mar. 1660, oyer and terminer, London 1653–4, Western circuit 1655, Mdx. Mar. 1660.

Commr. for Westminster Assembly 1643–8; member, committee of both kingdoms 1644–8; commr. for distressed captives 1645, abuses in heraldry 1646, plantations 1646, exclusion from sacrament 1646, bishops' lands 1646, indemnity 1647–9, counsel, sale of bishops' lands 1647–8; commr. for scandalous offences 1648; serjeant-at-law 1648–54, June–Nov. 1660, Protector's serjeant 1654–5, King's serjeant Nov. 1660–*d.*; c.j. Upper Bench 1655–9; commr. for trade 1655–7, relief of Piedmontese Protestants 1656, great seal 1656–8; contractor, sale of excise farms 1657; chairman, committee of ways and means 30 May–8 Sept. 1660.[3]

Glynne was descended from Tudur Goch who acquired Glynllifon by marriage under Edward III. His elder brother was the first of the family to sit, representing Caernarvonshire in 1624, 1625 and the Short Parliament. Glynne himself, a successful and adaptable lawyer, took a prominent part in the impeachment of Strafford, and remained at Westminster during the Civil War; but he was disabled as a Presbyterian moderate in 1647 and secluded at Pride's Purge. He resumed office under the Protectorate as a judge, in which capacity he tried and sentenced the Cavalier rebels in 1655. A strong supporter of the Humble Petition and Advice, he was summoned to the Other House in 1657.

Having resigned his judgeship on the overthrow of the Protectorate, he was less compromised than if he had served the Rump or the military regime.[4]

Glynne was returned for his native county at the general election of 1660, and listed by Lord Wharton as a friend, but excluded from the meetings of the Presbyterian cabal, at which he was 'so piqued . . . as to offer his services to the King'. Together with William Prynne* he was sent to thank Dr Reynolds, a conformable Presbyterian and future bishop, for his sermon at the opening of Parliament. A very active Member, he was appointed to 70 committees, and made eleven recorded speeches. He was appointed to the committees to consider the legal forms of the Restoration and the land purchases bill, and given special responsibility for the proclamation ordering officers of justice to perform their duties. He was particularly active over the continuity of judicial proceedings, in which he had his own ends to serve. He helped to draft a proviso for resuming the use of Latin in the courts, and acted as chairman of ways and means in the first session. A member of the committee for the indemnity bill, he helped to prepare for a conference on the regicides who had given themselves up, to draw up the clauses of exception and to consider two provisos. On 12 July he moved to reject the disbandment bill on a technicality. He was also appointed to the committee for settling ecclesiastical livings. When a bill was introduced to enable Sir George Booth* to sell land, Glynne pointed out that he had received none of the £10,000 voted to him as a reward, and was appointed to the committee. He took the chair to consider the Lords' amendments to the judicial proceedings bill, presented two reports, and returned it to the Upper House on 17 Aug. He also carried the bill for continuing the levy of excise and the indemnity bill, after reporting that the amendments agreed during its passage through the Commons had been made to cohere. He was added to the managers of the conference which followed. When the Lords sent down a petition from some maimed Cavaliers, Glynne protested that the Upper House 'ought not to meddle with matters of money', and was among those ordered to prepare a memorial on the subject. He helped to manage a conference on disbandment on 7 Sept., and reported draft addresses for the preservation of timber and the abolition of the court of wards. On the following day he was ordered to assist Heneage Finch* in drafting an assessment bill.[5]

During the recess Glynne, who had already sued out his pardon, received a copy of Wharton's case for modified episcopacy, though without the possible objections, circumstances and considerations, but he took no part in the debate when Parliament reassembled. He was replaced by Richard Rainsford I* as chairman of ways and means, and his hopes of regaining judicial office were dashed by a Welsh petition organized by Sir Thomas Myddelton*; but he was promoted to King's serjeant and knighted. He was given special responsibility with Edward King* and Nicholas Pedley* for an inquiry into obstructions in the poll-tax. He was appointed to the committees to prepare the impeachment of the author of the pamphlet *The Long Parliament Revived*, and to bring in two additional clauses in the bill for the abolition of feudal tenures, those to compensate the crown with a perpetual excise and to repeal Henry VIII's statute. After serving on the committee for the attainder bill, he secured on the report stage the deletion of the dangerously vague reference to 'divers others'. He helped to prepare reasons for the conferences on college leases and confirming civil marriages, and was appointed to the committee for the wine licences bill, though he opposed the attempt of (Sir) Thomas Clarges* to establish maximum prices. With Edward King* and Nicholas Pedley* he was given special responsibility for an inquiry into obstructions in the poll-tax, helped to manage a conference on the Lords' amendments, and closed his parliamentary career with a typical speech on the last day of the session: 'They could not justify taxing the commons and taking no care that the lords should pay too; though he was not much averse, and would agree with them rather than hinder the bill'.[6]

Glynne was reported to be seeking re-election in 1661 with the support of (Sir) John Carter*, but is unlikely to have gone to the poll. He added to the gaiety of the coronation by falling off his horse during the procession, 'which people do please themselves with, to see how just God is to punish that rogue at such a time'. His life was thought to be in danger, but he recovered to take part in the prosecution of Sir Henry Vane†. He died on 15 Nov. 1666, and in accordance with his will was buried with his first wife beneath the altar of St. Margaret's, Westminster.[7]

[1] Disabled 7 Sept. 1647 and readmitted 7 June 1648; did not sit after Pride's Purge, 6 Dec. 1648 and readmitted 21 Feb. 1660. [2] *Misc. Gen. et Her.* (ser. 2), i. 43–44; *Proc. Dorset Nat. Hist. and Arch. Soc.* lxviii. 60–62; *Vis. London* (Harl. Soc. xvii), 78. [3] *CSP Dom.* 1639–40, p. 351; 1655–6, p. 100; *CJ*, iv. 474; *Thurloe*, iii. 296. [4] *DWB.* [5] *Cal. Cl. SP.*, iv. 674; v. 41; *CJ*, viii. 1, 7, 10, 11, 13, 15, 20, 105, 123, 125, 128, 139, 140, 144, 148; Bowman diary, ff. 76v, 105; *Old Parl. Hist.* xxii. 467. [6] *Cal. Hawarden Deeds*, 92; *Cal. Wynn Pprs.* 358; *CJ*, viii. 179, 219, 221, 233; *Old Parl. Hist.* xxiii. 43, 68, 69, 79. [7] *Cal. Wynn Pprs.* 364; *Pepys Diary*, 23 Apr. 1661.

M.W.H./A.M.M.

GLYNNE, William (1638–90), of Bicester, Oxon. and Hawarden, Flints.

CAERNARVONSHIRE	1659
CAERNARVON BOROUGHS	1660

bap. 20 Jan. 1638, 1st s. of John Glynne* by 1st w. *educ.* L. Inn, entered 1652; Jesus, Oxf. 1654. *m.* 12 July 1659, Penelope, da. of Stephen Anderson of Eyworth, Beds., 4s. (2 *d.v.p.*) 2da. *cr.* Bt. 20 May 1661; *suc.* fa. 1666.

Commr. for assessment, Flints. Aug. 1660–1, 1673–4, 1679–80, 1689–*d.*, Oxon. Sept. 1660–1, 1663–80, 1689; j.p. Oxon. Mar. 1688–*d.*; sheriff, Oxon. 1668–9, Flints. 1672–3; dep. lt. Oxon. Feb. 1688–*d.*, Caern. 1689–*d.*

Glynne resided on the Oxfordshire estates settled on him at the time of his marriage by his father. His name appears on Lord Wharton's list of the Convention as a friend to be influenced by his father, and he was doubtless a court supporter, but he left no trace on its records. He may have become a Whig collaborator under James II, when he was recommended for local office in Oxfordshire. He was buried at Bicester on 8 Sept. 1690. His son, the second baronet, was returned for Oxford University in 1698 and for Woodstock in 1702 as a Tory.

J. E. Griffith, *Peds. of Anglesey and Caern. Fams.* 172; *Mems. St. Margaret Westminster*, 156; *Misc. Gen. et Her.* (ser. 2), i. 42.

M.W.H./A.M.M.

GODDARD, Edward (*d.* 1679), of Ogbourne St. Andrew, Wilts.

MARLBOROUGH	1679 (Mar.)

o.s. of Edward Goddard of Hartham Park, Corsham and Ogbourne St. Andrew. *m.* Elizabeth, da. of John Smith of South Tidworth, Hants, 6s. 1da. *suc.* fa. 1676.[1]

Commr. for assessment, Wilts. 1673–*d.*

Goddard came from an obscure branch of a prolific family, which had held land in Wiltshire since the 13th century, though none had previously sat in Parliament. His interest in politics was probably aroused by his brother-in-law John Smith*, and he was returned to the first Exclusion Parliament for Marlborough, two miles from his home. Shaftesbury marked 'Mr Goddard of Ogbourne' as honest. He was named to no committees, made no speeches, and was given leave to go into the country on 17 Apr. 1679; but he is listed as voting for the exclusion bill. He died on 10 June and was buried at Ogbourne St. Andrew. No later member of this branch of the family entered Parliament.[2]

[1] *Misc. Gen. et Her.* (ser. 4), iii. 212, 214; *Wilts. Vis. Peds.* (Harl. Soc. cv), 68; Aubrey and Jackson, *Wilts. Colls.* 83. [2] R. Jefferies, *Goddards of North Wilts*, 8, 41; *Coll. Top. et Gen.* v. 357.

J.P.F.

GODDARD, Richard (c.1590–1666), of the Inner Temple; Etchilhampton, Wilts. and Winchester, Hants.

WINCHESTER   1661–8 Oct. 1666 [new writ]

b. c.1590, o.s. of Richard Goddard† of Southampton by Elizabeth, da. of Ambrose Dauntsey of Potterne, Wilts. *educ.* I. Temple 1607, called 1616. *m.* (1) 25 July 1615, Mary, da. of Edward Nicholas of All Cannings, Wilts., 3s. 2da., 7 other ch.; (2) c.1641, Hester, da. of Edward Richards of Yaverland, I.o.W., wid. of John Nevey of Southampton, and Robert Mason† of Lincoln's Inn and Winchester, *s.p. suc. fa.* 1596.[1]

Bencher, I. Temple 1633, reader 1635, treasurer 1659–61; steward, New Forest by 1639–46, May 1660–*d.*; freeman, Portsmouth 1639, Winchester Sept. 1660; j.p. Hants and Wilts. 1640–6, Hants July 1660–*d.*; commr. for assessment, Hants Aug. 1660–*d.*; recorder, Winchester 1661–*d.*; commr. for corporations, Hants 1662–3, loyal and indigent officers 1662.[2]

Lt.-col. of horse (royalist) 1643–4.[3]

Goddard entered a short pedigree at the heralds' visitation of Wiltshire in 1623, but did not claim kinship with the prolific gentry family of that name. His father, a merchant of Dorset origin, represented Southampton in 1589. Although Goddard was registered at the Inner Temple as a Gloucestershire man, and resided in Wiltshire during his first marriage, and again during the Interregnum, his principal interests lay in the county of his birth. A practising lawyer, he was appointed steward of the New Forest before the Civil War, and acquired a little property there. His second wife, the step-mother of Sir Robert Mason*, brought him an annuity of £225, as well as an interest at Winchester. He raised a troop of horse for the King, but was taken prisoner at Christchurch by Sir William Waller I* at the end of 1644, and on his release settled at Salisbury. He was fined £862 10s. for his delinquency, and forbidden to follow his profession under the Protectorate; but his standing was shown by his election as treasurer of his Inn in 1659. By the following year he had taken up residence in Winchester, where he was elected recorder at the dissolution of the Convention, and shortly afterwards returned to the Cavalier Parliament at the general election of 1661 when he must have been about 70. An inactive Member, he was appointed to only eight committees, none of which was of political significance. He helped to consider the bills for abolishing damage clere in 1661 and for reforming the Marshalsea court in 1663. He was included in the list of court dependants in 1664. He attended a meeting of the benchers of the Inner Temple on 1 July 1666, but died a few months later.[4]

[1] *Wilts. Vis. Peds.* (Harl. Soc. cv), 69, 144; *PCC Adm. Acts* (Index Lib. lxxxi), 54; *Vis. Hants* (Harl. Soc. lxiv), 176; *Hants*

Mar. Lic. 1607–40, p. 61; C8/147/41; *Cal. Comm. Comp.* 1044; *Wilts. Arch. Mag.* xxiv. 78. [2] *CSP Dom.* 1638–9, p. 585; R. East, *Portsmouth Recs.* 169, 352; *Cal. Treas. Bks.* i. 243, 247; *HMC 11th Rep. III*, 55; Winchester corp. assembly bk. 4, ff. 145, 161. [3] Eg. 868, f. 17; G. N. Godwin, *Civil War in Hants*, 195; *Cal. Comm. Comp.* 994. [4] *Wilts. Arch. Mag.* xxiv. 78; xxvi. 388; *I. Temple Recs.* ii. 302, 331, 335; iii. 40; *HMC 7th Rep.* 100; PCC adm. act bk. 1667, f. 35v.

P.W.

GODDEN *see* **GODWIN**

GODFREY, Charles (c.1648–1715), of Windmill Street, Westminster and Huntercombe, Bucks.

MALMESBURY	1689		
CHIPPING WYCOMBE	26 Oct. 1691,	1695,	1698,
	1701	(Feb.),	1701
	(Dec.),	1702,	1705,
	1708,	1710	

b. c.1648, s. of Francis Godfrey of Little Chelsea, Mdx. *m.* c.1679, Arabella, da. of (Sir) Winston Churchill* of Minterne Magna, Dorset, 1s. *d.v.p.* 3da. *suc.* fa. 1688.[1]

Capt. R. Ft. Gds. (later Grenadier Gds.) 1674; lt.-col. of ft. regt. of Sir Thomas Slingsby* 1678; capt. Duke of Monmouth's Horse 1678; maj. Ld. Gerard's ft. 1679; col. of dgns. (later 5 Dgn. Gds.) Dec. 1688–93.

Commr. for assessment, Wilts. 1689–90; freeman, Chipping Wycombe 1691; j.p. Bucks. 1695–?*d.*, Mdx. by 1701–*d.*; dep. lt. Bucks. 1703–?*d.*[2]

Dep. constable of the Tower 1694–8; master of the jewels 1698–1704; clerk-comptroller of the green cloth 1704–*d.*[3]

Godfrey came of a recusant family, originating in Norfolk. His father, who had property in Oxfordshire, was commissioned ensign in the second Bishops' war, but was dismissed as a Papist. At the outbreak of the Civil War, however, he rejoined the army and saw much action. When taken prisoner at Naseby he had risen to the rank of lieutenant-colonel. He was probably the Francis Godfrey, Papist and delinquent, whose rent-charge of £10 p.a. was sequestrated in Norfolk in April 1648. Godfrey served with the Duke of Monmouth as a volunteer in the French service and distinguished himself in a gallant action at the siege of Maestricht in June 1673. He carried the news of its capture to London, for which, it was incorrectly rumoured, he was to receive a knighthood. Commissioned captain in the guards shortly thereafter, he embarked upon a military career and served in Flanders in 1678, but apparently left the army in the next year.[4]

About this time Godfrey married Arabella Churchill, a former mistress of the Duke of York, a marriage which was to prove fortunate. He was an associate of Monmouth, who may have been hidden in his house in Covent Garden in November 1679 on his return to England, and he carried a letter from the Duke to Charles II asking for an audience, a letter which enraged the King. After the Rye House Plot it was reported that Godfrey and William Jephson* had been arrested for denying belief in Monmouth's confession published in the *Gazette*. By 1687 he was resident at a large house in Windmill Street, and a member of the 'Treason Club' which met under the presidency of Lord Colchester (Richard Savage*) at the *Rose* tavern in Covent Garden. With Colchester, Henry Wharton* and Jephson, he was one of the first to join William of Orange and on 31 Dec. 1688 was rewarded with the command of a regiment of dragoons.[5]

Godfrey was returned for Malmesbury to the Convention on the Wharton interest. He was not an active Member, being named only to the committees to consider the first mutiny bill and to reverse the attainder of Sir Thomas Armstrong*. On 22 Nov. he was given permission to testify before the Lords' committee—the so-called 'murder committee'—appointed to discover 'who were the advisers and prosecutors of the murders' of the Hon. William Russell*, Colonel Algernon Sidney†, and Armstrong. His testimony was designed to prove that Lord Halifax had compelled Monmouth to sign the paper which had incriminated Russell and Sidney. He supported the disabling clause in the bill to restore corporations.[6]

After 1690 Godfrey voted with the Whigs. He took part in the campaigns of 1691–2 and his regiment fought well at the battle of Steinkirk. He gave up his commission, however, 'said to be disgusted', in March 1693. In 1698, when his brother-in-law the Duke of Marlborough (John Churchill II*) came back into favour, Godfrey was made master of the jewels and in 1704 a clerk of the green cloth. He died on 23 Feb. 1715, aged 66, when on a visit to Bath, and was buried in Bath Abbey. His son Francis, who represented St. Mawes in 1705, was also a soldier and rose to be a brigadier before his death in 1712. Two of his daughters were maids of honour to Queen Anne.[7]

[1] St. James Piccadilly rate bk. 1686–7; *Bucks. Sess. Recs.* ii. 128; Le Neve, *Mon. Angl. 1700–15*, pp. 240, 279–80; *DNB*; *CP*, v. 247; PCC 47 Exton. [2] *First Wycombe Ledger Bk.* (Bucks. Rec. Soc. xi), 231; *Bucks. Sess. Recs.* ii. 455. [3] *Cal. Treas. Bks.* xiii. 367; Luttrell, v. 464; *CSP Dom.* 1703–4, p. 277. [4] *Stevens Pprs.* (Oxf. Rec. Soc. xlii), 46; *Oxon. Charters* (Oxf. Rec. Soc. xlv), 86; P. Young, *Edgehill*, 218–19; W. Churchill, *Marlborough*, i. 97–98; *Williamson Letters* (Cam. Soc. n.s. viii), 64. [5] E. D'Oyley, *Monmouth*, 48; *HMC Ormonde*, n.s. v. 244; R. Morrice, *Entering Bk.* 1, p. 395; J. P. Carswell, *Old Cause*, 67–68; *HMC 7th Rep.* 226; *HMC Le Fleming*, 219. [6] *LJ*, xiv. 382; Foxcroft, *Halifax*, ii. 100. [7] R. Cannon, *Hist. Rec. 4 Dgn. Gds.* 12; Luttrell, iii. 36; v. 169; *CP*, v. 247.

B.D.H.

GODOLPHIN, Charles (c.1651–1720), of Westminster and Coulston, Wilts.

HELSTON   1681, 1685, 1689, 1690, 1695, 1698, 1701 (Feb.)

b. c.1651, 5th s. of Francis Godolphin*, and bro. of Sidney Godolphin I* and Sir William Godolphin, 1st Bt.* *educ.* Wadham, Oxf. matric 16 Mar. 1666, aged 15; M. Temple 1670, called 1677. *m.* lic. 27 June 1687, his cos. Elizabeth (*d.* 29 July 1726), da. of Francis Godolphin of Spargor, St Mabyn, Cornw. 1s. 1da. *d.v.p.*[1]

Assay-master of the stannaries 1681–*d.*; inspector of tin coinage Sept. 1688, commr. 1689; asst. R. Africa Co. 1690–1; commr. of customs 1691–1714, union with Scotland 1702; registrar of shipping 1702–*d.*[2]

J.p. Cornw. by 1701–?*d.*

Although Godolphin qualified as a barrister, there is no evidence that he practised. He had private means, investing £400 in the East India Company in 1676, though later he obtained a better yield from Royal Africa stock. He served under his elder brother Sidney at the Treasury and was returned with him for Helston in 1681. Both brothers attended the Oxford Parliament, but played no known part in it. Shortly after the dissolution Godolphin was given a post in the stannary administration with a salary of £200 p.a. He was re-elected in 1685, but was again totally inactive in James II's Parliament. His marriage brought him an estate in Wiltshire, besides expectations from his wife's wealthy uncle, (Sir) William Godolphin*.[3]

Godolphin was re-elected to the Convention, in which he was appointed to only eight committees, including the committee of elections and privileges, but made 15 recorded speeches. He voted to agree with the Lords that the throne was not vacant. On 20 Feb. 1689 he argued that the House had been elected merely to prepare for a Parliament, and read out his own return to prove his point. A member of the committee to draw up the coronation oath, he supported the inclusion of the phrase 'to preserve the Church, etc. as it is now established by law', declaring:

I would have tender consciences come in at the door and not pull down the rafters to come in at the roof. Those who stood to the Protestant religion were the bishops; those who were against it were those who managed Brent's regulation of corporations; and I would have no countenance given to them.

On 9 Apr. he was appointed to the committee to prepare an address of thanks to the King for his declaration to maintain the Church of England. On the bill of settlement he proposed an amendment to assert not only the Queen's merit, but her title to the succession 'that the monarchy might be looked upon as hereditary and not elective', and later in the debate strongly denied that he managed this as

Godolphin Family

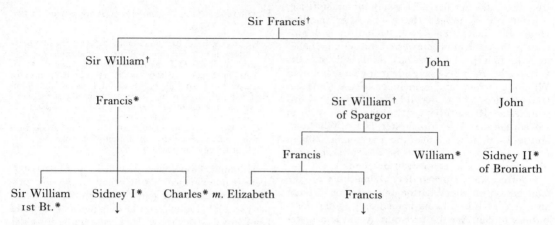

Sir Francis[†]

Sir William[†] — John

Francis[*]

Sir William[†] of Spargor — John

Francis — William[*] — Sidney II[*] of Broniarth

Sir William 1st Bt.[*] — Sidney I[*] — Charles[*] *m.* Elizabeth — Francis

'a stratagem from France', saying 'this proviso was suggested to me by no man'. He opposed the bill to suspend the Habeas Corpus Act, declaring 'some time ago we did arraign the Government of arbitrary power exercised against law. We go about now to establish arbitrary government by law.' He was given a month's leave of absence early in July, but he returned after the recess. He was named to the committee of inquiry into war expenditure, and in the supply debate of 9 Nov. proposed a land tax at the rate of 2s. in the pound.[4]

Godolphin continued to support the Government while his brother was in power. He gave up his seat in 1701 when it was declared incompatible with his place as chairman of the board of customs. He died on 10 July 1720, and was buried in Westminster Abbey.[5]

[1] F. G. Marsh, *Godolphin Fam.* 38; Vivian, *Vis. Cornw.* 184. [2] *Cal. Treas. Bks.* vii. 245; viii. 2060; ix. 266, 1191; xvii. 210, 245; xxviii. 242; xxix. 327. [3] *Cal. Ct. Mins. E.I. Co.* ed. Sainsbury, x. 405; Add. 28052, ff. 85, 90; *HMC 7th Rep.* 294; Marsh, 38. [4] Grey, ix. 105–6, 198, 237, 239–40, 295–6, 403; *CJ*, x. 65. [5] *Westminster Abbey Reg.* (Harl. Soc. x), 300.

E.C.

GODOLPHIN, Francis (1605–67), of Godolphin, Breage, Cornw.

HELSTON	1626
ST. IVES	1628
CORNWALL	1640 (Apr.)
HELSTON	1640 (Nov.)–22 Jan. 1644, 8 Aug. 1660

b. 25 Dec. 1605, 1st s. of Sir William Godolphin[†] of Godolphin by Thomasine, da. and h. Thomas Sidney

of Wrighton, Norf.; bro. of Sidney Godolphin[†]. *educ.* Exeter, Oxf. 1624. *m.* bef. 1635, Dorothy, da. of Sir Henry Berkeley[†] of Yarlington, Som., 6s. 7da. *suc.* fa. 1613; KB 23 Apr. 1661.[1]

Stannator, Penwith and Kerrier 1636, 1663; sheriff, Cornw. 1637–8, commr. of array 1642, j.p. July 1660–?d.; commr. for oyer and terminer, Western circuit July 1660, assessment, Cornw. Aug. 1660–d., dep. lt. 1662–d.; receiver, Devon and Cornw. by 1663–d.[2]

Gov. Scilly Is. 1640–6, June 1660–d.[3]

Godolphin was descended from John Knava, who assumed the name of Godolphin from his estate in the reign of Henry VII. The family first represented the county in 1539, and from 1570 leased the isles of Scilly from the crown. During the Civil War Godolphin held them for the King, until he escaped to France with the Prince of Wales in 1646. After the surrender of the islands he received a free pardon, but his estates in Norfolk and Cornwall were still under sequestration in 1648, presumably because he had not taken the Covenant. Though less notable for literature than his brother, he was a friend of Hobbes, who dedicated *Leviathan* to him, and corresponded with the future Archbishop Sancroft.[4]

Godolphin was ineligible at the general election of 1660; but when the Helston election was declared void after the Restoration he stood at the by-election for the borough, four miles from his home. Though he owned property in the town, he was involved in a double return with Sir Peter Killigrew[*], and seated on the merits of the return. In the Convention he was appointed only to the committee on the bill to prevent cursing and swearing. His income at this time was estimated at £1,000 p.a. He did not stand again, and his duties as custodian of such important state prisoners as Sir

Henry Vane[†] and John Wildman I[*] were mostly performed by deputy. He died suddenly on 22 Mar. 1667, 'much lamented' as 'a person of great integrity'.[5]

[1] F. G. Marsh, *Godolphin Fam.* 7–8. [2] Add. 6713, f. 167; *Cal. Treas. Bks.* i. 474. [3] *HMC De L'Isle and Dudley*, vi. 241; *Cal. Treas. Bks.* i. 231; *CSP Dom.* 1660–1, p. 71. [4] Gilbert, *Paroch. Hist. Cornw.* i. 133; Keeler, *Long Parl.* 187–8; M. Coate, *Cornw. in Gt. Civil War*, 32, 214; *CJ*, v. 41–42; *Cal. Comm. Comp.* 115, 117; Boase and Courtney, *Bibl. Cornub.* i. 177. [5] *CJ*, viii. 115, 177; Sir Tresham Lever, *Godolphin*, 7–8; *Western Antiq.* vii. 39; *CSP Dom.* 1661–2, pp. 169, 460; 1666–7, p. 584; 1667, p. 17; Add. 28052, f. 4.

M.W.H./E.C.

GODOLPHIN, Sidney I (1645–1712), of Whitehall.[1]

HELSTON	15 Oct. 1668
ST. MAWES	1679 (Mar.)
HELSTON	1679 (Oct.), 1681

bap. 15 June 1645, 3rd s. of (Sir) Francis Godolphin[*], and bro. of Charles Godolphin[*] and Sir William Godolphin, 1st Bt.[*]. *educ.* travelled abroad (Italy) 1664. *m.* 15 May 1675, Margaret (*d.* 9 Sept. 1678), da. and coh. of Thomas Blagge of Horningsheath, Suff., maid of honour to Queen Catherine of Braganza, 1s. *cr.* Baron Godolphin of Rialton 24 Sept. 1684; KG 6 July 1704; Earl of Godolphin 26 Dec. 1706; *suc.* bro. 1710.

Page of honour 1662–8; groom of the bedchamber 1670–8; envoy extraordinary to Louis XIV of France 1672, to the Spanish Netherlands and the Prince of Orange 1678; master of the robes 1678–9; ld. of Treasury 1679–84, 1687–90, first ld. 1684–5, 1690–6; sec. of state (south) May–Aug. 1684; PC 4 Feb. 1680–Feb. 1689, 20 Nov. 1690–*d.*; ld. chamberlain to Queen Mary of Modena 1685–Dec. 1688; member of council to Queen Catherine 1687–?91; one of the lds. justices 1695, 1696, 1701; ld. treasurer 1700–1, 1702–10.[2]

Cornet, Prince Rupert's Horse 1667.

Freeman, Portsmouth 1668, Liskeard 1685; commr. for assessment, Cornw. 1673–80; j.p. Cornw. 1680–*d.*, Mdx. 1680–5; ranger of Cranborne chase, Windsor forest July 1688–1700; ld. lt. and custos rot. Cornw. 1705–10.[3]

Godolphin became a page to Charles II at the age of 17, and was reckoned 'the silentest and modestest man that was perhaps ever bred in a court'. He formed a close friendship with Sunderland, with whom he travelled to Rome in 1664. On the occurrence of a vacancy at St. Mawes in the following year he wrote: 'I should think myself extremely happy if there could be anything done for me for love or money'. But with Joseph Tredenham[*] and Sir Vyell Vyvyan[*] in the field it is unlikely that his name was put to the electors. In 1668 his brother, the sitting Member for Helston, informed him of the death of his colleague, Sir Peter Killigrew[*]. Godolphin thanked him for his 'timely intimation of this vacant burgess-ship, which I set my heart upon extremely, and, if I can obtain it by your means, will be a very great furtherance to my pretensions here'. The family interest was exerted, 'though for a courtier', and Godolphin was eventually returned without a contest. At Court 'little Sidney Godolphin was never in the way and never out of the way', and he was no more obtrusive in the Commons. He was appointed to only eight committees in the Cavalier Parliament, including the committee of elections and privileges in four sessions, and made no recorded speeches. He was on both lists of the court party in 1669–71. A protégé of Lord Arlington (Sir Henry Bennet[*]), he undertook several diplomatic missions at this time, escorting the Duchess of Orleans to Dover for the secret treaty against the Dutch in 1670. As a reward he was made a groom of the bedchamber and granted a pension of £500 for life. The opposition writers assumed that his duties included pimping for his master, and after his death he was credited with great skill in discovering 'what were his prince's inclinations, which he was very ready to comply with'. Nevertheless it was as a connoisseur of horse-flesh that he chiefly valued his own services. Burnet comments approvingly on his 'true principles of religion and virtue', which made 'godly Godolphin' the butt of the libertines at Court; but he was a compulsive gambler, which kept him always a comparatively poor man.[4]

Godolphin was included in the Paston list of 1673–4 and the list of officials in the House in 1675. But he was one of the 'little things' at Court suspected of intriguing against Danby. When Sir Robert Viner attended the Commons to give evidence against the lord treasurer, Godolphin acted as teller for according the witness (in his capacity as lord mayor of London) the comfort and dignity of a chair. In the autumn sessions he was among those ordered to bring in a bill against the suspending power. Sir Richard Wiseman[*] noted him simply as 'of the bedchamber', while Shaftesbury classed him as 'doubly vile', and he was on both lists of the court party in 1678. After a diplomatic mission to William of Orange which kept him away from Westminster for most of the earlier sessions of 1678, he succeeded Laurence Hyde[*] as master of the robes, with a personal allowance of £500 p.a. His wife, celebrated by Evelyn for the nobility and purity of her life in a profligate Court, died of puerperal fever in September, and he remained a widower for the rest of his life. He was appointed to two important committees in the last session of the Cavalier Parliament, those to translate Coleman's letters and to consider the reception of foreign ambassadors at Court.[5]

Godolphin was returned for St. Mawes at the

first general election of 1679, probably on the Vyvyan interest, and marked 'vile' on Shaftesbury's list. His only committee in the first Exclusion Parliament was to inquire into abuses in the postal system, and he was absent from the division on the bill. Nevertheless, with Hyde and Sunderland, he represented such government as was possible after the fall of Danby. They were referred to scornfully as the 'Chits'; but Godolphin now embarked at the Treasury on a third career which spanned over 30 years with only brief intervals.

> He had a clear apprehension and despatched business with great method, and with so much temper that he had no personal enemies; but his silence begot a jealousy which has hung long upon him. . . . His incorrupt and sincere way of managing the concerns of the Treasury created in all people a very high esteem for him.

In the autumn election his brother made way for him in the family borough, which he represented jointly with Vyvyan in the second Exclusion Parliament. Before it met, he advised the King to send the Duke of York away and not to obstruct the bill. Ormonde was told that it was rushed up to the Lords on 'an assurance derived from the Duchess of Portsmouth, Secretary Sunderland and Mr Godolphin that it would infallibly pass, 55 votes being secured and his Majesty contrived into a passive neutrality'. After its rejection the King selected Godolphin to carry a message to the Commons expressing his determination to veto exclusion, but, like Sir Robert Carr*, he declined to execute the commission, and indeed took no known part in the business of this Parliament or its successor. He failed even to make advance arrangements for his own accommodation at Oxford, and according to his younger brother Charles, who had succeeded Vyvyan as his colleague for Helston, 'Privy Councillor Godolphin is lodged in a garret'. After the dissolution he advised William of Orange to visit England as soon as possible, writing: 'I am satisfied there is nothing that can so infallibly restore that good understanding between the King and your Highness, which is so necessary for you both'. The Duke of York, on the other hand, wrote that 'till Godolphin and all the rotten sheep are turned out, it will never be well'.[6]

Godolphin became secretary of state for a few months in 1684 on the resignation of Sir Leoline Jenkins*, but returned to the Treasury as first lord and was raised to the peerage when Lord Halifax (Sir George Savile*) arranged for Hyde (now Earl of Rochester) to be 'kicked upstairs'. On the accession of James II, Godolphin ordered that the taxes voted only for the life of his predecessor should continue to be collected. Nevertheless he lost his

office to Rochester, but regained it in 1687, and was sent with Halifax and the Earl of Nottingham (Daniel Finch*) to negotiate with William during the Revolution. To the fury of the Whigs he was retained at the Treasury by the new regime as 'the most reassuring guarantee of competence'. He was implicated in Jacobite intrigues, but formed a close alliance with Princess Anne and Lord Marlborough (John Churchill II*). In the judgment of the historian of the Treasury, it 'never fully recovered the professionalism that Godolphin had tried to nurture' before his dismissal with Marlborough in 1710. He died on 15 Sept. 1712 and was buried in Westminster Abbey. His only son Francis, who was sitting for Tregony as a Whig, succeeded to the title.[7]

[1] This biography is based upon Sir Tresham Lever, *Godolphin: His Life and Times*, except where otherwise indicated. [2] *Cal. Treas. Bks.* i. 719, 720; iii. 801; v. 1160; *CSP Dom.* 1668–9, p. 60; 1670, p. 263. [3] R. East, *Portsmouth Recs.* 359; *CSP Dom.* 1685, p. 66; *Cal. Treas. Bks.* viii. 1965; xvi. 342. [4] Burnet, ii. 250–1; J. P. Kenyon, *Sunderland*, 7, 11; Add. 28052, ff. 32, 42, 72; *CSP Dom.* 1688–9, p. 412; 1670, pp. 204, 214, 433; 1671–2, p. 291; *Bulstrode Pprs.* 228. [5] *HMC 14th Rep. IX*, 377; *CJ*, ix. 328; *CSP Dom.* 1677–8, pp. 640, 659; 1678, pp. 18, 242, 302. [6] *HMC Ormonde*, n.s. v. 281, 496; Burnet, ii. 250; *Temple Mems.* ed. Courtenay, ii. 69; *Sidney Diary*, ii. 210; *HMC Dartmouth*, i. 58. [7] Foxcroft, *Halifax*, ii. 205; H. Roseveare, *Treasury: Evolution of a British Inst.*, 76, 95.

E.C.

GODOLPHIN, Sidney II (1652–1732), of Broniarth, Mont. and Thames Ditton, Surr.

HELSTON	1685
PENRYN	30 Apr. 1690
HELSTON	1698, 1701 (Feb.), 1701 (Dec.), 1702, 1705, 1708, 1710, 1715
ST. MAWES	1722
ST. GERMANS	1727–22 Sept. 1732

bap. 12 Jan. 1652, 2nd but o. surv. s. of John Godolphin, DCL, judge of Admiralty 1653–9, of Clerkenwell, Mdx. by 2nd w. Mary, da. of William Tregose of St. Ives, Cornw. *educ.* I. Temple 1668. *m.* c.1673, Susanna (*d.* 10 Feb. 1724), da. of Rice Tanat of Abertanat, Salop, and coh. to her bro. Owen, 1s. *d.v.p.* 5da. *suc.* fa. 1678.[1]

J.p. Denb. 1678–89, Mont. 1678–90, Cornw. June 1688–?*d.*, Salop 1700–*d.*; commr. for assessment, Mont. 1679–80, 1689, Denb. 1689–90; dep. lt. Mont. Feb. 1688–9.

Capt. Earl of Bath's Regt. (later 10 Ft.) 1685, lt.-col. 1694–6; lt.-gov. Scilly Is. 1690, gov. 1700–*d.*; maj. Queen's Regt. (later 2 Ft.) 1700–2.

Auditor in the Exchequer 1702–*d.*[2]

Godolphin's father, a younger son, became a civilian, and was appointed judge of the Admiralty under the Commonwealth. His cousin William Godolphin* wished to resign his auditorship of the Welsh revenues in Godolphin's favour in 1677, but was prevented by his deputy, who had been granted the reversion. Godolphin was returned for Helston on the interest of another and more distant cousin, Sir William Godolphin, Bt.*, at the general election of 1685, but played no ascertainable part in James II's Parliament. He was commissioned in the regiment raised by the Earl of Bath to fight the Duke of Monmouth in the summer. He was absent from the meeting of Cornish magistracy to answer the lord lieutenant's questions on the repeal of the Test Act and Penal Laws, but presumably gave satisfaction elsewhere, for he was recommended as deputy lieutenant of Montgomery, where his wife had property. His part in the Revolution is unknown, but at the general election of 1689 he gave way to Sir John St. Aubyn, 2nd Bt.*, and he was disappointed in his application for the post of deputy governor of Guernsey, though he thought it 'morally impossible for anyone to come betwixt me and home in that affair'. However, in 1690 he was made lieutenant-governor of Scilly and re-entered Parliament as a placeman, usually voting with the Whigs. He died on 22 Sept. 1732 and was buried at Thames Ditton. His daughter married her cousin Henry, dean of St. Paul's, and their son Francis sat for Helston from 1741 until he succeeded to the peerage in 1766.[3]

[1] F. G. Marsh, *Godolphin Fam.*, 22–23, add. p. 2; Vivian, *Vis. Cornw.* 82; *Mont. Colls.* xiii. 119. [2] *Cal. Treas. Bks.* xvii. 239. [3] *CSP Dom.* 1676–7, p. 534; Add. 25564, ff. 3, 19; 29563, f. 410.

E.C.

GODOLPHIN, William (1635–96), of Spargor, St. Mabyn, Cornw.

CAMELFORD 17 Oct. 1665

bap. 2 Feb. 1635, 4th but 2nd surv. s. of Sir William Godolphin[†] (*d.*1663) of Spargor by 1st w. Ruth, da. of Sir John Lambe, dean of the Arches 1633–43, of Coulston, Wilts. *educ.* Westminster 1648, KS 1650; Christ Church, Oxf. 1651, MA 1661; I. Temple 1654. *unm.* Kntd. 28 Aug. 1668.[1]

Under-sec. of state (south) by 1662–5; sec. of embassy, Madrid 1666, envoy extraordinary 1668, ambassador 1671–8; auditor in the Exchequer 1668–90.[2]

FRS 1664.

Godolphin's father, the first cousin of Francis Godolphin*, sat for Helston in the Short Parliament. He commanded a royalist regiment of foot during the Civil War, and compounded under the articles of Scilly in 1647 on a fine of £330 at one-tenth. His elder brother Francis fought at the battle of Worcester and went into exile in France.[3]

Godolphin was one of Locke's closest schoolfriends; but he had much more in common with Sir Henry Bennet*, to whom he became under-secretary soon after the Restoration. He petitioned

for one of the seven auditorships in the Exchequer, pleading that his father had 'faithfully served his late and present Majesty at the hazard of life and ruin of fortune without recompense', and was granted a reversion. He was returned to the Cavalier Parliament at a by-election for Camelford on the last day but one of the Oxford session in 1665; but he probably never took his seat, since early in the following year he went to Spain with Lord Sandwich (Edward Montagu I*) and, except for a visit to England during the recess of 1668–9, seems to have remained there for the rest of his life. He was on both lists of the court party in 1669–71 among the Members to be engaged by the Duke of Buckingham. The influence of Bennet (now Lord Arlington) secured his promotion to ambassador and his knighthood. His Venetian colleague described him as experienced, profound and well-skilled in languages; he had 'arrived at his present position by his remarkable talents and by the skill with which he has conducted the most difficult transactions. . . . He favours the side of this crown [i.e. Spain], and hopes to profit thereby'. Godolphin did indeed acquire remarkable wealth in his adopted country after his conversion to Roman Catholicism in 1671. Two years later Sir Robert Southwell* reported to (Sir) Joseph Williamson* 'the very scandalous rumours that many merchants of Cadiz and Seville . . . declare touching our friend at Madrid, as if he and all his family but the cook were professed Romanists'. Godolphin denied his conversion in a letter which Arlington showed to the King, and retained his post. Sir Richard Wiseman* noted him in 1676 as a government supporter absent in the King's service, and Shaftesbury marked him 'doubly vile'. The author of *A Seasonable Argument* wrote that he had got £30,000 in boons, which is probably true, though not at the expense of the English tax-payer. He was on both lists of the court party in 1678 as 'in foreign parts', and was denounced by Titus Oates as one of the principal conspirators in the Popish Plot, who was to be rewarded with the office of lord privy seal. With considerable less plausibility Bedloe said that he was to have landed at Milford Haven with a Spanish army of 10,000 men. In a private letter to (Sir) Stephen Fox*, Godolphin himself commented, fairly enough: 'I cannot guess whether the purpose of my enemies be to make me appear in the world more of a fool or a traitor'. On 12 Nov. the House of Commons voted an address for his recall to answer the charges against him, and on the next day Williamson announced that the King had already despatched a letter of revocation. He retained the profits of his post in the Exchequer, which he had always performed by deputy, and he was not even expelled the House. But in 1680 he was made a grandee of Spain 'for his sufferings about the Plot'.[4]

After the accession of James II he contemplated a return to his native country on the grounds that 'his own presence can give best order to some parts of his estate, which suffereth ruin by his absence'. But the Government was too deeply committed to the French alliance to give him any encouragement. After the Revolution his auditorship of crown revenues in Wales was transferred to Charles Herbert*. On his deathbed 'surrounded by priests and Jesuits' he executed 'a notarial act' empowering four persons, including the procurator-general of the Jesuits, to make a posthumous will for the good of his soul. He died on 11 July 1696 and was buried in Madrid. His will was nullified by a private Act in 1698, which made over his assets in England to his heirs-at-law, his nephew Francis and his niece's husband Charles Godolphin*. But these represented only a quarter of his wealth, estimated at £80,000. Diplomatic pressure persuaded his bankers in Amsterdam and Venice to transfer his accounts to England; but his property in Madrid and Rome returned, presumably, whence it had come. Parliament further required that the heirs should satisfy the provisions of an earlier will made in 1669, bequeathing £3,000 to be distributed among poor scholars, decayed virtuous gentlemen, prisoners, and poor apprentices, as well as the poor of Camelford, Liskeard and St. Mabyn. Part of his wealth was eventually used to found and endow the Godolphin School for girls.[5]

[1] Vivian, *Vis. Cornw.* 187. [2] *Cal. Treas. Bks.* ii. 645; ix. 615. [3] *Cal. Comm. Comp.* 1559; M. Coate, *Cornw. in Gt. Civil War*, 96; *CSP Dom.* 1650, p. 149; 1651, pp. 96, 414, 478, 506; 1651–2, pp. 79, 171. [4] M. Cranston, *John Locke*, 22; *CSP Dom.* 1663–4, p. 417; 1673, p. 465; *CSP Ven.* xxxv. 20, 216; xxxviii. 248; Eg. 1509, ff. 281–3; 2539, f. 185; V. Barbour, *Arlington*, 149; *DNB*; *HMC Ormonde*, n.s. iv. 222, 471, 475, 577; Oates, *True Narrative* (1679); Grey, vi. 189, 193; *CJ*, ix. 539; Add. 51319, f. 53. [5] Add. 28051, f. 208; 28942, f. 254; F. G. Marsh, *Godolphin Fam.*, 19–25; *HMC Lords*, n.s. iii. 117–24; 9 Wm. III, c.19; *DNB*; *HMC 8th Rep.* pt. i (1881), 68, 90.

E.C.

GODOLPHIN, Sir William, 1st Bt. (c.1640–1710), of Godolphin, Breage, Cornw. and Suffolk Street, Westminster.

HELSTON   30 Oct. 1665, 1679 (Mar.)

b. c.1640, 1st s. of Francis Godolphin*, and bro. of Charles Godolphin* and Sidney Godolphin I*. *educ.* Christ Church, Oxf. 1655; travelled abroad (Italy) to 1661. *unm. cr.* Bt. 29 Apr. 1661; *suc.* fa. 1667.[1]

Dep. lt. Cornw. 1662–?96, 1702–*d.*, j.p. ?1667–July 1688, Oct. 1688–96, by 1701–*d.*; receiver, Devon and Cornw. 1667–89; stannator, Penwith and Kerrier 1673; col. of militia ft. Cornw. by 1679–?89.[2]

Gov. Scilly Is. 1667–81.[3]

Godolphin's father obtained a baronetcy for him on his return from his travels; but a bride was not so easily come by, since he was 'no courtier' and 'very modest'. He was defeated by Edward Nosworthy I* at a by-election at St. Ives in January 1665; but he was returned unopposed for the family borough of Helston nine months later, while his petition was still pending. An inactive Member of the Cavalier Parliament, he was appointed to only nine committees, including the committee of elections and privileges in three sessions. In April 1667, only a few days after he succeeded to the estate, the family mansion was burned down and his estate papers destroyed. His brother Sidney, already an accomplished courtier, obtained from the King a promise that he would be allowed to succeed to his father's offices. His attitude to the fall of Clarendon is not known, but in the following session he was appointed to the committees to inquire into the miscarriages of the war and to consider two drainage bills, one of which was promoted by Sir William Killigrew*. He took no further part in legislation, and never spoke, but he was entered as a court dependant in both lists of 1669–71. He received the government whip for the autumn session of 1675, and promised to attend, though not till after 21 Oct. He was marked 'absent', and on the working lists it was noted that the King would speak to his brother about him. However, during the recess Sir Richard Wiseman* noted that he 'went very well the last [session]', and Shaftesbury classed him as 'thrice vile' in 1677. It was alleged in *A Seasonable Argument* that he had '£1,200 p.a. out of the fee-farm rents', besides the governorship of Scilly. 'A most learned gentleman and an excellent divine', he was doubtful about the Test Act of 1678, and went to Bishop Gunning 'to be resolved whether mass were idolatry, as the Test expressed it'. The bishop assured Godolphin that he might take it; but he was absent from the call of the House in the following month.[4]

Godolphin was re-elected to the first Exclusion Parliament, and marked 'vile' on Shaftesbury's list. He voted against the bill, but was otherwise inactive, and did not seek re-election. He was allowed to transfer the governorship of the Scillies to another member of the family in 1681, and retired from public life. He was absent from the meeting of the Cornish magistracy in 1688 to answer James II's questions on the repeal of the Test Act and Penal Laws. At the Revolution he held £1,200 in East India stock. He died on 17 Aug. 1710 and was buried in Westminster Abbey, leaving an estate valued at £4,000 p.a. to his brother Sidney.[5]

[1] Add. 28052, f. 5. [2] *Cal. Treas. Bks.* i. 259; ix. 217; *CSP Dom.* 1667, pp. 47; 1679–80, p. 61; Add. 6713, f. 327. [3] *CSP Dom.* 1667, pp. 6, 43; 1680–1, p. 205. [4] Add. 28052, f. 5; *CJ,* viii. 623, 629; ix. 558; *CSP Dom.* 1667, p. 17; Sir Tresham Lever, *Godolphin,* 11; *Evelyn Diary,* v. 159. [5] F. G. Marsh, *Godolphin Fam.* 8; Add. 22185, f. 14; *Westminster Abbey Reg.* (Harl. Soc. x), 269; Luttrell, vi. 623.

E.C.

GODWIN (GODDEN), Sir John (c.1634–88), of London and Chatham, Kent.

QUEENBOROUGH   1685

b. c.1634. *m.* (2) lic. 13 June 1666, aged 32, Anne, da. of John Timbrell, anchor-smith, of Portsmouth, Hants, 2s. 1da. Kntd. c.1680.[1]

Lt. RN 1665–8; clerk in victualling office by 1669–79, surveyor-gen. 1679; commr. resident at Chatham 1679–86, special commr. 1686–*d.*; elder bro. Trinity House 1686–*d.*[2]

J.p. Kent 1680–*d.*, Essex, Hants, Mdx., Suff., Surr., Suss. and Westminster 1687–*d.*

Godwin may have been akin to the coachman who prosecuted Edward Hales I* for breach of the Test Act in the well-known collusive action designed to confirm the dispensing power; but the name in its less aristocratic form is so common in Kent that the matter must remain uncertain. He served under Jeremiah Smith both at sea, in the second Dutch war, and afterwards in the victualling office. He was appointed resident navy commissioner at Chatham in 1679, and returned for Queenborough in 1685, but he was not active in James II's Parliament, being appointed only to consider a naturalization bill. He gave affirmative answers on the repeal of the Test Act and Penal Laws, and was approved as court candidate in February 1688. But early on the morning of 3 Mar. his neighbour Sir John Berry found him in his London home 'in a weak and declining condition', and he was buried at St. Olave's Hart Street a week later. Nothing further is known of the family.[3]

[1] *London Mar. Lic.* ed. Foster, 559; *CSP Dom.* 1664–5, p. 14; *St. Olave Hart Street* (Harl. Soc. Reg. xlvi), 78, 79, 81. [2] *Cal. Treas. Bks.* v. 1209; *Cat. Pepysian Mss* (Navy Rec. Soc. xxvi), 60, 80, 355. [3] PCC 33 Exton; *St. Olave Hart Street,* 231.

B.D.H.

GOODRICKE, Francis (c.1621–73), of Manby, Lincs.

ALDBOROUGH   1659, 1660, 1661–18 Aug. 1673

b. c.1621, 9th but 3rd surv. s. of Sir Henry Goodricke of Ribston, Yorks., v.-pres. of the council in the north, by Jane, da. of Sir John Savile† of Methley, Yorks., baron of the Exchequer 1598–1607; bro. of Sir John Goodricke, 1st Bt.* *educ.* Aberdeen c.1638; L. Inn 1641,

called 1649. *m.* Hester, da. of Peter Warburton, j.c.p. 1649–55, of Hefferston Grange, Cheshire, *s.p.* Kntd. 3 Mar. 1662.[1]

J.p. Lincs. (Lindsey) July 1660–*d.*; commr. for assessment, Yorks. (W. Riding) Aug. 1660–*d.*, Lindsey Aug. 1660–1, Lincs. 1661–*d.*, co. Dur. 1666–*d.*, for oyer and terminer, Lincoln, 1661, corporations, Yorks. 1662–3; temporal chancellor, Durham dioc. 1664–*d.*; bencher, L. Inn 1670, reader 1672, treasurer Feb. 1673–*d.*[2]

Solicitor-gen. to Duke of York 1670–2, attorney-gen. 1672–*d.*; KC 1671.[3]

Goodricke, a practising lawyer, took no part in the Civil War and held no offices during the Interregnum. He was first returned for Aldborough, on the interest of his royalist brother, to Richard Cromwell's Parliament. He represented the same constituency in the Convention, when he was marked as a friend by Lord Wharton. An active Member, he was appointed to 50 committees, including the drafting committee, from which he reported to the House a bill to require the great seal to be issued in the King's name from 5 May 1660. Some 22 of his speeches have been recorded, which show him a firm Anglican, but a political moderate, with a strong sense of professional solidarity. On 18 June he moved to lay aside a motion to exclude from the indemnity bill all members of the high courts of justice and all who had made the instrument of government, and on 2 July he opposed the proposal of William Prynne* to disable decimators, major-generals and abjurors on the grounds that ''twas as dangerous as a hand-grenade in a barrel of gunpowder'. He also spoke against provisos not to pardon any who had enriched themselves from church lands or goods, to force all protectorate officials to refund their salaries, and to question lawyers who had prosecuted for the Commonwealth. During the debate on religion on 6 July he spoke in favour of referring the settlement to a committee of the whole House with the advice of a synod of divines. Three days later he supported the Anglican contention that the settlement should be based on the 39 Articles as well as the Old and New Testaments. On 11 July he favoured committing the bill of sales with modification in favour of 'all old tenants that were forced to buy or be turned out'. On 30 July during the debate on settling ministers he suggested a short bill to acquit the present possessors of all mean profits at Michaelmas, and was appointed to the committee. On 17 Aug. he brought in a bill for indemnifying officials in the courts of justice. In the second session he served on the committees for the attainder and excise bills, and spoke twice on the militia bill, describing it as 'one of the best and worst bills that could be made'. On 22 Nov. he moved to restrain the unlimited power of the deputy lieutenants. He took the chair for two estate bills. On 11 Dec. he was instructed to bring in a clause on behalf of the customs farmers for the indemnity bill. He spoke in support of a reward of £500 to the sister of John Lane* for her part in helping the escape of Charles II.[4]

Goodricke was re-elected in 1661, when his brother was returned for Yorkshire, and became a very active Member of the Cavalier Parliament. He was appointed to 259 committees and took the chair in 17, mostly for estate bills, including that promoted by Sir Edward Mosley*. He also acted as teller in nine divisions. In the first session he was named to the committees for the security, corporations and uniformity bills, and to those for the execution of those under attainder and to prepare reasons for a conference on the uniformity bill. Goodricke had married the daughter of the obliging Commonwealth judge before whom had been levied in 1651 the fine extorted from the dying Lady Powell by her husband and nephew (William Powell*), and he acted as teller for the adjournment of the great debate about annulling the fine on 28 Jan. 1662. He was one of five Members sent to intercede with the bishop of Ely on 15 Feb. 1662 on behalf of one of his tenants. He took the chair in grand committee on the militia bill, and acted as teller against an amendment from the Upper House requiring peers to be specially assessed. His committee on the alnage bill failed to report. With four other Members he was ordered to attend the King on the last day of the session with a resolution concerning the Mines Royal. On 10 July 1663 he carried up to the Lords an order for a day of national humiliation, and reminded them of legislation pending against Papists and nonconformists. He was teller on 16 May 1664 for retaining the reference to suits in ecclesiastical courts in the proviso to the conventicles bill. Before the next session he had become temporal chancellor of Durham, and in the supply debate of 15 Dec. he was teller for reducing the charge on that county and against reducing that on Norfolk, in both cases successfully. He acted as chairman on the bill for repairing Bridlington pier and as teller on its third reading, but it was rejected. In the 1666 session, he took the chair for the bills to enable the bishop of Durham to lease his lead mines to Humphrey Wharton* and to prevent theft and rapine on the northern borders. He was also nominated one of the managers of Lord Mordaunt's impeachment. After the fall of Clarendon he was appointed to the committees of inquiry into restraints on juries, the miscarriages of the Dutch war and the sale of Dunkirk, and he again

took the chair for the bishop of Durham's bill. On 29 Oct. 1667, although he had already spoken in Clarendon's defence, he was nominated to the committee which drew up the accusations against the chancellor. On 6 Nov. when the committee reported, he moved that the articles should be referred back 'to see how far they were true, because fame is too slender a ground to bring a man upon the stage'. Later in the same debate he opposed attempts to consider them without calling witnesses. On 9 Nov. he argued that the first article did not constitute treason, saying:

> the matter concerns life, therefore we should be wary in the exercise of legislative power. You are not tied to rules, but you are now a step towards judicature; the common law is *jus non scriptum*, and though every treason includes felony, yet not every felony treason. . . . There is a declaratory power whether a thing be treason or other felony, not whether it be treason, and could not be declared treason if not felony before. . . . So that I cannot think the article before you is treason, it not coming within the words of the statute.

He was appointed to the committee on the bill banishing Clarendon on 16 Dec. As a follower of Ormonde, he naturally agreed that the charges brought against Lord Orrery (Roger Boyle*) in 1669 constituted treason. He was appointed to the committee for punishing the assault on Sir John Coventry*, although he opposed a motion to lay aside all other business until it had passed. He agreed, however, that for the future assaults on Members of Parliament should be classed as felony and treason. This was his last recorded speech. His name appeared on both lists of the court party among those who usually voted for supply, and he became legal adviser to the Duke of York. He died on 18 Aug. 1673 and was buried at Ribston. In his will he left the manor of Walton Head and other estates in Yorkshire and Lincolnshire to his widow.[5]

[1] Clay, *Dugdale's Vis. Yorks.* i. 55; C.A. Goodricke, *Hist. Goodricke Fam.* 15; *CSP Dom.* 1638–9, pp. 543–4. [2] *HMC 8th Rep.* pt. 1 (1881), 275; Hutchinson, *Durham,* i. 553. [3] *HMC 8th Rep.* pt. 1 (1881), 230; *CSP Dom.* 1671–2, p. 58. [4] Bowman diary, ff. 4v, 42v, 46, 50v, 56, 57, 67v, 72, 110; *Old Parl. Hist.* xxiii. 14, 22, 37, 42, 53, 59. [5] *Milward,* 86, 120; *Dering,* 45; Goodricke, 15; *Clarendon Impeachment,* 18, 19, 30; Grey, i. 183, 325, 336; Harl. 7020, f. 47.

M.W.H./P.W.

GOODRICKE, Sir Henry, 2nd Bt. (1642–1705), of Ribston, Yorks.

BOROUGHBRIDGE   7 Nov. 1673, 1679 (Mar.), 1685, 1689, 1690, 1695, 1698, 1701 (Feb.), 1701 (Dec.), 1702–5 Mar. 1705

b. 24 Oct. 1642, 1st s. of Sir John Goodricke, 1st Bt.*, by

1st w. *educ.* travelled abroad (France) 1657–8. *m.* 1668, Mary, da. of William Legge I* of The Minories, London, *s.p. suc.* fa. as 2nd Bt. Nov. 1670.

Commr. for assessment, Yorks. (W. Riding) 1664–80, York 1673–9, W. Riding and York 1689–90; dep. lt. Yorks. 1664–Aug. 1688, Nov. 1688–?*d.*; j.p. (W. Riding) 1667–Sept. 1688, Nov. 1688–*d.*; freeman, Portsmouth 1675; commr. for recusants, Yorks. 1675; lt.-col. of militia ft. (W. Riding) 1677, col. Nov. 1688–?*d.*; gov. York Nov.–Dec. 1688.[1]

Col. of ft. 1678–9.

Envoy extraordinary to Spain 1678–82; lt. of the Ordnance 1689–1702; commr. for preventing the export of wool 1689–92; PC 13 Feb. 1690–*d.*

'A gentleman of fine parts naturally, and those improved by great reading and travel', Goodricke was successful for Boroughbridge, ten miles from his home, at a by-election in 1673, as an opponent both of the Duke of Buckingham and of the Court. A moderately active Member of the Cavalier Parliament, he was appointed to 52 committees, acted as a teller on three occasions and made some 16 recorded speeches. In the debate of 17 Jan. 1674 on the impeachment of Lord Arlington, he proposed that the last article should be presented to the King in order that he might decide what course to adopt, and he was co-opted to the committee to consider the articles of impeachment as a whole. He was appointed soon afterwards to the committee to consider the condition of Ireland. A rigid opponent of Catholicism who told the House that 'promotion and promoters of Popery ought to be punished by your opinion', he was named to the committee of 16 Apr. 1675 on the bill to exclude Roman Catholics from Parliament, and to three other committees directed against Popery. In the autumn session he joined in the outcry over the 'government whip', demanding a list of the recipients and inquiring on what authority the letters had been sent. In the following month he supported the motion, prompted by the appointment of (Sir) Edmund Jennings* as sheriff of Yorkshire, for an address against the pricking of MPs as sheriffs. He served on the committees for the bills to recall British subjects from French service and to extend habeas corpus. After the assault on Luzancy he helped to prepare the address protesting at the failure to apprehend the Jesuit St. Germain. In anticipation of a general election, after the prorogation, he canvassed for Lord Clifford (Charles Boyle*) as country candidate for Yorkshire.[2]

In February 1677, immediately before the new session, Goodricke, with his friend and colleague Sir John Reresby*, was converted to the support of Danby and the Court, and was accordingly classed 'thrice vile' by Shaftesbury. He regretted that the business of Dr Cary's treatment by the Lords had

been put before the Commons at a time when the King had desired that there be no discord between the Houses. In the debate of 13 Mar. he opposed the Lords' suggestion that the address to the King in favour of alliance against France should mention Sicily, as well as Flanders, as worthy of England's protection, and on 11 Apr. he expressed his satisfaction with the King's recent message in favour of an adjournment. He was teller against an explanatory bill on Irish cattle. In the earlier sessions of 1678 he helped to prepare a summary of foreign commitments and the address for the removal of counsellors, acting as teller for the address against Lauderdale. After the Popish Plot he led the opposition to Danby's impeachment, speaking twice on the lord treasurer's behalf, and on 21 Dec. during the debate on the articles of impeachment he acted as a teller for the adjournment.[3]

In the first general election of 1679 Goodricke supported the candidature of Danby's son, Edward Osborne*, for the county, and was himself returned for Boroughbridge. As an opponent of exclusion, he was marked 'vile' by Shaftesbury. A moderately active Member of the first Exclusion Parliament, he was appointed to four committees including the committee of elections and privileges. On 30 Apr. he spoke in favour of an address of thanks for the King's speech, and he voted against exclusion. He was defeated in August by Sir John Brookes*, a militant opponent of the Court. Soon afterwards he was sent as envoy to Spain, where he served until diplomatic relations were severed in 1682.[4]

On the accession of James II, Goodricke and Sir Roger Strickland* presented a loyal address from Aldborough. He regained his seat in the general election of 1685, and was listed among the Opposition. A very active Member, he twice acted as teller and helped to carry the address expressing satisfaction at the capture of Argyle. His 36 committees included that to draft the address promising support against Monmouth. He took the chair for a naturalization bill. After the recess he was teller against seeking the concurrence of the Lords to the address against the employment of Roman Catholic officers. In August 1688 he gave negative replies to the questions on the Penal Laws and Tests. In the months that followed he concerned himself deeply in the plans for a northern uprising in favour of the Prince of Orange, and his seat at Ribston Hall became the headquarters for the movement. It was he who summoned and addressed that meeting of the Yorkshire gentry at York on 22 Nov. which served as the occasion for the seizure of York by the insurgents. At the general election of 1689 he did his utmost to secure the return of Danby's son for Knaresborough.[5]

As the leader of Danby's Tory group Goodricke played an extremely active part in the Convention, serving on 77 committees, in four of which he took the chair, and making 29 recorded speeches. He did not vote with the rest of his party on the vacancy of the throne, but on 5 Feb. 1689 he was named one of the managers of the conference with the Lords. He served on the committee of 25 Feb. to consider alterations to the coronation oath and in the debates that followed was at pains to ensure that the clause requiring that the King defend the Protestant religion should be so phrased as not to preclude any later measures of comprehension. Danby described him to the King as 'capable of discharging any employment in the kingdom', and he was given a senior post in the Ordnance. On 22 Mar. he was co-opted to the committee to prepare the bill for settling the crown. Goodricke was chairman of the committee which drew up the address in favour of war with France, and spoke in defence of the publisher who had infringed parliamentary privilege by printing it. In the debate of 22 Apr. he spoke four times in opposition to the Lords' suggestion to exempt the clergy from the oaths of supremacy and allegiance. He took the chair in the committee for disarming Papists and carried up the bill. Though he opposed the toleration of Quakers, he was named to the committee for the bill. He was teller for agreeing with the Lords that the crown should retain the power to nominate custodes rotulorum. He advocated a general pardon for Protestants, and was one of the Members appointed on 22 June to prepare a bill of indemnity. In the days which followed he was the chief apologist for Danby, now Marquess of Carmarthen, over the arrest of his son, Peregrine Osborne*, and presented two reports from the committee to prevent the export of wool. He carried this bill also to the Lords. After the recess he was named to the committees of inquiry into the miscarriages of the war and the state of the revenue. He presented a statement on the condition of the Ordnance and a petition from suppliers. He sought in vain to adjourn the debate on Commissary Shales, and acted as teller for going into committee on supply. His hostility to the Quakers was undiminished, and he opposed their exemption from the double taxation imposed on non-jurors. On 10 Jan. 1690, during the debate on the bill to restore corporations, he led the Tory attack on the disabling clause, which was so widely drawn as to exclude all those who normally served, and acted as teller for bringing in candles to prolong the debate. He carried up a naturaliza-

tion bill and opposed reparations to Thomas Pilkington*.[6]

Goodricke retained office throughout the reign of William III and became a Privy Councillor. As a placeman he voted with the Court, and signed the Association in 1696. He died on 5 Mar. 1705 and was buried at Ribston. The next member of the family to enter Parliament was the fifth baronet, who was returned for Pontefract as a government supporter in 1774.

[1] Add. 28082, f. 81; 29674, f. 160; R. East, *Portsmouth Recs.* 361; R. Morrice, Entering Bk. 2, p. 631; SP31/4/124; Yale Lib. Osborn mss; Browning, *Danby*, i. 404; *Yorks. Arch. Jnl.* xxix. 266; *Reresby Mems.* 128, 527, 584; Eg. 1626, f. 56. [2] *Reresby Mems.* 89; Browning, *Danby*, i. 118; Grey, ii. 291, 361; iii. 370, 420; iv. 26; *Parl. Rep. Yorks.* (Yorks. Arch. Soc. rec. ser. xcvi), 171–2. [3] Browning, *Danby*, i. 207; Grey, iv. 170, 171, 172, 242, 348; vi. 350, 384; *CJ*, ix. 406, 478, 562. [4] Grey, vii. 161; *Parl. Rep. Yorks.* 172–3. [5] *London Gazette*, 12 Mar. 1685; *CJ*, ix. 745, 758; Eg. 3336, f. 140; *Reresby Mems.* 515, 526–8, 585–6; Add. 28875, f. 426. [6] Grey, ix. 197, 198, 218–19, 232, 258–9, 321–3, 358, 359, 360, 371–2, 373–4, 514; Eg. 3336, f. 151; *CJ*, x. 99, 101, 102, 153, 198, 205, 258, 278, 288, 295, 299, 303, 329, 338, 339.

P.A.B./P.W.

GOODRICKE, Sir John, 1st Bt. (1617–70), of Ribston, Yorks.

YORKSHIRE 1661–10 Nov. 1670 [new writ]

b. 20 Apr. 1617, 7th but 1st surv. s. of Sir Henry Goodricke, and bro. of Francis Goodricke*. *educ.* Jesus, Camb. 1633; Aberdeen 1635; travelled abroad (France) 1636–8. *m.* (1) 7 Oct. 1641, Catherine (*d.* Aug. 1644), da. and coh. of Stephen Norcliffe, counsellor at law, of York, 1s.; (2) c. 1635, Elizabeth (*d.*1691), da. of Alexander Smith of Stutton, Suff., wid. of William, 3rd Visct. Fairfax of Emly [I], of Gilling Castle, Yorks., 1s. *suc.* fa. 1641; *cr.* Bt. 14 Aug. 1641; *kntd.* Nov. 1641.[1]

Capt. of militia ft. Yorks. 1638, commr. of array 1642; j.p. (W. Riding) July 1660–d., dep. lt. c. Aug. 1660–d.; commr. for assessment (W. Riding) Sept. 1660–9, (N. Riding) 1661–9, York 1663–9, corporations, Yorks. 1662–3, loyal and indigent officers 1662, oyer and terminer, Northern circuit 1665.[2]

Capt. of ft. 1639; col. of horse (royalist) 1642–3.[3]

Goodricke's family originated in Lincolnshire in the 15th century, producing a Member for Grimsby in 1545. But he was descended from a younger son who managed Ribston for the Knights Hospitallers and bought the estate after the dissolution of the monasteries. His father deputized for Sir Thomas Wentworth† as president of the council in the north, and sent him to Aberdeen only because the discipline was stricter than in the English universities. He served under Sir Ferdinando Fairfax† in the first Bishops' war, and was regarded as a parliamentary sympathizer as late as the spring of 1642. But he was nominated to the commission of array, raised a regiment of dragoons, and himself took up arms for the King. He was taken prisoner early in 1643, and remained in captivity for almost three years. He compounded for £1,343, but in addition he had to settle £40 p.a. on the Church and to pay £200 to the committee for the advance of money. An efficient estate manager, with all his lands let 'upon the rack', he was able to take these modest penalties in his stride.[4]

Goodricke was returned as knight of the shire at the general election of 1661, and listed as a friend by Lord Wharton. A very active Member of the Cavalier Parliament, he was appointed to 205 committees, including the committee of elections and privileges in six sessions, acted as teller in seven divisions, and made ten recorded speeches. One of the strongest Anglicans in the House, he was instructed to list Members receiving the sacrament at the corporate communion of 26 May. In the opening session he was also named to the committees to bring in a bill to prevent mischief from Quakers and to consider the security bill, the bill restoring bishops to the House of Lords, the corporations bill, the bill of pains and penalties, and the bill for the execution of those under attainder. He helped to manage a conference on this last measure on 19 Feb. 1662, and made two reports on the bill for draining the Isle of Axholme. He carried this bill to the Lords, and also the Stour and Salwarp navigation bill. He was teller on the second reading for the bill to establish a 'court of conscience' for small claims in the London area, and was appointed to the committee. He also took the chair for an estate bill. In 1663 he was teller against adjourning the debate on the Declaration of Indulgence, and on the following day was among those ordered to bring in a bill to prevent the further growth of Popery, to consider a petition from the loyal and indigent officers, and to thank the King for his proclamation against Popish priests and Jesuits. In the next session he was named to the committee for the conventicles bill, and was sent to the Lords to ask for a conference. He was teller with his brother for retaining the reference to ecclesiastical courts in the bill. In the supply debate of 25 Nov. 1664 he supported the opposition demand for reversing normal procedure by discussing ways and means first; but in the Oxford session he proposed a gift of £100,000 to the Duke of York, as well as serving on the committee for the five mile bill. In October 1666 he was again among those ordered to make a list of Members receiving the sacrament, and helped to present a joint address for the prohibition of French imports.[5]

Goodricke opposed thanking the King for the dismissal of Clarendon; but he was appointed to the committees to inquire into restraints on jurors and the sale of Dunkirk and to consider the charges against Mordaunt and the public accounts bill. He spoke repeatedly in defence of the fallen minister, pointing out that a mere 'design' to alter the constitution was not treasonable. He gave offence during the debate of 16 Nov. by referring to the people as 'the beast with many heads'. He moved on 11 Mar. 1668 to lay aside the debate on religious comprehension and refer the matter to Convocation. He said of the dissenters:

> These persons would have a superstructure without a foundation. They propose nothing. Though at Hampton Court Conference the authority of truth stopped some men's mouths, yet the rest were never satisfied.

He was reckoned a friend by Ormonde, and classed by Sir Thomas Osborne* among the independent Members who usually voted for supply. He does not appear to have attended the 1669 session, though a new writ was not ordered till 10 Nov. 1670, and his will was proved later in the month.[6]

[1] C.A. Goodricke, *Hist. Goodricke Fam.* 17–25; *Roll of Alumni* (Aberdeen Univ. Studies, i), 12. [2] *CSP Dom.* 1638–9, pp. 301, 543; *HMC 8th Rep.* pt. 1 (1881), 275. [3] Goodricke, *Ribston*, 38, 41. [4] *Ribston*, 3; *CSP Dom.* 1638–9, p. 543; J. T. Cliffe, *Yorks. Gentry*, 46, 334; *Royalist Comp. Pprs.* (Yorks. Arch. Soc. rec. ser. xv), 73–80. [5] *CJ*, viii. 247, 296, 369, 374, 380, 384, 440, 565, 643; Add. 32094, f. 25; Bodl. Carte 34, f. 433. [6] *Milward*, 86, 119–20, 214; *Clarendon Impeachment*, 29; Grey, i. 41, 130; *Ribston*, 55.

P.W.

GOODWIN, Deane (1658–92), of the Middle Temple, and Bletchingley, Surr.

REIGATE 1679 (Mar.), 9 Dec. 1680, 1681

bap. 14 Jan. 1658, 2nd s. of Deane Goodwin (*d.*1661) of Bletchingley by Thomasine, da. of Sir Samuel Owfield[†], Fishmonger, of Covent Garden, Westminster, and Upper Gatton. *educ.* M. Temple 1674; travelled abroad (France) 1680. *unm. suc.* gdfa. John Goodwin*1674.[1]

Commr. for assessment, Surr. 1679–80.

Goodwin became his grandfather's heir on the death of his elder brother in 1670, and inherited a moiety of the manor of Reigate, on the strength of which he represented the borough in the three Exclusion Parliaments, being first elected within a couple of months of attaining his majority. Shaftesbury marked him 'honest', and he voted for exclusion. He acted as teller on 13 May 1679 for the motion to allow all Members to attend and vote at the committee for the repeal of the Irish Cattle Act, but he was given leave to go into the country eight days later, and throughout his parliamentary career he made no speeches and was appointed to no committees. He was defeated at the second election of 1679, and on 21 May 1680 he drew up his will 'intending shortly to travel and go into France and other countries beyond the seas'. Presumably he returned when the second Exclusion Parliament met and on his petition declared him duly elected. He was apparently returned unopposed in 1681, but five years later he sold his Reigate property to the crown for £4,400. He died on 13 May 1692, and was buried at Bletchingley, the last of the family to sit in Parliament.[2]

[1] Bletchingley par. reg.; *Vis. Surr.* (Harl. Soc. lx) 51; PCC 104 Fane. [2] Manning and Bray, *Surr.* i. 281; *CJ*, ix. 637, 673; *Cal. Treas. Bks.* viii. 979; Add. 5698, f. 166v.

J.S.C.

GOODWIN, John (c.1603–74), of Bletchingley, Surr. and Rowfant, Worth, Suss.

HASLEMERE	c. Feb. 1641
EAST GRINSTEAD	1654, 1656[1]
BLETCHINGLEY	1659, 1660

b. c.1603, 2nd s. of Edward Goodwin of Horne, Surr. by Susan, da. of Richard Wallop of Bugbrooke, Northants.; bro. of Robert Goodwin[†]. *educ.* I. Temple 1622, called 1630. *m.* by 1635, Katherine, da. and coh. of Sir Richard Deane, Skinner, of London, ld. mayor 1628–9, 1s. *d.v.p.* 2da.[2]

Commr. for sequestration, Surr. 1643, levying of money, Leics. and Surr. 1643, assessment, Surr. 1643–52, 1657, Jan. 1660–1, London 1652, Glos. 1657, accounts, Surr. 1643, defence 1643, 1645, execution of ordinances 1644, new model ordinance 1645; j.p. Surr. by 1646–53, 1656–July 1660, Glos. 1650–July 1660; bencher, I. Temple 1649–61; commr. for militia, Surr. 1649, Bucks., Glos. and Surr. 1659, Surr. Mar. 1660; steward of Wimbledon manor, Surr. 1649–May 1660.[3] Commr. for Great level of the fens 1649, obstructions 1649–51.

The surname of Goodwin occurs on the Surrey-Sussex borders in the Middle Ages; John Godwyn sat for Reigate in 1302 and Hugh Godewyn for Bletchingley in 1432. Goodwin's ancestry, however, cannot certainly be traced beyond his great-grandfather, who represented East Grinstead in the Reformation Parliament. Goodwin himself, a younger son who became a professional lawyer, married well and acquired property, mostly leasehold, as far afield as Warwickshire and Somerset. He was probably a Presbyterian, like his brother, but less prominent politically. A parliamentary supporter during the Civil War, he conformed after Pride's Purge and continued to prosper during the Interregnum. He did not sit after the return of the secluded Members in 1660, but was returned at the general election for Bletchingley, where he occupied the largest house in the borough. He was an inactive Member of the Convention, making no recorded speeches and being named only to the committee of elections and privileges and to those for the drainage of the fens and the prevention of profanity. Lord Wharton sent him a copy of the case for modified episcopacy. Goodwin did not stand himself in 1661, though he gave his interest at Reigate to the country candidates. He was disbenched by the Inner Temple for refusing to read, and seems to have been an object of local suspicion in Surrey, though his will, in which he nominated the rector of Bletchingley as a trustee, suggests that he accommodated himself to Anglicanism as easily as to Independency. He died on 18 Feb. 1674 and was buried at Worth.[4]

[1] Excluded. [2] *Vis. Surr.* (Harl. Soc. lx) 51. [3] *HMC 6th Rep.* 108; *Archaeologia*, x. 444. [4] J. Comber, *Suss. Genealogies Ardingly*, 226–7; Keeler, *Long Parl.* 190; D. Underdown, *Pride's Purge*, 374; *Surr. Hearth-Tax* (Surr. Rec. Soc. xvii) 65; *I. Temple Recs.* iii. 4; *CSP Dom.* 1661–2, p. 487; PCC 35 Bunce.

M.W.H.

GORE, Gerard (c.1653–c.1706), of Garlick Hill, London and Tunstall, Kent.

QUEENBOROUGH 1681

b. c.1653, o.s. of Robert Gore, mercer, of Maiden Lane, London. *m.* lic. 8 Feb. 1675, aged 22, Thomasine (*d.* 1 Jan. 1708), da. of Edward Hales I[*] of Chilston and coh. to her bro. Edward, 3s. 2da. *suc.* fa. 1668.[1] Commr. for assessment, Kent 1689–1705.

Gore, a cousin of Sir John Gore[*], came of a well-established London merchant family. It was presumably through his father-in-law's influence that he was returned for Queenborough as an opponent of the Court in 1681; but the 'Mr Gore' or 'George' whose name appears with some prominence in the records of the Oxford Parliament must have been William Leveson Gower[*]. He was defeated at Queenborough in 1690, but his name continued to appear on the Kent assessment commissions till 1707, when he was replaced by his son Robert. None of his descendants sat in Parliament.[2]

[1] G. E. Cokayne, *Lord Mayors and Sheriffs of London*, 74; E. R. Mores, *Hist. Tunstall*, 36. [2] Hasted, *Kent*, v. 409; *N. and Q.* (ser. 11), v. 174; *Misc. Gen. et Her.* (ser. 2), ii. 226, 349; Kent RO, Qb/RP, p. 1.

B.D.H.

GORE, Sir John (1621–97), of Sacombe, Herts.

HERTFORD 28 Feb. 1677

bap. 17 Apr. 1621, 1st s. of Ralph Gore, Merchant Taylor, of Milk Street, London by Agnes, da. and h. of Richard Young, Salter, of London, wid. of Christopher Merick of Northcote, Southall, Mdx. *educ.* M. Temple 1638. *m.* c.1642, Catherine, da. of Sir John Boteler, 1st Bt.[†], of Watton Woodhall, Herts., 3s., 3da. *suc.* fa. 1637; kntd. 18 Aug. 1660.[1]

J.p. Herts. July 1660–82, ?1687–*d.*, commr. for assessment Aug. 1660–80, 1689–90, loyal and indigent officers 1662, dep. lt. 1670–?82, 1687–*d.*, commr. for inquiry into recusancy fines 1687.[2]

Gore's grandfather was an Elizabethan alderman of London. Several branches of the family settled in Hertfordshire; Gore's cousin and namesake was elected for the county in 1656 but excluded from the House. Gore probably purchased Sacombe, five miles from Hertford, during the Interregnum. He is credited on the list of knights of the Royal Oak with an estate of £600 p.a., but it is not known whether he had done anything to earn the honour proposed for him. After the Restoration he is found acting as henchman to Thomas Fanshawe* in persecuting conventiclers. Perhaps this contributed to his defeat at Hertford by Edmund Feilde* in 1675, but he was successful in another by-election two years later. Shaftesbury entered him as 'worthy', but later altered it to 'vile'. But he appears in none of the lists of court supporters. He was named to only four committees, two for private bills, one to consider the debts of the Merchant Adventurers and the last for the preservation of fishing.[3]

Gore's views may have changed with age, for he was removed from the commission of the peace with the exclusionists in 1682, and his appointment to the commission of inquiry into recusancy fines in 1687 suggests known sympathy with dissenters. He had run into serious financial trouble, and just before the Revolution he contracted to sell Sacombe for £21,400. He died on 14 Sept, 1697, aged 77, and was buried with his wife's family at Watton at Stone. His children migrated to Ireland, but this branch of the Gore family does not seem to have produced any more Members of the English Parliament.[4]

[1] Boyd, London Units, 35016; Chauncy, Herts. ii. 58; Le Neve's Knights (Harl. Soc. viii), 107; Vis. Mdx. ed. Foster, 39; Lysons, Environs of London, iii. 323; Misc. Gen. et Her. ser. 2, ii. 246. [2] Cal. Treas. Bks. viii. 1695; CSP Dom. 1691–2, p. 118. [3] Vis. London (Harl. Soc. xv), 226; VCH Herts. iii. 425; HMC Verulam, 62. [4] CSP Dom. 1682, p. 218; HMC Lords, ii. 353–4; Misc. Gen. et Her. n.s. iv. 244.

J.P.F.

GORGES, Edward (1631–1708), of Charlton House, Wraxall, Som.

SOMERSET   1689

bap. 18 Dec. 1631, 1st s. of Samuel Gorges of Wraxall by Jane, da. of John Cottrell of Winford, wid. of George Allen of Wrington. educ. G. Inn 1648. m. 22 Sept. 1653, Grace (d. 9 Sept. 1698), da. of William Winter of Clapton-in-Gordano, 1s. d.v.p. 1da. suc. fa. 1671.[1]
  Commr. for sewers, Som. Aug. 1660, j.p. 1670–Feb. 1688, Oct. 1688–d., commr. for assessment 1673–80, 1689–90, recusants 1675, dep. lt. 1680–87, 1689–91.[2]

Gorges's ancestors gained possession of the manor of Wraxall and other Somerset properties by a fortunate marriage in the 13th century, and

had sat in Parliament for Somerset since Henry VI's reign. During the Civil War Gorges's father was a Royalist who paid £582 in composition for his estates, but was still able to build himself a new house during the Interregnum. After the Restoration he was named one of the projected knights of the Royal Oak, when his income was estimated at £600 p.a. Gorges himself, presumably a court supporter, held local office throughout the exclusion crisis. In 1687 he gave the same evasive answers as John Hunt* to the first two questions on the repeal of the Test Act and Penal Laws. He signed the declaration of support for the Prince of Orange at Crewkerne on 15 Nov. 1688, and was returned as knight of the shire in 1689. In the Convention, according to Ailesbury's list, he voted to agree with the Lords that the throne was not vacant. His only committee was on the bill for relief of poor prisoners, to which he was added on 30 May. He supported the disabling clause in the bill to restore corporations, and is not known to have stood again. He was buried at Wraxall on 8 Sept. 1708, the last of the senior line of his family. His estates passed to a granddaughter who married John Codrington, MP for Bath (with one interval) from 1710 to 1741.[3]

[1] G. S. Master, Colls. Par. Hist. Wraxall, 26–28. [2] Q. Sess. Recs. (Som. Rec. Soc. xxxiv), p. xii. [3] Cal. Comm. Comp. 971; E. Green, March of Wm. of Orange through Som. 57–58; CJ, x. 160.

I.C.

GORGES, Richard, 2nd Baron Gorges of Dundalk [I] (c.1619–1712), of Stetchworth, Cambs.

NEWTON   24 Oct. 1661

b. c.1619, 3rd but o. surv. s. of Edward, 1st Baron Gorges [I] of Longford Castle, Wilts. by 1st w. Katherine, da. and h. of Sir Robert Osborne of Kelmarsh, Northants., wid. of Edward Haselwood of Maidwell, Northants.; step-bro. of James Livingston*, 1st Earl of Newburgh [S]. educ. Clare, Camb. 1637; travelled abroad 1639–40. m. by 1654, Bridget, da. of Sir Henry Kingsmill of Sydmonton, Hants, 2s. d.v.p. suc. fa. Jan./Apr. 1657.[1]
  Surveyor-gen. Bedford level 1656–86, commr. of sewers 1662–3, bailiff 1663–5, 1666–1700, conservator 1700–d.; commr. for assessment, Lancs. 1663–4, 1673–9, Ely 1664–80, Cambs. 1673–80, Wilts. 1677–80, Cambs. Ely and Westminster 1689–90; j.p. Cambs. 1669–?87, Cambs. and Lancs. 1689–1702, Lincs. (Holland) and Mdx. by 1701–?d.[2]
  Commr. for plantations 1670–2, trade and plantations 1672–4.

Gorges's grandfather, a younger son, married the widowed Marchioness of Northampton about 1580, and the peerage followed in the next generation. But Gorges's father, who invested heavily in North American plantations and the drainage of the fens, was obliged to sell Longford Castle just before the

Civil War. In December 1640, Gorges himself stood for the neighbouring borough of Downton against Sir Anthony Ashley Cooper*; the decision on the double return in favour of his opponent was not reached until after the return of the secluded Members in 1660. The remaining estates in the west country were sequestrated by the Royalists in 1643, but neither Gorges nor his father was active in the Civil War.[3]

Gorges devoted the greater part of his long life to the drainage of the fens. He first appears at a meeting of the Adventurers in 1649, and on the death of Sir Cornelius Vermuyden, the Dutch engineer in charge of the whole project, was appointed surveyor-general.

> In his attention to the interest of the fens he was indefatigable. The Earl of Bedford placed great reliance upon his judgment, and entertained the highest opinion of his integrity.

In August 1659 Gorges obtained a pass overseas, but there is no record of contact with the exiled Court. Soon afterwards he is said to have accompanied Lord Bedford on his visit to the fens, where much damage had been done to the drainage works during the general breakdown of public order. New legislation was an urgent necessity for the Adventurers; a temporary Act was passed through the Convention for the maintenance of the works, but there were so many disputes with the dispossessed royalist Adventurers, headed by Samuel Sandys* and (Sir) William Tyringham*, that a permanent measure setting up a corporation and giving it power to levy rates would obviously require skilful and patient steering through the Lower House. In these circumstances it is surprising that Lord Bedford failed to find a seat for Gorges at the general election of 1661. Lord Treasurer Southampton recommended him in vain to Sir John Wolstenholme as 'a person every way qualified for that service, and one who, as he will be of public use, so particularly a very faithful and industrious servant for the place he represents'. Fortunately a vacancy soon occurred at Newton, where the patron, Richard Legh, was the son-in-law of a leading Adventurer, Thomas Chicheley*.[4]

Gorges was a moderately active Member of the Cavalier Parliament, with a total of 72 committees. He took every opportunity to familiarize himself with parliamentary procedure, helping to manage two conferences on street repairs in London and Westminster and acting as chairman of a naturalization bill. Meanwhile the Bedford level bill had been slowly proceeding through committee; by 12 May 1662 it was clear that it had no chance of becoming law before the end of the session, and a new

temporary bill was introduced. On the first reading it was rejected by 113 to 58, Gorges being one of the tellers for the minority. Two days later there occurred a 'difference' between Gorges, seconded by Chicheley on the one hand and Sandys and Tyringham on the other, whereby, the House was told, 'a mischief [was] like to ensue'. The four Members were ordered to wait on the King 'to give him satisfaction touching the difference'. Shortly after the adjournment a commission of sewers was issued that in fact gave the Adventurers the temporary power they were seeking.[5]

In 1663 the new Adventurers at last reached a compromise with the Sandys group, and the General Drainage Act was passed. Even then the establishment, represented by Gorges and Chicheley, met with some setbacks. Amendments in committee filled 34 sheets, and when they asked the House to reject them they were crushingly defeated by 96 votes to 13. The majority tellers were Henry Williams* and Roger Pepys*, who were not Adventurers and probably acted in the interests of the commoners and corporate towns. On 27 July the bill received the royal assent. Even so an explanatory bill was required in the next session; Pepys again opposed it, together with Lionel Walden I*, but the second reading was carried by 108 to 82. In 1667 the old Adventurers tried again; Sandys got their bill through the Commons over the opposition of Pepys, as well as Gorges and Chicheley, but it died in committee in the Upper House. In the next session a bill was introduced to compensate Sir John Cutts for damage to his lands caused by the drainage of the Bedford level; the House ordered that none of the parties principally interested should sit on the committee, but an exception was made for Gorges and Sandys, for once in agreement, who had spoken against it on the first reading. Thus unimpeded, Cutts's bill became law.[6]

Gorges was repeatedly named to drafting committees on other drainage bills and he occasionally spoke on other subjects, but he was not prominent. In 1668 he attacked toleration, but in the following year he was among those to be engaged for the Court by the Duke of York. In *A Seasonable Argument* he was alleged to be in receipt of a pension of £500, presumably a reference to the salary he enjoyed for two years as a member of the committee for plantations. His name appeared on the Paston list, the working lists, and the list of government speakers. For the autumn session of 1675 he received the government whip, and attended the court caucus. Sir Richard Wiseman* recommended that he should again be summoned to the next session, and Shaftesbury classed him 'doubly vile', but his name disappeared from the lists in 1678, though on 4 Feb. he spoke in defence of the royal prerogative over the proposed Dutch alliance. On 19 June he urged strong measures against the recusant (Sir) Solomon Swale*, saying that his excuses were inadmissible.[7]

Gorges did not sit again after the dissolution of the Cavalier Parliament. Presumably he opposed the repeal of the Test Act and Penal Laws, for his name seems to disappear from the Cambridgeshire commission of the peace in 1687. His means were straitened by the general deterioration of the fenland about this time, and by 1700 he no longer held the 400 acres required to qualify as a bailiff of the Bedford level. A man of scrupulous honour, though 'captious and peevish' in his old age, he was buried at Stetchworth on 27 Sept. 1712, aged 94, the last of this branch of the family.[8]

[1] Bridges, *Northants.* ii. 48; *Mon. Inscriptions from Cambs.* 155–6; S. Wells, *Drainage of the Bedford Level*, i. 329; *CSP Dom.* 1639, p. 166. [2] Wells, i. 328, 350, 456–81, 544. [3] Hoare, *Wilts.* Downton 30–32; Wells, i. 111; *Cal. Comm. Adv. Money*, 190; *Cal. Comm. Comp.* 3244. [4] Wells, i. 163, 328, 336–40; *Cal. Treas. Bks.* vii. 1539–40; *CSP Dom.* 1653–4, pp. 115–116; 1659–60, p. 563. [5] *CJ*, viii. 423, 427, 429, 430; *CSP Dom.* 1661–2, p. 383. [6] *CJ*, viii. 505, 579, 683; ix. 65; Wells, i. 388; *LJ*, xii. 100; *Milward*, 96, 223. [7] *Milward*, 217; *CSP Dom.* 1670, pp. 538–9; Grey, v. 65; vi. 107. [8] Le Neve, *Mon. Angl. 1700–15*, p. 251; *HMC 15th Rep. X*, 172; Add. 29564, f. 379.

I.C.

GORGES, Thomas (c.1618–70), of Batcombe, Som. and Heavitree, Devon.

TAUNTON 1654, 1656, 1659, 1660

> b. c.1618, 1st s. of Henry Gorges of Batcombe by Barbara, da. of Thomas Baynard of Colerne, Wilts.; bro. of John Gorges†. *educ.* L. Inn 1638, called 1647. *m.* (1) Mary, da. of Martin Sanford of Nynehead Court, Som., 3s. 1da.; (2) 23 Mar. 1658, Rose (*d.* 14 Apr. 1671), da. and coh. of Sir Jerome Alexander, j.c.p. [I], of Dublin, wid. of Roger Mallock of Cockington, Devon, 1s. 1da. *suc.* fa. c.1649.[1]
>
> Dep. gov. Maine 1640–3; commr. for assessment, Som. 1649–52, Devon and Som. 1657, Som. Jan. 1660; j.p. Som. 1649–53, 1656–July 1660, Devon 1657–July 1660; lt.-col. of militia horse, Som. 1650, commr. for scandalous ministers 1654; recorder, Taunton by 1655–?62; commr. for militia, Som. Mar. 1660.[2]
>
> Commr. for fraudulent debentures 1656–8.[3]

Gorges was the eldest of four forceful brothers from an obscure cadet branch of the family. His father played no part in the Civil War, but he himself interrupted his law studies at the behest of his distant cousin Sir Ferdinando Gorges to serve as deputy governor of Maine. He returned to England after a few years and became recorder of Taunton, which he represented throughout the Protectorate. A Presbyterian and a Cromwellian, especially after

his brother Robert became secretary to Henry Cromwell in Ireland, Gorges was re-elected in 1660, and included by Lord Wharton among his friends. An inactive Member of the Convention, he was named only to the committee of elections and privileges, and those to consider the bill to confirm land purchases and to inquire into the fraudulent conversion of public funds. He was given leave to go into the country on 20 June, and probably received a hint from his cousin Sir Edward Hyde† not to return. He settled on his wife's property near Exeter, and lost his recordership when the Taunton corporation was dissolved by the commissioners. He died on 21 Oct. 1670, lamenting 'few and evil have been my days', and was buried at Heavitree. His direct descendants emigrated or fell into obscurity, though his nephew Henry was returned for Herefordshire in 1698.[4]

[1] *Vis. Som.* (Harl. Soc. xi), 41; *Som. Wills*, vi. 57; R. Gorges, *Gorges Fam.* 197; Vivian, *Vis. Devon*, 547. [2] *Province and Court Recs. of Maine* (Maine Hist. Soc. i), 36–41; *CSP Dom.* 1649–50, p. 521; 1655–6, p. 33. [3] *CSP Dom.* 1656–7, p. 15; 1658–9, p. 3. [4] Gorges, 183–99; D. Underdown, *Som. in the Civil War*, 172–3; B. F. Cresswell, *Churches of Exeter*, 38.

M.W.H./I.C.

GORING, Charles (c.1668–1713), of Wappingthorn, Steyning, Suss.

BRAMBER 1689

> b. c.1668, 1st s. of Henry Goring II* by 1st w. *m.* 22 May 1700, Elizabeth (*d.*1741), da. and coh. of Richard Bridger* of Coombe Place, Hawsey, *s.p. suc.* gdfa. Henry Goring I* as 3rd Bt. 3 Apr. 1702.
>
> Commr. for assessment, Suss. 1689–90, j.p. 1702–*d.*

Goring was returned for Bramber, two miles from his home, on the family interest at the general election of 1689, although he can barely have been of age. He was described on the indenture as Charles Goring junior to distinguish him from his uncle. In the Convention, according to Anthony Rowe*, he voted to agree with the Lords that the throne was not vacant; but he served on no committees and made no recorded speeches. Although he took the oaths to the new regime, unlike his grandfather, he does not seem to have stood again. They were both alleged to have been involved in smuggling French wine into Sussex in 1698, but escaped prosecution. He was buried at Billingshurst on 13 Jan. 1713. His half-brother, who succeeded to the baronetcy, sat for Horsham and Steyning from 1707 to 1715.

Cal. Treas. Bks. x. 23; xii. 98; xiii. 69, 70, 172, 259; *Suss. N. and Q.* xi. 58–59.

B.M.C./J.P.F.

GORING, Henry I (1622–1702), of Highden, Washington, Suss.

SUSSEX   1660
STEYNING   1661, 1679 (Mar.)
SUSSEX   1685

b. 1 May 1622, o.s. of Henry Goring† of Highden by Mary, da. of Sir Thomas Eversfield of Denne Park, Horsham. *m.* 2 May 1642, Frances, da. of Sir Edward Bishopp, 2nd Bt.†, of Parham, 4s. (3 *d.v.p.*), 3da. *suc.* fa. 1655, Sir James Bowyer as 2nd Bt. Feb. 1680.[1]

J.p. Suss. July 1660–July 1688, Sept. 1688–9, dep. lt. Aug. 1660–May 1688, commr. for assessment Aug. 1660–80, 1689, sewers, W. Suss. Oct. 1660, oyer and terminer, Home circuit 1661, loyal and indigent officers, Suss. 1662, recusants 1675; common councilman, Chichester 1685–Oct. 1688.[2]

Goring came from a cadet branch of the Burton family. His father, who was MP for Arundel in the Short Parliament, was apparently neutral in the Civil War, serving on the commission of the peace from 1646 to 1650. Goring's own case is more dubious; he was probably the 'Henry Goring, gent.' captured by Sir William Waller I* at the surrender of Arundel Castle in 1644. No composition proceedings followed, and the county committee must have accepted that he was merely a visitor to the garrison, where his wife and mother-in-law had been living. Nevertheless, his sympathies were royalist, though he was, with good reason, 'very wary and shy' of Cavalier plotting during the Interregnum. At the Restoration he was nominated to the proposed order of the Royal Oak, with an income of £2,000 p.a.[3]

At the general election of 1660 Goring was returned for Steyning, four miles south-east of Highden, as well as for the county. An inactive Member, he was appointed only to the committee of elections and privileges and to that for the attainder bill, but doubtless supported the Government. He had to step down to the borough in 1661, and was again inactive in the Cavalier Parliament, serving on 46 committees at most. He was named to the committee for the five mile bill in the Oxford session. Goring was a firm friend to an extruded minister who kept a school in his former parish of Billingshurst, although later William Penn the Quaker complained that he and John Alford* made his life in Sussex 'uneasy'. He made default in attendance in 1666 and again in 1671, though noted as a supporter of Ormonde and listed by Sir Thomas Osborne* among the independent Members who had usually voted for supply. From 1673 there is the possibility of confusion with his son, but he was probably appointed to the committee to consider the dispute between Sir Thomas Byde* and the board of green cloth on 3 Feb. 1674 and to

the committee on illegal exactions six days later. He was marked with a query on the list of government supporters drawn up by Sir Richard Wiseman* but he was reckoned 'thrice vile' by Shaftesbury in 1677. According to *A Seasonable Argument* he was receiving a pension of £200 p.a. as well as 'court dinners'. He was on both lists of the court party in 1678, when his chief interest appears to have been burying in woollen. 'Mr Goring' was appointed to the committee to bring in a bill on 15 Feb. and to manage the conference on 10 May, as well as to three other committees on the subject. In this year he obtained the reversion of the Bowyer baronetcy, with precedence of its creation in 1627, and it was (by anticipation) as 'Sir Henry Goring' that he was found to have absented himself without leave on 11 Dec. and sent for in custody.[4]

Goring was re-elected at the first general election of 1679 and styled baronet on the Steyning return. Shaftesbury marked him 'vile'. It was probably he, rather than his son, who was allowed to go into the country on 8 Apr., since another charge of departure without leave in the following month was quickly withdrawn, and he was absent from the division on the first exclusion bill. He does not appear to have stood at the next two elections. With Sir William Morley* and James Butler* he was active in searching for arms after the Rye House Plot, and with his son petitioned for the grant of Up Park if it should be forfeited by Lord Grey of Warke. In 1685 he was not only himself returned for the county but secured the election of government nominees at New Shoreham and Bramber. His only committee in James II's Parliament was the elections committee, and he appears on Danby's list as in opposition. To the lord lieutenant's questions on the Tests and Penal Laws he answered that

> he must suspend his judgment till he hears (in case he be a Parliament man) the case argued in the House, upon which he may take his measures. ... He knows no person of the Church of England whom he can prefer as being for advancing what the King requires, and he cannot give his assistance for the choosing of any other.

A non-juror after the Revolution, he settled his land on his grandson to avoid double taxation. He died on 3 Apr. 1702 and was buried at Billingshurst.[5]

[1] Add. 5698, f. 258; PCC 94 Herne; *Suss. Arch. Colls.* v. 16. [2] C181/7/58; A. Hay, *Hist. Chichester*, 589. [3] *Suss. Arch. Colls.* v. 62–63; *Thurloe*, vii. 86. [4] *Suss. Arch. Colls.* li. 5. [5] *CSP Dom.* July–Sept. 1683, pp. 19, 231; 1685, p. 79; *Cal. Treas. Bks.* x. 23; Luttrell, ii. 87.

M.W.H./B.M.C.

GORING, Henry II (1646–85), of Wappingthorn, Steyning, Suss.

NEW SHOREHAM   11 Feb. 1673
BRAMBER   1679 (Mar.), 1679 (Oct.),
                                      1681
STEYNING   12 Mar. –10 June 1685

bap. 6 Apr. 1646, 2nd s. of Henry Goring I*. *educ.* Queen's, Oxf. 1662. *m.* (1) 17 Oct. 1667, Elizabeth, da. and coh. of Anthony Morewood of Alfreton, Derbys., 2s. (1 *d.v.p.*); (2) 2 Feb. 1676, Mary, da. and coh. of Sir John Covert, 1st Bt.*, of Slaugham, Suss., 3s. (1 *d.v.p.*).[1]

Jt. steward, honour of Peveril 1664–72; commr. for assessment, Suss. 1673–9, j.p. 1674–*d.*, sheriff 1681–2, dep. lt. 1685; common councilman, Chichester 1685.[2]

Capt. of ft. regt. of Lord Ibrackan (Henry O'Brien*) 1678–9.

Goring became his father's heir when his elder brother died of smallpox at Cambridge in 1661. The precise date of the purchase of Wappingthorn from the Leedes heirs has not been ascertained, but it is presumably connected with his father's claim of privilege on 4 Nov. 1670 against Barnaby Bowtell, one of the parties to a fine of the property in Trinity Term 1671. Goring was elected at the first subsequent vacancy for a West Sussex borough, but in view of the comments on his youth and inexperience in 1678, he was probably inactive, though in committee work he cannot be distinguished from his father. Marked 'thrice vile' on Shaftesbury's list, he achieved prominence in the last sessions of the Cavalier Parliament as an officer in the newly-raised forces by his outspoken and provocative support for the Government. On 20 Feb. 1678 he reflected on Sir Charles Harbord* for his grants of crown lands. On 29 Apr. he spoke of the 'committee of Popery', who, he said, had not done their duty 'in putting in the clause of not granting money till their minds be satisfied that all care and diligence is used to secure the Kingdom; and those that defend it should be called to the bar'. He was excused by Sir Thomas Littleton, 2nd Bt.* as 'a young gentleman not used to speak', but his next indiscretion was not so lightly passed over. Following Henry Powle* on 3 May he said:

> I desire a test from those gentlemen on that side of the House that they have no design of creeping into ministers' places when they are out; and if they will give me good security that they will act better, I will then be on their side. Till then, I think the ministers have done well.

Sir George Downing* pointed out that 'the gentleman is well descended, and but young in years and experience', but Littleton complained that he 'sat a great while in his place, smiling and laughing' before apologizing and denying any personal allu-

sion. 'The young gentleman is forward and zealous, but I would have no more said to him but an admonition in his place to forbear the like in the future'; and he was reprimanded by the Speaker (Robert Sawyer*) in the mildest terms. He continued to be treated with a tolerance which can only be explained by a total lack of support for his threatening propositions. On 1 June he said: 'Yesterday there was a grand committee for disbanding the army, but I see there is need of keeping it up, if these things are said here'. A fortnight later he openly wished for liberty 'to demand satisfaction out of doors'. In the final session he scoffed at Oates's charge that his cousin Sir William Goring (who was still under age) had received a commission as captain of horse at the time of the Popish Plot.[3]

Goring transferred to Bramber at the general election, and, although included in the 'unanimous club' of court voters, was returned to all three Exclusion Parliaments. According to Oates, 'Mr Goring was very lavish of his tongue in the country, that he had the King's ear and favour'. He was marked 'vile' on Shaftesbury's list. Meeting Oates in the lobby when the first Exclusion Parliament met, he denied that Sir John Gage, who had been arrested on Oates's information, was a traitor, and called the informer a rascal, a lying rogue and a base, impudent fellow. He defended the King's right to veto the re-election of Edward Seymour* with an appeal to precedent: 'I would know whether any person but a Privy Councillor usually proposes a Speaker'. On 24 Mar. 1679, Oates complained to the House of his conduct, but John Fagg I*, whom he called as a witness, had absented himself, and the matter was not pursued, the House no doubt accepting Goring's assertion that 'if I gave Oates ill language, he was even with me'. When Thomas Bennett* seemed to refer to his religion, he interrupted: 'I am as good a Protestant as Bennett, and I demand satisfaction', a fairly safe demand in view of Bennett's avoidance of the challenge from Edward Osborne* in the last Parliament. He voted against the exclusion bill, as he did again in 1680 when his was the only vote against it. He was given leave to go into the country on 23 Dec., made no further speeches, and served on no committees in any of the Exclusion Parliaments.[4]

Goring's loyalty was surely above suspicion, even though he was reluctant to 'meddle' in the attempt to intercept the Duke of Monmouth and his closest associates immediately after the discovery of the Rye House Plot. 'A most intimate friend of Lord Chief Justice Jeffreys', he was returned to James II's Parliament for Steyning, and became an active committeeman, serving on four committees, including those to hear the petition from hackney coachmen and to consider the bill to regulate them. With (Sir) Joseph Tredenham* he acted as teller against hearing the Buckinghamshire election case at the bar of the House, and was listed among the Opposition. But on 10 June 1685 he met the fate which he had so long been courting. After a quarrel in a theatre, he was mortally wounded by a younger son of Sir Edward Dering*. Danby can hardly have forgotten so spectacular and appropriate a demise, and must therefore have included him in his list of the Opposition before that date.[5]

[1] *Suss. Arch. Colls.* v. 67; Add. 5698, f. 258; Le Neve, *Mon. Angl. 1650–79*, p. 82; J. Comber, *Suss. Genealogies Ardingly*, 186. [2] *CSP Dom.* 1663–4, pp. 160, 513; 1671–2, p. 101; A. Hay, *Hist. Chichester*, 589. [3] *Suss. Arch. Colls.* liv. 52; *Fines of Manors* (Suss. Rec. Soc. xx), 464; Grey, v. 196, 282–4, 314–19; vi. 59, 91, 116. [4] Grey, vi. 419–20; vii. 9–10, 47, 55–56, 239; *HMC Ormonde*, n.s. v. 475; PRO 31/3, bdle. 142, f. 16. [5] *CSP Dom.* July–Sept. 1683, p. 37; *HMC Egmont*, ii. 153; *CJ*, ix. 717; Luttrell, i. 346; R. Morrice, Entering Bk. 1, p. 467.

B.M.C.

GORING, Percy (d.1697), of Parham, Suss. and Maidstone, Kent.

BRAMBER 17 May 1661, 1681

5th s. of Sir William Goring, 1st Bt.[†] (d.1658), of Burton, Suss. by Bridget, da. and h. of Sir Edward Francis[†] of Petworth, Suss. *m.* (1) Aug. 1656, Lady Mary Tufton (d.1663), da. of Nicholas Tufton[†], 1st Earl of Thanet, wid. of Sir Edward Bishopp, 2nd Bt.[†], of Parham, *s.p.*; (2) lic. 23 Apr. 1667, Elizabeth, da. of George Hall of Maidstone, wid. of Sir Thomas Taylor, 1st Bt., of Shadoxhurst, Kent, *s.p.*[1]

Capt. of militia horse, Suss. c. Apr. 1660–?d., j.p. Suss. July 1660–d., Kent 1682–9; commr. for assessment, Suss. 1661–80, Kent 1673–80, loyal and indigent officers, Suss. 1662, recusants 1675.[2]

Goring's family achieved county status in the late 15th century, and first represented Sussex in 1547. His father remained aloof during the Civil War, though he was appointed to two local commissions by Parliament in 1643–4; but his brother Henry was in arms for the King and was fined £250. Goring's first marriage connected him with the leading royalist families of Kent and Sussex, and in April 1658 he was accused of possessing a seditious pamphlet.[3]

Goring was recommended as a militia officer at the Restoration, and stood for Bramber at the general election of 1661. His maternal grandfather had been the seneschal of Petworth manor under the 4th Earl of Northumberland, and he owed his christian name and probably this election to the Percy family, though his wife's interest must have been helpful. He was involved in a double return with a local lawyer, and seated on the merits of the return. An inactive Member of the Cavalier Parlia-

ment, he was appointed to the committee of elections and privileges in six sessions and to only 14 others, most of which were for private bills. Lord Aungier (Francis Aungier*) included him among Ormonde's friends in the House in 1668. His name appeared on neither list of the court party in 1669–71, but he was on the Paston list and Secretary Coventry sent him the government whip in September 1675. On 4 Nov. he took part in the debate on providing and equipping ships for the navy. Impatient of the quibbling of some of his fellow-Members, he declared that he 'would have no tricks put upon ourselves nor cheats upon the nation', and gave offence by remarking that 'building of ships and not making them useful is like those who declared for the King and kingdom in the late times of rebellion'. He was on the working lists as one to be spoken to by the King, in December Sir Richard Wiseman* reported that he had 'given hopes' to 'Mr Goring', and at the end of the month he was granted a pension of £200 p.a. Wiseman regarded him as more dependable that his kinsman Henry Goring I*, and he was marked 'thrice vile' on Shaftesbury's list. On 28 Jan. 1678 Goring was the first speaker in the new session, when he moved for 'a short day' for considering the King's speech. He was on both the court and opposition lists in 1678.[4]

Goring's nephew, the 3rd baronet, became a Roman Catholic, and in October 1678 was accused of treason and imprisoned in the Tower. This may, perhaps, explain why Goring made way at the general election for his cousin Henry Goring II*. Although blacklisted in the 'unanimous club', he stood again for Bramber in the autumn of 1679, but 'consented to desist' in favour of Henry Sidney*, 'if he might have his charge reimbursed', which he reckoned to be £80. Sidney's agent reported that he had passed away his interest for ever, but he regained the seat in 1681, though he left no trace on the records of the Oxford Parliament.[5]

Goring sold some of his Sussex property later in the year, and in March 1683 he applied for appointment as cursitor baron of the Exchequer, but the post was given to (Sir) Richard May*. In February 1686 he petitioned for the grant of a fine of 1,000 marks which had been imposed on Sir Richard Newdigate*, 'his condition at present needing some post'. There is no evidence that he ever received it, but he was granted £424 8s. 10d. from secret service funds later in the year. Goring was a supporter of James II's religious policy, agreeing in 1688 to all three questions concerning the repeal of the Penal Laws and Test Act, and was recommended for continuance on the commission of the peace in Kent and Sussex. As further evidence of his straitened financial condition he petitioned after the Revolution for the post of muster-master in the Sussex militia, but it is not known whether he was ever appointed.[6]

Goring was buried on 17 Feb. 1697 in the chancel of Burton church.[7]

[1] *Vis. Suss.* (Harl. Soc. liii), 45–46; *Suss. N. and Q.* ix. 154–5. [2] SP29/42, f. 131. [3] Bodl. Rawl. A58, f. 401. [4] H. A. Wyndham, *Petworth Manor*, 6; J. W. Fitzwilliam, *Parham*, 62; Grey, iii. 402; v. 14; *Cal. Treas. Bks.* v. 415. [5] *CSP Dom.* 1678, p. 496; *Sidney Diary*, i. 115–16. [6] *Fines of Manors* (Suss. Rec. Soc. xix), 107; *CSP Dom.* Jan.-July 1683, p. 113; *Cal. Treas. Bks.* viii. 548; *Secret Service Moneys* (Cam. Soc. lii), 135; Kent AO, U269. [7] Add. 43446, f. 26.

B.M.C./B.D.H.

GOTT, Samuel (1614–71), of Battle, Suss.

WINCHELSEA	2 Oct. 1645[1]
SUSSEX	1656[2]
HASTINGS	1659
WINCHELSEA	1660

b. 20 Jan. 1614, 1st s. of Samuel Gott, Ironmonger, of London, by Elizabeth Russell. *educ.* Merchant Taylors' 1626–9; St. Catherine's, Camb. 1630, BA 1633; G. Inn 1633, called 1640, ancient 1658. *m.* c.1643, Joan (*d.*1681), da. and coh. of Peter Farnden of Sedlescombe, Suss., 1s. 2da. *suc.* fa. 1641.[3]

Commr. for exclusion from sacrament 1646, bishops' lands 1646, indemnity 1647–9, scandalous offences 1648.
Commr. for militia, Suss. 1648, Mar. 1660, scandalous ministers 1654, assessment, Suss. 1657, Jan. 1660–9, Winchelsea Aug. 1660–1; sheriff, Suss. 1658–Mar. 1659, j.p. Mar. 1660–70; commr. for sewers, Mdx. Aug. 1660.[4]

Gott, a Londoner by birth, moved to Sussex on his marriage, where he became an ironfounder and landowner, entering the Long Parliament as a recruiter for Winchelsea. He did not sit after Pride's Purge, but in spite of his professed aversion to public life he was twice returned to Protectorate Parliaments and appointed to local office. He was dejected by Cromwell's refusal of the crown. He regained his original seat at the general election of 1660.[5]

Gott was moderately active in the Convention, being named to 17 committees, of which the most important was for the indemnity bill, and making five speeches. In the debate on 16 July he took the Presbyterian side, though willing to accept 'primitive episcopacy', and he was appointed to the committee to inquire into unauthorized Anglican publications. He spoke twice in favour of sparing the lives of those regicides who had surrendered themselves, urging that banishment or imprisonment would be a more effective punishment as rendering them 'living monuments of their own wretchedness', and on 23 Aug. he was added to the conference managers. He also helped to manage the conference of 11 Sept. on settling ministers. Lord Wharton sent him a copy of the case for modified episcopacy with objections. After the recess he was appointed to the committees for the attainder bill and for the conference on the assessment.[6]

It is not known whether Gott stood at the general election of 1661, but he sought to ingratiate himself with the monarchy by reporting treasonable words to the Privy Council in June. A few months later, however, he was defeated in a by-election at Rye by his 'noble friend', the Anglican John Robinson I*. He was omitted from the commission of the peace on the passing of the second Conventicles Act, and was buried at Battle on 18 Dec. 1671. A man of scholarly tastes, he was the author of several religious and philosophical works. His son Peter was defeated at Hastings in 1689, but became a director of the Bank of England, and sat for the port in three later Parliaments as a court Whig.[7]

[1] Did not sit after Pride's Purge, 6 Dec. 1648, readmitted 21 Feb. 1660. [2] Excluded. [3] *Vis. Suss.* (Harl. Soc. lxxxix), 54; *Her. and Gen.* viii. 191. [4] C181/7/29. [5] E. Straker, *Wealden Iron*, 268; *Fines of Manors* (Suss. Rec. Soc. xix), 29, 115, 178; (xx), 422; *Suss. Arch. Colls.* xcii. 151; D. Underdown, *Pride's Purge*, 56, 212; A. Fletcher, *County Communities in Peace and War*, 67. [6] Bowman diary, f. 83; *Old. Parl. Hist.* xxii. 442, 448; *CJ*, viii. 226. [7] *Suss. Arch. Colls.* v. 96; lii. 279; PC2/55/252; *HMC 13th Rep. IV*, 243; *CSP Dom.* 1663, p. 16; PCC 3 Eure; *The Library* (ser. 3), i. 225–38.

M.W.H./B.D.H.

GOUGH, Sir Henry (1649–1724), of Perry Hall, Staffs.

TAMWORTH	1685, 1689, 1690, 1695, 17 Mar. 1699, 1701 (Feb.)
LICHFIELD	1705

b. 3 Jan. 1649, 1st s. of John Gough of Oldfallings by 2nd w. Bridget, da. of Sir John Astley of Wood Eaton, Oxon.; bro. of Sir Richard Gough†. *educ.* Christ Church, Oxf. 1666; M. Temple 1667. *m.* 1668, Mary, da. of Sir Edward Littleton, 2nd Bt.*, of Pillaton, Hall, Staffs., 10s. 5da. *suc.* fa. 1665; kntd. 7 Apr. 1678.[1]

J.p. Staffs. 1671–Mar. 1688, Oct. 1688–96, 1700–d., sheriff 1671–2, commr. for assessment 1673–80, 1689–90, recusants 1675.

Gough's grandfather 'a great usurer' of Welsh extraction, laid the foundation of the family estates in Staffordshire. His father served under Prince Rupert in the siege of Lichfield but held no command, and the county committee appear to have accepted that he acted by *force majeure*.[2]

In 1685 Gough told Lord Weymouth (Thomas Thynne I*) that he was willing to spend up to £200 against the Whig John Swinfen* at Tamworth, and he was returned unopposed, the first of the family to sit. In James II's Parliament he was named only to the committee for expiring laws. He was appointed a governor of King Edward VI's grammar school, Birmingham, under the new charter. But to the questions on the repeal of the Test Act and Penal Laws he replied that he could not determine his actions in advance if he were to be elected to Parliament, and could not bind himself to support any particular candidate.[3]

Gough had acquired a good interest among the 'commonalty' at Tamworth, and was re-elected in 1689. An inactive Member of the Convention, he voted to agree with the Lords that the throne was not vacant, and was named to nine committees, of which the most important was for restoring corporations (2 May). After the recess he was added to the committee of elections and privileges, and probably brought in a petition to confirm the school charter, for he was the first Member appointed to the committee to consider it. He afterwards voted consistently with the Tories, refusing to sign the Association of 1696. He died on 24 Jan. 1724, and was buried at Bushbury. A younger son, Henry, sat for Bramber as a government supporter from 1734 to 1751.[4]

[1] Shaw, *Staffs.* ii. 179, 188. [2] Erdeswick, *Staffs.* 355; *Cal. Comm. Comp.* 2844. [3] Bath mss, Thynne pprs. 27, f. 80; *King Edward's Sch. Recs.* (Dugdale Soc. xii), 185–6. [4] Thynne pprs. 28, ff. 231–2; *CJ*, x. 311; *Staffs. Parl. Hist.* (Wm. Salt Arch. Soc.), ii. 162–3.

A.M.M.

GOULD, James I (1593–1676), of Dorchester, Dorset.

DORCHESTER 1659, 1661–Feb. 1676

bap. 21 July 1593, 2nd s. of John Gould (*d.*1630) of Dorchester by Joan, da. of John Benvenewe of Abbotsbury, wid. of John Roy of Weymouth. *m.* 28 Apr. 1624 (with £500) Margery, da. of George Savage of Bloxworth, 6s. 2da.[1]

Mayor, Dorchester 1637–8, senior alderman 1661–*d.*; commr. for assessment, Dorset 1652, 1661–9, sheriff 1655–6, commr. for recusants 1675.[2]

Gould's father, the younger son of a Devonshire county family, became a merchant in Dorchester, and Gould inherited the business. A prominent opponent of ship-money, in the Civil War and Interregnum he took a more cautious line than most of his kinsmen or fellow-tradesmen. He advanced £300 to Parliament in 1643, but claimed to have been ousted from the administration of a charitable trust 'for his loyalty' in the fateful month of January 1649.[3]

Gould first sat for Dorchester in Richard Cromwell's Parliament, but was narrowly defeated by John Whiteway* at the general election of 1660. With all his family he signed the loyal address from

Dorset presented to the King. He was successful in 1661, at the age of 67, but he was not an active Member of the Cavalier Parliament. He was named to 18 committees, including three concerned with the woollen industry in 1661–2, those considering bills to prevent the import of wool-cards, to regulate the Yorkshire cloth trade and to prohibit the export of raw wool. He probably supported the country party, but after the 1668 session his name disappears from the Journals. He was clearly by this time a man of great wealth; rumour put his income at £10,000 a year. In August 1675 he was dismissed as very aged and sick, and he was buried on 15 Feb. 1676 at Holy Trinity, Dorchester.[4]

[1] Vivian, *Vis. Devon*, 421; Eg. 784, f. 41v.; *N. and Q.* clxvi. 422–3. [2] Hutchins, *Dorset*, ii. 354; C. H. Mayo, *Dorchester Recs.* 715; *Cal. Treas. Bks.* iv. 695. [3] SP16/319/89; *CSP Dom.* 1638–9, p. 421; Mayo, *Dorset Standing Committee*, 245; *Dorchester Recs.* 627. [4] *Dorchester Recs.* 436, 718; *Address of Nobility and Gentry of Dorset*; *CSP Dom.* 1675–6, p. 263; Hutchins, ii. 387; R. Granville, *Hist. Granville Fam.* 354; Soc. of Genealogists, Holy Trinity reg.

J.P.F.

GOULD, James II (c.1625–1707), of Dorchester, Dorset.

DORCHESTER 28 Feb. 1677, 11 Nov. 1680, 1681, 1690

b. c.1625, 1st s. of James Gould I*. *m.* bef. 2 July 1678, Mary, da. and coh. of William Bond of South Bestwall, wid. of John Baskett of Dewlish, 1da. *suc.* fa. 1676.[1]

Alderman, Dorchester 1676, mayor 1677–8, 1696–7; commr. for assessment, Dorset 1677–80, 1689–90, sheriff 1687–8, j.p. May 1688–9, 1700–*d.*; freeman, Poole 1689.[2]

Commr. for drowned lands 1690.[3]

Gould signed the loyal address from Dorset at the Restoration, but otherwise little is known of him before his father's death, when he succeeded him, both as alderman and Member. In the by-election he was returned unopposed. His only committee was for the prevention of wool exports, but he was noted by Shaftesbury as 'worthy'. He stood down in favour of his cousin Nicholas Gould* in 1679, but was again returned for Dorchester when Sir Francis Holles* succeeded to the peerage, and re-elected in 1681. In both the second and third Exclusion Parliaments he was entirely inactive.[4]

Gould was proposed as court candidate at Poole in 1688, and may have been a Whig collaborator. He failed to win a seat in the Convention, but regained it in 1690. He was buried at St. Peter's, Dorchester, on 11 Aug. 1707, the last of the Dorset Goulds to sit in Parliament. His daughter and heir married first Charles Churchill[†] and then the 2nd Earl of Abingdon (Montagu Venables-Bertie*).[5]

[1] Hutchins, *Dorset*, i. 602. [2] C. H. Mayo, *Dorchester Recs.* 718;

Hutchins, ii. 354; Poole archives B17. [3] *Cal. Treas. Bks.* ix. 794. [4] *Address of Nobility and Gentry of Dorset*; *CSP Dom.* 1676–7, p. 575. [5] Hutchins, ii. 387; iii. 483.

J.P.F.

GOULD, Nicholas (1635–91), of Lime Street, London and Upwey, Dorset.

DORCHESTER   1679 (Mar.), 1679 (Oct.)

WEYMOUTH AND

MELCOMBE REGIS   1690–28 Apr. 1691 [new writ]

b. 16 Mar. 1635, 3rd s. of John Gould (*d.*1644) of Upwey by Sarah, da. of William Every of Cothays, Som. *m.* 9 Jan. 1677, Elizabeth, da. of Benjamin Bale of Seaborough, Som., 2s. (1 *d.v.p.*) 3da.[1]

Commr. for assessment, Dorset 1679–80, 1690; mayor, Dorchester 1680–1; j.p. Dorset June 1688–9.[2]

Gould's father, the elder brother of James Gould I*, was probably the 'Captain Gold' of the Dorset militia who tried to rally his men against the Cavaliers in 1642. Gould himself became a London merchant, though he signed the loyal address from Dorset at the Restoration. He acquired a small property in Upwey, four miles from Dorchester, in 1678, and in the following year succeeded his cousin James Gould II* in the representation of the borough. Marked 'honest' on Shaftesbury's list, he was moderately active in the first Exclusion Parliament, though none of his six committees was of much political importance. He helped to consider measures to assist the cloth trade and reform the Post Office, and to investigate complaints against the customs. He voted for the first exclusion bill. In the succeeding Parliament he was totally inactive, perhaps because of his mayoral duties in Dorchester, and in 1681 he was returning officer for the borough. He was described as a dissenter in 1688, when James II's electoral agents accepted him as court candidate for Dorchester; but he failed to find a seat in the Convention. He was elected at Weymouth in 1690, but died in the following year. His sons died young, and the property (valued at a mere £1,200) eventually passed to his nephew and son-in-law, John Gould, who bought out Paul Methuen†, husband of the other coheir.[3]

[1] Hutchins, *Dorset*, ii. 842; *Dorset Nat. Hist. and Antiq. Soc. Proc.* liii. 130, 142. [2] Hutchins, ii. 354. [3] *HMC Hatfield*, xxii. 354; A. R. Bayley, *Civil War in Dorset*, 49; *Dorset Soc. Proc.* liii. 115, 130, 137, 142.

J.P.F.

GOULD, William (1640–71), of Downes, Crediton, Devon.

DARTMOUTH   22 Dec. 1670–24 Oct. 1671

b. 31 Mar. 1640, o. surv. s. of William Gould of Floyer's Hayes, Exeter by Anne, da. of John Browne† of Frampton, Dorset. *educ.* Wadham, Oxf. 1656; I. Temple 1657. *m.* Agnes, da. of Edmund Powell of Sandford-on-Thames, Oxon, 3s. (2 *d.v.p.*) 4da. *suc.* fa. 1644.[1]

J.p. Devon 1669–70.

Gould represented the senior male line of a crusader who was granted an estate in Somerset for his valour at the siege of Damietta in 1217. His father was a Parliamentarian in the Civil War; he sat on the county committee and for a time commanded the Plymouth garrison. Orphaned at the age of four, Gould was no doubt brought up by his maternal grandfather, a Rumper and an Independent, who complained in his will of his grandson's lack of respect.[2]

Gould was removed from the commission of the peace in May 1670 after only a year in office, presumably because of his opposition to the second Conventicles Act. But this did not prevent his election for Dartmouth seven months later on the interest of his first cousin John Upton*. During his one session in the Cavalier Parliament he was an inactive committeeman, being named only to the committee of elections and privileges and to the committee for the encouragement of fishing. But he made no less than four interventions in the supply committee, and gave proof of his interest in economic affairs. On 16 Jan. 1671 he opposed the suggested tax on interest:

> Whatever money is owing to the tradesmen, or any other man, is so much the less in his estate; so you will subject the business to uncertainty, and put persons to remove their money into other countries.

Sir Edward Dering* wrote on 20 Jan. that 'Mr Gould of Devonshire made a long and studied speech . . . dilating much upon the nature of manufactures, the advance of human industry, and the inconvenience of scanting men's shops'. Three days later he made 'a narrative of the business of the Mendip Hills' in opposition to a proposal for a tax on minings. With regard to the revenue from minerals, he said:

> It is affirmed that three-fourths is the labour of the men, and but one-fourth a fund for you. If a real profit, that's a rent; but if you will tax the mine barely, you must direct your commissioners how to do it.

Although Gould's attitude could not fairly be called obstructive (he expressed a preference for the poll tax), it is unlikely to have been relished by his fellow-Devonians Edward Seymour* and (Sir) Thomas Clifford*, who were in charge of the government programme on supply, and he must have attracted some notice as a useful, though prolix, opposition speaker. He died on 24 Oct. 1671, before the next session opened, and his branch of the Gould family became extinct in the male line in

1726 without further parliamentary representation.[3]

[1] Vivian, *Vis. Devon*, 422. [2] Vivian, 418–23; PCC 266 Pell. [3] Grey, i. 350, 367; *Dering*, 56–57.

J.P.F.

GOULSTON (GULSTON), Sir William (c.1641–87), of Whitechapel, Mdx. and Fairfield, Kent.

BLETCHINGLEY 1681
NEW ROMNEY 1685

b. c.1641, 2nd s. of Richard Goulston[†] of Wyddial, Herts. by Alice, da. of William Meggs, Draper, of Whitechapel. *m.* 24 Nov. 1674, Frideswide, da. of Robert Morris, yeoman, of Abingdon, Berks., 3s. 2da. Kntd. 8 Mar. 1680.[1]

Member, R. Africa Co. 1672, E.I. Co. 1675, committee 1684–5; commr. for assessment, Herts. 1679–80; j.p. Mdx. 1679–87; lt.-col. orange regt. of militia ft. London 1680–1; member, Hon. Artillery Co. 1681; jurat, New Romney 1685–*d.*[2].

Goulston's grandfather, of Leicestershire origin, became a protonotary of the court of common pleas and bought the Hertfordshire estate of Wyddial in 1628. His father, though apparently neutral in the Civil War, sat for Hertfordshire in Richard Cromwell's Parliament. Goulston, taking after his mother's family, became a London merchant and by 1671 was engaged in foreign trade. His association with the Africa and East India Companies must have been profitable; in the seventies he was trading briskly in the stock of the latter company. He owned property in Whitechapel, and his wife brought him the Norfolk manor of East Bradenham. He was one of the Middlesex grand jury that found a true bill against Lord Arundell of Wardour in the Popish Plot. Through his marriage to the niece of John Morris*, he became intimately connected with his senior partner, Sir Robert Clayton*, serving as his lieutenant-colonel in the London train-bands, and it was doubtless Clayton who secured his return for Bletchingley in 1681. He was named only to the committee of elections and privileges in the short Oxford Parliament. In April he lost his militia commission. Although empanelled as a juryman for the Fitzharris trial, he failed to appear. In July 1683 he was regarded as 'dangerous' by (Sir) Adam Browne*, whose son Ambrose had his eye on the constituency, though Goulston's connexion with so prominent a Whig as Clayton gave some grounds for distrust. But he can never have been seriously under suspicion, for he was not removed from the commission of the peace.[3]

Goulston inherited an interest at New Romney from his uncle Edward, who married a local heiress, and he leased the manor of Fairfield, 12 miles away,

from the Canterbury chapter. On 24 Mar. 1685 Sir Benjamin Bathurst* described him to the corporation as his very good friend. 'I know he hath a good interest in and near your town', he wrote, adding that if he were elected the King would be pleased. Fortified by this recommendation, the electors not only returned him to Parliament but chose him as one of the supporters of the canopy at the coronation. An active Member of James II's Parliament, he was named to 12 committees, including those appointed to inspect the accounts of the disbandment commissioners and to bring in the bill for the general naturalization of foreign Protestants. In August he was appointed a jurat of New Romney under the new charter, but he was removed from the Middlesex bench by order of the Privy Council early in 1687. He died later in the year, aged 46, and was buried at Wyddial on 23 Dec. 1687. In his will he was able to leave to each of his daughters a portion of £5,000, and his executors still held £5,500 East India stock at the Revolution. His cousin Edward sat for New Romney in William III's last Parliament as a Tory.[4]

[1] J. Cussans, *Herts. Edwinstree*, 121; *Le Neve's Knights* (Harl. Soc. viii), 335; *Misc. Gen. et Her.* n.s. i. 212–13. [2] *Sel. Charters* (Selden Soc. xxviii), 188; *Cal. Ct. Mins. E.I. Co.* ed. Sainsbury, x. 255; Guildhall Broadsheets, A9/1/9; Luttrell, i. 75; *Ancient Vellum Bk.* ed. Raikes, 110. [3] Blomefield, *Norf.* vi. 136; *HMC Lords*, i. 28; *State Trials*, viii. 333; *CSP Dom.* July–Sept. 1683, p. 172. [4] Hasted, *Kent*, viii. 380; PCC 176 Mico; *VCH Surr.* iv. 258; Kent AO, NR/ AEp, f. 52; *Arch. Cant.* xiii. 476; Cussans, 121; *Suss. Arch. Colls.* xv. 193; Luttrell, i. 75; Stowe 796, f. 196; PCC 4 Exton; Add. 22185, f. 14.

B.D.H.

GOUNTER (GUNTER), George (c.1646–1718), of Racton, Suss.

CHICHESTER 1685

b. c.1646, 2nd s. of George Gounter of Racton by Katherine, da. of Sir Lawrence Hyde[†] of Salisbury, Wilts. *educ.* Winchester 1656; New Coll. Oxf. matric. 15 Aug. 1665, aged 18. *m.* (1) 28 May 1695, Elizabeth (*d.* 3 Nov. 1700) da. of William Sherrington of East Hoe, Soberton, Hants, *s.p.*; (2) Judith, da. of Richard Nicoll of Norbiton Place, Kingston-on-Thames, Surr., 2s. (1 *d.v.p.*) 2da. *suc.* bro. by 1677.[1]

Fellow of New Coll. 1667–73; commr. for assessment, Suss. 1677–80, 1689–90, j.p. 1683–July 1688, Nov. 1688–?89; common councilman, Chichester 1685–Feb. 1688.[2]

Gounter's ancestors had been assessed for taxation in Racton as long ago as 1327, and held land there by 1428. Their only previous parliamentary experience was when Giles Gunter sat for Arundel in 1442. Gounter's father was already seriously indebted before the Civil War. He was appointed a commissioner of array and became a colonel of horse in the royalist army, compounding on the

Truro Articles at £580. He procured the ship in which Charles II escaped to France in 1651. He was assessed at a mere £100 p.a. by the decimators, and died shortly before the Restoration leaving a large family. Gounter obtained a royal recommendation for a scholarship to New College at the request of his uncle, the lord chief justice, and in 1669 his mother was granted a pension of £200 p.a. for 21 years. He doubtless opposed exclusion, since he was added to the commission of the peace in 1683, and was elected to James II's Parliament for Chichester, six miles from Racton. Later in the same month he was nominated to the corporation under the new charter. A moderately active Member, he was appointed to the committees on the bills for the rebuilding of St. Paul's, prohibiting the import of tallow candles, encouraging shipbuilding and establishing a land registry. He was probably a government supporter, since on 14 Dec. 1685 a payment of £150 was authorized in respect of the arrears of his mother's pension; but in 1688 he returned the following elaborate answers to the lord lieutenant's questions on the Test Act and Penal Laws:

> The bent of my inclination is to serve his Majesty in all things; but I must beg the freedom of suspending my opinion of what I shall or shall not do, supposing I should be a Member of Parliament, inasmuch as my yea and nay there would certainly follow the conviction of the present debate had then upon my judgment and conscience. . . . I shall always endeavour to choose such Members to serve in Parliament as I shall judge to be most likely to do the King and kingdom best service.

He was removed from office, and probably never stood again. He died in 1718. His son, who added the name of Nicoll to his own, sat for Peterborough as a government supporter from 1729 to his death four years later.[3]

[1] *Suss. N. and Q.* iii. 207; *VCH Hants*, iii. 264; *Wilts. N. and Q.* vi. 437. [2] A. Hay, *Hist. Chichester*, 589. [3] *VCH Suss.* iv. 115; *Cal. Comm. Comp.* 1237–8; Clarendon, *Rebellion*, v. 211; *Thurloe*, iv. 240; *CSP Dom.* 1661–2, p. 624; 1663–4, p. 407; 1668–9, p. 317; *Cal. Treas. Bks.* viii. 488.

B.M.C.

GOWEN see GEWEN

GOWER, Sir Thomas, 2nd Bt. (c.1605–72), of Stittenham, Sheriff Hutton, Yorks.

MALTON   18 Dec. 1661–3 Sept. 1672

b. c.1605, 1st s. of Sir Thomas Gower, 1st Bt., of Stittenham by Anne, da. and coh. of John Doyley[†] of Merton, Oxon. *educ.* Wadham, Oxf. matric. 7 Nov. 1617, aged 12; G. Inn 1621. *m.* (1) Elizabeth, da. of Sir William Howard of Naworth Castle, Cumb., *s.p.*; (2) settlement 29 Sept. 1631 (with £3,000), Frances, da. and coh. of Sir John Leveson[†] of Lilleshall, Staffs., 2s. (1 *d.v.p.*) 1da. Kntd. 24 June 1630; *suc.* fa. 20 Oct. 1651.[1]

Sheriff, Yorks. 1641–2, 1662–3, commr. of array 1642; j.p. (N. Riding) July 1660–*d.*, co. Dur. 1662–*d.*; commr. for assessment (N. Riding) Aug. 1660–9, oyer and terminer, Northern circuit 1661, corporations, Yorks. 1662–3, loyal and indigent officers 1662; dep. lt. (N. Riding) 1662–6; receiver of taxes, Yorks. by 1663–7; gov. York 1663–*d.*; steward, honour of Penrith 1670–2.[2]

Col. of dgns. ?1642–5.
Commr. for trade with Scotland 1668.[3]

Gower's ancestors were seated at Stittenham in the 12th century, and first sat for the county in 1338. Although his father was in trouble for insulting the council in the north in 1632, he was fined £200 for taking refuge in the Newark garrison, and the whole family was royalist in the Civil War. Gower himself diligently executed the orders of Parliament in the early months of 1642; but he was appointed to the commission of array, and advanced £1,200 to the King in August. He raised a regiment of dragoons, and was taken prisoner at Rowton Heath in 1645. (Sir) Thomas Fairfax* (3rd Lord Fairfax) testified that he had been plundered by the northern Cavaliers, and that his 'moderation towards the Parliament and their friends begot him a long imprisonment by the King'. He compounded for £730 on the Oxford articles. Fairfax was one of the trustees of Gower's marriage settlement, and Gower assisted him to raise the county against Lambert in 1659.[4]

Gower was defeated by Thomas Danby* at Malton, seven miles from Stittenham, in the general election of 1661, but he was awarded the seat on petition, though not until the eve of the Christmas recess. Listed as a friend by Lord Wharton, and initially a country Cavalier, he became a very active Member of the Cavalier Parliament. He was appointed to 389 committees, in six of which he took the chair, acted as teller in 11 divisions, carried nine bills or messages, and made 16 recorded speeches. Even during the remainder of the first session he made his mark. He carried up the bill to make void the conveyances unduly procured from Lady Powell and was named to the committee on the bill reversing Strafford's attainder. On 1 Mar. 1662 he took over temporarily from Robert Milward* as chairman of the committee of elections and privileges. Ten days later he was teller for extending the duty on Tyneside coal to exports from Sunderland. On 16 Apr. he was teller in a division on the uniformity bill, and was named to a small committee to check the text of the revised Prayer Book. He favoured giving ministers until Michaelmas to conform, and helped to prepare reasons for a conference. He was appointed to the committee for the additional corporations bill, which was left in his hands during the recess, and helped to present an address asking the King to hear the rival claimants to the Lindsey level. He was pricked for a second term as sheriff of Yorkshire in November, but given leave to attend the 1663 session, having assured the Government that 'there can be no dangerous design on foot in the county'. He was among those appointed to bring in a bill to prevent the growth of Popery, to hear a petition from the loyal and indigent officers, to consider the staple bill, and to provide remedies for meetings of sectaries. A member of the committee on the bill to make the lessee prove the lives in being, he opposed the motion of 23 Mar. to recommit it. He took over the chair of the committee on the long and complicated bill for draining the Bedford level, which had already proved too much for Henry North* and (Sir) George Reeve*, and, despite the insertion of two more provisos at the report stage, steered it to completion. He acted as teller on 23 July in a House reduced to under 50 against agreeing with the Lords on an amendment to the excise bill.[5]

The unrest in Yorkshire came to a head towards the end of Gower's shrievalty, and he had 'a hard part between those who believe nothing and those who believe too much'. His chief informer, Major Greathead, was exposed in September by an indiscretion in the office of Sir Henry Bennet*; but by this time the whole conspiratorial organization had been deeply penetrated, and Gower knew all the leaders and even the date of the rising. His chief problem was the unreliability of the militia, but on 10 Oct. he was able to report that 'almost all the heads of the fanatics are privately seized'. The failure of the plot has been ascribed 'to the unwearied watchfulness and to the excellent system of espionage instituted by Gower'. He attended the next session primarily in order to present a petition from his constituency, which has not been traced. He was listed as a court dependant, and added to the committee on the bill for the abolition of the legal charges known as 'damage clere', opposing a successful amendment on third reading. He was again among those ordered to consider an additional corporations bill, and helped to manage the conference of 13 May 1664 on the conventicles bill. In the next session he served on the committee for the bill for the repair and maintenance of Bridlington pier, and acted as teller for the motion for engrossment, which was heavily defeated. Together with Sir Jordan Crosland* he tendered unsuccessfully for the Yorkshire excise farm in 1665; but he succeeded in extracting from the hard-pressed Treasury

£2,250 owed to him by the crown. In the Oxford session he was probably appointed to the committee for the five mile bill, as well as to those for the prohibition of cattle imports and the attainder of English officers in the service of the enemy. He reported the bill for naturalizing Bennet's wife on 24 Oct. 1666, and helped to prepare reasons for prohibiting French imports and for desiring the cancellation of the Canary Company patent. As chairman of the committee of grievances he upheld the complaint against Lord Mordaunt and was named to the committees to draw up and manage his impeachment. On 29 Dec. he was sent to the Lords to desire a conference, which he helped to manage. His nomination to the abortive parliamentary accounts commission was approved by the House, and he was a manager of the conference on the bill of 24 Jan. 1667. He also helped to manage conferences on the bill to increase the amount of coinage and the plague bill. He was one of the Members to whom was committed the petition of the English merchants trading to France, and helped to present a joint address from both Houses on their behalf.[6]

Gower probably welcomed the fall of Clarendon, being among those appointed to bring in a public accounts bill, and to inquire into the miscarriages of the war, the sale of Dunkirk, and the further charges against Mordaunt. He spoke twice in the debates on Clarendon, helping to manage two conferences and to prepare for another, and served on the committee for the banishment bill. He took the chair for the estate bills promoted by his neighbour William Palmes* and the 3rd Earl of Clare (Gilbert Holles*). On 7 Dec. 1667 he carried up Palmes's bill together with a bill empowering the bishop of Durham to lease out the leadmines on his estate, and a message reminding the Lords of a bill to prevent abuses in removing cases from inferior courts by writ of *certiorari*. As chairman of the inquiry into the restraints on jurors he began an account of the misdeeds of (Sir) John Kelyng* on 9 Dec.; but 'the time of day being far spent, and the rest of the report being long', the House adjourned, and it was completed by Thomas Crouch* two days later, though Gower remained deeply concerned with the subject. He was sent to ask the Lords to continue sitting in the afternoon of 18 Dec. to facilitate the passage of the accounts bill, and he was among the Members ordered to examine the accounts of the loyal and indigent officers fund during the Christmas recess. When Parliament resumed, Gower was the first of those sent to the lord chief baron (Matthew Hale*) to inquire what had been done to ease sheriffs of their charges at the Exchequer. He was named to the committees on the bills to prevent the fining or imprisonment of jurors and to prolong the Conventicles Act, and took the chair for two more private bills. He 'justified' the bill to sever the entail on the estate of his colleague (Sir) Thomas Hebblethwaite* during the second reading debate, reported it on 13 Mar. 1668, and carried it to the Lords three days later. On 3 Apr. he was ordered to bring in a bill about the miscarriages of the judges in general. He opposed a bill to settle the Leveson estate, 'pretending that his son and Sir Richard Temple* had a right to that estate and inheritance', and the committee was ordered to have regard for their interests. On 28 Apr. he reported that it was possible, in the opinion of his committee, to relieve Brome Whorwood* of paying alimony by a private bill without breach of the Judicial Proceedings Confirmation Act of the Convention.[7]

Gower took little part in the next session, though he was among those appointed on 8 Dec. 1669 to consider a bill to prevent exorbitances and abuses in parliamentary elections. Although he was considered a friend by Ormonde, Sir Thomas Osborne* included him among the Members to be brought over to the Court by the Duke of Buckingham. On 26 Feb. 1670 he was ordered to bring in a bill to extend habeas corpus by forbidding the transportation of English prisoners overseas, and he served on the committee to consider it. He was again named to the committee for the conventicles bill, and given leave to revive the *certiorari* bill; but it never reached the floor of the House, probably because he had to concentrate on the bill for regulating juries, in which he took the chair. The bill was twice recommitted after debate, but on 26 Mar. he was able to carry it up. Gower, who had served on the commission to consider the balance of trade with Scotland, was the first Member named to the committee on the bill nominating commissioners to treat for union. He helped to prepare reasons for a conference on the juries bill in the autumn, and to manage the conference of 6 Feb. 1671 about the assault on Sir John Coventry*, when he argued: 'If a penalty for wearing a sword, should there not be a punishment for using it badly?' His last important committee was to inquire into the causes of the growth of Popery. He died on 3 Sept. 1672, and was buried at Sheriff Hutton. His younger son William, who had taken the name of Leveson Gower on inheriting the Trentham estate, failed to succeed him at Malton, but was returned for Newcastle-under-Lyme in 1675.[8]

[1] Collins, *Peerage*, ii. 445–6; *Royalist Comp. Pprs.* (Yorks. Arch. Soc. rec. ser. xviii), 129; *Yorks. Arch. Jnl.* xxvii. 153. [2] *HMC 8th Rep.* pt. 1 (1881), 275; *Cal. Treas. Bks.* i. 566; ii. 52; iii. 545; *CSP Dom.* 1663–4, p. 332; 1665–6, p. 397; 1672, p. 594. [3] *Bulstrode*

Pprs. 17. [4] *VCH N. Riding*, ii. 183; J. T. Cliffe, *Yorks. Gentry*, 301–2, 330, 334–5; *CSP Dom.* 1641–3, p. 365; 1665–6, p. 49; information from Brig. Peter Young; *Cal. Comm. Comp.* 1042–3; *Royalist Comp. Pprs.* 128–30. [5] *CJ*, viii. 336, 354, 409, 444, 506; *CSP Dom.* 1663–4, pp. 26, 43. [6] *CSP Dom.* 1663–4, pp. 225, 279, 293, 481; 1665–6, pp. 49, 80; *Trans. R. Hist. Soc.* (ser. 3), xi. 135–9; *Yorks. Arch. Jnl.* xxxi. 351–6; *CJ*, viii. 554, 606, 661, 664, 669, 674, 681, 685; Browning, *Danby*, ii. 30. [7] Grey, i. 21; *CJ*, ix. 21, 26, 35, 39; *Clarendon Impeachment*, 136; *LJ*, xii. 160, 174, 206; *Milward*, 204, 243, 246, 263. [8] *CJ*, ix. 130, 137, 140, 146; Grey, i. 383.

P.A.B./P.W.

GRAHAM, Richard (d.1691), of Clifford's Inn, London.

NEW WINDSOR 1685

m. by 1663, Elizabeth (*bur.* 4 Dec. 1669), 2s. (1 *d.v.p.*) 2da.[1]
  Principal, Clifford's Inn 1677–*d.*; commr. for encroachments, Tower liberties 1686, perambulation, New Forest 1686.[2]
  Gent. of the privy chamber 1682–5; commr. of excise and hearth-tax 1684–9; asst. solicitor to the Treasury 1685–9.[3]

Graham was described by Lord Preston (Sir Richard Grahme*) as his cousin, but his pedigree and education are alike obscure. In 1663 he had chambers in Clifford's Inn and was living in Fetter Lane. He acted as solicitor to the Earl of Burlington, whose son-in-law, Laurence Hyde*, is credited with bringing him to the notice of the Duke of York. He acted for the crown at the trial of Stephen College, the Protestant joiner, and helped to draw up the case against Shaftesbury. He and Philip Burton, whom he succeeded as assistant solicitor to the Treasury, were said by Burnet to be 'fitter men to have served in a court of inquisition than in a legal government'.[4]

Graham's career reached its peak in the next reign. His close connexion with the King by virtue of his office earned him a bad reputation. Luttrell calls him 'the famous Mr Graham, the tool in King James's time'; but Roger North* declared that he was well suited to the post of crown solicitor, except for 'a little north-country flattery and desire to oblige all that he could . . . and if he went too far in anything, it was not out of bad principle, but obedience and complaisance'. On royal recommendation, Graham was elected for Windsor in 1685. He was probably moderately active in James II's Parliament, being appointed by full name to the committees for prohibiting the import of gunpowder and for estimating the yield of a tax on new buildings, and he may have served on three others where he cannot be distinguished from James Grahme*. In 1686 he was granted a pension of £250 p.a. out of the Post Office. Sunderland recommended him for re-election as court candidate in

1688. At the Revolution he attempted to escape overseas with Burton and Sir Thomas Jenner*, but was captured and thrown into the Tower. He was released on bail by the King's bench on 25 Oct. 1689, but immediately ordered into custody by the Commons. Among other charges he and Burton, whom Burnet calls 'the wicked solicitors in the former reigns', were said to have

> practised packing and embracery of juries, as in the cases of the late Lord Russell [Hon. William Russell*], Algernon Sidney† esq. and others; and that they had divided amongst the juries of Middlesex in criminal cases, contrary to the law, several sums of money, and given them great entertainments. . . . By their malicious indictments, informations and prosecutions of quo warrantos, [they had] openly endeavoured the subversion of the Protestant religion and the government of this realm.

He was released on the prorogation of Parliament, but excepted from the Act of Indemnity. 'He never joyed after, and languished in his mind' till his death on 8 Dec. 1691. He was buried at St. Dunstan in the West.[5]

[1] Guildhall RO, St. Dunstan in the West par. reg.; PCC 227 Vere. [2] Cal. I. T. Recs. iii. 114; Cal. Treas. Bks. viii. 533, 995. [3] Carlisle, Privy Chamber, 195; Cal. Treas. Bks. vii. 1316–17; viii. 173–4; CSP Dom. 1685, p. 102; Luttrell, i. 450. [4] HMC 7th Rep. 308; CSP Ire. 1663–5, pp. 166, 398; North, Lives, iii. 126; Cal. Treas. Bks. vii. 13; CSP Dom. 1680–1, pp. 387, 401, 442, 506; Burnet, iii. 293. [5] Luttrell, i. 493, 595–6; ii. 311; North, iii. 126–7; Cal. Treas. Bks. viii. 948–9; CSP Dom. 1687–9, p. 276; 1689–90, p. 76; Burnet, iv. 26; CJ, x. 274; HMC Hastings, ii. 335; St. Dunstan in the West par. reg.

L.N./G.J.

GRAHAM see also GRAHME, James and Sir Richard, 3rd Bt.

GRAHME (GRAHAM), James (1650–1730), of Bagshot, Surr. and Levens, Westmld.[1]

CARLISLE	1685
APPLEBY	1702, 1705
WESTMORLAND	1708, 1710, 1713, 1715, 1722

b. Mar. 1650, 2nd s. of Sir George Grahme, 2nd Bt., of Netherby, Cumb. by Lady Mary Johnston, da. of James, 1st Earl of Hartfell [S]; bro. of Sir Richard Grahme*. educ. Westminster; Christ Church, Oxf. 1666; I. Temple, entered 1666. m. (1) lic. 23 Nov. 1675, Dorothy (d.1700), da. of the Hon. William Howard of Rivensby, Lincs., 3s. d.v.p. 2da.; (2) lic. 4 Mar. 1702, Elizabeth (d.1709), da. of Isaac Barton, merchant, of London, wid. of George Bromley of the Middle Temple, s.p.

Capt. Douglas's Ft. (French army) 1671–3, R. English regt. 1673–4; capt. of ft. to the 1st Earl of Carlisle (Charles Howard*) Mar.–Nov. 1673, Admiralty Regt. Jan.–Oct. 1675, Coldstream Gds. 1675–8; lt.-col. of ft. to Lord Morpeth (Edward Howard*) 1678–9.

Commr. for assessment, Westminster 1677–9; freeman, Portsmouth 1678, Edinburgh 1679, Stirling and Linlithgow 1681; keeper of Pirbright Walk, Windsor Forest 1680–2, Bagshot Park 1682–9; dep. lt. Windsor Castle and Forest 1685–9; freeman, New Windsor 1685, alderman 1685–Oct. 1688, mayor 1686–7; j.p. Westmld. by 1701–d.; mayor, Appleby 1717–18; dep. lt. Westmld. by 1722–d.[2]

Keeper of the privy purse to the Duchess of York c.1677, to the Duke of York by 1679, (as King) 1685–Dec. 1688; master of the buckhounds 1685–9.

Grahme was first commissioned in one of the Scottish regiments in the French service and fought in the Netherlands under Turenne and Monmouth. He fell in love with a granddaughter of the 1st Earl of Berkshire, and married her despite family opposition and 'great inequalities'. Although one of the notorious maids of honour at the Restoration Court, she became 'an excellent housewife [and] a prudent and virtuous lady', and it was no doubt through her that Grahme attained a post in the household of the Duke of York. He was sent to France in 1682 with Lord Feversham on a mission of compliment to Louis XIV, who presented him with his portrait set in diamonds.[3]

At the outset of the new reign Grahme was appointed privy purse and master of the buckhounds in succession to Baptist May* and John Carey* and was elected for Carlisle, where his elder brother, Lord Preston, had been nominated recorder under the new charter. He does not appear to have used his rank after leaving the army, and hence there is the possibility of confusion between his record in James II's Parliament and that of Richard Graham*. He was probably moderately active, however. He may have served on the committee of elections and privileges, helped to consider the bill to provide carriages for the navy and ordnance, and acted as teller against the bill for the general naturalization of Huguenot refugees. He fortified his interest at Carlisle by presenting the corporation with a mace, and bought Levens for £24,200. The famous topiary gardens there were laid out by Beaumont, the royal gardener.[4]

Grahme was approved as court candidate at Carlisle in 1688, but was rejected 'with great contempt' by the corporation. He accompanied James on his flight to Rochester and lent him 6,000 ducats on the security of his shares in the East India and Royal Africa Companies. In the following spring Grahme and his brother were sent to the Tower on suspicion of treason. Though he submitted to the new regime in 1690, ostensibly for patriotic reasons, and gave information to Secretary Nottingham (Daniel Finch*) about Jacobite activities, he was implicated in Preston's confession in the following year. He was obliged to give up the shares he had acquired from James, and received a royal pardon in February 1692. He returned to the Commons under Queen Anne, representing first Appleby and then Westmorland. After some years' wavering he went over to the Whigs in 1722. He died on 26 Jan. 1730 and was buried with his first wife at Charlton (Wiltshire), where his epitaph described him as a faithful servant both to King Charles and King James II. His heir was his daughter, who married her cousin, the 4th Earl of Berkshire.[5]

[1] Except where otherwise stated this biography is based on J. Bagot, *Col. James Grahme of Levens*. [2] R. East, *Portsmouth Recs.* 363; *First Hall Bk.* (Windsor Hist. Recs. i), 51, 169. [3] *HMC 7th Rep.* 347, 350; *Evelyn Diary*, iv. 69, 467–8. [4] R. Morrice, *Entering Bk.* 1, p. 456; *CJ*, ix. 738; *HMC Lords*, n.s. i. 365. [5] *CSP Dom.* 1687–9, p. 273; *HMC Lonsdale*, 98; *HMC Finch*, ii. 360, 391–2; iii. 149, 355; Luttrell, ii. 356.

E.C.

GRAHME, Ranald (c.1605–85), of Petty France, Westminster and Nunnington, Wath, Yorks.

LEOMINSTER   1661

b. c.1605, 3rd s. of Fergus Grahme *alias* Plumpe of Plomp, Kirkandrews Nether, Cumb. by Sybil, da. of William Bell of Blackyett House, Kirtlebridge, Dumfries. *m.* Susanna, da. of Sir William Washington of Packington, Leics., *s.p.*[1]

Member, Merchant Taylors' Co. 1629; commr. for assessment, Westminster Aug. 1660–80, Yorks. (N. Riding) 1661–80, Herefs. 1661–3, 1664–74, sewers, Westminster Aug. 1660, loyal and indigent officers, London and Westminster 1662, highways and sewers 1662; j.p. Yorks. (N. Riding) 1662–*d.*[2]

Servant of Charles I; commr. for Duke of Richmond's estate 1662.[3]

Grahme, a younger brother of the first baronet, was apprenticed to a London merchant in 1622, and became a woollen draper in Watling Street. He was listed as one of the wealthiest inhabitants of Cordwainer ward in 1640, the year in which he purchased the manor of Lewisham. Though a servant of Charles I, he seems to have avoided involvement in the Civil War. He fined for alderman in 1651, and in the following year was excused from serving as master of his company. He bought Nunnington for £9,500 in 1655, and his income was estimated at £1,000 p.a. As early as 1657 he was trying to persuade Thomas Fairfax*, 3rd Lord Fairfax, to declare for the King.[4]

Grahme married the sister of Col. Henry Washington, the royalist governor of Worcester, whose widow married Samuel Sandys I*. Together with his nephew George Legge* and Sir John Pakington, 2nd Bt.*, Grahme acted as trustee for Washington's four daughters. He owed his election at Leominster in 1661 to the Buckingham interest. He was not an active Member of the Cavalier Parliament, being appointed to only 47 committees, none of which was

of the first importance. He joined the other Herefordshire Members in petitioning for a post in the excise for Fitzwilliam Coningsby†, his defeated opponent in 1661, but he was so little known in the county that in 1670 a by-election campaign got well under way in the belief that he was dead. About this time he was noted by Sir Thomas Osborne* as one of those to be engaged for the Court by Buckingham. His name appeared on the Paston list and on the working lists, but his support, doubly useful owing to his 'command' over his heir presumptive, Sir Richard Grahme*, was considered doubtful; he was 'to be fixed' either through George Legge or Osborne himself, now Lord Treasurer Danby. But presumably he remained loyal to Buckingham in opposition, for in 1676 Sir Richard Wiseman* wrote:

> Mr Ranald Grahme went very ill, contrary to expectations, and I hear he does not repent of it. If I had got but half so much money as he hath done, and many others, by the crown, I would not have done as he and they do, many of them.

About this time he and his fellow-trustees had a grant of Ashdown forest, which they sold for £1,700 to Sir Thomas Williams* on behalf of the Washington family. In 1677, Shaftesbury, temporarily estranged from Buckingham owing to the latter's desertion of him in the Tower, noted Grahme as 'doubly vile'. Grahme's name is absent from the Journals in 1678, except when he obtained leave to go out of the House after Oates's examination on 28 Nov. He probably did not stand again, though he survived into the reign of James II, his name appearing on the commission of the peace for the North Riding. But he died soon after, his will being proved on 2 Dec. 1685. He had already made over Lewisham to Legge, but Nunnington went to Sir Richard Grahme, and there were extensive family and charitable bequests, totalling over £2,300.[5]

[1] Nicolson and Burn, *Westmld. and Cumb.* ii. 467. [2] Merchant Taylors Co. Ct. Bk. 12 Oct. 1629; C181/7/38; *N. Riding Recs.* vi. 97, 156; *Tudor and Stuart Proclamations* ed. Steele, i. 405. [3] Add. 21947, f. 7. [4] *CSP Dom.* 1638–9, p. 454; H. F. Waters, *Gen. Gleanings in Eng.*, 558; *Misc. Gen. et Her.* (ser 2), ii. 88; L. L. Duncan, *Hist. Lewisham*, 53; *VCH Yorks. N. Riding*, i. 546; *Thurloe*, vi. 706. [5] *Cal. Treas. Bks.* i. 329–30; BL Loan 29/79, Thomas Harley to Sir Edward Harley, 5 Dec. 1670; *CSP Dom.* 1675–6, p. 261; K. H. D. Haley, *Shaftesbury*, 431; PCC 150 Cann.

E.R.

GRAHME (GRAHAM), Sir Richard, 3rd Bt. (1648–95), of Netherby, Cumb.

COCKERMOUTH   8 June 1675, 1679 (Mar.), 1679 (Oct.), 1681

CUMBERLAND   1685

b. 24 Sept. 1648, 1st s. of Sir George Grahme, 2nd Bt., of Netherby, and bro. of James Grahme*. *educ.* Westminster 1660; Christ Church, Oxf. 1664; I. Temple, entered 1664. *m.* 2 Aug. 1670, Lady Anne Howard, da. of Charles Howard*, 1st Earl of Carlisle, 3s. (2 *d.v.p.*) 4da. *suc.* fa. 19 Mar. 1658; *cr.* Visct. Preston [S] 12 May 1681; *suc.* gt.-uncle Ranald Grahme* in Nunnington estate 1685.[1]

J.p. Cumb. and Yorks. (N. Riding) 1668–89, Westmld. 1680–9; capt. of militia horse, Cumb. and Westmld. 1672–89; commr. for assessment, N. Riding 1673–80, Cumb. and Westmld. 1677–80; recusants, Cumb. 1675; dep. lt. Cumb. and Westmld. 1675–87, N. Riding 1685–Feb. 1688; freeman, Portsmouth 1676; recorder, Carlisle 1684–Oct. 1688; ld. lt. Cumb. and Westmld. 1687–9.[2]

Envoy extraordinary to France 1682–5; master of the great wardrobe 1685–Dec. 1688; PC 21 Oct. 1685–Dec. 1688; chancellor to Queen Catherine of Braganza 1685–9; sec. of state (north) Oct.–Dec. 1688.[3]

Grahme's grandfather, from an obscure Scottish border family, became master of the horse to the first Duke of Buckingham, acquired the Netherby estate of 5,400 acres in 1624, and sat for Carlisle in two of Charles I's early Parliaments. He was wounded at the battle of Edgehill, and according to family tradition received a warrant for a peerage which was destroyed when his house was plundered by the forces of Parliament. He was taken prisoner in 1645 and compounded for £2,385. No doubt Grahme's father was also royalist in sympathy, but he does not seem to have been active.[4]

Grahme, 'a close student' at Oxford, 'had good learning and tolerable parts'. A firm Anglican, he hoped to succeed Sir Thomas Strickland* as MP for Westmorland on the passing of the Test Act, but withdrew with what dignity he could muster on learning that the seat was destined for the youthful (Sir) John Lowther III*. But two years later he was returned for Cockermouth at a by-election. He had property in the neighbourhood, and presumably enjoyed the powerful interest of his stepfather, Sir George Fletcher*. An inactive Member of the Cavalier Parliament, he was appointed to 18 committees, including those on the bills to prevent moor-burning and border rapine in his first session. He was noted on the working lists as under the influence of the Speaker (Edward Seymour*), and as 'heir to Mr Ranald Grahme, who can command him'. But his great-uncle was in opposition in 1675, and Grahme himself was marked 'thrice worthy' on Shaftesbury's list in 1677. In the spring session of 1678 he distinguished himself as leader of the attack on Lauderdale. He was appointed to the committees for summarizing foreign commitments and drafting the address for the removal of counsellors. When it was proposed to name Lauderdale in the address he acted as teller against a motion to

adjourn the debate, and three days later formally moved the resolution against the Scottish minister. But in the final session of the Parliament he was listed as a defaulter; a motion to excuse him was lost on division, and he arrived at Westminster too late to avoid the payment of £30 or £40 to the serjeant-at-arms for his fees.[5]

Grahme was re-elected for Cockermouth unopposed to the Exclusion Parliaments. A member of the Green Ribbon Club, he was classed as 'worthy' by Shaftesbury. He was moderately active in 1679, being appointed to seven committees, including those to state matters undetermined in the previous Parliament and to regulate elections. On 6 May he renewed the attack on Lauderdale:

> It was he who was instrumental to break the Triple League, to advise toleration, and to bring in Popery like a stream, and tyranny like a torrent, and who gave opprobrious and nasty terms to the House of Commons. It is he who has brought in arbitrary power on the other side Tweed.

He was again appointed to the committee to draw up an address for the removal of the obnoxious minister, and also to those to inquire into the shipping of artillery from Portsmouth and to consider the continuation of the ban on Irish cattle. But he was absent from the division on the exclusion bill, and on the appointment of his brother to the Duke of York's household he went over to the Court, refusing to sign the Yorkshire petition for frequent Parliaments. He was again moderately active in the second Exclusion Parliament, in which he was named to five committees and made four speeches. He helped to draw up the address for the defence of the Protestant religion on 27 Oct. 1680, but in the debate on exclusion he said:

> Before this bill pass, I would consider one thing very weighty; whether it is fit to condemn the Duke before he be heard or cited to appear, to take away his right before he be heard to speak for himself? Next, what will you do with his children, who are Protestant and innocent? . . . Through this matter a most dreadful civil war may arise, as in the quarrel between York and Lancaster.

If the consequence of the bill were to divide England from Scotland, he believed that he would be one of the first sufferers. It was necessary that a successor should be named and expedients offered, which could be freely debated only in committee. On 4 Nov. he was among those ordered to bring in a bill to prohibit imports of Scottish cattle, and he still believed in the Popish Plot. But he played no known part in the Oxford Parliament. Shortly afterwards he was raised to the Scottish peerage as Viscount Preston. He took his seat in the House of Lords at Edinburgh, and in 1682 he was sent as ambassador to France.[6]

Preston was recalled in 1685 to share with the inexperienced Lord Middleton (Charles Middleton*) in the management of James II's Parliament. He was elected knight of the shire for Cumberland unopposed, and became a very active Member, being appointed to 18 committees, including that to recommend expunctions from the Journals. He was the first to be appointed to the committee on the border bill on 6 June, and he helped to draft the loyal address on Monmouth's invasion and to prepare a bill for the general naturalization of Huguenot refugees. On 22 June he was sent to thank the King for news of the capture of the Scottish rebel, Argyll. With Middleton he was given leave to bring in a bill for the relief of London widows and orphans, and on 25 June he returned to the Lords the bill to prohibit imports of gunpowder. He reminded the House, when Parliament met again after the recess, that 'we have lately had an unfortunate proof how little we are to depend upon the militia', and urged supply for an increase in the standing army. He was among those ordered to draw up the address against Roman Catholic officers on 14 Nov., but he argued strongly for supply, and demanded that John Coke II should be sent to the Tower for describing the King's message as 'a few high words' designed to frighten Members out of their duty. He was given the office of master of the great wardrobe, although Ralph Montagu* had a life patent, and succeeded Lord Halifax (Sir George Savile*) as chancellor to the dowager queen.[7]

Preston supported James II's religious policy, and as lord lieutenant sought to extract favourable replies from the Cumberland and Westmorland magistrates with very little success. Nevertheless he apparently expected an English peerage for his efforts, and drafted a superb patent of creation for a barony of Liddel. On 25 Aug. 1688, with the arrangements for James's abortive Parliament under way, Sir John Lowther II* wrote: 'My Lord Preston was just now with me, and says he quits the county to Sir George and me'. He was now a formidable rival to Lord Sunderland, who endeavoured to check his aspirations to a seat in the Lords by writing on 13 Sept. that the King believed that Preston would secure his own election for Cumberland. But in the following month Preston took over the seals. He was one of the council of five left in London when the King joined the army in the west, and was summoned to the meeting of the peers at the Guildhall on 11 Dec., but refused to concur with their proceedings. The Earl of Clarendon (Henry Hyde*) presented him to William on 19 Dec., but he made little attempt to ingratiate himself with the new regime, and was dismissed from all his offices. He did not stand for the Convention, and on 8 Jan. 1689 James wrote to him from Versailles:

> I approve of what you have resolved as to yourself in staying in town till the Convention and the Parliament, as they call it, be over, and I think you can do me much more service by staying in England than in coming hither to me, at least at present. ... I need not recommend to you doing me what service you can, I am sure you will do it, and you that are acquainted with Members of both Houses may do me very much by speaking and consulting with such of them as you can trust.

A fortnight later he was awarded a Jacobite peerage. An imprudent demonstration outside Carlisle led to his arrest in March on a charge of fomenting disturbances, but he was released seven months later. When Montagu threatened to sue him for the profits of the great wardrobe during his intrusion, he claimed privilege as an English peer on the grounds that his patent was dated before the resolutions of Parliament had declared the throne to be vacant. But he was compelled to withdraw his claim and apologize, and on 28 Nov. 1690 Montagu was awarded £1,300 damages. An active plotter, Preston was arrested on his way to France on 1 Jan. 1691, and condemned to death later in the same month. By now a confirmed alcoholic, he saved his life by a full confession, involving not only Clarendon and Seymour, but Lord Dartmouth (George Legge*), Lord Weymouth (Thomas Thynne I*), and even his own brother. He was allowed to retire to the Yorkshire estate which he had inherited from his great-uncle. He died on 22 Dec. 1695, and was buried at Nunnington. 'An honest man, but no knower of men', was the verdict of a fellow Jacobite. 'Plausible to all to an equality ... he was thought more flattering than sincere. ... [He was] given so much to the bottle that it dulled much the good understanding that God had endowed him with.' None of his descendants sat in Parliament.[8]

[1] Scots Peerage, vii. 99. [2] H. R. Moulton, Cat. (1930), 317; CSP Dom. 1675-6, p. 470; R. East, Portsmouth Recs. 362; SP44/164/247; Westmld. RO, D/Ry 2832; Ellis Corresp. i. 338. [3] CSP Dom. 1685, p. 402; Luttrell, i. 361; Reresby Mems. 568. [4] Royalist Comp. Pprs. (Yorks. Arch. Soc. rec. ser. xv), 128-34; HMC 6th Rep. 321. [5] HMC Le Fleming, 102-3, 152; Ailesbury Mems. 278; Lauderdale Pprs. (Cam. Soc. n.s. xxxviii), 144; Grey, v. 381; CJ, ix. 477, 558. [6] Westmld. RO, D/Ry 2142, Fleming to Lamplugh, 22 Feb. 1679; Grey, vii. 188-9, 408-9; viii. 35; HMC 6th Rep. 321; Exact Coll. Debates, 43. [7] Burnet ed. Routh, iii. 40; Bramston Autobiog. (Cam. Soc. xxxii), 199; CJ, ix. 746; Grey, viii. 354-5, 364, 370. [8] HMC 12th Rep. IX, 91; HMC 6th Rep. 321; Westmld. RO, D/Ry 3250; CSP Dom. 1687-9, pp. 273, 1689-90, p. 40; Clarke, Jas. II, ii. 260, 441-3; Clarendon Corresp. ii. 231; HMC 7th Rep. 263; Luttrell, i. 509, 610; ii. 48, 152, 161, 220, 244; iii. 567; Ailesbury Mems. 278.

E.C.

GRANVILLE (GRENVILLE), Bernard (1631–1701), of The Mews Gatehouse, Westminster; Apps Court, Walton-on-Thames, Surr., and Marr, Yorks.

LISKEARD	18 May 1661
LAUNCESTON or SALTASH	1679 (Mar.)
SALTASH	1681
PLYMOUTH	1685
SALTASH	1689
LAUNCESTON	1690
LOSTWITHIEL	1695

b. 4 Mar. 1631, 4th but 2nd surv. s. of Sir Bevil Granville† (*d.*1643) of Stowe, Cornw. by Grace, da. of Sir George Smith† of Exeter, Devon; bro. of John, 1st Earl of Bath, and Denis, dean of Durham 1684–91. *educ.* academy at Angers 1651. *m.* lic. 25 Feb. 1664, Anne (*d.* 20 Sept. 1701), da. and h. of Cuthbert Morley of Hawnby, Yorks., 3s. 2da.[1]

Gent. of the bedchamber to the Duke of Gloucester May–Sept. 1660; equerry ?Sept. 1660–72; groom of the bedchamber 1672–Dec. 1688; envoy extraordinary to Genoa and Savoy 1675–6; jt. surveyor and receiver of green-wax fines 1677–9; master of the swans 1683–92; comptroller-gen. of wine licences 1685–90.[2]

Under-keeper, St. James's Park Aug. 1660–*d.*; commr. for assessment, Cornw. 1661–80, Westminster 1665–9, 1679–80, Surr. 1673–80, Cornw. and Yorks. (N. Riding) 1689–90, loyal and indigent officers, Cornw. 1662; jt. keeper of Petersham Walk, Surr. 1663–*d.*; recorder, Doncaster 1685–?Oct. 1688; freeman, Liskeard, East Looe, Plymouth and Plympton Erle 1685.[3]

Granville was in arms for the King in the second Civil War, assisting his brother in the defence of Scilly, after which he joined his uncle, Sir Richard Granville, in exile. On his return to England he endured five years' imprisonment. This, he later claimed, was for political offences, but he was certainly a debtor in the Fleet in 1659, and 'had £3,000 given him to fetch him out', or so it was said. On the eve of the Restoration he was acting as courier between his kinsman George Monck* and the exiled Court; but he was much less prominent than his brother and the pension of £500 which he expected did not at once materialize. He had to be satisfied with two minor posts and the reimbursement of his expenses.[4]

At the general election of 1661 Granville was returned for Camelford and Bodmin, but in neither case did he secure the mayor's signature to his indenture. While his petition for Camelford was still pending, he was returned at a by-election for Liskeard on a vacancy created by his brother-in-law, Peter Prideaux*, who chose to sit for Honiton. He was moderately active in the Cavalier Parliament, in which he was named to 89 committees, though few were of political importance. He was appointed to the committee on the bill to confirm the grants

made to Monck, now Duke of Albemarle (18 Mar. 1662), and added to that for the sale of the lands of his future father-in-law (19 Mar. 1663). He was listed as a court dependant in 1664. In 1666 his committees included that for the private bill promoted by his brother-in-law Sir Thomas Higgons*. He appealed to the House of Lords in 1667 against a Chancery decision concerning the mortgage of the Morley estate, but this was ultimately dismissed three years later. A friend of Ormonde and a King's servant, he was on both lists of the court party in 1669–71. He petitioned the King

for a pension to relieve his great extremity, or for payment of £2,000 lent by the father of his wife to the late King, before the rebels forced him from Whitehall. . . . [He] has exhausted himself in ten years' unprofitable employment, and, but for being a Member of Parliament, would end his days in the gaol where he spent five years in his Majesty's service.

He was appointed to the committees to receive information about the insolencies of nonconformists (5 Mar. 1668), to inquire into arrears of taxes owed by officials (24 Mar. 1670), and to consider the transfer of the Cornish assizes from Bodmin to Launceston (14 Mar. 1671). In 1672 he was made groom of the bedchamber with a pension of £500. In the list of excise pensions, however, he was put down for only £300 p.a. His name appeared on the Paston list and the list of officials in 1675, and he was given rank as an earl's younger son. In Italy on a diplomatic mission, he missed the autumn session; 'the King loseth a vote', as Sir Richard Wiseman* commented. Shaftesbury marked him 'thrice vile' in 1677, and the author of *A Seasonable Argument* alleged that he had 'got in boons at several times £20,000'. He was one of the syndicate headed by the Earl of Peterborough and Lord Yarmouth (Robert Paston I*) to whom was granted with dubious legality the right of farming the fines imposed in the Exchequer. In 1678 he was appointed to the committees to consider the bill for duchy of Cornwall leases and to prepare instructions for disbanding the army, and he was on both lists of the court party.[5]

At the first general election of 1679 Granville was returned both for Saltash and Launceston in contested elections, and marked 'vile' on Shaftesbury's list. Despite a petition from the unsuccessful candidates in the former constituency he occupied both seats for the duration of the first Exclusion Parliament. But he was not active, being appointed only to the elections committee that buried the Saltash petition, and to those to inquire into the decay of the woollen industry and abuses in the Post Office. He voted against exclusion, and, as one of the 'unanimous club', was defeated at Saltash in the autumn. The patent for green-wax fines was cancelled after Danby's fall, and in 1680 Granville experienced in his turn the frustration of an election petition that was never reported from committee. He regained his seat in 1681, but there is no evidence that he attended the Oxford Parliament.[6]

Lord Bath lost his place as groom of the stole to the Roman Catholic Earl of Peterborough under James II, but Granville, rather to his surprise, was not only allowed to retain his post in the bedchamber, but also given the office of comptroller-general of wine licence accounts, with a salary of £200 p.a. He gratefully expressed the hope that he might be returned 'to serve in the Parliament and prove his loyalty'. He was elected at Plymouth, where his brother was recorder, but no activity can definitely be ascribed to him in this Parliament, in which his nephew John also served. He was returned to the Convention for Saltash unopposed, and according to Ailesbury's list voted to agree with the Lords that the throne was not vacant. But he was otherwise probably inactive, for there are no references to 'Mr Granville' in the Journals until after his nephew's return at a by-election. He sat as a Tory in the next two Parliaments, refusing the Association in 1696. He died on 14 June 1701 and was buried at Lambeth.[7]

[1] Vivian, *Vis. Cornw.* 192; R. Granville, *Hist. Granville Fam.* 328, 336, 404; C66/3056; *Evelyn Diary*, iv. 11, 24; *London Mar. Lic.* ed. Foster, 586; *HMC 8th Rep.* pt. 1 (1881), 115. [2] *Cal. Cl. SP*, iv. 688; E. Handasyde, *Granville the Polite*, 5, 7, 11; *CSP Dom.* 1663–4, p. 677; *Cal. Treas. Bks.* iii. 1271; v. 795; vi. 121; viii. 124; ix. 873; *HMC 5th Rep.* 186; N. F. Ticehurst, *Mute Swan in England*, 65. [3] *CSP Dom.* 1660–1, p. 213; 1663–4, p. 75; 1685, pp. 65, 66, 87; *Plymouth Municipal Recs.* ed. Worth, 8. [4] Handasyde, 4; *CSP Dom.* 1659–60, pp. 269, 279; 1670, p. 617; 1671, p. 432; *Cal. Cl. SP*, iv. 688; v. 5, 9; *Cal. Treas. Bks.* i. 80. [5] *CJ*, viii. 250, 373; *HMC 8th Rep.* pt. 1 (1881), 115; *LJ*, xii. 321; *CSP Dom.* 1670, p. 617; 1675–6, pp. 246, 264; *Cal. Treas. Bks.* iii. 1271. [6] *CJ*, ix. 569, 645; *Cal. Treas. Bks.* vi. 121. [7] *HMC 5th Rep.* 186; *Cal. Treas. Bks.* viii. 124; J. Tanswell, *Hist. Lambeth*, 150–1.

J.S.C.

GRANVILLE (GRENVILLE), Bevil (1665–1706).

FOWEY   1685
LOSTWITHIEL   1690
FOWEY   1695, 1698

b. 3 Mar. 1665, 1st s. of Bernard Granville*, and bro. of Bernard Granville† and George Granville†, 1st Baron Granville of Bideford. *educ.* Trinity Coll. Camb. 1677; academies at Paris 1682–5. *unm.* Kntd. 28 May 1686; *suc.* fa. 1701.[1]

Capt. Earl of Bath's regt. (later 10 Ft.) 1685, maj. 1687, col. 1693–1703; gov. Pendennis Castle 1696–1703, Barbados 1703–6; maj.-gen. 1704.[2]
Master of the swans 1692–*d.*[3]
Freeman, Portsmouth 1686; j.p. Cornw. by 1701–*d.*[4]

Granville was returned unopposed for Fowey in 1685, on the interest of Lord Bath, his uncle, who had become recorder of the borough under its new charter. Though doubtless a Tory, he left no certain trace on the records of James II's Parliament. He became an army officer, and was knighted in the camp on Hounslow Heath in 1686. At the Revolution he was sent to Jersey to bring over the garrison to William of Orange. He disarmed the Papists on the island, and was returned for Lostwithiel in 1690 as a government supporter. Though he later moved with his uncle into opposition for a time, his military career did not suffer, and he signed the Association in 1696. Queen Anne made him governor of Barbados, but he died on the return voyage from the colony on 15 Sept. 1706.[5]

[1] Westminster City Lib., St. Martin in the Fields par. reg.; E. Handasyde, *Granville the Polite*, 10. [2] Luttrell, iii. 491; iv. 33; v. 175. [3] N. F. Ticehurst, *Mute Swan in England*, 65. [4] R. East, *Portsmouth Recs.* 368. [5] R. Granville, *Granville Fam.* 407, 409; *HMC Bath*, i. 121.

J.S.C.

GRANVILLE (GRENVILLE), Charles, Lord Lansdown (1661–1701).

LAUNCESTON   19 Nov. 1680
CORNWALL   1685

bap. 31 Aug. 1661, 1st s. of John, 1st Earl of Bath by Jane, da. of Sir Peter Wyche, merchant, of London; bro. of John Granville*. *educ.* travelled abroad 1676–8. *m.* (1) lic. 22 May 1678, Lady Martha Osborne (*d.* 11 Sept. 1689), da. of Sir Thomas Osborne*, 1st Duke of Leeds, *s.p.*; (2) 10 Mar. 1691, Isabella, da. of Henry de Nassau, 1st Lord of Auverquerque, Count of Nassau, master of the horse to William III, 1s. *summ.* to Lords in his fa.'s barony as Lord Granville, 16 July 1689; *suc.* fa. as 2nd Earl of Bath 22 Aug. 1701.[1]

Gent. of the bedchamber 1683–5, 1692–3; envoy extraordinary to Spain 1685–9.[2]
Freeman, Plymouth 1684, Bodmin, Liskeard, Plympton Erle and Tintagel 1685; commr. for assessment, Cornw. 1689; jt. ld. lt. Devon and Cornw. 1691–3; j.p. Cornw. by 1701–*d.*[3]

Lord Lansdown's ancestors can be traced back in the west country to the 12th century, and first sat in Parliament in 1388. He derived his courtesy title from the battle in which his grandfather, the royalist hero Sir Bevil Granville†, was slain. His father fought for the King in both wars, and was constantly engaged in royalist plots. As a kinsman of George Monck* he played a key role in the Restoration and was raised to the peerage. Throughout the remainder of the period, as lord lieutenant of Cornwall and warden of the stannaries, he managed the court interest in the local elections. He became a close friend and follower of Lord Treasurer Danby, whose daughter Lansdown married at the age of 17.[4]

Lansdown was first returned to Parliament in 1680, still under age, at a by-election for Launceston on the family interest. Doubtless a court supporter, he was appointed to no committees and made no speeches in the second Exclusion Parliament, and he did not stand in 1681. In the following year he left his wife, whom he had detected in an intrigue with her brother-in-law, William Leveson Gower*, and went abroad. He served with distinction in the Imperial army against the Turks, and in January 1684 he was honoured with the title of Count of the Holy Roman Empire, which Charles II ordered to be registered in the Office of Arms. On his return to England in May he applied unsuccessfully for the regiment formerly commanded by Lord Ossory (Thomas Butler*). He was given leave to serve under the Prince of Orange, 'who has been kind to him, and given him hopes of the first regiment of the King's subjects in the service of the States'. This, however, does not seem to have materialized, and in November Charles appointed him envoy extraordinary to Spain. The appointment was confirmed by James II when he succeeded to the throne, but before he left for Madrid he was elected knight of the shire. He was named to the committee of elections and privileges, but embarked for Spain on 13 May. He was recommended in his absence as court candidate for the county or for Launceston in 1688, but he did not return to England till the following March, delivering up his credentials to James at St. Germains on the way. Like his father, he accepted the new regime. He helped to carry William's train at the coronation, and was called up to the House of Lords a few months later.[5]

Lansdown's continued matrimonial difficulties led to a breach with Danby, and after 1690 he and his father were both reckoned among the Whig peers. In October he was only prevented from fighting a duel with Danby by the intervention of the King's guards. In 1692 he was appointed joint lord lieutenant of Cornwall and Devon with his father to help strengthen their defences. But in the following March he

> petitioned his Majesty for his arrears due on his embassy to Spain formerly, and, pressing more than ordinary for it, [he] was checked by the King, on which he resigned his place of the bedchamber to the King ... [and] that of lord lieutenant of Cornwall and Devon.

Lansdown succeeded to the earldom in 1701, but shot himself a fortnight later on 4 Sept. He was buried with his father at Kilkhampton. Luttrell wrote that ''tis said he had been melancholy for some time past', but the coroner's court returned a verdict of accidental death. His only son, the last of

the senior branch of the family, died of smallpox at the age of 19 on 17 May 1711.[6]

[1] *CSP Dom.* 1675-6, p. 559. [2] *CSP Dom.* Jan.–June 1683, p. 155; 1685, pp. 102-3; Luttrell, i. 507; ii. 343; iii. 65. [3] J. Wallis, *Bodmin Reg.* 169; *HMC 9th Rep.* pt. 1, p. 281; *CSP Dom.* 1685, pp. 66, 87; 1691-2, p. 231; 1693, p. 98; Luttrell, ii. 397; iii. 62; R. Granville, *Hist. Granville Fam.* 356; J. Maclean, *Trigg Minor*, i. 216; iii. 207. [4] Vivian, *Vis. Cornw.* 190-7; Granville, 26, 31, 55. [5] Browning, *Danby*, i. 449; Add. 29577, f. 503; *CSP Dom.* Jan.–June 1683, p. 137; 1684-5, pp. 6, 100-1, 221; 1685, p. 288; 1689-90, p. 34. [6] Luttrell, ii. 118; iii. 62, 65; v. 86-87.

P.W.

GRANVILLE (GRENVILLE), Hon. John (1665–1707), of Stowe, Cornw.

LAUNCESTON	1685
PLYMOUTH	10 July 1689, 1690, 1695
NEWPORT	1698
FOWEY	1701 (Feb.)
CORNWALL	1701 (Dec.), 1702–13 Mar. 1703

b. 12 Apr. 1665, 2nd s. of John, 1st Earl of Bath; bro. of Charles Granville*, Lord Lansdown. *educ.* Christ Church, Oxf. 1680. *m.* 15 Apr. 1703, Rebecca, da. of (Sir) Josiah Child, 1st Bt.*, of Wanstead, Essex, wid. of Charles Somerset*, Mq. of Worcester, *s.p. suc.* fa. in Potheridge estate 1701; *cr.* Baron Granville of Potheridge 13 Mar. 1703.

Freeman, Plympton Erle 1685; commr. for assessment, Devon 1690; chief commr. for Plymouth dock 1692–?96; j.p. Cornw. by 1701–d.; ranger of St. James's Park 1701–d.; recorder, Launceston 1701–d.; ld. prop. Carolina 1701–d.; ld. warden of the stannaries and steward of the duchy of Cornw. (jt.) 1701–2, (sole) 1702–5; ld. lt. and custos rot. Cornw. 1702–5.[1]

Capt. Earl of Bath's regt. (later 10 Ft.) 1687–Dec. 1688; capt. and brevet col. 1 Ft. Gds. 1689–90; gov. Deal by Apr.–Dec. 1690.[2]

Commr. of public accounts 1696–7; lt. of the Ordnance 1702–5; PC 18 June 1702–22 May 1707.[3]

Granville served with his elder brother in the Imperial army in 1683. He was returned in 1685 for Launceston, one of the boroughs of which his father was recorder. Though doubtless a Tory, he left no certain trace on the records of James II's Parliament. He was commissioned in his father's regiment, and recommended as court candidate for Launceston in 1688. Like the rest of his family he welcomed the Revolution, when his father became governor of Plymouth. He was returned for the borough at a by-election caused by the elevation of his friend Arthur Herbert* to the peerage, and survived a petition from one of James's Whig collaborators to become a moderately active Member. As 'Colonel Granville' he was appointed to only five committees in the Convention; but he probably acted as teller in four divisions, and made four speeches attacking the vile conditions in the navy. 'If you value not these complaints', he said, 'you may talk of raising money, but not of raising seamen.' In December 1689 he was added to the committees to consider the mutiny bill and to recommend ways of relieving wounded seamen and their dependants. He was probably twice teller against the disabling clause in the bill to restore corporations. He delivered a report from the mayor of Plymouth on victualling on 16 Jan., and again acted as teller against making reparations to (Sir) Thomas Pilkington*.[4]

Granville soon moved into opposition in 1690, and was dismissed at the time of Herbert's court-martial at the end of the year. One of the most influential of the country party, he 'expressed the most violent and unrelenting aversion to the whole administration' throughout the remainder of William III's reign. Under Anne, however, he succeeded his father as government manager of the Cornish boroughs, and was raised to the peerage. But he went into opposition again in 1705. He died on 3 Dec. 1707, after an apoplectic seizure, and was buried at St. Clement Danes.[5]

[1] *CSP Dom.* 1685, p. 87; 1702–3, pp. 391, 503–4; *HMC Hastings*, ii. 344; *Cal. Treas. Bks.* xvii. 412; xviii. 290; *London Gazette*, 23 Mar. 1702. [2] *CSP Dom.* 1686–7, p. 119; 1687–9, pp. 32, 376; 1689–90, p. 559; 1690–1, p. 190; J. Laker, *Hist. Deal*, 230, 234. [3] *HMC Kenyon*, 400; *CSP Col.* 1702–3, pp. 15–16; Luttrell, v. 174, 185; *Marlborough-Godolphin Corresp.* 788. [4] R. Granville, *Granville Fam.* 400–3; Grey, ix. 443; *CJ*, x. 323, 329, 339. [5] *Hatton Corresp.* (Cam. Soc. n.s. xxiii), 149; Burnet ed. Routh, v. 10–11.

J.S.C.

GRATWICK, Francis (d.1670), of Tortington, Suss.

SEAFORD   15 Mar.–c. July 1670

2nd s. of William Gratwick of Tortington by Amphillis, da. of Sir Benjamin Tichborne, 1st Bt.†, of Tichborne, Hants. *m.* Barbara, wid. of John Venables of Western Court, Bishop's Sutton, Hants, *s.p. suc.* bro. c.1665.[1]
 Commr. for assessment, Suss. 1664–9.

Gratwick came from a family which was widespread among the Sussex yeomanry in the 16th century. Its fortunes were made by the exertions of Roger Gratwick, ironmaster to Queen Elizabeth, who bought Tortington in 1587. Gratwick's grandfather acquired an interest in Seaford by purchasing the manor, and his uncle, another Roger, who served in the parliamentary army and sat for Hastings from 1645 to 1653, was four times bailiff of Seaford. Gratwick defeated Robert Morley* at a by-election in 1670, being returned by the mayor, jurats and freemen only, but may never have taken his seat. He died between 28 June, when he signed his will, and 15 Aug. when it was proved. After his death his election was declared void, and his nephew and

heir, Oliver Weekes, sold the Seaford property, though a great-nephew, Carew Weekes†, came in for Arundel in 1701.[2]

[1] *Vis. Suss.* (Harl. Soc. lxxxix), 56; PCC Adm. Act Bk. 1669, f. 12v; PCC 383 Wootton; *VCH Hants*, iii. 43. [2] *Suss. Arch. Colls.* lx. 34–43; E. Straker, *Wealden Iron*, 460; D. Underdown, *Pride's Purge*, 392–3.

B.D.H.

GRAY *see* GREY

GREGORY, William (1625–96), of How Caple, Herefs.

WEOBLEY   7 Mar. 1678, 1679 (Mar.)
HEREFORD   11 Jan.–18 Apr. 1689

b. 1 Mar. 1625, 2nd but o. surv. s. of Robert Gregory, vicar of Fownhope, 1619–43, by 1st w. Anne, da. of John Harvey of Bradstone, Glos. *educ.* Hereford Cathedral sch.; Staple Inn; G. Inn, entered 1640, called 1651; All Souls, Oxf. 1644. *m.* 1653, Catherine, da. and h. of James Smith of Tillington, Herefs., wid. of John Carpenter of The Homme, Dilwyn, Herefs., and of Humphrey Tomkyns, merchant, of London, 1s. *d.v.p.* 1da. *suc.* fa. 1643. Kntd. 26 July 1679.[1]
 ?Clerk to county committee, Herefs. 1644; dep. steward, Hereford by 1653–82, common councilman c.1662–82; commr. for assessment, Herefs. Jan. 1660–80, Hereford Jan. 1660–1, 1663–80, Glos. and Gloucester 1679–80, Herefs. and Hereford 1689–90, Glos. 1689, Serjeants' Inn 1690, militia, Herefs. Mar. 1660; j.p. Herefs. Mar. 1660–Mar. 1688, Oct. 1688–*d.*, chairman quarter sessions by 1663–?79; commr. for inquiry, Kingswood chase 1671; recorder, Gloucester 1672–87; bencher, G. Inn 1673, reader 1675.[2]
 Serjeant-at-law 1677; baron of the Exchequer 12 July 1679–86; j.c.p. 18 Apr.–8 May 1689; j.K.b. 8 May 1689–*d.*
 Speaker of House of Commons 17 Mar.–27 May 1679.

Gregory came from a minor gentry family settled in Herefordshire since the beginning of the century. A virulent account (in a private letter written shortly after he became recorder of Gloucester many years later) describes him as left virtually penniless on his father's death, and forced to enter the service of a local committeeman, the grandfather of Sir John Kyrle*. He then served as one of the clerks to the county committee before qualifying as a barrister. His fortune was founded on the stewardship of the Devereux estates, but his employment by the royalist Lady Hertford in this capacity did not prevent him from deputizing for the regicide Major-General Harrison as steward of Hereford. Nevertheless he voiced the demand for a poll in opposition to the court candidates in the 1656 election.[3]

Gregory's practice throve after the Restoration, and he became an extensive purchaser of land, acquiring How Caple in 1677. He first stood for Weobley in 1675 as the candidate of the country party, probably on the strength of his marital connexion with the Tomkyns family. He feared 'nothing so much as foul play from the sheriff', which duly occurred. His petition was delayed by the culprit's death, and meanwhile he was selected as country party candidate for Hereford, where he remained a member of the corporation. However, the Weobley election was declared void on 22 Feb. 1678, and Gregory was successful at the second attempt. Listed by Shaftesbury as 'doubly worthy', he was an active Member in the last nine months of the Cavalier Parliament, serving on 30 committees and making five speeches. He was one of the Members appointed to draw up reasons for a conference on the growth of Popery. He seconded the motion for an address for the removal of counsellors, and helped to draw it up. In the autumn session he was active over the Popish Plot. He served on the committee of inquiry, and took part in preparing the impeachment of Lord Arundell of Wardour, and (with three other Members, all strong opponents of the Court) the examination of Samuel Atkins, by which it was hoped to implicate Samuel Pepys* in the plot. He was appointed to the committee for excluding Papists from Parliament and to prepare reasons for disagreeing with the Lords' amendments to the bill. He was deeply concerned about the Roman Catholic officers in the army, reading to the House the dispensations granted to them by Secretary Williamson and taking part in the preparation of instructions for disbandment and devising punishments for recusants who accepted commissions. He helped to draw up the address on the present dangers of the nation, and was appointed to the committee of secrecy on 14 Dec. 1678.[4]

Gregory was re-elected to the first Exclusion Parliament and noted as 'worthy' on Shaftesbury's list. After some days of deadlock between King and Commons over the choice of a Speaker, he was proposed as a compromise candidate by the Hon. William Russell* and William Cavendish*, Lord Cavendish, and accepted, in spite of his plea of inexperience. Gregory was not a forceful Speaker; Oates's impertinence to the House was far more effectively rebuked by back-benchers like Sir Robert Southwell*, and Sir Richard Wiseman* replied to his questions 'rudely and surlily'. Gregory was chiefly anxious to expedite the disbandment of the army, and to facilitate this he lent himself to a court manoeuvre to carry up the supply bill to the Lords on a mere motion, without vote or debate, for which he was blamed by John Trenchard*. Gregory's elevation to the judicial bench had been

pressed by the preceding Speaker, Edward Seymour; but although there had been a vacancy at the Exchequer since the death of Timothy Littleton* in March, Gregory was not appointed to fill it till after the dissolution, thus disappointing Seymour's expectations of returning to the Speaker's chair.[5]

Although no longer eligible for the Commons, Gregory remained an active politician locally, much valued by the country party for his influence on Lord Scudamore (John Scudamore*). He thought it necessary, however, to re-insure himself with the Court, and he probably played some part, as was later alleged, in the surrender of Hereford's charter. He brought up the Herefordshire address against associations: 'The reason is said to be fear he should be removed, of which there has been strong report'. However, he remained in office for four years more, until dismissed by James II for declaring against the suspending and dispensing powers.

Gregory took a prominent part in organizing a loan in Herefordshire to William of Orange in December 1688, himself subscribing £30, and was returned for Hereford in the following month, despite some 'particular piques' the inhabitants had conceived against him. On the Ailesbury list he is recorded as voting to agree with the Lords that the throne was not vacant. A moderately active Member of the Convention in its opening months, he was appointed to seven committees, including those to amend the Lords' version of the declaration of rights, to suspend habeas corpus, to draw up new oaths of allegiance and supremacy, and to abolish the court of the marches. On 7 Mar. 1689 he opposed the motion for restoring corporations to their condition in 1660 by reminding the House that at that time 'the loyal nobility, gentry and commons were out of the magistracy'. Promoted to the King's bench shortly afterwards, he distinguished himself as one of the two judges who supported the opinion of Sir John Holt* that the surrender of the charters was neither illegal nor treasonable, whereupon a Whig peer alleged that Gregory 'in the very beginning had been most forward and active in procuring the surrender of Hereford'. When holding the assizes at Bristol in 1691 he was insulted by the Tory mob at the instigation of John Knight II*. He died in London on 28 May 1696, and was buried at How Caple, the only member of his family to sit in Parliament.[6]

[1] W. R. Williams, *Parl. Hist. Herefs.* 94; Cooke, *Herefs.* iii. 233; C. J. Robinson, *Mansions and Manors of Herefs.* 293, 310. [2] SP29/417/188; Cooke, 229–32; *Cal. Treas. Bks.* iii. 911; ix. 84, 111; *CSP Dom.* 1672, p. 12. [3] Robinson, 150; Bath mss, Thynne pprs. 20, f. 225; *HMC Portland*, iii. 208; *CSP Dom.* 1677–8, p. 64; *CJ*, ix. 444, 477, 538; Grey, v. 351; vi. 217–18. [4] Grey, vii. 2–3,

47, 217, 334; North, *Examen*, 460; Jones, *First Whigs*, 50; *HMC Finch*, ii. 47. [5] R. Morrice, Entering Bk. 3, p. 99; *Somers Tracts*, viii. 325; Luttrell, i. 166; *HMC Portland*, iii. 394; *Bramston Autobiog.* (Cam. Soc. xxii), 221–2; PC2/72/534. [6] C115/8903; BL Loan 29/184, f. 120; *HMC Portland*, iii. 417; Morrice, 2, p. 496; 3, p. 99; Luttrell, ii. 277.

E.R.

GRENVILLE *see* GRANVILLE

GRESHAM, James (c.1617–89), of Haslemere, Surr.

HASLEMERE   17–20 May 1661, 1679 (Mar.)

b. c.1617, 3rd but 2nd surv. s. of Thomas Gresham (*d.*1620) of North End, Fulham, Mdx. by 2nd w. Judith, da. of Sir William Garrard of Dorney, Bucks. *educ.* I. Temple 1636, called 1652. *m.* by July 1642, Anne (*d.*1700), da. of Sir Robert More of Loseley, Surr., 2s. *d.v.p.* 3da.[1]

J.p. Surr. July 1660–?Feb. 1688, ?Nov. 1688–*d.*, commr. for assessment 1661–80; freeman, Guildford 1662; commr. for charitable uses, Haslemere 1662, recusants, Surr. 1675.[2]

Gresham's grandfather, a younger son of the Titsey family, acquired property in Fulham by marriage and sat in three Elizabethan Parliaments. Gresham married the sister of Sir Poynings More[†], lord of the manor of Haslemere, before the Civil War, in which he took no part, his strongly royalist and Anglican views being in conflict with his brother-in-law's support of Parliament. By 1650 he was in occupation of a house on the outskirts of Haslemere as a tenant on the More estate. He was called to the bar in 1652, but there is no indication that he practised. His legal knowledge was of service, however, to his dubious electioneering activities, which may date back to 1659 when the borough regained the right to elect its own Members. At some time before the Restoration he was guilty of executing ten or 12 bogus conveyances to create votes, 'and the election being over, they were cancelled and delivered up'. At the general election of 1660 he caused the bailiff to sign and seal an indenture in his favour, though he had been outvoted three to one by Richard West[*]; but it never reached Chancery. Next year, however, there was a double return. Gresham and his colleague, Chaloner Chute[*], were allowed to sit on 17 May 1661, but they were unseated three days later on the merits of the election, and the bailiff was reprimanded by the Speaker. However, Gresham had the satisfaction of presenting West at quarter sessions for forcible entry and theft, and of obtaining a commission of charitable uses which obliged his rival to hand over the Haslemere charter to Sir William More[*]. 'A lover of antiquity' and an active j.p., though 'of

no estate in the county', Gresham was proposed for the order of the Royal Oak, with an annual income from his property in the Lincolnshire fens estimated at £800 p.a.[3]

Gresham took little part in politics for the next few years; but in 1676 he presented an almshouse to the borough, endowing it with the tolls of the market, which had shrunk to very small proportions, and were subject to litigation. He was returned with his nephew More at the first general election of 1679 and marked 'base' on Shaftesbury's list. He was given leave to go into the country on 16 Apr., but returned in time to be appointed to the committee of inquiry into the woollen industry (2 May) and another committee on a private bill. He was absent from the division on the exclusion bill. In the autumn election he was defeated by Denzil Onslow[*], but again he prevailed upon the bailiff to make a double return, which was decided against him. It is probable that his conduct was adversely criticized in the elections committee, for he did not stand again, though he accompanied his nephew and George Woodroffe[*] with the loyal address from Haslemere in 1681. When Onslow sued the bailiff for a false return, Gresham's spurious conveyances were produced by the prosecution. 'Endeavouring to say something by way of excuse', he was told by Lord Chief Justice Pemberton that 'it was too bad to be excused; and it was well an Act of general pardon had passed since this was done, else he should have answered it in another place'.[4]

Gresham drew up his will in January 1686, as 'a true and obedient son of the Church of England as it is a reformed member of the Holy Catholic Church'. He went on to declare that

> I do firmly believe that the high and sacred order of kings is of divine right, and that our lord the king is the supreme power within all his dominions and the fountain from which all lawful power (other than what is purely spiritual) must derive itself, and against which to set up, maintain or avow any coractive [*sic*] power either Papal or popular is treasonable against God and the king, and that he hath such an inherent right to tribute, custom and supply by the laws of God, nature and nations for the discharge of his office in the governing and protecting his subjects that can by no concessions or law be released, extinguished or alienated from his crown or office.

By a codicil dated 23 Oct. 1688 he bequeathed the tithes on his Lincolnshire property, over which he had developed conscientious scruples, to the vicar of Tetney, to revert to his own heirs 'if the mass, or any other vain or superstitious service of the Church of Rome shall be imposed'. He died on 4 Mar. 1689, aged 72, and was buried at Haslemere.[5]

[1] *Misc. Gen. et Her.* n.s. iv., 271–2; *Vis. Surr.* (Harl. Soc. lx), 53; *HMC 7th Rep.* 677. [2] Surr. RO (Guildford), 1083; Manning

and Bray, *Surr*. i. 657. [3] Swanton and Woods, *Bygone Haslemere*, 164, 251; Manning and Bray, i. 658; *Somers Tracts*, viii. 272; Surr. RO (Guildford) 985; *CJ*, viii. 253–6; *Q. Sess. Recs*. (Surr. Recs. vii), 210–11; Aubrey, *Antiqs. of Surr*. iv. 28; *HMC Lords*, i. 190. [4] Swanton and Woods, 160; *Somers Tracts*, viii. 271–2; *CJ*, ix. 650. [5] G. Leveson-Gower, *Gen. of Gresham Fam*. 105–8; *Haslemere* (Surr. Par. Reg. Soc. viii), 109; Manning and Bray, i. 661.

J.S.C.

GRESHAM, Marmaduke (1627–96), of Titsey, Surr.

EAST GRINSTEAD   1660
BLETCHINGLEY   1685

bap. 24 Jan. 1627, 2nd s. and h. of Sir Edward Gresham of Titsey, being o.s. by 2nd w. Mary, da. of Abraham Campion of Putney, wid. of Gabriel Wight of Brockham, Betchworth. *educ*. King's, Camb. 1645. *m*. lic. 18 Dec. 1647, Alice (*d*. 1 Sept. 1682), da. of Richard Corbet, bp. of Norwich 1632–5, 8s. (6 *d.v.p.*) 4da. *suc*. fa. 1647; *cr*. Bt. 31 July 1660.[1]

J.p. Surr. 1659–87, ?1689–*d*., Kent July 1660–80; commr. for militia, Surr. Mar. 1660; lt.-col. of militia ft. Apr. 1660; commr. for assessment, Surr. Aug. 1660–80, 1689–90, Kent 1661–80, recusants, Kent and Surr. 1675; dep. lt. Surr. ?1675–86.[2]

Gresham's ancestors were landowners in Norfolk by 1442, but the parliamentary history of the family begins under Henry VIII. The Titsey branch was established by Sir John Gresham, a London Fishmonger, who purchased the manor in 1535, with other property on the Kent-Surrey border. Gresham's grandfather sat for the local boroughs of Bletchingley and Gatton. His parents, though clearly 'malignant' at heart, took no part in the Civil War; they were assessed at £500 between them by the committee for the advance of money, but never paid. Gresham's elder half-brother was disinherited, and he succeeded to the Titsey estate in 1647. He was alleged to have supplied the Royalists in the second Civil War with horses, arms, men and money, and to have advised the Surrey men to shut up the Parliament doors and not let the Members out till their petition was granted. But no proceedings were taken, and he was not implicated in conspiracy, though he and his wife were doubtless responsible for the continuance of Anglican services at Titsey during the Interregnum.[3]

Gresham was returned for East Grinstead at the general election of 1660 on the Sackville interest, and probably at the instance of Lady Dorset, who also recommended him for a baronetcy as 'a Parliament man, eminent in the King's service, and worth £1,200 p.a.'. Lord Wharton also had hopes of him, committing him to the management of Sir Richard Onslow*, but he presumably voted with the Court. He was inactive in the Convention, being appointed to only one unimportant committee on 9 Nov., that to consider a petition from a former serjeant-at-arms. His baronetcy had already passed the seals, though the clerk of the Commons was unaware of it.[4]

Gresham is not known to have stood again until the exclusion crisis. He contested Bletchingley, five miles from Titsey, at both elections of 1679 without success. He was marked 'honest' on Shaftesbury's list and removed from the commission of the peace in Kent. The French ambassador suggested that on the surrender of the charter of London he might claim the site of the Royal Exchange, which had been founded by his collateral ancestor, Sir Thomas Gresham. He was successful at Bletchingley in 1685, but was appointed only to the committee of elections and privileges in James II's Parliament, and played no further part in politics. He died on 14 Apr. 1696 and was buried at Titsey. His son sat for Bletchingley in 1701–2.[5]

[1] *Misc. Gen. et Her*. n.s. iv. 301–5. [2] BL, M636/17, William Denton to Sir Ralph Verney, 4 Apr. 1660. [3] *Misc. Gen. et Her*. n.s. iv. 253; *Cal. Comm. Adv. Money*, 199, 1033–4, 1237; *CSP Dom*. 1660–1, p. 157. [4] *CSP Dom*. 1660–1, pp. 45, 81. [5] PRO 31/3, bdle. 156, f. 29.

M.W.H./B.M.C.

GREVILLE, Hon. Fulke (1643–1710), of The Castle, Warwick and Twickenham, Mdx.

WARWICK   28 Mar. 1664–17 Feb. 1677

b. aft. 2 Mar. 1643, 5th (posth.) s. of Robert Greville[†], 2nd Baron Brooke of Beauchamps Court, by Lady Katherine Russell, da. of Francis, 4th Earl of Bedford. *m*. lic. 12 Jan. 1665, Sarah, da. of Francis Dashwood, merchant, of London, 5s. (2 *d.v.p.*) 7da. *suc*. bro. as 5th Baron Brooke 17 Feb. 1677.

Commr. for assessment, Warws. 1664–74; recorder, Warwick 1677–*d*., Coventry 1682–1706; j.p. Warws. 1681–?*d*.[1]

Greville's family can be traced back as Warwickshire landowners to 1398, and first sat in Parliament in 1414. His father, an Independent and probably a republican, was killed by a royalist sniper while commanding the siege of Lichfield in the Civil War; but his brother, the 4th Lord Brooke, was one of the peers sent to The Hague in May 1660 to invite Charles II to return. Greville himself can scarcely have been of age when he was returned on the family interest for Warwick at a by-election in 1664. Though 'well-bred' and of 'very good capacity', he was 'always a man of pleasure' and a gambler, and he never became active in the Cavalier Parliament, defaulting on a call of the House in 1668. He was added to the committee of elections and privileges in three sessions, and named to one private bill committee and the committee on the bill to prevent the growth of Popery on 27 May 1675. He was probably in opposition under the Danby administration, but he succeeded to his brother's title and interest two days after the start of the 1677 session. As a peer he was marked 'doubly worthy' on Shaftesbury's list, and he voted for exclusion in 1680 and seems to have been popular with the dissenters in Coventry. But he played an active part in securing the surrender of the Warwick and Coventry charters, and supported Tory candidates in 1685. He was later listed among the opposition to James II, and after the Revolution he and his son Francis Greville[†] were described as 'great assertors of the prerogative in church and state'. He died on 22 Oct. 1710 and was buried in the family vault in St. Mary's, Warwick. Three of his sons sat for Warwick as Tories between 1690 and 1727.[2]

[1] *CSP Dom.* 1682, pp. 35–36; *Q. Sess. Recs.* (Warws. Recs. ix), p. xliii. [2] F. E. Greville, *Warwick Castle*, ii. 748; *CSP Dom.* 1676–7, pp. 459–60; 1682, pp. 8, 19; 1685, p. 72; Add. 34730, f. 40; Add. 41803, f. 33; *EHR*, lxix. 303.

A.M.M.

GREY (GRAY), Hon. Anchitell (c.1624–1702), of Risley, Derbys.

DERBY   16 Feb. 1665, 1679 (Mar.), 1679 (Oct.), 1681, 1689, 1690

b. c.1624, 2nd but 1st surv. s. of Henry Grey[†], 1st Earl of Stamford (*d.*1673), by Lady Anne Cecil, da. and coh. of William Cecil[†], 2nd Earl of Exeter; bro. of Hon. John Grey* and Thomas Grey[†], Lord Grey of Groby. *m.* by 1657, Anne (*d.* 2 June 1688), da. and coh. of Sir Henry Willoughby, 1st Bt., of Risley, wid. of Sir Thomas Aston, 1st Bt.[†] of Aston, Cheshire, 1s. *d.v.p.* 1da.[1]

Commr. for assessment, Derbys. 1657, Derbys. and Notts. Aug. 1660–80, 1689–90, Leics. Aug. 1660–1, 1677–9, Warws. 1677–80; sheriff, Notts. 1657–8; commr. for militia, Derbys. and Notts. Mar. 1660; j.p. Derbys. Mar. 1660–80, Derbys. and Notts. Feb. 1688–*d.*; dep. lt. Derbys. July 1660–?81, Feb. 1688–*d.*, Leics. 1667–?81, Notts. 1692–*d.*; commr. for loyal and indigent officers, Derbys. 1662, oyer and terminer, Midland circuit 1665.[2]

Gent. of the privy chamber extraordinary June 1660.[3]

Grey claimed descent from Anchitel de Grai, a Domesday tenant-in-chief in Oxfordshire, and his ancestors were certainly major landowners in Derbyshire in the 13th century. Several branches of the family were called to the House of Lords in the Middle Ages, but the first of his ancestors to sit in the Commons was his great-grandfather, who represented Essex in 1589. His father and his elder brother (who died in 1657) were ardent Presbyterians and Parliamentarians in the Civil War. But by 1659 the family was for 'King and Covenant', and Grey was arrested for complicity in the rising of his brother-in-law, Sir George Booth*.[4]

By his marriage Grey acquired an estate at Risley, six miles east of Derby, and he canvassed the borough while Roger Allestry* was on his deathbed in 1665. On 4 Feb. he wrote to his brother-in-law, Robert Bruce*:

> Lord Devonshire gave me his recommendatory letter to the corporation of Derby, which I thought it a respect due to my lord from me to crave at his hands, although the business in effect was concluded some days before. There is some difficulty, which is that Mr [John] Frescheville* may be taken off from urging me to stand for knight of the shire.... Mr Allestry is yet living, but is on the point of expiring every hour, so that while it pleases God to continue him I can make no further progress than give the corporation their fill of sack and tobacco.

He was returned unopposed, and continued to represent the borough, with one interval, for 30 years. He is seldom distinguished in the Journals from his namesakes in the House, but he was probably moderately active as a committeeman in the Cavalier Parliament. He may have been appointed to 78 committees, although few of them were of much political significance. In his only recorded speech, he 'made a fair excuse' for the absence of his colleague John Dalton* on 18 Jan. 1667, and three days later was appointed by full name to the committee for the illegitimization of the children of Lady Roos, whose husband (John Manners*) after his divorce married Grey's niece, Lady Diana Bruce. On 24 Jan. he carried a local estate bill to the Lords.[5]

With the proceedings against Clarendon in the next session Grey began the parliamentary diary which constitutes his real title to fame. No other individual has covered single-handed so long a span from 1667 to 1694, though the initial entries are considerably scrappier than the record kept by his colleague for the county, John Milward*. Much of the material about Commons debates used by Samuel Starkey for his news-letters about this time was apparently derived from Grey. It would seem that he was one of the country Members who seceded from the House after their defeat in two important divisions on 18 Feb. 1668, but he was noted as a friend of Ormonde, and Sir Thomas Osborne* listed him in 1669 among the Members to be engaged for the Court by the Duke of York. His was the first name on the committee appointed to consider a bill to settle the Derbyshire manor of Duffield Frith in 1670, and in the following year he probably carried up two more estate bills, one of which was promoted by his nephew Henry Booth*.[6]

Although others besides Sir Thomas Meres* must have observed Grey taking shorthand notes of the proceedings, it was only in 1674 that he was given any opportunity to use them for the benefit of the House by serving on the committee to inspect the Journals. He probably introduced the second bill to enable the spendthrift Derbyshire poet Charles Cotton to sell land in 1675, for he was the first Member named to the committee. In the autumn session he was appointed to the committees for the appropriation bill and the Derwent navigation bill. In retirement many years later he remembered that the latter had 'passed through my hands so far as twice reading to commitment, and summons to the country to be heard, but was extinguished on prorogation'. The great objection to the bill was that 'the price of corn in that market will depend wholly upon the Derby traders. . . . I confess I could not then balance that objection with any great conveniences to the country in other matters of trade.' When Coleman, the Duchess of York's secretary, was being examined by the committee of inquiry into the assault on the Protestant convert Luzancy, he said that he had shown his paper justifying the principal culprit to Francis Hawley* and Grey; but (Sir) John Malet* suppressed their names in his report to the House. During the subsequent long recess Sir Richard Wiseman* described Grey as 'my ancient acquaintance and friend; but I could never get him to go [right] as yet', and Francis Gwyn* later remembered him as 'a very angry man'. On 19 Feb. 1677 William Cavendish*, Lord Cavendish, informed the House that Grey had 'business of consequence' with one of the lords sent to the Tower for insisting that Parliament had been automatically dissolved. He was probably appointed to the committees to inquire into abuses in the collection of the hearth-tax, a particularly vexatious impost in an industrial neighbourhood, and to prevent the growth of Popery. In April 1678 either Grey or his brother was named to two important committees, those to inquire into the dangers from Popery and to summarize foreign commitments. When Grey's old acquaintance Coleman was arrested during the Popish Plot, he supplied a translation of one of the letters found in his possession, although not a member of the committee. In the *Debates* it is recorded that the compiler acted as teller for retaining the word 'traitorously' in Danby's impeachment; but in the Journals the name appears as May, thereby misleading Speaker Onslow into attributing at least part of the work to the court supporter, Richard May*.[7]

Grey was re-elected to the Exclusion Parliaments, and marked 'worthy' on Shaftesbury's list. He was probably moderately active in 1679, when he may have been sent to the Lords to desire conferences on Danby's attainder and the disbandment of the army, and served on five committees, including that to consider the bill for security against

Popery. He voted for the first exclusion bill. In 1680 he was removed from the commission of the peace by the interest of Sir Henry Every, who had been able to make little opposition in the August election. He may have again been moderately active in the second Exclusion Parliament, with seven possible committees, of which the most important was to take the disbandment accounts. He defeated John Coke II* in 1681, and in the Oxford Parliament he may have helped to prepare reasons for a conference on the loss of the bill of ease for Protestant dissenters. The new charter destroyed Grey's interest at Derby, and in 1685 he stood for the county. A local Tory wrote: 'I do not find any inclination to Mr Grey in the country', but he appears to have gone to the poll. In January 1688 he was expected to regain his seat at Derby, and he was restored to local office in the following month; but it seems unlikely that he became a Whig collaborator, since in September Coke replaced him as court candidate. During the Revolution he organized the defence of Derby against the Irish troops, and he was returned to the Convention with Coke, probably unopposed, in 1689. In this Parliament, however, he was for the first time definitely overshadowed by his brother. His account of the debates of 28–29 Jan. 1689 has been unfavourably compared with the notes taken by John Somers*. He may have served on as few as seven committees, of which the most important was for the suspension of habeas corpus. He was on leave from the House for the first half of April and almost the whole of July, but the gaps in the *Debates* suggest considerably longer absences, though he was among those ordered to inspect the Journals for references to the Popish Plot on 12 June. In the second session he was appointed to the committee on the state of the revenue, and supported the disabling clause in the bill to restore corporations.[8]

Grey continued to represent Derby in the next Parliament, despite increasing sufferings from gout. He died of cancer on 8 July 1702 and was buried at Little Wilne, leaving an estate valued at £4,000 p.a. to his daughter, who died unmarried in 1721.[9]

As a parliamentary reporter Grey lacked the trained analytical mind of Somers and the access to the court caucus of Sir Edward Dering* and Daniel Finch*. He seldom introduces an aside into his record of speeches, and even less often does he permit himself a comment. There is no doubt where his political sympathies lay, and some of the court spokesmen, such as (Sir) John Berkenhead* and Sir Leoline Jenkins*, clearly bored him. It must be remembered also that the *Debates* were not printed till many years after his death, and that we have no access to his manuscript, which has probably perished. Where comparison is possible, it does not seem that he was guilty of the grosser forms of partiality in his reporting, though his principles of selection are open to challenge.[10]

[1] Collins, *Peerage*, iii. 359; *IHR Bull.* v. 55–56. [2] J. C. Cox, *Three Centuries Derbys. Annals*, i. 42, 172–3; Yeatman, *Feudal Hist. Derbys.* ii. 227; *HMC Coke*, i. 177; *HMC Coke*, ii. 358; *CSP Dom.* 1691–2, p. 276. [3] LC3/2. [4] Nichols, *Leics.* iii. 682–3; D. Underdown, *Royalist Conspiracy*, 279; *Cal. Comm. Comp.* 3252. [5] *HMC 15th Rep. VII*, 174; *Milward*, 65–66. [6] D. T. Witcombe, *Cavalier House of Commons*, 99; *CJ*, ix. 197, 219. [7] *Pepys Naval Minutes* (Navy Rec. Soc. lx), 122; *HMC Ormonde*, n.s. vi. 437; *HMC Coke*, iii. 383–4; Grey, v. 5, 101; vi. 386; *HMC Lords*. i. 7. [8] *CJ*, ix. 594, 616; x. 63, 203; *HMC Lords*, i. 177; Add. 6705, f. 101; *HMC Rutland*, ii. 86–87; Browning, *Danby*, i. 426; Simpson thesis. [9] *HMC Coke*, ii. 449; *Jnl. Derbys. Arch. Soc.* xxii. 112; Luttrell, v. 194. [10] *IHR Bull.* v. 56.

E.R.E.

GREY, Edward (c.1611–76), of Ulgham Grange, Northumb. and Covent Garden, Westminster.

BERWICK-UPON-TWEED   22 June 1660, 1661–Feb. 1676

b. c.1611, 5th but 4th surv. s. of Sir Ralph Grey[†] (*d.*1623) of Chillingham, being 2nd s. by 2nd w. Dorothy, da. of Thomas Malet[†] of Enmore, Som., wid. of Sir Thomas Palmer of Fairfield, Stogursey, Som. *educ.* Univ. Coll. Oxf. matric. 18 Nov. 1625, aged 14; Christ's, Camb. 1626; G. Inn 1629. *m.* aft. 1640, Mary (*d.*1650), da. and coh. of Robert Delaval of Cowpen, Northumb., wid. of Robert Mitford of Seghill, Northumb., *s.p.*[1]

Col. of dgns. (royalist) 1642–6, 1648; capt. of King's Ft. Gds. (later Grenadier Gds.) 1661, maj. 1664, lt.-col. 1665–*d.*[2]

Freeman, Berwick 1648; j.p. Northumb. July 1660–*d.*, Westminster 1665–*d.*; commr. for assessment, Berwick Aug. 1660–74, Northumb. 1673–4, loyal and indigent officers, Northumb. 1662; commr. for hackney coaches, London and Westminster 1667–*d.*; dep. lt. Northumb. 1669–*d.*[3]

Gent. of the privy chamber by June 1660–*d.*; commr. for licensing pedlars 1665, loyal and indigent officers' accounts 1671.[4]

Grey's half-brother, the father of Thomas Grey*, was raised to the peerage in 1624. Grey himself inherited a modest patrimony, rated at only £272 p.a. in 1663, and despite his varied and expensive education failed to adopt a profession. He took the opposite side to his father's first family in the Civil War, serving as a colonel in the royalist army until the surrender of Newark. After subscribing to the Covenant and the negative oath he was allowed to compound at £389 10s. But he was in arms again in the second Civil War, and for a time commanded the royalist garrison of Berwick. 'There is not a man in the North of England', Sir Arthur Hesilrige[†] told the Commons, 'who hath done you more mischief than Colonel Grey.' His estate was sold by the treason trustees in 1652. Grey, who had fled abroad, returned in the same year, ostensibly to

make his peace with the republican regime, but actually to work for a restoration as one of the leaders of the 'action party'. He was arrested on 6 Feb. 1655; proof of his relations with the exiled Court was obtained, but he was reprieved from transportation on grounds of ill-health. In 1657 he accepted a pension of 10s. a week from the Protectorate, and dropped out of further conspiracy.[5]

Grey was, of course, ineligible as a Cavalier at the general election of 1660, but he was returned for Berwick at a by-election in June. In his only recorded speech he told the House why the Royalist conspirator Dr Hewitt had refused to plead at his trial in 1658. As 'Colonel Grey' he was appointed to the committees on the bill for the better observation of the Lord's day, and the Earl of Cleveland's estate bill. Shortly after the dissolution of the Convention, he was given a commission in the guards, and remained a serving officer until his death. He was re-elected to the Cavalier Parliament, and listed as a moderate by Lord Wharton. He was a moderately active Member, being appointed to 57 committees, including that for the corporations bill. Various small boons came his way, such as a share in the receipts from pedlars' licences and in moneys embezzled from the Vaudois relief fund, if he could discover any, and his name appears on both lists of the court party in 1669–71. He continued to take an interest in Northumberland affairs, serving on bills to prevent theft and rapine on the northern borders, and to prevent the import of corn upon pack-horses from Scotland, as well as on that to appoint commissioners to negotiate a union of the two kingdoms. In 1675 he was appointed to the committees for the prevention of illegal exactions and the suppression of pedlars. His name appeared on the Paston list and the list of court dependants, while on the working lists he was expected to influence his step-brother Peregrine Palmer*. He was buried at St. Paul, Covent Garden on 17 Feb. 1676.[6]

[1] *Hist. Northumb.* ix. 66; xiv. 328–9. [2] *HMC Ancaster*, 411. [3] J. Scott, *Berwick-upon-Tweed*, 210; C181/7/373; *CSP Dom.* 1668–9, p. 250; 1675–6, p. 173. [4] Carlisle, *Privy Chamber*, 165; *CSP Dom.* 1666–7, p. 40; 1671, p. 255. [5] *Royalist Compositions* (Surtees Soc. cxi), 215–17; *HMC Hodgkin*, 119; D. Underdown, *Royalist Conspiracy*, 59, 114, 131, 203; *CSP Dom.* 1655, p. 114; Hodgson, *Northumb.* pt. 3, i. 322. [6] Bowman diary, f. 58; *CSP Dom.* 1663–4, p. 677; *Cal. Treas. Bks.* ii. 214; *St. Paul Covent Garden* (Harl. Soc. Reg. xxxvi), 72.

M.W.H./G.H.

GREY (GRAY), Hon. John (c.1628–1709), of Bradgate, Leics. and Enville Hall, Staffs.

LEICESTER   1660, 2 Apr. 1677, 1679 (Mar.), 1679 (Oct.), 1681
STAFFORDSHIRE   1689, 1690, 1695

b. c.1628, 3rd s. of Henry Grey†, 1st Earl of Stamford, and bro. of Hon. Anchitell Grey* and Thomas Grey†, Lord Grey of Groby. *m.* (1) 6 May 1680, Mary (*d.* 10 Jan. 1682), da. and coh. of Sir Francis Wolryche, 2nd Bt., of Dudmaston Hall, Quatt, Salop, 1da.; (2) 2 Jan. 1683, Catherine (*d.* 21 Apr. 1691), da. of Edward, 7th Lord Dudley, 2s. 1da.; (3) Susanna, wid. of one Ball of Worcester, and of Edwin Skrymsher* of Aqualate, Staffs., *s.p. suc.* cos. Henry Grey in Staffs. estate 1686.[1]

Freeman, Leicester Apr. 1660; j.p. Leics. July 1660–80, Staffs. 1680–7, 1689–96, 1700–*d.*; commr. for assessment, Leics. Aug. 1660–1, 1663–80, Staffs. 1689–90; dep. lt. Staffs. 1689–96, by 1700–*d.*[2]

Chairman, ways and means 4–11 July 1689, committee of elections and privileges 25 Oct. 1689–5 Jan. 1691.

Grey was returned for Leicester, four miles from his home, at the top of the poll in 1660, and marked as a friend on Lord Wharton's list. He kept the corporation informed of the progress of the Restoration and the measures against the regicides, but he was not active in the Convention. As 'Mr Grey' he was appointed to ten committees, including the committee of elections and privileges. Probably in opposition to the Court, on 16 June he acted as teller against putting the question for excepting Sir William Roberts† from the benefits of the bill of indemnity. He was appointed to the committee on the bill to enable his brother-in-law, Sir George Booth*, to break the entail on his land, and after the recess on those to draw up an address for a day of fasting and humiliation and to consider the attainder bill. He was involved in a double return with the Cavalier Sir John Pretyman* at the general election of 1661. Grey was supported by the majority of the corporation, but his opponent was declared elected on the inhabitant franchise, and he was out of Parliament for 16 years.[3]

Grey was still unmarried when his father died in 1673, and appears to have managed the estate for his young nephew, the 2nd Earl of Stamford, whose matrimonial difficulties he exacerbated. On Pretyman's death in 1676 he wrote to Lord Roos (John Manners*) to ask for his support at Leicester, and was commended as 'a very loyal subject'. He defeated the lord chancellor's son, the Hon. Heneage Finch I*, at the cost of £800, and Shaftesbury marked him 'doubly worthy'. On taking his seat he hastened to report to the corporation on the anti-Papal zeal of the Lower House. With other Members he was reproved by the Speaker on 28 May 1677 for leaving his seat too hastily to attend the King in the Banqueting Hall 'before the King's message is reported . . . as if to get places at a show or a play'. No committees in the Cavalier Parliament can be definitely ascribed to Grey, and he was probably less active at this time than his long-serving elder brother. However, he may have acted as

teller against the adjournment with John Birch* on 3 June 1678, a day which is not reported in the *Debates.*[4]

Grey was re-elected to the Exclusion Parliaments, and classed as 'worthy' by Shaftesbury. He voted for the first exclusion bill, and was appointed to the committees of elections and privileges in 1680 and 1681. But no other activity can be certainly attributed to him in these Parliaments, and his politics may have begun to change after his adoption by a childless Staffordshire cousin. The family interest at Leicester was undermined by the new charter of 1684, and Grey is unlikely to have stood in the following year. His nephew was arrested after Monmouth's invasion, and would have been tried by his peers but for the prorogation of Parliament; but Grey himself was one of the churchmen removed from the Staffordshire commission of the peace in 1687. He signed the county petition for the removal of evil counsellors in 1688, and his nephews Lord Stamford and Lord Delamer (Henry Booth*) were among the first to take up arms for William of Orange.[5]

Grey was returned for Staffordshire at the general election of 1689, and played a much more prominent part in the Convention. A very active committeeman, he was probably appointed to 50 committees, and was much in demand as chairman. 'A plain but downright honest man', according to another nephew, Lord Ailesbury (Thomas Bruce*), he had been 'a downright Whig as all his family was; but he had been so by a principle and not by ambition'. He was 'truly convinced that he had been in a wrong way, and was deluded in former Parliaments' by Richard Hampden* and Hugh Boscawen*. According to Anthony Rowe* he voted to agree with the Lords that the throne was not vacant, but his name is not on Ailesbury's list. He was named to the committees for the suspension of habeas corpus, the first mutiny bill and the new oaths of supremacy and allegiance, and helped to draw up the address thanking William for his care of the Church. In the first session he was voted into the chair in grand committees on the bill to relieve London orphans, the militia bill, and the additional excise bill. On 31 May he was sent to ask the broad churchman William Wake to preach to the House. He was added to the committee to consider the Lords' amendments to the bill of rights and settlement on 26 June, and he acted as teller with Ailesbury's henchman, Thomas Christie*, on a proviso to the Wye navigation bill. He helped to draw up an address for access to the Privy Council records relating to Ireland and to consider the charges against William Harbord*. After reporting the excise bill on 10 July, he took the chair in a committee to insert some amendments, and carried it to the Lords. He acted as teller for the Tories on an amendment to the bill for restoring corporations (23 July), against accepting Harbord's explanations (29 July), and against going into supply committee (30 July). On 3 Aug. he was elected chairman of the important committee on the state of the nation, but before the recess he had time only to propose an inquiry into the balance of trade with France.[6]

When the House reassembled Grey replaced the Whig John Birch* as chairman of the committee of elections and privileges, from which he presented eight reports, as well as six from the grand committee on the state of the nation. He was also proposed as chairman of the supply committee by the Tories, but there was so large a majority for Hampden that they did not risk a division. He was appointed to the committees on the expenses and miscarriages of the war and the second mutiny bill. In the name of the grand committee he complained of the want of convoys and recommended the arrest of Commissary Shales, and on 27 Nov. he was among those appointed to draw up an address inquiring who was responsible for this appointment. On the next day, to the delight of the Tories, he had to recommend the unseating of his nephew, George Booth*, a disreputable Whig. He helped to draft the address asking for an allowance of £50,000 p.a. to Princess Anne and her husband. After the Christmas recess he took the chair for the bill to settle maintenances on the children of Sidney Wortley Montagu*, which he carried to the Lords on 13 Jan. 1690. He took the chair again in grand committee on the bills of indemnity and of pains and penalties.[7]

Grey became a Jacobite conspirator and refused to sign the Association in 1696. He died in February 1709. His son Harry succeeded as 3rd Earl of Stamford in 1720, and his grandson was returned for Leicestershire in 1738 as an opposition Whig.[8]

[1] *Staffs. Parl. Hist.* ii. 166–7; *Trans. Salop Arch. and Nat. Hist. Soc.* (ser. 4), iv. 116. [2] *Reg. Leicester Freemen*, i. 143; *HMC Lords*, i. 182, 189; *Staffs. Dep. Lts.* (Wm. Salt Arch. Soc. 1931), 234. [3] *CJ*, viii. 66; *Recs. Bor. Leicester* ed. Stocks, iv. 463, 465, 466. [4] *HMC Montagu*, 172–3; *HMC Rutland*, ii. 30, 33, 35, 40; *Recs. Bor. Leicester*, 546; Grey, iv. 389. [5] *CSP Dom.* 1685, pp. 307, 327; R. Morrice, Entering Bk. 2, p. 64. [6] *Ailesbury Mems.* 359; *CJ*, x. 131, 199, 205, 220, 256. [7] Morrice, 642; *CJ*, x. 286, 295, 296, 339. [8] *Ailesbury Mems.* 359; Le Neve, *Mon. Angl.* 1700–15, p. 164.

E.C.

GREY, Hon. Ralph (1661–1706), of Gosfield, Essex.

BERWICK-UPON-TWEED   1679 (Mar.), 1679 (Oct.), 1681, 1695, 6 Feb.–24 June 1701

b. 28 Nov. 1661, 2nd *s.* of Ralph, 2nd Baron Grey of Warke (*d.*1675) by Catherine, da. and h. of Sir Edward Ford of Harting, Suss., wid. of Hon. Alexander Colepeper of Wigsell, Kent. *educ.* St. Paul's 1677. *unm. suc.* bro. as 4th Baron 24 June 1701.[1]

Commr. for assessment, Berwick 1679–80, Northumb. 1689, Essex 1689–90; j.p. Northumb. by 1701–*d.* Auditor of land revenues, Wales 1692–1702; gov. Barbados 1697–1702.[2]

Grey's father, the younger brother of Thomas Grey*, was politically inactive, and died after holding the title for less than a year; but his brother, later created Earl of Tankerville, was conspicuous in opposition during the exclusion crisis and later. At the dissolution of the Cavalier Parliament it was reported that Grey would join with the crypto-Catholic Ralph Widdrington* to oppose (Sir) Ralph Delaval* and Sir John Fenwick* for Northumberland. 'I don't like the conjunction', wrote Sir William Frankland*; but the negotiations were probably aimed only at securing the neutrality of Widdrington at Berwick, where he was commander of the garrison. Grey duly defeated the court candidates in the family borough and continued to represent it in the Exclusion Parliaments, although under age. Shaftesbury marked him 'honest', and he voted for the bill, but he was otherwise totally inactive. Despite his brother's involvement in the Rye House Plot, Grey 'had not any way offended the Government', and Widdrington feared lest he might stand again for the borough in 1685. He made heavy sacrifices to enable the third lord to buy his pardon after participation in Monmouth's rebellion. 'A sweet-disposed gentleman', according to Macky, 'he joined King William at the Revolution, and is a zealous assertor of the liberties of the people.' In 1689 he was proposed for a post in the bedchamber which his father had held under Charles II, and as governor of Barbados. William refused both proposals at the time, but 'spoke kindly of him', and 'said he would be glad to find something for him'. After escaping from a debtors' prison in 1695, he regained his seat as a court Whig. He died of apoplexy on 20 June 1706, and was buried at Bocking, the last of the family.[3]

[1] *St. Paul Covent Garden* (Harl. Soc. Reg. xxxiii), 16. [2] *Cal. Treas. Bks.* ix. 1523, 1583; xvii. 239; *CSP Dom.* 1697, p. 135; *APC Col.* ii. 792. [3] *HMC Astley*, 42; PC2/71/302; *HMC Lords*, iv. 47; Macky, *Mems.* 103; Foxcroft, *Halifax*, ii. 213, 237; Carlisle, *Privy Chamber*, 183; Luttrell, iii. 484.

G.H.

GREY, Hon. Thomas (c.1625–72), of Gosfield Hall, Essex and Whitehall.

LUDGERSHALL   28 Oct. 1669–16 Feb. 1672

b. c.1625, 2nd s. of Sir William Grey† (*d.*1674), 1st Baron

Grey of Warke, by Cecilia, da. and coh. of Sir John Wentworth[†] of Gosfield. *unm.*[1]

J.p. Essex Apr.–July 1660, Northumb. July 1660–*d.*; commr. for assessment, Northumb. Aug. 1660–9.

Asst. R. Adventurers into Africa 1663, 1669, 1671, dep. gov. 1665, 1667–8, sub-gov. 1666, 1670; asst. R. Fishing Co. 1664; commr. for trade 1668–*d.*, plantations 1670–*d.*; gent. pens. by 1670–*d.*[2]

Grey came from a Northumberland family which can be traced back to the early 14th century and had represented the county under Richard II. Unlike many of their neighbours, they welcomed the Reformation, and Grey's father acted as Speaker of the House of Lords during the Civil War, though he refused to serve on the Council of State after the execution of Charles I. Grey's elder brother died young, and he became the heir to a settled estate of £6,000 p.a.; but he proved unmarriageable. On his paying his addresses to a highly eligible young lady in 1650, his prospective father-in-law, the Presbyterian Earl of Northumberland, wrote:

> We observed not only a very strange behaviour in him, but such a disordered melancholy as argued a mind not well composed. . . . I have neither had time nor knowledge enough to discover what it is that troubles his weak brain, but I believe it rather folly with some touch of a tame mopish madness than anything of witchcraft or love to his mother's chambermaid, as some report of him. . . . By that little which I have seen of him, if in the actions of his life he ever shows abilities, I am much deceived.

Nevertheless his father made over to him the manor of Epping, worth £1,200 p.a., and enabled him to recover Gosfield, which had been alienated by his maternal grandfather. After the Restoration he played a prominent part in the City and at Court. He invested £2,000 in the Africa company, on the board of which, according to William Coventry*, he was eager for war with the Dutch, being

> steered by the merchant party without perceiving it (being zealous for the company) and partly out of a desire to maintain a popularity with the merchants as well as the court party, so that he might be chosen the next sub-governor, of which he was ambitious, partly having nothing else to do and partly for the opportunity it gave him to make his court to his Royal Highness.

Nevertheless in 1665 he was unsuccessful at Berwick, where his uncle Edward Grey was the sitting Member. An associate of Buckingham, he probably inherited Presbyterian principles and sympathized with the anti-Anglican policy of the Cabal. But the Duke of Ormonde called him a 'worthy gentleman' after his attempt to reconcile Lord Ossory (Thomas Butler*) with Buckingham. Grey was returned for Ludgershall in 1669, presumably on the interest of the Roman Catholic Brownes, but no committees can be definitely ascribed to him, and he was

probably inactive, though listed as a court supporter by the Opposition. He was appointed to the council of trade, with a salary of £500 p.a., and it was even reported that he had been made a lord of the Treasury. But he was very ill of consumption and dropsy on 12 Feb. 1672, and died four days later. His will had been drawn up as long ago as 1655 with all the voluble piety of the period. In a codicil added shortly before his death he refers to his chambers and furniture in Whitehall.[3]

[1] *Northumb. County Hist.* xiv. 328–9. [2] *Sel. Charters* (Selden Soc. xxviii), 179, 183; T70/75; *CSP Dom.* 1670, p. 539; 1671–2, p. 176. [3] *HMC Salisbury*, xxii. 420, 423, 425; Morant, *Essex*, i. 47; ii. 382; *CSP Dom.* 1667–8, p. 453; 1671, p. 57; *Camb. Hist. Jnl.* xii. 113; Carte, *Ormond*, iv. 329; v. 64; North, *Lives*, iii. 250; *Nottingham's Chancery Cases* (Selden Soc. lxxix), 657; *HMC Buccleuch*, i. 465; *Hatton Corresp.* (Cam. Soc. n.s. xxii), 79; *Bulstrode Pprs.* 221; PCC 15 Eure.

B.D.H.

GRIFFIN, James (1667–1715), of Dingley, Northants.

BRACKLEY 1685

bap. 15 Dec. 1667, o.s. of Edward Griffin of Dingley, treas. of the chamber 1679–88, by Lady Essex Howard, da. and coh. of James, 3rd Earl of Suffolk. *m.* 29 Nov. 1684, Anne, da. and h. of Richard Rainsford II* of Dallington, Northants., 3s. 2da. *suc.* fa. as 2nd Baron Griffin of Braybrooke 10 Nov. 1710.

Capt. indep. tp. 1685; maj. (4) Horse Gds. 1686, lt.-col. Dec. 1688.

Groom of the bedchamber to James II 1685–1702, to the Old Pretender 1702.[1]

Griffin's ancestors had been landowners in the East Midlands since the reign of King John. His grandfather, a courtier, was the first of the family to become an MP, representing Downton both in the Short and Long Parliaments, and compounding in 1646 as a Royalist. Griffin was returned for Brackley at the age of 17 as a court candidate, probably on the Bridgwater interest. His only committee was to estimate the yield of the duty on French wines. He laid down his commission at the Revolution. He was arrested with his father in 1692 but released on bail, after which they seem to have gone to St. Germains. The father was a Protestant, but Griffin became a Roman Catholic. Nevertheless he had returned to England by 1704, when he promoted an estate bill. In 1708 his father was captured at sea on a Jacobite mission and died in the Tower. Griffin, 'a plain, drunken fellow', according to Swift, was allowed to succeed to the estates, but never assumed the title. He was buried at Dingley on 31 Oct. 1715. His son conformed in 1727 and sat in the House of Lords as a Tory, but no later member of the family was elected to the Lower House.[2]

[1] *Cal. Treas. Bks.* viii. 222; *HMC Stuart,* i. 171. [2] Nichols, *Leics.* ii. 587; Keeler, *Long Parl.* 196–7; *Cal. Comm. Comp.* 1206; Luttrell, ii. 477; vi. 321; *CSP Dom.* 1691–2, p. 319; *HMC Lords,* n.s. vi. 238–9.

E.R.E./J.P.F.

GRIFFITH, John (1662–87), of Cefnamwlch, Lleyn, Caern.

CAERNARVON BOROUGHS 1685

bap. 11 July 1662, o.s. of William Griffith*. *educ.* Jesus, Oxf. 1680. *m.* c.1683, Elizabeth, da. of Robert Bulkeley*, 2nd Visct. Bulkeley of Cashel [I], 2s. 1da.[1]

Dep. lt. Anglesey 1685–*d.*, Caern. 1686–*d.*; j.p. Caern. 1687–*d.*[2]

Griffith was returned for Caernarvon Boroughs in 1685, doubtless as a Tory, his father being incapacitated by age and infirmity, but left no trace on the records of James II's Parliament. He was noted as dead in the Welsh returns to the questions on the repeal of the Test Act and Penal Laws in 1687. His sons sat successively for the county from 1713 to 1740.

[1] *Cal. Wynn. Pprs.* 371; J. E. Griffith, *Peds. Anglesey and Caern. Fams.* 169; *Anglesey Antiq. Soc. Trans.* (1943), 23. [2] *CSP Dom.* 1686–7, p. 47; *Trans. Caern. Hist. Soc.* vii. 33.

A.M.M.

GRIFFITH, William (c.1620–88), of Cefnamwlch, Lleyn, Caern.

CAERNARVON BOROUGHS 1661

b. c.1620, 2nd s. of John Griffith† (*d.*1643) of Cefnamwlch by Margaret, da. and coh. of Sir Richard Trevor† of Trevalun, Denb. *educ.* Charterhouse 1631; L. Inn, entered 1638; All Souls', Oxf. 1639. *m.* Elizabeth, da. and h. of Arthur Davenport of Calveley, Cheshire, 1s. *d.v.p.* 4da. *suc.* bro. John Griffith† c.1650.[1]

Lt. of horse (royalist) 1643–6.[2]

J.p. Caern. 1643–6, July 1660–87; commr. for assessment, Caern. 1657, Aug. 1660–80, Anglesey 1673–80; sheriff, Caern. by Sept. 1661, dep. lt. 1661–Feb. 1688, col. of militia c.1663–?66.[3]

Griffith's ancestors had held Cefnamwlch since the 15th century and first served for Caernarvon Boroughs in 1604. His father, who sat for Beaumaris in the Long Parliament, was a Straffordian and a commissioner of array during the Civil War until his death at Oxford. His elder brother, a pictuesque character known as 'Prince Griffin', represented the county until expelled the House for attempted rape on 10 Aug. 1642, after which he received a commission in the parliamentary army; but he had to flee the country to avoid a murder charge in 1648, and died in Paris soon afterwards. Griffith himself was intended for the legal profession. He was taken prisoner during the Irish rebellion, but subsequently fought for the King in

the Caernarvonshire horse. Not only did he avoid sequestration, but he was also canvassed for his vote in the 1656 elections, when 'malignants' were generally 'ticketed'. His offer to serve as sheriff in the following year was not accepted, but he was appointed to the assessment commission.[4]

Griffith apparently had some thoughts of standing in 1660, but is unlikely to have gone to the poll against the Glynne interest. At the Restoration he offered to lease the Caernarvonshire and Flintshire fines at £20 p.a. He was elected to the Cavalier Parliament by agreement with Sir Richard Wynn*, whose convivial habits he shared. Although energetic in repressing local disaffection and dissent, he proved inactive in the House. He was appointed to only 13 committees, of which the most important was to recommend measures against conventicles in 1663. Nevertheless by promoting the transfer of the assizes to Caernarvon he left his mark on the statute book, though it was alleged that he had acted 'more out of design than any love to the town or the country'. His was the first name on the committee for the bill, which he carried to the Lords on 4 June. Although he had promised to attend, he was listed as a defaulter in 1666, and again in 1668 and 1671. On the last occasion he was vouched for by (Sir) John Berkenhead*, but Sir Trevor Williams* told Sir Robert Carr* that he was able to travel, and he was ordered to pay double taxation. On a list of government supporters drawn up by Sir Richard Wiseman he was noted as absent throughout the autumn session of 1675, and Shaftesbury marked him 'doubly vile'. Although never blacklisted, he is unlikely to have stood again. He failed to answer the questions on the Tests and Penal Laws, being 'aged and very infirm', and was removed from the lieutenancy. He died on 31 July 1688, aged 68.[5]

[1] J. E. Griffith, *Peds. Anglesey and Caern. Fams.* 169; *Cheshire Vis. Peds.* (Harl. Soc. xciii) 34. [2] N. Tucker, *Royalist Officers in North Wales,* 31. [3] *Cal. Wynn Pprs.* 364; *Cal. North Wales Letters* (Univ. Wales Bd. of Celtic Studies, Hist. and Law ser. xxiii) 161; NLW, Clenennau mss 726. [4] Keeler, *Long Parl.* 197–8; L. Inn Black Bks.* i. 375; *Cal. Wynn Pprs.* 346, 348. [5] *Cal. Wynn Pprs.* 355, 361, 368, 374, 383, 386; *CSP Dom.* 1660–1, p. 395; 1663–4, p. 312; *CJ,* viii. 482; *Trans. Caern. Hist. Soc.* vii. 33.

A.M.M.

GRIMSTON, Sir Harbottle, 2nd Bt. (1603–85), of Gorhambury, Herts.

HARWICH	20 Oct. 1628
COLCHESTER	1640 (Apr.), 1640 (Nov.)[1]
ESSEX	1656[2]
COLCHESTER	1660, 1661, 1679 (Mar.), 1679 (Oct.), 1681

b. 27 Jan. 1603, 2nd but 1st surv. s. of Sir Harbottle Grimston, 1st. Bt.†, of Bradfield Hall, Essex by Elizabeth, da. of Ralph Coppinger of Stoke, Kent. *educ.* Emmanuel, Camb. 1619; L. Inn 1621, called 1628. *m.* (1) 16 Apr. 1629, Mary (*d.* 21 May 1649), da. of Sir George Croke of Waterstock, Oxon. and coh. to her bro. Thomas, 6s. (5 *d.v.p.*) 2da.; (2) 1651, Anne (*bur.* 20 Sept. 1680), da. and h. of Sir Nathaniel Bacon of Culford, Suff., wid. of Sir Thomas Meautys† of Gorhambury, 1da. *suc.* fa. 19 Feb. 1648.[3]

Recorder, Harwich 1634–?48, by 1665–84, Colchester 1638–49; j.p. Mdx. by 1638–?48, 1656–62, by 1680–*d.*, Essex by 1639–?48, 1662–*d.*, Herts. 1656–*d.*, St. Albans borough and liberty 1656; dep. lt. Essex 1642–4, Herts. c. Aug. 1660–?66, 1680–1, commr. for assessment, Essex 1643–8, Colchester 1644–8, Herts. 1657, Jan. 1660, Essex, Herts., St. Albans and Mdx. 1660–80, Colchester 1667–80, sequestrations, Essex 1643, levying money, Essex and Colchester 1643, defence, eastern association 1643, new model ordinance, Essex 1645, militia, Essex 1648, Essex and Herts. Mar. 1660; bencher, L. Inn 1648, treas. 1658–9; commr. for oyer and terminer, London Nov. 1660; high steward, Colchester by 1661–84, St. Albans 1664–*d.*; commr. for recusants, Essex 1675.[4]

Commr. for both kingdoms 1644–8, scandalous offences 1646, indemnity 1647–8, obstructions 1648, exclusion from sacrament 1648, Isle of Wight treaty 1648; Councillor of State, 23 Feb.–31 May 1660; master of the rolls Nov. 1660–*d.*[5]

Speaker of House of Commons 25 Apr.–29 Dec. 1660.

Grimston came from a cadet branch of an ancient Yorkshire family which had settled in Suffolk in the early 15th century, and produced a Member for Eye in the Armada year. His father, who sat for Harwich in the Long Parliament, was a Parliamentarian in the Civil War and a Presbyterian elder. Grimston himself, a lawyer, shared his father's political and religious outlook and distinguished himself in opposition to Laud and the high church party. But, as one of those responsible for the treaty of Newport with the King, he was imprisoned at Pride's Purge. After marrying the daughter of the most celebrated gentleman-artist of the time he bought Gorhambury from her first husband's family for £10,000, and three years later his income was estimated at over £3,000 p.a.[6]

On the return of the secluded Members, Grimston was appointed to the Council of State and worked for the Restoration. At the general election of 1660 he stood unsuccessfully for Essex, but he was returned for Colchester on the corporation interest. Lord Wharton marked him as a friend, to be reserved to his own management. According to Clarendon his election as Speaker 'was contrived by those who meant well to the King, and he submitted to it out of a hope and confidence that the designs would succeed': but the Essex churchman (Sir) John Bramston* was less happy about the choice:

Ere we got into the House . . . they were seated (as they had contrived), and Mr [William] Pierrepont* had named Sir Harbottle Grimston for Speaker, and they were conducting him to the chair before many others were come into the House.

Grimston was described by the Venetian resident as 'a learned man, versed in affairs of state, upright, a Presbyterian but very moderate'. As Speaker it fell to him to answer the King's letter, and to welcome him to London on 29 May. He served on the commission for the trial of the regicides, and was rewarded with a life patent for the mastership of the rolls. The profitability of this 'very gainful employment' was increased by a private Act enabling him to lease out his official property, which was rushed through under the chairmanship of the Hon. William Montagu*. According to Burnet, for many years his chaplain at the Rolls, 'he was a just judge, very slow and ready to hear everything that was offered, without passion or partiality'.[7]

As his office had long ceased to be incompatible with a seat in the Commons, Grimston again stood for Essex in 1661, but withdrew after the first day's polling and was returned for Colchester. Wharton again listed him as a friend. But he was an inactive Member, making 22 recorded speeches and sitting on only 19 committees. In the opening session he was added to the managers of a conference on the security bill on 5 June, and two days later appointed to consider the bill restoring bishops to the House of Lords. He was the first to be appointed to a committee for regulating the fees of masters in Chancery, and on 10 July he served on a small committee to add a necessary proviso to the bill confirming the abolition of High Commission. He took no part in the Clarendon Code, but was among those appointed to bring in a bill against the growth of Popery in 1663. 'A very pious and devout man', according to Burnet, 'he was much sharpened against Popery, but had always a tenderness to the dissenters, though he himself continued still in the communion of the Church.' He was listed as a court dependant in 1664. In November of the same year a barrister named Bacon, who had had custody of his mother-in-law's property, was convicted for 'endeavouring' Grimston's death. He was involved in a painful dispute with Thomas Fanshawe* in 1666, in which he was reminded of his Civil War record, but Clarendon poured balm into his wounds, and perhaps in gratitude he temporarily resumed parliamentary activity. His name again stood first in the list of the committee on the bill for regulating hospitals and schools, and he was also among those ordered to receive information about the increase in Popery. He was included in both lists of the court party in 1669–71.[8]

It was the autumn session of 1675 that marked Grimston's move into cautious opposition. Listed as an official, he received the government whip in the form of a special letter from (Sir) Joseph Williamson*. But in his first recorded speech of the Parliament, he supported the bill to prevent illegal exactions. He declared that 'they do the King best service that resist and oppose these impositions', and was accordingly named to the committee. In the debate on the state of the kingdom he called for the election of a new Parliament, adding, however, that he

would not bind the King. He has had some experience of this mischief. There is as great a mischief in the length of this Parliament as if there were no Parliament. A standing Parliament is as inconvenient as a standing army.

After the prorogation Sir Richard Wiseman* advised that the lord chancellor should 'conjure' Grimston and his son, and when Parliament met again he weakly rejected the opposition contention that it had been automatically dissolved by the long recess. Nevertheless Shaftesbury accorded him the tepid rating of 'worthy'. On 20 Feb. 1677 he opposed the building of 30 warships 'till, like wise fathers in the case of children, we could tell whether we were able to support and keep them'.

He is against giving either supply or grievances the preference. He is for going the old Parliamentary way, hand in hand.... But people's purses will not be opened without redress of grievances. He may say that we have grievances, and heart-aching ones too.... We must strengthen people's hearts before we can lighten their purses.

On 3 Mar. he told the House that his colleague John Shaw* was suing the borough of Colchester for his parliamentary wages, and he was the first Member named to the committee to free constituencies from this liability. The mayor thanked him warmly for his efforts, though the bill never achieved a second reading, and Shaw successfully extracted several hundred pounds from the corporation. Grimston was appointed to two other committees of legal interest in this session, those to take affidavits in the country and to prevent frauds and perjuries. The bill for educating the King's children as Protestants aroused his old prejudices against the high church party:

He finds in this bill that there is an engrossing and appropriating the administration of this list to be given the King by the bishops exclusive to the Commons and peers of the realm. This power in the bill to the bishops is not in our power to give. It has been said that Parliaments are omnipotent; but as great as that power is there are things not in the power of Parliaments to give away.

On 4 Apr. he demanded that 'the good laws' against recusants should be put into execution, and his last committee in this Parliament was on a bill to expedite their conviction. He supported the first article of Danby's impeachment on 21 Dec. 1678, declaring:

When once confidence is broken betwixt the King and his people, nothing tends more to the destruction of both, and they are the worst of men that have brought us to this pass that we have no trust at home.... I say it was treason at common law before the statute of 25 Edward III, and this is a power reserved in Parliament by 25 Edward III to declare it treason now.[9]

Grimston continued to serve for Colchester in the Exclusion Parliaments. Shaftesbury again marked him 'worthy' and he was moderately active in 1679. He was appointed to seven committees and made 14 recorded speeches. When the King refused to accept Edward Seymour* as Speaker he asked the House: 'Shall we not have the liberty to choose our own servant fit for our own work?'. He attacked the Lords' bill for Danby's banishment, because it was not an attainder but a composition for the treason which the fallen minister had 'confessed' by his 'flight'. He was appointed to the committees to consider the Lords' amendments to the habeas corpus bill, and to prepare reasons on the illegality of Danby's pardon. In debate he declared:

I think this pardon is void in several respects and therefore needs no bill for revocation of it.... If this be admitted that the King can grant pardons thus, it is to no purpose to complain; our mouths are stopped with a pardon.

He did not speak in the exclusion debate, but voted for the bill. Although Barillon regarded him as one of the most considerable Members of the House, in the second and third Exclusion Parliaments he was totally inactive, both in committee and debate. He died of apoplexy on 2 Jan. 1685 and was buried at St. Michael's Church, St. Albans. Burnet began his epitaph:

His principle was that allegiance and protection were mutual obligations and that the one went for the other. He thought the law was the measure of both and that when a legal protection was denied to one that paid a legal allegiance, the subject had a right to defend himself.[10]

[1] Secluded at Pride's Purge 6 Dec. 1648, readmitted 21 Feb. 1660. [2] Excluded. [3] Morant, Essex, i. 464–5; Essex Rev. v. 203; Trans. St. Albans and Herts. Arch. Soc. (1933), 68. [4] S. Dale, Harwich, 222; SP44/335/241; Essex RO, 35/101–26; T/2/26; Harwich Charters (1798), 57; Foss, Judges, vii. 100; CSP Dom. 1637–8, p. 507; 1639, p. 57; 1680–1, p. 182; HMC 10th Rep. IV, 507–10; A. E. Gibbs, Corp. Recs. St. Albans, 7, 85. [5] CSP Dom. 1648–9, p. 277; CJ, vii. 849. [6] Vis. Essex (Harl. Soc. xiii), 205–8; Morant, i. 464–5; Keeler, Long Parl. 198–9; D. Underdown, Pride's Purge, 147; Trans. St. Albans and Herts. Arch. Soc. (1933), 68. [7] Bramston Autobiog. (Cam. Soc. xxxii), 114–15, 116–17; Clarendon, Rebellion, vi. 215; CJ, viii. 1; CSP Ven. 1659–61, pp. 140–1; CSP Dom. 1659–60, pp. 429–30; Old Parl. Hist. xxii. 263–7, 317–19; Hatton

Corresp. (Cam. Soc. n.s. xxiii), 43; *State Trials*, v. 986; Burnet, ii. 76. [8] *Bramston*, 119; *CJ*, viii. 265; Burnet, ii. 76; *HMC Verulam*, 56, 68; *HMC Heathcote*, 170–1. [9] *CSP Dom.* 1675–6, p. 341; Grey, iii. 322, 341; iv. 66, 110–11, 177, 284–6, 337–8; vi. 379–80; *Pepys Naval Minutes* (Navy Rec. Soc. lx), 296; *CJ*, ix. 391, 399; *EHR*, lxvi. 46–47. [10] Grey, vi. 409; vii. 61, 175–7; Luttrell, i. 324; Burnet, ii. 76.

M.W.H./G.H./G.J.

GRIMSTON, Samuel (1644–1700), of Gorhambury, Herts.

ST. ALBANS 15 May 1668, 1679 (Oct.), 1681, 1689, 1690, 1695, 1698–17 Oct. 1700

b. 7 Jan. 1644, 6th but o. surv. s. of Sir Harbottle Grimston, 2nd Bt.* *educ.* Clare, Camb. 1663; L. Inn 1668. *m.* (1) 14 Feb. 1670, Elizabeth (*d.* 6 Feb. 1672), da. of Heneage Finch*, later 1st Earl of Nottingham, 1da. *d.v.p.*; (2) 17 Apr. 1673, Lady Anne Tufton (*d.* 22 Nov. 1713), da. of John, 2nd Earl of Thanet, 1s. 1da. *d.v.p.* *suc.* fa. as 3rd Bt. 2 Jan. 1685.[1]

Commr. for assessment, Essex, Herts. and St. Albans 1673–80, Mdx. 1679–80, Essex and St. Albans 1689, Herts. and Westminster 1689–90; j.p. and dep. lt. Herts. 1689–*d.*[2]

Gorhambury, purchased by the Grimstons in 1652, carried an important political interest at St. Albans, and Grimston was returned for the borough at a by-election in 1668. He was described in *Flagellum Parliamentarium* as 'a silly son to the master of the rolls', and was entered on both lists of the court party in 1669–71 among those who had usually voted for supply. But he was inactive in the Cavalier Parliament, in which he was appointed to the committee of elections and privileges in three sessions, and to four other committees of secondary importance. He made no recorded speeches, but acted as teller on 16 Nov. 1675 for declaring it a breach of privilege to prick an MP as sheriff while the House was sitting, though, if so, it would have been his first wife's father who would have had to take the constitutional responsibility for the offence. He was included in the working lists, and in 1676 Sir Richard Wiseman* advised that his former father-in-law, the lord chancellor, should 'conjure' him. But Shaftesbury marked him 'worthy' in the following year. He stood unsuccessfully for Sudbury and St. Albans in February 1679, when Shaftesbury again classed him as 'worthy'. At St. Albans he was said to have 'appeared too late' and 'lost it by being too close-fisted'. He was returned for St. Albans to both the second and third Exclusion Parliaments, but was totally inactive.[3]

Grimston was a candidate again in 1685 and petitioned, but without success. He was returned to the Convention but left no trace upon its records. He continued to represent the borough as a country

Whig for the rest of his life. He died on 17 Oct. 1700, the last of his family, bequeathing his estates to his great-nephew, the grandson of (Sir) Capel Luckyn*, who assumed the name of Grimston and represented St. Albans as a Whig with one interval from 1710 to 1734.[4]

[1] Clutterbuck, *Herts.* i. 96; *Bulstrode Pprs.* 131; *CSP Dom.* 1671–2, p. 128; G. C. Williamson, *Lady Anne Clifford*, 480; Collins, *Peerage*, viii. 219. [2] *Herts. Sessions Bks.* vi. 522. [3] *Trans. St. Albans and Herts. Arch. Soc.* (1933), 68; BL, M636/32, John Stewkeley to Sir Ralph Verney, 6 Feb., John Verney to Sir Ralph Verney, 10 Feb. 1679. [4] *CJ*, ix. 722; *Trans. St. Albans and Herts. Arch. Soc.* (1927), 66, 102; (1933), 68; PCC 87 Dyer.

E.R.E./G.J.

GROSVENOR, Sir Thomas, 3rd Bt. (1655–1700), of Eaton Hall, Cheshire.

CHESTER 1679 (Mar.), 1679 (Oct.), 1685, 1690, 1695, 1698–2 July 1700

b. 20 Nov. 1655, 1st s. of Roger Grosvenor (*d.*1661) of Eaton by Christian, da. of Sir Thomas Myddelton* of Chirk, Denb. *educ.* travelled abroad 1670–3. *m.* 10 Oct. 1677, Mary (*d.* 10 Jan. 1730), da. and h. of Alexander Davies, scrivener, of Ebury, Mdx., 5s. (2 *d.v.p.*) 3da. *suc.* gdfa. Sir Richard Grosvenor, 2nd Bt.[†], 31 Jan. 1664.[1]

Freeman, Chester 1677, alderman 1677–Aug. 1688, Oct. 1688–93, 1697–*d.*, mayor 1684–5; commr. for assessment, Cheshire and Denb. 1677–80, Flints. 1679–80, Chester 1689, Cheshire 1689–90; j.p. Cheshire 1681–?*d.*, Mdx. and Westminster 1687–9; sheriff, Cheshire, Nov. 1688–9; mayor, Holt 1693–4.[2]

Capt. indep. tp. 1685, Earl of Shrewsbury's Horse 1685–7.

The Grosvenor family claimed to trace their descent back to the Conquest, and they were certainly well established in Cheshire by the time of Richard II. Grosvenor's grandfather was the first of the family to sit in Parliament, representing Cheshire in 1621, 1626 and 1628. He was a Royalist in the Civil War and compounded for his estates in 1646 for £1,250. In 1659 he was suspected of complicity in the rising of Sir George Booth*. Grosvenor's father was a militia commissioner in March 1660 and was nominated a knight of the Royal Oak, his income being estimated at £3,000 per annum. In 1661 he was killed in a duel.[3]

Grosvenor was granted the freedom of Chester in June 1677 at the second attempt, and three months later was elected alderman. Although he married a great heiress, the development of the Ebury estate lay in the future, and his wealth was derived chiefly from the Welsh mines inherited from his grandfather. He rebuilt Eaton Hall, some four miles from the city, 'a very noble hall, square and very regular, with many fine walks and trees planted about it'. Grosvenor was returned for Chester to the first Exclusion Parliament, apparently without opposition. He was an inactive Member, being named only to the committee for the bill for the speedier conviction of recusants. On 10 Apr. 1679 he wrote to the corporation that

this day I had a hard bout in the Commons about the bringing in of Irish cattle. I thought I should be pulled in pieces by my countrymen and the rest of my acquaintances for dividing in the House against them for the good of the city, the which I shall always prefer before my own interest.

He had been marked 'worthy' by Shaftesbury, but he was absent at the vote on the exclusion bill. He was re-elected in September but must have come out against exclusion as he was made a j.p. for the county in 1680. He left no trace on the records of the second Exclusion Parliament and is unlikely to have stood in 1681. In September 1684 he was foreman of the Cheshire grand jury which presented the Earl of Macclesfield and several other Whigs as dangerous to the King and kingdom because of their association with Monmouth and their alleged complicity in the Rye House Plot, and recommended that they be bound over to keep the peace. Macclesfield replied with an action of *scandalum magnatum* in the court of the Exchequer against Grosvenor and several other jurymen, but all were acquitted, the judge declaring that 'no action lies against an officer doing his duty'.[4]

Grosvenor was instrumental in procuring the surrender of Chester's charter and was named mayor in the new charter of November 1684, which he carried down to the city. He was returned to James II's Parliament without a contest, and was listed among the Opposition. He was again an inactive Member, being named only to the committee of elections and privileges and to that for estimating the yield of a tax on new buildings. On Monmouth's landing he raised a troop of horse, which was eventually incorporated into the Earl of Shrewsbury's regiment and stationed on Hounslow Heath. His wife had become a Roman Catholic, and, according to his son, Grosvenor

was closeted by the King, and proffered the regiment and a peerage for his assent [to the repeal of the Penal Laws], which he refused, preferring the religion and liberty of his country to all honours and power.

In any case he gave up his commission on 1 Apr. 1687, and on the next day, so his old friend Bishop Cartwright noted in his diary, he

came to me for satisfaction, whether in conscience he could submit to the taking off of the Penal Laws, to whom I read my papers, with which he declared himself well satisfied, but that he thought the King expected the taking off all Penal Laws, etc.

In August 1688 he was removed as alderman in the general purge of the corporation of Chester, and was not reappointed in the new charter. He was defeated in the 1689 election, and on 2 Sept. Charles Trelawny* reported that 'the frequent and great meetings of Roman Catholics every week at Sir Thomas Grosvenor's have occasioned his neighbours to complain of him'.[5]

Despite the handicap of his wife's religion, Grosvenor regained his seat in 1690. A Tory under William III, he nevertheless signed the Association in 1696 after an initial refusal. He died of a fever on 2 July 1700 and was buried at Eccleston. His son, the 4th Baronet, sat for Chester as a Tory from 1715 until his death.[6]

[1] C. T. Gatty, *Mary Davies and the Manor of Ebury*, i. 215, 222; *CSP Dom.* 1670, p. 149. [2] Chester corp. assembly bk. 2, ff. 185, 186, 198–200; 3, f. 59v; SP44/70, p. 75; PC2/72, pp. 723, 752; A. N. Palmer, *Town of Holt*, 150; *Diary of Bp. Cartwright* (Cam. Soc. xxii), 43. [3] Ormerod, *Cheshire*, ii. 383–4; *Cal. Comm. Comp.* 1187. [4] Gatty, i. 214; ii. 35; Chester corp. mayors' letters 4, f. 509; *Arch. Camb.* i. 412; lxxxiv. 198–9; L. A. Dasent, *Grosvenor Square*, 16–21; R. Morrice, Entering Bk. 1, pp. 421, 431, 456; *CSP Dom.* 1683–4, p. 391; *HMC Portland*, ii. 156. [5] Fenwick, *Chester*, 231–5; SP44/70, p. 75; T. Wotton, *Baronetage* (1741), i. 497–8; *Cartwright Diary*, 23, 43; Morrice, 1, p. 598; 3, p. 123; Grey, x. 79; *CSP Dom.* 1689–90, p. 238. [6] Chester corp. assembly bk. 3, f. 59v.

G.H./B.D.H.

GROVE, Thomas (c.1609–92), of Ferne, Donhead St. Andrew, Wilts.

MILBORNE PORT	c. Dec. 1645[1]
WILTSHIRE	1654, 1656
MARLBOROUGH	1659
SHAFTESBURY	1660

b. c.1609, 1st s. of Robert Grove of Mere by Honor, da. of Thomas South of Swallowcliffe. *educ.* M. Temple 1627. *m.* (1) 15 Dec. 1628, Mary, da. of John Low of Salisbury, wid. of John Grove of Shaftesbury, Dorset, *s.p.*; (2) Elizabeth, da. and coh. of Edward Lambert of Boyton, Wilts., wid. of Robert Henley of Leigh, Som., 3s. *suc.* fa. c.1642.[2]

Freeman, Poole 1642; commr. for assessment, Wilts. 1643, Dorset, Wilts. and Som. 1647–8, Som. 1649–50, Wilts. 1657, Jan. 1660–1, 1690; j.p. Dorset 1646–8, Dorset and Wilts. 1652–July 1660; commr. for militia, Som. and Wilts. 1648, Dorset and Wilts. Mar. 1660, scandalous ministers, Wilts. 1654.[3]

Commr. for scandalous offences 1648, trade 1655–6, relief of Piedmontese Protestants 1656.[4]

Grove claimed descent from a medieval Buckinghamshire family which produced a Member for Amersham in 1301. They had been connected with Shaftesbury since the 15th century, and his great-grandfather sat for the borough in 1545. Grove, enthusiastically described by Calamy as 'that ornament of his country for learning, piety and public spiritedness', was a Parliamentarian during the Civil War, and sat for Milborne Port as a recruiter until Pride's Purge. A staunch Presbyterian, he returned to public life under the Protectorate, and was named by the Dorset Quakers as one of their persecutors. Returned for Shaftesbury, four miles from his home, at the general election of 1660, he was listed by Lord Wharton as a friend, to be managed by John Thurloe[†] and Sir Wilfred Lawson*. An inactive Member of the Convention, he was named to 11 committees, including the committee of elections and privileges and that to consider the complaints of the intruded dons at Oxford about their expulsion by the Marquess of Hertford as chancellor of the university. He helped to prepare reasons for a conference about orders issued by the House of Lords. On 16 July, in his only recorded speech, he urged the House not to pass any resolution on religious discipline, saying that the King was now in consultation with divines. After the recess he was appointed to the committee on the bill for the prevention of profanity, and was added to that for restoring the dukedom of Somerset to Lord Hertford.[5]

Perhaps Grove hoped that his services on this last committee would assist his candidature at Marlborough in 1661. But he was to be disappointed, for he was opposed by Lord John Seymour* and defeated by one vote after three eve-of-poll desertions. He retired into private life, and held no office for the remainder of Charles II's reign. In 1670 he was prosecuted for keeping a conventicle in the cellars of Ferne. Under the Declaration of Indulgence both he and his son took out licences for Presbyterian chapels, but his conventicle was again raided in 1677. He received a few votes at Shaftesbury in the first general election of 1679, but he was not a serious candidate and in 1681 he promised his interest to Thomas Bennett*. He apparently became a Whig collaborator under James II, even though his son married the daughter of Dame Alice Lisle, the most prominent victim of the Bloody Assizes. The King's agent recommended that he be restored to the commission of the peace, and he was approved as court candidate for Wilton; but it is unlikely that he stood. He was buried at Donhead St. Andrew on 27 Jan. 1692, and the parliamentary history of the family was not renewed until 1865.[6]

[1] Did not sit after Pride's Purge 6 Dec. 1648, readmitted 21 Feb. 1660. [2] Hoare, *Wilts. Dunworth*, 58; *Wilts. Par. Reg.* v. 39; *Wilts. Arch. Mag.* xxxviii. 597, 627; PCC 6 Crane. [3] Hutchins, *Dorset*, i. 32; Christie, *Shaftesbury*, i. p. xxxiv. [4] *CSP Dom.* 1655–6, pp. 1, 100. [5] Hoare, 55; Calamy, *Nonconformists' Mem.* iii. 363; SP18/130/46; Bowman diary, f. 81. [6] *HMC 15th Rep. VII*, 162; *Ventris Reps.* ii. 41–44; *CSP Dom.* 1671–2, pp. 437, 552; *HMC Var.* i. 154; Wilts. RO, 413/435; *Pythouse Pprs.* ed. Day, 88; Hoare, 53.

M.W.H./J.P.F.

GRUBBE, Walter (1655–1715), of Eastwell House, Potterne, Wilts.

DEVIZES   1685, 1689, 1690

bap. 11 Aug. 1655, 2nd s. and h. of Thomas Grubbe of Potterne by Thomasine, da. of Walter Bourchier of Barnsley, Glos. *educ.* Trinity, Oxf. matric. 3 July 1672, aged 17; G. Inn 1673. *m.* lic. 7 Feb. 1678, Rebecca, da. of Randolph Brereton of London, *s.p. suc.* fa. c.1669.[1]
    Commr. for assessment, Wilts. 1679–80, 1689, j.p. 1680–June 1688, Oct. 1688–?*d.*, major of militia by 1688; freeman, Devizes to 1687.[2]

Grubbe's ancestors had been associated with Potterne since the 15th century, probably as tenants of the manor under the bishops of Salisbury. One of them sat for Devizes, two miles away, under Elizabeth, but they were not a regular parliamentary family, nor did they register their pedigree with the heralds before 1623. Neither Grubbe's grandfather nor father is known to have taken any part in the Civil War, though the latter served briefly on the commission of the peace during the Interregnum. Grubbe must have opposed exclusion, for he was made a j.p. in 1680, and returned for Devizes under the new charter in 1685. He left no trace on the records of James II's Parliament. He was displaced as freeman of Devizes by order in council on 23 Dec. 1687. To the lord lieutenant's questions on the repeal of the Test Act and Penal Laws, he replied:

> He will not declare his opinion till he comes into Parliament, and upon the debate of the House will govern himself to the best of his judgment to serve the King and kingdom. He will be for such [candidates] as are undoubtedly loyal.

Grubbe's confidence in re-election proved to be fully justified. In the Convention he voted to agree with the Lords that the throne was not vacant. An inactive Member, he was appointed to six committees, none of much political importance. He was re-elected in 1690, but this was the last appearance of his family in Parliament. He was buried at Potterne on 13 Sept. 1715.[3]

[1] Wilts. RO, Potterne par. reg.; *Vis. Glos.* ed. Fenwicke and Metcalf, 21; *London Mar. Lic.* ed. Foster, 596; information from Mr P. Montagu-Smith; PCC 36 Penn, 49 Fox. [2] *HMC Lords*, i. 192; PC2/72/562. [3] *Wilts. Arch. Mag.* xvi. 268–70; *Wilts. Vis. Peds.* (Harl. Soc. cv), 76; B. H. Cunnington, *Annals of Devizes*, ii. 195; information from Miss E. Crittall.

J.P.F.

GUEANE see GEWEN

GUISE (GUYSE), Sir John, 2nd Bt. (c.1654–95), of Elmore, Glos.

GLOUCESTERSHIRE   1679 (Mar.), 1679 (Oct.), 1681, 1689, 1690, 13–19 Nov. 1695

b. c. 1654, o.s. of Sir Christopher Guise, 1st Bt.†, of Elmore by 2nd w. Rachel, da. of Lucas Corsellis, merchant, of London. *educ.* Christ Church, Oxf. matric. 3 Dec. 1669, aged 15; travelled abroad (France) c.1675. *m.* settlement 10 July 1674, Elizabeth, da. of John Grobham Howe I* of Little Compton, Withington, Glos., 1s 2da. *suc.* fa. Oct. 1670.[1]

Commr. for assessment, Glos. 1673–80, 1689–90, j.p. 1674–80, 1689–*d.*, dep. lt. ?1674–81, 1689–*d.*; freeman, Gloucester 1675–84, 1686–?*d.*, mayor 1690–1; v.-adm. Glos. 1691–*d.*[2]

Col. of ft. Nov. 1688–9.

Guise's ancestors had held Elmore since 1274, and one of them represented the county as early as 1328. His father took no part in the Civil War, but was returned for Gloucestershire in 1654 and 1656, and accepted a baronetcy at the Restoration. Guise himself, according to his son,

> of all things loved popularity, and had an excellent way of managing the common people to obtain it. He was very healthy, of a robust make, an open countenance and cheerful, not displeased with the company of the meanest, nor unfit for that of the best, yet he was never so acceptable either to his equals or superiors as to those of less rank than himself. He was liberal and kind to his friends, stout and unrelenting to his enemies, yet very ready to forgive offences upon acknowledgment made.

In his youth, indeed, he was clearly of a quarrelsome and even violent disposition. He was returned for the county without a contest in the first election of 1679, and marked 'honest' on Shaftesbury's list. A moderately active Member of the first Exclusion Parliament, he was appointed to four committees, but did not speak. On 24 Mar. he was sent to ask for the Lords' concurrence to the resolution affirming the existence of 'a horrid and treasonable plot'. He served on the committees to examine the disbandment accounts, to consider the bill for the better discovery of recusants and to consider the complaint against John Robinson I*. He was teller for the unsuccessful motion that all who came to the committee for the continuance of the Irish Cattle Act should be allowed to vote. In view of his later Whig record, his last two mentions in this Parliament are surprising; he voted against exclusion and acted as teller against the election petition of Philip Foley* for Bewdley. He was re-elected in the autumn, though not without opposition, and was again moderately active as a committeeman in the second Exclusion Parliament, being appointed to five committees. He told the House on 17 Nov. 1680 that 'two of University College are Papists, and in the Plot'. He probably proposed the repeal of the Severn Fishery Act on 29 Nov., since his was the first name on the committee to bring in a bill for that purpose. On 20 Dec. he claimed privilege, on grounds unspecified, against a colleague on the Gloucester corporation. He spoke three times

in the debate on 7 Jan. 1681, wishing to postpone action against Laurence Hyde* but hoping that, if the House continued sitting, 'he will help us to a Privy Councillor or two', and moving against the Duchess of Portsmouth. There was opposition to his re-election in 1681 from the radicals, but he was again successful. Although he left no trace on the records of the Oxford Parliament, he was now clearly an exclusionist, and in June 1681 he and Sir Duncombe Colchester* were ordered to be removed from the lieutenancy.[3]

Guise was defeated in the general election of 1685 by the Court candidates. He was sent for in custody during Monmouth's invasion, and withdrew his election petition. After an affray in Gloucester with a hussar officer he took refuge in Holland, a country for which he always acknowledged gratitude and respect. He was noted in Danby's list among the Gloucestershire opponents of James II, and in October 1688 Richard Howe* found the county 'unanimous for Guise'. The Government was wrongly informed that he had returned there and was engaged in 'dangerous practices'. In fact he landed at Torbay with William of Orange in the following month, and was given a commission to raise an infantry regiment, with which he helped to secure Bristol. He was anxious to secure help from the dissenters, but was told that 'if they appeared, for one friend they made the Prince, they would make him twenty enemies'.[4]

Guise regained his seat in the Convention, in which he was a very active Member. He was appointed to 66 committees, from which he presented 11 reports, acted as teller in six divisions, and made 48 recorded speeches. He helped to draw up reasons for, as well as to manage, the conference on the state of the throne. He was among those appointed to inquire into the authors and advisers of grievances and to bring in the first mutiny bill. He was sent to Marshal Schomberg to ask for a guard for Members attending the coronation, and to the Lords to desire a conference on the oaths of allegiance. He was chairman of the committee for the bill to annul the attainder of Algernon Sidney†, which he carried to the Upper House on 8 May. He also took the chair for the petition from the Gloucestershire clothiers against alnage, and was given special responsibility for a bill to remedy the abuses, although when he presented it on 29 June it was ordered to lie on the table. He gave information to the House about the dispersal of Jacobite propaganda at Cambridge University and the arrest of Peregrine Osborne*. 'I am much concerned that this by a general silence should be passed over', he said. 'The breach of privilege seems plain; is it not a thing to be mended?' His remarks were clearly aimed at (Sir) Robert Sawyer*, as Member for the University, and the Earl of Nottingham (Daniel Finch*) as secretary of state. He made no secret of his objective of driving all Tories out of public life:

> Upon this maxim of policy I cannot agree to employ those I cannot trust, or put them in a capacity to do more mischief. What will all the people ruined by these men say to us? Pray, what have they deserved your favour for? For breaking all your laws?

For the Ecclesiastical Commission he blamed the then Privy Council, remarking that 'whoever does own such a Commission is never fit to serve the nation in any public capacity'. In July he took a prominent part in the consideration of Irish affairs, acting as chairman of three committees, those to inspect the Admiralty books, to ask for permission to inspect the Privy Council registers and to propose measures of relief for Protestant refugees. He brought the King's answer on 13 July, and on the same day reported from the committee of inquiry into the delays in relieving Londonderry, to which he was not formally appointed till nine days later. Together with William Sacheverell* and William Williams* he was ordered to inspect the minutes of the Irish committee on 17 July. He acted as teller against the exculpation of William Harbord* for the miscarriages in Ireland and for the adjournment of a debate on free trade in wool. He helped to manage the conference on the attainder bill, and on 2 Aug. proposed an address for the dismissal of Lord Halifax.[5]

During the recess Guise resigned his commission because of a quarrel with his second-in-command, the King remarking that 'he would by that prevent him from taking it away, which he was resolved to do'. He was also disappointed of the governorship of Portsmouth, which the Duke of Bolton (Charles Powlett I*) wanted for Richard Norton*. In the second session of the Convention he was a country Whig, openly critical of the Government as a whole. He was appointed to the committees of inquiry into the expenditure and miscarriages of the war, presenting four reports from the former. He was given special responsibility for the militia bill. He told the House on 11 Nov.: 'I do not doubt but it is absolutely necessary for your service to know the numbers of your forces in Ireland, the army here, and the fleet'. He helped to draw up the address for an inquiry, with which he attended the King. On 16 Nov. he said:

> I now hear what I have seen a good while. You give money for the war, and you know not whither it goes. . . . The best you can do is not to see your money diverted. I hope you will . . . appoint a committee to know the state of account of the nation, and you will see those that are honest.

(Sir) Henry Capel* questioned Guise's abilities in accounts, to which he retorted: 'I am as capable of reckoning 1, 2, 3 as another man'. He rejected the allegation of (Sir) Thomas Clarges* that the dissenters were republicans:

> I suppose the gentleman was not upon the spot when the charge was [made], but, I assure you, the Church of England ran away from us, and the dissenters stayed. I hear the word monarchy named; I would know who is against monarchy?

He was appointed to the committees for stating the condition of the revenue and restoring corporations, but obtained leave to go into the country on 23 Dec. because his wife was ill. He returned in time to act as teller for a proviso to the bill, and supported the disabling clause. He took the chair in the committee for the bill to indemnify those who had acted in the Revolution, which he twice carried to the Lords. In the debate on the condemnation of Sir Thomas Armstrong*, he expressed surprise 'that the House is not of the same opinion they were formerly of. . . . Did I think I sat in the House with a murderer, I would not sit till I had thrown him out.' In a further allusion to Sawyer, he exclaimed: 'The most abominable part of an attorney-general he has acted!'.[6]

Guise remained a country Whig in the next Parliament and was chosen one of the commissioners of public accounts. He died of smallpox immediately after his re-election in 1695. His son sat for Gloucestershire as a Whig under Queen Anne.[7]

[1] Bristol and Glos. Arch. Soc. Trans. iii. 72; Raymond and Guise Mems. (Cam. Soc. ser. 3, xxviii), 134. [2] Gloucester corp. council bk. 1656-86, pp. 645, 870, 918; 1690-1700, p. 12. [3] Bristol and Glos. Arch. Soc. Trans. ii. 260; iii. 50; Raymond and Guise Mems. 137-8; HMC Portland, iii. 352; CJ, ix. 621, 634; Grey, viii. 18; Gloucester corp. council bk. 1656-86, p. 870; HMC 12th Rep. IX, 113-15; CSP Dom. 1680-1, p. 350. [4] Raymond and Guise Mems. 135; HMC 12th Rep. IX, 89; R. Morrice, Entering Bk. 2, p. 42; 3, p. 47; CJ, ix. 721, 759; Grey, ix. 148, 358; 440; Bath mss. Thynne pprs. 18, f. 192; CSP Dom. 1687-9, pp. 303, 316; Luttrell, i. 482; Univ. Intell. 11 Dec. 1688. [5] CJ, x. 18, 20, 85, 98, 125, 166, 176, 190, 196, 204, 206, 212, 244, 245, 246; Grey, ix. 361, 369; Clarendon Corresp. ii. 284. [6] Foxcroft, Halifax, ii. 232; HMC Portland, iii. 431; CSP Dom. 1689-90, p. 278; CJ, x. 279, 282, 284, 286, 288, 304, 329, 330, 332, 338; Grey, ix. 406, 425-6, 427, 483, 526, 535. [7] Raymond and Guise Mems. 137; Luttrell, iii. 553.

J.P.F.

GULSTON see **GOULSTON**.

GUNTER see **GOUNTER**.

GURDON, John (1595–1679), of Assington, Suff.

IPSWICH	1640 (Apr.), 1640 (Nov.)
SUFFOLK	1654
SUDBURY	3 May 1660

b. 3 July 1595, 1st s. of Brampton Gurdon[†] of Assington by 1st w. Elizabeth, da. of Edward Barrett of Belhus, Aveley, Essex. *educ.* Emmanuel, Camb. 1611; G. Inn 1614. *m.* Anne, da. of Sir Calthorpe Parker[†] of Erwarton, Suff., 7s. 5da. *suc.* fa. 1648.[1]

Commr. for sewers, Suff. 1634, dep. lt. 1642, commr. for assessment 1643–52, 1657, Jan. 1660, 1679, sequestration 1643, defence, eastern assoc. 1643, new model ordinance, Suff. 1645, Westminster Abbey 1645, drainage of the fens 1649; j.p. Suff. 1649–July 1660, commr. for poor prisoners 1653, scandalous ministers 1654, militia 1659, Mar. 1660.[2]

Commr. for regulating excise 1645, exclusion from sacrament 1646, scandalous offences 1648, high court of justice 1649, obstructions 1651–2; Councillor of State 1650–2.

Gurdon's great-grandfather, of Essex origin, acquired the manor of Assington, five miles from Sudbury, early in the 16th century. His father, a parliamentary supporter and a Presbyterian elder, represented the borough in 1621. Gurdon, also an active Parliamentarian, inherited estates in Suffolk and Essex worth £1,400 p.a. A conformist Rumper, he absented himself from the King's trial but served on the Council of State.[3]

Gurdon was involved in a double return for Sudbury at the general election of 1660, and allowed to sit on 3 May. An inactive Member of the Convention, he was marked as a friend on Lord Wharton's list, but expressed his opposition to the Court by shaking his head, since he 'durst not speak', and was named to only three committees, including those to cancel all grants of offices and titles since 1642 and to establish a Post Office. He retired from public life at the dissolution. Assington Hall was licensed for Presbyterian worship in 1672. Gurdon was buried at Assington on 9 Sept. 1679.[4]

[1] *DNB*; J. J. Muskett, *Suff. Manorial Fams.* i. 282; Add. 19077, f. 78. [2] *HMC 9th Rep.* pt. 1, p. 312. [3] Copinger, *Suff. Manors*, i. 17–18 98, Keeler, *Long Parl.* 199–200; *Suff. and the Gt. Rebellion* (Suff. Rec. Soc. iii), 16; Add. 19077, ff. 70, 72. [4] *Voyce from the Watch Tower*, 121; *CSP Dom.* 1671–2, p. 414; *Vis. Eng. and Wales Notes* ed. Crisp, ix. 108.

M.W.H./P.W.

GURDON, Philip (c.1631–90), of Assington, Suff.

SUDBURY 1689, 20 Mar.–June 1690

b. c.1631, 3rd s. of John Gurdon*. *educ.* Colchester g.s. 1643; Emmanuel, Camb. 1650, BA 1653, MA (Queens') 1657. *m.* (1) lic. 19 Oct. 1669 (aged 38), Elizabeth (*d.*1670), wid. of Thomas Agge, merchant, of London, 1da.; (2) Margaret (*d.*1675), da. of Sir Andrew Jenoure, 2nd Bt., of Great Dunmow, Essex, *s.p.*; (3) lic. 20 July 1679, Rachel, da. of Sir Thomas Abdy, 1st Bt., of Felix Hall, Kelvedon, Essex, *s.p.*; (4) 20 Feb. 1690, Lucy, da. of Roger Hatton, Draper, of Mark Lane, London, wid. of Thomas Steward of Haslingfield, Cambs., *s.p. suc.* bro. 1683.[1]

Commr. for assessment, Suff. 1679–80, 1689–90.

Gurdon was probably a nonconformist in religion like his father, since he was not appointed to the commission of the peace after he succeeded to the family estates in 1683. Returned to the Convention for Sudbury he was appointed to no committees, made no recorded speeches, and was twice given leave to go into the country. He did not support the disabling clause in the bill to restore corporations. He was re-elected in 1690, but died shortly afterwards and was buried at Assington on 23 June. By the terms of his will his property in Suffolk, Yorkshire, Lincolnshire and London was divided between his brother and sister. His nephew John was elected at Sudbury in 1699.[2]

[1] J. J. Muskett, *Suff. Manorial Fams.* i. 282–8; *Vis. England and Wales Notes* ed. Crisp, ix. 108; Add. 19077, ff. 69, 77; *St. Martin Outwich* (Harl. Soc. Reg. xxxii), 45; *London Mar. Lic.* ed. Foster, 1287; *London Vis. Peds.* (Harl. Soc. xcii), 75; J. R. Woodhead, *Rulers of London*, 86; *Mon. Inscriptions from Cambs.* 77. [2] PCC 124 Dyke.

P.W.

GUY, Henry (1631–1711), of Tring, Herts. and King Street, Westminster.

HEDON 8 Mar. 1670, 1679 (Mar.), 1679 (Oct.), 1681, 1685, 1689, 1690, 1702

bap. 16 June 1631, o.s. of Henry Guy of Tring by Elizabeth, da. of Francis Wethered of Ashlyns, Berkhampstead, Herts. *educ.* G. Inn 1648; I. Temple 1652. *unm. suc.* fa. 1640.[1]

J.p. Herts. 1661–?d., St. Albans liberty 1682; commr. for highways, London and Westminster 1662, hackney coaches 1662–7, assessment, Herts. 1665–80, Yorks. (N. and E. Ridings) 1677–80, Westminster 1689, Herts. and E. Riding 1689–90; jt. farmer of excise, Yorks. by 1667–71; commr. for wine licences, London 1668–?71; freeman, Hedon 1669, Portsmouth 1684; commr. for recusants, E. Riding 1675; dep. lt. and maj. of militia ft. Herts. by 1680–9; member, Hon. Artillery Co. 1681; alderman, St. Albans 1685–Oct. 1688, mayor 1685–6.[2]

Cup-bearer to Queen Catherine of Braganza by 1669–75; groom of the bedchamber 1675–9; member, R. Fishery Co. 1677; receiver-gen. of fee-farm arrears 1677–9; sec. to the Treasury 1679–89, 1689, 1691–5; commr. of the stables 1682–5, customs 1690–1.[3]

Guy's father, a tenant on the crown estate, left his widow all his copyholds, valued at £200 p.a., for life. As she survived him by 50 years, Guy received at his coming of age only a lump sum of £1,800. He attached himself to the exiled Court, becoming a personal friend of Charles II and the companion of his pleasures. He applied for a post in the Queen's household when it was formed, and by 1667 he was associated with his uncle Francis Wethered in the farm of the Yorkshire excise. Their contract was renewed in the following year at an annual rent of £20,750. It was through this grant that he first acquired an interest at Hedon, which he fortified by gifts of plate to the corporation and the purchase of property in the borough.[4]

Returned to the Cavalier Parliament at a by-election in 1670, Guy was at once appointed to two committees on bills of personal interest, those providing for the sale of fee-farm rents and for reforming the assessment of wines for excise. Listed as a court supporter by the Opposition in 1671, he was described as 'a privy chamber man, who, for pimping, had the excise farm of Yorkshire, by which he got £50,000.' He helped to draft the clause transferring the additional impositions from the excise to the customs, and joined the syndicate formed by Lord St. John (Charles Powlett I*) which applied unsuccessfully for the customs farm. He contracted to purchase certain fee-farm rents, but there was a technical error in the conveyance. He attached himself to Lord Sunderland, though neither of them could obtain office under Danby's administration. However, Guy was transferred to the King's household in 1675 and listed as a court dependant. He was marked 'thrice vile' on Shaftesbury's list in 1677, when he acted as teller for the Court on the Newark election and for the Lords' proviso on the naturalization bill. In July Danby signed a warrant for Guy's appointment as receiver-general of fee-farm arrears, though it involved loss of treasury control. He was on both lists of the court party in 1678, when he was teller for the election of Robert Reeve* at Eye, and was named to committees for breaking the entail on the estates of Henry Hilyard* and of a Hertfordshire neighbour, and for building a new church in Westminster. But he was never an active Member, with only 18 committees in nine sessions.[5]

Despite his inclusion in the blacklist of the 'unanimous club', Guy was re-elected to the Exclusion Parliaments. Shaftesbury naturally classed him as 'vile', and he voted against the first exclusion bill, but otherwise left no trace on their records. On the fall of Danby he replaced Charles Bertie* as secretary of the Treasury, doubtless on Sunderland's recommendation. 'A polished figure, thoroughly acceptable at Court,' he retained this post for ten years, under several different commissions, thus breaking the tradition that the secretary would be replaced at every change in the Treasury. The reason was probably that whereas Bertie had handled the secret service money for Danby, Guy handled it directly for the King. The office was lucrative, and Guy's own estimate of his fees as £2,570 p.a. was almost certainly too low. He was probably receiving at least £3,500 p.a. before the death of Charles II and possibly as much as £5,000 p.a. after 1685. Moreover there were other ways of

turning the office to account. Lord Keeper Guilford (Francis North*) alleged that Guy and his friends made a fortune out of the Treasury by preventing the issue of funds to pay off exchequer tallies, buying them up at a discount, and then obtaining payment in full. Despite the somewhat unsavoury reputation he was acquiring in certain quarters, his friendship was much valued in others. In 1679 Henry Savile* wrote to Lord Halifax that Guy's

> steady friendship to me neither has, nor ever can, fail me, and if you knew him as well as I, whatever disadvantages his exterior may show to so nice a man as you, you would not find in England a fitter man to make a friend of.

In 1680 he received most acceptable compensation for the failure of his fee-farm grant, when the manor of Tring, part of the Queen's jointure, was transferred to him, and in 1683 it was even suggested that he should stand for Hertfordshire at the next election.[6]

Guy remained in favour under James II. In 1685 he brought in his associate Charles Duncombe* at Hedon, and become a moderately active Member of his Parliament, with eight committees, including the committee of elections and privileges. On 30 May he was sent to Lord Treasurer Rochester (Laurence Hyde*) to ask for the disbandment accounts, and he was appointed to the committee to inspect them. He also helped to consider a petition from the hackney coachmen and to estimate the yield of a tax on new buildings. Guy helped Sunderland, now lord president of the council, to oust Rochester from the Treasury in 1686, while at the same time safeguarding his own position. A correspondent wrote to the second Earl of Clarendon (Henry Hyde*) in November:

> If you saw what court Mr Guy makes, not only to my lord president, which is not new, but to others who are now in great credit, you would believe he were sure of keeping his place when the staff is in another hand.

Rochester fell and Guy remained. The King's agents reported in 1688 that he would be re-elected on his own interest. After the Revolution he stayed at his post throughout the winter of 1688–9, collaborating with the new regime.[7]

Guy did sit for Hedon in the 1689 Convention, but he was totally inactive apart from a speech on 20 Mar. in reply to a comment that secret service pensions 'were never heard of till Mr Guy's time'.

> I hear my name mentioned upon the head of great sums, though under the denomination of secret service. The reason was to ease the charge of the great seal. But, be it what it will, I am ready to give account, to a penny, of what I received.

He was dismissed in the following month.[8]

Guy was re-elected in 1690 and appointed to the customs commission, transferring to the Treasury in the following year. He managed Sunderland's interest in the Commons, but had to resign office after charges of corrupt practices in 1695 and lost his seat at the general election. He was returned to Queen Anne's first Parliament, but died on 23 Feb. 1711 and was buried at Tring, the only member of the family to sit. He left a fortune estimated at £40,000 in cash and £500 p.a. in land to the grandson of Sir William Pulteney*, the Whig statesman who became Earl of Bath in 1742.[9]

[1] Cussans, *Herts.* xiii. 82; Clutterbuck, *Herts.* i. 510. [2] *CSP Dom.* 1682, p. 218; 1685, p. 73; C181/7/151, 215; *Cal. Treas. Bks.* ii. 144, 348; iii. 1015; iv. 496; G. Poulson, *Holderness*, ii. 174; R. East, *Portsmouth Recs.* 366; Ancient Vellum Bk. ed. Raikes, 111; Clutterbuck, i. 52. [3] *CSP Dom.* 1675–6, p. 200; 1689–90, p. 514; *Cal. Treas. Bks.* v. 437; vii. 674; viii. 162–3, 404; *Savile Corresp.* (Cam. Soc. lxxi), 129; *Select Charters* (Selden Soc. xxviii), 198. [4] *DNB*; PCC 133 Coventry; Clutterbuck, i. 298; SP29/26/78; North, *Lives*, i. 196; *CSP Dom.* 1661–2, p. 388; *Cal. Treas. Bks.* vi. 857; Poulson, ii. 154, 174. [5] Harl. 7020, f. 46v; *Cal. Treas. Bks.* iii. 1259; v. 437, 674, 695; vi. 393; *CJ*, ix. 389, 416, 437; Kenyon, *Sunderland*, 15. [6] H. Roseveare, *Treasury: Evolution*, 72; Dalrymple, *Mems.* i. pt. 2, p. 146; *Savile Corresp.* 120; *VCH Herts.* ii. 383. [7] *CJ*, ix. 722; North, ii. 195; *Clarendon Corresp.* ii. 66; *Cal. Treas. Bks.* ix. 1–25; R. Morrice, Entering Bk. i, p. 388. [8] Grey, ix. 177. [9] Kenyon, 271; *HMC Lords*, n.s. iii. 399; *DNB*; Le Neve, *Mon. Angl.* 1700–15, p. 209.

P.W.

GUYBON, Sir Francis (c.1639–1705), of Thursford, Norf.

THETFORD 14 Feb. 1689, 3 May 1690

b. c.1639, 2nd but 1st surv. s. of Sir Thomas Guybon of Thursford by Barbara, da. of Sir William de Grey of Merton. *m.* (1) 2 Feb. 1669 (aged 30), Susanna, da. of Goldsmith Hodgson of Framfield, Suss., wid. of John Byne* of Rowdell, Washington, Suss., *s.p.*; (2) lic. 15 Feb. 1675, Isabella (*d.*1723), da. of Joachim Matthews† of Havering, Essex, 4s. 2da. *suc.* fa. 1666; kntd. 19 June 1682.[1]

J.p. Norf. 1668–Feb. 1688, 1689–*d.*; commr. for assessment, Norf. 1673–80, Norf. and Thetford 1689–90; capt. of militia horse, Norf. by 1676–?Feb. 1688, lt.-col. Nov. 1688–*d.*, dep. lt. by 1682–Feb. 1688, Nov. 1688–*d.*; freeman, King's Lynn 1682; sheriff, Norf. 1685–6.[2]

Guybon's ancestors acquired the manor of Thursford, five miles from Thetford, under Elizabeth, and one of them sat for King's Lynn in 1597. His father was a parliamentary supporter in the Civil War and held local office throughout the Interregnum, but signed the Norfolk address for a free Parliament in 1660.[3]

Guybon himself helped to disarm local Papists in 1679. He signed the address abhorring the 'Association' in 1682 and was knighted on the recommendation of Lord Yarmouth (Robert Paston*)

as a gentleman of £1,200 p.a. who 'in all instances manifests his loyalty'. He was absent from the meeting of deputy lieutenants at King's Lynn in February 1688 on the repeal of the Test Act and Penal Laws, 'but sent a letter whereby he desired not to answer any of the questions, not knowing but he might stand somewhere, and was resolved not to declare his opinion'. He was removed from local office, and when the King offered to restore him in October he followed the example of Sir John Holland* in refusing to join with those incapacitated under the Test Act.[4]

Guybon apparently did not stand at the general election of 1689, but he was successful at Thetford in a by-election caused by the decision of Sir Henry Hobart* to sit for the county. Although the return is dated a week after the division on the vacancy of the throne, he was blacklisted by Anthony Rowe* among those who voted to agree with the Lords. A moderately active Member of the Convention, he was named to 14 committees, including those to prevent excessive expenditure at parliamentary elections (25 Oct.), and to restore corporations (20 Dec.); but he is not recorded as speaking in the House. He stood successfully for re-election in 1690 as a court Tory. He died on 23 Jan. 1705 and was buried at Thursford, the last of the family to enter Parliament.[5]

[1] *Vis. Norf.* (Harl. Soc. lxxxv), 91; *Le Neve's Knights* (Harl. Soc. viii), 304; *The Gen.* n.s. xxiii. 7–8. [2] *HMC Lothian*, 127; Add. 28082, f. 79; Add. 36988, f. 305; *Norf. Ltcy. Jnl.* (Norf. Rec. Soc. xxx), 37, 38, 90, 124; *Lynn Freemen*, 193; Mason, *Norf.* 436. [3] Mason, 291; Blomefield, *Norf.* vii. 258; W. Rye, *Address from the Gentry of Norf.* (1660). [4] *Norf. Ltcy. Jnl.* 27, 89; Add. 36988, ff. 180, 187; *HMC Lothian*, 133, 135–6. [5] *Le Neve's Knights*, 304.

E.C.

GUYSE *see* **GUISE**

GWYN, Francis (c.1648–1734), of Llansannor, Glam. and Scotland Yard, Westminster.

CHIPPENHAM	1–6 Feb. 1673, 11 Feb. 1673
CARDIFF BOROUGHS	1685
CHRISTCHURCH	1689, 1690
CALLINGTON	1695
TOTNES	11 Jan. 1699, 1701 (Feb.)
CHRISTCHURCH	1701 (Dec.), 1702, 1705, 1708
TOTNES	1710, 1713
CHRISTCHURCH	9 Mar. 1717
WELLS	1722

b. c.1648, 1st s. of Edward Gwyn of Llansannor by Eleanor, da. of Sir Francis Popham† of Houndstreet, Som. *educ.* Christ Church, Oxf. 1666; M. Temple 1667. *m.*

18 Dec. 1690, Margaret (*d.*1709), da. and coh. of Edmund Prideaux* of Forde Abbey, Devon, 4s. 3da. *suc.* fa. bef. 1667.[1]

Commr. for assessment, Glam. 1673–9, 1689–90, Westminster 1677–80, 1689; protonotary and clerk of the crown, Brecon circuit 1677–*d.*; j.p. Glam. 1680–5, Brec., Glam. and Rad. 1687–?*d.*, Devon by 1700–?*d.*; chamberlain, Brecon 1681–90; freeman, Portsmouth 1682; recorder, Totnes 1708–*d.*; mayor, Christchurch 1719–20.[2]

Commr. for revenue [I] 1676–81; clerk of PC 1679–85; under-sec. of state (north) 1681–3; groom of the bedchamber 1683–5; jt. sec. to the Treasury 1685–6; commr. of public accounts 1696–7; sec. to ld. lt. [I] 1701–3; PC [I] 1703; ld. of trade 1711–13; sec. at war 1713–14.[3]

Gwyn's ancestors had been seated at Llansannor since the early 16th century. Though well-connected and claiming a descent from the Herberts, they seem to have played little part in Welsh politics. Gwyn's father avoided commitment in the Civil War, despite his marriage to the sister of the parliamentary colonel Alexander Popham*. Gwyn was first returned for Chippenham on the Popham interest on 1 Feb. 1673, but the election was disallowed because the writ had been issued by Lord Chancellor Shaftesbury during the recess. Ten days later he became the first of his family to enter Parliament by defeating the court lawyer, Vere Bertie, the return being upheld by the House against the recommendation of the elections committee under Sir Thomas Meres*. He was a moderately active Member of the Cavalier Parliament, in which he was appointed to 34 committees, and acted as teller in three divisions, but made no speeches. Although he had entered the House under the auspices of the country party, Ormonde described him as 'a man thoroughly devoted to the crown', and he was immediately added to the committee on the bill for the better observance of Charles I's martyrdom. His strong churchmanship led him into the following of Bertie's brother-in-law, Lord Treasurer Danby, though he was also often to be seen with Edward Seymour*. He was appointed to the committee to prevent the growth of Popery in 1675, and with (Sir) Edmund Jennings* he acted as teller for the motion to send Sir John Churchill* to the Tower on 4 June. In 1676 he was rewarded with a seat on the Irish revenue board, and included in Danby's list of servants and officers. His name also appears on the working lists and in Wiseman's account. He was made protonotary of the local circuit in 1677, and marked 'thrice vile' on Shaftesbury's list. In this session he was appointed to another committee against Popery and also to consider an estate bill promoted by (Sir) Edward Hungerford*. He was on both lists of the court party in 1678, but was appointed to the small committee entrusted with the examination of the Roman Catholic conspirator Coleman.[4]

Gwyn 'had behaved himself very dutifully' in the eyes of the Government and was naturally blacklisted in the 'unanimous club'. Defeated at both elections of 1679, he bought a clerkship of the Privy Council from Sir Robert Southwell* for £2,500, and became under-secretary to Lord Conway. In searching Shaftesbury's papers in 1681, he found the 'Association'; but when he gave evidence 'the jury asked him how it came there and who writ it'. It was reported that he also found a list of Whigs and Tories, the latter distinguished as 'men worthy', i.e. to be hanged; but this allegation depends upon the recollections of Lord Ailesbury (Thomas Bruce*). When he went out of office with Conway in 1683, a Glamorgan neighbour wrote:

There's Frank, who of late
Knew secrets of state,
Though now he's turned out of employment.
Since that he finds time
To ply women and wine,
Which will prove a more lasting enjoyment.

On 10 Jan. 1685 he sold his Privy Council office to Philip Musgrave*, and became secretary to the Earl of Rochester (Laurence Hyde*), who created for him a post at the Treasury with special responsibility for Irish finances. He remained attached to the Hyde interest for the rest of his political career.[5]

At the general election of 1685 Gwyn was recommended by his countryman, Sir Leoline Jenkins*, for Cardiff Boroughs. 'I dare take it upon me that he will serve our gracious King with all duty, and that poor country (as far as it shall come in his way) with great zeal.' Llansannor is two miles from Cowbridge, one of the more important contributory boroughs, and as a friend of Thomas Mansel II* he probably enjoyed the support of the leading family in the county. He was again moderately active in James II's Parliament, being named to seven committees, including those to inspect the disbandment accounts and to recommend expunctions from the Journals. A mature but hopeful bachelor, he acted as teller against the first reading of the clandestine marriages bill, but was appointed to the committee. He remained a government supporter in the second session, acting as teller for proceeding with supply before the King's message on the Roman Catholic army officers. But he lost his place at the same time as his patron at the end of 1686. Nevertheless he was approved as court candidate for Cardiff in 1688.[6]

Gwyn was an eye-witness of events at Salisbury during the Revolution, but returned to London after five days, and was given 'a very wholesome employment . . . that is like to be a very short one, which is secretary to the lords spiritual and temporal', who had assumed the government on James's collapse. On 25 Dec. he wrote to Lord Dartmouth (George Legge*) that:

the poor King . . . has acted so quite contrary to his interests that one would think his design was to spend the rest of his days in a cloister . . . and this second time of his going from Rochester was the day the Lords were to meet, and a great part of them would have been for an application to him in relation to a Parliament. But it is now all over. Neither he nor his (if the child be so) are like ever to set foot here again.

He asked for the admiral's interest at Portsmouth; but Richard Norton* had a superior claim, and Gwyn was returned for Christchurch on the Hyde interest.[7]

Gwyn was a very active Member of the Convention. He was named to 84 committees, in three of which he took the chair, and acted as teller in seven divisions, including that of 5 Feb. 1689 for agreeing with the Lords that the throne was not vacant. He was named to the committees to consider alterations in the coronation oath, to inquire into the authors and advisers of grievances, to approve the new oaths of allegiance and supremacy, to consider the bill of rights, to repeal the Corporations Act, and to draw up an address assuring the King of support for a war against France. He was chairman of the committee on the bill for the abolition of the court of the marches, which he carried to the Lords on 29 Apr. and again in its amended form two months later, telling them that 'all the gentlemen of his county have sent to desire this bill may pass'. On 1 May he reported on the claim of his future father-in-law Prideaux on the estate of Judge Jeffreys. He was appointed to the committees for restoring corporations and to inquire into the delays in relieving Londonderry. His only recorded speech was to defend Rochester's conduct in the debate on the indemnity bill of 1 July. He took the chair for the Lords bill to regulate the oaths taken by army officers, and was appointed to the committee on the attainder bill. On 23 July he acted as teller for an amendment to the bill for restoring corporations. He helped to prepare reasons for a conference on tithes on 19 Aug., but the measure was killed in a division on the same day, Gwyn acting as teller for the minority. In the second session he was somewhat less active. He was appointed to the committees to inquire into the expenses and miscarriages of the war, and acted as teller for the Tories against asking the King who was responsible for recommending Commissary Shales, and in one of the

divisions that led to the defeat of the disabling clause in the bill to restore corporations.[8]

Gwyn remained a Tory under William III and Anne, signing the Association in 1696 only after his election as commissioner of public accounts. He lost both his office and his seat on the Hanoverian succession, and after his return to the House in 1717 took little active part in politics, spending much of his time in antiquarian studies. His elder son sat for Christchurch from 1724 to 1727, and then succeeded him at Wells. He died on 14 June 1734, aged 86, and was buried in the chapel of Forde Abbey, which he had inherited in the right of his wife.[9]

[1] G. T. Clark, *Limbus Patrum*, 271; Hutchins, *Dorset*, iv. 528; *Cal. Treas. Bks.* vii. 1317. [2] W. R. Williams, *Great Sessions in Wales*, 156–7; J. P. Matthews, *Cardiff Recs.* v. 495–6; R. East, *Portsmouth Recs.* 366; PC2/78/63; *Trans. Devon Assoc.* lvi. 222. [3] *Cal. Treas. Bks.* v. 180; HMC Ormonde, n.s. iv. 565; CSP Dom. 1684–5, pp. 281–2. [4] Clark, 270; *CJ*, ix. 260–1, 533; HMC 6th Rep. 724; HMC Ormonde, n.s. vi. 737; Browning, *Danby*, i. 364. [5] HMC 6th Rep. 724; CSP Dom. 1679–80, pp. 90, 197; 1684–5, pp. 281–2; HMC Ormonde, n.s. iv. 565; *State Trials*, viii. 780–1; Luttrell, i. 146; *Ailesbury Mems.* i. 64; *NLW Jnl.* xxi. 172. [6] Carte 234, ff. 126–7; G. Holmes, *British Politics in the Age of Anne*, 261; *CJ*, ix. 740, 757; CSP Dom. 1687–9, p. 276. [7] *Fortnightly Rev.* xl. 358–64; HMC Dartmouth, iii. 139, 141–2. [8] *CJ*, x. 103, 216, 296, 329; Grey, ix. 380; HMC Lords, ii. 107. [9] Luttrell, iv. 74; *Hearne's Colls.* (Oxf. Hist. Soc. xliii), 194; (lxxii), 359; HMC Popham, 254–6.

B.D.H.

GWYNNE, George (c.1623–73), of Llanelwedd, Rad.

RADNORSHIRE 1654, 1656, 1660

b. c.1623, 1st s. of David Gwynne of Berrisbrook, Carm. by Joan, da. of George Morgan of Itton, Mon. *educ.* St. John's, Oxf. matric. 4 Dec. 1640, aged 17. *m.* Sybil, da. and h. of Roderick Gwynne of Llanelwedd, 2s. 6da. *suc. fa.* 1651.[1]

Commr. for militia, Rad. 1648, 1659, Mar. 1660; sheriff, Carm. 1650–1, Mon. 1662–3; commr. for assessment, Carm. 1652, Carm. and Rad. 1657, Mon. and Rad. Jan. 1660, Brec. and Rad. Aug. 1660–9; j.p. Brec. and Carm. 1653–8, Rad. 1653–*d.*, Mon. and Brec. July 1660–4; commr. for propagation accounts, S. Wales 1654, security 1656; dep. lt. Brec. and Rad. 1661–?*d.*; commr. for oyer and terminer, Wales 1661; receiver-gen. Mon. by 1664–?*d.*

Gwynne came from a Carmarthenshire family settled at Glanbran by the 15th century. His father was a royalist colonel in the Civil War, but as a younger son his estate was too modest to bring him within the scope of the commissioners for compounding. Gwynne himself does not seem to have been active, apart from signing the agreement between the Carmarthenshire gentry and the Pembrokeshire county committee in 1645. In 1650 his uncle made over to him most of his estates in Monmouthshire, but Gwynne apparently preferred to reside on his wife's inheritance in Radnorshire, where, in spite of his Cavalier background, he held local office and was twice chosen knight of the shire during the Interregnum.[2]

Gwynne was re-elected in 1660, but he was not an active Member of the Convention, being appointed only to the committees for the confirmation of marriages and the regulation of fees. He was named to the order of the Royal Oak with an estate of £1,500 p.a., but failed to secure the stewardship of the crown manors in Radnorshire, which was given to the Earl of Carbery. At the general election of 1661 he was apparently induced by Carbery to stand down in favour of the outsider, Sir Richard Lloyd I*, and with Griffith Jones* he tried to carry the borough for another courtier, probably (Sir) Allen Brodrick*, against Edward Harley*. He was active against conventicles and in the militia, but met with such frustration that in 1664 he begged to be allowed to lay down his commission, which exposed him to envy and malice. As receiver-general for Monmouth, he was ordered to be sent for in custody by the House for not paying over money received for loyal and indigent officers, but no further proceedings are recorded. His will, with a codicil, dated 14 Dec. 1672, was proved on 26 Nov. 1673, and suggests some pecuniary embarrassment in spite of his splendid estate. His debts totalled less than £500, but a mortgage on some messuages in Carmarthenshire had been forfeited, and the Monmouthshire lands were to be sold if necessary to pay debts, legacies and funeral expenses.[3]

[1] Bradney, *Mon.* i. 408; Jones, *Brec.* iv. 246–8; PCC 98 Pye. [2] *Old Wales*, ii. 326–7; J. R. Phillips, *Civil War in Wales*, ii. 154, 275–8; *Cal. Comm. Comp.* 1824; PCC 406 Alchin. [3] *CSP Dom.* 1660–1, p. 67; 1663–4, p. 573; BL Loan 29/79, Thomas Harley to Sir Edward Harley, 18 Mar., 30 Apr., 25 July 1661; *CJ*, viii. 541.

M.W.H./J.P.F.

GWYNNE, Rowland (c.1658–1726), of Llanelwedd, Rad.

RADNORSHIRE	1679 (Mar.), 1679 (Oct.), 1681, 1689
BRECONSHIRE	1690
BERE ALSTON	1695
BRECONSHIRE	1698, 1701 (Feb.), 1701 (Dec.)

b. c.1658, 1st s. of George Gwynne*. *educ.* St. John's, Oxf. matric. 16 July 1674, aged 15; G. Inn 1679. *m.* Mary, da. and h. of William Bassett, DCL, of Broviscan, Glam., *s.p. suc.* fa. c.1673; kntd. 28 May 1680.[1]

Commr. for assessment, Mon. and Rad. 1677–80, Brec. 1679–80, Mon., Brec., Brecon, Glam. and Rad. 1689–90; sheriff, Brec. Jan.–July 1688; steward of crown manors Rad. 1689–91; custos rot. Rad. 1689–1702, Brec. May–Oct. 1689; j.p. and dep. lt. Brec., Glam. and Rad. 1689–1710.[2]

Treasurer of the chamber 1689–92.[3]

FRS 1681.

Gwynne succeeded to a fine estate, and married an heiress. His income was computed at £1,000 p.a. but according to Lord Ailesbury (Thomas Bruce*) he 'spent all in a few years by eating and rioting'. He was returned for Radnorshire to all three Exclusion Parliaments, the sitting Member, Richard Williams*, making way for him by migrating to Breconshire. Marked 'honest' on Shaftesbury's list, he voted for exclusion, and served on the committees for the better attendance of Members, and for the encouragement of cloth exports to Turkey and of woollen manufactures. He can hardly have been prominent in opposition, for he received the honour of knighthood in the following year, probably to encourage him to attack the Harley interest in the borough seat. But in the second Exclusion Parliament he was very active, serving on 19 committees, the most important of which were for the address demanding the removal of Lord Halifax, the inquiry into the proclamation against petitioning and the bill for security against arbitrary power. On 7 Jan. 1681, in his maiden speech, he violently attacked the Marquess of Worcester (Henry Somerset*):

'Tis known what intimacy between him and the Duke of York. Fawns upon the Duke. Goes to him every morning before he goes to the King. If his parts were equal to his power his oppressions would be as great as the worst of them.

He concluded by moving for an address for Worcester's removal, and later 'aggravated' the motion against the Earl of Clarendon (Henry Hyde*). He was re-elected to the Oxford Parliament, but nothing is known of his activity there except that he was named to the committee of elections and privileges.[4]

On 8 Sept. 1683 Gwynne, accompanied by Lord Mordaunt, an equally ardent Whig, obtained a pass for Holland, and he spent the next five years in exile, though according to his sister Lady Hartstonge he was in London in the summer of 1686. Mordaunt wrote to William of Orange on 4 Sept. 1687: 'I am informed they are sending a privy seal for Sir Rowland Gwynne. As he loves talking of business, I fear he may have been indiscreet, or else it is to endeavour to frighten him from coming into England to stand for Parliament.' Mordaunt's information was correct, if somewhat premature; Gwynne was one of the Welsh opponents of James II's religious policy pricked for sheriff in January 1688, and on 30 Apr. he was summoned to return from the Continent on pain of outlawry. As he was still overseas in July the quarter sessions could not be held; he was fined £300 for neglect. He was exempted from the general pardon in September and his lands were seized. He came over with William in November and was reported, apparently by a fellow-countryman, to be going into Wales 'to make disturbances', despite his lack of military experience. On 26 Dec. 1688 he was one of the three Members of Charles II's Parliaments sent to ask William when it would be convenient for him to receive an address.[5]

Gwynne regained the Radnorshire seat at the general election, and became a moderately active Member of the Convention, acting as teller in four divisions, though he was named to only ten committees. He urged that the grand committee on the state of the nation should report without delay that the throne was vacant. On 21 Feb. 1689 he was sent with Lord Wiltshire (Charles Powlett II*) to desire the King to bestow a donative on his foreign troops. He was refused the mastership of the Household, and had to be content with the lesser post of treasurer of the chamber. He was among those ordered to inquire into the authors and advisers of grievances and to consider new oaths of supremacy and allegiance. On 9 Mar. he rebuked the House for minding little things and not great. 'I desire the King's speech may be read', he said, 'that we mind what we ought.' He was teller for adjourning the debate on imposing a sacramental test on corporations on 1 Apr., and on 31 May he was instructed to inform the Upper House that their amendments to the poll bill had been rejected. On 18 July he was added to the committee of inquiry into the delay in relieving Londonderry. After the recess he helped to draft the address inquiring who had recommended Commissary Shales. In the debate, he accused the privy councillors of misrepresenting the Commons to the King, remarking 'If you had taken more care in other messages, we might have fared better in the answers (the case of religion, the laws and the government)'. He was teller against the adjournment on restoring corporations on 2 Jan. 1690, and supported the disabling clause.[6]

Gwynne lost his post at Court in 1692 when his charges of corruption against Henry Sidney* were adjudged unfounded, but he remained a court Whig under William III, proposing the Association in 1696. Subsequently he withdrew to Hanover, only returning with George I in 1714, but his efforts to ingratiate himself with the new King were unsuccessful and he died a prisoner for debt on 24 Jan. 1726. The greater part of his estates seem to have passed to the senior branch of the family, one of whom sat for Radnorshire from 1755 to 1761.[7]

[1] W. R. Williams, *Old Wales*, i. 250, 379; G. T. Clark, *Genealogies of Glam.* 354. [2] Jones, *Brec.* i. 131; *Arch. Camb.* (ser. 3), iii. 189; *CSP Dom.* 1689–90, p. 89. [3] *CSP Dom.* 1689–90, p. 68; 1691–

2, p. 255; LS13/231/16. [4] *NLW Jnl.* xxi. 161; *Ailesbury Mems.* 554–5; *HMC 12th Rep. IX*, 114, 115. [5] *CSP Dom.* 1683–4, p. 193; 1687–9, pp. 176, 185, 354; *HMC Downshire*, i. 286; *Dalrymple Mems.* ii. bk. 5, p. 77; *Bramston Autobiog.* (Cam. Soc. xxxii), 319; Bodl. Fleming newsletter 20 Nov. 1688; *Ellis Corresp.* ii. 305–6. [6] *Hardwicke SP*, ii. 412; Foxcroft, *Halifax*, ii. 213; Grey, ix. 147, 458. [7] *Ailesbury Mems.* 555; *The Gen.* n.s. vii. 42.

J.P.F.

HACKET, Sir Andrew (c.1632–1709), of Moxhull, Wishaw, Warws.

TAMWORTH   1679 (Oct.)

> *b.* c.1632, 2nd but 1st surv. s. of John Hacket, bp. of Lichfield 1661–70 by 1st w. Elizabeth, da. of William Stebbins of Earl Soham, Suff. *educ.* Westminster; Trinity Coll. Camb. 1645, BA 1649, MA 1652; G. Inn 1653. *m.* (1) by 1662, Mary, da. of Joseph Henslow, bp. of Peterborough 1663–79, 1da.; (2) by 1665, Mary (*d.* 11 Dec. 1716), da. and coh. of John Lisle of Moxhull, 3s. 3da. *suc.* fa. 1670; *kntd.* 16 Jan. 1671.[1]
> Recorder, Tamworth 1670–May 1688; j.p. Warws. 1677–*d.*, commr. for assessment 1677–80, 1689, dep. lt. 1686–7, 1689–?*d.*, sheriff 1684–5.[2]
> Master in Chancery 1670–80.[3]

Hacket was the grandson of a Scottish household official in the service of Prince Henry. His father, chaplain to Bishop Williams, was so moderate an Anglican that he was invited to the Westminster assembly and retained his living at Cheam throughout the Interregnum. At the Restoration he became bishop of Lichfield and launched a successful appeal for £20,000 to rebuild the cathedral, which had been ruined in the Civil War. One-quarter of the sum came from his own pocket, and the building was reconsecrated at Christmas 1669.[4]

Hacket's second marriage brought him possession of Moxhull, ten miles from Tamworth, where he became recorder in 1670. As a master in Chancery, he was well placed to supervise a private bill to enable him to provide for his daughter by his first marriage, which was steered through the Commons by Thomas Crouch* in 1671. He first considered standing on the dissolution of the Cavalier Parliament, and on 26 July 1679 Thomas Thynne I* described him as 'a weak man, but honest', adding that 'the town being inclined to him, I have agreed he shall be my partner'. He was returned to the second Exclusion Parliament for Tamworth as a court supporter, but took no known part in its proceedings, and in 1681 desisted before the election for lack of support among the commonalty.[5]

As sheriff in 1685 he claimed to have been guaranteed a nomination at Tamworth which he offered to one of the candidates for the county in order to avoid a contest; but he does not appear to have been able to make good his promise. He had ceased to play an active part in the borough before the Revolution; but he accepted the new regime, and continued to hold county office. In his will he thanked God for two happy marriages and dutiful children, adding:

I have lived and do die a member of the true, ancient, reformed Church of England by law established, and my tender regards for the same make me to pray that it may long continue quiet under that establishment against all miscreants that dissent from it and make it their business to subvert apostolical government of the Church and the other monarchical government of the state.

He died on 19 Mar. 1709, the only member of his family to sit in the Commons, and was buried at Wishaw.[6]

[1] *Vis. Warws.* (Harl. Soc. lxii), 140; Dugdale, *Warws.* 936–7. [2] C. F. Palmer, *Hist. Tamworth*, p. xxiv. [3] T. D. Hardy, *Principal Officers of Chancery*, 95. [4] *DNB*; A. G. Matthews, *Walker Revised*, 49; *CSP Dom.* 1672, p. 279. [5] *CJ*, ix. 226; *Staffs. Parl. Hist.* (Wm. Salt Arch. Soc), ii. 147; *VCH Warws.* iv. 260; Spencer mss, Thynne to Halifax, 26 July 1679; Shaw, *Staffs.* i. 276. [6] Bath mss, Thynne pprs. 21, f. 148, 21 Feb. 1685; PCC 118 Lane.

A.M.M.

HADDOCK, Sir Richard (c.1629–1715), of Mile End, Wapping, Mdx.

ALDEBURGH 1679 (Mar.)
NEW SHOREHAM 1685

b. c.1629, s. of William Haddock, mariner, of Leigh-on-Sea, Essex by Anna Goodlad. *m.* (1) bef. 30 May 1657, Lydia, da. and coh. of John Stevens, master mariner, of Leigh-on-Sea, 1da.; (2) lic. 24 July 1671, Elizabeth (*d.* 26 Feb. 1710), da. of Nicholas Hurlestone, master mariner, of Rotherhithe, Surr., 3s. (1 *d.v.p.*) 2da. *suc.* fa. 1667; kntd. 3 July 1675.[1]

Lt. Commonwealth navy 1653, capt. 1656; capt. RN 1665–7, 1672–3; c.-in-c. Channel fleet 1682; adm. 1690.

Commr. for navy 1673–82, comptroller 1682–5, May 1688–*d.*, commr. for old accounts 1685–May 1688, victualling 1683–90.

Freeman, Portsmouth 1673, Dunwich 1679; elder bro. Trinity House 1675–*d.*, master 1687–8; commr. for assessment, Aldeburgh 1679–80, Mdx. 1689; j.p. Essex, Hants, Kent, Mdx., Suff., Surr. and Suss. 1680–?*d.*, Westminster 1687–9.[2]

Haddock came from a seafaring family whose name occurs at Leigh as early as 1327. His grandfather and father both served in the Commonwealth navy, where his own service began. After the Restoration he traded in the Mediterranean, but he served in the second and third Dutch wars in the Royal Navy, where he was popular with the seamen. As flag-captain to the Earl of Sandwich (Edward Montagu I*) he was one of the few who escaped from the *Royal James* at the battle of Sole Bay, and was rewarded with a seat on the navy board, for, as he told Samuel Pepys*, 'it is impossible for any

man by the bare wages and lawful profits of his place as commander at sea ever to lay up anything for his family'. He was returned for Aldeburgh with Henry Johnson* at the first general election of 1679 on the Admiralty interest, and marked 'base' on Shaftesbury's list. In the first Exclusion Parliament he was appointed only to the committee of elections and privileges and to that for the reform of the bankruptcy law. According to Roger Morrice he voted against exclusion, and he was not re-elected in the autumn. Although he remained a dissenter, and was reported as attending a conventicle in 1682, he was appointed comptroller and commissioner for victualling, and helped to present a loyal address from Dunwich after the Rye House Plot.[3]

On James II's accession Haddock was given the less responsible post of commissioner for old accounts. Nevertheless he was recommended to Henry Goring II* as court candidate for Shoreham in 1685, and probably returned unopposed. He was again inactive, being appointed only to the committees to provide carriages for the navy and ordnance and to prohibit the import of gunpowder. In May 1688 he was restored as comptroller, writing: 'However the King may choose to deal with me (which hitherto hath been extra kind), I shall never forsake my loyalty to him, even to my last breath'.[4]

It was alleged that Haddock had opposed the dispensing power, but he was continued in office after the Revolution only as 'a man so conversant with the affairs of the navy' that Johnson's son told the Commons 'the navy would stand still without him'. He was regarded with intense suspicion by the Whigs, and ordered into custody with Sir John Parsons* and his partners after complaints about the 'corrupt and unwholesome victuals' issued to the fleet. 'I must not call it injustice in that august assembly what they did to me', he commented bitterly 20 years later, reckoning that it had cost him about £100 in fees to the serjeant-at-arms 'and to lawyers soliciting the House of Commons, with expenses of entertainment whilst in custody'. But after a fortnight they were admitted to bail. He was removed from the victualling office, but, after Lord Torrington (Arthur Herbert*) had demonstrated his incapacity at the battle of Beachy Head, he was given joint command of the fleet which helped to reduce Cork and Kinsale. This was his last command at sea, but he retained his office of comptroller of the navy, unlike his loyalty to the Stuarts, to his last breath. He died on 26 Jan. 1715, aged 85, and was buried at Leigh. His son Nicholas, also a distinguished seaman, sat for Rochester from 1734 to 1746.[5]

[1] *DNB*; information from Miss Sonia P. Anderson; *London Mar. Lic.* ed. Foster, 602; PCC 26 Fagg; *CSP Dom.* 1675–6, p. 197. [2] R. East, *Portsmouth Recs.* 360; E. Suff. RO, EE6/1144/13. [3] P. Benton, *Hist. Rochford Hundred*, 351–2; *CSP Dom.* 1673, p. 92; *Pepys Naval Mins.* (Navy Rec. Soc. lx), 26; *CSP Dom.* 1682, p. 8; Luttrell, i. 278. [4] *CSP Dom.* 1685, p. 79; *Haddock Corresp.* (Cam. Soc. n.s. xxxi), 36. [5] Grey, ix. 445; *CJ*, x. 293, 302; *Haddock Corresp.* 51–52; Benton, 352.

B.M.C.

HALE, John (1614–91), of Bowringsleigh, West Alvington, Devon.

DEVON	1654, 1656[1]
DARTMOUTH	1659, 1660

bap. 19 Mar. 1614, 1st s. of John Hale, grocer, of Soper Lane, London and Harmer Green, Welwyn, Herts. by Elizabeth, da. of Humphrey Browne of Essex. *m.* by 1634, Anne, da. and coh. of Robert Halswell† of Goathurst, Som., 3s. (2 *d.v.p.*) 1da. *suc.* fa. 1620.[2]

Capt. of ft. (parl.) 1642.[3]

Receiver of tithe, Devon and Cornw. 1655; j.p. Devon 1656–65, 1667–70, 1673–6, commr. for assessment 1657, Jan. 1660–80, militia 1659, Mar. 1660, maj. of militia horse Apr. 1660; commr. for inquiry into Newfoundland govt. 1667.[4]

Hale came from a cadet branch of the Hertfordshire family. By his marriage he obtained not only an estate in Devon, but a valuable political connexion with Sir John Northcote*, who married his wife's cousin. A parliamentarian officer in the Civil War, he became under the Protectorate the first of the family to enter Parliament. He was re-elected to the Convention for Dartmouth, 15 miles from his home, and was marked on Lord Wharton's list as a friend. An inactive Member, he was named to only eight committees as 'Major Hale' and made no recorded speeches. On 1 Aug. 1660 he was among those ordered to bring in a bill for taking local accounts, and he helped to manage a conference on the poll-tax on 12 Sept. He did not stand again, and was three times removed from the commission of the peace, once for encouraging the constable of West Alvington to flout the jurisdiction of the Admiralty, and twice as a favourer of 'fanatics'. Presumably he was a conformist Presbyterian. His wife had succeeded to only one-third of the Bowringsleigh estate, but in 1658 he bought another third for £1,350, and in 1675 John Speccot I*, the son of the other coheir, agreed to divide the remainder. He may have been the 'old rebel knave' who played a prominent part in the country interest at the Devon election of 1681. He died in September 1691, leaving the estate burdened with a portion of £2,500 for his granddaughter, and his surviving son, who had a large family and debts of his own, was obliged to sell out. No other member of this branch of the family entered Parliament.[5]

[1] Excluded. [2] *Vis. Herts.* (Harl. Soc. xxii), 61; Soc. of Genealogists, Boyd's London Units, 14799; PCC 23 Dale, 352 Berkeley. [3] E. Peacock, *Army Lists*, 51. [4] Devon RO, 316M/ET1; HMC *Finch*, ii. 43; *Parl. Intell.* 16 Apr. 1660; *APC Col.* i. 433. [5] Lysons, *Devon*, 7; PC2/58/150; *Somers Tracts*, vii. 292; *Bagford Ballads* ed. Ebsworth, 966; Devon RO, 316M/TD/A9–10.

M.W.H./J.P.F.

HALE, Matthew (1609–76), of Alderley, Glos. and Lincoln's Inn.

GLOUCESTERSHIRE	1654
OXFORD UNIVERSITY	1659
GLOUCESTERSHIRE	Apr.–7 Nov. 1660

b. 1 Nov. 1609, o.s. of Robert Hale, barrister, of Lincoln's Inn by Joan, da. of Matthew Poyntz of Alderley. *educ.* Wotton-under-Edge (John Stanton); Magdalen Hall, Oxf. 1626; L. Inn 1628, called 1636. *m.* (1) by 1640, Anne, da. of Sir Henry Moore, 1st Bt., of Fawley, Berks., 4s. (3 *d.v.p.*) 6da.; (2) 18 Oct. 1667, Anne, da. of Joseph Bishop of Fawley, *s.p. suc.* fa. 1614; kntd. 30 Jan. 1662.[1]

Governor, Covent Garden precinct 1646; bencher, L. Inn 1648; j.p. Glos. 1656–d., commr. for militia 1659, oyer and terminer, Oxford circuit July 1660, assessment, Glos. 1664–d., Mdx. 1673–d.

Chairman, law reform commission 1652–3; judge of probate 1653–4; serjeant-at-law 1654; j.c.p. 1654–8; commr. for trade 1655–7; chief baron of the Exchequer 7 Nov. 1660–71; c.j.K.b. 1671–6.[2]

Hale, the outstanding lawyer of his generation, inherited a small estate of £100 p.a. Receiving a puritan education, he took no part in the Civil War, but assisted in the defence of Archbishop Laud and other Royalists. He was appointed chairman of the law reform committee by the Rump and raised to the bench by Cromwell, serving at the same time for his county in the first Protectorate Parliament, but he relinquished his judgeship on Cromwell's death.[3]

At the general election of 1660 Hale was invited to stand both for Oxford University and Gloucestershire, and returned for the county after a contest. Lord Berkeley 'bore all the charge of the entertainments on the day of his election, which was considerable'. A very active Member, he was appointed to 87 committees and made 14 recorded speeches in the Lower House of the Convention. Lord Wharton marked him as a friend, to be approached by himself, and he was clearly in opposition on several important issues. On the receipt of the King's letter, according to Burnet, he

moved that a committee might be appointed to look into the propositions that had been made and the concessions that had been offered by the late King during the war, particularly at the Treaty of Newport, that from thence they might digest such propositions as they should think fit to be sent over to the King.

The motion was unsuccessful, but Hale was appointed one of the managers of the conference with the Lords on the subject. He seconded the motion of Arthur Annesley* for the admission of Edmund Ludlow* to the House. He was named to the committees for the land purchases and indemnity bills, and helped to prepare for a conference on the regicides on 21 May. He was confirmed as serjeant-at-law on 22 June. He spoke in favour of naming a day to hear the petition from the intruded dons at Oxford, and was appointed to the committee. In a debate on the indemnity bill he moved 'to cement differences' by limiting the exceptions to 20, as originally drafted, and in accordance with the King's desire and the faith of the House. His first wife had come from a Roman Catholic family, and he advised against pressing the Papists to take the oaths 'for fear of making them desperate'. He opposed questioning lawyers who had appeared for the prosecution in the High Courts of Justice. He accepted the Thirty-Nine Articles, 'but thought it not fitting' to join them in the same paragraph with the Old and New Testaments, and urged the adjournment of the debate on 9 July without a division. He was given special responsibility for the tunnage and poundage bill and for bringing in a bill to appoint commissioners of sewers with Sir Anthony Irby* and Edward King*. On 28 July he moved for two bills to regularize Interregnum proceedings. The first, to confirm civil marriages, he brought in on 8 Aug., and two days later, with Nathaniel Bacon*, he was directed to bring in a bill restraining grants of ecclesiastical leases. Perhaps his most impressive speech was in the debate of 17 Aug. on the Lords' amendments to the indemnity bill. He agreed that 'there was never so high a crime' as the execution of Charles I.

> If there should be cause shown by the Lords you may alter your vote, but the question ... was whether the Lords had shown that cause. But here is the case. Now they are in your power, you cannot let them go.

He moved for a committee to state the facts, which was immediately ordered and to which he was appointed. He continued to urge that the regicides who had surrendered themselves voluntarily should be pardoned, 'for the honour of the King and the Houses'. To leave the decision to the King 'was but to take a thorn out of our foot to put into the King's'. He helped to manage the conference on 18 Aug., and was added to the committee to draft a petition on behalf of Lambert and Vane. On 5 Sept. he reported amendments to the ecclesiastical leases bill which he had prepared together with William Prynne* and Heneage Finch*. He was instructed to draft an order for preserving the timber in the

Forest of Dean, and he took part in the conference on settling ministers on 10 Sept. After the autumn recess, his was the first name among those ordered to bring in the bill for modified episcopacy, and he was also named to the committee for the attainder bill. But on the same day he was removed from the Commons by his appointment as chief baron.[4]

Hale served as a judge with great distinction until a few months before his death. His behaviour in Church, according to Baxter, was 'conformable but prudent'. He tried to mitigate the severity of the Conventicles Act wherever possible, and in 1668, together with Lord Keeper Bridgeman, drafted a comprehension bill. He died on 25 Dec. 1676, and was buried in the churchyard at Alderley. He had not greatly enriched his family, despite the studied simplicity of his life-style. His estate was worth under £900 p.a., and none of his descendants sat in Parliament.[5]

[1] Bristol and Glos. Arch. Soc. Trans. lxxiv. 199–202; Burnet, Life of Hale (1806), 130–2; Glos. Par. Regs. x. 55. [2] Whitelocke Mems. iii. 385. [3] Burnet, Life, 3–6. [4] J. B. Williams, Mems. of Hale (1835), 45–48; Burnet, Life, 37–38; Burnet, Hist. Own Time, i. 160; CJ, viii. 7, 74, 94, 95, 127, 142, 156; Voyce from the Watch Tower, 120; Bowman diary, ff. 25v, 43v, 54v, 57v, 65, 68, 102v, 128, 147, 153. [5] Burnet, Hist. i. 465; Burnet, Life, 110; Works of Hale ed. T. Thirwall, 89, 101, 104.

M.W.H.

HALE, William (c.1632–88), of King's Walden, Herts.

HERTFORDSHIRE   11 Nov. 1669, 1679 (Mar.), 1681

> b. c.1632, o.s. of Rowland Hale of King's Walden by Elizabeth, da. of Sir Henry Garway, Draper, of Broad Street, London, ld. mayor 1639–40. educ. Trinity Coll. Camb. 1649; G. Inn 1651. m. by 1659, Mary (d. 18 July 1712), da. of Jeremy Elwes of Broxbourne, Herts., 10s. (5 d.v.p.) 4da. suc. fa. 1669.[1]
> Commr. for militia, Herts. Mar. 1660, capt. of militia ft. Apr. 1660, maj. by 1677, lt.-col. by 1680, commr. for assessment Aug. 1660–74, 1679–80, j.p. 1661–83, ?1687–d., dep. lt. 1671–83, 1687–d.[2]

Hale was the great-grandson of a London Grocer who bought the manor of King's Walden in 1576. His mother was the daughter of a prominent City Royalist, but his father, apart from serving as sheriff in 1647–8, played no part in public life. Hale himself, according to his contemporary Chauncy,

> was endowed with excellent parts, great integrity and general learning; he was a good philosopher, a great historian, and used an excellent style in writing. [He] was firm to the established Church of England, a kind husband, a provident father, prudent in his house, and very faithful and steadfast to the interests of his country.

He was returned for the county at a by-election soon after succeeding to the estate, and was doubtless reckoned from the first as one of the country party. But he was not active in the Cavalier Parliament, being appointed to only 15 committees, acting as teller in three divisions, and making 16 recorded speeches. In his second session he was involved in a case of some constitutional importance, concerning the jurisdiction of the Lords over Members of the Commons. After successfully defending a suit brought against him in Chancery by Henry Slingsby of Kippax, the master of the Mint, Hale was formally notified that an appeal had been lodged with the Upper House. This apparently unprecedented situation was debated on 4 Mar. 1670, and the Lords were warned to have regard to the Commons' privileges; but a direct confrontation between the two Houses, such as was to occur over Shirley v. Fagg five years later, was averted when Slingsby discovered that action in Chancery was still open to him and withdrew his appeal. During the summer Hale and a neighbouring justice were severely reproved by the Treasury for issuing their own certificates of exemption from hearth-tax instead of using the printed forms emanating from the Government. 'We are likewise informed that you intend at the next quarter sessions to move the bench that the form of a certificate by you now allowed may be there agreed to be universally used in your county. It is advisable that you consider well before you propose it.' No reference to this matter appears in the county records. On 12 Dec. he was teller for adjourning rather than discussing supply. Hale seconded the motion of his neighbour (Sir) John Monson* on 10 Jan. 1671 for a bill to banish the assailants of Sir John Coventry*. 'If a man must be thus assaulted by ruffianly fellows', he said, 'we must go to bed by sunset, like the birds. . . . Would have them hanged, if they could be caught.'[3]

Hale took an interest in the bill of ease for Protestant dissenters in 1673. He suggested that the first step should be to discover what their complaints were, 'but it did not please the House'. He believed that 'we cannot better express our duty to the King than in coming as near to the Declaration [of Indulgence] as we can'. Hence he would leave the licensing of chapels to the crown, and spoke against clauses to exclude dissenters from the House and to require the renunciation of the Covenant. He helped to draw up the address on the state of Ireland. When he took his son over to France he was shocked at the heavy casualties sustained by English troops in the French service, 'and 'tis said in France they set the crown upon the King of France's head'. He was naturally appointed to the committees to search for precedents for Shirley v. Fagg, and to inspect the Lords' Journals about the Ouse naviga-

tion bill after they had summoned Sir John Napier* as a witness. He favoured the proposal of Henry Eyre* for no further supply bills, in view of the thinness of the House. 'If a motion should be put for a million of money', he said, 'there would be few to maintain the battle.' He was for sending the Four Lawyers to the Tower 'to avoid confusion'. Sir Richard Wiseman* described him as 'a discreet gentleman, too much governed by his uncle', William Garway*. When Parliament reassembled after the long recess in 1677, he acted as teller against the naming of grand committees, and urged that a resolution should be put to the House on the validity of the prorogation. Shaftesbury marked him 'thrice worthy'. He returned to the question of English forces in the French service, moving that those who had assisted in recruiting them should be declared enemies to the King and kingdom. 'They cannot be little ones about the King that suffer these things', he said. 'How can we think of securing Flanders whilst we are false to ourselves?' He ridiculed the Lords bill for educating the children of the royal family as Protestants:

> If ever we be so unhappy as to have a Popish prince, we must have recourse to our prayers and not contend with the crown for religion's sake. . . . He is against this bill, which is like empty casks for whales to play with, and rattles for children to keep them quiet.

He was outraged by the misuse of protections by Thomas Wanklyn* and moved for his expulsion from the House.[4]

Hale had 'so gained the hearts of the people that . . . the freeholders would choose him contrary to his inclinations' at the first general election of 1679, though he desired to be excused for reasons of health. He was marked 'worthy' on Shaftesbury's list and voted for exclusion. He was named to no committees, but when (Sir) Stephen Fox* produced the list of excise pensioners, he expressed the hope that they would clear themselves of receiving rewards for their votes. Hale refused all solicitation to stand for re-election in the autumn, but after nomination both by the exclusionist peers and the gentry consented to serve in 1681. He played no known part in the Oxford Parliament, but was removed from local office as a Whig two years later.[5]

Hale was a personal friend of Richard Hoare, the banker, and a cheque, or 'drawn note', of his is the earliest remaining in the archives of Hoare's Bank. He also became the principal partner in the Friendly Society, a mutual fire insurance fund, which competed with the Fire Office, founded by Nicholas Barbon†. James II sought to prevent competition between the two by giving each the exclusive right to issue new policies in alternate years. Hale was restored to the lieutenancy at the end of 1687 and may have been reckoned a Whig collaborator. But he died on 25 May 1688, aged 56, and was buried at King's Walden. His will suggests liquid assets predominating over his landed estates. He bequeathed to his younger sons and daughters legacies totalling £16,000 and annuities of £400 p.a. His eldest son died in the following year, but his grandson sat for Bramber and St. Albans as a Whig.[6]

[1] Clutterbuck, *Herts.* iii. 132-3; *Misc. Gen. et Her.* (ser. 1), iv. 134; PCC 94 Exton. [2] *Parl. Intell.* 16 Apr. 1660; *Herts. Recs.* i. 213; *CSP Dom.* 1671-2, p. 53; *CJ*, ix. 284. [3] Clutterbuck, iii. 132; Chauncy, *Herts.* ii. 207; *HMC 8th Rep.* pt. 1 (1881), p. 140; Grey, i. 223-5, 334; *CJ*, ix. 132; *Cal. Treas. Bks.* iii. 605-6. [4] Grey, ii. 38, 71, 93-94, 117; iii. 121-2, 160, 249; iv. 89, 255-6, 294; v. 51; *Dering*, 122; *CSP Dom.* 1673-5, p. 610. [5] Chauncy, ii. 207; Bodl. Carte 228, f. 134; Grey, vii. 331. [6] *Gent. Mag.* vii. 294-5; *Sel. Charters* (Selden Soc. xxviii), 208-10; Clutterbuck, iii. 135; PCC 94 Exton.

E.R.E.

HALES, Edward I (1630-96), of Chilston, Boughton Malherbe, Kent.

HYTHE   1679 (Oct.), 1681, 1689

bap. 18 Apr. 1630, o. surv. s. of Samuel Hales of Davington by Martha, da. and h. of Stephen Heronden of Staple Inn, Mdx. and Rochester, Kent. *educ.* Trinity Coll. Camb. 1646, BA 1650; G. Inn 1652. *m.* 22 May 1656, Elizabeth, da. of Sir John Evelyn I* of Lee Place, Godstone, Surr., 2s. (1 *d.v.p.*), 3da. *suc.* fa. 1638.[1]

Commr. for assessment, Kent 1657, Aug. 1660-1, 1663-80, Kent and Hythe 1689-90, militia, Kent Mar. 1660, j.p. Mar.-June 1660, 1662-70, 1679-80, 1689-*d.*, capt. of militia horse Apr. 1660-?70; commr. for sewers, Rother marshes Oct. 1660.[2]

Hales was the first cousin of Sir Edward Hales, 2nd Bt.* Although his father was a younger son, he was well provided for, and Hales added to his inheritance by the purchase of Chilston. His stepfather, William Kenwricke†, a violent republican, sat in Richard Cromwell's Parliament for Hythe, a borough with which the Hales family had long been associated before their move to North Kent at the beginning of the century. Hales himself stood there at the general election of 1660 and perhaps again in the following year, but was persuaded by Lord Chancellor Clarendon to stand down in favour of the courtier Sir Henry Wood* at the by-election which followed the death of Phineas Andrews*. He was rewarded by being restored to the commission of the peace, but again removed on the passing of the Conventicles Act in 1670. On Wood's death he renewed his candidature, but was narrowly defeated by the court candidate, Sir Leoline Jenkins*. After his petition had been rejected, he made over his interest to his local henchman, Julius Deedes*, and

transferred his attentions to Queenborough. In the elections of 1679 he was extremely active, canvassing Hythe on behalf of Sir Edward Dering* and the county on behalf of his son. He might have been chosen at Hythe in February but for his reluctance to oppose Deedes, and at New Romney he was 'greatly encouraged by the kindness of some there, but I'll put nothing to hazard'. His confidence over Queenborough proved unjustified, for his cousin Edward Hales II* declared himself pre-engaged to James Herbert*. His petition was never reported. Hales was promised a seat at Shoreham by (Sir) Henry Capel* in August, but Deedes stood down at Hythe for personal reasons, and he defeated Sir William Honeywood*, a court supporter. It may have been on his interest that William Glanville* contested Queenborough. Hales took a leading part in petitioning for the meeting of Parliament, and was for the third time removed from local office. But he was not an active Member, though he may have served on two committees in the second Exclusion Parliament, those for encouraging the export of leather and beer. The family interest did even better at the 1681 election, taking both seats at Queenborough, while Hales himself was unopposed at Hythe. But he left no trace on the records of the Oxford Parliament.[3]

Hales regained his seat after a contest in 1689, and helped to carry the canopy at the coronation. He is said to have acted as teller for continuing the debate on the queen dowager's servants on 28 Mar., but this was more probably John Hawles*, who may also have been responsible for the two speeches ascribed to him by Grey. On 6 Apr. 'Mr Hales' spoke against the Lords' bill to extend the definition of treason: 'something of poison lies concealed in this bill, and I would reject it'. On 8 May he opposed the proviso to the bill of settlement which would have allowed the Pretender to inherit the crown if he turned Protestant. An inactive Member, Hales was named to six committees in the Convention, of which the most important was to appoint new oaths for army officers. He was not listed as a supporter of the disabling clause in the bill to restore corporations, though doubtless a Whig. He was defeated at the general election and never stood again. He died on 9 Aug. 1696; his sons were short-lived, and in 1698 his daughters sold the estate.[4]

[1] E. R. Mores, *Hist. Tunstall*, 36; *Vis. Kent.* (Harl. Soc. liv), 90; *Arch. Cant.* xv. 65-67; *Misc. Gen. et Her.* (ser. 2), i. 296; ii. 37. [2] Add. 34152, f. 12; *Pub. Intell.* 2 Apr. 1660. [3] A. M. Everitt, *Community of Kent and the Gt. Rebellion*, 150, 310; Bodl. Carte 73, f. 369; Kent AO, U47/3, F3/7; Stowe 746, ff. 9, 14, 19-20; *Sidney Diary*, i. 79; Bath mss, Coventry pprs. 6, f. 230. [4] *Suss. Arch. Colls.* xv. 209; *Arch. Cant.* xiv. 67, 84; Hasted, *Kent*, v. 409.

B.D.H.

HALES, Edward II (1645–95), of Paulerspury, Northants. and Hackington, Kent.

CANTERBURY 1679 (Mar.), 1679 (Oct.)

b. 28 Sept. 1645, 1st s. of Sir Edward Hales, 2nd Bt.*, and bro. of John Hales*. *educ.* travelled abroad (France, Italy) 1657–64; Padua 1664. *m.* lic. 12 July 1669, Frances (*d.*1694), da. and h. of Francis Windebank, gent. usher to the Prince of Wales 1638–45, 5s. (1 *d.v.p.*), 7da. *suc.* fa. as 3rd Bt. bef. 8 Feb. 1684.[1]

Commr. for assessment, Kent 1673–80, Tenterden 1677–80, Canterbury 1679–80; j.p. Kent 1675–85, 1687–Nov. 1688, Mdx. ?1687–Nov. 1688; freeman, Canterbury 1679; dep. lt. Kent Feb.–Oct. 1688; commr. for inquiry into recusancy fines, Kent and Hants July 1688.[2]

Ld. of Admiralty 1679–84; lt.-gov. Dover Castle 1686–Dec. 1688; judge of Admiralty, Cinque Ports 1686–Dec. 1688; lt. Tower of London 1687–Nov. 1688.[3]

Col. (later 14 Ft.) 1685–Oct. 1688.

After the Revolution, mindful of the penalties of conversion as an adult, Hales declared that he had become a Papist at his tutor's instigation at the age of 12. But this is unlikely, though his religion was long 'disguised'. He matriculated at Padua in 1664. In 1675 he bought Hackington, on the outskirts of Canterbury, and resided there till his father went abroad. On his election to the first Exclusion Parliament, Shaftesbury marked him 'doubtful'. On 9 Apr. 1679 he had leave to go into the country for a week. 'Mr Hales' was among those Members appointed to draw up reasons for a conference on disbanding the army, but this may be a mistake for William Hale*. After receiving a seat on the board of Admiralty, he voted against the exclusion bill. He was re-elected in the autumn, though not without difficulty, and soon came under attack in the second Exclusion Parliament for 'a notorious Popish sermon' preached by his son's tutor in favour of the doctrine of purgatory. Hales protested weakly that he had discharged the man, and hoped that there would be no reflection on him. But neither he nor his father stood again, and his proposed appointment to the lieutenancy was dropped. He seems to have been totally inactive as a committeeman.[4]

Hales raised a regiment of foot during Monmouth's rebellion, and was formally reconciled to Rome on 11 Nov. 1685. A collusive action was brought by his coachman Godden to vindicate the dispensing power, which the King had used to allow him to keep his regiment. With Sir Nicholas Butler and (later) the Earl of Sunderland, Hales was the only notable official convert of the reign, and he was soon given responsible office to the limits of, and perhaps beyond his capacities. In November 1688 he planned to mount mortars in the Tower in order to bombard the City if signs of restiveness appeared. Even the King considered such a step counter-productive, and Hales was dismissed. The incident, long remembered by Londoners, throws light on his extreme unpopularity in his own county, which made him a poor choice as escort when James fled from London on 11 Dec. 1688. Hales was recognized, and the little party detained and treated with gross contempt at Faversham. Hales, lately the gaoler of the seven bishops in the Tower, was returned to it as a prisoner. His other chief responsibility, Dover Castle, had already fallen to 'the rabble'. After nine months' imprisonment, Hales and Obadiah Walker, the leading clerical apostate, applied for a writ of habeas corpus; but on 26 Oct. 1689 they were charged at the bar of the House with high treason, 'in being reconciled to the Church of Rome, and other high crimes and misdemeanours'. In his defence Hales sought to exculpate Walker from the responsibility for his own conversion with which he was credited by popular report, and to sow dissension between Anglicans and Presbyterians. To account for his taking the oaths and the Anglican sacrament under Charles II, he explained that when he was young he 'did not much consider the matter of religion, nor the obligations of oaths or conscience'. He was returned to the Tower, but released on bail at the dissolution. He was excepted from the Act of Pardon, and after discharging his bail joined James in France, rather as a friend than an adviser. His estate was valued at £3,000 p.a., less than half his father's assessment for decimation under the Protectorate. He was excepted from the Act of Indemnity, and created Earl of Tenterden in the Jacobite peerage. Though he applied for permission to return to England in 1694, he died in Paris in October 1695, and was buried at St. Sulpice. His son returned to the Church of England, but none of his descendants sat in Parliament.[5]

[1] *Arch. Cant.* xiv. 80; *N. and Q.* clxx. 164; R. Morrice, Entering Bk. 2, pp. 631–2; *CSP Dom.* 1657–8, p. 550; 1658–9, p. 210; *HMC Finch*, ii. 187. [2] *Roll of Freemen* ed. Cowper, 318; *Cal. Treas. Bks.* viii. 2028. [3] *CSP Dom.* 1686–7, p. 96; 1687–9, pp. 11, 364. [4] Morrice, loc. cit.; Burnet ed. Routh, iii. 97; North, *Lives*, ii. 260; Hasted, *Kent*, ix. 47; *HMC Finch*, ii. 56; *CSP Dom.* 1679–80, p. 532; Grey, viii. 17–18. [5] *CSP Dom.* 1685, p. 391; 1689–90, p. 375; J. R. Jones, *Revolution of 1688 in England*, 83, 93; *HMC 7th Rep.* 417; *HMC Dartmouth*, i. 211, 216, 231; Stow, *London*, i. 77; Clarke, *Jas. II*, ii. 255; *N. and Q.* (ser. 3), vi. 1–3; Morrice, loc. cit.; Bodl. Carte 208, f. 123; Luttrell, ii. 10–11; *London Recusant*, iii. 56–57.

B.D.H.

HALES, Sir Edward, 2nd Bt. (1626–c.84), of Tunstall Place, Kent and 43 King Street, Covent Garden, Mdx.

MAIDSTONE 3 Aug. 1660

QUEENBOROUGH 1661, 1679 (Mar.), 1679 (Oct.)

bap. 12 Feb. 1626, o.s. of Sir John Hales[†] (*d.*1639) of Woodchurch, Kent by Christian, da. and h. of Sir James Crowmer of Tunstall. *educ.* Magdalen Coll. Oxf. 1642. *m.* by 1645, Anne, da. and coh. of Thomas, 2nd Baron Wotton of Marley, 4s. *suc.* gdfa. Sir Edward Hales, 1st Bt.[†], 6 Oct. 1654.[1]

J.p. Kent June 1660–*d.*, dep. lt. June 1660–?*d.*, col. of militia ft. July 1660–9, commr. for assessment Aug. 1660–80, sewers, Rother marshes Oct. 1660, Medway marshes Dec. 1660; asst. Rochester Bridge 1661–80, warden 1661, 1668, 1675, commr. for corporations Kent 1662–3, recusants 1675.[2]

Hales's ancestors can be traced back in the Tenterden area of Kent to the 14th century. They rose through the law and a series of fortunate marriages, though none of them is known to have entered Parliament before 1605. Hales's grandfather sat for Queenborough in the Long Parliament and took the chair in the original county committee, but was sent to the Tower as a royalist suspect in 1643 and fined £6,000. Most of the Kentish Royalists were in his debt, and the sharp practice to which he was driven sowed a legacy of hatred for the purse-proud family not finally reaped till 1688. As heir to the greatest fortune in the county, Hales was drawn into the Kentish rising of 1648, of which he was the nominal leader, by his close friend Roger L'Estrange*. He escaped to Holland, but in his absence the Tunstall estate was released from sequestration at the cost of £2,000. Returning to England in 1651, he was of course under constant suspicion during the Interregnum. He was several times imprisoned, and after his grandfather's death paid no less than £604 p.a. as decimation tax.[3]

As a Cavalier Hales was ineligible for the general election of 1660, but was returned for Maidstone, eight miles from Tunstall, at a by-election. As soon as he had taken his seat he was selected to help raise a loan of £100,000 in the City. He was also appointed to the committee to give parochial status to Covent Garden, where his town house stood, but he was not otherwise active. At the general election he transferred himself to the family seat at Queenborough. An inactive Member of the Cavalier Parliament, he served on only 13 committees, none of them of political importance. In 1671 he complained of lack of ready money, but it was not until 1677 that he was given a pension of £500 p.a., which was regularly paid till 1679. Shaftesbury changed his assessment of 'worthy' to 'vile'. His name appears as a court supporter on the working lists and apparently in Wiseman's account, but he was otherwise ignored by the Opposition.[4]

Hales retained his seat in the first and second Exclusion Parliaments. He was again marked 'vile' on Shaftesbury's list and voted against the bill, but left no other trace on their proceedings. Outside

the House he was overshadowed by his son Edward Hales II*. In August 1681 he was given a pass for France, where he died between 6 Aug. 1683 and 8 Feb. 1684. It is a natural conjecture that he had become a Roman Catholic like his son, but there is no positive evidence for this.[5]

[1] *N. and Q.* clxx. 164; E. R. Mores, *Hist. Tunstall*, 36, 82; *Vis. Kent* (Harl. Soc. liv), 71; *Surv. of London*, xxxvi. 96. [2] *Twysden Ltcy. Pprs.* (Kent Recs. ix), 13; Kent AO, Hales mss; K. S. Martin, *Maidstone Recs.* 145; *Arch. Cant.* xvii. 173, 386–7; xxxiii. 103. [3] Hasted, *Kent*, vii. 205, 224; Keeler, *Long Parl.* 200–1; A. M. Everitt, *Community of Kent and the Great Rebellion*, 79, 147, 275, 283, 294; Clarendon, *Rebellion*, iv. 333–5, 342–4; *Cal. Comm. Comp.* 461; *CSP Dom.* 1651, p. 422; *Thurloe*, iv. 293; *Arch. Cant.* xxiii. 76; *Cal. Cl. SP*, iv. 326. [4] *CJ*, viii. 119; *CSP Dom.* 1671, p. 187; *Cal. Treas. Bks.* v. 709, 1541; *HMC Lindsey*, 103. [5] *CSP Dom.* 1680–1, p. 431; July–Sept. 1683, p. 259; *HMC Finch*, ii. 187.

M.W.H./B.D.H.

HALES, John (1648–1723), of the Inner Temple.

NEW SHOREHAM 1679 (Oct.), 1681

b. 2 Mar. 1648, 2nd s. of Sir Edward Hales, 2nd Bt.*, and bro. of Edward Hales II*. *educ.* Univ. Coll. Oxf. 1664; G. Inn, entered 1664; I. Temple 1665, called 1673. *unm.*[1]

Bencher, I. Temple 1692, reader 1695, treas. 1705–6.

Hales was at University College under Obadiah Walker, but unlike his brothers, who did not enjoy the benefits of such tuition, he is not known to have become a Roman Catholic. A professional lawyer, he took the Shoreham seat originally intended for his brother on the Admiralty interest at the second election of 1679. Presumably, like his father and brother, he opposed exclusion, but no committee work can be definitely ascribed to him, and on 4 Jan. 1681 he was listed as a defaulter. Nevertheless he was re-elected, though not without a contest. He passed the remainder of his life in the safe obscurity of the Temple, where he was buried on 8 Oct. 1723.[2]

[1] *Arch. Cant.* xiv. 80. [2] *HMC Finch*, ii. 56; PCC 61 Bolton; *Temple Church Recs.* 39.

B.M.C.

HALFORD, Sir Thomas, 3rd Bt. (c.1663–90), of Wistow Hall, Leics.

LEICESTERSHIRE 1689

b. c.1663, 1st s. of Sir Thomas Halford, 2nd Bt., of Wistow by Selina, da. of William Welby of Denton, Lincs. *educ.* G. Inn 1681. *unm. suc.* fa. c. June 1679.[1]

J.p., dep. lt. and commr. for assessment, Leics. 1689–*d.*

Halford's ancestor purchased the manor of Wistow in 1603. His great-grandfather, who had been created a baronet in 1641, was a Royalist in the Civil War, and compounded at £2,000 on an estate valued at £1,800 p.a. Unlike his distant cousin, Sir William Halford of Welham, Halford did not support James II's religious policy, and he was returned for the county as a Tory at the general election of 1689. According to Anthony Rowe* he voted to agree with the Lords that the throne was not vacant; but he was otherwise completely in-active in the Convention. He was buried at Wistow on 30 May 1690, the only member of this branch of the family to enter Parliament.[2]

[1] Nichols, *Leics.* ii. 873. [2] Nichols, ii. 869–70; *Cal. Comm. Comp.* 835–7.

E.C.

HALL, John (1632–1711), of Wells, Som. and The Hall, Bradford-on-Avon, Wilts.

WELLS   4 Nov. 1673, 27 Nov. 1680, 1681

bap. 17 May 1632, 1st s. of Sir Thomas Hall of Bradford by Catherine, da. of Sir Edward Seymour, 2nd Bt.[†], of Berry Pomeroy, Devon. *m.* (1) Susan, da. and h. of Francis Cox of Wells, *s.p.*; (2) lic. 1 Dec. 1670, Eliza-beth, da. of Sir Thomas Thynne* of Richmond, Surr., *s.p.*; 1da. illegit. by Rachel, da. of (Sir) George Wil-loughby* of Bishopstone, Wilts., wife of Thomas Bayntun of Little Chalfield, Wilts. *suc.* fa. 1663.[1]
   Gent. of the privy chamber by June 1660–85.[2]
   Commr. for assessment, Som. 1661–3, 1679–80, Wilts. 1664–80, Som. and Wilts. 1689–90; j.p. Som. 1662–Jan. 1666, Apr. 1666–80, Wilts. 1673–80, 1689–*d.*; capt.-lt. of militia horse, Som. by 1667; sheriff, Wilts. 1669–70; commr. for recusants, Som. 1675, in-quiry into recusancy fines, Wilts. Mar. 1688; dep. lt. Wilts. by 1696–*d.*[3]

Hall was the last of a family which took its name from the property in Bradford where they had resided since the middle of the 13th century. They were also landowners in Somerset, and two of them sat for Wells under the Lancastrians; but they were not a regular parliamentary family. Hall's father (under duress, by his own account) acted as a roy-alist commissioner during the Civil War, and was fined £660. Hall claimed to have expended a con-siderable sum in the Restoration, and was included in the Somerset list of knights of the Royal Oak with an income of £900 p.a. His preference for that county may not have been unconnected with the charms of the local milkmaids, which he described in detail to his friend, the lecherous Duke of Rich-mond. As sheriff of Wiltshire he wrote from Wells (without having obtained permission to leave the county) on 3 Jan. 1670, complaining of the financial burden imposed by that office, and in particular that Secretary Arlington (Sir Henry Bennet*) had ordered him to replace the keeper of the county gaol.[4]

Although Hall was a cousin of the Speaker, Edward Seymour*, it was as an opponent of the Government that he entered Parliament in 1673 as Member for Wells, where his brother-in-law Wil-liam Coward* was recorder. A more influential connexion at Westminster was another brother-in-law, Thomas Thynne II*. Hall was moderately active in the Cavalier Parliament, in which he was appointed to 31 committees and twice acted as teller. On 20 Jan. 1674 he urged that the House should divide on the impeachment of Arlington, failing to realize in his parliamentary inexperience that this was just what the secretary's friends wanted at this juncture. He never spoke in the House again, though he was added to the impeach-ment committee. In 1675 he was appointed to the committees for hindering Papists from sitting in Parliament and preventing the growth of Popery. On 6 Nov. he acted with Thynne as teller against the adjournment of the debate on building war-ships. On the working lists he was committed to the management of Secretary Williamson, who was intimate with the Duke of Richmond's sister, but Shaftesbury marked him 'doubly worthy'. He served on the committee for the estate bill of (Sir) Edward Hungerford* in 1677, as well as that for Thynne's bill in the following year. On 31 Jan. 1678, he complained to the House that he had been assaulted and wounded by a local attorney and bail-iff; one of the assailants was formally reprimanded on his knees by the Speaker and ordered to apolo-gize to Hall at quarter sessions, but nothing further is known of the incident. A few days later he accused the lord treasurer's servants of detaining the writ for the Westbury by-election. He was among those ordered to draw up an address for the removal of counsellors on 7 May, and in the last session he was added to the committee for the translation of Coleman's letters, and helped to draw up the address for their publication. He was probably a member of the Green Ribbon Club.[5]

Hall lost his seat at the general election, which he is not known to have contested, but he received the majority of votes from the scot-and-lot payers in the autumn and was seated on petition. Meanwhile he had been dismissed from local office. He leaves no further trace on the records of the second or third Exclusion Parliaments. As Thynne's executor, he tried to find a Whig purchaser for his Hindon burgages, and he was in good standing with the west country dissenters, the Bath Presbyterians hoping in 1683 that he might join with Sir Walter Long* against the court candidates. Lord Feversham, who occupied Hall's house during Monmouth's rebel-lion, described him to James II as 'none of the best affected, as your Majesty knows'. In 1688 he was made a commissioner for recusancy fines for Wiltshire, where, according to the King's electoral agents, he had an 'undoubted interest' and was 'esteemed right' as court candidate for the county. It is unlikely, however, that he stood again. His political retirement may have been due to a curious development in his private life. Hall had settled his nephew, Thomas Bayntun, on his estate at Chalfield, and, although he was at least twice Mrs Bayntun's age, and had had no children by two wives, he believed that he was the father of her younger daughter, baptized on 14 Apr. 1695 as 'Rachel Bayntun'. The scandal was apparently well hushed up, and Hall continued in local office, signing the Association in 1696 among the Wiltshire deputy lieutenants. Mrs Bayntun predeceased him, generously forgiving her husband all the wrongs he had done her, and Hall, who died between February and September 1711, left his estate to their daughter, who married the heir of the 1st Duke of Kingston (Evelyn Pierrepont*).[6]

[1] Dorset County Museum. Puddletown par. reg.; Som. Wills. iii. 56; Eg. 3653, f. 19; W. H. Jones, Bradford upon Avon, 192; The Gen. n.s. xxxiv. 44. [2] Carlisle, Privy Chamber, 164. [3] Q. Sess. Recs. (Som. Rec. Soc. xxxiv), p. xii; Bristol RO, AC/02/22; Cal. Treas. Bks. viii. 1805. [4] Jones, 52, 188; Cal. Comm. Comp. 1668; Add. 21947, f. 304; CSP Dom. 1670, p. 3. [5] Grey, ii. 318; Add. 28091, f. 67; CJ, ix. 485. [6] Bath mss, Thynne pprs. 24, f. 165, Davis to Ld. Weymouth, 1 Mar. 1690; CSP Dom. Jan.–June 1683, pp. 60, 314; HMC Sackville, Stopford-Sackville, i. 8; Coll. Top. et Gen. i. 17-19; Wilts. Arch. Mag. v. 365.

I.C.

HALL, Thomas (1619–67), of Worcester.

WORCESTER 1660

bap. 5 Aug. 1619, 1st s. of Richard Hall of Ludlow, Salop by Mary, da. of Richard Nash of Worcester. educ. Christ Church, Oxf. 1637; I. Temple 1638, called 1646. m. Elizabeth, da. of Robert Skinner, bp. of Worcester 1663-70, s.p. suc. fa. 1654.[1]

Town clerk, Worcester 1654–d.; commr. for assessment, Worcester 1657, Aug. 1660–d., Worcs. 1663-4; oyer and terminer, Western circuit July 1660; j.p. Worcs. July 1660-6.[2]

Hall's father, though not a member of Ludlow corporation, was of sufficient status to be named trustee of a local charity in 1634. He was then styled 'gentleman', which may mean that he was an attorney of the court of the marches. Such a background would account for Hall's 'jeering or taunting words against the Parliament' which was so hostile to the Ludlow court, though fortunately only one witness could be found to depose to seeing him 'ride in arms with a party of horse of the King's forces upon some design against the Parliament forces at Stanton Lacy' (where his father had a farm on long lease).

Hall's father retired to another farm of his when the court was finally abolished, but Hall himself, after qualifying as a barrister, settled in Worcester, which his uncle John Nash had represented in the Long Parliament, and became town clerk under the Protectorate. Hall was probably an Anglican, but, never having been convicted of delinquency, he was eligible at the general electionof 1660. He doubtless supported the Court in the Convention, but he was not an active Member, for he was named to only seven committees, of which the most important was for the navigation bill, and he made no recorded speeches. He was buried at St. Helen's, Worcester on 28 Sept. 1667. His property eventually passed through his sister to her nephew Thomas Vernon, Tory MP for the county from 1715 to 1721.[3]

[1] Ludlow Reg. (Salop Par. Reg. Hereford dioc. xiii), 158; PCC 391 Alchin; W.R. Williams, Worcs. Members, 98; Keeler, Long Parl. 284; Vis. Northants. (Harl. Soc. lxxxvii), 202. [2] Worcester chamber order bk. 1650-78, ff. 18, 69; Townshend's Diary (Worcs. Rec. Soc.), ii. 276. [3] Ludlow Reg. 385; SP23/166, ff. 209-10; Nash, Worcs. i. 327; Vis. Worcs. ed. Metcalfe, p. 97; PCC 33 Hene; Par. Bk. of St. Helen's Worcester ed. Wilson, ii. 139.

M.W.H./J.P.F.

HALSEY, Thomas (1655–1715), of Great Gaddesden, Herts.

HERTFORDSHIRE 1685, 1695, 1698, 1701 (Feb.), 1701 (Dec.), 1702, 1708, 1710, 1713

bap. 12 Mar. 1655, 7th but 2nd surv. s. of Sir John Halsey, master in Chancery (d.1670), of Great Gaddesden by Judith, da. and coh. of James Necton of London. educ. Magdalen Coll. Oxf. 1671; L. Inn, entered 1671. m. 4 Feb. 1679, Anne (d. 7 June 1719), da. and h. of Thomas Henshaw of Kensington, Mdx., 10s (1 d.v.p.) 4da. suc. bro. 1670.[1]

Commr. for assessment, Herts. 1679-80, 1689-90, St. Albans 1689; sheriff, Herts. 1679-80, capt. of militia ft. by 1680-?87, j.p. 1681-?Feb. 1688, Oct. 1688-?d., dep. lt. 1681-7, 1689-?d.; alderman, St. Albans 1685-?87.[2]

The Halseys were established in Hertfordshire in early Tudor times, and in 1545 were granted the rectory and advowson of Great Gaddesden, formerly belonging to Dartford Priory. Halsey's father who was legal adviser to the 2nd Earl of Bridgwater played no known part in the Civil War. He was a j.p. during the Protectorate, but was removed after the Restoration, though he held other local office.[3]

A strong Anglican and a Tory, Halsey was elected for Hertfordshire with government backing in 1685, the first of the family to sit, but he was totally inactive in James II's Parliament. He was doubtless opposed to the King's religious policy as he was removed from the lieutenancy in 1687. He sat in nine successive Parliaments from 1695 onwards, voting as a Tory under William III and Anne, though he signed the Association in 1696. He died on 25 May 1715 and was buried at Great Gaddesden. His grandson sat for Hertfordshire from 1768 to 1784.[4]

[1] Cussans, *Herts.* iii. pt. 1, p. 122; Westminster City Lib. St. Martin in the Fields par. reg. [2] *CSP Dom.* 1685, p. 73. [3] *Letters and Pprs. Hen. VIII*, xx. pt. 1, p. 213; Herts. RO, AH 1060. [4] Clutterbuck, *Herts.* i. 379, 381; *VCH Herts.* ii. 199; *CSP Dom.* 1685, p. 79; 1686–7, p. 314; 1687–9, p. 125.

E.R.E./G.J.

HALSEY *see also* HOWARD, George

HAMPDEN, John (1653–96), of Great Hampden, nr. Wendover, Bucks., and Great Russell Street, Bloomsbury, Mdx.

BUCKINGHAMSHIRE   1679 (Mar.), 1679 (Oct.)
WENDOVER   1681, 1689

bap. 21 Mar. 1653, 1st s. of Richard Hampden*. *educ.* M. Temple 1668; travelled abroad (France) 1670–3. *m.* (1) 5 May 1674, Sarah (*d.* Nov. 1687), da. of Thomas Foley I* of Witley Court, Worcs., wid. of Essex Knightley of Fawsley, Northants., 1s. 1da.; (2) Anne, da. and coh. of the Hon. Frederick Cornwallis, 1s. 1da. *suc.* fa. 1695. Commr. for assessment, Bucks. Northants and Oxon. 1679–80, Bucks. and Oxon. 1689–90; capt. London vol. horse 1689.[1]

Hampden was sent to study in France under the tutorship of Francis Tallents, an ejected Presbyterian minister. Burnet, who knew him well, described him as 'a young man of great parts, the learnedest gentleman I have ever known, for he was a critic both in Latin, Greek and Hebrew. He was a man of great heat and vivacity, but too unequal in his temper.' In France he adopted Father Richard Simon's critical view of the Old Testament, and became a professed free thinker. His political thinking was profoundly affected by the historian Mezeray, who told him that France had once enjoyed the same free institutions as England but lost them through the encroachment of kings.[2]

Returned for the county with his father's support in 1679, Hampden was appointed to the committee of elections and privileges in both Exclusion Parliaments. He was classed as 'honest' by Shaftesbury, spoke against the sale of Tangier on 9 Apr. and voted for the exclusion bill in May 1679. It is not likely that he attended the two following Parliaments, for in November 1680 he went over to France, though in 1681 he was elected for Wendover in his absence. He travelled through France, Switzerland and Germany, 'in all which places',

according to Lord Preston (Sir Richard Grahme*) 'he hath been extremely industrious to vilify and misrepresent our governors and Government, both in church and state'. According to the same authority, early in 1682 he was carrying on negotiations on behalf of his party with the French court through Father La Chaise, Louis XIV's confessor. He returned to England the following September, and was then said to have fallen under the influence of John Wildman I*. On the discovery of the Rye House Plot, Hampden was sent to the Tower on 8 July 1683, after William Howard* had testified that the first meeting of the Council of Six had been held at Hampden's house in Bloomsbury. As there was only one witness against him, he was tried not for high treason but for a misdemeanour and was fined £40,000 in February 1684. He could not pay this, 'offered several sums of money' but was told 'they would rather have him rot in prison than have the £40,000'. An estate of his in Buckinghamshire worth £700 p.a. and his manor of Preston in Northamptonshire were seized into the King's hands. After Monmouth's rebellion, a second witness appeared against him for his part in the Rye House Plot and he was transferred from the King's Bench prison to the Tower. Tried for high treason, he confessed to the plot, though not to the assassination part of the scheme, resigned himself entirely into the hands of James as 'the fountain of grace and mercy', and paid £6,000 to Jeffreys and Father Petre to secure a pardon. James, who had wanted his humiliation rather than his life, gave him a pardon and liberty. (Sir) John Bramston* commented 'the Whigs are extreme angry at him ... and they have reason on their side, for, as they truly say, he hath made good all the evidence of the plot, and branded the Lord Russell [Hon. William Russell*] and some others with falsehood, even when they died'. A contemporary commented: 'At last let out, he lost his goods, his estate, his wife and reputation'. Henceforth, the memory of his humiliation, wrote Burnet, 'gave his spirits a depression and disorder he could never quite master'. In a signed confession he attributed his misfortunes at this time to his having abandoned 'the certainty of the truths of the Christian religion ... to which I was principally drawn by that vanity and desire of vain-glory, which is so natural to the corrupted hearts of men'. Although he had lost much of his former influence with his party, he was trusted with secret communications with the Prince of Orange in 1688.[3]

After the Revolution, Hampden once again appeared in society and was described as 'a great beau'. He formed an attachment to Lady Monmouth, and King William told Halifax (Sir George Savile*) that what Hampden and Lady Monmouth contrived her husband, the first lord of the Treasury, executed. The King, who 'said young Mr Hampden was mad', did not think him fit for the embassy at The Hague, and sought instead to send him on a mission to Spain, which Hampden refused. Returned for Wendover in 1689, Hampden was appointed as John Hampden or Mr Hampden junior to 16 committees, including those to prohibit trade with France, to bring in a list of the essentials for securing religion, laws and liberty, to suspend the Habeas Corpus Act and to appoint the oaths of supremacy and allegiance. He took the chair in the committee which drew up the address promising support for the allies. On 14 Mar. he argued for a generous supply for the war and towards the expenses of the Dutch expedition to England. Later in the month, when an amendment was offered to the coronation oath for the King to maintain the Protestant religion professed by the Church of England, Hampden proposed unsuccessfully to maintain the Protestant religion, and the Church of England, 'and that will comprehend every man's sense'. In April he took the chair of a committee to draw up an address calling for a declaration of war against France, and did so in terms so partisan, with reflections on Charles II, that the House recommitted it under a different chairman. On the toleration bill on 15 May he argued that its provisions should be extended to all dissenters, not merely to Trinitarians. In November he gave evidence before the 'murder committee' of the House of Lords investigating the trials of the Whig leaders implicated in the Rye House Plot. Again he owned the reality of the conspiracy, said that William's expedition of 1688 was but a continuation of the Council of Six, showed particular hatred against Halifax, who he thought had initiated the prosecution against him, and said 'he looked upon himself as murdered, as truly as any of those whose case was under consideration, since few of the Lords, as he maintained, but would have preferred death to such sufferings he had undergone'. Halifax, who was shown to have interceded on Hampden's behalf, suggested that he should 'be contented with the honour of a confessor without pretending to that of a martyr'. On 6 Dec. he spoke for a proviso excepting Quakers from the penalties for refusing the oath of allegiance. On 14 Dec., he made a bitter attack on Halifax, Nottingham and Godolphin as the men responsible for the miscarriages of the war: 'that these men who came to Hungerford from King James, should be the greatest men in England, I leave the world to judge. . . . If we must be ruined again, let it be by

new men.' On 2 Jan. 1690 a contemporary reported that on reversing Walcot's attainder Hampden 'spoke much for the passing of the bill, and took occasion to make mention of some imputations laid upon him for what he said upon examination', when his father cut him short. According to the same authority, in this Parliament father and son were 'ordinarily opposite one to another'. He supported the disabling clause in the bill to restore corporations and wanted to except (Sir) Robert Sawyer* from the bill of indemnity, thinking the House too lenient with the prosecutors of the Whig martyrs. 'I ask whether nobody can be murdered but a King?'[4]

Hampden was defeated for Wendover in 1690 when his father opposed his readoption. In November 1691, much to his father's annoyance, he attacked the whole financial management, claiming that the commission of accounts last year had found great sums unaccounted for. The following year he was one of the four commissioners of public accounts (not being Members of Parliament) nominated by the Lords. He also declared that 'with a general excise and an army of 100,000 men, Englishmen will be as enslaved as Asia'. He published his views in a series of tracts, one written in collaboration with Wildman, and particularly attacked the King's refusal to give royal assent to the triennial bill. He was anxious to stand in 1695. In a pamphlet published as a guide to the electors, Halifax made a transparent attack on Hampden:

> there are some splenetic gentlemen who confine their favourable opinion within so narrow a compass that will not allow it to any man that was not hanged in the late reigns. Now by that rule one might expect they should rescue themselves from the disadvantage of being now alive, and by abdicating a world so little worthy of them get a great name to themselves, with the general satisfaction of all those they leave behind them.

Wharton's refusal to put him up as knight of the shire was said to have finally driven him to suicide. He cut his throat on 7 Dec. 1696, and died three days later. His elder son sat from 1701 to his death, representing Buckinghamshire in three Parliaments.[5]

[1] SP44/165/385. [2] Burnet ed. Airy, ii. 354; *DNB*. [3] Grey, vii. 100; Howell, *State Trials*, ix. 961, 1054–1127; xi. 479–495; *CSP Dom.* 1680–1, p. 86; *HMC 7th Rep.* 275, 278, 343; *HMC Lords*, ii. 294; *CSP Dom.* July–Sept. 1683, p. 80; 1684–5, pp. 253, 302; Macaulay, *Hist.* 696–7; *Bramston Autobiog.* (Cam. Soc. xxxii), 218; *HMC Hastings*, iv. 308–9; *DNB*; Calamy, *Life*, i. 386–90; Dalrymple, *Mems.* ii. bk. 5, p. 22. [4] *HMC Portland*, iii. 442; *Poems on Affairs of State*, v. 167; Foxcroft, *Halifax*, ii. 94–95, 97, 204, 229, 233; Grey, ix. 159, 190, 200, 322, 361, 536; Macaulay, 1426; *Clarendon Corresp.* ii. 277; R. Morrice, Entering Bk. 3, pp. 32, 89. [5] *HMC 7th Rep.* 200, 206, 219, 482; Luttrell, ii. 346; Foxcroft, *Halifax*, ii. 481–2; *Vernon-Shrewsbury Letters*, i. 121; *HMC Portland*, iii. 580.

L.N./E.C.

HAMPDEN, Richard (1631–95), of Great Hampden, nr. Wendover, Bucks.

BUCKINGHAMSHIRE	1656–10 Dec. 1657
WENDOVER	1660, 1661, 1679 (Mar.), 1679 (Oct.)
BUCKINGHAMSHIRE	1681
WENDOVER	1685, 1689
BUCKINGHAMSHIRE	1690, 22 Nov.–12 Dec. 1695

bap. 13 Oct. 1631, 2nd but 1st surv. s. of John Hampden† of Great Hampden by Elizabeth, da. of Edmund Symeon of Pyrton, Oxon. *m.* 11 Mar. 1652, Letitia, da. of William, 5th Baron Paget, 2s. (1 *d.v.p.*) 2da. *suc.* fa. 1643.

J.p. Bucks. 1653–?62, Feb. 1688–?*d.*; commr. for assessment, Bucks. 1657, Jan. 1660–80, Bucks. and Oxon. 1689–90, militia, Bucks. and Oxon. Mar. 1660; capt. of militia horse, Bucks. Apr. 1660, commr. for recusants 1675, dep. lt. Feb. 1688–?*d.*[1]

PC 14 Feb. 1689–3 May 1694; chairman of committees of supply and of ways and means 27 Feb. 1689–Oct. 1690; ld. of the Treasury 1689–94; chancellor of the Exchequer 1690–4.

Hampden's family had been seated on the Buckinghamshire estate from which they took their name since at least the reign of Edward the Confessor and first represented the county in 1352. His father, the celebrated opponent of ship-money under Charles I, died of wounds after the battle of Chalgrove Field, leaving an estate of over £1,500 p.a. Hampden supported the Protectorate, and was called to the 'other House' in 1657. Returned to the Convention for the family borough of Wendover, he was classed as a friend by Lord Wharton. But he made only two recorded speeches, in one of which he proposed that the moderate Presbyterian Baxter should be invited to preach to the House, and was appointed to seven committees, including those for settling ecclesiastical livings (30 July) and for supplying defects in the poll bill (13 Nov.). As Oliver Cromwell's kinsman he applied for confirmation of the grant of certain goods of the late Protector worth £400 to be recovered towards the satisfaction of a debt of £6,000.[2]

Hampden was again marked as a friend by Wharton on his re-election in 1661. He was moderately active in the Cavalier Parliament, serving on 86 committees, acting as teller in three divisions, and making 34 recorded speeches, often on procedural matters. He remained a Presbyterian, and was reported to the House on 3 July for failure to receive the sacrament. Baxter, who often stayed and preached at Great Hampden, described him as 'the true heir of his famous father's sincerity, piety and devotedness to God'. He was inactive during the administration of Clarendon, but on 25 Nov. 1667 he was appointed to the committee to examine the accounts of the French merchants. He was called to order on 7 May 1668 for urging dissolution. On 8 Apr. 1669 he supported the motion that the King should consult all Protestants, including dissenters, on remedies for the decay of trade. He took the chair for the bill to enable the coheirs of (Sir) John Fitzjames* to sell the estate. On 4 Feb. 1673 he seconded the motion that no writs should be issued for by-elections except on certificate from the Speaker. Two days later he urged an address to 'represent how grievous the war is, and how grateful peace', and to submit all to the King's judgment. In January 1674 he spoke in favour of a separate peace with the Dutch and a breach of the alliance with France. On 19 May 1675 he was appointed to the committee on the bill for appropriating the customs to the use of the navy, and in June he perused the Lords' Journals as chairman of the committee on the Ouse navigation bill. Sir Richard Wiseman* listed him in 1676 among the gentlemen of whom he had 'little cause to hope well', and Shaftesbury marked him 'thrice worthy'. He was appointed to the committee to prevent the growth of Popery (8 Mar. 1677). Hampden came to the fore with the Popish Plot, and the French ambassador reported to Louis XIV that he and William Harbord* were 'two of the most considerable Members of Parliament' whose services he had engaged. Between 1678 and 1680 he received 500 guineas from the French. Some of this money was distributed to Members by Coleman, the Duchess of York's secretary, and on 2 Nov. 1678 he was among the Members sent to examine Coleman in Newgate. When pressed in the House for details of Coleman's distribution of bribes to Members, Hampden replied that 'to the best of my remembrance, Coleman made great protestations that he knew no more, but he told you of three and four hundred pounds given the last session, and £2,500'. He was added to the committee to examine Coleman's papers, and appointed to that to receive evidence for the impeachment of Danby, though he was said to be among the 'Presbyterians' who were willing to drop the prosecution if the Parliament were dissolved and Danby resigned.[3]

In the first Exclusion Parliament Hampden was classed as 'worthy' by Shaftesbury. A very active Member, he was appointed to 38 committees, in seven of which he took the chair. He acted as teller in three divisions and made 21 recorded speeches. On 22 Mar. 1679 he was ordered to inform the Upper House that it was unparliamentary to demand a conference without specifying the subject. He was appointed to the committee to draw up Danby's attainder, and acted as chairman of the committees to draft the bill for regulating elections and the address for the execution of the Jesuit Pickering. On 27 Apr. he moved that 'the Duke of York being a Papist and the hopes of his coming to the crown have given the greatest countenance and encouragement to the present conspiracies and designs of the Papists against the King and the Protestant religion'. He was appointed to the committees to examine the disbandment accounts and to consider the habeas corpus amendment bill. On 5 May he reported reasons for the illegality of Danby's pardon, saying that if it were allowed 'accusing great men and accounting for money' would become impossible. He was also responsible as chairman for preparing for the conference on 10 May about the trials of the lords in the Tower, and for three inspections of the Lords' Journals. He strongly supported the exclusion bill:

> For us to go about to tie a Popish successor with laws for the preservation of the Protestant religion is binding Samson with withies; he will break them when he is awake. The Duke of York is the presumptive heir of the crown indeed; but if a man be likely to ruin the estate he may be heir to, we disinherit every day.

He was appointed to the committee and acted as teller for the second reading. On 26 May he reported the successful conference with the Lords on habeas corpus.[4]

In the second Exclusion Parliament Hampden was again very active. He was appointed to 51 committees, acting as chairman of three, and made 42 recorded speeches. He served on the committees to inquire into abhorring and to consider the exclusion bill, which he again supported in debate, 'since the succession of the crown had been often changed and yet continued hereditary. .... If the Dauphin or Infanta of Spain should become Protestant he doubted not but those kingdoms would be more impatient than we for this remedy'. He moved the second reading on 4 Nov. 1680 with the words: 'The Pope is your King when you have a Popish successor', under whom the Inquisition would soon be introduced. He reported the conference on the Irish plot, and on 27 Nov. brought in an address on the state of the kingdom; a correspondent of Ormonde's described it as 'the matter of the moment':

> It is not to be wondered at that it consisted of two sheets of paper, when 'tis considered what it contained, all the miscarriages past and present, in its close an assurance to the King that if he pleased to apply remedies, not only Tangier but all other his Majesty's necessary wants should be satisfied.

Hampden was one of the managers of Lord Stafford's prosecution, and chairman of the committee which drew up the address of 20 Dec. insisting on exclusion. He supported the bill to give toleration to Protestant dissenters. On 6 Jan. 1681 he was named to the committee for the bill to repeal the Corporations Act. He sat for the county in the Oxford Parliament. He was appointed as usual to the committee of elections and privileges, and made nine speeches. On 24 Mar. he spoke about the disappearance in the previous Parliament of the bill to repeal the Elizabethan statute against Protestant dissenters, and was appointed to prepare for a conference on 'the constitution of Parliaments in passing of bills'. He reported the proceedings to date on Danby's impeachment, and was appointed to the committees for the impeachment of Fitzharris and the exclusion bill, though the Duke of York included him among 'the most violent and cunning Members' who professed readiness to consider expedients.[5]

Hampden was returned to James II's Parliament for his borough. His sole committee was to prepare the address for the dismissal of Roman Catholic officers. Danby listed him among the eminent Parliamentarians in opposition 'most considerable for parts', and he maintained his attitude despite restoration to local office in 1688. In fact he was one of William's chief contacts among the Whigs, urging action before it became too late to shake James's position, and adding that nobody now favoured setting up a republic. He was chairman of the committee of Members of Charles II's Parliaments which drew up the address to William of 27 Dec.[6]

It is not always possible to distinguish Hampden from his son in the Convention, despite their increasingly divergent views. But he was clearly very active. The new regime gave him office with special responsibility for finance and for liaison with and between the Houses. He was chairman of the supply committee and seven other grand committees, from which he presented 50 reports. He brought 12 messages from the King, and was as often employed by the House as messenger to the Lords. He was named to 82 committees, in 15 of which he took the chair, and made 113 recorded speeches. On 22 Jan. 1689 he seconded the proposal that William should be asked to undertake the government pending the settlement of the succession, and took the chair of the committee to draw up the address. As chairman of the grand committee on the state of the nation, he reported on 28 Jan. that the throne was vacant, an opinion for which he was at once sent to desire the Lords' concurrence, and on the following day he brought the resolution that it had been found by experience to be inconsistent with the safety and welfare of a Protestant kingdom to be governed by a Popish prince. He was appointed to the committee to bring in a list of the essentials for securing religion, laws and liberties. On 4 Feb. he reported from the committee to prepare reasons for a conference on the state of the throne, declaring: 'I do not only serve the King as my prince, but—pardon my low expression—as one whom I love'. He twice reported from the conferences which followed, and also from that for the proclamation of the new sovereigns. On 1 Mar. he brought a message from the King about 'divers cabals against the Government about the town', and was appointed to the committee to bring in a temporary bill for the suspension of habeas corpus. Three days later he was sent to desire a conference on the address promising support to the King. He was appointed to the committee to inquire into the authors and advisers of the grievances of the last two reigns. He spoke in favour of an address on the Ipswich mutiny and took the chair in the drafting committee. It was on Hampden's recommendation that the King agreed to abolish the hearth tax, and he was appointed to the committee for the bill. He helped to manage the conference on the removal and disarming of Papists. Hampden, by his own account, was the only English politician whom William consulted on the religious settlement; he was willing to excuse beneficed clergymen from the new oath of allegiance, but, even as chairman of the committee to draw up reasons for a conference on the subject, he could not carry the Whigs with him. On 8 May he opposed the proviso to the bill of rights that nothing in it should 'prejudice the right of any Protestant Prince or Princess in their hereditary succession' on the grounds that it would enable James II's son to succeed if he became a convert. He carried the toleration bill to the Lords on 17 May and reported a conference five days later, making 'as few differences with the Lords as I can' in his anxiety to expedite the measure. On the bill of indemnity he thought that the precedent of 1660 should be followed by excepting a definite number of offenders: but here again the Whig pressure for the exclusion of all who could be inculpated under various categories was too strong for him. He was chairman of the grand committee for the suspension of habeas corpus, and carried the bill to the Upper House on 25 May. He invited Tenison to preach to the House on 5 June, and was ordered to thank him for his sermon. He reported three more conferences in the first session: those on the tea, coffee and chocolate duties, on the reversal of Titus Oates's conviction, and on the attainder of the Jacobite rebels in Ireland. He also carried the bills for repayment to the Dutch of their expenses in the liberation and for prohibiting trade with France, and acted as teller against the reference to the Quakers in the security bill. After the recess he secured as chairman of supply a grant of £2,000,000 'for a vigorous prosecution of the war with France, both by sea and land'. On 20 Dec. he attended the King with a request that Commissary Shales should be sent over from Ireland in custody, and on the next day he reported the address on the miscarriages of the war. In the debate on restoring corporations he supported the disabling clause, wishing 'that they who gave up charters might be liable to this penalty, though they were a majority'.[7]

Hampden regained the county seat at the general election, and sat for Buckinghamshire for the rest of his life as a court Whig and (until 1694) a member of the Government. He died on 12 Dec. 1695 and was buried at Great Hampden.[8]

[1] *Merc. Pub.* 12 Apr. 1660; *CP*, iv. 609–10; *DNB*; Lipscomb, *Bucks.* ii. 260; *CSP Dom.* 1694–5, p. 204; 1695, p. 112. [2] Keeler, *Long Parl.* 202; M. Sylvester, *Reliquae Baxterianae*, ii. 448; *CSP Dom.* 1660–1, p. 338. [3] *Milward*, 300; Grey, i. 130; vi. 132, 152; *Dering*, 104, 351; Witcombe, *Cavalier Parliament*, 163; Dalrymple, *Mems.* i. 357, 382; Browning, *Danby*, i. 312. [4] *CJ*, ix. 584, 605, 626; Grey, vii. 150–1, 183, 243–4; Clarke, *Jas. II*, i. 608. [5] Grey, vii. 421; viii. 302, 314–15; *HMC Ormonde*, n.s. v. 561; *HMC 12th Rep. IX*, 101; *HMC Finch*, ii. 106; *Jas. II*, i. 671. [6] J. R. Jones, *Revolution of 1688*, 169–70, 235–6; *Evelyn Diary*, iv. 635; Macaulay, *Hist.* 1337; Browning, *Danby*, i. 444; Grey, ix. 6. [7] R. Morrice, *Entering Bk.* 3, pp. 73, 74; Grey, ix. 53, 129–30, 168, 244–52, 419; *HMC Portland*, iii. 430; Macaulay, 1406; Browning, i. 447; Burnet, i. 213; Simpson thesis 1, pp. 175–6. [8] Luttrell, iii. 563.

L.N./M.W.H./E.C.

HAMPSON, Sir Denis, 3rd Bt. (c.1653–1719), of Taplow, Bucks.

CHIPPING WYCOMBE   1685

> b. c.1653, 1st s. of Sir Thomas Hampson, 2nd Bt., of Taplow by Mary, da. and coh. of Sir Anthony Dennys of Orleigh, Devon. *unm. suc.* fa. 22 May 1670.[1]
>
> Commr. for assessment, Bucks. 1673–80, 1689–90; j.p. Bucks. 1675–?1702, Oxon. 1700–?2; dep. lt. Bucks. 1680–?1702, Oxon. 1701–2; capt. of militia horse, Bucks. 1680–at least 1697, sheriff 1683–4; freeman, Chipping Wycombe 1684, alderman 1685–?Oct. 1688; freeman, New Windsor 1685.[2]

Hampson was the great-grandson of a London Merchant Taylor. His grandfather, who bought Taplow in 1635, tried to avoid involvement in the Civil War, but his estates were plundered by both sides. Accused of delinquency in 1647, he was not finally cleared until 1650. Hampson's father, still a student when hostilities began, was an unsuccessful candidate for Oxford in 1660.[3]

Hampson was a strong Tory and a high Anglican who harried the Quakers. In May 1683 he broke up a meeting at Wooburn, and sent 23 men to prison, directing that they should be indicted for riot. He was returned in 1685 for Wycombe, some ten miles from Taplow, apparently on the corporation interest, but left no trace on the records of James II's Parliament. He consented to the repeal of the Penal Laws and Test Acts, but declared that he would not trust fanatics. Yet he accepted the Revolution, took the oath of allegiance to William and Mary in 1689 and consequently continued to hold local office. He is not known to have stood again. He sold Taplow about 1700, and was buried at St. Sepulchre's, Holborn, on 10 Apr. 1719. His affairs were involved, letters of administration being granted to a creditor. A cousin inherited the baronetcy, but no other member of the family sat in Parliament.[4]

[1] *Vis. Bucks.* (Harl. Soc. lviii), 71–2; Lipscomb, *Bucks.* iii. 303. [2] J. Parker, *Wycombe*, 56; *CSP Dom.* 1679–80, p. 439; 1685, p. 45; Eg. 1626, f. 5; *First Hall Bk.* (Windsor Hist. Recs. i), 48. [3] Beaven, *Aldermen of London*, i. 131; ii. 46; *VCH Bucks.* iii. 242; *Cal. Comm. Adv. Money*, 154–6; *Oxford Council Acts* (Oxf. Hist. Soc. xcv), 255–6; Bath mss, Thynne pprs. 12, ff. 162–3. [4] *Quaker Minute Bk.* (Bucks. Rec. Soc. i), 125; W. Le Hardy, *Bucks. Sess. Recs.* i. 287; *VCH Bucks.* iii. 242; Prob. 6/95/69.

L.N./G.J.

HANMER, Sir John (*d.*1701), of Hanmer, Flints. and Whittingham Hall, Fressingfield, Suff.

FLINT BOROUGHS	1659
EVESHAM	29 Oct.–22 Nov. 1669, 7 Dec. 1669
FLINTSHIRE	1681
FLINT BOROUGHS	1685, 1689

1st s. of Sir Thomas Hanmer, 2nd Bt.* by 1st w. *educ.* travelled abroad (France, Portugal) 1644–51. *m.* c. June 1659, Mary (*d.* 11 Dec. 1709), da. and h. of Joseph Alston of Washbrooke, Suff., 1da. *d.v.p.* Kntd. 9 Aug. 1660; *suc.* fa. as 3rd Bt. 6 Oct. 1678.[1]

Commr. for assessment, Flints. 1657, Jan. 1660, 1661–74, 1679–80, 1689–90, Suff. Aug. 1660–1, 1673–80, 1689, Worcs. 1673–9; j.p. Flints. Mar. 1660–*d.*, Suff. July 1660–at least 1664; keeper of the game, N. Wales Dec. 1660; capt. of militia horse, Flints. 1661–?85; commr. for loyal and indigent officers, Suff. 1662; sheriff, Glos. 1664–5; commr. for recusants, Worcs. 1675; dep. lt. Flints. 1685–*d.*[2]

Gent. of the privy chamber (extraordinary) June 1660–?70; esquire of the body by 1670–85; commr. for revenue inspection [I] 1676–80; PC [I] 1695–*d.*[3]

Capt. Lord Gerard's Horse 1662–3, 1666–7, maj. 1678–9; capt. Duke of Buckingham's Ft. 1672–3; capt. of ft. [I] 1678–80; lt.-col. (later 11 Ft.) 1685, col. Dec. 1688–*d.*; gov. Cork 1692; brig. 1695.[4]

MP [I] 1695–9.

Hanmer spent much of his childhood and adolescence with his father in Roman Catholic countries, but, unlike his sister, who ended her life as a nun, he acquired only a distaste for the religion. During the Interregnum he advanced £600 for the King's

service, and at the Restoration he was knighted and given a post at Court. Although he married an heiress, and eventually also inherited the Baker estates in Gloucestershire and Suffolk, his extravagance entailed frequent outlawries. When he stood on the court interest for Evesham in 1669, he was described as 'a privy chamber man, vastly in debt, [who] had £500 to follow his election'. He defeated Sir James Rushout* on the corporation franchise, and again on the votes of the 'burgesses at large' after the first election had been declared void. He was an active Member of the Cavalier Parliament in which he was appointed to 89 committees, made 17 recorded speeches, and acted as government teller in 20 divisions. His first important committee was on the bill for suppressing conventicles (2 Mar. 1670), and in December he acted as teller for supply. At the end of the session he was listed among the government supporters. He was appointed to the committee for the test bill in 1673, but would have agreed with the Lords to permit the continuance of pensions to Roman Catholics. He also served on the committee to consider the bill of ease for Protestant dissenters. He served aboard the fleet in the Duke of Buckingham's regiment during the summer, and when Parliament reassembled insisted that only those articles of war which were agreeable to law had been read to home service troops. He favoured seeking the concurrence of the Lords, which was unlikely, for the address against Buckingham. When his regiment was disbanded, the King ordered proportional compensation to be found for him. He was granted a pension of £800 p.a. for three years, and his name appeared on the Paston list of court supporters.[5]

In the spring session of 1675 Hanmer was teller against the third paragraph of the address for the removal of Lauderdale and against a place bill. He was among those Members consulted by Danby on the eve of his impeachment. During the debate he moved for a summons to the witnesses to be called for the defence, and objected to setting up a committee to inquire into payments for secret service because the matter was already before the House. On 10 May he clashed with William Cavendish*, Lord Cavendish, over the result of a division in committee on the recall of British subjects in the service of Louis XIV, and only prompt action by Edward Seymour* averted serious disorder. He received the government whip for the autumn session, in which he was appointed to the committee for the appropriation bill. In the renewed debate on British troops in the French army he warned the House on 23 Oct.: 'If you withdraw these forces from France, you give the French encouragement to make peace. Having these men there, you keep the balance.' On the prorogation he was forced to leave the country to avoid arrest, but he was soon appointed to the Irish revenue commission. He was listed among the officials in the House and in Wiseman's account, and on the working lists he was marked 'to be sent for'. Protected by his privilege he duly landed at Chester for the 1677 session, together with George Weld*, Sir Cyril Wyche* and Lord Fitzharding (Maurice Berkeley*). He was marked 'doubly vile' on Shaftesbury's list and included among the government speakers, which he justified on 21 Feb. by supporting the grant of £600,000 for building warships, and remarking offensively that in a loyal country no man would mention a lesser amount. He was appointed to the committees to recall Englishmen from France, preventing the growth of Popery and drafting an address to promise assistance to the King in the event of war with France. After the debate, however, complaint was made that he, with other members of the government caucus, 'did not stir'. He was teller against imposing a permanent ban on Irish cattle, a reckless action if he ever intended to represent a Welsh constituency. Having served on the committee for the bill to ensure that children of the royal family should be brought up as Protestants, he vigorously opposed a more tolerant bill sent down by the Lords on 4 Apr., calling on the House to stand by

> our David against this Goliath; our bill against the Lords' bill. Ours will go up to the Lords triumphant in throwing out this, and warm your party in the Lords' House.[6]

Hanmer was again commissioned in the newly-raised forces in 1678, and when Parliament met he was appointed to the committee to draw up the address for reducing France to her 1659 frontiers, and acted as teller for adjourning the debate on Seymour's arbitrary conduct in the chair and for agreeing with the Lords on the address for war with France. In the debate of 29 Apr. he defended the Government's unpopular and ineffective foreign policy:

> The King has proceeded to war as much as he could, and the Dutch say they have been so wasted with the war that without [even] a preliminary from the French King they would go into a peace with him. . . . The King has all along intended war with the French, and has endeavoured to do it, and the alliances are not come up to it.

He was appointed to the committee to draw up the address for the removal of counsellors, which, he considered, exceeded its instructions by ignoring the position of the House of Lords:

> I would not have the committee, though men of great

parts, think that the House will always agree with them. I would have the address recommitted, they having no authority to do what they have done.

He was teller against the fourth paragraph of the address, and was summoned to the meeting of the government caucus on 30 May, in preparation for the debate on disbandment. He was appointed to the committee to report on arrears of pay.[7]

Hanmer had to leave London in October 1678 to attend his father's funeral. On the way, he wrote to Sir Charles Wheler* to assure Danby that he would return for the next session. He hoped to succeed his father as custos rotulorum of Flintshire, a place 'of very small value, but of some interest in the country, which I hope my lord thinks I shall be as ready to employ in his service as any man'. Although his hopes were not to be fulfilled, he had resumed his seat by 30 Oct., when he was added to the committee to translate Coleman's letters. He helped to draw up reasons for belief in the Popish Plot and an address to explain the committal of Secretary Williamson. On 21 Nov. he urged the House to allow the Duke of York to retain his seat in the Lords without taking the Test:

> You had better impeach the Duke than throw out this proviso and take him from his brother. Keep him here, and you may breathe the wholesome doctrines of the Church of England into him. And because I see the whole bill in danger if you throw out the proviso, and religion too, therefore I am against throwing it out.

He was appointed to the committee to prepare reasons against excepting a limited number of the servants of the Queen and the Duchess of York from the Test, and five days later acted as teller for the adjournment of the debate, a subject in which he was particularly interested because his half-brother was the Queen's solicitor-general. In his last speech, on 19 Dec. he sought in vain to divert attention from the attack on Danby's instructions to Ralph Montagu* by taking up a melodramatic allusion to poison in the speech of William Harbord*.[8]

Hanmer was on both lists of the court party in 1678, and was described in *A Seasonable Argument* as 'a prodigal gentleman of the horse . . . a commissioner of the excise and in command of a troop of horse in Ireland, who had £2,000 given him'. As one of the 'unanimous club', he probably did not stand at the first general election of 1679, and though he proposed to contest Flintshire in the autumn he seems to have desisted, and lost his post in Ireland in the following year. He was, however, successful in 1681, but left no trace on the records of the Oxford Parliament. He sat for the Boroughs in 1685, and was listed among the Opposition in James II's Parliament. He was a moderately active

Member, being appointed to the committees to recommend expunctions from the Journal, to inspect the disbandment accounts, to continue relief for the creditors of the late Earl of Cleveland, and to consider a petition from the hackney coachmen. He resumed his interrupted military career again during Monmouth's rebellion, and was absent with his regiment when the lord president questioned the magistracy about their attitude to the Test Act and Penal Laws. He must have given satisfaction to the Government, for he was retained in local office, and Sunderland ordered him to stand for the county in 1688. This confidence was ill-founded, for at the Revolution he accepted an offer of £5,000 from Danby to secure Hull for the Protestant cause. The Roman Catholic officers of the garrison were apprehended 'without effusion of blood and to the satisfaction of the town', and Hanmer was rewarded with the colonelcy of his regiment.[9]

Hanmer was re-elected for the Boroughs to the Convention, in which he was almost totally inactive. A court Tory, he did not vote to agree with the Lords that the throne was not vacant. His only speech was to attack the bailing of Brent, the 'Popish solicitor', and his only committee was for the toleration bill. He probably joined his regiment in Ireland soon afterwards, though he was absent sick from the parade in October 1688, when it was found to be 'very badly clothed'. His political career in Britain was over, but he fought at the battle of the Boyne and represented Carlingford in the Irish Parliament. He was buried at Hanmer on 12 Aug. 1701. His nephew, the fourth baronet, was the most distinguished politician of the family, acting as Speaker of Queen Anne's last Parliament and subsequently as leader of the Hanover Tories.[10]

[1] J. Hanmer, *Par. and Fam. of Hanmer*, 75–76, 122, 128; *East Anglian*, n.s. xii. 366. [2] *CSP Dom.* 1660–1, p. 431; 1661–2, p. 145; 1665–6, p. 215; T. Dingley, *Beaufort's Progress*, 88. [3] LC3/2; Hanmer, 123; *Cal. Treas. Bks.* v. 180; *HMC Ormonde*, n.s. v. 493–4; *CSP Dom.* 1695, p. 5. [4] *CSP Dom.* 1661–2, p. 577; 1665–6, p. 557; 1695, p. 5; *HMC Ormonde*, ii. 210, 215; n.s. v. 493–4; *Cal. Treas. Bks.* ix. 1664. [5] Hanmer, 123; 128; Copinger, *Suff. Manors*, iv. 36; vi. 224; *VCH Glos.* viii. 263; Harl. 7020, f. 46; *CJ*, ix. 182, 264, 303; G4ey, ii. 397; *CSP Dom.* 1673–5, pp. 207–8; 1675–6, p. 356. [6] *CJ*, ix. 322, 327, 408; *Dering Pprs.* 74, 82; Grey, iii. 336; iv. 126, 338; *Cal. Treas. Bks.* v. 180, 526; *CSP Dom.* 1676–7, p. 512; Eg. 3345, f. 35v. [7] *CJ*, ix. 436, 458, 479; Grey, v. 280, 369; *CSP Dom.* 1678, p. 194. [8] *CSP Dom.* 1678, p. 455; Grey, vi. 242, 350; *CJ*, ix. 548. [9] *Flints. Hist. Soc.* xiv. 44; *HMC Ormonde*, n.s. v. 493–4; *CSP Dom.* 1687–9, p. 276; Browning, *Danby*, ii. 142–3, 147–8; Add. 28053, f. 369; Clarke, *Jas. II*, ii. 230. [10] Grey, ix. 52; *CSP Dom.* 1689–90, p. 48; Hanmer, 131.

E.R.

HANMER, Sir Thomas, 2nd Bt. (1612–78), of Bettisfield, Flints.

FLINT BOROUGHS   1640 (Apr.)
FLINTSHIRE   1 Nov. 1669–6 Oct. 1678

b. 4 May 1612, 1st s. of Sir John Hanmer, 1st Bt.[†], of Hanmer by Dorothy, da. and coh. of Sir Richard Trevor[†] of Trevalun, Denb. *educ.* King's, Camb. 1627; travelled abroad 1638–40. *m.* (1) by 20 Feb. 1632, Elizabeth (*d.* c.1644), da. of Sir Thomas Baker of Whittingham Hall, Fressingfield, Suff. and h. to her bro. Thomas, maid of honour to Queen Henrietta Maria, 1s. 1da.; (2) 22 Nov. 1646, Susan, da. of Sir William Hervey[†] of Ickworth, Suff., 2s. *suc.* fa. 29 June 1624.[1]

Page of honour c.1625–7; cupbearer c.1642.[2]

J.p. Flints. 1632–44, July 1660–*d.*, custos rot. 1642–4, Aug. 1660–*d.*, commr. of array 1642–4, dep. lt. c. Aug. 1660–*d.*, commr. for assessment Aug. 1660–*d.*, loyal and indigent officers 1662.

Capt. of dgns. (royalist) 1642–4; gov. Chirk Castle 1643.[3]

Hanmer's family traced its descent from an English knight who settled in Flintshire under Edward I. They had represented Flintshire constituencies since the reign of Mary Tudor. Hanmer, a courtier, was an active Royalist at the outset of the Civil War, but obtained leave to go abroad with his wife and children on 15 May 1644, and was fined £984 by Parliament for his delinquency at the minimum rate of one-tenth. In 1646 he provided information about the King's negotiations with the Scots, and was later exempted from decimation for this 'signal service'. He was more interested in horticulture than in politics, being celebrated for the introduction of the Agate Hanmer tulip, though Roger Whitley* included him among the Welsh Royalists in 1658, and at the Restoration he was proposed as knight of the Royal Oak, with an estate of £3,000 p.a.[4]

After an interval of nearly 30 years. Hanmer was returned for Flintshire at a by-election in 1669. He was a moderately active Member of the Cavalier Parliament, in which he was named to 35 committees. Together with John Birch* and John Ratcliffe* he was ordered on the petition of the Chester corporation to bring in a bill for improving the navigation of the Dee. A persecutor of conventicles, he was appointed to the committees for both bills in 1670. He spoke in favour of a land tax on 1 Dec., and at the end of the session he was listed among the government supporters as a 'court cully', who had been 'entered in the bribe-master's books'. He spoke briefly on the Northumberland peerage case in 1674, and was appointed to his last committee on 20 Apr. 1675. Although he received the government whip for the autumn session, he was noted as absent by Sir Richard Wiseman* and 'wanting' on the working lists. Nevertheless he was listed among the government speakers and marked 'doubly vile' by Shaftesbury in 1677. According to *A Seasonable Argument* he was in receipt of a pension of £500 p.a., and he was listed among the court party in 1678. He died on 6

Oct. before the last session of the Parliament, and was buried at Hanmer. He was posthumously included in the 'unanimous club' of government supporters.[5]

[1] J. Hanmer, *Par. and Fam. of Hanmer*, 63–65, 77; Copinger, *Suff. Manors*, iv. 36. [2] Hanmer, 63; *Cal. Comm. Comp.* 943. [3] Hanmer, 65. [4] Hanmer, 14, 75–76; *Thurloe*, iv. 277; J. W. Stoye, *English Travellers Abroad*, 405. [5] *CJ*, ix. 109; Hanmer, 121; Grey, i. 315; ii. 401, 403; Harl. 7020, f. 48; Hanmer, 112.

A.M.M.

HANSES, Charles (c.1659–c.1697), of Gray's Inn.

WINCHESTER 1685

b. c.1659, 1st s. of John Hanses of Selby and York, Yorks. *educ.* Archbishop Holgate's sch. York; Magdalene and St. John's, Camb. 1677; G. Inn 1681, called 1683. *?unm.*

Freeman, Winchester 1685; judge-advocate, Jamaica 1693–?*d.*[1]

Hanses was recommended to Lord Halifax in 1681 as secretary and reader. 'He is a very good scholar, and of a modest, humble and ingenuous behaviour. He has studied the law a little, and may be capable to solicit any business in it. . . . My lord may have him upon easy terms, for his parents are but of moderate fortune.' Halifax apparently refused the bargain, for Hanses entered government service and was called to the bar after only two years' study at the special request of Judge Jeffreys. He assisted Roger L'Estrange* in his investigation of the press after the Rye House Plot and the treasury solicitors in preparing the case against Titus Oates, for which he received £1,800. After considerable pressure from the Court, he and L'Estrange were returned unopposed for Winchester in 1685, and he became an active Member of James II's Parliament. He was appointed to 12 committees, including those to recommend expunctions from the Journals and revivals of expiring laws. He was reappointed to the latter committee on 18 June, when it was instructed to bring in a clause to regulate printing. He was also named to the committees on the bills to prevent clandestine marriages and relieve poor debtors, and for the general naturalization of Protestant refugees. Towards the end of the year, he sought to connect himself by marriage with the Meux, a leading Isle of Wight family; but although he took out a licence, the marriage did not take place in the specified church.[2]

Hanses received no preferment from James II, and had broken with his government by the summer of 1688, when he helped Archbishop Sancroft to prepare his defence. He gave evidence in 1689 to the Commons committee appointed to pre-pare a case against his former superiors. He accepted the new regime, however, for on the recommendation of the Earl of Nottingham (Daniel Finch*) he was made judge-advocate of Jamaica. His name was removed from the lists of the Winchester electorate in 1698.[3]

[1] Winchester corp. assembly bk. 6, f. 13; *CSP Col.* 1693–6, p. 110. [2] Notts. RO, DDSR 219/11, Goodall to Clarges, 27 Apr. 1681; *Pension Bk. of G. Inn*, ii. 72; G. Kitchin, *Sir Roger L'Estrange*, 311; *HMC Kenyon*, 264; *CSP Dom.* 1684–5, p. 133; *Cal. Treas. Bks.* viii. 280; *Secret Services* (Cam. Soc. lii) 101; *Mar. Lic.* (Harl. Soc. xxx) 222. [3] *Collectanea Curiosa*, i. 363; Bodl. Tanner mss 28, f. 97; *CJ*, x. 148; *CSP Col.* 1693–6, p. 102; Winchester corp. assembly bk. 6, ff. 136, 143.

P.W.

HARBORD, Sir Charles (1596–1679), of Charing Cross, Westminster and Stanninghall, Norf.

LAUNCESTON 1661, 8 Mar.–25 May 1679

bap. 2 July 1596, 1st s. of William Harvord of Welton, Midsomer Norton, Som. by Dorothy, da. and h. of Richard Richmond *alias* Sheppard of Babington, Som., wid. of Edmund Tynte of Wraxall, Som. *educ.* Staple Inn; M. Temple 1624. *m.* (1) Anne (*d.* by 1623), da. and h. of Jasper Tyen, jeweller, of Fenchurch Street, London, *s.p.*; (2) Mary (*d.* 5 Sept. 1666), da. of Jan van Aelst of Sandwich, Kent, 6s. (3 *d.v.p.*) 3da. *suc.* fa. 1616; *kntd.* 29 May 1636.[1]

Surveyor-gen. 1631–42, June 1660–*d.*; commr. for inquiry into customs frauds 1632, prohibited exports 1635, Chatham chest 1635; auditor-gen. to the Prince of Wales 1636–42; commr. for revenue and member of council to Queen Henrietta Maria 1638–41, ?June 1660–*d.*, to Queen Catherine of Braganza ?1662–*d.*; commr. of trade Nov. 1660–8; trustee for sale of fee-farm rents 1670–3; commr. for loyal and indigent officers accounts 1671; chairman, supply committee 19–22 Oct. 1675; commr. for inquiry into the Mint 1677, 1678.[2]

Commr. for enclosure, Richmond Park 1634; j.p. Herts. and Mdx. 1636–42, Norf. Mar. 1660–*d.*, Mdx. 1667–*d.*; asst. to saltmakers' co., Gt. Yarmouth 1636; commr. for repairs, Tower of London 1638; keeper of New Lodge walk, Windsor Forest by 1640–2; commr. for assessment, Herts. 1640, Norf. 1661–*d.*, Mdx. and Westminster 1663–*d.*, oyer and terminer, Norf. circuit July 1660, sewers, Lincs. Aug. 1660, Ravensbourne Sept. 1660, pre-emption of tin, Devon and Cornw. 1662, loyal and indigent officers, London and Westminster 1662; conservator, Bedford level 1663–79; commr. for concealments, Mdx. and Surr. 1670, inquiry, Kingswood chase and Richmond Park 1671.[3]

Harbord's great-grandfather came out of Wales with Henry VII, or so he had heard. His father leased a farm of some 200 acres in Somerset from the duchy of Cornwall. Harbord described himself to his eldest son as a self-made man. He was said to have begun life as 'a poor solicitor of Staple Inn'; but he entered the service of Philip Herbert*, Earl of Montgomery, subsequently 4th Earl of Pembroke. He prospered sufficiently to advance £7,000 to the crown in 1629, and two years later became surveyor-general, though he retained chambers in Baynard's Castle till at least 1635, and acted as principal trustee for the Pembroke manor of Rickmansworth Moor, in Hertfordshire, until it was sold to Sir Richard Franklin* in 1655. It was presumably from his patron, who was warden of the stannaries and constable of St. Briavels, that he derived his life-long interest in the duchy of Cornwall and the Forest of Dean. He was involved in a double return at Bossiney in the autumn election of 1640, and as a petitioner witnessed something of the impeachment of Strafford. But his 'too good husbandry for the King' had made him enemies, he was too staunch an Anglican to take the Covenant, and on 28 Oct. 1642 he obtained a pass for Holland with his wife, children, servants and goods. His return was thought 'very uncertain', and he probably remained there until the outbreak of the first Dutch war. But without losing the esteem of the Royalists he succeeded in winning the good graces of the Protector, who protested to the governor of the Spanish Netherlands when some of Harbord's goods at Brugge were seized by the exiled Cavalier Sir Richard Grenville†. He acquired Stanninghall from the Roman Catholic Waldegraves during the Interregnum, and on the eve of the Restoration Sir Edward Hyde† was assured that Harbord would serve him on all occasions, 'and is generally trusted by the best'.[4]

Harbord was promptly reappointed to the surveyorship, with a reversion to his son William*, who also became auditor to the duchy of Cornwall. At the general election of 1661 he was returned on the duchy interest for Launceston and also for Hindon, which he gave up to Edward Seymour*. One of the most active Members of the Cavalier Parliament, he was appointed to 694 committees and delivered 65 reports, 15 of them from grand committee. He acted as teller in five divisions and as messenger from the Commons on 12 occasions, and made 123 recorded speeches. In the first session his committees included those to consider the security, corporations, and uniformity bills, against tumultuous petitioning, and the bill of pains and penalties. He took part in the inquiry into the shortfall in the revenue, and on 23 July was among those ordered to bring in an imposition upon sealed paper and parchment. Two days later he accompanied Sir Baynham Throckmorton* and others to Lord Treasurer Southampton with proposals for improving the Forest of Dean. A member of the committee on the bill to restore the bishops to the House of Lords, he was sent to inform the Upper House that the Commons agreed to their proviso on ecclesiastical jurisdictions. After the autumn

recess he was named to the committee on the bill for the execution of those under attainder. On behalf of the House he asked Dr Samuel Bolton, one of the canons of Westminster, to preach for the fast day of 15 Jan. 1662. As one of the committee for preventing mischief from Quakers, he helped to prepare reasons for a conference. He took the chair for the bill to regulate the pilchard fishery in the west of England, and before the prorogation he helped to redraft the Lords' expedient to the militia bill.[5]

Harbord's activity increased in the 1663 session. On 7 Mar. he recommended from the committee appointed to examine the working of the Corporations Act that the commissioners' powers should be extended for another year. Two days later he was given leave to bring in a bill to abolish concurrent leases of ecclesiastical property. He took the chair for a bill to punish the unlawful cutting and spoiling of woods, and he was later among those sent to ask the lord treasurer to name those responsible for damage to the Forest of Dean. He was also named to the committees to hear a petition from the loyal and indigent officers and to provide remedies against sectaries' meetings. But his most important work was done as chairman of the revenue committee from which he presented 12 reports. With Richard Kirkby* and William Yorke* he obtained from the King an order for the Exchequer to deliver deeds concerning impropriate rectories. He took the chair for the bills against pluralities and profanity, and he was the first Member named to the committee to consider the ecclesiastical leases bill which he had drafted. He was teller against a bill to prevent the sale of offices, and on 26 June he reported two more bills, one to legalize the transfer of bonds and the other to prevent butchers from selling live cattle. He had not been named to the latter committee, but was presumably co-opted in view of his concern over the practice as a Middlesex j.p. before the Civil War. Before the session ended he was able to carry the pluralities bill to the Upper House.[6]

Harbord was listed as a court dependant in 1664, when he was named to the committee to consider the conventicles bill, and given special responsibility for bringing in a bill to prevent licentiousness and restrain excessive expenditure. He set an excellent example himself when summoned to London to assist in the retrenchment of the Household by performing the journey from Norwich by public transport. He succeeded in steering his ecclesiastical leases bill through committee in this session, and also took the chair for a Gloucestershire estate bill. He was added to the committee for a

Cornish canal bill on 16 Jan. 1655, and reported it in the following month. He does not seem to have attended the Oxford session. As a Norfolk landlord, he opposed the bill to prohibit the import of Irish cattle, and he supported an inquiry into the Fire of London so vigorously that he was the first Member named to the committee. He was also among those appointed to receive information about the insolence of Popish priests. He took the chair for a private bill on behalf of the Earl of Cleveland, and on 31 Oct. 1666 seconded the proposal of (Sir) Thomas Clifford* 'for a general excise of all inland goods, which was much disliked'. Nevertheless he was approved as a member of the abortive parliamentary accounts commission. He took part in hearing a petition against the Canary Company, tabled estimates of the yield of a poll-tax, and helped to prepare reasons for conferences on both subjects. He was teller against hearing the petition from the merchants trading to France on 17 Jan. 1667. During the recess he was among those commissioned with (Sir) John Denham* to prepare plans for rebuilding the London Customs House.[7]

Harbord probably welcomed the dismissal of Clarendon, helping to draft the address of thanks, to reduce the charges against him into heads, and to consider the banishment bill, though he agreed with John Vaughan* that it was necessary 'to prepare some precedents and reasons to justify their proceedings'. Though he was not prominent in debate in this session, his committee activity attained another peak. On 6 Nov. 1667 he reported the proposals of the Duke of Albemarle (George Monck*) for improving security against highwaymen, and three days later he and Denham were recommended by a resolution of the House to put the laws into execution against hackney coachmen. He took the chair for the bills for the repair of highways and the relief of poor prisoners, and also for the public accounts bill. In this capacity he produced twenty names from which the House was to select nine commissioners; but 'the panel was very much disliked (and very justly) because many villains and enemies to the late King were nominated, especially Colonel [Edward] King* and Major [John] Wildman [I*]'. Before the Christmas recess he carried up the bill to naturalize prize ships. On 12 Feb. 1668 he was given special responsibility for bringing in a bill to protect the Forest of Dean. In a debate on the miscarriages of the war he said: 'The counsels were either weak or treacherous, . . . and if we declare them so he [the King] will know how to lay them aside and not use them for the future'. On 26 Feb. he reported on the receipts

from the poll-tax. He excused himself from taking the chair of the supply committee, but declared:

> If this House had not been, the necessity of money had not been. If you give him not now, you are never likely to aid him more. Weakening of ourselves and our allies is strengthening of our enemies. . . . What he can propose is only from observation and experience, being not a man of invention.

There was a strong inclination to vote him into the chair, but he was allowed to excuse himself in favour of Robert Steward*. Under his guidance the grand committee of grievances sent for Joseph Williamson* to give evidence against Ormonde; but eventually they could only agree on presenting the misconduct of a hearth-tax collector in Lincolnshire and the erection of a lighthouse at Milford Haven. He was named to the committees for extending the Conventicles Act and preventing the refusal of habeas corpus. As chairman of the trade committee he investigated the export of wool, and reported an address for wearing English manufactures. He was sent to the Lords to desire their concurrence, subsequently serving on the joint committee to present the address. After helping to manage a conference on taxing the newly-drained lands in the fens and to superintend the engrossment of the bill against thefts and robberies, he carried both bills to the Lords on 15 Apr. His proposal for charging interest on receivers who detained public moneys for over two months was referred to a committee, in which he took the chair and produced a bill before the session closed. More important, after repeated and rather unreasonable reminders from the House, he tabled on 6 May a list of grants and long leases of crown land made since 1640.[8]

In the next session Harbord and (Sir) John Berkenhead* were recommended to bring in a bill imposing the penalties of felony for kidnapping. He was among those sent to thank the dying Albemarle for his care in preserving the peace of the kingdom. A debate on his alienations report was ordered, but never took place. He was appointed to a committee to prepare reasons for a conference on a highways bill on 2 Apr. 1670, and a week later carried up a bill enabling the King to lease out duchy of Cornwall lands. In the winter session of 1670–1 he chaired the Boston navigation bill and no less than six private bills, including one to enable Christopher Monck* to re-convey several manors mortgaged to his late father. But despite his unrivalled reputation as a surveyor his computation of the total area of England at 76 million acres was wildly out. He was named to the committee on the bill to punish the assailants of Sir John Coventry*, although he opposed as unprecedented the resolution that no other bills should pass until it had gone through the Upper House. He opposed taxing offices at 2s. in the pound believing that 'you are not to look how a man is worth a thing, but that he is worth it, and has a share in the proportion of the government, and so must have his part in the tax'. Similarly he opposed a tax on mines: 'tin mines are not farmed, most cannot be farmed, and it will be a discouragement to the commodity'. With Sir Thomas Meres* he was ordered to bring in a bill to recover moneys due to the loyal and indigent officers, and he also helped to draft a bill to prevent the profanation of the Lord's day by arrests. He was the first Member named to the committee to consider this bill, took the chair, and carried it up. Harbord and Meres were ordered to hasten the clauses in the subsidy bill imposing double taxation on absent Members. It was resolved that defaulters should not take their seats until they had been heard at the bar of the House; but an exception was then made for Richard Norton*, to which

> it was well said by Sir Charles Harbord that we are masters of our orders indeed, but we are servants of our honour, and obliged to preserve that, which we should not do if we make such solemn orders one day and revoke them another, especially after we had put them in execution against some persons and then lay them aside as unreasonable against others in the very same case.

He helped to prepare reasons for a conference on the subsidy bill and the additional excise. He tried to stifle on a technicality the bill to transfer the Cornish assizes from his constituency to Bodmin, and later acted as teller with (Sir) John Coryton I* for an unsuccessful motion to appoint a further day for hearing witnesses in committee. He was reckoned a friend to Ormonde and a court dependant on both lists, while an opposition writer with old-fashioned tastes in drama called him 'the old Volpone . . . worth above £100,000, besides a most plentiful provision for his numerous family'. In fact only two of his sons held remunerative office.[9]

When Parliament met again during the third Dutch war Harbord warmly commended the proposal for a general naturalization bill, only regretting that it should be restricted to Protestants, and he was appointed to the drafting committee. On the Declaration of Indulgence he said that statute law could only be altered in Parliament, and that it had done the King 'more hurt among his father's friends than good to those indulged'. Nevertheless he showed himself conciliatory towards the dissenters. Admitting that there were many good things in the Covenant, and blaming the severity of the churchmen, he 'would have a bill for ease of

tender consciences in matters of religion'. He was chairman of the committee to prevent the growth of Popery that brought in the test bill, and carried it up to the Lords; but of the Queen he observed: 'she is a person of the most inoffensive carriage that ever was'. He also took the chair for the bills to rebuild the Navy Office, and to confirm the marriage settlement of Sir William Rich*. In the autumn session he was named to the committees to prepare the address against the Modena marriage and a general test bill. As chairman of the grand committee on the speech from the throne, it fell to him to recommend the refusal of supply. He showed himself hostile to Buckingham in the debates on the Cabal in 1674, though he thought he should be allowed to sell his mastership of the horse, which had cost 'a great sum of money', and on 26 Jan. he was added to the committee to consider the charges against his son's patron, Lord Arlington. He took the chair in grand committee to consider the announcement in the speech from the throne that overtures had been received from the Dutch 'in a more decent style than before'. He believed that 'the peace is of great use as proffered', and helped to prepare reasons for two conferences. Having been formerly engaged in 'contests with the judges', he was 'against making their places for life', but he was named to the committee. As chairman of the committee of grievances he reported that 'any standing force in this nation, other than the militia, is a great grievance and vexation to the people', and recommended that the Scottish army law and the powers of commitment by the Privy Council should be further investigated. He was appointed to both committees, and also took the chair in grand committee on the condition of Ireland. During the recess, at his son's suggestion, he very humbly petitioned for the reversion of four manors held in jointure by the Queen in East Anglia.[10]

Together with Meres and Robert Sawyer* Harbord was given special responsibility on 21 Apr. 1675 for drawing up a bill to expedite the conviction of popish recusants. He was one of Danby's most effective champions in the impeachment proceedings:

> He has had the honour to serve the King under seven or eight lord treasurers, and by the duty of his place he is to advise with all things relating to the revenue. . . . So far as he has been acquainted with the lord treasurer he has not found his understanding defective in it; and has wondered at it, that a young man and a country gentleman should understand it so soon. In this business would go as faithfully and as truly as any man. . . . He can disprove many of these things alleged.

He took the chair in the committee of the whole House to consider the King's answer to the address for the recall of British subjects in the French service, and was among those ordered to prepare a further address. In the case of Shirley v. Fagg he helped to draw up reasons for the Speaker's warrant to arrest the plaintiff and for the committal of the Four Lawyers. In the autumn session he was one of five Members sent to Colonel Thomas Howard to ask him whether he admitted responsibility for a paper describing Meres and William Cavendish*, Lord Cavendish, as 'bold and busy Members' and 'barbarous incendiaries'. As chairman of the grand committee on religion he proposed a committee of inquiry into dangerous books, and another to bring in a Lord's day observance bill, and was the first Member named to both committees. But his conduct in the chair over the government demand for supply to take off the anticipations in the revenue was more controversial. Burnet described him at this juncture as

> a very rich and covetous man, who knew England well; and his parts were very quick about him in that great age, being past eighty. . . . He had said the right way of dealing with the King and of gaining him to them was to lay their hands on their purses and to deal roundly with him. So his son said he seconded the motion, he meant that they should lay their hands on their purses, as he himself did, and hold them well shut.

During the debate in committee of the whole House on anticipations, Cavendish moved the previous question. The result was a tie, and Harbord, who had taken the trouble to obtain accurate information about the history of this device, correctly gave his casting vote for the Government so that business could proceed. But before the main question could be put several opposition Members entered the chamber, and the government programme was defeated by 172 votes to 165. Neither Burnet, who censured Harbord for his rashness, nor Lord Conway, who thought that he 'gave it against the King', seems to have understood the procedure. Danby, who had sat in the Commons for so many years, was not so easily misled; but he was probably incensed by Harbord's attack on the Stop of the Exchequer in the debate on appropriations and his declaration that the chamber of London afforded the best security, and replaced him as chairman of the supply committee by Sir John Trevor*. Nevertheless Harbord opposed penny-pinching by the opposition over the naval estimates. One of his sons had been killed at Sole Bay, and he told the House: 'If he sent a servant or son to sea, would send them in a ship safe for them to go in'. On a list of government servants in the House he was marked 'bad', and Sir Richard Wiseman* apparently thought that he should be reminded of his duty.[11]

Harbord dismissed the opposition contention that Parliament had been automatically dissolved by the long recess. 'All Parliaments are in being', he told the House on 15 Feb. 1677, 'till dissolved by the death of the King, or word of his mouth. There have been several prorogations of fifteen months.' Shaftesbury classed him as 'doubly vile', but he was appointed to the committees to consider the bills for recall from French service, better preservation of the liberty of the subject, and the Protestant education of the royal children, and helped to draft the address on the danger from French power. He took the chair for the bill to provide for the maintenance of the Northampton clergy, for the bill for the repair of Yarmouth pier, and for the frauds bill, perhaps the most important legal reform of the period. He helped to manage a conference on building warships and to draft an address promising a credit of £200,000 for the safety of the kingdom. In 1678 he was reckoned a government speaker and a court supporter. Although he declared that 'I have always been for the Church of England, and I will die in it', he supported a bill from the Lords to relax the Tests. Together with Meres, Sir Edward Dering* and Sir Francis Winnington* he was ordered to bring in a supply bill. When he was accused by Henry Goring II* of benefiting from the alienation of crown lands, he replied:

> The King has granted me four manors of £400 p.a. each, not a farthing profit to me as long as the queen lives. As I have saved the crown £80,000 at a time, I desired only a mark of my service, and that is all.

On 27 Mar. he was given leave to bring in a bill for better regulating of the poor, but he does not seem to have done so. He hoped to prepare reasons for a conference on the danger from Popery and to summarize England's alliances. He was named to the committee of inquiry into the Popish Plot and helped to prepare reasons for a conference. He was also among those ordered to investigate noises in Old Palace Yard, to prepare the impeachment of Lord Arundell of Wardour, and to examine the French translation of the *Gazette*. He helped to consider the bill to hinder Papists from sitting in Parliament, but warmly supported the Lords proviso to except the Duke of York. He was among those ordered to prepare reasons for disagreeing with the Upper House on further amendments relating to the servants of the Queen and the Duchess of York and to bring in a series of anti-Papal bills. He was still sufficiently trusted by the majority of the Commons to be included in the committee to devise means of surmounting the royal veto on the militia bill, and to be given custody of Coleman's papers. In the debate on Danby's impeachment he called on William Williams* to explain why the unusual venue of the drafting committee had not been communicated to several of its members.[12]

Harbord was re-elected to the first Exclusion Parliament and marked 'vile' on Shaftesbury's list. A moderately active Member, he was named to six committees and made two recorded speeches. On 22 Mar. 1679 he criticized the validity of Danby's pardon, asking:

> Did the King ever pardon anyone after an impeachment was against them? This way of pardoning, an impeachment depending, is one of the most dangerous consequence in the world, both to King and people.

He was among those ordered to inspect the profanity laws and to consider the bill to remove Papists from the London area. Still an indefatigable legislator, he was ordered to prepare bills to regulate the silver manufactory and to provide for the easier administration of oaths for burial in woollen. He was called up by John Maynard I* to give an account of the procedure in the trial of Strafford, apparently in the mistaken belief that he had served on the secret committee. He was absent from the division on the exclusion bill, though on the following day he was named to the committee on the bill for appointing certain times for the coinage of tin in Cornwall. But he died three days later, on 25 May, and was buried on his eldest son's estate at Besthorpe.[13]

[1] Information from Dr R. W. Dunning; *Survey of London*, xvi. 114; *Som. Wills*, vi. 100; G. S. Master, *Colls. Par. Hist. Wraxall*, 64; *Grantees of Arms* (Harl. Soc. lxvi), 113; Add. 12225, f. 50v; Blomefield, *Norf.* i. 495. [2] *Foedera*, viii. pt. 3, p. 222; ix. pt. 2, pp. 86, 187; *Grantees of Arms*, 113; *CSP Dom.* 1631–3, p. 253; 1635, pp. 514, 543; 1660–1, p. 572; 1671, p. 255; *Cal. Treas. Bks.* iii. 414; iv. 61; v. 751, 986. [3] *Foedera*, viii. (4), 98; ix. (2), 157; *CSP Dom.* 1635–6, p. 336; 1639–40, p. 419; 1641–2, p. 279; *Sel. Charters* (Selden Soc. xxviii), 149; C181/7/51; *Cal. Treas. Bks.* i. 411; iii. 607, 911, 1107; S. Wells, *Drainage of the Bedford Level*, i. 456–9. [4] Information from Dr R. W. Dunning; R. M. Bacon, *Mems. of Edward, Lord Suffield*, 1–2; Harl. 7020, f. 34v; *Grantees of Arms*, 112–13; *CSP Dom.* 1629–31, p. 17; 1634–5, p. 499; 1640–1, p. 297; Chauncy, *Herts.* ii. 344; Grey, ii. 101; vii. 203; *N. and Q.* cc. 193; *HMC 5th Rep.* 70; *Cromwell's Writings and Speeches* ed. Abbott, iii. 377–8; Blomefield, x. 466; *Cal. Cl. SP*, iv. 661. [5] *CJ*, viii. 246, 314, 343, 397. [6] *CJ*, viii. 448, 461, 471, 474, 516, 525, 527; *CSP Dom.* 1635–6, p. 336; 1663–4, pp. 103, 137. [7] *CJ*, viii. 545, 552, 554, 635, 661, 662; *Cal. Cl. SP*, v. 270; *Milward*, 3, 7, 35; *CSP Dom.* 1666–7, pp. 525–6. [8] *Milward*, 129, 164; *CJ*, ix. 23, 27, 39, 42, 48, 74, 77, 80, 90, 92; Grey, i. 75, 94, 100, 122; *CSP Dom.* 1667–8, pp. 44, 233; Bodl. Carte 36, f. 269; *LJ*, xii. 223. [9] *CJ*, ix. 100, 112, 166, 170, 189, 194, 210, 224, 225, 234; *HMC Hastings*, ii. 315; Grey, i. 323, 341, 360, 366; *Dering*, 40, 90; Harl. 7020, ff. 34v, 43. [10] *Dering*, 112; *CJ*, ix. 250, 266, 268, 272, 278, 285, 299, 305, 307, 309, 312; Grey, ii. 25, 31, 101, 118, 141, 266, 346, 419; *CSP Dom.* 1673–5, p. 214. [11] Grey, iii. 46, 358, 384, 416; *CJ*, ix. 334, 360, 362; Burnet, ii. 87–88; *HMC Hastings*, ii. 383. [12] Grey, iv. 70–71; v. 195–6; vi. 246, 372; *CJ*, ix. 402, 416, 418, 419, 564. [13] Grey, vii. 22, 203; *CJ*, ix. 607, 608; *HMC Ormonde*, n.s. v. 116; Blomefield, i. 495.

E.C.

HARBORD (HERBERT), William (1635–92), of the Middle Temple and Grafton Park, Northants.

DARTMOUTH	1661
THETFORD	1679 (Mar.), 1679 (Oct.), 1681
LAUNCESTON	1689, 1690–31 July 1692

b. 25 Apr. 1635, 2nd s. of Sir Charles Harbord* by 2nd w. *educ.* Leyden 1651; M. Temple 1655; travelled abroad (the Levant) 1656. *m.* (1) lic. 26 July 1661, Mary, da. and coh. of Arthur Duck†, DCL, of North Cadbury, Som., 3da.; (2) 21 Feb. 1678, Catherine, da. of Hon. Edward Russell of Corney House, Chiswick, Mdx., 1da.[1]

Commr. for sewers, Hatfield chase Aug. 1660, assessment, Som. 1661–9, 1677–80, Notts. 1663–4, Herts. 1664–9, Westminster 1664–79, Northants. 1673–9, Norf. and Thetford 1679–80, Som. and Thetford 1689, pre-emption of tin, Devon and Cornw. 1662; j.p. Herts. and St. Albans liberty 1668–80, Northants. 1689–d.; commr. for inquiry, Kingswood chase, Windsor and Richmond Park 1671, Whittlewood and Salcey Forests and Forest of Dean 1679, 1691; ranger, St. James's Park 1690–d.[2]

Auditor, duchy of Cornw. 1661–d.; trustee for sale of fee-farm rents (supernumerary) 1670–3; sec. to ld. lt. [I] 1673–7; PC [I] 1673; surveyor-gen. 1679–d.; commissary gen. Nov.–Dec. 1688; v.-treas. [I] 1689–d.; paymaster of the forces [I] 1689–90, PC 8 Mar. 1689–d.; commr. for reforming abuses in the army 1689, preventing exports of wool 1689–d.; ambassador to Turkey 1691–d.[3]

Capt. indep. tp. 1689–90.[4]

Harbord's elder brother married a Norfolk heiress, but although he also made a good match he seems, as 'own son to the old Volpone', to have been intended by his father for an official career at the Restoration. He was returned for Dartmouth at the general election of 1661 on the government interest. He succeeded Thomas Gewen* as auditor of the duchy of Cornwall and was granted the reversion of the office of surveyor-general after his father, who had thwarted a rival applicant by declaring that it was 'not a place to be granted in reversion'. A moderately active Member of the Cavalier Parliament, he acted as teller in, probably, 23 divisions, made 29 recorded speeches, and was appointed to about a hundred committees, including those in the first session for restoring the bishops to the House of Lords, the corporations and uniformity bills, and the bill for the execution of those under attainder. His father delegated to him the care of the crown woods and forests, in particular his lifelong efforts to improve the Forest of Dean. On 12 May 1662 Harbord, with the Hon. Edward Montagu*, Giles Hungerford* and John Bulkeley*, was sent to ask the lord treasurer to deposit with the clerk of the Commons the return of a survey of the forest undertaken at the request of the House. In the 1663 session his committees included those to consider the staple bill, to provide an income for the Duke of York, and to inquire into the conduct of Sir Richard Temple*. Though Harbord later claimed to be well-known on the bench as 'a severe enemy to fanatics' he was probably more sympathetic to the dissenters than his father. In the debate on the bill to prevent sectaries' meetings he was teller for a narrowly successful proviso against requiring those who refused the sacramental test to accept public office. He also acted as teller on the second reading of the bill to preserve the timber of the Forest of Dean and advance the revenue. Listed as a court dependant in 1664, he was appointed to the committee for the additional corporations bill and added to that for the Forest of Dean. He was twice teller against the adjournment in December 1666, and in the following month opposed hearing the report on the hemp and flax bill, perhaps because it might delay the proceedings against Mordaunt.[5]

Harbord became more prominent after the dismissal of Clarendon, helping to draft the address of thanks and to consider the additional charges against Mordaunt. He may also have been teller for the second reading of the bill for the creditors of the navy. He was among those ordered to bring in a bill for supply of timber, and on 29 Oct. 1667 he was added to the committee to consider the petition of Sir John Winter (with whom part of his mother's fortune had once been invested) and to inquire into the causes of the waste of timber in the Forest of Dean. On his voluminous report of 12 Feb. 1668 the House agreed that Winter, the queen mother's secretary, 'since his Majesty's happy restoration hath been the sole occasion of the waste and destruction of the timber'. Harbord was appointed to the committees to take the accounts of the taxes voted for the second Dutch war and to consider the bill to prevent abuses in the collection of the hearth-tax. On 2 Apr. he reported another bill for the preservation of the timber in the Forest of Dean, but after some debate one of the amendments concerning the disposal of coppice wood was re-committed, and it was Sir Baynham Throckmorton* who succeeded in completing the passage of the bill through the Commons. In November 1669 he was appointed to the committees to extend the Conventicles Act and to receive information about conventicles. He was teller for convicting Sir George Carteret* on the first observation from the public accounts commission. He took the chair for the bill to enable (Sir) Ralph Bankes* to sell his Welsh estate, and carried it to the Lords on 1 Mar. 1670. He was appointed to the committee on the bill to provide for the sale of the fee-farm rents, and was named as an additional trustee, though without salary.

Though he may have been teller for the bill to prevent transportation, the Opposition reckoned him among the court party at this time, describing him as 'under-surveyor, and a court contriver to cheat the King of his lands'.[6]

On 14 Feb. 1673 Harbord was teller for seeking the concurrence of the Lords to an address against the suspending power, and, in what appears to have been his maiden speech, declared that 'in this he takes the liberty rather to displease the King than to undo him'. The words gave offence to the Commons, and after some debate he was allowed to explain that 'he intended no reflection on the King'. The lesson was well-digested, and Harbord was henceforward careful to exonerate the King from his attacks on the Government. In the autumn session he told Edward Seymour* that his way of life disqualified him from the Speaker's chair: 'you expose the honour of the House in resorting to gaming-houses, with foreigners as well as Englishmen'. Although he helped to draw up the address against the Duke of York's second marriage, he was appointed secretary to the new lord lieutenant of Ireland, the Earl of Essex, with a pension of £500 p.a. during pleasure. He probably owed his post to the recommendation of Lord Arlington (Sir Henry Bennet*), and returned to Westminster for the 1674 session to act as teller against a motion for his patron's dismissal, being later added to the impeachment committee. He was probably teller for the second reading of a bill to reform the trial of peers. Essex told Lord Conway, who was concerned at Harbord's dependence on Arlington at this time:

> I take Will Harbord to be a very quick man for dispatch of business, and, having experience of his integrity towards me upon other occasions, I am confident he will be a very useful servant to me.

In September Essex assured Arlington that Harbord was ready to attend the King's service again in the next session. More sceptically, Conway wrote to Danby on 13 Mar. 1675 that Harbord

> desired me to acquaint your lordship with the great professions he made to serve you. He swore he would stick as close to your interests and concerns as your own lady and children should do, and that he would sooner abandon his own family than neglect his obligations to your lordship.

Sir John Coventry* expected Harbord to prove the charge against Danby of usurping the management of Irish affairs; but he told the House that he knew nothing of it, and defended the lord treasurer with the confident assertion that none of his predecessors had received less from the crown. The reverse side of these dutiful speeches is to be found in his letter to Essex of 1 May:

I am even weary of my life, to sit daily seven or eight hours in the House, and at last vote against my reason or steal away; and if that be found out, it gives offence also.

A more congenial task to one of Harbord's temperament was to act as teller for proceeding with the charges against Lauderdale. Later in the session he helped to prepare reasons for a conference on Shirley v. Fagg and to consider a bill to prevent the growth of Popery. In the autumn session he spoke and voted against supply, neatly reversing his father's appeal to Members to put their hands on their purses. He was marked 'bad' on the list of officials in the House, and Sir Richard Wiseman* reported bluntly: 'Mr Harbord disserves the King'.[7]

Harbord lost his Irish post on the recall of Essex, and was marked 'worthy' on Shaftesbury's list of 1677. His speeches in this session were principally directed against France. He quoted his brother's chief patron in the navy, Lord Sandwich (Edward Montagu I*), as saying to him: 'Will, if you will defend me against the French at Whitehall, I'll defend you against the King of France'.

> The King as to himself was the best man living, and the furthest from Popery.... He had in one of his speeches declared that there could not be a greater scandal laid upon him than to be reputed popishly affected.... We might address to the King that that person whoever, and how great soever he be, that was so reputed might for the satisfaction of the world make some public demonstration of the contrary.

This daring proposal, obviously aimed at the Duke of York, found no seconder. With regard to finance, Harbord said: 'Let us vote to supply the King from year to year, according to the emergencies that shall happen in case a war follows; but I doubt we shall not be so happy'. When French tariffs were mentioned in the committee of grievances he burst out:

> He is so transported with the French thus using us that it breaks his sleep.... He will not say that country gentlemen are able to judge of peace and war, but fundamentals can never vary, and one man may judge of them as well as another. The true balance of France and the house of Austria is our interest.

He helped to prepare an address for a speedy and strict alliance against the French, and acted as teller for a perpetual ban on cattle imports from Ireland, though as Norfolk landowners his father and two of his brothers would have benefited from the trade. On 25 May he said:

> England is not safe but by alliance with Holland.... Make a law to prohibit French trade. You need no wine, and few of his commodities; and France will grow poor, and we shall grow rich.

He was named to the committee to draft the address for reducing France to her 1659 frontiers; but renewed demands for supply found him in a quandary. 'A negative in this matter', he said on 5 Feb. 1678, 'would be of fatal consequence, I think as fatal as an affirmative.... I will never put a great sum of money in the ministers' hands till the King has need of it.' He seconded the motion of (Sir) John Holman* for a severance of diplomatic relations with France: 'I never hope we shall have a war whilst we have a French ambassador in England', he said. He was twice teller for the address for the removal of counsellors. 'Though for the people's sake I would have these men out of the ministry', he said, 'yet 'tis principally for the King's sake.... If I saw hands that must manage the money that I durst trust, I would give the King *carte blanche*; he might ask what he pleased.' He was appointed to the committee to enable the King to lease out duchy of Cornwall property, and helped to prepare reasons for a conference on burial in woollen. He was teller against accepting any obligation to repay the King £200,000 charged on the credit of the additional excise, and was named to the committee on the bill for hindering Papists from sitting in either House of Parliament. He warmly supported the test against corruption:

> I would have every gentleman of the House come to the table and protest that he has received no reward for anything he has done in Parliament, or for giving his vote. Or if any gentleman be in employment in the government and has been put out of his place for giving his vote here according to his conscience, or has been threatened, this is a great crime.[8]

Despite Harbord's ostentatious Gallophobia, his enmity to Danby and his eagerness to disband the army put him in touch with the French embassy, which promised him financial support. He assisted Ralph Montagu* in his election at Northampton. After the Popish Plot he was named to the committee to prepare the impeachment of Lord Arundell of Wardour. 'I profess I never go to bed', he said 'but I expect the next morning to hear of the King's being killed. There is nothing so necessary to you as the care of the King's person. I have not the honour to see the King often, and I know not what care is taken of him.' He urged that (Sir) Joseph Williamson*, whom he hoped to supplant at Thetford, should be expelled the House for countersigning commissions for Roman Catholic officers. He was among those ordered to prepare instructions for disbandment, speaking so strongly of the army that he had to apologize to those officers who were Members. He was even more useful to the French in securing the fall of Danby. As chairman of the committee to fetch Montagu's papers he produced the damning letters authorizing the ambassador to treat for peace and a French subsidy at a time when the Government was demanding supply for a war. He declared triumphantly:

> I hope now gentlemen's eyes were opened by the design on foot to destroy the government and our liberties. I believe, if the House will command Mr Montagu, he will tell you more now. But I would not press it now upon him, because poisoning and stabbing are in use.

He was appointed to the committee to prepare Danby's impeachment, and given 500 guineas by Barillon as a reward for his services.[9]

Harbord was never remarkable for courage, and on the dissolution of the Cavalier Parliament he took to flight. Unable to find a ship at Yarmouth, he concealed himself in the house of his youngest brother John at Gunton, though their political principles were different. In his absence he was defeated at Dartmouth; but he was returned with his rival Williamson for Thetford, and also on the duchy interest at Camelford. Marked 'worthy' on Shaftesbury's list, he was a very active Member of the first Exclusion Parliament, with 19 committee appointments and 15 recorded speeches. He defended the royal prerogative of denying approbation to the Commons choice of Speaker, attempting to divert the debate to the less controversial matter of the Popish Plot, but was called to order by Sir Harbottle Grimston*. He was named to the committee to draw up a state of the matters undetermined in the last Parliament, and stridently attacked the refusal of the Upper House to commit Danby: 'The Parliament has impeached the treasurer, and the Lords deny us justice, which their ancestors ever did us'. The awkward fact that Montagu's letters were countersigned by the King he brazenly dismissed:

> I believe the King will never allow those letters to have been by his own order, but that the treasurer has been well paid for it by somebody. I can never believe that the King is so ill a man that, when a war was depending, etc., he should order those letters to bargain for a peace.

He helped to manage a conference, to draw up the address protesting against Danby's pardon, and to consider the bill summoning the fallen minister to give himself up. During the debate, it was alleged, he remained at the door of the House, only allowing those believed to favour the Court to leave; 'the others he kept back almost by force'. He told the Commons on 27 Apr. that nothing had contributed more to the foiling of plots against the Protectorate than the banishment of Cavaliers from London; 'though it is not always convenient to take precedents from ill times', he proposed a similar measure against Roman Catholics. He wanted Lauderdale extradited to Scotland to face trial there, and helped

to prepare an address for his removal from Court. On 13 May he was added to the committee to draft another address promising revenge on the Papists if the King should come to any violent death; but he voted against the first exclusion bill, probably in the Orange interest. As chairman for the inquiry into the navy, he adjourned it into the City without informing court supporters such as (Sir) John Talbot*, although the House had refused his demand for a secret committee. He was thus able to report that Samuel Pepys* and Sir Anthony Deane* had betrayed naval secrets to the French. Of Pepys, whose place as secretary of the Admiralty he may have coveted, he said: 'By collateral proof I shall much convince the House that he is not of our religion; I am sorry I must say it of a man I have lived well withal'. They were sent to the Tower on 22 May, and Harbord was ordered to transmit the evidence against them to the attorney-general (Sir William Jones*). In the debate on corruption of Members in the previous Parliament he exclaimed indignantly: 'If a pensioner went not well, slash! He was put out of his pension'.[10]

After the prorogation Harbord told Henry Sidney* that 'the only thing that could be done for the good of this notion was to declare and make the Prince of Orange protector in case the succession fell into the hands of a Roman Catholic prince'. His re-election at Thetford in the autumn was assured by a bequest from his father to the poor, despite an attempt by Williamson to replace him by Sir John Bennet*. He also hoped to be returned for Launceston in case Sidney or Sir William Temple* should need a seat. Barillon acknowledged Harbord's outstanding services in driving Danby from office and his credit in the provinces, but thought that

> it would be difficult to employ him at present. . . . He would be more fit if a minister was to be attacked than he will be to speak in Parliament against an alliance which the Court would make and the other party hinder. . . . Mr Harbord . . . is a friend of Mr Montagu, but has not the same connexions with the Duke of Monmouth; on the contrary, he appears to be in the Prince of Orange's interest. . . . He is an active, vigilant man from whom I have very good informations, and who has a great desire to make his fortune by means of France.

When the second Exclusion Parliament met he was even more active, with 28 committee appointments, two tellerships, and over 50 speeches. As chairman for the address for preserving the Protestant religion at home and abroad, he was condemned by Barillon for presenting a report at variance with French interests. One of the few old Members to command a hearing in this Parliament, he had become a vociferous convert to exclusion. Though he was obliged to withdraw his absurd charge that the Duke of York had betrayed the English fleet at Sole Bay in 1672, when his brother Charles was killed, he built up a formidable indictment on other grounds. How could the vagaries of foreign policy, he asked, or the failure to complete the discovery of the Popish Plot be ascribed to the influence of any lesser man than the Duke of York? 'From what cause can such strange, unheard of effects proceed but from the power and influence of a Popish successor?' A member of the committee for the second exclusion bill, he moved on the report stage an additional clause that no King should marry a Popish queen:

> I have been told that we owe our misfortune of the Duke's being perverted by his mother; from her we derive that wound. If this bill should exclude the Duke's children from the crown that are Protestant, I am against it; it is unjust. I would not have them suffer for their father's fault.

As chairman of a committee to examine a priest who had taken the oath of allegiance, he urged 'that this man may have some encouragement'. He was among those instructed to draw up a reply to a message from the King urging the House to expedite matters concerning Popery and Plot, which he likened to Pharaoh's command to the Israelites to make bricks without straw:

> I am sorry I was forced to make use of that comparison, but, when all is at stake, no consideration can tie up a man's mouth in this place. I confess I am naturally warm, and I cannot but speak warmly in the matter.

A further remark 'that ladies do endeavour to subvert the government' helped to frighten the Duchess of Portsmouth into the exclusionist camp. On Tangier, he said that he would regret its abandonment to the French or the Moors, but at present it was a seminary for Popish priests and soldiers, and the safety of England was more important. When Montagu attacked Lord Halifax (Sir George Savile*), he said:

> I am satisfied in my conscience that I know he dissolved the last Parliament, and I can prove it. ... I am ashamed to see this man have advocates; whoever is so, deserves to appear at the bar.

Although this last expression was condemned by the veteran country Member John Birch*, Harbord helped to draw up two more addresses rejecting supply for Tangier and desiring the removal of Halifax. He urged the House to punish the most notorious offenders on the Somerset grand jury that had presented an abhorring address. One of the committee for Seymour's impeachment, he spoke so frequently, so bitterly, and so irrelevantly that

he had to deny that he coveted his victim's place as treasurer of the navy. In the interest of the republican Algernon Sidney†, he acted as teller for the narrow franchise at Amersham. He urged the abolition of *scandalum magnatum*, which protected bishops and judges, and was named to the committee to insert a clause to this effect in the bill to regulate the trial of peers. He helped to prepare the address of 20 Dec. insisting on exclusion. 'For the matter of supply he would be tender', though he told Barillon that a bill would be introduced to prohibit the raising of government loans on the London money market, and undertook to oppose any expression of support for an alliance against France. 'A true friend of the Church', by his own account, he attacked the clergy for preaching against exclusion, and urged the repeal of the Corporations Act. With less wit than Silius Titus*, he sought to stifle charges of place-hunting:

> So many artifices are used to asperse your Members against the public good that I move that no person may have any place during the Parliament without leave of the House, or else that he be incapable of being a Parliament man if he accept of it.

While professing great esteem for Laurence Hyde* he urged his dismissal, and when 'Sir George Downing* speaks well for him, Mr Harbord falls into a rage'. When the session ended without any supply, Barillon again rewarded him, as promised, with 500 guineas.[11]

With this handsome addition to his electoral resources, Harbord was returned for both Launceston and Thetford in 1681. After the Rye House Plot one of the Thetford corporation deposed to hearing Harbord declare that

> he was engaged with as many of the two Houses and persons of quality as were worth £500,000 a year, who were all resolved to stand by one another, and to go well-armed to Oxford, where he believed they should have a skirmish with the King and his guards, for they were resolved now to know what the King would be at, and, if they were forced to buy their liberties and religion of him, they would have better security than his word, for he had broken it so often that they would not take it for a groat. As to the exclusion bill, he foresaw it would not do their work, if it passed, and therefore they were resolved to seize the King and make him sign a warrant to take off the Duke of York, for that, if ever he should come to be King, he himself was sure to be hanged, and that the Duke was the right heir to the crown, but it was better for him to suffer than a great part of the kingdom.

In the Oxford Parliament Harbord was appointed to the committee of elections and privileges and to those to inspect the Journals relative to the proceedings against Danby and to prepare the impeachment of Fitzharris. He moved successfully that the Speaker (William Williams*) should be entrusted with publishing the resolutions of the Commons, and spoke twice against the expedients proposed to avoid exclusion, telling the House that 'the danger is not from Popery, but from the King's being encompassed with the Duke's creatures'. In a list of Northamptonshire Whigs drawn up in the following year, Harbord was described as a violent man and credited with an income of £3,000 p.a. Although he still officiated as surveyor-general, he was apparently unaware of the flourishing state of government finances, believing that 'the King must and would call a Parliament when poverty knocked at Whitehall gate a little harder, and then he should have a Parliament that would humble him'. He was among the 'dissatisfied and dangerous' gentlemen presented by the Northamptonshire grand jury at the summer assizes of 1683, and his arms were removed from Grafton Park by the deputy lieutenants, but restored to him on the orders of Sir Leoline Jenkins*. On the accession of James II he fled to Holland, but was ordered to return by privy seal in January 1686. He is said to have obeyed, but his salary was stopped in the following month, though the work of both his offices continued to be performed by his deputies, and in the summer he was present at the siege of Buda by the imperial army. Danby listed him among the eminent Members of Parliament, considerable for parts, but not to be trusted. Again summoned by privy seal in April 1688, he came over with William of Orange and was appointed commissary-general during the Revolution. He told the second Earl of Clarendon (Henry Hyde*) on 7 Dec. that, although 'he had drawn his sword against the King, ... he had no need of his pardon; but they would bring the King to ask pardon of them for the wrongs he had done'. Evidence was later given to a Commons committee that Harbord was chiefly responsible for the delay in sending the Prince's declaration to Ireland.[12]

Harbord was particularly anxious that James's election writs should be superseded, since otherwise the exiles would be handicapped by lack of time to canvass their former constituencies. However the general election of 1689 was held on the Prince's writs, and Harbord's interest ultimately carried both seats at Launceston and at Thetford. He was also returned for Scarborough on the Thompson interest, no doubt with the assistance of Sir John Hotham, 2nd Bt.*. The Thetford return was challenged by Williamson, and Harbord chose to sit for his Cornish constituency with his brother-in-law Edward Russell*. A moderately active Member of the Convention, he was appointed to 26 committees, in two of which he took the chair. He carried two bills to the Lords, twice acted as teller, and made 33 recorded speeches. He would not hear any question made of Parliament's power of deposition, which might tend to calling James back again, 'and then we are all ruined'. He helped to draw up the list of the essentials for securing law, liberty and religion, although he doubted the wisdom of giving it priority:

> You have an infallible security for the administration of the government; all the revenue is in your hands, which fell with the last King, and you may keep that back. Can he whom you place on the throne support the government without the revenue? Can he do good or harm without it? 'Tis reasonable that you should be redressed by laws; but unless you preserve your government, your papers cannot protect you. Without your sword, how will you be secured from the dangers from Ireland, and the mutiny of the army? All may be lost, whilst you are considering.

He helped to prepare reasons for insisting that the throne was vacant, and, drawing the attention of the House to the imminent French mobilization, acted as teller against yielding to the Lords. He became a Privy Councillor under the new regime, much to the alarm of the Tories, who feared that he would persuade the King that 'the faction are everything in this kingdom'. In this capacity he informed the House of the Ipswich mutiny, helped to prepare the address asking the King to suppress it, and took the chair for the first mutiny bill. He assured the supply committee that times had changed: 'The money you give will not be spent in debauchery and lewdness, but employed as you would have it'. On 21 Mar. he condemned as totally inadequate the motion of William Garway* to support the war in Ireland by a grant of £300,000 for six months. 'Persons have been sent into the north of Ireland, and there are not oats for your horses, only grass.... Money must be spent in bread, barley and beef. What with the levy-money and the arms, you will not have one shilling to keep them the rest of the time.' During his residence in Holland he had become intimate with Schomberg; he took the chair for his naturalization bill and carried it to the Lords; but his proposal to reward the veteran marshal out of the estates of those who had been 'the occasion of your misfortunes' found no support. He helped to draft the addresses thanking the King for his declaration to maintain the Church as by law established and offering assistance for a war with France. His name heads the list of the committee for the relief of distressed Irish Protestants. On 7 May the House took note of some hot words exchanged with Henry Bertie* about the Westbury election. Harbord had reflected on Bertie as a pensioner, being secured from the usual consequences by the consideration that 'the gentleman is of too much honour to engage one that has not the use of either of his hands'; but both had to promise the Speaker not to prosecute the quarrel. On the following day he acted as teller for the Whigs on a proviso to the bill of rights concerning the succession. He returned the toleration bill to the Lords on 22 May. Harbord had been the first to urge the punishment of the 'great offenders', by which he meant those who had changed their religion or given their opinion for the dispensing power. 'I am for catching the great fishes', he said; 'to catch little rogues is not worth your while.' He took a prominent part in the debates on the indemnity bill, moving that two of the judges should be hanged at the gate of Westminster Hall. He also thirsted for the blood of (Sir) Robert Sawyer* as counsel for the prosecution at the trial of Sir Thomas Armstrong*, 'a most barbarous thing' which had shocked 'all foreign nations where I have been'. When (Sir) Thomas Clarges* asserted that the timely despatch of a small force would have saved Ireland, Harbord retorted: 'I would ask that gentleman what 3,000 men he would have sent over. To send our own was not safe, and not fit to part with the Dutch.' He was appointed to the committee of inquiry into the delay in relieving Londonderry. His defence of the committal of Peregrine Osborne* by Lord Nottingham (David Finch*) was interrupted, and he declared 'something in passion': 'I speak my mind, and I care not two pence for those who interrupt me, be they who they will'. William had first taken Harbord for 'an extraordinary man of business', but he was now undeceived, according to Halifax. When Harbord complained of 'a false and scandalous report' that he had fraudulently converted to his own use 'great sums of money' raised during the Revolution, William commented privately that he himself could be the best witness of his guilt. A committee of inquiry was ordered by the Commons, but never reported. Harbord was more fortunate with the Londonderry committee; on 29 July Sir Thomas Littleton, 3rd Bt.* reported that 'no reflection whatsoever did rest upon him', and the House resolved to agree with the committee by 75 votes to 29.[13]

This whitewashing exercise may have been necessitated by Harbord's appointment as purveyor and paymaster of the forces in Ireland. He arrived in September, but owing to the gout was unable to attend his duties for a fortnight. Schomberg was soon as disillusioned over his capacity and integrity as the King, and obliged him to hand over the purveyance to Commissary Shales. 'Mr Harbord makes great profit out of the musters, the hospital, the artillery, and the payment of the troops', he

wrote on 14 Nov., and he later recounted with ill-concealed delight how the paymaster fell off his horse, whereupon 'five or six Enniskillen troopers began to strip and rob him, though he said who he was'. Perhaps it was this incident that determined him to throw up his duties: 'really winter campaigns will be too hard for me', he wrote to the King. He started for England without orders on 10 Dec. leaving the troops unpaid, for which, the King commented, 'in another country he would be hanged'. There is no evidence that he appeared again at Westminster, though he was listed among the supporters of the disabling clause in the bill to restore corporations. He was re-elected in 1690, but dismissed as paymaster as soon as Parliament adjourned. Rather than face an inquiry into his accounts, which showed a deficiency of £406,000, he obtained an appointment as ambassador to the Sublime Porte. He died 'of a malignant fever' at Belgrade on 31 July 1692 on his way to take up his duties, the last of his family to sit in Parliament. But his sister Catherine married William Cropley of Thetford, and their son, who took the name of Harbord on succeeding to the Gunton estate, sat for Norfolk as a government supporter from 1728 to 1734.[14]

[1] Soc. of Genealogists, R. P. Harbord, 'Hist. Harbord Fam.'; CSP Dom. 1651, p. 529; 1656, p. 583; Grey, v. 41; London Mar. Lic. ed. Foster, 621; Knightsbridge Chapel Reg. 75. [2] C181/7/21; Cal. Treas. Bks. i. 411; iii. 911, 923, 1161; v. 184, 196; ix. 1156, 1605, 1869; Northants. RO, FH 2226; CSP Dom. 1689-90, p. 82. [3] Cal. Treas. Bks. i. 233; iii. 431; ix. 213, 678, 1366; CSP Dom. 1673-5, pp. 55, 66; 1689-90, p. 97. [4] Cal. Treas. Bks. ix. 186, 1476; CSP Dom. 1689-90, p. 93. [5] Harl. 7020, f. 43; Cal. Treas. Bks. i. 233, 630; CSP Dom. 1660-1, p. 206; 1661-2, pp. 303, 420; CJ, viii. 509, 528, 659, 668, 688; Exact Coll. Debates, 162. [6] CSP Dom. 1639, p. 420; CJ, ix. 22, 108, 128, 142; Cal. Treas. Bks. iii. 431; Harl. 7020, f. 43. [7] Grey, ii. 76, 77, 188; iii. 91, 93; Essex Pprs. (Cam. Soc. n.s. xlvii), 143-4, 258, 322; Eg. 3329, f. 12; Stowe 207, ff. 362-3; CSP Dom. 1673-5, pp. 55, 66, 228, 354; HMC Hastings, ii. 383; Burnet, ii. 86-87. [8] Grey, iv. 176-7, 198-9, 387-8; v. 91-92, 241, 353; vi. 104-5; CJ, ix. 408, 477, 479, 492; Eg. 3345, f. 38v; Add. 28091, ff. 39v-40. [9] PRO 31/3, bdle. 141, ff. 28v, 35, 96; Grey, vi. 205, 224, 345, 349; CJ, ix. 559; Dalrymple, Mems. i. 381. [10] HMC 6th Rep. 389; Grey, vi. 428-9; vii. 23-24, 137-8, 194, 304, 331; CJ, ix. 574, 613, 626, 628; PRO 31/3, bdle. 146, f. 85v; Pepys Naval Mins. (Navy Rec. Soc. lx), 43; HMC 7th Rep. 472. [11] Sidney Diary, i. 8, 78-79; A. L. Hunt, Capital of East Anglia, 138-9; Dalrymple, i. 338, 358; PRO 31/3, bdle. 147, ff. 13, 75v, 86; bdle. 148, f. 45; HMC Ormonde, n.s. v. 467; CJ, ix. 642, 645, 646, 650, 655, 664, 677, 681; Exact Coll. Debates, 25, 74, 112, 162; Grey, vii. 397, 403, 417, 427, 439-40; viii. 7-8, 24, 26, 34, 93, 175, 222; HMC 12th Rep. IX, 99, 104, 113; HMC Finch, ii. 99. [12] CSP Dom. Jan.-June 1683, p. 276; July-Sept. 1683, pp. 281, 292; 1683-4, pp. 236-7; 1686-7, p. 9; 1687-9, p. 192; SP29/421/216; Somers Tracts, viii. 409; Cal. Treas. Bks. viii. 509; HMC 7th Rep. 500; Bramston Autobiog. (Cam. Soc. xxxii), 236; Clarendon Corresp. ii. 217, 219, 239; CJ, x. 243-4. [13] Clarendon Corresp. ii. 219; Grey, ix. 12, 36, 54, 164-5, 178, 184, 187, 227, 234-6, 246, 256, 269-70, 316, 331, 372, 379; CJ, x. 20, 49, 67, 83, 84, 124, 210, 243-4; Simpson thesis, 307; Foxcroft, Halifax, ii. 225, 226. [14] CSP Dom. 1689-90, pp. 264, 276, 300, 320, 351, 372; Kennett, Hist. iii. 542; Foxcroft, ii. 242; Luttrell, ii. 24, 551; Add. 51335.

E.C.

HARBY, Edward (c.1633–89), of Adstone, Northants.

NORTHAMPTONSHIRE   14 Jan.–8 May 1689

b. c.1633, 1st s. of Edward Harby† of Adstone by Eliza-
beth, da. of Henry Freeman of Higham Ferrers. *educ.*
Wadham, Oxf. 1652. *m.* Frances, da. of John Elmes of
Greens-Norton and h. to her bro. Richard Elmes of
Stow, Hunts., 1s. 1da. *suc.* fa. 1674.[1]
    Commr. for assessment, Northants. 1663–80, Hunts.
and Northants. 1689; capt. of militia ft. Northants.
1663–bef. 1680; j.p. Northants. 1664–85, 1687–*d.*,
Hunts. July 1688–?*d.*; sheriff, Northants. 1675–6;
commr. for wastes and spoils, Whittlewood and Salcey
Forests 1679, inquiry into recusancy fines, Leics.,
Northants., Rutland and Warws. Mar. 1688.[2]

Harby's ancestor acquired the ex-monastic property of Adstone in the mid-16th century. Harby's
father was a Parliamentarian in the Civil War;
returned for Higham Ferrers as a recruiter, he
acquiesced after some hesitation in Pride's Purge.
In 1660 a double return was decided against him,
and he retired into private life. He applied for a
licence for Presbyterian worship in 1672. Harby
himself must have conformed, since he was appointed to the commission of the peace in his
father's lifetime in 1664. He was listed as the only
active Whig j.p. in Northamptonshire in 1682, with
an income of £900 p.a. He was removed from the
bench in March 1685, when he stood for the county
unsuccessfully, but was restored in 1687. Returned
as knight of the shire to the Convention, he
probably never took his seat, dying on 8 May 1689,
aged 56. He was buried at Canons Ashby. No later
member of the family was elected to Parliament,
and his son sold Adstone in 1720.[3]

[1] *Vis. Northants.* (Harl. Soc. lxxxvii), 84–86; Lansd. 921, f. 65v;
VCH Hunts. iii. 101. [2] Add. 34222, f. 58; *Cal. Treas. Bks.* vi. 184;
viii. 1805. [3] Baker, *Northants.* ii. 19; Underdown, *Pride's Purge*,
375; *CSP Dom.* 1672, p. 198; SP29/421/216.

                                                      E.R.E.

HARCOURT, Sir Philip (1638–88), of Stanton
Harcourt, Oxon.

BOSTON   26 Oct. 1666
OXFORDSHIRE   1681

bap. 15 Dec. 1638, 1st s. of Sir Simon Harcourt of Stanton
Harcourt by Anne, da. of William, 5th Lord Paget.
educ. travelled abroad to 1659. *m.* (1) 21 Feb. 1661,
Anne (*d.* 23 Aug. 1664), da. of Sir William Waller I* of
Osterley Park, Mdx., 1s.; (2) 11 June 1672, Elizabeth
(*d.* 17 Aug. 1713) da. of John Lee, merchant, of An-
kerwyke, Bucks., 3s. (2 *d.v.p.*) 4da. *suc.* fa. 1642; kntd.
5 June 1660.[1]
    Commr. for militia, Oxon. Mar. 1660, assessment
1661–80, j.p. 1675–80; commr. for recusants, Lincs.
1675; freeman, Woodstock 1680.[2]

Harcourt's ancestors were established in Ox-

fordshire by the early 13th century, and first represented the county in 1322. But the property had
been seriously embarrassed by his grandfather 'in
chimerical pursuits', and his father was forced to
become a soldier of fortune. He returned from the
Low Countries to command a regiment of foot in
the Bishops' wars and the Irish rebellion, but was
mortally wounded in an attack on Kilgobbin Castle.
Harcourt's mother, a devout Puritan, remarried the
parliamentary general Waller and the family connexion was strengthened by his own marriage to
Waller's daughter. At the Restoration he received a
knighthood, presumably in recognition of his step-
father's services. Although he conformed to the
Church of England, his chaplains were Presbyterian.[3]

Harcourt owed his election for Boston in 1666 to
the sitting Member, Sir Anthony Irby*, who had
married his aunt. He was an inactive Member of
the Cavalier Parliament, in which he was named to
only 33 committees, and made seven recorded
speeches of little political significance. He was appointed to the committee for the private bill
promoted by Thomas Horde* in 1670, but became
more active in the early years of the Danby administration. He was appointed to the committee of inquiry into the state of Ireland in 1674, and to those
to appropriate the customs to the use of the navy,
to prevent the growth of Popery, and to report on
scandalous and dangerous books in 1675. He contributed to the debates in the autumn session on
the challenge to William Cavendish*, Lord Cavendish, from Thomas Howard, a Roman Catholic
who, he declared, had reflected on the whole House.
When it was proposed on 18 Nov. to request a conference with the Lords 'for avoiding the occasions
of reviving differences between the two Houses in
matters of appeal', Harcourt was teller for retaining
the last four words. In 1676 Sir Richard Wiseman*
observed that he had 'little hopes' of Harcourt and
Irby. The court party tried to exploit an incident
of 29 Mar. 1677 involving Harcourt and his friend
Andrew Marvell*, but the House accepted his explanation that 'Marvell had some kind of a stumble,
and mine was only a thrust, and the thing was accidental'. Shaftesbury marked him 'thrice worthy' at
this time. He spoke again briefly on 30 Apr. 1678
about an assault on a servant of Sir John Coventry*,
and on the same day he was appointed to the committee to summarize foreign commitments. 'Of a
generous and sweet nature', Harcourt apparently
had little stomach for the animosities of the last session of the Cavalier Parliament. He was given leave
to go into the country on 17 Dec. 1678, and made
way for William Ellys* at the general election.[4]

Harcourt stood unsuccessfully for Oxfordshire as an exclusionist in August 1679, and was removed from local office. Though he received no encouragement from Shaftesbury, he was successful in 1681, but left no trace on the records of the Oxford Parliament. At the time of the Rye House Plot it was reported that Sir William Waller II* was staying with him, but no action was taken. He died on 30 Mar. 1688 and was buried at Stanton Harcourt. His eldest son, a barrister, sat for Abingdon and other constituencies as a Tory from 1690 until he became lord keeper in 1710.[5]

[1] Lipscomb, *Bucks.* iv. 591; E. W. Harcourt, *Harcourt Pprs.* i. 188, 200, 247–8; ii. 4–5; *Knightsbridge Chapel Reg.* 42. [2] Woodstock council acts, 7 July 1680. [3] Lipscomb, 589; Harcourt, i. 111–13, 169–71; D. R. Lacey, *Dissent and Parl. Pols.* 404. [4] Grey, iii. 338, 353; iv. 329; v. 288; *Wood's Life and Times* (Oxf. Hist. Soc. xxi), 525–6. [5] *Wood's Life and Times*, 461; *CSP Dom.* Jan.–June 1683, p. 354; Lipscomb, 591; Bodl. Locke mss, c7/76.

L.N./G.J.

HARDRES, Thomas (c.1610–81), of Canterbury, Kent and Gray's Inn.

CANTERBURY   21 Apr. 1664, 1679 (Oct.)

b. c.1610, 4th s. of Sir Thomas Hardres (*d.* 1628) of Upper Hardres by Eleanor, da. and h. of Henry Thoresby of Thoresby, Yorks. *educ.* Staple Inn; G. Inn 1629, called 1636, ancient 1654. *m.* (1) lic. 21 Sept. 1639, Dorcas (*d.* 1643), da. and h. of George Bargrave of Bridge, Kent, 1s. 1da.; (2) by 1651, Philadelphia (*d.* 1690), da. of James Franklyn of Maidstone, Kent, wid. of Peter Manwood of Sandwich, Kent, 5s. (1 *d.v.p.*), 1da. Kntd. 17 May 1676.[1]

Steward, manor of Lambeth 1649–*d.*; bencher, G. Inn 1659, reader 1663, treas. 1666–8; j.p. Kent July 1660–*d.*; commr. for assessment, Canterbury Aug. 1660–1, Kent 1661–3, Kent and Canterbury 1663–80, sewers, E. Kent Sept. 1660; freeman, Canterbury 1661, common councilman 1662–*d.*, recorder 1664–75, 1675–*d.*; commr. for recusants, Kent 1675; steward of Chancery court, Cinque Ports ?1679–*d.*; chairman of quarter sessions, Kent by 1680–*d.*[2]

Serjeant-at-law 1669, King's serjeant 1676–*d.*[3]

Hardres may have been descended from a Domesday Book tenant on the manor from which the name was derived. Under Richard II William Hardres was three times returned for Canterbury, but they were not a regular parliamentary family. Hardres's eldest brother was an active member of the county committee, but went over to the King in the second Civil War. Hardres himself, a professional lawyer, paid £15 to the county committee as composition for delinquency, and was still under suspicion in 1656. Another brother became a prebendary of Canterbury at the Restoration.[4]

Hardres succeeded Francis Lovelace* both as recorder and MP for Canterbury. He was an inactive Member of the Cavalier Parliament, in which

he was named to 21 committees, all but two before 1673. He took the chair for a local estate bill to enable Lord Strangford (Philip Smythe*) to sell land, and carried it to the Lords on 12 Dec. 1666. Although not reckoned a court supporter in 1669–71, and a defaulter in attendance in the latter year, Hardres was a strong defender of the Church and the prerogative: 'I never thought that one fire would quench another', he wrote towards the end of his life, 'or that reformation in the Church would be wrought by heat in the state'. He was awarded the coif in 1669, but the strength of dissent in Canterbury rendered his relations with his constituency uneasy. 'A malicious observer . . . once trepanned me for my opinion concerning conventicles and nonconformists, making use of it to my prejudice above'. In 1675 the corporation resolved to replace him as recorder by Paul Barret*, as their charter gave them power to do. (Sir) Joseph Williamson* was informed of 'several affronts to Serjeant Hardres, a gentleman of an ancient, eminent family, and one learned in the law. . . . I implore your assistance . . . and real resentment of this high abuse to a gentleman who so little deserves it.' On 22 Apr. the House ordered that Barret, with the mayor and aldermen, should be sent for in custody. Although Sir Edward Dering* thought it 'a high strain of our privilege', they were not discharged until Hardres had been restored. He was not ungrateful to Danby, suggesting in the impeachment debate that the House should begin by determining which charges were criminal. In the debate on illegal imprisonment on 5 May, he declared that 'matters of treason here will be triable here'.[5]

Hardres received the government whip in the autumn, but at the end of the session Sir Richard Wiseman* noted that he 'went ill very often'. He was listed among those 'to be remembered' on the working lists, and during the long recess he was knighted and advanced to the rank of King's serjeant, after which Shaftesbury marked him 'doubly vile'. He was included in both lists of the court party in 1678, but left no further trace on the records of the Cavalier Parliament until he was ordered to be sent for in custody as an absentee in its closing weeks. As one of the 'unanimous club', he lost his seat at the general election, but regained it in August at the expense of the Whig William Jacob*. As chairman of quarter sessions, he refused to accept the petition for the immediate assembly of Parliament in January 1680, and when it did meet, he was once again in trouble as a defaulter. He may never have attended, and was not re-elected. He continued to have difficulty with the local nonconformists, writing:

If I must not only spend my time in his Majesty's service without any recompense, but be hectored out of my reason to comply with a fiery pretender to Reformation, I must quit that service unless I receive better encouragement.

He died on 18 Dec. 1681, aged 71, and was buried at Upper Hardres. His *Reports of Cases in the Exchequer* was published in 1693. His grandson represented Canterbury as a Tory under Queen Anne and George I.[6]

[1] *DNB*; *Dorm. and Ext. Baronetcies*, 242; *Canterbury Mar. Lic.* ii. 454; *Canterbury Cathedral Reg.* (Harl. Soc. Reg. ii), 122, 128; *St. George's Canterbury Par. Reg.* 38–39; PCC 125 Evelyn; W. Boys, *Sandwich*, 246. [2] C181/7/57; *Roll of Freemen* ed. Cowper, 318; J. B. Jones, *Annals of Dover*, 346; *CSP Dom.* 1682, p. 283. [3] H. W. Woolryche, *Eminent Serjeants*, 401. [4] Hasted, *Kent*, ix. 306; *Arch. Cant.* iv. 53–54; xxiii. 71; A. M. Everitt, *Community of Kent and the Great Rebellion*, 146, 243; *Cal. Comm. Comp.* 458. [5] *CJ*, viii. 644; ix. 194, 321, 327; *CSP Dom.* 1675–6, p. 70; 1680–1, p. 420; *Dering Pprs.* 75; Eg. 3345, f. 23v; Grey, iii. 105. [6] *CJ*, ix. 557, 699; Bath mss, Coventry pprs. 6, f. 230; *CSP Dom.* 1680–1, pp. 420, 442; *DNB*.

B.D.H.

HARE, Henry, 2nd Baron Coleraine [I] (1636–1708), of Longford Castle, Wilts. and Bruce Castle, Tottenham, Mdx.

OLD SARUM 1679 (Oct.)

bap. 21 Apr. 1636, 1st s. of Hugh, 1st Baron Coleraine [I], of Totteridge, Herts. and Longford Castle by Lady Lucy Montagu, da. of Henry Montagu[†], 1st Earl of Manchester. *m.* (1) Constantia, da. of Sir Richard Lucy, 1st Bt.[†], of Broxbourne, Herts., 2s. *d.v.p.* 1da.; (2) lic. 17 July 1682, Sarah (*d.* 2 Nov. 1692), da. and coh. of Sir Edward Alston, FRCP, of Great St. Helens, London, wid. of George Grimston of Gorhambury, Herts., and of Lord John Seymour*, 4th Duke of Somerset, *s.p.*; (3) 4 Aug. 1696, Elizabeth, da. of John Portman, Goldsmith, of the Unicorn, Lombard St., London, wid. of Robert Reade of Cheshunt, Herts., *s.p. suc.* fa. 2 Oct. 1667.[1]

J.p. Herts. ?1667–80, Mdx. and Wilts. by 1680–?*d.*; dep. lt. Wilts. 1668–June 1688, Oct. 1688–*d.*, Herts. by 1670–80, Mdx. 1697–*d.*; commr. for assessment, Wilts. 1673–80, 1689, Mdx. 1689–90; freeman, Salisbury 1683.[2]

Gent. of privy chamber 1668–85.[3]

Lord Coleraine was descended from a younger brother of the family of Sir Ralph Hare*, but his branch, enriched by the fortune accumulated in the court of wards by John Hare[†], was probably the wealthier. His father bought Longford Castle from the father of Richard Gorges* just before the Civil War, in which he played no active part, though forced to contribute £2,000 to the committee for the advance of money. Coleraine had antiquarian tastes, like many of his family, and does not seem to have played any part in politics before the exclusion crisis. His Wiltshire residence lies some six miles from Old Sarum, which his first wife's father had represented from 1647 to 1653. He replaced the country Member John Young* in the second Exclusion Parliament, in which he was a moderately active Member, with seven committees. The most important were to consider the proceedings of the judges in Westminster Hall, the disbandment accounts and the repeal of the Corporations Act. He probably opposed exclusion, as he held local office at least until the summer of 1688, when the lord lieutenant of Wiltshire reported him absent from the county when he was due to give his answers on the repeal of the Test Act and Penal Laws. Coleraine contested Wiltshire in 1690, but his petition was unsuccessful. He died on 4 July 1708 and was buried at Tottenham. His grandson, the third lord, sat for Boston from 1730 to 1734 as a Tory.[4]

[1] Foster, *London Mar. Lic.* 1121; *London Vis. Peds.* (Harl. Soc. xcii), 112. [2] *CSP Dom.* 1667–8, p. 608; 1697, p. 22; Hoare, *Wilts. Salisbury*, 478. [3] Carlisle, *Privy Chamber*, 181. [4] *Cal. Comm. Adv. Money*, 243–4; *Wilts. Arch. Mag.* lii. 1–3; *VCH Wilts.* v. 198.

J.P.F.

HARE, Sir Ralph, 1st Bt. (1623–72), of Stow Bardolph, Norf.

NORFOLK 1654, 1656[1]
KING'S LYNN 1660
NORFOLK 1661–28 Feb. 1672

b. 24 Mar. 1623, 1st s. of Sir John Hare[†] of Stow Bardolph by Margaret, da. of Sir Thomas Coventry[†], 1st Baron Coventry of Aylesborough. *educ.* Magdalen Coll. Oxf. 1638; travelled abroad (France) 1643–6. *m.* (1) lic. 26 Oct. 1647, Mary, da. and coh. of Sir Robert Crane, 1st Bt.[†], of Chilton, Suff., 1s. 6da.; (2) 30 Aug. 1660, Vere (*d.*1669), da. of Sir Roger Townshend, 1st Bt.[†], of Raynham Hall, Norf., *s.p.*; (3) lic. 12 July 1671, Elizabeth Chapman (*d.* 17 Mar. 1684) of Westminster, 1s. (posth.). *suc.* fa. 1637; *cr.* Bt. 23 July 1641.[2]

J.p. Norf. 1646–*d.*, commr. for assessment 1647–50, 1656, Jan. 1660–9, militia 1648, Mar. 1660, sheriff 1650–1; freeman, King's Lynn 1660; col. of militia ft. Norf. Apr. 1660–7, dep. lt. c. Aug. 1660–*d.*; commr. for sewers, Lincs. Aug. 1660, corporations, Norf. 1662–3, loyal and indigent officers 1662, oyer and terminer, Norfolk circuit 1665.[3]

Hare's ancestors were living in Suffolk in the 15th century, but the family was raised by Sir Nicholas Hare[†], Speaker of the 1539 Parliament and lord keeper under Mary, who bought Stow Bardolph in 1557. Hare was abroad for most of the Civil War, but held local office throughout the Interregnum and represented the county in two of the Protectorate Parliaments. He signed the Norfolk address for a free Parliament in 1660, and was returned for King's Lynn, some 12 miles from his home, presumably with the support of Edward Walpole*, his brother-in-law. Lord Wharton marked him as a friend, to be managed by Sir John Potts*, but he was not active in the Convention. He was named to five committees, including the committee of elections and privileges, and twice acted as teller. On 30 June he supported a complicated proviso to the indemnity bill to enable the courts to give relief from extorted releases and discharges, and on 24 July he opposed a proviso to the tunnage and poundage bill allowing the surveyor-general of customs to take the established fees. He was appointed to the committees for settling the revenue and the establishment of Dunkirk, and added after the recess to that considering the defects in the poll bill.[4]

Hare presumably gave satisfaction to the Court, for in 1661 he moved up to the county seat vacated by Sir Horatio Townshend*, another brother-in-law, and was returned unopposed. A moderately active Member of the Cavalier Parliament, he was named to 49 committees, and acted as teller in three divisions. Although no longer included in Wharton's list, he took no part in the Clarendon Code or in any other legislation of high political significance, though he was among those appointed to consider the bill restoring the temporal jurisdiction of the clergy and acted as teller against the proviso to the corporations bill to prevent any Member or unsuccessful candidate from acting as commissioner for the borough where he had stood. In 1663 he was appointed to the committees for hindering the growth of Popery, and acted as teller for an unsuccessful motion against deleting any commissioners' names from the subsidy bill. On matters of local interest he helped to consider the bill for repairing Wells quay and the estate bill promoted by Sir Jacob Astley*. His attitude to the fall of Clarendon is not known, though in 1667 he was appointed to committees for assigning debts in the Exchequer and preventing the growth of Popery, as well as one on a private bill promoted by Townshend to enable him to exchange land with the rector of East Raynham. In 1669 Sir Thomas Osborne* included him among the Members who might be engaged for the Court by the Duke of York. He died on 28 Feb. 1672 and was buried at Stow Bardolph.[5]

[1] Excluded. [2] The Gen. n.s. xxvii. 241; N. and Q. cc. 297; London Mar. Lic. ed. Foster, 625. [3] Lynn Freeman, 192; Parl. Intell. 9 Apr. 1660; Cal. Treas. Bks. i. 73; Blomefield, Norf. iii. 405. [4] Blomefield, vii. 440; Address from Gentry of Norf. ed. Rye, 29. [5] CJ, viii. 291, 524; Blomefield, vii. 445.

M.W.H./E.C.

HARE, Sir Thomas, 2nd Bt. (c.1658–93), of Stow Bardolph, Norf.

NORFOLK 1685

b. c.1658, 1st s. of Sir Ralph Hare, 1st Bt.*, by 1st w. educ. Caius, Camb. 1672. m. 20 Apr. 1680, Elizabeth,

da. of George Dashwood, merchant, of Hackney, Mdx., 4s. 5da. suc. fa. 28 Feb. 1672.[1]

Commr. for assessment, Norf. 1677–80, 1689, j.p. 1680–Feb. 1688; freeman, King's Lynn 1682; dep. lt. Norf. 1683–Feb. 1688.[2]

Although Lord Townshend (Sir Horatio Townshend*) had been his guardian, Hare became a pupil of Dr Robert Brady* at Cambridge and a high-flier for the prerogative. In February 1679 he personally attended the county election at the head of his tenants, and when it was declared void he again brought some 400 voters to the poll at the by-election. When Sir Christopher Calthorpe* asked to be excused from standing again, the court electoral agent wrote: 'Sir Thomas Hare, I am afraid, is too young, [but] otherwise as honest a gentleman as can be chosen'. He was nominated by the Earl of Yarmouth (Robert Paston*) as one of the court candidates in 1681, but defeated. He signed the loyal address from Norfolk in 1682 expressing abhorrence of the 'Association'. He was elected on the recommendation of his fellow deputy lieutenants in 1685, but left no trace on the records of James II's Parliament. To the lord lieutenant's questions in 1688:

> He thinks the Penal Laws may be reviewed, and some amendments made, but cannot consent to repeal them, nor the Tests. He will endeavour to choose those of the same mind. He is willing to live friendly and peaceably with all persuasions, whilst they continue loyal to the King and Government.

He was removed from the lieutenancy and the commission of the peace, and followed the example of Sir John Holland* in refusing to resume office in October 'in conjunction with persons unqualified and incapacitated by the laws of the realm'. He was apparently a non-juror after the Revolution. He died on 1 Jan. 1693, aged 35, and was buried at Stow Bardolph. A younger son was returned for Truro as a Tory to the last Parliament of Queen Anne.[3]

[1] H. Ellis, Hist. Shoreditch, 73. [2] Lynn Freemen, 192; Norf. Ltcy. Jnl. (Norf. Rec. Soc. xxx), 45. [3] PCC 143 Eure; Works of Sir Thomas Browne ed. Wilkin, i. 241; Add. 27447, f. 399; 27448, f. 5; 36988, ff. 144, 180; Norf. Arch. Soc. xxvii. 373–4; Norf. Ltcy. Jnl. 66, 89, 109; HMC Lothian, 133.

E.C.

HARFORD, Bridstock (1634–83), of Hereford.

HEREFORD 1679 (Mar.), 1679 (Oct.)

bap. 30 Sept. 1634, o.s. of Bridstock Harford, MD, of St. Owen's Street, Hereford by 1st w. Elizabeth, da. of Richard Hereford of Sufton, Herefs. educ. St. John's, Oxf. 1647, BA 1651; G. Inn 1650, called 1658. m. (1) Catherine, da. of Thomas Read of Ipsden, Oxon., 2s.

(1 *d.v.p.*) 1da.; (2) 6 July 1670, Dorothy, da. and coh. of John Davies of Mynachty, Rad., wid. of John Vaughan of Hergest, Herefs., *s.p.*; (3) 1680, Elizabeth, da. of Thomas Brydges of Old Colwall, Herefs., wid. of John Dannett of Bosbury, Herefs., 1da.[1]

Commr. for assessment, Hereford 1663–9, Herefs. 1673–80, Hereford, Mdx. and Rad. 1679–80; j.p. Herefs. by 1671–*d.*, Worcs. 1681–*d.*; alderman, Hereford by 1680–*d.*, dep. steward 1682–*d.*[2]

Harford's great-grandfather acquired several messuages in Hereford, formerly chantry property, under Edward VI. His father, a physician, served on most of the local assessment commissions during the Interregnum and was intermittently justice of the peace for the county, but does not appear to have held local office after the Restoration. Harford, a lawyer, and his father were described in 1663 as 'implacable enemies of the King'. Nevertheless the old doctor, on rebuilding the city hospital in 1675, put up the inscription: 'Fear God, honour the King, relieve the poor: these three are all'.[3]

On his return to the first Exclusion Parliament, Harford was noted by Shaftesbury as 'honest'. He was named only to the committee to examine abuses in the Post Office. Though he had disappointed expectations by voting against the exclusion bill, he was again elected to the second Exclusion Parliament, in which he was totally inactive. Although described by Secretary Jenkins as 'a worthy Member of the last Parliament', he did not stand in 1681. Under the new charter he replaced William Gregory* as deputy steward of Hereford. He died 'of a lingering distemper' in his father's lifetime on 10 Apr. 1683. His son, the last of the family, was elected mayor in 1697, but never entered Parliament.[4]

[1] W. R. Williams, *Parl. Hist. Herefs.* 93; *Arch. Camb.* ser. 6, ix. 295–7; C. J. Robinson, *Mansions and Manors of Herefs.* 163. [2] Herefs. RO Q. Sess. minute bk. 1665–89; *CSP Dom.* 1680–1, p. 176; Duncumb, *Herefs.* i. 360; SP29/417/188. [3] *Arch. Camb.* 283–4, 295; *CSP Dom.* 1663–4, p. 284. [4] *CSP Dom.* 1680–1, p. 186; Beaufort mss., Robert Price to Beaufort, 20 Apr. 1683; *Her. and Gen.* vii. 422.

E.R.

HARLACKENDEN, Thomas (1624–89), of Maidstone and Woodchurch, Kent.

MAIDSTONE 14 Jan. 1668

b. 28 Sept. 1624, o.s. of Walter Harlackenden of Woodchurch by Pauline, da. of Sir Thomas Colepeper† of Leeds Castle, Kent. *educ.* Univ. Coll. Oxf. 1640; travelled abroad (Holland) 1642–5. *m.* (1) Philippa, da. of John Colepeper†, 1st Baron Colepeper of Thoresway, 2s. 2da.; (2) 9 Sept. 1652, Elizabeth (*d.*1681), da. of Sir George Strode of Squerryes Court, Westerham, 1s. *d.v.p. suc.* fa. 1628.[1]

Capt. of militia, Kent Oct. 1660, col. by 1680–2;

commr. for sewers, Rother marshes Oct. 1660, corporations, Kent 1662–3, j.p. 1662–4, 1689–*d.*, commr. for assessment 1663–80, 1689–*d.*, receiver of taxes 1664–8, dep. lt. ?1673–82, commr. for recusants 1675.[2]

Harlackenden came of a minor gentry family, seated at Woodchurch since at least 1286. He was orphaned at the age of four and committed to the guardianship of his grandfather, who sent him abroad with a tutor on the eve of the Civil War. His first wife was the daughter of the royalist counsellor, and Harlackenden himself paid £20 to the Kent committee as composition for his own delinquency.[3]

Harlackenden signed the loyal address at the Restoration, and in 1663 published a pamphlet about Romney marsh, which earned for him from Evelyn the description of 'a witty gentleman'. But it was probably less his loyalty and his wit than the influence of John Strode II*, his brother-in-law, that earned for him nomination as receiver-general of the royal aid in Kent during the second Dutch war. In June 1667, 'great complaint being made of his not paying in duly', he was ordered to produce his accounts before the board of Treasury. In the following January he was returned at a by-election for Maidstone, where he seems to have resided; but membership of the House did not save him from dismissal. His parliamentary activity was minimal; he was added to the committee of elections and privileges in the next session and appointed to one other committee for a private bill. On 12 Dec. 1670 he was named in his absence by Sir George Downing* as one of four Members in debt to the crown. The amount was only £1,700, but on 27 Mar. 1671 a bill was introduced for the sale of his estates 'for satisfaction of a debt due to his Majesty'. The bill was steered through committee by Sir William Doyley*, whose son was a greater and more successful embezzler of public funds, and received the royal assent at the end of the session. His name appeared on the opposition list of court supporters and on the Paston list of 1673–4.[4]

Under Danby Harlackenden went over to the Opposition. Sir Richard Wiseman* marked him absent from the autumn session of 1675, later describing him as 'discontented'. On the working lists he was assigned to the lord treasurer's management, but neither the means nor the effect is certain. In *A Seasonable Argument* it was stated that 'his only livelihood is his pension', but this has not been traced. He mortgaged the estate in 1676 for £681 10s., but he remained 'a debtor to the King', as stated in *Flagellum Parliamentarium*, and on 14 Mar. 1677 Danby ordered a stay of process 'because of his attendance in Parliament'. Shaftesbury marked him 'doubly worthy', but then crossed it out, and he was black-listed among the 'unanimous club' of court supporters. Nevertheless he probably supported exclusion, for in 1680 it was noted that 'the lord lieutenant does not like him', two years later he was removed from the lieutenancy with the Whig leader, Sir Vere Fane*, by the King's express orders, and he reappeared on the commission of the peace after the Revolution. He died shortly afterwards and was buried at Woodchurch on 21 July 1689, the only member of his family to enter Parliament. In 1700 his son George was forced to sell what remained of the estate.[5]

[1] C142/480/86; N. and Q. cc. 193; Top. and Gen. i. 232; ii. 216; Misc. Gen. et Her. (ser. 2), v. 141; Frag. Gen. viii. 146. [2] Parl. Intell. 8 Oct. 1660; C181/7/60; Eg. 2985, f. 66; Cal. Treas. Bks. ii. 6, 565; iii. 180; CSP Dom. 1682, p. 223. [3] Top. and Gen. i. 236; SP23/233/143; Cal. Comm. Comp. 457. [4] Bodl. Wood mss 276A/162; Wood, Athenae, iv. 272–3; Evelyn Diary, iii. 422; Cal. Treas. Bks. ii. 6; iii. 180; Dering, 31–32; CJ, ix. 223, 227, 232, 235; Statutes, v. 751. [5] Cal. Treas. Bks. v. 570; CSP Dom. 1679–80, p. 533; Top. and Gen. i. 232; ii. 216.

B.D.H.

HARLEY, Edward (1624–1700), of Brampton Bryan, Herefs.

HEREFORDSHIRE 14 Nov. 1646,[1] 1656,[2] 1660
NEW RADNOR
BOROUGHS 1661, 1679 (Mar.)
HEREFORDSHIRE 1679 (Oct.), 1681, 1689, 8 Feb. 1693, 1695

b. 21 Oct. 1624, 3rd but 1st surv. s. of Sir Robert Harley† of Brampton Bryan, being 1st s. by 3rd w. Brilliana, da. of Sir Edward Conway†, 1st Visct. Conway; bro. of Robert Harley I*. educ. Gloucester sch.; Shrewsbury sch.; Magdalen Hall, Oxf. 1638–40; L. Inn 1641–2. m. (1) 26 June 1654 (with £3,000), Mary, da. and coh. of Sir William Button of Parkgate, Tawstock, Devon, 4da.; (2) 25 Feb. 1661, Abigail, da. of Nathaniel Stephens† of Eastington, Glos., 4s. (1 d.v.p.) 1da. suc. fa. 1656; KB 23 Apr. 1661.[3]

Capt. of horse (parliamentary) 1643, col. of ft. 1643–7, col. of horse 1660–1; gov. Monmouth 1644–5, Canon Frome 1645–6, Dunkirk May 1660–1.

Commr. for sequestrations, Herefs. 1643, execution of ordinances, Glos. 1644, assessment, Herefs. 1644, 1647–52, 1657, Jan. 1660, Herefs. and Rad. Aug. 1660–80, 1689–90, Leominster 1689; alderman, New Radnor c. 1647–80; commr. for militia, Herefs. 1648, 1659, Herefs., Worcs. and Rad. Mar. 1660, scandalous ministers, Herefs. 1654, j.p. 1656–82, July 1688–d., Rad. ?Mar. 1660–82, 1689–d.; custos rot. Herefs. Mar.–July 1660, Rad. Mar. 1660–82; dep. lt. Herefs. c. Aug. 1660–82, Herefs. and Rad. 1689–d.; col. of militia ft., Herefs. 1668–82, commr. for recusants 1675.[4]

Councillor of State 25 Feb.–31 May 1660.
FRS 1663–85.

Harley's ancestors had been resident at Brampton Bryan and Members of Parliament since the 14th century. His father, who restored the family fortunes by good estate management, prudent mar-

riages and the profitable office of master of the Mint, was a Presbyterian, and the only county magnate to take the parliamentary side in the Civil War. Harley himself had a distinguished war record, but he opposed the army in 1647 and was twice imprisoned. Unlike his brother, he took no part in royalist conspiracies. In 1656 he succeeded to the family property, valued at £1,500 p.a. In February 1660 he resumed his seat with the secluded Members and was elected to the Council of State. But he was still insistent on the abolition of episcopacy and on parliamentary control of the militia. It required court intervention with the old Cavaliers, and the support of Edward Massey* among the Presbyterian Royalists, to secure his return for Herefordshire at the ensuing general election.[5]

In the Convention, Harley was named to the committees for the abolition of the court of wards, for drawing up the instructions for the messengers to the King, and for the indemnity bill, and he took part in a conference on the King's reception. He received his commission as governor of Dunkirk from Charles II at Canterbury, and at once crossed over to take up his post, which Lord Gerard of Brandon offered to buy from him for £10,000. He returned to Westminster in June, and served on the committees for the Dunkirk establishment and for disbanding the army, and in the conference on settling ministers. In spite of his other duties he was a moderately active Member, sitting on 17 committees, but he made no recorded speeches. He failed to prevent the re-establishment of the court of the marches at Ludlow, though he obtained the signatures of Matthew Hale* and four other Herefordshire Members to his petition against it. It is perhaps an indication of his waning prestige just before the dissolution that the £7,200 required for the payment of the Dunkirk garrison was placed at the bottom of the list of charges on the excise.[6]

Harley made no attempt to defend his county seat in the general election of 1661. According to family tradition he was offered a peerage in the coronation honours, but he preferred to accept a KB and remain in the Lower House. His steward advised him not to contest the neighbouring borough of Leominster 'unless you come in by the interest of the Duke of Buckingham'. His brother Robert Harley I, who was steward of the crown estates in Radnorshire, made way for him in the borough seat; but even though another brother was recorder of New Radnor, (Sir) Allen Brodrick*, standing on the Earl of Carbery's interest, carried the election to a poll. 'The elections', as a sardonic old Royalist wrote to him, 'are in all places such as you would wish.' Nor were Harley's friends much kinder, and the sprightly Lady Clinton never tired of alluding to his new constituency by describing him as 'a good gentleman of Wales'. To fill up the cup, he was shortly afterwards required to surrender the governorship of Dunkirk, the King 'being continually disturbed because he is represented to be a notorious Presbyterian'. Harley's Protestant zeal was ill-adapted to the rule of a Catholic town, and the queen mother had complained of him.[7]

Although relieved of the burdens of office, Harley sat on only five committees in the first nine sessions of the Cavalier Parliament, and none of them was of political or religious importance. Although his correspondence shows that he was assiduous in attendance at the House, his total for the whole Parliament was only 38. Nor did he shine as an orator, and it is to be feared that Lady Clinton was teasing him again when on one occasion she professed to believe that 'had you been in the House of Commons . . . the Speaker had been argued into the chair'. His absence from the Oxford session, when the Five Mile Act was passed, led to the accusation that he 'countenanced factious persons'. Harley thought it necessary to explain to the lord chancellor that he had been incapacitated by gout, an excuse which surely would have earned Clarendon's sympathy, and professed:

> As for my religion, I thank God that I can truly say I have no opinion but what is consonant to the catholic faith and the doctrines of the Church of England, but what I have learned out of the scriptures and the writings of the ancient fathers.

If Clarendon had to pretend to be satisfied with this highly qualified statement, others were not. In 1668 the Marquess of Worcester (Henry Somerset*) explained to Arlington that he could not make Harley colonel of the Herefordshire militia in succession to Sir Edward Hopton* because he was a Presbyterian. 'Lord Arlington replied', according to Harley's brother Robert, 'that the King commanded the lord marquess to offer you the command of the regiment without more ado'. Harley, who depended for spiritual guidance largely on the moderate Presbyterian Richard Baxter, had no scruples about conforming, though when in London he attended Baxter's services and even proposed to lodge with him during one session of Parliament.[8]

Harley took little part in the impeachment of Clarendon, though he made his only recorded speech in the Cavalier Parliament to condemn the sale of Dunkirk. In 1668 he was appointed for the first time in this Parliament to a politically significant committee, one which was entrusted with a review of the militia laws. In the following year he was noted as one of the independent Members who had usually voted for supply, but his loyalty was put under severe strain by the renewal of the Conventicles Act. On 12 Mar. 1670, he wrote sorrowfully to his wife: 'That day before I came, to the grief of my soul the bill of conventicles passed the House of Commons'. But when the bill was reintroduced and amended in the next session, he was satisfied on the whole, writing: 'Blessed be to God the conventicles bill had a better issue. Most of the severe parts are left out.' Needless to say, his tolerant views did not extend to Popish priests, of whom one was brought before him in petty sessions in 1671, though he does not seem to have initiated any prosecution. While active during the Cabal ministry in making representations to the Government on behalf of Presbyterians, as well as preferring low churchmen to benefices in his gift, he himself took the Anglican sacrament in 1673.[9]

Harley was appointed to the committee for the suppression of Popery in 1675, and henceforward became increasingly intimate with Shaftesbury, who was his partner in the lease of a mine at Lyonshall. When the session closed amid general expectation of an imminent dissolution, he took the lead in nominating opposition candidates for all the Herefordshire seats, and he himself was adopted as a candidate for the county. Harley came up to London in the following February. The death of William Strode I* was about to involve him in an unpleasant lawsuit over the portions of Strode's daughters, in which his opponent was no less formidable a lawyer than John Maynard I*. But no doubt he seized the opportunity to report to Shaftesbury on the difficulty that had arisen in Herefordshire over the claim of Sir Herbert Croft* to the county seat, and he was certainly closeted with Shaftesbury when Secretary Williamson called at Exeter House to warn the opposition leader to desist from his political activities. Undeterred by this unfortunate encounter, Harley was noted by Shaftesbury in 1677 as 'thrice worthy'. He was one of the Members instructed to prepare reasons for a conference on the growth of Popery on 29 Apr. 1678, and after Oates's revelations he helped to investigate the murder of Godfrey, as well as the mysterious knocking noises heard in the night in Old Palace Yard. He did not succeed in finding another Guy Fawkes, but his services in promoting the fall of Danby were valued by the French ambassador at 300 guineas.[10]

There is no evidence that Harley stood for Herefordshire in February 1679, when Croft was returned. Indeed he had some difficulty in securing

re-election for Radnor Boroughs, but the committee of elections never reported on his opponent's
petition. Although Harley was permitted to take his
seat, he was only moderately active in the first Exclusion Parliament. He was named to five committees, none of much importance; but Maynard's
advocacy of lifting the ban on the import of Irish
cattle stirred him to unusual eloquence in defence
of the stock-breeding interest of the marcher
counties, and perhaps also for more personal
reasons. He justified Shaftesbury's description of
him as 'worthy' by voting for the exclusion bill.
But the Radnor burgesses, he learnt, were likely to
express themselves unkindly towards one that 'hath
deserved better from them' by easing the county of
£80 a month in taxes.[11]

This was probably some intrigue of Croft's, but
it backfired. Harley transferred himself to his own
county, and was returned unopposed with Lord
Scudamore (John Scudamore*) at the next general
election as knight of the shire. He employed his leisure while waiting for the second Exclusion Parliament to assemble in writing a pamphlet on religious
comprehension, which attacked the imposition of
rites and ceremonies. He was an active Member of
this Parliament, sitting on 16 committees. He took
the chair of the committee to consider the bill for
regulating elections, but apart from presenting his
report he did not speak in the House. He was again
returned unopposed to the Oxford Parliament, in
which he served only on the committee of elections
and privileges. But he was certainly present, for he
attended the meeting of Herefordshire Members in
Lord Scudamore's lodgings the morning after the
dissolution. On this occasion Shaftesbury is said to
have offered them both commands in a revolutionary army, and when Scudamore refused Harley
denounced him as a timorous spirit. The breach
became irreparable in the following summer, when
Harley was forced to choose between the support
of Scudamore and of Thomas Coningsby*, who had
run away with Lady Scudamore.[12]

Harley was naturally under suspicion during the
Tory reaction and was removed from all local office
in Feb. 1682, but his political activity did not decrease. He announced his candidature for Herefordshire in 1685, but withdrew without a poll.
During Monmouth's Rebellion he experienced a
few weeks of not uncomfortable detention. In 1687
Danby noted Harley as one of the eminent Parliament men, distinguished by ability rather than
wealth or interest, who were hostile to James II's
government. Efforts were made to win him over; in
1688 he was restored to the commission of the peace
but he refused, for the second time, a seat on the

Privy Council, and he urged the bishop of Hereford
not to read the Declaration of Indulgence. He took
up arms for William III in 1688, subscribed £50 to
a loan, and was chosen governor of Worcester by
the local gentry.[13]

Although a contest for Herefordshire was
expected, and John Dutton Colt* was holding a seat
in reserve for Harley he was in fact returned unopposed in 1689, though, unlike his younger colleague
Sir John Morgan*, he did not care to face the electors. Nor, when he reached London, did he find
the new regime particularly appreciative of his
services: 'Sir E.H. has met with many disappoint-
ments in his attendance upon the King', wrote one
of his younger sons. Within the House, however,
his influence over the Herefordshire Members was
undiminished, and he had the satisfaction of leading
them all to vote against the Lords' amendments to
the abdication vote on 5 Feb. He was named to 58
committees in the Convention, including those of
chief political importance, though he made no
recorded speeches. 'I was never so tied to a Parliament', he complained on 2 Apr. He served on the
committees for the mutiny and toleration bills. In
the latter he may have been active behind the
scenes, for before Parliament met he asked his son
to send him 'a sheet or two written by myself, being
a scheme of the ecclesiastical government of England'. He also took part in the inquiries into the
authors and advisers of grievances and the delays in
the relief of Londonderry. Harley's correspondence
shows that three less important committees were of
particular concern to him, those for refugee
Huguenot ministers, for the abolition of the court
of the marches (on which his name stands first) and
for the Wye and Lugg navigation. 'I hope the good
work goes on to your content', wrote a Leominster
clothier on 12 Apr., 'which you have so long
laboured in to make Wye and Lugg navigable.' In
the second session he was appointed to the inquiries
into the expenses and miscarriages of the war. He
served on the committee for the bill to restore corporations, and supported the disabling clause.[14]

Harley was defeated at the general election of
1690, and on his return to the House went into
opposition as a country Whig. He died on 8 Dec.
1700 and was succeeded by his son, Robert Harley
II*. He was never a political figure of national
importance, being content to control and guide the
elections and representatives of his county. Even
here he owed his influence less to his territorial
power, which was only moderate, than to his character. It was a political opponent, Herbert Aubrey*,
who wrote to him: 'That you are kind and good
all persons own', and his voluminous cor-

respondence confirms this contemporary verdict.[15]

[1] HMC Portland, iii. 147. Secluded at Pride's Purge, 6 Dec. 1648 and readmitted 21 Feb. 1660. [2] Excluded. [3] HMC Portland, iii. 247, 291; v. 641; Letters of Lady Brilliana Harley (Cam. Soc. lviii), 218. [4] HMC Portland, iii. 111, 117, 129, 140, 155, 306; Nottingham Univ. Lib. Pw2 Hy 114; Trans. Woolhope Field Club, xxxiv. 292; Portland mss BL Loan 29/80, Richard Jeffrey to Harley, 20 May 1682; CSP Dom. 1682, p. 77. [5] C. J. Robinson, Castles of Herefs. 8; Keeler, Long Parl. 203; HMC Portland, iii. 220, 226, 617; Cal. Cl. SP, iv. 580, 642; Add. 11051, f. 229; Symonds's Diary (Cam. Soc. lxxiv), 195. [6] BL Loan 29/88; CJ, viii. 234; HMC Portland, v. 641. [7] BL Loan 29/82, Samuel Shilton to Harley, 8 Feb. 1661; 29/79, letters of Thos. Harley, passim; 29/74, Lady Clinton to Harley, 23 Dec. 1676; HMC Portland, iii. 235, 250, 617. [8] BL Loan 29/83, Ralph Strettell to Harley, 24 Nov. 1674; Letters of Lady Brilliana Harley, 240–1; HMC Portland, iii. 306; D. R. Lacey, Dissent and Parl. Pols. 405–7. [9] Milward, 124; HMC Portland, iii. 313, 323, 336; CJ, ix. 469. [10] BL Loan 16, Mineral and Battery Works Society Order Bk., ff. 145, 151; CSP Dom. 1675–6, pp. 461, 529; BL Loan 29/87, Strode letters, passim; Dalrymple, Mems. ii. 317. [11] CJ, ix. 571, 577, 578; Grey, vii. 91; BL Loan 29/140, Harley to Robert Harley, 30 July [1679]; Nottingham Univ. Lib. Pw 2 Hy 114. [12] CSP Dom. 1682, p. 426. [13] BL Loan 29/140, Harley to Robert Harley, 12 Mar. 1685; 29/74, Harley to Bishop Croft, 20 June 1688; HMC Portland, iii. 384–5, 415, v. 644; R. Morrice, Entering Bk. 2, pp. 343, 347, 358; Hatton Corresp. ii. 113; BL Loan 29/184, f. 120. [14] BL Loan 29/184, f. 123, Colt to Harley, 14 Jan. 1689; 29/140, Harley to Robert Harley, 2 Apr. 1689; 29/49, James Powle to Harley, 12 Apr. 1689; Add. 40621, ff. 2, 10, 16, 18, 21; HMC Portland, iii. 398; v. 644. [15] BL Loan 29/50, Aubrey to Harley, n.d.

M.W.H./E.R.

HARLEY, Robert I (1626–73), of Walford, Herefs.

NEW RADNOR BOROUGHS   13 May 1647,[1] 1660

b. 6 Apr. 1626, 2nd surv. s. of Sir Robert Harley†, and bro. of Edward Harley*. educ. privately (Mr Simons). m. 8 Feb. 1671, Edith, da. of Thomas Pembrugge of Wellington, wid. of Thomas Hinton of Hayton, Salop, s.p. Kntd. 19 Nov. 1660.[2]

Cornet (parliamentary) 1643; capt. of arquebusquiers 1643–4, maj. 1644–7; lt. of horse Feb.–May 1660, col. July 1660–2.[3]

Commr. for assessment, Herefs. and S. Wales 1647, Rad. 1648, Herefs. and Hereford Jan. 1660, Herefs. and Rad. Aug. 1660, Rad. 1661–3, 1665–d.; j.p. Herefs. Mar.–July 1660, Rad. Mar. 1660–d.; steward of crown manors, Rad. July–Aug. 1660, 1672–d.; keeper of the seals and c.j. of the revenue court, Barbados 1663–4; receiver of fee-farm rents, Herefs., Worcs. and Staffs. 1670–1.[4]

Gent. of the privy chamber 1672–d.[5]

FRS 1663–d.

Harley was thanked by the House for his good service in suppressing the royalist rising led by Sir Henry Lingen* in August 1648, but like his father and brother he did not sit after Pride's Purge, and became an active Royalist. His connexion with (Sir) Thomas Fairfax* was particularly valuable, and he took some part in arranging the marriage of Fairfax's daughter to the Duke of Buckingham. He was in and out of prison during the Interregnum. He may have been the beneficial purchaser of crown or royalist lands in Radnorshire, however, since it was later asserted that he had acquired his interest there

'in the worst of times'. With Sir Horatio Townshend* he claimed the chief credit for Fairfax's rising in Yorkshire in 1659. He met George Monck* in Nottinghamshire on his march south and was expected in the Low Countries to report to the exiled Court. But he found better employment in assisting his old commanding officer Sir William Waller I* to provoke a mutiny among the troops sent to occupy the City, and then volunteered to serve as a subaltern under (Sir) Richard Ingoldsby* to suppress the last republican regiments in Suffolk.[6]

Harley was re-elected without difficulty for New Radnor, where his brother Thomas was recorder. He was an inactive Member of the Convention, being named to only seven committees. According to Lord Mordaunt, on 3 May he engaged in a hot dispute with William Morice I*, who opposed the King's immediate return to England. When Edmund Ludlow* took his seat, Harley advised him to avoid at all costs defending the execution of Charles I. On 29 June he was one of the Members instructed to prepare an order for settling a committee for the army. On 1 Sept. he was named to the committees for the Dunkirk establishment and for disbandment, and in the debate four days later he seconded the 'last in, first out' proposal of John Birch*. Shortly afterwards he crossed over to Dunkirk as his brother's deputy, where his high-handedness required all the diplomacy of the British minister in Brussels. He was back in the House by 27 Dec. 1660, acting as teller (for both sides, if the Journal is correct), and two days later urging that Sir William Lockhart (whose regiment he had been granted) deserved no favourable consideration.[7]

At the general election of 1661, Harley made way for his brother. He did not accompany his regiment to Tangier, where it was disbanded after incurring heavy casualties from the Moors. Henceforward his life was an almost uninterrupted series of disasters. His sectarian associates (including most of his former officers) brought him under suspicion. He obtained a post in the West Indies and set himself up as a planter, but within a few months quarrelled with the governor of Barbados, who had him arrested and shipped back to England. He returned broken in health and spirit. To his credit, he refused to fabricate evidence against Clarendon; but even his brother had to pronounce him unfit for public office. Religious fervour, combined with a burning sense of grievance and a defective education, make his letters almost unintelligible. He sold most of his property to Sir Thomas Williams*, and with the proceeds bought a revenue office which was abolished within a year. In 1672 he wrote to his brother that he was 'unresolved whether to come into the commission of bankrupts or no', but through Williams's intercession he was granted a pension of £500 p.a. and a post at Court. On the report of the death of Sir Richard Lloyd I* he expressed 'his desire to be chosen in his room . . . if it might receive a dispatch without great contest'. However, the report proved to be unfounded, and Lloyd was still alive when Harley died on 6 Nov. 1673. He was buried at Brampton Bryan.[8]

[1] Did not sit after Pride's Purge, 6 Dec. 1648, readmitted 21 Feb. 1660. [2] *Letters of Lady Brilliana Harley* (Cam. Soc. lviii), 11, 74; C. J. Robinson, *Mansions and Manors of Herefs.* 285; *HMC Portland*, iii. 320; Aubrey, *Brief Lives*, i. 288. [3] *HMC Portland*, iii. 114, 229; viii. 12; *CSP Dom.* 1644–5, p. 131; BL Loan 29/84, certificate of Sir William Waller; *Cal. Treas. Bks.* i. 597. [4] *CJ*, vi. 400; *CSP Dom.* 1660–1, pp. 140, 210, 398; 1671, p. 14; *HMC Portland*, viii. 8; BL Loan 29/180, f. 23. [5] Carlisle, *Privy Chamber*, 190. [6] *CSP Dom.* 1648–9, p. 248; 1659–60, p. 334; 1660–1, p. 348; *CJ*, vi. 679; D. Underdown, *Royalist Conspiracy*, 221, 224, 234, 309; *HMC Portland*, iii. 218; viii. 12. [7] *Cal. Cl. SP*, iv. 580; Lister, *Clarendon*, iii. 103; *Voyce from the Watch Tower*, 121; *Old Parl. Hist.* xxii. 473; xxiii. 80; *Nicholas Pprs.* (Cam. Soc. ser. 3, xxxi), 252–3. [8] *CSP Dom.* 1660–1, p. 409; Clarendon, *Life*, iii. 304–5; BL Loan 29/79, Thomas to Sir Edward Harley, 14 May [1661], 17 Mar. 1673; 29/181, f. 309v, Robert to Sir Edward Harley, 2 July 1672; *CSP Col.* 1661–8, p. 195; *HMC Portland*, iii. 284, 320, 376; viii. 13; *Letters of Lady Brilliana Harley*, p. xlix.

M.W.H./J.P.F.

HARLEY, Robert II (1661–1724), of Brampton Bryan, Herefs.

TREGONY	6 Apr. 1689
NEW RADNOR	12 Nov. 1690, 1695, 1698, 1701
BOROUGHS	(Feb.), 1701 (Dec.), 1702, 1705, 1708, 1710–23 May 1711

b. 5 Dec. 1661, 1st s. of Edward Harley*. *educ.* Shilton, Oxon. (Mr Birch) 1671–80; Sherwood Street Academy, London (M. Foubert) 1680–1; M. Temple 1682. *m.* (1) 14 May 1685, Elizabeth, da. of Thomas Foley I* of Witley Court, Worcs., 2s. (1 *d.v.p.*), 2da.; (2) 4 Oct. 1694, Sarah, da. of Simon Middleton of Edmonton, Mdx., *s.p. suc.* fa. 1700; *cr.* Earl of Oxford 23 May 1711; KG 26 Oct. 1712.[1]

Major of militia ft. Herefs. Dec. 1688–at least 1694, commr. for assessment Herefs. 1689–90, Salop 1690, sheriff Mar.–Nov. 1689; steward of crown manors, Rad. 1691–1714; dep. lt. Herefs. by 1694–? 1714, Rad. by 1701–?14; custos rot. Rad. 1702–14; j.p. Herefs. by 1702–14; steward, Sherwood Forest 1712–14.[2]

Commr. for public accounts 1691–7; sec. of state (north) 1704–8; PC 27 Apr. 1704–May 1708, 13 Aug. 1710–Sept. 1714; commr. for union with Scotland 1706; chancellor of the Exchequer 1710–11; ld. treas. 1711–14. FRS 1712.

Speaker of House of Commons 10 Feb. 1701–5 Apr. 1705.

Harley's education was purely nonconformist, his father changing his mind in 1678 about sending him to Oxford. Thomas Coningsby* wrote of him to

Harley's father on 27 Aug. 1681 in terms that the friends of his maturity would scarcely have employed, except sarcastically:

> I have been to wait upon your most sober and ingenious son, and Mr Foubert gives him such a character that I believe no young man in England ever had a better.

It is probable that Coningsby, who was fresh from the ignominious outcome of his escapade with Lady Scudamore, promised to bring Harley in at the next opportunity for Leominster. This was not in his power in 1685, but on 4 Oct. 1687 Thomas Harley wrote: 'It is spoken at Leominster that my nephew Harley would stand to be burgess there'. Harley was under arms with his father in the Protestant interest in December 1688, and was sent to report to William of Orange at Henley. But he was again disappointed at the ensuing general election, when the interest of John Dutton Colt* and his claims as a Whig martyr were too strong to be set aside. Harley now pinned his hopes on his father's old seat at New Radnor, in the vain expectation that the election of Richard Williams* would be declared void on petition. The promotion of (Sir) William Gregory* to the King's bench created a vacancy at Hereford, but he reluctantly decided that so large and open a constituency was beyond his means. Meanwhile, consumed by ambition, he was limited to the care of his father's estate and the ceremonial duties of a sheriff. But on the death of Charles Boscawen* his brother Hugh brought him in for Tregony unopposed.[3]

Harley took his seat as soon as he could secure permission to leave Herefordshire, and on 14 May he made his maiden speech, calling for justice on those responsible for the shambles in the west after Monmouth's Rebellion. He was an active Member of the Convention, sitting on 24 committees. He took part in drawing up the new oaths of allegiance and supremacy before obtaining three weeks' leave to attend to his county. In the second session he was named to the committees to prepare charges against the former treasury solicitors, to inquire into war expenditure and to consider the second mutiny bill. On 8 Nov. (immediately after giving up his shrievalty), he was ordered to take charge of presenting a bill to ease sheriffs in their accounts. He was teller for the address asking the King who had advised the appointment of Commissary Shales. He was appointed to the committee for restoring corporations, and supported the disabling clause. On 21 Jan. 1690 he spoke in favour of punishing offences rather than individuals responsible for tyrannical rule: 'if you take persons at random, possibly you may not take them that are most guilty'.[4]

Harley had made a promising start on orthodox Whig lines, but he was soon to follow his brother-in-law Paul Foley* into the new country party, which merged with the Tories. He was in office for most of Queen Anne's reign, for the last three years as prime minister. On the Hanoverian succession he was impeached on the motion of his local rival Coningsby, who, with a symmetry appropriate to the Augustan Age, thus brought down the curtain on the political career which 35 years earlier he had undertaken to promote. Harley died on 21 May 1724, but the Harleys continued as a great parliamentary family till 1802.

[1] *Dorm. and Ext. Peerages*, 265. [2] HMC Portland, iii. 361, 492; *CSP Dom.* 1696, pp. 488–9. [3] Portland mss BL Loan 29/183, f. 100, Coningsby to Sir Edward Harley, 27 Aug. 1681; 29/79, Thomas Harley to Sir Edward Harley, 4 Oct. 1687; Add. 40621, f. 18; *HMC Portland*, iii. 425, 432, 435, 436. [4] Grey, ix. 247, 544; *CJ*, x. 216, 296; *CSP Dom.* 1689–90, p. 103.

J.P.F.

HARRINGTON, Thomas (1635–at least 1690), of Boothby Pagnell, Lincs.

GRANTHAM 1685

bap. 9 Dec. 1635, 1st s. of John Harrington of Boothby Pagnell by Esther, da. of Sir Henry Gibbs of Honington, Warws. *educ.* travelled abroad (France) 1655–7. *m.* by 1664, Eleanor, 1da. *suc.* fa. by 1657.[1]

Commr. for assessment, Lincs. (Kesteven) Sept. 1660–3, 1665–80, enclosures, Deeping fen 1665; receiver of taxes, Lincs. 1677–8, sheriff 1677–8, capt. of militia horse by 1680, dep. lt. 1680–9; alderman, Grantham 1685–Oct. 1688.[2]

Capt. indep. tp. 1685, 4 Dgn. Gds. 1687–Dec. 1688.

Harrington was the last of a family established in the East Midlands by the 14th century, first representing Rutland in 1384. His grandfather, a royalist commissioner of array, compounded for £463 on the Newark articles for his delinquency in the Civil War. Harrington and his brother contracted with a Roman Catholic officer in the Earl of Dumbarton's regiment in 1676 'to raise twenty able and sufficient men to bear arms in the French king's service and land them at Calais or Dieppe'. But 'before they could get them near the sea-coast they quarrelled, mutinied, and ran away'. About the same time he presented a tankard to the corporation of Grantham, five miles from his home, with a promise 'that he would at all times serve the corporation to the utmost of his power'. But when Sir William Thorold*, whose grandson was married to Harrington's daughter and heir, died early in the following year, the court candidate was Sir Robert Markham*, and in 1680 he was arrested for debt by his uncle, a decayed London fishmonger. As a grand juryman in 1682, he assisted Markham in

procuring a loyal address. His loyalty earned the commendation of the Earl of Lindsey (Robert Bertie I*), and he was instrumental in the surrender of Grantham's charter in 1684. The corporation thanked him for his 'great trouble' in obtaining a new charter, in which he was nominated alderman.[3]

Harrington was returned for Grantham with his kinsman (Sir) John Thorold* as a Tory at the general election of 1685. A moderately active Member of James II's Parliament, he was appointed to five committees, including those to report on expiring laws and to recommend expunctions from the Journals. On Monmouth's landing Peregrine Bertie I* wrote: 'Tom Harrington has a troop given him, and many others of as little quality'. Nevertheless he was accepted for a permanent commission. He returned affirmative answers on the repeal of the Test Act and Penal Laws, and was ordered by Sunderland to stand for re-election in 1688.[4]

Harrington was a Jacobite after the Revolution, and on 19 May 1690 he was among those who had 'listed themselves in several regiments under pretence of commissions from the late King James', and were ordered by proclamation to give themselves up. The date of his death is unknown.[5]

[1] Lincs. AO, Boothby Pagnell par. reg.; *Lincs. Peds.* (Harl. Soc. li), 462; Add. 34015, f. 101. [2] *Cal. Treas. Bks.* v. 616; G. H. Martin, *Grantham Charters*, 178, 226. [3] *HMC Buccleuch*, i. 528; *Cal. Comm. Comp.* 1323; C10/201/38; C7/179/61; Lincs. AO, Monson mss, 7/11/37, 12/41; C7/544/52; *CSP Dom.* 1682, p. 138. [4] Add. 38012, f. 5; *CSP Dom.* 1687–9, p. 275. [5] *CSP Dom.* 1690–1, p. 23.

J.S.C.

HARRIS, Arthur (c.1650–86), of Hayne, Stowford, Devon.

OKEHAMPTON 2 Jan. 1671, 1679 (Mar.), 1679 (Oct.), 1681

b. c.1650, o.s. of John Harris† of Hayne by 2nd w. Cordelia, da. of John Mohun†, 1st Baron Mohun of Okehampton. *m.* lic. 5 June 1673, Theophila, da. of John Turner, serjeant-at-law, of Salisbury Court, London, *s.p. suc.* fa. 1657; *cr.* Bt. 1 Dec. 1673.[1]

Recorder, Okehampton 1671–81; j.p. Devon 1673–80, commr. for assessment 1673–80, recusants 1675.[2]

Harris came from a cadet branch of the Radford family which acquired Hayne, about ten miles from Okehampton, by marriage in the 16th century. His father, a Puritan, sat for Launceston in the Long Parliament until secluded at Pride's Purge. Though without the benefit of legal training, Harris was made recorder of Okehampton in 1671, and returned to the Cavalier Parliament at a by-election on the interest of his cousin, the 3rd Lord Mohun. An inactive Member, he was probably appointed to the committee of elections and privileges in February 1673, and to four others of minor importance. Although his politics were not known to Sir Richard Wiseman* in 1676, Mohun was one of the most prominent country peers, and Shaftesbury marked Harris 'worthy' in the following year. He three times acted as teller for the Opposition in 1678, for a committee of inquiry into charges of corruption (18 June), for the adjournment of the supply debate (25 June), and against excusing the women servants of the Duchess of York from the test (26 Nov.).[3]

Harris was re-elected to the Exclusion Parliaments, and was again considered 'worthy' by Shaftesbury. In the first Exclusion Parliament he acted as teller on 17 Apr. 1679 against paying into the Exchequer the supply granted specifically for disbandment, and voted for the bill. He was removed from the commission of the peace in 1680 and took no known part in the second Exclusion Parliament. He was admitted to the Green Ribbon Club in December, and went to great lengths to secure the re-election of Josias Calmady II*. He was among those appointed to bring in the third exclusion bill in the Oxford Parliament. He lost his recordership in the same year and is unlikely to have stood in 1685. He was buried at Lifton on 20 Feb. 1686. His estate passed in the following year to his cousin William, who was proposed as a court candidate for Penryn in 1688 and later sat for St. Ives and Okehampton.[4]

[1] Vivian, *Vis. Devon*, 449. [2] W. B. Bridges, *Okehampton*, 101, 104. [3] Keeler, *Long Parl.* 204. [4] *Prot. Dom. Intell.* 8 Feb. 1681.

J.S.C.

HARRIS, John (c.1633–77), of Lanrest, Liskeard, Cornw. and Radford, Plymstock, Devon.

LISKEARD   1661–Aug. 1677

b. c.1633, o.s. of John Harris† of Lanrest by 1st w. Elizabeth, da. and coh. of Emorb Johnson of South Petherton, Som. *educ.* Pembroke, Camb. 1649; I. Temple 1652. *m.* 4 Feb. 1666, Mary, da. of John Rashleigh† of Menabilly, Cornw., 1s. *suc.* fa. 1648.[1]
Commr. for assessment, Cornw. Aug. 1660–3, 1665–d., Devon 1661–3, recusants, Cornw. 1675; j.p. Devon Feb. 1677–d.

Harris's paternal ancestors had been seated at Lanrest since Tudor times, but do not appear to have been of the same stock as the Devonshire family with whom they intermarried and whose Radford estate they inherited. His father was recorder of Liskeard, where he was first elected in 1628, and he continued to represent the borough until disabled for royalism in 1644. His property was still under sequestration at his death. Harris

himself was accused by his footman of complicity in Booth's rising in 1659.[2]

Harris was returned for Liskeard at the general election of 1661, though he seems to have resided chiefly in Devon, and was known in Plymouth as 'the great Mr Harris'. But he did not acquire the epithet through his activity at Westminster. In 14 sessions of the Cavalier Parliament he was appointed to only three committees, of which the most important was to prevent meetings of sectaries (14 May 1663), and he defaulted on calls of the House in 1666, 1668 and 1671. In the opening sessions, when present, he was presumably a court supporter. He was entered on the working lists as under the influence of the Earl of Bath, but Sir Richard Wiseman* in 1676 included him among the Cornish Members of whom he could 'say little', and in the following year Shaftesbury classed him as 'worthy'. He died in August 1677, the last of his family to sit in Parliament. His widow married Shadrach Vincent*.[3]

[1] Vivian, *Vis. Devon*, 448; *Vis. Cornw.* 209; *Som. and Dorset N. and Q.* ii. 223; Keeler, *Long Parl.* 204–5; *Paroch. Hist. Cornw.* iii. 152. [2] J. Allen, *Hist. Liskeard*, 320, 470; Keeler, 205; *Cal. Comm. Comp.* 2893. [3] *Jnl. of James Yonge*, 150.

P.W.

HARRIS, Taverner (c.1656–85), of Soundess, Nettlebed, Oxon.

WALLINGFORD   1681

b. c.1656, o.s. of John Harris, barrister, of the Inner Temple and Silkstead, Hants by Mary, da. and h. of John Taverner of Soundess. *educ.* New Coll. Oxf. matric. 3 Nov. 1671, aged 15; I. Temple, entered 1671. *unm. suc.* fa. 1661.[1]
Commr. for assessment, Oxon. 1679–80, j.p. 1680–1; freeman, Woodstock 1680.[2]

Harris's grandfather, of Buckinghamshire origin, became warden of Winchester college in 1630. A Presbyterian, he sat in the Westminster Assembly. Harris's father, a lawyer, took no known part in the Civil War. He acquired a small estate seven miles from Wallingford by marrying a cousin. During the exclusion crisis, Harris himself became a member of the Green Ribbon Club and a friend of Thomas Tipping* and Lord Lovelace (John Lovelace*). With their support he was returned for Wallingford in 1681, but left no trace on the records of the Oxford Parliament. He was removed from the commission of the peace in June. He died of smallpox on 11 July 1685 and was buried at Compton, Hampshire, the only member of his family to enter Parliament. In his will he directed that his lands in Oxfordshire and Berkshire should be sold.[3]

[1] *Wood's Life and Times* (Oxf. Hist. Soc. xix), 239–40. [2] Wood,

(xxi), 544; Woodstock council acts (7 July 1680). [3] Wood, (xix), 240; (xxvi), 154; *Ath. Ox.* iii. 455; *Prideaux Letters* (Cam. Soc. n.s. xv), 105; PCC 87 Cann.

L.N./G.J.

HARRISON, Sir John (c.1590–1669), of Montague House, Bishopsgate, London and Balls Park, Herts.

SCARBOROUGH   1628
LANCASTER   1640 (Apr.), 1640 (Nov.)–4 Sept. 1643, 1661–28 Sept. 1669

b. c.1590, 12th s. of William Harrison, yeoman, of Aldcliffe Farm, Beaumont, Lancs. by Margaret, da. of Christopher Gardiner of Urswick, Lancs. *educ.* Warton g.s. *m.* (1) lic. 21 Aug. 1616, Margaret (*d.*1640), da. of Robert Fanshawe of Dronfield, Derbys., 3s. *d.v.p.* 2da.; (2) c.1645, Mary (*d.* 14 Feb. 1706), da. of Philip Shotbolt of Ardeley, Herts., 1s. 1da. Kntd. 4 Jan. 1641.[1]

Farmer of customs 1633–8, 1640–1, Sept. 1660–2, commr. 1662–7; gent. of privy chamber 1664–*d.*[2]

J.p. Herts. by 1641–?43, Sept. 1660–*d.*; commr. for levying money, Herts. 1643, loyal and indigent officers, London and Westminster 1662, assessment, Lancs. 1663–*d.*, Norf. 1664–*d.*

Harrison, a younger son of an obscure Lancashire family, came to London in his youth and was given a small place in the customs house by Lord Treasurer Salisbury. 'A great accountant, of vast memory, and an incomparable penman', he married into a leading Exchequer family and acquired an estate of £1,800 p.a., including the manor of Beaumont, near Lancaster. Returned for his native town in both elections of 1640, he was persuaded to rejoin the customs administration to enable Charles I to resist the Scots; but the Long Parliament refused to repay his advances to the crown, and fined him £10,800. During the Civil War he joined the Court at Oxford. When he petitioned to compound for his delinquency in 1648 his debts amounted to over £25,000, and a fine of a mere £1,000 was accepted.[3]

At the Restoration Harrison 'was most justly and meritoriously restored to his former condition ... and to the trust of a Member of Parliament'. Returned for Lancaster at the general election of 1661, he was listed as a friend by Lord Wharton, but never became an active Member of the Cavalier Parliament. He was named to 19 committees, including the committee of elections and privileges in the first seven sessions, and those to examine the shortfall in the revenue (18 June 1661) and to prevent frauds on the customs (29 Jan. 1662). The transfer of the customs to direct administration in 1662 was in accordance with Harrison's longstanding advice, and he was appointed to the board with a salary of £2,000 p.a. He was also one of the original Royal Adventurers into Africa. In 1663–4

warrants were issued for repayment of his loans to Charles I. He was not listed as a court dependant in 1664, although his support could hardly be doubted. In the Oxford session he was appointed to the committee for the five mile bill. His last committee was to hear a petition from the creditors of Sir Thomas Dawes, one of his partners in the customs farm (8 Apr. 1668). In the following year Sir Thomas Osborne* included him among the court dependants, but he died on 28 Sept. 1669 in his 80th year, and was buried at All Saints, Hertford, leaving his son property in four counties, though burdened with debts to the crown of £6,000.[4]

[1] Clutterbuck, *Herts.* ii. 186; *Fanshawe Mems.* 20; *The Gen.* n.s. xvii. 134; *London Mar. Lic.* ed. Foster, 635. [2] *Vis. London* (Harl. Soc. xv), 354; Stowe 326, ff. 52, 75–77; *Cal. Treas. Bks.* i. 226; iii. 1127; Carlisle, *Privy Chamber,* 174. [3] Keeler, *Long Parl.* 205–6; *Fanshawe,* 21, 39; Stowe 184, ff. 161–2; 326, ff. 75, 92; *Royalist Comp. Pprs.* (Lancs. and Cheshire Rec. Soc. xxix), 165; *Cal. Comm. Comp.* 1523. [4] Clutterbuck, ii. 157; *Sel. Charters* (Selden Soc. xxviii), 179; *CSP Dom.* 1663–4, pp. 50, 639, 676; 1665–6, p. 79; *Cal. Treas. Bks.* i. 226; *Fanshawe,* 328–9; *The Gen.* n.s. xvii. 134.

I.C.

HARRISON, Richard (1646–1726), of Balls Park, Herts.

LANCASTER   25 Oct. 1669, 1679 (Mar.)

b. Oct. 1646, 4th but o. surv. s. of Sir John Harrison* being o.s. by 2nd w.; half-bro. of William Harrison†. *educ.* Peterhouse, Camb. 1663; M. Temple, 1663. *m.* lic. 28 Apr. 1668 Audrey, da. of George, 4th Visct. Grandison of Limerick [I], 8s. 6da. *suc.* fa. 1669.[1]

Gent. pens. by 1671–bef. 1679.[2]

J.p. Herts. 1670–?Feb. 1688, Hertford 1687; collector of coal imposition, London 1672–87; commr. for assessment, Herts. and Mdx. 1673–80, Lancs. 1673–4, 1679–80, recusants, Lancs. 1675; capt. of militia ft. Herts. by 1680, lt.-col. 1681–?87, dep. lt. 1681–7.[3]

Harrison succeeded to an estate of £1,600 p.a.; but it was soon extended for a debt to the crown of £6,000. Sir John Shaw* and his father's other partners made their own arrangements with the Treasury, leaving Harrison to plead total ignorance of customs affairs and to extricate himself as best he could. Privilege of Parliament was the first essential if he was to escape arrest, and aided by his father's legacy of £100 to the poor of Lancaster, he succeeded without difficulty to his seat. His father-in-law, who was captain of the gentlemen pensioners, proved a tower of strength, and by enrolling him in his corps gave him protection during recesses. The salary was only £100 p.a.—'a small pension, proportionable to his understanding', as the opposition pamphleteer sneered—but it gave him a breathing space, and in 1672 Lord Grandison was able to take over the extent on his lands and to secure for him the office of collector of the tax on coal in London imposed to pay for the rebuilding of St. Paul's. By then the worst of Harrison's difficulties were over.[4]

Harrison was not an active Member of the Cavalier Parliament. He was appointed to only 16 committees and made no recorded speeches. He was not involved in any measures of political significance or of particular concern to his constituents, but he was named to two Hertfordshire estate bill committees, and took an interest in highway legislation, and a proposal for the relief of debtors. He received the government whip in 1675, but was subsequently 'doubted' by Sir Richard Wiseman*. However, according to the list of 1676 he was to be sent for to attend, and he was noted by Shaftesbury as 'doubly vile'. In 1678 he figures on both lists of court supporters.

Harrison was re-elected to the first Exclusion Parliament, but took no part in its proceedings so far as is known. Huntingdon marked him as a court supporter, but he was absent from the division on the exclusion bill. It is possible that Harrison's property at Lancaster had been sold by this time; in any case, whether because of the difficulty of maintaining the family interest in the borough from a distance or because he had been blacklisted in the 'unanimous club', he did not stand again. Presumably he opposed James II's religious policy, for he was removed from the lieutenancy in 1687. But he became a non-juror after the Revolution, and spent the remainder of his long life in retirement, though three of his sons sat for Weymouth, Hertford and Old Sarum under the Hanoverians. He died on 17 Jan. 1726 and was buried at All Saints, Hertford.[5]

[1] Clutterbuck, *Herts.* ii. 186; *London Mar. Lic.* ed. Foster, 636. [2] *Cal. Treas. Bks.* iii. 854. [3] *CSP Dom.* 1672, p. 622; 1680–1, p. 423; Chauncy, *Herts.* i. 521. [4] *Fanshawe Mems.* 22, 45; *CSP Dom.* 1671–2, p. 75; *Cal. Treas. Bks.* iii. 994, 1348; *VCH Lancs.* viii. 33. [5] *VCH Lancs.* viii. 60; *Herts. Recs.* i. 386.

I.C.

HART, Sir Richard (c.1637–1702), of Bristol and Hanham Hall, Bitton, Glos.

BRISTOL   1681, 9 Nov. 1685, 1689, 1690

b. c.1637, 1st s. of George Hart, linen-draper, of Bristol by Mary, da. of George Knight, mercer, of Bristol. *m.* (1) Margaret, 1s. *d.v.p.*; (2) lic. 11 Aug. 1673, aged 36, Anne, da. and coh. of Robert Nicholas† of Devizes, Wilts., wid. of Thomas Hulbert of Corsham, Wilts., 2s.; (3) c.1685, Elizabeth, da. of Richard Jones† of Stowey, Som., wid. of Henry Pinnell of Nash House, Bremhill, Wilts., 1s. *suc.* fa. 1658; kntd. 27 Oct. 1680.[1]

Member of merchant venturers, Bristol 1660, master 1675–7, treas. 1677–83; common councilman, Bristol 1664–80, sheriff 1668–9, mayor 1680–1, alderman 1681–6, Oct. 1688–*d.*; commr. for assessment, Glos. 1666–74, 1679–80, Bristol 1673–80, Glos. Bristol and Wilts. 1689–90, Som. 1690; sheriff, Wilts. 1676–7; j.p. Glos. 1682–7, ?1689–*d.*; dep. lt. Bristol 1685–6, commr. for port regulation 1690.[2]

Hart's father, of Devonshire origin, supported Parliament during the Civil War, serving on the Bristol corporation from 1645 to his death and as a decimator under the Protectorate. Hart was nominated to the common council in 1661, but refused to take the oaths until informed of the King's displeasure at such neglect and contempt. Thereafter he conformed, with increasing enthusiasm. He inherited property in Gloucestershire and Somerset, and acquired a life interest in Wiltshire by his second marriage; but he was primarily a merchant, with an interest in the Newfoundland fishery. He must have become a Tory before his mayoralty, during which he was knighted, and at the general election in 1681 he and Thomas Earle* defeated the Whigs Sir John Knight* and Sir Robert Atkyns*. He attended the Oxford Parliament, where he made no speeches and served on no committees, and on his return is said to have declared his support for exclusion. If true, this cannot have been known to Secretary Jenkins, who congratulated him in the following autumn on the successful outcome of the municipal elections. On handing over the mayoralty to Thomas Earle, he said:

> May the Church of England triumph over all her enemies, both popish and schismatic. May the King's days be prolonged, and the remainder from henceforth be a continual jubilee. And may there never want a man from the loins of our royal martyr Charles I to govern these kingdoms until time is swallowed by eternity.[3]

Hart led the opposition to the surrender of Bristol's charter in 1683, recognized as one of the 'good' aldermen by the Court, and retained his place on the bench. He did not stand at the general election of 1685, and his third wife, the sister of the Whig lawyer Sir William Jones*, claimed to have some hundreds of cheeses in stock to refresh Monmouth's followers if they had advanced a little further. On the death of Sir John Churchill* Hart stood for Bristol at a by-election, defeating the candidate proposed by the Duke of Beaufort (Henry Somerset*). The indenture never reached Chancery, and it is probable that he did not take his seat in James II's Parliament. He was removed from local office at Beaufort's instigation, but restored to the Bristol corporation when the new charters were withdrawn, and elected to the Convention, probably unopposed. He seconded the motion of his colleague Sir John Knight* for observing the anniversary of Charles I's execution, and voted to agree with the Lords that the throne was not vacant.

A moderately active Member, he was appointed to 19 committees, including those to hear complaints against customs officials and to consider restoring corporations. He probably introduced the bill for rebuilding Bristol gaol and establishing 'courts of conscience' for small claims at Bristol and Gloucester on 9 May 1689. The committee of most political importance to which he was nominated was to inquire into the delay in relieving Londonderry. In the second session he was among those instructed to inquire into the impressment of merchant seamen and to consider the second mutiny bill. He was given leave to go into the country for three weeks on 18 Dec., and was presumably absent from the division on the disabling clause in the bill to restore corporations. He was re-elected in 1690, but lost his seat five years later, and was detained for some weeks on suspicion of complicity in the Jacobite plot in 1696. He died on 16 Jan. 1702, and was buried in St. Nicholas, Bristol, the only member of his family to sit in Parliament.[4]

[1] *Bristol and Glos. Arch. Trans.* viii. 324; *The Gen.* n.s. xxxv. 132; PCC 376 Wootton. [2] *Merchant Venturers* (Bristol Rec. Soc. xvii), 30; A. B. Beaven, *Bristol Lists*, 186, 187, 201, 224, 225, 294; *CSP Dom.* 1685, p. 189; *Cal. Treas. Bks.* ix. 620. [3] *N. and Q.* (ser. 11) iv. 291–2; *HMC 5th Rep.* 328; Bristol RO, common council procs. 1659–75, ff. 68, 108–9; *CSP Dom.* 1672–3, pp. 218, 275; SP29/387/27, 417/242; SP44/62/300. [4] *CSP Dom.* Jan.–July 1683, pp. 150–1; PC2/71/287; R. Morrice, Entering Bk. 1, p. 560; 3, p. 443; *HMC 5th Rep.* 328; Luttrell, iv. 25.

J.P.F.

HARTOPP, Sir John, 3rd Bt. (1637–1722), of Stoke Newington, Mdx. and Freatby, Leics.

LEICESTERSHIRE 24 Apr. 1679, 1679 (Oct.), 1681

bap. 31 Oct. 1637, 3rd but o. surv. s. of Sir Edward Hartopp, 2nd Bt., of Freatby by Mary, da. of Sir John Coke[†] of Melbourne, Derbys., sec. of state 1625–40. *educ.* St. John's, Oxf. 1655; L. Inn 1656. *m.* 8 Nov. 1666, Elizabeth (*d.* 9 Nov. 1711), da. of Charles Fleetwood[†] of Feltwell, Norf., c.-in-c. 1659, 4s. (3 *d.v.p.*) 9da. *suc.* fa. Mar. 1658.[1]

Commr. for militia, Leics. 1659, Mar. 1660, assessment Jan. 1660–3, 1677–9, j.p. Mar.–July 1660, Feb. 1688–?*d.*, sheriff 1670–1.

Hartopp's ancestors were of little account before the Tudor period, receiving a grant of arms only in 1596. His grandfather was created a baronet in 1619, and sat for the county in 1628–9. His father raised a regiment for Parliament in the Civil War and continued to hold local office during the Interregnum. His mother became the third wife of the republican general Fleetwood in 1664, and two further intermarriages followed, including Hartopp's own. The entire family settled in the London suburbs, and attended the Independent conventicle of Dr John Owen in Leadenhall Street. Owen's

sermons were printed many years later from Hartopp's shorthand notes.[2]

Hartopp was defeated by Lord Roos (John Manners[*]) at the first general election of 1679. But he petitioned successfully, giving evidence on his own behalf at the bar of the House. The election was declared void, and he defeated his cousin John Coke II[*] at the by-election. He was classed as 'honest' by Shaftesbury and voted for exclusion, but his only committee in the first Exclusion Parliament was for a naturalization bill. Re-elected without a contest in the autumn, he was moderately active in the second Exclusion Parliament, with eight committees, including those to inquire into the conduct of Sir Robert Peyton[*], into abhorring, and the proceedings of the judges. He was also among those instructed to bring in bills to regulate parliamentary elections, to unite Protestants, and to reform the Post Office. He was again unopposed in 1681, but left no trace on the records of the Oxford Parliament.[3]

Hartopp's house at Stoke Newington was raided for a conventicle in April 1686, and he was listed among the opposition to James II as one considerable for interest in Leicestershire. Nevertheless he may have become a Whig collaborator. He was restored to the commission of the peace in 1688 and recommended as court candidate for the county. But he is not known to have stood again. He died on 1 Apr. 1722 and was buried at Stoke Newington. His funeral sermon was preached by Isaac Watts, for some years his family chaplain. His intention of leaving £10,000 for the instruction of candidates for the dissenting ministry was partially frustrated by his heirs. No later member of the family entered Parliament.[4]

[1] Nichols, *Leics.* ii. 123, 124, 128. [2] *Grantees of Arms* (Harl. Soc. lxvi), 117; G. F. Farnham, *Quorndon Recs. Supp.* 92; D. R. Lacey, *Dissent and Parl. Pols.* 408–9. [3] *HMC Ormonde*, n.s. v. 49–50; *Prot. Dom. Intell.* 11 Mar. 1681. [4] R. Morrice, Entering Bk. 1, p. 530; *DNB*.

E.C.

HARTOPP, Sir William (c.1626–at least 1692), of Rotherby, Leics.

LEICESTER 1661

b. c.1626, 1st s. of Sir Thomas Hartopp of Burton Lazars by 1st w. Dorothy, da. of Sir Thomas Bendish, 1st Bt., of Steeple Bumpstead, Essex. *educ.* Bumpstead (Mr Thorbeck); St. John's, Camb. adm. 20 Apr. 1642, aged 16; M. Temple 1646. *m.* (1) 12 Aug. 1649, Agnes (*bur.* 26 June 1667), da. of Sir Martin Lister[†] of Thorpe Arnold, Leics., 2s. 3da.; (2) settlement 4 Dec. 1668, Elizabeth, da. of John Poulett[†], 1st Baron Poulett of Hinton, wid. of William Ashburnham of Chiswick, Mdx., *s.p.* Kntd. 19 June 1660; *suc.* fa. 1661.[1]

Maj. of militia ft. Leics. Apr. 1660, j.p. July 1660–85; commr. for assessment, Leics. Aug. 1660–80, Leicester 1664–9, enclosures, Deeping fen 1665; dep. lt. Leics. 1667–?81, receiver of taxes 1677–8.[2]

Gent. of the privy chamber 1675–85; proofmaster of ordnance by 1692.[3]

Hartopp came of a strongly parliamentarian family. His father, a second cousin of Sir John Hartopp*, served on the Leicestershire county committee, acquired Rotherby in 1654, and after marrying the widowed mother of Sir Thomas Mackworth* held local office in Rutland throughout the Interregnum. Another cousin, and also brother-in-law, William Hartopp of Little Dalby, was probably a security commissioner under the Protectorate. But Hartopp himself apparently imbibed royalist views from the Mackworths, and was knighted at the Restoration.[4]

Hartopp was involved in a double return for Leicester at the general election of 1661, but his name was on both indentures and he took his seat at once. An inactive Member of the Cavalier Parliament, he was appointed to the committee of elections and privileges in nine sessions and to only eight others, none of them of major political significance, and he defaulted on a call of the House in 1668. He reported to the mayor of Leicester that when Parliament assembled for the 1674 session:

> There was great calmness in the House, and I hope it is a sign of unanimity in that place, the contrary to which can be no less than ruin to us all. . . . There was a very great appearance in the House of Commons, more numerous than I e'er did see it heretofore.

On receiving the government whip from (Sir) Joseph Williamson* for the autumn session of 1675, he replied:

> His Majesty being resolved of our meeting on the 13th, I hope they will be firm in his honour and happiness: I am certain my vote will ever be so. I hope to be in London on the 13th, and shall be very impatient till I have presented you my humble service.

But in December, Sir Richard Wiseman*, apparently unaware of his connexion with Williamson, wrote that he

> was a most steady man last sessions. He is acquainted with none of us, and I know not any that correspond with him. He ought to know by somebody how well the King approves and takes notice of his services.

Hartopp's name duly appeared on the working lists among the Members 'to be remembered', and he was assigned to the management of Sir Robert Carr*. He was made receiver of taxes in 1677, and marked 'doubly vile' on Shaftesbury's list. On 27 Dec. he wrote to Williamson

> I am very glad to hear of the approaching Parliament. At my first coming to London I shall give you my humble

respects, and shall heartily rejoice that some may be found to disappoint those that desire the overturning of this kingdom.

But in the event he was detained in the country by 'a violent fit of gout', and Williamson listed him among those Members 'wanting' in a debate. Nevertheless he was on both lists of the court party in 1678, and described in *A Seasonable Argument* as 'a pensioner of £200 p.a., and promised to be clerk of the kitchen. Threatens to sue his town for his wages because he hears they will choose him no more'.[5]

Hartopp did not in fact stand in 1679, and in a list of the Leicestershire commission of the peace in November 1680 it was noted that he was 'very much in debt, absconds, and goes by another name'. Ormonde obtained an Oxford fellowship for his younger son in 1684 on the grounds that Hartopp's 'loyalty and service to the King have reduced his income [by] £2,000 p.a.'. By 1692 he was serving as gentleman proofmaster in the Ordnance at £20 p.a. The date of his death has not been ascertained. His elder son retained some property in the county, but no later member of the family entered Parliament.[6]

[1] Nichols, *Leics.* ii. 267; *Reps. Assoc. Architectural Soc.* xxiv. 86; *Le Neve's Knights* (Harl. Soc. viii), 78; PCC 178 May. [2] *Merc. Pub.* 12 Apr. 1660; SP44/20/141A; *Cal. Treas. Bks.* v. 431. [3] Carlisle, *Privy Chamber*, 192; *HMC Lords*, iv. 190. [4] Nichols, ii. 128, 152, 267; iii. 397. [5] *Recs. Bor. Leicester* ed. Stocks, iv. 534; *CSP Dom.* 1675–6, p. 318; 1677–8, pp. 473, 571. [6] *HMC Lords*, i. 182–3; iv. 190; *CSP Dom.* 1683–4, p. 379; *HMC Ormonde*, n.s. iv. 638.

E.C.

HARVEY, Daniel (1631–72), of Coombe, Surr.

SURREY 1660

bap. 10 Nov. 1631, 4th but 1st surv. s. of Daniel Harvey, Grocer and merchant, of Croydon and London by Elizabeth, da. of Henry Kinnersley of London; cos. of (Sir) Eliab Harvey* and Michael Harvey*. *educ.* Croydon g.s.; Pembroke, Oxf. 1644; Caius, Camb. 1646. *m.* by 1651, Elizabeth, da. of Edward Montagu†, 2nd Baron Montagu of Boughton, 2s. 2da. *suc.* fa. 1649; kntd. 27 May 1660.[1]

Sheriff, Surr. 1654–5; commr. for militia, Northants. and Surr. Mar. 1660; j.p. Surr. Mar. 1660–d., Kingston-upon-Thames 1665; col. of militia horse, Surr. Apr. 1660, commr. for assessment. Aug. 1660–9, dep. lt. 1661–d.; jt. keeper of Hartleton walk, Richmond Park 1661–d., New Park by 1668–d.; commr. for corporations, Surr. 1662–3; freeman, Guildford 1662, commr. for oyer and terminer, Norfolk circuit 1665.[2]

Gent. of the privy chamber (extraordinary) July 1660; ambassador to Turkey 1668–d.[3]

Harvey's grandfather, a Kentish yeoman, had seven sons, of whom the most famous was the eminent physiologist William, who discovered the circulation of the blood. Another of Harvey's uncles

Harvey Family of Surrey, Essex and Dorset

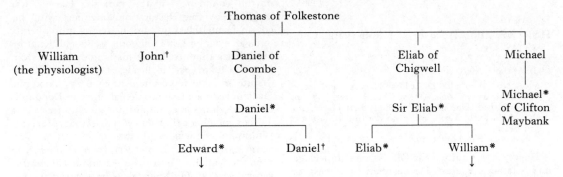

sat for Hythe in the Long Parliament, while his father, a Turkey merchant, earned the reputation of 'understanding the whole business of trade more exactly than most men', and acted as adviser to Archbishop Laud on business matters. Harvey's marriage was quickly followed by the acquisition of a Surrey estate, and his three sisters married Heneage Finch*, later 1st Earl of Nottingham, Sir Edward Dering, 2nd Bt.*, and Robert Bulkeley*, 2nd Viscount Bulkeley.[4]

Although the Harveys never took up arms for the King, they were royalist sympathizers during the Civil Wars and Interregnum, and Harvey's father was harassed until his death by the committee for the advance of money for his assessment of £5,000. Harvey himself was not politically active during the period except for his nomination as sheriff of Surrey, and with Francis Aungier* he defeated the Onslows at the county election of 1660. He made no recorded speeches in the Convention and was appointed to only five committees, including the committee of elections and privileges. A court supporter, he was knighted at the Restoration. He acted as teller in five divisions of which the most important were against agreeing with the Lords not to disable 16 prominent personalities of the Interregnum, and against a proviso to protect from further punishment those excepted from the indemnity bill. The measures in which he was interested include those to reduce interest to 6 per cent and to prevent the voluntary separation of married persons.[5]

Harvey did not stand for Parliament again, and he spent the last four years of his life as ambassador to Turkey, succeeding his kinsman the Earl of Winchilsea, while his wife remained at home and continued active in court intrigues throughout the reign of Charles II. He died in Constantinople in August 1672.[6]

[1] *Misc. Gen. et Her.* (ser. 2), iii. 330–1. [2] *Parl. Intell.* 23 Apr. 1660; *CSP Dom.* 1660–1, p. 210; 1661–2, p. 40; Add. 6167, f. 207. [3] LC3/2; *CSP Dom.* 1668–9, p. 135. [4] Keeler, *Long Parl.* 207–8; *Gen. Mag.* vii. 98; Clarendon, *Life*, i. 21–22; *VCH Surr.* iii. 502. [5] *HMC Laing*, i. 510. [6] *HMC Hastings*, ii. 159; *Misc. Gen. et Her.* (ser. 2), iii. 363.

M.W.H./J.S.C.

HARVEY, Edward (1658–1736), of Coombe, Surr.

BLETCHINGLEY   1679 (Mar.)
CLITHEROE   1705, 1708, 1710, 30 Mar. 1715

b. 30 Mar. 1658, 1st s. of Daniel Harvey*, and bro. of Daniel Harvey†. *m.* (1) 8 May 1679, his cos. Elizabeth (*d.* 15 Jan. 1696), da. of Sir Eliab Harvey* of Rolls Park, Chigwell, Essex, 3s. 8da.; (2) July 1702, Lady Elizabeth Newport (*d.* 7 Mar. 1724), da. of Francis Newport†, 1st Earl of Bradford, wid. of Sir Henry Lyttelton, 2nd Bt.*, of Hagley Hall, Worcs., *s.p.*; (3) 6 July 1725, Mary, da. and coh. of Edward Carteret†, postmaster-gen. 1721–39, *s.p. suc.* fa. 1672; cos. Michael Harvey* 1712.[1]

Commr. for assessment, Surr. 1679–80, j.p. 1689–?1715, dep. lt. 1701–15; high steward, Kingston-upon-Thames 1707–*d.*[2]

Harvey was returned after a contest for Bletchingley at the first general election of 1679, a month before reaching his majority. Considered 'honest' by Shaftesbury, he neither spoke nor sat on any committees in the first Exclusion Parliament. On 25 Apr. he was given leave to go into the country, but he returned to vote for exclusion. He did not sit again until the reign of Queen Anne. By this time he had become a Tory, and after the Hanoverian succession he was an ardent Jacobite, 'continually talking of designs to bring back the Stuarts'. He died at Dunkirk on 24 Oct. 1736. His son Michael sat for Milborne Port as a Tory with two intervals from 1717 to 1747, but ruined himself by expensive election contests.[3]

[1] *Misc. Gen. et Her.* (ser. 2), iii. 363. [2] Surr. RO, QS2/1/6/298; Manning and Bray, *Surr.* i. 342. [3] Manning and Bray, i. 402.

J.S.C.

HARVEY, Eliab (1659–81), of Rolls Park, Chigwell, Essex.

OLD SARUM   1679 (Mar.)

> *bap.* 2 Nov. 1659, 1st s. of Sir Eliab Harvey*, and bro. of William Harvey*. *educ.* Christ Church, Oxf. 1676. *m.* 23 Nov. 1680, Dorothy, da. of Sir Robert Dycer, 2nd Bt., of Hackney, Mdx., and h. to her bro. Sir Robert, 3rd Bt., *s.p.*[1]
> Freeman, Salisbury 1679.[2]

Harvey was returned for Old Sarum, under age, on his father's interest. He was marked 'honest' on Shaftesbury's list, and voted for exclusion, but was named to no committees and made no speeches. He never stood again, as the seat was required for his father in the second and third Exclusion Parliaments. In 1680 he married a 12-year-old heiress, with £1,700 p.a. in hand and £600 more in reversion. But he died on 3 June 1681, and was buried at Hempstead. The ecclesiastical court found that the marriage had not been consummated, and the widow married her brother-in-law William three months later.[3]

[1] *Misc. Gen. et Her.* (ser. 2), iii. 334, 383, 385. [2] Hoare, *Wilts.* Salisbury, 477. [3] Kent AO, Dering-Southwell corresp.

J.P.F.

HARVEY, Sir Eliab (1635–99), of Cokayne House, Broad Street, London and Rolls Park, Chigwell, Essex.

OLD SARUM	c. Oct. 1669[1]
ESSEX	1679 (Mar.)
OLD SARUM	1679 (Oct.), 1681, 1685
MALDON	7 Dec. 1693, 1695, 1698–20 Feb. 1699

> *bap.* 3 June 1635, 1st s. of Eliab Harvey, Grocer and merchant of Laurence Pountney Hill, London and Hempstead, Essex by Mary, da. of Francis West, Grocer of London, lt. of the Tower 1645–52; cos. of Daniel Harvey* and Michael Harvey*. *educ.* Merchant Taylors' 1643; Padua 1656. *m.* 7 Dec. 1658. Dorothy, da. of Sir Thomas Whitmore, 1st Bt.†, of Apley Park, Salop, 3s. (2 *d.v.p.*) 4da. Kntd. 27 May 1660; *suc.* fa. 1661.[2]
> Asst. Levant Co. 1670–2; commr. for assessment, Essex and Kent 1673–80, London 1677–80, Essex and Wilts. 1689–90; freeman, Salisbury 1679; lt. Waltham forest by 1681–d; j.p. Essex 1692–d., dep. lt. ?1692–d.[3]

Harvey's father was one of the wealthiest Royalists in the City, and sufficiently prominent for a reward to be offered for his capture in 1645. He escaped with a brief imprisonment and a payment of £885 to the committee for the advance of money,

no doubt owing to his marriage to the daughter of a London train-band officer standing second to none in the confidence of the radicals. Harvey was knighted at the Restoration, together with his cousin Daniel Harvey*; but he seems subsequently to have taken both his religion and his politics from his mother's family, hence his long exclusion from all but a token part in local government in Essex, despite an inherited estate estimated at £3,000 p.a. His failure to achieve municipal office in London is more puzzling, since he did not give up trade as a Turkey merchant till shortly before 1680. Harvey's Whitmore connexions doubtless gave him early warning of the death of (Sir) John Denham* in 1669, and after a contest he was returned for the vacant seat at Old Sarum. The interest is not known, but a decline in Harvey's balance with Robert Clayton* and John Morris* from £4,631 in 1669 to £2,156 in 1673 may signify a considerable outlay. He became a very active Member of the Cavalier Parliament in which he was appointed to 149 committees, acted as teller in 23 divisions, and made 44 recorded speeches. In his first session he was appointed, perhaps ironically, to the committee to prevent abuses in parliamentary elections, and in 1670 he took part in the inspection of treasury and admiralty accounts. On 1 Dec. he acted as teller against the land tax. In the debate arising out of the assault on Sir John Coventry*, he spoke in favour of suspending all other business.[4]

From the third Dutch war onwards Harvey's name is seldom absent from politically important committees, especially of an anti-Papal character. He was the first merchant, with no more than a primary education, to achieve prominence in debate from the opposition benches during the Cavalier Parliament. In the spring session of 1673, he acted as teller in three important divisions: against seeking the concurrence of the Lords in the address for ease to Protestant dissenters, against incapacitating dissenters from sitting in the Commons, and against adjourning the debate on the printing of grievances. On 8 Mar. he moved that the cancellation of the Declaration of Indulgence should be recorded in the Journal, and a week later he seconded the motion for leaving the supply bill on the table. During the summer, Sir Nicholas Armourer wrote to Secretary Williamson:

> I hope you will bring us peace against October. If not, look to it; my friend Sir Eliab Harvey, Sir Lewis and Robin Thomas will belt you all. There are close cabals and profound ones, as time will show.

Harvey was indeed, as his 'friend' forecast, one of the fiercest doves in the autumn session. He was among those appointed to prepare an address against the second marriage of the Duke of York, and to devise a test to distinguish between Papists and Protestants. On supply he said:

> Giving of money now is certainly to ruin King and kingdom. Give money, and you destroy the revenue of the nation, wool. You are letting the King of France be the merchant of the whole world. By falling out with Spain, we spoil the best trade we have. He [i.e. Harvey] has kept one hundred men at work upon the woollen manufacture, and now cannot keep one.

Before the adjournment he had time to express the hope that the House would declare the troops raised for the war to be a grievance, and when Parliament reassembled in January 1674, he was named to the committee to draw up an address on the subject. He moved for the banishment of Lauderdale and the removal of Buckingham from Court, and on 11 Feb. was among those appointed to examine a Scottish law which enabled the former to send forces south of the border. On the prorogation he was one of the 'guilty commons' who abandoned their dinner in the suburbs to seek safety in the City.[5]

In the spring session of 1675 Harvey introduced the bill to extend habeas corpus. He helped to draw up the addresses for the removal of Lauderdale and the recall of British subjects from the French service, which he had been the first to propose, and for which he acted as teller. He was chairman for the bill to naturalize the daughter of Sir James Rushout* which was lost owing to the quarrel between the Houses over Shirley v. Fagg, in which he was also prominent, being twice required to draw up reasons for a conference. On 3 June he was detailed to attend the conference demanded by the Lords in the Four Lawyers' case. In the autumn debate on the navy, Harvey's mercantile knowledge and statistical grasp made him a formidable opponent for Samuel Pepys*. 'We have 27 docks, slips, and launches', he remarked on 22 Oct. 'Would know whether, if all these should be employed, building merchant ships will not be stopped.' On 3 Nov. he assured the House that £14 per ton was an extravagant estimate for the cost of new warships. He was teller for a vote of no further supply that session on 8 Nov., and for tacking an appropriation clause to the supply bill. On 13 Nov. he informed the House that John Fagg I* had again been summoned to appear before the Lords. He was appointed to the committee for the liberty of the subject.[6]

In the 1677 session Harvey was marked 'thrice worthy' by Shaftesbury, and sat regularly with the chiefs of the opposition. On 26 Feb. he complained that 'the Speaker looks not so easily this way as the other'. He served on the committee to prevent il-

legal exactions, again acted as teller against supply for the navy, and opposed the issue of passes by the Navy Office to secure British ships from the Barbary corsairs, believing that 'this granting passes is to set up a particular office for particular men'. On 5 Mar. he carried the Rushout naturalization bill to the Lords, and he was later called on to manage a conference on the general principles of naturalization. He helped to draw up three addresses for international action to preserve the Spanish Netherlands, speaking in favour of and acting as teller for a specific reference to the Dutch. He was by now unmistakably hawkish:

> Never was a better time than now to break with France; for in the end of the summer France will make a peace, and then we shall be much more unfit for war than now. He is for war.

He served on the committee for educating the royal children as Protestants, and to counter a possible Papal fifth column in the hierarchy proposed that all church dignitaries should marry, or else be incapable of their preferments. On 14 Apr. he acted as teller against the Lords amendments to the supply bill.[7]

The rapidity of developments on the Continent in the early months of 1678 caught the Opposition off balance. Harvey began by helping to draw up an address demanding that France be reduced to her frontiers of 1659; but he was against permitting Secretary Jenkins to read a list of allowances for general officers, and condemned as unsatisfactory the Dutch alliance which he had so persistently demanded in the previous year. Although active as a teller, he did not speak on these subjects, concentrating on a demand for economic sanctions against the aggressor. He spoke as a merchant, he said, though his name does not appear in the 1677 *Collection* and he had leased his London house to the excise commissioners: 'By suffering French commodities to come, in that abundance, we do maintain his army to fight against us to doomsday'. On the other hand, he would give the Government no compensation for the loss of customs revenue if French imports were forbidden. It must have been a relief for Harvey to help draw up the comparatively straightforward reasons for a conference on burying in woollen on 8 May. In the last session of the Cavalier Parliament, Harvey was appointed to the committees to inquire into the Popish Plot, to draw up reasons for a conference, and to prepare the impeachment of Lord Arundell of Wardour. During November he helped to draft five addresses, those for the publication of Coleman's letters, for the administration of the oaths to the servants of the Queen and the Duchess of York, for the trial of the Popish priests under arrest, for the offer of rewards to informers, and for the raising of the militia. On Secretary Williamson's dispensations to Popish officers he remarked: 'If ministers do at this rate, you must not only send one minister to the Tower, but all'. On 29 Nov. he was one of the Members ordered to prepare instructions for disbanding the army. An amusing incident followed: his Hempstead tenants, no doubt well aware of their landlord's redcoat bogey, sent him word that they were afraid to pay him their rents because of the soldiers quartered in the neighbourhood, whereupon Harvey, without obtaining the leave of the House, went down to collect them in person. Consequently on 11 Dec. he was ordered among others to be sent for in custody and not to be re-admitted without paying the serjeant's fees. He was sufficiently annoyed to separate himself temporarily from his usual cronies, and on 16 Dec. he found himself sitting on the government benches next to his kinsman Daniel Finch*. But his estrangement from the country party was brief; on 19 Dec. he acted as teller for the impeachment of Danby, and two days later he was assigned to the congenial task of drawing up reasons for a conference on disbanding the army.[8]

Harvey was returned for Essex unopposed with Henry Mildmay* at the first general election of 1679, and marked 'worthy' on Shaftesbury's list. He was an active Member of the first Exclusion Parliament, with 16 committees and seven speeches. He was one of the managers of the conference on Danby's impeachment on 4 Apr., and was named to the committee for security against Popery. On 14 May he spoke against the adjournment:

> We have new councillors, but I fear we have so many old ones that we are on the same bottom still. . . . What is become of all this money we gave? We cannot set out twenty ships, and so the nation is ruined and undone. . . . We have not made one step towards the security of the Protestant religion, nor is one Popish priest hanged. Therefore, I would not adjourn the debate.

He was one of the Members appointed to search out precedents for the trials of the lords in the Tower, and to draw up a reply to the proposals of the Upper House. Although Harvey, like Mildmay, voted for exclusion, at the following general election he was prevailed upon by the Duke of Albemarle (Christopher Monck*) to desert Mildmay and join his interest with the moderate Sir Thomas Middleton*. Harvey was a keen sportsman, and the inducement was probably a promise of the lieutenancy of Waltham forest. He was crushingly defeated at the poll, finishing last with only 669 votes, and had to take refuge at Old Sarum, where

his interest now rested on a firm property basis. 'He will hardly recover the good reputation he formerly had', commented one of Shaftesbury's henchmen; and indeed he was never again a county Member. But his record in the second Exclusion Parliament shows no change in his politics and little decrease in his activity; he was named to 13 committees and spoke four times. He seconded the motion for an inquiry into abhorring, and was appointed to the committee, and he was one of the Members ordered to draw up the address for the preservation of the Protestant religion. Still smarting from the journalists' treatment of the Essex election, he spoke in favour of sending for the printer who had libelled Sir Edward Dering*. He took a prominent part in connexion with the bill to exempt Protestant dissenters from the Penal Laws, carrying it to the Upper House on 26 Nov. 1680 and later conveying the concurrence of the Commons with the Lords' amendments. He served on the committee to prepare bills for security against arbitrary power. In the debate on the King's speech rejecting exclusion, it was reported:

> Sir Eliab Harvey can give no more money if this be all we shall have . . . No mention of the bill of religion, nor that of association . . . He has been nicked before, and would not be nicked now. We have had fair words, but never any deeds.

He was appointed to the committee to draw up the reply.[9]

Harvey was again returned for Old Sarum in 1681 and 1685. No further speeches are recorded, but at Oxford he was appointed to the committee of elections and privileges and to those to inspect the Journals relative to Danby's impeachment, to prepare for a conference about the mysterious disappearance of the toleration bill in the last Parliament and to draw up Fitzharris's impeachment. In James II's Parliament he was appointed to the committee for relief of London widows and orphans, and perhaps, as 'Mr Hervey' to two others. He was noted as in opposition in 1687, but the King's electoral agents gave conflicting reports on him. Under Old Sarum, they noted that he and (Sir) Thomas Mompesson* 'have always favoured dissenters and been for liberty'. But under Essex they reported that the Roman Catholics and most of the dissenters preferred (Sir) Josiah Child*, Harvey enjoying the support only of the Church and the Presbyterian party. It is not known whether he went to the poll for either constituency in 1689; he certainly petitioned with Mompesson against the Old Sarum return, but this may have been on behalf of his son William Harvey*. When he again appeared in the House after two further unsuccessful attempts for Essex, he acted with the Tories, like most of his family under William III, refusing the Association in 1696. He died on 20 Feb. 1699, and was buried at Hempstead.[10]

[1] *CJ*, ix. 99, 102. [2] *Misc. Gen. et Her.* (ser. 2), iii. 330–4. [3] Information from H. Horwitz; Hoare, *Wilts. Salisbury*, 477; *CSP Dom.* 1680–1, p. 310; Essex RO, QS Rolls 472/1/17. [4] *Cal. Comm. Adv. Money*, 138–40; Grey, v. 213; *HMC Hastings*, ii. 370; Aubrey, *Brief Lives*, i. 298; Guildhall Lib. mss 6428; *Dering*, 45. [5] *CJ*, ix. 252, 266, 281; *Dering*, 134, 139; *CSP Dom.* 1673, p. 475; Grey, ii. 202, 216, 243, 254; *Letters to Williamson* (Cam. Soc. n.s. ix), 157. [6] *Dering Pprs.* 64; Grey, iii. 104, 329, 388; ix. 9; *CJ*, ix. 322, 338, 341, 352, 374. [7] Grey, iv. 157, 315, 319, 364; *CJ*, ix. 389, 414, 421, 424. [8] Grey, v. 210, 213; vi. 219; *CJ*, ix. 439, 475, 500; Aubrey, i. 295; *Cal. Treas. Bks.* iv. 537; Finch mss, 11, 16 Dec. 1678. [9] Grey, vii. 275; viii. 435; *HMC 13th Rep. VI*, 19; *CSP Dom.* 1671, p. 73; *VCH Wilts.* vi. 201; Finch mss, 27 Oct. 1680; *HMC 12th Rep. IX*, 99. [10] *CJ*, ix. 708; x. 11; *Universal Intelligencer*, 10 Jan. 1689; *Misc. Gen. et Her.* (ser. 2), i. 384.

J.P.F.

HARVEY, Francis (1611–1703), of Weston Favell, Northants. and the Middle Temple.

NORTHAMPTON   1656, 1659, 29 Mar.–21 June 1660, 22 May–13 June 1661

bap. 20 Dec. 1611, 1st s. of William Harvey of Weston Favell by Mary, da. of Lawrence Ball of Northampton. *educ.* St. Edmund Hall, Oxf. 1627; M. Temple 1629, called 1637. *m.* (1) 21 Dec. 1637, Elizabeth (*d.* 8 Jan. 1643), da. of Richard Lane, attorney-gen. to the Prince of Wales, of Kingsthorpe, Northants., 1s. *d.v.p.*; (2) Mary, 3s. (2 *d.v.p.*), 2da.; (3) lic. 7 Apr. 1665, Elizabeth, wid. of John Dickens, Haberdasher, of Crutched Friars, London, *s.p. suc.* fa. 1634.[1]

Dep. recorder and alderman, Northampton by 1657–?June 1660; commr. for assessment, Northants. 1657, Jan. 1660, j.p. 1657–70; bencher, M. Temple 1658, reader 1663, treas. 1667–8; commr. for militia, Northants. Mar. 1660.[2]

Harvey's grandfather, the younger son of a Norfolk family, became a duchy of Lancaster official and had settled in Northamptonshire by 1568. Harvey was named after his uncle, MP for Aldeburgh in 1597 and later a judge, and like him entered the legal profession. His small estate was only two miles from Northampton, of which he was a deputy recorder at the time of the general election of 1660. He stood on the corporation interest, but was unseated on petition without leaving any trace on the records of the Convention. He was again involved in a disputed election in 1661. He was allowed to sit on the merits of the return, but the election was declared void three weeks later before he had been nominated to any committees. By this time he had probably surrendered his place to Richard Rainsford I* and he did not stand again, though he supported Christopher Hatton* at the 1663 election. He was doubtless a nonconformist sympathizer, for he was dropped from the commission of the peace after the second Conventicles Act. In later life, he got into serious financial difficulties, and was forced to sell his estate to William Thursby†, reserving only the advowson for his son. He seems to have subsisted on a pension from the Middle Temple. He was buried in the Temple Church on 30 Apr. 1703, aged 91. His son, grandson and great-grandson all took orders in the Established Church and enjoyed the family living, and none of his descendants entered Parliament.[3]

[1] Bridges, *Northants.* i. 75; *Pepys Diary*, ii. 330; PCC 132 Laud. [2] J. C. Cox, *Northampton Bor. Recs.* ii. 106. [3] Bridges, i. 74–76; Add. 29551, f. 12; J. Cole, *Hist. Weston Favell*, 28.

M.W.H./E.R.E.

HARVEY, Michael (c.1635–1712), of Clifton Maybank, Dorset.

WEYMOUTH AND   1679 (Mar.), 1679 (Oct.), 1681,
MELCOMBE REGIS   1689, 1690, 1695, 1698, 1701 (Feb.)

b. c.1635, 1st s. of Michael Harvey, merchant, of Bishopsgate, London by Mary, da. of John Mellish, merchant, of London; *educ.* G. Inn, entered 1650; Emmanuel, Camb. 1651; Padua 1656. *m.* (1) c.1662, Susan, da. of William Underwood, merchant, of London, *s.p.*; (2) 1 Sept. 1664, Agnes, da. of Thomas Yeoman, *s.p. suc.* fa. 1643.[1]

J.p. Dorset July 1660–70, June 1688–?*d.*, commr. for assessment Aug. 1660–80, 1689–90, sheriff 1672–3, dep. lt. May 1688–1702.

Harvey's father, who died in the early days of the Civil War, had been reckoned one of the richest inhabitants of his ward in 1640. On Harvey's behalf the Clifton Maybank estate was bought in 1650 for £11,288—a good bargain since it had changed hands at £28,000 only 16 years before. The dominant influence on his boyhood was probably his stepfather, William Steele†, who rose to be lord chancellor of Ireland during the Protectorate and to receive a summons to the Cromwellian Upper House. Harvey became, in contrast to his cousins, an Independent in religion, but he conformed at the Restoration, and it was through him that the nonconformist plot at Sherborne in 1662 was discovered. Measures against the plotters were largely in the hands of that redoubtable Anglican Giles Strangways*, who supported Harvey at the Weymouth by-election of 1667 as candidate of the country party, against the courtier Sir John Coventry, nephew to the chancellor of the Exchequer, Lord Ashley (Sir Anthony Ashley Cooper*). 'I am sure Mr. Harvey is a sober man, a godly religious person, and our own countryman', proclaimed another of his supporters. Their zeal and ingenuity, and some highly irregular proceedings on the part of the sheriff, appeared at one time to have assured his triumph. But his return was finally rejected by the House on 20 Nov. 1667. In 1669 Harvey was reported to be keeping a conventicle in his house, and in the next year he either resigned or was removed from the commission of the peace. But on the death of Strangways in 1675 he was mentioned as a possible contender for the county. This must be attributed to the prestige conferred by his occupation of Clifton Maybank, whose previous owners, the Horseys, had frequently sat for Dorset for over 200 years. Harvey stood down in favour of the court candidate, Lord Digby (John Digby*), a step which must have materially contributed to the overwhelming defeat of his fellow-dissenter, Thomas Moore*. Moore had been put foward by Ashley, now Lord Shaftesbury and leader of the country party, and presumably Harvey was thus obtaining revenge for his defeat at Weymouth eight years before.[2]

But it was probably at least with the assent of Shaftesbury, who now described him as 'honest', that Harvey at last entered Parliament for Weymouth at the general election of February 1679. One of Lord Wharton's Presbyterian correspondents about this time calls him a 'fanatic'. He voted for exclusion, but was appointed only to the committee on the state of the navy in the first Exclusion Parliament. Shortly before its successor met he entertained the Duke of Monmouth at Clifton Maybank, thereby renewing an old family connexion, for Harvey's grandmother had given shelter to Lucy Walter in her house in Rotterdam shortly after the Duke's birth. Although he left no trace on the records of the next two Parliaments, he was now doubly a marked man, for his political as well as his religious connexions. At the Lent assizes of 1684 he was presented as disaffected, but refused to give security.[3]

Harvey was defeated at the general election of 1685, and his petition was never heard. When his former guest landed at Lyme, Harvey was at once arrested, though there is no evidence that he had any contact with the exiles. While he was under arrest, his brother and heir was on duty with the militia, and died of wounds received in a skirmish at Bridport. Harvey was soon released on giving 'assurance for dutiful and good behaviour'.[4]

Harvey was restored to the commission and made a deputy lieutenant in May 1688, when James II was gathering support from the dissenters. The government electoral agents reported that he had joined with Thomas Freke I* as candidate for Dorset, and they had 'so great interest that it is not to be supposed they can oppose them'. But by September he had fallen back on Weymouth, where he hoped also to bring in his cousin William Harvey*, both of them being described as 'right'. In this he failed, but he was able to regain his own seat, unlike most of the court candidates of 1688. An inactive Member of the Convention, Harvey probably served on nine committees, including those for the mutiny and corporation bills in the first session. His name appears on neither of the division lists, and he made no speeches. Harvey continued to sit for most of William III's reign and generally voted with the country party, though he did not refuse the Association in 1696. He died on 19 Feb. 1712, aged 77, and was buried at Bradford Abbas. His cousin Edward Harvey* succeeded to the estate.[5]

[1] *Misc. Gen. et Her.* (ser. 2), iii. 331, 362. [2] *Misc. Gen. et Her.* (ser. 2), ii. 37; *Cal. Comm. Adv. Money*, 138–40, 603; Eg. 784, f. 103; *Som. and Dorset N. and Q.* xxviii. 288–90; V. Pearl, *London and the Outbreak of the Puritan Revolution*, 150; SP29/61, ff. 91, 97; Hutchins, *Dorset*, ii. 435–6; *CSP Dom.* 1666–7, p. 473; 1675–6, p. 232; *CJ*, ix. 23; G. L. Turner, *Early Nonconformity*, i. 124. [3] D. R. Lacey, *Dissent and Parl. Pols.* 409; *Hist. and Biog. Tracts* ed. Smeeton, i. 2, 32; R. Morrice, *Entering Bk.* 1, p. 434. [4] *CJ*, ix. 718; *CSP Dom.* 1685, pp. 178, 281. [5] Hutchins, iv. 123.

J.P.F.

HARVEY, William (1663–1731), of Hempstead, Essex.

OLD SARUM	25 Mar. 1689, 1690, 1695, 1698, 1701 (Feb.), 1701 (Dec.), 1702
APPLEBY	1705
OLD SARUM	1708
WEYMOUTH AND MELCOMBE REGIS	18 Apr. 1711, 3 June 1714
ESSEX	31 May 1715–18 May 1716, 1722

bap. 18 Dec. 1663, 2nd but o. surv. s. of Sir Eliab Harvey*, and bro. of Eliab Harvey*. *educ.* St. Paul's sch.; Trinity Coll. Camb. 1680. *m.* 1 Sept. 1681, his bro.'s wid. Dorothy, da. of Sir Robert Dycer, 2nd Bt., of Hackney, Mdx., and h. to her bro. Sir Robert, 3rd Bt., 3s. (2 d.v.p.) 3da. *suc.* fa. 1699.

Commr. for assessment, Essex 1689–90, Wilts. 1690; lt. Waltham forest by 1700–*d.*; j.p. Essex by 1701–?*d.*, dep. lt. 1703–?*d.*

Harvey was approved, with his cousin Michael Harvey*, as court candidate for Weymouth in 1688. He was returned to the Convention for Old Sarum on his father's interest after a previous election had been declared void. He made no speeches and was clearly inactive as a committeeman, though his record cannot be distinguished from his cousin's. He did not support the disabling clause in the bill to restore corporations. He refused the Association in 1696, and was regarded as a Jacobite under the Hanoverians. He died on 31 Oct. 1731 and was buried at Hempstead. His son William had sat for Old Sarum from 1710 to 1713, while his grandson represented Essex as a Tory in three Parliaments.

Misc. Gen. et Her. (ser. 2), iii. 334; *Cal. Treas. Bks.* xvii. 107.

J.P.F.

HATCHER, John (1634–78), of Careby, Lincs.

STAMFORD   1660

bap. 23 Jan. 1634, o.s. of Thomas Hatcher*. *m.* 8 Apr. 1656, Elizabeth, da. of Sir Richard Anderson of Pendley, Herts., 4s. 4da. *suc.* fa. 1677.[1]
    Commr. for sewers, Lincs. 1659, Aug. 1660, assessment, Jan. 1660, 1661–3, 1664–d., (Kesteven) Aug. 1660–1, 1663–4, militia, Lincs. Mar. 1660; j.p. Lincs. (Kesteven) Mar. 1660–76; capt. of militia horse, Lincs. Apr. 1660, commr. for sewers, Aug. 1660, recusants 1675, sheriff 1676–7.[2]

Hatcher was too young to take any part in the Civil War and he first held local office in 1659. A Presbyterian like his father, he was returned for Stamford, five miles from his home, at the contested general election of 1660, and classed by Lord Wharton as a friend. An inactive Member of the Convention, 'Mr Hatcher' was named to only four committees, including those for the indemnity bill and the poll tax. He may have stood in 1661, and must have conformed to the Church of England. He acquired a useful connexion with the Court through Joseph Williamson*, to whom he offered a share in a local land purchase. Between 1665 and 1669 he received a weekly newsletter from Williamson and on three occasions asked him to help kinsmen of his to employment. After his removal from the commission of the peace in June 1676 on the complaint of Lord Lindsey (Robert Bertie I*), he wrote to Williamson:

> Last post I had notice of my being in the bill of sheriffs for this county, an office I had thought myself very secure from, since I have not been thought worthy to be in the commission of the peace, but when I consider how I have been treated in other matters, it does not seem so strange to me that I am put on this office or anything else that may be burdensome or chargeable to me. But my request is now to you, not as formerly to keep me off from being sheriff, but on the contrary to promote my being on, for, we being in our county, as in several others, under an agreement for sheriffs, I can defray the charge for £500 less than I could, were that agreement set aside. Another motive why I rather desire this office now is that having been engaged at Stamford for a burgesship there, which I find will be very chargeable, I could being made sheriff give over

prosecution of it, with a *salvo honore*. I should not presume to have requested your favour, did I not think it less trouble to you to make me sheriff than to keep me off.

He was duly made sheriff a few days later, but cast aside constitutional niceties, not only fighting the Stamford election but petitioning unsuccessfully against the result. He did not long survive his father, and was buried on 1 Jan. 1679 at Careby. No later member of the family entered Parliament.[3]

[1] *Lincs. Peds.* (Harl. Soc. li), 469; *Herts. Par. Reg.* ii. 65. [2] *Merc. Pub.* 19 Apr. 1660. [3] *CSP Dom.* 1664–5, pp. 41, 48, 419; 1665–6, pp. 50, 544; 1668–9, p. 198; 1676–7, p. 406; *HMC Finch*, ii. 44.

M.W.H./P.W.

HATCHER, Thomas (c.1589–1677), of Careby, Lincs.

LINCOLN	1624
GRANTHAM	1628
STAMFORD	1640 (Apr.), 1640 (Nov.)[1]
LINCOLNSHIRE	1654, 1656, 1659
BOSTON	1660

b. c.1589, 1st s. of Sir John Hatcher of Careby by Anne, da. of James Crewes of Fotheringay, Northants. *educ.* Emmanuel, Camb. 1603; L. Inn 1607. *m.* 14 Oct. 1617, Katherine, da. of William Ayscough of South Kelsey, Lincs., 1s. 1da. *suc.* fa. 1640.[2]
    J.p. Lincs. (Kesteven) c.1634–50, 1656–62, (Holland) 1656–July 1660; commr. for militia, Lincs. 1642, 1648, Mar. 1660, sequestration 1643, levying of money 1643, defence, eastern association 1643, assessment, Lincs. 1644–5, (Lindsey and Kesteven) 1647, Aug. 1660–1, (Lindsey) 1648, Lincs. 1649, 1657, Jan. 1660, 1661–3, 1664–d., new model ordinance 1645, oyer and terminer, Midland circuit July 1660.
    Capt. of horse (parliamentary) 1642, col. by 1645; gov. Lincoln 1644–5.[3]
    Commr. for Scotland 1643–6, exclusion from sacrament 1646, compounding 1647–8, scandalous offences 1648, Admiralty 1648.

Hatcher's great-grandfather, regius professor of physic and vice-chancellor of Cambridge University, acquired the manor of Careby and settled in Lincolnshire. He was himself the first member of his family to enter Parliament. A Puritan by religion, he was in opposition in the Parliaments of 1624 and 1628, and an active Parliamentarian in the Civil War. Though he abstained from the House after Pride's Purge, he sat in the Protectorate Parliaments, and did not return with the secluded Members in February 1660. He was defeated at the general election for the county, but Sir Anthony Irby* found him a seat at Boston. He was named as a manager in Lord Wharton's list of friends, although only a few Members are assigned to him and those mostly his kinsmen. An inactive Member, he made no recorded speeches and as 'Colonel Hatcher' he was appointed to only ten committees. He helped to draft the proclamation ordering officers of justice to perform their duties, and was appointed to the committees for the continuation of judicial proceedings and confirmation of the privileges of · Parliament. He was one of the commissioners deputed to administer the oaths of allegiance and supremacy to Members on 4 June. He was appointed to the committees to consider the petition from the intruded dons at Oxford and the estate bill of (Sir) William Wray*. Wharton sent him a copy of the case for modified episcopacy; but he apparently remained a rigid Presbyterian and was removed from the commission of the peace. He was buried at Careby on 11 July 1677.[4]

[1] Abstained after Pride's Purge, 6 Dec. 1648. [2] *Lincs. Peds.* (Harl. Soc. li), 469. [3] E. Peacock, *Army Lists*, 53; *CSP Dom.* 1644–5, p. 58; J. W. F. Hill, *Tudor and Stuart Lincoln*, 159. [4] Keeler, *Long Parl.* 208; *CSP Dom.* 1641–3, p. 475; 1644–5, p. 395; 1645–7, p. 16.

M.W.H./P.W.

HATTON, Hon. Christopher (1632–1706), of Kirby Hall, Northants.

NORTHAMPTON   9 Apr. 1663–4 July 1670

bap. 6 Nov. 1632, 1st s. of Christopher Hatton,[†] 1st Baron Hatton of Kirby by Elizabeth, da. and coh. of Sir Charles Montagu[†] of Cranbrook, Ilford, Essex. *educ.* privately (Dr Peter Gunning); travelled abroad (France) 1654. *m.* (1) 12 Feb. 1667, Lady Cicely Tufton (*d.* 30 Dec. 1672), da. of John, 2nd Earl of Thanet, 3da.; (2) by 27 Dec. 1675, Frances (*d.* 15 May 1684), da. of Sir Henry Yelverton, 2nd Bt.*, of Easton Maudit, Northants., 1s. *d.v.p.* 1da.; (3) Aug. 1685, Elizabeth, da. and coh. of Sir William Haslewood of Maidwell, Northants., 3s. 3da. *suc.* fa. as 2nd Baron Hatton 4 July 1670; *cr.* Visct. Hatton of Gretton 17 Jan. 1683.[1]

Steward of Higham hundred, Northants. Sept. 1660–97, 1702–*d.*; commr. for oyer and terminer, Midland circuit 1662, assessment, Mdx. and Northants. 1663–9; j.p. Northants. 1663–*d.*, dep. lt. 1670–?78, custos rot. 1681–Feb. 1689, Sept. 1689–*d.*; freeman, Portsmouth 1680.[2]

Gent. of privy chamber 1662–?70; gov. Guernsey 1670–*d.*[3]

Capt. Earl of Manchester's Ft. 1667; capt. of grenadiers, Earl of Huntingdon's Ft. 1687–Dec. 1688.[4]

Hatton came from a Cheshire family, established in Northamptonshire since the reign of Henry VIII, of which the most celebrated member was Queen Elizabeth's favourite. His father, a leading Royalist, was in exile for most of the Interregnum. Hatton himself was deep in Cavalier plotting in 1654, and the principal agent in bringing over his cousin Edward Montagu I* to the Stuarts. He received an express command from the King to

stand at the general election of 1660, but shrank from the penalties provided for Cavaliers and their sons by the last ordinance of the Long Parliament. But he stood at the invitation of Sir James Langham* and with the support of the dissenters at a by-election for Northampton in 1663, and was returned on petition. He was not an active Member, being appointed to only 27 committees in the Cavalier Parliament, mostly for private bills. Both in 1664 and 1669, he was noted as a court dependant, having been granted the governorship of Guernsey in reversion to his father, for whom he sometimes acted in his lifetime. He was regarded as one of Ormonde's friends. After succeeding to the peerage and a Northamptonshire estate valued at £1,370 p.a., he was given a pension of £1,000 p.a., necessitated by his father's extravagance. He took little further part in English politics, but he voted against exclusion and was rewarded with a step in the peerage. In 1687 he was numbered among the opponents of James II, but he seems to have played no part in the Revolution. He was one of the last peers to sign the Association in 1696. His death was reported on 24 Sept. 1706. Two of his sons succeeded to the peerage in turn, but he was the last of the family to sit in the Lower House.[5]

[1] E. A. Webb, *Recs. of St. Bartholomew Smithfield*, ii. 275; *HMC Bath*, ii. 81; *Nicholas Pprs.* (Cam. Soc. n.s.l), 89; *CSP Dom.* 1682, p. 568. [2] Sir Robert Somerville, *Duchy of Lancaster Official Lists*, 192; *HMC 5th Rep.* 188; *CSP Dom.* 1689–90, pp. 46, 268; R. East. *Portsmouth Recs.* 364. [3] Carlisle, *Privy Chamber*, 173. [4] *Hatton Corresp.* (Cam. Soc. n.s. xxiii), 89–90; Add. 29563, f. 353. [5] Baker, *Northants.* i. 194; *Nicholas Pprs.* 99, 153; Underdown, *Royalist Conspiracy*, 311; *Cal. Cl. SP*, iv. 589, 594, 651, 665; Add. 29551, ff. 8, 12; Add. 34222, f. 38v; *CJ*, x. 107; *HMC Lords*, n.s. ii. 213; Luttrell, vi. 90.

E.R.E.

HATTON, Sir Thomas, 2nd Bt. (1637–82), of Long Stanton, Cambs.

CAMBRIDGESHIRE   15 Jan. 1674

b. June 1637, 1st s. of Sir Thomas Hatton, 1st Bt.[†], of Long Stanton, and Gray's Inn, London by Mary, da. of Sir Giles Alington of Horseheath. *m.* c.1659, Bridget, da. of Sir William Goring, 1st Bt.[†], of Burton, Suss., 2s. 4da. *suc.* fa. 23 Sept. 1658.[1]

J.p. Cambs. July 1660–*d.*, commr. for assessment Aug. 1660–80; sheriff, Cambs. and Hunts. 1662–3; commr. for corporations, Cambs. 1662–3, pontage, Cambridge 1663, 1673, recusants, Cambs. 1675, dep. lt. 1681–*d.*[2]

Hatton's grandfather was the first of the family to reside at Long Stanton. His father, a younger brother of the 1st Lord Hatton, was imprisoned at Cambridge as a Royalist from the outset of the Civil War. He paid no taxes to the county committee except under compulsion and steadfastly refused to take the Covenant, but he could not be fined or sequestrated, and he was certainly not short of money during the Interregnum. Hatton crossed over to Flushing on the eve of the Restoration with Sir Richard Mauleverer*, but apparently returned empty-handed from the exiled Court. Little is known of him till 1674, when he narrowly defeated Gerard Russell* in a three-cornered contest for the county. He was expected, under the influence of (Sir) Thomas Chicheley*, to support the Court. In 1676, however, Sir Richard Wiseman* noted that Hatton had 'voted ill last session'; but he had 'good hopes' of him. These hopes were fully justified, for next year Shaftesbury marked him 'doubly vile', and in *A Seasonable Argument* he was attacked as 'a man of no estate but his pension'. No pension, however, can be traced, and Long Stanton remained in the family till the baronetcy became extinct in 1812. His name appeared on both lists of the court party in 1678. But he was appointed to only seven committees in the Cavalier Parliament, none of which was of any political importance, and was sent for as a defaulter in December. He was buried at Long Stanton on 19 Apr. 1682, the last of his family to sit in Parliament.[3]

[1] PCC 187 Pell; *Verney Mems.* ii. 65. [2] *Camb. Antiq. Soc. Procs.* xvii. 105; C. H. Cooper, *Annals of Cambridge*, iii. 513, 557. [3] Lysons, *Cambs.* 256; Aubrey, *Brief Lives*, ii. 284; *Cal. Comm. Adv. Money*, 322; *Cal. Comm. Comp.* 1352, 1869; *Pepys Diary*, 27 Apr. 1660.

E.R.E.

HAWARDE (HAYWARD), Sir William (c.1617–1704), of Tandridge Hall, Surr.

BLETCHINGLEY 1661

b. c.1617, 3rd s. of John Hawarde[†] (*d.*1631) of the Inner Temple and Tandridge, being 1st s. by 2nd w. Elizabeth, da. of William Angell, Fishmonger, of London, wid. of William Watts of the Middle Temple. *educ.* I. Temple 1635. *m.* 4 Sept. 1643 (with £1,250) Martha (*d.*1689), da. of John Acton, Goldsmith, of London and Elmley Lovett, Worcs., 4s. (1 *d.v.p.*) 6da. Kntd. 9 Sept. 1643.[1]

Gent. of the privy chamber 1641–6, June 1660–1702; trustee for sale of fee-farm rents 1670–3.[2]

J.p. Surr. July 1660–at least 1685, commr. for assessment Aug. 1660–80, corporations 1662–3, loyal and indigent officers 1662, oyer and terminer, Home circuit 1665, inquiry, Richmond Park 1671, rebuilding of Southwark 1677.[3]

Capt. Duke of Richmond's Horse 1666–7.

FRS 1665.

Hawarde's grandfather, a London Fishmonger, began acquiring property in and around Tandridge early in the reign of Elizabeth. His father, a lawyer, represented Bletchingley, four miles away, in the last two Parliaments of James I. Hawarde bought out his elder half-brother just before the Civil War, and became master of an estate of £600 p.a., including some of the burgages. As a courtier, he attended the King at Oxford and gave financial assistance, but was never in arms. He was fined £437 14s. at the rate of one-sixth, and remained under suspicion during the Interregnum. Later he claimed to have lost £10,000 by his loyalty.[4]

Hawarde was returned for Bletchingley in 1661 at the top of the poll. He was a moderately active Member of the Cavalier Parliament, in which he was appointed to about 70 committees, including those for the uniformity bill and the additional corporations bill. He was listed as a court dependant in 1664, and appointed to the committees for the five mile bill in 1665 and the continuance of the Conventicles Act in 1669. He was regarded as one of Ormonde's friends at this time, and included in the opposition list of court supporters. In *A Seasonable Argument* he was described as 'a commissioner in the sale of the fee-farm rents, by which he got £2,000; a privy chamber man, and a grant of £2,000 in money'. He was appointed to the committee to consider the claim of privilege brought by Sir Thomas Byde* against the board of green cloth in 1674. His name appeared on the Paston list, the working lists, and the list of government supporters prepared by Sir Richard Wiseman* at the end of the following year, and Shaftesbury marked him 'thrice vile'. Dugdale, his successful rival for appointment as Garter King of Arms in 1677, described him as 'a person well accomplished with learning, especially in honour and arms'. He was probably a strong churchman, acting as teller on the third reading of the bill to provide for the better repair of churches. He was on both lists of the court party in 1678, and was teller against the sixth paragraph of the address for the removal of evil counsellors on 10 May. He claimed never to have received a penny for 30 years in the service of the crown, and to be 'threatened with ruin on the rising of this Parliament'. He sold his estate in 1681 in exchange for an interest in the Broken Wharf waterworks, which he expected to bring in £300 p.a. He was buried at St. James, Piccadilly on 28 July 1704. Nothing is known of his descendants.[4]

[1] *Vis. Surr.* (Harl. Soc. lx), 58; *Vis. London* (Harl. Soc. xv), 4. [2] Carlisle, *Privy Chamber*, 144, 167, 197, 204; *Cal. Treas. Bks.* iii. 680; xviii. 27. [3] Manning and Bray, *Surr.* i. 36; *Cal. Treas. Bks.* iii. 1161. [4] W. P. Baildon, *Hawardes of Tandridge*, passim; *Cal. Comm. Comp.* 1238; *Surr. Arch. Colls.* xiv. 187; *CSP Dom.* 1671–2, p. 54. [5] *Life of Dugdale*, 32; *CJ*, ix. 417; *CSP Dom.* 1671–2, p. 54; U. Lambert, *Bletchingley*, i. 215; *HMC Lords*, iv. 323–5; Westminster City Lib. St. James Piccadilly par. reg.

J.S.C.

HAWLES, John (c.1645–1716), of Lincoln's Inn.

OLD SARUM	25 Mar. 1689
WILTON	1695
MITCHELL and BERE ALSTON	1698
TRURO	4 Mar. 1701
ST. IVES	1701 (Dec.)
WILTON	1702
STOCKBRIDGE	1705, 1708

b. c.1645, 2nd s. of Thomas Hawles of The Close, Salisbury, Wilts. by Elizabeth, da. and h. of Thomas Antrobus of Heath House, Petersfield, Hants. *educ.* Winchester; Queen's, Oxf. matric. 1662, aged 17; L. Inn 1664, called 1670. *unm.*; 1s. illegit. Kntd. 28 Nov. 1695.[1]

Commr. for assessment, L. Inn and Wilts. 1690; bencher, L. Inn 1692, treas. 1695.

KC 1694; solicitor-gen. 1695–1702; chairman, committee of elections and privileges 1695–6.[2]

Hawles's family moved from the Isle of Wight to Salisbury about the middle of the 16th century, and soon afterwards acquired an estate in Dorset. His father and his uncle were the leaders of the neutralist Clubmen in Wiltshire and Dorset respectively in 1645, while another uncle served as chaplain to the 5th Earl of Pembroke, becoming canon of Windsor at the Restoration. His father appears to have been active in the Old Sarum election of 1661, probably with the purely negative aim of preventing John Norden* from attaining parliamentary privilege. By 1672 the family was in embarrassed circumstances, and owed much to the friendship of John Wildman I*.[3]

Hawles, a professional lawyer, soon became known to Aubrey as 'an exceeding ingenious young gentleman', and made his name familiar to a wider public with his *Remarks upon the Trials of Edward Fitzharris*, which appeared in March 1689, and in the same month he was elected for Old Sarum, probably on the Pembroke interest. 'A great Williamite', he became a very active Member of the Convention, with 44 committees and 50 recorded speeches. In addition he was eight times given leave to attend the Lords as counsel. Although he can only just have taken his seat, he was probably the 'Mr Hales' who, on 28 Mar. 1689, was teller for adhering to the Commons' resolutions on the removal of Papists. He was among the Members appointed to draw up reasons for a conference on the oaths of supremacy and allegiance on 19 Apr. In his maiden speech on 8 May he opposed the proviso to the bill of settlement to preserve the rights of Protestant princes. He was in favour of suspending habeas corpus. He was twice appointed to inspect the Lords' Journals for entries concerning the

Popish Plot and the conviction of Titus Oates, which he described as 'the worst judgment ever given in law'. In the case of the Jacobite propagandists, he spoke in favour of impeachment rather than trial by common law, and was named to the committee. 'I do not think this to be a plain case of treason by 25 Edward III. I do say, no court can judge this offence to be treason; and that statute did plainly not bind the superior court of Parliament, but the inferior only.' On the indemnity bill he disclaimed any personal grievance, but asserted: 'If you go about to please those who have offended, you will anger twenty more that are injured'. He helped to draw up reasons for five more conferences in July and August, those on the Oates conviction, the bill of rights, the customs bill, the attainder bill and the bill for recovery of tithes. With Paul Foley* he was ordered to take care of the bill for security against Papists; he chaired the committee and carried the bill to the Lords.[4]

In the second session Hawles and Thomas Lee I* were given special responsibility for bringing in a bill to regulate imprisonment. He was appointed to the committees for the more effectual tendering of the oaths and to inquire into the miscarriages of the war. He spoke in favour of the address to inquire about the appointment of Commissary Shales, and helped to draw it up:

> We must make use of extraordinary means. If by a precedent we must find out unprecedented things, we shall never do it. If King James II was to come in again, he could not make a better choice of some persons in employment. The King is a stranger to us; councils have recommended persons who did it. It must be in the dark, and this is the best way to discover him and other persons.

He was appointed to the committees for the revenue and for discoveries of treason. Hawles does not seem to have worried about consistency of thought; on 21 Dec., in one and the same speech, he said: 'If there had been a reconciliation betwixt King James and the Prince of Orange, what would have become of the people? . . . When the Prince of Orange came in, they were for a regency, and that is a commonwealth.' He was again ordered to bring in the imprisonment bill on 31 Dec., and with Sir Thomas Littleton* to bring in a bill imposing the oath of allegiance on 9 Jan. 1690, to the committee for which he was later appointed. He is not recorded as speaking in the debates on the bill to restore corporations, although he supported the disabling clause. Probably he was reserving himself for a great effort against (Sir) Robert Sawyer* at whom he had been sniping intermittently ever since he had taken his seat:

Some say I encouraged this matter, and I have had hard words given me for it. As for Burton and [Richard] Grahme*, they only brought [Sir Thomas] Armstrong* up, etc.; but for an attorney-general, when he has that office, how comes it to pass that he must leave all rules of common honesty? I wish this gentleman had been as nice in spilling blood as we are in punishing it.

Hawles lost his seat at the general election, but was made KC to take part in the prosecution of the Lancashire Jacobites, and solicitor-general in 1695 while still out of the House. He was dismissed on the accession of Anne, remaining a Whig. His last public action was to assist in the prosecution of Dr Sacheverell. He inherited the family estates in Wiltshire and Dorset and died on 2 Aug. 1716, leaving no legitimate heir.[5]

[1] Hoare, *Wilts.* Salisbury, 402; Aubrey, *Brief Lives*, i. 305; *Antrobus Peds.* 11. [2] Luttrell, iii. 362. [3] Hutchins, *Dorset*, iii. 388-9; A. B. Bayley, *Civil War in Dorset* 262; Add. 34015, p. 105; S. S. Ollard, *Deans and Canons of Windsor*, 121; Bath mss, Thynne pprs. 10, f. 73, Hawles to Thynne, 9 Mar. 1661; C7/36/17. [4] Wood, *Athenae*, iv. 528-9; Grey, ix. 241, 267, 290, 305, 319; *CJ*, x. 252, 266, 267. [5] *CJ*, x. 276, 320, 328; Grey, ix. 330, 455, 507, 523, 534.

J.P.F.

HAWLEY, Francis, 1st Baron Hawley of Duncannon [I] (1608-84), of Buckland Sororum, Som. and Scotland Yard, Westminster.

MITCHELL   7 Dec. 1665

b. 14 Jan. 1608, 2nd s. of Sir Henry Hawley of Wiveliscombe by Elizabeth, da. of Sir Anthony Poulett of Hinton St. George. *m.* bef. 1646, Jane, da. of Sir Ralph Gibbs of Honington, Warws., 2s. *d.v.p. suc.* bro. 1624; *cr.* Bt. 14 Mar. 1644; Baron Hawley of Duncannon [I] 8 July 1645.[1]

Commr. of array, Som. 1642, j.p. 1643-6, July 1660-d.; commr. for sewers, Aug., Dec. 1660, assessment Aug. 1660-80, steward of crown manors Aug. 1660-75; freeman, Bath 1661, Portsmouth 1668; commr. for loyal and indigent officers, Som. and Bristol 1662; dep lt. Som. 1662-d.; recorder, Bath 1662-9; asst. R. Adventurers to Africa 1668, 1671, R. Africa Co. 1672-d.; steward, Artillery Co., London 1673; member, R. Fishing Co. 1677.[2]

Col. of horse (royalist) 1642-5, June-Nov. 1660; dep. gov. Bristol 1643-4; capt. R. Horse Gds. (The Blues) 1661-76; gov. Deal Castle 1672-4.[3]

Gent. of the bedchamber to the Duke of York by 1669-d.; trustee for fee-farm rents 1670-3; commr. for prizes 1672-4.[4]

Hawley's ancestors removed to Somerset in the reign of Henry VIII. His grandfather sat for Corfe Castle in three Elizabethan Parliaments as a servant of Lord Keeper Hatton. Hawley raised a troop of horse for the King in Somerset in 1642 and served, in his own words, as 'an officer of quality' under Rupert. He obtained the Speaker's licence to go into exile with the Prince in October 1645, and compounded for his estates in 1647. His fine, originally

set at £857, was reduced to £250 on his settling an annuity of £50 on the church. He seems to have intended to take part in the second Civil War, and was still abroad in 1650, after which nothing more is heard of him till 1660.[5]

Hawley was made colonel of a Cromwellian cavalry regiment at the Restoration, despite protests from the soldiers, until its disbandment. At the time of the Fifth Monarchist rising in 1661, he 'told the King that the better he was guarded, the more his enemies would fear him and his friends love him'. This support of a standing army, in opposition to the views of Clarendon and Southampton, earned him not only a commission in The Blues, but the esteem of the Duke of York, who reported the remark and then or later took him into his household. He was active in suppressing conventicles in Yorkshire, and was sufficiently prosperous to advance £1,600 to the King for his personal use in 1662-4.[6]

On the death of Sir John Stawell* Hawley announced his intention of standing for the county, but 'laid down the cudgels' owing to lack of support. He was, however, returned for Mitchell in November 1665, probably on the recommendation of the sitting Member, Matthew Wren*, though he was recalled for military duty while on his way to attend the election. An inactive Member of the Cavalier Parliament, he was appointed to 26 committees and acted as teller in five divisions, the first being against a proposal on 7 Dec. 1666 to enable public accounts to be taken on oath. In March 1670 he was among those ordered to consider the Lords' bill appointing commissioners for union with Scotland, the conventicles bill, and the bill to advance the sale of fee-farm rents. In his only recorded speech, on 1 Dec., he proposed a land-tax at the usual rate of £70,000 a month, of which he hoped to be appointed receiver for Gloucestershire and Somerset. After the Christmas recess he was teller against imposing double taxation on absentee Members and against appropriating the additional excise to paying off the existing debt. He was appointed to the committees on the bills to transfer the Cornish assizes from Launceston to Bodmin and to vest the fee-farm rents in trustees. He had already been appointed a trustee, at a salary of £400 p.a., and later received bounties of £1,200 for his services. He was included in both lists of the court party at this time as a dependant of the Duke of York, under whom he served, together with Wren, in the fleet during the third Dutch war. In the spring session of 1673 he was appointed to the committee for the Tone and Parret navigation bill, in which he was nominated a commissioner, and in the autumn he was teller against the motion for an address to remonstrate against the Duke's second marriage to a Roman Catholic. He was named on the Paston list and the list of officials in 1675, and appointed in both sessions to the bill to prevent the growth of Popery. Increasing infirmity compelled his surrender of the stewardship of the crown manors in Somerset and his army commission. But he continued to attend the House, and was one of the three Cornish Members in 1676 of whom Danby, in the opinion of Sir Richard Wiseman*, could be well assured. Shaftesbury marked him 'thrice vile', while the author of *A Seasonable Argument* described him as 'a court buffoon, [who] has got in boons £20,000'. He was on both lists of the court party in 1678, and is unlikely to have stood for the Exclusion Parliaments. At his death on 22 Dec. 1684 he was said to have been for some time bedridden. His grandson, the second baron, inherited property in Dorset, Devon and Berkshire as well as Somerset, and was returned for Bramber in 1713.[7]

[1] *Sale of Wards* (Som. Rec. Soc. lxvii), 24. [2] *CSP Dom.* 1660–1, p. 214; 1661–2, p. 511; 1663–4, p. 264; *Cal. Treas. Bks.* iv. 703; Bath council bk. 2, pp. 292, 491; R. East, *Portsmouth Recs.* 359. [3] *Bellum Civile* (Som. Rec. Soc. xviii), 19, 33; *Cal. Comm. Comp.* 1523; *Cal. Treas. Bks.* i. 66; iii. 1278; iv. 548. [4] *Cal. Treas. Bks.* ii. 414, 732. [5] *Vis. Som.* ed. Weaver, 113; Clarendon, *Rebellion,* ii. 297; *Cal. Cl. SP,* i. 285; *Cal. Comm. Comp.* 1523–4; *HMC 4th Rep.* 275; *CSP Dom.* 1650, p. 282. [6] *HMC 5th Rep.* 194; Clarke, *Jas. II,* i. 391; *CSP Dom.* 1663–4, pp. 468, 586; *Cal Treas. Bks.* i. 400, 581, 661. [7] Bristol RO, AC/C76–79; *CSP Dom.* 1665–6, p. 74; 1672, pp. 47, 428; 1676–7, p. 476; Grey, i. 315; *CJ,* ix. 203, 210, 284; *HMC 9th Rep.* pt. 2, p. 25; *Cal. Treas. Bks.* iii. 1164, 1210, 1347; iv. 703, 731; v. 820; PCC 5 Cann.

E.C.

HAWTREY, Ralph (c.1626–1725), of Eastcote House, Ruislip, Mdx.

MIDDLESEX 1685, 1689, 1690

> *b.* c.1626, 1st s. of John Hawtrey of Ruislip by Susannah, da. and coh. of Jacob James of London. *educ.* G. Inn, entered 1631. *m.* c.1650, Barbara, da. of Sir Robert de Grey of Merton, Norf., 6s. *d.v.p.* 4da. *suc.* fa. 1658.[1]
>
> J.p. Mdx. 1658–Feb. 1688, Sept. 1688–96, 1700–?*d.*, commr. for militia Mar. 1660, assessment Aug. 1660–80, 1689–90, oyer and terminer Nov. 1660, dep. lt. 1670–Jan. 1688, 1692–6, 1701–?*d.*, commr. for recusants 1675.[2]

Hawtrey came from a cadet branch of a family which acquired the Chequers estate in the reign of Edward I and represented Buckinghamshire in 1563. His father took no active part in the Civil War, but served on various Middlesex commissions during the Commonwealth and Protectorate. Hawtrey, however, became a Tory. He was foreman of the jury which acquitted Sir George Wakeman in July 1679, and intended to stand for the county in

the following month, but desisted on threats of being 'hissed out of the field', or worse. He was successful in 1685 and became an active Member of James II's Parliament. He was appointed to ten committees, including those to recommend the continuance of expiring laws, to estimate the yield of a tax on new buildings, and to consider a bill for the relief of poor debtors.[3]

Hawtrey presumably opposed the repeal of the Tests and Penal Laws, since he was removed from local office early in 1688. At the general election of 1689 he stood successfully with Sir Charles Gerard* against the Whigs Sir Robert Peyton* and William Johnson*. He was moderately active in the Convention, in which he was appointed to 15 committees. He voted to agree with the Lords that the throne was not vacant. He again helped to estimate the yield of new taxes, and was among those appointed to draft a clause in the additional excise bill. He was added to the committee to inquire into the delay in relieving Londonderry. In the second session he was named to the committees to restrain election expenses and to inquire into the miscarriages and the expenses of the war. He refused the Association in 1696, and died, the last of the Ruislip branch, on 5 Dec. 1725 'in the hundredth year of his age'.[4]

[1] F. W. Hawtrey, *Hawtrey Fam.* 42, 82–84; *Mdx. Peds.* (Harl. Soc. lxv), 4. [2] *CSP Dom.* 1691–2, p. 212; Luttrell, iv. 89. [3] Lipscomb, *Bucks.* ii. 192; BL, M636/33, John to Sir Ralph Verney, 24 July, 4, 25 Aug. 1679. [4] *Pol. State,* xxx. 614.

E.C.

HAY, William (1594–1664), of Little Horsted, Suss.

RYE   c. Jan. 1641
SUSSEX   1654
RYE   1656, 1659, 1660

> *b.* Dec. 1594, 2nd s. of John Hay (*d.*1605), counsellor at law, of Gray's Inn and Hurstmonceaux by 1st w. Mary, da. of William Morley of Glynde; bro. of Herbert Hay†. *educ.* Clare and Pembroke, Camb. 1612. *m.* Susan (*d.* 1640), da. of Barnaby Hodgson, yeoman, of Framfield, Suss., 4s. 2da.[1]
>
> Commr. for sequestration, Suss. 1643, assessment 1643–52, 1657, Jan. 1660–1, defence 1643, execution of ordinances 1644, militia 1648, 1659, Mar. 1660, j.p. 1644–*d.*; commr. for sewers, rapes of Lewes and Pevensey 1659, Sept. 1660.[2]
>
> Councillor of State 1651–2.[3]

Hay's grandfather was the first mayor of Hastings, but the family became of political importance only through their connexion with the Morley family, in which Hay and his brother, who sat for Arundel as a recruiter, were brought up. Hay bought the manor of Little Horsted in 1627, took

the parliamentary side in the Civil War, and conformed after Pride's Purge. He was re-elected in
1660 at Rye, no doubt on the combined interests of
his cousin Herbert Morley* and his nephew John
Fagg I*, with whom he sued for pardon shortly
afterwards. He was an inactive Member of the
Convention, except that as 'Mr Hayes' he may have
been among those appointed on 4 July to prepare
for a conference about three orders of the House of
Lords. With the eclipse of the Morley interest at
the Restoration, he is unlikely to have stood in 1661.
Although presumably an Independent in religion
he was not removed from the commission of the
peace, though whether this was due to his conformity or his insignificance cannot be determined. He
was buried at Little Horsted on 26 Dec. 1664. His
will, bequeathing £1,250 to his younger children,
indicates only moderate wealth, and none of his
descendants entered Parliament.[4]

[1] J. Comber, *Suss. Genealogies Ardingly*, 237; T. W. Horsfield,
Hist. Lewes, ii. 122; PCC 16 Hyde. [2] A. Fletcher, *County Com-
munity in Peace and War*, 353; C181/6/367, 7/55. [3] B. Worden,
Rump Parl. 281, 313; *CJ*, vii. 42, 220. [4] Keeler, *Long Parl.* 209;
Fines of Manors (Suss. Rec. Soc. xix), 227; D. Underdown, *Pride's
Purge*, 218; *Cal. Cl. SP*, v. 7; Add. 5697, f. 252.

M.W.H./B.D.H.

HAYNE, William (c.1665–98), of Dartmouth, Devon.

DARTMOUTH   1689, 1690, 1695

> b. c.1665, 1st s. of John Hayne, merchant, of Dartmouth,
> by Marcella, da. of Lawrence Wheeler, merchant, of
> Dartmouth. m. lic. 27 Aug. 1695, aged 30, Anne, da. of
> Henry Tichborne of Send, Surr., s.p. suc. fa. 1684.[1]
>   Commr. for assessment, Devon 1689–90.

Hayne's father became a partner in the shipping
firm headed by (Sir) John Frederick* in 1662; his
shares were then valued at £950. Under Frederick's
instructions he supported Joseph Williamson* in
the Dartmouth by-election of 1667 but, according
to a perhaps prejudiced source, ratted on him when
money was sent to the town in support of Walter
Yonge*. He was probably a nonconformist, leaving
money in his will to two of the local excluded
ministers.[2]

Hayne inherited land worth £500 p.a. and a personal estate of £30,000. He retained an interest in
his father's firm, now headed by Joseph Herne*,
but he also owned house property in Dartmouth
and a tenement in Blackawton, besides a long lease
of a farm in Brixham. Returned for Dartmouth as
a Tory at the general election of 1689, he was listed
by Anthony Rowe* as voting to agree with the
Lords that the throne was not vacant. But he left
no other record of his activities in the Convention.

He was reckoned a Tory in the next two Parliaments, but signed the Association in 1696. He died
shortly after making his will on 1 July 1698, having
doubled his landed wealth without impairing his
liquid assets. Although his heirs added considerably
to his estates in the neighbourhood of Dartmouth
by purchasing the property of John Upton*, no
other member of his family entered Parliament.[3]

[1] PCC 75 Hare, 102 Laud, 86 Pye, 167 Pett (not calendared);
London Mar. Lic. ed. Foster, 657; Manning and Bray, *Surr.* iii.
112. [2] PCC 102 Laud, 75 Hare; *CSP Dom.* 1666–7, pp. 373, 451,
497; *APC Col.* i. 462. [3] *APC Col.* ii. 167; PCC 167 Pett; Lysons,
Devon, 72; C8/572/21.

J.P.F.

HAYWARD see HAWARDE, Sir William and HOWARD, Thomas II

HEAD, John (c.1656–1711), of Langleys, Hamp-stead Norris, Berks.

STOCKBRIDGE   1685

> b. c.1656, o.s. of Thomas Head of Langleys. educ. New
> Inn Hall, Oxf. matric. 9 May 1672, aged 16. m. 4 Jan.
> 1687, Anna, da. of Richard Pococke of Chieveley, 1s.
> suc. fa. 1683.[1]
>   Sheriff, Berks. 1698–9, j.p. by 1701–d.

Head came from a long line of Berkshire yeomen
who had entered the ranks of the gentry only in the
last generation. The family were probably royalist
in sympathy during the Civil War. Head owned
property in Hampshire, including the manor of
Lickpit and meadowland in Sparsholt, seven miles
from Stockbridge; but this was hardly sufficient to
give him a natural interest. He defeated Oliver St.
John* at the general election of 1685, presumably
as a Tory. His only committee was to report on
expiring laws, and he does not seem to have stood
again, though he held local office after the Revolution. He died in 1711. His descendants continued
to rise in the social scale. After changing their name
to James they acquired a baronetcy in 1791 and a
peerage in 1884, but the next member of the family
to sit in Parliament was Sir Walter James in 1837.[2]

[1] *N. and Q.* clxxxv. 194–5; *Berks. Arch. Jnl.* li. 47; *VCH Berks.*
iv. 57, 78. [2] PCC 30 Barnes; *VCH Hants*, iv. 123.

J.P.F.

HEAD, Richard (c.1609–89), of Rochester, Kent.

ROCHESTER   2 Nov. 1667, 1679 (Mar.)

> b. c.1609, 2nd s. of Richard Head of Rochester by Anne,
> da. of William Hartridge of Cranbrook. m. (1) c.1639,
> Elizabeth, da. and coh. of Francis Merrick, merchant,
> of Rochester, 5s. d.v.p. 1da.; (2) bef. 1653, Elizabeth,
> da. and coh. of George Willey of Wrotham, 2s. d.v.p.

3da.; (3) aft. 1664, Anne, da. of William Kingsley, DD, archdeacon of Canterbury, wid. of John Boys of Hoad Court, Blean, *s.p. cr.* Bt. 19 June 1676.

Commr. for assessment, Kent 1661–80, Rochester 1663–4; alderman, Rochester 1662–*d.*, mayor 1663–4, June–Oct. 1671, 1683–4; j.p. Kent 1670–*d.*, commr. for recusants 1675; asst. Rochester bridge 1679–87, warden 1679, 1686.[1]

Head came of a yeoman family, and as a Royalist in the second Civil War compounded with the Kent committee on a modest fine of £10. But his first wife brought him a fleet of merchant ships and his second considerable property in Rochester. After the Restoration he was appointed to the corporation by the commissioners, granted arms in 1665, and returned for the city as a country candidate two years later. In the exalted company of Sir Frescheville Holles*, Sir Robert Howard* and William Love*, he brought in a proviso to the public accounts bill about the sale of seamen's tickets, and on 11 Mar. 1668 he acted as teller for a Kentish estate bill. But he failed to fulfil this promise of an active career in the House. He was appointed to only 14 committees in the Cavalier Parliament, including the committee of elections and privileges in two sessions, and he never spoke. Shaftesbury marked him 'worthy' in 1677, and on 28 Nov. 1678 he gave the House information at third hand about the Popish Plot. He defeated Sir Francis Clerke* at the general election, and was again classed as 'worthy' by Shaftesbury. In the first Exclusion Parliament he was moderately active, with eight committees, including those to consider the bill for security against Popery and to report on the proceedings of the Upper House on the impeachments of Danby and the Popish lords. He was absent from the division on the exclusion bill, and blacklisted in the 'unanimous club' of court supporters. Shortly before the autumn election it was predicted that:

> Sir John Banks* is like to carry it again for Rochester, and Sir Richard Head, who brought him in there by his interest last Parliament, will now be turned out.

It is not known whether Head actually went to the poll. It was reported that he intended to stand at the by-election following the death of Francis Barrell* before the meeting of the second Exclusion Parliament, but apparently the Speaker never issued the writ.[2]

In 1687 Head gave affirmative answers to the questions on the repeal of the Test Act and Penal Laws, and the King's agents recommended his retention on the commission of the peace. It was at his house in Rochester that James II stayed after his capture and also before his second flight. This, however, may have been due less to its owner's loyalty than to its size, although Lord Ailesbury

(Thomas Bruce*) called it only 'an indifferent good house'. For his hospitality Head was given an emerald ring by the King.[3]

Head died on 18 Sept. 1689, aged 80, and was buried in Rochester cathedral. In his will he left legacies totalling over £7,000 and mentioned land in a score of Kentish parishes; but no other member of the family entered Parliament.[4]

[1] Rochester Guildhall, AC2, ff. 66, 80v, 136, 214; information from Mr P. F. Cooper, Bridge Clerk, Rochester Bridge Trust. [2] J. C. Head, *Fams. Head and Somerville*, 8–9; *Grantees of Arms* (Harl. Soc. lxvi), 120; *CJ*, ix. 41; BL, M636/33, John Verney to Sir Ralph Verney, 4 Aug. 1679; *Dom. Intell.* 30 Sept. 1679. [3] *Ailesbury Mems.* 213, 220; F. Turner, *Jas. II*, 440. [4] Thorpe, *Reg. Roff.* 712; PCC 124 Ent.

B.D.H.

HEATH, John (1614–91), of Brasted Place, Kent.

CLITHEROE 1661

b. 2 May 1614, 3rd but 2nd surv. s. of Sir Robert Heath†, l.c.j.K.b. 1643–6, of Brasted by Margaret, da. and h. of John Miller of Tonbridge, Kent. *educ.* Clare, Camb. 1626; I. Temple 1626, called 1634. *m.* 24 Apr. 1664, Margaret, da. of Sir Matthew Mennes of Sandwich Priory, wid. of John Pretyman of Lodington, Leics., 1s. *d.v.p.* 1da. *suc.* fa. in Brasted estate 1649; kntd. 27 May 1664.[1]

KC 1642–9, 1653–July 1688; auditor, court of wards 1643–6; attorney-gen., duchy of Lancaster July 1660–?July 1688.[2]

Clerk of assize, Oxford circuit 1643–6, July–Nov. 1660; bencher, I. Temple 1660, treasurer 1673–4; j.p. Kent July 1660–Feb. 1688, Lancs. 1664–Apr. 1688; commr. for oyer and terminer, Home circuit July 1660, assessment, Kent Aug. 1660–80, Savoy liberty 1663–4, Lancs. and Mdx. 1663–9, Leics. 1664–79, corporations, Kent 1662–3, loyal and indigent officers, Kent and Lancs. 1662, recusants, Lancs. 1675; dep. lt. Kent 1680–Feb. 1688; recorder, Gravesend 1686–Oct. 1688.[3]

Heath came from a legal family of Tudor origin which reached its apogee in the person of his father, a leading spokesman for the Government in the early Parliaments of Charles I who was dismissed as chief justice of the common pleas in 1634. Nevertheless he joined the Court at Oxford in 1642, and as lord chief justice had a great deal of patronage at his disposal. Heath, who by his own account had given up a London practice worth £500 p.a., received from his father the clerkship of assize of the Oxford circuit, then vacant by death, and a post in the court of wards forfeited by an official who had elected to remain in London. The two posts were together worth some £1,200 p.a. He had already been put in possession of the Brasted estate acquired by his father under James I, his elder brother having married a Rutland heiress. He was not otherwise active in the Civil War, but was fined £152 for his delinquency. He was again a delinquent in the second Civil War. Most of the interregnum he passed in exile as the King's legal adviser, spending £4,000 of his own private patrimony 'without one penny help or allowance'. In 1659 he crossed over secretly to London, and together with Roger Whitley* was engaged in stirring up disaffection in the fleet.[4]

At the Restoration Heath was put in possession of the office of attorney of the duchy, granted him seven years before, he claimed, as an earnest of better things to come. But the yield was disappointing; in the first six months 'the King's wages, perquisites and all' amounted to only £94. 10s. He also established his claim to the clerkship of assize, though this required a direct order from the lord chancellor to Sir Thomas Malet, and was thus able to raise some much needed capital by selling it. His third post was less hopeful: not only did the Convention, despite a volley of petitions from Heath and his brothers, determine on the abolition of the court of wards, but they refused to adjudicate between the rival royalist and parliamentary claimants to office. Compensation of £1,200 was proposed, but no provision made for payment. On 11 Jan. 1661 Heath wrote to Clarendon to represent his unhappy position:

> Having received no fresh marks of his Majesty's favour since his return into England, I find the world looks on me at my return to my profession as one set aside . . . in so much as I am not willing to say how inconsiderable my practice hath been since my return.

He went on to suggest that he should be made serjeant-at-law; it was true that to combine this honour with the position of attorney of the duchy was unprecedented, but so were his sufferings, he claimed. Clarendon's reply has not been found, but it may well have been on his advice that Heath determined to use his duchy interest to enter Parliament. He was returned for Clitheroe at the general election of 1661, and at once assumed the active role expected of a minor official, although he made no recorded speeches. He was named to 293 committees in the Cavalier Parliament, including all the committees for the Clarendon Code, and those for the security bill, the bill of pains and penalites, and the bill for the execution of those under attainder. But his principal activity was in connexion with private legislation. He was chairman of the committees on two bills affecting duchy estates, one for Clitheroe itself; the other, for the manor of Rannes, he carried up to the Lords on 29 Nov. In 1662, he was chairman of the committee to consider the charges against James Philipps*. Heath was content to present the evidence, still preserved among his private papers, and leave the judgment to the House. He took part in managing four conferences

with the Lords in this session, including those on the execution of the regicides, the relief of loyal officers and the poor law. Undoubtedly his law had grown somewhat rusty during the Interregnum, and on being named reader at the Inner Temple he obtained a letter from the King to excuse him. Nevertheless in 1663 he acted as chairman of his most important committee, that for the repression of the meetings of sectaries, and he was also appointed to the revenue committee. His name appears on the list of court dependants in 1664.[5]

Heath's marriage to the niece of Sir John Mennes, the comptroller of the navy, and his subsequent knighthood did nothing to improve his finances. His wife's 'poor fortune had been miserable broken and still languishes under the horridest rapine and oppression that perhaps hath been heard of'. During her first marriage, while still under age, she had signed away her jointure to her father-in-law Sir John Pretyman*. Heath was reduced to petitioning the King for relief for 'my present very pressing wants, without which I should not adventure the seeming impudence of begging present money', and in May 1666 received a free gift of £1,000. Heath was again named to the principal committees of political importance in the autumn session of 1667; those for establishing free speech in Parliament, investigating the miscarriages of the war and the sale of Dunkirk, regulating official fees, inquiring into payments to loyal and indigent officers, and banishing Clarendon. In 1668 he was concerned with the habeas corpus bill and the working of the Conventicles and Militia Acts, but thereafter his activity declined sharply, though his name continued to appear on the lists of government supporters. This may be connected with the failure of his own private bill. His petition to reverse the conveyances of Lady Heath's property, stating that 'the petitioners have been for those four or five years locked up and obstructed in all the ordinary course of proceeding for their relief by Sir John Pretyman's privilege as Member of this House' was heard and committed on 10 Mar. 1670, and on the report, leave was given to bring in a bill. But this was rejected on the second reading by 45 votes to 28. The abolition of fee-farm rents further reduced the profits of his post; eventually he was granted £500 compensation. He served on the committee which produced the test bill in March 1673.[6]

Heath renewed his petition in the spring session of 1675, but it never emerged from committee. He was named on the Paston list and appointed to the committee to prevent the growth of Popery. His name appeared on the list of officials in the Commons, and he received the government whip for the autumn session. He was listed by Sir Richard Wiseman* as a court supporter, while in *A Seasonable Argument* he is called a heavy drinker and a suspected Papist. The latter charge is improbable. On Shaftesbury's list he was marked 'doubly vile'. He was appointed to another committee to consider the growth of Popery in 1677, but this was his last committee of political importance, apart from his appointment as one of the six Members to search Langhorne's study in the Inner Temple, from which as an ex-treasurer he could hardly have been excluded. He offered himself for re-election in 1679, but the corporation, though protesting themselves 'very sensible of the great service you have done for these many years', regretted that his letter came too late.[7]

There is no record of Heath's receiving any pension for his parliamentary services, as distinct from official fees and compensation. But on 19 June 1679 his former barber asserted that on his orders he had 'received several sums for his said master's use from the lord treasurer, and added to the said affirmation his opinion that it was a base, unworthy thing for any man to receive money for doing the King's business'. Nothing came of this, except that from 1680 for the remainder of the reign Heath no longer received his fees as KC. As far as is known he never stood for Parliament again. As a deputy lieutenant in Kent he replied to the lord lieutenant's questions on the repeal of the Test Act and Penal Laws on 26 Jan. 1688 that 'if he were a Parliament man, until he hears the debates he can give no resolution. . . . He will assist to the election of such as will take off the sanguinary laws, but not the Penal Laws and Tests in general.' Shortly afterwards he was dismissed from all his offices. Heath's attitude to the Revolution is not known, but he was probably a non-juror. He was buried at Brasted on 3 Nov. 1691; his modest estate was inherited by his daughter, who married George Verney, the clerical younger son of (Sir) Richard Verney*.[8]

[1] *Misc. Gen. et Her.* (ser. 5), iv. 157; Eg. 2979, f. 183. [2] W. R. Williams, *Lancaster Official Lists*, 35–36; *CSP Dom.* 1666–7, p. 410. [3] J. S. Cockburn, *Hist. Eng. Assizes*, 317; F. W. Jessup, *Sir Roger Twysden*, 172; *CSP Dom.* 1686–7, p. 323; Lancs. RO, QSC 63–96; Westmld. RO, Fleming mss 3190, Kenyon to Fleming, 16 Apr. 1688. [4] Eg. 2979, f. 32; J. Cave-Browne, *Hist. Brasted*, 16; *Cal. Comm. Comp.* 1471–2; *CSP Dom.* 1663–4, p. 165; D. Underdown, *Royalist Conspiracy*, 311; A. M. Everitt, *Kent and the Great Rebellion*, 306. [5] Eg. 2979, ff. 14, 26, 32; H. E. Bell, *Court of Wards*, 116; *CJ*, viii. 301, 305, 372; *Cal. I. T. Recs.* iii. 9; *Cal. Treas. Bks.* iii. 865. [6] Eg. 2979, ff. 175, 183; *CSP Dom.* 1665–6, p. 422; *CJ*, ix. 148, 150, 152. [7] Kent AO, U55 E100/112, Clitheroe corp. to Heath, 26 Feb. 1679. [8] Eg. 2979, f. 188; *Cal. Treas. Bks.* iv. 762.

I.C.

HEBBLETHWAITE, James (c.1652–1729), of Norton, nr. Malton, Yorks.

MALTON   18 Mar. 1678

b. c.1652, 1st s. of Thomas Hebblethwaite*. *m.* (1) Bridget (*d.* 13 June 1720), da. and h. of Sir William Cobb of Ottringham, Yorks., 5s. (4 *d.v.p.*) 6da.; (2) Mary, da. of one Lister, *s.p. suc.* fa. 1668.[1]
    Commr. for assessment, Yorks. (E. and N. Ridings) 1673–80, (E. Riding) 1689–90; mayor, Malton 1684–5; dep. lt. (E. Riding) ?1682–Apr. 1688, 1689–at least 1702.[2]

Hebblethwaite contested Malton with William Leveson Gower* at a by-election to the Cavalier Parliament in 1673. There was a double return, which was not resolved in his favour till 18 Mar. 1678. Shaftesbury marked him 'worthy', but he made no speeches, was appointed to no committees, and apparently never stood again. In answer to the lord lieutenant's questions on the Test Act and Penal Laws, he replied:

> If I shall be chosen a Member of Parliament, I conceive myself obliged to give my vote according to the reason of the debate of the House, and not otherwise. . . . If I do concern myself in the election of any to serve as a Member of Parliament, I shall give my vote for such as (to the best of my judgment) will serve the King and the whole kingdom faithfully and honestly. . . . I think myself obliged to live peaceably with all men, as becomes a good Christian and a loyal subject.

His example was followed by several others, including William Osbaldeston*, Sir Ralph Warton* and Matthew Appleyard*, and he was removed from the lieutenancy. He appears to have taken no further part in politics, and was buried at Norton on 10 Dec. 1729, the last of his family to sit in Parliament.

[1] Clay, *Dugdale's Vis. Yorks.* i. 267. [2] SP44/165/234.

P.A.B.

HEBBLETHWAITE, Thomas (1628–68), of Norton, nr. Malton, Yorks.

MALTON   1660, 1661–June 1668

bap. 19 June 1628, o.s. of James Hebblethwaite of Norton by 1st w. Anne, da. of Thomas Hungate of North Dalton. *educ.* Coxwold g.s.; St. John's, Camb. 1646; M. Temple 1647. *m.* Barbara, da. of Sir George Marwood, 1st Bt.[†], of Little Busby, 5s. (1 *d.v.p.*) 6da. *suc.* fa. 1653; kntd. 9 June 1660.[1]
    Commr. for militia, Yorks. Mar. 1660; j.p. (East and North Ridings) July 1660–d.; commr. for sewers (East Riding) Sept. 1660, assessment (E. Riding) Aug. 1660–d., (N. Riding) 1661–3, corporations, Yorks. 1662–3.[2]

Hebblethwaite's family came from Sedbergh, but had held the manor of Norton, adjoining Malton, since Elizabethan times. His grandfather was elected for the borough when its representation was restored in 1641. A passive Royalist, he was fined £500 for defection from the Long Parliament. His father seems to have taken no part in the Civil War. Hebblethwaite himself was returned for Malton in 1660. Lord Wharton noted that he was abroad, which probably means that he had joined the exiled Court, and he was knighted soon after the Restoration. Though doubtless a court supporter, he was not an active Member of the Convention, receiving leave to go into the country on 13 Aug. He returned after the recess, however, and was appointed to the committee on the bill for draining the great level of the fens.[3]

Hebblethwaite was re-elected in 1661. There was a contest for the junior seat, but his own return was not disputed. He was appointed to the committee for the uniformity bill, and served regularly on the committee of elections and privileges. But he was again an inactive Member of the Cavalier Parliament, in which his committee appointments totalled only 16. He soon joined the Opposition, being named to the committee on the bill to restrain abuses in the sale of offices in 1663. In 1665 he helped to consider the bill for maintaining Bridlington pier. On 29 Dec. 1666 he was teller for the successful adjournment motion which thwarted the government attempt to rush supply through a thin House. He was among those appointed to consider the estate bill promoted by his neighbour William Palmes* in the autumn session of 1667, and to take the accounts of the loyal and indigent officers fund during the Christmas recess. His own estate bill, to enable him to make provision for his large family, was read on 28 Feb. 1668, and the committee was instructed to ensure that the consent of Sir George and Lady Marwood had been obtained. On 13 Mar. Sir Thomas Gower* reported that the committee found no cause to make any alterations to the bill, and it passed the Commons three days later. The Lords saw fit to delete one proviso, and on 15 Apr. the Commons concurred. This was Hebblethwaite's last session, for he was buried at Norton on 21 June.[4]

[1] Clay, *Dugdale's Vis. Yorks.* i. 267, [2] C181/7/45; *HMC 8th Rep.* pt. 1 (1881), 275. [3] J. T. Cliffe, *Yorks. Gentry*, 37; Keeler, *Long Parl.* 209–10; *Royalist Comp. Pprs.* (Yorks. Arch. Soc. xviii), 2. [4] D. T. Witcombe, *Cavalier House of Commons*, 54–55; *CJ*, ix. 59, 78.

M.W.H./P.A.B.

HELE, John (1626–61), of Flanchford, Reigate, Surr.

REIGATE   1659, 1660

b. 3 Mar. 1626, o.s. of Nicholas Hele of Wembury, Devon and Easton in Gordano, Som. by 1st w. Dorothy, da. and h. of Edmund Stradling of Easton in Gordano. *educ.* Christ Church, Oxf. 1642; L. Inn 1644, called

1652. *m.* Dorothy, da. and coh. of Sir John Hobart, 2nd Bt.[†], of Blickling, Norf., wid. of his cos. Sir John Hele[†] of Clifton Maybank, Dorset, and of Hugh Rogers of Cannington, Som., *s.p. suc.* fa. 1640.[1]

J.p. Surr. 1659–*d.*, commr. for militia 1659, Mar. 1660, assessment Jan. 1660–*d.*, col. of militia ft. Apr. 1660; commr. for oyer and terminer, Home circuit July 1660.[2]

Hele's father, the sixth son of a successful lawyer from the old Devon family, married an heiress and sat for Liskeard in 1621 and 1624. In accordance with his last wishes, Hele's wardship was bought for 1,000 marks by his cousin, one of the Cavalier leaders in Dorset, whose rich widow he was later to marry. He was educated for the legal profession, but it is not clear whether he practised. He had bought the manor of Flanchford by 1656, and sat for Reigate in Richard Cromwell's Parliament. He was re-elected in 1660 and marked by Lord Wharton as a friend, though his known associates, such as Lord Falkland (Henry Carey*), were all Royalists. A moderately active Member of the Convention, he made no recorded speeches, but was named to 15 committees, including the committee of elections and privileges and those for cancelling all grants under the great seal since 1642, and for recommending poll-tax rates. On 30 May he acted as teller against agreeing to the Lords' amendments to the bill for continuing judicial proceedings. He was among those appointed to hear the petition from the intruded Oxford dons on 25 June and to prepare for a conference on three orders issued by the House of Lords on 4 July. In the second session he helped to consider bills to prevent profane swearing and marital separations. He died intestate on 25 Jan. 1661 before the next general election. His widow, who married the courtier Lord Crofts as her fourth husband 'after six weeks' mourning', renounced probate, and administration was granted on 18 Feb. 1661 to his nephew, the younger brother of Sir Humphrey Hooke*, who sold Flanchford to Sir Cyril Wyche* for £8,400.[3]

[1] *Sale of Wards* (Som. Rec. Soc. lvii), 176; Vivian, *Vis. Devon*, 464; *Som. Wills*, vi. 50–51; *HMC Lothian*, 85; PCC adm. act. bk. 1662, f. 15. [2] *Parl. Intell.* 23 Apr. 1660. [3] PCC 6 Evelyn; *CSP Dom.* 1640–1, p. 229; *Sale of Wards*, 177; *Surr. Arch. Colls.* xiv. 178; *Sess. Rolls* (Mdx. Recs. iii), 215; BL, M636/17, Smyth to Verney, 30 Jan. 1661; *HMC 5th Rep.* 185; Manning and Bray, *Surr.* i. 307.

M.W.H./J.P.F.

HELE, Thomas (1630–65), of Wigborough, South Petherton, Som.

PLYMPTON ERLE   1661–13 Sept. 1665

b. 6 Sept. 1630, 1st s. of Sir Thomas Hele, 1st Bt.*, by 1st w. *m.* (with £2,000) Amy, da. of Thomas Luttrell[†] of Dunster Castle, Som., *s.p.*[1]

Commr. for assessment, Devon 1661–*d.*, Som. 1665–*d.*

Hele was returned for Plympton on the family interest. An inactive Member of the Cavalier Parliament, he was named only to the committee (6 July 1661) to consider the charges against James Philipps*, but he probably supported the Government. He made his will in May 1664, 'considering my natural frailty', and died at Wigborough in his father's lifetime on 13 Sept. 1665. He was buried at South Petherton.[2]

[1] *Vis. Devon*, ed. Vivian, 466; *Som. Wills*, vi. 17. [2] PCC 107 Carr; *Trans. Devon Assoc.* xxxii. 554.

J.S.C.

HELE, Sir Thomas, 1st Bt. (c.1595–1670), of Flete House, Holbeton, Devon.

PLYMPTON ERLE	1626, 1628, 1640 (Apr.),
	c. 15 Nov. 1640–22 Jan. 1644
OKEHAMPTON	1661–7 Nov. 1670

b. c.1595, 2nd s. and h. of Thomas Hele of Flete by Bridget, da. of Sir Henry Champernowne† of Modbury. *educ.* I. Temple 1614. *m.* (1) 20 Nov. 1629, Penelope (*d.* 7 Sept. 1630), da. and coh. of Emorb Johnson of South Petherton, Som., 1s. *d.v.p.*; (2) 16 July 1632, Elizabeth (*bur.* 14 Mar. 1646), da. of Edward Elwes, Merchant Taylor, of London, 7s. (5 *d.v.p.*) 2da. *suc.* fa. 1624; *cr.* Bt. 28 May 1627.[1]

J.p. Devon 1626–46, July 1660–*d.*, sheriff Jan.–Oct. 1636, commr. of array 1642, assessment Aug. 1660–9, dep. lt. 1661–*d.*, commr. for oyer and terminer, Western circuit 1661, corporations, Devon 1662–3.[2]

Col. of horse (royalist) ?1642–6.[3]

Hele's ancestors had held land in Devon since at least the reign of Edward I, and had first sat for Plympton in 1355. Hele's elder brother was disinherited, and he succeeded to an estate not overvalued at £1,165 p.a. A ship-money sheriff, he was a Royalist in the Civil War. He took part in the siege of Plymouth and sat in the Oxford Parliament. The fine for his delinquency was assessed under the Exeter articles at £2,834; but he seems to have escaped payment by settling three rectories, worth £280 p.a., on their parishes. He was mentioned in the confession of a royalist agent under the Commonwealth, but he was not an active conspirator. He put up his son for Plympton in 1661, and was himself returned for Okehampton, probably on the Mohun interest. He was named to only four committees in the Cavalier Parliament, including those on the bills for restoring rectories (6 July 1661), in which he was personally concerned, and for the regulation of printing (19 Oct. 1665). He was absent from a call of the House in 1666 and was sent for in custody. He died on 7 Nov. 1670 and was buried at Holbeton. The baronetcy became extinct in 1677, but a great-nephew, who succeeded to the estate, was returned for Plympton in 1701.[4]

[1] *Vis. Devon*, ed. Vivian, 466; *Som. and Dorset N. and Q.* ii. 232; *VCH Northants. Fams.* 64–65; *Trans. Devon Assoc.* lxiv. 488, 490. [2] Keeler, *Long Parl.* 210; Exeter City Lib. DD63122, f. 356. [3] E. Warburton, *Mems. of Prince Rupert*, iii. 14. [4] Keeler, 210–11; *Cal. Comm. Comp.* 1239; *Cal. Comm. Adv. Money*, 699; *HMC Portland*, i. 584; *CJ*, viii. 663; *Trans. Devon Assoc.* lxiv. 488.

J.S.C./J.P.F.

HELYAR (HILLYARD), William (1662–1742), of East Coker, Som.

| ILCHESTER | 1689 |
| SOMERSET | 1715 |

b. 10 July 1662, 1st s. of William Helyar of East Coker by Rachel, da. and coh. of Sir Hugh Wyndham, 1st Bt., of Pilsdon, Dorset. *educ.* Trinity, Oxf. 1680; L. Inn 1683. *m.* 9 June 1690, Joanna (*d.* 11 Oct. 1714), da. and coh. of Robert Hole of South Tawton, Devon, 2s. 3da.; (2) 1719, Anne, da. of William Harbin of Newton Surmaville, Som., *s.p. suc.* fa. 1697.[1]

Commr. for assessment, Som. 1689–90, j.p. 1691–?*d.*, capt. of militia ft. by 1697, dep. lt. 1700–?*d.*, sheriff 1700–2.[2]

Helyar's family was founded by his great-grandfather, a notable ecclesiastical pluralist who became archdeacon of Barnstaple in 1605 and bought the manor of East Coker in 1616. His father, a royalist colonel, compounded at £1,522 16s. on the Exeter articles. After the Restoration he hunted down seditious conventicles, and in 1681 brought to the notice of Secretary Jenkins a book in support of Monmouth's claim to the throne. In 1685 he was in action against Monmouth, and he gave affirmative answers on the repeal of the Test Act and Penal Laws.[3]

Presumably it was Helyar and not his father who signed the declaration of support for William of Orange on 15 Nov. 1688. As 'William Helyar, junior' he was returned as a Tory for Ilchester, seven miles from his home, after a contest at the general election of 1689. He voted to agree with the Lords that the throne was not vacant. An inactive Member of the Convention, he was appointed to six committees, including both of those for the easier recovery of tithe, and that for reversing the attainder of Sir Thomas Armstrong*. He did not speak, but reported, presumably with approval, an anti-Dutch tirade of Edward Seymour* in December. Although still a Tory, he had no wish to sit in 1690, and persuaded John Hunt* to take his place. He was buried at East Coker on 8 Oct. 1742, the only member of his family to sit in Parliament.[4]

[1] Harbin, *Som. Members*, 190. [2] Som. RO, QJC103; Eg. 1626, f. 39. [3] Som. RO, Helyer mss 53, 77; A.G. Matthews, *Walker Revised*, 114; *Cal. Comm. Comp.* 125, 562, 1665; J. Batten, *South Som.* 159–62; Collinson, *Som.* ii. 341; *CSP Dom.* 1680–1, pp. 440–1; 1682, p. 97; *HMC 3rd Rep.* 97, 98, 100. [4] E. Green, *March of Wm. of Orange through Som.* 57–58; *Wood's Life and Times* (Oxf. Hist. Soc. xxvi), 316; Bodl. Ballard mss 38, f. 128; *Som. Wills*, iii. 21.

I.C.

HENLEY, Andrew (1622–75), of Bramshill, Hants.

PORTSMOUTH   8 May 1660

bap. 7 May 1622, 1st s. of Robert Henley of Henley, Som. and Soper Lane, London, chief clerk of K.b. 1629–42, by 2nd w. Anne, da. of John Eldred of Saxmundham, Suff.; bro. of Sir Robert Henley*. *educ.* M. Temple entered 1634, called 1646; Exeter, Oxf. 1639. *m.* (1) aft. 1648, Mary (*d.* 30 July 1666), da. of Sir John Gayer, merchant and Fishmonger, of London, ld. mayor 1646–7, 2s. 2da.; (2) 20 May 1672, Constance, da. of Thomas Bromfield, merchant and Haberdasher, of Coleman Street, London, wid. of Thomas Middleton of Stansted Mountfitchet, Essex, *s.p. suc.* fa. 1656; *cr.* Bt. 20 June 1660; kntd. 21 July 1660.[1]

Sheriff, Hants 1653–4; freeman, Portsmouth Apr. 1660, Winchester 1661; j.p. Hants July 1660–*d.*, commr. for assessment Aug. 1660–*d.*, col. of militia ft. Nov. 1660–?67, dep. lt. 1661–7; commr. of sewers, Bedford level 1662–3, conservator 1666–7, 1669–70; keeper of Frimley walk, Windsor forest 1670–*d.*; commr. for recusants, Hants 1675.[2]

Henley's father was first cousin of the half-blood of Henry Henley*; but by his successive occupation of two immensely lucrative offices, first as a Six Clerk in Chancery, and then as chief clerk of the King's bench (worth £22,500 by his own account), he outstripped the senior line both in wealth and status, acquiring considerable property in Somerset, Dorset and Hampshire, besides an 'adventure' of 5,500 acres in the fens. When he was sequestrated he claimed to have gone into the King's quarters not voluntarily but under constraint, and exhibited debts of £11,585, while his brother-in-law John Maynard I* produced counter-bonds from various creditors in the period 1629 to 1642 totalling £27,545. Nevertheless he paid the heavy fine of £9,000 within a month. Henley himself was said to have given £2,500 to needy Cavaliers. He bought some bishops' lands in Dorset and the manor of Great Bramshill in 1649, but he was probably never entirely free from debt.[3]

Although ineligible as the son of a Cavalier, Henley was 'incessantly importuned' to stand for Hampshire at the general election of 1660, and sent a message to Richard Norton* to the effect that he would not oppose him. An electoral bargain was struck:

Whereas we began to hold it doubtful whether I should carry it for knight of the shire or not, so it was agreed that Colonel Norton should decline his being burgess for Portsmouth and get me chosen there, and then I to decline being knight, so I am promised Colonel Norton's interest (who is governor) and not doubt but I shall [be] burgess of Portsmouth. But if I had been free and declared my mind sooner, I had undoubtedly been knight of the shire.

Henley was duly returned at a by-election for Portsmouth when Norton chose to sit for the county. He seems to have been a totally inactive Member of the Convention, though his baronetcy and knighthood suggest that he was expected to support the Court as a silent voter in divisions.[4]

Although both Norton and John Bulkeley* had promised to join with Henley at the next county election, in the changed circumstances of 1661 they were obliged to step down to borough seats, and he is not known to have stood again. He was desired by the lord lieutenant to stay in the country while most of the deputy lieutenants were attending Parliament 'in case any commotions should arise by any restless spirits endeavouring to beget new broils'. In 1662 he wrote to his Dorset agent: 'You know how I am pressed for money. . . . I have no other *intrada* but my rents to support myself.' Presumably he was extravagant, but it is not known what he spent his money on, except in paying a French chef, against which the rector of Eversley directed a sermon on the sin of gluttony. Henley was already involved in a dispute with the rector over tithes, and he also (more excusably) came into open conflict with Lord St. John (Charles Powlett I*) at a time and place that might have had very serious consequences. According to Samuel Pepys*:

My Lord St. John did, a day or two since, openly pull a gentleman in Westminster Hall by the nose, one Sir Andrew Henley, whilst the judges were upon their benches, and the other gentleman did give a rap over the pate with his cane, of which fray the judges, they say, will make a great matter.

Lord St. John was quickly pardoned, and was soon in a position to retaliate by dropping Henley from the lieutenancy. But Henley had to petition the King after a prosecution had been started against him in King's bench, and was not pardoned till 1668. In the following year he added to his debts by the purchase of Eversley manor. He died on 17 May 1675, and was buried at Eversley.[5]

[1] Soc. of Genealogists, Boyd's London Units 15608. [2] R. East, *Portsmouth Recs.* 206; Winchester corp. assembly bk. 4, f. 162; *Cal. Treas. Bks.* i. 82; Sloane 813, f. 50v; S. Wells, *Drainage of Bedford Level*, i. 350, 458–60; Harl. 1579, f. 186. [3] G. E. Aylmer, *The King's Servants*, 305–8; SP23/138, ff. 127–37; *Cal. Comm. Adv. Money*, 272; Grey, i. 6; *VCH Hants*, iv. 36, 40; Hutchins, *Dorset*, ii. 127. [4] Sloane 813, f. 16. [5] Sloane 813, ff. 49, 53, 79; *Cal. Treas. Bks.* i. 312; *Pepys Diary*, 29 Nov. 1666; *CSP Dom.* 1666–7,

p. 299; 1667, p. 263; 1667–8, pp. 371–2, 514; *VCH Hants*, iv. 34; C8/262/51; Eversley par. reg.

M.W.H./P.W.

HENLEY, Henry (c.1612–96), of Leigh, Winsham, Som. and Colway, Lyme Regis, Dorset.

SOMERSET 1653
DORSET 1654
LYME REGIS 1659
BRIDPORT 1660
LYME REGIS 1661, 1679 (Mar.), 1679 (Oct.), 1681

b. c.1612, 2nd but 1st surv. s. of Henry Henley of Leigh by Susan, da. of William Bragge of Sadborow, Thorncombe, Devon. *m.* (1) 28 Sept. 1636, Susan, da. of Thomas Moggridge, merchant, of Exeter, Devon, 2s. *d.v.p.*; (2) Bridget (*bur.* 9 Oct. 1657), da. of John Bampfield† of Poltimore, Devon, 2da. *suc.* fa. 1639.[1]

Col. (parliamentary) ?1643–6.[2]

Commr. for sequestrations, Som. 1643; assessment, Som. 1643, 1664–80, Som. and Dorset 1644–50, Dorset 1652, Jan. 1660–80, levying of money, Som. 1643, execution of ordinances, Som. and Dorset 1654; j.p. Som. 1646–54, Feb. 1688–9, Devon 1647–57, Dorset 1650–6, Mar.–July 1660, June 1688–9; commr. for rebuilding, Beaminster 1647, militia, Som. and Dorset 1648, Dorset Mar. 1660; elder, Ilchester classis 1648; sheriff, Dorset 1648–9; commr. for scandalous ministers, Som. 1654, recusants, Dorset 1675; freeman, Lyme Regis 1679; commr. for inquiry into recusancy fines, Som. Mar. 1688.[3]

Henley was descended from a Marian martyr in Taunton. His grandfather was granted arms in 1612 and acquired a dozen properties, mostly small, in south-west Somerset and west Dorset, as well as a couple of manors in Devon. Henley himself, though a Presbyterian in religion, belonged to the radical wing of the Parliamentarians in the Civil War, and in 1653 became the first of the family to enter Parliament. The senior branch rose less rapidly in rank and wealth than their Hampshire cousins, but they enjoyed a strong interest at Lyme, and also owned property in Bridport, for which Henley was returned at the general election of 1660. A moderately active Member of the Convention, he was named to 13 committees, including the committee of elections and privileges. The most important in the first session were to cancel all grants made by the crown since May 1642, and to settle ecclesiastical livings. Clearly in opposition to the Court, he warned Edmund Ludlow* of his danger under the indemnity bill, though he took no known part in debate. After the recess he was added to the committee to bring in a bill for modified episcopacy in accordance with the Worcester House declaration.[4]

With the re-establishment of the hostile Strangways interest at Bridport, Henley retreated to his own borough for the 1661 election, and was no doubt returned without a contest. Again a moderately active Member of the Cavalier Parliament, he made no recorded speeches, but acted as teller in three divisions and was named to 102 committees, including the elections committee in nine sessions. Lord Wharton listed him as a friend, and on 3 July he was reported to the House for not taking part in the corporate communion. He excused himself on grounds of health, and was ordered to bring in a sacrament certificate on the following Monday. Under the Clarendon administration he took no part in measures of political importance, but on 22 Nov. 1667 he was added to the committee of inquiry into the miscarriages of the second Dutch war. He was sufficiently emboldened by the advent of the Cabal to ask the Privy Council on behalf of his constituents for assistance for the repair of the Cobb and for redress against a customs official. In 1668 he was one of the tellers for religious comprehension and against the continuance of the Conventicles Act. In the next session he was among those appointed to inquire into customs fees, and acted with Andrew Marvell* as teller against the election of the churchman, Peregrine Palmer*, for Bridgwater. He kept an ejected minister as his chaplain, and after the Declaration of Indulgence in 1672 assisted him in building a Presbyterian chapel at Marshwood. He was less active in the early sessions of the Danby administration. Sir Richard Wiseman* indicated him as an opponent of the Court by placing his name at the foot of the list of Dorset Members, while Shaftesbury accorded him the accolade of 'thrice worthy'. In 1678 he was appointed to the committees to inquire into the conviction of Quakers for recusancy and to hinder Papists from sitting in Parliament.[5]

Henley continued to represent his notoriously disaffected constituency in the Exclusion Parliaments, and was marked 'worthy' on Shaftesbury's list. In 1679 he was moderately active, being appointed to five committees, of which the most characteristic was to bring in more effectual legislation for the enforcement of the puritan moral code, and he voted for the first exclusion bill. In the second Exclusion Parliament he was again moderately active. He was named to seven committees, including those to draw up an address for a national day of humiliation and to repeal the Corporations Act. There is no evidence that he took his seat in the Oxford Parliament or contested the 1685 election. He was accused of sending £300 to Monmouth during his rebellion, but appears to have become a Whig collaborator in 1688, when he was restored to the commission of the peace. He is unlikely to have stood again in view of his age, and was buried at Winsham on 10 June 1696, while his grandson was sitting for Lyme in Parliament.[6]

[1] *Vis. Glos.* ed. Fenwick and Metcalfe, 90; Hutchins, *Dorset,* ii. 72; *Proc. Dorset Nat. Hist. and Antiq. Soc.* lxiv. 65; Exeter City Lib. St. Kerrian par. reg.; *Som. and Dorset N. and Q.* iv. 103; C142/580/85. [2] *Ludlow Mems.* i. 86, 89. [3] *Q. Sess. Recs.* (Som. Rec. Soc. xxviii), 1; Harbin, *Som. Members,* 156; *Trans. Devon Assoc.* x. 313; C. H. Mayo, *Dorset Standing Committee,* 398; W. Prynne, *County of Som. Divided into Classes,* 8; Lyme Regis mss B1/10, f. 236; *Cal. Treas. Bks.* viii. 1804. [4] *Vis. Som.* (Harl. Soc. xi), 48–49; *N. and Q.* (ser. 11), iv. 177; *Som. and Dorset N. and Q.* v. 155; vii. 146; *Grantees of Arms* (Harl. Soc. lvi), 121; D. Underdown, *Som. in the Civil War,* 125, 172; Bridport corp. mss 21/2244; *Voyce from the Watch Tower,* 186. [5] *CJ,* viii. 289; ix. 77, 90, 119; *Cal. Treas. Bks.* ii. 312, 590; iii. 483; D. R. Lacey, *Dissent and Parl. Pols.* 410–11; *CSP Dom.* 1671–2, p. 411. [6] Lacey, 410; Lyme corp. mss. C. Wanklyn, 'Lyme Members', 145.

J.P.F.

HENLEY, Sir Robert (c.1624–92), of The Grange, Northington, Hants.

ANDOVER 1679 (Oct.)
HAMPSHIRE 16 Nov. 1691–15 Dec. 1692

b. c.1624, 2nd s. of Robert Henley of Henley, Som., and bro. of Andrew Henley*. *educ.* M. Temple 1634, called 1651. *m.* (1) 12 Feb. 1663, Catherine, da. of Sir Anthony Hungerford[†] of Blackbourton, Oxon., 1s. 1da.; (2) 1 Sept. 1674, Barbara, da. of John Every of Symondsbury, Dorset and coh. to her bro. John Every*, 2s. 3da. Kntd. 9 June 1663.[1]

Chief protonotary, K.b. May 1660–*d.*; assoc. bencher, M. Temple 1663; conservator, Bedford level 1666–9; j.p. Hants 1668–80; commr. for assessment, Hants 1673–80, Mdx. 1689–90, Dorset, Hants and Westminster 1690, recusants, Hants 1675.[2]

Henley was left £10,000 in his father's will, together with some houses in Lincoln's Inn Fields, and at the Restoration he was able to enjoy the reversion to the King's bench office, worth £4,000 a year. On his marriage he purchased an estate in Hampshire, 12 miles from Andover, for which he was returned as a country Member at the second general election of 1679 'to his great satisfaction', which must have been somewhat lessened when he was removed from the commission of the peace a few months later. An active Member, he was probably appointed to 13 committees in the second Exclusion Parliament, including those to receive information about the Popish Plot, and to draft the address urging the King to accept exclusion. On 4 Jan. 1681 he was reprimanded for default in attendance, and he was defeated at the next election. Nothing more is heard of him till the Revolution, but he was twice defeated in attempts to enter the Convention, at Andover at the general election, and for the county in February 1689. He was successful at a by-election for Hampshire in 1691, but died after little more than a year in the House on 15 Dec. 1692, and was buried at Northington. His son

Anthony, whose inheritance was said to be worth £3,000 p.a., was elected for Andover as a Whig in 1698.[3]

[1] Hutchins, *Dorset,* iii. 742; *N. and Q.* (ser. 10), ix. 141–3; St. Mary le Strand par. reg.; *Misc. Gen. et Her.* (ser. 5), viii. 215. [2] *CSP Dom.* 1661–2, p. 345; S. Wells, *Drainage of Bedford Level,* i. 458. [3] PCC 129 Berkeley; Luttrell, ii. 641; *VCH Hants,* iii. 395; iv. 196; BL, M636/33, Cary Gardiner to Sir Ralph Verney, 20 Aug. 1679; *N. and Q.* (ser. 10), ix. 496; R. H. Eden, *Northington Mem.* 5.

P.W.

HENLEY, Sir Robert, 2nd Bt. (bef. 1655–81), of Bramshill, Hants.

BRIDPORT 1679 (Oct.)

b. bef. 1655, 1st s. of Andrew Henley*. *unm. suc.* fa. 17 May 1675.[1]

Henley was probably only just of age when he succeeded to an estate worth £4,000 p.a. but heavily encumbered with his father's debts. He paid off few or none of these, but mortgaged the property for £20,000. On 4 Dec. 1678 his sister commenced a Chancery suit against him for the £3,000 portion bequeathed her by their father. No answer survives on the file; probably Henley's cousin, John Trenchard*, who was also the family lawyer, suggested that Parliament would provide a useful refuge. Henley owned considerable property in West Dorset, and in August 1679 he was elected for Bridport in succession to Trenchard's brother-in-law, John Every*. He was presumably attached to the country party, but it seems probable that the references in the second Exclusion Parliament are to his uncle, Sir Robert Henley*. The intervention of a second country candidate at Bridport in 1681 thrust Henley to the bottom of the poll, and his petition was never heard. He died on 7 Aug. 1681 and was buried at Eversley. His brother and heir served as sheriff of Dorset after the Revolution, but completed the ruin of the family by an unfortunate homicide. Bramshill was sold to Sir John Cope*, and in 1740 the baronetcy became extinct.[2]

[1] C8/262/51. [2] C8/293/86; Plymouth City Lib. Roborough mss 292; Hutchins, *Dorset,* ii. 127; *CJ,* ix. 707; Eversley reg.

J.P.F.

HENNING, Henry (c.1646–99), of Poxwell, Dorset.

WEYMOUTH AND 11 Nov. 1680, 1681, 1685,
MELCOMBE REGIS 1689, 1690

b. c.1646, o. (posth.) s. of Edmund Henning of Poxwell by Joan, da. of Henry Henley of Leigh, Winsham, Som. *m.* 1662, Ursula (*d.* 31 Dec. 1694), da. of Thomas

Achim of Pelynt, Cornw., 1s. *d.v.p.* 1da. *suc.* fa. at birth.[1]

Commr. for assessment, Dorset 1679–80, 1689–90, j.p. and dep. lt. May 1688–?*d.*

Henning represented the fifth generation of his family to reside at Poxwell since his ancestor, a Dorchester merchant, bought the estate in 1575, but he was the first to enter Parliament. His father in the closing months of the Civil War tore himself from his wife's embraces and entered the royalist garrison at Corfe Castle, where he died. Henning was born eight months later, a sickly child who was not expected to live. Although his uncle Henry Henley* was a member of the county committee, nothing could be done to prevent the sequestration of the estate, valued at £563 p.a., nor could he even obtain a favourable certificate. The fine was originally set at £1,137, and it was not until 1655 that it was reduced to £500 and paid.[2]

Henning's mother remarried a settler in Ireland and Poxwell was let. Nothing is known of Henning's life before 1678, when he bought a farm from (Sir) Winston Churchill*, with whose family the Hennings had long been associated. It is presumed that he shared Henley's exclusionist views, and he first entered Parliament at a by-election for Weymouth, six miles from his home, caused by the death of Thomas Browne*. At the succeeding general election the four sitting Members were returned unopposed, but Henning did well to survive the Tory challenge in 1685, particularly as he never spoke in the House nor served on any committee during this period. It is probable that his health was always indifferent. He may have been a Whig collaborator, as he was appointed to county office in 1688. Returned again in 1689, he was no more active than before. His name does not appear in either of the division lists in the Convention, and on 18 Mar. he obtained leave to go into the country for a month. He died on 26 Nov. 1699 and was buried at Poxwell, the only member of the family to enter Parliament. His daughter brought the property to her husband, Thomas Trenchard II*.[3]

[1] Hutchins, *Dorset*, i. 408. [2] Burke, *Fam. Recs.* 307; SP23/217/182–3; Add. 8845, p. 9; Dorset RO, D60/F1; *Cal. Comm. Comp.* 2055/6. [3] Dorset RO, D60/T103, f. 24; *Dorset Hearth-Tax* ed. Meekings, 80; Burke, *Gentry* (1846), 1415; PCC 132 Noel.

J.P.F.

HERBERT, Arthur (c.1648–1716), of Oatlands Park, Weybridge, Surr.

DOVER 1685

PLYMOUTH 17 Jan.–29 May 1689

b. c.1648, 3rd s. of Sir Edward Herbert[†] of Aston, Mont. by Margaret, da. and h. of Sir Thomas Smith[†], master of requests, of Parson's Green, Fulham, Mdx., wid. of Hon. Thomas Carey, groom of the bedchamber to Charles I; bro. of Charles Herbert* and Sir Edward Herbert*. *m.* (1) lic. 2 Nov. 1672, aged 25, Anne, da. of George Hadley, Grocer, of Southgate, Mdx., wid. of Walter Pheasant of Upwood, Hunts., *s.p.*; (2) c. 1 Aug. 1704, Anne, da. and coh. of Sir William Armine, 2nd Bt.[†], of Osgodby, Lincs., wid. of Sir Thomas Wodehouse of Kimberley, Norf., and of Thomas Crew*, 2nd Baron Crew, *s.p. cr.* Earl of Torrington 29 May 1689.

Lt. RN 1666, capt. 1666, v.-adm. 1678, adm. 1680–3, r.-adm. 1684–7; col. (later 15 Ft.) 1686–7; lt.-adm.-gen. (Dutch navy) Oct.–Nov. 1688; adm. of the fleet 1689–90; col. 1 Marine Regt. 1690.

Freeman, Portsmouth 1675, 1689, Dover 1684; member, R. Fisheries 1677; j.p. Kent 1689–?90; commr. for assessment, Surr. 1689; elder bro. Trinity House 1689–*d.*, master 1689–90; conservator, Bedford level 1694–1700, bailiff 1700–*d.*[1]

Ld. of the Admiralty 1683–4, first ld. 1689–90; groom of the bedchamber to the Duke of York 1684–5; master of the robes 1685–7; PC 26 Feb. 1689–23 June 1692.

Herbert entered the navy in 1663 and was first commissioned in 1666. He fought in both Dutch wars and saw service against the Algerian corsairs. His courage is not in dispute; he was several times wounded and lost the sight of one eye. But he was 'delivered up to pride and luxury', and according to the 1st Earl of Dartmouth (son of his rival George Legge*), 'the most universally hated by the seamen of any man that ever commanded at sea'. Samuel Pepys* was told that the seamen blessed God when he was transferred to another ship. He may have been a candidate for Montgomery Boroughs at one of the Exclusion elections, but if so he must have stood down in favour of another court supporter. He was made a supernumerary member of the board of Admiralty in 1683, joined the Duke of York's household in the following year and became master of the robes in the new reign. The annual income from his places was reckoned at £4,000, a great sum for a younger son of the family. Herbert was returned for Dover in 1685 as the nominee of the crown, but listed among the Opposition. He was named only to the committee on the bill repairing Great Yarmouth pier.[2]

Herbert had always been 'most passionately zealous in the King's service', his brother Sir Edward held the highest notions of passive obedience, and James confidently expected his assent to the repeal of the Test Act and Penal Laws. Herbert replied 'that he could not do it either in honour or conscience', but Burnet suggests that his unexpected obstinacy arose from jealousy of Legge, 'who he thought had more of the King's confidence than he himself had'. He was not only stripped of his offices, but also experienced great difficulty in

Herbert Family
of Montgomeryshire, Worcestershire and Shropshire

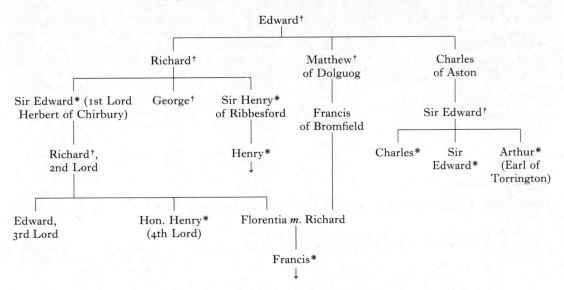

Herbert Family
of Wiltshire and Buckinghamshire

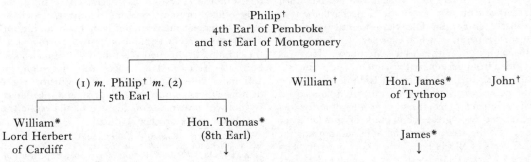

passing his accounts. He was in touch with Dykveldt, and in 1688 delivered the invitation to William of Orange, who put him in command of the invasion fleet. In this capacity he was at Plymouth during the general election of 1689, and was doubtless returned to the Convention without a contest.[3]

It is probable that fitting out the fleet prevented Herbert from taking his seat at once. He was made first lord of the Admiralty, and commanded the fleet at the indecisive skirmish of Bantry Bay on 1 May. The House agreed, however, that he should be formally thanked for his good services, and when he attended in his place on 21 May the Speaker told him that they looked upon his conduct in command 'as one of the bravest actions done in this last

age; and expect it will raise the reputation of the English valour to its ancient glory'. In reply, Herbert rather unexpectedly urged the House to make provision for seamen maimed in the service and defence of their country. A committee was set up accordingly, on which Herbert's name stood first. But he seems to have taken no further part in parliamentary proceedings before being raised to the peerage as Earl of Torrington a week later.[4]

Torrington was removed from the board of admiralty in January 1690 owing to a dispute with Lord Nottingham (Daniel Finch*). After his defeat off Beachy Head in June, he was dismissed the service and never employed again. However, he had been granted land in the fens valued at £3,000 p.a., and in 1696 he received his brother's forfeited estate at Oatlands. He died on 14 Apr. 1716, aged 67, the last of the Aston family, and was buried in Westminster Abbey. He left an estate valued at £6,000 p.a. to the impoverished 7th Earl of Lincoln, besides other legacies.[5]

[1] R. East, *Portsmouth Recs.* 361, 369; *Cal. Treas. Bks.* vi. 2; S. Wells, *Drainage of Bedford Level*, i. 467–82. [2] *Pepys Naval Mins.* (Navy Rec. Soc. lx), 36; PRO 30/53/8/12; Kent AO, NR/AEp/50; Burnet ed. Routh, iii. 101, 274. [3] Burnet, iii. 100–1; R. Morrice, Entering Bk. 2, pp. 81–82; Clarke, *Jas. II*, ii. 204; *Cal. Treas. Bks.* viii. 1657–8; Macaulay, *Hist.* 1054; *English Currant*, 28 Dec. 1688. [4] *CSP Dom.* 1689–90, p. 33; *CJ*, x. 138. [5] *Cal. Treas. Bks.* ix. 595; xi. 124–5; *Westminster Abbey Reg.* (Harl. Soc. x), 286; PCC 135 Fox.

B.D.H.

HERBERT, Charles (1644–91), of Aston, Mont.

MONTGOMERY   c. July 1685, 1689, 1690–12 July
BOROUGHS   1691

b. Aug. 1644, 1st s. of Sir Edward Herbert[†], and bro. of Arthur Herbert* and Sir Edward Herbert*. *unm. suc.* fa. 1657.[1]
   J.p. Mont. 1676–Mar. 1688, Oct. 1688–*d.*; commr. for assessment, Mont. 1679–80, 1689–90, Salop 1690.
   Capt. of ft. Admiralty Regt. 1678–9, lt. 1680–3, capt. 1683–7 (Prince George's Ft. 1685); col. (later 23 Ft.) 1689–*d.*
   Auditor of land revenues, Wales 1690–*d.*[2]

Herbert's father, first cousin to the 1st Lord Herbert of Chirbury, sat in the Long Parliament as royalist Member for Old Sarum until appointed attorney-general, in which capacity he prepared the impeachment of the Five Members. He was excluded from pardon by Parliament, and went into exile, dying in Paris, poor and friendless, in 1657. Clarendon wrote of him as an evil influence on Prince Rupert. Herbert's mother was described as one of the two 'great trumpeters of the Duke of York'. At the Restoration she obtained a grant for three years of all the King's new year presents, less £1,000. Herbert's own estate was small and he was unfortunate with his first army commission in 1678, as his company was promptly disbanded. But probably his younger brother persuaded the Duke of York to re-commission him in his regiment in 1680, though in a lower rank. He is said to have paid 800 guineas for a company three years later, and stood for Montgomery Boroughs at the general election of 1685, but was defeated by the Whig William Williams*. On his petition the election was declared void because the out-boroughs had not been polled. The return for the by-election does not survive, but Herbert took his seat in the House in the second session. During the debate on the army he asserted that 'the regiment he was of had not to his knowledge been guilty of any disorders'.

But he was appointed to no committees. He lost his commission in 1687 without compensation for opposing the introduction of Roman Catholic officers, and was absent when the questions on the Test Act and Penal Laws were put to the Montgomeryshire magistrates.[3]

Herbert was appointed governor of Ludlow by his cousin the Hon. Henry Herbert* during the Revolution, and re-elected to the Convention. He was probably an inactive Member, though as 'Captain Herbert' he was named to the committee to draw up the bill of rights, and was probably also appointed to the committees to prevent the education of Papists' children abroad, and to consider Lord Peterborough's estate bill. As a trustee for Peterborough's young nephew he gave evidence of his removal to France. He was in touch with the Hanoverian minister, and on 18 May 1689 he spoke in support of Princess Sophia's interest in the succession:

> I saw a letter of a sister of Prince Rupert's wherein she was complaining of great hardship done her children, that they were not regarded in the entail of the crown; therefore I move that they may be mentioned.

In August Herbert crossed over to Ireland with his regiment. At a review two months later William's Dutch experts commented: 'Colonel very assiduous, but too easy to the officers. Often he is the only officer present with his regiment, which he never quits, yet the regiment is in a bad condition.' The last comment applied only to the arms, since the clothing of the men was found to be good. Herbert was re-elected in 1690, but his regiment suffered severely at the battle of Aughrim, where he himself was captured by the Irish and murdered. By his will drawn up on the eve of the battle, he left Aston to his brother Arthur.[4]

[1] R. B. Gardiner, *Wadham Coll. Reg.* 159; C. J. Feret, *Fulham Old and New*, ii. 138. [2] *Cal. Treas. Bks.* ix. 615, 1523. [3] Keeler, *Long Parl.* 211; *CSP Dom.* 1651–2, p. 423; 1657–8, p. 288; *Cal. Cl. SP*, iv. 79; *Verney Mems.* ii. 461; *CJ*, ix. 715–16, 732; Christ Church Oxf. Evelyn mss; *HMC Downshire*, i. 242. [4] Eg. 2621, f. 77; *CJ*, x. 207; Grey, ix. 239; *Mont. Colls.* v. 485; xliii. 119–21; PCC 128 Vere.

L.N.

HERBERT, Sir Edward (1645–98), of Oatlands, Surr.

LUDLOW   15 Apr.–23 Oct. 1685

b. 10 June 1645, 2nd s. of Sir Edward Herbert[†] of Aston, Mont., and bro. of Arthur Herbert* and Charles Herbert*. *educ.* Winchester 1661; New College, Oxf. 1665; I. Temple 1667, called 1675, *unm.* Kntd. 19 Feb. 1684.[1]
   Gent. pens. 1671; KC [I] 1677; c.j. Tipperary [I] by 1681–3; KC 1682; c.j. Chester circuit 1683–5; solicitor-

gen. to the Duchess of York 1683–5; attorney-gen. to the Duke of York Jan.-Feb. 1685, to the Queen Feb.-Oct. 1685; PC 16 Oct. 1685–Dec. 1688; c.j.K.b. 23 Oct. 1685–7; commr. for ecclesiastical causes 1686–Oct. 1688; c.j.c.p. 1687–Dec. 1688.[2]

Fellow of New Coll. 1667–9; bencher, I. Temple 1682, reader 1685.

Herbert was elected to New College from Winchester on the recommendation of Charles II. Before qualifying as a barrister he went to Ireland in attendance on Lord Berkeley of Stratton. His application for a post in the Irish Chancery was unsuccessful, but he was appointed chief justice of Tipperary. A letter to Ormonde of 25 Feb. 1682 reported that:

> Mr Herbert, who finding his practice in Ireland not likely to answer his expectations hath during his last being to England resolved to settle at Westminster Hall, for which he hath encouragement from some grandees there, and Colonel [John] Churchill [II*] hath written him word from Scotland that his Royal Highness will take him into his service, if he were recommended from hence, where his practice of the law hath been.

He was duly given employment by the Duke of York, to whom his high notions of the royal prerogative commended him. As chief justice of Chester he was an important member of the council in the marches of Wales sitting at Ludlow, for which he was returned in 1685. He was appointed to six committees, including those on the bills for providing carriages for royal progresses, to rebuild the Earl of Powis's London house, and to repair Bangor cathedral. On the landing of Monmouth he took the chair of the committee on the bill for preserving the King's person, and carried it up to the Lords.[3]

On Herbert's appointment as lord chief justice in October, Lord Chancellor Jeffreys commended him for his 'ability, learning, integrity and resolution', and urged him to take 'the utmost vengeance of the law' upon the implacable enemies of the monarchy. In reply Herbert promised that he would 'particularly remember the obstinate and incurable Whigs'; and on the western circuit in 1686 he expressed disappointment that 'the most substantial escaped' after the Monmouth rebellion. He is chiefly remembered for his verdict in favour of the dispensation given to Edward Hales II*. However, as a member of the commission for ecclesiastical causes he had voted against a proposal that the expelled fellows of Magdalen College, Oxford, should be incapacitated, and he refused to abet the King's design of introducing martial law by declining to order the execution of a deserter from the army. He was therefore transferred to the common pleas before the trial of the Seven Bishops. In December 1688 he took out a pass to go beyond the seas, and joined James in exile, where in January

1689 he was given the new great seal struck for James in France and appointed lord chancellor. He accompanied James to Ireland and became a member of his Irish Privy Council. When he was proposed for exception from the indemnity in 1689, his old schoolfellow Sir John Holt* defended him:

> I have discoursed this point of dispensation with him, and I can say it was his own true opinion, for he aimed at nothing of preferment, and he went not so far as King James would have had him.

Before leaving England, Herbert had conveyed to his brother Charles Oatlands and 200 acres of land in Surrey which he held on a 99-year crown lease, but William seized it at the time of Herbert's outlawry. He was excepted from the Act of Indemnity in 1690, and created Earl of Portland in the Jacobite peerage. He died of apoplexy at St. Germain 5 Nov. 1698. Burnet wrote of him as 'a well-bred and virtuous man, generous and good-natured. He was but an indifferent lawyer'.[4]

[1] R. B. Gardiner, *Wadham Coll. Reg.* 159. [2] *DNB*; *Cal. Treas. Bks.* iii. 854; *HMC Ormonde*, n.s. vi. 31; *HMC Dartmouth*, iii. 125; *CSP Col.* 1685–8, pp. 194, 219. [3] *CSP Dom.* 1663–4, p. 647; 1671–2, pp. 62, 162; *HMC Ormonde*, n.s. vi. 326–7. [4] *DNB*; R. Morrice, *Entering Bk.* 1, pp. 483–4; *Reresby Mems.* 426–7; *Clarendon Corresp.* i. 426; Foss, *Judges*, vii. 222; Keeton, *Lord Chancellor Jeffreys*, 213, 367, 429, 439; *CSP Dom.* 1687–9, 417; *Trans. Salop Arch. Soc.* (ser. 2), vii. 484–5; *Parl. Hist.* v. 336; Clarke, *Jas. II*, ii. 488; *Cal. Treas. Bks.* viii. 1989; ix. 1591; *HMC Bath*, iii. 284; Burnet, iii. 97–98.

E.C.

HERBERT, Francis (c.1666–1719), of Oakly Park, nr. Ludlow, Salop.

LUDLOW   1689, 1698, 1701 (Dec.), 1715–27 Feb. 1719

b. c.1666, 1st s. of Richard Herbert of Bromfield, nr. Ludlow and Dolguog, Mont. by Florentia, da. of Richard Herbert†, 2nd Baron Herbert of Chirbury. *educ.* Christ Church, Oxf. matric. 26 Mar. 1683, aged 16; G. Inn 1687. *m.* lic. 1 Feb. 1702, Dorothy (*d.*1717), da. and h. of John Oldbury, merchant, of Broad Street, London, 6s. (4 *d.v.p.*) *suc.* fa. 1676.[1]

Freeman, Ludlow 1683, common councilman 1697–*d.*; j.p. Salop June 1688–?*d.*; commr. for assessment, Salop 1689–90, Mont. 1689; sheriff, Salop 1696–7, Mont. 1709–10.[2]

Herbert came from one of the less distinguished branches of the family. His grandfather was a commissioner of array for Charles I and compounded in 1646 on a fine of £318. His father, also a commissioner of array, was one of the proposed knights of the Royal Oak at the Restoration with estates valued at £700 p.a. Herbert succeeded at the age of ten under the guardianship of the Hon. Henry Herbert*, his maternal uncle, and Thomas Walcot*.[3]

Herbert was listed as in opposition to James II in

1687, but he was added to the Shropshire commission of the peace in the following June on the recommendation of his cousin, the Roman Catholic Marquess of Powis. He was returned as a Tory for Ludlow, two miles from his home, at the general election of 1689. According to Ailesbury's list he voted to agree with the Lords that the throne was not vacant. He was probably an inactive Member of the Convention, though he cannot usually be differentiated from Henry Herbert* and James Herbert*. As 'Mr Herbert of Ludlow' he was granted leave of absence for three weeks on 13 Apr. 1689. He wished to stand for Montgomery in 1690, but the family interest went to Charles Herbert*. After sitting in three more Parliaments as a Tory, he died on 27 Feb. 1719 and was buried at Bromfield. His sons Henry Arthur Herbert, later 1st Earl of Powis, and Richard Herbert represented Ludlow as Whigs under George II.[4]

[1] *Trans. Salop Arch. Soc.* (ser. 2), vii. 35–36. [2] Salop RO, Ludlow bor. recs. [3] *Her. and Gen.* i. 34; *Cal. Comm. Comp.* 1240; *Mont. Colls.* xx. 53; J. R. Burton, *Walcot Fam.* 63. [4] *Herbert Corresp.* (Univ. Wales, Bd. of Celtic Studies, Hist. and Law ser. xxi), 354.

E.C.

HERBERT, Henry (1654–1709), of Ribbesford, nr. Bewdley, Worcs. and Leicester Square, Westminster.[1]

BEWDLEY	10 Mar. 1677
WORCESTER	1681
BEWDLEY	1689, 1690–28 Apr. 1694

b. 24 July 1654, o. surv. s. of Sir. Henry Herbert*, being o.s. by 2nd w. *educ.* Trinity, Oxf. 1670; I. Temple 1671; L. Inn 1672. *m.* 12 Feb. 1678 (with £8,000), Anne (*d.* 24 Apr. 1716), da. and coh. of John Ramsey, Dyer, of London, 1s. *suc.* fa. 1673; *cr.* Baron Herbert of Chirbury 28 Apr. 1694.

Freeman, Bewdley 1670; commr. for assessment, Westminster, Salop, Worcs. and Mont. 1677–80, Bucks. 1679–80, Bucks., Salop, Worcs. and Worcester 1689–90; j.p. Worcs. 1677–80, 1689–*d.*, Rad. 1699–?*d.*, custos rot. Brec. 1695–1702; capt. of militia horse, Worcs. by 1697–?*d.* [2]

Ld. of trade 1707–*d.*

Though still under age, Herbert stood for Bewdley in 1673 in accordance with his father's deathbed wishes, but he was opposed by Thomas Foley I*, and it was not until 1677 that the House upheld his petition. On the working lists he was among those 'to be fixed'. Danby hastened to complete payment of the £1,448 which was owed to his father, and (Sir) Joseph Williamson*, who described him as 'a sober, discreet young man', helped to arrange a rich City marriage for him. But Shaftesbury marked him 'doubly worthy', and his sympathies clearly lay with the Opposition, though

he was not active in the Cavalier Parliament. He was probably appointed to six committees, including three of major political importance in the earlier sessions of 1678; those to examine the growth of Popery, to summarize England's commitments to her allies, and to draft an address for the removal of counsellors. He may also have acted as teller for the first paragraph of the draft address for the removal of Lauderdale of 8 May. He did not attend the final session, much to the regret of his cousin, the Hon. Henry Herbert*.[3]

At the first general election of 1679 Herbert again stood for Bewdley against the Foley interest; but he was defeated and his petition was rejected by the House. For the second election of 1679 Philip Foley* hoped to persuade him to stand for Bishop's Castle. Soon afterwards he was removed from the commission of the peace. In 1681 a seat was found for him at Worcester by the country party; but he left no traces on the records of the Oxford Parliament. He was on the Middlesex grand jury which in May found a true bill against Danby on Fitzharris's charge of complicity in the murder of Sir Edmund Berry Godfrey.[4]

Although Herbert was included in Danby's list of the Worcestershire opponents of James II, he was 'supposed right' as a candidate for Worcester by the King's electoral agents in September 1688. This is particularly surprising as he seems to have been in Holland, returning to England with the Prince of Orange in November. At the meeting of Members of Charles II's Parliaments he helped to draw up the address to the Prince and to ask him when it should be presented. At the general election of 1689 he regained his old seat at Bewdley unopposed. An active Member of the Convention, he was appointed by full name to 26 committees. He may have served on a dozen more, and acted as teller in eight divisions. He was among those instructed to inquire into the authors and advisers of grievances, to consider new oaths of allegiance and supremacy, and to inquire into the delay in relieving Londonderry. His only recorded speech was on the quarrel between William Harbord* and Henry Bertie*. He took the chair in the committee to draw up the address about the danger from France and Ireland, and made two reports, one requesting the appointment of a constable of Dover Castle, and the other inquiring about the strength of the Dutch navy. On 27 July he was sent to the House of Lords to desire a conference about Titus Oates. In the second session he was appointed to the committees to inspect expenditure on the war, to consider the mutiny bill and to examine the state of the revenue. He helped to prepare the addresses about the employment of Commissary Shales and making provision for Princess Anne. He supported the disabling clause in the bill to restore corporations, but acted as teller against extending it to James II's regulators. He was probably also teller for the expulsion of (Sir) Robert Sawyer* on 20 Jan. 1690.[5]

Herbert was re-elected for Bewdley in 1690, but raised to the peerage four years later. He remained a court Whig under William III, but did not achieve office till 1707. He died of a fever on 22 Jan. 1709, and was buried at St. Paul's, Covent Garden. His son and successor had been elected for Bewdley in the previous year.

[1] *Survey of London*, xxxiv. 490. [2] *Univ. Birmingham Hist. Jnl.* i. 105; Eg. 1626, f. 52. [3] *Epistolary Curiosities of Herbert Fam.* ed. Warner (1818), i. 100, 147; *Cal. Treas. Bks.* iv. 804; v. 726; *CSP Dom.* 1677-8, p. 410. [4] *CJ*, ix. 568, 634, 638; Add. 29910, f. 141; Eg. 2543, f. 251; Add. 28047, f. 285. [5] *CJ*, x. 186, 198, 296, 312, 323; Grey, ix. 236.

E.R.

HERBERT, Hon. Henry (c.1643–91), of Lymore, Mont. and Holborn, London.

MONTGOMERY BOROUGHS   Oct. 1665–9 Dec. 1678

b. c.1643, 4th but 2nd surv. s. of Richard Herbert[†], 2nd Baron Herbert of Chirbury (*d.*1655), by Lady Mary Egerton, da. of John Egerton[†], 1st Earl of Bridgwater. *m.* lic. 14 Dec. 1681, aged 38, Lady Katherine Newport, da. of Francis Newport[†], 1st Earl of Bradford, *s.p. suc.* bro. as 4th Baron Herbert of Chirbury 9 Dec. 1678.[1]

Ensign, King's Ft. Gds. [I] 1662; lt. of ft. Ludlow garrison 1665; capt. Admiralty Regt. 1667–80; col. own regt. (later 23 Ft.) Mar.–Apr. 1689.[2]

Commr. for assessment, Mont. 1673–8, j.p. 1677–80, custos rot. 1679–80, 1689–*d.*
Cofferer of the Household 1689–*d.*

Herbert was descended from the younger brother of the 1st Herbert Earl of Pembroke, executed as a Yorkist in 1469. His ancestors were seated at Montgomery Castle from the reign of Henry VIII till its destruction in 1649, and first sat for Montgomery Boroughs in 1542. Herbert's father was returned to the Long Parliament for this constituency, but was disabled, and fought in the Civil War as a royalist colonel. His delinquency fine was remitted in consideration of his losses sustained by the slighting of the castle. Herbert's elder brother, the 3rd Baron, was charged with complicity in Booth's rising, in which Herbert himself is also said to have been implicated. Herbert was returned at the first by-election after his coming of age. His record cannot always be distinguished from those of William Harbord* and the Hon. James Herbert*, but he was not active in the Cavalier Parliament. His duties as an army officer may have sometimes kept him from the House; he was appointed to no more than 18 committees, and never spoke. As 'Mr Henry Herbert' he served on the committee for the bill to regulate the Brecon frieze and cotton manufactures (3 Dec. 1669). After fighting a duel with John Churchill II* he was seconded to the French army in Lorraine in 1672. As 'Captain Herbert', he was named to the committee of elections and privileges on 7 Feb. 1673. Although personally anxious for peace with the Dutch, he served aboard the fleet in the summer under Sir Edward Spragge* and took part in the battle of the Schonveld. When Parliament reassembled he wrote: 'May God direct the King that . . . he may give his people some ease of mind that we shall not be overwhelmed with Popery'. The news of Shaftesbury's dismissal momentarily raised his spirits, but on 15 Nov. he lamented: ' '41, to our great trouble and grief, appears again in every action and circumstance almost'. In 1674 'Captain Herbert' was appointed to the committees to examine bills depending and to inquire into the state of Ireland.

He was marked 'bad' on the government list of 'officials' in the House in 1675; and 'worthy' on Shaftesbury's list in 1677. Either he or his cousin and namesake was appointed to the committee of 7 May 1678 to prepare an address for the removal of counsellors. He deplored his cousin's absence from the autumn session, 'when all lieth at stake, religion, King and government; a greater necessity can be never'.[3]

Herbert succeeded to the peerage in the closing weeks of the Cavalier Parliament, and became one of the most reliable country peers. As a petitioner he lost both his army commission and his local offices early in 1680. He voted for exclusion and for the condemnation of Lord Stafford, and signed the protestation over Fitzharris. At the Revolution he occupied Ludlow in the Protestant cause, and was made cofferer of the Household. He died on 21 Apr. 1691, leaving his property to his sister's son, Francis Herbert*; but his peerage was revived in 1694 for the benefit of Henry Herbert*.[4]

[1] *Herbert Corresp.* (Univ. of Wales, Bd. of Celtic Studies, Hist. and Law ser. xxi), 189; PRO 30/53/7/110; SP23/206/175. [2] *Epistolary Curiosities of Herbert Fam.* ed. Rebecca Warner (1818), i. 66–67; Bodl. Carte 31, f. 600; *HMC Ormonde*, i. 240; ii. 186. [3] Keeler, *Long Parl.* 212–13; *Cal. Comm. Comp.* 1682; *Hatton Corresp.* (Cam. Soc. n.s. xxiii), 66, 73; PRO 30/53/7/104, 108, 111, 112; *Epistolary Curiosities*, i. 147. [4] *Sidney Diary*, i. 253; *HMC Hastings*, iv. 303; *HMC Ormonde*, n.s. iv. 574; vi. 12; Clarke, *Jas. II*, ii. 233.

L.N.

HERBERT, Sir Henry (c.1595–1673), of Ribbesford, nr. Bewdley, Worcs.

MONTGOMERY BOROUGHS   1626
BEWDLEY   1640 (Apr.), 1640 (Nov.)–20 Aug. 1642, 1661–27 Apr. 1673

b. c.1595, 6th s. of Richard Herbert† (d.1596) of Montgomery Castle by Magdalen, da. of Sir Richard Newport of High Ercall, Salop; bro. of Sir Edward Herbert†, 1st Baron Herbert of Chirbury, and George Herbert†. *educ.* privately; travelled abroad (France) to 1618. *m.* (1) c.1625 (with £5,000), Susan, da. of Richard Sleford, Clothworker, of London, wid. of Edmund Plumer, Merchant Taylor, of London, 1s. *d.v.p.* 2da.; (2) by 1653, Elizabeth, da. of Sir Robert Offley of Dalby, Leics., 1s. 2da. Kntd. 7 Aug. 1623.[1]

Gent. of the privy chamber 1622–5, 1631–46; dep. master of the revels 1623–41, master 1641–2, May 1660–d,; member, council in the marches of Wales 1633–?46.[2]

J.p. Worcs. by 1636–46, July 1660–d., commr. of array 1642, sheriff 1648–9; commr. for assessment, Worcs. Aug. 1660–d., Mdx. 1661–d., Westminster and Bucks. 1663–d., Salop and Mont. 1665–d., loyal and indigent officers, Mdx. and Worcs. 1662.[3]

Herbert was the great-uncle of the Hon. Henry Herbert* and the youngest of a brilliant family. After marriage to a City widow he bought the mastership of the revels, with a salary of £500 p.a., for £3,000, and in 1627 he acquired the manor of Ribbesford, of which Bewdley had originally formed part. He was returned for the borough at both elections of 1640, but disabled as a royalist commissioner of array. Thereafter he sought, like his eldest brother, to maintain neutrality, but with even less success. He was plundered by both sides, and early in 1644 a Cavalier officer blew open the gates and the doors of Ribbesford with gunpowder, upbraided him as a traitor, and carried him off by force to sit in the Oxford Parliament. At the end of the first Civil War he petitioned to compound for an estate of £415 p.a., though its real value was almost double, and asked for debts of £3,000, loss of office, and four years' arrears of salary to be taken into consideration. He was fined £1,332 at one-third. For most of the Interregnum he lived in London and took no part in royalist conspiracy.[4]

Herbert is unlikely to have stood in 1660, but in 1661 his great-nephew, the 3rd Lord Herbert of Chirbury, proposed him as candidate for the borough seat in Montgomery. As tenant of Kerry rectory, he had some claim to be regarded as a local landowner, but he was not elected. However, he regained his Bewdley seat by defeating the Cavalier, Sir Ralph Clare†, and Lord Wharton listed him as a friend to be managed by Sir Richard Onslow*. A moderately active Member of the Cavalier Parliament, he was appointed to 90 committees. In the opening session he was named to the committees for the security and corporations bills, for preventing mischief from Quakers, for the bill of pains and penalties, and for the Stour and Salwarp navigation bill. In the course of his prolonged and unsuccessful struggle to reassert the authority of his office over

the theatres he was served with a subpoena on behalf of Michael Mohun, the leading man in the Theatre Royal. He claimed parliamentary privilege on 24 Jan. 1662, but the House ordered proceedings to be stayed three days later, and on 3 Feb. the court of common pleas awarded Herbert £48. In the 1663 session he was added to the committee for the regulation of printing and appointed to that for recommending remedies for meetings of dissenters. When he went out of town at the prorogation, one of his staff complained of his 'much attendance at the Parliament House'. Listed as a court dependant in 1664, he was named to the committees for the bills to cancel the conveyance by Sir John Pakington, 2nd Bt.*, of his Aylesbury property, and to erect a separate parish of St. James Piccadilly, as well as to that for the conventicles bill. On 20 Jan. 1665 he carried up the bill to enable Samuel Sandys I* and his son to sell part of their estate, and he was the first Member appointed to the committees on the bill for the true making of brick and tile and the bill for the Brixton navigation promoted by Lord Loughborough.[5]

Herbert's attitude to Clarendon's dismissal is unknown, and he was appointed to no further committees of political moment, though he took a keen interest in the rebuilding of London. He is recorded as making only four speeches. On 10 Dec. 1669 he opposed the attempt to suspend Sir George Carteret*, because he 'never remembers the suspension of any man but for things arising out of the House'. He argued cogently against double taxation of absentee Members in 1671, because it would condemn them unheard and expose the privileges of the Commons to the scrutiny of the Lords. He opposed the bill for a bridge at Putney on 4 Apr. because it looked like a monopoly and the House was too thin to consider so important a measure. He was on both lists of government supporters at this time as one of the Members who usually voted for supply. His last speech was in the debate on relief for 'tender consciences' on 14 Feb. 1673. He strongly opposed the extension of the bill to Papists, 'for they are not quiet and peaceable men as others are'. He died on 27 Apr. and was buried at St. Paul's, Covent Garden.[6]

[1] *Vis. Worcs.* (Harl. Soc. xc), 47; PCC 65 Dale, 67 Byrde. [2] Carlisle, *Privy Chamber*, 132; J. Q. Adams, *Dramatic Recs. of Sir Henry Herbert*, 8; *Arch. Camb.* (ser. 6), xvii. 195. [3] J. H. Gleason, *Justices of the Peace*, 217; *Townshend's Diary* ed. Bund, ii. 276. [4] *VCH Worcs.* iv. 308; Keeler, *Long Parl.* 211; SP23/186/518–43; *HMC 5th Rep.* 179. [5] PRO 30/53/7/76; L. Hotson, *Commonwealth and Restoration Stage*, 202–5; *CSP Dom.* 1661–2, p. 244; Adams, 129. [6] Grey, i. 213–14, 393, 417; ii. 35.

E.R.

HERBERT, James (1660–1704), of Tythrop House, Kingsey, Bucks.

QUEENBOROUGH 14 Apr. 1677, 1679 (Mar.), 1679 (Oct.)–8 Jan. 1681
WESTBURY   1685
QUEENBOROUGH   1689
AYLESBURY   28 Jan. 1696, 1698, 1701 (Feb.), 1701 (Dec.), 1702–11 Nov. 1704

bap. 27 Apr. 1660, 1st s. of Hon. James Herbert*. *educ.* travelled abroad (France) 1675–8. *m.* 1 July 1674, Lady Catherine Osborne, da. of Sir Thomas Osborne*, 1st Duke of Leeds, 3s. 4da. *suc.* fa. 1677.[1]
Dep. lt. Oxon. 1681–Feb. 1688, Bucks. 1685–Feb. 1688, Bucks. and Oxon. Oct. 1688–*d.*, Kent 1694–*d.*; j.p. Oxon. 1682–Mar. 1688, Oct. 1688–*d.*, Bucks. 1685–Feb. 1688, Sept. 1688–*d.*; freeman, Oxford 1684–Jan. 1688, Devizes 1684–Mar. 1688; commr. for assessment, Bucks., Kent and Oxon. 1689–90; maj. of militia ft. Oxon. by 1697–*d.*[2]
Receiver-gen. of prizes 1689–99, 1702–*d.*[3]

Though both under age and out of the country, 'very commendably employed in study or ingenious conversation or designing' in Paris, Herbert was returned for Queenborough unopposed within a fortnight of his father's death. His hereditary interest, coupled with the government interest he enjoyed as son-in-law to the lord treasurer, obliged his opponent to withdraw before the poll. Though he was not, as alleged in *A Seasonable Argument*, 'but fifteen years old', he did not take his seat until the following year, when he may have been appointed to one committee, on the bill for the new parish of St. James Piccadilly. He was marked 'doubly vile' on Shaftesbury's list, and his name appeared on both lists of the court party in 1678. Re-elected to the first Exclusion Parliament after a contest, he was marked 'vile' by Shaftesbury. He was appointed only to the committee of elections and privileges. According to the official list he voted against exclusion, but Roger Morrice put him down among the absentees. Despite the timely present of a new mace to the Queenborough corporation, Herbert's majority sank to one at the next election, and he was unseated in favour of William Glanville* without taking any ascertainable part in the proceedings of the second Exclusion Parliament. On its dissolution he renewed his candidature, but without success.[4]

After the Rye House Plot, 'young Mr Herbert' was active in searching for arms in Oxfordshire, and personally arrested Charlton, Shaftesbury's chief confidant, on the high road. At the general election of 1685, however, he seems to have covertly encouraged his Buckinghamshire tenants to vote for the Whig, the Hon. Thomas Wharton*, whilst he

transferred himself to Westbury, where he was returned, probably without a contest, on the Bertie interest, and included by his father-in-law among the Opposition in James II's Parliament. A moderately active Member, he was named to the elections committee and those for St. James Piccadilly and the Earl of Cleveland's creditors. To the questions put to him by the lord lieutenant of Oxfordshire about the repeal of the Test Act and Penal Laws, he replied: 'Though he should be ready to serve the King in anything else, he cannot consent. . . . He shall be for the electing of such as are of the same opinion.' In the abortive election of 1688 Herbert was returned for Queenborough, again presumably in his absence, for he took part in Danby's rising in the north, and was sent as his messenger to the Prince of Orange. The 1689 election confirmed his return for Queenborough. According to Ailesbury's list he voted to agree with the Lords that the throne was not vacant. But he became a court Tory and was made receiver-general of prizes. No committees or speeches can definitely be attributed to him in the Convention, but he was given leave to go into the country for a week on urgent business on 2 Dec. Herbert lost his seat at the general election, but sat for Aylesbury from 1696 to his death as a Tory, though he signed the Association in 1696. He died on 11 Nov. 1704. His son was elected for Queenborough in 1710 and for Oxfordshire after the Hanoverian succession.[5]

[1] *Mems. of St. Margaret's Westminster*, 261; *Cal. Treas. Bks.* iv. 826; v. 886; Westminster City Lib. St. Martin in the Fields par. reg.; PCC 49 Hale, 53 Gee. [2] *CSP Dom.* 1680–1, p. 515; 1683–4, p. 358; 1694–5, p. 128; *Bucks. Sess. Recs.* ed. Le Hardy, i. 165, 510; ii. 455; *Council Acts* (Oxf. Hist. Soc. n.s. ii), 162; PC2/72, ff. 579, 632; Eg. 1626, f. 36. [3] *Cal. Treas. Bks.* ix. 217; *CSP Dom.* 1699–1700, p. 210; Luttrell, v. 183. [4] Browning, *Danby*, ii. 554; HMC *14th Rep. IX*, 414; *Arch. Cant.* xxii. 185. [5] *CSP Dom.* July–Sept. 1683, pp. 153, 238, 244; Jones, *First Whigs*, 191; Browning, i. 368, 560; ii. 149, 154; Kent AO, Qb/RP, f. 1; Luttrell, v. 183; Le Neve, *Mon. Angl.* 1700–15, p. 92.

B.D.H.

HERBERT, Hon. James (c.1623–77), of Tythrop House, Kingsey, Bucks.

WILTSHIRE   12 May 1646[1]
QUEENBOROUGH   1659, 1660, 1661–3 Apr. 1677

b. c.1623, 6th but 2nd surv. s. of Philip Herbert†, 1st Earl of Montgomery and 4th Earl of Pembroke, by 1st w. Lady Susan Vere, da. and coh. of Edward, 17th Earl of Oxford; bro. of John Herbert†, Philip Herbert†, Lord Herbert of Cardiff and William Herbert†. *educ.* Jesus, Oxf. matric. 15 June 1638, aged 15; travelled abroad 1641–4. *m.* 3 Aug. 1646, Jane, da. and h. of Sir Robert Spiller† of Laleham, Mdx., 4s. 3da. *suc.* fa. in Sheppey estate 1650.[2]
Commr. for assessment, Wilts. 1647–8, Kent Aug.

1660–1, Oxon. Sept. 1660–1, Bucks. 1661–74, Kent and Oxon. 1664–74, militia, Wilts. 1648, Bucks., Oxon., Westminster and Wilts. Mar. 1660; j.p. Wilts. Mar.– July 1660, Bucks. Mar. 1660–*d.*, Oxon. 1662–*d.*; dep. lt. Bucks. c. Aug. 1660–*d.*; commr. for loyal and indigent officers, Oxon. 1662; receiver of taxes, Bucks. 1677–*d.*[3]

Herbert's father, one of James I's handsome young men, received, among other marks of favour, extensive grants of crown lands in Sheppey. Though the family was divided in the Civil War, he became one of the most prominent parliamentarian peers, sitting for Berkshire in the Rump after the abolition of the House of Lords. Herbert sat for Wiltshire in the Long Parliament as a recruiter, but held no office after Pride's Purge. He acquired by marriage an estate worth over £2,000 p.a. on the borders of Buckinghamshire and Oxfordshire, where he resided: but he inherited an interest at Queenborough, for which he was returned at the general election of 1660. An inactive Member of the Convention, he made no recorded speeches, was named to only five committees, and twice acted as teller. On 2 Apr. he was sent to the House of Lords to propose a day of thanksgiving. He was added to the committees for recovering the queen mother's jointure and examining John Thurloe†, and appointed to those for the prevention of swearing and marital separation. Herbert showed a great sense of personal loyalty towards Edmund Ludlow*, his colleague at the Wiltshire election of 1646, by offering £4,000 bail for him. Ludlow, with equal loyalty, took care that Herbert should not lose by it. On 10 Dec. he was instructed to secure the concurrence of the Lords in an order for the maintenance of the Dunkirk garrison. Lord Wharton marked him as a friend, and he may have acted with the Opposition.[4]

Herbert was re-elected in 1661, but he is seldom mentioned by full name in the Journals, and hence his record in the Cavalier Parliament cannot be entirely distinguished for those of William Harboard* and the Hon. Henry Herbert*. He was not an active Member, being appointed to no more than 57 committees, including those for the corporations and uniformity bills. He acted as teller against provisos to the indemnity bill and the bill of pains and penalties. He was probably in Opposition under the Clarendon administration, since a quo warranto was ordered in 1664 into his claim to a monopoly of oysters in his constituency, and in 1669 Sir Thomas Osborne* (later Lord Treasurer Danby) listed him among the Members to be gained for the Court by the Duke of Buckingham. He may have been sent to the Lords on 29 Mar. 1673 to desire a conference on the bill of ease for Protestant dissenters. In 1674 he was one of the Members who

reported Shaftesbury's assertion that he had seen a crucifix in the house of Samuel Pepys*, and he was apparently listed as in Opposition by Sir Richard Wiseman*. But his name appeared on the working lists, and the marriage of his son to Danby's daughter brought him into some prominence on the court side. On 21 Feb. 1677 he moved to give the King £800,000, the sum required by the Government. 'Had we given money the last meeting, we had not been outgone by the French in building of ships now', he said. Unfortunately he went on to second a motion made the day before, and was laughed at for his ignorance of procedure. But Danby gratefully put his name down for a receivership of taxes. He was named to the committee to consider the bill to prevent the growth of Popery, and on 26 Mar. he moved for an address for stricter alliances against France. This proposal was well supported, but the excitement may have been too much for him. He declared himself to be 'in perfect health' when he made his will on 2 Apr., but two days later he was dead. He was buried in Thame Church.[5]

[1] Did not sit after Pride's Purge, 6 Dec. 1648, readmitted 21 Feb. 1660. [2] Lipscomb, *Bucks.* i. 298; *PC Reg.* xii. 193; F. G. Lee, *Church of Thame*, 569–70; PCC 49 Hale; *Mems. St. Margaret's Westminster*, 221, 255. [3] *Cal. Treas. Bks.* v. 430. [4] Hasted, *Kent*, vi. 175–6; *EHR*, l. 245; *HMC Lords*, iii. 127; *Arch. Cant.* xxii. 185; *Voyce from the Watch Tower*, 164. [5] *CJ*, viii. 272, 306; ix. 197, 414; PC2/57/216; Grey, ii. 411, 429; iv. 112; Add. 28091, ff. 59–60; Eg. 3345, f. 38.

M.W.H./B.D.H.

HERBERT, Sir James (c.1644–1709), of Coldbrook Park, Mon.

?MONMOUTH   12 June 1685

b. c.1644, 2nd but o. surv. s. of Henry Herbert† of Coldbrook by Mary, da. of James Rudyard, Grocer, of London. *m.* 2 Dec. 1669, Judith, da. of Edward Mouse, Goldsmith, of Foster Lane, London, wid. of John Godden, laceman, of Stoke Newington, Mdx., 1da. *suc.* fa. 1656; kntd. 1 Aug. 1680.[1]

Commr. for assessment, Mon. 1664–80, 1689–90, j.p. 1667–96, 1700–*d.*, commr. for recusants 1675, sheriff 1678–9, dep. lt. 1685–Feb. 1688, Oct. 1688–9, by 1701–*d.*

Herbert was descended from a younger brother of the 1st Herbert Earl of Pembroke. The head of the Coldbrook branch had regularly sat for either county or borough since 1558. Herbert's father, thanks to his City connexions, was one of the few South Wales gentry to support Parliament consistently through the Civil War; during the Interregnum he sat on the Council of State and the high court of justice. But Herbert himself from his first appearance on the political scene supported the court party in Monmouthshire. He was proposed as a candidate for the county by-election of 1667 by the Marquess of Worcester (Henry Somerset*), but was defeated by Sir Trevor Williams*. As returning officer in 1679 Worcester relied on him to secure the return of his son (Charles Somerset*). Herbert took the lead in opposing the petitioning activities of John Arnold*, and on 18 Nov. 1680 was reprimanded by the House of Lords for his lack of zeal in prosecuting Papists, though with the qualification that his loyalty and protestantism were not impugned. Herbert is said to have been returned for the borough at a by-election in 1685 after Charles Somerset* had opted for another seat, but he left no trace in the records of James II's Parliament. He was severely rebuked by the Treasury in 1687 for oppressive use of his position on the bench to enforce feudal rights over his tenants. A secret correspondent of William of Orange, he gave negative replies on the repeal of the Test Act and Penal Laws, and was removed from the lieutenancy. Nevertheless he was approved as a court candidate for Monmouth in 1688. Refusing the Association in 1696, he is not known to have stood for Parliament again. He died on 6 June 1709, aged 65, leaving his estates to his only daughter, who married Sir Thomas Powell, MP for Monmouth from 1705 to 1708.[2]

[1] Bradney, *Mon.* i. 185–9; Soc. of Genealogists, Boyd's London Units 25022; *Inhabitants of London in 1638* ed. Dale, 92. [2] A. H. Dodd, *Studies in Stuart Wales*, 112; *CSP Dom.* 1678–9, p. 74; *CJ*, ix. 658; *HMC Finch*, ii. 77; *HMC Lords*, ii. 207–9; *Cal. Treas. Bks.* vii. 786; viii. 1396–7; *LJ*, xiii. 621, 675; Cobbett, *Parl. Hist.* iv. 1346; J. R. Jones, *Revolution of 1688*, 235; PC2/76/256; Bodl. Carte 130, f. 124.

J.P.F.

HERBERT, Hon. Thomas (c.1656–1733), of Wilton, Wilts.

WILTON 1679 (Mar.), 1679 (Oct.), 1681

b. c.1656, 3rd s. of Philip Herbert†, 5th Earl of Pembroke, being 2nd s. by 2nd w. Katherine, da. of Sir William Villiers, 1st Bt., of Brooksby, Leics.; half-bro. of William Herbert*, Lord Herbert. *educ.* Christ Church, Oxf. matric. 18 Mar. 1673, aged 16; travelled abroad (France, Italy) 1676–9, *m.* (1) 26 July 1684, Margaret (*d.* 27 Nov. 1706), da. and h. of (Sir) Robert Sawyer* of Highclere, Hants, 7s. 5da.; (2) 21 Sept. 1708, Barbara (*d.* 1 Aug. 1721), da. of Sir Thomas Slingsby, 2nd Bt.*, of Scriven, Yorks., wid. of Sir Richard Mauleverer, 4th Bt., of Allerton Mauleverer, Yorks., and of John Arundell*, 2nd Baron Arundell of Trerice, 1da.; (3) 14 June 1725, Mary, da. of Sir Scrope Howe*, 1st Visct. Howe [I], *s.p. suc.* bro. Philip as 8th Earl of Pembroke 29 Aug. 1683; KG 14 May 1700.[1]

Freeman, E. I. Co. 1678; commr. for assessment, Wilts. 1679–80; ld. lt. Wilts. 1683–*d.*, S. Wales and Mon. 1694–1715; j.p. and custos rot. Glam. 1683–1728, Pemb. 1683–1715; high steward, Wilton 1685–*d.*, Salisbury 1709–*d.*; elder bro. Trinity House 1691–1707, master 1692–4.[2]

Ambassador to the States General 1689, 1705; PC 14 Feb. 1689–*d.*, ld. pres. 1699–1702, 1702–8; first ld. of the Admiralty 1690–2, 1701–2; ld. privy seal 1692–9; one of the lds. justices 1695–1701, 1714; first plenip. Congress of Ryswick, 1697; ld. high admiral 1702, 1708–9; commr. for union with Scotland 1706–7; ld. lt. [I] 1707–8.

Col. of ft. (Dutch army) 1685, 2 Marine Regt. 1690–1.[3]

FRS 1685, pres. 1689–90.

As a younger son, Herbert is said to have 'applied himself to the law and knowledge of the constitution of his country', though he was not admitted to the inns of court. On his travels he became the friend and patron of Locke. He sat for Wilton, where the family interest had survived his brother's inroads on the estate, in the three Exclusion Parliaments, in which he served on no committees and made no speeches. He was marked 'doubtful' on Shaftesbury's list, and was absent from the division on the bill. After succeeding to the peerage as Lord Pembroke he led the Wiltshire militia at Sedgemoor, and was nominated by James II to command the British regiments in the Dutch service. Although he remained nominally lord lieutenant of Wiltshire for the rest of his life he refused to put the three questions on the repeal of the Test Act and Penal Laws, and was virtually superseded for the last months of James's reign by the Earl of Yarmouth (William Paston*). He was in touch with William of Orange, if only to desire his 'favourable opinion', but on the landing of the Dutch army he offered his services to James. He was one of the four peers sent to William on 11 Dec. 1688 to ask him to summon a free Parliament.[4]

After speaking and voting against the transfer of the crown in the Convention, he nevertheless took part in the coronation of William and Mary and held high office for the next 20 years, the perfect type of the court Tory. But he was not without principles; he opposed the execution of Sir John Fenwick*, protested against the Irish Forfeitures Act, and spoke in favour of the acquittal of Dr Sacheverell. On resigning office in 1709 he was given a pension of £3,000 p.a. Pembroke and Nottingham (Daniel Finch*) were the only Tory peers to insist on 'no peace without Spain' in 1711, and he was always a firm supporter of the Hanoverian succession. Burnet, his neighbour at Salisbury for a quarter of a century, describes him as

a man of eminent virtue, and of great and profound learning, particularly in the mathematics. This made him a little too speculative and abstract in his notions. He had great application, but he lived a little too much out of the world, though in a public station; a little more practice among men would give him the last finishing. There was somewhat in his person and manner that created him an universal respect, for we had no other man among us whom all sides loved and honoured so much as they did him.

As 'Long Tom' aged into 'Old Pem' his eccentricities became more pronounced, and he developed into something of a domestic tyrant. In spite of his expenditure on his collections—he was one of the leading virtuosi of his day—his long tenure of office and careful management of the estate greatly increased his wealth. He died on 22 Jan. 1733, and was buried in Salisbury Cathedral. Three of his sons sat for Wilton under the Hanoverians.[5]

[1] Cal. Treas. Bks. v. 382. [2] Cal. Ct. Mins. E.I. Co. ed. Sainsbury, xi. 192; CSP Dom. 1685, p. 99. [3] CSP Dom. 1689–90, p. 423; Luttrell, ii. 157. [4] Macky, Mems. 21; M. Cranston, John Locke, 166; Luttrell, i. 432, 467; Add. 34515, f. 33; CSP Dom. 1687–9, pp. 140, 379; Dalrymple, Mems. ii. bk. v. 113. [5] K. Feiling, Tory Party, 260, 324; D. Rubini, Court and Country, 167; G. Holmes, British Politics in the Age of Anne, 78, 253–4, 389; Burnet ed. Routh, iv. 361–2.

J.P.F.

HERBERT, William, Lord Herbert of Cardiff (1642–74).

GLAMORGAN   1661–11 Dec. 1669

b. 14 July 1642, 1st s. of Philip Herbert[†], 5th Earl of Pembroke, by 1st w. Penelope, da. and h. of Sir Robert Naunton[†] of Letheringham, Suff., wid. of Paul, 2nd Visct. Bayning of Sudbury; half-bro. of Hon. Thomas Herbert*. educ. privately; travelled abroad (France) 1658–9. unm. suc. fa. 11 Dec. 1669.[1]

Dep. lt. Wilts. and Glam. c. Aug. 1660–?70; freeman, Poole Nov. 1660; commr. for oyer and terminer, Wales 1661, assessment, Wilts. and Glam. 1661–9; j.p. and custos rot. Wilts. 1665–d., Glam. and Pemb. 1670–d.[2]

Lord Herbert's ancestors had been great landowners in South Wales since the 15th century, when they sat for the English border counties. His father represented Glamorgan in the Long Parliament, and as a Rumper presided over the Council of State in 1652. Reputedly a Quaker, he engaged the Anglican Sir Richard Fanshawe* as Herbert's bear-leader in 1658, and conformed to the restored monarchy at least to the extent of officiating in a minor capacity at the coronation of Charles II and as treasurer of the Royal Fishery. Herbert was returned for Glamorgan at the general election of 1661, the last of his family to sit for a Welsh constituency. The references to Lord Herbert in the Cavalier Parliament all seem to be to Henry Somerset*. He was listed as a friend on Lord Wharton's list, and assigned to the management of Sir Richard Onslow*. Nevertheless he was included by Sir Thomas Osborne* in the list of Members who usually voted for supply in 1669, shortly before he

succeeded to the title. He does not appear to have taken his seat in the House of Lords. He died on 8 July 1674, and was buried in Salisbury Cathedral.[3]

[1] Westminster City Lib. St. Martin in the Fields par. reg.; CSP Dom. 1658–9, p. 580. [2] Hutchins, Dorset, i. 32. [3] Keeler, Long Parl. 211–12; Fanshawe Mems. 87; HMC Hastings, ii. 150.

L.N.

HERBERT OF RAGLAN, Lord see **SOMERSET, Charles and Henry.**

HERBERT see also **HARBORD.**

HERLE, Edward (c.1617–95), of Prideaux, Luxulyan, Cornw.

BOSSINEY   1640 (Apr.)
FOWEY   1659, 1660
GRAMPOUND   1689

b. c.1617, 1st s. of Thomas Herle of Prideaux by Loveday, da. of Nicholas Glyn of Glynn, Cardinham; bro. of Thomas Herle*. m. (1) lic. 5 Feb. 1634, Mary (d.1673), da. and coh. of Nicholas Trefusis[†] of Landue, Lezant, 7s. (4 d.v.p.) 3da.; (2) 1680, Susanna, wid. of John Owen, Fishmonger, of Bread Street, London and Mortlake, Surr., s.p. suc. fa. 1644.[1]

Lt.-col. (parliamentary) to 1646.[2]

Sheriff, Cornw. Dec. 1646–Jan. 1648, v.–adm. 1647–9, commr. for assessment 1647–8, Jan. 1660, 1661–3, 1666–80, 1689–90, militia 1648, 1659, Mar. 1660, j.p. 1649–52, 1653–62, 1668–70, June 1688–d., maj. of militia horse Apr. 1660; stannator, Foymore 1673; dep. lt. Cornw. July 1688–?d.[3]

Herle's ancestors acquired Prideaux, five miles from Fowey, by marriage at the end of the 14th century, and first sat in Parliament for Liskeard in 1425. Herle's uncle was prolocutor of the Westminster Assembly, and he himself was doubtless a Presbyterian. In arms for Parliament in the first Civil War, he held office only intermittently during the Interregnum, and signed the Truro declaration for a free Parliament in December 1659.[4]

At the general election of 1660 Herle was returned for Callington, probably on the interest of Robert Rolle*, and for Fowey, where he was elected on the Treffry interest. Choosing to sit for the latter, he was marked as a friend on Lord Wharton's list. But he made no recorded speeches in the Convention, and probably served on no committees. He is unlikely to have stood in 1661, and was removed from the Cornish commission of the peace. After a further short period as j.p. from 1668 to 1670 he was again dismissed, presumably as an opponent of the Conventicles Act, though it was on the grounds of debt and ill-health that he was excused from serving as sheriff in 1671–2.[5]

Herle survived his eldest sons and his brother to become a Whig collaborator under James II. He was one of the dissenting magistrates restored to the county bench in 1688, and at the succeeding general election he was successful at Grampound. In the Convention he was named only to the committee on the bill for the easier recovery of tithes, and on 2 July 1689 he was granted leave to go into the country. Although presumably a Whig, he was not listed as a supporter of the disabling clause in the bill to restore corporations, and probably did not stand again. He was buried at Luxulyan on 20 Apr. 1695.[6]

[1] Vivian, *Vis. Cornw.* 218–20; J. R. Woodhead, *Rulers of London*, 124; PCC 5 Drax; Soc. of Genealogists, Lezant par. reg. [2] J. Sprigge, *Anglia Rediviva*, 304. [3] Boase and Courtney, *Bibl.Cornub.* iii. 1228–9; *CSP Dom.* 1649–50, p. 203; *Parl. Intell.* 9 Apr. 1660; Add. 6713, f. 377. [4] *DNB*; M. Coate, *Cornw. in the Gt. Civil War*, 219, 245, 308. [5] *CSP Dom.* 1671, p. 592; 1672–3, p. 126. [6] Vivian, 220.

M.W.H./P.W.

HERLE, Nicholas (1641–83), of Landue, Lezant, Cornw.

GRAMPOUND 1679 (Oct.), 1681

bap. 2 May 1641, 2nd s. of Edward Herle*. *m.* lic. 21 Oct. 1672, Elizabeth, da. and h. of Peter Read of Upton Pyne, Devon, 2s.[1]
Commr. for assessment, Cornw. 1666–9, 1677–80.

Herle's elder brother died young, and, on his marriage to a minor Devonshire heiress, Landue, which had belonged to his mother, and two-thirds of the estate, were settled on him. Returned to the second and third Exclusion Parliaments for Grampound, a borough frequently represented by the Herles, he was appointed to no committees and made no speeches in either Parliament. Nothing is known for certain about his politics, but as his family had earlier had Presbyterian and Parliamentarian sympathies he may have supported exclusion. He died of smallpox in his father's lifetime and was buried at St. Mary Aldermanbury on 20 Jan. 1683. His son, Edward, sat for Launceston as a Tory from 1713 to 1721.[2]

[1] Gilbert, *Paroch. Hist. Cornw.* iii. 41; Soc. of Genealogists, Exeter mar. lic.; C8/307/1. [2] Gilbert, iii. 122–3, 188; *St. Mary Aldermanbury* (Harl. Soc. Reg. lxii), 199.

P.W.

HERLE, Thomas (1622–81), of Luxulyan, Cornw.

GRAMPOUND 1659, 1660
TREGONY 1661

bap. 29 Dec. 1622, 2nd s. of Thomas Herle of Prideaux, and bro. of Edward Herle*. *educ.* Exeter, Oxf. 1639; M. Temple 1648. *unm.*

Commr. for assessment, Cornw. 1661–79, recusants 1675.

Herle, possibly a Presbyterian like his brother, does not seem to have taken any active part in the fighting during the Civil War, although his sympathies probably lay with the Parliamentarians. He was first returned to Parliament in 1659. In December of that year he was one of the Cornish gentry who met at Truro to issue a call for a free Parliament. Re-elected to the Convention for Grampound, he was not listed as a friend by Lord Wharton, nor was he an active Member. He made no recorded speeches, but probably served on four committees, of which the most important were for the Post Office and marital separation bills.

Returned for Tregony in 1661, presumably on the interest of Hugh Boscawen*, Herle was appointed to the committee for the corporations bill and only 17 others. He may have followed Boscawen's lead in politics, though he was sent the government whip by Secretary Coventry in 1675. His name did not appear on any other lists of court supporters, and in 1676 Sir Richard Wiseman* included him among the 19 Cornish Members of whom he could 'say very little', adding that most of them were Presbyterians from whom nothing could be hoped. In 1677 Shaftesbury classed him as 'worthy'. He acted as teller with John Fagg I* for the motion to give (Sir) John Otway* leave to go into the country on 10 March. In December 1678 he was absent from a call of the House, and he did not stand again. His will was proved on 14 June 1681.

Vivian, *Vis. Cornw.* 218–20; M. Coate, *Civil War in Cornw.* 29, 308; PCC 92 North.

M.W.H./P.W.

HERNE, Joseph (1639–99), of King's Arms Yard, Colman Street, London.

DARTMOUTH 28 Nov. 1689, 1690, 1695, 1698–26 Feb. 1699

bap. 17 Apr. 1639, 8th s. of Nicholas Herne, Merchant Taylor, of the Golden Bull, Cheapside, London, being 4th s. by 2nd w. Susan, da. of Richard Ironside, Leatherseller, of London; bro. of Sir Nathaniel Herne*. *m.* 23 July 1672 (with £5,000), Elizabeth, da. of (Sir) John Frederick* of Old Jewry, London, 7s. 3da. Kntd. 15 Sept. 1690.[1]
Freeman, E.I. Co. 1671, committee 1678–86, 1687–94, 1698–*d.*, gov. 1690–2; alderman of London 1686–7, dep. lt. 1689–?*d.*; member, Mercers' Co. by 1687–*d.*; commr. for assessment, London and Devon 1689–90; gov. Copper Miners' Co. 1691, Merchant Adventurers to N.W. America 1691; dep. gov. Royal Fishery [I] 1691–2; asst. Mines Co. 1693; commr. for Land Bank 1696; crown trustee for Exchequer bills 1697.[2]

Herne succeeded his father-in-law in 1685 as head of the leading firm in the peninsular trade, and by 1689 held £4,883 of East India stock. Appointed alderman of London in 1686, he was allowed to resign on 7 July 1687, probably in anticipation of the purge of Anglicans from the bench in the following month. Otherwise there is no evidence of his political attitude before or during the Revolution.[3]

Herne petitioned against the return of George Booth* for Dartmouth on 25 Oct. 1689, on the grounds of the irregular creation of freemen. His petition was upheld, and he took his seat on 28 Nov. Either at the time or shortly afterwards he took into partnership a London member of the Upton family, and thereby combined the interest of his own firm with that which had held one of the Dartmouth seats almost uninterruptedly since 1625. He did not speak, and his only committee in the Convention was appointed to consider the petition of the Royal Africa Company on the day of its final prorogation.[4]

Herne represented Dartmouth till his death. Although from 1690 he was heavily committed to the new regime financially, his parliamentary record is uncertain. In spite of Jacobite connexions he signed the Association in 1696. He died of a cerebral haemorrhage on 26 Feb. 1699, said to be worth £200,000. The Herne family continued to hold one seat at Dartmouth, and sometimes two, without intermission till 1722.[5]

[1] Vis. London (Harl. Soc. xv), 378; Inhabitants of London in 1638 ed. Dale, 60; Cal. Cl. SP, iii. 248; The Gen. n.s. xxvii. 67; J. R. Woodhead, Rulers of London, 89; PCC 77 Herne. [2] HMC Lords, iii. 47; CSP Dom. 1689–90, p. 488; 1690–1, p. 527; 1691–2, pp. 4, 113; Cal. Treas. Bks. xi. 16; xii. 8. [3] Cal. Co. Mins. E.I. Co. ed. Sainsbury, ix. 65; Add. 22185, f. 14; Cal. Treas. Bks. iv. 416; CSP Dom. Jan.–June 1683, p. 167. [4] Cal. Treas. Bks. ix. 847. [5] HMC Downshire, 484; HMC Portland, iii. 603.

J.P.F.

HERNE, Sir Nathaniel (c.1629–79), of Lothbury, London.

DARTMOUTH   1679 (Mar.)

b. c.1629, 5th s. of Nicholas Herne, being 1st s. by 2nd w.; bro. of Joseph Herne*. m. 1 Sept. 1656 (with £5,000), Judith, da. of John Frederick* of Old Jewry, London, 3s. 2da. Kntd. 9 Aug. 1674.[1]

Member, Barber-Surgeons' Company 1655, master 1674–5; member, Hon. Artillery Co. May 1660; committee, E.I. Co. 1666–d., dep. gov. 1672–4, gov. 1674–6, 1678–d.; sheriff, London 1674–5, common councilman 1675–6, alderman 1676–d.; commr. for assessment, London 1677–9, Mdx. and Devon 1679–d.; member Royal Fishery Co. 1677.[2]

Commr. for inquiry into the Mint 1677–8.[3]

Herne's family was of Norfolk origin, but his was the third generation to achieve civic office in London. A typically industrious apprentice, he married his master's daughter the year after the expiry of his indentures and was taken into partnership. The Spanish trade in which the firm was principally concerned was hard-hit by Cromwell's foreign policy, and Herne was probably the 'stout and active young citizen' concerned in Cavalier plots in the City in 1657.[4]

Herne first engaged in parliamentary politics in support of Joseph Williamson* at Dartmouth in 1667. Correctly anticipating Williamson's defeat, he offered to serve him also at Plympton. In both constituencies his interest was based on the extensive West Country connexions of his firm. A tireless worker (in one year he attended 215 out of 217 East India Company courts), Herne made himself useful both to the company and the Government in collecting foreign intelligence, though in the latter case under pledges of the strictest secrecy. His services were ill-rewarded when he stood for Dartmouth in 1673; court influence was used to intimidate his supporters and he was defeated by Josiah Child*. The election was quashed owing to an irregularity in the writ, but Herne was unable to regain more than one of his lost votes. He petitioned against the second election on the grounds of bribery, but no result is recorded.[5]

On appointment to municipal office, Herne showed the same indefatigable industry as in business. He could hardly find a day free for dinner with his old friend Williamson because of sessions business. Herne was personally commended by the King for his loyalty, vigilance and conduct in handling a weavers' riot against machines in 1675. But he declined to persecute conventiclers; inviting a dozen bishops to dinner, he told them bluntly that City merchants 'could not trade with their neighbours one day, and send them to gaol the next'. In the same year he gave evidence before the parliamentary committee to hear complaints against the East India Company. For all his experience and worldly knowledge, Herne was badly shaken by the Popish Plot. He wrote seriously to Sir Robert Southwell* 'to know if he should not send his wife and children out of town, for that the massacres of Paris and Ireland were enough talked of beforehand, but believed by none'.[6]

Meanwhile Herne had improved his interest at Dartmouth by arranging a public water supply for the town, one of his many charities, on which it was believed he spent not less than £1,000 p.a. He stood as a court supporter at the general election of February 1679, writing to Williamson: 'I glory in your favours, though they are alleged against me to keep me from an employment I am unfit for and desirous to avoid'. His name appears on Shaftesbury's list as 'base'. He was an active Member of the first Exclusion Parliament, sitting on 17 committees, of which the most important was for securing the King and kingdom against Popery. In the debate on a Tory pamphlet written in the character of a Jesuit by Dr John Nalson, Herne declared it to be 'against the doctrine of the Church of England, and there are such desperate hints in it that it is fit he should answer it at the bar'. Nevertheless he voted against the first exclusion bill.[7]

Herne died after a short illness on 10 Aug. 1679, aged 50. His executors held £10,838 of East India stock at the Revolution. The family interest at Dartmouth was re-established in 1689 by his brother Joseph.[8]

[1] *Vis. London* (Harl. Soc. xv), 378; *Grantees of Arms* (Harl. Soc. lxvi), 110; *The Gen.* n.s. xxvii. 67. [2] J. R. Woodhead, *Rulers of London*, 89. [3] *Cal. Treas. Bks.* v. 751, 986. [4] *Devon and Cornw. N. and Q.* ix. 180; A. T. Young, *Annals of Barber-Surgeons*, 554–5; *Cal. Cl. SP*, iii. 248, 373; iv. 634; D. Underdown, *Royalist Conspiracy*, 213. [5] *CSP Dom.* 1666–7, p. 440; 1671–2, p. 508; 1672, pp. 177–8, 260; *Cal. Ct. Mins. E.I. Co.* ed. Sainsbury, ix. 54, 224. [6] M. Sylvester, *Reliquiae Baxterianae*, iii. 172; *Life of Richard Kidder* (Som. Rec. Soc. xxxvii), 36; *CSP Dom.* 1675–6, pp. 198, 258–9, 262; *Cal. Ct. Mins. E.I. Co.* x. 241; *HMC Ormonde*, n.s. iv. 473. [7] *Devon and Cornw. N. and Q.* x. 159; Grey, vii. 104; *CSP Dom.* 1679–80, p. 77. [8] Add. 22185, f. 14.

J.P.F.

HERRYS, Edward (1612–62), of Great Baddow, Essex, and Lincoln's Inn.

MALDON 12 June 1660

bap. Sept. 1612, 1st s. of Edward Herrys of Great Baddow, by Elizabeth, da. of Robert Taverner of Aveley. *educ.* L. Inn 1628, called 1636. *m.* lic. 19 May 1645, Bridget, da. and h. of Thomas Glascock of Doddinghurst, wid. of Thomas Luther of Kelvedon Hatch, *s.p. suc.* fa. by 1648.[1]

Bencher, L. Inn 1648; commr. for militia, Essex Mar. 1660, j.p. July 1660–d., commr. for assessment Aug. 1660–1.[2]

Herrys came from a cadet branch of a family settled in Essex in early Tudor times which first entered Parliament in 1572. A lawyer, he took no known part in the Civil War. He was involved in a double return for the junior seat at Maldon with Henry Mildmay* at the general election of 1660. The election was declared void on 14 May, and Herrys was returned at the ensuing by-election after the Restoration. A firm Anglican, he was a moderately active Member of the Convention, in which he was named to 26 committees and spoke on ten occasions, chiefly on religious matters. He favoured committing the bill for the religious settlement and summoning Convocation. A member of the committee on the bill for settling

ecclesiastical livings, he seconded the motion of Heneage Finch* on 14 Aug. to recommit it, and was among those ordered to give directions to the clerk of the Commons for engrossing it. He opposed the Lords' arguments for excepting all the King's judges from the indemnity bill, and demanded a conference. In September he was appointed to the committees for settling the establishment of Dunkirk, for the supplementary disbandment bill and for preventing inconveniences from usurped grants.[3]

When Parliament met again after the recess Herrys opposed the motion for giving statutory force to the Worcester House declaration for modified episcopacy, but he was named to the committee to draw up a bill, as well as to those to bring in a supplementary poll bill, and to consider the attainder bill. On 16 Nov. he moved for a second reading of the militia bill. He opposed the bill for the restoration of the dukedom of Norfolk to the mad Earl of Arundel, declaring that 'it was promoted by his Lordship's brother, who was a known Papist and sought it for himself'. He was no friend to the corporation of London, opposing both the reimbursement of the City's expenses for the reception of the King, and the powers sought to raise money for the London militia, saying that 'it was only a design of some few officers of the city to promote the bill for their own advantage'. He is unlikely to have stood again. He was buried at Great Baddow on 3 Mar. 1662, the last of the family to serve in Parliament.[4]

[1] Great Baddow par. reg.; *Vis. Essex* (Harl. Soc. xiii), 415; Morant, *Essex*, i. 191; ii. 54; *London Mar. Lic.* ed. Foster, 672; PCC 84 Laud. [2] Essex RO, Q/SR 386–7. [3] *Vis. Essex*, 59; Morant, ii. 54, 74; *CJ*, viii. 3, 25; Bowman diary, ff. 55v, 66v, 134, 138, 154v. [4] *Old Parl. Hist.* xxiii. 5, 15, 32, 46, 50; Great Baddow par. reg.

M.W.H./G.H./G.J.

HERVEY, John (1616–80), of Ickworth, Suff. and Westminster.

HYTHE 1661

b. 18 Aug. 1616, 1st s. of Sir William Hervey† of Ickworth by 1st w. Susan, da. of Sir Robert Jermyn† of Rushbrooke; bro. of Sir Thomas Hervey*. *educ.* travelled abroad 1636; Leyden 1637. *m.* 1658 (with £30,000), Elizabeth, da. and h. of William Hervey†, 1st Baron Hervey of Kidbrooke, *s.p. suc.* fa. 1660.[1]

Gent. of the privy chamber ?1641–6; treasurer and receiver to Queen Catherine of Braganza 1662–d.[2]

Capt. of horse (royalist) 1642–6.[3]

J.p. Suff. July 1660–d.; commr. for assessment, Suff. Aug. 1660–d., Westminster 1661–d., Mdx. 1673–d., Norf. 1677–d., loyal and indigent officers, Suff. 1662, recusants 1675; member, Royal Fishery Co. 1677.[4]

FRS 1664–d.

Hervey's ancestors were originally seated in Bedfordshire, which they first represented in 1386. He was descended from a younger son who married the heiress of Ickworth about the middle of the 15th century. His father, who sat for Bury St. Edmunds in 1628-9, was neutral in the Civil War, but Hervey himself raised a troop of horse for the King. He compounded in 1646 on goods and chattels worth £240, and was fined £24 on the Exeter articles. Shortly before the Restoration, while engaged, according to a later account, in a royalist plot, he married a distant cousin, and when he succeeded to the family estate in September 1660 their combined income was £2,000 p.a. He appears to have left the management of the Suffolk estate to his brother, preferring a life at Court, where he had the support of his cousin, the Earl of St. Albans, and it soon became known that 'when we have a queen' Hervey would be appointed treasurer of her household.[5]

Hervey was returned for Hythe on the recommendation of the lord warden and the Earl of Sandwich (Edward Montagu I*) at the general election of 1661. An inactive Member of the Cavalier Parliament, he was named to only 20 committees, of which the most important were for the bill of pains and penalties (4 July 1661) and the bill to regulate the sale of offices and honours (18 May 1663). He acted as one of the trustees in the development of St. James's by Lord St. Albans, and was added to the committee on the bill for creating a separate parish. A patron of Cowley, he became a fellow of the Royal Society, and one of the principal shareholders in the Duke of York's theatre. He was listed as a court dependant in 1664 and on both lists of the court party in 1669-71. His name appeared on the Paston list and on the list of King's servants in 1675, though he was named to few committees after the fall of Clarendon, and his reluctant support for the Danby administration was the subject of a 'much talked of' anecdote. On the day after a reproof from the King for voting with the Opposition, he duly went into the government lobby. 'You were not against me to-day', the King remarked. 'No, sir', replied Hervey, 'I was against my conscience to-day.' Shaftesbury marked him 'doubly vile', and in *Flagellum Parliamentarium* he was called 'a court cully'. Although listed by the government managers as 'wanting' in a debate, he was on both lists of the court party in 1678. As one of the 'unanimous club', he probably never stood again, though his brother sat for Bury St. Edmunds in the Exclusion Parliaments. On 29 Nov. 1679 Sir Charles Lyttelton* wrote that he was not likely to live much longer, and he died on 18 Jan. 1680, aged 64. After legacies exceeding £12,000, he bequeathed the residue of his estate to his brother, on condition that he bought land to the value of £20,000. He was buried at Ickworth, where his memorial describes him as 'distinguished in character, powerful in intellect, bountiful in favour, impeccable in judgment, abundant in blessings'.[6]

[1] *Vis. Suff.* ed. Howard, ii. 195-6; *HMC Lords*, i. 264-5. [2] LC3/1; *Cal. Treas. Bks.* i. 464. [3] P. Young, *Edgehill*, 210. [4] *Sel. Charters* (Selden Soc. xxviii), 198. [5] J. Gage, *Hundred of Thingoe*, 293; *HMC 13th Rep. IV*, 457-8; SP23/184/881; *Cases in Chancery 1660-97*, ii. 180; *HMC 5th Rep.* 150. [6] *Survey of London*, xxix. 22; A. H. Nethercot, *Abraham Cowley*, 76, 297; L. Hotson, *Commonwealth and Restoration Stages*, 231; Burnet, ii. 80-81; *Hatton Corresp.* (Cam. Soc. n.s. xxii), 207; PCC 179 Bath; *Vis. Suff.* ii. 147.

B.D.H.

HERVEY, Sir Thomas (1625-94), of Ickworth, Suff.

BURY ST. EDMUNDS 1679 (Mar.), 1679 (Oct.), 1681, 1685, 1689

b. 25 May 1625, 3rd but 2nd surv. s. of Sir William Hervey[†] of Ickworth, and bro. of John Hervey*. *educ.* Pembroke, Camb. 1641. *m.* 21 July 1658, Isabella (*d.* 5 June 1686), da. of Sir Humphrey May[†] of Carrow Priory, Norf., chancellor of the duchy of Lancaster 1618-30, 3s. (1 *d.v.p.*) 3da. Kntd. by 1661; *suc.* bro. 1680.[1]

Commr. for assessment, Suff. 1661-80, Bury 1673-80, Suff. and Bury 1689-90; j.p. Suff. 1663-*d.*, dep. lt. by 1671-Apr. 1688, 1689-*d.*; ald. Bury St. Edmunds 1684-Oct. 1688.[2]

Commr. for navy 1664-8.[3]

Hervey is said to have 'ventured his life . . . in the service of the King and country in the time of Charles I', but he does not seem to have played a conspicuous part in the Civil War. During the Interregnum he occupied himself with courting his future wife, who was living in Bury St. Edmunds, but it was eight years before he was able to marry her. He was knighted either by Charles II in exile, or soon after the Restoration, and seems to have run the family estate after his father's death in September 1660, presumably because his elder brother did not care to leave London. This responsibility, however, did not prevent Hervey from buying a seat on the navy board from Lord Berkeley of Stratton in 1664 for £3,000. His colleague Samuel Pepys* found him 'a very droll' drinking companion, but disapproved of his working habits, particularly his absence during the plague. In November 1666 Pepys wrote that he

begins to crow mightily upon his late being at the payment of tickets; but a coxcomb he is and will never be better in the business of the navy.

During the inquiry into the miscarriages of the war, Hervey expected the Commons 'to make a great rout among us'. He accompanied Pepys to several of the hearings, but with the assurance of compensation for loss of office he left the defence of the naval administration to his colleague. When the board complained of his slow progress with auditing the accounts of Sir George Carteret*, Hervey was, according to Pepys:

> mighty angry, and particularly with me, but I do not care, but do rather desire it, for I will not spare him that we shall bear the blame, and such an idle fellow as he have £500 a year for nothing.

Nevertheless on his resignation in February 1668 he received £2,000 as royal bounty.[4]

Hervey was returned to the Exclusion Parliaments for Bury St. Edmunds, three miles from Ickworth. Presumably he stood on the family interest because his elder brother was unacceptable as a courtier and an absentee. Shaftesbury marked him 'base', but he missed the division on the first exclusion bill, served on no committees, and made no speeches. He was nominated to the corporation in the new charter of 1684 and re-elected in the next year as a Tory. Listed among the Opposition in James II's Parliament, he was appointed only to a private committee. The flight of Lord Dover at the Revolution encouraged him to attack both seats at the general election of 1689, but his son John was defeated by Sir Robert Davers*. In the Convention Hervey voted to agree with the Lords that the throne was not vacant, but his only committee was on the bill for the export of leather. He continued to take part in local affairs, but did not stand again. He died on 27 May 1694 and was buried with his wife at Ickworth. A memorial inscription describes them as 'most eminent examples of piety, charity and conjugal affection'. Their son sat for Bury St. Edmunds from 1694 as a Whig until he obtained a peerage through the good offices of the Duchess of Marlborough in 1703.[5]

[1] *Vis. Suff.* ed. Howard, ii. 195–7; A. Hervey, *Hervey Fam.* 89–99. [2] Add. 39246, ff. 23, 26, 30; SP44/335/128. [3] G. F. Duckett, *Naval Commrs.* 6. [4] Hervey, 101–5; Clarendon, *Life,* ii. 333; *Pepys Diary,* 7 June 1665, 10 Feb., 7 Nov. 1666, 26 June, 16 Nov. 1667; *CSP Dom. Add.* 1660–85, p. 223; *Cal. Treas. Bks.* ii. 247. [5] *IHR Bull.* liv. 203; *Vis. Suff.* ii. 147.

P.W.

HEVENINGHAM, Henry (1651–1700), of Hockwold, Norf. and Heveningham Hall, Suff.

THETFORD 26 Mar.–2 June 1685
DUNWICH 1695, 1698–26 Nov. 1700

b. 5 Jan. 1651, 2nd s. of Arthur Heveningham (*d.*1658) of Hockwold by w. Jane. *educ.* Pembroke, Camb. 1667; G. Inn 1669. *m.* lic. 1 July 1684, Frances, da. and coh.

of William Willoughby*, 6th Baron Willoughby of Parham, wid. of Sir John Harpur, 3rd Bt., of Swarkeston, Derbys., and of Charles Henry, 1st Earl of Bellomont [I], *s.p. suc.* bro. by 1669, cos. Sir William Heveningham in Suff. estate 1678.[1]

Freeman, Thetford 1682, mayor 1682–3, 1684–5; commr. for assessment, Derbys., Northants. and Norf. 1689; dep. lt. Suff. 1690–?*d.*; j.p. Derbys. 1693–*d.*, capt. of militia horse by 1697–*d.*[2]

Capt. indep. tp. 1685, Queen Dowager's Horse (later 6 Dgn. Gds.) 1686–Nov. 1688.[3]

Lt. gent. pens. 1689–*d.*[4]

Heveningham's ancestors had been seated on the Suffolk estate from which they took their name since the reign of King John, and represented the county in 1399. They were not a regular parliamentary family, however, and since the acquisition of Ketteringham in the 15th century their Norfolk interests had preponderated. The family was divided in the Civil War; Heveningham's uncle William was a strong Parliamentarian who sat in the high court of justice, while his father, a royalist colonel, was taken prisoner at the battle of Langport in 1645, and compounded with a fine of £400. According to Heveningham's mother, he was

> reduced to great poverty by imprisonment and sequestration, fined £600 for receiving a privy seal for £60 for the late King's service at Oxford, and dying left her and her children to the charge of his brother William, who within two months turned them out of doors and, but for friends, they must have perished.

At the Restoration she recovered her portion of £200 p.a. from her brother-in-law's estate, the remainder of which, though forfeited under the Act of Indemnity, was regranted to his wife.[5]

Heveningham succeeded his cousin in the Suffolk estates in 1678 under an entail, but continued to reside for some time at Hockwold, ten miles from Thetford. He acted as intermediary between the corporation and the Government in 1682, and was named as a 'burgess' in the new charter. He was serving a second term as mayor when he was elected to James II's Parliament, and listed among the Opposition. But he was unseated in favour of (Sir) Joseph Williamson* without taking any known part in its proceedings. On the invasion of the Duke of Monmouth he raised a troop of horse at Ipswich, and was later given a regular commission. Nevertheless he went over to the Prince of Orange in November 1688. He did not stand at the general election, but when Sir Henry Hobart* chose to sit for the county he wrote to the corporation of Thetford on 3 Feb. 1689:

> I hope my appearing so early and with hazard to my person and estate for the service of my country according to the Prince of Orange's declaration will give me an equal share, if not a preference, to any stranger that shall appear as candidate for your voices.

But he never regained his seat, though William gave him a post at Court worth £500 p.a. He sat for Dunwich as a court Whig in two later Parliaments, but died on 26 Nov. 1700, the last of the family, and was buried at Ketteringham.[6]

[1] Add. 19135, f. 268; *Mar. Lic.* (Harl. Soc. xxx), 171; Blomefield, *Norf.* ii. 185. [2] SP44/165/61, 166/138; *Norf. Official Lists* ed. Le Strange, 230; J. C. Cox, *Three Centuries of Derbys. Annals*, 43; Eg. 1626, f. 13. [3] *CSP Dom.* 1686–7, p. 169; 1687–9, p. 370. [4] Ibid. 1689–90, p. 25. [5] Copinger, *Suff. Manors*, ii. 92–96; Blomefield, v. 92–95; R. W. Ketton–Cremer, *Norf. in Civil War*, 188, 302; *CSP Dom.* 1660–1, p. 360; 1661–2, pp. 97, 158, 351, 624. [6] SP29/21/89; R. Morrice, Entering Bk. 2, p. 336; Add. 27448, f. 354; Luttrell, iv. 711; Add. 19135, f. 268.

E.C.

HEWER, William (1642–1715), of Gauden House, Clapham, Surr.

YARMOUTH I.o.W. 1685

b. 17 Nov. 1642, o.s. of Thomas Hewer, stationer, of London by Anne, sis. of Robert Blackburne of London, sec. of Admiralty 1652–June 1660. *unm. suc.* fa. 1665.[1]

Clerk, navy office July 1660–79; dep. judge-advocate of the navy 1677; member, R. Fishery Co. 1677; treas. of Tangier 1680–4; commr. of navy 1685–9; committee, E.I. Co. 1698–1709, dep. governor 1704–6, 1708–9, direction, 1709–13.[2]

Asst. Clothworkers' Co. 1684, master 1686–7; member of shipwrights' co., Rotherhithe 1686; j.p. Essex, Hants, Kent, Mdx., Suff., Surr., Suss. and Westminster 1687–9; commr. for assessment, Westminster 1689; dep. lt. Surr. 1702–*d.*[3]

Hewer's father supplied stationery to the Admiralty, but a more important influence on his career was his maternal uncle, who was at the centre of naval affairs during the Interregnum. At the Restoration he was succeeded by Samuel Pepys*, to whom he recommended Hewer as a clerk. Like his master he prospered in the service of the crown, and Blackburne, who had become secretary to the East India Company, obtained permission for him to indulge in one or two private trading ventures. By 1675 he was worth £16,500. He wrote to Pepys:

the kindness you are pleased to express towards me, and more particularly your regard of my mother, is such that I want words to express my thankfulness. . . . Living or dying, I shall remain to the end your faithful servant.

His gratitude stood the severe test of the exclusion crisis, when Pepys wrote from the Tower that he had received from Hewer 'all the care, kindness, and faithfulness of a son on this occasion, for which God reward him if I cannot'. Succeeding his master as treasurer of Tangier, he was able to purchase the fine house in Clapham built by the naval victualler, Sir Dennis Gawden, and by the Revolution held £3,500 in East India stock.[4]

On the accession of James II Hewer was made a naval commissioner, and elected at Yarmouth on the government interest. An active Member, he was appointed to 12 committees, including the committee of elections and privileges and those to recommend expunctions from the Journals and to estimate the yield of a tax on new buildings. His legislative interest covered the encouragement of ship-building, the relief of London widows and orphans, and the rebuilding of St. Paul's Cathedral. After the recess he helped to draw up the address against the employment of Roman Catholic officers. But in a speech sometimes attributed to William Ettrick* he moved for £700,000 to be raised by a tax on new buildings and a poll-tax. He must have given satisfaction to the Court, for he was retained on the navy board and was recommended to Sir Robert Holmes* as court candidate for Yarmouth in 1688. His name appeared on the panel for the jury at the trial of the Seven Bishops, although he was not called on to serve.[5]

On James's flight Hewer wrote to Pepys:

You may rest assured that I am wholly yours, and that you shall never want the utmost of my constant, faithful and personal service. . . . As all I have proceeded from you, so all I have and am is and shall be at your service.

The note was endorsed by Pepys as 'a letter of great tenderness at a time of difficulty'. Like Pepys, he was removed from office and arrested on suspicion of treason on 4 May 1689. He was released on bail in the following month and never brought to trial. But he was not re-employed in public office, though his former services were recognized by the grant of an allowance in 1701. By this time he was a prominent member of the East India board, and was able to afford Pepys permanent hospitality in his house. He died on 3 Dec. 1715 and was buried at Clapham, the only member of the family to enter Parliament.[6]

[1] Soc. of Genealogists, Boyd's London Units 22085; *Pepys Diary*, 17 July 1660; J. H. M. Burgess, *Chrons. of Clapham*, 17, 118. [2] *Cal. Treas. Bks.* vi. 2, 494; Add. 38871, ff. 13–17. [3] *CSP Dom.* 1686–7, p. 21. [4] G. E. Aylmer, *State's Servants*, 266–7; *Cal. Ct. Mins. E.I. Co.* ed. Sainsbury, ix. 113; A. Bryant, *Pepys*, ii. 148, 277–9, 302–3, 328; *Pepys Letters* ed. Heath, 74; Burgess, 114; Add. 22185, f. 14. [5] Lowther diary, f. 40; *CSP Dom.* 1687–9, p. 276; *Ellis Corresp.* ii. 2. [6] Bryant, iii. 148, 187, 250, 281; *CSP Dom.* 1700–2, p. 469.

P.W.

HEWLEY, Sir John (1619–97), of Wistow and Bell Hall, Naburn, Yorks.

PONTEFRACT 1659
YORK 1679 (Mar.), 1679 (Oct.), 1681

bap. 5 Aug. 1619, o.s. of John Hewley of Wistow by Dorothy, da. of John Wood of Copmanthorpe. *educ.* G. Inn 1639, called 1645, ancient 1662. *m.* Sarah (*d.* 23 Aug.

1710), da. and h. of Robert Worledge (Wolryche), attorney, of Ipswich, Suff. and Gray's Inn, 2s. *d.v.p.* *suc.* fa by 1630; kntd. 30 June 1663.[1]

J.p. Yorks. (W. Riding) 1646–July 1660, (W. and N. Ridings) 1663–80; commr. for assessment (W. Riding) 1649–52, 1657, W. Riding and York 1673–80, Yorks. 1689–90, security 1655–56; recorder, Pontefract c.1656–1661, Doncaster 1659–62; commr. for militia, Yorks. 1659, Mar. 1660; freeman, York 1659.[2]

Hewley's great-grandfather, of Cheshire origin, moved to Yorkshire, and settled at Wistow in Elizabethan times. Hewley himself was a sufficiently competent lawyer to be appointed counsel to the corporation of York, but most of his wealth was derived from a fortunate marriage. He held local office from the end of the Civil War to the Restoration, and became the only member of his family to enter Parliament, first sitting for Pontefract in 1659. He stood for re-election in 1660 on the corporation interest, but there was a double return which was decided in favour of his royalist opponents. He bought Bell Hall, five miles from York, in 1662, and was knighted in the following year. Although he maintained first an Independent and then a Presbyterian chaplain, he conformed and was restored to the West Riding bench in 1663. He entered his pedigree at the heralds' visitation in 1665, and leased his alum works at Skelton to the crown for 21 years at an annual rent of £400.[3]

When by-elections became due at both Aldborough and York in the autumn of 1673, Hewley was originally mentioned as a candidate for the former constituency, and as electoral agent for Lord Treasurer Danby's son, Edward Osborne*, in the latter. But with five other candidates in the field at Aldborough he soon desisted. Meanwhile Osborne, lacking corporation support, withdrew at York, and Hewley stood there himself against the country candidate, Sir Henry Thompson*, but was heavily defeated. Nevertheless he went up to London a year later 'as spruce as any bridegroom' to petition, and could not be persuaded by Andrew Marvell* to desist. His case was finally dismissed on 15 Mar. 1677.[4]

By 1679 Hewley had swung back into opposition. At the first general election he strongly supported the two exclusionist candidates for Yorkshire. He himself stood for Knaresborough against Sir Thomas Slingsby*, but after much consumption of alcohol desisted before the poll. At York, however, he defeated (Sir) Metcalfe Robinson* after intensive canvassing, and retained the seat throughout the Exclusion Parliaments. Shaftesbury classed him as 'doubtful', but Huntingdon correctly marked him as a supporter of the country party. A very active Member of the first Exclusion Parliament,

he was appointed to 34 committees. When the King rejected the Commons' choice of Edward Seymour* as their Speaker, Hewley asked:

> Shall we not have our tongue to speak our own words? ... The Speaker is our servant, and is he to obey his master, or not? Though the Speaker be the greatest commoner of England, yet he is not the greatest community of England. To have a servant imposed upon a man, though by the King himself, will not be suffered by any private master, or merchant; and shall the Commons of England endure it?

He was named to the committee of elections and privileges, and to those to consider bills for the extension of habeas corpus and the regulation of parliamentary elections. On 8 Apr. he was added to the committee to prepare reasons for Danby's attainder. Later bills with which he was concerned included those for the prevention of swearing, drunkenness and sabbath-breaking and for security against Popery. He was also among those ordered on 30 Apr. to inspect the disbandment accounts. On 5 May he urged that Danby should be tried despite his pardon, and he was appointed to two committees in this connexion later in the month. He took the chair of a committee on a private bill and carried it up to the Lords on 8 May, followed by another on the next day. He voted for the first exclusion bill. His removal from the commission of the peace after signing the York petition for the meeting of the second Exclusion Parliament seems to have sobered him, for when it did meet he was appointed only to the elections committee. In the Oxford Parliament, however, he was also among those named to conduct the inquiry into the loss of the bill of ease for Protestant dissenters and to prepare Fitzharris's impeachment. Doubtless a supporter of the Revolution, he subscribed £500 in November 1688 to Danby's voluntary contribution to William of Orange; but he never stood again. He died on 24 Aug. 1697, and was buried at St. Saviour's, York, the last of his family. His widow founded several local nonconformist charities.[5]

[1] Clay, *Dugdale's Vis. Yorks.* ii. 207–8. [2] *Trans. Unitarian Hist. Soc.* vi. 1, 4; *Thurloe*, iii. 402; Hunter, *S. Yorks.* i. 27; *Freemen of York* (Surtees Soc. cii), 121. [3] Clay, ii. 208; Add. 21417, f. 334; *VCH E. Riding*, iii. 77; D. R. Lacey, *Dissent and Parl. Pols.* 411–12; *Cal. Treas. Bks.* vi. 173. [4] Add. 28051, ff. 14–32; *CSP Dom.* 1675–6, p. 122; *Marvell* ed. Margoliouth, ii. 181, 183, 313, 317. [5] *HMC Var.* ii. 393; *HMC Astley*, 41, 42; Grey, vi. 435; vii. 175; Browning, *Danby*, i. 404; *DNB*.

E.C.

HICKMAN, Sir William, 2nd Bt. (1629–82), of Gainsborough, Lincs.

EAST RETFORD 1660, 1661, 1679 (Mar.), 1679 (Oct.), 1681

bap. 8 Jan. 1629, o.s. of Sir Willoughby Hickman, 1st Bt., of Gainsborough by Bridget, da. of Sir John Thornhaugh of Fenton, Notts. *educ.* I. Temple 1645. *m.* c.1652, Elizabeth, da. and h. of John Neville of Mattersey Priory, Notts., 5s. (3 *d.v.p.*) 8da. *suc.* fa. 28 May 1650.[1]

Sheriff, Notts. 1653–4; commr. for militia, Lincs. and Notts. Mar. 1660, assessment, Notts. Aug. 1660–80, Lincs. (Lindsey) Aug. 1660–1, 1663–4, Lincs. 1661–3, 1664–80; j.p. Lincs. (Lindsey) Mar. 1660–*d.*, Notts. June 1660–*d.*, Mdx. and Westminster 1679–?*d.*; commr. for oyer and terminer, Midland circuit July 1660; dep. lt. Lincs. and Notts. c. Aug. 1660–*d.*; commr. for sewers, Hatfield chase and Lincs. Aug. 1660; steward of Kirton manor, Lincs. Sept. 1660–*d.*; capt.-lt. of vol. horse, Notts. 1661; commr. for sewers, Hatfield chase 1668, concealments, Lincs. 1671, recusants 1675.[2]

Lt. indep. tp. of Lord Ogle (Henry Cavendish*) 1666–7.

Commr. for trade and plantations 1672–4, ordnance 1679–82.

Hickman's ancestors seemingly farmed the demesne lands of Woodford in Essex under the abbots of Waltham before the Reformation, after which they prospered greatly, though their ardent Protestantism drove them into exile under Mary. One of Hickman's great-uncles became chancellor of Peterborough and MP for Northampton in the last Parliament of Elizabeth. Another was the great-grandfather of Thomas Windsor*. Hickman's grandfather married a Willoughby and bought the manor of Gainsborough in 1596. His father was named to the county committee in 1643, but accepted a wartime baronetcy, and was fined £900 for being in the King's quarters, though he was never in arms. Hickman did not succeed to much wealth or social prestige; after the Restoration it was said 'the best of his estate [is] in the dues upon the fairs kept there, about £800 p.a., not more; but a late family'. He was connected with the Nottinghamshire gentry by birth, and acquired a small estate there by marriage, though his residence by his own computation stood ten yards outside the county. First returned for East Retford, some ten miles away, at the general election of 1660, though his eligibility under the Long Parliament ordinance was questionable, he held his seat for the rest of his life, so far as is known without a contest. He was not an active Member of the Convention, with 11 committees, none of much political importance, and no recorded speeches. He was presumably a supporter of the Court.[3]

Hickman was moderately active in the Cavalier Parliament, in which he was appointed to 167 committees and acted as teller in 13 divisions. About 40 of his speeches have been recorded. He was appointed to the committees for the corporations and uniformity bills and the bill of pains and penalties

in 1661, and for the five mile bill in 1665. He was regarded by the commoners of the Isle of Axholme as their friend and patron. He was active as local correspondent of the *London Gazette*, and as a cavalry officer in the second Dutch war. In 1667 he was named to the committees concerned with restraints imposed on juries, the miscarriages of the war and the banishment of Clarendon, and in 1668 to those for reviewing public accounts and the militia laws. He was reprimanded by the Treasury for failure to support the local excise farmer, but noted by Sir Thomas Osborne* in 1669 as one of the independent Members who usually voted for supply. On 3 Dec. he was teller for the unsuccessful motion declaring Sir George Carteret* guilty of negligence over the slop-sellers' accounts. About this time, Hickman himself acquired an interest in naval contracts, though only as trustee for the people of Gainsborough in the factory set up by Anthony Eyre* for the manufacture of sailcloth. On 28 Nov. 1670 he told the House: 'People will not make this canvas unless they have an inducement to it; and therefore [I] would have all French linen charged, as is now paid, with the additional duty at the custom house'. In November 1672 he was selected to fill a vacancy on the council of trade.[4]

In the days of the Clarendon Code, Hickman had something of the reputation of a persecutor, but his attitude changed, and on 14 Feb. 1673 he declared in the House that 'there did appear a general inclination for uniting Protestant subjects'. He hoped to find a formula renouncing the Covenant which tender consciences could accept. On 29 Jan. 1674 he was added to the committee to prepare a general test bill, and later in the same session he was among those appointed to consider the condition of Ireland. Now free of government office, in 1675 he opposed a vote of thanks for the speech from the throne and spoke in favour of appropriating a fixed proportion of the customs to the use of the navy, being named to both committees on this subject. He was also on the committees for preventing the growth of Popery, for examining dangerous and scandalous books on religion, for recalling British subjects from the French service, and for preserving the liberty of the subject. On 8 Nov. he seconded the motion of William Sacheverell* for no further supply, and he acted as teller against the adjournment on the penultimate day of the session. His activity follows the same pattern in 1677, when he was marked by Shaftesbury as 'doubly worthy'. With his customary lucidity, he faced the probability that a full-scale alliance with the Dutch would entail war with France, and accepted it 'if occasion be'. He was teller against omitting this passage from the address.[5]

Hickman's attitude towards the Danby administration hardened in 1678. He was teller against the report stage of the supply bill, and on 14 Mar. he said:

> We have done our parts in the House; we have given our advice several years against the growing greatness of the French king. Still we are in the same darkness as to the war with France as when we first met.

He helped to prepare reasons for a conference on the growth of Popery, and to draw up the address for the removal of counsellors. In the debate on the latter, he acted as teller for its fourth paragraph, remarking bitterly on 7 May: 'Plainly, I do not expect any good answer of our address whilst such are in power that have run reprimand upon reprimand upon a chain to all our addresses'. Such frustration explains how one of the coolest heads in the House could be prepared to swallow the Popish Plot in the autumn. He was the first Member appointed to the committee of inquiry, and carried up to the Lords the address for the removal of Papists from London. He helped to translate Coleman's letters, to search the chambers of Robert Wright* and to draw up reasons for believing in the Plot. He took part in preparing four addresses in November and December and in drafting instructions for disbanding the army. On 21 Dec. he was teller against adjourning the debate on the impeachment of Danby.[6]

Hickman is seen at his best in the Exclusion Parliaments, where he worked in close association with Lord Halifax (Sir George Savile*). It is an indication of the respect which he enjoyed and deserved that his speeches, though usually opposed to the orthodox country views of Anchitell Grey*, are fairly and clearly summarized in the *Debates*. In 1679 he was again moderately active, with ten committees, the most important of which were for the bill of security against Popery and to prepare for a conference on the impeachment of Danby. He had again been marked 'worthy' by Shaftesbury, but he soon revealed his well-grounded doubts about the practicability of exclusion. He reminded the House, with remarkable prescience, that the King might succeed in the plan revealed by Ralph Montagu* to make himself independent of Parliament with a French subsidy. He put his finger on a major constitutional difficulty by pointing out that the English Parliament could not exclude the Duke of York from the Scottish or Irish thrones. Finally he voted against the bill.[7]

In July, Hickman became one of the com-

missioners of the ordnance. Halifax was apprehensive lest he might have difficulty in securing re-election at East Retford, and urged Thomas Thynne I* to reserve a seat for him at Tamworth, but this was not required, even though a carriage accident on his way to his constituency prevented him from attending the election. In the second Exclusion Parliament he was appointed only to the committees for the regulation of elections and the removal of Papists from London. On 6 Nov. 1680 he seized on another weak point in the exclusion argument, the lack of agreement on an alternative successor:

> Here is nothing in the bill that the crown may devolve to the next successor. Suppose that two Protestants lay claim to the crown; if they divide, they may let in Popery at the end of it. Princes often leave those things doubtful, but Parliaments should leave them plain. I would have it left to the next right heir in succession.

Although Hickman's tactics seem obvious, to divide the supporters of Monmouth from those of William of Orange, they were too subtle for the Duke of York, who grumbled at his defence of the constitutionality of exclusion. The dangers of open opposition to exclusion were shown by the motion for the dismissal of Halifax on 17 Nov. Hickman was in some difficulty in defending his patron in his capacity as a councillor, for he had admitted (though as an exception) the use of 'common fame' against Arlington. But he skilfully steered the debate on to the other ground:

> You are now come to some particulars against this lord of what he should say in the Lords' House. But is that parliamentary to take notice of what is said there? What he said was in the last Parliament, which is dissolved, and did he not withdraw from the Council since the prorogation of this Parliament? Pray run not into such hasty resolutions against this lord till things are proved against him.

He acted as teller on a motion to adjourn, but in vain. He continued to defend Halifax at every opportunity, but he was in favour of impeaching Sir Francis North*, and he agreed with the anti-Papal legislative programme put forward by William Cavendish*, Lord Cavendish, on the defeat of the second exclusion bill in the Lords.[8]

In the Oxford Parliament, Hickman was named only to the committee of elections and privileges, and made no speeches. He was anxious to resign his seat at the ordnance board, but could not find a purchaser, and eventually the commission was dissolved only a few days before his death. He was buried at Gainsborough on 10 Feb. 1682.[9]

[1] *Lincs. Peds.* (Harl. Soc. li), 495. [2] *CSP Dom.* 1660–1, p. 279; 1667–8, p. 432; *Kingdom's Intell.* 7 Mar. 1661; C181/7/20, 76; *Cal. Treas. Bks.* iii. 912. [3] *Misc. Gen. et Her.* (ser. 5), v. 194–5; Allen, *Lincs.* ii. 12; *Cal. Comm. Comp.* 987; *Her. and Gen.* ii. 122; *Hut-*

chinson *Mems.* 96; *CSP Dom.* 1653–4, p. 402. [4] W. B. Stonehouse, *Isle of Axholme,* 103–4; *CSP Dom.* 1667, pp. 43, 236; 1670, p. 201; 1672–3, p. 114; *Cal. Treas. Bks.* ii. 382, 387; Spencer mss. Elizabeth Eyre to Ld. Halifax, 27 Sept. 1669; Grey, i. 311. [5] Calamy, *Nonconformists' Memorial,* iii. 91; Grey, ii. 27; iii. 98, 429; iv. 304; Dering, 125; *CJ,* ix. 342, 361, 382, 424; *Dering Pprs.* 59, 64, 83. [6] *CJ,* ix. 438, 479, 521, 524, 562; Grey, v. 225, 348. [7] Jones, *First Whigs,* 64, 65; Grey, vii. 100, 248. [8] *Cal. Treas. Bks.* vi. 140; Foxcroft, *Halifax,* i. 180; Spencer mss, Hickman to Halifax, 15, 30 Aug. 1679; Grey, ii. 327–8; vii. 427; viii. 22, 41, 67, 156, 281; Clarke, *Jas. II,* i. 609–10; *CJ,* ix. 655. [9] Spencer mss, John Millington to Halifax, 1 June 1681.

M.W.H./E.R.E.

HICKMAN, Sir Willoughby, 3rd Bt. (1659–1720), of Gainsborough, Lincs.

KINGSTON-UPON-HULL	1685
EAST RETFORD	1698, 15 Apr. 1701, 28 Nov. 1702, 1705–17 Jan. 1706
LINCOLNSHIRE	1713, 1715–28 Oct. 1720

b. 20 Aug. 1659, 3rd but 1st surv. s. of Sir William Hickman, 2nd Bt.* *m.* 11 Sept. 1683, Anne, da. of Sir Stephen Anderson, 1st Bt., of Eyworth, Beds., 5s. (3 *d.v.p.*) 6da. *suc.* fa. Feb. 1682.

Steward of Kirton manor, Lincs. 1682–9; dep. lt. Notts. 1682–Feb. 1688, Oct. 1688–?*d.*, Lincs. ?1682–Jan. 1688; j.p. Notts. 1689–?*d.*, Lincs. (Lindsey) by 1701–?*d.*; commr. for assessment, Lincs. 1689–90.

Hickman's cousin, Lord Plymouth, was high steward and governor of Hull in 1685. Hickman attended the governor's reception and was nominated court candidate, perhaps as compensation for not pressing his claim to succeed his father at East Retford. A moderately active Member of James II's Parliament, he was appointed to three committees, those for maintaining wool and corn prices, prohibiting the import of gunpowder and reforming the bankruptcy laws; but the anti-government speech in the supply debate sometimes ascribed to him was probably delivered by Sir William Honeywood*. He followed the example of (Sir) Henry Monson* in returning negative replies to the lord lieutenant's questions on the repeal of the Test Act and Penal Laws in Lincolnshire, and in Nottinghamshire, like Sir William Stanhope*, he answered curtly that he would do his duty. He was added to the Nottinghamshire commission of the peace in 1689 on the King's direction, but resigned his crown stewardship of Kirton to Nicholas Saunderson*, and it was nine years before he re-entered Parliament. Thenceforward he voted consistently as a Tory till his death on 28 Oct. 1720. He was the last of his family to sit in Parliament.

Lincs. Peds. (Harl. Soc. li), 495–6; *CSP Dom.* 1682, p. 282; 1685, p. 23; 1689–90, pp. 69–70; *Cal. Treas. Bks.* vii. 415; ix. 20; *HMC Lords,* n.s. x. 366; J. Tickell, *Kingston-upon-Hull,* 558.

P.A.B.

HIGGONS, Thomas (c.1624–91), of Greywell, Hants.

MALMESBURY	1659
NEW WINDSOR	1661
ST. GERMANS	1685

b. c.1624, 1st s. of Thomas Higgons, DD, rector of Westbury, Salop by 2nd w. Elizabeth, da. of Richard Barker of Haughmond Abbey, Salop. *educ.* St. Albans Hall, Oxf. matric 27 Apr. 1638, aged 14; M. Temple 1640; travelled abroad (Italy) c.1643–6. *m.* (1) c.1647, Elizabeth (*bur.* 16 Sept. 1656), da. of Sir William Powlett of Edington, Wilts., wid. of Robert, 3rd Earl of Essex, 2da.; (2) lic. 11 Nov. 1661, Bridget (*d.*1692), da. of Sir Bevil Granville[†] of Stow, Cornw., wid. of Simon Leach of Cadleigh, Devon, 3s. 3da. *suc.* fa. 1636; kntd. 17 June 1663.[1]

Commr. for assessment, Salop 1661–3, Hants 1661–80, 1689–90, Westminster 1663–9, Devon 1663–74; sub-commr. for prizes, Newcastle 1665–7; j.p. Hants 1665–*d.*[2]

Surveyor-gen. duchy of Cornw. 1668–*d.*; envoy extraordinary, Saxony 1668–9, Venice 1674–9.[3]

Higgons's ancestors were settled in Shropshire by the late 14th century. During the Civil War he travelled in Italy, where he acquired enough of the language to translate an account of Venetian triumphs over the Turks. He took up residence at Greywell after his marriage to Lady Essex, the widow of the parliamentary general, and avoided political involvement during the Interregnum, though he represented Malmesbury in Richard Cromwell's Parliament. His *Panegyric to the King,* published in 1660, earned him the praise of Edmund Waller I*, and probably marked him out for court favour.[4]

Higgons was returned for New Windsor at a contested election in 1661 on the corporation franchise. A moderately active Member of the Cavalier Parliament, he was appointed to 178 committees, seven of which he chaired. He was teller in 15 divisions, and made 22 recorded speeches. During the first session he married the sister of the newly created Earl of Bath, who had played a leading part in the Restoration. But he did not absent himself from Westminster during his second honeymoon, acting as teller for the unsuccessful motion to lay aside the bill for the execution of those under attainder on 26 Nov., which did not prevent his nomination to the committee. In 1663 he was appointed to the committees to consider the petition of the loyal and indigent officers, to prevent unlawful meetings of dissenters, and to consider the additional corporations bill. Listed among the court dependants in 1664, he was teller on 2 May for the unsuccessful motion for early consideration of a bill to enclose and improve commons and wastes, and three days later reported a similar bill, which had been languishing in committee, for the partition of lands. He was teller in two divisions on the assessment bill in 1664–5, and reported a proviso for better collection in respect of empty houses, as well as a bill to settle the Powlett estate in Hampshire. On 14 Feb. 1666 he was given leave to bring in a private bill to recover £4,550 owed to his first wife by the dowager Duchess of Somerset. Andrew Marvell*, describing the court party at this time, wrote:

Then comes the thrifty troop of privateers
Whose horses each with other interferes.
Before them Higgons rides with brow compact,
Mourning his countess, anxious for his Act.

His eldest son was the Countess of Thanet's godchild, and he took an active part in the bill to settle the family estate, reporting a conference on 28 Feb. and returning to the Lords to ask for another. His private bill was revived in the next session, and steered through committee against much opposition from Robert Steward*, but rejected on 11 Jan. 1667 as an infringement of the Act of Indemnity. In the same session his committees included that to prevent voluntary absence of Members, and he was teller for adjourning the debate on amendments to this bill. He was again teller on 29 Jan. 1667 for a motion which enabled the solicitor-general to join in, or rather to obstruct, the management of Lord Mordaunt's impeachment. On the fall of Clarendon, Higgons was named to the committees to bring in a public accounts bill, to inquire into the miscarriages of the war, to thank Prince Rupert and the Duke of Albemarle (George Monck*) for their part in the war, and to report on proceedings in Mordaunt's impeachment. As chairman of the committee of inquiry into the coal trade, he reported the colliers' complaints against the ballast monopoly and the abuses of the woodmongers, but acted as teller for deferring further debate till after Christmas. His first recorded speech was on 11 Dec. 1667 in defence of (Sir) John Kelyng* who was accused of bullying juries and other misconduct on the bench. Higgons declared:

that the judge was a man of choler and passion . . . but no ill man of bribery and corruption. Magna Carta he slighted not. . . . Desires it may be remembered what he has done and suffered for Magna Carta, and that his former life may be put into the balance with his present offence.

Two of his committees early in 1668 were those to take accounts of the poll tax and assessment voted for the war, and to prevent abuses in the collection of the hearth tax. In the debate for preservation of timber in the Forest of Dean he spoke much in defence of Sir John Winter, and was teller on 6 Apr.

for hearing his petition. It was no doubt to Lord Bath, who as groom of the stole enjoyed great interest at Court, that he owed his selection to deliver the garter to the Elector of Saxony, who gave him a 'great silver basin and ewer'.[5]

Higgons was included in both court party lists of 1669–71 among those who regularly voted for supply. On 12 Nov. 1670 he wrote to Lord Bath:

The King's business in Parliament hath gone on hitherto very prosperously, for they have voted a supply proportionable to his Majesty's occasions, even when they understood those occasions to require above two millions of money. . . . But your lordship will wonder when you shall know that this vote passed without contradiction, which is more than I ever yet saw in the like occasion. It is not but that there were some who had a good mind to oppose it, but finding much the greater part of the House for it, they were so wise as to give way to that which they could not hinder; so all that they can do now is by artifices to delay and obstruct the ways of raising this money by making all means ineffectual, which we can propose, to throw us upon a necessity of the land tax which the House does generally abhor as the most unsupportable of all taxes, and that which will give the greatest discontent to the people.

He was teller on 10 Dec. for preparing further instructions for the committee of the whole House regarding supply. When Steward introduced a bill to regulate wages, Higgons 'moved that as an expedient to make servants more tractable we might bring into this kingdom the use of negro slaves, but this was not relished by the House nor seconded by any'. Two days later he spoke in favour of taxing offices rather than land, declaring:

Tenants break and lands fall; offices are constant profit, and would have them higher rated.

In January 1671 he reported from the committee on Lord Stafford's estate bill and carried it to the Lords. As early as June 1672 the Venetian Government was informed that Higgons, 'a gentleman of very good parts', was to become England's envoy to the republic. Secretary Arlington (Sir Henry Bennet*) doubted his suitability, presumably because he was too intimate with the French ambassador. In the debate on Irish affairs in the spring session of 1673 he took it upon himself to defend the swaggering adventurer Richard Talbot, and it may be that he was retained in England even after he had been formally accredited as envoy in order to defend the equally unpopular Modena marriage in the autumn.

Marriage *in verbis de[i] praesenti* is indissoluble: the Princess is on the way. What the King does in his royal function is the act of the people, and the kingdom is bound, this House and every man by it. All kings are concerned in it, to preserve their supreme power. The law of nature is concerned in it, and nothing so against it. *Praeterita magis reprehendenda sunt quam corrigenda.*

We may lament it, and would have good laws against Popery, but would not have the honour of this nation concerned.

Higgons was one of the Members who kept the French embassy informed of proceedings in Parliament during this session, and he was named on the Paston list. Early in 1674 he served on committees to inquire into charges of corruption against Members, to consider the charges against Arlington, and to report on the state of Ireland. He finally left England as envoy at the end of April. He was noted as absent in the list of officials and government supporters, and Sir Richard Wiseman* regretted in 1676 that 'the King loseth a vote by it'. A contemporary account described him as 'a poor man's son' and the author of *A Seasonable Argument* correctly noted his salary at £500 p.a. and attributed to him £4,000 in gifts besides. He returned in May 1677, but his letters of appointment were not revoked until two years later, and Shaftesbury marked him 'thrice vile'. In the debate on foreign affairs of 14 Mar. 1678 he inquired:

To put the King upon a declaration of war, what can that hurt the French? It is not the King's fault that treaties were not sooner perfected. The King of France has a great fleet in the West Indies and our plantations there lie open. If you desire a declaration of war, judge the condition of those places; for your declaration of war will not help the confederates, and Spain will stand upon higher terms with you; and these are the reasons why we should not be so hasty to declare war against France.

He was teller on 27 Mar. for adjourning the debate on the growth of Popery, but was later appointed to the committee to draw up heads for a conference. His name appeared in the list of court party supporters in May. Among his later committees were those to bring in bills to secure the Protestant religion. On the outbreak of the Popish Plot he helped to draw up the address for printing Coleman's letters. But he defended the Lords' amendment to exempt the Duke of York from the bill to prevent Papists from sitting in Parliament, demanding:

Let gentlemen who are so earnest against this proviso consider. Should the Duke think himself disobliged and go beyond the sea and the French King support him with a hundred thousand men, could a greater blow be given to the Protestant religion? The heir of the crown to be in Popish hands, the Duke there, and all Catholic princes contribute to his restoration to the crown. What danger is there in his single person in the Lords' House? . . . As we tender union with the Lords, satisfaction to the King and the quiet of those that come after us, let us agree to the proviso.

He was then appointed to the committee to draw up reasons for a conference. Shortly before dissolution he staunchly defended Danby, exclaiming:

So great a minister of the King's to be impeached! I desire to see better reasons than yet have been offered before he be impeached. One thing is objected against him: his treating of peace with the King of France. It seems by the letter that the conditions were for an honourable peace, and why should any man be ashamed of it? For it is a very ordinary thing for Kings to get money from one another as in Edward IV's and Henry VII's time, and there is no ground of this accusation of treason against this Lord.[6]

Although Higgons was not blacklisted in the 'unanimous club' of court supporters, he did not stand for the Exclusion Parliaments. He was returned in 1685 for St. Germans by arrangement between his brother-in-law and Daniel Eliot*. He was moderately active in James II's Parliament, with three committees of secondary importance. On 12 June he reported a bill to repeal a clause in the Bedford Level Act. On the proposed repeal of the Penal Laws and Test Act, he wrote to the lord lieutenant in 1688 that having 'given his answer to the King, he had had his leave to stay in town'. He remained loyal to James II, but took no part in politics after the Revolution. He died of apoplexy in the court of King's bench on 24 Nov. 1691, after giving evidence for Bath in his claim to the Duke of Albemarle's estate, and was buried in Winchester Cathedral. His will showed debts of £4,650, but on the credit side he claimed that £1,640 was still due to him for his mission to Venice. His sons were Jacobites, and no other member of the family entered Parliament.[7]

[1] B. Botfield, *Stemmata Botevilliana*, 137; Guildhall Lib. mss 10091/25; Owen and Blakeway, *Hist. Shrewsbury*, ii. 235; *Salop Arch. and Nat. Hist. Soc. Trans.* (ser. 2), vii. 309. [2] Nat. Maritime Mus. Southwell mss, 17/15. [3] *CSP Dom.* 1667–8, pp. 108, 267; *Cal. Treas. Bks.* ii. 352; iii. 265; iv. 166. [4] *Vis. Salop.* (Harl. Soc. xxviii), 240; Botfield, 103; *Marvell* ed. Margoliouth, i. 145. [5] *CSP Ven.* 1671–2, p. 238; *CJ*, viii. 555, 558, 577, 582, 592, 684; ix. 22, 35, 39, 40; *Milward*, 28, 61–62, 132, 163, 171–3, 182; Grey, i. 63–64; *CSP Dom.* 1667–8, pp. 447, 564; PCC 213 Vere. [6] R. Granville, *Hist. Granville Fam.* 358; *Dering*, 33; Grey, i. 326; ii. 127, 192; v. 226; vi. 245, 350; *CJ*, ix. 194; *CSP Ven.* 1671–2, p. 238; 1673–5, p. 250; PRO 31/3, bdle. 129, f. 69; Harl. 7020, f. 33; *Cal. Treas. Bks.* iv. 428. [7] *HMC Hastings*, ii. 333; PCC 213 Vere; *State Trials*, xii. 1313; xiii. 192.

L.N./G.J.

HILDESLEY, John (c.1598–1681), of Hinton Admiral, nr. Christchurch, Hants.

HAMPSHIRE	1653
WINCHESTER	1654, 1656, 1659
CHRISTCHURCH	1660

b. c.1598. *m.* aft. 1641, Margaret (*d.* 14 Aug. 1679), wid. of Henry Tulse† of Hinton Admiral, *s.p.*[1]

Freeman, Lymington 1635, Winchester 1650–62; mayor, Christchurch 1637–8; commr. for defence, Hants 1645, assessment 1647–52, 1657, Jan. 1660, j.p. 1647–July 1660, commr. for militia 1648, Mar. 1660; recorder, Winchester 1651–2; commr. for scandalous ministers, Hants 1654, oyer and terminer, Western circuit 1655, security, Hants 1655–6; steward, Andover by 1656–c. Aug. 1660; sheriff, Hants 1656–7; commr. for wastes and spoils, New Forest 1672–3.[2]

Commr. for excise arrears 1653, army 1654–9; judge of probate 1654–9.

Hildesley, an attorney of unknown parentage, was three times elected mayor of Christchurch in the 1630s and eventually sworn in after the veto of Lord Arundell of Wardour had been overridden in King's bench. A strong Parliamentarian in the Civil War, he acquired corporation interest in other Hampshire boroughs during the Interregnum, held local and central office, and sat in all the Protectorate Parliaments. He was returned for Christchurch, three miles from Hinton Admiral, at the general election of 1660 with his step-son Henry Tulse*. Lord Wharton marked him as a friend, but his only committee in the Convention was for a private bill. Presumably in opposition to the restored monarchy, he was removed from the commission of the peace at the Restoration and never stood again. His house was licensed for Presbyterian worship in 1672. He died on 20 Jan. 1681, aged 83, and was buried in Christchurch Priory. He bequeathed the income from six messuages in Christchurch to be disposed of 'amongst pious, godly and learned nonconformist ministers'. His goods and chattels were inventoried at about £250, but he also held a mortgage on the lands of Dame Alice Lisle for £1,030. He was the only member of the family to sit in Parliament.[3]

[1] *The Gen.* n.s. x. 224, 225; *Ped. Reg.* ii. 263. [2] E. King, *Old Times Revisited*, 188; Winchester corp. ledger bk. 5, f. 7; *CSP Dom.* 1636–7, pp. 560–1; 1654, p. 385; 1655, p. 155; 1658–9, pp. 31, 362; *Cal. Comm. Comp.* 406; *Thurloe*, iii. 296, 363; Andover corp. recs. 2/JC/2; *Cal. Treas. Bks.* iii. 1204; iv. 124. [3] *CSP Dom.* 1636–7, pp. 560–1; 1637, p. 58; 1672, p. 299; *PC Reg.* i. 16–17; *The Gen.* n.s. x. 225; Hants RO, will proved 28 Feb. 1681.

M.W.H./P.W.

HILDYARD, Henry (1610–74), of Winestead, Yorks. and East Horsley, Surr.

HEDON 30 July 1660

b. 26 Jan. 1610, 1st s. of Sir Christopher Hildyard† of Winestead by Elizabeth, da. and h. of Henry Welby of Goxhill, Lincs. *educ.* Trinity Coll. Camb. 1626; I. Temple 1628. *m.* settlement 19 Aug. 1635, Lady Anne Leke, da. of Francis Leke†, 1st Earl of Scarsdale, 5s. 9da. *suc.* fa. 1634.[1]

J.p. Yorks. (E. Riding) 1634–?43, Lincs. (Lindsey) June 1660–d., Surr. 1666–d.; col. of militia ft. Yorks. to 1642; commr. of array, Yorks. 1642, assessment, Surr. Aug. 1660–d., (E. Riding) 1663–4; dep. lt. (E. Riding) c. Aug. 1660–d., sewers, Lincs. Aug. 1660, Yorks. (E. Riding) Oct. 1660.[2]

Chamberlain of Exchequer July 1660–d.; gent. of privy chamber 1670–d.[3]

Hildyard's ancestors acquired Winestead by marriage about the middle of the 15th century, and began to sit for Hedon, ten miles away, under Elizabeth. Hildyard himself was appointed a commissioner of array in 1642, but, unlike his brother Robert, a prominent royalist cavalry officer, he took no part in the actual fighting, since his only appearance in arms was as a colonel of foot in the Yorkshire trained bands in attendance on the King for about two weeks in July 1642. He signed the Yorkshire engagement in 1643. After this he retired to a house in Surrey which he had recently bought, where he 'lived peaceably' for the rest of the war and became friendly with Evelyn, the diarist. He petitioned to compound for an estate of over £2,000 p.a. in 1646 and was fined £4,660, but this was eventually reduced to a nominal sum in consideration of his debts, on condition that he made over the family house in Hull, which had been used as a magazine, to the corporation. He paid a further £150 in 1652 as part of the £300 he had been assessed as his proportion of the Yorkshire engagement.[4]

Hilyard remained under suspicion during the Protectorate, and was ineligible at the general election of 1660, but he was returned for the family borough at a by-election. An inactive Member of the Convention, he was named only to the committee on the bill for encouraging fen drainage. Undoubtedly a court supporter, he was rewarded with a sinecure office in the Exchequer, while his younger brother was created a baronet. It seems probable that his principal concern was to exert some leverage to secure the return of his house, to which end, according to Andrew Marvell*, he employed his interest in Parliament to continue Hull as a garrison. It was not until 21 Oct. 1661 that the corporation finally made over the house to him on payment of £300 which they had disbursed for repairs, but negotiations were far advanced by the dissolution of the Convention, and Hildyard did not stand again. He remained an active j.p. in Surrey, and when he died on 8 June 1674 he was buried at East Horsley. His estate was valued at £2,357 p.a., but his eldest son Henry, who had been converted to the Church of Rome by Obadiah Walker, was not mentioned in his will and was obliged to sever the entail by private Act and sell Winestead to the younger branch. The next member of the family to enter Parliament was the 3rd baronet, who sat for Bedwyn as a Tory from 1754 to 1761.[5]

[1] Clay, *Dugdale's Vis. Yorks.* iii. 331–6; *Winestead Reg.* (Yorks. Par. Reg. Soc. iv), 4; *Royalist Comp. Pprs.* (Yorks. Arch. Soc. rec. ser. xv), 104. [2] *Royalist Comp. Pprs.* 100; C181/7/44. [3] *CSP*

Dom. 1660–1, p. 138; Carlisle, *Privy Chamber*, 185. [4] G. Poulson, *Holderness*, ii. 467–72; *Royalist Comp. Pprs.* 98–99; *Cal. Comm. Adv. Money*, 902, 908; *Evelyn Diary*, ii. 551; *VCH Surr.* iii. 350; N. J. Miller, *Winestead and its Lords*, 74–76, 87. [5] *Surr. Arch. Colls.* xiv. 187; Miller, 141–2; *Evelyn Diary*, ii. 550; iv. 510; *Marvell* ed. Margoliouth, ii. 9, 11, 20, 334; *CSP Dom.* 1670, p. 299; 1675–6, p. 479; E. W. Brayley, *Top. Hist. Surr.* ii. 68.

M.W.H./P.W.

HILL, Sir Roger (1642–1729), of Denham, Bucks.

AMERSHAM	1679 (Mar.), 1679 (Oct.)
WENDOVER	15 July–21 Nov. 1702, 1705, 1708, 1710, 1713, 1715

b. 19 June 1642, 2nd but 1st surv. s. of Roger Hill[†] of Poundisford, Som., being o. surv. s. by 2nd w. Abigail, da. of Brampton Gurdon[†] of Assington, Suff. *educ.* Jesus, Camb. 1658; I. Temple 1658, called 1666. *m.* 11 July 1667, Abigail (*d.* 18 Aug. 1737), da. of John Lockey of Holmshill, Ridge, Herts., 3s. (1 *d.v.p.*) 2da. *suc.* fa. 1667; kntd. 18 July 1668.[1]

Gent. of the privy chamber 1668–85; filazer of c.p. by 1669–?74; freeman E. I. Co. 1679.[2]

Commr. for assessment, Bucks. 1673–80, 1689–90, sheriff 1673–4, j.p. 1689–93, 1702–*d.*, dep. lt. Feb.–June 1702.[3]

Although Hill claimed descent from a medieval knightly family and assumed their arms, his first certain ancestor was a Taunton merchant under Henry VIII. Two members of the family sat for the borough in Elizabethan Parliaments. Hill's father, who represented Bridport in the Long Parliament, refused to take part in the King's trial, but continued to sit in the Rump and became a judge during the Protectorate.[4]

Hill himself as a child witnessed the execution of Charles I, and perhaps in consequence was described in 1661 as 'very cavalierish ... as if he had been bred up in the use of it. If he lose his father's favour, woe to him.' But he was to develop into a violent Whig, who did not become a j.p. until the Revolution. He sold Poundisford and bought Denham manor and other properties from (Sir) William Bowyer* in 1670. Marked 'honest' by Shaftesbury in 1679, he was returned to the first Exclusion Parliament for Amersham, some 12 miles from Denham, but sat only on the committee for the better attendance of Members. He voted for exclusion. Barillon described Hill as an officer under Cromwell, perhaps confusing him with his father, and included him among the 'most considerable Members of the Lower House ... vehement against the Court'. Successful again in August, Hill was an active Member of the second Exclusion Parliament. He made no recorded speeches, but was appointed to 12 committees, including those to receive information concerning the

Popish Plot, and to repeal the Corporations Act. He was defeated in 1681 by the powerful Drake interest, which ignored the decision of the House to restrict the franchise to scot and lot payers only.[5]

After the Rye House Plot, Hill was described as 'a late untoward commoner, who has at all times vented himself most bitterly against the Government'. He was suspected of harbouring arms and traitors, and his house was searched by Samuel Starkey*, but nothing was proved against him. Through Ralph Montagu* he came to terms with Sir William Drake*, and again unsuccessfully contested Amersham in 1685, when Judge Jeffreys referred to him as 'a horrid Whig' and 'a fierce exclusioner'. He lent the Government £3,000 in that year, perhaps to buy his peace. He was mentioned as a possible candidate for Buckinghamshire in 1688, but James II's electoral agents did not fully understand his 'sentiments'. Although he supported the Revolution, he may have doubted its stability, for in 1689 he advanced only £500 to the new regime, compared with his investment of £2,000 in the East India Company. He did not sit in any of William III's Parliaments, partly because of a breach with the Wharton interest. He was buried at Denham on 29 Dec. 1729. His epitaph attests his fidelity to liberty and the Protestant religion. His sons did not long survive him, and the Denham estate passed to his great-grandson, Benjamin Way[†], who was returned for Bridport in 1765.[6]

[1] A. M. W. Stirling, *Ways of Yesterday*, 30–31, 43–45. [2] Carlisle, *Privy Chamber*, 179; *Cal. Ct. Mins. E.I. Co.* ed. Sainsbury, xi. 323. [3] *Bucks. Sess. Recs.* ed. Le Hardy, i. 510; *CSP Dom.* 1700–2, p. 519; 1702–3, p. 390. [4] *Vis. Som.* (Harl. Soc. xi), 50–51; Keeler, *Long Parl.* 215. [5] *East Anglian*, v. 5; *VCH Bucks.* iii. 258, 279; PRO 31/3, bdle. 146, f. 26; *CJ*, ix. 677. [6] *CSP Dom.* July–Sept. 1683, p. 378; 1685, p. 122; Add. 46500; Bodl. Carte 40, f. 172; R. Morrice, *Entering Bk.* 1, pp. 403, 423; *Cal. Treas. Bks.* viii. 2179; ix. 1986; Bucks. RO, Hill diary, ff. 51–53; Add. 22185, f. 14; Lipscomb, *Bucks.* iii. 456.

L.N./G.J.

HILLERSDEN, Thomas (1653–98), of Elstow, Beds.

BEDFORD	1689, 1690, 1695–Feb. 1698

b. 19 Oct. 1653, 1st s. of Thomas Hillersden of Elstow by Elizabeth, da. of John Huxley of Edmonton, Mdx. *educ.* Christ Church, Oxf. 1670; I. Temple 1670. *m.* lic. 12 July 1675, Mary (*d.* 6 Aug. 1693), da. of John Forth, Brewer, of Hackney, Mdx., 3s. 3da. *suc.* fa. 1657.[1]

J.p. Beds. 1675–80, ?1689–*d.*; commr. for assessment, Beds. 1677–80, Beds. and Bedford 1689–90; dep. lt. Beds. Feb.–June 1688, 1689–?*d.*, capt. of militia horse by 1697–*d.*[2]

Though said to be descended from the Devon family, Hillersden's ancestors were of little consequence until his great-grandfather purchased part of the site of Elstow abbey, just outside Bedford, in 1616. His father was too young to take part in the Civil War, but as a royalist sympathizer was assessed £9 10s. for decimation in 1655. Hillersden was connected with the St. Johns of Bletsoe through his step-father Sir William Beecher*, and married the daughter of a prominent London nonconformist. Like his step-father he signed the letter inviting the Hon. William Russell* to stand for the county at the second general election of 1679, and was removed from the commission of the peace in 1680. Regarded as a possible Whig collaborator, Hillersden was made a deputy lieutenant in February 1688, but was omitted in June. He was returned for the borough in 1689, but in the Convention he served only on the committee for disarming Papists, and he did not vote for the disabling clause. He continued to sit as a Whig under William III and signed the Association in 1696. He was buried at Elstow on 26 Feb. 1698. His son, also a Whig, represented the borough from 1707 to 1710 and the county from 1715 to 1722.[3]

[1] Beds. Par. Regs. i. (Elstow), 17; Beds. Hist. Rec. Soc. v. 82–91, 95; London Mar. Lic. ed. Foster, 685. [2] CSP Dom. 1687–9, pp. 141, 209; Eg. 1626, f. 4. [3] Beds. Hist. Rec. Soc. v. 75, 95; VCH Beds. iii. 281; Thurloe, iv. 513; J. R. Woodhead, Rulers of London, 72; J. Russell, Lord William Russell (1820), ii. 243; Beds. Par. Regs. i. 83.

L.N./G.J.

HILLERSDON, Richard (c.1639–1703), of Membland, Holbeton, Devon.

PLYMPTON ERLE 1679 (Mar.)

b. c.1639, 1st s. of Richard Hillersdon of Membland by Bridget, da. of John Harris of Lanrest, Liskeard, Cornw. educ. Exeter, Oxf. 1656. m. 11 May 1659, Anne, da. of Edward Nosworthy I* of Truro, Cornw., 1s. d.v.p. 2da. suc. fa. 1652.[1]

Commr. for assessment, Devon 1666–80, 1690–?d., j.p. 1670–87, July 1688–?d.

Hillersdon came from an old but minor gentry family which took its name from a hamlet in North Devon. One of them represented Plympton, five miles from Membland, in 1478; but they did not regularly sit in Parliament. Hillersdon's father took up arms for the King during the Civil War, compounding on his own discovery for £269. Hillersdon himself was returned for Plympton at the first general election of 1679, the last of his family to enter Parliament. Considered 'honest' by Shaftesbury, he voted for the first exclusion bill, but he was appointed to no committees and made no speeches. In the autumn election he made way for a more prominent opponent of the Court, John Pollexfen*, and he was sufficiently obscure to be allowed to remain on the commission of the

peace till 1687. He probably became a Whig collaborator under the influence of his brother-in-law, Edward Nosworthy II*. He was approved as a j.p. in July 1688, and his son was commissioned into a predominantly Roman Catholic regiment during the Revolution. Apparently Hillersdon himself accepted the new regime, and continued to hold local office even after he moved to Totnes. His son died in or before 1693, whereupon he seems to have made over Membland to his son-in-law Arthur Champernowne†. His other daughter married Courtenay Croker, who sat for Plympton as a Whig from 1695 to 1702. His name disappears from the commission of the peace in 1703.[2]

[1] Vivian, Vis. Devon, 447, 470; Lysons, Devon, 583; C8/543/110. [2] Lysons, 273; Cal. Comm. Comp. 2028; J. J. Muskett, Suff. Manorial Fams. i. 321; C7/156/74; H. R. Moulton, Cat. (1930), 200; Her. and Gen. viii. 380.

J.S.C.

HILLIARD see **HELYAR**

HINCHINGBROOKE, Visct. see **MONTAGU, Edward**

HINSON see **POWELL** formerly **HINSON, William**

HOBART, Sir Henry (c.1658–98), of Blickling Hall, Norf.

KING'S LYNN	1681
NORFOLK	1689
BERE ALSTON	14 May 1694
NORFOLK	1695

b. c.1658, 1st s. of Sir John Hobart, 3rd Bt.*, by 2nd w. educ. Thetford g.s.; St. John's, Camb. adm. 6 May 1674, aged 16. m. 9 July 1684, Elizabeth, da. and coh. of Joseph Maynard* of Clifton Reynes, Bucks., 1s. 8da. Kntd. 29 Sept. 1671; suc. fa. as 4th Bt. 22 Aug. 1683.[1]

Steward of duchy of Lancaster estates, Norf., Suff. and Cambs. 1680–d.; freeman, Lynn 1681; treas. King's Bench and Marshalsea prisons 1683–d.; j.p. and dep. lt. Norf. Feb. 1688–d., commr. for assessment 1689–90, v.–adm. 1691–d.[2]

Equerry 1689–?91; commr. of customs 1697–d.[3]

Hobart was knighted as a schoolboy of 13 during a royal visit to Blickling in 1671. Notwithstanding this unusual honour, he was returned for King's Lynn in 1681 as an opponent of the Court. In the Oxford Parliament he was named only to the committee of elections and privileges. After succeeding to an encumbered estate, he was defeated in the Norfolk election in 1685 and listed by Danby among the opposition to James II. Nevertheless in 1688 he was appointed to local office as a Whig collaborator, and the King's electoral agents reported that he would be proposed as court candidate for the county, his Presbyterian chaplain having 'engaged for him' that he was 'right by inclination' on the repeal of the Test Act and Penal Laws.[4]

At the general election of 1689 Hobart defeated Tory candidates both for Norfolk and Thetford. When the Convention met he opted to sit for the county, and moved that 'the votes of this House might be printed for the satisfaction of the nation in this juncture', but after debate the motion was laid aside. He may have been responsible for the excellent account of proceedings in the House on 28 Jan. On the next day he complained of the extravagant bail recently demanded and of the conduct of the lords lieutenant. A moderately active Member, he was among those instructed after the debate to bring in a list of the essentials for securing religion, law and liberty, and was appointed to 14 committees in all. He helped to prepare the address promising assistance in support of alliances abroad, in the reduction of Ireland, and in defence of the law and the Protestant religion (1 Mar.). He was added to the revived committee for the bill of rights and settlement (22 Mar.), and named to that to bring in the bill for religious comprehension (1 Apr.). On 8 May he was sent to the Lords to desire a conference on expediting the conviction and disarmament of Papists. Although he held a minor place at Court, he obtained the leave of the House on 28 June to go into the country for a month, and took an active part in disarming the local non-jurors. In the second session he acted as teller for an amendment to the address refusing to make any recommendations for service in Ireland. He served on the committee for the bill to restore corporations and supported the disabling clause. He lost his seat at the general election, but remained a court Whig until he died of wounds received in a duel on 21 Aug. 1698. He was buried at Blickling. His son sat for St. Ives as a Whig from 1715 to 1727 and then briefly for Norfolk, before being raised to the peerage in the coronation honours of George II.[5]

[1] *Vis. Norf.* ed. Bulwer, ii. 80–81. [2] Sir Robert Somerville, *Duchy of Lancaster Office-Holders*, 198; *Lynn Freemen*, 191; *HMC Lothian*, 89, 129; *Norf. Ltcy. Jnl.* (Norf. Rec. Soc. xxx), 92, 98; Ind. 24557. [3] LS13/231/28; Luttrell, ii. 252; iv. 239. [4] *HMC 11th Rep. VII*, 106; Hist. of Parl. Trust, W. W. Bean, 'List of Polls'. [5] R. Morrice, Entering Bk. 2, p. 437; *IHR Bull.* xlix. 243; *Hardwick SP*, i. 422; *CJ*, x. 125, 300; *HMC Lothian*, 136; *Vis. Norf.* ii. 99.

E.C.

HOBART, Sir John, 3rd Bt. (1628–83), of Blickling Hall, Norf.

NORFOLK   1654, 1656–10 Dec. 1657, 17 Feb. 1673, 5 May 1679, 1679 (Oct.), 1681

bap. 20 Mar. 1628, o.s. of Miles Hobart of Intwood by 1st w. Frances, da. of Sir John Peyton, 1st Bt., of Isleham, Cambs., wid. of Sir Philip Bedingfield of Ditchingham, Norf. *educ.* Emmanuel, Camb. 1644; L. Inn 1645. *m.* (1) 1647, his cos. Philippa (*bur.* 19 Jan. 1655), da. and coh. of Sir John Hobart, 2nd Bt.†, of Blickling, 1s. *d.v.p.*; (2) 3 June 1656, Mary, da. of John Hampden† of Great Hampden, Bucks., wid. of Robert Hammond of Chertsey, Surr., 4s. (1 *d.v.p.*) 1da. *suc.* fa. 1639, uncle as 3rd Bt. and in Blickling estate 20 Apr. 1647.[1]

Commr. for assessment, Norf. 1647–52, 1657, Aug. 1660–80, Norwich Aug. 1660–3, 1673–4; j.p. Norf. 1652–76, May–June 1679, commr. for scandalous ministers 1654, militia Mar. 1660, col. of militia ft. Apr. 1660–76; commr. for oyer and terminer, Norfolk circuit July 1660, sewers, Lincs. Aug. 1660; dep. lt. Norf. c. Aug. 1660–76, sheriff 1666–7; treas. King's Bench and Marshalsea prisons 1671–d.; commr. for recusants, Norf. 1675.[2]

Commr. for trade 1655–7, security 1656.

Hobart's ancestors can be traced back in Suffolk to 1389 and became armigerous in the following century. Their parliamentary record began with Sir James Hobart of Hales Hall, who sat for Ipswich in three Yorkist Parliaments and became recorder of Norwich in 1496. Blickling was purchased in 1616 by Hobart's grandfather, an even more successful lawyer. Hobart's uncle was a strong Parliamentarian in the Civil War, and Hobart himself sat in the Protectorate Parliaments for the county until called to the 'Other House'. Together with Sir Horatio Townshend* and Thomas Richardson* he presented the Norfolk address for a free Parliament in January 1660, but he was defeated at the general election. However, he was granted a royal pardon and proposed for the order of the Royal Oak with an estate of £1,000 p.a. In December it was reported that he would stand for Wendover with his brother-in-law Richard Hampden*, but as a stranger to the constituency he probably desisted before the poll.[3]

Hobart's son was knighted during a royal visit to Blickling in 1671, and in 1673, after an interval of 17 years, he was himself returned unopposed for the county, with Townshend's support and strong backing from the nonconformists. A Presbyterian minister, Dr John Collings, who kept a flourishing conventicle in Norwich, also acted as Hobart's man of business. He was at once added to the committee of elections and privileges, and appointed to consider the bill of ease for Protestant dissenters. (Sir) William Cook* wrote that he was 'very violent' for the bill, 'and by weekly letters to Mr Collings in

Norwich kept a correspondence with the nonconformist party'. He was named to the committees for ease of sheriffs and for a test to distinguish between Protestants and Papists in 1674, and for the prevention of illegal imprisonment on 22 Apr. 1675. In association with Townshend, he opposed the court candidate Robert Coke*, Danby's son-in-law, at King's Lynn, and was very active in promoting the election of Sir Robert Kemp* for the other county seat. He resigned from the lieutenancy when Townshend was replaced by Lord Yarmouth (Robert Paston*), and Charles II described him as one 'who will never be obliged', and had used his office 'against myself and Government'. Shaftesbury marked him 'thrice worthy' for the 1677 session, in which he acted as teller for candles to enable the debate on Irish cattle imports to continue. On 14 Nov. 1678 he was added to the committee to examine Coleman's papers, probably at the suggestion of his friend William Harbord*. It was said that throughout his service in the Cavalier Parliament he had never given a vote for the King. He was not recorded as speaking, but he was moderately active as a committeeman, with 28 committees.[4]

Hobart was defeated at the general election by the court candidates, but the hearing of his petition at the bar of the House was expedited through the efforts of Harbord and the Hon. William Russell*. His opponents were unseated, but an opposition motion to declare Hobart duly elected failed by five votes, perhaps because of rumours spread by the Paston faction that he attended conventicles and had defaulted on his sheriff's expenses. Elected at the head of the poll at the ensuing by-election, he reached London on 11 May 1679, ahead of his indenture, which had been delayed in the hope that a scrutiny of the poll books would give his opponents a majority. After the sheriff had been ordered into custody for this offence, Hobart was named to the committees to inquire into the shipping of artillery and to consider a naturalization bill. Again moderately active, he was unable to take his seat until after the division on the first exclusion bill, which he heartily supported. However, he did not emulate Harbord's persecution of the navy office, commenting that though Samuel Pepys* and Sir Anthony Deane* were 'neither my favourites', yet 'their offences are magnified beyond a due proportion'. His reputation as a conventicler, however, was putting his seat in jeopardy, and on 3 June he wrote to a supporter: 'I thank God my principles are such that I can and do with great satisfaction attend the public service of God Almighty according to the establishment of our Church'. Neverthe-

less a subscription was raised for him among the dissenters, and Collings arranged transport and accommodation for his supporters at the autumn election. He was returned with an increased majority, and became an active Member of the second Exclusion Parliament, undeterred by the loss of Townshend's support after a dispute over election expenses. His ten committees included those to inquire into abhorring and the conduct of the under-sheriff of Norfolk, to consider the bills for regulating elections and uniting Protestants, and to examine the disbandment accounts. Barillon listed him among the 'considerable' Members opposed to the Court, and described him as a Presbyterian and a republican. Now at the head of the country party in Norfolk, he was re-elected in 1681, though only by a narrow margin and with the help of the new sheriff. In the Oxford Parliament he was appointed only to the elections committee. His house was searched for arms after the Rye House Plot, and he died shortly afterwards, on 22 Aug. 1683, and was buried at Blickling.[5]

[1] Vis. Norf. ed. Bulwer, ii. 76–80; Cases in Chancery, i. 280. [2] Parl. Intell. 9 Apr. 1660; Cal. Treas. Bks. i. 73; HMC Lothian, 129. [3] Vis. Norf. ii. 60, 73; Blomefield, Norf. vi. 395; CSP Dom. 1659–60, p, 332; BL, M636/17, William Smith to Sir Ralph Verney, 27 Dec. 1660. [4] CSP Dom. 1672–3, p. 572; 1675–6, p. 54; 1679–80, p. 75; Bodl. Tanner 42, f. 148; HMC Finch, ii. 42; Norf. Arch. xxvii. 360–72; xxx. 97–98. [5] Durham Univ. Jnl. n.s. xxii. 53–56; Add. 36988, ff. 139, 149; Norf. Arch. xxvii. 373–4; Add. 37911, f. 12; HMC 12th Rep. IX, 184–5; Ketton-Cremer (Felbrigg) mss, Hobart to Windham, 3 June 1679, 20 Jan., 8 Mar. 1681, 14 Jan. 1683; PRO 31/3, bdle. 146, f. 27; HMC Lothian, 130.

E.C.

HOBY, John (c.1668–89), of Bisham Abbey, Berks.

GREAT MARLOW   8 Feb.–Dec. 1689

b. c.1668, 1st s. of Sir John Hoby, 2nd Bt. (d.1702), of Somerley, Hants by Mary, da. and h. of Thomas Long of Worton, Wilts. m. 23 Dec. 1686, aged 18, his cos. Elizabeth, da. and h. of Sir Edward Hoby, 1st Bt., of Bisham Abbey, s.p.[1]

Commr. for assessment, Berks. 1689.

Hoby's father, a younger son of Peregrine Hoby* and brother of Thomas Hoby*, acquired an estate in Hampshire by marrying an heiress, and succeeded to the baronetcy under a special remainder in 1675. Hoby himself was married, still under age, to his cousin, and had the use under the settlement of her dowry of £500 p.a. during his lifetime. He was returned for the family borough at a by-election in 1689, doubtless as a Whig, but his only appearance in the Journals was as an applicant for leave in May. He returned to Westminster, writing to his wife in August that the House was 'as good as a bagnio now, we are almost melted'. After the recess, he described the proceedings against George Churchill* on 18 Nov., but in the same letter he complained of 'a cruel cold', which soon proved fatal. He was buried at Bisham on 7 Dec. His nephew, the 4th baronet, was returned for Marlow in 1732 and sat as a Whig until his death 12 years later.[2]

[1] Soc. of Genealogists, All Hallows Staining par. reg. [2] 2 Wm. and Mary, c. 18, ss. i.; *CJ*, x. 145; *HMC Downshire*, i. 315, 319; *Bisham Par. Reg.* (Par. Reg. Soc. xv), 38.

L.N./G.J.

HOBY, Peregrine (1602–79), of Bisham Abbey, Berks.

GREAT MARLOW   Jan. 1641,[1] 1659, 1660, 1661

b. 1 Sept. 1602, illegit. s. of Sir Edward Hoby† of Bisham Abbey by Katharine Pinckney. *educ.* Eton 1612–16. *m.* 14 Apr. 1631, Katharine (*d.*1687), da. of Sir William Doddington† of Breamore, Hants, and coh. to her bro. Edward, 5s. (2 *d.v.p.*) 2da. *suc.* fa. 1617.[2]

Commr. for sewers, Berks. and Wilts. 1639; sheriff, Berks. 1640–1, commr. for assessment 1643–8, Sept. 1660–*d.*, sequestrations 1643, militia 1648, Mar. 1660, j.p. Mar. 1660–*d.*; commr. for oyer and terminer, Oxford circuit July 1660, recusants, Bucks. 1675.[3]

Bisham Abbey was acquired by Sir Philip Hoby in 1553, and Hoby's father represented Berkshire under Elizabeth. Hoby inherited the property despite his illegitimacy, and was brought up in the Calvinist household of Archbishop Abbot. He sat in the Long Parliament for Marlow, just across the river from his home, until Pride's Purge, after which he did not sit. He held no further local office until the eve of the Restoration. He regained his seat when the representation of Marlow was restored in 1659, and was re-elected to the Convention. Lord Wharton marked him as a friend, reserved for his own management. An inactive Member, he made no recorded speeches and was named to only seven committees, including those for settling the revenue, enabling soldiers to exercise trades, and taking accounts of public moneys.[4]

Hoby was re-elected in 1661, and again included in Wharton's list of friends. He was a moderately active committeeman in the Cavalier Parliament, but few of his 175 committees were of major political significance. He took no part in the Clarendon Code, but his only tellership on 7 May 1663 was for imposing on those who refused the oaths of allegiance and supremacy the status of recusant convicts. After the heralds' visitation of Berkshire in 1664, Hoby was given leave to use his father's arms, with a bordure for difference, as one 'generally known to be well deserving, not only for his good conversation and discreet demeanour, but also for a prudent discharge of his duty to his country, having been a burgess in Parliament for the town of

Marlow'. In 1666 his eldest son was created a baronet. Hoby's income about this time was estimated at £1,000 p.a. He was among those appointed to manage a conference on the impeachment of Lord Mordaunt on 29 Dec. 1666, but he probably went over to the Court temporarily under the Cabal, being listed by Sir Thomas Osborne* in 1669 among the independent Members who had usually voted for supply. On 23 Nov. 1667 he brought in a complaint about a young heir alleged to have been seduced by the Jesuits, but it turned out to be unfounded. In 1671 he was among the Members ordered to bring in a bill to prevent the growth of Popery, and added to the committee for considering an additional conventicles bill. In 1675 he was appointed to the committees on the bills to abolish *de heretico comburendo*, and to hinder Papists sitting in Parliament. Sir Richard Wiseman* listed him among six Buckinghamshire gentlemen of whom he had 'little cause to hope well', and Shaftesbury marked him 'worthy' in 1677. He is unlikely to have stood for re-election, however, for he was buried at Bisham on 6 May 1679.[5]

[1] Did not sit after Pride's Purge, 6 Dec. 1648. [2] *Eton Coll. Reg.* ed. Sterry, 175; *Vis. Berks.* (Harl. Soc. lvi), 228; *Bisham Par. Reg.* (Par. Reg. Soc. xv), 10, 11, 22, 23, 36, 39. [3] C181/5/271. [4] *VCH Berks.* iii. 147; Keeler, *Long Parl.* 217. [5] *Vis. Berks.* (Harl. Soc. lvii), 150; Salisbury Cathedral Library, Bp. Seth Ward, Liber Notitiae, f. 53; *Milward*, 136; *Bisham Par. Reg.* 37.

M.W.H./L.N./G.J.

HOBY, Thomas (1642–c.1706), of Bisham Abbey, Berks. and Breamore, Hants.

GREAT MARLOW   1681
SALISBURY   1689, 1690, 1695

bap. 7 Jan. 1642, 4th but 2nd surv. s. of Peregrine Hoby*. *educ.* L. Inn 1659. *m.* Anne, da. and h. of John Doddington of Breamore, wid. of Robert, 4th Baron Brooke of Beauchamps Court, *s.p.*[1]

Commr. for assessment, Berks. 1679–80, Hants, Wilts. and Salisbury 1689–90; j.p. and dep. lt. Hants and Wilts. 1689–*d.*; commr. for wastes and spoils, New Forest 1691.[2]

After two unsuccessful attempts to enter the second Exclusion Parliament, Hoby was returned for the family borough as a country candidate in 1681, and appointed to the committee to draw up the third exclusion bill. His marriage to his widowed cousin Lady Brooke brought him property in the Avon valley, downstream from Salisbury, for which he was returned to the Convention by the corporation, although apparently not a freeman. He probably served on most, if not all of the 19 committees to which 'Mr Hobby' was named, but did not speak. He was appointed to consider the attainder bill in the first session, and the mutiny bill in the second. He did not vote for the disabling clause in the bill to restore corporations, but he showed his support for the new regime with a loan of £5,000. He continued to sit for Salisbury as a Whig in the next two Parliaments. He was still active as a deputy lieutenant in 1705, but his will, bequeathing his lands to his elder brother, was proved on 14 Oct. 1707.[3]

[1] *Vis. Berks.* (Harl. Soc. lvi), 228; *Bisham Par. Reg.* (Par. Reg. Soc. xv), 11. [2] *Cal. Treas. Bks.* ix. 1988, 2180. [3] *HMC Lords*, n.s. iv. 411; vi. 419; PCC 230 Poley.

L.N.

HODGES, Hugh (1641–93), of Sherborne, Dorset and Lincoln's Inn.

BRIDPORT 1685

bap. 11 June 1641, 2nd but 1st surv. s. of Hugh Hodges, attorney, of Sherborne by Elizabeth, da. of Lawrence Swetnam of Sherborne. *educ.* Sherborne; Queen's, Oxf. 1658; L. Inn 1659, called 1666. *m.* Mary, da. of John Eastmont, clothier, of Sherborne, 1s. *suc.* fa. 1673.[1]

Jt. auditor of excise, Dorset 1662; gov. Sherborne sch. 1669, steward 1670–?1687; recorder, Dorchester 1671–d.; commr. for assessment, Dorset 1673–80, 1689–90; j.p. 1673–June 1688, Nov. 1688–d., commr. for recusants 1675; recorder, Bridport 1677–Aug. 1688, Oct. 1688–d., freeman 1685; bencher, L. Inn 1685; commr. for rebels' estates, Som. and Dorset 1685.[2]
Serjeant-at-law 1686–d.

Hodges's father, an attorney of Somerset origin, took part in the Civil War as clerk to the treasurer of the Cavalier armies in the west. He compounded for property worth £180 p.a. with debts of £950, chiefly due to an ambitious land purchase in 1638. During the Interregnum he acted in association with Thomas Chafe I* in buying back the Digby estates from the treason trustees.[3]

Hodges rapidly outstripped his father in the legal profession. The recusancy of the 2nd Earl of Bristol and the weakness of the 3rd (John Digby*, Lord Digby) enabled him to wield part of the vast influence which Sherborne Castle exercised in Somerset and Dorset. As chairman of quarter sessions 'he was very fierce all along against dissenters'. The only blemish on his record, from the government standpoint, was an episode in which he boxed the ears of an insolent tax-collector; but his loyalty could be vouched for by Digby and Thomas Strangways*, who advised the Bridport corporation to choose him as their recorder, an appropriate choice for a town where a tax-collector had been murdered a few years before. In 1680, Hodges was described by John Speke* as the Government's chief intelligencer in the area, predicting the speedy dissolution of the second Exclusion Parliament and denouncing

its conduct towards the King and Lord Halifax. He had been a subscriber to Williamson's newsletters as early as 1665, but it was his local intelligence system that enabled him to apprehend two of Shaftesbury's couriers at the time of the Rye House Plot.[4]

Hodges was returned for Bridport to James II's Parliament. As a moderately active Member, he was appointed to seven committees, of which the most important was for the general naturalization of Huguenot refugees. After the Bloody Assizes, Roger Morrice alleged that he became 'very much disturbed in his mind. . . . It is credibly reported that in his illness he often cried aloud, "Take down those quarters, for I must be hanged in their stead".' His delirium, if it ever occurred, must have been of short duration, for he was raised to the coif in the following year. His answers on the repeal of the Test and Penal Laws are not extant, but were presumably negative, for he was removed from county and municipal office.[5]

Hodges witnessed the return for the county election on 14 Jan. 1689, but otherwise nothing more is known of his career. He died on 16 Aug. 1693 and was buried in Sherborne Abbey, the only member of his family to sit in Parliament.[6]

[1] Dorset RO, Sherborne par. reg.; *Vis. Dorset* (Harl. Soc. cxvii), 4; Hutchins, *Dorset*, iv. 250; PCC 79 Pye. [2] *Cal. Treas. Bks.* i. 382; viii. 414; *Sherborne Reg.* 4; Hutchins, ii. 8, 361; Dorset RO, KG1148, 1496, 1147; *Dorset Hearth-Tax* ed. Meekings, 117; *CSP Dom.* 1685, p. 25. [3] SP23/185/866–79; *Cal. Comm. Comp.* 2170; *CSP Dom.* 1639–40, p. 151; 1656–7, p. 10; G. E. Aylmer, *King's Servants*, 90, 388; Hutchins, iv. 66. [4] R. Morrice, Entering-Bk. 1, p. 536; *CSP Dom.* 1665–6, p. 54; 1667–8, pp. 222, 224; 1675–6, p. 223; 1677–8, pp. 203, 254, 293; 1680–1, p. 92; July–Sept. 1683, pp. 64, 338. [5] Morrice, 536; PC2/72, pp. 567, 613. [6] Hutchins, iv. 251.

J.P.F.

HODY, John (c.1659–1729), of Northover, nr. Ilchester, Som.

ILCHESTER 1681

b. c.1659, 1st s. of John Hody of Northover by 2nd w. Susan, da. and coh. of Hugh Hody of Brixham, Devon. *educ.* Wadham, Oxf. matric. 19 July 1677, aged 18. *m.* 1s. *d.v.p.* 1da. *suc.* fa. 1702.[1]
Maj. of militia ft. Som. by 1679–at least 1697, commr. for assessment 1690–at least 1702.[2]

Hody's family originated in Dorset, providing an MP for Shaftesbury in 1421 and sitting repeatedly for Somerset under the Lancastrians. But the family declined rapidly in Tudor times and none had entered Parliament since the obscure William Hody† in 1589. Hody's mother was descended from a branch which had moved to Devon under Henry VI, while his father's ancestors had migrated to Crewkerne early in the 16th century. This branch was of so little consequence, however, that his father, a Royalist in the first Civil War, was never sequestrated, and compounded in 1650 for a mere £7. In the same year, however, he acquired North-over, just outside Ilchester, through his first wife, the Raymond heiress, but he never became a j.p. Hody was returned as John Hody junior for Ilchester as a moderate court supporter in 1681, probably as a stop-gap for the Phelips interest, but left no trace on the records of the Oxford Parliament. He joined William of Orange in 1688, but never stood again, though he survived into the reign of George II. He was buried at Northover on 6 Aug. 1729, the last of his family.[3]

[1] Hutchins, *Dorset*, ii. 233; *VCH Som*. iii. 226. [2] *CSP Dom*. 1679–80, p. 62; Eg. 1626, f. 39. [3] *Vis. Devon*, ed. Vivian, 491; *Cal. Comm. Comp*. 2647; *VCH Som*. iii. 226; E. Green, *Wm. III in Som*. 59; information from Dr R. W. Dunning.

I.C.

HOGHTON (HOUGHTON), Sir Charles, 4th Bt. (c.1644–1710), of Hoghton Tower, Lancs.

LANCASHIRE   1679 (Oct.), 1681, 1689

b. c.1644, 5th but 1st surv. s. of Sir Richard Hoghton[†], 3rd Bt., of Hoghton Tower by Lady Sarah Stanhope, da. of Philip, 1st Earl of Chesterfield. *educ.* privately (Adam Martindale). *m.* settlement 8 Mar. 1677 (with £5,000), Mary, da. of John, 2nd Visct. Massereene [I], 5s. (2 *d.v.p.*) 5da. *suc.* fa. 3 Feb. 1678.[1]

Freeman, Preston 1662, 1682; commr. for assessment, Lancs. 1677–80, 1689–90, dep. lt. 1680–?*d*., j.p. 1689–90, 1696–*d*., commr. for inquiry into superstitious uses 1693.[2]

Hoghton's ancestors acquired possession of the property to which they gave their name early in the 14th century, and served regularly as knights of the shire from 1322, with an interval due to recusancy under Elizabeth. His father, however, was a Presbyterian, who was in arms for Parliament in the Civil War, sitting for Lancashire as a recruiter until Pride's Purge, and again under the Protectorate. He conformed at the Restoration, but maintained dissenting ministers in his household as chaplains and tutors. In 1665 he was described as 'a very worthy person living in great repute in Lancashire' with an annual income of £2,500 or more. Hoghton's mother, 'a great patroness of religion and nonconformity', appears to have borne a strong resemblance to her brother Arthur Stanhope*. Hoghton was described as 'a proper man of person, very civil and judicious, given to no voice, a great scholar and mathematician' by a prospective father-in-law, but in spite of these admirable qualities the match fell through. A proposed union with Lord Wharton's daughter in 1671 also came to nothing. It was not until 1677 that he was provided with a wife of unimpeachable Presbyterian background.[3]

Hoghton succeeded to the family estates in the following year, but was not appointed to the commission of the peace, probably because his religious and political principles were too well known. He was returned for the county at the second general election of 1679 as a country candidate. A moderately active Member of the second Exclusion Parliament, he was named to the committees to inquire into abhorring, to encourage woollen manufactures, and to repeal part of the Severn Fishery Act. A private bill to rectify his marriage settlement was steered through committee and carried to the Lords by (Sir) John Otway*. Hoghton was re-elected in 1681 but probably failed to reach Oxford before the short-lived Parliament was dissolved. He did not stand in 1685, but he and Edward Rigby* provided the only support for Lord Brandon (Hon. Charles Gerard*) at the preliminary gentry meeting. He was returned unopposed to the Convention, in which he was named only to the committee for the relief of Protestant refugees from Ireland. He was not listed as supporting the disabling clause in the bill to restore corporations, and did not stand again. After presenting a nonconformist to the vicarage of Preston, he surrendered the advowson to the corporation, preferring to maintain a dissenting meeting-house at Tockholes. He died on 10 June 1710, aged 66, and was buried at Walton-on-the-Hill. His son, the 5th baronet, sat for Preston as a Whig in four Parliaments between 1710 and 1741.[4]

[1] *Vis. Lancs*. (Chetham Soc. lxxxv), 154; Croston, *Lancs*. iv. 182–5; *De Hoghton Deeds* (Lancs. and Cheshire Rec. Soc. lxxxviii), 252. [2] *Preston Guild Rolls* (Lancs. and Cheshire Rec. Soc. ix), 145, 187; Lancs. RO, QSC 103; T27/14/16. [3] *VCH Lancs*. vi. 37, 40–41; R. Halley, *Lancs. Puritanism and Nonconformity*, 126, 156, 298–9, 383–5; E. Broxap, *Civil War in Lancs*. 29; Bodl. Carte mss 75, f. 415, Pickering to Sandwich, 27 Dec. 1665; *De Hoghton Deeds*, 251–2; *CSP Dom*. 1676–7, p. 572. [4] *HMC Le Fleming*, 162; *CSP Dom*. July–Sept. 1683, p. 234; *CJ*, ix. 686; Westmld. RO, Fleming mss 2882, Kirkby to Fleming, 15 Mar. 1685; *De Hoghton Deeds*, 74, 252; *VCH Lancs*. vi. 44; vii. 86; Halley, 444–5.

I.C.

HOLLAND, Sir John, 1st Bt. (1603–1701), of Quidenham, Norf.

NORFOLK   1640 (Apr.)
CASTLE RISING   1640 (Nov.),[1] 1660
ALDEBURGH   1661

b. Oct. 1603, 1st s. of Sir Thomas Holland[†] of Quidenham by 1st w. Mary, da. of Sir Thomas Knyvett of Ashwellthorpe. *educ.* Christ's, Camb. 1620; M. Temple 1623. *m.* c. Aug. 1629, Alathea (*d.* 22 May 1679), da. and coh. of John Panton of Bryncunallt, Chirk, Denb., wid. of William, 4th Lord Sandys, 6s. (3 *d.v.p.*) 5da. *suc.* fa. 1626; *cr.* Bt. 15 June 1629.[2]

Capt. of militia ft. Norf. 1626, col. 1661–76; commr. for assessment, Norf. 1628, 1643–8, Aug. 1660–80, Suff. 1663–4, 1677–80, Aldeburgh 1663–79, Thetford

1664–80, Norf. and Thetford 1689–90; j.p. Norf. by 1635–48, Mar. 1660–76, May–June 1679, 1684–Feb. 1688, 1689–?d., Suff. 1647–8, Thetford 1666; dep. lt. Norf. 1638–43, c. Aug. 1660–76, commr. for sequestration 1643, levying of money 1643, eastern assoc. 1643, new model ordinance 1645, militia 1648, Mar. 1660, oyer and terminer, Norfolk circuit July 1660; alderman, Thetford by 1669–82; commr. for recusants, Norf. and Suff. 1675.[3]

Col. of ft. (parliamentary) 1642–3.[4]

Commr. for exclusion from sacrament 1646, scandalous offences 1648; Councillor of State 25 Feb.–31 May 1660.

Holland's great-great-grandfather, a retainer of the Howards, settled in Norfolk early in the 16th century, and his father sat for Thetford in 1621 and for the county three years later. Honest and moderate, Holland was much in demand as a conciliator. He was in arms for Parliament in the opening months of the war, but in 1643 he was allowed to join his wife, who was a Roman Catholic, in the Low Countries. He returned in 1645, and attended the King as a parliamentary commissioner at Holmby. He went overseas before Pride's Purge, and held no further office until the return of the secluded Members, when he was elected to the Council of State.[5]

Holland was returned to the Convention for Castle Rising on the Howard interest, and marked as a friend by Lord Wharton. A moderately active Member, he made ten recorded speeches, acted as teller in three divisions, and was named to 21 committees, including the committee of elections and privileges and the drafting committee. He was fourth in the ballot for the delegation to attend the King in Holland, and was appointed to the joint committees to draft their instructions and to prepare for the King's reception. After the Restoration he was teller for the motion to take accounts only from 1648, and helped to administer the oaths to Members. During the debates on the indemnity bill he urged that Bulstrode Whitelocke[†] should be included, because he had sent the King £500 and secured Lynn, where his son had commanded the garrison. On 30 June he was named to the committee to inquire into unauthorized Anglican publications. In the debate on the bill to confirm land purchases, he moved to except the queen mother's lands. On 31 July he supported the abolition of the court of wards, but objected to the imposition of an additional tax of £100,000 p.a. to provide compensation for the crown, because Norfolk was overassessed. He urged the rejection of a private bill to enable a Norfolk landlord to fell timber on his estate, but was named to the committee. He was also appointed to the committee for the Dunkirk establishment. Though a member of the revenue

committee, he claimed that it was dominated by Privy Councillors from the north and west, and attacked the report. He spoke in favour of the restitution of the dukedom of Norfolk to the head of the Howard family, and acted as teller for the bill. On 29 Dec. he was sent to remind the Lords of the fisheries bill.[6]

Holland 'expressed very much indifference' to an offer from Henry Howard to nominate him for reelection at King's Lynn, probably because it would involve him in a struggle with the Paston interest, and he 'positively refused' a suggestion from some of his friends that he should stand for the county in 1661. But he was returned for Aldeburgh on the Howard interest after a contest, and became an active Member of the Cavalier Parliament. He was named to 202 committees, including the committee of elections and privileges in eight sessions, and acted as teller in eight divisions. About 40 of his speeches are recorded, but half of them are found only among his own papers. If they were all actually delivered in the House, he was active in Opposition from the first. In the opening session he again helped to swear in his fellow-Members. He was one of the managers of the conference to receive the King's message about affairs in Scotland (20 May). An Erastian conformist, he objected to the constitutional position accorded to the Church in the preamble to the bill to restore the temporal jurisdiction of the clergy, and said: 'I think it will be much better for both [church and state] if the bishops would not entangle themselves with secular affairs'. Nevertheless he was appointed to the committee for the bill, and also to those to consider the corporations bill, to prevent mischiefs from Quakers, to consider the uniformity bill and the bill of pains and penalties, to draft a petition on behalf of Sir Arthur Hesilrige[†], and to attend the lord treasurer about the condition of the Forest of Dean. In the debate on the uniformity bill on 19 Apr. 1662 he spoke in favour of omitting the clause which condemned the Solemn League and Covenant. Explaining his position in the light of an earlier vote against any indulgence to dissenters, he said:

The question then was whether any indulgence should be granted the dissenters from the Act of Uniformity, to which I gave a negative, upon this ground that if it should be resolved in the affirmative, that then the doors would have been set so wide open, that no man could foresee what might or might not be brought in thereby, even that which might have shaken the very foundations of the Act of Uniformity, which I desire may be conserved entire, for we know that some of those that are concerned herein are of that temper that the more they gain, the more they will ask, that even granting begets an appetite of asking, and this was the reason of my negative to that question. But the question now being whether there shall be an indulgence granted only as to that clause touching the Covenant, which is but one particular of the Act of Uniformity and which is circumscribed and limited so that they cannot break into any part of the Act, I do, I confess, very much incline to give my affirmation to the question; and the rather to gratify the King, his Majesty having seemed so often and so passionately to desire . . . some indulgence towards those of different judgement.

He opposed the militia bill as establishing a standing army, and brought in an alternative which remained on the table. He acted as teller against a clause designed to protect the rights of the crown in the bill to regulate the manufacture of Norwich stuffs, and helped to manage a conference. On 19 May he was sent to desire a conference on the poor law, which he also helped to manage. In July he wrote to William Gawdy* that he was vexed at not being appointed a commissioner for corporations.[7]

In the 1663 session Holland was among those appointed to hear a petition from the loyal and indigent officers, to attend a conference on the Declaration of Indulgence, and to consider a bill against conventicles, though he seems to have attempted to distinguish between peaceful nonconformists and potential rebels. In 1664 he was again named to the committee for the conventicles bill. He spoke in favour of repealing the Triennial Act, though he had supported it in the Long Parliament.

I had rather never live to see a Parliament called, than to see a Parliament to be called and sit contrary to the good will of the King. For, Sir, it is not now as when this Act passed, for now, Sir, we have the sad and dear experience of that which was then incredible, I think, to most Englishmen (I am sure it was so with me) that, through the long sitting of a Parliament contrary to the good will of the King, greater and more desperate mischiefs have arisen both to the King and people than ever have or possibly can arise through the long intermission of Parliament, though those inconveniences be very great.

When Parliament met again in the autumn on the eve of the second Dutch war he urged the necessity of supply, but baulked at the figure of £2,500,000 proposed by (Sir) Robert Paston*. He acted (with (Sir) Edward Walpole*) as teller against Paston's motion, and (with Sir William Doyley*) for relief for Norfolk taxpayers; but he supported Paston's bill to regulate the Yarmouth herring trade. Holland was one of the Norfolk landowners who profited, directly or indirectly, by fattening Irish cattle for the London market, and accordingly spoke on 22 Sept. 1666 against the bill to prohibit their import. Nevertheless he was appointed to the committee. In the supply debates in this session he opposed both a general excise and a land-tax, but he supported the commutation of the hearth-tax

and was named to the committee to estimate the yield. Holland regarded his wife as a paragon in all respects but her religion, which was never allowed to influence his household or his politics, and he was appointed to a committee to receive information about the insolence of Popish priests and Jesuits.[8]

Although Holland opposed the motion to thank the King for dismissing Clarendon, he was appointed to the committee to draft the address. An adherent of the Townshend interest in Norfolk politics, he introduced a petition from Lord Townshend (Sir Horatio Townshend*) on 17 Oct. 1667 to exchange land with the rector of East Raynham, later reporting the bill and carrying it to the Lords. He was among those appointed to confer with the Duke of Albemarle (George Monck*) about security against highwaymen, to bring in a public accounts bill, to search for precedents for impeachment, and to reduce the charges against Clarendon into heads. He vigorously attacked the proceedings against the fallen minister:

I rise only now in discharge of mine own conscience in so tender a case as this is, in a case of blood, one drop whereof I would not have lie at my door for all the world. For when I have once given my vote for the impeachment of the Earl of Clarendon of high treason, I have done all that lieth in me to bring his head to the block; and this I cannot do upon no stronger inducement (as we now call them) than we have yet had to prove that article of treason, viz. the holding correspondence with the King and the discovery of his counsels to them, [the proof] amounting only to this, that two Members of this House inform you that there is a person that will make it good; but who or what this person is we know not.

After the Christmas recess he supported the Triple Alliance as affording grounds for the grant of supply, and the proposals for religious comprehension:

In the first place I crave leave to say that how true, how faithful, and how obedient a son soever I am to our mother, the Church of England as she is now established in doctrine, discipline and government, in whose bosom and communion I hope and desire to live and die, yet whilst I consider the present conjuncture of time and affairs, the dangerous divisions in matters of religion and God's worship that are among us, the necessity of uniting as much as possible may be for our preservation in the enlargement of the foundation of our common interest, and, whilst I consider the ill consequences that possibly may arise through the disappointment of his Majesty's expectation in what he tells us he conceives himself obliged at this present to recommend us, I cannot say, Sir, whilst I consider these and the like matters, but judge it very prudent to grant a relaxation of some things the law in force at present exacts and some indulgence of truly tender consciences, but not to that latitude as to let in all persons of all opinions, for that would amount to a general toleration.

He spoke against the bill to regulate alnage as detrimental to the new draperies, including Norwich stuffs, and with Thomas Richardson* acted as teller against it. Sir Thomas Osborne* included him in 1669 among the Members to be engaged for the Court by the Duke of York, but he took little further part in politics until the break-up of the Cabal.[9]

Holland was as much opposed to the third Dutch war as to its predecessor. When Lord Arlington (Sir Henry Bennet*) visited his country estate at Euston in August 1672 Holland 'thought himself obliged in good manners to visit him . . . desired to know the reason of the prorogation of Parliament', and obtained from the minister an assurance that he would do all he could to promote peace. When Parliament met in the following year he offered 'his almost traditional plea' for a reduction in Norfolk's assessment, but 'the House would give no ear to anything that might obstruct or delay supply'. Nevertheless he was appointed to the committee which produced the test bill and considered a bill of ease for Protestant dissenters. In his analysis of the House in the autumn session Sir William Temple* placed Holland at the head of the group who were for supply

> upon pretence of not exasperating the King . . . but with pretence of not perfecting it unless peace be made, though this be understood to be a way of securing the business of money under a show of moderation and popular aims.

In the debate of 20 Jan. 1674 he defended his neighbour Arlington, who thought that Englishmen were never happy except when King and Parliament agreed. 'A person that has these things planted in him cannot be dangerous', he argued. He approved the projected peace with Holland, though he wished Parliament had been consulted at the beginning of the war. But at two local by-elections in 1675 Holland, like Townshend, supported the country candidates, presenting on 3 May the petition of Simon Taylor*, who had been defeated by Robert Coke*, the lord treasurer's son-in-law, at King's Lynn, and mustering the Howard tenantry in his neighbourhood to vote for Sir Robert Kemp* for the county. In the autumn session he was appointed to the committees to inquire into dangerous books and to consider bills providing for the Protestant education of the royal children and the liberty of the subject. His name appeared on the working lists about this time among the Members to be influenced by Henry Coventry*, but his speech of 18 Oct. seriously disobliged the Court.

> If we consider that, after such supplies, never given before . . . now to have every branch of the revenue anticip-

ated; and not only that, but debts so great to the ruin of the people, and besides the King's wants so great as to be forced to break the credit of the Exchequer, to the ruin of widows, orphans, and numerous other people, as it puts so great a damage upon our English manufacture. . . . The charge of the government is greater than the nation can bear. [I] cannot but say the expenses of the Court may be reduced; especially the Treasury may be better managed. The truth is, the prodigal and excessive way of living now was unknown to our forefathers.

He went on to suggest that a petition should be presented to the King from both Houses,

> in which . . . we may represent to him the present poverty of the nation; together with the mischiefs of unseasonable prorogations, and that we be continued without prorogation till we have dispatched bills for the security of religion and property; and then declare that we will give supply to provide shipping and stores, to be equal if not stronger than our neighbours.

When Townshend was replaced as lord lieutenant by the Earl of Yarmouth (Robert Paston*) in 1676 Holland insisted on giving up his militia regiment, and in consequence was deprived of his other offices. Yarmouth was urged by (Sir) Henry Bedingfield* not to displace him because he was 'so considerable a man with the vulgar', and was led to believe by Howard, now Earl Marshal, that:

> if by my lord treasurer's means I could set him right in his Majesty's favour, I should do my lord treasurer, and in that way myself, a courtesy, and give the others a most unexpected defeat.

Meanwhile Arlington had requited Holland's good offices in the House by warning him that his speech of 18 Oct. 1675 had been represented to the King as seditious, and that William Ashburnham* claimed to remember hearing the same speech from him in the Long Parliament in 1640. When Parliament met again in 1677 after the long recess, Holland asked the House 'to consider a petition to the King to represent the ancient right and necessary privilege of freedom of speech in Parliament, and that he would be graciously pleased not to give any credit to such reports'. His case was weakened by Arlington's refusal to allow his name to be used, and for proof of Ashburnham's conduct he had to rely on (Sir) Edward Turnor*, who was dead, Sir Francis Clarke*, who remembered nothing, and Townshend, who was in the other House. Coventry ridiculed the allegation, and the House resolved in Ashburnham's favour. Though Shaftesbury marked Holland 'worthy', the lord treasurer now decided to act on Yarmouth's suggestion. On 29 Aug. Holland's son was awarded a secret service pension of £200 p.a. for his father's lifetime. He never addressed the House again, though he twice acted as teller with another Townshend henchman,

Sir Robert Kemp*, in the earlier sessions of 1678, once for a local estate bill and once against raising supply by subsidy. When the lord chancellor (Heneage Finch*), however, proposed restoring Holland to the Norwich commission of the peace, the King replied on 24 July that he saw no inconvenience in leaving him and Sir John Hobart* out, 'for there is no objection against it but in disobliging those [sic] sort of people who will never be obliged, and any countenance I give them is only used against myself and [my] Government'. In the final session of the Cavalier Parliament, Holland was appointed to the committees for the impeachment of Lord Arundell of Wardour, for examining Coleman's papers, and for the speedier conviction of recusants, and on 14 Dec. he was named to the committee of secrecy.[10]

Holland was expected to stand for Norfolk in 1679 as a country candidate, but he declined because of his wife's health, though he voted for the exclusionists, and was again removed from the commission of the peace. After proposing to Townshend in 1683 an arrangement to prevent further contests for the county he was restored to the bench when the 7th Duke of Norfolk became lord lieutenant. Nevertheless he stood with the Whig Sir Henry Hobart* in 1685 against the court candidates, even though they now enjoyed Townshend's support. To Norfolk's questions in 1688 he replied:

> He humbly conceives that if he should be chosen to serve in the next Parliament he could not (as his present judgment is) be for taking away the Penal Laws and the Tests, nor can contribute to the election of such as should; but he will live friendly with all persuasions as subjects of the same prince, and believes it to be his duty as a good Christian so to do.

For the fourth time in his career he was removed from local office, and in October he acted as spokesman of the Protestant magistrates who refused to sit 'with persons unqualified and incapacitated by the laws of the realm'. He accepted the Revolution and continued to act as j.p. into his ninetieth year. He died on 19 Jan. 1701, the last surviving Member of the Long Parliament, and was buried at Quidenham. His grandson, the 2nd baronet, represented Norfolk from 1701 to 1710 as a Whig.[11]

Owing to the fortunate preservation of Holland's speeches, many of them dating from the worst-recorded period of the Cavalier Parliament, he may have come to bulk larger to posterity than to his contemporaries. 'Upright and independent', in the words of a modern historian, 'what he is recorded as saying is almost uniformly sensible'. It is clear from other reports that he did not hesitate to take the unpopular side in debate, and his courage as an octogenarian is amply demonstrated by his resistance to the Tory landslide in 1685 and throughout James II's reign.[12]

[1] Secluded at Pride's Purge, 6 Dec. 1648, readmitted 21 Feb. 1660. [2] Blomefield, *Norf.* i. 335–6. [3] *Norf. SP* ed. Rye, 31, 137; *HMC Gawdy*, 190, 200; *CSP Dom. Add.* 1625–49, p. 508; 1667, p. 212; Bodl. Tanner mss 177, f. 14; R. W. Ketton-Cremer, *Norf. in the Civil War*, 120; A. L. Hunt, *Capital of East Anglia*, 47. [4] Ketton-Cremer, 198. [5] Blomefield, i. 341; Ketton-Cremer, 108, 223; Keeler, *Long Parl.* 219; D. Underdown, *Pride's Purge*, 60, 209. [6] *CJ*, viii. 53, 196, 234; Bowman diary, ff. 7, 74v, 112, 149; *IHR Bull.* xxix. 244–52; *Old Parl. Hist.* xxiii. 35, 64. [7] *Norf. Arch.* xxx. 130–9; *IHR Bull.* xxviii. 189–200; *CJ*, viii. 427, 429, 433. [8] D. R. Witcombe, *Cav. House of Commons*, 12, 19, 30; *IHR Bull.* xxviii. 201–2; Add. 32094, f. 25; *CJ*, viii. 463, 568, 578, 594, 627, 637; *Huntington Lib. Q.* xii. 137; *Milward*, 4, 307–12; Ketton-Cremer, 48. [9] Witcombe, 65; *CJ*, ix. 1, 7, 10, 84; *Milward*, 89, 312–19; *Clarendon Impeachment*, 19, 48; Add. 35865, f. 19v; Grey, i. 20, 22, 35. [10] Grey, ii. 324, 325; iii. 82, 294–5; iv. 73–77; Witcombe, 131; *Dering*, 112; *Essex Pprs.* (Cam. Soc. n.s. xlviii), 132; Add. 28621, f. 39; 27447, ff. 503–4; *HMC 6th Rep.* 371–2, 374, 378; *HMC Townshend*, 28, 29; *CJ*, ix. 383, 454, 506; *Cal. Treas. Bks.* v. 738; *HMC Finch*, ii. 42. [11] *CSP Dom.* 1679–80, pp. 66, 75; *HMC 12th Rep. IX*, 182–3; Hist. of Parl. Trust, W. W. Bean, 'List of Polls'; Add. 36988, f. 145; Add. 41656, f. 162; Norf. RO, Windham mss, ff. 2, 6–8, 12; *Norf. Ltcy. Jnl.* (Norf. Rec. Soc. xxx), 89; Blomefield, i. 336. [12] *IHR Bull.* xxviii. 189.

M.W.H./P.W.

HOLLES, Hon. Denzil (1599–1680), of Dorchester Priory, Dorset and Covent Garden, Westminster.

MITCHELL	3 Mar. 1624
DORCHESTER	1628, 1640 (Apr.), 1640 (Nov.),[1] 1660, 26 Mar.– 20 Apr. 1661

b. 31 Oct. 1599, 2nd s. of John Holles[†], 1st Earl of Clare, by Anne, da. of Sir Thomas Stanhope[†] of Shelford, Notts.; bro. of John Holles[†]. *educ.* Christ's, Camb. 1613; MA 1616; G. Inn 1615; travelled abroad 1618–21. *m.* (1) 4 June 1626, Dorothy (*d.* 21 June 1640), da. and h. of Sir Francis Ashley[†] of Dorchester Priory, 4s. (3 *d.v.p.*); (2) 12 Mar. 1642, Jane (*d.* 1666), da. and coh. of Sir John Shurley[†] of Isfield, Suss., wid. of Sir Walter Covert[†] of Slaugham, Suss., and of John Freke[†] of Cerne Abbey, Dorset, *s.p.*; (3) 14 Sept. 1666, Esther (*d.*1684), da. and coh. of Gideon Le Lou of Colombiers, Normandy, wid. of Jacques Richer of Combernon, Normandy, *s.p. cr.* Baron Holles of Ifield 20 Apr. 1661.[2]

Freeman, Dorchester 1628, Poole 1671; capt. W. Dorset militia 1636; commr. for sewers, Dorset 1638, oyer and terminer, Wilts. and Herts. 1640, Western circuit July 1660; j.p. Dorset 1640–8, Dorset and Wilts. Mar. 1660–*d.*; commr. for assessment, Dorset 1640–1, Dorset and Wilts. 1644, Surrey and Notts. 1645, Dorset, Notts., Surrey and Wilts. 1647, Dorset and Wilts. Aug. 1660–1; custos rot. Dorset 1641–2, Mar. 1660–*d.*; ld. lt. Bristol 1642; commr. for sequestration, Dorset and Wilts. 1643, execution of ordinances 1644, defence, Wilts. 1644, Surr. 1645, northern association, Notts. 1645; gov. Covent Garden precinct, 1646; commr. for appeals, Oxford University 1647, militia, Bristol, Dorset, Notts. and Wilts. 1648, Dorset and Wilts. Mar. 1660.[3]

Holles Family

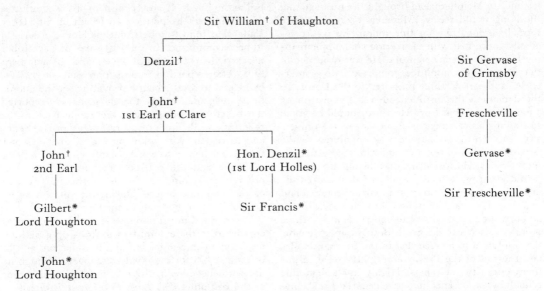

Sir William† of Haughton

Denzil†

John†
1st Earl of Clare

Sir Gervase
of Grimsby

Frescheville

John†
2nd Earl

Hon. Denzil*
(1st Lord Holles)

Gervase*

Gilbert*
Lord Houghton

Sir Francis*

Sir Frescheville*

John*
Lord Houghton

Commr. for treaty of Uxbridge 1644, religious propositions 1645, Admiralty 1645–8, propositions for relief of Ireland 1645, bishops' lands 1646, abuses in heraldry 1646, exclusion from sacrament 1646, indemnity 1647–9, compounding 1647–8, scandalous offences 1648; Councillor of State 25 Feb.–31 May 1660; PC 1 June 1660–7 Jan. 1676, 24 June 1679–*d.*; commr. for trade Nov. 1660–72, plantations Dec. 1660–70; asst. R. Africa Co. Dec. 1660; high steward, Queen Catherine of Braganza 1662–*d.*; ambassador, Paris 1663–6; plenip. Breda 1667.[4]

Holles had been a determined opponent of Charles I, both in and out of Parliament, and commanded a regiment against the King in the 1642 campaign. His brother changed sides no less than three times in the Civil War, and Holles himself soon became eager for a peaceful settlement. Bitterly hostile to Cromwell and the army, he was forced to take refuge in France in August 1647, and did not sit after Pride's Purge. Although an order was issued for the sequestration of his estates in 1651, and he was himself arrested by an over-enthusiastic militiaman at the time of Booth's rising, it seems clear that he had no connexion with Cavalier plotters of any kind. He is never mentioned among Mordaunt's Presbyterian contacts.[5]

Although Holles appears to have let his Dorchester house, which he had acquired by his first marriage, he was elected at the top of the poll there on 9 Apr. 1660. Few Members of the Convention could match his combined social and political prestige, and he was constantly employed on both formal and functional duties. He was named to 49 committees, and took the chair in five of them. He made 36 recorded speeches, and acted as teller in 11 divisions. He helped to manage ten conferences with the Lords, from six of which he presented reports, and carried eight bills and four messages to the Upper House.

Alarmed at the numerical weakness of the Presbyterians, he secured the chair for Sir Harbottle Grimston* in a thin House, and moved for the examination of the election returns. On 2 May he reported a draft reply to the King's letter. He was appointed to the committee on the bill for the abolition of the court of wards. He helped to draw up the instructions for the delegation to the King, and was given personal responsibility for carrying the letter from the Commons. The speech he made on delivering it to the King at The Hague was later subjected to aspersions, or so Holles claimed; but perhaps he only wanted an excuse for committing his eloquence to print. On 14 May he was nominated to a conference with the Lords about the protocol for the King's reception, but as this was the day he arrived in The Hague, he cannot have taken part. Perhaps this incident accounts for his complaint about the practice of naming absent Members to committees; he observed that it was against an order of the House to name such, unless any gentleman did move particularly for it.[6]

On Holles's return to Westminster, he was among those ordered to prepare clauses of exception to the indemnity bill, and was teller for limiting the number of those excepted to 20, apart from the regicides. He helped to administer the oath of allegiance to Members, and brought the message that the King would receive Members on 9 June for a formal pardon. During this month he was principally concerned with recovering and supplementing Henrietta Maria's jointure. He was chairman of the Commons committee, reported two conferences, and carried three messages to the Lords. In the debate on the intruded dons at Oxford on 25 June, he urged that Lord Hertford should be asked to stay his proceedings as chancellor of the university, and five days later he was appointed to the committee of inquiry into unauthorized Anglican publications. He was against imposing an oath that would 'destroy' Roman Catholics, but favoured the extension of double taxation to cover sectaries and fanatics. He was infuriated by the decision to adjourn the grand committee on religion for three months; when candles were brought in to enable the resolution to be recorded in the Journal, Holles and the rest of the Presbyterian party tried to put them out with their hats. Highly amused at this schoolboy exuberance in a sexagenarian, the King chose him to tell the Commons on the following morning that an assembly of divines would be speedily summoned to advise on the religious settlement, as the committee had recommended. He told the House on 27 July that 'if he thought the stopping the bill of indemnity at present were meant to injure the subject, he would not open his mouth for money, but [he] was assured the King would do and had done all he could to hasten the bill'. He was again sent with a message of thanks. On 30 July he was appointed to the committee on the bill for settling ministers. On the next day he was one of four prominent Members sent to the Lords for a conference, reporting on their return the lord chancellor's assurance that there was no deliberate delay over the indemnity bill. On 2 Aug. he reminded the House of the urgent problem of the navy debt, but for the rest of the month his activity was principally directed to expediting the indemnity bill. He helped to draw up reasons for another conference on 9 Aug., and four days later acted as teller for pardoning 16 of the excepted persons. He was one of the Members instructed to raise £10,000 in the City. From the next conference he reported that 'it was only concerning the poll bill', and was ordered to prepare reasons for maintaining the exclusive right of the Commons to name commissioners for taxes. On 17 Aug. he was among those ordered to establish the names of the regicides, as defined by the Lords, and he helped to manage the conference on the following day. He was teller for pardoning all treasons committed

before 1648, and on 28 Aug. carried the indemnity bill to the Lords. He was chairman of the committee which drafted the petition on behalf of Sir Henry Vane[†] and John Lambert, but the House ordered it to be recommitted. In the first week of September he carried up the college leases and disbandment bills. After reporting from a conference on 7 Sept. he helped to draft a clause providing for the guards to be disbanded before the garrisons. He reported the bill for securing the money collected for the relief of the Piedmontese Protestants on 10 Sept., and carried it, with other measures, to the Upper House. He helped to manage conferences on settling ministers and the poll-tax, and on 12 Sept. was ordered to remind the lords of the bill he had carried two days before. During the autumn recess he took part in the trials of the regicides.[7]

When the Convention reassembled, Holles was appointed to the committees to draw up a petition for a day of public fasting and humiliation, and to bring in a bill for modified episcopacy. Though he did not believe William Drake to be the real author of the pamphlet *The Long Parliament Revived*, he was named to the committee to prepare an impeachment. He reported from the conference of 22 Nov., announcing the King's intention of dissolving Parliament before Christmas. Two days later he was sent with three other Members to desire the lord chief justice to punish those responsible for defrauding the customs. On the attainder bill he expressed 'as great an abhorrence of that black crew as anyone', but did not want to punish their creditors, or their wives and children. He helped to draft the clause repealing Henry VIII's Statute of Liveries. He brought messages urging protection for the Jews and consideration of those enslaved by the Turks. Together with Arthur Annesley[*] he was given special responsibility for an address in favour of Sir John Lawson. He helped to prepare reasons for rejecting the lords' provisos to the college leases bill, one of which would have explicitly excluded the intruded dons from benefit, and helped to manage the last conference on disbandment.[8]

Holles was re-elected for Dorchester in 1661, and appointed to administer the oaths to Members of the new Parliament, but was raised to the peerage before it met. He employed both Anglican and Presbyterian chaplains after the Restoration; one of the latter was Roger Morrice, who remained in touch with him in later years. In the next few years he was chiefly employed in diplomacy, but on his return from Breda he was reported to be caballing with the Earls of Northumberland and Leicester, and other peers of Presbyterian sympathies, for the disbandment of the guards and the redress of other grievances. Nevertheless he entered a formal protest at the banishment of Clarendon without trial. He defended the jurisdiction of the Lords in Skinner's case in 1669, possibly in order to force a dissolution. His London house became a meeting place for the country party in the 1674 session. Alarmed by Danby's successes in the Lower House, he led the opposition to the non-resisting test in 1675, and was removed from the Privy Council. Although his attendance in the Upper House was increasingly interrupted by ill-health, his literary activity was unimpaired; his pamphlet *The Long Parliament Dissolved* supplied Shaftesbury with the argument that the long prorogation from 22 Nov. 1675 to 15 Feb. 1677 automatically dissolved Parliament.[9]

Holles displayed a more temperate attitude over the Popish Plot than might have been expected. He was now more closely associated with Halifax than Shaftesbury, and agreed to save Danby provided that the Cavalier Parliament was dissolved; but the real and effective leadership of the country party had now passed to younger men. On the exclusion issue he was similarly moderate, and was reported to exercise a restraining influence on the more respectable Whig leaders in the Lower House. His experiences in Paris made him 'difficult' about French bribes, and he had little direct contact with Ruvigny, though the latter remarked that 'in the affair of the lord treasurer and the disbanding of the army, no person was more useful to your Majesty than Lord Holles'. The prorogation of the second Exclusion Parliament greatly disturbed him, and almost the last act of his political life was to sign the petition of the peers against the delay in opening the session. Holles died on 17 Feb. 1680, and was buried at St. Peter's, Dorchester. He was succeeded by his son Francis, but it seems probable that the real heir to his political influence, at least in the West Country, was his step-son, Thomas Freke I*. The character by Burnet, who came to know Holles well during his embassy at Paris, is often quoted:

> Holles was a man of great courage, and as great pride. . . . He was faithful and firm to his side, and never changed through the whole course of his life. . . . He was well versed in the records of Parliament, and argued well, but too vehemently; for he could not bear contradiction. He had the soul of an old stubborn Roman in him. He was a faithful but rough friend, and a severe but fair enemy. He had a true sense of religion, and was a man of unblamable course of life, and of a sound judgment when it was not biassed by passion.[10]

[1] Disabled 27 Jan. 1648, readmitted 8 June, did not sit after Pride's Purge 6 Dec. and readmitted 21 Feb. 1660. [2] *APC 1617–18*, p. 100; Eg. 784, f. 88v. [3] C. H. Mayo, *Dorchester Recs.* 425; Dorset RO, D84 (official); Poole Archives, B17. [4] *Cal. Treas. Bks.* iv. 154;

PC2/55/30; SP29/47/116. [5] Keeler, *Long Parl.* 200; *CSP Dom.* 1651; pp. 127, 149; 1659–60, p. 165; *Cal. Comm. Comp.* 2772. [6] Mayo, 436; *Dorset Hearth-Tax* ed. Meekings, 19, 55; Clarendon, *Rebellion*, vi. 229; *Cal. Cl. SP*, iv. 675; *Somers Tracts*, vii. 417–19; *CJ*, viii. 8, 15, 22–23, 53. [7] *CJ*, viii. 58, 59, 65, 69, 73, 121, 139, 142, 153, 156, 162, 168; Bowman diary, ff. 25, 53, 69, 100; *Voyce from the Watch Tower*, 171; *State Trials*, v. 1027. [8] *Old Parl. Hist.* xxiii. 17, 38; *CJ*, viii. 187, 209, 214, 216, 219, 233. [9] Burnet, i. 175; ii. 117; PRO 31/3, bdle. 112, ff. 6, 233; bdle. 123, f. 20; bdle. 135, ff. 14, 57; *LJ*, xii. 168, 665; Clarke, *Jas. II*, i. 426; *Essex Pprs.* (Cam. Soc. n.s. xlvii), 168; Foxcroft, *Halifax*, i. 123; D. R. Lacey, *Dissent and Parl. Pols.* 466–9. [10] Burnet, i. 175; ii. 171, 187; Jones, *First Whigs*, 35; PRO 31/3, bdle. 141, ff. 49, 63v; bdle. 142, f. 40v; bdle. 143, f. 29v; Dalrymple, *Mems.* i. 337–40.

M.W.H./J.P.F.

HOLLES, Sir Francis, 1st Bt. (1627–90), of Aldenham, Herts.

LOSTWITHIEL	20 Jan. 1647[1]
WILTSHIRE	1654
DORCHESTER	1679 (Mar.), 1679 (Oct.)–17 Feb. 1680

b. 19 Aug. 1627, o. surv. s. of Hon. Denzil Holles*. *educ.* travelled abroad 1645; M. Temple 1648, called 1661; Clare, Camb. 1651. *m.* (1) 22 Aug. 1661 (with £6,000), Lucy (*d.* 15 Sept. 1667), da. of Sir Robert Carr, 2nd Bt., of Sleaford, Lincs., 2da.; (2) 9 June 1670, Anne (*d.* 8 Mar. 1682), da. and coh. of Sir Francis Pile, 2nd Bt.[†], of Compton Beauchamp, Berks., 1s. 1da. *cr.* Bt. 27 June 1660; *suc.* fa. as 2nd Baron Holles 17 Feb. 1680.[2]

J.p. Dorset 1647–8, 1650–?53, Mar. 1660–80, 1682–5, Wilts. 1653–80; commr. for assessment, Dorset and Wilts. 1648, 1657, Dorset Aug. 1660–80, Westminster 1673–80, militia, Dorset 1648, Mar. 1660.

Holles lived most of his life in the shadow of his irascible father. He took no known part in the Civil War, but sat for Lostwithiel as a recruiter until Pride's Purge, and for Wiltshire in the first Protectorate Parliament. When Francis Lascelles* was discharged from the House in 1660, he stood for Northallerton, probably on the interests of Thomas, 3rd Lord Fairfax, and Lord Fauconberg. But he was involved in a double return with George Marwood[†], which was never referred to the elections committee, and presumably did not sit. He is unlikely to have stood in 1661, and played no part in politics until the exclusion crisis. Although he never attended the Dorset quarter sessions between 1663 and 1674, and had long ceased to reside in the county, he was returned for Dorchester at both elections of 1679 as a member of the country party. On his entry to the House after an interval of 25 years he was marked 'honest' on Shaftesbury's list, and voted for exclusion; but his activities left no trace in the Journals. He succeeded to the peerage before the second Exclusion Parliament met. This time he seems to have abstained on exclusion, but he voted for acquitting Lord Stafford.[3]

Holles's house was searched for arms by the

Dorset deputy lieutenants during Monmouth's rebellion. He was marked as a court peer on Lord Willoughby's list in 1687, perhaps because of the extremely favourable decision given by Lord Chancellor Jeffreys in his protracted suit over his first wife's dowry. He was too infirm to attend the Convention at first, but took the oaths to the new regime on 16 Mar. 1689. Holles died on 1 Mar. 1690, and was buried at Isfield. His only son died under age and unmarried, and the estates passed to his cousin, the 4th Earl of Clare (John Holles*).[4]

[1] Did not sit after Pride's Purge, 6 Dec. 1648, readmitted 21 Feb. 1660. [2] A. Collins, *Hist. Colls. Noble Fams.* 169; PCC 210 Irby; *HMC Lords*, i. 177; ii. 73. [3] R. Carroll, 'Borough Rep. Yorks.' (Vanderbilt thesis, 1961), 398; *Dorset Hearth-Tax* ed. Meekings, 116. [4] R. Morrice, Entering Bk. 1, pp. 283, 548; 2, p. 14; *LJ*, xiv. 150, 216; *HMC Lords*, ii. 13.

J.P.F.

HOLLES, Sir Frescheville (1642–72), of Long Acre, Westminster and Carleton, Notts.

GREAT GRIMSBY   22 Nov. 1667–28 May 1672

b. 8 June 1642, s. of Gervase Holles* by 2nd w. *educ.* M. Temple 1659. *m.* lic. 24 Nov. 1662 (with £5,000), Jane, da. of Richard Lewis of Selston, wid. of Valentine Crome, merchant, of Fenchurch Street, London, *s.p.* Kntd. June 1666.[1]

Capt. of militia ft., Westminster 1663, maj. 1664–7; freeman, Portsmouth 1667; alderman, Grimsby 1667–*d.*, mayor 1669–70; j.p. Hants 1671–*d.*; bailiff of Burley walk, New Forest 1672–*d.*[2]

Gent. of privy chamber 1664–9, 1671–*d.*; capt. RN 1665–7, 1672; capt. 2 Ft. Gds. 1667–9.[3]

FRS 1672.

Holles married an 'old, foul wife' whom he soon discarded, though of course retaining her money. He inherited a full share of the martial spirit of the family. Before going on active service in command of a frigate in the second Dutch war, he composed his own epitaph, declaring his intent to require no other monument 'than what my sword should raise for me of honour and of fortune'. He lost an arm in the Four Days' battle of 1666, after which he was knighted. According to Henry Savile* he and Sir John Harman had 'got immortal fame, and are extremely in the favour of their generals and our sovereign'. But (Sir) William Penn* called him 'a conceited, idle, prating, lying fellow', and Samuel Pepys*, always hostile to gentlemen-captains, complained of his profanity and the indiscipline of his men. At the end of the war he received a bounty of £300, and was commissioned in the guards.[4]

Holles stood for Grimsby at a by-election in October 1667. His father already held the other seat, and Holles bragged to Pepys that his family had represented the borough for 140 years. He was defeated by Sir Philip Tyrwhitt*, but reversed the

result on petition. A moderately active Member of the Cavalier Parliament, he was appointed to 45 committees, acted as teller in five divisions, and made 20 speeches. On taking his seat he was added to the committee of inquiry into the miscarriages of the war. He was among those ordered to bring in a proviso to the public accounts bill on 17 Dec., and to take the accounts of the loyal and indigent officers fund over the Christmas recess. When the House resumed, Holles took the leading part in the attack on the naval administration to which his empty sleeve entitled him. A follower of Buckingham, he was particularly severe on (Sir) William Coventry*, whom he blamed for the division of the fleet in 1666. Together with Sir Richard Temple* he was rumoured to be sponsoring a petition for the repayment of the fees that Coventry had exacted for passing naval commissions. On 20 Feb. 1668 he told the House that 'the defect of provisions of victualling is as great a miscarriage as any', but he defended Lord Brouncker warmly over the discharge of seamen by ticket. He was among those ordered to receive information about illegal conventicles, but on 8 Apr., according to the Anglican John Milward*:

> Sir Frescheville Holles made a very long and impertinent speech [asking for toleration for] dissenters from the Church, and in conclusion moved to make an address to the King to take the business into [his] hands, and to call some principal persons of all the dissenters, and to receive proposals from them.

In the resumed debates on the miscarriages of the war, he wanted Harman to be given an opportunity of clearing himself from the charge of failure to press home the success off Lowestoft in 1665, and strongly attacked William Penn over the disposal of prize goods. He was one of those ordered to attend the Lords with the articles of Penn's impeachment.[5]

In the next session Holles urged that the public accounts commission should be ordered to prove their charges against Sir George Carteret*. He was appointed to the committees for the bills to improve the art of navigation and to settle the differences between Lady Lee and the coheirs of Sir Thomas Pope. He complained to the House that an attorney had described his opposition to Lady Lee's bill as 'a very unworthy and unhandsome action', but the words were denied and the matter referred to the committee of privileges. On 26 Nov. 1669 he compared the condition of the Dutch and English fleets, to the disadvantage of the latter, and he acted as teller against appointing a day to hear the charges against Lord Orrery (Roger Boyle*). His continued hostility to the Court did not escape attention, and his troop was given to Richard Kirkby*. In vain he offered his services to the French king, and, perhaps with a view to ingratiating himself, spoke against the proposed prohibition of brandy. He supported the bill to enable Lord Roos (John Manners*) to marry again, both in debate and division.[6]

During the recess Holles went to Ireland, presumably to escape his creditors; while there, he purchased timber for the Admiralty. When Parliament resumed, he was one of the five prominent Members who went over to the Court, and as 'one of the great councillors of state to the Duchess of Cleveland', he soon regained the favour of Charles II. He was appointed to the committees on the bills for the preservation of shipping and the continuance of the Conventicles Act. He paid two visits to the French Embassy in December 1670, offering to ensure that the grant of supply would not be made dependent on the maintenance of the Triple Alliance, and to engage two or three Members in the interests of France at £100 a head. 'A court projector, both body and soul', he proposed a poll-tax on 10 Dec., and opposed deferring supply until the bill to punish the assailants of Sir John Coventry* had passed. He acted as teller against the proposal to devote the additional excise to paying off the King's debts, and was appointed to consider the Lords' bill to prevent the disturbances of seamen and preserve naval stores. At the end of the session he was given £3,000 royal bounty 'for his virtues', and listed as a court supporter by the Opposition, who also believed him to have received 'a promise to be rear-admiral the next fleet and £500 p.a. pension'. He was indeed recalled to naval service at the outbreak of the third Dutch war, though not promoted. He took part in the attack on the Smyrna fleet under Sir Robert Holmes* in March 1672, but before the next campaign he made another will, ignoring his wife and father completely, and after legacies totalling £850 devoting the residue of his estate to the erection of a memorial in Westminster Abbey. He was killed at Sole Bay on 28 May. His executors, Sir Robert Clayton* and John Morris*, gave him a splendid funeral and presumably paid off the debt to the crown of £1,500 for timber not delivered.[7]

[1] *Cat. Ashmolean Mss*, 209; *Dugdale's Vis. Yorks.* ed. Clay, ii. 60; Hunter, *South Yorks.* i. 361; Harl. 7005, f. 82. [2] *HMC Buccleuch*, i. 540–2; R. East, *Portsmouth Recs.* 359; E. E. Gillett, *Hist. Grimsby*, 149; *HMC 14th Rep. VIII*, 291; *Cal. Treas. Bks.* iv. 1225. [3] *HMC Buccleuch*, i. 541; Carlisle, *Privy Chamber*, 188. [4] Harl. 7020, f. 35v; PCC 116 Eure; *Savile Corresp.* (Cam. Soc. lxxi), 10; *Pepys Diary*, 14, 17 June 1667; *Cal. Treas. Bks.* iii. 796. [5] *Pepys Diary*, 28 Sept. 1667, 11, 14, 18, 26 Feb., 24 Mar. 1668; *Milward*, 196, 248, 262, 294; Grey, i. 87, 136; *CJ*, ix. 42, 88. [6] Grey, i. 158, 189, 219, 252; *CJ*, ix. 109, 114, 150; Bodl. C37/1110; PRO 31/3, bdle. 125, f. 300v. [7] *CSP Dom.* 1670, pp. 373, 583; 1671–2, pp. 161, 206; 1672, pp. 288, 304; *Marvell* ed. Margoliouth, i. 290; ii. 305; Harl. 7020, f. 35v; PRO 31/3, bdle. 125, ff. 300v,

305; *Dering*, 27, 45; *CJ*, ix. 210; *Cal. Treas. Bks.* iii. 796; PCC 78 Pye; *Westminster Abbey Reg.* (Harl. Soc. x), 176.

P.W.

HOLLES, Gervase (1607–75), of Mansfield, Notts.

GREAT GRIMSBY 1640 (Apr.), 1640 (Nov.)–22 Aug. 1642, 1661–10 Feb. 1675

b. 9 Mar. 1607, 2nd but o. surv. s. of Frescheville Holles of Grimsby, Lincs. by 1st w. Elizabeth, da. and h. of John Kingston, merchant, of Grimsby. *educ.* Grimsby g.s. 1613; M. Temple 1628, called 1639; *m.* (1) 17 June 1630, Dorothy (d. 18 Jan. 1635), da. of John Kirketon of Grimsby, 1s. d.v.p. 2da.; (2) 4 Oct. 1637, Elizabeth (d. 21 Mar. 1662), da. of William Molesworth of Grimsby, 4s. d.v.p. suc. fa. 1630.[1]

Mayor, Grimsby 1636–7, 1638–9, 1663–4; j.p. Notts. 1641–4, commr. of array, Lincs. 1642, assessment 1661–3, 1664–9, 1673–4, (Lindsey) 1663–4, loyal and indigent officers 1662.[2]

Capt. of ft. (royalist) Aug. 1642, maj. Sept. 1642–3, col. 1643–4; gov. King's Lynn 1644; col. of ft. (French army) 1646–8.[3]

Master of requests June 1660–d.[4]

Holles came of a cadet branch of moderate means long associated with Grimsby. His property, encumbered with annuities, brought him in only £114 p.a., probably owing to debts incurred in rebuilding his house. Although called to the bar, he did not practise, devoting himself to antiquarian pursuits. He moved to Newark in 1640, but represented Grimsby in both Short and Long Parliaments until disabled for royalism. He joined the King's army early in the Civil War, and was commissioned colonel of foot in 1643, but laid down arms after a little over a year and surrendered himself to the parliamentary governor of Lincoln in November 1645. Unable to pay the composition fine of £738, he joined the French army, but returned for the second Civil War, when he was taken prisoner at the fall of Colchester. He lived in exile throughout the Interregnum, chiefly in Holland, but remaining in touch with the Court. Charles II gave him a commission in 1659, but shortage of money and the indiscretion of another Cavalier prevented him from leaving Rotterdam to take part in the royalist rising. On 21 Mar. 1660 Sir Edward Hyde† urged 'honest Gervase' to proceed to London forthwith and use his interest with his cousin, the 2nd Earl of Clare, to dispose Edward Rossiter* to the King's service. But owing to his debts he was unable to embark till May.[5]

At the Restoration Holles was given a mastership of requests, with an annuity of £100 p.a. He regained his seat at Grimsby at the general election of 1661, but he was not active in the Cavalier Parliament, in which he was appointed to only 21 committees. On 7 May 1662 he delivered a message from the King recommending the plight of English slaves in the Turkish dominions to the consideration of the House. He helped to consider the petition of the loyal and indigent officers in 1663. Listed as a court dependant in 1664, it was presumably Holles who was included in the deputation from the Commons to thank the King and the City for preserving the honour, safety and trade of the nation against the Dutch, although by a clerical error it was the name of his flamboyant son Frescheville that was entered in the Journals. He was appointed to the committee to investigate the miscarriages of the war in 1667, and urged by the 2nd Earl of Strafford to attend diligently at the House and in committee to hasten on the private bill of Gilbert Holles*; but he was not appointed to the committee. Unlike his son, who became the other Member for Grimsby during this session, there is no sign that he ever joined the Opposition. He was named to the committees for the continuance of the Conventicles Act and to receive information about seditious conventicles in 1669. He was included as a court dependant in both lists of 1669–71, and in an opposition pamphlet he was described as a 'pensioner at Court, and two places there', presumably in the expectation that he would succeed William Prynne* as keeper of the records. But 'his too much antiquated zeal against the delinquents in the House of Commons' was not in vogue, and the post was given to Sir Algernon May*. His name appeared on the Paston list, but he played little further part in Parliament. He died on 10 Feb. 1675 and was buried at Mansfield, the last of this branch of the family.[6]

[1] *Mems. Holles Fam.* (Cam. Soc. ser. 3, lv), pp. vii–xiv, 227–34. [2] *HMC 14th Rep. VIII*, 290–1; *HMC Buccleuch*, i. 526, 528, 530. [3] *HMC Buccleuch*, i. 526–7, 531–3. [4] Ibid. 539–40. [5] SP23/185/935–53; Keeler, *Long Parl.* 220–1; *Cal. Cl. SP*, ii. 257; iv. 667; *HMC Bath*, ii. 79, 144; *CSP Dom.* 1655–6, p. 395; 1659–60, p. 22; *HMC Buccleuch*, i. 539; *HMC 5th Rep.* 184. [6] *CJ*, viii. 423, 568; *HMC Bath*, ii. 151, 152; Harl. 7020, f. 35v; *HMC Hastings*, ii. 313; *CSP Dom.* 1673–5, p. 473; C. H. Josten, *Elias Ashmole*, 1412, 1420.

P.W.

HOLLES, Gilbert, Lord Houghton (1633–89), of Haughton, Notts. and Warwick House, Holborn, Mdx.

NOTTINGHAMSHIRE 1660

b. 24 Apr. 1633, 2nd but o. surv. s. of John Holles[†], 2nd Earl of Clare by Elizabeth, da. and coh. of Horace, 1st Baron Vere of Tilbury. *educ.* travelled abroad 1645. *m.* 9 July 1655, Grace, da. of Hon. William Pierrepont* of Thoresby, Notts., 3s. (1 *d.v.p.*) 4da. *suc.* fa. as 3rd Earl of Clare 2 Jan. 1666.

Commr. for militia, Notts. and Lincs. Mar. 1660,

j.p. Mar. 1660–?74; dep. lt. Notts. c. Aug. 1660–?74, commr. for sewers, Lincs. Aug. 1660, assessment, Notts. 1661–6.

Lord Houghton was descended from Sir William Holles, lord mayor of London 1539–40, who bought a large estate in Nottinghamshire. The next generation represented the county in the Parliament of 1553. The family was usually in opposition under the Stuarts. Houghton's father, the brother of Denzil Holles*, changed sides three times during the Civil War, and took no part in public affairs till the Restoration. 'Too much addicted to a natural melancholy', Houghton was used with great severity by his father, or so he alleged, his 'small allowance' of £900 p.a. being reduced by Commonwealth taxation to £500. He represented Nottinghamshire in the Convention together with his father-in-law. He made no speeches and was appointed to no committees, but presumably he voted with the Presbyterian opposition, and he was not re-elected. In the House of Lords from 1666 he acted regularly with the country party, achieving prominence on 26 Jan. 1674 when he moved that the King should be asked to withdraw from the debate. For a short time he was reckoned one of the 'most forward of the Hotspurs in the Upper House'. A strong Calvinist, he had never acted as j.p., which would have entailed conformity with the Church of England, and was probably removed from both commission and lieutenancy about this time. His journey abroad with his sons in September would have provided an excuse, though he returned in the following April. He signed the petition for the assembly of Parliament on 26 Jan. 1680, and was one of Monmouth's sureties in 1682. In September of the same year, he was fined £320 for permitting 16 unlawful conventicles to meet at a house in St. Clement Danes belonging to him. He gave evidence on behalf of Algernon Sidney[†]. He was reckoned among the opposition to James II, and signed the petition for a free Parliament on 16 Nov. 1688. His last years were saddened by domestic disagreements with his wife, 'she gadding usually from morning to night', while he had never much fancied 'Courts, Playhouse, Hyde Park by days nor St. James by nights, coffee houses, ordinaries, gaming houses or taverns'. Moreover her 'lazy trick' of sending all the table linen to the laundry had wasted and destroyed more of his linen in five years than in the previous 15. He died on 16 Jan. 1689 and was buried at Haughton.

Whitelocke Memorials, i. 498; *Hutchinson Mems.* 96; K. H. D. Haley, *Shaftesbury*, 358, 560, 658; *Letters to Williamson* (Cam. Soc. n.s. ix.), 156–7; *CSP Dom.* 1673–5, p. 345; 1675–6, p. 85; 1682, p. 430; July–Sept. 1683, p. 401; Burnet, ii. 402; PCC 42 Ent.

M.W.H./E.R.E.

HOLLES, John, Lord Houghton (1662–1711), of Haughton, Notts. and Warwick House, Holborn, Mdx.

NOTTINGHAMSHIRE 14–16 Jan. 1689

b. 9 Jan. 1662, 1st s. of Gilbert Holles*, 3rd Earl of Clare. *educ.* travelled abroad 1674. *m.* 1 Mar. 1690, Lady Margaret Cavendish, da. and coh. of Henry Cavendish*, 2nd Duke of Newcastle, 1da. *suc.* fa. as 4th Earl of Clare 16 Jan. 1689; *cr.* Duke of Newcastle 14 May 1694; KG 30 May 1698.[1]

J.p. custos rot. and ld. lt. Mdx. and Westminster 1689–92, 1711–*d.*, Notts. 1694–*d.*, Yorks (E. Riding) 1699–*d.*; high steward, East Retford 1689–*d.*, Dorchester 1701–*d.*; col. of militia ft. Notts. by 1697–*d.*; steward of Sherwood Forest 1699–*d.*; gov. Kingston-upon-Hull 1699–*d.*; ld. lt. Yorks. (N. Riding) 1705–*d.*[2] Gent. of the bedchamber 1689–91; commr. for Greenwich hospital 1695–*d.*; ld. privy seal 1705–*d.*; PC 29 Mar. 1705–*d.*; commr. for union with Scotland 1706; c.j. in eyre (north) 1711–*d.*

In 1681 Dryden dedicated *The Spanish Friar* to Lord Houghton with the words 'a Protestant play to a Protestant patron'. The patron's protestantism proved less fragile than the playwright's; he was in touch with Dykveld during the latter's mission to England in 1687, and was reckoned among the opponents of James II by Danby, whom he joined at York during the Revolution. He was returned for Nottinghamshire at the general election of 1689, but succeeded to the peerage before Parliament met. On the death of his father-in-law in 1691 he inherited the bulk of the Newcastle estates, but resigned all his posts on being refused the dukedom. When he acquired the estates of his cousin the 3rd Baron Holles in 1694, his income was reckoned at £40,000 p.a., and he was granted the coveted honour. 'A vapouring and wealthy Whig', he had no pretensions to administrative ability or statesmanship, but wielded enormous influence, controlling as many as ten Members in the Parliament of 1705. His accession to the Government and his continued loyalty to Harley in 1710 were thus of more importance than his 'modest talents' would otherwise justify. But he died after a hunting accident on 15 July 1711, leaving the Cavendish estates to his son-in-law, Edward Harley† (later 2nd Earl of Oxford) and the remainder of his property to his nephew Thomas Pelham, subsequently Duke of Newcastle and prime minister.[3]

[1] *CSP Dom.* 1673–5, p. 345. [2] *CSP Dom.* 1689–90, p. 137; *HMC Portland*, ii. 166; Eg. 1626, f. 33. [3] *HMC 7th Rep.* 420, *8th Rep.* pt. 1 (1881), 560; Feiling, *Tory Party*, 376, 419; G. Holmes, *British Politics in the Age of Anne*, 112, 225, 370.

E.R.E.

HOLLOWAY, John (1661–1721), of St. Aldate's, Oxford.

WALLINGFORD 1685

bap. 4 Oct. 1661, 1st s. of Sir Richard Holloway, j.K.b. 1683–July 1688, of Oxford by Alice, da. of John Smith†, maltster, of Kennington, Berks. *educ.* I. Temple, entered 1675, called 1682; St. John's, Oxf. 1676. *m.* 1da. *suc.* fa. 1699.[1]

Recorder, Wallingford 1683–1710, freeman 1685; j.p. Berks. 1685–?89, Oxon. by 1700–?*d.*; bencher, I. Temple 1708, reader 1712, treas. 1717.[2]

Holloway came from a family of lawyers settled in Oxford by Tudor times. His father, a fellow of New College, was expelled by the parliamentary visitors in 1648. After appearing for the prosecution in the trial of Stephen College, the 'Protestant joiner', he was made a judge in 1683, and concurred in the death sentence on Algernon Sidney† two months later. Holloway succeeded his father as recorder of Wallingford and was confirmed in office under the new charter of 1684. A Tory, he was returned for the borough in 1685, though some of the inhabitants petitioned against the election. A moderately active Member of James II's Parliament, he was appointed to the committee of elections and privileges and to two others, both for private bills. Holloway's father agreed with the defence of the Seven Bishops, and was dismissed by James immediately after their acquittal, but this did not save him from incurring the displeasure of Parliament in 1689. Holloway is unlikely to have stood again, though he accepted the Revolution and became a j.p. after his father's death. He was buried in the Temple Church on 13 Feb. 1721, the only member of his family to sit in Parliament.[3]

[1] *Wood's City of Oxford* (Oxf. Hist. Soc. xxxvii), 200; *Wood's Life and Times* (Oxf. Hist. Soc. xxi), 250; PCC 25 Noel. [2] *CSP Dom.* 1683–4, p. 71; J. K. Hedges, *Hist. Wallingford*, ii. 245; Berks. RO, Wallingford borough statute bk. 1648–1766, f. 128; Bodl. Carte 79, f. 681. [3] *Vis. Oxon.* (Harl. Soc. v), 290; M. Toynbee and P. Young, *Strangers in Oxford*, 53; *Visitors' Reg.* (Cam. Soc. n.s. xxix), 144; Wallingford borough statute bk. f. 127; *CJ*, ix. 716; *HMC Lords*, n.s. ii. 77, 88; Grey, ix. 344; *Temple Church Recs.* 37.

L.N./G.J.

HOLMAN, John (*d.*1700), of Banbury, Oxon. and Weston Favell, Northants.

BANBURY 1661, 1679 (Mar.), 1679 (Oct.), 1681

2nd s. of Philip Holman†, scrivener (*d.*1669), of London, and Warkworth, Northants. by Mary, da. and h. of John Pearte, Fishmonger, of London. *m.* 25 Sept. 1659, Jane, da. and coh. of Jacob de la Fortree of East Greenwich, Kent, 1da. *cr.* Bt. 1 June 1663.[1]

Gent. of the privy chamber 1662–85.[2]

Commr. for assessment, Northants 1665–80, Oxon. 1673–80, Herefs. 1677–80, Northants. and Oxon. 1689–90, rebuilding Northampton 1675, recusants, Oxon. 1675; asst. Banbury 1683–Oct. 1688; freeman, Oxford 1689; j.p. and dep. lt. Northants. aft. 1689–*d.*[3]

Holman came of a minor family settled at Godstone, Surrey, by 1542 which produced an MP for

Surrey under the Protectorate. His father bought a Northamptonshire estate adjoining Banbury in 1629. A Parliamentarian in the Civil War, he sat for the county in 1659, but continued to hold local office after the Restoration. Holman's elder brother changed his religion on his travels, married Lord Stafford's daughter, and was described as 'a melancholy and bigoted convert to the Church of Rome'.[4]

Holman resided in Banbury, where his father owned property, and was returned for the borough in 1661. He was totally inactive, apart from nomination to the committee of elections and privileges, during the opening sessions of the Cavalier Parliament; but he may have been among those ordered to bring in a public accounts bill on 15 Oct. 1667. He probably supported toleration, since a Presbyterian meeting-place was licensed on his Herefordshire property in 1672. His committees in 1674 and 1675 included those on bills for the better collection of the hearth-tax, for the export of leather, and for rebuilding Northampton. In grand committee on 8 Nov. 1675 he supported the proposal of Sir John Hotham, 2nd Bt.*, for a discriminatory tax on the Jews, declaring that 'in all places but here, the Jews have marks of infamy'. Five days later, he and Sir Charles Wheler* moved to recommend the French minister La Mott for preferment as a convert from Roman Catholicism. In the 1677 session he was marked 'thrice worthy' by Shaftesbury, and named to committees for levying a charge on Northampton buildings for the better support of the ministers there, and for preventing the growth of Popery. In the debate of 23 Feb. on regulating the power of Chancery, Holman referred to the Suffolk election case, declaring that if the judgment in Exchequer Chamber stood 'every Member may be returned here as the sheriffs please'. On 17 Mar. he said that if he were given a warrant he would undertake to prove that several Scotsmen had been forced into French service against their will. In the spring session of 1678 he urged the recall of the British ambassador from France. On 1 June he acted as teller for an addition to the proposal 'that the proceedings of this House have not occasioned a peace'. At the height of the Popish Plot scare, he declared on 8 Nov. 1678 that he was 'credibly informed there are forty Papists in the court of requests' in defiance of the King's proclamation to depart. Never an active Member, he had been named to 26 committees and made seven recorded speeches.[5]

Holman, a member of the Green Ribbon Club, was returned to the Exclusion Parliaments and again marked 'worthy'. In 1679 he was appointed to the committee to receive proposals concerning the royal fishery, but he was absent from the division on the exclusion bill. Together with Hotham and Sir Robert Peyton* he was deputed to fetch (Sir) Stephen Fox* from Whitehall on 23 May with his secret service accounts. He was moderately active in the second Exclusion Parliament, being named to five committees and speaking twice. He told the committee considering the bill for deporting Roman Catholics that 'he knew not his brother George Holman was a Papist, but that he was abroad in Paris and had been so for thirty years'. He added that his brother had often expressed hatred of the Jesuits, and his name was struck out of the bill. On 10 Dec. 1680 he reported on the search of Dr Day's former lodgings. He was also appointed to the committee to examine the disbandment accounts. His sole committee in 1681 was the elections committee. Although his property was not extensive, he was able to give £10,000 with his daughter when she married Sir William Portman*. He was nominated an assistant to Banbury corporation under the new charter, and not removed in the purges, although listed among the Opposition in 1687. After the Revolution he was mentioned as a possible candidate for Banbury in 1690, but he did not sit again. He was buried in London at St. Benet Fink on 22 May 1700, the last member of his family to serve in Parliament.[6]

[1] A. Beesley, *Hist. Banbury*, 481; *Vis. Essex* (Harl. Soc. xiii), 263; *Wandsworth Reg.* 11; PCC 215 Aylett. [2] Carlisle, *Privy Chamber*, 173. [3] SP44/66/308; *Oxford Council Acts* (Oxf. Hist. Soc. n.s. ii), 206. [4] *Vis. Surr.* (Harl. Soc. xliii), 95–96; Baker, *Northants.* i. 739, 740–1; *Index of Deeds* (Oxf. Rec. Soc. xlv), 112; *Wood's Life and Times* (Oxf. Hist. Soc. xix), 276. [5] *CSP Dom.* 1672–3, p. 261; C5/612/87; Grey, iii. 426; iv. 6, 140, 279; v. 241; vi. 167; Finch diary, 23 Feb. 1677. [6] Bodl. Carte 130, f. 288; *CJ*, ix. 629; *HMC Lords*, i. 228; *VCH Oxon.* x. 89; PCC 99 Noel; Guildhall Lib. mss, St. Benet Fink par. reg.

L.N./G.J.

HOLMES, Sir John (c.1640–83), of Yarmouth, I.o.W.

NEWTOWN I.o.W. 19 Feb. 1677, 1679 (Mar.), 1679 (Oct.), 1681

b. c.1640, yr. s. of Henry Holmes of Mallow, co. Cork, and bro. of Sir Robert Holmes*. *m.* lic. 6 Apr. 1668, aged 28, Margaret, da. of Robert Lowther, Draper, of London, 2s. 1da. Kntd. by 30 Apr. 1672.[1]

Lt. RN 1664, capt. 1665, r.-adm. 1673–8; capt. of ft. [I] 1675; capt. of Hurst Castle, Hants 1675–d., Walmer Castle, Kent ?1679–d.[2]

Keeper of New Park, New Forest by 1675–81; commr. for assessment, Hants 1677–9; 'chief burgess', Newtown 1677–d.; Mayor, Yarmouth 1678–9; freeman, Lymington 1679; j.p. Hants by 1680–d.[3]

Holmes first saw naval service as lieutenant to his brother in the Guinea expedition of 1664, and took part in the main battles of the second Dutch war. Samuel Pepys* was sorry to hear of his marriage to the sister of Anthony Lowther*, he being an idle rascal and proud, and worth little, I doubt, and she a mighty pretty, well-disposed lady, and good fortune; ... but the sport is Sir Robert Holmes doth seem to be mad too with his brother, and will disinherit him, saying that he hath ruined himself, marrying below himself and to his disadvantage.

Nevertheless he continued to serve under his brother, and was severely wounded in the attack on the Dutch Smyrna fleet in 1672. When not at sea he probably resided in the splendid mansion built by Robert at Yarmouth, and in 1675 he purchased the governorship of Hurst Castle on the other side of the Solent for £500. He was granted the governorship of the Isle of Wight in reversion to his brother, who outlived him.[4]

Holmes owed his first return for Newtown in 1677 to his brother. According to his opponent Sir William Meux he went down to the borough 'with one employed by the under-sheriff of Hampshire' on Saturday, the election was held on Monday, and 'on Thursday morning following [he] took his seat'. Several petitions were lodged against his return, but the House refused even to refer them to the elections committee. Shaftesbury marked him 'thrice vile', and in *A Seasonable Argument* he was described as

a cowardly, baffled sea-captain, twice poxed and once whipped with a dog-whip, as many gentlemen can testify; chosen in the night, without the head officer of the town and but one burgess; yet voted well elected last session.

He never became an active Member. In the Cavalier Parliament he was appointed to eight committees of secondary importance, and made no speeches. He was among those ordered to report on the pay due to the newly-raised forces (30 May 1678), and acted as teller for accepting the ordnance accounts. He was named to the committees to consider an explanatory bill for prohibiting French commodities and to investigate noises in Old Palace Yard after the Popish Plot. He was on both lists of the court party, though he went into opposition during the final session like his brother, but was not displaced.[5]

Holmes was re-elected to the Exclusion Parliaments, although blacklisted in the 'unanimous club', but appointed to no committees. Shaftesbury classed him as 'vile', and he voted against the bill. In June 1679 he fought a duel with John Churchill II*, his fellow-Member for Newtown, who conceived that Holmes had prejudiced him in the King's favour by relating a tale about 'beating an orange wench'. On 27 Nov. 1680 he was teller with Sir Thomas Armstrong* against referring to the committee for the encouragement of woollen

manufactures a petition against cane-bottomed chairs. He left no trace on the records of the Oxford Parliament. He died in London on 28 May 1683 and was buried at Yarmouth. His daughter married an Essex baronet, but nothing is known about his sons, apart from the annuities they received under their uncle's will.[6]

[1] *Le Neve's Knights* (Harl. Soc. viii), 3; *London Mar. Lic.* ed. Foster, 702; *CSP Dom.* 1671-2, p. 404. [2] *HMC Ormonde*, ii. 204; *CSP Dom.* 1675-6, p. 448; Jan.-June 1683, p. 300; *Cal. Treas. Bks.* vii. 706. [3] *Cal. Treas. Bks.* iv. 838; F. B. Kingdon, *Kingdon Fam.* 56; Bath mss, Coventry pprs. 5, f. 77; C. St. Barbe, *Recs. of Lymington*, 9. [4] *DNB*; *Pepys Diary*, 8 Apr. 1668; *CSP Dom.* 1675-6, p. 304; *Cal. Treas. Bks.* iv. 870. [5] *CSP Dom.* 1676-7, pp. 578-9; *CJ*, ix. 499; *HMC Ormonde*, n.s. iv. 290, 496. [6] *HMC 7th Rep.* 473; *CSP Dom.* Jan.-June 1683, p. 275; PCC 203 Fane.

P.W.

HOLMES, Sir Robert (c.1622-92), of Whitehall and Carisbrooke Castle, I.o.W.

WINCHESTER	26 Oct. 1669
NEWPORT I.o.W.	1679 (Mar.), 1685
YARMOUTH I.o.W.	1689
NEWPORT I.o.W.	1690-18 Nov. 1692

b. c.1622, 3rd *s.* of Henry Holmes of Mallow, co. Cork, and bro. of Sir John Holmes*. *unm.* 1 da. Kntd. 27 Mar. 1666.[1]

Cornet (royalist) by 1643; capt. RN July 1660, r.-adm. 1666-72; capt. of Sandown Castle, I.o.W. Oct. 1660-7, indep. co. I.o.W. 1669-87, Princess Anne's (later 8) Ft. 1687-9; gov. I.o.W. 1668-*d.*[2]

Page to Prince Rupert 1647.[3]

Freeman, Portsmouth 1661, 1666, Winchester 1669; j.p. Hants 1669-*d.*; v.-adm. Hants and I.o.W. 1669-May, 1692; keeper of Boldrewood walk, New Forest by 1675-?*d.*; 'chief burgess', Newtown 1677-*d.*, mayor 1680-4; commr. for assessment, Hants 1690.[4]

Holmes's grandfather, of Lancashire origin, fought in the Elizabethan wars in Ireland and was nominated provost of Mallow in the charter of 1612. Holmes himself was engaged in military affairs from his youth, serving in the Cavalier army in the Civil War. By 1647 he was in attendance on Rupert in France. He distinguished himself in Rupert's privateering fleet during the second Civil War, and then served as a mercenary soldier in France, Germany and Flanders. 'A very bold and expert man', he returned to England well ahead of his patron with the rank of major, and was rewarded with a naval commission and a military command in the Isle of Wight. His attack on the Dutch settlements on the Guinea coast in 1664, by which he was alleged to have got £40,000, began the second Dutch war. Promoted to rear-admiral, he distinguished himself by the destruction of the Dutch East India fleet in 1666. He remained in high favour with Rupert, and with the eclipse of Lord Sandwich (Edward Montagu I*) and (Sir) William

Penn* it was said that Holmes and his fellow-Irishman Sir Edward Spragge* governed most business of the navy. As a second string to his bow he attached himself to Buckingham, acting as his second in his notorious duel with the Earl of Shrewsbury.[5]

At the end of 1668 Holmes was appointed captain and governor of the Isle of Wight. 'He supported the dignity with much propriety, and by his constant residence acquired great popularity.' In the following year he was returned for Winchester at a by-election. A moderately active Member of the Cavalier Parliament, he was named to 35 committees, including the committee of elections and privileges in three sessions, twice acted as teller, and made four recorded speeches. He was among those appointed to consider bills to improve the art of navigation (18 Nov. 1669) and to encourage a device sponsored by (Sir) Philip Howard* for preserving ships (10 Nov. 1670). He was listed in the court party by the Opposition in 1671. Before the third Dutch war, he was ordered to intercept the Smyrna fleet in the Channel, but his attack was unsuccessful. He took part in the battle of Sole Bay, but received no further command at sea, despite pressure from Rupert. He was granted a pension of £500 per annum and fee-farm rents worth £600 per annum.[6]

When Buckingham was accused of responsibility for the attack on the Smyrna fleet, Holmes told the House on 14 Jan. 1674 that he had his orders from the Duke of York as lord high admiral. He was among those instructed to inquire into complaints about the press-gang a week later, and about abuses of the militia laws in the spring session of 1675. He was also appointed to a committee for granting Rupert a monopoly for his steel process. In a rowdy scene in the House on 10 May about British subjects in the French forces, he quarrelled with Lord Castleton (George Saunderson*). In the autumn he was named to the committees to bring in a bill regulating customs duties on various commodities, and to hear a petition from the Isle of Wight against the local customs officials for exacting several extraordinary fees. Information was given to the House that the collector of customs at Southampton had aspersed Holmes and the islanders by saying that 'the inhabitants were a company of mutinous persons, and the governor was ready upon all occasions to join with them'. The collector was sent for in custody, but released on making a full submission. Meanwhile Holmes had spoken twice on the naval programme, though he disappointed Samuel Pepys* by failing to support his demand for large ships. He hoped for a share 'in the trouble and danger of this fleet', and on 4 Nov. explained to the House:

> Whoever builds hulls must be at as great a charge for other materials as for hulls, and [he] sees not how you can come up to your vote unless you provide masts, sails, cables, standing and running rigging. He therefore moves to double the sum for your materials.

He acted as teller against an appropriation clause, and was included in the list of officials in the House. He was rewarded with over 3,000 acres of forfeited Irish estates. He was an eye-witness of the brush between Andrew Marvell* and Sir Philip Harcourt* on 21 Mar. 1677, and Shaftesbury marked him 'thrice vile'. In *A Seasonable Argument* he was described as

> first an Irish livery boy, then a highwayman, now bashaw of the Isle of Wight. Got in boons and by rapine £100,000. The cursed beginner of the two Dutch wars.

On 7 Feb. 1678 he was appointed to the committee to consider the papers tabled by the ordnance office and the Admiralty. He was teller against the address for the removal of counsellors on 10 May, and helped to prepare reports on the pay due to the newly-raised forces and defects in the prohibition of French imports. Although his name appeared on both lists of the court party, he went over to the Opposition in the final session, and was ordered by the King to return to his duties in the Isle of Wight. Hence he was probably absent from the debate on Danby's impeachment, and, unlike (Sir) Stephen Fox*, was able to keep his post, which he held on a life patent.[7]

Holmes was entrusted with the management of the government interest in the three Isle of Wight boroughs in the Exclusion elections, and was returned himself for Newport, two miles from his official residence, at the first general election of 1679. His only committee was to hear a petition from certain foreign merchants who claimed that their goods had been wrongfully condemned as prohibited French imports. It was expected that the Commons would demand his dismissal, Shaftesbury classed him as 'vile', and he voted against the committal of the first exclusion bill. Though his acquisition of the manor of Thorley from Thomas Lucy* gave him some claim to be regarded as a local landowner, he was blacklisted in the 'unanimous club', and replaced by John Leigh* of the country party in the second and third Exclusion Parliaments. He sought to reconcile the Duke of Monmouth with his father in 1682, but the duke repudiated that part of the message in which he 'refused to have anything to do with the Duke of York', and the King was very angry with Holmes for adding the offensive phrase. Threatened with a court martial for false musters in 1684, he deferred a hearing through his interest with William Blathwayte*, and seems to have escaped serious consequences.[8]

At the general election of 1685 Sunderland ordered Holmes to find a seat for the solicitor-general, the Hon. Heneage Finch I*; but he does not seem to have done so. He regained his own seat at Newport, but did not become an active Member of James II's Parliament. He was appointed only to the committees to examine the disbandment accounts and to propose remedies for the low price of wool and corn. He gave affirmative answers on the repeal of the Test Act and Penal Laws, and was recommended for re-election as court candidate. According to one report, he hoped for the command of the fleet in 1688, but it was given to Lord Dartmouth (George Legge*). He promised in September to keep a seat for Pepys in the Isle of Wight if he could, but warned him of the increase in discontent: 'I was never so afraid as I am at present', he wrote, 'for fear of those devils falling upon me'. At the general election of 1689 he was returned for Yarmouth, where he had built himself a handsome house. According to Anthony Rowe* he voted to agree with the Lords that the throne was not vacant; but he easily accommodated himself to the new regime and retained his governorship, despite a complaint from Sir Robert Dillington, 3rd Bt.*, about the quartering of soldiers at Knighton. His only committee was to draw up an address for the defence of the island and other vulnerable territories (18 June). On 25 Nov. he was given leave of absence for a month to attend the King's service, and he is unlikely to have been present for the divisions on the disabling clause in the bill to restore corporations. He was returned for Newport in 1690, but died on 18 Nov. 1692, aged 70, and was buried at Yarmouth. His younger brother, Sir John, had lost his favour by marrying beneath him, and it was his elder brother's son, Henry Holmes of Kilmallock, who inherited his property and interest on marrying his illegitimate daughter, and sat for Yarmouth as a Tory from 1695 to 1717.[9]

[1] Worsley, Hist. I.o.W. 267; Torrington Mems. (Cam. Soc. n.s. xlvi), 180. [2] R. Atkyns, Vindication (1669), 28; CSP Dom. 1660–1, p. 327; 1668–9, p. 118; Cal. Treas. Bks. ii. 167; Bulstrode Pprs. 61. [3] E. Warburton, Mems. Prince Rupert, iii. 241. [4] R. East, Portsmouth Recs. 356, 359; Winchester corp. assembly bk. 6, f. 53; Cal. Treas. Bks. iv. 838; Hants Field Club Pprs. ii. 100. [5] Add. 14294, f. 29; CSP Ire. 1611–14, p. 303; DNB; Warburton, iii. 351, 387; Worsley, 267; Harl. 7020, f. 38v; Clarendon, Life, iii. 80; Pepys Diary, 24 June 1666, 17 Jan., 3 Dec. 1668. [6] Worsley, 140; Cal. Treas. Bks. iv. 174, 247, 617; Williamson Letters (Cam. Soc. n.s. viii), 54; PRO 31/3, bdle. 127, f. 239. [7] Grey, ii. 259; iii. 381, 402; iv. 330; Morrah, 391; Dering Pprs. 82; CJ, ix. 367, 374, 556; Pepys Naval Mins. (Navy Rec. Soc. lx), 13; HMC 12th Rep. IX, 79; Finch diary, 10 Feb. 1679; PRO 31/3, bdle. 142, f. 2. [8] Pepys Further Corresp. ed. Tanner, 338, 342; HMC Ormonde, n.s. v. 96; vi. 316; PRO 31/3, bdle. 152, ff. 31–34; VCH Hants, v. 285; HMC Popham, 262; CSP Dom. 1683–4, p. 354. [9] CSP Dom. 1685, pp. 21, 97, 100; 1687–9, p. 276; Hatton Corresp. (Cam. Soc. n.s. xxiii), 91; Bryant, Pepys, iii. 269; Worsley, 140, 267; CJ, x. 112; Pepys Diary, 8 Apr. 1668; PCC 203 Fane.

P.W.

HOLT, James (1647–1713), of Castleton Hall, Rochdale, Lancs.

LANCASHIRE   1685

b. Oct. 1647, 4th but 2nd surv. s. of Robert Holt (*d.*1675) of Stubley Hall, Rochdale by 2nd w. Catherine, da. of John Bullock of Darley, Derbys. *educ.* Brasenose, Oxf. 1664, BA 1668, MA 1670. *m.* 24 Feb. 1679, Dorothy (*d.* 5 Mar. 1719), da. of Thomas Grantham of Goltho, Lincs. and Meaux, Yorks., and coh. to her bro. Vincent, 7da. *suc.* bro. 1676.[1]

Fellow of Brasenose 1668–77; commr. for assessment, Lancs. 1677–80, 1689–90, j.p. 1677–Apr. 1688, Oct. 1688–*d.*, dep. lt. 1685–7, 1689–*d.*[2]

Holt's ancestors can be traced back in Rochdale parish to the 14th century, and they acquired Castleton at the dissolution of the monasteries. His father, a ship-money sheriff, was induced by the Earl of Derby to assist the King's forces in the Civil War, and was fined £1,150 at one-sixth for his delinquency in 1646. He served on the commission for regulating corporations and in the militia after the Restoration, and died 'very rich'. Holt himself was educated for the Church, but succeeded to 'a vast estate' on his brother's death. He stood unsuccessfully for the county as a court candidate in September 1679, but was elected in 1685. The only member of his family to sit, he took no known part in James II's Parliament. He was removed from the lieutenancy as an opponent of the King's ecclesiastical policy, and in October 1688 he refused to serve under the Papist Lord Molyneux. In December he helped to call out the militia in defence of the Protestant cause, and stood for re-election in the following month with Lord Derby's support. His defeat by the Whig Lord Brandon (Hon. Charles Gerard*) apparently ended his political career, but he took the oaths to the new regime as a militia officer, and ordered the Wigan corporation to act against Jacobites and recusants in 1690. He died at York on 7 Jan. 1713, the last of the family, leaving bequests to Rochdale grammar school and to Brasenose, with which his family had been connected for several generations. He was buried in Rochdale parish church, where his epitaph describes him as well-instructed in sacred and secular learning, a faithful subject of the King [sic], an energetic upholder of the Church, and a despiser of the ignorant mob of fanatics.[3]

[1] H. Fishwick, *Rochdale*, 154; *Rochdale Par. Reg.* (Lancs. Par. Reg. Soc. lviii), 33, 477, 483; *Vis. Lancs.* (Chetham Soc. lxxxv), 151; *Brasenose Coll. Reg.* (Oxf. Hist. Soc. lv), 212; *Nonconformist Reg.* ed. Turner, 43; *Lincs. Peds.* (Harl. Soc. li), 423. [2] Lancs. RO, QSC 80–130; Cavendish mss 9/9. [3] *VCH Lancs.* v. 203–4, 222–4; H. Fishwick, *Rochdale*, 154, 271, 307–9; *Royalist Comp. Pprs.* (Lancs. and Cheshire Rec. Soc. xxix), 257–61; SP29/61/157; *Nonconformist Reg.* 55; O. Heywood, *Diaries*, ii. 137; *HMC Le Fleming*, 162; *HMC 11th Rep. VII*, 28; *HMC Kenyon*, 235, 289.

I.C.

HOLT, Sir John (1642–1710), of Bedford Row, Mdx. and Redgrave, Suff.

BERE ALSTON   31 Jan.–17 Apr. 1689

b. 30 Dec. 1642, 1st s. of Sir Thomas Holt[†] of Abingdon, Berks. and Gray's Inn by Susan, da. of John Peacock of Chawley, Berks. *educ.* Abingdon g.s.; G. Inn, entered 1652, called 1664, ancient 1676; Oriel, Oxf. 1658. *m.* lic. 28 June 1675, Ann, da. of Sir John Cropley, 1st Bt., of Clerkenwell, Mdx., *s.p. suc.* fa. 1686; kntd. 9 Feb. 1686.[1]

Bencher, G. Inn 1682; recorder and j.p. London 1686–7; gov. Charterhouse 1689; commr. for assessment, Mdx. and Serjeant's Inn 1690.[2]

King's serjeant 1686–9; l.c.j.K.b. 17 Apr. 1689–Feb. 1710; PC 26 Sept. 1689–*d.*; commr. of great seal Apr.– May 1700.

Holt was the grandson of a London merchant. His father, a lawyer, was both recorder and MP for Abingdon under the Protectorate; but he proved his loyalty during the exclusion crisis and was confirmed as recorder of Reading in the new charter of 1685. Holt followed his father's profession and appeared for the defence in several notable state trials, being appointed counsel for Danby in 1679 and for Lord Russell (Hon. William Russell*) in 1683. James II appointed him King's serjeant and recorder of London in 1686, but he lost the latter post for refusing to pronounce the death penalty on a deserter.[3]

At this juncture Holt began to play an increasing role in the political events which ensured the success of the Revolution. In December 1688 he was one of the lawyers summoned to advise the peers on their course of action, and he continued to act as assistant in the House of Lords when the Convention met. But when John Maynard I* chose to sit for Plymouth, Holt succeeded to his safe seat at Bere Alston. During his brief career in the Commons he was a very active Member, being appointed to 24 committees and speaking on at least five occasions, and he was involved in most of the important legislation. On 2 Feb. 1689 he was among those ordered to prepare reasons for a constitutional conference, and he helped to manage it three days later. In addition to speaking on this occasion he forcefully defended the position of William, moving

that the Prince of Orange may have the sole administration of the Government during the coverture. . . . The Prince has hazarded all for us; and if you make him consort only to the Queen, you will reduce him, upon her death, to a private condition.

He was added to the committee for bringing in a list of the essentials for preserving religion, law and liberty, but he defended the retention of a modified dispensing power. On 26 Feb. he spoke in favour of continuing revenue, remarking, 'I hope you will not say the King is dead as to the vacancy of the throne, and alive as to the revenue'. He was appointed to the committees to prepare the bill suspending habeas corpus, the first mutiny bill, and the religious comprehension bill, and he took the chair for reviving legal proceedings and removing Papists from the London area.[4]

Holt was made lord chief justice on 17 Apr. 1689, and retained this post until a month before his death, elevating its dignity in the eyes of Whigs and Tories alike, though witch-hunters grumbled at his incredulity. He died childless on 5 Mar. 1710, when the manor of Redgrave, along with other lands in Suffolk, Norfolk, Berkshire, Oxfordshire and Hertfordshire, passed to his brother. His great-nephew Rowland was returned for Suffolk as a Tory in 1759.[5]

[1] *Vis. Berks.* (Harl. Soc. lvi), 229; *Le Neve's Knights* (Harl. Soc. viii), 337; PCC 107 Lloyd; *HMC 11th Rep. VII*, 200. [2] *CSP Dom.* 1686–7, pp. 26, 302, 357; 1689–90, p. 59; *Clarendon Corresp.* ii. 275. [3] *DNB*; A. E. Preston, *St. Nicholas Abingdon*, 111; *CSP Dom.* July–Sept. 1683, pp. 377, 384; 1685, p. 403; *Bramston Autobiog.* (Cam. Soc. xxxii), 245, 276. [4] Cobbett, *Parl. Hist.* v. 70; Grey, ix. 75, 82, 115. [5] K. Thomas, *Religion and the Decline of Magic*, 547; PCC 161 Smith.

J.S.C.

HOLT, Richard (c.1635–1710), of Nursted House, Buriton, Hants.

LYMINGTON   1685, 1689
PETERSFIELD   1690, 1695

b. c.1635, o.s. of John Holt, brewer, of Portsmouth, Hants by Katharine, da. and h. of Anthony Brickett of Salisbury, Wilts. *educ.* St. John's, Oxf. 1652, BA 1655; M. Temple 1656. *m.* Margaret (*d.* 17 Aug. 1685), da. of Richard Whithed[†] of Norman Court, West Tytherley, Hants, 1da. *suc.* fa. 1670.[1]

Freeman, Portsmouth 1658, 1667, Lymington 1677; commr. for assessment, Wilts. and Salisbury 1673–4, Hants 1679–80, 1689–90; j.p. and dep. lt. Hants ?1689–*d*; commr. for wastes and spoils, New Forest 1692; lt.-col. of militia ft. Hants by 1697, col. 1699–*d.*[2]

Capt. of ft. regt. of Richard Norton* 1667.

Holt's grandfather, in his second term as mayor of Portsmouth in 1627, entered his pedigree at the College of Arms, claiming descent from the Lancashire family. Holt's father was also prominent in the municipal life of Portsmouth, serving as mayor in 1641–2 and again under the Commonwealth. He was victualler to the parliamentary navy, but he acquired manorial property in the county and seems to have retired to the Close at Salisbury before the Restoration. Holt himself was a country gentleman who was already living at Nursted in 1667, when he was temporarily commissioned in the army. He acquired an interest at Lymington by marriage. Probably an Independent in religion, he renounced the Covenant when he took out the freedom of the borough. He gave £10 towards building the new town hall in 1684 and was returned to James II's Parliament as a Whig. But he left no trace on its records.[3]

In April 1688 the royal electoral agents expected Holt and his colleague John Burrard* to be re-elected for Lymington, but believed that they would not comply with the King's ecclesiastical policy. By September, however, they had fully declared themselves in the court interest. They were returned to the Convention, but on 23 Feb. 1689 Holt was given leave to go into the country for his health, and he never became an active Member. The first of his eight committees was to inquire into the fall of rents, 4 May. On 1 June he told the House:

> We are beholden to Londonderry; if they had not made a good resistance, King James had been at Edinburgh before now. I never expect redress of these miscarriages, till we come to the root. If [the] Londonderry miscarriage be not redressed, it will come home to us. The old army we see is continued, and the new one laid aside. Those who were King James's creatures are now in office and employment, and in great ones.

He was nominated to the committee to inquire into the delay in sending relief. On 18 June he spoke against excepting Sir Edward Herbert* from the indemnity bill. He was among those ordered to inspect the Admiralty records on Irish affairs and to hear evidence about the trial and conviction of Titus Oates, after which he helped to manage a conference. In the second session he criticized the financial administration of the war:

> The present state of the nation is a state of war; all conclude that money is the sinews of war; I fear there have been great embezzlements, and I hope you will inquire into it—how it has been issued out. I have heard the stores are empty, and I believe there is a great want of money. . . . We have appropriated money for the stores and yards . . . but it has been like boys scrambling for nuts, some get three or four and others none at all. If we appropriate this money, it seems by that we are jealous, and why should we not inquire? You have been told by an honourable person how little there is, and how much wanting.

He was not listed as a supporter of the disabling clause in the bill to restore corporations; but after the Christmas recess he was named to the committees to reform the bankruptcy law and to regulate elections in the Cinque Ports.[4]

Holt transferred to Petersfield, two miles from his home, for the general election of 1690, and represented it in the next two Parliaments as a court Whig. He was buried at Buriton on 14 Apr. 1710, the only member of his family to sit in Parliament. His daughter brought Nursted to her husband, Henry Henley, MP for Lyme Regis (with two intervals) from 1690 to 1715.[5]

[1] *Wilts. Par. Reg.* v. 43; PCC 154 Essex, 76 Penn; B. Whitehead, *Hist. Whitehead Fams.* 23; R. Rawlinson, *Antiqs. Salisbury Cathedral*, 49. [2] R. East, *Portsmouth Recs.* 355, 359; E. King, *Old Times Revisited*, 190; *Cal. Treas. Bks.* ix. 1550; Eg. 1626, f. 45; *CSP Dom.* 1699–1700, p. 235. [3] *Vis. Hants* (Harl. Soc. lxiv), 228; East, 314; *CSP Dom.* 1648–9, pp. 374–5; *VCH Hants*, iii. 94; King, 75, 78. [4] Grey, ix. 280, 480; *CJ*, x. 217. [5] Hants RO, Buriton par. reg.; Collinson, *Som.* ii. 171.

P.W.

HOLTE, Sir Charles, 3rd Bt. (1649–1722), of Aston, Warws.

WARWICKSHIRE   1685

b. 22 Mar. 1649, 1st s. of Sir Robert Holte, 2nd Bt.*, by 1st w. *educ.* Magdalen Coll. Oxf. 1666, BA 1669, MA 1671, MD 1695. *m.* 5 Aug. 1680, Anne (*d.* Feb. 1739), da. and coh. of (Sir) John Cloberry* of Winchester, Hants, 4s. 8da. *suc.* fa. 3 Oct. 1679.[1]

  J.p. Warws. 1679–?*d.*, Staffs. 1681–?*d.*, Salop and Worcs. 1685–?96; dep. lt. Warws. by 1680–7, 1689–?*d.*; freeman, Winchester 1683; commr. for assessment, Warws. 1689–90.[2]

Holte was brought up by his uncle, William Brereton*, Lord Brereton, from whom he derived those principles of the love of God and his country 'which were to guide him in the splendid course of his life'. In this, politics played an altogether secondary role; his early years, after succeeding to the baronetcy, were principally devoted to rescuing the encumbered Aston estate by prudent management and rigid economy. He declined an invitation from the Warwickshire gentry to contest the county in 1681, though Sir Leoline Jenkins* wrote to him in 1684: 'Your affection for the public and your zeal for the King's service being so great . . . I wish you frequent occasions to approve yourself what you are'. The Birmingham nonconformists did not fail to supply such occasions, and Holte was particularly commended for his care and discretion in securing the surrender of the grammar school charter. Under the new charter of 20 Feb. 1685 he was appointed to the board of governors.[3]

Before the general election Holte wrote to Sunderland that 'our old disturbers are at work under the pretence of great loyalty'; but he was returned unopposed for Warwickshire to James II's Parliament. An active Member, he was named to 14 committees, including the committee of elections and privileges, and those to recommend expunctions from the Journals and to consider the general naturalization of Huguenot refugees. Danby added his name in pencil to his list of the Opposition. Holte seems to have evaded answering the three questions on the repeal of the Test Act and Penal Laws in Staffordshire and Worcestershire on the grounds that he could not leave home as he was expecting a visit from Sunderland. He did not stand again, though his name was retained on the Warwickshire commission of the peace after the Revolution. He seems to have cleared the estate by 1692, and occupied his later years with medical studies. 'By his skill in medical science, and by supplying the poor with medicine, he restored many to health who would have fallen a prey to disease, had he not charitably administered relief.' He died on 20 June 1722, and in accordance with his will was buried quietly at Aston:

> I never was fond of pompous funerals, which I ever esteemed as a gaudy show to entertain a mob and disorder a family. I have for several years lived retired, and do therefore earnestly desire that my burial may be private.

His grandson, Sir Lister Holte, was returned for Lichfield as a Tory in 1741.[4]

[1] A. Davidson, *Holtes of Aston*, 32–36. [2] *Warws. Recs.* vii. pp. xxix, xxxii; viii. p. xliii; ix. p. xviii; Worcs. RO, 186; Winchester corp. assembly bk. 5, f. 152. [3] Davidson, 36; Add. 34730, ff. 66–67, 74–75; Bath mss, Thynne pprs. 28, ff. 90–91, 231–2; *CSP Dom.* 1683–4, p. 376; 1684–5, pp. 90, 238; *Recs. King Edward's Sch.* (Dugdale Soc. xii), 196–7. [4] *CSP Dom.* 1685, pp. 32, 72; *HMC Lords*, n.s. iii. 474–7; Davidson, 36; PCC 28 Richmond.

A.M.M.

HOLTE, Sir Robert, 2nd Bt. (c.1625–79), of Aston, Warws.

WARWICKSHIRE 1661

b. c.1625, 1st s. of Edward Holte (*d.*1643) of Aston, groom of the bedchamber to Charles I, by Elizabeth, da. of John King, bp. of London 1611–21. *m.* (1) 23 May 1648 (with £4,000), Jane (*d.*1649), da. of Sir John Brereton of Brereton, Cheshire, 1s.; (2) Mary (*bur.* 18 June 1679), da. of Sir Thomas Smith[†] of Hatherton, Cheshire, wid. of George Cotton of Combermere, Cheshire, 4s. 3da. *suc.* gdfa. Dec. 1654.[1]

Sheriff, Warws. 1658–Nov. 1660; commr. for militia, Warws. and Coventry Mar. 1660, assessment, Warws. Aug. 1660–*d.*, dep. lt. c. Aug. 1660–*d.*, j.p. 1661–*d.*, commr. for corporations 1662–3, loyal and indigent officers 1662, oyer and terminer, Midland circuit 1662.[2]

Gent. of privy chamber 1671–?*d.*[3]

Holte's ancestors acquired Aston in 1367 and first entered Parliament in 1378, though they were not a regular parliamentary family. Holte's grandfather

disapproved strongly of his father's marriage, and Holte was brought up by his maternal uncle, Henry King, bishop of Chichester. Despite their personal differences, his father, who fought at Edgehill and died in the Oxford garrison, and his grandfather were both active Royalists in the Civil War. The Aston estate was not discharged from sequestration until February 1652, when a fine of £4,491 2s.4d. was paid. On his succession to the baronetcy two years later Holte was compelled to raise £5,000 on mortgage, and he was never free of debt. Nevertheless he built ten almshouses at Aston in 1655–6 in accordance with his grandfather's will. His High Church connexions were commemorated by Izaak Walton, who dedicated the second edition of his life of Donne in 1658 to 'my noble and honoured friend, Sir Robert Holte'. In the same year he was appointed sheriff of Warwickshire, in which capacity he conducted the county election of 1660.[4]

After suing out a pardon under the great seal, Holte was returned himself as knight of the shire in 1661. Listed by Lord Wharton as a friend, he was probably in opposition under Clarendon. An active Member of the Cavalier Parliament, he was named to 197 committees, including the committee of elections and privileges in the first nine sessions, acted as teller in 38 divisions, and made 32 recorded speeches. In the opening session he was appointed to the committees for restoring the bishops to the House of Lords, inquiring into the shortfall in revenue, considering the corporations bill and the bill of pains and penalties, and preventing tumultuous petitioning and mischief from Quakers. He was present at the demolition of the defences of Coventry on 22 July. After the autumn recess he was among those ordered to consider the execution of those under attainder, to bring in a militia bill, and to hear a petition from the wine retailers. On 2 Feb. 1662 he was teller against allowing sheriffs to charge their counties for the troopers in attendance at the assizes. In April he took the chair for an estate bill. He opposed exacting an oath from officials required to contribute to the relief of loyal and indigent officers, and twice acted as teller on the uniformity bill. He agreed with the Lords' amendment to bring the date forward from Michaelmas to Bartholomewtide, but opposed a compulsory payment of 20 per cent from new incumbents to their nonconformist predecessors. It was probably during these debates that he stigmatized the prayers and sermons of Baxter and Calamy as seditious. He was ordered to peruse the Lord's Day Observance Acts with (Sir) Francis Goodricke*, William Yorke* and William Prynne*, and to bring in a new bill to impose penalties for arrests on that day, a subject very close to his heart. He was teller for adjourning the debate on the militia bill on 3 May, and on the last day of the session he was one of the Members ordered to attend the King with an address on behalf of a petitioner against the Lindsey level bill.[5]

In the 1663 session Holte was among those appointed to consider a bill to hinder the growth of Popery, to inspect the laws regulating the sale of offices, and to devise remedies for sectaries' meetings. Though his Anglican convictions are beyond doubt, he supported a proviso to protect occasional conformists, and acted as teller for the second reading of an additional bill to regulate corporations. He was teller against the Lords amendments to the bill granting the profits of the Post Office and wine licences to the Duke of York. A member of the committee for the bill to recover excise arrears, he opposed it unsuccessfully on third reading with Giles Strangways*. In 1664 he was named to the committees to consider the conventicles bill, and to bring in bills regulating abuses and delays in the law-courts. He served on the committee to consider the private bill promoted by Sir Robert Carr*, but acted as teller against it. He was among those to whom a bill for the relief of poor prisoners was committed on 1 Feb. 1665. In the Oxford session he opposed the felony bill on second reading, but was named to the committee. He was also appointed to the committees for the five mile bill and the bill to prevent the import of foreign cattle and fish. On 28 Oct. he was sent to remind the Lords of this bill and added to the committee for the attainder of British officers in the service of the enemy. His activity increased in the next session, but he continued to work closely with the 'country Cavalier' Strangways. They were tellers against going into committee on supply on 17 Oct. 1666. Holte was willing to excuse from service on the abortive public accounts committee those who had wished the personnel to be drawn from outside Parliament, and he supported the higher estimate for the yield of the poll-tax. A member of the committee for a private bill on behalf of (Sir) Thomas Higgons*, he opposed the motion for engrossment on 21 Dec., and he acted as teller with Strangways for a short Christmas adjournment. When Parliament met again, he was teller for the country candidate in the Winchelsea election. A member of the committee to draw up the impeachment of Mordaunt, he was teller for adding Heneage Finch* and against allowing the defendant to sit within the bar during his trial. On 5 Feb. 1667 he was sent to desire a conference.[6]

Holte's colleague and friend Sir Henry Puckering* urged 'Bobsie' to attend the abortive session in July, but it is not known whether he did so. After the fall of Clarendon he probably went over to the Court, though he was always prepared to take an independent line where his constituents' interests were concerned. In his speech of 13 Dec. he

> justly reflected upon the Lords for their refusing to commit him [Clarendon] upon his impeachment, and now without any conference with us, or having any other special matter for it, [they] have sent us in a bill for his banishment upon his flight to avoid that impeachment.

In the debate on comprehension on 11 Mar. 1668 he complained that the nonconformists' desires had not been stated, and he spoke in favour of renewing the Conventicles Act. He was teller against desiring the King to receive proposals for uniting his Protestant subjects. On 1 Apr. he moved on behalf of his Birmingham neighbours that the forges of smiths and nailers should be exempt from hearth-tax; but Sir Thomas Osborne* included him among the Members who usually voted for supply. He was named to the committee for reviving the law against conventicles on 8 Dec. 1670, but he reacted violently to the assault on Sir John Coventry*:

> It is the greatest breach that ever was since the first constitution of Parliaments. ... His Majesty has a place here when he commands or does justice. If these persons are of his Guards, they that will not fear God will never honour the King. Guards have been the betrayers of the empire; the Praetorians did it. ... Would have his Majesty moved to inspect his Guards. Lords' noses are as ours are, unless they be of steel; it concerns the Lords as well as us.

On 6 Feb. 1671 'Sir Robert Holte informed the House that lately in the parish next to him in Warwickshire during the time of divine service five men armed with swords and pistols came into the church, and took away by force a gentleman out of the church, and carried him to prison, one of them being a bailiff arresting him'. The House, 'moved with just indignation at these abominations', ordered a bill to be brought in to prevent profanation of the Lord's day by arrest or otherwise, and Holte was the first Member named to the committee. He reported a Hampshire estate bill on 27 Feb. and carried it to the Lords. He was teller for an unsuccessful motion to appropriate supply to paying off debt. On 2 Mar. he urged the House to resolve the doubts over the liability of smiths' forges to hearth-tax, 'showing at large the trouble the country was in upon that account, and the uncertainty of the law in it, which was severally construed in several counties and by several judges'. A bill was ordered to remedy abuses, and Holte was given responsibility for expediting it, together with Thomas Crouch* and Sir Thomas Meres*. He suggested that 'those who would not abjure the Covenant might be taxed towards the satisfaction of those who had suffered for his Majesty'. He was recognized as the most determined opponent of conventicles in the West Midlands, and was well-briefed by local magistrates with the need to check their impudence and protect informers. Though he recognized the danger of malicious and vexatious indictments, he was teller for the new conventicles bill.[7]

During the following recess Holte was summoned before the Privy Council on a charge of encouraging opposition to the hearth-tax. 'The King', wrote Henry Coventry*, 'is much displeased to have so great a branch of his revenue endangered by one who always appeared loyal and affectionate.' Nevertheless he succeeded in smoothing down the Treasury, though Holte renewed his attack on the levy on smiths' forges when Parliament met again in 1673. In the same session he declared that the renunciation of transubstantiation devised by Brome Whorwood* for officials was unnecessary, and was named to the committee for the general naturalization bill. In 1674 his committees included those to consider habeas corpus reform and the power of commitment exercised by the Privy Council. He described the attack on Lord Arlington as 'a pretty way of hanging a man with a silken halter'. The minister had tried to preserve the Triple Alliance, he asserted, while the Council were responsible for advising war with the Dutch. But he was for the removal of Buckingham as an evil counsellor. His financial difficulties now drew him more closely to the Court. He attacked the place bill on 29 Apr. 1675: 'this bill is, in direct terms, that no man that serves the King shall be capable of being a Parliament man'. He acted as teller for a moderate reply to the message from the Lords on Shirley v. Fagg of 15 May, and was named to the committee on the bill for preventing the growth of Popery. He received the government whip from Secretary Williamson for the autumn session, replying that he would not 'fail to render an exact obedience to his Majesty's commands'. He was named to the committees for appropriating the customs to the use of the navy and hindering Papists from sitting in Parliament; but he had increasing difficulty in catching the Speaker's eye. After several attempts to speak in the debate of 6 Nov. on the naval programme, he exclaimed: 'he wonders a knight of Warwickshire may not be heard as well as another'. A brutal allusion by Sir Thomas Littleton, 2nd Bt.* to Holte's financial embarrassment probably helped to arouse the House's sympathy, and he was able to say that he 'knows it to be the opinion of the most substantial freeholders of that county that they would have the King be sufficiently supplied as to these ships'.[8]

At the end of the session Holte found it necessary to appeal for assistance to Osborne, now Lord Treasurer Danby.

> If my condition (by reason of my many sufferings for his late Majesty and our now dread sovereign) was bad enough before 'tis now by my late actings in Parliament for his service rendered much worse; it being not the least of my misfortunes that many of my creditors are persons (I fear) of not so loyal principles as I could wish, who, now the privileges of Parliament are expiring, threaten me with all the severity the law is master of.

Danby put him down for an excise pension, and according to *A Seasonable Argument* he received £1,000 as well as protection from his creditors. His name was included on the working lists, while Sir Richard Wiseman* listed him among the court party and Williamson among the government speakers. In *The Chequer Inn* he was depicted as reduced to the last extremities to maintain appearances:

> Holte, out of linen as of land,
> Had mortgag'd of his two one band,
>   To have the other wash'd.

One of his mortgages had passed into the unscrupulous hands of Andrew Fountaine*; but his most urgent creditor seems to have been the son of Peter Prideaux*. He was in a debtors' prison when Parliament reassembled on 15 Feb. 1677, but on the following day Puckering delivered a letter from him claiming privilege. Prideaux objected, on the ground that Holte might escape abroad, and the matter was referred to the committee of privileges. Meres recommended that his petition should be rejected, since he had been taken in execution before privilege began, but this view was reversed by the House after a division, with Puckering and (Sir) Henry Ford* acting as tellers for the majority. He took no part in the session, but Shaftesbury marked him 'thrice vile'. His swan-song as a parliamentary orator was delivered on 28 Jan. 1678, when he urged the House to debate the speech from the throne on the next day. Prideaux renewed his petition on 26 Mar., but Holte continued to sit, and was appointed to the committee for reform of the bankruptcy law on 27 May. His name appeared on both lists of the court party, and he did not stand again. He died intestate on 3 Oct. 1679, aged 54, and was buried in St. Clement Danes.[9]

[1] A. Davidson, *Holtes of Aston*, 29–32. [2] P. Styles, *Corp. of Warwick*, 25. [3] Carlisle, *Privy Chamber*, 188. [4] Davidson, 10, 21–23, 28, 30, 33; *Cal. Comm. Comp.* 2557; *VCH Warws.* vii. 562. [5] Davidson, 29; *CJ*, viii. 396, 403, 409, 414, 435; M. Sylvester, *Reliquiae*

Baxterianae, i. 380. [6] *CJ*, viii. 513, 517, 527, 532, 603, 615, 661, 664, 668, 674, 686. [7] Davidson, 29; *Milward*, 165, 225, 241; Grey, i. 110, 334; *CJ*, ix. 77, 210, 218, 230; *Dering*, 70, 86–87, 98; *CSP Dom.* 1671, p. 20. [8] *Cal. Treas. Bks.* iii. 774, 783, 1099, 1228–9; *CSP Dom.* 1672, pp. 626–7; 1672–3, pp. 3, 96; 1675–6, p. 323; *Dering*, 143; Grey, ii. 99, 306, 383; iii. 70, 412. [9] Eg. 3329, f. 49; *Poems on Affairs of State*, i. 258; Davidson, 33; *CJ*, ix. 384, 411; Grey, iv. 77; *CSP Dom.* 1676–7, p. 558; 1678, pp. 62–63.

A.M.M.

HONEYWOOD, John Lamotte (1647–94), of Markshall, Essex.

ESSEX 1679 (Oct.), 1681, 10 Jan. 1693–14 Jan. 1694

bap. 21 May 1647, 5th but 2nd surv. s. of Sir Thomas Honeywood[†] of Markshall by Hester, da. and coh. of John La Motte, Weaver, of London, wid. of John Manning, merchant, of Hackney, Mdx. *educ.* Christ's, Camb. 1665; I. Temple 1668. *m.* Elizabeth, da. and h. of Sir William Wiseman, 1st Bt.*, of Rivenhall, Essex, *s.p. suc.* bro. 1672.[1]

Commr. for assessment, Essex 1673–80, Kent 1679–80, Essex and Kent 1689–90; lt.-col. of militia ft. Essex by 1676–80, j.p. Apr. 1688–*d.*, sheriff 1689–90.[2]

Gent. of the privy chamber 1689–*d.*[3]

Honeywood came from a cadet branch of the Kentish family. His grandfather acquired Markshall in 1605. His father fought for Parliament in both wars, and was appointed to the high court of justice for the trial of Charles I in 1649, but did not attend. He represented Essex under the Protectorate until called to the 'Other House', and retired from politics at the Restoration. Honeywood himself, 'a chip of the old block', stood unsuccessfully for Maldon at the first general election of 1679, but was returned for the county in August after a fierce contest as an opponent of the Court. In the second Exclusion Parliament he was appointed only to the committees to inquire into abhorring and to consider extending the ban on Irish cattle. He was re-elected in 1681 and was nominated to the committee of elections and privileges at Oxford, but made no speeches in either Parliament. According to a newsletter, his nerve broke after the Rye House Plot; 'the eminent Honeywood has been with the King and the Duke, and was observed to come from them weeping. It is generally believed that he has made some discoveries.' A Tory pamphlet of the following year represented Titus Oates as saying that 'there would be no use for him' in another Parliament, and he did not stand in 1685.[4]

Honeywood may have been a Whig collaborator, since he was recommended for restoration to the commission of the peace in 1688. He stood unsuccessfully for the county at the general election of 1689, and his petition was rejected. He regained his seat at a by-election in 1693, but hanged himself on

14 Jan. 1694 after several other attempts at suicide, due to domestic differences. His widow, who was 'miserable to baseness', married Isaac Rebow*. His heir was his cousin Robert, who sat for Essex as a Whig from 1716 to 1727.[5]

[1] Morant, *Essex*, ii. 166–9; Soc. of Genealogists, H. Gwyn, Peds. 79. [2] *CSP Dom.* 1676–7, p. 115. [3] Carlisle, *Privy Chamber*, 202. [4] Morant, loc. cit.; *Bramston Autobiog.* (Cam. Soc. xxxii), 14; *CSP Dom.* July–Sept. 1683, p. 351; *The Essexian Triumviri* (1684). [5] *Bramston Autobiog.* 346, 377; *CJ*, x. 10, 75–77; Luttrell, iii. 254.

G.H.

HONEYWOOD, Sir William, 2nd Bt. (c.1654–1748), of Evington Place, Elmsted and Canterbury, Kent.

CANTERBURY 1685, 1689, 1690, 1695

b. c.1654, 1st s. of Sir Edward Honeywood, 1st Bt., of Evington Place by Elizabeth, da. of Sir John Maynard[†] of Tooting Graveney, Surr. *educ.* Jesus, Oxf. matric. 29 Mar. 1672, aged 17. *m.* lic. 12 July 1675, Anna Christiana, da. of Richard Newman of Tothill Street, Westminster, 2s. 3da. *suc.* fa. Sept. 1670.[1]

J.p. Kent 1675–Feb. 1688, Oct. 1688–*d.*; commr. for assessment, Kent 1677–80, Kent and Canterbury 1689–90; dep. lt. Kent 1679–Feb. 1688, Oct. 1688–at least 1701; freeman, Canterbury 1684, alderman 1684–7, mayor 1685–6, col. of militia ft. Kent by 1697.[2]

Commr. for excise appeals 1689–1714.[3]

Honeywood's ancestors were established in Kent by the reign of Henry III, and first sat for Hythe in 1393. Honeywood's grandfather served on the county committee till 1648, but his father is said to have sent £3,000 to Charles II in exile, for which he received a baronetcy at the Restoration, and Honeywood himself entered politics as a court supporter. He still held Scene Farm just outside Hythe, and in 1679 he strove to reactivate the family interest there. However, Sir Edward Dering* politely declined to assist, and he was defeated at both elections. He then transferred his attention to Canterbury, extending 'constant hospitality' for electoral purposes from his town house. He was nominated alderman in the new charter of 1684, and elected to James II's Parliament in the following year. An active Member, he was named to 12 committees, of which the most important was to recommend expunctions from the Journals. He was also among those appointed to consider the bill for supplying fresh water to Rochester and Chatham. After the recess he went into opposition on supply.

> The rebellion is suppressed. The army is urged to be small, but 'tis so thick officered that but filling up the troops, which is easily at any time to be done, increases their numbers one-third part more. I am for providing for them but one year only.

He was removed from the Canterbury corporation by order-in-council in December 1687 and from county office a few months later, after returning negative answers on the repeal of the Test Act Act and Penal Laws; but the King's electoral agents reported that his interest in the city was unshaken.[4]

During the Revolution Honeywood signed the deputy lieutenant's letter at Faversham, and his services were rewarded with a seat on the excise appeals board. Re-elected to the Convention, he was moderately active with 35 committees, including those on the bills for restoring corporations and regulating the oaths to be taken by army officers. On 8 July 1689, he was one of the Members ordered to hear charges of embezzlement against his wife's uncle, William Harbord*. In the second session he was appointed to the committees to inquire into the miscarriages of the war, to indemnify those who had acted in the Revolution, and to consider a compulsory oath of allegiance, and he was listed as supporting the disabling clause in the bill to restore corporations. Honeywood remained a court Whig until he lost his seat in 1698, but he retained his place till the Hanoverian succession. He died on 1 June 1748 at the age of 94, and was buried at Elmsted. His great-grandson, Filmer Honeywood, was elected for Steyning in 1784 and for Kent in 1790.[5]

[1] Wotton, *Baronetage*, iii (1), 108; Elmsted par. reg. [2] *Roll of Freemen* ed. Cowper, 319; *CSP Dom.* 1679–80, p. 232; PC2/72/555. [3] *Cal. Treas. Bks.* ix. 110; xxix. 193. [4] Hasted, *Kent*, viii. 36, 204–5; A. M. Everitt, *Community of Kent and the Great Rebellion*, 144, 147, 244; Stowe 746, f. 7; Lowther diary, f. 43. [5] *N. and Q.* (ser. 3), vi. 23.

J.P.F.

HOOKE, Sir Humphrey (1629–77), of King's Weston, Glos.

BRISTOL   30 Oct. 1666–16 Oct. 1677

b. 6 Aug. 1629, 1st s. of Thomas Hooke (*d.*1643) of Bristol by 1st w. Mary Burrus. *m.* Florence (*d.* 3 Sept. 1692), da. of Thomas Smith† of Long Ashton, Som., 2s. *d.v.p.* 1da. *suc.* gdfa. Humphrey Hooke† 1659; kntd. 21 Feb. 1661.[1]

Commr. for militia, Bristol Mar. 1660; j.p. Glos. July 1660–2, 1670–*d.*, sheriff 1661–2; keeper, Kingswood chase 1661–?*d.*; member of merchant venturers, Bristol 1661; commr. for assessment, Bristol 1661–4, 1666–9, Glos. 1663–74, loyal and indigent officers, Bristol 1662, col. of militia ft 1662–?*d.*, dep. lt. 1662–*d.*, alderman 1662–4, commr. for pressing seamen 1665, recusants, Glos. and Som. 1675.[2]

Hooke's grandfather, born in Chichester, was probably a cousin of John Hooke*. He became a Bristol merchant and represented the city in the Short and Long Parliaments until expelled as a monopolist. After the Civil War he was fined £669 as a royalist delinquent, but this was reduced to £125 in consideration of his contributions to the parliamentary forces. At the Restoration Hooke was

knighted and recommended for the order of the Royal Oak, with an income of £1,500 p.a., while his half-brother, who had inherited a Surrey estate, was created a baronet. Hooke married into a county family and took up residence at King's Weston, four miles from Bristol, although he did not sever all ties with his birthplace. At the general election of 1661 he was nominated, possibly against his will, in opposition to Lord Ossory (Thomas Butler*). There was a double return, but Hooke, who had signed Ossory's indentures, renounced his claim until his opponent was summoned to the Lords in 1666. He then renewed his petition, and was seated on the merits of the election.[3]

An inactive Member of the Cavalier Parliament, Hooke made no speeches and was appointed to only ten committees, none of which was of political importance, though in 1667 he took part in the inquiry into the shortage of timber in the Forest of Dean. His financial position was deteriorating, and, despite two defaults in attendance, he did not scruple to exact £77 from the corporation in 1669 for arrears of parliamentary wages, which he used to satisfy a debt to one of the aldermen, and he received the same reward from the merchant venturers as his very active colleague John Knight I* on the renewal of their charter in 1670. John Milward* described Hooke as 'a loyal person', but he was not on either list of the court party in 1669–71. In 1675, however, he received the government whip from Secretary Coventry, he was included among the court supporters on the working lists and by Sir Richard Wiseman*, and Shaftesbury marked him 'doubly vile'. He died on 16 Oct. 1677, heavily in debt to Thomas Earle* and others. His trustees, Hugh Smith* and William Cooke*, sold King's Weston to Sir Robert Southwell*.[4]

[1] F. W. Todd, *Humphrey Hooke of Bristol*, 47, 49, 55. [2] J. Latimer, *Bristol in the 17th Century*, 302; *Merchant Venturers* (Bristol Rec. Soc. xvii), 30; Bodl. Carte 32, f. 48; Bristol RO, AC/C74/35; *CSP Dom.* 1663–4, p. 301; 1664–5, p. 390; *CSP Ire* 1660–2, p. 634. [3] *Deposition Bks.* (Bristol Rec. Soc. vi), 248–9; *Vis. Hants* (Harl. Soc. lxiv), 84; Keeler, *Long Parl.* 221–2; *Cal. Comm. Comp.* 1629; *CJ*, viii. 250, 644. [4] *Merchants and Merchandise* (Bristol Rec. Soc. xix), 157; *Merchant Venturers*, 18, 71; *Milward*, 16; Todd, 199–202; Bristol RO, AC/C77/6.

J.P.F.

HOOKE, John (c.1605–85), of Bramshott, Hants.

HASLEMERE   Jan.–23 Mar. 1659
WINCHESTER   1660

b. c.1605, 1st s. of Henry Hooke of Bramshott by Margaret, da. of Cuthbert Lynde of Westminster. *educ.* Magdalen Coll. Oxf. 1623; M. Temple 1623. *m.* 8 Dec. 1631, Grissell (*d.* 4 Mar. 1687), da. of Sir Francis Clarke of Hitcham, Bucks., 2s. 1da. *suc.* fa. 1640.[1]

J.p. Hants 1636–*d.*, commr. for sequestration, Hants

1643, defence 1643, levying money 1644, assessment 1644–52, 1657, Jan. 1660–3, 1644–80, execution of ordinances 1644, militia 1648, 1659, Mar. 1660, sheriff Jan.–Nov. 1649, commr. for scandalous ministers 1658; freeman, Winchester Mar. 1660; commr. for recusants, Hants 1675.[2]

Hooke's grandfather, of Surrey origins, obtained a confirmation of arms in 1600 and bought the manor of Bramshott in 1610. As a nephew of John Pym[†], Hooke naturally supported Parliament throughout the Civil War; but he also complied with all succeeding governments, holding local office till his death some 40 years later. He was returned for Winchester at the top of the poll in the general election of 1660, and marked by Lord Wharton as a friend. In the Convention he made no speeches and was appointed to no committees, but he probably voted with the Opposition and did not stand again. Although approved as an ejector during the Protectorate, he conformed to the Church of England, and presented his younger son to the rectory in 1672. Presumably he opposed exclusion. He died on 14 May 1685 aged 80, the only member of this family to sit in Parliament, and was buried at Bramshott. The property was sold a few years later.[3]

[1] W. W. Capes, *Rural Life in Hants*, 333; *Bucks. Par. Reg.* v. 115; *Mdx. Par. Reg.* i. 10. [2] *CSP Dom.* 1658–9, p. 42; Winchester corp. assembly bk. 4, f. 137. [3] *Vis. Hants* (Harl. Soc. lxiv), 84; *Grantees of Arms* (Harl. Soc. lxvi), 128; *VCH Hants*, ii. 492; *Gent. Mag.* lxv. 594.

M.W.H./P.W./J.P.F.

HOPKINS, Richard I (c.1612–82), of Palace Yard, Earl Street, Coventry, Warws. and the Inner Temple.

COVENTRY 30 Mar.–31 July 1660, 14 Aug. 1660

b. c.1612, 3rd s. of Sampson Hopkins[†], draper (*d.*1622), of Coventry, being o.s. by 2nd w. Jane, da. of one Butts. *educ.* I. Temple, entered 1630, called 1639; Trinity Coll. Camb. 1631. *m.* Sarah, da. of William Jesson[†], dyer, of Coventry, 6s. (1 *d.v.p.*) 2da. Kntd. 1 Sept. 1660.[1]

Steward of borough court, Coventry 1647–*d.*; commr. for assessment, Coventry 1648–9, Aug. 1660–1, Warws. and Coventry 1650–2, Jan. 1660, 1661–80, Warws. 1657; j.p. Warws. 1649–*d.*; commr. for militia, Warws. and Coventry 1659, Mar. 1660; bencher, I. Temple 1660, reader 1664; dep. lt. Coventry 1661–*d.*; commr. for loyal and indigent officers, Warws. 1662.[2] Serjeant-at-law 1669–*d.*

Hopkins's ancestors were prominent in municipal affairs in Elizabethan Coventry, and his father, a Puritan, was the first of the family to enter Parliament, representing the borough in 1614 and 1621. Hopkins himself, a lawyer, was presumably a passive Parliamentarian in the Civil War. As legal adviser to the corporation since 1647, he was successful at a very confused general election in 1660.

He was named to the committee of elections and privileges and to that for the continuation of judicial proceedings (22 May). On 18 June he proposed the regicide Miles Corbet[†] for exception from pardon. When a speech attributed to his colleague Robert Beake* was printed, he was appointed to the committee of inquiry into this breach of privilege, and also to those to consider a petition from the intruded Oxford dons and a proviso to the indemnity bill concerning John Hutchinson*. Although describing himself as no favourer of the Papists, he thought that the proviso to the bill requiring its beneficiaries to take the oaths should be laid aside. The Coventry election was declared void on 31 July, but Hopkins, unlike Beake, was re-elected a fortnight later. He was knighted on the eve of the autumn recess when the corporation surrendered the crown lands which they had purchased in 1649 and presented the King with a basin and ewer and 50 pieces of gold. During the second session of the Convention, Hopkins was added to the committees on the bills to settle the militia, to explain the poll-tax and to establish the Post Office. He urged the House to give more time to debating the militia bill, reported the bill to enable George Faunt* to sever the entail on his estate, and seconded the motion for a grant of £1,000 to Jane Lane for assisting Charles II to escape after the battle of Worcester. But he was not an active Member, being appointed in all to nine committees and making four recorded speeches.[3]

Hopkins lost his seat at the general election of 1661, but remained the most active magistrate in the county. He was raised to the coif under the Cabal, but passed over for further promotion. When Lord Conway asked him in 1676 to curb his son's opposition to the Danby administration,

> Sir Richard Hopkins said he had no reason to concern himself in that matter, for there were two puisne serjeants-at-law to him already put over his head, and called up to the bench before him; but if, upon the death of any of the ancient judges, he might be preferred to be a judge in any of the King's courts he would not only make his son go right in the King's business, but several others of his friends that went in the House of Commons as perversely as his son did.

Danby replied that the King was resolved never 'to make such a fixed bargain', that could be boasted of to his disadvantage later, but added, 'he shall not fear to find the effects of the King's kindness to his satisfaction, if he demonstrate to his Majesty the effects of his service, and that, if he will not depend upon this assurance his Majesty had better want his assistance than lose many others by the umbrage which will be given by any other sort of proceeding'. He died on a visit to his sister-in-law at Lymington and was buried there on 16 July 1682.[4]

[1] *Staffs. Peds.* (Harl. Soc. lxiii), 130; PCC 47 Swann, 215 Grey, 109 Cottle; Burke, *Commoners*, iv. 120. [2] T. W. Whitley, *Parl. Rep. Coventry*, 100–1; *CSP Dom.* 1682, p. 478. [3] Coventry RO, A43, f. 22; Bowman diary, ff. 9v, 153v; B. Poole, *Coventry*, 79; *Old Parl. Hist.* xxiii. 15, 59; *CJ*, viii. 198. [4] *Sessions Order Bk.* (Warws. Recs. iv), p. xxvii; SP16/522/88 (misplaced); SP29/390/1; E. King, *Old Times Revisited*, 276.

M.W.H./A.M.M

HOPKINS, Richard II (c.1641–1708), of Palace Yard, Earl Street, Coventry, Warws.

COVENTRY   1 Nov. 1670, 1679 (Mar.), 1679 (Oct.), 1681, 1690, 1698

b. c.1641, 2nd but 1st surv. s. of Richard Hopkins I*, and bro. of Thomas Hopkins†. *educ.* Trinity Coll. Camb. 1657; I. Temple 1658, called 1665. *m.* 16 June 1670, Mary (*d.* 13 Oct. 1711), da. and coh. of Robert Johnson, Grocer, of Ilford, Essex, 1s. 1da. *suc.* fa. 1682.[1]

Master, drapers' co. of Coventry 1672–3, 1682–3, 1703–4; commr. for assessment, Warws. and Coventry 1673–80, 1689–90; j.p. Warws. 1690–*d.*[2]

Although Hopkins qualified himself to follow his father's profession there is no evidence that he practised. His long association with the Coventry drapers' company and his interest in the copperas industry suggests that he may have reverted to the mercantile pursuits of his grandfather. But he also purchased land, and his status as a gentleman was sufficiently established for him to cross swords with Sir John Hales when they quarrelled over their wives' inheritance. He soundly defeated a Royalist at a by-election in 1670, and became a moderately active Member of the Cavalier Parliament. He was named to 81 committees, including the committee of elections and privileges in four sessions, acted as teller in nine divisions, and made six speeches. In his first session he was among those appointed to bring in bills to prevent the growth of Popery and to regulate the hearth-tax. During the debate of 22 Feb. 1673 he favoured a further address from the King to demand a speedy answer on the suspending power. He served on the committees which produced the test bill and prepared a bill of ease for dissenters, remarking that the renunciation of transubstantiation was a test that no Papist would endure, but presented no difficulties to any Protestant. When John Grobham Howe I* charged Speaker Seymour with calling the House a company of curs, and cited Hopkins as a witness,

> Mr Hopkins said indeed he had heard the words, but he took them but as raillery, to which he himself had given the occasion; for telling the Speaker that he was very nimble, and had started from his seat as quick as a hare from her form, the Speaker replied he had reason to do so, when such curs were at his heels.

Hopkins defended Lord Arlington in the 1674 session, acting as teller for candles on 19 Jan. so that the debate could continue to the minister's advantage. He was named to the committees on the bills for the relief of those detained under habeas corpus, the prevention of illegal exactions, and the settling of fees and powers in judges' patents, and was among those ordered to conduct an inquiry into the condition of Ireland.[3]

In the spring session of 1675 Hopkins was again concerned with measures to prevent illegal imprisonment and exactions, and on 21 May he was appointed to the committee on the bill to hinder Papists from sitting in Parliament. Sir Robert Holte* told Secretary Williamson ironically that he 'need not doubt of enjoying the good company of Mr [John] Swinfen* and Dick Hopkins' in the autumn session, and indeed he acted as teller for the Opposition against supply. He was among those to whom a petition from the London Weavers' Company against machinery and foreign competition was committed. During the long recess which followed, Lord Conway ineptly tried to curb Hopkins's hostility to the court through his father, but the latter demanded a judgeship, which Danby refused. Hopkins was marked 'thrice worthy' on Shaftesbury's list in 1677. He was named to the committee for the recall of British subjects from the French service and acted as teller for the appropriation clause in the bill for building warships. He was also appointed to the committee for the Protestant education of the royal children, and helped to draw up two addresses on foreign affairs. In the earlier sessions of 1678 he was among those entrusted with inquiring into the conviction of Quakers for recusancy, preparing reasons for a conference on the growth of Popery, summarizing foreign commitments, and drawing up the address for the removal of counsellors. He was appointed to the committees to consider the bills for wearing woollen cloth, requiring burial in wool, and preventing its export, and he also served on the committee to investigate the breach of parliamentary privilege involved in the printing and distribution of arguments against these measures. In the last session of the Cavalier Parliament he was named to the committees to inquire into the Popish Plot, to prepare reasons for believing in it, and to translate Coleman's letters.[4]

Hopkins was re-elected to the Exclusion Parliaments and marked 'worthy' on Shaftesbury's list. He was moderately active in 1679, with seven committees, of which the most important were to bring in a bill to regulate parliamentary elections, to consider the bills for the speedier conviction of recusants and security against Popery, to prepare an address for the removal of Lauderdale, and to inquire into the shipping of artillery. He voted for the committal of the first exclusion bill. An active Member of the second Exclusion Parliament, he was appointed to 13 committees, including those for the inquiries into abhorring and the judges' proceedings. He was also among those to whom the address insisting on exclusion, the bill for Protestant unity, and the repeal of the Corporations Act were committed. On 7 Jan. 1681 he urged the postponement of the debate on Laurence Hyde*. In the short Oxford Parliament he was named only to the committee of elections and privileges.[5]

Hopkins was among those who welcomed the Duke of Monmouth to Coventry in 1682, and after the Rye House Plot Thomas Lucy* searched his house for arms, finding four cases of pistols, a blunderbuss and a small gun. Hopkins bid Lucy disarm him at his peril, but he was left with only one case of pistols, and Secretary Jenkins wrote that Hopkins's 'language and confidence is much wondered at'. He was defeated in 1685, but in 1687 James II on his way to Banbury races held court at Hopkins's magnificent town house, rejecting an offer from the loyal Anglican Sir Thomas Norton*. It is not known whether he became a Whig collaborator, but it may be significant that he apparently did not stand in 1689. A court Whig under William III, he died on 1 Feb. 1708 in his 68th year and was buried in St. Michael's Coventry. His son Edward, who also sat for the borough as a Whig, described him in his epitaph as 'a tender husband, an indulgent father, a sincere friend, a devout Protestant, and a true, loyal patriot; of the latter he gave proofs in the several Parliaments in which for many years he represented this city'.[6]

[1] Soc. of Genealogists, Coventry St. Michael bishops' transcripts; C5/45/82; Lipscomb, *Bucks.* i. 377; PCC 62 Barrett. [2] Coventry RO, drapers' co. order bk. 1671–1777, ff. 3, 31, 129. [3] T. W. Whitley, *Parl. Rep. Coventry*, 105; PCC 62 Barrett; *CSP Dom.* 1671, p. 452; Grey, ii. 48–49, 86, 287; *Dering*, 153. [4] *CJ*, ix. 365, 392; *CSP Dom.* 1675–6, p. 323; SP16/522/18 (misplaced). [5] *HMC 12th Rep. IX*, 113. [6] *CSP Dom.* 1682, p. 429; Jan.–June 1683, pp. 362, 374; July–Sept. 1683, p. 26; B. Poole, *Coventry*, 140, 405; Add. 41803, f. 53; Coventry RO, council bk. 1635–96, ff. 342–4.

A.M.M.

HOPTON, Sir Edward (c.1603–68), of Canon Frome, Herefs.

HEREFORD   16 May–23 July 1661

b. c.1603, 2nd s. and h. of Sir Richard Hopton of Rockhill by Elizabeth, da. of John Hopton, merchant, of Southampton and h. to her uncle Michael Hopton, merchant, of London and Canon Frome. *educ.* Shrewsbury 1614. *m.* (1) c.1625, *s.p.*; (2) 1654, Deborah, da. of Robert Hatton of Thames Ditton, Surr., wid. of Isaac Jones, Merchant Taylor of London and Petersham, Surr., 6s. (4 *d.v.p.*) 2da. Kntd. 4 June 1645; *suc.* fa. 1653.[1]

Yeoman of the stirrup 1634–?46; lt.-col. of ft. (royalist) 1643–4, col. 1644–6; gent. pensioner June 1660–*d.*[2]

Commr. for oyer and terminer, Oxford circuit July 1660; j.p. Herefs. July 1660–*d.*, dep. lt. c. Aug. 1660–*d.*, commr. for assessment Aug. 1660–*d.*, lt.-col. of militia ft. c. Oct. 1660–*d.*, commr. for loyal and indigent officers 1662.

Although Hopton claimed descent in the male line from the 12th-century Shropshire family (to which his mother unquestionably belonged), the Herefordshire Hoptons, who can be traced back to 1408, were of little account until Sir Richard, described as an usurer, acquired the ex-monastic estate of Canon Frome by marriage. They were quite unrelated to Sir Ralph Hopton†, the Cavalier general, and his forebears in Suffolk and Somerset. Hopton was bred a merchant, like most younger sons of the family, and entered the service of the East India Company as a purser's mate at Surat. From this lowly employment he was recalled in 1625 by his father, who had determined to disinherit his elder brother for marrying beneath him. Hopton seems to have escaped from an extremely difficult parent, first to a very humble court appointment, and then, after his first wife's death, to Ireland, perhaps as an army officer. His father was described by Henry Lingen* as the ringleader of the opposition to ship-money in the county, and during the Civil War favoured Parliament, though on 16 May 1643 he sued out a pardon at Oxford for all offences committed since the beginning of 1636. Two of Hopton's younger brothers served with distinction in the local parliamentary forces, but Hopton himself fought under his namesake in the King's army. He was second-in-command to Sir Matthew Appleyard* at the battle of Cheriton. He took care to keep well clear of Herefordshire during the war, though this did not save him from furious letters from his father when the local Royalists sequestrated the property. The old man, who had retained a power of revocation over the settlement of his estate, lived just long enough to free Hopton from liability to compound for his inheritance, valued at £1,500 p.a. With his brothers, he bought off the claim of his elder brother's son Richard for £4,000.[3]

Hopton lived in Surrey after his second marriage, and was accused of complicity in the local Cavalier movement there in 1659. At the Restoration he was proposed as a knight of the Royal Oak. His annual income was said to be £2,500, almost certainly an exaggeration. The Herefordshire Hoptons had no parliamentary tradition, though one of the Shropshire family had come south to sit for the county in 1305. But Hopton was prepared to contest a very expensive election in 1661, presumably in order to resist the revival of his nephew's claim to the Canon Frome estate. He was warmly supported by his father's old enemy Lingen, and the mayor was induced to make an obviously false return. He was allowed to take his seat on 16 May, but was named to no committees before the election was declared void two months later. It is improbable that he stood again, though he remained an active deputy lieutenant. When Richard Hopton introduced his bill into the Upper House in 1666, Hopton was compelled to the expense of retaining as counsel Heneage Finch* whose eloquence prevailed on the Lords to reject it. He died on 1 Apr. 1668. His grandson represented the county as a Tory in the first Parliament of George I.[4]

[1] M. Hopton, *Froma Canonnica*, 24, 53–54, 75; E. Calvert, *Shrewsbury Sch. Reg.* 242; Manning and Bray, *Surr.* i. 415. [2] Hopton, 32, 46, 57, 75; *Symonds Diary* (Cam. Soc. lxxiv), 196; *Bellum Civile* (Som. Rec. Soc. xviii), 81; Beaufort mss 600.2 (clerk of the cheque's bk.); *Trans. Woolhope Field Club*, xxxiv. 292. [3] *CSP Col.* (*E. Indies*), i. 503; ii. 17; iii. 16; W. Foster, *English Factories in India*, ii. 280, 294, 325; *CSP Dom.* 1637–8, p. 511; W. H. Black, *Docquets of Letters Patent*, 37. [4] *Cal. Comm. Comp.* 3249; *CSP Dom.* 1663–4, p. 454; Hopton, 66–75; *LJ*, xii. 7, 9, 27.

E.R.

HORDE, Thomas (1625–1715), of Cote, Bampton, Oxon.

OXFORDSHIRE   1679 (Oct.), 1681

b. 26 July 1625, 1st s. of Sir Thomas Horde of Cote by 1st w. Frances, da. of Sir Thomas Gardiner of Peckham, Surr. *m.* (1) by 1653, Barbara (*d.* 12 Aug. 1671), da. of Charles Trinder of Holwell, Oxon., wid. of William Rainton of Shilton, Berks., 5s. (4 *d.v.p.*) 7da.; (2) 22 Sept. 1673, Susannah (*d.* 12 Aug. 1680), da. of Sir Erasmus de la Fontaine of Kirby Bellars, Leics., 2da.; (3) bef. 1686, Mary (*d.*1717), da. of Jonathan Barford of Tooley Park, Leics., wid. of Paul Castelman of Coberley, Glos., *s.p. suc.* fa. 1663.[1]

Commr. for assessment, Oxon. Jan. 1660–80, Berks. 1679–80, Berks. and Oxon. 1689–90, militia, Oxon. Mar. 1660; j.p. Oxon. Mar. 1660–80, Feb. 1688–?*d.*, Berks. 1689–?*d.*; freeman, Oxford Sept. 1660; dep. lt. Oxon. Feb. 1688–1702.[2]

Horde claimed descent from a Shropshire family which first sent Members to Parliament in 1391. His great-grandfather, a London merchant, purchased Cote manor in 1553. The family took no known part in the Civil Wars; but Horde apparently came under suspicion in 1659 when a letter of his to Lord Falkland (Henry Carey*) was submitted for examination.[3]

Horde was a neighbour of (Sir) William Coventry*, who obtained for one of his younger sons a post in the dockyard at Chatham, and may have contributed to his political education, though they differed over exclusion. Horde did not stand in February 1679, but he was returned at the top of

the poll for the county at the contested election of August. In January 1680 he supported the petition for the meeting of the second Exclusion Parliament and was removed from local office. He made no speeches, but was moderately active as a committeeman, serving on four committees, including those to inquire into abhorring and to repeal the Corporations Act. Re-elected with Shaftesbury's approval after a lengthy poll, he was totally inactive in 1681. He lost his seat in 1685, and on Monmouth's invasion he was imprisoned for a time in Oxford Castle. He was presumably a Whig collaborator, being appointed to local office in February 1688. Again unsuccessful for the county in 1689 and for the city in 1690, he seems then to have retired from politics. His estate brought him in £648 p.a. about this time, and his investments another £500 or more. Although Wood described him as 'a most ill-natured man and of no religion', his will was markedly Protestant in tone, and he endowed charities for the benefit of debtors imprisoned in Oxford, including provision for an Anglican chaplain, for clothing the poor on his estate, and for teaching 20 poor children 'to read English until they can perfectly read the Bible'. He died on 6 Nov. 1715 and was buried at Bampton, the sole member of the Oxfordshire line to sit in Parliament.[4]

[1] A. H. Hord, *Hord Fam.* 26–28, 37–38; *Par. Colls.* (Oxf. Rec. Soc. ii), 18; *Top. and Gen.* i. 36; PCC 73 Fox; *Vis. Glos.* ed. Fenwick and Metcalfe, 37. [2] *Oxford Council Acts* (Oxf. Hist. Soc. xcv), 267. [3] *Top. and Gen.* i. 35–36; ii. 519; *CSP Dom.* 1659–60, p. 242. [4] *Gent. Mag.* n.s. xxxii. 594; *Wood's Life and Times* (Oxf. Hist. Soc. xxi), 476, 519, 544; (xxvi), 136, 145, 325; Bodl. Locke mss, CT/76; PCC 73 Fox; J. A. Giles, *Hist. Bampton*, pp. xciv–xcv; Hord, 26.

L.N./G.J.

HORNER, George I (1605–77), of Cloford, Som.

SOMERSET   2 Dec. 1645–2 June 1646, 13 July 1646,[1] 1660

bap. 3 Mar. 1605, 1st s. of Sir John Horner† of Mells by Anne, da. of Sir George Speke of White Lackington. *educ.* Lincoln, Oxf. 1623; L. Inn 1626, called 1633. *m.* Anne, da. of Sir Neville Poole† of Oaksey, Wilts., 4s. (1 *d.v.p.*) 4da. *suc.* fa. 1659; kntd. 25 June 1660.[2]

Commr. for assessment, Som. 1647–8, Aug. 1660–74, militia 1648, Mar. 1660, j.p. 1648–?9, Mar. 1660–*d.*; elder, Wells classis 1648; dep. lt. Som. June 1660–*d.*, commr. for sewers Aug., Dec. 1660, sheriff 1667–8, commr. for recusants 1675.[3]

Horner's family had been settled in Somerset since early in the 15th century, and at the dissolution of the monasteries picked the plum estate of Mells out of the monastic pie, a feat commemorated in the well-known nursery rhyme. His grandfather sat for the county in two Elizabethan Parliaments, and his father was one of the most active of the parliamentarian gentry during the Civil War. But Horner himself, though a Presbyterian, was described as 'a known neuter, if not worse', when he was elected as a recruiter. He took no part in politics during the Interregnum, and was regarded as a Royalist in 1659.[4]

Horner was returned for Somerset at the general election of 1660, and marked by Lord Wharton as a friend. Doubtless a court supporter, he was rewarded with a knighthood. He was named to no committees in the Convention, but on 28 July urged legislation to reduce the maximum rate of interest to 6 per cent. He is not likely to have stood again, and when he was pricked as sheriff in 1667, he was allowed to execute his office by deputy owing to ill health. He died on 9 Feb. 1677 and was buried at Cloford.[5]

[1] Did not sit after Pride's Purge, 6 Dec. 1648, readmitted 21 Feb. 1660. [2] Hutchins, *Dorset*, ii. 667; *Misc. Gen. et Her.* (n.s.) iv. 162–4. [3] *Q. Sess. Recs.* (Som. Rec. Soc. xxxiv), p. xiii; W. Prynne, *County of Som. Divided into Classes*, 7; Som. RO, Popham mss 167. [4] Collinson, *Som.* ii. 463; D. Underdown, *Som. in the Civil War*, 130; *CSP Dom.* 1659–60, p. 264. [5] Bowman diary, f. 102; *CSP Dom.* 1667–8, p. 244; Collinson, *Som.* ii. 206.

M.W.H./I.C.

HORNER, George II (1646–1707), of Mells, Som.

SOMERSET 1685, 1689

b. 1646, 2nd but 1st surv. s. of (Sir) George Horner I*. *educ.* L. Inn 1663. *m.* Elizabeth (*d.* 5 Sept. 1693), da. of Robert Fortescue of Buckland Filleigh, Devon, 3s. (1 *d.v.p.*) 4da. *suc.* fa. 1677.[1]

Commr. for assessment, Som. 1673–80, 1689–90, j.p. 1675–Feb. 1688, Oct. 1688–*d.*, lt.-col. of militia ft. by 1679, col. by 1681–?87, sheriff 1680–1, dep. lt. 1680–7, 1689–*d.*[2]

Horner opposed exclusion, and in 1681 it was reported that his militia regiment had been earmarked by the 'fanatics' for a more sympathetic commander. He was returned for the county in 1685, but left no trace on the records of James II's Parliament. He refused his consent to the repeal of the Test Act and Penal Laws and was deprived of local office. But he signed the Somerset declaration in favour of the Prince of Orange and was re-elected to the Convention. He was again entirely inactive, and is not recorded as voting to agree with the Lords on the abdication. He was given leave of absence on 6 Dec. 1689 and probably never stood again. He died on 11 Mar. 1707 and was buried at Mells. His son was returned for the county as a Tory in 1713 and 1727.[3]

[1] Hutchins, *Dorset*, ii. 667; Collinson, *Som.* ii. 464. [2] *Q. Sess. Recs.* (Som. Rec. Soc. xxxiv), p. xiii; *CSP Dom.* 1679–80, p. 62; 1680–1, p. 352. [3] *CSP Dom.* 1680–1, p. 352; E. Green, *March of Wm. of Orange through Som.*, 57–58.

I.C.

HOSKYNS, Sir John, 2nd Bt. (1634–1705), of Harewood, Herefs.

HEREFORDSHIRE 1685

b. 23 July 1634, 1st s. of Sir Bennet Hoskyns†, 1st Bt., of Harewood, by 1st w. Anne, da. of Sir John Bingley of Templecombe, Som. *educ.* Westminster; M. Temple, entered 1647, called 1653; Christ Church, Oxf. 1650. *m.* lic. 29 Aug. 1671, Jane, da. of Sir Gabriel Lowe of Newark, Ozleworth, Glos., 7s. (1 *d.v.p.*) 3da. Kntd. 24 Jan. 1676; *suc.* fa. 10 Feb. 1680.[1]

Commr. for assessment, Herefs. 1665–80, 1689–90; freeman, Lymington 1667; bencher, M. Temple 1671; j.p. Herefs. 1673–*d.*, dep. lt. 1683–9, 1691–*d.*[2]

Master in Chancery 1676–1703.[3]

FRS 1663–*d.*, pres. 1682–3, sec. 1685–7.

Hoskyns was descended from a substantial yeoman family which in Tudor times leased the demesnes of the Herefordshire manor of Monnington-on-Wye. His grandfather John Hoskins, the eminent Jacobean lawyer and wit, sat for Hereford in three Parliaments, and incurred the wrath of James I by a reference to Scottish favourites in 1614. His father, a Presbyterian, served for the same constituency as a recruiter until Pride's Purge and again under the Protectorate. He withdrew from public life at the Restoration, but was created a baronet in 1676.[4]

Hoskyns inherited the legal and intellectual tastes of his grandfather, his chief interests being 'philosophy and experiments'. His membership of the Rota Club, with its radical political tone, was a youthful indiscretion, but he was prominent in the Royal Society. 'One of the most hard-favoured men of his time ... his visage was not more awkward than his dress, so that, going, as his use was, on foot with his staff and an old hat over his eyes, he might be taken rather for a sorry quack than, as he was, a bright virtuoso.' As master in Chancery, his record was 'proof example that the office might be executed with integrity'. He helped to present a loyal address from Herefordshire approving the dissolution of Parliament in 1681, and attended a meeting of the Tory gentry at Holme Lacy in the following year. Returned unopposed for the county in 1685, he was a very active Member of James II's Parliament. His 23 committees included the committee of elections and privileges; but the most important were to take the disbandment accounts and to consider the general naturalization of Huguenot refugees. He was also concerned with four measures of legal reform: for the suppression of clandestine marriages, the amendment of the bankruptcy laws, the establishment of a land registry and the amelioration of the condition of insolvent debtors. He was chairman of the committee to establish a water supply for Rochester and Chat-

ham. There is no indication that he attended the
turbulent second session, and he does not seem to
have stood again.[5]

On the proposed repeal of the Test Act and Penal
Laws, the Duke of Beaufort (Henry Somerset*)
wrote to Hoskyns that 'his mind, I suppose, is
known to the King'. He was one of the three candidates for Herefordshire approved by Sunderland
in his letter of 13 July 1688, and he was retained in
county office. But he was not much affected by the
Revolution; he was soon restored to the lieutenancy
and his rights in Ascension Island (granted in 1684)
were confirmed. He died on 12 Sept. 1705 and was
buried at Harewood. His younger son, the 4th
baronet, sat for the county as a Whig from 1717 to
1722.[6]

[1] C. J. Robinson, *Mansions and Manors of Herefs.* 133. [2] C. St.
Barbe, *Recs. of Lymington*, 9; BL Loan 29/141, Sir Edward to
Robert Harley, 4 Aug. 1691. [3] T. D. Hardy, *Principal Officers of
Chancery*, 95. [4] *DNB.* [5] Aubrey, *Brief Lives*, i. 290, 294; North,
Lives, i. 372; *London Gazette*, 11 Sept. 1681; *CSP Dom.* 1682, p.
291; *CJ*, ix. 744. [6] Bodl. Carte 130, f. 24; *CSP Col.* 1681–5, p.
580; 1693–6, p. 218.

E.R.

HOSTE, James (1633–99), of Wood Hall, Sand-
ringham, Norf.

CASTLE RISING   1679 (Mar.), 1679 (Oct.), 1681

bap. 11 Aug. 1633, 2nd but 1st surv. s. of Theodore (Dier-
ick) Hoste, merchant, of Pudding Lane, London and
Mortlake, Surr. by Jane, da. of James Desmaistres,
Brewer, of Pudding Lane, London. *m.* 27 Apr. 1658
(with £2,000), Elizabeth, da. of Edmund Sleigh,
Mercer, of London, 1s. 3da. *suc.* fa. 1663.[1]

J.p. Norf. 1676–87, by 1690–?*d.*, commr. for assessment 1677–80, 1689–90.[2]

On both sides Hoste was of Protestant refugee
descent. His paternal grandfather fled from Flanders in 1568 and introduced the bleaching industry
to Surrey. His father was an elder in the Dutch
church, in which he was baptized, but as a merchant
stranger took no part in English politics, though he
was nominated to the London corporation for the
poor by the Rump. Hoste was apprenticed to his
other grandfather as a brewer, but probably did
not serve out his time. By 1676 he had bought
a Norfolk estate, valued at £2,000 p.a., and conformed to the Church of England. 'Well-beloved'
in the neighbourhood, he was returned for Castle
Rising, five miles from his home, to the three
Exclusion Parliaments. Lord Yarmouth (Robert
Paston I*), who frequently visited him, hoped that
he would support the Government, but Shaftesbury
marked him 'honest', and he voted for the bill.
Otherwise he left no trace on the records of Parliament. To Yarmouth's surprise, he signed the

loyal address abhorring the 'Association' in 1682,
and was not removed from the commission of
the peace until 1687. He was restored after the
Revolution, but did not stand again, though his son,
who married a sister of Robert Walpole*, was active
as a militia officer against the local Jacobites. He
'shot himself through the head with a pistol in his
closet', and was buried at Sandringham on 30 July
1699. His grandson sat for Bramber on the government interest from 1728 to 1734.[3]

[1] *Reg. Dutch Church Austin Friars*, 35; *Vis. London* (Harl. Soc.
xv), 395; *Inhabitants of London in 1638* ed. Dale, 102; *Mortlake
Par. Reg.* 22–27, 46, 72; *Vis. Surr.* (Harl. Soc. lx), 61. [2] *Norf.
Ltcy. Jnl.* (Norf. Rec. Soc. xxx), 115. [3] W. Rye, *Norf. Fams.* 366;
VCH Surr. ii. 368; J. H. Hessels, *Ecclesiae Londino-Batavae Arch-
ivum*, iii. 2277, 2463; Guildhall Lib. mss 5445/17; Blomefield,
Norf. ix. 569; *Works of Sir Thomas Browne* ed. Wilkins, i. 233;
CSP Dom. 1679–80, p. 66; Add. 36988, ff. 180, 182; *Norf. Ltcy.
Jnl.* 120; Luttrell, iv. 544.

P.W.

HOTHAM, Sir John, 2nd Bt. (1632–89), of Scor-
borough, Yorks.

BEVERLEY   1660, 1661, 1679 (Mar.), 1679 (Oct.),
1681, 11 Jan.–Mar. 1689

bap. 21 Mar. 1632, 1st s. of John Hotham[†] (*d.* 1645) by 1st
w. Frances, da. of Sir John Wray, 2nd Bt.[†], of Glentworth, Lincs. *educ.* Peterhouse, Camb. 1648. *m.* 8 Aug.
1650, Elizabeth, da. of Sapcote, 2nd Visct. Beaumont
of Swords [I], of Cole Orton, Leics., 4s. (2 *d.v.p.*) 3da.
suc. gdfa. 2 Jan. 1645.[1]

J.p. Beverley 1657, Yorks. (N. and E. Ridings) July
1660–70; commr. for militia, Yorks. Mar. 1660; col. of
militia horse (E. Riding) Apr. 1660–1, custos rot. July
1660–70; commr. for assessment (E. Riding) Aug.
1660–80, 1689, (N. Riding) 1661–80; dep. lt. (E. Riding)
c. Aug. 1660–?79, commr. for sewers Sept. 1660, corporations, Yorks. 1662–3, concealments 1671, recusants
(E. Riding) 1675; gov. Kingston-upon-Hull Jan. 1689–
d.[2]

Hotham's ancestors had been seated at Scorborough, four miles north of Beverley, since the 12th
century, and first represented the borough in 1307.
His father and grandfather initially supported Parliament during the Civil War, but were executed in
1645 for attempting to betray Hull to the Cavaliers.
The Scorborough estate, valued at £2,000 per
annum, was restored to Hotham without composition. He signed the Yorkshire petition for a free
Parliament in February 1660, and at the general
election he was returned for Beverley after promising to serve at his own charge. He continued to
represent the borough for the rest of his life, except
in James II's Parliament. An inactive Member of
the Convention, he was named only to the committees for cancelling all grants of titles and offices
since May 1642, for nominating commissioners of
sewers, and for inquiring into presentations to

crown livings. He obtained leave to go into the country on 20 Aug., and may not have attended the second session. His sympathies were probably with the Opposition, but he is unlikely to have opposed the Court on major issues, since he was appointed custos of the East Riding.[3]

Hotham was moderately active in the Cavalier Parliament with 133 committees, including the committee of elections and privileges in 12 sessions, six tellerships, and about 40 recorded speeches. He was among those ordered to devise remedies for the meetings of sectaries on 29 Apr. 1663; but in August he was implicated in the Yorkshire plot, and briefly imprisoned. He was appointed to the committee for the conventicles bill in the next session, but thereafter his activity declined, and he twice defaulted on calls of the House. He was removed from the commission of the peace in 1670, presumably as an opponent of persecution, and became much more active at Westminster. He was teller against supply on 17 Feb. and for the prohibition of foreign brandy a fortnight later, and was named to the committee of 3 Mar. on the bill to prevent the transportation of English prisoners overseas. After (Sir) Thomas Clarges* had given the House an account of the assault on Sir John Coventry*, 'Sir John Hotham began with an invective against the thing, but moved not what to do in it, but only to wreak our vengeance upon the assassins that had done this foul and horrid act'. He was added to the committee for drafting a bill to prevent the growth of Popery on 8 Feb. 1671, and acted as teller against a Lords proviso to the subsidy bill.[4]

Hotham gave voice to the impatience of the House on 22 Feb. 1673 at the delay in the King's reply to their address against the suspending power. In the autumn session he was among those charged with preparing an address against the Duke of York's marriage to the Roman Catholic Mary of Modena and with bringing in a general test bill to distinguish between Protestants and Papists. He hoped to ensure the disbandment of the newly-raised forces by a resolution against any further supply. He spoke repeatedly against a standing army, which he described as 'the monster that will devour all your liberties and properties'. In 1674 he was appointed to the committees to prevent illegal exactions, to inquire into the condition of Ireland, to prescribe the fees and powers in judges' patents, and to reform the collection of hearth-tax. In the spring session of 1675 he was named to committees to prevent the export of wool and to draw up a bill for suppressing the growth of Popery. In the debates on Danby's conduct of the Treasury he moved for some of the revenue to be appropriated

to the use of the navy, and suggested that the office was too big to be entrusted to a single man. He acted as teller against adjourning the debate on Lauderdale on 4 May, and was appointed to the committees to draft an address for the recall of British subjects from the service of France, and to consider the bill for hindering Papists from sitting in Parliament. In the autumn session he was named to the committee for the appropriation bill. After the government victory of 26 Oct. on supply, Hotham's allegation that several Members had been 'taken off' was so ill received by Sir Philip Musgrave* and others that, had he 'not explained himself very nicely, he would have been called to the bar'. Quite undaunted, he went on to support an inquiry into the government whip, and was named to the committee to devise a test to be taken by Members against corruption. He helped to manage a conference on the bill of recall from the French service, to draft an address on the failure to apprehend the violent Jesuit St. Germain, and to prepare reasons for avoiding the revival of differences between the Houses.[5]

Shaftesbury classed Hotham as 'thrice worthy' in 1677, when he acted as teller on the third reading for a bill to prevent frauds and abuses in the import of Irish cattle, and helped to draw up an address promising a credit of £200,000. 'None of my estate or blood shall be spared in this matter', he said, though he did not fail to remind the House of the resolution against a standing army. After stressing the need 'to abate the pride, assuage the malice, and confound the devices of the King of France', he was among those ordered to draw up an address for an alliance for this purpose. On 29 Jan. 1678 he helped to draw up another address requiring France to withdraw from all territories acquired since the Peace of the Pyrenees in 1659. He seconded the 'very worthy motion' of the Hon. William Russell* on 14 Mar. 'of going into a grand committee to consider the deplorable condition we are in'. He was twice among those appointed to prepare reasons for remedies to prevent the growth of Popery, and it was on his motion that the committee continued to sit during the April recess. When the House met again, he led the demand for the terms of the alliances, and he agreed with the sharp criticism of John Birch* that 'the leagues are not pursuant to our address, and are not for the good of the nation'. He supported a motion that any ministers who opposed the address for an alliance against France 'may be judged as enemies', and on 7 May he made a strong attack on Lauderdale:

Since I see Lauderdale pursues to act what he hath formerly advised, I am for removing him. I hear it said that Lauderdale is a true churchman and I know not what; and yet he is a man of no morality. I wonder the Church is not ashamed of such a proselyte. ... In Scotland if any man looks but discontented, then kill him, shoot him, eat him up! Will you have him do the same thing here? Are we weary of our properties? ... I am against an adjournment till this question be put off our hands for removing Lauderdale. ... I am a York-shireman (neighbour to Scotland), and there they fear the very looks of Lauderdale, that he should bring his army with him.

He was appointed to the committee to prepare the address demanding the removal of counsellors. When (Sir) Joseph Williamson* sought to obtain a grant of supply by surprise, Hotham commented: 'If these pranks go on, we shall be reduced to slavery'. After the Popish Plot he was appointed to the committees to prepare instructions for disbanding the army and to draw up an address protesting against private advices. He moved for the impeachment of the five popish lords. He was noted by Barillon as in receipt of a French bribe of 300 guineas.[6]

A very active Member of the first Exclusion Parliament, Hotham was appointed to 17 committees, including the elections committee, and those to take the disbandment accounts, to extend habeas corpus, and to provide for the speedier conviction of popish recusants. Shaftesbury marked him 'worthy', and he made six speeches. On 17 Apr. 1679 he moved that money voted for disbanding the army should not be placed in the Exchequer lest it should be directed to other uses. He was a member of the committee of 6 May to prepare the address to the King for the removal of Lauderdale, and two weeks later voted in support of the first exclusion bill. He showed great eagerness to exploit the revelations about the misuse of secret service payments, and was one of the party of Members to accompany (Sir) Stephen Fox* in his enforced visit to Whitehall for the books. A member of the committee of inquiry into the state of the navy, he was able to assure the House, on the authority of Titus Oates, that one of the servants of Samuel Pepys* was a Jesuit. Together with William Harbord* he made repeated visits to Pepys's discharged butler to obtain signed depositions against his former master.[7]

Hotham was even more active in the second Exclusion Parliament, with 26 committee appointments and 11 speeches, thus earning inclusion by Barillon among the most considerable Members of the Lower House. He was named to the elections committee and the committee of inquiry into abhorring, moving for the expulsion of Sir Robert

Cann* for publicly denying the existence of the Popish Plot. He was also among those ordered to bring in the second exclusion bill and a bill for uniting Protestants. After its rejection by the Lords Hotham broke the prolonged silence in the Commons by saying:

If the wisdom of this House has turned the affairs of Christendom, they have shown it particularly in the bill for excluding the Duke. Our only wisdom now is to preserve our wives and children, estates and religion and all that is dear to us. If these are not arguments to persuade gentlemen, I cannot hear better to be spoken to, nor do I know what to propose. But if it fare with other men as with me, I am not able to utter anything to secure us after this defeat of the bill. But yet I would not lose courage, but rally up our thoughts, and the way to consider well what to do is to adjourn till to-morrow, and let every man lay his hand upon his heart, and consider what to propose by that time.

Later in the day he urged the removal of Lord Halifax from the Privy Council as 'the great occasion of throwing out this bill'. On 13 Dec. he declared: 'I think there is not a Papist of quality in England but is guilty of cutting all your throats', and he was among those appointed to bring in bills to associate all Protestant subjects on the Elizabethan model, and for security against arbitrary power. He helped to prepare the address insisting on exclusion, and was named to the committee for the repeal of the Corporations Act. In the Oxford Parliament he was again named to the elections committee, and on 24 Mar. 1681 proposed that the resolutions of the House, with the rest of their proceedings, should be printed. He was among those ordered to prepare for a conference on the loss of the bill to repeal the Elizabethan statute against Protestant nonconformists.[8]

Hotham was implicated in Monmouth's confession after the Rye House Plot, but no action was taken against him. He quarrelled with the corporation of Beverley, and was defeated by Sir Ralph Warton* at the general election of 1685. His petition was never reported. Danby included him among the Opposition, and in 1687 he fled to Holland. Returning with the Prince of Orange in November 1688, he and Harbord showed much anxiety lest their electoral interest should have suffered from their absence. But he was invited to stand for Hull and Beverley, and was returned for the latter constituency both at the abortive election and at the general election of 1689. He played no known part in the Convention, and returned to Yorkshire after the coronation as governor of Hull. The bitter winter weather proved too much for him, however, and he was buried at South Dalton on 29 Mar. 1689.[9]

[1] Clay, *Dugdale's Vis. Yorks.* iii. 263. [2] Stowe 744, f. 4v; C181/7/44; *HMC 8th Rep.* pt. 1 (1881), 275; *Cal. Treas. Bks.* iii. 912; J. Tickell, *Kingston-upon-Hull*, 586. [3] A. M. W. Stirling, *The Hothams*, i. 20, 100; P. Saltmarshe, *Hothams of Scorborough*, 178–84; Keeler, *Long Parl.* 222–3; *Beverley Bor. Recs.* (Yorks. Arch. Soc. rec. ser. lxxxiv), 103. [4] *Reresby Mems.* 47; *CJ*, viii. 663; ix. 49, 123, 130, 210; *Dering*, 44. [5] *Dering*, 128; Grey, ii. 205–6, 390–1; iii. 36, 367; Eg. 3345, f. 34v; *Bulstrode Pprs.* 320; *CJ*, ix. 372. [6] *CJ*, ix. 415, 424; Eg. 3345, ff. 47v, 50v; Grey, iv. 364; v. 225, 273, 280, 322, 332–3, 359–60, 384; vi. 320; *Dalrymple Mems.* i. 382. [7] Grey, vii. 119, 305; *CJ*, ix. 629. [8] PRO 31/3, bdle. 146, f. 28; Grey, vii. 382; viii. 4, 30, 129, 292–3; *HMC Ormonde*, n.s. v. 496–7; Clarke, *Jas. II*, i. 619. [9] Clarke, i. 742; *CSP Dom.* July–Sept. 1683, p. 173; *Beverley Bor. Recs.* 108, 170–2; *CJ*, ix. 723; Stirling, 103–4; *Reresby Mems.* 525; *Clarendon Corresp.* ii. 219; Saltmarshe, 183–4.

P.A.B./P.W.

HOTHAM, Sir John, 3rd Bt. (1655–91), of Scorborough, Yorks.

BEVERLEY 7 May 1689

b. 2 Aug. 1655, 1st s. of Sir John Hotham, 2nd Bt.* *m.* 5 Feb. 1679, Catherine, da. and h. of John Heron, merchant, of Beverley, Yorks., *s.p. suc.* fa. Mar. 1689.[1]

Commr. for assessment, Yorks. (E. Riding) 1679–80, (E. and N. Ridings) 1689–90, j.p. (E. Riding) 1689–*d.*

Hotham's marriage alienated him from his parents, although the bride brought him property worth £300 p.a. and £2,000 in cash. Presumably a Whig collaborator, he was recommended to the King for the East Riding bench in 1688. In May 1689 he was returned for Beverley at the by-election caused by his father's death, but the House allowed him leave of absence on 23 July and he proved to be a totally inactive Member of the Convention. He did not stand again, and died suddenly in Amsterdam on 25 Aug. 1691. His cousin and heir, Sir Charles Hotham, sat for Scarborough and Beverley as a Whig from 1695 till his death in 1723.[2]

[1] Clay, *Dugdale's Vis. Yorks.* iii. 263; P. Saltmarshe, *The Hothams of Scorborough*, 188. [2] Saltmarshe, 186, 188–90; A.M.W. Stirling, *The Hothams*, 111–13.

P.A.B./P.W.

HOUGHTON, Lord see HOLLES, Gilbert and John

HOUGHTON, Sir Charles see HOGHTON

HOVELL, Sir William (c.1637–70), of Hillington Hall, Norf.

KING'S LYNN 1661–4 Mar. 1670

b. c.1637, o.s. of Sir Richard Hovell of Hillington by Dorothy, da. of Sir Thomas Chicheley† of Wimpole, Cambs. *educ.* Wimpole (Mr Bagg); Caius, Camb. matric. 10 Oct. 1649, aged 12, BA 1654; G. Inn 1655. *m.* 29 Apr. 1661, Ethelreda, da. and h. of Thomas Lilley, merchant, of South Lynn, Norf., 3s. (2 *d.v.p.*) 3da. *suc.* fa. 1654. Kntd. 5 June 1660.[1]

J.p. Norf. July 1660–*d.*, commr. for assessment Aug. 1660–9, maj. of militia horse Oct. 1660–?*d.*; freeman, King's Lynn 1661; commr. for sewers, Bedford level 1663.[2]

Capt. of ft. regt. of Lord Townshend (Sir Horatio Townshend*) 1667.

Hovell's grandfather purchased the manor of Hillington, seven miles from Lynn, in 1610. His father was one of the Royalists who occupied the town in 1643 and escaped without penalty on the terms signed by the parliamentary commander, the Earl of Manchester. Hovell himself was knighted at the Restoration, and was returned for Lynn at the general election of 1661 as a court supporter, probably through the influence of his father-in-law, one of the chief merchants in the town. He was not an active Member of the Cavalier Parliament, but he served under Townshend in the invasion scare during the second Dutch war, and may have gone into opposition. His first appearance in the Journals was as an additional member of the committee of elections and privileges in the next session, and he was also appointed to a private bill committee in the month before his death. He died on 4 Mar. 1670, and was buried at Hillington. A posthumous son failed to survive infancy, and no other member of the family entered Parliament.[3]

[1] *Vis. Norf.* (Harl. Soc. lxxxv), 22. [2] *Cal. Treas. Bks.* i. 77; *Lynn Freemen*, 170. [3] Blomefield, *Norf.* viii. 456; W. Richards, *Hist. Lynn*, 754–7; *Cal. Comm. Comp.* 2891; *Blomefield's Norf. Supp.* ed. Ingleby, 181; J. J. Muskett, *Suff. Man. Fams.* ii. 36.

E.C.

HOW, Sir Richard (c.1638–83), of Paris Garden, Southwark, Surr.

SOUTHWARK 1679 (Mar.), 1679 (Oct.), 1681

b. c.1638, o.s. of James How, woodmonger, of Paris Garden by w. Anne Haile. *m.* (1) 25 Aug. 1663, Anne Hart of Southwark, 1s. 2da.; (2) lic. 18 June 1678, aged 40, Sarah (*d.* 7 Apr. 1706), wid. of William Lewington of Lambeth, and of John Hill, Fishmonger, of London, *s.p. suc.* fa. 1667; kntd. 28 Oct. 1677.[1]

Member, Woodmongers' Co. c.1660; capt. of militia ft. Southwark Apr. 1660, maj. by 1672, col. 1681–*d.*; commr. for assessment, Southwark 1667–9, Surr. 1673–80, London 1679–80; alderman, London 11–25 June 1668, 1682–*d.*, sheriff 1678–9; member, Fishmongers' Co. 1669, prime warden 1680; j.p. Surr. 1670–*d.*; dep. lt. Mdx. and Southwark by 1672–*d.*; member, Eastland Co. 1672; commr. for recusants, Surr. 1675, rebuilding of Southwark 1677.[2]

How's father was born in the Forest of Dean, but he had settled on Bankside by 1613, and from 1622 his name figures regularly in the accounts of Paris Garden as scavenger, overseer of the poor, and coal-merchant. He was nominated by the Rump as militia commissioner in 1649, but seems to have avoided political commitment. How himself, as one of the churchwardens of St. Saviour's, strove to maintain control of the clergy, and in 1664 he was committed to the Fleet by the Privy Council for beating the afternoon lecturer and ejecting him from the pulpit in full view of a congregation of six thousand. He fined off for alderman of London in 1668, but when the new parish of Christ Church was created by Act of Parliament in 1670 he paid for a gallery in the church. He was made a county magistrate, and in view of his 'interest among the people' Joseph Williamson* suggested asking for his assistance in putting down conventicles in Southwark. In the business world he was best known as a fishmonger 'to be found every morning at Billingsgate', but he was also a lighterman and ship-owner, and he prospered sufficiently to allow each of his daughters a £4,500 portion. Described to the Government as 'active and honest' in 1672, he was knighted six years later, although still refusing municipal office.[3]

How represented Southwark in the three Exclusion Parliaments, and was initially classed by Shaftesbury as 'honest'. According to Roger Morrice he voted for the first exclusion bill, but the official list puts him in the opposite lobby, and this is more probably correct, for he enjoyed court support in the October election, and in the same month acted as one of the stewards at the feast of the artillery company held in honour of the Duke of York. His only committee was in the second Exclusion Parliament, when he was among those to whom a Surrey petition against the ecclesiastical courts was referred. Cries of 'no abhorrers' greeted How and Peter Rich* at the hustings in 1681, but they were re-elected. He stood unsuccessfully as court candidate for alderman of Bishopsgate ward in September. He helped Rich to suppress conventicles in Southwark, and in March 1682 he sat on the jury which fined Thomas Pilkington* £800 in an action of scandalum magnatum. In June of that year he was put in nomination by the Tory lord mayor to succeed Thomas Bludworth* as alderman of Aldersgate, and was chosen out of the two successful candidates by the court of aldermen. He was accused of using the trained bands 'to terrify' the Whig voters at the election of the sheriffs of London that summer. He died intestate on 22 July 1683, the only member of his family to sit in Parliament.[4]

[1] London Mar. Lic. ed. Foster, 682, 718; PCC 106 Carr; The Gen. n.s. vii. 94; Le Neve's Knights (Harl. Soc. viii), 329; Manning and Bray, Surr. i. 635; C10/221/55. [2] J. R. Woodhead, Rulers of London, 94; Parl. Intell. 9 Apr. 1660; CSP Dom. 1678, p. 392. [3] PCC 106 Carr; Surr. Arch. Colls. xvi. 97, 122; PC2/57/164; Survey of London, xxii. 102; CSP Dom. 1671, pp. 569, 581; SP29/307/3; C10/221/55. [4] HMC Lindsey, 32; G. G. Walker, Hon. Artillery Co. 92; Trial of Slingsby Bethell (1681); CSP Dom. 1680-1, p. 40; 1682, pp. 75, 141; July–Sept. 1683, p. 201; Luttrell, i. 191, 194; Case of Thomas Pilkington (1689); C10/221/55.

E.C.

HOWARD, Charles (1628–85), of Naworth Castle, Cumb. and Hinderskelfe, Yorks.

WESTMORLAND 1653
CUMBERLAND 1654, 1656–10 Dec. 1657, 1660

b. 4 Feb. 1628, 2nd s. of Sir William Howard of Naworth by Mary, da. of William, 4th Lord Eure; bro. of Philip Howard*. educ. travelled abroad (Holland) 1646–7. m. c.Dec. 1645, Anne, da. of Sir Edward Howard†, 1st Baron Howard of Escrick, 3s. (2 d.v.p.) 3da. suc. bro. 1644; cr. Earl of Carlisle 30 Apr. 1661.[1]

J.p. Cumb. 1647–59, Northumb. 1652–9, Yorks. (N. and E. Ridings) 1653–9, co. Dur. and Westmld. 1656–9, Cumb., co. Dur., Essex, Northumb. and N. and E. Ridings Mar. 1660–d., Mdx. 1675–d.; sheriff, Cumb. 1649–50; commr. for assessment, Cumb. 1649–50, Cumb., Northumb. and Yorks. 1652, 1657, Aug. 1660–1, Dumfries, Selkirk and Roxburgh 1657, Jan. 1660, oyer and terminer, Yorks. 1653–4, Northern circuit June 1660, scandalous ministers, Cumb., Westmld., Northumb. and co. Dur. 1654, security, Cumb. and Westmld. 1655–6, statutes, Durham college 1656; freeman Newcastle-upon-Tyne 1656, Portsmouth 1680; alderman, Carlisle ?1658–d., mayor 1677–8; commr. for militia, Cumb., Northumb., Westmld. and Yorks. Mar. 1660; custos rot. Cumb. July 1660–d., ld. lt. Cumb. and Westmld. Oct 1660–d., co. Dur. 1672–4; v.-adm. Cumb., co. Dur., Northumb. and Westmld. 1661–d.; jt. c.-in-c. of militia, Cumb., Westmld., Northumb. and co. Dur. 1667; warden of Barnard Castle, Teesdale forest and Marwood chase, co. Dur. 1672–d.[2]

Capt. of Gds. 1651–Jan. 1655, Sept. 1655–6; col. of horse Jan.–Sept. 1655, Feb.–Oct. 1660; dep. maj.-gen. Cumb., Northumb. and Westmld. 1655–6; col. of ft. 1656–9, 1673–4; gov. Carlisle 1658–9, Feb.–Nov. 1660, 1678–d.; capt. indep. tp. 1666–7; lt.-gen. 1667.

Councillor of State Apr.–Dec. 1653, [S] 1655–8; commr. for trade 1656–7, 1668–72, security [S] 1656; PC 2 June 1660–21 Apr. 1679; farmer of wine customs [I] 1660–81; member, R. Adventurers into Africa 1661–72, asst. 1670; ambassador to Russia, Poland, Denmark and Sweden 1664, Sweden 1668; commr. for prizes 1664–7; member, Society of Mines Royal 1667, R. Fishery Co. 1677; dep. earl marshal 1673–d.; gov. Jamaica 1678–81.[3]

Howard's great-grandfather, 'Belted Will of Naworth', was a younger son of the fourth Duke of Norfolk who inherited the Dacre estates. Howard was brought up as a Roman Catholic, and by resisting capture by a parliamentary force during the first Civil War made himself a technical Royalist. On his marriage he became a Presbyterian, and was allowed to compound both for his wardship and his delinquency for £4,000. His loyalty to Parliament during the second Civil War was at first in doubt, but he fought with great distinction at Worcester as captain of Cromwell's guards. Changing to Independency, he assumed 'a high profession of religion, to the pitch of praying and preaching at their meetings', and held office throughout the Protectorate, being called up to the 'Other House' in 1657. But he was probably in touch with the exiled Court through his brother-in-law, William

Howard (Norfolk) Family

Thomas, 4th _m._ (2)
Duke of Norfolk

Lord William
of Naworth

Philip

Sir William

Philip* →

Charles*
(1st Earl of Carlisle)

Edward,
Visct. Morpeth*

Charles,
Visct. Morpeth* →

Thomas, 1st Earl
of Suffolk

Sir Edward†
(1st Baron Howard
of Escrick)

Hon. William*

Sir Thomas†
(1st Earl of
Berkshire)

Hon. Philip* →

Sir Robert*

Thomas I*

Theophilus†
(2nd Earl)

Hon. Thomas*

Howard*. He was dismissed by the Rump in 1659 and arrested with good reason during Booth's rising. On the fall of the military regime he was again given a regiment. George Monck* made him governor of Carlisle, and in April 1660 he was among the officers who undertook that the army would no longer 'meddle in any affairs of state'.[4]

Howard was returned for Cumberland at the general election of 1660 and became a moderately active Member of the Convention. As 'Lord Howard' or 'Colonel Howard' he was appointed to 23 committees, and acted as teller in four divisions, while seven speeches may probably be ascribed to him. He was among those appointed to consider the Declaration of Breda and to conduct the poll to choose Members to carry the reply, reporting the figures on 7 May. He was also on the committees to consider the indemnity bill and to inquire into unauthorized Anglican publications. He now changed religion for the third time, declaring on 17 July that:

> As monarchy had been so long interrupted by rebellion and faction, so had episcopacy by schism and heresy, and that no one that spoke against episcopacy offered anything better.

On 13 Aug. he helped to raise the £100,000 loan in the City. He opposed double taxation of Popish recusants, because of their 'constant allegiance to the King'. Of the regicides who had surrendered themselves he said:

> The late King clothed them in scarlet, and had turned their iron into brass, their brass into silver, and themselves into gold. That this prince should be murdered at his own door would make them seek out such a punishment for it as the exquisiteness of a woman could invent. But the honour of the House being engaged, he moved . . . to banish and immure them that they should never see the sun more, which would be worse than death.

In September Howard was chiefly concerned with the disbandment of the army. He was appointed to the committee for the bill and helped to manage a conference. He also served on the committee for the bill to exempt ex-soldiers from the apprenticeship regulations in corporate towns, which he carried to the Lords.[5]

In the second session, Howard was appointed to the committee for the attainder bill. On 16 Nov. he moved for some course to be taken with moss-troopers, and obtained a first reading for his bill to prevent theft and rapine on the northern borders. He proposed that the author of The Long Parliament Revived should be punished 'by being tied up to the gallows while his book was burning below it', and was appointed to the committee for his impeachment. On 21 Nov. he acted as teller against the motion to grant the excise for the King's life only,

and as Privy Councillor he brought the message of thanks for settling the revenue. He described the bill for modified episcopacy brought in on 28 Nov. as of the highest importance, and moved a second reading in three days' time. He was appointed to the committee for restoring the title of Duke of Norfolk to the head of his family, acted as teller on the third reading, and carried it to the Lords.[6]

Howard was too unpopular among the northern Royalists to stand again in 1661, but was given a peerage in the coronation honours. As Viscount Morpeth and Earl of Carlisle he exercised considerable interest in these boroughs, for which his brother and son sat in the Cavalier Parliament and later. His marriage had broken up before the Restoration, after which, according to Burnet, he 'ran into a course of vice'. He was granted a lease of a Northumberland colliery in 1663 and an excise pension of £1,000 p.a. in 1667. Nevertheless he was reckoned one of Clarendon's leading opponents in the House of Lords, and subsequently an associate of Shaftesbury. In February 1674 he moved that any member of the royal family who married a Roman Catholic without the consent of Parliament should be excluded from the succession. It was afterwards rumoured that he was to be turned out of the Council, but he remained there for another four years. He soon parted company with Shaftesbury, for as Burnet commented, 'he loved to be popular, and yet to keep up an interest at Court, and so was apt to go forward and backward in public affairs'. In 1678 he recovered the governorship of Carlisle, and was appointed governor of Jamaica at a salary of £2,500 p.a. He stayed in the island less than three years, and after encountering many difficulties with the local assembly sailed home, never to return, in May 1680. Thereafter he decided to 'live as a country gentleman in Cumberland'. He voted against the second exclusion bill on 15 Nov. 1680, but next month, like most of the Howards, found his kinsman Lord Stafford guilty of treason. He apparently co-operated in remodelling the Carlisle charter in 1684, and was reappointed to the corporation. He died on 24 Feb. 1685, and was buried in York Minster.[7]

[1] C142/774/15; LJ, viii. 296, 499. [2] Ferguson, Cumb. and Westmld. Members, 23, 296; Thurloe, iii. 562; Reg. of Freemen (Newcastle Recs. Committee iii), 71; R. East, Portsmouth Recs. 364; S. Jefferson, Hist. Carlisle, 447; CSP Dom. 1655–6, p. 297; 1667, p. 214; Cal. Treas. Bks. iii. 1234. [3] CSP Ire. 1669–70, pp. 390–1. [4] LJ, viii. 296, 469, 497; Cal. Comm. Adv. Money, 1237; Cary, Mems. Civil War, ii. 363; Burnet, i. 271–2; Cal. Cl. SP, iii. 153, 173; iv. 169, 209, 511, 609; CSP Ven. 1659–61, pp. 90, 138. [5] Bowman diary, ff. 82v, 140; Old Parl. Hist. xxii. 441–2; CJ, viii. 157, 161. [6] Old Parl. Hist. xxiii. 15, 20, 28; CJ, viii. 187, 194, 196. [7] Williamson Letters (Cam. Soc. n.s. ix), 158; HMC Le Fleming, 30; CSP Dom. 1663–4, pp. 76, 133; Cal. Treas. Bks. i. 736; Eg. 2539, ff. 197, 205; K. W. D. Haley, Shaftesbury, 357–8, 376; F.

Cundall, *Govs. of Jamaica*, 80–88; Cumb. RO, Fleming mss 2370, Lowther to Fleming, 25 Jan. 1681.

M.W.H./E.C.

HOWARD, Charles, Visct. Morpeth (c.1669–1738).

MORPETH 1689, 1690–23 Apr. 1692

b. c.1669, o.s. of Edward Howard*, 2nd Earl of Carlisle. *m.* lic. 25 July 1688, aged 19, Lady Anne Capel (*d.* 14 Oct. 1752), da. of Arthur, 1st Earl of Essex, 2s. 3da. *educ.* Morpeth g.s. *suc.* fa. as 3rd Earl 23 Apr. 1692.[1] Commr. for assessment, Cumb. and Northumb. 1689–90; gov. Carlisle 1693–*d.*; ld. lt. Cumb. and Westmld. 1694–1712, 1714–*d.*, Tower Hamlets 1717–22; custos rot. Cumb. and Westmld. 1700–14, 1715–*d.*; mayor, Carlisle 1700–1; constable, Tower of London 1715–22, Windsor Castle 1724–30.[2] Gent. of the bedchamber 1700–2; dep. earl marshal 1701–6; PC 19 June 1701–*d.*; first ld. of the Treasury 1701–2, May–Oct. 1715; commr. for union with Scotland 1706; one of the lds. justices 1714; master of the foxhounds and harriers 1730–*d.*

Consummation of Lord Morpeth's marriage was deferred 'through the greenness of their years'. Twelve days after the landing of William of Orange he was given leave 'to sail to Flanders with his governor', and he does not seem to have played any part in the Revolution. He was returned to the Convention two months later, still under age, on the family interest; but he left no trace on its records, and was not listed as supporting the disabling clause in the bill to restore corporations. A moderate Whig, he was re-elected in 1690, but succeeded to the peerage two years later. 'A gentleman of great interest in the country and very zealous for its welfare, [he] hath a fine estate and a very good understanding, with a grave deportment.' He held high office in Whig administrations both before and after the Hanoverian succession. He died on 1 May 1738 and was buried at Castle Howard (formerly Hinderskelfe) in the splendid mausoleum built for him by his friend Vanbrugh.[3]

[1] Hodgson, *Northumb.* pt. 2, iii. 402. [2] S. Jefferson, *Hist. Carlisle*, 448. [3] *Ellis Corresp.* ii. 46; *CSP Dom.* 1687–9, p. 356; Macky, *Mems.* 59.

G.H.

HOWARD, Edward, Visct. Morpeth (1646–92).

MORPETH	27 Sept. 1666, 1679 (Mar.)
CUMBERLAND	1679 (Oct.)
CARLISLE	1681

b. 27 Nov. 1646, o. surv. s. of Charles Howard*, 1st Earl of Carlisle. *educ.* travelled abroad (Germany) 1665. *m.* lic. 27 Apr. 1668, Elizabeth, da. and coh. of Sir William Uvedale†, treas. of the chamber, of Wickham, Hants, wid. of Sir William Berkeley, RN, 1s. 1da. *suc.* fa. as 2nd Earl of Carlisle 24 Feb. 1685.[1]

Commr. for assessment, Cumb. 1664–80, Northumb. 1673–80; j.p. Cumb. 1667–May 1688, Oct. 1688–*d.*, ld. lt. (jt.) 1668–85, (sole) 1689–*d.*; dep. gov. Carlisle 1678–85, alderman by 1680–June 1688, Oct. 1688–*d.*, mayor 1683–4.[2] Capt. of ft. 1667; cornet, English Gens d'Armes (French army) 1667; col. of ft. 1678–9.[3]

Lord Morpeth, while still under age, was designed by his father to succeed Lord Ogle (Henry Cavendish*) as Member for Northumberland. But when the vacancy failed to materialize he took the seat at Morpeth promised to Joseph Williamson*. An inactive Member of the Cavalier Parliament, he was appointed to only 13 committees, his principal interest being the prevention of theft and rapine in the northern counties. He carried to the Lords a bill for this purpose on 21 Dec. 1666, and later served on four similar committees. In 1669 Sir Thomas Osborne* included him among the Members who had usually voted for supply, and his name appears on the Paston list. He did not speak in the House, except on 8 Nov. 1675 to present the petition of his Roman Catholic uncle Col. Thomas Howard, who had been sent to the Tower for circulating a scandalous attack on William Cavendish*, Lord Cavendish. He was among those 'to be remembered' on the working lists, and noted as under his father's influence. But Sir Richard Wiseman* reckoned him a court supporter, and Shaftesbury marked him 'doubly vile'. He was on the government list of the court party in 1678, and was given one of the newly-raised regiments.[4]

At the dissolution of the Cavalier Parliament Lord Morpeth, who was acting lord lieutenant of Cumberland during his father's absence in Jamaica, agreed to stand jointly with Sir John Lowther II* for the county and to share expenses. No opposition was expected, and they were duly adopted at a gentry meeting, but Morpeth had quarrelled with Sir George Fletcher* and Sir Richard Grahme*, two of the most influential local personages, and on 13 Feb. 1679 (Sir) Christopher Musgrave* wrote to (Sir) Joseph Williamson* that 'the last post brought news that Lord Morpeth will not stand for the county, which occasions much discourse'. He was re-elected at Morpeth, and again marked 'vile' on Shaftesbury's list. In the first Exclusion Parliament he was appointed only to the committee of elections and privileges and to the inquiry into the woollen industry. According to Roger Morrice he voted against the committal of the exclusion bill. In the autumn election he was returned for Cumberland, but his only committee in the second Exclusion Parliament was to bring in a bill to restrict imports of Scottish cattle. He had exacerbated his quarrel with Fletcher by procuring his removal from county office, and consequently was faced with opposition to his re-election in 1681. His father, returning from Jamaica, soon realized that Fletcher could not be defeated in Cumberland, and persuaded Morpeth's uncle (Sir) Philip Howard* to make way for him at Carlisle; but he played no known part in the Oxford Parliament. He succeeded as second earl shortly before the next general election.[5]

Lord Carlisle was listed among those who opposed James II in 1687, pledged his service to William of Orange in July 1688, and was appointed lord lieutenant after the Revolution. 'A cripple with the gout', he died on 23 Apr. 1692, and was buried at Wickham.[6]

[1]*Naworth Accounts* (Surtees Soc. clxviii), 76; Westminster City Lib., St. Martin in the Fields par. reg.; *Cal. Cl. SP*, v. 176; Berry, *Hants Genealogies*, 75. [2] *Bulstrode Pprs.* 76; *CSP Dom.* 1677–8, p. 677; Luttrell, i. 512; Ferguson, *Cumb. and Westmld. Members*, 581; S. Jefferson, *Hist. Carlisle*, 447. [3] *HMC Le Fleming*, 53. [4]*CSP Dom.* 1665–6, p. 186; 1666–7, p. 308; Grey, iii. 147. [5]*HMC Le Fleming*, 169–71, 178, 396; *CSP Dom.* 1677–8, pp. 414; *CSP Dom.* 1679–80, p. 82; *HMC Dartmouth*, i. 75–76; Westmld. RO, D/Ry 2126, 2285, 2375. [6]*CSP Dom.* 1687–9, p. 233; *EHR*, xxx. 93.

E.C.

HOWARD formerly **HALSEY, George** (1622–71), of Fitzford, Tavistock, Devon.

TAVISTOCK   27 Apr. 1660, 16 May 1661–17 Sept. 1671

b. Feb. 1622, illegit. s. of Mary, da. and h. of Sir John Fitz of Fitzford, w. of Sir Charles Howard of Clun Castle, Salop, prob. by George Cuttford of Walreddon, Whitchurch, Devon. *m.* 10 Sept. 1655, Mary, da. of Richard Burnby of Bratton Clovelly, Devon, 1s. *d.v.p.*[1]
  Commr. for militia, Devon Mar. 1660, assessment Sept. 1660–9; portreeve, Bere Alston 1661–2; j.p. aft. 1666–69.[2]

Howard's mother came from a minor gentry family which represented Tavistock in several Parliaments in the 15th century. When her father, 'a very comely person', committed suicide after a short but violent career, she inherited an estate of £1,000 p.a. and 'a haughty and imperious nature'. 'A lady of extraordinary beauty' with one of the best fortunes in the west country, she was four times married. By her third husband, Sir Charles Howard, a younger son of the 1st Earl of Suffolk, she had two daughters. But at the time of Howard's birth, in 'some obscure place near London', they had been separated for 18 months, and the real father was probably a servant called George Cuttford, whom Lady Howard made her steward, addressing him affectionately as 'honest Guts'. The child was christened George Halsey, which was the maiden name of Cuttford's mother, and his existence was successfully concealed until he was nine years old. Lady Howard became a widow a few months after his birth and in 1628 married a professional soldier, Sir Richard Granville. By him she had a son and a daughter, but this marriage too broke up in a few years, and during the Civil War, in which Granville played a notable if not altogether creditable part as a Cavalier, they were living apart. She continued to reside in London, and was accordingly regarded as a parliamentary sympathizer. After the war, when Granville was banished, she resumed residence at Fitzford.[3]

Howard was completely overshadowed by the colourful personality of his mother, whose evil deeds made her a prominent figure in Devon folklore. He continued to live with her after his marriage and to manage her estates, reduced to £500 p.a. by her generosity to Cuttford. He was returned to the Convention on the family interest at Tavistock and probably with the support of John Maynard I* at Bere Alston, but in each case on a double return. On 27 Apr. 1660 he was allowed to hold both seats until the merits of the elections should be decided, and chose to serve for the former borough on 30 May. He was marked by Lord Wharton as an Anglican and presumably supported the Court, though he was probably totally inactive both as committeeman and speaker. He was re-elected to the Cavalier Parliament for both boroughs, again on double returns. On 16 May 1661 he was declared elected for Tavistock, but allowed also to occupy the Bere Alston seat on the merits of the return. When this was also awarded to him on 29 Jan. 1662 he chose to sit for Tavistock, and acted as returning officer at the by-election. He was an inactive Member, being appointed to only three private bill committees. He was listed as a court dependant in 1664, possibly by confusion with his namesake, subsequently 4th Earl of Suffolk, who was a pensioner of the Duke of York. He died on 17 Sept. 1671, and was buried at Tavistock. His mother died in the following month, bequeathing the Fitzford estate to her cousin Sir Willian Courtenay*.[4]

[1] *Trans. Devon Assoc.* xxii. 102; cii. 93, 96–97; Vivian, *Vis. Devon*, 119. [2] *Trans. Devon Assoc.* xxii. 103. [3] Ibid. xxii. 74; cii. 87, 92–93, 101; Clarendon, *Rebellion*, iii. 419; iv. 65–66. [4] *Trans. Devon Assoc.* xxii. 66–67.

M.W.H./J.S.C.

HOWARD, Philip (c.1631–86), of Leicester Fields, Westminster and Sissinghurst, Kent.

MALTON   7 Mar. 1659, 1660
CARLISLE   1661, 1679 (Mar.), 1679 (Oct.)

b. c.1631, 3rd s. of Sir William Howard (*d.*1642) of Naworth Castle, Cumb., and bro. of Charles Howard*,

1st Earl of Carlisle. *m.* lic. 23 Apr. 1668, Elizabeth, da. and h. of Sir Robert Newton, 1st Bt., of London, wid. of Sir John Baker, 3rd Bt., of Sissinghurst, 1s. Kntd. 27 May 1660.[1]

Capt. Life Gds. Jan. 1660–*d.*; gov. Jamaica 1685–*d.*[2]

Commr. for militia, Yorks. Mar. 1660; j.p. Yorks (N. Riding) July 1660–*d.*, Westminster 1665–*d.*, Kent 1672–*d.*; commr. for assessment, Westminster Aug. 1660–1, 1673–4, Cumb. 1661–80, Carlisle 1663–4, sewers, Westminster Aug. 1660; dep. lt. Kent 1668–?72; farmer of excise, South Wales 1671–4; receiver of hearth-tax, Kent 1671–4; member, R. Fishery Co. 1677.[3]

Howard, like his brother, was active in the Restoration. Standing on the Eure interest, he retained his seat for Malton at the general election of 1660. As commander of Monck's guards, he met the King at Dover, and was knighted. Apart from helping to manage the conference on the poll tax on 12 Sept. and serving on the committee to restore the dukedom of Norfolk to the head of the Howard family, he played no known part in the Convention.[4]

At the general election of 1661 Howard was returned for Carlisle, from which his brother took his title. He was appointed to only 25 committees in the Cavalier Parliament, of which the most important was for the uniformity bill, and acted as teller in four divisions. Samuel Pepys* considered Howard not only one of the finest persons he had ever seen, but also 'of great parts and very courteous. . . . He discourses as well as ever I heard man, in few words and handsome', but he does not seem to have shone as a parliamentary orator, and no speeches of his are recorded for the whole of this Parliament. On 16 Apr. 1662 he was ordered to carry to the Upper House the bill for preventing theft and rapine on the northern borders. He was marked as a court dependant in 1664. Howard had been brought up as a Roman Catholic, and his younger brothers were known to be ardent adherents of that church. His religion was always suspect, though the information laid against him in 1664 by Macedo, who also accused (Sir) John Bramston*, was not to be taken seriously. Two years later a protestant convert called L'Heure alleged that Howard had tried to dissuade him from changing his religion, and the charge was brought before the House by (Sir) Edward Hungerford*. Fortunately for Howard, he had just returned from service aboard the fleet with Monck, now Duke of Albemarle, thus certifying both his military ability and his sound Protestantism, and the House dismissed the allegation as a lie. Hungerford was not without interested motives, for he was in dispute with Howard and his partner, Francis Watson, over an invention for sheathing hulls with lead. They were granted a patent of monopoly for 14 years in 1668,

but sought an extension to 31 years, which required a private Act. On 25 Nov. 1670 (Sir) Thomas Higgons* reported in favour of the patent, but the general tenor of the debate was hostile, and the bill was recommitted. Under a new chairman, (Sir) John Berkenhead*, the bill made good progress and received the royal assent at the end of the session. Howard was reckoned one of Ormonde's friends, and as a dependant appeared on both lists of the court party in 1669–71.[5]

Howard's marriage to a wealthy widow proved unfortunate. She tricked him over her jointure, and they separated. Some ruffians whom he had hired from the bear-garden beat two of her servants to death, and he had need of his parliamentary immunity. It was said that his military command enabled him to keep her 'under a guard' at little cost. Even after Lord Carlisle went into opposition with Shaftesbury in 1673, Howard remained a government supporter, with his name on the Paston list. He was given a pension of £400 p.a. as compensation for loss of the South Wales excise farm, and according to *A Seasonable Argument* received altogether £4,000 'in patents and boons'. He served with the French army in the spring of 1674, but when his youngest brother John was killed in action in the following year he showed, unlike his brother Thomas, no resentment at the gleeful attitude of William Cavendish*, Lord Cavendish, and Sir Thomas Meres*. He was reckoned among the King's servants in the House, Sir Richard Wiseman* wrote that he was 'not doubted' by Danby, and his name appeared on the working lists, though (Sir) Joseph Williamson* noted that he was 'to be questioned' on one occasion. He was marked 'thrice vile' by Shaftesbury, but omitted from *Flagellum Parliamentarium*, perhaps because Andrew Marvell* had once been Lord Carlisle's secretary. In the debate on foreign policy on 25 May 1678 he acted as teller for the Court, and he was on both lists of the court party in that year. He had an angry dispute with Monmouth at a review in Hyde Park, and was threatened with being cashiered. As a Westminster justice he took the deposition of his disreputable nephew, Capt. Charles Atkins, on the Popish Plot.[6]

Howard was re-elected for Carlisle to the first and second Exclusion Parliaments. He was classed as 'vile' by Shaftesbury, and voted against the bill. When (Sir) Stephen Fox* produced his list of excise pensioners, Howard protested that he had come in 'upon a valuable consideration'; but otherwise he made no speeches, and was appointed to no committee in either Parliament. He stood down in 1681 in favour of his nephew Lord Morpeth

(Edward Howard*). In the following November he was arrested for a debt of £3,000, but the suit was dismissed as insolent and vexatious. He was appointed governor of Jamaica, where he owned a plantation, in 1685, and granted 200 of Monmouth's followers to transport and sell there; but his departure was delayed by his creditors and he died in England in April 1686. Although he was said to have been reconciled to Rome on his deathbed, he was buried in Westminster Abbey. His son Philip was elected for Morpeth in 1698 and for Carlisle in 1701.[7]

[1] *London Mar. Lic.* ed. Foster, 716. [2] *Cal. Cl. SP*, iv. 526; *CSP Col.* 1681–8, p. 751. [3] C181/7/37; *Twysden Ltcy. Pprs.* (Kent Recs. x), 64; *Cal. Treas. Bks.* iii. 833; iv. 49; *Sel. Charters* (Selden Soc. xxviii), 198. [4] *HMC Popham*, ii. 137–8; *Verney Mems.* ii. 145. [5] *Pepys Diary*, 1 Apr., 15 Aug., 21 Nov. 1666; *Bramston Autobiog.* (Cam. Soc. xxxii), 144; *Milward*, 45; *CJ*, viii. 653; ix. 183; *CSP Dom.* 1667–8, p. 479; *Dering*, 12–13. [6] E. C. Legh, *Lady Newton, Lyme Letters*, 37; *Harl.* 7020, f. 42; *CSP Dom.* 1670, p. 154; 1673–5, p. 11; 1678, p. 271; *Cal. Treas. Bks.* iv. 472; *Arch. de Guerre* 397, f. 25; *HMC Rutland*, ii. 51; *North, Examen*, 245. [7] *CSP Dom.* 1679–80, p. 82; 1685, p. 330; F. Cundall, *Govs. of Jamaica*, 99–101; *Ellis Corresp.* i. 35–36, 99, 105; *Westminster Abbey Reg.* (Harl. Soc. x), 216.

M.W.H./E.C.

HOWARD, Hon. Philip (1629–1717), of Charlton House, Wilts. and Westminster.

MALMESBURY 13 Feb. 1662
WESTMINSTER 1689

bap. 5 Mar. 1629, 7th s. of Thomas Howard[†], 1st Earl of Berkshire, by Lady Elizabeth Cecil, da. of William Cecil[†], 2nd Earl of Exeter; bro. of Sir Charles Howard[†], Visct. Andover, Sir Robert Howard* and Thomas Howard[†]. *m.* bef. 1679, Mary (*d.*1698), da. of one Jennings, 2s. 2da.
Gent. to the Princess Royal ?1650–4; gent. of the bedchamber to the Duke of York Dec. 1660–82; housekeeper, Excise Office May–Dec. 1702.[1]
Capt. Duke of Gloucester's tp. July–Sept. 1660; lt. indep. tp. 1667; capt. R. Ft. Gds. (later Grenadier Gds.) 1668–82.[2]
Commr. for assessment, Wilts. 1665–79, Westminster 1690, recusants, Wilts. 1675; receiver of taxes, London and Mdx. 1677–80; dep. lt. Mdx. 1689–?d.; lt. vol. horse, London 1689–at least 1692; j.p. Westminster 1690–?d., col. of militia ft. by 1697–?d.[3]

Howard's grandfather, a younger son of the 4th Duke of Norfolk, acquired Charlton by marriage in 1598 and was created Earl of Suffolk. Howard went abroad in 1650 and entered the service of the Princess Royal in Holland. He returned in 1654, coming under suspicion as a royalist agent, which he does not seem to have deserved, though he brought a letter from The Hague to the House of Commons on 23 May 1660. At the Restoration, he entered the Duke of York's household and, with Sir Charles Berkeley II*, applied for a patent of monopoly for the manufacture of glass. He was

successful in 1662 at a by-election for Malmesbury, two miles from his father's residence at Charlton. An inactive Member of the Cavalier Parliament, he was probably appointed to 19 committees, besides acting as teller in ten divisions. Within a few months of his taking his seat the King had to be addressed to compose a dispute between him and Lord Ossory (Thomas Butler*). He was granted the King's third of a lawful prize in 1664, and marked as a court dependant. He was appointed to the committee for the naturalization of the Marquis de Blanquefort in the Oxford session. In 1666 he was serving aboard the fleet as a volunteer, where, according to Thomas Bruce*, it was common report that 'Mr Howard ran down into the hull of the ship' whenever the fighting began. However that may be, and his subsequent record makes it highly improbable, he was given a commission in the following year. 'A great talker of nothing', his only recorded speech in the House was during the debate on Clarendon's impeachment, when he urged that the judges should be asked to declare the law of treason. His name appeared on both lists of the court party in 1669–71. He was given £400 as a royal boon, and began to act as a teller for the Court. On 8 Apr. he carried up the bill for the better collecting of fines and forfeitures. He was teller against the word 'unanimous' in the address against the suspending power on 26 Feb. 1673, after which he again went to sea, losing his arm at the battle of Texel. He was included on the Paston list, and as one of the King's servants in the House in 1675, twice acting as teller for supply in the autumn session. In 1677 he was appointed to the committees for the Duke of Norfolk's bill, and for the recall of British subjects from the French service. He was again teller for the Court against the Dutch alliance on 25 May, and was marked 'doubly vile' on Shaftesbury's list. The authors of *A Seasonable Argument* and *Flagellum Parliamentarium* described him as 'not born to a farthing' and the recipient of a pension of £300. He was given a receivership of taxes, in which capacity he was commended by the Treasury, and later received a special gratification of £200 'for his extraordinary pains and charges'. In 1678, however, he appears only on the government list of the court party; by this time he had married a woman of means and could afford to take an independent line. Nevertheless he was anxious that Lauderdale should know that he had voted for him, and acted as teller for the Court in three more important divisions, on the removal of counsellors on 7 May, on the tax on new buildings on 25 June, and on the removal of Papists from Court on 26 Nov.[4]

It is not known whether Howard stood at the first

general election of 1679, but he petitioned the second Exclusion Parliament. The constituency is not stated, but he may have contested Malmesbury as an exclusionist. He was still well enough at Court for the King to stand godfather to his younger son in 1681, but in the following year, as an associate of the Duke of Monmouth and the Earl of Clare (Gilbert Holles*), he lost all his places. Later James II stopped his pension. Hence he was able to stand in 1689 for Westminster, where he had been born, as 'an eminent Protestant sufferer'. He was appointed to at least five committees in the Convention, of which the most important was to inquire into the authors and advisers of grievances. He also served on the committees of an explanatory bill about tanning, for the bankruptcy bill, and for two private bills promoted by the Duke of Norfolk. King William granted him a pension of £400 p.a., and readily accepted his offer to reconcile his brother Sir Robert with Lord Halifax (Sir George Savile*); but nothing came of it. He thirded the address of thanks for the King's speech on 19 Oct., and a week later was commissioned lieutenant to John Hampden* in the ultra-Whig London volunteer horse. Defoe was his cornet. He supported the disabling clause in the bill to restore corporations. He lost his seat at the general election, and probably did not stand again. He retained his pension, but his circumstances were so embarrassed that he was compelled to ask for an advance of £40 to pay for his wife's funeral. He died at the age of 88 in September 1717 and was buried at St. Martin in the Fields, where he had been baptized. His great-grandson succeeded to the earldoms of Suffolk and Berkshire in 1783.[5]

[1] Thurloe, ii. 568. [2] Parl. Intell. 23 July 1660. [3] Cal. Treas. Bks. v. 617, 1099; vi. 452; xvii. 219, 433; SP44/165/285; Luttrell, ii. 242; Eg. 1626, f. 31. [4] CSP Dom. 1650–1, p. 551; 1660–1, p. 386; 1663–4, p. 452; 1666–7, p. 149; 1670, p. 41; 1672, p. 47; 1673, p. 523; Whitelocke Mems. iv. 414; Ailesbury Mems. 323–4; CJ, viii. 427; Add. 35865, p. 19; Lauderdale Pprs. (Cam. Soc. n.s. xxxviii), 132. [5] CSP Dom. 1682, pp. 40, 429–30; Orange Gazette, 7 Jan. 1689; R. Morrice, Entering Bk. 2, p. 617; Cal. Treas. Bks. xiii. 73.

E.C.

HOWARD, Sir Robert (1626–98), of Lincoln's Inn Fields, Mdx.; the Receipt Office, Westminster and Ashtead, Surr.[1]

STOCKBRIDGE   1661
CASTLE RISING   1679 (Mar.), 1679 (Oct.), 1681, 1689, 1690, 1695

bap. 19 Jan. 1626, 6th s. of Thomas Howard†, 1st Earl of Berkshire, and bro. of Charles Howard†, Visct. Andover, Hon. Philip Howard*, and Thomas Howard†. m. (1) 1 Feb. 1645, Anne (d. c.1656), da. of Sir Richard Kingsmill of Malshanger, Church Oakley, Hants, 3s.

(2 d.v.p.) 3da.; (2) 10 Aug. 1665, Lady Honoria O'Brien (d. 19 Sept. 1676), da. of Henry, 5th Earl of Thomond [I], wid. of Sir Francis Englefield, 3rd Bt., of Wootton Bassett, Wilts., s.p.; (3) c.1678, Mary (d. by 3 Aug. 1682), da. of Jacob Uphill of Wards, Dagenham, Essex, s.p.; (4) 26 Feb. 1692, Annabella, da. of John Dyves of Bromham, Beds., clerk to the PC, s.p. Kntd. 29 June 1644.

Lt.-col. of horse (royalist) by 1644; col. of ft. 1667.[2]

Serj.-painter June 1660–3; clerk of the patents June 1660–4; commr. for discovery of crown property Oct. 1660; sec. to the Treasury 1671–3; auditor of receipt 1673–d.; PC 13 Feb. 1689–d.[3]

J.p. Hants July 1660–?d., Wilts. by 1667–?89, Westminster 1689–d.; commr. for assessment, Hants Aug. 1660–79, Westminster 1661–3, 1664–9, 1677–80, Wilts. 1667–79, Mdx., Westminster and Surr. 1689–90; dep. lt. Hants c. Aug. 1660–?76, Wilts. 1675–83; col. of militia ft. Hants Nov. 1660–?76; commr. for highways and sewers, London and Westminster 1662; steward, honour of Pontefract and manors of Spalding, Barton and Hitchin 1672; gamekeeper, manor of Oatlands 1675–d.[4]

Howard, a Royalist like his father and brothers, was knighted in the field in the Civil War. He was not required to compound for his delinquency, and took up residence in Hampshire with his first wife's family. In 1657 the farm of the post-fines in the Exchequer (originally granted to his father in 1625) was renewed to him by the Protectorate at an increased rent. Lord Berkshire's interest was soon to be taken over by (Sir) Robert Clayton*, with whom Howard became closely linked. As a cousin of Mordaunt he came under suspicion as a conspirator in 1658, and was imprisoned for a time in Windsor Castle. Mordaunt sent him to The Hague on the eve of the Restoration, remarking that he had great influence over Sir Charles Wolseley* and Sir Anthony Ashley Cooper*, while Dr Morley recommended him as well-affected to King and Church. Howard always made good use of his opportunities at Court; not only was his lease confirmed and enlarged to cover all the greenwax fines, but he was also granted two minor offices as serjeant-painter of the works and clerk of the patents in Chancery. Meanwhile his first book was passing through the press, a volume of indifferent poetry including such topical subjects as panegyrics on the King and George Monck*.[5]

At the general election of 1661 Howard was successful at Stockbridge, an open borough about 16 miles from Malshanger. There was a double return, but his name was on both indentures and he took his seat in the Cavalier Parliament at once. A very active Member, he was named to 289 committees, in 14 of which he took the chair, acted as teller in 20 divisions, carried seven bills and 12 messages to the Lords, and delivered some 250 recorded speeches. His most important committees in the first session were for restoring the bishops to the Upper House, inquiring into the shortfall in the revenue, preventing tumultuous petitioning, and considering the uniformity bill. He was deeply concerned in providing compensation for the Marquess of Winchester, the most prominent sufferer among the Hampshire Royalists, whose son Lord St. John (Charles Powlett I*) was perhaps his most intimate friend. He helped to manage a conference and to present a petition to the King on his behalf. On 21 Nov. he was among those sent to ask when the King would receive an address asking for precautions to be taken against the former Commonwealth soldiers. After the Christmas recess he twice requested conferences about the mischiefs that might arise from the Quakers' refusal to take lawful oaths, and helped to prepare reasons. His chief interest in this session, however, was the improvement of highways in the metropolitan area. A bill for this purpose made no progress until he was added to the committee on 19 Feb. 1662. He at once took the chair, and reported it to the House a month later. In the light of the debate, provision was made for widening some notorious bottle-necks, and on 24 Mar. he was able to carry the amended bill to the Lords. In the Upper House, further amendments were inserted to reduce the number of hackney coaches and to restrict the loading and unloading of goods vehicles; but Howard successfully resisted them, taking the chair in the committee to prepare reasons and reporting the subsequent conference. As a manager of another conference, this time on the Prayer Book, he supported the motion to agree on the text before proceeding further with the uniformity bill. In the closing days of the session he helped to manage conferences on the militia bill and the distribution of £60,000 to the loyal and indigent officers, and to present an address asking the King to adjudicate on the rival projects for draining the Lindsey level. In the 1663 session his most important committee was to hear a petition alleging maldistribution of the indigent officers fund; but he was also among those to whom was committed the bill to compose the differences between St. John and his father. 'Willing to bring the stage to be a place of some credit, and not an infamous place for all persons of honour to avoid', he achieved considerable success in the early years of the Restoration as a dramatist of impeccable morality, and acquired a quarter-share in the Drury Lane theatre. His satire on the parliamentarian sequestrators, The Committee, became one of the most popular of Restoration comedies. His circumstances were now sufficiently easy to permit him to dispose of his rather undignified offices, though he retained the lucrative

farms. A court dependant still in 1664, he did not abandon his former fellow craftsmen of the Painter-Stainers Company; he probably introduced a bill on their behalf on 3 May, for he was the first Member named to the committee, and when it was revived in December he acted as teller for it. In the Oxford session he was appointed to the committee for the five mile bill, and made his first recorded speech. A supporter of friendship with Spain, he was undeterred by the presence of the French ambassador from speaking of him 'very slightingly' in the House, which was thought to be 'very unparliamentary'. He remained in high favour with the King, who offered his help in arranging his second marriage to a wealthy widow with a strong interest at Wootton Bassett.[6]

It was the 1666-7 session that brought Howard into prominence in the Opposition, together with Sir Richard Temple*, Edward Seymour*, and William Garway*. He took part in preparing or managing conferences on imports from France, the Canary Company, and the charges against Mordaunt. 'Of birth, state, wit, strength, courage Howard presumes', wrote Andrew Marvell'*, and Samuel Pepys* was astonished to hear that one of the King's servants had been responsible for the public accounts commission clause in the poll-bill, though he was excused from serving on it himself. He was chairman of the committee to prepare reasons for insisting that Irish cattle imports should be declared a nuisance, acted as teller for retaining the word (which would preclude the King from suspending the prohibition of imports), and reported three conferences. He also reported a conference about empowering the accounts commissioners to take evidence on oath, and acted as teller for a motion deploring the petition from the Lords to the King while the matter was still before Parliament. Meanwhile his second marriage had proved a disastrous failure, and soon after the session closed his wife begged the King to relieve her from his ill usage. Her petition was referred to Lord Chancellor Clarendon, who had 'no mind to have anything to do with the knight' after his unruly behaviour in the House, and proceedings languished.[7]

Howard first became a frequent speaker in the House after the dismissal of the lord chancellor, for which he helped to draw up an address of thanks. He was also among those instructed to bring in another accounts bill, which he denied would be 'fishing in troubled waters', and to inquire into the sale of Dunkirk. He urged that Clarendon should be committed immediately on common fame, even though he might be innocent: 'his inconvenience, to be imprisoned only for a few days; ours, to let a person go free with such a charge ... If the charge be not true, every Member that delivered the charge [is] exposed to ruin.' Witnesses would not testify before a Commons committee, he alleged, for fear of an action of *scandalum magnatum*. He was appointed to the committee to reduce the charges into heads. On the first charge, of advising the dissolution of Parliament and military rule, he and the Hon. John Vaughan* had 'heard from persons of quality that it would be proved'. He urged unsuccessfully that the accusation of secret correspondence with the Protectorate should stand, despite the Act of Indemnity. When all the original charges had been dismissed, Vaughan was inspired by the Austrian ambassador to accuse Clarendon of betraying the King's counsels to his enemies during the second Dutch war. (Sir) John Bramston* inquired sceptically whether the information came from a subject or an enemy, to which Howard replied virtuously: 'I would not have brought you information from one of the King's enemies, nor did I ever converse with them during the war'. He helped to manage a conference on the impeachment. On 18 Nov. 1667 he informed the House that John Ashburnham I* had received £400 for procuring a licence to unlade wines from France. He was sent to the Lords three days later to desire a free conference on Clarendon, which he helped to report. He ascribed the continued refusal of the Upper House to commit the fallen minister without a specific charge to the malign influence of the spiritual lords. On 4 Dec. he was one of five Members sent to the Painted Chamber to hear Clarendon's letter explaining his flight. On returning to the Lower House he described it as 'a scandalous, seditious and malicious paper. ... The account in it of affairs [is] all false.' He would rather have been guilty of Clarendon's crimes, he said, than of those imputed in the letter to the Commons. He was sent to the Lords again to desire a conference on burning the letter, and attended another conference to hear why they opposed a proclamation for apprehending its author (who had already escaped to France). He supported the banishment bill, and was named to the committee, where he hoped to 'add all severities, except that of attainder', (because that might injure the interests of Clarendon's son-in-law, the Duke of York).[8]

During the recess Howard, Vaughan and Sir Thomas Littleton, 2nd Bt.*, were 'brought over to the Court, and did undertake to get the King money'. According to Pepys the undertakers had difficulty in securing a hearing when Parliament met again in February 1668; but John Milward*

recorded that Howard 'spoke well' in a debate on the miscarriages of the war, declaring that the failure of the 1666 campaign was due not to faulty intelligence but to evil counsel. A henchman of Buckingham's at this time, he had no reason to avoid reflections on his patron's rival, Lord Arlington. He supported Temple's triennial bill: 'should the people see this bill thrown out, what would they say who have given so much money?' he asked. Despite the rejection of the bill, he moved on 19 Feb. to raise £300,000 by a wine-tax: 'believes his Majesty's revenue managed with all prudence, and would not have a prince confined in his methods'. The defeat of the comprehension proposal on 4 Mar. would, he believed, 'work a despair in the nonconformists', and he seconded the proposal of Sir Nicholas Carew* for selling the lands of cathedral chapters. His principal activity in the second half of the session was devoted to the impeachment of (Sir) William Penn* for failure to follow up the victory in 1665 and malversation of prize goods. In an eloquent speech he strove to transfer the description 'undertaker' from himself to those who, like William Coventry*, acted in Penn's defence. He dismissed the plea of superior orders:

> Should an admiral command a person to be apprehended, and also to pick his pocket, to bring a woman, and violate her by the way? A man may be commanded to sink a ship, but not to rob the King. You have inducements to believe all this; and remember yourselves that lately, in a less matter than this, you came to an impeachment; and if this man be not impeached I could wish Lord Clarendon never had been.... This Member was the man that pursued the Hollander; when they offered themselves as a sacrifice to anybody that would be conqueror, this bait of the prizes came in the way, and this worthy Member, with the rest, minded his business, which was to plunder.

He was among those ordered to prepare articles of impeachment, and on 24 Apr. was sent to the Lords to request a conference. On the same day he was named to the committee on a bill to prevent the refusal of writs of habeas corpus. Meanwhile Lady Howard through her trustee Randolph Egerton* had presented her petition to the House; but Howard renounced his privilege, and no action was taken. His standing was unaffected; on the next day he was named to the committee to prepare an appropriation clause in the wine duties bill, and on 2 May he warned the House over Skinner's case: 'the Lords may be so raised in point of their judicature that at last all causes will be brought [there] originally, if you suffer this'. He wound up the session by complaining that 'no bills were passed to redress the grievances of the subject', enumerating the accounts bill, the bill to reform the collection of hearth-tax, the additional Irish cattle bill, and the habeas corpus bill, together with the punishment of Henry Brouncker* and Penn, and the disputed jurisdiction of the House of Lords, but omitting the failure to renew the Conventicles Act.[9]

The House was still in session when Howard received unwelcome publicity as 'Sir Positive At-All' in Shadwell's play, *The Sullen Lovers*. In the *dramatis personae* the character was described as 'a foolish knight that pretends to understand everything in the world, and will suffer no man to understand anything in his company; so foolishly positive that he will never be convinced of an error, though never so gross'. The Duke of York, for one, vouched for the accuracy of the portrait. In the following year Howard was involved in an even more pointed personal satire, a play called *The Country Gentleman* aimed at Coventry and his satellite Sir John Duncombe*; but the most damaging scene, which led to a challenge and to Coventry's dismissal, was supplied by Buckingham. The play was suppressed, and Howard wrote no more for the stage. Throughout the 1669 session he led the attack on Sir George Carteret* with all the venom at his command, alleging that punishment was required to reassure the allies. 'A man of spirit, dissatisfied with the Court', he defended Lord Orrery (Roger Boyle*) against the charge of treason brought by Ormonde's friends. But his most notable achievement in this session was subsequently expunged from the Journals. Alarmed at the precedent set in Skinner's case, he urged the Commons on 4 Dec. to take a strong line against the jurisdiction of the Lords, and was voted into the chair of a committee to prepare reasons for a conference. During the Christmas recess Howard brought together some 60 of the Opposition in a tavern to agree on a programme for the next session, involving the continued pursuit of Carteret and an outcry against Lauderdale's Scottish army. He failed to make any headway with either, but he was ordered, with (Sir) Thomas Lee I* and (Sir) Robert Atkyns*, to bring in a habeas corpus bill. A supporter of religious comprehension (not toleration, which he described as 'a spot in any government'), he was anxious to retain the suspending power in the renewed conventicles bill. 'He thinks the King does everything well, and would have him given this.' His own matrimonial difficulties failed to gag him in the debate on enabling Lord Roos (John Manners*) to divorce his wife. 'He has that charity for women that he believes none so bad . . . Lady Roos stands convicted of known and proven adulteries'. After supporting a ban on imports of brandy, he took the

chair for the bill. He acted as teller on 2 Apr. 1670 against the first reading of a private bill introduced by (Sir) John Heath* to recover Lady Heath's jointure from Sir John Pretyman*, and a few days later he reported a bill to sell up Pretyman, who was in major default at the Exchequer.[10]

It may have been the failure of the Opposition in this session that prompted Howard to revert to the Court; he was one of the five 'recanters' that took their leave of the country party in the autumn. He was twice sent to remind the Lords of the brandy bill, and on 7 Nov. he offered the sceptical House to farm all the new taxes under discussion for £500,000. A hostile account described him as 'projector-general' to the royal mistress, the Duchess of Cleveland, 'undertakes to get money for the Court, out of which he is to have snips', and 'the grand esquire of the law-tax bill'. Although unable to excuse the bumptious conduct of the prominent London dissenter Jekyll, he persuaded the intolerant majority to discharge him. After the attack on Sir John Coventry* during the Christmas recess, he was among those ordered to bring in a bill to punish the assailants, being 'persuaded that [there is] no gentleman in England but desires their room more than their company'; but he was against deferring all other business until the bill passed, and against extending it by making all cases of nose-slitting felonies. He twice acted as teller against the revived conventicles bill. When the preamble to the subsidy bill was under discussion, he opposed defining the purpose of the grant as for a war. He played a prominent part in the negotiations with the Lords over supply. On 6 Mar. 1671 he reported reasons for not fixing the price of beer and ale in the additional excise bill, helped to manage a conference, told the Commons that their view had prevailed, and returned the bill to the Upper House. A more serious dispute arose over the Lords' attempt to reduce the sugar duty, which Howard regarded as unconstitutional:

> The balance of all these things is the right of both Houses. Whether the Lords lower or not, it is their rate, and the Commons give it not. We, the Commons, give, and the Lords make it less; then we give not. If the Commons cannot say they give, their title will be yielded.

He twice reported conferences on the additional impositions bill which failed to resolve the dispute. He also took the chair for preparing reasons for retaining the colonial governors' oaths in the tobacco bill, and helped to manage the conference. Both bills were lost on the prorogation. Howard was now listed in the court party by the Opposition, and his tax-farming projects naturally did not escape attention.[11]

Undeterred by these sardonic allusions, Howard formed a syndicate with his friend Lord St. John, Sir William Bucknall*, Sir John Bennet* and others to farm the customs and certain other revenues for five years from Michaelmas 1671; but they overplayed their hand, and the contract was abruptly cancelled. Howard was no loser, however; he almost immediately stepped into the shoes of Sir George Downing* as secretary of the Treasury. 'Must he always gain by being against the King?' asked (Sir) John Berkenhead*, who was fortunately unaware that only this appointment prevented Howard's old associate Ashley Cooper (now lord chancellor and Earl of Shaftesbury) from pressing his claim to the Speakership. Howard could scarcely be expected to maintain his predecessor's standards of administration, though he proudly informed the Commons on 7 Feb. 1673 that, 'since he had the honour to serve the King in the revenue, the comings-in [have been] more and goings-out less'. For his other new role as government spokesman he was better equipped, warmly supporting the Declaration of Indulgence, which, he observed, invaded neither life, liberty nor estate. 'Is it an argument', he asked 'that the Church of England is unsupported unless every man be compelled to everything in it?' Nevertheless he was twice among those ordered to draft addresses against the suspending power. He served on the committee that produced the test bill, though he disapproved of a sacramental test in the forces. On 15 Mar. he reported and returned to the Lords a bill to settle Chudleigh rectory on the lord treasurer (Thomas Clifford*) and his trustees. On the bill of ease for dissenters he supported a Lords amendment to leave the King a discretionary power. By 'ostentation of his pretended usefulness to his Majesty's service in the House of Commons' (to use the words of a disappointed rival) he obtained a life patent in reversion of the auditorship of the receipt, to which he succeeded on the death of (Sir) Robert Long* in July. Not only was this post highly lucrative, it also carried with it an official residence within easy hobbling distance of the Palace of Westminster, no unimportant consideration for one who was to be reduced to crutches by the gout for most of the rest of his life. Clifford's successor Danby initially welcomed the appointment because it enabled him to appoint his own brother-in-law, Charles Bertie*, as secretary to the Treasury. On the eve of the next session, Howard asked an astrologer whether King and Commons would 'unite in a good correspondency', and received a reassuring reply; but he did little to assist in fulfilling the prophecy. On 30 Oct. he said:

Without a thorough care we shall be in a worse condition for religion than before. . . . It is necessary that where any fountain is it may be pure; and he would have the Protestant religion pull up the very roots of Popery, wherever they grow.

He was among those entrusted with preparing a general test bill and an address against the marriage of the Duke of York, now revealed as a Roman Catholic, to Mary of Modena. An observer commented on the address:

Many of the House imagine the thing not very displeasing to the King because Sir Robert Howard promoted it, and with expressions of his not only desiring the duke should not marry a Roman Catholic, but wishing none of that profession might ever be married to any of the royal family.

In this policy Sir William Temple* believed that Howard was acting as Shaftesbury's principal lieutenant in the Commons, with the further objective of passing a bill to enable the King to marry again, beget a legitimate heir, and cut the Duke out of the succession. But he still supported the Government over supply, and opposed the resolution declaring the standing army a grievance.[12]

In the 1674 session Howard moved the vote of thanks for the speech from the throne. Anxious to moderate the attacks not only on Buckingham, but also on Lauderdale and Arlington, he warned the Commons against condemning ministers unheard: 'starting the name of a man here to blow him up is as much beneath the judgment as dignity of the House'. The activities of Bernard Howard, the youngest brother of the 5th Duke of Norfolk, kept the elder branch of the family continuously in the limelight at this time. When he petitioned for exemption from the recusancy laws, Howard described his cousin as a man of 'honour and gallantry', but he could not support his demand for the return from Italy of the mad duke, 'a sad spectacle' who would be 'in some measure ignominious to his family' if he were in England. In this speech he reflected the attitude of Norfolk's heir, Henry Howard, also a Roman Catholic, but master of the family parliamentary interest. Conscious as Howard was that election expenses had grown 'beyond all bounds' at such open boroughs as Stockbridge, he was probably already turning his eyes towards Castle Rising, one of the family seats. When Pepys, the sitting Member, was accused of Popery by (Sir) Robert Thomas*, Howard urged the House to facilitate the production of witnesses to support the charge. On a less parochial subject he disagreed with the Lords' resolution that the Dutch proposals formed 'upon the whole' an acceptable basis for peace, and helped to manage a conference which agreed to omit the phrase. He was also appointed to committees to consider a general test bill and to inquire into the condition of Ireland. 'It is an easy commonplace to rant against a standing army', he told the House, and proposed instead an address for the disbandment of the newly-raised forces only. He feared that the bill to give judges security of tenure during good behaviour would encourage them to 'arbitrary peevishness when they are old'. At the opening of the spring session of 1675 he moved a successful amendment to the vote of thanks for the speech from the throne. When Giles Strangways*, who had obtained a valuable reversion in the Exchequer for his son, reflected on Members who spoke one way in office and another way out of office, Howard pretended to believe that he was a self-accuser, 'having a very good interest in a very good office, I'll assure you'. '*Sic dixit* Sir Positive', commented one diarist for the information of Danby, who had long been anxious to turn him out. In his evidence on the lord treasurer's impeachment he did little harm, though he was soon to have reason for regretting his confident assertion that 'no man can cheat in the Exchequer' when it was revealed by one of the tellers that he had himself connived at extensive embezzlement. He was one of several Members formerly numbered among Lauderdale's friends who turned against him in this session, demanding that Thomas Dalmahoy* should prove that Burnet had been suborned, and later observing: 'perhaps the House is inflamed by the Duke of Lauderdale's high carriage'. Although he opposed the appropriation of the customs to the use of the navy, he was appointed to committees for this purpose in both the spring and autumn sessions. He spoke frequently on the dispute over the Lords' jurisdiction, helping to manage a conference on Shirley v. Fagg, to prepare reasons for a conference about the case of Arthur Onslow* (Norfolk's principal trustee), and to attend a conference on the Four Lawyers, although he had been called to order for attempting to excuse Serjeant Pemberton. Another of his Roman Catholic kinsmen made himself conspicuous in October, when Colonel Thomas Howard of the Naworth branch described William Cavendish*, Lord Cavendish, and Sir Thomas Meres* as incendiaries. Howard could only defend his cousin as 'one so little versed in business that he may err in his answer'. His statement on the public debt, though voluble as ever, can have left the House little wiser, but he acted as teller against lodging the revenue appropriated for the building of warships with the corporation of London instead of in the Exchequer.[13]

At the close of the session Danby marked Howard 'bad' on a list of officials in the Commons, and set

about collecting evidence to warrant his dismissal. Though the defaulting teller, who was the son of Sir William Doyley*, was prepared to swear to his complicity in his frauds, Howard stood on his rights under his patent and refused to resign without a public trial. In 1676 he sold Wootton Bassett to Laurence Hyde* for £36,000, of which £8,000 went to Howard's estranged wife, who died later in the year, cutting him off with a shilling. The author of *A Seasonable Argument*, who valued his post in the Exchequer at £3,000 p.a., commented: 'many great places and boons he has had, but his whore Uphill spends all, and now refuses to marry him'. She did not remain obdurate for much longer, and the result was a striking *mésalliance*, though Evelyn may have been mistaken in describing her as an actress. When it was suggested to the House on 15 Feb. 1677 that the long recess had automatically dissolved Parliament, Howard said: 'You are upon the most dangerous debate that may be, and from which no good consequence can arise', and Shaftesbury marked him 'vile'. He was appointed to the committees on the bills for the recall of British subjects from the French service, though he disliked the severity of the provisions, and for preventing the growth of Popery. He attacked the bill for the Protestant education of the royal children because it gave too much power to the bishops: 'it is but a charitable opinion, and no more, that the bishops will not make an ill use of this power'. But he acted as teller for the Court over the Newark election, and repeatedly defended the royal prerogative in foreign affairs, opposing the address of 29 Mar. because 'he would have all things left out of it that are of present pressure on the King'. He served on the committee to draw up a further address for an alliance with the Dutch, but needed the protection of the chair when he proposed a similar amendment on the report stage. It was not until November that he was required to appear before the Privy Council to answer the charges of embezzlement in the Exchequer. Minor irregularities were proved, but young Doyley was scarcely a credible witness, and Howard, after a bold and able defence 'declaring himself not to be a man that raised any great hasty fortune', was allowed to retain his post. In this capacity, the historian of the Treasury asserts, he 'contributed more than most to the degeneration of the late seventeenth century Exchequer'. Gout probably restricted his activity in 1678, both in debate and committee; but he was on both lists of the court party, and (Sir) Joseph Williamson* was fully justified in listing him among the government speakers, though he had taken to sitting with the Opposition, and one group of

Danby's enemies met regularly at his official quarters. Unable to oppose appropriation any longer, he continued to speak for supply with the necessary precautions and he was among those ordered on 30 Apr. to summarize England's international commitments. In the debate of 11 May on the navy he could not resist a jibe at Pepys, who, he said, 'speaks rather like an admiral than a secretary'.[14]

After the Popish Plot Howard urged the offer of £5,000 reward for the discovery of Godfrey's murderers. He was among those ordered to prepare the impeachment of Lord Arundell of Wardour and to draft an address for the apprehension of four suspects denounced by Oates. When Williamson was sent to the Tower for countersigning commissions to Roman Catholic officers, he commented: 'It is hard that the honourable gentleman should be singled out in the middle betwixt the original and the execution'. But on the following day he reported an address asking the King not to release his unpopular minister. He defended the Lords' proviso exempting the Duke of York from the bill to disable Papists from sitting in Parliament, but helped to prepare reasons for disagreeing with the other amendments from the Upper House. He was the first Member named to draw up an address for the removal of the Queen from Whitehall, and he was also among those charged with preparing instructions for the disbandment of the army. When the militia bill was vetoed he denied that it threatened to impinge on the prerogative, and he helped to draw up an address against 'private advices'. When Danby sought to forestall the production by Ralph Montagu* of his instructions to ask for a French subsidy by seizing his papers, Howard proposed that some Members should accompany Montagu to the place where he had hidden them, and he voted for Danby's impeachment.[15]

Howard neatly destroyed Pepys's interest at Castle Rising by reviving 'all my old charge of being a Papist, and the new one of having a hand in the late plot'. Although himself blacklisted in the 'unanimous club', he represented the borough in the three Exclusion Parliaments. He was no more than moderately active as a committeeman in 1679, with only six appointments, but he delivered 18 speeches, most of which were aimed at Danby. On 21 Mar. he said:

> Now I can speak; formerly I wanted courage and honesty to do it. This maxim has raised some people to the height they are at; to do ill and put it upon the King. The worst action of the world is selling a Parliament of England to be laid to the charge of the King. . . . Draw up your own condition to him, and represent to him the counsels that have enclosed him, . . . that the King and you may be joined and knit, never to be dissolved.

This climax was little to the taste of the extremist William Sacheverell*, who coldly announced that he agreed with only one point in the speech, the attack on Danby, and Shaftesbury classed him as 'vile'. Nevertheless Howard was anxious not to discourage Oates, and as a former 'chief of the patents' repeatedly attacked Danby's pardon and the right of the bishops to vote on its legality. He was among those appointed to inspect the disbandment accounts. Silius Titus* relied on him to prove that Bertie had a book of secret service payments, but all Howard would say when it came to the point was that 'no man is so unwise but he would keep notes of what he does'. On 14 May he told the House: 'The Exchequer has been managed in such an extravagant way that the nation is at the mercy of the money-lenders. . . . Had common law been observed in it, things had not come to this pass. There is not a shilling due of the revenue to find the King bread for a year'. He was absent from the division on the exclusion bill.[16]

The dissolution of the first Exclusion Parliament was followed by an acrimonious pamphlet war between Danby and Howard over the management of the Exchequer. In 1680 he bought the Ashtead estate from Henry Howard, now the 6th Duke of Norfolk, and built on it a new house. He also published anonymously *The Life and Reign of Richard II*, always a sensitive subject for English monarchs. When the second Exclusion Parliament met he joined in the attack on abhorring and probably served on the committee of inquiry. 'Some of no knowledge in the law advised the King to this', he declared. 'Saying prayers and meeting together at this rate may be a riot towards Heaven.' Though much less active, with only four committee appointments and four speeches, he now committed himself to exclusion, and spoke against the court attempt to drive a wedge into the Opposition by naming the Duke of York's children as successors to the crown:

> I tremble to hear so much discourse about the King's death and naming him a successor. Certainly the like was never known in any former age, but rather it was looked on as so dangerous a thing to be discoursed of, as that none durst attempt it . . . and therefore I hope we shall never go so far as to put it into an Act. I am for showing a great respect for the Duke and his children, but I think we are first bound in duty to the King, and therefore ought first to show our respects to him. Some persons, in my poor opinion, have showed so much zeal for the Duke's interest, that I am afraid they have forgot their allegiance to the King. Can he ever be safe, so long as it is the interest of every Papist in England to kill him, which it will be, so long as there is hopes of a Papist to succeed to the throne? And therefore I think we cannot answer the permitting of any delay in an affair of so great importance, and I humbly move you that the bill now be committed.

He was among those ordered on 10 Nov. to draw up an address insisting on exclusion. There is no evidence that he attended during the proceedings against Lord Stafford, though he later warmly approved of his cousin's execution. In the Oxford Parliament he was anxious to discover how the bill to repeal the Elizabethan statute against Protestant nonconformists had miscarried, and was among those instructed to prepare reasons for a conference. As chairman of the committee to find a more convenient place for the Commons to meet in, he recommended the Sheldonian. The refusal of the Lords to accept the impeachment of Fitzharris he considered 'not only a subverting the constitution of Parliaments but of the Protestant religion also', and he hoped that the Lower House would resolve accordingly 'with the same calmness of mind that every man does wish that loves his religion'.[17]

At the general election of 1685 Howard stood down at Castle Rising in favour of his son Thomas. He was required to give evidence to the parliamentary committee to inspect the disbandment accounts, but otherwise he succeeded in staying out of politics until the flight of James II. He then wrote to William urging him not to negotiate and assuring him of the support of the City, with which he was in close contact through Clayton, and of Norfolk, where the 7th duke, a Protestant, was 'appearing very considerable'. He came in to the Prince at Windsor on 16 Dec. 1688 with Henry Powle*, and after a long private interview they were entrusted with a letter to the corporation of London. At the general election of 1689 he regained his seat at Castle Rising, while his son was returned for Bletchingley on Clayton's interest. An active Member of the Convention and a strong Whig, he was named to 40 committees and made 74 recorded speeches. Perhaps the most celebrated of his career was delivered on 29 Jan., when he was the first to assert the vacancy of the throne and the breach of the social contract:

> I am sure we have a divine right to our lives, estates, and liberty. The original of power was by pact by agreement from the people, and sure none ever intended perfectly to enslave themselves and their posterity. But we have seen violences offered to our very constitution. I look upon it therefore to be above a demise; a very abdication of the King, who, before he went, lopped both church and state. By liberty of conscience he let in the Romish religion. He left nothing unattempted that might entirely ruin us. In my opinion the right is therefore wholly in the people, who are now to new-form themselves again under a governor yet to be chosen. What should we do when a king so much detests his people as to carry away, as much as in him lies, all justice from us by withdrawing the seals and making no provision for the government in his absence?

He was among those entrusted with drawing up a list of the essentials for religion, law and liberty, and reasons for disagreeing with the Lords over the vacancy of the throne. 'All things are not so clear as we could wish', he said, 'but let us preserve ourselves, which is the supreme law; if we part with the crown being vacant, we part with all.' He helped to manage the free conference of 6 Feb. when the Lords gave way, and to draft amendments to the declaration of rights.[18]

Under the new regime Howard became a Privy Councillor, while retaining his post as auditor of the receipt. After tabling the accounts of the treasury solicitors, he announced that they 'were willing to discover something necessary for the service of the House', and he was sent with Clayton and Sir John Holt* to examine them. On 25 Feb. he told the Commons: 'I would have an Act to take away any obligation to take the sacrament upon accepting any office; it is profaning the sacrament'. He urged the House to grant William an adequate revenue for life: 'when a popish king has received such testimony of kindness from a Parliament as to have the revenue for life, if a prince come in to save your religion and laws [and] should not have the same confidence, it will be thought a great coldness'. He was the first Member appointed to prepare a bill for regulating the Exchequer, which came to nothing. On 1 Mar. he brought in an account of the revenue, and took the chair in a committee to prepare an address of thanks to the King for relinquishing the hearth-tax. His name again stands first on the list of the important committee to inquire into the authors and advisers of grievances. He urged the House to publish their resolutions, lest unauthorized accounts should mislead the public. When a bill was sent down from the Lords to annul the attainder of the Hon. William Russell*, Howard was stimulated to an emotional speech by the ill-timed attempt of the Hon. Heneage Finch I* to defend his part in the trial:

> I cannot name Lord Russell without disorder. I would neglect all things to read this bill a second time. Perhaps the learned gentleman may tell us how large the law is then; 'tis a sufficient thing to name that noble lord. I am not able to say more; but pray read the bill.

He was named to the committee, and also helped to prepare the address asking the King to suppress the Ipswich mutiny. On 20 Mar. he tabled the estimates, and he was among those ordered to draw up an address promising assistance for a war against France. He strongly supported imposing the oaths of loyalty to the new regime on the bishops, and was added to the managers of a conference on the subject. On 27 Apr. he tabled a long report on the standing charges on the revenue. He defended the suspension of habeas corpus as a necessity, and was among those appointed to consider the bills enabling the Duke of Norfolk to develop the grounds of Arundel House and confirming Clayton's purchase of Bletchingley. He also took part in the inquiry into the delay in relieving Londonderry and the impeachment of four Jacobite propagandists. But his chief concern in the remainder of the first session was the rehabilitation of Oates, in which he was able to combine his hostility to the Papists and the peers. The name of the arch-perjuror was hissed when he first mentioned it on 4 June, whereupon he continued:

> Such gentlemen as did it I shall not be reconciled to, unless they favour whipping and perpetual imprisonment, and no confirmation of the Popish Plot. . . . With all my heart let Oates be brought to trial for perjury, but nothing can be more fatal to the English nation than that his testimony should be sufficient against Lord Stafford, and yet he be convicted of perjury.

A week later he reported indignantly that according to their Journals the Lords had found no viciousness or defect in the judgment against Oates, and moved for a bill to reverse it. He wished the House to define offences deserving exception from indemnity and to leave the naming of offenders to a committee, though he was anxious to deprive Bishop Crew. He was disappointed, however, with the evidence: 'I wish they would tell us no more stories of the dead; I see they must bear all,' he burst out, adding a few days later, rather unconvincingly: 'I do not speak to still the charity of anybody'. Forgetful of his own vociferous support of the dispensing power, he insisted that the judgment of Sir Edward Herbert* in Godden v. Hales was criminal, though it might be pardoned for his brother's sake. On 3 July he was named to the committees to consider the Oates bill and to prepare an address asking for access to the records of the Privy Council concerning Ireland. He reported on 12 July that the King had consented to the release on bail of Colonel John Richards, the brilliant engineer officer whose potential services in the Irish campaign far outweighed the disadvantage of his religion, and was sent to return thanks for a message deferring further supply till after the recess. He was the first Member appointed to prepare reasons for disagreeing with the Lords about Oates.[19]

In the second session of the Convention Howard was appointed to the committees of inquiry into the expenditure and miscarriages of the war, though he was apprehensive of their outcome. 'Should you, out of good husbandry, strike off ten thousand men from Ireland, I believe you will give great satisfaction to King James', he warned the House. He was

named to the committee for the second mutiny bill. Most of his speeches related to the unsatisfactory condition of the army in Ireland. He thought that 'melancholy complaints will do us no service', and recognized that 'I have been rather too warm upon persons formerly'; though he had a low opinion of Commissary Shales, he advised the House not to inquire who had recommended him for employment. He seconded the vote of thanks to the King for the message of 30 Nov. and regarded the refusal of the House to nominate commissioners to go into Ireland as contradictory. He was named to the committees to inquire into the state of the revenue and to draw up an address for provision for Princess Anne. Though he professed dislike of the revival of party labels, he supported the disabling clause in the bill to restore corporations, and attacked those Churchmen who had supported the doctrine of non-resistance:

> I arraign those that arraign the Church of England of such doctrines; these men prepared corporations to deliver up their charters. The false representations of the Church of England's doctrine made way for those misfortunes that followed. . . . I have abhorred what was done in the late times, but rather than no mark of incapacity shall be put upon these men, I would part with the whole bill.

His last committee was to consider the bill to impose a general oath of allegiance.[20]

Howard was re-elected to the next two Parliaments as a court Whig. Surviving another pamphlet war over his anti-clerical *History of Religion* in 1694–6 and another scandal at the Exchequer in 1697, he died on 3 Sept. 1698 and was buried in Westminster Abbey. Howard's reputation has suffered from his frequent changes of party in the Cavalier Parliament, but his speeches, which reveal a more powerful mind than his published works, are less inconsistent. It is clear that his loathing of Popery, surprising in view of his family connexions and his sophisticated background, was deep and genuine and to it he united a better-founded fear of French ambitions in Europe. Unlike many of the country party, he saw that these could only be resisted by a strong executive, and he was always anxious to promote mutual confidence between King and Parliament, both under Charles and William. Only his official life cannot be defended; never more than a minor poet, at the Exchequer he was little short of a major disaster.

[1] This biography is based on H. J. Oliver, *Sir Robert Howard*, and the *Commons Journals*. [2] *Symonds Diary* (Cam. Soc. lxxiv), 24. [3] *CSP Dom.* 1660–1, pp. 55, 76, 607; 1663–4, pp. 58, 677; *Cal. Treas. Bks.* iv. 83. [4] Mdx. RO, WJP/CP3; *Cal. Treas. Bks.* i. 82, iii, 1262; *Tudor and Stuart Proclamations* ed. Steele, i. 405; *CSP Dom.* 1675–6, p. 354. [5] *HMC 10th Rep. IV*, 210; *Cal. Cl. SP*, v. 17–18, 25, 30; *Cal. Treas. Bks.* i. 619; Stow, *Survey of London* (1720), i. bk. 1, p. 179. [6] *CJ*, viii. 314, 356, 367, 389, 401, 402,

406, 432, 433, 531, 573; PRO 31/3, bdle. 116, f. 115; Bodl. Carte 34, f. 429. [7] Clarendon, *Life*, ii. 321; *CJ*, viii. 637, 661, 669, 670, 671, 673, 678; Marvell ed. Margoliouth, i. 147; *Pepys Diary*, 8 Dec. 1666. [8] Grey, i. 3, 17–18, 46; *Milward*, 102, 131; *Clarendon Impeachment*, 18, 21, 23, 47, 80, 128–9; *CJ*, ix. 21, 25, 32, 39. [9] *Pepys Diary*, 14 Feb. 1668; *Milward*, 183, 202, 281, 283, 298–9; Grey, i. 83, 92, 106, 108, 138, 147, 149, 153. [10] *Pepys Diary*, 8 May 1668; Grey, i. 157–8, 176, 183, 204, 209, 217, 222, 253; PRO 31/3, bdle. 123, f. 58; bdle. 124, f. 123; *CJ*, ix. 129, 147, 155. [11] *Marvell*, ii. 305; *CJ*, ix. 166, 192, 214, 236, 238; Grey, i. 278–9, 304, 335, 342, 394, 439; *Dering*, 12, 45; Harl. 7020, f. 39. [12] *CSP Dom.* 1671, pp. 407, 526; 1673, p. 18; D. R. Chandaman, *Eng. Pub. Revenue*, 27; Grey, ii. 11, 21, 80, 166, 201–2, 218; E. C. Legh, Lady Newton, *Lyme Letters*, 52; K. W. D. Haley, *Shaftesbury*, 215; *HMC Lindsey*, 182; C.H. Josten, *Ashmole*, 1340; *Williamson Letters* (Cam. Soc. n.s viii), 120; (ix), 52; *Essex Pprs.* (Cam. Soc. n.s. xlvii), 130, 132. [13] Grey, ii. 234, 243–4, 265, 287, 333, 358, 375, 386, 393–4, 411, 418; iii. 54, 69, 101, 114, 217, 248, 299, 303; *Dering Pprs.* 59; Eg. 3345, f. 25v; *HMC Laing*, i. 402; *CJ*, ix. 342, 344, 352, 361, 365. [14] *HMC Rutland*, ii. 28; *HMC 11th Rep. VII*, 13; *HMC 7th Rep.* 467; Grey, iv. 67, 131, 291, 333; v. 82, 315, 388; Add. 28091, f. 65v; *CJ*, ix. 387, 403; Eg. 3345, f. 65v; *HMC Ormonde*, n.s. iv. 383, 386; *Hatton Corresp.* (Cam. Soc. n.s. xxii), 152; H. Roseveare, *Treasury: Foundations of Control*, 50. [15] Grey, vi. 122–3, 220, 249–50, 304, 343; *CJ*, ix. 542, 543, 551; *HMC 12th Rep. IX*, 79. [16] *Pepys Further Corresp.* 341; Grey, vii. 34, 48, 171, 233, 271, 279; Add. 28046, f. 115. [17] Grey, vii. 269–70; viii. 301, 325–6; ix. 287; *Exact Coll. Debates*, 59–60; *CJ*, ix. 641, 650, 708, 710. [18] *CJ*, ix. 751; x. 18, 20; *Clarendon Corresp.* ii. 228; Clarke, *Jas. II*, ii. 301–2; *IHR Bull.* xlix. 250–1; Grey, ix. 62–63. [19] *CJ*, x. 32, 34, 46, 98, 176; Grey, ix. 111, 126, 145, 152, 219–20, 269, 286–7, 289, 300, 310, 324, 342–3. [20] Grey, ix. 391, 439, 451, 452, 456, 466, 470, 485, 519–20.

P.W.

HOWARD, Thomas I (1651–1701), of Ashtead, Surr.

CASTLE RISING	1685
BLETCHINGLEY	1689, 1690, 1695
CASTLE RISING	1698, 11 Jan.–4 Apr. 1701

bap. 21 Feb. 1651, 3rd but o. surv. s. of Sir Robert Howard* by 1st w. *m.* 31 Aug. 1683 (with £5,500), Lady Diana Newport, da. of Francis Newport†, 1st Earl of Bradford, 3s. (2 *d.v.p.*) 1da. *suc.* fa. 1698.[1]
    Teller of the Exchequer 1689–d.[2]
    Commr. for assessment, Surr. 1689–90; j.p. Norf. by 1690–d., Surr. by 1701–d.; dep. lt. Norf. and Surr. by 1701–d.

Howard's father as auditor of the Exchequer secured for him the reversion of a valuable office in 1674 and a pension of £50 p.a. When Howard married it was agreed that as long as his father remained a widower he and his wife should live with him at Ashtead on an allowance of £500 p.a. He was returned in 1685 for Castle Rising, the borough which his father had represented in the Exclusion Parliaments, on the interest of the 5th Duke of Norfolk, the head of the family. He was not active in James II's Parliament, in which he was appointed only to the committee on the bill for the relief of insolvent debtors. An opponent of the Court, he acted as teller in favour of hearing the Buckinghamshire election case at the bar of the House. When Sir William Clifton* asked if complaints about a standing army included the Beefeaters,

Howard retorted that at least they were established by Act of Parliament.[3]

Howard's reversion had still not fallen in at the Revolution, but one of the tellers was incapable of office under the Test Act. An order was obtained for the admission of Howard in his place, his sureties including Sir Robert Clayton*, who had a controlling interest at Bletchingley. He was elected to the borough for the Convention, in which he probably became a moderately active Member, though there is some possibility of confusion with his cousin, the Hon. Philip Howard*. He may have served on 17 committees, including the committee of elections and privileges in the first session, and those to inquire into the authors and advisers of grievances, and the delay in relieving Londonderry. He supported the disabling clause in the bill to restore corporations, and was named to the committee on the bill to discharge the 6th Duke of Norfolk of certain payments as trustee under his father's will. A court Whig under William III, he died on 4 Apr. 1701 and was buried at Ashtead. His only surviving son died at the age of 14 in the following year.[4]

[1] H. J. Oliver, *Sir Robert Howard*, 7–8, 250; F. E. Paget, *Recs. of Ashtead Estate*, 69. [2] *Cal. Treas. Bks.* viii. 2146, 2151. [3] *Cal. Treas. Bks.* iv. 633; Grey, x. 191; *HMC Lords*, iii. 387; Oliver, 250–1; *CJ*, ix. 717; Lowther debates, f. 26. [4] *Cal. Treas. Bks.* viii. 2146, 2151; Paget, 69–70.

J.C./P.W.

HOWARD (HAYWARD), Thomas II (c.1655–82), of Fletherhill, Rudbaxton, Pemb.

| HAVERFORDWEST | 1681 |

b. c.1655, o.s. of James Hayward of Fletherhill by Joanna, da. of Evan Gwynne of Moel Ifor, Llandyssul, Card. *m.* lic. 9 Aug. 1678, Anne, da. of Sir Erasmus Philipps†, 3rd Bt., of Picton, Pemb., wid. of Thomas Bowen of Trefloyn, Penally, Pemb., *s.p. suc.* fa. 1668.[1]
    Commr. for assessment, Pemb. 1677–80, Haverfordwest 1679–80; j.p. Pemb. and Haverfordwest 1677–d.

Howard's ancestors acquired Great Rudbaxton, some three miles from Haverfordwest, by 1580. His grandfather was appointed to the county committee in 1644, but they did not belong to the major gentry. Howard presumably opposed exclusion, for he remained on the commission of the peace from 1677 until his death. His marriage into the Philipps family in 1678 undoubtedly enhanced his status. He defeated Thomas Owen* in 1681, but left no trace on the records of the short Oxford Parliament. He was killed in a duel on 7 July 1682 and buried at Rudbaxton, the only member of his family to sit in Parliament. The estate passed to his sister, Mary Tasker.[2]

[1] NLW mss 1387, f. 19; PCC 1 King; *Bristol Mar. Bonds* (Bristol and Glos. Arch. Soc. Recs. i), 112. [2] S. R. Meyricke, *Vis. Wales*,

i. 179; *West Wales Hist. Recs.* iv. 205; x. 10–11, 18–24; *Trans. Carm. Antiq. Soc.* xx. 86.

L.N./G.J.

HOWARD, Hon. Thomas (1621–c.81), of Pall Mall, Westminster.

NEW WOODSTOCK   16 Feb. 1674

bap. 8 July 1621, 2nd s. of Theophilus Howard†, 2nd Earl of Suffolk, by Lady Elizabeth Home, da. and coh. of George, 1st Earl of Dunbar [S]. *m.* by 1649, Walburga, illegit. da. of Jan Polyander van der Kerchhove, lord of Henvliet, Zeeland, 1s. *d.v.p.*[1]
   Col. of horse (royalist) c.1643–5; master of horse to the Princess Royal by 1647–Dec. 1660; capt. of horse, Dutch army 1647–at least 1656; lt.-col. of ft. Holland regt. 1665–74.[2]
   Freeman, Woodstock 1673; commr. for assessment, Berks. 1673–9, Oxon. 1677–9, recusants, Oxon. 1675.[3]

Howard's father, as warden of the Cinque Ports, nominated him as court candidate for Rye before he was 19, but he was not elected, and when his father died a few months later, he was left virtually unendowed. The 3rd Earl sided with Parliament in the Civil War till he was impeached in 1647, but Howard fought as a Royalist. After the battle of Naseby he retired to Holland, where he was taken into the service of the Princess Royal and given a commission in the Dutch army. He made periodic visits to England, one of them in the company of the royal mistress, Lucy Walter. He was suspected of sending information to his brother-in-law, Lord Broghill (Roger Boyle*), and in 1658 George Downing* reported that he had 'perfectly gained' him. Sir Edward Hyde† angrily denounced him as a spy, and his hopes of a peerage were dashed, but the King remarked only that he 'earns his wages very easily, for all he informs is of his own invention'. Certainly the letters which Downing obtained from him cannot have been of much use to the Protectorate Government. At the Restoration a pension of £500 was settled on his wife, from whom he was living apart, but nothing was done for Howard himself until the outbreak of the second Dutch war, when he came over from Zeeland as second-in-command of the newly-formed Holland regiment. This was soon followed by the marriage of his only son to the King's natural daughter by Lady Shannon, and his future as a courtier seemed assured. With his younger brother he was granted the right to levy a shilling for every ton of ship's ballast in any Irish port, though the opposition of Dublin made this ineffective.[4]

   Howard's election at Woodstock in 1674 was probably procured by John Lovelace*, his partner in obtaining a lease of crown property in Lincolnshire some four years before. On laying down his

commission he received an excise pension of £300 p.a. He was not an active Member of the Cavalier Parliament, with only eight committees, none of which was of any political importance. He was noted as an official in 1675, perhaps by confusion with his cousins of the Berkshire or Escrick families. But in August his pension was stopped until he had made good his soldiers' pay, which he had detained. His name appeared on the working lists and Wiseman's account, but Shaftesbury marked him 'worthy', no doubt because of his elder brother's politics and his own association with Lovelace. However, he was included in the court party in both lists of 1678, and as one of the 'unanimous club' probably did not stand for re-election. He died between 17 Jan. 1680 and 10 June 1682, when he was omitted from the entail on the Suffolk estates.[5]

[1] C6/282/86; *Misc. Gen. et Her.* (ser. 2), v. 142; H. K. S. Causton, *Howard Pprs.* 650. [2] *CSP Dom.* 1644–5, p. 54; 1645–7, p. 577; 1664–5, p. 469; 1675–6, p. 275; F. J. G. ten Raa and F. de Bas, *Het Staatsche Leger*, iv. 205; v. 53. [3] Woodstock council act bk. 5 Feb. 1673. [4] *HMC 13th Rep. IV*, 209; Clarendon, *Rebellion*, iii. 76; Thurloe, v. 160, 169; vii. 428, 444–5; *Cal. Cl. SP*, iv. 121, 173, 219, 245, 444; Carte, *Orig. Letters and Pprs.* ii. 319; *CSP Dom.* 1651–2, pp. 65, 90; 1661–2, p. 140; 1664–5, p. 234; 1671, p. 225; 1675–6, p. 275. [5] *Cal. Treas. Bks.* iii. 533; iv. 577; *HMC Ormonde*, n.s. v. 264; *CP.*

L.N.

HOWARD, Hon. William (c.1630–94), of Lincoln's Inn.

WINCHELSEA   1660

b. c.1630, 2nd s. of Sir Edward Howard†, 1st Baron Howard of Escrick (*d.*1675), by Mary, da. of Sir John Boteler†, 1st Baron Boteler of Brantfield. *educ.* Corpus, Camb. 1646; L. Inn 1648, called 1654. *m.* 21 July 1661, Frances, da. of Sir James Bridgeman of Whitley, Yorks., 4s. (3 *d.v.p.*) 2da. *suc.* bro. as 3rd Baron Howard of Escrick 24 Aug. 1678.[1]
   Tpr. Life Gds. by 1653–6.
   Commr. for oyer and terminer, Home circuit July 1660, assessment, Westminster 1661–3.
   Gent. of privy chamber 1672–?78.[2]

Howard's father, the youngest son of the 1st Earl of Suffolk, married into the Villiers 'kindred' and was raised to the peerage in 1628. He was one of the most constant attendants in the House of Lords during the Civil War, and after its abolition sat on the Council of State and in the Rump as MP for Carlisle till expelled for corruption in 1651, after which he took no further part in public life. Howard himself, 'a person of very extraordinary parts, sharpness of wit, readiness and yet volubility of tongue, and yet an Anabaptist ... sucked in the opinions that were most prevalent', in his adolescence. Although undersized and misshapen, he joined up in the ranks of Cromwell's lifeguard while still eating his dinners at Lincoln's Inn. But after a few years he was dismissed as a Leveller, and became preacher in an Anabaptist congregation. 'After some few days' conference' he prevailed on John Wildman I* and other leading Levellers to lay aside their 'vain and idle prejudices' against the monarchy. As their emissary, he visited the King at Brugge in 1656, and offered his humble associates as pawns 'in a desperate game at chess' for the modest price of £2,000. But even this was beyond the resources of the exiled Court, and Howard returned empty-handed, only to be arrested through Wildman's treachery and imprisoned until Oliver's death. On his release, he resumed correspondence with Sir Edward Hyde†, who urged him to stand for Richard Cromwell's Parliament, but he is not known to have done so.[3]

Howard was a nephew of William Ashburnham*, and his return for Winchelsea in 1660 was probably on the Ashburnham interest, but he was not an active Member of the Convention, serving on one committee at most, that for preserving the Forest of Dean, and probably acting as teller against the tanning bill on 18 Dec. Hyde, however, now Lord Chancellor Clarendon, had not forgotten his services to the Restoration, particularly among the sectaries. He was granted £500 out of smuggling fines and, with his younger brother Sir Cecil Howard, £1,500 for secret service. He was used to obtain a confession from a prisoner suspected of importing seditious literature and allowed to sell a couple of baronetcies. After failing to extract £900 from the keeper of the King's Bench prison for a technical breach of habeas corpus, he went to Ireland, and at the King's request was given the standing of a KC. He reappeared in the House of Commons in 1668, opening the case for the Irish Adventurers. John Milward* found him 'a well-spoken young man, but indeed too fine and affected'. In a speech of 'full two hours' he charged Richard Rainsford I* with unjustly favouring the Irish, and 'received a sharp reprimand from the Speaker'. Returning to Ireland, he was appointed leading counsel to the Earl of Meath, a tool of his kinsman, the 2nd Duke of Buckingham, against Ormonde. Meath advanced him money to extract him from a debtors' prison, and he crossed to England again and sold another baronetcy. When Meath tried to recover his money, Howard became a gentleman of the privy chamber. He soon grew weary of lurking about Whitehall to avoid arrest, and was recruited to du Moulin's organization. He was sent to the Tower on 28 June 1672, but released in October, and spent the remainder of the third Dutch war as a double agent in England and Holland.[4]

Howard succeeded to the peerage on the eve of the Popish Plot, but not to the estate, which had been sold to Sir Henry Thompson* in 1668. A member of the Green Ribbon Club, he voted for exclusion, and (like most of his family) for the condemnation of his distant cousin, Lord Stafford. He was again imprisoned in 1681 on a false charge made by Fitzharris, who summoned him as a witness for the defence at his own trial. According to Burnet he owed his liberty largely to the unremitting efforts of Algernon Sidney*. A member of the Council of Six, he warmly approved the project of 'lopping' the royal brothers in the theatre, 'for then they will die in their calling'. He was one of the last to be arrested after the discovery of the Rye House Plot, being found hiding in a chimney. 'As soon as he was taken, he fell a-crying: and at his first examination he told, as he said, all he knew.' He implicated John Hampden*, and was the chief witness against William Russell*, Lord Russell, and the only witness against his benefactor Sidney. On 2 Dec. 1683 a warrant was issued for his pardon and he was allowed to retire into obscurity like his father before him. He was buried in York Minster on 24 Apr. 1694. His son, the last of the Escrick branch, sat in the Lords as a Tory.[5]

Howard's extraordinary career provided ample material for the moralist and the satirist. Against Clarendon's assessment in his early years may be set Burnet's: 'a man of learning . . . who had run through many parties in religion. . . . [He] did some service at the Restoration, but was always poor and ready to engage in anything that was bold'.[6]

[1] *Temple Church* (Harl. Soc. Reg. n.s. i), 58. [2] Carlisle, *Privy Chamber*, 190. [3] *CSP Dom.* 1672, p. 302; *Thurloe*, v. 393; Clarendon, *Rebellion*, vi. 74–78; *Cal. Cl. SP*, iv. 98; D. Underdown, *Royalist Conspiracy*, 193–4, 198. [4] *Cal. Cl. SP*, iv. 518; *CSP Dom.* 1659–60, p. 326; 1661–2, pp. 87, 158, 175, 203, 288, 327; 1663–4, p. 45; 1665–6, p. 154; 1668–9, p. 647; *CSP Ire.* 1663–5, p. 611; *Milward*, 264, 273; Carte, *Ormond*, iv. 378; K. H. D. Haley, *Wm. of Orange and the Eng. Opp.* passim. [5] *VCH E. Riding*, iii. 20; *State Trials*, viii. 370–2; Burnet, ii. 294, 370, 402; *CSP Dom.* 1683–4, p. 129. [6] Burnet, ii. 63–64.

M.W.H./B.D.H.

HOWARD see also **DANVERS** alias **VILLIERS, Robert**

HOWE, George Grobham (c.1627–76), of Berwick St. Leonard, nr. Hindon, Wilts.

HINDON   1660, 1661–26 Sept. 1676

b. c.1627, o.s. of George Howe of Berwick St. Leonard by Dorothy, da. of Humphrey Clarke of Bradgate, Kent. *educ.* L. Inn 1646. *m.* 1650, Elizabeth, da. of Sir Harbottle Grimston, 2nd Bt.*, of Gorhambury, Herts., 4s. (3 *d.v.p.*) 7da. *suc.* fa. 1647; *cr.* Bt. 20 June 1660.[1]

Howe Family

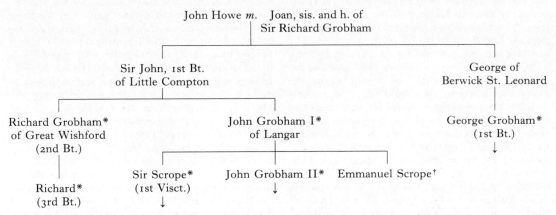

John Howe *m.* Joan, sis. and h. of Sir Richard Grobham

Sir John, 1st Bt. of Little Compton

George of Berwick St. Leonard

Richard Grobham* of Great Wishford (2nd Bt.)

John Grobham I* of Langar

George Grobham* (1st Bt.) ↓

Richard* (3rd Bt.)

Sir Scrope* (1st Visct.) ↓

John Grobham II* ↓

Emmanuel Scrope†

J.p. Wilts. 1649–52, 1656–*d.*, commr. for scandalous ministers 1654, assessment 1657, Jan. 1660–*d.*, militia Mar. 1660, corporations 1662–3, dep. lt. 1662–*d.*, col. of militia ft. by 1673–*d.*; commr. for recusants, Glos. and Wilts. 1675.[2]

Howe's father inherited Berwick St. Leonard, a mile from Hindon, from the Grobham family. Though anything but an active Parliamentarian in the Civil War he stood for the borough in 1645, but the double return was decided in favour of Edmund Ludlow* at his death. Howe's marriage suggests Presbyterian leanings, and he was marked as a friend by Lord Wharton, but he held local office during most of the Interregnum. His return at the general election of 1660 was not in dispute, and he seems to have taken his seat from the first, being named on 26 Apr. to the committee of elections and privileges. But as his name stands last on the list, it may represent an addition made by the clerk on the instructions of Howe's father-in-law, the Speaker, who was also responsible for his baronetcy. Howe was inactive in the Convention, with only seven committees: there would have been even fewer if he had not represented Grimston's interests in two matters: the appointment of a minister for Harwich and his power (as master of the rolls) to grant leases. Howe spoke in the debate on the poll bill on 10 Dec. to suggest that the sums charged on clergymen should be specified. Howe was again returned in 1661, probably unopposed, but was no more active in the Cavalier Parliament. He was named to only 26 committees in 14 sessions, and made no recorded speeches. Outside Parliament he co-operated in the suppression of conventicles, but he took no part in preparing the Clarendon Code. In 1666 he acted as teller for the committal of a bill to regulate hospitals and free schools. With an income estimated at £1,500 p.a., he had so much

improved his interest at Hindon that in 1673 he was reported to intend bringing in his cousin Richard Howe* for the second seat. He appears on the working lists of 1675 as under Grimston's influence. He died on 26 Sept. 1676. His son and successor, Sir James Howe, sat for Hindon in several Parliaments as a Tory between 1693 and 1709.[3]

[1] *Wilts. Vis. Peds.* (Harl. Soc. cv), 75; Hoare, *Wilts.* Branch and Dole, 46; *Som. and Dorset N. and Q.* viii. 47–48. [2] Hoare, Salisbury, 449; *Cal. Treas. Bks.* i. 692; Salisbury Cathedral Lib. Bp. Seth Ward, Liber Notitiae, f. 53. [3] *Wilts. Arch. Mag.* xxvi. 356; Brunton and Pennington, 23; *CSP Dom.* 1660–1, p. 45; 1661–2, p. 155; *Old Parl. Hist.* xxiii. 47; *CJ*, viii. 626; Hoare, *Repertorium Wiltonense*, 16; Bath mss, Thynne pprs. 14, f. 395.

M.W.H./J.P.F.

HOWE, John Grobham I (1625–79), of Little Compton, Withington, Glos. and Langar, Notts.

GLOUCESTERSHIRE 1654, 1656, 1659, 1661

b. 25 Jan. 1625, 2nd s. of Sir John Howe, 1st Bt., of Little Compton by Bridget, da. of Thomas Rich, master in Chancery, of North Cerney, Glos.; bro. of Richard Grobham Howe*. *educ.* L. Inn 1645. *m.* by 1648, Lady Annabella Scroope (*d.* 20 Mar. 1704), illegit. da. of Emmanuel, 1st Earl of Sunderland 4s. 5da.[1]

J.p. Wilts. 1646–?49, Glos. 1650–3, Mar. 1660–*d.*, Notts. July 1660–*d.*; commr. for assessment, Glos. 1649–52, Aug. 1660–*d.*, Gloucester 1661–9, Notts. 1661–*d.*, Yorks. (N. Riding) 1665–79; commr. for militia, Glos. and Notts. Mar. 1660; capt. of militia horse, Glos. Apr. 1660, dep. lt. c. Aug. 1660–*d.*, commr. for loyal and indigent officers 1662, recusants 1675.[2]

It is difficult to distinguish Howe's record from his father's until comparatively late in life. It seems, however, that it was Howe who was the active royalist plotter in the closing years of the Interregnum, since the estates in Nottinghamshire which he held in his wife's right were sequestrated after Booth's rising. His father was rewarded with a baronetcy at the Restoration and his wife was legitimized. Howe was successful in a contested election in 1661, but proved an inactive Member of the Cavalier Parliament, in which he was appointed to only 40 committees. Listed by Lord Wharton as a friend, he was clearly a reluctant conformist, obtaining leave to go into the country on 20 May 1661, and thereby evading compliance with the resolution of the House that all Members should receive the sacrament on the following Sunday. He was appointed to the committee on the bill for preventing dangers from schismatics, but took no part in the Clarendon Code. On 7 Dec. 1666 he acted as teller for an unsuccessful motion seeking leave to speak against the compulsory taking of the sacrament. He was included by Sir Thomas Osborne* in 1669 among those Members to be engaged by the Duke of Buckingham for the Court. A claim of privilege which he made in 1671 led to the apprehension of the under-sheriff of Gloucestershire by order of the House, and at the Cirencester by-election in the same year he quarrelled violently with Thomas Master I*, striking him with an iron-tipped cane in the presence of many of the local gentry.³

Howe first took a prominent part in the House in the attacks on the Speaker (Edward Seymour*) in the brief autumn session of 1673. He alleged that Seymour had called the House a company of curs. He thought it was a grievance to have a Privy Councillor in the chair, and was reluctant to vote money to be paid to him in his capacity as treasurer of the navy. On 13 Jan. 1674 he supported the motion for the dismissal of Lauderdale, alleging that he had been 'solicitor from Scotland to bring the late King to the block'; but he was compelled to acknowledge that his story of Buckingham's seizing the bridle of Charles II's horse 'to the great danger of the King's person' was unfounded. He moved to vote Lord Arlington (Sir Henry Bennet*) innocent, declaring him the victim of a malicious prosecution instigated by Buckingham, and was appointed to the committee to examine the charges. On 28 Jan. he was sent with Peregrine Bertie I* to desire the lord chief baron, (Sir) Edward Turnor*, to expedite the passing of the accounts of Arlington's brother, Sir John Bennet*, who had recently married Howe's daughter. An attempt was made to discredit him on Master's evidence that he had said 'he hoped this session might be worth five thousand guineas to him; but whether in relation to Irish cattle coming in again' the witness did not remember. He failed to obtain leave to go into the country on 21 Feb. to answer a charge of riotous behaviour at the Cirencester election. In his absence, the attorney-general (Sir Francis North*) for the prosecution

suggested that the assize court should act as 'somewhat of a limited Star Chamber ... for the punishment of such enormous crimes', but (Sir) Matthew Hale* sentenced him only to a fine of 500 marks.⁴

Howe was responsible for bringing to the notice of the House on 25 Oct. 1675 the challenge to William Cavendish*, Lord Cavendish. His last important committees were in the same session, those to prevent the growth of Popery and to secure the liberty of the subject. In the working lists he was committed to the management of Osborne himself, now Lord Treasurer Danby, to whom Sir Richard Wiseman* wrote significantly: 'Your lordship knows who can influence him'. The influence was presumably successfully exerted, for when Parliament met again in 1677 Howe 'moved to stand by the King with our lives and fortunes'. Nevertheless Shaftesbury marked him 'worthy', and his name was not on either list of the court party in 1678. On 3 May he declared that he was glad to hear a reference to pensions:

> We are named to be the greatest rogues and villains, and 'tis said commonly ... that we take money to betray our country. I would have some committee to draw up a test about persons that receive pensions.

But it passed off, and he is not known to have attended the House again. He was buried at Langar on 27 May 1679.⁵

¹ *Vis. England and Wales Notes* ed. Crisp, xiii. 96–106. ² *Parl. Intell.* 16 Apr. 1660. ³ *Cal. Cl. SP*, iv. 78, 573; *Ludlow Mems.* ii. 86; *Cal. Comm. Comp.* 755, 3252; *CJ*, viii. 289; ix. 193; P. Ventris, *K.B. Reps.* 209. ⁴ *Dering*, 153, 158; Grey, ii. 210, 241, 247, 280, 281, 288, 374–5; *CJ*, ix. 301; Ventris, 209. ⁵ Grey, iii. 337; v. 318; Eg. 3345, f. 47vᵛ; Notts. RO, Langar par. reg.

J.P.F.

HOWE, John Grobham II (c.1657–1722), of Stowell, Glos.

CIRENCESTER	1689, 1690, 1695
GLOUCESTERSHIRE	1698, 1701 (Feb.), 1702

b. c.1657, 2nd s. of John Grobham Howe I*, and bro. of Sir Scrope Howe* and Emmanuel Scrope Howe†. *m.* lic. 30 Apr. 1683, Mary, da. and coh. of Humphrey Baskerville of Pontrilas, Herefs., wid. of Sir Edward Morgan, 3rd Bt.*, of Llantarnam, Mon., 1s. 1da.¹
V.-chamberlain to Queen Mary II 1689–92; commr. for public accounts 1701–2; PC 21 Apr. 1702; paymaster of guards and garrisons 1702–14.²
Dep. lt. Glos. and Mon. 1689–?92; keeper of Pall Mall 1689–92; commr. for assessment, Glos., Herefs., Mon. and Som. 1689–90, Lincs. and Staffs. 1690; j.p. Glos. ?1689–96, 1700–?d., v.-adm. 1702–12.

In his early years, Howe, 'a young amorous spark of the Court', acquired some reputation as an author of lampoons. In 1678 he falsely boasted of enjoying the favours of the Duchess of Richmond, and was banished from Court; but he retained his reputation as a gallant and was frequently mentioned in the satiric verse of the period. His name was first mentioned in a political context in 1687, when he was included in the Gloucestershire opposition. He was returned for Cirencester at the general election of 1689, although he did not acquire Stowell, nine miles away, until later in the year. He took no great part in the routine business of the House, being named to only 24 committees, 'but before he had been a Member three weeks, his volubility, his asperity, and his pertinacity had made him conspicuous'. He made the first of over 70 recorded speeches on the day that the Convention met, in the debate on an address of thanks to the Prince of Orange. 'I think it [as] proper for us to say by whose means we were brought into Popery and slavery, as by whom we were brought out.' But the drafting committee, on which he served, did not agree. In the debate on the state of the nation on 22 Jan. he urged somewhat paradoxically that 'the King's tyranny had before his departure put an end to his government', and reflected very much on the Hon. Heneage Finch I*. When Dr Sharp, preaching before the House on the anniversary of Charles I's execution, used the customary prayer for the King, Howe complained on 30 Jan. that:

> This prayer of Dr Sharp's, to put a contradiction on your vote, will encourage the priests to knock your brains out. The vote we made is contrary to passive obedience, and this man preaches it up.

His zeal for the Revolution was rewarded with the highly inappropriate post of vice-chamberlain to the Queen. His next important committee was that of 25 Feb. to recommend alterations in the coronation oath. On the following day he informed the House that

> I received a letter from my corporation last night which acquaints me, with all the terror that can be expressed, that the soldiers are so insolent there, that, contrary to the interest of the King and Queen, they proclaim King James. 'Tis time to prevent these insolencies; they drank King William's and Queen Mary's damnation. I believe the justices will not redress this. The clergy are got into cabals, and they would not appear at the proclamation. I believe the black coats and the red coats to be the grievances of the nation. I would willingly satisfy the poor people I represent.

After demanding on 5 Mar. an inquiry into the grievances reported to the House and 'who were the authors and advisers thereof', he was named to the select committee. When news was brought of the Ipswich mutiny, he urged sending Dutch troops to suppress it. As a concession to the dissenters, he favoured the coronation oath proposed by William Garway* which would bind the sovereign to accept changes in the established Church. 'If you do not

add the words moved', he told the House, 'it will be thought the King has taken an oath without any consideration for what these men [the dissenters] have suffered.' Howe was constantly in search of subversive elements in the army, and on 21 Mar. he gleefully produced information that a discharged officer had forecast the return of King James within six months. Unfortunately for him the information was proved to be false and malicious, and his credulity was rebuked by his fellow Whigs. When William told the House that he was ready to pass an act of general oblivion, Howe agreed, provided that those concerned withdrew into obscurity, and he helped to draw up the address of thanks.[3]

In the debate of 1 June on the failure to relieve Londonderry, Howe demanded the removal from office of all who had ever been impeached, declaring that:

> King William came over and delivered us from these counsels; if we be delivered to these men, who formerly gave the ill counsel, and were of the Privy Council to King James, they are not fit to be counsellors to King William. If you deprive him of these servants, who would draw the King into the same inconvenience they did King James, I hope affairs will go on much better.

He was named to the committee of inquiry, and not even a message from William himself through Dykvelt could persuade him to change his tune. Two days later he moved that the House should proceed with the indemnity bill:

> As for offenders, I would shake them off gently from my hand like a viper, but when it is on the ground I would tread upon it, and destroy it, that it may hurt no more.

He obtained a resolution from the House that pardons were not pleadable against impeachments, and supported the proposal of Sir Robert Howard* to reverse the judgment against Titus Oates, 'who has saved the nation', declaring that 'possibly it is in the interest of some persons that no witnesses may be believed'. He acted as teller for excepting from indemnity those East India Company officials responsible for martial law on St. Helena, and helped to inspect the Journals for references to the Popish Plot. He continued to speak frequently on the indemnity bill, in an attempt to discredit those who had held high office in the last reign. 'He that was against abdicating King James, and [declared] the throne not vacant is not fit to be trusted in King William's Council.' On the succession bill he suggested that, instead of the Privy Council, the House of Commons should be summoned on the demise of the crown to administer the Test to the new sovereign, because 'it would content the people'. He supported the address for the dismissal of Halifax and Carmarthen, exclaiming: 'I would keep out that filthy trimming trick, to disoblige our friends and oblige our enemies.'[4]

In the second session Howe was named to the committees to inquire into the expenses of the war and to consider the mutiny and desertion bill. He thought 'there would be no good effect' of the address to ask who had recommended Commissary Shales. Though he was eager to find out the 'great men' behind the appointment, he declined to name them when challenged. In the debate on the state of the nation on 14 Dec. he said, in a speech that could not have been delivered in any previous Parliament:

> I think the worst state of the nation is to throw the [words] fanatic and Papist at one another's heads. The Church of England have so well vindicated themselves from Popery that I hope we shall show ourselves not the men we are represented to ruin the Church, and ruin monarchy. I know not what religion does here; that is for the pulpit.

He acted as teller for recommitting the bill to restore corporations in order to save the disabling clause. 'I cannot let so useful a clause be lost', he said, and sought to make it more acceptable by applying it only to mayors and recorders, but in vain.[5]

In the next Parliament Howe continued to attack those politicians who had been identified with James II, but in 1692 he was dismissed from office and became as violent a Tory as he had been a Whig. Returned to favour under Queen Anne he was again dismissed from office on the Hanoverian succession. He died on 11 June 1722, and was buried at Stowell. His son represented Gloucester and Wiltshire under the first two Hanoverians as a Tory until 1735, when he became a supporter of Walpole, and was created Baron Chedworth in 1741.[6]

[1] *DNB*; *Vis. England and Wales Notes* ed. Crisp, xiii. 103. [2] Luttrell, ii. 390; *Cal. Treas. Bks.* xvii. 424; *HMC Cowper*, ii. 430; *HMC Var.* viii. 34. [3] *Poems on Affairs of State* ed. Ellis, ii. 123; iii. 309; *VCH Glos.* viii. 176; Macaulay, *Hist.* 1334; Grey, ix. 4, 24, 37, 112, 138–9, 165, 183, 187, 188. [4] Grey, ix. 198, 276–7, 279–80, 282, 287, 349, 352, 362; Macaulay, 1674–5; *IHR Bull.* xlix. 250, 259; *CJ*, x. 168; R. Morrice, Entering Bk. 2, p. 590. [5] Grey, ix. 415–16, 462, 484, 516; *CJ*, x. 329. [6] Browning, *Danby*, i. 497; *Hist. Reg. Chron.* vii. 30.

B.D.H.

HOWE, Richard (c.1652–1730), of Chedworth, Glos.

HINDON	1679 (Mar.), 1679 (Oct.)
TAMWORTH	1685
CIRENCESTER	1690, 1695
WILTSHIRE	1701 (Feb.), 1702, 1705, 1708, 1710, 1713, 1715, 1722

b. c.1652, 2nd but o. surv. s. of Richard Grobham Howe*. *educ.* Christ Church, Oxf. matric. 13 July 1667, aged

16. *m.* 12 Aug. 1673, Mary, da. of Sir Henry Frederick Thynne, 1st Bt., of Kempsford, Glos., *s.p. suc.* fa. as 3rd Bt. 1 May 1703.

Commr. for assessment, Wilts. 1677–80, Glos. and Wilts. 1689–90; j.p. Glos. by 1680–7, ?1689–96, Glos. and Wilts. 1700–?*d.*; dep. lt. Glos. 1702–?14.

Howe was returned to the first and second Exclusion Parliaments for the family borough of Hindon. He was marked 'honest' by Shaftesbury and voted for the bill, but was otherwise inactive. By 1681 he was probably an opponent of exclusion. He stood down at Hindon under a family arrangement and declined contesting Appleby on the Lowther interest. But he obtained his father's consent to run again in 1685 on condition that he bore all the expenses himself. 'I need not tell your lordship how ill that will suit with my condition', he wrote to his brother-in-law Lord Weymouth (Thomas Thynne I*). His efforts to induce the Tory Robert Hyde* to join with him at Hindon proving fruitless, he hoped that the Whig Henry Powle* would consent to combine interests with him at Cirencester, but in the end it was Weymouth who found him a seat at Tamworth. Howe was appointed to only one committee in James II's Parliament, that to consider reform of the bankruptcy laws, but Weymouth was sufficiently pleased with his performance to recommend him again to the electors in 1688, though James's electoral agents disapproved. He did not however go to the poll in 1689, and, when he returned to Parliament, it was on his own interest. A strong Tory who refused the Association in 1696, and later a Jacobite sympathizer, he died on 3 July 1730. His heir was his cousin, the eldest son of John Grobham Howe II*.

Hoare, *Wilts.* Branch and Dole, 49; Cumb. RO, LW2/D10, Lowther to Lowther, 22 Jan. 1681; *HMC Bath*, iv. 368; Bath mss, Thynne pprs. 18, ff. 178, 179, 189; 28, f. 231; PC2/76, f. 253.

J.P.F.

HOWE, Richard Grobham (1621–1703), of Great Wishford, Wilts.

WILTSHIRE	1656
WILTON	1659, 27 June 1660
WILTSHIRE	4 May 1675, 1679 (Mar.)
HINDON	1679 (Oct.), 1681
WILTON	1690

b. 28 Aug. 1621, 1st s. of Sir John Howe, 1st Bt., of Little Compton, Withington, Glos., and bro. of John Grobham Howe I*. *educ.* Hart Hall, Oxf. 1640; L. Inn 1641. *m.* (1) by 1642 (with £4,000), Lucy (*d.*1658), da. of Sir John St. John, 1st Bt.†, of Lydiard Tregoze, Wilts., 5s. (4 *d.v.p.*) 4da.; (2) Anne, da. of John King, bp. of London 1611–12, wid. of John Dutton† of Sherborne, Glos., *s.p.* Kntd. c.1665; *suc.* fa. as 2nd Bt. c.1671.[1]

J.p. Wilts. 1650–2, 1656–80, ?1689–*d.*; commr. for

assessment, Wilts. 1657, Jan. 1660–80, Glos. 1673–80, Glos. and Wilts. 1689–90, militia, Wilts. Mar. 1660; capt. of militia horse, Wilts. Apr. 1660, sheriff 1668–9, dep. lt. 1670–?June 1688, Oct. 1688–d.; freeman, Salisbury 1672, Wilton 1685; commr. for rebels' estates, Wilts. 1686.[2]

Gent. of the privy chamber (extraordinary) July 1660.[3]

Howe's grandfather, of an obscure Somerset family, obtained a grant of arms in 1625. His father acted as a royalist commissioner for contributions, but changed sides in May 1645, the parliamentary committee of Wiltshire accepting a modest composition of £120. This did not debar him from local office in Gloucestershire during the Interregnum. Great Wishford, which is within three miles of Wilton, was settled on Howe in 1648. He sat for the borough when its representation was restored in 1659; but at the next general election he was involved in a double return with the mayor, who was a friend of the royalist secretary of state, Sir Edward Nicholas†. He came into the House at a by-election after the mayor's return had been declared void, and was noted by Lord Wharton as a friend. He was not an active Member of the Convention, in which he was named to only four committees, those for a naturalization bill, reducing the rate of interest, settling the militia, and inserting the excise clauses in the bill to abolish the court of wards. He was unable to retain his seat in 1661 and was out of Parliament for 14 years, during which little is known about him. He is described as a knight in 1667, with an income of £1,500 p.a., but this seems to have been before he succeeded his father, who had been created a baronet at the Restoration. In 1673 his cousin (Sir) George Grobham Howe* was said to be intending to bring him in for Hindon, but before any vacancy occurred there a higher honour came his way. Lord Cornbury (Henry Hyde*) succeeded to the peerage, and Howe was elected to fill the vacancy as knight of the shire on the nomination of the lord lieutenant (Lord John Seymour*). He was again inactive, with six committees, of which the most important, in the year of his election, were for preventing the growth of Popery and promoting the liberty of the subject. He appeared on the working lists as under the lord treasurer's influence, but Shaftesbury marked him 'doubly worthy', and he acted as teller for the Opposition in a debate on supply on 10 Apr. 1677.[4]

Howe was re-elected for the county to the first Exclusion Parliament, and again noted as 'worthy' by Shaftesbury. He was appointed to the committee of elections and privileges and to that for expiring laws. According to Roger Morrice he voted for exclusion, but the official list placed him in the

other lobby, probably correctly, for he surrendered the county seat in August to his first wife's brother, Sir Walter St. John*, and sat for the family borough of Hindon in the second and third Exclusion Parliaments; but he was totally inactive. He does not appear to have stood at the general election of 1685, though when Thomas Bruce* succeeded to the peerage in October he prepared to stand again for the county; but there is no trace of a by-election. Although he had been removed from the commission of the peace in 1680, he was apparently still, or again, deputy lieutenant in 1688, when the lord lieutenant was told:

> He will not be for taking off any Penal Laws or Tests till he comes into the House of Commons. He will not contribute to the electing such Members as shall. Declares he will live friendly with all persons whatsoever, and added, when the Parliament met, he hoped an accommodation would be to the King's content.

He again failed to find a constituency in 1689, but sat for Wilton in the next Parliament. He died on 3 May 1703.[5]

[1] *Vis. Eng. and Wales Notes* ed. Crisp, xiii. 94–96; Add. 23682, f. 3. [2] *Merc. Pub.* 12 Apr. 1660; Hoare, *Wilts.* Salisbury, 473; *CSP Dom.* 1685, p. 99; *Cal. Treas. Bks.* viii. 546. [3] LC3/2. [4] *Wilts. Arch. Mag.* xxvi. 346; Hoare, *Repertorium Wiltonense*, 16; Bath mss, Thynne pprs. 12, f. 25; 14, f. 395. [5] Bath mss, Thynne pprs. 18, f. 175.

M.W.H./J.P.F.

HOWE, Sir Scrope (1648–1713), of Langar, Notts.

NOTTINGHAMSHIRE   24 Mar. 1673,   1679 (Mar.),   1679 (Oct.),   1681,   1689,   1690,   1695,   1710–26 Jan. 1713

b. Nov. 1648, 1st s. of John Grobham Howe I*, and bro. of John Grobham Howe II* and Emmanuel Scrope Howe†. *educ.* Christ Church, Oxf. 1665. *m.* (1) 20 Apr. 1672 (with £10,000), Lady Anne Manners, da. of John Manners†, 8th Earl of Rutland, 2s. *d.v.p.* 3da.; (2) lic. 15 July 1698, Juliana, da. of William Alington*, 3rd Baron Alington of Killard [I], 2s. 3da. Kntd. 11 Mar. 1663; *suc.* fa. 1679; *cr.* Visct. Howe [I] 16 May 1701.[1]

Commr. for assessment, Glos. and Notts. 1673–80, Notts. 1689–90; j.p. Notts. 1674–80, Feb. 1688–d.; dep. lt. Notts. Feb. 1688–d., Leics. 1690–bef. 1701; commr. for inquiry into recusancy fines, Notts., Derbys. and Lincs. Mar. 1688; capt. of militia horse, Notts. by 1697–?d.[2]

Comptroller of excise 1693–1710.[3]

Stimulated by the example of Lord Deincourt (Robert Leke*), Howe eloped with the sister of John Manners* in the spring of 1672. It was five years before her family was finally reconciled to the match and paid over her portion, through the good offices of Lord Shaftesbury (Sir Anthony Ashley Cooper*). In the meantime his standing in

Nottinghamshire, where he enjoyed an estate of £3,000 p.a., was unimpaired. His success at a by-election in the following year marked a gain for the country party. But he was not an active Member of the Cavalier Parliament, with a mere dozen committee appointments and speaking briefly and infrequently. With Robert Pierrepont* and John Man* he gave evidence against Lauderdale in 1673. In 1675 he was appointed to two committees for excluding Papists from Parliament and discouraging the growth of Popery, and acted as teller for the motion to appropriate the customs to the use of the navy. He earned the mark of 'thrice worthy' on Shaftesbury's list in 1677 by complaining to the House about the necessity for Members to obtain permission before visiting the opposition lords in the Tower. He again acted as teller for the country party on the motion on 5 Feb. 1678 deprecating irregular adjournments of the House. On 5 Dec. he carried the impeachment of Lord Stafford to the Upper House, and a fortnight later he was one of four Members entrusted with collecting the papers of Ralph Montagu* from their hiding-place.[4]

Howe was re-elected to all three Exclusion Parliaments, and marked 'worthy' by Shaftesbury. He made no speeches and was not active in committee. In the first Exclusion Parliament he was appointed to the committee of elections and privileges, but he was ordered to be sent for in custody as a defaulter on a call of the House on 25 Apr. 1679. He was later appointed to the committee to secure the better attendance of Members, as well as to the inquiry into the decay of woollen manufactures, but he probably paired for the division on the exclusion bill, since he did not apply for leave to go into the country until the last day of the session. In June 1680 he encouraged the Middlesex grand jury to present the Duke of York as a Popish recusant. In the second Exclusion Parliament he was appointed to a minor committee of inquiry into the Popish Plot, and at Oxford only to the elections committee. He offered to stand bail for Shaftesbury in 1682, and his arms were seized after the Rye House Plot. He had rashly laid himself open not only to an action of *scandalum magnatum* for calling the Duke of York a Popish dog, but even to charges of treason, since information was laid that he had promised to place his wealth at Monmouth's command. John Millington* wrote to Halifax that he now

associated himself with Sir William Clifton* and the loyal gentlemen, cursing my Lord Shaftesbury that ever he was born; but this is looked upon to palliate from words he hath lately spoken, highly reflecting upon the Government and especially the Duke of York.

He promised to 'walk very inoffensively and duti-

fully' in future, and when he was charged in the King's bench in January 1685 the indictment was withdrawn. His name was put forward as Whig candidate for the county at the general election, but the Duke of Newcastle (Henry Cavendish*) obliged him to sign a formal withdrawal. After the election Newcastle wrote to Sunderland: 'I believe he will be very loyal', and his arms were restored to him. As James II's reign proceeded, Howe grew closer to the Tories, describing Lord Clarendon (Henry Hyde*) as behaving extremely well. He was in contact with Dykvelt in 1687, and was reckoned an opponent of James II by Danby. Nevertheless the Government still had hopes of him as a Whig collaborator, adding him to the lieutenancy and the commission of the peace, and inserting his name among the miscellaneous batch of dissenters and Roman Catholics to inquire into recusancy fines.[5]

At the Revolution Howe raised a troop of horse for William of Orange and occupied Leicester, but Halifax found 'nothing particular intended' as a reward for his services. He regained his seat at the general election of 1689, and became an inactive Member of the Convention. He was appointed to eight committees, including those to inquire into the sending of children abroad to be educated as Papists and to inspect the Journals about the Popish Plot. After the recess he was added to the committee for reversing the attainder of Sir Thomas Armstrong*, and was teller for recommitting the proposed grant to Princess Anne. A member of the committee on the bill for restoring corporations, he twice acted as teller for the disabling clause. He remained a Whig throughout William's reign. He died on 26 Jan. 1713, and was buried at Langar. His son sat for the county from 1722 to 1732 as a Whig.[6]

[1] *Vis. Eng. and Wales Notes* ed. Crisp, xiii. 96–100. [2] *Cal. Treas. Bks.* viii. 1806; Eg. 1626, f. 33. [3] *Cal. Treas. Bks.* x. 152; xxiv. 356. [4] *HMC Buccleuch*, i. 317, 330; *Savile Corresp.* (Cam. Soc. lxxi), 57; Add. 41803, f. 84; Grey, ii. 236; K. H. D. Haley, *Shaftesbury*, 420. [5] Haley, 522, 658; *HMC 7th Rep.* 479; *Sidney Diary*, i. 237; Add. 41803, f. 84; Spencer mss, Millington to Ld. Halifax, 30 July 1683; R. Morrice, Entering Bk. 1, p. 452; *CSP Dom.* 1684–5, p. 298; 1685, p. 105; Luttrell, i. 326; *HMC Rutland*, ii. 109; *HMC 8th Rep.* pt. 1 (1881), 560. [6] *HMC 9th Rep.* pt. 2, p. 460; Foxcroft, *Halifax*, ii. 213; *CJ*, x. 311, 323, 329.

E.R.E.

HULTON, William (1625–94), of Over Hulton, Deane, Lancs.

CLITHEROE   16 July 1660

b. 9 Sept. 1625, o.s. of Adam Hulton of Over Hulton by Grace, da. of Edmund Howarth of Howarth. *m.* 1656, Anne, da. and h. of William Jessop†, clerk of the Council 1654–May 1660, of Holborn, Mdx., 5s. (1 *d.v.p.*) 1da. *suc.* fa. 1652.[1]

J.p. Lancs. 1658–Apr. 1688, Oct. 1688–*d.*, commr. for militia 1659, Mar. 1660, assessment Aug. 1660–1, 1673–4, 1689–90.[2]

Hulton was ultimately of Welsh descent, but his ancestors had been established on the property from which they took their name since the 12th century. They espoused the more radical version of Protestantism under Elizabeth, but never achieved the status of county magnates. During the Civil War Hulton's grandfather raised forces for Parliament from his estates, and it was probably his father who was the Capt. Hulton imprisoned by the Royalists in Chester Castle in 1643. Nevertheless Hulton would scarcely have harboured parliamentary aspirations before he became the son-in-law of one of the most powerful servants of the Protectorate. At the general election of 1660 he was defeated at Clitheroe by William White*, who had a majority of the freemen; but the House seated him on petition on the burgage franchise. An inactive Member of the Convention, he was named only to the committee on a bill to nominate commissioners of sewers. His father-in-law was acting as clerk of the Commons, and Hulton certainly stayed in town long enough to hear that the King at the request of the House had consented to grant him a life patent, for at the end of the first session he wrote to a Lancashire neighbour that the bill for settling ministers in their livings had passed, adding that any benefit from it must be ascribed only to the King and Commons. It is not known whether he attended the second session, when Sir Allen Brodrick* was sent to ask the lord chancellor to expedite the passing of Jessop's patent. Cromwellians were out of fashion, however, and when the Cavalier Parliament met another clerk had been appointed. Neither was Hulton in the House, and indeed he never stood again, so far as is known, though dissenters found him an active and sympathetic county magistrate. He died on 27 Mar. 1694 and was buried at Deane, the only member of the family to sit in Parliament.[3]

[1] *Vis. Lancs.* (Chetham Soc. lxxxv), 159; Croston, *Lancs.* iii. 142; Lancs. RO, Hulton mss 46/1, 2; G. E. Aylmer, *State's Servants*, 237; *Deane Par. Reg.* (Lancs. Par. Reg. Soc. liv), 473. [2] Lancs. RO, QSC 59–113. [3] *VCH Lancs.* v. 26; R. Halley, *Puritanism and Nonconformity in Lancs.* 7, 164; *HMC Kenyon*, 61, 63, 67, 158; *CJ*, viii. 90, 169, 230; O. C. Williams, *Clerical Organization of the House of Commons*, 8; O. Heywood, *Diaries*, i. 197; *Deane Par. Reg.* 478.

M.W.H./I.C.

HUNGERFORD, Edward (1632–1711), of Corsham, Wilts.; Broadwater, Suss. and Hungerford House, the Strand, Westminster.

CHIPPENHAM	1659, 1660, 17 May–20 June 1661, 21 Aug. 1661, 1679 (Mar.), 1679 (Oct.), 1681
NEW SHOREHAM	1685, 1689, 1690
STEYNING	1695, 1698, 1701 (Feb.), 1702

b. 20 Oct. 1632, 1st s. of Anthony Hungerford† of Blackbourton, Oxon. by Rachel, da. of Rice Jones of Asthall, Oxon. *educ.* Queen's, Oxf. 1649. *m.* (1) bef. 1661, Jane (*d.* 18 Mar. 1664), da. and h. of Sir John Hele† of Clifton Maybank, Dorset, 1s. *d.v.p.* 2da.; (2) 3 Feb. 1666, Jane (*d.* 18 May 1674), da. of Hugh Culme of Burlescombe, Devon, and h. to her bro. Richard, *s.p.*; (3) July 1679, Jane (*d.*1703), da. and h. of George Digby of Sandon, Staffs., wid. of Charles, 4th Baron Gerard of Gerard's Bromley, 1s. *suc.* fa. 1657; KB 23 Apr. 1661.[1]

Commr. for militia, Wilts. 1659, Som. and Wilts. Mar. 1660, assessment, Som. and Wilts. Jan. 1660–80, Oxon. Jan. 1660–1, 1665–80, Devon 1663–9, Westminster 1679–80, Oxon. and Wilts. 1689–90, Staffs. and Suss. 1690; j.p. Oxon. and Wilts. Mar. 1660–80, Som. 1661–80, Staffs. 1692–?1703, Suss. by 1701–?3; capt. of militia horse, Wilts. Apr. 1660, dep. lt. c. Aug. 1660–81, commr. for sewers, Som. Dec. 1660, loyal and indigent officers Wilts. 1662, oyer and terminer, Western circuit 1665, inquiry, Kingswood chase 1671; committee, Hudson's Bay Co. 1674–5; commr. for recusants, Wilts. 1675.[2]

Hungerford's family were established in Wiltshire in the 12th century, representing the county from 1322. Sir Thomas Hungerford in 1377 was the first Speaker formally mentioned as such in the parliament rolls. Hungerford's father, a younger son, sat for Malmesbury in the Long Parliament, until disabled as a Royalist. In compounding for his delinquency he claimed that he had been brought to Oxford by force to attend the Parliament there, and had surrendered immediately after his release. As a reversioner to the principal estates of the family, which came to him in 1653, he was fined £2,532 at one-tenth. Hungerford became the most notorious spendthrift of the age. On one occasion he is said to have paid 500 guineas for a wig. He sat in Richard Cromwell's Parliament for Chippenham, where he owned the manor of Sheldon, but his brother Anthony, a royalist agent, brought Charles II a handsome contribution from him, 'not three men of the nation having made the like present' according to Sir Edward Hyde†. In addition Hungerford helped to bring up the Oxfordshire petition for a free Parliament in February 1660, and clearly favoured the Restoration.[3]

Hungerford was re-elected for Chippenham in 1660 and listed as a friend by Lord Wharton. But he was probably less active in the Convention than his uncles Giles and Henry, being appointed by full name only to the committee for St. Nicholas hospital, Harnham. He was re-elected in 1661 and dubbed a knight of the Bath at the coronation. In the Cavalier Parliament he was named to the original elections committee, but Sir Hugh Speke* offered another indenture for Chippenham and the election was declared void. Hungerford regained the seat later in the year at a by-election after Speke's death. A moderately active Member, he made no recorded speeches, but was named to a further 72 committees, including those for an additional corporations bill in 1664 and to receive information about the insolence of Popish priests and Jesuits in 1666. His income about this time was reckoned at £4,000 p.a. but already by 1667 he was claiming privilege to avoid appearing in a suit in the Exchequer. He was one of the deputation sent to the King on 23 Apr. 1668 with the resolution in favour of wearing English manufactures. Sir Thomas Osborne* included him in 1669 among those who had usually voted for supply, and Charles described him as 'deserving well for his loyalty'. He was deeply involved with Sir John Pretyman*, from whom he bought the valuable Sussex manor of Broadwater. Through his brother-in-law, James Hayes†, who was secretary to Prince Rupert, he became one of the original adventurers of the Hudson's Bay Company. Despite his town house, Hungerford was irregular in his attendance, making default in three sessions. He was added to the committee to draw up articles of impeachment against Lord Arlington (3 Feb. 1673), and rather ironically appointed to that to devise means for compelling better attendance (31 Jan. 1674). He was busiest in the two sessions of 1675, being named to the committees on the bills for preventing illegal exactions (26 Apr.), hindering Papists from sitting in Parliament (28 May) and appropriating the customs to the use of the navy (21 Oct.). Although he had received the government whip for the autumn session, and his name appeared on the working lists, by 1677 Shaftesbury regarded him as 'worthy', and on 22 Feb. he was appointed to the committee on the bill for the recall of British subjects from the French service. Meanwhile a private bill, inspired by the very successful development of Covent Garden as a market by the Earl of Bedford, was passing through the Lords. It was brought down to the Commons on 26 Mar., and passed through all the remaining stages in a fortnight, Henry Eyre* taking the chair in the committee. Hungerford was thus empowered to demolish his house in the Strand and let the site, and in the following year he was granted the right to hold a market there on three days a week; but it did not flourish, and he eventually sold out to (Sir) Stephen Fox*.[4]

The remainder of Hungerford's long parliamentary career was chiefly motivated by his need for privilege to elude his creditors. He retained his seat in the Exclusion Parliaments, though he was opposed in both 1679 elections by Francis Gwyn*. Shaftesbury again marked him 'worthy', and he voted for the bill but was otherwise totally inactive. In January 1680, together with Thomas Thynne II* and Sir Walter St. John*, he brought up the Wiltshire petition for the immediate assembly of the second Exclusion Parliament, which was 'roughly' received by the King. In the summer he was one of the exclusionists who planned to have the Duke of York presented as a recusant by the Middlesex grand jury. Not unnaturally he was dismissed as j.p. and deputy lieutenant. After the Rye House Plot, Farleigh Castle, his Somerset home, was searched for arms, and 'a considerable parcel of armour' was discovered.[5]

Hungerford lost his interest in Wiltshire when he sold Corsham and much else to Richard Kent* in 1684. But in 1685 and 1689 he was returned for New Shoreham, some four miles from Broadwater. Presumably he favoured the Revolution, but he was totally inactive in both Parliaments. He sheltered himself from his creditors in his London house, but was twice ordered to attend the Convention to answer petitions against him. An associate of Robert Harley II*, he was a country Whig under William III. He died in 1711 and was buried in St. Martin in the Fields, the last of the senior branch of the Hungerfords to sit in Parliament.[6]

[1] R. C. Hoare, *Hungerfordiana*, 31, 67; *Vis. Oxon.* (Harl. Soc. v), 258; *Vis. Devon* ed. Vivian, 263; *Staffs. Peds.* (Harl. Soc. lxiii), 73; *Le Neve's Knights* (Harl. Soc. viii), 213; Add. 29910, f. 140. [2] *Merc. Pub.* 12 Apr. 1660; *Company Minutes* (Hudson's Bay Rec. Soc. v), 237; *Cal. Treas. Bks.* iii. 911. [3] Keeler, *Long Parl.* 225; *Cal. Comm. Comp.* 867; *Cal. Cl. SP.* iv. 559; *CSP Dom.* 1659–60, p. 361. [4] Hoare, *Repertorium Wiltonense*, 15; *CJ*, viii. 478; ix. 26, 49, 143, 192, 416; *CSP Dom.* 1668–9, p. 224; 1678, p. 308; *Fines of Manors* (Suss. Rec. Soc. xix), 67; E. E. Rich, *Hudson's Bay Co.* (Hudson's Bay Rec. Soc. xxi), 39; *HMC Hodgson*, 11; *Survey of London*, xviii. 44. [5] *Wilts. Arch. Mag.* xlvii. 67; *Hatton Corresp.* (Cam. Soc. n.s. xxii), 219; *HMC Ormonde*, n.s. v. 340; *CSP Dom.* July–Sept. 1683, pp. 398–9, 401. [6] Aubrey and Jackson, *Wilts. Colls.* 79; PC2/71/294; *CJ*, x. 83, 165; *HMC Portland*, viii. 27–28.

B.D.H.

HUNGERFORD, Sir George (c.1637–1712), of Cadenham, Bremhill, Wilts.

CRICKLADE	1661
CALNE	1679 (Mar.), 1679 (Oct.), 1681
WILTSHIRE	1695, 1698, 1701 (Feb.)

b. c.1637, 2nd but 1st surv. s. of Edward Hungerford of Cadenham by Susan, da. of Sir John Pretyman of Driffield, Glos. *educ.* Christ Church, Oxf. 1653; L. Inn 1656. *m.* 5 Apr. 1665, Frances (*bur.* 16 Aug. 1715), da. of Charles Seymour*, 2nd Baron Seymour of Trowbridge, 4s. (2 *d.v.p.*) 3da. Kntd. bef. Apr. 1661; *suc.* fa. 1667.[1]

Commr. for assessment, Wilts. 1661–80, 1689–90, corporations 1662–3, dep. lt. 1672–5, by 1696–?d., commr. for recusants 1675, inquiry into recusancy fines Mar. 1688, j.p. 1689–?d.[2]

Hungerford came from a cadet branch of the family, which had been seated at Cadenham for five generations. A direct ancestor, Robert, sat for Calne, some five miles away, in 1553. Hungerford's father apparently took no part in the Civil Wars, but both father and son sent their servants to a rendezvous near Bath for the abortive royalist rising in the summer of 1659. No action seems to have been taken against them by the Government. Returned unopposed to the Cavalier Parliament for Cricklade, where his family owned property, Hungerford was an inactive Member, being named to but 15 committees in the first nine sessions, of which only that for the bill against restraints on jurors (19 Feb. 1668) was of any importance. On 21 Feb. 1671 he was sent for in custody as a defaulter. But Shaftesbury marked him 'doubly worthy' in 1677, and he made his first recorded speech on 12 Mar., when he 'jestingly desired that the question might be that the excise might be continued for three years for payment of pensions and nothing else'.[3]

Hungerford really found his tongue, however, in the summer session of 1678. He was strongly in favour of disbanding the newly-raised forces, 'that army that has done so much ill', but loath to grant the necessary supply. He clearly distrusted the King. On 1 June he was rash enough to say that 'the army was pretended to be raised against France, but the world says, and I believe, there never was intended a war'. This caused a furore; Sir Thomas Littleton, 2nd Bt.* demanded that the words should be written down, and, after various interpretations of them, Hungerford begged the House's pardon, asserting that he 'intended no reflection on the King nor on any particular person'. On 8 June, however, when the King in his message to the House reported that peace was at hand but that supply was needed to maintain the forces, Hungerford said that 'at the latter end of a session, now we are going into the country, this demand of the King's is the most extraordinary thing that ever was done'. A week later, having heard that Danby had sent his agent, Christian, to Aldborough to procure the election of Sir Thomas Mauleverer* against the Whig Ruisshe Wentworth*, Hungerford 'moved that this Christian might receive condign punishment for being employed by the lord treasurer to spend the public money in poisoning corporations'. Danby, it was said, threatened 'a dreadful revenge for this affront'.[4]

In the last session of the Cavalier Parliament Hungerford revealed his intense anti-Catholic feelings. He was added to the committees to investigate the mistranslation of the *Gazette* and to examine Coleman's papers. He deplored the King's request for allowing the Duchess of York to keep her priests: 'the misfortunes of the last King were much from a Popish marriage', he said. On 18 Nov. he urged sending (Sir) Joseph Williamson* to the Tower for countersigning commissions of Roman Catholic officers. When the proviso exempting the Duke of York from the bill to exclude Papists from both Houses was accepted by a narrow margin on 21 Nov., 'Sir George Hungerford immediately moved for a bill to disable a Papist to succeed to the crown; but whether this was as an effect of rage for the loss of the foregoing question or that matters were not yet ripe, no man seconded this motion'. This seems to be the first formal motion aimed at the exclusion of the Duke of York from the throne. On the next day he expressed his scepticism about resistance to the King if he chose to dispense with laws against Papists, and on 9 Dec. he renewed his concern about the disbanding of the army, desiring to add to the bill a proviso 'to make it treason to pay the money granted for disbanding the army to any other use of the revenue'. The Speaker asked the House if they would 'make treason in a rider of a bill without any other solemnity', several Members spoke against it and the bill was not altered. Hungerford's last recorded action in the Cavalier Parliament was on 19 Dec. when he served as teller for proceeding with the impeachment of Danby. He was understandably listed as 'doubly worthy' by Shaftesbury and became a member of the Green Ribbon Club.[5]

Hungerford was returned to the Exclusion Parliaments for Calne. On 22 Mar. 1679 he urged the House to proceed with the impeachment of Danby despite his pardon. A moderately active committeeman in the first Exclusion Parliament, he was named to four committees, including those for the security bill and the bill to prevent illegal exactions. In the heated debate over exclusion on 11 May he intervened on the side of the extremists:

> I know no law that can bind in this case, unless we can tell who shall be Prince of Wales. If you do anything, you must appoint a person to succeed the King, and I can never think that the Protestant princes will join with us in defence of our religion, unless a third person be named to succeed to the crown. Then the German and French Protestants will join with you, and there is a million of them in France. We ought to do something materially to secure our religion, and it must be either

that the King may have an heir to succeed him, or a third person must be named. As long as the Duke is heir to the crown, the kingdom is unsafe, and I believe that the queen will never be capable to children; for when she came into England she had something given her, to be always a red-lettered woman. But something must be done.

He opposed unsuccessfully the motion for adjourning the violent debate of 14 May on the King's request for money for the fleet.

We are told that the affairs of Christendom are now on foot, since the general peace, and therefore a navy is necessary. The best way of treating is when they see a good union, that they may trust us. We have deceived the Dutch, in taking the Smyrna fleet; and the King owning my lord treasurer's letters that treated for a peace, for money, with the French when we were preparing for war. When they see a confidence betwixt the King and this House they will trust us.

He voted for the committal of the exclusion bill.[6]

In the second Exclusion Parliament Hungerford was named to five important committees, including those to consider the exemption of Protestant dissenters from the Penal Laws, and to prepare the addresses advising the King of the dangerous state of the kingdom and demanding the dismissal of Halifax. On 15 Dec. 1680, during the debate on naming the Duke of York in the exclusion bill, he reminded the House, somewhat irrelevantly, that 'in the Holy League of France the Duke of Guise excluded Henri IV by name'. He was added to the committee to examine the disbandment accounts, and appointed to that for the repeal of the Corporations Act. On 7 Jan. 1681, in the long debate on the necessity of persuading the King to agree to exclusion, he appealed to Scripture: 'desires the King may be told part of our Saviour's sermon on the mount, that if thy hand, foot, or eye offend thee, it might be cut off, rather than the whole body perish'. In the short Oxford Parliament Hungerford was named to no committees, but on 25 Mar. 1681, he urged that Sir Leoline Jenkins* should be called to the bar for flatly refusing to carry Fitzharris's impeachment to the Lords, exclaiming: 'I never heard such words uttered in Parliament before'.[6]

Hungerford probably did not stand in 1685, but he may have become a Whig collaborator under James II, when he was nominated to the commission of inquiry into recusancy fines. On 19 April 1688, the King's electoral agents reported that Calne 'hath yet proposed only Sir George Hungerford, in whom they had a confidence that he is right'. He represented the county from 1695 to 1702 as a country Whig, though he signed the Association.[7]

Hungerford had inherited an estate of £1,000

p.a., but at his death his affairs were 'much entangled', due largely to the expenses, estimated at more than £2,700, of the 'groundless and unchristian suit' brought against him by his younger son Walter. His eldest son George, who was elected for Calne in 1695, had died in 1697. Hungerford was buried at Bremhill on 9 May 1712. Walter Hungerford, who had sat for the borough briefly in 1701, was defeated in 1715, and did not recover the seat till 1734.[8]

[1] Le Neve's Knights (Harl. Soc. viii), 313; PCC 128 Carr. [2] Add. 32324, f. 149; CSP Dom. 1672–3, p. 101; Wilts. N. and Q. vi. 349. Cal. Treas. Bks. viii. 1805. [3] D. Underdown, Royalist Conspiracy, 264; Cal. Cl. SP, iv. 308–10; Grey, iv. 237. [4] Grey, vi. 31, 52, 59–61, 72; CSP Dom. 1678, p. 245. [5] Grey, vi. 194, 223, 262, 325; Leics. RO, Finch mss, 21 Nov. 1678. [6] Grey, vii. 20, 239, 275. [7] Ibid. viii. 168, 305; HMC 12th Rep. IX, 111. [8] Hoare, Repertorium Wiltonense, 16; PCC 82 Aston.

M.W.H./B.D.H.

HUNGERFORD, Giles (1614–85), of Freefolk, Hants and East Coulston, Wilts.

WHITCHURCH   1660, 1661
DEVIZES   1679 (Oct.)

bap. 25 Sept. 1614, 5th s. of Sir Anthony Hungerford[†] of Stokke House, Great Bedwyn, Wilts. and Blackbourton, Oxon., being 4th s. by 2nd w. Sarah, da. and coh. of Giles Crouch, Haberdasher, of Cornhill, London, wid. of William Wiseman of Woolstone, Uffington, Berks.; bro. of Henry Hungerford*. educ. Oxf. 1631; M. Temple 1634, called 1641. m. (1) 23 May 1654, Frances, da. of Sir George Croke[†], j.K.b. 1628–41, of Waterstock, Oxon., coh. to her bro. Thomas, and wid. of Richard Jervoise[†] of Freefolk, s.p.; (2) by 1673, Margaret (d. 4 Dec. 1711), da. of Sir Thomas Hampson, 1st Bt. of Taplow, Bucks., 1da. Kntd. 27 Nov. 1676.[1]

J.p. Hants and Mdx. 1659–July 1660, Wilts. 1666–d.; commr. for militia, Hants and Mdx. Mar. 1660, assessment, Hants Aug. 1660–9, Mdx. 1661–9, Wilts. 1666–80, Glos. 1677–9, Berks. 1677–80, recusants, Hants 1675.

Hungerford was brought up with his brother Henry and likewise became a barrister. But nothing more is heard of him until at the age of 40 he married the widow of Richard Jervoise, MP for Whitchurch in the Long Parliament, and went to live on her jointure, within a couple of miles of the borough. Hungerford, too, was returned for Whitchurch in 1660, but he was probably inactive in the Convention, though marked by Lord Wharton as a friend. His only speech was on the bill to make reparations to the royalist Marquess of Winchester, part of whose estate had been granted to Sir Thomas Jervoise[†] and Robert Wallop* in 1649. It is not clear whether he declared an interest, but he urged the rejection of the bill, 'and said the grant was not prejudicial to my lord' because if he had refused his consent his whole estate would have been sold by the Long Parliament. His only certain committee was for this bill.[2]

Hungerford was re-elected in 1661 and became an active Member of the Cavalier Parliament. He was appointed to 171 committees, taking the chair in nine, and acted as teller in six divisions. Clearly an opponent of the Clarendon administration, he was probably too hostile to Roman Catholicism to join the Earl of Bristol's followers in the Commons. Although no longer included by Wharton among his friends, his antipathy towards the dignitaries of the Church was no doubt responsible for his selection to deliver a copy of the petition from George Lowe* to the treasurer of Salisbury Cathedral, and to ask the master of St. Cross to afford the vicar of Twyford a competent maintenance. He took no part in the Clarendon Code, except to act as teller for postponing a debate on the uniformity bill on 15 Apr. 1662. He was among those Members instructed to ask the lord treasurer to enable the House to consider the survey of the Forest of Dean and to ask the King to forbear any grants of mines royal pending legislation. In 1663 he reported that the complaints of the hackney coachmen against extortion by the clerk and messenger attached to the licensing commission were well-founded. He reported several amendments from the committee on the Marquess of Worcester's steam engine, designed to protect future inventions. He took the chair for the mines royal bill, but it was recommitted on report. As chairman of the committee to confirm the King's arbitration between Lord Winchester and his son (Charles Powlett I*), he obtained an order to compel a scrivener to deliver to him the relevant documents, and reported the bill on 21 May.[3]

Hungerford seems to have conformed to the Church of England after his first wife's death, becoming a Wiltshire j.p. in 1666. His estate was valued at only £500 p.a., but this was before his purchase of East Coulston, six miles from Devizes. As chairman of the committee set up to receive information about the insolence of Popish priests and Jesuits, he presented two reports to the House, and was sent to the Lords to request their concurrence in an address. On the fall of Clarendon he was appointed to the committees to inquire into the sale of Dunkirk and the miscarriages of the second Dutch war, and to ascertain how far the revenue had been applied to the purposes for which it was granted. In his only recorded speech, on 28 Feb. 1669, he complained that the orders of the navy board for the paying off of seamen had not been carried out. He helped to consider the bill for regulating juries, and to inspect the Conventicles and

Militia Acts in 1670. In 1674 he was added to the committee to devise a general test, appointed to the inquiry into the state of Ireland, and took the chair for the bill to prevent illegal exactions. In November 1675 he was teller for the Opposition on two divisions, the effects of which were to continue the debate on appropriating supply for the use of the navy and to remind the Lords of the bill to hinder Papists from sitting in Parliament. He was also appointed to the committees to prevent the growth of Popery and to preserve the liberty of the subject. During the long recess he accepted a knighthood, but it is not clear that this affected his politics, though his activity was reduced. In the last three sessions of the Cavalier Parliament he was named to only three committees. But in 1677 Shaftesbury marked him 'doubly worthy', and he acted as teller for denying the court supporter, Sir Robert Holte*, protection against his creditors. On 14 Nov. 1678 he was added to the committee to examine Coleman's papers.[4]

It is not known whether Hungerford stood in February 1679, but in August he was elected for Devizes. The return was, however, challenged by the Court candidates on such unassailable grounds that he did not venture to take his seat, though the petition was never reported. It was presumably owing to this passivity that he was not removed from the commission of the peace, although his nephew, (Sir) Edward Hungerford*, had become one of the most prominent local Whigs. He appears to have contested Devizes again in 1681, but this time his opponents were elected, and his petition was not reported. He died on 7 Mar. 1685, and was buried in Salisbury Cathedral. His will shows extensive purchases of land, including the manor of Hungerford, which he had acquired from his nephew, and when his daughter married the 2nd Lord Lexinton in 1691, she was said to be worth £30,000.[5]

[1] Wilts. Vis. Peds. (Harl. Soc. cv), 93; Vis. London (Harl. Soc. xv), 207; VCH Berks. iv. 549; Add. 33412, f. 82v; J. Harris, Epitaphs in Salisbury Cathedral, 47–48. [2] Bowman diary, f. 129. [3] CJ, viii. 304, 406, 421, 460, 470, 475, 477, 483. [4] Hoare, Repertorium Wiltonense, 16; VCH Wilts. viii. 236; CJ, viii. 641, 642; ix. 313, 373, 377, 411; Grey, i. 229. [5] CJ, ix. 707; PCC 66 Cann.

B.D.H.

HUNGERFORD, Henry (1611–73), of Standen, Wilts.

GREAT BEDWYN	27 July 1646[1]
WILTSHIRE	1656[2]
GREAT BEDWYN	1659
MARLBOROUGH	1660

bap. 23 July 1611, 4th s. of Sir Anthony Hungerford† (d. 1627) of Stokke House, Great Bedwyn, Wilts. and

Blackbourton, Oxon., being 3rd s. by 2nd w.; bro. of Giles Hungerford*. *educ.* Queen's, Oxf. 1631; L. Inn 1635, called 1642. *unm.*[3]

Commr. for execution of ordinances, Wilts. 1644, assessment 1647–8, 1657, Jan. 1660–*d.*, militia 1648, Mar. 1660, j.p. Mar. 1660–*d.*

Hungerford and his younger brother were brought up by their half-brother, Sir Edward Hungerford[†], subsequently a parliamentary commander in the Civil War. A barrister and a Presbyterian, he was elected for Great Bedwyn as a recruiter, but did not sit after Pride's Purge and was excluded from the second Protectorate Parliament. At the general election of 1660 he was returned by a narrow majority for Marlborough, nine miles from Standen, where he lived with his widowed sister, Sarah Goddard, and her family. He was marked by Lord Wharton as a friend. His record in the Convention cannot always be distinguished from those of his brother and his nephew Edward Hungerford*, but he was certainly the most experienced, and probably the most active 'Mr Hungerford' in the House. In the opening weeks of the Parliament he was appointed by full name to the elections committee and to those preparing the bill for the abolition of the court of wards and considering the indemnity bill; and he may have later served on 17 others, and made nine speeches. The Seymour interest was normally dominant in his constituency, and he appears to have challenged it at every opportunity, suggesting that Lord Hertford, as chancellor of Oxford University, should be told of the debate occasioned by his expulsion of the intruded dons. In the debate on the indemnity on 27 July he declared that 'the Lords give great cause of jealousy in retarding the bill', and proposed asking the King to hasten them. In the name of 'prudence and moderation', he urged the committal of the bill to settle ecclesiastical livings, and was named to the committee. He was appointed by full name to the committees on the bills for reparations to the royalist Marquess of Winchester and Earl of Bristol. His brother, who had married the widow of Richard Jervoise[†], was adversely affected by the first of these bills, and one or other of the brothers acted as teller against an order for the committee to sit.[4]

When Parliament reassembled after the recess, Hungerford lost no time in ingratiating himself with the Court by proposing a grant of £10,000 to Princess Henrietta and a day of fasting for the death of the Duke of Gloucester. But on 28 Nov. he made what seemed to the Anglican Seymour Bowman* a very long speech in favour of giving statutory form to the Worcester House declaration for modified episcopacy:

All those who pretended so much loyalty should agree with the King's desire, that they might all go down to the country and be well accepted there; which (he said) they could not better deserve than by setting this great affair in order before the dissolution.

Although Hertford, the lord lieutenant of Wiltshire, had died in October, Hungerford attacked the exorbitances of the lieutenancy, 'averring to his knowledge in some places 2s. 9d. a day was exacted for each trooper'. On the proposal to reward Jane Lane for assisting Charles II to escape after the battle of Worcester, he remarked tartly that 'by the many gifts they were bestowing he thought the House was making its will, and moved rather to give the money to the poor at the door'. He concluded his parliamentary career by acting as teller against receiving the report from the committee appointed to consider the case of another royalist sufferer, the Earl of Cleveland.[5]

Hungerford did not stand again, although he apparently remained on the Wiltshire commission of the peace until his death. Presumably, therefore, he conformed to the Church of England and raised no objections to enforcing the Conventicles Act in 1670. He died on 27 May 1673, and was buried at Hungerford at the cost of £200. In accordance with his will his brother and sister expended a further £150 on a memorial, which declared that 'he lived a single, pious and unspotted life, [and] employed his time in the service of God and his country'.[6]

[1] Did not sit after Pride's Purge, 6 Dec. 1648, readmitted 21 Feb. 1660. [2] Excluded. [3] *Wilts. Vis. Peds.* (Harl. Soc. cv), 93. [4] *Wilts. N. and Q.* ii. 357; Bowman diary, ff. 25v, 99v, 108v; *CJ*, viii. 106, 134, 140; *HMC 7th Rep.* 117. [5] *Old Parl. Hist.* xxiii. 1, 2, 28, 51–52, 59; *CJ*, viii. 226. [6] Hoare, *Repertorium Wiltonense*, 16; PCC 77 Pye; Hoare, *Hungerfordiana*, 71.

M.W.H.

HUNT, John (c.1639–1721), of Compton Pauncefoot, Som.

MILBORNE PORT	26 Feb. 1677, 1679 (Mar.), 1679 (Oct.), 1681, 1685, 1689
ILCHESTER	1690, 1695
SOMERSET	1698, 1701 (Feb.)
MILBORNE PORT	5 Feb. 1702, 8 Dec. 1702

b. c.1639, 1st s. of Robert Hunt*. *educ.* L. Inn 1658. *m.* (1) lic. 26 Oct. 1672, Elizabeth (*d.* 13 Jan. 1698), da. and coh. of Charles Roscarrock* of Trevenna, St. Neot, Cornw., *s.p.*; (2) Elizabeth (*d.* 9 Sept. 1758), da. of Edmund Lloyd of London, 4s. 1da. *suc.* fa. 1680.[1]

Commr. for assessment, Som. 1665–80, 1689–90, j.p. 1680–Feb. 1688, Oct. 1688–*d.*, dep. lt. 1680–7, 1689–?1714, capt. of militia ft. by 1683–?87, lt. col. by 1697–?1714, commr. for rebels' estates 1686.[2]

Hunt was proposed for the order of the Royal

Oak at the Restoration with an income of £1,500 p.a., presumably representing his father's estate rather than his own. He controlled both seats at Milborne Port, three miles from his home, for which he was first returned at a by-election in 1677. An inactive Member of the Cavalier Parliament, he was marked 'worthy' on Shaftesbury's list and appointed to four committees of no political importance in its closing sessions. Hunt's grandfather had helped Sir John Bankes[†] to acquire and defend his Dorset estates, and Hunt himself sat on the committee for the bill to enable the family trustees to sell some of them. Although Shaftesbury still regarded him as 'worthy' in 1679, he abstained from the division on the first exclusion bill, and his choice of Henry Bull* to replace William Lacy* as his colleague in the second Exclusion Parliament indicates that he had gone over to the Court. He left no trace on the records of the Exclusion Parliaments, except to obtain leave to go into the country.[3]

Hunt was among the most active Somerset justices in the suppression of conventicles. A moderately active Member of James II's Parliament, he was named to four committees, including that to examine the disbandment accounts. He took part as a militia officer in the Sedgemoor campaign. His violent hostility to the King's ecclesiastical policy brought him before the Privy Council after an altercation with the sheriff at the Bruton quarter sessions in 1687. To the lord lieutenant's questions on the repeal of the Test Act and Penal Laws, Hunt, together with Edward Gorges* and John Sanford*, replied 'that they know not what they shall do till they hear the debates', but would 'promote the elections of the fittest men they can'. He was removed from local office, and great efforts were made to oust him from his seat, but he was re-elected in 1689. In the Convention he voted to agree with the Lords that the throne was not vacant. An inactive Member, he was appointed to ten committees, including those to consider the abolition of the hearth-tax, to prepare a bill for making the militia more effective, and to inquire into the charges against William Harbord*. He remained a Tory under William III and Anne, though he signed the Association in 1696. He died on 26 Apr. 1721, aged 82, and was buried at Compton Pauncefoot, the last of the family to sit in Parliament.[4]

[1] Phelps, *Som.* ii. 409–11; Soc. of Genealogists, Exeter Mar. Lic. [2] *Q. Sess. Recs.* (Som. Rec. Soc. xxxiv), p. xiii; Som. RO; *CSP Dom.* Jan.–June 1683, p. 194; T27/9/186–7; Eg. 1626, f. 39; *Cal. Treas. Bks.* viii. 545. [3] Bankes mss, till 39, bdle. D, Hunt to Bankes, Jan. 1649; *CJ*, ix. 634. [4] *CSP Dom.* Jan.–June 1683, p. 194; 1687–9, p. 135; *HMC 3rd Rep.* 99, 100.

I.C.

HUNT, Robert (c.1609–80), of Speckington, Yeovilton, Som.

ILCHESTER	15 Feb. 1641–5 Feb. 1644
SOMERSET	1659
ILCHESTER	1660

b. c.1609, 1st s. of John Hunt of Forston, Charminster, Dorset and Compton Pauncefoot, Som. by Catharine, da. of Alexander Popham of Huntworth, North Petherton, Som. *educ.* Rampisham, Dorset (Mr Howlett) 1619–25; Caius, Camb. adm. 5 Oct. 1625, aged 16; M. Temple, entered 1625, called 1633. *m.* 24 Sept. 1635, Elizabeth (*d.* 24 Sept. 1675), da. of John Browne[†] of Frampton, Dorset, 3s. (1 *d.v.p.*) 5da. *suc.* fa. 1660.[1]

J.p. Som. by 1640–3, 1654–9 Mar. 1660–*d.*, 1654–6, commr. for scandalous ministers 1654, security 1655, assessment 1657, 1661–*d.*, militia Mar. 1660, sewers Aug. 1660, dep. lt. 1666–*d.*, commr. for recusants 1675.[2]

Hunt's father, from a Dorset yeoman family became a lawyer, entering the service of Francis Bacon and acquiring an estate in Somerset of £1,000 p.a. He bought Speckington, three miles from Ilchester, in 1618, and Compton Pauncefoot during or soon after the Civil War. He was named to the county committee, but retired from public life after the Royalists overran Somerset in 1643. Hunt himself, a barrister, was returned to the Long Parliament for Ilchester, the first of the family to sit. He was disabled in 1644 for residing in the King's quarters, and the local sequestrator claimed that he had attended the Oxford Parliament; but he was able to prove that he had advanced £100 to the parliamentary cause, and the House cleared him of delinquency. As sheriff during the Interregnum he was responsible for the trial of the Royalists after Penruddock's rising and the elections to the second Protectorate Parliament, discharging both tasks with such reliability and impartiality that he was elected for the county to Richard Cromwell's Parliament.[3]

Hunt was returned for Ilchester at the general election of 1660. An inactive Member of the Convention, he was named to eight committees, of which the most important were to consider a bill confirming the privileges of Parliament, to inquire into the publication of parliamentary proceedings, and to hear a petition from the intruded dons at Oxford. In the second session he was appointed to the committee on the bill to supply defects in the poll-tax. After losing his seat at the general election to Edward Phelips*, he petitioned against the other successful candidate, Henry Dunster*, but allowed the petition to drop. 'The most reputed justice in Somerset', Hunt personally uncovered 'a hellish knot of witches' despite official discouragement. He welcomed the peace with Holland in 1674, but criticized the working of the Irish Cattle Act. He probably opposed exclusion, joining forces with Phelips at the first general election of 1679. There was a double return, but they never took their seats, the House declaring in favour of the country candidates. Hunt died on 20 Feb. 1680 and was buried at Compton Pauncefoot.[4]

[1] Phelps, *Som.* i. 409–10; *Som. Wills.* iv. 73; v. 108. [2] *Q. Sess. Recs.* (Som. Rec. Soc. xxviii), p. xxi; (xxxiv), p. xiii; C181/7/24; Som. RO, DD/Pot. 162. [3] *Proc. Dorset Nat. Hist. and Arch. Soc.* liv. 104–11; Aubrey, *Brief Lives,* i. 71; *VCH Som.* iii. 170; D. Underdown, *Som. in the Civil War,* 118, 124; Keeler, *Long Parl.* 226; *Som. Arch. and Nat. Hist. Soc. Procs.* xvi. pt. 2, p. 19; *Cal. Comm. Adv. Money,* 758; *Som. Assize Orders* (Som. Rec. Soc. lxx), 57–8. [4] *CJ,* viii. 358; ix. 570, 581; K. Thomas, *Religion and the Decline of Magic,* 547; *CSP Dom.* 1673–5, pp. 183–4, 195; Phelps, i. 410.

M.W.H./E.C.

HUNTINGTON, Richard (*d.*1690), of King Street, Great Yarmouth, Norf.

GREAT YARMOUTH 1679 (Mar.), 1679 (Oct.)

m. (1) 10 Nov. 1644, Rose (*d.* 8 Sept. 1678), da. of Robert Wakeman, draper, of Yarmouth, 4s. (1 *d.v.p.*) 2da.; (2) settlement 11 Oct. 1679, Hannah (*d.*1686), da. of Henry Watts, hosier, of Norwich, and wid. of John Hawes, apothecary, of Norwich, *s.p.*[1]
  Freeman, Yarmouth 1646, lt. of militia ft. 1648–70, capt. 1670–82, alderman by Dec. 1660–84, Oct. 1688–d.; commr. for assessment, Yarmouth 1663–4, 1677–80, 1689–d., Norf. 1679–80; bailiff, Yarmouth 1666–7, 1676–7.[2]

Huntington, who probably came from a Suffolk yeoman family, was apprenticed to his brother Robert, a Yarmouth merchant, in or before 1640, and may subsequently have served under him in the eastern association and the New Model Army. His means were probably modest, and he appears to have become a freeholder in the borough only after his second marriage. His brother publicly resigned his commission in 1648 in protest at Cromwell's attitude to Parliament and the monarchy; but Huntington himself 'joined with all the late usurped governments and was very zealous for them ... and his cabal were the only instruments of Sir William Doyley* being made a burgess', i.e. MP for Yarmouth in the Convention and Cavalier Parliament. It was doubtless Doyley who ensured that he survived the purge of the corporation after the Restoration. Huntington attended Anglican services, but refused either to kneel for prayer or to stand for the creed; while his first wife, despite her lameness, was 'a constant frequenter' of the Independent conventicle. His election as bailiff in 1666 marked the turn of the tide in Yarmouth politics; the Clarendon Code became a dead letter in the town, as Huntington 'made it his business to find out occasions to make void the law'. He was no

doubt emboldened by the emergence of his brother as an excise commissioner. In July 1667 the corporation sent him to London with (Sir) James Johnson* to promote a bill for the repair of the pier and haven. When it appeared that the renunciation of the Covenant would be enforced on the corporation, Huntington and Johnson invoked the assistance of the lord lieutenant, Lord Townshend. In the summer of 1670 one of the churchwardens of St. Nicholas, supported by Sir Thomas Medowe*, complained that Huntington had evaded taking action against a seditious conventicle almost next door to his home, and the Privy Council referred the petition to Townshend. But Huntington had made friends with the Roman Catholic Henry Howard (who was managing the family interest for his brother, the mad Duke of Norfolk); and by this means Townshend was induced not only to dismiss the churchwarden's complaint but to promote the negligent magistrate to captain in the borough militia. When Medowe protested, he was required to resign his own commission.[3]

Huntington first stood for Parliament at the by-election caused by Doyley's death, his candidature being adventitiously assisted by an incident in which he personally arrested a naval officer who had murdered a butcher in an affray with the constables. Though the only account of the affair comes from a hostile source, it is clear that Huntington acted with singular promptitude and courage. The same government informer described him as 'a person never worthy of any honour, that has not a house or a foot of land ... so necessitated that he begged an employment of the town which he still keeps', and he was defeated by Medowe, though only by 15 votes. But at both elections of 1679 he was successful as a candidate of the 'partial conformists'. Classed as 'honest' on Shaftesbury's list, he voted for the first exclusion bill, but left no other trace on the records of Parliament. He gave way to Johnson in 1681, and lost his militia commission in the following year. An order was made by the lieutenancy for the search of his newly-purchased house for arms after the Rye House Plot, but apparently withdrawn. He signed the surrender of the charter, which he had initially opposed. He was 'confined at home by sickness' when the accession of James II was proclaimed, but apparently contested the general election of 1685. No longer an alderman, he was elected by the freemen with George England*, but they did not petition against the return of Sir William Cook* and (Sir) John Friend* by the corporation. They were again elected to the abortive Parliament of 1688, but at the general election of 1689 he was replaced by his son-in-law Samuel

Fuller*. His religious outlook may have mellowed with the years, for he allowed the 'Arminian' Dean Davies to minister to him on his deathbed. He died of gangrene, and was buried in the parish church of St. Nicholas on 24 Jan. 1690. He left no will, the funeral expenses were apparently met by Fuller, and nothing is known of his sons.[4]

[1] C. J. Palmer, *Perlustration of Yarmouth*, ii. 52–53; PCC 183 Aylett, 47 Dycer; Gt. Yarmouth, St. Nicholas par. reg.; *Yarmouth Freemen*, 97, 100, 111; Norf. RO, Norwich consistory court wills, 569 Calthorpe; H. Swinden, *Hist. Yarmouth*, 862. [2] *Yarmouth Freemen*, 77; Swinden, 574; *Cal. Treas. Bks.* i. 74; *CSP Dom.* 1670, p. 474; 1679–80, p. 32; Yarmouth bor. recs. assembly bks. [3] Clarendon, *Rebellion*, iv. 260; *Thurloe*, i. 94–98; *CSP Dom.* 1668–9, p. 96; 1670, pp. 358, 440, 473–4, 512–13, 519; 1675–6, p. 568; 1676–7, pp. 155–6; *Cal. Treas. Bks.* i. 728. [4] *CSP Dom.* 1677–8, pp. 349, 496, 555; *Perlustration*, ii. 53; *Norf. Ltcy. Jnl.* (Norf. Rec. Soc. xxx), 46; Add. 27447, f. 324; 27448, ff. 231, 281; 36988, f. 239; *HMC 9th Rep.* pt. 1, p. 301; Palmer, *Hist Yarmouth*, 214, 215; *Diary of Dean Davies* (Cam. Soc. lxviii), 72, 76–77; St. Nicholas par. reg.

E.C./B.D.H.

HUNTINGTOWER, Lord *see* **TOLLEMACHE, Lionel**

HUSSEY, Charles (1626–64), of Caythorpe, Lincs.

LINCOLNSHIRE 1656, 1661–2 Dec. 1664

bap. 30 Oct. 1626, 3rd but 1st surv. s. of Sir Edward Hussey, 1st Bt.[†] (*d.*1648), of Honington by Elizabeth, da. of George Anton[†] of Lincoln; bro. of Thomas Hussey.[†] *educ.* G. Inn 1646. *m.* lic. 10 Apr. 1649, Elizabeth, da. of Sir William Brownlow, 1st Bt.[†], of Humby, 3s. 6da. *cr.* Bt. 21 July 1661.[1]

Commr. for assessment, Lincs. 1652, 1657, Jan. 1660, 1661–3, (Kesteven) Aug. 1660–1, 1663–*d.*, militia, Lincs. 1659, Mar. 1660; j.p. (Kesteven) Mar. 1660–*d.*; commr. for sewers, Lincs. Aug. 1660, loyal and indigent officers, 1662, complaints, Bedford level 1663.[2]

Hussey's family had held property in Lincolnshire since at least the reign of Henry VI, first entering Parliament in 1467. The whole family was royalist in the Civil War. His father was fined £8,750 as a commissioner of array, his uncle died in the Newark garrison, and his brother John was killed at Gainsborough. Hussey, too young to have committed himself, was appointed to local office during the Interregnum, and represented the county in the second Protectorate Parliament. As the son of a Royalist, he may have been considered ineligible at the general election of 1660.[3]

Hussey regained his seat at the general election of 1661, and was created a baronet shortly afterwards. An active Member in the opening sessions of the Cavalier Parliament, he was appointed to 82 committees and acted as teller in five divisions. In the first session he was named to the committees to examine the Journals of the Long Parliament and to consider the security and schismatics bills, but he took no part in the principal measures of the Clarendon Code, though he was added to the revived committee for the execution of those under attainder and appointed to that for the additional corporations bill. With Lord Herbert of Raglan (Henry Somerset*), Sir Anthony Irby* and Robert Long* he was given leave on 29 Nov. to bring in a bill for the more effectual draining of the Lincolnshire fens. He introduced a petition from the commoners in the soke of Bolingbroke and East Holland as one of their friends and patrons on 28 Jan. 1662, and with Lord Willoughby de Eresby (Robert Bertie I*) acted as teller for its committal. His interest in the Lindsey level was questioned by the Adventurers, and he appears to have been unable to prove his title at the bar of the House.[4]

When Parliament met again in 1663, Hussey was among the leaders of the opposition. He was appointed to the committees to consider the defects in the Corporations Act and the petition from the loyal and indigent officers. He took the chair for the bill to prevent abuses in the sale of offices, and on 12 June acted as teller against supply with Sir Richard Temple*. When the King denounced Temple as an 'undertaker', Hussey produced a politely incredulous report from the committee of inquiry. Meanwhile the Lindsey level bill had been revived. Hussey acted as teller against the recompense proposed for the Adventurers on 4 July, and against the adjournment of the debate on 22 July. In the third session he was teller for an unsuccessful proviso to the repeal of the Triennial Act. He was one of the opposition speakers in the debate of 21 Apr. 1664 'pretending as great a fervency' to war with the Dutch as any in the House, but urging the appointment of a council of war (see John Vaughan*). He was appointed to the committee of elections and privileges in the fourth session, but died in London on 2 Dec., and was buried at Caythorpe, leaving an estate valued at some £2,500 p.a. His early death and the scanty records of these sessions prevent any conclusion on his politics. His opposition to the Clarendon administration may have been based on principle, or he may have been a mere *frondeur* eager to avenge his defeat over the Lindsey level drainage bill.[5]

[1] R. E. G. Cole, *Hist. Doddington*, 97. [2] C181/7/76. [3] *Lincs. Peds.* (Harl. Soc. li), 526–31; Cole, 90–95. [4] *CJ*, viii. 352, 402, 418; W. B. Stonehouse, *Isle of Axholme*, 103–4. [5] *CJ*, viii. 496, 507, 538; Bodl. Carte 215, f. 30; *Her. and Gen.* ii. 222.

J.S.C./J.P.F.

HUSSEY, Sir Edward, 3rd Bt. (c.1662–1725), of Caythorpe, Lincs.

LINCOLN   28 May 1689, 1690, 1698, 1701 (Dec.), 1702

b. c.1662, 2nd s. of (Sir) Charles Hussey*, 1st Bt. *educ.* Trinity Coll. Camb. adm. 18 May 1675, aged 13; M. Temple 1676. *m.* (1) by 1680, Charlotte (*d.* 30 Aug. 1695), da. and h. of Daniel Brevint, dean of Lincoln, 5s. *d.v.p.* 7da.; (2) 31 May 1698, Elizabeth, da. and h. of Sir Charles de Vic, 2nd Bt., of Guernsey, 3s. (2 *d.v.p.*) 1da. *suc.* bro. as 3rd Bt. Apr. 1680, cos. Sir Thomas Hussey* of Honington as 3rd Bt. 19 Dec. 1706.[1]

J.p. Lincs. (Kesteven) 1682–Feb. 1688, Oct. 1688–?*d.*; freeman, Lincoln 1689; commr. for assessment, Lincs. 1689–90.[2]

Hussey presumably opposed exclusion, for he was appointed to the commission of the peace as soon as he came of age, and he was one of those who presented a congratulatory address from Lincolnshire on James II's accession. The Earl of Lindsey (Robert Bertie I*) in January 1688 expected him to be elected at Boston, but like his cousin he followed the lead of (Sir) Henry Monson* in refusing consent to the repeal of the Test Act and Penal Laws. He was removed from local office, and is not known to have stood at the general election of 1689. But when Monson was expelled the House as a non-juror, Hussey quickly purchased the freedom of Lincoln and was elected in his place. An active Member of the Convention, he was appointed to 23 committees, and made two recorded speeches. On 12 Aug. he was named to the committee for the security bill. In the debate on the succession on 6 Nov. he said:

> There is a clause in the bill that I do not understand. 'That no Papist shall succeed to the crown, none of the Church of Rome, and no Protestant shall be put by'. Charles I was thought a Papist; Charles II by many was reckoned popishly affected; and I fear, as there was Spanish gold stirring in Court and Parliament in James I's time, why may not these things happen again? I hear of no test to the King to distinguish him from a Papist; must the muzzle be set upon the King when the Council please? This may prevent a Lutheran from coming to the crown, because he comes not up to all the points of our religion. I fear it may be like the bill of oaths, which the greatest lawyers of England understand not. There is a clause in the bill 'that the King shall not suspend laws, etc.' What if a murder be committed and a man wrongfully condemned, shall he be hanged for want of the King's power to pardon? I stand not up to oppose the bill, but I would have it explained and moderated.

He was appointed to the committees for the second mutiny bill and for the bill to restore corporations, in which, presumably for local political reasons, he supported the disabling clause. On 10 Jan. 1690, he was placed on the committee charged with the bill of indemnity, and in debate 11 days later he

seconded the motion of Peregrine Bertie* to except William Williams*. A country Whig under William III, he voted with the Tories under Anne. In 1706 he inherited the Honington estate, and a second baronetcy. He died on 19 Feb. 1725, the last of his family to sit in Parliament.[3]

[1] *Lincs. Peds.* (Harl. Soc. li), 531. [2] *Lincs. AO,* L/1/1/1/6. [3] *London Gazette,* 23 Mar. 1685; Grey, ix. 396–7, 539; C. Holmes, *17th Cent. Lincs.* 257.

J.S.C.

HUSSEY, Sir Thomas, 2nd Bt. (1639–1706), of Doddington, Lincs.

LINCOLN   1681
LINCOLNSHIRE   1685, 1689, 1690, 1695

bap. 14 Jan. 1639, 2nd but 1st surv. s. of Thomas Hussey† (*d.*1641) of Gonerby by Rhoda, da. and coh. of Thomas Chapman, Draper, of Soper Lane, London and Wormley, Herts. *educ.* Wormley (Mr Lovelace); Christ's, Camb. 1655. *m.* 22 Feb. 1661, Sarah (*d.*19 July 1697), da. of (Sir) John Langham, 1st Bt.*, of Crosby Place, Bishopsgate, London and Cottesbrooke, Northants. 6s *d.v.p.* 4da. *suc.* gdfa. Sir Edward Hussey, 1st Bt.† 22 Mar. 1648.[1]

Commr. for militia, Lincs. Mar. 1660, capt. of militia horse Apr. 1660; j.p. Lincs (Kesteven) July 1660–Feb. 1688, (Lindsey) 1662–Feb. 1688, (Kesteven and Lindsey) Oct. 1688–*d.*; commr. for assessment (Kesteven) Aug. 1660–1, 1663–4, Lincs. 1661–3, 1664–80, 1689–90, sewers, Hatfield chase and Lincs. Aug. 1660, dep. lt. Lincs. c. Aug. 1660–Jan. 1688, Oct. 1688–?1700, commr. for loyal and indigent officers 1662; freeman, Lincoln, 1664; sheriff, Lincs. 1668–9, commr. for recusants 1675.[2]

Hussey's father, the elder brother of Charles Hussey*, was returned to the Long Parliament for Grantham, but died before his political sympathies could be demonstrated. Hussey succeeded to an estate of about £2,500 p.a., and took up residence at Doddington, some five miles from Lincoln. He welcomed the Restoration, contributing £60 towards a loan to the King. He stood for the county in 1665 at the by-election occasioned by his uncle's death, and again after the dissolution of the Cavalier Parliament, but was twice defeated by Sir Robert Carr*. In August 1679 he was said to be 'hovering' over both county and city, finally withdrawing in favour of Henry Monson*. He defeated Monson at Lincoln in 1681, finishing at the head of the poll, but left no trace on the records of the Oxford Parliament. He moved up to a county seat in 1685, but in James II's Parliament he was appointed only to the committees to consider expiring laws and to establish a land registry. A speech sometimes attributed to him on the standing army was probably delivered by Thomas Howard*. He was listed by Danby as a member of the Opposition, but in January 1688 the Earl of Lindsey (Robert Bertie I*) expected him to stand for re-election against the Whig Sir William Ellys*. He gave the same negative answer as his old rival Monson on the repeal of the Test Act and Penal Laws, and was removed from local office.[3]

Hussey was among the last of the Lincolnshire magnates to join the Revolution. On 11 Dec. Lindsey wrote: 'If Sir Thomas Hussey wed the cause, his interest will do much to make this country unanimous'. Re-elected to the Convention, but again inactive, he did not vote to agree with the Lords that the throne was not vacant, and he was probably a court Tory. Of his six committees, the most important were in the second session, those for the second mutiny bill and reversing Walcot's attainder. He remained a Tory under William III, though he did not refuse to sign the Association in 1696. He died on 19 Dec. 1706, and was buried at Honington.[4]

[1] *Lincs. Peds.* (Harl. Soc. li), 520; R. E. G. Cole, *Hist. Doddington*, 100. [2] *Merc. Pub.* 19 Apr. 1660; C181/7/20. [3] Keeler, *Long Parl.* 226–7; *Her. and Gen.* ii. 122; Cole, 101; *The News*, 12 Jan. 1665; BL, M636/32, John to Sir Ralph Verney, 19 Feb. 1679; Spencer mss, Hickman to Halifax, 15 Aug. 1679. [4] *HMC 11th Rep.* VII, 28.

J.S.C.

HUTCHINSON, John (1615–64), of Owthorpe, Notts.

NOTTINGHAMSHIRE	16 Mar. 1646
NOTTINGHAM	Apr.–9 June 1660

bap. 18 Sept. 1615, 2nd but 1st surv. s. of Sir Thomas Hutchinson[†] of Owthorpe by 1st w. Margaret, da. of Sir John Byron[†] of Newstead Abbey, Notts. *educ.* Nottingham g.s. to 1628, 1631–2; Lincoln g.s. 1628–31; Peterhouse, Camb. 1632–6, BA 1634; L. Inn 1636–8. *m.* 3 July 1638, Lucy, da. of Sir Allen Apsley, lt. of the Tower 1617–30, 4s. (1 *d.v.p.*) 4da. *suc.* fa. 1643.[1]

J.p. Notts. 1642–June 1660, commr. for defence of associated counties 1642, sequestration 1643, levying of money 1643, assessment 1644–52, 1657, northern assoc. 1645; freeman, Nottingham 1645; commr. for militia, Notts. 1648, c.-in-c. militia 1650, sheriff 1658–Feb. 1660; commr. for militia, Leics. and Notts. 1659, Mar. 1660, assessment Jan. 1660; custos rot. Notts. Mar.– June 1660.[2]

Lt.-col. of ft. (parliamentary) 1642–3, col. 1643–7; gov. Nottingham 1643–7.[3]

Commr. for exclusion from sacrament 1646, scandalous offences 1648; member, high court of justice 1649; Councillor of State 13 Feb. 1649–51.

Hutchinson's ancestors had been minor Nottinghamshire landowners for five generations. They had intermarried with the leading county families, but Hutchinson's father, three times elected knight of the shire, was the first of the family to enter Parliament. He was nominated royalist com-

missioner of array and parliamentary commissioner for sequestrations, but probably acted in neither capacity. He continued to sit at Westminster as a member of the peace party till his death in August 1643, when he left everything he could to his second family and away from his more radical elder sons. Hutchinson became an Independent under his wife's influence, took up arms for the Parliament and was 'as zealous against the late King at the time of his trial as any other of his judges'. But he opposed the Protectorate, standing unsuccessfully against the court candidates for Nottinghamshire in 1656. During the Civil War and the Interregnum he had made few enemies among his own class, and by 'improving all opportunities against the honest party', notably Sir Henry Vane[†], he was able through his connexions at Court to await the Restoration with complacency, if not with the enthusiasm that his friends alleged. He had some thoughts of standing for the county again in 1660, but desisted at the request of William Pierrepont*, and was brought in for Nottingham by his colleague Arthur Stanhope*, who 'laboured more for the colonel than for himself'.[4]

Hutchinson duly went up to Westminster for the opening of Parliament. He had made no speeches and sat on no committees when he was called on to explain his participation in the high court of justice. 'If he had erred', he told the House on 12 May, 'it was the inexperience of his age and the defect of his judgment. . . . He had made shipwreck of all things but a good conscience; and as to that particular action of the King, he desired them to believe he had that sense of it that befitted an Englishman, a Christian and a gentleman.' This conditional penitence contrasted unfavourably with the tearful performance of Richard Ingoldsby*, nor could Hutchinson seriously claim to have assisted the Restoration, and with the other regicides he was suspended from sitting. Though the Commons insisted on his privilege when the Lords issued an order to secure his person and estate, both were now in danger, and in a letter calendared under 5 June Mrs Hutchinson either persuaded him to sign, or, according to her own account, forged his signature to a much humbler statement, in which he expressed his concern that 'in the surprise of being proceeded against as a fugitive by the late proclamation, after claiming the benefit of the King's pardon, he did not speak in the House with a sufficient sense of his guilt'. His royalist brother-in-law Sir Allen Apsley* was working hard for him behind the scenes. In the debate on the indemnity bill Roger Palmer* and Heneage Finch* spoke warmly in his favour, and he was merely discharged from sitting and declared incapable of holding public office. To the House of Lords he made a 'humble and sorrowful acknowledgment of those crimes whereunto seduced judgment, and not malice nor any other self-respect, unfortunately betrayed him', attaching to it a charitably mendacious certificate of his long-standing crypto-royalism signed by Sir Anthony Ashley Cooper* and eight others of impeccable loyalty. Meanwhile the Lower House on the recommendation of Edward King* added to the indemnity bill a proviso to compel Hutchinson to refund certain grants made to him by the Long Parliament at the expense of the Newark Royalists, but this, with other similar clauses, was struck out by the Lords. In its place two of the Nottinghamshire Cavaliers brought in a separate bill to raise £2,680 and damages out of his estate. Hutchinson employed Finch as his counsel, but the bill passed the Lords, despite his eloquence and the partiality of Lord Dorchester in the chair of the committee, only to be rejected by the Commons on the second reading by 85 votes to 45.[5]

Hutchinson had succeeded in preserving his life, liberty and estate, but not for long. True, the Newark bill again failed in the first session of the Cavalier Parliament; but he was a marked man, and when his name was mentioned in connexion with the Derwentdale Plot in 1663 he was ordered to be arrested. After 11 months' imprisonment he died on 11 Sept. 1664. His own family, loaded with debt, vanished into obscurity, but his half-brother Charles, who bought the estate from them in 1671, was prominent on the Whig side during the Nottingham charter riot, and sat for the borough from 1690 till his death.[6]

[1] *Hutchinson Mems.* 23, 29, 31, 32, 46; *Nottingham Bor. Recs.* v. 131. [2] *Hutchinson Mems.* 80, 343; *Nottingham Bor. Recs.* v. 239; *CSP Dom.* 1650, p. 506; A. C. Wood, *Notts. in the Civil War*, 181. [3] *Hutchinson Mems.* 116, 132, 167, 276. [4] Keeler, *Long Parl.* 227–8; *Voyce from the Watch Tower*, 175; *Thurloe*, v. 299; *Hutchinson Mems.* 362–5. [5] *Hutchinson Mems.* 367–8; *CJ*, viii. 24, 41, 56, 60, 84, 86, 205; *CSP Dom.* 1660–1, p. 39; *HMC 7th Rep.* 120; Bowman diary, f. 61v; *HMC Var.* vii. 371–2; *Cal. Comm. Adv. Money*, 882, 942; *LJ*, xi. 118–19, 167. [6] *CJ*, viii. 371; *HMC Portland*, ii. 144; *CSP Dom.* 1682, pp. 437–8.

M.W.H./J.P.F.

HUXLEY, James (1614–c.1672), of Dornford, Wootton and Oxford, Oxon.

OXFORD   1660

bap. 6 Nov. 1614, 3rd s. of George Huxley, Haberdasher (*d.*1627), of Wyer Hall, Edmonton, Mdx. by Catherine, da. of John Robinson, Mercer, of London. *educ.* G. Inn 1632. *m.* Elizabeth, da. of Sir Robert Barkham, merchant, of Wainfleet St. Mary, Lincs. and Tottenham, Mdx., 2da.[1]

Freeman, Oxford Mar. 1660; j.p. Oxon. July 1660–?*d.*, Oxford Aug. 1660–?*d.*; commr. for assessment, Oxon. and Oxford Aug. 1660–1, Oxford 1661–3.[2]

Huxley's father, of Cheshire origin, bought Wyer Hall in 1609. Huxley himself was described by Wood as a Presbyterian, but he played no known part in the Civil War. It is not clear when he first came into Oxfordshire, but by 1660 he was living in a house (probably rented) behind Pembroke College 'on the south side'. Elected to the Convention for Oxford after a contest, he made no recorded speeches, and was appointed to only nine committees of secondary importance, including those to consider an additional clause in the judicial proceedings bill and the bills to levy arrears of assessment and to prevent swearing and cursing. He probably voted with the Presbyterian Opposition. He was mentioned as a candidate in 1661, but did not go to the poll. He is said to have been a great improver of clover on his Dornford estate. He also owned lands in Huntingdonshire and Somerset, but these were not extensive. His will, signed on 31 Oct. 1672, was proved on 28 Feb. 1673. He was the only member of the family to sit in Parliament.[3]

[1] *Ped. Reg.* i. 118; ii. 31; *Misc. Gen. et Her.* (ser. 2), i. 188; PCC 106 May. [2] *Oxford Council Acts* (Oxf. Hist. Soc. xcv), 254. [3] *Mdx. Peds.* (Harl. Soc. lxv), 111; *Wood's Life and Times* (Oxf. Hist. Soc. xix), 311, 399; *Hearth-Tax Returns* (Oxf. Rec. Soc. xxi), 127; *HMC Hastings*, ii. 166; *Ped. Reg.* i. 122.

M.W.H./L.N./G.J.

HYDE, Edward, Visct. Cornbury (1661–1723).

WILTSHIRE   1685, 1689, 1690
CHRISTCHURCH   1695, 1698, 1701 (Feb.)

b. 28 Nov. 1661, o.s. of Henry Hyde*, 2nd Earl of Clarendon. *educ.* Christ Church, Oxf. 1675; Académie Foubert, Paris 1676; Padua 1678. *m.* 10 July 1688, Catherine, *suo jure* Baroness Clifton of Leighton Bromswold (*d.* 11 Aug. 1706), da. and h. of Henry O'Brien*, Lord Ibrackan, of Great Billing, Northants., 1s. *d.v.p.* 1da. *suc.* fa. as 3rd Earl of Clarendon 31 Oct. 1709.[1]

Lt.-col. R. Dgns. 1683, col. 1685–9.

Gent. of the horse to Prince George of Denmark 1683, master of the horse 1685–90; gov. New York and New Jersey 1701–8; PC 13 Dec. 1711; envoy extraordinary to Hanover May–Aug. 1714.[2]

J.p. Berks. 1680–?1701, Oxon. 1685–?1701; freeman, King's Lynn 1687; commr. for assessment, Wilts. and Westminster 1689–90.[3]

Lord Cornbury became an army officer and a member of Prince George's household in 1683. Two years later he was returned for Wiltshire as a court supporter, although Thomas Bruce* complained that he had to empty his purse to bring in one of a family so unpopular in that county. An inactive Member of James II's Parliament, he was appointed to the committee for a private bill promoted by the Duke of Ormonde, and added to the committee to bring in a bill for regulating hackney coaches. After active service at the battle of Sedgemoor, he was given command of his regiment. Several matches proposed for him fell through, owing to the embarrassed circumstances of the family, and he eloped, much to his father's distress, with Lady Clifton, 'a young woman oddly bred, no manner of advantage, and an unavoidable charge'. He 'began the general defection' from James in November 1688, although few of his men followed him. At a meeting of the gentry on 5 Dec. at Salisbury, then occupied by the invaders, his readoption for the county was agreed on, and he was returned to the Convention in the following month, though he was defeated at Reading. In the debate on the state of the nation on 28 Jan. 1689 he desired an explanation of the declaration that James had abdicated and left the throne vacant, and he was one of three Members to vote against it. According to Anthony Rowe* he also voted to agree with the Lords on this question on 5 Feb. He was again inactive in Parliament, in which he was named to the committee of elections and privileges in both sessions and that to consider the first mutiny bill. He was deprived of his commission in July, and voted against the motion for the dismissal of Lord Halifax. After the recess he was appointed to the committee of inquiry into the miscarriages of the war. He demanded parliamentary confirmation of Princess Anne's pension, and on 17 Dec. acted as teller against recommitting the bill to increase her income.[4]

Cornbury continued to sit in the Commons as a Tory until he became governor of New York, though he did not refuse the Association in 1696. He died 'in obscurity and deep in debt' on 31 Mar. 1723, and was buried in Westminster Abbey. His title was inherited by his cousin, the 2nd Earl of Rochester.

[1] *CSP Dom.* 1676–7, p. 304; *Savile Corresp.* (Cam. Soc. lxxi), 42. [2] *CSP Dom.* July–Sept. 1683, p. 215; LS13/231/24. [3] *Lynn Freemen*, 198. [4] *Ailesbury Mems.* 99–100; *HMC Stopford-Sackville*, i. 18; *Clarendon Corresp.* ii. 180, 216, 283; Clarke, *Jas. II*, ii. 215; *IHR Bull.* xlix. 261; *HMC 11th Rep. VII*, 202; Foxcroft, *Halifax*, ii. 89; R. Morrice, Entering Bk. 3, p. 43.

L.N.

HYDE, Hon. Edward (1645–65), of the Middle Temple, London.

SALISBURY 16 May 1664–10 Jan. 1665

bap. 1 Apr. 1645, 3rd s. of Sir Edward Hyde[†], 1st Earl of Clarendon, and bro. of Henry Hyde* and Laurence Hyde*. *educ.* Christ Church, Oxf. 1660; M. Temple 1661, called 1664. *unm.*[1]

Freeman, Salisbury 1662; student of Christ Church by 1665; commr. for oyer and terminer, Western circuit 1665.[2]

Hyde's father became high steward of Salisbury in 1662, and seems to have nominated his son as the only candidate in whose favour he could decline, without offence, to support (Sir) Thomas Clarges*. Hyde thus entered Parliament, presumably unopposed, shortly after his 19th birthday. In spite of his youth he was not inactive, serving on at least four committees in his only session. His was the first name on the committee for the bill to make the Avon navigable from Christchurch to Salisbury. He died on 10 Jan. 1665 and was buried in Westminster Abbey.[3]

[1] *Westminster Abbey Reg.* (Harl. Soc. x), 161; North, *Lives*, i. 59; *Cal. Cl. SP*, v. 393. [2] Hoare, *Wilts.* Salisbury, 449. [3] North, *Lives*, i. 59; *Cal. Cl. SP*, v. 393.

J.P.F.

HYDE, Sir Frederick (1614–77), of Teddington, Mdx.

HAVERFORDWEST c. Sept. 1666–Apr. 1677

b. 28 June 1614, 10th but 8th surv. s. of Sir Lawrence Hyde[†] (*d.*1642), attorney-gen. to Queen Anne of Denmark, of Salisbury, Wilts. by Barbara, da. of John Baptist Castilion of Benham Valence, Berks.; bro. of Sir Robert Hyde[†], c.j.K.b. 1663–5, and Alexander Hyde, bp. of Salisbury 1665–7. *educ.* M. Temple 1631, called 1638. *m.* Anne (*d.* 27 June 1687), da. of Nathaniel Tomkins[†], clerk of the Queen's council, of Holborn, Mdx., *s.p.* Kntd. 23 July 1663.[1]

Bencher, M. Temple June 1660; commr. for assessment, Mdx. 1664–*d.*, Bucks. 1665–9, Haverfordwest 1673–*d.*, Pemb., Pembroke and Tenby 1673–4; j.p. Hants July 1660–*d.*, Bucks. and Herts. 1665–*d.*; commr. for oyer and terminer, Western circuit 1662, c.j. S. Wales circuit 1666–*d.*[2]

Serjeant-at-law Oct. 1660; serjeant-at-law to Queen Catherine of Braganza by 1669–*d.*

Hyde was the first cousin of Lord Chancellor Clarendon, and came of a strongly Anglican royalist family. His elder brother Robert, MP for Salisbury in the Long Parliament, joined the King at Oxford. His father-in-law was hanged in 1643 for participation in the plot devised by Edmund Waller I* for betraying London to the Royalists, and another brother, Henry, was executed in 1650. Hyde himself seems to have taken no part in the Civil War. At the Restoration, his brother became a judge and Hyde himself serjeant-at-law. Six years later he succeeded Sir William Morton* both as Welsh judge and as Member for Haverfordwest. Hugh Owen (Sir Hugh Owen, 2nd Bt.*) petitioned against the return; the committee recommended that the election should be declared void, but the House voted in favour of the sitting Member. In an enigmatic passage, Andrew Marvell* describes him as contending with (Sir) Solomon Swale* 'for the command of politics or sots' in the court party. He was not an active member of the House, sitting on only ten committees, of which the most important

Hyde Family of Wiltshire and Hampshire

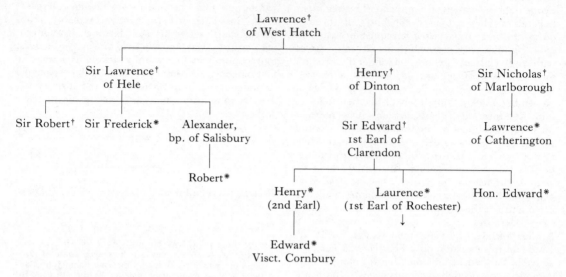

were to amend the articles of impeachment against Henry Brouncker* and to consider the condition of Ireland. He was included in both lists of the court party in 1669–71, as one who might be engaged by the Duke of York and his friends, and later his name appears on the Paston list, the list of officials in the House, and on Wiseman's list. He was buried in the Temple on 3 May 1677. He left some property in Wiltshire and Dorset, but his will indicates that he was not a wealthy man.[3]

[1] *Vis. Wilts.* (Harl. Soc. cv), 99; *Wilts. N. and Q.* vi. 344, 436; Lipscomb, *Bucks.* iii. 185. [2] W. R. Williams, *Great Sessions in Wales*, 175. [3] Keeler, *Long Parl.* 228; *CJ*, ix. 26; *Marvell* ed. Margoliouth, i. 145; Harl. 7020, f. 48; PCC 49 Hale.

L.N./G.J.

HYDE, Henry (1638–1709).

LYME REGIS   18 June 1660
WILTSHIRE   1661–19 Dec. 1674

b. 2 June 1638, 1st s. of Edward Hyde†, 1st Earl of Clarendon, and bro. of Hon. Edward Hyde* and Laurence Hyde*. *educ.* M. Temple 1661. *m.* (1) Jan. 1661, Theodosia (*d.* Mar. 1662), da. of Arthur Capel†, 1st Baron Capell of Hadham, 1s.; (2) 19 Oct. 1670, Flower (*d.* 17 July 1700), da. and h. of William Backhouse of Swallowfield, Berks., wid. of William Bishop of South Warnborough, Hants, and of her cos. Sir William Backhouse, 1st Bt., of London, *s.p.* styled Visct. Cornbury 20 Apr. 1661; KB 23 Apr. 1661; *suc.* fa. as 2nd Earl of Clarendon 19 Dec. 1674.[1]

Commr. for assessment, Wilts. Aug. 1660–74, Mdx. 1661–3, 1664–74, Oxon. 1663–74, Berks. and Westminster 1673–4; keeper, Windsor Forest and bailiff of Clewer manor, Berks. Nov. 1660–4; commr. for oyer and terminer, Wales 1661; j.p. Wilts. 1661–75, Mdx.

1661–bef. 1680, Oxon. 1661–89, Berks. 1670–89; dep. lt. Wilts. 1661–2, Oxon. 1663–89; commr. for loyal and indigent officers, Wilts. 1662; capt of militia horse, Oxon. by 1663; custos rot. Oxon. 1663–89; ranger of Wychwood Forest, Oxon. 1674–*d.*; high steward, Reading 1674–?*d.*, Salisbury 1683–*d.*, Oxf. Univ. 1686–*d.*; keeper, Somerset House 1679–?89; searcher of customs, Gravesend 1681–5; gov. New River Co. by 1682.[2]

Commr. for trade Nov. 1660–8; private sec. to Queen Catherine of Braganza 1662–5, ld. chamberlain 1665–8, 1670–5, treas. and receiver-gen. by 1680–6; PC 8 Jan.–21 Apr. 1679, 26 May 1680–9; ld. privy seal Feb.–Sept. 1685; ld. lt. [I] 1685–7; commr. for licensing pedlars 1686–7.[3]

Hyde's great-grandfather, the younger son of a minor gentry family which had never distinguished itself in its native Cheshire, became an Exchequer clerk and a client of Sir John Thynne, subsequently sitting for Malmesbury in 1559 and acquiring an estate in Wiltshire. During the Interregnum Hyde joined his father, the historian and statesman, in exile on the Continent, 'so that he was generally half the day writing in cipher or deciphering, and was so discreet as well as faithful that nothing was ever discovered by him'. After the Restoration he was returned at a by-election for Lyme Regis, and became a moderately active Member of the Convention. Before his brother Laurence joined him in the House, he certainly served on six committees, including two concerned with unauthorized publications, and later possibly on eight others, of which the most important was for the Dunkirk establishment, attending the House of Lords with a draft order on the subject on 12 Sept. 1660. In the second session, 'Mr Hyde' was among those instructed to recommend a form of prayer for use in the House. In the debate on the pamphlet *The Long Parliament Revived* on 20 Nov. he wanted its author to be asked whether he had submitted it for examination by the proper authorities, and four days later he was sent with three senior Members to ask the lord chief justice to punish offences against customs officials. One of the brothers was teller for the second reading of the tanning bill, and was sent to the Lords to desire a conference on the college leases bill.[4]

Although the family property in Wiltshire was apparently occupied by Nevil Maskelyne*, Hyde was returned for the county at the general election of 1661, sharing with Charles Seymour* a bill of £191 7s. 2d. In the Cavalier House of Commons, under the courtesy title of Lord Cornbury, he was a moderately active Member, being appointed to 101 committees, acting as teller in nine divisions, and making 25 recorded speeches. In the opening session he was appointed to the committees for the security bill and the bill to restore the temporal jurisdiction of the clergy. He carried the latter bill to the House of Lords on 13 June, and again after amendment a week later. He also served on the committees for the corporations and uniformity bills. He was teller for the second reading of the bill for the execution of those under attainder, and was appointed to the committee. On the King's marriage he was appointed to the new Queen's household, first as her private secretary and then, in succession to the 2nd Earl of Chesterfield, as chamberlain. After the division on the Declaration of Indulgence on 25 Feb. 1663, a Roman Catholic correspondent assumed that Cornbury had voted on the opposite side to his brother and John Bulteel*, that is, presumably, in the minority against debating it. He was appointed to the committee for the Witney grammar school bill. He was listed as a court dependant in 1664, and during the first session was appointed to the committee for the additional corporations bill and acted as teller for retaining the reference to courts of equity in the conventicles bill. In the next session he was among those sent to thank the King and the City for providing for the defence of the country against the Dutch, and on 28 Jan. 1665 he carried to the Lords a bill to make the Avon navigable from Christchurch to Salisbury. He was one of the Members appointed to attend the King on 30 Oct. 1666 with a resolution against imports from France, and he twice acted as teller against the proposal to extend favour to all the merchants who had failed to comply. Andrew Marvell* alleged that he was the first to flee from Chatham during the Dutch attack on the Medway, and pictured him as leading

the peers' sons to reinforce the court party in the House astride a hobby horse, perhaps an allusion to his activities in the Oxfordshire militia.[5]

Cornbury was less prominent than his brother in his father's defence. But on 22 Nov. 1667 he moved that the charges against him should be specified and sent to the Lords, and he defended the acquisition of the lease of Witney. He was already out of favour at Court on suspicion of assisting the Duchess of Richmond to escape the King's pursuit, and was now ordered to withdraw, though his post was not filled. After the Christmas recess he was appointed to the committee to inspect the militia laws. His name was on both lists of the court party in 1669–71, when he took part in all the measures against conventicles. During the negotiation of the secret treaty of Dover he was restored to his post through the mediation of the Duchess of Orleans. In 1673 he was appointed to the committee for the test bill and helped to manage a conference, though he felt compelled to defend an English priest in the Queen's household and brought in a proviso for her servants 'not so happily worded as he could have wished'. He wished the bill of ease for Protestant dissenters to apply only to nonconformists who renounced the Covenant, and although he was put on the committee at the end of the list, he acted as teller for the indefinite adjournment of the debate when the bill returned from the Lords. In contrast, his was the first name on the committee to draw up an address on the state of Ireland. In the autumn session he seconded the motion of (Sir) William Coventry* for redress before supply, instancing as a grievance that 'some men have been under prejudice for giving votes'.[6]

With the break-up of the Cabal, Cornbury seized the opportunity to pay off old scores against his father's enemies. He did not speak in the debate on Lauderdale in 1674, but of Buckingham he said:

> Suppose he should acquit himself of all the great matters concerning the King, yet here is a crime in the face of the sun, a murder, and his living with that miserable woman [Lady Shrewsbury] in perpetual adultery.

But it was against Lord Arlington (Sir Henry Bennet*) that he was most 'malicious' and 'inveterate'. He acted as teller for the address for his dismissal, and on 20 Jan. said:

> [I] will not enlarge on his religion, but he might have made distinction between Protestants and Papists. He had so great a hand in all these things that there seems much more against him than either of the rest. Buckingham proposed the alliance with France, but Arlington promoted it.

Cornbury's standing in the House was now so high that he was employed as messenger to ask the latitudinarian Whichcott to preach, and to ask the concurrence of the Lords in an address for peace, as well as helping to prepare reasons for two conferences.[7]

Cornbury succeeded as second Earl of Clarendon on his father's death later in the year. But he was already in the scriveners' books to the tune of £19,860, and he was never able to extricate himself from debt, though always ready with a plausible excuse and a promise. Building, planting and collecting were apparently the only causes of his extravagance. He remained in opposition during the Danby administration, and was dismissed on an obvious pretext in 1675. He went over to the Court during the Exclusion crisis, returning Tories for his borough of Christchurch. He voted against the bill in 1680, after which the Commons resolved that he was a promoter of Popery. He resided chiefly on his second wife's property at Swallowfield, which gave him an interest at Reading, some six miles distant. James II appointed his former brother-in-law first lord privy seal and then lord lieutenant of Ireland; but his authority was undermined by the Roman Catholic commander-in-chief Tyrconnel, who took over from him. He assisted with the defence of the Seven Bishops, and, after castigating the royal policy in the council of peers, he followed his son's example by going over to the Prince of Orange. But he opposed the transfer of the crown, and was imprisoned as a Jacobite in 1690-1. 'Though he almost wanted bread to eat', he refused employment and remained a strict non-juror. His father's palatial house in Piccadilly had already been demolished, and Cornbury had to be conveyed to his brother, though the transaction was kept secret to save appearances. He died of asthma on 31 Oct. 1709 and was buried in Westminster Abbey. He was one of the principal informants used by Burnet for his *History*, in which he is described as 'the most beloved of all the family, for he was humble and obliging, but peevish and splenetic, [and] his judgment was not [to] be much depended on'.[8]

[1] *Vis. Berks.* (Harl. Soc. lvi), 160-1; C. C. E. Russell, *Swallowfield and its Owners*, 137. [2] *CSP Dom.* 1660-1, p. 368; 1663-4, p. 280; 1664-5, p. 50; 1679-80, p. 299; 1685, p. 403; Russell, 142, 190; C. Coates, *Hist. Reading*, App. xiv; Hoare, *Wilts*. Salisbury, 699; *HMC Ormonde*, n.s. vii. 476; *Cal. Treas. Bks.* vi. 508; vii. 226; viii. 512. [3] *CSP Dom.* 1661-2, p. 396; 1686-7, pp. 16, 387; *Evelyn Corresp.* ed. Wheatley, iii. 320; *Cal. Treas. Bks.* vi. 508; viii. 689, 1114. [4] Clarendon, *Life*, i. 1-2; Burnet, i. 463; *Old Parl. Hist.* xxiii. 20; *CJ*, viii. 215, 228. [5] *Cal. Cl. SP*, v. 270, 305; Add. 32324, f. 74; *CJ*, viii. 320, 564, 681; *Marvell* ed. Margoliouth, i. 146, 155. [6] *Pepys Diary*, 22 Nov. 1667; *Milward*, 152; Burnet, i. 452-3; *Marvell*, ii. 64; Eg. 2539, f. 203; *CSP Dom.* 1670, p. 263; Grey, ii. 81, 204; *CJ*, ix. 263, 268, 280. [7] Grey, ii. 252, 297, 320; *CJ*, ix. 296, 298, 300; *Williamson Letters* (Cam. Soc. n.s. ix), 127, 135, 153. [8] Guildhall RO, 6428; Burnet, i. 462-3; *Evelyn Diary*, iv. 339; *Clarendon Corresp.* i. 181-3; *Hearne's Colls.* (Oxf. Hist. Soc. vii), 297.

L.N.

HYDE, Laurence (1642–1711) of St. James's Square, Westminster and Vasterne Park, Wootton Bassett, Wilts.

NEWPORT	20 Aug. 1660
OXFORD UNIVERSITY	1661
WOOTTON BASSETT	1679 (Mar.), 1679 (Oct.)

bap. 15 Mar. 1642, 2nd s. of Edward Hyde[†], 1st Earl of Clarendon, and bro. of Hon. Edward Hyde* and Henry Hyde*. *educ.* M. Temple 1660. *m.* bef. 14 June 1665, Lady Henrietta Boyle (*d.* 12 Apr. 1687), da. of Richard, 2nd Earl of Cork [I] and 1st Earl of Burlington, 1s. 4da. *cr.* Visct. Hyde of Kenilworth 23 Apr. 1681, Earl of Rochester 29 Nov. 1682; KG 29 June 1685.[1]

Freeman, Portsmouth 1661; commr. for assessment, Westminster 1677-9, Oxf. Univ. 1677-80, Wilts. 1679-80; j.p. Oxon. 1680-?85, St. Albans 1686; keeper, Richmond New Park 1683-?d.; recorder, Salisbury 1685-Oct. 1688; custos rot. Herts. 1686-9; ld. lt. Herts. 1687-9, Cornw. 1710-d.; high steward, Oxf. Univ. 1709-d.[2]

Master of the robes 1662-79; ambassador to Poland Nov.-Dec. 1676; plenip. at Nymwegen and envoy to The Hague 1677-8; ld. of Treasury Mar. 1679, first ld. Nov. 1679-84; PC 19 Nov. 1679-Dec. 1688, 1 Mar. 1692-d., ld. pres. 1684-5, 1710-d.; gent. of the bedchamber 1680-5; gov. Merchant Adventurers 1684-c.92; ld. treas. 1685-7; postmaster-gen. and chancellor to Queen Mary of Modena 1685-9; commr. for ecclesiastical affairs 1686-7; ld. lt. [I] 1700-3.[3]

Hyde was first returned for Newport in 1660 after William Morice I* had chosen to sit for Plymouth. No sooner had he taken his seat than his father, the lord chancellor, recommended him as a candidate for Oxford University at the next general election. He was created MA and returned unopposed, though still under age, to the Cavalier Parliament. He was probably named to no committees before 1663, although he may have been sometimes confused in the Journals with his cousin Lawrence Hyde*. He then seems to have become moderately active, sitting on perhaps 67 committees and acting as teller in eight divisions. Although a much abler man than his elder brother, and an excellent draftsman, he spoke ungracefully, and only eight speeches can be attributed to him. On succeeding Lord Mansfield (Henry Cavendish*) as master of the robes in 1662, he 'was thought the smoothest man in Court', though easily provoked into a rage, when 'he would swear like a cutter'. On 28 Mar. 1663 a Roman Catholic wrote that presumably Hyde and his brother had voted on opposite sides in the division over debating the Declaration of Indulgence. One of the cousins helped to consider the bill against unlawful meetings of dissenters and the charge against Sir Richard Temple*, and both were appointed to the committees for the bills against pluralities and the sale of offices in the same session. Hyde was listed with his cousin as a court dependant in 1664, probably serving on the committee for the additional corporations bill, and acting as teller with Thomas Clifford* against a proviso for the punishment of hearth-tax collectors. In the Oxford session he was appointed to the committee for the attainder of English officers in the Dutch service. He was among those ordered on 30 Oct. 1666 to attend the King with the resolution against French imports. When a proclamation was issued accordingly, he was teller against allowing merchants to land goods purchased before the prohibition, but he was on the opposite side to his brother on the proposal to extend favour to all who had failed to comply. He was appointed to the committee on the private bill for the illegitimization of Lady Roos's children, which some saw as a first step to enabling the King to marry again and cut out Hyde's nieces from the succession.[4]

Hyde defended his father in the impeachment proceedings in one of his rare speeches, which, 'for its greatness and worthiness', led Edmund Waller I* to compare him to Brutus:

> I shall endeavour to show myself not so much a son of the Earl of Clarendon as a Member of this House, and I assure you that, if he shall be found guilty, no man shall appear more against him than I; if not, I hope everyone will be for him as much as I. Let every man upon his conscience think what of this charge is true, for I believe that, if one article be proved, he will own himself guilty of all.

On 16 Nov. 1667 he moved that Clarendon should be brought to trial rather than 'set the two Houses at difference'. But, according to Burnet, 'during all the dispute concerning his father, he made his court so dexterously that no resentments appeared on that head'. After the Christmas recess he was appointed to the committees to inspect the militia laws and for the continuation of the Conventicles Act. He was named to the committees to receive information about seditious conventicles in 1669 and to suppress them in the following year. He acted as teller against hearing the report on customs fees in the outports on 26 Mar. 1670, and was appointed to the committee for union with Scotland. Unexpectedly, in the next session he spoke in favour of a tax on offices, and acted as teller against an indemnity for offences against the Conventicles Act. As a placeman, he was included in both lists of the court party in 1669–71, and was alleged in *Flagellum Parliamentarium* to have received £1,000 p.a. in crown lands. He took no part in the attack on the Cabal and its policies in 1673–4, but was included in the Paston list and the King's servants in the autumn session of 1675, when he was appointed to the committee on the bill for the liberty of the subject.[5]

According to *A Seasonable Argument*, Hyde had received £20,000 in boons, and in 1676 he was sufficiently opulent to lease a town house from (Sir) Thomas Clarges* and to purchase Wootton Bassett from Sir Robert Howard* at the rumoured price of £36,000. He was marked 'thrice vile' on Shaftesbury's list, and entered on the working lists as possessing influence over his cousin. He acted as teller against the adjournment of the debate on Irish cattle on 5 Apr. 1677, but he was frequently out of the country on diplomatic business, and was so noted on the government list of supporters in May 1678. He returned at the time of the Popish Plot, and was among those appointed to examine Coleman, to translate his letters, and to search Langhorne's chambers. The proposal to exclude the Duke of York from the House of Lords brought Hyde to his feet, Daniel Finch*, who had been a Member since 1673, noting that it was the first time he had heard him in the House:

> If the bills to be prepared by the Parliament might pass into law, the chief objection that was insisted on would cease. Now (he said) we had more than ordinary assurance that they would pass without any obstruction, as was feared, and therefore desired them they would stay. That there was great discourse of French counsels, but 'twas apparent that now the Duke had no such inclinations and 'twas a great misfortune no notice should be taken of any such thing by the House when there was some colour for such an objection, and that it should be now when there is none.

Although he also acted as teller against adhering to the proposal, he was appointed one of the managers of the conference.[6]

Listed by the Whigs as one of the 'unanimous club' of Court supporters, Hyde was reckoned to stand little chance of re-election for the University. But his recent purchase had given him control at Wootton Bassett, which he fortified with a new charter, and he was returned at both elections of 1679. When the Treasury was put in commission on the fall of Danby, Hyde was appointed to the board, and distinguished himself by 'always early plodding at the scrutiny of accounts and estimates before the other lords came'. In the first Exclusion Parliament, for which Shaftesbury marked him 'vile', he was appointed only to the elections committee, and his only speech was confined to a defence of his father's record, but he voted against the bill. On his return from the autumn election he was made a privy councillor and promoted first lord. Together with Sidney Godolphin I* and the 2nd Earl of Sunderland, he formed the triumvirate of 'Chits', so called because of their youth, who directed the Government. In the second Exclusion Parliament he brought three messages from the

King, but was appointed to no committees. Despite his infirmities of temper, to which over-indulgence in wine contributed, he became one of the leading debaters for the Court, making 14 speeches. On 27 Oct. 1680 he declared himself unable to credit the informer Dangerfield, who had contradicted himself before the Council, though the House had ordered the publication of his *Narrative of the Popish Plot*. Following the vivacious Silius Titus* in the debate on exclusion on 2 Nov., it was only with difficulty that he could make himself heard:

> I am sorry to see a matter of so great importance managed in this House with so much bitterness on one hand and with so much jesting and mirth on the other. ... It is to me very unpleasant to hear a prince, that hath so well deserved of this nation by fighting our battles and so often appearing for us in war, so upbraided. ... I believe the Duke is convinced that it cannot be reasonable from him to expect to come to the crown upon such terms as if he had not given those apprehensions and jealousies. ... Does any man think that this bill will pass the Lords, and the King too? ... I cannot apprehend that our case is so desperate but that we may secure ourselves some other way without overturning foundations.

When the bill was introduced he denied the assertion of George Vernon* that no good Protestant could be against it, and complained that the rights of the Duke's children had been studiously ignored. When he pointed out that the Irish troops in the Tangier garrison had taken the oaths, and must therefore be 'far from Popery', the House only laughed. On the proposed address for the removal of Lord Halifax, he said: 'I am against this summary way of justice because I do not know whose turn it may be next. If it should be my turn, I would take leave and kiss your hands.' His resolute affirmation that he would never be ashamed of his opposition to the bill, either in Parliament or elsewhere, soon brought on him the fate that he expected. Though the Hon. William Russell* in moving for his removal referred only to his relationship to the Duke, other speakers warned him that 'if he did value the pleasure of the House, he must change his measures as to the bill of exclusion', like Godolphin and Sunderland, to which he replied in tears that he could only follow his conscience. 'What becomes of liberty of speech', inquired William Cavendish*, Lord Cavendish, 'if he may be questioned for what he says here?' But his name was added to Halifax's without a division.[7]

Hyde did not stand at the general election and was raised to the peerage after the dissolution of the Oxford Parliament, which he was supposed to have advised. He was the only minister cognisant of the negotiations for the French subsidy, and in the following year he was created Earl of Rochester.

Although his probity as a financier was beyond suspicion, and he was invariably kind to his family and dependants, his haughtiness and over-confidence made him vulnerable; and when Lord Halifax (Sir George Savile*) was able to prove that the Treasury had been defrauded by the excise farmers, he was promoted to the sinecure office of lord president. He served on James II's ecclesiastical commission, but contemptuously rebutted the arguments put forward for his conversion to the church of Rome. He was dismissed from central government office, though with a handsome pension. It is said that as lord lieutenant of Hertfordshire he browbeat the local gentry into compliance with the repeal of the Test Act and Penal Laws, though this charge was not brought against him after the Revolution. Although he was slighted by William of Orange when he came in at Windsor on 16 Dec. 1688, and spoke in the Lords in favour of a regency, he took the oaths to the new regime without delay; and it was agreed without a division to include him in the indemnity bill. He remained the leader of the high church party to his death, devising a formula which enabled them to sign the Association in 1696. He died on 2 May 1711 and was buried in Westminster Abbey. His son Henry, the last of the family, sat for Launceston as a Tory from 1692 until succeeding to the title.[8]

[1] *Clarendon Corresp.* i. 625; *Cal. Cl. SP*, v. 492. [2] R. East, *Portsmouth Recs.* 357; Hoare, *Wilts. Salisbury* 712; *CSP Dom.* 1683–4, p. 23. [3] *CSP Dom.* 1661–2, p. 367; 1685, p. 299; 1686–7, pp. 202, 358; 1687–9, p. 220; *Cal. Treas. Bks.* ix. 279; information from E. K. Newman and S. P. Anderson. [4] Burnet, i. 463; *CSP Dom.* 1660–1, p. 275; *Cal. Cl. SP*, v. 305; *CJ*, viii. 550, 675, 681. [5] Burnet, i. 458, 463; North, *Lives*, i. 302; *Pepys Diary*, 19 Nov. 1667; *Clarendon Impeachment*, 8; Grey, i. 41; *Dering*, 39; *CJ*, ix. 147. [6] *Survey of London*, xxix. 136; *HMC 7th Rep.* 467; Finch diary, 4 Nov. 1678; *CJ*, ix. 543. [7] *HMC Le Fleming*, 155; *HMC Ormonde*, n.s. iv. 310; v. 281; *CSP Dom.* 1679–80, pp. 279–80; North, loc. cit.; *Sidney Diary*, i. 71–72; Grey, vii. 366, 401–3; viii. 6, 30, 281, 283; *Exact Coll. Debates*, 33–34, 90; Clarke, *Jas. II*, i. 604–5; *HMC 12th Rep. IX*, 113. [8] *Burnet Supp.* ed. Foxcroft, 145, 220, 224; North, op. cit. ii. 202–3; Macaulay, *Hist.* 976–7; *Clarendon Corresp.* ii. 227; Grey, ix. 383

L.N.

HYDE (HIDE), Lawrence (c.1610–82), of Hinton Daubney, Catherington, Hants.

WINCHESTER 1661

b. c.1610, 3rd but 2nd surv. s. of Sir Nicholas Hyde†, l.c.j.K.b. 1627–31, of Marlborough, Wilts. and Hinton Daubney by Maria, da. of Arthur Swayne of Sarson, Amport, Hants. *educ.* M. Temple 1629, called 1637. *m.* c.1652, Alice, da. of Sir John Glanville†, Speaker of the House of Commons Apr.–May 1640, of Broad Hinton, Wilts., 2s. 2da. *suc.* bro. Arthur 1654.[1]

J.p. Hants July 1660–d., commr. for assessment Aug. 1660–80; freeman, Winchester Sept. 1660, Portsmouth 1668; capt. of militia ft. Hants Nov. 1660–d., commr. for corporations 1662–3, loyal and indigent officers

1662, oyer and terminer, Western circuit 1665; dep. lt. Hants. ?1676–d.[2]

Hyde's father, a strong upholder of the prerogative, sat for Old Sarum in 1597 and bought Hinton Daubney in 1604. Hyde's career before succeeding to the estate, valued at about £750 p.a., is obscure. He was educated for the bar, like his father; but he was described as 'clerk' when captured with the Dorset clubmen in 1645, and a few months later, when arrested as a royalist suspect in Southwark, he called himself a merchant. He compounded in 1649 lest he 'might be questioned for something said or done in the first war', and was fined £93. After the battle of Worcester, he helped Lord Wilmot in the escape of Charles II.[3]

Hyde's election for Winchester was no doubt a compliment to his cousin, Lord Chancellor Clarendon. His career in the Cavalier Parliament overlaps that of Clarendon's son, his namesake, but he was probably inactive. He was listed by Lord Wharton as a friend in 1661. He may have served on 44 committees, most of them before his cousin came of age, including those on the security and uniformity bills, and on four private bills prompted by the marquess of Winchester and the bishop of the diocese. Both the cousins were appointed to consider the bills against pluralities and the sale of offices in 1663, and listed as court dependants in 1664. Hyde was not mentioned in the court party lists of 1669–71, but received the government whip in 1675. On the working lists he was to be managed by his cousin and Henry Coventry*, and he was noted as a government supporter by Sir Richard Wiseman*. Shaftesbury marked him 'doubly vile', and according to *A Seasonable Argument* he was 'a constant court dinner man'. He was included in the opposition list of the 'unanimous club', and did not stand again, dying in September 1682. None of his descendants sat in Parliament.[4]

[1] *Wilts. Vis. Peds.* (Harl. Soc. cv), 100; *Wilts. N. and Q.* vi. 344; *VCH Hants*, iii. 96–97; C. J. Hyde, *Hundred of Bosmere*, 152. [2] *Cal. Treas. Bks.* i. 82; *CSP Dom.* 1679–80, p. 61; Winchester corp. assembly bk. 4, f. 142; R. East, *Portsmouth Recs.* 169, 359. [3] *VCH Hants*, iii. 96–100; *Som. and Dorset N. and Q.* viii. 437; *Cal. Comm. Comp.* 1184; *Cal. Comm. Adv. Money*, 961–2; SP23/212/616, 230/226; A. Fea, *Flight of the King*, 166, 169. [4] PCC 224 Fane; Rylands Lib. Eng. mss.

P.W.

HYDE, Robert (1650–1722), of Dinton, Wilts.

HINDON   23 Feb. 1677, 1685, 1689, 1690, 1695
WILTSHIRE   1702, 1705, 1708, 1710, 1713, 1715, 10–20 Apr. 1722

b. 10 Oct. 1650, 2nd but o. surv. s. of Alexander Hyde, bp. of Salisbury 1665–7, by Mary, da. of Robert Townson, bp. of Salisbury 1620–1. *educ.* Magdalen Hall, Oxf. 1666; M. Temple 1667, called 1673. *m.* (1) 4 May 1674, Lady Finetta Pope (*d.* 16 Oct. 1700), da. of Thomas, 3rd Earl of Downe [I], and coh. to her bro. Thomas, 4th Earl, 2s. 1da. *d.v.p.*; (2) 26 Jan. 1704, Arundell, da. of Thomas Penruddock* of Compton Chamberlayne, Wilts., *s.p. suc.* uncle Sir Robert Hyde†, c.j.K.b. 1663–5, at Dinton and Heale 1665, fa. 1667.[1]

J.p. Wilts. 1672–June 1688, Oct. 1688–*d.*, commr. for assessment 1677–80, 1689–90, dep. lt. 1685–June 1688, Oct. 1688–*d.*; freeman, Salisbury 1680, Wilton 1685–May 1688; commr. for rebels' estates, Wilts. 1686.[2]

Hyde's father was the elder brother of Sir Frederick Hyde*. Hyde himself seems to have passed his early manhood chiefly at Dinton, the lease of which had been settled on him by his uncle. Returned to the Cavalier Parliament at a by-election in 1677, he was accused in *A Seasonable Argument* of selling his vote to the Court for £1,000 before he even took his seat, and Shaftesbury marked him 'thrice vile'. But Danby did not list him as a court supporter in 1678, which seems to dispose of the allegation, whatever the Opposition thought. Probably his only committee was for the estate bill of John Bankes†, whom he remembered in his will as one of his worthy friends. He was included in the list of the 'unanimous club', and probably did not stand in 1679, though with his kinsman Thomas Lambert* he was commended at the assizes in 1680 for his zeal in seeking out Papists. In 1681 he was invited to contest Shaftesbury, but refused in order to concentrate on Hindon, where, however, the Thynne interest was too strong for him. The sale of burgages after the death of Thomas Thynne II* in the following year and the acquisition of West Hatch, two miles from Hindon, in 1683 strengthened Hyde's interest in the borough. He was returned with Lambert to James II's Parliament, probably unopposed, but was appointed only to the committee for the encouragement of woollen manufactures. To the lord lieutenant's questions in 1688:

> He will not declare what he will do, before he comes into the House of Commons. He will not contribute to the election of such Members as shall be for taking away Penal Laws and Tests, by reason 'twould declare his opinion beforehand. With all his heart he will live friendly with all persons of what persuasions soever, and is for a toleration.

The King's electoral agents wrote that Hyde had the chief interest at Hindon, and he was duly returned to the Convention. After voting to agree with the Lords that the throne was not vacant, he obtained leave to go into the country on 6 Mar. 1689. But he may have served on the committee of elections and privileges in the second session. Hyde continued to sit for Hindon as a Tory till 1698, though he did not refuse the Association. He represented the county from 1702 till his death ten days after the general election of 1722, being regarded as a possible Jacobite under the Hanoverians. His estates passed under entail to a cousin and namesake, the last of this branch of the family, who never sat in Parliament and died shortly afterwards.[3]

[1] *Wilts. N. and Q.* vi. 388–9; Baker, *Northants.* i. 708; *N. and Q.* (ser. 2), vi. 65; PCC 95 Coke, 158 Marlborough. [2] Hoare, *Wilts. Salisbury,* 477; PC2/68/381, 72/678; *CSP Dom.* 1685, p. 99; *Cal. Treas. Bks.* viii. 546. [3] *Pythouse Pprs.* 93–94; H. R. Moulton, *Cat.* (1930), 245.

J.P.F.

HYDE, William (1635–94), of Langtoft, Lincs.

STAMFORD 1679 (Mar.), 1679 (Oct.), 1681, 1689, 1690–21 Nov. 1694

b. 10 Nov. 1635, o.s. of Humphrey Hyde of Langtoft by Sarah, da. and h. of Thomas Gibson of Barleythorpe, Rutland. *educ.* Queens', Camb. 1652. *m.* 18 Aug. 1658, Mary (*d.* 21 Mar. 1672), da. of Sir Thomas Trollope, 1st Bt., of Casewick, Lincs., 3s. 1da. *suc.* fa. 1637.[1]

Sheriff, Rutland 1658–Nov. 1660; commr. for assessment, Rutland Jan. 1660, 1664–9, 1679–80, Kesteven Aug. 1660–1, Lincs. 1661–3, 1664–74, 1679–80, 1689–90; j.p. Lincs. (Kesteven) July 1660–Feb. 1688, (Holland) 1663–Feb. 1688, (Kesteven and Holland) Oct. 1688–*d.*; capt. of militia horse, Lincs. Aug. 1660–81, 1689–*d.*, commr. for sewers, 1660, oyer and terminer, Lincoln 1661.[2]

Hyde was the grandson of a London merchant and customs farmer. His father, a younger son, acquired property and connexions in Lincolnshire and Rutland by marriage. As sheriff of Rutland Hyde was responsible for conducting the general election of 1660, and signed the congratulatory address to the King at the Restoration. But he took no known part in politics until the Exclusion Parliaments, in all of which he sat for Stamford, six miles from Langtoft. He defeated the Berties at the first general election of 1679 on the interest of his friend the 5th Earl of Exeter (John Cecil*). He was classed as 'honest' by Shaftesbury, but took no known part in the Exclusion Parliaments and was absent from the division on the bill. He may have gone over to the Court, for he remained on the commission of the peace, and when he lost his militia commission in 1681 Sir Leoline Jenkins* wrote, by 'express command from his Majesty, to inquire the cause'. He went abroad with Lord Exeter in 1683, and did not stand in 1685. In 1687 he was listed among the Northamptonshire opposition to James II, and in Lincolnshire he returned the same negative answers on the repeal of the Test Act and Penal Laws as (Sir) Henry Monson*. It was probably of him that Lord Lindsey (Robert Bertie I*) wrote: 'This is one of the worst of them, fit to be turned out'. He was indeed removed from local office, but regained his seat at the general election of 1689. He was again totally inactive in the Convention, being given leave to go into the country on 12 July. Though presumably a Whig, he was not listed as a supporter of the disabling clause in the bill to restore corporations. Re-elected in 1690, he died on 21 Nov. 1694 and was buried at Langtoft. According to his daughter-in-law 'he was the delight of his country, honoured with the title of honest . . . a senator most faithful to his God, king and country'. No other member of the family entered Parliament.[3]

[1] *Lincs. Peds.* (Harl. Soc. li), 537–8. [2] SP29/26/73; *CSP Dom.* 1680–1, p. 506; *CJ,* x. 214. [3] *VCH Rutland,* i. 201; *HMC 13th Rep. VI,* 13; *CSP Dom.* 1680–1, p. 506; 1683–4, p. 192; Blore, *Rutland,* 51.

P.W.

IBRACKAN, Lord *see* O'BRIEN, Henry

INCE, William (*d.*1679), of Chester.

CHESTER 1660

o. surv. s. of Nicholas Ince, maltster, of Chester by Ellen, da. of Richard Spenser of Chester. *m.* (1) 25 Sept. 1626, Priscilla Hanley of Chester, 1da.; (2) 31 Dec. 1627, Anne (*d.*1644), da. of Thomas Thropp, merchant, of Chester, at least 5s. (3 *d.v.p.*) 3da.; (3) lic. 17 Apr. 1665, Sarah Chamberlaine, wid., of Chester, *s.p. suc.* fa. 1653.[1]

Freeman, Chester 1626, common councilman 1626–39, sheriff 1634–5, alderman 1639–*d.*, treasurer 1641–2, mayor 1642–3, commr. for assessment 1661–*d.*[2]

The Ince family had a long association with Chester, having enjoyed the freedom of the city since the beginning of the 16th century. Ince, a clothier, and his father, who had been mayor in 1626–7, were royalist sympathizers; both lent the King money in 1642. As mayor, Ince protected the parliamentary leader, Sir William Brereton[†], from the royalist mob, and hence survived the purge of the corporation at the end of the Civil War. His moderation made him an acceptable choice at the general election of 1660, but he left no trace on the records of the Convention. He died on 27 Jan. 1679 and was buried at Holy Trinity, Chester, the only member of his family to sit in Parliament.[3]

[1] *Funeral Certs.* (Lancs. and Cheshire Rec. Soc. vi), 172; *Cheshire Sheaf* (ser. 3), xxi. 78; *Mar. Lic.* (Lancs. and Cheshire Rec. Soc. lvii), 73; (lxv), 145; Ormerod, *Cheshire,* i. 328; *Holy Trinity Chester Par. Reg.* 25–32, 37, 54, 108. [2] *Freemen of Chester* (Lancs. and Cheshire Rec. Soc. li), 112; Chester corp. assembly bk. 2, ff. 12, 13v, 34, 50v, 119, mayors' letters 3, no. 404. [3] *Cal. Chester Council Mins.* (Lancs. and Cheshire Rec. Soc. cvi), 120, 124; Lysons, *Cheshire,* 564.

M.W.H./G.H./B.D.H.

INGOLDSBY, Richard (1617–85), of Waldridge, Dinton, Bucks.

WENDOVER	4 Oct. 1647
BUCKINGHAMSHIRE	1654, 1656–10 Dec. 1657
AYLESBURY	1660, 1661, 1679 (Mar.), 1679 (Oct.), 1681

bap. 10 Aug. 1617, 2nd s. of Sir Richard Ingoldsby (*d.* 1656) of Lenborough by Elizabeth, da. of Sir Oliver Cromwell† of Hinchingbroke, Hunts.; bro. of Francis Ingoldsby† and Henry Ingoldsby†. *educ.* Thame g.s., Oxon.; G. Inn 1638. *m.* by 1650, Elizabeth (*d.*1675), da. of Sir George Croke†, j.K.b. 1628–41, of Waterstock, Oxon., and coh. to her bro. Thomas, wid. of Thomas Lee of Hartwell, Bucks., 1s. 1da. KB 23 Apr. 1661.[1]

Capt. of ft. (parliamentary) 1642, col. 1645–55; col. of horse 1655–9, Feb.–Dec. 1660; capt. of horse 1667.[2]

J.p. Bucks. 1645–70, Oxon. 1649–?Mar. 1660; commr. for militia, Bucks. 1648, 1655, 1659, Mar. 1660, assessment, Bucks. and Oxon. 1649–52, 1657, Bucks. Jan. 1660–80, scandalous ministers, Bucks. 1654, security 1656–7, dep. lt. c. Aug. 1660–80, commr. for corporations 1662–3, recusants 1675.[3]

Member, high court of justice 1649; Councillor of State 1652–3; commr. for trade 1656–7; gent. of the privy chamber 1661–85.[4]

Ingoldsby's ancestors had held the manor of Lenborough since the 15th century, but he was the first of his family to sit in Parliament. His father and at least six of his brothers were active on the parliamentarian side during the Civil War and Interregnum. His kinship with the Cromwells earned him a regiment in the New Model Army, and he was able to purchase Waldridge, five miles from Aylesbury, in 1650. He sat in Cromwell's 'Other House', but became an active Royalist when the Rump deprived him of his regiment in 1659. He claimed unconvincingly that his signature on Charles I's death-warrant had been procured by force, but was told that, as a regicide, he would have to earn his pardon. As 'the most popular man in the army' when restored to his command by George Monck*, he soon had ample opportunity to work his passage.[5]

Ingoldsby was returned to the Convention for Aylesbury on the interest of his step-son, Thomas Lee I*, defeating the unrepentant regicide, Thomas Scott†. He was entitled to the sole credit for the re-capture of Lambert, and received a vote of thanks from the House on 26 Apr. 1660; but a fortnight later he appeared, bathed in tears, to express his penitence for the King's execution. He did not speak again, and was appointed to only two committees, of no political significance, those for the drainage of the fens and to enable the master of the rolls to make leases. Nevertheless Lord Wharton marked him as a friend reserved for his own management. Sir George Booth* obtained leave for him to petition the Lords for a debt owed to him by his fellow-regicide, Sir Hardress Waller†, whose daughter had married his brother, and on 7 Dec. Lord Aungier (Francis Aungier†) presented a proviso to the indemnity bill on his behalf.[6]

Ingoldsby was re-elected in 1661, given a place at Court, and made a knight of the Bath for the coronation. An inactive Member of the Cavalier Parliament, he was appointed to only 27 committees. He was still listed among Wharton's friends, but also remained in favour at Court. Sir Henry Bennet* wrote to Ormonde to support his case before the commissioners of settlement in Ireland, while on his behalf the claims of a devoted Royalist to a lease of the Lincolnshire manor of Ingleby, bought 'during the late times', were overridden. He was named to the committees for the private bills on behalf of the younger children of Bulstrode Whitelocke†, and to enable Ingleby to be sold. He was reckoned a court dependant in 1664 and a friend of Ormonde, and in 1669 Sir Thomas Osborne* included him among those to be engaged for the Court by the Duke of York. 'Honest Dick Ingoldsby', in his cousin's unfortunate phrase, could 'neither pray nor preach', and for some time he maintained an Independent chaplain in his household for these purposes. Later Samuel Pepys* included him among the Presbyterians commissioned to raise troops of horse after the Dutch raid on the Thames; but he must have conformed, at least until the Conventicles Act, when he lost his place on the commission of the peace. When Osborne took office as Lord Treasurer Danby, Ingoldsby, doubtless under Lee's influence, moved into Opposition. His first important committee was for the liberty of the subject (13 Nov. 1675). He was included on the working lists among Members to be influenced by the King in person; but Sir Richard Wiseman* saw 'little cause to hope well' of him. Shaftesbury marked him 'worthy' in 1677, and he was appointed to the committee for the recall of British subjects from the French service. During the Popish Plot alarm he was among those Members appointed to investigate the sounds of knocking heard in Old Palace Yard, and on the proposal to call out the militia he made his only recorded speech:

> I think the horse of the militia are most convenient to be employed. That charge lies upon the gentlemen only. The foot are useless, and mostly lying upon the poorer sort. The horse can be everywhere in the county.[7]

Ingoldsby was re-elected to the Exclusion Parliaments, and again marked 'worthy' on Shaftesbury's list. He was given leave to go into the country for a fortnight on 1 May 1679, but returned in time to vote for the bill. But he was named to no committees and made no speeches. He was defeated in 1685, but did not join in Lee's petition, although it was reported that they had a majority of six to one over the Tories. On the news of Monmouth's landing he was sent to the Tower, but released later in the month. He died on 9 Sept. 1685 and was buried with his wife at Hartwell. His grandson sat for Aylesbury as a government supporter from 1730 to 1734.[8]

[1] Lipscomb, *Bucks.* ii. 169. [2] E. Peacock, *Army Lists*, 43; *CSP Dom.* 1641–3, pp. 379–98; 1667, p. 396; *Pepys Diary*, 13 June, 6 July 1667. [3] *Thurloe*, iii. 583; *CSP Dom.* 1655, p. 93; 1679–80, p. 438; Huntington Lib. Stowe mss, 2/452. [4] *CSP Dom.* 1652, p. 505; 1655–6, p. 327; Carlisle, *Privy Chamber*, 172. [5] *DNB*; *VCH Bucks.* ii. 278; iii. 483; D. Underdown, *Royalist Conspiracy*, 255; Clarendon, *Rebellion*, vi. 222–3; *Cal. Cl. SP*, iv. 666. [6] *Cal. Cl. SP*, iv. 626, 628; 675; *Hutchinson Mems.* 323–4; *HMC 7th Rep.* 96; Bowman diary, f. 54; *Old Parl. Hist.* xxiii. 42. [7] Bodl. Carte 32, f. 153; 46, f. 15; *CSP Dom.* 1663–4, pp. 98, 117; *Ludlow Mems.* ii. 63; D. R. Lacey, *Dissent and Parl. Pols.* 414–15; *Pepys Diary*, 13 June 1667; Grey, vi. 214. [8] *HMC Frankland*, 61; *CSP Dom.* 1685, pp. 241, 268; Lipscomb, ii. 169.

M.W.H./L.N.

INGRAM, Sir Thomas (1614–72), of Sheriff Hutton, Yorks. and Isleworth, Mdx.

THIRSK   1640–6 Sept. 1642, 1661–13 Feb. 1672

bap. 23 June 1614, 4th but 2nd surv. s. of Sir Arthur Ingram[†] (*d.*1642), of Templenewsam, Yorks., being o.s. by 2nd w. Alice, da. of William Ferrers, Mercer, of London, wid. of John Holliday of Bromley, Mdx. *m.* 1637, Frances, da. of Thomas Belasyse[†], 1st Visct. Fauconberg, 1da. *d.v.p.* Kntd. 16 Oct. 1636.[1]

Commr. of array, Yorks. 1642; j.p. Mdx. July 1660–d.; dep. lt. Yorks. (N. Riding) Aug. 1660–1, 1666–d., Mdx. 1662–d.; commr. for assessment Mdx. Aug. 1660–9, (N. Riding) 1661–9, Westminster and duchy of Lancaster 1663–4, corporations, Yorks. 1662–3, loyal and indigent officers, Mdx., London, Westminster and Yorks. 1662, highways and sewers, London and Westminster 1662, oyer and terminer, London 1665.[2]

Gent. of privy chamber June 1660–?4; commr. for trade Nov. 1660–8; chancellor, duchy of Lancaster 1664–d.; PC 17 Aug. 1664–d.[3]

Ingram's grandfather, a Yorkshireman by birth, became a prosperous London linen-draper. As a businessman and revenue farmer his father built up a great fortune, which he invested in land, and sat in Parliament from 1609 till his death just before the Civil War. An estate of £1,800 p.a. was settled on Ingram at his marriage, by which he acquired an interest at Thirsk. Unlike his father, he was a Royalist in the Long Parliament, and he became an active commissioner of array. He took refuge in the Newark garrison, claiming to have lost £5,000 by plunder, and compounded at £2,933 in 1649. He sent £1,000 to the exiled Court in June 1659, and on the eve of the Restoration was engaged

in negotiations with the leading Presbyterians.[4]

Ingram regained his seat in 1661. He was a moderately active Member of the Cavalier Parliament, in which he was appointed to 54 committees, including those for the corporations, uniformity and regicides bills. On 20 Mar. 1662 he reported the bill for expediting public accounts, but this remained his only chairmanship. He was listed among the court dependants in 1664, carried a Lincolnshire estate bill to the Lords on 11 May, and as 'Sir Arthur Ingram' was appointed to the committee for the conventicles bill. His activity decreased after his appointment as chancellor of the duchy on a life patent, though on 30 Oct. 1666 he was among those ordered to attend the King with a resolution against the import of French goods. An adherent of Clarendon, he was 'ill looked on' at Court after 1667; but as a placeman he was included in both lists of the court party in 1669–71. He died on 13 Feb. 1672, and was buried in Westminster Abbey. His elder brother had been given a Scottish peerage at the Restoration, and his nephew, the third Viscount Irvine, was returned for Scarborough in 1693 as a Whig.[5]

[1] Foster, *Peds. Yorks. Fams. W. Riding*; *Chamberlain Letters* ed. McClure, i. 545; *Paver's Mar. Lic.* (Yorks. Arch. Soc. xl), 114. [2] *Yorks. Arch. Jnl.* i. 95; H. B. M'Call, *Fam. of Wandesford*, 291; *HMC 8th Rep.* pt. 1 (1881), 275; *Tudor and Stuart Proclamations* ed. Steele, i. 405. [3] Carlisle, *Privy Chamber*, 170; *CSP Dom.* 1663–4, p. 664. [4] J. T. Cliffe, *Yorks. Gentry*, 30; A. F. Upton, *Sir Arthur Ingram*, 207–8; Keeler, *Long Parl.* 229–30; *Royalist Composition Pprs.* (Yorks. Arch. Soc. xviii), 124–6; *Cal. Cl. SP*, iv. 250, 599. [5] Add. 36916, f. 118.

P.A.B./P.W.

IRBY, Sir Anthony (1605–82), of Whaplode, Lincs. and Westminster.

BOSTON   6 May 1628, 1640 (Apr.), 1640 (Nov.),[1] 1656,[2] 1659, 1660, 16 May 1661, 1679 (Oct.), 1681

b. by 17 Jan. 1605, 1st s. of Sir Anthony Irby of Whaplode by Elizabeth, da. of Sir John Peyton[†] of Isleham, Cambs. *educ.* L. Inn, entered 1620; Emmanuel, Camb. 1620. *m.* (1) 1623, Frances, da. of Sir William Wray[†], 1st Bt., of Glentworth, Lincs., 1da.; (2) Margaret (*d.* July 1631), da. of Sir Richard Smythe[†] of Leeds Castle, Kent, *s.p.* (3) by 1633, Margaret (*d.* 28 Nov. 1640), da. of Sir Edward Barkham[†] of Southacre, Norf., ld. mayor of London 1621–2, 3da.; (4) 19 Aug. 1641, Catherine, da. of William, 5th Lord Paget, 1s. 5da. Kntd. 2 June 1624; *suc.* gdfa. 1625.[3]

Recorder, Boston 1624–37; commr. for sewers, Lincs. 1625, Lincs. and Westminster Aug. 1660; j.p. (Holland and Lindsey) by 1634–49, Lincs. Mar. 1660–70; dep. lt. Lincs. by 1636–44, July 1660–1, sheriff 1637–8; commr. for sequestration (Holland) 1643, levying of money, Lincs. 1643, eastern assoc. 1643, assessment (Holland and Lindsey) 1644, 1648, Lincs. 1645, 1649, 1657, Jan. 1660, 1661–3, 1664–79, (Holland) 1647, Mdx. 1648, Westminster Aug. 1660–3,

1664–80, new model ordinance, Lincs. 1645, militia, Lincs. 1648, Lincs. and Westminster Mar. 1660; col. of militia ft. Lincs. Apr. 1660; commr. for complaints, Bedford level 1663, enclosures, Deeping fen 1665, concealments, Lincs. 1671, recusants 1675.[4]

Capt. of dgns. (parliamentary) 1642–5.[5]

Commr. for regulating excise 1645, with Scottish army 1645, for exclusion from sacrament 1646, bishops' lands 1646, compounding 1647–50, scandalous offences 1648, maimed soldiers Dec. 1660–1.[6]

Irby's ancestors acquired a strong interest at Boston under the Tudors, and regularly represented the borough from 1554. Irby was a consistent opponent of the Stuarts until Pride's Purge, but he was included by a royalist agent in 1659 among the Lincolnshire Presbyterians who 'pretend now to be better disposed, either out of a sense of what they have done ill, or hatred to the now governing faction'.[7]

Irby was re-elected in 1660, marked as a friend by Lord Wharton, and probably voted with the Presbyterian Opposition. One of the most active Members of the Convention, he was named to 87 committees, acted as teller in 15 divisions, and delivered about 30 recorded speeches. His committees before the Restoration included the committee of elections and privileges, the drafting committee, the committee for the bill to continue Parliament and the joint committee on the King's reception. He helped to manage a conference on the proclamation against the Irish rebels, to consider a bill to confirm parliamentary privileges, and to administer the oaths to Members. A member of the committee for the indemnity bill, he was among those instructed to draft the clauses of exception. He was teller for the successful motion to limit the number of those penalized to 20, over and above the regicides, against excepting Sir William Roberts* and for excepting Major Richard Creed. He acted as teller against requiring the refund of gifts and salaries, spoke against a proviso directed at the Protector's legal advisers, especially William Ellys*, and was appointed to the committees to consider the provisos concerning John Hutchinson* and preserving purchasers' estates. He was teller for committing the petition from the intruded dons at Oxford, favoured an inquiry into unauthorized Anglican publications, and was named to both committees. He was among those instructed to prepare for a conference on three orders issued by the House of Lords. He supported the motion of Sir Anthony Ashley Cooper* to adjourn the committee on religion for three months. He carried up the sewers bill on 23 July, and was ordered with Edward King* and Matthew Hale* to bring in a bill for nominating commissioners. He moved for a vote of thanks to Edward Montagu I* for bringing in the King, and opposed a levy on imports of cattle from Scotland. He spoke in favour of the bill to settle ministers in their livings, and was appointed to the committee. He was also named to the revenue committee, and added to the committee for the navigation bill. He twice urged that the King should be desired to purge the Popish lords from the Upper House, and moved for conferences on the delay in proceeding with the indemnity bill and the position of those regicides who had given themselves up. On 21 Aug. he carried up a bill to indemnify certain officials in the courts of justice, and he opposed the exception of Sir Arthur Hesilrige† from the indemnity. After the speech from the throne of 29 Aug. he said that 'it was not proper to have the Act of Indemnity passed and raise money at one breath', and secured the postponement of any further consideration of supply. He was among those to whom the disbandment bill was committed, and took the chair for the bill to restore the Earl of Inchiquin to his honours and estates.[8]

During the recess Wharton sent Irby a copy of the case for modified episcopacy 'with some circumstances', and as soon as Parliament reassembled he 'moved to return the King most hearty thanks for his great care of the church government in his late gracious declaration concerning ecclesiastical affairs, and to make an Act confirming it'. He supported the attainder bill, provided that suitable provision was made for creditors, and was named to the committee. He helped to bring in the militia bill, which he wished to commit to the whole House. He did not speak in the debate of 27 Nov. on religion, but acted as teller for a second reading of the bill to give statutory effect to the Worcester House declaration. He took the chair for the bill to enable (Sir) William Wray* to break the entail on his estate, which he carried to the Lords, and also for the Earl of Donegal's petition.[9]

Irby was involved in a double return at the general election of 1661, but took his seat on the merits of the return. Wharton again listed him as a friend, and he continued to maintain Presbyterian chaplains, though he conformed himself. He remained very active in the Cavalier Parliament, with 613 committee appointments, seven tellerships, and 13 recorded speeches. His most important committees in the opening session were for the bills to prevent tumultuous petitioning and mischief from Quakers, the uniformity bill, and the bill of pains and penalties. He opposed the bill to regulate printing. Together with (Sir) Charles Hussey*, Lord Herbert of Raglan (Henry Somerset*) and Robert Long* he was ordered on 29 Nov. to bring in a bill for effectually draining the Lincolnshire fens, and in the following month he helped to manage two conferences of minor importance, on swearing witnesses before parliamentary committees and on the Lords' additions to the bill confirming private Acts. He was teller for hearing Hussey's case over the Lindsey level at the earliest possible moment, and helped to prepare for a conference on the Quakers bill. In 1664 he was named to the committee for the conventicles bill and took the chair for a Lincolnshire estate bill. He was sent to ask Dr William Outram, rector of St. Margaret's, Westminster, and described by Baxter as one of the best and ablest of the conformists, to preach to the House on the sixteenth anniversary of the execution of Charles I. He took the chair on the bill for the drainage of Deeping fen and returned it to the Lords.[10]

Irby's response to the dismissal of Clarendon was probably favourable. He was named to the committees to inquire into the charges against Mordaunt, to consider the public accounts bill, and to reduce into heads the accusations against the fallen minister. After the Christmas recess he moved unsuccessfully to go into committee on supply, and was appointed to the committees to bring in a new militia bill and extend the Conventicles Act. His committee work in 1669 included the consideration of a bill to prevent electoral abuses, and he was listed by Sir Thomas Osborne* among the Members who usually voted for supply. In April 1670 he helped to prepare reasons for conferences on the highways bill and the Yarmouth pier bill, acting as teller against a Lords proviso on behalf of Norwich. In a debate on ways and means on 15 Dec. he urged that officials should be rated higher than landowners 'because they pay no taxes to church or poor'. He was ordered to prepare reasons for a conference on the bill to improve navigation between his constituency and the Trent. He helped to prepare reasons on the bill to prevent frauds in the sale of cattle and to manage the conference of 18 Apr. 1671.[11]

In the debate of 6 Feb. 1673 on the writs issued by Cooper (now Lord Chancellor Shaftesbury) during the recess, Irby 'moved that it might be referred to a committee to examine and report the precedents', but his motion was rejected on a division. He was appointed to the committee to consider the bill of ease for Protestant dissenters, and ordered with three other elderly Members to bring in a bill for the better observation of the Lord's day. He took the chair for the last time for the repeal of a clause in the Cattle Sales Act to prohibit the sale of fat cattle by jobbers. In 1674 he was among those appointed to consider the charges

against Lord Arlington, to prepare a general test bill and to report on the condition of Ireland. In a debate on foreign policy he urged an alliance with the Protestant powers, which was omitted from the address lest it might offend the Spaniards, and he was ordered to prepare for a conference on the terms of peace with the Dutch. He opposed the enfranchisement of Newark:

> You have sat here twelve years and had no news of this borough. If, the Parliament sitting, boroughs be made, there may be as many new Members sent as we are already, and what will be the consequence of that?

In the spring session of 1675 he was named to the committees on bills for appropriating the customs to the use of the navy and preventing the growth of Popery. In the autumn he was sent with four other Members to ask Colonel Thomas Howard whether he would admit responsibility for distributing an attack on William Cavendish*, Lord Cavendish. He was also among those ordered to inspect dangerous books, and to consider bills to hinder Papists from sitting in either House of Parliament, to recall British subjects from the French service, and to preserve the liberty of the subject. In a debate on supply he declared from his experience 'for these 47 or 48 years' that the smaller sum should be moved first, and obtained a standing order to that effect. During the recess Sir Richard Wiseman* admitted that he had little hope of Irby, and argued that Sir Christopher Wray* must be ill-disposed towards the government 'or Sir Anthony Irby would not so well approve of him'. Shaftesbury classed him as 'doubly worthy', and he was named to the committee of 30 Apr. 1678 to summarize alliances. He was teller against giving leave to Sir William Killigrew* to bring in his perennial bill for the drainage of Lindsey level and against the Lords bill to prevent the poaching of deer. Osborne, now Lord Treasurer Danby, believed that his enemies sometimes caballed at Irby's house in Westminster. After the Popish Plot he was named to the committee of inquiry. He was also appointed to the committees to consider the bill to hinder Papists from sitting in Parliament, to examine Coleman's letters, and to prepare instructions for disbanding the newly-raised forces. He defended the right of the Commons to send Secretary Williamson to the Tower without informing the King.[12]

Irby was re-elected to the Exclusion Parliaments. Shaftesbury marked him 'worthy', and he remained very active in 1679, with 26 committee appointments, including the elections committee and those to inspect the disbandment accounts, and to consider the extension of habeas corpus and security against Popery. Invited to inform the House of the procedure in the trial of Strafford, he remained silent; but he voted for exclusion. An active Member of the second Exclusion Parliament, he was named to 12 committees, of which the most important were to inquire into the conduct of Sir Robert Peyton* and into abhorring. There is no evidence that he attended the Oxford Parliament. He died on 2 Jan. 1682, and was buried at St. Margaret's, Westminster. Though he had reduced the Whaplode estate from over £4,000 a year to a quarter of that sum, the Irbys remained a great parliamentary family. His grandson Edward, who sat for Boston as a Whig under Queen Anne, was created a baronet, and his great-grandson took the name of the constituency as his title on being raised to the peerage in 1761.[13]

[1] Secluded at Pride's Purge, 6 Dec. 1648, and readmitted, 21 Feb. 1660. [2] Excluded. [3] Wards 7/36/160; Collins, *Peerage*, vii. 303–5; *Arch. Cant.* xx. 78; *Mdx. Par. Reg.* ii. 148. [4] *Lincs. N. and Q.* xiii. 81; C181/4/30, 7/37; *CSP Dom.* 1636–7, p. 149; *Merc. Pub.* 19 Apr. 1660; *Cal. Treas. Bks.* iii. 912. [5] E. Peacock, *Army Lists*, 54. [6] *CJ*, viii. 213. [7] Keeler, *Long Parl.* 230–1; Eg. 2541, f. 362. [8] *CJ*, viii. 47, 59, 66, 67, 74, 81, 103, 159; Bowman diary, ff. 36, 57v, 58, 86, 96, 100v, 105v, 116, 131v, 134; *Old Parl. Hist.* xxii. 462. [9] *Old Parl. Hist.* xxiii. 4–5, 7, 22; *CJ*, viii. 177, 182, 194, 223. [10] D. R. Lacey, *Dissent and Parl. Pols.* 415–16; *CJ*, viii. 313, 327, 332, 402, 560, 605, 610, 611. [11] *Milward*, 223; *CJ*, ix. 153, 237; Grey, i. 326. [12] *Dering*, 108; *CJ*, ix. 275, 482, 513; Grey, ii. 357, 369–70; iii. 387; iv. 75; vi. 233. [13] Grey, vii. 203; Keeler, 231; *Her. and Gen.* ii. 122.

M.W.H./P.W.

IRELAND, Gilbert (1624–75), of Hale Hall, Childwall, Lancs.

LANCASHIRE   1654, 1656
LIVERPOOL   1659, 1660, 1661–30 Apr. 1675

b. 11 July 1624, 1st s. of John Ireland of Hutt, Childwall by Elizabeth, da. of Sir Thomas Hayes, Draper, of London, ld. mayor 1614–15. *m.* 26 Jan. 1646, Margaret (*d.* 1 July 1675), da. and h. of Thomas Ireland of Bewsey Hall, Warrington, *s.p. suc.* fa. 1633; kntd. 16 June 1660.[1]

Capt. of horse (parliamentary) by 1644–6; gov. Liverpool 1655–?59.[2]

Commr. for northern assoc. Lancs. 1645, defence 1645; elder, Walton classis 1646; j.p. Lancs. 1647–?59, Mar. 1660–d.; sheriff 1647–9, commr. for militia 1648, 1651, 1655, Mar. 1660, col. of militia ft. 1650–9, commr. for assessment 1652, 1657, Aug. 1660–74, scandalous ministers 1654, dep. lt. c. Aug. 1660–2, 1673–d., commr. for corporations 1662–3; mayor, Liverpool 1674–d.[3]

Member, high court of justice 1651.[4]

Ireland's ancestors had held manorial property in the parish of Childwall since 1279, and first represented Lancashire in 1337. His great-uncle and uncle sat for Liverpool, ten miles down the Mersey, in early Stuart Parliaments. Ireland himself, a Presbyterian, was in arms for Parliament in both wars,

leading his militia regiment in the Worcester campaign. He bought land from the treason trustees, sat for the county under the Protectorate, and voted for offering the crown to Oliver Cromwell. The Rump deprived him of his commission in May 1659, and he was deeply implicated in the royalist rising under Sir George Booth*, saving himself only by a timely change of front.[5]

Ireland was re-elected for Liverpool after a contest in 1660. An inactive Member of the Convention, he was added on 9 May to the committee of elections and privileges, and named to six others in the first session, including those for the indemnity bill and the confirmation of parliamentary privileges. Presumably a court supporter, he was knighted at the Restoration. But on 6 July, in his only recorded speech, he urged the House to pardon those lawyers who had served the Protector. There is no evidence that he attended the second session.[6]

During the Interregnum Ireland had been of assistance to the Earl of Derby, who appointed him one of his deputy lieutenants and probably supported him in another contested election in 1661. Lord Wharton listed him among his friends in the Cavalier Parliament, but he was again inactive. He was named to the elections committee in five sessions, to five private bill committees, and to only three others. In the opening session he was among those appointed to inquire into the shortfall in the revenue and to consider the bill restoring the bishops to the House of Lords. He acted as teller against a proviso to the militia bill, and was dropped from the lieutenancy in 1662, though against Derby's own inclinations. His last committee was for the relief of loyal and indigent officers, to which he was added on 1 Dec. 1666.[7]

Ireland, described as 'a man of unbounded hospitality', with a haughty disposition and a stately demeanour, is said to have ruined both his health and his fortune at the Liverpool by-election of 1670. He was certainly much courted by the principal candidates and invited to 'treat the town' at their expense. He worked assiduously but without success first for the son of Humphrey Wharton* and then for Ormonde's candidate, Sir George Lane, and in the following year the Opposition listed him as a court supporter, though he defaulted on a call of the House. He was still consulted over measures of local interest, such as the Weaver navigation bill, and the corporation begged him to appear in Parliament to support complaints against the lighthouse patent; but there is no evidence that he did so. He was restored to the lieutenancy in 1673 and completed the rebuilding of Hale in the following year. In October 1674 he was elected mayor, but he had served out barely half his term of office when he died of apoplexy on 30 Apr. 1675. He was buried in Hale chapel, 'the last of his house' according to his epitaph, which ignored the recusant branches of the family. He left the income from lands worth between £300 and £500 p.a. to trustees for 30 years to pay off a debt of £2,500. A nephew, Gilbert Aspinall, inherited Hale, while on his widow's death a few months later Bewsey Hall passed to Richard Atherton*.[8]

[1] Wards 7/84/117; *Vis. Lancs.* (Chetham Soc. lxxxv), 165; G. E. Cokayne, *Lord Mayors and Sheriffs of London*, 71; W. Beamont, *Hale and Orford*, 58. [2] *Moore Mss* (Lancs. and Cheshire Rec. Soc. lxvii), 167, 207; *Cal. Comm. Comp.* 1369; *Thurloe*, iii. 359. [3] Beamont, 58, 127; Lancs. RO, QSC44-72; *CSP Dom.* 1650, p. 505; 1651, p. 480; 1655, p. 78; 1659-60, p. 24; SP29/61/157; *Moore Rental* (Chetham Soc. xii), 132. [4] *CSP Dom.* 1651, p. 523. [5] *VCH Lancs.* iii. 142-4; *Cal. Comm. Comp.* 643, 2625; *CSP Dom.* 1659-60, pp. 24, 114, 147; *Cal. Cl. SP*, iv. 312; D. Underdown, *Royalist Conspiracy* 274; *Civil War in Cheshire* (Chetham Soc. n.s. lxv), 164, 172. [6] *HMC 10th Rep. IV*, 116-17; Bowman diary, f. 58. [7] *CJ*, viii. 304; SP29/61/85. [8] W. Gregson, *Frags.* 202; Beamont, 102, 107, 122-6; *HMC Lords*, iii. 265-6; *VCH Lancs.* iii. 437.

M.W.H./I.C.

ISHAM, Sir Justinian, 2nd Bt. (1611-75), of Lamport Hall, Northants.[1]

NORTHAMPTONSHIRE 1661-2 Mar. 1675

b. 20 Jan. 1611, o.s. of Sir John Isham, 1st Bt., of Lamport by Judith, da. of William Lewin†, dean of the arches, of Otterden, Kent. *educ.* Uppingham; Christ's, Camb. 1627-8; M. Temple 1628; travelled abroad (Holland) 1633-4. *m.* (1) 10 Nov. 1634 (with £4,000) Jane (*d.* 4 Mar. 1639), da. of Sir John Garrard, 1st Bt., of Lamer Park, Wheathampstead, Herts., 1s. *d.v.p.* 4da.; (2) Aug. 1653, Vere (*d.* 29 Oct. 1704), da. of Sir Thomas Leigh, 2nd Bt.†, 1st Baron Leigh of Stoneleigh, 6s. (1 *d.v.p.*) 2da. *suc.* fa. 8 July 1651.[2]

J.p. Northants. July 1660-d., dep. lt. c. Aug. 1660-d., commr. for oyer and terminer, Midland circuit July 1660, assessment, Northants. 1661-74, loyal and indigent officers 1662.

FRS 1673.

Isham's ancestors took their name from a Northamptonshire village, and their pedigree can be traced back to an escheator under Richard II. They first sat in Parliament in 1554, and Isham's great-grandfather, a merchant adventurer of London, bought Lamport in 1560. Isham's father was neutral during the Civil War, though he was obliged to contribute over £1,000 to the parliamentary forces and an attempt was made to convict him of delinquency a few months before his death. Isham himself, though acting as solicitor to the parliamentary general, the Earl of Essex, was in the King's quarters during the war, but never bore arms. He compounded at £1,100 for the Leicestershire manor of Shangton, which had been settled on him. On his father's death he found him-

self master of some £1,700 p.a., and could indulge his scholarly and artistic tastes, which unfortunately stood in the way of his rather ponderous courtship of Dorothy Osborne. However, his second marriage soon brought him the requisite heir, and indeed a large family, whose education he carefully superintended. Although he took no part in royalist conspiracy, his strong Anglican convictions exposed him to the suspicions of the Interregnum authorities, and he was twice imprisoned. At a meeting of the Northamptonshire gentry before the general election of 1661, he agreed to stand for the county, with some reluctance because 'a provoked person, having suffered by sequestration, imprisonment, etc.' might be subject to exception by those who had been active on the other side. He defeated Richard Knightley*, but owing to ill-health he was not an active Member of the Cavalier Parliament. He was named to only 22 committees, of which the most important was for the uniformity bill, and made no recorded speeches. His name appears on no list of government supporters, which suggests that he soon went into opposition, probably out of disgust at the licentiousness of the Restoration Court. He died of the stone at Oxford on 2 Mar. 1675, and was buried at Lamport.[3]

[1] This biography is based on Sir Gyles Isham, *Duppa-Isham Corresp.* (Northants. Rec. Soc. xvii). [2] *VCH Northants. Fams.* 158-60. [3] *HMC 3rd Rep.* 254; M. E. Finch, *Wealth of Five Northants. Fams.* (Northants. Rec. Soc. xix), 36; Northants. RO, IC 510; *Genealogists' Mag.* xiii. 41.

E.R.E.

ISHAM, Sir Justinian, 4th Bt. (1658-1730), of Lamport Hall, Northants.

NORTHAMPTON	1685, 1689, 9 Mar. 1694, 1695
NORTHAMPTONSHIRE	1698, 1701 (Feb.), 1701 (Dec.), 1702, 1705, 1708, 1710, 1713, 1715, 1722, 1727-13 May 1730

b. 11 Aug. 1658, 3rd s. of Sir Justinian Isham, 2nd Bt.*, being 2nd s. by 2nd w. *educ.* Christ Church, Oxf. 1674; L. Inn 1677. *m.* 16 July 1683, Elizabeth (*d.* 22 Aug. 1713), da. of Sir Edmund Turner of Stoke Rochford, Lincs., 8s. (3 *d.v.p.*) 6da. *suc.* bro. 26 July 1681.[1]

Dep. lt. Northants, 1681-8, 1689-?d.; j.p. Northants. 1683-Feb. 1688, 1689-?d., Leics. 1711-?d.; commr. for assessment, Northants. 1689-90.[2]

Isham was one of those recommended in 1683 to replace the Whigs who had been dismissed from the commission of the peace. He was returned to the first of his 15 consecutive Parliaments for Northampton in 1685, and was listed by Danby among the Opposition. He was appointed to only two committees, one for the relief of the Earl of Cleveland's creditors and the other for the repeal of the Bedford Level Act so far as it affected Northamptonshire. In reply to the lord lieutenant's questions on the Test Act and Penal Laws, he said that he would not stand; but he was dismissed from county office. He took an active part in the Revolution, signing warrants to raise the militia and serving as cornet under Bishop Compton in Princess Anne's escort at Nottingham. He was probably returned without a contest in 1689 by arrangement with Edward Montagu II*, with whom he kept up a political correspondence. After voting to agree with the Lords that the throne was not vacant he probably left Westminster, serving on no committees in the Convention and making no speeches. He was given leave on 14 Dec. 1689, but a week later Montagu wrote urging him to return, 'for I really believe there will be more need than ordinary of so good a man as you'. Whether or not Isham returned in time to vote against the disabling clause in the bill to restore corporations is not known, but he lost his seat at the general election. He sat in the House as a Tory without any further interruption from 1694 till his death on 13 May 1730, when his son succeeded him as knight of the shire.[3]

[1] VCH Northants. Fams. 160–1. [2] CSP Dom. 1680–1, p. 557. [3] CSP Dom. 1682, p. 618; Hatton Corresp. (Harl. Soc. n.s. xxiii), 116; Northants. RO, IC 1440.

E.R.E.

JACOB, William (c.1623–92), of Canterbury, Kent.

CANTERBURY   1679 (Mar.)

b. c.1623, s. of John Jacob, physician, of Canterbury. educ. Christ Church, Oxf. matric. 27 Mar. 1640, aged 17, MD 1660; Leyden 1645. unm.
  Freeman, Canterbury May 1660; commr. for assessment, Kent and Canterbury 1679–80, 1689–91.

Jacob's few known connexions lay entirely among the local professional classes, and he is said to have been unrelated to the philologist Henry Jacob (1608–52), who came of Kentish yeoman stock. Nevertheless when the latter was expelled from Oxford by the parliamentary visitors, he sheltered him in his house in Canterbury until his death, and was rewarded by becoming the protagonist in one of the most popular ghost stories of the period. He was allowed to practise as a doctor among the Dutch prisoners of war in 1653. His brother Israel, an apothecary, became a common councilman in 1655, but he himself held no municipal office, and was given the freedom of the city at the Restoration. He may have assisted in the election of Heneage Finch*, who doubtless obtained for him the royal mandate to the university for the grant of an MD, and two

years later he was licensed to practise medicine in the city. In 1670 the corporation entertained him at a collation 'for his love and favour in repairing Wincheap Gate'. After his election to the first Exclusion Parliament, he prudently made his will before setting out for Westminster. Shaftesbury marked him 'honest', and he became a moderately active Member. He was appointed to seven committees, including those for the security bill and the habeas corpus amendment bill. He was given leave for a week on 21 May, but is said to have voted for exclusion on the next day. He was replaced by a court supporter, (Sir) Thomas Hardres*, in August, and probably never stood again. In 1682 he was described as a well-known exclusionist, who favoured fanatics and factions in the city. His name disappeared from the assessment commission after 1691, and his will was proved by his brother on 30 Mar. 1692.

DNB; Roll of Freemen ed. Cowper, 319; Wood, Athenae Oxon. iii. 330–3; CSP Dom. 1653–4, p. 537; 1682, p. 250; information from Miss A. M. Oakley; Hasted, Kent, xii. 650; Kent AO, RC56/135.

B.D.H.

JAMES, Roger (c.1620–1700), of Reigate, Surr.

REIGATE   1661, 1679 (Mar.), 1679 (Oct.), 1689

b. c.1620, o.s. of Sir Roger James[†] of Reigate by Margaret, da. of Anthony Aucher of Bishopsbourne, Kent. educ. Clare, Camb. 1637; I. Temple 1638; Leyden 1648. m. by 1649, his cos. Elizabeth, da. of Sir Anthony Aucher of Bishopsbourne, 2s. (1 d.v.p.) 2da. suc. fa. 1636.[1]
  Elder, Reigate classis 1647; j.p. Surr. 1659–80, 1690–?d., commr. for militia Mar. 1660, oyer and terminer, Home circuit July 1660, sewers, Surr. and Kent Aug. 1660, assessment, Surr. Aug. 1660–80, 1689–90, recusants 1675, rebuilding of Southwark 1677.[2]

James was descended from a Dutch brewing family originally called van Haestricht which migrated to London about 1540 and adopted the surname of James. James's father was knighted in 1613, purchased the rectory manor of Reigate in 1614, and was returned to Parliament for the borough in 1625. James himself was apparently a Presbyterian and was not appointed to the commission of the peace until 1659.[3]

At the general election of 1660 James was involved in a double return at Gatton, and listed as a friend by Lord Wharton. He received the same number of votes as Thomas Turgis* and William Oldfield*, but did not sit before the election was declared void. At the by-election he made way for Sir Edmund Bowyer*. He was successful in 1661 for Reigate, where he had a large house at the east end of the town. He was appointed to only 34 committees in the Cavalier Parliament, of which the most important was on the bill for hindering Papists from sitting in either House of Parliament (28 May 1675). Despite his inactivity in the House, however, his political allegiance was well known, and Shaftesbury considered him 'thrice worthy' in 1677. James was again returned for Reigate at both elections of 1679. Marked 'worthy' on Shaftesbury's list of the first Exclusion Parliament, he was appointed to the committee of elections and privileges, and voted for the exclusion bill. Although the autumn election was contested, James's own return was not questioned. But he was left out of the commission of the peace in the purge of exclusionist justices in 1680, and took no known part in the second Exclusion Parliament.[4]

James was not elected in 1681 or 1685 because of the eclipse of the country party in Reigate. He was returned to the Convention, however, in a contested election, though again there was no opposition to his return. He was not named to any committees, but was given leave to go into the country for a fortnight on 23 Apr. 1689. Although presumably a Whig, he was not listed as a supporter of the disabling clause in the bill to restore corporations. James unsuccessfully contested the Reigate seat in 1695 and did not sit again. He died on 25 July 1700 and 'was buried late at night privately according to his own appointment' at Reigate, the last member of his family to enter Parliament.[5]

[1] *Misc. Gen. et Her.* (ser. 4), v. 106; *Vis. Surr.* (Harl. Soc. lx), 65. [2] *Q. Sess. Recs.* (Surr. Rec. Soc. xxxv), 12; C181/7/31. [3] *Returns of Aliens* (Huguenot Soc. x), 136; Shaw, *Eng. Church*, ii. 434. [4] *CJ*, viii. 13; Aubrey, *Antiqs. Surr.* iv. 192. [5] W. Hooper, *Reigate*, 196.

M.W.H./J.P.F.

JAY, Christopher (c.1605–77), of Norwich, Norf.

NORWICH 1661–21 Aug. 1677

b. c.1605, 3rd s. of John Jay (d.1619) of Holverston, being 2nd s. by 2nd w. Lucy, da. of one Johnston. m. by 1631, Judith (bur. 7 Nov. 1675), da. of William Browne of Norwich, 8s. (5 d.v.p.) 4da.[1]
  Freeman, Norwich 1627, common councilman to 1649, sheriff 1653–4, alderman 1654–d., mayor 1657–8; commr. for assessment, Norwich Jan. 1660–d., Norf. Aug. 1660–d., militia, Norwich Mar. 1660, lt.-col. of militia ft. Apr. 1660–d., dep. lt. Sept. 1660–d.; commr. for oyer and terminer, Norfolk circuit Oct. 1660; receiver-gen. Norf. and Hunts. 1664–7, 1669–71; commr. for recusants, Norf. 1675.[2]
  Gent. of privy chamber 1668–?d.[3]

Since Elizabethan times Jay's family had enjoyed a footing both in Norfolk and London. His elder brother was squire of Holverston, while his uncle, a Draper, became alderman of London. Jay himself was a draper of Norwich, and held municipal office in that city. In 1647 he leased the manor of Hindol-

veston from the dean and chapter, only to be dispossessed by the 'usurped powers'. His sympathies were Anglican and royalist; he spent £165 on repairs to the cathedral to preserve it from ruin, and he signed the Norfolk address to George Monck* for a free Parliament in 1660. Sir Edward Nicholas† was his cousin by marriage, and he was recommended for the order of the Royal Oak with an income somewhat improbably estimated at £1,500 p.a.[4]

Indeed Jay was by no means the most prominent Royalist on the corporation in 1661, and his election to the Cavalier Parliament was probably due to the belief that his connexion with the Government could be of use to his constituency. So far was this from being the case that it could not even prevail on the dean of Norwich to renew his lease of Hindolveston, and a few months later Nicholas was removed from office. He was a moderately active but totally inconspicuous Member, with 141 committee appointments, mostly concerned with trade. In the opening session he was among those to whom the corporations bill was committed, and he was also named to the committees on the bills for the regulation of Norwich stuffs and the alnage, the prevention of wool exports, and the repair of the walls of Norwich. In 1663 he was appointed to committees to hear a clothiers' petition, to review the Printing Act, and to consider a bill to hinder the growth of Popery, and the staple bill. His most important committee in 1664 was for the conventicles bill. The Hindolveston dispute had been left to the law, and Jay repeatedly claimed privilege to protect his interests. In an attempt to strengthen his finances he became receiver-general of crown revenue, including the hearth-tax for Norfolk and Huntingdonshire. But it was ominous that on 1 Feb. 1665 he was for the first time appointed to a committee to consider a bill for the relief of poor prisoners. On 1 Oct. 1666 he was among those ordered to inquire into the Canary Company patent.[5]

The new brooms on the Treasury commission were not slow to sweep Jay out of office. His arrest was ordered for arrears in his hearth-tax accounts on 5 June 1667, and in the following month he was suspended from duty, and replaced by Sir Edmund Poley*. He took his place in the House in October, and was named to the committees to consider the bill for assigning debts in the Exchequer and the petition from the merchants trading to France. He was given a post at Court in 1668; but a warrant was again issued for his arrest on 25 June 1669, by which time his debt to the crown totalled £4,335. He was released and restored to office on agreeing to assume responsibility for a debt owed to the father of Robert Foley* for ironmongery supplied to the navy. He was listed by Sir Thomas Osborne* in September among those Members who usually voted for supply. On 20 Aug. 1670 the prosecution of his sureties was ordered, in view of his parliamentary immunity. But when he applied to the House for privilege in a case where his servant had been arrested and his sheep driven away he found the committee unsympathetic. Job Charlton* reported that as the major offence had occurred five years since, he had lost his privilege by default; but Lord Cramond (Thomas Richardson*) and Sir John Pettus* divided the House, and it was agreed that his sheepwalk should be restored to him. He was not named by Sir George Downing* among Members in debt to the crown, but he was appointed to the committee for the bill to sell up Thomas Harlackenden*. At the end of the session he was finally dismissed; his chattels were seized by the sheriffs of Norwich and sold for £300. But he still owed Foley £1,000. He took refuge in the Temple during the long recess, but he was apparently evicted, for by July 1672 the ironmonger, whose own finances were almost as desperate, had cast him into Norwich gaol. He missed the next session, but was apparently released on making over all his property in Norwich and elsewhere to his creditors. He received the government whip from Secretary Williamson for the autumn session of 1675, but he was unable to attend through an illness that brought him to death's door. His name appeared on the working lists and on the list of court supporters prepared by Sir Richard Wiseman* in 1676. On 23 Mar. it was noted that he was 'in a low condition', and Osborne (now Lord Treasurer Danby) minuted that £200 was to be accepted for the final discharge of his debt to the crown. Shaftesbury classed him as 'thrice vile', and in *A Seasonable Argument* he was described as 'a prisoner in the King's bench, an old decrepit lecher [who] has £50 a session'. He was highly indignant when he overheard the country propagandist Ayliffe say in a Fleet Street coffee house that MPs voted for supply for a guinea a day and their dinners, and threatened to report him to the Commons. Almost his last committee was for the relief of insolvent debtors (14 Mar. 1677), and he died on 21 Aug., the only member of the family to sit in Parliament.[6]

[1] E. C. Cust, *Recs. Cust Fam.* i. 180, 211–12. [2] *Freemen Norwich* ed. Millican, 59; J. T. Evans, *17th Cent. Norwich*, 203; H. Le Strange, *Norf. Official Lists*, 113; *Merc. Pub.* 12 Apr. 1660; *Cal. Treas. Bks.* i. 73, 74, 627; ii. 24; iii. 279, 903. [3] Carlisle, *Privy Chamber*, 182. [4] Blomefield, *Norf.* iv. 315–16; W. Rye, *Norf. Fams.* i. 401; *CSP Dom.* 1661–2, pp. 234–5; *Address from Gentry of Norf.* ed. Rye, 30. [5] *CSP Dom.* 1661–2, pp. 54, 181, 234–5, 316–17; *CJ*, viii. 440, 547. [6] *Cal. Treas. Bks.* ii. 7, 24; iii. 96, 137, 139,

274, 654, 903, 1032, 1162, 1266; iv. 82; v. 169; *CJ*, ix. 159, 174, 269; *Dering*, 18–19; *HMC 6th Rep.* 374, 382; *CSP Dom.* 1676–7, p. 569.

P.W.

JEFFREYS, John (c.1623–89), of The Priory, Brecon.

BRECONSHIRE	27 Nov. 1661–31 Jan. 1662
BRECON	1 Apr. 1679, 1679 (Oct.), 1681, 22 June 1685

b. c.1623, 1st s. of Jeffrey Jeffreys of Abercynrig by Margaret, da. of Gregory Price of The Priory, Brecon. *educ.* I. Temple 1640; G. Inn 1641. *m.* Mary, da. of Edward Bassett of Fledborough, Notts., 1 da. *suc.* fa. by 1647.[1]

Lt.-col. of ft. (royalist) to 1645; lt. of horse [I], regt. of Francis, Lord Aungier 1663, capt. 1664–78; constable of Dublin Castle 1673–80.[2]

J.p. Brec. July 1660–*d.*, dep. lt. c. Aug. 1660–*d.*; commr. for assessment, Brec. Aug. 1660–80, Brecon 1677–80; maj. of militia horse, Brec. by 1661–?4, commr. for loyal and indigent officers 1662, col. of militia ft. by 1679–at least 1684; capital burgess, Brecon by 1679–?*d.*; master of Kilmainham hospital 1684–?*d.*[3]

Jt. registrar of claims [I] 1665–70.[4]

MP [I] 1665.

Jeffreys, the grandson of a Brecon mercer, fought as a Royalist in the Civil War, compounding for his estate in 1648 for £380 10*s.* He claimed to have been always active in the King's service except when prevented by strict imprisonment, and his name appeared on the list drawn up by Roger Whitley* in 1658 as a lieutenant-colonel of foot. At the Restoration he was nominated for the order of the Royal Oak, with an estate of £600 p.a. He applied for a tellership of the Exchequer, but the candidate proposed by Edward Progers* was preferred. He defeated Progers at a by-election for Breconshire in 1661, and became the only member of his family to enter Parliament. But he had taken no part in the proceedings of the Cavalier Parliament when the election was declared void, after which he stood down in favour of his opponent, probably at the wish of the Duke of Ormonde, who gave him a commission in the Irish army. It was said on his arrival in Ireland that 'his estate in Wales was so encumbered by his loyalty to the crown that he had to remove hither in hopes to redeem it'. Abercynrig had to be sold in 1664, but in the following year Jeffreys was made joint registrar to the commissioners appointed under the Act of Explanation, a post believed to be worth at least £8,000. He sat in the Irish Parliament and his fortunes probably improved, although he was still not clear of debt in 1672.[5]

Jeffreys intended to stand for the county again at the first general election of 1679, but he again withdrew in favour of Progers. With government support, he challenged the country candidate Thomas Mansel I* in the borough, where he had probably inherited the Priory from his cousin Sir Herbert Price*. There was a double return, but Jeffreys was allowed to take his seat. He knew too much about the informer Bedloe to attach credence to the Popish Plot; marked as a court supporter on Huntingdon's list, he was absent from the division on the first exclusion bill. He was inactive in the 1679 Parliament, in which he was appointed only to a committee for the continuation of the Irish Cattle Act and another for a private bill. He was re-elected in October, when he was described as one of the capital burgesses. In the second Exclusion Parliament he was moderately active, being appointed to six committees, including those to draw up an address for a fast, to audit the disbandment accounts, and to consider a bill for relief from arbitrary fines. He left no trace on the records of the Oxford Parliament, but in the following summer it was stated that he had been lately 'very serviceable to his Majesty in the county where he lives'. Sir Leoline Jenkins*, who had known him for over 40 years, persuaded Ormonde to accept him as the first master of the new military hospital at Kilmainham, although a serving officer would have been preferred. 'He hath spent all his time and almost all his estate in the King's service, and he hath done it with a very clear reputation.' He was returned in 1685 at a by-election when the Marquess of Worcester (Charles Somerset*) chose another seat, but was again appointed to no committees. He was in Ireland when the Breconshire magistrates were questioned on the repeal of the Test Acts and Penal Laws, and in some apprehension about his place; but James II acknowledged his 'faithful services and sufferings', and ordered him to stand again for Brecon. It is not known whether he contested the general election of 1689. He died shortly afterwards and was buried at Carmarthen on 24 Apr. His daughter, who had already contravened his wishes over his funeral and her own marriage, completed her disobedience by selling the Priory to the Jeffreys family of Llywel, who were of a different stock. They sat for the borough as Tories for most of the period from 1695 to 1713.[6]

[1] Jones, *Brec.* iv. 273; *Vis. Notts.* (Harl. Soc. iv), 42; *CSP Ire.* 1663–5, p. 255; SP23/207/473. [2] J. R. Phillips, *Civil War in Wales*, ii. 286; *HMC Ormonde*, i. 218, 268; n.s. iii. 165. [3] SP 29/34/21; J. Dingley, *Beaufort's Progress*, 200; *HMC Ormonde*, n.s. vii. 215. [4] *CSP Ire.* 1663–5, p. 663. [5] *Cal. Comm. Comp.* 1674; *CSP Dom.* 1660–1, p. 9; Bodl. Carte 33, ff. 7, 203; *CSP Ire.* 1663–5, p. 662; 1666–9, p. 106; J. Lloyd, *Hist. Mems. Brec.* 55–56. [6] *CSP Dom.* 1679–80, pp. 64, 74, 84; 1680–1, p. 600; Jan.–June 1683, pp. 89–90; 1686–7, p. 212; 1687–9, p. 276; SP23/207/471; *HMC Ormonde*, n.s. iv. 275; vi. 89, 93; vii. 482; *Trans. Hist. Soc. West Wales*, xiv. 18.

L.N.

JENKINS, Sir Leoline (c.1625–85), of Jesus College, Oxford and Hammersmith, Mdx.

HYTHE	2–6 Feb. 1673, 11 Feb. 1673
OXFORD UNIVERSITY	1679 (Oct.), 1681, 17 Mar.–1 Sept. 1685

b. c.1625, s. of Llewellyn Jenkins, yeoman, of Llanblethian, Glam. *educ.* Cowbridge g.s.; Jesus, Oxf. matric. 4 June 1641, aged 16, DCL 1661; advocate, Doctors' Commons 1664. *unm.* Kntd. 7 June 1670.[1]

Fellow of Jesus c. Aug. 1660, principal 1661–73; commissary, Bridgnorth peculiar 1661, Canterbury dioc. 1663; dep. prof. of civil law, Oxford Univ. 1662, assessor to chancellor's court 1662–7; j.p. Oxford 1662–?73; registrar, Westminster Abbey 1663–5; commr. for assessment, Oxon. 1664–79, Kent and Glam. 1673–80, London 1677–80; judge of Admiralty, Cinque Ports ?1667–*d.*; freeman, Portsmouth 1682, 1685; master, Salters' Co. 1684–*d.*[2]

Dep. dean of the arches 1665–*d.*; judge-asst. court of Admiralty 1665, judge 1668–73; judge, prerogative court of Canterbury 1669–80; commr. for union with Scotland 1670; plenip. congress of Köln 1673–4, Nymwegen 1675–9; PC 11 Feb. 1680–*d.*; sec. of state (north) 1680–1, (south) 1681–4.

Jenkins was the son of 'a good, plain countryman' whose landlord, Sir John Aubrey, had him educated for the Church. His studies were interrupted by the Civil Wars, and he may, like other undergraduates, have taken up arms for the King. In 1648 he removed to Aubrey's house, where he met Gilbert Sheldon, who was to become his friend and patron. There he taught the sons of a few gentlemen in the neighbourhood until he was indicted at quarter sessions in 1651 for keeping 'a seminary of rebellion and sedition'. He returned to Oxford and with his pupils set himself up in a house in the High Street, which in consequence came to be known as the Little Welsh Hall. In 1655, under suspicion of royalist activity, he took his pupils with him to the continent and travelled in France, Holland and Germany for three years. On his return he lived with Sir William Whitmore* at Apley Park, where he applied himself to the study of civil law. At the Restoration he returned to Oxford. Elected a fellow of Jesus, he succeeded as principal a few months later, and was largely responsible for the reform and reorganization of the College.[3]

On Sheldon's elevation to the primacy he summoned Jenkins from his college 'merely for his merit and ability's sake' to preside in the Admiralty court, although he had never practised as a civilian. Samuel Pepys* found him at this early stage in his public career 'very rational, learned and uncorrupt. ... A very excellent man, both for judgement [and] temper, yet majesty enough.' He probably succeeded Sir Edmund Peirce* as judge of Admiralty in the Cinque Ports in 1667, and two years later was knighted for his successful negotiations with the French over the queen mother's estate. After the death of Sir Henry Wood* in 1671 he stood for Hythe on the court interest, and was returned during the recess. When Lord Chancellor Shaftesbury's writs were declared void, he was re-elected after a contest, and three days later added to the committee of elections and privileges. He was named to six other committees in his first session, but on 22 Mar. 1673 his opponent, Edward Hales I*, petitioned. Hearing was deferred till the second Thursday of the next session, which lasted only nine days. When the House met again in 1674 Jenkins was absent at the congress of Köln, though he was included in the Paston list, and his friends obtained a further postponement though only by a narrow majority. When he resumed his seat in the spring session of 1675, he was appointed to the elections committee and to 16 others, including that to draw up the address for the removal of Lauderdale. Hales's petition was finally dismissed on 28 Apr., and on 14 May Jenkins helped to draw up a further address for the recall of British subjects from the French service. On 28 May he made his only recorded speech in this Parliament, in support of the unsuccessful motion to adjourn on the case of Arthur Onslow*, which involved the appellate jurisdiction of the Lords. In his usual portentous manner, he told the House 'that by voting [that] the Lords had no power of judging appeals, we did take away and avoid all the judgements they had made for these 55 years, which was of dangerous consequences'. He was named to the committee to prepare reasons, and three days later sent to the Upper House to request a further conference. He was included in the lists of officials and government speakers, and, after the summer recess, helped to manage the conference of 10 Nov. on British subjects in the French service. On the next day he was appointed to his last committee in this Parliament, that for the appropriation of the customs to the use of the navy. A week later he was named as a defaulter, but his name was struck off the list, presumably because he was preparing to attend the congress of Nymwegen. He remained abroad until the summer of 1679, but Shaftesbury listed him as 'thrice vile' in 1677, and in *A Seasonable Argument* he was described as

> Son of a tailor, judge of the admiralty, was in hopes to be archbishop of Canterbury, employed in four embassies ... indefatigable industry in promoting a peace for France ... He affirmed in the House of Commons that, upon necessity, the King might raise money without Act of Parliament.

He was named on both lists of the court party in 1678 but sent for as a defaulter on 17 Dec.

On 11 Feb. 1679 Henry Coventry* wrote to Jenkins at Nymwegen: 'We at Court take it for granted that you will be Member as burgess for Windsor, though the election is not yet past, but I think it pretty secure'. However the seat was more urgently required for John Ernle I*, and Jenkins was not returned to the first Exclusion Parliament. On his recall from Nymwegen he was immediately elected for Oxford University, though not without opposition. He was made a Privy Councillor, and persuaded by Sunderland to accept Coventry's secretaryship, being informed by the King that he could 'be assisted in the making up the £6,500' which Coventry was to receive. Whatever his merits as a diplomat and civilian, Jenkins was a disastrous choice as spokesman for the Court in the Commons, as even his admirers admitted. Roger North* called him 'the most faithful drudge of a secretary the Court ever had; and Lord Ailesbury (Thomas Bruce*), while praising his abilities and industry as an administrator, allowed that 'he was but heavy in his discourse and uttering his sentiments in Council and in the House of Commons'.[4]

Jenkins was named to only four committees in the second Exclusion Parliament, those appointed to prepare the address for the pardon of the Whig journalist Harris and for the bills for the abolition of courts martial in Wales, the repeal of the Corporations Act and the prohibition of bequests for superstitious uses. In his capacity as secretary he carried messages almost daily to and from the King, though it was recognized that as a messenger to the Commons he would be unacceptable, especially if called on to announce the King's determination to veto exclusion. He spoke against the bill at every reading, and urged 'expedients'. On 2 Nov. 1680, in the debate on the motion to appoint a committee to draft a new exclusion bill, he said

> I desire the difference may be considered betwixt 'extremity' and 'expedients'. The bill to exclude the Duke, is the extremity. Though expedients have been offered and not accepted, yet it is hard to refuse hearing them; the rather, in regard that the King in the last Parliament did offer an expedient. Pray consider, whenever this bill does pass, whether it must not be supported by a standing army.

Two days later he spoke against the second reading:

> I crave leave to speak against the second reading of this bill till I am satisfied that it is for the service of the Crown and the safety of the nation; till I am satisfied with the justice of it, whether it be natural to exclude the Duke before you hear him. In reason we ought to do as we would be done by. Popery here is a crime and punished by a law already made, but here is now a law for this Prince alone to be excluded. Consider whether

it be just to make a new law for one person. . . . Farther, this bill, as it is drawn, does change the very essence and being of the monarchy. Consider whether you do not reduce it to an elective monarchy. In the essence of the monarchy the Duke is heir to the Crown and this bill is against primogeniture. . . . Consider if this bill is consistent with the oath of allegiance we have all taken. By the blessing of God, the King has not his Crown by designation: he is not an elective monarch . . . I took it [the oath] ten, twenty years ago, and if I am asked what is meant in that oath by 'heirs and successors', I answer, the next heir to the Crown is the Duke in case the King have no children. . . . I believe it is not in the power of man to absolve me from that oath. When God gives us a King in his wrath, it is not in our power to change him; we cannot require any qualifications; we must take him as he is. Thus allegiance binds my faith nothing at all so long as the King is alive, but my oath binds me to his successor. . . . It is a fundamental maxim not to enter into an uncertain for a certain mischief, and upon these considerations, pray lay this bill aside.

On 22 Nov. Jenkins spoke against the address for the removal of Halifax, and two days later defended Sir Francis North* for his draft of the proclamation against petitioning. On 9 Dec. he came under attack for his part in the arrest of one Norris, who was alleged to have information concerning the Popish Plot. The debate lasted two days and the House ordered Jenkins to withdraw, and resolved that his action 'was illegal and arbitrary, and an obstruction to the evidence for the discovery of the horrid Popish Plot'. On 7 Jan. 1681, three days before the dissolution, Jenkins made one more attempt to avoid exclusion:

> Why then should we be so bent upon it, seeing the great difficulties of obtaining it are so visible? . . . It is strange to me that no arguments will prevail to aim at some other thing, that so we may get something which must be better than to have this Parliament be broken for want of taking what we may get. For supposing the worst, that we should not get anything that should be sufficient to prevent the Duke's coming to the Crown, yet we may get such laws as may be sufficient to secure our religion, though he should come to it. And would it not be much better to spend our time in making laws which we have reason to believe may be granted, than to spend our time in pursuing what we are not likely to get? Some good laws added to what we have, and the numbers of people which we have in this nation, Protestants, would in my opinion be an impregnable fence against Popery.[5]

Jenkins was returned unopposed to the third Exclusion Parliament. He was named to no committees. On 24 Mar. he spoke against printing the votes of the House. 'It is against the gravity of this assembly', he said, 'and it is a sort of appeal to the people.' On the next day the House, in a spirit of ridicule, ordered him to carry the impeachment of Fitzharris to the Lords. He thrice refused, but after cries of 'To the bar', he apologized to the House and carried up the message. On the last day of the

Parliament, he moved against the first reading of the exclusion bill. He repeated his usual arguments and concluded: 'Perhaps I am too tedious, and not willingly heard. This bill is against our religion, against the government and wisdom of the nation, and I hope you will throw it out.' His motion was not seconded. He regarded the dissolution as inevitable, but 'a sad misfortune'.[6]

As secretary of state Jenkins was active in investigating plots and rumours of plots against the government. He was a witness (though a rather ineffective one) against Shaftesbury in his trial in Nov. 1681, and played a principal role in the election of the Tory sheriffs of London in 1682 and in the quo warranto proceedings against the City. His health, however, was failing and he resigned on 4 Apr. 1684. He was re-elected in 1685, again unopposed, but was named to no committees in James II's Parliament, and probably did not attend. He died on 1 Sept. 1685 at his house in Hammersmith and was buried in the chapel of Jesus College. Already a generous benefactor in his lifetime, he left to the college the major part of his estate, which, due to his incorruptibility, was worth less than £1,000 per year. There can be no doubt of Jenkins's loyalty to his Church and his King. As he wrote to the archbishop of Armagh, 'It is from the Church I have learnt my duty to the King, and 'tis to her I shall always endeavour to approve myself'. Burnet wrote of him:

> He was a man of exemplary life, and considerably learned, but he was dull and slow. He was suspected of Popery, though very unjustly, but he was set in every punctilio of the Church of England to superstition, and was a great assertor of the divine right of monarchy, and for carrying the prerogative high. He neither spoke nor wrote well.[7]

[1] This biography is based on William Wynne, Life (1724). [2] R. East, Portsmouth Recs. 368; J. S. Watson, Hist. Salters' Co. 146. [3] Aubrey, Brief Lives, ii. 7; Jenkins, Life of Mansell, 17–21. [4] Pepys Diary, 26, 27 Mar. 1667; CSP Dom. 1673, p. 223: 1673–5, p. 277; 1675–6, p. 448; Dering Pprs. 94; Add. 25119, ff. 142, 143; Rex, Univ. Rep. 282; Kenyon, Sunderland, 43; HMC Ormonde, n.s. iv. 578; North, Lives, i. 301; Ailesbury Mems. 42. [5] Temple Mems. ed. Courtenay, ii. 69; Grey, vii. 403, 418–20; viii. 15–16, 45–6, 67–8, 122–3, 125. [6] Rex, 288; Grey, viii. 288, 339; Sidney Diary, ii. 186. [7] J. Levin, London Charter Controversy, 22–26; K. W. D. Haley, Shaftesbury, 680, 688; State Trials, viii. 804; Rex, 296; PCC 136 Cann; CSP Dom. 1679–80, pp. 488–90; Burnet, ii. 257.

B.D.H.

JENKINSON, Sir Robert, 2nd Bt. (c.1655–1710), of Walcot, Oxon.

OXFORDSHIRE   1689, 1690, 1695, 1698, 1701 (Feb.), 1701 (Dec.), 1702, 1705, 1708–30 Jan. 1710

b. c.1655, 1st s. of Sir Robert Jenkinson†, 1st Bt., of Walcot by Mary, da. of Sir John Bankes[†], c.j.c.p. 1641–4, of Corfe Castle, Dorset. *educ.* Brasenose, Oxf. matric. 11 Nov. 1671, aged 17; I. Temple 1672. *m.* 14 Feb. 1684, Sarah (*d.* 8 Aug. 1709), da. and h. of Thomas Tomlins, Grocer, of London and Bromley, Mdx., 9s. 5da. *suc.* fa. 1677.[1]

Commr. for assessment, Oxon. 1679–80, Oxon. and Oxford 1689–90; freeman, Woodstock 1680, Oxford 1684; j.p. Oxon. 1680–Mar. 1688, Oct. 1688–96, Oxon. and Oxford, 1700–*d.*; dep. lt. Oxon. 1681–Feb. 1688, 1689–96, 1702–*d.*[2]

Jenkinson came from a family of mercantile origin which had settled in Oxfordshire shortly before the Civil War, and maintained neutrality, though with some difficulty. His father, however, served on local commissions from 1647 and sat for the county in the three Protectorate Parliaments. He was created a baronet in 1661 and continued to hold local office till his death.[3]

Jenkinson himself, a churchman and an opponent of exclusion, was appointed to the commission of the peace and the lieutenancy in 1680–1. To the lord lieutenant's questions in 1688 he replied that he could not say that, if it should be his chance to be a Parliament man, he could give his consent to taking off either the Penal Laws or Tests, and was removed from county office. In 1689 he stood as Tory candidate for Oxfordshire and headed the poll. He voted to agree with the Lords that the throne was not vacant, but he was not an active Member of the Convention, making no recorded speeches and being appointed only to the committee to restore the university charters. Despite allegations of Jacobitism and his refusal of the Association in 1696, he held his seat for the remainder of his life, and passed it on to his son, the 3rd baronet. He died on 30 Jan. 1710 and was buried at Charlbury.[4]

[1] *Misc. Gen. et Her.* (ser. 2), v. 9–10, 63; *East Anglian*, n.s. xiii. 323; Soc. of Genealogists, St. Botolph Aldersgate par. reg. [2] Woodstock council acts, 1679–99 (6 Sept. 1680); *Oxford Council Acts* (Oxf. Hist. Soc. n.s. ii), 163; Bodl. Carte 79, f. 68o. [3] *Misc. Gen. et Her.* (ser. 2), v. 7–8; *Cal. Comm. Comp.* 3152. [4] Bodl. G. A. Oxon 4/6/2.

L.N./G.J.

JENNENS, William I (1614–c.87), of Plymouth, Devon.

SALTASH 1679 (Oct.)

bap. 4 Sept. 1614, 3rd s. of Abraham Jennens, merchant (*d.*1650) of Plymouth by Judith, da. of Nicholas Shere of Plymouth. *educ.* Leyden 1628. *m.* by 1651, Elizabeth, da. of Robert Trelawny[†], merchant, of Plymouth, 2s. *d.v.p.* 2da.[1]

Commr. for assessment, Devon Sept. 1660–80, Plymouth 1677–9; mayor, Plymouth 1662–3, alderman to 1684; sheriff, Cornw. 1677–8.[2]

Jennens's father was established at Plymouth as a Spanish merchant and naval victualler by 1600. He was also engaged in the colonization of New England. Neither Jennens nor his father, from whom he inherited £20,000, appears to have been active in the Civil War. But, perhaps in consequence of a double marriage alliance with the royalist Trelawnys and his responsibility for the completion of Charles church, he was nominated mayor of Plymouth by the commissioners for corporations, and was later described as 'a most furious justice' against conventicles, 'very busy' in breaking them up and 'making sport' for the soldiers. Prince Cosmo of Tuscany lodged in his house on his visit in 1669. When he was appointed sheriff of Cornwall in 1677, the corporation supported his petition to be excused as the 'eldest magistrate and standing justice for Plymouth, . . . being also 70 years old [*sic*], in ill health, and unable to travel. His estate in Cornwall is not worth £30 a year, and he lives by his trade as a merchant of Plymouth.' Nevertheless his excuses were not accepted. His business interests were widespread, including the purchase of lead from William Blackett* on Tyneside and its export to Marseilles. He stood for Saltash at the first general election of 1679. His father had owned property in the town, but he probably depended on the interest of his son-in-law Edward Nosworthy II* as a country candidate. Shaftesbury marked him 'worthy', but he was not returned, and his petition was never reported. He was successful in September, but took no known part in the second Exclusion Parliament, and may have retired before the next election. 'A crafty, spiteful man', he opposed the surrender of the Plymouth charter in 1684, and did not stand for James II's Parliament. His will, dated 14 May 1685, was proved three years later. No other member of the family sat in Parliament.[3]

[1] *Plymouth St. Andrew Reg.* (Devon and Cornw. Rec. Soc.), 18, 181, 263; E134/25 and 26 Chas. II Hil. 10; Eg. 2761, f. 67; Devon RO, 11262/Z1. [2] L. F. W. Jewitt, *Hist. Plymouth*, 224–5. [3] R. N. Worth, *Hist. Plymouth*, 83–84; H. F. Whitfeld, *Plymouth and Devonport*, 95, 121; *CSP Dom.* 1677–8, p. 480; L. Magalotti, *Travels of Cosmo III*, 113; PC2/65/374; Jewitt, 236; PCC 62 Exton.

J.P.F.

JENNENS, William II (c.1666–1709), of Long Wittenham, Berks.

WALLINGFORD 21 Feb. 1689, 1690, 1695, 1698, 1701 (Feb.), 1701 (Dec.), 1702, 1705, 1708–Feb. 1709

b. c.1666, 3rd but 1st surv. s. of Richard Jennens of Long Wittenham by w. Elizabeth. *educ.* G. Inn 1683. *m.* lic. 15 June 1696, aged 30, Mary, da. and coh. of Richard Spencer, Vintner and Turkey merchant, of Berry

Street, Aldgate, London and Newington, Surr., wid. of Edward Wiseman of East Locking, Berks., 2s. 1da. *suc.* fa. 1696.[1]

Freeman, Wallingford Sept. 1688, Woodstock 1703; commr. for assessment, Berks. 1689, j.p. by 1701–*d.*, dep. lt. 1703–?*d.*[2]

Jennens was descended from a Berkshire yeoman family which was established at Harwell by the end of the 16th century, but played no known part in the Civil War. His grandfather, who died in 1667, described himself as a gentleman in his will, though his property at Harwell and Long Wittenham was only leasehold. Jennens was involved in a double return for Wallingford, five miles from his home, at the general election of 1689, and was not seated until after the division on agreeing with the Lords that the throne was not vacant. He left no trace on the records of the Convention, but was undoubtedly a Tory under William III and Anne, refusing the Association in 1696. He died heavily in debt and was buried at Long Wittenham on 9 Feb. 1709, the only member of his family to sit in Parliament.[3]

[1] *Berks. Arch. Jnl.* xxxv. 136; PCC 23 Foot, 49 Bond, 259 Box; *London Mar. Lic.* ed. Foster, 760; Woodhead, *Rulers of London*, 154; *HMC Lords*, n.s. viii. 338. [2] Berks. RO, Wallingford borough statute bk. 1648–1766, f. 150; Woodstock council acts (27 Sept. 1703). [3] *VCH Berks.* iii. 491; PCC 169 Carr, 77 Lane; *CJ*, x. 11, 32; Salisbury Dioc. RO, Long Wittenham bishops' transcripts.

L.N./G.J.

JENNER, Sir Thomas (c.1638–1707), of Petersham, Surr.

RYE 1685–2 Jan. 1686

b. c.1638, 1st s. of Thomas Jenner of Mayfield, Suss. by Dorothy, da. of Jeffrey Glyde of Dallington, Suss. *educ.* Tonbridge g.s.; Queens', Camb. 1655; I. Temple 1656, called 1663. *m.* 1 Jan. 1661, Anne (*d.*1698), da. and h. of James Poe of Swinden Hall, Kirkby Overblow, Yorks., 11s. (8 *d.v.p.*) 2da. *suc.* fa. 1668; kntd. 4 Oct. 1683.[1]

Jt. steward, Windsor Castle 1672–3; commr. for assessment, Surr. 1673–80, London 1679–80; bencher, I. Temple 1682; recorder, London 1683–6; j.p. Kent, Mdx., Suss. and Westminster 1683–9; dep. lt. London 1685–9.[2]

Serjeant-at-law 1683, King's serjeant 1684–6; baron of the Exchequer 2 Jan. 1686–July 1688; commr. for ecclesiastical causes 1687–Oct. 1688; j.c.p. July 1688–9.

Jenner came of a widespread Sussex yeoman family. His father was presumably an Independent and a parliamentary supporter, becoming a j.p. and the mainstay of the county militia during the Interregnum. Jenner appears to have combined his legal studies with service to the Roman Catholic zealot, Lord Powys; but after qualifying as a barrister he did not question the establishment. His practice was not impressive, but as 'a very loyal, zealous gentleman', he was appointed recorder of London under the new charter, acted for the prosecution in several state trials, and was nominated by James II for Rye in 1685. An active Member, he was named to ten committees, none of which was of much political importance, but including those on the bills for regulating hackney coaches, rebuilding St. Paul's, and relieving London widows and orphans. He must have given satisfaction to the Government, for he was raised to the bench early in the New Year and gave his opinion in favour of the dispensing power. In his diary for November 1687 he wrote:

> I did not seek any public place, because I never thought myself proper for such employ, my conversation having been most among the middle sort of men, not with great or honourable persons, which rendered me less capable of those great and most difficult affairs. Always doubtful of my own sufficiency to acquit myself in great matters and that they would be too high for me, yet of duty and too much obedience I did submit to it.

As a member of the second ecclesiastical commission he was unable to avoid taking a prominent part in the attack on Magdalen. When the president protested against these proceedings 'there was a tumultuous hum, or acclamation, made by the bystanders'; whereupon Jenner bound him over to appear in the King's bench. But he did not vote for the expulsion of the remaining fellows. It was rumoured that 'he would have his quietus', but he was merely transferred to the bench of common pleas.[3]

The Revolution ended Jenner's public career. He fled with James, but was captured at Faversham and sent to the Tower. When he appeared before the Commons on 28 Oct. 1689 he was

> charged with giving his opinion on the dispensing power, acting in the ecclesiastical commission, and particularly against Magdalen College. He answered that he could not deny what they charged him with; that what he had acted amiss he hoped would be less aggravated against him because his temptations were great, he had a wife and ten children and but a small estate; he had been nine or ten months in prison, that this was the first time he had heard what he was charged with; he was not prepared to give an answer but desired time.

According to Morrice he might have been discharged four days later, but for one Member, who described the judges as 'more than double offenders', and alleged that no man had been 'more forward and active in the Magdalen College business'. In his own defence Jenner said that:

> The business of the dispensing power did not come originally before him. ... Lord Chief Justice Herbert [Sir Edward Herbert*] required their opinion, and the authority of others inclined him to be of their minds, etc.; that his name was put into the ecclesiastical com-

mission without his knowledge when he was in the country, etc.; that he was against the legality of the commission, but was over-voted.

He was released when the Convention was prorogued, but excepted from the Act of Indemnity in 1690. He resumed his legal practice, and successfully pleaded a pardon from James II when accused of extracting £3,000 from dissenters, not returned into the Exchequer. He died on 1 Jan. 1707 and was buried at Petersham, the only member of his family to sit in Parliament.[4]

[1] *DNB*: Manning and Bray, *Surr.* i. 442; PCC 33 Hene. [2] *CSP Dom.* 1671–2, p. 325; 1673, p. 223; 1685, p. 56; *HMC Lords*, iii. 46. [3] *Suss. Arch. Colls.* xxiv. 35; *Thurloe*, iv. 240; *Herbert Corresp.* (Univ. Wales, Bd. of Celtic Studies, Hist. and Law ser. xxi), 31; *HMC 7th Rep.* 366; *Evelyn Diary*, iv. 342; Kent AO, NR/AEp/50; *Magdalen Coll. and James II* (Oxf. Hist. Soc. vi), 134, 211; Macaulay, *Hist.* 952; R. Morrice, Entering Bk. 2, p. 649; *CSP Dom.* 1686–7, pp. 112–13. [4] Clarke, *Jas. II*, ii. 254; *Hatton Corresp.* (Cam. Soc. n.s. xxiii), 124; Morrice, 646, 649, 670; Luttrell, ii. 612; iii. 37.

B.D.H.

JENNINGS, Edmund (1626–91), of Ripon, Yorks.

RIPON 1659, 3 May 1660, 27 Mar. 1673, 1679 (Mar.), 1685, 1690–Sept. 1691

bap. 30 Nov. 1626, 1st s. of Jonathan Jennings (*d.*1649) of Ripon by Elizabeth, da. and coh. of Giles Parker of Newby; bro. of Jonathan Jennings*. *educ.* Silsden; Ripon g.s.; Sidney Sussex, Camb. 1641; L. Inn 1646. *m.* Margaret, da. of Sir Edward Barkham, 1st Bt.†, of Tottenham, Mdx. and Southacre, Norf., 4s. 3da. *suc.* gdfa. 1651; kntd. by 17 Aug. 1660.[1]

J.p. liberty of Ripon 1658–?Sept. 1688, Yorks. (W. Riding) Mar. 1660–?Sept. 1688, Nov. 1688–*d.*, (N. Riding) 1683–?Feb. 1688; commr. for militia, Yorks. 1659, Mar. 1660, assessment (W. Riding) Jan. 1660–80, 1689–90, alderman, Ripon 1662–85, mayor 1663–4; dep. lt. (W. Riding) 1667–?87; commr. for concealed lands, Yorks. 1670, recusants (W. Riding) 1675; sheriff, Yorks. 1675–6.[2]

Commr. for prizes Mar. 1691–*d.*[3]

Jennings's grandfather was granted arms in 1641 and became a passive Royalist in the Civil War. His father, a lawyer who settled in Ripon, was an active commissioner of array, compounding on a fine of £156. Jennings represented Ripon in Richard Cromwell's Parliament, the first of the family to sit, and hence considered himself eligible under the Long Parliament ordinance at the general election of 1660. He was involved in a double return with the republican general John Lambert† but was seated by the House on the merits of the return on 3 May. Classed as a friend by Lord Wharton, he was probably appointed to only three committees in the Convention and may have voted with the Opposition. In the debate of 16 July he supported the motion of Sir Anthony Ashley Cooper* to defer

discussion of religious discipline for three months. He opposed the Lords' amendment to the bill of indemnity for the total exception of all who sat in judgment on Charles I. Granted leave of absence on 28 Aug., he returned for the second session, and on 30 Nov. was a teller against receiving the report on the marital separation bill.[4]

Jennings lost his seat in 1661, when the Archbishop of York's interest was re-established, but he was nominated alderman by the commissioners for corporations, and during his mayoralty promoted measures for the more stringent observance of the sabbath. He regained his seat at a by-election in 1673 and became a very active Member of the Cavalier Parliament. He was appointed to 113 committees, in four of which he took the chair, spoke 34 times in debate and acted as a teller in 13 divisions. A consistent supporter of the Court, and a 'creature' of Danby's, he did not countenance the attacks on Buckingham and Arlington in January 1674, and in 1675 resisted similar attacks both on Lauderdale and on Danby. In both sessions he was named to anti-papal committees, and on 12 May he reported a bill to ascertain the hearth-tax. In the autumn he was appointed to the committee for appropriating the customs to the use of the navy. In the debate of 27 Oct. he supported demands for Members to declare and refund any money paid them by reason of their offices or otherwise, and on 8 Nov., during the debate on supply, he opposed the motion for a land tax. Two days later he was named to the committee on the bill for recall of British subjects from the French service. The Opposition affected to consider his selection as sheriff of Yorkshire, which was alleged to be worth £1,000, as a breach of privilege, and carried a motion to that effect by 157 votes to 101. A committee was appointed to consider the proper way of discharging him, but Parliament was prorogued on 22 Nov. before any further action could be taken. His name appeared on both the working lists and the list of the court party in 1675 prepared by Sir Richard Wiseman*, and he was included among the court speakers. The author of *A Seasonable Argument* alleged that he had been promised a pension and a place at Court.[5]

Jennings was a teller for Sir Richard Temple* for the chair of the supply committee on 21 Feb. 1677, and on the following day he was among those to whom the bill to prevent illegal exactions was committed. He was appointed to the committee of 8 Mar. on the bill to prevent the growth of Popery, and on 27 Mar. was a teller in favour of committing the Lords bill for the Protestant education of the royal children. Shaftesbury classed him as 'vile'. He was among those ordered to thank Sprat for his sermon on the anniversary of the royal martyrdom on 30 Jan. 1678. He was an advocate of supply for war against France, and on 29 Apr. he resisted opposition demands for deferring it until measures had been taken against Popery. He twice criticized general attacks on the King's counsellors as pointless unless the offenders were mentioned by name, and on 19 Mar. was a teller in favour of accepting the Lords' amendments to the address in favour of war with France. In July he again chaired a committee on the hearth-tax. He was a member of the committee on the bill to exclude Roman Catholics from Parliament, but in the debate of 21 Nov. supported the proposal to exempt the Duke of York from the terms of the bill, saying 'the headache coming from an ill stomach, to cut off the hair and apply oils to the head will do no good'. Five days later he supported the suggestion of a search for all Papists who had remained in London in defiance of the royal proclamation. In the debate of 21 Dec. on Danby's impeachment, Jennings spoke three times in his patron's defence. He was listed as a government supporter by both Court and Opposition in 1678.[6]

Re-elected to the first Exclusion Parliament Jennings was noted as 'base' by Shaftesbury. An active Member, he was named to 12 committees, including those for summoning Danby to give himself up and the bill for regulating elections. He twice sought to hasten proceedings against the Popish lords in the Tower, and in the debate of 11 May attacked the expedient of exclusion as unnecessary, advocating instead a bill to banish all Papists who would not conform to the Church of England. Ten days later he voted against the bill. A warrant had been issued for the appointment of Jennings as joint surveyor of the customs at a salary of £1,000 p.a. in place of Charles Osborne*, but never took effect, though Sir John Reresby* included Jennings among several 'put into good places at Court by means of his lordship [Danby]', who 'were all displaced' on the treasurer's fall.[7]

Jennings was defeated in August by the exclusionist Christopher Wandesford,* and did not regain his seat until 1685. A very active Member of James II's Parliament, he was appointed to 18 committees, taking the chair for the bills for a new parish in Soho and to forbid the import of tallow candles. He went into Opposition in the second session. After a long and great silence on 14 Nov. 'he broke the ice' by moving for the presentation of an address for the discharge of Roman Catholic officers from the army, and was appointed to the drafting committee. Two days later, during the debate on supply, he argued that the House should grant the relatively meagre sum of £200,000. 'Giving all at once is doubting the affection of the people.' The royal agents reported in 1688 that as a Ripon j.p. he 'absolutely disallowed our commission and did conceive it inimical to answer to any questions of that nature not offered in Parliament'. In fact he asked the commissioners:

> Whether for any man to deliver an opinion or resolution out of Parliament to endeavour the repeal of laws made for the security of the King and government be not an endeavouring an alteration of the government,

and was not such an attempt 'criminal'? Although he had thus refused to answer in writing he did inform the agents orally that

> he could not positively say how he should vote in the House, if elected, until he had informed his judgement by the debates, but at present thought that some Penal Laws might be repealed, but that the Tests should not be repealed.

He was defeated at the Ripon election of 1689, but sat in the Parliament of 1690 as a government supporter and placeman. He died early in September 1691 and was buried in St. Clement Danes. He was succeeded by his son, Jonathan, both in his estates and in the parliamentary representation of Ripon.[8]

[1] Clay, *Dugdale's Vis. Yorks.* ii. 200–1; *CJ*, viii. 125. [2] *Ripon Millenary Rec.* ed. Harrison, ii. 66; SP29/130/139; SP44/20/197; Yale Univ. Lib. Osborn mss; *Cal. Treas. Bks.* iii. 634. [3] *Cal. Treas. Bks.* ix. 1060, 1371. [4] *Grantees of Arms* (Harl. Soc. lxvi), 138; *Royalist Comp. Pprs.* (Yorks. Arch. Soc. rec. ser. xviii), 13–15, 58–59; Bowman diary, ff. 86, 151v. [5] PRO31/3, bdle. 162, f. 188v; *CJ*, ix. 335; Grey, ii. 248, 274, 305; iii. 25, 47, 369, 426; iv. 16–27. [6] *CJ*, ix. 511; Grey, v. 161, 243, 244, 286–7, 335–6, 387; vi. 242, 277, 367, 369, 373; Finch mss, f. 61. [7] Grey, vii. 131, 240–1, 297; *Cal. Treas. Bks.* v. 1271, 1306; vi. 14, 49, 294; *Reresby Mems.* 175–6. [8] Grey, viii. 361, 363; *Bramston Autobiog.* (Cam. Soc. xxxii), 213; *HMC Astley*, 66–67; Browning, *Danby*, ii. 207.

M.W.H./P.A.B./P.W.

JENNINGS, Sir Jonathan (c.1632–1707), of Ripon, Yorks.

RIPON 1659, 1689, 1690

b. c.1632, 2nd s. of Jonathan Jennings of Ripon, and bro. of Edmund Jennings*. *educ.* Ripon g.s.; G. Inn, entered 1649; Christ's, Camb. adm. 28 June 1650, aged 17. *m.* Anne, da. of Sir Edward Barkham, 1st Bt.†, of Tottenham, Mdx. and Southacre, Norf., 1da. Kntd. 18 Mar. 1678.[1]

Commr. for militia, Yorks. 1659, Mar. 1660; alderman, Ripon 1662–87, mayor 1664–5; commr. for assessment, Yorks. (W. Riding) 1663–1680, 1689–90; j.p. (W. Riding) 1674–Sept. 1688 (W. and N. Ridings), Nov. 1688–?*d.*; liberty of Ripon 1678–?*d.*; capt. of militia ft. (W. Riding) by 1677; sheriff, Yorks. Nov. 1689–Jan. 1690; dep. lt. (W. Riding) by 1700–*d.*[2]

Capt. of ft. regt. of Sir Henry Goodricke* 1678–9.[3]

Commr. for prizes 1691–9.[4]

Jennings represented Ripon with his brother in Richard Cromwell's Parliament and was nominated alderman by the commissioners for corporations. A nonconformist minister described him as 'a debauched person' and 'mad against protestant dissenters'. In a duel in 1675 he killed the archbishop's registrar George Aislabie (father of the Whig statesman). He was convicted of manslaughter at the assizes, but obtained a pardon and was knighted three years later. He was a signatory of the Yorkshire petition of 1683 expressing abhorrence of the Rye House plot, and remained on the Ripon corporation under its remodelled charter in 1686. He came to oppose the ecclesiastical policies of James II, however, and in 1688, refusing to answer the questions of the King's agents on the Penal Laws and Test Act, he 'laid his hand on his breast and told us he could not in his conscience own our commission'.[5]

After a lapse of 30 years, Jennings was successful for Ripon in 1689 on the family interest. A Tory, he voted to agree with the Lords that the throne was not vacant. Four of his speeches in the Convention are recorded, but he was not an active Member, being named to only seven committees. In the debate of 15 Mar. he gave evidence of Popish activities in the neighbourhood of his constituency. He was added to the committee to inspect the new oaths of allegiance and supremacy on 8 June, and appointed to that to regulate army officers' oaths. As a Yorkshire Member, he served on the committee for the Bathurst estate bill, which he reported and carried to the Lords on 20 June. He acted as teller for reading the London petition against the sacramental test. During the debate on the indemnity bill on 1 July he attacked the record of Sir Thomas Jenner* on the ecclesiastical commission. He was named to the committees to examine a petition from the inhabitants of a Yorkshire village against their Roman Catholic landlord, and to inquire into the charges against William Harbord*.[6]

Jennings may not have attended the second session of the Convention, as he had been pricked for sheriff. When he was absent from the call of the House on 7 Jan. 1690, this was declared a breach of privilege, and the King appointed (Sir) Christopher Wandesford* in his place. On 24 Jan. a petition was read alleging that Jennings had committed a certain William Brownrigg to York Castle in 1681 for informing Shaftesbury's steward that witnesses were being suborned. Jennings was given a month to appear to answer the complaint, but Parliament was prorogued three days later. He was re-elected in 1690 as a Tory, and buried in Ripon Minster on 27 Jan. 1707.[7]

[1] Clay, *Dugdale's Vis. Yorks.* ii. 201. [2] Ripon corp. mins. 1607–66, f. 548; *Ripon Millenary Rec.* ed. Harrison, ii. 67–68; Add. 29674, ff. 160–1. [3] *Cal. Treas. Bks.* vi. 336. [4] Ibid. ix. 1371; xiv. 301, 401. [5] *Diary of Oliver Heywood* ed. Turner, ii. 287, 292–3; iii. 209–11; *Ripon Millenary Rec.* ii. 67–68; *CSP Dom.* 1686–7, p. 300; *Reresby Mems.* 311. [6] Grey, ix. 165, 387; *CJ*, x. 197. [7] *CJ*, x. 325, 335, 342; Clay, ii. 201.

P.A.B./P.W.

JENNINGS, Richard (c.1616–68), of Sandridge, Herts.

ST. ALBANS c. Aug. 1642,[1] 1659, 1660, 1661–May 1668

b. c.1616, 1st s. of Sir John Jennings† of Sandridge by Alice, da. of Sir Richard Spencer† of Offley. *educ.* I. Temple 1634; travelled abroad (Italy) 1637–40; Padua 1639. *m.* lic. 18 Dec. 1643, 'aged 24', Frances, da. and coh. of Sir Gifford Thornhurst, 1st Bt., of Agnes Court, Kent, 4s. (2 *d.v.p.*) 5da. *suc.* fa. 1642.[2]

Commr. for assessment, Herts. 1643–8, Herts. and St. Albans Aug. 1660–d., sequestrations, Herts. 1643, levying of money 1643, defence of eastern assoc. 1643; j.p. Herts. by 1644–8, 1658–July 1660, St. Albans 1658–d., commr. for militia, Herts. 1648, Mar. 1660.[3]

Jennings was the great-great-grandson of Bernard Jennings (*d.*1552), Master of the Skinners' Company. Sandridge, less than two miles from St. Albans, had been in the family since 1571. His father, first elected for St. Albans in 1628, resisted the forced loan and tried to evade ship-money. Jennings succeeded his father as MP for St. Albans in the Long Parliament, and like him took the popular side. Though he does not appear to have been in arms, he was captured by Royalists and imprisoned for a time, but exchanged in January 1646. He did not sit after Pride's Purge, and seems to have taken no further part in politics until the close of the Interregnum. Returned to Parliament again in 1659, he retained the seat until his death.[4]

Jennings was an inactive Member of the Convention. He made no recorded speeches and was appointed to only four committees, those for impropriate rectories, for the attainder bill, for considering the petition of the surveyor-general of customs, and for settling wine licences. In the Cavalier Parliament his record was even more unimpressive and he was appointed to only three committees. He was classed as a friend by Lord Wharton in 1661, to be managed by Sir Richard Onslow*. He presented a Presbyterian to Sandridge in that year, but the minister conformed in 1662, and Jennings apparently followed his example. His estate, including Holywell Manor just outside the borough of St. Albans, was valued for militia purposes at £715 p.a. He was in trouble with the Privy Council in 1666 for failing to do justice to the excise farmers against one of the influential Gape family in his constituency. He was buried in the Abbey Church of St. Albans on 8 May 1668, the last of his branch of the family to sit in Parliament. His sons were short-lived, and in 1684 John Churchill II*, the husband of his formidable daughter, Sarah, bought out the other coheir and acquired the whole estate.[5]

[1] Did not sit after Pride's Purge, 6 Dec. 1648, readmitted 21 Feb. 1660. [2] Misc. Gen. et Her. (ser. 5), viii. 89–90; PC Reg. i. 177; London Mar. Lic. ed. Foster, 760. [3] Herts. Recs. vi. 523. [4] Misc. Gen. et Her. (ser. 5), viii. 89, 103; VCH Herts. ii. 433; Keeler, Long Parl. 233–4; CJ, iv. 410, 413. [5] W. Urwick, Nonconformity in Herts. 331–2; HMC Verulam, 103; PC2/58/406; Misc. Gen. et Her. (ser. 5), viii. 107; VCH Herts. ii. 433; Som. Arch. and Nat. Hist. Soc. Jnl. xxx, pt. 2, p. 44.

M.W.H./E.R.E.

JEPHSON, William (c.1647–91), of Boarstall, Bucks.

EAST GRINSTEAD	1679 (Oct.)
CHIPPING WYCOMBE	1689, 1690–7 June 1691

b. c.1647, 2nd s. of William Jephson[†] (d.1658) of Froyle, Hants by Alice, da. and coh. of Sir John Dynham of Boarstall. educ. M. Temple 1665, called 1673. m. by 1674, his cos. Mary, da. of William Lewis* of The Van, Glam. and Boarstall, and coh. to her bro. Edward Lewis*, s.p.[1]

Commr. for assessment, Bucks. 1677–80, Bucks. and Chipping Wycombe 1689–90; freeman, Chipping Wycombe 1689; j.p. and dep. lt. Bucks. 1689–d.[2]

Private sec. to William of Orange Dec. 1688–9; sec. to the Treasury 1689–d.[3]

Jephson's ancestors held the manor of Froyle from the dissolution of the monasteries until 1652. His great-uncle and his grandfather, who acquired extensive property in Ireland, both represented Hampshire in Jacobean Parliaments. His father, a Presbyterian, sat for Stockbridge in the Long Parliament until Pride's Purge, serving in the parliamentary forces both in Ireland and England, and subsequently rallying to the Protector, who sent him to Sweden as envoy in 1657. Jephson's elder brother succeeded to the Irish estates, and Jephson himself, although a qualified barrister, is not known to have practised after marrying a Buckinghamshire heiress. He joined the Green Ribbon Club, and became a follower of the Hon. Thomas Wharton*, to whom he wrote on 14 July 1679 that through John Clayton* he had been introduced to Robert Goodwin[†], who had an interest at East Grinstead.

> I was this day with Major Clayton to wait upon Mr Goodwin (who is in town) to thank him and his daughter for their civilities in the last business of Grinsted (not designing to speak of any new matter to him); but before my parting, she began and made the offer of their assistance, and he then confirmed it.

He was also offered the support of the Borlase and Lovelace interests at Marlow to oppose (Sir) Humphrey Winch*, and of the dissenters at Great Yarmouth. But with additional support from Lord Dorset (Charles Sackville*), who was reckoned his friend, he felt justifiably confident of carrying East Grinstead, and he was duly returned with Goodwin Wharton*. But he took no ascertainable part in the proceedings of the second Exclusion Parliament. Edward Dering* canvassed Rye on his behalf at the next general election, but soon discovered that his candidature was hopeless. After the Rye House Plot it was reported that Jephson and Charles Godfrey*, another Wharton henchman, had been arrested for denying the genuineness of Monmouth's confession in the Gazette. He stood unsuccessfully with Henry Wharton* at Malmesbury in 1685, and their petition was never reported.[4]

Jephson, together with Wharton, Godfrey and Lord Colchester (Richard Savage*), was among the first to join William of Orange in 1688, and was appointed private secretary to the prince, who would have thought him qualified to act as secretary of state if he had been more of a linguist. He opposed the cancellation of James II's writs for elections, but was overborne by the more violent Whigs. He attended the meeting of Members of Charles II's Parliaments on 26 Dec. and helped to draw up the address asking William to summon a convention. He was returned for Wycombe on the Wharton interest, and became a moderately active Member, with 18 committee appointments. He presented the letter from his master on 22 Jan. 1689 which replaced the usual speech from the throne, and was appointed to the committee to bring in a list of the essentials for securing religion, laws and liberties. He also helped to draw up the address promising assistance in defence of the Protestant religion, and to consider the bill to punish mutiny and desertion. After his appointment as secretary of the Treasury in July he was ordered to explain how Jacobites arrested in England had later appeared in arms in Ireland, and two days later he was able to satisfy the Commons that no passes had been issued to them. He told the House on 14 Dec. that he had rewarded the captain of the ship which broke the boom at Londonderry, and on the same day he was appointed to the committee to examine the state of the revenue. He supported the disabling clause in the bill to restore corporations, and was re-elected in 1690, but died of a malignant fever on 7 June 1691. He was the last of the family to sit for an English constituency, though his brother's descendants regularly represented Mallow both before and after the Act of Union.[5]

[1] Lipscomb, Bucks. i. 66; HMC Egmont, i. 332. [2] First Wycombe Ledger Bk. (Bucks. Rec. Soc. xi), 224. [3] Luttrell, i. 492. [4] VCH Hants, ii. 502; Keeler, Long Parl. 234; Bodl. Carte 103, ff. 221–2;

Savile Corresp. (Cam. Soc. lxxi), 130; CSP Dom. 1680–1, p. 209; R. Morrice, Entering Bk. 1, p. 395; CJ, ix. 720. ⁵ Wood's Life and Times (Oxf. Hist. Soc. xxvi), 282, 363; Foxcroft, Halifax, ii. 202; Clarendon Corresp. ii. 221; CJ, x. 217, 220; Grey, ix. 481; Luttrell, ii. 242.

L.N.

JERMYN, Thomas (1633–1703), of Rushbrooke, Suff. and Spring Gardens, Westminster.

BURY ST. EDMUNDS 1679 (Mar.), 1679 (Oct.), 1681

bap. 10 Nov. 1633, 2nd but 1st surv. s. of Thomas Jermyn† of Rushbrooke by Rebecca, da. and h. of William Rodway, merchant, of London. *m.* 1659, Mary, da. of Henry Merry of Barton Blount, Derbys.; 1s. *d.v.p.* 5da. *suc.* fa. 1659, uncle Henry Jermyn† as 2nd Baron Jermyn of St. Edmundsbury 2 Jan. 1684.

Capt. of ft. Jersey garrison 1661–79; capt. of grenadiers (later 12 Ft.) 1685–7; lt.-gov. Jersey 1662–79, gov. 1684–*d.*[1]

Commr. for assessment, Suff. 1673–80, j.p. 1674–*d.*, commr. for recusants 1675.

Jermyn's family acquired the manor of Rushbrooke, three miles south-east of Bury St. Edmunds, in the 13th century, and first sat for the county in 1584. Though the estates in Suffolk, Norfolk and Lincolnshire were estimated at £1,500 p.a., the family were much at Court in the 17th century. His grandfather and father together represented Bury in the Long Parliament. The former, comptroller of the Household from 1639 to 1641, was disabled in 1644, while in 1651 the latter paid a fine of £2,750 for his delinquency. Jermyn's uncle, raised to the peerage in 1643, remained in exile with the queen mother, presided over her household, and according to some sources privately married her. Jermyn himself may have been among the exiles in Paris around 1650, but he probably returned to England shortly afterwards, and attended his father's deathbed in 1659.[2]

After the Restoration Jermyn fared less well than his uncle, who was created Earl of St. Albans, and his younger brother Henry, master of the horse to the Duke of York. He was given a commission in the garrison of Jersey, whence he despatched a privateer in the second Dutch war. He took virtually no part in Suffolk affairs until the Exclusion Parliaments, in which he represented Bury. Classed as 'base' by Shaftesbury, he duly voted against the first exclusion bill. He presumably continued to oppose exclusion, but he made no recorded speeches and was not appointed to any committees.[3]

In 1684 Jermyn succeeded his uncle as governor of Jersey, and also in his peerage under a special remainder, although the estates were divided with his brother, a Roman Catholic who was created

Lord Dover by James II. He supported the Revolution, signing the Association in 1696. He died at his house in Westminster on 1 Apr. 1703, the last of his family to sit. The estates, valued at £15,000 p.a. were divided between his four surviving daughters, and Rushbrooke was eventually bought by his son-in-law, Sir Robert Davers, 1st Bt.*[4]

¹ CSP Dom. 1671, p. 533; 1679–80, p. 212; Add. 1660–85, p. 74. ² Rushbrooke Par. Regs. (Suff. Green Bks. vi), 303–10; Keeler, Long Parl. 234–5; Cal. Comm. Comp. 1869. ³ CSP Dom. 1666–7, p. 499; Add. 1660–70, pp. 682, 722; Bulstrode Pprs. 304. ⁴ CSP Dom. 1665–6, p. 119; 1684–5, p. 154; 1695, p. 230; Luttrell, i. 464; ii. 651; HMC Finch, ii. 429, 454; Rushbrooke Par. Regs. 306–10; HMC Dartmouth, i. 229.

P.W.

JERVOISE, Thomas (1616–93), of Herriard, Hants.

HAMPSHIRE 29 Nov. 1680, 19 Feb. 1689

b. 16 Mar. 1616, 2nd but 1st surv. s. of Sir Thomas Jervoise† of Britford, Wilts. by 1st w. Lucy, da. and coh. of Sir Richard Powlett of Herriard. *educ.* L. Inn 1638. *m.* 30 July 1657, Mary, da. of George Purefoy† of Wadley, Berks., 2s. 4da. *suc.* fa. 1654.[1]

Capt. of horse (parliamentary) 1643–6.

Commr. for assessment, Hants 1649–52, Aug. 1660–80, Hants and Wilts. 1689–90; j.p. Hants 1652–56, 1658–80, ?1689–*d.*, commr. for militia 1659, Mar. 1660, capt. of militia horse Apr. 1660, sheriff 1666–7; commr. for wastes and spoils, New Forest 1672–3; dep. lt. Hants 1673–6, 1689–*d.*; freeman, Winchester 1689.[2]

The Jervoise family was founded by a London Mercer who bought Britford in 1538. Jervoise's father, a Puritan and eventually an Independent, acquired Herriard by marriage, and with it a strong interest at Whitchurch, which he represented as a country Member in every Parliament from 1621 to 1653. He supported Parliament in the first Civil War and sat in the Rump. During the Civil War, Jervoise was in arms for Parliament. He was present at the siege of Corfe Castle and was taken prisoner before Basing House in 1644. In 1645 he served under Fairfax throughout the campaign of the New Model Army in the West. Presumably reconciled to the Restoration, he was appointed to the militia commission and the commission of the peace in March 1660. He was removed in 1680 as an exclusionist, but returned to Parliament later in the year at a by-election for Hampshire. He made no speeches and served on no committees. He did not stand again until after the Revolution, when he was returned at a contested by-election for the county. He was again totally inactive in the Convention. He was given leave for a month to recover his health on 29 Nov., and did not vote for the disabling clause in the bill to restore corporations, though he was presumably a Whig. He did not stand again, and died on 13 May 1693. He was buried at Herriard. His son Thomas had been returned for Stockbridge in 1691, subsequently sitting for Hampshire in four Parliaments as a Whig.[3]

[1] *The Ancestor*, iii. 1–5. [2] *Parl. Intell.* 30 Apr. 1660, 1673, p. 462; *Cal. Treas. Bks.* iii. 1204; iv. 124; Eg. 2557; Winchester corp. assembly bk. 6, f. 38. [3] *The Ancestor*, iii. 5; Clarendon, *Rebellion*, iii. 414.

P.W.

JESSON, William (c.1617–61), of Little Park Street, Coventry, Warws.

COVENTRY 14 Aug. 1660

b. c.1617, 1st s. of William Jesson† of Coventry by Elizabeth, da. of John Barker, draper, of Coventry. *educ.* I. Temple 1635. *m.* (1) Anne, da. of Sir Edward Pinchon of Writtle, Essex, 2s. 1da.; (2) aft. 1651, Frances, da. and coh. of Richard Cresheld†, serjeant-at-law, of Mattishall, Norf., *s.p. suc. fa.* 1651.[1]
    Commr. for assessment, Warws. and Coventry 1657, Coventry Sept. 1660–*d.*, militia 1659, Mar. 1660.

Jesson's ancestors had lived in Coventry for three generations. His father, a dyer by trade, was mayor in 1631, and distinguished himself in opposition to Charles I both in church and state. A Presbyterian, he represented the borough in the Short and Long Parliaments until Pride's Purge, and served on the county committee. Jesson inherited an estate of £600 p.a. and does not seem to have engaged in trade. At the general election of 1660 he probably stood jointly with his brother-in-law Richard Hopkins I*, but he was defeated by Robert Beake*. The election was declared void on 31 July, and Jesson was successful at the by-election. He took no known part in the Convention, but probably voted with the Presbyterian Opposition. He stood for re-election with Hopkins in 1661, but they were defeated by the royalist candidates. He died soon afterwards; his will, proved on 1 Aug., mentions losses sustained through bad debts. His son completed the ascent through the ranks of the gentry with removal to a country seat in Leicestershire, a knighthood and a second marriage to a Villiers; but no later member of the family entered Parliament.[2]

[1] *Vis. London* (Harl. Soc. xvii), 11; *Vis. Essex* (Harl. Soc. xiii), 470; PCC 215 Grey; C8/320/61. [2] *VCH Warws.* viii. 249; Keeler, *Long Parl.* 238; D. Underdown, *Pride's Purge*, 114; PCC 132 May; Nichols, *Lincs.* ii. 197; iii. 909.

A.M.M./J.P.F.

JOHNSON, George (1626–83), of Bowden Park, Lacock, Wilts.

DEVIZES 30 Oct. 1669, 1681

b. 6 Mar. 1626, 1st s. of William Johnson of Bowden Park by Elizabeth, da. of Thomas Baynard of Wanstrow, Som. *educ.* M. Temple 1645, called 1654. *m.* c.1659, Mary, da. of James Oeils, merchant, of London, 9s. 3da. *suc.* fa. 1664.[1]
    Commr. for assessment, Dorset 1665–9, Wilts. 1666–80; j.p. Wilts. 1668–*d.*; freeman, Devizes 1670; bencher, M. Temple 1670, reader 1675, treas. 1679–80; member, council in the marches of Wales 1674; second justice, Chester circuit 1674–81; commr. for recusants, Wilts. 1675.[2]

Johnson's father migrated from Bedfordshire to Wiltshire early in the 17th century and took a lease of Bowden Park, ten miles from Devizes, from the Fane family. He was disclaimed by the heralds at their visitation of 1623. Johnson became a lawyer, but both he and his father appear to have remained neutral in the Civil War. The foundations of his political career were laid in 1655, when Vere Bertie, brother-in-law of Sir Thomas Osborne*, entered his chambers. Johnson and his father bought the freehold of Bowden Park in 1662 from the 2nd Earl of Westmorland. The estate was estimated at £800 p.a., but, according to Aubrey, Johnson trebled its value by marling and skilful management. He was an active local magistrate, but he did not neglect his legal practice, either in London or Wiltshire. He was returned for Devizes at a by-election in 1669. For a lawyer he was surprisingly inactive in the House, with only 15 committees, none of them of political importance. On 13 Feb. 1673, immediately before Bertie's petition against the Chippenham return, he was appointed to the committee for the prevention of abuses in elections. Apart from the committee of elections and privileges in the next session, this was his last appearance in the Journals of the Cavalier Parliament. But he continued to attend the House in the interests of Osborne, now Earl of Danby and lord treasurer. 'I cannot possibly stir', he wrote on 30 Apr. 1675, 'till we have acquitted my lord treasurer of all those crimes exhibited against him in certain articles of impeachment.' He received the government whip in 1675, and in the same year he appears among the officials in the Commons. On the working lists he was marked as possessing influence over Jeffrey Daniel*. In *A Seasonable Argument* he was described as 'a lawyer and a Welsh judge, the treasurer's solicitor, and an impudent—; has the reversion of the master of the rolls, but some say that is only in trust for Baron Bertie'. He was marked 'thrice vile' by Shaftesbury, and appeared on both lists of the court party in 1678. On 16 Nov. he defended (Sir) Job Charlton*, his senior colleague on the Chester circuit, against an accusation of failing to bring priests and Jesuits to trial, but this was his only speech in Parliament.[3]

It is not known whether Johnson stood at the next general election, but he was defeated in September 1679 only by the malpractices of the mayor. Meanwhile Danby in the Tower was becoming anxious about the mastership of the rolls. Johnson indeed held the reversion to Sir Harbottle Grimston* in trust, though for Edward Osborne*, not Bertie. On 12 Jan. 1681 Danby wrote to the King from the Tower: 'I have some reason to doubt that Mr Johnson doth design to take some advantage against me by reason of my present circumstances'. Confirmation of Danby's suspicions is provided by Aubrey, who wrote that if Johnson had 'lived to have been master of the rolls, I had been one of his secretaries, worth £600 p.a.'. It is not known whether this breach with the fallen treasurer assisted Johnson to regain his seat in 1681. At Oxford he was appointed only to the elections committee. He retired from the bench later in the year. Sir Francis North* complained: 'George Johnson gets a pension likewise, and sells the place with the pension; so the King gives a pension to be sold, and it must be continued because it is bought'. Johnson died on 28 May 1683 of a malignant fever, contracted in drawing up a will, and was buried at Lacock.[4]

[1] London Vis. Peds. (Harl. Soc. xcii), 83; Aubrey, Brief Lives, ii. 9; PCC 114 Drax. [2] Devizes bor. recs. bk. C; CSP Dom. 1673-5, p. 111; Cal. Treas. Bks. iv. 468. [3] Vis. Beds. (Harl. Soc. xix), 206; Wilts. Arch. Mag. xxxix. 112; Hoare, Repertorium Wiltonense, 16; Aubrey and Jackson, Wilts. Colls. 94; CSP Dom. 1670, p. 384; 1672-3, p. 445; HMC 15th Rep. VII, 176; Grey, vi. 202. [4] HMC 14th Rep. IX, 421; Aubrey, ii. 9; CSP Dom. 1680-1, p. 405; Dalrymple, Mems. i. (1) p. 149; T. Dingley, Hist. from Marble (Cam. Soc. xcvii), pp. ccccxcvii, ccccci.

J.P.F.

JOHNSON, Henry (1623–83), of Blackwall, Mdx. and Friston, Suff.

ALDEBURGH 1679 (Mar.)

bap. 25 Jan. 1623, 1st s. of Francis Johnson of Aldeburgh by Mary, da. of Peter Pett of Deptford, Kent. *m.* 13 Dec. 1648, Dorothy, da. and h. of William Lord of Melton, Kent, 2s. 3da. *suc.* fa. 1636; kntd. 8 Mar. 1680.[1]
    Commr. for sewers, Mdx. 1647, Havering and Dagenham levels Sept. 1660, assessment, Mdx. and Suff. 1677-80, Aldeburgh 1679-80; capt. of militia ft. Mdx. by 1678–d.[2]
    Yr. bro. Trinity House Aug. 1660; member, R. Adventurers into Africa 1663, R. Africa Co. 1672; committee, E.I. Co. 1683–d.[3]

Johnson was descended from a merchant family. His great-grandfather settled at Aldeburgh and represented the borough in Parliament in 1597. His maternal grandfather was a member of the Kentish shipbuilding family, and in 1639 he was apprenticed to his cousin Phineas Pett. He took no part in the Civil War and by 1651 he was building ships for both the merchant service and the Commonwealth navy at Deptford. He bought the East India Company's shipyard and docks at Blackwall in 1655 for £4,350. Thereafter he became one of the leading shipbuilders and owners of the time. He lived at Blackwall in the house at the entrance to the dockyard, which he eventually rebuilt.[4]

After the Restoration Johnson continued to prosper, building ships for, among others, the Royal Navy and the East India Company, in which he held £1,200 stock. He had £1,388 on deposit at the Stop of the Exchequer, but two years later he bought Friston estate, three miles from Aldeburgh, from Thomas Bacon*, and rebuilt the Hall. Samuel Pepys* found his prosperity unaccountable since he was 'never famous for building the best or biggest ships'.[5]

Returned for Aldeburgh at the first general election of 1679, Johnson was classed as 'doubtful' on Shaftesbury's list. A moderately active Member of the first Exclusion Parliament, he was appointed to six committees, including that to examine the disbandment accounts. His claim on the Exchequer was hastily settled with an excise pension of £83 p.a., and according to Roger Morrice he voted against exclusion. He is not known to have stood again. In February 1680 he and two partners unsuccessfully tendered for a three-year lease of the excise farm, but he received some compensation in the following month, when the King knighted him in his own house at Blackwall. In 1681 he made some proposals for the tin farm, again unsuccessfully. He died at Bath and was buried on 19 Nov. 1683 in the East India Company chapel at Poplar, to the building of which he had been a major contributor. In the funeral sermon he was described as being

religiously inclined; not only free from the gross debaucheries and sinful excesses of this atheistical and corrupt age ... but very serious in his discourses, grave and exemplary in his whole deport. No encourager of faction or rebellion, no friend to or favourer of profaneness or irreligion, but on the contrary a countenancer of religion and loyalty ... Sir Henry Johnson was one who both feared God and honoured the King.

Under his will almshouses were built at Poplar for six ships' carpenters, though it was not until 1756 that they were used for the purpose he had intended.[6]

[1] Vis. Mdx. ed. Foster, 67; H. Green and R. Wigram, Chrons. Blackwell Yard, 9, 18, 24. [2] Green and Wigram, 11; C191/7/48; CSP Dom. 1678, p. 440. [3] Add. 22183, f. 4; Sel. Charters (Selden Soc. xxviii), 179, 188; Add. 38871, f. 8. [4] East Anglian, n.s. iii. 198; W. Foster, John Company, 148-51; Cal. Ct. Mins. E.I. Co. ed. Sainsbury, iv. 307; v. 34; Econ. Hist. Rev. (ser. 2), v. 198; CSP

Dom. 1651–2, pp. 552, 567; 1653–4, pp. 470, 507; 1655, p. 441. [5] *CSP Dom.* 1665–6, p. 26; 1667, p. 140; *Cal. Ct. Mins. E.I. Co.* viii. 117, 327; ix. 311; Copinger, *Suff. Manors*, v. 131; *Pepys Naval Mins.* (Navy Rec. Soc. lx), 163. [6] *Cal. Treas. Bks.* v. 1268; vi. 448; vii. 128; Green and Wigram, 24; S. Peck, *Funeral Sermon*, 26; Lysons, *Environs*, iii. 470.

P.W.

JOHNSON, Sir Henry (c.1659–1719), of Blackwall, Mdx. and Friston, Suff.

ALDEBURGH   1689, 1690, 1695, 1698, 1701 (Feb.),
               1701 (Dec.), 1702, 1705, 1708, 1710,
               1713, 1715–29 Sept. 1719

b. c.1659, 1st s. of Henry Johnson*, and bro. of William Johnson*. *m.* (1) 20 May 1686, Anne, da. and h. of Hugh Smithson, Haberdasher, of Old Exchange Precincts, London, 1da.; (2) 11 Mar. 1693, Martha (*d.* 18 July 1745), *suo jure* Baroness Wentworth, da. and h. of John Lovelace*, 3rd Baron Lovelace of Hurley, *s.p. suc.* fa. 1683; kntd. Mar. 1685.[1]
   Capt. of militia ft. Tower Hamlets by 1683, col. by Aug. 1688–at least 1697; j.p. Mdx. 1685–7, 1689–*d.*, Berks. 1695–*d.*, Suff. by 1701–*d.*; committee E.I. Co. 1684–91, 1698–1702; dep. master of shipwrights' co. Rotherhithe 1686; commr. for encroachments, Tower of London 1686, assessment, Mdx., Suff. and Aldeburgh 1689–90; dep. lt. Tower Hamlets 1689–?*d.*, Mdx. 1692–?*d.*, Berks. and Oxon. 1702–?*d.*, elder bro. Trinity House 1700–*d.*, master 1707–9; commr. for sewers, Tower Hamlets 1712.[2]

Johnson negotiated his first contract to build a ship for the East India Company when still under age. 'An ingenious young gentleman', according to Samuel Pepys*, he was nevertheless 'above all personal labour' and 'too well provided for to work much'. With this last comment Johnson would have strongly disagreed, evading all his life so far as he could the charitable bequests in his father's will. Roger L'Estrange* described him in 1683 as a disciple of Ferguson the plotter, apparently confusing him with his neighbour Thomas Johnson of Mile End, subsequently Whig candidate for Middlesex. In fact Johnson was a Tory and a churchman, knighted by James II in 1685, and removed from local office two years later. In addition to the Blackwall yard which he had inherited, he owned shares in 38 merchant ships and held £3,675 East India stock at the Revolution. Nothing but the threat of a quo warranto could shake his interest at Aldeburgh, where he had 'almost revived the town by building three half-parts of fishing vessels (when all their shipping was lost) and adventuring them to sea with the principal of the townsmen'. As colonel of the Tower Hamlets militia during the Revolution he was responsible for conveying Judge Jeffreys to the safety of his last earthly lodging.[3]

Johnson and his brother represented Aldeburgh in the Convention and its 11 succeeding Parliaments. A moderately active Member, he voted to agree with the House of Lords that the throne was not vacant, and was appointed to 14 committees. He was the first Member named on 20 Mar. 1689 to the committee to prepare defence estimates for times of peace, and he was among those entrusted with repealing the Corporations Act and inquiring into exactions by customs officials and the affairs of the East India Company. In November, after the recess, he was appointed to three more committees of inquiry, into the expenses of the war, the administration of martial law on St. Helena, and the activities of the press gang. When it was proposed to remove Sir Richard Haddock* from the victualling office, Johnson declared, in his only recorded speech:

> I believe the navy will stand still without Sir Richard Haddock, he is a man so conversant in the affairs of the navy. You have been offered security for his appearance. He was against the dispensing power and was turned out by King James.

Johnson remained a Tory after 1690, though he signed the Association in 1696. After his second marriage he resided chiefly on the Wentworth estates in the south Midlands. He died of gout at Bath on 29 Sept. 1719, aged 60, and was buried in the Wentworth vault at Toddington, though in a manner sufficient to distinguish his common clay from the remains of his noble kinsmen. His vast wealth and interest were inherited by his son-in-law, the 1st Earl of Strafford of the second creation.[4]

[1] *East Anglian*, iii. 198; Add. 22187, f. 96; J. R. Woodhead, *Rulers of London*, 153. [2] *CSP Dom.* July–Sept. 1683, p. 49; 1686–7, p. 21; Eg. 1626, f. 60; Add. 22187, ff. 116, 127; Mdx. RO, MJP/CP5a; information from Henry Horwitz; SP44/165/305; *Cal. Treas. Bks.* viii. 533; *HMC Townshend*, 211. [3] *Cal. Ct. Mins. E.I. Co.* ed. Sainsbury, x. 314; *Cat. Pepysian Mss* (Navy Recs. Soc. xxvi), 78; Lysons, *Environs*, iii. 470; *CSP Dom.* July–Sept. 1683, pp. 49, 125; *Econ. Hist. Rev.* ii. 263; Add. 22185, f. 14; E. Suss. RO, Winterton mss, Godfrey to Turnor, 3 Dec. 1688; Add. 22183, f. 140. [4] Add. 22185, f. 14; Grey, ix. 445; *Wentworth Pprs.* 280; W. C. Hutton, *Fam. of Wentworth*, 137.

P.W.

JOHNSON, Sir James (1615–at least 1688), of South Quay, Great Yarmouth, Norf.

GREAT YARMOUTH   1681

bap. 16 July 1615, 2nd s. of Thomas Johnson† (*d.*1661) of Yarmouth by Margaret, da. of Thomas Thompson of Yarmouth. *m.* Dorothy, da. of Augustine Scottow, grocer, of Norwich, 2s. Kntd. 22 Sept. 1671.[1]
   Freeman, Yarmouth 1641, common councilman to 1649, alderman by Aug. 1660–2; commr. for assessment, Norf. Aug. 1660–1, 1677–80, Yarmouth Sept. 1660–3, 1673–80; j.p. Norf. 1673–80; commr. for inquiry into recusancy fines, Norf., Suff. and Cambs. Mar. 1688.[2]

Johnson's great-grandfather served as bailiff of Yarmouth in 1589, and his father represented the borough in 1626. Johnson himself, with his elder brother, was the first to take up arms against the King. But during the second Civil War his father was among those commissioned to hold the port by the Prince of Wales, and organized a noisy demonstration 'for Prince Charles and Captain Johnson'. He was allowed to compound for his delinquency at £234, and after the second return of the Rump signed the Norfolk address to George Monck* for a free Parliament.[3]

At the Restoration Johnson moved and carried a loyal address from the Yarmouth corporation. He served as admiralty agent in the port until the end of the second Dutch war, securing two contracts for frigates for local ship-builders. He also acted as electoral agent for Sir William Doyley*, but he was among the Presbyterians removed from the corporation at the instigation of Sir Thomas Medowe* in 1662, though he continued to exact precedence as an alderman when he attended the parish church. In August 1668 he accompanied Richard Huntington* to London to promote a private bill for the repair of the pier and haven, and he was one of the commissioners named in the Act. He was again associated with Huntington in consulting the lord lieutenant, Sir Horatio Townshend*, about the renunciation of the Covenant required from new members of the corporation. His contribution to a collection for nonconformist ministers was modest, and he described himself as 'much straitened in his affairs' when he applied to the Admiralty for £527 for goods supplied, moneys laid out, and other services over a period of three-and-a-half years. The King, on his visit to Yarmouth in 1671, was received at Johnson's house, the finest in the town, and 'observed to feed very heartily on our sea-made herrings'. No ill consequences followed, and at Townshend's instance hospitality was rewarded with a knighthood. Johnson 'nobly entertained' less august visitors to Yarmouth, and his credit was still good as far afield as Amsterdam, Frankfurt, Venice and Vienna.[4]

As a 'partial conformist' he was determined to stand at the first general election of 1679, but was defeated by (Sir) William Coventry*. 'A sober and understanding person', he was returned as an exclusionist in 1681, and in a speech to the electors said: 'Besides the honour of your service, it seems there is profit; such good masters are you to provide wages for those you are pleased to employ, but of these I do hereby acquit you'. This was a rather barren renunciation, since Great Yarmouth had paid no wages to MPs since the Restoration. John-

son played no known part in the Oxford Parliament; but on 22 June it was reported to Sir Leoline Jenkins* that he had been heard to remark that 'the King of France can whore well and govern well; our King could whore well but not govern'. He was convicted for seditious words at Norwich assizes in August 1682 and fined £500, subsequently reduced to £200 by the King's direction. An order was issued after the Rye House Plot to search his house for arms, but apparently never executed.[5]

Under James II Johnson became a Whig collaborator. In January 1688 he produced an order-in-council removing six aldermen and 11 common councilmen. In April the King's agents recommended him as a court candidate for Yarmouth, and in September advised that to 'secure' his election the precept should be delivered to him 'and not executed until the change of mayor'. After the Revolution he lapsed into obscurity, and none of his descendants entered Parliament. The date of his death is unknown; but he is said to have 'lived well, spent much, and died poor'.[6]

[1] Yarmouth St. Nicholas par. reg.; *Le Neve's Knights* (Harl. Soc. viii), 266; PCC 7 Laud; P. Millican, *Freemen of Norwich*, 76. [2] *Yarmouth Freemen*, 73; H. Swinden, *Hist. Yarmouth*, 576; Yarmouth bor. recs. assembly bks.; *CSP Dom.* 1668–9, p. 111; *Cal. Treas. Bks.* viii. 1805. [3] *CSP Dom.* 1671, p. 491; Rushworth, *Hist. Colls.* vii. 1207; *Cal. Comm. Comp.* 1896; *Address from the Gentry of Norf.* ed. Rye. [4] C. J. Palmer, *Perlustration of Yarmouth*, ii. 368–9; iii. 376; *CSP Dom.* 1660–1, pp. 40–41; 1664–5, p. 295; 1667, p. 468; 1668–9, pp. 77, 96, 111, 287; 1670, p. 620; 1671, pp. 491, 517; SP29/233/50. [5] *CSP Dom.* 1679–80, p. 66; 1680–1, p. 338; Swinden, 909; *Works of Sir Thomas Browne* ed. Wilkin, i. 306; *EHR*, lxvi. 38; *Cal. Treas. Bks.* vii. 665, 753; *Norf. Ltcy. Jnl.* (Norf. Rec. Soc. xxx), 46. [6] Palmer, iii. 370; PC3/72/570; *Le Neve's Knights*, 266.

E.C./B.D.H.

JOHNSON, Nathaniel (c.1645–1713), of Newcastle-upon-Tyne, Northumb. and Kibblesworth, Lamesley, co. Dur.

NEWCASTLE-UPON-TYNE 1 Dec. 1680, 1681, 1685

b. c.1645, 1st s. of William Johnson, merchant, of Newcastle by Margaret, da. of William Sherwood, merchant, of Newcastle. *m.* 1s. 1da. *suc.* fa. 1678; kntd. 28 Dec. 1680.[1]

Dep. treas. Barbados by 1668; jt.-farmer of hearth-tax 1679–84; gov. Leeward Isles 1686–9, Carolina 1702–8.[2]

Member of eastland co. Newcastle 1668, merchant adventurers 1669, freeman 1673; j.p. co. Dur. 1674–?86; collector of hearth-tax, Cumb., Westmld., Northumb. and co. Dur. by 1675; commr. for assessment, co. Dur. 1677–9, Newcastle 1679–80, carriage of coals, Newcastle 1679; capt. of militia ft. Newcastle by 1680–?Feb. 1688; member, Hon. Artillery Co. 1681; mayor, Newcastle 1681–2, alderman 1682–June 1688.[3]

Johnson was the grandson of a Scottish blacksmith. His father, who served as mayor of Newcastle and sequestrator during the Interregnum, acquired a small estate in Durham and recorded his pedigree at the heralds' visitation of the county in 1666. Though he attended a Presbyterian conventicle after the Restoration, Johnson himself grew up a staunch Anglican. He went out to the West Indies as a young man, serving for a time as deputy to William Willoughby*. But by 1675 he had become a local hearth-tax official, and in 1678 he formed a syndicate, which included Anthony Rowe*, to farm and manage the whole tax for five years from Michaelmas 1679.[4]

Johnson was first returned for Newcastle at a by-election in 1680. A court supporter, he was knighted later in the month, and became a moderately active Member of the second Exclusion Parliament. He was added to the committee on the bill for export of beer, ale and mum, and appointed to that for reforming the collection of hearth-tax. When Laurence Hyde*, who as first lord of the Treasury had modified the terms of the hearth-tax lease in the farmers' favour, was attacked in the House as a friend of the Duke of York, Johnson defended him, rather clumsily. 'The Treasury being poor', he said on 7 Jan. 1681, 'it is an improper time to spend time on removing a treasurer.' He was re-elected to the Oxford Parliament, but left no trace on its records. In October 1681 he presented a loyal address from the lieutenancy and militia of Newcastle, approving the dissolution. A friend of Count Königsmarck, he acted as surety and interpreter at his trial for the murder of Thomas Thynne II*. After the Rye House Plot he induced the vintner Shepherd to turn king's evidence.[5]

Johnson appears to have been designated governor of the Leeward Islands on the lapse of the hearth-tax farm. Although rumour assigned a scandalous profit to the syndicate, Johnson himself complained that his 'circumstances were very strait and pinching'. However he did not take up his post till 1686, and meanwhile played a leading part in the surrender of Newcastle's charter, after which the Duke of Newcastle (Henry Cavendish*) was rightly confident that he would be re-elected. Again moderately active in James II's Parliament, he was named to nine committees, of which the most important were to recommend expunctions from the Journals and to consider the bill for the general naturalization of Huguenot refugees.[6]

As governor of the Leeward Islands Johnson conformed to the King's religious policy. He disestablished the Church and was thanked by the Roman Catholics for his 'impartiality'. He proclaimed William and Mary as King and Queen when news of the Revolution was received, but requested permission to retire into private life.

I have no liking for the Romish faith, as you know, and hope to live and die a Protestant; and it is from the doctrines of the Church of England that I learned the scruples which oblige me to ask for my dismission.

He settled in Carolina, where he had a large estate, and experimented with the culture of silkworms. On the death of James he took the oaths and was appointed governor of the proprietors of the colony, which he defended with conspicuous courage and success against French and Spanish; but he was criticized as a tool of the High Church party in enforcing the sacramental test for office-holders, and was dismissed in 1708. He died in 1713. His son sold Kibblesworth in 1729 on his appointment as governor of South Carolina; and no other member of the family sat in Parliament.[7]

[1] Surtees, *Dur.* ii. 218; *Le Neve's Knights* (Harl. Soc. viii), 343. [2] *APC Col.* i. 503; *Cal. Treas. Bks.* v. 1151; *CSP Col.* 1685-8, p. 229; 1689-92, p. 43; 1702, p. 398. [3] *Newcastle Merchant Adventurers* (Surtees Soc. ci), 295; *Reg. of Freemen* (Newcastle Recs. iii), 89; *HMC Le Fleming*, 115; 120; *Cal. Treas. Bks.* v. 1205; *Ancient Vellum Bk.* ed. Raikes, 111. [4] *Cal. Comm. Comp.* 694; *CSP Dom.* 1655-6, p. 25; *Barnes Mems.* (Surtees Soc. l), 409; Luttrell, i. 25. [5] *HMC 12th Rep. IX*, 114; *HMC Buccleuch*, i. 334; *London Gazette*, 31 Oct. 1681; Luttrell, i. 170; *CSP Dom.* 1682, p. 212; July-Sept. 1683, p. 99; *Dom. Intell.* 2 Mar. 1682; *Hatton Corresp.* (Cam. Soc. n.s. xxiii), 15. [6] J. C. Jeaffreson, *A Young Squire of the 17th Century*, ii. 99; *CSP Col.* 1689-92, pp. 43, 88, *CSP Dom.* Jan.-June 1683, pp. 30, 130; 1683-4, pp. 314, 333; 1685, p. 25. [7] *CSP Dom.* 1686-7, p. 228; *CSP Col.* 1685-8, p. 470; 1689-92, pp. 43, 87, 111; *Dict. Amer. Biog.* x. 111.

G.H.

JOHNSON, William (c.1660–1718), of Blackwall, Mdx.

ALDEBURGH 1689, 1690, 1695, 1698, 1701 (Feb.), 1701 (Dec.), 1702, 1705, 1708, 1710, 1713, 1715–Nov. 1718

b. c.1660, 2nd s. of Henry Johnson*, and bro. of Sir Henry Johnson*. *educ.* Leyden 1678. *m.* by 1687, Agneta, da. of Hartgill Baron, clerk of the privy seal, of Windsor, Berks., 3s. 8da.[1]

Asst. R. Africa Co. 1687–9; commr. for assessment, Mdx., Suff. and Aldeburgh 1689–90; dep. lt. Tower Hamlets 1689–at least 1702; committee E.I. Co. 1690–91, 1698–9, 1702–5; elder bro. Trinity House 1709–*d.*; commr. for sewers, Tower Hamlets 1712.[2]

Gent. of privy chamber 1690–1702; capt.-gen. of Guinea 1716–*d.*[3]

Johnson was sent out to Bengal as a factor for the East India Company. Described as both 'ingenious' and 'hopeful', he distinguished himself by spying on the interlopers, and carrying tales to the governor, Hedges. His cousin, a captain of one of the company's ships, wrote:

If there is money to be got I am sure [he] will do it as soon as anyone in this place, . . . for he does take the greatest delight in business that ever I see. . . . Those that are his friends love him as if he were their brother, and those that are his enemies fear him as being too cunning for them. . . . He has got the love of the natives to such a height that they would do anything for him.

When Hedges was recalled in 1683 for suppressing a critical report to (Sir) Josiah Child*, which Johnson, his only friend in India, had opened and brought to him, the court wrote:

Mr Johnson we look upon as a young man whose heat and youth was intemperately drawn in and managed by Mr Hedges . . . and therefore, as well in respect to his father, deceased, who hath left him a great estate, we do not require you to send him home.

He returned to England of his own volition, however, and set up as a merchant, trading to Africa and the Peninsula. He was able to buy himself a manorial property in Suffolk, but lived chiefly near his brother's shipyard at Blackwall.[4]

Johnson was returned for Aldeburgh in 1689 on his brother's interest, and held the seat for the rest of his life. A Tory in politics, he voted to agree with the Lords that the throne was not vacant, but he was not active in the Convention. His six committees included those to consider the management of the East India trade, the bill for restoring corporations, and a petition from the Royal Africa Company. Although he remained a Tory after 1690, like his brother, he signed the Association in 1696. After the Hanoverian succession he accepted an appointment as governor of Guinea under the Royal Africa Company, and died at Cape Coast Castle in November 1718. In his will he estimated his personal estate at £20,000. His son Henry, the author and traveller, considered standing for Aldeburgh in 1734, writing to the Earl of Strafford that 'my name may somewhat facilitate my election, as those people are under some obligation to our family'. But none of his descendants entered Parliament.[5]

[1] East Anglian, iii. 198; Add. 22187, f. 219; Hedges Diary (Hakluyt Soc. lxxiv), 249; PCC 218 Tenison; The Ancestor, x. 163. [2] Add. 22187, f. 127; SP44/165/305; information from Henry Horwitz; HMC Townshend, 211. [3] Carlisle, Privy Chamber, 206. [4] Add. 22186, ff. 22, 27; Hedges Diary (Hakluyt Soc. lxxiv), 141, 163, 186; (lxxv), p. cciii; Copinger, Suff. Manors, v. 171. [5] Add. 22187, f. 219; Hist. Reg. Chron. iii. 43; PCC 218 Tenison; DNB; Add. 22221, f. 509.

P.W.

JOLLIFFE (JOLLEY), John (1613–80), of Threadneedle Street, London.

HEYTESBURY   1660, 24 May 1661

bap. 29 Aug. 1613, 2nd s. of Thomas Jolliffe, mercer, of Leek, Staffs., being 1st s. by 2nd w. Elizabeth, da. of Edward Mainwaring of Whitmore, Staffs. m. (1) 27 June 1650, Rebecca (bur. 23 June 1674), da. of Walter Boothby, Haberdasher, of London and Tottenham, Mdx., 3s. (2 d.v.p.) 5da.; (2) lic. 30 Apr. 1675, Anne, da. of John Gurdon* of Assington, Suff., wid. of Samuel Brandling of Ipswich, Suff., 1s.[1]

Member, Skinners' Co. 1642, asst. 1656, master 1661–2; asst. Levant Co. 1650–78, treas. 1659–61, dep. gov. 1662–71, gov. 1672–3; committee, E.I. Co. 1657–8, July 1660–d., dep. gov. 1665–7; alderman, London 23–28 Sept. 1658, councilman 1660, auditor 1662–4; commr. for assessment, London Aug. 1660–d., Mdx. 1673–d.; gov. Muscovy Co. by 1663–74; asst. R. Fishing Co. 1664; commr. for recusants, Wilts. 1675.[2]

Commr. for trade Nov. 1660–8, trade with Scotland 1668, marine treaty with the United Provinces 1674.[3]

Jolliffe was apprenticed first to a leading London Grocer, and then to his kinsman Matthew Cradock, MP for London and a leader of the puritan opposition in the early days of the Long Parliament. His half-brother, the head of the family, was an active member of the Staffordshire committee. But Jolliffe himself was of a timorous disposition and seems to have taken no part in the Civil War or in public affairs until the eve of the Restoration. He was already one of the leading merchants in the Mediterranean trade, but he preferred to fine off for alderman of London in 1658. When George Monck* was ordered by the Rump to destroy the defences of London, Jolliffe spoke to him 'to very good purpose, as became so prudent and discreet a citizen'. He owed his two returns for Heytesbury to his widowed niece, whose two sons William Ashe* and Edward Ashe* were too young to stand in 1660 and 1661. A moderately active Member of the Convention, he was appointed to 25 committees. He was twice instructed in May 1660 to use his credit in the City for the benefit of the Government, and he was appointed to the committee preparing the indemnity bill. He was active throughout the Parliament over excise, having been one of the common councilmen of London appointed to prepare a petition against it. On 4 July he spoke against imposing double poll-tax on recusants. In the second session he was named to the committee on the attainder bill. On 21 Nov. he spoke against compensating the crown for the abolition of the court of wards with a grant of excise, but nevertheless was appointed to the committee for drafting a clause accordingly.[4]

Jolliffe and his kinsman Sir Joseph Ashe* were involved in a double return with two Cavaliers at the general election of 1661, which was declared void; but he was successful at the by-election. He was again moderately active in the Cavalier Parliament; the majority of his 151 committees and all his half-dozen recorded speeches were concerned with trade. In spite of a strong laisser faire attitude, he probably had as much contact with Whitehall as any merchant of the Restoration period, chiefly through William Coventry* who valued him as an 'oracle' in matters of commerce. Nevertheless, he appears on no list of government supporters in the House. Described as a 'fair trader', he was proposed as a commissioner for customs frauds, and named to a parliamentary committee in 1662. His only committee of political consequence during Clarendon's administration was for the conventicles bill in 1664. He was among the first to leave London during the plague, gravely inconveniencing the East India Company, of which he was deputy governor at the time. He attended the Oxford session with Thomas Kendall*, where he acted as teller against the second reading of the Irish cattle bill; nevertheless he was appointed to the committee. The Great Fire interrupted his communications with the Court, for he held it unsafe to venture into the ruins, but he wrote to express the high obligations of the East India Company towards Lord Arlington, and he was one of the merchants called in to advise on the paying off of the fleet in 1667, to which he apparently advanced £5,000. He was chosen to attend the negotiations at Breda on behalf of the company, but excused. He was appointed on 25 Nov. to the committee considering the petition from the merchants trading with France. On 12 Dec. he introduced the petition of Alexander Fitton, who had married a kinswoman of his, against Lord Gerard of Brandon, and was appointed to the committee. Four days later he acted as teller for the adjournment of the debate on controlling the price of coal. He was among the Members appointed to assist Sir Charles Harbord* in his report on alienations of crown lands.[5]

Presumably Jolliffe followed Coventry into opposition in 1669. In the winter session of 1670 he spoke against the proposed ban on imports of brandy, for fear of depriving the planters. On 11 Apr. he was appointed to attend a conference with the Lords on the shipping bill. He made several speeches in the supply committee during the next session. He opposed any increase of taxes on Venetian exports, because the English woollen trade was beginning to thrive. All the spices brought into England every year, he claimed, were not worth £12,000. He dissented from the patriotic enthusiasm of William Love* for the English silk industry: 'knows not what we may prophesy in the business, but as yet we have not that trade so fully as to carry on the manufacture'. With regard to bankers, he 'would charge these people, but in intelligible terms'. Jolliffe seems to have initially approved of the third Dutch war, forwarding naval intelligence from his factor at Leghorn; but on 1 Aug. 1673 Sir Nicholas Armorer wrote to (Sir) Joseph Williamson*:

We expect the olive branch from you, and Mr Jolliffe wants it much. If you keep not things well with him,

Lord George Berkeley will have him all to himself, for I observe them very dear together.

He was therefore an appropriate choice as one of the commissioners for the marine treaty with the Dutch in 1674. Although at East India House he attended 116 out of 117 committees in 1672–3, more than any other member, and as governor of the Muscovy Company he was planning the revival of the caviar trade, he may have begun to reduce his activities in other directions. After 28 years he retired from the court of assistants of the Levant Company, and the increasing political acrimony in Parliament may have been distasteful to him. Shaftesbury awarded him only a single 'worthy', and he served on no committees in the final session of the Cavalier Parliament. It is improbable that he stood again. He died 'somewhat suddenly' on 2 Jan. 1680, and was buried at St. Martin Outwich. He had not invested in land, and his personal estate (including £2,500 in the East India Company) was valued at £34,323. He left £200 to 'poor ministers' to be distributed on the advice of Dr Jacombe, his second wife's kinsman, and he seems himself to have had nonconformist sympathies. His son, Sir William Jolliffe, sat for Petersfield as a Whig from 1734 to 1741.[6]

[1] H. G. H. Jolliffe, *Jolliffes of Staffs.* 6–8; *Vis. Mdx.* ed. Foster, 20; Rylands Lib. Eng. mss 305, f. 91; *Mdx. Par. Reg.* ix. 40; *Mar. Lic.* (Harl. Soc. xxxiv), 140; *Vis. England and Wales Notes* ed. Crisp, ix. 111; *St. Martin Outwich* (Harl. Soc. Reg. xxxii), 3, 39, 41, 44, 100, 102, 104. [2] J. R. Woodhead, *Rulers of London*, 99; *Sel. Charters* (Selden Soc. xxviii), 183; PC2/56/453. [3] *Bulstrode Pprs.* 63; *CSP Dom.* 1673–5, p. 287. [4] Guildhall RO, 11593/1, f. 16; *Cal. Ct. Mins. E. I. Co.* ed. Sainsbury, v. 189; Keeler, *Long Parl.* 144–5; *Vis. Staffs.* (Wm. Salt Arch. Soc. v. (2), 100; *Committee at Stafford* (Staffs. Rec. Soc. ser. 4, i), 352; *Cal. Comm. Adv. Money,* 394; *HMC Popham,* 216; Guildhall RO, common council jnl. 2 Mar. 1660; Bowman diary, f. 52v; *Old Parl. Hist.* xxiii. 21. [5] *Pepys Diary,* 18 Oct. 1664; *HMC Finch,* i. 414; *Cal. Treas. Bks.* i. 304, 735; ii. 101, 291; *Cal. Ct. Mins. E.I. Co.* vii. 168, 313, 332; *CSP Dom.* 1666–7, p. 174; 1667, p. 30; *Milward,* 164. [6] Grey, i. 219; 292–3, 311, 352; *Dering,* 3; *CSP Dom.* 1673, p. 475; 1675–6, p. 241; R. Morrice, Entering Bk. 1, p. 245; Woodhead, 99; PCC 6 Bath; *HMC Finch,* i. 411.

J.P.F.

JONES, Edward (c.1659–96), of Buckland, Brec.

BRECONSHIRE 24 June 1685, 1689, 1695–Dec. 1696

b. c.1659, 4th but 1st surv. s. of Edmund Jones[†] of Llandewi Yscyrid, Mon. and Gray's Inn by Gladys, da. and coh. of Edward Games of Buckland. *educ.* G. Inn, entered 1669, called 1682; Merton, Oxf. matric. 29 Mar. 1672, aged 13. *m.* Margaret (*d.* 12 Apr. 1695), da. of Roger Oates of Cefntilly, Mon., 7s. (6 *d.v.p.*) 2da. *suc.* fa. 1683.[1]

J.p. Brec. 1684–Mar. 1688, Oct. 1688–*d.*; dep. lt. Brec. 1685–Feb. 1688, 1689–*d.*, Mon. 1686–?87; bailiff, Brecon 1685–6, mayor Feb.–Sept. 1686, alderman 1686–Oct. 1688; commr. for assessment, Brec. 1689–90, sheriff 1693–4.[2]

Jones's father, a lawyer of obscure family, was an

active commissioner of array in the first Civil War, and compounded for £70 6s.8d. He married into an old Breconshire family, and became recorder of Brecon in 1650, MP for the county in 1654 and attorney-general for South Wales under the Protectorate. He was allowed to retain the recordership after the Restoration. Jones, also a lawyer, was returned for the county at a by-election in 1685, when the Marquess of Worcester (Charles Somerset*) chose to sit for Gloucestershire. He was doubtless elected as a Tory, but he was probably totally inactive in James II's Parliament. He was appointed mayor of Brecon under the new charter, but refused consent to the repeal of the Test Acts and Penal Laws and was removed from county office. He was re-elected to the Convention, in which he voted to agree with the Lords that the throne was not vacant. Otherwise he was totally inactive. He was replaced by the Whig (Sir) Rowland Gwynne* at the next general election. He regained his seat in 1695, but refused the Association in the following year. He died in December 1696, and was buried at Llansantffraid. His son Roger was returned for the borough as a Tory in 1713, but became a Whig two years later.[3]

¹ Jones, *Brec.* iii. 204; iv. 281. ² *CSP Dom.* 1686–7, pp. 42, 141; Jones, iv. 274, 306. ³ Jones, iv. 272; *Cal. Comm. Comp.* 1524; A. H. Dodd, *Studies in Stuart Wales*, 150; W. R. Williams, *Parl. Hist. Wales*, 18.

L.N.

JONES, Griffith (c.1630–80), of Trewern, Llanfihangel Nant Melan, Rad.

NEW RADNOR BOROUGHS   1679 (Oct.)–Feb. 1680

> *b.* c.1630, 1st s. of Richard Jones of Trewern. *m.* (1) da. of Edmund Weaver* of Above Eign, Hereford, 2s. 1da.; (2) lic. 18 Dec. 1677, Anna, da. of one Howard of Holborn, Mdx. *suc.* gdfa. Richard Jones† c.1659.[1]
>
> J.p. Rad. 1656–*d.*, commr. for assessment 1657, Jan. 1660–*d.*, militia Mar. 1660; alderman, New Radnor by 1661–*d.*; dep. lt. Rad. 1661–*d.*, capt. of militia ?1661, commr. for loyal and indigent officers 1662.[2]

Jones's family was of sufficient status to provide one of the first sheriffs of Radnorshire in 1548–9, and they had been associated with New Radnor since its charter of 1562. Trewern, three miles away, was in their day a spacious mansion well adapted to hospitality. Jones's grandfather sat for the county in 1628 and the boroughs in the Short Parliament. 'About 70 years of age and an unwieldy gentleman', he supported the Royalists in the Civil War as a commissioner of array to the extent of subscribing warrants for raising money and pressing men. He was only too eager to submit to Parliament in October 1645, in revenge for which the local Cavalier commander swooped on Tre-

wern, took him prisoner and plundered him down to the rings off his wife's fingers. After this alarming experience he was allowed to compound at Goldsmiths' Hall for a mere £72. He was still alive in 1658, but probably died before the Restoration.[3]

As a member of the New Radnor corporation, Jones tried with George Gwynne* to find a candidate to oppose Edward Harley* in 1661. Afterwards Harley's brother wrote: 'Griffith Jones and others of the 25 pretend they will send up an indenture by themselves, and that they will question the election, but that I suppose is but a crack'. Jones's estate was probably no more than £300 p.a. and his affairs became steadily more involved during the seventies. In April 1679 he mortgaged most of his property to Sir Herbert Croft*, probably in order to obtain funds for ousting Harley at New Radnor. This he succeeded in doing, but died before the second Exclusion Parliament met. His elder son of the same name stood by at the by-election, but the double return was never decided. By 1690 Trewern had been sold. Jones's younger son, an army officer, restored the family fortunes, but although his great-grandson acquired a baronetcy for diplomatic services, none of his descendants entered Parliament.[4]

¹ E.134/20 Chas. II Mich. 29; NLW, Penybont mss; C6/19/75; E134/2 Wm. & Mary E.20, deposition of Henry Bull; *London. Mar. Lic.* ed. Foster, 772; C6/113/72; E134/29 Chas. II. Mich 14. ² BL Loan 29/79, Thos. Harley to Sir Edw. Harley, 30 Apr. 1661; Hereford City Lib., Phillips mss, Bull of Harpton ped. ³ *Trans. Rad. Soc.* xxxvii. 41; *Arch. Camb.* (ser. 3), iv. 2; SP23/205, ff. 965–85. ⁴ C5/508/15; C6/246/66.

J.P.F.

JONES, John (c.1610–92), of Lothbury, London and Hampton, Mdx.[1]

LONDON   1656,[2] 1659, 1661

> *b.* c.1610. *educ.* Shrewsbury ?*m.* 15 Apr. 1632, Elizabeth Smith of London, 1da.[3]
>
> Member, Grocers' Co. by 1633, asst. May 1660; member, Hon. Artillery Co. 1641, July 1660; capt. of militia ft. London 1642–?47; common councilman 1645–7, elder of 7th classis 1646, commr. for militia 1647, assessment, Mdx. Jan. 1660, London and Mdx. 1661–80, Surr. 1661–73, Mdx. 1689–90, recusants, London 1675.[4]

Jones was born of obscure parentage in the parish of St. Chad, Shrewsbury and educated at the local grammar school. He came to London in 1629 and became a successful Grocer, ranking in the third class of 'able inhabitants' in 1640. A militant Presbyterian, he served as an officer in the train-bands during the Civil War; but he supported a negotiated settlement with the King, and was put under arrest in 1647, which subsequently enabled him to claim that he had 'sufficiently expressed his loyalty in the worst times'. Though holding neither company nor municipal office, he was elected for London to the second and third Protectorate Parliaments.[5]

At the general election of 1661 it was estimated that Jones received about 3,800 votes out of 4,000 on a show of hands, with particularly strong support in the common council. Though the Government was disappointed at this crushing Presbyterian victory over the court candidates, the official view was that 'Jones of late years hath been esteemed both honest and able', and he was the only City Member not listed as a friend by Lord Wharton. He never held municipal office again, but he was the last London MP to receive wages, which he continued to draw throughout the Cavalier Parliament, and, on the grounds of 'his attendance upon public affairs', he was excused without the usual fine from serving as warden of his Company. He was probably an active Member, though until 1670 he is not usually distinguishable from Thomas Jones I*. He may have served on 244 committees, the majority being concerned with trade. He was teller in ten divisions, and made 18 recorded speeches. In the opening session 'Mr Jones' was named to the committees to consider the security bill and to inquire into the shortfall of the revenue. 'Captain Jones' (as he was still occasionally described) served on the committee for confirming the pawnbrokers' register, and it was presumably he who carried the bill to the Lords. After the autumn recess he may have helped to consider the bill for the execution of those under attainder and the additional corporations bill. With Sir Richard Ford* he undertook on 6 Dec. to give notice to the petitioners against the Dover harbour bill that the committee was prepared to consider 'a more fitting and reasonable way for the raising of money for the repair of the said harbour'. Jones's name usually occurs near the end of the list, but on 3 Mar. 1662 it stands first on the committee for the bill to regulate abuses in the packing of butter, and he probably introduced a petition on the same day from London tradesmen dealing in butter and cheese. He acted as teller against extending the imposition on Newcastle coals, London's principal fuel, to those shipped from Wearside. In 1663 he was among those ordered to bring in a bill for the better maintenance of the clergy in corporate towns, perhaps an indication that his religious opinions were evolving towards Anglicanism. But it is unlikely that he favoured the activities of the commissioners for corporations. He was among those ordered to consider the petition of his Shrewsbury namesake and the bill to restore the clerk of the chamber of London. Though he acted (with Sir William Thomp-

son*) as teller against the bill concerning the grant of offices in London on 30 June, he was named to the committee. He probably contributed to the great debate on trade initiated by Sir George Downing* in this session, for he was the first Member appointed to inspect the Import of Madder Act and to consider the bill to regulate the trade of weaving. On the report stage of the bill to vest in the Duke of York the profits of the postal service and the power of granting wine licences, he was teller on 6 July for an unsuccessful proviso on behalf of vintners' apprentices and the Haberdashers' Company, and later helped to manage a conference. He was among those sent to ask the King for a proclamation 'for the punctual and effectual execution and observance of the Act of Navigation', and for the withdrawal of dispensations from it. In 1664 'Mr Jones' acted as teller against another corporations bill and as manager of a conference on the conventicles bill. He was teller with his fellow-Grocer (Sir) John Frederick* in two divisions affecting the assessment of London in January 1665, and he was nominated to the abortive parliamentary accounts commission.[6]

Apart from serving on the committee for the accounts bill, Jones took no part, direct or indirect, in the proceedings against Clarendon. His chief activity in this session was over Irish cattle. He was named to the committee to review the Act, reporting on 9 Dec. 1667 that fresh legislation was necessary to prevent resale, and he also took the chair for the additional bill. On behalf of the merchants, he opposed a bill to fix the price of wine and punish adulteration, and he feared that an increase in customs duties would invite Spanish retaliation against English exports. 'The Dutch', he said, 'ease all commodities inwards in the customs, which invites all trade to them.' Having by now acquired a modest estate in Middlesex, he was able to complain of unjust taxation: 'he pays for his goods more than for his land in the country ratably'. Hearth-tax and excise, he thought, were particularly burdensome to corporations. He urged the House not to renew the Conventicles Act, and opposed legislation to reduce interest. He described the slitting of the nose of Sir John Coventry* as 'this horrid, un-English act . . . his soul trembles at the sad consequences'. By sitting day and night on the bill to punish the assailants, the House would give satisfaction to the country without delaying supply. He seconded the motion of Sir Trevor Williams* for the rejection of the subsidy bill. On 23 Feb. 1671 he made 'a long, sharp speech' against the additional excise on ale and beer, a very unpopular measure in the City. On the proposed bridge over the Thames at Putney, he declared:

This bill will question the very being of London; next to the pulling down the borough of Southwark, nothing can ruin it more. All the correspondences westward, for fuel and grain and hay, if this bridge be built, cannot be kept up. The water there is shallow at ebb; the correspondences of London require free passage at all times, and, if a bridge, a sculler can scarce pass at low water. It will alter the affairs of watermen to the King's danger and to the nation's.

He acted as teller against the bill.[7]

During the third Dutch war Jones was among those appointed to draft a bill for the general naturalization of foreign Protestants; but when the bill was brought in he acted as teller against committing it with another London Member, William Love*. In the debate on the speech from the throne on 12 May 1674, he produced a catalogue of grievances from his constituency. Speaking no longer as a merchant, but as a man in the street, he said:

The imposition upon coals is hard upon the rich, but destructive to the poor; thousands had died for the want of them, but for the favourableness of the weather. He has known London these 45 years, and never knew that impudence in meetings that the Papists have now. . . . Protections from the Lords' House and this ruin trade, together with shutting up the Exchequer; how can we secure that the Exchequer be not stopped to-morrow again?

He described the Leather Export Act as more of a burden than a tax of £70,000 a month, and he qualified as 'a great paradox' the assertion of Josiah Child* that the increase of building had improved the value of London houses. In 1675 he was named to committees on bills to relieve poor prisoners (12 May) and to prevent the growth of Popery (27 May) and illegal exactions (21 Oct.). Sir Richard Wiseman* professed himself unable to answer for the London Members in his report of 1676, but believed that 'the ascertaining the interest of the bankers' debt' could only be beneficial. But his name appeared on no other government list. Shaftesbury initially classed him as 'doubly worthy' in 1677, but altered it to 'vile', probably after Jones's speech of 4 Feb. 1678, when he approved supply to assist the allies against the French 'if there be reason for it'. He was appointed to the committee to reform the bankruptcy laws (27 Mar.), and acted as teller against limiting the benefit of the poor prisoners bill to those owing less than £500. After the Popish Plot he was named to the committee to hinder Papists from sitting in Parliament.[8]

On the dissolution of the Cavalier Parliament Jones retired to his country estate, though he remained an assistant of the Grocers' Company under the new charter of 1684. He died on 21 May 1692 and was buried at the cost of £600 at St. Bartholomew by the Exchange. His personal estate, exclusive of bad debts, amounted to some £20,000, the bulk of which went to charity. His executors paid out over £1,000 to his poor relations, and substantial sums to his Company and the London hospitals. Smaller bequests went to his school and the parishes where he was born and had resided. He left £100 each for the relief of Huguenot refugees and the redemption of English slaves in Africa. He endowed five Shropshire parishes and Hampton school, prescribing that the Anglican catechism should be taught there.[9]

[1] This biography is based on B. Garside, *Hist. Hampton Sch.* 131–56. [2] Excluded. [3] *London Top. Soc.* i. 44; Garside, 251–2. [4] Guildhall Lib. mss 11588/4, f. 493; *Ancient Vellum Bk.* ed. Raikes, 61, 81. [5] Grey, ii. 234; *Misc. Gen. et Her.* (ser. 2), ii. 53; *Studies in London Hist.* ed. Hollaender and Kellaway, 323–4. [6] *CSP Dom.* 1660–1, pp. 539, 542; *HMC Finch*, i. 120; *EHR*, lxvi. 35; *CJ*, viii. 305, 384, 531, 554, 564, 581, 588, 661. [7] *CJ*, ix. 55, 79, 230; *Milward*, 192, 197, 225; Grey, i. 96, 107, 276, 336–7, 415; *Dering*, 49, 83. [8] *CJ*, ix. 275; 509; Grey, ii. 234–5; iii. 10; v. 68; *Dering Pprs.* 63. [9] SP44/335/202; Garside, 112.

E.C.

JONES, Richard, 1st Earl of Ranelagh [I] (1641–1712), of St. James's Square, Westminster.

PLYMOUTH	1685
NEWTOWN I.o.W.	1689, 1690
CHICHESTER	1695
MARLBOROUGH	1698, 1701 (Feb.)
WEST LOOE	1701 (Dec.), 1702–1 Feb. 1703

b. 8 Feb. 1641, o.s. of Arthur Jones†, 2nd Visct. Ranelagh [I], by Lady Katherine Boyle, da. of Richard, 1st Earl of Cork [I]. *educ.* privately (John Milton); Oxf. Univ. 1656; travelled abroad (France and Italy) 1657–60. *m.* (1) 28 Oct. 1662, Elizabeth (*d.* 1 Aug. 1695), da. and coh. of Francis, 5th Baron Willoughby of Parham, 1s. *d.v.p.* 3da.; (2) 9 Jan. 1696, Lady Margaret Cecil (*d.* 21 Feb. 1728), da. of James Cecil*, 3rd Earl of Salisbury, wid. of John, 2nd Baron Stawell of Somerton, *s.p. suc.* fa. as 3rd Visct. Ranelagh 7 Jan. 1670; *cr.* Earl of Ranelagh 11 Dec. 1677.[1]

Gov. Roscommon Castle 1661–*d.*; constable, Athlone Castle 1674–*d.*; capt. of horse [I] by 1675–at least 1682, ft. [I] 1678–80.[2]

Chancellor of the Exchequer [I] 1668–74; PC [I] 1668–at least 1685; gent. of the privy chamber 1670, bedchamber 1679–85; ld. of the Treasury [I] 1670–5; v.-treas. [I] 1674–82; paymaster-gen. 1685–1702; PC 1 Mar. 1692–*d.*; member, R. Fishery Co. [I] 1692; supt. of buildings and works 1700–2; gov. Queen Anne's bounty 1704, commr. for South Sea Co. subscriptions 1711.[3]

J.p. Mdx. 1676–87; treas. Chelsea hospital 1686–1702; commr. for assessment, Hants 1690; ranger, Cranborne chase 1700–*d.*, Bagshot park by 1702–6.[4]

MP [I] 1661–2.
FRS 1663–82.

Lord Ranelagh's great-grandfather, of Lancashire origin, settled in Ireland, where he became Archbishop of Dublin and lord chancellor. His father, a drunken oaf, sat for Weobley in the Long Parliament until disabled for residing in the King's quarters. His mother, a strong-minded woman of eminent piety, extracted an allowance of £6 a week from Parliament for herself and her children, and consigned her only son to Milton's savage puritan discipline, which improved his intellect at the expense of his morals and religion. Burnet thought him one of the ablest men ever born in Ireland, 'capable of all affairs even in the midst of a loose run of pleasure and much riot'. On his return from his travels he was elected to the Dublin Parliament for Roscommon, and achieved conspicuous success with 'a set and studied harangue' against the land settlement. Ormonde tried to buy him off with the post of chancellor of the Exchequer, at a salary of £200 p.a., and a seat on the Privy Council; but on his father's death he moved to England, declaring that 'he will humour nobody, but stand on his own legs'. He shrewdly attached himself to the rising star Sir Thomas Osborne*, becoming one of his most intimate confidants, and formed a syndicate to farm the whole of the Irish revenues. A no less valuable friend was the Duchess of Portsmouth, who derived most of her income from this source and fought Ranelagh's battles at Court. Moreover 'he had a pleasantness in his conversation that took much with the King'. With Edward Seymour* too he shared a taste for womanizing that seems to have brought friendship rather than rivalry, and served him well in the Commons. But so vast a concession could not escape criticism. Ranelagh's uncle Lord Orrery (Roger Boyle*) refused to raise the subject, but on 20 Feb. 1674 the whole arrangement was bitterly attacked at Westminster by two other Irish peers, Lord Ibrackan (Henry O'Brien*) and Francis Aungier*, Lord Aungier. As the House was in committee Seymour was out of the chair, and was able to defend his crony as 'a worthy person, a loyal subject, a good Christian, and true to his friend'. This appears to have ended the debate, but the farm was not renewed, and Ranelagh began to look round for a seat. When a vacancy occurred at Cockermouth in the following year he hoped to be returned 'by the favour and help of Lady Northumberland'. Seymour undertook that he should have the writ, but his friend Lord Conway could not persuade Orlando Gee* to stand down, and he never went to the poll. He remained vice-treasurer of Ireland, and was promoted a step in the Irish peerage, but his position was undermined when Ormonde resumed the lord lieutenancy and declared his intention of probing his deliberately tangled accounts.[5]

Even before the dissolution of the Cavalier Parliament the serious illness of William Ashburnham*

had promised an early vacancy at Ludgershall, and the King and the Duke of York had 'done their parts to get my Lord Ranelagh chosen in his place'. Ashburnham in fact lived on for another year, but at the first general election of 1679 the King ordered William Legge II* to desist in Ranelagh's favour, 'for that his Majesty wanted speakers in the House'. He was defeated, and declared himself 'so much mortified as to resolve not to pretend anywhere else'. He was closely associated with the 'new undertakers' who had succeeded Stephen Fox* as the crown agents in the money market. Their enterprise collapsed ignominiously in 1679, and with them Ranelagh was reported to be 'all to pieces'. As a safeguard against his creditors he purchased a place at Court; but Ormonde added to his embarrassment by pressing for a settlement of his accounts. He was allowed to resign in 1682 and granted £16,000 as compensation.[6]

Ranelagh was at last successful at the general election of 1685, when he was returned for Plymouth by the Earl of Bath under the new charter, though by his own confession he 'did not know one person in that town'. An active Member of James II's Parliament, he was appointed to 12 committees, including those to recommend expunctions from the Journals and to draft the loyal address promising support against the Duke of Monmouth. On 22 June he carried to the Lords the bills to legalize the collection of revenue derived from the Post Office and the excise since the death of Charles II, and to enable the King to lease out the duchy of Cornwall lands. After the recess he spoke effectively in favour of granting £1,200,000 for defence:

> I do not intend to arraign the militia, but seeing a soldier is a trade and must (as all other trades are) be learned, I will show you where the militia has failed, viz. at Chatham and in June last when the late Duke of Monmouth landed and had but 83 men and £300 in money, who in spite of the militia, nay in spite of such other force as the King could spare hence, brought it so far as he did. If the King of France had landed then, what would have become of us? I say the militia is not insignificant, but an additional force is necessary.

He was among those ordered to draft the address against the employment of Roman Catholic officers in the army, but he cannot have voted for it, as he almost immediately succeeded Charles Fox* as paymaster on the recommendation of Lord Treasurer Rochester (Laurence Hyde*). The French ambassador wrote that he had 'distinguished himself in the recent Parliament in favour of the Court'. He was certainly most handsomely rewarded, for with the vast increase in the standing army the post was already worth £4,000 p.a. and the income continued to rise.[7]

Ordered in June 1688 by Sidney Godolphin I*
to stand for re-election at Plymouth, Ranelagh protested his lack of personal contacts there, only to be
told that 'the King's interest should supply that'. It
is unlikely that he contested the seat at the general
election of 1689, but he was returned for the Isle of
Wight borough of Newtown, no doubt with the
assistance of Sir Robert Holmes*. He voted to agree
with the Lords that the throne was not vacant, but
quickly rallied to the new regime, and retained his
office, now valued by his own reckoning at £6,910
p.a. net. A moderately active Member of the Convention, he made five recorded speeches and was
appointed to 15 committees, including the committee of elections and privileges in both sessions, and
those to inquire into the authors and advisers of
grievances, to consider the mutiny bills and to
provide for the relief of Protestant refugees from
Ireland. On 1 July he spoke against excepting
Lord Rochester from the indemnity bill, although he
admitted that membership of the ecclesiastical
commission was a crime. Later in the month he
was named to the committees to inquire into the
collection of the non-hereditary revenue after
Charles II's death and to prepare reasons for rejecting the Lords' amendments to the customs
duties proposed for tea, coffee and chocolate. After
the recess he was appointed to the committee of
inquiry into war expenditure, and made several
contributions to the debate, correcting the figures
produced by (Sir) Thomas Clarges* and assuring
the House that a replacement for Commissary
Shales had been sent to Ireland. He was also named
to the committees for giving security to Irish Protestants and attainting the Jacobites in Ireland.[8]

Ranelagh remained in Parliament as a placeman
under William and Anne. 'He had the art of
pleasing masters of very different tempers and
interests so much', wrote Burnet, 'that he continued above thirty years in great posts.' 'A bold
man', according to Macky, 'and very happy in
jests and repartees', he 'often turned the humour
of the House of Commons when they have
designed to have been very severe'. But in 1703 he
was expelled the House and dismissed from office
for misappropriating £72,000 of public money. 'A
great epicure and prodigiously expensive', he
'built more fine houses and laid out more on household furniture and gardening than any other nobleman in England.' He died in poverty and despair
on 5 Jan. 1712 and was buried in Westminster
Abbey. His cousin and heir did not assume the title
until 1759, after which he took his seat in the Irish
House of Lords; but no later member of the family
sat at Westminster.[9]

[1] R. Vaughan, *Hist. Protectorate*, ii. 174. [2] *HMC Ormonde*, ii.
202, 206, 216, 224, 229. [3] *HMC Ormonde*, n.s. v. 122; *Hist. King's
Works*, v. 35. [4] *Cal. Treas. Bks.* viii. 801; xvi. 342; xvii. 424, 973;
xx. 549; xxvi. 95. [5] *DNB*; Keeler, *Long Parl.* 238–9; *Cal. Comm.
Comp.* 1659; Burnet, i. 480; ii. 110; *CSP Ire.* 1663–5, pp. 682–3,
688; 1666–9, pp. 654, 662; Browning, *Danby*, i. 118, 134–5; *CSP
Dom.* 1671, pp. 257, 423; *Conway Letters* ed. Nicolson, 440; Grey,
ii. 441–5; *CJ*, ix. 312; *Essex Pprs.* (Cam. Soc. ser. 3, xxiv), 15, 28–
29; *HMC Ormonde*, n.s. iv. 29. [6] *HMC Ormonde*, n.s. iv. 153, 317,
439; vi. 218, 265, 351; *CSP Dom.* 1679–80, p. 90; Bodl. Carte 39,
f. 65; *Cal. Treas. Bks.* vii. 1330–2. [7] *Ellis Coresp.* ii. 20; Grey, viii.
355, 364; *Clarendon Coresp.* ii. 343; PRO31/3, bdle. 162, f. 207;
C. Clay, *Public Finance and Private Wealth*, 225. [8] *Ellis Coresp.* ii.
20; Clay, 131; Grey, ix. 383, 389, 428, 454. [9] Burnet, ii. 110;
Macky, *Mems.* 82.

P.W.

JONES, Samuel (c.1610–73), of Petersham, Surr.
and Courteenhall, Northants.

SHREWSBURY 1656,[1] 1660

b. c.1610, 2nd s. of Isaac Jones, Merchant Taylor, of
Austin Friars, London and Petersham by Elizabeth, da.
of Richard Prince of Abbey Foregate, Shrewsbury,
Salop. *educ.* Shrewsbury 1622. *m.* (1) by 1647, Margaret, da. of Timothy Middleton of Stansted Mountfitchet, Essex, *s.p.*; (2) lic. 1 June 1669, Mary, da. of Peter
Tryon of Bulwick, Northants., *s.p.* *suc.* fa. in Shrewsbury property 1652; kntd. 2 Sept. 1660; *suc.* bro. Sir
William Jones of Berwick, Salop 1663.[2]

Col. of ft. (parliamentary) 1643–5.[3]

Commr. for defence, Surr. 1643, assessment, Surr.
1644, 1657, Westminster 1652, Salop and Denb. Aug.
1660–1, Northants. Aug. 1660–9, Oxon. 1665–9; j.p.
Surr. 1644–52, Northants. 1662–*d.*; sheriff, Northants.
1652–3, Salop 1663–4, Oxon. 1669–70; commr. for
militia, Salop 1659, Salop and Northants. Mar. 1660;
col. of militia ft. Northants. 1661–?*d.*; sec. and auditor
to council in the marches of Wales 1663–*d.*[4]

Gent. of privy chamber 1667–*d.*[5]

Jones's grandfather, of Denbighshire origin,
became a wealthy Shrewsbury merchant, serving
four terms as bailiff of the borough. His father
moved to London and acquired considerable property in his native county and in Surrey. He was
ordered into custody during the Civil War for failure to pay his assessment to the committee for the
advance of money, but Jones himself commanded
a regiment under the Presbyterian Earl of Manchester. His services were not required by the New
Model Army, but he held local office under the
Commonwealth. To the property in Shrewsbury
and Surrey that he inherited under his father's will,
he added Courteenhall and other purchases, bringing his total income up to £3,000 p.a.[6]

Jones became the first of his family to enter Parliament when he was returned for Shrewsbury in
1656. He regained his seat at the general election of
1660, probably owing chiefly to the interest of his
cousin Thomas Jones I* with the Presbyterian corporation, and he was classed as a friend by Lord
Wharton. Nevertheless he had already begun to

work his passage with the offer of a loan to the exiled Court, and in the Convention he was to reveal himself as an ultra-Royalist. A moderately active Member, he made 18 recorded speeches, and acted as teller in four divisions. He was named to 29 committees, including those for the land purchases bill and the bill of indemnity, to both of which his attitude was anything but cordial. On 24 May he was one of five Members sent into the City to raise £2,000 'for the present service of his Majesty', but 'finding difficulty therein', as John Frederick* reported, they agreed to advance the whole amount themselves, for which they received the thanks of the House.[7]

After the Restoration Jones was among those commissioned to administer the oaths of allegiance and supremacy to his fellow-Members. He played a prominent and generally harsh part in the debates on the indemnity bill. On 8 June he was among those ordered to establish the names of those who had sat in judgment on Charles I before the day of the verdict, and he acted as teller against limiting the number of those to be excepted from the bill. On individual cases, he was against putting the question on William Sydenham† and Bulstrode Whitelocke†, against pardoning the clerical agitator Hugh Peter, against reading a petition from Oliver St. John†, and against extending the period of grace for the regicides to give themselves up. He was entrusted with reporting the debts charged on the Exchequer on 20 June. For settling religion he first proposed a committee of the whole House, and then, three days later, a synod of divines. On 4 July he 'urged very strongly' that Protectorate officials should be compelled to refund their salaries. He moved against the purchasers of crown lands and the property of cathedral chapters, 'but to consider the soldiers under General [George] Monck*'. On 26 July he was ordered to draft an address for negotiations with the Dutch over the discriminatory taxes imposed on imported cloth. On the following day he was named to the committee for the navigation bill, and urged the House to proceed with supply. With regard to ecclesiastical livings, he proposed that the intruded ministers should be given till Michaelmas to quit, and should divide the profits with the incumbents. He was appointed to the committees to consider the bill for settling ministers, and also to estimate the revenue necessary to 'maintain the splendour and grandeur of the kingly office'. But his speeches were becoming less acceptable to the House. Robert Shapcote*, falsely accused by him of sitting in a high court of justice, contemptuously 'desired that, if Colonel Jones were not careful of other men's credit, he would be

of his own'. A strong supporter of the Lords' amendments to the indemnity bill, Jones demanded extravagantly: 'What will the world say to [hear us] speak for the King's murderers?' Called to order by another Devonian, Sir John Northcote*, he was obliged to explain that 'he did not reflect upon any person'. On 23 Aug. he reported a Shropshire estate bill, and on 4 Sept. he carried his draft address on Dutch taxation, as amended on the floor of the House, to the Lords. Two days later he returned, to remind them of a number of bills awaiting completion, including the bill for settling ministers and the navigation bill, and he helped to manage the conference of 11 Sept. on disbanding the army.[8]

For his loyalty Jones had already been rewarded with a knighthood before the House rose for the autumn recess. In the second session he was added to the committee to bring in a militia bill 'that they might know, he said, how to govern and be governed'. He proposed on 19 Nov. that the crown should be compensated for the loss of feudal revenues with a grant of excise, and a week later he was teller for a bill to empower the corporation of London to levy a rate for the militia. But a proposal from Heneage Finch* to include him among those to be rewarded for their services and sufferings only 'set the House into laughing'. He provided further light relief during the debate on the bill to encourage the fisheries, in which a clause had been inserted to make Wednesday a meatless day.

> Sir Samuel Jones offered a proviso to it that all travellers on the road might have liberty to have flesh dressed at their inns.... Sir William Doyley* jestingly said that it was fit Sir Samuel Jones and his family only should be excepted out of the bill for this motion. The bill passed without the proviso.[9]

Jones's concern to maintain the standards of hospitality at the English roadside inn was natural in view of his widespread estates, which must have required constant travelling. But his interest was not commensurate, and he was unable to find a seat in the Cavalier Parliament. Though he inherited further property in Shropshire in 1663 as well as an office in the court in the marches, in Northamptonshire he seems to have been even less able to command respect than at Westminster. He died on 3 Jan. 1673, aged 63, and was buried at Courteenhall. Under his will he endowed almshouses on his Shropshire estate and a school at Courteenhall, besides leaving £500 to be used for interest-free loans to young tradesmen in Shrewsbury. Jones was the last of this branch of the family, although he stipulated that his heirs should assume the name. His widow married Charles Bertie*.[10]

[1] Excluded. [2] Vis. London (Harl. Soc. xvii), 18; Le Neve's Knights

(Harl. Soc. viii), 109; *Misc. Gen. et Her.* (ser. 3), ii. 262; *London Mar. Lic.* ed. Foster, 775. [3] *CSP Dom.* 1644–5, pp. 160, 343. [4] Add. 34222, f. 20; *Trans. Salop Arch. Soc.* (ser. 4), viii. 106–7. [5] Carlisle, *Privy Chamber*, 179. [6] *Trans. Salop Arch. Soc.* (ser. 4), xii. 214; *Cal. Comm. Adv. Money*, 142; PCC 129 Bowyer; Bridges, *Northants.* i. 353; *Cal. Cl. SP*, v. 7. [7] Owen and Blakeway, *Hist. Shrewsbury*, i. 482; *Cal. Cl. SP*, v. 7; *CJ*, viii. 45. [8] *CJ*, viii. 59, 63, 69, 106; Bowman diary, ff. 10v. 28, 39, 49v, 56, 68v, 71, 99, 109, 137, 147, 152. [9] *Old Parl. Hist.* xxiii. 18, 24, 53, 58, 68; *CJ*, viii. 181, 192. [10] *EHR*, xlvi. 249–51; *Trans. Salop Arch. Soc.* (ser. 4), viii. 97–114.

M.W.H./E.C.

JONES, Thomas I (1614–92), of Shrewsbury, Salop and Cerreghwfa, Mont.

SHREWSBURY 1660, 1661–13 Apr. 1676

b. 13 Oct. 1614, 2nd s. of Edward Jones (*d.*1648) of Shrewsbury and Sandford by Mary, da. of Robert Powell of Whittington Park; bro. of William Jones†. *educ.* Shrewsbury 1627; Emmanuel, Camb. 1629; L. Inn 1629, called 1636. *m.* c.1640, Jane, da. of Daniel Bavand of Chester, 5s. 6da. Kntd. 26 Oct. 1671; *suc.* nephew William 1679.[1]

Alderman, Shrewsbury 1638–62, town clerk Apr. 1660–2; bencher, L. Inn May 1660; j.p. Salop July 1660–87; commr. for assessment, Salop Aug. 1660–80, 1689–90, Shrewsbury 1663–4, Mont. Aug. 1660–1, 1663–80, 1689, Caern. and Denb. 1673–4, Mdx. 1677–9, oyer and terminer, Wales 1661; second justice, N. Wales circuit 1662–70, c.j. 1670–6; commr. for recusants, Salop 1675; freeman, Preston 1682.[2]

Serjeant-at-law 1669, King's serjeant 1671; j.K.b. 13 Apr. 1676–83; l.c.j.c.p. 1683–6.

Jones's ancestors had been prominent in Shrewsbury municipal life since Elizabethan times. His father was steward of the borough, and his elder brother William recorder. Jones himself, after qualifying as a barrister, set up in practice in his home town and was nominated to the corporation in the charter of 1638. While Shrewsbury remained a royalist garrison Prince Rupert resided at his house. He was taken prisoner when the town was surprised by the Parliamentarians in February 1645. But the commissioners for corporations later alleged that he had

> declared himself against the commission of array in the time of the wars, which was the dispute between the King and the Parliament, and refused to find a dragoon for the King's service, for which he was committed by Sir Francis Ottley, then governor of Shrewsbury; which commitment Mr Jones afterwards brought two men to testify to before the Parliament's committee in that town as an argument of his good affection to them. His brother, that was of the Parliament's party and recorder of the town in the time of the rebellion, declared him then publicly upon the bench at a quarter sessions a man well-affected to the Parliament.[3]

Jones's cousin, Col. Samuel Jones*, was elected for Shrewsbury in 1656, the first of the family to sit in Parliament, and they were returned together at the general election of 1660. On the next day

Jones was elected town clerk. 'A great countenancer of the Presbyterian party' he was marked as a friend by Lord Wharton, and probably voted with the Opposition. But he was not active in the Convention, with no recorded speeches and only five committees, the committee of elections and privileges, and those to prepare the clauses of exception to the indemnity bill and to consider a naturalization bill, a Shropshire estate bill, and the wine licences bill. He advised the corporation how to evade the Act by filling up their vacancies and was alleged to have described the arrest of three local radicals after the Fifth Monarchist rising in London as unlawful.[4]

Re-elected for Shrewsbury in 1661, Jones is seldom distinguished in the Journals from John Jones*, but he probably remained inactive in the Cavalier Parliament. He was certainly appointed to 38 committees, including those to consider the uniformity bill and to inquire into the shortfall in the revenue in the first session. In August 1662 he was made a Welsh judge; but in the same month he was removed from corporation office in his constituency by the commissioners as politically unreliable, and in particular for giving 'encouragement to the factious ministers there (he being a Parliament man) to preach so boldly and seditiously as they did, and to refuse all along to read the common prayers'. His petition to the House was referred on 5 Mar. 1663 to a committee including all the Shropshire Members, which was ordered to report 'with what speed they can', but never did so. He probably took the chair for a Montgomeryshire estate bill in 1665.[5]

Jones went over to the Court under the Cabal, being promoted to chief justice of the North Wales circuit, knighted, and made a King's serjeant. The Opposition reckoned him among the court party in 1671, describing him (perhaps ironically) as 'almost famished for preferment, and a great wheedler to the projectors', and his name appeared on the Paston list in 1673/4. He became more active in 1675, receiving the government whip for both sessions from Secretary Coventry. He was among those ordered to draw up reasons for demanding the removal of Lauderdale, but he opposed an address against the pardon granted to the Scottish minister: 'If we have not a confidence in the King's mercy, he knows not whether we can have confidence in anything'. He also helped to prepare reasons for four conferences on the disputes over the judicature of the Lords. He was listed among the officials and government speakers in the House, and apparently designed by Danby as chairman of the supply committee in the autumn session. 'Jones being very forward to take the chair, [Sir Thomas] Meres* gave him a check, and said he would rather

have [Sir Charles] Harbord* for his modesty.'
During the recess Sir Richard Wiseman* listed
Jones among the court supporters in the Commons,
but Danby had apparently concluded that he would
be more useful elsewhere and he was made a high
court judge.[6]

Roger North* described Jones as

a very reverend and learned judge, a gentleman, and impartial, but being of Welsh extraction was apt to be
warm, and when much offended often shewed his heats
in a rubor of countenance set off by his grey hairs, but
appeared in no other disorder, for he restrained himself
in due bounds and temper, and seldom or never broke
the laws of his gravity.

In 1677 he refused to interfere with the commitment of Shaftesbury to the Tower by the House
of Lords, and but for the dissolution of the second
Exclusion Parliament he would have been impeached for discharging the Middlesex grand jury
to prevent the presentment of the Duke of York as
a Popish recusant. When an action for extortion was
brought against Serjeant Topham in 1682 by an
Abhorrer, Jones was one of the judges who rejected
his plea that he had only acted on the orders of the
Commons. He pronounced judgment against the
corporation of London in the quo warranto proceedings in 1683, and succeeded Sir Francis North*
as chief justice of common pleas. But he was
removed by James II for ruling against the dispensing power. According to his son Jones told the
King that:

he was not sorry for himself to be laid aside, being old
and worn-out in his service, but that his Majesty should
expect such a construction of the law from him as he
could not honestly give; and that none but indigent,
ignorant, or ambitious people would give their judgments as he expected.

After the Revolution the Commons resolved that
his judgment against Topham was a breach of their
privileges. He was taken into custody on 19 July
1689, but released on the prorogation a fortnight
later. He died in May 1692 and was buried at St.
Alkmund's, Shrewsbury. His grandson Thomas
was returned for the borough in three elections as a
Whig.[7]

[1] PCC 162 King, 140 Fane; *Trans. Salop Arch. Soc.* (ser. 4), xii.
215–17. [2] Owen and Blakeway, *Shrewsbury*, i. 407, 543; W. J. Williams, *Gt. Sessions in Wales*, 104; *Preston Guild Roll* (Lancs. and
Cheshire Rec. Soc. ix), 190. [3] *Trans. Salop Arch. Soc.* (ser. 4), i.
299; xii. 214–16. [4] Owen and Blakeway, i. 543, 551; *Trans. Salop
Arch. Soc.* (ser. 4), i. 297–8. [5] *Trans. Salop Arch. Soc.* (ser. 4), i.
296–7; *CJ*, viii. 444, 595. [6] Harl. 7020, f. 38; Grey, iii. 217, 301;
Dering Pprs. 94, 95, 97. [7] R. North, *Examen*, 563; *HMC Finch*, ii.
103; *HMC 12th Rep. IX*, 103; *Reresby Mems.* 422; *CJ*, x. 227;
State Trials, xii. 831–4.

E.C.

JONES, Thomas II (*d.*1711), of Lincoln's Inn.

EAST GRINSTEAD 1685

2nd s. of Thomas Jones I*. *educ.* G. Inn; L. Inn 1669. *m.*
by 1666, Jane, da. of Thomas Wilkinson of Kirkbrigg,
Yorks., 3s. 2da.[1]
KC 1683–?89; bencher, L. Inn 1683, treas. 1685, librarian 1695.[2]

Jones was destined to follow his father at the bar,
but his education seems to have followed a peculiar
course, for there is no trace either of his entry at
Gray's Inn, whence he transferred to his father's
Inn as an utter barrister, nor of his call at Lincoln's
Inn. He took silk when his father became chief justice of the common pleas in 1683, and was returned
as court candidate for East Grinstead two years
later. It was probably he, rather than Edward
Jones*, who was a moderately active committeeman
in James II's Parliament, being named to eight
committees, of which the most important was to
recommend expunctions from the Journals. In 1686
he took charge of the prosecution of William Williams*, who jibed: 'Mr Jones will never leave persecuting me till he has made me as beggarly as himself'.[3]

After the Revolution, Jones remained a high
Tory, and probably a Jacobite, as alleged by the
notorious informer William Fuller. He was counsel
for Matthew Crone in 1690, but left the country in
February 1692, and a few months later his father
judged it wisest to alter his will, appointing trustees
for the estate which had been devised to him. He
had returned to England before Fenwick's plot,
when his chambers, which had a private entrance
from Chancery Lane, were used for meetings by
Father Charnock, the leader of the assassins. When
Charnock was arrested, he asked for Jones as his
counsel, but he was indisposed. He died on 8 Oct.
1711, and was buried in Lincoln's Inn Chapel. His
nephew Thomas was three times returned for
Shrewsbury as a Whig, but none of his direct descendants in the male line sat in Parliament.[4]

[1] *Le Neve's Knights* (Harl. Soc. viii), 269; *L. Inn Black Bks.* iii.
61, 141, 150, 191; *Dugdale's Vis. Yorks.* ed. Clay, i. 85. [2] Luttrell,
i. 247. [3] R. Morrice, Entering Bk. 2, p. 114. [4] *CSP Dom.* 1689–90,
p. 147; 1691–2, p. 145; 1696, p. 74; 1700–2, p. 482; PCC 140
Fane; Ailesbury, *Mems.* 356; *L. Inn Black Bks.* iii. 225; Luttrell,
iv. 26; *Lexington Pprs.* 182; *L. Inn Reg.* 647.

B.M.C.

JONES, Sir William (1630–82), of Southampton Square, Bloomsbury, Mdx. and Ramsbury, Wilts.

PLYMOUTH 3 Nov. 1680, 1681

bap. 3 July 1630, 2nd s. of Richard Jones† (*d.*1692) of
Stowey Court, Chew Magna, Som. by Joyce Wood-

ward. *educ.* G. Inn 1647, called 1655. *m.* lic. 11 Sept.
1661, Elizabeth, da. of Edmund Alleyn of Hatfield
Peverel, Essex, wid. of John Robinson of Denston Hall,
Suff., 2s. (1 *d.v.p.*) 2da. Kntd. 15 July 1671.[1]

Standing counsel, Exeter 1668; bencher, G. Inn
1671, reader 1674; j.p. Mdx. 1674–?*d.*; commr. for
assessment, Berks. 1677–80, Mdx. and Westminster
1677–9.[2]

KC 1671; solicitor-gen. 1673–5; attorney-gen. 1675–
9.

Jones's family had held the small estate of Stowey
Court since Elizabethan times. His father was a
parliamentary supporter during the Civil War, held
county office throughout the Interregnum, and
represented Somerset in the first Protectorate Parliament. Jones became a lawyer, and by 1671 he
was reckoned among the most learned of his profession. With the Duke of Buckingham's support
he looked for and achieved rapid advancement, and
built up a considerable estate on the Berkshire-
Wiltshire borders from his earnings; but his manic-
depressive temperament put him always one step
behind his rival Sir Francis North*. As early as
1676 he was 'much in with that knot' of opposition
politicians, including Sir Thomas Player* and
Silius Titus*, but he remained a crown lawyer until
October 1679, leading for the prosecution in the
Popish Plot trials. For his resignation from this
lucrative post, in which he earned 'no less than
£6,000 per annum', he gave as his reasons ill-health
and the death of his infant son, but it was also
asserted that 'he was very weary of the Plot
prosecutions'. He remained politically inactive for
another 12 months, refusing all crown appointments, but declining also to sign the petition for
the meeting of Parliament. Indeed as late as October 1680 some considered him 'a firm friend to the
Court'.[3]

Hence it is not surprising that a pamphleteer
should inquire how 'a very worthy knight dwelling
in Southampton Square (though otherwise of very
great abilities)' could be 'sufficiently qualified for a
burgess of Plymouth', when Jones stood for the
borough on the death of John Sparke*, probably
on the interest of John Maynard I*. But on his
election he at once joined the leaders of the Opposition in the House, despite his total lack of parliamentary experience. A very active Member of the
second Exclusion Parliament, he was named to 31
committees and delivered some 50 recorded
speeches. His oratorical skill was enhanced by the
slight west-country accent that he affected. His
commitment to exclusion was total. In his maiden
speech he declared:

> I have as much respect for the Duke as any person, but I
> must have respect to religion above all things.... The
> question is whether a Popish prince can inherit the

crown of England without a loss of all our laws? ... We
do not punish the Duke as a criminal, but we are preventing the evil that is likely to befall us from the religion he professes.... It is for the benefit of the King
and Protestant religion that this bill pass and I am for
it.

The fact that such a notoriously timid soul, who
shrank from the dangers which other men courted,
could speak so vigorously for the bill 'made people
generally conclude that the thing was certain and
safe and would at last be agreed on all parts'. On 11
Nov. he reported an address attacking the 'pernicious counsels' of those who had advised prorogation.
He denounced the proclamation against petitioning
as taking away 'the very liberty of Englishmen',
insinuating that his rival North was the real author
of the proclamation. He was appointed to the committee for the impeachment of Edward Seymour*.
As one of the principal managers of Lord Stafford's
impeachment, he was described as 'mighty sweet in
words, but sour enough in sense'. He maintained
that 'the Parliament of England has power over all
the subjects of England; we may banish them out of
any place', and was appointed to a small committee
on 15 Dec. 1680 to bring in a bill to expel all the
considerable Papists 'out of the King's dominions'.
He supported the idea of an association, but not as
a substitute for exclusion, on which he never
wavered. 'Without the exclusion bill,' he said 'there
can be no expedient, but what will leave us in that
miserable condition of having first or last a contest
with our lawful King.... If the act does not pass to
exclude the Duke, an act of association would be
treason when the Duke becomes King.' He was the
only lawyer on the committee appointed on 24 Dec.
to bring in a bill repealing the Corporations Act,
and he spoke in favour of relaxing the laws against
Protestant dissenters, because 'the Papists have
offered them larger terms than this, and if they are
refused some liberty now, the Papists' hopes will
be more upon this sort of people'.[4]

After the failure of the Opposition in the second
Exclusion Parliament, it was widely rumoured that
some of their leaders would privately come to
terms, and that Jones would at last be made chief
justice of the common pleas. But nothing came of
it, and after his re-election he remained firmly
committed to exclusion in the Oxford Parliament.
He was appointed to the committees to draw up the
articles of impeachment against Fitzharris and the
third exclusion bill. He argued with Burnet against
a regency, and he stated in the House that

> it is less evil or injustice to take away from him both the
> crown and power than to leave him both but the
> name ... but if this can be made effectual, I am as
> willing to exclude the Duke's power as name.... If

there must be an army to maintain the bill of exclusion, there must be four armies to maintain the expedient.

Jones was appointed to a total of five committees during the week-long Parliament. On 26 Mar. he reported reasons for a conference on the loss of the bill of ease for dissenters, and he was on his feet making his seventh and last speech, in support of the Fitzharris impeachment, when Black Rod knocked at the door. After the Parliament was dissolved Jones published *A Just and Modest Vindication of the Proceedings of the Two Last Parliaments of King Charles II*, in which he claimed that the King's declaration was composed by a Frenchman, and that the dissolution was due solely to the 'influence of a few evil men on the King's mind'. In defence of the Parliaments Jones stated that

> never did men husband their time to more advantage; they opened the eyes of the nation; they showed them their danger with a freedom becoming Englishmen; they asserted the people's right of petitioning; they proceeded vigorously against the conspirators discovered and heartily endeavoured to take away the very root of the conspiracy; they had before them as many great and useful bills as had been seen in any Parliament, and it is not to be laid at their doors that they proved abortive.[5]

Perhaps Jones 'grew weary of the restless party' after the Oxford Parliament, as one friend observed. He certainly was less active and, it is claimed, his dislike of Shaftesbury became obsessive. Nevertheless, he was often seen 'locked up' with his friend Lord Russell (Hon. William Russell*) and the Prince of Orange in the last year of his life, and he undertook to help in the defence of London's charter. Jones died 'very rich' on 2 May 1682, an event seen by some as a victory for the Court and by others as a loss to the City. Thomas Pelham*, who had married his daughter, and Dean Tillotson were his executors. His nephew Richard, who inherited the Ramsbury estate, was returned for Marlborough as a Tory in 1712.[6]

[1] F. A. Wood, *Hist. Chew Magna*, 176; *Le Neve's Knights* (Harl. Soc. viii), 250; Morant, *Essex*, ii. 99, 132. [2] Exeter corp. act bk. II, f. 74. [3] *DNB*; Harbin, *Som. Members*, 162; Burnet, ii. 106; *VCH Berks*. iii. 253; iv. 120, 160, 212, 248; *CSP Dom*. 1675–6, p. 562–3; 1677–8, p. 426; 1679–80, p. 263; *Ailesbury Mems*. i. 36; R. North, *Examen*, 508–10, 514, 515, 540; *HMC 7th Rep*. 476; *HMC Ormonde*, n.s. iv. 544, 569; v. 454; *HMC Le Fleming*, 163. [4] J. Thirsk and J. P. Cooper, *17th Cent. Econ. Problems*, 408; Burnet, ii. 343; Temple, *Works*, ii. 549, 582–3; Grey, vii. 451, 459, 465–6; viii. 61, 62, 63, 65, 66, 68, 70, 161, 167–8, 216; *Exact Coll. Debates*, 192; *HMC Ormonde*, n.s. v. 515; *HMC 12th Rep. IX*, 110. [5] *HMC Ormonde*, n.s. v. 562; vi. 48; Grey, viii. 320, 339; Burnet, ii. 282; *HMC Finch*, ii. 99. [6] *Ailesbury Mems*. i. 36; North, 508; *CSP Dom*. 1682, p. 40; Dalrymple, *Mems*. pt. 1, bk. 1, p. 73; *HMC Hastings*, ii. 392; PRO 31/3, bdle. 149, f. 104; *HMC Astley*, 51; Temple, 549; PCC 58 Cottle.

J.S.C.

KAYE, Sir John, 2nd Bt. (c.1641–1706), of Woodsome, Yorks.

YORKSHIRE   1685, 1689, 1690, 1695, 1701 (Feb.), 1702, 1705–8 Aug. 1706

b. c.1641, 1st s. of Sir John Kaye, 1st Bt., of Woodsome by 1st w. Margaret, da. and coh. of John Moseley of Northcroft. *educ*. M. Temple 1659. *m*. bef. 1664, Anne, da. of William Lister of Thornton, 5s. (2 *d.v.p.*) 2da. *suc*. fa. 25 July 1662.[1]

J.p. Yorks. (W. Riding) by 1663–Sept. 1688, Nov. 1688–*d*.; commr. for assessment (W. Riding) 1663–80, (W. and E. Ridings) 1689–90, (N. Riding) 1690, Lincs. 1689; dep. lt. (W. Riding) 1664–?Sept. 1688, Oct. 1688–*d*., lt.-col. of militia ft. by 1678–?Sept. 1688, col. Oct. 1688–?*d*.; freeman, Preston 1682.[2]

Kaye's family acquired Woodsome in the reign of Henry VII. His grandfather was elected for Eye in 1610. His father owned an estate worth £1,000 a year before the Civil War, including fulling mills and coal mines. He raised a regiment of horse for the King, and compounded in 1645 for only £500 in view of £3,000 debts; but he held county office again after the Restoration.[3]

Kaye stood at the first general election of 1679 against the exclusionist candidate Lord Clifford (Charles Boyle*) with the support of Lord Latimer (Edward Osborne*) and Sir Richard Grahme*. However, at the county meeting on 7 Feb. he withdrew to save the county trouble and expense. Clifford and Henry Fairfax*, Lord Fairfax, the other candidate, attempted unsuccessfully to find him a seat at Aldborough. In the autumn he stood again, alone, against Clifford and Fairfax. Sir John Reresby was active on his behalf, and nearly 6,000 supporters came to the election in York, but he desisted after a three-day poll, probably owing to the enormous costs involved. He was unsuccessful at Pontefract in 1681. In the years 1682–4 he took part in breaking up conventicles in Yorkshire, but he was not harsh to the nonconformists, one of whom described him as 'a man of great mildness and moderation and a swaying man'. He was returned unopposed for the county in 1685 and listed among the Opposition. A moderately active Member of James II's Parliament, he was added to the committee to recommend expunctions from the Journals when it was revived on 3 June, and appointed to six others of secondary importance.[4]

Kaye gave negative replies to the questions on the repeal of the Test Act and Penal Laws, and was removed from the commission of the peace. Nevertheless he was expected to be re-elected. During the Revolution he was chosen colonel of about seven thousand volunteers. Many of them were persuaded by Danby and the Hon. Thomas Fairfax* to declare for the Prince of Orange, but Kaye refused, and took no part in the abortive election of 24 Dec. Before the general election in the following month, Danby and 22 of his friends attempted to dissuade Kaye from standing for the county, but he was returned unopposed. Again moderately active in the Convention, he did not vote to agree with the Lords that the throne was not vacant. Of his 13 committees, the most important in the first session were to bring in a bill to regulate the militia (24 Apr.) and to prepare reasons for a conference on disarming Papists (7 May). After the recess he was among the Members entrusted with the second mutiny bill, the inquiry into the state of the revenue, and the bill for the security of Irish Protestants. A letter of his of 6 Feb. 1690 to the mayor of Leeds shows that he was a strong opponent of the disabling clause in the bill to restore corporations. He was classed as a government supporter in 1690–2, signed the Association in 1696, and appears to have been a moderate Tory under Anne. He died on 8 Aug. 1706, aged 65, and was buried at Almondbury. His eldest son represented Yorkshire as a Tory from 1710 to his death in 1726.[5]

[1] Clay, *Dugdale's Vis. Yorks.* i. 74. [2] Add. 29674, f. 160; Browning, *Danby*, ii. 20; Yale Lib. Osborn mss; *Reresby Mems.* 584; *Bradford Antiquary* n.s. vi. 404; *Preston Guild Rolls* (Lancs. and Cheshire Rec. Soc. ix), 190. [3] J. T. Cliffe, *Yorks. Gentry*, 53, 97, 356; *Royalist Comp. Pprs.* (Yorks. Arch. Soc. rec. ser. xviii), 2. [4] *HMC Astley*, 38–40; *HMC Var.* ii. 166–7, 393; O. Heywood, *Diaries*, iii. 119–20; *Reresby*, 185–8, 276; *Dom. Intell.* 26 Sept. 1679; *Parl. Rep. Yorks.* (Yorks. Arch. Soc. rec. ser. xcvi), 94. [5] *Reresby*, 584–5; *Yorks. Arch. Jnl.* x. 61, 163, 164; *Parl. Rep. Yorks.* 94, 174; *Camb. Hist. Jnl.* v. 249.

E.C.

KEATE, Sir Jonathan, 1st Bt. (1633–1700), of The Hoo, Kimpton, Herts.

HERTFORDSHIRE 1679 (Oct.)

bap. 14 Feb. 1633, 2nd but 1st surv. s. of Gilbert Keate, Grocer, of Water Lane, London, being 1st s. by 2nd w. Elizabeth, da. of Gilbert Armstrong of Rempstone, Notts. *m.* (1) 1 May 1655, Susannah (*d.* 11 June 1673), da. and h. of Thomas Hoo of Kimpton, 2s. (1 *d.v.p.*) 3da.; (2) lic. 17 Mar. 1675, Susannah (*d.* 13 Jan. 1720), da. of John Orlebar, Merchant Taylor, of London, *s.p. suc.* fa. 1658; *cr.* Bt. 12 June 1660.[1]

Commr. for militia, Herts. Mar. 1660, j.p. July 1660–70, bef. 1696–*d.*; commr. for assessment, Herts. 1664–80, 1689–90, Kent 1673–9; sheriff, Herts. 1665–6; commr. for concealments, Mdx. and Surr. 1670.[2]

Keate came from a cadet branch of a family settled in Berkshire in the early 16th century. His father was apprenticed to a London Grocer and prospered as a ship-owner, sugar-refiner, and a substantial investor in the East India Company. He was not active during the Civil War, and after one nomination as an assessment commissioner in 1648 he fined for alderman in 1650. As a merchant he

chartered ships to the Commonwealth and Protectorate. Keate himself also became a merchant, and during the Interregnum imported sugar from Barbados. He retired from business after his wife inherited the Hoo estate, rebuilt the mansion there, and later acquired two adjacent manors. At the Restoration he was granted a baronetcy and appointed to the commission of the peace; but he was removed in 1670, presumably as a opponent of the second Conventicles Act.[3]

Keate was returned for the county at a contested election in August 1679, doubtless as an exclusionist. A moderately active Member of the second Exclusion Parliament, he made no recorded speeches, but he was appointed to five committees, including those to inspect the law concerning the anniversary of the Gunpowder Plot, to draw up an address for a fast, and to examine the disbandment accounts. He is not known to have stood again. Though he conformed to the Anglican church, an ejected Presbyterian minister served him at an unknown period, and he maintained a Congregationalist chaplain from 1683 to 1688. He appears to have been restored as a j.p. after the Revolution, and signed the Association in 1696. He died on 17 Sept. 1700 and was buried at Kimpton, the only member of his family to sit in Parliament.[4]

[1] *St. Dunstan in the East* (Harl. Soc. Reg. lxix), 67; (lxxxiv), 46, 73; *London Mar. Lic.* ed. Foster, 781; Clutterbuck, *Herts.* iii. 73. [2] *Cal. Treas. Bks.* iii. 607. [3] *Vis. Berks.* (Harl. Soc. lvii), 162–3; *Inhabitants of London in 1638* ed. Dale, 50; *Cal. Co. Mins. E. I. Co.* ed. Sainsbury, ii. 262; v. 153; *CSP Dom.* 1651–2, p. 526; 1652–3, p. 137; 1655, p. 545; *CSP Col.* i. 432; ii. 14; *VCH Herts.* ii. 407; iii. 30, 31; Clutterbuck, iii. 77. [4] D. R. Lacey, *Dissent and Parl. Pols.* 417; *Herts. Recs.* vi. 523; Clutterbuck, ii. 192; iii. 77.

E.R.E./G.J.

KELLAND, Charles (1660–95) of Painsford, Ashprington, Devon.

TOTNES 1681

b. 6 May 1660, 2nd but 1st surv. s. of John Kelland*. *educ.* Exeter, Oxf. 1679; M. Temple 1680. *m.* (1) 30 Oct. 1684 (with £5,000), Margaret, da. and coh. of Thomas Drewe† of Broadhembury Grange, 1s. 2da.; (2) 23 Aug. 1694, Bridget, da. of Richard Coffin of Portledge, 1da. *suc.* fa. 1692.[1]

J.p. Devon c.1681–July 1688, 1694–*d.*

Kelland was chosen with his father to represent Totnes in the third Exclusion Parliament, but neither left any trace on its records. If he reached Oxford in time, he probably voted with the country party. He was not re-elected in 1685, when Sir Edward Seymour* resumed his seat. His answers on the repeal of the Test Act and Penal Laws were negative, like his father's, and he is not known to have stood again. He was buried at Ashprington on

5 July 1695. His only son never sat in Parliament and died unmarried at the age of 22, but his brother-in-law, Arthur Champernowne, was returned for Totnes in 1715 and his nephew Kelland Courtenay in 1734.

[1] Vivian, *Vis. Devon*, 504; Devon RO, 118M/T30.

J.P.F.

KELLAND, John (c.1635–92), of Painsford, Ashprington, Devon.

TOTNES   1679 (Mar.), 1681, 1685

> b. c.1635, 1st s. of John Kelland of Totnes and Painsford by Susanna, da. of Thomas Fownes of Plymouth. *educ.* Exeter, Oxf. 1652; M. Temple 1652. *m.* by 1657, his cos. Bridget, da. of John Fownes of Whitleigh, 2s. 3da. *suc.* fa. 1679.[1]
> J.p. Devon 1677–81, 1682–July 1688, Oct. 1688–d., Dartmouth 1680–1, 1684; commr. for assessment, Devon 1679–80, 1689–90, sheriff 1683–4; freeman, Totnes to 1684, alderman and j.p. 1684–Jan. 1688.[2]

Kelland's ancestors had been Totnes merchants for three generations. His father, who bought Painsford three miles away in 1647, was a wealthy man with many debtors, one of whom charged him with delinquency in the Civil War; his royalism was only notional, but he had to pay a fine of £663. He was active in the court interest at the Ashburton by-election of 1677.[3]

Nevertheless, when Kelland was returned for Totnes at the first general election of 1679, doubtless by agreement with the Seymours, Shaftesbury marked him 'honest'. An inactive Member of the first Exclusion Parliament, he was appointed only to the committees for the habeas corpus amendment bill, for preventing illegal exactions and for reforming the collection of hearth-tax, and he voted for exclusion. He gave way in August to Edward Seymour*, whose indentures he witnessed, and in the Oxford Parliament, when the Seymours temporarily abandoned Totnes, he left no trace.[4]

Kelland, who rebuilt the chapel at Painsford, was clearly an Anglican. He became an alderman of Totnes in 1684, and after a bitter dispute with the leader of the local dissenters over 'a piece of ground of very small value' he was re-elected for the borough in 1685 as a Tory. His only committee in James II's Parliament was on the bill to prevent the export of wool. Towards the end of the year his casual attitude towards perfecting his accounts as sheriff brought him a severe rebuke from the Treasury. He was removed as alderman of Totnes on 22 Jan. 1688, and returned the same negative answer as Sir Edward Seymour* on the repeal of the Test Act and Penal Laws. His attitude to the Revolution is not known. He died on 7 Oct. 1692,

aged 57, and was buried at Ashprington, the last of the family to sit in Parliament.[5]

[1] Vivian, *Vis. Devon*, 508; E. A. Webb, *Recs. of St. Bartholomew Smithfield*, ii. 468–9. [2] *Trans. Devon Assoc.* viii. 365, 367; SP44/335/198. [3] *Cal. Comm. Comp.* 1878, 2810; *Trans. Devon Assoc.* xcviii, 214. [4] *HMC 15th Rep. VII*, 106. [5] W. G. Hoskins, *Devon*, 322; *Cal. Treas. Bks.* viii. 500; PC2/72/581.

J.P.F.

KELYNG, John (1607–71), of Hatton Garden, London and Southill, Beds.[1]

BEDFORD   1661–18 June 1663

> *bap.* 19 July 1607, o.s. of John Kelyng of Hertford by Alice, da. of Gregory Waterhouse of Halifax, Yorks. *educ.* Trinity Coll. Camb. 1623; I. Temple 1624, called 1632. *m.* (1) by 1634, Martha (*d.* 18 July 1660), da. of Sir Thomas Boteler of Biddenham, Beds., 4s. (3 *d.v.p.*) 4da.; (2) Mary (*d.* 24 Sept. 1667), da. of William Jesson, Draper, of London, wid. of Oliver Boteler of Harrold, Beds., 1da.; (3) 23 Mar. 1668, Elizabeth, da. of Sir Francis Bassett of Tehidy, Illogan, Cornw., *s.p. suc.* fa. 1642; kntd. 21 Jan. 1662.[2]
> Steward of borough court, Hertford 1637–44; bencher, I. Temple May 1660; j.p. Beds. July 1660–d.; commr. for oyer and terminer, Norfolk circuit July 1660, assessment, Beds. Aug. 1660–9, Bedford 1661–3; freeman, Bedford 1661; commr. for loyal and indigent officers, Beds. 1662.[3]
> Serjeant-at-law July 1660, King's serjeant 1661–3; j.K.b. 18 June 1663, c.j. 1665–d.

No connexion has been found between Kelyng and John Keling[†], the crown lawyer who sat for Newcastle-under-Lyme in 1625–6, though they were both barristers of the Inner Temple. Kelyng succeeded his father as steward of Hertford, refused the Protestation in 1642, and was imprisoned by the Long Parliament for inciting the grand jury to oppose the militia ordinance. Clarendon described him as 'a person of eminent learning [and] eminent suffering, [who] never wore his gown after the rebellion, but was always in gaol'. He probably leased Southill during the Interregnum, though the freehold was not purchased until 1667.[4]

Kelyng was one of the first group of serjeants to be appointed after the Restoration, and acted as crown counsel at the trials of the regicides Francis Hacker[†] and William Heveningham[†]. He was involved in a double return with Sir Samuel Luke* at Bedford in 1661, and seated on the merits of the return. Although a bigoted Anglican, he was listed by Lord Wharton among his friends. A moderately active Member of the Cavalier Parliament, he was appointed to 53 committees. Early in the first session he was among those given the responsibility for drawing up a proviso to the security bill and managing a conference. His other committees included those for the corporations bill and the bill of pains and penalties. He was among those instructed to peruse a proviso to the bill against mischief from Quakers and to prepare reasons for a conference. He was largely responsible for drafting the uniformity bill, reporting a conference on 10 Apr. 1662. He served on the committee to consider the bill for the execution of those under attainder, and his conduct of the prosecution of Sir Henry Vane† has been condemned as 'unfeelingly harsh and insulting'. On 2 Apr. 1663 he attended a conference to receive the King's answer to the petition of both Houses against priests and Jesuits. He was appointed to the committees to provide remedies against meetings of dissenters, to bring in a bill for restricting the grant of offices to loyalists, and to inquire into the conduct of Sir Richard Temple*. During the session he was raised to the bench, on which his conduct seems to have been marked by lack of discretion, violent outbursts of temper, and an insulting manner generally. Charged with mishandling juries, aiding arbitrary government, and having 'undervalued, vilified and condemned Magna Carta', he appeared at the bar of the House on 13 Dec. 1667. After hearing 'a very modest and fair answer to two or three of the charges against him', the Commons declared that 'the precedents and practice of fining or imprisoning jurors is illegal', but decided to proceed no further 'out of particular respect to him and the mediation of a great many'. Shortly before his death he appeared before the Lords to apologize publicly to Lord Holles (Denzil Holles*) for affronting him during a trial in the King's bench. He died in his house in Hatton Garden and was buried on 13 May 1671 at St. Andrew, Holborn, the only member of his family to sit in Parliament.[5]

[1] This biography is based on E. Stockdale, 'Sir John Kelyng, Chief Justice of the King's Bench 1665–71', (Beds. Hist. Rec. Soc. lix), 43–53. [2] Le Neve's Knights (Harl. Soc. viii), 150. [3] Chauncy, Herts. i. 492; Bedford Corp. Minute Bk. (Beds. Hist. Rec. Soc. xxvi), 148. [4] CJ, ii. 597; VCH Beds. iii. 258. [5] CJ, viii. 250, 279; ix. 4, 35, 37; Burnet, i. 326; Milward, 88, 159–60, 162–3, 166–9; Pepys Diary, 17 Oct., 13 Dec. 1667; HMC Kenyon, 81; LJ, xii. 452.

L.N./G.J.

KEMP, Sir Robert, 2nd Bt. (1628–1710), of Gissing Hall, Norf. and Ubbeston, Suff.

NORFOLK 10 May 1675
DUNWICH 1679 (Oct.), 1681

b. 2 Feb. 1628. 1st s. of Sir Robert Kemp, 1st Bt., of Gissing, gent. of the privy chamber to Charles I, by Jane, da. of Sir Matthew Browne of Betchworth Castle, Surr. educ. Corpus, Camb. 1644. m. (1) 15 July 1650, Mary (d. June 1655), da. of Thomas Kerridge of Shelley Hall, Suff., 1s. 2da. d.v.p.; (2) 20 Nov. 1657, Mary, da. and h. of John Sone of Ubbeston, 3s. 2da. suc. fa. 20 Aug. 1647.[1]

J.p. Norf. Mar. 1660–76, May–June 1679, 1687–Apr. 1688, 1689–?d., Suff. July 1660–80, 1687–July 1688, 1689–d.; lt.-col. of militia horse, Norf. Apr. 1660–?76; dep. lt. Norf. c.Aug. 1660–76, Suff. 1689–?94, by 1701–d.; commr. for assessment, Norf. and Suff. Aug. 1660–80, 1689–90, Dunwich 1689, recusants, Norf. and Suff. 1675; alderman, Dunwich 1684–June 1688, Oct. 1688–94, 1694–d., bailiff 1685–6, 1695–6, 1698–9, 1701–2, recorder 1686–June 1688, Oct. 1688–94.[2]

Kemp's ancestors acquired Gissing by marriage in 1324 and sat for Castle Rising and Eye in the reign of Elizabeth. His father, a courtier, raised a troop of horse for the King in 1642 and was rewarded with a baronetcy, but he fled abroad without taking any part in the Civil War, and his estate, valued at £1,200 p.a., was discharged from sequestration in 1644. He advanced £100 and three horses worth £30 to Parliament in 1646; but after the Restoration Kemp applied for the advowson of Gissing on the plea that his father had been 'plundered and sequestered in the service of the late King'.[3]

Kemp's request was not gratified until 1673, perhaps because he was known to have absorbed his mother's puritan principles. His wives were conspicuous for their prudence and piety, and he was probably influenced by the views on comprehension of his close friend Sir John Hobart*. It was said that he left the bench when 'gaol appeals from the fanatics' came up, and made it his business 'to compliment the dissenters whensoever he met with them'. When he was put up for the county by Lord Townshend (Sir Horatio Townshend*) in 1675, he was strongly supported by the large nonconformist element in Norfolk, and he was reported to have declared that 'he feared none but the drunken clergy'. Although his success cost him £1,500 he never became an active Member. In the Cavalier Parliament he was appointed to only nine committees, including in his first session the committee of elections and privileges and that to bring in a bill to prohibit the use of the suspending power in religious affairs. The result of the Norfolk by-election was ascribed to the influence of Townshend as lord lieutenant, and during the long recess he was replaced by Lord Yarmouth (Robert Paston*), under whom Kemp refused to serve. He was consequently removed from all his Norfolk offices; the King, resenting the useless sacrifice of a crown living, remarked that Kemp would never be 'obliged', and had used his position on the bench 'against myself and Government'. Shaftesbury marked him 'worthy' in 1677. In the following year he acted as teller with Sir John Holland* for a local estate bill, and was named to the committee. Two of more consequence followed in June 1678; he was against accepting the ordnance accounts, and (again with Holland) against supply. In the final session he may have moved for a committee to inspect the Journals, for he was the first Member named to it.[4]

Kemp did not stand again for Norfolk; but since his second marriage he had acquired property in and around Dunwich and established an interest there. He was returned unopposed for the borough to the second and third Exclusion Parliaments, presumably as a country Member; but he was appointed to no committees and made no speeches. He appears to have gone over to the Court by 1683, when he brought up a loyal address from Dunwich abhorring the Rye House Plot, and he was nominated to the corporation in the new charter, and restored to the commission of the peace by James II. To the lord lieutenant's questions in 1688 he replied:

> If he be chosen knight or burgess he will be for taking away the Penal Laws and the Tests, so far as shall be consistent with the safety of the Church of England. He will be for choosing such as he believes will proceed in the method afore mentioned.... He is for living friendly with all mankind so long as they continue loyal, and is for liberty of conscience so far as the Church of England may be supported.

These answers were not deemed satisfactory, and he was removed from all local office. He was out of the county in October when the former magistrates in Norfolk declared themselves unable to act with persons incapacitated by the Test Act. He accepted the Revolution, but does not seem to have stood again, though he was actively concerned in the disputes between the old and new corporations at Dunwich. He died on 26 June 1710 in his eighty-third year, and was buried at Gissing. His son, the third baronet, sat as a Tory for Dunwich under Queen Anne and for Suffolk under George II.[5]

[1] Blomefield, *Norf.* i. 166, 179. [2] *Parl. Intell.* 9 Apr. 1660; *Cal. Treas. Bks.* i. 77; E. Suff. RO, EE6/1144/13; *HMC Var.* vii. 104, 105; *CSP Dom.* 1685, p. 15; PC2/72/689; information from Dr O. G. Pickard. [3] Blomefield, i. 177; F. A. Kemp, *Kemp Fam.* 38–39; *Cal. Comm. Comp.* 115; *Cal. Comm. Adv. Money*, 475, 476; *CSP Dom.* 1661–2, p. 625. [4] *CSP Dom.* 1673–5, p. 46; E. Bohun, *Diary and Autobiog.* 257; Kemp, 39; *HMC Townshend*, 28; *HMC 6th Rep.* 372; *HMC Finch*, ii. 42, 45; *HMC 7th Rep.* 532; Bodl. Tanner mss 43, f. 148; *CJ*, ix. 454, 499, 506. [5] Copinger, *Suff. Manors*, ii. 170–1; *HMC Var.* vii. 103–5; *Norf. Ltcy. Jnl.* (Norf. Rec. Soc. xxx), 88; Blomefield, i. 166.

E.C.

KEMPTHORNE, Sir John (c.1620–79), of Portsmouth, Hants.[1]

PORTSMOUTH 1679 (Mar.)

b. c.1620, 2nd. s. of John Kempthorne, attorney, of Witchcombe, Ugborough, Devon by Agnes, da. of Toby Simon of Diptford, Devon. *m.* 1649, Joanna (*d.* 1691), 3s. 1da. Kntd. 24 Apr. 1670.

Yr. bro. Trinity House Nov. 1660, elder bro. 1666, master 1674–5; commr. resident at Portsmouth 1675–d., freeman 1676.[2]

Capt. RN 1664, r.-adm. 1666, v.-adm. 1673–4.

Kempthorne was from an old Devonshire gentry family named Ley, one of whom took the name of Kempthorne in the 14th century from the farm on which he had settled. His father is said to have served as a cavalry officer in the royalist army. Kempthorne himself went to sea, serving his apprenticeship in the coastal trade; but by his own account he was abroad from 1644 to 1656. During this time he married a maidservant in the Commonwealth embassy at Istanbul, and rose to command several of the Levant Company ships. He was commissioned in the Royal Navy on the eve of the second Dutch war, in which he served as flag-captain to Prince Rupert at the battle of Lowestoft and to the Duke of Albemarle (George Monck*) in the Four Days' battle, and was promoted rear-admiral. He remained in the royal service after the Peace of Breda, though he was at the same time one of the leading ship-owners in the Mediterranean trade, and he was knighted in 1670 for his successful defence of a convoy against the Algerian corsairs. In the third Dutch war, he took a prominent part in the battle of Sole Bay and was further promoted. He was wounded at the battle of Texel in 1673, and retired in the following year when England made peace, with a pension of £200.[3]

Kempthorne was not long unemployed, for in 1675 he succeeded Sir Anthony Deane* as navy commissioner at Portsmouth and superintendent of the dockyard. He became a freeman of the borough and formed a friendship with the governor, George Legge*. At the dissolution of the Cavalier Parliament he stood for Portsmouth with Legge's support, ignoring a letter from Samuel Pepys* ordering him to make way for John Ernle*. He was nevertheless marked 'base' on Shaftesbury's list. An inactive Member of the first Exclusion Parliament, he was named only to the committee of elections and privileges and to that for preventing illegal exactions. He did not vote in the division on the exclusion bill, nor did he stand for re-election in August, perhaps for reasons of health, for he died on 19 Oct. 1679 and was buried at Portsmouth. In his will he bequeathed shares in five ships to his three sons, who all became captains in the Royal Navy, though he was the only member of the family to serve in Parliament.[4]

[1] This biography is based on G. A. Kempthorne, 'Sir John Kempthorne and His Sons' in the *Mariner's Mirror*, xii. 289–310, with further information from Miss Sonia Anderson. [2] R. East,

Portsmouth Recs. 362. ³ Add. 34015, p. 40; CSP Dom. 1668–9, p. 630.
⁴ Pepys Further Corresp. 344–5.
P.W.

KEMYS, Sir Charles, 3rd Bt. (1651–1702), of Cefn Mabli, Glam.; Llanfair Discoed, Mon. and Denmark Street, St. Giles in the Fields, Mdx.

MONMOUTHSHIRE   1685
MONMOUTH   1690
MONMOUTHSHIRE   1695

b. 18 May 1651, 1st s. of Sir Charles Kemys, 2nd Bt., of Cefn Mabli by 3rd w. Margaret, da. of Sir George Whitmore, ld. mayor of London 1631–2, of Balmes, Hackney, Mdx. educ. Wadham, Oxf. 1669. m. (1) 1677, Mary (d.1699), da. of Philip, 4th Baron Wharton, wid. of William Thomas of Wenvoe, Glam., 2s. (1 d.v.p.) 2da.; (2) 30 Dec. 1701, Mary, da. of William Lewis* of Bletchington, Oxon., coh. to her bro. Edward Lewis*, and wid. of William Jephson* of Boarstall, Bucks., and of Sir John Aubrey, 2nd Bt.†, of Llantriddyd, Glam., s.p. suc. fa. c. June 1658.¹

Commr. for assessment, Mon. and Glam. 1673–80, 1689–90, j.p. Mon. 1682–Apr. 1688, Oct. 1688–d., Glam. 1689–d., Bucks. 1702–d.; lt. of militia horse, Mon. by 1684–Feb. 1688; dep. lt. Mon. and Glam. 1685–Feb. 1688, Glam. Oct. 1688–d., Mon. Oct. 1688–9, by 1701–d., Bucks. 1702–d.; v.-adm. Mon. by 1700–d.²

Kemys's ancestors had been seated at Cefn Mabli since the 15th century, but his grandfather, MP for Monmouthshire in 1628, was the first to enter Parliament; a man of gigantic strength and stature, he was killed at Chepstow Castle in the second Civil War. Kemys's father was likewise a Royalist in both wars, and was fined £3,500. Kemys succeeded to an estate of £1,200 p.a., only two-thirds of its former value, and even before his first marriage, into a notoriously Whiggish aristocratic family, was described as 'unsettled'. His wife proved a 'doughty' Puritan, but he was himself remarkable chiefly for his addiction to the bottle. Returned for Monmouthshire in 1685 as a follower of the Tory Duke of Beaufort (Henry Somerset*), he was moderately active in James II's Parliament, being appointed to the committee of elections and privileges and to three others of minor significance. He returned negative answers to Beaufort's questions on the repeal of the Test Act and Penal Laws, and was removed from local office. He was not elected in 1689, but in the next two Parliaments voted with the court Whigs. He died in December 1702, and was succeeded by his son, a Jacobite who sat for Monmouthshire with one interval from 1713 to 1734.³

¹ G. T. Clark, Limbus Patrum, 51, 412–14; PCC 383 Wootton. ² Old Wales, i. 87. ³ W. R. Williams, Parl. Hist. Wales, 127; Cal. Comm. Comp. 1276; SP29/398/185; Beaufort mss, Lord to Lady Worcester, 11 Dec. 1681; NLW Jnl. xxi. 161, 166, 167–8.

J.P.F.

KENDALL, James (1647–1708), of Birdcage Walk, Westminster and Killigarth, Cornw.

WEST LOOE   1685, 1689, 1695, 1698, 1701 (Feb.), 1701 (Dec.)
LOSTWITHIEL   17 Jan. 1706, 17 May–10 July 1708

bap. 17 June 1647, 4th but 3rd surv. s. of Thomas Kendall*. educ. M. Temple 1666; L. Inn 1666 unm. 1s.¹

Cornet, R. Horse Gds. 1675; lt.-col. of ft, regt. of Lord Morpeth (Edward Howard*) 1678–9, capt. Coldstream Gds. 1680–5.

Freeman, Portsmouth 1678; commr. for assessment, Cornw. 1689–90, j.p. by 1701–d.²

Gov. and v.-adm. Barbados 1689–94, member of council 1694–5; ld. of Admiralty 1696–9.³

Kendall, a younger son, became a professional soldier, although he inherited his father's West Indian plantations. He was returned to Parliament for West Looe in 1685 as a Tory on the interest of his elder brother, who had acquired the nearby manor of Killigarth by marriage and had unsuccessfully contested the borough in the last three elections. In James II's Parliament he was moderately active with four committees, including those on the bills for regulating hackney coaches and for the relief of insolvent debtors. He was probably at first a court supporter, and in September he was granted a hundred of the western rebels sentenced to transportation. At the opening of the second session he switched to the Opposition. On 13 Nov. he voted against the government motion to proceed with supply before debating the King's message about Roman Catholic officers in the army, which was lost by one vote. The Earl of Middleton (Charles Middleton*)

seeing many go out upon the division against the Court who were in the service of the Government, went down to the bar, and as they were told in, reproached them to their faces for voting as they did; and a Captain Kendall being one of them, the Earl said of him there, 'Sir, have not you a troop of horse in his Majesty's service?'. 'Yes, my lord', says the other, 'but my brother died last night, and has left me £700 a year'.

He lost his commission, but as his niece's guardian he controlled the manor of Killigarth, and continued to represent West Looe, with one interval, till 1702.⁴

Kendall was closely linked with the Earl of Rochester (Laurence Hyde*) in the closing years of James II's reign. Together with Francis Gwyn* he accompanied him to Spa in 1687, and to Salisbury during the Revolution. Unlike his comrades, he went over to William of Orange; but according to Ailesbury's list he voted to agree with the Lords that the throne was not vacant. Probably again a moderately active Member in the Convention, although the Journals do not distinguish him from

Walter Kendall*, he may have served on 18 committees, including those appointed to inquire into the authors and advisers of grievances in the last two reigns, and into the delay in relieving Londonderry. His only speech was in the debate on the indemnity bill on 18 June 1689, when he asked favour for Sir Edward Herbert* for the sake of his brother. On 5 July he was appointed governor of Barbados, but did not leave to take up his post till the following spring. He acted as teller on 29 July for accepting the report of the committee which exonerated William Harbord* from charges of malversation. He was one of five Members instructed on 9 Aug. to bring in a bill to ease the plantations of the duties imposed in 1685. In the second session he was appointed to the committees for the second mutiny bill and restoring corporations.[5]

Kendall did not stand for re-election in 1690. He left for Barbados on 9 Mar., returning five years later. He was appointed to the board of Admiralty in 1696, and sat as a court Whig. He died on 10 July 1708, leaving an estate of £40,000, chiefly in the West Indies, to his mistress.[6]

[1] *Westminster Abbey Reg.* (Harl. Soc. x), 264; *Cal. Treas. Bks.* xv. 169–70; Vivian, *Vis. Cornw.* 258–62. [2] R. East, *Portsmouth Recs.* 363. [3] *CSP Dom.* 1689–90, pp. 178, 247; 1693, p. 78; 1696, p. 46; 1699–1700, p. 190; *CSP Col.* 1693–6, p. 220. [4] *CSP Dom.* 1685, p. 329; Burnet, ed. Routh, iii. 92; *Reresby Mems.* 403; T. Bond, *Looe,* 156–9. [5] *Ellis Corresp.* i. 314; *Fortnightly Rev.* xl. 358; *HMC Stuart,* vi. 50; Grey, ix. 341. [6] *CSP Dom.* 1689–90, p. 540; *HMC Downshire,* i. 472; Luttrell, iii. 58, 478; vi. 327.

P.W.

KENDALL, John (1631–at least 1702), of Treworgey, Duloe, Cornw.

EAST LOOE 1659
WEST LOOE 1660
EAST LOOE 1681

bap. 7 Aug. 1631, 2nd but 1st surv. s. of John Kendall of Treworgey by w. Mary. *educ.* L. Inn 1649. *suc* fa. 1641.[1]

J.p. Cornw. 1653–July 1660, June 1688–?1700, commr. for poor prisoners 1653, assessment 1657, Jan. 1660, 1663–80, 1689–1700, militia Mar. 1660, lt.-col. of militia ft. Apr. 1660; freeman, West Looe 1672, East Looe 1678.[2]

Kendall's ancestors were established at Treworgey, two miles from Looe, early in the 14th century, first entering Parliament for Launceston in 1330. Kendall held local office under the Protectorate, and sat for East Looe in Richard Cromwell's Parliament. He transferred to West Looe in 1660 but left no trace on the records of the Convention, though he probably opposed the Court, since he lost his place on the commission of the peace at the Restoration. He is unlikely to have stood in 1661,

but he joined his cousin Thomas Kendall of Killigarth in challenging the Trelawny interest in the exclusion elections. He was twice defeated at East Looe in 1679, but won the seat in 1681 after the death of Jonathan Trelawny I*, probably without a contest. Presumably an exclusionist, he again left no trace on the records of the Oxford Parliament. He may have become a Whig collaborator, since he was restored to the commission of the peace in February 1688 and recommended as court candidate for East Looe. It is unlikely that he ever stood again, however, since his circumstances were now embarrassed and after the Revolution he was compelled to part with his whole estate. He was not named to the Cornish tax commission of 1701, though he was still alive, for in July 1702 his cousin James Kendall* left him a small legacy. He died childless, the last of this branch of the family.[3]

[1] Vivian, *Vis. Cornw.* 259. [2] *Parl. Intell.* 9 Apr. 1660; A. L. Browne, *Corp. Chrons.* 189. [3] *Paroch. Hist. Cornw.* i. 302; *Westminster Abbey Reg.* (Harl. Soc. x), 264.

M.W.H./P.W.

KENDALL, Thomas (1609–66), of Chiswick, Mdx.

DARTMOUTH 7 Apr. 1664–Dec. 1666

bap. 13 Aug. 1609, 2nd s. of Thomas Kendall of Lostwithiel, Cornw. by Elizabeth, da. of Arthur Arscott of Tetcott, Devon. *m.* (with £500) Grace, da. of John Modyford, merchant, of Exeter, Devon, 4s. (1 *d.v.p.*).[1]

Commr. for arbitration of Dutch and English shipping losses 1654; committee, E.I. Co. 1659–63, 1665–d., dep. gov. 1663–5; commr. for trade Nov. 1660–d., plantations Dec. 1660–d.[2]

Commr. for assessment, Mdx. 1664–d.

Kendall was a younger son of a cadet branch of the Kendalls of Treworgey, of whom nothing is known before the Protectorate, when he appeared as head of a company engaged in the East India trade. His West Indian interests became even more important, and by his death he had acquired half-shares in plantations in Barbados and Jamaica.[3]

Kendall first stood for Lostwithiel at the general election of 1660, but although his brother was returning officer he finished at the bottom of the poll. He was elected, not without opposition, at Dartmouth at a by-election in 1664, no doubt largely on the strength of his position on the board of trade, though he may also have enjoyed the support of the Duke of Albemarle (George Monck*) to whom he was related through his brother-in-law, Sir Thomas Modyford. In four sessions, he was named to only nine committees, the most important being that set up at Oxford for the preservation of prize goods; but if he was only moderately active in Parliament, he was energetic enough elsewhere in forwarding the interests of his business associates and political supporters: 'Mr Kendall . . . would never get protection or convoy for any ship but for those that stuck by him and opposed all those that [?sought] any of the contrary party'. Kendall died rather suddenly about Christmas 1666; he presented a report to the court of the East India Company on 21 Dec., but within a week canvassing had begun for his Dartmouth seat.[4]

Kendall's will reveals associations with two figures of the radical opposition. Thomas Papillon* was named as a trustee, and it was apparently drawn up and witnessed by Edward Nosworthy I*.[5]

[1] Vivian, *Vis. Cornw.* 262; PCC 23 Carr; V. L. Oliver, *Caribbeana*, iv. 337. [2] *Cal. Ct. Mins. E.I. Co.* ed. Sainsbury, v. 333; vi. 305; vii. 30, 141, 218. [3] Scott, *Jt. Stock Cos.* i. 247; *APC Col.* i. 304. [4] *HMC Var.* i. 336; SP29/266/129C; *Cal. Ct. Mins. E.I. Co.* vii. 101, 269; *CSP Dom.* 1666-7, p. 374; SP29/266/129C. [5] PCC 23 Carr.

J.P.F.

KENDALL, Walter (1626-96), of Pelyn, Lanlivery, Cornw.

LOSTWITHIEL 1679 (Mar.), 1679 (Oct.), 1681, 1689, 1690

bap. Oct. 1626, 1st s. of Nicholas Kendall of Pelyn by Emlyn, da. and coh. of Thomas Treffrey of Lostwithiel, Cornw. *m.* 17 July 1650, Joan (*bur.* 29 Apr. 1716), da. of Sir Alexander Carew, 2nd Bt.[†], of Antony, Cornw., *s.p. suc.* fa. 1641.[1]

Lt.-col. of ft. (royalist) by 1646.[2]

Commr. for assessment, Cornw. 1660-80, j.p. 1662-80, 1685-July 1688, Nov. 1688-?*d.*; stannator, Blackmore 1673, 1686.[3]

Kendall was descended from a branch of the Treworgey family seated at Pelyn, one mile from Lostwithiel. His ancestors had represented the borough since the reign of Richard II, and were equally prominent in municipal office; his cousin Walter (1608-93), the elder brother of Thomas Kendall*, who lived in the town, served seven terms as mayor between 1642 and 1687. His great-uncle Nicholas Kendall[†] was killed fighting for the King, and Kendall himself, despite his youth, was commissioned in the regiment of Sir Charles Trevanion[†]. He was denounced as a delinquent in 1649, and compounded in the following year on a fine of £150.[4]

Kendall was returned for Lostwithiel to all three Exclusion Parliaments with his brother-in-law, Sir John Carew*. Classed as 'doubtful' by Shaftesbury, he was appointed only to the committee of elections and privileges in 1679, and voted against the exclusion bill. Perhaps because Carew, whose return he had procured, was an exclusionist, he was among the gentlemen 'of estate and worth' put out of the

Cornish commission of the peace in 1680. He took no known part in the second and third Exclusion Parliaments, but he joined the syndicate headed by Francis Robartes* 'of knights and burgesses of this present Parliament for Cornwall', which applied for the Tangier victualling contract. Although his cousin was charter mayor in 1685, Kendall is not known to have stood for James II's Parliament. He was recommended by Lord Bath as court candidate for the borough in 1688; but he gave the same evasive answers as Carew on the repeal of the Test and Penal Laws, and was again removed. He regained his seat in the Convention, but the references to 'Mr Kendall' in the Journal are probably to James Kendall*, though he may have been added to the committee for the bill reversing 'Julian' Johnson's degradation. He was granted leave of absence on 6 July 1689, but he was back in Westminster on 2 Jan. 1690 when he complained that his servant had been arrested and was still being held in custody. There is no record of his having voted or spoken in this Parliament. He was re-elected in 1690 and buried at Lanlivery on 5 July 1696. The next member of the family to sit was Nicholas Kendall, who represented East Cornwall in every Parliament between the first and second reform bills.[5]

[1] Vivian, *Vis. Cornw.* 260. [2] Information from Brigadier Peter Young. [3] *HMC Var.* i. 337; Add. 6713, ff. 121, 377. [4] Gilbert, *Paroch. Hist. Cornw.* iii. 22, 178; F. M. Hext, *Mems. Lostwithiel*, 96; Vivian, 262; M. Coate, *Cornw. in the Gt. Civil War*, 72; *Cal. Comm. Adv. Money*, 1121; *Cal. Comm. Comp.* 2240. [5] *HMC Lords*, i. 176; *Cal. Treas. Bks.* vii. 149; *HMC Var.* i. 328; Gilbert, iii. 22.

E.C./B.D.H.

KENT, John (c.1612-69), of the Market Place, Devizes, Wilts.

DEVIZES 1661-Aug./Sept. 1669

b. c.1612, o.s. of John Kent of Devizes by Anne, da. of Jerome Potticarie of Stockton. *educ.* Oriel, Oxf. matric. 20 June 1628, aged 16; M. Temple 1630. *m.* 1642, Jane, da. of Sir Humphrey Lynde[†] of Cobham, Surr., 1s. *suc.* gdfa. John Kent[†] 1630.[1]

Commr. for assessment, Wilts. Aug. 1660-*d.*; j.p. Devizes 1661, alderman 1662-*d.*[2]

Kent's grandfather, an attorney of Cheshire origin, became town clerk of Devizes towards the end of Elizabeth's reign, represented the borough in 1597, and registered his pedigree with the heralds in 1623. Kent himself, or some other member of the family, was removed as town clerk during the Interregnum 'for his loyalty'; but his marriage to the sister-in-law of Robert Nicholas[†] the Cromwellian judge, probably saved him from more serious consequences. Returned after a contest at the general election of 1661 he was a moderately active Member of the Cavalier Parliament, with 65 committees. Few of these were of political importance, but he was probably a court supporter. In 1661 he was appointed to the committees for the uniformity bill and for cancelling the conveyance of Devizes Castle (with other property) by Dame Mary Powell during the Interregnum (see William Powell*). He was named to the committees to examine defects in the Corporations Act in 1663 and to attaint English officers in Dutch service in 1665. His will, dated 30 July 1669, was proved on 2 Oct. His son John was appointed alderman of Devizes under the charter of 1684, but returned negative answers on the repeal of the Test Act and Penal Laws, and no later Member of the family sat in Parliament.[3]

[1] *Wilts. Vis. Peds.* (Harl. Soc. cv), 105; PCC 27 St. John, 125 Coke; *Wilts. Arch. Mag.* xli. 92; *Wilts. N. and Q.* iii. 36. [2] Add. 32324, f. 149. [3] *CSP Dom.* 1661–2, p. 286.

J.P.F.

KENT, Richard (c.1643–90), of Westminster and Corsham, Wilts.

CHIPPENHAM 25 Aug. 1685,[1] 25 Feb.–23 Nov. 1690

b. c.1643, 3rd s. of Robert Kent (*d.* c.1658) of Winterbourne Dauntsey by w. Dorothy. *m.* lic. 12 Feb. 1666, aged 23, Bridget (*bur.* 10 Aug. 1692), da. of one Harris of Westminster, 1s. *d.v.p.* 1da.[2]

Clerk, Pay Office 1661–74; receiver-gen. and cashier of excise 1674–6, commr. 1675–6; receiver-gen. and cashier of customs 1677–89; six clerk in Chancery July–Aug. 1682.[3]

J.p. Wilts. Oct. 1688–*d.*; commr. for assessment Mdx. 1689, Wilts. 1689–*d.*

Kent came from a minor Wiltshire family unrelated to John Kent*. His uncle bought the manor of East Boscombe in 1629, and was in arms as a Royalist in the Civil War. Another uncle was removed from his rectory of Fisherton Anger by Parliament, and Kent's father was also 'engaged in the wars' on the King's side. He fled to France, but returned and was condemned to death 'and in the end lost his life'.[4]

Kent himself came up to London at the age of 15, 'a mere country lad, very ignorant both in telling money and keeping accounts'. Entering the Pay Office under Stephen Fox*, he learnt fast, and by 1666 had established an account under his own name with Edward Backwell*. Though still in government employ, he went into partnership with Charles Duncombe* to take over Backwell's bank at the sign of The Grasshopper after the Stop of the Exchequer. 'It seems', writes Dr Clay, 'that Duncombe furnished most of the capital and Kent

provided the contacts with government circles and the knowledge of government methods.' In 1674 Danby appointed him receiver-general of the excise, ostensibly in order to ensure better liaison with the Pay Office, but actually with the aims of establishing an important new credit at the Government's disposal, and (it was suspected) of facilitating the bribery of Members. Kent's patent became the focal point of the opposition attack on Danby in the following year, and although the lord treasurer weathered the storm he seems to have thought it discreet to supersede him in 1676. By now *The Grasshopper* was well on the way to dominating the money-market, and in 1677 Kent became receiver-general of the customs, a post held until the Revolution, at the increased salary of £1,000 p.a. According to Sir Francis North*, an acid critic of Danby's financial policy, he had offered

> to lend a great sum of money to pay off the clamorous debts that lie upon the customs so that they are anticipated for a great time and no ready money to be expected. He finds out the creditors and gives them his own security at time, or buys their debts beforehand. To secure him, he is made cashier of the customs, and only advanceth with one hand to receive with the other.

On 27 May 1679 he gave evidence to the first Exclusion Parliament about payments to Members, but the only sums he could recall were £1,000 paid to Sir Richard Wiseman* and £500 to Sir Courtenay Pole*.[5]

In 1684 Kent bought Corsham, one of the principal estates of the extravagant (Sir) Edward Hungerford*, and with it the manor of Sheldon, which formed the western side of the parish of Chippenham. He improved his interest in the borough by paying the fees for its new charter, and was returned at a by-election during the autumn recess of James II's Parliament. During the brief second session he was named only to the committee to calculate the yield of an imposition on French wines. In August 1688 the King's electoral agents noted that 'Mr Richard Kent of the Customs House' and Henry Bayntun II* enjoyed the chief interests at Chippenham, and recommended him for the Wiltshire commission of the peace. Sunderland ordered him to stand for re-election, presumably in conjunction with (Sir) John Talbot*, but he objected to the cost, and is unlikely to have gone to the poll in 1689. He regained the seat at the next general election, but died on 23 Nov. 1690. To his wife and daughter, neither of whom survived him long, he left an annuity of £500 and a portion of £10,000, and no less than £2,000 to the poor of Winterbourne Monkton, his birthplace. His nephew sold Corsham to Richard Lewis* in 1694, and Sheldon to Sir Richard Hart*, and no other member of this family entered Parliament.[6]

[1] F. C. Goldney, *Chippenham Recs.* 72. [2] *Wilts. N. and Q.* vii. 232–3; *Mar. Lic.* (Harl. Soc. xxiii), 112. [3] C. Clay, *Public Finance and Private Wealth*, 141–3; *Cal. Treas. Bks.* iii. 265, 685; iv. 807; v. 113, 443; viii. 2168; T. D. Hardy, *Principal Officers of Chancery*, 111. [4] Hoare, *Wilts.* Ambresbury, 112; *Cal. Comm. Comp.* 995; A. G. Matthews, *Walker Revised*, 375; *Wilts. N. and Q.* vii. 229. [5] Clay, 82, 141–2; F. G. Hilton Price, *Handbk. of London Bankers*, 108–9; C. D. Chandaman, *Eng. Pub. Revenue*, 65, 72; Grey, iii. 56; Dalrymple, *Mems.* i. pt. 2, p. 146; Blackett diary. [6] Aubrey and Jackson, *Wilts. Colls.* 79; *Wilts. Arch. Mag.* iii. 28–29; Goldney, 71; *CSP Dom.* 1687–9, p. 276; *Ellis Corresp.* ii. 20; Luttrell, ii. 132; *Wilts. N. and Q.* vii. 233–5.

B.D.H.

KERR (CARR), Charles, 2nd Earl of Ancram [S] (1624–90), of Kew, Surr. and Lincoln's Inn Fields, Mdx.[1]

MITCHELL   c. Mar. 1647[2]
THIRSK   13 July 1660
WIGAN   1661, 1679 (Mar.), 1679 (Oct.), 1681, 1685

b. 6 Aug. 1624, 2nd s. of Robert Kerr[†], 1st Earl of Ancram [S], being 1st s. by 2nd w. Lady Anne Stanley, da. of William, 6th Earl of Derby, wid. of Sir Henry Portman, 2nd Bt.[†], of Orchard Portman, Som. *educ.* travelled abroad 1638–41. *m.* bef. 1 May 1662, Frances, da. of Sir Henry Knollys of Grove Place, Nursling, Hants, wid. of Sir Edward Manfield of Cliveden, Bucks., 1s. *d.v.p. suc.* fa. Dec. 1654.[3]

Commr. for sequestrations, Surr. 1648, militia 1648, Mar. 1660; j.p. Berks. and Surr. Mar. 1660–80, Bucks. Mar.–July 1660, 1665–?80, Beds., Essex, Hants., Kent, Lancs. and Westminster to 1680; commr. for sewers, Westminster Aug. 1660, assessment, Lancs. and Surr. 1661–80, Berks. and Bucks. 1663–80, loyal and indigent officers, Surr. 1662.[4]

Gent of the privy chamber 1666–85; PC [S] 1681.[5]

The first Earl of Ancram came from a cadet branch of a well-known Scottish border family. Under Charles I he became keeper of the privy purse, and sat for Preston in 1627. He took no active part in the Civil War, but on 27 May 1647 Parliament ordered that he should be given £1,500 and a pension. Nevertheless he had to take refuge from his creditors abroad. Ancram himself was arrested at the time of Booth's rising, and may have been regarded as a Presbyterian in 1660; according to Burnet he was of no principles either as to religion or virtue, but had 'studied the most in divinity of any man of quality I ever knew'. He inherited little except his mother's house at Kew. On 1 Apr. 1660, he warned the Council of State that the Republicans in Richmond were planning to disturb the Surrey election, and advised sending a troop of horse to keep guard.[6]

Ancram was returned for Thirsk at a by-election to the Convention on the interest of his kinsman, the Earl of Derby, in succession to the Hon. Wil-liam Stanley*, who chose to sit for Liverpool. His only recorded speech in 1660 was a sharp attack on Sir Arthur Hesilrige[†] during the debate on the bill of indemnity, but he was named to eight commit-tees, being particularly prominent in the financial provisions for the royal family. On 21 Sept. he wrote to the Queen of Bohemia:

> I thought myself a very happy person that I was one of that number who at the close of our adjournment did strive to manifest our duty and service to your Majesty ... I have since the rising of the Parliament (according as I was by the House ordered) made it my business to secure this money forthwith to your Majesty by getting an alderman of London to advance it.

On 7 Nov. Ancram carried to the Lords the order for a grant to Princess Henrietta. Three days later he acted as teller against the marital separation bill.[7]

Ancram was returned for Wigan in 1661, again on Derby's interest, and proved an active Member in the Cavalier Parliament. He was appointed to 212 committees, in four of which he took the chair, acted as teller in 32 divisions, and delivered 16 reported speeches. He was a teller for the corpora-tions bill on 5 July 1661, and was added to the committee on the bill for the execution of those under attainder on 10 Jan. 1662. Shortly afterwards he was in Paris, perhaps in attendance on the queen mother, and he was probably married there. This marriage to the sister of Thomas Knollys* rein-forced his links with the Court, for his wife's father had been comptroller of the household to Charles I, and she herself became lady of the bedchamber to Catherine of Braganza. From her first husband, a recusant, she enjoyed a comfortable jointure, which Ancram was not long in selling or mortgag-ing. It is an indication of Ancram's tolerance that about the same time he arranged the marriage of his portionless sister to the Fifth Monarchist Nath-aniel Rich[†] who had opposed the Restoration, and secured the release of the prominent Quaker Isaac Pennington. Although without legal education, he acted as chairman of the committee for the abolition of the legal charges known as damage clere in 1663. Ancram was noted as a court dependant in 1664, when his long and fruitless association with Lau-derdale had already begun. Later he was described as 'a needy Scots lord, therefore a knave'. He was chairman of the committees for reversing the attainder for felony of his kinsman, Sir Charles Stanley, and enabling him to pay his debts.[8]

Ancram became more active politically on the fall of Clarendon. He was among those ordered to report on the proceedings against Lord Mordaunt and to draw up heads of the accusations against

Clarendon. On 30 Oct. 1667 he spoke against the impracticable bill to prevent the growth of Popery, and on the next day he delivered Prince Rupert's narrative of the Four Days' battle. He took the chair in the committee to assess taxation in the Bedford level. In 1669 he assisted in a review of the militia laws. On 3 Mar. 1670 he was appointed to the committee against transportation of English prisoners. In the supply debate on 10 Nov., he urged putting the King in a position to stand well with his neighbours. In the debate on the Duke of York's marriage to Mary of Modena in 1673, he repeatedly urged that it was beyond the power of Parliament to hinder, and hoped they would not affront a man who had fought their battles. He showed his caution by announcing that he would have preferred a Protestant match, though in private he was supplying the Duke with arguments in favour of papal infallibility for use against Burnet. Ancram remained a steady supporter of the Court, his name appearing on the Paston list, but he did not resist the rising tide against Popery. He was appointed to the committees for the general test bill in 1673, and for educating the children of the royal family as Protestants. 'He depended on Duke Lauderdale, but hated him, because he did nothing for him.' He spoke twice in his patron's defence in the debates of 1675, but was named to the committee to draw up the address for his removal. He was teller against the demand for the withdrawal of all British subjects from France, and his services to the Court were rewarded by a pension of £500 for life. Although a member of the committee to draw up an address for an anti-French alliance in 1677, he was marked by Shaftesbury as 'thrice vile'. He again resisted an attack on Lauderdale on 7 May 1678, in language reminiscent of his Presbyterian youth, and was appointed to the committee to pen the address demanding the removal of counsellors. Three days later, when that committee reported the terms of the address, he supported the motion for an adjournment. He served on the committees to inquire into the Popish Plot and to consider the bill for the exclusion of Papists from Parliament.[9]

In the first Exclusion Parliament Ancram was described by Shaftesbury as 'vile'. He was appointed to five committees, including the committee to examine what proportion of the money voted for disbanding the army still remained in the Exchequer, and that of 8 May on the bill requiring better attendance by Members. On 21 May he was a teller against the second reading of the first exclusion bill; but he was removed from the commissions of the peace in 1680, presumably because of his wife's recusancy. He had acquired sufficient personal interest in Wigan to survive even the loss of Derby's support. Roger Bradshaigh II* said of him that his constituents were 'daily more obliged in many particulars than any town that I have known hath been to any burgess that ever served them, not only in time of Parliament, but every day in the interval of every Parliament'. Ancram was re-elected to both the second and third Exclusion Parliaments, probably without a contest, though totally inactive in both, and also took his seat in the Scottish House of Lords in 1681. He presented a loyal address from the Wigan corporation and was plainly regarded as manager for the court interest in the borough. An embarrassing incident was narrowly averted in 1683 when one of his step-sons, 'in which family there is no great store of money', tried to set himself up as an informer in the Popish Plot. The evidence he produced was not only untimely but clumsily forged and planted, and it took all Ancram's influence to keep him out of the pillory.[10]

Ancram was again returned unopposed for Wigan in 1685. An impeccable courtier, he was naturally in favour with James II. He was a moderately active Member, with six committees, of which the most important was to examine army accounts. He spoke against the general naturalization bill on the specious grounds that it imposed conformity on Protestant refugees. On 15 June he carried Monmouth's attainder to the Lords. In the second session he was appointed to the committee to draw up the address for the removal of Roman Catholic officers, but acted as teller against obtaining the concurrence of the Lords. He was not at first molested after the Revolution, but in November 1689 a warrant was issued for his arrest. He died in needy circumstances and was buried at Kensington on 10 Sept. 1690, his title falling to his nephew, the Whig 1st Marquess of Lothian.[11]

[1] HMC Popham, 172; Ancram and Lothian Corresp. ed. D. Laing, 458; Manning and Bray, Surr. i. 446; Survey of London, iii. 52. [2] Did not sit after Pride's Purge on 6 Dec. 1648, readmitted 21 Feb. 1660. [3] Richmond Par. Reg. (Surr. Par. Reg. Soc. i), 16; CSP Dom. 1637–8, p. 466; 1680–1, p. 367; C10/139/65; Corresp. 458; Hants Field Club Pprs. i. 126; Add. 38175, f. 33. [4] C181/7/37. [5] Carlisle, Privy Chamber, 177; CSP Dom. 1680–1, p. 386. [6] Scots Peerage, v. 464–8; Whitelocke Mems. ii. 147; CSP Dom. 1659–60, p. 96; Burnet, ii. 28–29; HMC Popham, 172. [7] Old Parl. Hist. xxii. 444; Add. 18744, f. 15. [8] Corresp. 458–60, 464; C5/437/78; Lipscomb, Bucks. iii. 241; Add. 23117, f. 108. [9] Milward, 104; PRO 31/3, bdle. 125, f. 288; Grey, ii. 192; v. 360; Burnet, ii. 28, 29; CSP Dom. 1675–6, p. 558; Lauderdale Pprs. (Cam. Soc. n.s. xxxviii), 141. [10] Burnet, ii. 28; HMC Kenyon, 169–70; London Gazette, 23 May 1681; CSP Dom. Jan.–June 1683, pp. 208–9, 257; 1683–4, p. 85. [11] CSP Dom. 1685, p. 119; 1689–90, p. 312; North, Lives, iii. 181; Kensington Par. Reg.

J.P.F.

KILDARE, 17th Earl of [I] *see* **FITZGERALD, Wentworth**

KILLIGREW, Peter (c.1634–1705), of Arwennack, St. Budock, Cornw.

CAMELFORD   5 May–12 June 1660

b. c.1634, o.s. of Sir Peter Killigrew*. *educ.* Queen's, Oxf. 1650; travelled abroad 1653; Padua 1654. *m.* lic. 24 Dec. 1662, Frances (*d.* Apr. 1711), da. of Sir Roger Twysden, 2nd Bt.†, of Roydon Hall, East Peckham, Kent, 2s. *d.v.p.* 2da. *suc.* uncle Sir William Killigrew as 2nd Bt. June 1665, fa. 1668.[1]

Gent. of privy chamber by June 1660–89.[2]
J.p. Cornw. 1669–July 1688, Oct. 1688–?*d.*, commr. for assessment 1673–80, 1689–90; jt. receiver-gen. duchy of Cornw. 1673–*d.*; commr. for recusants, Cornw. 1675; recorder, Falmouth 1680–*d.*[3]

Killigrew stood for the open borough of Camelford at the general election of 1660, and was seated with Samuel Trelawny* on the merits of the return. He was classed as a friend by Lord Wharton, but he made no recorded speeches in the Convention and was appointed to no committees before the election was declared void. He did not stand at the by-election, nor did he sit again, though he lived for another 45 years. He was active in local affairs, and seems to have enjoyed a measure of royal favour. He hoped to succeed his father as MP for Helston in 1668, but his interest could not prevail against his fellow-courtier Sidney Godolphin I*. He continued to receive his father's £300 p.a. pension, which had been extended to cover his life. In 1673 he and John Tregagle* were appointed joint receivers of the duchy of Cornwall for life, although by a private agreement he was to receive up to £300 a year out of the office and leave its functions, salary and profits to Tregagle. In the following year he took part in an investigation into the coinage of tin and the laws of the stannaries. He continued his father's efforts to develop Falmouth, where, by 1676, a new quay had been built, to which, despite their strong opposition, the neighbouring ports of Truro, Penryn and Helston had to bring most of their goods.[4]

Killigrew remained on the Cornish commission of the peace in 1680 and was presumably opposed to exclusion. In June 1688, he was marked as 'absent' in the returns of the royal agents on the answers to the questions on the Test Act and Penal Laws, and his name was not included in the list of proposed justices of the peace. In 1697 he was reprimanded for failure to render any account of duchy revenues since the Revolution. He retired to Ludlow, but in 1702 he was found to be £3,133 in debt to the crown, and proceedings were commenced against him. He died on 8 Jan. 1705, aged 71, and was buried at Falmouth. His son had been killed in a duel by Walter Vincent II*, and Arwennack was inherited by his daughter, whose husband,

Martin Lister, assumed the name of Killigrew and wrote a history of the family.[5]

[1] Vivian, *Vis. Cornw.* 269; *London Mar. Lic.* ed. Foster, 792. [2] Carlisle, *Privy Chamber*, 165, 198. [3] *CSP Dom.* 1672–3, p. 621; 1679–80, p. 540. [4] *CJ*, viii. 12, 62; Add. 28052, f. 72; *CSP Dom.* 1667–8, p. 441; 1668–9, pp. 645–6; *Cal. Treas. Bks.* iii. 993, 1601; iv. 226–7; v. 854; vi. 807–8; *HMC 8th Rep.* pt. 1 (1881), 142, 254. [5] *Cal. Treas. Bks.* xiii. 26, 146; xvii. 366; xviii. 87; Gilbert, *Paroch. Hist. Cornw.* i. 389, 398.

M.W.H./P.W.

KILLIGREW, Sir Peter (c.1593–1668), of Arwennack, St. Budock, Cornw.

ORKNEY, SHETLAND AND
    CAITHNESS   1659[1]
HELSTON   1661–July 1668

b. c.1593, 4th s. of John Killigrew of Arwennack by Dorothy, da. of Thomas Monck of Potheridge, Merton, Devon. *m.* c. Oct. 1625, Mary, da. of Thomas Lucas† of Colchester, Essex, 1s. 1da. Kntd. 29 Dec. 1625; *suc.* bro. 1633.[2]

Gent. of the privy chamber 1633–?42.[3]
J.p. Cornw. 1655–*d.*, commr. for assessment 1657, Aug. 1660–*d.*, militia Mar. 1660; gov. Pendennis Castle Mar.–Sept. 1660; dep. lt. Cornw. 1662–*d.*[4]

Killigrew's ancestors were holding manorial property in Cornwall under Henry III, and first represented a Cornish borough in 1553. Killigrew, like so many of his family, made his career at Court. He acted as diplomatic courier during Prince Charles's visit to Spain in 1623, and on his marriage the prince (now Charles I) settled on him and his wife a pension of £200 p.a. In 1633 he inherited the Arwennack estate, reduced by litigation and extravagance to £800 p.a., and accepted employment from Parliament as a messenger during the Civil War. He was rewarded by the Rump with the grant of a market at Smithwick on Carrick Roads, where he continued the development begun by his father. He held local office under the Protectorate, and his cousin George Monck* secured his return to Richard Cromwell's Parliament for a Scottish constituency, and his appointment as governor of Pendennis on the return of the secluded Members. He was twice involved in double returns for Helston in 1660; Lord Wharton marked him as a friend, but he was never allowed to sit, in spite of favourable recommendations from the elections committee. He brought the King a letter of thanks from Monck for the Declaration of Breda and expressions of loyalty from the fleet. In September he surrendered Pendennis to Richard Arundell* in exchange for a pension of £300.[5]

Successful at Helston in the general election of 1661, Killigrew was again listed by Wharton as a friend, to be managed by himself and Sir Richard

Onslow*. An inactive Member of the Cavalier Parliament, he was appointed to only ten committees. Listed as a court dependant in 1664, he obtained a charter for Smithwick under the name of Falmouth, and arranged for the transfer of the customs house from Penryn. He raised money to build and endow a church dedicated to King Charles the Martyr, and promoted a bill to make it parochial. After passing the Lords, it was steered through committee in the Commons by John Coryton I*. Some amendments were made, and Killigrew helped to manage a successful conference. On 1 Dec. he was ordered to attend the committee of privileges on a charge of 'affronting and assaulting Sir Richard Everard*', but no report was made. On 20 Feb. 1665 he was named to a committee to permit the payment of interest in excess of the legal maximum of 6 per cent on crown loans. Appropriately enough for so indefatigable a traveller, he died at Exeter on the road to London. It was reported on 5 Aug. 1668 that his body was to be returned to Falmouth for burial in the church that he had founded.[6]

[1] N. and Q. clxvi. 65. [2] Vivian, Vis. Cornw. 268–9; CSP Dom. 1625–6, pp. 111, 152. [3] Carlisle, Privy Chamber, 134; LC3/1. [4] Cal. Cl. SP, iv. 609; CSP Dom. 1668–9, p. 646. [5] Gilbert, Paroch. Hist. Cornw. i. 388–90; Jnl. R. Inst. Cornw. iii. 269, 282; CSP Dom. 1619–23, p. 611; 1625–6, p. 152; 1644–5, p. 255; 1668–9, p. 646; Cal. Comm. Adv. Money, 192; HMC Popham, 226; CJ, viii. 115, 203; Pepys Diary, 9 May 1660. [6] CSP Dom. 1660–1, p. 387; 1661–2, p. 63; 1667–8, p. 522; Cal. Treas. Bks. i. 383.

M.W.H./P.W.

KILLIGREW, Sir William (1606–95), of Westminster.

PENRYN   1628
RICHMOND   9 Apr. 1664

> bap. 28 May 1606, 1st s. of Sir Robert Killigrew[†] of Kempton Park, Sunbury, Mdx. by Mary, da. of Sir Henry Woodhouse[†] of Hickling, Norf. educ. St. John's Oxf. 1623; travelled abroad c.1626–8. m. c.1625, Mary, da. of John Hill of Honiley, Warws., 3s. (1 d.v.p.) 1da. Kntd. 12 May 1626; suc. fa. 1633.[1]
> Col. W. Cornw. militia ?1628–35; commr. for recusants, Yorks. (W. Riding) 1675.[2]
> Gov. Pendennis Castle 1633–5; capt. of horse gds. (royalist) 1642.[3]
> Gent. usher of the privy chamber by 1640–6, May 1660–2; v.-chamberlain to Queen Catherine of Braganza 1662–85.[4]

Killigrew's grandfather, a younger son of the Arwennack family, served Elizabeth as groom of the privy chamber, and his father was vice-chamberlain to Henrietta Maria. Killigrew himself, 'a person of much honesty and very good ability', has to be distinguished from the younger brother of Sir Peter Killigrew*, a professional soldier who after long service in the Danish and Dutch armies was created a baronet at the Restoration, and commanded the Duke of York's regiment till his death in 1665. A courtier like so many of his family, Killigrew exhausted his resources in an attempt to drain the Lindsey level for the Earl of Lindsey in partnership with Robert Long* and others. After a riot in 1641 he was never able to regain possession of his property there. During the Civil War he commanded the servants' troop of the royal bodyguard. He compounded for his delinquency in 1649 on the Oxford articles with the nominal fine of £3 6s.8d. After his sale of Kempton Park in 1651 he wrote: 'my wants do drive me live wherever I am welcome', and he had to live apart from his wife after 30 years of marriage with 'never one discontent or anger between us'. The republican general John Lambert[†] sheltered him from his creditors on the former crown property at Nonsuch, and another Yorkshire officer, Adam Baynes[†], though an entire stranger, contributed to his relief. In April 1660 he advised Charles II to accept the 'golden fetters' of a restoration on terms.[5]

Killigrew's brother Thomas, who had lived in exile throughout the Interregnum, became manager of Drury Lane under patent when the theatres reopened, and Killigrew himself enjoyed some success as a playwright. He regained his position at Court, and petitioned the Lords for reinstatement in his Lincolnshire estate. He was recommended for Penryn by the Duke of York at the general election of 1661, but without effect. On the King's marriage he was appointed to the post held by his father under Charles I, and his wife also became one of the Queen's servants. Their combined salary was £800 p.a., but off-duty life at Whitehall may not have been altogether congenial to a respectable middle-aged couple, and they appear to have resided with another brother, Henry, who was a canon of Westminster. In 1663 two rival bills for drainage of the Lindsey level were introduced in the Commons, which on 6 May resolved in Killigrew's favour. But the judicial clauses gave trouble, and the bill foundered in committee. Killigrew may have acquired some acquaintance in Yorkshire through his benefactors Lambert and Baynes; but it was probably on the Wandesford interest that he was returned for Richmond at a by-election in 1664. A moderately active Member of the Cavalier Parliament, he was appointed to 53 committees, including the committee of elections and privileges in eight sessions, and made five speeches. The bulk of his parliamentary activity was directed towards the regaining of his rights in the Lindsey level, with the support of the 3rd Earl of Lindsey (Robert Bertie I*). He served on committees for settling reclaimed marshlands in both sessions of 1664, and acted as teller against the bill on 18 Feb. 1665. He was named to the committee for Falmouth church, built by his cousin, on 9 May. He first brought in his own Lindsey level bill on 28 Nov. 1666, and a week later it was ordered to be read 'the first bill after his Majesty's business is dispatched', but it made no progress this session. One of the few items of constituency interest in which Killigrew is known to have concerned himself was the bill to enable the bishop of Durham to lease certain lead mines to Humphrey Wharton* for three lives.[6]

Killigrew displayed little interest in the proceedings against Clarendon. On 14 Nov. 1667 'an ancient bill was revived and brought in for the draining of the Lindsey level, ... mainly opposed by Sir Robert Carr*, and as stoutly maintained by Sir William Killigrew and others; it was laid aside for the present', but given a first reading on the following Saturday, and committed on 28 Nov., though adverse comment was aroused by the reservation of 114,000 acres for Killigrew and his partner, Sir Henry Heron of Cressey Hall. After the Christmas recess Killigrew was added to the committee to report on business depending, and five days later the House resolved to agree with the committee to hear the matter the following week. On 28 Mar. 1668 Carr secured a fortnight's adjournment in a thin House on the Speaker's casting vote, but Killigrew succeeded in reducing this to ten days after 'a great stir and stiff debate about it'. However the need to hear the evidence at the bar of the House retarded progress. He was named to the committee to receive information about seditious conventicles in 1669, and again served on the committee for bills depending on this and the following sessions. His bill was again committed on 1 Mar. 1670, but with both Killigrew and Carr serving on the committee it is hardly surprising that it was never reported. Killigrew and his partners succeeded in buying up their opponents' counsel, a breach of professional etiquette which the House refused to consider a disqualification. On 21 Feb. 1671 it was resolved to give a month's notice to possible objectors through the high constables of four wapentakes and the incumbents of 21 parishes. Hearings began promptly, and on 27 Mar. all parties and persons were discharged from further attendance. Nothing more was heard of the bill, though Killigrew was included on both lists of government supporters as a court dependant.[7]

Killigrew was again given leave to bring in a bill for settling Lindsey level on 11 Feb. 1673, but it advanced no further than first reading. Its prospects were scarcely enhanced by his speech against the test bill, though it must have been recognized that he spoke of the Queen's household only as in duty bound. 'You will bring in more Portuguese if the English Papists be turned out, and they will never understand one another how to serve the Queen', he concluded, rather feebly. He was named on the Paston list in 1673-4 and the list of officials in 1675. Nevertheless, on 21 May he was appointed to his most important committee, on the bill to hinder Roman Catholics from sitting in Parliament. His perennial bill appeared again in the autumn session, and notice was again given to local objectors, but two days later Parliament was prorogued. Shaftesbury classed him as 'thrice vile' in 1677, but the Lindsey level bill made steady progress until it came up for hearing on 13 Mar. 1678, with a passionate statement of Killigrew's wrongs printed and circulated to Members. Two days later a motion to hear counsel for the 'country' was defeated by 138 votes to 108, and the bill was killed by the prorogation of 13 May. Its indefatigable promoter sought leave to reintroduce it on the second day of the next session, which was granted by a mere nine votes on a division. It was read on 7 June, and the House resolved in favour of a second reading, but no date was fixed, and no more was heard of it. Killigrew was included in the government list of court supporters, and on 21 Nov. in the debate on excluding the Duke of York from the House of Lords he made his last and shortest speech. 'I dread taking the Duke from the King', he began, and burst into tears. In the closing days of the Parliament he was ordered, together with the officers of the green cloth, to prepare a list of Papists resident in the royal palaces.[8]

Although not blacklisted in the 'unanimous club' of court supporters, Killigrew is unlikely to have stood again. In 1684 he published anonymously *The Artless Midnight Thoughts of a Gentleman at Court*, in which he described himself as having 'for many years built on sand, which every blast of cross fortune has defaced'; but now he had laid new foundations on the rock of his salvation. His continued interest in the Lincolnshire fens was, he assured (Sir) Stephen Fox*, for the King's benefit, not his own. In 1685 Killigrew and Heron, who had married Long's great-grand-niece, petitioned the Commons and leave was once again given to bring in a bill for the draining of the Lindsey level. By now his importunity had become a standing joke in the House. 'It used to be jestingly said: "The session is not long-lived, for Sir William Killigrew's bill is come in".' On second reading it was rejected by a vast margin. Killigrew was buried in the Savoy

Chapel, of which his brother Henry was master, on 17 Oct. 1695. Little seems to be known of his direct descendants, though his nephew Henry had become an admiral after the Restoration, and sat as a Tory under Queen Anne.[9]

[1] Vivian, *Vis. Cornw.* 270; Wood, *Athenae*, iv. 691; Add. 21423, f. 193. [2] Wood, iv. 691. [3] *CSP Dom.* 1628-9, p. 31; 1635, p. 72; Clarendon, *Rebellion*, ii. 348; *Merc. Aul.* 14 July 1643. [4] Wood, iv. 691; *Cal. Treas. Bks.* i. 583. [5] Boase and Courtney, *Bibl. Cornub.* 296-7; Carte, *Ormond*, vi. 305; F. J. G. ten Raa and F. de Bas, *Het Staatsche Leger*, iv. 242; v. 96, 481; *CSP Dom.* 1633-4, p. 35; W. H. Wheeler, *Fens of S. Lincs.* 142-3, 252-3; *Cal. Comm. Comp.* 1557-8; *VCH Mdx.* iii. 55; Add. 21423, ff. 80, 85; 21425, f. 173; Thurloe, vii. 888-90. [6] *DNB*; *HMC 7th Rep.* 129, 130; Adm. 2/1745, f. 39; *Cal. Treas. Bks.* i. 690, 691; *CJ*, viii. 477, 605, 652, 658; *CSP Dom.* 1678, p. 142. [7] *Milward*, 128, 140, 238, 246, 254-5; *CJ*, ix. 20, 21, 27, 51, 70, 206-7, 222, 224; *Lincs. Peds.* (Harl. Soc. li), 489. [8] Grey, ii. 141; vi. 243; *CJ*, ix. 363, 381, 453, 455, 482, 490, 564; *CSP Dom.* 1678, pp. 142-5. [9] Add. 51319, f. 61; *CJ*, ix. 725, 739; North, *Lives*, iii. 185.

P.A.B./J.P.F.

KING, Edward (c.1606-81), of Ashby de la Launde, Lincs.

GREAT GRIMSBY 1660

b. c.1606, 2nd but 1st surv. s. of Richard King of Ashby by Elizabeth, da. of Anthony Colly of Glaston, Rutland. *educ.* G. Inn 1623, called 1646, ancient 1650. *m.* Anne, da. of Sir Edward Ayscough[†] of Stallingborough, Lincs., 2s. 4da. *suc.* fa. 1653.[1]

Capt. of ft. (parliamentary) 1643, col. by 1644-5; gov. Boston 1643-5.[2]

Sheriff, Lincs. 1643-4, commr. for levying money 1643, defence, eastern assoc. 1643, assessment, Lincs. 1644, 1661-3, (Kesteven) Aug. 1660-1, 1663-4; dep. lt. Lincs. 1644-5; freeman, Grimsby 1645, recorder 1646-d.; commr. for sewers, Lincs. 1658, Aug. 1660, militia Mar. 1660; j.p. Kesteven Mar. 1660-3; col. of militia ft. Lincs. Apr. 1660.[3]

Commr. for disbandment Sept. 1660-1, maimed soldiers Dec. 1660-1.[4]

King's grandfather, a Londoner of Suffolk origin, bought Ashby in 1580. His father avoided commitment in the Civil War, but King was in arms for Parliament. He took part in the first attack on Newark, and was indicted for treason at the Lincolnshire assizes in 1643. Although a rigid Presbyterian, he quarrelled with Lord Willoughby of Parham, but was regarded with suspicion by Cromwell, and in 1645 his commissions were cancelled at the request of the county committee. Later in the year he stood unsuccessfully for Grimsby against (Sir) William Wray*, and he became recorder of the borough in succession to a Royalist. In 1647 he was in trouble for obstructing the collection of taxes; he held no further county office until the eve of the Restoration, and in 1659 Gervase Holles* included him among the Lincolnshire Royalists.[5]

King was returned for Grimsby on his corporation interest at the general election of 1660, and became one of the most active Members of the Convention, with special interest in the indemnity proceedings, the religious settlement, and the disbandment of the army. He was named to 83 committees, in eight of which he took the chair, acted as teller in 24 divisions, and made 45 recorded speeches. 'Factious and fanatical enough', he was marked by Lord Wharton as a friend, but won over to the Court a few days before the opening of Parliament by a leading London Royalist, who was soon able to report with satisfaction that 'none act more vigorously for the King in the House than [William] Prynne* and King', who were 'resolved to drive on as fast as possible'. On 26 Apr. he proposed in barely veiled language that they should render unto Caesar the things that were Caesar's, 'which was acclaimed as a good motion', though not by George Monck*, who told King that 'he could not promise to keep the people quiet if such motions were made'. But on Mordaunt's advice he moved on the following day 'the stopping all private business till the public was settled, and to adjourn for a day or two'. He was seconded by Heneage Finch*, anxious to secure time for the Declaration of Breda to arrive before the elections committee could question the return of Cavaliers and their sons, contrary to the Long Parliament ordinance. On 15 May he was named to the committees to examine John Thurloe[†] and to consider the indemnity bill. As chairman of the committee to prepare measures against recusants he reported a proclamation against Jesuits and seminary priests and carried it to the Lords on 29 May.[6]

After the Restoration King was among those ordered to draft clauses of exception to the indemnity bill and to administer the oaths of allegiance and supremacy to his fellow-Members. On 8 June he was appointed to the committees to prepare a proviso about those regicides who had obeyed the proclamation to give themselves up and to establish the names of those who had sat in judgment on Charles I without signing the death sentence. He was teller against allowing a full pardon to William Lenthall[†] and Sir William Roberts[†] and for the soldiers William Sydenham[†], William Boteler[†] and Richard Creed[†]. But he favoured excepting all members of the high court of justice and spoke against reading a petition from Oliver St. John[†]. On 22 June he acted as teller against reading the bill to confirm land purchases, though at a later stage he spoke for committing it. He favoured referring the petition from the intruded dons at Oxford and the unauthorized issue of Anglican publications to special committees, on both of which he served. As chairman of the committee for the impropriate rectories surrendered by Royalists as part of their compositions, he desired to prevent their immediate return, and was empowered to take over their management from the trustees for the maintenance of ministers. He was named to the committees to consider the surest and speediest way to satisfy Monck's claim on the revenue and to recommend an establishment for Dunkirk. On 29 June he was ordered to bring in a naturalization bill.[7]

King opposed requiring the beneficiaries of the indemnity bill to go through the expensive process of suing out a pardon under the great seal, but he supported a wide measure of political disablement: ''Twas not prudence to set up those in power that now lie under our feet, nor that any in the House that are guilty of such crimes should plead their own causes'. His speeches are not normally remarkable for colourful expressions, but on the proposal to compel Protectorate officials to refund their salaries he observed succinctly that ''twas fit such sponges should be squeezed', and he acted as teller for the proviso. He was among those ordered to prepare reasons for a conference on three orders issued by the Upper House and to consider two provisos to the indemnity bill on 7 July. Four days later he reported that John Hutchinson* should be compelled to refund the rewards granted to him by the Long Parliament at the expense of the Newark Royalists, and the proviso was added to the bill. He urged that religious doctrine and ecclesiastical discipline should be discussed separately, saying that 'no man could tell what the discipline according to law was', and he supported Prynne's motion that the grand committee on religion should not meet again until further orders. On 21 July he introduced a petition from divers ministers in sequestrated livings, for which he obtained a reading only by a narrow majority. Together with Sir Anthony Irby* and Matthew Hale* he was ordered to bring in a bill for nominating commissioners of sewers. His speech of 27 July suggests that his honeymoon with the restored monarchy was nearing its end: 'though he could not but admire his Majesty's goodness, yet he desired to hasten the bill of indemnity'. He was named to the committee for the bill to enable Wray to sell land for payment of debts and to the revenue committee.[8]

After urging the House 'to remove all scandalous ministers, but not to press the 39 Articles', King took the chair in the committee for settling ecclesiastical livings. There appears to have been a small Anglican majority on this committee, but by adroit use of his powers he was able to ensure that only constant refusal of the sacraments should be deemed a disqualification. On 4 Aug. he reported a bill to set up a disbandment commission. He was teller against the Lords' amendment to the disablement clause of the indemnity bill, and helped to manage a conference; but when it was objected that the Commons were obliged in honour to defend the lives of those regicides who had come in on the proclamation, he declared unanswerably that 'God had infatuated them to bring them to justice'. On 16 Aug. he carried an order to the Lords appointing a new treasurer for the maimed soldiers in Ely House and the Savoy. But for most of the month his prime concern was the ecclesiastical livings bill; he reported it on 14 Aug., and after long debate warded off a renewed Anglican attempt on the floor of the House to prevent denial of the sacrament to those who were not scandalous or ignorant. He brought in a bill for a temporary restraint on ecclesiastical leases, and opposed an inquiry into presentations to crown livings. On the last day of the month the main bill was ordered to be engrossed, and King was among those entrusted with directing the clerk of the Commons over any difficulties that might arise in the process, and with managing a conference. On 6 Sept. he obtained an order from the House empowering the disbandment commissioners to obtain assistance from the civil authorities, and was nominated to the commission. He was among those ordered to amend the instructions so that the garrisons should be disbanded last, and helped to manage a conference.[9]

During the recess Wharton sent King a copy of the case for modified episcopacy, with objections and answers, but he took no part in the debate. On most other matters in the second session he acted with the Opposition. He moved for an inquiry into the present state of the revenue before any additional supply, and on 3 Dec. he was ordered with Nicholas Pedley* and John Glyn* to take care of an inquiry into obstructions in levying the poll-tax. If London obtained an Act to impose a rate for expenditure on the King's reception, he argued, 'they must do the same favour to every city and county that desired it', and he acted as teller against the bill. He complained of the arbitrary power of the lords lieutenant, and seconded Andrew Marvell* in denouncing the fees of £150 extorted from Milton by the serjeant-at-arms. On 18 Dec. he objected that the report by John Birch* on the debts of the army and navy had not been authorized by the committee. Though generally unsympathetic to royalist claims for compensation, he obtained an order for the sister of Sir Edward Seymour* to recover £3,571 sequestrated from the customs farmers in 1644. Together with Prynne and John Barton* he was ordered to bring in a bill to recover £10,000 for charitable purposes from the prize commissioners and maintenance trustees. He was teller against a proviso to the college leases bill precluding fellows and scholars from claiming restoration to their places. He considered that compensation for officials of the court of wards should be left entirely to the King, and was named to the committee to consider the Lords' amendments to the bill. He was among those ordered to prepare reasons on the bill for confirming marriages. Assisted by Prynne and Birch, he prepared a bill to recover arrears of excise, and steered it successfully through committee. But this did not prevent him from again taking issue with Birch over his proposal for a general excise on all foreign commodities, which, he again claimed, had not been approved by the committee. Although resigned to the celebration of Christmas, he seconded the unsuccessful motion of Robert Shapcote* for a session on Boxing Day.[10]

King did not stand for re-election in 1661, and was described as 'a great abettor of sectaries and nonconformists'. But his arrest by the deputy lieutenants during the second Dutch war was, he asserted, merely an act of personal revenge on the part of Sir Robert Carr*. He was released after three months, but in February 1666 he was committed to the Tower for refusing to give security to the deputy lieutenants for his peaceable demeanour,

> by entering into a bond for £2,000 . . . to appear where he should be directed by the lord lieutenant or any two deputy lieutenants after 20 hours notice in writing left at his house, to discover all plots, conspiracies etc. and to abstain from all conventicles and seditious meetings.

He claimed such conditions were 'illegal, infamous and servile'. He bribed his way out of prison, and was defeated by Sir Henry Belasyse* in a by-election in 1667, after which he may have moved to London, where two of his daughters were living. In 1670 he was described as appearing 'daily upon the Exchange, not merely to promote sedition but rebellion and treason also' in his zeal against the renewal of the Conventicles Act. When a licence was granted for a Presbyterian meeting at his house in Ashby in 1672 it was reported that

> for many years he has endeavoured to protect those questioned for non-conformity . . . in the ecclesiastical court at Lincoln, where at common law he has counselled or set on above 90 actions.

He died at Ashby in 1681, the only member of his family to sit in Parliament.[11]

[1] Lincs. Peds. (Harl. Soc. li), 565–6. [2] Hutchinson Mems. 122; Cal. Comm. Comp. 2308; CJ, iv. 66; Whitelocke Mems. i. 252. [3] E. Gillett, Grimsby, 129; HMC 14th Rep. VIII, 283, 286; C181/6/322, 7/76; Merc. Pub. 19 Apr. 1660. [4] CJ, viii. 154, 213. [5] E. Trollope,

Sleaford, 202; Gillett, 129–30, 133; CSP Dom. 1644, p. 295; 1644–5, pp. 307, 595; Eg. 2541, f. 362. [6] Bramston Autobiog. (Cam. Soc. xxxii), 115; Cal. Cl. SP, iv. 680, 682; v. 6, 7, 13; CJ, viii. 48. [7] CJ, viii. 61, 63, 65, 66, 67, 72, 74, 76, 77; Bowman diary, ff. 5, 28, 36. [8] Bowman diary, ff. 38v, 44, 50, 74, 82v, 91, 92v, 99; CJ, viii. 81, 86, 99. [9] Bowman diary, ff. 109v, 115a, 134, 151v; CJ, viii. 111, 118, 124, 129, 138, 154, 163, 165. [10] Old Parl. Hist. xxiii. 25, 50, 51, 54, 58, 61, 64–65, 67; CJ, viii. 207, 215; 217, 219, 222, 225. [11] J. W. F. Hill, Tudor and Stuart Lincoln, 178–9; C. Holmes, 17th Cent. Lincoln, 223–6; CSP Dom. 1664–5, p. 565; 1665–6, pp. 247, 296; 1668–9, p. 44; 1670, pp. 226, 235; 1671–2, pp. 568, 587; 1672, pp. 536, 538–9; Gillett, 133–4.

M.W.H./P.W.

KING, Thomas (d.1688), of London.

HARWICH 1659, 1661

> m. (1) 18 Jan. 1647, Mary, da. of Charles Gooch, merchant, of Great Yarmouth, Norf., 1s.; (2) Alice, 2s.[1]
> Freeman, Yarmouth 1647; commr. for assessment, Essex Aug. 1660–79, Harwich 1663–79, corporations, Essex 1662–3; dep. collector of hearth-tax, Suff. 1666–7; commr. for recusants, Essex 1675.[2]
> Gent. of privy chamber 1671–85.

Nothing is known of King before 1647 when he married into a prominent Yarmouth merchant family and became a victualler to the parliamentary navy. But he later claimed that during the second Civil War he 'ventured estate and liberty to relieve the King with provisions from Yarmouth in Colchester siege'. He transferred his business activities to Harwich in 1650, where several families of the name were already established. But he never attained municipal office, and there is no evidence that he was related to a namesake who served as mayor in 1651–2, while he described Captain John King, who commanded the Harwich garrison under the Protectorate, as a villain. His own newly-built house and warehouse, he complained, were wrested from him by Cromwell in 1657 to make way for a new dockyard, and he apparently moved to London, though he represented the borough in Richard Cromwell's Parliament.[3]

King regained his seat in 1661, and became a moderately active Member of the Cavalier Parliament. He was appointed to 110 committees and thrice acted as teller. Under the Clarendon Administration his activities were almost entirely mercantile. As the 'moving spirit' in the Royal Fishery project, it was probably King who introduced into the House on 5 Mar. 1662 a bill to confirm the charter. He was one of the four Members ordered to compare the texts. In the same session he acted as teller against including tin in the bill to prevent customs fraud and for a temporary suspension of the Merchant Adventurers' monopoly of cloth exports. He moved the rejection of a proviso to the hearth-tax bill proposed by Sir Thomas Littleton, 2nd Bt.*, and his Harwich premises were restored to him, though he did not retain them long. But he was regarded with such suspicion in government circles that he deemed it necessary to inform Clarendon by letter that he was not the brother of the Presbyterian Edward King*. His proposals for the fisheries, he asserted, would increase trade, employ the poor, promote seamanship and encourage shipping. He suggested a joint stock company to build fishing busses, offered to lay out money himself, provided he got royal financial backing, and advised bringing over Dutch families to promote the project. Lord Treasurer Southampton encouraged the scheme, with the result that in September the Government advanced £9,000, to be supplemented by a voluntary subscription, for the construction of ten busses at Harwich and Deptford. King served on committees to consider improvements in the customs and defects in the hearth-tax in 1663, and on those to settle the disputes over the Yarmouth herring trade (24 Nov. 1664) and a petition on naval debts (14 Jan. 1665). Meanwhile Samuel Pepys* had prepared a highly critical report on the finances of the Royal Fishery. Only £1,076 of the voluntary subscription had been paid in, but more had been collected, of which King retained £429 and the Earl of Pembroke, the nominal governor, a considerable sum. According to Pepys, instead of handing over the money, King had 'insinuated in his accounts' that he had assigned to the Fishing Company the lease of his house in Harwich, which was said to be worth £700. 'It may be fit', wrote Pepys, 'to inquire whether this house was not long ago otherwise disposed of by him, and is since fallen to his Majesty and now actually employed by the officers of the navy in his Majesty's service.' Pepys also drew attention to another instance whereby King was defrauding the Company, and finally suggested improved methods of collection and accounting.[4]

King's financial unreliability was now notorious. As a deputy collector of the hearth-tax for Suffolk, he was accused by his partners of withholding funds during the three-year farm, but he seems to have escaped any serious consequences. Probably an opponent of Clarendon, in 1667 he was named to the committees to inquire into the sale of Dunkirk, to report on the proceedings in Lord Mordaunt's impeachment, to consider the public accounts bill, to hear a petition from Cirencester against the hearth-tax, and to examine the case of the French merchants. He was named to committees to consider a petition for the encouragement of navigation, to bring in a bill for the use of prize ships and to consider the bills for settling the balance of trade with Scotland. He was teller on 9 Mar. 1670 for the

unsuccessful motion to proceed with the debate on union with Scotland before considering the conventicles bill. He was twice among those appointed to bring in a bill to regulate the making of brandy, and helped to consider four bills for the repair of Yarmouth pier and harbour. On 2 Apr. 1670 he was among those charged with preparing reasons for the rejection of the Lords' proviso on behalf of Norwich. As a Member who had usually voted for supply he was on both lists of the court party in 1669–71, and he was given further protection against his creditors by a post in the privy chamber. He was less active politically after the collapse of the Cabal ministry. His principal committees in 1673 were to consider the bill for the prevention of abuses in parliamentary elections, to bring in the general naturalization bill, and to draft an address on the state of Ireland. In 1674 he was added to the committee for the general test bill and appointed to that to consider the charges of corruption brought by Thomas Master I*. In the debate of 26 Apr. 1675 on Danby's impeachment he declared, in his only recorded speech, that

> he would take time to consider of these articles, and not proceed hastily upon them. He has known great good the Lord Treasurer has done. He has paid off the navy and the army. These articles are high and should be well considered of.

In 1675 he served on the committees for appropriating the customs to the use of the navy, and for considering a test to vindicate Members from accusations of corruption. He was granted £300 p.a. from the excise 'over and above all the money he had received'. His subservience to the Court and his notorious penury were satirized in *The Chequer Inn*, a poem on the Members trying to prevent Danby's impeachment

> But King, God save him, though so crammed,
> The cheer into his breeches rammed,
> That buttery were and larder;
> And of more provand to dispose,
> Had sewed on too his double hose,
> For times, thou knowest, grow harder.

At the end of the parliamentary session in November 1675, King, driven by financial necessity, first entered a claim for £238 6s. parliamentary wages, on the grounds that constant attendance in Parliament necessitated residence 'in and about the cities of London and Westminster, whereby his own private affairs were neglected'. He was included in the working lists, and in 1676 Sir Richard Wiseman* considered him 'a certain vote'. Shaftesbury marked him 'thrice vile', and in *Flagellum Parliamentarium* he was described as 'a poor beggarly fellow who sold his vote to the treasurer for £50 bribe'. The author of *A Seasonable Argument*, even more contemptuously, called him 'a pensioner for £50 a session, etc., meat and drink, and now and then a suit of clothes'. The corporation alleged inability to meet King's claim, though in 1677 they deposited £90 with Sir Anthony Deane* to be invested on their behalf. During the winter he almost died of pleurisy, but 'crept to the House' to vote for the Government in a vital division. He appeared on both lists of the court party in 1678. Among his later committees were those to take account of the additional excise and to inquire into the Popish Plot.[5]

King is unlikely to have stood again, and his rejection by the Harwich corporation led him to revive his claim for parliamentary wages, now increased to £383 6s. On 2 Dec. 1679 he petitioned for a writ in Chancery which was granted three months later. But the claim was settled out of court by the 2nd Duke of Albemarle (Christopher Monck*). King continued to receive secret service payments until his death. Between February 1680 and April 1688 he received £2,486, either 'in consideration of his pretension to interest money' for a debt due to him from Charles I, or 'as of free gift and royal bounty'. He died between April and October 1688, in which latter month £50 bounty was paid to his widow. His son Thomas, an army officer, sat for Queenborough with one interval from 1696 to 1722.[6]

[1] *Yarmouth Freemen* (Norf. Arch. Soc. 1910), 56, 78; PCC 157 Romney; *Secret Service Moneys* (Cam. Soc. lii), 207; *Al. Carthusiani*, 39. [2] *CJ*, viii. 287; *Cal. Treas. Bks.* ii. 62; iii. 291, 1201. [3] *Cal. Cl. SP*, v. 217, 219; *CSP Dom.* 1650, pp. 79, 82; *Cal. Treas. Bks.* i. 368. [4] PC2/56/25; *Pepys Diary*, 10, 25 Oct. 1664; *CJ*, viii. 390, 399; *Cal. Cl. SP*, v. 217, 219, 234; *VCH Essex*, ii. 286–7; *Cal. Treas. Bks.* i. 338; *CSP Dom.* 1661–2, pp. 477, 499; J. R. Elder, *Royal Fishery Companies*, 103–4. [5] *Cal. Treas. Bks.* ii. 62; iii. 291, 1201; iv. 871; v. 335; *Pepys Diary*, 9 Nov. 1667; *CJ*, ix. 153; Grey iii. 44; *Poems on Affairs of State*, i. 258; Harwich bor. recs. 57/3, 17, 19; 98/4/113; Eg. 3338, f. 103. [6] Harwich bor. recs. 57/5; 68/5; 98/4/66; 133/8; G. W. Sanders, *Orders in Chancery*, i. 353; *EHR*, lxvi. 47–48; *Secret Service Moneys*, passim.

G.H./G.J.

KINGDON, Lemuel (c.1654–86), of Whitehall and Great Russell Street, Bloomsbury, Mdx.

KINGSTON-UPON-HULL	1679 (Mar.)
NEWTOWN I.o.W.	1679 (Oct.)
YARMOUTH I.o.W.	1681
GREAT BEDWYN	1685–Feb. 1686

b. c.1654, o.s. of Richard Kingdon of Cornhill, London and Hackney, Mdx. by w. Jane. *m.* lic. 20 June 1677, aged 23, Theodosia, da. and h. of Thomas Carpenter of Upper Chilston, Herefs. and Lincoln's Inn, 1s. 4da. *suc.* fa. 1675.[1]

Dep. paymaster of the forces 1676–9; jt. farmer of hearth-tax surplus 1681–*d.*; commr. for revenue [I] 1682–*d.*; PC [I] 1682–*d.*[2]

Commr. for assessment, Hull and Herefs. 1679–80; keeper of New Park, New Forest 1681–*d.*[3]

Kingdon's father, who was probably of Cornish origin, was described as a 'precious, good man' and 'a very faithful servant' of the Protectorate, under which he held numerous offices, including those of commissioner of claims in Ireland and comptroller of prizes during the war with Spain. At the Restoration he sued out his pardon and passed easily into the service of the Stuarts as auditor of army accounts, returning to the prize office during the second Dutch war. He joined the syndicate formed by Lord Ranelagh (Richard Jones*) to farm the Irish revenues, and also served on the excise commission in England. With two of his colleagues on the board, Sir John James and Major Richard Huntington, he helped Danby to undermine the virtual monopoly of government credit exercised by (Sir) Stephen Fox*, though he died before Fox's dismissal in 1676. Thereupon Kingdon himself was nominated by his father's surviving partners to take charge of the Pay Office as deputy to Sir Henry Puckering*, whose functions were almost entirely social. He seems to have envisaged himself as an intermediary with Shaftesbury, and was also in touch with the Duke of Buckingham and John Wildman I*. In 1677 he married a 16-year-old heiress, giving her age as 18 on the licence and claiming the consent of her mother, who had long been dead.[4]

Kingdon's duties had brought him into close contact with the Duke of Monmouth, especially during the Flanders campaign, and at the first general election of 1679 Monmouth, as high steward of Hull, recommended him to the corporation and freemen, who would have appreciated his puritan background. He was duly returned, and classed as 'base' on Shaftesbury's list. On 1 Apr. he presented the disbandment accounts to the House, and was named to the committee to inspect them, a curious arrangement since he was inevitably the principal witness. Sir Richard Cust* reported that he had assured the committee that the whole of the £200,000 voted for paying off the newly-raised forces had been properly disbursed. Yet because payment had not been made

strictly pursuant to the letter of the Act, many would have reflected upon others, particularly Mr Kingdon, the paymaster (as a Member of the House), who found out an expedient to stop their mouths who were opened widest against him by offering to advance £3,000 on the security of the second payment of this new Act, which would be enough to pay off all the common soldiers what is allowed them to carry them home, being ten a man, this not going either to pay for their clothes or quarters. Thus a little water well applied served to quench as fierce a flame as hath yet been kindled, to the great disappointment of those who designed to improve it further.

Kingdon's bluff may have saved the Government, but with the pay of the remaining forces now ten months in arrears, his own position was desperate, and he and his partners were facing ruin. He was absent from the division on the exclusion bill, and on 28 May the paymastership was restored to Fox, who passed it on to his son. Nevertheless Kingdon offered himself for re-election; but, finding that the Hull corporation 'were not so well satisfied with me as I was in good hopes I had deserved', he availed himself of the interest of his neighbour Sir Robert Holmes*, who had 'fallen into a great intrigue with his wife' and returned him for Newtown. Much to Holmes's annoyance, Kingdon was obliged to quit his official residence in Whitehall, and on 26 Jan. 1680 the *London Gazette* announced that tallies in his hands could not be assigned until his accounts had been cleared. In the second Exclusion Parliament he was not appointed to any committees, but he twice intervened in the debate of 25 Nov. to defend Ranelagh's crony, Edward Seymour*, denying that the newly-raised forces had been kept in being, either by Seymour's advances or his own payments, after their disbandment had been voted. In 1681 he was returned for Yarmouth, another Isle of Wight borough under Holmes's control. Undaunted by the collapse of the 'undertaking', he launched into a new speculation with his wife's kinsman William Bridges and a third partner named Trant. Aware, presumably, that he was out of favour with the Treasury board, on which Fox was now sitting, he made use of a certain John Genew, who leased the farm of the hearth-tax surplus on 12 Mar., and nine days later made it over to Kingdon's syndicate. On the same day Kingdon was named to the committee of elections and privileges at Oxford, and he was also among those ordered to find a more convenient place for the Commons to meet.[5]

Holmes's interest in the Kingdon family was by no means at an end, and in September 1681 he conveyed New Park in the New Forest to Kingdon, with life reversions to his wife and Bridges. In 1682 he was appointed to the Irish revenue commission, with a salary of £1,000 p.a. and left to take up his post, borrowing £6,157 from his mother, presumably to secure a departure unimpeded by clamorous creditors. He dominated the board with his 'imperious, governing temper'; but he was a great success socially, winning the confidence of Lord Arran (Lord Richard Butler*), who asked his father Ormonde to show Kingdon 'all the favour you justly can, for I think he deserves it'. In the closing weeks of Charles II's reign the disposal of the hearth-tax surplus came under scrutiny, and it was reported that Kingdon and his partners had been dismissed and required to refund several thousand pounds of which they had cheated the crown. The King's death failed to interrupt the inquiry, and Kingdon must have considered that a seat in Parliament would be a valuable safeguard. At the general election of 1685 he was returned for Bedwyn as a placeman, on the interest of Thomas Bruce*, Lord Bruce. A moderately active Member of James II's Parliament, he was named to eight committees, of which the most important was again to inspect the disbandment accounts. On 11 July his farm of the hearth-tax surplus was extended for five years on payment of £30,000. Presumably he voted with the Court in the stormy second session, for when Charles Fox* was dismissed it was reported that Kingdon might return to the Pay Office as deputy to Ranelagh, the new paymaster. But by January 1686 he was ill beyond hope of recovery, and on 19 Feb. he was buried at St. Giles in the Fields. He left his affairs in great confusion, and legacies of £6,000 could not be paid in full. The 2nd Earl of Clarendon (Henry Hyde*) wrote: 'I am not surprised at any ill thing which is discovered of Kingdon, because I never had a good opinion of the man, knowing so much of his father and of his own beginning'. With notable impartiality, he left his children to the joint guardianship of the Tory Seymour and the Whig John Hawles*, if his widow should remarry. He was the only member of the family to sit in Parliament.[6]

[1] F. B. Kingdon, *Kingdon Fam.* 33, 47, 49; *London Mar. Lic.* ed. Foster, 798; *L. Inn Adm. Reg.* i. 254; C. J. Robinson, *Mansions and Manors of Herefs.* 192. [2] *Cal. Treas. Bks.* v. 128; vi. 70; viii. 596–7; *CSP Dom.* 1682, pp. 500, 515. [3] Kingdon, 56. [4] Ibid. 35–47; C. Clay, *Pub. Finance and Private Wealth*, 94–95, 103; *HMC 11th Rep. VII*, 12; Kingdon, 67. [5] *CSP Dom.* 1676–7, p. 505; 1677–8, p. 242; 1679–80, pp. 53, 378; *HMC Ormonde*, n.s. v. 76; *CJ*, ix. 610; Bodl. Carte 39, f. 65; Clay, 121, 124; Hull corp. letters, 955; Grey, viii. 81–82, 85; *Cal. Treas. Bks.* viii. 596–7. [6] Kingdon, 56, 66; *Clarendon Corresp.* i. 319, 328; *HMC Ormonde*, n.s. vii. 152; Luttrell, i. 326; *HMC Egmont*, ii. 145–6, 172; *Cal. Treas. Bks.* viii. 4, 261, 396–7; *N. and Q.* ser. 10, xii. 408; *Ellis Corresp.* i. 12, 39, 45, 50; PCC 5 Exton.

P.W.

KIRKBY, Richard (c.1625–81), of Kirkby Ireleth, Lancs.

LANCASTER 1661, 1679 (Mar.), 1679 (Oct.), 1681

b. c.1625, 1st s. of Roger Kirkby† of Kirkby Ireleth by Agnes, da. of Sir John Lowther† of Lowther, Westmld. *educ.* Muncaster g.s. (Mr Rutter); St. John's, Camb. adm. 24 Apr. 1640, aged 14; G. Inn 1640. *m.* (1) Elizabeth, da. and coh. of David Murray, tailor, of Westminster, 1s. 2da.; (2) Isabel, da. of Sir William Huddlestone of Millom Castle, Cumb., 2s. 1da.; (3) bef. 29

Mar. 1661, Helena, da. of Greville Maxey of Bradwell, Essex, wid. of Thomas Eden of Doreward's Hall, Bocking, Essex, 1s.; (4) unknown. *suc.* fa. 1643.[1]

Commr. for assessment, Lancs. Aug. 1660–80, Essex 1664–74, Suff. 1664–79; col. of militia ft. Lancs. by 1661–*d.*, dep. lt. 1662–*d.*, commr. for corporations 1662–3, loyal and indigent officers 1662; freeman, Preston 1662; j.p. Lancs. by 1663–*d.*, custos rot. by 1664–*d.*, receiver of assessments 1664–9; sub.-commr. of prizes, Hull 1665–6, 1672–4; constable, Lancaster Castle 1667–74; commr. for licensing hackney-coaches, London and Westminster 1675–?*d.*[2]

Surveyor of woods, duchy of Lancaster (north) Sept. 1660–74; gent. of the privy chamber 1668–*d.*[3]

Capt. 1 Ft. (Grenadier) Gds. 1669–74.

Kirkby's ancestors were established at Kirkby Ireleth in Furness by the 12th century, but Kirkby's father, who represented Lancaster in both the Short and Long Parliaments until disabled, was the first of the family to be elected. Although inclined to puritanism, he was one of the most energetic royalist commanders in the north until his early death. Kirkby himself served in the Cavalier army under the Marquess of Newcastle, and was fined £750 for his delinquency.[4]

Kirkby took no part in politics until the Restoration, when he was proposed as a knight of the Royal Oak, with an estate of £1,500 p.a. He and his friend Roger Bradshaigh I* tried unsuccessfully to persuade the new Government to override the Earl of Derby's almost hereditary claim to the lord lieutenancy of Lancashire in favour of Lord Gerard of Brandon. He was returned at the general election of 1661 for Lancaster, a borough which he and his son were to represent continuously, with one break of ten months, in 11 Parliaments until 1702. An active Member till disabled by gout and financial troubles, Kirkby was named to 285 committees in the Cavalier Parliament, taking the chair in seven. He acted as teller in 12 divisions, but spoke infrequently. In the opening session he was named to the committees for the corporations, uniformity and regicides bills, and again for the additional corporations bill in 1662. But when it came to enforcing the new laws at Lancaster, Kirkby was for moderation 'to gratify those who had elected him burgess of Parliament'. He served on the committee to examine the printer of a scandalous pamphlet against Edward Rigby*, who later repaid him by steering his estate bill through Parliament. He was one of the small committee appointed on 16 May 1662 to consider the Lords' proviso on the distribution of £60,000 to Cavalier officers. In 1663 he acted as teller for two provisos to the conventicles bill, helped to manage a conference on relief from the Act of Uniformity, and took the chair for a naturalization bill and a charity bill. In the next

session he was teller for the Court in a division on the repeal of the Triennial Act, and was appointed to the committee for the conventicles bill. In the last session of the Clarendon administration he took part in the conference on the Canary patent and acted as teller (against Bradshaigh) for the unsuccessful motion to agree with the Lords over the impeachment of Mordaunt. He also chaired in committee an estate bill and a bill on Welsh replevins.[5]

Kirkby's parliamentary activity reached its height in the sessions immediately following the fall of Clarendon. He had his own grievance against the late administration; the reduction in the number of prize commissioners in 1666 had a disastrous effect on his personal finances. An attempt to form a regiment came to nothing, and the Treasury, who were having great difficulty with his brother over his accounts as receiver of hearth-tax, turned a deaf ear to his request for a seat on the excise board. Perhaps he would have been more successful if he had persuaded (Sir) John Otway* to stand down in favour of Joseph Williamson* at the Preston by-election, but his influence did not extend so far. On 23 Oct. 1667 Kirkby was one of seven Members sent to Prince Rupert and the Duke of Albemarle (George Monck*) to ask about the division of the fleet in 1666 and the failure to fortify the Medway. Two days later he and (Sir) Thomas Clifford* were instructed to obtain from Secretary Arlington an explanation of the breakdown of naval intelligence during the war. Since Lord Derby seems to have regarded Arlington as a friend, the probability is that Kirkby was less well-disposed to him, and his nomination was intended to prevent the secretary's creature Clifford from sweeping too much under the carpet. He was named to the chief political committees in this session, including that for the banishment of Clarendon, though he took no part in the impeachment. Kirkby was popular in the House, and an allegation that he had been bribed to present a petition from the vintners was dismissed with contempt. On 10 Mar. 1668, he was forced to ask the House for protection against his creditors for the first time. Perhaps this was not unconnected with his request for leave to bring in a bill on chancery fees three days earlier. On 11 Mar. he moved that the Declaration of Breda should be read to the House; it is not clear to what end, for he was hostile to dissenters. In April he acted as teller for the Court in two divisions on the supply bill. He took the chair in committees on three estate bills in the 1668 session.[6]

Kirkby again spoke against toleration in 1670, relating his distasteful experience as a militia officer ordered to suppress conventicles. 'His company were pelted with stones, and they followed him a long mile pelting him, and told him they came to put the devil's laws, and not God's, in execution. . . . They threaten justices and officers, and you will not only have suits, but all about your ears.' He was one of the Members named by Sir George Downing* as a debtor to the crown, but as this was known to have been incurred only as security for his brother the effect was to win the House's sympathy for him. He was reckoned a friend to Ormonde, and one of the Members to be gained for the Court by the Duke of York. He strove to appease the uproar over the assault on Sir John Coventry*: 'a greater offence than this we petitioned the King to pardon, which was his father's murder'.[7]

The third Dutch war brought Kirkby some financial relief as a prize official. But he had again to appeal for parliamentary privilege on 30 Oct. 1673. Four days later he spoke against the disbandment of the army. His name appeared on the Paston list, and he was appointed to the committee for the general test bill in 1674. But with the prorogation he had to take refuge from his creditors in Gray's Inn, pathetically writing to Williamson:

> With justice I may pretend to my sovereign's kindness, for I have ventured my life, spent my estate and ruined my children already for him. Surely either in the navy, excise or customs an employment may fall for me ere long.

Kirkby received only £200 (against the £500 with which he was credited in *A Seasonable Argument*) and was forced to sell his commission and most of his offices. Nevertheless he was still regarded as a court dependant. He served on the committee to restrain the growth of Popery in the spring session of 1675, and received the government whip for the autumn session. He was named to the committee for the recall of British subjects from French service; but this was probably his last appearance in the Cavalier Parliament. He was classed as a court supporter by Sir Richard Wiseman* in 1676, and as 'thrice vile' on Shaftesbury's list in 1677; but both in 1677 and 1678 he was detained in the country with gout, and the opposition did not blacklist him in the 'unanimous club'.[8]

In the succeeding general election Kirkby's brother was very active in marshalling the freeholders for the country candidates in Lancashire, together with Rigby, but Kirkby's own politics were unaffected, and he was marked as 'court' on Huntingdon's list. He was named to only two committees in the first Exclusion Parliament, the committee of elections and privileges and that for the better attendance of Members. He voted against the exclusion bill. In 1680 he served only on the committee for the removal of Papists from the metropolitan area. His financial position had further deteriorated, and he wrote that he had 'neither bread nor clothes, nor money nor credit to purchase them, so that, unless his Majesty compassionates him, he will be unable to appear in Parliament, but must starve or perish in prison or the streets'. He was probably absent from the Oxford Parliament, and died on 9 Sept. 1681.[9]

[1] *Vis. Lancs.* (Chetham Soc. lxxxv), 169; *HMC Fleming*, 370, 397; Morant, *Essex*, ii. 157. [2] *CSP Dom.* 1661–2, pp. 173, 524, 532, 553; 1663–4, p. 337; 1665–6, pp. 443–4; 1667–8, p. 108; 1668–9, p. 629; 1671–2, p. 362; 1673–5, p. 353; 1675–6, p. 173; 1678, p. 510; Lancs. RO, QSC 63–83; *Cal. Treas. Bks.* vii. 1424; *Preston Guild Rolls* (Lancs. and Cheshire Rec. Soc. ix), 147. [3] Sir Robert Somerville, *Duchy of Lancaster Official Lists*, 80, 136; Carlisle, *Privy Chamber*, 182. [4] *VCH Lancs.* viii. 392–6; Keeler, *Long Parl.* 240; *Royalist Comp. Pprs.* (Lancs. and Cheshire Rec. Soc. xxxvi), 43–46. [5] SP29/61/85; *CSP Dom.* 1661–2, p. 517; *CJ*, viii. 461, 479, 509, 514, 533, 538, 654, 660, 662, 686. [6] *CSP Dom.* 1665–6, pp. 443–4; 1666–7, p. 497; 1667, p. 543; 1667–8, p. 108; *HMC Kenyon*, 79; *Cal. Treas. Bks.* ii. 113; viii. 1230; *Milward*, 62, 135, 210, 214; *CJ*, ix. 59, 60, 88, 89, 94. [7] Grey, i. 305, 323, 343. [8] Grey, ii. 221; *CSP Dom.* 1673–5, p. 355; 1675–6, p. 173; 1677–8, pp. 396, 584. [9] Westmorland RO, Fleming mss 2150; *CSP Dom.* 1680–1, p. 697.

I.C.

KIRKBY, Roger (c.1649–1709), of Kirkby Ireleth, Lancs.

LANCASTER 1685, 21 Nov. 1689, 1690, 1695, 1698, 1701 (Feb.), 1701 (Dec.)

b. c.1649, 1st s. of Richard Kirkby* by 1st w. *m.* 7 Aug. 1692, Catherine, da. and coh. of Sir John Baker, 3rd Bt., of Sissinghurst, Kent, 1s. *d.v.p. suc.* fa. 1681.[1]

Ensign, 1 Ft. (Grenadier) Gds. 1670–5; capt. of ft., regt. of Sir Charles Wheler* 1678–9, Chester garrison 1685, regt. of Sackville Tufton* (later 15 Ft.) by 1687–?89; gov. Chester 1693–1702.[2]

Freeman, Preston 1662, 1682; j.p. Lancs. 1684–?d., commr. for assessment 1689–90; dep. lt. Lancs. 1689–?96, Lancs. and Flints by 1701–?d.; col. of militia ft. Lancs. 1689–?d., sheriff 1708–d.[3]

Kirkby inherited his father's debts as well as his political principles. As a magistrate he was active in enforcing the laws against nonconformity. His military career was intermittent, and it was as a civilian that he was first returned for Lancaster on his natural interest at the general election of 1685. A moderately active Member of James II's Parliament, he was appointed to four committees, of which the most important was to take the disbandment accounts. Recommissioned during Monmouth's rebellion, 'trusty Captain Kirkby' declared himself enthusiastically in favour of the repeal of the Test Act and Penal Laws. But he was probably moved neither by conviction nor loyalty, for he had had the misfortune to kill a brother officer in a duel a few days earlier, and his pardon might depend on his acceptance of the King's religious policy.[4]

Kirkby was ordered to stand for re-election as court candidate in 1688, but he was defeated at the general election, and the House refused to receive his petition. Though he was compelled to mortgage Kirkby Ireleth to a London banker, he regained his seat at the by-election caused by the death of Curwen Rawlinson* later in the year. Although he was accused of 'putting the town and country to the great charge of many hundred pounds needlessly and unreasonably at this time of great taxes for buying solders' clothes at his own rate and by his own bespeaking', as colonel of militia he enjoyed the support of the Gerard interest and with it the nonconformist vote. He turned to his advantage 'a contest between the governing part of the town and the *mobile* about an assessment', and 'by his hectoring and swaggering for the *mobile*' fairly drove his opponent out of the borough. An inactive Member of the Convention, he was named to only three committees, including that for settling the militia, to which he was added on 4 Jan. 1690. He was not listed as a supporter of the disabling clause, but he sat in all the remaining Parliaments of William III's reign as a court Whig. He died on 8 Feb. 1709, aged 59, and was buried in St. Martin in the Fields. He had never been able to redeem his estate, and no later members of the family entered Parliament.[5]

[1] *Hunter's Peds.* (Harl. Soc. lxxxviii), 102; *Kent Par. Reg.* ii. 115. [2] *CSP Dom.* 1693, p. 31; *Cal. Treas. Bks.* xviii. 1184. [3] *Preston Guild Rolls* (Lancs. and Cheshire Rec. Soc. ix), 147, 190; Lancs. RO, QSC 86–130; *HMC Kenyon*, 411; *CSP Dom.* 1689–90, p. 138; Eg. 1626, f. 25; Luttrell, vi. 407. [4] *HMC Kenyon*, i. 172; *HMC Le Fleming*, 205, 206. [5] *CSP Dom.* 1687–9, p. 276; Westmld. RO, D/Ry3442; Bodl. Rawl. D863, ff. 33–49; *VCH Lancs.* viii. 396; Harl. 6835, f. 31.

I.C.

KIRKE, Percy (*d.*1691), of Whitehall.

WEST LOOE   1689

s. of George Kirke† (*d.*1675), keeper of Whitehall Palace, by 2nd w. Mary, da. of Aurelian Townsend, gent. of the privy chamber, of Barbican, London. *m.* bef. 1684, Lady Mary Howard, da. of George, 4th Earl of Suffolk, 1s. 2da.[1]

Ensign, Admiralty Regt. 1666; cornet, R. Horse Gds. (The Blues) 1670, lt. 1674, capt.-lt. 1675, capt. 1679; lt. 1 R. English Regt. (French army) 1675, maj. 1675–8; lt.-col. 2 Tangier Regt. (4 Ft.) 1680–2, col. 1 Tangier Regt. (Queen's Ft.) 1682–*d.*; gov. Tangier 1682–4, Londonderry 1689; brig. 1685, maj.-gen. Nov. 1688, lt.-gen. 1690–*d.*[2]

Freeman, Portsmouth 1683; keeper, Whitehall Palace 1687–*d.*; commr. for reforming abuses in the army 1689; groom of the bedchamber 1689–*d.*[3]

Kirke's father, a Scottish immigrant, served

Charles I both before and after his accession, sat for Clitheroe in 1626, and was naturalized in 1628. His first wife was Cornish by birth, the daughter of Sir Robert Killigrew†. He remained loyal to the King during the Civil War, and in 1646 married at Oxford the daughter of a court playwright, Charles himself giving the bride away. A few months later he compounded for £660, but was compelled to pay a further £325 for under-valuation. At the Restoration he became groom of the bedchamber and keeper of Whitehall. Kirke's parents and sisters were all the subject of scandalous report at the court of Charles II.[4]

Kirke, a professional soldier, was first commissioned in the Duke of York's regiment in the second Dutch war, and then served under his brother-in-law, the Earl of Oxford, in The Blues. He was seconded to the Duke of Monmouth in 1672, and fought in the French army during and after the third Dutch war. Assisted by Charles Trelawny*, he raised a new regiment for Tangier, which from its badge of the paschal lamb was to be ironically nicknamed 'Kirke's Lambs'. That impeccable moralist, Samuel Pepys*, officially condemned the drunken and dissolute way of life which Kirke both condoned and practised in Tangier, as well as 'his exactions on poor merchants, letting nothing be sold till he had the refusal'. Kirke returned to England when Tangier was abandoned in 1684, fought at Sedgemoor, and became notorious for his excesses after Monmouth's rebellion, which James afterwards came to suspect were deliberately inflicted to make him odious to his subjects. According to Burnet:

Kirke, who had commanded long in Tangier, was become so savage by the neighbourhood of the Moors there, that, some days after the battle, he ordered several of the prisoners to be hanged up at Taunton without so much as the form of law, he and his company looking on from an entertainment they were at. At every new health another prisoner was hanged up. And they were so brutal that observing the shaking of the legs of those whom they hanged, it was said among them they were dancing, and upon that music was called for. This was both so illegal and so inhuman that it might have been expected that some notice would have been taken of it. But Kirke was only chid for it.

In fact the only reproofs which Kirke is recorded as receiving were for taking free quarter, and freeing, doubtless corruptly, 'several persons who were actually in the late rebellion or abetting the same'. Nothing in his life suggests any firm attachment to the Protestant religion, which James confidently urged him to desert for the Church of Rome; but Kirke is said to have successfully pleaded a prior engagement to the ruler of Morocco to embrace Islam if he should ever change his religion. He retained his commission, and was promoted major-general on the landing of William of Orange, though he was already secretly committed to the Revolution. A fortnight later he was arrested on suspicion of plotting with Trelawny to arrest James at Warminster and hand him over to his son-in-law; but positive evidence was lacking, and he was discharged. Trelawny and about 30 of the 'Lambs' had already joined the invaders, and Kirke soon followed them.[5]

At the general election of 1689 Kirke was returned for West Looe on the Trelawny interest. A court Tory in the Convention, he did not vote against the transfer of the crown, and was appointed only to the committees for the bill to suspend habeas corpus and the first mutiny bill. He was soon called away to take command of the force which broke the siege of Londonderry. He died in Brussels on active service on 31 Oct. 1691. His son was also a distinguished soldier, but no other member of the family sat in Parliament.[6]

[1] *DNB*; *Westminster Abbey Reg.* (Harl. Soc. x), 295. [2] J. Childs, *Army of Charles II*, 245-6. [3] R. East, *Portsmouth Recs.* 367; Luttrell, i. 413; LS13/231/17; *CSP Dom.* 1689-90, p. 97; *Cal. Treas. Bks.* ix. 330. [4] *Chamberlain Letters*, ii. 480; *Denizations and Naturalizations* (Huguenot Soc. xviii), 41; G. E. Aylmer, *King's Servants*, 142; *Cal. Comm. Comp.* 1469-70; *CSP Dom.* 1661-2, p. 244; *Bulstrode Pprs.* 304. [5] *CSP Dom.* 1672-3, p. 601; Burnet, iii. 58-59, 122, 279; Clarke, *Jas. II*, ii. 44-45; *CSP Dom.* 1685, pp. 262, 279; 1687-9, pp. 361-3; Luttrell, i. 354, 483; Burnet, *Supp.* 532. [6] *CSP Dom.* 1689-90, pp. 59, 81; Luttrell, ii. 299.

P.W.

KNATCHBULL, John (c.1636-96), of Mersham Hatch, Kent.

NEW ROMNEY   1660
KENT   1685, 1689, 1690

b. c.1636, 1st s. of Sir Norton Knatchbull, 1st Bt.*. *educ.* Trinity Coll. Camb. 1652; I. Temple 1655. *m.* 17 Jan. 1659, Jane, da. and coh. of Sir Edward Monyns, 2nd Bt., of Waldershare, 3s. *d.v.p.* 9da. *suc.* fa. 5 Feb. 1685.
Commr. for militia, Kent Mar. 1660, maj. of militia horse Apr. 1660-at least 1685; freeman, New Romney Apr. 1660; commr. for assessment, Kent Aug. 1660-80, for sewers, Denge marsh Oct. 1660, Walland marsh Dec. 1660, 1689-90, corporations, Kent 1662-3, dep. lt. by 1670-Feb. 1688, 1689-*d.*, commr. for recusants 1675, j.p. 1680-Feb. 1688, 1689-*d.*[1]
Commr. for privy seal 1690-2.[2]

Knatchbull was returned with his father for New Romney at the general election of 1660, but was named to no committees in the Convention and made no recorded speeches. With the revival of government interest in 1661 he lost his seat to a courtier, Sir Charles Berkeley II*. It is perhaps surprising at first sight that he should fail to find a seat in any of the Exclusion Parliaments after his father had retired from public life. But his marriage

had drawn him into kinship with Lord Treasurer Danby, the other Monyns coheir having married Peregrine Bertie I*, and his brother was secretary to the lord chancellor (Heneage Finch*), which would have made his candidature unacceptable during the exclusion crisis. He was a prudent man, both politically and financially, maintaining a credit balance of between £4,000 and £6,000 at Hoare's Bank. He was warmly backed by the Court for the county seat in 1685, but was nevertheless listed by Danby among the Opposition. An active Member of James II's Parliament, he was appointed to 15 committees, of which the most important were to recommend expunctions from the Journals and to consider the bill for the general naturalization of Huguenot refugees.[3]

In answer to the lord lieutenant's questions on the repeal of the Test Act and Penal Laws, Knatchbull reserved his judgment for the debates in the House. 'He does not think it proper to assist to the election of such as will previously declare their opinions.' He was removed from local office, though the King's election agents described him in the same terms as Sir William Twysden*. Knatchbull's diary is a valuable source for the Revolution in Kent. He refused to serve as deputy lieutenant to the Roman Catholic Lord Teynham, and on 11 Dec. 1688 was ordered by the Privy Council to seize all Jesuits and other suspects in Kent. He paid his respects, rather unwillingly, to the captured King at Faversham, but signed the 'Association' and was returned for the county unopposed.[4]

Knatchbull sat in the Convention as a Whig and was a moderately active Member, being named to 27 committees. He was added to the committee of inquiry into the delay in relieving Londonderry, and on 17 Aug. 1689 was ordered to carry the bill for preventing the export of wool to the Lords. After the summer recess he was appointed to the committees to consider the bill for restoring corporations and to investigate the miscarriages of the war. His was the first name on the committee for the bill for the Greenwich 'court of conscience' for small claims, but his report was rejected by the House on 25 Nov. In the debate on restoring corporations he supported the disabling clause, without which he considered the bill 'too large'. He was appointed to the committees for enforcing a general oath of allegiance and declaring the rights of election in the Cinque Ports. He was re-elected at the general election, and made a commissioner of the privy seal at the instance of Lord Halifax. He died on 15 Dec. 1696 and was buried at Mersham. His nephew was elected for Rochester in 1702 and for Kent in 1713 and 1722.[5]

[1] *Pub. Intell.* 2 Apr. 1660; Kent RO, NR/AC2, f. 429. [2] *CSP Dom.* 1689–90, p. 471; Luttrell, ii. 326. [3] Stowe 746, f. 14; *CSP Dom.* 1675–6, p. 462; 1685, p. 26; H. M. Knatchbull-Hugessen, *Kentish Fam.* 95; *CJ,* x. 238. [4] *N. and Q.* (ser. 3), vi. 1–3, 21–23, 41–42, 81; *Camb. Hist. Jnl.* ii. 48–62; Add. 33923, f. 456. [5] Add. 33923, ff. 465–75.

B.D.H.

KNATCHBULL, Sir Norton, 1st Bt. (1602–85), of Mersham Hatch, Kent.

KENT   1640 (Apr.)
NEW ROMNEY   1640 (Nov.),[1] 1660, 1661

b. 26 Dec. 1602, 1st s. of Thomas Knatchbull of Maidstone by Eleanor, da. and coh. of John Astley of Maidstone. *educ.* Eton 1615–18; St. John's, Camb. 1619; M. Temple 1624. *m.* (1) lic. 22 Oct. 1630, Dorothy, da. of Thomas Westrowe, Grocer, of London, 3s. 1oda.; (2) lic. 27 Nov. 1662, Dorothy, da. of Sir Robert Honeywood† of Charing, Kent, wid. of Sir Edward Steward of Barking, Essex, *s.p. suc.* fa. 1623; uncle Sir Norton Knatchbull† in Mersham Hatch estate 1636. Kntd. 30 July 1641; *cr.* Bt. 4 Aug. 1641.[2]

J.p. Kent by 1634–44, Mar. 1660–d., commr. for levying money 1643, militia Mar. 1660; freeman, New Romney Apr. 1660; commr. for assessment, Kent Aug. 1660–80, Kent 1662–3, sewers, E. Kent Sept. 1660, Denge marsh Oct. 1660, Walland marsh Dec. 1660, corporations, dep. lt. 1662–d., commr. for recusants 1675.[3]

Mersham Hatch, 15 miles north of New Romney, had been in Knatchbull's family since 1485, but they did not enter Parliament till 1609, when his uncle and namesake was successful at Hythe in a by-election. Knatchbull originally sympathized with the opposition to Charles I, but in 1643 he was fined 1,000 marks for neglecting the service of the House and the county committee, and he showed his distaste for militant Presbyterianism by his long delay in taking the Covenant. Although he did not sit after Pride's Purge, he could be described as well-affected to the regime in 1656; but during the Interregnum he devoted himself principally to Hebrew studies, publishing in 1659 his *Animadversiones in Libros Novi Testamenti,* which won him a great reputation. At the general election in the following year his old constituency of New Romney conferred on him the unique honour of electing him together with his son, on condition that they both took out their freedom. He was named to only five committees in the Convention, of which the most important was for settling ecclesiastical livings. He probably voted with the Court.[4]

Re-elected in 1661, Knatchbull was, until his years began to tell on him, a moderately active Member of the Cavalier Parliament, serving on 33 committees. He took no part either in the Clarendon Code or in the measures against its author. In 1668 he acted as teller for the Lords' bill to ascertain the rates of subsidies and alnage, and was appointed to the committee for amending habeas corpus. Sir Thomas Osborne* included him in 1669 as one of the Members to be engaged by the Duke of Buckingham. On 5 Mar. 1673 Knatchbull was named to the committee for preventing abuses in elections, but this was probably the last session he attended. Sir Richard Wiseman* listed him with a query as a government supporter in December 1675, noting that he had been absent, while two years later Shaftesbury marked him 'doubly vile', probably because his younger son was secretary to the lord chancellor (Heneage Finch*). He died on 3 Feb. 1685, aged 83, and was buried at Mersham.[5]

[1] Did not sit after Pride's Purge, 6 Dec. 1648, readmitted 21 Feb. 1660. [2] C142/398/114. [3] Keeler, *Long Parl.* 242; Kent AO, NR/AC2, f. 429. [4] Keeler, 242; *CSP Dom.* 1655–6, p. 289. [5] *CJ,* ix. 84; *HMC Finch,* ii. 16.

M.W.H./B.D.H.

KNIGHT, John (1613–83), of Temple Street, Bristol, Glos.

BRISTOL   1660, 1661, 1679 (Mar.), 1679 (Oct.)

bap. 24 Nov. 1613, 3rd but 2nd surv. s. of George Knight, mercer (*d.*1659), of Bristol by Anne, da. of William Deyos of Bristol. *m.* 9 Apr. 1640, Martha, da. of Thomas Cole, merchant, of Bristol, 3s. 8da. Kntd. 5 Sept. 1663.[1]

Member, merchant venturers of Bristol 1639, master 1663–4, commr. for assessment Jan. 1660–80, militia, Mar. 1660, common councilman June 1660–2, commr. for loyal and indigent officers 1662, alderman 1662–d., mayor 1663–4, sub-commr. for prizes 1665–7, dep. lt. 1670–?*d.*; commr. for recusants, Som. 1675.[2]

Knight came from a merchant family which had held municipal office in Bristol since 1579. His father took no part in the Civil War, but was forced to retire from the bench of aldermen in 1656 because of his disaffection to the regime. Knight, a grocer by trade, was also royalist in sympathy and refused the oaths during the Interregnum. He was returned to the Convention for the city, and proved a moderately active committeeman, with 25 appointments to his credit, but a frequent speaker; 31 of his speeches were recorded. On the religious issue, he soon showed himself a zealous Anglican, urging the imposition of double poll-tax on both Papists and fanatics 'thereby to know the King's friends from his enemies'. He was appointed to the committees for settling ecclesiastical livings, re-enacting the Navigation Act, and reducing interest to 6 per cent. In the debate on the indemnity bill on 18 Aug. 1660, he spoke in favour of excepting all the regicides, whose lives were 'but as a bucket of water to the ocean, in regard that so many more are to receive benefit by the Act of Pardon'. His was the first name on the committee for the bill to enable disbanded soldiers to trade in corporate towns without apprenticeship. During the recess he was elected sheriff, but succeeded in obtaining his discharge by pleading the burden of his parliamentary duties. He spoke with increasing confidence in the second session. On 7 Nov. he moved the second reading of the bill, which he had previously introduced, to prevent the export of wool and fuller's earth. He opposed the marital separation bill 'because there were already laws against it; and said they ought not to be so severe on the female kind'. He sought to fend off the excise by proposing a six months' assessment to clear the naval debt, and a land tax at the modest rate of 2d. in the £. With an eye to Bristol's import trade, and in accordance with the desires of the merchant venturers, he supported the bill to prohibit the cultivation of tobacco in England. On 7 Dec. he told the House that he had heard a sermon from Hugh Peters urging the execution of the King long before 1647. Knight's status as a taxation expert was recognized when he was added to the managers of a conference on the assessment bill on 22 Dec.[3]

Knight was re-elected in 1661 without opposition, and became the most prominent provincial merchant in the earlier sessions of the Cavalier Parliament. Lord Wharton included him in his list of friends. A very active Member by any standards, he was appointed to 624 committees, taking the chair in 16, acted as teller in 20 divisions, and made about 60 recorded speeches. In the first session he served on the committees for the execution of those under attainder, to check the text of the revised Book of Common Prayer and to examine the Lords' amendments to the uniformity bill, but he was naturally most prominent in trade matters. He was teller against reading the report on alnage, and against imposing a levy on coal shipped from Sunderland as well as Newcastle. He took the chair for the bills to remedy abuses in the packing of butter, another matter in which the local merchant venturers were interested. As chairman of the grand committee on trade he reported on 24 Mar. 1662 in favour of abolishing the monopoly of the London Merchant Adventurers, and acted as teller for a motion to that effect. His name stood first on the bill to curb the activities of the notorious Bristol 'spirits' who kidnapped children to serve as labourers in the plantations. He again took the chair for the bill to prohibit the export of wool and fuller's earth, which he carried to the Lords on 28 Apr. In this capacity he also recommended the expansion of the linen industry to reduce unemployment. In 1663 he was chairman for the bill

to improve the collection of excise, and on attending the lord treasurer to complain of the activities of one of the local commissioners was accused by another of prejudicing the King's revenue by his speeches in committee. He continued his campaign against the Merchant Adventurers by acting as teller on 20 Dec. 1664 against a measure to give relief to their creditors. He also opposed the bill for the repair of Hartlepool pier and a proviso to the bill to except government loans from the statutory limitation on interest. He served on all the committees for the Clarendon Code, and took strong action against the Bristol Quakers during his mayoralty. In the 1666 session he acted as teller for the motion to refer the petition of Sir Humphrey Hooke* to the elections committee, and spoke against the proposal of John Birch* to impose an excise on tobacco. He was one of the Members appointed to prepare reasons for a conference on prohibiting French imports and to attend the King with the address. He also helped to draw up reasons against the Canary Company patent.[4]

On the fall of Clarendon, Knight was appointed to the committees for the public accounts bill and the French merchants' petition, but sought to divert the impeachment proceedings by informing the House of large sums received by Henry Brouncker* and others, and to cast the blame for English losses in the West Indies on the Presbyterian Lord Willoughby of Parham. He took the chair in the committee to consider the balance of trade with Scotland. He was among those sent on 27 Nov. 1667 to ask the King to take care of the relief and repatriation of English prisoners in Holland. He was appointed to the committee for the banishment of Clarendon. On instructions from his constituents, he pressed for the naturalization of prize ships, and chaired the committee for the bill. He continued to oppose the tobacco excise as 'the only way to destroy that plantation, and by that means to transport the trade into Holland', and delivered 'a long, impertinent speech' against the additional wine duty. In 1669 he defended Sir George Carteret*, urging the House to hear his counsel on matters of fact as well as law, and pointing out that if his accounts were unsatisfactory, the Exchequer must have been at fault to allow them. On 1 Dec. he acted as teller for the motion to appoint a day for the accusers of Lord Orrery (Roger Boyle*) to make out their charges. He was appointed to the committees to prevent the transportation of prisoners overseas and to nominate commissioners for union with Scotland. On 7 Nov. 1670 he again attacked the tobacco duties:

This commodity yields £140,000 per annum, one-third part of the customs of England. The port of Bristol has 6000 tons of shipping. The King gains £5 a head by every man that goes into the plantations. It employs half the ships of Bristol. Many leave their tobacco at the custom house, for want of money to pay the custom.

Knight was chairman of the committees of inquiry into the conduct of the London dissenters and the payment of the wine duties. His reference to the affairs of Sir Henry Thompson* provoked Andrew Marvell* into describing him in a private letter as 'a talkative wine merchant'. After the attack on Sir John Coventry* Knight spoke in favour of deferring all other business until the bill for punishment of the culprits had been passed, and was appointed to the committee to consider the Lords' amendments. But when he complained to the House that he had himself been assaulted during the exercise of his duty as a magistrate by his cousin and former partner the father of John Knight II*, Job Charlton* reported on 28 Mar. 1671 that it was not a breach of privilege, though this opinion was immediately reversed by the House without a division and the offender committed to the serjeant-at-arms. At the end of the session Knight was included in the opposition list of the court party.[5]

In the 1673 session, Knight moved for the suspension of the election writs issued by Lord Chancellor Shaftesbury during the recess, and spoke against giving consideration to the dissenters' complaints. He took the chair for an estate bill to enable the dean and chapter of Bristol to exchange an advowson with George, Lord Berkeley. He helped to draw up reasons for peace with Holland in 1674, and to consider the bill for a general test. In the summer of 1675 he was appointed one of the managers of a conference on the Four Lawyers. He received the government whip in the autumn, and was included on the working lists, among the government speakers, and in Wiseman's account. He was appointed to the committee for the appropriation bill, though he thought it damaging to the navy, and acted as teller for the adjournment on 11 Nov. He took the chair for the Ebury manor estate bill promoted by John Tregonwell*, and carried it to the Lords on 16 Nov. with a reminder about the bill to hinder recusants from sitting in Parliament. He was also appointed in this session and its successors to the committees for the recall of British subjects from French service, and other measures put forward by the Opposition, with whom concern at the growth of French power led him increasingly to act.[6]

In 1677, Shaftesbury first marked Knight 'vile', but altered it to 'worthy' after he had moved for an address against the issue of passes to merchant ships and given information about recruitment in Ireland for the French army. He introduced a bill to prevent abuses in the import of Irish cattle, with a 'retrospect' reflecting on Hugh Smith*. But his most important parliamentary work to date was in connexion with the better preservation of the liberty of the subject. He reported from the committee on 21 Mar. and carried the bill to the Lords three days later. Nevertheless he received a small payment from the French subsidies on 21 May. He opened the debate on the King's speech on 29 Jan. 1678 with a request for a statement on England's foreign commitments, and was appointed three months later to the committee to prepare a summary of them. On 3 May he spoke on the negotiations with the Dutch:

When Hannibal is at the gates, we should consider what at present is to be done. Here have been forces raised by Act of Parliament in order to an actual war with France. The confederates did depend upon it. Do you intend to have them lost, and Flanders totally lost, this summer? If you go not on, what will you do with the army you have raised? This treaty is not indeed pursuant to your advice, but it is seasonable at this time to advise the King, and he will stand by your advice. It is every man's safety that is now the case. If you intend good to the Church, state, King, and kingdom, speedily help yourselves.

He joined in the attack on Lauderdale five days later. By the following month his political and financial distrust of the Government had come to exceed his alarm at the international situation. He opposed the navy vote, and in answer to the King's demand for a further £300,000 p.a. declared that the existing revenue would be sufficient if it were better managed, and in particular freed from the burden of pensions upon it. 'At this rate we shall be Normans, and wear wooden shoes.' He was chairman of the committees for a private bill and for the bill to permit the export of leather, which he alleged would benefit the landed interest by raising the price. On the outbreak of the Popish Plot he was appointed to the committee of inquiry, and took the chair for the bill to hinder Papists from sitting in Parliament, which he carried to the Lords on 28 Oct. Three days later he was one of the four Members who searched the chambers of Robert Wright*. As chairman of the committee to translate Coleman's letters, he produced a licence to 'dispense with the taking of oaths' over the seal of Cardinal Barberini, and told the House: 'I believe Coleman had more communication and interest with ministers than the Parliament had'. When Ralph Montagu* produced Danby's letters on 19 Dec., Knight exclaimed: 'Take such evil counsellors from the King that have done these things, and he, and his posterity, and we all shall flourish; else we shall be destroyed. I move for impeachment.' Finally on 27 Dec. he acted as teller against the adjournment of the debate on the respite for three Jesuits convicted of Godfrey's murder.[7]

Knight was returned, probably unopposed, to the first Exclusion Parliament, and again marked 'worthy' on Shaftesbury's list. He made nine speeches and was appointed to 39 committees. He opposed any compromise on the right of the Commons to choose their own Speaker. On 22 Mar. he was among those ordered to bring in a security bill. He denounced Danby's pardon, on the grounds that 'when a man comes to be tried, then is his proper time to plead his pardon. This man must come to trial, to show the world how ill a minister he has been to the King.' He was again appointed to the committee for the habeas corpus bill. When it became clear that Danby intended to rely on the legality of his pardon, Knight said: 'I know nothing of law but self-preservation. I would therefore move, seeing there is such a pardon, to bring in a bill of attainder against him.' He urged the House to lay their hands upon their hearts, and consider, in his favourite metaphor, that Danby was but 'a bucket to the ocean in comparison of the safety of the nation'. On the exclusion issue he said:

> It is impossible that the Protestant religion should be pre-served under a Popish prince, as inconsistent as light and darkness. . . . If the Pope gets his great toe into England, all his body will follow. Something must be done, but I dare not venture to propose what.

Indeed he did not even dare to vote for the exclusion bill, probably preferring to pair with his Tory colleague, Sir Robert Cann*. But the House was still prepared to include him among the Members entrusted on 24 May with drawing up reasons on the trial of the lords in the Tower, and he was re-elected unopposed. Before Parliament met he attended the deathbed of Bedloe, who solemnly affirmed that all the information he had given about the Popish Plot was true. In the second Exclusion Parliament Knight remained very active. He was appointed to 22 committees, of which the most important was to inquire into abhorring, and made nine speeches. He gave evidence that Cann had publicly declared his disbelief in the Popish Plot. Cann replied: 'As for the credit of Sir John Knight in Bristol, it is such that a jury of twelve men, his neighbours, will not believe his testimony'. Anti-Popish zeal brought to Knight's defence so unlikely a champion as the Presbyterian Richard Hampden*, who remarked sarcastically:

> It is strange that the corporation of Bristol should send

Knight hither to serve in Parliament, and not believe his testimony. This is downright recrimination. No man of the last Parliament but knows that Knight was as diligent and faithful, as equal and impartial, as any man in the examination of the Plot. But at this time of the day, when all the rage of the Papists is against you, a Member to be called all to naught, whose credit is so well known here!

Knight objected to the proposal to prescribe the succession in the second exclusion bill 'as if you suppose the King should not have an heir of his own'. He was in favour of the address against Lord Halifax (Sir George Savile*), but thought that the House should be 'sure of proof' before impeaching Edward Seymour*. His involvement in high politics did not lead him to neglect the mundane interests of his constituents, and he opposed the proposal to allow Protestant refugees to practise their trades in corporate towns without going through an apprenticeship. 'Take care', he warned the House, 'that this bill of naturalization give them not more privilege than the King's subjects.' On his return to his constituency he was met by 196 of the most eminent and loyal persons of Bristol on horseback 'to testify their respects to him for his faithful service in the last Parliament'. Nevertheless he was defeated at the general election of 1681, and his petition had not been reported before the dissolution of the Oxford Parliament. He was indicted for his part in the irregular election of a Whig alderman, and led the opposition to the surrender of the charter, but died in December 1683 before he could be displaced. He was buried in the Temple church. His will suggests only moderate wealth, and nothing seems to be known of his descendants.[8]

Knight was described by Roger North as 'the most perverse, clamorous old party man in the whole city or nation'. Although coloured by political hostility this description seems more convincing than Hampden's equally partisan eulogy in 1680. Nevertheless Knight must be given credit for his industry as a Member, and his readiness to voice his opinions on a wide variety of subjects other than his own business interests in an assembly largely composed of his social superiors. The absurd conclusion of his 1679 speech on exclusion may be untypical, but unlike Birch he does not not seem to have overcome the defects in his education, and he had little real influence in the House.[9]

[1] Bristol RO, St. Nicholas par. reg.; *St. Augustine Par. Reg.* (Bristol and Glos. Recs. iii), 75; *Le Neve's Knights* (Harl. Soc. viii), 175; PCC 542 Pell. [2] *Merchant Venturers of Bristol* (Bristol Rec. Soc. xvii), 29; A. B. Beaven, *Bristol Lists*, 200, 201, 204; PRO 30/24, bdle. 40, no. 39, ff. 15–16. [3] *Bristol and Glos. Arch. Soc. Trans.* lxviii. 110–13, 129; J. Latimer, *Annals of Bristol in the 17th Century*, 265; *CSP Dom.* 1649–50, p. 84; Beaven, 199; Bowman diary, ff. 69v, 150v; *CJ*, viii. 146; *Old Parl. Hist.* xxiii. 6, 9, 10, 18, 32, 43; *Merchant Venturers*, 244. [4] *CJ*, viii. 375, 384, 390, 399,

409, 410, 469, 522, 602, 607, 631, 639, 662; R. Mortimer, *Early Bristol Quakerism*, 9; *Milward*, 30. [5] *Milward*, 109, 139, 228, 230; Grey, i. 33, 181; *CJ*, ix. 20, 41, 163, 184; *Merchant Venturers*, 194; *Marvell* ed. Margoliouth, ii. 305; *Dering*, 45. [6] Grey, ii. 3; iii. 317; *Dering*, 123; *CJ*, ix. 269, 352, 361, 375. [7] Grey, iv. 159, 206–7, 256; v. 17, 305–6, 366; vi. 74, 98, 314, 350; *CJ*, ix. 402, 472, 494, 495, 519, 523, 550, 564; Bristol RO, AC/C77/2, Southwell to Smith, 13 Mar. 1677; Browning, *Danby*, i. 201. [8] Grey, vi. 415; vii. 168, 238; 380–2; viii. 50, 88, 226; *CJ*, ix. 642, 706; *Bristol Charters* (Bristol Rec. Soc. xii), 50; *Merchants and Merchandise* (Bristol Rec. Soc. xix), 64–71; *Prot. Dom. Intell.* 15 Feb. 1681; SP29/422/218. [9] North, *Examen*, 253.

M.W.H./J.P.F.

KNIGHT, Sir John (*d.*1718), of The Hill, Bristol and Congresbury, Som.

BRISTOL   1689, 1690

2nd but 1st surv. s. of John Knight, sugar refiner, of St. Augustine's Back, Bristol by 1st w., da. of one Parsons of Som. *m.* Anne, da. of Thomas Smith[†] of Long Ashton, 1s. 2da. *suc.* fa. 1678; kntd. 12 Mar. 1682.[1]

Member of merchant venturers, Bristol 1675, warden 1681–2; freeman, Bristol 1675; common councilman 1679–85, Oct. 1688–1702, sheriff 1681–2, mayor 1690–1; commr. for assessment, Bristol 1679–80, 1689–90, Som. 1689; dep. lt. Bristol 1685–?86, commr. for port regulation 1690.[2]

Knight's father, the first cousin of John Knight*, seems to have left Bristol during the Civil War and invested in land reclamation in the fens. He returned during the Commonwealth and founded a sugar refinery. Although described as a 'fanatic', he refused to serve on the corporation during the Interregnum. He accepted office in 1664, but, like Sir Richard Hart*, only under duress.[3]

Knight passed his youth as a factor on his father's plantation in the West Indies, where he acquired a bad reputation for 'rude behaviour and insolence'. Both the West Indian property and the fenland adventure were inherited by his younger half-brother, leaving Knight only the Bristol sugar business and a small estate at Congresbury worth about £140 p.a. which had been in the family since Elizabethan times. The resultant lawsuits are unlikely to have improved his finances. In a natural reaction against his father's religious sympathies he showed great severity to the dissenters during his shrievalty. The local Quakers complained of his brutality to the King, whose only response was to confer on him the honour of knighthood. 'Eminent for integrity and loyalty' he led the intrigues against the recorder, (Sir) Robert Atkyns*. As a henchman of the Duke of Beaufort (Henry Somerset*) he undertook to secure a majority on the corporation for the surrender of the charter; but there were several defections among the moderate Tories, ascribed to 'a jealousy of Sir John Knight's having too great a sway', and the motion was narrowly defeated. In consequence the governorship of the

Leeward Islands which he had been promised never came his way, much to the relief of the inhabitants. Unabashed, he 'set himself up for a Parliament man, personally desiring votaries with promises and menaces, whereby he put our citizens in a great ferment by dividing the loyal men one against the other'. In the closing months of Charles II's reign, however, he was removed from the corporation at his own request 'as the only expedient to secure him from envy and ruin', and did not contest the general election of 1685. He stood at the by-election in December in opposition to Beaufort's candidate, the town clerk; but both were defeated by Sir Richard Hart*. In the following April Knight, no less zealous against Papists than against dissenters, personally took part in the arrest of a priest at mass, to the King's displeasure at his 'pretended zeal'. Shortly afterwards he was assaulted by Roman Catholics in the street, which encouraged him in 'some extravagancies, as to go armed with blunderbusses, like an armadillo, and to expose the Popish religion with odious figures and representations'. He was summoned before the Privy Council and tried in November 1686 for seditious practices and 'creating and encouraging fears in the hearts of his Majesty's subjects', but was acquitted by a Bristol jury.[4]

Knight resumed his seat on the common council on the restoration of Bristol's charter in October 1688, and was elected to the Convention, probably unopposed. An active Member, he was appointed to 40 committees and made five recorded speeches. On 28 Jan. he demanded immediate action to regularize the constitutional position. As an Anglican stalwart, he moved that the House should observe the anniversary of Charles I's execution, and was instructed to ask Dr Sharp to preach. Sharp gave offence by praying for James II, but Knight pointed out that he was obliged to do so by the Book of Common Prayer, and moved a vote of thanks for the sermon, which he and Thomas Done* were ordered to convey. He helped to draw up the address for preventing ships from going to France and to consider the balance of trade. He voted to agree with the Lords that the throne was not vacant. He was appointed to the committees for the removal of Papists from the metropolitan area, to prepare a comprehension bill, and to consider the bill for the disarming of Papists. In the debate on the corn bounty bill on 3 Apr. he acted as teller for extending the measure to peas and beans. He was among those appointed to hear complaints against customs officials, to consider the bill for the export of beer, ale and mum, and to draw up an address of thanks for the King's declaration to maintain the Church. He probably introduced the bill for the export of leather on 20 Apr. He served on the committee for the bill to rebuild Bristol gaol and to establish 'courts of conscience' for small claims at Bristol and Gloucester. In the second session he was appointed to the committees to inquire into the expenditure and miscarriages of the war. On 4 Nov. he asked leave of the House 'to go into the country for his own security, for he could not safely abide here. . . . At a committee a noble lord had laughed at him and offered him other abuses, and after that challenged him, and required satisfaction from him, all which he patiently bore.' The House ordered Lord Brandon (Hon. Charles Gerard*) to attend in his place to answer Knight's accusation, but nothing seems to have been done, and Knight was still at Westminster on 9 Dec., when he acted as teller against an additional clause to the supply bill forbidding reductions in tax assessments.[5]

Knight was re-elected in 1690, and distinguished himself by a violent attack on immigrants, especially Dutchmen. He did not stand in 1695, and was arrested as a Jacobite conspirator in the following year, but the evidence was insufficient to bring him to trial. He was defeated at the general election of 1698, and resigned from the common council four years later. His last years were spent in poverty on his Somerset property, where he died in February 1718. Nothing is known of his descendants.[6]

[1] Vis. Glos. 1682–3, p. 105. [2] Merchant Venturers (Bristol Rec. Soc. xvii), 32; A. B. Beaven, Bristol Lists, 203–5, 208, 225; CSP Dom. 1685, p. 189; Cal. Treas. Bks. ix. 620. [3] Bristol and Glos. Arch. Soc. Trans. lxviii. 112–15, 135–6. [4] Ibid. 128, 159; J. Besse, Sufferings of the Quakers (1753), i. 59; J. Latimer, Bristol in the 17th Century, 423, 426; North, Examen, 253; CSP Dom. 1682, pp. 120, 134; Jan.–June 1683, pp. 150–1; 1686–7. pp. 118, 136, 163, 164; Bristol RO, common council procs. 1670–87, ff. 159–61; SP29/421/50, 422/127, 436/180; HMC Ormonde, n.s. vii. 404; HMC Portland, iii. 396; R. Morrice, Entering Bk. 1, p. 538; HMC Downshire, i. 172–3; Luttrell, i. 379, 389; PC2/71/283. [5] Morrice, 2, pp. 443, 646; Hardwick SP, i. 411; CJ, x. 14, 16; Grey, ix. 38. [6] Somers Tracts, x. 591–6; Luttrell, iv. 31, 38, 78, 106; Latimer, Bristol in the 18th Century, 120.

J.P.F.

KNIGHT, Nathan (1643–94), of Ruscombe, Berks.

READING   1679 (Mar.), 1679 (Oct.), 1681

bap. 4 Jan. 1643, o.s. of Walter Knight, attorney, of Reading and Staple Inn by w. Naomi. educ. Univ. Coll. Oxf. 1659; L. Inn 1660, called 1667. m. lic. 28 Oct. 1667, Margaret (d.1705), da. and coh. of William Strode of Ruscombe, 3s. 3da. suc. fa. 1670.[1]

Commr. for assessment, Berks. 1673–80, 1689–90, Wilts. and Oxon. 1679–80; freeman, Reading 1679.[2]

Knight's father was sworn one of the attorneys of the Reading court in 1629. Presumably a parliamentary supporter in the Civil War, he was given responsibility for keeping courts on sequestrated manors in Berkshire in 1651. Knight himself became a barrister, but he may not have taken his profession very seriously, for in the year of his call he married an heiress and went to live on her property at Ruscombe, five miles from Reading. He seems to have been under suspicion as early as 1668, when his arrest and solitary confinement were ordered, but the nature of the charge has not been ascertained. He received a grant of arms in 1670. He was returned with John Blagrave* to the Exclusion Parliaments, and marked 'honest' on Shaftesbury's list. But in 1679 he was appointed only to the elections committee and two others of no political significance, and he was absent from the division on the exclusion bill. Unopposed in the autumn election, he left no trace on the records of the second Exclusion Parliament, but was named to the elections committee and that to draw up the third exclusion bill in the Oxford Parliament. In 1683, after the Rye House Plot, Knight and Blagrave were among those 'notoriously disaffected to the Government', who attended a Whig meeting at a Reading tavern on the invitation of Lord Lovelace (John Lovelace*). Presumably a Whig collaborator in 1688, he was nominated as court candidate for the borough with the support of the dissenters; but he did not go to the poll in 1689, and he was unsuccessful in the following year. His will, proved in June 1694, shows that he held lands in Oxfordshire, Hampshire and Dorset, as well as in Berkshire, but he was the only member of his line to sit in Parliament.[3]

[1] Berks. RO, St. Lawrence, Reading, par. reg.; Lond. Mar. Lic. ed. Foster, 804; Frag. Gen. viii. 94; PCC 129 Box. [2] Berks. RO, Reading corp. diary, 4 Feb. 1679. [3] Reading Bor. Recs. ii. 480; Cal. Comm. Comp. 480; VCH Berks. iii. 204; CSP Dom. 1667–8, p. 524; July–Sept. 1683, pp. 377, 389; Grantees of Arms (Harl. Soc. lxvi), 147; R. Morrice, Entering Bk. 2, p. 292; Reading corp. diary, 19 Feb. 1690; PCC 129 Box.

L.N./G.J.

KNIGHT, Ralph (c.1619–91), of Langold, Yorks. and Langwith, Notts.[1]

SUTHERLAND, ROSS AND CROMARTY   21 Mar. 1659[2]
MORPETH   1660

b. c.1619, o.s. of William Knight of Newbury, Berks. by Alice Worthington. m. (1) 23 June 1646, Faith (d. 18 Apr. 1671), da. and h. of William Dickinson, vicar of Rotherham, Yorks., 8s. (3 d.v.p.) 7da.; (2) lic. 17 May 1687, Elizabeth, wid. of John Rolleston of Sookholme, Notts., s.p. Kntd. May/June 1660.[3]

Maj. of ft. (parliamentary) 1643–5; capt. of horse 1645, maj. 1647, col. 1659–Dec. 1660; capt. indep. tp. 1667; lt.-col. Duke of Buckingham's Ft. 1673–4.[4]

J.p. Yorks. (W. Riding) 1653–87, Notts. Mar. 1660–87, 1689–d., Westminster July 1660–87; commr. for

militia, Notts. Mar. 1660, assessment (W. Riding) Aug. 1660–1, 1663–80, 1689–90, Northumb. Aug. 1660–1, Notts. Aug. 1660–3, 1664–9, 1677–80, sewers, Westminster Aug. 1660, recusants (W. Riding) 1675; dep. lt. Notts. ?1676–Feb. 1688, Oct. 1688–d., (W. Riding) 1677–?87, lt.-col. of militia ft. ?1679–87.[5]
Commr. for security [S] 1656.

Apart from the vague account of his parentage which Knight gave to the heralds in 1663, nothing is known of him before he was commissioned in the parliamentary army during the Civil War. He continued to serve throughout the Interregnum, and bought Langold in 1650. On the second expulsion of the Rump in 1659, George Monck* sent Knight and John Cloberry* to negotiate with the military regime. They were persuaded by Sir Anthony Ashley Cooper* and Sir Arthur Hesilrige† to advise the recall of the Rump. Knight, described as a great friend of the Presbyterian Earl of Manchester, took part in Monck's invasion of England, and was recommended by him to the electors of Morpeth. A moderately active Member of the Convention, he was appointed to 16 committees, acted as teller in five divisions and made nine recorded speeches. Although he stood to lose £900 p.a. in land and salary, he took the lead in restoring discipline and promoting the Restoration in the army. He was ordered to convey the House's appreciation of the thanksgiving sermon preached by Monck's chaplain on 10 May. He was given permission to attend the reception of the King on Blackheath on 28 May at the head of his regiment, which, to avoid accidents, he ordered not to shoot until the royal party had passed. On the following day he commanded the guard which gave Members passage from the House to Whitehall. He was knighted, and given a pension of £600 p.a. 'for good service' until lands of equivalent value should be settled on him.[6]

In the House, Knight sometimes acted as spokesman for Monck, though he was less prominent in this capacity than Thomas Clarges*. He intervened several times in the debates on the indemnity bill in defence of his old comrades, even the most unpopular. He was teller for the motion to put the question on excepting Major-General William Boteler†, pointed out that Major-General James Berry† had no property to forfeit, and defended the conduct of General Charles Fleetwood†. On 7 July he was appointed to the committee to consider the proviso about Colonel John Hutchinson*. He opposed the imposition of penal taxation on recusants, and on 11 July reminded the House of Monck's request for expedition of the land settlement. On the religious issue he declared himself a supporter of episcopacy, though loth to see many ministers turned out of their livings by the imposi-

tion of the Thirty-Nine Articles. He opposed the bill to enable Sir George Booth* to alienate part of his entailed property on 30 July: ' 'Twas not fit for a worthy person that had done such service should be forced to sell his lands to pay those debts which he contracted for the good of the nation'. On 1 Aug. he presented a report on the repayment of three bills of exchange drawn by the Commonwealth representatives at the Sound since the Restoration. On the report of the conference with the Lords on 23 Aug. he spoke in favour of allowing Hesilrige the benefit of the indemnity bill. He was appointed to the committees for the disbandment bill and for the bill to exempt discharged soldiers from apprenticeship. In the second session he acted as teller for the second reading of the bill to prevent marital separation and against hearing a complaint against the militia.[7]

Knight probably did not stand again. His circumstances prospered despite his large family. In 1671 he commuted his pension for a lump sum of £8,000, and in 1675 he bought the Nottinghamshire manor of Warsop. Described as a rich Presbyterian, he supported the country candidates for Yorkshire in 1679. But it is probable that his opinions had moved to the right: Danby called him 'my old friend', he was helpful to Lady Danby when her husband was in the Tower, and he made no protest at the renewed persecution of dissenters in 1682. He evaded the questions on the Tests and Penal Laws in Nottinghamshire on the grounds that he was no longer in the commission of the peace, to which he was restored after the Revolution. He died on 21 Apr. 1691, aged 71, and was buried at Firbeck, the only member of his family to sit in Parliament.[8]

[1] Notts. County Recs. ed. Copnall, 10. [2] Thurloe, vii. 600. [3] Clay, Dugdale's Vis. Yorks. 9–10; Notts. Mar. Lic. (Index Lib. lviii), 403; Thoroton, Notts. iii. 369. [4] J. Hunter, South Yorks. i. 298. [5] Reresby, Mems. 345; Yorks. Arch. Jnl. xxix. 285. [6] Christie, Shaftesbury, i. 196; Cal. Cl. SP, iv. 625; Nicholas Pprs. (Cam. Soc. ser. 3, xxxi), 195; Clarendon Corresp. i. 57; Baker, Chron. 697, 711; CJ, viii. 20, 48; HMC 13th Rep. VI, 3–4; Cal. Treas. Bks. i. 51. [7] CJ, viii. 64, 181, 185; Bowman diary, ff. 5v, 70, 74, 86v, 103v; Old Parl. Hist. xxii. 444. [8] Clarendon Corresp. i. 57; Hunter, i. 298; HMC Portland, ii. 153; HMC Lindsey, 60; Reresby, 188, 271.

M.W.H./J.P.F.

KNIGHT, Sir Richard (1639–79), of Chawton, Hants.

LYMINGTON 11 Feb. 1678

b. 21 Nov. 1639, o.s. of Richard Knight of Chawton by Elizabeth, da. of John Fielder of Burrow Court, Berks. educ. Queen's, Oxf. 1657; G. Inn 1658; travelled abroad. m. c.1667, Priscilla, da. and h. of Sir Robert

Reynolds[t] of Elvetham, Hants, *s.p. suc.* fa. 1642; kntd. 10 Jan. 1668.[1]

Lt. of militia horse, Hants Nov. 1660, capt. 1668–*d.*, lt.-col. of ft. by 1679, dep. lt. 1669–*d.*; freeman, Portsmouth and Winchester 1669, Lymington 1677; commr. for assessment, Hants 1673–*d.*, wastes and spoils, New Forest 1679.[2]

Knight's ancestors had been substantial yeomen in Chawton since the reign of Edward II, and bought the freehold of the demesne in 1551. His great-uncle, John Knight, sat for Lymington in 1593. Knight's father died before the Civil War, and he himself only came of age after the Restoration. But his sympathies were royalist; he was given a commission in the militia, though he never became a j.p. He was probably the 'Edward Knight, esquire of Chawton' included in the list of proposed knights of the Royal Oak with an estate of £1,000 p.a. He was returned for Lymington at a contested by-election towards the end of the Cavalier Parliament. He was appointed to no committees, but marked 'doubly vile' by Shaftesbury, and entered on the government list of the court party. It is not known whether he stood for the first Exclusion Parliament, but he was unsuccessful for Hampshire against the country candidates on 11 Aug. 1679. 'What with a former indisposition and present drinking, poor man, he died the next day after.' He was the last of the male line, but his heirs all took the name of Knight, two of them sitting for Midhurst in the 18th century.[3]

[1] W. A. Leigh and M. G. Knight, *Chawton Manor*, 91, 93; Wards 7/97/86. [2] *Cal. Treas. Bks.* i. 82; v. 303; R. East, *Portsmouth Recs.* 360; Winchester assembly bk. 5, f. 61; E. King, *Old Times Revisited*, 190; *CSP Dom.* 1679–80, p. 61. [3] Leigh and Knight, 183, 200; *Dom. Intell.* 5 Sept. 1679; BL, M636/33, John Stewkley to Sir Ralph Verney, 3 Sept. 1679.

P.W.

KNIGHTLEY, Richard (c.1610–61), of Fawsley, Northants.

NORTHAMPTON	1640 (Apr.), 1640 (Nov.)[1]
NORTHAMPTONSHIRE	1659
ST. GERMANS	1660

b. c.1610, o.s. of Richard Knightley of Burgh Hall, Staffs. and Fawsley by Jane, da. of Sir Edward Littleton[t] of Pillaton, Staffs. *educ.* Lincoln, Oxf. matric. 24 Oct. 1628, aged 18, BA 1631, MA 1633; G. Inn 1633. *m.* (1) c.1637, Elizabeth (*d.*1643), da. of John Hampden[t] of Great Hampden, Bucks., 1s. 1da.; (2) 22 July 1647, Anne, da. of Sir William Courteen, merchant, of London, wid. of Hon. Essex Devereux of Leigh Court, Warws., 1s. 2da. *suc.* fa. 1650; KB 23 Apr. 1661.[2]

Commr. for forests, Northants. 1641, assessment, Northants. 1643–8, 1657, Jan. 1660–*d.*, Rad. 1647–8, Westminster Aug. 1660–*d.*, sequestration, Northants. 1643, levying of money 1643, new model ordinance 1645, appeals, Oxf. Univ. 1647, militia, Northants.

1648, Northants. and Westminster Mar. 1660, drainage, Bedford level 1649; j.p. Mdx. 1655–?Mar. 1660; Westminster 1655–*d.*, Northants, 1656–*d.*; commr. for oyer and terminer, Midland circuit July 1660.[3]

Commr. for regulating excise 1645, relief of Ireland 1645, sale of bishops' lands 1646; member, committee of both kingdoms May–Dec. 1648; Councillor of State 25 Feb.–31 May 1660; commr. for maimed soldiers Dec. 1660–1,[4]

Knightley was descended from a certain Nicholas Maucovenant, who was seated in the 12th century on the Staffordshire estate from which the family later derived their surname. Fawsley was acquired in 1415, and their long parliamentary record began four years later with the return of Richard Knightley for Northamptonshire. Strongly puritan under Elizabeth, they were consistent in opposition to the early Stuarts, though Knightley's father, after nomination to the committee for the midland association in 1642, led a retired life. Knightley himself was a Parliamentarian and an unenthusiastic Presbyterian during the Civil War, but he opposed the trial of Charles I, and was imprisoned at Pride's Purge. He sat for the county in Richard Cromwell's Parliament, and both in May and December 1659 supported the efforts of William Prynne* to open the Rump to the secluded Members. When they were eventually readmitted by George Monck* he was appointed to the Council of State.[5]

Knightley stood for Northamptonshire in 1660 with another Presbyterian, John Crew*; but when some of the electors

> told him they hoped that he would be instrumental to the bringing in the King and that it should be honourably, he replied, 'Will you have him brought in on horseback?' This being bruited about the field, such offence was taken at the answer that his whole party immediately deserted him, and chose Sir Harry Yelverton*.

He was returned for St. Germans, however, on the interest of John Eliot*, and listed by Lord Wharton as a friend. Lord Mordaunt included him in the 'cabal of Suffolk House', whose main aim was to use their interest in the Commons to disband the greater part of the standing army. An active Member, he made 28 recorded speeches, and was appointed to 48 committees in the Convention, including the drafting committee and the joint committees to instruct the messengers to the King and to prepare for his reception. On 26 May he was named to the committee for dealing with the maimed soldiers, widows and orphans, so that 'the kingdom may be most eased of the charge', and he was later appointed to the commission for this purpose. On the same day he informed the Upper House that the Commons agreed to their amendments to the assessment ordinance.[6]

After the Restoration Knightley was one of those appointed to administer the oaths of allegiance and supremacy to the other Members. He proposed that the £20,000 voted to Monck should be charged on the assessment, and was appointed to the committee to hear the petition from the intruded Oxford dons. More moderate than Prynne on the indemnity bill, both in particular and general cases, he spoke in favour of Richard Salway†, who had joined with him in redeeming the forfeited estate of his Staffordshire cousins, the Littletons, and against excluding those who had abjured the monarchy or signed the Instrument of Government. He wished all petitioners to be heard, but he acted as teller for an unsuccessful proviso to permit Royalists to recover debts and rents not paid in to the Commonwealth. On religious questions he generally followed the Presbyterian line, supporting Prynne's complaint of 30 June about unauthorized Anglican propaganda. On 2 July he urged that the supply debate should be deferred until more progress had been made with the indemnity bill, and objected to Prynne's proposal to disable a large number of Cromwellian officials on the grounds that 'the proviso is too large, and not to be mended'. He also opposed another proviso to exclude those who would not take the oaths. When it was proposed to require the clergy to assent both to the Protestant faith according to the scriptures and the government of the church according to law, he moved 'silently to glide off this clause, and not put it to the question'. He wished 'to let the discipline alone to the consideration of the King and divines', but agreed that the bill for settling ministers in their livings should be referred to a committee, on which he served. When the indemnity bill returned to the Commons, he twice spoke against the Lords' amendment to exclude all the King's judges. He was named to the committee to establish how far the amendments reached, and urged a conference before putting them to the vote. He was against double taxation of recusants, whether Catholic or Protestant. He spoke in favour of a grant of £10,000 to Sir George Booth*, but wished the House to lay aside for the present a bill to compensate the royalist Marquess of Winchester.[7]

Knightley continued to be an active Member in the second session. On 6 Nov. he moved for a settlement of the militia, and took the chair in the committee to bring in a bill. Wharton sent him a copy of the case for modified episcopacy 'with some circumstances', and he supported the bill to give effect to the Worcester House declaration. He urged rejection of the bill to prevent wives from leaving their husbands. His first report of the bill

to make Covent Garden a parish was recommitted, but he was able to carry it up on 11 Dec. He favoured compensating the crown for the loss of feudal revenues by a land tax rather than an excise, and opposed any grants to officials of the court of wards. He urged the Lords to concur in acknowledging a debt of £1,387 for provisions supplied to Dunkirk on the orders of the Council of State on which he had served, and on 20 Dec. carried up a naturalization bill.[8]

In 1661 Knightley was again unsuccessful for Northamptonshire, thanks to the machinations of the sheriff, Sir William Dudley*. He was created knight of the Bath for the coronation of Charles II but his reluctant participation in the Popish ceremony hastened his end, and he died shortly afterwards in London on 29 June. He was buried at Fawsley. His son inherited an estate valued, for matrimonial purposes, at £2,000 p.a., but the next member of the family to enter Parliament was Valentine Knightley, who sat for the county as a Tory from 1748 to 1754.[9]

[1] Secluded at Pride's Purge, 6 Dec. 1648, readmitted 21 Feb. 1660. [2] VCH Northants. Fams. 189–90. [3] Keeler, Long Parl. 243. [4] CJ, viii. 213. [5] VCH Northants. Fams. 173, 180; DNB; D. Underdown, Pride's Purge, 64, 233. [6] Add. 15750, f. 47; Bath mss, Thynne pprs. 12, ff. 162–3; Cal. Cl. SP, iv. 674. [7] Bowman diary, ff. 5, 7, 20v. 28, 36v, 41, 43, 53, 69, 86, 104, 110, 129v, 134, 140, 147, 153; CJ, viii. 79, 106, 127. [8] Old Parl. Hist. xxiii. 2, 9, 14, 16, 18, 27, 32, 49, 61; CJ, viii. 179, 184, 193, 199. [9] Northants. RO, IC515; Voyce from the Watch Tower, 288; Pepys Diary, 17 May 1662.

M.W.H./P.W.

KNOLLYS, Thomas (c.1612–79), of Grove Place, Nursling, Hants.

SOUTHAMPTON 1659, 31 Oct. 1670, 1679 (Mar.)

b. c.1612, 2nd s. of Sir Henry Knollys (d.1638) of Grove Place, clerk-comptroller of the green cloth, by Catherine, da. of Sir Thomas Cornwallis of Portchester, groom-porter 1597–1618. educ. Peterhouse, Camb. 1628, BA 1632, MA 1635; I. Temple 1635. m. by 1659, Anne, da. of William Duncombe of Battlesden, Beds., wid. of Sir William Crayford of Beckerings Park, Ridgmont, Beds., 1s. 4da. suc. bro. 1648.[1]

Fellow of Peterhouse 1634–6; commr. for assessment, Hants 1657, Aug. 1660–d., Southampton 1677–d.; j.p. Hants 1659–d., Dorset and Wilts. 1675–d.; commr. for militia, Hants Mar. 1660, corporations 1662–3; freeman, Portsmouth 1662; verderer, New Forest by 1667–d.; sub-commr. for prizes, Portsmouth 1672–4; commr. for recusants, Hants 1675, wastes and spoils, New Forest 1676.[2]

Commr. for sick and wounded seamen 1673–4.[3]

Knollys's ancestors had been in Hampshire since the reign of Henry VIII, but they were of little account until his father entered the service of the Stuarts and obtained a crown grant of Nursling, five miles from Southampton, in 1630. Knollys's elder brother, who was created a baronet in 1642, was a Royalist in the Civil War, and compounded at one-tenth for £1,250 in 1645, though only one moiety of the fine had been paid when Knollys succeeded to the estate. Knollys himself, under his father's will, inherited a portion of £1,200 to be 'laid out in purchasing and obtaining of some office', for which his expensive education had sufficiently qualified him; but he became a merchant and apparently took no part in the Civil War. He accepted the Protectorate, holding county office and representing Southampton in 1659, the first member of his family to sit.[4]

Although Knollys was not re-elected for 11 years he supported the Restoration, acting as commissioner for corporations in 1662. In the same year a private bill to enable him to sell his brother's Isle of Wight estate was steered through the House by his brother-in-law, Sir John Duncombe*. Returned as a court supporter at a by-election in 1670, probably unopposed, he was not an active Member of the Cavalier Parliament, being appointed to only 14 committees, including the committee of elections and privileges in three sessions. None of the remainder was of political moment, and all except two were in his first session. Their purposes included the encouragement of an invention, sponsored by (Sir) Philip Howard*, to protect ships' hulls, the preparation of a bill to prevent the export of wool, and the preservation of naval stores from unruly seamen. During the third Dutch war Knollys served as a local prize commissioner and succeeded Bullen Reymes* as commissioner for sick and wounded, and when peace was made he was compensated with an excise pension of £200 p.a. He was named on the Paston list, and received the government whip from Secretary Coventry in 1675, though his reliability as a court supporter was 'doubted' by Sir Richard Wiseman* when Duncombe fell out with Lord Treasurer Danby. Nevertheless he was described in *A Seasonable Argument* as 'the treasurer's kinsman' with '£400 p.a. pension', marked 'thrice vile' by Shaftesbury in 1677, and included among the court supporters on the government list of 1678.[5]

Knollys successfully defended his seat at the first general election of 1679 and was marked 'vile' on Shaftesbury's list. He took no known part in the proceedings of the first Exclusion Parliament, and was absent from the division on the bill, although he was probably in London. He was named to the Commons as a pensioner by (Sir) Stephen Fox*, and would undoubtedly have figured in the opposition list of the 'unanimous club' of court supporters if he had not died soon afterwards. He was buried in Westminster Abbey on 3 June 1679. The next member of the family to enter Parliament was Henry Knollys, who sat for St. Ives on the Powlett interest from 1722 to 1734.[6]

[1] *Misc. Gen. et Her.* ii. 20; F. A. Blaydes, *Gen. Beds.* 179, 408; PCC 87 King. [2] *HMC 11th Rep. III*, 55; Woodward, *Hants*, ii. 113; *Cal. Treas. Bks.* ii. 91; iii. 207; v. 303, 431; R. East, *Portsmouth Recs.* 360; Nat. Maritime Mus. Dartmouth mss 6/1. [3] PC2/63/368. [4] *Misc. Gen. et Her.* ii. 19; *VCH Hants*, iii. 434; *Cal. Comm. Comp.* 1065; G. E. Aylmer, *King's Servants*, 82. [5] *CJ*, viii. 368; *Evelyn Diary*, iii. 602. [6] Grey, vii. 324; *Westminster Abbey Reg.* (Harl. Soc. x), 197.

P.W.

KNOLLYS, William (c.1620–64), of Rotherfield Greys, Oxon.

OXFORDSHIRE Apr./May 1663–Sept. 1664

b. c.1620, 1st s. of Sir Robert Knollys† of Rotherfield Greys by Joanna, da. of Sir John Wolstenholme, farmer of the customs, of Stanmore, Mdx. and Nostell Priory, Yorks. *educ.* St. Edmund Hall, Oxf. matric. 25 Nov. 1636, aged 16; M. Temple 1639. *m.* 23 May 1642, Margaret, da. of John Saunders†, counsellor at law, of Reading, Berks., 2s. (1 *d.v.p.*) 3da. *suc.* fa. 1659.[1]

J.p. Oxon. July 1660–*d.*, Berks. 1661–*d.*; commr. for assessment, Oxon. Aug. 1660–*d.*, Oxford 1663–*d.*; dep. lt. Oxon. c. Aug. 1660–*d.*, commr. for corporations 1662–3, loyal and indigent officers 1662; freeman, Oxford 1662; jt. farmer of excise, Oxon. 1662–*d.*[2]

Knollys came from a cadet branch of a family established in Hertfordshire by the 14th century, which first leased Rotherfield Greys in 1514 and later acquired the freehold. His great-grandfather, Sir Francis Knollys†, sat in the Reformation Parliament and represented Oxfordshire seven times under his kinswoman Elizabeth. The estate, worth about £800 p.a. but seriously encumbered, was settled on trustees for Knollys's benefit at his marriage. By absenting himself for five weeks from his house during the Civil War to escape 'the violence and disorders of the soldiers', he became a technical delinquent, though he had contributed £550 to the county committee, and even before his offence the parliamentary forces at Henley had felled timber to the value of £2,000, besides defacing the house for military purposes. He compounded for £1,100 in 1648. He apparently remained quiet during the Interregnum, but early in 1660 was among the Oxfordshire gentry who signed the address for a free Parliament.[3]

Knollys was a partner in the local excise farm in 1662, and was returned for the county after a contested by-election in the following year. During his brief service in the Cavalier Parliament he was an active Member. He was appointed to 14 committees, of which the most important were to prevent unlawful meetings of dissenters and to consider the additional bill to regulate the excise. He was buried on 4 Sept. 1664 at Rotherfield Greys. His son, the last of this branch of the Knollys family, died six years later.[4]

[1] F. G. Lee, *Church of Thame*, 595; Rotherfield Greys par. reg. [2] A. Ballard, *Chrons. Woodstock*, 92; *Oxford Council Acts* (Oxf. Hist. Soc. xcv), 293, 305; *Cal. Treas. Bks.* i. 425. [3] Lee, 595; *Her. and Gen.* viii. 297, 299; *Cal. Comm. Comp.* 996; SP 23/175/653-4, 657; Bodl. Wood, 276A/221. [4] *CJ*, viii. 506; *Cal. Treas. Bks.* vii. 1109, 1253-4; PCC 60 Mico.

L.N./G.J.

KNYVETT, Thomas (1656–93), of Ashwellthorpe, Norf.

DUNWICH	1685
EYE	1689

bap. Feb. 1656, 1st s. of Sir John Knyvett of Ashwellthorpe by Mary, da. and coh. of Sir Thomas Bedingfield[+] of Darsham, Suff. *educ.* St. Catherine's, Camb. 1672. *unm. suc.* fa. 1673.[1]

Col. of militia ft. Norf. 1676–Feb. 1688, Nov. 1688–d., dep. lt. 1677–Feb. 1688, Oct. 1688–d.; commr. for assessment, Norf. 1677–80, Norf., Suff. and Eye 1689–90; j.p. Norf. by 1680–Feb. 1688, Nov. 1688–d.; alderman, Dunwich 1685–June 1688, Oct. 1688–d., bailiff Dec. 1688–9.[2]

Knyvett's ancestors were lords of the Northamptonshire manor of Southwick by the end of the 12th century. But the real founder of the family fortunes was Sir John Knyvett, lord chancellor from 1372 to 1377, whose son sat for Huntingdonshire in 1397. The family was established in Norfolk by the middle of the 15th century. Knyvett's grandfather, *de jure* 5th Lord Berners, a Royalist during the Civil War, was taken prisoner at Lowestoft by Cromwell in March 1643 and his property sequestrated, but he was discharged in 1644, largely as a result of the intervention of Cromwell himself, and excused from decimation in 1655. In his later years he lived with his son-in-law, John Rous I*, in Suffolk. Knyvett's father married into a Suffolk family with a strong interest at Dunwich, and was dubbed knight of the Bath at the coronation of Charles II.[3]

Knyvett himself began to take part in local affairs after the appointment as lord lieutenant of his kinsman, Lord Yarmouth (Robert Paston*), to whom he wrote:

> I must now let your lordship know how proud I am of the honour of being publicly known to be your lordship's relation and friend, and that I rule myself on nothing so much as that pleasing consideration of our country's common consent in concluding your lordship to have no little kindness for me.

In May 1676 Yarmouth appointed him colonel of the militia regiment formerly commanded by Sir John Holland*, and other local offices followed.

He signed the loyal address from Norfolk abhorring the 'Association' in 1682. In 1685 he was appointed to municipal office in Dunwich under its remodelled charter and returned unopposed to Parliament for the borough in the ensuing election, no doubt on the Rous interest. A Tory in politics, he left no trace on the records of James II's Parliament. In 1688 he told the lord lieutenant that he thought it 'reasonable the Penal Laws be reviewed and amended, but not to repeal the Tests'. He was removed as alderman of Dunwich by order in council in June 1688, but elected bailiff in December. He did not take part in the contested election in the following month, nor did he sign the return. He was himself elected to a seat left vacant at Eye by the return of his cousin, Sir John Rous*, for Suffolk. According to Anthony Rowe* he voted to agree with the Lords that the throne was not vacant; but his only committee in the Convention was on a private bill to discharge the Duke of Norfolk of certain payments. He remained an active deputy lieutenant, taking the oaths to the new regime on 30 Sept. 1689, but he did not stand again. He died unmarried on 28 Sept. 1693 and was buried at Ashwellthorpe. His sister established her claim to the Berners peerage in 1720, but he was the last of the family to sit in either House.[4]

[1] *CP*, ii. 156–7. [2] *Norf. Ltcy. Jnl.* (Norf. Rec. Soc. xxx), 9, 37, 63, 90; *HMC Lothian*, 125; *CSP Dom.* 1679–80, p. 32; 1685, p. 15; *HMC Var.* vii. 104; E. Suff. RO, EE6/1144/13. [3] *VCH Northants.* ii. 591; Blomefield, *Norf.* i. 376–9; ii. 157–9; *CSP Dom.* 1655–6, pp. 344–5, 390; *Knyvett Letters* (Norf. Rec. Soc. xx), 33, 40; Thurloe, iv. 705. [4] *HMC 6th Rep.* 378; Add. 36988, f. 180; Add. 27447, f. 357; PC2/72/689; *Norf. Ltcy. Jnl.* 99.

P.W.

KYNASTON, Edward I (1641–93), of Albrightlee, nr. Shrewsbury, Salop.

SHREWSBURY	1679 (Mar.), 1679 (Oct.), 1681, 1685

b. 25 Mar. 1641, 1st s. of Roger Kynaston of Hordley by Rebecca, da. of Sir John Weld, town clerk of London 1613–41, of Willey. *educ.* Jesus, Oxf. 1659. *m.* by 1664, Amy, da. and h. of Thomas Barker of Haughmond Abbey, Salop, 6s. (2 *d.v.p.*) 2da. *suc.* fa. 1684.

Alderman, Shrewsbury 1664–Jan. 1688, Oct. 1688–d., mayor 1664–5; sheriff, Mont. 1665–6, Salop 1682–3; commr. for assessment, Salop 1673–80, 1689–90, j.p. 1680–June 1688, Nov. 1688–d.[1]

Settled in Shropshire since the 14th century, Kynaston's family acquired Hordley in the reign of Henry VI. His father, who was sheriff of Shropshire in 1640, took the side of the King in the Civil War, and compounded in March 1647 on a fine of £921 at one-sixth. Kynaston acquired by marriage very extensive property in and around Shrewsbury, and fixed his residence at Albrightlee, one of his wife's properties lying within the liberties of the town. He became an alderman under the 1664 charter, and was prominent in local affairs.[2]

Kynaston stood unsuccessfully for Shrewsbury at a by-election in March 1677. Returned for the borough to all three Exclusion Parliaments, he was classed as 'doubtful' by Shaftesbury. In 1679 he was appointed to only two committees, the first to bring in a new poor law (30 Apr.), the other for a naturalization bill (17 May). He was absent from the division on the exclusion bill. In the second and third Exclusion Parliaments he was appointed to no committees, but was given leave of absence for the recovery of his health on 2 Dec. 1680. He was active in securing the surrender of the Shrewsbury charter in June 1684 and was reappointed alderman under the new charter in 1685. Returned to James II's Parliament, and listed by Danby among the Opposition, he was appointed to no committees, but probably acted as teller against the clandestine marriages bill with Francis Gwyn*. In reply to Lord Chancellor Jeffreys, he wrote: 'I cannot in conscience comply with Your Lordship's proposals in taking off the Penal Laws or Tests. I shall always continue my allegiance to my King and live peaceably with my neighbours.' He was removed from municipal and county office, but his attitude to the Revolution has not been ascertained. He was buried at Hordley on 15 Aug. 1693. His son John represented Shrewsbury and Shropshire as a Tory in the next four reigns.[3]

[1] *Trans. Salop Arch. Soc.* (ser. 4), xii. 218; *Mont. Colls.* xv. 6; Owen and Blakeway, *Shrewsbury*, i. 487. [2] Burke, *Gentry* (1937); *Mont. Colls.* xv. 5; *Cal. Comm. Comp.* 1024; Owen and Blakeway, i. 487, 493. [3] Owen and Blakeway, i. 493–4; *Trans. Salop Arch. Soc.* (ser. 1), ii. 397; (ser. 4), xii. 218; PC2/72/567.

E.C.

KYNASTON, Edward II (1643–99), of Oteley Park, Salop.

SHROPSHIRE   1685, 1689, 1690, 1695, 1698–May 1699

bap. 24 Aug. 1643, 3rd s. of Edward Kynaston of Oteley by Katherine, da. of Sir John Hanmer, 1st Bt.†, of Hanmer, Flints. *educ.* Ruthin g.s. c.1654. *m.* Elizabeth, da. and coh. of Sir Robert Broke, 1st Bt.*, of Nacton, Suff., 3s. 4da. *suc.* bro. 1661.[1]

Commr. for assessment, Salop 1661–80, Flints. and Salop 1689–90; j.p. Salop 1671–June 1688, Nov. 1688–96, commr. for recusants 1675, dep. lt. 1683–Mar. 1688, Oct. 1688–96.

Kynaston belonged to a cadet branch of the family, which had produced a knight of the shire in 1554. His grandfather, Sir Francis Kynaston†, was commissioner of array for Charles I, and his father, an esquire of the body to the King, compounded

in 1647 on a fine of £2,000 reduced to £1,500.[2]

After the Rye House Plot Kynaston, a Tory, helped to search for arms in the houses of William Leveson Gower*, William Forester* and other Whig suspects. On his election for the county in 1685 he was described to Sunderland as 'very loyal'. No committee work in James II's Parliament can be ascribed to him, and he was probably totally inactive. He was absent when the questions on the repeal of the Test and Penal Laws were put to the Shropshire magistracy, and was removed from office. Re-elected to the Convention, he voted to agree with the Lords that the throne was not vacant, but otherwise was again inactive. He continued to act with the Tories, and refused to sign the Association in 1696, for which he was removed from the commission of the peace. His death was reported on 23 May 1699. He was the last of this branch of the family to sit in Parliament.[3]

[1] *Trans. Salop Arch. Soc.* (ser. 4), xii. 4–5; *Vis. Salop* (Harl. Soc. xxix), 299; J. R. Burton, *Walcot Fam.* 59–60. [2] *Trans. Salop Arch. Soc.* (ser. 4), xi. 164–5; *Cal. Comm. Comp.* 1024. [3] *CSP Dom.* July–Sept. 1683, p. 18; 1685, p. 103; *Trans. Salop Arch. Soc.* (ser. 4), xii. 5; Luttrell, iv. 519.

E.C.

KYRLE, Sir John, 2nd Bt. (c.1617–80), of Much Marcle, Herefs.

HEREFORDSHIRE   23 Sept. 1668

b. c.1617, 1st s. of Francis Kyrle of Much Marcle by 1st w. Hester, da. of Sir Paul Tracy, 1st Bt., of Stanway, Glos. *educ.* Christ Church, Oxf. matric. 25 Nov. 1636, aged 19; I. Temple 1638. *m.* 16 Dec. 1647, Rebecca, da. of Daniel Vincent, merchant, of Ironmonger Lane, London, 4da. *suc.* gdfa. Apr. 1650.[1]

Commr. for assessment, Herefs. 1650–2, 1657, Jan. 1660–d., j.p. Mar. 1660–d., dep. lt. 1661–2, commr. for loyal and indigent officers 1662, oyer and terminer, Oxford circuit 1665, recusants, Herefs. 1675.[2]

Gent. of the privy chamber (extraordinary) July 1660.[3]

Kyrle came from the junior line of a Herefordshire family dating back to the 14th century. To the senior line belonged Walter Kyrle, MP for Leominster in the Short and Long Parliaments and a Rumper, his nephew the Roundhead Colonel Robert Kyrle, who bore an unenviable reputation for treachery and plunder, and his son the philanthropist, celebrated by Pope as the 'Man of Ross'. The Much Marcle branch were also parliamentarian in sympathy, though they are said to have owed their baronetcy to the good offices of Archbishop Laud. Kyrle's grandfather, the 1st baronet, though pardoned for rebellion on 10 Feb. 1643, was appointed a commissioner for sequestrations, and served with Kyrle's father on the assessment commission from the end of the Civil War to their deaths. Kyrle succeeded them in this capacity, but was proposed as knight of the shire in 1660 by Lord Scudamore as 'one who had never been of either side', though it is not known whether he went to the poll. His omission from the lieutenancy in 1662 suggests that he was out of favour with the new regime, but he was elected for the county in 1668 on the death of Scudamore's son, largely through the efforts of (Sir) Edward Harley*. He proved an inactive Member, probably infrequent in attendance owing to indifferent health. He was named to only nine committees and made no recorded speeches. On 2 Mar. 1670 he acted as teller in favour of adjourning the debate on supply in order to expedite the second reading of the conventicles bill. Sir Richard Wiseman* reported him as generally absent in 1675, and better absent than present from the Government's point of view, and on Shaftesbury's list of 1677 he was marked 'worthy'. Kyrle did not stand again and died on 4 Jan. 1680. His eldest daughter brought the Much Marcle estate to her husband, Sir John Ernle*.[4]

[1] C. J. Robinson, *Mansions and Manors of Herefs.* 280–1; W. R. Williams, *Parl. Hist. Herefs.* 56; *Vis. London* (Harl. Soc. xvii), 312; PCC 40 Pile. [2] Cooke, *Herefs.* iii. 26–28, 184–9; W. H. Black, *Docquets of Letters Patent*, 5; Add. 11044, f. 251; 11051, ff. 233–4. [3] LC3/2. [4] *Her. and Gen.* vii. 422.

E.R.

LACY, William (c.1648–95), of Hartrow, Stogumber, Som.

MILBORNE PORT   1679 (Mar.)

b. c.1648, 1st s. of William Lacy of Hartrow by Sarah, da. and coh. of Nicholas Hole of Upton Pyne, Devon. *educ.* Queen's, Oxf. matric. 25 May 1666, aged 18; M. Temple 1666. *m.* Susanna, da. of Robert Hunt* of Compton Pauncefoot, Som., 1da. *suc.* fa. 1690.[1]
   Commr. for assessment, Som. 1677–80, capt. of militia by 1679–?87, sheriff 1691–2, j.p. 1693–*d.*[2]

Lacy came from a minor gentry family which had resided at Hartrow since the first decade of Elizabeth's reign. His father was nominated to the assessment commission of 1657 and was serving as sheriff at the Restoration; he was proposed for the order of the Royal Oak, with an estimated income of £1,000 p.a. Lacy was the only member of his family to enter Parliament, and doubtless owed his seat to his brother-in-law and colleague, John Hunt*. Before the first Exclusion Parliament met, Shaftesbury marked him 'doubtful', but he voted for the bill. He served on no committees and made no speeches, but his vote lost him Hunt's support, and he never sat again. Lacy's father described himself in 1687 as 'very decrepit', and it was

probably Lacy who held a captain's commission in the militia under Ralph Stawell*, and signed the letter describing how the regiment had gone over *en masse* to Monmouth in 1685. His father agreed to assist and contribute to the election of such Members as should be for taking off the Penal Laws and Tests, and was retained on the lieutenancy and the commission of the peace, while Lacy himself was proposed as court candidate for Milborne Port in 1688. Nevertheless he does not seem to have hesitated to accept local office on his father's death after the Revolution. He died in 1695, leaving most of his estate to his daughter.

[1] H. C. Maxwell Lyte, *Some Som. Manors*, 174–7. [2] *CSP Dom.* 1679–80, p. 62; *HMC Sackville*, i. 1–2.

I.C.

LAKE, Lancelot (1609–80), of Canons Park, Stanmore, Mdx.

MIDDLESEX   1660, 1661

bap. 10 Feb. 1609, 3rd s. of Sir Thomas Lake[†] (*d.*1630) of Canons Park, sec. of state 1616–19, by Mary, da. and coh. of Sir William Ryder, ld. mayor of London 1660–1; bro. of Sir Arthur Lake[†] and Sir Thomas Lake[†]. *educ.* Hart Hall, Oxf. 1622, BA 1625; L. Inn 1626, called 1633; assoc. bencher 1649. *m.* by 1637, Frances, da. of Sir Thomas Cheke[†] of Pirgo, Havering, Essex, 6s. (4 *d.v.p.*) 2da. *suc.* bro. 1653; kntd. 6 June 1660.[1]
   Farmer of coal duties, Newcastle-upon-Tyne 1630–Dec. 1660; j.p. Mdx. 1647–?49, Mar. 1660–*d.*, commr. for militia 1648, Mar. 1660, sewers, Ravensbourne 1657, Sept. 1660, Essex 1658, Oct. 1660, assessment, Mdx. Jan. 1660–*d.*, Westminster 1663–5, oyer and terminer, Mdx. July 1660; dep. lt. Mdx. Aug. 1660–*d.*; commr. for loyal and indigent officers, London and Mdx. 1662, recusants, Mdx. 1675.[2]
   Commr. for loyal and indigent officers accounts 1671.[3]

Lake's grandfather is said to have been a shopkeeper in Southampton, but his father, despite his 'mean birth' and 'meaner breeding', became clerk of the signet to Queen Elizabeth and first entered Parliament as MP for Malmesbury in 1593. He bought Canons in 1604, represented the county in 1614, and held office as secretary of state until he became involved in a particularly unsavoury scandal at the Jacobean court. As a younger son, Lake succeeded to his father's share in the farm of the duty of 12*d.* a chaldron imposed on coal shipped from Tyneside to London. The family took no part in the Civil War, though after the Restoration Lake claimed to have advanced £2,700 to the King at York and to have brought him military intelligence. His receipts from the coal farm were interrupted in 1645 when the Scots took Newcastle, but restored two years later, and a charge of delinquency in 1650 collapsed after Lake had tampered with the witnesses, or so it was alleged. He succeeded to Canons under a family settlement in 1653, to the exclusion of the daughter of his brother Sir Arthur, who had married Melchior de Sabran, the French representative in London during the Civil War.[4]

Lake was successful for Middlesex at the contested general election of 1660. A moderately active Member of the Convention, he was named to 36 committees. His chief concerns were to secure the renewal of his farm of the coal duties, in which he failed despite repeated petitions, and to obstruct the naturalization of his 12-year-old great-nephew René de Sabran, who as an alien was precluded from claiming any land under the family settlement. In this he was more successful; a bill passed the Lords, but never got beyond first reading in the Commons. Lake was, of course, a court supporter, and was rewarded with a knighthood. Lord Wharton marked him as a friend, but in his only recorded speech he spoke in favour of a religious settlement according to the 39 Articles. His most important committees in the first session were to consider the bills for settling ministers in their livings and for reducing interest to six per cent, and to report on the exceptions to the indemnity bill. After the recess he was among those to whom the attainder bill was committed. On 9 Nov. he was sent with (Sir) Francis Gerard* to ask the lord chamberlain to keep the Banqueting Hall clear when the House attended to thank the King for the Worcester House declaration on modified episcopacy. He was named to the committee to draw up the excise clauses in the bill to abolish the court of wards.[5]

Lake was re-elected in 1661 with Sir Thomas Allen*, with whom he worked closely for most of the Cavalier Parliament. A very active backbencher, he was appointed to 581 committees, including the committee of elections and privileges in 11 sessions, and acted as teller in 19 divisions. But only 13 speeches were recorded in his name, he took the chair in committee only once, managed only one conference, and carried only one message. In the first session he was named to the committees for the security bill, restoring bishops to the House of Lords, the inquiry into revenue, the uniformity bill, and the bill of pains and penalties. When the Sabran naturalization bill was reintroduced Lake was given leave to be represented by counsel at the bar of the House. Presumably it was suggested that Sabran, like his younger brother, was being educated by the Jesuits, and the bill was dropped. Two more nieces, the daughters of Lake's eldest brother Sir Thomas, petitioned the Lords during the winter for payment of £3,000 portions, but no action appears to have

been taken. In April 1662 Lake succeeded Edward Rigby* in the chair on the highways bill, and helped to manage a conference. He was also named to the committee to consider an additional corporations bill (10 May). In 1663 he was among those ordered to report on defects in the Corporations Act, and to consider the bill to provide remedies against sectaries. He was teller against the retrospective clause in the bill to regulate abuses in the sale of offices. In 1664 he was named to the committee for the conventicles bill, and together with Allen secured the rejection of a bill to regulate building in the suburbs. But the City Members were too strong for him over a petition from St. Martin's le Grand on 13 Jan. 1665. Later in the month Lake twice opposed tax reliefs for London, and with Allen secured a proviso to the supply bill for the equal assessment of new buildings and offices in Middlesex and Westminster. He opposed the bill to enable the maximum rate of interest to be exceeded on government loans. In the Oxford session Lake was appointed to the committee for the five mile bill. The Lords gave a first reading to a bill introduced on behalf of Lady Bergavenny, Sabran's guardian, to settle his claims on the payment of £550 by Lake, but again it proceeded no further.[6]

On the fall of Clarendon Lake was appointed to the committees to inquire into the miscarriages of the second Dutch war, the sale of Dunkirk, and the charges against Mordaunt. He was among those sent to ask the Duke of Albemarle to secure the highways against thieves and robbers, and instructed to consider the public accounts bill and the further examination of the French merchants. When there was opposition to the nomination to the accounts commission of Sir James Langham*, 'a very weak man' whose only qualification appeared to be 'florid Latin', Lake acted as teller on his behalf, presumably because Langham's daughter was married to his son. On 18 Feb. 1668 he spoke 'very well' against the coercive clause in the triennial bill introduced by Sir Richard Temple*. 'This bill', he said, 'would make the lord keeper a traitor if he did not obey it; and I say ... he is a traitor if he do obey it.' He was among those ordered to take the accounts of the revenue voted for the war and to bring in a militia bill. In the debate on the bill to prevent thefts and robberies he was teller for an additional clause giving 80 days for the apprehension of thieves. He seconded a motion for raising a loan of £100,000 in the City; but he opposed confirmation of the allotments already made in Thames Street and the bill to raise money for rebuilding London after the Fire by a tax on coal. A friend to Ormonde, he was listed by Sir Thomas Osborne* among those Members who usually voted for supply. He was named to all the committees against conventicles in this period.[7]

Lake was named to the committee that produced the test bill against Roman Catholics, and he also served on the committee to consider a bill of ease for Protestant dissenters, although he had declared himself against giving it 'any consideration at all', and urged that the shilling fine for absence from church on Sunday should be retained. On 14 Apr. 1675 he was appointed to the committee to draw up an address for the removal of Lauderdale, remarking in the debate that 'the Scots engaged against the King formerly by their oaths. They are, he thinks, Scotchmen still, and would not believe them, though they take the oaths.' In the same session he was appointed to the committees for appropriating the customs to the use of the navy and hindering the growth of Popery, and in the autumn he was among those ordered to bring in a bill against the suspending power in religion and to consider a bill hindering Papists from sitting in Parliament. Nevertheless his name appeared on the working lists, and Sir Richard Wiseman* confidently described Lake and Allen as 'my particular friends'. Shaftesbury classed him as 'thrice vile' in 1677, when the Commons added a proviso in his interest to the bill for the general naturalization of the children of English subjects abroad during the late troubles. The author of *A Seasonable Argument* described him as 'much in debt' and 'a notorious cuckold', adding that he had been promised that 'his elder brother's son' should never be naturalized. His name appeared on the government list of the court party in May 1678, but on 24 Oct. he was again included in a committee to exclude Papists from both Houses of Parliament. He was given leave of absence for a week on 18 Dec., and never stood again, although he was not blacklisted in the 'unanimous club'. He was buried at Little Stanmore on 4 May 1680. His youngest son Warwick Lake sat for the county from 1698 to 1705.[8]

[1] *St. Martin in the Fields* (Harl. Soc. Reg. xxv), 38; Lipscomb, *Bucks.* ii. 76–77; *Le Neve's Knights* (Harl. Soc. viii), 63–64; Lysons, *Environs*, iii. 413–14. [2] *CSP Dom.* 1628–9, p. 475; *Cal. Comm. Comp.* 2261; C181/6/228, 297; 7/51, 59. [3] *CSP Dom.* 1671, p. 255. [4] *Cal. Comm. Comp.* 2261; *CSP Dom.* 1653–4, pp. 310, 377, 391, 459; 1661–2, p. 616; *Cal. Comm. Adv. Money*, 186, 1205–6; *HMC 7th Rep.* 112. [5] *Cal. Cl. SP*, iv. 644; *CSP Dom.* 1661–2, p. 616; 1665–6, p. 117; 1673, p. 233; *HMC 7th Rep.* 112; Bowman diary, f. 68v; *CJ*, viii. 180. [6] *CJ*, viii. 290, 404, 413, 434, 559, 582, 588, 593, 602; *DNB* (Sabran); *HMC 7th Rep.* 152, 162, 180, 182; *LJ*, xi. 693. [7] *CJ*, ix. 36, 64, 95; Burnet, i. 483; *Milward*, 190, 223, 287. [8] *Dering*, 122–3; *Grey*, ii. 147; iii. 26; *CSP Dom.* 1677–8, p. 75; *HMC 9th Rep.* pt. 2, p. 84; Lysons, iii. 413.

M.W.H./E.C.

LAMBERT, Thomas (c.1638–92), of Boyton, Wilts.

HINDON 1679 (Mar.), 1685

b. c.1638, o.s. of Edmund Lambert of Keevil by Elizabeth, da. of Robert Cole of Willingale Doe, Essex. *educ.* Pembroke, Camb. adm. 9 Apr. 1656, aged 18. *m.* lic. 6 Dec. 1664, Eleanor, da. of Edward Topp of Stockton, Wilts., 3s. 4da. *suc.* fa. 1643.[1]

Commr. for assessment, Wilts. 1661–80, Wilts. and Salisbury 1689–90; capt. of militia ft. Wilts. by 1661, col. by 1685–?June 1688, j.p. 1669–June 1688, Oct. 1688–*d.*, dep. lt. 1683–June 1688, Oct. 1688–*d.*, commr. for rebels' estates 1686.[2]

Lambert was head of a minor gentry family, not akin to the Lamberts of Maiden Bradley. They had held land in Wiltshire since 1560, when his great-great-grandfather, a London alderman, purchased Boyton. His grandfather sat for Hindon, some five miles away, in 1625 and 1626. His father was probably a Royalist, as he was appointed j.p. under a commission issued at Oxford in April 1643, but he died too soon to take any active part in the Civil War. Lambert was undoubtedly an Anglican; his uncle and namesake became archdeacon of Salisbury after the Restoration, and he himself, as a militia officer, was reported to be active against Anabaptists and separatists in 1661. Returned for Hindon in February 1679, he was noted as 'doubtful' by Shaftesbury, but on Huntingdon's list he is marked as an opponent of the Court. An inactive Member, he was named to three committees of no political importance, and voted against exclusion. With Robert Hyde* and two other justices of the peace, he was ordered to be publicly commended at the assizes in 1680 for zeal in seeking out Papists. He regained his seat in 1685 but left no trace on the records of James II's Parliament. On the repeal of the Test Act and Penal Laws, he replied to Lord Yarmouth (William Paston*) that:

> Since his Majesty has been pleased to give a toleration for liberty of conscience, [he] is for securing it by law as his Majesty and his great council shall think fit. For the test, he has not so well considered of it, yet is doubtful.

This answer was construed unfavourably by the regulators, and he was removed from local office. Yarmouth considered Lambert to have great interest at Hindon, but prevailed on him not to stand, and he declared himself 'incapacitated' to help in the election of Members supporting the Government's policy. Apparently he kept his word to the lord lieutenant and did not contest the 1689 election. He died in 1692. His son Edmund sat for Hindon from 1708 to 1713 and for Salisbury from 1715 to 1722 as a Tory.[3]

[1] Hoare, *Wilts.* Heytesbury, 203; *The Gen.* n.s. xxxii. 208. [2] Add. 32324, f. 125; *London Gazette,* 19 Mar. 1685; *Cal. Treas. Bks.* viii. 546. [3] PC2/68/381.

J.P.F.

LAMBTON, William (1640–1724), of Lambton, co. Dur.

DURHAM CO.   1685, 1689, 1690, 1695, 1701 (Feb.), 1701 (Dec.), 1710

bap. 21 June 1640, 1st s. of Henry Lambton of Lambton by Mary, da. of Sir Alexander Davison of Blakiston. *educ.* Queen's, Oxf. 1659. *unm. suc.* fa. 1693.[1]
   Commr. for carriage of coals, port of Newcastle-upon-Tyne 1679; commr. for assessment co. Dur. 1689–90, v.-adm. ?1690–?*d.*, j.p. and dep. lt. by 1701–*d.*[2]

Lambton's family had held the property from which they took their name since at least the middle of the 14th century. His grandfather, a commissioner of array, was killed at Marston Moor, and his father, also a Royalist, compounded for the estate, including the valuable collieries. He supported the enfranchisement of Durham, but was appointed attorney-general to Bishop Crew and deputy recorder of Newcastle under the new charter. Lambton himself became the first of the family to enter Parliament when he was elected for the county in 1685 as a Tory without a contest. A moderately active Member of James II's Parliament, he was appointed to five committees, including those on the bills to prevent theft and rapine on the northern borders, to continue expiring laws, and to relieve insolvent debtors.[3]

Lambton's father returned the same evasive answer as (Sir) Ralph Delaval* on the repeal of the Tests and Penal Laws, and was removed from local office in 1688. But Lambton himself was re-elected to the abortive Parliament, and again to the Convention a month later without opposition. According to Anthony Rowe* he voted to agree with the Lords that the throne was not vacant. An inactive Member, he was named to nine committees, of which the most important was for removing Papists from the metropolitan area (20 Mar.). He remained a Tory under William III, though he signed the Association in 1696. He died in 1724, and was succeeded by his nephew Henry, who sat for the city of Durham as a Whig from 1734 till his death in 1761.[4]

[1] Surtees, *Dur.* ii. 174. [2] *Cal. Treas. Bks.* v. 1205; J. Spearman, *Inquiry into Ancient and Present State of Dur.* (1729), 33–34. [3] Surtees, ii. 174–5; *Cal. Comm. Comp.* 987; *HMC Le Fleming,* 210; *CSP Dom.* 1684–5, p. 241; *The Gen.* n.s. xxii. 21; Hutchinson, *Dur.* i. 549. [4] C. Sharp, *Parl. Rep. Dur.* 17; Spearman, 35.

G.H.

LAMPLUGH, Richard (c.1632–1705), of Ribton Hall, Bridekirk, Cumb.

CUMBERLAND   1679 (Mar.)

b. c.1632, o.s. of Thomas Lamplugh of Beverley, Yorks. and Ribton Hall by Eleanor, da. of Richard Barwis of Grange, Westward, Cumb. *educ.* Queen's, Oxf. 1650; G. Inn 1650, called 1657. *m.* (1) by 1668, Frances, da. of Sir Christopher Lowther, 1st Bt., of Whitehaven, Cumb.; (2) by 1682, Maria, da. of Abraham Moline, merchant, of London and Dovenby, Cumb. and coh. to her bro. Abraham, 2s. (1 *d.v.p.*) 1da. *suc.* fa. 1670.[1]
   Commr. for assessment, Cumb. Jan. 1660, 1663–4, 1666–80, 1689–90, j.p. Mar.–July 1660, 1665–May 1688, Oct. 1688–*d.*, sheriff 1690–1.

Lamplugh's family had held the Cumberland village from which they took their name since the reign of Henry II, and first represented the county in 1384. The senior branch was royalist in the Civil War, but Lamplugh's father, whose direct ancestors had resided in Yorkshire for several generations, acted as treasurer for sequestrations to the Cumberland county committee and built Ribton Hall. After the Restoration he retired into private life. As the first cousin of Thomas Lamplugh, for whom (Sir) Joseph Williamson* obtained the bishopric of Exeter in 1676, Lamplugh was not without friends in the court party, and relations with the head of the family were strengthened by marriage alliances. Nevertheless he would hardly have been considered a possible knight of the shire but for the last-minute withdrawal of Lord Morpeth (Edward Howard*) just before the first general election of 1679. He was returned with his brother-in-law Sir John Lowther II*, defeating an ultra-royalist candidate. Shaftesbury correctly classed him as 'honest'; he voted for the first exclusion bill, unlike Lowther, but was appointed to no committees and did not speak. He refused to stand again in the autumn, giving way to the anti-exclusionist Lord Morpeth. In 1685 he voted for the Whig candidates at Cockermouth, but remained on the commission of the peace until 1688. On 22 Jan. he wrote to Sir Daniel Fleming* that he was laid up with the gout and unable to attend the lord lieutenant at Penrith, but he answered the questions on the repeal of the Test Act and Penal Laws with a written negative, 'unless I can see the Protestant interest secured by a new law', and was dismissed. He accepted the Revolution, serving as sheriff under William and Mary, but never stood again. He was buried at Bridekirk on 24 Mar. 1705, the only member of this branch of the family to sit in Parliament.[2]

[1] *Cumb. and Westmld. Antiq. and Arch. Soc. Trans.* n.s. xxxvii. 115; xxxix. 84–85. [2] Ibid. xxxviii. 104–5; xxxix. 82; *Cal. Comm. Comp.* 257; Cumb. RO, Lowther to Lamplugh, 22 July 1679; Westmld. RO, D/Ry 2890; *HMC Le Fleming,* 209.

E.C.

LANE, John (1609–67), of Bentley, Staffs.

LICHFIELD 1661–31 Aug. 1667

b. 8 Apr. 1609, 1st s. of Thomas Lane of Bentley by 1st w. Anne, da. of Walter Bagot of Blithfield. *m.* Atalanta (*d.* c.1644), da. and h. of Thomas Anson, counsellor at law, of Dunston, 1s. 8da. *suc.* fa. 1660.[1]

Col. of ft. (royalist) 1642–6; gov. Stafford 1643, Rushall 1644; col. of ft. 1667.[2]

Commr. for assessment, Staffs. Aug. 1660–*d.*, j.p. Sept. 1660–*d.*, dep. lt. 1661–*d.*, commr. for loyal and indigent officers 1662.[3]

Lane came from a minor gentry family which had been seated at Bentley since 1427. His father, a passive Royalist, compounded in 1646 for £225. Lane himself was in arms for the King from the beginning of the Civil War until the surrender of Ashby-de-la-Zouch, compounding at £252 16s. He is said to have been on his way to Worcester with a company of foot when he was told of the royalist defeat. The part which the Lane family, especially his sister Jane, played in Charles II's escape is well known. He visited the exiled Court in the following year, and was described by Clarendon as 'a very plain man in his discourse and behaviour, but of fearless courage and integrity superior to any temptation'. He was imprisoned on his return to England, and again during the rising of Sir George Booth*, but released on 14 Sept. 1659 on entering into a £400 bond. He was listed among the proposed knights of the Royal Oak at the Restoration with an estate valued at £700 a year, and the Convention voted his sister (who later married Sir Clement Fisher*) a reward of £1,000.[4]

Lane was returned for Lichfield at the head of the poll at the general election of 1661. He was not an active Member of the Cavalier Parliament, being named to only ten committees of secondary importance, including the committee of elections and privileges in three sessions. 'Very loyal, orthodox and stout, intelligent and active', he played a much more prominent part locally in taking precautions against possible republican plotters. Listed as a court dependant in 1664, he was granted £2,000 in February 1667 for his eminent services during the Civil War, and given a regiment during the Dutch invasion scare in the summer; but he died on 31 Aug. He was buried at Wolverhampton, the only member of his family to sit in Parliament.[5]

[1] Shaw, *Staffs.* ii. 157; *Staffs. Peds.* (Harl. Soc. lxiii), 151. [2] *Committee at Stafford* (Staffs. Rec. Soc. ser. 4, i), p. lxiii; *CSP Dom.* 1644, pp. 177, 179; 1667, p. 182; *Cal. Comm. Comp.* 112. [3] *Staffs. Justices of the Peace* (Wm. Salt Arch. Soc. 1912), 337. [4] Shaw, ii. 95; *Staffs. Parl. Hist.* (Wm. Salt Arch. Soc.), ii. 128–9; *Cal. Comm. Comp.* 112, 1424; SP23/227/599, 603; Clarendon, *Rebellion*, v. 199, 201; H. M. Lane, *Lanes of Bentley Hall*, 3–6; *CJ*, viii. 222. [5] *Gentry of Staffs.* (Staffs. Rec. Soc. ser. 4, ii), 22; *CSP Dom.* 1663–4, pp. 152, 155, 346; 1666–7, pp. 525, 600; Shaw, ii. 157.

A.M.M.

LANGDON, Walter (*d.*1677), of Keverell, nr. East Looe, Cornw.

EAST LOOE 18 Feb. 1673–16 Feb. 1677

o.s. of Walter Langdon of Keverell by Joanna, da. of John Roscarrock of Roscarrock, St. Endellion, wid. of William Prideaux of Gurlyn, St. Erth. *m.* Rhoda, da. of William Martin of Lindridge, Bishop's Teignton, Devon, and coh. to her bro. William, 1da.[1]

Commr. for assessment, Cornw. 1663–74; stannator of Foymore 1663; j.p. Cornw. 1670–*d.*; freeman, East Looe 1672; sub-commr. of prizes, Plymouth 1672–4; commr. for recusants, Cornw. 1675.[2]

Langdon's ancestor John, who sat for Truro in 1419, married the heiress of Keverell. They were not a regular parliamentary family, but Langdon's grandfather was first sent for in custody by the Commons, and then knighted by the King, for his efforts to impede the return of the country candidates at the county election of 1628. His father acted as commissioner of array and went into exile at the end of the Civil War, leaving the care of his family and estate, valued at £700 p.a., to a parliamentarian uncle. He returned in 1652, and his fine was reduced to £441, doubtless through the influence of Francis Langdon, a Baptist who represented Cornwall in the Barebones Parliament. After the Restoration he received £966 as royal bounty to compensate him for his losses.[3]

Langdon himself married the sister-in-law of Thomas Clifford*, who obtained for him a post in the local prize office during the third Dutch war at a salary of £400 p.a. He was returned to the Cavalier Parliament for East Looe as a court supporter at a by-election in 1673, and set out for London shortly afterwards. But his only committee was on the bill to enable Sir Francis Drake, 3rd Bt.*, to settle a jointure on his wife and make provision for his younger children (31 Jan. 1674). After Clifford's fall he was assigned to the management of (Sir) Joseph Williamson* on Danby's working lists, and received the government whip for the autumn session of 1675; but according to Sir Richard Wiseman* he failed to attend. He predeceased his father by a few months on 16 Feb. 1677 and was buried at St. Martin's-by-Looe as 'the last of the male line of that loyal, ancient and honourable family'. The estate was sold by his widow to John Buller* for £6,000.[4]

[1] Vivian, *Vis. Cornw.* 275; Soc. of Genealogists, Exeter mar. lic., 30 Mar. 1635; J. Maclean, *Trigg Minor*, i. 563; ii. 224. [2] A. L. Browne, *Corp. Chrons.* 190; *CSP Dom.* 1673, p. 7; *Cal. Treas. Bks.* iii. 1246. [3] T. Bond, *Sketches of Looe*, 184; M. Coate, *Cornw. in Gt. Civil War*, 31, 371, 379; *Cal. Comm. Comp.* 2244, 3298; *CSP Dom.* 1661–2, p. 544; 1663–4, pp. 45, 368, 456; *Baptist Quarterly*, xxviii. 252. [4] *CSP Dom.* 1673, p. 7; Bond, 21; C7/42/54.

P.W.

LANGFORD, Humphrey (c.1636–85), of Langford Hill, Marhamchurch, Cornw.

CAMELFORD   28 Apr.–24 June 1685

b. c.1636, o.s. of William Langford (*d.*1686) of Langford Hill by Elizabeth, da. of Hugh Prouse of Chagford, Devon. *educ.* King's, Camb. 1655; G. Inn 1655. *m.* 1da.[1]

Commr. for assessment, Cornw. 1677–80, j.p. 1680–*d.*; mayor and coroner, Tintagel 1684–*d.*[2]

The Cornish Langfords can be traced back to the 14th century. Langford's father seems to have avoided commitment during the Civil War and Interregnum, but in 1672 he was granted a long lease of a duchy of Cornwall manor. As Langford was added to the Cornish commission of the peace in 1680, and confirmed as mayor of Tintagel under the new charter he must have opposed exclusion. In the latter capacity he conducted the 1685 election at Bossiney, while he was himself returned to James II's Parliament for Camelford. He was appointed only to the committee on the bill to enable the inhabitants of Soho to build St. Anne's church. He died on 24 June during the session and was buried in Westminster Abbey, the only member of the family to enter Parliament. On his father's death in the following year his daughter brought the estate to her husband, one of the Devon Langfords.[3]

[1] Vivian, *Vis. Cornw.* 277; *Westminster Abbey Reg.* (Harl. Soc. x), 213; J. Maclean, *Trigg Minor*, iii. 166. [2] Maclean, iii. 206–7. [3] *Cal. Treas. Bks.* ii. 1168, 1213, 1224; Vivian, *Vis. Cornw.* 277; *Vis. Devon*, 521; *Westminster Abbey Reg.* 213.

P.W.

LANGHAM, Sir James (c.1621–99), of Lincoln's Inn Fields, Mdx. and Cottesbrooke, Northants.

NORTHAMPTONSHIRE   1656
NORTHAMPTON   1659, 29 Apr.–13 June 1661, 21 Feb.–26 Apr. 1662

b. c.1621, 1st s. of John Langham*, and bro. of Sir William Langham*. *educ.* Emmanuel, Camb. 1638; L. Inn 1640. *m.* (1) lic. 8 Dec. 1647, aged 26, Mary (*d.*1660), da. and coh. of Sir Edward Alston, FRCP, of Great St. Helens, London, 3s. *d.v.p.* 2da.; (2) lic. 18 Nov. 1662 (with £10,000), Lady Elizabeth Hastings (*d.* 28 Mar. 1664), da. of Ferdinando Hastings†, 6th Earl of Huntingdon, *s.p.*; (3) lic. 13 Apr. 1667, Lady Penelope Holles (*d.*1684), da. of John Holles†, 2nd Earl of Clare, *s.p.*; (4) Dorothy, da. of John Pomeroy of Devon, *s.p.* Kntd. 25 May 1660; *suc.* fa. as 2nd Bt. 13 May 1671.[1]

Commr. for assessment, Northants. 1657, Jan. 1660–1, 1663–80, 1689, j.p. 1657–82, 1689–*d.*; commr. for militia 1659, Mar. 1660; member, Hon. Artillery Co. July 1660; sheriff, Northants. 1664–5.[2]

Commr. for public accounts 1667–70.

FRS 1677.

Langham sat for the county in the second Protectorate Parliament and for the borough in its successor; but he is not known to have stood for re-election in 1660. He accompanied his father to The Hague and was knighted there. At the general election of 1661, he was returned on both indentures, but the election was declared void a few weeks later. He regained his seat at the by-election caused by the death of Sir Charles Compton*. An inactive Member of the Cavalier Parliament, he was appointed to four committees, three on commercial matters and the fourth to provide increased maintenance for clergymen in towns. On 13 Mar. 1662 he acted as teller with Thomas Lee I* for an unsuccessful proviso to the militia bill. But 11 days later the elections committee agreed to receive a petition from Sir William Dudley* and on 26 Apr. Langham's election was again declared void. He did not stand again, realizing that his interest was insufficient to defeat Dudley, but eventually prevailed on Christopher Hatton* to contest the by-election with the support of 'the generality of the sober and discreet party'.[3]

After his third marriage Langham lived chiefly in London. His was the only name proposed for the public accounts commission set up after the second Dutch war that encountered serious opposition. Burnet described him as 'a very weak man, famous only for his readiness of speaking florid Latin, which he attained to a degree beyond any man of his age'; but he was accepted after a division. In 1670 his only surviving child married Henry Booth*, and there can be no doubt where his religious and political sympathies lay, though he canvassed energetically and expensively for the court candidate, Sir William Bucknall*, at the Liverpool by-election. He and his wife were reported to frequent Baxter's conventicle, and in 1677 he visited Shaftesbury in the Tower. Removed from the commission of the peace in 1682, he was included in the list of Northampton Whigs with an income of £3,000 p.a. He died in Lincoln's Inn Fields on 22 Aug. 1699, and was buried at Cottesbrooke.[4]

[1] *VCH Northants. Fams.* 216–17; *Vis. Northants.* (Harl. Soc. lxxxvii), 16. [2] Northants. RO, FH2226; *Ancient Vellum Bk.* ed. Raikes, 82. [3] J. C. Cox, *Northampton Bor. Recs.* ii. 345; Add. 29551, ff. 8, 12; *CJ*, viii. 269–70, 414. [4] *Survey of London*, iii. 92; Burnet, i. 483; *CJ*, ix. 36; *CSP Dom.* 1670, p. 330; 1677–8, p. 268; W. Beamont, *Hale and Orford*, 104; *HMC Dartmouth*, i. 15; SP29/421/216; Luttrell, iv. 552.

E.R.E.

LANGHAM, John (1584–1671), of Crosby Place, Bishopsgate, London, and Cottesbrooke, Northants.

LONDON   1654
SOUTHWARK   1660

bap. 20 Apr. 1584, 1st s. of Edward Langham of Guilsborough by Anne, da. of John West, yeoman, of Cotton End, Hardingstone. *m.* c.1620 (with £3,000), Mary (*d.* 8 Apr. 1652), da. of James Bunce[†] of Gracechurch Street, London, 6s. (3 *d.v.p.*) 5da. *suc.* fa. 1607; kntd. 16 May 1660; *cr.* Bt. 7 June 1660.[1]

Asst. Levant Co. 1621–32, 1634–8, treas. 1632–4, gov. 1654; member, Hon. Artillery Co. 1621; committee, E.I. Co. 1626–7, 1628–42; asst. Grocers' Co. 1632; sheriff, London 1642–3, alderman 1642–9, 4–18 Sept. 1660, commr. for militia 1645, 1647, assessment, Northants. 1657, Jan. 1660, London and Northants. Aug. 1660–1, London 1668–9, oyer and terminer, London July 1660.[2]

Capt. of ft. (parliamentary) 1642–3, col. 1643–5.
Commr. for excise 1643; trustee for bishops' lands 1646.[3]

Langham, the grandson of a Northamptonshire yeoman, was apprenticed to Sir Richard Napier, a Turkey merchant, in whose service he spent many years in the Near East. On his return he became a prominent member of the Levant and East India Companies. One of the wealthiest London merchants of his day, he bought the manor of Cottesbrooke in 1639. A staunch Presbyterian, he commanded one of the London train-band regiments in the Civil War; but he was imprisoned in the Tower in 1647 as an opponent of the New Model Army, and furnished money for royalist conspiracy under the Commonwealth. He represented London under the Protectorate, the first of his family to sit.[4]

Langham was associated with the City group, headed by Richard Browne I[*] and John Robinson I[*], which paved the way for the Restoration. He was returned for Southwark at the general election of 1660, apparently unopposed, and classed as a friend by Lord Wharton. In May he helped to draft the assessment ordinance and to raise two loans in the City, for which he received the thanks of the House. He also subscribed £5,310 out of the £50,000 to be presented to the King at The Hague, where he was knighted as one of the delegation that brought the City's answer to the Declaration of Breda. He advanced a further £10,000 towards paying off the navy, and on 13 Aug. he was appointed to the committee to raise £100,000 in the City. But he was granted leave of absence four days later, and took no further part in the Convention. The King ordered him to be restored as alderman, but he was discharged in consideration of his age and infirmity, and also excused from acting as one of the treasurers of the poll bill. He did not stand in 1661, though a poll was demanded at Southwark on his behalf, probably without his consent. He never conformed, and employed dissenting chaplains at Crosby Place. He died on 16 May 1671 and was buried at Cottesbrooke.[5]

[1] *VCH Northants. Fams.* 215–18. [2] J. R. Woodhead, *Rulers of London*, 105; *Ancient Vellum Bk.* ed. Raikes, 33. [3] *List of London Militia* (1642). [4] V. Pearl, *London and the Outbreak of the Puritan Revolution*, 321–3; R. Sharpe, *London and the Kingdom*, ii. 266, 273, 308; *HMC Portland*, i. 585. [5] D. Underdown, *Royalist Conspiracy*, 299; *CJ*, viii. 127, 280; *CSP Dom.* 1661–2, p. 601; D. R. Lacey, *Dissent and Parl. Pols.* 417–18.

M.W.H./E.C.

LANGHAM, Sir William (c.1625–1700), of Walgrave, Northants.

NORTHAMPTON   1679 (Oct.), 1681, 1689, 1690

b. c.1625, 4th but 2nd surv. s. of John Langham[*], and bro. of Sir James Langham[*]. *educ.* Emmanuel, Camb. 1642, BA 1646; Leyden 1647; Padua 1649, MD by 1652. *m.* (1) 2 Sept. 1657, Elizabeth (*bur.* 3 Nov. 1657), da. of Sir Anthony Haslewood of Maidwell, *s.p.*; (2) 19 June 1659, Alice (*d.*1664), da. of Sir George Chudleigh, 1st Bt.[†], of Ashton, Devon, wid. of John Rolle[†], merchant, of London, and Widdicombe House, Stokenham, Devon, 2da.; (3) 10 July 1666, aged 40, Martha, da. of Herbert Hay[†] of Glyndebourne, Suss., wid. of David Polhill of Chipstead Place, Kent, 3s. (2 *d.v.p.*). Kntd. 14 Dec. 1671; *suc.* bro. as 3rd Bt. 22 Aug. 1699.[1]

Fellow of Peterhouse, Camb. 1646–50; commr. for assessment, Northants. Jan. 1660–1, 1663–80, 1689–90, j.p. July 1660–70, 1675–82, 1689–d., sheriff 1671–2.[2]
Commr. for preventing export of wool 1689–92.

Langham studied medicine at several universities, qualified at Padua, and took up practice on his return to England. Walgrave, which his father bought in 1655 for £8,630, was settled on him on his marriage. He was removed from the Northamptonshire commission of the peace in 1670, no doubt as an opponent of the Conventicles Act. A country Member like his elder brother, he represented Northampton in the second and third Exclusion Parliaments, but, apart from his appointment to the committee of elections and privileges on 25 Oct. 1680, he left no trace on their records. In February 1683 he was fined £100 for not prosecuting conventicles. He was presented as ill-affected by the Northamptonshire grand jury, and his house was searched for arms. He regained his seat at the general election of 1689, but he was again inactive and seems to have been absent for most of the first session of the Convention. He took no part in the inquiries into the East India Company, though he was one of the four largest investors, with a holding of £18,200. He was named to nine committees in the second session, including those for compensation to such Whig sufferers as Sir Trevor Williams[*], John Arnold[*], Edmund Prideaux[*] and the widow and children of Sir Thomas Armstrong[*]. He supported the disabling clause in the bill to restore corporations. Re-elected for Northampton in 1690, he succeeded to the baronetcy in 1699 and died on 29 Sept. 1700. The next member of the family to enter Parliament was his great-grandson, the 7th baronet, who was returned for the county in 1784.[3]

[1] *Vis. Northants. Fams.* 218–19. [2] Northants. RO, FH2226. [3] Bridges, *Northants.* ii. 128; *Somers Tracts*, viii. 409; R. Morrice, Entering Bk. 1, p. 355; *CSP Dom.* July–Sept. 1683, p. 300; Add. 22185, f. 14.

E.R.E./J.P.F.

LANSDOWN, Lord *see* GRANVILLE (GRENVILLE), Charles

LASCELLES, Francis (1612–67), of Stank Hall, Kirby Sigston, Yorks.

THIRSK	6 Oct. 1645
NORTH RIDING	1653, 1654, 1656
NORTHALLERTON	c. Apr.–9 June 1660

bap. 23 Aug. 1612, 1st s. of William Lascelles *alias* Jackson (*d.*1624) of Stank Hall by Elizabeth, da. of Robert Wadeson of Yafforth; bro. of Thomas Lascelles*. *educ.* G. Inn 1629. *m.* 1626, Frances (*d.*1658), da. of Sir William St. Quintin, 1st Bt., of Harpham, 5s. (2 *d.v.p.*) 10da. *suc.* gdfa. 1628.[1]

J.p. Yorks (N. Riding) 1640–July 1660, commr. of array 1642, sequestrations 1643, assessment 1643–9, 1657, Jan. 1660, Yorks, 1650, 1652, northern assoc. (N. Riding) 1645, scandalous ministers 1654, security, Yorks. 1655–6, subscriptions, Durham college 1656, militia, Yorks. 1659, Mar. 1660.[2]

Capt. of ft. (parliamentary) 1642–4; col. 1644–5, 1648, 1651; capt. of horse 1644–5.[3]

Member, high court of justice 1649.

Lascelles is a name of great antiquity in Yorkshire, and the senior branch already held estates in the North Riding in the 12th century. But Lascelles's grandfather, who bought the Stank estate in 1608, was not able to connect up his pedigree with the medieval family. Lascelles served in the parliamentary army in both wars, but by his own account 'exercised his command with moderation', and became the first of his family to sit when he was returned for Thirsk as a recruiter, 'in order, as he supposed, to a better settlement under his Majesty'. He served as one of Charles I's judges, but refused to sign the death warrant. Nevertheless he continued to sit in the Rump and represented the North Riding under the Protectorate. He had presumably become a Royalist, for in February 1660 he urged the readmission of the secluded Members.[4]

At the general election of 1660 Lascelles was returned with his brother for Northallerton, two miles from his home. But he was under no illusions about the future, and immediately crossed over to the Low Countries to lodge a petition for a pardon, which he delivered on 8 Apr. at Breda, claiming (inaccurately) that he had held no command during the Interregnum nor purchased any crown lands. He was still abroad when Lord Wharton drew up his list of the Convention, but he was granted his pardon on 5 June. According to Edmund Ludlow* he owed his life to his son's marriage to a Popish lady, one of the Irish Talbots high in favour at Court; but in any case he was not a regicide. On 9 June he was disabled from sitting without having taken any known part in the proceedings of the House. Under the Act of Indemnity he was fined one year's income and incapacitated from office, and he remained under suspicion. In November 1661 his letters were opened in the post on the Duke of Buckingham's instructions. The Anabaptist conspirators met at Stank Hall in 1663, but found him 'not to be dealt with'. Nevertheless he was taken into custody for a time. He was buried at Kirby Sigston on 28 Nov. 1667. His son Daniel sat for Northallerton in 1702.[5]

[1] T. D. Whitaker, *Loidis and Elmete*, 168–9; *Yorks. Arch. Jnl.* xvii. 167. [2] *N. Riding Recs.* iv. 177; *Thurloe*, iii. 402; *CSP Dom.* 1655–6, p. 262. [3] *Parl. Rep. Yorks.* (Yorks. Arch. Soc. rec. ser. xcvi), 58–59; SP18/71/55/8. [4] *VCH Yorks. N. Riding*, i. 407; *Parl. Rep. Yorks.* 59–60; *Ludlow Mems.* ii. 217. [5] *CSP Dom.* 1659–60, pp. 408–9; 1660–1, p. 38; 1663–4, pp. 16, 18; *CJ*, viii. 60; *Voyce from the Watch Tower*, 175; *HMC Var.* ii. 117; SP29/86/68, 99/110.

M.W.H./P.A.B.

LASCELLES, Thomas (1624–97), of Mount Grace Priory, East Harlsey, Yorks.

NORTHALLERTON	1660, 1689, 1690, 1695–Nov. 1697

bap. 5 Aug. 1624, 4th s. of William Lascelles *alias* Jackson of Stank Hall, and bro. of Francis Lascelles*. *m.* Ruth, 3s. (1 *d.v.p.*) 4da.[1]

Capt. of ft. (parliamentary) 1644–at least 1652.[2]

J.p. Yorks. (N. and E. Ridings) 1652–Oct. 1660, (N. Riding) 1690–?*d.*; commr. for assessment (N. Riding) 1657, Aug. 1660–1, 1673–80, 1689–90, militia, Yorks. Mar. 1660, maj. of militia ft. ?1689–*d.*; bailiff, Northallerton by 1679–c.1685.[3]

Housekeeper, Excise Office 1693–*d.*[4]

Lascelles was in arms for the Parliament like his elder brother. He bought the bishop of Durham's manor of Northallerton in 1649 and Mount Grace four years later from the royalist Conyers Darcy*. These purchases seem to have crippled his financial resources, especially after the return of episcopal estates at the Restoration. He was returned with his brother for Northallerton, six miles from his home, at the general election of 1660, and classed as a friend by Lord Wharton, but played no known part in the Convention. He was cognisant of the Anabaptist plot in 1663, and was imprisoned in York Castle. He was again arrested during the second

Dutch war on a charge of 'turbulent and seditious practices'. Though he did not stand himself during the exclusion crisis, his interest returned two opponents of the Court at Northallerton and he acted as returning officer in all three elections. After the Rye House Plot arms were found in his house. He may have become a Whig collaborator, for in September 1688 the King's electoral agents reported that 'Mr Thomas Lascelles, that hath the interest of the place, will take care another good man shall be chosen' at Northallerton. But in fact he was himself elected to the Convention, resuming his seat after a lapse of 28 years. He was not an active Member, being appointed only to the committees to inquire into the charges against William Harbord*, to settle a maintenance on the children of Sidney Wortley Montagu*, and to inspect the Poor Laws. Although doubtless a Whig, he was not listed among the supporters of the disabling clause in the bill to restore corporations. He continued to represent the family borough as a court Whig for the rest of his life, becoming a placeman in 1693. He was buried at Northallerton on 4 Nov. 1697. None of his descendants sat in Parliament.[5]

[1] T. D. Whitaker, *Loidis and Elmete*, 167–8; *Yorks. Arch. Jnl.* vii. 481. [2] *Cal. Comm. Comp.* 2872. [3] Add. 29674, f. 161; Eg. 1626, f. 53. [4] *Cal. Treas. Bks.* x. 182; xiii. 158. [5] *Cosin Corresp.* (Surtees Soc. lv), 18–19; *VCH Yorks. N. Riding*, ii. 29; *Yorks. Arch. Jnl.* vii. 480; *CSP Dom.* 1663–4, p. 16; 1664–5, p. 201; 1667–8, p. 273; SP29/86/68; *HMC Astley*, 38; *HMC Var.* ii. 117; *Cal. Treas. Bks.* xiii. 158.

P.A.B./P.W.

LATIMER, Visct. *see* **OSBORNE, Edward**

LAUGHARNE, Rowland (c.1607–75), of St. Brides, Pemb.

PEMBROKE BOROUGHS 1661–Nov. 1675

b. c.1607, 1st s. of John Laugharne of St. Brides by Janet, da. of Sir Hugh Owen of Bodowen, Anglesey and Orielton, Pemb. *m.* bef. 1643, Anne (*d.*1681), da. of Sir Thomas Button of Cottrell, St. Nicholas, Glam., 3s. (2 *d.v.p.*) other ch. *suc.* fa. c.1638.[1]

C.-in-c. Pemb. (parliamentary) 1642, Card. and Carm. 1644, Glam. 1646; gov. Pembroke Castle 1644; maj.-gen. (parliamentary) 1644–6, (royalist) 1648.[2]

Commr. for assessment, Pemb. 1647, Aug. 1660–74; common councilman, Haverfordwest 1651–at least 1659; j.p. Pemb. July 1660–?70, 1672–*d.*, Haverfordwest 1662; dep. lt. Pemb. c. Aug. 1660–*d.*, commr. for loyal and indigent officers 1662.[3]

Gent. of the privy chamber June 1660–*d.*[4]

The Laugharne family could trace its origin back to the 14th century, but it became well established in Pembrokeshire only in Tudor times. After serving in his youth as page to the 3rd Earl of Essex,

Laugharne became a prominent Parliamentarian. He fought a series of campaigns in south-west Wales and reduced most of the area to obedience. Among the rewards for his service was the grant in February 1646 of the forfeited estates of John Barlow of Slebech. In 1648 Laugharne changed sides and supported the royalist revolt in South Wales, with disastrous consequences for himself and his estate. Forced to yield Pembroke garrison in July, he was sentenced to death, but reprieved. In 1649 he lost the Slebech estate, but his fine of £712 was remitted in 1655.[5]

Laugharne claimed to have spent 'most times in prison till your Majesty's happy Restoration'. At the time of Booth's rising he had to give security for good behaviour to the Pembrokeshire commissioners. He was proposed by Sir Thomas Myddelton* as commander of the Royalists in South Wales in February 1660, though he was then in town. Laugharne offered himself as a candidate for Haverfordwest at the general election, but he was not seriously considered. On 10 Dec. he was granted £3,000 in consideration of his heavy losses during the Civil Wars and consequent debts, but he never received even half the sum.[6]

Laugharne was returned on the interest of his cousin Sir Hugh Owen, 1st Bt.*, for Pembroke Boroughs in his absence in 1661, but he was an inactive Member of the Cavalier Parliament who made no recorded speeches and was named to only 20 committees. Their subjects included bills for regulating the weaving trade, poor relief and Lord's day observance. Throughout his parliamentary career he was in real distress. In March 1662, when he estimated his losses at £37,630, he was granted £500, and in 1663 a pension of £500 p.a. for life, but this was paid very irregularly, and he and his wife were constantly driven to petition for their arrears. He was listed among the court dependants in 1664, when he was given £125 to prevent 'immediate starvation'. In 1666 his debts were said to be £8,000. On 14 Mar. 1670 he claimed privilege over the seizure of his cattle by the under-sheriff of Pembrokeshire. Later that year his wife said that he had been obliged 'to pawn his cloak and sword, and has only 3s. in the world'. He was included on the Paston list, as a King's servant in 1675, and on the working lists, but he was buried at St. Margaret's, Westminster on 16 Nov. His grandson John Laugharne† sat for Haverfordwest as a Tory from 1702 to 1715.[7]

[1] *DWB*; *Cases in Court of Chivalry* (Harl. Soc. cvii), 119. [2] A. L. Leach, *Civil War in Pemb.* 41, 88, 99–100, 175. [3] *CSP Dom.* 1667, p. 587; 1667–8, p. 54; *Cal. Recs. Haverfordwest* (Univ. Wales, Bd. of Celtic Studies, Hist. and Law ser. xxiv), 95–96, 134. [4] Carlisle, *Privy Chamber*, 169. [5] *DWB*; *Cal. Comm. Comp.* 2106; *LJ*, viii.

199; *CJ*, vi. 305–6. [6] SP29/270/51; *CSP Dom.* 1659–60, p. 140; 1666–7, p. 402; *Cal. Cl. SP*, iv. 254, 549; *Cal. Recs. Haverfordwest*, 165–8; *LJ*, xi. 204. [7] *CSP Dom.* 1661–2, p. 313; 1666–7, p. 402; 1670, p. 405; *Cal. Treas. Bks.* i. 587; v. 33, 102, 1331; *Secret Service Moneys* (Cam. Soc. lii), 3, 10, 14, 17, 23, 31; Add. 18730, f. 4v.

L.N./G.J.

LAWLEY, Sir Francis, 2nd Bt. (c.1626–96), of Spoonhill, Salop and Canwell Priory, Staffs.

MUCH WENLOCK   1659, 1660
SHROPSHIRE   1661

*b.*c.1626, 1st s. of Sir Thomas Lawley, 1st Bt.[†], of Spoonhill, and Twickenham, Mdx. by Anne, da. of John Manning of London, and coh. to her bro. John Manning of Cralle Place, Warbleton, Suss. *m.* by 1650, Anne, da. of Sir Thomas Whitmore, 1st Bt.[†], of Apley Park, Salop, 3s. 6da. *suc.* fa. 19 Oct. 1646.[1]

Commr. for militia, Salop Mar. 1660; j.p. Salop Mar. 1660–June 1688, Nov. 1688–*d.*, Staffs. and Warws. July 1660–89; dep.-lt. Salop c. Aug. 1660–June 1688, Staffs. 1677–Feb. 1688; commr. for assessment, Salop and Staffs. Sept. 1660–80, 1689–90, Warws. Sept. 1660–1, Essex, Warws. and Mont. 1677–80, Mont. 1689; capt. vol. horse, Salop 1661, commr. for corporations 1662–3, loyal and indigent officers 1662, recusants 1675.[2]

Gent. of the privy chamber by June 1660–*d.*; member, Society of Mineral and Battery Works 1674, dep. gov. 1677–81, asst. 1687–Dec. 1688; commr. for customs 1677–9; member, Society of Mines Royal by 1685, dep. gov. 1689; master of the jewel house 1690–*d.*[3]

One of Lawley's family sat in the Commons for Bridgnorth in 1429. But their principal interest, fortified by the purchase of Wenlock Priory during the Reformation, lay in Wenlock, which Lawley's father represented in the first three Parliaments of Charles I. He was created a baronet in 1641, but lived quietly at Twickenham during the Civil War. He was assessed at £800 by the committee for the advance of money, but this was reduced to £200 in view of his 'being much in debt, and one-third of his lands under power of the King's army, and his service and good affection to the state'. Although Lawley's step-father was no less a person than John Glynne*, he remained inactive during the Interregnum, and his younger brother was apparently a Royalist. He was returned for Wenlock in 1659 and 1660, but was totally inactive in the Convention, being mentioned only as a claimant of privilege on 6 Dec. 1660.[4]

At the general election of 1661 Lawley was chosen with Sir Richard Ottley* as, in Lord Newport's judgment, 'the two most fittest to be knights of the shire for Shopshire'. He seems to have taken part in the coronation festivities, but he was an inactive Member of the Cavalier Parliament, in which he was named to only 43 committees. In a survey of Staffordshire gentlemen in 1663, when he was

37 years of age, he was described as 'loyal and orthodox' and 'of reasonable good parts', with an estate of about £8,000 p.a. He was apparently hostile to Clarendon, serving on the committee for the impeachment of Lord Mordaunt, but in 1669 Sir Thomas Osborne* listed him among the Members to be engaged by the Duke of Buckingham, and as long as Osborne was lord treasurer, Lawley was a dependable supporter of the Court. He received the government whip in 1675, and made two speeches on 26 Oct. against an opposition attempt to receive money appropriated for naval supply in the chamber of London. He was described as one 'of my lord treasurer's creatures' in 1676, was contemptuously dismissed in *A Seasonable Argument* as 'a pensioner, one of the horses in Madame Fontelet's coach', perhaps a reference to the Duchess of Portsmouth, and was naturally considered 'thrice vile' by Shaftesbury in 1677. In that year he was named to the committees on the bills to prevent the growth of Popery and to provide for the Protestant education of the children of the royal family. He was included in 1678 in both court and opposition lists as a member of the court party.[5]

With the fall of Danby Lawley was dismissed from his position with the customs, carrying an annual salary of £1,200. As one of the 'unanimous club' he was defeated at Wenlock in both elections of 1679. When he stood in 1681 for Lichfield, about eight miles from his Staffordshire property, a Tory thought he had as good a chance as any, but the Whigs were confident that he 'can do us no hurt', and he did not go to the poll. He remained in touch with the Government, and in 1683 intervened to prevent the re-grant of a charter to Walsall, 'the most factious place in the county'. He procured loyal addresses from Staffordshire and Shropshire on the accession of James II, reporting to Sunderland that he found 'all persons very forward to serve his Majesty'. Trusting in government support at Lichfield, and in 'the assurances and invitation of the greatest part of the town', he spread his electoral activities widely in the two counties, securing his son's return at Wenlock, and appearing only occasionally in his own constituency. On 4 Apr. 1685, returning to Lichfield from the election of 'two very loyal persons' for Shropshire, he found that he was in danger of losing the election unless the King ordered Thomas Orme* to desist. To his dismay, Sunderland replied that 'his Majesty thinks it too late to interpose in the matter of your election as you desire'. At the poll he was 'very ill dealt with, and many of his votes rejected'; but his petition was unsuccessful, though his old patron listed him among the parliamentary Opposition.[6]

Lawley was absent for the questions on the Penal Laws and Test Act in both Staffordshire and Shropshire in 1688. He accepted the Revolution, was appointed master of the jewel house, and continued as a gentleman of the privy chamber. He died on 25 Oct. 1696, leaving land in Berkshire, Kent, Lincolnshire and Sussex in addition to Shropshire.[7]

[1] *Trans. Salop Arch. Soc.* (ser. 3), ii. 331; *Vis. Salop* (Harl. Soc. xxix), 314; Shaw, *Staffs.* ii. 21; *Cal. Cl. SP*, ii. 244. [2] SP29/41/85; Bodl. Ch. Salop 146. [3] Carlisle, *Privy Chamber*, 166, 172, 197, 204; *Trans. Salop Arch. Soc.* (ser. 4), i. 296; BL Loan 16; *CSP Dom.* 1677-8, p. 86; 1689-90, p. 552; *Cal. Treas. Bks.* v. 769; vi. 12. [4] *Cal. Cl. SP*, ii. 244. [5] *HMC 5th Rep.* 150; *Gentry of Staffs.* (Staffs. Rec. Soc. ser. 4, ii), 21; *Evelyn Diary*, iii. 280; *Hatton Corresp.* (Cam. Soc. n.s. xxii), 122; Grey, iii. 357; *CSP Dom.* 1666-7, p. 507. [6] *Cal. Treas. Bks.* v. 1219; *HMC Finch*, ii. 53; *HMC Dartmouth*, i. 56; *CSP Dom.* 1682, p. 166; Jan.-June 1683, pp. 31, 95, 143, 203; 1685, pp. 103, 108, 121, 123; Bath mss, Thynne pprs. 21, f. 171; *Trans. R. Hist. Soc.* (ser. 4), xix. 180-3; *Staffs. Rec. Soc.* lxxi. 218-25. [7] PCC 131 Bond.

M.W.H./J.S.C.

LAWLEY, Thomas (c.1650-1729), of Spoonhill, Salop.

MUCH WENLOCK 1685

b. c.1650, 1st s. of Sir Francis Lawley, 2nd Bt.* *m.* (1) Rebecca, da. and coh. of (Sir) Humphrey Winch, 1st Bt.*, of Hawnes, Beds., 9s. (8 *d.v.p.*) 2da.; (2) 3 Mar. 1712, Elizabeth Perkins, wid., 1s. 1da. *suc.* fa. as 3rd Bt. 25 Oct. 1696.[1]

Commr. for assessment, Staffs. 1689-90, j.p. 1690-?d.

Lawley was returned for Wenlock in 1685 on the family interest, but was completely inactive in James II's Parliament. It was reported in 1688 that his father had settled Spoonhill on him, but he was repeatedly defeated at Wenlock and never regained his seat, though he lived to be nearly 80. He executed a codicil to his will on 22 Oct. 1729, and died before the end of the year. His grandson was returned for Warwickshire as a Whig in 1780.[2]

[1] Shaw, *Staffs.* ii. 21. [2] *Salop Arch. Soc. Trans.* (ser. 3), ii. 335; PCC 344 Abbott.

J.S.C.

LAWRENCE, Nathaniel (c.1627-1714), of Colchester, Essex.

COLCHESTER 1685

b. c.1627, s. of Thomas Lawrence, clothier, of Colchester. *m.* by 1661, Martha (d. 18 June 1677), da. of Richard Greene, linen-draper, of Colchester, at least 1s. 2da.[1]

?Ensign, Colchester militia by 1651, common councilman 1656-9, 1669-71, alderman 1671-Jan. 1688, 1693-?d., mayor 1672-3, 1679-80, 1683-4, 1709; commr. for assessment, Colchester 1679-80, 1690, Essex 1689-90; j.p. Essex 1680-Apr. 1688, Oct. 1688-d., lt. of militia horse 1680.[2]

Lawrence's father, of yeoman stock, was a parliamentary sympathizer during the Civil War, serving as mayor in 1643-4 and actively supporting the Protectorate. Lawrence himself followed his father's trade as a clothier, and as an ensign in the train-bands is alleged to have fought for the Commonwealth at the battle of Worcester. He was nominated to the corporation by the Protector in the charter of 1656. He regained office in 1669 and became an occasional conformist. It was said that he

> never brought a common prayer book to church or made any response after the parson, or say [sic] amen to any of the prayers of the Church, for he seldom comes until the prayers are almost over.

He was accused of maintaining a family pew in one of the local conventicles, and declaring at elections of magistrates that dissenters were 'as honest and good men as the Churchmen'. But he was not involved in exclusion politics, and during his third term as mayor complied with the Government's demand for surrender of the charter. He was confirmed as alderman, and when the 2nd Duke of Albemarle (Christopher Monck*) brought the new charter down in November 1684, the way was 'spread with Colchester bays of Mr Lawrence's for his grace and the company to walk on'.[3]

Lawrence was thus one of the few dissenters returned in 1685. But he was totally inactive in James II's Parliament, being given leave of absence on 19 June. He gave evasive answers to the first two questions on the repeal of the Test Act and Penal Laws, declaring that; 'If he be chosen a Member of Parliament, he will discharge his trust the people shall put in him; as to an election, he hopes he may have his liberty of voting'. He was among the first to be removed from the corporation in 1688, and apparently never sought re-election. He was not restored to municipal office until the new charter of 1693. He served again as mayor for about two months in 1709 on the death in office of the then holder. Lawrence died on 5 May 1714, aged 87, and was buried in St. James, Colchester, the only member of his family to sit in Parliament.[4]

[1] Morant, *Essex*, Colchester, app. 22; *Trans. Essex Arch. Soc.* xiii. 268, 270; *Essex Rev.* vi. 172; PCC 119 Aston. [2] *Essex Rev.* v. 208; Colchester Castle, Colchester assembly bk. 2, ff. 33, 47; PC2/72/581; G. Rickword, *Bailiffs and Mayors of Colchester*, 17, 18. [3] *Essex Rev.* v. 208; Stowe 835, ff. 37v-44; Bdl. Rawl. mss, Essex 1, ff. 113-17, 120-2, 126-8; *CSP Dom.* 1655, pp. 202-3, 354; 1655-6, p. 253; 1684-5, p. 216; *VCH Essex*, ii. 398. [4] PC2/72/581; Stowe 835, f. 65v; *CSP Dom.* 1693, pp. 186, 296, 344; Morant, app. 22.

G.H./G.J.

LAWSON, Wilfred (c.1636–aft. 1679), of Brayton, Aspatria, Cumb.

COCKERMOUTH 1659, 1660

b. c.1636, 2nd s. of Sir Wilfred Lawson*. *educ.* G. Inn 1654, called 1660. *m.* Sarah, da. of William James of Washington, co. Dur., and coh. to her bro. William, 2s. 1da.[1]

Commr. for militia, Cumb. Mar. 1660, assessment Aug. 1660–1, 1673–80, sheriff 1678–9.

Lawson's father bought Brayton in 1658 and settled it on him, with five other Cumbrian manors. He was returned to Richard Cromwell's Parliament for Cockermouth on the family interest, and re-elected in 1660, defeating the Earl of Northumberland's candidate by a wide margin. Lord Wharton marked him as a friend in the Convention, and he probably voted with the Opposition; but he was appointed only to the committee for the confirmation of parliamentary privileges. He gave way to his father at the general election of 1661, and apparently never stood again. As sheriff in 1679 he seems to have assisted the election of the exclusionist Richard Lamplugh*. Nothing further is known of him, except that he predeceased his father. His son sat for Cumberland as a Tory with one brief interval from 1701 to 1734.[2]

[1] Hutchinson, *Cumb.* ii. 241; Surtees, *Dur.* i. 216. [2] *Northern Hist.* v. 62.

M.W.H./G.H.

LAWSON, Sir Wilfred (c.1610–88), of Isel, Cumb.

CUMBERLAND 1659, 1660
COCKERMOUTH 1661

b. c.1610, o.s. of William Lawson of Isel by Judith, da. and h. of William Bewley of Hesket. *educ.* Queen's, Oxf. matric. 21 Nov. 1628, aged 17. *m.* Jane (*d.* 8 June 1677), da. of Sir Edward Musgrave, 1st Bt., of Hayton Castle, 5s. (2 *d.v.p.*) 8da. Kntd. 26 Feb. 1641; *suc.* fa. c.1654; *cr.* Bt. 31 Mar. 1688.[1]

Commr. of array, Cumb. 1642; j.p. Cumb. ?1642–May 1643, Cumb. and Westmld. Oct. 1643–*d.*; commr. for assessment, Cumb. 1644–52, 1657, Aug. 1660–80, militia, Cumb. 1648, Cumb. and Westmld. Mar. 1660; mayor, Carlisle 1652–3, 1657–8; sheriff, Cumb. 1653–7, capt. of militia to 1659, Oct. 1660, dep. lt. c. Aug. 1660–*d.*, commr. for recusants 1675.[2]

Col. (parliamentary) by 1644.[3]
Commr. for security [S] 1656.

Lawson's great-uncle acquired Isel by marriage in Elizabethan times, first representing Cumberland in 1593. His father, who inherited the estate in 1632, was a ship-money sheriff, but sat on the county committee in the Civil War. Lawson himself, though knighted in 1641 and nominated to the commission of array, took up arms for Parliament,

and was appointed commander-in-chief for Cumberland in 1644. He held local office throughout the Interregnum, and sat for the county in Richard Cromwell's Parliament. But his loyalty to the Rump was suspect, and he was imprisoned with Charles Howard* after Booth's rising.[4]

Lawson was re-elected for Cumberland in 1660 after a stiff contest with Sir George Fletcher*. Lord Wharton marked him as a friend, entrusting him with the management of the Cumbrian and some of the west-country Members. An inactive Member of the Convention, he was appointed to 11 committees, including the committee of elections and privileges and those for the land purchases and indemnity bills. After the Restoration he was named to the committees to inquire into impropriate rectories and unauthorized Anglican publications. On 7 July (Sir) Christopher Clapham* introduced a proviso to the indemnity bill requiring Lawson to make reparations to Sir Jordan Crosland* and his wife for the plunder of Rydal. Lawson, in his only recorded speech, 'made his defence, saying he never saw any plate or moneys', and the House accepted this convenient myopia. He received Wharton's statement of the case for modified episcopacy, but took no part in the proceedings, though he was appointed to two committees of minor importance in the second session.[5]

At the general election of 1661 Lawson had to step down to a borough seat at Cockermouth, where he enjoyed a strong burgage interest. Wharton again marked him as a friend, but he proved to be one of the least active Members of the Cavalier Parliament, and apparently veered towards the Court. He left no trace in the Journals till the 1666 session when he was added to the elections committee, and appointed to those to inquire into the charter of the Canary Company and to consider a bill for the relief of poor prisoners. His only other committee was the elections committee in 1673, and he three times defaulted on calls of the House. He received the government whip in 1675 and was described by Sir Richard Wiseman* as 'well known to my Lord Ogle [Henry Cavendish*] and my Lord Carlisle [Charles Howard*]'. On the working lists he was assigned to the management of (Sir) Joseph Williamson*, but Shaftesbury marked him 'worthy' in 1677. He did not stand again, and presumably opposed exclusion, since he remained a j.p. and deputy lieutenant till his death. To the lord lieutenant's questions in 1688 he replied:

In case I shall be chosen knight of the shire or burgess of a town when the King shall think fit to call a Parliament, I shall (God willing) be for taking off the Penal Laws and Tests. . . . I will assist and contribute to the election of such Members as shall be for taking off the Penal Laws and Tests to the best of my knowledge.

He was rewarded with a baronetcy, but died on 13 Dec. 1688, aged 79, and was buried at Isel. His grandson, the 2nd baronet, was returned for Cockermouth as a Tory in 1690.[6]

[1] Nicolson and Burn, *Cumb. and Westmld.* ii. 96; *Northern Hist.* v. 47. [2] *HMC Portland*, i. 186; Cumb. RO, D/MH/1. [3] *CSP Dom.* 1644-5, pp. 98, 614. [4] Nicolson and Burn, ii. 95; *Northern Hist.* v. 39, 47; *Cal. Cl. SP*, iv. 376. [5] *CSP Dom.* 1659-60, p. 415; *HMC Le Fleming*, 24; *CJ*, viii. 84; Bowman diary, f. 62v. [6] Westmld. RO, D/Ry 3228, 3314.

M.W.H./G.H./E.C.

LAWTON, John (1656-1736), of Lawton, Cheshire.

NEWCASTLE-UNDER-LYME   1689, 1695, 27 Feb. 1706, 1 Feb. 1709

bap. 7 May 1656, 1st s. of William Lawton of Lawton by Hester, da. of Sir Edward Longueville, 1st Bt., of Wolverton, Bucks. *m.* (1) by 1679, Anne (*d.* 1 July 1717), da. of George Montagu* of Horton, Northants., 7s. (6 *d.v.p.*) 8da.; (2) his cos. Mary, da. of Edward Longueville of Iver, Bucks., wid. of Sir Edward Longueville, 3rd Bt., of Wolverton, 1s. *suc.* fa. 1693.[1]

Commr. for assessment, Staffs. 1689-90, Cheshire 1690; mayor, Newcastle 1692-3; j.p. Cheshire 1695-*d.*, Staffs. by 1701-*d.*; capt. of militia horse, Cheshire by 1697; steward, Newcastle manor 1698-1702, 1707-10, 1716-17; dep. lt. Cheshire and Staffs. by 1701-?*d.*[2]

Lawton's ancestors took their name from a Cheshire manor, part of which had been in their hands since at least the reign of Henry III. A younger son sat for Callington in 1584 and for Chester 20 years later, but they were not a regular parliamentary family. Lawton's father during the Civil War took shelter with the King's forces in Shropshire, but evidence was given that he was 'no designer, nor malicious' in the royalist cause. Burdened with many children and debts of £4,523, he was allowed to compound for £680.[3]

Lawton and his father attended the Duke of Monmouth on his Cheshire progress in 1682. With the support of Sir John Bowyer* he was returned in 1689 for Newcastle-under-Lyme, six miles from his home. An inactive Member of the Convention, he was named to only five committees, including two for attainting Jacobites. He did not vote for the disabling clause in the bill to restore corporations, but acted consistently as a court Whig in later Parliaments. He died on 10 June 1736, when his son was sitting for Newcastle as a government supporter, and inherited an estate of £1,800 a year.[4]

[1] Ormerod, *Cheshire*, iii. 17. [2] Eg. 1626, f. 8; Somerville, *Duchy of Lancaster Office Holders*, 168. [3] Ormerod, iii. 11; *Cal. Comm. Adv. Money*, 786; *Cal. Comm. Comp.* 1024. [4] *Vis. Northants.* (Harl. Soc. lxxxvii), 142; *CSP Dom.* 1682, p. 383; *Staffs. Parl. Hist.* (Wm. Salt Arch. Soc.), ii. 169.

A.M.M.

LEACH, Sir Simon (c.1652-1708), of Cadleigh, Devon.

OKEHAMPTON   1685, 1702

b. c.1652. o.s. of Simon Leach of Cadleigh by Bridget, da. of Sir Bevil Granville† of Stowe, Cornw. *m.* 18 June 1673, Mary, da. of Thomas Clifford*, 1st Baron Clifford of Chudleigh, *s.p. suc.* fa. 1660; KB 23 Apr. 1661.[1]

Commr. for assessment, Devon 1677-80, 1689-90, j.p. 1678-89, 1703-*d.*, dep. lt. May 1688-9, 1703-*d.*

Capt. indep. tp. 1685, Earl of Peterborough's Horse 1687-Dec. 1688.

Leach's great-grandfather and namesake, the son of a Crediton blacksmith, acquired Cadleigh about 1600 and was the first of the family to rise to prominence in Devon. Leach's father was too young to take part in the Civil War, but he married into a leading royalist family, and was arrested in January 1660 for his involvement in royalist disturbances at Exeter. He died a few months later, and Leach was one of several children given the order of the Bath at the coronation of Charles II. He owed his marriage not so much to his fortune as to his piety, and to fitting the 'humour' of his father-in-law, the fallen lord treasurer.[2]

Okehampton lies on the opposite side of Dartmoor from Leach's home, and he had no known connexion with the borough. His return in 1685 must be attributed to his uncle, the Earl of Bath, who was the principal government election manager in the west country. Leach was totally inactive in James II's Parliament, but he raised a troop of horse against the Duke of Monmouth, and was paid £500 'bounty' out of the secret service money. He was given a regular commission in the Earl of Peterborough's regiment in 1687. In April 1688 the King's agents reported that Leach 'hath the greatest interest' in Okehampton and that if he 'be a right man and will engage his interest for Mr [Josias] Calmady [II*], this election will be safe'. Although he followed the lead of Sir Edward Seymour* in refusing to assent to the repeal of the Test Act and Penal Laws until they had been debated in Parliament, he was included in the new list of deputy lieutenants, no doubt through the influence of his wife's family. In September James's agents still anticipated Leach's election 'and that he will have an influence for the election of another fit man'. His commanding officer considered that he had a better chance than William Barlow*, and Sunderland ordered him to stand.[3]

Leach was under suspicion after the Revolution, and when his brother-in-law, the 2nd Lord Clifford, was arrested in Exeter in 1692 it was announced that Leach himself was 'taken in the west'. He was not active again politically until after the death of William III, when he regained his seat and was restored to the commission of the peace and the lieutenancy. He was buried at Cadleigh on 30 June 1708, but he had sold the estate before his death, and no other member of the family sat in Parliament.[4]

[1] Vivian, *Vis. Devon* 526; C. Hartmann, *Clifford of the Cabal*, 276. [2] *Devon and Cornw. N. and Q.* ii. 29–36; *CSP Dom.* 1659–60, p. 366; *Williamson Letters* (Cam. Soc. n.s. viii), 51. [3] *Moneys for Secret Services* (Cam. Soc. lii), 117; Add. 34079, f. 158; *CSP Dom.* 1687–9, p. 276. [4] Luttrell, ii. 459.

J.S.C.

LE DESPENSER, Lord *see* FANE, Charles

LEE, Sir Francis Henry, 4th Bt. (1639–67), of Quarrendon, Bucks. and Ditchley, Oxon.

MALMESBURY 1660, 1661–4 Dec. 1667

bap. 17 Jan. 1639, 2nd s. of Sir Francis Henry Lee, 2nd Bt., of Quarrendon by Ann, da. of Sir John St. John, 1st Bt.[†], of Lydiard Tregoze, Wilts. *educ.* Hayes, Mdx. (Dr Thomas Triplett); travelled abroad 1654–7; académie du Veaux, Paris, 1655–6. *m.* by 1663, Lady Elizabeth Pope, da. and h. of Thomas, 2nd Earl of Downe [I], 2s. (1 *d.v.p.*). *suc.* bro. Sir Henry Lee, 3rd Bt.[†], 21 Mar. 1659.[1]

Commr. for assessment, Oxon. Jan. 1660–*d.*, Bucks. 1661–*d.*, militia, Bucks. and Oxon. Mar. 1660; j.p. Oxon. Mar. 1660–*d.*, Bucks. July 1660–*d.*; commr. for corporations, Oxon. 1662–3.[2]

Originally of a Cheshire family, Lee's ancestors had been at Quarrendon since the beginning of the 14th century, taking a crown lease of the manor in 1499, and regularly representing Buckinghamshire from 1542. Lee's father died at York on active service in the first Bishops' war, and in 1644 his mother married Henry Wilmot[†] (later 1st Earl of Rochester). In 1654 Lee visited the exiled Court at Aachen, and in May 1659 he promised to aid Lord Falkland (Henry Carey*) in the abortive Cavalier rising, after which he seems to have gone abroad again.[3]

Lee's mother, as guardian to his nieces, enjoyed one of the principal interests at Malmesbury. On 2 Mar. 1660 she wrote to Sir Ralph Verney*:

the town of Malmesbury sent to my son Lee that if he would come in person they did hope to choose him, though there were at least 13 that did sue to be chosen for that town, so my son means to go thither at the election for fear of the worst.

The worst did not occur, and Lee was returned. An inactive Member of the Convention, he was named to the committee of elections and privileges and to five others, of which the most important was that entrusted with recommending the legal forms necessary for the Restoration (1 May). Doubtless a court supporter, he was proposed for the order of the Royal Oak with an estate of £3,000 p.a.[4]

Lee was re-elected in 1661, but was equally inactive in the Cavalier Parliament. He was named to 17 committees, including the committee of elections and privileges in seven sessions. He was not among those appointed to consider the corporations bill, but acted as teller for the unsuccessful motion that all Members should be able to attend and vote in the committee. On 18 May 1663 he was teller against giving retrospective effect to the bill to prevent abuses in the sale of offices. His only important committee was for the five mile bill. He died on 4 Dec. 1667. His widow married the 3rd Earl of Lindsey (Robert Bertie I*), and his son, after marriage with a natural daughter of Charles II, was created Earl of Lichfield. The next member of the family to sit in the Commons was his great-grandson, who represented Oxfordshire as a Tory from 1740 to 1743.[5]

[1] PCC 105 Penn (will of Thomas Triplett); Add. 34015, f. 123; *Thurloe*, ii. 528, 569; *Cal. Cl. SP*, iv. 166; *Nicholas Pprs.* (Cam. Soc. n.s. l), 263. [2] A. Ballard, *Chrons Woodstock*, 92. [3] Lipscomb, *Bucks.* ii. 404–5; *VCH Bucks.* iv. 101; *Bucks. Recs.* ii. 207; *Verney Mems.* i. 148–9; D. Underdown, *Royalist Conspiracy*, 265; *Cal. Cl. SP*, iv. 609. [4] *Burton's Diary*, iv. 402; *Verney Mems.* ii. 156–7. [5] *CJ*, viii. 277.

B.D.H.

LEE, Henry (c.1657–1734), of Dane John, nr. Canterbury, Kent.

CANTERBURY	1685, 1689, 1690
HINDON	22 Dec. 1697
CANTERBURY	1698, 1701 (Feb.), 1701 (Dec.), 1702, 1705, 1710, 1713

b. c.1657, 2nd s. of John Lee *alias* Warner, DD (*d.*1679), archdeacon of Rochester, being 1st s. by 3rd w. Anne, da. of Henry English of Maidstone. *educ.* Balliol, Oxf. matric. 4 July 1673, aged 16; I. Temple 1676. *m.* lic. 13 Oct. 1679, Dorothy (*d.* 28 July 1727), da. of (Sir) George Grobham Howe*, 1st Bt., of Berwick St. Leonard, Wilts., 4s. (2 *d.v.p.*) 4da. 3 other ch. *suc.* half-bro. 1699.[1]

Alderman, Canterbury 1684–Jan. 1688, freeman 1685, mayor 1687–Jan. 1688; dep. lt. Kent 1684–Feb. 1688, 1694–?1714; lt.-col. of militia ft. Canterbury by 1684–?Feb. 1688, col. by 1697–?1714; j.p. Kent 1689–?1715.[2]

Commr. for victualling 1704–6, 1711–14.[3]

Lee's grandfather, an attorney of New Inn, married the sister and heir of John Warner, the munificent bishop of Rochester from 1637 to 1666. His father took orders and managed to retain his living in Kent from 1642 to his death long after the Restoration. Lee bought the manor of Dane John, just outside the walls of Canterbury, in 1680 and was nominated to the corporation under the new charter. He was first returned for the city in 1685, and, except in the third Parliament of William III, retained the seat for 30 years. An active Member of James II's Parliament, 'Colonel Lee' was appointed to 11 committees, including those for the supply of fresh water to Chatham and Rochester, to reform the bankruptcy laws, to establish a land registry, to relieve poor debtors, and for the general naturalization of Huguenot refugees. A churchman and a Tory, Lee was removed from the mayoralty in January 1688, and from county office after replying to the lord lieutenant's questions that:

> Although his private opinion be for taking off the Penal Laws and the Tests, yet, if he should be a Parliament man, he does not know upon hearing the debates what reasons he may have for altering it. . . . As near as he can, he shall assist to the election of an honest man, but for his opinion relating to the Penal Laws and Tests he thinks it not proper for him to examine.

The King's electoral agents correctly judged that his interest in the city, thanks to his constant hospitality, remained unshaken. He rallied to the Prince of Orange in the autumn, and was duly re-elected to the Convention. An inactive Member, he was appointed only to the committee of elections and privileges and to that to consider the charges against William Harbord*, though he may have been the 'Mr Lee' who acted with (Sir) Joseph Tredenham* as teller against printing the votes of the House. He is said to have supported the disabling clause in the bill to restore corporations; but this may have been an error for Thomas Lee II*, as he remained a Tory under William III and Anne. His son Henry Lee Warner was returned for Hindon in 1711, but after the Hanoverian succession the family moved to Norfolk and abandoned parliamentary ambitions. He died on 6 Sept. 1734, and was buried at Little Walsingham.[4]

[1] Vis. Kent (Harl. Soc. liv), 98; E. L. Warner, Life of John Warner, 66–67; HMC Lords, n.s. iv. 425. [2] Hasted, Kent, xi. 26; Canterbury Archives, A/C7, f. 81; Roll of the Freemen ed. Cowper, 31; CSP Dom. 1684–5, p. 153; Eg. 1626, f. 22. [3] Beatson, Pol. Index, ii. 94–95; Luttrell, v. 411; vi. 54. [4] Warner, 76, 80; Hasted, xi. 150; N. and Q. (ser. 3), vi. 2; Blomefield, Norf. ix. 274; Gent. Mag. iv. 511.

B.D.H.

LEE, Richard (1625–1704), of Winslade, Clyst St Mary, Devon.

BARNSTAPLE 24 Dec. 1680, 1681, 1689

bap. 20 Aug. 1625, 4th but 1st surv. s. of William Lee of Pinhoe by Jane, da. of John Michell of Topsham. *m.* 22 Aug. 1655, Mary, da. of William Sydenham of Winford Eagle, Dorset, 2s. (1 *d.v.p.*) 2da. *suc.* fa. 1663.[1]

Commr. for assessment, Devon 1657, Jan. 1660, 1677–80, 1689–90, capt. of militia ft. Apr. 1660, by

1697–?*d.*; alderman, Barnstaple to Jan. 1688, recorder Sept. 1688–?*d.*; commr. for inquiry into recusancy fines, Cornw. Devon and Dorset Mar. 1688; j.p. Devon June–July 1688, 1689–1703, jt. receiver of taxes 1690–1.[2]

Lee came from a minor gentry family that first registered its pedigree with the heralds in 1620. Nothing is known of his father's politics or his own before he married the sister of the powerful Cromwellian, William Sydenham†, and he held no office from the return of the secluded Members till 1677. He first stood for Barnstaple at the October election of 1679, and obtained over a hundred signatures to his indenture. But the mayor returned the court supporter Arthur Acland*. When the second Exclusion Parliament met, Lee was seated on petition, and he was re-elected in 1681; but he left no further trace on the records of either Parliament. Although he was displaced from the corporation in January 1688 and from the county bench in the summer, he was approved as court candidate by the Whig collaborator Nathaniel Wade, and described as 'right' on the repeal of the Test Act and Penal Laws, as well as 'of great interest' in the borough. He was nominated as recorder in the new charter in September, and elected to the Convention. He was probably inactive again, and was not listed as a supporter of the disabling clause in the bill to restore corporations. He lost his seat at the general election, but acted for a year as receiver of taxes for Devon and Exeter with John Elwill* before being replaced by the Tory Christopher Bale*. When he was removed from the county bench under Queen Anne, his estate was reckoned at only £600 p.a., though it was claimed that he had £5,000 in cash. His will was proved in December 1704. No other member of the family entered Parliament, and by 1720 Winslade had passed into other hands.[3]

[1] Vivian, Vis. Devon, 527; Hutchins, Dorset, ii. 703; PCC 175 Ash; Trans. Devon Assoc. lxxii. 263–4. [2] Parl. Intell. 7 May 1660; Eg. 1626, f. 11; T. Wainwright, Barnstaple Recs. i. 75, 82; PC2/72/588; CSP Dom. 1687–9, p. 275; Cal. Treas. Bks. ix. 604, 975. [3] Add. Ch. 32899; CJ, ix. 637, 693; HMC Portland, iv. 134; PCC 175 Ash.

J.S.C.

LEE, Thomas I (1635–91), of Hartwell, nr. Aylesbury, Bucks.

AYLESBURY	1660, 1661, 1679 (Mar.), 1679 (Oct.), 1681
BUCKINGHAMSHIRE	1689
AYLESBURY	1690–19 Feb. 1691

bap. 26 May 1635, 1st s. of Thomas Lee of Hartwell by 2nd w. Elizabeth, da. of Sir George Croke, j.K.b. 1628–41, of Waterstock, Oxon., and coh. to her bro. Thomas. *m.* by 1660, Anne (*d.*1708), da. of Sir John Davis of

Pangbourne, Berks., 4s. (1 *d.v.p.*) 6da. *suc.* fa. 1643; *cr.* Bt. 16 Aug. 1660.[1]

Commr. for assessment, Bucks. Jan. 1660–3, 1664–80, 1689–*d.*, Kent. 1673–9, militia, Bucks. Mar. 1660, j.p. Mar. 1660–70, 1680–7, 1689–*d.*; commr. for oyer and terminer, Home circuit July 1660; dep. lt. Bucks. c. Aug. 1660–?70, 1680–?86, 1689–*d.*, commr. for corporations 1662–3, recusants 1675.[2]

Ld. of Admiralty 1679–80, 1689–*d.*; chairman, committee of elections and privileges 25–28 Mar. 1681.

Lee's ancestors, though not of the same stock as the Quarrendon family, had been settled in Buckinghamshire since the 15th century. They were of little account until they acquired Hartwell by marriage in 1617. Lee's father, who died in the autumn of 1643, had taken no known stance in the Civil War. His mother married Richard Ingoldsby*, but, in spite of thus acquiring kinship with the Protector, Lee was not appointed to county office until the second return of the Rump. He was elected a few months later for Aylesbury, together with his stepfather, the first of his family to enter Parliament. Lord Wharton marked him as a friend to be managed by himself; but he was not active in the Convention, being appointed only to the committees for continuing judicial proceedings and confirming parliamentary privilege, a matter which was to become his principal interest. He acted as teller for the second reading of the public accounts bill on 1 Aug. 1660. He was presumably a court supporter at this stage, though his baronetcy may have been earned more by Ingoldsby's services to the Restoration than by his own. They were re-elected in 1661, probably without a contest, and again listed as friends by Wharton. In the opening session of the Cavalier Parliament, he was appointed to the committees for the security and uniformity bills, and acted as teller for a rejected proviso to the militia bill on 13 Mar. 1662. A private bill to vary the terms of his marriage settlement passed through the House in the same session. Although a personal friend of Clarendon and a commissioner for corporations, by 1666 he was sufficiently consistent in Opposition to earn the commendation of Andrew Marvell*:

> Lee, equal to obey or to command,
> Adjutant-general was still at hand.

He was teller against adding £54,000 to the estimates, and for describing Irish cattle as a 'nuisance'. He was among those ordered to attend the King with a resolution against imports from France, and nominated to the abortive parliamentary public accounts commission. He helped to manage conferences on the impeachment of Lord Mordaunt and the import of Irish cattle.[3]

Lee opposed the address of thanks for the dismissal of Clarendon, but was appointed to the committees to inquire into restraints on juries and to reduce the charges against the former lord chancellor into heads. On 5 Dec. 1667, in his first recorded speech, he urged the Commons not to engage in a futile war of words with the Lords over impeachment procedure. He helped to prepare reasons for a conference on freedom of speech in Parliament, and to consider the banishment bill. After the Christmas recess he was twice sent with messages to the public accounts commission at Brooke House. Samuel Pepys* considered him one of the 'professed enemies' of the Navy Office, who on 5 Mar. 1668 prevented a vote in its favour because the House was not full. In the debate on religion on 8 Apr. Lee proposed the abolition of the new oaths. 'Many have fallen from the Church since they were imposed', he said; 'it is probable, if taken away, they may return.' He urged that grievances should go 'hand in hand' with supply. Believing that there was far more than 'common fame' against (Sir) William Penn*, he helped to prepare the articles of impeachment and deliver them to the Lords. He was also among those who presented the address of 23 Apr. for wearing English manufactures. An increasingly effective speaker in the 1669 session, he pressed the charges against Sir George Carteret*, and hoped that 'the King and his subjects may be the better' for the revelations that might be expected from the dispute between Ormonde and Lord Orrery (Roger Boyle*). Together with Robert Atkyns* he was ordered to take care of a bill to prevent electoral abuses and extravagance, and he was chiefly responsible for the bill to prevent the transportation of prisoners overseas. In a debate on the third reading he assured the House: 'It does not take away the King's powers at all, but secures the subject'. On 4 Mar. 1670 he moved for a conference about the appeal to the Upper House against William Hale*, and carried a message urging the Lords to have regard to the privileges of the Commons. He was also concerned at the Lords' proviso to the second conventicles bill reserving all prerogative powers ever exercised by the King or his predecessors. 'What this proviso may reach he knows not. . . . The precedent is of such dangerous consequence that you may shake Magna Carta in this breach.' He was among those appointed to prepare reasons for a conference. When the Act was passed, he resigned or was removed from the bench rather than enforce it. In the next session he consistently opposed supply, acting as teller in three divisions, and demanding pathetically over the proposal to extend excise to home brewing: 'Will you make poor labouring men drink water?'. For all his tolerance, he condemned the 'foolish zeal' of the dissenter Jekyll. The attack on Sir John Coventry* brought Lee into further prominence. 'We come to provide for the Commons of England, as well as a particular Member', he told the House. 'We are upon occasion of speaking exposed to that [which] other men are not.' He favoured the deferment of all other business until a measure to punish the assailants had passed both Houses, and was desired to take care of the bill, which he carried to the Lords on 14 Jan. 1671. He was chairman of the committee to consider the amendments made in the Upper House, and on 4 Feb. was sent to request a conference about them. Outraged by the unprofessional conduct of the radical lawyer Ayliffe over the Lindsey level case, he was teller for expelling him from the parliamentary bar. In the debate on the conventicles bill, he was teller for including a clause of indemnity for previous offences. He helped to manage five conferences in this session, and on 22 Apr. presented a major report on the differences between the Houses over supply procedure.[4]

When Parliament met again in 1673, Lee, to the general surprise, seconded the motion of William Garway* for a grant of £1,200,000, without which, it was privately alleged, the session could not have been kept alive. At the time he dismissed rumours of bribery with the jocular remark that if he had any guineas he had earned them by his assiduity in attending the House. On his deathbed, however, he implicitly admitted receiving money from Lord Treasurer Clifford, though not from Clarendon or Danby. In the debate on the suspending power on 10 Feb. he declared that the King had been misinformed:

> Could something happen that no mortal man could foresee, and the King raise money; were necessity so great that all men may see it, no Parliament would question it. It is not the first time the King has been deceived in prerogative. Hopes that in this he will be advised by the two Houses of Parliament.

He was teller for the resolution declaring that the Penal Laws could be suspended only by Parliament, and took part in drafting an address to that effect. Four days later he moved for a measure to unite Protestants, and in the following month he was sent to remind the Lords of the bill of ease for dissenters, and helped to prepare reasons for a conference on it. In the debate on the Modena marriage on 30 Oct. he said: 'If it be so far gone as is said, we can only lament it, but let us show our distaste for it', and he was appointed to the committee to draw up an address. Though he had previously argued that the House should not interfere with wars and alliances, he considered that Lord Arl-

ington (Sir Henry Bennet*) ought to be removed from office for advising an offensive war with the Dutch without consent of Parliament. Lee was disposed to consider the petition of Bernard Howard for exemption from the recusancy laws, craving his friends' pardon if he differed from them. 'This gentleman tells you he will live quietly', he observed, 'and yet cannot change his religion, being born to it.' He continued to press for the extension of habeas corpus, declaring that 'no penalty is too great for unlawful prisons', and carrying the bill to prevent illegal imprisonment to the Lords. He objected to the narrowness of the franchise in the Newark charter, and distrusted the standing army. 'In the militia of England lies your strength and safety', he told the House. 'The army, by rules of war, are bound to obey superior officers; if commanded to break your law, they must do it.' In supporting the proposal for judges to hold office during good behaviour, instead of at the King's pleasure, he said: 'When the judge is safe for doing right, he will do the better; no danger of not giving a right judgment'. None of these speeches can have been gratifying to the Court, though with his usual fairmindedness he encouraged Samuel Pepys* to rebut the charges of Popery brought against him after his election for Castle Rising. At the unexpected prorogation he was one of the 'guilty Commons' who took hasty refuge in the City.[5]

As one of the committee which drew up the address for the removal of Lauderdale in the spring session of 1675, Lee was dissatisfied with Burnet's reluctant evidence against his former patron, and desired to question him further at the bar of the House. The historian retaliated with a distinctly unflattering description. He brought in a bill to prevent the sending of prisoners beyond the reach of habeas corpus. On 21 Apr. he took the chair in the grand committee on the growth of Popery. He supported, both in debate and in division, the bill to oblige Members to submit to re-election on accepting office. On 5 May he reported his illegal imprisonment bill. When violence threatened over a disputed division in committee on British subjects in the French service, he approved the action of Edward Seymour* in resuming the chair himself without a formal motion, and proposed that every Member present should engage himself to proceed no further with the challenges that had passed. On the following day he himself acted as teller in an equally close but orderly division in favour of recalling all British subjects. He took a leading part in the disputes between the Houses that consumed the remainder of the session. He drew the case of Arthur Onslow* to the attention of the Commons, urging them not to become entangled in controverting the Lords' claim to appellate jurisdiction, but to confine themselves to the assertion of their own privilege. 'He thinks it in no man's power to waive privilege to your destruction.' He twice reported on entries in the Lords Journals, and took the chair in no less than seven committees to prepare reasons for conferences. When deadlock was reached, he remarked: 'Though the Lords have not so much land left as formerly their ancestors and predecessors had, yet they have enough to preserve the Government, and he hopes in this matter of judicature they will change their minds'. In the autumn session he told the House that he would 'represent to the King the present condition of the kingdom, but was none of those "meek and humble reformers". ... Did never think that all advices from hence were appeals to the people. Knows not how else the ill management of his counsellors shall be represented to him.' He was twice teller: for candles in order to prolong the debates on the motions for no further supply in that session, and an appropriation clause to the bill for building 30 warships. He helped to manage a conference on British subjects in the French service, and to prepare reasons for avoiding the revival of differences between the Houses. At the end of the session Sir Richard Wiseman* had 'little cause to hope well' of Lee, but added that he had been invited to Hartwell, which would at least increase his knowledge of the Opposition in Buckinghamshire.[6]

When Parliament met again in 1677 after the long recess, Lee was not prepared to support the contention of William Sacheverell* that it had been automatically dissolved; but he was much concerned that Shaftesbury, who marked him 'worthy', and four other peers had been committed to the Tower for insisting that so long a prorogation was illegal. He helped to manage three conferences, including that on the defence of the Spanish Netherlands. He condemned the imprisonment without a charge of Shaftesbury's cousin and agent, Harrington, for refusing to incriminate himself before the Privy Council. He helped to draw up the addresses offering security for a government loan of £200,000 and urging the speedy conclusion of alliances against France. On 28 May he told the Speaker that, whatever the King's commands, he had no power to adjourn the House against its own wishes; but Seymour suddenly sprang out of the chair and removed the mace. Lee had been excluded from the counsels of the opposition leaders in this session, and during the summer he was 'extremely surprised with a most large hamper of wine' from (Sir) Joseph Williamson*. 'It is enough', he wrote,

'to set up a country gentleman for a year's expense of wine, and to call in his neighbours too to drink Mr Secretary's health'; but not enough, it seems, to alter his politics. In the earlier sessions of 1678 he helped to draft addresses for reducing France to her boundaries of 1659 and declaring war on her immediately, and to prepare reasons for a conference on the growth of Popery. Lee's admiration for Seymour had long vanished, and when he was temporarily replaced by Robert Sawyer* in April he told Williamson that he hoped the new Speaker would be less pernicious than the old. He helped to summarize foreign commitments and to draw up the address for the removal of counsellors, although denying the charge of Henry Goring II* that MPs on the opposition benches desired to creep into the ministers' places. 'I am loath to tell you what fears the people have of an army, and what reason the people have for it', he said, and he took an active part in discussions between the Houses over disbandment. He was teller on 20 June for appropriating the new imposts on wine and vinegar to the use of the navy, and, fortified by an unknown hand with a list of Quakers convicted of recusancy, he supported a bill to distinguish Papists from Protestant dissenters. In the final session he was appointed to the committees to inquire into the Popish Plot, to consider the bill for disabling Papists from sitting in Parliament, to examine Coleman, and to prepare reasons for believing in the Plot, which he thought 'as clear as the sun that shines'; he hoped that some reference to it would be included in the Prayer Book. He took part in preparing six addresses, saying: 'While we smooth the way to the King, let us not smooth ourselves out of our religion'. He described the Lords' proviso to enable the Duke of York to retain his seat as 'an unfortunate reflection on the Duke, brought on by them that shelter Popery under his name', and was named to the committee to prepare reasons for a conference. He reported a conference on disbandment on 9 Dec., and helped to prepare reasons for another. He was responsible for the proposal that the Christmas recess should be reduced to two days, which he carried to the Lords. He had been a very active Member of the Cavalier Parliament, in which he was appointed to 465 committees, taking the chair in 12, acted as teller in 40 divisions, and made more than five hundred recorded speeches.[7]

Lee was re-elected to the Exclusion Parliaments, and marked 'worthy' on Shaftesbury's list. His attitude to Seymour had changed again: he took a leading part in forcing him into the chair against the King's wishes, and objected to any compromise over the choice of a Speaker. He was most anxious to instruct new Members about the Plot and the proceedings of the previous Parliament: 'gentlemen that were not here then, and who live in the country, will scarcely believe what they will find', he said. He was appointed to the committee of secrecy, and helped to prepare five addresses and manage three conferences. He was among those sent to the lord chancellor to inquire into the circumstances of Danby's pardon and instructed to prepare an address of protest. He was appointed to the committee on the habeas corpus amendment bill, reported from a conference on Danby on 10 Apr., and was among those entrusted with the consideration of the Lords' amendments on habeas corpus. On 5 May he reported that there was no reason for the further detention of Brent, the 'Popish solicitor'. He helped to prepare reasons for a conference on Danby's pardon. 'I am sure', he told the House, 'the pardon is illegal, or ought to be.' On 11 May he was appointed to the joint committee on the trial of the lords in the Tower. One of those who 'could not keep pace' with the exclusionists, he was appointed to the new Admiralty commission, and kept uncharacteristically silent in the debate on exclusion; but he voted for the bill. Again a very active Member, he made 45 speeches and was appointed to 37 committees.[8]

Although he had been a frequent contributor to naval debates, Lee seldom attended the Admiralty board, and resigned in February 1680, convinced that 'at this age and under his inexperience he could never hope to arrive at any useful knowledge of it'. His moderation was appreciated by the Government, and in April he even replaced his step-father on the Buckinghamshire lieutenancy. Scarcely less active in the second Exclusion Parliament, he made 35 speeches and was appointed to 32 committees, including those to inquire into abhorring, to repeal the laws against Protestant dissenters, to manage a conference on the Irish plot, and to draft the address for the removal of Lord Halifax. Recalling his long-standing friendship with Seymour, he warned the House of the absurdity of his impeachment:

> It is a matter of so great weight, an impeachment, that the Commons ought not lightly to accuse. Impeachment is your weapon, and you must not blunt it. If you are mistaken in one part, you may be in another; and it will be a fatal thing to go to the Lords with a mistake.

He served on the joint committee for Lord Stafford's trial, helped to prepare the address insisting on exclusion, and on 24 Dec. moved the total repeal of the Corporations Act. He was regarded as one of the leaders of the party of expedients, but on 7 Jan. 1681 he at last admitted that there was no viable alternative to exclusion. In the Oxford Parliament he was voted into the chair of the elections committee, but had no time to present any reports before the dissolution. He was among those appointed to prepare for a conference on the disappearance of the bill to relieve dissenters and to recommend a more convenient place for sitting. After taking part in drafting Fitzharris's impeachment, Lee was greatly shocked at the refusal of Sir Leoline Jenkins* to carry the articles to the Lords. 'I would not have said one word', he remarked implausibly, 'but that the very being of Parliament is in this case. It is to no end to sit here any longer if this be suffered.' He made two more speeches, and was appointed to the committee to bring in the third exclusion bill before the brief session ended.[9]

Lee retained local office during the Tory reaction, and kissed James II's hand on his accession. He was therefore well placed, as Judge Jeffreys complained, to assist the election campaign of the Whig candidates for Buckinghamshire. It was suggested that Lord Treasurer Rochester (Laurence Hyde*) might influence him. Lee and Ingoldsby were themselves defeated at Aylesbury, though they claimed a majority of six to one, and Lee's petition was never reported. In the list of the Opposition in 1687 he was classified among the eminent Parliament men who were useful, but not to be trusted. It was suspected that he might agree to collaborate with the King's religious policy, but he was in touch with Dutch agents during the summer of 1688 and refused to commit himself over the Tests. 'Always against persecution, and an able man of parts and temper', the King's electoral agents correctly expected him to stand for Buckinghamshire, leaving the Aylesbury seat to his son. He attended the meeting of Members of Charles II's Parliaments on 26 Dec., looking 'very grum', and helped to draw up the address asking the Prince of Orange to undertake the administration.[10]

As knight of the shire in the Convention, Lee was still a very active Member, though 'with a state of body very infirm'. He was named to 67 committees, in three of which he took the chair, and made 84 recorded speeches. As one of the committee which drew up the list of essentials for securing religion, law and liberty, he had the satisfaction of abolishing the right of the crown to raise troops, as he had urged. He was among those ordered to prepare reasons for maintaining that James had abdicated, and to manage the conference on that subject. On his reappointment to the Admiralty board he disturbed William by his doubts over the legality of pressing seamen. He was probably responsible for drafting the temporary bill for the detention of

Jacobite suspects, since he was the first to be appointed to the committee on second reading. He also helped to prepare the first mutiny bill and the declaration of rights, and to manage a conference on the removal of Papists from the metropolitan area. He was anxious lest the new coronation oath should 'too much tie up the legislature' from making changes in the Church. He helped to prepare reasons on the new oaths of supremacy and allegiance, and reported from the conference of 22 Apr. His suggestion that the King rather than the House should find a reward for Schomberg appears to have been resented, the veteran marshal comparing the performance of Lee and Lord Carberry (John Vaughan*) at the Admiralty unfavourably for 'truth and zeal' with that of the French minister of marine. He helped to manage a conference on the toleration bill, and to examine the Journals for references to the Popish Plot. On the indemnity issue he favoured excluding only a few individuals by name. In his account of shipping on 17 June, he modestly disclaimed, as Member for an inland county, any technical expertise. He was ordered to take care of the declaration on religion which the Lords had proposed for each sovereign on succeeding to the throne, and he helped to inquire into the scandalous reports about William Harbord* and to prepare reasons for reversing the judgment on Titus Oates.[11]

After the recess Lee presented a state of the navy for the ensuing year, and was appointed to the committee of inquiry into the miscarriages of the war. Defending the Admiralty, he admitted his own ignorance of naval matters, but appealed to common sense:

> Losses must be, and yet great fleets at sea, and you masters of the sea. Great numbers of ships were lost when the French fleet came not out. If merchants will go ship by ship, and not in company, all the fleet cannot protect them.

He helped to draft the address to inquire who had recommended Commissary Shales, but he could not conceal his concern at the vague and negative nature of parliamentary criticism, while a Whig lawyer complained that Lee wanted information about Shales to be given to the Privy Council rather than to Parliament. Together with John Hawles* he was ordered to bring in a bill for regulating imprisonment. His proposal to defer for six days the third reading of the bill to restore corporations 'was taken very ill' by the extreme Whigs, who suspected 'an intention to bring in a rider that may defeat the main design of the bill'. He was listed as a supporter of the disabling clause, but he was 'absent and really sick' from the crucial debate of 10 Jan. 1690, in

which it was rejected. He continued to favour moderation over the indemnity bill. 'I would forget and forgive', he said on 21 Jan. 'I do recommend heartily not to proceed in general terms. Where there are faults, and these evidently proved, I would have them punished, but not to involve all England.' Having 'utterly destroyed his interest' in the country Whigs, he had to return to his borough for the next Parliament. He died of dropsy on 19 Feb. 1691, and was buried at Hartwell.[12]

According to Burnet, Lee 'valued himself upon artifice and cunning, in which he was a great master, without being out of countenance when it was discovered'. He does not seem to have been an eloquent speaker, and was always anxious to adjourn the debate when the dinner-hour approached. He kept a magnificent table at his country house, which he naturally preferred to town life. His part in the struggle for habeas corpus was second only to that of (Sir) Thomas Clarges*. His tolerance was broad and sincere, and extended even to Roman Catholics provided that they abstained from politics. Always careful of the privileges of the House, he must rank among the most eminent parliamentarians of his time.[13]

[1] Lipscomb, *Bucks.* ii. 307, 324. [2] *CSP Dom.* 1679–80, p. 439; Huntington Lib. Stowe mss 2/452. [3] Lipscomb, ii. 148, 305; *Cal. Cl. SP*, iv. 626; *CJ*, viii. 380, 634, 644, 654, 659, 661, 669, 670; Grey, x. 366; *Marvell* ed. Margoliouth, i. 148. [4] *Clarendon Impeachment*, 119; *CJ*, ix. 59, 72, 88, 100, 129, 133, 134, 140, 189, 207, 227; *Pepys Diary*, 5 Mar. 1668; Grey, i. 130, 137, 171, 274, 305, 348, 394; x. 366; *Milward*, 255; *Dering*, 45. [5] Burnet, ii. 16, 92; *HMC Portland*, iii. 460; E. C. Legh, Lady Newton, *Lyme Letters*, 52; Grey, i. 394; ii. 19, 30, 192, 317, 335, 358, 365, 370, 391–2, 415, 426; iii. 68; *CJ*, ix. 251, 274, 284, 296, 305; *Williamson Letters* (Cam. Soc. n.s. ix), 157. [6] Grey, iii. 30, 70, 129, 140, 177, 194, 227, 347; Burnet, ii. 92; *Dering Pprs.* 64; *CJ*, ix. 327, 335, 336, 349, 370, 372, 373. [7] Grey, iv. 93, 263, 390; v. 250, 262, 314; vi. 171, 187, 237, 250; *CJ*, ix. 398, 502, 506, 555; *CSP Dom.* 1677–8, p. 318; 1678, p. 110; Finch diary, 18 Dec. 1678; Browning, *Danby*, i. 229. [8] *HMC Ormonde*, n.s. iv. 346; v. 98; Grey, vi. 426; vii. 5, 300; *CJ*, ix. 574. [9] *Pepys Naval Mins.* (Navy Rec. Soc. lx), 259; *HMC Ormonde*, n.s. iv. 578; v. 275; vi. 5; *CSP Dom.* 1679–80, p. 439; Grey, viii. 224, 255, 305; *CJ*, ix. 648; *HMC 12th Rep. IX*, 104; Bath mss, Thynne pprs. 17, f. 117. [10] *CSP Dom.* 1685, pp. 122–3; *HMC Astley*, 61; *CJ*, ix. 725; *HMC 7th Rep.* 501; Add. 34515, f. 82; *Clarendon Corresp.* ii. 236. [11] *Pepys Naval Mins.* 259; Grey, ix. 35, 204, 227, 324, 336; *CJ*, x. 20, 69, 199; Foxcroft, *Halifax*, ii. 206; *CSP Dom.* 1689–90, p. 201. [12] *CJ*, x. 278, 320; Grey, ix. 414, 489, 541; R. Morrice, Entering Bk. 3, pp. 37, 77, 84; *CSP Dom.* 1690–1, p. 275; *Pepys Naval Mins.* 259. [13] Burnet, ii. 92; Grey, iii. 425; viii. 224; x. 164; Finch diary, 19 Nov. 1678.

M.W.H./L.N.

LEE, Thomas II (c.1661–1702), of Hartwell, nr. Aylesbury, Bucks.

AYLESBURY   1689, 1690, 1695, 1698–7 Feb. 1699,
                 1701 (Feb.), 1701 (Dec.)

b. c.1661, 1st s. of Thomas Lee I*. *m.* by 1686, Anne, da. and coh. of Thomas Hopkins, Cutler, of Botolph Lane, London, 4s. 1da. *suc.* fa. as 2nd Bt. 19 Feb. 1691.

J.p. Bucks. 1689–d., Berks. 1690–d.; dep. lt. Bucks. 1689–d., commr. for assessment 1689–90; freeman, Chipping Wycombe 1691.

Lee was returned for Aylesbury on his father's interest at the general election of 1689. He was not an active Member of the Convention, serving on five committees at most, though even for these there is the possibility of confusion with Henry Lee* and Richard Lee*. The most important committee ascribed to 'Mr Lee' was on the bill to prevent the sale of offices. He may also have acted as teller for the adjournment on 19 July, and have been among the Members appointed after the recess to hear the petition from the widow and daughters of Sir Thomas Armstrong*. It may have been he, rather than Henry Lee*, who voted for the disabling clause in the bill to restore corporations, for he remained a court Whig under William III. He was buried at Hartwell on 13 Aug. 1702. His sons all sat in Parliament as Whigs, with varying degrees of independence.

Lipscomb, *Bucks.* ii. 307; J. R. Woodhead, *Rulers of London*, 93; *Bucks. Sess. Recs.* i. 510; ii. 88, 454; *First Wycombe Ledger Bk.* (Bucks. Rec. Soc. xi), 233.

L.N.

LEGARD, John (c.1631–78), of Ganton, Yorks.

SCARBOROUGH   4 Apr.–21 June 1660, 25 July 1660

b. c.1631, 1st s. of John Legard (*d.*1638) of Ganton by Mary, da. and h. of John Dawnay of Brompton Potter. *educ.* Clare, Camb. 1649; M. Temple 1650. *m.* (1) 18 Oct. 1655, Grace, da. of Conyers Darcy of Hornby Castle (later 1st Earl of Holdernesse), 1da.; (2) 12 Aug. 1658, Frances, da. and coh. of Sir Thomas Widdrington* of Cheeseburn Grange, Stamfordham, Northumb., 4s. 2da. *suc.* gdfa. 1643; *cr.* Bt. 29 Dec. 1660.[1]

Commr. for assessment, Yorks. (E. Riding) 1657, Aug. 1660–3, 1664–d., j.p. 1658–d.; commr. for militia, Yorks. 1659, Mar. 1660, sewers (E. Riding) 1659, Sept. 1660, oyer and terminer, Northern circuit July 1660; bailiff, Scarborough 1669–70; dep. lt. (E. Riding) 1671–d.[2]

Legard's family became armigerous in 1564, and his great-grandfather, a London Haberdasher of Yorkshire origin, bought Ganton in 1583. His grandfather supported Parliament at the outset of the Civil War, and he himself held county office during the Interregnum. But he assisted Thomas Fairfax*, 3rd Lord Fairfax, in the seizure of York in January 1660, and signed the Yorkshire petition for a free Parliament. He was returned for Scarborough at the general election on the interest of Vice-Admiral Lawson, 'though he had a lesser number of voices'. The first of the family to sit, he was marked as a friend by Lord Wharton. Unseated by William Thompson*, he was elected a month

later for the same constituency to fill the seat vacated by Luke Robinson*. He played no known part in the Convention, but presumably supported the Court, since he was rewarded with a baronetcy at the dissolution. He was buried at Ganton on 1 July 1678, and the family parliamentary record was not resumed until 1874, when the 11th baronet was returned for Scarborough.[3]

[1] Clay, *Dugdale's Vis. Yorks.* ii. 402. [2] C181/6/404, 7/44; T. Hinderwell, *Scarborough*, 162. [3] J. D. Legard, *Legards of Anlaby and Ganton*, 89–90, 94–96, 160–1; SP18/219/49; *CJ*, viii. 70.

M.W.H./P.A.B.

LEGGE, George (c.1647–91), of Pall Mall, Westminster.

LUDGERSHALL   1–6 Feb. 1673, 12 Feb. 1673
PORTSMOUTH   1679 (Mar.), 1679 (Oct.), 1681

b. c.1647, 1st s. of William Legge I*, and bro. of William Legge II*. *educ.* Westminster; King's, Camb. 1664. *m.* c. Nov. 1667, Barbara (*d.* 28 Jan. 1718), da. and h. of Sir Henry Archbold of Abbots Bromley, Staffs., 1s. 7da. *suc.* fa. 1670; *cr.* Baron Dartmouth 2 Dec. 1682.[1]

Capt. RN 1667, 1672–3; capt. of ft. 1669–78, col. 1678–9, 1685–9 (R. Fusiliers, later 7 Ft.); lt.-gov. Portsmouth 1672–3, gov. 1673–82; gen. of artillery 1678; adm. 1683–4; constable of the Tower 1685–9; adm. of the fleet Oct. 1688–9.[2]

Groom of the bedchamber to the Duke of York 1668–73; lt. of the Ordnance 1672–81; master 1681–9; master of the horse to the Duke of York 1673–85, (as King) 1685–Dec. 1688; PC 3 Mar. 1682–9; master, Trinity House 1683–5, elder bro. 1685–d.[3]

Keeper, Alice Holt and Woolmer forests, Hants 1670–d.; freeman, Portsmouth 1672, 1682, Newcastle-upon-Tyne 1682; commr. for assessment, Hants and Staffs. 1673–80, Westminster 1679–80; j.p. Hants 1674–89, dep. lt. 1685–9; ld. lt. Tower Hamlets 1685–9; high steward, Kingston-upon-Thames 1685–9; recorder, Lichfield 1686–Oct. 1688; common councilman, Berwick-on-Tweed 1686–Oct. 1688; master, shipwrights' co. of Rotherhithe, Surr. 1686–7.[4]

During the second Dutch war Legge first saw service as a volunteer under his cousin, Sir Edward Spragge*, and was almost immediately given a commission, much to the disgust of William Penn*, who had risen the hard way. He entered the Duke of York's household and became one of his closest friends. He returned to the sea during the third Dutch war, took part in most of the engagements, and inherited from Spragge a bitter dispute with Sir Robert Holmes*.[5]

Legge was elected for Ludgershall in 1673, no doubt chiefly on the interest of the Roman Catholic Brownes and with court backing. The original return was among those declared void by the House when it met, but he was re-elected within a week, probably unopposed. He delivered his maiden speech three days later, telling the House of desertions in the fleet 'upon the rumour that the Parliament would give the King no money'. But he was not an active Member of the Cavalier Parliament, in which he made only three more speeches and was named to seven committees. On the passing of the Test Act he succeeded the Duke of York as governor of Portsmouth. His name appeared on the Paston list, and in the 1674 session he was among those appointed to hear complaints from the Newcastle coal fleet against the pressing of seamen. In committee on 2 Nov. 1675 he urged the building of more second-rates for the navy. 'Supposed to be a Papist' by the author of *A Seasonable Argument*, though quite without grounds, he was alleged to have received £40,000 in boons. He was listed among the officials in the Commons, and noted on the working lists as possessing influence over Ranald Grahme*. Shaftesbury marked him 'thrice vile', and his name appeared on both lists of the court party in 1678. He was appointed to the committees to consider the reports from the Admiralty and Ordnance on 7 Feb. and to examine payments due to the forces (including his own regiment) which were to be disbanded.[6]

Although one of the 'unanimous club', Legge's exercise of government patronage at Portsmouth was undisturbed, and he was returned for the borough to the Exclusion Parliaments with colleagues of his own choice. His letter of excuse for preferring Sir John Kempthorne* to the court nominee John Ernle I* at the first election of 1679 was described by Henry Coventry* as 'too witty for a governor and too plain dealing for a courtier'. He was marked 'vile' on Shaftesbury's list, and in the first Exclusion Parliament was appointed only to the committee of elections and privileges and to that for the reform of the bankruptcy laws. He strove to allay fears caused by the movement to Portsmouth of artillery which the Whigs claimed was more suitable for a marching army than a garrison. He told the House on 12 May that the guns were needed to prevent a surprise attack and scandalized many Members by his expressions of great respect for the Duke:

> Ten times that preparation of artillery will not serve a land army. . . . I am the Duke of York's servant, and I will serve him affectionately, but I have been bred amongst them that speak no language but my own, and I will live and die as a Protestant, and am as loyal as my family has always been.

He voted against the exclusion bill, and spoke against it in the second Exclusion Parliament:

> It is my misfortune to lie under the disreputation of being a Papist, but have now an opportunity of showing myself

otherwise, in declaring that I am against this bill, for I think there is none but Papists that are of opinion that a man may be disinherited for his religion. I have also an opportunity to show my duty to my master, in declaring that those reproaches which have been cast upon him are in my opinion very unjust, because I believe he abhors the thoughts of doing those actions that have been imputed to him, and therefore do think it very hard that because he may differ with us in points of religion, [that] therefore his reputation should thus be called in question in this House.

In the Upper House the Earl of Salisbury urged the cancellation of his appointment as lieutenant-general of the Ordnance, on the grounds of his 'too great addiction to the Duke'. Legge again spoke against exclusion at Oxford on 26 Mar. 1681, but was appointed to no committees in either Parliament. Throughout the crisis he remained in touch with the Duke, and retained his favour even after urging him to return to the church of his baptism. In the wreck of the *Gloucester* in 1682 he saved the Duke's life by preventing with drawn sword the overcrowding of the escape boat. Raised to the peerage as Lord Dartmouth, he was entrusted with the evacuation of Tangier in 1683–4. After successfully accomplishing this mission, he made his only venture into high politics, proposing a truly national party independent of the Halifax and Sunderland factions, and 'averse to fanaticism on one hand, and to Popery and a French interest on the other'. The scheme was enthusiastically supported by Danby, out of office since his impeachment, but its proposer lacked the strength or suppleness needed to bring it into effect.[7]

Although Dartmouth had had to give up his Portsmouth command, much to the Duke's regret, when he became master-general of the Ordnance, he feasted the corporation on his way to Tangier, and was able to secure his brother's election for the borough in 1685. His interest at Lichfield, originally acquired by marriage and strengthened by his good relations with the corporation, he gave to the candidate nominated by Lord Weymouth (Thomas Thynne I*). From the outset of the new reign he warned the King of the danger from William of Orange, and when Dutch intentions became unmistakable he was given command of the fleet. But he failed to intercept the invaders, who landed in Torbay while the English ships lay becalmed. Dartmouth wrote to James of 'the great torment I am in, for not being able to serve you better'. The King professed satisfaction with his admiral's conduct, but privately referred to 'the conflicts, which my Lady Dartmouth owned he had, betwixt his religion and loyalty'. When he refused to send the infant Prince of Wales to France, James became convinced that loyalty had been worsted. On 11 Dec. 1688 Dartmouth wrote to William:

> Out of a duty to my country and the reformed religion of the Church of England ... I readily embrace the fair invitation given me by your highness's particular letter ... to dispose the fleet under me to join with your highness's.

He brought the ships back to the Nore and handed over command. In spite of the intercession of John Churchill II* he was stripped of all his offices by the new regime. But he took the oath of allegiance on 2 Mar. 1689, and remained active in the Lords until denounced by Lord Preston (Sir Richard Grahme*) for sending naval intelligence to St. Germains. He was thrown into the Tower, where he died of apoplexy on 25 Oct. 1691, aged 44. He was buried with his father at Holy Trinity. His son became a leading Tory peer in the reign of Queen Anne, and three of his grandsons sat in the Lower House under the Hanoverians.[8]

[1] *HMC Dartmouth* i. 16; iii. 115. [2] *Bulstrode*, 120; *CSP Dom.* 1668–9, p. 526; 1672–3, p. 184; 1678, p. 148; Jan.–June 1683, p. 331; 1684, p. 388; *Cal. Treas. Bks.* iv. 373. [3] *CSP Dom.* 1672–3, p. 229; 1679–80, p. 264; 1682, p. 7; 1685, p. 8; *HMC Dartmouth*, iii. 114. [4] *CSP Dom.* 1671, p. 120; 1685, p. 266; 1686–7, pp. 21, 231; R. East, *Portsmouth Recs.* 360; Manning and Bray, *Surr.* i. 342. [5] *HMC Dartmouth*, i. 25; *Pepys Diary*, 28 Jan. 1668; *Bulstrode Pprs.* 317. [6] Grey, ii. 108; iii. 377, 379, 381. [7] *HMC Dartmouth*, i. 30, 36; Grey, vii. 262–4; viii. 328–9; *HMC Ormonde*, n.s. iv. 512–13; *Exact Coll. Debates* 98–99; Reresby, *Mems.* 335; Browning, *Danby*, i. 360. [8] *HMC Dartmouth*, i. 72, 122, 190, 266, 275; *CSP Dom.* July–Sept. 1683, p. 315; 1685, p. 121; Clarke, *Jas. II*, ii. 58–59, 177, 208, 233; *HMC Finch*, iii. 10; Luttrell, ii. 298.

P.W.

LEGGE, William I (c.1608–70), of The Minories, London.

SOUTHAMPTON 1661–13 Oct. 1670

b. c.1608, 1st s. of Edward Legge of Geashill, King's Co. by Mary, da. of Percy Walsh of Moyvalley, co. Kildare. *m.* lic. 2 Mar. 1642, 'aged 26', Elizabeth (*d.* 14 Dec. 1688), da. of Sir William Washington of Packington, Leics., 3s. (1 *d.v.p.*) 2da. *suc.* fa. 1616.[1]

Cornet (Dutch army) 1627; capt. of ft. (Swedish army) by 1632; lt.-gen. of artillery 1639–40; maj. of cuirassiers (royalist) 1642–4; col. of ft. 1644–6; gov. Chester 1644, Oxford 1644–5; capt. of ft. June 1660–d.; lt.-gov. Portsmouth 1662–d.[2]

Master of the armouries 1636–46, June 1660–d.; groom of the bedchamber 1645–7, June 1660–d.; lt. of the Ordnance June 1660–d.[3]

Commr. for excise, Oxon. 1645; asst. R. Adventurers into Africa Dec. 1660–d.; commr. for assessment, Westminster 1661–4, Hants and Oxon. 1664–9; keeper, Alice Holt and Woolmer forests, Hants 1661–d.; freeman, Portsmouth 1662; commr. for corporations, Hants 1662–3, loyal and indigent officers, Westminster 1662; woodward, Chute forest, Wilts. 1663–d; j.p. Mdx. 1666–d.[4]

Legge was descended from a Protestant family of London origin which settled in Ireland under the Tudors. A professional soldier, he fought in the Protestant cause in the Thirty Years' War, returning to England as an expert in fortifications, and taking part in the second army plot against Parliament in 1641. He served with distinction in the Civil War under Rupert. He was allowed to attend Charles I in captivity as groom of the bedchamber, and accompanied him on his flight to the Isle of Wight; but unlike John Ashburnham* and Sir John Berkeley† he 'never fell under the least imputation or reproach' for its disastrous consequences. 'He was a very punctual and steady observer of the orders he received, but no contriver of them', according to Clarendon; 'and though he had in truth a better judgment and understanding than either of the other two, his modesty and diffidence of himself never suffered him to contrive bold counsels.' In February 1649 he compounded at £40 for his delinquency, but he was captured at sea in July on a mission for the new King and imprisoned until 1653, when he was allowed to go into exile. Returning to England in 1658, he became an active royalist conspirator, and was again imprisoned after Booth's rising.[5]

At the Restoration Legge was made lieutenant of the Ordnance, which brought him in £2,000 p.a., and granted leaseholds in Ireland worth about £500 p.a. An award of £2,000 on the Irish customs was still unpaid at his death. On the Duke of York's recommendation, he was elected at Southampton in 1661, and became a moderately active Member of the Cavalier Parliament. He was appointed to 96 committees, acted as teller in five divisions, and was five times sent as a messenger from the Commons to the King. In the opening session he helped to consider the uniformity bill and to manage the conference on the Lords' proposal that all municipal charters should be called in. During the autumn recess he went to Ireland, but he returned in time to be sent by the House on 22 Nov. to ask the King for the return of the remaining regicides to the Tower, and to be appointed to the committees for the execution bill and for the relief of loyalists. He was among those ordered to provide remedies against nonconformist meetings in 1663, and in the same session he acted as teller against making a retrospection in the bill to prevent abuses in the sale of offices for an immediate grant of supply, and for the additional bill to recover arrears of excise. In 1664 he was listed as a court dependant, and named to the committees for the conventicles bill and the additional corporations bill. He attended the Oxford session, and was appointed to the committee for the five mile bill. The ordnance office was not exempt from criticism during the second Dutch war, all the more so because Legge was widely suspected of Popery. He produced his accounts to the House on 26 Sept. 1666, and was appointed to the committee to bring in a bill to prevent the embezzlement of powder and ammunition. He was teller for an unsuccessful motion on 11 Oct. to increase the estimates by £54,000. He was among those sent to the King with an address on behalf of the merchants trading with France on 29 Jan. 1667 and to Rupert and Albemarle after the fall of Clarendon with a vote of thanks for their services. He was named to the committees on the bill for uniting parishes in Southampton (11 Mar. 1668), the bill to prevent electoral abuses (8 Dec. 1669), and the conventicles bill (2 Mar. 1670). He died on 14 Oct. 1670, in his 63rd year, and was buried at Holy Trinity Minories.[6]

[1] Collins, *Peerage*, iv. 107, 109, 114; Foster, *London Mar. Lic.* 835. [2] *Misc. Gen. et Her.* (ser. 5), ix. 118; Collins, iv. 110–11, 113; E. Peacock, *Army Lists*, 15. [3] *Foedera*, ix. pt. 2, p. 86; *CSP Dom.* 1660–1, p. 75; 1671–2, p. 59. [4] W. H. Black, *Docquets of Letters Patent*, 263; *CSP Dom.* 1661–2, p. 409; R. East, *Portsmouth Recs.* 357, 365; *HMC 11th Rep. III*, 55; Collins, iv. 114. [5] *HMC Ormonde*, n.s. v. 9; *CSP Dom.* 1637–8, p. 590; 1639–40, pp. 134, 167; 1649–50, p. 235; *Whitelocke Mems.* i. 134–5; Clarendon, *Rebellion*, iii. 131; iv. 266; *Cal. Comm. Comp.* 1583; *Cal. Cl. SP*, iv. 294; D. Underdown, *Royalist Conspiracy*, 218, 259. [6] *CSP Dom.* 1666–7, p. 467; 1667, p. 207; 1671, p. 88; *CSP Ire.* 1660–2, pp. 261, 639, 661; Adm. 2/1745, f. 31; *CJ*, viii. 311, 486, 501, 532; ix. 6; *Pepys Diary*, 13 June 1667; Le Neve, *Mon. Angl.* 1650–78, p. 144.

P.W.

LEGGE, William II (c.1650–c.1697).

PORTSMOUTH 1685

b. c.1650, 2nd s. of William Legge I*, and bro. of George Legge*. *m.* Mary, da. of one Poole, wid. of one Townshend, *s.p.*[1]

Lt. of ft. Admiralty Regt. 1666–7; ensign, Barbados Ft. 1667; cornet, R. Horse Gds. (The Blues) 1674, capt. 1676–85; lt.-col. Queen's Horse 1685–Dec. 1688; gov. Kinsale 1686–91.[2]

Page of honour 1668–76; groom of the bedchamber (supernumerary) 1676–85; envoy to Brussels and Cassel 1680; superintendent of royal parks 1685–90.[3]

Freeman, Portsmouth 1675; j.p. Hants and Suss. 1687–9.[4]

A murderer while still in his teens and 'a profane, wild creature' of whom the decorous Evelyn could say little good, Legge held various employments in the army and at Court. His brother nominated him as court candidate for Ludgershall in February 1679, but the King ordered him to resign his interest to Lord Ranelagh (Richard Jones*). In 1680 he was sent on a complimentary mission to the governor of the Spanish Netherlands and the landgrave of Hesse-Cassel. In the following year he paid his addresses to the young widow of a successful lawyer, Thomas Syderfin of the Middle Temple;

but she was abducted from her coach and taken to France by a rival. Diplomatic representatives secured her return, and in July 1682 it was reported that Legge had married her; but this is not confirmed by the family pedigree. On the execution of Sir Thomas Armstrong* he was granted the personal estate, later valued at £12,700, but it is doubtful whether this ever took effect.[5]

At the general election of 1685 Legge was returned for Portsmouth, where his brother had served as governor from 1673–82. An inactive Member of James II's Parliament, he was appointed only to the committees for a naturalization bill and for the improvement of tillage. His appointment as governor of Kinsale in 1686 was warmly welcomed by Lord Rochester (Laurence Hyde*), but by the spring of 1688 he had returned to Hampshire, replying in the affirmative to the three questions on the repeal of the Test Act and Penal Laws. He was approved as court candidate, but on 13 Dec. Lady Dartmouth wrote to her husband: 'Your brother Will went with his regiment to the Prince of Orange upon the first news of the King's absenting'. Roger Morrice believed that his purpose was to resign his commission, 'having in a good measure had his education and rise from his Majesty'. A false report of his suicide in 1694 was widely credited because he had 'as good reason to be discontented as any man I know'. He died in Dublin some time before 28 June 1698, aged 47.[6]

[1] Collins, *Peerage*, iv. 115. [2] *HMC Downshire*, i. 135. [3] *CSP Dom.* 1668–9, p. 60; 1676–7, p. 70; *Cal. Treas. Bks.* vi. 748; vii. 486; viii. 171, 1712; ix. 1329, 1599. [4] R. East, *Portsmouth Recs.* 362. [5] *CSP Dom.* 1666–7, p. 527; *Evelyn Diary*, v. 182; *HMC Ormonde*, n.s. iv. 317; *HMC 7th Rep.* 353, 497; *Cal. Treas. Bks.* vii. 1308, 1373. [6] *Clarendon Corresp.* i. 326; *HMC Ormonde*, n.s. vii. 416; *HMC Dartmouth*, i. 234; R. Morrice, Entering Bk. 2, p. 430; A. Boyer, *Wm. III*, i. 310; *HMC Portland*, iii. 551; *Cal. Treas. Bks.* xvii. 831.

P.W.

LEGH, Peter (1669–1744), of Lyme, Cheshire.

NEWTON 1685

b. 22 Aug. 1669, 1st s. of Richard Legh*, and bro. of Thomas Legh†. *educ.* G. Inn, entered 1673. *m.* lic. 21 Dec. 1686, Frances (*d.* 8 Feb. 1728), da. of Piers Legh† of Bruche, Poulton, Lancs., and h. to her half-bro. Piers, 1s. *d.v.p. suc.* fa. 1687.[1]

Freeman, Preston 1682, Liverpool 1686; dep. lt. Cheshire Nov. 1688–9; j.p. Lancs. 1689–94, 1702–15; commr. for assessment, Cheshire and Lancs. 1689–90.[2]

Legh was elected for the family borough at the age of 15 owing to his father's unwillingness to sit again. When James II's Parliament assembled, his uncle Sir John Chicheley* wrote:

This morning we met and took the oaths, after which I carried my nephew into our House, where I found several Members took notice of his youthfulness; but to keep us the better in countenance the Lord Plymouth's son [Thomas Windsor*] appeared, whose looks did not so well qualify him for a law-maker as Peter's.

Lord Willoughby de Eresby (Robert Bertie II*) was prompted to move for the expulsion of minors from the House, but no action was taken, and Legh remained, circumspectly avoiding attention by total inactivity.[3]

Legh politely refused to serve under Lord Molyneux, the Roman Catholic lord lieutenant of Lancashire. He never stood for Parliament after the Revolution, though his younger brother Thomas sat for Newton from 1701 to 1713. The leading spirit of the Cheshire Club, a society of Jacobite country gentlemen, he was arrested in 1694, at the time of the Lancashire Plot, and again in 1696, but on each occasion the prosecution broke down for lack of witnesses. He was buried at Winwick on 16 Jan. 1744. His heir was his nephew, who sat for Newton as an opposition Member from 1743 to 1774.[4]

[1] Croston, *Lancs.* iv. 388-9; *London Mar. Lic.* ed. Foster, 830. [2] *Preston Guild Roll* (Lancs. and Cheshire Rec. Soc. ix), 191; Wahlstrand thesis; Lancs. RO, QSC103-13, 130. [3] E. C. Legh, Lady Newton, *House of Lyme*, 330-1. [4] Legh, *Lyme Letters*, 153; *House of Lyme*, 354, 360-7; *CSP Dom.* 1694-5, pp. 214, 322; *HMC Kenyon*, 361, 363-6.

I.C.

LEGH, Richard (1634-87), of Lyme, Cheshire.

CHESHIRE 1656, 1659
NEWTON 1660, 1661

b. 7 May 1634, 2nd but 1st surv. s. of Thomas Legh, DD (*d.*1639), rector of Walton on the Hill, Lancs. 1631-9, by Lettice, da. of Sir George Calveley of Lea, Cheshire, and coh. to her bro. Sir Hugh; bro. of Thomas Legh*. *educ.* Winwick g.s.; St. John's, Camb. 1649; G. Inn 1653. *m.* lic. 31 Dec. 1660, Elizabeth (*d.*1728), da. of Sir Thomas Chicheley* of Wimpole, Cambs., 6s. 7da. *suc.* uncle 1643.[1]

Commr. for assessment, Cheshire 1657, Cheshire and Lancs. Aug. 1660-79, militia Mar. 1660, j.p. June 1660-*d.*, dep. lt. 1662-*d.*; freeman, Preston 1662, Liverpool 1686; commr. for recusants, Lancs. 1675.[2]

Legh's ancestors had held Lyme since 1398, and one of them represented Lancashire in 1491-2. A series of early deaths in the family prevented any of them from taking part in the Civil War; but Legh was brought up as a Presbyterian and sat for Cheshire in the second and third Protectorate Parliaments. He was deeply obnoxious to the republicans, and after the dissolution in 1659 he was imprisoned at York, thereby escaping involvement in the rising of Sir George Booth*, in which one of his cousins of the Bruche branch was killed.[3]

At the general election of 1660 Legh made way

for Booth in Cheshire, and was returned for Newton, where he owned a large part of the township. In the Convention he was added to the committee of elections and privileges on 9 May, but appears to have been otherwise totally inactive. He signed the loyal address from Cheshire at the Restoration, and was proposed for the order of the Royal Oak, with an income of £4,000 p.a.[4]

Legh strengthened his interest at Newton by purchasing the old feudal barony of Makerfield, and was re-elected in 1661. But he proved an equally inactive Member of the Cavalier Parliament, with no more than seven committees in 17 sessions. His attendance was affected by his wife's reluctance to part with him and his own increasingly indifferent health. Although a correspondent of Sir Henry Bennet* as early as 1663, he seems to have had no inclinations towards toleration. A conformist himself, he was eager to 'trounce the rogue Jolly', an Independent pastor who had been arrested for keeping a conventicle; but he was equally suspicious of Popish influences at Court. In view of the ill-feeling in the Commons during the session of 1666-7, he expected a dissolution, and in the next session he was for the first time added to the elections committee. Sir Thomas Osborne* included him in 1669 among those Members to be engaged for the Court by the Duke of York, and he supported the Duke's candidate, Robert Werden*, at the Chester by-election of 1673. But he was deeply disturbed by the Declaration of Indulgence; in the ensuing session he was named to his first legislative committees, those for the bill of ease for dissenters and the encouragement of the glass industry, and produced a creditable summary of the debate. The withdrawal of the Declaration prompted him to write to his brother:

> This day, I thank God, is the most glorious I have seen this ten years as to our public affairs. . . . I pray let the parson give thanks for it publicly. . . . The King told us he was sorry any mistake had happened among us; for his part he would never again be guilty.

On 22 Apr. 1675 he was appointed to the committee on the bill to prevent illegal imprisonment, but he received the government whip from Secretary Coventry for the autumn session. However, he did not attend, for which Sir Richard Wiseman* blamed his father-in-law, 'for I understand he expected his summons, which Sir Thomas never gave him'. The Duke of York visited Lyme in 1676, and his host was marked 'doubly vile' by Shaftesbury during the next session. He was still regarded by the Government as a supporter in 1678, though (Sir) Joseph Williamson* listed him among those 'wanting' in an important debate. He defaulted on a call of the House on 18 Dec., and was ordered up in custody, arriving in time for the conference on committing Osborne (now Lord Treasurer Danby) for his impeachment.[5]

Legh never stood again, but he continued to exercise his patronage at Newton during the exclusion elections, returning his brother-in-law Sir John Chicheley* and another kinsman, Andrew Fountaine*, although the latter was an exclusionist. He supported his cousin Peter Bold* at the Lancashire election of February 1679, and in the autumn his interest contributed to the success of William Banks II* at Wigan. He kept a watchful eye on the Duke of Monmouth's progress through Cheshire in 1682, and was asked to stand for the county again in 1685 after an interval of 26 years. But he pleaded ill health, adding:

> Several worthy gentlemen might take it ill from me, and indeed it looks a little vain in me to stand here to put them out, when I can with ease come in at my own place, where I design to put in my own son.

Fountaine accordingly had to make way for the youthful Peter Legh* at Newton. In the Lancashire election he was canvassed on behalf of Lord Colchester (Richard Savage*), one of Monmouth's adherents, but refused his support. He died on 31 Aug. 1687 and was buried at Winwick. His funeral sermon was preached by the father of the future Jacobite leader, William Shippen†, who commended his constant cheerfulness and his splendid hospitality.[6]

[1] Croston, *Lancs.* iv, 388–9; *London Mar. Lic.* ed. Foster, 831. [2] Lancs. RO, QSC62–96; *Preston Guild Rolls* (Lancs. and Cheshire Rec. Soc. ix), 148, 191; Wahlstrand thesis, 58. [3] Ormerod, *Cheshire*, iii. 677–8; E. C. Legh, Lady Newton, *House of Lyme*, 191, 204, 211. [4] *House of Lyme*, 209; *VCH Lancs.* iv. 134. [5] Legh, *Lyme Letters*, 21, 23, 52, 73; *CSP Dom.* 1661–2, p. 596; 1663–4, p. 306; 1672–3, p. 484; D. T. Witcombe, *Cav. House of Commons*, 58; *House of Lyme*, 246–7, 249, 252, 283. [6] Rylands Lib. Legh mss, Bold to Legh, 22 Jan. 1678; Colchester to Legh, 14 Feb. 1685; *House of Lyme*, 218, 219, 291, 300, 346–7; *Lyme Letters*, 327–8; *HMC Kenyon*, 179; *CSP Dom.* 1682, p. 460.

M.W.H./I.C.

LEGH, Thomas (1636–97), of Blackley, Lancs. and Lyme, Cheshire.

LIVERPOOL   1685

b. 6 Oct. 1636, 3rd but 2nd surv. s. of Thomas Legh, DD, and bro. of Richard Legh*. *educ.* Winwick g.s. *unm.*

Commr. for assessment, Cheshire Aug. 1660–1, 1663–80, Lancs. and Cheshire 1689–90; freeman, Liverpool 1662, Preston 1673; j.p. Lancs. 1672–83; receiver of taxes 1673–4; steward, Newton by 1679–at least 1689; sheriff, Lancs. 1682–4; dep. lt. Cheshire 1689–*d.*[1]

Legh spent most of his life managing the family estate, though he inherited the manor of Blackley

and property in Liverpool. He was instrumental in obtaining the new charter for the borough in 1677, and acted as returning officer at Newton from 1679 to the end of the period. He supported the Tory candidate at the Macclesfield mayoral election in 1682, and although the Gerard interest was too strong for him, he managed to persuade the townsmen to confer the freedom of Macclesfield on Judge Jeffreys, whom he then entertained at Lyme. In the following year he obtained a loyal address from the corporation of Liverpool, congratulating the King on his escape from the Rye House Plot.[2]

In the election of 1685, Legh stood for Liverpool, with the support of Lord Derby, against Thomas Norris* and the 'fanatical party'. Returned after a contested election, he became a moderately active Member of James II's Parliament, serving on nine committees, of which the most important was to recommend expunctions from the Journals. Although a devoted Royalist, Legh was also a staunch Protestant and opposed James II's attempts to undermine the Anglican Church. After the second session he rejoiced that the Test had been 'vigorously and bravely adhered to by the House of Commons to their immortal fame', commenting that 'had we suffered such a breach in the mounds of our Church, a spring-tide of Popery would have raged, for the oaths of allegiance and supremacy are already sweetened to go delicately down, but the Test cannot be dispensed with'.[3]

Legh did not sit again, but devoted himself to his duties in the country. He accepted the Revolution, and on several occasions advised his nephew, Peter Legh*, to abandon his extreme Jacobite position and take the oath to the new regime. He died on 22 Sept. 1697 and was buried at Macclesfield.[4]

[1] *Preston Guild Rolls* (Lancs. and Cheshire Rec. Soc. ix), 148, 191; *Cal. Treas. Bks.* iv. 102, 108; Lancs. RO, QSC 79–113; SP44/335/509. [2] PCC 108 Brent; E. C. Legh, Lady Newton, *House of Lyme*, 248; *CSP Dom.* 1682, pp. 458–9; July–Sept. 1683, p. 105. [3] Rylands Lib. Legh mss, Thomas to Richard Legh, 9 Mar., 5 Dec. 1685; Picton, *Liverpool Municipal Recs.* 240; *HMC Kenyon*, 103; Legh, *Lyme Letters*, 137. [4] Croston, *Lancs.* iv. 388–9.

I.C.

LEIGH, John (c.1651–89), of Northcourt, Shorwell, I.o.W.

NEWPORT I.o.W.   1679 (Oct.), 1681

b. c.1651, 2nd but o. surv. s. of Sir John Leigh*. *m.* 7 Oct. 1669, Anne (*d.*1719), da. of John Every of Wootton Glanville, Dorset, and coh. to her bro. John Every*, 3s. (1 *d.v.p.*) 8da. *suc.* fa. c.1666.[1]

Commr. for assessment, Hants 1677–80.

Leigh probably belonged to the Green Ribbon Club like his brother-in-law. He replaced the courtier Sir Robert Holmes* at Newport, five miles from Shorwell, in the second Exclusion Parliament, no doubt as a country Member, and also represented the borough at Oxford; but he made no speeches and was appointed to no committees. He gave way to Holmes in 1685. He drew up his will on 23 Jan. 1689 (and hence without a regnal year), and was buried at Shorwell shortly afterwards. Provision for his debts and his large family gave him much concern, and the will was left unproved during the lifetime of the principal executor, Sir Robert Henley*. His widow then undertook the administration, and apparently cleared the Northcourt estate by selling off her own inheritance. His son was returned for Newtown in 1702.[2]

[1] Berry, *Hants Genealogies*, 122–3; *Misc. Gen. et Her.* (ser. 5), viii. 215. [2] PCC 10 Coker; *VCH Hants*, v. 283; Hutchins, *Dorset*, iii. 743.

P.W.

LEIGH, Sir John (c.1598–c.1666), of Northcourt, Shorwell, I.o.W.

YARMOUTH I.o.W.   1640 (Nov.),[1] 1660

b. c.1598, 1st s. of Barnaby Leigh of Northcourt by 1st w. Elizabeth, da. and coh. of Hugh Bampfield of North Cadbury, Som. *educ.* Christ Church, Oxf. matric. 25 Oct. 1616, aged 18. *m.* by 1629, Anne, da. of William Bulkeley of Nether Burgate, Fordingbridge, Hants, 2s. (1 *d.v.p.*) 3da. Kntd. 1 Sept. 1628; *suc.* fa. 1622.[2]

Col. of militia ft. I.o.W. 1642–at least 1647, dep. lt. 1643; commr. for sequestrations, Hants 1643, levying money 1643, assessment, I.o.W. 1647–8, Aug. 1660–1, Hants 1648, 1652, 1657, Jan. 1660–1, Hants and I.o.W. 1664–*d.*; j.p. Hants 1650–3.[3]

Leigh's grandfather bought Northcourt in 1586, and improved a modest fortune by good husbandry and frugality. In 1640 Leigh became the first of the family to sit in Parliament. On receiving a militia commission from the Earl of Pembroke, he returned from Westminster to the Isle of Wight, which was undisturbed by the Civil War. He ceased to sit at Pride's Purge, but his only service on the commission of the peace was under the Commonwealth. He was re-elected for Yarmouth at the general election of 1660, and marked as a friend on Lord Wharton's list, where he is wrongly called 'Sir George'. But he was no more active in Parliament than in local government, perhaps sharing his grandfather's reluctance to differ in opinion from his neighbour. He made no speeches in the Convention and was named to no committees. It is not known whether he stood in 1661. He died about 1666.[4]

[1] Did not sit after Pride's Purge, 6 Dec. 1648, readmitted 21 Feb. 1660. [2] Berry, *Hants Genealogies*, 122; PCC 69 Campbell. [3] *CJ*, ii. 775; *HMC Portland*, i. 594; *Royalist's Notebook* ed. Bamford, 110. [4] *VCH Hants*, v. 280; *Oglander Mems.* ed. Long, 142–6; Keeler, *Long Parl.* 249–50; Berry, 122.

M.W.H./P.W.

LEIGH, Sir Thomas (1616–62), of Hamstall Ridware, Staffs.

STAFFORDSHIRE   1661–5 Apr. 1662

b. 15 July 1616, 2nd s. of Thomas Leigh[†] (*d.*1672), 1st Baron Leigh of Stoneleigh, by Mary, da. and coh. of Sir Thomas Egerton[†] of Dodleston, Cheshire. *educ.* Camb. *m.* (1) settlement 9 July 1642, with £6,000, Anne (*d.* bef. 1 June 1647), da. of Richard Brigham of Lambeth, Surr. 1da.; (2) by 1652, Jane, da. of Patrick Fitzmaurice, 18th Baron of Kerry [I], 1s. 3da. Kntd. 22 Aug. 1642.[1]

J.p. Staffs. July 1660–*d.*, commr. for assessment Aug. 1660–*d.*, dep. lt. c. Aug. 1660–*d.*; surveyor of woods, honour of Tutbury Sept. 1660–*d.*[2]

Leigh was descended from a lord mayor of London who obtained a grant of the Cistercian abbey of Stoneleigh from Queen Elizabeth. His father, who sat for Warwickshire in 1628, was an active commissioner of array, rewarded with a peerage in 1643. But Leigh, on whom the Staffordshire estate, valued at £423 13s.4d. p.a., was settled at his marriage, was only a passive Royalist. However, by leaving his home to live in the Cavalier garrison at Lichfield, he incurred the penalties of delinquency. The joint fines of father and son were fixed at £5,642 in April 1647. Although his father was arrested as a precautionary measure during Booth's rising, Leigh himself was not disturbed.[3]

Under the Long Parliament ordinance Leigh was forbidden to stand at the general election of 1660, but he was returned for Staffordshire in the following year. In his committee record there is the possibility of some confusion with Thomas Lee I*, but he was probably an active Member in his one session of the Cavalier Parliament, with 73 committees. He was appointed to those for the corporations and uniformity bills and the bills of pains and penalties, and on 22 Nov. 1661 he was one of the delegation sent to ask the King to make John Lambert[†] and Sir Henry Vane[†] available to stand trial. He died on 5 Apr. 1662, and the Leigh interest in Staffordshire died with him. He was said to have contracted sundry debts in the King's service, but a private bill for the sale of Hamstall Ridware met so much opposition that it was dropped. However the family never resided there again. His grandson Charles came in for Warwick as a Tory under Queen Anne.[4]

[1] *Vis. Warws.* (Harl. Soc. xii), 81; (lxii), 11; *HMC 5th Rep.* 182. [2] Sir Robert Somerville, *Duchy of Lancaster Official Lists*, 166. [3] *VCH Warws.* vi. 234; Shaw, *Staffs.* i. 155*–158*; *HMC 5th Rep.* 47–48, 182; *Cal. Comm. Comp.* 1134–6; SP23/200/777, 793, 799, 800; *Cal. Comm. Adv. Money*, 1304; *Cal. Cl. SP*, iv. 306. [4] *HMC 8th Rep.* pt. 1 (1881), 150; Dugdale, *Diary*, 109; Shaw, i. 156*; PC2/59/14–15.

A.M.M.

LEIGHTON, Robert (1628–89) of Wattlesborough, Alberbury, Salop and Bausley, Mont.

SHREWSBURY 1661

bap. 30 Dec. 1628, 1st s. of Edward Leighton of Wattlesborough by Abigail, da. and h. of William Stevens of Shrewsbury. *educ.* Shrewsbury 1638. *m.* c.1650, Gertrude, da. of Edward Baldwin of Diddlebury, Salop, 7s. (4 *d.v.p.*) 5da. *suc.* fa. 1632.[1]

Commr. for assessment, Salop 1657, Aug. 1660–80, Mont. 1661–80, Salop and Mont. 1689; j.p. Salop July 1660–80, 1682–5, Mont. 1675–85, Sept. 1688–?*d.*; capt. of militia ft. Salop 1660–?80, 1682–?5, commr. for recusants 1675, sheriff 1687–Nov. 1688; dep. lt. Mont. Sept. 1688–?*d.*[2]

Leighton came from a junior branch of a Shropshire family that had first represented the county in the 14th century. At the Restoration, he was one of the proposed knights of the Royal Oak with an income of £800 p.a. Returned for Shrewsbury, nine miles from his home, at the general election of 1661, he was an inactive Member of the Cavalier Parliament. He was appointed to only 13 committees, including the committee of elections and privileges in two sessions and those on the bills to regulate the weaving trade (15 Mar. 1663) and for the better collection of the hearth-tax (4 May 1675). He defaulted from a call of the House on 13 Feb. 1668, and was fined £40, and he was also absent without leave on 21 Feb. 1671 and 17 Dec. 1678. Classed as 'thrice worthy' by Shaftesbury in 1677, he does not appear in any list of the court party. In 1680 he was removed from the commission of the peace and the militia, presumably as an exclusionist, but he hoped to stand against William Leveson Gower* for the county in 1681, and was restored at the King's command in the following year. He was absent when the questions on the repeal of the Test Act and Penal Laws were put to the Montgomeryshire magistrates, but he must have been regarded as a potential Whig collaborator, since he was added to the lieutenancy in June 1688. He was buried at Alberbury on 27 Apr. 1689. His eldest son was created a baronet and represented Shropshire under William III and Shrewsbury under Queen Anne.[3]

[1] *Trans. Salop Arch. Soc.* (ser. 1), ix. 414; (ser. 4), xii. 217; *Mont. Colls.* viii. 99. [2] SP29/41/85. [3] *Trans. Salop Arch. Soc.* (ser. 1), ix. 416; (ser. 3), viii. 162; (ser. 4), iii. 287–9; Owen and Blakeway, *Shrewsbury*, i. 243; *VCH Salop*, iii. 257; *CSP Dom.* 1682, p. 81.

E.C.

LEKE, Sir Francis, 1st Bt. (1627–79), of The Chauntry, Newark, Notts.

NOTTINGHAMSHIRE 29 Oct. 1666

bap. 1 Nov. 1627, 1st s. of William Leke of Newark by 1st w. Elizabeth, da. of Sir Guy Palmes† of Ashwell, Rutland. *educ.* travelled abroad c.1645. *m.* c.1643, Frances, da. of Sir William Thorold, 1st Bt.*, of Marston, Lincs., 1s. 4da. *suc.* fa. 1651; kntd. by 17 Oct. 1661; *cr.* Bt. 15 Dec. 1663.[1]

Trooper (royalist) c.1643–5; capt. Lord Gerard's Horse 1666–7; gov. Gravesend and Tilbury 1670–*d.*[2]

J.p. Notts. July 1660–*d.*, commr. for assessment, Notts. Aug. 1660–*d.*, Newark 1663–4, Essex and Kent 1673–4, Derbys. 1677–*d.*, Essex 1679–*d.*; dep. lt. Notts. c. Aug. 1660–*d.*, sheriff Nov. 1660–1, commr. for corporations 1662–3, loyal and indigent officers 1662.[3]

Leke's father was half-brother to the 1st Earl of Scarsdale. He appears to have taken no part in the Civil War, but Leke himself, a married man at 16, rode as a trooper in the Belvoir garrison for two years. On returning from travel he was denounced as a delinquent, and on his father's death had to pay a fine of £2,352. He declared his income at £1,077 p.a., a good figure for a cadet branch. He became an army officer in 1662, but continued to act as deputy lieutenant in Nottinghamshire, in which capacity he was responsible for the arrest of John Hutchinson* in 1663. For this service he was created a baronet, and marked out for a responsible post. Returned for the county at a by-election in 1666, he was soon named to consider a bill for preventing and punishing the voluntary absence of Members, but his only other committees were two for indigent officers, two for taxes in the Bedford level, one on the export of horses, two private bills and six for elections and privileges. His appointment as governor of the block-houses on either side of the mouth of the Thames made him in effect controller of shipping between London and the Continent, half customs official, half policeman, and until his son was old enough to deputize for him he could seldom leave his post. He was on both lists of the court party in 1669–71 among those to be engaged by the Duke of Buckingham, on the Paston list in 1673–4, and the list of King's servants in 1675. Shaftesbury noted him as 'thrice vile' in 1677, and he appears again on both lists of court supporters in 1678. On 14 May he sat on his first committee since 1673, which was for his father-in-law's estate bill, but this was also his last. He probably did not stand again, and died at Gravesend in the first week of October 1679. His son, who was appointed to succeed him in his official posts, died unmarried a few years later without entering Parliament.[4]

[1] *Her. and Gen.* vii. 495; SP23/221/918; *CSP Dom.* 1661–2, p. 113. [2] SP23/221/908; *CSP Dom.* 1661–2, p. 577; 1670, p. 142. [3] C. Brown, *Hist. Newark*, ii. 139. [4] SP23/221/909–18; *Hutchinson Mems.* 343–8; *CSP Dom.* 1679–80, p. 326.

E.R.E.

LEKE, Robert, Lord Deincourt (1654-1707), of Duke Street, Westminster.

NEWARK 1679 (Mar.)

b. 9 Mar. 1654, 1st s. of Nicholas, 2nd Earl of Scarsdale, by Lady Frances Rich, da. of Robert Rich†, 2nd Earl of Warwick. *educ.* travelled abroad 1668. *m.* Feb. 1672, Mary (*d.* 17 Feb. 1684), da. and coh. of Sir John Lewis, 1st Bt., of Ledston, Yorks, 1da. *d.v.p. summ.* to Lords in his fa.'s barony as Lord Deincourt 22 Oct. 1680; *suc.* fa. as 3rd Earl of Scarsdale 27 Jan. 1681.[1]

Capt. gent. pens. 1677-83; groom of the stole to Prince George of Denmark 1685-7.

Keeper, Sherwood Forest 1677-?90; ld. lt. Derbys. 1685-7, j.p. by 1701-?*d.*[2]

Capt. Lord Gerard's Horse 1678-9, indep. tp. 1685; col. Princess Anne's Horse 1685-7.

Lord Deincourt's ancestors had been prominent in the North Midlands since the reign of John, and first represented Nottinghamshire in 1362. His grandfather, though no courtier, rather reluctantly supported the King in the Civil War, but his father claimed parliamentary sympathies. Deincourt began a highly successful career among the opposite sex by eloping with the daughter of a wealthy Eastern merchant, 'a very handsome young woman' if the Duke of York's judgment is to be trusted. He was returned for Newark on the interest of his cousin Sir Francis Leke* at the general election of February 1679. He was an inactive Member of the first Exclusion Parliament, being appointed only to the committee of elections and privileges. Shaftesbury marked him 'base', but he abstained from the division on the exclusion bill. On 11 Aug. 1679 Lord Halifax wrote to Henry Savile*: 'Your friend my Lord Deincourt will try at Newark, but saith he will not be at any charge, which maketh me doubt his success'. Instead Deincourt was called up to the House of Lords, where his father consistently voted with the country party. Father and son took opposite sides both on the second exclusion bill and the condemnation of Lord Stafford.[3]

Deincourt succeeded to the earldom before the next Parliament, and with the Tory reaction was made lord lieutenant of Derbyshire, where the principal family estates lay. Under James II he was given a post in Prince George's household, and a regiment; all his officers were Protestant except two subalterns. He was dismissed from all his posts for opposing James's policy on the repeal of the Test Act and Penal Laws, and at the Revolution he took up arms against James. In the Convention he voted for a regency. He took the oaths on 1 Apr. 1690, but was arrested as a Jacobite in 1692 and refused the Association in 1696. As a High Churchman, he took part in the coronation of Queen Anne, but held no further office. He died on 27 Dec. 1707 and was succeeded by his nephew, a Jacobite, on whose death the peerage became extinct.[4]

[1] *CSP Dom.* 1667-8, p. 477; *Cal. Treas. Bks.* viii. 1526. [2] *Savile Corresp.* (Cam. Soc. lxxi), 57. [3] Thoroton, *Notts.* i. 48, 390; Clarendon, *Rebellion*, ii. 332-4; *CSP Dom.* 1671-2, p. 147; 1683-4, p. 281; *Savile Corresp.* 118; Northants RO, Finch-Hatton mss 2893 D; Bodl. Carte 80, f. 823. [4] *CSP Dom.* 1687-9, pp. 110, 111; 1691-2, pp. 276, 319; Feiling, *Tory Party*, 236, 249, 319; *LJ*, xiv. 444; *HMC Cowper*, iii. 15.

E.R.E.

LENNARD, Sir Stephen, 2nd Bt. (1637-1709), of West Wickham, Kent.

WINCHELSEA 1681
KENT 1698, 1708-15 Dec. 1709

bap. 2 Mar. 1637, 3rd but 1st surv. s. of Stephen Lennard, 1st Bt., of West Wickham by 3rd w. Anne, da. of Sir John Oglander† of Nunwell, I.o.W. *m.* settlement 30 Dec. 1671, Elizabeth, da. of Delalyne Hussey of Shapwick, Dorset, wid. of John Roy of Woodlands, Dorset, 1s. 3da. *suc.* fa. Jan. 1680.[1]

Commr. for assessment, Kent and Surr. 1677-80, Kent 1689-90; dep. lt. Kent 1679-Feb. 1688, 1689-*d.*, j.p. 1680-Feb. 1688, Oct. 1688-*d.*, col. of militia by 1683-?Feb. 1688, ?Oct. 1688-*d.*[2]

Lennard's great-grandfather, who was custos brevium of the court of common pleas under Elizabeth, acquired the large manor of West Wickham and other estates in Kent. His grandfather sat for Fowey in 1593 and his great-uncle for Rye in 1597. His father, who was created a baronet in 1642, was in arms for the King in both Civil Wars according to information given to the committee for the advance of money; but presumably proof was lacking, as no composition proceedings followed. At the Restoration Lennard was proposed as a knight of the Royal Oak, his income being estimated at £1,000.[3]

Lennard probably opposed exclusion, for he was appointed to the commission of the peace in 1680 and defeated the country candidate Robert Austen* at Winchelsea in the following year. He played no known part in the short Oxford Parliament, but in August 1681 he testified to disloyal statements made by Edward Dering*. He avoided answering the lord lieutenant's questions on the repeal of the Test Act and Penal Laws by a plea of illness, and was removed from local office. A county Member under William III and Anne, he was listed as a court Whig. He died suddenly on 15 Dec. 1709 and was buried at West Wickham. His son sat for Hythe as a Whig under George I.[4]

[1] *Dorm. and Ext. Baronetcies*, 310. [2] Eg. 1626, f. 22. [3] *Cal. Comm. Adv. Money*, 1310. [4] *CSP Dom.* 1680-1, p. 395; Luttrell, vi. 524.

B.D.H.

LENTHALL, John (c.1625–81), of Burford Priory, Oxon. and Besselsleigh, Berks.

GLOUCESTER	25 Nov. 1645
ABINGDON	1659, 27 Apr.–23 May 1660

b. c.1625, o. surv. s. of William Lenthall[†] of Burford Priory, Speaker of the House of Commons, by Elizabeth, da. of Ambrose Evans of Loddington, Northants. *educ.* Corpus, Oxf. matric. 12 Sept. 1640, aged 15; L. Inn 1640, called 1647, assoc. bencher 1651. *m.* (1) Mary, da. and coh. of Sir William Ashcombe of Alvescot, Oxon., 1s. *d.v.p.*; (2) Mary, da. of John Blewett of Holcombe Rogus, Devon, wid. of Sir James Stonhouse, 2nd Bt., of Amerden Hall, Debden, Essex, 1s. 1da.; (3) Katherine (*d.*1692), da. of Eusebius Andrews of Edmonton, Mdx., *s.p. suc.* fa. 1662; kntd. 13 Mar. 1678.[1]

Six clerk in Chancery 1643–54; member, high court of justice 1649; commr. for the army 1652–3, Admiralty Feb.–July 1660.[2]

Commr. for appeals, Oxf. Univ. 1647, assessment, Berks., Glos., Gloucester and Oxon. 1647–52, Berks. 1657, Oxon. Jan. 1660, 1677–80, militia, Glos., Berks., Gloucester and Oxon. 1648, Oxon. 1659, Berks. and Oxon. Mar. 1660; j.p. Berks. and Oxon. 1650–3, Mdx. and Westminster 1653–9; freeman, Abingdon 1659; sheriff, Oxon. 1672–3.[3]

Gov. Windsor Castle 1659–June 1660; col. of ft. Feb.–June 1660.[4]

Lenthall's father came from a cadet branch of the family, but, as a successful lawyer earning £2,500 p.a. at the bar, he was able to purchase Besselsleigh, four miles from Abingdon, in 1634, and became the first of the family to sit; his career as the compliant Speaker of the Long Parliament is well known. Lenthall, described by Anthony à Wood as 'the grand braggadocio and liar of the age' and by Edmund Ludlow* as 'a better orator than his father', entered his father's profession and followed his dexterous political course to the best of his abilities. He refused to take part in the trial of Charles I, but sat in the Rump, and was 'knighted' by the Protector.[5]

Lenthall stood for Abingdon at the general election of 1660 on the corporation interest against the Royalist, Sir George Stonhouse*. He was warned not to 'act against the interest and settlement of the nation, according to the known laws of the land', and to 'comport himself to that rule or be no Member for that place'. There was a double return, but Lenthall's indentures were signed by the mayor, and he was allowed to sit, having already been appointed to the committee of elections and privileges. In the debate on the bill of indemnity on 12 May, he made the only serious attempt to exculpate the regicides, saying that 'he that first drew his sword against the King committed as high an offence as he that cut off the King's head'. 'Herein he behaved himself', wrote the wife of John Hutchinson*, 'with so much courage and honour as ever was matched at that time in England.' But this was not the view of the Presbyterians. He was called to the bar of the House, where the Speaker told him that 'there is much of poison in the words, and that they were spoken out of design to set this House on fire'. He took no further part in the Commons, and was unseated on the merits of the election on 23 May. He was deprived of office after the Restoration, and in November 'apprehended for hiring a man that was used to work in tobacco-pipe clay privately to take an impression of the great seal of England'. He was released on £3,000 bail, though it was later alleged that he had to make over some of his property to Lord Chancellor Clarendon. But when the matter was raised in Parliament after Clarendon's fall the House decided that in fact Lenthall was endeavouring to cheat his step-children out of their portions, and a bill was introduced to right them. He was probably reconciled to the monarchy by his third wife, the daughter of a Cavalier martyr. He was knighted in 1678, and Charles II took 'a little repast' at Burford Priory before the meeting of the Oxford Parliament. Lenthall died later in the same year on 9 Nov. 1681 and was buried at Besselsleigh, the last of his line to sit in Parliament.[6]

[1] *Vis. Berks.* (Harl. Soc. lvii), 169–70; Burke, *Gentry* (1952), 150a. [2] T. D. Hardy, *Principal Officers of Chancery*, 109. [3] Abingdon bor. mins. 1, p. 165. [4] *CJ*, vii. 814. [5] Wood, *Athenae*, iii. 604, 609; *VCH Berks.* iv. 396; *N. and Q.* xii. 359; D. Underdown, *Pride's Purge*, 230. [6] *Voyce from the Watch Tower*, 171–2; *Nicholas Pprs.* (Cam. Soc. ser. 3 xxxi), 202; *Hutchinson Mems.* 322; *CJ*, viii. 3, 24, 42; ix. 74; *Parl. Intell.* 28 Nov. 1660; *CSP Dom.* 1660–1, p. 468; 1661–2, pp. 170, 265, 379; *Wood's Life and Times* (Oxf. Hist. Soc. xxi), 530, 559; *Milward*, 152; *VCH Berks.* iv. 396.

M.W.H./G.J.

LENTHALL, William (*d.*1702), of Latchford, Great Haseley, Oxon.

WALLINGFORD	1679 (Oct.)
CRICKLADE	1681

o. surv. s. of Edmund Lenthall (*d.*1668) of Latchford by Elizabeth, da. of Sir William Wade[†], lt. of the Tower, of Hampstead, Mdx. *m.* (1) 1651, Stephana, da. of Sir Stephen Harvey of Northampton, *s.p.*; (2) by 1679, Lucy, da. of Edmund Dunch[†] of Little Wittenham, Berks., *s.p. suc.* gdfa. 1669.[1]

Commr. for assessment, Berks. 1657, Oxon. Jan. 1660, 1664–80, 1689–90; j.p. Oxon 1673–80, Surr. 1673–*d.*; freeman, Wallingford and Woodstock 1679.[2]

Gent. of the privy chamber 1668–85; marshal of the King's Bench prison 1669–?87, by 1690–?97.[3]

Lenthall's ancestor, of Herefordshire origin, acquired Latchford, some dozen miles north of Wallingford, by marriage in the 15th century. Lenthall's grandfather, the elder brother of the Speaker of the Long Parliament, acquired an unenviable reputation as marshal of the King's Bench prison. His father apparently avoided active participation in the Civil War, but held local office from 1648 throughout the Interregnum and after the Restoration. Lenthall's parliamentary career was probably due entirely to his second wife's family, who found him two seats to enable him to evade his creditors. In August 1679 he defeated the court candidate John Stone* at Wallingford, and a few months later he was removed from the Oxfordshire commission of the peace as an exclusionist. After the death of his brother-in-law Hungerford Dunch*, he transferred to Cricklade and was returned in 1681, though he had to swallow a loyal address after the election. Totally inactive in both Parliaments, he is unlikely to have stood again, as his financial circumstances became desperate.[4]

In 1684 Lenthall mortgaged the profits of the prison for £3,000, thereby increasing his total debt to Sir John Cutler* to £10,000. After the Revolution Robert Wright* was charged with removing Lenthall and his deputy from office in an illegal manner, and he was again officiating as marshal in 1690. Under a clause of the Prison Act of 1697 he was forbidden to make any grant of the office without the consent of Cutler's executor until the debt should be paid. Lenthall was still on the Surrey commission of the peace in 1702, but died, childless and intestate, before 27 Feb., when letters of administration were granted to Cutler's son-in-law, the 2nd Earl of Radnor (Charles Bodvile Robartes*). In 1708 Radnor obtained a private Act for the sale of the whole of Lenthall's property in part satisfaction of the debt, then totalling over £20,000.[5]

[1] Misc. Gen. et Her. (ser. 5), i. 226; Burke, Gentry (1952), 1509; Le Neve's Knights (Harl. Soc. viii), 324; Bodl. Great Haseley par. reg. [2] Berks. RO, Wallingford borough statute bk. 1648–1766, f. 109; Woodstock council acts, 6 Sept. 1679. [3] CSP Dom. 1670, p. 318; HMC Lords, ii. 434. [4] Berry, County Genealogies, 60; W. Rendle, Old Southwark and its People, 89; J. M. Dalton, Mss of St. George's Chapel, 351; Bodl. Ch. Oxon. C2/2839; Prot. Dom. Intell. 15 Mar. 1681. [5] Statutes, vii. 275; HMC 7th Rep. 420; Prob. 6/78, ff. 25–27; HMC Lords, n.s. vii. 547–8; Par. Colls. (Oxon. Rec. Soc. iv), 166.

L.N./G.J.

L'ESTRANGE, Sir Nicholas, 4th Bt. (1661–1724), of Hunstanton, Norf.[1]

CASTLE RISING   1685

b. 2 Dec. 1661, 1st s. of Sir Nicholas L'Estrange, 3rd Bt., of Hunstanton, being o.s. by 1st w. Mary, da. of John Coke† of Mileham. educ. Norwich g.s. 1669–72; Scarning 1672–7; Christ Church, Oxf. 1677–9. m. 2 Dec. 1686 (with £4,000), Anne, da. of Sir Thomas Wodehouse of Kimberley, 3s. (1 d.v.p.) 2da. suc. fa. 13 Dec. 1669.

J.p. Norf. 1680–Feb. 1688, dep. lt. 1681–Feb. 1688,

Nov. 1688–9; freeman, King's Lynn 1682; col. of militia ft. Norf. 1683–Feb. 1688, Oct. 1688–9.[2]

L'Estrange's ancestors had been seated at Hunstanton, 11 miles from Castle Rising, since the reign of Henry I, and first represented the county in the Parliament of 1547. The whole family, including his great-uncle Roger L'Estrange*, was strongly royalist in the Civil War and had to pay heavy compensation to their parliamentarian neighbours. Orphaned at the age of eight, L'Estrange became the ward of John Coke I*, who handled the Hunstanton estate as carelessly as his own. But his second guardian, Sir Christopher Calthorpe*, was more conscientious, and imbued L'Estrange with his high Tory views. He signed the loyal address abhorring the 'Association' in 1682. Returned to James II's Parliament for Castle Rising, his only committee was on the bill for relieving imprisoned debtors. But Danby apparently included him among the Opposition. He gave negative replies on the repeal of the Test Act and Penal Laws, and was removed from the lieutenancy. He refused, like Sir John Holland*, to sit with magistrates incapacitated under the Test Act; but he was on duty with his militia regiment at Lynn when the Prince of Orange landed in the west. He would not stand again after the Revolution, and resigned all his employments, much to the annoyance of the Duke of Norfolk, the lord lieutenant, by whom he was much harassed during the next few years. He was tried as a nonjuror in 1696, but acquitted on a technicality, and Dean Prideaux hoped to persuade him to take the oaths, describing him as:

a man of parts, virtue, and prudence. . . . He is one of the worthiest gentlemen of the country and a very fit person to serve in Parliament, and, would he qualify himself for it, would certainly be chosen for the county.

L'Estrange was able to clear off the encumbrances on the estate, and, with an income of £1,900 in 1701, to relieve the hardships suffered by his greatuncle in his old age. He remained a non-juror, his name being sent to the Pretender as a Jacobite supporter in 1721. He died on 18 Dec. 1724. His heir had become a Roman Catholic, and no later member of the family entered Parliament.[3]

[1] This biography is based on Norf. Arch. xxxiv. 314–29. [2] Norf. Ltcy. Jnl (Norf. Rec. Soc. xxx), 34, 63; Lynn Freemen, 193. [3] Blomefield, Norf. x. 320; R. W. Ketton-Cremer, Norf. in the Civil War, 188; DNB; Add. 36988, f. 180; Prideaux Letters (Cam. Soc. n.s. xv), 172, 174, 183; G. Kitchin, Sir Roger L'Estrange, 370; Stuart mss 65/10.

P.W.

L'ESTRANGE, Roger (1616–1704), of High Holborn, Mdx.[1]

WINCHESTER   1685

b. 17 Dec. 1616, 3rd s. of Sir Hamon L'Estrange† (*d.*1653) of Hunstanton, Norf. by Alicia, da. and coh. of Richard Stubbs of Sedgeford, Norf. *educ.* Eton c.1632; Sidney Sussex, Camb. 1634; G. Inn 1637. *m.* by 1680, Mary (*d.* 7 Apr. 1694), da. of Sir Thomas Dolman* of Shaw, Berks., 2s. (1 *d.v.p.*) 1da. Kntd. 30 Apr. 1685.

Commr. for loyal and indigent officers, Norf. 1662; j.p. Mdx. Apr.–Dec. 1680, Mdx. and Westminster 1683–9; freeman, Winchester 1685.[2]

Surveyor of the press 1662–79, 1684–9.[3]

Only a small portion of L'Estrange's colourful career was devoted to parliamentary politics. A younger son of an ancient Norfolk family, conspicuous both for its loyal sufferings and its literary tastes, he first fought for the Stuarts in the Bishops' wars. He was sentenced to death by John Mylles* at a court-martial in 1643 for attempting to seize King's Lynn, and played a prominent part in Kent in the second Civil War. In exile he took service for a time in a cardinal's household, where his musical talents were appreciated but his devotion to his Church could not be shaken. He was pardoned by the Protector in 1653, and lived for the next few years in such style that some believed him to have also been granted a pension. He began his career as a pamphleteer with an attack on the military regime and their London allies in December 1659, and after the Restoration complained bitterly of the neglect of loyal Cavaliers by the Court. He was appointed surveyor of the press in 1662, and confirmed in office by Sir Henry Bennet* under the Press Act in the following year. His post carried no salary, but gave him powers of search and censorship with the sole right to publish 'narratives' not exceeding two sheets of paper. He thus supplanted (Sir) John Berkenhead* as the chief government propagandist. He could not equal his predecessor in learning, grace, wit or dignity, but he far surpassed him in virulence, especially directed against the nonconformists, who retaliated, so far as they were able, by styling him 'the dog Towser', a monster of profanity, drunkenness, and depravity. His reporting of the second Dutch war failed to satisfy the Court, and in 1665 his news-books were superseded by the foundation of the *Gazette* under the editorship of Joseph Williamson*. L'Estrange was compensated with a pension of £300, which he was required to earn by tracking down the authors and printers of seditious libels. In this task, which involved him in a prolonged dispute with the Stationers' Company, he enjoyed very little success, and he lost office when the Press Act expired in May 1679.[4]

L'Estrange was the first to publish even a whisper of doubt about the wilder aspects of the Popish Plot, and was accused by one of Oates's crazier satellites not only of attempting to corrupt a witness, but also of the obligatory charge of Popery. The accusation was dismissed by the Privy Council, 'His Majesty speaking very well of him'; but when the second Exclusion Parliament met the House of Lords recommended his removal from the commission of the peace, and he fled abroad. He returned early in 1681, and began to publish *The Observator*, which perhaps did more than any other news-sheet to turn the tide against the exclusionists and win the propaganda battle for the Court. In particular he devoted himself to the exposure of Oates's fabrications. His post as surveyor of the press was revived in 1684, and he was rewarded by James II with a knighthood. At the general election of 1685 he was recommended as court candidate for Winchester by the Roman Catholic recorder, Bernard Howard, and returned without a contest when two local Tories were persuaded to withdraw. A moderately active Member, he was appointed to nine committees, including the committee of elections and privileges, and those to recommend expunctions from the Journals (a congenial task for a censor) and to consider the bills for regulating hackney coaches and providing carriages for the navy and ordnance. Although he defended the Declaration of Indulgence in 1687, the King was persuaded to offer him as a sacrifice to nonconformist hatred, and his news-sheet was suppressed. During the Revolution he was arrested on a charge of 'writing and dispersing treasonable papers', he was excluded from the Act of Indemnity in 1690, and twice taken into custody by the new regime. A nonjuror, he supported himself by his pen, though his wife gambled away much of his earnings, and he required assistance from his great-nephew, Sir Hamon L'Estrange. His last years were saddened by the conversion of his daughter to the Church of Rome. He died on 12 Dec. 1704 and was buried at St. Giles in the Fields. His only son died unmarried a few months later without entering Parliament.[5]

[1] This biography is based on G. Kitchin, *Sir Roger L'Estrange.* [2] Winchester corp. assembly bk. 6, f. 13. [3] *CSP Dom.* 1661–2, p. 282; 1663–4, p. 240. [4] Ibid. 1664–5, p. 420; 1665–6, p. 17; P. Fraser, *Intell. of Secs. of State,* 49. [5] Luttrell, i. 57; *HMC Lords,* i. 167, 246–51; *LJ,* xiii. 630; *HMC 11th Rep. VII,* 111–14.

P.W.

LEVESON, Richard (1659–99), of Wolverhampton, Staffs.

LICHFIELD I.o.W.   1685
NEWPORT I.o.W.   13 Dec. 1692

b. 12 July 1659, 1st s. of Robert Leveson (*d.* 1709) of Wolverhampton by Sarah, da. of John Povey of Hounslow, Mdx. *unm.*; 2s.[1]

Groom of the bedchamber 1685–Dec. 1688.[2]

Capt. R. Dgns. June 1685, Queen's Dgns. (3 Hussars) Aug. 1685, lt.-col. 1687, col. Dec. 1688–94; gov. Berwick-on-Tweed 1691–d.; brig. of horse 1691; col. of horse (later 2 Dgn. Gds.) 1694–d.; maj.-gen. 1696.[3]

Commr. for assessment, Staffs. 1689.

Leveson's ancestors had held property in and around Wolverhampton since the reign of Edward I, first sitting for Newcastle-under-Lyme in 1432, but since Elizabethan times they had been overshadowed by a vigorous cadet branch, the maternal ancestors of William Leveson Gower*. His grandfather, the royalist governor of Dudley during the Civil War, nevertheless enjoyed a rent-roll of over £1,000 a year. He died in exile in 1651, and his unsettled property was sold by the treason trustees. His father succeeded to a diminished estate of £600 or £700 a year; 'loyal, orthodox, active, stout and of very good parts', he was proposed as a knight of the Royal Oak at the Restoration.[4]

Either Leveson or his father appears to have contemplated standing in 1679, but was defeated by the determination of Thomas Thynne I* 'to keep out Lord Danby's friends'. Through his mother he was related to Thomas Povey†, treasurer to the Duke of York from 1660 to 1668. He was appointed groom of the bedchamber when the Duke succeeded to the throne, and approved as court candidate for Lichfield. He was returned after a contest but appointed to no committees in James II's Parliament. On Monmouth's invasion he was commissioned in the army and given leave to go into the country on 19 June 1685, doubtless to recruit. It was reported that he would not concur with the King's religious policy, but his father, a deputy lieutenant for the county, freely consented to the lord lieutenant's questions on the repeal of the Test Act and Penal Laws, and he was himself ordered to stand for re-election in 1688. On the pretext of searching for Percy Kirke* and other deserters he went over to William of Orange at Warminster during the Revolution, and was excepted from amnesty by James II.[5]

Leveson remained a professional soldier under the new regime, serving with distinction in Ireland and sitting for an Isle of Wight borough as a placeman. He died in March 1699, and his father, the last of the family, sold the property soon afterwards.[6]

[1] *Wolverhampton Par. Reg.* (Staffs. Par. Reg. Soc.), i. 234; PCC 148 Lane; *Vis. Staffs.* (Wm. Salt Arch. Soc. v. pt. 2), 202–3; *Staffs. Parl. Hist.* (Wm. Salt Arch. Soc.), ii. 161. [2] *CSP Dom.* 1685, p. 144. [3] Luttrell, ii. 215. [4] Shaw, *Staffs.* ii. 167, 169; *Cal. Comm. Comp.* 89, 511, 2483–6; *Gentry of Staffs.* (Staffs. Rec. Soc. ser. 4, ii), 22. [5] Foxcroft, *Halifax*, i. 179; *CSP Dom.* 1685, p. 121; 1687–9, pp. 277, 361; R. Morrice, Entering Bk. 2, p. 62; Clarke, *Jas. II*, ii. 224, 435. [6] *Staffs. Parl. Hist.* (Wm. Salt Arch. Soc.), ii. 161; Shaw, ii. 163.

A.M.M.

LEVESON GOWER, William (c.1647–91), of Trentham, Staffs.

NEWCASTLE-UNDER-LYME	21 Apr. 1675, 1679 (Mar.), 1679 (Oct.)
SHROPSHIRE	1681
NEWCASTLE-UNDER-LYME	1689, 1690–22 Dec. 1691

b. c.1647, 2nd but o. surv. s. of Sir Thomas Gower, 2nd Bt.*, of Stittenham, Yorks. *educ.* Pocklington g.s. 1656, aged 9. *m.* c.1669, Lady Jane Granville (*d.* 27 Feb. 1696), da. of John, 1st Earl of Bath, 3s. (2 *d.v.p.*) 2da. *suc.* cos. Francis Leveson (formerly Fowler) in Staffs. and Salop estate 1668, nephew as 4th Bt. 8 Oct. 1689.[1]

J.p. Yorks (N. Riding) 1669–81, Staffs. and Salop 1678–81, ?1689–d.; commr. for assessment, N. Riding and Salop 1673–80, Staffs. 1677–80, 1689, Salop 1689–90, (N. Riding) 1690, recusants, Yorks. 1675; dep. lt. Staffs. 1677–80, 1689–d.; steward, manor of Newcastle 1678–84.[2]

A younger son, Leveson Gower, according to a hostile account, 'had a great estate fall to him by chance; but honesty and wit never came by accident'. His marriage gave him a strong link with the Court, and Lord Arlington wrote on his behalf when he first stood for Malton in his native Yorkshire. After a double return with James Hebblethwaite*, he renounced the seat when he was elected two years later for Newcastle-under-Lyme, five miles from Trentham. A moderately active Member of the Cavalier Parliament, he was named to 12 committees, spoke nine times, and acted as a teller in four divisions. Sir Richard Wiseman* included him among the government supporters in 1676, and in the next session Shaftesbury classed him as 'doubly vile'. In the supply committee on 21 Feb. 1677 he asked:

> Has the King invaded any man's property, or shed any man's blood in vain? You need not be jealous of property and religion. It goes hard with the King to retrench his house and the pensions, and he has parted with his revenue to pay the bankers' debt, and moves therefore that we may supply the King with £600,000 for building ships.

But his principal concern in his early years in the House was to maintain the exclusion of foreign cattle. He twice acted as teller against proposals to modify the Act, but was nevertheless named to the repeal committee. Included on the government working lists among those 'to be remembered', he was enabled to consolidate his interest at Newcastle by the grant of the stewardship of the crown manor. His name was on both lists of the court party in 1678. He acted as teller for supply on 15 June, and in the final days of the Parliament he strove to divert the attack on Danby, not without some danger to himself:

I would not provoke the King, by this way of proceeding, to govern by arbitrary power and an army. I would know why the committee have not despatched the articles against the five lords in the Tower.[3]

Although blacklisted in the 'unanimous club', Leveson Gower was returned for Newcastle to all three Exclusion Parliaments. Shaftesbury marked him 'vile' in 1679, when he was moderately active, with three committees and as many speeches. During the dispute over the choice of a Speaker he inquired 'roughly' whether any address had ever been made without one, and was again called to order. When the speech from the throne of 22 Mar. about the proceedings against Danby was reported, Leveson Gower said:

If the Speaker had remembered all the King's speech he would have reported all. The King said he has given this lord his pardon before the Parliament met, and has done no more than he did to the Duke of Buckingham and Lord Shaftesbury. And I think, if he be so removed as you are told by the King, that the nation is not in danger, and the King says he will pardon him again and again.

He was appointed to the committee to examine the disbandment accounts, and on 27 Apr. moved that none of the Queen's servants should be exempted from the Test Act. He acted as teller for continuing the prohibition of Irish cattle, and was named to the committee for the bill. He was also appointed to the committee for reform of the bankruptcy laws. But before the Parliament ended he had gone over to the Opposition, voting for the exclusion bill, though his rivalry with Sir John Bowyer* for control of Newcastle led him to support court candidates in the autumn elections.[4]

In the second Exclusion Parliament Leveson Gower was again moderately active as a committeeman. He was among those instructed to draw up an address on the state of the kingdom. He was fair-minded enough to object to the proposal to commit Edward Seymour* without examining the charges that had been raked up against him. 'Nothing less than a firm union among all Protestants in this nation can be sufficient', he believed, though he still described the Church of England as 'the unspotted spouse of our blessed Saviour'. But he complained that 'the promises made to the nation at Breda are not kept', and was compelled to explain, amid protestations of loyalty, that he was blaming not the King, but his ministers. He supported the bill to banish all considerable Papists, 'excepting no one man in England whatsoever', though he feared that 'such bills as these will not do our business, because they will not destroy that footing which they have at Court'. He was added to the committee for the disbandment accounts, and

appointed to that to prevent bequests for superstitious uses. By now one of the strongest exclusionists in the House, he helped to draft the address rejecting the King's expedients to resolve the deadlock, and on 7 Jan. 1681 he said:

If the Lords had been left to themselves they would have passed this bill as well as we. But there is a great reason why we have not this bill passed. Persons near the King are interested for the Duke, and so long as they are at Court we shall not have this bill. ... The Court has become the nursery of all manner of vices transplanted into all England, and those are become only fit for the Court that are so. I would have the House freely express themselves about persons about the King, who hinder those things. ... I move that we may give no money till we are better secured of our religion and property, which I can see no way for but by this bill.

In the memoirs of James II he is reported as having averred at this time that, though some men would perhaps endeavour to make their peace with the Duke, he would perish first; 'wherefore my opinion is we should break up, and each man return to his country and let the people see how we are used and I doubt not but they will soon join with us, their swords in their hands, and they will let the Duke know we defy him and all his popish adherents'.[5]

At the general election of 1681 Leveson Gower was returned for Shropshire, where he had inherited extensive estates from his uncle, as well as for his borough. At Oxford he chose the county seat, and was named to the committee of elections and privileges. In the first of his four speeches he favoured publication of the resolutions of the House. On the proposal to bring in the exclusion bill again he declared:

I hope the King will now come up to what he has said in his speech. My liberty and property are dear to me, and I will support the King's prerogative too; and those people that are briars and thorns scratch you in your intentions against popery, which I see we cannot prevent without this bill, and therefore I am for it.

Two days later he returned to the subject:

If any gentlemen have expedients to preserve the Protestant religion without this bill of exclusion, they would do well to propose them, and they will deserve well of this House; and if they seem to them to give security then I should be glad to hear them.

Later in the same debate he urged that the King should be given reasons for excluding his brother from the succession to the throne:

I do think that the administration of the government has been in such hands since the King came in that, though the ministers have been shifted, yet the same principles of government remain to this day. ... The King of France made war with Holland for his glory, and our ministers to get taxes from us to make the King absolute: such violations as never were done upon the rights of the people!

As usual, he ignored calls to order, and as 'Mr George' he was appointed to the committee to bring in the bill.[6]

Early in 1682 Leveson Gower was named as one of the dissenters' supporters in Staffordshire. The Duke of Monmouth visited Trentham immediately before his arrest at Stafford in September, when his host was among those who offered to stand bail. After the Rye House Plot information was obtained that he had purchased considerable quantities of fire-arms, but he was apparently more successful than William Forester* in concealing them. He lost his stewardship in 1684, and was defeated at Newcastle in the following year, though he petitioned in both sessions of James II's Parliament. But in September 1688 he was recommended for county office as a Whig collaborator, and approved as court candidate for his borough, though he later affected to believe that the regulators' intervention was 'on purpose to keep me out'. During the Revolution it was reported that Trentham had been attacked, and horses and arms carried away for the Protestant cause.[7]

Leveson Gower was in fact one of the court candidates able to overcome this handicap at the general election of 1689, and in the Convention he sat again for Newcastle. An active Member, he delivered 19 recorded speeches and was appointed to 50 committees. Still a strong Anglican, on 1 Feb. he moved successfully to thank the two archbishops for their defence of the Protestant religion, and was instructed to deliver the message himself. But he was equally committed to the Revolution, despite his earlier hesitancy, and on the following day he helped to prepare reasons for insisting that the throne was vacant. At the end of the month he carried up the resolution of the Commons to assist William with their lives and fortunes, and on the next day he was among those appointed to draft the address to this effect and to consider the suspension of habeas corpus. He was also named to the committees to inquire into the authors and advisers of grievances, to consider the first mutiny bill, and to examine prisoners of state. He helped to draw up the address for war with France and to prepare reasons for a conference on disarming Papists. His nephew, who had been given a regiment, was under orders for Ireland, and on 1 June he desired to know why the forces sent to relieve Londonderry had returned without effecting their purpose. He was appointed to the committee of inquiry, and a month later he was added to the committee to consider the Lords' proviso on the succession. He assured the House that the Seven Bishops were too good Christians to desire any exceptions from the

indemnity bill on their account. He helped to draft the address asking for permission to inspect the Privy Council records about Ireland and to investigate the charges of malversation against William Harbord*. On 19 July he was teller against the adjournment. He took part in the attack on Lord Halifax in the House, for which he was denied the peerage that would naturally have come his way, especially after succeeding to Stittenham when his nephew died on active service.[8]

Leveson Gower moved for a vote of thanks for the speech from the throne which opened the second session, and was sent to carry it to the King with the Privy Councillors. He helped to conduct the inquiries into the miscarriages of the war and the state of the revenue. In the debate on Commissary Shales he said: 'I am for taking out all the deer in this King's park that were in King James's park'. Nevertheless he was moving back towards the Tories. A vehement champion of Princess Anne, he took the chair in the committee to draw up an address for her maintenance. Although not listed as a supporter of the disabling clause in the bill to restore corporations, he was appointed to the committee on the bill to enforce a general oath of allegiance, and reported on 24 Jan. 1690 that the imprisonment of three informers on a warrant from a Middlesex j.p. was illegal.[9]

Leveson Gower sat as a Tory in the opening sessions of the next Parliament, but died on 22 Dec. 1691. His son succeeded him as Tory MP for Newcastle until raised to the peerage in 1703.[10]

[1] Staffs. Peds. (Harl. Soc. lxiii), 109; Yorks. Arch. Jnl. xxv. 62; HMC 5th Rep. 196; Hist. Pirehill (Wm. Salt Arch. Soc. n.s. xii), 79. [2] Staffs. Dep. Lts. (Staffs. Rec. Soc. 1931), 285; Somerville, Duchy of Lancaster Official Lists, 168. [3] Staffs. Parl. Hist. (Wm. Salt Arch. Soc.), ii. 127-8; HMC 5th Rep. 197; Grey, iv. 112; vii. 386; CJ, ix. 406, 415. [4] Grey, vi. 412; vii. 21-22, 142; CJ, ix. 621. [5] Grey, viii. 89, 104-5, 157, 266; Exact Coll. Debates, 181-2, 263; HMC 12th Rep. IX, 100, 110; Clarke, Jas. II, i. 621. [6] Grey, viii. 294, 296, 313, 322-3; CJ, ix. 711. [7] CSP Dom. 1682, p. 381; July-Sept. 1683, pp. 18, 65; Bodl. Carte 216, ff. 189-90; CJ, ix. 716, 760; Grey, ix. 108; Ellis Corresp. ii. 334-5. [8] Grey, ix. 40, 276, 378; CJ, x. 16, 37, 162; Foxcroft, Halifax, ii. 228. [9] R. Morrice, Entering Bk. 2, p. 617; CJ, x. 271, 316, 343; Grey, ix. 464, 501-2. [10] Staffs. Parl. Hist. (Wm. Salt Arch. Soc.), ii. 127-8.

A.M.M.

LEWES (LEWIS), Thomas (c.1657-96), of West Wycombe, Bucks. and Stanford-upon-Soar, Notts.

CHIPPING WYCOMBE   1679 (Mar.), 1679 (Oct.), 1681, 1689, 1690, 1695-16 Mar. 1696

b. c.1657, 1st s. of Thomas Lewes, Vintner, of Little St. Helens, London by 2nd w. Elizabeth, da. of Francis Dashwood, merchant, of London. m. lic. 13 July 1687, aged 30, Anne (*d.* 18 Jan. 1695), da. of Sir Matthew Andrews* of Ashley Hall, Walton-on-Thames, Surr., 3s. (2 *d.v.p.*) 2da.[1]

Commr. for assessment, Bucks. 1690.

Lewes's father was reckoned one of the wealthiest merchants trading to Aleppo after the Restoration. He bought West Wycombe in 1670, but Lewes himself seems to have resided chiefly in Nottinghamshire. However, he was returned for Wycombe to the Exclusion Parliaments, appearing as 'Thomas Lewis junior' on the list drawn up by Sir Ralph Verney*. He was marked 'honest' by Shaftesbury in 1679, and voted for the bill. A moderately active Member, he may have served on five committees in the first Exclusion Parliament, including those to receive proposals for the Royal Fishery, to bring in a bill for the encouragement of woollen manufactures, and to consider the export of cloth to Turkey. In the second Exclusion Parliament he was appointed to the committee of elections and privileges, and to those to examine the proceedings of the judges in Westminster Hall and to take the accounts of the disbandment commissioners. He intervened in the debate of 17 Nov. 1680 on Tangier to urge that the naval base should not be given up, lest it fall into the hands of the French. He left no trace on the records of the Oxford Parliament. He contested Wycombe again in 1685, but his petition was not reported. Lewes's father was 'supposed to be a dissenter' when recommended for the Buckinghamshire commission of the peace and lieutenancy in 1688, but, with Lewes and his wife, was solely responsible for the 'reparation, ornaments and beauty' of Stanford church. Lewes himself regained his seat in the Convention, but he was not active. He probably served on five committees, including those to consider the abuses in alnage and the bill for restoring corporations in the second session, and he supported the disabling clause. He continued to sit for Wycombe till his death from apoplexy on 16 Mar. 1696. His father, who survived him, sold West Wycombe to the Dashwoods to pay his debts, but his son Francis sat for East Retford from 1713 to 1715.[2]

[1] J. R. Woodhead, *Rulers of London*, 108–9; *London Mar. Lic.* ed. Foster, 843; *The Topographer*, ii. 243; PCC 122 Pyne. [2] *Verney Mems.* ii. 261; *VCH Bucks.* iii. 637; BL, M636/71; *Exact Coll. Debates 1680*, p. 120; Luttrell, iv. 20.

L.N.

LEWIS, Edward (1650–74), of The Van, Glam. and Boarstall, Bucks.

DEVIZES 30 Oct. 1669–July 1674

b. 30 July 1650, 1st s. of William Lewis*. *educ.* travelled abroad 1663–6. *unm. suc.* fa. 1661.[1]

Dep. lt. Glam. 1670–*d.*; freeman, Devizes 1670; j.p. Mon., Glam. and Brec. 1672–*d.*; commr. for assessment, Mon. and Glam. 1673–*d.*[2]

Still under age and a stranger to the borough, Lewis was returned at a by-election for his father's old seat at Devizes. An inactive Member, his only certain appearances in the records of Parliament were on the committee of elections and privileges in 1669 and 1670, but either he or his uncle Richard Lewis* served on five others. His name does not appear on either list of court supporters in 1669–71. 'Mr Lewis of the West' was reported to be courting a daughter of Sir George Sondes* in 1670; but neither his will nor the codicil, executed on 4 July 1674, mentions a wife. He died in London before 23 July 1674, when the will (but not the codicil) was proved by his brother-in-law William Jephson*, who inherited the Buckinghamshire estate. Lewis's younger brother had predeceased him, and the Welsh lands went to Richard Lewis.[3]

[1] G. T. Clark, *Limbus Patrum*, 50; *CSP Dom.* 1663–4, p. 191. [2] *CSP Dom. Add.* 1660–70, p. 178. [3] *HMC Rutland*, ii. 17; PCC 14 Bunce; *VCH Bucks.* iv. 12.

J.P.F.

LEWIS, John (c.1660–1720), of Coedmor, Card.

CARDIGANSHIRE	1685, 1689
CARDIGAN BOROUGHS	11 Dec. 1693, 1695
CARDIGANSHIRE	1698
CARDIGAN BOROUGHS	1701 (Feb.)

b. c.1660, 1st s. of James Lewis of Coedmor by Catherine, da. of Richard Harrison of Hurst, Berks. *m.* 1680, Elizabeth (*d.*1734), da. and coh. of Lodowick Lewis† of Llangorse, Brec., 1s. *d.v.p.* 4da. *suc.* fa. 1669.[1]

Sheriff, Brec. 1683–4, Card. 1710–11; dep. lt. Card. 1683–?Feb. 1688, 1689–?*d.*; j.p. Card. 1684–Apr. 1688, Oct. 1688–?*d.*, Brec. and Pemb. by 1701–*d.*; commr. for assessment, Card. 1689–90, capt. of militia horse by 1697–?*d.*[2]

The Lewis family of Coedmor were prominent in Cardiganshire by Elizabethan times, first representing the county in 1604. Lewis's grandfather 'of inoffensive, facile constitution' sat in five Parliaments before the Civil War and again in the second Protectorate Parliament. His father married into a royalist family just before the Restoration, and was proposed as a knight of the Royal Oak with an estate of £700 p.a. Lewis inherited the heavily encumbered Coedmor estate as a child. He was brought up by his uncle in Berkshire, where he continued to reside. By his marriage to the granddaughter of Sir William Lewis* he acquired an estate in Breconshire. Despite non-residence, he was six times elected for either the county or borough seat in Cardiganshire, though his first return in 1685 was probably due to the minority of the Trawscoed heir. He served on no committees in James II's Parliament, and his politics at this date are hard to determine, but he may have been a moderate Tory. He was noted as living in Berkshire when the King's questions on the repeal of the Test Act and Penal Laws were put, and was removed from local office. He defeated John Vaughan† with the support of the Pryce interest in 1689, but no committee work can be ascribed to him in the Convention, and his name figures on neither division list. He was a court Whig after regaining his seat in 1693. 'Indolent in his affairs', he was obliged to sell Coedmor in 1700. He was buried at Hurst on 26 Jan. 1720, the last of the family.[3]

[1] *Ceredigion*, vi. 164; *Vis. Berks.* (Harl. Soc. lvi), 219. [2] Eg. 1626, f. 60. [3] *Ceredigion*, vi. 150–3, 157, 159; Berks. RO, Hurst par. reg.

L.N./G.J.

LEWIS, Richard (c.1627–1706), of Edington Priory, Wilts. and The Van, Glam.

WESTBURY 1660, 1661, 1679 (Mar.), 1679 (Oct.)– 26 Nov. 1680, 1685, 1689, 1690, 1695, 1698, 1701 (Feb.)

b. c.1627, 3rd s. of Sir Edward Lewis of Edington Priory and The Van by Lady Anne Sackville, da. of Robert Sackville†, 2nd Earl of Dorset, wid. of Edward, Lord Beauchamp; bro. of William Lewis*. *m.* Mary, da. and h. of Giles James of Sherston, Wilts., 3s. (2 *d.v.p.*) 2da. *suc.* nephew Edward Lewis* in Glam. estate 1674.[1]
Commr. for assessment, Wilts. Jan. 1660–80, Mon. and Glam. 1677–80, Mon., Wilts. and Glam. 1689–90, militia, Wilts. Mar. 1660; j.p. Wilts. July 1660–June 1688, Oct. 1688–96, Glam. ?1674–82, 1685–96, Glam. and Wilts. 1700–*d.*; lt.-col. of militia ft. Wilts. 1661, col. 1681, commr. for corporations 1662–3, dep. lt. 1668–June 1688, Oct. 1688–96, by 1701–?*d.*, sheriff 1681–2; freeman, Devizes ?1684–7; commr. for rebels' estates, Wilts. 1686.[2]

Lewis represented Westbury, four miles from Edington, in every Parliament except one from the Restoration till the death of William III. In the Convention he served on a committee for a private bill, and perhaps three others. His mother lived with him until her death in 1664, and Lord Wharton marked him as a stronger Anglican than his brother, presumably having regard to the influence of her Seymour kinsfolk. He was again inactive in the Cavalier Parliament, serving on 50 committees at the most. He was appointed to the committee for the London to Bristol canal in 1662, and took part in the consideration of defects in the Corporations Act in 1663. On 24 Nov. 1666 he acted as teller for the unsuccessful motion to name the mayor of Cambridge in the plague bill before the vice-chan-

cellor of the University. After succeeding to the family estate, he was reckoned to enjoy an income of £1,400 p.a. He was appointed to two important committees in November 1675, those for the recall of British subjects in French service and hindering the growth of Popery. He was considered a court supporter by Sir Richard Wiseman* and marked 'doubly vile' by Shaftesbury. In 1677 he was named to the committee for the education of children of the royal family as Protestants. His name does not appear on either list of the court party in 1678, but Shaftesbury considered him 'vile' at the general election. He probably sat on no committees in the first Exclusion Parliament, but voted against the bill. With Thomas Lambert* and Robert Hyde* he was commended at the assizes in 1680, on the King's instructions, for his zeal in seeking out Papists; but he was unseated on petition in the second Exclusion Parliament and probably did not stand in 1681.[3]

Lewis was asked to use his utmost endeavours in 1685 to secure the return of loyal Members. He himself regained his seat, but was totally inactive in James II's Parliament. He was listed among the Opposition and displaced as freeman of Devizes by order-in-council in 1687. To the lord lieutenant's questions he replied that he was 'for liberty of conscience as far as it may consist with the peace of the nation, and will not declare what he will further do as to the repealing the Tests till the House of Commons meets. He will not concern himself one way or the other in any election.' The lord lieutenant considered him to have one of the two chief interests in Westbury, though 'a very near man' who would 'spend little or nothing'. This remarkable tribute to Lewis's personal popularity in a notoriously corrupt borough was silently confirmed by the King's electoral agents, who could only hope against hope that he might be 'inclined to be right'. He was duly returned in 1689, and, according to Anthony Rowe*, voted to agree with the Lords that the throne was not vacant; but the committee references to 'Mr Lewis' are probably to Thomas Lewes*. He retained his seat at Westbury even after his lease of Edington fell in and he moved to Corsham. In 1696 he was removed from the lieutenancy for refusing the Association. He died on 1 Oct. 1706, 'in his eighty-third year', and was buried at Corsham. His son Thomas sat for various Hampshire and Wiltshire constituencies, first as a Tory, but from 1726 as 'an humble servant' of Walpole.[4]

[1] *Wilts. Arch. Mag.* xx. 291; G. T. Clark, *Limbus Patrum*, 52; *Wilts. N. and Q.* i. 229. [2] Add. 32324, f. 125; Hoare, *Wilts. Salisbury*, 449; *CSP Dom.* 1672–3, p. 107; 1680–1, p. 209; *Cal. Treas. Bks.* viii. 546. [3] *Wilts. Arch. Mag.* lviii. 387; SP29/398/185; PC2/68, f. 381. [4] *CSP Dom.* 1685, p. 21; B. H. Cunnington, *Annals*

of Devizes, i. 181; HMC Portland, iv. 176; Aubrey and Jackson, Wilts. Colls. 79; VCH Wilts. viii. 242; Misc. Gen. et Her. (ser. 2), iv. 333.

M.W.H./J.P.F.

LEWIS, William (c.1625–61), of Bletchington, Oxon. and The Van, Glam.

DEVIZES 1660

b. c.1625, 2nd s. of Sir Edward Lewis (d.1630) of The Van and Edington Priory, Wilts., and bro. of Richard Lewis*. educ. Jesus, Oxf. matric. 12 Oct. 1638, aged 14; travelled abroad (France, Italy) 1642–6. m. 24 June 1649, Margaret, da. and h. of Lawrence Banastre of Boarstall, Bucks., 2s. 2da. suc. bro. 1647.[1]

Commr. for assessment, Oxon. Jan. 1660–d., militia Mar. 1660, j.p. Mar. 1660–d., dep. lt. c. Aug. 1660–d.

Lewis was head of a very old, but thoroughly Anglicized Glamorgan family, distinguished chiefly for prudent marriages, but not previously aspiring to a seat in Parliament. His father, a courtier, married the widow of the 1st Earl of Hertford's heir, and bought the remainder of a long lease of Edington in 1629, dying there in the following year. Lewis's mother was careful to preserve neutrality in the Civil War, sending her eldest sons abroad lest their uncles, the Marquess of Hertford and the 4th Earl of Dorset, should engage them in the royalist cause. The Glamorgan committee testified in 1648 that Lewis was well-affected and had made large contributions to their funds; but it was probably a paternal uncle of the same name who sat with them throughout the Interregnum. Lewis's marriage to a Buckinghamshire heiress enabled him to buy an estate at Bletchington in 1656 for £10,000. He probably owed his election for Devizes, ten miles from Edington, to his mother, whose lavish hospitality at the Priory was notable chiefly for her excellent brew of beer. As she also secured the return for Westbury of another son, it is impossible to distinguish his record in the Convention, but he was clearly inactive. Lord Wharton seems to have regarded him as a moderate Anglican. One or other of the brothers was appointed to the committees for altering the entail on Lord Hertford's estates, attainting Oliver Cromwell, and considering the petition of a former serjeant-at-arms; but they made no speeches. He lost his seat at the general election, and died later in the same year. His widow brought Bletchington and other lands worth in all £38,000 to her second husband, the 5th Duke of Richmond; but on her death in 1667 the Boarstall estate went to her son Edward Lewis*.[2]

[1] Cal. Comm. Adv. Money, 569–70; London Mar. Lic. ed. Foster, 843; Evelyn Diary, ii. 557. [2] G. T. Clark, Limbus Patrum, 45, 50; VCH Wilts. viii. 242; Cal. Comm. Adv. Money, 728; VCH Bucks. iv. 12; VCH Oxon. vi. 59; Wilts. Arch. Mag. xx. 254, 292; PCC 181 May; CSP Dom. 1663–4, p. 528.

M.W.H./J.P.F.

LEWIS, Sir William, 1st Bt. (1598–1677), of Llangorse, Brec. and Bordean House, East Meon, Hants.

PETERSFIELD	1640 (Apr.), 1640 (Nov.)[1]
BRECONSHIRE	1660
LYMINGTON	1661–c. Nov. 1677

b. 26 Mar. 1598, 1st s. of Lodowick Lewis of Trewalter, Brec. by Elizabeth, da. and h. of William Watkins of Llangorse. educ. Univ. Coll. Oxf. 1613, BA 1616; L. Inn 1616. m. c. Feb. 1622, Mary (d. Feb. 1636), da. of Robert Calton of Goring, Oxon., wid. of Sir Thomas Neale of Warnford, Hants, 1s. d.v.p. 2da. suc. fa. 1614; cr. Bt. 14 Sept. 1628.[2]

Sheriff, Brec. 1619–20, 1636–7; j.p. Hants 1627–?47, Brec. 1647, Hants and Brec. Mar. 1660–d.; dep. lt. Hants by 1640–2, Brec. c. Aug. 1660–74; commr. for assessment, Hants 1643–7, Brec. 1647, Rad. Jan. 1660, Hants and Brec. Aug. 1660–d., sequestration, Hants 1643, levying of money 1643, defence 1643, execution of ordinances 1644; freeman, Portsmouth 1644, 1662, Lymington 1661; commr. for appeals, Oxford Univ. 1647, militia, Hants 1648, Hants and Brec. Mar. 1660; custos rot. Brec. Aug. 1660–d.; commr. for recusants, Hants 1675.[3]

Gov. Portsmouth (parliamentary) 1642–3.[4]

Commr. for excise 1645, Admiralty 1645–8, abuses in heraldry 1646, exclusion from sacrament 1646, bishops' lands 1646, obstructions 1648, scandalous offences 1648; Councillor of State 25 Feb.–31 May 1660.

Lewis, the grandson of a Brecon mercer, inherited a Welsh estate of £600 p.a.; but on his marriage to a Hampshire widow he leased a small property, three miles from Petersfield, from the bishop of Winchester. A ship-money sheriff and a devout Presbyterian, he was returned for the borough at both elections of 1640, the first of his family to enter Parliament. He was appointed governor when Portsmouth capitulated to the parliamentary forces in 1642, and served on the Hampshire committee during the first Civil War. But he was forced by the army to withdraw from Parliament in 1647, and treated with particular severity at Pride's Purge, being unable to obtain his release till 1651. He was out of politics till the return of the secluded Members, when he was elected to the Council of State. He was reckoned at this time among the leaders of the moderate Presbyterian group which aimed at a conditional restoration.[5]

Lewis was elected for his native county in 1660, and listed by Lord Wharton as a friend. When the Convention met, he seconded the nomination of the 'rigid' Protectorate official Jessop as clerk of the Commons, but he undertook privately not to call in question the elections of Cavaliers and their sons, contrary to the last ordinance of the Long Parliament. An active Member, he took a prominent part in devising the legislation necessary for the Restoration. He made 25 recorded speeches and was appointed to 61 committees, helping to manage five conferences and to prepare for four others, and acted as teller in three divisions. He also took a prominent part in preparing for the Restoration. He was among those ordered to draft a reply to the King's letter, to consider the necessary legal forms and to prepare an answer to the Declaration of Breda, and he was twice sent to the Lords to ensure that the two Houses kept in step. He helped to draft the instructions for the messengers to the King, and served on the joint committee to arrange for his reception. He was appointed to the committee for the indemnity bill on 15 May, and helped to manage a conference on the regicides four days later and to prepare for another. He was on the drafting committees for a letter to congratulate the King on his safe arrival and for a petition for a day of thanksgiving. In the proceedings on the indemnity bill he was teller for the motions to except no more than 20 from the benefits of its provisions and for imposing no more penalty on Francis Lascelles* than on John Hutchinson*. He was appointed to the committees to inquire into the publication of parliamentary proceedings and of unauthorized Anglican works, and to propose names for the army commission. On 2 July he urged that the indemnity bill should be passed before supply was granted 'that people may be more willing to pay'. He spoke 'excellently' against the proposal to except those who would not take the oath of supremacy, 'though he were no friend to the Papists'. On 11 July he had the satisfaction, with Arthur Annesley*, of carrying the bill to the Lords. On the report from the grand committee for religion on 20 July he seconded the motion of Sir Anthony Ashley Cooper* for an address for a synod. In the debate on settling ecclesiastical livings on 30 July 'Sir William Lewis said 'twas impossible to come *per saltum* to the old government, but to let it alone to the King's consideration, and not press so earnestly for the subscribing the articles'. It was at once agreed to refer the matter to a committee, to which he was appointed. He was also named to the revenue committee. On 4 Aug. William Wilde* was ordered to hand over to Lewis for the use of his constituency an acquittance given by the former assessment commissioners. When the King reminded Parliament of the urgency of providing for the pay of the army and navy, Lewis hoped that this would encourage the Lords to expedite the passing of the indemnity bill, and he was among those appointed to prepare for a conference; but he could not accept the Lords' arguments for expanding the scope of the bill. He also helped to draft the protestation on the missing college leases bill, to manage the con-

ference on the indemnity bill on 22 Aug., and to consider the establishment for Dunkirk.[6]

After the recess, Lewis was appointed to the committees for the attainder bill and for the bill to prevent marital separation, although he had urged the House to reject it. On 16 Nov. he moved for more time to consider the militia bill. Wharton sent him a copy of the case for modified episcopacy, but he took no part in the debate. He was among those ordered to prepare for a conference on the college leases bill. On 22 Dec. he 'very handsomely' moved for a composition of the dispute about the excise bill between John Birch* and Edward King*. He carried the assessment bill to the Lords, and on the last day of the session proposed that part of the excise should be used for redeeming English slaves in Algiers.[7]

Lewis was unable to find a seat on his own interest in 1661. He was returned for Lymington after a contest, probably on the interest of John Bulkeley*, and again listed by Wharton as a friend. He was again an active Member of the Cavalier Parliament, with 206 committees, including those for the corporations and uniformity bills and the bill of pains and penalties, to which he succeeded in annexing a proviso in his own interests. In the first session he also helped to manage conferences on the bill to confirm private Acts, the corporations bill, the execution of those under attainder, and the loyal and indigent officers fund, and to prepare reasons on the poor law amendment bill. His only chairmanship was on Colfe's charities in 1664.[8]

On the dismissal of Clarendon, Lewis was appointed to the committees to draw up an address of thanks, to prepare a public accounts bill, to report on restraints on juries, to inquire into the miscarriages of the war, to establish precedents for impeachment, to reduce the charges against the fallen minister into heads, and to consider the bill to prevent the growth of Popery. His contributions to debate were not calculated to assist Clarendon's enemies; he emphasized the need to proceed legally, found nothing to substantiate the gravest charge of saying that the King was unfit to govern, and doubted whether the article on the sale of Dunkirk was properly based, because the bill to annex the town did not receive the royal assent. He blamed faulty intelligence for the losses in the Four Days' battle, and laid the responsibility at the door of Lord Arlington (Sir Henry Bennet*). Of the thirty or so speeches attributed to him by the diarists, however, most concerned points of procedure and order. It was presumably on procedural grounds rather than from intolerance that he opposed the reading of the Declaration of Breda in the House on 11 Mar. 1668, although no links with the Presbyterians can be traced at this time. Sir Thomas Osborne* listed him among the Members who usually voted for supply. He was among those instructed to consider the bill to prevent abuses in parliamentary elections in 1669 and to examine the debts of the navy in 1670. In 1674 he was appointed to the committees to consider the charges against Arlington and to prepare a general test. He moved to retain the petition of Bernard Howard 'till the rest of the bills of Popery come in'. His last important committee was for hindering Papists from sitting in Parliament, on the bill introduced in the autumn session of 1675. There is no evidence that he attended again after the long recess, although he had presumably moved into opposition, for Shaftesbury marked him 'thrice worthy'. His will was proved on 28 Nov. 1677. His only son, Lodowick Lewis†, who had sat with him in the Long Parliament as recruiter for Brecon, had predeceased him, and the estate was divided among his granddaughters, one of whom married John Lewis*.[9]

[1] Disabled 27 Jan. 1648, readmitted 8 June, secluded at Pride's Purge 6 Dec., readmitted 21 Feb. 1660. [2] Wards 7/51/264; PCC 102 Lawe. [3] CSP Dom. 1640, p. 438; R. East, Portsmouth Recs. 353, 357; E. King, Old Times Revisited, 178. [4] Ludlow Mems. i. 34; G. N. Godwin, Civil War in Hants, 76. [5] Keeler, Long Parl. 250-1; Eg. 1048, f. 74; D. Underdown, Pride's Purge, 195, 346; Clarendon, Rebellion, vi. 191. [6] Cal. Cl. SP, iv. 675, 686; CJ, viii. 11, 19, 38, 59, 60, 106, 115; Bowman diary, ff. 40v, 54v, 90v, 110v, 134. [7] Old Parl. Hist. xxiii. 13, 15, 65, 80; CJ, viii. 219, 233. [8] CJ, viii. 301, 332, 335, 355, 426, 431, 554. [9] Milward, 100; 214; Grey, i. 18; ii. 361; Clarendon Impeachment, 44; Jones, Brec. iii. 65.

M.W.H./P.W.

LEWIS see also LEWES

LEWKNOR, John I (1624–69), of Westdean, nr. Chichester, Suss.

MIDHURST   1661–3 Dec. 1669

b. 11 Mar. 1624, o.s. of Richard Lewknor of Westdean by Mary, da. of Thomas Bennet, Mercer, of Cheapside, London and Babraham, Cambs. educ. M. Temple, entered 1638; St. John's, Oxf. 1639. m. lic. 19 Apr. 1649, Anne, da. and coh. of George Mynne, clerk of the hanaper, of Woodcote, Epsom, Surr., 1s. 3da. suc. fa. 1635; KB 23 Apr. 1661.[1]

Capt. of dgns. (royalist) 1643–6.[2]
J.p. Suss. July 1660–d., dep. lt. c. Aug. 1660–d., commr. for assessment Aug. 1660–d., sewers, W. Suss. Oct. 1660, loyal and indigent officers, Suss. 1662; freeman, Portsmouth 1667.[3]

Lewknor's ancestors had been Sussex gentry since the reign of Edward I, first representing the county in 1336. His uncle sat for Chichester in the Long Parliament and commanded a Cavalier regiment in the Civil War. Lewknor's own involvement

was less voluntary, as he told the commissioners for compounding. During the advance of Hopton's army into Sussex in 1643, a disorderly party of parliamentary soldiers sacked his house and assaulted him, with 'no other allegation or pretext against him, save that he had some of his name on the adverse party'. Lewknor took refuge with the Cavaliers, and was in arms until the surrender of Barnstaple in 1646. He was denied the benefit of the articles, and ordered to pay £1,440 to compound for his delinquency; but the fine was discharged on his settling £150 p.a. for the support of the local clergy. He was looked upon as a person who would engage for the King in 1651, but apparently took no part in royalist conspiracy during the Interregnum. His estate was assessed for decimation purposes at £700 p.a.[4]

At the general election of 1661 Lewknor was returned for Midhurst, the family borough, six miles from his home. He was appointed only to five committees, consisting of the committee of elections and privileges for the first three sessions of the Cavalier Parliament and those to establish a registry of pawnbrokers in 1661 and to inquire into the decay of trade in 1664. On 15 Dec. 1666 he defaulted at a call of the House, but shortly before his death he was included by Sir Thomas Osborne* among those who had usually voted for supply. He died on 3 Dec. 1669, and was buried at Westdean. His widow married Sir William Morley*.[5]

[1] Vis. Suss. (Harl. Soc. lxxxix), 72; Add. 5699, f. 202v. [2] List of Officers Claiming (1663), 72. [3] C181/7/58; R. East, Portsmouth Recs. 359. [4] Suss. Arch. Colls. iii. 92; Keeler, Long Parl. 251; SP23/186, ff. 593, 596; HMC Portland, i. 578; Thurloe, iv. 240. [5] J. Comber, Suss. Genealogies Lewes, 156.

B.M.C.

LEWKNOR, John II (1658–1707), of Westdean, nr. Chichester, Suss.

SUSSEX   1679 (Mar.)
MIDHURST   1679 (Oct.), 1685, 1689, 1690, 1695, 1698, 1701 (Feb.), 1701 (Dec.), 1702

b. 24 Apr. 1658, o.s. of John Lewknor I*. educ. Christ Church, Oxf. 1673; M. Temple 1675. m. lic. 27 Aug. 1679, Jane, da. of Charles Marescoe, merchant, of London, s.p. suc. fa. 1669.[1]

Commr. for assessment, Suss. 1677–80, 1689–90, j.p. 1680–96, 1700–d., dep. lt. 1685–?89; common councilman, Chichester 1685–Oct. 1688.[2]

As Lewknor's epitaph recorded, he was still under age when he was returned to the first Exclusion Parliament as knight of the shire. Marked 'base' on Shaftesbury's list, he voted against the bill. At the autumn election of 1679 he transferred to the family borough of Midhurst, but throughout the period he served on no committees and made no speeches. On 7 Jan. 1681 he was given leave to go into the country, but at the next election, two months later, he was replaced by William Montagu II*, already or soon to become his wife's paramour. He was appointed to the Chichester corporation under the new charter. By 1685 Lewknor had discovered the intrigue and spent highly to defeat his rival at Midhurst. He was to retain this seat in the next seven Parliaments. Montagu and his father had to give security of £1,500 against further misconduct; but in December the couple eloped.[3]

To the lord lieutenant's questions in 1688, Lewknor replied that he would 'consent readily to the abrogating of the Penal Laws and Tests, provided that the Church of England may be secured by Act of Parliament in her legal rights and possessions'. This was construed as a favourable answer; he remained in local office, and was recommended to the Roman Catholic Viscount Montagu as court candidate for Midhurst. In the Convention, according to Ailesbury's list, he voted to agree with the Lords that the throne was not vacant. He is also said to have supported the disabling clause in the bill to restore corporations, perhaps to prevent Whig opposition to his bill to illegitimize his wife's children, which was never reported from committee. He later acted with the Tories, at first refusing to sign the Association in 1696. He died on 19 Feb. 1707, and was buried at Westdean. His cousin and heir, William Knight[†], sat for Midhurst from 1713 to his death.[4]

[1] J. Comber, *Suss. Genealogies Lewes*, 156; *London Mar. Lic.* ed. Foster, 844; PCC 114 Penn. [2] *HMC Lords*, i. 190; PC2/76/49, 78/67; A. Hay, *Hist. Chichester*, 589. [3] G. Eland, *Shardeloes Pprs.* 83–90; Bodl. Rawl. mss B378, ff. 103–203; Add. 24852, ff. 10–12. [4] *CJ*, x. 336; Add. 5699, f. 203.

B.M.C.

LIDDELL, Henry (c.1644–1723), of Ravensworth Castle, co. Dur.

DURHAM	1689, 1695
NEWCASTLE-UPON-TYNE	1701 (Feb.), 1701 (Dec.), 1702, 2 Jan. 1706, 1708

b. c.1644, 1st s. of Sir Thomas Liddell, 2nd Bt., of Ravensworth by Anne, da. of Sir Henry Vane[†] of Raby Castle. *educ.* I. Temple 1662; travelled abroad 1662–5. *m.* by 1670, Catherine (*bur.* 24 Feb. 1704), da. of Sir John Bright,[†] 1st Bt., of Badsworth, Yorks., 5s. (1 *d.v.p.*) 1da. *suc.* fa. as 3rd Bt. Nov. 1697.[1]

Commr. for assessment, co. Dur. 1677–80, co. Dur. and Yorks. (W. Riding) 1689–90; j.p. co. Dur. 1680–7, Nov. 1688–?*d.*, (W. Riding) by 1701–?*d.*; dep. lt. co. Dur. 1701–?*d.*, sheriff 1721–2.[2]

Liddell was descended from an Elizabethan merchant adventurer of Newcastle. His grandfather acquired the Ravensworth estate with its valuable

collieries in 1607, and was fined £4,000 as a royalist commissioner of array during the Civil War. But his father married the daughter of the radical enthusiast, the younger Sir Henry Vane; he became a devout Presbyterian and took no part in politics.[3]

Liddell's appointment to the commission of the peace in his father's lifetime in 1680 suggests that he had reverted to his grandfather's politics, and opposed exclusion. He was removed in 1687 by order of the Privy Council but reinstated after the Dutch invasion. He was returned for the city of Durham at the abortive election in December 1688, and became the first member of the family to enter Parliament when he defeated the Tory William Tempest* in the following month. Nevertheless according to Ailesbury's list he voted to agree with the Lords that the throne was not vacant. He was an inactive Member of the Convention, being appointed only to the committees to consider abuses in alnage and to settle allowances on the children of Sidney Wortley Montagu*. He did not stand in 1690, and went to Holland in August. He was a court Whig under William III and Anne. He died on 1 Sept. 1723, and was buried at Kensington. A younger son sat for Berwick-upon-Tweed from 1727 to 1740, and his grandson and heir represented Morpeth from 1734 as a government supporter until raised to the peerage in 1747.[4]

[1] Surtees, *Dur.* ii. 212–13; *CSP Dom.* 1661–2, p. 509. [2] Dur. RO, sessions order bks. 7; *CSP Dom.* 1700–2, p. 255. [3] Surtees, ii. 209, 212–13; *Cal. Comm. Comp.* 892; R. Welford, *Men of Mark 'twixt Tyne and Tweed*, iii. 42, 44. [4] C. Sharp, *Parl. Rep. Dur.* (1831), 35–36; *CSP Dom.* 1690–1, p. 96; Surtees, ii. 213.

G.H./G.J.

LINDFIELD, Gilbert (d.1680), of Upper Brook Street, Ipswich, Suff.

IPSWICH	22 Jan. 1674, 1679 (Mar.), 1679 (Oct.)–8 Dec. 1680 [new writ]

m. Bridget, da. of John Smythier, merchant, of Ipswich.[1]

Chamberlain, Ipswich 1652–3, common councilman 1658, portman 1663, bailiff 1665–6, 1671–2, 1678–9; capt. of militia ft. Suff. by 1661, maj. by 1676; commr. for assessment, Ipswich 1663–d., recusants, Suff. 1675.[2]

Nothing is known of Lindfield's origins, but he married the daughter of an Ipswich portman, and became one of the strongest supporters of the Restoration on the corporation. He signed the Suffolk petition for a free Parliament, helped to set up the royal arms in the town hall, and was reappointed 'portman', or alderman, in the charter of 1665. An innkeeper by trade, his premises at the sign of the *Greyhound* were of moderate dimensions, with only nine hearths; but they were licensed to retail wine, and chosen by the commissioners for the royal aid for the county as their meeting-place in 1665. He was himself a militia officer and one of the most active members of the corporation, being among those chosen to strike copper farthings for local use in 1669.[3]

Lindfield was first returned for the borough at a by-election to the Cavalier Parliament, taking his seat on 3 Feb. 1674. A moderately active Member, he was named to 35 committees, none of them of major political significance. The first was for a Suffolk charity bill sponsored by Sir John Pettus*. One of the comparatively few genuine 'burgesses' in the House, he was chiefly interested in naturalization bills, the suppression of pedlars, and the export of wool and leather. A court supporter, he was entrusted on the working lists to the management of the Speaker (Edward Seymour*), but Sir Richard Wiseman* apparently doubted his reliability. Shaftesbury classed him as 'doubly vile', and he was on both lists of the court party in 1678. Although blacklisted in the 'unanimous club', he was twice re-elected in 1679. In the first Exclusion Parliament Shaftesbury marked him 'vile'. His only committee was on the bill for exporting leather, and he voted against the committal of the exclusion bill. The corporation granted him £20 in 1680 for his services in Parliament, but he may never have taken his seat in the second Exclusion Parliament. A new writ was ordered on 8 Dec.[4]

[1] F. Haslewood, *Mon. Inscriptions from St. Matthew's*, 2. [2] *East Anglian*, n.s. ii. 99; iv. 218; vii. 91, 186, 347; viii. 302; information from Mr W. Serjeant, Suff. County Archivist. [3] *Suff. and the Gt. Rebellion* (Suff. Rec. Soc. iii), 129; *East Anglian* n.s. vi. 318; vii. 373; viii. 12; R. Canning, *Principal Charters of Ipswich*, 33; *Hearth Tax Returns* (Suff. Green Bks. xi), 171; Add. 39246, f. 21. [4] Add. 25335, f. 9.

P.W.

LINGEN, Sir Henry (1612–62), of Stoke Edith, Herefs.

HEREFORD   20 Nov. 1660, 9 Apr.–23 July 1661, 24 Sept. 1661–Jan. 1662

b. 23 Oct. 1612, 1st s. of Edward Lingen of Stoke Edith by Blanche, da. of Sir Robert Bodenham of Rotherwas. *educ.* M. Temple 1629. *m.* 3 Apr. 1626 (with £1,000), Alice, da. of Sir Walter Pye† of The Mynde, Much Dewchurch, 3s. (1 *d.v.p.*) 6da. *suc.* fa. 1635; kntd. 6 July 1645.[1]

J.p. Herefs. by 1634–46, July 1660–*d.*, sheriff 1638–9, 1643–4, commr. of array 1643, oyer and terminer, Oxford circuit July 1660, assessment, Herefs. Aug. 1660–*d.*, Hereford 1661–*d.*; dep. lt. Herefs. c. Aug. 1660–*d.*

Col. of ft. (royalist) 1643–6, 1648; gov. Goodrich Castle 1645–6.[2]

Lingen's ancestors had been seated in Herefordshire since the reign of Henry III, though their acquisition of Stoke Edith, six miles from the county town, was comparatively recent. They first represented the county under Edward III. Lingen's father, a Roman Catholic, was imprisoned by the council in the marches, first for refusing to pay alimony to his estranged wife, and then on the grounds of insanity, but he was restored to his property by order of the Privy Council. Lingen, who was himself brought up as an Anglican by the first Lord Scudamore, was one of the ship-money sheriffs, and during the Civil War he was the most energetic royalist commander in the county, and the last to surrender. His fine of £4,270 was set at the maximum rate and was later increased to £6,008 after he had taken part in the second Civil War, in which he was seriously wounded. He remained an active Royalist throughout the Interregnum, and was proposed as a knight of the Royal Oak at the Restoration, with an estate of £2,000 p.a.[3]

Lingen, debarred as a Cavalier from standing at the general election of 1660, supported the candidature of Thomas Prise* for the county. He was himself returned at a by-election for Hereford, where he was highly esteemed, but was totally inactive in the Convention. There was no opposition offered to him personally in 1661, but he insisted on the mayor's returning Sir Edward Hopton* to the second seat. There was a double return with Herbert Westfaling*, but Lingen was allowed to take his seat in the Cavalier Parliament at once, and on 11 May was named to the committee of elections and privileges. Though not an active Member, he was also appointed to the committees on the bills for confirming public acts and restoring advowsons. From the elections committee (Sir) Job Charlton* recommended that only Hopton's election should be declared void, which would have enabled Lingen to retain the parliamentary privilege that he required to shelter him from his creditors; but the House resolved to quash the whole election. Lingen was re-elected with Westfaling, but left no further trace in the Journals, dying of smallpox at Gloucester on his way home for the Christmas recess. He was buried at Stoke Edith on 22 Jan. 1662. After his death, his widow was granted some compensation for his losses, but his sons died without issue, and in 1670 Stoke Edith was sold to Paul Foley* for £6,100.[4]

[1] C. J. Robinson, *Mansions and Manors of Herefs.* 179–80; Wards 7/88/70; *Her. and Gen.* v. 137. [2] J. Webb, *Civil War in Herefs.* i. 300; ii. 280. [3] Duncumb, *Herefs.* ii. 184–5; T. Coningsby, *Manor of Marden*, i. 529; CSP Dom. 1634–5, pp. 60, 91, 373; *Cal. Comm. Comp.* 1525–6; *Cal. Cl. SP*, i. 440; D. Underdown, *Royalist Conspiracy*, 35, 242. [4] *HMC Portland*, iii. 220; *Military Mem. of Col. Birch* (Cam. Soc. n.s. vii), 141; R. Johnson, *Ancient Customs of Hereford*, 149–53; *CJ*, viii. 251, 308; Coningsby, i. 538.

M.W.H./E.R.

LISLE, William (c.1632–1716), of the Middle Temple, London and Evenley, nr. Brackley, Northants.

BRACKLEY 1659, 1660, 1679 (Mar.), 1681

b. c.1632, 1st s. of Tobias Lisle, Grocer, of Cannon Street, London and Saffron Hill, Mdx. by Susan, da. of Richard Trist of Maidford, Northants. *educ.* Magdalen Coll. Oxf. 1651; M. Temple 1650, called 1659. *m.* 9 Nov. 1661, Elizabeth, da. of John Aylworth of the Middle Temple and Polsloe, Devon, 5s. 5da. *suc.* fa. 1659, uncle William Lisle† at Evenley 1665.[1]
    Lt. vol. horse, Northants. 1662, capt. of militia 1663, col. ?1673–bef. 1680, commr. for assessment 1665–80, 1689–90, j.p. 1689–*d.*[2]
    Master in Chancery June–Nov. 1665.[3]

Lisle's grandfather, who claimed to be an off-shoot of the Northumberland family, settled in Brackley in Elizabethan times, and acquired the advowson of St. Peter's. His uncle sat for the borough in the first Parliament of James I, and served on the Northamptonshire assessment committee during the Civil War and the Commonwealth. Lisle's father, a woollen draper ranked in the third class of wealthy citizens in 1640, was a Presbyterian elder; but he accepted the Protectorate, serving as j.p. for Middlesex after his retirement from business until his death. Lisle was presumably sent to Magdalen because the college was one of the principal landowners in Brackley. He became a lawyer, and represented the borough, two miles from his uncle's home, in Richard Cromwell's Parliament. To strengthen the family interest for the 1660 election, his uncle executed a will on 12 Mar. 'in the 12th year of the reign of our sovereign lord Charles II', bequeathing £120 to the poor of the borough to be disposed of by the mayor with Lisle's advice. John Crew* was one of the trustees with whom Lisle's bond to perform the will was deposited. Lisle was duly returned to the Convention, probably as one of the Presbyterian Opposition, though he served on no committees and made no recorded speeches, and he did not stand for re-election in 1661. But he achieved recognition in county society by serving under Sir Roger Norwich* in a volunteer troop raised to supervise the demolition of the defences of Northampton and winning some reputation as a gentleman jockey.[4]

Lisle abandoned his profession when he succeeded to the Evenley estate, valued at £700 p.a., but he does not seem to have been appointed to the commission of the peace until after the Revolution, perhaps owing to scruples of conscience over the oath. However, he regained his seat on the dissolution of the Cavalier Parliament. Unmarked on Shaftesbury's and Huntingdon's lists, he was named only to the committee for the privilege case

between Sir William Blackett* and Humphrey Wharton*, and was absent from the division on the exclusion bill. He lost his seat at the general election, but regained it in 1681. He left no trace on the records of the Oxford Parliament, but after its dissolution he was described as 'a violent man in Parliament, served for Brackley and it is feared will be chose again'. He was one of the Northamptonshire Whigs presented as disaffected by the grand jury in 1683. Although he lived for another 30 years, neither he nor any other member of his family appears to have stood for Parliament again. He died on 12 July 1716, aged 84, and was buried at Evenley.[5]

[1] *Vis. Northants.* (Harl. Soc. lxxxvii), 122–4; Baker, *Northants.* i. 612; *Smith's Obituary* (Cam. Soc. xliv), 50. [2] SP29/26/75; Add. 34222, f. 56; Northants. RO, FH 2226. [3] T. D. Hardy, *Principal Officers of Chancery*, 94. [4] Baker, i. 574–6; *Misc. Gen. et Her.* (ser. 2), ii. 51; *Fourth London Classis Reg.* ed. Surman, 2; PCC 29 Hyde; *Diary of Thomas Isham*, 151, 231. [5] SP29/421/216; *Somers Tracts*, viii. 410.

M.W.H./E.R.E.

LITTLETON, Edward (1653–1705), of Pillaton Hall, Staffs.

STAFFORDSHIRE 1685

bap. 17 Sept. 1653, 1st s. of Sir Edward Littleton, 2nd Bt.*, by 1st w. *educ.* Queen's, Oxf. 1670. *m.* 24 Jan. 1671, Susannah, da. of Sir Theophilus Biddulph*, 1st Bt., of Westcombe Park, Greenwich, Kent, 3s. 6da.[1]
    Commr. for assessment, Staffs. 1673–80, Staffs. and Herefs. 1689–90, sheriff, Staffs. 1680–1; j.p. Staffs. 1687–*d.*, Herefs. by 1701–*d.*; dep. lt. Staffs. 1689–?*d.*, Herefs. by 1694–?*d.*[2]

Although Littleton was only 17 when he married, he probably took up residence at once in the family home, his father and step-mother moving to Tamworth. He was more interested in racing than in politics, and was nominated as candidate for the county at a gentry meeting in 1685 without any effort on his part. It was even suggested that a subscription should be taken to finance his election expenses. He is not known to have spoken and he was appointed only to the committee on the bill for relief of poor debtors. To the lord lieutenant's questions on the Test Act and Penal Laws he replied that he could neither consent to their repeal nor promise to vote for candidates who would. There is no evidence, however, that he was removed from the commission of the peace, and he presumably supported the Revolution, since he was added to the lieutenancy in 1689. He is not known to have stood again. He died on 24 Jan. 1705 in his father's lifetime. His grandson sat for the county from 1784 till his death in 1812.[3]

[1] J. C. Tildesley, *Hist. Penkridge*, 28; Lysons, *Environs*, iv. 477.

Littleton (Lyttelton) Family

Sir Thomas (the jurist)

Thomas of Spetchley — John

Sir Edward of Henley
- Timothy*
- Sir Edward† (Lord Lyttelton)

Thomas of Stoke

Sir Adam, *m.* Etheldreda Poyntz, 1st Bt.

Sir Thomas, 2nd Bt.*

Sir Thomas, 3rd Bt.*

Richard† of Baxterley

Sir Edward† of Pillaton

Sir Edward

Sir Edward†

Sir Edward†

Sir Edward, 1st Bt.†

Sir Edward, 2nd Bt.*

Edward* →

Sir William of Frankley

John

Sir John†

Gilbert†

John

Sir Thomas, 1st Bt.†

Sir Charles Lyttelton* →

Sir Henry Lyttelton, 2nd Bt.*

[2] *Staffs. Dep. Lts.* (Wm. Salt Arch. Soc. 1931), 285. [3] Wm. Salt Lib. D1721/3/291, Littleton to Bagot, 6 Mar. 1685, Broughton to Bagot, 7 Mar. 1685, Sneyd to Bagot, 18 Mar. 1685; *Staffs. Parl. Hist.* (Wm. Salt Arch. Soc.), ii. 157-8.

A.M.M.

LITTLETON, Sir Edward, 2nd Bt. (c.1632–1709), of Pillaton Hall and The Moat House, Tamworth, Staffs.

STAFFORDSHIRE 5 Mar. 1663

b. c.1632, o.s. of Sir Edward Littleton, 1st Bt.[†], of Pillaton Hall by 1st w. Hester, da. of Sir William Courten, merchant, of London. *educ.* Shrewsbury 1644. *m.* (1) c.1650, Mary (*d.*1665), da. of Sir Walter Wrottesley, 1st Bt., of Wrottesley, 3s. (2 *d.v.p.*) 6da.; (2) by 1674, his cos. Joyce, da. of Edward (or George) Littleton of Shuston, Church Eaton, 5s. 2da. *suc.* fa. Aug. 1657.[1]

Commr. for oyer and terminer, Oxford circuit July 1660; j.p. Staffs. July 1660–Mar. 1688, Oct. 1688–*d.*; dep. lt. Staffs. c. Aug. 1660–80, 1689–1703, Herefs. by 1701–?3; commr. for assessment, Staffs. Aug. 1660–80, Herefs. and Staffs. 1689–90; capt. vol. horse, Staffs. by 1662, commr. for recusants 1675.[2]

Gent. of privy chamber 1671–85, 1692–1702.[3]

Littleton was descended from the great lawyer through his second son, who married the heiress of Pillaton and sat for Ludlow in 1491–2. His father, a ship-money sheriff, was returned for Staffordshire at both elections of 1640 as a supporter of the country party. He served on the county committee, but went over to the King in 1643, and sat at Oxford. He was taken prisoner at the fall of Worcester in 1646, but was unable to compound owing to his debts. However, the family trustees, Richard Knightley* and Richard Salway[†], bought back his forfeited estates.[4]

Littleton was included among the Staffordshire Royalists by Roger Whitley* in 1658. In a list of the county gentry drawn up in 1662, when he was 30, he was described as loyal, orthodox and sober, but of only ordinary parts. His estate was valued at £1,500 p.a. On 1 Nov. Lord Brooke, the lord lieutenant, wrote to Lord Chancellor Clarendon that he had persuaded all parties among the gentry to agree on Littleton as knight of the shire in succession to Sir Thomas Leigh*, but that he would be ineligible if he were pricked as sheriff. He avoided the unpopular office, and was elected to the Cavalier Parliament, probably unopposed, four months later. An inactive Member, he was appointed to the committee of elections and privileges in four sessions, and to only seven others. In his first session he helped to consider the additional bill for the relief of loyal and indigent officers and to conduct the inquiry into the conduct of Sir Richard Temple*, and in 1664 he was among those to whom a petition from navy creditors was entrusted. His last committee was on 13 Nov. 1670, and shortly afterwards he purchased the Moat House at Tamworth, where he lived with his second wife, though the legitimacy of their three eldest children was apparently doubtful. On the working lists he was noted as under the influence of his colleague, Randolph Egerton*, but Shaftesbury marked him 'doubly worthy'. On 13 Dec. 1678 he was sent for in custody as a defaulter.[5]

It is unlikely that Littleton stood again. He may have supported exclusion, since he was dropped from the lieutenancy in 1680, and it was his son who represented the county in James II's Parliament. He evaded the questions on the repeal of the Test Act and Penal Laws, and was removed from the commission of the peace. But he accepted the Revolution. He was buried at Tamworth on 31 July 1709. His will does not mention his grandchildren by his first wife.[6]

[1] *Gentry of Staffs.* (Staffs. Rec. Soc. ser. 4, ii), 21; J. E. Auden, *Shrewsbury Sch. Reg.* 26; *Staffs. Peds.* (Harl. Soc. lxiii), 157–8. [2] *Gentry of Staffs.* 21; *Staffs. Hist. Colls.* (1931), 285. [3] Carlisle, *Privy Chamber*, 188, 208. [4] Keeler, *Long Parl.* 254; *Staffs. Parl. Hist.* (Wm. Salt Arch. Soc.), ii. 58–61; *Cal. Comm. Comp.* 2080–2. [5] *Gentry of Staffs.* 21; *Cal. Cl. SP*, v. 279; Shaw, *Staffs.* i. 422. [6] *Staffs. Parl. Hist.* (Wm. Salt Arch. Soc.), ii. 121–2; Add. 28176, f. 228.

A.M.M.

LITTLETON alias POYNTZ, Sir Thomas, 2nd Bt. (c.1621–81), of Stoke St. Milborough, Salop and Lincoln's Inn Fields, Mdx.

MUCH WENLOCK 1640 (Apr.), 1640 (Nov.)–5 Feb. 1644, 1661
EAST GRINSTEAD 19 Apr. 1679
YARMOUTH I.o.W. 1681

b. c.1621, 1st s. of Sir Adam Littleton, 1st Bt., of Stoke St. Milborough by Etheldreda, da. and h. of Thomas Poyntz of North Ockenden, Essex. *educ.* I. Temple, entered 1636, called 1642; Jesus, Oxf. matric. 15 June 1638, aged 16. *m.* lic. 6 Oct. 1637, aged 17, Anne, da. and h. of Edward Littleton[†], 1st Baron Lyttelton of Mounslow, 2s. *suc.* fa. Sept. 1647.[1]

Commr. of array, Salop 1642, assessment 1661–3, 1664–74, Westminster 1661–80, Mdx. 1661–3, 1673–80, Essex 1664–80, corporations, Salop 1662–3; conservator, Bedford level 1665–8; commr. for concealments, Mdx. and Surr. 1670, recusants, Salop 1675; j.p. Mdx. and Westminster by 1680–*d.*[2]

Jt. treas. of the navy 1668–71, victualler 1671–3; commr. for trade 1668–72, union with Scotland 1670; ld. of Admiralty 1680–*d.*[3]

The Shropshire Littletons were descended from the youngest son of the great 15th-century lawyer. Unlike their cousins of the Staffordshire and Worcestershire branches, they did not enter Parliament before Stuart times. Littleton's father was apparently neutral in the Civil War, though his interest as recorder of Wenlock facilitated Littleton's return for the borough in both elections of 1640. Under the influence of his father-in-law, the lord keeper, he became an active Royalist, compounding in 1646 at £307 after settling tithes of £180 p.a. on the local churches.[4]

Littleton signed the Cavalier declaration of 1660 disclaiming animosity towards their former enemies. He is unlikely to have defied the Long Parliament ordinance by standing at the general election, but regained his seat in 1661. A very active Member of the Cavalier Parliament, he was appointed to 381 committees, in nine of which he took the chair, acted as teller in 18 divisions, and made 304 speeches. In the opening session, he was named to the committees for the uniformity bill and the execution of those under attainder, and took the chair for a Shropshire estate bill. A 'country Cavalier', he moved an unsuccessful proviso to the hearth-tax in grand committee in March 1662. He helped to manage two conferences on the bill for the repair of highways in London and Westminster, and twice acted as teller for the Bedford level bill. On 17 May he was sent to the Lords to ask for a conference on the militia bill. In 1663 he took part in the inquiry into the conduct of Sir Richard Temple*, and acted unsuccessfully as teller against the bill to prevent sectarian meetings. He took the chair for the bill to settle the poor in the parishes of their birth, and carried up the staple bill on 25 July. In 1664 he sought to postpone debate on the repeal of the Triennial Act, and helped to manage a conference on the conventicles bill. On the outbreak of the second Dutch war he would have granted only one-fifth of the £2,500,000 demanded by the Government. He reported a deficiency of £5,000 in the accounts of the loyal and indigent officers fund on 20 Dec., for which the receiver for Cornwall was responsible. In the Oxford session he was named to the committee for the five mile bill. In pursuit of office he had attached himself to Lord Arlington (Sir Henry Bennet*), and by promoting the ban on Irish cattle imports he helped to undermine the position of Clarendon's ally, Ormonde; as chairman of the committee he gave his casting vote for the bill. In 1666 he acted as teller for a bill for the preservation of naval stores and was named to the delegation from the House to ask the King to prohibit the import of French goods. He helped to prepare reasons for the ban on Irish cattle and the withdrawal of the Canaries Company patent, and was named to the abortive parliamentary accounts commission. He resisted the government proposals for the additional excise, both in debate and divi-

sion, earning from Andrew Marvell* the sobriquet of 'great Littleton'. He attended conferences on the conduct of Clarendon's friend Lord Mordaunt, and on the coinage and plague bills, and reported a bill for the better attendance of those Members who had not followed his example by taking up permanent residence in London. By now he was accounted one of the foremost speakers in the Commons, and (Sir) William Penn* described him to Samuel Pepys* as 'the usual second to the great [John] Vaughan*'. Burnet, who later became his next-door neighbour in Lincoln's Inn Fields, wrote:

> Littleton was the ablest and vehementest arguer of them all. He commonly lay quiet till the end of a debate; and he often ended it, speaking with a strain of conviction and authority that was not easily resisted. . . . A man of strong head and sound judgment, he had just as much knowledge in trade, history, and the disposition of Europe and the constitution of England as served to feed and direct his own thoughts, and no more.[5]

The fall of Clarendon opened up new vistas for the ambitious, and Littleton took a leading part in the next session. He helped to draft the address of thanks for the chancellor's dismissal, and served on all the principal committees of inquiry into the late administration. Clarendon, he said, 'being chief minister of state, and taking upon him the sole management of the Government, must either be guilty, or be able to clear himself by laying it justly upon others'. He chaired the committee to reduce the charges into heads, and undertook to prove five of them himself. On 18 Nov. he reported reasons why the Lords should order Clarendon's arrest, and was sent to desire a conference. After the fallen minister's flight he was named to the committee for the banishment bill. Despite his Cavalier background he was one of the leaders of the 'Presbyterian' party in Parliament; he declared on 11 Mar. 1668 that 'so long as the Church was true to itself, the nonconformists never hurt the Church', and that the causes of all religious controversies were the 'new ceremonies' introduced by Laud. A week later he spoke against excepting the clergy from paying the subsidy. He helped to prepare Penn's impeachment and to carry it up, and was among those ordered to prepare a clause in the supply bill appropriating the new revenue to the use of the summer fleet. In November Arlington obtained for him the lucrative post of treasurer of the navy, though he had to share the office with Buckingham's candidate, Sir Thomas Osborne*. He was included as a placeman in both lists of the court party at this time, and when Parliament met again in the autumn of 1669, a pamphlet, *The Alarum*, was distributed to Members, in which he was described as 'an angry man against the Court until silenced by a good place, and is now content that everything should be let alone, having got what he grumbled for'. He repeatedly spoke for supply in 1670, declaring that the money granted two years before had proved quite inadequate to the needs of the navy. He helped to manage conferences on the new impositions and on cattle frauds, and took the chair on the bill to preserve naval stores in April 1671; but during the recess Osborne succeeded in evicting him from his office on charges of malad-ministration and corruption, though he received a valuable victualling contract as compensation.[6]

For the remainder of the Cavalier Parliament Littleton, was in opposition, and had a hand in all their favourite measures. Vaughan had been removed to the judicial bench, but the Arlington group had been reinforced by Henry Powle*. Burnet judged that Littleton and Powle were 'the men that laid the matters in the House with the greatest care'. In February 1673 he acted as a teller for a motion to search for precedents for the issue of by-election writs while Parliament was not in session. He helped to prepare the address against the suspending power, but supported easing Prot-estant dissenters by statute. In the autumn session Arlington's followers attacked the choice of Edward Seymour* as Speaker, and Sir Edward Dering* reported:

> Sir Thomas Littleton in a set speech moved that we might have another Speaker, because he was a Privy Council-lor and so not proper to be trusted with the secrets of the House; secondly, because being in that high sphere he was now above the place of Speaker, nor was it fit he, who was now one of the governors of the world, should be servant to the House of Commons; thirdly, that he had other eminent places and employment which would take up his time so much as he could not attend the service of the House with that diligence he ought to do; and lastly, that the House had formerly occasion to question the management of the treasury of the Navy, and if it should have to again it would be a very unkind thing that he who is questioned should sit in the chair at the debates, when it was not fit he should so much as hear the debates.

Next month, at a meeting at the Admiralty to con-sider renewing the contract for victualling the navy, Osborne used the words 'a cheat upon the King' to describe the last contract. Littleton retorted 'no more cheat than he that said it', and Osborne told Littleton that 'he would deal with him elsewhere, that he was a cheat or knave, and he would prove it'. Littleton lost the contract. His accounts as treasurer and as victualler of the navy were never cleared, and though Osborne, now Lord Treasurer Danby, began proceedings against him, they came to nothing. In January 1674 he moved for the dis-

missal of Danby's ally Lauderdale, and opposed the impeachment of his own patron, Arlington, though he was added to the committee on 26 Jan. 1674. He reported reasons for a conference on the address accepting peace with Holland. He incensed (Sir) Robert Thomas* by failing to substantiate the charge of Popery against Pepys. But before the next session Danby wrote to the King:

> Sir Thomas Littleton, who besides the great knaveries already known to his Majesty both in Parliament and his offices, and near £90,000 brought in post abstracts to his accounts, sets himself industriously, not only to traduce me in all kinds, but is in perpetual cabals against his Majesty to prepare fuel for the Parliament, and that nothing should be believed which his Majesty does say.

It was even alleged that Littleton had resorted to bribery to procure evidence against his former col-league, though the witness of course denied it. On 14 Apr. 1675 he was appointed to the committee to draw up an address for the removal of Lauderdale. A fortnight later, when he was pressing for Danby's impeachment, Giles Strangways* observed: 'I am not for a general accusation, when I have heard some gentlemen speak one way when they have of-fices, and another when they have none, and fall out when they cannot agree about sharing the revenue among them'. Littleton suspected an allusion to him-self, but eventually agreed to let the matter drop.

> I beware saying anything in my own concern, though injured in the highest manner, even by erasing of a record and patent detrimentally taken from me, and a bargain broke made upon a valuable consideration, and I exposed to utter ruin and a statute of bankruptcy taken out against me to be tried Friday next. Pray God forgive the promoters of it. I had an office at Court, but it was at the time when the Triple League was newly entered into, and no religion nor property like to be invaded or in danger at all; but as soon as the French League was made, I lost the favour of a great man. But I would have you take notice that the great men are gone more from me than I from them, and no man runs greater hazards for the service of his country than I do at this time.

He continued to press for Danby's impeachment, and demanded an examination of secret service accounts. He supported a motion for recalling Brit-ish subjects from the French service, and reported an address on 20 May. He took part in three con-ferences on the disputes over the Lords' jurisdic-tion. In the autumn session he reported the refusal of Col. Thomas Howard to confirm or deny his challenge to William Cavendish*, Lord Cavendish, and acted as teller against the adjournment of a debate on appropriation. Classed as 'worthy' by Shaftesbury in 1677, he feared that the bill for edu-cating the royal children as Protestants under the bishops' supervision would 'rather promote than hinder Popery', because we have had a sort of clergy ever since Archbishop Laud's time too much addicted to Popery. Archbishop Laud professed that it was the best way for us to unite with the Papists, and that was his whole endeavour; and men of that leaven are still in the Church.

He seconded a motion for an alliance against France, though he was himself on close terms with the French ambassador from whom he received a bribe of £500. He helped to draw up two addresses on foreign policy in this session, and took a leading part in the stormy debates of 1678 that shattered Danby's court party. He was among those instructed to draw up the addresses on the terms of peace (28 Jan.) and for the removal of counsellors (7 May). In the closing session he was named to the committee to inquire into the Popish Plot and helped to draw up reasons for believing in it. On 14 Nov. he reported an address for administering the oaths to the servants of the Queen and the duchess of York. He again helped to draw up Danby's impeachment, though he subscribed privately to the undertaking given by Denzil Holles* that it would be dropped if Parliament were dissolved, and the minister dismissed.[7]

Littleton's continuous residence in London had undermined his interest at Wenlock. He was defeated at the general election, but Powle brought him in at a by-election for East Grinstead. A moderately active Member of the first Exclusion Parliament, he was appointed to nine committees and made eight speeches, but he was one of the Members 'accounted the greatest zealots' in the last Parliament who could not keep pace with the tide of hostility towards the Court. He helped to prepare reasons for disallowing Danby's pardon and addresses for the removal of Lauderdale and the calling up of the militia in the home counties. He took part in a conference on the trial of the lords in the Tower, but opposed the exclusion bill, both in debate and division, as 'the most impractical thing imaginable'. He was unable to find a seat in the second Exclusion Parliament, but was given a place on the board of Admiralty. With Seymour and Laurence Hyde* he formed 'the triumvirate of ministers' reckoned as 'too high-spirited' to brook the dominance of Lord Halifax (Sir George Savile*). In 1681 he was defeated at Truro, but Sir Leoline Jenkins* instructed Sir Robert Holmes* to find him a seat in the Isle of Wight, and he was returned for Yarmouth. In the Oxford Parliament he was appointed to the committee to draw up the impeachment of Fitzharris. As an 'expedient' to break the deadlock on exclusion, he proposed that on the King's death his authority should devolve on the Princess of Orange:

A regency has been proposed to secure the administration of the Government in Protestant hands, so as not to alter the constitution of the monarchy; and this alters the constitution of the monarchy the least imaginable, to have a regency in the room of the King, and the monarchy goes on.

He died on 14 Apr. 1681 and was buried at North Ockendon.[8]

[1] *Trans. Salop Arch. Soc.* (ser. 3), ii. 327. [2] Bodl. Ch. Salop 146; S. Wells, *Drainage of Bedford Level*, i. 457–9; *Cal. Treas. Bks.* iii. 607. [3] *CSP Dom.* 1668–9, p. 56; 1671, p. 169; Browning, *Danby*, i. 65; *Bulstrode Pprs.* 17. [4] Keeler, *Long Parl.* 254–5; *Trans. Salop Arch. Soc.* (ser. 3), ii. 327–9; *Cal. Comm. Adv. Money*, 113, 428. [5] *DNB; Cal. Cl. SP*, v. 217; *CJ*, viii. 401, 416, 433, 507, 514, 532, 562, 580, 630, 669, 674, 683, 687; Bodl. Carte mss 34, f. 44; *Marvell* ed. Margoliouth, i. 148; *Pepys Diary*, 18 July 1666; Burnet, i. 425–6; ii. 84. [6] *Milward*, 98, 99, 332–5; *CJ*, ix. 15, 21, 22, 26, 33, 233, 237; Burnet, ii. 84; *Survey of London*, v. 75; Grey, i. 112–13, 118, 270–1; Clarke, *Jas. II*, i. 436; *CSP Dom.* 1668–9, pp. 403–4; 1671, pp. 489, 498; 1672, pp. 566–7; Browning, *Danby*, i. 84–87. [7] *CJ*, ix. 248, 302, 310, 343, 356, 540; Grey, ii. 103, 106, 238, 297; iii. 88–90, 134; iv. 294; *Dering*, 152; Browning, i. 155–7, 159–60; iii. 1, 8; *HMC 13th Rep. VI*, 276; *Cal. Treas. Bks.* vi. 238, 257; Eg. 3345, ff. 24, 38; Dalrymple, *Mems.* ii. 123, 289–90, 314–17; Burnet, ii. 188. [8] *HMC 13th Rep. VI*, 20; *CJ*, ix. 617; Grey, vi. 255; viii. 317; *HMC Ormonde* n.s. v. 98; vi. 7.

E.C.

LITTLETON *alias* **POYNTZ, Sir Thomas,** 3rd Bt. (1647–1710), of North Ockendon, Essex and Stoke St. Milborough, Salop.

NEW WOODSTOCK	1689,	1690,	1695,
	1698,	1701	(Feb.),
	1701 (Dec.)		
CASTLE RISING	1702		
CHICHESTER	1705		
PORTSMOUTH	14 Dec. 1708–1 Jan. 1710		

b. 3 Apr. 1647, 2nd but 1st surv. s. of Sir Thomas Littleton *alias* Poyntz, 2nd Bt.* *educ.* St. Edmund Hall, Oxf. 1665; I. Temple 1666, called 1671. *m.* 6 Sept. 1682, Anne (*d.* 21 July 1714), da. of Benjamin Baun *alias* Baron of Westcote, Glos., *s.p. suc.* fa. 12 Apr. 1681.[1]

Freeman, Woodstock 1686, Oxford 1691; j.p. Mdx. 1689–*d.*, Essex, Oxon., Oxford and Salop by 1701–*d.*; commr. for assessment, Essex, London, Westminster, Oxon. and Salop 1689–90, Mdx. 1690; common councilman and recorder, Woodstock 1695–*d.*; dep. lt. Oxon. by 1701–2.[2]

Commr. of prizes 1689–90; clerk of the Ordnance 1689–96; chairman of supply committee and ways and means 16 Nov. 1693–7 July 1698; ld. of Treasury 1696–9; treas. of navy 1699–*d.*[3]

Speaker of House of Commons 6 Dec. 1698–19 Dec. 1700.

Although clearly a Whig sympathizer, Littleton was expelled from the Green Ribbon Club in November 1678 'during his father's life'. His unopposed election to the Convention for New Woodstock was presumably due to the influence there of his kinsman, Sir Littleton Osbaldeston, 1st Bt.* An ultra-Whig at the outset, Littleton became one of the chief supporters of government policy.

He was very active, sitting on 91 committees, 11 of which he chaired. He made 31 recorded speeches, helped to manage nine conferences, and was six times teller. An ardent supporter of the Revolution, he was appointed, early in the session, to committees to bring in a list of essentials for securing religion, laws and liberties, and to prepare reasons on the state of the throne, declaring on 2 Feb. 1689:

> The Lords cannot expect that we, who have said the throne is vacant, should not intend to fill it up. The best way is to go on and fill it up and put all out of doubt.

As one of the managers of the conference, he told the House that:

> If the administration of the Government should only be in the Prince, the great design of the Kingdom will be frustrated. The power of the Parliament of England being once asserted, it will establish our foreign affairs. If it be not a time now to strengthen our interest against France, we shall never be preserved but fall into the same misfortune we were in in the late King's time.

He was appointed to the committee for amending the Lords' resolution. On 1 Mar. in the debate on the King's message about conspiracy against the Government, he declared:

> 'Tis of great consequence what advice the Lords and Commons shall give in this. In the meantime, I desire the King may make no proceeding against these men, and I would add thanks to the King for asking your advice: a thing not very usual in this place.

After this, having served only two months in the House, he was appointed chairman of the committee for the suspension of habeas corpus, twice carrying the amended bill to the Lords. He favoured the unsuccessful motion for printing the votes of the House, stating that:

> England has from the clerks all you do, but not the truth of what you do, and it is fit England should know both. In former Parliaments when they were invading and undermining the people they were ashamed of it, but we are now under a King that preserves our liberties. ... It is fit the people should know the good things transacted between the King and this House. Such a union may have great influence both abroad and at home.

In the debate on supply of 11 Mar., Littleton spoke in favour of temporary settlement of the revenue, saying:

> The King does not expect that you should settle the revenue immediately, without great caution and consideration. Therefore, that the King may be in no inconvenience, settle it for three months, which will be so far from a distrust that it is kindly and gratefully done by the people, and the King will take it well from you.

He spoke in favour of comprehension on 25 Mar. and was appointed to the committee for the bill. On 14 May he was voted into the chair of the committee of the whole House on the indemnity bill against Thomas Done* and Sir William Williams*, and delivered four reports on the subject. In April and May, he helped to manage conferences on the oaths of allegiance and supremacy and on the poll tax. When (Sir) Thomas Clarges* expressed anxiety about the bill for continuing the suspension of habeas corpus on 24 May, Littleton replied:

> I think there is a necessity of such a bill: the peace of the Government depends upon it now there are a sort of people disturbing the Government. I observe how tender the Government is now; in the last reign, everything was 'conspiring the death of the King'.

On 3 June he reported from the committee to inquire into delays in the relief of Londonderry. He was made a commissioner of prizes on 19 June but held the post for only a year. He was chairman of the committee to prepare reasons for the conference on reversing the judgments against Titus Oates, and reported from the conference on 22 July.[4]

In the second session, Littleton was appointed to the committees to restore and confirm corporations and to inquire into the miscarriages of the war, when he advocated the rooting out and punishment of offenders, such as Sir Richard Haddock*, according to their degree of guilt. In the debate of 27 Nov. for removing John Shales as commissary-general of provisions, Littleton as a place holder was opposed to the particular demand that an address be sent to the King requesting him to dismiss those who had recommended Shales's appointment. In the closing months of the Convention he brought in the bill for reversing the attainder of Thomas Walcot*, chaired the committee for reversing the attainder of Sir Thomas Armstrong*, served as teller in three divisions over disputed elections and was given special responsibility, with John Hawles*, to prepare a bill for enforcing a general oath of allegiance. In the bill to restore corporations he supported the more moderate form of the disabling clause to affect only 'such as forcibly delivered up the charters without consent of the majority'. He wound up the debate of 20 Jan. 1690 on annulling Armstrong's attainder with an effective speech which led to the expulsion of (Sir) Robert Sawyer*. On 22 Jan. he was appointed to ask Dr Tillotson to preach on the anniversary of Charles I's execution, evidence of his high standing in the House. Owing chiefly to his effectiveness as a speaker he achieved rapid promotion in succeeding Parliaments. He voted consistently as a court Whig under William, but was sufficiently flexible under Anne to hold office till his death on 1 Jan. 1710. He was buried at North Ockendon. Although the baronetcy then became extinct, his estates were inherited by a cousin, James, who sat as a Whig in several Parliaments between 1710 and 1723.[5]

[1] *Glos. Par. Regs.* xiv. 144. [2] Woodstock council acts; *Oxford Council Acts* (Oxf. Hist. Soc. n.s. ii), 219. [3] SP44/165/212; *CSP Dom.* 1689–90, p. 516; 1696, p. 154; *Cal. Treas. Bks.* xx. 248. [4] *CJ*, x. 18, 39, 43, 44, 93, 127, 130, 136, 138, 143, 145, 161; Grey, ix. 49, 76, 130, 145, 156–7, 192, 271; R. Morrice, Entering Bk. 2, p. 556. [5] Grey, ix. 416, 446, 454, 520, 537–8; *CJ*, x. 287, 307, 322, 327, 328; Morrice, 3, p. 73.

L.N./G.J.

LITTLETON, Timothy (c.1608–79), of Henley, Salop and St. Giles in the Fields, Mdx.

LUDLOW 1660, 1661–1 Feb. 1670

b. c.1608, 7th s. of Sir Edward Littleton (*d.*1622) of Henley, Salop. c.j. N. Wales circuit 1621–2, by Mary, da. of Edmund Walter of Ludlow, c.j. S. Wales circuit 1581–94; bro. of Edward Littleton[†], 1st Baron Lyttelton of Mounslow. *educ.* I. Temple 1626, called 1635. *m.* (1) 23 July 1631, Elizabeth (*bur.* 27 June 1667), ?1s. *d.v.p.*; (2) lic. 30 June 1668, aged 60, Elizabeth (*d.*1684), da. of one Ayliffe, wid. of one Gibbons, *s.p.* Kntd. 29 June 1671.[1]

Serjeant-at-law 1640; baron of the Exchequer 1 Feb. 1670–*d.*

Bencher, I. Temple 1640; second justice, N. Wales circuit 1644–7, c.j. Aug. 1660–70; member, council in the marches of Wales 1644; j.p. Anglesey, Caern. and Merion. 1644–6, Sept. 1660–*d.*, Salop Aug. 1660–*d.*; commr. for association, Salop 1645; recorder, Ludlow 1656–75, Bewdley 1660–70; commr. for assessment, Salop 1657, Sept. 1660–*d.*, Mdx. 1673–9; oyer and terminer, Oxford circuit July 1660, corporations, Salop 1662–3.[2]

Littleton's father was a younger son of the Shropshire branch of the family, and his eldest brother was lord keeper from 1641 till his death at Oxford in the Civil War. It was doubtless to this connexion that he owed his appointment as a Welsh judge in 1644; but he can hardly have been regarded as a royalist delinquent, since he never compounded. He was allowed to serve as recorder of Ludlow under the Protectorate, and was named to the county assessment commission. Returned for the borough at the general election of 1660, he was not an active committeeman in the Convention, being named only to the committee of elections and privileges and seven others. His eight speeches suggested a moderate attitude towards the Restoration. He opposed penalties for those who had collaborated under the Protectorate, though he agreed that the bill of indemnity should not apply where the oaths of allegiance and supremacy were refused. He seconded a motion to empower the King to nominate army and excise commissioners. He was appointed to the committee on the bill to settle ministers in their livings, though on the first reading he complained that "twas to continue all scandalous

ministers out, and not to remove all scandalous that were in', and later he was among those ordered to direct the clerk of the Commons in any difficulties arising over the engrossment. He helped to manage the conference of 31 Aug. on the King's message announcing the recess. As chairman for the bill to confirm the land purchases, he reported the case of Thomas Gewen*. An Anglican and a court supporter, he was rewarded with promotion to the chief justiceship of his circuit.[3]

Littleton was re-elected in 1661 after a contest, but he was even less active in the Cavalier Parliament, with nine committees in eight sessions. Of these, three (all in the first session) were on private bills, and he was named to the elections committee in each of the first four sessions. Though he took no part in politically sensitive legislation, he was listed as a court dependant in 1664. He is last mentioned in the Journals on 22 Nov. 1666, when he and Thomas Jones I* testified on the sanity of John Bodvile,* whose estates were claimed under a disputed will by Robert Robartes*. Nevertheless Sir Thomas Osborne* included him in 1669 among the Members who usually voted for supply, and in the following year he became a high court judge. He was buried in the Temple church on 2 Apr. 1679.[4]

[1] *Trans. Salop Arch. Soc.* (ser. 2), xi. 324; (ser. 4), iii. 309–11; *London Mar. Lic.* ed. Chester, 850; C7/304/17; PCC Hare. [2] W. R. Williams, *Gt. Sessions in Wales*, 96–97; W. H. Black, *Docquets of Letters Patent*, 145; *CSP Dom.* 1645–7, p. 80; 1675–6, p. 247; Bodl. Ch. Salop 146. [3] Bowman diary, ff. 51, 52, 57v, 76, 105; *CJ*, viii. 106, 144, 152. [4] *Temple Church Recs.* 23.

M.W.H./J.S.C.

LITTLETON *see also* **LYTTELTON**

LIVINGSTON, Charles, 2nd Earl of Newburgh [S] (c.1666–94), of Cirencester, Glos.

CIRENCESTER 1685

b. c.1666, 1st s. of James Livingston*, 1st Earl of Newburgh [S], by 2nd w. *m.* lic. 12 Sept. 1692, aged 26, Frances (*d.* 23 Sept. 1736), da. of Francis, Lord Brudenell, 1da. (posth.); 1s. illegit. *suc.* fa. 4 Dec. 1670.[1]

Capt. indep. tp. June 1685; guidon 2 Horse Gds. July 1685, lt. 1687–Dec. 1688.

Dep. lt. Glos. Feb. 1688–9.

Lord Newburgh was not long in following his father's example, fighting his first duel with another adolescent in 1681. He was returned as junior Member for Cirencester on his own interest at the contested election of 1685, doubtless as a Tory. Still under age, he was an inactive Member of James II's Parliament, being named only to the committee to recommend expunctions from the Journals when it was revived on 3 June. On the news of Monmouth's invasion, he raised a troop of cavalry, ignoring the requirements of the Test Act, and was 'shot dangerously in the belly' in a skirmish near Pensford on 24 June. He was commissioned in The Blues, but given leave to go abroad for six months in February 1688. Presumably he was expected to support the King's religious policy, for he was made a deputy lieutenant, but he was not approved as a court candidate, perhaps because of his wildness. Instead, Sunderland wrote to him on 13 Sept. to ask for his interest at Cirencester with his tenants and officers for Henry Powle* and John Chamberlain, 'intending to stand with the King's approbation'. He attended the King at Rochester in order to lay down his commission. He was under constant suspicion as a Jacobite after the Revolution, and spent a month in the Tower in 1690. He died on 6 Nov. 1694, and was buried at Cirencester. His posthumous daughter brought the earldom into the Radclyffe family, but his widow, who had a fortune of £12,000, sold the Cirencester property to Sir Benjamin Bathurst*.[2]

[1] C6/84/55; *Scots Peerage*, vi. 453. [2] Luttrell, i. 150; ii. 238, 477, 619; *Collectanea* (Oxf. Hist. Soc. xxxii), 255; *HMC Ormonde*, n.s. vii. 344; *CSP Dom.* 1687-9, p. 154; 1690-1, pp. 69, 336; 1691-2, pp. 318, 319; SP44/56/433; *HMC Kenyon*, 211; Clarke, *Jas. II*, ii. 268.

B.D.H.

LIVINGSTON, James, 1st Earl of Newburgh [S] (c.1622–70), of Cirencester, Glos.

CIRENCESTER 1661–4 Dec. 1670

b. c.1622, o. s. of Sir John Livingstone, 1st Bt., of Kinnaird, Perth by Jane, da. of Richard Sproxton of Wakefield, Yorks., wid. of William Marwood of Little Busby, Yorks.; step-bro. of Richard Gorges*, 2nd Baron Gorges of Dundalk [I]. *educ.* Merton, Oxf. matric. 17 Dec. 1638, aged 16; travelled abroad (France) c.1642–6. *m.* (1) 1648, Lady Catherine Howard (*d.* c.1650), da. of Theophilus Howard†, 2nd Earl of Suffolk, wid. of Lord George Stuart, 9th Seigneur d'Aubigny, 1da.; (2) c. May 1660, Anne (*bur.* 26 May 1692), da. of Sir Henry Poole† of Sapperton, Glos., 2s. *suc.* fa. as 2nd Bt. Mar. 1628; *cr.* Visct. Newburgh [S] 13 Sept. 1647, Earl of Newburgh [S] 31 Dec. 1660.[1]

Lt.-col. Life Gds. [S] 1650–1; col. of horse (Spanish army) 1656–8; capt. of the bodyguard [S] 1661–70.

PC [S] 1661–*d.*; v.-adm. [S] 1666–8; gent. of the privy chamber 1668–*d.*[2]

Commr. for loyal and indigent officers, Glos. 1662, assessment, Glos. 1663–9, Gloucester 1663–4; j.p. Glos. and Lincs. 1664–*d.*

Lord Newburgh's ancestry cannot be traced with certainty beyond his great-grandfather, who was elected provost of Stirling in 1553. His father was groom of the bedchamber to James I, from whom

he received generous grants of land in Scotland. About 1642 he himself was sent to France to be brought up, in accordance with Charles I's instructions. He joined the King at Newcastle in 1646, was given a Scottish peerage, and married into the royal family. After planning to rescue the King on his way to Windsor in December 1648 before his trial, he fled to Holland, but accompanied Charles II to Scotland in 1650, subscribed to the Covenant, and took his seat in the Scottish House of Lords. Escaping abroad again after the battle of Worcester, he relieved the tedium of exile by duelling and a brisk correspondence with the Scottish Royalists. He commanded one of the English regiments which fought under the Spaniards at the battle of the Dunes.[3]

Newburgh continued his military career after the Restoration, becoming captain of the bodyguard in Scotland. He was given a Scottish earldom, with a special remainder to his heirs 'whomsoever', and received many other favours, which continued throughout his life. By his second marriage he became lord of the manor of Cirencester, for which he was returned, apparently unopposed, at the general election of 1661. An inactive Member of the Cavalier Parliament, he was named to only 29 committees and took no part in the Clarendon Code, though he was appointed to the committee on the bill for the execution of those under attainder. He had property in the Lincolnshire fens, although his title was disputed by his stepson, the Duke of Richmond and was appointed to committees for no less than five land reclamation bills. During 1662 he was in Scotland, assisting Lord Middleton in the establishment of episcopacy and incurring the lasting enmity of Lauderdale. He was reported as particularly 'severe against those who refuse to abjure the Covenant, not only removing them from office, as in England, but imprisoning them'. He was back at Westminster for the second session, and on 5 May 1663 was appointed to the committee to bring in the bill restricting offices to loyalists. In 1664 he was on the list of court dependants, and the House resolved that his interest should be taken care of under his brother-in-law's estate bill. As vice-admiral, he was in Scotland from February to December 1666, chiefly concerned with the suppression of the Pentland Rising.[4]

After the fall of Clarendon Newburgh was among those appointed to consider the balance of trade with Scotland. In April 1668 he was twice teller for reading the Lords' bill to ascertain the alnage duties, which had been granted to Richmond. Sir Thomas Osborne* included him among the Members who had usually voted for supply. He resigned his commission early in 1670, on the grounds of 'corpulency and goutishness'. His dispute with his stepson came to a head in the same year, with both parties issuing writs of ejectment and claiming privilege, but a collision between the Houses was averted by Newburgh's death on 4 Dec. 'One of the finest gentlemen of his age, with untainted principles of loyalty and honour', he was buried at St. Margaret's, Westminster.[5]

[1] Scots Peerage, vi. 452; Misc. Gen. et Her. (ser. 5), iii. 210. [2] Carlisle, Privy Chamber, 182. [3] Scots Peerage, vi. 446–7; DNB; Clarendon, Rebellion, iv. 478–9; v. 9; vi. 44; State Trials, v. 1019; Clarke, Jas. II, i. 326–7, 345; Cal. Cl. SP, iv. 69. [4] Rudder, Glos. 354, 660; Reg. PC Scotland (ser. 3), i. 215; ii. 137; CSP Dom. 1663–4, p. 264; HMC Hastings, ii. 144; CJ, viii. 551. [5] CJ, ix. 83, 84; Grey, i. 288–92; HMC 8th Rep. pt. 1 (1881), 146.

B.D.H.

LLOYD, Isaac (c.1628–75), of Lincoln's Inn, and Kilgetty, Pemb.

HAVERFORDWEST   1661–23 May 1663

b. c.1628, 3rd s. of David Lloyd of Ynys y borde, Carm. by Joyce, da. of Thomas Vaughan of Llether Cadfan, Carm. educ. L. Inn 1646, called 1653. m. c.1656, Elizabeth, da. of John Wogan of Wiston, Pemb., wid. of Maurice Canon of Kilgetty, s.p.[1]
   Commr. for assessment, Pemb. 1657, Aug. 1660–74, Haverfordwest Aug. 1660–3; j.p. Pemb. 1658–July 1660, Haverfordwest Sept. 1660–2, 1666–d.; commr. for militia, Pemb. 1659, Carm. Mar. 1660.

Lloyd's ancestors had resided on their small Carmarthenshire estate since early Tudor times. He became a lawyer, acquired by marriage a property 12 miles from Haverfordwest, and held county office under the Protectorate. At the general election of 1661 he was returned for the borough on the interest on the Presbyterian corporation. During his two years in the Cavalier Parliament he was not active. He was appointed to only six committees, including those to prevent the export of leather and to suppress profanity and licentiousness. On 8 May 1663 he successfully claimed privilege over an action of ejectment, but his election was declared void a fortnight later. His restoration to the borough bench in 1666 suggests that he had undertaken not to stand against the court candidate at the by-election caused by the promotion of Sir William Morton*. He died on 20 Apr. 1675 and was buried in Lincoln's Inn Chapel, the only member of the family to enter Parliament.[2]

[1] Information from Major Francis Jones, Wales Herald; West Wales Hist. Recs. ii. 67. [2] S. R. Meyricke, Vis. Wales, i. 234; Haverfordwest Lib., Francis Green pprs. 9, pp. 335, 347.

L.N./G.J.

LLOYD, John (c.1617–64), of Fforest Brechfa, Carm. and Woking, Surr.

CARMARTHENSHIRE   16 Apr. 1646,[1] 1660

b. c.1617, 2nd but 1st surv. s. of Griffith Lloyd of Fforest Brechfa by Joan, da. of John Wogan of Stonehall, Pemb. educ. G. Inn 1635. m. c.1646, Beatrix (d. 26 Mar. 1668), da. of Francis Annesley[†], 1st Visct. Valentia [I], wid. of James Zouche of Woking, 2s. 3da. suc. fa. 1659; cr. Bt. 28 Feb. 1662.
   Col. (parliamentary) to 1644.
   Commr. for assessment, Carm. 1647–8, 1657, Aug. 1660–d., Pemb. 1652, 1657, Aug. 1660–1, Surr. 1657, 1661–d.; j.p. Hants and Surr. 1647–9, Carm. and Surr. Mar. 1660–d., commr. for militia, Carm. and Surr. 1648, Mar. 1660; elder, Guildford classis 1648; custos rot. Carm. Mar.–July 1660, dep. lt. 1661–d.[2]

Lloyd's family was established at Fforest Brechfa by Tudor times. After the Restoration he was described as

a person constant to his principles and resolute in his undertakings when he apprehendeth justice or honour to be concerned. He bore arms under the Earl of Essex for King and Parliament, and when that pretence was laid aside, he laid aside the sword, [and] refused, though tendered, to bear any office, civil or military, under the various governments that sprung afterwards.

He was probably strongly influenced both in religion and politics by his brother-in-law, Arthur Annesley*. A recruiter to the Long Parliament and a Presbyterian elder, he did not sit after Pride's Purge, and during the Interregnum concentrated on improving his wife's Surrey estate. He wrote to his Surrey neighbour, Sir Richard Weston, to inquire about the value of clover with which he was experimenting. He was re-elected in 1660 on the Golden Grove interest. An inactive Member of the Convention, he was named only to the committee of elections and privileges and to that for the assessment bill on 7 May, but he doubtless voted with the Court. He is unlikely to have stood again, though he was created a baronet in 1662. He died on 1 Jan. 1664, and was buried at Woking, the only member of his family to sit in Parliament.[3]

[1] Did not sit after Pride's Purge, 6 Dec. 1648, readmitted 21 Feb. 1660. [2] J. Buckley, Carm. Sheriffs, 38, 86; West Wales Hist. Recs. vii. 3; Manning and Bray, Surr. i. 139. [3] Nat. Lib. Wales Jnl. xi. 143; D. Underdown, Pride's Purge, 178, 394; Agricultural Hist. Rev. xxii. 160–1.

L.N./G.J.

LLOYD (FLOYD), Sir Richard I (1606–76), of Esclus Hall, Denb.

MONTGOMERY BOROUGHS	1628
NEWCASTLE-UNDER-LYME	1640 (Apr.)
RADNORSHIRE	1661–6 Nov. 1676

b. 23 Feb. 1606, 1st s. of Evan Lloyd of Dulasau, Penmachno, Caern. by Janet, da. of Roderick ap Ieuan of

Pennarth, Llanystumdwy, Caern. *educ.* Wadham, Oxf. 1624, BA 1624; G. Inn 1618, called 1635. *m.* 24 Sept. 1632, Margaret, da. of Ralph Sneyd of Keele, Staffs., 1s. *d.v.p.* 3da. *suc.* fa. 1626; kntd. 7 Oct. 1642.[1]

Reader, Barnard's Inn 1639; attorney-gen. N. Wales 1640–7, July 1660–71; commr. of array, Denb. and Rad. 1642; c.j. Brecon circuit July 1660–*d.*; j.p. Brec., Caern., Denb., Glam. and Rad. July 1660–*d.*; commr. for assessment, Denb. and Caern. Aug. 1660–*d.*, Glam. and Merion. 1661–*d.*, Rad. 1661–3, 1665–*d.*, Brec. 1665–9, loyal and indigent officers, Caern., Denb., Merion. and Rad. 1662; dep. lt. Denb. 1674–*d.*[2]

Col. of dgns. (royalist) 1642–7; gov. Holt Castle 1645–7.[3]

Lloyd's ancestors had been lords of Penmachno in the later middle ages. Lloyd, a crown lawyer, was one of the most zealous Royalists in North Wales. Under his command, Holt held out for the King longer than any other garrison except Harlech, and he was rewarded with exceptionally favourable terms on its surrender. He was allowed to go into exile, and his estate, valued at £300 p.a., was granted to his wife. He seems to have established himself at Calais, but took no part in royalist activities during the Interregnum, which would doubtless have jeopardized this grant.[4]

Lloyd was almost as much a foreigner in Glamorgan or Radnorshire as an Englishman would have been. Nevertheless at the general election of 1661 he was returned for both Cardiff and Radnorshire, thanks to his post as chief justice of the circuit. He chose the county seat on 24 May 1661, and was listed as a moderate by Lord Wharton. Although he organized support for the court of the marches, a *bête noire* of the borough Member (Sir) Edward Harley*, he was not active in the Cavalier Parliament. No speeches are recorded, and he was named to only 18 committees. He was one of the Members appointed to examine the Journals of the Long Parliament, and recommend erasures of treasonable and scandalous passages, and he was on the committee for the corporations bill. He acted as chairman for one private bill committee in the opening session. His leisure hours, it may be inferred from Samuel Pepys*, were spent in the convivial company of old Cavaliers like Giles Strangways* and John Robinson I*. His last appearance in the Journals was when he was added to the committee of elections and privileges in 1669. He was marked as a court supporter on the opposition list in 1671, but in July 1672 and March 1673 he was reported dead. He was one of the officials absent from the 1675 sessions, but he did not die till 5 May 1676. His grandson died in childhood, the last of the family, and his estates after much litigation were divided, Esclus falling to the heirs of his son-in-law, Sir Henry Conway*.[5]

[1] J. E. Griffith, *Peds. Anglesey and Caern. Fams.* 330; C142/426/91; A. N. Palmer, *Wrexham Parish Church*, 188; *Wadham Reg.* i. 55. [2] *Pens. Bk. G. Inn*, i. 336; W. R. Williams, *Gt. Sessions in Wales*, 137–8; CSP Dom. 1660–1, p. 142; 1671, p. 275. [3] *List of Officers Claiming* (1663), 50. [4] *Evelyn Diary*, ii. 560; iii. 16, 55; *Whitelocke Mems.* ii. 96. [5] CSP Dom. 1661–2, p. 36; *Pepys Diary*, 17 Mar. 1663; *Arch. Camb.* (ser. 4, vi), 266–8.

J.P.F.

LLOYD, Sir Richard II (c.1634–86), of Southampton Buildings, Bloomsbury, Mdx.

DURHAM   1679 (Oct.), 1681, 1685–28 June 1686

b. c.1634, 4th but 3rd surv. s. of Andrew Lloyd† (*d.*1663) of Aston Hall, Oswestry, Salop by Margaret, da. of Thomas Powell of Whittington Park, Salop. *educ.* Shrewsbury 1648; G. Inn 1655; All Souls, Oxf. BCL 1659, DCL 1662; advocate, Doctors' Commons 1664. *m.* Elizabeth, da. of John Jones, apothecary, of the Strand, Westminster, 8s. (5 *d.v.p.*) 3da. Kntd. 16 Jan. 1677.[1]

Fellow of All Souls 1655–?64; chancellor, Lichfield dioc. by Dec. 1660–?69, Durham dioc. (spiritual) 1676–*d.*; judge of Admiralty, Hants and I.o.W. 1669–85; freeman, E.I. Co. 1676; commr. for assessment, London 1679–80; j.p. co. Dur. 1680–*d.*; common councilman, Berwick-upon-Tweed 1685–*d.*[2]

Advocate, high court of Admiralty 1674–85, judge 1685–*d.*; dean of the arches 1684–*d.*[3]

Lloyd's family, of Denbighshire origin, appear to have settled in the Oswestry area in Elizabethan times. His father, a parliamentary colonel, and one of the 'best affected and most zealous patriots' on the Shropshire committee, was returned for the county in 1656, but excluded from the first session of this Parliament. Lloyd, however, was a devout Anglican and a Tory. A civil lawyer, he stood high in favour with Nathaniel Crew, bishop of Durham, who made him spiritual chancellor of the diocese and brought him in for the city after a contest at the second general election of 1679. On 21 Dec. 1680 he spoke against the bill for uniting the Protestants: 'This bill seems to look one way, but doth look another; and hopes that nobody will easily, at one blow, part with so ancient and so excellent a liturgy'. Nevertheless this was the only committee to which he was appointed in the second Exclusion Parliament. He was re-elected unopposed in 1681, but left no trace on the records of the Oxford Parliament.[4]

Lloyd was moderately active in James II's Parliament, in which he was named to five committees. He took the chair on the bill for the repair of Bangor Cathedral and carried it to the Lords. Presumably he gave satisfaction to the King in the first session, for on 1 Oct. 1685 he was appointed to preside in the high court of Admiralty. 'New brooms sweep clean', Sir William Trumbull* was informed a few months later; 'in a little time there will be no occasion for an advocate.' But he was taken ill early in the new year and died on 28 June 1686, aged 52. Bishop Crew described his loss as irreparable, and was sure that as dean of the arches there could hardly be 'a fitter person for learning, loyalty and integrity'. He was buried at St. Benet, Paul's Wharf. Lloyd's will shows that he had put most of his savings into East India and Royal Africa Company stock. His eldest son followed the same profession, becoming master of Trinity Hall, Cambridge in 1710, but none of his descendants entered Parliament, though his nephew Robert sat for Shropshire as a high Tory from 1699 to 1708.[5]

[1] *Le Neve's Knights* (Harl. Soc. viii), 314; J. E. Auden, *Shrewsbury Sch. Reg.* 34; information from Mr J. S. G. Simmons; PCC 98 Lloyd. [2] *Llandaff Recs.* ii. 5; Hutchinson, *Dur.* ii. 256; *HMC Downshire*, i. 192; Ind. 24557; *Cal. Ct. Mins. E.I. Co.* ed. Sainsbury, x. 310; *CSP Dom.* 1685, p. 67. [3] Haydn, *Dignities*, 420, 423. [4] *Vis. Salop* (Harl. Soc. xxix) 339; *Trans. Salop Arch. Soc.* ser. 4, xi. 183–4; J. R. Phillips, *Civil War in Wales*, ii. 123; C. E. Whiting, *Nathaniel Lord Crewe*, 109; *HMC 12th Rep. IX*, 102. [5] *CJ*, ix. 753; *HMC Downshire*, i. 77, 189; Whiting, op. cit. 146; *Paul's Wharf* (Harl. Soc. Reg. xli), 90; Strype, *Hist. London*, ii. 384.

G.H.

LODER, Thomas (1652–1713), of Prince's Harwell and Balsdon Park, Kintbury, Berks.

GREAT BEDWYN 1685

b. 30 Aug. 1652, 1st s. of John Loder of Welford and Hinton Waldrist by Mary, da. and h. of Thomas Barrett of Balsdon Park. *educ.* Brasenose, Oxf. 1670, BA (Queen's) 1675. *m.* bef. 17 Nov. 1679 (with £5,000), Elizabeth, da. of Sir Jonathan Raymond[†], Brewer, of Houndsditch, Mdx. and Barton Court, Kintbury, 1da. *suc.* fa. 1701.[1]

Commr. for assessment, Berks. 1690–d.

Loder's ancestors had held the manor of Prince's Harwell since 1557, raising themselves from yeoman status to the ranks of the gentry by enterprising husbandry combined with careful bookkeeping; but none had aspired to a seat in Parliament. His father apparently ignored a request from Charles I for a loan during the Civil War, and was named to three local commissions during the Protectorate; after the Restoration he acquired much of the property of the profligate republican, Henry Martin[†], allowing him £2 a week (subsequently halved) for 'necessaries'. Loder's mother brought into the family the Balsdon Park estate, about seven miles from Great Bedwyn, which was entailed on him in 1682. He married the daughter of a Tory alderman of London by another Kintbury heiress. Returned to James II's Parliament for Great Bedwyn, Loder left no trace on its records. His father was appointed a deputy lieutenant in March 1688, but Loder seems to have held no local office

till after the Revolution. Much of his property appears to have passed to his father-in-law, who sat for Great Bedwyn from 1690 to 1695. He died in 1713, the only member of the family to sit in Parliament. His great-granddaughter eventually brought the Raymond estate to Charles Dundas, MP for Berkshire from 1794 to 1832.[2]

[1] Kintbury par. reg.; C7/297/89. [2] *VCH Berks.* iii. 488; iv. 207, 211, 464–5; C5/56/41; *CSP Dom.* 1673, p. 235; J. R. Whitehead, *Rulers of London*, 136; PCC 44 Dyer; Lysons, *Berks.* 305; *Berks. Arch. Jnl.* lxii. 68.

J.P.F.

LONG, Sir James, 2nd Bt. (1616–92), of Draycot Cerne, Wilts.

MALMESBURY 1679 (Mar.), 1679 (Oct.), 1681, 1690–22 Jan. 1692

b. c. Sept. 1616, o.s. of Sir Walter Long[†] of Draycot Cerne by Lady Anne Ley, da. of James Ley[†], 1st Earl of Marlborough. *educ.* L. Inn 1634. *m.* by 1640, Dorothy (*d.*1710), da. of Sir Edward Leach[†] of Shipley, Derbys., 1s. *d.v.p.* 5da. *suc.* fa. 1637, uncle (Sir) Robert Long* as 2nd Bt. and in Yorks. estate 13 July 1673.[1]

Capt. of horse (royalist) 1642, col. 1644–6.[2]

Sheriff, Wilts. (royalist) 1644–5; commr. for assessment, Wilts. 1664–80; 1689–90, Yorks. (W. and N. Ridings) 1679–80; j.p. Wilts. 1671–*d.*, dep. lt. 1675–?*d.*, commr. for recusants 1675.[3]

Gent. of privy chamber 1673–85.[4]

FRS 1663.

Long's ancestors had regularly represented Wiltshire constituencies since 1414, and purchased Draycot Cerne in 1438. Aubrey called Long his 'honoured friend' and 'a gentleman absolute in all numbers', including specifically the handling of horse and sword; but his career as a royalist cavalry commander was far from glorious. He compounded for £810 on the Oxford articles, and was reported to be in France with his uncle. But in 1650 he was described as 'a very active man formerly', and during the Interregnum he abandoned politics for entomology and falconry. A 'great historian and romancer', he told Aubrey how

Oliver Protector, hawking at Hounslow Heath, discoursing with him, fell in love with his company, and commanded him to wear his sword and to meet him a-hawking, which made the strict Cavaliers look on him with an evil eye.[5]

Although Long was not in the commission of the peace during the second Dutch war he was asked to inquire into reports of military activity in the Chippenham area. He had 'more interest than anyone upon the Avon', and was named as a commissioner in two navigation bills; but he informed John Vaughan* that this was without his consent, and they were both dropped. The Yorkshire estate to which he succeeded in 1673 included property near Boroughbridge, which he twice contested unsuccessfully in by-elections to the Cavalier Parliament. At the general election, however, he returned to his native county, and represented Malmesbury in all three Exclusion Parliaments. Shaftesbury marked him 'vile', but he was probably less interested in party politics than in social and economic issues. On 10 Apr. 1679 he was added to the committee of inquiry into the pamphlets issued in defence of Danby, and later he was among those ordered to search for precedents for punishing false returns. But most of his committees were of more direct interest to his constituents, dealing with such subjects as the poor law, the decay of the woollen industry, and abuses in the collection of the hearth-tax and the excise. Altogether he was a moderately active Member of the first Exclusion Parliament, with 11 committees. But he made no speeches, although Aubrey thought him an 'admirable extempore orator', and he was absent from the division on the first exclusion bill.[6]

Again moderately active in the second Exclusion Parliament, Long was named to six committees, of which the most important were on the bills to regulate parliamentary elections and to remove Papists from the London area. In the Oxford Parliament he was named only to the committee of elections and privileges. By now clearly an opponent of exclusion, he gave evidence in 1682 at the trial of Edward Whittaker, 'the true Protestant attorney', of treasonable words.[7]

Long seems not to have stood in 1685. When questioned by the lord lieutenant in 1688, he declared that he was

> of opinion that toleration is best, and is for taking away the Penal Laws provided there be a clause inserted against atheism [and] blasphemy; and for the repealing the Tests he totally relies upon the King's sense in Parliament.

In April 1688 James II's agents reported that he would be chosen knight of the shire, with strong nonconformist support, described him as 'right', and recommended that he should be continued in the lieutenancy. In September Thomas Freke II* reported that there was 'discourse of' him for Wiltshire, but it is unlikely that he stood at the general election of 1689, either for county or borough, though he strongly supported the new regime. He was, however, returned for Malmesbury in 1690, and was regarded as 'doubtful' by the Government. He died suddenly 'of an apoplexy' on 23 Jan. 1692 and was buried at Draycot Cerne. His grandson, the 5th baronet, sat for Chippenham under Queen Anne and for Wootton Bassett and Wiltshire after the Hanoverian succession as a high Tory.[8]

[1] *Wilts. Inquisitions* (Index Lib. xxiii), 241; *Misc. Gen. et Her.* n.s. iii. 58. [2] *Army Lists* ed. Peacock, 12; *Ludlow Mems.* i. 470. [3] *Wilts. Arch. Mag.* iii. 220. [4] Carlisle, *Privy Chamber*, 191. [5] *Wilts. Arch. Mag.* iii. 179; *Ludlow Mems.* i. 470–1, 474–5; Clarendon, *Rebellion*, iv. 12; *Cal. Comm. Comp.* 1457; *HMC Pepys*, 207; *HMC Portland*, i. 589; Aubrey, *Brief Lives*, ii. 36. [6] *CSP Dom.* 1666–7, pp. 182, 230, 465, 488; Eg. 2231, ff. 209–10; *VCH Yorks. N. Riding*, i. 365, 367; ii. 102; *CJ*, ix. 290; Aubrey, ii. 36. [7] Luttrell, i. 233. [8] Bath mss, Thynne pprs. 24, f. 39; *CSP Dom.* 1689–90, pp. 178, 352; *HMC Hastings*, ii. 339.

B.D.H.

LONG, Robert (c.1600–73), of Westminster and Nonsuch, Surr.

DEVIZES	17 Mar. 1626, 1628
MIDHURST	1640 (Apr.)
BOROUGHBRIDGE	1661–13 July 1673

b. c.1600, 4th but 3rd surv. s. of Sir Walter Long[†] (*d.*1610) of South Wraxhall, Wilts., being 2nd s. by 2nd w. Catherine, da. of Sir John Thynne[†] of Longleat, Wilts.; bro. of Sir Walter Long[†]. *educ.* L. Inn 1619, called 1627. *unm. cr.* Bt. 1 Sept. 1662.[1]

Sec. to Ld. Treas. Marlborough by 1626–8; servant to Charles I by 1633; commr. for preventing export of butter 1636, compounding with tobacco planters 1636; jt. commissary for the army in the north 1639; receiver of recusancy forfeitures (south) 1639–46; surveyor-gen. to Queen Henrietta Maria 1641–6, by 1661–9, treas. and receiver-gen. 1671–*d.*; auditor of the receipt in the Exchequer 1643–6, 1662–*d.*; sec. to Charles II as Prince of Wales 1645–9; sec. of state 1649–52; PC 14 May 1649–Jan. 1652, 3 July 1672–*d.*; commr. for trade and plantations 1672–*d.*[2]

Commr. for corporations, Yorks. 1662–3, assessment, Westminster 1663–*d.*, Surr. 1665–*d.*; jt. keeper of Somerset House 1664–*d.*; j.p. Surr. 1666–*d.*[3]

Long, the younger son of a prominent Wiltshire family, entered public life as secretary to his kinsman, the 1st Earl of Marlborough (James Ley[†]). He was granted the reversion of the auditorship of the receipt to the long-lived Sir Robert Pye[†], for whom he substituted at Oxford during the Civil War. He accompanied Prince Charles to the west country as his secretary, and was also surveyor-general to Henrietta Maria, whose religion he seems to have adopted. The ablest of the Louvre group of royalist exiles, he was a bitter enemy of Sir Edward Hyde[†] until he was dismissed in 1652. Besides a farm in Wiltshire which he had inherited, he had acquired substantial interests in the Lincolnshire fens and the former forest of Galtres, which were sold by the treason trustees. He was in England in 1654, but seems to have lived chiefly at Rouen till the Restoration.[4]

Long had recovered his office as surveyor-general of the queen mother's estate by 1661, and presumably also his Yorkshire property. He was returned for Boroughbridge at the general election, but did not become an active Member of the Cavalier Parliament, being appointed to 43 committees, none of which was of much political importance. He retained his interest in the drainage of the Lincolnshire fens, in association with Sir William Killigrew*, and was named to several committees. When his Exchequer reversion at last fell in he was created a baronet, with special remainder to his nephew. He showed himself 'exceptional among 17th-century Exchequer officials in having a conscientious devotion to the personal performance of his duties', and in 1663 he was appointed to the parliamentary committee to propose improvements in the revenue. In the same year his application for a long lease of Nonsuch was granted, nominally in reversion to the queen mother; but as she was now permanently resident in France he probably moved in at once. It is unlikely, however, that his old quarrel with Hyde, now Lord Chancellor Clarendon, had been made up, and his name was significantly absent from the list of court dependants in 1664. During the great plague the Exchequer was moved to Nonsuch, and it is not clear whether Long was able to attend the Oxford session; but during the next recess Samuel Pepys* found him 'mighty fierce in the great good qualities of payment in course', provision for which had been inserted by Sir George Downing* in the supply bill.[5]

Long was the first Member named to the inquiry into the loyal and indigent officers fund on 2 Oct. 1666, and his high standing in the House at this time is shown by his selection, together with Lord Ancram (Charles Kerr*), to ask the dean of Westminster and the rector of St. Margaret's to preach at the fast, to return thanks for the sermons, and to urge publication. As chairman of the committee for naval and ordnance accounts he reported on 15 Oct. that the papers tabled by Sir Philip Warwick* were substantially correct. When the Treasury was put into commission in 1667, with Downing as the driving-force, Long entered on the most constructive period of his career. As the key official in the lower Exchequer 'he was the Treasury's principal executive ... receiving a steady flow of instructions and returning a regular sequence of information. ... If any one man could work out the current Exchequer balance between income and expenditure, it was the auditor of the receipt.' Perhaps the additional burden of administration precluded Long from playing much part henceforth in the House. Presumably he welcomed the fall of his old enemy Clarendon, but he was not even among those appointed to consider legalizing the transfer of Exchequer bills. Whether by accident or design 'the very first sum mentioned in the account brought in by Sir Robert Long of the disposal of the poll-bill money is £5,000 to my Lord Arlington [Sir Henry

Bennet*] for intelligence; which was mighty unseasonable, after they [the Commons] had so much cried out against his want of intelligence'. His only other recorded intervention in debate was on 19 Jan. 1671 when he told (Sir) Thomas Lee I* that interest on crown loans above the legal maximum of 6 per cent was authorized not by the Exchequer but by privy seal. His last committee, not unsuitably, was on the bill to sell up the defaulting tax-collector Thomas Harlackenden* two months later. He was on both lists of the court party in 1669–71 as a dependant, and was described in a hostile account as having gained at least £50,000 by managing the queen mother's affairs. He continued to build up his Yorkshire estate, but died after a long illness on 13 July 1673 and was buried in Westminster abbey. He bequeathed £300 to his niece's husband, Sir Richard Mason*, to be expended for the good of his soul, as well as his lease of Worcester Park; but the bulk of the estate descended with the baronetcy to his nephew, Sir James Long*.[6]

[1] Misc. Gen. et Her. n.s. iii. 58; Wilts. Vis. Peds. (Harl. Soc. cv), 118. [2] CSP Dom. 1627–8, p. 299; 1633–4, p. 35; 1635–6, pp. 240, 377; 1638–9, p. 572; 1639, p. 119; 1640–1, p. 528; 1641–3, p. 494; Add. 1625–49, p. 722; 1660–1, p. 478; Cal. Treas. Bks. iii. 867; Clarendon, Rebellion, iv. 22; v. 2, 323. [3] HMC 8th Rep. pt. 1 (1881), 275; CSP Dom. 1663–4, p. 661. [4] Strafford Letters ed. Knowler, ii. 149; DNB; Cal. Comm. Comp. 2105, 3257, 3293; Cal. Cl. SP. ii. 379; iv. 696; CSP Dom. 1631–3, pp. 404–5; Wilts. Inquisitions (Index Lib. xxiii), 394. [5] Cal. Treas. Bks. i. 167, 183; CJ, viii. 322, 458, 507, 526; CSP Dom. 1661–2, p. 473; 1663–4, p. 105; 1664–5, p. 492; H. Roseveare, The Treasury 1660–1870, p. 30; Pepys Diary, 28 Nov. 1665. [6] CJ, viii. 627, 630, 633, 635; Roseveare, 30; Milward, 194; Pepys Diary, 21 Feb. 1668; Grey, i. 357; Harl. 7020, f. 46v; VCH N. Riding i. 365; ii. 102; Williamson Letters (Cam. Soc. n.s. viii), 106; Cal. Treas. Bks. iii. 659; PCC 30 Pye.

                        J.P.F.

LONG, Sir Walter, 2nd Bt. (c.1626–1710), of Whaddon, nr. Melksham, Wilts. and James Street, Covent Garden, Westminster.

BATH   1679 (Oct.)

b. c.1626, 1st s. of Sir Walter Long†, 1st Bt., of Whaddon by 1st w. Mary, da. and coh. of Robert Cox, Grocer, of London. *educ.* Magdalen Hall, Oxf. matric. 12 June 1640, aged 14; L. Inn 1644. *unm. suc.* fa. 27 Nov. 1672.[1]
    Commr. for assessment, Wilts. Aug. 1660–1, 1663–80, 1689–90, j.p. 1671–80, 1689–*d.*, commr. for recusants 1675; freeman, Bath 1679.[2]

Long's ancestors had held the manor of Whaddon, nine miles from Bath, since 1555. They were apparently not of the same stock as the older Draycot family. One of them sat for Westbury in 1571, but it was Long's father who achieved prominence in Opposition in the early Parliaments of Charles I. The chief Presbyterian whip in the Long Parliament, he was expelled by the army in 1647, but resumed his seat on the return of the secluded Members, and received a baronetcy at the Restoration.[3]

Long was returned for Bath by the Presbyterian faction at the second general election of 1679 with a majority of one over Sir William Bassett* on the third poll. He was removed from the commission of the peace as an exclusionist, but in the second Exclusion Parliament he was named only to the committee of elections and privileges. He was defeated by Bassett at the general election of 1681, and in 1689 received only three votes. He died on 21 May 1710, aged 84, and was buried at Whaddon. There was no heir to the baronetcy, but his estate, valued at £4,000 p.a., was inherited by a nephew, the younger son of Sir Philip Parker*, who assumed the name of Long.[4]

[1] Wilts. N. and Q. ii. 28; PCC 109 Dale; Wilts. Inquisitions (Index Lib. xxiii), 229; St. Mary Woolchurch Haw Reg. 323; E134/29 Chas. II/Easter 31/8. [2] Bath council bk. 2, p. 750. [3] VCH Wilts. vii. 172; Wilts. Vis. Peds. (Harl. Soc. cv), 116; Keeler, Long Parl. 256–7; D. Underdown, Pride's Purge, 69, 82, 210. [4] Bath council bk. 2, p. 812; 3, p. 86; CSP Dom. Jan.–June 1683, p. 60; Misc. Gen. et Her. (ser. 2), ii. 326; Luttrell, vi. 585.

I.C.

LONGFORD, 1st Viscount [I] and 1st Earl of see AUNGIER, Francis

LOVE, William (c.1620–89), of St. Mary Axe, London.

LONDON   1661, 1679 (Mar.), 1679 (Oct.), 1681, 9 Jan.–26 Apr. 1689 [new writ]

b. c.1620, 1st s. of William Love of Aynho, Northants. by Mary, da. of John Uvedale of Linford, Bucks. m. lic. 1 Feb. 1651, Elizabeth (bur. 3 Aug. 1694), da. of Sir John Burgoyne, 1st Bt.†, of Sutton, Beds., 3s. 1da. suc. fa. by 1662.[1]

Member, Drapers' Co. 1650, master 1660–1; asst. Levant Co. 1653–70, dep. gov. 1661–2; committee, E.I. Co. 1657–62; commr. for militia, London 1659, alderman 1659–62, sheriff 1659–60, commr. for assessment Jan. 1660, 1673–80, 1689, recusants 1675, dep. lt. 1689–d.[2]

Councillor of State 2 Jan.–25 Feb. 1660; member, corp. for propagation of the Gospel in New England 1661; commr. for trade 1668–72.[3]

Love came from a minor gentry family which acquired property in Aynho in Elizabeth's reign. He spent many years of his early life in the Mediterranean, returning with 'a very great estate' during the Interregnum, and becoming a leading light in the Levant Company and an alderman of London in 1659. In this capacity he opposed the appeal to George Monck* from the militia officers as 'inimical to the government of the Commonwealth'. But on the second return of the Rump

he was appointed to the Council of State and the board of customs, though from this post he immediately resigned as 'having other great employment upon him'. He did not sign the petition of the common council for the return of the secluded Members, though he served on the delegation that presented it to the Rump. As sheriff of London he was ineligible at the general election of 1660. He was unable to prevent the return of four Royalists, but according to Edmund Ludlow* the selection of a jury for the regicides had to be deferred until his term of office had expired.[4]

Love was among those accused with John Wildman I* of attending republican conclaves where candidates for the general election of 1661 were approved. His own return for London was greeted with consternation at Court, since he was 'esteemed rather inclined to the Levellers than monarchical government'. In religion he was considered a Congregationalist, and Lord Wharton listed him among his friends in the Cavalier Parliament, though he accepted the 39 Articles and seems to have been anxious to achieve comprehension. When he refused to attend the corporate communion of 26 May, Thomas Clifford* 'fell on' him, alleging that he had contracted 'Popish principles' during his long residence abroad, a charge to which his reminiscences of religious colloquy with the Jesuits at Rome certainly gave some colour. He was suspended from the House until he should produce a sacrament certificate. He was one of the two London aldermen removed by the commissioners for corporations as having been 'faulty in the late troubles'. On 5 Mar. 1663 the Commons gave him a month to produce his certificate, and further pressure was put on him by nominating him to a committee on a bill to restore the clerk of the London chamber to office. He probably absented himself, however, for this was his only committee during the Clarendon administration, and in 1667 Daniel Finch* wrote that he had never taken the Anglican sacrament. In 1668 it was represented to Lord Winchilsea, who had been appointed ambassador to Constantinople by the Levant Company on the King's recommendation, that Love was 'a traitor and a schismatic', who 'either doth or would rule the whole company', that he had been responsible for sending a nonconformist as chaplain to the factory at Smyrna, and that he opposed granting Winchilsea unlimited use of company money. Love wrote to Winchilsea

I am more puzzled to guess at the accusations than to justify myself. Was it that I am a nonconformist? If by that term they mean one who concurs not in every point of church government (for in doctrinals I am a Protestant throughout), I dare not disown it.

Winchilsea urged the Government that Love should be

> removed on this occasion out of the company, where his factious disposition gives more disturbance than assistance to their affairs, though perchance that may be too light a punishment for one who hath formerly expressed so great a dislike, and now so great a contempt for monarchy.

Love, however, retained his influence in the court of the company, and it was Winchilsea who had to make peace with him.[5]

After the dismissal of Clarendon, Love resumed attendance in the House, and later claimed that he 'could produce the very speeches I then took in shorthand, both those against him and those for him'. These notes probably formed the basis for *Proceedings in the House of Commons touching the Impeachment of Edward, Earl of Clarendon*, published in 1700. On 16 Oct. 1667 Love imputed 'the sinking of trade to the severity of proceedings in the oath of renouncing the Covenant'. He was appointed to the committees to consider the bill for preventing the growth of Popery and to continue the inquiry into the affairs of the merchants trading with France. With Thomas Bludworth* and Samuel Sandys I* he was ordered on 26 Nov. to examine a witness who accused Edward Backwell* of defrauding the revenue. He was among those to whom the bill for naturalizing prize ships was committed, and he helped to draft a proviso to the public accounts bill, and to inquire into taxes unpaid by office-holders in London and Middlesex. After the Christmas recess he was appointed to an accounts committee. Although he disclaimed parliamentary wages 'because he thinks he never deserved any', he was in fact an active constituency Member under the Cabal. He was named to the committee to investigate proposals for bringing down the price of the timber, and to consider the bill to regulate the rebuilding of London after the Great Fire. In grand committee on 29 Feb. 1668 he told the House that he regarded taxing retailers as a Spanish inquisition and encouraging a black economy; and he was twice appointed to committees to estimate the yield of additional customs duties. On 22 Apr. he opposed a bill for lowering the rate of interest because

> it would be a means to obstruct the bringing in of silver, for whereas other commodities yield ten in the hundred bullion and silver will not yield above four, which will take away the chiefest means to make money plentiful. He said in Turkey money was generally at ten in the hundred, sometimes at forty in the hundred, and in Turkey there was a great store (if not greater) as in any other country whatsoever. He also said that whereas it was alleged that money was so plentiful in Turkey because interest was low, it was clean contrary, for the interest there was low because money was plentiful.

He was one of the dissenters appointed to the remodelled council of trade in October, probably at the instance of Lord Ashley (Sir Anthony Ashley Cooper*), with whom he had been associated before the Restoration. He did not directly oppose the extension of the Conventicles Act in 1669, but when the House was reminded of the rejoicings in Rome at the execution of Laud, he insisted that the Jesuits had regarded him as their greatest rival in the introduction of Popery: 'what we bring about in an age, he would do in a year or two'. He supported the suspension of Sir George Carteret*: 'the consequence of his negligence and ignorance is such that the King may have the ill effects when he shall set out his fleet again'. In the debate on brandy on 1 Mar. 1670 he agreed with John Jones* that prohibition would only lead to bootlegging, especially in the colonies. He was named to the committee for the bill to strengthen habeas corpus by forbidding transportation of English subjects overseas. He offered a proviso to the second conventicles bill to allow nonconformists to teach in schools provided that they took the oaths, subscribed to the 39 Articles, and obtained a licence from a magistrate. He was appointed to the committees to consider a bill to recover arrears of money given for the London poor (31 Mar. 1670), to inspect the naval accounts (31 Oct.), and to hear a petition from London artificers (9 Dec.). He was one of five Members instructed to amend the penal clause in the additional imposition bill (15 Mar. 1671) so that persons in possession of prohibited goods would have to prove their innocence. On 27 Mar. he introduced a bill to perpetuate the paving and draining powers granted to the corporation under the Rebuilding of London Acts, and was named to the committee.[6]

When the proposal to relieve Protestant dissenters was under debate in February 1673 it was asked, doubtless by arrangement, whether anybody could explain what they desired. Many of their previous demands were abandoned to facilitate the passing of the test bill and the definitive exclusion of Roman Catholics from public life.

> Alderman Love stood up, and said that he was acquainted with many of them; that he knew they did not desire to be admitted to any offices of honour or profit in the church or kingdom, which was not reasonable to expect without being entirely conformable to the established church, that they did not desire to be exempted from any offices of charge or burden, nor from any taxes or payment of parish duties, nor from tithes, but only from the penalties of the laws made against them, and that they might have leave to worship God in public places to be appointed by the magistrate with the doors open, and, if the House thought fit, in public churches at such times as no other worship or service was there.

The House 'heard him very well', apart from the last proposal. The next day he moved 'for a general indulgence by way of comprehension', and he was named to the committee on the bill of ease. He opposed the bill for the general naturalization of foreign Protestants, however. Like most dissenters, he supported Arlington in January 1674, but wished to ask Buckingham 'who advised that the army should be appointed to draw up towards London to awe this House, to make us vote what they pleased'. He was named to a committee to bring in an electoral reform bill in the same session. On 26 Oct. 1675 he supported the motion that the money voted for the navy should be paid into the chamber of London rather than into Exchequer:

> You must put it into the City's, or some secure hands, or you are never like to have it rightly employed. Merchants' ships are built cheaper than the King's ships, because they may get their money how they can. 'Tis well known that it can be done for seven or eight pounds per ton, if the carpenters be assured of their money. The merchants pay not the third penny of what the King gives now, and there is no reason but the King's money should go as far as another man's money, if the workmen were paid as they ought to be.

Although Love no longer held office in the Levant Company, he still identified himself with their interests, and in particular their resentment at the competition of the East India Company. On 9 Nov. he was among those instructed to consider a complaint against their over-successful rivals. Four days later he probably introduced a petition from the London weavers complaining of foreign imports and the introduction of machinery, since he was the first Member named to the committee. Sir Richard Wiseman*, as government whip, was unable to answer for him in 1676.[7]

After the long prorogation Love was appointed to the committees for the bills to recall British subjects from the French service and to prevent illegal exactions (22 Feb. 1677). In the debate on the liability of corporations for parliamentary wages, he proudly declared that 'he never received any wages from the City, nor demanded any'. In the grand committee of grievances he seconded the attack of John Knight* on the cost of passes to secure merchantmen against the Barbary corsairs. He estimated that ten or twelve thousand pounds was given annually 'to private persons', and complained that passes had to be renewed every year. A select committee on which Love served was appointed to consider how to remedy these complaints. He admitted that it would be irregular to receive a petition from the brewers of his constituency against the additional excise while the supply bill was under dis-

cussion, but 'he thought it fitter for this House to reject it than himself'. One-third of the 240 brewers in London, he said, had failed in the last six years. When the bill for building 30 warships was reported, Love and Sir William Thompson* acted as tellers for a successful motion to reduce the assessment of London. Ashley, now Earl of Shaftesbury, classed him as 'doubly worthy'. On 19 Feb. 1678 he was named to a committee to estimate the yield of a tax on new buildings in the suburbs. When it was alleged that Quakers had been convicted of recusancy and subjected to the same penalties as Roman Catholics, Love said:

> They may come under the notion of Papists to have the better quarters. I have had some Quakers that would renounce according to the Test, etc., and there are thousands that will. I would not have them be encouraged to seek better quarters by being under the notion of Romanists.

He was appointed to the committee of inquiry. On 30 May, on the second reading of the bill to encourage the wearing of woollens, a petition from the Levant Company was presented and referred to a select committee, of which Love was a member. He was also named to the committee to consider the bill for reforming the hearth-tax, but on the report stage he and Thompson acted as tellers for recommitting it. He was reported about this time as attending a great Presbyterian conventicle in Cutlers' Hall. After the Popish Plot he was named to the committee of inquiry, and also to those to consider the bill to prevent Roman Catholics from sitting in Parliament and to investigate the mistranslation of the *Gazette*.[8]

Re-elected to the Exclusion Parliaments, Love was marked 'worthy' on Shaftesbury's list. A very active Member in 1679, he was named to 28 committees and made three recorded speeches. He was appointed to the committees to examine the disbandment accounts, and to consider the bills for the speedier conviction of recusants and for regulating elections. On 7 Apr. 1679 he was one of a small committee ordered to bring in a bill annexing Tangier to the crown. Two days later, heedful of the rumour that the King intended to sell the outpost to the French, he said

> If the French have that, they will have as good an advantage as they that have the Sound. If Tangier were under water I should be glad of it, but seeing we have it, it is not for us to say that it is of no matter if it were gone. If it were in the hands of the Dutch or the Spanish galleys, your trade is gone. . . . It may be worth millions to the French; they may then put what impositions upon our trade they please.

He was appointed to the committees to bring in a bill banishing Papists from the London area, to examine naval miscarriages, to draw up the address for the dismissal of Lauderdale, and to consider the bill to secure the better attendance of Members. On 13 May he was added to the committee to bring in an address promising revenge if the King should meet a violent death. He was named to the committees to inquire into the excise laws, and, as might be expected, to consider the bill for the export of cloth to Turkey. He voted for exclusion.[9]

Love was again very active in the second Exclusion Parliament, being appointed to 34 committees and making ten recorded speeches. On 27 Oct. 1680 he was among those appointed to the committee to inquire into abhorring, and presented a petition for the removal of Sir George Jeffreys as recorder of London for threatening petitioners and jurors, declaring:

> I was some years past in that Parliament (which, I thank God, we are rid of) where a man was still a Presbyterian, or this, or that, if he spoke plainly of miscarriages. The Act passed in that Parliament for regulating corporations sets us all together by the ears. These petitioners in the City for the sitting of Parliament were constrained; ... till a common hall was called they could do nothing. Now, I thank God, we are in a Protestant Parliament, and both those of this or that persuasion will spend their blood for the Protestant religion. The whole body of the City of London are of the same mind, and will join heart and hand with you, as these gentlemen that serve with me will attest.

He was named to the committees to bring in a comprehension bill and to repeal the Elizabethan law against Protestant dissenters. He led the attack on the East India Company, now increasingly unpopular with the country party because of the close links formed with the crown under the guidance of (Sir) Josiah Child*.

> The East India Company have been very industrious to promote their own trade, but therein have given a great blow to the trade of the nation. The Indians knew little of dyeing goods, or ordering them so as to be fit for our European markets, until the company sent from hence Englishmen to teach them. For the cheapness of wages and materials in the Indies must enable the Indians to afford their manufactured goods cheaper than any we can make here, and therefore it is probable the trade will increase prodigiously.... They have already spoiled the Italian and Flanders trade with their silks and calicoes; now they will endeavour to spoil the Turks' trade by bringing abundance of raw silk from the Indies, so that ere long we shall have no need of having silk from Turkey, and, if not, I am sure we shall not be able to send any cloths or other goods there.

When the House debated the King's request for a supply for Tangier, Love reversed his previous attitude. He never shrank from contradicting himself, but in this case he may have reckoned that no power would buy Tangier if it were on offer:

> I am a merchant, and all my trade is in the Mediterranean sea. I was bred there.... I have passed by Tangier. All men have admired the expense of it, for it never was and never will be a place of trade.

He alleged that the proposal for a supply to repair the mole was due to 'Popish counsels', and helped to draw up the Commons answer. In the debate on the premature dismissal of the Westminster grand jury to prevent a petition, he urged the broadening of the investigation, and he was named to the committee to examine the proceedings of the judges. When it was proposed to impeach Edward Seymour*, Love recalled the record he had made of Clarendon's impeachment, and argued against the necessity of producing witnesses:

> I shall speak only to the question. If I were convinced in the reason and equity of it, I should not be against commitment. I have refreshed my memory ... out of my notes.... It was then said: 'Now you have heard the articles read, for the honour of the House you are to know where and when the crimes were committed, and by whom they will be proved'. Says Seymour himself: 'That is the way to invalidate all your testimony, by publishing the witnesses, who by corruption or menace may be taken off'.

He was among those appointed to bring in bills for security against arbitrary power on 17 Dec., and a week later he said: 'I hope we shall now take all dissenters in to save the nation with heart, hand and shoulder to unite against Popery. Let the House make it their interest to bring all in.' On the same day he was named to the committees to bring in the repeal of the Corporations Act. In the Oxford Parliament Love was appointed to the committee of elections and privileges and to the committee to prepare for a conference with the Lords on the failure of the bill of ease for Protestant dissenters to receive the royal assent.[10]

Understandably Love did not stand in 1685. He supported the Revolution, subscribing £500 to the new regime on 8 Jan. 1689. He was returned to the Convention, and in its first three months he was moderately active, with nine committee appointments. On 29 Jan. he was among those ordered to draft an address for stopping shipping to France and to consider reducing trade with France to the level of barter. On 26 Feb. he was appointed to the committee to bring in a bill for regulating elections, and on the next day he expressed the hope that the House would 'consent to such a revenue as may make the King great to all the world'. It was later remembered that he had attacked the East India Company as bringing the profits of trade to investors, such as country gentlemen, 'unto which they are not entitled by their education'. He urged an investigation into the shrieval elections in London in 1682, and he was appointed to the committee of inquiry into the authors and advisers of the quo warranto proceedings and other grievances. His last committee, fittingly enough, was on a bill to prevent the export of wool. Shortly thereafter a group of Tory Members attempted unsuccessfully to engineer the expulsion of Love and all other nonconformists from the House. He was buried on 1 May 1689 at St. Andrew Undershaft. None of his descendants entered Parliament.[11]

[1] London Vis. Peds. (Harl. Soc. xcii), 92, 192; PCC 67 Ent. [2] J. R. Woodhead, Rulers of London, 110. [3] CJ, vii. 798, 801, 802; PC2/55/217. [4] Bridges, Northants. i. 136; Narrative Procs. Militia Officers (1660); Guildhall Lib. mss 507; Guildhall RO, common council jnl. 40, p. 216; Voyce from the Watch Tower, 198. [5] M. Ashley, John Wildman, 178; HMC Finch, i. 120, 356, 377–8, 382, 422; HMC Popham, 166; CJ, viii. 289, 444; Grey, i. 213; viii. 217; Finch diary; D. R. Lacey, Dissent and Parl. Pols. 419–20. [6] Grey, i. 2, 99, 162, 213, 216, 219, 228; iv. 180; viii. 84, 217; Milward, 270–1; K. H. D. Haley, Shaftesbury, 113, 255–6; CJ, ix. 225. [7] Haley, 324–5; Dering, 123; Grey, ii. 48, 260; iii. 358; CJ, ix. 275; A. C. Wood, Hist. Levant Co. 102. [8] Grey, iv. 180, 207–8, 225; v. 254; Add. 28091, f. 41; CJ, ix. 416, 512; CSP Dom. 1678, p. 246. [9] Grey, vii. 100. [10] Grey, vii. 374; viii. 14, 59, 95–96, 216–17; Exact Coll. Debates, 67–68; Wood, 102. [11] Lacey, 224; Grey, ix. 124, 139; Bank of England, Morice mss, Nicholas to Humphrey Morice, 25 Mar. 1709; R. Morrice, Entering Bk. 2, p. 505.

E.C./B.D.H.

LOVELACE, Francis (1594–1664), of Canterbury, Kent and Gray's Inn.

CANTERBURY 1661–Feb. 1664

bap. 22 Sept. 1594, 1st s. of Lancelot Lovelace of Canterbury and Gray's Inn by Mary, da. and coh. of William Cayser of Hollingbourne. educ. G. Inn, entered 1609, called 1620; St. John's, Camb. 1612. m. lic. 5 July 1624, Anne (d.1679), da. of Goldwell Rogers of Canterbury, 5s. (1 d.v.p.) 3da. suc. fa. 1640.[1]

Freeman, Canterbury 1636, recorder 1638–43, July 1660–d., common councilman Oct. 1660–d.; recorder, Dover 1640–54, ?July 1660–d.; j.p. Kent by 1641–?44, Mar. 1660–d.; counsel, Cinque Ports 1647–d.; bencher, G. Inn 1650, reader 1663; steward, St. Augustine's liberty July 1660–3, courts of Chancery and Admiralty, Cinque Ports ?July 1660–d.; commr. for assessment, Canterbury Aug. 1660–d., Kent 1661–d., sewers, E. Kent Sept. 1660, Denge marsh Oct. 1660, corporations, Kent 1662–3.[2]

Lovelace's ancestors had held property in Kent since the 14th century, and the elder branch, to which Richard Lovelace the Cavalier poet belonged, first represented Canterbury in 1567. 'By their deep knowledge in the municipal laws', according to a contemporary, 'the family deserved well of their country', and in 1638 Lovelace, a professional lawyer, succeeded his father as recorder. He has to be distinguished from his cousin, the poet's brother, and from the governor of New York, one of the Berkshire family. He was removed from office in 1643 as a royalist sympathizer; but in 1647 he was one of the moderates who strove to

allay the disturbances in the city caused by the attempt of the county committee to suppress the celebration of Christmas. When the parliamentary forces regained control, he was imprisoned in Leeds Castle for a few months, and he signed the Kentish petition for a free Parliament in the following year. He was described as 'very active against Parliament' in the second Civil War, and compounded for £50 on a property he had purchased in Chartham, though this had apparently been sequestrated because of the vendor's delinquency rather than his own.[3]

Lovelace again signed a Kentish petition for a free Parliament in January 1660 and regained his recordership at the Restoration. He petitioned successfully for the stewardship of the liberty of St. Augustine, near Canterbury, on the grounds of the sequestration, imprisonment, and loss of office which he had suffered for his loyalty. In a fulsome speech of welcome to the King and the queen mother in October he described the Act of Indemnity as inaugurating a golden age. He was returned for the city on the corporation interest in 1661. Much activity could not be expected of a Member making his parliamentary debut at the age of 66, and only three committees can be definitely attributed to him, including that for the corporations bill, though he may have sat on 14 others. In 1663 he resigned his stewardship in favour of Sir Anthony Aucher*, with whom he worked closely in local affairs. Both were little disposed to credit alarming accounts of seditious activities. Lovelace was buried at St. Margaret's, Canterbury on 1 Mar. 1664, the last of the Kentish family to sit in Parliament.[4]

[1] Arch. Cant. x. 216–19; Canterbury Mar. Lic. ed. Cowper, ii. 626; Vis. Kent (Harl. Soc. xlii), 126. [2] Roll of the Freemen ed. Cowper, iii. 320; Hasted, Kent, xii. 611; J. B. Jones, Annals of Dover, 346; Black and White Bks. (Kent Recs. xix), 481; CSP Dom. 1660–1, p. 139; 1663–4, pp. 215, 502; Eg. 2985, f. 66; C181/7/56. [3] Arch. Cant. x. 185, 216; A. M. Everitt, Community of Kent and the Great Rebellion, 231–5; Cal. Comm. Adv. Money, 892; Cal. Comm. Comp. 458, 2391. [4] CSP Dom. 1660–1, p. 139; 1663–4, pp. 189, 208, 502; Arch. Cant. x. 219.

B.D.H.

LOVELACE, Hon. John (c.1642–93), of Water Eaton, Oxon. and Hurley, Berks.

BERKSHIRE 1661–25 Sept. 1670

b. c.1642, 1st s. of John, 2nd Baron Lovelace of Hurley by Lady Anne Wentworth, da. and h. of Thomas, 1st Earl of Cleveland. educ. Wadham, Oxf. 1655, MA 1661. m. 28 Aug. 1662, aged 20, Martha, da. and coh. of Sir Edmund Pye, 1st Bt.*, of Bradenham, Bucks., 1s. d.v.p. 3da. suc. fa. as 3rd Baron 25 Sept. 1670.[1]

Commr. for oyer and terminer, Oxford circuit 1661, assessment, Berks. 1661–9, Oxon. 1664–9, loyal and indigent officers, Berks. 1662; j.p. Berks., Bucks. and Oxon. 1663–7, by 1670–80, Beds., Essex, Herts., Kent and Westminster to 1680, Woodstock 1675, Mdx. and Oxon. 1689–d.; dep. lt. Berks. 1662–7, by 1670–80, Oxon. by 1670–83, 1689–d.; steward and lieutenant, Woodstock manor and park 1670–8, 1692–d.; freeman, Chipping Wycombe 1672, Oxford 1680; common councilman, Woodstock 1673–?81; high steward, Wallingford 1689–d., Wycombe 1689–93.[2]

Capt. of gent. pensioners 1689–d.; c.j. in eyre (south) 1689–d.[3]

Col. of ft. Mar.–Sept. 1689.

The descent of the Berkshire Lovelaces can be traced with certainty only from 1518. An ancestor, John Lovelace[†], purchased Hurley in 1545 and sat for Reading in 1554. Lovelace's father joined Charles I at Oxford in August 1643. He compounded for £7,057 7s.5d. in 1652 and was said to have contracted debts of £20,000 in the King's service, leaving his estates seriously encumbered. At the Restoration he was made lord lieutenant of Berkshire and a Privy Councillor.[4]

Lovelace's election for Berkshire in 1661 under age was presumably a tribute to his father. He sat for nine years in the Lower House of the Cavalier Parliament, but he was not active, serving on no more than 34 committees, probably including those for the corporations bill, the uniformity bill and the bill for the execution of those under attainder, for which he was the first to be named. On 13 May 1662 he may have acted as teller in a division on the Lords' amendments to the bill for regulating the Norfolk cloth trade. He probably sat on the committee to consider remedies against meetings of dissenters in April 1663. On 18 May he acted as teller for an additional clause to forbid the sale of titles in the bill to prevent abuses in sales of offices, but he was not named to the committee. He was listed among the court dependants in 1664. But soon afterwards he was in trouble with the Privy Council for beating a collector of hearth-tax, and in 1666 Andrew Marvell* included him among the Opposition. He was appointed to the committee for the bill to prevent cattle imports. After helping to consider a bill to extend the time allowed to his grandfather, Lord Cleveland, for the redemption of mortgages, he carried it to the Lords. On 7 Jan. 1667 he was teller against imposing double taxation on nonconformists. He took no known part in the attack on Clarendon, and probably went over to the Court soon afterwards. His name appeared on both lists of 1669–71 among those who had usually voted for supply. On 23 Feb. 1670 he carried to the Lords a private bill settling the estates of an Oxfordshire landowner, the Earl of Downe.[5]

'A man of good natural parts, but of very ill and very loose principles', Lovelace had already shown signs of inheriting his father's alcoholic tendencies, and in 1670 he also inherited his title and debts. He was among the opposition peers in 1675, and became a member of the Green Ribbon Club. He played a prominent part in Whig electioneering during the exclusion crisis, notably at Woodstock and Oxford, and voted for the second bill in the House of Lords. After the Rye House Plot he was arrested at a Whig meeting in Reading, attended by John Blagrave* and Nathan Knight* among others, but he was quickly released on bail. He paid a flying visit to Holland in September 1688, and played a prominent part in the Revolution. He was taken prisoner at Cirencester on 11 Nov. at the head of a party of horse attempting to join William of Orange, who made him captain of his gentlemen pensioners and chief justice in eyre south of the Trent. He sold Water Eaton to his son-in-law, Sir Henry Johnson*, in 1692, and died in Lincoln's Inn Fields on 27 Sept. 1693. He was buried at Hurley, but this estate was also sold by his creditors. A cousin inherited the title, but no later member of the family sat in the Lower House.[6]

[1] Mar. Lic. (Harl. Soc. xxiv), 63. [2] HMC Le Fleming, 47; CSP Dom. July–Sept. 1683, p. 162; 1691–2, p. 515; Cal. Treas. Bks. iii. 845; v. 1230; First Wycombe Ledger Bk. (Bucks. Rec. Soc. xi), 198; Woodstock council acts, 5 Feb. 1673; Oxford Council Acts (Oxf. Hist. Soc. n.s. ii) 126; J. K. Hedges, Hist. Wallingford, ii. 241; L. J. Parker, Wycombe, 84. [3] CSP Dom. 1689–90, pp. 11, 18. [4] VCH Berks. iii. 155; Cal. Comm. Comp. 1188–9; HMC 9th Rep. pt. 2, p. 92. [5] PC2/59/379; EHR, li. 635–6; Marvell ed. Margoliouth, i. 147; CJ, viii. 638. [6] Hearne's Colls. (Oxf. Hist. Soc. xiii), 349; CSP Dom. July–Sept. 1683, pp. 88, 91, 107, 389; Luttrell, i. 266, 461, 464; Ashmole, Berks. ii. 478; Wood's Life and Times (Oxf. Hist. Soc. xxvi), 431.

L.N./G.J.

LOWE, George (c.1600–82), of Calne, Wilts. and Pennyfarthing Street, Oxford.

CALNE 1640 (Nov.)–5 Feb. 1644, 1661

b. c.1600, 4th but 2nd surv. s. of Richard Lowe[†], barrister, (d.1624), of Shrewsbury, Salop and Calne by 2nd w. Mary, da. and coh. of Charles Wotton, merchant, of Salisbury, Wilts., wid. of John Vennard of Salisbury. m. (1) 1s. d.v.p.; (2) c.1651, Jane (d. 9 Sept. 1655), da. of Martin Wright, goldsmith, of Oxford, wid. of Acton Drake of Shorthampton Lodge, Charlbury, Oxon., 1s. d.v.p. suc. mother in Calne property 1640.[1]

J.p. Oxon. 1646–53, Wilts. July 1660–c.63; commr. for assessment, Oxon. 1649–52, Wilts. Aug. 1660–3, 1673–80, Oxford 1661–79, Salisbury 1673–4, corporations, Wilts. 1662–3; bailiff, Oxford 1665, assistant 1666–d.; commr. for recusants, Wilts. 1675.[2]

Clerk of petty bag 1666–80.[3]

Lowe's father, of Shropshire origin, acquired an interest at Calne through his second wife and represented the borough in the Addled Parliament. His uncle and godfather, a prominent London merchant, also sat for the borough in the first three

Parliaments of Charles I, and it may have been from him that Lowe derived the funds which enabled him to buy out his half-brother's interest in the lease of the prebendal manor before his father's death. Later he joined with his mother in renewing the lease on the eve of the Civil War at the cost of £4,000. In her will she required her other children to renounce their claims to the Calne property in his favour, and bequeathed £100 to the poor of the borough. It is therefore hardly surprising that he was elected to the Long Parliament a few months later. Lowe's brother married the sister of Sir Edward Hyde[†], and during the Civil War he himself sat at Oxford, though he alleged that he acted under constraint, having visited the King's quarters on business as a trustee and left before the vote declaring the Members at Westminster as traitors. He surrendered to Edward Massey[*] two months later, but according to the officer who took him into custody he was so popular in Calne that four or five hundred of his neighbours would have rescued him if he had given the word. His voluntary and early submission earned him leniency from the committee for compounding; he was fined at a tenth instead of a third, and on his release he became a j.p. for Oxfordshire, though how he formed a connexion with that county has not been ascertained. His second wife, whom he married some years later, was widow of the steward of the Danvers estates, which lay principally in Wiltshire; but the head of the family, the Earl of Danby of the first creation, lived near Oxford, and this may have been the link.[4]

Lowe regained his seat at the general election of 1661, though his lease was about to expire. On 17 July he complained to the House that the treasurer of Salisbury refused to renew it, although he had been a great sufferer for the royalist cause, and had spent 'for preservation of his estate and in improvement and otherwise above £4,000'. Giles Hungerford[*], John Ernle[*] and Jeffrey Daniel[*] were ordered to mediate between Lowe and the treasurer, but the result of their mission is not known. Lowe was not an active Member of the Cavalier Parliament, being named to only 26 committees, the most important being to consider the bill for the execution of those under attainder in 1661 and to hear the petition of the loyal and indigent officers in 1663. He occupied himself principally with the municipal affairs of Oxford, in which his brother-in-law William Wright[*] exercised great influence, and in 1668 he was voted the thanks of the corporation 'for his constant help to the mayor and his brethren in the negotiations between the university and the city now happily finished'. Sir Thomas Osborne[*] included him in 1669 as one of the Members who might be engaged for the Court by the Duke of York and his friends; but his support was probably lost by the Stop of the Exchequer. He had £2,900 on deposit with the London bankers at the time, little or none of which had been recovered when he drew up his will nine years later. Nevertheless, he received the government whip for the autumn session of 1675, although he is not known to have attended either then or later. Shaftesbury marked him 'worthy' in 1677, but also numbered him among the court stalwarts. He is unlikely to have stood again, dying on 19 Nov. 1682, 'aged 88'. On his memorial in St. Aldates, Oxford, it is said that

he exerted himself for forty years, more or less, in the illustrious court of senators (commonly called Parliament) no less to the approbation of individuals than to the advantage of the public.

His heir was his nephew Sir Edward Lowe, a master in Chancery, to whom he bequeathed houses in Oxford and Salisbury, but the family has not been further traced.[5]

[1] *Wilts. Vis. Peds.* (Harl. Soc. cv), 121; *Wood's Life and Times* (Oxf. Hist. Soc. xix), 196, 198–9; (xxi), 353; PCC 70 Cobham, 62 Eure; *VCH Wilts.* vi. 128, 185; Vivian, *Vis. Devon*, 293. [2] A. L. Stedman, *Marlborough and Upper Kennet Country*, 156; *Oxford Council Acts* (Oxf. Hist. Soc. xcv), 329; (n.s. ii), 1, 24, 41, 79, 92, 112, 130. [3] T. D. Hardy, *Principal Officers of Chancery*, 127–8. [4] PCC 70 Cobham, 71 Byrde, 109 Coventry, 83 Grey; W. H. Rich Jones, *Fasti*, 347; Keeler, *Long Parl.* 257–8; *Wilts. Arch. Mag.* xxiv. 309–12; SP23/177, ff. 319–25, 343–7. [5] *CJ*, viii. 304; *Oxford Council Acts* (Oxf. Hist. Soc. n.s. ii), 19; PCC 135 Cottle; Le Neve, *Mon. Angl. 1680–99*, p. 37.

B.D.H.

LOWE, John (c.1628–67), of Shaftesbury, Dorset.

SHAFTESBURY 1661–10 Oct. 1667 [new writ]

b. c.1628, 1st s. of John Lowe, barrister, of Salisbury, Wilts. by Mary, da. and coh. of William Grove of Shaftesbury. *educ.* M. Temple 1646–7. *m.* by 1655, Helen (*d.* 6 Oct. 1661), da. and coh. of Lawrence Hyde[†] of Heale, Wilts., 1s. 1da. *suc.* fa. c.1636; kntd. 19 Apr. 1661.[1]

J.p. Wilts. July 1660–2; commr. for assessment, Wilts. Aug. 1660–*d.*, Dorset 1661–*d.*, Salisbury 1661–3, 1664–*d.*

Lowe came from a legal family. His grandfather, of Herefordshire origin, settled in Wessex, sat for Wootton Bassett in 1597, and registered his pedigree at the 1623 visitation of Wiltshire. His father, also a lawyer, was returned as a ship-money resister shortly before his death, but his offence seems to have been accidental. No inquisition post mortem was held, as an informer pointed out, but in any case Lowe would not have been liable to wardship, as none of his grandfather's land was held in chief by knight service. Lowe's mother married Dr

Humphrey Henchman, a royalist clergyman, who became bishop of Salisbury after the Restoration. Both Henchman and Lowe's mother-in-law actively assisted Charles II in his escape after the battle of Worcester. As stepson of the bishop of the adjoining diocese and a cousin by marriage of Lord Chancellor Clarendon, Lowe had outstanding claims to represent his fellow-townsmen in 1661, and he was knighted before the coronation. But soon afterwards he was struck off the commission of the peace, probably because Henchman had cause to regard him as unsound in religion. His ward Francis Anchitell, whose religious education had been specifically commended to his care, became a Roman Catholic, and Lowe described himself in his will as a member of the holy catholic church. No attempt was made to expel him from the Cavalier Parliament, in which he was an inactive Member. He was appointed to only 21 committees in six sessions, of which the most important were to regulate the fees of masters in Chancery in 1661 and to secure better observation of the Lord's day in 1663. He died during the 1667 recess, leaving Henry Whittaker* 'my fellow burgess in Parliament' as one of his executors. His son received a few votes in both elections of 1679, but, died in the following year without issue.[2]

[1] Wilts. Vis. Peds. (Harl. Soc. cv), 120; J. Harris, Epitaphs in Salisbury Cathedral, 7; M.T. Recs. 947; VCH Hants, iii. 414; PCC 143 Hene; CSP Dom. 1635–6, p. 147. [2] CSP Dom. 1635, p. 535; 1640–1, p. 235; Wilts. Inquisitions (Index Lib. xxiii), 326–9; A. Fea, Flight of the King, 249; PCC 65 May, 143 Hene; Wilts. RO, 413/445; VCH Hants, iii. 414.

J.P.F.

LOWTHER, Anthony (1641–93), of Marske, Yorks. and Walthamstow, Essex.

APPLEBY 1679 (Mar.), 1679 (Oct.)

bap. 15 May 1641, 2nd but 1st surv. s. of Robert Lowther, Draper, of London by 2nd w. Elizabeth, da. of William Holcroft of Basingstoke, Hants. m. 15 Feb. 1667, Margaret (d. 5 Dec. 1719), da. of (Sir) William Penn* of Walthamstow, 6s. (2 d.v.p.) 3da. suc. fa. 1655.[1]
Commr. for assessment, Yorks. (N. Riding) 1661–80, 1689–90, Essex 1663–4, Westmld. 1679–80; j.p. Yorks. (N. Riding) 1662–bef. 1680, Feb. 1688–?d.; freeman, Hartlepool 1671.[2]
FRS 1663–82.

Lowther's father, the youngest son of a large family, became a London merchant. Although he was named by the Long Parliament as one of the sequestrators of his parish church and to a charitable committee during the Civil War, he complained of their proceedings and was probably out of sympathy with their cause. In 1649, together with his nephew, Sir John Lowther I*, he bought

Marske for £13,000 and developed the alum deposits. He served briefly as alderman in 1650–1. Lowther received a great portion with his plain wife, and their life-style attracted the envy of Samuel Pepys*, who watched them closely for venereal symptoms. He was first nominated for Appleby on the family interest in 1668, but was very ready to withdraw in favour of Joseph Williamson*. But in 1679 he was brought in by his cousin, Sir John Lowther III*. Shaftesbury marked him 'honest', but he probably paired with his colleague Richard Tufton* for the division on the exclusion bill. Though he was re-elected in September he left no trace on the records of either Parliament. He refused to stand in 1681 and retired into private life. His reappointment to the North Riding commission of the peace in February 1688 was no doubt due to his brother-in-law, William Penn. He died on 27 Jan. 1693 and was buried at Walthamstow. His son was created a baronet in 1697 and sat for Lancaster in the first Parliament of Queen Anne.[3]

[1] Trans. Cumb. and Westmld. Antiq. and Arch. Soc. n.s. xliv. 103, 107–12; Vis. Hants (Harl. Soc. lxiv), 197. [2] Add. 29674, f. 161; C. Sharp, Hist. Hartlepool, 72. [3] Cal. Comm. Adv. Money, 668–9; R. B. Turton, Alum Farm, 191; Trans. Cumb. and Westmld. Antiq. and Arch. Soc. n.s. xliv. 102; Pepys Diary, 28 July 1661, 15 Feb., 15 May, 13 Sept. 1667; CSP Dom. 1667–8, pp. 174, 213; Westmld. RO, D/Ry2129, Lowther to Fleming, 30 Jan. 1679; Cumb. RO, LW2/D10, Lowther to Lowther, 22 Jan. 1681; Mon. Inscriptions (Walthamstow Antiq. Soc. xxvii), 19.

L.N.

LOWTHER, John (c.1628–68), of Hackthorpe, Westmld.

APPLEBY 1661–Jan. 1668

b. c.1628, 1st s. of Sir John Lowther I*, 1st Bt., by 1st w.; bro. of Richard Lowther* and half-bro. of Robert Lowther†. educ. G. Inn 1646. m. (1) by 1653, Elizabeth (d. c.1661), da. and coh. of Sir Henry Bellingham, 1st Bt., of Hilsington, 1s. 2da.; (2) lic. 25 Feb. 1667, aged 39, Mary, da. of William Wythens of Southend, Eltham, Kent, 1s.[1]
Commr. for assessment, Westmld. Aug. 1660–d.; steward of Richmond and Marquess fees, barony of Kendal Dec. 1660–d.; capt. of militia ft. Cumb. and Westmld. by 1661–d.; commr. for corporations, Westmld. 1662–3, loyal and indigent officers 1662.[2]

Lowther was too young to take part in the first Civil War, but in his own words, perhaps exaggerated, he 'endured perpetual imprisonment for his loyalty' from 1648 to the Restoration. After paying fines of £194, he took up arms in 1651 and fought at Worcester. He was involved in Booth's rising, and again imprisoned till the return of the secluded Members. The compounding commissioners expressed some disquiet at the vigour displayed by their local agents, who replied that 'he is such a known delinquent that he is not likely to

Lowther Family

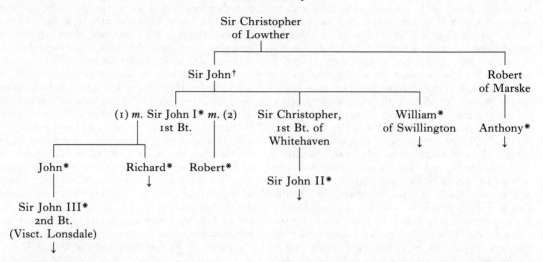

Sir Christopher
of Lowther

Sir John†   Robert
                                of Marske

(1) *m.* Sir John I* *m.* (2)   Sir Christopher,   William*   Anthony*
       1st Bt.   1st Bt. of   of Swillington   ↓
                      Whitehaven   ↓

John*   Richard*   Robert*
            ↓   Sir John II*

Sir John III*   ↓
2nd Bt.
(Visct. Lonsdale)
↓

defend himself'. He was nominated to the order of the Royal Oak with an income of £4,000 p.a., which presumably included his expectations from his father.[3]

Lowther was returned for Appleby at the general election of 1661, and became a moderately active Member of the Cavalier Parliament. During most of the first session, there is the possibility of confusion with his uncle, William Lowther*, but he was certainly appointed to 40 committees and twice acted as teller. His sister had married Sir Christopher Wandesford, and on 11 Jan. 1662 he was appointed to a committee for establishing a family trust. In the same session he helped to consider the measure for preventing theft and rapine on the northern borders which his father had opposed in the previous Parliament. Nevertheless they were not on good terms, and the King recommended Lowther for 'the greater measure of fatherly favour' in view of his 'loyalty, fidelity and valour during the late wars'. He was particularly active in the 1663 session, in which he was appointed to the committees to consider the petition from the loyal and indigent officers and to recommend remedies for the meetings of dissenters. A supporter of the Clarendon administration, he acted as teller against the retrospective clause in the bill to prevent abuses in the sale of offices, and was appointed to the committee of inquiry into the conduct of Sir Richard Temple*. He was teller on 1 Apr. 1664 for the bill to settle certain Hampshire marshlands on Lady Wandesford, and was appointed to the committee. The bill

failed, and the lands were granted to Clarendon's physician, William Quatremaine*. Thereafter Lowther took little part in Parliament. His last committee was again on behalf of the loyal and indigent officers, to which he was added on 12 Dec. 1667. He died on or about 8 Jan. 1668.[4]

[1] *Vis. Cumb. and Westmld.* ed. Foster, 85; Collins, *Peerage*, v. 703; *London Mar. Lic.* ed. Foster, 865. [2] *Cal. Treas. Bks.* i. 98, 145; SP29/445/115; Westmld. RO, Appleby memo. bk. 12 Jan. 1663. [3] *Cal. Comm. Comp.* 1025, 3265; *CSP Dom.* 1651, p. 478; 1659–60, p. 126; 1660–1, p. 71; SP23/264/49. [4] *CSP Dom.* 1661–2, p. 351; *CJ*, viii. 486; Cumb. RO, Lonsdale mss.

L.N.

LOWTHER, Sir John I, 1st Bt. (1606–75), of Lowther Hall, Westmld.

WESTMORLAND   1628, 1660

b. 20 Feb. 1606, 1st s. of Sir John Lowther† of Lowther Hall by Eleanor, da. of William Fleming of Rydal; bro. of William Lowther*. *educ.* I. Temple 1621, called 1630. *m.* (1) by 1628, Mary, da. of Sir Richard Fletcher of Hutton, Cumb., 5s. 6da.; (2) Elizabeth, da. of Sir John Hare† of Stow Bardolph, Norf., wid. of Woolley Leigh of Addington, Surr., 3s. 3da. *suc.* fa. 1637; *cr.* Bt. c.1638.[1]

Recorder, Kendal 1636–48; j.p. Westmld. by 1641–?48, by 1655–6, Cumb. Westmld. and Yorks. (N. Riding) July 1660–*d.*; commr. of array, Cumb. and Westmld. 1642, oyer and terminer, Northern circuit July 1660, assessment, Westmld. Aug. 1660–*d.*, (N. Riding) 1661–*d.*, Cumb. 1663–*d.*, dep. lt. c. Aug. 1660–*d.*; steward of Richmond and Marquess fees, barony of Kendal Sept.–Dec. 1660; sheriff, Cumb. 1661–2; commr. for loyal and indigent officers, Westmld. 1662, charitable uses. Cumb. and Westmld. 1670, recusants, Cumb., Westmld. and N. Riding 1675.[2]

Col. (royalist) ?1642–4; gov. Brougham Castle to 1644.[3]

Lowther's ancestors had been seated at the village from which they took their name since at least the reign of Edward I, and from 1305 regularly represented the county. Lowther himself claimed in his old age to have been first elected as knight of the shire in his minority, but it is probable that his memory played him false. He and his father sat together for Westmorland in 1628–9, a highly unusual distinction for any family, however eminent. 'A man of rigid virtue, temperate and grave, bred from his youth to a great frugality and privacy of living', he was twice defeated by Sir Philip Musgrave* in 1640. Though a royalist commissioner and a colonel in the Civil War, he claimed never to have borne arms against Parliament. He took the Covenant on the approach of the parliamentary forces, and was recommended for reappointment as j.p. He admitted an income of £1,418 p.a., and was fined £1,500, which, even allowing for the vast taxes and free quarter extorted by the Scots, was at least £400 under value. He was again appointed to the commission of the peace under the Protectorate, but probably refused to serve.[4]

Lowther was returned as representative of the barony at the general election of 1660, though his eligibility under the Long Parliament ordinance must have been dubious. A moderately active Member of the Convention, he was appointed to 25 committees, including those to consider the indemnity bill and to prepare for a conference on three orders issued by the House of Lords. He also helped to consider the bill for settling ecclesiastical livings and was named to the revenue committee. On 17 Aug. he was among those ordered to report on the amendments to the indemnity bill, and after the recess he was appointed to the committee for the attainder bill. In his only recorded speech, on 16 Nov., he opposed the bill introduced by Charles Howard* to deal with Scottish moss-troopers, urging that peace might be kept on the borders as it formerly had been.[5]

Lowther did not stand again, though he remained very active in local administration and continued to expand his estate. He was particularly severe on Quakers, but his gentry neighbours were even more frightened of him, unless their estates were invulnerable to his take-over bids. He died on 30 Nov. 1675 and was buried at Lowther. Sir Daniel Fleming* computed the value of his property in Westmorland, Cumberland, and the North Riding at £80,000, and he left £20,000 to his widow to provide for his second family.[6]

[1] Collins, *Peerage*, v. 704–5; E. Bellasis, *Westmld. Church Notes*, ii. 180. [2] *Boke off Recorde* (Cumb. and Westmld. Antiq. and Arch. Soc. extra ser. vii), 29; *HMC Portland*, i. 186; *CSP Dom.* 1655, p. 94; 1660–1, p. 284; Westmld. RO, D/Ry 1124. [3] SP23/186/408; *HMC Lonsdale*, 89. [4] Collins, v. 696; *HMC Le Fleming*, 104; Cumb. RO, D/Lons.; SP23/173/127. [5] *Old Parl. Hist.* xxiii. 15. [6] *CSP Dom.* 1663–4, p. 586; 1664–5, p. 120; Bellasis, ii. 180; *Flemings at Oxford* (Oxf. Hist. Soc. xliv), 479.

M.W.H./L.N.

LOWTHER, Sir John II, 2nd Bt. (1642–1706), of Whitehaven, Cumb. and Southampton Square, Bloomsbury, Mdx.

CUMBERLAND   18 Jan. 1665, 1679 (Mar.), 1679 (Oct.), 1681, 1685, 1689, 1690, 1695, 1698

bap. 20 Nov. 1642, 2nd but o. surv. s. of Sir Christopher Lowther, 1st Bt., of Whitehaven by Frances, da. and h. of Christopher Lancaster of Sockbridge, Westmld. *educ.* Balliol, Oxf. 1657–8. *m.* 6 Mar. 1659, Jane, da. of Woolley Leigh of Addington, Surr., 2s. 3da. *suc.* fa. Apr. 1644.[1]

J.p. Cumb. July 1660–May 1688, Oct. 1688–*d.*, Westmld. July 1660–*d.*, Mdx. 1670–87; dep. lt. Cumb. and Westmld. c. Aug. 1660–May 1688, Oct. 1688–*d.*; commr. for assessment, Cumb. and Westmld. Aug. 1660–80, 1689–90, Mdx. 1673–9; capt. of militia ft. Cumb. and Westmld. by 1661–bef. 1685; member, R. Africa Co. 1672; commr. for recusants, Cumb. 1675; v.-adm. Cumb. and Westmld. 1686–1702; commr. for Greenwich hospital 1694.[2]

Ld. of Admiralty 1689–96.

FRS 1664.

The former monastic estate of Whitehaven was acquired by Lowther's grandfather in 1631 and settled on his father, the younger brother of Sir John Lowther I*. Harbour works began before the Civil War, in which Lowther's father served as a royalist colonel and commissioner of array. At the Restoration Lowther obtained a confirmation of his right to hold a market at Whitehaven. He then set about vigorously developing the collieries and salt-pans on his estates, and, to provide an outlet for them, transformed Whitehaven into a thriving seaport with 2,222 inhabitants by 1693. He also planned a carrier service to connect with London through Kendal. As a member of the Royal Society and a friend of (Sir) Joseph Williamson* he was interested in education, and built, at his own expense, a school at Whitehaven to teach grammar, navigation and mathematics.[3]

Lowther was successful for Cumberland at a contested by-election in 1665. An active Member of the Cavalier Parliament, he was appointed to at least 141 committees. He was naturally interested in projects for improving harbours, and was named to committees for Bridlington, Great Yarmouth, Boston and Dover. In political matters he initially followed the lead of his uncle, William Lowther*;

he was nominated to the abortive commission of public accounts in 1666 and helped to draft the address of thanks for the dismissal of Clarendon in 1667. In the same session he was appointed to the committee on freedom of speech in Parliament, and added to that to hear the petition from the merchants trading to France. Sir Thomas Osborne* listed him in 1669 among the Members who had usually voted for supply. He was among those ordered to examine the lists of debts brought in by the Treasury and the Navy Office on 31 Oct. 1670. A firm Anglican, he helped to consider the additional conventicles bill later in the year, and to prepare a bill against the growth of Popery in 1671; but he was among those ordered on 27 Feb. 1673 to bring in a bill of ease for Protestant dissenters. He was appointed to the committees to inquire into the condition of Ireland in 1674 and to consider appropriating the customs to the use of the navy in the spring session of 1675. By the autumn he could no longer be relied on by the Government. He was named to committees for the recall of British subjects from French service and preventing the growth of Popery, and acted as teller against adjourning the debate on appropriation. However, Sir Richard Wiseman* judged that Lowther and his colleague Sir George Fletcher* 'must be well-known' to Lord Ogle (Henry Cavendish*) and the Earl of Carlisle (Charles Howard*), and in 1677 Shaftesbury marked him 'doubly vile'. In this session he was appointed to the committees for the extension of habeas corpus, and for preventing abuses in the import of Irish cattle and the collection of hearth-tax. His constituents had already complained to him about the inequitable burden of the hearth-tax on Cumberland, while in October he and Fletcher granted a warrant to the constables of Brough to seize and slaughter as illegal imports 18 bullocks recently purchased from Lord Carlisle's son (Edward Howard*). For the remainder of the period it is seldom possible to distinguish Lowther in Parliament from his cousin, Sir John Lowther III*. His activity probably decreased, and he was on neither list of the court party in 1678. The prosperity of Whitehaven was threatened by a proposal to build a rival harbour on crown land in the neighbourhood, but though it was stated on 1 Mar. that the King was favourably disposed to Lowther's petition for a grant of the land to himself, it took over a year to pass the seal.[4]

Lowther was re-elected to the Exclusion Parliaments, promising in his election address of February 1679 to serve the freeholders, who had 'sufficiently owned my diligence', with 'the same attendance, industry and zeal as before', and again defeating an ultra-royalist candidate. Nevertheless he was marked 'vile' on Shaftesbury's list. He was probably appointed to the committee of inquiry into the Post Office, and spoke on 14 Apr. in favour of a grant for the militia.

> I find that something is still recommended to hinder the consideration of our defence and safety. It is not the interest of gentlemen now to put a difference between the King and his people. We have sat all this while and done nothing but the proceedings against the Earl of Danby. Must we not think of our safety because there are faults? And must we still infer that money is not to be given? To say, because there are not alliances with Holland, shall we lay aside all considerations? Pray let not this motion of the militia be stifled.

On the same day the House granted him unlimited leave, but he returned to justify Shaftesbury's opinion of him by voting against the exclusion bill. Re-elected after another contest in the autumn, he was appointed to no committees and made no speeches in the second Exclusion Parliament. Faced again with the possibility of a contest in 1681 he wrote to his cousin:

> My health is such as I dare not venture upon a journey at this time of year, or not upon a journey wherein I know I must be stirring when I come there, for the country has little regard either to a man absent or inactive.

He even considered transferring to Carlisle on the Howard interest, and Sir George Fletcher, with whom he had joined interests in the county, confided to Sir Daniel Fleming*: 'I have done all I could to serve Sir John, but I find he will be the worst befriended in his own neighbourhood'. Fortunately, however, his opponents desisted, and he enjoyed the hitherto unaccustomed luxury of an unopposed return. But he never took his seat in the Oxford Parliament, writing to Fleming from London on 27 Mar.:

> We are here surprised with the dissolution of the Parliament yesterday early in the morning, the Commons not having had above two days for business, the rest form. They all despaired of sitting long from the time they heard the King's speech; but proceeded in the usual methods, and first entered upon the business of the succession where all expedients were heard but concluded in a bill of exclusion of the Duke of York. They also ordered a bill in behalf of Protestant dissenters and another for banishing all the principal Papists in England. . . . What offence the King took at these proceedings or what other reason he had is only known to himself.

Now clearly in good standing at Court, Lowther took a positive interest in naval construction; and when he applied for permission to levy a toll of a penny a ton at Whitehaven, where he had recently spent £500 on enlarging the pier, (Sir) Robert Sawyer*, the attorney-general, reported with the utmost alacrity in favour of the grant.[5]

Lowther was re-elected to James II's Parliament unopposed, but it is probable that the majority of the committee references are to his cousin, the head of the family. He was listed among the Opposition, and was removed from the Middlesex commission of the peace in 1687 after being closeted by the King. Nevertheless he was still attending Court as late as April 1688. In spite of the envy he had contracted 'for serving so often as I have done', he was 'quietly elected' in his absence in 1689. No committees can be definitely ascribed to him in the Convention, in which he was completely overshadowed by his cousin, who obtained for him a seat on the Admiralty board. He supported the disabling clause in the bill to restore corporations, and became a court Whig under William III. He was buried at St. Bees on 17 Jan. 1706. His second son James sat for Cumberland as an independent Whig in every Parliament but one between 1708 and his death in 1755.[6]

[1] Trans. Cumb. and Westmld. Antiq. and Arch. Soc. i. 294–5; ix. 333–58; HMC Le Fleming, 409. [2] SP29/11/22; Sel. Charters (Selden Soc. xxviii), 188; Ind. 24557. [3] Hutchinson, Cumb. ii. 48–49; CSP Dom. 1660–1, p. 198; Flemings at Oxford (Oxf. Hist. Soc. xlii), 149; HMC Le Fleming, 198–9. [4] CJ, viii. 661; ix. 373; CSP Dom. 1675–6, pp. 369, 562–3; 1677–8, pp. 414–15; Cal. Treas. Bks. v. 924, 1262–3. [5] Cumb. RO, LW2/D10; Grey, vii. 110; HMC Le Fleming, 181; Westmld. RO, D/Ry2395, 2405; Pepys Naval Mins. (Navy Rec. Soc. lx), 80, 220; Cal. Treas. Bks. vii. 1237–8. [6] Bramston Autobiog. (Cam. Soc. xxxii), 269; R. Morrice, Entering Bk. 2, p. 52; Clarendon Corresp. i. 168; Yale Univ. Lib. Osborn mss 71/6/20, Lowther to Lowther, 15 Dec. 1688.

E.C.

LOWTHER, Sir John III, 2nd Bt. (1655–1700), of Lowther Hall, Westmld.

WESTMORLAND   29 Mar. 1677, 1679 (Mar.), 1681, 1685, 1689, 1690, 1695–28 May 1696

b. 25 Apr. 1655, 1st s. of John Lowther* by 1st w., and half-bro. of William Lowther†. educ. Kendal g.s. 1668; Sedbergh 1669; Queen's, Oxf. 1670–2; I. Temple, entered 1671, called 1677; travelled abroad (France) 1672–4. m. 3 Dec. 1674, Katharine (d.1713), da. of Sir Henry Frederick Thynne, 1st Bt., of Kempsford, Glos., 5s. (2 d.v.p.) 7da. suc. gdfa. Sir John Lowther I* 30 Nov. 1675; cr. Visct. Lonsdale 28 May 1696.[1]

J.p. Westmld. 1675–d., Cumb. 1689–d.; commr. for assessment, Cumb. Westmld. and Yorks. (N. Riding) 1677–80, 1689–90; custos rot. Westmld. 1678–May 1688, Oct. 1688–d.; gov. Carlisle 1689–90; ld. lt. Westmld. 1689–94; gov. Ironmakers' Co. 1693.[2]

PC 19 Feb. 1689–d.; v.-chamberlain 1689–94; first lord of the Treasury Mar.–Nov. 1690, second ld. Nov. 1690–2; ld. privy seal 1699–d.; one of the lds. justices 1699, 1700.[3]

FRS 1699–d.

The care devoted to Lowther's education was not, as he himself admitted, matched by its success, because his tutors, through their social awkwardness, could not win his respect. Nevertheless his grandfather was determined to bring him before the world at the first opportunity. With the passing of the Test Act in 1673 it was only a matter of time before Sir Thomas Strickland* should be disabled, and a vacancy created for Westmorland. But Sir George Fletcher* argued so strongly against the candidature of a minor in these circumstances that no action was taken. On succeeding to the title Lowther was very anxious to join the 'knot' of opposition politicians meeting on Sunday nights, but his application was vetoed by Sir William Jones*. After at length procuring Strickland's disablement in 1677, he was returned in his absence and without a contest, and marked 'worthy' by Shaftesbury. On 7 Apr. he wrote to his cousin Sir Daniel Fleming*:

I am afraid I brought ill luck with me into the House, for neither things foreign nor domestic have gone well since. . . . The Prince of Orange's army is wholly routed in attempting the siege of St. Omer and himself forced to retire to Ypres; which how much it concerns us you yourself can sufficiently judge. As to our domestic concerns, we have ordered the matter so that the contrary party took advantage of our party's absence, and have voted an Act to be brought in for the repeal of the Irish Act, which prohibits the importation of Irish cattle. I hope I shall not send you every post so bad news, although by what I see there's little likelihood there should be any good.

Although the Journals do not distinguish Lowther from his cousin, Sir John Lowther II*, he was probably moderately active in the Cavalier Parliament; he may have served on 18 committees, and acted twice as teller for the Opposition. But he and Fletcher were absent from the House in March 1678, when they were visited by the Scottish covenanting peer, Lord Cassilis. (Sir) Christopher Musgrave* commented that they expected to do 'better service to their party' as a result, and when Parliament met again in May Lowther and Sir Richard Grahme* successfully opposed the adjournment of the debate on Lauderdale. After the Popish Plot he was appointed to the committee on the bill for disabling Papists from sitting in either House of Parliament. He made his maiden speech on 19 Dec., when it was revealed that the King had ordered the seizure of the papers of Ralph Montagu*:

For aught I know Montagu may be served as Sir Edmund Berry Godfrey was; therefore I would not have him go out of the House for the papers. He knows by what practice these negotiations with France have been done. I am of opinion we shall not sit here to-morrow. I move therefore to have the papers sent for now.

Two days later he acted with Anchitell Grey* as teller against adjourning the debate on Danby's impeachment.[4]

Lowther was re-elected to the first Exclusion

Parliament, and again marked 'worthy' on Shaftes-bury's list. But he was an inactive Member, and was absent from the division on the bill. He did not stand again in September 1679, but resumed his seat in the Oxford Parliament, in which he was probably appointed to the committee of elections and privileges. But it was James II's Parliament that brought him to the fore. On 27 May 1685 he moved for a committee to consider the proper way of applying to the King for the return of the forfeited charters and the restoration of the customary franchise. He was supported by two young men of his own age, though without previous parliamentary experience, Lord Willoughby (Robert Bertie II*) and Sir Richard Myddelton*, and it was only by considerable manoeuvring that the Government managed to stifle the debate. A very active Member, he may have been appointed to 18 committees. He carried the naturalization and tithe bills to the Lords, and was named to the committee for the general naturalization of Protestant refugees. He was much alarmed by the attempt to extend the definition of treason to cover any proposal to alter the succession, but succeeded in emasculating the bill in committee. He was of course included among those in Opposition to James II. He drafted, in consultation with Fleming, the answers to the lord lieutenant's questions on the Test Act and the Penal Laws that were given by at least 15 of the Cumberland justices:

> If I be chosen a Member of Parliament, I think myself obliged to refer my opinion concerning the taking away the Penal Laws and Tests to the reasons that shall arise from the debate of the House. If I do give my interest for any to serve in Parliament, it shall be for such as I shall think loyal and well-affected to the King and the established Government. I will live friendly with those of several persuasions, as a loyal subject and a good Christian ought to do.

During the Revolution he intercepted a cargo of arms designed for the garrison of Carlisle, and with his friends produced a petition for a free Parliament. 'The sun doth not always shine upon the same men', he wrote on 5 Dec. 1688. 'Some rays may fall upon me upon this change of weather.'[5]

At the general election of 1689 Lowther was returned unopposed, and also brought in Henry Wharton* 'whose family have a great claim, not only on account of their great estates, but much more for their well deserving upon this great occasion from all good Protestants'. Danby had already recommended him to William for office, and he was now also assured of Whig support. By his own account, however, he 'went up to London to serve there, out of curiosity to see what would become of us in so extraordinary conjuncture'. As a

committeeman he was only moderately active in the Convention. He may have served on 18 committees, and made 28 recorded speeches. Although his only known intervention in the constitutional debate was to urge the House to proceed deliberately, he considered the regency proposal absurd, or so he later wrote. After the transfer of the crown his colleague's brother, the Hon. Thomas Wharton*, 'surprised' him with the offer of the vice-chamberlain's place, worth £1,500 p.a. and demanded an immediate answer:

> I had a great family of daughters that wanted education, to be had only in London, which I knew must bring me thither for some time, and I had experienced the expense of living there, so that I considered the advantage proposed to me would be a great ease in that respect.

On his acceptance, he was also summoned to the Privy Council and appointed lord lieutenant of Cumberland and Westmorland, and governor of Carlisle. He was named to the committee on the Lords' bill for removing disputes about the legality of the Convention. On 27 Feb. he reminded the supply committee of dangers at home and abroad, and urged them to show their confidence in the King. He spoke in favour of the temporary suspension of habeas corpus, and was appointed to the committee for the bill. He was also among those entrusted with the inquiry into the authors and advisers of grievances, the preparation of the first mutiny bill, the alteration of the oaths, and the drafting of an address for the suppression of the mutiny at Ipswich. But most of his energy was reserved for the indemnity bill, which he first proposed during the debate of 15 Mar.:

> I would put men out of doubt, and make as many friends as we can. Therefore I move that whether, as you made a strict inquiry into grievances, there may not as well be an Act of Oblivion at the same time, and, at the same time, that you address the King to proclaim his pardon to such as shall surrender themselves and return to their obedience and duty.

'We have got the Government settled', he remarked on 15 June; 'I would punish for the future, and pardon all that is past.' In respect of his uncle, Sir Francis Wythens*, he was justifiably afraid that excuses would be unwelcome, but he did his best:

> He lost his place for his opinion about hanging the soldier who ran from his colours. He was never corrupt; he never took a shilling. I perceive I am ill heard upon this subject, but I leave him to your mercy.

He helped to consider the address on the dangers from France and Ireland, and rose in the King's opinion when he argued, on Elizabethan precedent, against naming Princess Sophia in the bill of succession, although it is not clear that he went so far as to mention the Nassau family, as William thought.

He claimed the principal responsibility for the passing of the tithe bill, though he was not on the committee.[6]

Lowther was given leave for five weeks on 18 July, but it was not until 8 Aug. that he arrived in the country, and discovered to his consternation, 'not having been bred to any military skill', that the garrison of Carlisle was to be totally withdrawn; but Shrewsbury at once reassured him that another regiment was on its way. After the recess he defended the Privy Councillors against (Sir) Rowland Gwynne*, who accused them of misrepresenting the House to the King:

I am not so fond of my own opinion as not only to relinquish it, but obey you, contrary to my own sense. I would not only relinquish the service of the Council, but retire, if you think not well of me.

He was appointed to the committees for reversing two of the attainders pronounced after the Rye House Plot, and for stating the condition of the public revenue. He probably voted against the disabling clause in the bill to restore corporations, having previously expressed dismay at the multitude of persons involved in such a measure, and was chosen as spokesman for the meeting at the *Devil* tavern on 29 Jan. 1690 to assure the King of an adequate supply if the Convention were dissolved and a new Parliament called. When it met he was made first lord of the Treasury, and leader of the House. His honesty and moderation were respected, but he was not a ready debater, and his assumption that the wisdom of the House lay on his side, and its weakness on the other, was apt to be ill received. He continued to support William, in or out of office, for the rest of his life, and was raised to the peerage in 1696. After suffering much from ill health, he died on 10 July 1700, aged 45, and was buried at Lowther. His sons were all Whigs, the youngest, Anthony, representing the county from 1722 to 1741.[7]

[1] Collins, *Peerage*, v. 705–8. [2] *EHR*, xxx. 93–94; *Sel. Charters* (Selden Soc. xxviii), 229. [3] *EHR*, xxx. 91. [4] Collins, v. 705; *HMC Le Fleming*, 104, 134; Westmld. RO, D/Ry 1854, Lowther to Fleming, 7 Apr. 1677; *CSP Dom.* 1676–7, pp. 562–3; 1678, p. 5; *CJ*, ix. 477, 562; Grey, vi. 346–7. [5] *Lonsdale Mems.* 5, 7, 9, 16–17; *CJ*, ix. 731, 741; Jefferson, *Cumb.* i. 373; *HMC 11th Rep. VII*, 27; *HMC Le Fleming*, 226. [6] *HMC Le Fleming*, 226, 250; *EHR*, xxx. 92–93; *Hardwick SP*, ii. 412; Yale Univ. Lib. Osborn mss 71/6/20, Lowther to Lowther, 29 Dec. 1688; Grey, ix. 124, 134, 168–9, 319, 343, 345; Foxcroft, *Halifax*, ii. 225. [7] *CSP Dom.* 1689–90, pp. 219, 222; Grey, ix. 39, 154, 313. 458; Macaulay, *Hist.* 1792–3, 1797–8.

L.N.

LOWTHER, Richard (1638–1703), of Maulds Meaburn, Westmld.

APPLEBY 1689

bap. 15 Nov. 1638, 3rd but 1st surv. s. of Sir John Lowther I*, 1st Bt., of Lowther by 1st w., and bro. of John Lowther* and half-bro. of Robert Lowther†. *educ.* Queen's, Oxf. 1655; I. Temple 1655; travelled abroad (France) 1656. *m.* (1) Mary, da. of Sir Amos Meredith, 1st Bt., of Ballinakill, Queen's Co., *s.p.*; (2) 13 Dec. 1679, Barbara, da. and coh. of Robert Prickett of Wressell Castle, Yorks., 3s. 1da. *suc.* fa. at Maulds Meaburn 1675.[1]

Capt. of ft. [I] 1663–c.69[2]

Alderman, Appleby 1678–85, Oct. 1688–*d.*, mayor 1680–1; commr. for assessment, Westmld. 1679–80, 1689–90; maj. of militia ft. Cumb. and Westmld. by 1685–?*d.*; collector of customs, Newcastle-upon-Tyne 1689–*d.*; j.p. and dep. lt. Westmld. by 1701–*d.*[3]

Lowther, a younger son, was intended for the common law, but he was 'too much given to tennis' and, by his own admission, a 'vexatious' charge on his travels to his unfortunate bear-leader, Joseph Williamson*. Even his autocratic father had to admit defeat, and packed him off to Ireland, where he succeeded Sir Thomas Wharton* as captain of foot. Under his father's will he inherited Maulds Meaburn, four miles from Appleby, of which he became an alderman. He also received an allowance of £200 p.a. from his nephew, Sir John Lowther III*, who showed great patience with his 'infinite irresolution'. He first stood for Parliament at a by-election in 1678 for the 'Bottom' of Westmorland, but as his nephew was already sitting for the barony, his candidature was not well received. So good a family friend as Sir Daniel Fleming* would spend only 4s. making votes for him in Kendal and Kirkby Lonsdale, and another half-crown during the poll at Appleby. Although his own expenses of nearly £600 much exceeded his current ability, he seems to have contemplated a petition against Allan Bellingham*, and even proposed to stand again at the general election.[4]

Lowther was removed from the Appleby corporation under the new charter. He signed the Westmorland petition for a free Parliament on 2 Dec. 1688, and was returned for Appleby on the family interest in the following month. According to Anthony Rowe* he voted to agree with the Lords that the throne was not vacant. Nevertheless in July he was given a post in the customs. This appointment later obliged his nephew to fight a duel with the official, a warm partisan of the Stuarts, whom he had displaced. He was appointed to no committees in the Convention and made no recorded speeches. When he stood again for the county in 1701 Fleming said of him that 'he hath been so well affected to King William that ... he keepeth not any in his family that is dissatisfied to the King or Protestant religion', and Sir John Lowther II* wrote: ' 'Twould be impossible for any but cousin

Richard Lowther to fail of success'. He was buried at Lowther on 20 Nov. 1703. His grandson James inherited the Lowther and Whitehaven estates, and sat in the House from 1757 to 1784, when he was raised to the peerage.[5]

[1] *Lowther Reg.* 34; Collins, *Peerage*, v. 704; Ormerod, *Cheshire*, iii. 708; Clay, *Dugdale's Vis. Yorks.* iii. 520. [2] *HMC Ormonde*, i. 293; ii. 187, 195. [3] Westmld. RO, Appleby memo. bk.; D/Ry 2832 (militia, 5 Feb. 1685); Eg. 1626, f. 7; *Cal. Treas. Bks.* ix. 165; xviii. 457. [4] *CSP Dom.* 1655–6, pp. 333, 387; 1656–7, p. 159; 1677–8, p. 684; PCC 20 Bence; Cumb. RO, Lowther Jnl.; *HMC Le Fleming*, 142–5; *Flemings at Oxford* (Oxf. Hist. Soc. xliv), 488, 489; Westmld. RO, D/Ry 2137. [5] *HMC 11th Rep. VII*, 27; Westmld. RO, D/Ry, Fleming to freeholders, 23 Nov. 1700; Cumb. RO, Lowther to Lady Lonsdale, 19 Sept. 1700; *Lowther Reg.* 155.

L.N.

LOWTHER, William (c.1612–88), of Swillington, Yorks.[1]

PONTEFRACT   16 May 1660, 1661

b. c.1612, 3rd s. of Sir John Lowther† of Lowther, Westmld., and bro. of Sir John Lowther I, 1st Bt.* *m.* by 1636, Jane, da. of William Busfield, merchant, of Leeds, Yorks., 5s. (1 *d.v.p.*) 9da. Kntd. 30 Dec. 1661.

J.p. Yorks. (W. Riding) 1632–43, July 1660–*d.*, commr. for assessment Aug. 1660–80 capt. of militia ft. 1661–?76, commr. for corporations 1662–3, loyal and indigent officers 1662, dep. lt. (W. Riding) 1667–76, commr. for concealed lands, Yorks. 1670, recusants (W. Riding) 1675.[2]

Commr. for customs 1671–9.

Designed by his father for a mercantile career, Lowther had established himself by 1636 in Leeds, the thriving centre of the Yorkshire woollen industry. At the outset of the Civil War he helped to raise a loan of £5,000 to the King under the Yorkshire Engagement, and contributed to the Marquess of Newcastle's Cavalier forces, allegedly under duress. From 1643 to 1645 he was in Rotterdam, where he had business interests, and on his return compounded for stock and investments worth £1,000 (excluding 'debts desperate'). After paying a fine of £200 he resumed his business in Rotterdam. He is said to have contributed to the support of the exiled Court, but finally returned to England in or before 1653, when he bought several Yorkshire manors. He retired from trade at this time, though he exploited the coal and lime deposits on his property.[3]

Although ineligible under the Long Parliament ordinance, Lowther was involved in a double return with Sir John Hewley*, at Pontefract, seven miles from Swillington, at the general election of 1660. He was seated on the merits of the election and classed by Lord Wharton as a friend. An active Member of the Convention, he was appointed to 53 committees, twice acted as teller, and made four

recorded speeches. He was in touch with the Court before the Restoration, urging, despite his staunch churchmanship, that every effort should be made to win over Edward Bowles, whom he described as the Presbyterian patriarch of the north. He was among those ordered to consider the libel on Sir Richard Temple* and to prepare reasons for a conference on three orders issued by the House of Lords. On 11 July he opposed the bill to confirm sales of land, quoting the old proverb: 'He that eats the King's goose may be choked with the feathers'. He was appointed on 30 July to the committee for settling ministers in ecclesiastical livings. He tried to insert a proviso in the indemnity bill to cover the Yorkshire Engagement, but withdrew it when he was included in a committee to bring in an accounts bill. His speech on 22 Aug. apparently persuaded the House to agree with the Lords in leaving Sir Henry Vane† liable to the death penalty under the indemnity bill. He acted as teller against a naturalization bill on 30 Aug., and was named to the committee for the Dunkirk establishment. When Parliament met again after the recess he moved that the whole House might attend the King with a vote of thanks for his declaration in favour of a modified episcopacy. He was appointed to the committee for the attainder bill, and on 20 Dec. acted as teller for a proviso to prevent the intruded dons from taking advantage of the bill to confirm college leases.[4]

Lowther was re-elected to the Cavalier Parliament, in which he was very active. He was probably appointed to 564 committees, in four of which he took the chair. He acted as teller in five divisions, and made 12 recorded speeches. In the earlier sessions, as one of the few Members who combined mercantile experience with unimpeachable loyalty to crown and Church, he was particularly prominent, serving on all the committees for the Clarendon Code, though Wharton still listed him among the moderates. During the exceptionally mild winter the local markets had been frequently disturbed by Quaker nudists, many of them ex-officers, crying 'Woe to Yorkshire!' and abusing the Government. Lowther, who had moved in the Wakefield sessions for the suppression of these unseemly practices, was among those ordered to bring in a bill to prevent ill consequences from the activities of the schismatics. On 31 May 1661 he was sent to the Lords to ask for their concurrence for a day of public humiliation in respect of the immoderate rain, and he helped to manage a conference on the corporations bill. At the end of the year he was knighted, and acted as one of the managers of the conference of 7 Jan. 1662 on the 'traitorous design'. He took the chair for the bill to

regulate the West Riding woollen industry, which
he reported on 31 Jan. He was sent on 13 Feb. with
Sir Baynham Throckmorton, 2nd Bt.*, and Sir
William Doyley* to ask the lord treasurer to expedite his report on the Forest of Dean. After being
added to the committee for the execution of those
under attainder, he served on the deputation to ask
the King to return Vane and John Lambert† to the
Tower to await trial. He was among those appointed
to consider the Lords' proviso to the bill against
schismatics, and to prepare reasons for a conference
on it. He acted as teller for referring a petition from
the salt-makers of the north-east to the revenue
committee. On 3 Mar. he carried a bill for the relief
of maimed soldiers to the Lords, and on the following day a bill to discharge James Scudamore*
from a gambling debt, which he had chaired in
committee. On 25 Feb. 1663 he was teller against
adjourning the debate on the Declaration of Indulgence, and he was named to the committee for preparing a bill to prevent the further growth of
Popery. He was one of four Members instructed on
26 Mar. to inquire about Cavaliers' deeds remaining in the Exchequer, and he also served on the
committee of inquiry into Temple's conduct. In
1664 he assisted William Prynne* to establish the
correct title of the Triennial Act, and acted as teller
for a proviso to the hearth-tax collection bill about
punishing the misbehaviour of officials. He was one
of the Members instructed to thank the King and
the City for defending the honour, safety and trade
of the nation against the Dutch. He acted as teller
against bills for relieving the creditors of the Merchant Adventurers and regulating the manufacture
of tobacco pipes. On 1 July 1665 he wrote to Sir
Philip Warwick* to complain of the insolence of
Presbyterian and other conventiclers, and in the
Oxford session his was the first name on the committee for the five mile bill. It is clear that during
the second Dutch war, if not before, he moved into
Opposition as a 'country Cavalier'. He acted as
chairman of the parliamentary accounts committee,
from which he presented an admirably lucid report
on the debts of the navy on 17 Oct. 1666. He helped
to manage a conference on the subject, and he was
the first Member nominated to the abortive public
accounts commission in the following month. He
was among those ordered to prepare reasons against
the patent of the Canary Company and to manage
conferences on the impeachment of Lord Mordaunt, and the bill to encourage coinage. On 21
Jan. 1667 he was sent to ask the Lords to fix a day
for proceeding with Mordaunt's trial.[5]

Lowther took the chair in the committee appointed to draw up an address on 10 Oct. 1667, and
four days later presented a draft including an expression of thanks for the dismissal of Clarendon.
He was among those ordered to bring in an accounts bill, to report on freedom of speech in Parliament, to inquire into the miscarriages of the war,
to consider further charges against Mordaunt, and
to reduce into heads the accusations against Clarendon. On 6 Nov. he cited the *Historical Collections* of
John Rushworth* to prove that 'an impeachment
may be justly drawn by the Commons against a peer
by public fame'. He helped to draw up reasons for
committing Clarendon and for freedom of speech,
and was appointed to the committee on the bill to
banish the fallen minister. Sir Thomas Osborne*
included him in 1669 among those Members to be
engaged for the Court by the Duke of Buckingham,
who had made him a deputy lieutenant. On 10 Nov.
1670 he recommended the postponement of the new
customs farm till the alterations proposed by Sir
Robert Howard* had been considered. On 17 Mar.
1671 he urged that 'all gentlemen who had lent any
money to the King in the late wars might be satisfied', and five days later, in a debate on conventicles, supported a clause to forbid the fining
of juries by judges because 'it is harder to corrupt
twelve men than one judge'. Although his name
continued to appear on committees directed against
both conventicles and Papists, a major speech on 5
Apr. confirms that his attitude towards nonconformists was becoming less rigid:

> Is the Church nothing but discipline? The Church of
> Christ is the doctrine of Christ; the ceremonies are the
> Church of men. As great men as the Church has had
> have dissented in discipline, though they have not pub-
> lished it. The Church is built upon the state of England,
> and the commonwealth bears the Church, not the
> Church the commonwealth. A great prelate, consider-
> ing how to recover the honour of the Church, says,
> 'How came the Church by that honour? By piety and
> humility, and by pride and insolence lost it'.

Lowther was not included by the Opposition among
the court party at the end of the session, but in
September he was appointed to the new customs
commission with a salary of £2,000 p.a.[6]

Lowther helped to draw up the address against
the suspending power in 1673, and was appointed
to the committee which produced the test bill. He
was also named to committees to consider the state
of Ireland (20 Feb. 1674), for the recall of British
subjects from the French service (10 Nov. 1675),
and for the better preservation of the liberty of the
subject (5 Mar. 1677). He was included among the
officials in the House and on the working lists, and
in *A Seasonable Argument* he was described as 'a
man whose honesty and integrity oftener fail him
than his wit'. Nevertheless Shaftesbury marked him

'worthy' in 1677, and Anchitell Grey* mentioned him, together with Henry Savile* and Sir Cyril Wyche*, as losing his place for voting with his conscience. His salary had in fact been reduced to £1,200 when the customs commission was renewed in 1675, but Osborne (now Lord Treasurer Danby) could not persuade the King to replace him by one of his wife's family, though he was removed from the lieutenancy. In his last recorded speech, on 23 Feb. 1678, he opposed the proposal to tax the East India Company, because 'that company does furnish the King with as many brave ships as any body of men do'. His name remained on the government list of court supporters, and he was appointed to the committees for hindering Papists from sitting in Parliament, preparing reasons for a conference on colliers, and translating Coleman's letters.[7]

Although not on the opposition list of the 'unanimous club' of court supporters, Lowther did not stand again. Nor was he reappointed to the customs commission in 1679, presumably because of his age. He died on 20 Feb. 1688, and was buried at Kippax. His son sat for Pontefract as a Whig from 1695 to 1698.

[1] This biography is based on *Trans. Cumb. and Westmld. Antiq. and Arch. Soc.* xlii. 67–76. [2] Stowe 744, f. 53; *HMC 8th Rep.* pt. 1 (1881), 275; *Cal. Treas. Bks.* iii. 634. [3] *Royalist Comp. Pprs.* (Yorks. Arch. Soc. xv), 146–7. [4] *Cal. Cl. SP*, v. 30; Bowman diary, f. 73v; *HMC 7th Rep.* 117; *CSP Dom.* 1660–1, p. 472; *Old Parl. Hist.* xxii. 443; xxiii. 5. [5] *Kingdom's Intelligencer*, 6 June 1662; *CSP Dom.* 1660–1, p. 472; 1664–5, p. 458; *CJ*, viii. 311, 368, 373, 374, 537, 550, 580, 584, 655, 661, 669, 674; *Milward*, 26–27. [6] *Milward*, 117; Grey, i. 280–1, 408, 420; *Dering*, 98; *Bulstrode*, 202; *Cal. Treas. Bks.* iii. 1120. [7] Grey, v. 200, 381; *Cal. Treas. Bks.* iv. 869; v. 1219; Browning, *Danby*, ii. 40, 70.

M.W.H./P.W.

LUCKYN, Capel (1622–80), of Messing Hall, Essex.

HARWICH   Apr. 1648,[1] 1660, 4 Apr. 1664

bap. 8 May 1622, 1st s. of Sir William Luckyn, 1st Bt., of Little Waltham by 1st w. Mildred, da. of Sir Gamaliel Capel of Rookwood Hall, Abbess Roding. *educ.* Bishop's Stortford; Caius, Camb. 1639; L. Inn 1640, called 1647. *m.* 20 Jan. 1648, Mary (*d.* 18 Mar. 1719), da. of Sir Harbottle Grimston, 2nd Bt.*, of Gorhambury, Herts., 6s. (3 *d.v.p.*) 7da. Kntd. 2 June 1660; *suc.* fa. as 2nd Bt. Feb. 1661.[2]

Commr. for militia, Essex 1648, Mar. 1660, j.p. Mar. 1660–*d.*; commr. for assessment, Essex Aug. 1660–*d.*, Harwich 1664–79, recusants, Essex 1675.[3]

Luckyn's ancestors can be traced back as Essex yeomen to 1454, but his grandfather was the first to style himself a gentleman. His father bought Little Waltham about 1624 and was created a baronet in 1629. Luckyn and his father were probably neutral in the Civil War; the latter was assessed at £700 by the committee for the advance

of money in 1644, but no proceedings were taken. Nevertheless Luckyn became the first of the family to enter Parliament when he was elected as a recruiter for Harwich on his father-in-law's interest in 1648, but he did not sit after Pride's Purge, and took no part in politics during the Interregnum. In 1650 he acquired Messing Hall, which became his principal residence.[4]

Luckyn was re-elected at the general election of 1660 and became a moderately active Member of the Convention, in which he was named to 17 committees, but made no recorded speeches. Lord Wharton classed him as a friend, but he was doubtless a court supporter, being rewarded with a knighthood in June. His chief interests were apparently ecclesiastical; in the first session he was among those ordered to inquire into impropriate rectories, to provide maintenance for a minister in his constituency, to settle ministers in their livings, and to provide for observation of the Lord's day. After the recess he was appointed to committees for the prevention of profanity, the establishment of a chapel of ease in Waltham forest, and to enable his father-in-law to make leases as master of the rolls. On 17 Dec. he acted as teller for the third reading of the bill to restore Lord Arundell of Wardour's estate.

Luckyn is unlikely to have stood in 1661, but he successfully contested a by-election in 1664. There was a double return, but he must have taken his seat by 9 Dec. when he was appointed to a private bill committee. An inactive Member of the Cavalier Parliament, he was appointed to only 14 committees of no major political importance and again made no recorded speeches. He was among those to whom the public accounts bill was committed on 11 Dec. 1666. He was included in both lists of 1669–71 among the Members who usually voted for supply, but he later veered towards the Opposition. Sir Richard Wiseman* commented that he was governed by his father-in-law, and Shaftesbury marked him 'worthy' in 1677. His later committees included those to consider a bill to prevent simoniacal contracts and to bring in a bill to remedy inconveniences in the poor laws. He was three times teller in 1678: for naming subsidy commissioners in the House (26 June), for putting the question on the expulsion of (Sir) Jonathan Trelawny I* from the House (21 Nov.), and for excusing Sir John Duncombe* for his default in attendance (18 Dec.). Luckyn's health had given grounds for anxiety since 1674, and he did not stand again. He died on 23 Jan. 1680 and was buried at Messing. His grandson changed his name to Grimston on succeeding to the Gorhambury estate and sat for St. Albans as a Whig.[5]

[1] Did not sit after Pride's Purge, 6 Dec. 1648, readmitted 21 Feb. 1660. [2] Great Baddow par. reg.; *VCH Herts. Peds.* 177–81. [3] Essex RO, 35/101–20; Q/SR 414–39; T/2 26. [4] *VCH Herts. Peds.* 176, 177, 178; *Cal. Comm. Adv. Money*, 405; D. Underdown, *Pride's Purge*, 153; *Trans. Essex Arch. Soc.* n.s. vi. 210, 212–14. [5] *CJ*, viii. 558; Harwich bor. recs. 98/4/26, *VCH Herts. Peds.* 179.

M.W.H./G.H./G.J.

LUCY, Sir Fulk (c.1623–77), of Henbury, Cheshire.

WARWICK   1659

CHESHIRE   16 May 1664–26 Aug. 1677

b. c.1623, 6th s. of Sir Thomas Lucy[†] (d.1640) of Charlecote, Warws. by Alice, da. and h. of Thomas Spencer of Claverdon, Warws.; bro. of Richard Lucy*. *m.* c.1656, Isabel, da. and h. of William Davenport of Henbury, 8s. (2 d.v.p.) 5da. Kntd. by 1661.[1]

Commr. for assessment, Cheshire 1657, 1661–d., Westminster 1677–d., militia, Cheshire Mar. 1660, j.p. Mar. 1660–d.

Capt. Lord Gerard's Horse 1666–7.[2]

Lucy acquired an estate in Cheshire by marrying the heiress of a cadet branch of a prominent county family. He was knighted soon after the Restoration, being so styled in the assessment commission of 1661. But he had connexions with the dissenters, and his return for the county at a by-election in 1664 was probably a defeat for the Court. An inactive Member of the Cavalier Parliament, he was named to only 35 committees. On 21 Dec. 1666 he carried the estate bill of Henry Mildmay* to the Lords. In the autumn of 1667 he was appointed to the committees to report on defects in the Act against the import of Irish cattle and to consider the additional bill which was recommended. He carried another private bill on 11 Mar. 1670, that for settling the Leigh estate, and introduced the Weaver navigation bill in December. He was appointed to the committee on the bills for better observance of the Lord's day in 1671 and preventing abuses in parliamentary elections in 1673. On the working lists it was suggested that Lucy's support might be gained through the influence of Philip Meadows, the Cromwellian diplomat and a distant connexion by marriage. But soon afterwards (Sir) Joseph Williamson* described Lucy as 'very bitter against the lord treasurer', and Sir Richard Wiseman* noted that he was 'touchily and peevishly angry ... and watcheth who bids most for him'. Lord Gerard of Brandon, his partner in the Weaver canal project, and Gilbert Gerard II* were recommended to manage him, presumably with success, for when Parliament reassembled in 1677 Shaftesbury marked him 'vile'. He died of a fever on 26 Aug., aged 54. His son later inherited the family estate in Warwickshire and sold Henbury; but none of his descendants sat in Parliament.[3]

[1] Ormerod, *Cheshire*, iii. 708. [2] *CSP Dom.* 1665–6, p. 557. [3] A. Fairfax-Lucy, *Charlecote and the Lucys*, 142, 171–3, 187, 420; W. Beamont, *Hale and Orford*, 124; *CSP Dom.* 1675–6, pp. 562–3; BL Loan 29/83, Strettell to Harley, 1 Sept. 1677; *Vis. Warws.* (Harl. Soc. lxii), 93–94.

G.H.

LUCY, Sir Kingsmill, 2nd Bt. (c.1650–78), of Faccombe, Hants and Great Newport Street, Westminster.

ANDOVER   31 Jan.–6 Feb. 1673, 10 Feb. 1673–19 Sept. 1678

b. c.1650, o.s. of Sir Richard Lucy, 1st Bt.[†], of Broxbourne, Herts. by 2nd w. Jane, da. and coh. of Thomas Chapman, Draper, of Soper Lane, London and Wormley, Herts. *educ.* Sidney Sussex, Camb. adm. 12 June 1663, aged 12, BA 1666; L. Inn 1667. *m.* 14 May 1668, aged 19, Theophila, da. of George, 9th Lord Berkeley of Berkeley Castle, Glos., 1s. 2da. *suc.* fa. 6 Apr. 1667.[1]

Committee, E.I. Co. 1671–2, 1673–4; commr. for assessment, Hants and Westminster 1673–d., recusants, Hants 1675.[2]

FRS 1668–d.

Lucy's father, a younger son of the Charlecote family, went abroad early in the Civil War, but returned to be elected as a recruiter for Old Sarum. He abstained from the House after Pride's Purge, but represented Hertfordshire under the Protectorate. He acquired an interest at Andover by the purchase of Faccombe, eight miles to the north, in 1655.[3]

Through his father-in-law Lucy became concerned with the East India Company both as member and stockholder, though he also invested in land in the Netley area. He was first returned for Andover on 31 Jan. 1673, but the writ was declared invalid when Parliament met. Though at once re-elected, he never became an active Member, serving on only nine committees, and speaking twice. He was among those appointed to consider the bill for hindering Papists from sitting in Parliament on 28 May 1675, and in the debate three days later on the King's answer to the address for the removal of Lauderdale, he said:

> We have pressed the King so often for the removal of the Duke of Lauderdale, and for answer we have only had a civil denial. If there be a reason to cease this prosecution would hear it. If he has expiated his former ill actions by anything lately done it would much prevail with him by such a demeanour to forget what is past. Has no reason to think his principles are changed when he calls those that were against the Declaration deserters of the King. Since the first address for his removal he has had increase of honour, and a pension as if in defiance of us. He believes him dangerous and obnoxious to the Government, and as such a one would have him removed.

He acted as teller for the motion to present a further address. In the autumn session he was named to the committees for appropriating the customs to the use of the navy and for considering the petition from the Isle of Wight against customs officers. He was noted about this time as being under the influence of the Cromwellian diplomat Philip Meadows, who married his guardian's daughter. On 11 Apr. 1677 he seconded the motion of Lord Ibrackan (Henry O'Brien*) for resuming work on legislation after the adjournment, but he must have gone over to the Government soon afterwards, for Shaftesbury marked him 'doubly vile', and in *A Seasonable Argument* he was said to have been given £1,000 (though no payment can be traced in any existing account) and promised a place at Court, which he did not live long enough to claim. He signed his will with a mark on 19 Sept. 1678 and was buried at Faccombe on the following day, the last of his branch of the family to enter Parliament.[4]

[1] *The Gen.* n.s. xxxiv. 5; *Fire Court* ed. P. E. Jones, ii. 219; PCC 47 Carr, 112 Reeve; *Survey of London*, xxxiv. 345. [2] *Cal. Ct. Mins. E.I. Co.* ed. Sainsbury, ix. 30, 225. [3] *N. and Q.* cc. 298; D. Underdown, *Pride's Purge*, 379; *VCH Hants*, iv. 316. [4] *Cal. Ct. Mins. E.I. Co.* viii. 158, 400; ix. 306–7, 309, 311, 313; x. 400, 404; xi. 332; Grey, iii. 211; Eg. 3345, f. 47v.

A.M.M.

LUCY, Richard (c.1619–77), of Charlecote Park, Warws.

WARWICKSHIRE	1653, 1654, 1656, 1659
YARMOUTH I.o.W.	1660, 1661–21 Dec. 1677

b. c.1619, 3rd s. of Sir Thomas Lucy† of Charlecote, and bro. of Sir Fulk Lucy*. *educ.* Queen's, Oxf. matric. 17 Sept. 1634, aged 14; travelled abroad 1637–40; G. Inn 1652. *m.* Elizabeth, da. and h. of John Urrey of Thorley, I.o.W., 4s. (3 *d.v.p.*) 2da. *suc.* bro. 1658.[1]

Sheriff, Warws. 1646–7; commr. for assessment, Warws. 1648–52, Hants 1649–52, Warws. and Hants 1657, Jan. 1660–d., I.o.W. 1663–4, Westminster 1677–d., militia, Warws. and Coventry 1648, Warws. Mar. 1660; j.p. Warws. by 1649–d., Hants 1649–July 1660; commr. for scandalous ministers, Warws. 1654, oyer and terminer, Western circuit 1655, Midland circuit July 1660; capt. of militia ft. Warws. Apr. 1660, dep. lt. c. Aug. 1660–d.; recorder, Stratford-on-Avon 1672–d.; commr. for recusants, Hants 1675.[2]

Commr. for army 1653–9, Feb.–May 1660, excise arrears 1653–4; judge of probate 1654–9; member, high court of justice.[3]

Lucy's ancestors had held Charlecote since the 12th century and first sat for Warwickshire in 1312. His eldest brother was a royalist colonel, but Lucy himself is not known to have taken part in the Civil War. Before succeeding to the property he was a salaried official under the Commonwealth and Protectorate. He acquired an interest in the Isle of Wight by marriage, and was first returned for Yar-

mouth, one mile from Thorley, in 1659, though he chose to sit for Warwickshire. Again elected for the borough in 1660, he was moderately active in the Convention, being appointed to 17 committees, of which the most important was for the indemnity bill. On 24 May he recorded his acceptance of the King's pardon 'with humble and hearty thankfulness', and promised to 'continue his loyal and obedient subject'. He made no speeches, but he was marked as a friend on Lord Wharton's list and probably voted with the Opposition, and his name was struck out of the disbandment commission. He was re-elected with his brother-in-law Edward Smythe* in 1661. Again moderately active in the Cavalier Parliament, he was named to 59 committees. His only recorded speech, made in the debate on the five mile bill on 30 Oct. 1665, suggests that he retained some nonconformist sympathies, for he objected to the second part of the oath to be imposed on dissenting ministers and schoolmasters: 'there would be no danger to the crown from them that should take the first part'. In 1671 he sold Highclere to Robert Sawyer*. He was added to the committee to consider the general test bill on 12 Feb. 1674, but otherwise seems to have avoided involvement in political controversy. He was noted in 1675 on the working lists as under the influence of the distinguished ex-Cromwellian, Lord Orrery (Roger Boyle*). He visited Shaftesbury in the Tower in 1677, and was marked by him 'thrice worthy'. He died on 21 Dec., aged 58.[4]

[1] *Vis. Warws.* (Harl. Soc. lxii) 94; *PC Reg.* iii. 10. [2] *Thurloe*, iii. 296; *Merc. Pub.* 5 Apr. 1660; *CSP Dom.* 1671–2, p. 153. [3] G. E. Aylmer, *State's Servants*, 238. [4] W. F. Lucy, *Lucy Fam.* 36–37; *VCH Hants*, v. 285; *CJ*, viii. 116, 154; *CSP Dom.* 1659–60, p. 445; 1675–6, pp. 562–3; 1677–8, p. 267; Bodl. Carte 80, f. 757v.; *VCH Hants*, iv. 278.

A.M.M.

LUCY, Thomas (c.1655–84), of Charlecote Park, Warws.

YARMOUTH I.o.W.	28 Dec. 1678, 1679 (Mar.)
WARWICK	1679 (Oct.), 1681

b. c.1655, 2nd but o. surv. s. of Richard Lucy*. *educ.* G. Inn, entered 1667. *m.* Catherine, da. of Robert Wheatley, poulterer, of Holborn, London and Bracknell, Berks., 1da. *suc.* fa. 1677.[1]

Recorder, Stratford-on-Avon 1678–d.; commr. for assessment, Warws. and Westminster 1679–80; j.p. Warws. 1680–d., sheriff 1682–3, dep. lt. 1683–d.[2]

Capt. Duke of Monmouth's Ft. 1678–9, R. Horse Gds. (The Blues) 1679–d.

Lucy, an army officer, succeeded to his father's seat at Yarmouth only two days before the Cavalier Parliament was prorogued. Shaftesbury at once marked him 'vile', possibly because of his marriage to a Roman Catholic of obscure family, 'rich only in beauty', and addicted to gambling; but he is unlikely to have sat, though on 2 Jan. 1679 his privilege was infringed by a distraint on his coach and horses. He was re-elected to the first Exclusion Parliament, and again marked 'vile'. He was named to the committee of elections and privileges, and according to the list in the state papers voted against the exclusion bill, though Morrice included him among the absent Members. By the autumn he had disposed of his Isle of Wight property to Sir Robert Holmes*, and he was returned for Warwick, six miles from Charlecote, no doubt with the support of Lord Brooke (Fulke Greville*). A moderately active Member of the second Exclusion Parliament, he was one of those instructed to examine a convicted priest in Newgate on 3 Nov. 1680 and to draft an address for a day of fasting and humiliation. On 9 Dec. he reported that the search of Sheridan's lodgings in York Buildings had failed to reveal any suspicious papers. His last committee was on the bill to disarm Papists and expel them from the metropolitan area; but on 21 Dec. he had leave to go into the country. He was re-elected in 1681, but left no trace on the records of the Oxford Parliament.[3]

As sheriff of Warwickshire Lucy was responsible after the Rye House Plot for searching the homes of prominent Whigs, among them Arbury, where, according to Sir Richard Newdigate*, he carried out the task politely. Hearing that in Coventry three-quarters of the people were as disaffected as any in the nation, he caused the oath of allegiance to be administered to the suspects. He secured the surrender of the Stratford charter and its return without alteration. He died of smallpox on 1 Nov. 1684 and was buried at Charlecote. His heir was his cousin, the son of Sir Fulk Lucy*, but the estate was diminished by a bequest of £10,000 to his daughter, and no later Member of the family entered Parliament. In 1684 his widow caused a court scandal by marrying Charles II's illegitimate son, the Duke of Northumberland.[4]

[1] *Vis. Warws.* (Harl. Soc. lxii), 94; Luttrell, i. 373. [2] A. Fairfax-Lucy, *Charlecote and the Lucys*, 164–5. [3] *HMC Portland*, iii. 395; M. E. Lucy, *Lucy Fam.* 37–38; *CJ*, ix. 582; *VCH Hants*, v. 285. [4] Newdigate-Newdegate, *Cavalier and Puritan*, 215–17; *CSP Dom.* Jan.–June 1683, pp. 362, 374; *VCH Warws*. iii. 352; Fairfax-Lucy, 167, 170; *Evelyn Diary*, iv. 505; *HMC Rutland*, ii. 107–10.

A.M.M.

LUDLOW, Edmund (c.1617–92), of South Court, Maiden Bradley, Wilts.[1]

WILTSHIRE 12 May 1646
HINDON 1659, 3–18 May 1660

b. c.1617, 1st s. of Sir Henry Ludlow† of Maiden Bradley by Elizabeth, da. and coh. of Richard Phelips of Winterbourne Whitchurch, Dorset. *educ.* Blandford g.s.; Trinity, Oxf. matric. 10 Sept. 1634, aged 17, BA 1636; I. Temple 1637–42. *m.* c.1649, Elizabeth, da. of William Thomas of Wenvoe, Glam., *s.p. suc.* fa. 1643.

Cuirassier, lord general's life gd. (parliamentary) 1642–3; capt. of horse 1643–4, maj. 1644, col. 1644–5; gov. Wardour Castle 1644; lt.-gen. of horse [I] 1650–5; c.-in-c. [I] 1659–Jan. 1660.

Commr. for executing ordinances, Wilts. 1644, defence 1644, assessment 1644–52, 1657, Jan. 1660; sheriff 1644–5; j.p. Wilts. 1646–Mar. 1660, Mdx. 1649–?51; commr. for militia, Westminster 1649, Wilts. 1659.

Commr. for exclusion from sacrament 1646, scandalous offences 1648, high court of justice 1649; Councillor of State 1649–51, May–Dec. 1659; commr. for civil affairs [I] 1650–4, adventurers [I] 1654, army Oct.–Dec. 1659.

Ludlow's family was founded by a Lancastrian household official who acquired property in Wiltshire about the middle of the 15th century and sat for Ludgershall in six Parliaments. They later acquired an evil reputation as encroaching landlords. Ludlow's father, a younger son, inherited little freehold land besides the small manor of Yarnfield, holding South Court on a lease for lives from the Devonshire Seymours. Both father and son were extreme opponents of the Stuarts, but Ludlow, though a regicide and a religious experimentalist, was almost as hostile to the Protectorate. He bought the manor of East Knoyle (in which Hindon was comprised) at the sale of capitular lands in 1650, and represented the borough in Richard Cromwell's Parliament. He was made commander-in-chief in Ireland by the Rump in 1659, but accepted Lambert's military regime. He refused to sit in the Long Parliament after the return of the secluded Members.[2]

When the Long Parliament dissolved itself Ludlow 'resolved to repair into the country, as well to withdraw myself from under the eyes of those in power, as for the raising of what moneys I could among my tenants'. He had agreed with Edward Bayntun I* to oppose Sir Anthony Ashley Cooper*, 'who had now most clearly discovered himself to be what I always suspected him to be', in the Wiltshire election; but Bayntun desisted before he arrived. He concealed himself in lodgings in Salisbury, but not so effectively as to prevent a report that he had been elected for the city, rather through fear than love, it was suggested. At East Knoyle 'I found the present tenants do dally with me, reserving the day of payment to half a year after, in which time they hoped to have another landlord more agreeable to their temper'. But by the generality of the electors at Hindon he was received with 'much affection and heartiness', and assured that Edward

Seymour* (who in any case was ineligible as a Cavalier's son under the Long Parliament ordinance) 'would not desire their voices in case I would serve for them'. He did not dare appear at the election; but he was told that 'of about twenty-six who had any right to give voices, nineteen appeared for me'. The bailiff accordingly returned Ludlow with George Grobham Howe*, who was unopposed; but the agents of (Sir) Thomas Thynne II*, 'making up in quantity what they wanted in quality', procured enough subscription among the rabble to furnish a plausible double return. When John Lambert† escaped from the Tower Ludlow told his emissary that he was 'not free to engage against others till we agreed for what', and discovered that 'the Lord had deprived me at present of an opportunity of appearing in the field, or indeed of being any way active for him'.[3]

On 3 May Edward Turnor* reported that Ludlow ought to sit on the merits of the return. But only the weight and influence of Arthur Annesley* and Matthew Hale* could persuade the House, in the name of justice, to accept the report, and he was ordered to attend within a week. Ludlow, who was now in hiding at a friend's house in Holborn, was quickly informed of these resolutions, and on Annesley's advice took his seat on 5 May, immediately withdrawing into the Speaker's chamber, possibly by prior arrangement, since Sir Harbottle Grimston* was Howe's father-in-law. He received good advice about his conduct from Robert Harley I* and John Maynard I*; but Richard Norton* and John Swinfen* reproached him for the 'paring and straitening' of the Parliamentarian party, which had brought it to its present condition, and even the absent-minded Sir George Booth*, having saluted him very civilly on his first entrance, 'bent his brows' on him. He remained with Cooper in the Speaker's chamber during the ballot for messengers to the King, being 'resolved to have no hand in the setting up of this exploded idol', but attended the elections committee in the afternoon. This appears to have been his only attempt to perform his parliamentary duties in the Convention. On 18 May he was unseated on the merits of the election.

Ludlow was among the regicides excepted from pardon by the resolution of 9 June, in which it was declared that they should not be subject to the death penalty. He surrendered himself to the Speaker on 20 June, and on the following day the House ordered that he should remain in the custody of the serjeant-at-arms. Annesley, finding Ludlow unrepentant, washed his hands of the obstinate regicide, but he still had many friends in the House. The

Hon. James Herbert* stood security for Ludlow, who ensured that he should suffer no loss by substituting four men of straw, since he had no intention of remaining in England any longer than it took to settle his affairs. Warned by Francis Swanton* and Henry Henley* that as soon as the bill was passed he would be committed to the Tower, he took ship and arrived in France about the middle of August. In 1662 he moved to Vevey, in the canton of Lausanne, where, with one brief interval, he was to reside for the remainder of his life. Though all his property in England had been forfeited, he was well supplied with funds on his wife's account. In the early years of the Restoration, his name was constantly mentioned in connexion with republican plots, and he contemplated taking service with the Dutch in 1665; but inaction had become second nature to him, and he never went further afield than Lyon. The daring Colonel Blood, hoping to entice him into activity, 'found him very unable for such an employment, only that he was writing a history (as he called it) which he told the Colonel would be as true as the gospel'. Since the discovery of part of his manuscript at Warwick Castle, it has been recognized that the *Memoirs* published in 1698–9 were unscrupulously, though skilfully, edited to minimize the apocalyptic element. But as a valuable source for local history during the Civil War, for the kaleidoscopic politics of 1659–60, and above all for their unconscious revelation of the author's personality and the impracticability of the republican doctrinaires, they have always been highly regarded. In August 1689 Ludlow reappeared in England, to the consternation of Seymour, who feared that the forfeiture of his estates might be reversed. On 6 Nov. Seymour's brother-in-law (Sir) Joseph Tredenham* moved for an address to the King to issue a proclamation for his expulsion. Nobody spoke in Ludlow's defence, though Whigs like Sir John Guise*, John Hawles* and John Birch* sought to delay the vote by technicalities and buffoonery. Without waiting for the proclamation, Ludlow quietly withdrew to Holland, and thence to Vevey, where he died in November 1692.[4]

[1] This biography is based on Sir Charles Firth's edition of the *Ludlow Mems.* and *A Voyce from the Watch Tower* (Cam. Soc. ser. 4, xxi). [2] Hoare, *Wilts. Mere* 136*, Heytesbury 16; *VCH Wilts.* iv. 46; Keeler, *Long Parl.* 260–1; S. Gale, *Cathedral of Winchester*, 23. [3] *Cal. Cl. SP*, iv. 628. [4] *CJ*, viii. 61, 70; *CSP Dom.* 1676–7, p. 577; Grey, ix. 397–8.

M.W.H./J.P.F.

LUKE, Sir Samuel (1603–70), of Woodend, Cople, Beds.

BEDFORD   6 Aug. 1641,[1] 1660

bap. 27 Mar. 1603, 1st s. of Sir Oliver Luke† of Woodend by 1st w. Elizabeth, da. and coh. of Sir Valentine Knightley of Fawsley, Northants. *educ.* Eton 1617–19; travelled abroad 1623. *m.* 2 Feb. 1624, Elizabeth, da. of William Freeman, Haberdasher and merchant, of London, 6s. (1 *d.v.p.*) 4da. Kntd. 20 July 1624; *suc.* fa. c.1651.[2]

Freeman, Bedford 1625; commr. for sewers, Beds. 1636; j.p. Bedford 1640, Sept. 1660, Beds. Mar. 1660–6; commr. for midland assoc. Beds. 1642, assessment 1643–8, Aug. 1660–3, sequestrations 1643, levying of money 1643, new model ordinance 1645, militia 1648, Mar. 1660, col. of militia ft. Apr. 1660.[3]

Capt. of horse (parliamentary) 1642; col. of dgns. 1643; scoutmaster-gen. 1643–5; gov. Newport Pagnell 1643–5.[4]

Commr. for scandalous offences 1646, indemnity 1647–8, exclusion from sacrament 1648.

Luke was descended from a Tudor judge who acquired Woodend by marriage. His father represented either the county or the borough almost continuously from 1597 to Pride's Purge, but the family fortunes were in decline before the Civil War. Father and son were both Presbyterians, and as scoutmaster-general for the parliamentary forces Luke achieved distinction for his diligence and skill in espionage. As one of the tellers for the treaty of Newport, he was imprisoned for a few days after Pride's Purge, and 'refused all public employment ever since till the sitting of the secluded Members'.[5]

Luke was returned in 1660 for Bedford, three miles from his residence, together with Humphrey Winch*, his tenant and kinsman. He was listed as one of Lord Wharton's friends, but made no recorded speeches in the Convention, and was appointed to only six committees, of which the most important were for the confirmation of parliamentary privileges and for settling the establishment of Dunkirk. After the recess he was named to the committee on the bill for the sale of the lands of Lord Cleveland, who recommended him as deputy lieutenant with the implication that he had been involved with Richard Browne I* in a royalist conspiracy so secret that it was unknown even to Edward Massey*; but nothing is known of this, and the recommendation failed. Luke lost his seat to John Kelyng* in 1661. He has usually been identified with the principal character in Butler's Cavalier satire *Hudibras*, which appeared in the following years with enormous success. He was obliged to alienate Hawnes, one of his principal estates, to Sir George Carteret*, and was buried at Cople on 30 Aug. 1670, the last of the family to sit in Parliament.[6]

[1] Secluded at Pride's Purge, 6 Dec. 1648, readmitted 21 Feb. 1660. [2] *Beds. N. and Q.* i. 353; *Vis. Beds.* (Harl. Soc. xix), 180; *APC* 1621–3, p. 468; *Coll. Top. et Gen.* iii. 85; v. 363; *St. Michael's Cornhill* (Harl. Soc. Reg. vii), 224. [3] *Beds. N. and Q.* iii. 94; *Min.*

Bk. Bedford Corporation (Beds. Hist. Rec. Soc. xxvi), 1, 3, 17; C181/5/74, 373; *LJ*, v. 493; *Merc. Pub.* 12 Apr. 1660. [4] *Jnl. of Sir Samuel Luke* (Oxon. Rec. Soc. xxix), pp. v–vi; *CJ*, iii. 156. [5] *VCH Beds.* iii. 239; Keeler, *Long Parl.* 261–2; Beds. Hist. Rec. Soc. xviii. 29; xxvii. 39, 43; D. Underdown, *Pride's Purge*, 147; *Jnl. of Sir Samuel Luke*, p. v; SP29/11/142. [6] SP29/11/142; *CJ*, viii. 250; *VCH Beds.* 340–1; Beds. RO, CRT 110/35/14; *Pepys Diary*, 17 May 1667; *Coll. Top. et Gen.* v. 363.

M.W.H./L.N./G.J.

LUTTRELL, Francis I (1628–66), of Dunster Castle, nr. Minehead, Som.

SOMERSET 1656

MINEHEAD 1660, 1661–23 Feb. 1666 [new writ]

bap. 1 Nov. 1628, 4th but 2nd surv. s. of Thomas Luttrell† (*d.*1644) of Dunster by Jane, da. of Sir Francis Popham† of Littlecote, Wilts.; bro. of Alexander Luttrell†. *educ.* L. Inn 1646, called 1653. *m.* 8 Oct. 1655, Lucy, da. of Thomas Symonds of Whittlesford, Cambs., 3s. *suc.* bro. 1655.[1]

J.p. Som. 1657–9, Mar. 1660–*d.*, commr. for assessment, Som. 1657, Jan. 1660–*d.*, Cornw. 1663–*d.*, militia, Som. Mar. 1660, col. of militia ft. Apr. 1660, commr. for sewers, Aug., Dec. 1660, dep. lt. 1675–*d.*[2]

Luttrell's ancestors had held extensive property in Somerset since 1232, and first entered Parliament in 1360. In 1405 they acquired Dunster, two miles from Minehead, and regularly represented the borough from its enfranchisement in 1563. Luttrell's father held Dunster Castle for Parliament until forced to surrender to Francis Wyndham*, his elder brother served on the county committee during the Civil War and under the Commonwealth, and he himself, despite his youth, found it advisable to sue out a pardon at Oxford in 1644. He qualified as a barrister, but succeeded to the estate two years later, married a granddaughter of John Pym†, and represented the county in the second Protectorate Parliament. At the Restoration he was proposed for the order of the Royal Oak, with an income estimated at £1,500 p.a.; but Lord Wharton marked him as a friend both in 1660 and 1661. He was returned to the Convention for the family borough, but he was appointed to no committees and did not speak. He was re-elected to the Cavalier Parliament, in which he was named to only two committees, one, in 1661, for easing sheriffs in their accounts, the other, in 1663, for the better observance of the Lord's day. He was buried at Dunster on 14 Mar. 1666. He left several young children to the guardianship of (Sir) Charles Pym* and Sir Francis Popham*.[3]

[1] H. C. Maxwell Lyte, *Hist. Dunster*, 179, 184, 201, 202. [2] *Q. Sess. Recs.* (Som. Rec. Soc. xxxiv), p. xiv; *Merc. Pub.* 26 Apr. 1660. [3] Maxwell Lyte, 64, 80, 169, 183, 200, 203; D. Underdown, *Som. in the Civil War*, 43, 51; W. H. Black, *Docquets of Letters Patent*, 155.

M.W.H./I.C.

LUTTRELL, Francis II (1659–90), of Dunster Castle, Som.

MINEHEAD 1679 (Mar.), 1679 (Oct.), 1681, 1685, 1689, 5 Mar.–25 July 1690

bap. 16 June 1659, 2nd s. of Francis Luttrell I*, and bro. of Alexander Luttrell†. *educ.* Christ Church, Oxf. 1676. *m.* 15 July 1680, Mary, da. and h. of John Tregonwell of Milton Abbas, Dorset, 1s. 3da. *suc.* bro. 1670.[1]

Commr. for assessment, Som. 1679–80, Som. and Dorset 1689–90, j.p. Som. 1680–Feb. 1688, Oct. 1688–*d.*, Dorset 1682–7, Apr. 1688, Nov. 1688–*d.*; dep. lt. Som. 1681–7, Dorset 1685–7; col. of militia ft. Som. 1681–?87, v.-adm. 1685–?*d.*, commr. for rebels' estates 1686.[2]

Col. of ft. Nov. 1688–*d.*

Luttrell's mother defended the estate vigorously during his minority from the encroachments of neighbours and the attempts of the inhabitants of Minehead to escape the control of its lords. Luttrell went up to Oxford in 1676 and, according to Anthony à Wood, almost became a peer while still an undergraduate, when the bishop of Oxford was granted the patent for an earldom by which he might raise the money for completing the great gate of Christ Church. Luttrell did not secure the peerage, however, perhaps because he was unable to pay the £1,000 required, though according to Wood, he already enjoyed an income of £4,000 p.a.[3]

Luttrell was still under age when he was first elected in 1679 for the family borough of Minehead, which he continued to represent until his death. In the first Exclusion Parliament he was appointed only to the committee of elections and privileges and is not known to have spoken. Shaftesbury expected his support, classing him as 'honest', but he did not vote for the exclusion bill, having been given leave of absence nine days before the division. In the second Exclusion Parliament he was appointed to two committees, one of which was for the bill for the discovery of estates settled to superstitious uses on 7 Jan. 1681. In the Oxford Parliament no activity is recorded.[4]

Luttrell acquired by marriage the ex-monastic properties of the elder branch of the Tregonwell family in Somerset and Dorset, which were estimated to bring in £2,500 p.a. As a j.p. he was hostile to nonconformists. Elected again for Minehead in 1685, he took no known part in James II's Parliament, but he was probably a court supporter. During the summer he commanded a militia regiment against the Duke of Monmouth, but was unable to distinguish himself as most of his men deserted.[5]

By 1687, James II's religious policy was causing Luttrell's allegiance to falter, and he refused his consent to the repeal of the Test and Penal Laws; in consequence he was deprived of his deputy lieutenancy and was removed from the commission of the peace. In November 1688 he raised a regiment in support of William of Orange and was given a permanent commission after the Revolution, although he had voted to agree with the Lords that the throne was not vacant. He was otherwise inactive in the Convention. He died on 25 July 1690 while with his regiment at Plymouth waiting to go overseas. His brother inherited his seat as well as a seriously encumbered estate, representing Minehead until his death in 1708.[6]

[1] H. C. Maxwell Lyte, *Hist. Dunster*, 204, 205, 215. [2] *Q. Sess. Recs.* (Som. Rec. Soc. xxxiv), p. xiv; *HMC Lords*, i. 189; Som. RO, Q/JC 99, 100; Dorset Q. Sess. minute bk. 1669–87; *CSP Dom.* 1680–1, pp. 277, 290; 1685, p. 165; *Cal. Treas. Bks.* viii. 545; Ind. 24557. [3] Som. RO, Luttrell mss A/4; *Wood's Life and Times* (Oxf. Hist. Soc. xxi) 421. [4] *CJ*, ix. 620. [5] Maxwell Lyte, 205; *CSP Dom.* 1682, pp. 97–98; Jan.–June 1683, p. 194; *HMC 3rd Rep.* 96; *HMC Sackville*, 1–2; *Bramston Autobiog.* (Cam. Soc. xxxii) 185. [6] *HMC Le Fleming*, 223; *Hatton Corresp.* (Cam. Soc. n.s. xxiii) 106, 108, 110; Maxwell Lyte, 206, 215–16, 218, 220.

I.C.

LUTTRELL, Narcissus (1657–1732), of Holborn, London, and Little Chelsea, Mdx.

BOSSINEY 1679 (Oct.)
SALTASH 30 Oct. 1691

b. 12 Aug. 1657, 3rd but o. surv. s. of Francis Luttrell of Gray's Inn by Catherine, da. of Narcissus Mapowder of Holsworthy, Devon, and coh. to her bro. Anthony. *educ.* Sheen, Surr. (Mr Aldrich); G. Inn, entered 1673, called 1680, ancient 1706; St. John's, Camb. 1674. *m.* (1) lic. 25 Feb. 1682, Sarah (*d.* 9 July 1722), da. of Daniel Baker, merchant, of Hatton Garden, Mdx., 1s.; (2) 13 May 1725, Mary, da. of John Bearsley of Wolverhampton, Staffs., 1s. *d.v.p. suc.* fa. 1677.[1]

Commr. for assessment, Cornw. and Mdx. 1690; j.p. Mdx. 1693–1702; bencher, G. Inn 1702–6.

Luttrell inherited a small property at Trethurffe, near Truro. Proud of his kinship with the Luttrells of Dunster Castle he collated the family muniments, but he was a collector by nature, and, for all his learning and industry, published nothing. With a private income of £300–£475 p.a., he soon abandoned 'the practice of the law', and amassed a large collection of books, pamphlets, and manuscripts, which Shaftesbury and Locke both consulted. From 1678 he compiled his *Brief Relation of State Affairs*, first used by Macaulay, but not printed until 1857.[2]

Returned for Bossiney at the autumn election of 1679, Luttrell was appointed to no committees and made no speeches in the second Exclusion Parliament, though he is said to have been 'one of the warm promoters of the exclusion bill'. He was probably the 'Mr Luttrell' whom the townsmen of Barnstaple preferred as a court candidate in 1688. He sat as a Whig in the second Parliament of William III, when he kept a valuable parliamentary diary. With increasing prosperity he was able to purchase a house at Chelsea from the third Earl of Shaftesbury in 1710. He died on 27 June 1732 after a long illness and was buried at Chelsea, the last of this branch of the family to sit in Parliament.[3]

[1] Vivian, *Vis. Devon*, 537–41; H. C. Maxwell Lyte, *Hist. Dunster*, 521–5; *Dunster and its Lords*, 44–45. [2] *Hist. Dunster*, 518–25; *N. and Q.* clii. 111; ccvii. 452; *Bk. Collector*, vi. 16. [3] *Hist. Dunster*, 521–5; *DNB*; *N. and Q.* clii. 111; information from Prof. H. Horwitz.

E.C.

LUTWYCHE, Sir Edward (1634–1709), of Lutwyche Hall, Easthope, Salop.

LUDLOW 14 Nov. 1685–21 Apr. 1686

b. 6 Sept. 1634, o.s. of William Lutwyche of Lutwyche Hall by Elizabeth, da. of Richard Lister of Rowton Castle. *educ.* Shrewsbury 1644; L. Inn 1652; G. Inn 1654, called 1661, ancient 1671. *m.* by 1659, Anne, da. of Sir Timothy Tourneur of Bold, 2s. (1 *d.v.p.*) 3da. *suc.* gdfa. 1638; kntd. 14 Nov. 1684.[1]

J.p. Salop 1673–89, Cheshire 1684–5; commr. for recusants, Salop 1675, assessment, Salop 1677–80, Cheshire and Chester 1677–9; recorder and alderman, Chester 1684–5; c.j. Chester circuit Nov. 1685–6.[2]

Serjeant-at-law 1683, King's serjeant 1684; j.c.p. 21 Apr. 1686–9.

Lutwyche's family had resided at the property from which they took their name since at least 1418. One of them sat for Bridgnorth in four Elizabethan Parliaments. A successful provincial lawyer, Lutwyche succeeded Sir Edward Herbert* as Member for Ludlow at a by-election in 1685 held two days before the issue of the writ, and Parliament was prorogued before he could be appointed to any committees. In the following year he was promoted to the court of common pleas. As one of the judges who had supported the dispensing power, though not in ecclesiastical cases, he was excepted from the Act of Indemnity in 1690. He returned to his practice, though he was fined as a non-juror at the York assizes in 1693, and continued at the bar until 1704. He died in June 1709 and was buried at St. Bride's, Fleet Street. His son Thomas, also a lawyer, sat as a Tory for various constituencies from 1710 to 1734.[3]

[1] *Le Neve's Knights* (Harl. Soc. viii), 391; J. E. Auden, *Shrewsbury Sch. Reg.* 26. [2] W. R. Williams, *Gt. Sessions in Wales*, 43; *CSP Dom.* 1685, p. 393. [3] *Vis. Salop* (Harl. Soc. xxix), 345–7; Grey, ix. 312; Luttrell, iii. 83; vi. 452; Le Neve, *Mon. Angl.* 1700–15, p. 181.

E.C.

LYTTELTON (LITTLETON), Sir Charles (c.1629–1716).

BEWDLEY 1685

b. c.1629, 7th but 2nd surv. s. of Sir Thomas Lyttelton, 1st Bt.†, of Hagley Hall, Worcs. by Catherine, da. and h. of Sir Thomas Crompton of Driffield, Yorks.; bro. of Sir Henry Lyttelton, 2nd Bt.* *m.* (1) Catherine (*d.* 26 Jan. 1663), da. of Sir William Fairfax of Steeton, Yorks., wid. of Martin Lister† of Thornton, Yorks., 1s. *d.v.p.*; (2) lic. 23 May 1666, aged 36, Anne, da. and coh. of Thomas Temple of Frankton, Warws., maid of honour to Queen Catherine of Braganza, 5s. (4 *d.v.p.*) 8da. Kntd. c. Apr. 1662; suc. bro. as 3rd Bt. 24 June 1693.[1]

Lt. (royalist) 1648; lt.-gov. of Jamaica 1662–4; maj. of ft. Admiralty Regt. 1664–5, lt.-col. 1665–8, col. 1668 (Duke of York's Ft. 1673–85, Prince George's Ft. 1685–9), brig. Nov. 1688; gov. Harwich and Landguard Fort 1667–72, 1673–80, Sheerness 1680–90.[2]

Cup-bearer 1650–?55, May 1660–75; asst. R. Adventurers into Africa 1664–6, 1668; jt. agent for Jamaica 1682–?89.[3]

Freeman, Harwich 1671, sub-commr. for prizes 1672–4; commr. for assessment, Harwich 1677–9, Surr. 1689; dep. lt. Kent 1682–?89; alderman, Bewdley 1685–1706; j.p. Kent Feb. 1688–9, Worcs. July 1688–9, ?1700–*d.*[4]

Too young to fight in the Civil War, Lyttelton first saw service in the siege of Colchester in 1648. He was made cup-bearer to the King in Scotland in 1650, but by 1655 he was back in England and imprisoned in the Gatehouse. Hence he was unable to take part in Penruddock's rising, but in August 1659 he and his brothers made an unsuccessful attempt on Shrewsbury, after which he attended the King in France. At the Restoration he was given £500, and knighted shortly before sailing for Jamaica as lieutenant-governor. For most of the time he was acting governor, but his brother, wife and infant son all fell victim to the climate, and in 1664 he returned to England and became a professional soldier. He was 'very industrious in his own person' in building fortifications at Harwich, and soon came to be regarded by the corporation as a friend at Court. He served aboard the fleet in 1673 and commanded the English forces at Bruges in 1678. At the dissolution of the Cavalier Parliament he described himself as 'trying to creep in at Harwich'; but the Admiralty had other ideas. Lyttelton was transferred to Sheerness early in 1680, and, on the death of Francis Barrell*, Sir Francis Clerke* was confident that Lyttelton would succeed him as Member for Rochester, but the writ was never issued. As joint agent for Jamaica, he presented a loyal address in 1683.[5]

Lyttelton was returned for Bewdley, four miles from his brother's favourite residence at Upper Arley, on the day that the new charter was received in 1685, doubtless unopposed. He was a moderately active Member of James II's Parliament, serving on seven committees, of which the most important were to recommend erasures in the Journals and to examine the accounts of the disbandment commissioners. He was on garrison duty during Monmouth's rebellion, but in the autumn he was transferred to Somerset to replace Percy Kirke*. On 7 Oct. he described to Lord Hatton (Christopher Hatton*).

> the violence of our predecessors to the country in all kinds, both as to the persons as well as the goods, such as I have scarce known practised at any time in our former Civil Wars, and which I cannot but believe we shall hear more of when the Parliament meets.... The country looks, as one passes, already like a shambles.

Nevertheless Lyttelton cannot have opposed the Court in the second session, as he kept his regiment. Early in 1688 he inherited the Sheen estate of Henry Brouncker*,

> to whom he had no manner of relation but an ancient friendship contracted at the famous siege of Colchester forty years before. It is a pretty place, a fine garden and well-planted, and given to one worthy of them, Sir Charles being an honest gentleman and a soldier. . . . He is married to one Mrs Temple (formerly maid of honour to the late Queen), a beautiful lady, and has many fine children, so that none envy him his good fortune.

Lyttelton complied with all the lord lieutenant's questions on the repeal of the Test Act and Penal Laws, and was approved as court candidate for Bewdley. He served James to the last, even after his eldest son had gone over to William, and his regiment was deemed so hostile to the new regime that it was disbanded in February 1689, Lyttelton declaring himself 'quite weary of serving any longer, and very willing to resign'. Nevertheless he took the oaths as governor of Sheerness, where he remained till July 1690. He surrendered his commission at the sacrifice of £500–£600 a year on the grounds that his business would not permit the constant attendance required in wartime, but really because (as he said): 'I began to find myself pressed to sign an address of renouncing my late master, which (however I had sufficiently done in effect) would have been so odious an ingratitude I despised any advantage to oblige me to'. The confession of Lord Preston (Sir Richard Grahme*) in the following year implicated Lyttelton, while governor, in correspondence with St. Germains, but no action was taken against him till 1696. He seems to have been soon released, and by the end of the reign he was on the Worcestershire commission of the peace. He died on 2 May 1716 aged 87. His only surviving son sat for the county as a Whig from 1721 to 1734.[6]

[1] Nash, *Worcs.* i. 493; Clay, *Dugdale's Vis. Yorks.* ii. 136; *CSP Col.* 1661–8, pp. 83, 106. [2] *CSP Dom.* 1672–3, p. 263; 1679–80, pp. 128, 380; *Hatton Corresp.* (Cam. Soc. n.s. xxiii), 100, 157. [3] *Cal. Cl. SP.* ii. 84; *CSP Dom.* 1675–6, p. 4; *CSP Col.* 1681–5, p. 308. [4] S. Dale, *Harwich and Dovercourt*, 224; *CSP Dom.* 1671–2, p. 484; 1682, p. 527; 1685, p. 138; *Univ. Birmingham Hist. Jnl.* i. 112, 113, 126. [5] *CSP Dom.* 1655, p. 575; 1661–2, p. 178; 1667, p. 16; 1668–9, p. 271; 1678, p. 131; 1679–80, p. 380; 1680–1, p. 68; 1687–9, p. 275; *Cal. Cl. SP.* iv. 236, 312–13, 350, 389, 396, 460; *Williamson Letters* (Cam. Soc. n.s. viii), 36; *Hatton Corresp.* (Cam. Soc. n.s. xxii), 171; Luttrell, i. 246. [6] *Hatton Corresp.* (Cam. Soc. n.s. xxiii), 60, 130, 157, 222, 223; *Evelyn Diary*, iv. 575–6; Nash, i. 501; *HMC Finch*, iii. 342.

J.P.F.

LYTTELTON (LITTLETON), Sir Henry, 2nd Bt. (c.1624–93), of Hagley Hall, Worcs. and Upper Arley, Staffs.

LICHFIELD   21 Feb. 1678, 1679 (Mar.)

b. c.1624, 5th but 1st surv. s. of Sir Thomas Lyttelton, 1st Bt.†, of Frankley, Worcs., and bro. of Sir Charles Lyttelton*. *educ.* Balliol, Oxf. matric. 12 Sept. 1640, aged. 16. *m.* (1) Philadelphia (*d.* 2 Aug. 1663), da. and coh. of Hon. Thomas Carey, groom of the bedchamber to Charles I, *s.p.*; (2) Lady Elizabeth Newport, da. of Francis Newport†, 1st Earl of Bradford, *s.p. suc.* fa. 22 Feb. 1650.[1]

Sheriff, Worcs. 1654–5; j.p. Worcs. 1654–5, July 1660–?*d.*, Salop July 1660–June 1688, Sept. 1688–*d.*; commr. for oyer and terminer, Oxford circuit July 1660, assessment, Worcs. Aug. 1660–80, Salop 1673–80, Lichfield 1679–80, Salop, Staffs. and Worcs. 1689–90; dep. lt. Worcs. 1661–?89, Staffs. 1677–Feb. 1688; capt. vol. horse, Worcs. 1661, commr. for loyal and indigent officers 1662, recusants, Salop and Worcs. 1675; freeman, Worcester 1683; alderman, Bewdley 1685–*d.*[2]

Lyttelton was descended from Thomas Heuster *alias* Woodcote of Lichfield who married the heiress of Frankley and sat for Worcestershire in the Parliament of 1431, and from the eminent jurist Sir Thomas Littleton, who took his mother's name. Lyttelton's father garrisoned Frankley for the King; it was demolished by Prince Rupert when it was no longer tenable, and its owner, taken prisoner by the Earl of Essex, was obliged to compound at £4,000 for his delinquency.[3]

Lyttelton himself joined the royalist army at Worcester in 1651, and was imprisoned for two years in the Tower. On release he joined the Action party of royalist conspirators in the Midlands; his appointment as sheriff provided an excuse for the purchase of arms in 1654–5, but, deterred perhaps by his brother's arrest, he did nothing during Penruddock's rising. Lyttelton and Lord Mordaunt married sisters, and in consequence he was more prominent in 1659. He was arrested, but treated with great respect. Charles II sent him an appreciative letter from Brussels:

> I am very well informed how much and how often you

have suffered for me, and how much I am beholden to all your relations; and you may be very sure I have the sense of it that I ought to have, of which you shall one day have evidence. In the meantime, cherish your health, and prepare for better times that we shall enjoy together.[4]

At the Restoration Lyttelton served on the grand jury which found a true bill against the regicides, and was granted the East India Company shares held by Robert Tichborne, which he sold for £3,000. 'Dry and illiberal' and 'troubled with fits of the spleen', he refused both an invitation to stand for Worcestershire in 1661 and a peerage. He preferred to live on his Staffordshire property, where the produce of his vineyards was pronounced 'altogether indistinguishable from the best French wines by the most judicious palates'. He made inquiries about the vacancy at Bewdley in 1673, but it was not until five years later that he was returned, 'at vast expense' for Lichfield, where his sisters lived. He was marked 'doubly worthy' by Shaftesbury, but served on no committees and made no speeches. During the debate on the Popish Plot of 28 Nov., he and one of the Gorings were reported to be copying out Bedloe's information in the Speaker's chamber; their papers were torn up, but no further action was taken.[5]

At the first general election of 1679, Lyttelton was re-elected for Lichfield, probably unopposed. His brother reported that

he might have been knight of the shire for Worcestershire with less charge, I imagine. But my Lord Windsor seemed to oppose him for Sir Francis Russell*. Since, Sir Francis refusing to stand, my Lord would have had my brother; he then, being so far engaged for Lichfield, would not quit them.

Shaftesbury again marked him 'worthy', but he was totally inactive in Parliament, being absent from the division on the exclusion bill. He does not seem to have stood at the next general election, and declined an invitation from Lichfield in 1681. His opinions were probably shifting towards the Government. In August 1683 he reported on the suspicious purchase of 12 cannon by two tenants of Philip Foley* and Thomas Foley II*; but a government expert found that they were worn out and fit only for scrap. He became an alderman of Bewdley under the new charter, no doubt to facilitate the election of his brother Charles. He gave unconditional consent to the three questions on the Penal Laws as put to him by the lord lieutenant of Worcestershire, where he was living at the time, but refused to stand as court candidate there because 'his intent lay in another county'. But he is not known to have stood again for Lichfield. He died on 24 June 1693, aged

69, and was buried at Arley. His widow married Edward Harvey*.[6]

[1] Nash, *Worcs.* i. 493; Vivian, *Vis. Devon*, 155. [2] *Townshend's Diary* (Worcs. Rec. Soc.), iii. 276; SP29/21/48; *Hatton Corresp.* (Cam. Soc. n.s. xxii), 23; *CSP Dom.* 1685, p. 138. [3] *The Gen.* n.s. xxxvii. 20–22; *Cal. Comm. Adv. Money*, 782. [4] *Cal. Comm. Comp.* 750, 2898–9; D. Underdown, *Royalist Conspiracy*, 130; *Cal. Cl. SP*, iv. 350; Nash, i. 499. [5] *State Trials*, v. 987; *Townshend's Diary*, i. 292; *Cal. Ct. Mins. E.I. Co.* ed. Sainsbury, vi. 27, 85, 104, 108–9, 360, 371; *Hatton Corresp.* 24, 36, 174; *Plot, Staffs.* 380; Erdeswick, *Survey of Staffs.* 388; *Epistolary Curiosities of Herbert Fam.* ed. Warner, i. 97. [6] *Hatton Corresp.* 174; *HMC Dartmouth*, i. 56; *CSP Dom.* July–Sept. 1683, pp. 318, 332, 382.

A.M.M.

LYTTON, Rowland (c.1615–74), of Knebworth, Herts.

HERTFORDSHIRE 1656,[1] 1659, 1660

b. c.1615, o.s. of Sir William Lytton[†] of Knebworth by 1st w. Anne, da. and h. of Stephen Slaney of Norton, Salop. *educ.* Hertford sch.; Sidney Sussex, Camb. matric. 24 Jan. 1632, aged 17; I. Temple 1633; travelled abroad (Italy) 1635–6. *m.* (1) Judith (*d.* 13 May 1659), da. and coh. of Thomas Edwards, Mercer, of London and Wadhurst, Suss., 2s. 2da.; (2) settlement 12 June 1661, Rebecca (*d.* 23 Mar. 1686), da. and coh. of Thomas Chapman, Draper, of Soper Lane, London and Wormley, Herts., wid. of Thomas Playters of Sotterley, Suff., and of Sir Richard Lucy, 1st Bt., of Broxbourne, Herts., 1da. Kntd. 27 June 1660; *suc.* fa. Aug. 1660.[2]

Commr. for new model ordinance, Herts. 1645, assessment 1645–50, 1657, Jan. 1660–*d.*; j.p. Herts. and Mon. 1656–July 1660, St. Albans 1656–Sept. 1660; commr. for militia, Herts. 1659, Mar. 1660, sheriff 1662–3, dep. lt. 1670–*d.*

Originating in Derbyshire, Lytton's ancestors had been reckoned among the foremost gentry of Hertfordshire since Sir Robert Lytton* acquired Knebworth in 1492 and became knight of the shire in 1495. Lytton's father sat for the county in the Long Parliament until imprisoned as a Presbyterian at Pride's Purge.[3]

Lytton himself served on the county committee, but was regarded as hostile to the Protectorate in 1656. Nevertheless he was re-elected for the county to Richard Cromwell's Parliament and again in 1660. He was an inactive member of the Convention, making no recorded speeches and serving on only three committees, those for the indemnity bill, for cancelling all grants since May 1642, and for settling the militia. Presumably a court supporter, he was rewarded with a knighthood; but the ascendancy of the Cavaliers, headed by Thomas Fanshawe*, drove him from county office. He probably did not stand again, though he was reappointed deputy lieutenant in 1670 and served until his death. After settling the bulk of his estates, he left

£5,000 as a portion to his only unmarried daughter. He died on 1 Nov. 1674 and was buried at Knebworth. The family became extinct in the male line without further parliamentary honours.[4]

[1] Excluded. [2] Clutterbuck, *Herts.* ii. 377–8, 384; PC2/44/390; *Vis. London* (Harl. Soc. xv), 249; *The Gen.* n.s. xxxiv. 4–5. [3] *VCH Herts.* iii. 315; Keeler, *Long Parl.* 263–4, D. Underdown, *Pride's Purge*, 211. [4] *VCH Herts.* iv 13; PCC 129 Bunce; Clutterbuck, ii. 384.

M.W.H./E.R.E./G.J.